DISCARD

McGraw-Hill's
Dictionary
of
American Idioms
and
Phrasal Verbs

Richard A. Spears, Ph.D.

McGraw·Hill

New York   Chicago   San Francisco   Lisbon   London   Madrid   Mexico City
Milan   New Delhi   San Juan   Seoul   Singapore   Sydney   Toronto

Library of Congress Cataloging-in-Publication Data

Spears, Richard A.
    McGraw-Hill's dictionary of American idioms and phrasal verbs / Richard A. Spears.
        p.   cm.
    Includes index.
    ISBN 0-07-140858-4 (acid-free paper)
      1. English language—United States—Idioms—Dictionaries.   2. English
language—United States—Verb phrase—Dictionaries.   3. Figures of speech—
Dictionaries.   4. Americanisms—Dictionaries.

    PE2839 .S636   2004
    423'.13'0973—dc22   2004061047

1 2 3 4 5 6 7 8 9 0   HPC/HPC   0 9 8 7 6 5 4

ISBN 0-07-140858-4

Interior design by Terry Stone   3 9082 09690 9398

This book is printed on acid-free paper.

Contents

About This Dictionary *v*

How to Use This Dictionary *ix*

Acknowledgments *xv*

Terms and Symbols *xvii*

Dictionary *1*

Phrase-Finder Index *783*

About This Dictionary

All languages have phrases that cannot be understood literally and, therefore, cannot be used with confidence. They are opaque or unpredictable because they don't have expected, literal meaning. Even if you know the meaning of all the words in a phrase and understand all the grammar of the phrase completely, the meaning of the phrase may still be confusing. A phrase or sentence of this type is said to be idiomatic. This dictionary is a collection of the idiomatic phrases and sentences that occur frequently in American English. Many of them occur in some fashion in other varieties of English also.

Many overlapping terms have been used to describe the idiomatic phrases included here: verbal collocations, idioms, idiomatic expressions, clichés, proverbs, set phrases, fixed phrases, phrasal verbs, common phrases, prepositional verbs, and phrasal/prepositional verbs. They all offer the same kinds of problems to the speaker and writer of English. They are unclear because the meaning of the phrase is not literal or predictable. Phrasal verbs, also called *two-word verbs*, are idiomatic expressions because the second element of the verb (the adverb or preposition) is not necessarily predictable. For instance, why the word *up* in *call up a friend*? Why not say *call on a friend* or *call in a friend*? Actually, those are three separate, unpredictable combinations, and they each mean something completely different. For example, you can *call up a friend* on the telephone, *call on a friend* to have a visit, and *call in a friend* to come and help you with something.

Although there are some entries that are very casual or informal English, slang and idioms should not be confused. Some slang is also idiomatic, and some idioms are also slang, but generally they refer to different aspects of language. There are a few slang terms in this dictionary, because they are also fairly commonly known idioms.

GOALS OF THE DICTIONARY

A major goal of this dictionary is to make certain that each definition of a phrase illustrates the meaning of the phrase and matches it in syntax. The major exceptions are definitions that begin with "a phrase" or "an expression." Similarly, the examples for each sense must match the definition in meaning and syntax. The best use of the entries is to study the entry head, definition, and example carefully. Look for the meaning that is common to all three. If the diligent user can see the elements of meaning shared by the entry phrase, the definition, and the example(s), the dictionary entry has done its task well.

A second goal is to provide the learner with enough information about the many forms that an idiom might take to allow the user to recognize it in a variety of contexts and to be able to use it in speech and writing.

A third goal is to make the details accessible to the learner. Idiomatic expressions and their variants are complex and unpredictable. There are many synonyms and near synonyms. General cross-referencing in the body of the dictionary will help users find synonymous phrases. The Phrase-Finder Index provides a powerful tool for locating entry forms embedded in other entries and partially remembered phrases. The form of the entry is quite straightforward, consisting of entry, definition, comments (if any), and examples. Senses are numbered and may include variants *in addition to* those found in the entry head. A minimum of abbreviations and symbols are used, and these are explained in the section "Terms and Symbols." The user who understands the meaning of **entry head**, **variable**, and **wild card term** is equipped to understand everything that follows.

WHO CAN BENEFIT FROM THIS DICTIONARY?

The dictionary will prove useful for native speakers who are looking for synonymous idiomatic phrases. Many phrases can be expressed in a variety of ways, and this dictionary, through cross-referencing, can lead the native speaker to equivalent forms with the same or similar meaning. The index provides a means for a writer to find the most appropriate phrase for a given purpose. Native speakers can find most of what they want by looking up words representing key ideas in the index and following the references to phrases in the dictionary itself.

Likewise, near-native speakers who need help with phrasal verbs and common idiomatic phrases will find this reference very useful. Speakers and writers trained in British English will find this dictionary a good reference for checking on the American form and meaning of expressions previously encountered in British English.

The format of the dictionary is designed to provide the information needed by learners who are attempting to read and write conventional American English. It contains far more detail and specificity than is required by people who have heard, spoken, and written standard American English all their lives. For instance, a dictionary designed for native speakers of English might include the subentries **bail out** and **see through**. However, there are major differences in meaning between the idiomatic expressions that can be based on these words.

bail out (of something) "jump out"

bail someone **out (of** something) "post bond to get a person out of jail"

bail something **out (of** something) "remove water from a boat"

bail something **out** "empty a boat (of accumulated water)"

see something **through** "work at something until it is finished"

see through something "see through something that is transparent"

see through something "detect a trick or deception"

These differences may never be revealed if the entry heads are just **bail out** and **see through**, with no object indicated. This dictionary presents the additional details that a native speaker already knows. The information needed for the learner includes whether the verb can take an object and, if so, what kind of object (human, nonhuman, or both) is needed. The learner also needs to know what additional prepositional phrases are required or optional for the correct use of the expressions.

PHRASE ORIGINS

A surprising number of phrases have literary or Biblical origins. The works of Shakespeare, in particular, have provided many memorable phrases that are in constant use around the world. When the source is the Bible or Shakespeare, as well as other authors, that is noted in the dictionary entries. Most of the phrasal or two-word verbs are due to the Germanic origins of English. The choice of which particle (the second part of a two-word verb) is an ancient problem.

There are many instances, recorded in this dictionary, of a figurative phrasal verb being derived from a more literal interpretation of the same phrasal verb. In these instances, the phrasal verbs (or two-word verbs) appear in both figurative and literal senses in the same entry. One sense helps the user understand the other sense. In this case, the figurative sense has its origin in the literal sense. In entries where this occurs, the literal senses are marked *Lit.* and the figurative senses are marked *Fig.*

A high percentage of the entries in this dictionary have their origins in a figurative usage where there is no matching literal sense. That is why they offer special difficulty in understanding. Wherever necessary or possible there is a note in the entry suggesting what a figurative entry is based on or alluding to. Sometimes the relationship is completely obvious and no explanation is offered.

Quite a few of the similes (for example, **as busy as a beaver**) are contrived and appear to be part of an ever-expanding repertory of colorful and quaint comparisons. Similarly, the senses marked *Rur.* (rural) are often contrived and may appear more often as colorful expressions in writing than they ever did in real life. That these rural-sounding expressions actually had a rural origin can be debated. Nor can all the similes be taken seriously. They are included because they might be encountered by the learner and their listing here might be useful for a writer—if nothing more than as something to be avoided.

There is another kind of "origin" that needs to be mentioned. There are a few idioms that seem to invite very clever but totally baseless tales of origin. Many of these tales are quite popular and widely known. Two examples of such "story" idioms involve **sleep tight** and **a dead ringer**. The first is associated with sleeping on a tightly strung, rope-supported mattress, and the second refers to a corpse ringing a bell. The details depend on the teller of the tale. Such tales of origin are very entertaining to many people. The idioms on which these stories are based are included in this dictionary, but the tale is neither told nor debunked here.

There are many additional phrases that are just the customary patterns used to say things in both casual and more formal situations. Common greetings and responses are included in this category, and these expressions have their origins in the functions they were meant to serve.

WHEN WERE THEY FIRST USED?

Users often have an interest in dating the origins of a phrase. It is possible to put a specific date on the early use of a *word* by consulting a historical dictionary, such as the *Oxford English Dictionary*. That will show the earliest usage recorded in the books and other documents that have been consulted for the creation of the dictionary. Some phrases and idioms may be included in the entries and quotations, but that is not the primary focus of a historical dictionary. As more and more data become available in a searchable, digital format, it is possible to find examples of the early uses of specific phrases more easily. A very careful writer of historical novels or screenplays will be interested in making sure that a certain word or phrase was actually in use during the period in question. The *OED* can be helpful in determining this kind of information. An early date for a phrase (or word) does not necessarily indicate the earliest use of the item nor the period of widespread comprehension in the population, however.

This dictionary offers the user help in seeing semantic relationships and allusions, but it has goals that are quite different from those of a historical dictionary. The major concern here is contemporary usage, and it probably reflects idiomatic English over the last 50 years. The older members of the native-speaking population know more of the entries than the younger people, but the latter will learn more as they age. Probably 75 percent of the entries are widely known, conventional English for 75 percent of the educated, native-speaking adult population.

How to Use This Dictionary

For most users, most of the time, a single instruction will be enough, and that is to start with the Phrase-Finder Index.

> In the index, look up a major word in the idiom, preferably a verb, and go to the most appropriate dictionary entry listed in the right-hand column. If no appropriate entry is listed at the verb, try an adverb, preposition, or other word.

Further hints can be found at the beginning of the Phrase-Finder Index. The organization and philosophy of the dictionary is discussed in much greater detail below.

ALPHABETIZATION

In the dictionary, phrasal verbs (or two-word verbs) and their related prepositional verbs are alphabetized on the verb. All other idiomatic expressions are alphabetized in their complete forms with no inversion of parts. Entries are not listed by "key word" unless the "key word" is the first word. On the other hand, the index lists *all* the key words in a phrase. In that way, the key word is the user's choice and not the compiler's choice. All alphabetizing is word by word, rather than letter by letter. Initial *a*, *an*, and *the* are ignored in the alphabetization. Significant variants are cross-referenced to a main **entry head**. In most instances, an object of a verb or preposition is shown by a **wild card term**, either someone, something, someone or something, or some other expression such as some amount of money. Showing whether an object is human, nonhuman, or of some other semantically limited category is essential to explaining meaning and distinguishing the senses. **Wild card terms** are included in the alphabetization. In the Phrase-Finder Index, you are shown

which entry head to look up. Those entry heads will include **wild card terms**. It is much easier to look up these expressions in the dictionary itself if the **wild card terms** are included in the alphabetization.

OVERCOMING OPAQUE AND UNPREDICTABLE PHRASES

There are three general reasons why idiomatic expressions are problems for students, writers, and other adults wishing to expand their skills with conventional American English. The three problems involve (1) difficulties with extracting the core of the idiomatic expression from a sentence or paragraph, (2) the variable nature of idioms, and (3) the basic opaque nature of these phrases. There is little that can be done about opacity other than use a dictionary, but there is some information about the other problems that can help the user. What follows will explain the organization of the dictionary and the way the peculiarities of English phrases have been handled here. It is not necessary to be able to understand the following discussion to use the dictionary.

EXTRACTING THE IDIOMATIC PART OF A SENTENCE

Idiomatic phrases are usually found included within a sentence, and it is difficult to extract the core of the idiom so that it can be looked up in a dictionary. These expressions are often learned in a list, and, unfortunately, the form of the expression presented in the list is probably only one of many variants. In the real world, these expressions are never seen or heard except in a complete sentence. In order to look them up in a dictionary, they have to be extracted from the sentence in which they are found. You cannot look up a phrase that is found within a sentence unless you know the boundaries of the phrase. Here are some hints for extracting idiomatic phrases.

Simplify the Grammar

Entries in the dictionary and index use the singular form of the noun and the present tense (bare) verb. The index actually lists both regular and irregular forms when there are both. For instance **old wives' tale** is listed in the index under "old," "wife," "wives," and "tale." In order to look something up in either section, the user will save time by using the simplest form. There are more items to choose from at the simplest form.

Look for Nonliteral Meanings

Look for something in the sentence that is not understandable literally. For instance, "Sue is known for thinking ahead of her time." How can Sue think ahead of or in front of time? Only figuratively. Mentally extract the nonliteral phrase, "thinking ahead of her time." Try to match "think ahead of her time" to a phrase in the index by looking at "think" and scanning down to "think ahead" where you find **think ahead of one's time** or the shorter ***ahead of one's time**.

Ignore Immediate Context

The parts of a sentence that refer to specific places, things, measurements, and activities are not likely to be items you can look up in the index. Examine the sentence "It's almost 6:00, and you, Tom, and I have to thrash this contract out before we can meet the President of Acme Widgets for dinner at 8:00." Ignore the specifics that relate only to this time and place: "6:00," "Tom," "you," "I," "President of Acme Widgets," "dinner at 8:00." That leaves "thrash this contract out." Look up "thrash" in the index and find **thrash** something **out**, and it seems to explain the meaning of the sentence perfectly. There are things that can cause confusion, though. "Dinner at 8:00" is a common and well-known phrase. "Acme" is a (once) common name for a company, and "widget" is a common imaginary name for a product. Those words are not in the index, however.

VARIATION IN IDIOMATIC EXPRESSIONS

Idioms are sometimes called *fixed phrases*. In the real world, many idiomatic expressions are found in many variations, and this makes them hard to use and even harder to find in a dictionary. What follows is a discussion of the seven kinds of variation shown in this dictionary. Unfortunately, many idiomatic expressions exhibit more than one kind of variation. Fortunately, use of the Phrase-Finder Index to find a particular idiom will eliminate most of the problems caused by variation. It is important to know how the variants are related to each other so you do not think that three variants of a single phrase might have three different meanings. Knowing what the core of an idiomatic expression is, and how it can vary, makes it possible to recognize it and use its variants in a far greater number of contexts.

Grammatical Variation

In idioms in general, nouns can be plural or singular and verbs can occur in a variety of tenses and aspects. Many phrases can appear equally well in the negative or affirmative and undergo question inversion. Use the index to find the simplest form. This will lead you to the appropriate entry, even if the entry contains nouns or verbs that do not vary, such as **old wives' tale**, which is never singular. Here are some sentence examples of grammatical variation:

> The tape wouldn't adhere to the door.
> Why won't this glue adhere to the doors?
> The adhesive adhered to the door easily.
> That old glue has adhered to the front of
>   the door nicely.
> That old tape has adhered to it nicely.

The thing that all the example sentences have in common is that they all have the verb *adhere* plus a prepositional phrase beginning with *to*. The object of *to* can be a variety of nouns or pronouns. The elements each example shares are: **adhere to something**, and that is the form of the entry in this dictionary. The general rule is to simply reduce the noun to singular and the verbs to present tense and look up the results in the index.

The Transposable Adverb

Adverbs in certain phrases can swap places with the direct object of a transitive verb. This cannot be done if the object of the verb is a pronoun. Although the result may, in some instances, look like a prepositional phrase, it is not. In the following example containing "down the door," the word *down* is an adverb that stands between the verb and its direct object:

> She broke *down* the door with an axe.
> She broke the door *down* with an axe.

> Please hammer the nail *in*.
> Please hammer *in* the nail.

But you cannot say:

> *She broke down it.
> *Please hammer in it.

The entry head **break** something **down**[†] contains a dagger ([†]) that indicates that the "down" can be transposed to a position just after the verb. Any word marked with the dagger can be transposed to a position immediately following the verb except when the object of the verb is a pronoun. Only the adverbs followed by [†] can be swapped in this manner.

Prepositions That Become Adverbs

There is both a noun *hammer* and a verb *hammer*. Similarly, some particles can function as either prepositions or adverbs, depending on how they are used. Prepositions have objects. *Out* is a preposition in "Run out the door." It is an adverb in "Put the cat out." Some prepositional verbs (verb + prepositional phrase) can become phrasal verbs (verb + adverb) by "losing" the object of the

preposition. In the phrase **add** something **into** something, *add* has both an object of the verb and a prepositional phrase. Without the object of the preposition, the remaining preposition, in this case *in*, functions as an adverb, as in **add** something **in**. Examine the following sets of sentences. Note the transposable adverb in the second and third examples.

> Add the flour into the eggs.
> Add the flour *in*.
> Add *in* the flour.

> Boil the wax out of the cloth.
> Boil the wax *out*.
> Boil *out* the wax.

In this dictionary, these pairs are presented as variants of the same entry. Usually it is necessary to express this variation in two parts. Then, the cross-referencing or the index will lead the user to the longer entry, which is then followed by the shorter one. Note that the adverb is marked transposable in the entry heads below. The relationship between these two varieties of phrasal verb is very common in English around the world. The pairs of entries are listed as follows:

> **add** something **into** something
> and **add** something **in**[†]

> **boil** something **out of** something
> and **boil** something **out**[†]

Note that the prepositions *into* and *out* do not have daggers, indicating that they cannot be transposed to the position immediately after the verb.

Idioms with a Limited Verb Choice

There are a number of expressions in the dictionary that consist of a phrase that is likely to be preceded by one of a limited list of verbs. These expressions can usually stand alone, at least in casual conversations. The core meaning is the same regardless of the choice of initial verb. The members of the limited set of verbs that can come before the expression are not predictable. This kind of variation is similar to **wild card terms**. Here are examples of the sets of limited sets of verbs.

> *be* ahead of Tom
> *get* ahead of Tom
> *keep* ahead of Tom
> *remain* ahead of Tom
> *stay* ahead of Tom

> *keep* clear of the doors
> *remain* clear of the doors
> *stand* clear of the doors

If each of these idiomatic expressions were a separate entry, it would be repetitive and difficult for the user to see that they include the same basic phrase. Therefore, the core of the entry is preceded by an asterisk (*****), as with ***ahead of** someone and ***clear of** something. Within the entry, a list of the appropriate verbs is given at the asterisk (*****). The index lists all of the variations, and the most common ones are given cross-references in the dictionary itself. Many of them are found after *be*, *get*, and *have* and are cross-referenced from the index only. There are some expressions that must begin with *be*, *get*, or *have* and these are alphabetized in the dictionary under their initial word.

Optional Elements

Various additional words or phrases can be used optionally within a single idiomatic expression. These words or phrases occur often with the idiom in question, but they are not required. They are included as part of the idiomatic pattern since they are so typical of conventional usage. Often, idiomatic expressions seem difficult simply because they are shortened versions of a longer expression that would be easier to understand in its full form. There are many instances of optional prepositional phrases. The following examples illustrate optional words:

> At last, I am able to breathe freely again.
> At last, I am able to breathe again.

> all joking aside
> joking aside

In this dictionary, optional elements are enclosed in parentheses.

The word *freely* is the optional element in the first pair of examples, and *all* is optional in the second set. Their entries are:

> **able to breathe (freely) again**
> **(all) joking aside**

Variable Classes or Wild Card Terms

Idiomatic phrases include both fixed and variable classes of words. The variable classes can be very broad, such as **someone**, which refers to any person, or **something**, which refers to any thing, object, or group. Many idiomatic phrases are very particular as to whether they include either **someone** or **something**. Others can refer to people or things, **someone** or **something**, without distinction. In this dictionary, these groups are called **wild card terms**. They can be thought of as aliases or proxies for the members of the classes of words they describe. Wild card terms appear in a unique type style. In a few instances, the expression always contains the real word *someone* or *something* and in these instances, special type is not used, as with **pick on someone your own size**. The following examples show the kinds of things that wild card terms can stand for:

> associate with *new friends* (**someone**)
> associate with *them* (**someone**)
> associate with *a bunch of different people* (**someone**)
> associate with *the Smiths* (**someone**)
> play *the radio* at full blast (**something**)
> play *my new record* at full blast (**something**)
> play *his huge stereo* at full blast (**something**)
> play *all the audio stuff in the whole dorm* at full blast (**something**)

The variable classes are represented in these examples by **someone** or **something** as in **associate with** someone or **play** something **at full blast**. The wild card term indicates that any member of the specified class can be used. There are dozens of wild card terms of this kind. All of the wild card terms are descriptive of the kind of words or phrases they can stand for. Here are some of the most common wild card terms with one example of each:

a direction "east by northeast"
a period of time "about an hour"
doing something "eating bread and butter"
some amount of money "about three bucks"
somehow "without much effort"
someone "Fred"
some place "the kitchen"
something "a toaster"
sometime "at noon"

and someone or something, which can be either someone or something.

Note: Wild card terms are mostly nouns, pronouns, and noun phrases. There is no way that these variables could be listed in an index. Therefore, the user is advised to save time by first looking up a verb, adverb, or preposition rather than a noun or pronoun.

Random and Unpatterned Variation

Some expressions differ by only a word or two and are otherwise essentially synonymous. This is more confusing when not all the senses in an entry share the same synonyms, as in the first example where the full entry is quoted. In this entry, only the first sense has a variant.

give someone **a lift 1.** and **give** someone **a ride** *Fig.* to provide transportation for someone. □ *I've got to get into town. Can you give me a lift?* **2.** *Fig.* to raise someone's spirits; to make a person feel better. □ *It was a good conversation, and her kind words really gave me a lift.*

Other entries with variants of this type are:

ache for someone or something
and **hurt for** someone or something

amount to the same thing
and **come to the same thing**

Equivalent forms of an idiomatic expression are combined into a single entry where possible. The second and any subsequent expression are joined by *and* to the first. Sometimes a numbered sense has additional variants. These are introduced by *and.*

If the variants apply to all senses, they are listed at the beginning of the entry. If they apply only to some senses, the restricted form appears after the sense number, as with **give** someone **a ride** above.

Acknowledgments

The compiler has included idiomatic phrases drawn from or suggested by Anne Bertram in the McGraw-Hill publications, *NTC's Dictionary of Proverbs and Clichés*, *NTC's Dictionary of Euphemisms*, and *NTC's Dictionary of Folksy, Regional, and Rural Sayings*, as well as other McGraw-Hill special-purpose dictionaries. In addition, I am very grateful for help from my coworkers for their counseling, writing, and editing skills, as applied to various components and stages of this dictionary. They are Carla (White) Kirschenbaum, Nancy L. Dray, Michelle Davidson, Garret Lemoi, Steven R. Kleinedler, and Frank Abate. I also wish to thank Mark and William Pattis for providing appropriate atmosphere, support, and encouragement for the creation of specialized dictionaries.

Terms and Symbols

☐ is a box that marks the beginning of an example.

~ is a "swung dash" that is an abbreviation for the **entry head**.

† is a "dagger" that is seen in some **entry heads**. It shows that the adverb that precedes is one that can occur instead just after the verb in the same **entry head**. This means that the *out* in **ace** someone **out**† can also be **ace out** someone.

[....] enclose a partial entry that is followed by an instruction about where to find the whole entry or a comment. These brackets are also used to enclose information needed to understand a definition.

and indicates that an **entry head** has variant forms that are the same or very similar in meaning as the **entry head**. One or more variant forms are preceded by *and*.

Cliché refers to an overused expression that is trite and tiresome.

Entry head is the first phrase or word, in boldface type, of an entry. It is the phrase or word that the definition explains.

Euph. means "euphemistic," making something sound or seem "nicer" than some other word might.

Fig. means "figurative." When the meaning of an **entry head** is not literal, it is marked *Fig.* Some are more figurative than others. Some entries contain both literal and figurative senses.

Go to means to search for and read the entry indicated. **Go to previous** means to read the entry immediately above. **Go to next** means to read the entry that follows.

Inf. means "informal." This is used for expressions that are casual but not as intrusive as those marked *Sl.*, "slang."

Jocular refers to an expression that is said in a joking or humorous way.

Lit. means "literal," the normal or expected interpretation of a word or phrase. Some entries contain both literal and figurative senses.

Prov. means "proverbial," in the manner or nature of a proverb.

Rur. means "rural" and refers to country or folksy expressions.

See also means to consult the entry indicated for additional information or to find expressions similar in form or meaning to the entry containing the **See also** instruction.

Simile refers to expressions containing as or like, such as **dry as dust**.

Sl. means "slang," very informal, colorful, playful, or intrusive alternates for more common words.

Variable is an element that stands for a class of items, usually nouns or pronouns. Many expressions must include a noun that is a person, a noun that is a thing, or both. These classes are indicated in the **entry head** as someone, something, or someone or something. There are many other variables, such as some place or sometime, whose meaning is obvious.

Wild card term is a term that represents a **variable**, such as someone, something, or someone or something.

*an A for effort *Fig.* acknowledgement for having tried to do something, even if it was not successful. (*Typically: **get** ~; **give** someone ~.) □ *The plan didn't work, but I'll give you an A for effort for trying.*

A man's gotta do what a man's gotta do. Go to You got to do what you got to do.

Abandon hope, all ye who enter here. *Prov.* If you come in, be prepared for the worst. (Describes a hopeless situation or one somehow similar to hell. Often used jocularly. This is the English translation of the words on the gate of Hell in Dante's *Inferno*.) □ *This is our cafeteria. Abandon hope, all ye who enter here!*

abandon oneself **to** something to yield to the comforts or delights of something. □ *The children abandoned themselves to the delights of the warm summer day.*

abandon ship 1. *Lit.* to leave a sinking ship. □ *The captain ordered the crew and passengers to abandon ship.* **2.** *Fig.* to leave a failing enterprise. □ *A lot of the younger people are abandoning ship because they can get jobs elsewhere easily.*

abandon someone or something **to** someone or something to leave a person, living creature, or thing to the care of someone or something; to give up someone or something to someone or something. (Usually with the thought that the abandoned person or thing will not receive the best of care.) □ *They had to abandon the dogs to the storm.*

abbreviate something **to** something **1.** and **abbreviate** something **as** something to make specific initials or an acronym out of a word or phrase. □ *The phrase was abbreviated to ABC.* **2.** to make something into a shorter version of itself. □ *The act has been abbreviated to just a few minutes.*

the **ABCs of** something *Fig.* the basic facts or principles of something. □ *I have never mastered the ABCs of car maintenance.*

abduct someone **from** someone or something to take away or kidnap a person from someone or from a particular place, usually in secret. □ *The thugs abducted the child from her mother.*

abet someone **in** something to help someone in some deed; to help someone do something illegal. □ *Surely you do not expect me to abet you in this crime!*

abide by something to follow the rules of something; to obey someone's orders. □ *John felt that he had to abide by his father's wishes.*

abide with someone to remain with someone; to stay with someone. (Old and stilted. Primarily heard in the church hymn *Eventide*.) □ *You are welcome to abide with me for a while, young man.*

able to breathe (easily) again and **able to breathe (freely) again 1.** *Lit.* able to breathe clean, fresh air with no restriction or obstruction. □ *After I got out of the dank basement, I was able to breathe easily again.* **2.** *Fig.* able to relax and recover from a busy or stressful time; able to catch one's breath. (*Able to* can be replaced with *can*.) □ *Final exams are over, so I can breathe easily again.*

able to breathe (freely) again Go to previous.

able to cut something *Fig.* to be able to manage or execute something. (Often negative. *Able to* can be replaced with

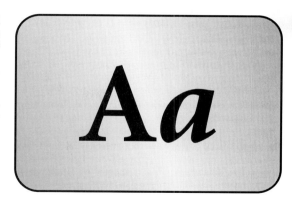

can.) □ *We thought he could handle the new account, but he is simply not able to cut it.*

able to do something to have the strength or skill to do something. (*Able to* can be replaced with *can*.) □ *Are you able to carry those bags by yourself?*

able to do something **blindfolded** and **able to** do something **standing on** one's **head** *Fig.* able to do something very easily, possibly without even looking. (*Able to* can be replaced with *can*.) □ *Bill boasted that he could pass his driver's test blindfolded.*

able to do something **standing on** one's **head** Go to previous.

able to do something **with** one's **eyes closed** *Fig.* able to do something very easily, even without having to think about it or look at it. (Always affirmative. *Able to* can be replaced with *can*.) □ *It's easy. I can do it with my eyes closed.*

able to fog a mirror *Fig. Inf.* alive, even if just barely. (Usually jocular. Alludes to the use of a small mirror placed under the nose to tell if a person is breathing or not. (*Able to* can be replaced with *can*.) □ *Look, I don't need an athlete to do this job! Anybody able to fog a mirror will do fine!*

able to make an event able to attend an event. (*Able to* can be replaced with *can*.) □ *I don't think I'll be able to make your party, but thanks for asking me.*

able to take a joke to be able to accept ridicule good-naturedly; to be able to be the object or butt of a joke willingly. (*Able to* can be replaced with *can*.) □ *Better not tease Ann. She can't take a joke.*

able to take just so much and **able to take only so much** able to endure only a limited amount of discomfort or unpleasantness. (*Able to* can be replaced with *can*.) □ *Please stop hurting my feelings. I'm able to take just so much.*

able to take only so much Go to previous.

abound in something to be rich and abundant in something; to have plenty of something. (A bit formal.) □ *The entire area abounds in game and fish.*

abound with someone or something to be plentiful with particular persons, other living beings, or objects. □ *The world abounds with talented people who are too shy to develop their talents.*

A

about as exciting as watching (the) paint dry Go to exciting as watching (the) paint dry.

***about** one's **business** busy doing something. (*Typically: **be** ~; **get** ~; **go** ~.) □ *Why are you still in the house? It's time to be about your business.* □ *Why are you just standing there? You'd better get busy doing something!*

***about to** do something in the process of doing something. (*Typically: **be** ~; **get** ~.) □ *I'd better be about my yard work.*

***an about-face (on** someone or something**)** *Fig.* a reversal of attitude or action. (*Typically: **do** ~; **have** ~.) □ *She did an about-face on her rule about not eating in the living room. Now we can do it if we want.*

***above and beyond (**something**)** more than is required; greater than the required amount. (*Typically: **be** ~; **go** ~.) □ *The English teacher helped students after school every day, even though it was beyond the call of duty.*

above average higher or better than the average. □ *Max's grades are always above average.*

above (doing) something [of someone] too mature or honorable to do something. □ *I thought you were above doing something so thoughtless.*

above one's **bend** and **above** one's **huckleberry** *Rur.* beyond one's ability. □ *Fixing those new cars with computers in them is above my bend.* □ *Joe's a good cook, but fancy desserts are above his huckleberry.*

above one's **huckleberry** Go to previous.

above par better than average or normal. □ *His work is above par, so he should get paid better.*

above reproach not deserving of blame or criticism. □ *Some politicians behave as though they are above reproach.*

above someone at a higher rank than someone else; serving as someone's supervisor. □ *Ron is above Ginney, but he treats her like an equal.*

above someone or something to be in a position that is higher than someone or something. □ *The plane is now directly above us.*

***above suspicion** [for one] to be honest enough that no one would suspect one; in a position where one could not be suspected. (This is a translation of words attributed to Julius Caesar, who divorced his wife, Pompeia, on the grounds of her possible involvement in a public scandal; Caesar stated, "Caesar's wife must be above suspicion.") (*Typically: **be** ~; **keep** oneself ~; **remain** ~.) □ *The general is a fine old man, completely above suspicion.*

above the law not subject to the law; immune to the law. □ *None of us is above the law. We have to obey all of them.*

aboveboard in the open; visible to the public; honest. □ *Don't keep it a secret. Let's make certain that everything is aboveboard.*

***abreast of** someone or something **1.** *Lit.* keeping even with someone or something. (*Typically: **be** ~; **get** ~; **keep** ~; **stay** ~.) □ *I had to run hard to stay abreast of Sally.* **2.** *Fig.* knowing the news about someone or something. (*Typically: **be** ~; **get** ~; **keep** ~; **stay** ~.) □ *The press corps has to keep abreast of the president.*

abscond with someone or something to steal or run away with someone or something; to **make off with** someone or something in secret. □ *The boys absconded with all the dessert.*

Absence makes the heart grow fonder. *Prov.* You will like someone or something better if that person or thing is far away. □ *Ever since Carla's boyfriend moved away, she can't stop thinking about him. Absence makes the heart grow fonder.*

absent oneself **from** someone or something to remain away from or avoid someone or some place. □ *Fred absented himself from the meeting, which he was certain would be boring.*

***absent without leave** absent from a military unit without permission; absent from anything without permission. (*AWOL* is an abbreviation. This is a serious offense in the military. *Typically: **be** ~; **go** ~.) □ *The soldier was taken away by the military police because he was absent without leave.*

an absent-minded professor a bumbling professor who overlooks everyday things. □ *Fred is such an absent-minded professor. He'd forget his head if it wasn't screwed on.*

Absolute power corrupts absolutely. *Prov.* One who has total authority is very likely to abuse his position. (This phrase was used by the British historian Lord Acton: "Power tends to corrupt and absolute power corrupts absolutely.") □ *We thought that Johnson would be a responsible mayor, but within a year of taking office, he was as bad as all the rest. Absolute power corrupts absolutely.*

Absolutely not! a strong denial or refusal. (Compare this with Definitely not!) □ *Bob: Can I please have the car again tonight? Father: Absolutely not! You can't have the car every night!*

absolve someone **from** something and **absolve** someone **of** something to prove that an accused person is innocent of something; to demonstrate that someone is not responsible for something. □ *Bob attempted to absolve himself of the crime.*

absorb oneself **in** someone or something *Fig.* [for someone] to become very interested or preoccupied with something or someone else's interests. □ *Tom would often absorb himself in his children's activities on weekends.*

absorb someone **in(to)** something [of a person or a group of people] to include someone in all the activities of the group; to integrate someone into something. □ *The club absorbed the new members into the organization.*

absorb something **in(to)** something [of matter or substance] to draw something into itself. □ *The sponge absorbed all the moisture into its fibers.*

absorb something **with** something to soak up a fluid with something. □ *Henry absorbed the spilled milk with a sponge.*

abstain from something to avoid some activity or the use of some substance, such as alcohol, drugs, sex, or food. □ *They abstained from hard liquor and any other kind of intoxicants.*

abstain from voting to choose not to vote either for or against a proposition or nominee. □ *I will have to abstain from voting since I cannot make up my mind.*

abstract something **from** someone or something to steal something from someone or something. (Formal.) □ *The officer was found guilty of abstracting a rather large amount of money from the company.*

abstract something **from** something to take the important information from a longer document; to extract the essentials or the gist from a piece of complicated writing. □ *Can you abstract a shorter article from this material?*

abut on something [particularly of the edge of an area of land] to meet or touch something along one boundary or at one point. □ *Our land abuts on the shopping center's parking lot.*

abut (up) against something to rest firmly against something solid. □ *The end of the board abutted against the foundation.*

accede to something **1.** to agree to the terms or demands that someone has stated. □ *We cannot accede to your demands.* **2.** to assume a position of power or authority; to begin serving in one's official capacity. □ *She acceded to the office of mayor in January.*

accept someone **as** something to consent to receive or consider someone as a particular type of person or a person who can serve a particular role. □ *Sally finally accepted herself as the only possible peacemaker in the dispute.*

accept something **as** something **1.** to agree that something will serve in payment of a debt or in return for something. □ *This receipt shows that we have accepted your money as payment on your debt.* □ *This money has been accepted as reimbursement for the expenditure.* **2.** to resign [oneself] to something that cannot be changed. □ *I must accept what you say as the final decision.*

accept the blame for something Go to the **blame for** something.

acceptable damage and **acceptable losses** *Euph.* casualties or destruction inflicted by an enemy that is considered minor or tolerable. □ *At present, the enemy's first-strike capability would produce acceptable damage.* □ *The general indicated that the fifty thousand casualties were within the range of acceptable losses.*

acceptable losses Go to previous.

*access to someone or something permission to approach someone or something; the right to use someone or something. (*Typically: **get** ~; **have** ~; **give** someone ~.) □ *Can you get access to a computer?*

accidentally-on-purpose *Inf.* deliberate, but meant to look like an accident. □ *Then, I accidentally-on-purpose spilled water on him.*

Accidents will happen. *Prov.* It is impossible to completely prevent things from going wrong. (Often used to console someone who has made a mistake or caused an accident.) □ *Child: Mommy, I spilled grape juice all over the carpet! Mother: Don't cry, honey. Accidents will happen.* □ *Jill: I'm so embarrassed. I was just tapping on your window to wake you up. I didn't mean to break it. Jane: Accidents will happen.*

acclimate someone or an animal **to** something and **acclimatize** someone or an animal **to** something to cause a person or other living thing to become used to a different climate or environment. □ *We will help acclimate Henry to the new building.* □ *We need to acclimatize the fish to the new aquarium.*

acclimatize someone or an animal **to** something Go to previous.

accommodate oneself **to** something to adapt oneself to something, such as someone else's needs or a new environment. □ *Please try to accommodate yourself to our routine.*

accommodate someone **with** something to provide something special for someone; to do something that provides for someone's needs or desires. □ *We will try to accommodate you with an earlier flight.*

accompanied by something with something extra to go along with something else; with something to complement something else. □ *Dessert was accompanied by a fine white wine.*

accompany someone **on** a journey **1.** [for someone] to go with someone on a trip, journey, adventure, etc. □ *Would you please accompany me on my next trip?* **2.** [for something] to be brought with someone on a trip, journey, etc. □ *My cameras always accompany me on my travels.*

accompany someone **on** a musical instrument to provide complementary instrumental music for someone's musical performance. □ *Sally accompanied the singer on the piano.*

accompany someone **with** something to use a particular musical instrument to play music that goes along with someone else's musical performance. □ *She accompanied Mary with her flute.*

accord with something to agree with or match up with something; to **jibe with** something. □ *Does this accord with what you heard?*

according to all accounts and **by all accounts** from all the reports [that are available]; according to what everyone is saying. □ *According to all accounts, the police were on the scene immediately.* □ *By all accounts, it was a very poor performance.*

according to Hoyle according to the rules; in keeping with the way something is normally done. (Alludes to the rules for playing games. Edmond Hoyle wrote a widely used book with rules for card games. This expression is usually used for something other than games.) □ *That's wrong. According to Hoyle, this is the way to do it.*

according to one's **own lights** according to the way one believes; according to the way one's conscience or inclinations lead one. □ *John may have been wrong, but he did what he did according to his own lights.*

according to someone or something as said or indicated by someone or something. □ *According to the weather forecast, this should be a beautiful day.*

according to something in proportion to something. □ *You will get paid according to the number of hours that you work.*

account for someone or something to know the state of or whereabouts of someone or something. (Usually in reference to some person or thing placed in one's charge.) □ *They cannot account for three of the passengers.*

account for something to explain something. □ *Your explanation accounts for everything that has happened.*

A

accredit something **to** someone to assign or attribute a deed to someone; to assign or attribute praise to someone. (Often passive.) □ *We can accredit this great success to Fred and his committee.*

accrue to someone or something [used of interest paid on money] to be credited to an account or to a person's account. □ *Interest will accrue to your account as long as the account is active.*

accuse someone **of** something to charge someone with a crime, a violation of rules or instructions, or doing something wrong. □ *Please don't accuse me of forgetting to lock the door.*

accustom someone **to** someone or something to get someone used to someone or something. □ *I think we can accustom Fred to the new rules without difficulty.*

***accustomed to** someone or something and ***accustomed to** doing something used to someone or something; used to or in the habit of doing something. (*Typically: **be** ~; **become** ~; **grow** ~.) □ *The children are accustomed to eating late in the evening.*

ace in the hole and someone's **ace in the hole** *Fig.* something important held in reserve. □ *The twenty-dollar bill I keep in my shoe is my ace in the hole.*

ace in(to something**)** to be lucky in getting admitted to something. □ *I aced into the history class at the last minute.*

ace out to be fortunate or lucky. □ *Freddy aced out at the dentist's office with only one cavity.*

ace out (of something**)** to get out of something through luck; to evade or avoid something narrowly. □ *I just aced out of having to take the math test!*

ace someone **out†** to maneuver someone out; to win out over someone. □ *Martha aced out Rebecca to win the first place trophy.*

ache for someone or something and **hurt for** someone or something *Fig.* to desire someone or something very much. (So much that it "hurts.") □ *Jim ached for the sight of Mary, whom he loved deeply.*

Achilles' heel *Fig.* a weak point or fault in someone or something otherwise perfect or excellent. (From the legend of Greek hero Achilles, who had only one vulnerable part of his body, his heel; as an infant his mother had held him by one heel to dip him in the River Styx to make him invulnerable.) □ *He was very brave, but fear of spiders was his Achilles' heel.*

aching heart *Fig.* the feeling of pain because of love that is lost or has faded away. (Described as being in the heart, where love is said to reside.) □ *I try to tell my aching heart that I don't love him.*

the **acid test** *Fig.* a test whose findings are beyond doubt or dispute. □ *The senator doesn't look too popular just now, but the acid test will be if he gets reelected.*

acknowledge someone **as** something to agree or announce publicly that a person holds a particular office or station, or that a person has particular qualities. □ *She found it difficult to acknowledge herself as a failure.*

acknowledge someone **to be right** to admit or state that someone is correct about something. □ *Bill said that the car was useless, and the mechanic acknowledged him to be right.*

acknowledge something **as** something to agree or announce publicly that something is as previously stated. □ *The president acknowledged the statement as the truth.*

acknowledge (the) receipt of something to report receiving something, such as a package, letter, or notice. □ *The company acknowledged receipt of the merchandise I returned.*

acquaint someone **with** something to introduce someone to an unfamiliar thing; to become familiar with something; to get to know something; to tell someone the facts [about someone or something]. (See also **acquainted with** someone; **acquainted with** something.) □ *It took a month for the new attorney to acquaint herself with the facts in the case.*

***acquainted with** someone [of a person] known to someone; [of a person] having been introduced to someone. (*Typically: **be** ~; **become** ~; **get** ~.) □ *We are only acquainted with each other. We are certainly not what you would call close friends.*

***acquainted with** something familiar with something; able to understand or recognize something. (*Typically: **be** ~; **become** ~; **get** ~.) □ *Tom is fully acquainted with the way we do things.*

acquiesce to someone or something to give in to someone or someone's wishes; to agree, perhaps reluctantly, to someone's ideas or requests. □ *We are willing to acquiesce to your demands.*

acquire a taste for something Go to a **taste for** something.

acquit someone **of** something to establish someone's innocence of a criminal charge or the blame for some wrongdoing. □ *The investigator acquitted Wally of the charges.*

across the board *Fig.* [distributed] equally for everyone or everything. □ *The school board raised the pay of all the teachers across the board.*

act as one Go to **as one**.

act as someone to perform in the capacity of someone, temporarily or permanently; to serve in some special capacity, possibly temporarily. □ *This is Mr. Smith. He'll act as manager from now on.*

act for someone **1.** to represent someone in an official capacity; to represent the interests of someone. □ *Don't worry. I am acting for the owner. I am his real estate agent.* **2.** to take action when the proper person fails to take action. □ *I had to act for her since she was out of town.*

act full of oneself Go to **full of** oneself.

act high-and-mighty Go to **high-and-mighty**.

act in earnest Go to **in earnest**.

act like a cold fish Go to a **cold fish**.

act like oneself **again** Go to oneself **again**.

an **act of faith** an act or deed demonstrating religious faith; an act or deed showing trust in someone or something. □ *For him to trust you with his safety was a real act of faith.*

an **act of God** an occurrence or an event for which no human is responsible; an act of nature such as a storm, an earthquake, or a wildfire. □ *Will your insurance com-*

pany pay for damage caused by earthquakes and other acts of God?

an **act of war 1.** *Lit.* an international act of warlike violence for which war is considered a suitable response. □ *To bomb a ship is an act of war.* **2.** *Fig.* any hostile act between two people. □ *"You just broke my stereo!" yelled John. "That's an act of war!"*

act out to behave badly. (Usually used to describe young people.) □ *Your son has been acting out in the classroom, and his teacher feels that professional intervention is desirable.*

act something **out**[†] **1.** to perform in real life a role that one has imagined in a fantasy. □ *When I was onstage, I was really acting an old fantasy out.* □ *I acted out an old fantasy onstage.* **2.** to convert one's bad feelings into action rather than words. □ *Don't act your aggressions out on me!* □ *She acted out her aggression.* **3.** to demonstrate or communicate something through gestures or action rather than words. □ *Act your request out, if you can't say it.* □ *She had a sore throat and had to act out her request.*

act tough on someone Go to **tough on** someone.

act up [for a thing or a person] to behave badly. □ *This car is acting up again.*

act (up)on something **1.** to take action on a particular problem. (*Upon* is more formal and less commonly used than *on*.) □ *I will act on this immediately.* **2.** to take action because of some special information. □ *The police refused to act upon his complaint because he was an ex-convict.* **3.** to perform on something, usually the stage (in a theater). □ *Ken has never acted on the stage or in front of a camera.*

act within one's **rights** Go to **within** one's **rights**.

act young at heart Go to **young at heart**.

Act your age! Behave more maturely! (A rebuke for someone who is acting childish. Often said to a child who is acting like an even younger child.) □ *Child: Aw, come on! Let me see your book! Mary: Be quiet and act your age. Don't be such a baby!*

Actions speak louder than words. *Prov. Cliché* What you do is more significant than what you say. □ *You keep saying that you'll do your fair share of the housework. Remember that actions speak louder than words.*

adapt someone or something **to** something to cause someone or something to change, adjust to, or get used to something else. □ *Can't you adapt yourself to my way of doing things?*

adapt something **for** something to change or alter something for use with something else. □ *Has this furnace been adapted for natural gas?*

adapt something **from** something to derive something from something else; to create by modifying something else. □ *I adapted my new musical from a novel.*

adapt something **to** something to convert something to fit or work with something else. □ *We converted our furnace to natural gas.*

adapt to something to adapt or get used to someone or something. □ *Please try to adapt to our routine.*

add fuel to the fire and **add fuel to the flame** *Fig.* to make a problem worse; to say or do something that makes a bad situation worse; to make an angry person get even angrier. (Alludes to causing a flame to grow larger when fuel is added.) □ *Shouting at a crying child just adds fuel to the fire.*

add fuel to the flame Go to previous.

add insult to injury *Fig. Cliché* to make a bad situation worse; to hurt the feelings of a person who has already been hurt. □ *First, the basement flooded, and then, to add insult to injury, a pipe burst in the kitchen.* □ *My car barely started this morning, and to add insult to injury, I got a flat tire in the driveway.*

add something **into** something and **add** something **in**[†] to introduce something into something else. □ *Now, add the eggs into the mixture.* □ *Add in some more eggs.*

add (something) **on(to)** something and **add** (something) **on**[†] to extend something by providing more (of something). (This use of *on* with *add* is colloquial.) □ *You added nearly one thousand dollars onto the total.* □ *You added on a thousand dollars to the total!* □ *You added too much on.*

add (something) **to** something to increase the intensity or amount of something by giving more (of something) to it. □ *You added too much sugar to my coffee.*

add something **together** to sum or total two or more things. □ *Add these two together and tell me what you get.*

add something **up**[†] to sum or total a set of figures. (See also **add up (to** something).) □ *Please add these figures up again.* □ *I didn't add up these figures!*

add up (to something) **1.** *Lit.* [for a set of figures] to equal a total. □ *These figures don't add up to the right total!* **2.** *Fig.* [for facts or explanations] to make sense. (Considering facts as if they were figures.) □ *Your explanation just doesn't add up!*

add up to the same thing Go to **amount to the same thing**.

addict someone **to** something to cause someone to become habituated to something, usually alcohol or some another drug. □ *The hospital personnel were thought to have addicted John to morphine.* □ *She ended up addicting herself to the substance.*

address comments or remarks **to** someone to say something directly to a specific person or group of persons. (See also **address** oneself **to** someone; **address** oneself **to** something.) □ *George addressed his remarks to everyone.*

address oneself **to** someone to speak directly to a particular person, rather than someone else. □ *I did not address myself to you!*

address oneself **to** something to turn one's complete attention to something, such as a problem or an issue. (See also **address** something **to** someone.) □ *Please address yourself to these current, pressing problems.*

address someone **as** a specific title or attribute **1.** to talk to or write to a person, using a particular title. □ *They addressed Abraham Lincoln as "Mr. President."* **2.** to treat a person you are talking with in a particular manner. □ *You should address him as your equal.*

address something **to** someone to write someone's name and address on an envelope, package, letter, etc. □ *Gilbert addressed the envelope to Walter.*

A

adhere to something **1.** *Lit.* to stick to something. □ *The stamp won't adhere to the envelope.* **2.** *Fig.* to follow or "stick to" a particular course of action, plan, or set of beliefs. □ *If you don't adhere to the proper routine, you will confuse the other workers.*

adjourn for a time to bring a meeting to a temporary close so the participants can take part in some other activity. □ *We must adjourn for the day.*

adjourn to some place to bring a meeting to a temporary close so the participants can move to another place (where the meeting will be started again). □ *We adjourned to the sitting room.*

adjust (oneself) to someone or something to make changes in one's opinion or attitude toward someone or something, such as a change in one's life or environment. □ *Can't you adjust yourself to your new office?*

adjust something **to** something to make something fit something else; to alter something to make it suitable for something else. □ *The builder adjusted the plans for the new house to the requirements of the fire marshal.*

administer something **to** someone or an animal to present or apply something to a person or an animal. □ *The vet administered the drug to the cow.*

admire someone **for** something to have a positive feeling toward someone because of something. □ *I really admire you for your courage.*

admire to do something *Rur.* to want to do something, to be happy to do something. □ *He asked her to the dance. She said she would admire to go with him.*

admit someone **(in)to** some place to allow someone to enter some place. □ *They refused to admit us into the theater.*

admit something **into** something to allow something to be introduced into something else. □ *You cannot admit this document into the body of evidence!*

admit something **to** someone to confess something to someone. □ *Harry admitted his error to his uncle.*

admit to something to acknowledge or confess something; to acknowledge or confess to having done something. □ *Max would not admit to anything.*

admonish someone **for** something to warn or scold someone mildly for doing something. □ *The nurse admonished the patient for not eating her dinner.*

adopt someone **as** something to choose someone as something. □ *The committee will adopt Jane as its candidate.*

adopt something **as** something to take on something, such as a policy or principle, as one's own. □ *I will adopt this policy as my own.*

adore someone **for** doing something to be in awe of someone for doing something well. □ *Everyone adores Sally for her wonderful sense of humor.*

adore someone **for** having something to be in awe of someone because of a particular trait or feature. □ *Robert adores Mary for her smiling eyes.*

adorn someone or something **with** something to decorate or ornament someone or something with something. □ *They adorned the room with garlands of flowers.*

adulterate something **with** something to dilute or taint something with some other substance. □ *They adulterated the wine with some sort of drug.*

advance something **to** someone or something **(against** something**)** to make an early payment of a sum of money promised or owed to a person or organization. □ *We advanced the money to Tom against his next month's salary.*

advance to(ward) someone or something to move forward in the direction of someone or something. □ *The line of people slowly advanced to the door of the theater.*

advance (up)on someone or something to move toward someone or something. (Typically in military maneuvers or in team sports, such as American football. *Upon* is more formal and less commonly used than *on*.) □ *They advanced upon the town, firing their rifles and shouting.*

advanced in years Go to up in years.

*the **advantage of** someone and *the **advantage over** someone; *an **advantage over** someone; *the **advantage over** someone; *the **edge on** someone; *the **edge over** someone a position superior to that of someone else; a status wherein one controls or has superiority or authority over someone else. (*Typically: **get** ~; **give** someone ~; **have** ~.) □ *She'd gotten an advantage over me at the start of the competition.* □ *I got an edge on Sally, too, and she came in second.*

advertise for someone or something to advertise one's intention to purchase something or hire a particular type of person. □ *Did you advertise for a new receptionist?*

advertise something **for** a price to make known by public notice that something is to be sold at a particular price. □ *Is this the one that was advertised for a dollar?*

advertise something **for** something to make known by public notice, such as broadcast or print notice, that something is available for purchase or rent. □ *Was this apartment advertised for rent?*

advise against something to suggest that something not be done. □ *Lisa always advises against hasty actions.*

advise someone **about** someone or something to inform someone about someone or something; to counsel someone about someone or something. □ *Bill needs to advise the committee about Karen's request.*

advise someone **against** doing something to encourage or counsel someone not to do something. □ *I advised Bill against quitting his job.*

advise someone **of** something to inform someone of specific facts or some other information. □ *I hope you will advise Larry of the details of the proposal.*

advise someone **on** someone or something to provide someone with specific advice about someone or something. □ *Would you please advise me on what kind of computer to buy?*

affiliate (someone or something**) to** someone or something and **affiliate (**someone or something**) with** someone or something to cause a person or thing to be associated with some other person or thing. □ *He did not want to affiliate his club to the other clubs.* □ *We tried to affiliate John with other people who shared his interests.*

affiliate (someone or something) with someone or something Go to **affiliate** (someone or something) **to** someone or something.

affinity for someone or something a strong preference for something; a strong liking for something. □ *Mary's affinity for classical music accounts for her large collection of recordings.*

affix one's **signature to** something to sign one's name on something. □ *I affixed my signature to each of the documents.*

affix something **to** someone or something to fasten or attach something to someone or something. □ *Please affix these tags to your luggage.*

afflict someone **with** someone to burden someone with an annoying person. □ *I was foolish enough to afflict myself with my young cousin for the weekend.*

afflict someone **with** something **1.** *Lit.* to cause someone to suffer from a disease or disability. □ *The virus has afflicted everyone in the valley.* **2.** *Fig.* to burden someone with trouble. □ *We were afflicted with all the worry that comes with raising a teenager.*

afraid of one's **own shadow** *Fig.* easily frightened; always frightened, timid, or suspicious. (An exaggeration.) □ *After Tom was robbed, he was even afraid of his own shadow.*

after a fashion in a manner that is just barely adequate; poorly. □ *He thanked me—after a fashion—for my help.* □ *Oh, yes, I can swim, after a fashion.*

After a storm comes a calm. and **After the storm comes a calm.; The calm after a storm.** *Prov.* Things are often calm after an upheaval. □ *Jill: I can't believe how peaceful the office is today, when yesterday everyone was either being fired or threatening to quit. Jane: After a storm comes a calm.*

after all 1. anyway; in spite of what had been decided. (Often refers to a change in plans or a reversal of plans.) □ *It looks like Tom will go to law school after all.* **2.** recalling or considering the fact that. □ *Don't punish Tommy! After all, he's only three years old.*

after all is said and done *Cliché* when everything is settled or concluded; finally. □ *After all is said and done, it will turn out just as I said.*

after hours after the regular closing time; after any normal or regular time, such as one's bedtime. □ *John got a job sweeping floors in the library after hours.*

*after someone or something **1.** *Lit.* following someone or something. (*Typically: be ~; come ~.*) □ *Tom comes after Mary in the line.* **2.** *Fig.* in pursuit of someone or something. (*Typically: be ~; chase ~; run ~.*) □ *The dog is after a rabbit.*

after the fact after something has happened; after something, such as a crime, has taken place. (Originally a legal phrase.) □ *John is always making excuses after the fact.*

after the fashion of someone or something and **after the style of** someone or something in the manner or style of someone or something. □ *She walks down the street after the fashion of a grand lady.* □ *The parish church was built after the style of a French cathedral.*

after the style of someone or something Go to **after the fashion of** someone or something.

After while(, crocodile). *Inf.* Good-bye till later.; See you later. (The word *crocodile* is used only for the sake of the rhyme. It is the response to **See you later, alligator**.) □ *Mary: See you later, alligator. Bill: After while, crocodile.*

After you. Please go ahead of me.; Please pass through ahead of me. □ *Bob stepped back and made a motion with his hand indicating that Mary should go first. "After you," smiled Bob.*

again and again repeatedly; again and even more [times]. □ *He knocked on the door again and again until I finally answered.*

Again(, please). Say it one more time, please. □ *Tom: I need some money. I'll pay you back. Bill (pretending not to hear): Again, please. Tom: I said I need some money. How many times do I have to say it?*

against all odds despite very low probability; in a most unlikely way. □ *Against all odds, she managed to win the trophy.*

*against someone or something **1.** in opposition to someone or something; in competition with someone or something. (*Typically: be ~; run ~; stand ~.*) □ *I am against everything you stand for.* □ *She ran against me in the election.* **2.** to the disadvantage of someone or something; in opposition to someone or something. (*Typically: be ~; go ~; run ~; turn ~.*) □ *When did the trial go against us?*

against someone's **will** without a person's consent or agreement. □ *You cannot force me to come with you against my will!*

against the clock *Fig.* in a race with time; in a great hurry to get something done before a particular time. □ *In a race against the clock, they rushed the accident victim to the hospital.*

*against the grain 1. *Lit.* across the alignment of the fibers of a piece of wood. (*Typically: be ~; cut ~; go ~; run ~; saw ~.*) □ *You sawed it wrong. You sawed against the grain when you should have cut across it.* □ *You went against the grain and made a mess of your sanding.* **2.** *Fig.* running counter to one's feelings or ideas. (*Typically: be ~; go ~.*) □ *The idea of my actually taking something that is not mine goes against the grain.*

Age before beauty. a jocular and slightly rude way of encouraging someone to go ahead of oneself; a comical, teasing, and slightly grudging way of indicating that someone else should or can go first. □ *"No, no. Please, you take the next available seat," smiled Tom. "Age before beauty, you know."*

The **age of miracles is past.** *Prov.* Miracles do not happen nowadays. □ *I'm afraid this old vacuum cleaner can't be fixed. The age of miracles is past.*

age out (of something) [for an adult] to grow [mentally or in years] out of certain behavior or out of a group or classification that is based on age. (Jargon.) □ *Most of them tend to age out at about 35.*

agitate against someone or something to stir up active dissatisfaction about someone or something. □ *The students were agitating against the closing of the old cafeteria.*

A

agitate for something to stir up active support for something. □ *The committee agitated for a change, but nothing was done.*

agonize (oneself) over someone or something to fret or anguish about someone or something. □ *Now, now, don't agonize yourself over the situation. Time cures all.*

agree to disagree *Cliché* [for two or more parties] to calmly agree not to come to an agreement in a dispute. □ *We have accomplished nothing except that we agree to disagree.*

agree to something to consent to something; to allow something to be done; to approve something. □ *If you don't agree to my leaving early, I'll just do it anyway.*

agree (up)on someone or something to agree to the choice of someone or something. □ *Let's try to agree upon a date.*

agree with someone **1.** *Lit.* to hold the same opinion or judgment as someone else. □ *I simply do not agree with you!* **2.** *Fig.* [for something] to be acceptable to someone as food. (Usually negative, referring to the disagreeable consequences of eating bad food.) □ *Onions do not agree with me.*

agree (with someone**) (about** someone or something**)** and **agree (with** someone**) ((up)on** someone or something**)** [for two or more parties] to agree with one another about the facts concerning someone or something. □ *I agree with you about Judy; she is brilliant.* □ *He agreed with Sam upon a time for the meeting.*

agree with something **1.** *Fig.* [for something] to look good or go well with something else. □ *This dress does not agree with these shoes, does it?* **2.** *Fig.* [for something] to be in accord with something else. □ *Your analysis agrees with mine.*

agree (with something**) (in** something**)** [for grammatical features] to match or go together with other grammatical features. □ *The subject and the verb agree in number.*

(Ah) shucks! and **(Ah) shoot!** *Rur.* Darn! (A mild oath.) □ *Ah, shucks! I forgot to call Grandma.* □ *Tom: We can't get chocolate ice cream. The store's all out. Jane: Shucks.* □ *Ah, shoot! I missed my favorite TV show.*

*ahead of one's **time** *Fig.* having ideas or attitudes that are too advanced to be acceptable in the present. (*Typically: **be** ~; **think** ~.) □ *Sue's grandmother was ahead of her time in wanting to study medicine.*

*ahead of schedule *Fig.* having done something before the time given on a schedule or before the expected time. (*Typically: **be** ~; **finish** ~.) □ *I want to be able to finish the job ahead of schedule.*

*ahead (of someone or something**)** farther forward than someone or something. (*Typically: **be** ~; **get** ~; **keep** ~; **remain** ~; **stay** ~.) □ *I managed to get ahead of everyone else in line and get tickets for everyone.* □ *Try to stay ahead of that big truck we just passed.*

*ahead of something ahead or on target with one's work schedule or responsibilities. (*Typically: **be** ~; **get** ~; **keep** ~; **remain** ~; **stay** ~.) □ *By the end of the week, I usually can get ahead of my duties, but not by much.* □ *Jerry can't seem to get ahead of his work.*

*ahead of the game being early; having an advantage in a competitive situation; having done more than neces-sary. (*Typically: **be** ~; **get** ~; **keep** ~; **remain** ~; **stay** ~.) □ *Without the full cooperation of my office staff, I find it hard to stay ahead of the game.* □ *If being ahead of the game is important to you and to your business, lease a mobile phone from us.*

*ahead of time beforehand; before the announced time. (*Typically: **arrive** ~; **get there** ~; **leave** ~; **show up** ~.) □ *If you show up ahead of time, you will have to wait.* □ *Be there ahead of time if you want to get a good seat.*

*(a)hold of someone or something **1.** *Lit.* [get/have] a grasp of someone or something. (*Typically: **get** ~; **have** ~; **take** ~.) □ *I got hold of him and dragged him back from the edge just in time.* □ *I took ahold of his hand and held on tight.* **2.** *Fig.* [get/have] contact with someone or something; [get/have] the location of someone or something. (*Typically: **get** ~.) □ *I got hold of a replacement part in Peoria. They are shipping it to us today.* □ *Try to get ahold of a plumber, would you?* **3.** *Fig.* [get/have] contact with someone or a group on the telephone. (*Typically: **get** ~.) □ *I got hold of her just as she was going out the door.* □ *I was able to get ahold of the factory and cancel the order.*

aid and abet someone *Cliché* to help someone; to incite someone to do something, possibly something that is wrong. (Originally a legal phrase.) □ *He was scolded for aiding and abetting the boys who were fighting.*

aid someone **in** doing something to help someone do something. □ *He aided her in fixing up the back bedroom.*

aid someone **in** something to help someone in some kind of trouble. □ *Will you aid me in this difficulty?*

aim for something and **aim at** something to strive toward a particular goal; to direct oneself or one's energies toward something. □ *You should aim for success.* □ *Aim at getting this done on time.*

aim for the sky Go to reach for the sky.

Aim for the stars! and **Reach for the stars!** Aspire to something!; Set one's goals high! □ *Aim for the stars, son! Don't settle for second best.* □ *Set your sights high. Reach for the stars!*

aim something **at** someone or something to point or direct something at someone or something. □ *Wally aimed the hose at Sarah and tried to soak her.*

aim to do something *Rur.* to intend to do something. □ *I didn't aim to hurt your feelings, sugar, you know I didn't.*

ain't fittin' to roll with a pig *Rur.* is or are filthy or uncouth. □ *After a day's work in the hot sun, Clyde ain't fittin' to roll with a pig.*

ain't got a grain of sense and **ain't got a lick of sense** *Rur.* is or are foolish. □ *Mary spends money like there's no tomorrow. She sure ain't got a grain of sense.* □ *I wouldn't trust Jim to take care of my kids. He ain't got a lick of sense.*

ain't got a lick of sense Go to previous.

ain't got the brains God gave a squirrel and **ain't got the sense God gave geese** *Rur.* is or are very foolish. □ *There goes John, running around barefooted in the snow. He ain't got the brains God gave a squirrel.* □ *No use trying to explain anything to Jane. She ain't got the sense God gave geese.*

ain't got the sense God gave geese Go to previous.

Ain't it the truth? *Rur.* or *Jocular* That is true.; Isn't that true? (Used to agree with a statement someone has made.) □ *Jane: I swear, life can be a trial sometimes. Bill: Yes, Lordy. Ain't it the truth?*

ain't particular 1. *Rur.* doesn't or don't care. □ *Tom: Would you rather have ice cream or cheese on your apple pie? Mary: Whatever you're having. I ain't particular.* **2.** *Rur.* doesn't or don't have a preference. □ *Jane ain't particular. She'll use any old brand of soap.*

*the air *Fig.* a dismissal. (*Typically: **get** ~; **give** someone ~.) □ *Whenever I get around Tom, I end up getting the air.*

air one's **belly** *Fig. Sl.* to empty one's stomach; to vomit. □ *I had a bad case of food poisoning and was airing my belly for most of the night.*

air one's **dirty linen in public** and **wash** one's **dirty linen in public** *Fig.* to discuss private or embarrassing matters in public, especially when quarreling. (This *linen* refers to sheets and tablecloths or other soiled cloth.) □ *They are arguing again. Why must they always air their dirty linen in public?* □ *She will talk to anyone about her problems. Why does she wash her dirty linen in public?*

air one's **grievances** *Fig.* to complain; to make a public complaint. □ *I know how you feel, John, but it isn't necessary to air your grievances over and over.*

air one's **lungs 1.** *Rur.* to swear. □ *Don't pay those old cowboys no mind. They're just airin' the lungs.* □ *I could tell John was working on his old car 'cause I could hear him out in the garage, airin' his lungs.* **2.** *Rur.* to talk, gossip, or brag. □ *The ladies just love to air their lungs whenever they get together.*

air one's **paunch** *Sl.* to vomit. □ *He got so nauseous that he spent much of the night airing his paunch.*

air one's **pores** *Sl.* to undress oneself; to become naked. □ *Me and Wilbur, that's my brother, both fell in the creek and had to air our pores a while so our pants could dry out.*

air out [for something] to remain in the fresh air and become fresher. □ *The pillows are airing out on the balcony.*

air something **out**† to freshen something up by placing it in the open air; to freshen a room by letting outside air move through it. □ *I'll have to air out the car. Someone has been smoking in it.*

alert someone **to** something to make someone aware of trouble or potential trouble. □ *The auditors alerted us to some problems with the accounts.*

alienate someone **from** someone or something to cause someone to feel negative about someone or something. □ *The teacher alienated the entire class from the subject of calculus.*

alight from something to get off something; to get down off something. □ *Almost three hundred people alighted from the plane.*

alight (up)on someone or something to land on something; [for a bird or other flying animal] to come to rest on something. (*Upon* is more formal than *on*.) □ *A small bird alighted on the branch directly over my head.* □ *It alighted upon the branch and began to sing.*

align oneself **with** someone or something *Fig.* to bring oneself into agreement with someone or someone's ideas; to associate oneself with someone or someone's cause. □ *She sought to align herself with the older members.*

align something **with** something to adjust, straighten, or arrange something in reference to something else. □ *Try to align this piece with the one next to it.*

*alike as (two) peas in a pod very similar. (Compare this with like (two) peas in a pod. *Also: **as** ~.) □ *These two books are as alike as peas in a pod.*

alive and kicking and **alive and well** *Fig.* well and healthy. □ *Jane: How is Bill since his illness last month? Mary: Oh; he's alive and kicking.* □ *The last time I saw Tom, he was alive and well.*

alive and well Go to previous.

alive with people or things *Fig.* covered with, filled with, or active with people or creatures. □ *Look! Ants everywhere. The floor is alive with ants!*

all agog surprised and amazed. □ *He sat there, all agog, as the master of ceremonies read his name as the winner of first prize.*

all and sundry *Cliché* everyone; one and all. □ *Cold drinks were served to all and sundry.*

all around Robin Hood's barn going somewhere by an indirect route; going way out of the way [to get somewhere]; by a long and circuitous route. □ *We had to go all around Robin Hood's barn to get to the little town.*

all at once 1. *Lit.* all at the same time. □ *The entire group spoke all at once.* **2.** *Fig.* suddenly. □ *All at once the little girl fell out of her chair.*

(all) at sea (about something**)** *Fig.* to be confused; to be lost and bewildered. (Alludes to being lost at sea.) □ *When it comes to higher math, John is totally at sea.*

*(all) balled up troubled; confused; in a mess. (*Typically: **be** ~; **get** ~.) □ *John is all balled up because his car was stolen.*

(all) beer and skittles all fun and pleasure; easy and pleasant. (Skittles is the game of ninepins, a game similar to bowling. Fixed phrase.) □ *For Sam, college was beer and skittles. He wasted a lot of time and money.*

all better (now) improved or cured. (Juvenile.) □ *I fell off my tricycle and bumped my knee. Mommy kissed it, and it's all better now.*

all by one's **lonesome** *Rur.* all alone; by oneself. □ *Mary's folks went out and left her all by her lonesome.*

All cats are gray in the dark. *Prov.* When in the dark, appearances are meaningless, since everything is hard to see or unseen. □ *I don't care if my date is ugly. All cats are gray in the dark.*

all day long throughout the day; during the entire day. □ *We waited for you at the station all day long.*

*(all) dolled up *Fig.* dressed up and well-groomed. (Usually used of females. *Typically: **be** ~; **get** ~.) □ *I have to get all dolled up for the dance tonight.*

*(all) dressed up dressed in one's best clothes; dressed formally. (*Typically: **be** ~; **get** ~; **get** someone ~.) □ *I really hate to get all dressed up just to go somewhere to eat.*

A

all dressed up and nowhere to go and **all dressed up with nowhere to go** completely ready for something that has been postponed or has failed to materialize. (May be literal or figurative.) □ *Tom: I just heard that your company is closed today. Fred: Gee, I'm all dressed up and nowhere to go.* □ *The space shot was cancelled, so all the astronauts are all dressed up with nowhere to go.*

all ears *Fig.* listening eagerly and carefully. □ *Well, hurry up and tell me. I'm all ears.*

all eyes and ears *Fig.* listening and watching eagerly and carefully. □ *Be careful what you say. The children are all eyes and ears.* □ *Tell us quick. We are all eyes and ears!*

(all) for someone or something *Fig.* (completely) in favor of someone or something; supporting someone or something. □ *I'm all for your candidacy.* □ *I'm for the incumbent in the upcoming election.*

(all) for the best good in spite of the way it seems; better than you think or than it appears to be. (Often said when someone dies after a painful illness.) □ *I'm very sorry to hear of the death of your aunt. Perhaps it's for the best.* □ *I didn't get into the college I wanted, but I couldn't afford it anyway. It's probably all for the best.*

all gone used up; finished; over with. □ *Oh, the strawberry jelly is all gone.* □ *We used to have wonderful parties, but those days are all gone.*

All good things must (come to an) end. *Prov.* All experiences, even pleasant ones, eventually end. □ *It's time to leave the party, honey. All good things must end.* □ *We've had a lovely visit, but all good things must come to an end.*

all hell broke loose all sorts of wild or terrible things happened. □ *When the boss left early for the weekend, all hell broke loose.*

***(all) het up** *Rur.* very angry or upset. (All "heated" up. *Typically: **get** ~; **be** ~.) □ *The boss got all het up when I said my project would be late.* □ *Jane gets real het up when folks tease her about her freckles.*

***all hours (of the day and night)** *Fig.* very late in the night or very early in the morning. (*Typically: **until** ~; **till** ~; **at** ~.) □ *Why do you always stay out until all hours of the day and night?* □ *I like to stay out till all hours.*

all in completely tired. □ *I'm all in. I need some rest.* □ *After their 10-mile hike the campers were all in and very hungry.*

all in a day's work part of what is expected; typical or normal. □ *I don't particularly like to cook, but it's all in a day's work.* □ *Cleaning up after other people is all in a day's work for a busboy.*

all in all considering everything that has happened; in summary and in spite of any unpleasantness. □ *All in all, it was a very good party.* □ *All in all, I'm glad that I visited New York City.*

all in good time at some future time; in the near future; in good time; soon. (This phrase is used to encourage people to be patient and wait quietly.) □ *When will the baby be born? All in good time.* □ *Mary: I'm starved! When will Bill get here with the pizza? Tom: All in good time, Mary, all in good time.*

(all) in one breath *Fig.* spoken very rapidly, usually while one is very excited. □ *Ann said all in one breath, "Hurry, quick! The parade is coming!"* □ *Jane was in a play, and she was so excited that she said her whole speech in one breath.*

all in one piece *Fig.* safely; without damage. □ *Her son came home from school all in one piece, even though he had been in a fight.* □ *The package was handled carelessly, but the vase inside arrived all in one piece.*

(all) in the family restricted to one's own family, as with private or embarrassing information. □ *Don't tell anyone else. Please keep it all in the family.* □ *He only told his brother because he wanted it to remain in the family.*

(all) joking aside and **(all) kidding aside** being serious for a moment; in all seriousness. □ *I know I laugh at him but, joking aside, he's a very clever scientist.* □ *I know I threatened to leave and go round the world, but, joking aside, I do need a vacation.*

(all) kidding aside Go to previous.

***all kinds of** someone or something *Fig.* a great number of people or things; a great amount of something, especially money. (*Typically: **be** ~; **have** ~.) □ *There were all kinds of people there, probably thousands.* □ *The Smith family has all kinds of money.*

all manner of someone or something *Fig.* all types of people or things. □ *We saw all manner of people there. They came from every country in the world.* □ *They were selling all manner of things in the country store.*

all my eye (and Betty Martin) nonsense; not true. □ *Jane is always talking about her wonderful childhood, but it's all my eye.* □ *He pretends to have great plans, but they're all my eye and Betty Martin.*

all night long throughout the whole night. □ *I couldn't sleep all night long.* □ *John was sick all night long.*

all oak and iron bound and ***sound as a barrel** *Rur.* in good health; feeling good. (*Also: **as** ~.) □ *Tom: How are you today? Bill: All oak and iron bound, thank you.* □ *Jane made a wonderful recovery from her surgery, and now she's as sound as a barrel.*

all of a size *Rur.* all of the same size. □ *I tried to pick out the biggest tomato, but they were pretty much all of a size.* □ *The houses in that neighborhood are all of a size.*

all of a sudden suddenly. □ *All of a sudden lightning struck the tree we were sitting under.* □ *I felt a sharp pain in my side all of a sudden.*

all or nothing 1. *Lit.* everything or nothing at all. □ *Sally would not accept only part of the money. She wanted all or nothing.* □ *I can't bargain over trifles. I will have to have all or nothing.* **2.** *Fig.* [the best] time to choose to do something or not to do it. □ *It was all or nothing. Tim had to jump off the truck or risk drowning when the truck went into the water.* □ *Jane stood at the door of the airplane and checked her parachute. It was all or nothing now. She had to jump or be looked upon as a coward.*

all over 1. and **(all) over with** finished. □ *Dinner is all over. I'm sorry you didn't get any.* □ *It's all over. He's dead now.* **2.** everywhere. □ *Oh, I just itch all over.* □ *She's spreading the rumor all over.*

(all) over again starting over completely again; going through something completely yet another time. □ *Do I have to go through this all over again?* □ *Please start over again for those who came in late.*

all over creation and **all over hell and half of Georgia; all over hell and gone; to hell and gone** *Rur.* everywhere. □ *Little Billy had his toys spread out all over creation. It took forever to clean up after him.* □ *They're looking all over creation, trying to find the missing man.* □ *Tom has traveled all over hell and half of Georgia trying to find the man who done him wrong.*

all over hell and gone Go to previous.

all over hell and half of Georgia Go to all over creation.

*all over (some place**)** found in every place; available in all locations. (*Typically: **be** ~; **spread** ~.) □ *The window shattered and shards of glass were all over the place.* □ *There are ants all over the cake!*

all over the earth and **all over the world** *Fig.* everywhere. □ *Gravity acts the same all over the earth.* □ *Human nature is the same all over the world.*

all over the world Go to previous.

all over town 1. *Lit.* in many places in town. □ *Our dog got loose and ran all over town.* □ *Jane looked all over town for a dress to wear to the party.* **2.** *Fig.* known to many; widely known. □ *Now keep this a secret. I don't want it all over town.* □ *In a short time the secret was known all over town.*

all right 1. an indication of agreement or acquiescence. (Often pronounced *aright* in familiar conversation.) □ *Father: Do it now, before you forget. Bill: All right.* □ *Tom: Please remember to bring me back a pizza. Sally: All right, but I get some of it.* **2.** *Inf.* a shout of agreement or encouragement. (Usually **All right!**) □ *Alice: Come on, let's give Sally some encouragement. Fred: All right, Sally! Keep it up! You can do it!* □ *"That's the way to go! All right!" shouted various members of the audience.* **3.** well, good, or okay, but not excellent. (This phrase has all the uses that *okay* has.) □ *I was a little sick, but now I'm all right.* □ *His work is all right, but nothing to brag about.* □ *All right, it's time to go.* **4.** beyond a doubt; as the evidence shows. □ *The dog's dead all right. It hasn't moved at all.* □ *The train's late all right. There must be a problem up the line.*

All right for you! That's the end of being friendly with you!; That's the last chance for you! (Usually said by a child who is angry with a playmate.) □ *All right for you, John. See if I ever play with you again.* □ *All right for you! I'm telling your mother what you did.*

all right with someone agreeable to someone. □ *If you want to ruin your life and marry Tom, it's all right with me.* □ *I'll see if using the car is all right with my father.*

All righty. *Inf.* All right.; OK. □ *Tom: Let's go to the state fair. Bill: All righty, let's do that.* □ *Everybody ready? All righty, then, let's get started.*

All right(y) already! *Inf.* an impatient way of indicating agreement or acquiescence. □ *Alice: All right already! Stop pushing me! Mary: I didn't do anything!* □ *Bill: Come on! Get over here! Bob: All righty already! Don't rush me!*

All roads lead to Rome. *Prov.* There are many different routes to the same goal. □ *Mary was criticizing the way that Jane was planting the flowers. John said, "Never mind, Mary, all roads lead to Rome."* □ *Some people learn by doing. Others have to be taught. In the long run, all roads lead to Rome.*

All's fair in love and war. *Prov. Cliché* In some situations, such as when you are in love or waging war, you are allowed to be deceitful in order to get what you want. (Often said as an excuse for deception.) □ *I cheated on the entrance exam, but I really want to get into that school, and all's fair in love and war.* □ *To get Judy to go out with him, Bob lied and told her that her boyfriend was seeing another woman. All's fair in love and war.*

All's well that ends well. *Prov. Cliché* An event that has a good ending is good even if some things went wrong along the way. (This is the name of a play by Shakespeare.) □ *I'm glad you finally got here, even though your car had a flat tire on the way. Oh, well. All's well that ends well.* □ *The groom was late for the wedding, but everything worked out all right. All's well that ends well.*

*(all) set (to do something**)** prepared or ready to do something. (*Typically: **be** ~; **get** ~.) □ *Are you set to cook the steaks?* □ *Yes, the fire is ready, and I'm all set to start.*

*all shook up *Sl.* excited; disturbed and upset. (See also shook up. *Typically: **be** ~; **get** ~.) □ *She stole my heart, and I'm all shook up.* □ *They were all shook up after the accident.*

all show and no go *Sl.* equipped with good looks but lacking action or energy. (Used to describe someone or something that looks good but does not perform as promised.) □ *That shiny car of Jim's is all show and no go.* □ *He's mighty handsome, but I hear he's all show and no go.*

(all) skin and bones Go to nothing but skin and bones.

*all spruced up freshened up; tidied up; cleaned up. (*Typically: **be** ~; **get** ~; **get** someone or something ~.) □ *Let's get the yard all spruced up for spring.*

all sweetness and light *Cliché* very kind, innocent, and helpful. □ *She was mad at first, but after a while, she was all sweetness and light.* □ *At the reception, the whole family was all sweetness and light, but they argued and fought after the guests left.*

All systems (are) go. *Cliché* Everything is ready. (Originally said when preparing to launch a rocket.) □ *The rocket is ready to blast off—all systems are go.* □ *Tom: Are you guys ready to start playing? Bill: Sure, Tom, all systems go.*

all talk (and no action) talking often about doing something, but never actually doing it. □ *The car needs washing, but Bill is all talk and no action on this matter.* □ *Bill keeps saying he'll get a job soon, but he's all talk and no action.* □ *Bill won't do it. He's just all talk.*

All that glistens is not gold. Go to next.

All that glitters is not gold. and **All that glistens is not gold.** *Prov.* Just because something looks attractive does not mean it is genuine or valuable. (Often said as a warning.) □ *Hollywood may look like an exciting place to live, but I don't think you should move there. All that glitters is not gold.* □ *I know Susie is popular and pretty, but don't be fooled by that. All that glitters is not gold.*

All the best to someone. Go to Give my best to someone.

all the livelong day all day long. □ *Well, of course you get to feeling stiff, sitting in front of a computer all the livelong day.* □ *I'd go crazy if I had to stay at home all the livelong day.*

A

*all the marbles *Fig.* all the winnings, spoils, or rewards. (*Typically: **end up with** ~; **get** ~; **win** ~; **give** someone ~.) □ *Somehow Fred always seems to end up with all the marbles. I don't think he plays fair.*

all the more reason for doing something and **all the more reason to** do something with even better reason or cause for doing something. (Can be included in a number of grammatical constructions.) □ *Bill: I don't do well in calculus because I don't like the stuff. Father: All the more reason for working harder at it.* □ *Bob: I'm tired of painting this fence. It's so old it's rotting! Sally: All the more reason to paint it.*

all the rage *Fig.* in current fashion; being a current fad. □ *A new dance called the "floppy disc" is all the rage.* □ *Wearing a rope instead of a belt was all the rage in those days.*

all the same and **just the same** nevertheless; anyhow. □ *They were told not to bring presents, but they brought them all the same.* □ *His parents told him to stay home, but John went out just the same.*

all the same (to someone**)** and **just the same (to** someone**)** of no consequence to someone—one way or the other; [of a choice] immaterial to someone. □ *It's all the same to me whether we win or lose.* □ *If it's just the same to you, I'd rather walk than ride.* □ *If it's all the same, I'd rather you didn't smoke.*

all the time 1. *Lit.* throughout a specific period of time. □ *Bill was stealing money for the last two years, and Tom knew it all the time.* □ *All the time through December and January, Jane held down two jobs.* **2.** *Fig.* at all times; continuously. □ *Your blood keeps flowing all the time.* □ *That electric motor runs all the time.* **3.** *Fig.* repeatedly; habitually. □ *She keeps a handkerchief in her hand all the time.* □ *He whistles all the time. It drives me crazy.*

all the way 1. *Lit.* from the beginning to the end; the entire distance, from start to finish. □ *The ladder reaches all the way to the top of the house.* □ *I walked all the way home.* **2.** *Fig.* with everything on it, as with a hamburger with pickles, onion, catsup, mustard, lettuce, etc. □ *I'd like one double cheeseburger—all the way.* □ *Make mine all the way.* **3.** *Sl.* [progressing] up to and including sexual intercourse. □ *They went all the way on their date last night.*

all the way live *Sl.* very exciting; excellent. □ *Man, this place is all the way live.* □ *Oh, Tiffany is just, like, all the way live!*

all there *Fig.* alert, aware, and mentally sound. (Usually negative.) □ *After talking with Larry today, I get the feeling that he's not quite all there.* □ *You do such foolish things sometimes! I wonder if you're all there.*

all things being equal Go to other things being equal.

All things must pass. and **All things will pass.** *Fig.* Everything comes to an end eventually. □ *You'll get over this setback. All things must pass.*

all things to all men and **all things to all people** *Fig.* [for someone or something] liked or used by all people; [for someone or something] everything that is wanted by all people. □ *You simply can't be all things to all people.* □ *The candidate set out to be all things to all men and came off looking very wishy-washy.*

all things to all people Go to previous.

All things will pass. Go to All things must pass.

all thumbs *Fig.* very awkward and clumsy, especially with one's hands. □ *Poor Bob can't play the piano at all. He's all thumbs.* □ *Mary is all thumbs when it comes to gardening.*

all to the good for the best; to one's benefit. □ *He missed the train, but it was all to the good because the train had a wreck.* □ *It was all to the good that he died without suffering.*

all told *Fig.* totaled up; including all parts. □ *All told, he earned about $700 last week.* □ *All told, he has many fine characteristics.*

*all tore up (about something**)** *Inf.* very upset and sorry about something. (The correct *torn* can also be used. *Typically: **be** ~; **get** ~.) □ *When Jim's dog was lost, he was all tore up about it.* □ *I'm all tore up about denting your car like that. I'd be more than happy to pay for fixing it.*

*(all) tuckered out *Rur.* tired out; worn out. (*Typically: **be** ~; **get** ~.) □ *Poor John worked so hard that he's all tuckered out.* □ *Look at that little baby sleeping. She's really tuckered out.*

all vine and no taters *Rur.* to be all display with no real value. □ *She's a good-looking woman, but really she's all vine and no taters.* □ *Don't be fooled by Jim's flowery promises. They're all vine and no taters.*

all walks of life *Fig.* all social, economic, and ethnic groups. □ *We saw people at the airport from all walks of life.* □ *The people who came to the street fair represented all walks of life.*

(all) well and good good; desirable. □ *It's well and good that you're here on time. I was afraid you'd be late again.* □ *It's all well and good that you're passing English, but what about math and science?*

all wet 1. *Lit.* completely wet. □ *I fell in and got all wet.* **2.** *Fig.* mistaken; wrongheaded; on the wrong track. □ *That's not the correct answer, John. You're all wet.* □ *If you think that prices will come down, you're all wet.*

all wool and a yard wide *Fig.* trustworthy and genuinely good. (A description of good quality wool cloth.) □ *Mary's a fine human being—all wool and a yard wide.* □ *I won't hear a word against Bill. He's all wool and a yard wide.*

all wool and no shoddy *Rur.* one hundred percent good quality. □ *Everything Mary sells is the best there is, all wool and no shoddy.* □ *John's a good man through and through—all wool and no shoddy.*

All work and no play makes Jack a dull boy. *Prov.* It is not healthy for someone to work all the time and never play. (Often used to exhort someone to stop working, or to justify why you have stopped working. You can substitute the name of the person you are addressing for *Jack.*) □ *Don't come to the office this weekend. All work and no play makes Jack a dull boy.* □ *I'd like to take a week's vacation next month. All work and no play makes Jack a dull boy.*

all year round *Fig.* throughout all the seasons of the year; during the entire year. □ *The public swimming pool is enclosed so that it can be used all year round.* □ *In the South they can grow flowers all year round.*

allocate something **to** someone or something and **allocate** something **between** someone or something; **allocate** something **among** someone or something to give or assign something to someone or something. (*Between* with two, *among* with three or more.) □ *The committee allocated the surplus cheese to the elderly people in the community.* □ *David allocated the money among all the members.* □ *He allocated the work between Fred and George.* □ *We had to allocate the money between the philanthropy and social committees.*

allot something **to** someone or something to give or assign something to someone or something. □ *We will allot a share of the proceeds to charity.* □ *I allotted a small portion of the work to Fred.*

*an **all-out effort** a very good and thorough effort. (*Typically: **begin** ~; **have** ~; **make** ~; **start** ~.) □ *We need to make an all-out effort to get this job done on time.* □ *The government began an all-out effort to reduce the federal budget.*

all-out war total war, as opposed to limited military actions or threats of war. □ *We are now concerned about all-out war in the Middle East.* □ *Threats of all-out war caused many tourists to leave the country immediately.*

allow for someone or something **1.** to plan on having enough of something (such as food, space, etc.) for someone. □ *Mary is bringing Bill on the picnic, so be sure to allow for him when buying the food.* □ *Allow for an extra person when setting the table tonight.* **2.** to plan on the possibility of something. □ *Allow for a few rainy days on your vacation.* □ *Be sure to allow for future growth when you plant the rosebushes.*

Allow me. and **Permit me.** Please let me help you. (Typically said by someone politely assisting another person, as by opening a door or providing some personal service. In **Allow me**, the stress is usually on *me*. In **Permit me**, the stress is usually on *-mit*.) □ *Tom and Jane approached the door. "Allow me," said Tom, grabbing the doorknob.* □ *"Permit me," said Fred, pulling out a gold-plated lighter and lighting Jane's cigarette.*

allow some elbow room Go to some elbow room.

allow someone or something **in†** Go to next.

allow someone or something **into** a place and **allow** someone or something **in†** to permit someone or something to enter some place. □ *Will they allow you in the restaurant without a tie?* □ *They won't allow in too many visitors.*

allow someone **up (from** something**)** to permit someone to arise or get up. (Fixed phrase.) □ *He knocked Peter down and would not allow him up from the ground.* □ *The doctor won't allow you up!*

allow something **for** something **1.** to allocate a share or a suitable amount of something, such as time, money, space, etc., for some activity or goal. □ *I allowed only an hour for lunch.* □ *They did not allow enough money for their expenditures this month.* **2.** to give consideration to circumstances or contingencies. □ *We allowed room for expansion when we designed the building.* □ *Allowing for his youth and lack of experience, I forgave him completely for his oversight.*

alloy something **with** something **1.** *Lit.* to combine one molten metal into another molten metal. □ *Is it possible to alloy copper with nickel?* □ *The copper has been alloyed with nickel.* **2.** *Fig.* to combine one quality or attribute with another. □ *She alloyed her courage with a helping of wisdom.* □ *Her courage has been alloyed with wisdom.*

allude to someone or something to refer to someone or something; to make an implication about someone or something. □ *I did not mean to allude to someone you disliked so much.* □ *I alluded to the accident only once.*

ally oneself **to** someone or something to unite or affiliate oneself with someone or something. □ *She sought to ally herself to the older members.* □ *Jane allied herself to the teacher almost immediately.*

ally (oneself) **(with** someone) **(against** someone or something**)** to unite with someone in opposition to someone or something. □ *Sally allied herself with John against the committee.* □ *We allied with the older ones against the younger ones.* □ *They allied themselves against the attackers.*

the **almighty dollar** *Fig.* the U.S. dollar, or the acquisition of money, when viewed as more important than anything else. □ *Bill was a slave to the almighty dollar.* □ *It's the almighty dollar that drives Wall Street thinking.*

(almost) jump out of one's **skin** and **nearly jump out of** one's **skin** *Fig.* to react strongly to shock or surprise. □ *Oh! You really scared me. I nearly jumped out of my skin.* □ *Bill was so startled he almost jumped out of his skin.*

almost lost it *Fig.* to nearly lose one's temper, composure, or control, as out of anger. □ *I was so mad, I almost lost it.* □ *When he saw the dent in his fender, he almost lost it.*

(a)long about a certain time near a particular time. □ *We arrived in town long about midnight and went right to the hotel.* □ *Along about his thirteenth birthday, Tom decided he was old enough to leave home.*

along in years Go to up in years.

along similar lines Go to along those lines.

along these lines Go to next.

along those lines and **along these lines; along similar lines** similarly; in nearly the same way. □ *We will deal with the other students along similar lines.*

along with someone or something in addition to someone or something; together with someone or something. □ *Jane went to the mall along with David.* □ *I ate some chocolates along with some fruit.*

alongside (of) someone or something as compared with a person or a thing. (The things being compared need not be beside one another. *Of* is normally used before pronouns.) □ *Our car looks quite small alongside of theirs.* □ *My power of concentration is quite limited alongside of yours.*

*aloof from** someone or something being remote or distant from someone or something. (*Typically: **be** ~; **keep** ~; **remain** ~; **stay** ~.) □ *She tends to keep aloof from the rest of us.* □ *Ken stays aloof from other committee members between meetings.*

alpha and omega both the beginning and the end; the essentials, from the beginning to the end; everything, from the beginning to the end. □ *He was forced to learn the alpha and omega of corporate law in order to even talk to the lawyers.* □ *He loved her deeply. She was his alpha and omega.*

A

alphabet soup initialisms and acronyms, especially when used excessively. □ *The names of these government agencies are just alphabet soup.* □ *Just look at the telephone book! You can't find anything because it's filled with alphabet soup.*

also-ran someone of no significance. (From horse racing, used of a horse that finishes a race but that does not finish among the money winners.) □ *Oh, he's just another also-ran.* □ *Ignore the also-rans.*

alternate between someone **and** someone else and **alternate between** something **and** something else to choose or change between two persons or things alternately. □ *The job will alternate between Gil and Ed.* □ *The maid will alternate between the first floor and the second floor.*

alternate with something **1.** [for someone] to serve as a substitute for someone. □ *I alternated with Fred as the lead in the school play.* □ *They asked Harry to alternate with Ron on the team.* **2.** [for something] to appear repetitively and regularly in a sequence with something else. (For instance, A alternates with B in the sequence ABABAB.) □ *In this design the straight lines alternate with the circles.* □ *The red dots alternate with the blue ones.*

always chasing rainbows tending to look for something (more) exciting and (more) rewarding but without realistic expectations. □ *He can't seem to settle down and enjoy life. He's always chasing rainbows.*

Am I glad to see you! I am very glad to see you! (Not a question. There is a stress on *I* and another on *you.*) □ *Bill: Well, I finally got here! John: Wow! Am I glad to see you!* □ *Tom (as Bill opens the door): Here I am, Bill. What's wrong? Bill: Boy, am I glad to see you! I need your help right now.*

Am I my brother's keeper? Go to **I am not my brother's keeper.**

Am I right? *Inf.* Isn't that so? Right? (A way of demanding a response and stimulating further conversation.) □ *John: Now, this is the kind of thing we should be doing. Am I right? Sue: Well, sure. I guess.* □ *Fred: You don't want to do this for the rest of your life. Am I right? Bob: Yeah. Fred: You want to make something of yourself. Am I right? Bob: I suppose.*

amalgamate something **with** something to unite something with something else; to merge two things. □ *We will amalgamate this company with another firm.* □ *How long has our local been amalgamated with the national union?*

amalgamate with something to join with something; to merge with something. □ *Our group decided to amalgamate with another group.* □ *The groups did not amalgamate after all.*

amble along (something**)** to walk along slowly and casually somewhere. □ *They ambled along the path.* □ *I was just ambling along, minding my own business, when I tripped.*

ambulance chaser a lawyer who hurries to the scene of an accident to try to get business from injured persons. □ *The insurance companies are cracking down on ambulance chasers.*

*American as apple pie *Cliché* quintessentially American. (*Also: **as** ~.) □ *A small house with a white picket fence is supposed to be as American as apple pie.*

amount to much to be as good as something; to be any good. □ *His fine plans don't amount to much, since he won't work for them.* (Usually negative.) □ *She's a nice girl, but she'll never amount to much.*

amount to something **1.** *Lit.* [for someone or something] to become worthwhile or successful. □ *I hope Charles amounts to something some day.* □ *I doubt that this business will ever amount to anything really profitable.* **2.** *Fig.* [for something] to be the equivalent of something. □ *Why, doing this amounts to cheating!* □ *Your comments amount to treason.* **3.** and **amount (up) to** something [for a sum of money] to increase [to a large amount]. □ *Is that everything you want to buy? That amounts to twenty dollars.* □ *These charges amount up to a lot.*

amount to the same thing and **come to the same thing; add up to the same thing** *Fig.* to be the same [as something]. □ *Borrowing can be the same as stealing. If the owner does not know what you have borrowed, it amounts to the same thing.* □ *With cars—whether they're red or blue—it comes to the same thing.*

amount (up) to something Go to **amount to** something.

amuse someone **with** something to entertain or interest someone with something. □ *Try to amuse the child with this little toy.* □ *She was able to amuse herself with the puzzle for a while.*

ancient history *Fig.* someone or something from so long ago as to be completely forgotten or no longer important, as a former relationship. □ *Bob? I never think about Bob anymore. He's ancient history.* □ *His interest in joining the army is now ancient history.*

and all that jazz and all that stuff; and all that nonsense. □ *I need some glue, paper, string, and all that jazz to make a kite.* □ *She told me I was selfish, hateful, rude, ugly, and all that jazz.*

and change plus a few cents; plus a few hundredths. (Used in citing a price or other decimal figure to indicate an additional fraction of a full unit.) □ *This one only costs ten bucks and change.* □ *The New York Stock Exchange was up seven points and change for the third broken record this week.*

And how! *Inf.* I agree! □ *I am really excited you are here. And how!* □ *Bill: I am pleased you are here. Bob: Me, too! And how!*

and so forth and **and so on** with additional related or similar things mentioned (but not specified). □ *She told me everything about her kids and so forth.* □ *I heard about problems at work and so forth.* □ *He told me about all his health problems, including his arthritis and so on.* □ *I need some help getting ready for dinner, setting the table, and so on.*

and so on Go to **and so forth.**

and something **to spare** and **with** something **to spare** *Fig.* with extra left over; with more than is needed. □ *I had as much flour as I needed with some to spare.* □ *Fred said he should have enough cash to last the week—with money to spare.*

and that's a fact *Fig.* and that is true. (Used to emphasize a statement.) □ *John ain't no friend of mine, and that's a fact.* □ *I'll be glad when this day is over, and that's a fact.*

And that's that. That is final and nothing more needs to be said. □ *I refuse to go with you and that's that!*

and the like and other similar things. □ *Whenever we go on a picnic, we take potato chips, hot dogs, soda pop, and the like.* □ *I'm very tired of being yelled at, pushed around, and the like.*

and them Go to **and those**.

and then some and even more; and more than has been mentioned. □ *John is going to have to run like a deer and then some to win this race.* □ *The cook put the amount of salt called for into the soup and then some.*

and this and that and more; and other miscellaneous things. □ *Mom sent me some pillowcases, some sheets, a couple of blankets, and this and that.* □ *The repairman tightened some screws, fiddled with some bolts, and this and that.*

and those and **and them** *Rur.* and some other people; and other friends or family members. □ *But if we invite Jill, Mary and them will want to come.* □ *Jim and those was sayin' nasty things about me.*

and what have you and more things; and other various things. □ *Their garage is full of bikes, sleds, old boots, and what have you.* □ *The merchant sells writing paper, pens, string, and what have you.*

And you? and **Yourself?** a way of redirecting a previously asked question to the asker or someone else. □ *Bill: Do you want some more cake? Mary: Yes, thanks. Yourself? Bill: I've had enough.* □ *Jane: Are you enjoying yourself? Bill: Oh, yes, and you?*

angle for something **1.** *Lit.* to fish for something, as with a fishhook and line. □ *Fred was angling for a big bass.* □ *I am angling for whatever I can catch.* **2.** *Fig.* to scheme or plan to get something; to "fish" for something. □ *She is just angling for a larger settlement from her former employer.* □ *Are you angling for a raise in pay?*

angle off (to(ward) something**)** to turn or move toward something at an angle. □ *The road angles off to the right.* □ *The sailboat angled off toward the direction the wind was blowing.*

angry enough to chew nails Go to **mad enough to chew nails (and spit rivets)**.

annex something **to** something [for a governmental body of a town or city] to attach a parcel of land onto an existing parcel of land through legal proceedings. □ *The village annexed some adjacent land to itself.* □ *The adjoining lot was annexed to the site to allow for a bigger building.*

annex to something [for the owner of a parcel of land] to have land attached to an adjacent town or city. □ *Our community doesn't want to annex to Adamsville.* □ *The town voted to annex to the neighboring city of Smithton.*

announce (one's **support) for** someone or something to declare one's political support for someone or something. □ *The senator announced for the Supreme Court nominee.* □ *Our club announced for the incumbent candidate.*

announce something **to** someone to tell something publicly to someone. □ *The president announced his nominee for attorney general to the media.* □ *When was the news announced to the public?*

anoint someone **with** something to pour or rub oil on a person's head as an honor or blessing; to put a liquid onto oneself. (Mostly in biblical references.) □ *They anointed the king with oil and praised him greatly.* □ *He anointed himself with a menthol rub that was meant to help his cold symptoms.*

another country heard from *Fig.* yet another person adds to the conversation. Used when someone joins a discussion other people are having, especially unexpectedly. (Used sarcastically, implying that the new speaker is not welcome in the discussion.) □ *Alan: You ought to take a vacation tomorrow. You really look tired. Fred: I am not tired and I don't need a vacation. Jane: But you do seem awfully short-tempered. Fred: Well, well, another country heard from!* □ *Brother: Let's go to the movies. Father: I'm too busy to drive you to the movies. Sister: I want to go to the movies, too. Let's go to the movies! Father: Oh, splendid. Another country heard from.*

(another) nail in someone's or something's **coffin** *Fig.* something that will harm or destroy someone or something. (Alludes to the sealing of a coffin with nails.) □ *Every word of criticism that Bob said about the boss was another nail in his coffin.* □ *Losing their biggest customer was the final nail in the company's coffin.*

another pair of eyes and a **fresh pair of eyes** *Fig.* another person to examine something closely in addition to anyone previously. □ *As soon as we can get a fresh pair of eyes on this manuscipt, we will find the last of the typos.*

answer back (to someone**)** and **answer** someone **back** to talk back (to someone); to argue (with someone). (Fixed phrase.) □ *I wish you wouldn't answer back to me that way.* □ *Please don't answer me back like that!* □ *Don't answer back or I'll ground you for a week!*

answer for someone **1.** *Lit.* to speak for another person. □ *I can't answer for Chuck, but I do have my own opinion.* □ *I will answer for my friend in his absence.* **2.** *Fig.* to vouch for someone; to tell of the goodness of someone's character. □ *Mr. Jones, who had known the girl all her life, answered for her. He knew she was innocent.* □ *I will answer for Ted. He could not hurt a flea.*

answer for someone or something *Fig.* to explain or justify the actions of someone or some act; to take responsibility or blame for someone or something. □ *You will have to answer for your children's bad behavior.* □ *I will answer only for my own misdeeds.*

answer someone **back** Go to **answer back (to** someone**)**.

answer someone's **purpose** and **serve** someone's **purpose** to fit or suit someone's aim or goal. □ *This piece of wood will answer my purpose quite nicely.* □ *The new car serves our purpose perfectly.*

answer the call 1. *Euph.* to die. □ *Our dear brother answered the call and has gone to his eternal rest.* **2.** and **answer the call (of nature)** *Euph.* to find and use the toilet. □ *We stopped the car long enoug for Jed to answer the call of nature.* □ *You had better answer the call of nature when you feel it coming.*

answer the call (of nature) Go to **previous**.

answer the door *Fig.* [after hearing the doorbell or a knock] to go to the door to see who is there. □ *Would you please answer the door. I am busy.* □ *I wish someone would answer the door. I can't stand to hear the knocking.*

answer to someone **1.** *Fig.* to explain or justify one's actions to someone. (Usually with *have to*.) □ *If John can-*

A

not behave properly, he'll have to answer to me. □ *The car thief will have to answer to the judge.* **2.** *Fig.* [in the hierarchy of the workplace] to be under the supervision of someone; to report to someone. (See also **report to** (someone or something).) □ *You will answer directly to Mr. Wright.* □ *I answer only to the boss.*

answer to the description of someone *Fig.* to match a particular set of physical or facial characteristics. □ *Chuck answers to the description his sister gave us.* □ *The man in police custody answers to the description of the burglar.*

answer to the name (of) something to respond to a particular name. □ *I answer to the name Walter.* □ *She answers to the name of Claire.*

***ants in** one's **pants** *Fig.* nervousness and agitation. (on the image of someone suffering great discomfort as if having actual ants in the pants. *Typically:* **get ~; have ~; give** one **~.**) □ *I always get ants in my pants before a test.* □ *I wonder if all actors get ants in their pants before they go onstage.*

any fool thing any ridiculous thing; anything that should be viewed as unimportant. □ *He'll buy his wife any fool thing she wants.* □ *Bill can get distracted by any fool thing.*

Any friend of someone('s) **(is a friend of mine).** *Cliché.* I am always pleased to meet a friend of someone I know. (A pleasant response when meeting or being introduced to a friend of a friend.) □ *Fred: Well, nice to meet you, Tom. Any friend of my brother is a friend of mine. Tom: Thanks, Fred. Nice to meet you too.* □ *John: Thank you so much for helping me find Sue's address. Sally: You're welcome. Any friend of Sue's.*

any number of someone or something *Fig.* a large number; a sufficiently large number. (Used when the exact number is not important.) □ *Any number of people can vouch for my honesty.* □ *I can give you any number of reasons why I should join the army.* □ *I ate at that diner any number of times and never became ill.*

any old thing *Fig.* just anything, not necessarily old. □ *Just give me one. I don't care which. Just give me any old thing.*

any port in a storm *Fig.* when one is having serious trouble, one must accept any solution, whether one likes the solution or not. □ *I don't want to live with my parents, but it's a case of any port in a storm. I can't find an apartment I can afford.* □ *He hates his job, but he can't get another. Any port in a storm, you know.*

any Tom, Dick, and Harry Go to (every) Tom, Dick, and Harry.

Anyone I know? and **Anybody I know?** a coy way of asking *who?* □ *Sally: Where were you last night? Jane: I had a date. Sally: Anyone I know?* □ *Bill: I've got a date for the formal next month. Henry: Anybody I know?*

Anything new down your way? *Rur.* Has any interesting event happened where you live? □ *Bill: Anything new down your way? Bob: Nothing worth talking about.* □ *Mary: Hi, Sally. Anything new down your way? Sally: No, what's new with you? Mary: Nothing much.*

Anything you say. *Fig.* Yes.; I agree. □ *Mary: Will you please take these blouses over to the cleaners? Bill: Sure, anything you say.* □ *Mother: You're going to finish your homework before you watch TV, right? Child: Anything you say, Mom.*

Anytime you are ready. and **Anytime you're ready.** a phrase indicating that the speaker is waiting for the person spoken to to make the appropriate move or action. □ *Mary: I think it's about time to go. Bill: Anytime you're ready.* □ *Surgeon: Shall we begin the operation? Nurse: Anytime you're ready, Doctor.*

apologize (to someone) **(for** someone) to make an apology to someone for someone else's actions. □ *Would you please apologize to Wally for Tom?* □ *I apologized for Frank to the hostess.* □ *I had to apologize for Frank.* □ *I had to apologize to the hostess.* □ *He was never able to apologize to himself for his past errors.*

appeal against something to ask a court of appeals to change a ruling made by a lower court. □ *My lawyer appealed against the judgment.* □ *We will file an appeal against the court ruling.*

appeal (to a court) **(for** something) to plead to a court of appeals for a favorable ruling. □ *She appealed to the court for a retrial.* □ *She appealed for an injunction to the circuit court.* □ *She appealed for a retrial.*

appeal to someone to please or attract someone. □ *Fast food doesn't appeal to me.* □ *The idea of a vacation to Florida this winter appeals to me a lot.*

appear as something **1.** to act a certain part in a play, opera, etc. □ *Madame Smith-Franklin appeared as Carmen at the City Opera last season.* □ *The actor refused to appear as a villain in the play.* **2.** [for something] to be seen or occur in a particular form or with particular characteristics. □ *The tumors appear as shadows on the X-ray.* □ *The first signs of the disease appear as a fever and a rash.*

appear at some place to perform at a particular place. □ *She is appearing at the Bijou all month.* □ *I will appear at Carnegie Hall soon.*

appear at some time to arrive at a particular time. □ *I am due to appear at the council at noon.* □ *I will appear at the meeting whenever my plane gets in.*

appear before someone **1.** to show up in the presence of someone, suddenly. □ *The deer appeared before us with no sound or other warning.* □ *A frightful specter appeared before me.* **2.** to have a trial or hearing with a particular judge or court. □ *You have to appear before Judge Cahill tomorrow.* □ *Have you ever appeared before the Supreme Court?*

appear before something to arrive in advance of the appointed time or before some event. □ *Please appear at least ten minutes before you are due.* □ *It is best to appear shortly before the time of your interview.*

appear for someone to represent or substitute for a person who is absent. □ *I will appear for you in the council.* □ *Who is going to appear for my lawyer, who is ill?*

appear in court to go to a court of law as a participant. □ *She has to appear in court tomorrow.* □ *I have to appear in court for my traffic violation.*

appear in something **1.** to be seen in some performance. □ *The singer will appear in the opera with the rest of the chorus.* □ *I will appear in Aida.* **2.** to be seen wearing something. □ *I wouldn't appear in that in public!* □ *Would you want to appear in a wrinkled suit?*

appear out of nowhere Go to out of nowhere.

appear to be rooted to the spot Go to rooted to the spot.

appear to someone [for something] to make an appearance before someone. □ *My late grandmother appeared to me in a dream.*

appear to someone **that...** *Fig.* to seem to someone that... □ *It appears to me that you are always late.*

appear to the naked eye Go to the naked eye.

appear under the name of some name [for an actor] to perform under a special name. □ *She is appearing under the name of Fifi.* □ *I appeared under the stage name Rex Righteous.*

appear (up)on something to arrive and be seen on something. (*Upon* is more formal and less commonly used than *on.*) □ *A fly appeared on the sterile bandages.* □ *A small bird appeared on our mailbox.*

Appearances can be deceiving. *Prov.* Things can look different from the way they really are. □ *Edward seems like a very nice boy, but appearances can be deceiving.* □ *Jane may look like she doesn't understand you, but she's really extremely bright. Appearances can be deceiving.*

append something **(on)to** something to attach something to something; to hang something onto something. □ *Please append these tassels onto the hem of your coat.* □ *Append this sentence to the last paragraph.*

appertain to something [of a responsibility or privilege] to belong to something as a right. □ *Do these rights appertain to a third cousin of the deceased?* □ *The statement doesn't make sense. It appertains to no one as it is stated.*

An **apple a day keeps the doctor away.** *Prov.* Apples are so nutritious that if you eat an apple every day, you will not ever need to go to a doctor. □ *Remember to take an apple in your lunch today. An apple a day keeps the doctor away.* □ *Grandma always fed us lots of apples when we visited her. She believed that an apple a day keeps the doctor away.*

the **apple of** someone's **eye** *Fig.* someone's favorite person or thing; a boyfriend or a girlfriend. □ *Tom is the apple of Mary's eye. She thinks he's the greatest.* □ *John's new car is the apple of his eye.*

apple-polisher *Fig.* a flatterer. □ *Doesn't that wimpy apple-polisher know how stupid he looks?* □ *Everybody at my office seems to be an apple-polisher but me.*

apples and oranges *Fig.* two entities that are not similar. (Used especially in reference to comparisons of unlike things.) □ *You can't talk about Fred and Ted in the same breath! They're like apples and oranges.* □ *Talking about her current book and her previous bestseller is like comparing apples and oranges.*

apply oneself **to** something to work hard and diligently at something. □ *You should apply yourself to your studies.* □ *She applied herself to her work and the time passed very rapidly.*

apply something **to** something **1.** *Lit.* to put something onto the surface of something. □ *Apply the decal to the surface of the glass.* □ *Apply the paint evenly to each surface.* **2.** *Fig.* to use something, such as force, effort, etc., on something or in the performance of some task. □ *Apply more effort in your school work.* □ *An even greater effort has been applied to make sure we finish on time.*

apply to someone or something [for rules, laws, etc.] to affect someone or something; to be relevant to someone or something. □ *Does this rule apply to me?* □ *These policies apply only to very large companies.*

apply (to someone or something**) (for** something**)** to ask for something from someone or an organization. □ *You must apply to the proper office for permission.* □ *I applied to seven colleges for admission.*

apply within to ask about something [inside some place]. (Usually part of a sign or announcement posted outside a place.) □ *The sign outside the office read, "Apply within."* □ *If you are interested in working here, please apply within.*

appoint someone **to** something to select or assign someone to serve in a particular role. (Usually focusing on the role of the person or on a group of persons with similar roles.) □ *I am going to appoint you to the position of treasurer.* □ *Fred tried to appoint himself to the board of directors, but it violated the by-laws.*

apportion something **out**† **(among** some people**)** to divide something and distribute it among people. □ *He apportioned the cake out among the guests.* □ *He apportioned out the applications among all those in the waiting room.*

appraise something **at** something to study something and place a monetary value on it. □ *They appraised the house at twice what it is worth.* □ *The diamond ring was appraised at a very high price.*

apprentice someone **to** someone to assign someone to work at a certain trade and learn from someone experienced. □ *She apprenticed her son to a local diesel mechanic.* □ *I apprenticed myself to a printer and learned what it means to get really dirty.*

apprise someone **of** something to inform someone of something. □ *I hope you will apprise me of any change.* □ *Have you been apprised of the new rule?*

approach someone **about** someone or something to ask someone about someone or something, usually with tact and caution. □ *Wally has been acting strangely. I will approach Judy about him.* □ *She approached Tom about the broken window.*

appropriate something **for** something **1.** to allot a certain amount of money for a particular purpose. □ *They will appropriate $10,000 for the exhibit at the fair.* □ *A large sum was appropriated for the expenses.* **2.** *Euph.* to take something [from someone else] and use it as something else or for a purpose different from what was intended. □ *Walter appropriated a truck for an ambulance.* □ *It was necessary to appropriate your laptop for connecting to the Internet.*

approve of someone or something to take a favorable view of someone or something. □ *I approve of the way you have remodeled the kitchen.* □ *I don't approve of your foul language.*

April showers bring May flowers. *Prov.* Although rain in April is annoying, it starts the flowers growing. □ *Child: I hate all this rain. Why does it have to rain? Mother: April showers bring May flowers.* □ *Although it was a dreary, rainy day, we felt cheerful, since April showers bring May flowers.*

A

arbitrate between someone **and** someone else to mediate between two disagreeing parties; to help two disagreeing parties to resolve their differences. □ *Jane was called upon to arbitrate between the workers and the manager.* □ *I arbitrated between Fred and his ex-wife.*

arbitrate in a dispute to mediate or negotiate a settlement in a dispute. □ *She refuses to arbitrate in this dispute.* □ *I will arbitrate in this little disagreement.*

arch (oneself) over to bend or curve over. (*Oneself* includes *itself*.) □ *The tree arched over in the wind.* □ *Arch yourself over gracefully and then straighten up.* □ *The tree arched itself over in the windstorm.*

arch over someone or something to bend or curve over someone or something; to stand or remain bent or curved over someone or something. □ *The trees arched gracefully over the walkway.* □ *A lovely bower of roses arched over the bride.*

arch something **over** someone or something to place something above someone or something to form an arch or archway. □ *The cadets arched their swords over the bridal couple.* □ *The willow arched its long drooping branches over the tiny cabin.*

(Are) things getting you down? Are everyday issues bothering you? □ *Jane: Gee, Mary, you look sad. Are things getting you down?* □ *Tom: What's the matter, Bob? Things getting you down? Bob: No, I'm just a little tired.*

(Are you) doing okay? and **You doing okay? 1.** How are you? □ *Mary: Doing okay? Bill: You bet! How are you?* □ *Bill: Hey, man! Are you doing okay? Tom: Sure thing! And you? 2.* How are you surviving this situation or ordeal? □ *Mary: You doing okay? Bill: Sure. What about you? Mary: I'm doing fine.* □ *Tom: Wow, that was some turbulence we just hit! Are you doing okay? Mary: I'm still a little frightened, but I'll make it.*

(Are you) feeling okay? Do you feel well? □ *Tom: Are you feeling okay? Bill: Oh, fair to middling.* □ *Susan: Are you feeling okay? Mary: I'm still a little dizzy, but it will pass.*

(Are you) going my way? If you are traveling in the direction of my destination, could I please go with you or can I have a ride in your car? □ *Mary: Are you going my way? Sally: Sure. Get in.* □ *"Going my way?" said Tom as he saw Mary turn toward him.*

(Are you) leaving so soon? and **You leaving so soon?** a polite inquiry made to a guest who has announced a departure. (Appropriate only for the first few guests to leave. It would seem sarcastic to say this to the last guest to leave or one who is leaving very late at night.) □ *Sue: We really must go. Sally: Leaving so soon? Sue: Fred has to catch a plane at five in the morning.* □ *John (seeing Tom at the door): You leaving so soon? Tom: Yes, thanks for inviting me. I really have to go. John: Well, good night, then.*

(Are you) ready for this? a way of presenting a piece of news or information that is expected to excite or surprise the person spoken to. □ *Tom: Boy, do I have something to tell you! Are you ready for this? Mary: Sure. Let me have it!* □ *Tom: Now, here's a great joke! Are you ready for this? It is so funny! Alice: I can hardly wait.*

(Are you) ready to order? Would you please tell me what you want as your meal? (A standard phrase used in eating establishments to find out what a customer wants to eat.) □ *The waitress came over and asked, "Are you ready to order?"* □ *Tom: I know what I want. What about you, Sally? Are you ready to order? Sally: Don't rush me!*

(Are you) sorry you asked? Now that you have heard (the unpleasant answer), do you regret having asked the question? (Compare this with **You'll be sorry you asked.**) □ *Father: How are you doing in school? Bill: I'm flunking out. Sorry you asked?* □ *Mother: You've been looking a little down lately. Is there anything wrong? Bill: I probably have the flu. Are you sorry you asked?*

argue against someone or something **1.** *Lit.* [for someone] to make a case against someone or something; to oppose the choice of someone or something in an argument. □ *I am preparing myself to argue against the case.* □ *Liz argued against Tom as the new president, but we chose him anyway.* **2.** *Fig.* [for something, such as facts] to support a case against someone or something in an argument; [for something, such as facts] to support a case against the choice of someone or something in an argument. □ *I have uncovered something that argues against continuing this friendship.* □ *His own remarks argue against his qualifications for the office, but he probably will be elected anyway.*

argue back to argue with or oppose someone; to **answer back (to** someone); to **talk back (to** someone). (Usually said of persons who are supposed to listen and obey without comment.) □ *Please don't argue back all the time.* □ *I wish you children did not argue back so much.*

argue for someone or something to make a case in favor of someone or something; to speak on behalf of someone or something in an argument. □ *Are you prepared to argue strongly for this proposal?* □ *We will argue for our candidate in the debate.*

argue one's **way out of** something and **argue** one's **way out** to talk and get oneself free of a problem. □ *You can't argue your way out of this!* □ *It's a problem, and there is no way that you can argue your way out.*

argue someone **down**† to defeat someone in a debate. □ *Sally could always argue him down if she had to.* □ *She tries to argue down everyone she meets.*

argue someone **into** doing something to convince or persuade someone to do something. □ *She was unable to argue the manager into attending.* □ *She was unable to argue herself into doing something so unpleasant.*

argue something **down**† **1.** *Lit.* to reduce something, such as a bill or a price, by arguing. □ *I tried to argue the price down, but it did no good.* □ *Tom could not argue down the bill.* **2.** *Fig.* to urge the defeat of a proposal or a motion in a meeting through discussion. □ *I am prepared to argue the proposal down in court.* □ *She will argue down the proposal in the council meeting.*

argue something **out**† to settle something by discussing all the important points. □ *We are going to have to argue this out some other time.* □ *Must we argue out every single detail of this contract?*

argue (with someone) **(over** someone or something) and **argue (with** someone) **(about** someone or something) to dispute or quarrel over someone or something with someone. □ *Are you going to argue with her over something so simple?* □ *I wish you wouldn't argue over money with me.*

□ *We always argue about who should drive.* □ *Don't argue with me!*

argue with something to challenge or dispute something; to dispute someone's statement of fact. □ *I won't argue with your conclusions.* □ *It is not a good idea to argue with the facts.*

arguing for the sake of arguing and **arguing for the sake of argument** arguing simply to be difficult or contrary. □ *You are just arguing for the sake of arguing. You don't even know what the issue is.* □ *He is annoying, because he is always arguing for the sake of argument.*

arguing for the sake of argument Go to previous.

arise from something and **arise out of** something **1.** *Lit.* to get up from something. □ *What time did you arise from bed?* □ *I arose out of my slumbers at dawn.* **2.** *Lit.* [for something] to drift upward from something. □ *The smoke arose from the burning oil wells.* □ *The smoke arose out of the exhaust pipe.* **3.** *Fig.* to be due to something; to be caused by something. □ *This whole problem arose from your stubbornness.* □ *The labor problem arose out of mismanagement.* **4.** *Fig.* [for someone] to come from poor or unfortunate circumstances. □ *She arose from poverty to attain great wealth.* □ *She arose out of squalor through her own hard work.*

*****arm in arm** *Fig.* [of persons] linked or hooked together by the arms. (*Typically: **go ~; stroll ~; walk ~**.) □ *The two lovers walked arm in arm down the street.* □ *They skated arm in arm around the rink.*

arm (someone **against** someone or something) (**with** something) to equip someone with whatever is needed to fight against someone or something. □ *They armed themselves against the enemy with guns and ammunition.* □ *The government armed the soldiers with the new guns.*

*****armed and dangerous** *Cliché* [of someone who is suspected of a crime] having a gun or other lethal weapon and not being reluctant to use it. (This is part of a warning to police officers who might try to capture an armed suspect. *Typically: **be ~; be regarded as ~; be presumed to be ~**.) □ *The murderer is at large, presumed to be armed and dangerous.* □ *The suspect has killed once and is armed and dangerous.*

armed to the teeth *Fig.* heavily armed with deadly weapons. □ *The bank robber was armed to the teeth when he was caught.* □ *There are too many guns around. The entire country is armed to the teeth.*

An **army marches on its stomach.** *Prov.* An army needs a regular supply of food in order to keep on fighting. □ *The invading army will soon have to pull back. An army marches on its stomach, and they're out of food.*

*****around** someone or something **1.** enclosing someone or something. (*Typically: **be ~; go ~; circle ~**.) □ *The white picket fence is around the house and the yard.* □ *Jimmy was crying loudly. A ring of children circled around him, singing "Happy Birthday."* **2.** near someone or something in this vicinity. (*Typically: **be ~; hang ~; live ~**.) □ *How long have you been around here?* □ *I don't like people like that hanging around me.*

*****(a)round the bend 1.** *Fig.* crazy; having lost sanity. (*Typically: **be ~; go ~**.) □ *I think this job is sending me around the bend.* □ *She sounds like she's round the bend*

already. **2.** intoxicated from alcohol or drugs. (*Typically: **be ~; go ~**.) □ *One more of those, and you'll be around the bend.* □ *From the glassy look in her eyes, I'd say she is completely round the bend now.*

(a)round the clock *Fig.* continuously for twenty-four hours at a time. □ *The priceless jewels were guarded around the clock.* □ *Grandfather was so sick that he had to have nurses round the clock.*

arouse someone **from** something to activate a person out of a state of rest, sleep, or inaction. □ *I could not arouse her from her sleep.* □ *She aroused herself from a deep sleep.*

arrange for someone **to** do something to make plans for someone to do something. □ *I will arrange for Charles to fix what he broke.* □ *I arranged for the plumber to install a new water heater.*

arrange for something to prepare or plan for something. □ *We will arrange for a celebration.* □ *John arranged for it.*

arrange some music **for** something to prepare or adapt music for particular instruments or for a particular musical key. □ *Paul arranged the piece for piano.* □ *This piece was arranged for the guitar by Frank's brother.*

arrange something **for** some time to plan something for a particular time. □ *We will arrange a picnic for the afternoon.* □ *I will arrange an appointment for the noon hour.*

arrange something **for** someone or something to prepare or plan something for someone or something. □ *They arranged a reception for Frank.* □ *We arranged a dance for the holiday.*

arrange something **with** someone or something to prepare or plan something that will include someone or something. □ *We arranged entertainment with clowns and a musician.* □ *I will arrange a fancy dinner with wine and cloth napkins.* □ *Paul arranged a meeting with the opposition.*

arrive ahead of time Go to ahead of time.

arrive at a decision and **reach a decision** to make a decision; decide. □ *Have you arrived at a decision yet?* □ *We will reach a decision tomorrow.*

arrive back (some place) Go to back (some place).

arrive in force Go to in force.

arrive in the (very) nick of time Go to in the (very) nick of time.

arrive on a wing and a prayer Go to on a wing and a prayer.

arrive on the scene Go to come on the scene.

arrive (some place) **at** some time to reach some place at a particular time. □ *We will arrive at the border at noon.* □ *They arrived at seven o'clock in the evening.*

arrive (some place) **from** some other place to reach or come to a place from another place. (If the first *some place* is missing, the place is either *here* or must be inferred.) □ *They arrived here from New York yesterday.* □ *They arrived from Charleston last week.*

arrive (some place) **in** something to reach or come to a place in a particular kind of vehicle. □ *They arrived here in their car.* □ *We arrived at the museum in a bus.*

arrive some place **in a body** Go to in a body.

A

arrive (somewhere**) at the stroke of** some time Go to arrive (somewhere) (up)on the stroke of some time.

arrive (somewhere**) (up)on the stroke of** some time and **arrive** (somewhere**) at the stroke of** some time to reach a place at a particular instant of time. (*Upon* is more formal and less commonly used than *on*.) □ *She arrived home on the stroke of midnight.* □ *We all arrived at the stroke of two.*

arrive (up)on the scene (of something**)** and **arrive at the scene (of** something**)** to reach the location of an event in progress. (*Upon* is formal and less commonly used than *on* and *at*.) □ *The police arrived on the scene of the crime.* □ *They arrived upon the scene of a frightening accident.* □ *What did they do when they arrived at the scene?*

Art is long and life is short. *Prov.* Works of art last much longer than human lives.; Life is too short to learn everything you need to know about a particular discipline. □ *Alan: You ought to do something besides paint pictures in your spare time. Come out with us, have some fun. Bob: Having fun will not win me immortality. Only my paintings can do that. Art is long and life is short.* □ *I always feel a sense of awe when I look at the Babylonian statues in the art museum. They were made thousands of years ago. Art is long and life is short.*

as a duck takes to water *Cliché* easily and naturally. □ *She took to singing just as a duck takes to water.* □ *The baby adapted to the bottle as a duck takes to water.*

as a (general) rule usually; almost always. □ *He can be found in his office as a general rule.* □ *As a general rule, Jane plays golf on Wednesdays.* □ *As a rule, things tend to get less busy after supper time.*

as a last resort as the last choice; if everything else fails. □ *Call me at home only as a last resort.* □ *As a last resort, the doctor will perform surgery.*

As a man sows, so shall he reap. Go to As you sow, so shall you reap.

as a matter of course normally; as a normal procedure. □ *The nurse takes your temperature as a matter of course.* □ *You are expected to make your own bed as a matter of course.*

as a matter of fact actually; in addition to what has been said; in reference to what has been said. □ *As a matter of fact, John came into the room while you were talking about him.* □ *I'm not a poor worker. As a matter of fact, I'm very efficient.*

as a result (of something**)** because of something that has happened. □ *As a result of the accident, Tom couldn't walk for six months.* □ *We couldn't afford to borrow money for a house as a result of the rise in interest rates.*

as a rule in general; usually. □ *As a rule, men should wear tuxedos at formal dinners.* □ *As a rule, the bus picks me up at 7:30 every morning.*

as a token (of something**)** symbolic of something, especially of gratitude; as a memento of something. □ *He gave me a rose as a token of his esteem.* □ *Here, take this gift as a token of my appreciation.*

as all get out *Rur.* very much; as much as can be. □ *I'm tired as all get out.*

as an aside [said] as a comment that is not supposed to be heard by everyone. □ *At the wedding, Tom said as an aside, "The bride doesn't look well."* □ *At the ballet, Billy said as an aside to his mother, "I hope the dancers fall off the stage!"*

as bad as all that as bad as reported; as bad as it seems. (Usually expressed in the negative.) □ *Come on! Nothing could be as bad as all that.* □ *Stop crying. It can't be as bad as all that.*

as far as anyone **knows** and **so far as** anyone **knows; to the best of** one's **knowledge** to the limits of anyone's knowledge. (The *anyone* can be replaced with a more specific noun or pronoun.) □ *As far as anyone knows, this is the last of the great herds of buffalo.* □ *Far as I know, this is the best spot to sit.* □ *Q: Are the trains on time? A: To the best of my knowledge, all the trains are on time today.*

as far as it goes as much as something does, covers, or accomplishes. (Usually said of something that is inadequate.) □ *Your plan is fine as far as it goes. It doesn't seem to take care of everything, though.* □ *As far as it goes, this law is a good one. It should set stiffer penalties, however.*

as far as possible and **so far as possible** as much as possible; to whatever degree is possible. □ *We must try, as far as possible, to get people to stop smoking in buses.* □ *As far as possible, the police will issue tickets to all speeding drivers.* □ *I'll follow your instructions so far as possible.*

as far as someone **is concerned** and **so far as** someone **is concerned** from the point of view of someone. □ *Bob: Isn't this cake good? Alice: Yes, indeed. This is the best cake I have ever eaten as far as I'm concerned.* □ *As far as we are concerned, anything at all would be fine for dinner.*

as far as something **is concerned** and **so far as** something **is concerned** having to do with something; pertaining to something; as for something. □ *This bill? As far as that's concerned, the committee will have to take care of it.* □ *As far as the roof's concerned, it will just have to last another year.*

as for someone or something and **as to** someone or something regarding someone or something. □ *As for the mayor, he can pay for his own dinner.* □ *As for this chair, there is nothing to do but throw it away.*

as good as one's **word** obedient to one's promise; dependable in keeping one's promises. □ *He was as good as his word. He lent me the books as he said he would.* □ *She said she would babysit and she was as good as her word.*

As I live and breathe! *Fig.* How amazing! (Said on seeing or experiencing something surprising.) □ *As I live and breathe, here we are again!* □ *Well, as I live and breathe, it's Harry Smith!*

as I see it and **in my opinion; in my view** *Fig.* the way I think about it. □ *Tom: This matter is not as bad as some would make it out to be. Alice: Yes. This whole affair has been overblown, as I see it.* □ *Bob: You're as wrong as can be. John: In my view, you are wrong.*

as I was saying and **like I was saying** to repeat what I've been saying; to continue with what I was saying. (The first form is appropriate in any conversation. The second form is colloquial, informal, and familiar. In addition, this use of *like* for *as*, in the second form, is objected to by many people.) □ *Bill: Now, Mary, this is one of the round* *ones that attaches to the wire here. Bob (passing through the room): Hello, you two! I'll talk to you later. Bill: Yeah, see you around. Now, as I was saying, Mary, this goes here on this wire.* □ *Tom: I hate to interrupt, but someone's car is being broken into down on the street. Fred: As I was saying, these illegal practices must stop.*

as it is the way things are; the way it is now. □ *"I wish I could get a better job," remarked Tom. "I'm just getting by as it is."* □ *Mary: Can we afford a new refrigerator? Fred: As it is, it would have to be a very small one.*

as it were as one might say; as could be said. (Sometimes used to qualify an assertion that may not sound reasonable.) □ *He carefully constructed, as it were, a huge submarine sandwich.* □ *The Franklins live in a small and, as it were, exquisite house.*

as long as 1. and **so long as** since; because. □ *As long as you're going to the bakery, please buy some fresh bread.* □ *So long as you're here, please stay for dinner.* **2.** and **so long as** if; only if. □ *You may have dessert so long as you eat all your vegetables.* □ *You can go out this evening as long as you promise to be home by midnight.* **3.** for a specified length of time. □ *You may stay out as long as you like.* □ *I didn't go to school as long as Bill did.*

as luck would have it by good or bad luck; as it turned out; by chance. □ *As luck would have it, we had a flat tire.* □ *As luck would have it, the check came in the mail today.*

*as one as if acting or moving as a single person. (*Typically: **act ~; move ~; speak ~.**) □ *All the dancers moved as one.* □ *The chorus spoke as one.*

as soon as at the moment that; at the time that; when. □ *I fell asleep as soon as I lay down.* □ *John ate dinner as soon as he came home.*

as such in the way something is; as someone or something is. □ *I cannot accept your manuscript as such. It needs revisions.* □ *You are new to this job, and as such, I will have to train you.*

As the twig is bent, so is the tree inclined. *Prov.* A grown person will act the way he or she was taught to act as a child. □ *Alice's parents thought it was cute when she threw tantrums, and you'll notice that she still throws tantrums now that she's grown up. As the twig is bent, so is the tree inclined.* □ *Don't encourage your son to be so greedy. As the twig is bent, so is the tree inclined.*

as usual as is the normal or typical situation. □ *John ordered eggs for breakfast, as usual.* □ *He stood quietly as usual, waiting for the bus to come.*

as we speak and **even as we speak** *Cliché* just now; at this very moment. □ *"I'm sorry, sir," consoled the agent at the gate, "the plane is taking off as we speak."* □ *Tom: Waiter, where is my steak? It's taking a long time. Waiter: It is being grilled even as we speak, sir—just as you requested.*

as well also; in addition. □ *Could I have a second helping of potatoes as well?* □ *I'm feeling tired, and dizzy as well.*

as well as someone or something **1.** in addition to someone or something. □ *Mary and Jane are coming to the party, as well as Tom.* □ *I'm studying biology and chemistry, as well as history.* **2.** to the same high degree as someone or something; as much as someone or something else.

□ *Mary's parents treated me as well as they treat her.* □ *I did as well as you on the test.*

As you make your bed, so you must lie (up)on it. and **As you make your bed, so you must lie in it.; As you make your bed, so must you lie in it.** *Prov.* You have to suffer the consequences of what you do. (Often used as a rebuke.) □ *Tom insisted on taking a trip to Florida in August, after we all told him how hot it was then. Now that he's there, all he does is complain about the heat. As you make your bed, so must you lie upon it.* □ *You were the one who chose these house painters because they were cheap. I told you they'd do a terrible job. As you make your bed, so must you lie in it.*

As you sow, so shall you reap. and **As a man sows, so shall he reap.** *Prov.* Things will happen to you good or bad, according to how you behave. (Biblical.) □ *You should stop being so cruel to other people. As you sow, so shall you reap.* □ *Fred built an immense fortune by swindling others, but lost it all when someone swindled him. As a man sows, so shall he reap.*

ascertain something **from** someone or something to find out or learn with certainty information from someone or something. □ *I need to ascertain some facts from you.* □ *A few facts have been ascertained from the interview.*

ascribe something **to** someone or something to attribute something to someone or something; to assert that something has been caused by someone or something. □ *Please do not ascribe that attitude to my friends.* □ *We ascribed the offensive action to Jill and only Jill.*

aside from someone or something not including someone or something. □ *Aside from a small bank account, I have no money at all.* □ *Aside from Mary, Nancy, Craig, and Phil, I have no friends on campus.*

ask about someone or something Go to **ask around (about** someone or something**)**.

ask after someone to inquire about the health and well-being of someone. □ *Hermione asked after you when I saw her today.* □ *I asked after Molly and her family.*

ask around (about someone or something**)** and **ask about** someone or something to request information (about someone or something) from a number of different sources. □ *I don't know the answer. I'll ask around about it.* □ *Ask about, will you? Find out what people are thinking.* □ *Please ask around about her.*

ask for a knuckle sandwich Go to a **knuckle sandwich**.

ask for someone or something to request someone or something; to ask that someone come forth. □ *The police are at the door asking for Henry.* □ *The child asked for a glass of water.*

ask for something bad or dire to act badly, such that one will bring on bad consequences. □ *If you keep misbehaving, you'll be asking for punishment.* □ *You're really asking for it!*

ask for the moon *Fig.* to make outlandish requests or demands for something, such as a lot of money or special privileges. □ *She's asking for the moon, and she's not going to get it.* □ *Don't ask for the moon. Be reasonable!*

ask for trouble and **look for trouble** *Fig.* to seem to be trying to get into trouble; to do something that would

A

cause trouble; to do or say something that will cause trouble. □ *Stop talking to me that way, John. You're just asking for trouble.* □ *The guard asked me to leave unless I was looking for trouble.*

Ask me no questions, I'll tell you no lies. Go to next.

Ask no questions and hear no lies. and **Ask me no questions, I'll tell you no lies.** If you ask me that, my answer might not be the truth. (Implies that you will likely tell a lie, because you do not want to tell the truth.) □ *What am I going to give you for your birthday? Ask no questions and hear no lies.* □ *Maybe I like Greg, and maybe I don't. Ask me no questions, I'll tell you no lies.*

ask someone **back 1.** [for a host or hostess] to invite someone to come again (at a later time or to another similar event). □ *After the way you behaved, they'll never ask us back.* □ *They had been asked back a number of times, but they never came.* **2.** [for someone who has been a guest] to invite a previous host or hostess to come to an event. □ *We've had the Smiths to dinner five times. I think it's time they asked us back.* □ *I don't care if they ask us back or not.*

ask someone **down†** to invite someone to come to one's home [for a visit]. (Usually said when someone must go to a lower level, travel south, down a hill, or into the country for the visit.) □ *Sam asked us down for Friday evening. Shall we go?* □ *We asked down some old friends for the evening.*

ask someone **for** something **1.** to request something from someone. □ *The diners asked the waiter for a type of wine the restaurant didn't have.* □ *A special wine was asked for by a number of patrons.* **2.** and **ask** someone **to** something to invite someone to something. □ *Janet asked us to a party Friday evening.* □ *Janet asked us for dinner.*

ask someone **in** Go to next.

ask someone **in(to)** some place and **ask** someone **in** to invite someone inside some place. □ *We asked them into the house.* □ *We stopped our friends in the hallway and asked them in.*

ask someone **out†** **(for** something**)** Go to next.

ask someone **out (to** something**) 1.** and **ask** someone **out†** **(for** something**)** to invite someone to go out (to something or some place) [on a date]. □ *He asked her out to dinner, but she had other plans.* □ *She couldn't go, so he asked out someone else.* □ *Liz asked Carl out for dinner.* **2.** to invite someone for a visit to a place in the country or some other location remote from the center of things. □ *Tom must be tired of the city. Let's ask him out to our place.* □ *I don't want to ask out everyone in the whole family again.* □ *Oh, let's ask him out anyway.*

ask someone **over** to invite someone who lives close by to come to one's home [for a visit]. (Either to a house or apartment.) □ *Can we ask Tom over?* □ *He has been asked over a number of times.*

ask someone **to** something Go to **ask** someone **for** something.

ask someone **up†** to ask someone to come to one's home for a visit. (Usually said when someone must travel north, up a hill, or to an apartment on a higher floor for the visit.) □ *Let's ask Judy up for the weekend.* □ *We asked up a few old friends.*

ask something **of** someone or something to request or demand something from someone, something, or a group. □ *I*

want to ask something of you. □ *We will ask that of the board of directors.* □ *You should ask that of your database.*

asking price the price that someone puts on an item being offered for sale. □ *I think your asking price is a little high.*

*****asleep at the switch** *Fig.* not attending to one's job; failing to do one's duty at the proper time. (Alludes to a technician or engineer on a train sleeping instead of turning whatever switches are required. *Typically: **be** ~; **fall** ~.) □ *The security guard fell asleep at the switch and a robber broke in.* □ *If I hadn't been asleep at the switch, I'd have noticed the car being stolen.*

aspire to something to seek or aim for something better. □ *She aspires to a job more challenging than her current position.* □ *I aspire to far greater things.*

assail someone **with** something **1.** *Lit.* to attack someone with something, such as a weapon. □ *The crook assailed the officer with the officer's own club.* □ *The riot police were assailed with stones and bottles.* **2.** *Fig.* to pester or annoy someone with questions, requests, demands, etc. □ *Don't assail me with all your complaints.* □ *She assailed herself with constant guilty rebukes.*

assault and battery a violent attack [upon someone] followed by a beating. (A technical legal charge.) □ *Richard was charged with two counts of assault and battery.* □ *Dave does not go out at night because he does not want to be a victim of assault and battery.*

assault the ear *Fig.* [for sound or speech] to be very loud or persistent. □ *That loud music assaults the ears!* □ *I can't hear you with all that traffic noise assaulting my ears.*

assent to something to agree to something. □ *I assent to what you suggest.* □ *She will not assent to our request.*

assess something **at** something to estimate or value something at some figure. □ *They assess the value of our house at half what it would sell for.* □ *The house was assessed at far more than its true worth.*

assign someone or something **to** someone or something to designate someone or something as belonging to someone or something else. □ *They assigned the new car to Roger.* □ *They assigned the new worker to the mail room.*

assign something **to** someone to attribute something to someone; to blame something on someone. □ *We were forced to assign the blame to Robert.* □ *They assigned the responsibility for the accident to the driver of the car.*

assimilate someone or something **into** something to cause someone or something to be absorbed into something. (As when a person or thing joins a group.) □ *We sought to assimilate Arnold into the community.* □ *The manager had to assimilate the new policies into the list of current ones.* □ *They assimilated themselves into the general population.*

assimilate with some people to join or mix in with people and become accepted by them. □ *It's easy for Karen to assimilate with new people.* □ *I want to assimilate rapidly with the other people in my class.*

assist in something to help with something. □ *May I assist in this?* □ *Please assist in this task.*

assist (someone**) at** something to serve as a helper or assistant in some procedure. (This usually refers to a surgical procedure.) □ *Will you assist at surgery this morning?* □ *I would be happy to assist you at the procedure.*

assist someone **in** something to help a particular person working on a task. □ *Please assist Greg in the committee's assignment.* □ *We assisted him in the whole procedure.*

assist someone **with** someone or something to help someone manage someone or something, especially with lifting or physical management. □ *Assist me with Jane, won't you?* □ *Will you assist me with this heavy box?* □ *Sally assisted herself with the math problem. She did it on her own.*

associate oneself **with** someone or something to join someone or something as a partner or friend. □ *I wanted to associate myself with a prestigious law firm.* □ *She associated herself with people of low repute.*

associate someone or something **with** someone or something to link someone or something [in one's mind] to someone or something else. (*Something* and *someone* can occur in all possible combinations.) □ *I always associate Walter with pizza for some reason.* □ *I associate pizza with stringy cheese.*

associate with someone to be friendly with someone; to be acquainted with someone socially in a work setting. □ *We seek to associate with persons like ourselves.* □ *I like to associate with interesting people.*

assume a low profile Go to a low profile.

assume liability for something to accept the responsibility for paying a cost. □ *Mr. Smith assumed liability for his son's student loans.* □ *The store assumed liability for the injured customer's hospital bills.*

assure someone **of** something to guarantee something to someone; to promise someone that something will happen or that a particular state exists. □ *I want to assure you of our good intentions.* □ *Frequently, she had to assure herself of her basic worth.*

astound someone **with** something to shock or amaze someone with something. □ *She astounded us with her skill.* □ *He astounded himself with his sudden burst of strength.*

at a dead end *Fig.* having reached an impasse; able to go no further forward. □ *I can't go on. I'm at a dead end.* □ *We are at a dead end; the project is hopelessly stalled.*

***at a fast clip** Go to next.

***at a good clip** and ***at a fast clip** rapidly. (*Typically: **go** ~; **move** ~; **run** ~; **travel** ~.) □ *We were moving along at a good clip when a state trooper stopped us.*

at a loss (for words) *Fig.* unable to speak; speechless or befuddled. □ *I was so surprised that I was at a loss for words.* □ *Tom was terribly confused—really at a loss.*

at a moment's notice and **on a moment's notice** with very little advance notice; with just a little bit of warning. □ *They are always asking us to produce reports at a moment's notice.*

at a premium at a high price; priced high because of something special. □ *Sally bought the shoes at a premium because they were of very high quality.* □ *This new sports car sells at a premium because so many people want to buy it.*

at a set time at a particular time; at an assigned time. □ *Each person has to show up at a set time.* □ *Do I have to be there at a set time, or can I come whenever I want?*

at a sitting at one time; during one period. (Usually refers to an activity that takes place while a person is seated.) □ *The restaurant could feed only sixty people at a sitting.* □ *I can read about three hundred pages at a sitting.*

at a snail's gallop Go to next.

at a snail's pace and **at a snail's gallop** very slowly. □ *Things are moving along at a snail's pace here, but we'll finish on time—have no fear.* □ *Poor old Wally is creeping at a snail's gallop because his car has a flat tire.*

at a stretch continuously; without stopping. □ *We all had to do eight hours of duty at a stretch.* □ *The baby doesn't sleep for more than three hours at a stretch.*

at all without qualification. (See the examples for word order variations.) □ *It really wasn't very cold at all.* □ *It really wasn't at all cold.* □ *Tom will eat anything at all.*

at all costs and **at any cost** *Fig.* regardless of the difficulty or cost; no matter what. □ *I intend to have that car at all costs.* □ *Mary was going to get that job at any cost.*

at all hours (of the day and night) Go to all hours (of the day and night).

at all times constantly; continuously. □ *You must keep your passport handy at all times when you are traveling in a foreign country.* □ *When you're in a crowd, you must watch your child at all times.*

at an early date soon; some day soon. □ *The note said, "Please call me at an early date."* □ *You are expected to return the form to the office at an early date.*

at an end having come to a stop; having reached the end. □ *Things are now at an end.* □ *It's over between us. It's at an end. Good-bye.*

at any cost Go to at all costs.

at any rate in any case; anyway. □ *At any rate, what were we talking about?* □ *At any rate, I don't think you should quit your job.*

***at bay** *Fig.* at a distance. (*Typically: **be** ~; **keep** someone or something ~; **remain** ~.) □ *I have to keep the bill collectors at bay until I get my paycheck.* □ *The mosquitoes will not remain at bay for very long.*

at best and **at most** in the most favorable view; in the most positive judgment; as the best one can say. □ *At best we found their visit pleasantly short.* □ *The dinner was not at all pleasant. At best the food was not burned.* □ *At most there were three people in line ahead of me.*

at close range very near; in close proximity. (Usually used in regard to shooting.) □ *The hunter fired at the deer at close range.* □ *The powder burns tell us that the gun was fired at close range.*

at cross-purposes with opposing viewpoints; with goals that interfere with each other. □ *We are arguing at cross-purposes. We aren't even discussing the same thing.* □ *Bill and Tom are working at cross-purposes. They'll never get the job done right.*

at death's door very near the end of one's life. (Often an exaggeration.) □ *I was so ill that I was at death's door for three days.* □ *The family dog was at death's door for three days, and then it finally died.*

23

A

at ease without worry or anxiety. □ *The performer is at ease on the stage.* □ *After she had met a few people, Mary felt at ease with the group.*

at every turn everywhere; everywhere one looks. □ *There is a new problem at every turn.* □ *Life holds exciting adventures at every turn.*

at face value from outward appearance; from what something first appears to be. (From the value printed on the "face" of a coin or bank note.) □ *Don't just accept her offer at face value. Think of the implications.* □ *Joan tends to take people at face value and so she is always getting hurt.*

at fault to blame [for something]; serving as the cause of something bad. □ *I was not at fault in the accident. You cannot blame me.*

at first initially; at the very beginning. □ *He was shy at first. Then he became more friendly.* □ *At first we chose the red one. Later we switched to the blue one.*

at first blush Go to next.

at first glance and **at first blush** when first examined; at an early stage. □ *At first glance, the problem appeared quite simple. Later we learned just how complex it really was.* □ *He appeared quite healthy at first glance.* □ *At first blush, she appeared to be quite old.*

at first light at dawn; when the first light of dawn appears. □ *We will be ready to leave at first light.*

***at full blast** using full power; as loudly as possible. (*Typically: **be on** ~; **play** ~; **play** something ~; **run** ~; **run** something ~.) □ *The neighbors had their televisions on at full blast.* □ *The car radio was on at full blast. We couldn't hear what the driver was saying.*

at full speed and **at full tilt; at full throttle** as fast as possible. □ *The motor was running at full speed.* □ *John finished his running at full tilt.* □ *When the horse reached the back stretch he was at full throttle.*

at full strength at the strongest amount, dilution, power, loudness, etc. □ *You should use this medicine at full strength, even if it tastes bad.*

at full throttle Go to at full speed.

at full tilt Go to at full speed.

***at great length** for a long period of time. (*Typically: **explain** ~; **question** someone ~; **speak** ~.) □ *The lawyer questioned the witness at great length.*

at half-mast and **at half-staff** [of a flag] halfway up or down its flagpole. □ *The flag was flying at half-mast because the general had died.* □ *Americans fly flags at half-staff on Memorial Day.*

at half-staff Go to previous.

at hand close by in time or space. □ *I don't happen to have your application at hand at the moment.* □ *With the holiday season at hand, everyone is very excited.*

at hazard in danger; at risk. □ *He is not willing to have much of his money at hazard in the stock market.* □ *Your life is at hazard unless you wear a helmet when you ride your motorcycle.*

at home at or in one's dwelling. □ *Is Mary at home, or is she still at work?* □ *What time will she be at home?*

at home with someone or something **1.** *Lit.* in one's home with someone or something. □ *She's at home with her mother.* □ *Bob's not alone. He's at home with the cats.* **2.** *Fig.* comfortable with someone or something; comfortable doing something. □ *Tom is very much at home with my parents.* □ *Mary seems to be at home with her job.*

at it again doing something again. □ *I asked Tom to stop playing his trumpet, but he's at it again.* □ *They are at it again. Why are they always fighting?*

at its best Go to at one's best.

at large 1. free; uncaptured. (Usually said of criminals not in custody.) □ *At noon, the day after the robbery, the thieves were still at large.* □ *There is a murderer at large in the city!* **2.** in general; according to a general sample. □ *Truck drivers at large don't like the new speed restriction on the highway.* □ *Students at large felt that discipline was too strict.* **3.** representing the whole group rather than its subsections. (Always refers to a special kind of elective office.) □ *He ran for representative at large.* □ *She represented shareholders at large on the governing board.*

at last finally; after a long wait. □ *The train has come at last.* □ *At last, we have gotten something to eat.*

at least anyway; in spite of difficulties. □ *At least we had a good evening, even though the afternoon was rainy.* □ *At least we came away with some of our money left.*

at least so many no less than; no fewer than. □ *There were at least four people there that I knew.* □ *I want to spend at least three weeks in Mexico.*

at leisure and **at one's leisure** at one's convenience. □ *Choose one or the other at your leisure.* □ *Please drop by at your leisure.*

at length 1. after some time; finally. □ *At length, the roses bloomed, and the tomatoes ripened.* □ *And at length, the wizard spoke.* **2.** and **at some length** for quite a long time. □ *He spoke to us about the problem at some length.* □ *He described the history of his village at length.*

at liberty free; unrestrained. □ *The criminal was set at liberty by the judge.* □ *You're at liberty to go anywhere you wish.* □ *I'm not at liberty to discuss the matter.*

at loggerheads (with someone**)** and **at loggerheads over** something *Fig.* in conflict with someone; having reached an impasse (about something). □ *Tom is at loggerheads with Bill.* □ *We are at loggerheads with each other.* □ *The twins were at loggerheads over who should take the larger room.*

at (long) last after a long wait; finally. □ *At last the hostages were released.* □ *Sally earned her diploma at long last after six years in college.*

***at loose ends** restless and unsettled; unemployed. (*Typically: **be** ~; **leave** someone ~.) □ *Just before school starts, all the children are at loose ends.* □ *Jane has been at loose ends ever since she lost her job.*

at most Go to at best.

at night during the night. □ *Most people sleep at night.* □ *Mary studies at night.*

at odds (with someone**)** and **at odds over** something in opposition to someone; at loggerheads (with someone). □ *Mary is always at odds with her father about how late she can stay out.* □ *John and his father are always at odds over what to watch on TV.*

at once immediately; right now. □ *We must leave at once!* □ *You must come here at once; it is an emergency.*

at one fell swoop and **in one fell swoop** *Fig.* in a single incident; as a single event. (This phrase preserves the old word *fell*, meaning "terrible" or "deadly.") □ *The party guests ate up all the snacks at one fell swoop.* □ *When the stock market crashed, many large fortunes were wiped out in one fell swoop.*

at one's best 1. and **at its best** to the utmost; to the highest degree possible. □ *This restaurant serves gourmet food at its best.* □ *The singer was at her best when she performed ballads.* **2.** in the best of health; displaying the most civilized behavior. (Often in the negative.) □ *He's at his best after a good nap.* □ *I'm not at my best when I'm angry.*

at one's leisure Go to at leisure.

at one's wit's end *Fig.* at the limits of one's mental resources. □ *I'm at my wit's end with this problem. I cannot figure it out.* □ *Tom could do no more. He was at his wit's end.*

at peace 1. relaxed and happy. □ *I am always at peace when I sit in my rocking chair.* □ *When the warm breeze is blowing, I am at peace.* **2.** *Euph.* dead. □ *It was a long illness, but she is at peace now.* □ *At last, Uncle George is at peace.*

at play [at this moment] involved in playing. (See also at work.) □ *The children are at play, and I am doing household chores.* □ *Whether I am at work or at play, I try to be pleasant to people.*

at present now; at this point in time. □ *We are not able to do any more at present.* □ *We may be able to lend you money next week, but not at present.*

at random by chance; haphazard. □ *The lottery numbers are chosen at random.* □ *As a prank, the children dialed phone numbers at random.*

at regular intervals [of things in a series] at points that are equally distant from each other. □ *You will find service stations at regular intervals along the highway.* □ *There are street lights at regular intervals on the main street of town.*

at rest 1. not moving; not active. □ *After the hectic day, the office was finally at rest at 8:00 P.M.* □ *When the car is at rest, you can get into the backseat.* **2.** *Euph.* dead. □ *After a long, weary life, Emily is at rest.* □ *There he is, at rest in his coffin.*

***at risk** in a situation where there is risk or hazard; in danger. (*Typically: **be ~; put** someone or something ~.) □ *I refuse to put my family's welfare at risk by quitting my job.* □ *Your whole future is at risk if you don't stop smoking.*

at sea 1. *Lit.* on the sea; away on a voyage on the ocean. □ *The ship is at sea now, and you can't disembark.* □ *I spent many happy days at sea on my cruise.* **2.** *Fig.* confused; at a loss. □ *Bill was at sea over the calculus problem.* □ *Reading economic theory leaves me feeling at sea.*

at sea level at the level of the surface of the ocean. □ *It is easier to breathe at sea level than in the mountains.* □ *Boats on the ocean are at sea level, but those on rivers are not.*

at sixes and sevens lost in bewilderment; at loose ends. □ *Mrs. Smith is at sixes and sevens since the death of her husband.* □ *Bill is always at sixes and sevens when he's home by himself.*

at some length Go to at length.

at some time sharp exactly at the time named. □ *You must be here at noon sharp.* □ *The plane is expected to arrive at seven forty-five sharp.*

at someone being argumentative or contentious with someone. □ *She is always at him about something.* □ *I wish you weren't at me all the time over finances.*

at someone's beck and call ready to obey someone. □ *What makes you think I wait around here at your beck and call? I have to leave for work, you know!* □ *It was a fine hotel. There were dozens of maids and waiters at our beck and call.*

at someone's doorstep and **on someone's doorstep** *Fig.* in someone's care; as someone's responsibility. □ *Why do you always have to lay your problems at my doorstep?* □ *I shall put this issue on someone else's doorstep.* □ *I don't want that problem on my doorstep.*

at someone's earliest convenience as soon as it is possible for someone to do something. (This is also a polite way of saying *immediately*.) □ *Please stop by my office at your earliest convenience.* □ *Bill, please have the oil changed at your earliest convenience.*

at someone's mercy Go to at the mercy of someone.

at someone's request due to someone's request; on being asked by someone. □ *At his mother's request, Tom stopped playing the saxophone.* □ *At the request of the police officer, Bill pulled his car over to the side of the road.*

at someone's service *Fig.* ready to help someone in any way. □ *The count greeted me warmly and said, "Welcome to my home. Just let me know what you need. I'm at your service."* □ *The desk clerk said, "Good morning, madam. I'm at your service."*

at stake *Fig.* ready to be won or lost; at risk; hanging in the balance. □ *That's a very risky investment. How much money is at stake?* □ *I have everything at stake on this wager.*

at that rate in that manner; at that speed. □ *If things keep progressing at that rate, we'll be rich by next year.* □ *At that rate we'll never get the money that is owed us.*

at the appointed time at the expected or assigned time. □ *The cab pulled up in the driveway at the appointed time.* □ *We all met at the hotel at the appointed time.*

at the bottom of the hour *Fig.* on the half hour; the opposite of **at the top of the hour**. (Alludes to the big hand of a clock pointing to the 6. Typically heard on television or the radio.) □ *Hear the news headlines at the bottom of the hour.* □ *We will have an interview with Harry Kravitz at the bottom of the hour.*

at the bottom of the ladder and **on the bottom rung (of the ladder)** *Fig.* at the lowest level of pay and status. (Alludes to the lowness of the bottom rung of a ladder.) □ *Most people start work at the bottom of the ladder.* □ *After Ann got fired, she had to start all over again on the bottom rung.*

at the break of dawn Go to next.

at the crack of dawn and **at the break of dawn** *Fig.* at the earliest light of the day. □ *Jane was always awake at*

A

the crack of dawn. □ *The birds start singing at the break of dawn.*

at the drop of a hat *Fig.* immediately; instantly; on the slightest signal or urging. (Alludes to the dropping of a hat as a signal.) □ *John was always ready to go fishing at the drop of a hat.* □ *If you need help, just call on me. I can come at the drop of a hat.*

at the eleventh hour *Fig.* at the last possible moment. (Just before the last clock hour, 12) □ *She always turned her term papers in at the eleventh hour.* □ *We don't worry about death until the eleventh hour.*

at the end of nowhere *Fig.* at a remote place; at some distance from civilization. (An exaggeration.) □ *They live way out in the country at the end of nowhere.* □ *The police will never find us here, at the end of nowhere.*

at the end of one's **rope** and **at the end of** one's **tether** *Fig.* at the limits of one's endurance. □ *I'm at the end of my rope! I just can't go on this way!* □ *These kids are driving me out of my mind. I'm at the end of my tether.*

at the end of one's **tether** Go to previous.

at the end of the day 1. *Lit.* at the time when work or one's waking hours end. (See also **by the end of the day.**) □ *I will have an answer at the end of the day.* □ *Will this be finished at the end of the day or before?* **2.** *Fig.* when everything else has been taken into consideration. □ *At the end of the day you will have to decide where you want to live.* □ *The committee interviewed many applicants for the post, but at the end of the day made no appointment.*

at the expense of someone or something *Fig.* to the detriment of someone or something; to the harm of someone or something. □ *He had a good laugh at the expense of his brother.* □ *He took a job in a better place at the expense of a larger income.*

at the forefront (of something**)** and **in the forefront (of** something**)** *Fig.* at the place of greatest activity; vital or important to some activity. □ *I interviewed Max Brown, the director who is in the forefront of the movie industry.* □ *The university I go to is at the forefront of computer technology.*

at the height of something *Fig.* at the most intense or forceful aspect of something. □ *At the height of his career, Tom was known around the world.* □ *At the height of the party, there were 50 people present.*

at the helm (of something**)** *Fig.* in the position of being in control of something. □ *The president is at the helm of the company.* □ *Things will go well with Anne at the helm.*

at the last gasp *Fig.* at the very last; at the last chance; at the last minute. (Refers to someone's last breath before death.) □ *She finally showed up at the last gasp, bringing the papers that were needed.* □ *We got there at the last gasp, just before our names were called.*

at the last minute *Fig.* at the last possible chance; in the last few minutes, hours, or days. (Often an exaggeration.) □ *Please don't make reservations at the last minute.* □ *Why do you ask all your questions at the last minute?*

at the latest not beyond the time mentioned. □ *Please pay this bill in ten days at the latest.* □ *I'll be home by midnight at the latest.*

at the mercy of someone and **at** someone's **mercy** *Fig.* under the control of someone; without defense against someone. □ *We were left at the mercy of the arresting officer.* □ *Mrs. Franklin wanted Mr. Franklin at her mercy.*

at (the) most no more than the amount mentioned. □ *A: How far away is the beach? B: Ten miles at most.* □ *At the most, there were only 15 people in the audience.*

at the outset *Fig.* at the very beginning. □ *At the outset, we were told everything we had to do.* □ *I learned at the outset of the project that I was to lead it.*

at the point of doing something Go to **on the point of** doing something.

at the present time and **at this point (in time)** *Cliché* now; at present. (Used often as a wordy replacement for *now.*) □ *We don't know the location of the stolen car at the present time.* □ *The patient is doing nicely at the present time.*

at the rear of something located at the back part of something. □ *I keep my tools at the rear of my garage.* □ *There's a stream at the rear of my property.*

at the same time 1. *Lit.* during the same moment; simultaneously. □ *We arrived at the same time.* □ *Too many things are happening at the same time, and I am confused.* **2.** *Fig.* nevertheless; however; along with that. □ *Bill was able to pay for the damage. At the same time, he was very angry about the accident.* □ *We agree to your demands. At the same time, we object strongly to your methods.*

at the top of one's **game** *Fig.* good and as good as one is likely to get. (Usually of sports.) □ *I guess I was at the top of my game last year. This year, I stink.*

at the top of one's **lungs** Go to next.

at the top of one's **voice** and **at the top of** one's **lungs** *Fig.* very loudly. □ *Bill called to Mary at the top of his voice.* □ *How can I drive safely when you're all screaming at the top of your lungs?*

at the top of the hour *Fig.* at the exact beginning of an hour. (Alludes to the big hand on a clock pointing to the 12. Often heard on television or the radio. See also **at the bottom of the hour.**) □ *Every class in my school starts at the top of the hour.* □ *Our next newscast will be at the top of the hour.*

at the (very) outside at the very most. □ *The car repairs will cost $300 at the very outside.* □ *I'm now on my way and I'll be there in three hours at the outside.*

at the wheel 1. operating the wheel that turns a ship's rudder; at the helm. □ *The cabin boy was at the wheel with the captain close by.* **2.** operating the steering wheel of a car. □ *Bobby was at the wheel when the car went off the road.*

at (the) worst in the most negative or pessimistic view. □ *At worst, Tom can be seen as greedy.* □ *Ann will receive a ticket for careless driving, at the worst.*

at the zenith of something *Fig.* at the highest point of something; at the pinnacle of something. □ *Tragically, at the zenith of his career, the teacher died suddenly.* □ *The scientist was at the zenith of her career when she made her discovery.*

at this juncture at this point; at this pause. □ *There is little more that I can say at this juncture.* □ *We can, if you wish, at this juncture, request a change in venue.*

at this point (in time) Go to **at the present time.**

at this rate at this speed; if things continue in the same way. (Usually of a pessimistic view.) □ *Hurry up! We'll never get there at this rate.* □ *At this rate, all the food will be gone before we get there.*

at this stage (of the game) *Fig.* at the current point in some event or situation; currently. □ *We'll have to wait and see. There isn't much we can do at this stage of the game.* □ *At this stage, we are better off not calling the doctor.*

at times sometimes; occasionally. □ *I feel quite sad at times.* □ *At times, I wish I had never come here.*

at will whenever one wants; freely. □ *You're free to come and go at will.* □ *The soldiers were told to fire their guns at will.* □ *You can eat anything you want at will.*

at work 1. at one's place of work. □ *I'm sorry to call you at work, but this is important.* □ *She's at work now. She'll be home at supper time.* **2.** working [at something]; busy [with something]. (See also **at play.**) □ *Tom is presently at work on his project. He'll be finished in a half hour.* □ *Don't disturb me when I'm busy at work.*

atone for something to make amends for an error. □ *You must atone for the bad things you have done.*

attach oneself to someone **1.** *Fig.* to become emotionally involved with someone. □ *Fred seems to have attached himself to a much older woman, who has captured his attention.* □ *Somehow, Susan has attached herself emotionally to Tom, and she is distraught over his being away.* **2.** *Fig.* to follow after someone; to become a constant companion to someone. □ *Andy's little brother attached himself to Andy and his friends—much to Andy's distress.* □ *John attached himself to his older brother and drove him crazy.*

attach oneself to something **1.** *Lit.* to connect or secure oneself to something. □ *During the storm, Tony attached himself to the helm and proceeded to steer the boat.* □ *The caterpillar attached itself to a branch and began to spin its cocoon.* **2.** *Fig.* to choose to associate with a particular thing, group, or organization. □ *Ron attached himself to a volleyball team that practices at the school.* □ *The manager attached himself to the luncheon club and became a regular fixture there.*

attach to someone *Fig.* [for blame, importance, guilt, fault, etc.] to become "fixed" onto someone or an organization. □ *A lot of guilt attaches to Henry for his part in the plot.* □ *Most of the blame for the accident attaches to Roger.*

attach to something [for something] to be meant to fit onto or into something. □ *This one attaches to this other one right at this point.* □ *This part should have attached to the back of the desk, but it didn't fit.*

attached to someone or something **1.** *Lit.* connected to someone or something. □ *The patient has a tube attached to his arm.* □ *A little shelf is attached to the wall.* **2.** *Fig.* fond of someone or something. □ *John is really attached to his old-fashioned ideas.* □ *I'm really attached to my long-time girlfriend.*

attack in force Go to **in force.**

*an **attack (of** an illness)** a bout of some sickness; an instance or acute case of some disease. (*Typically: **have** ~; **produce** ~; **suffer** ~.) □ *Mr. Hodder had an attack of stomach upset that forced him to stay at home.*

attend to someone to listen to someone. □ *Please attend to your teacher's instructions.* □ *Attend to the announcement of the new flight departure time.*

attend to someone or something to take care of the needs of someone or something; to respond to a request or demand from someone or something. □ *Please attend to your wounded friend.* □ *Would you please attend to the action points of this memo?*

attest to something to certify or bear witness to a fact. □ *I cannot attest to what you have reported.* □ *The witness attested to the suspect's presence at the scene of the crime.*

attire someone **in** something to dress someone in something. □ *The mother attired her children in new, clean clothes.* □ *She attired herself in her finest garments.*

attract someone or something **to** someone or something else to draw or pull someone or something to someone or something else. □ *The poster attracted a large number of people to the concert.* □ *The shouting attracted a lot of attention from the people who were nearby.*

attribute something **to** someone or something to ascribe something to someone or something; to believe that someone or something is the source of something. □ *We attribute our success to your good advice.* □ *I attribute all these ill-mannered memos to Andrew.*

attune someone or something **to** someone or something else *Fig.* to bring someone or something into accord with someone or something else; to adjust someone or something to someone or something else. (Usually metaphorical. Not used for musical tuning.) □ *You should try to attune yourself to our needs and direction.* □ *Try to attune your comments to the level of your audience.*

auction something **off**† to sell something [to the highest bidder] at an auction. □ *He auctioned his home off.* □ *He auctioned off his home.* □ *The duke was forced to auction off his ancestral home to pay his taxes.*

audition for something to try out for a part in something. (In a setting in which one's singing, speaking, or playing is heard and judged.) □ *I plan to audition for the lead role in the school play.* □ *Liz auditioned for The Mikado.*

audition someone **for** something to allow someone to try out for a part in a performance; to judge someone's singing, speaking, or playing potential for a part in a performance. □ *Will you audition anyone else for the part?* □ *Have you been auditioned for a part in the school play?*

augur well for someone or something to indicate or predict good things for someone or something. (Usually in the negative.) □ *This latest economic message does not augur well for the stock market.* □ *I am afraid that this poll data does not augur well for the incumbent in the election.*

avail oneself **of** something to help oneself by making use of something that is available. □ *We availed ourselves of Tom's goodwill and let him repair the fence.* □ *The campers availed themselves of the first chance in a week to take a shower.*

avenge oneself **(on** someone or something**) (for** something**)** and **avenge** oneself **(against** someone or something**) (for**

something) to get even with, or take revenge against someone or something for some hurt or damage. □ They avenged themselves on the enemy for the surprise attack. □ He avenged himself against the storekeeper for the false charges. □ Mary avenged herself for her ex-husband's neglect to pay child support. □ Tom avenged himself on Bill for Bill's previous insults.

avenue of escape *Fig.* the pathway or route along which someone or something escapes. □ The open window was the bird's only avenue of escape from the house. □ Bill saw that his one avenue of escape was through the back door.

average out (at something) and **average out (to** something) to equal something as the average of a set of figures. □ The figures averaged out at what was expected. □ Will the charges average out to a reasonable figure? □ Over time, our expenses will average out to a low monthly outlay.

average something **up**† to calculate the average of a set of figures. □ Please add these figures and average them up. □ Please average up all the monthly expenses for the previous year. □ Will you please average these figures up on the calculator?

avert something **(away) from** someone or something to turn or divert something away from someone or something. □ We will attempt to avert attention from the problems. □ She averted her eyes from Bill when he walked by.

avoid someone or something **like the plague** *Fig.* to ignore or keep away from someone or something totally. □ What's wrong with Bob? Everyone avoids him like the plague. □ I don't like opera. I avoid it like the plague.

(Aw) shucks! *Rur.* Gosh!; a mild oath. □ Shucks, ma'am. It wasn't anything at all. □ Aw shucks, I ain't never been this close to a woman before.

awake(n) from something to wake up from something, such as a dream or a deep sleep. □ Tom awakened from a deep sleep at the sound of the phone ringing. □ At dawn, she awoke from her slumbers.

awake(n) someone **from** something to cause someone to wake up from something. □ The crowing of the rooster awakened Sally from her slumbers. □ She awakened herself from a deep sleep when she fell out of bed.

awake(n) someone **to** something to make someone alert to something, such as a problem or a need. □ We need to awaken the voters to the need for more taxes. □ They awakened themselves to their callousness and began to treat other people better.

awake(n) to something to wake up while experiencing something. □ Mary awoke to the smell of freshly brewed coffee. □ I love to awaken to music.

award something **(to** someone**) (for** something**)** and **award (**someone**)** something **(for** something**)** to give a prize or reward to someone (for something). □ The committee awarded a plaque to Andy for his loyalty. □ They awarded prizes for efficiency to two different people.

award something **to** someone or something [for a judge or other legal entity] to decide in favor of a person or group. □ The judge awarded the judgment to the plaintiff. □ The jury awarded a large sum to the smaller company.

*****away from it all** at a place where one can avoid completely what one is leaving behind. (*Typically: **be ~; get ~.**) □ I need a few days off to get away from it all. □ Everyone needs to get away from it all every now and then.

*****away from** one's **desk** *Fig.* not available for a telephone conversation; not available to be seen or spoken to. (Sometimes said by the person who answers a telephone in an office. It means that the person whom the caller wants is not immediately available due to personal or business reasons. *Typically: **be ~; step ~.**) □ I'm sorry, but Ann is away from her desk just now. Can you come back later? □ Tom has stepped away from his desk, but if you leave your number, he will call you right back.

*****away (from** someone or something**)** avoiding someone or something; maintaining a physical distance from someone or something. (*Typically: **get ~; keep ~; stay ~.**) □ Please keep away from me if you have a cold. □ Stay away from the construction site, Timmy.

awkward as a bull in a china shop Go to a bull in a china shop.

*****awkward as a cow on a crutch** and *****awkward as a cow on roller skates** very clumsy or off balance. (*Also: **as ~.**) □ When Lulu was overweight, she was awkward as a cow on a crutch. □ Tom will never be a gymnast. He's as awkward as a cow on roller skates!

*****awkward as a cow on roller skates** Go to previous.

the **ax** Go to the sack.

a **babe in arms 1.** *Lit.* a very young baby that is carried by an adult. □ *I have known that since I was a babe in arms!* □ *A young mother with a babe in arms stood in line with the rest of the students.* **2.** *Fig.* an innocent or naive person. □ *He's a babe in arms when it comes to taking girls out.* □ *Mary has no idea how to win the election. Politically she's a babe in arms.*

A **babe in the woods** *Fig.* a naive or innocent person; an inexperienced person. (Like a child lost in the woods.) □ *Bill is a babe in the woods when it comes to dealing with plumbers.* □ *As a painter, Mary is fine, but she's a babe in the woods as a musician.*

babysit for someone and **babysit (with)** someone **1.** to attend and care for a child for a period of time. □ *I'm looking for someone to babysit for my cousin.* □ *Will you babysit with my cousin?* **2.** to attend and care for a child for someone for a short period of time. □ *Would you mind babysitting Roger for me for a few minutes?* □ *Sure, I will babysit for you.*

back and fill *Fig.* to act indecisively; to change one's direction repeatedly; to reverse one's course. (Originally nautical, referring to trimming the sails so as to alternately fill them with wind and release the wind, in order to maneuver in a narrow space.) □ *The president spent most of his speech backing and filling on the question of taxation.* □ *The other candidate was backing and filling on every issue, depending on whom she was addressing.*

back and forth in one direction and then the other repeatedly; from one place to another repeatedly. □ *We tossed the ball back and forth between us.* □ *The tiger paced back and forth in its cage.*

back at it (again) doing something again. (Usually said in criticism.) □ *I thought you stopped smoking, but I see you are back at it again.*

***back (at** someone**)** repaying someone for a bad deed. (*Typically: **get** ~; **have** ~.) □ *Tom called me a jerk, but I'll get back at him.* □ *I don't know how I'll get back for her insult, but I will.*

back away (from someone or something**)** and **back off (from** someone or something**) 1.** *Lit.* to move backwards from a person or thing; to withdraw physically from someone or something. □ *You should back away from the fire.* □ *Please back off from the man who is threatening you.* **2.** *Fig.* to begin to appear uninterested in someone or something; to withdraw one's interest from someone or something. □ *The board of directors began to back away from the idea of taking over the rival company.* □ *Tom backed off from the whole idea of investing in stocks.*

back down (from someone or something**)** to yield to a person or a thing; to fail to carry through on a threat. □ *Jane backed down from her position on the budget.* □ *It's probably better to back down from this situation; looks like you are at a disadvantage.*

back down (on something**)** to lessen or drop an earlier rigid position on something; to yield something in an argument. □ *She backed down on her demands.* □ *In the end, she backed down.*

back down (something**)** to go down something backwards, such as a ladder or inclined driveway. □ *Harry backed*

down the ladder safely. □ *Looking behind him, he backed down slowly.*

back East to or from the eastern United States, especially the northeastern or New England states. (Used even by people who have never been in the East.) □ *Sally felt that she had to get back East for a few days.* □ *Tom went to school back East, but his brother attended college in the Midwest.*

***back in(to) (the) harness** *Fig.* back doing one's job. (*Typically: **be** ~; **get** ~.) □ *I don't look forward to getting back into the harness next Monday.* □ *When my vacation is over, I have to get back into harness the very next day.* □ *I'm not looking forward to having to get back in harness after my trip abroad.*

***back in(to) circulation 1.** *Fig.* back enjoying one's social contacts; back continuing to make new friends and develop a social life. (*Typically: **be** ~; **get** ~.) □ *After her illness, Kristine looked forward to getting back into circulation.* □ *I want to get back in circulation and have some fun.* **2.** *Fig.* becoming available for dating again. (*Typically: **be** ~; **get** ~.) □ *Now that Fred and Amy are through, Amy is getting back into circulation.* □ *Now that you're divorced, are you going to get back into circulation?*

back into someone or something to move backwards, bumping into someone or something; to move a car backwards into something, such as a garage or a parking space. (See also **back** someone or something **into** someone or something.) □ *I'm sorry. I didn't mean to back into you.* □ *I backed into the potted plant.*

the **back of the beyond** the most remote place; somewhere very remote. □ *John hardly ever comes to the city. He lives at the back of the beyond.* □ *Mary likes city life, but her husband likes to live in the back of the beyond.*

back off (from someone or something**)** Go to **back away (from** someone or something**)**.

***back on** one's **feet 1.** *Lit.* standing up again after a fall. (*Typically: **be** ~; **get** ~.) □ *She struggled to get back on her feet after she fell.* **2.** *Fig.* recovered from an illness and out of one's sickbed. *Typically: **be** ~; **get** ~.) □ *I will go back to work as soon as I get back on my feet.* □ *I want to get back on my feet as soon as possible.* **3.** *Fig.* recovered from anything, especially financial problems. (*Typically: **be** ~; **get** ~.) □ *I can't afford to buy a car until I get a job and get back on my feet.* □ *I'll get back on my feet as soon as I start working again.*

B

*back on track *Fig.* running according to schedule again. (*Typically: **get** ~; **get** something ~; **have** something ~; **put** something ~.) □ *I hope we can have this project back on track by the end of the week.*

back oneself **into a corner** *Fig.* to manage to get oneself into a position where there is limited escape. (Ranging from literal to figurative.) □ *He tells different stories to different people. Finally he backed himself into a corner and had to admit his lies.*

back onto someone or something to go backwards, moving or rolling onto someone or something. □ *The motorcycle backed onto my toe.* □ *Don't back onto anything as you go down the driveway!*

back-order something [for a merchant] to order something that is not in stock and make delivery to the customer when the goods become available. □ *The store didn't have the replacement part for my vacuum cleaner, so the manager back-ordered it for me.* □ *The shop had to back-order some of the items on my list.*

back out (of something) **1.** *Lit.* [for someone or something] to move out of something backwards. □ *The rabbit tried to back out of its burrow.* □ *The rabbit backed out.* **2.** *Fig.* [for someone] to withdraw from something, such as an agreement, negotiations, an argument, etc. □ *Are you going to try to back out of our agreement?* □ *You won't back out, will you?*

back over someone or something [for a car or other vehicle] to roll backwards over someone or something. □ *Sandy backed over her brother's bicycle.* □ *She almost backed over her brother.*

*back (some place**)** returned to some place; at some place again. (*Typically: **be** ~; **get** ~; **arrive** ~.) □ *I can't wait till we get back home.* □ *When will we get back? Is it much farther?*

back someone **for** something to support or endorse someone for something, such as a public office. □ *We all back Tom for president.* □ *I am backing Jane for treasurer.*

back someone or something **into** someone or something to guide or move someone or something backwards into someone or something. □ *Don't back your car into anyone.* □ *Using hand signals, the attendant backed all the cars into the parking spaces.*

back someone or something **off (from** something**)** to guide or move someone or something a short distance from something. □ *I backed the car off from the curb a tiny bit.* □ *Using signals, I backed the car off from the crushed bicycle.*

back someone or something **onto** someone or something to guide or move someone or something backwards onto someone or something. □ *I backed the car onto the flowers accidentally.* □ *Using hand signals, the mechanic helped the driver back the car onto the ramp.*

back someone or something **out**[†] **(from** something**)** to back someone or something out of something. □ *Judy backed out the car from the parking place.* □ *She backed it out from its space.*

back someone or something **out of** something and **back** someone or something **out**[†] to guide or move someone or something backwards out of something or some place. □ *Judy backed the car out of the garage.* □ *Please back out the car.* □ *Don backed Fred out of the garage.*

back someone or something **up to** someone or something and **back** someone or something **up**[†] to guide or move someone or something backwards to someone or something. □ *She backed the car up to the end of the street.* □ *Using hand signals, Todd helped back Mary up to the gas pump.* □ *He backed up the motor home carefully.*

back someone **up**[†] to provide someone with help in reserve; to support someone. □ *Don't worry. I will back you up when you need me.* □ *Will you please back up Nancy over the weekend?*

back something **up**[†] **1.** *Lit.* to drive a car backwards. □ *Will you back your car up a little?* □ *I will back up the car.* **2.** *Lit.* to cause objects to obstruct a pathway or channel and cause a slowdown in the flow. □ *The wreck backed the cars up for a long way.* □ *Some dead branches and leaves backed the sewer up.* **3.** *Fig.* to give additional support or evidence about something. (To support or strengthen the facts.) □ *My story of the crime will back your story up.* □ *That backs up my story, all right.*

back the wrong horse *Fig.* to support someone or something that cannot win or succeed. □ *I don't want to back the wrong horse, but it seems to me that Jed is the better candidate.* □ *Fred backed the wrong horse in the budget hearings.*

back to basics return to basic instruction; start the learning process over again. □ *Class, you seem to have forgotten the simplest of facts, so it's back to basics for the first week of classes.*

back to square one *Fig.* back to the beginning. (As with a board game.) □ *Negotiations have broken down, and it's back to square one.* □ *We lost our appeal of the lower court decision, so back to square one.*

back to the drawing board *Fig.* time to start from the start; it is time to plan something over again. (Plans or schematics are drawn on a drawing board. Note the variations shown in the examples.) □ *It didn't work. Back to the drawing board.* □ *I flunked English this semester. Well, back to the old drawing board.*

back to the salt mines *Cliché* time to return to work, school, or something else that might be unpleasant. (The phrase implies that the speaker is a slave who works in the salt mines.) □ *It's one o'clock and lunch break is over. Back to the salt mines.* □ *School starts in the fall, so then it's back to the salt mines again.*

back up 1. *Lit.* [for objects] to obstruct and accumulate in a pathway or channel. □ *Something clogged the sewer and it backed up.* **2.** *Fig.* to refuse to go through with something; to back out (of something). □ *Fred backed up at the last minute, leaving me to do the job alone.*

back up (to someone or something**)** to move backwards to someone or something. (See also **back** someone or something **up to** someone or something.) □ *The bus backed up to the end of the parking space.*

back up (to something**)** to go back to something said in a conversation. □ *Wait—back up a little. What did you say that phone number was?* □ *Let's back up to what you just said and go over that point again.*

backfire on someone *Fig.* [for something, such as a plot] to fail unexpectedly; to fail with an undesired result. □ *Your plot backfired on you.* □ *I was afraid that my scheme would backfire on me.*

backhanded compliment and **left-handed compliment** an unintended or ambiguous compliment. □ *Backhanded compliments are the only kind he ever gives!* □ *And I think his left-handed compliments are all given by accident, too!*

the **backroom boys** Go to the **boys in the back room**.

backseat driver *Fig.* an annoying passenger who tells the driver how to drive; someone who tells others how to do things. □ *I don't need any backseat driver on this project.* □ *Stop pestering me with all your advice. Nobody likes a backseat driver!*

back-to-back 1. *Lit.* adjacent and touching backs. □ *They started the duel by standing back-to-back.* □ *Two people who stand back-to-back can manage to see in all directions.* **2.** *Fig.* following immediately. (Actually such things are front to back, with the "end" of one event followed in time by the beginning of another.) □ *The doctor had appointments set up back-to-back all day long.* □ *I have three lecture courses back-to-back every day of the week.*

*****bad blood (between** people**)** unpleasant feelings or animosity between people. (*Typically: **be ~; have ~.**) □ *There is bad blood between Fred and Jim. They cannot be civil to one another.* □ *There is no bad blood between us. I don't know why we should quarrel.*

a **bad egg** Go to a **rotten egg**.

A **bad excuse is better than none.** *Prov.* If you offer some explanation for an unwanted action, there is a slight chance that it will be accepted and you will therefore not be in trouble, but if you have no explanation at all, you do not even have that slight chance. □ *Fred: I can't believe we played cards till midnight! What will I tell my wife when she asks why I'm so late getting home? Bill: Tell her something came up at the office. Fred: But that's a lousy excuse. She'll never believe it. Bill: A bad excuse is better than none.*

a **bad hair day** a bad day in general. (As when one's inability to groom one's hair in the morning seems to color the events of the day.) □ *I'm sorry I am so glum. This has been a real bad hair day.* □ *It's just one bad hair day after another.*

Bad money drives out good. *Prov.* If there is counterfeit or inflated currency in circulation, people will hoard their genuine currency; worthless things will drive valuable things out of circulation. (This principle is also known as *Gresham's Law*.) □ *When the government reduced the amount of copper in the pennies it produced, we saw that bad money drives out good; everyone saved copper pennies and only spent the less pure ones.* □ *Ever since cheap, flimsy furniture began to be manufactured in large quantities, it has been very difficult to find solid, well-made furniture. Bad craftsmanship, like bad money, drives out good.*

Bad news travels fast. *Prov.* Information about trouble or misfortune disseminates quickly (more quickly than good news). □ *John: Hi, Andy. I'm sorry to hear you got fired. Andy: How did you know about that already? It only happened this morning. John: Bad news travels fast.* □ *I*

called my mother to tell her about my car accident, but my aunt had already told her. Bad news travels fast.

a **bad penny** a worthless person. □ *Wally is a bad penny. Someday he'll end up in jail.* □ *My little brother is a real bad penny. Every time he shows up, he wants to borrow money.*

A **bad penny always turns up.** *Prov.* A worthless person always comes back to the place he or she started out. □ *Jill: I just found out that Tom left town after we fought last Saturday. What if I never see him again? Jane: Don't worry. A bad penny always turns up.*

a **bad time** Go to a **hard time**.

bad times and **difficult times; trying times; hard times; tough times** a period that offers difficulties, such as when there is not enough food, money, or work. □ *We went through trying times when Perry was out of work, but we all bounced back.*

badger someone **into** something *Fig.* to pester someone into doing something. □ *Don't try to badger us into doing it.* □ *My brother and I were badgered into cleaning out the garage.*

badger someone or something **to death** *Fig.* to bother and annoy someone or some group. □ *If you don't tell him what he wants to know, he will badger you to death until he finds out.*

bad-mouth someone or something to say negative things about someone or something. □ *Mr. Smith was always bad-mouthing Mrs. Smith. They just didn't get along.* □ *John bad-mouths his car constantly because it is too small for him.*

bag and baggage and **part and parcel** with one's luggage; with all one's possessions. □ *Sally showed up at our door bag and baggage one Sunday morning.* □ *All right, if you won't pay the rent, out with you, bag and baggage!* □ *Get all your stuff—part and parcel—out of here!*

Bag it! and **Bag your face!** *Sl.* Be quiet!; Shut up and go away! □ *Mary: Sally, you look just terrible! What happened? Sally: Bag it! Mary: Sorry I asked!* □ *Bill: Did I ever tell you about the time I went to Germany? Sue: Give it a rest, Bill. Bag it!* □ *Sue: Can I borrow your car again? Mary: Bag your face, Sue! Sue: Well, I never!*

bag of bones an extremely skinny person or animal with bones showing. (The skin is the figurative bag.) □ *I've lost so much weight that I'm just turning into a bag of bones.* □ *Get that old bag of bones off the racetrack!*

bag of tricks *Fig.* a collection of special techniques or methods. □ *What have you got in your bag of tricks that could help me with this problem?* □ *Here comes Mother with her bag of tricks. I'm sure she can help us.*

bag on someone *Sl.* to criticize someone. □ *Stop bagging on me! I'm tired of all your complaining.* □ *If you are going to bag on everyone all the time, I don't want to hear about it.*

bag some rays Go to **catch some rays**.

Bag that! *Sl.* Forget that! □ *Bag that! The number I gave you was wrong.* □ *There are four—no, bag that!—six of the red ones and three blue ones.*

Bag your face! Go to **Bag it!**

bail out (of something) 1. *Lit.* to jump out of an airplane with a parachute. □ *John still remembers the first time he* bailed out of a plane. □ When we get to 8,000 feet, we'll all bail out and drift down together. We'll open our parachutes at 2,000 feet. **2.** *Fig.* to abandon a situation; to get out of something. □ John got tired of school, so he just bailed out. □ Please stay, Bill. You've been with us too long to bail out now.

bail someone or something **out†** *Fig.* to rescue someone or something from trouble or difficulty. (Based on **bail** someone **out of jail.**) □ The proposed law was in trouble, but Senator Todd bailed out the bill at the last minute. □ I was going to be late with my report, but my roommate lent a hand and bailed me out at the last minute.

bail someone **out of jail** and **bail** someone **out†** **1.** *Lit.* to deposit a sum of money that allows someone to get out of jail while waiting for a trial. □ John was in jail. I had to go down to the police station to bail him out. □ I need some cash to bail out a friend! **2.** *Fig.* to help someone who is having difficulties. □ When my brother went broke, I had to bail him out with a loan.

bail something **out†** **1.** to remove water from the bottom of a boat by dipping or scooping. □ Tom has to bail the boat out before we get in. □ You should always bail out a boat before using it. **2.** to empty a boat of accumulated water. □ Would you bail this boat out? □ I will bail out the boat.

bait and switch *Fig.* a deceptive merchandising practice where one product is advertised at a low price to get people's attention [the bait], but pressure is applied to get the customer to purchase a more expensive item. □ Walter described how the store used bait and switch, since they never seemed to have in stock the bargains that they advertised. □ Wilbur accused the merchant of bait and switch practices and stalked out of the store.

bake something **from scratch** Go to from scratch.

a **baker's dozen** thirteen. (Bakers often added an extra item to an order for a dozen.) □ We ended up with a baker's dozen each of socks and undershirts on our shopping trip.

the **balance of power** the situation where the power held by one governing body or adversary is balanced by the power of another. □ The balance of power was threatened when China captured our airplane.

balance out to equal out; to become even or fair. □ These things all balance out in the end. □ Don't worry. Things will balance out.

balance something **against** something else to consider one thing in reference to another; to weigh one possibility against another possibility. □ We will have to balance all the good he did against all the bad. □ The good will be balanced against the bad in the final reckoning.

balance something **with** something else to offset something with something else; to **balance** something **against** something else. □ The teacher tends to balance a harsh grading scheme with a strong sense of fair play. □ Roger balanced the spicy soup with a bland first course. □ They balanced his bad behavior with the good, but still felt he was much too rude.

balance the accounts 1. *Lit.* and **balance the books** to determine through bookkeeping that accounts are in balance, that all money is accounted for. □ Jane was up all night balancing the accounts. □ The cashier was not allowed

to leave the bank until the manager balanced the books. **2.** *Fig.* to get even [with someone]. □ Tom hit Bob. Bob balanced the accounts by breaking Tom's toy car. □ Once we have balanced the accounts, we can shake hands and be friends again.

bald as a baby's backside Go to next.

***bald as a coot** and ***bald as a baby's backside** completely bald. (*Also: **as** ~.) □ If Tom's hair keeps receding like that, he'll be bald as a coot by the time he's thirty. □ Fred: Now, I'll admit my hair is thinning a little on the top, but— Jane: Thinning? You're not thinning, you're as bald as a baby's backside!

***baleful as death** promising evil; very threatening. (*Also: **as** ~.) □ The wind's moan was as baleful as death. □ His voice sounded baleful as death.

balk at something to resist and object to something; to shy away from doing something. □ I hope they don't balk at finishing their work. □ They will probably balk at it.

ball and chain 1. a wife. (Mostly jocular.) □ I've got to get home to my ball and chain. □ My ball and chain is mad at me. **2.** a person's special burden; a job. (Prisoners sometimes were fettered with a chain attached to a leg on one end and to a heavy metal ball on the other.) □ Tom wanted to quit his job. He said he was tired of that old ball and chain. □ Mr. Franklin always referred to his wife as his ball and chain.

the **ball is in** someone's **court** *Fig.* to be someone else's move, play, or turn. (From tennis.) □ The ball's in your court now. You do something. □ I can't do anything as long as the ball is in John's court.

ball of fire and **fireball** an energetic and ambitious person; a go-getter. □ That guy is a real ball of fire when it comes to sales. □ I don't want to hire some young fireball. I need wisdom and thoughtfulness.

ball someone or something **up†** to interfere with someone or something; to mess someone or something up. □ Who balled this television up? □ Someone balled up the television.

ball something **up†** to roll something up into a ball. (Alluding to something, such as rope, being tangled up and so useless.) □ She balled the clay up and stuck it to the clown's face as a nose. □ Why are you balling up the paper?

a **ballpark figure** *Fig.* an estimate; an off-the-cuff guess. □ I don't need an exact number. A ballpark figure will do.

the **balls of** one's **feet** the bottom part of the feet just behind the toes. □ Mary got blisters on the balls of her feet from playing tennis. □ The dancer balanced on the balls of his feet.

ban someone **from** something **1.** to prohibit someone from doing something. □ We banned everyone from smoking. □ Everyone has been banned from smoking. **2.** to prohibit someone from entering something or some place. (The same as **bar** someone **from** some place.) □ They banned us from the building. □ The manager banned the children from the theater.

band together (against someone or something) to unite in opposition to someone or something; to unite against someone or something. □ We must band together against the enemy. □ Everyone banded together to finish the cleanup work.

bandage someone or something **up**† to wrap bandages on someone or on someone's wounds. □ *We should bandage the wounds up first.* □ *We should bandage up the wounds first.* □ *I have to bandage him up before we can move him.* □ *She bandaged herself up with the supplies she kept in her backpack.*

bandy something **about**† to spread something, such as someone's good name, around in an unfavorable context; to toss words around in a gossipy fashion. (*Bandy* means to toss or hit something back and forth.) □ *Just stop bandying words about and start telling the truth!* □ *There is no need to keep bandying about those rumors.*

bandy with someone to argue [with someone]; to argue by "playing catch with words." (*Bandy* means to toss or hit something back and forth.) □ *Why are you bandying with me?* □ *She has been bandied with enough. Give her a straight answer.*

bang against someone or something to knock or strike against someone or something. □ *The shutter banged against the side of the house.* □ *The board banged against me and hurt my shin.*

bang (away) at something to hit at something repeatedly, causing harm or making noise. □ *Someone is banging away at the door.* □ *Stop banging at the door.*

(bang) dead to rights in the act; (guilty) without question. □ *We caught her dead to rights with the loot still on her.* □ *There he was, bang dead to rights with the smoking gun still in his hands.*

bang for the buck value for the money spent; excitement for the money spent; a favorable cost-to-benefit ratio. (Expressed as an amount of **bang for the buck**.) □ *I didn't get anywhere near the bang for the buck I expected.* □ *How much bang for the buck did you really think you would get from a twelve-year-old car—at any price?*

bang into someone or something to knock or bump into someone or something. □ *Why did you bang into me with your car?* □ *I banged into the door by accident.*

bang on someone or something to strike someone or something repeatedly. (Especially to beat on a person or a drum.) □ *Please stop banging on that drum!* □ *Max was banging on Lefty when the cops arrived.*

bang one's **head against a brick wall** Go to **beat** one's **head against the wall.**

bang someone or something **around**† to knock someone or something about; to beat or strike someone or something. □ *Let's bang him around a little and see if that will change his mind.* □ *Why are you banging around my friend?* □ *Don't bang those pans around.* □ *He banged himself around badly in the car wreck.*

bang someone **up**† to beat someone up; to assault someone; to damage someone. □ *The crooks banged him up a little bit.* □ *The crash banged up the passengers in the car.* □ *She banged herself up badly.*

bang something **against** someone or something to strike something against someone or something. (Usually refers to striking with something that can make a banging noise.) □ *She banged the spoon against the pan to call everyone to dinner.* □ *He banged the pan against me and made me very angry.*

bang something **in**† to crush something; to dent or collapse something. □ *Who banged the side of the washing machine in?* □ *Who banged in the side of the washing machine?*

bang something **into** someone or something to strike someone or something with something. □ *Mark banged his fist into the cushion and swore.* □ *He banged the pole into Liz by accident.*

bang something **out**† to play something on the piano, loudly, banging on the keys; to type something on a keyboard by pounding on the keys. □ *Let me bang this melody out and see if you can guess who wrote it.* □ *Please bang out the school song good and loud.* □ *I banged out the newspaper story and just barely made my deadline.*

bang something **up**† to crash or wreck something; to damage something. □ *Don't bang my best skillet up!* □ *Who banged up my best skillet?*

bang the drum for someone or something Go to **beat the drum for** someone or something.

banish someone or something **from** some place to ban or evict someone or something from some place. □ *The town council banished motorcycles from all the parks in town.* □ *The new law banished vagrants from the train station.*

bank on something *Fig.* to be so sure of something that one can trust it as one might trust a bank with one's money. □ *I will be there on time. You can bank on it.* □ *I need a promise of your help. I hope I can bank on it.*

bank something **up**† **(against** something**) 1.** to heap or mound up something so that it presses against something. □ *Walter banked the coals up against the side of the furnace.* □ *He banked up the coals against the side.* □ *Tim banked the coals up.* **2.** to heap or mound up something to guard against something. □ *They had to build barriers to hide behind. They banked dirt and rubble up against the oncoming attackers.* □ *Who banked up this dirt against the flood?* □ *The river was rising, so we banked some dirt up.*

banker's hours *Fig.* short work hours: 10:00 A.M. to 3:00 P.M. □ *When did you start keeping banker's hours?* □ *There aren't many bankers who keep banker's hours these days.*

baptism of fire *Fig.* a first experience of something, usually something difficult or unpleasant. □ *My son's just had his first visit to the dentist. He stood up to this baptism of fire very well.* □ *Mary's had her baptism of fire as a teacher. She was assigned to the worst class in the school.*

bar none with no exceptions. (Follows an assertion.) □ *This is the best of all, bar none.*

bar someone **from** some place to prevent someone from entering some place. (See also **ban** someone **from** something.) □ *Please don't bar me from the movie theater. I will be quiet from now on.* □ *They were barred from the concert for smoking.*

bare one's **soul (to** someone**)** *Fig.* to reveal one's innermost thoughts to someone; to tell another person exactly how one feels about someone or something. □ *Mary bared her soul to Jane and Jane told Mary her problems also.* □ *You don't have to bare your soul to me. Just tell me why you are crying.*

bare one's **teeth** Go to **show** one's **teeth.**

the **bare** something the smallest or least possible. □ *Bob did the bare minimum of work to pass the class.* □ *Food, clothing, and shelter are the bare necessities of life.*

bare something **to** someone to reveal or disclose something to someone. □ *I have to know a guy pretty well before I will bare my innermost thoughts to him.* □ *Our criminal involvement was bared to the judge.*

bare-bones *Cliché* limited; stripped down; lacking refinements or extras. □ *This one is the bare-bones model. It has no accessories at all.*

barf out *Sl.* to become deranged, to a greater or lesser degree. □ *Terry barfed out when he heard about the damage Nick had done to his car.* □ *Yuck! I thought I was going to barf out.*

barf someone **out** *Sl.* to disgust someone. (Fixed order.) □ *You just barf me out!* □ *I barf myself out every time I look in the mirror.*

bargain (for someone or something**) (with** someone**)** Go to bargain **(over** someone or something**) (with** someone**).**

bargain for something and **bargain on** something to plan for something; to expect something. □ *We knew the project would be difficult, but we didn't bargain for this kind of trouble.* □ *I bargained on an easier time of it than this.*

bargain on something Go to previous.

bargain (over someone or something**) (with** someone**)** and **bargain (for** someone or something**) (with** someone**)** to negotiate with someone about obtaining someone or something. □ *I refuse to bargain over money with Dan.* □ *We will bargain with the supplier over prices.* □ *You can't bargain over Claire with Jeff as if she were a car!*

bargaining chip *Fig.* something to be used (traded) in negotiations. □ *I want to use their refusal to meet our terms as a bargaining chip in future negotiations.* □ *I need to have a few bargaining chips ready when we get down to drawing up the contract.*

barge in (on someone or something**)** *Fig.* to break in on someone or something; to interrupt someone or something. □ *Oh! I'm sorry. I didn't mean to barge in on you.* □ *They barged in on the church service and caused a commotion.* □ *Please don't interrupt me! You can't just barge in like that!*

barge in(to some place**)** *Fig.* to go or come rudely into some place. (See also barge **into** someone or something.) □ *He just barged right in without knocking.* □ *Don't barge in like that, without letting us know you're here!*

barge into someone or something *Fig.* to bump or crash into someone or something, possibly on purpose. □ *She just barged into me and nearly knocked me over.* □ *Tom tripped, barged into the water cooler, and hurt his knee.*

bark at someone *Fig.* to speak harshly to someone. □ *Don't bark at me like that over such a trivial mistake!* □ *Ken barked at the children for being noisy.*

bark at someone or something *Lit.* [for a dog] to make a characteristic sharp sound at someone or something. (See also bark **at** someone.) □ *The dog is barking at the traffic again.* □ *Their guard dog was barking at me.*

bark something **out at** someone and **bark** something **at** someone; **bark** something **to** someone; **bark** something **out†** **(to** someone**)** *Fig.* to say something harshly to some-

one. □ *The sergeant barked the orders out at the recruits.* □ *He barked an order at his staff.* □ *The teacher barked a reprimand out to the class.* □ *He barked out the order clearly and loudly.*

bark up the wrong tree *Fig.* to make the wrong choice; to ask the wrong person; to follow the wrong course. (Alludes to a dog in pursuit of an animal, where the animal is in one tree and the dog is barking at another tree.) □ *If you think I'm the guilty person, you're barking up the wrong tree.* □ *The hitters blamed the team's bad record on the pitchers, but they were barking up the wrong tree.*

A **barking dog never bites.** *Prov.* Someone who makes threats all the time seldom carries out the threats. □ *Old Mrs. Smith keeps saying she'll call the police if we walk on her lawn, but don't worry. A barking dog never bites.* □ *My boss threatens to fire me at least once a week, but a barking dog never bites.*

barrel along to move along rapidly. □ *The car was barreling along at a fairly rapid clip.* □ *Don't barrel along so fast that you miss the turn.*

barrel in(to some place**)** *Fig.* to move into a place rapidly and with great force. □ *Tony barreled into the room and interrupted the card game.* □ *He just barreled in without knocking.*

a **barrel of fun** *Fig.* a tremendous amount of fun. □ *Jill is just a barrel of fun in class.* □ *We had a barrel of fun at your party.*

barrel out (of some place**)** to move rapidly out of a place; to burst out of a place. □ *The kids barreled out of town as fast as they could go.* □ *They heard the police siren and quickly barreled out.*

barter for something and **barter over** something to trade [something] for something else; to acquire something by exchanging goods or services, not by using money. □ *I want to barter for a large amount of cloth.* □ *Will you barter for this month's rent?* □ *We will not barter over what you owe us.*

barter something **away†** to trade something away; to lose something of value in a trade. □ *Don't barter my car away!* □ *Don't barter away anything of such high value.*

barter something **for** something else to trade something for something else. □ *He sought to barter the car for a large computer.* □ *She bartered the piano for a settee.*

barter something **off†** to get rid of something by trading it for something else. □ *See if you can barter that old desk off.* □ *She bartered off the used bookshelf.*

barter with someone to enter into trading with someone without using money; to bargain with someone. □ *Are you willing to barter with me, or is this strictly a cash transaction?*

base one's **opinion on** something to make a judgment or form an opinion from something. □ *You must not base your opinion on one bad experience.* □ *I base my opinion on many years of studying the problem.*

base something **(up)on** someone or something to ground something, such as one's opinion, decision, or thinking, on someone or something; to found one's ideas or attitude on something. (*Upon* is more formal and less commonly used than *on*.) □ *I base my opinion on many, many facts.* □ *I based my opinion upon my own seasoned judgment.*

bash someone or something **around**[†] to treat someone or something roughly (physically or figuratively); to beat on or abuse someone or something (physically or otherwise). □ *Stop bashing me around, and let's talk.* □ *The robber acted as though he was about to bash around his victims.*

bash something **against** someone or something to strike something against someone or something. □ *He accidentally bashed his head against a beam.* □ *She bashed her sore elbow against Ted's forehead and both of them were hurt.*

bash something **in**[†] to crush something inward or to the inside. □ *Don't bash the door in!* □ *It sounds like someone is bashing in the door.*

bash something **up**[†] to crash something; to strike something and damage it. □ *She bashed the car up badly.* □ *How did she bash up the car?*

bask in something *Fig.* to enjoy or revel in something, such as praise, fame, etc. (Alludes to a person or animal resting in the warming rays of the sun.) □ *Alice enjoyed basking in her newfound fame.* □ *Lily loves basking in praise.*

a **basket case** *Fig.* a person who is a nervous wreck. (Formerly referred to a person who is physically disabled in all four limbs because of paralysis or amputation.) □ *After that all-day meeting, I was practically a basket case.* □ *My weeks of worry were so intense that I was a real basket case afterwards.*

bat something **around**[†] **1.** *Lit.* to knock something around with a bat or something similar. □ *Terry spent a little time batting a ball around, then he went home.* □ *Let's bat around some balls before we go home.* **2.** *Fig.* to discuss something back and forth. □ *Let's bat this around a little bit tomorrow at our meeting.* □ *Do you want to bat around this matter a little more?*

ba(t)ch (it) to live alone like a bachelor. □ *I tried to bach it for a while, but I got too lonely.* □ *I didn't want to batch, but I had to.*

bathe someone or something **in** something **1.** *Lit.* to cleanse someone or something in something; to coat someone or something all over with some liquid. (In a container of liquid or the liquid itself.) □ *She bathed the baby in warm water.* □ *Liz bathed her injured hand in cold water.* □ *She bathed herself in the warm spring water and took a long nap under a tree.* **2.** *Fig.* to blanket or spread over someone or something, as with light, vapor, color, etc. □ *The candles bathed her in a soft glow.* □ *The red of the sunset bathed the trees in an eerie light.*

batten down the hatches *Fig.* to prepare for difficult times. (From a nautical expression meaning, literally, to seal the hatches against the arrival of a storm. The word order is fixed.) □ *Here comes that contentious Mrs. Jones. Batten down the hatches!* □ *Batten down the hatches, Congress is in session again.*

batter someone or something **up**[†] to damage or harm someone or something. □ *Max threatened to batter Lefty up within an inch of his life.* □ *Who battered up this desk?*

batter something **down**[†] to smash or break down something, such as a wall, door, or any defensive structure. □ *Do they have to batter anything down as part of the construction project?* □ *They battered down the wall as a first step in enlarging the house.*

battle against someone or something **1.** *Lit.* to wage a fight against someone or something; to attempt to defeat someone or something. □ *The army battled against the enemy until both sides were exhausted.* **2.** *Fig.* to struggle with someone or something. □ *We are battling against the ancient enemies of ignorance and hatred.* □ *I am tired of battling against Karen.*

battle for something **1.** *Lit.* to fight to gain something. □ *The army battled for the town until they had defeated its defenders.* **2.** *Fig.* to attempt to win or gain something by struggling or arguing. □ *Both of them battled for Kristina's attention.*

battle of the bulge the attempt to keep one's waistline slim. (Jocular. Alludes to a World War II battle.) □ *She appears to have lost the battle of the bulge.* □ *I've been fighting the battle of the bulge ever since I turned 35.*

a **battle royal** a classic, hard-fought battle or argument. □ *The meeting turned into a battle royal and everyone left angry.*

battle something **out**[†] **1.** *Lit.* to fight about something to a conclusion. □ *They battled the matter out and came to an agreement.* □ *The two young toughs went into the alley to battle out their differences.* **2.** *Fig.* to argue something to a conclusion; to struggle to reach a conclusion. □ *The Senate and the House disagree on the bill, so they will have to battle a compromise out.*

battle (with someone**) (over** someone or something**)** *Fig.* to argue or struggle with someone over someone or something. (Not meant to involve physical fighting.) □ *Why do you always have to battle with me over practically nothing?* □ *You shouldn't battle over just anything for the sake of argument!*

bawl someone **out**[†] to scold someone in a loud voice. □ *The teacher bawled the student out for arriving late.* □ *Principals don't usually bawl out students.*

bay at something to howl at something. (Usually said of a dog, wolf, or coyote.) □ *The dogs were baying at the moon.* □ *We heard a coyote in the distance, baying at the moon.*

Be careful. 1. an instruction to take care in a particular situation. □ *Bill: I'm going to the beach tomorrow. Sally: Be careful. Use lots of sunscreen!* □ *Jane: Well, we're off to the Amazon. Mary: Heavens! Be careful!* **2.** a way of saying good-bye while cautioning someone to take care. □ *John: See you around, Fred. Fred: Be careful.* □ *Alice: Well, I'm off. John: Bye, Alice, be careful.*

be for doing something Go to next.

be for someone or something and **be for** doing something supporting or in favor of someone or something. □ *I'm for abandoning the scheme.* □ *Mary is running for office, and the whole family is for her.*

be game to be ready for action; to be agreeable to participating in something. □ *"I'm game," David replied when I suggested we go for a long hike.* □ *We're going to the park to play football. Are you game?*

be given precedence over someone or something Go to **precedence over** someone or something.

Be good. a departure response meaning "good-bye and behave yourself." □ *Jane: Well, we're off. Be back in a week. Mary: Okay, have fun. Be good. Jane: Do I have to?* □ *Tom: Bye. Be good. Bill: See you next month.*

B

Be happy to (do something**).** Go to (I'd be) happy to (do something).

be in aid of to be intended to help, cure, or resolve. □ *What is all this in aid of?* □ *I don't understand what your comments are in aid of.*

Be just before you're generous. *Prov.* Do what you ought to do before you do things that you want to do; pay your debts before you give money away. □ *Jill: It's payday! I can't wait to go out and buy my niece that nice toy train set for her birthday. Jane: But, Jill, we have bills to pay. Be just before you're generous.*

Be my guest. Help yourself.; After you. (A polite way of indicating that someone else should go first, help himself or herself to something, or take the last one of something.) □ *Mary: I would just love to have some more cake, but there is only one piece left. Sally: Be my guest. Mary: Wow! Thanks!* □ *Jane: Here's the door. Who should go in first? Bill: Be my guest. I'll wait out here. Jane: You're so polite!*

be one's **brother's keeper** to be responsible for someone else. (Used of others besides just real brothers.) □ *I can't force these kids to go to school and get an education so they can get jobs. I am not my brother's keeper.* □ *You can't expect me to be my brother's keeper. Each of us should be responsible for himself!*

be one's **own man** and **be** one's **own master** to be someone who is not controlled by other people; to be an independent person. □ *Bert longed to be his own master, but at the same time feared losing the security he had as the employee of a large company.* □ *When I go away to college, I'll be my own man. My parents won't be able to tell me what to do anymore.*

be one's **own master** Go to previous.

Be quiet! Stop talking or making noise. (Regarded as a bit harsh or overbearing, but made polite with *please.*) □ *Bill (entering the room): Hey, Tom! Tom: Please be quiet! I'm on the phone.* □ *Tom: Hey, Bill! Bill: Be quiet! You're too loud. Tom: Sorry.*

be so bold as to do something and **make so bold as to** do something to dare to do something. □ *Would you care to dance, if I may make so bold as to ask?* □ *She was so bold to confront her rival.*

be that as it may *Cliché* even if what you say is true. □ *I am sorry to hear about your troubles, but, be that as it may, you still must carry out your responsibilities.* □ *Be that as it may, I still cannot help you.*

be the last person (to do something**)** to be the most unlikely person of whom one could think in a particular situation; to be the most unlikely person to do something. (Also literal.) □ *Mary is the last person you should ask to chair the meeting—she's so shy.*

Be there or be square. *Sl.* Attend or be at some event or place or be considered uncooperative or not "with it." □ *There's a bunch of people going to be at John's on Saturday. Be there or be square.*

be too and **be so** to be something (despite any information to the contrary). (An emphatic form of *is, am, are, was, were.*) □ *Mother: Billy, you aren't old enough to be up this late. Billy: I am too!* □ *I was so! I was there exactly when I said I would be!*

Beam me up, Scotty! Get me out of here!; Take me away from this mess! (From the late 1960s television program *Star Trek.*) □ *This place is really crazy! Beam me up, Scotty!* □ *I've heard enough! Beam me up, Scotty!*

beam someone or something **up**[†] **(to** some place**)** to transport someone or something (up) to something. (Originally in the context of a *Star Trek* adventure, but also used jocularly.) □ *The captain asked the first mate to beam him up.* □ *Please beam up the crew, Roger.* □ *Beam me up so I can see your penthouse suite!*

beam up *Sl.* to die. (Alluding to the television program *Star Trek.*) □ *Pete Dead? I didn't think he was old enough to beam up.* □ *I was so exhausted after climbing four flights that I was afraid I would beam up.*

bear a grudge (against someone**)** and **have a grudge (against** someone**); hold a grudge (against** someone**)** to continue feeling an old resentment for someone; to harbor continual anger for someone. □ *She bears a grudge against the judge who sentenced her.* □ *I have a grudge against my landlord for not fixing the leaky faucet.*

bear a resemblance to someone or something to have a degree of similarity to someone or something. □ *This wallet bears a strong resemblance to the one I lost last month.* □ *Do you think that Wally bears any resemblance to his sister Mary?*

bear down (on someone or something**)** to press down on someone or something. □ *Bear down on the pen. You have to make a lot of copies.* □ *Don't bear down too hard or you'll break it.*

bear fruit 1. *Lit.* [for a plant or tree] to yield fruit. □ *Our apple tree didn't bear fruit this year.* **2.** *Fig.* to yield results. □ *I hope your new plan bears fruit.* □ *We've had many good ideas, but none of them has borne fruit.*

bear in mind that... to remember [something]; to consider [something]. □ *Bear in mind that the trip will be expensive.* □ *I asked the teacher to bear in mind that I am just a beginner.*

bear off (of something**)** to turn off a road or course. □ *Bear off the main road to the left.* □ *Don't bear off too sharply.*

bear one's **cross** and **carry** one's **cross** *Fig.* to handle or cope with one's burden; to endure one's difficulties. (This is a biblical theme. It is always used figuratively except in the biblical context.) □ *It's a very painful disease, but I'll bear my cross.* □ *I can't help you with it. You'll just have to carry your own cross.*

bear someone or something **in mind** Go to keep someone or something in mind.

bear someone or something **up**[†] to hold someone or something up; to support someone or something. □ *Will this bench bear me up?* □ *This bench is so sturdy it would bear up an elephant.*

bear someone **up**[†] to sustain or encourage someone. □ *Your encouragement bore me up through a very hard time.* □ *I will bear up the widow through the funeral service as well as I can.*

bear something **out**[†] [for facts or evidence] to support or confirm a story or explanation. □ *The facts don't bear this out.* □ *Her story bears out exactly what you said.*

bear the blame for something Go to the blame for something.

bear the brunt (of something**)** to withstand the worst part or the strongest part of something, such as an attack. □ *I had to bear the brunt of her screaming and yelling.* □ *Why don't you talk with her the next time she complains? I'm tired of bearing the brunt of her objections.*

bear up (against something**)** to withstand something. □ *She was unable to bear up against the criticism.* □ *Ken bore up against the challenge of his disabling injury well.*

bear up (under something**) 1.** *Lit.* to hold up under something; to sustain the weight of something. □ *How is the new beam bearing up under the weight of the floor?* □ *It isn't bearing up. It broke.* **2.** *Fig.* [for someone] to remain brave under a mental or emotional burden. □ *Jill did not bear up well under problems with her family.* □ *Jill bore up quite well amid serious difficulties.*

bear (up)on something [for information or facts] to concern something or be relevant to something. (*Upon* is formal and less commonly used than *on.*) □ *How do those facts bear on this matter?* □ *They do not bear upon this matter at all.*

bear watching to need close, attentive observation or monitoring. □ *This problem will bear watching.* □ *This is a very serious disease, and it will bear watching for further developments.*

bear with someone or something to be patient with someone or something; to wait upon someone or something. (Especially through difficulties.) □ *Please bear with me for a moment while I try to get this straightened out.* □ *Can you bear with the committee until it reaches a decision?*

beard the lion in his den and **beard** someone **in** his **den** *Prov.* to confront someone on his or her own territory. □ *I spent a week trying to reach Mr. Toynbee by phone, but his secretary always told me he was too busy to talk to me. Today I walked straight into his office and bearded the lion in his den.* □ *If the landlord doesn't contact us soon, we'll have to beard him in his den.*

beat a dead horse Go to flog a dead horse.

beat a (hasty) retreat to withdraw from a place very quickly. □ *We went out into the cold weather, but beat a retreat to the warmth of our fire.* □ *The dog beat a hasty retreat to its own yard.*

beat a path to someone's **door** *Fig.* [for people] to arrive (at a person's place) in great numbers. (The image is that so many people will wish to come that they will wear down a pathway to the door.) □ *I have a new product so good that everyone will beat a path to my door.* □ *If you really become famous, people will beat a path to your door.*

beat about the bush Go to beat around the bush.

beat against someone or something to strike against someone or something. □ *The wind beat against the sides of the house.* □ *Max beat against Lefty's jaw with his quick jabs.*

beat around the bush and **beat about the bush** *Fig.* to avoid answering a question; to stall; to waste time. □ *Stop beating around the bush and answer my question.* □ *Let's stop beating about the bush and discuss this matter.*

beat at something to strike out at something. □ *He beat at his attacker to no avail.* □ *Lily beat at the snake, but didn't harm it.*

beat down (on someone or something**)** to fall on someone or something. □ *The rain beat down on us for an hour.* □ *The rock slide beat down on the car and totally ruined the body.*

Beat it! *Inf.* Go away!; Get out! □ *Bill: Sorry I broke your radio. Bob: Get out of here! Beat it!* □ *"Beat it, you kids! Go play somewhere else!" yelled the storekeeper.*

beat on someone or something to pound or hammer on someone or something. □ *She beat on him until he let her go.* □ *Stop beating on that drum!*

beat one's **brains out**† **(to** do something**)** to try very hard to do something. □ *If you think I'm going to beat my brains out to do this, you are crazy.* □ *I beat out my brains to do this for you!* □ *I won't beat my brains out again for you!*

beat one's **gums** to waste time talking a great deal without results. (As if one were toothless.) □ *I'm tired of beating my gums about this over and over.* □ *You're just beating your gums. No one is listening.*

beat one's **head against the wall** and **bang** one's **head against a brick wall** *Fig.* to waste one's time trying hard to accomplish something that is completely hopeless. □ *You're wasting your time trying to figure this puzzle out. You're just beating your head against the wall.* □ *You're banging your head against a brick wall trying to get that dog to behave properly.*

beat oneself **up** *Fig.* to be overly critical of one's behavior or actions; to punish oneself with guilt and remorse over past actions. (Not a physical beating. Fixed order.) □ *It's over and done with. There's no need to beat yourself up.* □ *He's beating himself up over his role in the accident.*

beat someone **down**† *Fig.* to defeat or demoralize someone. □ *The constant bombing finally beat them down.* □ *The attackers beat down the defenders.*

beat someone **down to size** and **knock** someone **down to size** *Fig.* to make a person more humble, sometime by actual physical beating. □ *If you keep acting so arrogant, someone is going to beat you down to size.* □ *It's time someone knocked you down to size.* □ *I'll try to be less arrogant. I don't want anyone to beat me down to size.*

beat someone **into (doing)** something to beat a person until the person agrees to do something or to assume a particular attitude. □ *They had to beat John into submission before he gave up.* □ *Max threatened to beat Lefty into helping him rob the candy store.*

beat someone **into** something *Fig.* to beat a person until the person turns into a particular physical state, such as a pulp, a mess, etc. □ *Fred threatened to beat Mike into a pulp if he didn't do as he was asked.* □ *Mike beat Fred into a bloody mess.*

beat someone or something **back**† to drive someone or something back to where it came from. □ *We beat them back to where they were before the war started.* □ *The army beat back the defenders and saved the town.* □ *They were able to beat the wolves back and make an escape.*

beat someone or something **off**† to drive someone or something away by beating. □ *They beat the enemy off.* □ *The* *army beat off the savage attack, saving the town.* □ *I was able to beat off the intruder.*

beat someone or something **out†** to beat someone or something; to win over someone or something. □ *The other team beat us out readily.* □ *They beat out every other team in the league, too.* □ *I will win! You will not beat me out!*

beat someone **out†** to outdistance someone; to perform better than someone. □ *We have to beat the other company out, and then we'll have the contract.* □ *I beat out Walter in the foot race.*

beat someone's **brains out 1.** to hit or batter someone severely. □ *She threatened to beat my brains out.* □ *Those thugs nearly beat his brains out.* **2.** to drive oneself hard (to accomplish something). □ *I beat my brains out all day to clean this house, and you come in and get dirt on the carpet!* □ *Don't beat your brains out. Just give it a good try.*

beat someone **to** something to get to something before someone else; to claim something before someone else does. (See also **beat** someone **into** something.) □ *You beat me to it and took the last cookie.* □ *Ken beat John to the door.*

beat someone **to the punch** and **beat** someone **to the draw** *Fig.* to do something before someone else does it. □ *I wanted to have the new car, but Sally beat me to the punch.* □ *I planned to write a book about using the new software program, but someone else beat me to the draw.*

beat someone **up†** to harm or subdue a person by striking him. □ *The robber beat me up and took my money.* □ *I really wanted to beat up that intruder.*

beat something **down† 1.** to break something in; to break through something. □ *Don't beat the door down! I'm coming!* □ *Please don't beat down the door!* **2.** to flatten something. □ *Sam beat the veal down to the thickness of a half an inch.* □ *First you beat down the meat to a very thin layer.*

beat something **into** someone and **beat** something **in†** *Fig.* to use physical abuse to get someone to learn something; to work very hard to get someone to learn something. (Beating something into someone or someone's head.) □ *Do I have to beat this into your head? Why can't you learn?* □ *Why do I have to beat in this information?* □ *Can't you learn by yourself? Does someone have to beat it in?*

beat something **into** something to beat or whip something with a utensil, until it changes into something else. □ *Beat the white of the egg into stiff peaks.* □ *Beat the batter into a smooth consistency.*

beat something **up† 1.** to whip up something, such as an egg. □ *Beat the egg up and pour it in the skillet.* □ *Beat up another egg and do the same.* **2.** to ruin something; to damage something. □ *The banging of the door has really beat this wall up.* □ *The frequent pounding of the door handle beat up the wall.*

beat the clock *Fig.* to do something before a deadline; to finish before the time is up. (Alludes to accomplishing something before a clock reaches a specific time.) □ *Sam beat the clock, arriving a few minutes before the doors were locked.* □ *They were afraid they would be late and hurried in order to beat the clock.*

beat the drum for someone or something and **bang the drum for** someone or something *Fig.* to promote or support someone or something. (As if one were beating a

drum to get attention.) □ *I spent a lot of time beating the drum for our plans for the future.* □ *The senator is only banging the drum for his special interests.*

beat the gun *Fig.* to manage to do something before the ending signal. (Originally from sports, referring to scoring in the last seconds of a game just before the referee fires a gun to signal the end of the game.) □ *The field goal beat the gun and was in the air just in time.* □ *Tom tried to beat the gun, but he was one second too slow.*

beat the hell out of someone and **beat the living daylights out of** someone; **beat the pants off (of)** someone; **beat the shit out of** someone; **beat the socks off (of)** someone; **beat the stuffing out of** someone; **beat the tar out of** someone **1.** *Fig.* to defeat someone very badly. (Caution: the use of the word *shit* is considered vulgar and is offensive to many people. *Of* is usually retained before pronouns.) □ *Our team beat the hell out of the other side.* □ *We beat the stuffing out of the other side.* **2.** *Fig. Inf.* to batter someone severely. (Alludes to physical violence, not the removal of someone's pants. *Of* is usually retained before pronouns.) □ *The thugs beat the living daylights out of their victim.* □ *If you do that again, I'll beat the pants off of you.* □ *Before the boxing match Max said he would beat the socks off Lefty.*

beat the (natural) stuffing out of someone Go to kick the (natural) stuffing out of someone.

beat the pants off (of) someone Go to beat the hell out of someone.

beat the rap *Sl.* to evade conviction and punishment (for a crime). □ *He was charged with drunk driving, but he beat the rap.* □ *The police hauled Tom in and charged him with a crime. His lawyer helped him beat the rap.*

beat the shit out of someone Go to beat the hell out of someone.

beat the socks off (of) someone Go to beat the hell out of someone.

beat the stuffing out of someone Go to beat the hell out of someone.

beat the tar out of someone Go to beat the hell out of someone.

beat up on someone to batter someone, usually physically. □ *Lefty beat up on Max and made a mess of him.* □ *Don't beat up on me, you bully!*

Beauty is in the eye of the beholder. *Prov.* Different people have different ideas about what is beautiful. □ *Bob: I can't believe Ted bought that ugly old car. Fred: He loves it. Beauty is in the eye of the beholder.* □ *Jill: Have you seen Mary's pictures of her new baby? He looks pretty ugly, to my eyes. Jane: Beauty is in the eye of the beholder.*

Beauty is only skin-deep. *Prov.* A person who looks beautiful may not have a pleasing personality; a person's good looks may not last. □ *Fred: I hope Nancy will go out with me. She's so beautiful! Jane: I hate to disappoint you, but in Nancy's case, beauty is definitely only skin-deep.* □ *Don't be so proud of your pretty face. Beauty is only skin-deep.*

beckon to someone to signal someone to come. □ *Wally beckoned to Sally, and she came over to him.* □ *Lily beckoned to Max and he turned his back on her.*

become of someone or something to happen or occur to someone or something. □ *Whatever became of Joe and his friends?* □ *I don't know what became of my other plaid sock.*

*becoming on someone [of clothing] complimentary to someone; [of clothing] enhancing one's good looks. (*Typically: **be ~; look ~**.) □ *The dress you wore last night is not becoming on you.* □ *That color is very becoming on you.*

bed down (for something) to lie down to sleep for a period of time. □ *After she had bedded down for the night, the telephone rang.* □ *All the chickens bedded down hours ago.*

bed down some place to sleep somewhere; to find a place to sleep somewhere. □ *I need to bed down somewhere for the night.* □ *Can I bed down here with you?*

a **bed of roses** a luxurious situation; an easy life. □ *Who said life would be a bed of roses?* □ *If I had a million bucks, I would be in a bed of roses.*

bed (someone or something) **down**† (some place) to put someone or something into a bed or on bedding some place. □ *We bedded the kids down on mattresses on the floor.* □ *We bedded down the horses for the night.*

bed-and-breakfast a type of lodging for travelers or tourists offering a place to sleep and breakfast the next morning, typically in a small inn or private home. □ *We visited six European countries and stayed in a bed-and-breakfast every night.* □ *I had to take a bed-and-breakfast because the hotels in the city were much too expensive.*

bedeck someone or something **with** something to decorate someone or something with something. □ *She bedecked herself with garlands of daisies.* □ *Karen bedecked the room with flowers.*

*a bee in one's **bonnet** a single idea or a thought that remains in one's mind; an obsession. (*Typically: **get ~; have ~; give** one **~**.) □ *I have a bee in my bonnet over that cool new car I saw, and I can't stop thinking about it.* □ *I got a bee in my bonnet about swimming. I just wanted to go swimming all the time.*

beef about someone or something *Sl.* to complain about someone or something. □ *Stop beefing about Karen.* □ *He is always beefing about his working conditions.*

beef something **up**† to add strength or substance to something. □ *Let's beef this music up with a little more on the drums.* □ *They beefed up the offer with another thousand dollars.*

been around have had many experiences in life. □ *You don't need to warn me about anything! I've been around.*

been had and **was had; have been had 1.** (of a woman) been copulated with; been made pregnant. □ *I've been had, and I'm going to have the baby.* □ *When she said she had been had, I didn't know it happened on her honeymoon.* **2.** been mistreated, cheated, or dealt with badly. □ *Look at this cheap shirt that I paid $30 for! I was had!* □ *I've been had by that lousy gyp joint.*

beer up *Sl.* to drink a lot of beer. □ *Those guys are out there beering up like mad.* □ *Stop beering up and go home!*

before long soon. □ *Billy will be grown-up before long.* □ *If we keep spending so much, before long we'll be without any money.*

*before someone ahead of or in front of someone in order. (*Typically: **be ~; get ~; go ~**.) □ *Who is before Mary?* □ *I am before all of you.*

*before someone's **time** happening before someone was born or old enough to know what was going on. (*Typically: **be ~; happen ~; occur ~**.) □ *Of course I don't remember it. It was before my time.* □ *All that happened before your time.*

before you can say Jack Robinson and **quicker than you can say Jack Robinson** *Fig.* almost immediately. (Often found in children's stories.) □ *And before you could say Jack Robinson, the bird flew away.* □ *I'll catch a plane and be there quicker than you can say Jack Robinson.*

before you know it almost immediately. □ *I'll be there before you know it.* □ *If you keep spending money like that, you'll be broke before you know it.*

beg for someone or something to plead to be given someone or something. □ *He missed Jane a lot and was just begging for her to return to him.* □ *Jane begged for another helping of ice cream.*

beg of someone to request earnestly of someone. (Usually added to a request.) □ *Please help me. I beg of you.* □ *I beg of you to help me.*

beg off (on something) to ask to be released from something; to refuse an invitation. □ *I'm sorry, but I'll be out of town on the day of your party. I'll have to beg off on your invitation.* □ *I have an important meeting, so I'll have to beg off.*

beg something **from** someone to plead for something from someone. □ *She begged the amount of a telephone call from someone who walked by.* □ *I begged a dollar from a kind lady who went by.*

beg something **of** someone to request earnestly that someone do something or grant something. □ *Please help me. I beg it of you.* □ *She begged a favor of Max.*

beg something **off**† to decline an invitation politely. □ *She begged the trip to the zoo off.* □ *We all begged off the dinner invitation.*

beg the question 1. to carry on a false argument where one assumes as proved the very point that is being argued, or more loosely, to evade the issue at hand. (Essentially a criticism of someone's line of argument.) □ *Stop arguing in circles. You're begging the question.* □ *A: Why do two lines that are equidistant from one another never meet? B: Because they are parallel. A: You are begging the question.* **2.** to invite the (following) question. (This reinterpretation of **beg the question** is incorrect but is currently in widespread use.) □ *His complaints beg the question: Didn't he cause all of his problems himself?*

beg to differ (with someone) *Fig.* to disagree with someone; to state one's disagreement with someone in a polite way. (Usually used in a statement being made to the person being disagreed with.) □ *I beg to differ with you, but you have stated everything exactly backwards.* □ *If I may beg to differ, you have not expressed my position as well as you seem to think.*

beggar (all) description to defy description; to be unable to be described. □ *The house was a horrible mess. The place beggared description.* □ *Our reaction to the proposal beggars description. We were deeply disturbed for days.*

B

Beggars can't be choosers. *Prov.* If someone gives you something you asked for, you should not complain about what you get. □ *I asked Joe to lend me his bicycle, and he sent me this old, rusty one. But beggars can't be choosers.* □ *Jill: Let me wear your green dress; I don't like the blue one you lent me. Jane: Beggars can't be choosers.*

begin an all-out effort Go to **an all-out effort.**

begin by doing something to start out by doing something first. □ *We will begin by painting the house.* □ *She began by opening the door.*

begin to see daylight *Fig.* to begin to see the end of a long task. □ *I've been working on my thesis for two years, and at last I'm beginning to see daylight.* □ *I've been so busy. Only in the last week have I begun to see daylight.*

begin to see the light *Fig.* to begin to understand something. (See also **see the light (at the end of the tunnel).**) □ *My algebra class has been hard for me, but I'm beginning to see the light.* □ *I was totally confused, but I began to see the light after your explanation.*

begin with someone or something to start off a sequence with someone or something. □ *Let's have dinner begin with a nice clear soup.* □ *I will begin with Liz and take Frank next.*

beginner's luck absolute luck; the luck of an inexperienced person. (Referring to surprisingly good luck.) □ *I could never have accomplished this if I had practiced a lot. My win was just beginner's luck.*

the **beginning of the end** *Fig.* the start of the termination of something or of someone's death. □ *When he stopped coughing and grew still, I knew it was the beginning of the end.* □ *The enormous debt we ran up marked the beginning of the end as far as our standard of living was concerned.*

beguile someone **into** something to charm someone into doing something. □ *You can't beguile me into stealing for you!* □ *I beguiled Tom into driving me to the airport.*

beguile someone **out of** something **1.** to charm someone out of doing something. □ *I will try to beguile them out of doing it.* □ *He beguiled her out of leaving.* **2.** to charm something away from someone. □ *She's trying to beguile the old man out of a substantial amount of his money.* □ *Max beguiled the old lady out of her rings.*

beguile someone **with** something to charm or fascinate someone with something. □ *She beguiled her date with tales of her luxurious lifestyle.* □ *He spent the evening beguiling her with stories of the Old West.*

***behind bars** in jail. (*Typically: **be** ~; **put** someone ~.*) □ *Very soon, you will be behind bars for your crimes.* □ *Max should be behind bars soon for his conviction on burglary charges.*

behind closed doors in secret; away from observers, reporters, or intruders, usually in a closed room. □ *They held the meeting behind closed doors, as the law allowed.* □ *Every important issue was decided behind closed doors.*

***behind schedule** having failed to do something by the appointed time, especially the time given on a written plan. (*Typically: **be** ~; **fall** ~; **get** ~.*) □ *We have to hurry and finish soon or we will fall behind schedule.* □ *The project is behind schedule by six months.*

behind someone's **back** without someone's knowledge; secret from someone. □ *Please don't talk about me behind my back.* □ *She sold the car behind his back, while he was away on vacation.*

***behind the eight ball 1.** *Fig.* in trouble; in a weak or losing position. (Alludes to the eight ball in pool, which in certain games cannot be touched without penalty. *Typically: **be** ~; **get** ~; **have** someone ~; **put** someone ~.*) □ *I'm behind the eight ball again and can't see how to relieve my dilemma.* □ *John is behind the eight ball because he started writing his term paper far too late.* **2.** *Fig.* broke. □ *Sorry, I'm really behind the eight ball this month. I can't make a contribution.* (*Typically: **be** ~; **get** ~; **have** someone ~; **put** someone ~.*) □ *I was behind the eight ball again and couldn't make my car payment.*

behind the scenes without receiving credit or fame; out of public view. (Referring originally to those who worked on a theatrical piece but do not appear on the stage.) □ *The people who worked behind the scenes are the real heroes of this project.* □ *I worked behind the scenes in the play.* □ *We should thank the people who are behind the scenes of our success.*

behind the times old-fashioned. □ *Sarah is a bit behind the times. Her clothes are quite old-fashioned.* □ *Our 90-year-old state senator is a bit behind the times.*

Behind you! Look behind you!; There is danger behind you! □ *"Behind you!" shouted Tom just as a car raced past and nearly knocked Mary over.* □ *Alice shouted, "Behind you!" just as the pickpocket made off with Fred's wallet.*

behoove one **to** do something *Cliché* [for someone] to be obliged to do something. □ *It behooves you to apologize to her for how you insulted her.* □ *It behooves me to make up for all the help you have given me.*

belabor the point to spend too much time on one item of discussion. □ *I don't want to belabor the point, but the sooner we get this matter settled, the better.* □ *If the speaker would agree not to belabor the point further, I will place it on the agenda for resolution at the next meeting.*

belch out to burst, billow, or gush out. □ *Smoke belched out of the chimney.*

belch something **up**† to cause the release of something that goes upward. □ *The fire belched flames and smoke up.* □ *The volcano belched up clouds of poison gasses.*

believe in someone or something to trust or have faith in someone or something; to accept a fact or what someone says as truth. □ *You must believe in your own abilities.* □ *I believe in myself and my talent.*

believe it or not (you may) choose to accept something as true or not; it may seem amazing but it's true. □ *It's late, but believe it or not, I just got home from work.* □ *I'm over fifty years old, believe it or not.*

Believe nothing of what you hear, and only half of what you see. *Prov.* Rumors are usually false, and sometimes the things you see can be misleading as well; be very skeptical until there is proof. □ *Jill: I heard the football team is losing its best player. He has not been at practice for two days. Jane: Believe nothing of what you hear, and only half of what you see.* □ *The paper reported that the city government is going bankrupt, but I believe nothing of what I hear, and only half of what I see.*

believe something **of** someone to accept a statement about someone as truth. □ *What a terrible thing for Jill to do. I can't believe it of her.* □ *I can believe anything of Max. He's such a conniving person.*

Believe you me! *Inf.* You really should believe me!; You'd better take my word for it! □ *Alice: Is it hot in that room? Fred: It really is. Believe you me!* □ *Sue: How do you like my cake? John: Believe you me, this is the best cake I've ever eaten!*

bell, book, and candle things that are miraculous or that signal that something unusual or bizarre may soon happen. (Alluding originally to the items used when performing the rite of excommunication from the Roman Catholic Church.) □ *Look, I can't work miracles! Do you expect me to show up at your house with bell, book, and candle, and make everything right? You have to take charge of your own destiny!* □ *On the top shelf of the tiny used-book store, Jim saw a bell, book, and candle sitting in a row, and he knew he was going to find some very interesting reading material.*

bellow something **out** † to cry something out loudly with great force. □ *Don't just say it. Bellow it out!* □ *Bellow out your name so we know who you are!*

bells and whistles *Fig.* extra, fancy add-ons or gadgets. □ *I like cars that are loaded with all the bells and whistles.* □ *All those bells and whistles add to the cost.*

belly out [for a sheet of fabric, such as a ship's sail] to fill out in the wind. □ *The sails bellied out as the ship turned to catch the wind.* □ *When the sails bellied out, we began to move forward.*

belly up 1. intoxicated by alcohol. □ *Fred was boiled—belly up—glassy-eyed.* □ *After four beers, I was belly up, for sure.* **2.** *Sl.* (of a business) bankrupt; dead. (Like a dead fish that floats belly up.) □ *That's the end. This company is belly up.* □ *After the fire the firm went belly up.*

belly up (to something**)** to move up to something, often a bar. (Usually in reference to nudging one's way to a bar.) □ *The man swaggered in and bellied up to the counter and demanded my immediate attention.* □ *As he bellied up, he said, "Do you know who I am?"*

belong to someone or something to be owned by someone or something. □ *This one belongs to me.* □ *This desk belongs to the company. You can't take it home!*

belong under something to be classified under some general category. □ *This one belongs under the other category.* □ *This file belongs under A.*

below average lower or worse than average. □ *Tom's strength is below average for a child his size.* □ *Dad asked why my grades are below average.*

below par not as good as average or normal. □ *I feel a little below par today. I think I am getting a cold.* □ *His work is below par, and he is paid too much money.*

below someone ranking below someone. □ *I am below Terri, but my scores are better than Carol's.* □ *I am below everyone in the class.*

*below someone or something positioned under or lower than someone or something. (*Typically: **be** ~; **lie** ~; **sink** ~; **sit** ~.) □ *The sun is below the horizon.* □ *The swimming hole is below the dam.*

belt a drink **down** † *Fig.* to drink an alcoholic drink rapidly. (See also **belt** someone or something **down**.) □ *She belted a couple of drinks down and went out to face her guests.* □ *How many drinks did Gloria belt down?*

belt someone or something **down** † to secure someone or something with a belt or strap. □ *Please belt the child's seat down and put the child in it.* □ *Did you belt down the kids?*

belt someone **up** † to secure someone with a belt, such as a seat belt in a car. □ *I had to belt her up because the seat belt was so complicated.* □ *We belted up the kids securely.*

belt something **out** † *Fig.* to sing or play a song loudly and with spirit. □ *When she's playing the piano, she really belts the music out.* □ *She really knows how to belt out a song.*

belt the grape *Sl.* to drink wine or liquor heavily and become intoxicated. □ *He has a tendency to belt the grape—every afternoon after work.* □ *She's been belting the grape more than her husband wants.*

belt up Go to **buckle up**.

bend back to lean or bend backwards. □ *He bent back to pick up the book, and he fell.* □ *When she bent back, she ripped something.*

bend before something to bend under the pressure of moving air. □ *The trees bent before the wind.* □ *Our roses bent gracefully before the breeze.*

bend down to curve downward; [for someone] to lean down. □ *Please bend down and pick up the little bits of paper you just dropped.* □ *The snow-laden bushes bent down.*

bend forward to lean forward; to curve forward. □ *The tree bent forward in the wind.* □ *I bent forward to pick up the pencil.*

bend in to curve or turn inward. □ *The shore bent in about a mile to the west.* □ *The side of the shed bent in under the force of the wind.*

bend one's **elbow** and **bend the elbow; lift** one's **elbow** to take a drink of an alcoholic beverage; to drink alcohol to excess. □ *He's down at the tavern, bending his elbow.* □ *Paul gets lots of exercise. I saw him bend his elbow thirty times at a bar yesterday.*

bend over [for someone] to bend down at the waist. □ *I bent over and picked up the coin.* □ *When he bent over, something ripped.*

bend over backwards (to do something**)** Go to **fall over backwards (to** do something**)**.

bend over backwards (to do something**) (for** someone**)** *Fig.* to work very hard to accomplish something for someone; to **go out of** one's **way (to** do something**) (for** someone**)**. (See also **fall over backwards (to** do something**)**.) □ *He will bend over backwards to help you.* □ *I bent over backwards for you, and you showed no thanks!*

bend someone or something **back** † to curve or arch someone or something backward. □ *We bent the child back a little so we could examine the spider bite.* □ *Ouch! Don't bend back my hand!* □ *Bend the branch back so we can get a better view.*

bend someone **out of shape** *Fig.* to make someone angry. □ *The cheating that was going on really bent Joe out of shape.* □ *Why do you let yourself get bent out of shape? Chill, man, chill.*

bend someone's **ear** *Fig.* to talk to someone, perhaps annoyingly. (As if talking so much that the other person's ear is moved back.) □ *Tom is over there, bending Jane's ear about something.* □ *I'm sorry. I didn't mean to bend your ear for an hour.*

bend something **out of shape** to distort something by twisting or bending. □ *Jill bent the spring out of shape.* □ *I bent the coat hanger out of shape by hanging my leather jacket on it.*

bend the elbow Go to bend one's elbow.

bend the law and **bend the rules** *Fig.* to cheat a little bit without breaking the law. (Jocular.) □ *I didn't break the rules. I just bent the rules a little.* □ *Nobody ever got arrested for bending the law.*

bend the rules Go to previous.

beneath contempt exceedingly contemptible. □ *What you have done is beneath contempt.* □ *Your rude behavior is beneath contempt.*

beneath one's **dignity** too rude or coarse for a polite person to do. □ *That kind of thing is beneath my dignity, and I hope yours as well.* □ *I would have thought something like that to be beneath your dignity.*

beneath someone too shameful for a polite person to do. □ *That kind of thing is beneath Fred. I'm appalled that he did it.* □ *That sort of foul language is beneath you!*

*****beneath** something under something. (*Typically: **be** ~; **sit** ~.) □ *What is that beneath the table?* □ *The cat is beneath the piano.*

benefit by something and **benefit from** something to profit or gain by something. □ *We hope to benefit by the collapse of our competition.* □ *We will all benefit from the new tax laws.*

benefit from something Go to previous.

*****the **benefit of the doubt** a judgment in one's favor when the evidence is neither for one nor against one. (*Typically: **get** ~; **have** ~; **give** someone ~.) □ *I was right between a B and an A. I got the benefit of the doubt—an A.* □ *I thought I should have had the benefit of the doubt, but the judge made me pay a fine.*

bent on doing something *Fig.* determined to do something. □ *I believe you are bent on destroying the entire country.* □ *I am bent on saving the planet.*

bent out of shape 1. *Fig.* angry; insulted. □ *Man, there is no reason to get so bent out of shape. I didn't mean any harm.* □ *I got bent out of shape because of the way I was treated.* **2.** intoxicated by alcohol or drugs. □ *I was so bent out of shape I thought I'd never recover.* □ *I've been polluted, but never as bent out of shape as this.*

bequeath something **to** someone to will something to someone; to leave something to someone. □ *My uncle bequeathed some furniture to me.* □ *I will bequeath this watch to my grandson.*

bereft of someone or something left without someone or something. (*Bereft* is the past participle of *bereave*, functioning here as an adjective.) □ *Tom was bereft of all hope.* □ *The child was bereft of his parents.*

beset someone **with** something to surround someone with harassment; to harass someone with something. □ *Please*

do not beset them with problem after problem. □ *They beset us with requests for money.*

beside oneself **(with** something) *Fig.* in an extreme state of some emotion. □ *I was beside myself with joy.* □ *Sarah could not speak. She was beside herself with anger.*

beside the point and **beside the question** irrelevant; of no importance. □ *That's very interesting, but beside the point.* □ *That's beside the point. You're evading the issue.*

beside the question Go to previous.

besiege someone or something **with** something **1.** *Lit.* to attack someone or a group with something. □ *We besieged the enemy with bombs and bullets.* **2.** *Fig.* to overwhelm someone or something with something □ *They besieged us with orders for the new book.* □ *We besieged the company with complaints.*

besmirch someone or something **with** something to dirty or soil someone or someone's reputation with something. □ *Please don't continue to besmirch Alice with that gossip.* □ *You have besmirched my reputation with your comments.* □ *He besmirched her with vile gossip in order to turn people against her.*

The **best defense is a good offense.** *Prov.* If you attack your opponents, they will be so busy fighting off your attack that they will not be able to attack you. (Often associated with sports. Often pronounced with the accent on the first syllable, similar to *offense*.) □ *The team mostly practiced offensive moves because the coach believed that the best defense is a good offense.* □ *Jim thought that the best defense is a good offense, so he always tried to pass other drivers before they could pass him.*

The **best is the enemy of the good.** *Prov.* If you are too ambitious and try to make something better than you are capable of, you may ruin it. □ *Bob: After I revise it a few more times, my novel will be the best ever written. Alan: I don't think you should revise it any more. Remember, the best is the enemy of the good.* □ *In fund-raising as in other areas, the best is the enemy of the good. If you ask someone for a larger contribution than he can possibly give, he may give you nothing at all.*

*****the **best of both worlds** a situation wherein one can enjoy two different opportunities. (*Typically: **enjoy** ~; **have** ~; **live in** ~.) □ *When Don was a fellow at the university, he had the privileges of a professor and the freedom of a student. He had the best of both worlds.* □ *Donna hated to have to choose between retirement and continuing working. She wanted to do both so she could live in the best of both worlds.*

the **best of** someone Go to the better of someone.

the **best part of** something almost all of something; a large part of something; the major part of something. □ *The discussion took the best part of an hour.* □ *The best part of the meeting was taken up by budgetary matters.*

The **best things come in small packages.** and **Good things come in small packages.** *Prov.* Small packages often contain valuable things. (Sometimes said of petite or short people.) □ *Jill: I'm upset at George. He only gave me this tiny box for my birthday. Jane: Don't get upset till you know what's in it. Good things do come in small packages.* □ *Child: I hate being so short. Grandmother: You shouldn't. The best things come in small packages.*

The **best things in life are free.** *Prov.* The most satisfying experiences do not cost any money. □ *Don't be gloomy because you're broke. The best things in life are free.* □ *Yesterday I took my children to the zoo. We didn't spend a penny, but we had a wonderful time. The best things in life are free.*

the **best-case scenario** *Cliché* the optimum outcome being considered. (Compare this with the **worst-case scenario**.) □ *Now that we've seen the negative angle, let's look at the best-case scenario.* □ *In the best-case scenario, we're all dead eventually—but then that's true of the worst-case scenario also.*

The **best-laid plans of mice and men oft(en) go astray.** and The **best-laid schemes o' mice an' men gang aft a-gley.** *Prov.* Things often go wrong even though you have carefully planned what you are going to do. (The *gang aft a-gley* version is Scots dialect, and comes from Robert Burns' poem "To a Mouse.") □ *Jill: I reserved a hotel room for us three weeks ago, but now the clerk says he has no record of our reservation. So much for our fun weekend in the city. Jane: Well, these things happen. The best-laid plans of mice and men oft go astray.* □ *I had all the arrangements made for my party, and then the guest of honor got sick and I had to call the whole thing off. The best-laid schemes of mice and men gang aft a-gley.* □ *If a little rain can ruin the best-laid plans of mice and men, think what an earthquake might do!*

bestow something **on** someone to give something to someone; to present something to someone. □ *The mere presence of the queen bestowed wisdom and grace on the court.* □ *Fine gifts were bestowed on the visiting prince.*

bet on someone or something to wager on someone or something. □ *Are you really going to bet on that horse?* □ *I bet on Paul. He is the fastest runner.*

bet one's **bottom dollar** and **bet** one's **life** *Fig.* to be quite certain (about something). (A *bottom dollar* is the last dollar.) □ *I'll be there. You bet your bottom dollar.* □ *I bet my bottom dollar you can't swim across the pool.* □ *You bet your life I can't swim that far.*

bet one's **life** Go to previous.

bet someone **dollars to doughnuts** *Fig.* to bet something of value against something worth considerably less. □ *I bet you dollars to doughnuts that she is on time.* □ *He bet me dollars to doughnuts that it would snow today.*

bet something **on** someone or something to wager something on someone or something. □ *I bet one thousand dollars on that horse!* □ *Fred bet a few bucks on his favorite football team.*

bet the farm Go to sell the farm.

bet with someone to make a bet or wager with someone. □ *No, I won't bet with you. That's not my style.* □ *Max will bet with anyone.*

betroth someone **to** someone to promise someone in marriage to someone else. □ *The king betrothed his daughter to a prince from the neighboring kingdom.* □ *She betrothed herself to one of the peasant boys from the village.*

Better be an old man's darling than a young man's slave. *Prov.* A young woman should prefer to marry an old man who dotes on her rather than a young man who may treat her badly. □ *When Mr. Nash proposed to me, I* thought he was too old, but my mother advised me, "Better be an old man's darling than a young man's slave." □ *When Marion's friends objected that her fiancé was much too old for her, she said, "Better be an old man's darling than a young man's slave."*

Better (be) safe than sorry. *Prov. Cliché* You should be cautious—if you are not, you may regret it. □ *It may be time-consuming to check the oil in your car every time you buy gasoline, but better safe than sorry.* □ *Bob: I don't need a tetanus shot just because I stepped on a nail. Mary: I still think you should get one. Better be safe than sorry.*

Better be the head of a dog than the tail of a lion. *Prov.* It is better to be the leader of a less prestigious group than to be a subordinate in a more prestigious one. □ *Joe: I can be the headmaster of a small secondary school, or I can be a teacher at a famous university. Which job offer do you think I should take? Nancy: Better be the head of a dog than the tail of a lion.* □ *A professional writing workshop had asked Bob to join, but he elected to stay with his amateur group, since he thought it better to be the head of a dog than the tail of a lion.*

Better keep still about it. and Someone **had better keep still about it.; Better keep quiet about it.;** Someone **better keep quiet about it.** A particular person ought not to tell about or discuss something. (The *someone* can stand for any person's name, any pronoun, or even the word *someone* meaning "you-know-who." If there is no *Someone* had, the phrase is a mild admonition to keep quiet about something.) □ *Mary: I saw you with Bill last night. Jane: You'd better keep quiet about it.* □ *Jane: Tom found out what you're giving Sally for her birthday. Bill: He had better keep quiet about it!*

Better late than never. *Prov. Cliché* Doing something late is better than not doing it. □ *I'm sorry I'm late to the party. Better late than never, right?* □ *Jill: Lisa's birthday was two weeks ago. Should I send her a card now? Jane: Better late than never.*

better left unsaid [refers to a topic that] should not be discussed; [refers to a thought that] everyone is thinking, but would cause difficulty if talked about in public. (A typical beginning for this phrase might be *It is, That is, The details are,* or even *Some things are.* See the examples.) □ *Mary: I really don't know how to tell you this. Bob: Then don't. Maybe it's better left unsaid.* □ *Bill: I had such a terrible fight with Sally last night. I can't believe what I said. Bob: I don't need to hear all about it. Some things are better left unsaid.*

Better luck next time. 1. an expression that comforts someone for a minor failure. (Said with a pleasant tone of voice.) □ *Bill: That does it! I can't run any farther. I lose! Bob: Too bad. Better luck next time.* □ *Mary: Well, that's the end of my brand new weight lifting career. Jane: Better luck next time.* **2.** an expression that ridicules someone for a failure. (Said with rudeness or sarcasm. The tone of voice distinguishes ② from ①.) □ *Sally: I lost out to you, but I think you cheated. Mary: Better luck next time.* □ *Sue: You thought you could get ahead of me, you fool! Better luck next time! Joan: I still think you cheated.*

*the **better of** someone and *the **best of** someone triumph over someone. (*Typically: **get ~; have ~.**) □ *Bill got*

B

the best of John in the boxing match. □ *I tried to get the bet-ter of Tom in the golf match, but he won anyway.*

better off (doing something) and **better off (if** something **were done)** in a better position if something were done. □ *She'd be better off selling her house.* □ *They are better off flying to Detroit than driving.*

better off (somewhere) and **better off (if** one **were** some-where else**)** in a better position somewhere else. □ *They would be better off in a cheaper apartment.* □ *We'd all be better off if we were in Florida.* □ *I know I'd be better off in a warmer climate.*

Better the devil you know than the devil you don't know. *Prov.* If you have to choose between a familiar but unpleasant situation and an unfamiliar situ-ation, choose the familiar one because the unfamiliar sit-uation may turn out to be worse. □ *Jill: I hate my job so much that I'm thinking of asking for a transfer. Jane: I'd advise against it. Better the devil you know than the devil you don't know.* □ *Although she was unhappy in her mar-riage, Donna never considered pursuing romances with other men. "Better the devil you know than the devil you don't know," was her philosophy.*

between a rock and a hard place and **between the devil and the deep blue sea** *Fig.* in a very difficult position; facing a hard decision. □ *I couldn't make up my mind. I was caught between a rock and a hard place.* □ *He had a dilemma on his hands. He was clearly between the devil and the deep blue sea.*

between jobs and **between projects** *Euph.* unem-ployed. □ *Interviewer: Tell me about your current position. Job candidate: I'm between jobs right now.* □ *When Jill was between projects, she took a computer class at the commu-nity college.*

between life and death *Fig.* in a position where living or dying is an even possibility. (Especially with *caught* or *hovering*.) □ *And there I was on the operating table, hov-ering between life and death.* □ *The mountain climber hung by his rope, caught between life and death.*

between projects Go to **between jobs.**

between someone **and** someone else and **between** some-thing **and** something else *Fig.* [of a choice] existing between a selection of people or a selection of things. □ *The choice is between Fred and Jill.* □ *It's between chocolate cake and cherry pie.*

between something **and** something else Go to previous.

between the devil and the deep blue sea Go to between a rock and a hard place.

between you (and) me and the bedpost and **between you and me and these four walls** *Fig.* a somewhat affected way of signaling that you are about to tell a secret. □ *Alan: What's wrong with Ellen these days? She seems so touchy. Jane: Between you and me and the bed-post, I've heard that her boyfriend is seeing someone else.* □ *Jill: How much did you get for your used car? Jane: Well— between you and me and these four walls—five thousand dollars.*

between you and me and these four walls Go to previous.

betwixt and between 1. *Lit.* between (people or things). □ *I liked the soup and the dessert and all that came*

betwixt and between. □ *I sat betwixt and between all the actors who weren't on stage.* **2.** *Fig.* undecided about some-one or something. □ *I wish she would choose. She has been betwixt and between for three weeks.* □ *Tom is so betwixt and between about getting married. I don't think he's ready.*

a **bevy of beauties** *Cliché* a group of very attractive women, as found in a beauty contest. □ *A whole bevy of beauties waltzed past the old man, but he didn't even notice.*

Beware of Greeks bearing gifts. *Prov.* Do not trust an opponent who offers to do something nice for you. (A line from the story of the Trojan horse, as told in Vergil's *Aeneid.*) □ *Jill: I can't believe Melanie brought me cookies today, when we've been fighting for weeks. Jane: Beware of Greeks bearing gifts. She probably has ulterior motives.* □ *When the rival company invited all his employees to a Christmas party, Tom's first impulse was to beware of Greeks bearing gifts, but then he upbraided himself for being para-noid.*

beware of someone or something to be cautious and watch-ful about someone or something. □ *Beware of Ted. He's acting irrational.* □ *You should beware of the dog.*

beyond a reasonable doubt almost without any doubt. (A legal phrase.) □ *The jury decided beyond a reasonable doubt that she had committed the crime.* □ *He was also found guilty beyond a reasonable doubt.*

*****beyond help** and *****beyond repair** beyond the help of anything; not able to be fixed. (*Typically: **be ~; get ~**.) □ *The poor dog that was hit by a truck is beyond help.* □ *This old car is beyond repair.*

beyond me completely missing or surpassing my under-standing. □ *I'm confused. All this is beyond me.*

beyond measure *Fig.* in an account or to an extent more than can be quantified; in a very large amount. □ *They brought in hams, turkeys, and roasts, and then they brought vegetables and salads beyond measure.* □ *They thanked all of us beyond measure.*

beyond one's **depth 1.** *Lit.* in water that is too deep. □ *Sally swam out from the beach until she was beyond her depth.* □ *Jane swam out to get her even though it was beyond her depth, too.* **2.** *Fig.* beyond one's understanding or capabilities. □ *I'm beyond my depth in calculus class.* □ *Poor John was involved in a problem that was really beyond his depth.*

beyond one's **ken** outside the extent of one's knowledge or understanding. □ *Why she married that shiftless drunk-ard is beyond our ken.* □ *His mean attitude to others is quite beyond my ken.*

beyond one's **means** more than one can afford. □ *I'm sorry, but this house is beyond our means. Please show us a cheaper one.* □ *They feel that a Caribbean cruise is beyond their means.*

beyond repair Go to **beyond help.**

beyond some emotional response in too extreme a state to feel or care. □ *Do what you want. You have hurt me so much, I am beyond caring.* □ *The dying patient is beyond feeling. It doesn't matter now.*

*****beyond** someone or something **1.** on the other side of something. (*Typically: **be ~; get ~**.) □ *When we get beyond this bad road, I'll have to check the tires.* □ *I have to get beyond the large gentleman standing in the hall.*

2. finished with someone or something; having solved the problems relating to someone or something. (*Typically: **be** ~; **get** ~; **move** ~.) □ *Things will be better when we get beyond this financial crisis.* □ *When the country gets beyond the current situation, things will have to get better.*

beyond the pale *Fig.* unacceptable; outlawed. (A *pale* is a barrier made of wooden stakes.) □ *Your behavior is simply beyond the pale.* □ *Because of Tom's rudeness, he's considered beyond the pale and is never asked to parties anymore.*

beyond the shadow of a doubt Go to without a shadow of a doubt.

beyond words *Fig.* more than one can say. (Especially preceded by *grateful, shocked,* and *thankful.*) □ *Sally was thankful beyond words.* □ *I don't know how to thank you. I'm grateful beyond words.*

bias someone **against** someone or something to prejudice someone against someone or something. □ *Please avoid biasing everyone against me.* □ *One bad experience biased all of us against that brand of sausage.*

bicker (with someone**) (about** someone or something**)** and **bicker (with** someone or something**) (over** someone or something**)** to argue with someone about someone or something. □ *Why are you always bickering with her about absolutely nothing?* □ *Please don't bicker with us over these small details.*

bid adieu to someone or something *Cliché* to say good-bye to someone or something. (The word *adieu* is French for *good-bye* and should not be confused with *ado.*) □ *Now it's time to bid adieu to all of you gathered here.* □ *He silently bid adieu to his favorite hat as the wind carried it down the street.*

bid something **down**† to lower the value of something, such as stock, by offering a lower price for it each time it comes up for sale. □ *We bid the price down and then bought all of it.* □ *I could see that the traders were bidding down the price, but I didn't want to take the risk.*

bid (something**) for** something and **bid (**something**) on** something to offer an amount of money for something at an auction. □ *I bid a thousand for the painting.* □ *I didn't want to bid for it.* □ *I wouldn't bid a cent on that rickety old table!*

bid (something**) on** something Go to previous.

bid something **up**† to raise the price of something at an auction by offering higher and higher prices; to increase the value of something, such as shares of stock, by offering a higher price for it each time it comes up for sale. □ *Who is bidding the price up on that painting?* □ *Someone bid up the price on each piece at auction and then backed off.*

bide one's **time** to wait patiently. □ *I've been biding my time for years, just waiting for a chance like this.* □ *He's not the type just to sit there and bide his time. He wants some action now.*

big and bold large and capable of getting attention. (Usually refers to things, not people.) □ *The big and bold lettering on the book's cover got lots of attention, but the price was too high.* □ *She wore a brightly colored dress. The pattern was big and bold and the skirt was very full.*

The **Big Apple** New York City. □ *We spent the weekend in the Big Apple.*

***big around as a molasses barrel** Rur.* very big around. (*Also: **as** ~.) □ *He ate till he was as big around as a molasses barrel.* □ *The athlete's chest was big around as a molasses barrel.*

***big as all outdoors** Cliché* very big, usually referring to an indoor space of some kind. (*Also: **as** ~.) □ *You should see Bob's living room. It's as big as all outdoors!* □ *The new movie theater is as big as all outdoors.*

***big as life (and twice as ugly)** and ***large as life (and twice as ugly); bigger than life (and twice as ugly)** Cliché* a colorful way of saying that a person or a thing appeared, often surprisingly or dramatically, in a particular place. (*Also: **as** ~.) □ *The little child just stood there as big as life and laughed very hard.* □ *I opened the door, and there was Tom as large as life.* □ *I came home and found this cat in my chair, as big as life and twice as ugly.*

a **big break** Go to lucky break.

big bucks a very large amount of money. □ *He earns big bucks for doing almost nothing.*

a **big drink of water** and a **tall drink of water 1.** *Fig.* a very tall person. □ *Tim is sure a big drink of water.* □ *Kelly grew into a tall drink of water.* **2.** *Fig.* a boring person or thing. (A pun on "hard to take.") □ *She is a big drink of water, but she could be worse.* □ *The lecture was a big drink of water.*

***the big eye 1.** a flirtatious look or gaze; a long look to get another's attention. (*Typically: **get** ~; **give** someone ~.) □ *Look at that pretty girl giving you the big eye.* □ *I thought she was cute, so I gave her the big eye.* **2.** obvious eye contact with someone. (*Typically: **get** ~; **give** someone ~.) □ *Tom gave me the big eye to let me know he wanted to talk to me.* □ *I tried to give her the big eye, but she never looked my way.*

a **big frog in a small pond** an important person in the midst of less important people. (Alludes to a large frog that dominates a small pond with few challengers.) □ *I'd rather be a big frog in a small pond than the opposite.* □ *The trouble with Tom is that he's a big frog in a small pond. He needs more competition.*

***a big hand for** something lots of applause for something. (*Typically: **get** ~; **have** ~; **give** someone ~.) □ *She got a big hand for singing so well.* □ *They always give the acrobats a big hand.*

***a (big) head** a hangover. (*Typically: **get** ~; **have** ~; **give** someone ~.) □ *Oh, man, that booze gave me a big head!* □ *Tom has a head this morning and won't be coming into work.*

big man on campus *Sl.* an important male college student. (Often derisive or jocular.) □ *Hank acts like such a big man on campus.* □ *Let some big man on campus do the dirty work for a change.*

the **big moment** and the **moment everyone has been waiting for** the special time that everyone has been waiting for. □ *The big moment has come. I will now announce the winner.* □ *This is the moment everyone has been waiting for. Now we will learn the name of the big winner.*

big of someone generous; kind or forgiving. (Sometimes sarcastic.) □ *He gave me some of his apple. That was very* *big of him.* □ *It was big of Sally to come over and apologize like that.*

*the big picture the whole story of something; a complete view of something. (*Typically: **get ~; have ~; give** someone **~; know ~; see ~; show** someone **~.**) □ *The sales manager gave us all the big picture this morning, and I'm more confused than ever.*

*a big send-off a happy celebration before departing. (*Typically: **get ~; have ~; give** someone **~.**) □ *I had a wonderful send-off before I left.* □ *John got a fine send-off as he left for Europe.*

big with someone famous with or desired by someone or some group. □ *This kind of pizza is supposed to be big with people in Chicago.* □ *Rock concerts are big with the kids.*

bigger than life (and twice as ugly) Go to big as life (and twice as ugly).

The **bigger they are, the harder they fall.** *Prov.* When prominent people fail, their failure is more dramatic. □ *After the newspapers reported that the mayor cheated on his wife, he lost the election and he can't get any kind of job. The bigger they are, the harder they fall.* □ *Jackson used to be very wealthy, but he lost every cent in the stock market crash. The bigger they are, the harder they fall.*

The **biggest frog in the puddle** and The **biggest toad in the puddle** *Prov.* The most important or powerful person in some small, unimportant group. (See also a **big frog in a small pond.**) □ *Jill: Elaine seems to be obsessed with becoming class president. Jane: Yes, she really wants to be the biggest frog in the puddle.* □ *The people in my office don't care about doing their work; mostly they compete over who will be the biggest toad in the puddle.*

The **biggest toad in the puddle** Go to previous.

bilk someone **out of** something to get something away from someone by deception. □ *The crooks bilked the old lady out of a fortune.* □ *I was bilked out of my life's savings!*

bill someone **for** something to ask someone for payment for something in writing. □ *Just bill me for the balance.* □ *She billed them for her expenses and then tried to deduct the expenses from her income tax.*

billow out 1. [for something, such as smoke] to burst and flow outward. □ *At the site of the fire, smoke billowed out.* □ *Clouds of ash billowed out of the volcano.* **2.** [for a sheet of cloth] to fill with the wind. (Especially a ship's sail.) □ *The sail billowed out and we moved forward.* □ *Her skirt billowed out when the wind caught it.*

bind someone or something **down**[†] to tie or secure someone or something to something. □ *Bind the tarpaulin so it won't get away.* □ *We will bind down the patient tightly.* □ *They bound the hatch down so it could not be opened.*

bind someone or something **together**[†] to tie the parts of something together; to tie a number of things or people together. □ *Can you bind together all three parts?* □ *Bind these two bandits together and lead them to jail.*

bind someone or something **up**[†] **(in** something**)** and **bind** someone or something **up**[†] **(with** something**)** to tie someone or something up in something. □ *They bound the books up in leather straps.* □ *I will bind up the larger sticks in strong cord.*

bind someone or something **up**[†] **(with** something**)** Go to previous.

bind someone **over**[†] **(to** someone or something**)** to deliver someone to some legal authority; to deliver someone to some legal authority. (A legal usage.) □ *They bound the suspect over to the sheriff.* □ *The sheriff will bind over the suspect to the county jail.*

binge and purge to overeat and vomit, alternatively and repeatedly. (A symptom of the condition called bulimia.) □ *She had binged and purged a number of times before she finally sought help from a doctor.* □ *Terry had been bingeing and purging for a number of years and was very, very thin.*

A **bird in the hand is worth two in the bush.** *Prov.* Having something for certain is better than the possibility of getting something better. □ *I might get a better offer, but a bird in the hand is worth two in the bush.* □ *Bill has offered to buy my car for $3,000 cash. Someone else might pay more, but a bird in the hand is worth two in the bush.*

a **bird's-eye view 1.** *Lit.* a view seen from high above. □ *We got a bird's-eye view of Cleveland as the plane began its descent.* □ *From the top of the church tower you get a splendid bird's-eye view of the village.* **2.** *Fig.* a brief survey of something; a hasty look at something. □ *The course provides a bird's-eye view of the works of Mozart, but it doesn't deal with them in enough detail for your purpose.* □ *All you need is a bird's-eye view of the events of World War II to pass the test.*

the **birds and the bees** *Euph.* sex and reproduction. (See also the **facts of life.**) □ *My father tried to teach me about the birds and the bees.* □ *He's twenty years old and doesn't understand about the birds and the bees!*

Birds in their little nests agree. *Prov.* People who live together should try hard to get along peacefully. (Usually used to admonish children not to fight with each other.) □ *Brother: She called me a name! Sister: I did not! He's a liar! Father: Now, now, kids—birds in their little nests agree.* □ *Let's not argue about this, guys. Birds in their little nests agree.*

Birds of a feather flock together. *Prov.* Similar people tend to associate with each other. □ *I always thought Amy was pretentious, and now she's going out with that snobbish boy, Louis. Birds of a feather flock together.* □ *George: Why do you think Donald is dishonest? Ned: All his friends are dishonest. Birds of a feather flock together.*

a **bit much** beyond what is needed or tolerable. □ *The speech she gave in acceptance of the award was a bit much. She went on and on.*

a **bit of the action** Go to a **piece (of the action).**

*a bit off and ***a little off** a little crazy; a little out of whack. (*Typically: **be ~; find** someone **~.**) □ *This guy's a little off, but he is harmless.*

bitch about someone or something *Inf.* to complain about someone or something. (Use discretion with *bitch*, a word many consider coarse or vulgar.) □ *You are always bitching about your girlfriend.* □ *Stop bitching about your job so much.*

a **bitch of a** someone or something *Inf.* a really difficult person or thing. (Use discretion with *bitch*, a word many consider coarse or vulgar.) □ *What a bitch of a day!* □ *He is really a bitch of a boss.*

bitch someone **off**† *Sl.* to make someone angry. (Use discretion with *bitch*, a word many consider coarse or vulgar.) □ *You really bitch me off, do you know that?* □ *That foul temper of yours could bitch off anybody.*

bitch someone or something **up**† *Inf.* to mess someone or something up. (Use discretion with *bitch*, a word many consider coarse or vulgar.) □ *Who bitched these cards up?* □ *I never bitch up anything!*

bite back (at someone or something**) 1.** *Lit.* to defend an attack by biting at someone or something. (Usually an animal.) □ *I threatened the dog and the dog bit back.* **2.** *Fig.* to fight back at someone; to return someone's anger or attack; to speak back to someone with anger. □ *She is usually tolerant, but she will bite back if pressed.* □ *Yes, she will bite back.*

bite into something **1.** *Lit.* to press one's teeth into something. □ *As he bit into the apple, the juices ran down his chin.* □ *Lily bit into the sandwich and smiled.* **2.** *Fig.* [for the wind or something similar] to blow sharply against someone, causing a stinging pain. □ *The cold wind bit into poor Wally, who only has a light jacket.* □ *The frigid air bit into my exposed skin.*

bite off more than one **can chew 1.** *Lit.* to take a larger mouthful of food than one can chew easily or comfortably. □ *I bit off more than I could chew, and nearly choked.* **2.** *Fig.* to take (on) more than one can deal with; to be overconfident. □ *Ann is exhausted again. She's always biting off more than she can chew.*

bite on someone *Sl.* to copy something that someone else has done; to dress the same way someone else does. □ *Nobody will bite on Sally. She has terrible taste.* □ *Jennifer is always biting on Anne, who is a careful dresser.*

bite on something **1.** to chew on something; to grasp something with the teeth. □ *The injured cowboy bit on a leather strap while they tried to fix his dislocated shoulder.* **2.** to respond to a lure; to **fall for** something. (Can refer literally to fishing, or be used figuratively.) □ *Do you think the fish will bite on this?* □ *No one would bite on that bait. Try another approach.*

bite one's **nails 1.** to use one's teeth to remove parts of one's fingernails as a means of shortening them. □ *Stop biting your nails! Use clippers!* **2.** to literally bite one's nails from nervousness or anxiety; to be nervous or anxious. □ *I spent all afternoon biting my nails, worrying about you.* □ *We've all been biting our nails from worry.*

bite one's **tongue 1.** *Lit.* to bite down on one's tongue by accident. □ *Ouch! I bit my tongue!* **2.** *Fig.* to struggle not to say something that you really want to say. □ *I had to bite my tongue to keep from telling her what I really thought.* □ *I sat through that whole silly conversation biting my tongue.*

bite someone's **head off** *Fig.* to speak sharply and with great anger to someone. (Fixed order.) □ *Don't bite my head off! Be patient.* □ *I'm very sorry I lost my temper. I didn't mean to bite your head off.*

bite something **off**† to remove something in a bite. □ *Ann bit a piece off and chewed it up.* □ *She bit off a piece.*

bite the big one *Sl.* to die. □ *I was so tired that I thought I was going to bite the big one.* □ *I hope I am old and gray when I bite the big one.*

bite the bullet *Sl.* to accept something difficult and try to live with it. □ *You are just going to have to bite the bullet and make the best of it.* □ *Jim bit the bullet and accepted what he knew had to be.*

bite the dust 1. *Sl.* to die. □ *A shot rang out, and another cowboy bit the dust.* □ *The soldier was too young to bite the dust.* **2.** *Sl.* to break; to fail; to give out. □ *My old car finally bit the dust.* □ *This pen is out of ink and has bitten the dust.*

bite the hand that feeds one *Fig.* to do harm to someone who does good things for you. (Does not involve biting.) □ *I'm your mother! How can you bite the hand that feeds you?* □ *She can hardly expect sympathy when she bites the hand that feeds her.*

Bite the ice! *Sl.* Go to hell! □ *If that's what you think, you can just bite the ice!* □ *Get away from me! Bite the ice!*

*a **bite (to eat)** to get something to eat; to get food that can be eaten quickly. (*Typically: **get** ~; **grab** ~; **have** ~.) □ *I need a few minutes to grab a bite to eat.* □ *Bob often tries to get a bite between meetings.*

Bite your tongue! *Fig.* an expression said to someone who has just stated an unpleasant supposition that unfortunately may be true. □ *Mary: I'm afraid that we've missed the plane already. Jane: Bite your tongue! We still have time.* □ *Mary: Marry him? But you're older than he is! Sally: Bite your tongue!*

bitten by the same bug *Fig.* having the same need, desire, or obsession. □ *Bob and I were both bitten by the same bug and ended up getting new cars at the same time.*

a **bitter pill to swallow** *Fig.* an unpleasant fact that has to be accepted. (Does not involve pills or swallowing.) □ *It was a bitter pill for her brother to swallow when she married his enemy.* □ *We found his deception a bitter pill to swallow.*

blab something **around**† *Inf.* to gossip something to others; to spread some news or secret. □ *It's true, but don't blab it around.* □ *Did you blab around everything I told you to keep to yourself?*

blab something **out**† *Inf.* to speak out freely about something that is a secret. □ *Don't just blab it out!* □ *Don't blab out the names of the people who were there!*

black-and-blue *Fig.* bruised, physically or emotionally. □ *I'm still black-and-blue from my divorce.* □ *What is that black-and-blue mark on your leg?*

*black as a skillet** and *black as a stack of black cats; *black as a sweep; *black as coal; *black as night; *black as pitch; *black as the ace of spades** completely dark or black. (*Also: **as** ~.) □ *I don't want to go down to the cellar. It's as black as a skillet down there.* □ *Her hair was black as a stack of black cats.* □ *After playing in the mud all morning, the children were as black as night.* □ *The stranger's clothes were all black as pitch.*

*black as** one **is painted** as evil as described. (Usually negative. *Also: **as** ~.) □ *The landlord is not as black as he is painted. He seems quite generous to me.* □ *Young people are rarely black as they are painted in the media.*

B

black as pitch Go to black as a skillet.

black as the ace of spades Go to black as a skillet.

a **black eye 1.** *Lit.* a bruise near the eye from being struck. (*Typically **have** ~; **get** ~; **give** someone ~.) □ *I got a black eye from walking into a door.* □ *I have a black eye where John hit me.* **2.** *Fig.* harm done to one's character. (*Typically **have** ~; **get** ~; **give** someone ~.) □ *Mary got a black eye because of her constant complaining.* □ *The whole group now has a black eye, and it will take years to recover our reputation.*

*a **black mark beside** one's **name** *Fig.* something negative associated with a person. (*Typically: **get** ~; **have** ~; **give** one ~.) □ *I did it again! Now I've got still another black mark beside my name!*

black out 1. *Lit.* [for lights] to go out. □ *Suddenly the lights blacked out.* □ *The power went dead and everything blacked out from the heat.* **2.** *Fig.* to pass out; to become unconscious. □ *After I fell, I must have blacked out.* □ *I think I am going to black out.*

the **black sheep of the family** *Fig.* the worst member of the family. □ *Mary is the black sheep of the family. She's always in trouble with the police.* □ *He keeps making a nuisance of himself. What do you expect from the black sheep of the family?*

black something **out**[†] **1.** *Lit.* to cut or turn out the lights or electric power. □ *The lightning strike blacked the entire town out.* □ *The manager blacked out the whole building during the emergency to prevent an explosion.* **2.** *Fig.* to prevent the broadcast of a specific television or radio program in a specific area. □ *Will they black the game out around here?* □ *They blacked out the basketball game in this area.*

blackmail someone **into** doing something to force a person to do something by threatening to reveal some secret about the person. □ *Are you trying to blackmail me into doing what you want?* □ *They blackmailed me into doing it.*

*the **blame for** something the responsibility of having done something wrong or caused something bad to happen. (*Typically: **accept** ~; **bear** ~; **shoulder** ~; **take** ~.) □ *I absolutely refuse to shoulder the blame for the entire fiasco!*

blame someone **for** something to hold someone responsible for something; to name someone as the cause of something. □ *Please don't blame Jill for it.* □ *She blamed herself for everything that went wrong.*

blame something **on** someone to say that something is someone's fault; to place the guilt for something on someone. □ *Don't blame it on me.* □ *I blamed it all on someone else.*

blanch at something *Fig.* to cringe at something; to become pale at the thought of something. □ *Jill blanched at the thought of swimming in that cold water.* □ *Lily blanched at the sight before her.*

blanch with something *Fig.* to become pale with some emotion, such as anger or fear. □ *He saw the injury and blanched with fear.* □ *Lily blanched with anger as Max walked out.*

a **blank check** freedom or permission to act as one wishes or thinks necessary. □ *He's been given a blank check with regard to reorganizing the work force.* □ *The new manager has been given no detailed instructions about how to train the staff. He just has a blank check.*

blank something **out**[†] **1.** *Lit.* to erase something, as on a computer screen. □ *Who blanked out the information that was on my screen?* □ *Please blank your password out as soon as you type it.* **2.** *Fig.* to forget something, perhaps on purpose; to blot something out of memory. □ *I'm sorry, I just blanked your question out.* □ *I blanked out your question. What did you say?*

blanket someone or something **with** something *Fig.* to cover someone or something with something. □ *They blanketed the flames with a layer of foam.* □ *The children blanketed Jimmy with leaves and pretended he was lost.*

blast off (for some place) **1.** [for a space vehicle] to take off and head toward a destination. □ *The rocket blasted off for the moon.* □ *Will it blast off on time?* **2.** *Sl.* [for someone] to leave for a destination quickly. □ *Ann blasted off for the library so she could study.* □ *I've got to blast off. It's late.*

blast something **off** something else to remove something from something else with a powerful charge, pressure, or force. □ *They blasted the writing off the wall with a stream of sand.* □ *We will have to blast the paint off the wall.*

blaze a trail 1. *Lit.* to make and mark a trail. □ *The scout blazed a trail through the forest.* **2.** *Fig.* to do early or pioneering work that others will follow up on. □ *Professor Williams blazed a trail in the study of physics.*

blaze away (at someone or something) [for gunfire] to fire continually at someone or something. □ *The guns blazed away at the oncoming ducks.* □ *The cowboy blazed away at his opponent in the gunfight.*

blaze down (on someone or something) [for the sun or other hot light] to burn from above onto someone or something. □ *The sun blazed down on the people on the beach.* □ *The stage lights blazed down on the set while the actors rehearsed.*

blaze up 1. *Lit.* [for flames] to expand upward suddenly. □ *The fire blazed up and warmed all of us.* □ *As the fire blazed up, we moved away from the fireplace.* **2.** *Fig.* [for trouble, especially violent trouble] to erupt suddenly. □ *The battle blazed up again, and the fighting started to become fierce.* □ *As the battle blazed up, the cowards fled into the hills.*

blaze with something to burn with some quality, such as great heat or sound. □ *The sun blazed with unbelievable heat.* □ *The fire blazed with much crackling.*

bleach something **out**[†] to remove the color or stain from something. □ *Wally bleached his jeans out so they looked more stylish.* □ *Can you bleach out this stain?*

bleed for someone *Fig.* to feel the emotional pain that someone else is feeling; to sympathize or empathize with someone. □ *I just bled for him when I heard his sad story.* □ *We bled for her as she related her recent woes.*

bleed from something for blood to emerge from a wound or other source. □ *He was bleeding from a number of wounds.* □ *He bled from his mouth and nose.*

bleed someone **white** and **bleed** someone **dry** to take all of someone's money; to extort money from someone. □ *The creeps tried to bleed me white.* □ *Richard got a picture* of Fred and Joan together and tried to *bleed* both of them dry by threatening to show it to their spouses.

bleed to death to die from the loss of blood. □ *If something isn't done, he will bleed to death.* □ *I cut my finger. I hope I don't bleed to death.*

bleeding heart *Fig.* someone, usually considered politically liberal or leftist, who is very emotional about certain political issues, such as endangered species, downtrodden people, the suffering poor, etc. □ *Bob is such a bleeding heart. No cause is too far out for him.*

bleep something **out**[†] to replace a word or phrase in a radio or television broadcast with some sort of covering tone. (This is sometimes done to prevent a taboo word or other information from being broadcast.) □ *He tried to say the word on television, but they bleeped it out.* □ *They tried to bleep out the whole sentence.*

blend in (with someone or something**)** to mix well with someone or something; to combine with someone or something. □ *Everyone there blended in with our group.* □ *This color doesn't blend in with the upholstery fabric I have chosen.*

blend in(to something**)** to combine nicely with something; to mix well with something. □ *The oil won't blend into the water very well.* □ *It simply won't blend in.*

blend something **into** something else and **blend** something **in**[†] to mix something evenly into something else. □ *We should blend the strawberry jam into the peanut butter slowly.* □ *You should blend in some more jam.*

blend something **together (with** something**)** to mix something evenly with something else. □ *Blend the egg together with the cream.* □ *Blend the ingredients together and pour them into a baking pan.*

Bless one's **lucky star.** and **Bless** one's **stars.** *Prov.* Be thankful for a lucky thing that happened. (Also **Bless my stars!,** a mild interjection of surprise.) □ *I bless my lucky star that I met you, dear.* □ *I was in a car crash yesterday, and I bless my stars that no one was hurt.* □ *Alan: Look, honey! I gave the house a thorough cleaning while you were away. Jane: Bless my stars!*

Bless one's **stars.** Go to previous.

bless someone or something **with** something [for God or fate] to give someone or something a valuable gift. □ *God has blessed us with a bountiful harvest.* □ *Nature blessed the morning with a gentle rain.*

blessed event *Fig.* the birth of a child. □ *My sister is expecting a blessed event sometime in May.* □ *The young couple anxiously awaited the blessed event.*

Blessed is he who expects nothing, for he shall never be disappointed. *Prov.* If you do not expect good things to happen, you will not be disappointed when they fail to happen. □ *Ellen: This is going to be the best vacation we've ever had; we're going to have fun every minute of every day. Fred: Blessed is he who expects nothing, for he shall never be disappointed.* □ *Jill: Do you think you'll win the contest? Jane: I like to keep in mind that blessed is he who expects nothing, for he shall never be disappointed.*

a **blessing in disguise** *Fig.* something that at first seems bad, but later turns out to be beneficial. □ *Tony's motorcycle accident was a blessing in disguise, because he got*

enough insurance money from the other driver to make a down payment on a house. □ *Dad's illness was a blessing in disguise; it brought the family together for the first time in years.*

a **blight on the land** *Fig.* something that harms the land or the enviornment. □ *Your garage is ugly! No, it's a blight on the land!*

blimp out to overeat; to eat too much and gain weight. □ *I blimp out almost every weekend.* □ *If I could stop blimping out, I could lose some weight.*

***blind as a bat 1.** completely blind. (Bats are not really blind. *Also: **as** ~.) □ *He lost his sight in an accident and is as blind as a bat.* **2.** not able to see well. □ *I'm as blind as a bat without my glasses.* **3.** unwilling to recognize problems or bad things. □ *Connie is blind as a bat when it comes to her daughter's disgraceful behavior.*

The **blind leading the blind** *Prov.* Someone who is not capable of dealing with a situation is guiding someone else who is not capable of dealing with it. (See also a **case of the blind leading the blind.**) □ *Jill: Mike is helping me fill out my tax forms this year. Jane: Is he a tax expert? Jill: He read a book about income tax once. Jane: Sounds to me like the blind leading the blind.* □ *Nathan offered to be my guide through Philadelphia, but since he'd never been there before either, it was a case of the blind leading the blind.*

blind luck Go to **pure luck.**

blind someone **to** something *Fig.* to prevent someone from seeing or understanding something. □ *The king blinded his subjects to what was going on by controlling what appeared in the newspapers.* □ *The lies and confusion blinded Jill to what was happening.* □ *She blinded herself to all his faults.*

blink at something **1.** *Lit.* to open and close the eyelids quickly, one or more times. □ *I blinked at the bright light and finally had to close my eyes.* □ *Don't blink at me while I am trying to take your picture.* **2.** *Fig.* to overlook something, such as a mistake. (As if one had blinked one's eyes rather than seeing the error.) □ *I just can't blink at that kind of behavior.* □ *We can't blink at what evil you did.*

blink one's **tears back**[†] *Fig.* to try to keep from crying. □ *She blinked back her tears and went on.* □ *He blinked his tears back and endured the pain.*

bliss out *Sl.* to be overcome with happiness. □ *She blissed out at the concert, because she loves that kind of music.*

bliss someone **out**[†] *Sl.* to cause someone to be overcome with happiness. □ *This kind of sunny weather just blisses me out.* □ *The lovely weather blissed out everyone after the long winter.*

blitz someone **out**[†] *Sl.* to shock or disorient someone. □ *The accident blitzed her out for a moment.* □ *The second act blitzed out the audience and thrilled them to pieces.*

blitzed out *Sl.* shocked or disoriented. □ *Ann was totally blitzed out by the events of the day.* □ *They were totally blitzed out by the bad news.*

block someone or something **in** some place and **block** someone or something **in**[†] to place an obstacle that prevents someone or something from getting out of something. □ *I can't get out of my parking space. Someone blocked me in my space.* □ *Don't block in any of the other cars in the garage.*

B

block someone **up**[†] to constipate someone. □ *That food always blocks me up.* □ *He blocked himself up by eating something he shouldn't.* □ *That vile stuff would block up anybody!*

block something **off**[†] to prevent movement through something by putting up a barrier; to close a passageway. □ *Sam blocked the corridor off with a row of chairs.* □ *He used some chairs to block off the hallway.*

block something **out**[†] **1.** to obscure a clear view of something. □ *The trees blocked the sun out.* □ *The bushes blocked out my view of the car that was approaching.* **2.** to lay something out carefully; to map out the details of something. □ *She blocked it out for us, so we could understand.* □ *Let me block out this project for you right now.*

block something **up**[†] to obstruct something; to stop the flow within a channel. □ *The heaps of debris blocked the channel up.* □ *The leaves blocked up the drain.*

blood and guts 1. *Fig.* strife; acrimony. □ *There is a lot of blood and guts around here, but we get our work done anyway.* □ *Cut out the blood and guts and grow up.* **2.** *Fig.* acrimonious. (This is hyphenated before a nominal.) □ *There are too many blood-and-guts arguments around here.* □ *Old blood-and-guts Wally is making his threats again.*

Blood is thicker than water. and **Blood runs thicker than water.** *Prov.* People who are related have stronger obligations to each other than to people outside the family. □ *My friends invited me to go camping on Saturday, but I have to go to my cousin's wedding instead. Blood is thicker than water, after all.* □ *If you ever need help, don't ask your friends. Come home and ask us, your family. Blood runs thicker than water.*

blood, sweat, and tears *Fig.* the signs of great personal effort. □ *There will be much blood, sweat, and tears before we have completed this project.* □ *After years of blood, sweat, and tears, Timmy finally earned a college degree.*

Blood will have blood. *Prov.* People will use violence to get revenge for violent acts; murderers will themselves be murdered. □ *Although no one suspected him of the murder he had committed, Parker lived in fear. He had heard that blood will have blood.* □ *I am afraid that the two gangs will never stop killing each other. Blood will have blood.*

Blood will tell. *Prov.* A person whose ancestors had certain characteristics, often bad ones, will eventually turn out to be similar. □ *Lisa's father was a gambler, and now Lisa has started to gamble, too. Blood will tell.* □ *William went to all the best schools, but he's just as vulgar as the rest of his family. Blood will tell.*

bloody but unbowed *Fig.* showing signs of a struggle, but not defeated. (Originally referring to the head. From the poem *Invictus* by William Earnest Henley.) □ *Liz emerged from the struggle, her head bloody but unbowed.* □ *We are bloody but unbowed and will fight to the last.*

blossom forth 1. *Lit.* [for a plant] to burst into flower. □ *All the trees blossomed forth at the same time.* □ *Each spring my tulips blossom forth in all their glory.* **2.** *Fig.* [for someone or a concept] to develop or grow quickly. □ *A wonderful idea blossomed forth and caught on quickly.* □ *That summer she suddenly blossomed forth into a young woman.*

blossom into something **1.** *Lit.* [for a plant] to develop into full bloom. □ *The bush blossomed into beautiful red roses.* □ *Imagine this brown old bulb blossoming into a lovely flower.* **2.** *Fig.* [for someone or a concept] to develop into something. □ *She blossomed into a lovely young lady.* □ *The idea blossomed into a huge real estate development.*

blossom out 1. *Lit.* [for a plant or tree] to become covered with flowers. □ *The apple tree blossomed out for the last time.* **2.** *Fig.* [for someone or a concept] to develop fully, physically and intellectually. □ *She blossomed out in her studies and her excellent grades showed it.* □ *In her last year in school, she blossomed out.*

a **blot on the landscape** *Fig.* a sight that spoils the look of a place. □ *That monstrosity you call a house is a blot on the landscape. You should have hired a real architect!*

blot someone or something **out**[†] *Fig.* to forget someone or something by covering up memories or by trying to forget. □ *I try to blot those bad thoughts out.* □ *I tried to blot out those unhappy days.*

blot someone **out**[†] *Sl.* to kill someone. (Originally underworld slang.) □ *Sorry, chum, we got orders to blot you out.* □ *The gang blotted out the only living witness before the trial.*

blot something **out**[†] to make something invisible by covering it. (See also blot someone or something out.) □ *Don't blot the name out on the application form.* □ *Who blotted out the name on this form?*

blow a bundle (on someone**)** Go to **drop a bundle (on** someone**).**

blow a fuse 1. to burn out the fuse on an electrical circuit and lose power. □ *The microwave oven blew a fuse, so we had no power.* □ *You'll blow a fuse if you use too many appliances at once.* **2.** and **blow** one's **fuse; blow a gasket; blow** one's **cork; blow** one's **lid; blow** one's **top; blow** one's **stack** *Fig.* to explode with anger; to lose one's temper. □ *Come on, don't blow a fuse.* □ *Go ahead, blow a gasket! What good will that do?*

blow away [for something light] to be carried away by the wind. □ *The leaves blew away on the autumn winds.* □ *My papers blew away!*

blow hot and cold *Fig.* to be changeable or uncertain (about something). □ *He keeps blowing hot and cold on the question of moving to the country.* □ *He blows hot and cold about this. I wish he'd make up his mind.*

blow in 1. Go to blow in (from some place). **2.** Go to blow in(to some place) (from some place). **3.** [for something] to cave in to the pressure of moving air. □ *The door blew in during the storm.* □ *The window blew in from the wind.*

blow in (from some place**)** [for a wind] to move air in from some place. □ *A huge mass of frigid air blew in from Canada.* □ *When the cold air blew in, we were dressed in short sleeves.*

blow in(to some place**) (from** some place**)** *Sl.* [for someone] to arrive at a place suddenly, or surprisingly, or with a casual air. □ *We blew into town about midnight from Detroit.* □ *It was late when we blew in from Detroit.* □ *What time did you blow in?*

blow into something to force air into something. □ *He blew into the balloon.* □ *I blew into the box, hoping to get some of the little bits of paper out.*

Blow it out your ear! *Sl.* Go away!; Leave me alone! □ *Oh, blow it out your ear, you cornball!* □ *You are not cool, you're just weird! Blow it out your ear!*

blow itself out [for a storm or a tantrum] to lose strength and stop; to subside. (Fixed order.) □ *The storm blew itself out.* □ *Eventually, the hurricane blew itself out.*

blow off 1. *Lit.* [for something] to be carried off something by moving air. □ *The leaves of the trees blew off in the strong wind.* □ *My papers blew off the table.* **2.** *Lit.* [for a valve or pressure-maintaining device] to be forced off or away by high pressure. (See the examples.) □ *The safety valve blew off and all the pressure escaped.* □ *The valve blew off, making a loud pop.* **3.** *Fig.* [for someone] to become angry; to lose one's temper; to **blow off (some) steam.** □ *I just needed to blow off. Sorry for the outburst.* □ *I blew off at her.* **4.** *Sl.* to goof off; to waste time; to procrastinate. □ *You blow off too much.* □ *All your best time is gone—blown off.* **5.** *Sl.* a time-waster; a goof-off. (Usually **blow-off.**) □ *Fred is such a blow-off! Get busy. I don't pay blow-offs around here.* **6.** *Sl.* something that can be done easily or without much effort. (Usually **blow-off.**) □ *Oh, that is just a blow-off. Nothing to it.* □ *The test was easy—a blow-off.* **7.** and **blow someone or something off**† *Sl.* to ignore someone or something; to skip an appointment with someone; to not attend something where one is expected. □ *He decided to sleep in and blow this class off.* □ *It wasn't right for you to just blow off an old friend the way you did.* **8.** and **blow someone off**† *Sl.* to ignore someone in order to end a romantic or other relationship. □ *She knew that he had blown her off when he didn't even call her for a month.* □ *Steve blew off Rachel before he started seeing Jane.* **9.** *Sl.* the final insult; an event that causes a dispute. (Usually **blow-off.**) □ *The blow-off was a call from some girl named Lulu who asked for Snookums.* □ *When the blow-off happened, nobody was expecting anything.* **10.** *Sl.* a dispute; an argument. (Usually **blow-off.**) □ *After a blow-off like that, we all need a break.* □ *There was a big blow-off in the office today.*

blow off (some) steam Go to let off (some) steam.

Blow on it! *Sl.* Cool it!; Take it easy! □ *It's all right, Tom. Blow on it!* □ *Hey, man. Relax. Blow on it!*

blow on something to force air across something especially with a puff of breath. □ *Jill blew on the hot soup.* □ *Blow on the fire to make it burn hotter.*

blow one's **cookies** Go to blow (one's) lunch.

blow one's **cool** Go to lose one's cool.

blow one's **cork** Go to blow a fuse.

blow one's **fuse** Go to blow a fuse.

blow one's **groceries** Go to blow one's lunch.

blow one's **lid** Go to blow a fuse.

blow one's **lines** Go to fluff one's lines.

blow (one's) lunch and **lose** one's **lunch; blow** one's **cookies; blow** one's **groceries** *Sl.* to vomit. □ *I almost lost my lunch, I ran so hard.* □ *I wanted to blow my lunch, that's how rotten I felt.* □ *He got carsick and blew his cookies all over the front seat.*

blow one's **nose** to expel mucus and other material from the nose using air pressure from the lungs. □ *Excuse me,* *I have to blow my nose.* □ *Bill blew his nose into his hand-kerchief.*

blow one's **own horn** and **toot** one's **own horn** *Fig.* to brag. □ *Gary sure likes to toot his own horn.* □ *"I hate to blow my own horn," said Bill, "but I am always right."*

blow one's **stack** Go to blow a fuse.

blow one's **top** Go to blow a fuse.

blow over *Fig.* [for something] to diminish; to subside. (As with a storm or a temper tantrum.) □ *Her display of temper finally blew over.* □ *The storm will blow over soon, I hope.*

blow someone **a kiss** to pantomine the sending of a kiss to a person visible nearby by kissing one's hand and "blowing" the kiss toward the person. □ *As she boarded the train she blew him a kiss, and he waved back.*

blow someone **away 1.** *Sl.* [for something shocking or exciting] to overwhelm a person; to excite a person very much. □ *The amount of the check blew me away.* □ *The loud noise from the concert blew me away.* **2.** *Sl.* to murder someone, usually by gunfire. □ *Mr. Big ordered Lefty to blow Max away.* □ *Max tried to blow Lefty away.*

blow someone or something **away**† [for the wind] to carry someone or something away. □ *The wind almost blew her away.* □ *It nearly blew away all the houses.*

blow someone or something **down**† [for a rush of air] to knock someone or something over. □ *The wind blew Chuck down.* □ *The tornado blew down many buildings.*

blow someone or something **out of the water** *Fig.* to destroy utterly someone or something, such as a plan. (Alludes to a torpedo or other weapon striking a ship and causing a great explosion that makes pieces of the ship fly out of the water.) □ *I will blow him out of the water if he shows up around here.* □ *The boss blew the whole idea out of the water.*

blow someone or something **over** [for the wind] to move strongly and upset someone or something. □ *The wind almost blew us over.* □ *The tornado blew the shed over.*

blow someone or something **to bits** Go to blow someone or something to smithereens.

blow someone or something **to kingdom come** *Fig.* to destroy someone or something by means of an explosion. □ *You'd better get that gas leak fixed or it will blow you and your car to kingdom come.*

blow someone or something **to pieces** Go to next.

blow someone or something **to smithereens** and **blow** someone or something **to bits; blow** someone or something **to pieces** *Lit.* to explode someone or something into tiny pieces. (See also blow something to smithereens.) □ *The bomb blew the ancient church to smithereens.* □ *The explosion blew the tank to bits.* □ *The explosion blew the car to pieces.*

blow someone or something **up**† **1.** *Lit.* to destroy someone or something by explosion. □ *The terrorists blew the building up at midday.* □ *They blew up the bridge.* **2.** *Fig.* to exaggerate something [good or bad] about someone or something. □ *I hope no one blows the story up.* □ *The media always blows up reports of celebrity behavior.* □ *The press blew the story up unnecessarily.*

blow someone **out** *Sl.* to kill someone, especially with gunshots. (Fixed order.) □ *Lefty set out to blow Max out once and for all.* □ *Lefty wanted to blow Max out too.*

blow someone **over**† **1.** *Lit.* [for the wind or an explosion] to knock someone over. □ *The force of the wind nearly blew me over.* □ *The wind blew over the old tree.* **2.** *Fig.* to surprise or astound someone. (Fixed order.) □ *Her announcement just blew me over.* □ *The whole event just blew me over.*

blow someone's **brains out**† *Sl.* to kill someone with a gun. □ *Careful with that gun, or you'll blow your brains out.* □ *Max was so depressed that he wanted to blow out his brains.*

blow someone's **cover** *Sl.* to reveal someone's true identity; to ruin someone's scheme for concealment. □ *The dog recognized me and blew my cover.* □ *I didn't mean to blow your cover by calling out to you.*

blow someone's **doors off**† *Sl.* [for a driver] to speed past another vehicle. □ *Wow, he almost blew my doors off!* □ *The truck passed us and blew off our doors!*

blow someone's **mind 1.** *Sl.* to disturb or distract; to destroy the function of one's brain. □ *It was a terrible experience. It nearly blew my mind.* □ *She blew her mind on drugs.* **2.** *Sl.* to overwhelm someone; to excite someone. □ *It was so beautiful, it nearly blew my mind.* □ *The loud guitar music was so wild. It blew my mind.*

blow someone **to** something *Sl.* to pay for something or someone, such as a meal, a movie, a drink, etc. □ *Let me blow you to a meal.* □ *I think I'll blow myself to a fancy dessert.*

blow something *Sl.* to ruin or waste something. □ *I had a chance to do it, but I blew it.* □ *He blew the whole five dollars on candy.*

blow something **out**† to extinguish a flame with a puff of breath. □ *I blew the candle out.* □ *I blew out the candles one by one.*

blow something **out of (all) proportion** Go to out of (all) proportion.

blow something **to smithereens** and **blow** something **to bits; blow** something **to pieces** *Fig.* to destroy an idea or plan by exposing its faults. (See also blow someone or something to smithereens.) □ *The discovery blew my case to pieces.* □ *The opposing lawyer blew my case to smithereens.*

blow something **up**† **1.** to inflate something. □ *He didn't have enough breath to blow the balloon up.* □ *They all blew up their own balloons.* **2.** to have a photograph enlarged. □ *How big can you blow this picture up?* □ *I will blow up this snapshot and frame it.*

blow something **wide open** and **bust** something **wide open** *Sl.* to expose corrupt practices or a secret plan; to put an end to corruption. □ *The press is trying to blow the town wide open, and the feds are trying to hush them up so they can move about in secret.* □ *I'm going to bust this racket wide open.*

blow the joint *Sl.* to get out of a place, usually in a hurry or without delay. □ *Come on, let's blow the joint before there's trouble.* □ *They blew the joint about an hour ago.*

blow the lid off (something) *Sl.* to expose something to public view. □ *The police inspector blew the lid off the work of the gang of thugs.* □ *The investigation blew the lid off the scandal.*

blow the whistle (on someone) 1. *Fig.* to report someone's wrongdoing to someone (such as the police) who can stop the wrongdoing. (Alludes to blowing a whistle to attract the police.) □ *The citizens' group blew the whistle on the street gangs by calling the police.* □ *The gangs were getting very bad. It was definitely time to blow the whistle.* **2.** *Fig.* to report legal or regulatory wrongdoing of a company, especially one's employer, to authorities. □ *She was fired for blowing the whistle on the bank's mismanagement of accounts, but she then sued the bank.*

blow up 1. *Lit.* [for something] to explode. □ *The bomb might have blown up if the children had tried to move it.* □ *The firecracker blew up.* **2.** *Fig.* to burst into anger. □ *I just knew you'd blow up.* □ *So she blew up. Why should that affect you so much?* **3.** *Fig.* an angry outburst; a fight. (Usually **blowup**.) □ *After the third blowup, she left him.* □ *One blowup after another from you. Control your temper!* **4.** *Fig.* an enlarged version of a photograph, map, chart, etc. (Usually **blowup**.) □ *Here's a blowup of the scene of the crime.* □ *Kelly sent a blowup of their wedding picture to all her relatives.* **5.** *Fig.* the ruination of something; the collapse of something. (Usually **blowup**.) □ *The blowup in the financial world has ruined my chances for early retirement.* □ *After the blowup at the company, the top managers called one another to compare notes.* **6.** *Fig.* to fall apart or get ruined. □ *The whole project blew up. It will have to be canceled.* □ *All my planning was blown up this afternoon.* **7.** [for a storm] to arrive accompanied by the blowing of the wind. □ *A terrible storm blew up while we were in the movie theater.* □ *I was afraid that a rainstorm was blowing up.*

blow up in someone's **face 1.** *Lit.* to blow up or explode suddenly. □ *The bomb blew up in the terrorist's face.* □ *The firecracker blew up in his face and injured him.* **2.** *Fig.* [for something] to get ruined while someone is working on it. □ *All my plans blew up in my face.* □ *It is terrible for your life to get ruined and blow up in your face.*

a **blow-by-blow account** and a **blow-by-blow description** *Fig.* a detailed description (of an event) given as the event takes place. (This referred originally to reporting on boxing.) □ *I want to listen to a blow-by-blow account of the prizefight.* □ *The lawyer got the witness to give a blow-by-blow description of the argument.*

a **blow-by-blow description** Go to previous.

blown (up) *Sl.* intoxicated. □ *I guess I'm a little too blown up to drive.*

blue around the gills Go to pale around the gills.

blue blood 1. *Fig.* the blood [heredity] of a noble family; aristocratic ancestry. □ *The earl refuses to allow anyone who is not of blue blood to marry his son.* □ *Although Mary's family is poor, she has blue blood in her veins.* **2.** *Fig.* a person of aristocratic or wealthy ancestry. □ *Because his great-grandparents made millions, he is regarded as one of the city's blue bloods.*

blue collar of the lower class or working class; of a job or a worker, having to do with manual labor. (Also, when used as an attributive adjective, often **blue-collar**. Compare this with *white collar*. Alludes to the typical color of work shirts worn by mechanics, laborers, etc.) □ *His parents were both blue-collar workers. He was the first person in his family to go to college.* □ *They bought a house in a nice, settled, blue-collar neighborhood.*

*the **blues 1.** sadness; a mood of depression. (*Typically: **get** ~; **have** ~.) □ *You'll have to excuse Bill. He's getting the blues thinking about Jane.* □ *I get the blues every time I hear that song.* **2.** a traditional style of popular music characterized by lyrics expressing hardship, lost love, etc. □ *Buddy had been singing the blues ever since the Depression.*

bluff one's **way out (of** something) to get out of a difficult situation by deception or cunning. □ *I will try to bluff my way out of this mess.*

bluff someone **into** something to mislead or deceive someone into doing something. □ *Are you trying to bluff me into giving up without a fight?* □ *I won't be bluffed into revealing the whereabouts of the safe.*

bluff someone **out (of** something) to get something away from someone through deception. □ *We bluffed her out of her share of the pie.* □ *I bluffed Liz out of her rightful turn to drive.*

blurt something **out**† **(at** someone) to say something to someone without thinking. (Usually to say something that should not be said.) □ *It was a secret. Why did you blurt it out?* □ *Why did you blurt out our hiding place?*

blush with something [for someone's cheeks] to redden from a particular emotion or reaction. □ *She blushed with shame.* □ *You could see that Lily was blushing with anger, even though she tried to conceal it.*

board someone or an animal **out**† to send someone or an animal away to live, temporarily. (Usually said of a school-age child or a pet.) □ *They decided to board Billy out.* □ *They boarded out the dog while they were on vacation.*

board something **up**† to enclose or seal a building or part of a building with boards or panels. □ *We will have to board this house up if we can't sell it.* □ *Should I board up the house while I am away that season?*

board with someone to live with someone temporarily, usually while paying to do so. □ *I will board with my aunt when I go to school in Adamsville.* □ *I do not wish to board with relatives.*

boast about someone or something and **boast of** someone or something to speak highly about someone or something that one is proud of. □ *I just have to boast about my grandchildren. Do you mind?* □ *Is he boasting about his car again?* □ *I don't like to boast of what I did.*

bode somehow **for** someone or something to foretell or portend fortune or misfortune for someone or something. (Typically with *ill* or *well*.) □ *Things do not bode well for the stock market.* □ *Things do not bode well for your future at this job.*

bodily functions *Euph.* anything the body does automatically or as a normal occurrence, especially urinating and defecating. □ *The dog needed to go outside and perform her bodily functions.* □ *It is not polite to discuss bodily functions at the dinner table.*

the **body politic** the people of a country or state considered as a political unit. □ *The body politic was unable to select between the candidates.*

bog down to become encumbered and slow. (As if one were walking through a bog and getting stuck in the mud. Often preceded by a form of **get**.) □ *The process bogged down and almost stopped.* □ *The truck got bogged down in the mud soon after it started.*

*bogged down** stuck; prevented from making progress. (*Typically: **be** ~; **get** ~; **become** ~.) □ *The students became bogged down with the algebra problems.* □ *The Smiths really got bogged down in decorating their house.*

boggle at something to be amazed at something, particularly something large or surprising. □ *The audience boggled at the size of the loss.* □ *I boggled at the damage to my car.*

boggle someone's **mind** to confuse someone; to overwhelm someone; to **blow** someone's **mind**. □ *The immense size of the house boggles my mind.* □ *She said that his arrogance boggled her mind.*

boil down to something **1.** and **boil down** *Lit.* [for a liquid] to be condensed to something by boiling. □ *Boil this mixture down to about half of what it was.* **2.** *Fig.* [for a complex situation] to be reduced to its essentials. □ *It boils down to the question of who is going to win.* □ *It boils down to a very minor matter.*

boil over [for a liquid] to overflow while being boiled. (See also **boil over (with** something).) □ *The sauce boiled over and dripped onto the stove.* □ *Don't let the stew boil over!*

boil over (with something) *Fig.* [for someone] to erupt in great anger. □ *The boss boiled over with anger.* □ *Things got out of hand and the crowd's passions boiled over.*

boil something **away**† **1.** *Lit.* to boil a liquid until it is gone altogether. □ *She left the kettle on and boiled the water away.* □ *Boil away some of that water.* **2.** *Lit.* to remove a volatile chemical from a solution by boiling. □ *Boil the alcohol away or the sauce will be ruined.* □ *You should boil away some of the liquid.*

boil something **down**† **1.** *Lit.* to condense or thicken something, such as a liquid. □ *I have to boil this gravy down for a while before I can serve it.* □ *You boil down the sauce and I'll set the table.* **2.** *Fig.* to reduce a problem to its simple essentials. □ *If we could boil this problem down to its essentials, we might be able to solve it.* □ *We don't have time to boil down this matter. This is too urgent.*

boil something **out**† Go to next.

boil something **out of** something and **boil** something **out**† to remove something from something by boiling. □ *I boiled the wax out of the cloth.* □ *You can boil out the stain.*

boil something **up**† *Rur.* to cook a batch of food by boiling. □ *She boiled some beans up for dinner.* □ *She boiled up some potatoes.*

boil with something *Fig.* to show the heat or intensity of one's anger. □ *You could see that she was just boiling with anger.* □ *Tom was boiling with rage when we got there.*

*bold as brass** very bold; bold to the point of rudeness. (*Also: **as** ~.) □ *Lisa marched into the manager's office, bold as brass, and demanded her money back.* □ *The tiny* *kitten,* as bold as brass, *began eating the dog's food right under the dog's nose.*

bollix something **up**[†] *Inf.* to ruin something; to mess something up. □ *Please don't bollix my stereo up.* □ *Who bollixed up the folded laundry?*

bolster someone **up**[†] *Fig.* to give someone emotional support and encouragement. □ *We bolstered her up the best we could, but she was still unhappy.* □ *I don't mind bolstering up people who are depressed.*

bolster something **up**[†] to give added support to something. □ *The carpenter bolstered the shelf up with a nail or two.* □ *I had to bolster up the door or it would have fallen in.*

a **bolt from the blue** *Fig.* a sudden surprise. (Alludes to a stroke of lightning from a cloudless sky.) □ *Joe's return to Springfield was a bolt from the blue.* □ *The news that Mr. and Mrs. King were getting a divorce struck all their friends as a bolt from the blue.*

bolt out (of some place**)** to run out of some place very quickly. □ *Frank bolted out of the room in a flash.* □ *I bolted out after him.*

bolt something **down**[†] **1.** *Lit.* to fasten something down securely with bolts. □ *Did anyone bolt the washing machine down?* □ *Someone should bolt down this washing machine.* **2.** *Fig.* to eat something too rapidly. □ *Don't bolt your food down.* □ *She bolted down her dinner and ran out to play.*

bomb out (of something**)** *Sl.* to flunk out of or fail at something, especially school or a job. □ *She was afraid she would bomb out of school.* □ *Her brother bombed out the year before.*

bomb someone **out**[†] to cause people to flee by bombing their homes and towns. □ *The planes bombed the villagers out.* □ *The attack bombed out everyone for miles around.*

bomb something **out**[†] to destroy a place by bombing. □ *I hope they don't bomb the village out.* □ *The planes bombed out the factory.*

bombard someone or something **with** something to cast or shoot something at someone or something. (See also **bombard** someone **with questions.**) □ *The boys bombarded their friends with snowballs.* □ *Gerald bombarded his friends with criticism.*

bombard someone **with questions** *Fig.* to ask someone many questions, one after another. □ *The press bombarded the president with questions.* □ *The company spokesperson was bombarded with leading questions.*

bone of contention *Fig.* the subject or point of an argument; an unsettled point of disagreement. □ *We've fought for so long that we've forgotten what the bone of contention is.* □ *The question of a fence between the houses has become quite a bone of contention.*

bone up (on something**)** to study something thoroughly; to review the facts about something. □ *I have to bone up on the state driving laws because I have to take my driving test tomorrow.* □ *I take mine next month, so I'll have to bone up, too.*

boo someone **off the stage** and **boo** someone **off**[†] to jeer and hoot, causing a performer to leave the stage. □ *The rude audience booed the performer off the stage.* □ *The audience booed off the comedian.*

booby prize a mock prize given to the worst player or performer. □ *Bob should get the booby prize for the worst showing in the race.*

boogie down (to somewhere**)** *Sl.* to hurry (to somewhere); to go (somewhere). □ *So, why don't you boogie down to the store and load up with goodies for the weekend?* □ *I'm gonna boogie down and see what's going on.*

book (on) out *Sl.* to leave in a hurry; to depart very suddenly and rapidly. □ *I'm in a hurry, so I've got to book out right now.* □ *Let's book on out of this place as soon as we can.*

book someone **on** something to reserve a place for someone on some travel conveyance. □ *They booked us on a direct flight to San Juan.* □ *He booked himself on a flight to Manaus.*

book someone **through (to** some place**)** to make transportation arrangements for someone that involve a number of changes and transfers. □ *The travel agent booked me through to Basra.* □ *I would be happy to book you through if you would like.*

book something **up**[†] to reserve all the available places. □ *The travel agency booked all the good seats up.* □ *Who booked up all these seats?*

boom out [for a loud sound] to sound out like thunder. □ *His voice boomed out such that everyone could hear.* □ *An explosion boomed out and frightened us all.*

boom something **out**[†] [for someone] to say something very loud; to shout. □ *Will someone with a loud voice boom the names out?* □ *The announcer boomed out the names of the players.*

boost someone **up**[†] to give someone a helpful lift up to something. □ *She boosted me up so I could get into the window.* □ *They boosted up the child for a better view.*

*the **boot** dismissal from employment or from a place that one is in. (*Typically: **get** ~; **give** someone ~ .) □ *I guess I wasn't dressed well enough to go in there. They gave me the boot.* □ *I'll work harder at my job today. I nearly got the boot yesterday.*

boot someone or an animal **out**[†] and **kick** someone or an animal **out**[†] **1.** *Lit.* to send or remove someone or an animal from a place forcefully, often by kicking. □ *I kicked the cat out and then went to bed.* □ *Tom kicked out the dog.* **2.** *Fig.* to force someone or something to leave some place. □ *We booted out the people who didn't belong there.* □ *The doorman booted the kid out.*

boot something **up**[†] to start up a computer. □ *She booted her computer up and started writing.* □ *Please go boot up your computer so we can get started.*

boot up [of a computer] to begin operating; to start up one's computer. □ *He turned on the computer and it booted up.* □ *Try to boot up again and see what happens.*

booze it up *Sl.* to drink heavily; to drink to get drunk. (Fixed order.) □ *She wanted to get home and booze it up by herself.* □ *He boozes it up every Friday after work.*

booze up *Sl.* to drink heavily. □ *Those guys are always boozing up.* □ *Stop boozing up and go home.*

border (up)on something **1.** *Lit.* [for something] to touch upon a boundary. (*Upon* is more formal and less commonly used than *on*.) □ *Our property borders on the* *lakeshore.* □ *The farm borders upon the railroad tracks.* **2.** *Fig.* [for some activity or idea] to be very similar to something else. (Not usually physical objects. *Upon* is formal and less commonly used than *on.*) □ *This notion of yours borders upon mutiny!* □ *That plan borders on insanity.*

bore someone **stiff** and **bore** someone **to death; bore** someone **to tears** *Fig.* to be exceedingly dull and uninteresting. (*Stiff* means "dead.") □ *The play bored me stiff.* □ *The lecture bored everyone to death.*

bore someone **to death** Go to previous.

bore someone **to tears** Go to bore someone stiff.

bore the pants off of someone *Fig.* to be exceedingly dull and uninteresting to someone. □ *You bore the pants off of me!* □ *The lecture bored the pants off of everybody.*

bore through someone *Fig.* [for someone's gaze] to seem to penetrate the person being gazed or stared at. □ *Her stare bored right through me.*

bore through something to pierce or drill through something. □ *The drill bit could not bore through the steel plate.*

bored silly and **bored to distraction; bored stiff; bored to death; bored to tears** very bored; extremely dull and uninteresting (Usually an exaggeration.) □ *I was bored silly at the lecture.* □ *The dull speaker left me bored to distraction.* □ *I am bored to tears. Let's go home.*

bored to distraction Go to previous.

born and bred Go to next.

born and raised and **born and bred** born and nurtured through childhood, usually in a specific place. □ *She was born and raised in a small town in western Montana.* □ *Freddy was born and bred on a farm and had no love for city life.*

born on the wrong side of the blanket *Rur.* [of a child] illegitimate. □ *All his life, Edward felt that people looked down on him because he was born on the wrong side of the blanket.* □ *Just between you and me, I suspect Mrs. Potter's oldest child was born on the wrong side of the blanket.*

born out of wedlock born to an unmarried mother. □ *The child was born out of wedlock.* □ *In the city many children are born out of wedlock.*

born with a silver spoon in one's **mouth** *Fig.* born into wealth and privilege. □ *James doesn't know anything about working for a living; he was born with a silver spoon in his mouth.* □ *Most of the students at the exclusive private college were born with silver spoons in their mouths.*

borrow something *Euph.* to steal something. □ *The bank robber borrowed a car to drive out of state.* □ *I discovered that my office mate had been borrowing money out of my wallet when I wasn't looking.*

borrow something **from** someone to request and receive the use of something from someone. □ *Can I borrow a hammer from you?* □ *Sorry, this hammer was borrowed from my father.*

borrow trouble *Fig.* to worry needlessly; to make trouble for oneself. □ *Worrying too much about death is just borrowing trouble.* □ *Do not get involved with politics. That's borrowing trouble.*

bosom buddy and **bosom pal** a close friend; one's closest friend. □ *Of course I know Perry. He is one of my bosom pals.*

bosom pal Go to previous.

boss someone **around**† to give orders to someone; to keep telling someone what to do. □ *Stop bossing me around. I'm not your employee.* □ *Captain Smith bosses around the whole crew. That's his job.*

botch something **up**† to mess something up; to do a bad job of something. □ *You really botched this up.* □ *I did not botch up your project.*

both sheets in the wind intoxicated. (A ship's sheets are the ropes or lines that control the sails. See also **three sheets in the wind**.) □ *She's both sheets in the wind at the moment.* □ *She's not just both sheets in the wind—they're all in the wind.*

bother about something to care about something; to take the trouble to deal with something. □ *Please don't bother about this mess. I'll clean it up.* □ *Don't bother about it.*

bother one's **(pretty little) head about** someone or something *Rur.* to worry about something. (Stereotypically polite Southern talk to a woman; often said facetiously or patronizingly.) □ *Now, don't bother your pretty little head about all this.* □ *Don't bother your head about me.*

bother someone **with** someone or something and **bother** someone **about** someone or something to annoy someone with someone or something; to worry someone about someone or something. (Either a physical annoyance or a mental annoyance.) □ *Don't bother me with that!* □ *Don't bother yourself about the bill. I'll pay it.*

bother with someone or something to take the time or trouble to deal with someone or something. (Usually negative.) □ *Please don't bother with Jill. She can take care of herself.* □ *Don't bother me with your problems.*

the **bottle** drinking alcohol. □ *His friends thought he was a bit too fond of the bottle.* □ *She tried to stay away from the bottle, but she never could manage it for long.*

bottle something **up**† **1.** *Lit.* to put some sort of liquid into bottles. □ *She bottled her homemade chili sauce up and put the bottles in a box.* □ *She bottled up a lot of the stuff.* **2.** *Fig.* to constrict something as if it were put in a bottle. □ *The patrol boats bottled the other boats up at the locks on the river.* □ *The police bottled up the traffic while they searched the cars for the thieves.* **3.** and **bottle** something **up**† **(inside (**someone**))** *Fig.* to hold one's feelings within; to keep from saying something that one feels strongly about. □ *Let's talk about it, John. You shouldn't bottle it up.* □ *Don't bottle up your problems. It's better to talk them out.* □ *Don't bottle it up inside you.* □ *Don't bottle up all your feelings.*

the **bottom fell out (of** something**)** *Fig.* a much lower limit or level of something was reached. □ *The bottom fell out of the market and I lost a lot of money.*

the **bottom line 1.** *Lit.* the last figure on a financial profit-and-loss statement, or on a bill. □ *What's the bottom line? How much do I owe you?* □ *Don't tell me all those figures! Just tell me the bottom line.* **2.** *Fig.* the result; the final outcome. □ *I know about all the problems, but what is the bottom line? What will happen?* □ *The bottom line is that you have to go to the meeting because no one else can.*

the **bottom of the barrel** and the **bottom of the heap** *Fig.* the location of persons or things of the very lowest quality; someone or something of the lowest quality. (The fruit at the bottom of a barrel of apples is likely to be bruised from the weight of the other apples.) □ *That last secretary you sent me was really the bottom of the barrel.* □ *I don't need any candidates from the bottom of the heap.*

the **bottom of the heap** Go to previous.

bottom out *Fig.* to reach the lowest or worst point of something. □ *All my problems seem to be bottoming out. They can't get much worse.* □ *Interest rates bottomed out last February.*

Bottoms up! and **Here's looking at you.; Here's mud in your eye.; Here's to you.** *Inf.* an expression said as a toast when people are drinking together. (Alludes to the bottoms of the drinking glasses.) □ *Bill: Bottoms up. Tom: Here's mud in your eye. Bill: Ah, that one was good. Care for another?*

bounce along 1. *Lit.* to move along bouncing. (As might be done by a ball.) □ *The ball bounced along and finally came to rest.* □ *The beach ball sort of bounced along until it came to the water.* **2.** *Fig.* [for someone] to move along happily. □ *He was so happy that he just bounced along.* □ *He stopped bouncing along when he saw all the work he had to do.*

bounce back (from something**) 1.** *Lit.* [for something] to rebound; [for something] to return bouncing from where it had been. □ *The ball bounced back from the wall.* □ *A rubber ball always bounces back.* **2.** and **bounce back (after** something**)** *Fig.* [for someone] to recover after a disability, illness, blow, or defeat. (See also **rebound from** something.) □ *She bounced back from her illness quickly.* □ *She bounced back quickly after her illness.*

bounce for something Go to **spring for** something.

bounce off ((of) something**)** to rebound from something. (*Of* is usually retained before pronouns.) □ *The ball bounced off the wall and struck a lamp.* □ *It hit the wall and bounced off.*

bounce out (of something**)** to rebound out of or away from something. □ *The ball bounced out of the corner into my hands.* □ *The ball bounced out of the box it had fallen into.*

bounce something **around**† **(with** someone**)** to discuss something with a number of people; to move an idea from person to person like a ball. □ *I need to bounce this around with my family.* □ *I need to bounce around something with you.*

bounce something **back and forth 1.** *Lit.* to bat, toss, or throw something alternately between two people. (Usually a ball.) □ *The two guys bounced the ball back and forth.* □ *John and Timmy bounced it back and forth.* **2.** *Fig.* to discuss an idea back and forth among a group of people. □ *Let's bounce these ideas back and forth awhile and see what we come up with.* □ *The idea was bounced back and forth for about an hour.*

bounce something **off (of)** someone or something **1.** *Lit.* to make something rebound off someone or something. (*Of* is usually retained before pronouns.) □ *She bounced the ball off the wall, turned, and tossed it to Wally.* □ *She bounced the ball off of Harry, into the wastebasket.* **2.** and

bounce something **off**† *Fig.* to try an idea or concept out on someone or a group. (*Of* is usually retained before pronouns.) □ *Let me bounce off this idea, if I may.* □ *Can I bounce something off of you people, while you're here?*

bounce up and down to spring up and down due to natural elasticity or from being jostled or thrown. □ *The ball bounced up and down for an amazingly long time.* □ *I bounced up and down in the back of that truck for almost an hour.*

bound and determined *Cliché* very determined; very committed or dedicated (to something). □ *We were bound and determined to get there on time.* □ *I'm bound and determined that this won't happen again.*

bound for somewhere headed for a specific goal or destination. □ *Bill accidentally got on a bus bound for Miami.* □ *Our baseball team is bound for glory.*

bound hand and foot with hands and feet tied up. □ *The robbers left us bound hand and foot.* □ *We remained bound hand and foot until the police found us and untied us.*

bound to do something certain to do something; destined to do something. □ *Jill's bound to do a good job.* □ *We are bound to tell the truth.*

bound up with someone or something deeply concerned or involved with someone or something. □ *He's so bound up with his work, he has time for nothing else.* □ *Andrew is bound up with his girlfriend and has time for no one else.*

bow and scrape *Fig.* to be very humble and subservient. □ *Please don't bow and scrape. We are all equal here.* □ *The salesclerk came in, bowing and scraping, and asked if he could help us.*

bow before someone or something **1.** *Lit.* to bend or curtsy in respect to someone or something. □ *I will not bow before any king or queen.* □ *Henry insisted that I bow before him.* **2.** *Fig.* to submit to someone or something; to surrender to someone or something. □ *Our country will never bow before a dictator's demands.* □ *We will not bow before such a corrupt politician.*

bow down (to someone or something**)** and **bow to** someone or something **1.** *Lit.* to bend or curtsy to someone or something. □ *Do you expect me to bow down or something when you enter?* □ *He bowed down low to the duchess.* □ *She faced forward and bowed to the altar.* **2.** *Fig.* to submit to someone or something; to yield sovereignty to someone or something. □ *I will not bow down to you, you dictator!* □ *We will never bow to a foreign prince.*

bow out (of some place**)** to bow as one departs from a place. □ *The servant bowed out of the room.* □ *The servant departed, bowing out as he left.*

bow out (of something**)** *Fig.* to retire or resign as something. □ *It's time to bow out as mayor.* □ *I think I will bow out and leave this job to someone else.*

bow to someone's **demands** *Fig.* to yield to someone's demands; to agree to do something that someone has requested. □ *In the end, they had to bow to our demands.* □ *We refused to bow to their demands that we abandon the project.*

bow to the porcelain altar *Sl.* to vomit, especially as a result of drinking too much alcohol. (The *porcelain altar* is a euphemism for a toilet bowl.) □ *He spent the whole* night bowing to the porcelain altar. □ I have the feeling that I will be bowing to the porcelain altar before morning.

bowl someone **over 1.** *Lit.* to knock someone over. (Fixed order.) □ *We were bowled over by the wind.* □ *Bob hit his brother and bowled him over.* **2.** *Fig.* to surprise or overwhelm someone. (Fixed order.) □ *The news bowled me over.* □ *The details of the proposed project bowled everyone over.*

bowl up to fill a pipe bowl with smokable material. □ *The detective bowled up and struck a match.* □ *Roger bowled up, but forgot to light his pipe.*

box someone **in**[†] *Fig.* to put someone into a bind; to reduce the number of someone's alternatives. (See also the following entry.) □ *I don't want to box you in, but you are running out of options.* □ *I want to box in the whole staff, so they'll have to do it my way.*

box someone or something **in**[†] to trap or confine someone or something. □ *He boxed her in so she could not get away from him.* □ *They tried to box in the animals, but they needed more space.* □ *Don't try to box me in.*

box someone **up**[†] to confine someone in a small area. □ *Please don't box me up in that little office.* □ *The boss boxed up Fred in a tiny office.* □ *Why the president boxes himself up in such a little office is beyond me.*

box something **up**[†] to place something in a box. □ *Please box the books up and put them into the trunk of the car.* □ *Please box up four of these for me.*

boxed in *Fig.* in a bind; having few alternatives. □ *I really feel boxed in around here.* □ *I got him boxed in. He'll have to do it our way.*

boxed on the table *Sl.* died on the (operating) table. (Medical.) □ *The surgeon did the best job possible, but the patient boxed on the table.* □ *Another patient boxed on the table. That's three this month.*

boxed (up) 1. *Sl.* intoxicated. □ *I am way boxed, and I feel sick.* □ *She got boxed up on gin.* **2.** *Sl.* in jail. □ *I committed the crime, and I was boxed for a long time for it.* □ *Pat was boxed up for two days till we got bond money.*

Boy howdy! *Rur.* an exclamation of excited surprise. □ *Bob: Well, I finally got here. Fred: Boy howdy! Am I glad to see you! □ Bill: How do you like my horse? Fred: That's one fine-looking filly! Boy howdy!*

the **boys in the back room** and the **backroom boys** *Fig.* any private group of men who make decisions, usually political decisions. (See also **smoke-filled room.**) □ *The boys in the back room picked the last presidential candidate.* □ *The backroom boys have decided too many things in the past. Their day is over.*

Boys will be boys. *Prov.* Boys are expected to be irresponsible or boisterous. (Also said ironically about men.) □ *You can't blame David for breaking the window with his baseball. Boys will be boys.* □ *My husband can't resist driving eighty miles an hour in his new sports car. Boys will be boys.*

brace oneself **for** something **1.** *Lit.* to hang onto something or prop oneself against something in preparation for something that might cause one to fall, blow away, wash away, etc. □ *Hold onto the rail. Brace yourself. Here comes another huge wave.* **2.** *Fig.* to prepare for the shock or force of something. □ *Brace yourself for a shock.* □ *As the boat*

leaned to the right, I braced myself for whatever might happen next.

brace someone or something **up**[†] to prop up or add support to someone or something. □ *They braced the tree up for the expected windstorm.* □ *They braced up the tree again after the storm.*

brace up to take heart; to be brave. □ *Brace up! Things could be worse.* □ *I told John to brace up because things would probably get worse before they got better.*

brag about someone or something to boast about someone or something; to talk proudly about someone or something. □ *He bragged about how selfish he was.* □ *Jill brags a lot about her kids.*

brain someone *Fig.* to strike a person hard on the skull as if to knock out the person's brains. (Often said as a vain threat.) □ *I thought he was going to brain me, but he only hit me on the shoulder.* □ *If you don't do it, I'll brain you.*

brainwash someone **with** something to drive specific knowledge or propaganda into someone's brain, by constant repetition and psychological conditioning. □ *The dictator brainwashed his people with lie after lie.* □ *You have brainwashed yourself with your own propaganda.*

branch off (from something**)** to separate off from something; to divide away from something. □ *A small stream branched off from the main channel.* □ *An irrigation ditch branched off here and there.*

branch out (from something**) 1.** *Lit.* [for a branch] to grow out of a branch or trunk. (Having to do with plants and trees.) □ *A twig branched out of the main limb and grew straight up.* □ *The bush branched out from the base.* **2.** *Fig.* to expand away from something; to diversify away from narrower interests. □ *The speaker branched out from her prepared remarks.* □ *The topic was very broad, and she was free to branch out.*

branch out (into something**)** *Fig.* to diversify and go into new areas. □ *I have decided to branch out into some new projects.* □ *Business was very good, so I decided to branch out.*

(brand) spanking new very new; just purchased and never before used. □ *My car is spanking new.* □ *Look at that brand spanking new car!*

brass someone **off**[†] *Sl.* to make someone angry. (Primarily military. As angry as the "brass," or officers, might get about something.) □ *You really brass me off.* □ *The private brassed off the sergeant.*

brave something **out**[†] to endure something; to put up with something courageously. □ *I don't know if all the men can brave the attack out.* □ *The soldiers braved out the attack.*

The bread always falls on the buttered side. *Prov.* When things go wrong, they go completely wrong. □ *Not only did my phone break, but it broke today—today of all days, when I'm expecting a really important call. The bread always falls on the buttered side.* □ *When the painting fell off the wall, it landed on a priceless porcelain vase and broke it. The bread always falls on the buttered side.*

bread and water *Fig.* the most minimal meal possible; a meal as once was given to prisoners. (Usually used in reference to being in prison or jail.) □ *Wilbur knew that if he got in trouble again it would be at least a year on bread*

B

and water. □ *This dinner is terrible again. I would rather have bread and water! Why don't we ever have pizza?*

Bread is the staff of life. *Prov.* Food is necessary for people to survive. □ *Miranda likes to give money to charities that feed people. "Other services are important," she reasons, "but bread is the staff of life."* □ *Jill: Want to go to lunch with us, Bob? Bob: No. I must work on my novel while inspiration lasts. Jill: Don't forget to eat. Bread is the staff of life, you know.*

bread-and-butter letter a letter or note written to follow up on a visit; a thank-you note. □ *When I got back from the sales meeting, I took two days to write bread-and-butter letters to the people I met.* □ *I got sort of a bread-and-butter letter from my nephew, who wants to visit me next summer.*

*****a **break** a chance; another chance or a second chance. (*Typically: **get** ~; **have** ~; **give** someone ~.) □ *I'm sorry. Please don't send me to the principal's office. Give me a break!* □ *I got a nice break. They didn't send me to prison.*

break a code to figure out a code; to decipher a secret code. □ *The intelligence agents finally broke the enemy's code.* □ *When they broke the code, they were able to decipher messages.*

break a habit and **break the habit; break** one's **habit** to end a habit. □ *I was not able to break the habit of snoring.* □ *It's hard to break a habit that you have had for a long time.*

break a law and **break the law** to fail to obey a law; to act contrary to a law. □ *Lisa broke the law when she drove the wrong way on a one-way street.* □ *If you never break the law, you will never get arrested.*

Break a leg! *Fig.* Good luck! (A special theatrical way of wishing a performer good luck. Saying "good luck" is considered by actors to be a jinx.) □ *"Break a leg!" shouted the stage manager to the heroine.* □ *Let's all go and do our best. Break a leg!*

break a record to destroy a previously set high record by setting a new one. □ *The athlete broke all the school records in swimming.* □ *The league record was broken after thirty years.*

break a story [for a media outlet] to be the first to broadcast or distribute the story of an event. □ *The Tribune broke the story before the Herald could even send a reporter to the scene.*

break against something [for something] to crash against something. □ *The waves broke against the barrier.* □ *The glass broke against the side of the sink.*

break away (from someone) and **break free (from** someone); **break loose (from** someone) **1.** *Lit.* to get free of the physical hold of someone. □ *I tried to break away from him, but he was holding me too tight.* □ *She broke free from him, at last.* □ *I broke free from the intruder.* **2.** *Fig.* to sever a relationship with another person, especially the parent-child relationship. □ *He found it hard to break away from his mother.* □ *She was almost thirty before she finally broke free.*

break bread with someone *Fig.* to eat a meal with someone. □ *Please come by and break bread with us sometime.* □ *I would like to break bread with you.*

break camp to close down a campsite; to pack up and move on. □ *Early this morning we broke camp and moved on northward.* □ *Okay, everyone. It's time to break camp. Take those tents down and fold them neatly.*

break down 1. *Lit.* [for something] to fall apart; [for something] to stop operating. □ *The air-conditioning broke down, and we got very warm.* □ *The car broke down on the long trip.* **2.** *Fig.* [for one] to lose control of one's emotions; [for one] to have an emotional or psychological crisis. □ *He couldn't keep going. He finally broke down.* □ *I was afraid I'd break down.* **3.** Go to next.

break down (and cry) to surrender to demands or emotions and cry. □ *Max finally broke down and confessed.* □ *I was afraid I would break down and cry from the sadness I felt.*

break even for income to equal expenses. (This implies that money was not made or lost.) □ *Unfortunately, my business just managed to break even last year.* □ *I made a bad investment, but I broke even.*

break for something **1.** to stop working for something else, such as lunch, coffee, etc. □ *We should break now for lunch.* □ *I want to break for coffee.* **2.** to run suddenly toward something; to increase dramatically one's speed while running. □ *At the last moment, the deer broke for the woods.* □ *The deer broke for cover at the sound of our approach.*

break free (from someone) Go to **break away (from** someone).

break ground (for something) to start digging the foundation for a building. □ *The president of the company came to break ground for the new building.* □ *This was the third building this year for which this company has broken ground.* □ *When do they expect to break ground at the new site?*

break in (on someone) **1.** to burst into a place and violate someone's privacy. □ *The police broke in on him at his home and arrested him.* □ *They needed a warrant to break in.* **2.** to interrupt someone's conversation. (See also **break in (on** something).) □ *If you need to talk to me, just break in on me.* □ *Feel free to break in if it's an emergency.*

break in (on something) to interrupt something; to intrude upon something. (See also **break in (on** someone).) □ *I didn't mean to break in on your discussion.* □ *Please don't break in on us just now. This is important.*

break into a gallop [for a horse] to begin to gallop; [for a horse] to speed up to a gallop. □ *The pony broke into a gallop, racing to get home.* □ *Near the stables, the horse broke into a fast gallop.*

break into something to begin to perform or utter suddenly, especially with song, speech, chattering, tears, etc. □ *Suddenly, she broke into song.* □ *As soon as the movie started, the people behind me broke into loud chattering.*

break in(to something or some place) to force entry into a place criminally; to enter some place forcibly for the purpose of robbery or other illegal acts. □ *The thugs broke into the liquor store.* □ *They broke in and took all the money.*

break in(to) tears Go to **break out in(to) tears.**

Break it up! Stop fighting!; Stop arguing! (Fixed order.) □ *Tom: I'm going to break your neck! Bill: I'm going to mash in your face first! Bob: All right, you two, break it up!*

When the police officer saw the boys fighting, he came over and hollered, "Break it up! You want me to arrest you?"

break loose (from someone**)** Go to break away (from someone).

break new ground *Fig.* to begin to do something that no one else has done; to pioneer [in an enterprise]. □ *Dr. Anderson was breaking new ground in cancer research.* □ *They were breaking new ground in consumer electronics.*

break off (from something**)** [for a piece of something] to become separated from the whole. □ *This broke off from the lamp. What shall I do with it?* □ *This piece broke off.*

break off (with someone**)** and **break with** someone to end communication with someone; to break up (with someone); to end a relationship with someone, especially a romantic relationship, or to create a break between adult members of a family. □ *Terri has broken off with Sam.* □ *We thought she would break with him pretty soon.*

break one's **arm patting oneself on the back** Go to have calluses from patting one's own back.

break one's **back (to** do something**)** Go to break one's neck (to do something).

break one's **balls to** do something Go to bust (one's) ass (to do something).

break one's **habit** Go to break a habit.

break one's **neck (to** do something**)** and **break** one's **back (to** do something**)** *Fig.* to work very hard to accomplish something. □ *I broke my neck to get here on time.* □ *There is no point in breaking your back. Take your time.*

break one's **stride** to deviate from a rhythmic stride while walking, running, or marching. (See also put one off one's stride.) □ *After I broke my stride, I never could pick up enough speed to win the race.*

break one's **word** not to do what one said one would do; not to keep one's promise. (Compare this with keep one's word.) □ *Don't say you'll visit your grandmother if you can't go. She hates people to break their word.* □ *If you break your word, she won't trust you again.*

break out 1. to burst forth suddenly, as with a fire, a riot, giggling, shouting, etc. □ *A fire broke out in the belfry.* □ *A round of giggling broke out when the teacher tripped.* **2.** *Sl.* to leave. □ *It's late, man. Time to break out.* □ *We broke out a little after midnight.* **3.** Go to break out (in pimples); break out (of something); break out (with something).

break out in a cold sweat *Lit.* or *Fig.* to become frightened or anxious and begin to sweat. □ *I was so frightened, I broke out in a cold sweat.* □ *Larry broke out in a cold sweat when he cut his hand.*

break out in a rash [for the skin] to erupt with a rash. (See also break out in a cold sweat; break out (with a rash).) □ *I knew Dan had the chicken pox, because he broke out in a rash and had a dry cough.* □ *The baby breaks out in a rash all the time.*

break out (in pimples) to erupt with something such as a rash, a cold sweat, or pimples. □ *After being in the woods, I broke out in a rash. I think it's poison ivy.* □ *I hate to break out like that.* □ *Whenever I eat chocolate, I break out in pimples the next day.*

break out in(to) tears and **break in(to) tears** to start crying suddenly. □ *I was so sad that I broke out into tears.* □ *I always break into tears at a funeral.*

break out (of something**) 1.** *Lit.* to escape from something, often by destructive means, especially from prison. □ *The convicts plotted to break out of prison.* □ *You don't have the guts to break out of jail!* **2.** *Fig.* to escape from something in one's life that is too confining. □ *I was 16 years old when I finally broke out of my rigid upbringing.* □ *She just couldn't break out of her old patterns of behavior.*

break out (with a rash**)** [for the skin] to erupt with pimples, hives, or lesions, from a specific disease such as measles, chicken pox, rubella, etc. □ *Nick and Dan broke out with chicken pox.* □ *They both broke out at the same time.*

break out with something to utter or emit laughter, a shout, or a cry. □ *The kids broke out with a cheer.* □ *They broke out with laughter every time they saw the lady with the red wig.*

break over something [for waves] to lift high and tumble over a barrier. □ *The waves broke over the rocks at the shore.* □ *Huge waves broke over the bow of the ship.*

break silence to give information about a topic that no one was mentioning or discussing. □ *The press finally broke silence on the question of the plagiarized editorial.*

break someone **down†** to force someone to give up and tell secrets or agree to do something. □ *After threats of torture, they broke the spy down.* □ *They broke down the agent by threatening violence.*

break someone **in†** to train someone to do a new job; to supervise someone who is learning to do a new job. □ *Who will break the new employee in?* □ *I have to break in a new receptionist.*

break someone or something **of** something to cause someone or something to stop practicing a habit. □ *We worked hard to break the dog of making a mess on the carpet.* □ *I don't think I can break her of the habit.* □ *Tom broke himself of biting his nails.*

break (someone's**) balls** and **break (**someone's**) stones; bust (**someone's**) balls; bust (**someone's**) stones 1.** *Sl.* to wreck or ruin (someone); to overwork someone; to overwhelm someone. (Potentially offensive. Use only with discretion.) □ *The boss acts like he's trying to break everybody's balls all the time.* □ *No need to break my balls. I'll do it!* **2.** *Sl.* to kid or tease (someone). □ *Don't sweat what I said—I was just bustin' balls.* □ *Hey, relax, he didn't mean it. He was just breakin' your stones!*

break someone's **fall** to cushion a falling person; to lessen the impact of a falling person. □ *When the little boy fell out of the window, the bushes broke his fall.* □ *The old lady slipped on the ice, but a snowbank broke her fall.*

break someone's **heart** *Fig.* to cause someone great emotional pain. □ *It just broke my heart when Tom ran away from home.* □ *Sally broke John's heart when she refused to marry him.*

break someone's **stones** Go to break (someone's) balls.

break someone **up†** to cause a person to laugh, perhaps at an inappropriate time. □ *John told a joke that really broke*

Mary up. □ *The comedian's job was to break up the audience by telling jokes.*

break something **away**[†] **(from** something**)** to break a part or piece of something away from the whole. □ *She broke a bit away and popped it into her mouth.* □ *Todd broke away a piece from the bar of candy.*

break something **down**[†] **1.** *Lit.* to tear something down; to destroy something. □ *They used an ax to break the door down.* □ *We broke down the wall with big hammers.* **2.** *Fig.* to destroy a social or legal barrier. □ *The court broke a number of legal barriers down this week.* □ *They had to break down many social prejudices to manage to succeed.*

break something **down**[†] **(for** someone**)** *Fig.* to explain something to someone in simple terms or in an orderly fashion. (Alludes to breaking a complex problem into smaller segments which can be explained more easily. See also **break** something **down (into** something**).**) □ *She doesn't understand. You will have to break it down for her.* □ *I can help. This is a confusing question. Let me break down the problem for you.*

break something **down**[†] **(into** something**) 1.** to reduce a compound or its structure to its components. □ *Heat will break this down into sodium and a few gases.* □ *Will heat break down this substance into anything useful?* □ *We broke it into little pieces.* **2.** to reduce a large numerical total to its subparts and explain each one. □ *She broke the total down into its components.* □ *Please break down the total into its parts again.* □ *I'll break the total down for you.* **3.** to discuss the details of something by examining its subparts. (See also **break** something **down (for** someone**).**) □ *Let's break this problem down into its parts and deal with each one separately.* □ *Breaking down complex problems into their components is almost fun.* □ *Let's break this issue down and discuss it.*

break something **free (from** something**)** to force something to detach from something; to get something out of the hold of something else. □ *I broke the gun free from her grasp.* □ *Someone broke the light fixture free from its mounting.*

break something **in**[†] **1.** *Lit.* to crush or batter something to pieces; to **break** something **down.** □ *Why are you breaking the door in? Here's the key!* □ *Who broke in the door?* **2.** *Fig.* to use a new device until it runs well and smoothly; to wear shoes, perhaps a little at a time, until they feel comfortable. □ *I can't drive at high speed until I break this car in.* □ *I want to go out this weekend and break in the car.* □ *The new shoes hurt her feet because they were not yet broken in.*

break something **loose from** something to loosen a part of something; to loosen and remove a part of something. □ *The mechanic broke the strap loose from the tailpipe.* □ *The bracket was broken loose from the wall.*

break something **off (of)** something and **break** something **off**[†] to fracture or dislodge a piece off something. (*Of* is usually retained before pronouns.) □ *He broke a piece of the decorative stone off the side of the church.* □ *He didn't mean to break off anything.* □ *This fragment was broken off of that.*

break something **on** something to strike and break something against something else. □ *She broke the glass on the countertop.* □ *He broke his arm on the steps.*

break something **out (of** something**)** to remove something from something else by force. □ *Carefully, she broke the gemstone out of the side of the rock face.* □ *She broke the gemstone out carefully.*

break something **to pieces** to shatter something. □ *I broke my crystal vase to pieces.* □ *I dropped a glass and broke it to pieces.*

break something **to** someone to disclose some news or information to someone. (Often said of unpleasant news.) □ *I hate to be the one to break this to you, but there is trouble at home.* □ *We broke the bad news to Ken gently.*

break something **up**[†] **1.** *Lit.* to destroy something. □ *The storm broke the docks up on the lake.* □ *The police broke up the gambling ring.* **2.** *Fig.* to put an end to something. □ *The police broke the fight up.* □ *Walter's parents broke up the party at three in the morning.*

break something **up**[†] **(into** something**)** to break something into smaller pieces. □ *We broke the crackers up into much smaller pieces.* □ *Please break up the crackers into smaller pieces if you want to feed the ducks.*

break something **off**[†] **1.** to end a relationship abruptly. (See also **break off (with** someone**).**) □ *I knew she was getting ready to break it off, but Tom didn't.* □ *After a few long and bitter arguments, they broke off their relationship.* **2.** Go to **break** something **off (of)** something.

break the back of something *Fig.* to end the domination of something; to reduce the power of something. □ *The government has worked for years to break the back of organized crime.* □ *This new medicine should break the back of the epidemic.*

break the bank *Fig.* to use up all one's money. (Alludes to casino gambling, in the rare event when a gambler wins more money than the house has on hand.) □ *It will hardly break the bank if we go out to dinner just once.* □ *Buying a new dress at a discount price won't break the bank.*

break the habit Go to **break a habit.**

break the ice 1. *Fig.* to attempt to become friends with someone. □ *He tried to break the ice, but she was a little cold.* □ *A nice smile does a lot to break the ice.* **2.** *Fig.* to initiate social interchanges and conversation; to get something started. □ *It's hard to break the ice at formal events.* □ *Sally broke the ice at the auction by bidding $20,000 for the painting.*

break the law Go to **break a law.**

break the news (to someone**)** to tell someone some important news, usually bad news. (See also **break** something **to** someone.) □ *The doctor had to break the news to Jane about her husband's cancer.* □ *I hope that the doctor broke the news gently.*

break the silence to make a noise interrupting a period of silence. □ *The wind broke the silence by blowing the door closed.*

break the spell 1. to put an end to a magic spell. □ *The wizard looked in his magic book to find out how to break the spell.* **2. to do something that ends a desirable period of figurative enchantment.** □ *At the end of the second movement, some idiot broke the spell by applauding.*

break through (something) 1. *Lit.* to break something and pass through. □ *The firefighters broke through the wall easily.* □ *The robbers broke through the glass window of the shop.* **2.** *Fig.* to overcome something. □ *Tom was able to break through racial barriers.* □ *The scientists broke through the mystery surrounding the disease and found the cause.*

break through (to someone or something) to force [one's way] through an obstruction and reach someone or something on the other side. □ *The miners broke through to their trapped friends.* □ *They broke through the thin wall easily.*

break up 1. *Lit.* [for something] to fall apart; to be broken to pieces. (Typically said of a ship breaking up on rocks.) □ *In the greatest storm of the century, the ship broke up on the reef.* □ *It broke up and sank.* **2.** Go to **break up (with someone). 3.** [for married persons] to divorce. □ *After many years of bickering, they finally broke up.* **4.** [for a marriage] to dissolve in divorce. □ *Their marriage finally broke up.* **5.** to begin laughing very hard. □ *The comedian told a particularly good joke, and the audience broke up.* □ *I always break up when I hear her sing. She is so bad!*

break (up) (into something) to divide into smaller parts. □ *The glass broke up into a thousand pieces.* □ *It hit the floor and broke up, flinging bits everywhere.*

break up (with someone) to end a romantic relationship with someone. □ *Tom broke up with Mary and started dating Lisa.* □ *We broke up in March, after an argument.*

break wind *Euph.* to expel gas from the anus. □ *Someone in the bus broke wind. It smelled terrible.* □ *He broke wind with an embarrassing noise.*

break with someone Go to **break off (with someone).**

breaking and entering the crime of forcing one's way into a place. (A criminal charge.) □ *Wilbur was charged with four counts of breaking and entering.* □ *It was not an act of breaking and entering. The thief just opened the door and walked right in.*

the **breaking point 1.** *Lit.* the point at which something will break. □ *The mule's back was strained to the breaking point with masses of bundles and straw.* **2.** *Fig.* the point at which nerves or one's mental state can endure no more. □ *My nerves are at the breaking point.*

a **breath of fresh air 1.** *Lit.* an influx of air that is not stale or smelly, especially from outdoors. □ *You look ill, John. What you need is a breath of fresh air.* **2.** *Fig.* a portion of air that is not "contaminated" with unpleasant people or situations. (This is a sarcastic version of ①.) □ *You people are disgusting. I have to get out of here and get a breath of fresh air.* □ *I believe I'll go get a breath of fresh air. The intellectual atmosphere in here is stifling.* **3.** *Fig.* a new, fresh, and imaginative approach (to something). (Usually with *like.*) □ *Sally, with all her wonderful ideas, is a breath of fresh air.* □ *The decor in this room is like a breath of fresh air.*

breathe a sigh of relief 1. *Lit.* to sigh in a way that signals one's relief that something has come to an end. □ *At the end of the contest, we all breathed a sigh of relief.* **2.** *Fig.* to express relief that something has ended. □ *With the contract finally signed, we breathed a sigh of relief as we drank a toast in celebration.*

breathe down someone's neck 1. *Fig.* to keep close watch on someone; to watch someone's activities intently. (Alludes to someone standing very close behind a person.) □ *I can't work with you breathing down my neck all the time. Go away.* □ *I will get through my life without your help. Stop breathing down my neck.* **2.** *Fig.* [for someone or something] to represent an approaching deadline. □ *The project deadline is breathing down my neck.* □ *The due date for this paper is breathing down my neck.*

breathe easy to assume a relaxed state after a stressful period. □ *After this crisis is over, I'll be able to breathe easy again.* □ *He won't be able to breathe easy until he pays off his debts.*

breathe in to inhale; to take air into the lungs. □ *Now, relax and breathe in. Breathe out.* □ *Breathe in deeply; enjoy the summer air.*

breathe into something to exhale into something; to expel one's breath into something. □ *I was told to breathe into a tube that was connected to a machine of some type.*

breathe one's last *Euph.* to die. □ *She breathed her last at about two o'clock that afternoon.* □ *Cradled in his wife's arms, he breathed his last.*

breathe out to exhale. □ *Now, breathe out, then breathe in.* □ *The doctor told me to breathe out slowly.*

breathe something in† to take something into the lungs, such as air, medicinal vapors, gas, etc. □ *Breathe the vapor in slowly. It will help your cold.* □ *Breathe in that fresh air!*

breathe something into something to revive something; to introduce something new or positive into a situation. □ *Her positive attitude breathed new life into the company.* □ *The project breathed a new spirit into the firm.*

breathe something (of something) (to someone) to tell something to someone. (Usually in the negative.) □ *Don't breathe a word of this to anyone!* □ *I won't breathe a word!*

breathe something out† to exhale something. □ *At last, he breathed his last breath out, and that was the end.* □ *Breathe out your breath slowly.*

breathe (up)on someone or something to exhale on someone or something. (*Upon* is more formal and less commonly used than *on.*) □ *Please don't breathe upon the food.* □ *Don't breathe on me!*

Breeding will tell. *Prov.* One's character or lack of it will become known. □ *From the beginning, he appeared to be courteous, and now he clearly has proven himself to be so. Breeding will tell.*

breeze along *Fig.* to travel along casually, rapidly, and happily; to go through life in a casual and carefree manner. □ *Kristine was just breezing along the road when she ran off onto the shoulder.* □ *We just breezed along the highway, barely paying attention to what we were doing.* □ *Don't just breeze along through life!*

breeze away to leave quickly or abruptly. □ *She said nothing more. She just breezed away.* □ *I breezed away without stopping to say good-bye.*

breeze in (from some place) Go to **sweep in (from some place).**

breeze in(to some place) to enter a place quickly, in a happy and carefree manner. □ *She breezed into the con-*

ference room and sat down at the head of the table. □ *Jerry breezed in and said hello.*

breeze off to leave quickly or abruptly. □ *Don't just breeze off! Stay and talk.* □ *Lily breezed off in a huffy manner.*

breeze out (of some place**)** to leave a place quickly. □ *She was here for a moment and then suddenly breezed out.* □ *She breezed out of the room in an instant.*

breeze through (something**) 1.** *Fig.* to complete some task rapidly and easily. □ *I breezed through my calculus assignment in no time at all.* □ *It was not hard. I just breezed through.* **2.** *Fig.* to travel through a place rapidly. □ *They breezed through every little town without stopping.* □ *We didn't stop. We just breezed through.*

Brevity is the soul of wit. *Prov.* Jokes and humorous stories are funnier if they are short. □ *Dale took ten minutes to tell that joke; he obviously doesn't know that brevity is the soul of wit.* □ *The comedian was in the middle of a long, tedious story when someone in the audience shouted, "Brevity is the soul of wit!"*

brew a plot *Fig.* to plot something; to make a plot. □ *The children brewed an evil plot to get revenge on their teacher.* □ *We brewed a plot so that we would not have to help with dinner.*

brew something **up†** **1.** *Lit.* to brew something, as in making coffee or tea. □ *Can somebody brew some coffee up?* □ *Let me brew up a pot of tea, and then we'll talk.* **2.** *Fig.* to cause something to happen; to foment something. □ *I could see that they were brewing some kind of trouble up.* □ *Don't brew up any trouble!*

brew up *Fig.* to build up; [for something] to begin to build and grow. (Typically said of a storm.) □ *A bad storm is brewing up in the west.* □ *Something serious is brewing up in the western sky.*

bribe someone **into** doing something to pay money to get someone to do something. □ *You can't bribe me into doing anything!* □ *Max bribed Lily into leaving early.*

brick something **up†** to fill up an opening with bricks. □ *He bricked the doorway up.* □ *Why did he brick up the opening?*

bricks and mortar buildings; the expenditure of money on buildings rather than something else. (The buildings referred to can be constructed out of anything.) □ *The new president of the college preferred to invest in new faculty members rather than bricks and mortar.* □ *Sometimes people are happy to donate millions of dollars for bricks and mortar, but they never think of the additional cost of annual maintenance.*

brick(s)-and-mortar [of commercial establishments] based in buildings rather than relying on online sales over the Internet. □ *Many of the dot-com business owners have never been involved in a brick-and-mortar business.*

bridge over something to make a bridge or passage over something. □ *They bridged over each of the streams as they came to them.* □ *I think we can bridge over this little river in a few days if we work hard.*

bridge the gap 1. *Lit.* to make a bridge that reaches across a space. □ *The engineers decided to bridge the gap with a wooden structure.* **2.** *Fig.* to do or create something that will serve temporarily. □ *We can bridge the gap with a few temporary employees.*

bridle at someone or something *Fig.* to show that one is offended by someone or something. □ *She bridled at the suggestion that she should go.* □ *Tony bridled at Max. Max was going to have to be dealt with.*

brief someone **about** someone or something and **brief** someone **on** someone or something to tell someone a summary with the essential details about someone or something. □ *We need to brief the president about the latest event.* □ *I have to brief Michael on the new procedures at work.*

bright and breezy cheery and alert. □ *You look all bright and breezy this morning.* □ *Bright and breezy people on a gloomy day like this make me sick.*

bright and early very early in the morning or the workday. □ *Yes, I'll be there bright and early.* □ *I want to see you here on time tomorrow, bright and early, or you're fired!*

*****bright as a button** intelligent; quick-minded. (Usually used to describe children. *Also: as ~.) □ *Why, Mrs. Green, your little girl is as bright as a button.* □ *You can't fool Jane. She may be only six years old, but she's bright as a button.*

*****bright as a new pin** bright and clean; shiny. (*Also: as ~.) □ *After Joe cleaned the house, it was as bright as a new pin.* □ *My kitchen floor is bright as a new pin since I started using this new floor wax.*

*****a** **bright idea** a clever thought or new idea. (*Typically: have ~; get ~; give someone ~.) □ *Now and then I get a bright idea.* □ *John hardly ever gets a bright idea.*

brighten up to become brighter; to lighten, especially with sunshine. □ *The sky is brightening up a little.* □ *When the morning sky brightens up just a little, the birds begin to sing.*

bright-eyed and bushy-tailed *Fig.* awake and alert. (Often used ironically, as in the first example. The idea is that one is like a frisky animal, such as a squirrel.) □ *Jill: Hi, Jane! How are you on this beautiful morning? Jane: Bright-eyed and bushy-tailed, just as you might expect, since I've only had three hours of sleep.* □ *Despite the early hour, Dennis was bright-eyed and bushy-tailed.*

brim over (with something**)** and **brim with** something to overflow with something. □ *The basket was brimming over with flowers.* □ *I was brimming with confidence after my recent success.*

brim with something Go to previous.

brimming with something *Fig.* full of some kind of happy behavior. □ *The volunteer workers were brimming with goodwill.* □ *The smiling children were brimming with joy.*

bring a charge against someone or something to file a complaint against someone or a group; to begin a legal process against someone or a group. (A charge can also be charges even if only one charge is involved.) □ *We brought a charge against the town council.* □ *Sam brought charges against Jeff.*

bring a dog to heel to make a dog heel; to make a dog stand or follow close to one's heels. □ *A quiet command from his owner brought Fido to heel.*

bring a verdict in† [for a jury] to deliver its decision to the court. □ *Do you think they will bring a verdict in today?* □ *The jury brought in their verdict around midnight.*

bring an amount of money **in**† to earn an amount of money; to draw or attract an amount of money. □ *My part-time job brings fifty dollars in every week.* □ *She brings in a lot of money from her executive's salary.*

bring down the curtain (on something**)** Go to **ring down the curtain (on** something**)**.

bring home the bacon *Fig.* to earn a salary; to bring home money earned at a job. □ *I've got to get to work if I'm going to bring home the bacon.* □ *Go out and get a job so you can bring home the bacon.*

bring one **out of** one's **shell** and **get** one **out of** one's **shell; bring** one **out; get** one **out** *Fig.* to make a person become more open and friendly. (Alludes to a shy turtle being coaxed to put its head out of its shell.) □ *We tried to bring Greg out of his shell, but he is very shy.* □ *He's quiet, and it's hard to get him out of his shell.*

bring one **to** one's **feet** and **bring** something **to its feet** to make someone or an audience rise up applauding or cheering in approval or in salute to someone or something. (Usually refers to an audience.) □ *The finale brought the audience to its feet.* □ *Liz was brought to her feet by the playing of the national anthem.*

bring one **to** one's **senses** to cause someone to return to normal [after being out of control or irrational]. □ *A gentle slap in the face brought him to his senses.* □ *Liz was brought to her senses quickly.*

bring one **to** oneself to cause one to become rational; to cause one to act normal. □ *A glass of ice water thrown in her face brought Sally to herself.* □ *I was brought to myself by some smelling salts.*

bring out the best in someone to cause someone to behave in the best manner. □ *This kind of situation doesn't exactly bring out the best in me.* □ *Good weather brings out the best in me.*

bring someone **around**† **1.** *Lit.* to bring someone for a visit; to bring someone for someone (else) to meet. □ *Please bring your wife around sometime. I'd love to meet her.* □ *You've just got to bring around your doctor friend for dinner.* **2.** and **bring** someone **around (to consciousness)** *Fig.* to bring someone to consciousness. □ *The doctor brought around the unconscious man with smelling salts.* □ *The boxer was knocked out, but his manager brought him around.* **3.** and **bring** someone **around (to** one's **way of thinking); bring** someone **around (to** one's **position)** *Fig.* to persuade someone (to accept something); to manage to get someone to agree (to something). □ *The last debate brought around a lot of voters to our candidate.* □ *I knew I could bring her around if I just had enough time to talk to her.*

bring someone **back out** [for an applauding audience] to succeed in bringing a performer back onto the stage for a curtain call or encore. □ *They brought her back out about seven times, cheering and applauding.* □ *She was brought back out repeatedly for curtain calls.*

bring someone **back to reality** to force someone to face reality. □ *The rain shower brought her back to reality.* □ *Liz was brought back to reality by a rude shock.*

bring someone **before** someone or something to bring a person to an authority, such as a judge, for criticism or discipline. □ *They brought Terri before the committee for her*

explanation. □ *I brought you before me to explain your side of the story.*

bring someone **down**† **1.** *Lit.* to assist or accompany someone from a higher place to a lower place. □ *Please bring your friends down so I can meet them.* □ *She brought down her cousin, who had been taking a nap upstairs.* □ *Aunt Mattie was brought down for supper.* **2.** *Fig.* to bring someone to a place for a visit. □ *Let's bring Tom and Terri down for a visit this weekend.* □ *We brought down Tom just last month.* □ *They were brought down at our expense for a weekend visit.* **3.** *Fig.* to restore someone to a normal mood or attitude. (After a period of elation or, perhaps, drug use.) □ *The bad news brought me down quickly.* □ *I was afraid that the sudden change of plans would bring down the entire group.*

bring someone **down to earth** *Fig.* to help someone face reality; to help someone who is euphoric become more realistic. □ *The events helped bring us all down to earth.* □ *I hate to be the one to bring you down to earth, but things aren't as good as you think.*

bring someone **in**† **(on** something**)** to include someone in some deed or activity. □ *I'm going to have to bring a specialist in on this.* □ *Please bring in several specialists to advise on this case.* □ *Let's bring an expert in before we go any further.*

bring someone **into the world** *Fig.* to deliver a baby; to attend the birth of someone. □ *The doctor who brought me into the world died last week.* □ *I was brought into the world by a kindly old doctor.*

bring someone **on**† **1.** *Lit.* to bring someone out onto the stage. □ *Now, for the next act, I'm going to bring a chorus on, and I'm sure you'll love them.* □ *Bring on the clowns!* **2.** *Fig.* to arouse someone romantically or sexually. □ *Ted sought to bring Sally on, but she was uninterested.* □ *He tried to bring on one of the guests.*

bring someone or an animal **back to life** and **bring** someone or an animal **back**† to make someone or some living creature come back to life. □ *There was nothing that would bring Jimmy's cat back. It was truly dead.* □ *Not even a magician could bring back the cat.*

bring someone or something **along**† **(to** something**)** to bring someone or something with one to some event. □ *I brought my uncle along to the party.* □ *Please bring along your camera to the show.*

bring someone or something **back**† to make someone or something return. (See also **bring** something **back to life.**) □ *Would you please bring the child back?* □ *Bring back my child!*

bring someone or something **forth**† to present or produce someone or something. □ *Bring the roast turkey forth!* □ *Bring forth the roast turkey!*

bring someone or something **forward** to introduce someone or something; to move someone or something into a more visible position. □ *Please bring him forward so that we can examine him.* □ *Please bring your chair forward so I can see you.*

bring someone or something **in**† Go to **bring** someone or something **in(to)** some place.

bring someone or something **into action** to activate someone or something; to cause someone or something to function as intended. □ *The threats brought the police into action.* □ *A kick in the side brought the television set into action.*

bring someone or something **into contact with** someone or something to cause things or people to touch or associate with one another. □ *She hasn't been the same since I brought her into contact with the child who had chicken pox.* □ *Don't bring your hand in contact with the poison ivy.* □ *Don't bring him into contact with Fred.*

bring someone or something **into disrepute** to dishonor or discredit someone or something. □ *This embarrassing incident will bring the entire committee into disrepute.* □ *My bankruptcy brought me into disrepute.*

bring someone or something **into line (with** someone or something**) 1.** Lit. to make someone or something even with someone or something. □ *I brought the books into line with the others on the shelf.* □ *I brought Jimmy into line with the other scouts.* **2.** Fig. to make someone or something conform to someone or something. □ *We brought Ted into line with the guidelines.* □ *Sam brought his proposal into line with the company standards.*

bring someone or something **into prominence** to cause someone or something to become famous or renowned. □ *The award brought Mike into national prominence.* □ *The current national need for engineers brought our school into prominence.* □ *A terrible scandal brought Lily into prominence.*

bring someone or something **in(to)** some place and **bring** someone or something **in**† to permit or assist someone or something to enter something or some place. □ *Do you mind if I bring my sister in here with me?* □ *Please bring in your sister.*

bring someone or something **into view** to cause someone or something to be seen or to be visible. □ *A bright light brought the sleeping cattle into view.* □ *Please bring your child into view.*

bring someone or something **out**† Go to **bring** someone or something **out of** something.

bring someone or something **out in droves** Fig. to lure or draw out people or other animals in great number. □ *The availability of free drinks brought people out in droves.* □ *The fresh grass sprouts brought the deer out in droves.*

bring someone or something **out of** something and **bring** someone or something **out**† to cause someone or something to emerge from something or some place. □ *The explosion brought the people out of their homes.* □ *The noise brought out all the people.*

bring someone or something **out of the woodwork** Go to **out of the woodwork.**

bring someone or something **to a halt** to cause someone or something to stop immediately. □ *The explosion brought the lecture to a halt.* □ *I brought the visitor to a halt at the front gate.*

bring someone or something **to life** Fig. to give vigor or vitality to someone or something; to reactivate someone or something. (See also **bring** something **back to life.**) □ *A little singing and dancing would have brought the play to life.* □ *Some coffee will bring you to life.*

bring someone or something **to light** Fig. to present or reveal someone or something to the public. □ *The news-*

paper story brought the problem to light. □ *I have brought some interesting facts to light in my article.*

bring someone or something **to** someone's **attention** to make someone aware of someone or something. □ *Thank you for bringing this to my attention.* □ *I am grateful for your bringing her to my attention.*

bring someone or something **to trial** to bring a crime or a criminal into court for a trial. □ *At last, the thugs were brought to trial.* □ *We brought the case to trial a week later.*

bring someone or something **under control** Go to under control.

bring someone or something **under** one's **control** to achieve dominion over someone or something. □ *The dictator was at last able to bring the army under his control.* □ *Harry could not bring Ron under his control.* □ *Walter could not be brought under Lily's control.*

bring someone or something **under** someone or something to assign someone or something to someone or something; to put someone or something under the management of someone or something. □ *I had David brought under me, so I could keep an eye on his day-to-day work.* □ *David was brought under my jurisdiction.*

bring someone or something **up**† **1.** Lit. to cause someone or something to go up with one from a lower place to a higher place. □ *We brought them up and let them view the city from the balcony.* □ *Why did you bring up Tom? Wasn't he comfortable down there?* **2.** Fig. to mention someone or something. □ *Why did you have to bring that up?* □ *Why did you bring up Walter? I hate talking about him!* **3.** Fig. to raise someone or something; to care for someone or something up to adulthood. □ *We brought the dog up from a pup.* □ *We brought up the puppies carefully and sold them for a good profit.*

bring someone or something **up to** something to raise someone or something to a particular standard, level, expectation, etc. □ *What do I have to do to bring Billy up to grade level?* □ *The lab was brought up to standards quickly.*

bring someone or something **up-to-date** to modernize someone or something. □ *We brought the room up-to-date with a little paint and some modern furniture.* □ *I can bring you up-to-date with a new hairdo.*

bring someone or something **within range (of** someone or something**)** to cause someone or something to be in someone's or something's [gun] sights. □ *Don't bring the hunters within range of the farmer's gun sights.* □ *The bait brought the geese within range of Jeff and his friends.*

bring someone **out of the closet** Go to out of the closet.

bring someone **out (on** something**)** Lit. to make someone come onto the stage from the stage sides or wings. (See also **bring** someone **on.**) □ *Let's applaud loudly and bring her out on stage again.* □ *Lily was brought out on stage by the applause.*

bring someone **over**† **from** some place to bring someone from a place, from nearby, or from a great distance. □ *They brought over the neighbors from across the street.* □ *A soprano was brought over from Moscow.*

bring someone **over**† **((to)** some place**)** to bring a person for a visit to some place. □ *Why don't you bring her over to our place for a visit?* □ *You should bring over your girlfriend for a visit.*

bring someone **over**[†] **to** something to bring someone for a visit and a meal or other event. □ *Please bring your friend over to dinner sometime.* □ *I want to bring over my husband sometime.*

bring someone **through** something to help someone endure something, such as a disease, an emotional upset, or a stressful period. □ *The doctor brought Tom through the sickness.* □ *Liz was brought through the ordeal by her friends.*

bring someone **to** to help someone return to consciousness. □ *We worked to bring him to before he went into shock.* □ *He was finally brought to by the smelling salts.*

bring someone **to a boil** *Fig.* to make someone very angry. □ *This really brought her to a boil. She was fit to be tied.* □ *Lily was really brought to a boil by the news.*

bring someone **to account** *Fig.* to confront someone with a record of misdeeds and errors. □ *The committee decided to bring Martha to account.* □ *Martha was brought to account by the committee.*

bring someone **to** do something to cause someone to do something; to encourage someone to do something. □ *What brought you to do this?* □ *I was brought to do this by a guilty conscience.*

bring someone **to heel** *Fig.* to cause someone to act in a disciplined fashion; to force someone to act in a more disciplined manner. □ *She tried to bring her husband to heel, but he had a mind of his own.* □ *He was brought to heel by his demanding wife.*

bring someone **to justice** *Fig.* to punish someone for a crime. □ *The police officer swore she would not rest until she had brought the killer to justice.* □ *Years later, the rapist was found out and finally brought to justice.*

bring someone **together 1.** *Lit.* to cause people to gather into a group. □ *He brought everyone together in the drawing room.* □ *They were brought together in a large conference room.* **2.** *Fig.* to attempt to get people to agree with one another. □ *I tried to bring them together, but they are too stubborn.* □ *They could not be brought together on a price.*

bring someone **up**[†] **for** something **1.** to suggest someone's name for something. □ *I would like to bring Beth up for vice president.* □ *I will bring up Beth for this office if you don't.* **2.** to put someone's name up for promotion, review, discipline, etc. □ *We brought Tom up for promotion.* □ *The boss brought up Tom, too.*

bring someone **up**[†] **on** something to provide something while raising a child to adulthood. □ *She brought her children up on fast food.* □ *You shouldn't bring up your children on that kind of entertainment!*

bring someone **up sharply** and **bring** someone **up short** to surprise or shock someone; to make someone face something unpleasant, suddenly. □ *The slap in the face brought me up sharply.* □ *The loud bang brought me up short.*

bring someone **up short** Go to previous.

bring someone **up to speed on** someone or something Go to **up to speed**.

bring someone **up-to-date (on** someone or something**)** to inform someone of the latest information about some-

thing. □ *Let me bring you up-to-date on what is happening in the village.* □ *Please bring me up-to-date.*

bring something **about**[†] to make something happen. □ *Is she clever enough to bring it about?* □ *Oh, yes, she can bring about anything she wants.*

bring something **all together** to organize something; to coordinate something or some event. □ *The party was a great success. Janet was the one who brought it all together.* □ *It was a difficult conference to organize, but Sam brought it all together.*

bring something **around**[†] **(to** someone or something**) 1.** to move something, such as a vehicle, from one place to another, especially so it can be used. □ *Would you kindly have James bring the car around?* □ *Tony will bring around the car to us.* **2.** to distribute something to someone or a group. (Said by a person who intends to receive what is brought.) □ *Please bring the snacks around to us.* □ *Carl is bringing around the snacks to us.*

bring something **away**[†] **(from** something**) 1.** to come away from some event with some important insight or information. □ *I brought some valuable advice away from the lecture.* □ *She brought away some valuable advice from the meeting.* **2.** to move something away from something. (A request to move something away from something and toward the requester.) □ *Bring the pitcher of water away from the fireplace.* □ *Bring away the pitcher from the fireplace when you get up.*

bring something **back**[†] to restore an earlier style or practice. □ *Please bring the good old days back.* □ *Bring back good times for all of us.*

bring something **back to life** *Fig.* to restore vitality to something, such as a performance, a story, etc. (See also **bring** someone or an animal **back to life**.) □ *The third act of the play had a clever twist that brought the whole drama back to life.*

bring something **back**[†] **(to** someone**)** to remind someone of something. □ *The funeral brought memories back.* □ *The warm winds brought back the old feeling of loneliness that I had experienced so many times in the tropics.*

bring something **before** someone or something to bring a matter to the attention of someone or a group. □ *I wanted to bring this matter before you before it got any worse.* □ *I will have to bring this matter before the committee.*

bring something **crashing down (around** one**) 1.** *Lit.* to cause a structure to collapse and fall (on oneself). □ *He hit the tent pole and brought the tent crashing down.* □ *When she removed the last vertical board, she brought the shed crashing down around her.* **2.** *Fig.* to destroy something, such as one's life and well-being, that one has a special interest in; to cause someone's basic orientation to collapse. □ *She brought her whole life crashing down around her.*

bring something **down**[†] **1.** *Lit.* to move something from a higher place to a lower place. □ *Bring that box down, please.* □ *And while you're up there, please bring down the box marked "winter clothing."* **2.** to lower something, such as prices, profits, taxes, etc. □ *The governor pledged to bring taxes down.* □ *I hope they bring down taxes.* **3.** *Fig.* to defeat or overcome something, such as an enemy, a government, etc. □ *The events of the last week will probably* *bring the government down.* □ *The scandal will bring down the government, I hope.*

bring something **down**† **on** one('s **head**) **1.** *Lit.* to cause something to fall onto one's head. (See also **bring** something **crashing down (around** one).) □ *He jarred the shelves and all the books were brought down on his head.* □ *When he hit the wall of the hut, he brought down the roof on himself.* **2.** *Fig.* to cause the collapse of something or some enterprise onto oneself. □ *Your bumbling will bring everything down on your head!* □ *Your mistakes have brought down the whole thing on your own head.*

bring something **down to** something to make a concept simpler to understand by bringing it to a simpler level of understanding. □ *Why don't you bring all this down to my level?* □ *Everything was brought down to the child's level.*

bring something **home to** someone **1.** *Lit.* to return home with a gift for someone. □ *I brought a box of candy home to the children.* □ *The candy was brought home to Lily by Ken.* **2.** *Fig.* to cause someone to realize something. □ *My weakness was brought home to me by the heavy work I had been assigned to do.* □ *The hard work really brought my frailty home to me.*

bring something **into being** to cause something to be; to create something. □ *How can I bring my new scheme into being?* □ *The new scheme was brought into being by a lot of hard work.*

bring something **into blossom** to make a plant or tree bloom. □ *The special plant food brought the rosebush into blossom.* □ *The roses were brought into blossom by the lovely weather.*

bring something **into focus 1.** *Lit.* to make something seen through lenses sharply visible. □ *I adjusted the binoculars until I brought the bird sharply into focus.* □ *The flowers were brought into focus by adjusting the controls.* **2.** *Fig.* to make something clear and understandable. □ *I think we will have a better discussion of the problem if you will say a few words to bring it more sharply into focus.* □ *Please try to bring your major point into focus earlier in the essay.*

bring something **into play 1.** *Lit.* [in a ball game] to put the ball into the action of the game, such as after a time-out. □ *Fred brought the ball into play when he bounced it in from the sidelines.* **2.** *Fig.* [for the shares of a company] to become the subject of a takeover bid. □ *The recent drop in the value of that stock brought the company into play.* □ *The company was brought into play by a news story about their new product line.* **3.** *Fig.* to cause something to become a factor in something. □ *Now, this recent development brings some other factors into play.* □ *Something else was brought into play by the strange event.*

bring something **into question** to cause something to be doubted; to cause something to be questioned. □ *What you have just told me seems to bring the wisdom of the trip into question.* □ *Your presence here has been brought into question.*

bring something **into service** to begin to use something; to start something up. □ *They are bringing a much larger boat into service next month.* □ *A newer machine will be brought into service next year.*

bring something **off**† to cause something to happen; to carry out a plan successfully. □ *Do you think you can bring it off?* □ *She brought off her plan without a hitch!*

bring something **on**† **1.** to cause something to happen; to cause a situation to occur. □ *What brought this event on?* □ *What brought on this catastrophe?* **2.** to cause a case or an attack of a disease. □ *What brought on your coughing fit?* □ *Something in the air brought it on.*

bring something **on** someone to cause something to go wrong for someone. □ *You brought it on yourself. Don't complain.* □ *Max brought this problem on all of us.*

bring something **out** † **1.** to issue something; to publish something; to present something [to the public]. □ *I am bringing a new book out.* □ *I hear you have brought out a new edition of your book.* **2.** Go to **bring** something **out of** someone.

bring something **out**† **(in** someone) to cause a particular quality to be displayed by a person, such as virtue, courage, a mean streak, selfishness, etc. □ *You bring the best out in me.* □ *This kind of thing brings out the worst in me.*

bring something **out in the open** Go to **out in the open.**

bring something **out of mothballs** *Fig.* to bring something out of storage and into use; to restore something to active service. □ *They were going to bring a number of ships out of mothballs, but the war ended before they needed them.*

bring something **out of** someone and **bring** something **out**† to cause something to be said by a person, such as a story, the truth, an answer, etc. □ *We threatened her a little and that brought the truth out of her.* □ *This warning ought to bring out the truth!*

bring something **to a boil** to heat liquid to its boiling point; to make something boil. □ *First, you must bring the soup to a boil.*

bring something **to a climax** Go to next.

bring something **to a close** and **bring** something **to an end; bring** something **to a climax** to end something; to cause something to reach its final point and stop. □ *I think it is time to bring this matter to a close.* □ *The incident has been brought to a climax.*

bring something **to a dead end** to cause something to reach a point from which it can go no further. □ *The accident brought the project to a dead end.* □ *The study was brought to a dead end by the loss of federal funding.*

bring something **to a head** to cause something to come to the point when a decision has to be made or action taken. □ *The latest disagreement between management and the union has brought matters to a head. There will be an all-out strike now.* □ *It's a relief that things have been brought to a head. The disputes have been going on for months.*

bring something **to a standstill** to cause a process or a job to reach a point at which it must stop. □ *The accident brought the work to a standstill.* □ *The strike brought construction to a standstill.*

bring something **to a successful conclusion** to complete something successfully. □ *They brought the battle to* *a successful conclusion.* □ *The case was brought to a successful conclusion by the prosecutor.*

bring something **to an end** Go to bring something to a close.

bring something **to fruition** to make something come into being; to achieve a success. □ *Do you think you can bring this plan to fruition?* □ *The plan was brought to fruition by the efforts of everyone.*

bring something **to its feet** Go to bring one to one's feet.

bring something **to light** *Fig.* to make something known. □ *The scientists brought their findings to light.* □ *We must bring this new evidence to light.*

bring something **to mind** Go to call something to mind.

bring something **to rest** to cause a machine, vehicle, or process to stop. □ *Jill brought the car to rest against the curb.* □ *The car was brought to rest against the curb.*

bring something **to someone's aid** to bring something with which to help someone. □ *The officer brought medical supplies to our aid.* □ *An ambulance was brought to the injured man's aid.*

bring something **to someone's attention** to make someone aware of something; to mention or show something to someone. □ *I would like to bring this problem to your attention.* □ *If there is something I should know about, please bring it to my attention.*

bring something **to the fore** to move something forward; to make something more prominent or noticeable. □ *All the talk about costs brought the question of budgets to the fore.* □ *The question of budget planning was brought to the fore.*

bring something **together**† to assemble things; to gather things together. □ *Thank you for bringing everything together so we can begin work.* □ *We brought together all the tools that we needed.*

bring something **up**† **1.** *Lit.* to vomit something up; to cough something up. □ *See if you can get him to bring the penny up.* □ *I did, and he brought up a nickel instead!* **2.** *Fig.* to mention something. □ *Why did you have to bring that problem up?* □ *Then they brought up the question of money.*

bring something **up to speed** Go to up to speed.

bring something **up to the minute** Go to up to the minute.

bring something **(up)on** oneself to be the cause of one's own trouble. (*Upon* is more formal and less commonly used than *on*.) □ *It's your own fault. You brought it upon yourself.* □ *You brought it all on yourself.*

bring something **with** (*Inf.* or regional.) to carry something along with [oneself]. □ *Are you going to bring your umbrella with?* □ *I brought it with. Don't worry.*

bring something **within a range** to adjust something into a particular range; to adjust a parameter. □ *Let's try to bring your cholesterol within the normal range with diet.* □ *It was brought within the normal range by an expensive drug.*

bring the house down† **1.** *Lit.* to cause a house to collapse. □ *The most severe earthquake in years finally brought the house down.* □ *The earthquake brought down all the*

houses on the hillside. **2.** *Fig.* [for a performance or a performer] to excite the audience into making a great clamor of approval. □ *Karen's act brought the house down.* □ *She really brought down the house with her comedy.*

bring up the rear to move along behind everyone else; to be at the end of the line. (Originally referred to marching soldiers. Fixed order.) □ *Here comes John, bringing up the rear.* □ *Hurry up, Tom! Why are you always bringing up the rear?*

bristle at something *Fig.* to show sudden anger or other negative response to something. (Alludes to a dog or cat raising the hair on its back in anger or as a threat.) □ *She bristled at the suggestion.* □ *I knew Lily would bristle at the appearance of Max.*

bristle with anger Go to next.

bristle with rage and **bristle with anger; bristle with indignation** *Fig.* to demonstrate one's anger, rage, or displeasure with a strong negative response. (Alludes to a dog or cat raising the hair on its back in anger or as a threat.) □ *She was just bristling with anger. I don't know what set her off.* □ *Walter bristled with rage as he saw the damage to his new car.*

broach something **with** someone and **broach** something **to** someone to mention something to someone; to bring up an idea to someone. □ *I hate to be the one to have to broach this to you, but your trousers are torn.* □ *This delicate matter must be broached with Mr. Rogers.*

***broad as a barn door** very broad or wide. (*Also: **as ~**.) □ *Jim's backside is as broad as a barn door.* □ *The weight lifter's chest is broad as a barn door.*

broad in the beam 1. *Lit.* [of a ship] wide at amidships. □ *This old tub is broad in the beam and sits like a ball in the water, but I love her.* **2.** *Fig. Inf.* with wide hips or large buttocks. □ *I am getting a little broad in the beam. It's time to go on a diet.* □ *John is just naturally broad in the beam.*

broaden out to become wider; to expand. □ *The river broadened out and became deeper.* □ *The road broadens out here.*

broaden something **out**† to make something wider; to expand something. □ *Now, broaden this part out a little, so it looks like a cloud, not a painted pillow.* □ *Broaden out the river in your painting so it looks very wide.* □ *The photographic view of the valley can be broadened out by using a different lens.*

broken dreams wishes or desires that cannot be fulfilled. □ *We all have our share of broken dreams, but they were never all meant to come true anyway.*

a **broken reed** an unreliable or undependable person. (On the image of a useless, broken reed in a reed instrument.) □ *You can't rely on Jim's support. He's a broken reed.* □ *Mr. Smith is a broken reed. His deputy has to make all the decisions.*

brood about someone or something and **brood on** someone or something; **brood over** someone or something to fret or be depressed about someone or something. □ *Please don't brood about Albert. He is no good for you.* □ *There's no need to brood on Jeff. He can take care of himself.*

browbeat someone **into** something *Fig.* to bully or intimidate someone into something. □ *It won't do any good to* *try to browbeat me into it.* □ *I was browbeaten into doing it once. I refuse to do it again.*

***brown as a berry** very brown from the sun; quite suntanned. (*Also: **as ~**.) □ *She was out in the sun so much that she became as brown as a berry.*

brown out [for the electricity] to diminish in power and dim the lights, causing a brownout. (Something less than a *blackout*, when there is no power.) □ *The power kept browning out.* □ *The lights started to brown out, and I thought maybe there was a power shortage.*

brown someone **off**† *Sl.* to make someone angry. (See also **browned (off)**.) □ *You really brown me off!*

browned (off) *Sl.* angry. □ *I am really browned off at you!* □ *The boss really got browned—to say the least; he fired me!*

browse among something **1.** [for an animal] to wander about among plants and trees, selecting and eating some. □ *The deer were browsing among the vegetables in my garden.* □ *The cows were browsing among the grasses in the field.* **2.** [for someone] to look at or survey different items of reading material. □ *I browsed among the books on the rack until I found what I wanted.* □ *I browsed among the books for something suitable.*

browse on something [for an animal] to feed on some kind of plant material. □ *The deer browsed on the tender shoots in my garden.* □ *The rabbit browsed on my carrots.*

browse over something and **browse through** something [for someone] to glance through written or printed material quickly or curiously. □ *Why don't you browse over this and call me about it in the morning?* □ *I want to browse through this magazine quickly.* □ *When it has been browsed through by everyone, throw it away.*

browse through something Go to previous.

bruit something **about** to spread a rumor around; to gossip something around. □ *You really shouldn't bruit that incident about, you know.* □ *The story was bruited about all over the office.*

brush by someone or something and **brush past** someone or something to push quickly past someone or something. □ *She brushed by the little group of people standing there talking.* □ *I brushed by the plant, knocking it over.*

brush over someone or something *Fig.* to deal lightly with an important person or matter; to just barely mention someone or something. □ *I want to hear more. You only brushed over the part I was interested in.* □ *You only brushed over the bit about your girlfriend. Tell us more about her.*

brush past someone or something Go to **brush by** someone or something.

brush someone **off**† **1.** *Lit.* to remove something, such as dust or lint, from someone by brushing. □ *The bathroom attendant brushed Mr. Harris off and was rewarded with a small tip.* □ *The porter had never brushed off such a miserly man before.* **2.** *Fig.* to reject someone; to dismiss someone. (As if someone were mere lint.) □ *He brushed her off, telling her she had no appointment.* □ *He brushed off Mrs. Franklin, who was only trying to be nice to him.*

brush someone or something **aside**† **1.** *Lit.* to push or shove someone or something out of the way. □ *Don't just brush*

me aside. I almost fell over. □ *I brushed aside the branch, not realizing it was poison ivy.* **2.** *Fig.* to cast someone or something away; to rid oneself of someone or something; to ignore or dismiss someone or something. □ *You must not brush this matter aside.* □ *The clerk brushed aside the old man and moved on to the next person in line.*

brush something **away**† **(from** something**)** to remove something from something by brushing; to get dirt or crumbs off something by brushing. □ *He brushed a bit of lint away from Tom's collar.* □ *She brushed away the crumbs from the table.*

brush something **down**† to clean and groom fur or fabric by brushing. □ *Why don't you brush your coat down? It's very linty.* □ *I brushed down my trousers, and they looked much better.*

brush something **off** someone or something and **brush** something **off**† to remove something from someone or something by brushing. □ *I brushed a little lint off her collar.* □ *I brushed off the lint that was on her collar.*

brush something **up**† to improve one's knowledge of something or one's ability to do something. (See also **brush up (on** something**)**.) □ *I need to brush my French up a little bit.* □ *I need to brush up my French.*

brush (up) against someone or something to touch someone or something lightly in passing. □ *I brushed up against the freshly painted wall as I passed.* □ *I guess I brushed against Walter as I walked by.*

brush up (on something**)** to improve one's knowledge of something or one's ability to do something. □ *I need to brush up on my German.* □ *My German is weak. I had better brush up.*

a **brush with death** *Fig.* an instance of nearly dying. □ *After a brush with death, Claire seemed more friendly and outgoing.*

***the **brush-off** *Fig.* rejection; being cast aside and ignored. (*Typically: **get ~; give** someone **~**.) □ *Don't talk to Tom. He'll just give you the brush-off.* □ *I went up to her and asked for a date, but I got the brush-off.*

bubble over 1. *Lit.* [for boiling or effervescent liquid] to spill or splatter over the edge of its container. □ *The pot bubbled over and put out the flame on the stove.* □ *The stew bubbled over.* **2.** *Fig.* [for someone] to be so happy and merry that the joy "spills over" onto other people. □ *She was just bubbling over, she was so happy.* □ *Lily bubbled over with joy.*

bubble up (through something**)** [for a liquid] to seep up or well up through something, such as from between rocks, through a crack in the floor, or through a hole in the bottom of a boat. □ *The water bubbled up through a crack in the basement floor.*

buck for something *Sl.* to work ambitiously for something, such as a promotion. □ *I'm just bucking for recognition and, of course, a 20 percent raise.* □ *You can tell by her attention to the boss that she's bucking for promotion.*

buck someone **off**† [for a horse or similar animal] to rear up in an attempt to shake off its rider. □ *The horse tried to buck Sharon off, but she held on tight.* □ *The horse bucked off its rider.*

The **buck stops here.** The need to act or take responsibility, that other people pass on to still other people, ultimately ends up here. (An expression made famous by U.S. President Harry Truman, about the finality of decisions a president must make. See also **pass the buck**.) □ *After everyone else has avoided making the decision, I will have to do it. The buck stops here.*

buck up to cheer up; to perk up. □ *Come on, now, buck up. Things can't be all that bad.* □ *She began to buck up when I showed her the results of the tests.*

buckle down (to something**)** to settle down to something; to begin to work seriously at something. □ *If you don't buckle down to your job, you'll be fired.* □ *You had better buckle down and get busy.*

buckle someone **in**† to attach someone securely with a vehicle's seat belts. (This includes airplane seat belts.) □ *Don't forget to buckle the children in.* □ *Did you buckle in the children?*

buckle someone or something **down**† to attach someone or something down with straps that buckle together. □ *They stopped to buckle the load down again.* □ *Did you buckle down the kids?*

buckle someone or something **up**† to attach someone or something securely with straps that buckle together. (This emphasizes the completeness and secureness of the act.) □ *Buckle the children up before we leave.* □ *Buckle up your shoes.*

buckle under 1. *Lit.* [for something] to collapse. □ *With heavy trucks on it, the bridge buckled under.* □ *The table buckled under.* **2.** *Fig.* [for someone] to collapse or give in under the burden of heavy demands or great anxiety. □ *With so much to worry about, she buckled under.* □ *I was afraid she would buckle under.*

buckle under something to collapse under or from the weight of something. □ *The bridge buckled under the weight of the truck and collapsed.* □ *The table finally buckled under.*

buckle up and **belt up** to buckle one's seat belt, as in a car or plane. □ *Please buckle up so our flight can begin.* □ *I wish you would obey the law and belt up.*

bud out [for a flowering plant or tree] to develop buds. □ *How early in the spring do the trees bud out around here?* □ *The trees bud out in early spring.*

a **budding genius** a very bright and promising young person. □ *Harry is a budding genius, but he seems like a fairly normal teenager.*

buddy up (to someone**)** to become overly familiar or friendly with someone. □ *Don't try to buddy up to me now. It won't do any good.* □ *He always tries to buddy up, no matter how coldly you treat him.*

buddy up (with someone**)** to join with another person to form a pair that will do something together or share something. □ *I buddied up with Carl, and we helped each other on the hike.* □ *Carl and I buddied up, and we shared a canoe.*

budget something **for** someone or something to set aside a certain amount of money for someone or something. □ *Did you budget some money for the holiday party?* □ *I budgeted a few hundred a month for Andrew's college expenses.*

buff something **down**† to polish or smooth something by buffing. □ *I buffed the newly waxed table down with a cloth.* □ *I'm going to go out and buff down the car.*

buff something **up**† to polish something to a shine. □ *He buffed his shoes up and went out for the evening.* □ *He buffed up the antique silver platter.*

buffet someone or something **from** someone or something **to** someone or something *Fig.* to shift someone or something back and forth between people, things, or places, as if being tossed around by the waves of the sea. □ *The state agency buffeted the orphan child from one relative to another.* □ *The office staff buffeted the memo from one desk to another.*

bug off 1. *Sl.* to cease bothering [someone]. □ *Hey, bug off! Your comments are annoying.* □ *I wish you would bug off!* **2.** *Sl.* Get out!; Go away! (Usually **Bug off!**) □ *Bug off! Get out of my sight!* □ *Bug off and leave me alone!*

bug out 1. *Sl.* to pack up and leave or retreat. □ *Orders are to bug out by oh-nine-hundred.* □ *Okay, everybody, move it! We're bugging out.* **2.** *Sl.* to get out of somewhere fast. □ *I gotta find a way to bug out of here without getting caught.* □ *Okay, the downpour has stopped. Let's bug out.*

bug someone to irritate someone; to bother someone. □ *Go away! Stop bugging me!* □ *Leave me alone. Go bug someone else.*

buggy whip Go to horse and buggy.

build a better mousetrap to develop or invent something superior to a device that is widely used. (From the old saying, "If you build a better mousetrap, the world will beat a path to your door.") □ *Harry thought he could build a better mousetrap, but everything he "invented" had already been thought of.*

build a case (against someone**)** and **gather a case (against** someone**)** to put together the evidence needed to make a legal or disciplinary case against someone. □ *The police easily built a case against the drunken driver.* □ *As soon as we gather the case against her, we can obtain a warrant to arrest her.*

build a fire under someone Go to a **fire under** someone.

build castles in Spain Go to next.

build castles in the air and **build castles in Spain** *Fig.* to daydream; to make plans that can never come true. □ *Ann spends most of her time building castles in Spain.* □ *I really like to sit on the porch in the evening, just building castles in the air.*

build down [for traffic] to reduce in volume or diminish. □ *At about six, the going-home traffic begins to build down.* □ *When traffic builds down, I leave for home.*

build one's **hopes on** someone or something to make plans or have aspirations based on someone or something. □ *I have built my hopes on making a success of this business.* □ *I built my hopes on John's presidency.*

build on(to) something and **build on** to add to something by constructing an extension. □ *Do you plan to build onto this house?* □ *Yes, we are going to build on.*

build out onto something to extend a building onto a particular space. □ *We can build out onto the adjacent lot after we purchase it.* □ *We built out onto the area over the old patio.*

build someone **in**† Go to next.

build someone **into** something and **build** someone **in**† to make a person an integral part of an organization or a plan. □ *The mayor built his cronies into the organizational structure of the town.* □ *He built in his relatives as part of the administration.*

build someone or something **up**† **1.** *Lit.* to make someone or something bigger or stronger. □ *Tom is lifting weights to build himself up for basketball.* □ *Tom needs to build up his upper body.* **2.** *Fig.* to advertise, praise, or promote someone or something. □ *Theatrical agents work very hard to build up their clients.* □ *Advertising can build a product up so much that everyone will want it.*

build someone or something **up**† **(from** something**)** to transform someone or something from a lowly start to a higher state. □ *I built up this business from nothing.* □ *The publicity agent built this politician up from a cheap party hack.*

build someone or something **up**† **(into** someone or something**)** to develop or advance someone or something into a particular [desirable] kind of person or thing. □ *The publicity people built her up into a singer whom everyone looked forward to hearing.* □ *The agent built up the local band into a top national act.*

build someone **up**† **(for** something**)** *Fig.* to prepare someone for something; to bring a person into a state of mind to accept some information. □ *We built them up for the challenge they were to face.* □ *We had to build up the woman before breaking the bad news.*

build something **in**† Go to next.

build something **into** something and **build** something **in**† **1.** to integrate a piece of furniture or an appliance into a building's construction. □ *We will build this cupboard into the wall about here.* □ *We are going to build in a chest of drawers.* □ *Then we will build another one in.* **2.** to make a particular quality a basic part of something. □ *We build quality into our cars before we put our name on them.* □ *We build in quality.* **3.** to make a special restriction or specification a part of the plan of something. □ *I built the restriction into our agreement.* □ *The lawyer built in the requirement that payments be by certified check.*

build something **on**† Go to next.

build something **on(to)** something and **build** something **on**† to construct an extension onto a building. □ *We are going to build a garage onto this side of the house.* □ *We will build on a new garage.* □ *The people next door are not going to build anything on.*

build something **out of** something to construct something from parts or materials. □ *She built a tower out of the blocks.* □ *They will build the bridge out of reinforced concrete.*

build (something) **out**† **over** something and **build** (something) **over** something to construct something so that it extends over something else, such as water or some architectural feature. □ *We built a deck out over the pond.* □ *We built the deck over the pond.*

build (something) **over** something Go to previous.

build something **to order** to build an individual object according to a special set of specifications. □ *I am having them build a new house to order—just for us.* □ *The car will be built to order.*

build something **up**† **1.** *Lit.* to add buildings to an area of land or a neighborhood. □ *They are really building this area up. There is no more open space.* □ *They built up the area over the years.* **2.** *Fig.* to develop, accumulate, or increase something, such as wealth, business, goodwill, etc. □ *I built this business up through hard work and hope.* □ *She built up a good business over the years.* **3.** *Fig.* to praise or exalt something; to exaggerate the virtues of something. □ *The master of ceremonies built the act up so much that everyone was disappointed when they saw it.* □ *He built up the act too much.*

build something **(up)on** something **1.** *Lit.* to construct something on the base of something else. (*Upon* is formal and less commonly used than *on*.) □ *The ancients built their houses upon the houses of earlier people.* **2.** *Fig.* to add to and develop something that already exists. □ *We have a good reputation and we must build on it.* □ *He has to build on his strong friendships with the customers.*

build up to increase; to develop. □ *The storm clouds are building up. Better close the windows.*

build up to something **1.** [for a person] to lead up to something or advance to doing or saying something. □ *I can tell you are building up to something. What is it?* **2.** [for a situation] to develop into something. □ *The argument is building up to something unpleasant.*

build (up)on something **1.** to construct something on a particular space. (*Upon* is more formal and less commonly used than *on*.) □ *Are you going to build upon this land?* □ *Yes, we will build on it.* **2.** to start with something and add to it. (*Upon* is more formal and less commonly used than *on*.) □ *Our progress has been good so far. Let's build on it.* □ *We will build upon the success of our forebears.*

built like a brick outhouse and **built like a brick shithouse** *Fig.* well-built—either strong or full-sized. (Built more strongly than is typical. The second form is potentially offensive. Use only with discretion.) □ *Look at that guy's muscles—he's built like a brick shithouse.* □ *This garage is built like a brick outhouse. It'll last for years.*

bulge out to swell outward; to extend out into a lump or mound. □ *The puppy's tummy bulged out, full of food.* □ *The bag of grass clippings bulged out heavily.*

bulge with something to be swollen with something. □ *The bag was bulging with gifts and candy.* □ *The chipmunk's cheeks bulged with the nuts it had found.*

*a **bull in a china shop** *Prov.* a very clumsy creature in a delicate situation. (*Typically: **as awkward as** ~; **like** ~.) □ *I never know what to say at a funeral. I feel like a bull in a china shop, trampling on feelings without even meaning to.* □ *Lester felt like a bull in a china shop; reaching for an orange, he made several elaborate pyramids of fruit tumble down.*

bulldoze into something *Fig.* to move clumsily into something. □ *Don't just bulldoze into me! Watch where you are going!* □ *Todd bulldozed into the wall, denting it badly.*

bulldoze through something *Fig.* to push clumsily and carelessly through something. □ *Don't just bulldoze through your work!* □ *I wish you wouldn't bulldoze through the room.*

Bully for you! **1.** an expression that praises someone or someone's courage. (Dated, but still heard.) □ *The audi-*

ence shouted, "Bravo! Bully for you!" □ Bob: I quit my job today. Sally: Bully for you! Now what are you going to do? Bob: Well, I need a little loan to tide me over. **2.** a sarcastic phrase belittling someone's statement or accomplishment. □ Bob: I managed to save three dollars last week. Bill: Well, bully for you! □ Mary: I won a certificate good for a free meal! Sally: Bully for you!

A **bully is always a coward.** *Prov.* Bullies will only intimidate people who are much weaker than they are, because they are afraid of losing a fight. □ Child: Dad, Joey keeps picking on me. How can I make him stop? Father: Try fighting back. A bully is always a coward. □ Bill took advantage of the younger children, but he was quiet and docile around the older ones. A bully is always a coward.

bully someone **into** something to harass or threaten someone into doing something. □ The coach tried to bully them into agreeing to stay late and practice. □ Don't try to bully me into your way of doing things.

bum around (with someone**)** to spend or waste a lot of time with a particular person. □ He used to bum around with Ted a lot. □ They bummed around together all summer.

bum out *Sl.* to have a bad experience. (Originally referred to a bad experience with drugs.) □ Are you going to bum out again tonight? □ Man, is he bummed out!

*the **bum's rush** hurrying someone out of a place. (As someone might quickly escort a vagrant from a fancy restaurant. *Typically: **get ~; give** someone **~.**) □ The young customer in the jewelry store was getting the bum's rush until he pulled out an enormous roll of bills. □ Bill got the bum's rush at the restaurant because he didn't have a tie on.

bum someone **out**† *Sl.* to disappoint someone. □ This menial job really bums me out. □ The bad movie bummed out the entire audience.

bum something **off** someone *Sl.* to beg or borrow something from someone. □ Can I bum a cigarette off you? □ You can't bum anything off me that I don't have.

*a **bum steer** misleading instructions or guidance; a misleading suggestion. (*Bum* = false; phony. *Steer* = guidance, as in the steering of a car. *Typically: **get ~; have ~; give** someone **~.**) □ Wilbur gave Ted a bum steer and Ted ended up in the wrong town. □ I got a bum steer from the salesman, and I paid far more than I needed to for a used car.

bumble through something to get through something clumsily. □ I guess I will have to bumble through this speech again. □ Lily bumbled through her song and fled from the stage.

bummed (out) *Sl.* discouraged; depressed. □ I feel so bummed. I think I need a nice hot bath. □ When you're feeling bummed out, think how much you've accomplished.

bump along 1. and **bump along** something *Lit.* to travel along a rough road. □ We bumped along on the dirt road to the lake. □ We bumped along the road, hanging onto our hats. **2.** *Fig.* [for some plan or situation] to move along awkwardly and unevenly. □ The whole project bumped along to an uncertain conclusion. □ The plan bumped along for a while and then we all gave it up.

bump into someone and **run into** someone **1.** *Lit.* to move inadvertently or crash into someone. □ Excuse me. I didn't mean to bump into you. □ The child on the bicycle nearly bumped into me. **2.** *Fig.* to chance on someone; to meet someone by chance. (Not normally with physical contact.) □ Guess who I bumped into downtown today? □ I ran into Bill Jones yesterday.

bump someone **off**† and **knock** someone **off**† *Sl.* to kill someone. □ They tried to bump her off, but she was too clever and got away. □ The crooks threatened to bump off the witness to the crime.

bump someone or something **up**† **1.** *Lit.* to damage or batter someone or something. □ The crash into the wall bumped the race driver up a little. □ The accident bumped up the passengers a little. **2.** *Fig.* to raise someone or something to a higher category or level. (As if pushing someone into a higher category.) □ I wanted to fly first class, but they wouldn't bump me up. □ The ticket agent bumped up both of my friends, but not me.

Bump that! *Sl.* Forget that! □ Bump that! I was wrong. □ I gave you the wrong number. Bump that!

bump (up) against someone or something to strike someone or something accidentally, usually relatively gently. □ The car bumped up against the curb. □ The door has bumped against the wall and scratched the paint.

bumper to bumper [of traffic] close together and moving slowly. □ The traffic is bumper to bumper from the accident up ahead.

a **bunch of fives** *Sl.* a punch from a closed fist. □ How would you like a bunch of fives right in the kisser? □ He ended up with a bunch of fives in the gut.

bunch someone or something **up**† to pack or cluster things or people together. □ Bunch them up so you can squeeze them into the sack. □ Kelly bunched up the roses and put them in a vase.

bunch up to pack together or cluster. □ Spread out. Don't bunch up!

bundle from heaven Go to next.

bundle of joy and **bundle from heaven** *Fig.* a baby. □ We are expecting a bundle of joy next September. □ When your little bundle from heaven arrives, things will be a little hectic for a while.

a **bundle of nerves** a very nervous person. □ I was a bundle of nerves before my dental appointment.

bundle off to leave in a hurry; to take all one's parcels or baggage and leave in a hurry. □ She got ready and bundled off after her bus. □ Her arms full, Lily bundled off in a rush.

bundle (oneself) up (against something**)** to wrap oneself up in protective clothing or bedding as protection against the cold. □ Please bundle yourself up against the frigid wind. □ Bundle up before you go outside.

bundle someone **into** something **1.** to put someone, usually a child, into heavy outdoor clothing. □ Bill bundled Billy into his parka. □ Tom bundled himself into his parka and opened the door to go out. **2.** and **bundle** someone **in** to put someone, usually a child, into bed. □ She bundled Sarah into bed after reading her a story. □ June pulled the sheets back and bundled Sarah in.

B

bundle someone **off**† **(to** some place) *Fig.* to send someone, usually a child, somewhere. □ *Robert bundled the children off to school.* □ *They bundled off the kids and were able to relax.*

bundle someone **up**† **(against** something) to wrap someone up in protective clothing or bedding against the cold. □ *Wally bundled Billy up against the winter storm.* □ *You had better bundle up the children against the bitter wind.*

bundle someone **up**† **(in** something) to wrap someone up in protective clothing or bedding. □ *Bill bundled Billy up in his parka.* □ *Bill bundled up Mary in her parka.*

bundle something **off**† **(to** someone or some place) to send something off in a bundle to someone. □ *He bundled his laundry off to his mother, who would wash it for him.* □ *Mary bundled off the package to her brother.*

bung something **in**† to cram or bang something into something. □ *He bunged the cork into the barrel.* □ *With a heavy blow, he bunged in the cork.*

bung something **up**† to damage someone or something by blows. □ *Don't let the watermelon roll around in the trunk of your car. You don't want to bung it up.* □ *Last time I put up the storm windows, I really bunged up my hands.*

bunged up battered or bruised. □ *It used to be a nice table, but it got all bunged up.* □ *What happened to Jane? Her face was bunged up.*

bungle something **up**† to botch something; to mess something up. □ *Please don't bungle this job up.* □ *Tom was careless and he bungled up the job.*

bunk down (for the night) to bed down for the night; to go to bed. □ *Where are you going to bunk down for the night?* □ *I'm tired and ready to bunk down.*

bunk (up) together [for two or more people] to share a bed, a bedroom, or a tent. □ *Shall we bunk together?* □ *My tent is big and you can bunk up with me.*

bunk (up) with someone to share a bed, a bedroom, or a tent with someone. □ *Are you going to bunk up with Fred?* □ *I'll bunk with Todd.*

buoy someone or something **up**† to keep someone or something afloat. □ *Use this cushion to buoy yourself up.* □ *The log buoyed up the swimmer until help came.* □ *The air trapped in the hull buoyed the boat up.*

buoy someone **up**† *Fig.* to support, encourage, or sustain someone. □ *The good news buoyed her up considerably.* □ *Her good humor buoyed up the entire party.*

burden someone or something **with** someone or something to bother or weigh down someone or something with someone or something. □ *Please don't burden us with the bad news at this time.* □ *I don't want to burden the school with a troublesome child.*

burden someone **with** something to give unpleasant information to someone; to give someone some bad news. □ *I hate to burden you with this, but your cat ran away.* □ *I wish I had not been burdened with all the facts.*

burgeon out to develop and grow rapidly; to burst forth. □ *The flowers burgeoned out and made the garden beautiful again.* □ *When the trees have burgeoned out, spring is really here.*

burn something **to a crisp** to burn something totally or very badly. □ *The cook burned the meat to a crisp.*

burn away 1. [for something] to burn until there is no more of it. □ *All the oil burned away.* □ *The logs burned away and the fireplace was cooling down.* **2.** for something to keep on burning. □ *The little fire burned away brightly, warming the tiny room.* □ *The candle burned away, giving a tiny bit of light to the huge room.*

burn down 1. [for a building] to be destroyed by fire. □ *The barn burned down.* □ *There was a fire, and the old factory was burned down.* **2.** [for a fire] to burn and dwindle away. □ *The flame burned down and then went out.* □ *As the fire burned down, it began to get cold.*

burn for someone or something to desire someone or something very much. □ *Jim said he was burning for Sally.* □ *I was just burning for another look at her.*

burn (itself) out 1. [for a flame or fire] to run out of fuel and go out. □ *Finally, the fires burned themselves out.* □ *The fire finally burned out.* **2.** [for an electrical or mechanical part] to fail and cease working. □ *The motor finally burned itself out.* □ *The light bulb burned out.*

Burn not your house to fright the mouse away. *Prov.* Do not do something drastic when it is not necessary. □ *Ellen: I don't like the shape of my nose; I think I'll have surgery to make it look better. Jane: But you can make your nose look better just by using different makeup. Don't burn your house to fright the mouse away.* □ *When someone pointed out a small flaw in Bob's latest painting, Bob wanted to tear the whole painting to shreds. "Now, now, Bob," his friends said, "burn not your house to fright the mouse away."*

burn off [for some excess volatile or flammable substance] to burn away or burn up. □ *A film of oil on the surface of the water was burning off, making dense black smoke.* □ *The alcohol burned off and left a delicious flavor in the cherries jubilee.*

burn one's **bridges (behind** one) **1.** *Lit.* to cut off the way back to where you came from, making it impossible to retreat. □ *The army, which had burned its bridges behind it, couldn't go back.* □ *By blowing up the road, the spies had burned their bridges behind them.* **2.** *Fig.* to act unpleasantly in a situation that you are leaving, ensuring that you'll never be welcome to return. □ *If you get mad and quit your job, you'll be burning your bridges behind you.* □ *No sense burning your bridges. Be polite and leave quietly.* **3.** *Fig.* to make decisions that cannot be changed in the future. □ *If you drop out of school now, you'll be burning your bridges behind you.* □ *You're too young to burn your bridges that way.*

burn one's **bridges in front of** one *Fig.* to create future problems for oneself. (A play on **burn** one's **bridges (behind** one).) □ *I made a mistake again. I always seem to burn my bridges in front of me.* □ *I accidentally insulted a math teacher whom I will have to take a course from next semester. I am burning my bridges in front of me.*

burn (oneself) out *Fig.* to do something so long and so intensely that one gets sick and tired of doing it. (See also **burn** someone **out**.) □ *I burned myself out as a competitive swimmer. I just cannot stand to practice anymore.* □ *Tom burned himself out in that boring job.*

burn someone **at the stake 1.** *Lit.* to set fire to a person tied to a post (as a form of execution). □ *They used to burn witches at the stake.* **2.** *Fig.* to chastise or denounce someone severely or excessively. □ *Stop yelling. I made a simple mistake, and you're burning me at the stake for it.* □ *Sally only spilled her milk. There is no need to shout. Don't burn her at the stake for it.*

burn someone **down**[†] *Sl.* to humiliate someone. □ *Man, don't you ever burn me down like that again!* □ *You just want to burn down everybody to make yourself seem better.*

burn someone **in effigy** to burn a dummy or other figure that represents a hated person. □ *For the third day in a row, they burned the king in effigy.* □ *Until they have burned you in effigy, you can't really be considered a famous leader.*

burn someone **out**[†] *Fig.* to wear someone out; to make someone ineffective through overuse. (See also **use** someone **up**.) □ *Facing all these problems at once will burn Tom out.* □ *The continuous problems burned out the office staff in a few months.*

burn someone **out of** something and **burn** someone **out**[†] to burn down a home(stead) or place of business. □ *Lightning struck and burned the farmer out of his home.*

burn someone **up**[†] **1.** *Lit.* to destroy someone by fire. □ *The house fire burned the victims up.* □ *The fire burned up both of them.* **2.** *Fig.* to make someone very angry; to make someone endure the "heat" of rage. □ *You really burn me up! I'm very angry at you!* □ *The whole mess burned up everyone.*

burn something **away**[†] to remove or destroy something by burning. □ *The doctor burned the wart away.* □ *The doctor burned away the wart.*

burn something **down**[†] [for a fire] to destroy a building completely. □ *The fire burned the barn down.* □ *It burned down the barn.*

burn something **in**[†] *Fig.* to run a piece of new electronic equipment for a while to make certain that all the electrical parts will last a long time. □ *Please burn this computer in for a couple of hours before you deliver it.* □ *The technician burned in the computer.*

burn something **into** something and **burn** something **in**[†] **1.** *Lit.* to engrave, brand, or etch marks or letters into something by the use of great heat. □ *She burned her initials into the handle of the umbrella.* □ *She burned in her initials.* **2.** *Fig.* to implant something firmly in someone's head, brain, memory, etc. □ *She burned the information into her head.* □ *The events of the day burned in sad memories.*

burn something **off**[†] Go to next.

burn something **off** something and **burn** something **off**[†] to cause excess volatile or flammable substance to burn until there is no more of it. □ *We burnt the gasoline off the water's surface.* □ *Why did you burn off the gasoline?*

burn something **out**[†] **1.** to burn away the inside of something, getting rid of excess deposits. □ *The mechanic burned the carbon out of the manifold.* □ *He burned out all of the carbon deposits.* **2.** to wear out an electrical or electronic device through overuse. □ *Turn it off. You're going to burn the motor out!* □ *He burned out the motor.*

burn something **up**[†] to destroy something by fire; [for fire] to consume something. □ *Take this cardboard and burn it up.* □ *The fire burned up the papers and left no trace.*

burn the candle at both ends *Fig.* to work very hard and stay up very late at night. (One end of the candle is work done in the daylight, and the other end is work done at night.) □ *No wonder Mary is ill. She has been burning the candle at both ends for a long time.* □ *You'll wear out if you keep burning the candle at both ends.*

burn the midnight oil *Fig.* to stay up working, especially studying, late at night. (Alludes to working by the light of an oil lamp late in the night.) □ *I have a big exam tomorrow so I'll be burning the midnight oil tonight.* □ *If you burn the midnight oil night after night, you'll probably become ill.*

burn up to become destroyed or consumed by fire. □ *The wood burned up and left only ashes.* □ *The deed burned up in the fire.*

burn with a low blue flame 1. *Lit.* [of a properly adjusted gas burner] to burn and put off heat. □ *Each burner on the stove burns with a low blue flame giving the maximum amount of heat per BTU.* **2.** *Fig.* to be quietly and intensely angry. □ *She just sat there with her steak in her lap, burning with a low blue flame.* □ *She was quiet, but everyone knew she would soon burn with a low blue flame.* **3.** *Fig.* to be heavily intoxicated with alcohol. (Alludes to the irritability of a person who is very drunk.) □ *Yeah, he's burning with a low blue flame.* □ *He's not just drunk, he's burning with a low blue flame.*

burn with something **1.** [for a fire] to burn with a particular quality. □ *The building burned with great ferocity.* □ *The fire burned with a lot of crackling and popping.* **2.** [for someone] to experience intense and consuming feelings of a particular quality. □ *Fred is just burning with anger.* □ *Why is he burning with envy?*

burned to a cinder burned very badly. [Very often used figuratively.] □ *I stayed out in the sun too long, and I am burned to a cinder.* □ *This toast is burnt to a cinder.*

burned up *Fig.* very angry. (From the heat of anger. See also **burn** someone **up**.) □ *My new assistant's mistakes are so maddening! I've never been so burned up in my life.* □ *I'm really burned up at Bob's behavior.*

a **burning question** and the **burning question** *Fig.* a question whose answer is of great interest to everyone; a question that needs very much to be answered, as a fire needs to be extinguished. □ *There's a burning question that needs to be answered: Why did you leave your wife of only one month?*

A **burnt child dreads the fire.** *Prov.* If something has hurt you once, you avoid it after that. (See also **once bitten, twice shy.**) □ *Jill: Let's go ride the roller coaster! Jane: No, thanks. I got sick on one of those once, and a burnt child dreads the fire.* □ *Ever since Cynthia rebuffed me so rudely, I've avoided asking her for anything; a burnt child dreads the fire.*

burst See also entries at **bust.**

burst at the seams 1. *Fig.* to be very full and burst, perhaps at the seams. (Alludes to something that would burst at the seams if overfilled.) □ *I am so full from dinner! I'm ready to burst at the seams.* □ *The room was so full it was bursting at the seams.* **2.** *Fig.* [for someone] to strain from holding in pride or laughter as if one might burst. □ *Tom* *nearly burst at the seams with pride.* □ *We laughed so hard we just about burst at the seams.*

burst forth to come forth explosively. □ *The words burst forth and frightened everyone.* □ *The blossoms burst forth in the first warm days of the year.*

burst in (on someone or something**)** to enter a room, interrupting someone or some activity. (Often without knocking or seeking permission to enter.) □ *Tom burst in on his sister and her boyfriend while they were kissing.* □ *I must ask you not to burst into my office again. Whatever it is can wait.*

burst in ((up)on someone or something**)** *Fig.* to intrude or come in thoughtlessly and suddenly and interrupt someone or something. (*Upon* is formal and less commonly used than *on.*) □ *I didn't mean to burst in on you.* □ *She feared that someone would burst in upon her.*

burst in (with something**)** to interrupt with some comment. □ *Ted burst in with the good news.* □ *He burst in to tell us about his new car.*

burst into flame(s) [for something] to catch fire and become a large fire quickly. □ *As soon as the flame reached the curtains, the entire wall seemed to burst into flames.* □ *The two cars burst into flames soon after the collision.*

burst into sight *Fig.* to come into view suddenly. (As if the sight appeared as suddenly as an explosion.) □ *The sun finally burst into sight at the horizon.* □ *Suddenly, a tiger burst into sight and caught the hunter off guard.*

burst in(to some place**)** *Fig.* to intrude or come in thoughtlessly and suddenly. □ *Ted burst into the room and sat down right in the middle of the meeting.* □ *Wasn't it very annoying of him to just burst in?*

burst into something Go to burst out into something.

burst into tears and **burst out crying** *Fig.* to begin to cry suddenly. □ *After the last notes of her song, the audience burst into tears, such was its beauty and tenderness.* □ *The children burst into tears on hearing of the death of their dog.*

burst onto the scene *Fig.* to appear suddenly in a location. □ *When Charles burst onto the scene, no one was prepared for the news he brought.* □ *The police suddenly burst onto the scene and arrested everyone in the room.*

burst out to explode outward; to break open under force. □ *The door burst out and released the trapped people.* □ *When the glass burst out, Gerald was cut by some splinters.*

burst out crying Go to burst into tears.

burst out doing something to begin to do something suddenly, such as cry, laugh, shout, etc. □ *Suddenly, she burst out singing.* □ *Ted burst out laughing when he read the joke.*

burst out into something and **burst into** something **1.** *Fig.* [for plants or trees] to open their flowers seemingly suddenly and simultaneously. (*Burst* indicates suddenness.) □ *The flowers burst out into blossom very early.* □ *They burst into blossom during the first warm day.* **2.** *Fig.* [for someone] to begin suddenly doing a particular activity, such as crying, laughing, chattering; to begin an activity such as laughter, chatter, tears, etc. □ *Suddenly, she burst out into laughter.* □ *The child burst into tears.*

burst out laughing to begin to laugh suddenly. □ *The entire audience burst out laughing when the clown took a*

fall. □ *Every time I think of you sitting there with a lap full of spaghetti, I burst out laughing.*

burst out (of some place**)** to come out of a place very rapidly, like an explosion. □ *Everyone burst out of the burning building.* □ *Suddenly, the windows all burst out.*

burst out (of something**)** *Fig.* to seem to explode out of something; to become [suddenly] too big for something, such as clothes, a house, etc. □ *She is practically bursting out of her dress.* □ *The butterfly burst out of the chrysalis.*

burst out with something *Fig.* to utter something loudly and suddenly. (Compare this with burst in (with something).) □ *The child burst out with a scream.* □ *Lily burst out with song.*

burst someone's **bubble** *Fig.* to destroy someone's illusion or delusion; to destroy someone's fantasy. □ *I hate to burst your bubble, but Columbus did not discover Canada.* □ *Even if you think I am being foolish, please don't burst my bubble.*

burst through something to break through or penetrate something with force. □ *The tank burst through the barrier easily.* □ *The workers burst through the wall after a lot of hard work.*

burst (up)on someone *Fig.* [for an idea] to strike someone suddenly. (As if an idea had burst forth. *Upon* is formal and less commonly used than *on.*) □ *After thinking all morning long, this really tremendous idea burst upon me.* □ *It burst on me like a bolt of lightning.*

burst (up)on the scene to appear suddenly somewhere; to enter or arrive suddenly some place. (*Upon* is formal and less commonly used than *on.*) □ *The police suddenly burst upon the scene.* □ *They burst on the scene and took control.*

burst with excitement *Fig.* to have a strong feeling of excitement. □ *Joe was just bursting with excitement because of his triumph.* □ *The new toys had the children all bursting with excitement.*

burst with joy *Fig.* [for someone] to be full to the bursting point with happiness. (To be so filled with joy as if to burst.) □ *When I got my grades, I could have burst with joy.* □ *Bill was not exactly bursting with joy when he got the news.*

burst with pride to be full as if to the bursting point with pride. □ *My parents were bursting with pride when I graduated from college.* □ *I almost burst with pride when I was chosen for the first prize.*

bury one's **head in the sand** and **hide** one's **head in the sand; have** one's **head in the sand** *Fig.* to ignore or hide from obvious signs of danger. (Alludes to an ostrich, which is believed incorrectly to hide its head in a hole in the ground when it sees danger.) □ *Stop burying your head in the sand. Look at the statistics on smoking and cancer.*

bury oneself **in** something **1.** *Fig.* to become very busy with something. □ *She stopped taking phone calls and buried herself in her work.* □ *He tended to bury himself in his work.* **2.** *Fig.* to hide oneself some place. (Alludes to burying oneself in a cave or something similar.) □ *He buried himself in the back of the little shop and worked quietly.* □ *The lizard buried itself in the sand.*

bury someone or something **away (some place)** to bury or hide someone or something some place. □ *The dog buried the bone away under a bush.* □ *The ex-dictator was buried away in an unmarked grave.*

bury someone or something **in** something **1.** *Lit.* to inter someone or something in a grave, the ground, a vault, a tomb, etc. □ *They buried the old man in the family vault.* □ *Thousands of war veterans are buried in the national cemetery.* **2.** *Fig.* to hide or conceal someone or something from view in some place. □ *The office manager buried Tom at a small desk in the back room.* □ *Someone buried the manual typewriter in a room full of old junk.*

bury someone or something **under** something to bury someone or something beneath something, sometimes to hide or conceal it. □ *Joe buried the money under a stone in the forest.* □ *They buried Aunt Mary under a pine tree.*

bury the hatchet *Fig.* to make peace. □ *Let's stop arguing and bury the hatchet.* □ *Tom and I buried the hatchet and we are good friends now.*

bush out [for a plant, bush, beard, head of hair] to develop many small branches or hairs. □ *His beard bushed out and really needed trimming.* □ *I hope the hedge bushes out nicely this year.*

a **bushel and a peck (and some in a gourd)** *Rur.* a great deal or amount. (Usually used to answer the question, "How much do you love me?") □ *Mary: How much do you love me? Tom: A bushel and a peck and some in a gourd.* □ *We knew that Grandpa loved us a bushel and a peck.*

The **busiest men have the most leisure.** and The **busiest men find the most time.** *Prov.* Industrious people get their work done efficiently and therefore have time to do what they want. □ *Fred: How does Phil do it? He produces more than the rest of us, but he also manages to pursue all his hobbies. Alan: The busiest men have the most leisure.* □ *As the town's only doctor, Bert worked extremely hard, yet he always had time to play with his children and go out with his wife. The busiest men find the most time.*

*the **business 1.** harassment; a scolding; general bad treatment. (*Typically: **get ~; give** someone **~**.) □ *The guys have been giving me the business about my new hairstyle.* □ *Sam was giving Tom the business about being late all the time.* **2.** *Sl.* an execution. (Underworld. *Typically: **get ~; give** someone **~**.) □ *The mob wanted to give him the business for confessing to the federal prosecutor.*

business as usual having things go along as usual. □ *Even right after the flood, it was business as usual in all the stores.* □ *Please, everyone, business as usual. Let's get back to work.*

Business before pleasure. *Prov.* You should finish your work before starting to relax and enjoy yourself. □ *Alan: Hi, Ted. Shall we get something to drink? Ted: Business before pleasure, Alan. Do you have the reports I asked you to bring?* □ *I'd love to go water-skiing with you now, but I have a few things to do in the office first. Business before pleasure, I'm afraid.*

the **business end of** something the part or end of something that actually does the work or carries out the procedure. □ *Keep away from the business end of the electric*

drill so you won't get hurt. □ *Don't point the business end of that gun at anyone. It might go off.*

a **busman's holiday** leisure time spent doing something similar to what one does at work. (Alludes to a bus driver going on a bus tour for his vacation or on a day off.) □ *Tutoring students in the evening is a busman's holiday for our English teacher.* □ *It's a bit of a busman's holiday to ask her to be wardrobe mistress for our amateur production in the summer. She's a professional dressmaker.*

bust a bronco to ride and thus tame a wild horse so that it can be ridden. (*Bust* is a nonstandard form of *burst*.) □ *In them days, I made my living busting broncos.* □ *That was the meanest bronco I ever seen. Nobody could bust 'im.*

bust a gut Go to **split a gut.**

bust a gut (to do something) *Fig.* to work very hard; to strain oneself to accomplish something. (The word *gut* is considered impolite in some circumstances. *Bust* is a nonstandard form of *burst*.) □ *I don't intend to bust a gut to get there on time.* □ *I busted a gut to get there the last time, and I was the first one there.*

bust a move *Sl.* to leave (a place). □ *Let's go. Time to bust a move.* □ *Let's bust a move. Lots to do tomorrow.*

bust ass out of some place *Sl.* to get out of some place in a hurry. (Potentially offensive. Use only with discretion.) □ *I had to bust ass out of the house and run all the way to school.* □ *Bob busted ass out of the classroom and headed for home.*

bust (one's) ass (to do something) and **break** one's **balls to** do something; **bust** one's **butt to** do something; **bust** one's **nuts to** do something *Sl.* to work very hard to do something. (The expressions with *balls* and *nuts* are said typically, but not necessarily, of a male. Potentially offensive. Use only with discretion.) □ *I've been busting my nuts to get this thing done on time, and now they don't want it!* □ *The new boss expects you to bust your nuts every minute you are at work at the warehouse.*

bust one's **butt to** do something Go to previous.

bust out laughing *Fig.* to start laughing suddenly. (See also **burst out laughing.** *Bust* is a nonstandard form of *burst*.) □ *I busted out laughing when I saw him in that get-up.* □ *The bridegroom was so nervous, it was all he could do not to bust out laughing.*

bust out (of some place) *Sl.* to break out of some place, especially a prison. (*Bust* is a nonstandard form of *burst* meaning 'break' here.) □ *Somehow the gangsters busted out of prison and left the country.* □ *They busted out together.*

bust (some) suds 1. *Sl.* to drink some beer. (*Bust* is a nonstandard form of *burst*. See also **crack some suds.**) □ *Let's go out and bust some suds.* □ *I'm tired of busting suds. Let's play cards.* **2.** *Sl.* to wash dishes. (*Bust* is a nonstandard form of *burst*.) □ *I don't want to spend the rest of my life busting suds.* □ *You get into that kitchen and bust some suds to earn your allowance.*

bust someone **one** *Sl.* to punch someone; to give someone a punch, probably in the face. (*Bust* is a nonstandard form of *burst* meaning 'hit' here.) □ *You better shut up, or I'll bust you one!* □ *You want me to bust you one? I will if you do that again.*

bust someone **out of** some place and **bust** someone **out**[†] **1.** *Sl.* to help someone escape from prison. (*Bust* is a nonstandard form of *burst* meaning 'break' here.) ☐ *Lefty did not manage to bust Max out of prison.* ☐ *Lefty wanted to bust out some of his friends.* **2.** *Sl.* to expel or force someone to withdraw from school. (*Bust* is a nonstandard form of *burst* meaning 'break' here.) ☐ *The dean finally busted Bill out of school.* ☐ *The dean busted out the students with very low grades.*

bust (someone's) **balls** Go to break (someone's) balls.

bust (someone's) **stones** Go to break (someone's) balls.

bust someone **up**[†] **1.** *Sl.* to cause lovers to separate; to break up a pair of lovers, including married persons. (See also **bust** something **up**. *Bust* is a nonstandard form of *burst* meaning 'break (apart)' here.) ☐ *Mary busted Terri and John up.* ☐ *Mary busted up Terri and John.* **2.** *Sl.* to beat someone up; to batter someone. (*Bust* is a nonstandard form of *burst* meaning 'hit' here.) ☐ *You want me to bust you up?* ☐ *Max busted up Lefty pretty badly.*

bust someone **wide open** *Sl.* to beat someone severely. (An exaggeration. *Bust* is a nonstandard form of *burst*.) ☐ *If you ever take a step onto my property, I'll bust you wide open.* ☐ *Jim threatened to bust Bill wide open.*

bust something **up**[†] **1.** *Inf.* to break or ruin something; to break something into smaller pieces. (*Bust* is a nonstandard form of *burst* meaning 'break' here.) ☐ *Who busted this plate up?* ☐ *Don't bust up the plates! Be careful!* **2.** *Sl.* to ruin a marriage by coming between the married people. (See also **bust** someone **up**. *Bust* is a nonstandard form of *burst* meaning 'break' here.) ☐ *He busted their marriage up by starting rumors about Maggie.* ☐ *He busted up their marriage.*

bust something **wide open** Go to blow something wide open.

bust up 1. *Sl.* [for lovers] to separate or break up. (*Bust* is a nonstandard form of *burst* meaning 'break' here.) ☐ *Tom and Alice busted up for good.* ☐ *They busted up last week.* **2.** *Sl.* [for something] to break up due to natural causes. (*Bust* is a nonstandard form of *burst* meaning 'break (apart)' here.) ☐ *The rocket busted up in midair.* ☐ *I saw it bust up.*

bustle about doing something to go about doing something busily and energetically. ☐ *Greg bustled about all day, doing the chores.* ☐ *Lily bustled about, getting dinner ready.*

bustle about some place to move about some place very busily, or as if busy. ☐ *They were all bustling about the kitchen, getting the feast ready.* ☐ *Veronica was bustling about outside, cleaning up the yard.*

bustle around to move about very busily. ☐ *The people were bustling around, trying to get things ready for the picnic.* ☐ *I wish you would stop bustling around.*

bustle off to leave in haste. ☐ *Well, I have to bustle off or I'll miss my flight.* ☐ *I hate to bustle off so soon.*

bustle someone **off**[†] to help someone leave; to send someone out or away. ☐ *The cops bustled the crook off.* ☐ *They bustled off the three men who were fighting.*

*busy as a beaver (building a new dam) and ***busy as a bee; *busy as a one-armed paperhanger; *busy as Grand Central Station; *busy as a cat on a hot tin roof; *busy as a fish peddler in Lent;**

*busy as a cranberry merchant (at Thanksgiving); *busy as popcorn on a skillet very busy. (**Also:* **as ~**.) ☐ *My boss keeps me as busy as a one-armed paperhanger.* ☐ *I don't have time to talk to you. I'm as busy as a beaver.* ☐ *When the tourist season starts, this store is busy as Grand Central Station.* ☐ *Sorry I can't go to lunch with you. I'm as busy as a beaver building a new dam.* ☐ *Prying into other folks' business kept him busy as popcorn on a skillet.*

busy as a cranberry merchant (at Thanksgiving) Go to previous.

busy as a fish peddler in Lent Go to busy as a beaver (building a new dam).

*busy as a hibernating bear not busy at all. (**Also:* **as ~**.) ☐ *Tom: I can't go with you. I'm busy. Jane: Yeah. You're as busy as a hibernating bear.* ☐ *He lounged on the sofa all day, busy as a hibernating bear.*

busy as a one-armed paperhanger Go to busy as a beaver (building a new dam).

busy as Grand Central Station Go to busy as a beaver (building a new dam).

busy as popcorn on a skillet Go to busy as a beaver (building a new dam).

busy oneself **with** someone or something to occupy one's time by dealing with someone or something. ☐ *Tony busied himself with helping Sam.* ☐ *Mrs. Wilson busied herself with little Jimmy.*

busy someone **with** someone or something to keep someone busy dealing with someone or something. ☐ *You should busy the children with some activity.* ☐ *We will busy Randy with cleaning up the garage.*

but for someone or something if it were not for someone or something. ☐ *But for the railing, I'd have fallen down the stairs.* ☐ *But for the children, Mrs. Smith would have left her husband years ago.*

but good severely; thoroughly. ☐ *She told him off but good.* ☐ *Joe beat up Bill but good.*

butt in (on someone or something**)** to interrupt someone or something. ☐ *Pardon me for butting in on your conversation, but this is important.* ☐ *John butted in on Tom and Jane to tell them that the mail had come.*

butt into something to intrude upon something; to break into a conversation. ☐ *Please don't butt into my conversation; I'm on the phone.* ☐ *I don't like my conversations being butted into by perfect strangers!*

the **butt of a joke** the reason for or aim of a joke, especially when it is a person. ☐ *Poor Fred was the butt of every joke told that evening.*

butt out to exit [as abruptly as one has intruded]. (Compare this with butt in (on someone or something). Usually a command.) ☐ *Butt out! Leave me alone!* ☐ *Please butt out of my life!*

butt (up) against someone or something to press against someone or something firmly. ☐ *This board is supposed to butt up against the one over there.* ☐ *The goat butted against Fred, but didn't hurt him.*

butter someone **up**[†] and **butter up to** someone to flatter someone; to treat someone especially nicely in hopes of receiving special favors. (See also **spread** something **on**

thick; soft soap.) □ *A student tried to butter the teacher up.* □ *She buttered up the teacher again.*

Butter wouldn't melt (in someone's **mouth).** *Prov.* Someone is acting as if innocent. □ *By the time her parents came home, Emily had cleaned up all evidence of having broken the valuable figurine, and she looked as though butter wouldn't melt in her mouth.* □ *Jane: How can you suspect George of playing that practical joke on you? He looks so innocent. Jill: Yes, butter wouldn't melt, I'm sure.*

***butterflies in** one's **stomach** a nervous feeling in one's stomach. (*Typically: **get** ~; **have** ~; **give** someone ~.) □ *Whenever I have to speak in public, I get butterflies in my stomach.* □ *She always has butterflies in her stomach before a test.* □ *It was not frightening enough to give me butterflies in my stomach, but it made me a little apprehensive.*

button something **down**[†] to fasten something down with buttons. □ *Button your collar down. You look too casually dressed.* □ *Please button down your collar.*

button something **up**[†] to fasten something with buttons. □ *Button your shirt up, please.* □ *I will button up my shirt.*

button up 1. *Lit.* to fasten one's buttons. □ *Your jacket's open. You'd better button up. It's cold.* □ *I'll button up in the car.* **2.** *Fig.* to get silent and stay silent. (See also **button (up)** one's **lip.**) □ *Hey, button up! That's enough out of you.* □ *I wish you would button up and stop gossiping.*

button (up) one's **lip** *Fig.* to stop talking. (Fixed order.) □ *Please button up your lip!* □ *Will you button your lip? I don't want the news to get out.*

buttress something **up**[†] **1.** *Lit.* to brace something; to provide architectural support for something. □ *We have to buttress up this part of the wall while we work on it.* □ *The workers buttressed the wall up with heavy timbers.* **2.** *Fig.* to provide extra support, often financial support, for something. □ *We rounded up some money to buttress the company up through the sales slump.* □ *The loan buttressed up the company for a few months.*

buy a pig in a poke *Fig.* to buy something without looking inside first. □ *If you don't get a good look at the engine of a used car before you buy it, you'll wind up buying a pig in a poke.* □ *I just took the salesman's word that this camera worked. I guess I bought a pig in a poke.*

buy a round (of drinks) and **buy the next round (of drinks)** to buy a drink for each person present, with the expectation that one or more of those persons will later do likewise. □ *Which one of you guys is going to buy the next round?*

buy in(to something**) 1.** *Lit.* to purchase shares of something; to buy a part of something the ownership of which is shared with other owners. □ *I bought into a company that makes dog food.* □ *Sounds like a good company. I would like to buy in.* **2.** *Fig.* to agree with; to accept an idea as worthwhile. □ *The committee liked my proposal and decided to buy into my plan.* □ *Do you think you can get the whole board to buy in?*

buy it Go to **buy the farm.**

buy one's **way in(to** something**)** to achieve entry or membership in something often by paying money. □ *Do you think you can buy your way into this fraternity?* □ *I'm sure I can buy my way in with my family connections.*

buy one's **way out (of** something**)** to get out of trouble by bribing or influencing someone to ignore what one has done wrong. □ *You can't buy your way out of this mess, buster!* □ *You made this mess and you can't buy your way out!*

buy some food **to go** Go to **to go.**

buy someone **off**[†] to bribe someone to ignore what one is doing wrong. □ *Do you think you can buy her off?* □ *The mobster tried to buy off the jury.*

buy someone or something **out**[†] to purchase full ownership of something from someone or a group. □ *We liked the company, so we borrowed a lot of money and bought it out.* □ *Carl bought out the owners of the company.*

buy someone's **wolf ticket** *Sl.* to challenge someone's boast or taunt. □ *He wants me to buy his wolf ticket bad.* □ *He's such a fighter. He'll buy anybody's wolf ticket.*

buy something *Fig.* to believe something someone says; to accept something to be a fact. □ *It may be true, but I don't buy it.* □ *I just don't buy the idea that you can swim that far.*

buy something **at** something **1.** to purchase something at a particular place or at a particular type of sale, such as a store, an auction, a clearance sale, etc. □ *I bought this table at an auction.* □ *This was bought at an auction.* **2.** to purchase something at a particular price or for a particular level of price. □ *I bought shares in General Motors at forty and a half.* □ *The shares were bought at a good price.*

buy something **back**[†] **(from** someone**)** to repurchase something that one has previously sold from the person who bought it. □ *Can I buy it back from you? I have decided I need it.* □ *He bought back his book from George.*

buy something **for a song** Go to **for a song.**

buy something **(from** someone**) (for** something**)** to purchase something from someone at a particular price, or for a particular type of payment, such as for cash, for practically nothing, etc. □ *I bought the car from Mark for a reasonable price.* □ *I bought it for a reasonable price from Mark.*

buy something **on credit** to purchase something now and pay for it later (normally plus interest). □ *Almost everyone who buys a house buys it on credit.* □ *I didn't have any cash with me, so I used my credit card and bought a new coat on credit.*

buy something **on time** to buy something on credit. □ *Tom: That's an awful fancy TV. Are you sure you can afford it? Jane: I'm buying it on time.* □ *I bought the sofa on time, but I paid cash for the chairs.*

buy something **out**[†] to buy all that is available of a particular item. □ *The kids came in and bought all our bubble gum out.* □ *They bought out the bubble gum in a single hour.*

buy something **sight unseen** to buy something without seeing it first. □ *I bought this land sight unseen. I didn't know it was so rocky.* □ *It isn't usually safe to buy something sight unseen.*

buy something **up**[†] to buy all of something; to buy the entire supply of something. □ *He bought the oranges up from all the groves.* □ *He bought up all the oranges and drove up the price.*

B

buy the big one *Euph.* to die. □ *I don't plan to buy the big one for at least another thirty years.* □ *She conked out for good—you know, bought the big one.*

buy the farm and **buy it** *Sl.* to die; to get killed. (The farm is a burial plot.) □ *I'll pass through this illness; I'm too young to buy the farm.* □ *He lived for a few hours after his collapse, but then he bought it.*

buy the next round (of drinks) Go to buy a round (of drinks).

buy time to postpone an event hoping that the situation will improve. □ *You are just stalling to buy time.* □ *Maybe I can buy some time by asking the judge for a continuance.*

buy trouble *Fig.* to encourage trouble; to bring on trouble. (As if certain acts would pay for or cause difficulties that would have to be suffered through.) □ *I don't want to buy trouble. I have enough already.* □ *Saying something insulting to him is just buying trouble.*

buzz along to move or drive along fast. □ *The cars were buzzing along at a great rate.* □ *Traffic is sure buzzing along.*

buzz for someone to sound a signal for someone. □ *Please buzz for the bell captain.* □ *I buzzed for my secretary and waited for a reply.*

buzz in(to some place**)** *Fig.* to come into a place rapidly or unexpectedly. □ *The child buzzed into the shop and bought a nickel's worth of candy.* □ *I just buzzed in to say hello.*

buzz off *Fig.* to leave quickly. □ *I've got to buzz off. Bye.* □ *It's time for me to buzz off.*

buzz someone **into** a place and **buzz** someone **in**† *Fig.* to push a button that opens a door latch electrically, allowing someone to use the door and enter. (The process creates a buzz while the latch is open.) □ *My secretary will buzz you in.* □ *Please buzz in our guest.* □ *Oh, hello. I will buzz you into the lobby. Then take the elevator to apartment 310.*

buzz with something *Fig.* [for a place] to be busy or filled with something. □ *The room buzzed with excitement.* □ *The office had better be buzzing with moneymaking activity when I get there.*

by a hair('s breadth) and **by a whisker** *Fig.* just barely; by a very small distance. □ *I just missed getting on the plane by a hair's breadth.* □ *I made it onto the last flight by a hair!*

by a mile *Fig.* by a great distance. (Usually an exaggeration.) □ *You missed the target by a mile.* □ *Your estimate of the budget deficit was off by a mile.*

by a show of hands [of a vote taken] expressed by people raising their hands. □ *We were asked to vote for the candidates for captain by a show of hands.* □ *Bob wanted us to vote on paper, not by a show of hands, so that we could have a secret ballot.*

by a whisker Go to by a hair('s breadth).

by all accounts Go to according to all accounts.

by all appearances apparently; according to what one sees or how things seem. □ *She is, by all appearances, ready to resume work.* □ *By all appearances, we ought to be approaching the airport.*

by all means certainly; yes; absolutely. □ *I will attempt to get there by all means.* □ *Bob: Can you come to dinner tomorrow? Jane: By all means. I'd love to.*

by all means of something trying to do something by the use of every possible manner of something. □ *People will be arriving by all means of transportation.* □ *The surgeon performed the operation by all means of instruments.*

by and by at some time in the future; as time passes. □ *The weather's sure to clear up by and by.* □ *You may think your heart is broken, but you'll feel better by and by.*

by and large generally; usually. (Originally a nautical expression.) □ *I find that, by and large, people tend to do what they are told to do.* □ *By and large, rosebushes need lots of care.*

by ankle express *Fig.* on foot. □ *After my horse was stolen, I had to go by ankle express.* □ *It's a five-minute drive, forty minutes by ankle express.*

by any means by any way possible. □ *I need to get there soon by any means.* □ *I must win this contest by any means, fair or unfair.*

by any stretch of the imagination as much as anyone could imagine; as much as is imaginable. (Often negative.) □ *I don't see how anyone by any stretch of the imagination could fail to understand what my last sentence meant.*

by brute strength by great muscular strength. □ *The men moved the heavy door by brute strength.*

by chance accidentally; randomly; without planning. □ *I found this book by chance at a book sale.* □ *We met by chance in a class in college.*

by check by using a check for payment. □ *He paid for the book by check.* □ *You will be paid by check.*

by choice due to conscious choice; on purpose. □ *I do this kind of thing by choice. No one makes me do it.* □ *I didn't go to this college by choice. It was the closest one to home.*

by coincidence by an accidental and strange similarity; by an unplanned pairing of events or occurrences. □ *We just happened to be in the same place at the same time by coincidence.* □ *By coincidence, the circus was in town when I was there. I'm glad because I love circuses.*

By cracky! *Rur.* By God! (A mild oath, often used to express surprise or approval.) □ *Jim said he'd get the whole house painted this weekend, and by cracky, that's just what he did.* □ *By cracky! That thunder sure was loud.*

by day and **by night** during the day; during the night. (Often used in simultaneous clauses for contrast.) □ *By day, Mary worked in an office; by night, she took classes.* □ *Dave slept by day and worked by night.*

by dint of something because of something; due to the efforts of something. (*Dint* is an old word meaning 'force,' and it is never used except in this phrase.) □ *They got the building finished on time by dint of hard work and good organization.* □ *By dint of much studying, John got through college.*

by fits and starts Go to fits and starts.

by force of habit owing to a tendency to do something that has become a habit. □ *After I retired, I kept getting up and getting dressed each morning by force of habit.*

By godfrey! By God! (A mild oath.) □ *By godfrey, Jim's brother is a big man!* □ *Those cats sure do make a lot of noise, by godfrey.*

by guess and by golly Go to next.

by guess and by gosh and **by guess and by golly** *Rur.* by estimating; without careful planning. □ *Jane: Did you have a plan for putting up that toolshed? Tom: Nope, we just sort of did it by guess and by gosh.* □ *Grandma always made dresses by guess and by golly, without using a pattern, and they always turned out just fine.*

by hand made by human hands and handheld tools as opposed to a machine. □ *This fine wooden cabinet was made by hand.* □ *I carved this figurine by hand.*

by herself and **by himself 1.** with no one else present; alone. □ *She hates to go to strange places by herself.* □ *He sat by himself at a table big enough for six people.* **2.** with the help of no one else. □ *The two-year-old boy can get dressed by himself.* □ *Susan is unable to get there by herself.*

by hook or (by) crook by any means, legal or illegal. □ *I'll get the job done by hook or by crook.* □ *I must have that house. I intend to get it by hook or crook.*

by itself with the help of nothing else; without the addition of anything else. □ *Will this food be enough by itself for all of us?* □ *Can the dog get out of the house by itself?*

by leaps and bounds *Fig.* rapidly; by large movements forward. □ *The brush we cut back last fall is growing by leaps and bounds.* □ *The profits of my company are increasing by leaps and bounds.* □ *He is gaining by leaps and bounds.*

by main strength and awkwardness *Rur.* by force or brute strength. □ *Tom: How did you get that piano up the stairs? Mary: By main strength and awkwardness.* □ *By main strength and awkwardness, we got all the luggage crammed into the car.*

by means of something using something; with the use of something. □ *I opened the bottle by means of a bottle opener.* □ *I was able to afford a car by means of a loan.*

by mistake in error; accidentally. □ *I'm sorry. I came into the wrong room by mistake.* □ *I chose the wrong road by mistake. Now we are lost.*

by myself 1. with no one else present; alone. □ *I sat at the table by myself.* □ *I will not be at the party. I will be at home by myself tonight.* **2.** without the help of anyone else. □ *I did it all by myself.* □ *Can you eat that whole pie by yourself?*

by night Go to by day.

by no means absolutely not; certainly not. □ *I'm by no means angry with you.* □ *Bob: Did you put this box here? Tom: By no means. I didn't do it, I'm sure.*

by oneself 1. with no one else present; alone (of two or more people). □ *Must one sit by oneself or may one join another group?* □ *One just hates eating by oneself, doesn't one?* **2.** with the help of no one else. □ *One is expected to do it by oneself.* □ *Can one do this by oneself?*

by ourselves 1. with no one else present; alone. □ *Do we have to sit here by ourselves? Can't we sit with Mary and Max?* □ *We like to eat by ourselves, so we can talk about private matters.* **2.** with the help of no one else. □ *We can do it by ourselves.* □ *Can we lift this by ourselves, or do we need some help?*

by return mail and **by return post** by a subsequent mailing (back to the sender). (A phrase indicating that an answer is expected very soon, by mail.) □ *Since this bill is overdue, would you kindly send us your check by return mail?* □ *I answered your request by return post over a year ago. Please check your records.*

by return post Go to previous.

by rote [of learning or memorizing] done as habit and without thinking. □ *I simply memorized the speech by rote. I don't know what it means.* □ *The student learns everything by rote and doesn't really understand the concepts.*

by shank's mare *Fig.* by foot; by walking. (*Shank* refers to the shank of the leg.) □ *My car isn't working, so I'll have to travel by shank's mare.* □ *I'm sore because I've been getting around by shank's mare.*

*by the book and ***by the numbers** following the rules exactly. (Alludes to a (numbered) book of rules. *Typically: go ~; do something ~; play ~; run something ~.*) □ *The judge of the contest ran things strictly by the rules and disqualified us on a small technicality.* □ *Everyone insisted that we go by the numbers and not accept the proposal.*

by the by Go to by the way.

by the day one day at a time. □ *I don't know when I'll have to leave town, so I rent this room by the day.*

by the dozen in groups of 12. (Compare this with **by the dozens.**) □ *Eggs are normally sold by the dozen.*

by the dozens *Fig.* many; by some fairly large, indefinite number. (Similar to but implying less than *hundreds*. Compare this with **by the dozen.**) □ *Just then people began showing up by the dozens.* □ *I baked cookies and pies by the dozens for the charity bake sale.*

by the end of the day by the time when the workday is over; by the time that the sun goes down. □ *Will this task be completed by the end of the day?* □ *We have to do all these things by the end of the day.*

by the handful in amounts equal to a handful; in quantity. □ *Billy is eating candy by the handful.* □ *People began leaving by the handful at midnight.*

by the hour at each hour; once each hour. □ *It kept growing darker by the hour.* □ *I have to take this medicine by the hour.*

by the month one month at a time. □ *Not many apartments are rented by the month.* □ *I needed a car for a short while, so I rented one by the month.*

by the nape of the neck by the back of the neck. (Mostly said in threats.) □ *He grabbed me by the nape of the neck and told me not to turn around if I valued my life. I stood very still.* □ *If you do that again, I'll pick you up by the nape of the neck and throw you out the door.*

by the numbers Go to by the book.

by the same token *Cliché* a phrase indicating that the speaker is introducing parallel or closely contrasting information. □ *Tom: I really got cheated! Bob: You think they've cheated you, but, by the same token, they believe that you've cheated them.* □ *Some say he is a real charmer, but by the same token others are put off by his manner.*

*by the seat of one's **pants** Fig. by sheer luck and use of intuition. (*Typically: **fly ~; make it ~**.) □ *I got through school by the seat of my pants.* □ *Pilots who are in fog and using only instruments are flying by the seat of their pants.*

by the skin of one's **teeth** Fig. just barely. (By an amount equal to the thickness of the (imaginary) skin on one's teeth.) □ *I got through calculus class by the skin of my teeth.* □ *I got to the airport a few minutes late and missed the plane by the skin of my teeth.* □ *Lloyd escaped from the burning building by the skin of his teeth.*

by the sweat of one's **brow** Fig. by one's efforts; by one's hard work. □ *Tom raised these vegetables by the sweat of his brow.* □ *Sally polished the car by the sweat of her brow.*

by the unit Fig. each; per. (Used to designate the unit of measure, but not the rate of a measure.) □ *Lettuce is sold by the head.* □ *Gas is sold by the gallon.*

by the way and **by the by 1.** a phrase indicating that the speaker is adding information. (*By the by* is not as frequent.) □ *Tom: Is this one any good? Clerk: This is the largest and, by the way, the most expensive one we have in stock.* □ *Bill: I'm a realtor. Is your house for sale? Alice: My house is not for sale, and, by the way, I too am a realtor.* **2.** a phrase indicating that the speaker is casually opening a new subject. □ *Bill: Oh, by the way, Fred, do you still have that hammer you borrowed from me? Fred: I'll check. I thought I gave it back.* □ *Jane: By the by, don't you owe me some money? Sue: Who, me?*

by the week one week at a time. □ *I plan my schedules by the week.* □ *Where can I rent a room by the week?*

by the year one year at a time. □ *Most apartments are available by the year.* □ *We budget by the year.*

by themselves 1. with help from no one else. □ *Do you think they can do it by themselves?* □ *Mike and Max cannot lift the piano by themselves.* **2.** with no one else present; alone (of two or more people). □ *They are sitting there by themselves. Let's sit with them.* □ *They enjoy spending the evening at home by themselves.*

by virtue of something because of something; due to something. □ *She's permitted to vote by virtue of her age.* □ *They are members of the club by virtue of their great wealth.*

by way of something 1. passing through something (as a place); via something. □ *He came home by way of Toledo.* □ *She went to the bank by way of the drugstore.* **2.** in illustration; as an example. □ *By way of illustration, the professor drew a picture on the board.* □ *He read them a passage from Shakespeare by way of example.*

by word of mouth by speaking rather than writing. □ *I learned about it by word of mouth.* □ *I need it in writing. I don't trust things I hear about by word of mouth.*

by yourself 1. with no one else present; alone. □ *Do you want to sit here by yourself, or can I sit here too?* □ *Don't sit at home by yourself. Come to the movie with me.* **2.** with the help of no one else. □ *Can you really do all this cooking by yourself?* □ *Bill, can you lift this box by yourself?*

by yourselves 1. with no one else present; alone (of two or more people). □ *Are you two going to stand here by yourselves all evening?* □ *Don't sit home by yourselves. Come to the party.* **2.** with the help of no one else. □ *Can you three do this by yourselves?* □ *I expect you guys to get there by yourselves.*

Bye for now. Go to **Good-bye for now.**

cadge something **from** someone and **cadge** something **off** someone *Sl.* to beg or borrow something from someone. □ *Go cadge some sugar from the lady next door.* □ *I cadged this jacket off a friendly guy I met.*

Caesar's wife must be above suspicion. *Prov.* The associates of public figures must not even be suspected of wrongdoing. (The ancient Roman Julius Caesar is supposed to have said this when asked why he divorced his wife, Pompeia. Because she was suspected of some wrongdoing, he could not associate with her anymore.) □ *Jill: I don't think the mayor is trustworthy; his brother was charged with embezzlement. Jane: But the charges were never proved. Jill: That doesn't matter. Caesar's wife must be above suspicion.* □ *When the newspapers reported the rumor that the lieutenant governor had failed to pay his taxes, the governor forced him to resign, saying, "Caesar's wife must be above suspicion."*

cage someone or something **in**[†] **1.** *Lit.* to enclose someone or something in a cage. □ *We caged the monkey in, but it threw a fit.* □ *We are going to have to cage in the dogs.* **2.** *Fig.* to confine someone or something. □ *Please don't cage me in this tiny room!* □ *The health authorities virtually caged in the quarantined population until they could all be tested.*

cage someone or something **up**[†] **(in** something**)** to enclose or confine someone or something in something or someplace. □ *They caged the lions up in strong containers for the trip across country.* □ *How long did it take to cage up the lions securely?*

cajole someone **into** something to coax or persuade someone to do something. □ *They tried to cajole us into helping them move.* □ *You can't cajole me into doing that!*

cajole someone **out of** something **1.** to coax or persuade someone not to do something. □ *Try and cajole her out of going there.* □ *I cajoled her out of leaving so soon.* **2.** to coax or persuade someone to give up something or give away something. □ *She tried to cajole him out of his inheritance.*

cake someone or something **with** something to cover someone or something with a thicker layer of clumps of a substance such as mud, dirt, blood, etc. □ *The attendant caked her with hot mud at the beginning of the arthritis treatment.* □ *All the motocross racers were heavily caked with mud.* □ *She caked herself with green mud to remove her wrinkles.*

calculate on something *Rur.* to think about or plan on something. □ *Let me calculate on this a little bit.* □ *He's busy calculating on a serious problem.*

calculate something **into** something and **calculate** something **in**[†] to include something in one's calculations. □ *Did you calculate the cost of the cake into the total?* □ *Yes, I calculated in all the costs.*

call a halt to something to demand that something be stopped. □ *We must call a halt to this childish behavior.* □ *The manager called a halt to all overtime.*

call a meeting to ask that people assemble for a meeting; to request that a meeting be held. □ *The mayor called a meeting to discuss the problem.* □ *I'll be calling a meeting of the library board to discuss the new building project.*

call a meeting to order and **call the meeting to order** to announce that a meeting is about to begin. □

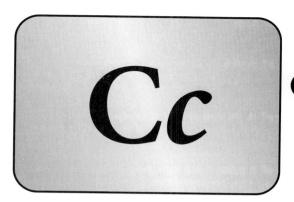

The chair called the meeting to order. □ *The meeting will be called to order at noon.*

call a spade a spade *Fig.* to call something by its right name; to speak frankly about something, even if it is unpleasant. (Considered offensive by some. Use only with discretion.) □ *Well, I believe it's time to call a spade a spade. We are just avoiding the issue.* □ *Let's call a spade a spade. The man is a liar.*

Call again. Please visit this shop again sometime. (Said by shopkeepers and store clerks.) □ *"Thank you," said the clerk, smiling, "Call again."* □ *Clerk: Is that everything? John: Yes. Clerk: That's ten dollars even. John: Here you are. Clerk: Thanks. Call again.*

call (all) the shots to decide on the course of action; to be in charge. □ *Why do you have to call all the shots?* □ *Do what you're told. I'll call the shots.*

call around (about someone or something**)** to telephone a number of different people in succession about something. □ *I'll call around about Tom and see if I can find out anything.*

call at some place to visit some place; [for a ship] to put into port at a place. □ *I called at the druggist's for some medicine.* □ *Our ship will call at seven ports during the voyage.*

call attention to someone or something to cause someone, including oneself, or something to be noticed or observed. □ *I think he dresses like that simply to call attention to himself.*

call back 1. to call [someone] again on the telephone at a later time. □ *Call back later, please.* □ *I will call back when you are not so busy.* **2.** to return a telephone call received earlier. □ *The note says I am to call back. What did you want?* □ *This is Bill Wilson calling back.*

call for someone or something **1.** to need, require, or demand something or the services of someone. □ *The recipe calls for two cups of flour.* □ *This job calls for someone with experience.* **2.** to arrive to collect or pick up a person or a thing. (Used especially when you are to pick someone up and are acting as an escort.) □ *I will call for you about eight this evening.* □ *The messenger will call for your reply in the morning.* **3.** to shout for or request someone or something. □ *I called for Ted, but he didn't hear me.* □ *I stood on the porch and called for the dog.*

call hogs *Rur.* to snore. □ *I couldn't sleep at all last night, with Cousin Joe calling hogs in the next room.* □ *Joe calls hogs so loud the windows rattle.*

call in sick to call one's place of work to say that one is ill and cannot come to work. (See also **report in sick**.) □ *Four of our office staff called in sick today.* □ *I have to call in sick today.*

call in (to some place**)** to telephone to some central place, such as one's place of work, as to check for messages. □ *I have to call in to the office at noon.* □ *I will call in whenever I have a chance.*

call it a day to quit work and go home; to say that a day's work has been completed. □ *I'm tired. Let's call it a day.* □ *The boss was mad because Tom called it a day at noon and went home.*

call it a night to end what one is doing at night and go [home] to bed. □ *At midnight, I called it a night and went to bed.* □ *Guest after guest called it a night, and at last we were alone.*

call it quits to quit; to resign from something; to announce that one is quitting. □ *Okay! I've had enough! I'm calling it quits.* □ *Time to go home, John. Let's call it quits.*

Call my service. Please don't call me directly, but through my answering service. (Not a friendly or encouraging invitation.) □ *Good to talk to you, but I gotta go now. Call my service.* □ *I can't talk now. Call my service.*

Call no man happy till he dies. and **Count no man happy till he dies.** *Prov.* You cannot tell if a person's life has been happy on the whole until that person's life is over; no matter how happy someone is now, something bad may happen to destroy his or her happiness. □ *Alan: You must be very happy with your new wife. Bill: Call no man happy till he dies.* □ *Jill: That movie star must be the happiest person in the world. He's rich, people love him, and he likes his work. Jane: Count no man happy till he dies.*

the **call of nature** *Euph.* the need to go to the lavatory. □ *Stop the car here! I have to answer the call of nature.* □ *There was no break in the agenda, not even for the call of nature.*

call on someone to court someone. □ *Jim's calling on the new cook over at the Browns'.* □ *In the old days, a boy had to ask a girl's father for permission to come call on her.*

call on something *Fig.* to draw on something, such as a particular quality or talent. □ *This project calls on all the creative skills you can gather together.* □ *It calls on everything you've got.*

call out (to someone**)** to speak loudly to get someone's attention. □ *Mike called out to Tom that there was a telephone call for him.* □ *I heard someone call out, but I could see no one.*

call someone **about** something to call someone on the telephone, seeking information about someone or something. □ *I'll call Maggie about Ted and see what she knows.* □ *Let me call the manager about this.*

call someone **away**[†] **(from** something**)** to ask someone to come away from some place or from doing something. □ *The boss called Kathy away from her office.* □ *The principal called away the teacher from the classroom.* □ *Why did you call Kathy away?*

call someone **back**[†] **1.** to call someone again on the telephone. □ *Since she is not there, I will call her back in half an hour.* □ *Carl called back Mary after his meeting was over.* **2.** to return a telephone call to a person who had called earlier. □ *I got his message; I will call him back tomorrow.* □ *I have to call back my friend now.* **3.** Go to **call** someone or something **back**.

call someone **by a name** to address someone by a particular kind of name. □ *They call me by my first name.* □ *Don't call me by my nickname!*

call someone **down**[†] to reprimand a person; to bawl someone out. □ *The teacher had to call down Sally in front of everybody.* □ *"I wish you wouldn't call me down in public," cried Sally.*

call someone **forth**[†] to call to someone to come out or come forward. □ *The principal called Wally forth.* □ *Please call forth Wally again.*

call someone **forward** to call to someone to come to the front, and to the attention of everyone present. □ *The teacher called the student forward to recite.* □ *Don't call me forward. I am not prepared.*

call someone **in**[†] **(for** something**) 1.** to request that someone come to have a talk. □ *The manager called Karen in for a private meeting.* □ *The police called in Gary for questioning.* **2.** to request a consultation with a specialist in some field. (The person called probably will not "come in," but will work at another place.) □ *We will have to call a heart specialist in for a consultation.* □ *We called in another specialist for an opinion.*

call someone **names** to call someone by an abusive or insulting name. □ *Billy cried when the other kids called him names.* □ *John was punished for calling his teacher names.*

call someone **on the carpet** and **haul** someone **on the carpet** *Fig.* to reprimand a person. (When done by someone of clear superiority. Haul is stronger than *call*.) □ *One more error like that and the big boss will call you on the carpet.* □ *I'm sorry it went wrong. I really hope the regional manager doesn't call me on the carpet again.*

call someone or an animal **off** someone or something and **call** someone or an animal **off**[†] to request that someone or an animal stop bothering or pursuing someone or something; to call a halt to an attack by someone or an animal. □ *Please call your dogs off my brother.* □ *Call off your spying on me, or else!*

call someone or something **back**[†] to call out that someone or something should come back. □ *As she left, the clerk called her back.* □ *The clerk called back the customer.*

call someone or something **in**[†] **1.** to call on the special talents, abilities, or power of someone or something. □ *They had to call a new doctor in.* □ *Yes, they had to call in a specialist.* **2.** Go to **call** someone or something **into** something.

call someone or something **into question** to cause someone or something to be evaluated; to examine or reexamine the qualifications or value of someone or something. □ *Because of her poor record, we were forced to call Dr. Jones into question.* □ *We called Dr. Jones's qualifications into question.*

call someone or something **into** something and **call** someone or something **in**[†] to call to a person or a pet to come into something or some place. □ *Would you please call Jeff into the house?* □ *Please call in Jeff.*

call someone or something **out**† to request the services of someone or a group. (See also **call** someone **up**; **call** someone **out**.) □ *Things got bad enough that the governor called the militia out.* □ *The governor called out the militia.*

call someone or something **up**† to call someone, a group, or a company on the telephone. □ *I will call them up and see what they have to say.* □ *Please call up the supplier.*

call someone **out**† to challenge someone to a fight. □ *Wilbur wanted to call him out, but thought better of it.* □ *Why did you call out that guy? He used to be a prizefighter!*

call someone **over (to** some place**)** to request that someone come to where one is. □ *I will call her over to us, and you can ask her what you want to know.* □ *Call over the waitress so we can order.* □ *I called Ted over.*

call someone's **attention to** something and **call** something **to** someone's **attention** to bring something to someone's notice; to make someone recognize some fact. □ *May I call your attention to the sign on the door?* □ *He called to our attention the notice on the wall.*

call someone's **bluff** to demand that someone prove a claim or is not being deceptive. □ *All right, I'll call your bluff. Show me you can do it!* □ *Tom said, "You've made me really angry, and I'll punch you if you come any closer!" "Go ahead," said Bill, calling his bluff.*

call someone **to account** to ask one to explain and justify one's behavior, policy, performance, etc. □ *The sergeant called the police officer to account.* □ *I called my workers to account for the accident.*

call someone **to attention** to demand that someone assume the formal military stance of attention. □ *The officer called the platoon to attention.* □ *The sergeant called us to attention.*

call someone **together** to request that people come together for a meeting. □ *Please call everyone together and we'll discuss this.* □ *I called all the players together.*

call someone **up**† to request that someone or a group report for active military service. (See also **call** someone or something **out**.) □ *The government called the reserve units up for active service.* □ *They called up another battalion.*

call something **(back) in** and **call** something **in**† to formally request (usually by mail) that something be returned. □ *The car company called many cars back in for repairs.* □ *They called in a lot of cars.*

call something **down**† **(on** someone**)** *Fig.* to invoke some sort of divine punishment onto someone. □ *The preacher sounded as though he was calling down the wrath of God on us.* □ *Moses called down a plague on the Pharoah.*

call something **down**† **(to** someone**)** to shout something to a person on a lower level. □ *The worker called a warning down to the people below.* □ *She called down a warning to them.*

call something **forth**† [for an event] to draw a particular quality or induce a particular behavior. □ *The battle called extraordinary courage forth from the soldiers.* □ *It called forth great courage.*

call something **in**† Go to **call** something **(back) in**.

call something **off**† to cancel an event. □ *It's too late to call the party off. The first guests have already arrived.* □ *Because of rain, they called off the baseball game.*

call something **out**† **1.** to draw on something, such as a particular quality or talent. □ *It's times like these that call the best out in us.* □ *These times call out our best effort.* **2.** to shout out something. □ *Who called the warning out?* □ *You should call out a warning to those behind you on the trail.*

call something **square** to pronounce a debt or obligation to have been paid, balanced, or ended. □ *Thanks for the hundred bucks. I think we can call it square now.*

call something **to mind** and **bring** something **to mind** to bring something into someone's mind; to cause something to be remembered. □ *Your comment calls something unpleasant to mind.* □ *This photo album calls our vacation to mind.*

call something **to** someone's **attention** Go to **call** someone's **attention to** something.

call something **up**† to summon information from a computer. □ *John used his laptop to call the information up.* □ *With a few strokes on the computer keyboard, Sally called up the figures she was looking for.*

call the dogs off† **1.** *Lit.* to order hunting or watch dogs to abandon their quarry. □ *They robber gave up and the guard called the dogs off.* □ *Call off the dogs!* **2.** *Fig.* to stop threatening, chasing, or hounding [a person]. □ *Tell the sheriff to call off the dogs. We caught the robber.* □ *Okay, you've caught me! Please call your dogs off!*

call the meeting to order Go to **call a meeting to order**.

call (the) roll and **take (the) roll** to call the names of people from a list of those enrolled, expecting them to reply if they are present. □ *After I call the roll, please open your books to page 12.* □ *I will take roll, and then we will do arithmetic.*

call the shots and **call the tune** *Fig.* to make the decisions; to decide what is to be done. □ *Sally always wants to call the shots, and Mary doesn't like to be bossed around. They don't get along well.* □ *Sally always wants to call the tune.*

call the tune Go to previous.

call to someone to shout to get someone's attention. □ *I called to Fred, but he didn't hear me.* □ *Did you hear me call to you?*

call (up)on someone **1.** to visit someone. (*Upon* is formal and less commonly used than *on*.) □ *My mother's friends call upon her every Wednesday.* □ *Let's call on Mrs. Franklin this afternoon.* **2.** to choose someone to respond, as in a classroom. □ *The teacher called upon me, but I was not ready to recite.* □ *Please don't call on me. I can't remember a thing.*

call (up)on someone **(for** something**)** to choose someone to do or to help with some particular task. (*Upon* is formal and less commonly used than *on*.) □ *Can I call upon you for help?* □ *You can call on me at any time.*

call (up)on someone **(to** do something**)** to choose someone to do something. (*Upon* is formal and less commonly used than *on*.) □ *I call upon all of you to make your feelings* *known to your elected representatives.* □ *I called on George for his help, but he refused.*

called to straw *Rur.* about to begin labor and childbirth. □ *Susan was called to straw when she was only seven months along.* □ *Nancy's nine months pregnant and could be called to straw any day now.*

the **calm before the storm** Go to the lull before the storm.

calm down to relax; to become less busy or active. □ *Now, now, calm down. You look so nervous.* □ *Please calm down. Nothing bad is going to happen.*

calm someone or an animal **down**† to cause someone or an animal to be less active, upset, or unsettled. □ *Please try to calm yourself down!* □ *Can you calm down your yapping dog?*

camp in the boondocks Go to in the boondocks.

camp in the boonies Go to in the boondocks.

camp it up [for performers] to overact or behave in an affected manner. □ *The cast began to camp it up in the second act, and the critics walked out. (Fixed order.)* □ *There is no need to camp it up. Play it the way it was written.*

camp out to live out of doors temporarily in a tent or camping vehicle, as on a vacation or special camping trip. □ *I love to camp out in the winter.*

campaign against someone or something **1.** to crusade or battle against someone or something. □ *Currently, I am campaigning against littering.* □ *Sarah is campaigning against crooked politicians.* **2.** to run one's political campaign against someone or something. □ *I campaigned against the incumbent and won.* □ *John spent a lot of time campaigning against Sarah for class president.*

campaign for someone or something to support actively someone or someone's candidacy for political office. □ *I would be very happy to campaign for you.* □ *I want to campaign for the winning candidate.*

Can do. I can definitely do it. (The opposite of No can do.) □ *Jane: Will you be able to get this finished by quitting time today? Alice: Can do. Leave it to me.* □ *Bob: Can you get this pack of papers over to the lawyer's office by noon? Bill: Can do. I'm leaving now. Bye.*

Can I help you? Go to Could I help you?

Can I leave a message? Go to Could I leave a message?

Can I see you again? Go to Could I see you again?

Can I see you in my office? Go to Could I see you in my office?

Can I speak to someone? Go to Could I speak to someone?

Can I take a message? Go to Could I take a message?

Can I take your order (now)? Go to Could I take your order (now)?

Can I tell her who's calling? Go to Could I tell him who's calling?

Can I use your powder room? Go to Could I use your powder room?

Can it! Shut up! □ *I've heard enough of your arguing. Can it!* □ *That's enough complaining from you! Can it!*

can (just) whistle for something *Fig.* can just forget about having something. □ *The last time Mary came over for dinner, she was downright rude. If she wants dinner at my house again, she can just whistle for it!* □ *I asked the boss for a promotion. He told me I could whistle for it.*

a **can of worms *Fig.* a very difficult issue or set of problems; an array of difficulties. (*Typically:* **be ~; open ~** .) □ *This political scandal is a real can of worms.* □ *Let's not open that can of worms!*

can take it to the bank *Fig.* able to depend on the truthfulness of my statement: it is not counterfeit or bogus; to be able to **bank on** something. □ *Believe me. What I am telling you is the truth. You can take it to the bank.* □ *This information is as good as gold. You can take it to the bank.*

Can we continue this later? Go to Could we continue this later?

Can you excuse us, please? Go to Could you excuse us, please?

Can you hold? Go to Could you hold?

Can you imagine? Can you believe that?; Imagine that! □ *She wore jeans to the wedding. Can you imagine?* □ *Billy was eating the houseplant! Can you imagine?*

Can you keep a secret? Go to Could you keep a secret?

cancel each other out† [for the opposite effects of two things] to balance each other. □ *The cost of the meal you bought and what I owed you cancel each other out, so we're even.* □ *They canceled out each other.*

cancel out (of something**)** to withdraw from something. □ *I hate to cancel out of the event at the last minute, but this is an emergency.* □ *It's too late to cancel out.*

cancel someone **out**† Go to next.

cancel someone **out of** something and **cancel** someone **out**† **1.** to eliminate someone from something (as from a list of names). □ *We had to cancel them out.* □ *We canceled out all the people who did not show up.* **2.** *Sl.* to eliminate someone; to kill someone. □ *The drug lord threatened to cancel out his former partner for testifying against him.*

cancel someone's **Christmas** *Sl.* to kill someone; to destroy someone. (Underworld or jocular; the idea is that the dead person will not live until Christmas.) □ *If he keeps bugging me, I'm gonna cancel his Christmas.* □ *Willie threatened to cancel Richard's Christmas if Richard didn't pay up.*

cancel something **out**† to balance the effects of something. □ *Sending flowers might cancel the bad feelings out.* □ *The last payment canceled out the debt.*

a **candidate for a pair of wings *Euph.* someone who is likely to die; someone who is close to death. (Jocular. *Typically:* **be ~; look like ~** .) □ *Whenever Jane wants to cross the street, she just walks out into traffic without looking. She's a candidate for a pair of wings, I say.* □ *Tom: How's Bill doing? I heard he was sick. Jane: Not good, I'm afraid. He looks like a candidate for a pair of wings.*

cannot See the expressions listed at **can't** and also those at not able.

cannot carry a tune Go to can't carry a tune.

cannot help doing something not able to refrain from doing something; not able not to do something. □ *Anne is such a good cook, I can't help eating everything she serves.* □ *Since John loves to shop, he can't help spending money.*

cannot see (any) further than the end of one's **nose** Go to see no further than the end of one's nose.

cannot see the forest for the trees Go to next.

cannot see the wood for the trees and **cannot see the forest for the trees** *Prov.* Cannot perceive the overview or important things because of concentrating too much on details. □ *The information presented in this textbook is so disorganized that I can't see the wood for the trees.* □ *The politician's opponents claimed that she couldn't see the forest for the trees, because she spent so much time trying to solve minor problems.*

cannot stomach someone or something Go to not able to stomach someone or something.

[can't] See the expressions listed at **not able**, as well as those listed below.

can't call one's **soul** one's **own** *Fig.* working for other people all the time. □ *Jane has to work two jobs and take care of both her aging parents. She can't call her soul her own.* □ *Between supporting his family and working off his brother's bad debts, Bob really can't call his soul his own.*

can't carry a tune and **cannot carry a tune; can't carry a tune in a bushel basket; can't carry a tune in a bucket; can't carry a tune in a paper sack** *Fig.* [to be] unable to sing a simple melody; lacking musical ability. □ *I wish that Tom wouldn't try to sing. He can't carry a tune.* □ *I don't know why Mary's in the choir. She can't carry a tune in a bushel basket.* □ *Joe likes to sing in the shower, though he can't carry a tune in a bucket.* □ *I'd try to hum the song for you, but I can't carry a tune in a paper sack.*

can't carry a tune in a bucket Go to previous.

can't carry a tune in a bushel basket Go to can't carry a tune.

can't carry a tune in a paper sack Go to can't carry a tune.

can't do anything with someone or something not [to be] able to manage or control someone or something. (Also with *cannot.*) □ *Bill is such a discipline problem. I can't do anything with him.* □ *My hair is such a mess. I just can't do anything with it.*

can't find one's **butt with both hands (in broad daylight)** *Sl.* is stupid or incompetent. (Use caution with *butt*, which is often considered crude.) □ *Why did they put Jim in charge? He can't find his butt with both hands!* □ *Tom: Jane seems like a bright girl. Bill: You've got to be kidding! She couldn't find her butt with both hands in broad daylight!*

can't hack it unable to do the job. □ *I thought delivering papers would be an easy job, but I just can't hack it.* □ *If you can't hack it, let me know, and I'll help you out.*

can't help but do something [to be] unable to choose any but one course of action. (Also with *cannot.*) □ *Her parents live nearby, so she can't help but go there on holidays.* □ *Bob is a tennis fan and can't help but travel to Wimbledon each year.*

can't hit the (broad) side of a barn *Rur.* cannot aim something accurately. □ *You're way off. You couldn't hit the broad side of a barn.* □ *Please don't try to throw the paper into the wastebasket. You can't hit the side of a barn.*

can't hold a candle to someone *Fig.* not [to be] equal to someone; unable to measure up to someone. (Also with *cannot.*) □ *Mary can't hold a candle to Ann when it comes to athletics.* □ *As for singing, John can't hold a candle to Jane.*

can't make heads or tails (out) of someone or something *Fig.* [to be] unable to understand someone or something. (Also with *cannot.*) □ *John is so strange. I can't make heads or tails of him.* □ *Do this report again. I can't make heads or tails out of it.*

Can't say (a)s I do(, can't say (a)s I don't). *Rur.* I am not sure. □ *Tom: Do you know Mr. Smith? Mary: Well, I can't say as I do, can't say as I don't.* □ *Jane: What do you think of my cousin? Do you like him? Mary: Can't say's I do, can't say's I don't.*

can't say boo to a goose *Rur.* shy and not talkative. □ *I was surprised to see Joe so talkative at the party. Usually he can't say boo to a goose.* □ *She's a quiet little kid. Can't say boo to a goose.*

can't see a hole in a ladder stupid or drunk. □ *No use asking her questions. She can't see a hole in a ladder.* □ *After the big party, Joe needed someone to drive him home. He couldn't see a hole in a ladder.*

can't see beyond the end of one's **nose** Go to see no further than the end of one's nose.

can't see one's **hand in front of** one's **face** *Fig.* [to be] unable to see very far, usually due to darkness or fog. (Also with *cannot.*) □ *It was so dark that I couldn't see my hand in front of my face.* □ *Bob said that the fog was so thick he couldn't see his hand in front of his face.*

can't see straight *Fig.* cannot function (often because of strong emotion). □ *I am so mad I can't see straight.* □ *She left me so frustrated that I couldn't see straight.*

can't stand (the sight of) someone or something and **can't stomach** someone or something *Fig.* [to be] unable to tolerate someone or something; disliking someone or something extremely. (Also with *cannot.*) □ *I can't stand the sight of cooked carrots.* □ *Mr. Jones can't stomach the sight of blood.* □ *None of us can stand this place.* □ *Nobody can stand Tom when he smokes a cigar.*

can't stomach someone or something Go to previous.

can't wait (for something **(to** happen**))** to be very eager, as if to be unable to endure the wait for something to happen. □ *I am so eager for my birthday to come. I just can't wait.*

can't wait (to do something**)** to be very eager, as if to be unable to endure the wait until it is possible to do something. □ *I'm glad it's almost summertime—I just can't wait to go swimming!*

cap and gown the academic cap or mortarboard and the robe worn in formal academic ceremonies. □ *We all had to rent cap and gown for graduation.* □ *I appeared wearing my cap and gown, but I had shorts on underneath because it gets so hot at that time of year.*

capable of doing something having the ability to do something. □ *Do you think Tom is capable of lifting 200 pounds?* □ *No one I know is capable of such a crime!*

capitalize on something *Fig.* to build on something; to exploit something, such as an opportunity of talent, to one's own benefit. □ *Let's try to capitalize on the strength of the economy and invest for the future.* □ *Capitalize on your experience in the field and you'll do well in the interview.*

capitulate to someone or something to surrender or submit to someone or something. □ *The general finally capitulated to the enemy.* □ *I won't capitulate in this argument.*

captain of industry *Fig.* a high-ranking corporation officer; a wealthy and successful capitalist. □ *The captains of industry manage to hang on to their money no matter what.* □ *It's fun to see those captains of industry drive up in their limousines.*

capture someone's **imagination** *Fig.* to intrigue someone; to interest someone in a lasting way; to stimulate someone's imagination. □ *The story of the young wizard has captured the imagination of the world's children.*

***a card** *Fig.* an entertaining and clever person who says or does funny things. (*Typically: **act like** ~; **be** ~.) □ *He is such a card. Always making jokes.* □ *Mary is a card, and she has to learn to take things seriously sometimes.*

card-carrying member *Fig.* an official member of some group, originally, the communist party. □ *Bill is a card-carrying member of the electricians union.*

the **cards are stacked against** one [informal] luck is against one. (See also **stack the deck (against** someone or something).) □ *I have the worst luck. The cards are stacked against me all the time.* □ *How can I accomplish anything when the cards are stacked against me?*

care about someone or something **1.** to hold someone or something dear; to prize someone or something. □ *I really care about you.* □ *I care very much about my family.* **2.** to have even minimal regard for someone or something. (Does not imply any of the tender feelings expressed in ①.) □ *Don't you care about animals?* □ *I care about what happens in Washington.*

care for someone to feel tenderly toward someone; to love someone. □ *I care for you a great deal, Walter.* □ *I care for you too, Alice.*

care for someone or something to take care of someone or something. □ *Will you care for my cat while I am away?* □ *I would be happy to care for your child.*

care for something to like the taste of some kind of food or drink. (Usually used with a negative.) □ *I don't care for sweet potatoes.* □ *I don't care for sweet desserts.*

care nothing about someone or something to have no regard or respect for someone or something. □ *You have hurt me with your insults. I care nothing about you!* □ *She cares nothing about your money!*

care nothing for someone or something not to like someone or something. □ *She cares nothing for your suggestion.* □ *Sarah cares nothing for Jeff.*

care to do something to want to do something; to be willing to do something. □ *I really don't care to see that movie.* □ *Would you care to go out for dinner?*

careful not to do something using care to avoid some difficulty or difficulties. □ *Please be careful not to discuss politics with Mr. Brown.* □ *Please be careful not to leave the house unlocked.*

careful (with something**)** treating or handling something with caution. □ *Please be careful with the vase. It's old and valuable.* □ *That's too big a load. Be careful!*

carp about someone or something to complain about someone or something. □ *You are always carping about all your petty problems at work.* □ *Stop carping about Randy!*

carp at someone **(about** someone or something**)** to complain to someone about someone or something. □ *Why are you always carping at me about your family?* □ *You are always carping at Joan about her brother.*

carp at someone or something to criticize someone or something. □ *Poor Clara is carping at Bill's carelessness again.* □ *Please stop carping at me.*

carry (a lot of) weight (with someone or something**)** *Fig.* to be very influential with someone or some group of people. □ *Your argument does not carry a lot of weight with me.* □ *The senator's testimony carried a lot of weight with the council.*

carry a secret to the grave and **carry a secret to** one's **grave** *Fig.* to never reveal a secret, even to the day of one's death. □ *John carried our secret to his grave.* □ *Trust me, I will carry your secret to the grave!*

carry a torch (for someone**)** and **carry the torch (for** someone**)** *Fig.* to be in love with someone who is not in love with you; to brood over a hopeless love affair. □ *John is carrying a torch for Jane.* □ *Is John still carrying a torch after all this time?*

carry coals to Newcastle *Prov.* to do something unnecessary; to do something that is redundant or duplicative. (Newcastle is an English town from which coal was shipped to other parts of England.) □ *Mr. Smith is so rich he doesn't need any more money. To give him a gift certificate is like carrying coals to Newcastle.*

carry on to behave badly or mischievously. □ *The children always carry on when the teacher's out of the room.* □ *Stop carrying on and go to sleep!*

carry on (about someone or something**)** to make a great fuss over someone or something; to cry (especially for a long time or uncontrollably) about someone or something. (Note the variation in the examples.) □ *Billy, stop carrying on about your tummy ache like that.* □ *The child carried on endlessly when his mother scolded him.* □ *When the soldier finally came home, his wife cried and carried on for hours.* □ *Calm down. There's no need to carry on so.*

carry on somehow to manage to continue or endure, in spite of problems. □ *Even though we did not have a lot of money, we managed to carry on somehow.* □ *Don't worry about us. We will carry on somehow.*

carry on (to something**)** to continue on to some place or some time. □ *Please keep reading. Carry on to the next page.* □ *Please carry on with your report.*

carry on (with someone**)** to flirt with someone; to have a love affair with someone. □ *It looks like Linda is carrying on with James.*

carry on (with something**)** to continue doing something. (Compare this with **carry** something **on.**) □ *Please carry on with your singing.* □ *Tom carried on with his boring speech for twenty minutes.*

carry on without someone or something to manage to continue without someone or something. □ *I don't know how we will be able to carry on without you.* □ *We can't carry on without a leader!*

carry one's **cross** Go to **bear** one's **cross.**

carry one's **(own) weight** and **pull** one's **(own) weight** *Fig.* to do one's share; to earn one's keep. (The *weight* is the burden that is the responsibility of someone.) □ *Tom, you must be more helpful around the house. We each have to carry our own weight.* □ *Bill, I'm afraid that you can't work here anymore. You just haven't been carrying your weight.*

carry over to extend into another time period or location. □ *I don't like for bills to carry over into the next month.* □ *Please do not let the paragraph carry over.*

carry over (to something**) 1.** [for a sum or other figure] to be taken to another column of figures. □ *This amount carries over into the next column.* □ *Yes, this number carries over.* **2.** to last or continue until another time. □ *Will this enthusiasm carry over to the following week?* □ *Of course, it will carry over.*

carry someone **along**[†] **(with** someone**)** [for someone's enthusiasm or power] to affect other people and persuade them. □ *The excitement of the play carried the audience along with the actors.* □ *She carried along the audience with her all the way.*

carry someone **along**[†] **(with** something**)** [for something] to transport someone as it moves along. □ *The flood carried us along with the debris.* □ *The rushing water carried along everything with it.*

carry someone **around**[†] **(with** oneself**) 1.** *Lit.* to be the source of transport for someone, usually a child. □ *I'm tired of carrying this baby around with me everywhere. Can't I buy a baby carriage?* □ *I always carry around my child with me.* **2.** *Fig.* to have in mind the memory or a sense of presence of another person with oneself. □ *I have been carrying my dead grandfather around with me for years.* □ *She carries around her brother with her in her memories.*

carry someone **away**[†] [for someone or something] to cause a person to lose control. □ *The excitement of the parade carried us all away.* □ *The fervor of the speech carried away the whole crowd.*

carry someone **back (to** some time**)** to return someone, mentally, to a former time; to remind someone of an earlier time. □ *This carries me back to the times of knights and jousting.* □ *This article about the Sixties really carries me back.*

carry someone or something **about** and **carry** someone or something **around** to carry someone or something with one; to carry someone or something from place to place. □ *Do I have to carry these books about all over campus?* □ *You are too heavy, sweetie. I don't want to carry you around all day.*

carry someone or something **away**[†] to take or steal someone or something. □ *Someone carried our lawn furniture away while we were on vacation.* □ *The kidnappers carried away the child when no one was looking.*

carry someone or something **into** some place and **carry** someone or something **in**[†] to lift and move someone or something to some place. □ *Will you carry the baby into the bedroom?* □ *Let me carry in the packages.*

carry someone or something **off**[†] to take or steal someone or something. □ *The kidnappers carried the child off.* □ *They carried off the child.*

carry someone or something **out**[†] to lift up and move someone or something out. □ *Help me carry the baby and her things out.* □ *Let's carry out the dishes and set the table.*

carry someone or something **over**[†] **from** something to transport someone or something from somewhere, usually a great distance or another country. □ *The ship carried the travel club over from Spain.* □ *They carried over all my furniture from Paris.*

carry someone or something **over to** something to lift and move someone or something to another place. □ *Please carry this over to the window.* □ *Could you carry Timmy over to his bed, please? He's asleep.*

carry someone or something **through** something to lift up and move someone or something through something. □ *We will have to carry him through the crowd to the ambulance.* □ *Jane carried the groceries through the doorway.*

carry someone **somewhere** *Rur.* to take or escort someone somewhere. □ *Friday nights, Joe always carries his wife to town.* □ *"May I carry you home?" the young man asked Jane.*

carry someone **through (**something**)** to sustain someone (as someone's expenses or needs) during something. □ *Can this amount carry you through the week?* □ *Yes, this will carry me through.*

carry something **along**[†] **(with** someone**)** to bring or take something with one; to have something with one and have it handy at all times. □ *You should carry this emergency phone list along with you whenever you travel.* □ *Please carry along this package when you go.*

carry something **around**[†] **(with** one**)** to have something on one's person at all times. □ *He carries a backpack around with him.* □ *Max carries around his checkbook with him.*

carry something **back**[†] to take something back to where it came from. □ *Did you bring this here? If so, carry it back.* □ *Please carry back the empty box after you take out all the books.*

carry something **down**[†] to take something from a higher to a lower place. □ *Would you go up to the attic and carry the trunk down?* □ *Why should I carry down the trunk?*

carry something **forward** to take a figure from one column or category to another. □ *Now, carry this figure forward into the tens column.*

carry something **off**[†] **1.** *Lit.* to take something away with oneself; to steal something. □ *Someone carried off my books!* □ *I think someone carried off the lawn chairs last night.* **2.** *Fig.* to make a planned event work out successfully. □ *It was a huge party, but the hostess carried it off beautifully.* □ *The magician carried off the trick with great skill.*

carry something **on**[†] **1.** to do something over a period of time. (Compare this with **carry on (with** something.) □ *Do you think you can carry this on for a year?* □ *I will carry on this activity for three years if you want.* **2.** to continue to do something as a tradition. □ *We intend to carry this celebration on as long as the family can gather for the holidays.* □ *We will carry on this tradition for decades, in fact.* **3.** Go to **carry** something **onto** something.

carry something **on** someone's **shoulders** Go to **on** someone's **shoulders**.

carry something **onto** something and **carry** something **on**[†] to take something onto a vehicle. □ *Do you plan to carry this bag onto the plane?* □ *I'd like to carry on two bags.* □ *Can I carry them both on?*

carry something **out**[†] to perform a task; to perform an assignment. □ *"This is a very important job," said Jane. "Do you think you can carry it out?"* □ *The students didn't carry out their assignments.*

carry something **over**[†] to let something like a bill extend into another period of time. □ *We'll carry the amount of money due over into the next month.* □ *Yes, please carry over the balance.*

carry something **over**[†] **(until** some time**)** and **carry** something **over**[†] **(to** some time**)** to defer something until a particular time. □ *Can we carry this discussion over until later?* □ *We will carry over our discussion to tomorrow.*

carry something **with*** Go to next.

carry something **with** one and **carry** something **with*** to have something with one or on one's person. (*The second form is informal.) □ *Do you always carry that bag with you?* □ *I always carry a pen with.*

carry the ball 1. *Lit.* to be the player who is relied on to gain yardage, especially in football. □ *It was the fullback carrying the ball.* □ *Yes, Tom always carries the ball.* **2.** *Fig.* to be in charge; to be considered reliable enough to make sure that a job gets done. □ *We need someone who knows how to get the job done. Hey, Sally! Why don't you carry the ball for us?* □ *John can't carry the ball. He isn't organized enough.*

carry the day and **win the day** to be successful; to win a competition, argument, etc. (Originally meaning to win a battle.) □ *Our team didn't play well at first, but we won the day in the end.* □ *Preparation won the day and James passed his exams.*

carry the torch 1. *Fig.* to lead or participate in a (figurative) crusade. □ *The battle was over, but John continued to carry the torch.* □ *If Jane hadn't carried the torch, no one would have followed, and the whole thing would have failed.* **2.** Go to **carry a torch (for** someone**)**.

carry the weight of the world on one's **shoulders** *Fig.* to appear or behave as if burdened by all the problems in the whole world. □ *Look at Tom. He appears to be carrying the weight of the world on his shoulders.* □ *Cheer up, Tom! You don't need to carry the weight of the world on your shoulders.*

carry through (on something**)** Go to **follow through (on** something**)**.

carry weight (with someone**)** *Fig.* to have influence with someone; [for an explanation] to amount to a good argument to use with someone. □ *That carries a lot of weight with the older folks.* □ *What you say carries no weight with me.*

cart someone or something **off**[†] to take or haul someone or something away. (When used with *someone* the person is treated like an object.) □ *The police came and carted her off.* □ *Let's cart off these boxes.*

***carte blanche** *Fig.* freedom or permission to act as one wishes or thinks necessary. (*Typically: **get** ~; **have** ~; **give** someone ~.) □ *He's been given carte blanche with the reorganization of the workforce.* □ *The manager has been given no instructions about how to train the staff. He has carte blanche from the owner.*

carve someone or something **up**[†] to damage someone or something by careless or purposeful cutting (of a person, can be figurative). □ *Someone carved the tabletop up. Who did it and why?* □ *The boxer wanted to carve up his opponent.*

carve something **from** something to shape by cutting something off or out of something with a knife. □ *Can you carve an elephant from a bar of soap?*

carve something **in**[†] Go to **carve** something **into** something.

carve something **in stone** *Fig.* to fix some idea permanently. (See also **carved in stone**.) □ *No one has carved this one approach in stone; we have several options.*

carve something **into** something **1.** and **carve** something **in**[†] to cut letters or symbols into something. □ *He carved his initials into a tree.* □ *He carved in the letters one by one.* **2** to create a carved object by sculpturing raw material. □ *Ken carved the apple into a tiny snowman.*

carve something **out**[†] to hollow something out by carving; to make something hollow by carving. □ *Can he carve a bowl out of such soft wood?* □ *He carved out the bowl of the pipe and then began to sand it.*

carve something **out**[†] **(of** something**)** to remove something from the inside of something else by carving or cutting. □ *She carved the insides out.* □ *She carved out the insides of the pumpkin.*

carve something **up**[†] to divide something up, perhaps carelessly. □ *The peace treaty carved the former empire up into several countries.* □ *You can't just carve up one country and give the pieces away.*

carved in stone and **engraved in stone; written in stone** *Fig.* permanent or not subject to change. (Often in the negative.) □ *Now, this isn't carved in stone yet, but this looks like the way it's going to be.* □ *Is this policy carved in stone, or can it still be modified?*

the **case** the [current] instance; an actual situation. □ *I think Bill is a vegetarian, and if that is the case, we should not serve him meat.* □ *Susie believes trees can talk, but that is not the case.*

a **case in point** a specific example of what one is talking about. □ *Now, as a case in point, let's look at nineteenth-century England.* □ *Fireworks can be dangerous. For a case in point, look at what happened to Bob Smith last Fourth of July.*

a **case of mistaken identity** the incorrect identification of someone. □ *I am not the criminal you want to arrest. This is a case of mistaken identity.*

*a case of something **1.** an instance of something. (*Typically: **be ~; have ~.**) □ *This is a case of police brutality. They should not have injured the suspect.* **2.** an occurrence of a disease. (*Typically: **be ~; look like ~; treat ~.**) □ *I am suffering from a case of the flu.*

a **case of the blind leading the blind** *Fig.* a situation where people who don't know how to do something try to teach other people. □ *Tom doesn't know anything about cars, but he's trying to teach Sally how to change the oil. It's a case of the blind leading the blind.* □ *When I tried to show Mary how to use a computer, it was a case of the blind leading the blind.*

case someone or something **out†** *Sl.* to look someone or something over carefully, with a view to additional activity at a later time. □ *He came into the room and cased all the lighting fixtures out.* □ *He cased out the fixtures to see which ones to replace.* □ *John cased the girls out.*

case the joint 1. *Sl.* to look over some place to figure out how to break in, what to steal, etc. (Underworld.) □ *First of all you gotta case the joint to see where things are.* □ *You could see he was casing the joint the way he hung around.* **2.** *Sl.* to look a place over. □ *The dog came in and cased the joint, sniffing out friends and foes.* □ *The old lady entered slowly, casing the joint for someone of her own age, and finally took a seat.*

cash flow problem a lack of hard currency. □ *My real estate business has a temporary cash flow problem.* □ *Due to his cash flow problem, he was unable to pay his employees that month.*

cash in (on something**)** *Fig.* to earn a lot of money at something; to make a profit at something. □ *This is a good year for drug stocks, and you can cash in on it if you're smart.* □ *It's too late to cash in on that particular clothing fad.*

Cash is king. *Prov.* It is best to keep one's investment money in cash. (Said when the prices in the securities markets are too high. It is better to build up cash and wait for a break in the market.) □ *Things look a little pricey now. I'd say that cash is king for the moment.* □ *I'm holding a little cash for a little bottom fishing, but I wouldn't say that cash is king.*

Cash is trash. *Prov.* It is unwise to keep one's investment money in cash. (Said when there are good opportunities in securities and it is foolish not to invest cash.) □ *If you've got money sitting around in savings while the market is steaming ahead, you are losing dollars. Right now cash is trash.* □ *Cash is trash. Get into the market or you stand to lose a bundle.*

cash money *Rur.* money in bills and coins. □ *You could make cash money selling your quilts, you really could.* □ *Joe wants cash money for his old TV set. He won't let me have it on credit.*

cash on the barrelhead and **cash on the line** *Rur.* cash at the time of purchase. □ *Jonson's store doesn't give credit. Everything is cash on the barrelhead.* □ *They offered me fifty thousand dollars cash on the line for Aunt Nancy's old house.*

cash on the line Go to previous.

cash (one's **chips) in† 1.** *Lit.* to turn in one's gaming tokens or poker chips when one quits playing. □ *When you leave the game, you should cash your chips in.* □ *Cash in your chips before you go.* □ *I'm going to cash in.* **2.** *Fig.* to quit [anything], as if one were cashing in gaming tokens; to leave or go to bed. □ *I guess I'll cash my chips in and go home.* □ *Well, it's time to cash in my chips and go home.* □ *I'm really tired. I'm going to cash in.* **3.** and **cash** one's **checks in†** *Euph.* to die; to finish the "game" of life." □ *There's a funeral procession. Who cashed his chips in?* □ *Poor Fred cashed in his chips last week.*

cash or credit [a purchase made] either by paying cash or by putting the charges on a credit account. □ *When Fred had all his purchases assembled on the counter, the clerk asked, "Cash or credit?"* □ *That store does not give you a choice of cash or credit. They want cash only.*

cash something **in†** to exchange something with cash value for the amount of money it is worth. □ *I should have cashed my insurance policy in years ago.* □ *It's time to cash in your U. S. savings bonds.*

cash something **in† (for** something**)** to exchange a security for money; to convert a foreign currency to one's own currency; to turn gaming tokens or poker chips in for money. (See also **cash (**one's **chips) in.**) □ *I cashed the bonds in for a cashier's check.* □ *I cashed in my bonds for their face value.*

cash-and-carry a method of buying and selling goods at the retail level where the buyer pays cash for the goods and carries the goods away. (As opposed to paying on credit or with the cost of delivery included.) □ *Sorry, we don't accept credit cards. This is strictly cash-and-carry.* □ *I bought the chair cash-and-carry before I realized that I had no way to get it home.*

cast a spell (on someone**) 1.** *Lit.* to enchant someone with a magic spell. □ *The wizard cast a spell on the frog, turning it into a prince with bad skin.* **2.** *Fig.* to intrigue and delight someone. □ *She is a real beauty. She cast a spell on every man she met.*

cast around for someone or something and **cast about for** someone or something to seek someone or something; to seek a thought or an idea. (Alludes to a type of person or thing rather than a specific one.) □ *John is casting around for a new cook. The old one quit.* □ *Bob is casting about for a new car.*

cast aspersions on someone to make a rude and insulting remark. □ *I resent your casting aspersions on my brother and his ability!* □ *It is rude to cast aspersions on people in general.*

cast doubt(s) (on someone or something**)** to cause someone or something to be doubted. □ *The police cast doubt on my story.* □ *How can they cast doubt? They haven't looked into it yet.* □ *The city council cast doubt on John and his plan.*

cast in the same mold *Fig.* [of two or more people or things] very similar. □ *The two sisters are cast in the same mold—equally mean.* □ *All the members of the family are cast in the same mold and they all had success as entertainers.*

cast off (from something**)** [for the crew of a boat or ship] to push away from the dock or pier; to begin the process of navigating a boat or ship. □ *The crew cast off from the dock.* □ *It's time to cast off.*

Cast one's **bread upon the waters.** *Prov.* Act generous because you feel it is right and not because you expect a reward. (Biblical.) □ *Joseph is casting his bread upon the waters, supporting Bob while he works on his novel.* □ *Cast your bread upon the waters; make a generous contribution to our cause.*

cast one's **eyes down**† *Fig.* to tilt one's head or gaze downward. (Usually a sign of shame or to appear not to have seen someone.) □ *She cast her eyes down as they saw each other again.* □ *He cast down his eyes in shame.*

cast one's **lot in**† **(with** someone or something**)** to join in with someone or a group. □ *He cast his lot in with the others.* □ *She cast in her lot with the others.* □ *She cast in with a questionable crowd.*

cast (one's**) pearls before swine** *Fig.* to waste something good on someone who doesn't care about it. (From a biblical quotation.) □ *To sing for them is to cast pearls before swine.* □ *To serve them French cuisine is like casting one's pearls before swine.*

cast one's **vote** to vote; to place one's ballot in the ballot box. □ *The citizens cast their votes for president.* □ *The wait in line to cast one's vote was almost an hour.*

cast someone **as** something **1.** *Lit.* to choose someone to play a particular role in a play, opera, film, etc. □ *The director cast her as the young singer.* □ *They cast me as a villain.* **2.** *Fig.* to decide or fantasize that someone is going to follow a particular pattern of behavior in real life. □ *I'm afraid my teachers cast me as a dummy when I was very young.* □ *They cast me as someone who would not succeed.*

cast someone **aside**† and **cast** someone **off**†; **cast** someone **away**† *Fig.* to dispose of someone; to reject or discard someone. □ *He simply cast his wife aside, and that was it.*

cast someone or something **up**† [for the waves] to bring up and deposit someone or something on the shore. □ *The waves cast the wreckage up, and it was found on the shore.* □ *The waves cast up the wreckage of a boat.*

cast something **aside**† and **cast** something **off**†; **cast** something **away**† to throw something away. □ *You can't just cast aside a new coat that you've only worn once.*

cast something **back (**some place**)** to throw something back somewhere. □ *I cast the fish back in the water.* □ *Cast back those stones and all the others you took from the pile.*

cast something **down**† to hurl or throw something down. □ *She cast the glass down, breaking it into a thousand pieces.* □ *She cast down the tray and all that was on it.*

cast something **off**† Go to **cast** someone or something **aside**†.

cast the first stone *Fig.* to make the first criticism; to be the first to attack. (From a biblical quotation.) □ *Well, I don't want to be the one to cast the first stone, but she sang horribly.* □ *John always casts the first stone. Does he think he's perfect?*

cast-iron stomach *Fig.* a very strong stomach that can withstand bad food or anything nauseating. □ *If I didn't have a cast-iron stomach, I couldn't eat this stuff.* □ *Fred— known for his cast-iron stomach—ate ten whole hot peppers.*

A **cat can look at a king.** *Prov.* No one is so important that an ordinary person cannot look at him or her; everyone has the right to be curious about important people. □ *Jane: I get so angry at those people who read tabloid mag-*azines. *The private lives of television stars are none of their business. Alan: Don't be so hard on them. A cat can look at a king.* □ *Fred: You shouldn't stare at me like that. I'm your boss. Jill: A cat can look at a king.*

A **cat has nine lives.** *Prov.* Cats can survive things that are severe enough to kill them. (You can also refer to a particular cat's *nine lives.*) □ *Jill: My cat fell off a third-floor balcony and just walked away. How can he do that? Jane: A cat has nine lives.* □ *I think my cat used up one of her nine lives when she survived being hit by that car.*

A **cat in gloves catches no mice.** *Prov.* Sometimes you cannot get what you want by being careful and polite. □ *Jill: I've hinted to Mary several times that I need her to pay me the money she owes, but she just ignores me. Jane: A cat in gloves catches no mice, Jill. Tell her bluntly that you need the money.*

the **cat is out of the bag** *Fig.* the secret has been made known. (See also **let the cat out of the bag.**) □ *Now that the cat is out of the bag, there is no sense in pretending we don't know what's really happening.*

catapult someone or something **into** something **1.** *Lit.* to throw someone or something into a place using a catapult. □ *The soldiers catapulted the huge stone into the fortress.* **2.** *Fig.* to thrust or force someone or something into something, such as fame, glory, front-page news, etc. □ *The success catapulted her into the spotlight.* □ *The scandal catapulted the contractual arrangements into public scrutiny.*

catch a glimpse of someone or something Go to **catch sight of** someone or something.

catch a whiff of something Go to a **whiff of** something.

catch (a)hold of someone or something to grasp or seize someone or something. □ *See if you can catch hold of the rope as it swings back and forth.* □ *I couldn't catch ahold of her.*

catch cold and **take cold** *Fig.* to contract a cold (a common respiratory infection.) (Use with *catch* is more frequent.) □ *Please close the window, or we'll all catch cold.* □ *I take cold every year at this time.*

catch forty winks and **take forty winks; have forty winks** *Fig.* to take a nap; to get some sleep. □ *I'll just catch forty winks before getting ready for the party.* □ *I think I'll go to bed and take forty winks. See you in the morning.*

catch hell Go to **hell.**

catch hell (about someone or something**)** and **get hell (about** someone or something**); catch hell (for** something**)** to be scolded (about someone or something.) □ *This isn't the first time Bill's caught hell about his drinking.* □ *We knew we were gonna catch hell when Ma saw how we'd ruined her garden.* □ *Somebody is going to catch hell for this!*

catch it to get into trouble and receive punishment. □ *I know I'm going to catch it for denting mom's car when I get home.* □ *Bob hit Billy in the face. He really caught it from the teacher for that.*

Catch me later. and **Catch me some other time.** Please try to talk to me later. □ *Bill (angry): Tom, look at this phone bill! Tom: Catch me later.* □ *"Catch me some other time," hollered Mr. Franklin over his shoulder. "I've got to go to the airport."*

Catch me some other time. Go to previous.

catch (on) fire to ignite and burn with flames. □ *Keep your coat away from the flames, or it will catch fire.* □ *The curtains blew against the flame of the candle and caught on fire.*

catch on (to something) *Fig.* to figure something out. (See also **get onto** someone.) □ *I finally caught on to what she was talking about.* □ *It takes a while for me to catch on.*

catch on (with someone) *Fig.* [for something] to become popular with someone. □ *I hope our new product catches on with children.* □ *I'm sure it will catch on.*

catch one off (one's) guard Go to catch someone off guard.

catch one's breath *Fig.* to struggle for normal breathing after strenuous activity. □ *The jogger stopped to catch her breath.* □ *It took Jimmy a minute to catch his breath after being punched in the stomach.*

catch one's death (of cold) and **take one's death (of cold)** *Fig.* to contract a cold, a common respiratory infection; to catch a serious cold. (See also **catch cold**.) □ *If I go out in this weather, I'll catch my death of cold.* □ *Dress up warm or you'll take your death.*

catch one with one's pants down *Fig.* to discover someone in the act of doing something that is normally private or hidden. (Literal uses are possible.) □ *Some council members were using tax money as their own. But the press caught them with their pants down and now the district attorney will press charges.*

catch onto someone or something Go to onto someone or something.

catch onto something [for something] to snag on or get grabbed by something else. (See also **onto** something.) □ *This little piece has to catch onto this gear each time it comes around.* □ *A few threads of my shirt caught onto the cactus needles and ruined the whole thing.*

catch sight of someone or something and **catch a glimpse of someone or something** to see someone or something briefly; to get a quick look at someone or something. □ *I caught sight of the plane just before it flew out of sight.* □ *Ann caught a glimpse of the robber as he ran out of the bank.*

catch some rays and **bag some rays** *Fig.* to get some sunshine; to tan in the sun. □ *We wanted to catch some rays, but the sun never came out the whole time we were there.* □ *I went to Hawaii to bag some rays.*

catch some Zs and **cop some Zs; cut some Zs** to get some sleep. (In comic strips, Zs are used to show that someone is sleeping or snoring.) □ *I gotta catch some Zs before I drop.* □ *Why don't you stop a little bit and try to cop some Zs?*

catch someone at a bad time to attempt to speak or deal with someone at a time inconvenient for that person. □ *I'm sorry. You look busy. Did I catch you at a bad time?*

catch someone at something and **catch someone doing something** to discover someone doing something, especially something bad or shameful. □ *We caught her at her evil deeds.* □ *Don't let me catch you doing that again!*

catch someone by surprise Go to take someone by surprise.

catch someone doing something Go to catch someone at something.

catch someone flat-footed Go to catch someone red-handed.

catch someone in the act (of doing something) to discover someone doing a [bad] deed at the very moment when the deed is being done. (See also **caught in the act.**) □ *I caught her in the act of stealing the coat.* □ *He was caught in the act of taking money from the cash box.*

catch someone napping and **catch someone off balance; catch someone up short** to come upon someone who is unprepared; to surprise someone. (See also **asleep at the switch.**) □ *The enemy soldiers caught our army napping.* □ *The thieves caught the security guard napping.* □ *I didn't expect you so soon. You caught me off balance.* □ *The teacher asked a trick question and caught me up short.* □ *The robbers caught Ann off balance and stole her purse.*

catch someone off guard and **catch one off (one's) guard** *Fig.* to catch a person at a time of carelessness. □ *Tom caught Ann off guard and frightened her.* □ *She caught me off my guard, and my hesitation told her I was lying.*

catch someone or something in something to trap someone or something in something. □ *We caught David in the snare by accident.* □ *My platoon was caught in an enemy ambush.*

catch someone out† to discover the truth about someone's deception. □ *The investigator tried to catch me out, but I stuck to my story.* □ *The teacher caught out the student and punished him immediately.*

catch someone red-handed and **catch someone flat-footed** to catch a person in the act of doing something wrong. (See also **caught red-handed.**) □ *Tom was stealing the car when the police drove by and caught him red-handed.* □ *Mary tried to cash a forged check at the bank, and the teller caught her red-handed.*

catch someone's eye and **get someone's eye 1.** *Fig.* to establish eye contact with someone; to attract someone's attention. □ *The shiny red car caught Mary's eye.* □ *When Tom had her eye, he smiled at her.* **2.** *Fig.* to appear and attract someone's interest. □ *A small red car passing by caught my eye.* □ *One of the books on the top shelf caught my eye, and I took it down to look at it.*

catch someone up in something [for excitement or interest] to extend to and engross someone. □ *The fireworks caught everyone up in the excitement.* □ *The accident caught us all up in the resultant confusion.*

catch someone up (on someone or something) to tell someone the news of someone or something. (Fixed order.) □ *Oh, please catch me up on what your family is doing.* □ *Yes, do catch us up!* □ *I have to take some time to catch myself up on the news.*

catch someone up short Go to catch someone napping.

catch someone with something 1. to discover or apprehend someone with something—usually something stolen or illicit. □ *They caught Elizabeth with the earrings she shoplifted.* □ *Don't let them catch you with the money!* **2.** to apprehend someone with the aid of something. □ *The state trooper caught the speeder with radar.* □ *The cops caught Lefty with the help of an informer.*

catch something *Fig.* to see or listen to something. □ *I will try to catch that new movie this weekend.* □ *Did you catch that radio program about cancer last night?*

catch something **from** someone to get a disease from someone. □ *I hope my children catch the chicken pox in kindergarten. Better to have it while you are young.* □ *I don't want to catch a cold from you.*

catch something **on** something to snag something on something. □ *I caught the pocket of my trousers on the drawer pull and almost ripped it off.* □ *He caught the sleeve of his uniform on a branch.*

catch something **up†** **in** something to ensnare and capture something in something. □ *We caught a large number of fish up in the net.* □ *We caught up many fish in the net.*

catch the devil Go to the **devil.**

catch the next wave and **wait for the next wave** *Fig.* to follow the next fad. □ *He has no purpose in life. He sits around strumming his guitar and waiting to catch the next wave.*

a **catch to it** a hidden problem associated with it. □ *It sounds good at first, but there's a catch to it. You have to pay all costs up front.*

catch up (on someone or something**)** to learn the news of someone or something. □ *I need a little time to catch up on the news.* □ *We all need to catch up on what Tony has been doing.* □ *I need some time to catch up.*

catch up (on something**)** to bring one's efforts with something up-to-date; to do the work that one should have done. □ *I need a quiet time so I can catch up on my work.* □ *He started school late and now has to catch up.*

catch up (to someone or something**)** and **catch up (with** someone or something**)** to move faster in order to reach someone or something who is moving in the same direction. □ *The red car caught up with the blue one.* □ *Bill caught up with Ann, and they walked to the bank together.*

catch up with someone Go to **up with** someone.

catch up (with someone or something**)** Go to **catch up (to** someone or something**).**

catch wind of something Go to **get wind of** something.

catch-as-catch-can the best one can do with whatever is available. □ *We went hitchhiking for a week and lived catch-as-catch-can.* □ *There were ten children in our family, and every meal was catch-as-catch-can.*

cater to someone or something **1.** *Lit.* to provide for or care for someone or something. □ *I believe that we can cater to you in this matter.* □ *Our company caters to larger firms that do not wish to maintain a service department.* **2.** *Fig.* to provide special or favorable treatment for someone or something. □ *I'm sorry, but I cannot cater to you and not to the others.* □ *We do not have the time to cater to special requests.*

caught in the act and **caught red-handed** *Fig.* seen doing something illegal or private. (See also **catch** someone **in the act (of** doing something**)** and **catch** someone **red-handed.**) □ *Tom was caught in the act and cannot deny what he did.* □ *Many car thieves are caught red-handed.*

caught in the crossfire 1. *Lit.* trapped between two lines of enemy fire. □ *I was caught in the crossfire and dove into a ditch to keep from getting killed.* **2.** and **caught in the middle** *Fig.* caught between two arguing people or groups, making it difficult to remain neutral. □ *Bill and Ann were arguing, and poor Bobby, their son, was caught in the middle.*

caught short 1. left without any money temporarily. □ *I'm caught a little short. Can I borrow a few bucks?* **2.** pregnant and unmarried. □ *Both of Jane's sisters got caught short before they graduated high school.*

caught unaware(s) surprised and unprepared. □ *Sorry. You startled me when you came up behind me. I was caught unaware.* □ *The clerk was caught unawares, and the robber emptied out the cash register before the clerk could sound the alarm.*

caught up in something and **caught up with** something deeply involved with something; participating actively or closely in something. □ *Wallace is caught up in his work and has little time for his son, Buxton.*

cause a commotion Go to **cause (quite a) stir.**

cause hard feelings Go to **hard feelings.**

cause lean times (ahead) Go to **lean times (ahead).**

cause qualms (about someone or something**)** Go to **qualms (about** someone or something**).**

cause (quite) a stir and **cause a commotion** to cause people to become agitated; to cause trouble in a group of people; to shock or alarm people. □ *When Bob appeared without jacket and tie, it caused a stir at the state dinner.* □ *The dog ran through the church and caused quite a commotion.*

cause (some) eyebrows to raise and **cause some raised eyebrows** *Fig.* to shock people; to surprise and dismay people. (The same as **raise some eyebrows.**) □ *John caused eyebrows to raise when he married a woman half his age.* □ *If you want to cause some eyebrows to raise, just start singing as you walk down the street.*

cause some raised eyebrows Go to previous.

cause (some) tongues to wag *Fig.* to cause people to gossip; to give people something to gossip about. □ *The way John was looking at Mary will surely cause some tongues to wag.* □ *The way Mary was so scantily dressed will also cause tongues to wag.*

caution someone **about** someone or something and **caution** someone **against** someone or something to warn someone against someone or something. □ *Haven't I cautioned you about that before?* □ *Hasn't someone cautioned you about Daniel?*

cave in [for a roof or ceiling] to collapse. □ *The roof of the mine caved in when no one was there.* □ *The tunnel caved in on the train.*

cave in (to someone or something**)** *Fig.* to give in to someone or something. □ *Finally, the manager caved in to the customer's demands.* □ *I refuse to cave in under pressure from my opponent.*

cavil at someone to find fault with someone; to complain about someone constantly. □ *Will you never cease caviling at all of us?* □ *There is no need to cavil at me day and night!*

cease and desist to completely stop doing something. (A legal phrase.) □ *The judge ordered the merchant to cease* and desist the deceptive practices. □ When they were ordered to cease and desist, they finally stopped.

cede something **to** someone to grant a parcel of land to someone. □ We refuse to cede that land to you. □ They ceded the land to the city for a park.

celebrate someone **for** an accomplishment to honor someone for having done something. □ The people celebrated the astronaut for a successful journey. □ She was celebrated widely for her discovery.

cement something **on**† Go to next.

cement something **on(to)** something and **cement** something **on**† to fasten something onto something with glue or household cement. □ Cement this handle back onto the cup. □ Now, cement on the other handle. □ I will cement it on for you.

cement something **together** to fasten something together with glue or household cement. □ Use this stuff to cement the vase together. □ Will you cement these parts together?

censure someone **(for** something**)** to criticize someone formally for having done something. □ Please don't censure us for doing our duty. □ The legislature proposed to censure one of its members.

center around someone or something to make someone or something the central point in something; to be based on someone or something. □ Your salary increases center around your ability to succeed at your job. □ The success of the picnic centers around the weather next week.

the **center of attention** the focus of people's attention; the thing or person who monopolizes people's attention. □ She had a way of making herself the center of attention wherever she went.

center on someone or something to focus on someone or something in particular. □ Let us center on the basic problem and try to solve it. □ I want to center on Liz and her contributions to the firm.

center something **on** someone or something to base something on someone or something. □ Let us center the discussion on Walter. □ Our whole meeting was centered on the conservation question.

a **certain party** someone you know but whom I do not wish to name. □ I spoke to a certain party about the matter you mentioned. □ If a certain party finds out about you-know-what, what on earth will you do?

certain sure Rur. very sure. □ Tom: Are you sure you saw Bill at work today? Mary: Certain sure. □ If you keep hanging around with them no-good kids, you'll get in a heap of trouble for certain sure.

Certainly not! Go to Definitely not!

chafe at something Fig. to be irritated or annoyed at something. □ Jane chafed at the criticism for a long time afterward. □ Jerry chafed for a while at what Ken had said.

A **chain is no stronger than its weakest link.** Prov. A successful group or team relies on each member doing well. □ George is completely out of shape. I don't want him on our ball team; a chain is only as strong as its weakest link.

the **chain of command** Fig. the series or sequence of holders of responsibility in a hierarchy. □ The only way to get things done in the military is to follow the chain of command. Never try to go straight to the top.

chain someone or an animal **up**† to bind someone or an animal in chains. □ We will have to chain him up until the police get here. □ Please chain up your dog.

chain someone or something **down**† to fasten someone or something down with chains. □ They chained down the bicycle rack so no one could steal it. □ We chained the toolshed down so a strong wind would not blow it over.

chain something **to** something to connect things together with chains. □ We chained all the bicycles to one another so no one could steal them. □ We will have to chain the lawn furniture to a tree if we leave it out while we are on vacation.

chain something **up**† to lock or secure a door or gate with chains. □ Please chain the gate up again when you come through. □ Yes, chain up the gate.

chalk something **out**† 1. Lit. to draw a picture of something in chalk, especially to illustrate a plan of some type. □ The coach chalked the play out so the players could understand what they were to do. □ Our team captain chalked out the play. 2. Fig. to explain something carefully to someone, as if one were talking about a chalk drawing. □ She chalked out the details of the plan over the phone.

chalk something **up**† 1. Lit. to write something on a chalkboard. □ Let me chalk this formula up so you all can see it. □ I'll chalk up the formula. 2. Fig. to add a mark or point to one's score. See also chalk something up (against someone).) □ Chalk another goal for Sarah. □ Chalk up another basket for the other side.

chalk something **up**† **(against** someone**)** Fig. to blame someone for something; to register something against someone. □ I will have to chalk another fault up against Fred. □ She chalked up a mark against Dave.

chalk something **up**† **(to** something**)** Fig. to recognize something as the cause of something else. □ We chalked her bad behavior up to her recent illness. □ I had to chalk up the loss to inexperience.

challenge someone **on** something to dispute someone's statement, remarks, or position. □ I think Fred is wrong, but I won't challenge him on his estimate.

challenge someone **to** something to dare someone to do something; to invite someone to compete at something. □ I challenge you to a round of golf. □ Jerry challenged us to a debate of the issues.

champ at the bit and **chomp at the bit** 1. Lit. [for a horse] to bite at its bit, eager to move along. □ Dobbin was champing at the bit, eager to go. 2. Fig. to be ready and anxious to do something. □ The kids were champing at the bit to get into the swimming pool. □ The dogs were champing at the bit to begin the hunt.

chance something to risk doing something; to try doing something while being aware of the risk involved. □ I don't usually ride horses, but this time I will chance it. □ Bob didn't have a ticket, but he went to the airport anyway, chancing a cancellation.

chance (up)on someone or something to find someone or something by accident; to happen on someone or something. (Upon is formal and less commonly used than on.) □ I chanced upon a nice little restaurant on my walk today. □ I chanced on an old friend of yours in town today.

chances are the likelihood is (followed by a clause stating what is likely). □ *Chances are that she would have been late even if she had left on time.*

change back (from something**)** to return to the original form, state, or selection, from some other form, state, or selection. □ *We are going to change back from our position of last month.* □ *We didn't like our new plumber, so we changed back.*

change back ((in)to someone or something**)** to return to the original form. □ *The crisis in Congress changed back to a minor matter within a week.* □ *Then Superman changed back into mild-mannered Clark Kent.*

change hands [for something] to be sold or passed from owner to owner. (From the "point of view" of the object that is passed on.) □ *How many times has this lot changed hands in the last ten years?* □ *We built this house in 1970, and it has never changed hands.*

change horses in midstream and **change horses in the middle of the stream** *Fig.* to make major changes in an activity that has already begun; to choose someone or something else after it is too late. (Alludes to someone trying to move from one horse to another while crossing a stream.) □ *I'm already baking a cherry pie. I can't bake an apple pie. It's too late to change horses in the middle of the stream.* □ *The house is half-built. It's too late to hire a different architect. You can't change horses in midstream.* □ *Jane: I've written a rough draft of my research paper, but the topic doesn't interest me as much as I thought. Maybe I ought to pick a different one. Jill: Don't change horses in midstream.*

change horses in the middle of the stream Go to previous.

change into someone or something to alter one's or its state to another state. □ *The ugly witch changed into a lovely maiden.* □ *An insect larva changes into a cocoon.*

the **change (of life)** menopause. □ *The change of life affects each woman differently.* □ *Jill started the change when she was forty-seven.*

a **change of pace** an addition of some variety in one's life, routine, or abode. □ *Going to the beach on the weekend will be a change of pace.* □ *The doctor says I need a change of pace from this cold climate.*

a **change of scenery** a move to a different place, where the surroundings are different. □ *I thought I would go to the country for a change of scenery.* □ *A change of scenery would help me relax and organize my life.*

change off [for people] to alternate in doing something. □ *Tom and I changed off so neither of us had to answer the phone all the time.* □ *Let's change off every 30 minutes.*

change out of something to take off a set of clothing and put on another. □ *I have to change out of these wet clothes.* □ *You should change out of your casual clothes and put on something more formal for dinner.*

change over (from someone or something**) (to** someone or something**)** to convert from something to something else; to convert from someone to someone else. □ *We decided to change over from oil to gas heat.* □ *We changed over to gas from oil.*

change places with someone to trade or exchange situations or locations with someone. □ *He has a much higher salary, but I wouldn't change places with him for the world.* □ *Juan decided to change places with Ken in the bus.*

change someone or something **into** someone or something to make someone or something change form or state. □ *The wizard claimed he could change a horse into a unicorn.* □ *He suddenly changed himself into a smiling friend rather than the gruff old man we had long known.*

change someone's **mind** to cause a person to think differently (about someone or something). □ *Tom thought Mary was unkind, but an evening out with her changed his mind.* □ *I can change my mind if you convince me that you are right.*

change someone's **tune** to change the manner of a person, usually from bad to good, or from rude to pleasant. □ *The teller was most unpleasant until she learned that I'm a bank director. Then she changed her tune.* □ *"I will help change your tune by fining you $150," said the judge to the rude defendant.*

change something **back†** to cause something to return to the original or a previous form. □ *Whoever changed the television channel should change it back.* □ *Change back the channel to the game!*

change something **with** someone to trade or exchange something with someone. □ *I changed coats with Fred and his is much warmer.* □ *Will you change seats with me?*

change the channel *Sl.* to switch to some other topic of conversation. □ *Just a minute. I think you changed the channel. Let's go back to the part about you owing me money.* □ *Let's change the channel here before there is a fight.*

change the subject to begin talking about something different. □ *They changed the subject suddenly when the person whom they had been discussing entered the room.* □ *We'll change the subject if we are embarrassing you.*

change to something to convert to something; to give up one and choose another. □ *We will change to standard time in the fall.* □ *I decided to change to gas for heating and cooking.*

channel something **in(to** something**) 1.** *Lit.* to divert water or other liquid through a channel into something. □ *The farmer channeled the irrigation water into the field.* **2.** *Fig.* to divert something, such as energy, money, effort, into something. □ *The government channeled a great deal of money into rebuilding the inner part of the city.* □ *I can't channel any more of our workforce into this project.*

channel something **off† 1.** *Lit.* to drain off water or some other liquid through a channel. □ *The front yard is flooded, and we will have to channel the water off.* □ *Let's channel off the water before it gets too deep.* **2.** *Fig.* to drain off or waste energy, money, effort, etc. □ *Unemployment channeled their resources off.* □ *The war channeled off most of the resources of the country.*

chapter and verse *Fig.* very specifically detailed, in reference to sources of information. (A reference to the method of referring to biblical text.) □ *He gave chapter and verse for his reasons for disputing that Shakespeare had written the play.* □ *The suspect gave chapter and verse of his associate's activities.*

character assassination *Fig.* seriously harming someone's reputation. □ *The review was more than a negative* *appraisal of his performance. It was total character assassination.*

charge at someone or something to move quickly forward to attack someone or something. □ *The elephant charged at the hunter.* □ *I was afraid that the water buffalo was going to charge our vehicle.*

charge down on someone or something [for an animal or vehicle] to race or move quickly against someone or something. □ *The angry elephant charged down on the hunters.* □ *The speeding truck charged down on the small shed.*

charge in(to some place**)** to move quickly or run wildly into a place. □ *The people charged into the store on the day of the sale.* □ *They all charged in trying to be first in line.*

Charge it to the dust and let the rain settle it. *Rur.* Do not expect to be paid for this. (A humorous answer to a question like, "Who is going to pay for this?") □ *Tom: Who's going to pay me all that money you owe? Mary: Charge it to the dust and let the rain settle it!*

***charge (of** someone or something**)** control of someone or something; the responsibility for caring for someone or something. (*Typically: **take ~; have ~; give** someone **~**.) □ *How long have you had charge of this office?* □ *He took charge of the entire company.*

charge off to move quickly or run away. □ *He got angry and charged off.* □ *Juan charged off to talk to the boss.*

charge out (of some place**)** to move quickly or stomp out of some place. □ *Carol charged out of the house, trying to catch Sally before she got on the bus.* □ *Juan got mad and suddenly charged out.*

charge someone or something **(with)** something to make someone or a group pay the cost of something. □ *I will have to charge Bill with the cost of repairs.* □ *The manager will charge your account with about forty dollars.*

charge someone **up**[†] to excite someone; to make a person enthusiastic about something. (See also **charged up**.) □ *The speaker charged up the crowd.* □ *He reread the report, hoping to charge himself up enough to make some positive comments.*

charge someone **with** something **1.** to place criminal charges against someone. □ *The police charged Max with robbery.* **2.** to order someone to do a particular task. □ *The president charged him with organizing the meeting.* □ *We charged her with locating new office space.*

charge something **against** something to debit or assign the cost of something against something. □ *Can I charge this item against the entertainment account?* □ *Don't even try to charge it against your business expenses.*

charge (something**) for** someone to demand an amount of money to pay for someone's ticket, fare, admission, treatment, etc. □ *Tickets are expensive. They charged sixty dollars for each seat.* □ *I didn't realize they charged for children.*

charge (something**) for** something to set a price in payment for something. □ *You are charging too much for this.* □ *You really shouldn't charge for it at all.*

charge something **off as** something to consider something a legitimate expense and deduct it from one's taxes; to assign something to the tax loss category in accounting.

□ *I will have to charge this off as a loss.* □ *Try to charge it off as a business expense.*

charge something **on** something **1.** to put the cost of something on a credit card or credit account. □ *I would like to charge this purchase on my credit card.* □ *What card do you want to charge it on?* **2.** to demand the payment of interest or a penalty on something. □ *They charged an enormous amount of interest on the loan.* □ *The bank charged a penalty on the late payment.*

charge something **up**[†] **1.** *Lit.* to apply an electrical charge to a battery. □ *How long will it take to charge this battery up?* □ *It takes an hour to charge up your battery.* **2.** *Lit.* to load or fill something under pressure or with special contents, such as a fire extinguisher. □ *We had to send the extinguishers back to the factory, where they charged them up.* □ *How much does it cost to charge up an extinguisher?* **3.** *Fig.* to reinvigorate something. □ *What can we do to charge this story up?* □ *A murder in the first act would charge up the play.* **4.** Go to next.

charge something **up to** someone or something and **charge** something **up**[†] to place the cost of something on the account of someone or a group. (Also without *up*.) □ *I will have to charge this up to your account.* □ *Do you have to charge this to my account?* □ *Are you ready to charge up the total to my bill?*

charged up 1. *Lit.* [of something such as a battery] full of electrical power. □ *The battery is completely charged up.* □ *If the battery isn't charged, the car won't start.* **2.** *Fig.* [of someone] excited; enthusiastic. □ *The crowd was really charged up.* □ *Tom is so tired that he cannot get charged up about anything.*

Charity begins at home. *Prov.* You should take care of family and people close to you before you worry about helping others. □ *I don't think our church should worry so much about a foreign relief fund when there are people in need right here in our own city. Charity begins at home.* □ *If you really want to make the world a better place, start by being polite to your sister. Charity begins at home.*

***a **charley horse** a painful, persistent cramp in the arm or leg, usually from strain. (*Typically: **get ~; have ~; give** someone **~**.) □ *Don't hike too far or you'll get a charley horse.*

charm someone **with** something to enchant or fascinate someone with something. □ *He charmed her with stories of his house on the beach.* □ *She charmed him with her bright smile.*

charm the pants off someone *Fig.* to use very charming behavior to persuade someone to do something. (Use with caution.) □ *She is so nice. She just charms the pants off you.* □ *He will try to charm the pants off you, but you can still refuse to take the job if you don't want to do it.*

chart something **out**[†] **(for** someone or something**)** to lay out a plan or course for someone or something. □ *The navigator charted the course out for the captain.* □ *The captain charted out the course for us.*

chase after someone or something Go to **after** someone or something.

chase around after someone or something to look here and there for something; to seek someone or something in many different places. □ *I don't want to have to spend* a whole day chasing around after exotic ingredients for this recipe of yours. □ I chased around after Roger and never found him.

chase someone or an animal **in**† Go to next.

chase someone or an animal **in(to)** some place and **chase** someone or an animal **in**† to drive someone or an animal into a place of confinement. □ They chased all the cattle into the corral. □ The cowboys chased in the cattle.

chase someone or something **around**† to follow someone or something around in pursuit. (There is an implication that the person or thing pursued is attempting to elude whatever is in pursuit.) □ The dog chased us around in play. □ It chased around all the children.

chase someone or something **(away**†**) from** some place and **chase** someone or something **out of** some place to drive someone or something away from or out of a place. □ The police sirens chased the thief from the building. □ We chased away all the children from the pond.

chase someone or something **down**† to track down and seize someone or something. □ Larry set out to chase the pickpocket down. □ The police chased down the suspect.

chase someone or something **out of** some place Go to chase someone or something **(away**†**) from** some place.

chase someone or something **up**† to seek someone or something out; to look high and low for someone or something. □ I will chase Tom up for you. □ I will try to chase up a buyer for your car.

chase someone or something **up** something to drive someone or an animal up something, such as a tree, a hill, a cliff, etc. □ The ranchers chased the mountain lion up a tree. □ The bull chased the rodeo clown up into the stands.

chat about someone or something to talk idly or informally about someone or something. □ We need to chat about Molly. □ I want to chat about your expenditures a little.

chatter about someone or something to talk idly and actively about someone or something. □ All the guests were chattering about something or other. □ People are chattering about you and Claire. Do you want to know what they are saying?

chatter (away) (at someone or something**) 1.** Lit. to talk incessantly or noisily to or at someone or something. □ The parrot was chattering away at its reflection in the mirror. □ The kids were chattering away. □ Stop chattering at me! **2.** Fig. [for a small animal, such as a squirrel] to try to scare off someone or something. □ The little squirrel chattered away at the crow. □ The crow came close and the squirrel chattered away again.

chatter from something [for one's teeth] to shake noisily with a chill from the cold, the dampness, a fever, etc. □ My teeth were chattering from the extreme cold. □ It was a terrible illness. My teeth chattered from the chills that followed the fever.

cheat at something to use deception while competing [against someone]. □ They say she cheats at cards. □ The mob is likely to cheat at getting the contracts.

cheat on someone to commit adultery; to be unfaithful to one's spouse or lover. □ "Have you been cheating on me?" cried Mrs. Franklin. □ He was caught cheating on his wife.

cheat someone **out of** something to get something from someone by deception. □ Are you trying to cheat me out of what is rightfully mine? □ She cheated herself out of an invitation because she lied about her affiliation.

Cheats never prosper. and **Cheaters never prosper.** Prov. If you cheat people, they will not continue to do business with you, and so your business will fail. □ Customer: You charged me for ten artichokes, but you only gave me nine. Grocer: Too bad. You should have counted them before you paid for them. Customer: Cheats never prosper, you know.

check back (on someone or something**)** to look into the state of someone or something again at a later time. □ I'll have to check back on you later.

check back (with someone**)** to inquire of someone again at a later time. □ Please check back with me later.

check in (at something**)** to go to a place to record one's arrival. □ When you get there, check in at the front office.

check in (on someone or something**)** Go to look in (on someone or something).

check in (with someone**)** to go to someone and indicate that one has arrived some place. □ Please check in with the desk clerk.

check in(to something**) 1.** to sign oneself into a place to stay, such as a hotel, hospital, motel, etc. □ She checked into a private hospital for some kind of treatment. □ They checked into the first motel they came to on the highway. **2.** Go to look into something.

check on someone or something to look into the legitimacy or condition of someone or something. □ Sarah will check on the matter and report to us. □ I will check on Jeff while he's not feeling well.

check out [for someone or something] to prove to be correctly represented. □ Everything you told me checks out with what other witnesses said.

check out (of something**)** and **check out (from** something**)** to do whatever is necessary to leave a place and then depart. (check out (of something) is more frequent.) □ I will check out of the hotel at about noon. □ I will check out from the office and come right to where you are.

check out the plumbing Euph. to go to the bathroom. (The order is fixed.) □ I think I'd better check out the plumbing before we get on the highway.

Check, please. and **Could I have the bill?; Could I have the check?** Could you give me the check or the bill for this food or drink? □ When they both had finished their dessert and coffee, Tom said, "Check, please." □ Bill: That meal was really good. Waiter! Could I have the check, please. Waiter: Right away, sir.

check someone **in**† to record the arrival of someone. □ Ask the guard to check you in when you get there. □ Tell the guard to check in the visitors as they arrive.

check someone or something **off**† to mark or cross out the name of a person or thing on a list. □ I am glad to see that you were able to come. I will check you off. □ I checked the items off. □ I checked off the recent arrivals.

check someone or something **out**† to evaluate someone or something. □ That stock sounds good. I'll check it out. □ I'll check out the competition.

check someone or something **out**[†] **(of** something**)** to do the paperwork necessary to remove someone or something from something or some place. □ *I will have the manager check you out of the hotel and send you the bill.* □ *The librarian checked out the computer to me.*

check someone or something **over**[†] to examine someone or something closely. □ *You should have the doctor check you over before you go back to work.* □ *The doctor checked over the children who had shown the worst symptoms.* □ *The mechanic checked the car over.*

check someone or something **through (**something**)** to allow one to pass through something after checking one's identification, tickets, passes, etc. (Fixed order.) □ *The guard checked us through the gate, and we went about our business.* □ *We checked them through security.*

check someone's **bags through (to** some place**)** and **check** someone's **luggage through (to** some place**)** to have one's luggage sent directly to one's final destination. □ *Please check these bags through London to Madrid.*

check something **in**[†] **1.** to record that someone has returned something. □ *I asked the librarian to check the book in for me.* □ *Did the librarian check in the book?* **2.** to take something to a place, return it, and make sure that its return has been recorded. □ *I checked the book in on time.* □ *Did you really check in the book on time?* **3.** to examine a shipment or an order received and make certain that everything ordered was received. □ *I checked the order in and sent a report to the manager.* □ *Tim checked in the order from the supplier to make sure that everything was there.*

check something **out**[†] to examine or try something; to think about something. □ *It's something we all have to be concerned with. Check it out.* □ *Check out the new comedy show on tonight.*

check that cancel that; ignore that (last remark). □ *Check that. I was wrong.* □ *At four, no, check that, at three o'clock this afternoon, the shipment arrived and was signed for.*

check through something to examine something or a collection of things. (Usually refers to papers or written work, or to details in the paperwork.) □ *Check through this and look for missing pages.* □ *I'll check through it for typographical errors also.*

check up (on someone or something**)** to determine the state of someone or something. □ *Please don't check up on me. I can be trusted.* □ *I see no need to check up.*

check with someone **(about** something**)** to ask someone about something. □ *You should check with the concierge about the bus to the airport.* □ *Please check with your agent.*

checks and balances a system, as in the U.S. Constitution, where power is shared between the various branches of government. □ *The newspaper editor claimed that the system of checks and balances built into our Constitution has been subverted by party politics.*

***a **checkup** a physical examination by a physician. (*Typically: **get** ~; **have** ~; **give** someone ~.) □ *She got a checkup yesterday.* □ *I'm going to have a checkup in the morning. I hope I'm okay.*

cheek by jowl *Fig.* side by side; close together. □ *The pedestrians had to walk cheek by jowl along the narrow streets.* □ *The two families lived cheek by jowl in one house.*

cheer for someone or something to give a shout of encouragement for someone or something. □ *Everyone cheered for the team.* □ *I cheered for the winning goal.*

cheer someone or something **on**[†] to encourage someone or a group to continue to do well, as by cheering. □ *We cheered them on, and they won.* □ *We cheered on the team.* □ *Sam cheered Jane on.*

cheer someone **up**[†] to make a sad person happy. □ *When Bill was sick, Ann tried to cheer him up by reading to him.* □ *Interest rates went up, and that cheered up all the bankers.*

cheer up [for a sad person] to become happy. □ *After a while, she began to cheer up and smile more.* □ *Cheer up! Things could be worse.*

cheese someone **off**[†] *Sl.* to make someone very angry. □ *You sure know how to cheese Laurel off.* □ *Bobby cheesed off every person in the club.*

***cheesed off** *Sl.* angry; disgusted. (*Typically: **be** ~; **get** ~; **get** someone ~.) □ *Clare was really cheesed off at the waiter.* □ *The waiter was cheesed off at the cook.*

cherry-pick something *Fig.* to choose something very carefully. (As if one were closely examining cherries on the tree, looking for the best.) □ *We have to cherry-pick the lumber we want to use for the cabinetry. Nothing but the best will do.*

chew (away) at something to gnaw or chew something for a period of time. □ *The puppy chewed away at the leather belt all night.*

chew on someone or something **1.** to gnaw at something. □ *The dog was chewing on my shoe.* **2.** Go to **chew** something **over.**

chew one's **own tobacco** *Rur.* to mind one's own business. □ *Sally: You seem awfully happy all of a sudden. How come? Tom: Chew your own tobacco.* □ *I'm just sitting here chewing my own tobacco, not bothering anybody.*

chew one's **cud** *Fig.* to think deeply; to be deeply involved in private thought. (Alludes to the cow's habit of bringing food back from the first stomach into the mouth to chew it, called chewing the cud.) □ *He's chewing his cud about what to do next.*

chew someone or something **up**[†] to damage or ruin someone or something by pinching, grinding, biting, etc. □ *Stay away from the mower blade or it will chew you up.* □ *The lawn mower chewed up the flowers.*

chew someone **out**[†] and **eat** someone **out**[†] *Fig.* to scold someone. □ *The sergeant chewed the corporal out; then the corporal chewed the private out.* □ *The boss is always chewing out somebody.*

chew something **away**[†] to gnaw something off; to gnaw at something until it's all gone. □ *You can see what's left of it. Most of it has been chewed away by some animal.* □ *Your puppy chewed away the top of my shoe!*

chew something **off** something and **chew** something **off**[†] to bite or gnaw something off something. □ *The puppy chewed the heel off my shoe.* □ *The puppy chewed off the heel and mangled the tongue.*

chew something **over**[†] **1.** *Inf.* to talk something over; to discuss something. □ *We can chew it over at lunch.* □ *Why don't we do lunch sometime and chew over these matters?*

2. and **chew on** something *Fig.* to think something over. □ *I'll have to chew it over for a while. I'm not sure now.* □ *I have to chew on all this stuff for a day or two. Then I'll get back to you.*

chew something **up**† to grind food with the teeth until it can be swallowed. □ *You had better chew that stuff up well.* □ *Please chew up your food well.*

chew the fat and **chew the rag** *Fig.* to chat or gossip. □ *Sit yourself down and let's chew the fat for a while.* □ *We were just chewing the rag. Nothing important.*

chew the rag Go to previous.

chicken feed *Fig.* a small amount of anything, especially of money. (See also **for chicken feed.** Compare this with **for peanuts.**) □ *Of course I can afford $800. That's just chicken feed.* □ *It may be chicken feed to you, but that's a month's rent to me.*

chicken out (of something) *Inf.* to manage to get out of something, usually because of fear or cowardice. □ *Come on! Don't chicken out now!* □ *Freddy chickened out of the plan at the last minute.*

chicken out on someone *Inf.* to decide not to do something for or with someone. □ *Come on, don't chicken out on me now!* □ *Ken chickened out on us and won't be going with us.*

chicken-hearted cowardly. □ *Yes, I'm a chicken-hearted softie. I never try anything too risky.*

The **chickens come home to roost.** *Prov.* You have to face the consequences of your mistakes or bad deeds. □ *Jill: Emily found out that I said she was incompetent, and now she won't recommend me for that job. Jane: The chickens have come home to roost, I see.*

chide someone **for** something to tease or scold someone for doing something. □ *Maria chided Gerald for being late.*

chief cook and bottle washer *Fig.* the person in charge of practically everything (such as in a very small business). □ *I'm the chief cook and bottle washer around here. I do everything.*

The **child is father of the man.** and The **child is father to the man.** *Prov.* People's personalities form when they are children; A person will have the same qualities as an adult that he or she had as a child. (From William Wordsworth's poem, "My Heart Leaps Up.") □ *In Bill's case, the child was father of the man; he never lost his childhood delight in observing nature.*

child's play something very easy to do. □ *The test was child's play to those who took good notes.* □ *Finding the right street was child's play with a map.*

Children and fools tell the truth. *Prov.* Children have not yet learned, and fools never did learn, that it is often advantageous to lie. □ *Fred: What will I tell Ellen when she asks why I'm so late getting home? Alan: Tell her the truth—we were out having a few drinks. Fred: Children and fools tell the truth, Alan.*

Children should be seen and not heard. *Prov.* Children should not speak in the presence of adults. (Often used as a way to rebuke a child who has spoken when he or she should not.) □ *You may come out and meet the party guests if you'll remember that children should be seen and not heard.*

chill out and **cool out** *Sl.* to calm down. □ *Before we can debate this matter, you're all gonna have to chill out. So sit down and stop bickering.* □ *Everybody cooled out after the emergency, and everything was fine.*

chill someone's **action** *Sl.* to squelch someone; to prevent someone from accomplishing something. □ *Freddie is trying to chill my action, and he'd better stop and leave me alone.*

***chilled to the bone** *Fig.* very cold. (*Typically: **be ~; get ~.**) □ *I got chilled to the bone in that snowstorm.* □ *The children were chilled to the bone from their swim in the ocean.*

chime in (with something) *Fig.* to add a comment to the discussion. □ *Little Billy chimed in with a suggestion.* □ *He chimed in too late; the meeting was breaking up.*

chin music *Fig. Inf.* talk; conversation. □ *Whenever those two get together, you can be sure there'll be plenty of chin music.* □ *Bill just loves to hear himself talk. He'll make chin music for hours at a time.*

a **chink in** one's **armor** *Fig.* a special weakness that provides a means for attacking or impressing someone otherwise invulnerable. (Alludes to an opening in a suit of armor that allows a weapon to penetrate.) □ *Jane's insecurity is the chink in her armor.* □ *The boss seems mean, but the chink in his armor is that he is easily flattered.*

chip away [for something] to break off or break away in small chips. □ *The edges of the marble step chipped away over the years.* □ *Some of the stone figures had chipped away so badly that we couldn't see what they were.*

chip (away) at something to break off tiny pieces of something little by little. □ *The mason chipped away at the bricks.* □ *He chipped at the block of marble gently.*

chip in (on something) and **chip** something **in**† **(on** something) **1.** to contribute a small amount of money to a fund that will be used to buy something. □ *Could you chip in a dollar on the gift, please?* **2.** chip in (on **something**) **(for** someone) to contribute money toward a gift for someone. □ *Would you please chip in on the present for Richard?* □ *Will you chip in for Randy?*

chip in (with something) **(on** something) **(for** someone) and **chip in (with** something) **(for** something) **(for** someone); **chip** something **in**† **(on** something) **(for** someone) to contribute money for a gift for someone. □ *Would you like to chip in with a little cash on a gift for Carol?* □ *I will chip in a little with you on a gift for Carol.* □ *Would you chip in with a few bucks for a gift for Carol?* □ *Would you chip a few bucks in on a gift for Carol?* □ *Would you care to chip in on a gift for the teacher?* □ *Yes, I'd be happy to chip in.*

a **chip off the old block** *Fig.* a person (usually a male) who behaves in the same way as his father or resembles his father. □ *John looks like his father—a real chip off the old block.* □ *Bill Jones, Jr., is a chip off the old block. He's a banker just like his father.*

***a chip on** one's **shoulder** *Fig.* a bad attitude that tends to get someone easily upset. (*Typically: **get ~; have ~; give** one ~.) □ *Why did you get so angry at the slightest criticism? You seem to have a chip on your shoulder.*

chip something **away**† **(from** something) to break off tiny pieces of something. □ *Many years of heavy use chipped* the marble steps away. □ Someone chipped away little bits of the marble from that step.

chip something **in**[†] **(on** something**)** Go to chip in (on something).

chip something **in**[†] **(on** something**) (for** someone**)** Go to chip in (with something) (on something) (for someone).

chips and dip potato chips, or some other kind of crisp snack food, and a sauce or dressing to dip them into before eating them. □ There were tons of chips and dip and all kinds of cold drinks available for everyone.

chisel in (on someone or something**)** Sl. to use deception to get a share of something. □ I won't chisel in on your deal. □ You had better not chisel in!

chisel someone **out of** something and **chisel** something **out of** someone; **chisel** something **from** someone to get something away from someone by cheating. □ The scam tried to chisel pension money out of retired people.

chock full of something Fig. very full of something. □ These cookies are chock full of big chunks of chocolate.

choke on something to gag and cough on something stuck in the throat. □ The dog choked on the meat. □ The restaurant patron began to choke on a fish bone.

choke someone **off**[†] to prevent someone from continuing to talk. (A figurative use; does not imply physical choking.) □ The opposition choked the speakers' debate off before they finished. □ Why did they want to choke off the speakers?

choke someone **up**[†] Fig. to cause someone to feel like starting to cry. □ Sad stories like that always choke me up. □ The movie was sad and it choked up most of the audience.

choke something **back**[†] to fight hard to keep something from coming out of one's mouth, such as sobs, tears, angry words, vomit, etc. □ I tried to choke the unpleasant words back, but I could not. □ She choked back her grief, but it came forth nonetheless. □ I could hardly choke my tears back.

choke something **down**[†] to eat something, even though it is hard to swallow or tastes bad. □ The cough medicine tasted terrible, but I managed to choke it down. □ She choked down four of those pills all at once.

choke something **off**[†] **1.** Lit. to restrict or strangle a living creature's windpipe. □ The tight collar on the cat tended to choke its airstream off. □ The collar choked off its airstream. **2.** Fig. to put an end to debate or discussion; to stop the flow of words from any source. □ Are they going to choke the debate off? □ The chair tried to choke off debate but failed.

choke something **up**[†] **1.** to clog something up; to fill up and block something. □ Branches and leaves choked the sewer up. □ Rust choked up the pipes. **2.** to cough or choke until something that has blocked one's windpipe is brought up. □ The old man choked up the candy that was stuck in his windpipe. □ He choked up the chunk of meat and could breathe again.

choke up 1. to feel like crying. □ I choked up when I heard the news. □ He was beginning to choke up as he talked. **2.** to become emotional or saddened so that one cannot speak. □ I choked up when I heard about the disaster. □ I was choking up, and I knew I would not be able to go on.

chomp at the bit Go to champ at the bit.

choose among someone or something to make a choice of a person or thing from a variety of possibilities. □ We will choose among the names on the list you gave us. □ I need to choose among the car models available.

choose between two people or things to choose one from a selection of two persons or things in any combination. □ For dessert, you can choose between chocolate and vanilla ice cream. □ I am unable to choose between promoting John and hiring one of the others.

choose from someone or something to make a selection from a group of persons or things. □ You will have to choose from these people only. □ Ron chose from the items in the catalog.

choose someone **as** something to select someone to be something. □ We will choose her as our representative. □ I chose Sam as my assistant.

choose someone or something **for** something to select someone or something for a particular purpose, office, title, etc. □ I chose red for the color or the carpet. □ I will choose Alice for office manager.

choose something **for** someone to select something for someone, perhaps as a gift. □ I will probably choose flowers for your mother. □ I chose a funny card for his birthday.

choose (up) sides to select from a group to be on opposing sides for a debate, fight, or game. (Fixed order.) □ Let's choose up sides and play basketball. □ The children chose up sides and began the game.

chop someone **off**[†] Fig. to stop someone in the middle of a sentence or speech. (Abruptly, as if actually chopping or cutting.) □ I'm not finished. Don't chop me off! □ The moderator chopped off the speaker.

chop someone or something **(up**[†]**) (in(to)** something**)** to cut something up into something smaller, perhaps with an axe or a cleaver. □ The butcher chopped up the beef loin into small fillets. □ I chopped up the onion into little pieces.

chop something **back**[†] to prune vegetation; to reduce the size of plants by cutting. □ Why don't you chop those bushes back while you have the shears out? □ Chop back the bushes, please.

chop something **down**[†] **1.** Lit. to cut down something, such as a tree, with an ax. □ Please don't chop my favorite tree down. □ Don't chop down this tree! **2.** Fig. to destroy something, such as a plan or an idea. □ The committee chopped the idea down in its early stages. □ They chopped down a great idea!

chop something **off (of)** something and **chop** something **off**[†] to cut something off something, as with an axe or saw. (Of is usually retained before pronouns.) □ We chopped the dead branches off the tree. □ You should chop off the other branch.

chortle about someone or something and **chortle over** someone or something to chuckle or giggle about someone or something funny. □ I was chortling about Elaine's silly puppy for a long time. □ Elaine chortled about me and my dislike for cats.

chortle with something Go to chuckle with something.

chow (something) down Sl. to eat something, usually quickly or without good manners. □ We can chow this *pizza down in about two minutes!* □ *I found a box of cookies and chowed it down before anybody knew what I was doing.*

Christmas comes but once a year. *Prov.* Since Christmas only happens once a year, we should treat it as a special time by being good to others or by indulging children. □ *Christmas comes but once a year, so we urge you to give to those less fortunate through this Christmas charity campaign.*

chuck it in *Inf.* to quit; to give up. (Fixed order.) □ *I was so depressed, I almost chucked it in.* □ *If I didn't have to keep the job to pay my bills, I'd have chucked it in long ago.*

chuck someone or something **away**† to push or shove someone or something out of the way quickly or roughly. □ *She chucked the children away and ran to lock the door to protect them.* □ *He chucked away his clothes in a drawer.* □ *The rock star approached, and the guard chucked the teenagers away.*

chuck someone **out of** some place and **chuck** someone **out**† to throw someone out of some place. □ *The bouncer chucked the drunks out of the tavern.* □ *He chucks out about three drunks a night.*

chuck someone **under the chin** to tap someone, as a child, lightly under the chin, as a sign of affection. □ *He said hello to little Mary and chucked her under the chin.* □ *Please don't chuck me under the chin! I am not a child, you know!*

chuck something **away**† to throw something away; to dispose of something. □ *Would you please just chuck this garbage bag away?* □ *I don't want to chuck away any paper that's been used on only one side.*

chuck something **down**† *Sl.* to eat something very quickly. □ *Don't just chuck your food down. Enjoy it!* □ *I'll be with you as soon as I chuck down this hamburger.*

chuck something **into** something and **chuck** something **in**† to pack something into something. □ *She chucked her clothes into the suitcase and left.* □ *Just chuck in all your clothes and let's go.*

chuck something **over** something to throw something over something. □ *Here, chuck this over the wall, and let's go.* □ *If you chuck another can over the fence, I will file a complaint.*

chuck something **up**† to vomit something up. □ *Don't give chocolate to the dog. It will just chuck it up later.* □ *The dog chucked up the grass it had eaten.*

chuckle about someone or something and **chuckle over** someone or something to giggle about someone or something. □ *I had to chuckle about Wally and his story about that broken-down old car.* □ *We chuckled over how angry Jed was.*

chuckle with something and **chortle with** something to giggle in some manner because one is gleeful or happy. □ *He chuckled with unsuppressed mirth at the antics of the strangely dressed people.* □ *Sally chortled with glee at the thought of Ken slipping on the ice.*

chug along 1. *Lit.* [for a train engine] to labor along slowly. (Steam locomotives made the sound "chug, chug.") □ *The train chugged along to the top of the hill.* **2.** *Fig.* to move along at a steady pace. □ *We chugged along for two hours but finally made it home.*

chum up to someone to try or seem to become friendly with someone. □ *Todd chummed up to Martin.* □ *I don't want to have to chum up to anyone I don't want to work with.*

chum up with someone to become friendly with someone. □ *He seems to have chummed up with Fred.* □ *Juan quickly chummed up with all the guys in his class.*

a **chunk of change** *Fig.* a lot of money. □ *Tom's new sports car cost a real big chunk of change!*

chunk something *Rur.* to throw something. □ *The kids were out chunking rocks into the lake.* □ *Somebody chunked a snowball at me!*

Church ain't out till they quit singing. *Rur.* things have not yet reached the end. □ *Charlie: No way our team can win now. Mary: Church ain't out till they quit singing. There's another inning to go.*

church key a two-ended device used to remove bottle tops and to pierce a hole in can lids. □ *I'm looking for the church key so I can open this beer.* □ *She opened the can of tomato juice with the church key.*

churn something **out**† to produce something in large numbers, perhaps carelessly. □ *We churn toys out by the thousand.* □ *This factory can churn out these parts day and night.*

churn something **up**† to stir up a liquid; to mix up material suspended in water. □ *The oars of our boat churned the shallow water up, leaving little clouds of sediment in our wake.* □ *The oars churned up the mud.*

circle around (over someone or something**)** [for a plane or a bird] to fly around above someone, something, or some place. □ *The plane circled around over us for a few minutes and then went on.* □ *It circled around over the field.*

circle around someone or something Go to **around** someone or something.

circulate among someone or something to move at random within a gathering of people or things. □ *Karen circulated among the guests, serving drinks.* □ *The guests circulated among the various rooms in the house.*

circulate something **through** something to route something through something; to make something travel through something. □ *Walter circulated the memo from the boss through the department.* □ *I would like for you to circulate this through the members of the club.*

circulate through something **1.** *Lit.* [for a fluid in a closed system of pipes or tubes] to flow through the various pathways of pipes and tubes. □ *Cold water circulates through the entire building and keeps it cool.* □ *Blood circulates through the veins and arteries, reaching all parts of the body.* **2.** *Fig.* to move through a group of people or an area, from person to person. □ *Rumors circulated through the department about Tom's retirement.* □ *Please circulate through the room and hand out these papers to each person.*

Circumstances alter cases. *Prov.* In unusual situations, people are allowed to do unusual things. □ *Cashier: I'm sorry, this store does not accept personal checks. Customer: But I need this medicine, and I don't have any cash. I've shopped at this store for fifteen years. Surely you can trust me this once. Cashier: Well, all right. Circumstances alter cases.*

cite someone **for** something **1.** to honor someone for doing something; to give someone a citation of honor for doing something good. □ *The town council cited her for bravery.* □ *They cited Maria for her courageous act.* **2.** to charge or arraign someone for breaking a law; to issue a legal citation to someone for breaking a law. □ *An officer cited the driver for driving too fast.* □ *The housing department cited the landlord for sanitary violations.*

city slicker someone from the city who is not familiar with country ways. □ *Them city slickers think we're stupid just because we talk different.* □ *The city slicker didn't know the first thing about fishing for trout.*

Civility costs nothing. and **Courtesy costs nothing.** *Prov.* It never hurts you to be polite. □ *Always greet people politely, no matter what you think of them. Civility costs nothing.* □ *Why not write Mildred a thank-you note? Courtesy costs nothing.*

claim a life *Fig.* [for something] to take the life of someone. □ *The killer tornado claimed the lives of six people at the trailer park.* □ *The athlete's life was claimed in a skiing accident.*

claim something **for** someone or something to declare rights to or control of something for someone, or that something is the property of someone, a group, or a nation. □ *The small country claimed the mountainous area for itself.* □ *Roger claimed all the rest of the ice cream for himself.*

claim something **for** something to make a claim for money in payment for damages. □ *David claimed one thousand dollars for the damaged car.* □ *She claimed a lot of money for the amount of harm she experienced.*

clam up to say nothing. (Closing one's mouth in the way that a clam closes up.) □ *The minute they got him in for questioning, he clammed up.* □ *You'll clam up if you know what's good for you.*

clamber onto something and **clamber in(to** something**); clamber on** to climb onto something clumsily. □ *The kids clambered onto the tractor and tried to start it.* □ *The wagon stopped and the kids clambered on.* □ *All the campers clambered into the bus.*

clamber up (something**)** to climb up something, especially in a particular way. □ *The wall climbers clambered up the wall quickly.* □ *Tricia clambered up the ladder and cautiously went down again.*

clamor against someone or something to raise a great outcry against someone or something. □ *The protestors clamored against the mayor.* □ *The citizens clamored against the new taxes.*

clamor for someone or something to raise a great outcry for someone or something. □ *Everyone was clamoring for Mark. They just loved him.* □ *The children were clamoring for ice cream.*

clamp down (on someone or something**)** to become strict with someone; to become strict about something. □ *Because Bob's grades were getting worse, his parents clamped down on him.* □ *The police have clamped down on speeders in this town.*

clamp something **on(to)** something and **clamp** something **on** to press or squeeze something onto something else. □ *Clamp this board onto the workbench.* □ *Clear a place* near the edge of the table, and then clamp on the meat grinder.

clap eyes on someone or something to see someone or something, perhaps for the first time; to set eyes on someone or something. □ *I wish she had never clapped eyes on her fiancé.* □ *I haven't clapped eyes on a red squirrel for years.*

clap someone **in(to)** some place to shove or push someone into a place, usually jail. □ *Be good or the sheriff will clap you into jail.* □ *The cops clapped Max into a cell.*

clap something **on(to)** something to slap or attack something onto something else. □ *The police came and clapped a sign onto the car saying it was abandoned.* □ *Do not clap any signs on my fence.*

clap something **out** to clap the rhythmic beat of something in order to learn it. (Said of music.) □ *All right, now. Let's clap the rhythm out.* □ *We'll clap out the rhythm in time with our singing.*

clap something **together** to slap two things, usually hands, together so that they make a noise. □ *The boys clapped their hands together whenever a goal was scored.* □ *One of the orchestra members clapped two blocks of wood together periodically, making a very loud noise.*

clash against something to wage a battle or attack against someone or something. □ *The troops clashed against the enemy.* □ *We clashed against the opposite side for over three days.*

clash (with someone**) (over** someone or something**)** to fight or argue with someone about someone or something. □ *The customer clashed with the pharmacist over the price of the medicine.* □ *I clashed over my pay increase with the school principal.*

clash with something [for the color of something] to conflict with or mismatch another color. □ *This red carpet clashes with the purple of the drapes.* □ *This red does not clash with purple. It looks gorgeous.*

clasp someone or something **to** something to hold on to and press someone or something to a part of one's body. □ *He clasped a wad of cloth to the bleeding wound.* □ *She clasped the child to her breast and hugged him.*

class someone or something **with** someone or something to group someone or something with someone or something considered similar. □ *Please don't class this car with anything you've ever driven before.* □ *The sportswriters classed this team with some of the all-time best in history.*

clatter around and **clatter** something **around** to move around among things, making noise. □ *Stop clattering around! It's late.* □ *I wish you would not clatter those dishes around.*

claw one's **way to the top** *Fig.* to climb to the most prestigious level of something ruthlessly. □ *He was the type of hard-hitting guy who claws his way to the top.* □ *She clawed her way to the top, fighting at every step.*

claw something **off** someone or something and **claw** something **off** to rip or tear something off from someone or something. □ *We saw a guy clawing his burning clothes off himself.* □ *He clawed off his burning clothes.*

*clean as a hound's tooth and ***clean as a whistle** **1.** *Rur. Cliché* very clean. (*Also:* **as** ~.) □ *After his* mother scrubbed him thoroughly, the baby was as clean as a hound's tooth. □ The car was as clean as a whistle after the Girl Scouts washed it. **2.** *Rur. Cliché* innocent and free from sin or wrong. (*Also: **as** ~.) □ Jane's record was clean as a whistle; she had never committed even the smallest infraction.

clean as a whistle Go to previous.

*a **clean bill of health** *Fig.* a physician's determination that a person is in good condition, especially following an illness, surgery, etc. (*Typically: **get** ~; **have** ~; **give** someone ~.) □ Sally got a clean bill of health from the doctor. □ Now that Sally has a clean bill of health, she can go back to work.

clean one's **act up**[†] to reform one's conduct; to improve one's performance. □ We were told to clean our act up or move out. □ I cleaned up my act, but not in time. I got kicked out.

clean one's **plate** Go to clean up one's plate.

clean out (of something) Go to fresh out (of something).

clean someone or something **down**[†] to clean someone or something by brushing or with flowing water. □ He was covered with mud, and we used the garden hose to clean him down. □ Please clean down the sidewalk.

clean someone or something **out of** something and **clean** someone or something **out**[†] to remove people or things from something or some place. □ Someone should clean those bums out of political office. □ Let's clean out the garage this weekend; I can't get the car in.

clean someone or something **up**[†] to get someone or something clean. □ Please go into the bathroom and clean yourself up. □ I'll clean up the kids before we leave for dinner. □ Can you clean this place up a little?

clean someone **out**[†] **1.** *Fig.* to get or use up all of someone's money. □ The bill for supper cleaned me out, and we couldn't go to the flick. □ The robbers cleaned out all the bank's cash. **2.** *Fig.* to empty someone's bowels. □ That medicine I took really cleaned me out. □ Whatever was in that stew cleaned out every kid in the entire scout camp.

clean someone's **plow** *Rur.* to beat someone up. □ If Joe crosses me one more time, I'll clean his plow for sure. □ Somebody must have really cleaned Bill's plow last night. He had two black eyes this morning!

clean something **off**[†] and **clean** something **off** something to take something off something; to remove something such as dirt or dirty dishes. □ Please clean the table off and put the dishes in the kitchen. □ I'll clean off the table. □ Judy cleaned the writing off the wall.

clean something **out**[†] to remove dirt or unwanted things from the inside of something. □ Someone has to clean the garage out. □ I'll clean out my closet tonight.

a **clean sweep** a broad movement clearing or affecting everything in its pathway. (See also make a clean sweep. Usually figurative.) □ The manager and everybody in accounting got fired in a clean sweep of that department. □ Everybody got a pay rise. It was a clean sweep.

clean the floor up[†] **with** someone *Fig.* to beat someone up. □ If you don't shut up, I'll clean up the floor with you. □ You won't clean the floor up with me!

clean up (on something) *Fig.* to make a lot of money on something. □ The promoters cleaned up on the product. □ If we get this invention to market soon, we can clean up.

clean (up) one's **plate** to eat all the food on one's plate. □ You have to clean up your plate before you can leave the table. □ Mom said we can't watch TV tonight unless we clean our plates.

clean-cut having to do with a person (usually male) who is neat and tidy. □ He's a very clean-cut guy, and polite too. □ He's sort of clean-cut looking, but with curly hair.

cleaned out 1. *Fig.* broke; with no money. □ I'm cleaned out. Not a cent left. □ Tom's cleaned out. How will he pay his bills now? **2.** *Fig.* with one's digestive tract emptied. □ That medicine really left me cleaned out.

Cleanliness is next to godliness. *Prov.* It is very important to keep yourself clean. □ Child: How come I have to take a bath? Mother: Cleanliness is next to godliness. □ The woman sitting next to me on the bus had obviously never heard that cleanliness is next to godliness.

***clear as a bell** very clear, as with the sound of a bell. (*Also: **as** ~.) □ I fixed the radio, so now all the stations come in clear as a bell. □ Through the wall, I could hear the neighbors talking, just as clear as a bell.

***clear as crystal 1.** *Cliché* very clear; transparent. (*Also: **as** ~.) □ The stream was as clear as crystal. □ She cleaned the windowpane until it was clear as crystal. **2.** *Cliché* very clear; easy to understand. (*Also: **as** ~.) □ The explanation was as clear as crystal. □ Her lecture was not clear as crystal, but at least it was not dull.

***clear as mud 1.** *Cliché* not clear at all. (*Also: **as** ~.) □ Your swimming pool needs cleaning; the water is clear as mud. **2.** *Cliché* not easy to understand. (*Also: **as** ~.) □ This physics chapter is clear as mud to me. □ I did all the reading, but it's still as clear as mud.

clear as vodka Go to clear as crystal.

***clear of** something without touching something; away from something. (*Typically: **keep** ~; **move** ~; **remain** ~; **stand** ~.) □ Please stand clear of the doors while the train is moving. □ Make sure the dog moves clear of the driveway before backing the car up.

clear off ((of) some place) to depart; to get off someone's property. □ Clear off my property! □ Clear off, do you hear?

clear out (of some place) to get out of some place. □ Will you all clear out of here? □ Please clear out!

***clear sailing** and ***smooth sailing** *Fig.* a situation where progress is made without any difficulty. (*Typically: **be** ~; **have** ~.) □ Once you've passed that exam, it will be clear sailing to graduation. □ Working there was not all smooth sailing. The boss had a very bad temper.

clear someone **of** something to show that a person is innocent; to exonerate someone of a crime. (See also clear someone's name.) □ An investigation cleared me of any wrongdoing. □ They were unable to clear themselves of the charges.

clear someone or something **out of** some place and **clear** someone or something **out**[†] to make someone or something leave a place. □ Please clear all the people out of here. □ Clear out the people quickly, please.

clear someone's **name** to prove that someone is not guilty of a crime or misdeed. (See also **clear** someone of something.) □ *I was accused of theft, but the real thief confessed and I cleared my name.*

clear something **away**[†] to take something away. □ *Please clear the children's toys away.* □ *Would you clear away the dishes?*

clear something **for publication** to approve the release of something so it can be published. □ *The government refused to clear the story for publication.* □ *I want to clear this for publication as soon as possible.*

clear something **from** some place to take something away from a place. □ *Please clear all these papers from the desk.* □ *Would you clear the dishes from the table?*

clear something **off** something and **clear** something **off**[†] to take something off something. □ *Please clear the dishes off the table.* □ *I'll clear off the dishes.*

clear something **up**[†] **1.** to make something more clear. □ *Let the muddy water stand overnight so it will clear up.* □ *A strong wind blew in and cleared up the smoke in the air.* **2.** to explain something; to solve a mystery. □ *I think that we can clear this matter up without calling in the police.* □ *First we have to clear up the problem of the missing jewels.* **3.** to cause a rash or inflammation to return to normal; to cause skin to "clear." □ *There is some new medicine that will clear your rash up.* **4.** to cure a disease or a medical condition. □ *The doctor will give you something to clear up your congestion.*

clear something **with** someone or something to get someone's approval for something. □ *You will have to clear this expenditure with the main office.* □ *I will clear your trip with Dad.*

clear the air 1. *Lit.* to get rid of stale or bad air. □ *Open some windows and clear the air. It's stuffy in here.* **2.** *Fig.* to get rid of doubts or hard feelings. □ *All right, let's discuss this frankly. It'll be better if we clear the air.*

clear the decks 1. *Lit.* [for everyone] leave the deck of a ship and prepare for action. (A naval expression urging seaman to stow gear and prepare for battle or other action.) □ *An attack is coming. Clear the decks.* **2.** *Fig.* get out of the way; get out of this area. □ *Clear the decks! Here comes the teacher.* □ *Clear the decks and take your seats.*

clear the table to remove the dishes and other eating utensils from the table after a meal. (Compare this with **set the table**.) □ *Will you please help clear the table?* □ *After you clear the table, we'll play cards.*

Clear the way! Please get out of the way, because someone or something is coming through and needs room! □ *The movers were shouting, "Clear the way!" because they needed room to take the piano out of the house.*

clear up 1. [for the sky] to become more clear or sunny. □ *Suddenly, the sky cleared up.* □ *When the sky cleared up, the breeze began to blow.* **2.** [for something] to become more understandable. □ *At about the middle of the very confusing lecture, things began to clear up.* □ *I was having trouble, but things are beginning to clear up.* **3.** [for a rash or skin condition] to clear the skin and return to normal. □ *I'm sure your rash will clear up soon.* **4.** [for a minor illness] to improve or become cured. □ *His cold cleared up after a couple of weeks.*

cleave to someone to be sexually faithful, usually to one's husband. (Biblical. As in the traditional marriage ceremony, "And cleave only unto him.") □ *She promised to cleave only to him for the rest of her life.*

click with someone **1.** [for something] to be understood or comprehended by someone suddenly. □ *His explanation clicked with Maggie at once.* **2.** [for someone or something new] to catch on with someone; to become popular or friendly with someone very quickly. □ *The new product clicked with consumers and was an instant success.* □ *I clicked with Tom the moment I met him.*

climb down (from something**)** to dismount something; to come down from something. □ *The child climbed down from the roof.* □ *Please climb down!*

climb on Go to **climb on(to)** something.

climb on the bandwagon Go to **on the bandwagon**.

climb on(to) something and **climb on** to ascend to or mount something. □ *I climbed onto the side of the truck.* □ *Tommy climbed on the truck.*

climb out (of something**)** to get, crawl, or move out of something. □ *He climbed out of the wreckage and examined himself carefully for injuries.* □ *He climbed out very carefully.*

climb the wall(s) *Fig.* to be very agitated, anxious, bored, or excited. □ *He was home for only three days; then he began to climb the wall.* □ *I was climbing the walls to get back to work.*

climb up (something**)** to ascend something; to scale something. (Fixed order.) □ *The hikers took two hours to climb up the hill.* □ *The adventurer tried to climb up the side of the cliff.*

cling to someone or something **1.** *Lit.* to hold on tight to someone or something. □ *The child clung tightly to his mother.* □ *As she drifted in the sea, she clung to a floating log.* **2.** *Fig.* to hold onto the thought or memory of someone or something; to have a strong emotional attachment to or dependence on someone or something. □ *Her immigrant parents clung to the old ways.* □ *Harold clung to the memory of his grandmother.*

cling together [for two or more people or animals] to hold on tightly to each other. □ *The two children clung together throughout the ordeal.* □ *The baby baboon and its mother clung together and could not be separated.*

clip someone's **wings** *Fig.* to restrain someone; to reduce or put an end to someone's privileges. (Alludes to clipping a bird's wings to keep it from flying away.) □ *You had better learn to get home on time, or I will clip your wings.* □ *My mother clipped my wings. I can't go out tonight.*

clip something **from** something to cut something out of or away from something; to cut something off something. □ *I clipped the picture from the magazine.* □ *I clipped the straggly hairs from his head.*

clip something **on(to)** someone or something and **clip** something **on**[†] to attach something to someone or something with a clip. □ *I clipped a little name tag onto him before I put him on the plane.* □ *I clipped on a name tag.*

clip something **out of** something and **clip** something **out**[†] to remove something from something by clipping or cutting. □ *Please clip the article out of the magazine.* □ *Could you clip out the picture, too?*

cloak someone or something **in secrecy** *Fig.* to hide or conceal someone or something in secrecy. □ *Patrick cloaked his activities in secrecy.* □ *The agents cloaked the spy in secrecy, making her identity a mystery.*

cloak-and-dagger involving secrecy and plotting. □ *A great deal of cloak-and-dagger stuff goes on in political circles.* □ *A lot of cloak-and-dagger activity was involved in the appointment of the director.*

clock in to record one's time of arrival, usually by punching a time clock. □ *What time did she clock in?* □ *She forgot to clock in today.*

clock out to record one's time of departure, usually by punching a time clock. □ *I will clock out just before I go home.* □ *Jim clocked out early Tuesday to go to the doctor.*

clock someone **in** to observe and record someone's time of arrival. □ *The manager says he clocked you in at noon. That's a bit late, isn't it?*

clock someone or something **at** something to measure the speed of someone or something to be a certain figure. □ *I clocked the runner at a record speed for the race.* □ *Karen clocked the race at three minutes flat.*

clock someone **out** to observe and record someone's time of departure. □ *Jane clocked herself out and went home.*

clock someone **at speeds of** some amount Go to **speeds of** some amount.

clock something **up**† **1.** to record the accumulated hours, miles, etc., of some device or machine. (The recording is usually done by a meter of some type such as a speedometer, an elapsed time meter, etc. □ *She must have clocked two hundred flying hours up in six months.* □ *She clocked up a lot of hours.* **2.** to reach a goal that is worthy of being recorded. (Typically sports journalism. Compare this with **chalk** something **up.**) □ *Patrick clocked a fantastic number of points up this year.* □ *He sure clocked up a lot of goals.*

clock-watcher someone—a worker or a student—who is always looking at the clock, anticipating when something will be over. □ *There are four clock-watchers in our office.* □ *People who don't like their jobs can turn into clock-watchers.*

clog someone **up**† [for some kind of food] to constipate someone. □ *This cheese clogs me up. I can't eat it.* □ *This food clogs up people who eat it.*

clog something **up**† [for something] to obstruct a channel or conduit. □ *The leaves clogged the gutters up.* □ *They clogged up the gutter.*

clog something **with** something to block or obstruct a channel or conduit with something. □ *The neighbors clogged the creek with their brush and leaves.* □ *Please don't clog the drain with garbage.*

clog up [for a channel or conduit] to become blocked. □ *The canal clogged up with leaves and mud.*

close a deal and **close the deal** to formally conclude bargaining; to bring negotiating to an end by reaching an agreement. □ *We negotiated the terms of the agreement, and this afternoon we will close the deal.*

close a sale and **close the sale** to complete the sale of something; to seal a bargain in the sale of something. □ *The salesman closed the sale and the customer drove off in a brand new car.*

*close as two coats of paint *Cliché* close and intimate. (**Also:* **as** ~.) □ *When Tom and Mary were in high school, they were as close as two coats of paint.* □ *All their lives, the cousins were close as two coats of paint.*

close at hand within reach; handy. □ *I'm sorry, but your letter isn't close at hand. Please remind me what you said in it.* □ *When you're cooking, you should keep all the ingredients close at hand.*

Close, but no cigar. *Cliché* Some effort came close to succeeding, but did not succeed. (Alludes to not quite winning a cigar as a prize.) □ *Jill: How did you do in the contest? Jane: Close, but no cigar. I got second place.*

a **close call** Go to a **close shave**.

close chewer and a tight spitter *Rur.* someone who hates to spend money; a cheapskate. □ *He's a close chewer and a tight spitter. Everything about him looks run-down, but he's probably the richest man in the county.*

close down and **shut down** [for someone] to close a business, office, shop, etc., permanently or temporarily. □ *This shop will have to close down if they raise taxes.* □ *The fire department closed down all the stores on the block because of the gas leak.*

close enough for government work and **good enough for government work** sufficiently close; done just well enough. (Alludes to the notion that work for the government is not done with care or pride.) □ *I didn't do the best job of mending your shirt, but it's close enough for government work.*

close enough to use the same toothpick *Rur.* very close. (Used to describe close friends.) □ *We've been friends since we were five years old. We're close enough to use the same toothpick.*

close (in) around someone or something to move to surround someone or something. □ *The police closed in around the thieves.* □ *We closed in around the enemy camp.*

close in for the kill and **move in for the kill 1.** *Lit.* to move in on someone or something for the purpose of killing. □ *The wolves closed in for the kill.* □ *When the lions closed in for the kill, the zebras began to stampede.* **2.** *Fig.* to get ready to do the final and climactic part of something. □ *The car salesman closed in for the kill with contract and pen in hand.*

close in (on someone or something**) 1.** *Lit.* to move inward on someone or something. □ *The cops were closing in on the thugs.* □ *They closed in quietly and trapped the bear.* **2.** *Fig.* [for threats or negative feelings] to overwhelm or seem to surround someone or something. □ *My problems are closing in on me.* □ *I feel trapped. Everything is closing in.*

close on something to formally complete the sale and transfer of property, especially real estate. □ *We closed on the new house on April 16.* □ *We were able to close on our old house on June 2.*

close one's **eyes to** something and **shut** one's **eyes to** something **1.** *Lit.* to close one's eyes to avoid seeing something unpleasant. □ *I had to close my eyes to the carnage about me. I couldn't bear to look.* **2.** *Fig.* to ignore something; to pretend that something is not happening. □

Maria simply shut her eyes to the bad morale in her department.

Close only counts in horseshoes (and hand grenades). *Prov.* Coming close but not succeeding is not good enough. □ *I came close to winning the election, but close only counts in horseshoes and hand grenades.*

close ranks to move closer together in a military formation. □ *The soldiers closed ranks and marched on the enemy in tight formation.*

close ranks (behind someone or something**)** to support someone or something; to back someone or something. □ *We will close ranks behind the party's nominee.* □ *Let's close ranks behind her and give her the support she needs.*

close ranks (with someone**)** to join with someone in a cause, or agreement. □ *We can fight this menace only if we close ranks.* □ *Let's all close ranks with Ann and adopt her suggestions.*

a **close shave** and a **close call** a narrow escape. (See also **have a close shave**.) □ *Wow, that was a close shave. I thought the guard would spot us.* □ *The speeding car passed only a few inches from us—a real close call.*

close someone or something **down**† to force someone or someone's business, office, shop, etc., to close permanently or temporarily. □ *The health department closed the restaurant down.* □ *They closed down the same place last year, too.*

close someone or something **in (something)** to contain someone or something in something or some place; to seal someone or something inside something. □ *Don't close the bird in such a small cage.* □ *Don't close me in! Leave the door open.*

close someone **out of** something and **close** someone **out**† to prevent someone from getting into something, such as a class, a room, a waiting list, etc. □ *They closed me out of the class I wanted.* □ *I got in, but they closed out everyone after me in line.*

close someone **up**† to close a surgical wound at the end of a surgical procedure. □ *Fred, would you close her up for me?* □ *Fred closed up the patient.*

close something **down**† and **shut** something **down**† to make something stop operating; to put something out of business. □ *The police closed the illegal casino down.* □ *The manager shut down the factory for the holidays.*

close something **off**† to prevent entrance into something; to **block** something **off**. □ *Please don't close this passageway off.* □ *They closed off the passageway anyway.*

close something **out**† **1.** to sell off a particular kind of merchandise with the intention of not selling it in the future. □ *These are not selling. Let's close them out.* □ *They closed out all of last season's merchandise.* **2.** to prevent further registration in something. □ *We are going to have to close this class out.* □ *The registrar closed out the class.*

close something **to** someone to prevent someone or some type of person from participating in or attending something. □ *We closed membership to anyone who signed up late.* □ *They had to close the registration to nonresidents.*

close something **up**† **1.** to close someone's business, office, shop, etc., temporarily or permanently. □ *Tom's restaurant nearly went out of business when the health depart-*

ment closed him up. □ *The health department closed up the restaurant.* **2.** to close something that is open, such as a door or a box. □ *Please close the door when you leave.*

close the books on someone or something *Fig.* to declare that a matter concerning someone or something is finished. (The *books* here originally referred to financial accounting records.) □ *It's time to close the books on Fred. He's had enough time to apologize to us.*

close the deal Go to **close a deal**.

close the door on someone or something Go to **shut the door (up)on** someone or something.

close the door to someone or something Go to **shut the door (up)on** someone or something.

close the sale Go to **close a sale**.

close to home *Fig.* affecting one personally and intimately. □ *Her remarks were a bit too close to home. I took her review as a personal insult.*

***close to** someone friendly or intimate with someone. (*Typically: **be** ~; **get** ~.) □ *She is very shy and really won't let anyone get close to her.* □ *It is difficult to get close to a loner like Wally.*

***close to** someone or something **1.** near someone or something. (*Typically: **get** ~; **stand** ~; **sit** ~; **move** ~.) □ *Don't get close to me. I have a cold.* □ *If you get close to the fire, you may get burned.* **2.** approximating someone or something in some quality or measure. (*Typically: **be** ~; **get** ~.) □ *This brand of frozen fish does not even get close to that brand in flavor and freshness.* □ *Tom doesn't even get close to Nancy when it comes to artistic ability.*

close up 1. *Lit.* [for an opening] to close completely. □ *The door closed up and would not open again.* □ *The wound will close up completely in a day or so.* **2.** *Fig.* [for a place of business] to close for business. □ *The store closed up and did not open until the next day.*

close up shop *Fig.* to quit working, for the day or forever. (Fixed order.) □ *It's five o'clock. Time to close up shop.* □ *I can't make any money in this town. The time has come to close up shop and move to another town.*

close with someone or something to end a performance with a particular act or event. □ *The show is almost over and we will close with Sarah Miles, who will announce her own song title.* □ *The evening closed with a magic act.*

closefisted (with money) Go to **tightfisted (with money)**.

closet someone **with** someone to put someone into a private room with someone else for the purposes of conducting business. □ *She closeted herself with the president and finally, once and for all, had her say.*

clothe someone **in** something to dress someone in something. □ *She clothed her children in the finest garments.* □ *He clothed himself in his tuxedo for the wedding.*

Clothes make the man. *Prov.* People will judge you according to the way you dress. □ *Jim was always careful about how he dressed. He believed that clothes make the man.*

cloud over 1. *Lit.* [for the sky] to fill with clouds; [for the sun] to be obscured by clouds. □ *It was beginning to cloud over, so we went inside.* □ *The sky clouded over and it began to get chilly.* **2.** *Fig.* [for something once clear] to become opaque; to become clouded. □ *My vision seemed to cloud over, and I could see very little.* □ *The mirror clouded over as the steam rose from the hot water in the sink.*

cloud up 1. *Lit.* [for the sky] to get cloudy, as if it were going to rain. □ *All of a sudden it clouded up and began to rain.* □ *It usually clouds up at the top of the mountain.* **2.** *Fig.* [for someone] to grow very sad, as if to cry. □ *Whenever Mary got homesick, she'd cloud up. She really wanted to go home.*

clown around (with someone**)** *Fig.* to join with someone in acting silly; [for two or more people] to act silly together. □ *The boys were clowning around with each other.* □ *The kids are having fun clowning around.*

clue someone **in**[†] **(on** something**)** to inform someone of something. □ *Please clue me in on what's been going on.* □ *Clue in those guys before it's too late.*

clunk down [for something] to drop or fall, making the sound "clunk." □ *A large piece of metal clunked down right in front of me.* □ *A tree branch clunked down on the roof and damaged a few shingles.*

clunk something **down**[†] to drop or place something heavily on something so that it makes a clunking noise. □ *He clunked the big box down on the table.* □ *He clunked down all his school books on the table.*

cluster around someone or something [for a group of people or things] to bunch together, surrounding someone or something. □ *The birds clustered around the chimney top to keep warm.* □ *The kids clustered around the police officer.*

cluster someone or something **around** someone or something to bunch people or things together around someone or something. □ *She clustered the cups around the punch bowl.* □ *Karen clustered the children around the fire.*

cluster together to bunch or group together. □ *All of the bats clustered together on the roof of the cave.* □ *The children clustered together in small groups here and there on the playground.*

clutch at someone or something to grasp at or grab for someone or something. □ *He clutched at the roots of the trees along the bank, but the flood swept him away.* □ *Karen clutched at me, but lost her grip.*

clutch at straws *Fig.* to continue to seek solutions, ideas, or hopes that are insubstantial. □ *When you talk of cashing in quick on your inventions, you are just clutching at straws.* □ *That is not a real solution to the problem. You are just clutching at straws.*

clutch someone or something **to** something to grasp and hold someone or something to something. □ *She clutched the baby to her bosom.* □ *Lee clutched the ice pack to his head.*

clutch (up) to become very tense and anxious; to freeze with anxiety. □ *I have been known to clutch before a big game.* □ *Just relax, play your game, and you won't clutch!*

clutter something **up**[†] to mess something up; to fill something or some place up with too many things. □ *Heaps of newspapers cluttered the room up and made it a fire hazard.* □ *Who cluttered up this house?*

coach someone **for** something to train or drill someone in preparation for doing something. □ *Elliott coached his*

roommate every night for the contest. □ *Juan coached Alice for the play.*

coalesce into something [for two or more things] to blend or fuse and become one thing. □ *The fading colors coalesced into a gray blur.* □ *In the distance, the crowd coalesced into a single blob.*

coast along to roll or move along with little or no effort. □ *We just coasted along on the flat prairie.* □ *We coasted along until we came to the bottom of the hill.*

The coast is clear. There is no visible danger. □ *I'm going to stay hidden here until the coast is clear.* □ *You can come out of your hiding place now. The coast is clear.*

coast-to-coast from the Atlantic to the Pacific Oceans (in the continental U.S.A.); all the land between the Atlantic and Pacific Oceans (considered in either direction). □ *My voice was once heard on a coast-to-coast radio broadcast.* □ *Our car made the coast-to-coast trip in eighty hours.*

coat and tie [for men] a jacket or sports coat and necktie. (A respectable but less than formal standard of dress.) □ *My brother was not wearing a coat and tie, and they would not admit him into the restaurant.* □ *I always carry a coat and tie in my car just in case I have to dress up a little for something.*

coat someone or something **with** something to put a layer of something on someone or something. □ *Her manager coated her with grease before she began the Channel swim.* □ *The cook coated the chicken with batter and dropped it into the hot fat.*

coax someone or an animal **in(to)** something **1.** to urge or persuade someone or an animal to go into something. □ *We coaxed the lion into the cage with fresh meat.* □ *The teacher coaxed the child into the kindergarten classroom.* **2.** to urge or persuade someone or an animal into doing something. □ *We coaxed her into singing for us.* □ *Janet coaxed the dog into sitting up and begging.*

coax someone or an animal **out of** something **1.** to urge or persuade someone or an animal to give something up. □ *He almost wouldn't sell it, but I coaxed him out of it.* □ *I coaxed the cat out of the canary it was holding in its mouth.* **2.** to urge or persuade someone or an animal to come out of something. □ *She coaxed the puppy out of the carton.* □ *Janet coaxed the child out of the closet with a promise of a piece of cake.*

coax someone **to** do something to urge someone to do something. □ *The kids coaxed her to let them go swimming.* □ *Can I coax you to try some of this pie?*

cobble something **up**[†] and **cobble** something **together** to make something or put something together hastily or carelessly. □ *Who cobbled this thing up? Take it apart and start over.* □ *The kids cobbled up their model planes badly.* □ *It looks like you cobbled together that report just last night.*

cock a snook at someone to show or express defiance or scorn at someone. □ *He cocked a snook at the traffic cop and tore up the ticket.* □ *The boy cocked a snook at the park attendant and walked on the grass.*

cock of the walk someone who acts more important than others in a group. □ *The deputy manager was cock of the* walk until the new manager arrived. □ *He loved acting cock of the walk and ordering everyone about.*

cock-and-bull story a hard-to-believe, made-up story; a story that is a lie. □ *Don't give me that cock-and-bull story.* □ *I asked for an explanation, and all I got was your ridiculous cock-and-bull story!*

*cocky as the king of spades boastful; overly proud. (*Also: **as** ~.) □ *He'd challenge anyone to a fight. He's as cocky as the king of spades.* □ *She strutted in, cocky as the king of spades.*

coerce someone or an animal **into** something to force or compel someone or an animal to do something. □ *I could not coerce her into coming along with us.* □ *You cannot coerce a cat into anything.*

coexist with someone or something to exist agreeably or tolerably with or at the same time as someone or something. □ *I decided that I would have to coexist with your policies, despite my objections.* □ *It is hard for cats to coexist with dogs.*

coffee and coffee and a doughnut or a pastry. □ *I'll have coffee and.* □ *We stopped at a little shop for coffee and.*

coffee and Danish a cup of coffee and a Danish sweet roll. □ *A few of us like to have coffee and Danish before we start work.* □ *Coffee and Danish is not my idea of a good breakfast!*

coffee-table book a book that is more suitable for display than for reading, typically, an oversize, illustrated book left on the coffee table for visitors to examine. □ *This book is more of a coffee-table book than an art book. I prefer something more scholarly.* □ *We purchased a coffee-table book for Jan's birthday.*

cogitate on something *Rur.* to think about something. □ *Cogitate on this idea for a while.* □ *I will have to cogitate on this for a few days. I'll get back to you.*

cohabit with someone **1.** [for an unmarried person] to live with a person of the opposite sex. □ *They were cohabiting with one another for several years.* **2.** *Euph.* to copulate with someone. □ *She had been cohabiting with him, and she admitted it in court.*

coil (itself) around someone or something [for something or an animal] to wrap itself around someone or something. □ *The monkey's tail coiled itself around the branch.* □ *The huge python coiled around poor Roger.*

coil (itself) up [for something] to wrap or roll itself into a coil. □ *The snake coiled itself up, trying to hide.* □ *It coiled up, ready to strike.*

coil (itself) up into something [for something] to wrap or twist itself into a particular shape. □ *The frightened snaked coiled itself up into a knot.* □ *The spring coiled up into its original shape.*

coil something **up†** to roll or twist something into a coil. □ *Maria coiled the strip of stamps up and put them in the little dispenser.* □ *Please coil up the rope.*

coin a phrase *Fig.* to create a new expression that is worthy of being remembered and repeated. (Often jocular.) □ *He is "worth his weight in feathers," to coin a phrase.*

coincide with something to agree with or match something; [for something] to happen at the same time as something else. □ *This pattern coincides with the pattern*

we see in the carpet. □ *My birthday sometimes coincides with Thanksgiving Day.*

*cold as a welldigger's ass (in January) and ***cold as a welldigger's feet (in January)**; ***cold as a witch's caress**; ***cold as marble**; ***cold as a witch's tit**; ***cold as a welldigger's ears (in January)** very, very cold; chilling. (Use caution with *ass*. *Also: **as** ~.) □ *Bill: How's the weather where you are? Tom: Cold as a welldigger's ass in January.* □ *By the time I got in from the storm, I was as cold as a welldigger's feet.* □ *The car's heater broke, so it's as cold as a welldigger's ears to ride around in it.* □ *She gave me a look as cold as a witch's caress.*

cold as a welldigger's feet (in January) Go to previous.

cold as a witch's tit Go to cold as a welldigger's ass (in January).

cold as marble Go to cold as a welldigger's ass (in January).

coldcock someone to knock someone unconscious. □ *He hit him once and looks like he coldcocked him.* □ *She coldcocked him with her walking stick.*

cold comfort no comfort or consolation at all. □ *She knows there are others worse off than her, but that's cold comfort.* □ *It was cold comfort to the student that others had failed as he had done.*

*cold feet *Fig.* fear of doing something; cowardice at the moment of action. (*Typically: **get** ~; **have** ~; **give** someone ~.) □ *The bridegroom got cold feet on the day of the wedding.* □ *Sally said I should try skydiving, but I had cold feet.*

*a cold fish *Fig.* a person who is distant and unfeeling. (*Typically: **act like** ~; **be** ~.) □ *Bob is so dull—a real cold fish.* □ *She hardly ever speaks to anyone. She's a cold fish.*

Cold hands, warm heart. *Prov.* People whose hands are usually cold have kind and loving personalities. □ *Nancy: I don't like holding hands with Joe. His hands are so cold. Jane: Cold hands, warm heart.*

cold, hard cash cash, not checks or credit. □ *I want to be paid in cold, hard cash, and I want to be paid now!* □ *Pay me now! Cash on the barrelhead—cold, hard cash.*

cold-shoulder to ignore someone; to give someone a cool reception. (See also the **cold shoulder**.) □ *The hostess cold-shouldered me, so I spilt my appetizers in the swimming pool.* □ *Tiffany cold-shouldered the guy who was trying to flirt with her.*

*the cold shoulder *Fig.* an attitude of rejection. (*Typically: **get** ~; **give** someone ~.) □ *If you greet her at a party, you'll just get the cold shoulder.* □ *I thought that Sally and I were friends, but lately I've been getting the cold shoulder.*

cold sober Go to stone (cold) sober.

cold turkey *Sl.* immediately; without tapering off or cutting down gradually. (See also **go cold turkey**. Originally drug slang. Now used of breaking any habit.) □ *Tom stopped smoking cold turkey.* □ *She gave up her drinking habit cold turkey and had no ill effects.*

collaborate with someone or something to work together on something with someone or a group. □ *I will collaborate with Amy on this research.* □ *I was forced to collaborate with a totally uninformed committee.*

collapse into something **1.** *Lit.* to fall down into something with suddenness, as if out of energy. □ *She was so tired, she collapsed into the chair.* □ *Juan collapsed into a chair and fell fast asleep.* **2.** *Fig.* [for someone] to fall into a particular kind of despair. □ *The poor man collapsed into a deep depression.* □ *Scott collapsed into his own personal brand of grieving.*

collapse under someone or something to cave in under the weight of someone or something. □ *The grandstand collapsed under the weight of the spectators.* □ *The bridge collapsed from the force of the flood.*

collar-and-tie men *Rur.* businessmen who wear dress shirts and ties. □ *After Jim graduated from college, he went off to join the collar-and-tie men.* □ *Us working folks at the plant have an awful time getting the collar-and-tie men to see our point of view.*

collate something **with** something to compare or match something with something. □ *Try to collate these figures with that other list.* □ *I can't collate these notations with the spreadsheet they go with.*

collect around someone or something to gather around someone or something; to accumulate around someone or something. □ *The guests collected around the table that held the birthday cake.* □ *The children collected around the birthday boy.*

collect (money) for someone or something to solicit money for the benefit of someone or something. □ *I would like to collect some money for Fred, who is in the hospital.* □ *I am collecting for the church building fund.*

collect (money) for something to solicit money that is owed. □ *I'm collecting money for payment on your loan.* □ *Someone is calling to collect for the newspaper delivery.*

collect on something to take or receive payment on a debt or promise. □ *I have come to collect on your debt.* □ *I will have to assign your account to an agency to collect on this bill.*

collect one's **thoughts** *Fig.* to take time to think through an issue; to give some thought to a topic. □ *I'll speak to the visitors in a moment. I need some time to collect my thoughts.*

collect something **from** someone **1.** to gather up something from someone; to gather money from someone. □ *I'm here to collect used clothing from you.* □ *She is out collecting donations from the neighbors.* **2.** to take a medical specimen from a person. □ *I am here to collect a urine specimen from the patient.* □ *The phlebotomist collected the specimen from Todd and left the room.*

collect something **up**† to gather something up. □ *Collect your things up, and let's go.* □ *I collected up all my luggage and left.*

collide with someone or something to crash with or bump into someone or something. □ *The bus collided with a truck.* □ *Maria collided with Alice, but neither was hurt.*

collude with someone or something to plot or conspire with someone or a group. □ *The CEO colluded with the board of directors in the scandal.*

color something **in**† to paint or draw color on a pattern or outline. □ *Here is a sketch. Please color it in.* □ *Color in the sketch, please.*

comb something **for** someone or something *Fig.* to look all over or all through something for a particular person or thing. □ *The police combed the entire neighborhood for the criminals.* □ *I combed the entire house for the missing paper.*

comb something **out of** something and **comb** something **out**† to remove substances or knots and snarls from something by combing. □ *I had to comb the gum out of her hair.* □ *It took me over an hour to comb out the gum.*

comb through something *Fig.* to look through something, examining it thoroughly. □ *I combed through all my belongings, looking for the lost papers.* □ *The vet combed through the dog's coat, looking for tick bites.*

combine something **against** someone or something to join something together in opposition to someone or something. □ *We will combine forces against the enemy.* □ *Our game plan combined our various talents against the opposite team.*

combine something **with** something to mix something with something else. □ *I want to combine the red flowers with the pink ones for a bouquet.* □ *First, combine the eggs with the sugar.*

come a cropper *Fig.* to have a misfortune; to fail. (Meaning 'fall off one's horse.') □ *Bob invested all his money in the stock market just before it fell. Boy, did he come a cropper.* □ *Jane was out all night before she took her final. She really came a cropper.*

come aboard and **go aboard** to get onto a boat or ship. □ *Please come aboard. We are shoving off now.* □ *Please ask everyone to go aboard.*

come about 1. to happen. □ *How did this damage come about?* □ *This came about due to the windstorm.* **2.** [for a ship or boat] to turn. □ *Look how easily this boat comes about.* □ *Now, practice making the boat come about.*

come across 1. to be compliant. □ *Oh, she'll come across, just you wait; she'll do what we want.* **2.** to agree; to yield. □ *How can we get him to come across?*

come across as someone or something **(to** someone**)** Go to next.

come across like someone or something **(to** someone**)** and **come across as** someone or something **(to** someone**)** to appear or seem like someone or something to other people. □ *You always come across like a madman to people.* □ *She comes across like the Queen of the Nile to most people who meet her.*

come across someone or something and **run across** someone or something to find someone or something; to discover someone or something. □ *John came across a book he had been looking for.* □ *Where did you run across that lovely skirt?*

come across (to something**)** to agree to something; to yield to someone else's position. □ *He came across to our point of view.* □ *Will a sign-on bonus get him to come across?*

come across (with something**)** to deliver what is expected of one. □ *You had better come across with what you owe* me. □ *You owe me money, and I wish you would come across.*

come after someone or something Go to after someone or something.

Come again. 1. Please come back again sometime. □ *Mary: I had a lovely time. Thank you for asking me. Sally: You're quite welcome. Come again.* □ *"Come again," said Mrs. Martin as she let Jimmy out the door.* **2.** *Rur.* (usually **Come again?**) I didn't hear what you said. Please repeat it. □ *Sally: Do you want some more carrots? Mary: Come again? Sally: Carrots. Do you want some more carrots?*

come along (with someone**)** to come with or go with someone. □ *Please come along with me to the store.* □ *Come along, let's go.*

Come and get it! and **Come 'n' get it!** Dinner's ready. Come eat! □ *The camp cook shouted, "Time to eat! Come and get it!"*

come apart to break apart; to break up. □ *The missile came apart in midair.* □ *I was afraid our car would come apart on that rough road.*

come apart at the seams Go to fall apart at the seams.

come (a)round 1. finally to agree or consent (to something). □ *I thought he'd never agree, but in the end he came around.* □ *She came round only after we argued for an hour.* **2.** to return to consciousness; to wake up. □ *He came around after we threw cold water in his face.* □ *The boxer was knocked out, but came round in a few seconds.*

come around (for a visit) Go to come around (to visit).

come around (to doing something**)** to agree to do something eventually, after a long wait. □ *Finally, she came around to painting the kitchen.* □ *She hesitated for a long time, but eventually we got Lynn to come around.*

come around (to some place**) 1.** to come to some place for a visit. □ *You must come around to our place for a while.* □ *Do come around and have dinner with us sometime.* **2.** and **come around (to visit)** and **come around (for a visit)** to pay a casual visit to someone. □ *Why don't you come around to visit next week?* □ *Why don't you come around for a visit? You are welcome any time.*

come as no surprise will not be surprising [for someone] to learn [something]. □ *It will come as no surprise for you to learn that the company is losing money this year.* □ *It came as no surprise that the president had been lying.*

come at someone or something **1.** to make a threatening move toward someone or something. □ *The gorilla came at the cage and shook the bars.* □ *Walter came at the cake as if he were going to snatch the whole thing.* **2.** to attack someone or something. □ *The elephant came at us and we moved away.* □ *The cat came at the mouse and pounced on it.*

come away empty-handed to return without anything. □ *All right, go gambling. Don't come away empty-handed, though.* □ *Go to the bank and ask for the loan again. This time don't come away empty-handed.*

come away (from someone or something**)** to move away from someone or something. □ *Please come away from the fire. You will get burned if you don't.* □ *Come away! You can walk with me for a while.*

come away with someone to go away or travel away with someone. □ *Come away with me for a ride in the country.* □ *Come away with me and we'll find a nice place to eat.*

come back to return; to return to an advantageous or favorable state or condition. □ *Walter practiced every day, hoping to come back from his injury.* □ *When will the good old days come back?*

Come back and see us. and **Come back and see me.** Come visit us [or me] again. (Often said by a host or hostess to departing guests.) □ *Bill: Good night. Thanks for having me. Sally: Oh, you're quite welcome. Come back and see us.* □ *Bob: I enjoyed my visit. Good-bye. Mary: It was very nice of you to pay me a visit. Come back and see me.*

Come back anytime. Please come and visit us again. You're always welcome. (Often said by a host or hostess to departing guests.) □ *Mary: So glad you could come. Bill: Thank you. I had a wonderful time. Mary: Come back anytime.* □ *Bob: Thanks for the coffee and cake. Bye. Mary: We're glad to have you. Please come back anytime.*

come back (from some place**)** to return from a place. □ *When will you come back from Detroit?* □ *Please come back soon.*

come back to haunt one and **return to haunt** one *Fig.* [for a bad memory] to recur; for the consequences of a bad decision to affect one negatively later. □ *I never dreamed that a little thing like a traffic ticket could come back to haunt me years later.*

come back (to someone**)** [for a memory] to return to someone's consciousness. □ *Everything you said suddenly came back to me.* □ *All the old memories came back to me and made me feel very sad.*

come back (to someone or something**)** to return to someone or something. □ *Please come back to me. I'm lonely.* □ *Come back to your home!*

Come back when you can stay longer. Come back again sometime when your visit can be longer. (Often said by a host or hostess to departing guests.) □ *John: I really must go. Sue: So glad you could come. Please come back when you can stay longer.* □ *Bill: Well, I hate to eat and run, but I have to get up early tomorrow. Mary: Well, come back when you can stay longer.*

come before someone or something **1.** [of persons or things in an order or a line] to be in front of or in advance of someone or something. □ *This one comes before that one.* □ *She comes before me.* **2.** [for one] to present oneself in the presence of someone or a group. □ *Thank you for coming before this committee with your testimony.* □ *The judge said I would have to come before her again next month.* **3.** [for an issue] to be raised before someone, a board, committee, etc.; [for an issue] to appear on the agenda of someone or a deliberative body. □ *The matter of the broken windows came before the school board at last.* □ *The question came before the business manager.*

come between someone **and** someone else **1.** *Lit.* to be in between two people. □ *That's my place, there. I come between Maria and Lynn.* □ *In the line of contestants, I come between Bob and Bill.* **2.** *Fig.* to interfere in someone else's romance; to break up a pair of lovers. □ *Don't come between Terri and Jeff.*

come between something **and** something else to have a position between one thing and another. □ *April comes between March and May.* □ *This volume comes between numbers fourteen and sixteen.*

come by (some place) to stop some place for a visit. □ *Can you come by our place for a few minutes on the way home?* □ *Please come by sometime.*

come by something **1.** *Lit.* to travel by a specific means, such as a plane, a boat, or a car. □ *We came by train. It's more relaxing.* □ *Next time, we'll come by plane. It's faster.* **2.** *Fig.* to find or get something. □ *How did you come by that haircut?* □ *Where did you come by that new shirt?*

come by something **honestly 1.** *Fig.* to get something honestly. (See also **come by** something.) □ *Don't worry. I came by this Swiss watch honestly.* □ *I have a feeling she didn't come by it honestly.* **2.** *Fig.* to inherit something—such as a character trait—from one's parents. □ *I know I'm mean. I came by it honestly, though.* □ *She came by her kindness honestly.*

come clean (with someone**) (about** something**)** *Fig.* to be honest with somebody about something. □ *I want you to come clean with me about your financial status.* □ *Sam will come clean with me. I know he will.*

come close (to someone or something**) 1.** *Lit.* to approach very near to someone or something. □ *Come close to me and keep me warm.* □ *I didn't touch it, but I really came close that time.* **2.** *Fig.* to approximate someone or something in a specific quality. □ *When it comes to kindness, you don't even come close to Jane.* □ *You don't come close to the former owners in caring for your property.*

come down 1. *Sl.* to happen. □ *Hey, man! What's coming down?* □ *When something like this comes down, I have to stop and think things over.* **2.** a letdown; a disappointment. (Usually **comedown**.) □ *The loss of the race was a real comedown for Willard.* □ *It's hard to face a comedown like that.* **3.** *Sl.* to begin to recover from the effects of alcohol or drug intoxication. □ *She came down slow from her addiction, which was good.* □ *It was hard to get her to come down.* **4.** [for something] to descend (to someone) through inheritance. □ *All my silverware came down to me from my great-grandmother.* □ *The antique furniture came down through my mother's family.*

come down (from some place**)** Go to **down** (from some place).

come down (from something**) 1.** to come to a lower point from a higher one. □ *Come down from there this instant!* □ *Come down, do you hear?* **2.** to move from a higher status to a lower one. (See also **come down in the world**.) □ *He has come down from his original position. Now he is just a clerk.* □ *He has come down quite a bit.*

come down (hard) (on someone or something**)** *Fig.* [for someone] to scold or punish someone or a group severely. □ *The judge really came down on the petty crooks.* □ *The critics came down much too hard on the performance.*

come down in the world to lose one's social position or financial standing. □ *Mr. Jones has really come down in the world since he lost his job.* □ *If I were unemployed, I'm sure I'd come down in the world, too.*

come down to earth 1. *Lit.* to arrive on earth from above. □ *An angel came down to earth and made an announcement.* **2.** *Fig.* to become realistic; to become alert to what is going on around one. □ *You have a fit of enthusiasm, John, but you must come down to earth. We can't possibly afford any of your suggestions.*

come down to some place to come to some place in the south or in a lower altitude for a visit. (Assumes a perspective of a visitor from a northern state of the U.S.) □ *Come down to our place in Florida this winter if you want.*

come down to something to be reduced to something; to amount to no more than something. □ *It comes down to whether you want to go to the movies or stay at home and watch television.* □ *It came down to either getting a job or going to college.*

come down with something to become or to be sick with some illness. □ *Susan came down with a bad cold and had to cancel her trip.* □ *I didn't go to work because I came down with the flu.*

come for someone to arrive to get someone. □ *I have come for Amy. Is she ready?* □ *The mothers came for their children at about five o'clock.*

come forth to come out; to move forward and appear. □ *Please come forth and meet your cousins.* □ *All the stage crew came forth and received some applause.*

come forward 1. *Lit.* to move oneself forward. □ *Come forward and stand before the whole class.* **2.** *Fig.* to present oneself to offer evidence in court voluntarily. □ *Why did you not come forward earlier in the trial?* □ *I was afraid to come forward during the trial.*

come forward (with something**)** to bring something, such as information, to someone's attention. □ *Colleen came forward with a new idea.* □ *I hope you each can come forward with something useful.*

come from behind to advance from a losing position. (Alludes to being behind in a score or in a race.) □ *Our team came from behind to win the game.* □ *The horse I bet on came from behind and almost placed second.*

come from far and wide to arrive from everywhere; to arrive from many directions and great distances. □ *People came from far and wide to attend the annual meeting.* □ *The deer came from far and wide to lick the salt block we had put out.*

come from nowhere to come as a surprise with no warning. □ *The dogs came from nowhere and attacked my cat.* □ *The whole set of problems came from nowhere. There was no way we could have foreseen them.*

come from some place Go to **from** some place.

come from someone or something to arrive from someone or something; [for something] to have originated with someone or something. □ *Did this letter come from Alice?* □ *A notice came from the Internal Revenue Service.*

come full circle *Fig.* to return to the original position or state of affairs. □ *The family sold the house generations ago, but things have come full circle and one of their descendants lives there now.*

come hell or high water *Fig.* no matter what happens. (Use *hell* with caution.) □ *I'll be there tomorrow, come hell* *or high water.* □ *Come hell or high water, I intend to own my own home.*

come home from some place to arrive home from another place. □ *The soldiers came home from the war.* □ *When will you come home from the office?*

come home (to roost) 1. *Lit.* [for a fowl or other bird] to return to its home, as for a night's rest. □ *The chickens come home to roost in the evening.* **2.** *Fig.* [for a problem] to return to cause trouble [for someone]. (See also **come home to** someone.) □ *As I feared, all my problems came home to roost.*

come home to someone *Fig.* [for a fact] to be recognized suddenly by someone. □ *Suddenly, it came home to me that you thought I was Ronald.* □ *The importance of the events of the day finally came home to me.*

come home to someone or something to arrive home and find someone or something there. (See also **come home to** someone.) □ *I like to come home to a happy house.* □ *I look forward to coming home to you.*

come in 1. to enter. (Often a command or polite request.) □ *Please come in.* □ *If you will come in and have a seat, I will tell Betty that you are here.* **2.** to arrive; [for a shipment of something] to arrive. □ *New models come in almost every week.* □ *When do you expect a new batch to come in?* □ *The tomatoes will come in at the end of July.* □ *The election results came in early in the evening.* **3.** [for a broadcast signal] to be received satisfactorily. □ *Can you hear me? How am I coming in?* □ *You are coming in all right.*

come in a certain position to finish in a certain position or rank. □ *Fred came in fourth in the race.* □ *He was afraid he would come in last.*

Come in and make yourself at home. Please come into my home and make yourself comfortable. □ *Sue: Oh, hello, Tom. Come in and make yourself at home. Tom: Thanks. I will.*

Come in and sit a spell. and **Come in and set a spell.; Come in and sit down.; Come in and take a load off your feet.** *Rur.* Please come in and have a seat and a visit. (The variant with *set* informal or folksy.) □ *"Hi, Fred," smiled Tom, "Come in and sit a spell."* □ *Tom: I hope I'm not intruding. Bill: Not at all. Come in and set a spell.*

come in for something to be eligible for something; to be due something. □ *You are going to come in for a nice reward.* □ *Your report came in for a lot of criticism at the last board meeting.*

come in handy [for something] to be useful. □ *I think that this gadget will come in handy in the kitchen.*

come (in) on a wing and a prayer Go to **on a wing and a prayer.**

come in on something Go to **in on** something.

come in out of the rain 1. *Lit.* to seek shelter from the rain. □ *Come in out of the rain! You'll get wet.* **2.** *Fig.* to wake up to reality; to **come down to earth.** (See also **doesn't have enough sense to come in out of the rain.**) □ *Hey, man! Come in out of the rain! Don't you see that your boss is taking advantage of you!*

come in useful to be useful. □ *Your report has come in useful a number of times.*

come into a (small) fortune Go to **come into (some) money.**

come into being to begin existence. □ *This idea came into being during the last decade.* □ *When did this organization come into being?*

come into bloom and **come into blossom 1.** [for a flower] to bloom. □ *This rose comes into bloom later in the summer.* □ *When do they normally come into blossom?* **2.** [for a plant, bush, or tree] to begin to have many blossoms. □ *When do these bushes come into bloom?* □ *They come into blossom in June.*

come into blossom Go to previous.

come into conflict [for things or people] to conflict or to be at odds with one another. □ *The various policies came into conflict at the last moment.* □ *Bill and Bob came into conflict over almost everything.*

come in(to) contact (with someone or something**) 1.** *Lit.* to touch someone or something, probably unknowingly. □ *How many people have come into contact with the sick man?* □ *He came in contact with almost no one.* **2.** *Fig.* to meet up with and learn about someone or something. □ *Have you ever come into contact with trigonometry before?* □ *I have never come in contact with anything so difficult.*

come into effect to become valid, effective, or operable. □ *When did these rules come into effect?* □ *They came into effect while you were on vacation.*

come into existence to begin existence; to begin to be. □ *This country came into existence in the early part of the fifteenth century.* □ *When did this little town come into existence?*

come into fashion to become stylish or fashionable. □ *Do you think that a design like this will ever come into fashion?* □ *That kind of dance will never come into fashion.*

come into focus Go to **in focus.**

come in(to) heat and **come in(to) season** [for a female animal] to enter into the breeding season. □ *This animal will come into heat in the spring.* □ *When did your dog come in season?*

come into one's or its **own** to become independent; to be recognized as independent and capable, usually after much effort or time. □ *Maria is coming into her own as a concert pianist.*

come into play to become an important factor in something; to go into force. □ *All your hard practice and preparation will now come into play in the finals.*

come into power Go to **in power.**

come into prominence to become notable; to become renowned. □ *She first came into prominence during the late forties, when she starred in a few movies.* □ *Wally came into prominence when he won the state championship.*

come into season 1. [for a game animal] to be subject to legal hunting. □ *When do ducks come into season around here?* □ *Deer came into season just yesterday.* **2.** Go to **come in(to) heat.**

come into service to begin to be used; to begin to operate and function as designed. □ *When did this elevator* come into service? □ *I think that this machine came into service during World War II.*

come into sight and **come into view** to become visible; to move closer so as to be seen. □ *The tall buildings of the city came into sight first.* □ *A large herd of elephants came into view in the distance.*

come into (some) money and **come into a (small) fortune** to get some money unexpectedly, usually by inheritance. □ *She came into a lot of money when she turned twenty.* □ *I hope I can come into some money some day.*

come into someone's **possession** Go to in someone's possession.

come into the world *Fig.* to be born. □ *I came into this world nearly seventy years ago.* □ *Little Timmy came into the world on a cold and snowy night.*

come into view Go to come into sight.

come Monday *Rur.* when Monday comes. (Can be used with other expressions for time, as in *come next week, come December, come five o'clock.* See the second example.) □ *Joe plays so hard on the weekend that come Monday, he's all worn out.* □ *You may think that putting up storm windows is a bother, but come December, you'll be glad you did it.*

Come 'n' get it! Go to Come and get it!

come naturally (to someone**)** to be natural and easy for someone. □ *Her ability to deal easily with people comes naturally to her.*

come of age Go to of age.

come off *Inf.* to happen; to take place. □ *What time does this party come off?* □ *How did your speech come off?* □ *It came off very well.*

Come off it! 1. *Inf.* Stop acting arrogantly! (See also **come off ((of)**something**).)**) □ *Come off it, Tiff. You're not the Queen of England.* **2.** *Inf.* Give up your incorrect point of view! □ *Come off it! You're wrong, and you know it!*

come off ((of) something**) 1.** [for something] to detach from, fall off, or drop off something. (See also **Come off it!.** *Of* is usually retained before pronouns.) □ *The paint came off the west side of the house because of the hot sun.* □ *A wheel came off Timmy's tricycle.* **2.** to get down off something; to get off something. (*Of* is usually retained before pronouns.) □ *Come off the roof immediately.* □ *Please come off of that horse!*

come off second best to be second to someone or something; to get the poorer end of a bargain. □ *As usual, he came off second best with a little less prize money than the winner.* □ *I don't want to come off second best again.*

come on 1. Stop it!; Stop doing that. (Usually **Come on!**) □ *Mary: Are you really going to sell your new car? Sally: Come on! How dumb do you think I am?* **2.** please oblige me. □ *Mother: Sorry. You can't go! Bill: Come on, let me go to the picnic!* □ *"Come on," whined Jimmy, "I want some more!"* **3.** to hurry up; to follow someone. □ *If you don't come on, we'll miss the train.* **4.** [for electricity or some other device] to start operating. □ *After a while, the lights came on again.* □ *I hope the heat comes on soon.* **5.** to walk out and appear on stage. □ *You are to come on when you hear your cue.* **6.** *Fig.* [for a pain] to begin hurting; [for a

disease] to attack someone. □ *The pain began to come on again, and Sally had to lie down.* **7.** [for a program] to be broadcast on radio or television. □ *The news didn't come on until an hour later.*

come on as something to appear to be something; to project one's image as something. □ *The senator comes on as a liberal, but we all know better.* □ *He comes on as a happy guy, but he is miserable.*

come on (duty) to begin to work at one's scheduled time. □ *When did you come on duty tonight?* □ *What time does she come on?*

Come (on) in. and **come on in(to)** something Enter.; Come into this place. (A polite invitation to enter someone's home, office, room, etc. It is more emphatic with on.) □ *Bob: Hello, you guys. Come on in. We're just about to start dinner.* □ *Bill: Come in. Nice to see you. Mary: I hope we're not too early. Bill: Not at all.* □ *Come on into the house and have a cold drink.*

Come on in, the water's fine! 1. *Lit.* Get into the water and swim! (Usually a polite command.) □ *As Todd swam along, he said to Rachel, "Come on in. The water's fine."* **2.** *Fig.* to begin to do anything. □ *You will like skiing. Come on in, the water's fine.* □ *I think you would like working here, and I'm happy to offer you the job. Come on in, the water's fine.*

come on like gangbusters Go to come on strong.

come on somehow to advance in some fashion, manner, rate, or degree. □ *Darkness comes on early these days.* □ *The illness comes on by degrees.*

come on strong and **come on like gangbusters** to seem aggressive; to impress people initially as very aggressive and assertive. □ *She has a tendency to come on strong, but she's really a softie.* □ *The new president comes on strong at first.*

come on the scene and **arrive on the scene 1.** *Lit.* to arrive at a place. □ *When we came on the scene, the ambulances were already there.* □ *The police arrived on the scene and began directing traffic.* **2.** *Fig.* to become part of a situation. □ *She thought she was in love with Harry until Bob came on the scene.*

come on (to someone**)** *Sl.* to attempt to interest someone romantically or sexually. □ *He was trying to come on to me, but I found him unappealing.*

come on(to) someone or something to find someone or something by accident; to happen onto someone or something. □ *When I was out on my walk, I came on a little shop that sells leather goods.* □ *I came onto an old friend of yours downtown today.*

come out 1. *Lit.* to exit; to leave the inside of a place. □ *Please come out. We have to leave.* □ *When do you think they will all come out?* **2.** *Fig.* to result; to succeed; to happen. □ *I hope everything comes out fine.* □ *It will come out okay. Don't worry.* **3.** *Fig.* to come before the public; [for a book] to be published; [for a report] to be made public. □ *A new magazine has just come out.* □ *When will your next book come out?* **4.** *Fig.* to become visible or evident. □ *His pride came out in his refusal to accept help.* □ *The real reason finally came out, and it was not flattering.* **5.** *Fig.* [for a young woman] to make a social debut. (Now only done in certain U.S. regions.) □ *Does your daughter *plan to come out this year?* **6.** *Fig.* to reveal one's homosexuality. (See also **out of the closet.**) □ *Herbie finally came out when he was forty-five.*

come out against someone or something to announce or reveal that one is opposed to someone or something. □ *Our governor came out against the new tax bill.*

come out ahead to end up with a profit, benefit, or advantage. □ *It was a tricky deal, and no one came out ahead of anyone else.* □ *I never come out ahead after paying my bills.*

come out at an amount and **come out to** an amount to result in a certain amount, as the result of mathematical computation. □ *The total charges came out at far more than we expected.*

come out at someone or something and **come out toward(s)** someone or something to emerge and attack someone or something. □ *The dogs came out at us, but we got away.* □ *Betsy's bulldog came out toward my bike as I rode by.*

come out badly [for efforts at something] to have a bad result. □ *I hope trying to get back together with Joan doesn't come out badly.*

come out for someone or something and **come out in favor of** someone or something to announce or reveal that one supports someone or something. □ *The defense lawyers all came out for the judge's ruling.* □ *Roger came out for Lynn, who was running for mayor.* □ *I thought the mayor would come out in favor of more public housing.*

come out (in bloom) Go to **out (in blossom).**

come out (in blossom) Go to **out (in blossom).**

come out in droves Go to **out in large numbers.**

come out in force Go to **out in force.**

come out in large numbers Go to **out in large numbers.**

come out in something **1.** *Lit.* to come outside wearing something in particular. □ *You shouldn't come out in that skimpy jacket.* □ *I didn't mean to come out in my pajamas. I just wanted to get the newspaper.* **2.** *Fig.* to break out with a rash. □ *The baby has come out in a rash again.*

come out in the open Go to **out in the open.**

come out in the wash *Fig.* to work out all right. (Alludes to a clothing stain that can be removed by washing.) □ *Don't worry about that problem. It'll all come out in the wash.* □ *This trouble will go away. It'll come out in the wash.*

come out in(to) the open and **come (out) into the open 1.** *Lit.* [for someone or something] to move from a concealed position to an open area. □ *Sooner or later, she will have to come out in the open.* □ *The deer finally came into the open.* **2.** *Fig.* [for someone who has been hiding] to appear in public. □ *The thief came out into the open and was recognized by one of the witnesses to the crime.* □ *The FBI agents finally came into the open.*

come out in(to) the open with something *Fig.* to make something known publicly. □ *The auditors came out into the open with the story of the bankruptcy.* □ *After much fuss about its secret dealings, the city council came out in the open with the whole story.*

come out of a clear blue sky and **come out of the clear blue sky; come out of the blue** suddenly; without warning. □ *Then, out of a clear blue sky, he told me he was leaving.* □ *My sister Mary appeared on my doorstep out of the blue, after years with no word from her.*

come out of left field [for a problem or dilemma] to come from an unexpected place. (See also **out of left field.**) □ *This new problem came out of left field. We were really surprised.* □ *Your remarks came out of left field. I can't understand your complaint.*

come out of nowhere Go to **out of nowhere.**

come out of one's **shell** *Fig.* to become more friendly; to be more sociable. (Alludes to a shy turtle putting its head out of its shell.) □ *Come out of your shell, Tom. Go out and make some friends.*

come out (of someone or something**)** to emerge from someone or something. □ *Did that pile of books really come out of just one office?* □ *The lion came out of its den.*

come out (of something**) 1.** and **come out from** something *Lit.* to exit from something. □ *When will they come out of that meeting?* □ *The people came out from the houses and celebrated.* **2.** *Fig.* to result from something. □ *Nothing at all came out of our discussions.*

come out of the blue Go to **come out of a clear blue sky.**

come out of the closet Go to **out of the closet.**

come out (of) the little end of the horn *Rur.* to lose a great deal; to end with less than one started with. (See also **end up with the short end of the stick.**) □ *After the stock market crash, plenty of folks came out the little end of the horn.*

come out of the woodwork Go to **out of the woodwork.**

come out on something [for someone] to do well or poorly on a business venture. □ *How did you come out on the Adams project?* □ *We came out ahead on the Adams project, but for the quarter we came out with a loss overall.*

come out on top *Fig.* to end up being the winner. □ *I knew that if I kept trying, I would come out on top.* □ *Harry came out on top as I knew he would.*

come out smelling like a rose *Fig.* to succeed; to do better than anyone else in some situation. □ *Everyone else in the firm lost money in the real estate deal, but Bob came out smelling like a rose.* □ *If I can just finish my research paper on time, I'll come out smelling like a rose by the end of the school year.*

come out to an amount Go to **come out at** an amount.

come out to be to end up being a certain way. □ *I do not know what this sculpture will come out to be.* □ *When I start writing a poem, I never know what it will come out to be.*

come out well to end up well. □ *I hope things come out well.* □ *Everything will come out well in the end.*

come out with something **1.** to publish something. □ *When are you going to come out with a new edition?* □ *The publisher decided not to come out with the book.* **2.** to express or utter something. □ *He came out with a strong dissenting opinion.* □ *It was over an hour before the president came out with an explanation.*

come over 1. to join this party or side; to change sides or affiliation. □ *Tom was formerly an enemy spy, but last year he came over.* □ *I thought that Bill was a Republican. When did he come over?* **2.** to come for a visit. □ *See if Ann wants to come over.* □ *I can't come over to visit now. I'm busy.*

come over someone [for something] to affect a person, perhaps suddenly. (See also **come over** someone or something.) □ *I just don't know what came over me.* □ *Something came over her just as she entered the room.*

come over someone or something to move over and above someone or something. (See also **come over** someone.) □ *A cloud came over us and rained like fury.* □ *Darkness came over the city and streetlights blinked on.*

come rain or (come) shine Go to next.

come rain or shine and **come rain or (come) shine** no matter whether it rains or the sun shines; in any sort of weather. (See also **rain or shine.**) □ *Don't worry. I'll be there come rain or shine.* □ *We'll hold the picnic—rain or shine.*

Come right in. Come in, please, you are very welcome here. □ *Fred (opening door): Well, hi, Bill. Bill: Hello, Fred. Good to see you. Fred: Come right in. Bill: Thanks.*

come (right) on top of something *Fig.* [for something] to happen immediately after something else. □ *The accident expenses came right on top of the costs of her illness.* □ *The bad news came on top of some other problems we were having.*

come short of something *Fig.* to do something almost; to fail to achieve something completely. □ *The workers came short of finishing the job on time.* □ *We came short of our goal for the year.*

come someone's **way** [for something] to come to someone. □ *I wish a large sum of money would come my way.* □ *I hope that no bad luck comes my way.*

come through 1. [for someone] to do what one is expected to do, especially under difficult conditions. □ *You can depend on Jane. She'll always come through.* □ *Tom came through at the last minute with everything we needed.* **2.** [for something] to be approved; [for something] to gain approval. □ *Our mortgage loan approval finally came through!* □ *Your papers came through, and you can be sure that the matter has been taken care of.* **3.** Go to **come through (for** someone or something**). 4.** Go to **come through** something. **5.** Go to **come through (with** something**).**

come through (for someone or something**)** *Fig.* to produce or perform as promised for someone or a group. □ *You knew I would come through for you, didn't you?* □ *The team came through for its loyal fans again.*

come through something and **come through** *Fig.* to pass through something. □ *Please come through the entrance slowly.* □ *Please chain the gate up again when you come through.*

come through something **(with flying colors)** *Fig.* to survive something quite well. (See also **with flying colors.** *Colors* here refers originally to flags.) □ *Todd came through the test with flying colors.* □ *Mr. Franklin came through the operation with flying colors.*

come through (with something**)** to produce or deliver something as promised. □ *Finally, Bob came through with*

the money he had promised. □ *I knew he would come through.*

come to to become conscious; to wake up. □ *We threw a little cold water in his face, and he came to immediately.*

come to a bad end *Fig.* to have a disaster, perhaps one that is deserved or expected; to die an unfortunate death. □ *My old car came to a bad end. Its engine seized up.* □ *The dishonest merchant came to a bad end.*

come to a boil 1. *Lit.* [for a liquid] to reach the boiling point. □ *The soup came to a boil and the chef reduced the flame.* **2.** *Fig.* [for a problem or situation] to reach a critical or crucial stage. (Alludes to water reaching an active boil.) □ *Finally, things really came to a boil.* □ *Everything came to a boil after Mary announced her engagement.* **3.** *Fig.* [for someone] to get very angry. □ *Fred was coming to a boil and clearly he was going to lose his temper.*

come to a climax Go to next.

come to a close and **come to an end; come to a climax** to end; to progress to an ending. □ *The celebration came to an end about midnight.*

come to a conclusion 1. to reach a decision. □ *We talked for a long time but never came to any conclusion.* □ *Can we come to a conclusion today, or do we have to meet again?* **2.** [for a process] to reach the end and be finished. □ *At last, the yearlong ordeal of buying a house came to a conclusion.* □ *I was afraid that the opera would never come to a conclusion.*

come to a dead end and **reach a dead end 1.** *Lit.* to reach a point where one can go no farther and can go in no new direction. □ *The road comes to a dead end about a mile farther.* **2.** *Fig.* to have run out of possible ideas, solutions, energy, etc. □ *I've come to a dead end. I'm fresh out of ideas.* □ *The committee reached a dead end on the matter and tabled the whole business.*

come to a halt to stop; to slow down and stop. □ *Slowly, the train came to a halt.* □ *After the bus came to a halt, more people got on.*

come to a head *Fig.* [for a problem] to reach a critical or crucial stage. □ *At the end of the week, everything came to a head and Sam was fired.*

come to a pretty pass *Fig.* to encounter a difficult situation. (This *pretty* expresses irony.) □ *This project has come to a pretty pass. I don't know how we can possibly finish on time.* □ *Mary had come to a pretty pass. She quit her job to be with her husband, and then he left her.*

come to a standstill [for something] to slow down and finally stop; to stop completely. (Usually refers to something that is progressing, such as work, traffic, negotiations.) □ *As the strike began, the production line came to a standstill.* □ *At the height of rush hour, traffic comes to a standstill.*

come to a stop [for someone or something] to stop moving or happening. □ *The bus finally came to a stop so I could get off.* □ *The dog's barking finally came to a stop.*

come to a turning point Go to a **turning point.**

come to an end Go to **come to a close.**

come to an impasse *Fig.* to reach a deadlock, stalemate, etc., in a situation. (Alludes to a blocked roadway.) □ *The committee has come to an impasse in its deliberations.*

come to an understanding (with someone**)** Go to reach an understanding with someone.

come to an untimely end *Fig.* to come to an early death. ☐ *Poor Mr. Jones came to an untimely end in a car accident.* ☐ *Cancer caused Mrs. Smith to come to an untimely end.*

come to attention to assume a formal military posture, standing very straight. ☐ *Almost immediately, the soldiers came to attention.*

come to blows (over someone or something**)** and **come to blows (about** someone or something**)** to reach the point of fighting about someone or something. ☐ *Let's not come to blows over this silly disagreement.*

come to fruition *Fig.* to occur or turn out as suspected or intended. ☐ *When will all of these good things come to fruition?* ☐ *Our hard work and the end we planned for will soon come to fruition.*

come to grief *Fig.* to experience something unpleasant or damaging. ☐ *In the end, he came to grief because he did not follow instructions.*

come to grips with someone or something *Fig.* to begin to deal with someone or something difficult or challenging in a sensible way. ☐ *We must all come to grips with this tragedy.* ☐ *I cannot come to grips with Ed and his problems.*

come to harm to experience something bad; to get damaged or harmed. ☐ *I sincerely hope that you do not come to harm.* ☐ *I hope no one comes to harm.*

come to life 1. *Lit.* to act as if alive after a period of seeming not to be alive. ☐ *As the anesthetic wore off, the patient came to life.* ☐ *After CPR, the child came to life.* **2.** *Fig.* to become vigorous or lively. ☐ *About midnight, the party really came to life.* ☐ *The actors didn't come to life until the middle of the second act.*

come to light *Fig.* [for something] to become known or to be discovered. ☐ *Many surprises have come to light since then.* ☐ *Nothing new has come to light since we talked last.*

come to mind *Fig.* [for a thought or idea] to enter into one's consciousness or be remembered. ☐ *Do I know a good barber? No one comes to mind right now.* ☐ *Another idea comes to mind. Why not check in the phone book?*

come to much 1. to amount to a large amount of money. (Usually used with a negative.) ☐ *The bill did not come to much, considering what we had for dinner and drinks.* **2.** to count for much; to be important or meaningful. (Usually negative.) ☐ *No one thought he would come to much.* ☐ *All that discussion did not come to much.*

come to naught Go to come to nothing.

come to no good to end up badly; to come to a bad end. ☐ *The street gang leaders came to no good in the end.*

come to nothing and **come to naught** to amount to nothing; to be worthless. ☐ *So all my hard work comes to nothing.* ☐ *Yes, the whole project comes to naught.*

come to one's **feet** to stand up. ☐ *The audience came to its feet, cheering.* ☐ *Fred came to his feet to greet Roger.*

come to one's **senses** to begin thinking sensibly. ☐ *I'm glad he finally came to his senses and went on to college.* ☐ *I wish you would come to your senses and look for a better job.*

come to oneself to begin acting and thinking like one's normal self. ☐ *I began to come to myself and realize the wrong I had done.* ☐ *Please come to yourself and stop acting so strangely.*

come to pass to happen; to take place. ☐ *And when do you think all these good things will come to pass?* ☐ *Do you think it will really come to pass?*

come to rest to stop; to slow down and stop. ☐ *The ball rolled and rolled and finally came to rest.* ☐ *Where did the ball come to rest?*

come to someone's **assistance** to arrive and provide assistance to someone. ☐ *A kindly truck driver came to our assistance, and we were able to call for help.* ☐ *I hope someone will come to my assistance soon.*

come to someone's **attention** and **come to** someone's **notice** to be told to, revealed to, or discovered by someone. ☐ *It has come to my attention that you are not following the rules.* ☐ *Your comments have just come to my notice.*

come to someone's **notice** Go to previous.

come to someone's or something's **rescue** to rescue or save someone or something. ☐ *The paramedics came to our rescue at once.* ☐ *A big donor came to the college's rescue.*

come to something to end up being helpful or significant. (See also **amount to** something; **when it comes to** something.) ☐ *Do you think this work will come to anything?* ☐ *I don't think this will come to what we were promised.*

come to terms (about someone or something**)** and **come to terms (on** someone or something**)** [for two or more people] to reach an accord on someone or something. ☐ *Ed and Alice came to terms about money.* ☐ *They did not come to terms on the price.*

come to terms (with someone or something**) 1.** to come to an agreement with someone. ☐ *I finally came to terms with my lawyer about his fee.* ☐ *Bob, you have to come to terms with your father.* **2.** to learn to accept someone or something. ☐ *She had to come to terms with the loss of her sight.* ☐ *She couldn't come to terms with her estranged husband.*

come to the fore *Fig.* to become prominent; to become important. ☐ *The question of salary has now come to the fore.* ☐ *Since his great successes as a prosecutor, he has really come to the fore in city politics.*

come to the job with something and **come to the position with** something; **come to the task with** something to bring a particular quality to a task or job. ☐ *She comes to the job with great enthusiasm.* ☐ *Ann comes to this position with a lot of experience.*

come to the point and **get to the point** to get to the important part (of something). ☐ *He has been talking a long time. I wish he would come to the point.* ☐ *We are talking about money, Bob! Come on, get to the point.*

come to the position with something Go to come to the job with something.

come to the same thing Go to amount to the same thing.

come to the task with something Go to come to the job with something.

come to think of it I just remembered. □ *Come to think of it, I know someone who can help.* □ *I have a screwdriver in the trunk of my car, come to think of it.*

come to this to result in this situation. (Usually said out of surprise.) □ *Who would believe it would come to this?* □ *So, it has come to this?*

come together 1. to touch together; to meet. □ *The ends of the boards just came together. They were almost too short.* □ *We came together in the park, just as we had agreed.* **2.** to attend something together; to arrive at an event together. □ *Alice and I are going to come together.* □ *We will come to the party together.*

come together (on something**)** to discuss and agree on something. □ *I hope we can come together on a price.* □ *I'm sure we can come together.*

come true to materialize as expected or hoped. □ *Jane's wishes had come true.* □ *Dave wondered if his dreams would ever come true.*

come under something to be classed in the category of something. □ *This request comes under the category of a plain nuisance.* □ *Your proposal comes under the heading of new business and is out of order.*

come under the hammer and **go under the hammer** *Fig.* [for something] to be auctioned. □ *The house at the corner is coming under the hammer next week.* □ *The repossessed farm will go under the hammer.*

come unglued *Fig.* to lose emotional control; to break out into tears or laughter. □ *When Sally heard the joke, she almost came unglued.* □ *When the bank took away my car, I came unglued and cried and cried.*

come up 1. *Lit.* to come from a lower place to a higher one. □ *You can come up now. They are gone.* □ *Come up and enjoy the view from the tallest rooftop in the county.* **2.** *Lit.* to come near; to approach. □ *He came up and began to talk to us.* □ *A heron came up while we were fishing, but it just ignored us.* **3.** *Fig.* to come to someone's attention. □ *The question of what time to be there never came up.* □ *The matter came up, but it was never dealt with.*

come up a storm *Rur.* to become stormy. □ *It came up a storm as I was on my way home, and I got soaked to the skin.*

come up against someone or something Go to up against someone or something.

come up for air 1. *Lit.* to lift one's head out of the water to breathe. □ *After staying under water for almost a minute, Jason had to come up for air.* **2.** *Fig.* to stop what one is doing for a different activity or rest. □ *Whenever you get off the phone and come up for air, I have a question for you.* □ *I want you to go to the store for me when you come up for air.* **3.** *Fig.* to stop kissing for a moment and breathe. □ *Don't those kids ever come up for air?* □ *When are you two going to come up for air?*

come up for auction Go to up for auction.

come up for reelection Go to up for reelection.

come up for sale Go to up for sale.

come up for something to be eligible for something; to be in line or sequence for something. □ *She comes up for reelection in April.* □ *How soon does your driver's license come up for renewal?*

come (up) from behind to advance in competition; to improve one's position relative to the positions of other things or people. □ *The horse was working hard to come up from behind.* □ *Lee was losing in the election, but he began to come from behind in the last week.*

come up heads and **come up tails** *Fig.* [for a tossed coin] to turn out to be either heads or tails. □ *We tossed a coin, and it came up heads.* □ *The coin came up tails.*

come up in the world Go to move up in the world.

come up smelling like a rose and **come up smelling like roses** *Fig.* to end up looking good or respectable after being involved in some difficult or notorious affair. □ *I was surprised that my congressional representative came up smelling like a rose after his colleagues investigated him.*

come up tails Go to come up heads.

come up through the ranks *Fig.* to rise to a position of leadership by working up through the sequence of lower positions. □ *He came up through the ranks to become a corporate executive.* □ *The general came up through the ranks. There is no other way to become a general.*

come up to someone's **expectations** to be as good as someone expected. □ *Sorry, but this product does not come up to my expectations and I want to return it.*

come up to someone's **standards** to meet or be equal to someone's standards or requirements. □ *Does this ice cream come up to your standards?* □ *Ann's concert recital did not come up to her own standards.*

come up with someone or something to find or supply someone or something; to manage to find or improvise something. □ *I came up with a date at the last minute.* □ *My mom is always able to come up with some yummy snack for me in the afternoon.*

come (up)on someone or something to find or happen on someone or something. (See also happen (up)on someone or something.) □ *I came upon Walter while I was in the bookstore.* □ *I came on this little store near Maple Street that has everything we need.*

come what may *Cliché* no matter what might happen. □ *I'll be home for the holidays, come what may.* □ *Come what may, the mail will get delivered.*

come with (someone or something**)** to depart in the company of someone or something; to travel with someone or a group. □ *Come with me. We'll go to my place.* □ *Are you going to come with the tour?* □ *Are you going to come with?*

come with the territory and **go with the territory** *Fig.* to be expected under circumstances like this. (Alludes to the details and difficulties attendant to something like the assignment of a specific sales territory to a salesperson. When one accepts the assignment, one accepts the problems.) □ *There is a lot of paperwork in this job. Oh, well, I guess it comes with the territory.* □ *There are problems, but they go with the territory.*

come within a hair('s breadth) of someone or something Go to come within an inch of someone or something.

come within an ace of something to come very close to [doing] something. □ *I came within an ace of leaving school. I'm glad you talked me out of it.* □ *Donna came within an ace of having an accident.*

come within an inch of doing something *Fig.* almost to do something; to come very close to doing something. □ *I came within an inch of going into the army.* □ *I came within an inch of falling off the roof.*

come within an inch of someone or something and **come within a hair('s breadth) of** someone or something to come very close to someone or something. □ *The bullet came within an inch of Heather.* □ *The car came within a hair of the bus.*

come within earshot (of something) Go to within earshot (of something).

come within range Go to within range.

come within range (of something) Go to within range (of something).

come within something **1.** to be in the category of something; to be under the domain of someone or something. □ *This comes within the domain of the treasurer.* □ *This matter doesn't come within my area of expertise.* **2.** to be inside a stated range, such as price, time, weight, range, etc. □ *This comes within my price range. I'll take it.*

come-hither look an alluring or seductive look or glance, usually done by a woman. □ *She blinked her bedroom eyes and gave him a come-hither look.* □ *She had mastered the come-hither look, but was not ready for the next part.*

***comfortable as an old shoe** *Cliché* very comfortable; very comforting and familiar. (*Also: as ~.) □ *My old house may seem small to you, but I think it's cozy. It's as comfortable as an old shoe.*

Coming events cast their shadows before. *Prov.* Significant events are often preceded by signs that they are about to happen. (From Thomas Campbell's poem, "Lochiel's Warning.") □ *If you pay attention to the news, you can generally tell when something momentous is about to happen. Coming events cast their shadows before.*

coming out of one's **ears** *Fig.* very numerous or abundant. (As if people or things were coming in great numbers from many sources including unlikely ones.) □ *I've got phone and e-mail messages coming out of my ears.* □ *We are very busy at the factory. We have orders coming out of our ears.*

Coming through(, please). Please let me pass through. (Often said by someone trying to get through a crowd of people, as in a passageway or an elevator. Compare this with **Out, please.**) □ *Tom: Coming through, please. Sue: Give him some room. He wants to get by.* □ *Mary (as the elevator stops): Well, this is my floor. Coming through, please. I've got to get off.*

coming up a cloud *Rur.* getting ready to rain. □ *Look at that sky! It's comin' up a cloud!*

commence with someone or something to start a procedure affecting a number of people or things by choosing a particular person or thing first. □ *Each meeting commences with a reading of the minutes of the last meeting.* □ *The doctor interviews with Lynn and took everyone else in the order in which they had arrived.*

commend someone **for** something to praise someone for doing something. □ *The committee commended Ralph for his good work.*

commend someone or something **to** someone or something to recommend or speak well of someone to someone or a group. □ *I commend Walter to your organization. He would make a fine employee.* □ *We commended your organization to Martha, who may wish to become a member.*

comment about someone or something and **comment (up)on** someone or something to make a remark about someone or something. □ *There is no need to comment upon this event.* □ *Please don't comment on Liz's problems.*

commiserate with someone to share one's misery with another person who is also miserable. □ *I stopped by Bruce's house to commiserate with him on being laid off.*

commit oneself **on** something to agree to something; to promise or pledge to do something. □ *I'm sorry, but I can't commit myself on this matter until I know more details.*

commit oneself **to** someone or something to devote oneself to someone or something; to be faithful to someone or something. □ *He committed himself to his wife.* □ *She settled down and committed herself to her job.*

commit oneself **to** something **1.** to agree to something; to promise or pledge to do something. □ *Yes, I will commit myself to the repair of the door frame.* □ *Will you commit yourself to finishing on time?* **2.** to promise to support and assist something. □ *I can't commit myself to your cause at the present time. Maybe next month when I am less busy.* □ *She committed herself to being there on time.*

commit someone or something **for** something to promise someone or something for a particular purpose or time. □ *I can't commit myself for Friday night.* □ *We are unable to commit any more funds for your project.*

commit someone or something **to** something to pledge or assign someone or something to something. □ *The boss committed Ralph to the task.* □ *I cannot commit any more money to your project.*

commit something **to memory** to memorize something. □ *Do we have to commit this poem to memory?* □ *The dress rehearsal of the play is tomorrow night. Please make sure you have committed all your lines to memory by that time.*

commit to someone to marry or enter into an exclusive relationship with another person. □ *Jane says she loves me, but she's not ready to commit to any one person.* □ *If you can't commit to me, then this relationship is over.*

commode-hugging drunk *Sl.* heavily alcohol intoxicated; drunk and vomiting. □ *Willie got commode-hugging drunk in the space of two hours.*

***common as an old shoe** and ***common as dirt** low class; uncouth. (*Also: as ~.) □ *That ill-mannered girl is just as common as an old shoe.* □ *Despite Mamie's efforts to appear to be upper class, most folks considered her common as dirt.*

common as dirt Go to previous.

a **common thread (to all this)** *Fig.* a similar idea or pattern to a series of events. □ *All of these incidents are related. There is a common thread to all this.*

commune with something *Fig.* to experience wordless or spiritual communication with something. □ *She went on long walks to commune with nature.* □ *He enjoyed going off on a retreat to commune with his inner self.*

communicate something **to** someone to say or write something to someone; to tell someone something. □ *Will you please communicate my regards to her?* □ *I intend to communicate your request to the front office this morning.*

communicate with someone **1.** *Lit.* to correspond or talk with a person. □ *I have to communicate with Wally first.* □ *As soon as I have communicated with Fred, I can give you an answer.* **2.** *Fig.* to make oneself understood with a person. (Often used with a negative.) □ *I just don't seem to communicate with Sam, no matter what I do.* □ *We just can't seem to communicate with each other.*

commute between places to travel between the place where one works and the place where one lives. □ *I have to commute between Chicago and Detroit every week.* □ *Mary has commuted between New York City and New Jersey for years.*

commute from some place to travel to work from some place. □ *I commute from way out in the country.* □ *Betty commutes from only a few miles away and will be here very soon.*

commute something **into** something to change something into something. □ *No one, as it turns out, can commute lead into gold.* □ *I had hoped to commute this argument into a sensible discussion, but it is hopeless.*

compare notes on someone or something to share observations on someone or something. □ *We took a little time to compare notes on our ancestors and have discovered that we are cousins.*

compare someone or something **to** someone or something to liken people or things to other people or things; to say that some people or things have the same qualities as other people or things. (See the comment at **compare** someone or something **with** someone or something.) □ *I can only compare him to a cuddly teddy bear.* □ *He compared himself to one of the knights of the round table.*

compare someone or something **with** someone or something to consider the sameness or difference of sets of things or people. (This phrase is very close in meaning to **compare** someone or something **to** someone or something, but for some connotes stronger contrast.) □ *Let's compare the virtues of savings accounts with investing in bonds.* □ *When I compare Roger with Tom, I find very few similarities.* □ *Please compare Tom with Bill on their unemployment records.*

compartmentalize something **into** something to segment or divide something into smaller things; to assign the parts of something into categories. □ *We will have to compartmentalize this large area into a number of smaller offices.* □ *His brain seems to be compartmentalized into a number of different centers.*

compel someone **to** do something to force someone to do something; to drive someone to so something. □ *You can't compel me to do that.* □ *She compelled herself to try, even though she was ill.*

compensate for something to counterbalance or counteract something; to make up for something. □ *Your present kindness will not compensate for your previous rudeness.*

compensate someone **for** something to pay someone [back] money for something. □ *Don't worry. I will com-*

pensate you for your loss. □ *Let us compensate you for your expenses.*

compete against someone to contend against someone; to play against someone in a game or contest. □ *I don't see how I can compete against all of them.* □ *She refused to compete against her own brothers.*

compete against something to struggle against something; to seem to be in a contest with something. □ *It was hard to be heard. I was competing against the noise of construction.* □ *Please stop talking. I do not wish to compete against the audience when I lecture.*

compete for someone or something to contend against or contest [someone] for someone or something; to struggle for someone or something [against a competitor]. □ *They are competing for a lovely prize.* □ *Ed and Roger are competing for Alice's attention.*

compete in something to enter into a competition. □ *I do not want to compete in that contest.* □ *Ann looked forward to competing in the race.*

compete with someone or something to contend against someone, something, or a group; to play in a competition against someone, something, or a group. □ *I can't compete with all this noise.* □ *We always compete closely with our crosstown rivals, Adams High School.*

compile something **from** something to make up something from something; to collect and consolidate something from something. □ *She compiled a book of poetry from verses written by her friends.* □ *Lynn compiled a picture book from family photographs going back almost a century.*

complain about someone or something to protest someone or something; to grouch about someone or something. □ *Oh, stop complaining about the weather.* □ *You are always complaining about me.*

complain of something to moan and suffer from a disease; to report the symptoms of a disease or health condition. □ *Kenneth complained of a headache and general weakness.* □ *The patient was complaining of a headache.*

complain to someone to grouch or protest to someone. □ *Don't complain to me.* □ *I will complain to the manager.*

compliment someone **on** something to say something nice to someone about something connected to that person. □ *I was pleased with Alice's work and complimented her on it.* □ *They complimented me on my new tie.*

comply with something to conform to something; to obey guidelines or regulations; to agree to something. □ *I hope you decide to comply with our rules.* □ *I am happy to comply with your request.*

comport oneself **with** some manner to behave in a certain manner. □ *I hope you are able to comport yourself with better behavior next time.* □ *The old man was able to comport himself with dignity.*

composed of something assembled or made out of something. □ *This cloth is composed of a number of different kinds of fibers.* □ *The committee is composed of people from every department.*

compound something **with** something to unite some substance with another; to mix something with something else. □ *Can this unpleasant medicine be compounded with something to make it palatable?*

compress something **into** something **1.** to squeeze or press something into something, such as a mold or container. □ *We compressed the tomatoes into the jar.* □ *I cannot compress any more clothing into the suitcase.* **2.** to form something into a shape by applying pressure. □ *He compressed the mass of paper into a tight ball.* □ *The clay was compressed into the shape of a brick upon the application of pressure to the mold.*

comprised of someone or something made up of someone or something. (The use of *of* after *comprise* is regarded as bad grammar by some.) □ *The committee was comprised of representatives from all areas.* □ *The dessert was comprised of a number of different delicious substances.*

compromise on someone or something **(with** someone) and **compromise (on** someone or something**) with** someone to reach agreement with someone on a disputed matter concerning someone or something; to make concessions to someone on some point concerning someone or something. □ *I intend to compromise on this matter with them.* □ *Are you going to compromise with me on this issue?*

compute something **at** something to calculate the total of something to be a certain figure. □ *I compute the total at nearly three thousand dollars.* □ *The tax department computed the penalty at an enormous amount.*

con someone **into** something to deceive someone into doing something. □ *The dishonest contractor conned her into buying a new furnace even when her old one was fine.* □ *You are just conning yourself into believing your plan will work.*

con someone **out of** something to trick someone out of money or something of value. □ *Anne conned her little sister out of her allowance.* □ *Dave conned me out of my autographed baseball.*

conceal someone or something **from** someone or something to hide someone or something from someone or something. □ *Are you trying to conceal something from me?* □ *I cannot conceal Roger from the police.* □ *We could not conceal the present from mom.*

concede something **to** someone or something to yield something to someone or a group; to grant something to someone or something. □ *At midnight, Ronald conceded the election to his opponent.*

concede to someone or something to yield to someone or a group; to give in to someone or a group. □ *In the end we conceded to the demands of the petition.* □ *I will not concede to you.*

*conceited as a barber's cat *Rur.* very conceited; vain. (*Also:* **as** ~.) □ *Ever since he won that award, he's been as conceited as a barber's cat.*

conceive of someone or something to think of or invent the notion of someone or something. □ *Who on earth ever conceived of doing this?* □ *Edison conceived of many very useful things that we now use every day.*

conceive of someone or something **as** someone or something to think of someone as being someone else; to think of something as being something else. □ *I can't conceive of you as a pilot.* □ *I can conceive of this grassy spot as a very interesting setting for a cottage.*

concentrate at some place to gather thickly at a place. □ *The moths concentrated at the window at night, attracted by the light.* □ *All the thirsty children concentrated at the water fountain.*

concentrate someone or something **at** something to cause people or things to gather at a place; to cause people or things to convene or converge at a place. □ *You shouldn't concentrate all the guards at one entrance.* □ *The general concentrated all the big guns at the entrance to the valley.*

concentrate something **on** someone or something to focus something on someone or something; to center on someone or something. □ *Let's try to concentrate our efforts on finishing this job today.* □ *She concentrated her attention on Lynn.*

concentrate (up)on someone or something to focus one's thinking on someone or something; to think intensely about someone or something. (*Upon* is formal and less commonly used than *on.*) □ *Please concentrate upon Jeff. He is the one we should discuss.* □ *Try to concentrate on your work more.*

concern oneself **about** someone or something and **concern** oneself **over** someone or something to turn one's thoughts and consideration to someone or something. □ *I hope you will concern yourself over your work a little more.* □ *Please don't concern yourself about me. I'll do okay.*

concern someone **in** something to bring someone into some matter; to engage someone in something; to occupy someone with something. □ *Don't concern Dave in our party planning. He doesn't know anything about entertaining.* □ *The wrong committee was concerned in this from the very beginning.*

concern someone **with** someone or something to busy someone with someone or something; to worry someone with thoughts of someone or something. □ *I hope Jennifer does not concern herself with this matter.* □ *Try to concern him with something other than his work.*

concur on someone or something **(with** someone) and **concur (on** someone or something**) with** someone to agree with someone about someone or something. □ *I certainly do concur on this matter with all of you.* □ *I concur with you on Tom.* □ *We concurred with the committee on you as our choice for the job.* □ *We concurred on the plans with the council.*

condemn someone **as** something to blame or judge someone as being something bad. □ *The team condemned Larry as a traitor.* □ *Max was condemned as a common thief.*

condemn someone **for** something to blame or judge someone for something or for having done something. □ *I really can't condemn her for doing it. I would have done the same too.* □ *Don't condemn yourself for the accident. It was no one's fault.*

condemn someone **to** something [for a judge] to sentence someone to something; to relegate someone to a particular punishment. □ *By confessing, he condemned himself to many years in prison.* □ *I don't want to condemn you to a life of unpleasantness.*

condense something **(in)to** something to compress or reduce something to something; to shrink or abridge something into a smaller version. □ *Condense this into half its original volume.* □ *You should condense this novel to a short story.*

condescend to do something to agree to do something that is humbling or belittling. □ *I will not condescend to respond to that remark.* □ *"Will you condescend to join us for dinner?" teased Bob.*

condescend to someone to talk down to someone; to treat people as if they were below oneself; to patronize someone. □ *Please do not condescend to me.* □ *There is no need to condescend to the children. They are just small, not stupid.*

condition someone or something **to** something **1.** to train or adapt someone or an animal to do something. □ *I conditioned the dog to beg for a treat.* □ *Over the years, he had conditioned himself to run for hours at a stretch.* **2.** to train or adapt someone or an animal to something. □ *We could never condition the cat to the finer points of domestication.* □ *I conditioned myself to the extreme cold.*

conduct someone **away (from** someone or something**)** to lead someone away from someone or something. □ *The usher conducted the gentleman away from the front of the auditorium.* □ *Can you conduct Fred away from the area?* □ *Please conduct him away.*

conduct someone **into** something and **conduct** someone **in**[†] to lead someone into something or some place. □ *The usher conducted the gentleman into the hall.* □ *The host was pleased to conduct in the guest of honor.*

conduct someone **out of** something and **conduct** someone **out**[†] to lead someone out of something or some place. □ *The usher conducted the gentleman out of the hall.* □ *The cop conducted out the gang of rowdy youths.*

confederate with someone or something to organize, join, or unite with someone or a group. □ *A number of states confederated with one another and formed a loose association.* □ *I confederated with the neighbors and we filed a joint complaint.*

confer on someone or something **(with** someone**)** and **confer (on** someone or something**) with** someone; **confer with** someone **(about** someone or something**); confer (with** someone**) about** someone or something to discuss someone or something. □ *Let us confer on this matter with the headmaster.* □ *I want to confer with you on how to handle the problem.* □ *I need to confer with you about Walter.*

confer something **(up)on** someone to grant something, such as an academic degree, to someone, usually in a ceremony. (*Upon* is more formal than *on*.) □ *The university conferred an honorary degree upon her.* □ *They conferred degrees on 300 graduates this year.*

confer with someone **(about** someone or something**)** Go to **confer on** someone or something **(with** someone**)**.

confess something **to** someone and **confess to** someone to admit something to someone; to admit having done something to someone. □ *Tom confessed his involvement to the boss.* □ *Max confessed to the police.*

confess to something to admit having done something. □ *He will not confess to the crime.* □ *In the end, Max confessed to it.*

confide in someone to trust someone with one's secrets or personal matters. □ *Sally always confided in her sister Ann.* □ *She didn't feel that she could confide in her mother.*

confide something **in** someone and **confide** something **to** someone to tell a secret or private matter to someone, trusting that the person will not reveal the secret. □ *I learned not to confide anything secret in Bob.* □ *Tom really needed to confide his inner fears to someone.*

confine someone or an animal **to** something to limit someone or an animal to a particular place; to imprison someone or an animal in a particular place. □ *Would you please confine the dog to the basement?* □ *She confined herself to the small room for over a year because of her fear of crowds.*

confine someone or an animal **within** something to contain someone or an animal within something. □ *We were unable to confine the dog within the yard.* □ *Could you confine all your car-repair mess within the garage?*

confine something **to** someone or something to limit something or the doing of something to a person or a thing. □ *Please try to confine your comments to John.* □ *Can we confine tonight's discussion to the agenda?*

confirm someone **in** something to perform a religious rite that ties one more closely to one's religion. □ *They confirmed her in the church this morning.*

confiscate something **from** someone or something to seize or impound something from someone or a group. □ *The police confiscated all the stolen property from the suspect's garage.* □ *The dean confiscated the beer from the dormitory.*

conflict with something to clash with something. (Does not refer to fighting.) □ *This date conflicts with my doctor's appointment.* □ *As far as I can tell, the date you suggest does not conflict with anything.*

conform to something to agree with or behave within guidelines or regulations. □ *I hope that your policies will conform to our guidelines.* □ *Does my casual dress conform to your regulations?*

conform with something to match or agree with a model, plan, or set of specifications. (Compare this with **conform to** something.) □ *Does this part conform with the specifications?* □ *This one conforms with them quite well.*

confront someone **with** something to face someone with incriminating evidence, charges of wrongdoing, or criticism. □ *The angry husband confronted his wife with the evidence of her financial irresponsibility.* □ *The police confronted Wilson with the witness's statement.*

confuse someone **about** something to cause someone to be puzzled or bewildered about something. □ *She confused me about the time of the concert.* □ *I wish you wouldn't confuse me about those things.*

confuse someone or an animal **with** something to use something to bewilder or confuse someone or an animal. □ *You have confused me with your clever talk.* □ *You confused the dog with your orders.*

confuse someone **with** someone else and **confuse** something **with** something else to mix someone up with someone else; to mistake someone or something with something else. □ *I'm afraid you have confused me with my brother.* □ *Don't confuse the old ones with the new ones.*

congratulate someone **(up)on** something to compliment or wish happiness to someone because of something. (*Upon* is formal and less commonly used than *on*.) □ *I want to congratulate you on your recent success.* □ *I congratulate you on your new job!*

conjecture on something to speculate on or guess about something. □ *I will not even conjecture on the outcome.* □ *Dave conjectured on what might happen next.*

conjure someone or something **up**† **1.** *Lit.* to make someone or something appear, seemingly by the use of magic. □ *The magician conjured seven white doves up.* □ *Then an old wizard conjured up a horse.* **2.** *Fig.* to manage to locate someone or something. □ *I think I can conjure a pencil up for you.* □ *Do you think you can conjure up a large coffee urn in the next half hour?* **3.** *Fig.* to manage to think up or imagine someone or something in one's mind. □ *Can you conjure a vision of grandma up?* □ *All I could do was to conjure up happy memeories.*

conk off and **conk out 1.** *Sl.* (from years ago.) to fall asleep. □ *I conked off about midnight.* □ *I was so tired that I nearly conked off.* □ *I was afraid I would conk out while I was driving.* **2.** *Sl.* (always **conk out.**) [for something] to break down; to quit running. □ *My car conked out finally.* □ *I hope my computer doesn't conk out.*

conk out Go to previous.

connect someone or something **(up) to** someone or something and **connect** someone or something **(up) with** someone or something **1.** *Lit.* to connect people or things in any combination, physically or by wires. □ *The nurse connected Maggie up to the electrocardiograph.* □ *Eric connected the machine to the wall plug.* □ *The receptionist connected my call up to Susan.* **2.** *Fig.* to make a mental connection between people and things in any combination. □ *I connected myself up to a person with similar interests.* □ *I often connect up Bob to sailing, because I first met him on a boat.* **3.** *Fig.* to argue that someone or something is linked to a criminal or a criminal act. □ *I can connect Eric to the crime.* □ *The police connected the stolen goods to Susan.*

connect (up) to something to attach to something; to attach or link something to some electrical device or electrical signal. □ *When we finish the house, we will connect up to the utilities.* □ *We have to connect to the Internet ourselves.*

connect (up) with someone or something **1.** to form an association with someone or a group. (The *up* is informal.) □ *Let's connect up with some other people and form an organization through which we can express our views.* □ *We need to connect with like-minded people that can help us with our problems.* **2.** to meet with someone or a group; to communicate with someone or a group, especially over the telephone. □ *I tried to connect up with Bob over the phone, but I could never reach him.* □ *We could not connect with the council to discuss these matters.*

connect (with someone**)** *Fig.* to meet someone; to talk to someone on the telephone. □ *Let's try to connect on this matter tomorrow.* □ *We finally connected and discussed the matter fully over dinner.*

connect (with the ball) [for a batter] to hit a baseball. □ *Wally connected for a double.* □ *He swung, but didn't connect with the ball.*

connive at something **(with** someone**)** and **connive (at** something**) with** someone to scheme at something (with someone); to plot something (with someone). □ *Are you conniving at something with Ronald?* □ *Are you and Ronald*

conniving with Tom at something I should know about? □ *Stop conniving with people!*

Consarn it! *Rur.* Damn it! (A mild oath.) □ *Consarn it! I can't find my keys.* □ *That's the second batch of muffins I've burned today, consarn it!*

Conscience does make cowards of us all. *Prov.* People sometimes fear to do what they want or what they believe is necessary because they think it is wrong. (From Shakespeare's play, *Hamlet.*) □ *Alan: I really want to go to the ball game with you guys this afternoon, but it just doesn't seem right to skip work to do it. Fred: Conscience does make cowards of us all, right, Alan?*

conscript someone **into** something to call someone into military service; to draft someone. □ *The war-torn country was even conscripting children into the army.* □ *Fred was conscripted into the army.*

consecrate someone or something **to God** to pledge someone to the service of God; to dedicate something to the glory or service of God. □ *They consecrated the new church building to the glory of God.*

consent to something to agree to permit something to happen. □ *I will not consent to your marriage.* □ *There is no need for you to consent to anything.*

consider someone **(as)** something to think of a person as a particular type of person. □ *I don't consider you as a possible candidate.* □ *I consider myself an excellent cook.*

consider someone **for** something to think about offering someone a job, office, or other responsibility. □ *Would you consider David for the job?* □ *I could not possibly consider you for the position.*

consign something **to** someone or something **1.** to entrust something to someone, something, or some place. □ *We consigned all the toughest assignments to our top employees.* □ *What shipping company should we consign these boxes to?* **2.** to assign something for shipment to a place. □ *Bill consigned this batch to Denver.*

consist of someone or something to include people or things; to be made up of people or things. □ *This bread consists of flour, water, sugar, oil, and yeast.* □ *The U.S. Senate consists of two elected officials from each state.*

console someone **on** something to comfort someone about something. □ *I want to console you on your recent loss.* □ *They consoled Fred on the continuing difficulties he was having.*

console someone **with** something to use something to comfort someone. □ *We consoled her with a sympathy card and flowers.* □ *He sat down and consoled himself with a beer or two.*

consort with someone **1.** to associate with someone. □ *It is said that she consorts with thieves.* □ *No one worth anything would consort with Max.* **2.** *Euph.* to have sex with someone. □ *Over the years it is rumored that she consorted with numerous young men.*

*****conspicuous by** one's **absence** *Cliché* noticeably absent (from an event). (*Typically: **be** ~; **made** ~.*) □ *How could the bride's father miss the wedding? He was certainly conspicuous by his absence.*

conspire with someone **(against** someone or something**)** and **conspire (with** someone**) against** someone or some-

thing to join with someone in a plot against someone or something else. □ *The CEO conspired with the board of directors against the stockholders.* □ *Ed conspired with Sam against the plan.*

Constant dropping wears away a stone. and **Constant dripping wears away a stone.** *Prov.* Persistence accomplishes things. □ *Jill: How did you get Fred to give you a raise? Jane: I just kept asking him for it every week. Constant dropping wears away a stone.*

constrain someone **from** doing something to prevent someone from doing something; to hold someone back from doing something. □ *I hope this doesn't constrain you from trying out for the play.* □ *His handicap did not constrain him from finishing the race.*

construct something **from** something and **construct** something **out of** something to build something using something. □ *Do you want to construct the house from wood?* □ *Shall we construct the building out of stone?*

construe something **as** something to interpret something to mean something. □ *Please do not construe this as criticism.* □ *We mistakenly construed her comments as positive.*

consult (with) someone **(about** someone or something**)** to ask someone about someone or something. □ *Please consult with me about all your plans.* □ *You should consult the architect about your needs.* □ *Please consult with me first.*

*****contact with** someone a link to someone resulting in communication. (*Typically: **be in** ~; **have** ~; **make** ~.) □ *I have had no contact with Bill since he left town.* □ *Tom made contact with a known criminal last month.*

contaminate someone or something **with** something to get someone or something dirty with something; to pollute someone or something with something. □ *Something in the hospital contaminated the patient with a serious infection.* □ *The campers learned not to contaminate the outdoors with anything they carried in.*

contend against someone or something to fight or compete against someone or something. □ *Do we have to contend against all this criticism?* □ *Ed refuses to have to contend against Eric.*

contend with a problem to put up with a difficulty; to struggle with the problems caused by someone or something. □ *I cannot contend with your temper anymore.* □ *I wish we did not have to contend with this changeable weather.*

contend with someone **(for** something**)** and **contend (with** someone**) for** something to fight someone for something; to compete with someone to win something. □ *I don't want to have to contend with Sally for the award.* □ *I don't want to have to contend for the job with Ed.*

content oneself **with** someone or something to be satisfied with (usually less of) someone or something. □ *You will just have to learn to content yourself with fewer nice vacations now that you have kids entering college.*

A **contented mind is a perpetual feast.** *Prov.* If you are mentally at peace, you will always feel that you have enough of everything, and will not have to strive to get more. □ *Jill: Lillian doesn't make very much money, but she seems to be happy all the time. I wonder how she manages that? Jane: A contented mind is a perpetual feast.*

continue by doing something to keep going by starting to do something else or the next step. □ *You are doing very well in this piano lesson. Please continue by playing the other sonata.* □ *After the interruption, Wally continued by explaining his position on the trade negotiations.*

continue one's **losing streak** Go to a **losing streak.**

continue with something to keep doing whatever was being done before. □ *Oh, please continue with your discussion.* □ *Do you mind if I continue with my knitting as we talk?*

contract something **out**† to make an agreement with someone to do a specific amount of work. (Rather than doing it oneself or in one's own place of business.) □ *I will contract this out and have it done by consultants.* □ *I contracted out this kind of job the last time.*

contract with someone **(for** something**)** and **contract (with** someone**) for** something to make an agreement with someone to produce or supply something, or to do something. □ *I will have to contract with an expert for that part of the project.* □ *We contracted with a local builder for a new kitchen.* □ *Did you contract for plumbing work with Eric?*

a **contradiction in terms** a statement containing a seeming contradiction. □ *A wealthy pauper is a contradiction in terms.* □ *A straight-talking politician may seem to be a contradiction in terms.*

contrary to something in spite of something that seems to suggest otherwise; regardless of something else. □ *Contrary to what you might think, I am neat and tidy.* □ *Contrary to public opinion, my uncle is well and healthy.*

contrast someone or something **with** someone or something else and **contrast** someone or something **to** someone or something else to examine people or things in a way that will show their differences. □ *Contrast Sally with Sam, for instance, to see real differences.* □ *Contrast the busy geometry of a Gothic cathedral to the simple lines of an old Saxon castle.*

contrast with someone or something **1.** to be different from someone or something. □ *Bill's cheery attitude really contrasts with the gloom of his twin brother, Bob.* □ *This stiped tie really contrasts with that polka-dot shirt.* **2.** [for a color or pattern, etc.] to show a marked difference with or complement another. □ *The black one contrasts nicely with the white one.*

contribute something **(to** someone**) (for** someone or something**)** to donate something to someone for the benefit of someone or something. □ *I hope you will contribute at least a dollar to Mary for Tom's birthday present.* □ *Will you contribute a dollar for Tom to Mary when she comes around?* □ *Can you contribute a dollar for the gift?*

contribute to something **1.** to donate something to some cause. □ *Please contribute to the fund for the needy.* **2.** to add to or exacerbate something. □ *The dry weather contributed to the failure of the crops.*

*****control over** someone or something the power to direct or manage someone or something. (*Typically: **get** ~; **have** ~; **give** someone ~.) □ *I have no control over*

Mary. I can't stop her from running away. □ Who gave you control over what goes on in this house?

control the purse strings and **hold the purse strings** *Fig.* to be in charge of the money in a business or a household. □ *I control the purse strings at our house.* □ *Mr. Williams is the treasurer. He controls the purse strings.*

convalesce from something to recuperate from a disease, operation, or injury. □ *I spent three weeks in bed convalescing from the flu.* □ *Donna needed some time to convalesce from her surgery.*

converge (up)on someone or something **1.** *Lit.* to gather near or around someone or something. (*Upon* is formal and less commonly used than *on*.) □ *Everyone converged on the wounded sailor.* □ *The shoppers converged on the store as it opened for the big sale.* **2.** *Fig.* to meet on someone or something; to grow together so as to focus on someone or something. (*Upon* is formal and less commonly used than *on*.) □ *Even political enemies converged on the matter of simplifying the tax code.* □ *Our discussions converged on Eric.*

converse with someone (**about** someone or something) and **converse (with** someone) **about** someone or something to talk about someone or something. □ *Please converse with Ted about that.* □ *I need to converse about last night with you.* □ *The principal needs to converse with you.*

convert from something (**(in)to** something) and **convert (from** something) **(in)to** something to change from one thing into another. □ *We converted from oil to natural gas to heat our house.* □ *I had hoped he would convert from an impatient youth into a relaxed gentleman. He did not.*

convert someone or something (**from** something) **(in)to** something) to change someone or something from something into something else. □ *Can we convert you from a meat eater into a vegetarian?* □ *Would you be willing to convert your oil furnace to a gas one?*

convey something (**from** someone or something) (**to** someone or something) to carry or transport something from someone or something to someone, something, or some place. □ *I conveyed the box from the table to the basement.* □ *Please convey every good wish from those of us in the Midwest to those on the East Coast.* □ *Would you convey my blessings to the newlyweds?*

convict someone **of** something to pronounce someone guilty of something. □ *In the end, they convicted her of theft.* □ *The police wanted to convict Max of the crime.*

convince someone **of** something to persuade someone that something is true. □ *You will never convince me of what you say.* □ *I will probably convince myself of the need to find a better job.*

convulse someone **with** something to cause someone to quake or jerk because of pain or emotion. (Can be physical or figurative; see examples.) □ *He convulsed with abdominal pain from something he ate.* □ *The audience was convulsed with laughter.*

cook someone's **goose** *Fig.* to damage or ruin someone. □ *I cooked my own goose by not showing up on time.* □ *Sally cooked Bob's goose for treating her the way he did.*

cook (something**) out†** to cook food out of doors. □ *Shall we cook out some chicken tonight?* □ *Yes, let's cook out.*

cook something **to perfection** to cook something perfectly. □ *John cooked my steak to perfection.* □ *The entire dinner was cooked to perfection!*

cook something **up† 1.** *Lit.* to prepare a batch of some kind of food by cooking. □ *Fred cooked a batch of beans up for the ranch hands.* □ *He cooked up some food for dinner.* **2.** *Fig.* to devise or concoct something. □ *Fred cooked up a scheme that was supposed to earn him a lot of money.* □ *I don't have a plan right now, but I think I can cook one up.*

cook something **up† (with** someone) *Fig.* to arrange or plan to do something with someone. (The *something* is usually the word *something*. See also **cook** something **up.**) □ *I tried to cook something up with Karen for Tuesday.* □ *I want to cook up something with John.* □ *Let's see if we can cook something up.*

cook the accounts and **cook the books** to cheat in bookkeeping; to make the accounts appear to balance when they do not. □ *Jane was charged with cooking the accounts of her mother's store.* □ *It's hard to tell whether she really cooked the accounts or just didn't know what she was doing.*

cook the books Go to previous.

cook up a storm Go to up a storm.

cooked up contrived. (This is hyphenated before a nominal.) □ *The whole thing seems so cooked up.* □ *What a cooked-up story! Of course, you don't believe it.*

cooking with gas doing [something] exactly right. □ *That's great! Now you're cooking with gas!* □ *I knew she was finally cooking with gas when she answered all the questions correctly.*

*cool as a cucumber extremely calm; imperturbable. (**Also: as ~.*) □ *Joan felt nervous, but she acted as cool as a cucumber.* □ *The politician kept cool as a cucumber throughout the interview with the aggressive journalist.*

cool, calm, and collected *Cliché* [of a person] very calm and poised. □ *James did very well in his TV appearances. He stayed cool, calm, and collected.* □ *The bad news didn't seem to distress Jane at all. She remained cool, calm, and collected.*

cool down Go to cool off.

Cool it! *Inf.* Calm down!; Take it easy! □ *Don't get mad, Bob. Cool it!* □ *Cool it, you guys! No fighting around here.*

cool off and **cool down 1.** *Lit.* to lose or reduce heat. □ *I wish my soup would cool off. I'm hungry.* □ *It'll cool down this evening, after dusk.* **2.** *Fig.* to let one's anger die away. (As the "heat" of anger declines.) □ *I'm sorry I got angry. I'll cool off in a minute.* □ *Cool off, Tom. There is no sense getting so excited.* **3.** *Fig.* to let one's passion or love die away. (As the "heat" of passion declines.) □ *Ted: Is Bob still in love with Jane? Bill: No, he's cooled off a lot.*

cool one's **heels** *Fig.* to wait (for someone); to wait for something to happen. □ *I spent an hour cooling my heels in the waiting room while the doctor saw other patients.* □ *All right, if you can't behave properly, just sit down here and cool your heels until I call you.*

cool out Go to chill out.

cool someone **down†** and **cool** someone **off† 1.** *Lit.* to cool someone by reducing the heat or applying something cold. □ *Here, have a cold drink. Cool yourself down.* □ *The ice* *finally cooled down the feverish child.* □ *We need to cool off the pudding in a hurry.* **2.** *Fig.* to reduce someone's anger. (Reducing the "heat" of anger.) □ *I just stared at him while he was yelling. I knew that would cool him down.* □ *The coach talked to them for a long time. That cooled them off.* **3.** *Fig.* to reduce someone's passion or love. (Reducing the "heat" of passion.) □ *When she slapped him, that really cooled him down.* □ *Seeing Mary was too intense, so Bill cooled himself off by breaking it off for a while.*

cool someone out† *Sl.* to calm someone; to appease someone. □ *Cool yourselves out, you people. We gotta be sensible.* □ *The manager appeared and tried to cool out everybody, but that was a waste of time.*

cooled out *Sl.* calm; unabashed. □ *Ted is a really cooled out kind of guy.* □ *When she's cooled out, she's great.*

cooler heads prevail *Fig.* the ideas or influence of less emotional people prevail. (Used of a tense situation.) □ *One hopes that cooler heads will prevail and soon everything will calm down.*

coop someone or something up† to confine someone or something in a small place. □ *Don't coop me up. I can't stand small places.* □ *We had to coop up the dogs for a while.*

cooperate with someone (on something) and **cooperate (with someone) on something** to work together in harmony with someone on something. □ *Please cooperate with me on this project.* □ *Can you cooperate on this with me?* □ *I hope we can cooperate on this.*

co-opt someone into something to convince someone of a differing view to adopt one's position or philosophy. □ *They tried to co-opt the students into rioting.* □ *There is no point in trying to co-opt them into it. They are too clever.*

coordinate something with something 1. to make something harmonize with something else. □ *I want to coordinate my hat with my shoes.* □ *Is this tie coordinated with my jacket?* **2.** to synchronize something with something else. □ *Let us coordinate our actions in this matter.* □ *I think we should coordinate our departure times with that of Fred.*

cop a packet to become badly injured; to be wounded severely. (Originally military.) □ *My uncle copped a packet in Normandy.* □ *If you want to cop a packet or worse, just stand up in that shallow trench, son.*

cop a plea *Fig.* to plead guilty to a lesser charge to avoid a more serious charge or lessen time of imprisonment. □ *He copped a plea and got off with only two months in the slammer.*

cop a squat *Sl.* to sit down. □ *Hey, man! Come in and cop a squat here next to me.* □ *Cop a squat and crack a tube.*

cop an attitude *Sl.* to take a negative or opposite attitude about something. □ *My teenage son copped an attitude when I asked why he seemed to be sneaking around.*

cop onto something *Sl.* to understand or become aware of something. □ *I think I'm copping onto the significance of this at last.* □ *Try to cop onto what I'm saying, Otto.*

cop out (of something) and **cop out (on something) 1.** *Sl.* to withdraw from doing something. □ *Are you copping out of this job?* □ *No, I'm not copping out!* **2.** *Sl.* to break one's promise about doing something. □ *You said you would and now you are copping out of it.* □ *I'm not copping out.*

I just can't find the time. **3.** *Sl.* to plead guilty (to a lesser charge). □ *Frank copped out and got off with a night in the cooler.*

cop out (on someone) *Sl.* to break one's promise to someone. (See also previous.) □ *Come on! Don't cop out on me!* □ *You promised me you would do it! Don't cop out now!*

cop out (on something) Go to **cop out (of something)**.

cop some Zs Go to **catch some Zs**.

cop something from someone or something *Sl.* to steal or swipe something from someone or something. □ *Some thug copped my watch from me.* □ *Max copped food from a number of stores.*

cope with someone or something to endure someone or something; to manage to deal with someone or something. □ *I don't think I can cope with any more trouble.* □ *I can't cope with your being late for work anymore.*

copulate with someone [for someone] to have sexual intercourse with someone. □ *He said he wanted to copulate with whom?*

copy something down† **(from someone or something)** to copy onto paper what someone says; to copy onto paper what one reads. □ *Please copy this down from Tony.* □ *Ted copied down the directions from the invitation.* □ *Jane copied the recipe down from the cookbook.*

copy something out† Go to **copy something out of something**.

copy something out† **(by hand)** to copy something in handwriting. □ *I have to copy this out again. I lost the first copy.* □ *Please copy out this article for me.*

copy something out of something and **copy something out**† to copy something onto paper from a book or document. □ *Did you copy this out of a book?* □ *I did not copy this paper or any part of it out of anything.* □ *I copied out most of it.*

cordon something off† to mark off an area where people should not go with a rope, tape, ribbon, etc. □ *The police cordoned the scene of the crime off, and we could not even get close.* □ *They cordoned off the area.*

cork high and bottle deep *Rur.* very drunk. □ *By the time the party was over, he was cork high and bottle deep.*

cork something up† **1.** *Lit.* to close and seal a bottle with a cork. □ *I think we should cork this up and save it for later.* □ *Cork up the bottle for later.* **2.** *Fig.* to stop up one's mouth and be quiet. □ *Cork it up and listen!* □ *Cork up your mouth!*

corner the market on something and **corner the something market** *Fig.* to develop or obtain a monopoly of something. □ *The company sought to corner the market on frozen yogurt.* □ *Standard Oil had the oil market cornered at the end of the nineteenth century.*

corral someone or something *Fig.* to herd someone or something into a corral or other enclosed space. □ *It took the cowboys two hours to corral the mustangs.* □ *The nursery school teacher herded the kids off the playground and corraled them in the classroom.*

correlate something with something to match or equate something with something else. □ *Can you correlate her comment with what she said yesterday?* □ *The scientist could not correlate the new data with his hypothesis.*

correlate with something to match or equate with something. □ *This does not correlate with your earlier story.* □ *What she said yesterday does not correlate with what she is saying today.*

correspond to something to match up with something; to harmonize with something. □ *This pin on this part corresponds to the receptacle on the other part it fits into.*

correspond with someone (**about** someone or something) **correspond (with** someone) **about** someone or something to write letters back and forth with someone about someone or something. □ *I will have to correspond with the manager about that.* □ *I corresponded about this with my brother.* □ *I corresponded with my brother for over a year.* □ *We corresponded about Fred.*

cost a king's ransom Go to a king's ransom.

cost a pretty penny and **cost an arm and a leg; cost the earth** *Fig.* to be expensive; to cost a lot of money. □ *Mary's dress is real silk. It must have cost a pretty penny.* □ *Taking care of a fancy car like that can cost a pretty penny, let me tell you.* □ *It cost an arm and a leg, so I didn't buy it.* □ *A house that size with an ocean view must cost the earth!*

cost an arm and a leg Go to previous.

cost something **out**† to figure out the total cost of some set of costs or a complex purchase of goods or services. □ *Give me a minute to cost this out, and I will have an estimate for you.* □ *Do you have time to cost out these specifications this week?*

cost the earth Go to cost a pretty penny.

cotton (on)to someone or something *Rur.* to begin to like or agree to someone or something quickly. □ *She began to cotton to Fred, despite his country ways.* □ *She cottoned onto Jane's way of thinking.*

cotton up to someone *Rur.* to try to make friends with someone; to flatter or fawn on someone in hopes of favorable treatment. □ *James set out to cotton up to the parents of his friends.* □ *Just watch her cotton up to the teacher!*

a **couch potato** a lazy individual, addicted to television-watching. □ *All he ever does is watch TV; he's become a real couch potato.* □ *Couch potatoes can tend to become very fat and unhealthy, you know.*

couch something **in** something to express something in carefully chosen or deceptive words. □ *He tended to couch his explanations in arcane vocabulary.* □ *She couched her words in an overly polite manner.*

cough one's **head off** *Fig.* to cough long and hard. (See also laugh one's head off.) □ *I had the flu. I nearly coughed my head off for two days.*

cough something **out**† to say something while coughing. □ *He coughed the words out, but no one could understand him.* □ *He coughed out the name of his assailant.*

cough something **up**† **1.** to get something out of the body by coughing. □ *She coughed some matter up and took some more medicine.* □ *She coughed up phlegm all night.* **2.** *Euph.* to vomit something. □ *The dog coughed the rabbit up.* □ *The dog coughed up the food it had eaten.* **3.** *Sl.* to produce or present something, such as an amount of money. □ *You will cough the money up, won't you?* □ *You*

had better cough up what you owe me, if you know what's good for you.

could do with someone or something to want or need someone or something; to benefit from someone or something. □ *I could do with a nice cool drink right now.* □ *I could do with some help on this project.*

could fight a circle-saw (and it a-runnin') *Rur.* eager to fight. □ *He was so mad he could fight a circle-saw and it a-runnin'.* □ *She's a good watchdog. She could fight a circle-saw.*

Could I be excused? Would you give me permission to leave?; Would you give me permission to leave the table? (Also used with *can* or *may* in place of *could*.) □ *Bill: I'm finished, Mom. Could I be excused? Mother: Yes, of course, when you use good manners like that.*

(Could I) buy you a drink? 1. *Lit.* Could I purchase a drink for you? (An offer by one person—usually in a bar—to buy a drink for another. Then the two will drink together. Also used with *can* or *may* in place of *could*.) □ *When Sally and Mary met at the agreed time in the hotel bar, Sally said to Mary, "Could I buy you a drink?"* **2.** *Fig.* Could I make you a drink? (A slightly humorous way of offering to prepare and serve someone a drink, as in one's home. Also used with *can* or *may* in place of *could*.) □ *Bill: Come in, Fred. Can I buy you a drink? I've got wine and beer. Fred: Great. A beer would be fine, thanks.*

Could I call you? 1. I am too busy to talk to you now. Do you mind if I telephone you later on? (Usually in a business context. Also used with *can* in place of *could*. *May* is too polite here.) □ *Sally: I can't talk to you right now. Could I call you? Tom: Sure, no problem.* □ *Bill: I've got to run. Sorry. Can I call you? Bob: No, I'm leaving town. I'll try to get in touch next week.* **2.** Do you mind if I call you and ask for another date sometime?; Do you mind if I call you sometime (in order to further our relationship)? (Usually in a romantic context. Also used with *can* or *may* in place of *could*.) □ *Mary: I had a marvelous time, Bob. Bob: Me, too. Can I call you? Mary: Sure.* □ *Bob: I had a marvelous time, Mary. May I call you? Mary: Maybe in a week or two. I have a very busy week ahead. I'll call you, in fact.*

Could I come in? Do you mind if I enter? (A polite request. Also used with *can* or *may* in place of *could*.) □ *Tom (standing in the doorway): Hello, I'm with the Internal Revenue Service. Could I come in?* □ *Bill: Hi, Tom. What are you doing here? Tom: Could I come in? I have to talk to you. Bill: Sure. Come on in.*

Could I get by, please? Would you please allow me space to pass by? (Also used with *can* or *may* in place of *could*. *May* is almost too polite.) □ *Poor Bill, trapped at the back of the elevator behind a huge man, kept saying, "Could I get by, please?"* □ *"Can I get by, please?" Jane said, squeezing between passengers on the crowded bus.*

(Could I) get you something (to drink)? an expression offering a drink, usually an alcoholic drink. (Compare this with **(Could I) buy you a drink?** Also used with *can* or *may* in place of *could*.) □ *Bill: Hi, Alice! Come on in! Can I get you something to drink? Alice: Just a little soda, if you don't mind.* □ *Waiter: Get you something to drink? John: No, thanks. I'll just order dinner now.*

(Could I) give you a lift? Can I offer you a ride to some place? (Also used with *can* or *may* in place of *could*.) □ *Bill stopped his car at the side of the road where Tom stood. "Can I give you a lift?" asked Bill.* □ *John: Well, I've got to leave. Alice: Me, too. John: Give you a lift? Alice: Sure. Thanks.*

Could I have a lift? and **How about a lift?** Would you please give me a ride (in your car)? (This usually refers to a destination that is the same as the driver's or on the way to the driver's destination. Also used with *can* or *may* in place of *could*.) □ *Bob: Going north? Could I have a lift? Bill: Sure. Hop in. Bob: Thanks. That's such a long walk to the north end of campus.* □ *Sue: Can I have a lift? I'm late. Mary: Sure, if you're going somewhere on Maple Street.*

Could I have a word with you? Go to I'd like (to have) a word with you.

Could I have someone **call you?** Could I take a message so your call can be returned? (A question asked by someone who answers the telephone when the person the caller is seeking is not available. The *someone* can be a person's name or a pronoun, or even the word *someone*. Also used with *can* or *may* in place of *could*.) □ *Tom: Bill's not here now. Could I have him call you? Bob: Yeah. Ask him to leave a message on my machine. Tom: Sure.* □ *"Could I have her call you?" asked Mrs. Wilson's secretary.*

Could I have the bill? Go to Check, please.

Could I help you? and **Can I help you?; May I help you?** Could I assist you? (Said by shopkeepers, clerks, food service workers, and people who answer the telephone.) □ *The clerk came over and said, "Could I help you?"* □ *Clerk: May I help you? Mary: No thanks, I'm just looking.*

Could I join you? and **(Do you) care if I join you?; (Do you) mind if I join you?** Will you permit me to sit with you? (An inquiry seeking permission to sit at someone's table or join someone else in some activity. Also used with *can* or *may* in place of *could*.) □ *Tom came into the cafe and saw Fred and Sally sitting in a booth by the window. Coming up to them, Tom said, "Could I join you?"*

Could I leave a message? and **Can I leave a message?** Can I request that a message be written down for a person who is not available to come to the telephone. □ *Bill: Can I talk to Fred? Mary: He's not here. Bill: Could I leave a message? Mary: Sure, I can leave a message for him.*

Could I see you again? and **Can I see you again?; May I see you again?** Could we go out again sometime? □ *Tom: I had a wonderful time, Mary. Can I see you again? Mary: Call me tomorrow, Tom. Good night.* □ *"Could I see you again?" muttered Tom, dizzy with the magic of her kiss.*

Could I see you in my office? and **Can I see you in my office?** I want to talk to you in the privacy of my office. (Typically said by a supervisor to a lower-ranking employee.) □ *"Mr. Franklin," said Bill's boss sort of sternly, "Could I see you in my office for a minute? We need to talk about something."*

Could I speak to someone? and **Can I speak to** someone?; **May I speak to** someone? the phrase used to request to talk to a particular person, usually on the telephone. (Also used with *talk* in place of *speak*.) □ *Tom*

(answering the phone): Good morning, Acme Air Products. With whom do you wish to speak? Bill: Can I speak to Mr. Wilson? Tom: One moment. □ *Sally: May I speak to the manager, please? Clerk: Certainly, madam. I'm the manager.*

Could I take a message? and **Can I take a message?; May I take a message?** the phrase used on the telephone to offer to take a message and give it to the person the caller is seeking. □ *Bill: Can I talk to Fred? Mary: He's not here. Could I take a message for him?*

Could I take your order (now)? and **Can I take your order (now)?; May I take your order (now)?** an expression used by food service personnel to determine if the customer is ready to order food. □ *Waiter: May I take your order now? Mary: Of course. Jane, what are you going to have? Jane: I'm still trying to decide. Waiter: I'll be back in a minute.* □ *Waiter: Can I take your order? Mary: Yes, we're ready.*

Could I tell him who's calling? and **Can I tell her who's calling?; May I tell him who's calling?** a question asked by people who answer the telephone to find out politely who is asking for someone. (*Him* or *her* can be replaced by a person's name or by a plural pronoun.) □ *Mary (on the phone): Hello. Could I speak to Bill Franklin? Sally: Could I tell him who's calling? Mary: It's Mary Peters. Sally: Oh yes, he's expecting your call. I'll get him for you.*

Could I use your powder room? and **Can I use your powder room?; May I use your powder room?; Where is your powder room?** *Euph.* a polite way to ask to use the bathroom in someone's home. (Alludes to a woman powdering her nose. Sometimes used jocularly by men. See also powder one's nose.) □ *Mary: Oh, Sally, could I use your powder room? Sally: Of course. It's just off the kitchen, on the left.* □ *Tom: Nice place you've got here. Uh, where is your powder room? Beth: At the top of the stairs.*

Could we continue this later? and **Can we continue this later?** Could we go on with this conversation at a later time? □ *As Mary and John were discussing something private, Bob entered the room. "Could we continue this later?" whispered John. "Yes, of course," answered Mary.*

Could you excuse us, please? and **Can you excuse us, please?; Would you excuse us, please?; Will you excuse us, please?** We must leave. I hope you will forgive us. (A polite way of announcing a departure.) □ *Bill: Could you excuse us, please? We simply must rush off. Alice: So sorry you have to go. Come back when you can stay longer.*

Could you hold? and **Can you hold?; Will you hold?** Do you mind if I put your telephone call on hold? □ *"Could you hold?" asked the operator.* □ *Sue: Hello. Acme Motors. Can you hold? Bob: I guess. Sue (after a while): Hello. Thank you for holding. Can I help you?*

Could you keep a secret? and **Can you keep a secret?** I am going to tell you something that I hope you will keep a secret. (Also used with *can* in place of *could*.) □ *Tom: Could you keep a secret? Mary: Sure. Tom: Don't tell anybody, but I'm going to be a daddy.* □ *Sue: Can you keep a secret? Alice: Of course. Sue: We're moving to Atlanta.*

couldn't be happier totally happy. □ *They both couldn't be happier since they got married.*

could(n't) care less [one is] unable to care at all; it does not matter at all. □ *John couldn't care less whether he goes to the party or not.* □ *I could care less if I live or die.*

couldn't hit a bull in the ass with a bass fiddle *Rur.* unable to aim; very clumsy. (Jocular. Use with caution.) □ *Tom: Is Jane a good shot? Charlie: She couldn't hit a bull in the ass with a bass fiddle.*

couldn't pour water out of a boot (if there was instructions on the heel) *Rur.* stupid. □ *I won't say Jim is dumb, but he couldn't pour water out of a boot.* □ *Jane couldn't pour water out of a boot if there was instructions on the heel—and she's the smartest one in her family!*

Councils of war never fight. *Prov.* A group of people charged with crucial decisions often cannot act decisively. □ *We tried to convince the boss not to form a committee, but to decide himself. We knew that councils of war never fight.*

counsel someone **about** something to give advice to someone about something. □ *Will you counsel George about which tires to buy?*

counsel someone **against** something to advise someone against doing something. □ *The lawyer counseled her against suing the government.* □ *I was counseled against going for a walk alone at night.*

count against someone [for something] to be held against someone; [for something] to weigh against someone. □ *I hope this mistake doesn't count against me.* □ *Don't worry, it won't count against you at all.*

count down to count backwards to an event that will start when zero is reached. □ *The project manager was counting down—getting ready for the launch of the rocket.* □ *I can still hear the captain counting down: "Five, four, three, two, one, zero, blast off!"*

count for something to be valid for something; to be worth something. □ *Doesn't all my work count for anything?* □ *Your positive attitude counts for a lot as far as I'm concerned.*

count from something **(up) to** something to say or list the numbers from one number to some other number. □ *Now, count from 100 up to 300 by threes.* □ *Timmy can count from 1 to 40.*

count heads and **count noses** *Fig.* to count people. □ *I'll tell you how many people are here after I count heads.* □ *Let's count noses so we can be sure everyone is back on the bus.*

Count no man happy till he dies. Go to Call no man happy till he dies.

count noses Go to count heads.

count off [for a series of people, one by one] to say aloud the next number in a fixed sequence. □ *The soldiers counted off by threes.* □ *The sergeant told them to count off.*

count on someone or something to rely on someone or something; to depend on someone or something. □ *We can count on Bill to get the job done.* □ *Can I count on this car to start every morning of the year?*

count one's **chickens before they hatch** *Fig.* to plan how to utilize good results of something before those results have occurred. (The same as **Don't count your** chickens before they are hatched.) □ *You may be disappointed if you count your chickens before they hatch.*

count someone **among** something to consider someone as a particular type of person or part of a particular group. □ *I count her among my closest friends.* □ *Rachel counted herself among the luckiest people alive.*

count someone **in (for** something) and **count** someone **in (on** something); **count** someone **in†** to include someone as part of something. □ *Please count me in for the party.* □ *Do count me in on it.* □ *Count in everybody who said they would attend.*

count someone or something **as** something to consider someone to be a particular type of person. □ *I count Todd as one of the possible candidates.* □ *I count this entry as a definite prizewinner.*

count someone or something **off†** to count people or things, to see if they are all there. (See also count off.) □ *Let's count them off to see who's missing.* □ *Count off each person, one by one.* □ *I counted each one off.*

count someone or something **up†** to count things or people to see how many there are. □ *Let's count them up and see how many we have.* □ *I counted all the guests up, and there are too many to seat.* □ *Please count up all these books and tell me how many there are.*

count someone **out (for** something) to exclude someone from something. □ *Please count me out for the party next Saturday. I have other plans.* □ *You should count the whole family out. We are going to the beach for the weekend.*

count something **against** someone to regard something in a negative way against someone. □ *I'm afraid we must count this against you as an unexcused absence.* □ *Don't count that last strike against the batter.*

count something **as** something to treat or think of something as being a certain thing. □ *I count this as a win.* □ *Did you count that one as a fair ball?*

count something **in†** to include something in a count of something. □ *Did you count the tall ones in?* □ *Did you count in the tall ones in the corner?*

count something **out†** **1.** to disregard something; to eliminate a possibility. □ *We'll have to count out the possibility of his being elected.* □ *Never count it out. It can always happen.* **2.** to give out things, counting them one by one. □ *She counted the cookies out, one by one.* □ *She counted out the cookies to each child.*

count up to something **1.** to say or list the numbers from zero on up to a certain number. □ *Can you count up to a million?* □ *I can count up to any number you name, and I will do it if you will stay around to listen.* **2.** to equal a specified total; to add up to something. □ *That counts up to a lot.* □ *The money we earned today counts up to just enough to pay for the electricity we used today.*

count (up)on someone or something to rely on someone or something. (*Upon* is formal and less commonly used than *on*.) □ *Can I count upon you to do the job?* □ *You can count on me.*

count with someone to be important to someone. □ *Your cooperation really counts with me.* □ *All my efforts do not count with her.*

counter someone or something **with** something to refute someone or something with something. □ *She countered our evidence with an eyewitness.* □ *I countered Nancy with a better argument.*

counter with something to say something in refutation of something; to strike back with something. □ *Aren't you going to counter with an argument?* □ *He countered with a punch in the jaw.*

a **country mile** *Rur.* a great distance. □ *The batter knocked that ball a country mile.* □ *I had to walk a country mile to the next gas station.*

a **couple of** two; two or three; a few; some; not many. □ *Bill grabbed a couple of beers from the refrigerator.* □ *I hung a couple of pictures on the wall.*

couple someone **with** someone to join one person with another to make a pair. □ *I coupled Todd with Amy for the dinner party.*

couple something **(on)to** something and **couple** something **on(to** something); **couple** something **on**† to attach something to something. □ *Couple this connector to that one.* □ *The railroad worker coupled on the next car in line.* □ *Couple the green one onto the red one.*

couple something **together** to attach two parts of something together. □ *Couple these two cars together and put them on track seven.* □ *You have to couple the ends of the two hoses together before you turn on the water.*

couple something **with** something to join one thing with another to make a pair. □ *We coupled the budget issue with the staffing issue for our agenda.*

couple up (with someone) [for one person] to join another person to form a pair. □ *I decided to couple up with Larry.* □ *Larry and I coupled up with each other.* □ *By midnight, they all had coupled up and were dancing.*

couple with someone *Euph.* to have sexual intercourse with someone. □ *They coupled with each other in a night of passion.*

couple with something to connect or join to something. □ *This railroad car will couple with the engine.* □ *These cars did not couple with the others properly, and there was almost an accident.*

course of action the procedures or sequence of actions that someone will follow to accomplish a goal. □ *I plan to follow a course of action that will produce the best results.* □ *The board planned a course of action that would reduce costs and eliminate employees.*

The **course of true love never did run smooth.** *Prov.* People in love with each other often have to overcome difficulties in order to be together. (From Shakespeare's play, *A Midsummer Night's Dream.*) □ *Jill: What am I going to do? My boyfriend's job is transferring him to Texas, and I have to stay here. Jane: The course of true love never did run smooth.*

course through something to run, race, or flow rapidly through something. □ *I believe, sometimes, that ice water courses through your veins.* □ *No, perfectly red blood courses through them.*

Courtesy costs nothing. Go to Civility costs nothing.

cover a lot of ground 1. *Lit.* to travel over a great distance; to investigate a wide expanse of land. □ *The* prospectors covered a lot of ground, looking for gold. □ *My car can cover a lot of ground in one day.* **2.** *Fig.* to deal with much information and many facts. □ *The history lecture covered a lot of ground today.*

cover for someone **1.** to make excuses for someone; to conceal someone's errors. □ *If I miss class, please cover for me.* □ *If you're late, I'll cover for you.* **2.** to handle someone else's work. □ *Dr. Johnson's partner agreed to cover for him during his vacation.*

cover someone **in** something to place something over someone or something to serve as clothing or concealment. □ *The designer had covered her in see-through fabric that was very revealing.*

cover someone or something **against** something **1.** to cover someone or something as protection against something. □ *You should cover your ears against the cold.* □ *I covered little Jimmy against the night's drafts.* □ *I covered myself against the driving rain.* **2.** *Rur.* [for an insurer] to provide insurance on someone or something against some peril. □ *The insurance policy covered us against losses.* □ *This policy covers your car against theft.*

cover someone or something **for** something [for an insurer] to provide protection to someone or something for a particular price. □ *One company will cover the car for about a thousand dollars.* □ *This policy covers you for a few dollars a week.*

cover someone or something **up**† to place something on someone or something for protection or concealment. □ *Cover the pie up, so Terry won't see it.* □ *Cover up Jimmy so he doesn't get cold.*

cover someone's **tracks (up)**† to conceal one's trail; to conceal one's past activities. □ *She was able to cover her tracks up so that they couldn't pin the charges on her.* □ *It's easy to cover up your tracks when the investigators botch their job.* □ *The robber failed to cover his tracks.*

cover something **up**† **1.** *Lit.* to place some sort of cover on something. □ *Please cover up that mess with a cloth.* □ *Cover it up.* **2.** *Fig.* to conceal a wrongdoing; to conceal evidence. □ *They tried to cover the crime up, but the single footprint gave them away.* □ *She could not cover up her misdeeds.*

cover the territory 1. *Lit.* to travel or deal with a specific large area. □ *The sales manager was responsible for all of the eastern states and personally covered the territory twice each year.* **2.** *Fig.* to deal with all matters relating to a specific topic. □ *That lecture really covered the territory in only an hour.*

cover the waterfront to deal with every detail concerning a specific topic. □ *Her talk really covered the waterfront. By the time she finished, I knew much more than I wanted to know.*

cover (up) for someone to conceal someone's wrongdoing by lying or concealing the evidence of wrongdoing. □ *Are you covering up for the person who committed the crime?* □ *I wouldn't cover for anyone.*

cow chip and **cow pie; cow patty; cow flop** *Inf.* a piece of cow manure. □ *The pioneers didn't have much wood, so they burned dried cow chips.* □ *How did that big ol' cow pie get in the middle of my flower bed?* □ *Tom slipped on a cow patty.*

cow juice *Sl.* milk. □ *Here's a little cow juice to pour on your cereal.*

cow paste *Rur.* butter. □ *Would you kindly pass the cow paste?*

cow patty Go to cow chip.

cow pie Go to cow chip.

cow someone **into** something to intimidate someone into doing something through the use of guilt or shame. □ *You can't cow me into doing it. Those tricks don't work on me.* □ *You can cow Wally into almost anything.*

Cowards die many times before their death(s). *Prov.* Cowards are often afraid that they are going to die, so that they often feel what it is like to die, while brave people only feel the fear of death when they are really about to die. (From Shakespeare's play, *Julius Caesar*.) □ *Every time Nina went out alone, she was always afraid. Cowards die many times before their deaths.*

cower (away) from someone or something to pull away from someone or something in fear. □ *The coyote cowered away from the fire.*

cower down (from something**)** and **cower down (with** something**)** to crouch down, displaying an emotion, such as fear. □ *They cowered down with sheer terror.* □ *I would cower down from fright in a similar situation.*

cower from something to draw back from the fear of something. □ *The wolves cowered from the flames.* □ *Some excited hyenas cowered from the lions as they passed by.*

cozy up (to someone**) 1.** *Lit.* to snuggle up to someone as if to get warm. □ *The children cozied up to their mother.* □ *They cozied up to each other.* **2.** *Fig.* to try to get in good with someone; to try to increase one's influence with someone by being extra nice and friendly. □ *The salesman tried to cozy up to the customer.*

crack a book *Fig.* to open a book to study. (Usually used with a negative.) □ *I never cracked a book and still passed the course.* □ *Sally didn't crack a book all semester.*

crack a bottle open[†] *Fig.* to open a bottle of liquor. □ *Let's crack open a bottle and celebrate.* □ *He cracked a bottle open and poured a little for everyone to try.*

crack a joke to tell a joke. □ *She's never serious. She's always cracking jokes.* □ *Every time Tom cracked a joke, his buddies broke up laughing.*

crack a smile to grin; to smile. □ *I was tellin' my best jokes, but Jim never cracked a smile.* □ *She looked surprised, and then cracked a big, beautiful smile.*

a **crack at** someone Go to a try at someone.

a **crack at** something Go to a try at something.

crack down (on someone or something**)** to put limits on someone or something; to become strict about enforcing rules about someone or something. □ *The police cracked down on the street gangs.* □ *They cracked down once last year too.*

crack open [for something brittle] to break or split open. □ *The egg cracked open and a chick worked its way out.* □ *The side of the mountain cracked open and molten lava flowed out.*

crack some suds *Sl.* to drink some beer. □ *Let's go out tonight and crack some suds.* □ *The guys wanted to watch the game and crack some suds.*

crack someone or something **up**[†] to damage someone or something. (See also **crack** someone **up**.) □ *Who cracked my car up?* □ *Who cracked up my car? Who was driving?* □ *The accident cracked him up a little.*

crack someone **up**[†] to make someone laugh very hard; to make someone break out laughing. □ *You and your jokes really crack me up.* □ *That comedian really knows how to crack up an audience.*

crack something **up**[†] to crash something; to destroy something (in an accident). □ *The driver cracked the car up in an accident.* □ *The pilot cracked up the plane.*

crack something **(wide) open 1.** *Lit.* to crack or split something. □ *An incredible eruption cracked the volcano wide open.* **2.** *Fig.* to expose and reveal some great wrongdoing. □ *The police cracked the drug ring wide open.* □ *The newspaper story cracked the trouble at city hall wide open.*

crack the door (open) and **crack the window (open)** to open the door or window a very small amount. □ *I cracked open the door to peek out.* □ *Just crack the window a bit to let some air inside.*

crack the window (open) Go to previous.

crack under the strain *Fig.* to have a mental or emotional collapse because of continued work or stress. □ *He worked 80-hour weeks for a month and finally cracked under the strain.*

crack up 1. to have a wreck. □ *The plane cracked up and killed two of the passengers.* □ *Whose car cracked up on the expressway?* **2.** to break out in laughter. □ *The whole audience cracked up.* □ *I knew I would crack up during the love scene.* **3.** *Sl.* to have a mental or emotional breakdown. □ *The poor guy cracked up. It was too much for him.* □ *You would crack up, too, if you had been through all he went through.* **4.** an accident; a wreck. (Usually **crack-up.**) □ *There was a terrible crack-up on the expressway.* □ *There were four cars in the crack-up.*

cracked *Fig.* solved; understood. (*Typically: **get** something ~; **have** something ~.) □ *I've got the mystery cracked!* □ *After I get it cracked, the rest'll be easy.*

cracked up to be something and **cracked up to be; cracked up as** something alleged or understood to be something. □ *She was cracked up to be a pretty good player.* □ *She was cracked up as a pretty good golfer.* □ (Used with the negative.) *He is not the problem solving CEO that he was cracked up to be.*

cram for a test Go to next.

cram for an examination and **cram for a test** *Fig.* to study very hard for an exam. □ *I have to go cram for a test now.* □ *If you would study during the school term, you would not have to cram.*

cram someone or something **into** something and **cram** someone or something **in**[†] to stuff or crush someone or something into something. □ *Can you really cram seven kids into that car?* □ *He crammed in his clothes and closed the drawer.*

cram someone or something **with** someone or something to fill someone or something by stuffing with someone or

129

something. □ *You won't be happy till you cram all of us with cake and ice cream.* □ *He crammed his drawer with his socks.*

cramp someone's **style** *Fig.* to limit someone in some way. □ *I hope this doesn't cramp your style, but could you please not hum while you work?* □ *To ask Bob to keep regular hours would really be cramping his style.*

crank someone **up**[†] *Fig.* to motivate; to get someone started. (See also **crank** something **up**.) □ *See if you can crank up your brother and get him going on time today.* □ *Some mornings, I can't crank myself up enough to get to work on time.*

crank something **out**[†] *Fig.* to produce something quickly or carelessly; to make something in a casual and mechanical way. □ *John can crank a lot of work out in a single day.* □ *The automated production line could really crank out parts, but the quality was shoddy.*

crank something **up**[†] **1.** to get a machine or a process started. (Alludes to turning the starting crank of an early automobile.) □ *Please crank the machinery so the workers can start working.* □ *Let's crank up the drill and make a few holes here in the wall.* **2.** to increase the volume of an electronic device. □ *He cranked it up a little more and CRACK, there went both speakers!* □ *Kelly cranked up his stereo until we were nearly deafened.*

crap out *Sl.* to die. □ *Max almost crapped out from the beating he took.* □ *The old dog just crapped out. What shall we do?*

crap out (of something**)** to lose on a roll of the dice in a dice game called craps and leave the game and the other players. (See also **crap out (of** something**) (on** someone**).**) □ *Wally crapped out of the game early in the evening.*

crap out (of something**) (on** someone**) 1.** *Sl.* to withdraw from doing something with someone, unexpectedly, perhaps because of fear or cowardice. □ *Are you going to crap out of this game on me?* **2.** *Sl.* to quit doing something with someone or withdraw because of exhaustion. □ *Don't crap out of this on me! Pull yourself together!* □ *Don't crap out on me!*

crash and burn 1. *Lit.* [for a plane or car] to crash and burst into flames. □ *The small plane crashed and burned just after it took off.* **2.** *Fig.* to fail spectacularly. □ *Poor Chuck really crashed and burned when he made his presentation at the sales meeting.*

crash around to move around in a noisy way □ *Stop crashing around. I'm trying to study.* □ *The people upstairs were crashing around and I couldn't get any sleep.*

a **crash course in** something a short and intense training course in something. □ *I took a crash course in ballroom dancing so we wouldn't look stupid on the dance floor.*

crash down (around someone or something**)** and **crash down (about** someone or something**) 1.** and **crash in (on** someone or something**)** *Lit.* [for something] to collapse on someone or something. □ *The walls crashed in around the burning house.* □ *The branches of the tree crashed down on the roof.* □ *The old barn crashed down.* **2.** *Fig.* [for the structure and stability of one's life] to fall apart. □ *Her whole life crashed down around her.* □ *Everything he was familiar with crashed down about him.*

crash into someone or something to bump or ram into someone or something accidentally or roughly. □ *The student crashed into the door when it opened suddenly.* □ *The car crashed into a bus.*

crash out (of some place**)** to break out of some place, such as a prison. □ *Max and Lefty crashed out of the state prison last week, but they were captured.* □ *They crashed out at midnight.*

crash something **together** to bring things together with great force, making a loud noise. □ *Fred crashed the cymbals together and the sound could have wakened the dead.* □ *Don't crash those pans together. It drives me crazy.*

crash through something to break through something forcefully. □ *The cows crashed right through the fence.*

crash to the floor to fall onto the floor and make a crashing sound. □ *The tray of dishes crashed to the floor.* □ *Everything crashed to the floor and was broken.*

crash together to ram or move together with great force. □ *The two cars crashed together, making a loud noise.* □ *The ships crashed together, opening a gaping hole in the side of one of them.*

crash with someone *Sl.* to spend the night at someone's place. □ *I don't need a hotel room. I can crash with Tom.* □ *There is no room for you to crash with me.*

crave to do something *Rur.* to want to do something eagerly. □ *I don't crave to ride the roller coaster, thank you.* □ *The kids have been craving to see that movie for weeks.*

crawl across something and **crawl along** something [for someone] to move across something on hands and knees; [for an insect or something similar] to walk across something. □ *The wounded officer had to crawl across the open area to get to safety.* □ *The caterpillar crawled across the leaf and stopped at the end.* □ *She crawled along the catwalk, fearing to look down.*

crawl along something Go to previous.

crawl back to someone *Fig.* to go back to someone humbly, perhaps asking for forgiveness. □ *I knew you would come crawling back to me!* □ *I wouldn't crawl back to him for all the tea in China.*

crawl in(to something**) 1.** *Lit.* to enter a place crawling or creeping. □ *The cat crawled into the room and meowed.* □ *The baby crawled in and tried to stand up.* **2.** *Fig.* to dress quickly in some kind of clothing. □ *I crawled into my pants and threw on a shirt.* □ *He finally found his pants and crawled in.* **3.** *Fig.* to get into bed. □ *At about ten o'clock, she crawled into bed.* □ *She pulled back the covers and crawled in.*

crawl out to get out by crawling. □ *The bears finally woke up and crawled out.* □ *In the cave, I injured my leg and I had to crawl out.*

crawl out (from under someone or something**)** Go to **out (from under** someone or something**).**

crawl out (of something**)** to get out of something by crawling. □ *The injured man crawled out of the overturned car.* □ *Donna crawled out of the cave.*

crawl over something to cross over something by crawling. □ *We crawled over the pile of boxes.* □ *Timmy crawled over the carpet and stood up at the coffee table.*

crawling with some kind of creature [of a surface] covered with insects or animals, moving about. □ *The basement was crawling with rats!* □ *We came home and found the kitchen floor crawling with ants.*

crawling with someone *Fig.* [of a surface] covered with many people or members of a class of people moving about. □ *The place was crawling with police and FBI agents.* □ *The city was crawling with tourists making it almost impossible to go from place to place.*

crazy about someone or something and **mad about** someone or something; **nuts about** someone or something; **crazy for** someone or something *Fig.* very fond of someone or something. □ *Ann is crazy about John.* □ *He's crazy about her, too.* □ *I'm mad about their new song.*

***crazy as a betsy bug** and ***crazy as a peach-orchard boar**; ***crazy as a loon** *Rur.* acting as if insane. (*Also: **as** ~.) □ *Tom: Susan says she's really the Queen of England. Bill: She's crazy as a betsy bug.* □ *Jill: David's a little eccentric, isn't he? Jane: Crazy as a loon, I'd say.* □ *What's wrong with Jim? He's acting as crazy as a peach-orchard boar.*

crazy as a loon Go to previous.

crazy as a peach-orchard boar Go to crazy as a betsy bug.

crazy bone Go to funny bone.

crazy for someone or something Go to crazy about someone or something.

crazy in the head stupid or insane. □ *Be quiet, Jed. You are just crazy in the head.* □ *Am I crazy in the head, or did I just see someone walking a leopard on a leash?*

A **creaking door hangs longest.** and A **creaking gate hangs longest.** *Prov.* Sickly people often live longer than healthy ones. □ *Jill: I'm worried that my grandmother may not live much longer. She's been sick for so many years. Jane: Well, if it's any comfort, I've heard that a creaking door hangs longest.*

A **creaking gate hangs longest.** Go to previous.

the **cream of the crop** *Fig.* the best of all. □ *This particular car is the cream of the crop.* □ *These three students are very bright. They are the cream of the crop in their class.*

crease something **up**† to get creases or folds into something that is supposed to be flat; to wrinkle one's clothing. (Very similar to *messed up.*) □ *You will crease your jacket up if you don't sit up straight.* □ *I was sitting so long that I creased up my pants.*

create a scene Go to make a scene.

create a stink (about something) and **make a stink (about** something); **raise a stink (about** something) *Fig.* to make a major issue out of something; to make much over something; to make a lot of complaints and criticisms about something. □ *Tom created a stink about Bob's remarks.* □ *Why did he make a stink about that?* □ *Tom is always trying to raise a stink.*

create an uproar and **make an uproar** to cause an outburst or sensation. □ *The dog got into church and made an uproar.* □ *Her poodle created an uproar in the restaurant.*

creature comforts things that make people comfortable. □ *The hotel room was a bit small, but all the creature comforts were there.*

***credit (for** something) **1.** praise or recognition for one's role in something. (*Typically: **get** ~; **have** ~; **give** someone ~.) Especially with **a lot of** ~, **much** ~.) □ *Mary should get a lot of credit for the team's success.* □ *Each of the team captains should get credit.* **2.** praise or recognition of someone for having a particular quality. (*Typically: **get** ~; **have** ~; **give** someone ~.) □ *We give her a lot of credit for her ability to get people to work out their differences.* □ *We will give credit to Sharon for her good humor.* **3.** credit granted to someone's account for some other financial transaction. (*Typically: **get** ~; **have** ~; **give** someone ~.) □ *I will give you credit for the returned merchandise.* □ *We got credit for the check Brian sent us.*

credit someone or something **for** something to give someone or something the praise deserved for doing something. □ *We must credit Sarah for her efforts on our behalf.* □ *We have to credit all the rain we've had for saving the crops.*

credit someone or something **with** something **1.** *Lit.* to record a payment, deposit, etc., to the account of someone or something. □ *I will credit you with this payment as you request.* □ *Your account has been credited with this adjustment.* **2.** *Fig.* to give someone or something well-deserved praise for doing something or having something. □ *We have to credit Jeff with saving us a lot of money.* □ *We will credit the weather with part of the success of the picnic.*

credit something **to** someone or something **1.** *Lit.* to record a sum owed to the account of someone or something. □ *I will credit this payment to your account.* □ *I am afraid that I accidentally credited your payment to George.* **2.** *Fig.* to give someone or something well-deserved praise. □ *The entire organization credited much praise to Jeff.* □ *We had to credit much of our success to simple good luck.*

a **credit to** someone or something of value or benefit to someone or something; of enough value or worth as to enhance someone or something. □ *I always want to be a credit to my school.* □ *John is not what you would call a credit to his family.*

creep across something **1.** *Lit.* to move across something slowly and carefully; to sneak across something. □ *The soldiers crept slowly across the rope bridge.* □ *The cat crept across the floor, stalking the mouse.* **2.** *Fig.* [for light, fog, etc.] to move slowly across a place or an area. □ *A heavy fog crept across the coastal areas.* □ *The spotlight crept across the stage from one side to the other, as if looking for the performer.*

creep along something to move along something slowly and carefully; to sneak along something. □ *Creep along the side of the building until you reach the door.* □ *The cat crept along the narrow kitchen counter.*

creep away to travel away slowly and carefully; to sneak away. □ *The boys were completely ashamed and crept away.* □ *The cat crept away quietly.*

creep by *Fig.* [for time] to pass slowly. □ *The minutes crept by as I awaited Mrs. Barron's telephone call.* □ *I know the days will creep by until we finally get our test results.*

creep in(to something) to go into something or a place slowly and carefully; to sneak into something or a place. □ *The cat crept into the bedroom.* □ *Max planned to creep into the house and take cash and jewelry.*

creep out (from under someone or something**)** Go to out (from under someone or something**).**

creep out (of something**)** to go out of something or a place slowly and carefully; to sneak out of something or a place. □ *A little mouse crept out of the cupboard.* □ *The fox crept out of the henhouse, carrying a chicken.*

creep out of the woodwork Go to out of the woodwork.

creep over someone or something **1.** *Lit.* [for something, such as an insect] to walk or crawl over someone or something. □ *A huge ant crept over me, and I just lay there.* **2.** *Fig.* [for darkness] to move slowly over someone or something. □ *The shadows crept over the picnic and made everyone realize what time it was.* □ *Dusk crept over us.*

creep under something to move slowly and carefully underneath something; to sneak underneath something. □ *The dog crept under the table to escape punishment.* □ *The chipmunk crept under a pile of leaves and disappeared.*

creep up [for darkness] to move gradually and slowly [toward someone or something]. □ *Dusk crept up and swallowed us in darkness.*

creep up on someone or something to sneak up on someone or something. □ *Please don't creep up on me like that. You scared me to death.* □ *The cat crept up on the mouse.*

***the **creeps** and ***the **willies** a state of anxiety or uneasiness. (*Typically: **get** ~; **have** ~; **give** someone ~.) □ *I get the creeps when I see that old house.* □ *I really had the willies when I went down into the dark basement.*

crib something **from** someone or something to cheat by copying something from someone or something. □ *It appears that you cribbed this directly from the person sitting next to you.*

a **crick in** one's **back** a twisted or cramped place in the back that causes pain. □ *I can't move! I've got a crick in my back!* □ *I had a crick in my back all night and I couldn't sleep.*

a **crick in** one's **neck** *Fig.* a twisted place or a cramp in the neck that causes pain. □ *I got a crick in my neck from sleeping in a draft.* □ *When I read on the plane, I get a crick in my neck.*

Crime doesn't pay. *Prov.* Crime will ultimately not benefit a person. □ *No matter how tempting it may appear, crime doesn't pay.*

cringe away from someone or something and **cringe from** someone or something to pull back or away from someone or something, as from fear. □ *The child cringed away from the teacher.* □ *Why did you cringe away from the dentist's chair?* □ *The cat cringed from the fire.* □ *The child cringed from the huge dog.*

cringe before someone or something to cower or recoil in the presence of someone or something. □ *Jeff cringed before the wrath of the policeman.*

crinkle up to wrinkle up. □ *Her nose crinkled up when she laughed.*

criticize someone **for** something to reprimand or censure someone for something. □ *I hope you don't criticize me too severely for my part in this matter.* □ *Maria criticized Ken for not being there on time.*

crock someone or something **up**[†] *Sl.* to damage or harm someone or something. □ *The accident crocked me up a bit.* □ *I really crocked up my car last night.*

***crooked as a barrel of fish hooks** and ***crooked as a fish hook; *crooked as a dog's hind leg** very dishonest. (*Also: **as** ~.) □ *Don't play cards with him. He's as crooked as a barrel of fish hooks.* □ *Mary says all politicians are crooked as a dog's hind leg.*

crooked as a dog's hind leg Go to previous.

crop out to appear on the surface; [for something] to reveal itself in the open; to begin to show above the surface. □ *A layer of rock cropped out at the edges of the desert.*

crop someone or something **out**[†] [for a photographer] to cut or trim out someone or something from a photograph. □ *The photographer cropped Mr. Jones out of the picture.* □ *See if you can crop out the ugly fence at the side of the house.*

crop up to appear without warning; to happen suddenly; [for something] to begin to reveal itself in the open. □ *Some new problems cropped up at the last minute.*

cross a bridge before one **comes to it** and **cross that bridge before** one**comes to it** *Fig.* to worry excessively about something before it happens. (Note the variations in the examples. See also **cross that bridge when** one **comes to it.**) □ *There is no sense in crossing that bridge before you come to it.* □ *She's always crossing bridges before coming to them. She needs to learn to relax.*

cross from some place **to** some place to move across something from one point to another. □ *We crossed from one side of the hall to the other, looking for a seat.* □ *I have to cross from Illinois to Missouri over a rickety old bridge.*

cross one's **fingers** Go to keep one's **fingers crossed (for** someone or something**).**

cross one's **heart (and hope to die)** *Fig.* a phrase said to pledge or vow that the truth is being told. □ *It's true, cross my heart and hope to die.* □ *It's really true—cross my heart.*

cross over 1. to cross something such as a river or a street. □ *This is a very wide river. Where do we cross over?* □ *Let's cross over here where it's shallow.* **2.** to change sides, from one to another. □ *Some players from the other team crossed over and joined ours after the tournament.* **3.** *Euph.* to die. □ *Uncle Herman crossed over long before Aunt Helen.*

cross over into some place to go from one place into another, by crossing a border, river, mountain range, etc. □ *The refugees crossed over into Switzerland.* □ *We crossed over into Missouri at dawn.*

cross over something to go some place by crossing a border, river, mountain range, etc. □ *Do we want to cross over the river at this point?* □ *How do we cross over the highway?*

cross paths (with someone**)** *Fig.* to meet someone by chance and not by choice. □ *The last time I crossed paths with Fred, we ended up arguing about something inconsequential.*

cross someone to oppose someone. □ *You best not cross Jim. He has a very bad temper.* □ *This is the last time you cross me, you hear?*

cross someone or something **off (of)** something and **cross** someone or something **off**[†] to eliminate a name from a list or record. (*Of* is usually retained before pronouns.) □ *We* will have to cross her off of our list. □ *We crossed off Sarah.* □ *I crossed the sweater off the list of what I needed to buy.*

cross someone or something **out†** to draw a line through the name of someone or something on a list or record. □ *You can cross me out. I'm not going.* □ *Please cross out Sarah's name.* □ *I crossed the sweater out. It was an error.*

cross someone's **mind** Go to **pass through** someone's **mind**.

cross someone's **palm with silver** *Fig.* to pay money to someone in payment for a service. (A fortune-teller might ask for a potential customer to cross her palm with silver. Used in that sense or jocularly for something like tipping a porter.) □ *I crossed his palm with silver, but he still stood there.* □ *You will find that things happen much faster in hotels if you cross the staff's palms with silver fairly often.*

cross someone **up†** to give someone trouble; to defy or betray someone; to spoil someone's plans. (Also without up.) □ *You really crossed up Bill when you told Tom what he said.* □ *Please don't cross me up again.*

cross something **with** something **1.** to go across something, using a particular type of vehicle. □ *The explorers crossed the river with their Jeep.* □ *We can't cross this stream with the canoes. It's too fast.* **2.** to interbreed something with something else. □ *The farmer crossed this smaller breed of chicken with the meatier one.* □ *It is possible to cross a horse with a donkey.*

cross swords (with someone) *Fig.* to become the adversary of someone. □ *Gloria loved an argument and was looking forward to crossing swords with Sally.*

cross that bridge when one **comes to it** *Fig.* to delay worrying about something that might happen until it actually does happen. (Usually used in the phrase, "Let's cross that bridge when we come to it," a way of telling someone not to worry about something that has not happened yet. □ *Alan: Where will we stop tonight? Jane: At the next town. Alan: What if all the hotels are full? Jane: Let's cross that bridge when we come to it.*

cross the Rubicon *Fig.* to do something that inevitably commits one to following a certain course of action. (Alludes to the crossing of the River Rubicon by Julius Caesar with his army, which involved him in a civil war in B.C. 49.) □ *Jane crossed the Rubicon by signing the contract.* □ *Find another job before you cross the Rubicon and resign from this one.*

Cross the stream where it is shallowest. *Prov.* To do things in the easiest possible way. □ *Jill: How can I get Fred to give me permission to start this project? Jane: Cross the stream where it is shallowest. First ask Fred's boss for permission; I'm sure she'll give it to you. Then Fred will have to agree.*

Crosses are ladders that lead to heaven. *Prov.* Having to endure trouble can help you to be virtuous. □ *When Mary was diagnosed with cancer, her mother consoled her by saying that crosses are ladders that lead to heaven, and that though she might have to suffer in this world, she would surely be rewarded in the next.*

cross-examine someone to question someone in court who has already been questioned by the opposing side; to question a suspect or a witness at great length. □ *The*

lawyer plans to cross-examine the witness tomorrow morning. □ *The police cross-examined the suspect for three hours.*

crouch around [for people or other creatures] to stoop or squat within an area. □ *Everyone crouched around, hoping the bomb would fall somewhere else.* □ *The baboons crouched around, grooming one another.*

crouch down to stoop or huddle down. □ *Crouch down here, next to me.* □ *Suddenly, Tex crouched down and reached for his pistol.*

crow about something and **crow over** something **1.** *Lit.* [for a rooster] to cry out or squawk about something. □ *The rooster was crowing about something—you never know what.* **2.** *Fig.* [for someone] to brag about something. □ *Stop crowing about your successes!* □ *She is crowing over her new car.*

crow bait *Rur.* someone or an animal that is likely to die; a useless animal or person. □ *That old dog used to hunt good, but now he's just crow bait.*

crow over something Go to **crow about** something.

crowd around someone or something to flock or swarm around someone or something. □ *The children crowded around the department store Santa, eager for their chance at talking to him.* □ *Everyone crowded around the radio to listen.*

crowd in Go to **crowd in(to)** some place.

crowd in (on someone or something**)** to press or crush around someone or something. □ *Please don't crowd in on the guest of honor.* □ *Can you keep them back from me? I don't like it when they crowd in.* □ *The people crowded in on us and frightened us a little bit.* □ *Don't crowd in on the display case. It is an antique.*

crowd in(to) some place and **crowd in** to push or squeeze into some place. □ *Please don't try to crowd into this place.* □ *Too many people are trying to crowd in.*

crowd someone or something **in(to)** something and **crowd** someone or something **in†** to push or squeeze someone or something into a place or a container. □ *They tried to crowd a dozen people into that tiny room.* □ *Then they crowded in one more.* □ *They all tried to crowd themselves into the same room.*

crowd someone or something **out of** something and **crowd** someone or something **out†** to push or force someone, something, or an animal out of something. □ *Don't crowd your brother out of line!* □ *Don't crowd out my favorite plants with all your rosebushes!*

crowd someone or something **together** to push or squeeze people or things together. □ *See if you can crowd them together and get more in the row.* □ *I am afraid that I crowded the plants together too much.*

crowd something **with** someone or something to pack too many people or things into something. □ *The ushers crowded the room with visitors.* □ *Aunt Victoria had crowded the room with the busy trappings of a bygone era.*

crowd through (something**)** [for a number of people] to push through something. □ *The little group of revelers crowded through the door.* □ *They all tried to crowd through.*

crowd together to pack tightly together. □ *The tenants crowded together in the lobby.* □ *All the kittens crowded together to keep warm.*

crown someone **with** something **1.** *Lit.* to place a crown on someone's head. □ *They crowned the prince with the heavily jeweled royal crown.* **2.** *Fig.* to strike someone on the head with something. □ *She crowned him with a skillet.* □ *The carpenter crowned himself with a board he knocked loose.*

crown something **with** something *Fig.* to place something on the very top of something. (As if crowning royalty.) □ *The chef crowned the cake with golden icing.*

cruise around in something to drive or ride around in something. □ *Would you like to cruise around in a car like that?* □ *They really liked cruising around in the motorboat.*

cruising for a bruising and **cruisin' for a bruisin'** *Sl.* asking for trouble. □ *You are cruising for a bruising, you know that?* □ *Who's cruisin' for a bruisin'?*

crum something **up**† and **crumb** something **up**† *Sl.* to mess something up. □ *Who crummed the bird feeder up?* □ *Now don't crum up this deal.* □ *Who crumbed up my room?*

crumble away to break away in little pieces. □ *The marble pillar was crumbling away because of the acidic rain.* □ *One of my teeth is just crumbling away.*

crumble into something to break apart and fall down into bits and pieces. □ *The base of the pillar suddenly crumbled into dust.* □ *The bones crumbled into dust as the body was lifted from the box.*

crumble something **up**† **(into** something**)** to crunch up or break up something into pieces. □ *Now, crumble the dried bread up into crumbs.* □ *Crumble up the bread into crumbs.*

crumble up to break up into little pieces. □ *The cake, which was very dry, crumbled up when I tried to cut it.* □ *The paper of the old book crumbled up when I turned the pages.*

crumped out *Sl.* intoxicated. □ *She was too crumped out to drive herself home.* □ *Are you crumped out again?*

crumple something **up**† to fold up or crush someone or something. □ *Walter crumpled the paper up.* □ *He crumpled up the paper.*

crumple up to fold up; to collapse. □ *She was so frightened that she just crumpled up.* □ *Fran crumpled up in a dead faint.*

crunch someone or something **up**† to break someone or something up into pieces. □ *That machine will crunch you up. Stay away from it!* □ *A number of blows with the hammer crunched up the rocks into pebbles.* □ *Try to crunch the larger chunks up.*

crunch something **down**† to press or crush something down, breaking it with a crunching noise. □ *Sally crunched the flower pot down, breaking it.* □ *She crunched down the fragile glass in the box accidentally.*

crusade against someone or something to campaign or demonstrate against someone or something. □ *You are always crusading against one cause or another.* □ *Ed started crusading against Eric and the latter threatened suit.*

crusade for someone or something to campaign or demonstrate for someone or something. □ *I can hardly crusade for the defeat of a friend.* □ *Ed went on a crusade for Eric, hoping to get him elected.*

*a **crush on** someone infatuation with someone. (*Typically: **get** ~; **have** ~.) □ *Mary thinks she's getting a crush on Bill.* □ *Sally says she'll never have a crush on anyone again.*

crush someone or something **down**† **1.** *Lit.* to press or force someone or something down. □ *Crush the leaves down so you can put more into the basket.* □ *Crush down the leaves and fill the basket higher.* **2.** *Fig.* to suppress someone or something. □ *The dictator crushed the opposition down ruthlessly.* □ *He crushed down all political opposition.* □ *The army crushed the peasants down ruthlessly.*

crush someone or something **to** something to press or squeeze someone or something into a particular state, such as death, a pulp, nothing, etc. □ *The anaconda crushed the tapir to death.* □ *Donna crushed the bananas to a pulp and put them into the cake batter.*

crush something **in**† to force something inward; to break something in. □ *The beam nearly crushed Jason's head in.* □ *He tried to crush in the door.*

crush something **(in)to** something to grind or break something into bits and pieces. □ *He crushed the fennel seeds into a powder.* □ *The roller crushes the rocks to bits.*

crush something **out** **1.** to put out a cigarette or small flame by crushing. □ *She crushed her cigarette out and put the butt into the sink.* □ *Please crush out your cigarette.* **2.** Go to next.

crush something **out of** someone or something and **crush** something **out**† to press or squeeze something from someone or something. □ *He crushed the juice out of the grapes.* □ *He thought that the weight of the lumber would crush the life out of him.* □ *Robert crushed out the juice.*

crush something **up**† to reduce the mass of something by crushing. □ *Crush this up and put it in the sauce.* □ *Crush up a clove of garlic and put it in the sauce.*

crush something **up**† **(into** something**)** to press or grind something with great force until it is reduced to something smaller. □ *The chef crushed the almonds up into a powder and sprinkled them on the dessert.* □ *The machine crushed up all the glass into tiny bits.*

crush (up) against someone or something to press hard against someone or something. □ *The crowd crushed up against the people standing in line.* □ *The eager theatergoers crushed against the lobby doors.*

crushed by something *Fig.* demoralized; having hurt feelings. □ *The whole family was completely crushed by the news.* □ *I was just crushed by your attitude. I thought we were friends.*

*the **crux of the matter** and *the **root of the matter**; *the **heart of the matter** the central issue of the matter. (*Crux* is an old word meaning "cross." *Typically: **be at** ~; **get at** ~; **go to** ~; **look at** ~.) □ *All right, this is the crux of the matter.* □ *It's about time that we got to the heart of the matter.*

cry all the way to the bank *Fig.* to make a lot of money on something that one ought to be ashamed of. □ *Jane: Have you read the new book by that romance novelist? They say it sold a million copies, but it's so badly written that the author ought to be ashamed of herself. Alan: I'm sure she's* *crying all the way to the bank.* □ *That dreadful movie had no artistic merit. I suppose the people who produced it are crying all the way to the bank.*

cry before one **is hurt** *Fig.* to cry or complain needlessly, before one is injured. □ *Bill always cries before he's hurt.* □ *There is no point in crying before one is hurt.*

cry bloody murder *Fig.* to scream as if something very serious has happened, especially unnecessarily. □ *Now that Bill is really hurt, he's crying bloody murder.* □ *There is no point in crying bloody murder about the bill if you knew the restaurant was expensive.*

cry crocodile tears Go to shed crocodile tears.

cry for someone or something **1.** to weep for the absence or loss of someone or something. □ *No need to cry for me. Take care of yourself.* □ *She cried for her lost cat.* **2.** to shout a demand for someone or something. □ *She cried for help, but no one heard her.* □ *Tony cried for Walter, but he did not hear.* **3.** to cry or bawl, signaling the need or want for someone or something. (As done by a baby.) □ *The baby cried for a bottle.* □ *Little Jimmy was crying for his mother.*

cry in one's **beer** *Fig.* to feel sorry for oneself. □ *She calls up, crying in her beer, and talks on and on about her problems.* □ *Don't cry in your beer. Get yourself straightened out.*

cry one's **eyes out** *Fig.* to cry very hard. □ *When we heard the news, we cried our eyes out with joy.* □ *She cried her eyes out after his death.*

cry one's **heart out** and **sing** one's **heart out; play** one's **heart out; sob** one's **heart out** *Fig.* to do something with vigor or intensity. □ *She suffered such grief—alone and sobbing her heart out.* □ *The bird sang its little heart out each morning.*

cry oneself **to sleep** to weep until sleep overtakes one. □ *The baby finally cried herself to sleep.*

cry out (against someone or something**)** to shout in anger against someone or something. □ *The crowd cried out against the police.* □ *She cried out against Eric, who had insulted her grossly.*

cry out for someone or something **1.** to shout praise or encouragement for someone or something. □ *Everyone in the street cried out for the mayor to make an appearance.* **2.** to shout out demands for someone or something. □ *The children cried out for ice cream.* □ *The mob was crying out for justice when they heard the unpopular sentences of the judge.*

cry out (in something**)** and **cry out (with** something**)** to scream or shout in pain, joy, anger, etc. □ *The child cried out in pain.* □ *On seeing his father, the overjoyed little boy cried out.*

cry over someone or something to weep because of someone or something. □ *There's no need to cry over it. Things will work out.* □ *She is still crying over her lost love.*

cry over spilled milk *Fig.* to be unhappy about what cannot be undone. (See also **It's no use crying over spilled milk.**) □ *He is always crying over spilled milk. He cannot accept reality.* □ *It can't be helped. Don't cry over spilled milk.*

cry (something**) out**† **(to** someone or an animal**)** to yell something to someone or an animal. □ *She cried a warning out* to the others. □ *Sally cried out a warning to the people behind her.* □ *The trainer cried a command out to the runaway horse.*

cry uncle Go to holler uncle.

cry wolf *Fig.* to cry or complain about something when nothing is really wrong. (From the story wherein a child sounds the alarm frequently about a wolf when there is no wolf, only to be ignored when there actually is a wolf.) □ *Pay no attention. She's just crying wolf again.* □ *Don't cry wolf too often. No one will come.*

a **crying need (for** someone or something**)** *Fig.* a definite or desperate need for someone or something. □ *There is a crying need for someone to come in and straighten things out.* □ *All the people in that area have a crying need for a local hospital.*

a **crying shame** *Fig.* a very unfortunate situation; a real shame. □ *It's a crying shame that people cannot afford adequate housing.* □ *That your father could not attend graduation was a crying shame.*

cuddle up (to someone or something**)** and **cuddle up (with** someone**)** to nestle or snuggle close to someone or something to get warm or to be intimate. □ *Let's cuddle up to the warmth, near the fireplace.* □ *She cuddled up with him and went to sleep.*

cuddle up with a (good) book and **curl up (with a (good) book)** to snuggle into a chair or bed comfortably to read a book. □ *I want to go home and cuddle up with a good book.* □ *She went home and curled up with a good book.*

cuddle up (with someone**)** Go to cuddle up (to someone or something).

cue someone **in**† **1.** *Lit.* to give someone a cue; to indicate to someone that the time has come. □ *Now, cue the orchestra director in.* □ *All right, cue in the announcer.* **2.** *Fig.* to tell someone what is going on. (Almost the same as **clue** someone **in (on** something**).)** □ *I want to know what's going on. Cue me in.* □ *Cue in the general about the troop movement.*

cull someone or something **out of** something and **cull** someone or something **out**† to eliminate someone or something from a group. □ *We will cull the older pigeons out from the flock.* □ *They culled out the slower runners from the team.*

culminate in something to climax in something; to end with something. □ *The contest culminated in a victory for the best band.* □ *The play-offs culminated in a big win for the Chicago team.*

culturally advantaged *Euph.* rich; upper-class. □ *I can't deny I had a culturally advantaged upbringing.* □ *The charity appealed to culturally advantaged people to donate time and money to those less fortunate.*

culturally deprived and **culturally disadvantaged** *Euph.* poor; lower-class. □ *Joe is working at a summer camp for culturally deprived children.* □ *Jane grew up in a culturally disadvantaged neighborhood.*

culturally disadvantaged Go to previous.

culture vulture someone whom one considers to be excessively interested in the (classical) arts. □ *She won't go to a funny film. She's a real culture vulture.* □ *They watch only highbrow television. They're culture vultures.*

cunning as a fox Go to sly as a fox.

cup one's **hands together** to put one's hands together to form a sort of cup. □ *He cupped his hands together and scooped up the water.* □ *You have to cup your hands together if you want a drink.*

curdle someone's **blood** *Fig.* to frighten or disgust someone severely. □ *The story was scary enough to curdle your blood.* □ *The terrible scream was enough to curdle my blood.*

cure someone **of** something to rid someone of a disease, ailment, bad habit, or obsession. □ *I hope that the doctor prescribes something to cure him of that chronic cough.* □ *Will you please try to cure yourself of your constant interrupting?*

cure something **of** something to eliminate the cause of a malfunction in a machine or a device. (See also **cure** someone **of** something.) □ *I think I have cured the stapler of jamming all the time.* □ *I can't seem to cure the committee of procrastination.*

Curiosity killed the cat. *Prov.* Being curious can get you into trouble. (Often used to warn someone against prying into other's affairs.) □ *Jill: Where did you get all that money? Jane: Curiosity killed the cat.*

curl someone's **hair** and **make** someone's **hair curl** *Fig.* to frighten or alarm someone; to shock someone with sight, sound, or taste. □ *Don't ever sneak up on me like that again. You really curled my hair.* □ *The horror film made my hair curl.*

curl something **up**† to roll something up into a coil. □ *She curled the edges of the paper up while she spoke.* □ *Why did she curl up the paper?*

curl up and die *Fig.* to die. (Often jocular.) □ *When I heard you say that, I could have curled up and died.* □ *No, it wasn't an illness. She just curled up and died.*

curl up (in(to) something) **1.** to roll into a coil. □ *The snake curled up into a neat coil.* □ *It curled up so we couldn't get at it.* **2.** [for one] to bend one's body into a resting place, such as a chair or a bed. □ *Colleen curled up in the chair and took a nap.* □ *She curled up and took a nap.*

curl up (with a (good) book) Go to cuddle up with a (good) book.

curl up with someone or an animal to snuggle up to someone or something. □ *She curled up with her husband and fell asleep.* □ *Elaine curled up with the family dog to keep warm.*

curly dirt and **house moss; slut's wool** puffs of dirt and dust. □ *How long has it been since you swept under this bed? There's a mountain of curly dirt under here!* □ *No one's been in this room for an age. Look at all the cobwebs and curly dirt.* □ *She was a terrible housekeeper. House moss collected in all the corners of her rooms.*

curry favor with someone to try to win favor from someone. □ *The lawyer tried to curry favor with the judge.* □ *It's silly to curry favor with the boss. Just act yourself.*

curse at someone or something to swear at someone or something; to use foul language at someone or something. □ *He cursed at the jammed toaster and pounded his fist on the counter in anger.* □ *Please don't curse at me.*

curse someone **for** something to damn someone for doing something; to invoke evil upon someone for doing something. □ *She cursed her mother for ever having borne her.* □ *Over and over, she cursed herself for ever having come there.*

curse someone or something **under** one's **breath** Go to under one's breath.

curse someone or something **with** something **1.** to damn someone or something with something, especially a verbal curse. □ *She cursed him with the fervent wish that he rot in hell.* □ *She cursed the day he was born with an unprintable oath.* **2.** to afflict or oppress someone or something with something. □ *His upbringing cursed him with a strong sense of guilt.* □ *The political scandal cursed the town with a dismal reputation for years.*

curse under one's **breath** Go to under one's breath.

curtain something **off**† to separate something or some place with a drape, screen, or curtain. □ *We curtained this part of the room off, so please sleep over there.* □ *We will curtain off part of the room.*

curtains for someone or something the death, end, or ruin of someone or something. (From the lowering or closing of the curtains at the end of a stage performance.) □ *If the car hadn't swerved, it would have been curtains for the pedestrians.* □ *If they can't get into the export market, it's curtains for the whole company.*

curtsy to someone [for a woman] to dip or bow in deference to someone. □ *Of course, I curtsied to the queen! Do you think I'm an anarchist?* □ *The little girls curtsied after they did their dance number.*

curve to something to bend or bow toward something, some direction, or some place. □ *The road curved to the left.* □ *One of her toes curves to the right.*

cuss a blue streak *Rur.* to curse a great deal. □ *When she dropped the brick on her toe, she cussed a blue streak.* □ *Bill could cuss a blue streak by the time he was eight years old.*

cuss someone **out**† to curse at someone. □ *Dad cussed me out for losing the money he gave me.* □ *The little kid cussed out his brother, shocking his grandmother.*

The customer is always right. *Prov.* In order to keep customers happy, the people who serve them should always obey their wishes. (Often cited as a principle of good business dealings; customers sometimes say it to the people serving them in order to try to get good service.) □ *When I began working at the gift shop, my boss told me, "Remember, the customer is always right, no matter how stupid or rude you may think he is being."*

cut a big swath Go to cut a wide swath.

cut a deal to arrange a deal; to negotiate an agreement. □ *Maybe we can cut a deal. Let's talk.* □ *The two lawyers cut a deal that left me with my car, although she got the house.*

cut a fine figure to look good; to look elegant. (Usually said of a male.) □ *Tom really cuts a fine figure on the dance floor.* □ *Bill cuts a fine figure since he bought some new clothes.*

cut a long story short Go to make a long story short.

cut a wide swath and **cut a big swath** to seem important; to attract a lot of attention. □ *In social matters, Mrs. Smith cuts a wide swath.* □ *Bob cuts a big swath whenever he appears in his military uniform.*

a **cut above average** better than average. (See also a **cut above** something. The *cut* is a degree or notch.) □ *John isn't the best mechanic in town, but he's a cut above average.*

a **cut above** something a measure or degree better than something else. (See also a **cut above average**. The *cut* is a degree or notch.) □ *Your shirt is beautiful, but mine is a cut above yours.*

cut across something **1.** and **cut across** *Lit.* to travel across a particular area; to take a shortcut across a particular area. □ *Please don't cut across the neighbor's yard anymore.* **2.** *Fig.* to reach beyond something; to embrace a wide variety; to slice across a figurative boundary or barrier. □ *His teaching cut across all human cultures and races.* □ *This rule cuts across all social barriers.*

cut against the grain Go to **against the grain**.

cut along something to make a cut following a line or guide. □ *Please cut along the dotted line.* □ *My hand is too shaky to cut along the line neatly.*

cut and dried fixed; determined beforehand; usual and uninteresting. (Can be hyphenated before nominals.) □ *I find your writing quite boring. It's too cut and dried.* □ *The lecture was, as usual, cut and dried.*

cut and paste 1. *Lit.* to cut something out of paper with scissors and paste it onto something else. □ *The teacher told the little children that it was time to cut and paste, and they all ran to the worktables.* □ *Mary made a tiny house by cutting and pasting little strips of paper.* **2.** *Fig.* something trivial, simple, or childish. □ *I hate this job. It's nothing but cut and paste.* □ *I don't mind doing things that have to be done, but I hate to waste my time on cut and paste.*

cut and run *Sl.* to run away quickly. (Alludes to cutting loose a ship's or boat's anchor and sailing away in a hurry.) □ *Wilbur decided to cut and run when he heard the police sirens.* □ *As soon as I finish what I am doing here, I'm going to cut and run. I've got to get home by six o'clock.*

cut around something to move rapidly around something, such as a corner, pole, beam, etc. □ *The cat cut around a corner and escaped from the dog.* □ *The speeding car cut around the light pole and almost hit it.*

cut at someone or an animal to thrust a knife or something similar at someone or an animal. □ *The hoodlum cut at me, but I dodged the blade.* □ *He cut at the dog, but it had no effect on the vicious animal.*

cut at something and **cut away at** to cut on something to slice something. □ *He cut at the chair leg carefully, trying not to remove too much.* □ *Dad cut away at the turkey and asked us what part we wanted.*

cut back to turn back; to reverse direction. □ *Suddenly, the bull cut back in our direction and began chasing us.* □ *The road cuts back about a mile ahead, and it goes west again.*

cut back (on something) to reduce the use, amount, or cost of something. □ *You are all going to have to cut back on water usage.* □ *You simply must cut back on office expenses.*

cut back to someone or something [for a film or television camera] to return to a picture of someone or something. □ *Suddenly, the camera cut back to the reporter, who—unprepared—just stood there.* □ *The scene cut back to the veranda overlooking the bay.*

cut both ways to affect both sides of an issue equally. □ *Remember that your suggestion that costs should be shared cuts both ways. Your division will have to reduce its budget as well.* □ *If our side cannot take along supporters to the game, then yours cannot either. The rule has to cut both ways.*

cut class and **cut school** to skip a school class or a day of school without an excuse. □ *As a joke, one day all the students cut their math class and went to lunch.* □ *Jane was grounded after she cut school last Friday.*

cut corners *Fig.* to take shortcuts; to save money or effort by finding cheaper or easier ways to do something. □ *They're always finding ways to cut corners.* □ *I won't cut corners just to save money. I put quality first.*

cut down (on something) to reduce the amount of something or of doing something; to use or buy less of something. □ *You will have to cut down on the time it takes you to get ready in the morning.* □ *The doctor told him to cut down on his drinking.*

cut from the same cloth and **made from the same mold** *Fig.* sharing a lot of similarities; seeming to have been created, reared, or fashioned in the same way. □ *She and her brother are cut from the same cloth. They both tell lies all the time.* □ *Father and son are made from the same mold and even sound alike on the telephone.*

cut in (ahead of someone or something**)** to move quickly and carelessly into line ahead of someone, as in a line of people or in traffic. □ *A red car cut in ahead of me and nearly caused me to run off the road.* □ *Careful! Don't cut in ahead of that car!*

cut in (on someone**) 1.** *Lit.* [for someone] to ask to replace one member of a dancing couple. □ *Excuse me, may I cut in?* □ *Please don't cut in.* **2.** *Fig.* [for someone] to interrupt someone who is talking. □ *While Gloria was telling us her story, Tom kept cutting in on her.* □ *I'm talking. Please don't cut in!*

cut in (on something**) 1.** *Lit.* to interrupt something, especially some sort of electronic transmission. □ *I didn't mean to cut in on your announcement.* □ *Who cut in on my telephone call?* **2.** *Fig.* to join in something even when not invited. □ *Can I cut in on this little party?*

cut in (with something**)** to interrupt [someone] with a comment; to speak abruptly, interrupting what someone else is saying. □ *Jimmy cut in with a particularly witty remark.* □ *Must you always cut in while others are talking?*

cut in(to something**)** to slice something; to gouge something. □ *We cut into the watermelon and found it to be spoiled.* □ *It was a beautiful apple, but when she cut in, she found out that she had been cheated.*

Cut it out! *Inf.* Stop doing that!; Stop saying that! (Fixed order.) □ *Sue: Why, I think you have a crush on Mary! Tom: Cut it out!* □ *"Cut it out!" yelled Tommy as Billy hit him again.*

cut loose (with something**)** Go to **let go (with** something**)**.

cut no ice (with someone) *Sl.* to have no influence on someone; to fail to convince someone. □ *I don't care who you are. It cuts no ice with me.* □ *So you're the mayor's daughter. It still cuts no ice.*

cut off 1. to stop by itself or oneself. □ *The machine got hot and cut off.* □ *Bob cut off in midsentence.* **2.** to turn off a road, path, highway, etc. □ *This is the place where you are supposed to cut off.* □ *When you come to a cutoff on the left, continue on for about mile.*

cut one's **coat according to** one's **cloth** and **cut** one's **coat to suit** one's **cloth** *Prov.* to plan one's aims and activities in line with one's resources and circumstances. □ *We would like a bigger house, but we must cut our coat according to our cloth.* □ *They can't afford a vacation abroad—they have to cut their coat according to their cloth.*

cut one's **coat to suit** one's **cloth** Go to previous.

cut one's **eyes at** someone or something *Rur.* to glance at someone or something. □ *He cut his eyes at me to see if I was looking.* □ *She cut her eyes at the TV for a second.*

cut one's **eyeteeth on** something *Fig.* to grow up experiencing something; to have had the experience of dealing with something [successfully] at a very early age. □ *My grandfather taught me how to fish, so I cut my eyeteeth on fishing.* □ *Fred cut his eyeteeth on writing; both his parents were authors.*

cut one's **losses** to do something to stop a loss of something. □ *I knew I had to do something to cut my losses, but it was almost too late.* □ *Sell some of the high-priced stuff to cut your losses.*

cut one's **nose off to spite** one's **face** *Prov.* to hurt yourself in an attempt to hurt someone else. (Often in the form, "Don't cut off your nose to spite your face.") □ *Isaac dropped out of school because he wanted to make his father angry; years later, he realized that he had cut off his nose to spite his face.*

cut one's **(own) throat** *Fig.* [for someone] to bring about one's (own) failure. □ *If I were to run for office, I'd just be cutting my throat.* □ *Judges who take bribes are cutting their own throats.*

cut one's **wolf loose** *Sl.* to go on a drinking bout; to get drunk. □ *I'm gonna go out and cut my wolf loose tonight.* □ *You're going to cut your wolf loose too often and really get into trouble.*

cut (oneself**) loose (from** someone or something**)** to get out from under the domination of someone or something. □ *At last, she cut herself loose from her mother.* □ *She had to cut loose from home.* □ *Everyone wished that Todd would cut himself loose from his mother.*

cut oneself **on** something to slice one's flesh with something accidentally. □ *Careful, you will cut yourself on that knife.* □ *Careful! Don't cut yourself on that broken glass.*

cut out to depart; to leave in a hurry. □ *Good-bye. I have to cut out now.* □ *It's time I was cutting out. I'm late already.*

cut out (for some place**)** and **light out (for** some place**)** to leave quickly for some place. □ *The kids all cut out for home.* □ *When they heard their mother call, the Wilson kids cut out for home.*

cut out for someone or something to run hurriedly toward someone or something. □ *At the last minute, he cut out for the gate, which was closing very fast.* □ *The child cut out for his mother, who had come to get him at school.*

cut out for something suited for something. □ *She was bright and she loved to read. Her folks thought she was cut out for being a schoolteacher.* □ *He did his best, but he just wasn't cut out for farming.*

cut out to be something destined to be something or a particular type of person. (See also **cut out for** something.) □ *I don't think I was cut out to do this.* □ *We weren't cut out to be laborers.*

cut school Go to cut class.

cut some Zs Go to catch some Zs.

cut someone **a break** and **cut** someone **some slack** *Sl.* to give someone a break; to allow someone a reprieve from the consequences of an action. □ *Come on, cut me a break! I'm a good guy!* □ *I was only a few minutes late! Cut me a break! Don't dock my pay!* □ *Cut me some slack and I'll be sure to pay you all I owe in a month.*

cut (someone**) a check** to write a check; to have a computer print a check. (Used in business especially of machine-made checks.) □ *We will cut a check for the balance due you later this afternoon.* □ *We will cut you a check as soon as possible.*

cut someone **dead** to ignore someone totally. □ *Joan was just about to speak to James when he walked away and cut her dead.* □ *Jean cut her former husband dead.*

cut someone **down**† to kill someone with a weapon, such as a sword, or with gunfire, etc. □ *The bandits cut the bystanders down and fled.* □ *The gunman cut down an innocent pedestrian.*

cut someone **down (to size)** and **take** someone **down (to size)** *Fig.* to make a person humble; to put one in one's place. □ *John's critical remarks really cut me down to size.* □ *Jane is too conceited. I think her new boss will take her down to size.*

cut someone **in**† **(on** something**)** *Sl.* to permit someone to share something, such as profits or loot. □ *Max refused to cut in his partner Lefty.* □ *We can't cut you in. There's not enough.*

cut someone **off**† **at the pass** *Fig.* to block someone's effort to get away; to thwart someone's efforts. □ *They are ahead now, but we'll cut them off at the pass.* □ *Try to cut off the bandits at the pass!*

cut someone **off**† **without a penny** *Fig.* to end someone's allowance; to fail to leave someone money in one's will. □ *Mr. and Mrs. Franklin cut their son off without a penny after he quit school.* □ *They cut off both of their sons without a penny.* □ *We learned, when Uncle Sam's will was read, that he cut off his own flesh and blood without a penny.*

cut someone or something **loose from** something to sever the connection between people or things, in any combination. □ *Wally cut the child loose from the tree where his playmates had tied him up.* □ *I cut the cord loose from the anchor by mistake.*

cut someone or something **off**† **(from** something**)** to block or isolate someone or something from some place or something. □ *They cut the cattle off from the wheat field.* □ *The enemy tanks cut off the troops from their camp.*

cut someone or something **off**† **(short)** *Fig.* to interrupt someone or something; to prevent someone from continuing to speak. (See also **chop** someone **off**.) ☐ *In the middle of her sentence, the teacher cut her off short.* ☐ *Bob cut off Mary when she was trying to explain.*

cut someone or something **out**† to eliminate someone or something. ☐ *They cut out the free coffee with lunch at the cafeteria.* ☐ *We have to cut Chuck out. There are too many better men on the team.*

cut someone or something **to** something **1.** *Lit.* to chop or slice up someone or something, especially to bits or pieces. ☐ *The chef cut the carrots to bite-size pieces.* ☐ *The lawn mower will cut you to bits if you get under it.* **2.** *Fig.* to destroy an argument; to destroy someone's argument. ☐ *The lawyer heard her argument and cut her to bits.* ☐ *She cut the argument to pieces.*

cut someone or something **up**† *Fig.* to criticize someone or something severely. ☐ *Jane is such a gossip. She was really cutting Mrs. Jones up.* ☐ *The professor really cut up my essay.*

cut someone or something **with** something and **cut** someone or something **on** something to slice someone or something with or on something. ☐ *Don't cut yourself on that sharp blade.* ☐ *He cut the bread with a dull knife and crushed it.*

cut someone's **water off**† *Fig.* to squelch someone; to thwart someone. (Fixed order.) ☐ *Well, I guess that cuts your water off!* ☐ *That sure cuts off my water!*

cut someone **some slack** Go to **cut** someone **a break.**

cut someone **to ribbons 1.** *Lit.* to cut or slice someone severely. ☐ *He broke a mirror and the glass cut his hand to ribbons.* **2.** *Fig.* to criticize someone severely. ☐ *The critics just cut her acting to ribbons!*

cut someone **to the bone** Go to next.

cut someone **to the quick** and **cut** someone **to the bone 1.** *Lit.* to slice the flesh of someone or some animal clear through to the underlying layer of flesh or to the bone. ☐ *With the very sharp knife, David cut the beast to the quick in one blow.* ☐ *He cut his finger to the quick with the sharp knife.* **2.** *Fig.* to injure someone emotionally. (See also **cut** something **to the bone.**) ☐ *Your heartless comments cut me to the quick.* ☐ *Her remarks cut him to the bone.*

cut someone **up**† **1.** *Lit.* to gash or carve on someone by cutting. ☐ *The thugs cut him up badly, just for talking back.* ☐ *They cut up their victim into pieces.* **2.** *Fig.* to cause someone severe emotional distress. ☐ *That rebuke really cut me up.* ☐ *The critic really cut up the performer.*

cut someone **up** *Fig.* to make someone laugh. ☐ *That comedian's routine really cut me up.* ☐ *Tommy's rude noises cut the whole class up, but not the teacher.*

cut something **away**† **(from** something**)** to separate something from something by cutting. ☐ *The doctor cut the wart away from the patient's foot.* ☐ *She cut away the loose thread.*

cut something **back**† to prune plants; to reduce the size of plants, bushes, etc. ☐ *Let's cut these bushes back. They're getting in the way.* ☐ *Don't cut back my roses!*

cut something **down**† **1.** *Lit.* to chop something down; to saw or cut at something until it is felled. ☐ *Stop cutting the banners down!* ☐ *Don't cut down that tree!* **2.** *Fig.* to destroy someone's argument; to destroy someone's position or standing. ☐ *The lawyer cut the testimony down quickly.* ☐ *The lawyer cut down the witness's story.* **3.** to reduce the price of something. ☐ *They cut the prices down to sell the goods off quickly.* ☐ *I wish they would cut down the prices in this store.*

cut something **down**† **to** something to reduce something to a manageable size. ☐ *We cut the program down to size and it was very enjoyable.* ☐ *We cut down the program to a half hour.*

cut something **from** something to remove something from something by cutting. ☐ *She carefully cut the blossoms from the bush.* ☐ *A few blossoms were cut from the bush.*

cut something **into** something **1.** and **cut** something **in**† to mix something, usually a soft baking ingredient, into something else. (See also **fold** something **into** something.) ☐ *Carefully cut the butter into the flour mixture.* ☐ *Now, cut in some more butter.* **2.** to slice or chop something into very small pieces, bits, etc. ☐ *We cut the meat into one-inch cubes for the stew.*

cut something **off**† **1.** to shorten something. ☐ *Cut this board off a bit, would you?* ☐ *Cut off this board a little, please.* **2.** to turn something off, such as power, electricity, water, the engine, etc. ☐ *Would you please cut that engine off?* ☐ *Cut off the engine, Chuck.*

cut something **on** something **1.** to slice something on or against something, accidentally. ☐ *I cut my finger on the knife.* ☐ *Maria cut her foot on the broken glass.* **2.** to slice something that is lying on something else. ☐ *I cut the tomatoes on the cutting board your mother gave us.*

cut something **out**† **1.** to stop doing something. (Usually a command. See also **Cut it out!**) ☐ *Cut that noise out!* ☐ *Cut out that noise!* ☐ *Now, cut that out!* **2.** Go to next.

cut something **out of** something and **cut** something **out**† to cut a pattern or shape from cloth, paper, sheet metal, etc.; to remove something from something by cutting; to excise something from something. (When both *out* and *of* are used, no direct object can intervene.) ☐ *Sam cut a pig out from the paper.* ☐ *I cut the picture out of a magazine.* ☐ *I cut out the shape of the moon from the paper.*

cut something **to the bone 1.** *Lit.* to slice deep to a bone. ☐ *The knife cut John to the bone. He had to be sewed up.* ☐ *Cut each slice of ham to the bone. Then each slice will be as big as possible.* **2.** *Fig.* to cut down severely (on something). (*To the bone* emphasizes the severity of the cutting.) ☐ *We cut our expenses to the bone and are still losing money.* ☐ *Congress had to cut expenditures to the bone in order to balance the budget.*

cut something **with** something to dilute something with something else. ☐ *They cut the liquor with cold water.* ☐ *Please cut this with some soda. It's too sweet, otherwise.*

cut teeth [for a baby or young person] to have new teeth emerging through the gums. ☐ *Billy is cranky because he's cutting teeth.* ☐ *Ann cut her first tooth this week.*

cut the cheese and **cut the mustard** *Sl.* to release intestinal gas. (Crude. Use caution with the topic.) ☐ *Who cut the cheese?* ☐ *People who cut the mustard in the car have to get out and walk.*

Cut the comedy! and **Cut the funny stuff!; Cut the shit!** Stop acting silly and telling jokes!; Be serious! (Use *shit* with caution, as it is considered vulgar.) □ *John: All right, you guys! Cut the comedy and get to work! Bill: Can't we ever have any fun? John: No.* □ *Bill: Come on, Mary, let's throw Tom in the pool! Mary: Yeah, let's drag him over and give him a good dunking! Tom: Okay, you clowns, cut the funny stuff! I'll throw both of you in!*

cut the deadwood out 1. *Lit.* to prune away and remove the dead branches from a tree or bush. □ *They cut a lot of the deadwood out to save the tree.* □ *You have to cut out the deadwood to make room for new growth.* **2.** *Fig.* to remove unproductive persons from employment. □ *This company would be more profitable if management would cut out the deadwood.* □ *When we cut the deadwood out, all our departments will run more smoothly.*

cut the dust *Fig.* to take a drink of liquor. □ *I think I'll stop in here and cut the dust.* □ *I want to cut the dust. Can I have a snort?*

Cut the funny stuff! Go to Cut the comedy!

cut the ground out† from under someone *Fig.* to destroy the foundation of someone's plans or someone's argument. □ *The politician cut the ground out from under his opponent.* □ *Congress cut out the ground from under the president.*

cut the mustard Go to cut the cheese.

cut the pie up† *Fig.* to divide something up. (Can refer to an actual pie or anything that can be divided into varying portions.) □ *It all depends on how you cut the pie up.* □ *How should I cut up the pie?*

Cut the shit! Go to Cut the comedy!

cut through red tape *Fig.* to eliminate or neutralize something complicated, such as bureaucratic rules and procedures. □ *I will try to cut through all the red tape for you so you get your visa on time.* □ *I am sure someone can help us cut through all this red tape.*

cut through something to penetrate something by cutting; to slice through something. □ *The worker cut through the steel door with a torch.* □ *Walter cut through the rind of the watermelon.*

cut to someone or something to shift the radio, movie, or television audience's attention abruptly to someone or something new. □ *Suddenly, the engineer cut to the announcer.* □ *The technical director cut to a remote unit that was covering an accident.* □ *The camera cut to scenes of Atlanta burning.*

cut to the chase *Sl.* to focus on what is important; to abandon the preliminaries and deal with the major points. □ *All right, let's stop the idle chatter and cut to the chase.* □ *After a few introductory comments, we cut to the chase and began negotiating.*

cut up 1. to act wildly; to show off and be troublesome; to act like a clown. □ *Tom, Billy! Stop cutting up, or I'll send you to the principal's office.* □ *If you spent more time studying than cutting up, you'd get better grades.* **2.** Go to next.

cut up (about someone or something**)** *Sl.* emotionally upset about someone or something. □ *She was all cut up about her divorce.* □ *You could see how cut up she was.*

cut your peaches *Rur.* go on with what you were doing. □ *Stop gawking and cut your peaches.* □ *There's no need for you to follow me around. Go cut your peaches.*

*cute as a bug's ear very cute. (*Also: **as** ~.) □ *That little baby is cute as a bug's ear.*

the **cutting edge** *Fig.* the most forward part of a trend; the leading part of a trend. (Alludes to the edge of a sword. See also **on the cutting edge.** See also **on the bleeding edge.**) □ *Fred's invention put him on the cutting edge of the computer chip business.*

dab at something to touch or pat something. □ *The painter dabbed at the canvas, making little changes here and there.* □ *Don't just dab at the wall, spread the paint on!*

dab something **off†** Go to next.

dab something **off (of)** something and **dab** something **off†** to pat or wipe something off something. (*Of* is usually retained before pronouns.) □ *Please dab the butter off your chin.* □ *Please dab off the butter.* □ *Dab the moisture off of the apples.*

dab something **on(to)** something and **dab** something **on†** to pat or spread carefully something onto something else. □ *Dab some medicine onto the scratch.* □ *Dab on some medicine.*

dabble at something to play at doing something; to do something halfheartedly. □ *Don't just dabble at your history paper. Settle down and do it right.* □ *She dabbles at painting.*

dabble in something to be involved in something in a casual manner. □ *She dabbled in local politics for a while.* □ *I want to dabble in something new for a while.*

Dad fetch my buttons! *Rur.* What a surprise!; Goodness me! □ *Dad fetch my buttons! It's a letter from Aunt Rita!* □ *Dad fetch my buttons, I never was so happy in all my life!*

the **daddy of them all** and the **granddaddy of them all** *Fig.* the biggest or oldest of all; the patriarch. □ *This old fish is the granddaddy of them all.* □ *This tree is the daddy of them all. It's been here since the place was built.*

daily dozen *Fig.* physical exercises done every day. □ *My brother always feels better after his daily dozen.* □ *She would rather do a daily dozen than go on a diet.*

the **daily grind** [someone's] everyday work routine. □ *I'm getting very tired of the daily grind.* □ *When my vacation was over, I had to go back to the daily grind.*

dally over something to waste time or take too long doing something. □ *Don't dally over your food. Eat your dinner.* □ *I wish you wouldn't dally over your homework.*

dally with someone to flirt with someone; to waste time with someone of the opposite sex. (Old.) □ *Sam is dallying with that Johnson girl again.* □ *Stop dallying with her and get back to your studies!*

dam something **up†** to erect a barrier in a river, stream, brook, etc. □ *We are going to have to dam this stream up to make a pond for the cattle.* □ *Let's dam up this stream.* □ *Why is this river dammed up?*

Damn it to blue blazes! *Rur.* Damn it. (An oath.) □ *Damn it to blue blazes, I told you I can't lend you any more money!* □ *"Damn it to blue blazes! I give up!" Joe shouted, flinging his tools aside.*

a **(damn) sight better** *Rur.* much better. □ *Mary can sing a damn sight better than Tom can.* □ *You look a sight better with your hair cut short.*

damn someone or something **with faint praise** *Fig.* to criticize someone or something indirectly by not praising enthusiastically. □ *The critic did not say that he disliked the play, but he damned it with faint praise.* □ *Mrs. Brown is very proud of her son's achievements, but damns her daughter's with faint praise.*

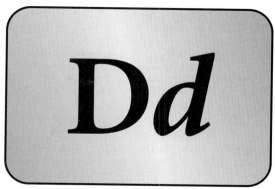

damn someone **with** something **1.** *Lit.* to curse someone with words. □ *She damned him with curse after curse.* □ *Maria damned Joe with the worst curses she could think of.* **2.** *Fig.* to denounce or defeat someone in a particular way. □ *She damned him with her insincere words of praise.* □ *She damned herself with the evidence she had hoped would save her.*

Damned if you do, damned if you don't. *Prov.* No matter what you do, it will cause trouble. □ *If I use this money to pay the rent, I won't have enough left over for food. But if I don't use the money to pay the rent, my landlord will evict me. Damned if I do, damned if I don't.* □ *Helen: If I invite Shirley to the party, I'm sure she'll get drunk and make an unpleasant scene. But if I don't invite her, she'll never forgive me. Jane: Damned if you do, damned if you don't, huh?*

damp off [for seedlings] to die from too much water. □ *All the new plants damped off, and we had to buy some from the nursery.* □ *The little seedlings damped off and withered away.*

damp something **down†** **1.** *Lit.* to make something damp. □ *Damp the clothes down before you iron them.* □ *Please damp down the clothes first.* **2.** *Fig.* to reduce the intensity of a flame, usually by cutting down on the air supply, as with a damper. □ *Please damp the woodstove down.* □ *Damp down the air supply or you are going to end up with a raging inferno.*

dampen someone's **spirits** Go to someone's **spirits**.

dance at someone's **wedding** to celebrate in honor of someone at someone's wedding. □ *I will dance at your wedding—if you invite me, of course.* □ *If you think I will dance at your wedding, you had better be nicer to me!*

dance on air *Fig.* to be very happy; to be euphoric enough as if to dance on air. □ *I was so happy, I could have danced on air.* □ *She was just dancing on air, she was so happy.*

dance out of step (with someone or something**)** Go to out of step (with someone or something).

dance out of time (with someone or something**)** Go to out of step (with someone or something).

dance to a different tune Go to next.

dance to another tune and **dance to a different tune** *Fig.* to shift quickly to different behavior; to change one's behavior or attitude. □ *After being yelled at, Ann danced to another tune.* □ *A stern talking-to will make her dance to a different tune.*

dance to something to respond to music or rhythm with dancing. □ *I can't dance to that fast beat!* □ *That music is horrible. No one can dance to that.*

dance with death *Fig.* to attempt to do something that is very risky. □ *The crossing of the border into enemy territory was like dancing with death.* □ *You are dancing with death in your effort to cross that narrow ledge.*

dance with someone to perform social dancing with another person. □ *Do you think you would like to dance with Wally?* □ *Would you please dance with me?*

dangle from something to hang from something. □ *A number of colorful glass balls dangled from the branches of the tree.* □ *Some loose threads dangled from the bottom of his jacket.*

dangle something **before** someone and **dangle** something **in front of** someone **1.** *Lit.* to tempt someone by dangling a tempting object in front of them. □ *Don't dangle that string of pearls in front of me unless you intend to give them to me!* **2.** *Fig.* to lure someone with something. □ *He dangled the keys before Wally, hoping to get him to drive.* □ *He dangled the money in front of Eric, hoping to make him change his mind.*

dangle something **from** something to hang something loosely from something else. □ *She dangled a few small bells from the bottom of her skirt during the holidays.* □ *I dangled a bit of fish from the window so I could see how high the cat would jump.*

dangle something **in front of** someone Go to **dangle** something **before** someone.

dare someone **(to** do something**)** to challenge someone to do something. □ *Sally dared Jane to race her to the corner.* □ *You wouldn't do that, would you? I dare you.*

dark horse *Fig.* someone or something whose abilities, plans, or feelings are little known to others. (From a race horse about which little or nothing is known.) □ *It's difficult to predict who will win the prize—there are two or three dark horses in the tournament.* □ *Everyone was surprised at the results of the election. The dark horse won.*

the **dark side of** someone or something *Fig.* the negative and often hidden aspect of someone or something. □ *I had never seen the dark side of Mary before, and I have to tell you that I was horrified when she lost her temper.*

darken someone's **door** *Fig.* [for an unwelcome person] to come to someone's door seeking entry. (As if the visitor were casting a shadow on the door. Formal, or even jocular.) □ *Who is this who has come to darken my door?* □ *She pointed to the street and said, "Go and never darken my door again!"*

The **darkest hour is just before the dawn.** and **It's always darkest just before the dawn.** *Prov.* When things are extremely bad, it may signal that they are about to get much better. □ *Jill: I feel like giving up. I don't have a job, my boyfriend left me, and they're raising the rent for my apartment. Jane: It's always darkest just before the dawn.*

darn tooting and **darn tootin'** absolutely. □ *You're darn tooting I'll be there. I wouldn't miss it for the world.*

dart a glance at someone or something to shoot a quick look at someone or something. □ *She darted a glance at him and looked quickly away.* □ *He darted a glance at the door and looked even more uncomfortable.*

dart about to move about quickly. □ *The little fish were darting about everywhere.* □ *People were darting about, to and fro, during the noon rush hour.*

dart across something to run quickly over something. □ *A small animal darted across the road in front of the car.* □ *I tried to dart across the street, but the traffic was too heavy.*

dart in and out [for something moving] to move quickly between two things, or into a number of things, and move away again. □ *On the highway, a small car was darting in and out of the two right lanes of traffic.* □ *A small bird darted in and out of the bush, probably going into a nest inside.*

dart out (of something**) (at** someone or something**)** to move quickly out of something toward someone or something. □ *The ferret darted out of its burrow at the children.* □ *The snake darted out at the frog.* □ *The mouse darted out of its hole.*

dash a letter off† Go to next.

dash a note off† and **dash a letter off**† to write a note or letter quickly and send it off. □ *I have to dash this letter off, then I will be with you.* □ *I'll dash off a note to her.*

dash across something to run quickly across some area. □ *John dashed across the busy street and ran in the door.* □ *The dog dashed across the yard and confronted the meter reader.*

dash away and **dash off** to run away; to leave in a hurry. □ *I must dash away. See you tomorrow.* □ *Juan had to dash away to an appointment.* □ *Ken dashed off and left me behind to deal with the angry customer.*

dash cold water on something Go to **pour cold water on** something.

dash off Go to **dash away**.

dash out (for something**)** [for someone] to leave a place in a hurry to get something. □ *Harry dashed out for some cigarettes.* □ *Excuse me. I just have to dash out.*

dash over (for something**)** [for someone] to come by quickly for something such as a brief visit. □ *I just dashed over for a cup of sugar. Can you spare it?* □ *I needed some sugar, so I just dashed over.*

dash someone or something **against** someone or something to throw or fling someone or something at or against someone or something. □ *Sam dashed the bottle against the floor, shattering it.* □ *Alice dashed the box against Ed, throwing him off balance.*

dash someone's **hopes** *Fig.* to ruin someone's hopes; to put an end to someone's dreams or aspirations. □ *Mary dashed my hopes when she said she wouldn't marry me.*

dash something **off**† to make or do something quickly. □ *I will dash this off now and try to take more time with the rest of them.* □ *I will see if I can dash off a cherry pie before dinner.*

dash something **to pieces** to break something into small pieces. □ *She dashed the glass to pieces on the floor—she was so mad.* □ *The potter dashed the imperfect pot to pieces.*

date back (to someone or some time**)** to have origins that extend back to the time of someone or something. □ *This part of the palace dates back to Catherine the Great.* □ *This is old! It really must date back.*

date from something to have an existence that extends from a particular time. □ *This building dates from the beginning of the last century.* □ *These books date from the 1920s.*

daub something **on(to)** something and **daub** something **on**† to smear or paint something onto something else. □ *The painter daubed a bit of yellow onto the canvas.* □ *Daub on a bit of yellow here.* □ *She daubed the medicine on.*

daub something **with** something to smear or paint something with something sticky, such as paint, grease, makeup, etc. □ *The mechanic daubed the part with grease and put it back where it came from.* □ *The end of the chair leg was daubed with glue and set into place.*

Davy Jones's locker the bottom of the sea, especially when it is a grave. □ *They were going to sail around the world, but ended up in Davy Jones's locker.* □ *Most of the gold from that trading ship is in Davy Jones's locker.*

dawdle about to waste time in a place; to waste time talking idly. □ *Don't dawdle about. Get moving.* □ *Tim has been dawdling about all morning.*

dawdle along to move along slowly and casually. □ *The boys dawdled along on their way to school.* □ *We were just dawdling along, talking about life. We didn't know we were late.*

dawdle over something to waste time when one should be doing a particular task; to loaf while doing something. □ *Don't dawdle over your hamburger. The lunch period ends in two minutes.* □ *Don't dawdle over it. Get it done.*

dawdle something **away**† to waste a particular amount of time; to let a period of time slip away, wasted. □ *You didn't finish your work because you dawdled most of your time away.* □ *You dawdle away too much time daydreaming.*

dawn (up)on someone *Fig.* [for a fact] to become apparent to someone; [for something] to be suddenly realized by someone. (*Upon* is formal and less commonly used than *on*.) □ *Then it dawned upon me that I was actually going to have the job.* □ *On the way home, it dawned on me that I had never returned your call, so when I got home I called immediately.*

day after day every day; daily; all the time. □ *He wears the same clothes day after day.* □ *She visits her husband in the hospital day after day.*

day and night and **night and day** all the time; around the clock. □ *The nurse was at her bedside day and night.* □ *The house is guarded night and day.*

day in and day out and **day in, day out** on every day; for each day. □ *She watches soap operas day in and day out.* □ *They eat nothing but vegetables, day in, day out.*

a **day late and a dollar short** late and ill-prepared. □ *Tommy, you seem to show up a day late and a dollar short all the time. You need to get organized.*

*the **day off** a day free from working. (*Typically: **get** ~; **have** ~; **give** someone ~; **take** ~.) □ *The next time I get a day off, we'll go to the zoo.* □ *I have the day off. Let's go hiking.*

***day one** the very beginning; the very first day. (*Typically: **from** ~; **since** ~.) □ *You haven't done anything right since day one! You're fired!* □ *She was unhappy with her new car from day one.*

a **day person** a person who prefers to be active during the daytime. (Compare this with a **night person**.) □ *I am strictly a day person. Have to be in bed early.*

daydream about someone or something to have daytime fantasies about someone or something. □ *Poor Alice is always daydreaming about Albert.* □ *John is daydreaming about running away to Tahiti.*

daylight robbery *Fig.* the practice of blatantly or grossly overcharging. □ *It's daylight robbery to charge that amount of money for a hotel room!* □ *The cost of renting a car at that place is daylight robbery.*

days running and **weeks running; months running; years running** days in a series; months in a series; etc. (Follows a number.) □ *I had a bad cold for five days running.* □ *For two years running, I brought work home from the office every night.*

day-tripper a tourist who makes excursions lasting just one day. □ *At about 4:00 P.M. the day-trippers start thinning out.* □ *Being a day-tripper is hard on your feet sometimes.*

dead ahead straight ahead; directly ahead. □ *Look out! There is a cow in the road dead ahead.* □ *The farmer said that the town we were looking for was dead ahead.*

dead and buried 1. *Lit.* dead and interred, and soon to be forgotten. □ *Now that Uncle Bill is dead and buried, we can read his will.* **2.** *Fig.* gone forever. □ *That kind of old-fashioned thinking is dead and buried.*

dead and gone 1. *Lit.* [of a person] long dead. □ *Old Gert's been dead and gone for quite a spell.* □ *When I'm dead and gone, I hope folks remember me at my best.* **2.** *Fig.* [of a thing] gone long ago. □ *That kind of thinking is dead and gone.* □ *The horse-and-buggy days are dead and gone.*

***dead as a dodo** and ***dead as a doornail; deader than a doornail** dead; no longer in existence. (*Also: **as** ~.) □ *That silly old idea is dead as a dodo.* □ *When I tried to start my car this morning, I discovered that the battery was deader than a doornail.*

dead as a doornail Go to previous.

dead broke completely broke; without any money. □ *I'm dead broke—not a nickel to my name.* □ *I've been dead broke for a month now.*

a **dead cat on the line** *Rur.* [for something to be] wrong. □ *I'm afraid there's a dead cat on the line over at Martha's place. I haven't heard from them for days.* □ *Bill has a kind of sixth sense. He can tell a dead cat on the line before anybody knows there's something wrong.*

dead center at the exact center of something. (See also **on dead center**.) □ *The arrow hit the target dead center.* □ *When you put the flowers on the table, put them dead center.*

dead certain very sure. (*Dead* means *absolutely*.) □ *I'm dead certain that horse will win. I bet two hundred on it myself.* □ *I didn't believe the rumor at first, but Bill's dead certain that it's true.*

dead drunk very intoxicated; totally inebriated. □ *They were both dead drunk. They could only lie there and snore.* □ *Marty stumbled off the bar stood dead drunk.*

a **dead duck** *Fig.* someone or something that is certain to die or fail. □ *If I fail that test, I'm a dead duck.* □ *When* *the outlaw drew his pistol, the sheriff knew he was a dead duck.*

dead easy very easy. □ *This whole job is dead easy.* □ *It was so dead easy, Frank did it with one hand.*

dead from the neck up 1. *Fig.* stupid. (With a "dead" head.) □ *She acts like she is dead from the neck up.* **2.** *Fig.* no longer open to new ideas. □ *Everyone on the board of directors is dead from the neck up.*

a **dead giveaway** something that reveals a fact or an intention completely. □ *The car in the driveway was a dead giveaway that someone was at home.*

dead in someone's or an animal's **tracks** *Fig.* exactly where someone or something is at the moment; at this instant. (This does not usually have anything to do with death. The phrase is often used with *stop*.) □ *Her unkind words stopped me dead in my tracks.* □ *When I heard the rattlesnake, I stopped dead in my tracks.*

dead in the water stalled; immobile. (Originally nautical.) □ *This whole company is dead in the water.* □ *The project is out of funds and dead in the water for the time being.*

dead letter 1. a piece of mail that is returned to the post office as both undeliverable and unreturnable. □ *At the end of the year, the post office usually has bushels of dead letters.* □ *Some of the dead letters are opened to see if there is an address inside.* **2.** an issue, law, or matter that is no longer important or that no longer has force or power. □ *His point about the need for education reform is a dead letter. It is being done now.* □ *This point of law is a dead letter since the last Supreme Court ruling on this matter.*

a **dead loss** a total loss. □ *My investment was a dead loss.* □ *This car is a dead loss after the accident.*

dead meat *Fig.* dead; as good as dead. (Usually an exaggeration.) □ *If you don't do exactly as I say, you are dead meat!*

Dead men tell no tales. *Prov.* Dead people will not betray any secrets. □ *The club members liked to hold their secret meetings in a graveyard, since dead men tell no tales.* □ *Gangster: Mugsy is going to tell the police that we robbed the bank. How can we stop him? Henchman: Dead men tell no tales.*

dead on exactly right; on target. □ *That's a good observation, Tiffany. You are dead on.* □ *Your criticism is dead on!*

dead on one's **feet** and **dead on its feet** *Fig.* exhausted; worn out; no longer useful. □ *Ann is so tired. She's really dead on her feet.* □ *He can't teach well anymore. He's dead on his feet.* □ *This inefficient company is dead on its feet.*

a **(dead) ringer (for someone) *Fig.* very closely similar in appearance to someone else. (*Typically: **be ~; look like ~**.) □ *You are sure a dead ringer for my brother.* □ *Isn't he a ringer for Chuck?*

dead serious absolutely serious; not joking. □ *Tom: You're funning me. Bill: No, I'm dead serious.* □ *Mary has threatened divorce a hundred times, but this time she says she's dead serious.*

dead set against someone or something totally opposed to someone or something. □ *I'm dead set against the new tax proposal.* □ *Everyone is dead set against the mayor.*

dead to the world 1. sound asleep. □ *After all that exercise, he's dead to the world.* □ *He's dead to the world, and I can't rouse him.* **2.** intoxicated. □ *Six beers and he was dead to the world.* □ *By midnight almost everybody at the party was dead to the world.*

dead wrong completely wrong. □ *I'm sorry. I was dead wrong. I didn't have the facts straight.*

deaden something **with** something to dull or anesthetize pain with something. □ *The doctor deadened the area with an injection before she began to stitch.* □ *I will deaden the pain with a local anesthetic.*

deader than a doornail Go to dead as a dodo.

deadly dull very dull. □ *The lecture was deadly dull, and I went to sleep.* □ *Her story was really deadly dull. I am sorry I was awake for part of it.*

deaf and dumb unable to hear or speak. (Used without any intended malice, but no longer considered polite. Sometimes euphemized as "hearing and speech impaired.") □ *Fred objected to being called deaf and dumb.* □ *Aunt Clara—she was deaf and dumb, you know—lived to be over 100.*

****deaf as a post** deaf. (*Also: **as ~**.) □ *When my cousin was a teenager, she played her drum set without ear protection, and she was as deaf as a post by the age of twenty-five.* □ *Mark can't hear you even if you shout; he's deaf as a post.*

deal in something to buy and sell something. □ *My uncle is a stockbroker. He deals in stocks and bonds.* □ *My aunt deals in antiques.*

deal someone **in**† Go to deal someone into something.

deal someone **into** something and **deal** someone **in**† **1.** *Lit.* to pass out cards to someone, making that person a player in a card game. □ *Can you deal me into this hand?* □ *Deal in anyone who wants to play.* □ *Deal me in!* **2.** *Fig.* to permit someone to take part in something. □ *Let's deal him into this project.* □ *Yes, deal in this guy.* □ *Should we deal her in?*

deal someone **out of** something and **deal** someone **out**† **1.** *Lit.* to skip someone when dealing a hand of cards. □ *Please deal me out of the next hand. I have to go make a telephone call.* □ *They dealt out the old lady because she would not pay attention to the game.* **2.** *Fig.* to remove someone from participation in something. □ *They dealt me out at the last minute.* □ *They dealt out Fred, too.*

deal something **out**† to pass something out piece by piece, giving everyone equal shares. □ *The manager dealt the proposals out, giving each person an equal number to read.* □ *I'll deal out some more proposals.*

deal the race card Go to the the race card.

deal with someone *Sl.* to kill someone. □ *"Spike, you deal with that cop," said the crime boss.* □ *The agent planned how best to deal with the rebel leader without getting caught.*

deal with someone or something to manage someone or something. □ *This is not a big problem. I think I can deal with it.* □ *I am sure I can deal with Jill.*

dear departed *Euph.* a dead person, as referred to at a funeral. □ *Let's take a moment to meditate on the life of the dear departed.*

a **Dear John letter** a letter a woman writes to her boyfriend telling him that she does not love him anymore. □ *Bert got a Dear John letter today from Sally. He was devastated.*

Dear me! an expression of mild dismay or regret. □ *Sue: Dear me, is this all there is? Mary: There's more in the kitchen.* □ *"Oh, dear me!" fretted John, "I'm late again."*

Death is the great leveler. *Prov.* Death makes everyone equal, because it does not spare anyone, not even the wealthy, famous, or talented. (Also the cliché: **the great leveler,** death.) □ *The wealthy tycoon lived as though he were exempt from every law, but death is the great leveler and came to him the same as to everyone else.* □ *We hoped that the brilliant pianist would entertain us with her music for many decades, but death, the great leveler, did not spare her.*

death on something **1.** *Fig.* very harmful; very effective in acting against someone or something. □ *This road is terribly bumpy. It's death on tires.* □ *The sergeant is death on lazy soldiers.* **2.** *Fig.* accurate or deadly at doing something requiring skill or great effort. □ *John is death on curve balls. He's our best pitcher.* □ *The boxing champ is really death on those fast punches.*

debate on something to hold a long and disciplined discussion on a particular subject. □ *We can debate on this all night if you think we will settle anything in the end.* □ *Are they still debating on the question?*

debate (with someone**) about** something **1.** to enter into a long and disciplined discussion on a particular subject with someone. □ *Our team debated with the other team about the chances for world peace.* □ *The candidates debate about taxes tomorrow.* □ *We will debate with them about health care.* **2.** *Fig.* to argue with someone about something. □ *I do not intend to debate with you about that matter.* □ *Tom did not agree to debate about it.*

debit something **against** someone or something to record a charge for something against someone's account or against a particular category of an account. □ *I will have to debit this against your account.* □ *The clerk debited the charge against you.*

debit something **to** someone or something to make a charge for something to someone or something. □ *To whose account can we debit this charge?* □ *Let's debit it to Jane.*

debit something **with** something to charge something for something. □ *They debited Fred's account with the whole expense.* □ *The bank debited my checking account with the cost of the new checks.*

deceive someone **into** something to trick someone into doing something. □ *She deceived me into giving her my car keys.* □ *You can't deceive me into doing what I don't want to do.*

deceive someone **with** something to cheat someone with something or with deceptive words. □ *You cannot deceive me with your promises.* □ *You are just deceiving yourself with fancy talk.*

decide against someone or something to rule against someone or something; to make a judgment against someone or something. □ *We decided against Tom and chose Larry instead.* □ *Jane decided against the supplier.*

decide among someone **and** someone else and **decide among** something **and** something else to choose from three or more people; to choose from three or more things. □ *I couldn't decide among all the choices on the menu.* □ *I will decide among Fred, Tom, and Alice.*

decide between someone **and** someone else and **decide between** something **and** something else to choose one from two people; to choose one from two things. □ *I could not decide between Tom and Wally.* □ *We could not decide between those two.*

decide for someone or something to rule in favor of someone or something; to make a judgment for someone or something. □ *The jury decided for the plaintiff.* □ *The judge decided for me.*

decide in favor of someone or something to determine that someone or something is the winner. □ *The judge decided in favor of the defendant.* □ *I decided in favor of the red one.*

decide (up)on someone or something to choose someone or something; to make a judgment about some aspect of someone or something. (*Upon* is formal and less commonly used than *on*.) □ *Will you please hurry up and decide upon someone to vote for?* □ *I decided on chocolate.*

deck someone or something **out**† **(in** something**)** and **deck** someone or something **out (with** something**)** to decorate someone or something with something. □ *Sally decked all her children out for the holiday party.* □ *She decked out her children in Halloween costumes.* □ *Tom decked the room out with garlands of flowers.*

declare (oneself**) against** someone or something to state one's opposition to someone or something publicly. □ *I must declare myself against the amendment.* □ *The politician declared himself against whatever the voters were already against.*

declare (oneself**) for** someone or something to state one's support of someone or something. □ *Susan declared herself for Mary's candidacy.* □ *I have not yet declared for any particular policy.* □ *Todd declared himself for the candidacy of Mary Brown for mayor.*

declare war against someone or something and **declare war on** someone or something **1.** *Lit.* to formally announce that one will fight a war with someone or some country. □ *A group of countries declared war against the aggressor.* **2.** *Fig.* to announce a serious campaign against a type of person or a serious problem. □ *The president declared war against crime and criminals.* □ *The pressure group declared war on waste.*

decorate someone **for** something to award someone a medal or ribbon for doing something important or brave. □ *The town decorated her for her heroic act.* □ *She was decorated for her heroism.*

decorate something **with** something to adorn or ornament something with something. □ *I will decorate the cake with roses made of sugar.* □ *Can I decorate your car with streamers for the parade?*

dedicate someone or something **to** someone or something **1.** to reserve someone or something for the use of someone or something. □ *The manager dedicated new assistants to the exclusive use of the legal department.* □ *The committee dedicated a corner in the library to books on agri-*

culture. **2.** to pledge someone or something to someone, something, a deity, or religious purposes. □ *The elders dedicated the building to the glory of God.* □ *He dedicated himself to the prosecution of justice.*

deduce something **from** something to infer or conclude something from a set of facts. □ *Can I deduce a bit of anger from your remarks?* □ *I deduce nothing from everything I have heard today.*

deduct something **from** something else to subtract an amount from another amount. □ *Are you going to deduct this from your income taxes?* □ *Mr. Wilson deducted the discount from the bill.*

deed something **(over) to** someone to grant something, such as land, to someone; to transfer legal title to something to someone. □ *Grudgingly, he deeded the land over to Walter.* □ *He deeded the property to his niece.*

deem it (to be) necessary and **deem that it is necessary** to decide that something is necessary. □ *Mary deemed that it was necessary to leave town that night.* □ *Lisa deemed it necessary to go home.*

deep-six someone or something *Sl.* to get rid of someone or something; to dispose of someone or something. (Refers originally to burying someone or something six feet deep, the standard depth of a grave.) □ *Take this horrible food out and deep-six it.* □ *That guy is a pain. Deep-six him so the cops will never find him.*

deface something **with** something to mutilate or spoil the appearance of something with something. □ *Someone defaced the wall with spray paint.* □ *Please don't deface the facilities.*

default on something to fail to act in some way regarding something, such as failing to make a payment, thereby losing one's right to the thing in question. □ *You are not going to default on your loan, are you?* □ *She defaulted on her mortgage payments and lost the house.*

defect from something to run away from something; to forsake something. □ *Thousands of soldiers defected from the army.* □ *Roger would never think of defecting from the armed services.*

defect to something to forsake one group and take up with another. □ *Will he defect to the other side?* □ *David defected to a small East European country.*

defend someone or something **against** someone or something **1.** to stand against an attack; to provide a defense against attack. □ *Don't worry, I will defend you against any muggers.* □ *We defended ourselves against the attack.* □ *The army defended the town against the enemy soldiers.* **2.** to advocate the cause of someone or something against someone or something else. □ *The lawyer defended her against the plaintiff.* □ *She defended the company against the suit.*

defend someone **with** something to repel danger from someone with something. □ *Here, defend yourself with this club.* □ *Mary defended herself with karate.*

defer to someone or something **(on** something**)** to yield to someone or something on some question or point. □ *I will defer to Mary on that question.* □ *She would not defer to the committee on anything.*

define something **as** something to label something as being something. □ *I define that kind of behavior as just plain*

rude! □ *We have to define that comment as careless and unthinking.*

Definitely not! and **Certainly not!** No, without any doubt at all. (Compare this with **Absolutely not!**) □ *Bill: Will you lend me some money? Bob: No way! Definitely not!* □ *Bob: Have you ever stolen anything? Fred: Certainly not!*

deflect something **away from** someone or something to divert someone or something away from someone or something; to cause someone or something to veer away from someone or something. □ *The press secretary deflected the reporter's questions from the candidate.* □ *The emergency deflected the boss's attention away from my mistake.*

defraud someone **out of** something to cheat someone out of something. □ *The crooked contractor defrauded the town out of a fortune.* □ *The clerk defrauded the employer out of a great deal of money.*

degenerate into something to decay into something; to break down into something. □ *The peace rally degenerated into a riot.* □ *I was afraid that the party would degenerate into a drinking contest.*

deign to do something to lower oneself to do something. □ *She will never deign to join in with us.* □ *I expect that he will not deign to have dinner with us.*

delegate someone **to** something to appoint someone to something; to appoint someone to be something. □ *I will delegate Jane to be our representative.* □ *Donna was delegated to attend the conference.*

delegate something **to** someone to assign a task to someone; to appoint someone to do a specific task. □ *I will have to delegate this job to Sam, who knows how to do these things.* □ *The job was delegated to Sally.*

delete something **from** something to remove something from something; to cross something out from something. □ *Will you please delete this paragraph from the contract?* □ *The line was deleted from the sales agreement.*

deliberate about someone or something and **deliberate on** someone or something to think about someone or something; to consider what to do about someone or something. □ *How long do you intend to deliberate about Carol?* □ *We will deliberate about this matter as long as it takes to do it right.* □ *Let's deliberate on this for a while.*

deliberate on someone or something Go to previous.

deliberate over someone or something to discuss and argue about someone or something. □ *We will deliberate over this question tomorrow.* □ *We have been deliberating over Karen long enough.*

delight in someone or something to take great pleasure in someone or something. □ *I delight in your interest in my work.* □ *We all delight in James. What a fine boy!*

delight someone **by** something to please someone with something; to please someone by doing something. (See also **delight** someone **with** something.) □ *You delighted me by agreeing to join us.* □ *I was delighted by your proposal.*

delight someone **with** something to please someone with something, such as a gift. □ *We delighted Alice with a gift of money.* □ *She was delighted with the gift.*

deliver someone **from** someone or something to save or rescue someone from someone or something. □ *The hero* delivered the children from a fiery death. □ Thank you for delivering me from a very boring meeting by calling me to the telephone.

deliver someone **of** something to free someone from some burden or problem; to liberate someone from some confinement. □ He was looking for someone to deliver him of his burdensome responsibility. □ He was delivered of his burden.

deliver someone or something **to** someone or something to transfer someone or something to someone or something; to yield over someone or something to someone or something. □ When will you deliver the deed to me? □ I will deliver the deed to you when I have your check.

deliver something **under pressure** Go to under pressure.

deliver something **up† to** someone to render or yield something to someone. □ Will you please deliver the documents up to Jane? □ Will you please deliver up the documents to Jane?

delude someone **into** something to fool someone into thinking something. □ You can't delude me into believing you. □ Todd deluded himself into believing he was back at home.

delude someone **with** something to fool or trick someone with something. □ She deluded us with her clever talk. □ Don't delude yourself with false hopes.

deluge someone or something **with** something **1.** Lit. to flood someone or something with water or something similar. □ The swollen river broke the dam and deluged the town with billions of gallons of water. **2.** Fig. to overwhelm someone or something with something; to "flood" someone or something with something. □ The reporters deluged us with questions.

delve into something to examine or study something carefully; to enter into the examination or study of something. □ He delved into the solution of the problem facing him. □ I am just now delving into a study of the Trojan War.

demand something **from** someone or something and **demand** something **of** someone or something to command that something be received from someone or a group or something; to demand that someone or a group or something do something. □ The muggers demanded money from everyone. □ The petitioners demanded a response from the board of directors. □ She demanded too much of her automobile.

demand something **of** someone or something Go to previous.

demonstrate against someone or something to make a public show against someone or something. □ The citizens demonstrated against the new policies. □ A number of protestors demonstrated against the mayor.

demonstrate for someone or something to make a public show in favor of someone or something. □ We will all demonstrate for Walter's candidacy. □ A number of supporters demonstrated for the mayor.

demonstrate something **to** someone to show someone how something works. □ Would you please demonstrate this DVD player to me? I may want to buy it. □ The new products were demonstrated to the board of directors in advance.

demote someone **from** something **(to** something**)** and **demote** someone **(from** something**) to** something to lower someone's rank from one rank to another. □ The manager demoted Bill from cashier to clerk. □ The army demoted her from lieutenant to sergeant.

demur at something to dispute something; to challenge something. □ I fear I must demur at your suggestion that I am aloof and condescending. □ Alice demurred at the suggestion that she was late.

a **den of iniquity** a place filled with criminal activity or wickedness. □ The town was a den of iniquity and vice was everywhere. □ Police raided the gambling house, calling it a den of iniquity.

denounce someone **as** something to criticize someone as something; to publicly call someone something bad. □ The mayor denounced her opponent as a crook. □ Anne was denounced as a cheater.

denounce someone **for** something to criticize someone publicly for doing something. □ The candidate denounced the governor for raising taxes. □ Donna denounced the mayor for incompetence.

dent something **up†** to mar or make depressions in something. □ I don't want to dent my car up. It's still new. □ He dented up my new bike!

denude someone or something **of** something to strip something from someone or something. □ The prison guards denuded the new prisoner of his garments. □ The wind denuded the trees of their leaves.

deny someone or something **to** someone to prevent someone from having someone or something. □ Would you deny her children to her after all these long months? □ I would not deny food to a starving man.

depart for some place to leave for some place. □ When shall we depart for the airport? □ When do we depart for St. Petersburg?

depart from some place to leave from some place or something; to set out from some place or something. □ When will you depart from here? □ We departed from Moscow on time.

depart this life Euph. to die. □ He departed this life on April 20th, 1973. □ She departed peacefully, in her sleep.

depend (up)on someone or something to rely upon someone or something. (Upon is formal and less commonly used than on.) □ Can I depend on you to do this right? □ You can depend upon me for help.

depict someone **as** something to show someone as something; to make someone appear to be something. □ He did report the fire, but it is going too far to depict him as a hero. □ The artist depicted himself as a much younger man than he really was.

deplete something **of** something to use up all of a certain thing that something has. □ They will deplete the soil of its nutrients by planting the same crop over and over.

deport someone **(from** some place**) (to** some other place**)** to expel or exile someone from one place to another, usually back to their prior country of residence. □ The government deported Jane from this country to her homeland. □ They deported Tom to Brazil from this country.

deposit something **in(to)** something to put something into something. □ *Please deposit your chewing gum into the wastebasket.* □ *You should deposit your money in the bank.*

deprive someone **of** something to take something away from someone. □ *If you don't behave, I will deprive you of your driving rights.* □ *They deprived themselves of a good time by pouting.*

deputize someone **as** something to assign someone the temporary power to act in some official capacity. □ *The sheriff deputized Chuck as an aid during the uprising.* □ *Chuck was deputized as an officer of the law.*

derive from something to come from something; to evolve from something. (Usually in reference to a word and its etymological history.) □ *This word derives from an ancient Celtic word.* □ *What does the English word skirt derive from?*

derive something **from** someone or something to draw or abstract something from someone or something. □ *She derives a lot of spiritual support from her religion.* □ *She derives her patience from her mother.*

derive something **from** something to show how something is descended from something else. □ *Is it possible to derive this word from Greek?* □ *Is this word derived from Latin?*

descend from someone or some group [for a living creature] to come from a particular set of ancestors. □ *I descend from a large family of Dutch traders.* □ *Wally is descended from Daniel Boone.*

descend from something to move down from something. □ *The bird descended from the top of the tree to a lower branch.* □ *Take care when you descend from the ladder.*

descend into something to go down into something. □ *The butler descended into the cellar for another bottle of wine.* □ *Fred descended into the canyon on an organized tour.*

descend to something **1.** *Lit.* to go down to something. □ *I must descend to the lower level to greet the guests.* □ *Gerald descended to the front door to see who was there.* **2.** *Fig.* to condescend to do something; to stoop to doing something; to lower oneself to do something bad. □ *I refuse to descend to the performance of such menial duties.* □ *I will not descend to a life of crime.*

descend (up)on someone or something **1.** *Lit.* [for something] to come down or fall upon someone or something. □ *Flakes of fluffy snow descended upon the gentle slopes.* **2.** *Fig.* [for people] to arrive or come to someone or something in great numbers. □ *The petitioners descended upon the mayor's office in droves.*

describe someone or something **as** something to describe or portray a person or a thing as something or as being in some particular state. □ *Would you describe her as a woman of average height?* □ *We described the building as a collection of contemporary architectural clichés.*

describe someone or something **to** someone to characterize or portray a particular person or thing to someone. □ *Will you describe her to me, please?* □ *Please describe yourself to me so I will know you.*

desensitize someone **to** something to make someone less sensitive to something. □ *The doctor wanted to desensitize the allergic child to pollen.* □ *I took injections to desensitize me to house dust.*

desert a sinking ship and **leave a sinking ship** *Fig.* to leave a place, a person, or a situation when things become difficult or unpleasant. (Rats are said to be the first to leave a ship that is sinking.) □ *I hate to be the one to desert a sinking ship, but I can't work for a company that continues to lose money.* □ *There goes Tom. Wouldn't you know he'd leave a sinking ship rather than stay around and try to help?*

Desert and reward seldom keep company. *Prov.* If you deserve a reward, you are not necessarily going to get it. □ *Jill: I worked so hard on that project, and Fred is taking all the credit for it. Jane: You know how it goes; desert and reward seldom keep company.*

desert someone or something **for** someone or something else to leave someone for someone else; to leave something or some place for some other thing or place. □ *She deserted her husband for another man.* □ *Many retirees have deserted northern states for the warmer climates of the South.*

desert someone or something **to** someone or something to abandon someone or something to someone or something; to let someone or something have someone or something. □ *Who deserted this child to her horrible fate?* □ *Sam deserted his land to the horde of grubby prospectors.*

deserve better from someone or something to merit better treatment from someone. □ *We deserve better from someone who is supposed to be our friend.* □ *I deserve better from Bill.*

deserve credit for something [for someone] to be owed recognition for doing something. □ *He certainly deserves credit for the work he did on the project.*

design something **for** someone to conceive of something for someone; to draw up plans of something for someone. □ *Ann designed a new kitchen for us.* □ *Would you design a book cover for me?*

design something **for** something to conceive of something that is to be part of something else; to draw up plans for something that is to be part of something else. □ *The engineers designed a cure for the rattling problem.* □ *Bob, the computer programmer, designed a fix for the bug in the program.* □ *She designed a system of shelving for the library.*

designate someone or something **as** something to choose or name someone or something as something. □ *Alice will designate Andrew as our representative.* □ *She designated herself as the head of the committee.*

Desires are nourished by delays. *Prov.* The longer you have to wait for something you want, the more eager you will be to get it. □ *The longer I had to postpone my trip to San Francisco, the more eagerly I wanted to go. Desires are nourished by delays.*

desist from something to stop doing something. □ *You must desist from further attempts to contact your wife.* □ *I wish you would desist from calling me Willie.*

despair of something to give up all hope of something. □ *Do not despair of his returning; I think we will see him again.* □ *I despair of ever seeing her again.*

Desperate diseases must have desperate remedies. *Prov.* If you have a seemingly insurmountable problem, you must do things you ordinarily would not do in order to solve it. □ *Fred: All my employees have been surly and morose for months. How can I improve their morale? Alan: Why not give everyone a raise? Fred: That's a pretty extreme suggestion. Alan: Yes, but desperate diseases must have desperate remedies.*

despise someone **for** something to hate someone for something or for doing something. □ *I just despise him for running away!* □ *She despised herself for her dishonest actions.*

despoil something **of** something to make something, such as a town, tomb, or building, lose value by stealing from it; to rob something of something. □ *The vandals despoiled the castle of much of its furnishings.* □ *The land was despoiled of its fertility by overplanting.*

destine someone **for** something to determine that someone should receive or achieve something in the future. □ *Her many talents destined her for a distinguished career.* □ *Larry's intelligence destined him for big things.*

destined for something predetermined to achieve or become something. □ *I know I am destined for a job that is better than this.* □ *We are destined for death in the long run.*

detach someone or something **from** someone or something to separate or disconnect someone or something from someone or something. □ *The high command detached Wallace from his platoon.* □ *The technician detached the sensors from Harry's chest.*

detail someone **for** something to choose someone to do a particular task. (Originally military.) □ *Sam detailed Private Bailey for guard duty.* □ *Donna was detailed for some extra work.*

detail someone **to** someone or something to assign someone to someone or a group. (Military.) □ *I will detail Private Bailey to that job.* □ *The general detailed a lieutenant to the platoon that was going to the front.*

detect something **in** something to recognize or identify something in something. □ *Can you detect the anger in her voice?* □ *I detect a bit of sarcasm in your comments.*

·**deter** someone or something **from** something to prevent or discourage someone or a group from doing something. □ *We can't seem to deter them from leaving.* □ *They were not deterred from their foolish ways.*

determine the root of the problem Go to the root of the problem.

detract from someone or something to lessen or diminish someone or something. □ *The large pieces of furniture detracted from the lovely design in the carpet.* □ *Alice's quiet demeanor did not detract from her grace and beauty.*

develop from someone or something **(into** someone or something**)** and **develop (from** someone or something**) into** someone or something to grow or evolve out of someone or something into someone or something else. □ *Her interest in music developed from a childlike curiosity to a full-fledged professional career.* □ *The flower developed from a little knot of a bulb.*

deviate from something to wander away from something, such as a path, road, etc.; to vary from the normal procedure. □ *Please do not deviate from the path. You will crush the wildflowers.* □ *I will not deviate one inch from the route you have prescribed.* □ *They did not deviate from her instructions.*

*the **devil** *Fig.* a severe scolding. (*Typically: **get** ~; **catch** ~; **give** someone ~.) □ *Bill is always getting the devil about something.* □ *I'm late. If I don't get home soon, I'll catch the devil!*

The **devil can cite Scripture for his own purpose.** Go to next.

The **devil can quote Scripture for his own purpose.** and The **devil can cite Scripture for his own purpose.** *Prov.* Evil people sometimes try to win the confidence of good people by quoting persuasive passages of Scripture.; Just because someone can quote Scripture to support his or her argument does not mean that the argument is virtuous. (*Scripture* usually refers to the Bible, but it can refer to other religious writings.) □ *Sadie: Dad, you really ought to give me permission to go out with Nathan. He's such a polite boy, and he can even quote the Bible. Father: The devil can quote Scripture for his own purpose.*

The **devil finds work for idle hands to do.** *Prov.* If you do not have useful work to do, you will be tempted to do frivolous or harmful things to get rid of your boredom. □ *Knowing that the devil finds work for idle hands to do, Elizabeth always made sure that her children had plenty of chores to keep them occupied.*

The **devil is not so black as he is painted.** *Prov.* No one is as bad as people say he is. (Implies that people are saying too many bad things about someone.) □ *I can't believe that actress is as coldhearted as the gossip columns say she is. The devil is not so black as he is painted.*

The **devil looks after his own.** *Prov.* Evil people are often prosperous or well taken care of. (Implies that they must be getting their prosperity from the devil, since they are not earning it by being good and deserving.) □ *Jane: I don't understand why the corner store is still in business. They cheat everybody! Alan: Well, the devil looks after his own.*

a **devil of a job** and the **devil's own job** the most difficult task. □ *We had a devil of a job fixing the car.* □ *It was the devil's own job finding a hotel with vacancies.*

a **devil of a time** and the **devil's own time** a very difficult time. □ *I had a devil of a time with my taxes.* □ *This cold has been giving me a devil of a time.* □ *Fixing the car seemed easy, but I had the devil's own time doing it.*

The **devil's children have the devil's luck.** *Prov.* Evil people often seem to have good luck. □ *The police thought they had trapped the murderer, but he escaped. The devil's children have the devil's luck.*

the **devil's own job** Go to a devil of a job.

the **devil's own time** Go to a devil of a time.

devil someone or an animal **for** something *Fig.* to bother or harass someone or an animal for something. □ *The child kept deviling her mother for an ice-cream cone.* □ *The kittens continued to devil the mother cat for their dinner.*

Devil take the hindmost. Go to Every man for himself (and the devil take the hindmost).

devil-may-care attitude and **devil-may-care manner** a very casual attitude; a worry-free or carefree attitude. □ *You must get rid of your devil-may-care attitude if you want to succeed.* □ *She acts so thoughtless—with her devil-may-care manner.*

devil-may-care manner Go to previous.

devolve (up)on someone or something [for something, such as a task] to be passed on to someone or a group. (*Upon* is formal and less commonly used than *on*.) □ *This job, I am afraid, devolves upon you and you alone.* □ *The task of repairing the damage devolved on Diane.*

devote oneself **to** someone or something to dedicate or give oneself over to someone or something. □ *Do you agree to devote yourself to this task?* □ *She devoted herself to raising her children.*

devote someone or something **to** someone or something to dedicate someone or something to the use or benefit of someone or something. □ *I will devote a few of my people to your project.* □ *Sarah devoted all of her time to Roger.*

dial the wrong number Go to the wrong number.

dialogue with someone to talk with someone. □ *I look forward to dialoguing with you tomorrow.* □ *The supervisor sets aside time to dialogue with each and every person in the department once a week.*

a **diamond in the rough** *Fig.* a person who has good qualities despite a rough exterior; a person with great potential. □ *Sam looks a little scruffy, but he's a diamond in the rough.* □ *He's a diamond in the rough—a little hard to take at times, but very smart and helpful.*

diarrhea of the jawbone Go to next.

diarrhea of the mouth and **diarrhea of the jawbone** *Fig.* constant talking; a "disorder" involving constant talking. □ *Wow, does he ever have diarrhea of the mouth!* □ *You're getting diarrhea of the jawbone again.*

dibs on something a claim on something. (See also have dibs on something; put one's dibs on something.) □ *I've got dibs on the yellow one!* □ *Dibs on the front seat!*

dicker with someone **(for** something**)** and **dicker with** someone **(over** something**)** to bargain with someone for something; to haggle with someone for something. □ *I don't want to stand here dickering with you for a cheap trinket.* □ *I don't want to waste time dickering with them over a few dollars.*

dictate (something**) to** someone **1.** to speak out words to someone who writes them down; to speak words into a recording device to be written down later by someone. □ *Walter dictated a letter to his secretary.* □ *Please come in so I can dictate to you.* **2.** to lay out or spell out the exact terms of something to someone; to act as a dictator. □ *You can't dictate the rules to us.* □ *Please don't dictate to me.*

did everything he could 'cept eat us *Rur.* acted very hostilely. □ *When it came time to pass sentence on the criminal, the judge did everything he could 'cept eat him.*

did you hear? Go to have you heard?

diddle someone **out of** something to cheat someone into giving up something. □ *The boys diddled the old man out of a few bucks.* □ *He was diddled out of his last dime.*

diddle something **out of** someone *Sl.* to get something from someone by deception. □ *We diddled about forty bucks out of the old lady who runs the candy shop.* □ *They diddled Larry's last dime out of him.*

diddle with something to play with something; to toy with something. □ *Here, don't diddle with that watch.* □ *Stop diddling with your nose, Jimmy!*

didn't care a whit and **don't care a whit** didn't care at all. □ *Sally thought Joe liked her, but he didn't care a whit about her.* □ *I don't care a whit what you do with my old clothes.*

didn't care too hard *Rur.* didn't mind. □ *Dad said he didn't care too hard if I took the dog out with me.* □ *If you don't care too hard, I'll shut this window.*

didn't exchange more than three words with someone to say hardly anything to someone. (The number may vary.) □ *I know Tom was there, but I am sure that I didn't exchange more than three words with him before he left.* □ *We hardly exchanged more than two words the whole evening.* □ *Sally and Liz didn't have enough time to exchange more than five words.*

didn't invent gunpowder *Rur.* did not do anything terribly important. □ *He may be the class president, but he didn't invent gunpowder.* □ *What's all this fuss about a movie star? She didn't invent gunpowder!*

die a natural death 1. *Lit.* [for someone] to die by disease or old age rather than by violence or foul play. □ *I hope to live to 100 and die a natural death.* □ *The police say she didn't die a natural death, and they are investigating.* **2.** *Fig.* [for something] to fade away or die down. □ *I expect that all this excitement about the scandal will die a natural death.* □ *Most fads die a natural death.*

die away *Fig.* to fade away. □ *The sound of the waterfall finally died away.* □ *When the applause died away, the tenor sang an encore.*

die back [for vegetation] to die back to the stems or roots. □ *The hedge died back in the winter but regenerated leaves in the spring.* □ *This kind of grass dies back every year.*

die behind the wheel to die in an automobile accident in a car that one is driving. □ *Poor Fred died behind the wheel in a horrible collision.*

die by one's **own hand** *Euph.* to commit suicide. □ Jane: *I just heard that Bill died. I didn't know he was sick.* Dan: *He wasn't sick. He died by his own hand.* □ *She died at the age of fifty, by her own hand.*

die by something to perish by a particular cause or device. (Often refers to execution as a death sentence.) □ *He died by electrocution.* □ *She was condemned to die by hanging.*

die down to fade to almost nothing; to decrease gradually. □ *The fire died down and went out.* □ *As the applause died down, a child came on stage with an armload of roses for the singer.*

die for someone or something **1.** *Lit.* to perish for the benefit or glory of someone or something. □ *He said he was willing to die for his country.* □ *She would die for her child if necessary.* **2.** *Fig.* to experience great physical or emotional desire for someone or something. □ *He was just dying for Jane, but she would have nothing to do with him.* □ *Freddie was dying for a glass of water—he was so thirsty.*

die from curiosity Go to die of curiosity.

die from something Go to die of something.

die in one's **boots** and **die with** one's **boots on** *Fig.* to go down fighting; to die in some fashion other than in bed; to die fighting. (Popularized by western movies. Heroes and villains of these movies said they preferred death in a gunfight to showing cowardice or giving up.) ☐ *I won't let him get me. I'll die in my boots.*

die in something to perish in a particular calamity or accident. ☐ *They both died in an automobile accident.* ☐ *Wally did not want to die in the war.*

The **die is cast.** *Prov.* A process is past the point of no return. (The *die* is one of a pair of dice. The *cast* means thrown. This phrase [in Latin] was said by Julius Caesar when he crossed the Rubicon with his legions, starting a civil war.) ☐ *After that speech favoring reform of the education system, the die is cast. This is now a campaign issue.* ☐ *The die is cast. There is no turning back on this point.*

die laughing 1. *Lit.* to meet one's death laughing—in good spirits, revenge, or irony. ☐ *Sally is such an optimist that she'll probably die laughing.* ☐ *Bob tried to poison his rich aunt, who then died laughing because she had taken Bob out of her will.* **2.** *Fig.* to laugh very long and hard. ☐ *The joke was so funny that I almost died laughing.* ☐ *The play was meant to be funny, but the audience didn't exactly die laughing.*

die of a broken heart *Fig.* to die of emotional distress. ☐ *I was not surprised to hear of her death. They say she died of a broken heart.* ☐ *In the movie, the heroine appeared to die of a broken heart, but the audience knew she was poisoned.*

die of boredom *Fig.* to be very bored. ☐ *No one has ever really died of boredom.* ☐ *We sat there and listened politely, even though we almost died of boredom.*

die of curiosity and **die from curiosity** *Fig.* to experience a strongly felt need to know about something. ☐ *I was just dying of curiosity!* ☐ *I almost died from curiosity to finish the book and see how the mystery was solved.*

die of something and **die from** something to perish from an injury or a particular disease. ☐ *The doctors did all they could, but he finally died of cancer.* ☐ *What did it die from?*

die of throat trouble *Sl.* to be hanged. (Old.) ☐ *He died of throat trouble after the posse caught up with him.* ☐ *The cattle rustler died of throat trouble.*

die off [for a living thing] to perish one by one until there are no more. ☐ *Most of the larger lizards died off eons ago.* ☐ *It would be really bad if all the owls died off.* ☐ *The cucumber blossoms all died off.*

die on someone **1.** *Lit.* [for a patient] to die under the care of someone. ☐ *Get that medicine over here fast, or this guy's gonna die on me.* ☐ *Come on, mister, don't die on me!* **2.** *Fig.* [for something] to quit running for someone. ☐ *My car died on me, and I couldn't get it started.* ☐ *My CD player died on me, and I had to listen to the radio.*

die on the vine Go to wither on the vine.

die out 1. *Lit.* [for a species or family] to perish totally because of the failure to produce offspring. ☐ *I am the last one in the family, so I guess our line will die out with me.* ☐ *The owls might die out if you ruin their nesting area.* **2.** *Fig.* [for an idea, practice, style, etc.] to fade away through time. ☐ *That way of doing things died out a long time ago.* ☐ *It died out like the horse and buggy.*

die with one's **boots on** Go to die in one's boots.

differ from something [for something] to be different from something else. ☐ *No, this one differs from the one you saw*

because it has a bigger handle. ☐ *How does this one differ from that one?*

differ in something [for people or things] to be different in a specific way or in specific ways. ☐ *They differ only in the color of their eyes and the size of their shoes.* ☐ *They differ in size and shape.*

differ (with someone**) about** something and **differ (with** someone**) on** something **1.** [for someone] to disagree with someone about something. ☐ *I must differ with you about that.* ☐ *We differ about that.* ☐ *I don't differ with you on that point.* **2.** [for someone] to argue with someone about something. ☐ *Tom was differing with Terry rather loudly about which one of them was going to carry the flag.* ☐ *Let's stop differing with each other on these simple things!*

***different as night and day** *Cliché* completely different. (*Also: **as** ~.) ☐ *Although Bobby and Billy are twins, they are as different as night and day.* ☐ *Birds and bats appear to be similar, but they are different as night and day.*

Different strokes for different folks. *Prov.* Different people like different things.; Different people live in different ways. ☐ *My neighbor spends all his free time working in his garden. I would never want to do that, but different strokes for different folks.*

differentiate between someone or something **and** someone or something else **1.** to recognize the difference between people or things in any combination. (Usually refers to two entities.) ☐ *In your painting, I cannot differentiate between the costume of the figure in front and the flowers in the background.* ☐ *Can't you differentiate between Billy and his brother?* ☐ *I can't differentiate between a donkey and a burro.* **2.** to establish or create the difference between people or things. ☐ *Why don't you paint in some highlights to differentiate between the figure in the foreground and the flowers in the background?*

differentiate someone or something **from** someone or something else **1.** to recognize the difference between people and things; to tell the difference between people and things. ☐ *How do you differentiate this one from that one?* ☐ *Can you differentiate Bill from Bob?* **2.** to make people and things different. ☐ *I will differentiate this one from that one by painting this one red.* ☐ *The twins' mother used different-colored clothing to differentiate Bill from Bob.*

The **difficult is done at once; the impossible takes a little longer.** *Prov.* Tasks that are only difficult are done immediately, harder tasks take longer. (Describes a very competent group or person.) ☐ *The secretary in our office is extremely capable. She has a little sign on her desk that says, "The difficult is done at once; the impossible takes a little longer." In her case, it's not a joke.*

difficult times Go to bad times.

diffuse something **through** something else to distribute or scatter something through something else. ☐ *The chemical process diffused the purple color through the liquid.* ☐ *Let us try to diffuse the medication through the bloodstream as rapidly as possible.*

diffuse through something to spread or scatter through something. ☐ *The smell diffused through the office through the ventilating system.* ☐ *The dye diffused through the water rapidly.*

dig at someone or something **1.** *Lit.* to poke or jab at someone or something. □ *Don't dig at me all the time. My side is getting sore where you jabbed me.* □ *Stop digging at the wall! Look at the hole you've made!* **2.** *Fig.* to make a cutting remark about someone or something. □ *She is always digging at her husband's laziness.* □ *Fred was digging at the company he works for.*

dig deep Go to next.

dig down and **dig deep 1.** *Lit.* to excavate deeply. □ *They are really having to dig deep to reach bedrock.* □ *We are not to the buried cable yet. We will dig down some more.* **2.** *Fig.* to be generous; to dig deep into one's pockets and come up with as much money as possible to donate to something. (As if digging into one's pocket.) □ *Please dig down. We need every penny you can spare.* □ *Dig down deep. Give all you can.*

dig for something **1.** *Lit.* to excavate to find something that is buried. □ *They are digging along the river bank for a special kind of clay.* □ *I want to dig for gold in Alaska.* **2.** *Fig.* to go to great pains to uncover information of some kind. □ *The police were digging for some important information while they questioned Mike "Fingers" Moran.* □ *There is no point in digging further for the name of the inventor. I have it right here.*

dig in(to something**) 1.** *Lit.* to use a shovel to penetrate a mass of something. □ *He dug into the soft soil and made a hole for the roots of the bush.* □ *He grabbed a shovel and dug in where he thought the tree ought to go.* **2.** *Fig.* to begin to process something; to go to work on something. □ *I have to dig into all these applications today and process at least half of them.* □ *Jed got out the stack of unanswered mail and dug in.* **3.** *Fig.* to begin to eat food. □ *We dug into the huge pile of fried chicken.* □ *I stuck the corner of my napkin in my collar and dug in.*

dig one's **heels in**† *Fig.* to refuse to alter one's course of action or opinions; to be obstinate or determined. □ *The student dug her heels in and refused to obey the instructions.* □ *I'm digging in my heels. I'm not going back.*

dig one's **own grave** *Fig.* to be responsible for one's own downfall or ruin. □ *If you try to cheat the bank, you will be digging your own grave.* □ *Those politicians have dug their own grave with their new tax bill. They won't be reelected.*

dig out (of something**)** to channel or excavate one's way out of something. □ *The miner had to dig out of the cave-in.* □ *They were too exhausted to dig out.*

dig some dirt up† **(on** someone**)** *Fig.* to find out something bad about someone. □ *If you don't stop trying to dig some dirt up on me, I'll get a lawyer and sue you.* □ *The citizens' group dug up some dirt on the mayor and used it against her at election time.*

dig someone or something **in** something to poke someone or something in something, such as the ribs, the side, the cheek, etc. □ *He dug Wally in the ribs as he finished telling the joke.* □ *Jed dug the cow in its side with a stick, trying to make it move into the barn.*

dig someone or something **out of** something and **dig** someone or something **out**† to excavate in order to get someone or something out of something; to dig about in order to get someone or something out of something. □ *She dug out the roots of the tree.* □ *The dog dug itself out of the rubble of the fallen building.*

dig someone or something **up**† *Fig.* to go to great effort to find someone or something. (There is an implication that the thing or person dug up is not the most desirable, but is all that could be found.) □ *Mary dug a date up for the dance next Friday.* □ *I dug up a recipe for roast pork with pineapple.* □ *I dug up a carpenter who doesn't charge very much.*

dig something **into** something and **dig** something **in**† to stab or jab something into something. □ *Dig your fork into that heavenly cake!* □ *He dug in his fork.*

dig something **out**† *Fig.* to work hard to locate something and bring it forth. □ *They dug the contract out of the file cabinet.* □ *I dug out an old dress and wore it to the Fifties party.*

Dig up! *Sl.* Listen carefully! □ *John: All right, you guys! Dig up! You're going to hear this one time and one time only!* □ *Bill: Dig up! I'm only going to say this once. Bob: What was that? Bill: I said listen!*

dig up one's **tomahawk** *Rur.* to get angry. (A jocular reversal of *bury the tomahawk.* Fixed order.) □ *When Joe saw the mess we made, he dug up his tomahawk and went looking for us.*

digress from something [for a speaker or writer] to stray from the subject. □ *I am going to digress from my prepared text.* □ *You will pardon me if I digress from my point a little.*

dilate on something *Fig.* to speak or write in great detail on some subject. □ *I am sure you do not wish me to dilate further on this matter.* □ *If you do not see my point, I would be pleased to dilate on this matter further.*

Diligence is the mother of good luck. *Prov.* If you work carefully and constantly, you will be far more likely to be successful, as if luck had come your way. □ *Mimi: I'll never get work as an actress; I always have such bad luck at auditions. Jane: Keep working at it. Diligence is the mother of good luck.*

dilly-dally (around) with someone or something to waste time frivolously with someone or something. □ *Stop dilly-dallying around with your friends.* □ *He is always dilly-dallying around with his work.*

dim down [for the lights] to go dim. □ *The lights dimmed down for a few seconds.* □ *Open the stage curtain when the house lights dim down.*

dim out [for a light] to grow dim and go out altogether. □ *The lights dimmed out twice during the storm.* □ *I was afraid that the lights would dim out completely.*

dim something **down**† to make lights dim; to use a dimmer to make the lights dimmer. □ *Why don't you dim the lights down and put on some music?* □ *Let me dim down the lights and put on some music.*

dim something **up**† to use a dimmer to make the lights brighter. (Theatrical. A dimmer is a rheostat, variable transformer, or something similar. The expression, a seeming contradiction, is the opposite of **dim** something **down.**) □ *As the curtain rose, the electrician dimmed the lights up on a beautiful scene.* □ *You dimmed up the lights too fast.*

a **dime a dozen** *Fig.* abundant; cheap and common. □ *People who can write good books are not a dime a dozen.* □ *Romantic movies are a dime a dozen.*

din something **into** someone and **din** something **in**† to repeat something over and over to someone. (As if one could "hammer" words into someone.) □ *The teacher dinned it into her constantly, but it did no good.* □ *He dinned in the same message over and over.*

dine at some place to eat at a place. □ *We really like to dine at the small cafe on the corner.* □ *I hope we can dine at a fine restaurant for our anniversary.*

dine in to eat at home rather than at a restaurant. □ *I think we will dine in tonight.* □ *I am tired of dining in. Let's go out.*

dine off something to make a meal of something; to make many meals of something. □ *Do you think we can dine off the leg of lamb for more than one meal?* □ *I hope we dine off the turkey only one more time.*

dine on something to eat something. □ *We are dining on roast beef tonight.* □ *What will we be dining on tonight?*

dine out Go to eat (a meal) out.

dinged out *Sl.* intoxicated. □ *Gary is dinged out and can't drive.*

dink someone **off**† *Sl.* to make someone angry. □ *Whatever you do, don't dink her off!* □ *Why did you have to start out your speech by dinking off the entire audience?*

Dinner is served. It is time to eat dinner. Please come to the table. (As if announced by a butler; often jocular.) □ *Sue: Dinner is served. Mary (aside): Aren't we fancy tonight?* □ *"Dinner is served," said Bob, rather formally for a barbecue.*

dip into one's **savings** *Fig.* to take out part of the money one has been saving. (See also **dip in(to** something).) □ *I had to dip into my savings in order to pay for my vacation.* □ *I went to the bank and dipped into savings. There wasn't much left.*

dip in(to something) **1.** to reach into a liquid. □ *I dipped into the dishwater, looking for the missing spoon.* □ *I dipped in and there it was.* **2.** to reach into a substance, usually to remove some of the substance. □ *I dipped into the sour cream with a potato chip and brought out an enormous glob.* □ *He grabbed the jar of peanut butter and dipped in.* **3.** [for something] to sink or lower into a liquid. □ *The oars dipped into the water and came out again.* □ *The lower branches sagged down to the water and dipped in.*

dip something **in(to)** something and **dip** something **in**† to put something into a substance in order to take some of it. □ *Tom dipped some of the bread into the cheese sauce.* □ *Dip in the bread again and get some more cheese on it.*

dip to something to decline to a lower level quickly or briefly. □ *The temperature dipped into the lower twenties overnight.* □ *The stock market dipped to a very low level during the day Friday.*

direct someone's **attention to** someone or something to focus someone's regard or concern on someone or something; to cause someone to notice someone or something. □ *May I direct your attention to the young man in the purple costume?* □ *The announcer directed our attention to the magician who was coming on stage.*

direct something **against** someone or something to aim a critical remark or a weapon at someone or something. (Very close to **direct** something **at** someone or something.) □ *We directed the guns against the occupied village.* □ *Ted said he had directed his remark against Judy.*

direct something **at** someone or something to aim something at someone or something. (Very close to **direct** something **against** someone or something.) □ *Are you directing your remarks at me?* □ *Please direct the hose at the bushes.*

direct something **to** someone to address, designate, or send something to someone. □ *Shall I direct the inquiries to you?* □ *Please direct all the mail to the secretary when it is delivered.*

direct something **to(ward)** someone or something to send, throw, push, or aim something at someone or something. □ *Tom directed the ball toward Harry.* □ *Should I direct this inquiry to Alice?*

dirt cheap extremely cheap. □ *Buy some more of those plums. They're dirt cheap.* □ *In Italy, the peaches are dirt cheap.*

dirty crack a rude remark. □ *Who made that dirty crack?* □ *Another dirty crack like that and I'll leave.*

dirty deal an unfair deal. □ *That was a dirty deal. I feel cheated.* □ *I got a dirty deal at that shop, and I won't go back.*

dirty dog a low and sneaky person. □ *That dirty dog tried to cheat in the card game!*

***a dirty look** *Fig.* an angry face or a frown. (*Typically: **get** ~; **give** someone ~.) □ *Anne gave me a dirty look.* □ *I got a dirty look from the teacher when I cracked a joke in class.*

dirty old man a lecherous old man. (Usually jocular.) □ *Jimmy, what you call flirting will make some girls call you a dirty old man!* □ *What a terrible joke. You are a dirty old man!*

dirty one's **hands** Go to get one's hands dirty.

dirty something **up**† *Rur.* to get something dirty. □ *Those pants are brand-new! Don't dirty them up!* □ *Don't dirty up your brand-new pants!*

a **dirty word 1.** a swearword; an obscene or blasphemous word; a four-letter word. □ *You are not allowed to use dirty words in your school essays.* □ *My aunt is offended by the use of dirty words.* **2.** something that is disliked or disapproved of. □ *Since Tom broke off his engagement, his name is a dirty word in the village.* □ *Socialism is a dirty word in that house.*

dirty work 1. *Fig.* unpleasant or uninteresting work. □ *My boss does all the traveling. I get all the dirty work to do.* □ *She's tired of doing all the dirty work at the office.* **2.** *Fig.* dishonest or underhanded actions; treachery. □ *She knew there was some dirty work going on when she saw her opponents whispering together.* □ *The company seems respectable enough, but there's a lot of dirty work that goes on.*

disabuse someone **of** something to rid someone of an incorrect idea. □ *Please allow me to disabuse you of that assumption.* □ *Please disabuse yourself of the notion that you are perfect.*

disagree with someone [for food or drink] to upset someone's stomach. □ *Milk always disagrees with me.* □ *Onions disagree with my husband, so he never eats them.*

disagree (with someone) **(about** someone or something) and **disagree (with** someone) **(on** someone or something) to hold views about someone or something that are opposed to someone else's views. □ *I take it you disagree with me about Tom.* □ *Don't disagree about Tom with me.* □ *I disagree about this with almost everyone.* □ *I disagree with you.*

disappear from something to vanish from something or some place, especially from *sight*, *view*, or *the face of the earth*; to have been taken away from something. □ *Jack disappeared all of a sudden last week, as if from the face of the earth.* □ *The car pulled away and disappeared from sight down the road.*

disappoint someone **with** someone or something to displease someone with someone or something. □ *I hope I haven't disappointed you with the modest size of the donation.* □ *I disappointed myself with my performance.*

disappointed at someone or something and **disappointed in** someone or something becoming sad because of someone or something. □ *I am really disappointed at what you did.* □ *I am very disappointed in you. That was a terrible thing to do.* □ *They were disappointed in the outcome.*

disappointed in someone or something Go to previous.

disapprove of someone or something to object to someone or something. □ *I disapprove of her choice for maid of honor.* □ *Do you disapprove of me?*

a **disaster of epic proportions** *Cliché* a very large disaster. (Often jocular.) □ *The earthquake was responsible for a disaster of epic proportions.* □ *Your late arrival caused a disaster of epic proportions.*

disbar someone **from** something to take the right to practice law away from a lawyer. □ *The state board disbarred Todd from practicing law in his own state.* □ *Sally was also disbarred from practicing law.*

discern between someone or something **and** someone or something to detect the difference between people and things. □ *I cannot discern between the dark trees and the dark sky behind them.* □ *I cannot discern between the person and the background.*

discern someone or something **from** something else to detect the difference between someone or something and something else. □ *I can hardly discern Tom from the busy background in this picture.* □ *I can't discern anything from that cluttered scene.*

discern something **from** someone or something to learn or determine something from someone or something. □ *We discerned a lot from the eyewitnesses.* □ *We discerned a lot from our discussions with the past president.*

discharge someone **from** something **1.** to fire someone from a job. □ *The manager discharged Walter from his position with the bank.* □ *Walter was discharged from his job.* **2.** to permit a person to leave a place, such as a hospital or the armed service. □ *They discharged her from the hospital today.* □ *She was well enough to be discharged from the hospital.*

discharge something **from** something to fire a round from a gun. □ *I discharged two bullets from the gun accidentally.* □ *Randy discharged about twenty rounds from his automatic rifle.*

discharge something **into** something to let something out of something into something else. □ *She discharged some nitrogen from the tank into the laboratory by accident.* □ *The technician discharged oxygen into the atmosphere.*

discipline someone **for** something to punish or chastise someone for doing something. □ *I will have to discipline you for fighting.* □ *Mary was disciplined for taking part in the fiasco.*

disclose something **to** someone to tell or reveal something to someone. □ *Tony refused to disclose the location of the papers to me.* □ *Please disclose the names to me at once.*

disconnect someone or something **from** someone or something to break the connection between things or people. □ *The telephone operator disconnected Larry from his caller.* □ *He disconnected himself from the cords of his parachute.*

discourage someone **from** something to dissuade someone from doing something. □ *I hope I can discourage Tom from leaving.* □ *I do not want to discourage you from further experimentation.*

discourse (up)on someone or something to lecture about someone or something. (*Upon* is formal and less commonly used than *on*.) □ *I would like to discourse upon this matter awhile.* □ *The committee chose to discourse on Tom and his latest fiasco rather than deal with the budgetary problems it faces.*

Discretion is the better part of valor. *Prov.* It is good to be brave, but it is also good to be careful.; If you are careful, you will not get into situations that require you to be brave. □ *Son: Can I go hang gliding with my friends? Father: No. Son: But they'll say I'm chicken if I don't go! Father: Discretion is the better part of valor, and I'd rather have them call you chicken than risk your life.*

discriminate against someone or something to single out a type of person or thing for special negative treatment or denial of equal treatment; to act in a prejudicial manner against someone or something. □ *This law discriminates against short people.* □ *You discriminate against people in wheelchairs.*

discriminate between someone **and** someone else or something **and** something else to distinguish between people or between things. □ *I find it hard these days to discriminate between my friends and my enemies.* □ *Can you discriminate between this shade of pink and that one?*

discuss someone or something **with** someone to talk about someone or something with someone. □ *I need to discuss Mickey with you.* □ *We need to discuss compensation with the boss.*

the **disease to please** an obsessive need to please people. □ *I, like so many, am afflicted with the disease to please. I am just too nice for my own good.*

disembark from something to get off a ship, plane, or train. □ *We disembark from the ship in Manaus.* □ *At what time do we expect to disembark from the plane?*

disengage (oneself) from someone or something to detach oneself from someone or something; to untangle oneself from someone or something. □ *I wanted to disengage* myself from the person I was talking to and go home. □ We disengaged from the argument.

disengage something **from** something to detach something from something. □ Sally disengaged the locking mechanism from the cupboard door and peeked in. □ The coupling was disengaged from the boxcar, and the car separated and rolled away.

disentangle someone or something **from** someone or something to untangle someone or something from someone or something. □ I helped disentangle Tony from the coils of ropes he had stumbled into. □ They worked feverishly to disentangle the dolphin from the net. □ He disentangled himself from the net.

disguise someone **in** something to conceal someone's identity in a costume or makeup. □ We disguised her in men's clothing and got her across the border. □ She disguised herself in a clown suit.

disguise someone or something **as** someone or something to dress or make someone up to appear to be someone or something. □ We disguised the child as a witch. □ We disguised Gerald as a pumpkin.

***disgusted at** someone or something severely disappointed at someone or something. (*Typically: **be** ~; **get** ~; **grow** ~.) □ We were disgusted at her incessant lying. □ Sam was disgusted at her.

***disgusted with** someone or something severely disappointed over someone or something. (*Typically: **be** ~; **get** ~; **grow** ~.) □ I am totally disgusted with Ellen. □ We are all disgusted with the fall in the company's profits.

dish on someone Sl. to gossip about or slander someone. □ Stop dishing on her. She never hurt you! □ They spent an hour dishing on Wally.

dish something **out†** 1. Lit. to serve up food to people. □ I'll dish it out, and you take it to the table. □ Careful how you dish out the mashed potatoes. There may not be enough. 2. Fig. to distribute information, news, etc. □ The press secretaries were dishing reports out as fast as they could write them. □ The company dishes out propaganda on a regular basis. 3. Fig. to give out trouble, scoldings, criticism, etc. □ The boss was dishing criticism out this morning, and I really got it. □ The teacher dished out a scolding to each one who was involved in the prank.

dish the dirt Sl. to spread gossip; to gossip. □ Let's sit down, have a drink, and dish the dirt. □ David goes down to the tavern to dish the dirt.

disinclined to do something unwilling to do something. □ I am disinclined to allow you to leave class early. □ They were disinclined to allow us to enter the country.

dislodge someone or something **from** someone or something to loosen and remove someone or something from someone or something. □ We were unable to dislodge her from office. □ Gene was able to dislodge the bone from his throat.

dismiss someone **(from** something) **(for** something) to discharge someone from employment for some reason; to fire someone from a job for some cause. □ We will have to dismiss him from employment for absenteeism. □ She was dismissed from the bank for making many errors in one month.

dismiss something **as** something to put something out of one's mind or ignore something as something. (The second something can be a noun or an adjective.) □ I dis-

missed the whole idea as foolishness. □ It was not possible to dismiss the whole matter as a one-time happening. □ Molly dismissed the whole event as accidental.

dismount from something to get down from something, such as a horse, bicycle, etc. □ She dismounted from her horse and fled into the house. □ Please dismount from the bicycle and wheel it into the shed.

dispatch someone **from** some place to send someone from some place. □ I dispatched a messenger from here over an hour ago. □ A telegram will be dispatched from my office first thing in the morning.

dispatch someone or something **to** someone or something to send someone or something to someone, something, or some place. □ I will dispatch a new copy of the damaged book to you immediately. □ Gene will dispatch a messenger to you.

dispense something **(to** someone) **(from** something) to distribute something to someone from something or some place. □ The nurse dispensed aspirin to everyone from a large bottle. □ The nurse dispensed aspirin from a large bottle to anyone who asked for it.

dispense with someone or something to get rid of someone or something; to brush someone or something aside. □ I think we will dispense with that subject for the rest of the day. □ We will have to dispense with the expensive gifts this year.

display something **to** someone to show something to someone. □ The peacock displayed his tail feathers to the other birds. □ Would you please display the artwork to the committee?

dispose of someone Sl. to kill someone. (See also **dispose of** someone or something.) □ Max suggested that he would dispose of Lefty if Lefty continued to be a pest. □ The boss ordered Max to dispose of Lefty.

dispose of someone or something to get rid of someone or something. (See also **dispose of** someone.) □ How can I dispose of this bothersome customer? □ Where shall I dispose of this wastepaper?

dispossess someone **of** something to separate someone from a possession. □ Do you intend to dispossess us of our home? □ They were dispossessed of the only possessions they had.

dispute something **with** someone to argue with someone about something, such as an amount of money. □ The customer disputed the amount of the check with the waiter. □ Please don't feel like you have to dispute every bill with the supplier.

disqualify someone or something **for** something and **disqualify** someone or something **from** something to invalidate someone's or something's claim to something. □ Does being late for practice disqualify me for the team? □ This loss disqualifies our team, doesn't it? □ Does it disqualify us from competition?

dis(s) (on) someone Sl. to belittle someone; to show disrespect for someone. (From either a nonstandard transitive verb disrespect or from dismiss [as insignificant]. Dis is also a slang transitive verb.) □ Gary is such a complainer. All he does is diss on people. □ Please stop dissing my little sister. She didn't do any of those things.

*dissatisfied with someone or something unhappy with someone or something. (*Typically: **be ~; grow ~.**) □ *We are quite dissatisfied with the service provided by the dealer.* □ *I am not dissatisfied with you.*

dissent from something to disagree with something. □ *We have chosen to dissent from the decision the rest of you made.* □ *Fred dissented from almost everything that everyone else agreed on.*

dissociate oneself **from** someone or something to break one's association or relationship with someone or something. □ *They decided to dissociate themselves from our organization.* □ *I was forced to dissociate myself from her.* □ *We advised her to dissociate herself from the gang.*

dissolve in something [for a substance] to break down in a liquid and disperse in the liquid. (Compare this with **dissolve into** something.) □ *Salt will dissolve in warm water.* □ *This material will not dissolve in oil.*

dissolve into something **1.** *Lit.* [for a substance to change from a solid state into another state; [for a substance] to melt or liquefy something. (Compare this with **dissolve in** something.) □ *In a hot pan, the sugar dissolved into syrup.* **2.** *Fig.* [for someone] to begin suddenly to display laughter, tears, giggles, gales of laughter, etc. (See also **dissolve in** something.) □ *The children dissolved into tears.* □ *The clown's appearance made the audience dissolve into laughter.* **3.** *Fig.* [for a film or television picture] to fade away into some other picture. □ *The scene dissolved into a shot of the interior of the castle.* □ *At this point in the script, dissolve to a face shot of Walter.*

dissolve something **in** something to cause a substance to break down in a liquid and disperse in the liquid. (See also **dissolve in** something.) □ *First, dissolve the salt in some warm water.* □ *Dissolve this medicine in water.*

dissolve something **into** something to cause a film or television picture to fade away into some other picture. (See also **dissolve into** something ③.) □ *The director dissolved the picture into the next scene.* □ *At this point, the opening scene should be dissolved into a side shot of the exterior.*

dissuade someone **from** something to discourage someone from (doing) something. □ *I hope to dissuade her from getting married until she graduates.* □ *I could not dissuade him from his plan.*

Distance lends enchantment (to the view). *Prov.* Things that are far away from you appear better than they really are. □ *Jill: High school was the happiest time of my life. Jane: But that was fifteen years ago. I think distance lends enchantment to the view.*

distance oneself **from** someone or something **1.** *Lit.* to separate oneself physically from someone or something. □ *She wanted to distance herself from the fighting in the corridor.* □ *I distanced myself from her from then on.* **2.** *Fig.* to "separate" oneself ideologically from someone or something. □ *She felt that he would want to distance himself from her radical politics.* □ *He had to distance himself from those policies if he wanted to be reelected.* □ *I will feel better when I can distance myself from that part of my life.*

distill something **from** something to derive product from something by heating and condensation. □ *They distilled the lighter components from the raw oil.* □ *The alcohol was distilled from fermented grain.*

distinguish between someone or something **and** someone or something else **1.** to perceive the difference between different people and things, in any combination. □ *Can't you distinguish between Tom and your real enemies?* □ *He can't distinguish between a good used car and that wreck over there!* **2.** to create or emphasize the difference between people and things, in any combination. □ *Try to distinguish between the figure in the foreground and the flowers in the background in your painting.* □ *I used red to distinguish between the new part and the old.*

distinguish oneself **among** someone to make oneself stand out from other people because of one's achievements. □ *I hope someday to distinguish myself among my peers.* □ *He distinguished himself among his classmates by his many talents.*

distinguish someone or something **from** someone or something else **1.** to tell the difference between different people and things, in any combination. □ *I cannot distinguish Billy from Bobby.* □ *She could not distinguish basil from oregano.* **2.** to delineate or emphasize the boundary between people and things, in any combination. □ *I cannot distinguish the blue scarf from the sky in the background.* □ *We could not distinguish the leaves of the bushes from the leaves of the trees as we moved farther away.*

distract someone **from** something to turn or divert someone's attention from something. □ *I hate to distract you from your work, but I have some important news.* □ *You haven't distracted me from anything.*

distribute something **(all) around** to give shares of something to people. □ *I distributed many gifts all around to everyone.* □ *We distributed the drinks around.*

distribute something **among** someone or something to give out shares of something to three or more people. □ *We must distribute the money among the various charities.* □ *The food was distributed among the people who showed up.*

distribute something **between** someone to give out shares of something to two people. □ *He distributed the remaining cake between Dave and Don.* □ *Please distribute the magazines between the two boys.*

distribute something **over** something to spread something over something or over an area. □ *Distribute the icing over the entire cake.* □ *Walter distributed the sand over the icy spots.*

distribute something **to** someone to give out something to someone. □ *Can you distribute this clothing to the needy people who live around here?* □ *I will distribute the ice cream to the party guests.*

dive in with both feet and **jump in with both feet** *Fig.* to become completely involved with something quickly, especially something new. □ *I had never done anything like this before, but I just jumped in with both feet and learned it in no time.*

dive in(to something**) 1.** *Lit.* to plunge into something; to jump into something headfirst. □ *Don't dive into that water! It's too shallow.* □ *David walked to the edge of the pool and dived in.* **2.** *Fig.* to start immediately on some business or activity with energy. □ *I can't wait to dive into the next project.* □ *Clara dives into her work eagerly every morning.*

dive off ((of) something**)** to jump off something headfirst. (*Of* is usually retained before pronouns.) □ *Rachel dived off of the rock into the river.* □ *She dived off the high diving board.*

diverge from something to move in a different direction from something. □ *Her line of thinking diverged from generally accepted thought on this point.* □ *The driveway diverges from the main road beyond the fence, straight ahead.*

diverge to something to turn to a particular direction. □ *A narrow road diverged to the left.* □ *A narrower channel diverged to the left of the island.*

divert someone or something **from** someone or something to turn someone or something aside or away from someone or something. □ *We could not divert his attention from his mother.* □ *I could not divert the woman from her interest in the book.*

divert someone or something **to** someone or something to channel or redirect someone or something to someone or something. □ *The farmers diverted the stream to a different channel.* □ *The guards diverted the museum visitors to the great hall.*

divert something **into** something 1. to channel something into something. □ *We will have to divert the runoff water into the culvert.* □ *Let's divert this stream into the ditch.* 2. *Euph.* to steal something and keep it some place. □ *He diverted the funds into a secret bank account.* □ *She diverted her clients' stock dividends into her own investment portfolio.*

divert something **onto** something to channel something onto the surface of something. □ *Temporarily, they diverted the southbound traffic onto the side streets.*

divest someone or something **of** something to take something away from someone or something. □ *The judge divested the company of its foreign holding.* □ *The court divested her of her stocks.*

divide and conquer to cause the enemy to divide and separate into two or more factions, and then move in to conquer all of them. □ *Mary thought she could divide and conquer the board of directors, but they had survived such tactics many times, and her efforts failed.* □ *Sam led his men to divide and conquer the enemy platoon, and his strategy succeeded.*

divide by something to perform mathematical division by a particular number. □ *Can you divide by sixteens?* □ *Add this figure to the next column and divide by twenty.*

divide someone **against** someone or something to cause people to separate into two groups, one of which opposes someone or something. □ *The issue divided the children against their parents.* □ *The argument divided the president against the board of directors.*

divide something **between** people or things to give shares of something to specific people or groups. (In a strict sense, only between two entities. Informally, between two or more.) □ *I will have to divide the toys between the two children.* □ *He divided the tasks between the day crew and the night crew.*

divide something **by** something to perform mathematical division on something, using a particular number. □ *Now, divide this sum by the figure in column seven.* □ *Can you divide 1,400 by 59?*

divide something **fifty-fifty** and **split** something **fifty-fifty** to divide something into two equal parts. (The *fifty* means 50 percent.) □ *Tommy and Billy divided the candy fifty-fifty.* □ *The robbers split the money fifty-fifty.*

divide something **into** something 1. and **divide** something **in** something to separate something into parts. □ *I will divide it into two parts.* □ *I will divide the cake in half.* □ *If you divide the pie in fourths, the pieces will be too big.* 2. to do mathematical division so that the divisor goes into the number that is to be divided. □ *Divide seven into forty-nine and what do you get?* □ *If seven is divided into forty-nine, what do you get?*

divide something **(off†) (from** something or animals**)** 1. to separate something from something else. □ *Let's divide the chickens off from the ducks and put the chickens in the shed.* □ *We divided off the chickens from the ducks.* 2. to separate something from something else, using a partition. □ *We divided the sleeping area off from the rest of the room.* □ *A curtain was used to divide off a sleeping area.*

divide something **(up†) (between** someone or something**)** and **divide** something **(up†) (among** someone or something**)** to give something out in shares to people or groups. (More informal with *up*. *Between* with two; *among* with more.) □ *Please divide this up between the visitors.* □ *Cut the birthday cake and divide it up among all the party guests.* □ *Please divide up this pie between the children.*

divide something **with** someone to share something with someone. □ *I will divide a piece of cake with you.* □ *They refused to divide the ice cream with us.*

divided between something separated into different categories. □ *The applicants for the job seemed to be divided between the overqualified and the underqualified.* □ *The dogs were divided evenly between terriers and poodles.*

divided on someone or something having differing opinions about someone or something. □ *Our opinions are divided on what is going to happen.* □ *We were divided on Ann. Some of us wanted to choose her; some did not.*

divorce oneself **from** something to separate oneself from something, such as an idea, policy, philosophy, etc. □ *She was not able to divorce herself from long-held prejudice.* □ *You should divorce yourself from those limiting ideas.*

divulge something **to** someone to reveal something to someone. □ *Promise that you will not divulge any of this to anyone.* □ *She refused to divulge their names to us.*

divvy something **up (between** someone**)** and **divvy** something **up (among** someone**); divvy** something **up†** to divide something up between two people or among three or more people. (*Between* is for two and *among* is for more than two.) □ *Would you like to divvy this money up?* □ *Please divvy up this money between you.* □ *Let's divvy up the leftovers among all the dinner guests.*

do a double take to react with surprise; to have to look twice to make sure that one really saw correctly. □ *When the boy led a goat into the park, everyone did a double take.* □ *When the nurse saw that the man had six toes, she did a double take.*

do a dump on someone or something Go to **dump on** someone or something.

do a fade *Sl.* to leave; to sneak away. □ *Richard did a fade when he saw heard the police siren.* □ *It's time for me to do a fade.*

do a flip-flop (on something**)** and **do an about-face** *Fig.* to make a total reversal of opinion. □ *Without warning, the government did a flip-flop on taxation.* □ *The candidate had done an about-face on the question of deductions last year.*

do a job on someone or something **1.** *Euph.* to defecate on someone or something. (Note the variation in the second example.) □ *The puppy did a job on the living-room carpet.* □ *It's supposed to do its job on the newspapers in the basement.* **2.** *Sl.* to damage someone or something; to mess up someone or something. □ *The robbers really did a job on the bank guard. They beat him when they robbed the bank.* □ *The puppy did a job on my shoes. They are all chewed to pieces.*

do a land-office business *Fig.* to do a large amount of buying or selling in a short period of time. □ *The ice-cream shop always does a land-office business on a hot day.* □ *The tax collector's office did a land-office business on the day that taxes were due.*

do a number on someone or something *Sl.* to damage or harm someone or something. □ *The teacher did a number on the whole class by giving them a pop quiz.* □ *Tom did a number on Mary when he went out with Ann.*

do a one-eighty and **turn one hundred and eighty degrees 1.** *Lit.* to turn around and go in the opposite direction. □ *When I hollered, the dog did a one-eighty and headed back to its own yard.* **2.** *Fig.* to radically reverse a decision or opinion. □ *His political philosophy turned one hundred and eighty degrees when he grew a little older.*

do a slow burn *Fig.* to be quietly angry. (See also **burn with a low blue flame**.) □ *I did a slow burn while I was waiting in line for a refund.*

do a snow job on someone *Sl.* to deceive or confuse someone. (As if to blind someone with snow.) □ *Don't try to do a snow job on me. I know all the tricks.* □ *She thought she did a snow job on the teacher, but it backfired.*

do a takeoff on someone or something to perform a parody on someone or something. □ *The comedian did a takeoff on the president, and everyone thought it was terribly funny.*

do a three-sixty and **turn three-hundred and sixty degrees 1.** *Lit.* to turn completely around. □ *I was really lost. I did a three-sixty in the middle of the street because I couldn't make up my mind which way to go.* **2.** *Fig.* to reverse a decision or an opinion and then return to one's original stance. □ *Over time, he did a three-sixty in his thinking about integration.*

do an about-face (on someone or something**)** Go to **do a flip-flop (on** something**).**

do an errand Go to **run an errand**.

Do as I say, not as I do. *Prov.* Take my advice, even though I am acting contrary to it. (Sometimes used as an apology for behaving hypocritically.) □ *Jill: Why are you walking on the grass when I told you not to? Jane: But you're walking on the grass. Jill: Do as I say, not as I do.*

do as something [for something] to serve as something; to be usable as something. □ *This spoon will do as a small shovel.* □ *This jacket will not do as formal wear.*

Do as you would be done by. Go to **Do unto others as you would have them do unto you.**

do away with oneself *Euph.* to commit suicide. (See also **do away with** someone or an animal; **do away with** something.) □ *The doctor was afraid that Betty would do away with herself.* □ *I wouldn't think of doing away with myself.*

do away with someone or an animal *Euph.* to kill someone or an animal. (See also **do away with** oneself; **do away with** something.) □ *The crooks did away with the witness.* □ *I was there, too. I hope they don't try to do away with me.*

do away with something to get rid of something. □ *This chemical will do away with the stain in your sink.* □ *The time has come to do away with that old building.*

do business with someone to trade or bargain with someone; to conduct commerce with someone. □ *You sound reasonable. I think I can do business with you.* □ *I am sure we can do business with one another.*

do credit to someone and **do** someone **credit** to add positively to the reputation of someone. □ *Your new job really does credit to you.* □ *Yes, it really does you credit.*

do dope Go to next.

do drugs and **do dope** to take illegal drugs; to use illegal drugs habitually. □ *Sam doesn't do drugs, and he doesn't drink.* □ *Richard started doing dope when he was very young.*

do for someone **1.** to provide for someone; to take care of or serve someone. □ *Do you expect me to stay home and do for you for the rest of my life?* □ *I can't do for all of them!* **2.** to suffice for someone; to be sufficient for someone. □ *Will this amount of sweet potatoes do for you?* □ *Yes, this will do for me fine.* **3.** See also **done for.**

do for something to serve as something; to substitute as something. □ *I think that this stone will do nicely for a doorstop.* □ *This stick will just not do for a stirring spoon.*

(Do) have some more. a polite invitation to take more of something, usually food or drink. □ *Bill: Wow, Mrs. Franklin, this scampi is great! Sally: Thank you, Bill. Do have some more.* □ *Jane: What a lovely, light cake. Mary: Oh, have some more. Otherwise the boys will just wolf it down.*

Do I have to paint (you) a picture? Go to next.

Do I have to spell it out (for you)? and **Do I have to paint (you) a picture?; Do I need to paint you a picture?** *Fig.* What do I have to do to make this clear enough for you to understand? (Shows impatience.) □ *Mary: I don't think I understand what you're trying to tell me, Fred. Fred: Do I have to spell it out for you? Mary: I guess so. Fred: We're through, Mary.* □ *Sally: Would you please go over the part about the square root again? Mary: Do I have to paint you a picture? Pay attention!*

Do I make myself (perfectly) clear? Do you understand exactly what I mean? (Very stern.) □ *Mother: You're going to sit right here and finish that homework. Do I make myself perfectly clear? Child: Yes, ma'am.* □ *Sue: No, the answer is no! Do I make myself clear?*

Do I need to paint you a picture? Go to Do I have to spell it out (for you)?

do it *Euph.* to have sex. □ *I hear that Bill and Jane did it in the back of his car.* □ *He did it for the first time when he was seventeen.*

do justice to something **1.** *Fig.* to do something well; to represent or portray something accurately. □ *Sally did justice to our side in the contract negotiations.* □ *This photograph doesn't do justice to the beauty of the mountains.* **2.** *Fig.* to eat or drink a great deal. □ *Bill always does justice to the turkey on Thanksgiving.* □ *The party didn't do justice to the roast pig. There were nearly ten pounds left over.*

Do not let the sun go down on your anger. Go to next.

Do not let the sun go down on your wrath. and **Do not let the sun go down on your anger.** *Prov.* Do not stay angry with anybody; calm your anger by the end of the day. □ *Son: Billy broke my bicycle, and I'm never going to speak to him again. Mother: Now, now, don't let the sun go down on your wrath.* □ *I was very upset by what you did, but I don't want to let the sun go down on my anger. Let's make up.*

Do not wash your dirty linen in public. *Prov.* Do not talk about your private family problems in public. □ *Grandson: How are we going to make Dad stop drinking? Grandmother: Hush! Don't wash your dirty linen in public.*

do one's **bit** Go to do one's part.

do one's **business** *Euph.* to defecate or urinate. □ *Do you need to do your business before we get in the car?* □ *The cat did her business on the sofa again.*

do one's **duty 1.** to do one's job; to do what is expected of one. □ *Please don't thank me. I'm just doing my duty.* □ *Soldiers who fight in wars are doing their duty.* **2.** *Euph.* to defecate or urinate. □ *We're not leaving this restroom until you do your duty.* □ *She did her duty in the potty, just like a big girl!*

do one's **(level) best** to do something as well as one can. □ *Just do your level best. That's all we can ask of you.* □ *Tom isn't doing his best. We may have to replace him.*

do one's **(own) thing** to do what one wants; to do what pleases oneself no matter what others think. □ *She's going to start doing her own thing for a change.* □ *I've always done my thing, and I don't see any reason to change to your view now.*

do one's **part** and **do** one's **bit** to do one's share of the work; to do whatever one can do to help. □ *All people everywhere must do their part to conserve energy.* □ *I always try to do my bit. How can I help this time?*

do one's **utmost (to** do something**)** to make one's best effort at doing something. □ *We will do our utmost to make the guests to feel welcome.*

do oneself **proud** to have done a very fine job. □ *That's super! You've done yourself proud!* □ *I feel like I've done myself proud by earning high honors.*

do or die *Fig.* trying as hard as one can. □ *I was determined to get there—do or die.* □ (Used as an attributive) *He has the obsessive do-or-die attitude.*

do's and don'ts the rules; the things that should be done and those that should not be done. □ *I must admit that a lot of do's and don'ts at this company are hard for me to understand.* □ *Better learn the do's and don'ts immediately.*

Do sit down. Don't stand on ceremony.; Please sit down. (A polite phrase encouraging people to resume their seats after rising for an introduction or out of deference.) □ *Tom rose when Mary approached the table, but she said graciously, "Do sit down. I just wanted to thank you again for the lovely gift."* □ *Tom: Hello, Bill. Bill (rising): Hi, Tom. Tom (standing): Do sit down. I just wanted to say hello.*

do so Go to do too.

do some fine coin *Sl.* to make a large sum of money. □ *When I get my big break, I'm going to do some fine coin.* □ *Richard did some fine coin on that last housepainting job.*

do somehow **by** someone to treat someone in a particular manner. (Do not confuse this with a passive construction. The *someone* is not the actor but the object.) □ *Tom did all right by Ann when he brought her red roses.* □ *I did badly by Tom. I fired him without good reason.*

do somehow **for** someone to benefit or harm someone in some degree. □ *This jacket does fine for me. I don't need a different one.* □ *This meal does okay for me. I'm satisfied.*

do someone **a favor** and **do** someone **a good turn** to perform a helpful service to someone. □ *Would you please do me a favor and take this letter to the post office?* □ *My neighbor did me a good turn by lending me his car.*

do someone **a good turn** Go to previous.

do someone **a heap of good** Go to do someone a power of good.

do someone **a kindness** to do a kind deed for a person. □ *My neighbor did me a kindness when he cut my grass.* □ *I am always happy to have the opportunity of doing someone a kindness.*

do someone **a power of good** and **do** someone **a heap of good** *Rur.* to be very good for someone. □ *You should take a vacation. It'd do you a power of good.* □ *Just hearing your voice does me a heap of good.*

do someone **credit** Go to do credit to someone.

do someone **damage** *Fig.* to harm someone, physically or otherwise. □ *I hope she doesn't plan to do me damage.* □ *They did us damage by telling the whole story to the newspapers.*

do someone **dirt(y)** *Rur.* to do something bad or dishonest to someone. □ *He sure did his wife dirty, leaving her like that.* □ *She did me dirt when we divided up the things mother left us.*

do someone **(down)** *Rur.* to treat someone badly. □ *I ain't speaking to Mary. Not after the way she did me down.*

do someone **good** to benefit someone. □ *A nice hot bath really does me good.* □ *A few years in the army would do you good.*

do someone **in 1.** to make someone tired. □ *That tennis game really did me in.* □ *Yes, hard activity will do you in.* **2.** to cheat someone; to **take** someone **in.** □ *The scam artists did the widow in by talking her into giving them all the money in her bank account.* **3.** *Sl.* to kill someone. □ *The crooks did the bank guard in.* □ *They'll probably do the witnesses in soon.*

do someone **one better** Go to go (someone) one better.

do someone or something **up**[†] to make someone or something attractive; to decorate or ornament someone or something. □ *Sally did Jane up for the party.* □ *Would you do up this present for Jane? It's her birthday.*

do someone **out of** something to swindle something away from someone; to defraud someone of a right or of property. □ *Are you trying to do me out of what's mine?* □ *Max tried to do her out of everything she had.* □ *I did myself out of a week's vacation by quitting when I did.*

do someone **over**[†] and **make** someone **over**[†] to buy a new wardrobe for someone; to redo someone's hairstyle, makeup, etc. □ *Sally's mother did Sally over for the play tryouts.* □ *The designer made over Sally completely.*

do someone **proud** to make someone proud. □ *Bill's kids sure did him proud at the boat race.* □ *Mary resolved she would do her friends proud.*

do someone's **bidding** to do what is requested. □ *The servant grumbled but did his employer's bidding.* □ *Am I expected to do your bidding whenever you ask?*

do someone's **heart good** *Fig.* to make someone feel good emotionally. □ *It does my heart good to hear you two are back together.* □ *When she sent me a get-well card, it really did my heart good.*

do something **about** someone or something to manage or deal with someone or something. □ *Can you please do something about Bob? He is too noisy.* □ *We were not able to do anything about the excessive rent increase.*

do something **by hand** to do something with one's hands rather than with a machine. □ *The calculator was broken so I had to do the calculations by hand.* □ *All this tiny stitching was done by hand. Machines cannot do this kind of work.*

do something **by the book** Go to by the book.

do something **from scratch** Go to from scratch.

do something **hand in hand** Go to hand in hand.

do something **in**[†] to destroy something. □ *The huge waves totally did in the seaside community.* □ *The fire did the wooden building in.*

do something **over**[†] **1.** and **make** something **over**[†] to rebuild, redesign, or redecorate something. □ *We did our living room over for the holidays.* □ *We made over the family room because it was looking shabby.* **2.** and **do** something **over**[†] **(again)** to repeat something; to do something again. □ *I am afraid that you are going to have to do over the complete series again.* □ *Would you do this one over, please?*

do something **the hard way** to accomplish something in the most difficult manner, rather than by an easier way. □ *I made it to this job the hard way. I came up through the ranks.* □ *She did it the hard way. She had no help from her parents.*

do something **to excess** to do too much of something; to consume too much of something. □ *Anne often drinks to excess at parties.* □ *John smokes to excess when he works.*

do something **up**[†] **1.** to fasten, zip, hook, or button some item of clothing. □ *Would you do my buttons up in back?* □ *Please do up my buttons.* **2.** to wrap up something, such as a package, gift, etc. □ *I have to do this present up before*

the party guests get here. □ *Do up the presents quickly. They are coming up the walk.* **3.** to arrange, fix, repair, cook, clean, etc., something. □ *I have to do the kitchen up before the guests get here.* □ *Do up the kitchen now, please.*

do something **up brown** to do something just right or with great effect. (Fixed order.) □ *Whenever they put on a party, they do it up brown.* □ *He was determined to cause a scandal, and he really did it up brown.*

do something **with a vengeance** *Fig.* to do something with vigor; to do something energetically as if one were angry. □ *Bob is building that fence with a vengeance.* □ *Mary is really weeding her garden with a vengeance.*

do something **with** someone or something **1.** *Lit.* to use someone or something in some way. □ *Can you do something with this bracket, or shall I throw it away?* □ *We can't do anything with the new secretary. Find us another.* **2.** *Fig.* to improve or refresh someone or something. □ *I would like to do something with this room. It is so drab.* □ *I can't do anything with this child! Keep him at home.* **3.** *Fig.* to manage as well as possible with someone or something; to **make do with** someone or something. □ *We will just have to do whatever we can with what we have.* □ *We will do the best we can with this employee until you find a better one.*

Do tell. a response to one of a series of statements by another person. (The expression can indicate disinterest. Each word has equal stress. See also **You don't say.**) □ *Bill: The Amazon basin is about ten times the size of France. Mary: Do tell.*

do the dishes to wash the dishes; to wash and dry the dishes, knives, forks, glasses, etc., after a meal. □ *Bill, you cannot go out and play until you've done the dishes.* □ *Why am I always the one who has to do the dishes?*

do the honors to act as host or hostess and serve one's guests by pouring drinks, slicing meat, making (drinking) toasts, etc. □ *All the guests were seated, and a huge juicy turkey sat on the table. Jane turned to her husband and said, "Bob, will you do the honors?" Bob smiled and began slicing thick slices of meat from the turkey.* □ *The mayor stood up and addressed the people who were still eating their salads. "I'm delighted to do the honors this evening and propose a toast to your friend and mine, Bill Jones. Bill, good luck and best wishes in your new job in Washington."*

do the trick to do exactly what is needed. □ *This new paint scraper really does the trick.* □ *Is this envelope large enough to do the trick?*

do time *Sl.* to serve a sentence in prison; to serve a specific amount of time in prison. □ *Lefty had done time on a number of occasions.* □ *You'd better talk and talk fast if you don't want to do time.*

do too and **do so** to do something (despite anything to the contrary). (An emphatic way of saying *do.*) □ *Bob: You don't have your money with you. Bill: I do too!* □ *He does so! I saw him put it in his pocket.* □ *She did too take a cookie. I saw her do it.*

Do unto others as you would have them do unto you. and **Do as you would be done by.** *Prov.* You should treat other people the way you want them to treat you. (From Luke 6:31; it is also known as "The Golden Rule.") □ *Mother: Don't call your playmates names. Child:*

Why not? Mother: Because you should follow the Golden Rule: Do unto others as you would have them do unto you. □ *It's hard to be kind to people sometimes, but I try to remember to do as I'd be done by.*

Do we have to go through all that again? Do we have to discuss that matter again? (Compare this with **Let's not go through all that again.**) □ *Bill: Now, I still have more to say about what happened last night. Sally: Do we have to go through all that again?* □ *Sally: I can't get over the way you treated me at our own dinner table. Fred: I was irritated at something else. I said I was sorry. Do we have to go through all that again?*

Do what? What did you say?; You want me to do what? □ *Charlie: My mama's coming to visit, so I want you to cook a fancy dinner. Mary: Do what?* □ *A: Let's perambulate. B: Do what? A: Let's take a walk.*

do with *someone or something* to do as well as possible with someone or something; to **make do with** *someone or something.* □ *I will just have to do with the car I now have.* □ *Can she do with just one chair for a while?*

do without Go to go without.

do without (*someone or something***)** to manage or get along without someone or something that is needed or expected. □ *I guess I will have to do without dinner.* □ *Yes, you'll do without.*

(Do you) care if I join you? Go to Could I join you?

(Do) you eat with that mouth? and **(Do) you kiss your momma with that mouth?** *Sl.* Do you actually eat with the mouth you use to talk that filth?; Do you actually use that filthy mouth to kiss your mother? (A phrase said to someone who talks dirty all the time.) □ *That's a lot of foul talk. Do you eat with that mouth?* □ *After the suspect finished swearing at him, the police officer said, "Do you kiss your momma with that mouth?"*

Do you expect me to believe that? That is so unbelievable that you do not expect me to believe it, do you? (Said with impatience or strong doubt. Compare this with **You can't expect me to believe that.**) □ *Bill: I'm going to quit my job and open a restaurant. Mary: That's silly. Do you expect me to believe that?* □ *Mary: Wow! I just got selected to be an astronaut! Sally: Do you expect me to believe that? Mary: Here's the letter! Now do you believe me?*

Do you follow? *Fig.* Do you understand what I am saying?; Do you understand my explanation? □ *Mary: Keep to the right past the fork in the road, then turn right at the crossroads. Do you follow? Jane: No. Run it by me again.*

(Do you) get my drift? Do you understand what I mean?; Do you understand what I am getting at? □ *Father: I want you to settle down and start studying. Get my drift? Bob: Sure, Pop. Whatever you say.* □ *Mary: Get out of my way and stop following me around. Do you get my drift? John: I guess so.*

(Do you) get the picture? Do you understand the situation?; Do you know what this means you have to do? □ *Bill: I want to get this project wrapped up before midnight. Do you get the picture? Tom: I'm afraid I do. Bill: Well, then, get to work.* □ *Fred: I want you to straighten up and get moving. Get the picture? Bill: I got it.*

(Do you) hear? *Rur.* Do you hear and understand what I said? □ *John: I want you to clean up this room this instant!*

Do you hear? Sue: Okay. I'll get right on it. □ *Bob: Come over here, Sue. I want to show you something, you hear? Sue: Sure. What is it?*

(Do) you kiss your momma with that mouth? Go to (Do) you eat with that mouth?

(Do) you know what? and **You know what?** an expression used to open a conversation or switch to a new topic. □ *Bob: You know what? Mary: No, what? Bob: I think this milk is spoiled.* □ *Bob: Know what? Bill: Tell me. Bob: Your hair needs cutting. Bill: So what?*

(Do) you know what I mean? Go to next.

(Do) you know what I'm saying? and **You know what I'm saying?; (Do) you know what I mean?; You know what I mean?** Do you understand me?; Do you agree? □ *Sue: This is, like, really great! You know what I'm saying? Mary: Yeah, I've been there. It's great.*

(Do) you mean to say *something?* and **(Do) you mean to tell me** *something?* Do you really mean to say what you said? (A way of giving someone an opportunity to alter a comment. The *something* represents a quote or a paraphrase.) □ *Mary: I'm leaving tomorrow. Sally: Do you mean to say you're leaving school for good? Mary: Yes.* □ *Bob: Do you mean to tell me that this is all you've accomplished in two weeks? Bill: I guess so. Bob: I expected more.*

(Do) you mean to tell me *something?* Go to previous.

Do you mind? 1. You are intruding on my space!; You are offending me! (Impatient or incensed. Essentially, "Do you mind stopping what you are doing?") □ *The lady behind her in line kept pushing against her every time the line moved. Finally, Sue turned and said sternly, "Do you mind?"* □ *All through the first part of the movie, two people in the row behind John kept up a running conversation. Finally, John rose and turned, leaned over into their faces, and shouted, "Do you mind?"* **2.** Do you object to what I am about to do? □ *Mary had her hand on the lovely silver cake knife that would carry the very last piece of cake to her plate. She looked at Tom, who stood next to her, eyeing the cake. "Do you mind?" she asked coyly.* □ *"Do you mind?" asked John as he bumped Sally and ran through the door.*

(Do you) mind if...? a polite way of seeking someone's permission or agreement. □ *Mary: Do you mind if I sit here? Jane: No, help yourself.* □ *Tom: Mind if I smoke? Bill: I certainly do. Tom: Then I'll go outside.*

(Do you) mind if I join you? Go to Could I join you?

Do you read me? 1. *Fig.* an expression used by someone communicating by radio, asking if the hearer understands the transmission clearly. □ *Controller: This is Aurora Center, do you read me? Pilot: Yes, I read you loud and clear.* □ *Controller: Left two degrees. Do you read me? Pilot: Roger, Sir, G'day.* **2.** *Fig.* Do you understand what I am telling you? (Said sternly, as when giving an instruction, and used in general conversation, not in radio communication.) □ *Mary: I want you to pull yourself together and go out and get a job. Do you read me? Bill: Sure. Anything you say.* □ *Mother: Get this place picked up immediately. Do you read me? Child: Yes, ma'am.*

(Do you) want to know something? and **(You want to) know something?** an expression used to open a conversation or switch to a new topic. □ *John: Do you want to know something? Sue: What? John: Your hem is* *torn.* □ *Bill: Hey, Tom! Know something? Tom: What is it? Bill: It's really hot today. Tom: Don't I know it!*

(Do you) want to make something of it? and **You want to make something of it?** Do you want to start a fight about it? (Rude and contentious.) □ *Tom: You're really bugging me. It's not fair to pick on me all the time. Bill: You want to make something of it?* □ *Bob: Please be quiet. You're making too much noise. Fred: Do you want to make something of it?*

(Do) you want to step outside? an expression inviting someone to go outdoors to settle an argument by fighting. □ *John: Drop dead! Bob: All right, I've had enough out of you. You want to step outside?* □ *Bill: So you're mad at me! What else is new? You've been building up to this for a long time. Bob: Do you want to step outside and settle this once and for all? Bill: Why not?*

dock someone or something **for** something to subtract money from someone or someone's account for payment of a debt or as punishment; to withhold money from someone's pay in payment of a debt or for recompense. □ *I will have to dock you for any breakage you cause.* □ *I was docked for being absent for half a day.*

dock (something) **at** some place to bring a boat or ship to a dock. □ *Let's dock our boat at the left side of the pier.* □ *We docked at the marina overnight.*

dock something **from** something to withhold money from an amount due to someone. □ *I will have to dock this from your paycheck.* □ *The boss docked ten dollars from my monthly pay.*

Doctor Livingstone, I presume? *Jocular* You are who I think you are, are you not? □ *Oh, there you are. Doctor Livingstone, I presume?*

doctor's orders something that one is strongly advised to do as ordered or as if ordered by a doctor. □ *I have to spend a month in Arizona. Doctor's orders.* □ *I'm doing this on doctor's orders, but I don't like it.*

doctor someone **up**[†] to give someone medical treatment, especially first aid. □ *Give me a minute to doctor Fred up, and then we can continue our walk.* □ *I'll doctor up Fred with a bandage; you can go on ahead.*

dodder along to walk along unsteadily, as in old age. □ *Both of the elderly ladies doddered along very slowly.* □ *We dodder along because we can't go any faster.*

dodge behind something to duck behind something; to move quickly and evasively behind something. □ *She dodged behind a tree to hide from Mark.* □ *The turkey dodged behind a tree to elude the hunter.*

Does it work for you? Is this all right with you?; Do you agree? (Can be answered by (**It**) **works for me.**) □ *Bill: I'll be there at noon. Does it work for you? Bob: Works for me.* □ *Mary: We're having dinner at eight. Does it work for you? Jane: Sounds just fine.*

doesn't care who knows it doesn't try to conceal something. (Also with *don't. Don't* used with all persons is folksy.) □ *Jane dyes her hair, and she doesn't care who knows it.* □ *Yeah, my old man's in jail. I don't care who knows it!*

doesn't have enough sense to bell a cat and **doesn't have enough sense to come in out of the rain** acts foolish. (Also with *don't. Don't* used with

all persons is folksy.) □ *I should've known Mary would mess things up completely. She doesn't have enough sense to bell a cat.* □ *Look after Joe and make sure he doesn't get into trouble. You know he doesn't have enough sense to bell a cat.* □ *I ain't surprised that Jim spends a hundred dollars a week on the lottery. Everyone knows he don't have enough sense to come in out of the rain.*

doesn't have enough sense to come in out of the rain Go to previous.

doesn't have the sense God gave geese and **doesn't have the sense God gave him (or her)** *Prov.* Doesn't have basic common sense. (Also with *don't. Don't* used with all persons is folksy.) □ *Mary's going out in this incredibly cold weather without a hat or gloves. She doesn't have the sense God gave geese.* □ *It was obvious that the man was a swindler, but George gave him all his money anyway. I swear, George doesn't have the sense God gave him.*

doesn't have the sense God gave him (or her) Go to previous.

doesn't know beans (about something**)** does not know anything. (Also with *don't. Don't* used with all persons is folksy.) □ *Bill doesn't know beans about car engines.* □ *Don't ask your daddy for advice about child rearing. He doesn't know beans.*

doesn't know his ass from a hole in the ground and **doesn't know his ass from his elbow** doesn't know anything; acts ignorant. (Use *ass* with caution. Also with *don't. Don't* used with all persons is folksy.) □ *That teacher doesn't know his ass from a hole in the ground.* □ *She's supposed to be an expert, but she doesn't know her ass from her elbow.*

doesn't know his ass from his elbow Go to previous.

dog and pony show *Fig.* a display, demonstration, or exhibition of something—such as something one is selling. (As in a circus act where trained dogs leap onto and off of trained ponies.) □ *Gary went into his standard dog and pony show, trying to sell us on an upgrade to our software.* □ *Don't you get tired of running through the same old dog and pony show at every trade show?*

The **dog ate my homework.** a poor excuse for something that someone has failed to do on time. (From an excuse a student might give for failing to turn in homework on time. Occurs in many variations.) □ *The dog ate my homework, so I have nothing to turn in.* □ (Used as an attributive.) *Bob was late with his report and had nothing but his typical dog-ate-my-homework excuses.*

dog days the hottest days of summer, usually during July and August. (Named for *Sirius,* the 'dog star.') □ *Bill spent the dog days lying out in his hammock.* □ *I hate doing yard work in the dog days.*

Dog does not eat dog. *Prov.* One disreputable person will not harm other disreputable people. □ *Ellen: My lawyer did such a bad job that I want to hire another lawyer to sue him. Jane: You'll never find a lawyer to take on that job. Dog does not eat dog.*

dog in the manger one who unreasonably prevents other people from doing or having what one does not wish them to do or have. (From one of Aesop's fables in which a dog—which cannot eat hay—lay in the hayrack [manger] and prevented the other animals from eating the hay.) □ *Jane is a real dog in the manger. She cannot drive, but she will not lend anyone her car.* □ *If Martin were not such a dog in the manger, he would let his brother have that dinner jacket he never wears.*

Dog my cats! *Rur.* My goodness!; What do you know! (An exclamation of surprise.) □ *Dog my cats! Somebody painted my house green!* □ *Well, dog my cats—it hasn't rained once all month!*

dog-eat-dog *Fig.* a situation in which one has to act ruthlessly in order to survive or succeed; ruthless competition. □ *It is dog-eat-dog in the world of business these days.* □ *Universities are not quiet peaceful places. It's dog-eat-dog to get a promotion.*

dog-faced liar *Rur.* a terrible liar. □ *Suzy said Jimmy was a dog-faced liar.* □ *If Joe says that, he's a dog-faced liar.*

a **doggy bag** a bag or other container used to carry uneaten food home from a restaurant. (As if it is for the dog.) □ *I can't eat all of this. Can I have a doggy bag, please?*

dole something **out†** (**to** someone) to distribute something to someone. □ *The cook doled the oatmeal out to each camper who held out a bowl.* □ *Please dole out the candy bars, one to a customer.* □ *She doled it out fairly.*

doll someone **up†** to dress someone up in fancy clothes. □ *She dolled her children up for church each Sunday.* □ *She dolls up all her kids once a week.*

dollar for dollar considering the amount of money involved; considering the cost or value. (Often seen in advertising.) □ *Dollar for dollar, you cannot buy a better car.* □ *Dollar for dollar, this laundry detergent washes cleaner and brighter than any other product on the market.*

done and gone *Rur.* gone. □ *She's not here. She's done and gone.* □ *Jed was done and gone before dawn.*

done by mirrors and **done with mirrors** *Fig.* illusory; purposefully deceptive. (See also **smoke and mirrors.**) □ *The whole legislative budgetary process is done with mirrors.* □ *The company's self-review was done by mirrors and didn't come off too bad, despite our falling stock price.*

a **done deal** a completed deal; something that is settled. □ *It's too late. It's a done deal.* □ *The sale of the property is a done deal. There is nothing that can be done now.*

done for finished; dead. □ *I'm afraid that animal hit by the car is done for.* □ *The goldfish looked as if it was either done for or sunning its tummy.*

*done in exhausted. (*Typically: **be ~; get ~.**) □ *I'm really done in! I think I'll go to bed.* □ *After all that lifting, Gerald was done in and breathing hard.*

done 'n' did *Rur.* already did. □ *Tom: Guess I better take the garbage out. Bill: No need. I done 'n' did it.* □ *Mary done 'n' did the chores for you.*

done over *Sl.* beat; outscored. □ *The other team was done over, and they showed it in their lackluster play.*

done to a T cooked just right. □ *Yummy! This meat is done to a T.* □ *I like it done to a T, not too done and not too raw.*

done to a turn 1. well-cooked; nicely cooked. □ *The entire meal was done to a turn.* □ *The turkey was done to a turn.* **2.** *Inf.* beaten. □ *When Wilbur's opponent was done to a turn, Wilbur was declared the winner.*

done told you *Rur.* have already told you something. □ *I done told you not to touch that pan, and you went and did it anyhow.* □ *Sally done told you to leave that dog alone.*

done with mirrors Go to done by mirrors.

done with someone or something finished with someone or something. □ *Mary is done with Bill. She has found another boyfriend.* □ *I can't wait until I'm done with school forever.* □ *I agree. I'll be glad when we are done with all these exams.*

don't amount to a bucket of spit *Rur.* is not worth anything. □ *Joe's a shiftless cuss. He don't amount to a bucket of spit.* □ *All your pretty promises don't amount to a bucket of spit.*

Don't ask. It is so bad, I do not wish to be reminded or talk about it, so do not ask about it. □ *John: How was your class reunion? Alice: Oh, heavens! Don't ask.* □ *Tom: What was your calculus final exam like? Mary: Don't ask.*

Don't ask me. Go to How should I know?

Don't be gone (too) long. Good-bye. Hurry back here. □ *Tom: I've got to go to the drugstore to get some medicine. Sue: Don't be gone too long. Tom: I'll be right back.* □ *"Don't be gone long," said Bill's uncle. "It's about time to eat."*

Don't be too sure. I think you are wrong, so do not sound so certain.; You may be wrong. (Compare this with **Don't speak too soon.**) □ *Bill: I think I've finally saved up enough money to retire. John: Don't be too sure. Inflation can ruin your savings.*

Don't bite off more than you can chew. *Prov.* Do not commit yourself to doing more than you can actually do. □ *I don't think you ought to take dance lessons three times a week; you're already working two jobs. Don't bite off more than you can chew.*

Don't bother. Please don't do it. It is not necessary, and it is too much trouble. □ *Mary: Should I make some dinner for you? Bill: No, don't bother; it's late.* □ *Sue: Do you want me to save this spoonful of mashed potatoes? Jane: No, don't bother. It isn't worth it. Sue: I hate to waste it.*

Don't bother me! Go away!; Leave me alone! □ *Tom: Hey, Bill! Bill: Don't bother me! I'm busy. Can't you see?* □ *"Don't bother me! Leave me alone!" the child shouted at the dog.*

Don't breathe a word of this to anyone. This is a secret or secret gossip. Do not tell it to anyone. (Breathing a word is fig. for whispering.) □ *Bill: Have you heard about Mary and her friends? Sally: No. Tell me! Tell me! Bill: Well, they all went secretly to Mexico for the weekend. Now, don't breathe a word of this to anyone.*

Don't call us, we'll call you. *Cliché* a formulaic expression said to applicants who have just interviewed or auditioned for a job or part. □ *Thank you, Eddie Evans. Don't call us, we'll call you.* □ *Stupendous, Gloria, just stupendous. What glamour and radiance! Don't call us, we'll call you.*

don't care a whit Go to didn't care a whit.

Don't change horses in midstream. Go to change horses in midstream.

Don't count your chickens before they are hatched. *Prov. Cliché* Do not act as though something has turned out favorably for you until it has really turned out that way. □ *Jill: When I get my raise, I'll use the extra money to go on vacation. Jane: But you don't know for sure that you're going to get a raise. Don't count your chickens before they are hatched.*

Don't cry before you are hurt. *Prov.* Do not be upset about a bad thing that might happen; only be upset when something bad really does happen. □ *Fred: What am I going to do? There's a possibility that my job will be eliminated! Jane: Don't cry before you are hurt. They haven't eliminated you yet.*

Don't cry over spilled milk. Go to It's no use crying over spilled milk.

Don't do anything I wouldn't do. an expression said when two friends are parting. □ *Bill: See you next month, Tom. Tom: Yeah, man. Don't do anything I wouldn't do.*

Don't even look like something! Do not even appear to be doing something! (The *something* can be thinking about something or actually doing something.) □ *Mary: Are you thinking about taking that last piece of cake? Bob: Of course not. Mary: Well, don't even look like you're doing it!* □ *John: You weren't going to try to sneak into the theater, were you? Bob: No. John: Well, don't even look like it, if you know what's good for you.*

Don't even think about (doing) it. Do not do it, and do not even think about doing it. □ *John reached into his jacket for his wallet. The cop, thinking John was about to draw a gun, said, "Don't even think about it."*

Don't even think about it (happening). Do not think about something like that happening, as the mere thought of it is so bad. (Compare this with **Don't even think about (doing) it.**) □ *Mary: Oh, those cars almost crashed! How horrible! Fred: Don't even think about it.* □ *Sally: If the stock market crashes, we'll lose everything we have. Sue: Don't even think about it!*

Don't forget to write. Go to Remember to write.

Don't get your bowels in an uproar! Do not get so excited! □ *Bill: What have you done to my car? Where's the bumper? The side window is cracked! Bob: Calm down! Don't get your bowels in an uproar!*

don't give a continental *Rur.* does not care at all. (Also with *doesn't. Don't* used with all persons is folksy.) □ *I don't give a continental if I never see him again.* □ *Mary's kids can do whatever they want. She doesn't give a continental.*

don't give a hoot (in hell's hollow) *Rur.* to not care one bit. (Also with *doesn't. Don't* used with all persons is folksy.) □ *Mary: Joe left town. Are you sorry to see him go? Tom: No! I don't give a hoot in hell's hollow.* □ *She's a devil-may-care young woman, doesn't give a hoot about anything.*

Don't give it a (second) thought. Go to Think nothing of it.

Don't give it another thought. Go to Think nothing of it.

Don't give me any of your lip! *Fig.* Don't talk back! □ *Do as I tell you and don't give me any of your lip!*

Don't give me that line! and **Don't hand me that (line)!** Don't tell me those lies! □ *Don't give me that line! I know the truth! You're lying to me!*

Don't give up! Do not stop trying!; Keep trying! □ *John: Get in there and give it another try. Don't give up! Bill: Okay. Okay. But it's hopeless.* □ *Jane: I asked the boss for a raise, but he said no. Tom: Don't give up. Try again later.*

Don't give up the ship! *Fig.* Do not give up yet!; Do not yield the entire enterprise! (Fixed order. Alludes to the words on a flag made by Captain Oliver Hazard Perry in the Battle of Lake Erie during the War of 1812.) □ *Bill: I'm having a devil of a time with calculus. I think I want to drop the course. Sally: Keep trying. Don't give up the ship!* □ *Bill: Every time we get enough money saved up to make a down payment on a house, the price of houses skyrockets. I'm about ready to stop trying. Sue: We'll manage. Don't give up the ship!*

Don't give up without a fight! *Fig.* Do not yield easily.; Keep struggling and you may win.; Do not give up too soon. (Also with *don't. Don't* used with all persons is folksy.) □ *Sue: She says no every time I ask her for a raise. Mary: Well, don't give up without a fight. Keep after her.*

Don't give up your day job. Go to Don't quit your day job.

Don't hand me that (line)! Go to Don't give me that line!

Don't have a cow! Calm down!; Don't get so excited! (Made famous in the television show, *The Simpsons*.) □ *Chill out, man! Don't have a cow!* □ *Aw, don't have a cow, Dad!*

don't have a pot to piss in (or a window to throw it out of) *Fig.* doesn't have anything of value; very poor. (Use with caution.) □ *When Ed was a young man, he didn't have a pot to piss in.* □ *Jane's folks don't have a pot to piss in or a window to throw it out of.*

Don't hold your breath. *Fig.* Do not stop breathing waiting for something to happen that won't happen. (Meaning that it will take longer for it to happen than you can possibly hold your breath.) □ *Tom: The front yard is such a mess. Bob: Bill's supposed to rake the leaves. Tom: Don't hold your breath. He never does his share of the work.* □ *Sally: Someone said that gasoline prices would go down. Bob: Oh, yeah? Don't hold your breath.*

Don't I know it! I know that very well! □ *Mary: Goodness gracious! It's hot today. Bob: Don't I know it!* □ *Sue: You seem to be putting on a little weight. John: Don't I know it!*

Don't I know you from somewhere? a way of striking up a conversation with a stranger, as at a party or other gathering. □ *Bill: Don't I know you from somewhere? Mary: I don't think so. Where did you go to school?* □ *Henry: Don't I know you from somewhere? Alice: No, and let's keep it that way.*

Don't judge a book by its cover. and **You can't tell a book by its cover.** *Prov.* Do not draw a conclusion about someone or something just from outward appearances. □ *Just because Sam dresses sloppy doesn't mean he's a bad person. Don't judge a book by its cover.* □ *Jill: How can you be so sure this will be a boring movie? Jane: The poster for it is so boring. Jill: Don't judge a book by its cover!*

Don't knock it. Don't criticize it. □ *You don't want any okra? Don't knock it.*

don't know whether to eat it or rub it on *Rur.* do not know what to do with something. (Used to describe a kind of food one does not recognize or that looks unusual.) (Also with *doesn't. Don't* used with all persons is folksy.) □ *That sure was a fancy dessert Mary served. I didn't know whether to eat it or rub it on.* □ *What kind of sauce is this? I don't know whether to eat it or rub it on!*

Don't let it go any further. and **Don't let it out of this room.** Don't tell this secret to anyone else. (Also literal.) □ *This is a strict secret. Don't let it go any further.* □ *I'll tell you what you what to know, but don't let it go out of this room.*

Don't let it out of this room. Go to previous.

Don't let someone or something **get you down.** Do not allow yourself to be overcome or disappointed by someone or something. □ *Don't let their constant teasing get you down.* □ *Don't let Tom get you down. He's not always unpleasant.*

Don't let the bastards wear you down. Don't let those people get the best of you. (Exercise caution with *bastard.*) □ *Bill: The place I work at is really rough. Everybody is rude and jealous of each other. Tom: Don't let the bastards wear you down.* □ *Jane: I have to go down to the county clerk's office and figure out what this silly bureaucratic letter means. Sue: You might call them on the phone. In any case, don't let the bastards wear you down.*

Don't look a gift horse in the mouth. *Prov.* Do not look for defects in a gift. □ *Jill: I wonder why Grandma gave me this table. Maybe it has one leg shorter than the others. Jane: Don't look a gift horse in the mouth.* □ *Mike: This letter says I just won a trip to Hawaii. I bet there's some kind of catch. Keith: Don't look a gift horse in the mouth.*

Don't make me laugh! That is a stupid suggestion! □ *You a judge? Don't make me laugh!* □ *Don't make me laugh. Tom could never do that.*

Don't make me say it again! and **Don't make me tell you again!** I have told you once, and now I'm mad, and I'll be madder if I have to tell you again. (Typically said to a child who will not obey.) □ *Mother: I told you thirty minutes ago to clean up this room! Don't make me tell you again!*

Don't make me tell you again! Go to previous.

Don't make two bites of a cherry. *Prov.* Do not leave a simple job half-done. □ *Tom: I washed the dishes and left them in the rack. I'll put them away tomorrow. Mary: Oh, come on. Don't make two bites of a cherry.*

Don't mention it. You are welcome and your thanks are not necessary. □ *A: Thank you so much! B: Don't mention it.*

Don't mind me. Don't pay any attention to me.; Just ignore me. (Sometimes sarcastic.) □ *Bill and Jane were watching television when Jane's mother walked through the room, grabbing the newspaper on the way. "Don't mind me," she said.*

Don't push (me)! 1. *Lit.* I can move on my own, so don't shove me! □ *I can't move any faster than this. Don't push me!* **2.** *Fig.* Don't put pressure on me to do something! □ *Sue: You really must go to the dentist, you know. John: Don't push me. I'll go when I'm good and ready.*

Don't put all your eggs in one basket. *Prov.* Do not risk everything on one undertaking. □ *Keep your day job while you pursue your acting career at night, just in case the acting doesn't go so well. You know—don't put all your eggs in one basket.*

Don't put off for tomorrow what you can do today. *Prov.* Do not procrastinate. □ *Father: Take out the garbage. Child: I'll do it in the morning. Father: It only takes a minute. Don't put off for tomorrow what you can do today.*

Don't put the cart before the horse. *Prov.* Do not do things in the wrong order. (This can imply that the person you are addressing is impatient.) □ *Tune the guitar first, then play it. Don't put the cart before the horse.*

Don't quit trying. Go to Keep (on) trying.

Don't quit your day job. and **Don't give up your day job.** Don't quit your regular job in hopes that you can support yourself doing this task that you do not do very well. □ *I saw your comedy act at the nightclub. Don't quit your day job!* □ *So, you laid the bricks in this wall. Well, don't quit your day job.*

Don't rush me! Don't try to hurry me! □ *Bill: Hurry up! Make up your mind! Bob: Don't rush me! Bill: I want to get out of here before midnight.* □ *Bill: The waiter wants to take your order. What do you want? Jane: Don't rush me! I can't make up my mind. Waiter: I'll come back in a minute.*

Don't say it! I don't want to hear it!; I know, so you don't have to say it. □ *John (joking): What is that huge pile of stuff on your head? Bill: Don't say it! I know I need a haircut.*

Don't speak too soon. I think you may be wrong. Don't speak before you know the facts. (Compare this with **Don't be too sure.**) □ *Bill: It looks like it'll be a nice day. Mary: Don't speak too soon. I just felt a raindrop.* □ *Tom: It looks like we made it home without any problems. Bill: Don't speak too soon, there's a cop behind us in the driveway.*

Don't spend it all in one place. *Prov.* a phrase said after giving someone some money, especially a small amount of money. □ *Fred: Dad, can I have a dollar? Father: Sure. Here. Don't spend it all in one place.* □ *"Here's a quarter, kid," said Tom, flipping Fred a quarter. "Don't spend it all in one place."*

Don't stand on ceremony. Do not wait for a formal invitation.; Please be at ease and make yourself at home. (Some people read this as "Don't remain standing because of ceremony," and others read it "Don't be totally obedient to the requirements of ceremony.") □ *Come in, Tom. Don't stand on ceremony. Get yourself a drink and something to eat and introduce yourself to everyone."*

Don't start (on me)! Do not complain! □ *Yes, I know it's a mess. Don't start!* □ *Don't start on me, I'm sorting it out.*

Don't stay away so long. *Rur.* Please visit more often. (Said upon the arrival or departure of a guest.) □ *John: Hi, Bill! Long time no see. Don't stay away so long! Bill: Thanks, John. Good to see you.* □ *Mary: I had a nice time. Thanks for inviting me. Sally: Good to see you, Mary. Next time, don't stay away so long.*

Don't sweat it! *Inf.* Don't worry about it! □ *No problem. Don't sweat it!* □ *Don't sweat it! We'll take care of it.*

Don't take any wooden nickels. *Prov.* Be careful and do not let anyone cheat you. (Often used as a jocular way of saying good-bye.) □ *Tom: So long. Bill: Don't take any wooden nickels.* □ *Good luck in college. Don't take any wooden nickels.*

Don't teach your grandmother to suck eggs. *Prov.* Do not try to instruct someone who is more experienced than you. (Extremely casual; potentially rude.) □ *Bob told the seasoned guitar player that she was holding the guitar incorrectly. "Don't teach your grandmother to suck eggs," she replied.*

Don't tell a soul. Please do not tell anyone this gossip. □ *Bill: Is your brother getting married? Sally: Yes, but don't tell a soul. It's a secret.* □ *Mary: Can you keep a secret? John: Sure. Mary: Don't tell a soul, but Tom is in jail.*

Don't tell me what to do! Do not give me orders. □ *Sue: Next, you should get a haircut, then get some new clothes. You really need to fix yourself up. Sally: Don't tell me what to do! Maybe I like me the way I am!*

Don't that (just) beat all! Go to If that don't beat all!

Don't throw the baby out with the bathwater. *Prov.* Do not discard something valuable in your eagerness to get rid of some useless thing associated with it. □ *Jill: As long as I'm selling all the books Grandpa had, I might as well sell the bookcases, too. Jane: Don't throw the baby out with the bathwater. You can use the bookcases for something else.*

Don't touch that dial! 1. *Lit.* Do not change your radio or television dial, but continue to listen to this station. (From broadcasts in the days when tuning was done with a dial.) □ *Don't touch that dial. Stay tuned for The Adventures of Blondie.* **2.** *Fig.* Do not change anything or divert your attention. □ *Don't touch that dial. Remember what you hear in today's lecture. It will be on the test.*

Don't waste my time. Do not take up my valuable time with a poor presentation.; Do not waste my time trying to get me to do something. □ *Bob: I'd like to show you our new line of industrial-strength vacuum cleaners. Bill: Beat it! Don't waste my time.* □ *"Don't waste my time!" said the manager when Jane made her fourth appeal for a raise.*

Don't waste your breath. You will not get a positive response to what you have to say, so don't even say it.; Talking will get you nowhere. □ *Alice: I'll go in there and try to convince her otherwise. Fred: Don't waste your breath. I already tried it.* □ *Sally: No, I won't agree! Don't waste your breath. Bill: Aw, come on. At least hear me out.*

Don't waste your time. You will not get anywhere with it, so don't waste time trying. □ *Mary: Should I ask Tom if he wants to go to the convention, or is he still in a bad mood? Sally: Don't waste your time. Mary: Bad mood, huh?* □ *Jane: I'm having trouble fixing this doorknob. Mary: Don't waste your time. I've ordered a new one.*

Don't work too hard. an expression said at the end of a conversation after or in place of *good-bye*. □ *Mary: Bye, Tom. Tom: Bye, Mary. Don't work too hard.*

Don't worry (about a thing). Do not become anxious about something.; Everything will be all right. □ *"Don't worry, Fred," comforted Bill, "everything will be all right."* □ *Bill: I think I left the car windows open. Sue: Don't worry, I closed them.* □ *"Don't worry about a thing," the tax collector had said. "We'll take care of everything." Or was it "We'll take everything?"*

Don't worry your (pretty little) head about it. *Rur.* Do not worry about it. (Said condescendingly, and can cause offense.) □ *Mary: How are you going to get another job if you don't start looking for one? Tom: Now don't worry your pretty little head about it. Just leave it to me.* □ *Tom: What are we going to do if we can't find an apartment? Sally: Don't worry your head about it. We'll find one, one way or another.*

Don't you know it! You can be absolutely sure about that!; You're exactly right, and I agree with you. (This is not a question.) □ *Alice: Man, is it hot! Fred: Don't you know it!* □ *Bob: This is the best cake I have ever eaten. The cook is the best in the world! Bill: Don't you know it!*

Don't you wish! Don't you wish that what you have just said were really true? □ *Mary: I'm going to get a job that lets me travel a lot. Sally: Don't you wish!* □ *Sally: Sorry you lost the chess game. It was close, but your opponent was top-notch. Bob: Next time, I'll do it! I'll win the next round. Sally: Don't you wish!*

doom someone or something **to** something to destine someone or something to something unpleasant. □ *The judgment doomed her to a life in prison.* □ *Your insistence on including that rigid clause doomed the contract to failure.*

doomed to something condemned to something; facing something as a future or as a consequence [of something]. □ *The project was doomed to failure from the start.* □ *I am doomed to a life of hard work and low pay.*

A **door must be either shut or open.** *Prov.* If you have only two alternatives, you must choose one or the other; you cannot have both. □ *Either you're going to marry that girl, or you're not. A door must be either shut or open.*

doors open up (to someone**)** opportunities become available to someone. □ *After Ann made a few inquiries, doors began to open up to me.* □ *An agent helps. After I got one, all sorts of doors opened up.*

door-to-door 1. *Lit.* having to do with movement from one door to another or from one house to another. □ *John is a door-to-door salesman.* □ *We spent two weeks making a door-to-door survey.* **2.** *Fig.* by moving from one door to another or one house to another. □ *Anne is selling books door-to-door.* □ *We went door-to-door, collecting money.*

dope someone or an animal **up**† to give drugs to someone or an animal. □ *Her parents doped her up with medicine so she would sleep through the night.* □ *It's dangerous to dope up a child night after night.* □ *The trainer got caught doping the horse up.*

dope something **out**† **1.** *Sl.* to figure something out. □ *He spent a lot of time trying to dope the assignment out so he could understand it.* □ *It's hard to dope out a physics assignment after midnight.* **2.** *Sl.* to explain something carefully. □ *He doped it all out to them very carefully so that no one would be confused.* □ *He doped out the information slowly and patiently.*

dork off *Sl.* to waste time; to goof off. □ *Stop dorking off and get busy.* □ *The whole class was dorking off and the teacher got furious.*

a **dose of** one's **own medicine** Go to a **taste of** one's **own medicine.**

dose someone or an animal **with** something to give medicine to someone or an animal. □ *You should dose the child with a little nonaspirin painkiller.* □ *She dosed the horse with a mild tranquilizer.*

doss down (for some time**)** *Sl.* to lie down to sleep for a period of time. □ *Chuck dossed down for a few hours before the evening performance.* □ *It's midnight: time to doss down.*

dot something **with** something to put little bits or dots of something on something. □ *She dotted her face with red marks to make it look as if she had measles.* □ *The chef dotted the cake with blobs of buttery icing.*

dote (up)on someone or something to adore or spoil someone or something; to like very much. (*Upon* is formal and less commonly used than *on*.) □ *His aunt simply dotes upon him.* □ *Mary dotes on vanilla ice cream.*

double as someone or something [for someone] to serve in two capacities. □ *The chairman will have to double as CEO until we find a new one.* □ *This table doubles as a desk during busy times.*

double back (on someone or something**)** [for a person or animal] to reverse motion, moving toward (rather than away from) someone or something. (Refers primarily to a person or animal that is being pursued by someone or a group.) □ *The deer doubled back on the hunter.* □ *The robber doubled back on the police, and they lost track of him.* □ *I doubled back on my own trail.*

double Dutch 1. language or speech that is difficult or impossible to understand. □ *This book on English grammar is written in double Dutch. I can't understand a word.* □ *Try to find a lecturer who speaks slowly, not one who speaks double Dutch.* **2.** a game of jumping rope using two ropes swung simultaneously in opposite directions. □ *The girls were playing double Dutch in the schoolyard.*

double in brass (as something**)** *Fig.* to serve in two capacities. (Alludes to a musician who could play the brass instruments as well as other instruments.) □ *Wally was our bookkeeper and doubled in brass as a clerk.*

double over [for a person] to bend at the waist. □ *Suddenly, he doubled over and collapsed.* □ *The people in the audience doubled over with laughter.*

double someone **over**[†] to cause someone to bend at the waist. □ *The blow to the back of the head doubled Steve over.* □ *The wind almost doubled over the children running for home.*

double something **over**[†] to fold something over. □ *Double the paper over twice, then press it flat.* □ *Double over the cloth a few times before you pack it away.*

double up (on someone or something**)** [for people] to deal with someone or something in pairs. □ *We are going to have to double up in this job.* □ *We will double up and get it done.*

double up (with laughter) *Fig.* to laugh so hard that one bends over. □ *We all just doubled up with laughter.* □ *I doubled up when I heard the punch line.*

double up (with pain) to bend at the waist with severe pain. □ *The man doubled up with pain when he was stabbed.* □ *He hurt so bad that he doubled up.*

double up (with someone**)** to share with someone. □ *We don't have enough books. Tom, will you double up with Jane?* □ *When we get more books, we won't have to double up anymore.*

a **double whammy** a double dose of something; a strong or powerful helping of something. □ *When the Federal Reserve Board raised the interest rates, I got a double whammy. My stocks went down and my bonds did too.*

double-cross someone to betray someone. (Originally a more complicated switching of sides in a conspiracy wherein the *double-crosser* sides with the victim of the conspiracy—against the original conspirator.) □ *Don't even think about double-crossing me!* □ *Richard double-crossed Mr. Big a few years back.*

a **double-edged sword** Go to a **two-edged sword**.

doubting Thomas someone who will not easily believe something without strong proof or evidence. (Can be said of a man or a woman. From the biblical account of the apostle Thomas, who would not believe that Jesus had risen from the dead until he actually touched the risen Christ.) □ *Mary won't believe that I have a dog until she sees it. She's such a doubting Thomas.*

douse someone or something **with** something to splash or drench someone with something. □ *She doused her brother with a bucket of cold water.* □ *They had to keep dousing the porpoise with cold water to keep it healthy.*

dovetail something **into** something *Fig.* to fit something neatly into something; to make something interlock nicely with something else. □ *She dovetailed her story into mine perfectly and the police let us go.*

dovetail with something **1.** *Lit.* to interlock tightly with something using a dovetail joint. □ *The side of the drawer dovetails with the front of the drawer.* **2.** *Fig.* to fit neatly into something. □ *Your story doesn't dovetail with mine very well.*

down and dirty 1. crude and carelessly done. □ *(Used as an attributive.) The last time he painted the kitchen, it was a down and dirty job because he thought we were moving.* *Fig.* coarse; mean-spirited. □ *The campaign for governor really got down and dirty in the final week.*

down by some amount having a score that is lower, by the specified amount, than someone else's score or the other team's score. □ *At halftime, the home team was down by 14 points.* □ *Down by one run, the team scored two runs in the ninth inning and won the game.*

down for something having one's name written down for something. □ *Am I down for an evening appointment?* □ *You are down for Friday.*

*****down for the count 1.** and *****out for the count** [of a boxer] knocked down by an opponent's punching and remaining down until the last count, or even beyond. (*Typically: be ~; go ~.) □ *Wally is down for the count. Chris is the winner.* **2.** eliminated from something or an activity for a period of time, perhaps permanently. (*Typically: be ~; go ~.) □ *I can't continue with this course. I'm down for the count.* □ *I'm down for the count. I have the flu.*

*****down in the dumps** *Fig.* sad or depressed. (*Typically: be ~; get ~.) □ *I've been down in the dumps for the past*

167

few days. □ *Try to cheer Jane up. She's down in the dumps for some reason.*

down in the mouth *Fig.* sad-faced; depressed and unsmiling. □ *Since her dog died, Barbara has been down in the mouth.* □ *Bob has been down in the mouth since he was laid off from his job.*

down on one's **luck** without any money; unlucky. □ *Can you lend me twenty dollars? I've been down on my luck lately.* □ *The gambler had to get a job because he had been down on his luck and hadn't won enough money to live on.*

***down on** someone or something against someone or something. (*Typically: **be** ~; **get** ~.) □ *You've been down on us all lately.* □ *I'm down on computers lately.* □ *Everyone sure got down on fast food.*

down one for the road Go to one for the road.

***down pat** learned or memorized perfectly. (*Typically: **get** something ~; **have** something ~.) □ *I have practiced my speech until I have it down pat.* □ *Tom has his part in the play down pat. He won't make any mistakes.*

down South to or at the southeastern United States. □ *I used to live down South.* □ *We are going down South for the winter.*

down the chute *Fig.* gone; wasted; ruined. □ *A lot of money went down the chute on that deal, and all for nothing.* □ *I just hate to see all that effort go down the chute.*

down the drain *Fig.* gone; wasted. □ *Well, there's 400 bucks down the drain.* □ *A lot of money went down the drain in that Wilson deal.*

Down the hatch. I am about to drink this.; Let's all drink up. (Said as one is about to take a drink, especially of something bad-tasting or potent. Also used as a jocular toast.) □ *Bob said, "Down the hatch," and drank the whiskey in one gulp.* □ *Let's toast the bride and groom. Down the hatch!*

down the little red lane *Fig.* down someone's throat; down a child's throat. □ *This really tasty medicine has to go down the little red lane.* □ *The last spoonful of that stuff that went down the little red lane came right back up.*

down the road 1. *Lit.* farther along on this same road. □ *Just continue down the road until you come to a little church. Turn left there.* **2.** *Fig.* in the future. □ *We don't know what things will be like a few months down the road.*

down the road a piece and **down the road a stretch** *Rur.* a short distance down the road. □ *Smith's Dry Goods Store? It's down the road a piece, on the left-hand side.* □ *I'm not sure we're lost. Let's go on down the road a stretch and see if we recognize anything.*

down the road a stretch Go to previous.

down the street a short distance away on this same street. □ *Sally lives just down the street.* □ *There is a drugstore down the street. It's very convenient.*

down the tube(s) *Fig.* ruined; wasted. □ *His political career went down the tubes after the scandal. He's lost his job.* □ *The business went down the tube.*

down to a gnat's eyebrow *Fig.* down to the smallest detail. □ *He described what the thief was wearing down to a gnat's eyebrow.* □ *No use trying to sneak anything out of the refrigerator. Mom knows what's in there, down to a gnat's eyebrow.*

down to chili and beans *Rur.* very poor; down to one's last penny. □ *Mary and Tom aren't doing too well. They're down to chili and beans.* □ *Many's the time I was down to chili and beans, but I always pulled through.*

***down to the last** bit of money having only a small amount of money left. (*Typically: **be** ~; **get** ~.) □ *I'm down to my last nickel.* □ *Lily is down to her last dollar.*

down to the last detail considering all of the details. □ *Jean planned the party very carefully, down to the last minute.* □ *Mary wanted to be in charge of everything right down to the last detail.*

down under Australia and New Zealand. □ *I've always wanted to visit down under.* □ *We spent Christmas down under.*

***down with a disease** ill; sick at home. (Can be said about many diseases. *Typically: **be** ~; **come** ~; **get** ~.) □ *Tom isn't here. He's down with a cold.* □ *Sally is down with the flu.*

***down (with** someone**)** *Sl.* friends with someone; okay or on good terms with someone. (*Down* = okay. *Typically: **be** ~; **get** ~.) □ *It's okay. I'm down with Chuck.* □ *Chuck and I are down.*

Down with someone or something! Do away with someone or something!; I am opposed to someone or something! □ *Down with higher taxes! Down with corporate tax breaks!* □ *Down with tyrants!*

down-and-out 1. having no money or means of support. □ *There are many young people down-and-out in the city.* □ *John gambled away all his fortune and is now completely down-and-out.* **2.** someone who is impoverished. □ *There were a couple of down-and-outs sleeping under the railway bridge.* □ *The down-and-out touched Martin for a fiver.*

***down-at-the-heels 1.** *Lit.* [of shoes] worn on the bottom of the heels. (*Typically: **be** ~; **get** ~.) □ *This pair is a little down-at-the-heels, but I only use them for gardening.* **2.** *Fig.* worn down; showing signs of use or age. (*Typically: **be** ~; **get** ~.) □ *He is a little down-at-the-heels, but give him a new suit of clothes and he'll look just great.* □ *This jacket is a little down-at-the-heels.*

downgrade someone or something **to** something to decrease the status of someone or something to something. □ *In effect, this downgrades your project to unimportant.* □ *I didn't mean to downgrade you to the assistant status.*

downhill all the way *Fig.* easy the entire way. □ *Don't worry about your algebra course. It's downhill all the way after this chapter.* □ *The mayor said that the job of mayor is easy—in fact, downhill all the way.*

downhill from here on *Fig.* easy from this point on. □ *The worst part is over. It's downhill from here on.* □ *The painful part of this procedure is over. It's downhill from here on.*

down-home as one would find in rural, especially southern, America. □ *She speaks with a kind of down-home accent that sounds more friendly than the typical, urban northener.*

downtime the time when a computer or some other system is not operating. (Computer jargon.) □ *I can't afford a lot of downtime in the system I buy.* □ *We had too much downtime with the other machine.*

down-to-earth 1. *Fig.* direct, frank, and honest. □ *You can depend on Ann. She's very down-to-earth.* □ *It's good that she's down-to-earth and will give us a frank response.* **2.** *Fig.* practical; not theoretical; not fanciful. □ *Her ideas for the boutique are always very down-to-earth.* □ *The committee's plans for the village are anything but down-to-earth.*

*down-to-the-wire *Fig.* waiting until the very last moment; right up to the deadline. (*Typically: **be ~; get ~**.) □ *It came down-to-the-wire before I turned the proposal in.* □ *We went right down-to-the-wire on that one.*

doze off (to sleep) to slip away into sleep. □ *I dozed off to sleep during the second act of the opera.* □ *I was so comfortable that I just dozed off.*

draft someone **for** something to select someone for something or to do something. □ *We drafted a bunch of the boys for moving tables.* □ *The committee drafted some of the members for kitchen work.*

draft someone **into** something **1.** *Lit.* to conscript someone into the armed services. □ *The draft board drafted Scott into the army.* □ *Todd was drafted into the army.* **2.** *Fig.* to convince someone to participate in something. □ *She drafted some of the boys into helping her move tables.* □ *They were drafted into helping.*

drag behind to follow along close behind someone. □ *His little brother came along, dragging behind.* □ *Stop dragging along behind!*

drag on and **drag out** to go on slowly for a very long time; to last a very long time. □ *The lecture dragged on and on.* □ *Why do these things have to drag on so?* □ *How much longer do you think his speech will drag out?*

a **drag (on** someone**)** a burden (to someone). □ *I wish you wouldn't be such a drag on your friends.* □ *I don't want to be a drag on the department.*

*a **drag (on** something**)** *Sl.* a puff or any kind of cigarette. (*Typically: **have ~; take ~**.) □ *She had a drag on her cigarette and crushed it out on the sidewalk.*

drag one's **feet (on** or **over** something**)** and **drag** one's **heels (on** or **over** something**)** to progress slowly or stall in the doing of something. □ *Why is she taking so long? I think she is just dragging her feet on this matter.* □ *I didn't mean to drag my feet on this decision.* □ *If the planning department had not dragged their heels, the building would have been built by now.* □ *You must not drag your heels over this; we must get finished.*

drag out Go to **drag on.**

drag someone **in†** (**on** something**)** to force someone to join something or participate in something. □ *Don't drag me in on this.* □ *Let's try to drag in some of the others on this.*

drag someone or something **down† 1.** *Lit.* to pull someone or something to the ground or to a lower level. □ *The lions dragged the antelope down and made dinner out of it.* □ *They dragged down the boxes from the closet shelf.* **2.** *Fig.* to debase someone or something; to corrupt someone or something. □ *The bad acting dragged the level of the performance down.* □ *The bad acting dragged down the level of the performance.*

drag someone or something **into** something and **drag** someone or something **in† 1.** *Lit.* to haul or pull someone or something into something or some place. □ *She dragged*

in the child to make him put on this jacket. □ *Despite his broken leg, he dragged himself into the shelter.* **2.** *Fig.* to involve someone or a group in something. □ *Please don't drag me into your argument.* □ *Don't drag the committee into this discussion.* □ *It is a serious dispute, and please don't drag me in.*

drag someone or something **off of** someone or something and **drag** someone or something **off†** to pull or remove someone or something off someone or something. (The *of* is informal.) □ *The police officers dragged the boys off the top of the wall.* □ *The cops dragged off the boys and took them home.*

drag someone or something **off†** (**to** someone or something) to haul someone or something away to someone, something, or some place. □ *The cops dragged her off to jail.* □ *They dragged off the criminal to the judge.*

drag someone or something **on(to)** something and **drag** someone or something **on†** to pull or lead someone or something to a particular place, such as a stage, platform, dance floor, etc. □ *The master of ceremonies dragged her onto the stage for another bow.* □ *Then he dragged on the next performer.*

drag someone or something **over to** someone or something and **drag** someone or something **over†** to pull or haul someone or something to someone or something. □ *He dragged the chair over to the window so he could sit and watch the children.* □ *Drag over a chair and sit down.*

drag someone or something **through** something **1.** and **drag** someone or something **through** *Lit.* to pull someone or something through an opening. □ *I dragged my brother through the opening into the room.* □ *We dragged the sofa through the window because we couldn't get it through the door.* **2.** *Fig.* to debase someone or something. □ *I don't want you to drag me through a drawn-out divorce.* □ *She dragged herself through all sorts of trouble in her autobiography.*

drag someone **through the mud** *Fig.* to insult, defame, and debase someone. □ *The newspapers dragged the actress through the mud week after week.* □ *The columnist felt it was her duty to drag people through the mud.*

drag someone **up†** to force someone to come up or to come and stand nearby. □ *He wouldn't come on his own, so I dragged him up.* □ *You will have to drag him up. He is too tired to walk by himself.* □ *The reporter dragged up a homeless man to interview.*

drag something **away (from** something**)** and **drag** something **away†** to push or pull something away from something or some place. □ *He dragged the sofa away from the wall so he could clean behind it.* □ *He had to drag away the sofa in order to plug in the lamp.* □ *We worked together to drag it away.*

drag something **behind** one to pull something that is behind one. □ *The child dragged the wooden toy behind him.* □ *What is that you are dragging behind you?*

drag something **out† 1.** to make something last for a long time. □ *Why does the chairman have to drag the meeting out so long?* □ *Don't drag out the meetings so long!* **2** Go to next.

drag something **out of** someone and **drag** something **out†** to force someone to reveal something; to extract an answer or information out of someone laboriously. □ *Why don't* *you just tell me? Do I have to drag it out of you?* □ *We had to drag out the information, but she finally told us.*

drag something **up**† to pull something close, such as a chair, stool, etc., to sit in. □ *Please drag a chair up and sit down.* □ *Drag up a chair and sit for a while.*

dragged out *Sl.* exhausted; worn out. □ *I feel so dragged out. I think I need some sleep.* □ *After the game, the whole team was dragged out.*

dragoon someone **into** something to force someone into doing something. □ *We dragooned the boys into helping us.* □ *She was trying to dragoon some of the men into setting up the banquet tables.*

drain away [for something] to flow away. □ *All the water drained away and exposed the mud and rocks on the bottom of the pond.* □ *When the water drained away, we found three snapping turtles in the bottom of the pond.*

drain from something to flow out of something. □ *All the dirty oil drained from the engine.* □ *The milk drained from the leaky container and covered the bottom of the refrigerator.*

drain out to flow out or empty. □ *All the milk drained out of the container onto the bottom of the refrigerator.* □ *All the oil drained out of the crankcase.*

drain someone or something **of** something *Fig.* to exhaust someone or something of something, such as energy, motivation, etc. □ *This day has drained me of all my motivation.* □ *The first performance drained the cast of all its energy.*

drain something **away**† **(from** something**)** to channel some liquid away from something. □ *Drain all of the standing water away from the foundation of the house.* □ *Drain away the water from the foundation.*

drain something **from** someone or something to cause something to flow out of someone or something. □ *The farmers drained the water from the flooded fields.* □ *The doctor drained the fluids from Roger after his operation.*

drain something **of** something to empty something out of something. □ *He drained the glass of the remaining beer.*

drain something **off** something and **drain** something **off**† to cause or permit something to flow from the surface or contents of something. □ *Drain some of the broth off the chicken.* □ *Drain off the fat at the bottom of the pan.*

drain something **out of** something and **drain** something **out**† to cause something to flow from something; to empty all of some liquid out of something. □ *She drained the last drop out of the bottle.* □ *She drained out all the water in the pot.*

drape oneself **over** something to sprawl on a piece of furniture. □ *He draped himself over the armchair and dropped off to sleep.* □ *He came in and casually draped himself over grandmother's antique chair.*

drape over **(**something**)** [for cloth] to cover something and hang down. □ *The robe draped over her knees, but she was still cold.* □ *The tablecloth draped over and reached down to the floor.*

drape someone or something **in** something to wrap or cover someone or something in something. □ *They draped her in golden silks, but she still looked like a country girl.* □ *They draped the tables in polka-dot cloth for the party.*

drape someone or something **with** something to hang something on or over someone or something. □ *They draped each guest with a makeshift toga.* □ *They draped the statue with a brightly colored loincloth.*

drape something **around** someone or something to wrap or hang something around someone or something. □ *She draped the shawl around her shoulders and felt a little warmer.* □ *Mother draped a towel around Timmy after his bath.*

draw a bead on someone or something and **get a bead on** someone or something **1.** *Lit.* to locate someone or something in the sights of a gun. □ *Fred drew a bead on the target and pulled the trigger.* □ *The hunter drew a bead on the deer.* **2.** *Fig.* to prepare to deal with or obtain someone or something. □ *As soon as I get a bead on how widespread the problem really is, I will set up a meeting about it.*

draw a blank 1. *Fig.* to get no response; to find nothing. □ *I asked him about Tom's financial problems, and I just drew a blank.* □ *We looked in the files for an hour, but we drew a blank.* **2.** *Fig.* to fail to remember something. □ *I tried to remember her telephone number, but I could only draw a blank.* □ *It was a very hard test with just one question to answer, and I drew a blank.*

draw a line between something **and** something else and **draw the line between** something **and** something else *Fig.* to separate two things; to distinguish or differentiate between two things. (Also with *the.*) □ *I draw a line between just bumping into people and actually striking them.* □ *It's very hard to draw a line between slamming a door and just closing it loudly.*

draw a line in the sand *Fig.* to create or declare an artificial boundary and imply that crossing it will cause trouble. □ *Todd drew a line in the sand by giving his roommate an ultimatum about his sloppiness—he had to start cleaning up after himself or move out.*

draw against an amount of money to withdraw money from something in advance. □ *I can draw against my allowance—at least a small amount.* □ *You cannot draw against your salary.*

draw ahead (of someone or something**)** to pull or move ahead of someone or something in motion. □ *I drew ahead of the car in front of me.* □ *The horse I was racing against drew ahead.*

draw apart (from someone or something**)** and **draw away (from** someone or something**)** to pull back or away from someone or something. □ *Don't draw apart from the rest of us.* □ *Please don't draw away from me. I won't bite.* □ *She drew away slowly and left the room.*

draw away (from someone or something**)** Go to previous.

draw blood 1. *Lit.* to hit or bite (a person or an animal) and make a wound that bleeds. □ *The dog chased me and bit me hard, but it didn't draw blood.* □ *The boxer landed just one punch and drew blood immediately.* **2.** *Fig.* to anger or insult a person. □ *Sally screamed out a terrible insult at Tom. Judging by the look on his face, she really drew blood.* □ *Tom started yelling and cursing, trying to insult Sally. He wouldn't be satisfied until he had drawn blood, too.*

draw fire from someone Go to **draw** someone's **fire.**

draw for something and **draw lots** to choose lots for something, without looking; to draw a token for something from a set of tokens concealed in something. (The tokens are typically slips of paper, one of which is marked as the winner. See also **draw straws**.) □ *Let's draw for the prize. The winner gets it.* □ *We will draw for a winner from the five finalists.* □ *The players drew lots to determine who would go first.*

draw in one's **horns** and **pull in** one's **horns** *Fig.* to back down from a fight. □ *For a minute it looked like they were gonna start sluggin' each other, but then they drew in their horns.* □ *We tried to calm him down and get him to pull in his horns.*

draw interest 1. to appear interesting and get (someone's) attention. (Note the variation in the examples.) □ *This kind of event isn't likely to draw a lot of interest.* □ *What kind of show will draw public interest?* **2.** [for money] to earn interest while on deposit. □ *Put your money in the bank so it will draw interest.* □ *The cash value of some insurance policies also draws interest.*

draw lots Go to **draw for** something.

draw near 1. and **draw near (to** someone or something**)** *Lit.* to come near to someone or something. □ *Draw near to me, and let me look at you.* □ *Draw near to the table and look at this.* **2.** *Fig.* [for a particular time] to approach. □ *The time to depart is drawing near.* □ *As the time for her speech drew near, Ann became more and more nervous.*

draw on someone or something and **draw upon** someone or something to use someone or something in some beneficial way; to extract from a resource, reserve, etc. □ *I may have to draw on your advice in order to complete this project.* □ *If there is some way you can draw on me to your advantage, let me know.* □ *By the end of the contest I had drawn upon all the energy I had.*

draw (oneself**) aside** [for someone] to move aside. □ *I drew myself aside so the children could pass.* □ *He drew himself aside so Maggie could pass.*

draw oneself **up (to** something**)** to stand up straight to one's full height. (Fixed order.) □ *Walter drew himself up to his six-foot height and walked away.* □ *She drew herself up and walked away.*

draw people or things **together**[†] to pull people together; to pull things together. □ *She drew her toys together in preparation for leaving.* □ *She drew together all the people she wanted to talk to.*

draw some kind of attention **away**[†] **(from** someone or something**)** to capture attention or praise due to someone or something. □ *Her sterling performance drew attention away from the big star in one of the other roles.* □ *She drew away too much notice by her late arrival at the party.*

draw someone **aside**[†] to pull or steer someone aside. □ *The teacher drew Bob aside to have a word with him.* □ *Harry drew aside someone he could trust and expressed his fears.*

draw someone or an animal **out of** something and **draw** someone or an animal **out**[†] to lure someone or an animal out of something or some place. □ *I thought the smell of breakfast would draw him out of his slumber.* □ *The catnip drew out the cat from under the front porch.*

draw (someone or something**) from** something to sketch (someone or something) from a particular source, such as memory, real life, a photograph, etc. □ *He is a very good artist. He can draw from a photograph or a painting.* □ *I will try to draw him from memory.*

draw someone or something **into** something and **draw** someone or something **in**[†] **1.** *Lit.* to pull someone or something into something; to attract someone or something in. □ *She drew the child into the shoe store and plunked her down.* □ *Liz opened the door and drew in the children who were all bundled in their parkas.* **2.** *Lit.* to sketch a picture, adding someone or something into the picture. □ *She drew a little dog into the lower corner of the picture.* □ *I drew in a large tree and the ruins of an abbey.* □ *She drew herself into the scene.* **3.** *Fig.* to involve someone or something in something. □ *Don't draw me into this argument.* □ *This is not the time to draw that argument into the discussion.*

draw someone or something **out of** some place and **draw** someone or something **out**[†] to pull someone or something out of a place. □ *We drew him out of the crawl space where he lay hiding.* □ *We drew the concealed microphone out of the cabinet.*

draw someone or something **to(ward)** someone or something to pull someone or something to someone or something. □ *She drew him toward her and kissed him.* □ *Todd drew the child toward the light.*

draw someone **out on** someone or something and **draw** someone **out about** someone or something; **draw** someone **out**[†] to bring out someone's private thoughts about someone or something. □ *I tried to draw him out on this matter, but he would not say any more.* □ *I tried to draw out the speaker, but she would not elaborate on what she had said.* □ *Fred wanted to draw out information about the company's plans, but the controller had nothing to say.*

draw someone's **attention to** someone or something to attract someone to notice or focus on someone or something. □ *Now, I would like to draw your attention to Fred, the gentleman we have all heard so much about.* □ *Could I draw your attention to the statue standing at the entrance?*

draw (someone's**) fire (away) from** someone, something, or an animal and **draw (**someone's**) fire away**[†] to attract the attention of someone firing a gun away from the target, hoping to protect the target; to make oneself a target in order to protect someone or something. (Can be verbal "fire," such as questions, etc.) □ *The mother bird drew fire away from her chicks.* □ *The hen drew away the hunter's fire.* □ *The president drew fire away from Congress by proposing a compromise.*

draw someone **together** to make people seek one another for emotional support. □ *The tragic accident drew the family all together.* □ *Do you think the crisis actually will draw us closer together?*

draw something **apart**[†] to pull something, such as curtains or drapes, open or apart. □ *She drew the curtains apart and looked out the window.* □ *She drew apart the curtains a little bit.*

draw something **down**[†] to pull something down. □ *She drew the shades down to cut off the bright sunlight.* □ *She drew down the shades.*

draw something **forth**† to pull something forward or where it can be seen. □ *Carl drew a booklet forth and began to show it to the people sitting on either side of him.* □ *She drew forth her pocketknife and threatened the bandit.*

draw something **off**† **(from** something**)** to remove a portion of a liquid from something; to cause something to flow from something. □ *The steward drew some wine off from the cask.* □ *He drew off some wine.*

draw something **out**† **1.** to make something have greater length. □ *Bill drew the taffy candy out into a long string.* □ *He drew out a long strand of melted cheese and tried to drop it into his mouth.* **2.** to extend something in time. □ *Do we have to draw this thing out? Let's get it over with.* □ *Stop drawing out the proceedings.* **3.** *Lit.* to draw a picture to make something more clear. □ *Here, I'll draw it out so you can see what I mean.* □ *Please draw out the concept on paper. I can't follow your explanation.* **4.** Go to next.

draw something **out of** someone and **draw** something **out**† to get some kind of information from someone. □ *He kept his mouth closed, and we couldn't draw anything out of him.* □ *We were able to draw out the information we wanted.*

draw something **over** someone or something to cover someone or something with something. □ *She drew the blanket over the sleeping baby.* □ *Polly drew some plastic over her work and left for the day.*

draw something **to** to close or nearly close something, such as curtains, drapes, etc. □ *She drew the drapes to and turned on the lights.* □ *Please draw the door to as you leave, but don't shut it all the way.*

draw something **to a close** to make something come to an end. □ *It is time we drew this evening to a close.* □ *Ann drew the meeting to a close with a few words of encouragement.*

draw something **to** someone's **attention** to make someone aware of something. □ *Please draw this error to the clerk's attention.*

draw something **up**† **1.** *Lit.* to pull something close by, such as a chair, stool, etc. □ *Draw a chair up and sit down.* □ *She drew up a pillow and sat on the floor.* **2.** *Fig.* to draft a document; to prepare a document. □ *Who will draw a contract up?* □ *I will draw up a contract for the work.*

draw straws for something *Fig.* to decide who gets something or must do something by choosing straws from an unseen set of straws of different lengths. (The person who gets the shortest straw is chosen. See also **draw lots.**) □ *We drew straws for the privilege of going first.* □ *Let's draw straws for it.*

draw the line (at something**)** to set a limit at something; to decide when a limit has been reached. □ *You can make as much noise as you want, but I draw the line at fighting.* □ *It's hard to keep young people under control, but you have to draw the line somewhere.*

draw the line between something **and** something else Go to **draw a line between** something **and** something else.

draw to a close to end; to come to an end. □ *This evening is drawing to a close.* □ *It's a shame that our vacation is drawing to a close.*

draw up to pull up more tightly; to shrink up. □ *When they got wet, his trunks drew up and became very tight.* □ *This cheap underwear has a tendency to draw up.*

draw (up) alongside someone or something and **draw (up) alongside** to move up even with someone or something in motion. □ *The police officer drew up alongside us and ordered us to pull over.* □ *A car drew up alongside us.*

draw upon something Go to **draw on** someone or something.

a **drawing card** *Fig.* an attraction that helps bring patrons to a place of entertainment. □ *The comedian was a real drawing card at the night club.*

*****drawn and quartered** *Fig.* to be dealt with very severely. (Now fig. except in historical accounts; refers to a former practice of torturing someone guilty of treason, usually a male, by disemboweling and dividing the body into four parts. *Typically:* **be ~; have** someone **~.** Fixed order.) □ *Todd was practically drawn and quartered for losing the Wilson contract.* □ *You were much too harsh with Jean. No matter what she did, she didn't need to be drawn and quartered for it!*

drawn like a moth to a flame *Fig.* attracted [to someone or some event] instinctively or very strongly, as a moth is drawn to the light of a flame. □ *Customers were drawn to the sale like a moth to a flame. They came from all over and bought up everything in the store.*

dream about someone or something and **dream of** someone or something to have mental pictures about someone or something, especially in one's sleep. □ *I dreamed about you all night last night.* □ *I dreamed of a huge chocolate cake.*

a **dream come true** *Fig.* a wish or a dream that has become a reality. □ *My vacation to Hawaii was like a dream come true.* □ *Having you for a friend is a dream come true.*

Dream of a funeral and you hear of a marriage. and **Dream of a funeral and you hear of a wedding.** *Prov.* If you dream that a person has died, you will learn that person is to be married. □ *Alan: I had a dream last night that my sister was killed. Jane: Dream of a funeral and you hear of a marriage.*

Dream of a funeral and you hear of a wedding. Go to previous.

dream of doing something *Fig.* to have a fantasy of doing something. (See also **dream about** someone or something.) □ *I dream of owning a house like that.* □ *Clara dreamed of sailing off into the sunset with Roger.*

dream of someone or something Go to **dream about** someone or something.

Dream on. What you are expecting or wanting to happen is nothing but fantasy. □ *You want to get promoted to general manager? Dream on.* □ *You, an opera singer? Dream on.*

dream something **away**† *Fig.* to waste away a period of time having fantasies. □ *I just want to sit in the sun and dream the day away.* □ *Don't dream away your life!*

dream something **up**† *Fig.* to invent something; to fabricate something. (The *something* can be the word *something*.) □ *I don't know what to do, but I'll dream something up.* □ *Please dream up a solution for this problem.*

dredge someone or something **up**† **1.** *Lit.* to scoop something up from underwater. □ *The workers dredged the lifeless body up from the cold black water.* □ *They dredged up* the mud from the riverbed. **2.** *Fig.* to use some effort to seek and find someone or something. □ *I will see if I can dredge a date up for Friday.* □ *Can you dredge up a date for me?* □ *I don't have a wrench here, but I'll see if I can dredge one up from the basement.*

drench someone or something **in** something and **drench** someone or something **with** something to soak someone or something in something. □ *A sudden summer shower drenched them in sheets of rain.* □ *My raincoat was drenched with droplets from the foggy night air.*

dress for someone to clothe oneself to please someone. □ *I don't dress for you! Don't tell me how I should look!* □ *Sally says she dresses for her friends, but she really dresses for herself.*

dress for something to clothe oneself suitably for some occasion or activity, or for success. □ *Finally, I learned to dress for success.* □ *I can wear my tuxedo if you want me to dress for the formal dinner.*

dress (oneself) **up** to dress in fancy dress. □ *They dressed themselves up in their finest.* □ *Please dress up for the dance.*

dress someone **down**† to bawl someone out; to give someone a good scolding. □ *The drill sergeant dressed down the entire squadron for failing inspection.* □ *I'm really late. I know my parents will dress me down when I get home.*

dress someone or something **up**† to make someone or something appear fancier than is actually so. □ *The publicity specialist dressed the actress up a lot.* □ *They dressed up the hall so it looked like a ballroom.*

dress someone or something **up**† **(in** something**)** to clothe, decorate, or ornament someone or something in something. □ *She dressed her dolls up in special clothing.* □ *She dressed up her dolls in tiny outfits.*

dress someone **up**† **(as** someone or something**) to dress someone to look like or impersonate someone or something.** □ *She dressed her little girl up as a witch for Halloween.* □ *She dressed up her little girl as a fairy.*

dress (up) **as** someone or something to dress in the manner of someone or something. □ *I am going to dress up as a ghost for Halloween.* □ *Larry will dress up as the pumpkin from Cinderella.*

dressed to kill and **dressed (up) fit to kill** *Fig.* dressed in fancy or stylish clothes. (See also **dressed (up) fit to kill.**) □ *Wow, look at Sally! She's really dressed to kill.* □ *A person doesn't go on vacation dressed to kill.* □ *When Joe came to pick Mary up for the movie, he was dressed up fit to kill and carrying a dozen roses.*

dressed to the nines and **dressed to the teeth** *Fig.* dressed very stylishly with nothing overlooked. □ *She showed up for the picnic dressed to the nines.* □ *Clare is usually dressed to the teeth in order to impress people.*

dressed to the teeth Go to previous.

dressed (up) fit to kill Go to **dressed to kill.**

a **dressing-down** a harsh scolding. □ *The boss gave the entire sales crew a powerful dressing-down for missing their forecast.*

drift along to float along; to be carried along on no particular course. □ *The boat just drifted along lazily with the current.* □ *The project drifted along until we received the leadership we needed.*

drift apart (from each other**) 1.** *Lit.* [for floating things] to separate as they drift. □ *The boats drifted apart from one another.* □ *The boats drifted apart in the waves.* **2.** *Fig.* [for people] to lead their lives without contact with each other having been together or friendly. □ *He drifted apart from his friends.* □ *As the years went by, they drifted apart.*

drift away (from someone**)** *Fig.* [for someone] to begin to be less of a friend and more like a stranger. (See also **drift away (from** someone or something**).**) □ *He began drifting away from me a few months ago, and I haven't seen him at all in the last three weeks.*

drift away (from someone or something**)** [for floating people, animals, or things] to move away from a particular person or thing, on the surface of water. (See also **drift away (from** someone**).**) □ *We watched the boat drift away from us.* □ *He was drifting away on the ice block and there was nothing we could do.*

drift back (to someone**)** *Fig.* [for someone] to return to one's friendship or romantic involvement slowly. (See also **drift back (to** someone or something**).**) □ *Finally he drifted back to her and they made up.*

drift back (to someone or something**)** to move back to someone or something slowly, on the surface of water. □ *The canoe drifted back to shore.* □ *My little boat finally drifted back to me.*

drift in(to something**)** to move slowly and gradually into something. □ *The people drifted slowly into the hall.* □ *The boats drifted into the shore on the tide.*

drift off to move slowly away. □ *The boat slowly drifted off and was gone.* □ *The clouds drifted off and the sun came out.*

drift off course Go to **off course.**

drift off to sleep *Fig.* to fall asleep gradually. □ *At last, he drifted off to sleep.* □ *During that boring lecture, I drifted off to sleep a number of times.*

drift out to move out of a place slowly. □ *After there was no more food, the people drifted out, one by one.* □ *The boat drifted out and almost got away.*

drift toward someone or something to move slowly and gradually toward someone or something. □ *The clouds drifted toward us, and we could see that a storm was coming.* □ *As the clouds drifted toward us, we could feel the humidity increase.*

drift with something **1.** *Lit.* to float along with something; to be carried along at the same rate as something. □ *He paddled the canoe into the center of the stream and let it drift with the current.* **2.** *Fig.* to "move along" passively with events and ideas. □ *He is not very decisive and is as likely as not to drift with the tide of sentiment.*

drill down (to something**)** to bore downward to something or some distance. □ *We drilled down to a layer of water-bearing sand, hoping to make a well.* □ *They had to drill down to bedrock to make a base for the piers that hold the building up.*

drill in(to something**)** to bore into or penetrate something. □ *The worker drilled into the wall in three places.* □ *Please don't drill into the wall here, where it will show.*

drill someone **in** something to give someone practice in something. □ *Now, I am going to drill you in irregular* verbs. □ *The teacher drilled the students in the use of the passive.*

drill something **into** someone or something and **drill** something **in**† *Fig.* to force knowledge into someone or something. □ *Learn this stuff! Drill it into your brain.* □ *Drill in this information so you know it by heart!*

drink like a fish *Fig.* to drink alcohol excessively; to be in the habit of drinking alcohol excessively. □ *Jeff really drank like a fish at the party on Saturday.* □ *I worry about Nancy; she drinks like a fish.*

drink someone **under the table** *Fig.* to be able to drink more alcohol than someone else. □ *I bet I can drink you under the table.*

drink something **down**† to drink something; to consume all of something by drinking it. □ *Here, drink this down, and see if it makes you feel better.* □ *Drink down this medicine.*

drink something **in**† *Fig.* to absorb something; to take in information, sights, a story, etc. □ *Terry and Amy drove up to the top of the hill to drink the sights in.* □ *They drank in the beautiful view.*

drink something **up**† to drink all of something that is served or that is on hand. □ *Who drank all the root beer up?* □ *I drank up the root beer.*

drink to excess *Euph.* to drink too much alcohol; to drink alcohol continually. □ *Mr. Franklin drinks to excess.* □ *Some people drink to excess only at parties.*

drink to someone or something to toast someone or something; to take an alcoholic drink in honor of someone or something. □ *I'll drink to that!* □ *Let us drink to our guest of honor, Wallace J. Wilson!*

Drink up! Finish your drink!; Finish that drink, and we'll have another! □ *Okay, drink up! It's closing time.* □ *Drink up, and let's get going.*

drip in(to something) [for a liquid] to fall into something drop by drop. □ *The water dripped into the bowl we had put under the leak.* □ *Is the water still dripping in the bathtub?*

drip something **into** something and **drip** something **in**† to make something fall into something drop by drop. □ *Alice dripped a little candle wax into the base of the candlestick.* □ *Don't pour it all into the jar. Drip in a little at a time.*

drip with something **1.** *Lit.* to be heavy or overloaded with something to the point of overflowing. □ *The foliage dripped with the heavy morning dew.* □ *Her clothing dripped with seawater as she climbed back onto the deck.* **2.** *Fig.* [for someone's speech] to show certain states of mind or attitudes. □ *Her voice dripped with sarcasm.* □ *The old lady's voice dripped with sweetness and affection.*

drive a coach and horses through something *Fig.* to expose weak points or "holes" in an argument, alibi, or criminal case by [figuratively] driving a horse and carriage through them. (Formal. Emphasizes the large size of the holes or gaps in the argument.) □ *The barrister drove a horse and carriage through the witness's testimony.* □ *The opposition will drive a coach and horses through the wording of that government bill.*

drive a hard bargain to work hard to negotiate prices or agreements in one's own favor. □ *All right, sir, you drive*

a hard bargain. I'll sell you this car for $12,450.* □ *You drive a hard bargain, Jane, but I'll sign the contract.*

drive a price **down**† *Fig.* to force the price of something down. □ *The lack of buyers drove the price down.* □ *The lack of buyers drove down the price.*

drive a price **up** and **force** something **up**† to force the price of something upwards. □ *Someone is buying a lot of gold and driving the price up.* □ *They are driving up the price.*

drive a wedge between someone **and** someone else *Fig.* to cause people to oppose one another or turn against one another. □ *The argument drove a wedge between Mike and his father.*

drive at something to be making a point; to be hinting at something; to work up to making a point. □ *What are you driving at? What's the point?* □ *I could tell Mary was driving at something, but I didn't know what it was.*

drive away to leave some place driving a vehicle. □ *They got in the car and drove away.* □ *They drove away and left us here.*

drive back to go in a vehicle back to where it started. □ *Mary drove back and parked the car where it had been when she started.* □ *You drive us there and I'll drive back.*

drive between something **and** something else to go in a vehicle between things or places. □ *I can't drive between work and home in less than thirty minutes.* □ *The cab driver drove between the airport and downtown more than twelve times in one day.*

drive down (to some place) to go in a vehicle to a relatively lower place or to a place in the south. □ *We are going to drive down to Houston for the weekend.* □ *We were going to fly to Florida, but it will be nice to drive down.*

drive into someone or something to strike someone or something while driving. □ *She drove into the garage and damaged the wall.* □ *Accidentally, Fred drove into Max.*

drive in(to something) to enter something or some place by driving. □ *She drove right into the garage and stopped the car before she realized that she was not at her own house.* □ *She drove in and looked around.*

drive into the middle of nowhere Go to in the middle of nowhere.

drive off to leave somewhere, driving a vehicle. □ *She got in her car and drove off.* □ *Please don't drive off and leave me!*

drive on to continue driving; to continue with one's journey. □ *We drove on for a little while.* □ *The traffic jam is breaking up, so we can drive on.*

drive one **out of** one's **mind** *Fig.* to make someone go crazy; to frustrate someone. □ *You are driving me out of my mind with your nagging.* □ *Henry was driven out of his mind by all the negative comments.*

drive out (to some place) to go in a vehicle to a place that is away from one's home, away from a city, etc. □ *We drove out to a little place in the country for a picnic.* □ *Why don't you drive out this weekend? We would love to have you here.*

drive over (to some place) to go in a vehicle to some place that is neither close by nor far away. □ *Let's drive over to Larry's place.* □ *Yes, let's drive over. It's too far to walk.*

Drive safely. an expression used to advise a departing person to be careful while driving. □ *Mary: Good-bye, Sally. Drive safely. Sally: Good-bye. I will.* □ *"Drive safely!" everyone shouted as we left on our trip.*

drive someone **around** something to transport a person in a vehicle on a tour of something or some place. □ *Fred will drive you around the city to see the sights.* □ *He spent an hour driving himself around town.*

drive someone **around the bend** *Fig.* to make someone angry or very frustrated. □ *This tax stuff is about to drive me around the bend.* □ *Gert will drive us all around the bend with her constant complaining.*

drive someone **back on** something to force someone to tap reserves of something. □ *The hard times drove them back on their life savings.* □ *The challenges of being a corporate executive drove her back on all her personal resources.*

drive someone **back to** someone to force someone to return to someone, such as a spouse, lover, parent, etc. □ *Her bad experience with her new friend drove her back to her husband.* □ *Being homeless was no fun, and soon Wally was driven back to his parents.*

drive someone **batty** and **drive** someone **bonkers; drive** someone **nuts** *Fig.* to annoy or irritate someone. □ *You are certainly annoying! You're going to drive me batty.* □ *This cold is driving me bonkers.* □ *These tax forms are driving me nuts.*

drive someone **bonkers** Go to previous.

drive someone **crazy** and **drive** someone **insane; drive** someone **mad 1.** *Lit.* to force someone into a state of insanity or mental instability. □ *The sound of the wind howling drove me crazy.* □ *The dog's constant barking drove me insane.* **2.** *Fig.* to annoy or irritate someone. □ *This itch is driving me crazy.* □ *All these telephone calls are driving me mad.*

drive someone **down (to** some place**)** to transport someone to some place (as in town or away from home), or to a relatively lower place or to a place in the south. □ *She drove herself down to the hospital.* □ *We have to drive Andrew down to school in the fall.*

drive someone **insane** Go to **drive** someone **crazy.**

drive someone **into a corner 1.** *Lit.* to force someone into the place where two walls intersect. □ *They drove him into a corner and captured him there.* □ *When he is driven into a corner, he will fight.* **2.** *Fig.* to force someone into a position or state where there are few choices and no escape. □ *You have driven me into a corner, so I guess I have to give in.* □ *Todd was driven into a corner when everyone disagreed with him.*

drive someone **mad** Go to **drive** someone **crazy.**

drive someone **nuts** Go to **drive** someone **batty.**

drive someone **on**[†] **(to** something**)** to make someone move onward toward some kind of success. □ *She said her parents drove her on to finish law school.* □ *They drove on their daughter to great things.* □ *The thought of earning a large salary drove him on.*

drive someone or an animal **away**[†] **(from** something or some place**)** to repel someone or an animal from something or some place. □ *We drove the monkeys away from the pineapples.* □ *We drove away the monkeys from the fruit.*

drive someone or an animal **out of** something and **drive** someone or an animal **out**[†] to force or chase someone or an animal out of something or some place. □ *We drove them all out of the country.* □ *We drove out the troublesome kids.*

drive someone or something **back**[†] to force someone or something away; to force someone or something to retreat. □ *The infantry drove the attackers back into the desert.* □ *They drove back the invading army.* □ *We drove them back to the border.*

drive someone or something **off**[†] to repel or chase away someone or something. □ *The campers drove the cows off before the animals trampled the tents.* □ *They drove off the cows.*

drive someone **out**[†] Go to **force** someone **out of office.**

drive someone **out of office** Go to **force** someone **out of office.**

drive someone **to despair** *Fig.* to depress someone; to frustrate someone. □ *Sometimes raising an infant drives me to despair!* □ *The recent problems drove her to despair.*

drive someone **to distraction** *Fig.* to confuse or perplex someone. □ *Can't you see you're driving her to distraction?* □ *The problems I am having with my boss are driving me to distraction.*

drive someone **to** do something to force someone to do something. □ *Poverty drove him to steal.* □ *She drove herself to earn a living.*

drive someone **to drink** *Fig.* [for someone or something] to cause someone to turn to alcohol as an escape from frustration. □ *Being a Cubs fan is enough to drive you to drink.* □ *She was driven to drink by the problems she had with her teenage son.*

drive someone **to the brink** Go to next.

drive someone **to the edge** and **drive** someone **to the brink** *Fig.* to drive someone almost insane; to drive someone close to doing something desperate. □ *Your trouble with the police has driven me to the brink! The next time you are arrested, I will not get you out of jail.*

drive someone **to the wall** Go to **force** someone **to the wall.**

drive someone **up the wall** *Fig.* to annoy or irritate someone. □ *Stop whistling that tune. You're driving me up the wall.* □ *All his talk about moving to California nearly drove me up the wall.*

drive someone **up (to** some place**)** to transport someone to a place on a higher level or to a place in the north. □ *Ralph drove Sally up to the cabin.* □ *He was going to drive her up last week, but could not.*

drive something **around** something **1.** to steer or propel something around something. □ *Wally drove the small car around the post easily.* □ *Please drive your truck around the corner carefully.* **2.** to go in a vehicle through different parts of a place. □ *He drove his new car around town, hoping everyone would see it.* □ *We drove the car around the parade route twice so everyone could get a good look at it.*

drive something **down**[†] **(to** some place**)** to transport a vehicle to a place by driving it there. □ *I will drive the car down to the college and leave it there for you.* □ *I'll drive down* the car and meet you. □ Do I have to drive the car down? Can't you fly up here and get it?

drive something **home** and **drive** something **home†** (to someone) *Fig.* to emphasize an important point about something (to someone). □ *The teacher repeated the point three times just to drive it home.* □ *I hope this really drives the importance of safety home to you.* □ *The accident drove home the importance of wearing seatbelts to everyone concerned.*

drive something **into** someone or something to strike someone or something while driving. □ *He drove the truck right into the abutment.* □ *She drove the car into the side of the garage.*

drive something **into** something and **drive** something **in†** **1.** to steer or guide a vehicle into something. □ *Liz drove the car into the garage.* □ *She drove in the car.* **2.** to pound or hammer something into something. □ *Using a heavy mallet, he drove the stake into the hard earth.* □ *With a mighty hammer blow, she drove in the nail.*

drive something **into the ground** Go to run something into the ground.

drive through (something) to go in a vehicle from one side of something to the other; to pass through something while driving. □ *We drove through some nice little towns on the way here.* □ *We didn't stop. We just drove through.*

drive up (to some place) to arrive some place in a vehicle. □ *She drove up to the door and stopped.* □ *Sally drove up and honked.*

*the **driving force (behind** someone or something) the person or a thing that motivates or directs someone or something. (*Typically: **be** ~; **become** ~; **serve as** ~.) □ *Making money is the driving force behind most businesses.* □ *Ambition is the driving force behind Tom.* □ *Love can also be the driving force.*

drizzle down (on someone or something) to rain on someone or something. □ *The light rain drizzled down on the garden.* □ *The rain drizzled down and soaked us because we had no umbrella.*

drone on (about someone or something) to lecture or narrate in a low-pitched, dull, and boring manner. □ *The dull old professor droned on about Byron—or was it Keats? □ It was Shelley and, yes, he did drone on.*

drone something **out†** to make a loud and low-pitched noise; to say something in a low-pitched and monotonous manner. □ *The announcer droned the winning numbers out.* □ *She droned out the winning numbers.*

drool (all) over someone or something **1.** *Lit.* to drip saliva on someone or something. □ *You're drooling all over my plate! □ The dog drooled all over my hand.* **2.** *Fig.* to envy or desire someone or something. (Alludes to drooling from hunger.) □ *The boys stood there, drooling over the fancy sports car.* □ *Wally Wilson spent many hours drooling over photographs of Marilyn.*

drop a bomb(shell) and **explode a bombshell; drop a brick** *Fig.* to announce shocking or startling news. □ *They really dropped a bombshell when they announced that the mayor would resign.* □ *Friday is a good day to drop a bomb like that. It gives the business world the weekend to recover.* □ *They must choose their words very carefully when* they explode a bombshell like that. □ *They really dropped a brick when they told her the cause of her illness.*

drop a brick Go to previous.

drop a bundle (on someone) and **blow a bundle (on** someone) *Inf.* to spend a lot of money pleasing or entertaining someone. □ *I blew a bundle on the candidate, and it didn't help me at all.* □ *Over the years, I've dropped a bundle on clients at that restaurant.*

drop a bundle (on something) *Inf.* to pay a lot of money for something. □ *Pete dropped a bundle on this car.* □ *I always buy old used cars. I've never dropped a bundle on any car.*

drop a hint *Fig.* to give a tiny or careful hint about something. □ *Mary dropped a hint that she wanted a new ring for her birthday.*

drop across someone or something [for something long or wide] to fall on and lay on someone or something. □ *A snake dropped across the hood of the tourist bus as it passed under a tree.* □ *As I lay sleeping, a ceiling panel dropped across me and woke me up.*

drop around (for something) to come for a casual visit that includes something such as tea, dinner, a drink, etc. □ *Drop around for a drink sometime.* □ *Yes, please drop around.*

drop around (sometime) and **drop by (sometime)** to come and visit (someone) at some future time. (Similar to drop in (on someone).) □ *Nice to see you, Mary. You and Bob must drop around sometime.* □ *Please do drop around when you're out driving.*

drop away 1. *Lit.* to fall off; to fall away. □ *The leaves were still dropping away from the trees in November.* □ *The dead branches dropped away from the tree.* **2.** *Fig.* [for a group of people] to decline in number over time through disinterest or attrition. □ *His friends gradually dropped away as the years passed.* □ *As the other contenders dropped away, Mary's chances for election improved.*

drop back 1. to fall back to an original position. □ *His arm raised up and then dropped back.* □ *The lid dropped back to its original position as soon as we let go of it.* **2.** to go slowly and lose one's position in a march or procession. □ *He dropped back a bit and evened up the spacing in the line of marchers.* □ *He got tired and dropped back a little.*

drop behind (in something) to fail to keep up with a schedule. □ *I don't want to drop behind in my work.* □ *She is dropping behind and needs someone to help her.*

drop behind (someone or something) **1.** *Lit.* to reduce speed and end up after someone or a group, at the back of a moving line. □ *I dropped behind the rest of the people, because I can't walk that fast.* □ *I dropped behind the speeding pack of cars and drove a little slower.* **2.** *Fig.* to fail to keep up with the schedule being followed by someone or a group. □ *My production output dropped behind what it should have been.* □ *I stayed later at work to keep from dropping behind.*

drop below someone or something to fall to a point lower than someone or something. □ *The gunman dropped below the cowboy's hiding place and got ready to take a shot.* □ *The temperature dropped below the freezing point.*

drop by (sometime) Go to **drop around** (sometime).

drop by the wayside and **fall by the wayside 1.** *Lit.* to leave a march or procession in exhaustion to recover beside the pathway. □ *A few of the marchers dropped by the wayside in the intense heat.* **2.** *Fig.* to fail to keep up with others. □ *Many of the students will drop by the wayside and never finish.* □ *Those who fall by the wayside will find it hard to catch up.*

drop dead 1. to die suddenly. □ *I understand that Tom Anderson dropped dead at his desk yesterday.* □ *No one knows why Uncle Bob suddenly dropped dead.* **2.** Go away and stop bothering me. (Usually **Drop dead!**) □ *If you think I'm going to put up with your rudeness all afternoon, you can just drop dead!* □ *Drop dead! I'm not your slave!*

drop down 1. [for someone] to fall down or stoop down. □ *Suddenly, Ted dropped down, trying not to be seen by someone in a passing car.* □ *I dropped down as soon as I heard the loud sounds.* **2.** [for something] to fall from above. □ *The tiles on the ceiling dropped down, one by one, over the years.* □ *The raindrops dropped down and gave the thirsty plants a drink.*

drop down (on someone or something) to fall on someone or something. □ *The leaves dropped down on the newly mowed lawn.* □ *The wind blew a mighty gust and a thousand leaves dropped down.*

drop everything *Fig.* to stop doing whatever you are doing. □ *Drop everything and go outside. The house is on fire.* □ *Do you expect me to drop everything and come and pick you up at school?*

drop in (on someone) and **drop in (to say hello)** to pay someone a casual visit, perhaps a surprise visit. □ *I hate to drop in on people when they aren't expecting me.* □ *You're welcome to drop in at any time.*

drop in one's tracks 1. to collapse from exhaustion. □ *I was so tired, I dropped in my tracks.* □ *Kelly almost dropped in her tracks from overwork.* **2.** to die instantly. □ *Finally, one day, he worked so hard that he dropped in his tracks.* □ *I know that someday I will just drop in my tracks.*

Drop in sometime. Visit my home or office sometime when you are nearby. □ *Bob: Bye, Bill, nice seeing you. Bill: Hey, drop in sometime. Bob: Okay.* □ *"Drop in sometime," said Bob to his uncle.*

a **drop in the bucket** and a **drop in the ocean** *Fig.* an insignificant contribution toward solving a large problem. □ *Jane: We need to stop spending so much. Alan: OK. I'll buy a cheaper brand of toothpaste. Jane: But that's just a drop in the bucket.* □ *Many companies donated food and medicine to help the survivors of the earthquake, but it was just a drop in the ocean of what was needed.*

a **drop in the ocean** Go to previous.

drop in (to say hello) Go to drop in (on someone).

Drop it! Go to Drop the subject!

drop like flies *Fig.* to faint, sicken, collapse, or die, in great numbers like houseflies dying in a large group. □ *It was a terrible year for the flu. People were dropping like flies.*

drop names and **drop someone's name** to mention a name or the names of important or famous people as if they were personal friends. (See also **drop someone's name**.) □ *Mary always tries to impress people by dropping the name of some big-time executives she claims to know.*

□ *Bill's such a snob. Leave it to him to drop the names of all the local gentry.*

drop off 1. *Lit.* [for a part of something] to break away and fall off. □ *The car's bumper just dropped off—honest.* □ *I lifted boxes until I thought my arms would drop off.* **2.** *Fig.* to decline. □ *Attendance at the meetings dropped off after Martin became president.* □ *Spending dropped off as the recession became worse.*

drop off (to sleep) *Fig.* to go to sleep without difficulty; to fall asleep. □ *I sat in the warm room for five minutes, and then I dropped off to sleep.* □ *After I've eaten dinner, I can drop off with no trouble at all.*

drop one's drawers to lower one's pant or underpants. □ *The boys dropped their drawers and jumped in the creek.*

drop one's teeth *Fig.* to react with great surprise. □ *I almost dropped my teeth when she told me her news.* □ *They dropped their teeth when I told them I was married.*

drop out of sight 1. *Lit.* to fall behind something and be seen no longer. □ *The pen dropped out of sight behind the sofa nevermore to be seen.* **2.** *Fig.* to disappear from public view; [for someone] to go into hiding. □ *The robbers dropped out of sight and the crime was never solved.*

drop out (of something) 1. *Lit.* to fall out of something. □ *One by one, the skydivers dropped out of the plane.* □ *The marshmallows dropped out of the bag.* **2.** *Lit. or Fig.* [for the bottom of something] to break loose and drop. □ *The bottom dropped out of the box, spilling everything everywhere.* □ *The bottom dropped out of the stock market, and we lost a lot of money.* **3.** *Fig.* [for someone] to resign from or cease being a member of something; [for someone] to leave school. □ *Sally dropped out of school for some unknown reason.* □ *But why did she drop out?*

drop over to come for a casual visit. □ *We would love for you to drop over.* □ *I would really like to drop over soon.*

drop someone 1. *Sl.* to knock someone down; to punch and knock down a person. □ *Fred dropped Willie with one punch to the jaw.* **2.** *Fig.* to stop being friends with someone, especially with one's boyfriend or girlfriend. □ *Bob finally dropped Jane. I don't know what he saw in her.* □ *I'm surprised that she didn't drop him first.*

drop someone a few lines Go to next.

drop someone a line and **drop someone a few lines; drop someone a note** to write a letter or a note to someone. (The line refers to lines of writing.) □ *I dropped Aunt Jane a line last Thanksgiving.* □ *She usually drops me a few lines around the first of the year.* □ *Drop me a note when you get a chance.*

drop someone or something down† to let someone or something fall. □ *He dropped his pants down, revealing the swimming trunks beneath.* □ *The rescuer dropped down the baby and the doctor caught it.* □ *Sam went to the well and dropped a rock down.*

drop someone or something from something 1. *Lit.* to release someone or something from some higher point. □ *Galileo proved that two objects of different weights dropped from the same height will reach the ground at the same time.* **2.** *Fig.* to exclude someone or something from something. □ *We had to drop Sally from our guest list.* □ *The professor was forced to drop the failing students from the course.*

drop someone or something **into** something and **drop** someone or something **in**† to let someone or something fall into something. □ *He dropped a quarter into the slot and waited for something to happen.* □ *He dropped in a quarter.* □ *Johnny Green dropped a cat into a well.* □ *He went to the well and dropped a coin in.*

drop someone or something **like a hot potato** *Fig.* to disassociate oneself with someone or something instantly. □ *When we learned of the conviction, we dropped him like a hot potato.* □ *I dropped the idea like a hot potato when the big boss said he didn't like it.*

drop someone or something **off**† Go to **drop** someone or something **off** something.

drop someone or something **off**† (some place) **1.** *Lit.* to let someone or a group out of a vehicle at a particular place; to deliver someone or something some place. □ *Let's drop these shirts off at the cleaners.* □ *Let's drop off Tom and Jerry at the hamburger joint.* **2.** *Fig.* to give someone or a group a ride to some place. □ *Can I drop you off somewhere in town?* □ *I dropped off the kids at the party.*

drop someone or something **off** something and **drop** someone or something **off**† to let someone or something fall from something; to make someone or something fall from something. □ *They dropped the feather off the top of the building.* □ *Jake dropped off a feather and it fell to the ground.*

drop someone or something **on** someone or something to release something so it falls on someone or something. □ *Poor Alice dropped an iron on her toe.* □ *I accidentally dropped the baby on the floor.*

drop someone or something **out of** something and **drop** someone or something **out**† to let someone or something fall out of something. □ *She dropped the paper out of the window.* □ *Max threatened to drop Lefty out of the open door of the plane.* □ *I opened the window and dropped out the caterpillar.*

drop someone's **name** Go to **drop names**.

drop something **across** something to let something fall in such a way that a span is bridged; to let something fall in such a way that a pathway is blocked. □ *Let's drop a little rug across the threshold.* □ *They dropped a huge boulder across the road so no one could pass.*

drop something **on** someone **1.** *Lit.* to let something fall on someone. □ *The bricklayer dropped some mortar on me.* **2.** *Fig.* to give someone some bad news. (As if dropping a burden on someone.) □ *Sally dropped some really bad news on Walter.* □ *I'm sorry I had to drop it on you like that.*

drop the ball 1. *Lit.* [in a ball game of some type] to let the ball get away or fall out of one's grasp. □ *Good grief! Bill dropped the ball, just as he was about to score!* **2.** *Fig.* to make a blunder; to fail in some way. □ *Everything was going fine in the election until my campaign manager dropped the ball.* □ *You can't trust John to do the job right. He's always dropping the ball.*

drop the other shoe *Fig.* to do the deed that completes something; to do the expected remaining part of something. (See also **wait for the other shoe to drop**.) □ *Mr. Franklin has left his wife. Soon he'll drop the other shoe and divorce her.* □ *Tommy has just failed three classes in school.*

We expect him to drop the other shoe and quit altogether any day now.

Drop the subject! and **Drop it!** *Fig.* Do not discuss it further! □ *Bill: Sally, you're gaining a little weight. I thought you were on a diet. Sally: That's enough! Drop the subject!* □ *Bill: That house is a mess. I wonder who lives there. Mary: That's my aunt's house. Just what did you want to know about it? Bill: Oh, drop it! Sorry I asked.*

drop up (some place) to come for a visit to a place that is relatively higher or in the north. □ *Drop up and see us sometime.* □ *Please drop up when you can.*

drop-dead gorgeous *Sl.* very good-looking. □ *Perry's girlfriend is drop-dead gorgeous. How can a twit like him hold onto a looker like that?*

drown in something **1.** *Lit.* to be asphyxiated in some liquid. □ *Wouldn't you hate to drown in that nasty, smelly water?* □ *I am not choosy about what I don't want to drown in.* **2.** *Fig.* to experience an overabundance of something. □ *We are just drowning in cabbage this year. Our garden is full of it.* □ *They were drowning in bills, not money to pay them with.*

drown one's **sorrows** Go to next.

drown one's **troubles** and **drown** one's **sorrows** *Fig.* to try to forget one's problems by drinking a lot of alcohol. □ *Bill is in the bar, drowning his troubles.* □ *Jane is at home, drowning her sorrows.*

drown someone **in** something *Fig.* to inundate someone with something. (See also **drown in** something.) □ *I will drown you in money and fine clothes.* □ *Mike drowned the nightclub singer in fancy jewels and furs.*

drown someone or an animal **in** something to cause someone or an animal to die of asphyxiation in a liquid. □ *He accidentally drowned the cat in the bathtub.* □ *She drowned herself in the lake.*

drown someone or an animal **out**† [for a flood] to drive someone or an animal away from home. □ *The high waters almost drowned the farmers out last year.* □ *The water drowned out the fields.*

drown someone or something **out**† [for a sound] to be so loud that someone or something cannot be heard. □ *The noise of the passing train drowned out our conversation.* □ *The train drowned us out.*

A **drowning man will clutch at a straw.** *Prov.* When you are desperate, you will look for anything that might help you, even if it cannot help you very much. □ *Scott thinks this faith healer will cure his baldness. A drowning man will clutch at a straw.*

a **drug on the market** and a **glut on the market** something that is on the market in great abundance. □ *Right now, small computers are a drug on the market.* □ *Twenty years ago, small transistor radios were a glut on the market.*

drum on something to tap, thump, or beat on something in rhythm. □ *Who is drumming on the table?* □ *Please stop drumming on the wall.*

drum someone **out**† Go to next.

drum someone **out of** something and **drum** someone **out**† *Fig.* to expel or send someone away from something, especially in a formal or public fashion. □ *They drummed Bill* out of the bridge club for having a bad attitude. □ The corps drums out a few cadets each year.

drum something **into** someone and **drum** something **into** someone's **head; drum** something **in**† Fig. to teach someone something intensely. □ Her mother had drummed good manners into her. □ She drummed in good manners day after day.

drum something **out**† to beat a rhythm, loudly and clearly, as if teaching it to someone. □ Drum the rhythm out before you try to sing this song. □ Drum out the rhythm first.

drum something **up**† to obtain something by attracting people's attention to one's need or cause. □ I shall try to drum up support for the party. □ You shall have to drum up new business by advertising. □ I need to do something to drum some business up.

drunk and disorderly a criminal charge for public drunkenness accompanied by bad or offensive behavior. □ The judge fined Richard for being drunk and disorderly. □ In addition to being convicted for driving while intoxicated, Richard was found guilty of being drunk and disorderly.

*drunk as a lord and ***drunk as a skunk** very drunk. (*Also: **as** ~.) □ After his fifth cocktail, Michael was as drunk as a lord. □ Judy bought herself a case of beer and proceeded to get as drunk as a skunk.

drunk as a skunk Go to previous.

dry as a bone Go to next.

*dry as dust and ***dry as a bone 1.** Cliché very dry. (*Also: **as** ~.) □ The bread is as dry as dust. □ When the leaves are as dry as a bone, they break into powder easily. **2.** Cliché very dull; very boring. (*Also: **as** ~.) □ This book is as dry as dust. I am going to stop reading it. □ Her lecture was dry as dust—just like her subject.

dry out 1. Lit. to become dry. □ The clothes finally dried out in the wet weather. **2.** Fig. to allow alcohol and the effects of drunkenness, especially if habitual, to dissipate from one's body. □ He required about three days to dry out completely. □ He dried out in three days.

dry run Fig. an attempt; a practice or rehearsal. □ We had better have a dry run for the official ceremony tomorrow. □ The children will need another dry run before their procession in the pageant.

dry someone or something **off**† to remove the moisture from someone or something. □ Please dry your feet off before coming in. □ Dry off your feet before you come in here!

dry someone **out**† Fig. to cause someone to become sober; to cause someone to stop drinking alcohol to excess. □ If the doctor at the clinic can't dry him out, no one can. □ The hospital will dry out Mary and start treatment.

dry something **out**† to make something become dry. □ Dry this out and put it on immediately. □ Dry out your jacket in the clothes dryer.

dry something **up**† **1.** to cause moisture to dry away to nothing. □ Dry this spill up with the hair dryer. □ Will the hair dryer dry up this mess? **2.** to cure a skin rash by the use of medicine that dries. □ Let's use some of this to try to dry that rash up. □ This medicine will dry up your rash in a few days.

dry spell Rur. a period with no rain. □ The dry spell killed the crops. □ We ain't had such a long dry spell since 1988.

dry up 1. Lit. [for something] to dry away to nothing. □ Finally, the water on the track dried up, and the race was able to continue. □ When will the fields dry up so we can plant? **2.** Fig. [for someone] to be quiet or go away. □ Dry up, you jerk! □ I wish you would dry up!

dry-gulch someone to ambush someone. □ The outlaw dry-gulched the traveler and took everything he had. □ The posse planned to dry-gulch the outlaw by waiting outside his favorite saloon.

dub something **in**† to mix a new sound recording into an old one. □ The actor messed up his lines, but they dubbed the correct words in later. □ They dubbed in his lines.

dub something **over**† to record a replacement sound over another sound in a recording. □ They had dubbed over all the dialog in the movie. □ It doesn't matter if you say a word wrong on the tape. We can dub it over.

duck and cover 1. Lit. to bend down and seek protection against an attack. □ When the gunfire started, we had to duck and cover or get killed. **2.** Fig. to dodge something, such as an issue or a difficult question, and attempt to shield oneself against similar issues or questions. □ The candidate's first reaction to the question was to duck and cover. □ The debaters were ducking and covering throughout the evening.

duck down to stoop down quickly, as if to avoid being hit. □ He ducked down when he heard the gunshot. □ Duck down and get out of the way.

duck out (of some place**)** Fig. to sneak out of some place. □ She ducked out of the theater during the intermission. □ When no one was looking, she ducked out.

duck out (of something**)** Fig. to evade something; to escape doing something. □ Are you trying to duck out of your responsibility? □ Fred tried to duck out of going to the dance.

duck soup Fig. very easy; an easy thing to do. □ For Maria, knitting a sweater is duck soup. □ Jill: This jar is stuck. Could you open it for me? Jane: Sure. Duck soup.

dude (oneself**) up** Sl. to dress in fancy or stylish clothing. □ I have to go dude myself up for the party. □ I'm not going to dude up tonight. □ Why don't you dude yourself up so we can go out tonight?

duded up Sl. dressed up. □ She got all duded up in her fanciest dancing dress. □ He hates fancy clothes. He didn't even get duded up for his own wedding.

duke it out Sl. to have a fistfight. □ John told George to meet him in the alley so they could duke it out.

duke someone **out**† Sl. to knock someone out. □ Wilbur tried to duke the guy out first. □ Bob duked out the mugger with a jab to the cheek.

*dull as dishwater and ***dull as ditchwater** very uninteresting. (*Also: **as** ~.) □ I'm not surprised that he can't find a partner. He's as dull as dishwater. □ Mr. Black's speech was as dull as dishwater.

dull as ditchwater Go to previous.

dummy up Sl. to refuse to talk. □ Jill dummied up when they got her into the station. □ John dummied up right away when the police arrived.

dump a load Go to dump one's load.

dump on someone or something **1.** to snow on someone or something. □ *Well, it dumped on us again last night.* □ *The cold front dumped on the northeast again today.* **2.** and **do a dump on** someone or something; **dump all over** someone or something *Sl.* to criticize someone or something; to destroy someone or something. □ *There is no need to do a dump on me. I didn't wreck your car.* □ *The boss— mad as a wet hen—dumped all over me.*

dump one's **load 1.** *Sl.* to empty one's stomach; to vomit. □ *He's had too much to drink and is dumping his load.* **2.** and **dump a load** *Sl.* to defecate. (Crude. Potentially offensive. Use only with discretion.) □ *He had to go dump a load.* □ *He dumped his load and settled back down to work.*

dump something **on** someone *Fig.* to pour out one's troubles to someone. □ *She dumped all her grief on her friend, Sally.* □ *I wish you wouldn't dump all your problems on me.*

dumped on 1. snowed on. □ *The entire Midwest was dumped on with about ten inches of snow.* □ *Our town really got dumped on last night.* **2.** *Sl.* maligned; abused. □ *I really feel dumped on by all the bad reviews in the press.* □ *The jerk who designed this stupid congested stairway hasn't been dumped on enough.*

dun someone **for** something to harass someone to pay a bill or deliver something. □ *If you don't pay the bill, they will dun you for it day and night.* □ *My job is to dun people for payment of their bills.*

dunk someone or something **into** something and **dunk** someone or something **in**[†] to submerge someone or something in something, fully or partially. □ *They dunked him into the pool as a way of celebrating.* □ *Liz pulled the cup of coffee toward herself and dunked in her doughnut.* □ *She dunked herself into the cold water for just a minute.*

a **dust bunny** and a **dust kitten**; a **turkey's nest** *Fig.* a clump of dust and lint. □ *She swept the dust bunnies out from under the bed.* □ *There's a huge dust kitten behind the chiffarobe.* □ *He hasn't cleaned in weeks. There are turkey's nests in every corner.*

a **dust kitten** Go to previous.

dust someone **off**[†] *Sl.* to punch or beat someone. □ *We dusted them off one by one.* □ *We had to dust off all those big guys.*

dust someone or something **off**[†] to wipe or brush the dust off someone or something. □ *Dust this vase off and put it on the shelf.* □ *Please dust off this vase.*

dust someone's **pants** *Sl.* to spank someone, usually a child. □ *My dad will dust my pants if he hears about this.* □ *I'm too old for somebody to dust my pants.*

dust something **out**[†] to brush the dust out of something. □ *Dust this cabinet out and put the china back in.* □ *Please dust out this cabinet.*

Dutch auction an auction or sale that starts off with a high asking price that is then reduced until a buyer is found. (Viewed by some as insulting to the Dutch.) □ *Dutch auctions are rare—most auctioneers start with a lower price than they hope to obtain.* □ *My real estate agent advised me to ask a reasonable price for my house rather than get involved with a Dutch auction.*

Dutch courage unusual or artificial courage arising from the influence of alcohol. (Viewed by some as insulting to the Dutch.) □ *It was Dutch courage that made the football fan attack the policeman.* □ *It will take a bit of Dutch courage to make an after-dinner speech.*

Dutch treat a social occasion where one pays for oneself. (Viewed by some as insulting to the Dutch.) □ *"It's nice of you to ask me out to dinner," she said, "but could we make it a Dutch treat?"* □ *The office outing is always a Dutch treat.*

Dutch uncle a man who gives frank and direct advice to someone. (In the way an uncle might, but not a real relative.) □ *I would not have to lecture you like a Dutch uncle if you were not so extravagant.* □ *He acts more like a Dutch uncle than a husband. He's forever telling her what to do in public.*

duty bound (to do something**)** forced by a sense of duty and honor to do something. □ *Good evening, madam. I'm duty bound to inform you that we have arrested your husband.* □ *No one made me say that. I was duty bound.*

dwell in an ivory tower Go to in an ivory tower.

dwell (up)on someone or something to remain on the [important] subject of someone or something for a long time. (*Upon* is formal and less commonly used than *on*.) □ *I can't dwell upon this subject anymore.* □ *There is no need to dwell on Sarah further.*

dwell (up)on something to live on something, such as the planet Earth. (*Upon* is more formal than *on*.) □ *This is the largest turtle that dwells upon the earth.* □ *Many creatures dwell on this earth.*

dwindle away (to something**)** and **dwindle down (to** something**)** to shrink, contract, or diminish to something. □ *The noise dwindled away to nothing.* □ *It just dwindled down and was gone.*

dwindle down (to something**)** Go to previous.

dyed-in-the-wool [of someone] permanent or extreme. □ *My uncle was a dyed-in-the-wool farmer. He wouldn't change for anything.* □ *Sally is a dyed-in-the-wool socialist.*

dying to do something *Fig.* very eager to do something. □ *I'm just dying to go sailing in your new boat.* □ *After a long hot day like this one, I'm just dying for a cool drink.*

dying to know (something**)** *Fig.* very eager to know something. □ *I'm just dying to know how your weekend went.*

eager beaver someone who is very enthusiastic; someone who works very hard. □ *New volunteers are always eager beavers.* □ *The young assistant gets to work very early. She's a real eager beaver.*

eagle eye acute eyesight; an intently watchful eye. (From the sharp eyesight of the eagle.) □ *The students wrote their essays under the eagle eye of the headmaster.* □ *The umpire kept his eagle eye on the tennis match.*

*an earful *Fig.* a great amount of discussion, criticism, gossip, or complaint. (*Typically: **get** ~; **have** ~; **give** someone** ~.) □ *She was really mad about something, and I sure got an earful.* □ *Sue was standing around the corner while Jim and Mary were arguing and got an earful.*

early bird 1. *Fig.* a person who gets up early. □ *I never miss sunrise. I'm an early bird.* □ *The early birds were up at dawn and ready for breakfast.* **2.** *Fig.* a person who arrives early. □ *The early birds get the best seats.* □ *There were some early birds who arrived before the party was set to start.* **3.** *Fig.* having to do with early arrival. (Usually hyphenated.) □ *Early-bird arrivals will be given a free cup of coffee.* □ *The early-bird special this week is a free six-pack of iced tea for the first 100 visitors.*

The **early bird catches the worm.** *Prov.* If you wake up and get to work early, you will succeed. (Sometimes used to remark that someone is awake and working surprisingly early, as in the first example.) □ *Fred: What are you doing in the office at 7:30 A.M.?* Jane: *The early bird catches the worm.* □ *I didn't expect to see you studying at the library at this hour of the morning. The early bird catches the worm, huh?*

early on early; at an early stage. □ *We recognized the problem early on, but we waited too long to do something about it.* □ *This doesn't surprise me. I knew about it early on.*

Early ripe, early rotten. and **Soon ripe, soon rotten.** *Prov.* A child with extraordinary talent or intelligence will probably lose those qualities by the time he or she grows up. □ *Jill: Philip was such a fine young boy; I'm surprised he's become such a good-for-nothing adult. Jane: Early ripe, early rotten.* □ *Jane: You must be very proud of your little boy. He seems so mature for his age. Ellen: I'm afraid it won't last. You know what they say: "Soon ripe, soon rotten."*

Early to bed and early to rise, makes a man healthy, wealthy, and wise. *Prov.* Going to bed early and waking up early is good for success. □ *Grandmother: I don't think it's good for you to be staying out so late, dear. Early to bed and early to rise— Grandson: Makes a man healthy, wealthy, and wise. Yeah, Grandma, I know.* □ *Host: Don't leave so soon! The party's just beginning. Guest: It's past my bedtime, I'm afraid. Host: Early to bed, early to rise, huh?*

earmark something **for** someone or something *Fig.* to reserve something for someone or something. □ *Tom earmarked the best of the steaks for his special guests.* □ *I have earmarked this chair for the family room.*

earn one's **keep** to help out with chores in return for food and a place to live; to earn one's pay by doing what is expected. □ *I earn my keep at college by shoveling snow in the winter.* □ *Tom hardly earns his keep around here. He should be fired.*

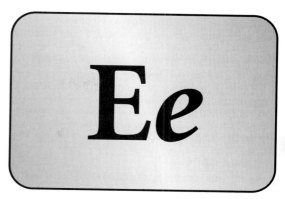

earn one's **spurs** *Fig.* to prove oneself. □ *After that rodeo, all the cowboys agreed that Sally had earned her spurs.* □ *He felt that he had earned his spurs when he received his Ph.D.*

ease away (from someone or something**)** to pull away from someone or something slowly and carefully. □ *The great ship eased away from the pier.* □ *The ship eased away slowly.*

ease back (on something**)** to move something back slowly and carefully. (Usually refers to a throttle or some other control on an airplane or other vehicle.) □ *Ann eased back on the throttle and slowed down.* □ *Please ease back on the volume control a little. You will deafen us.*

ease off [for something] to diminish. □ *The rain began to ease off.* □ *The storm seems to have eased off a little.*

ease off (from someone or something**)** to move away from someone or something, slowly and carefully. □ *Ease off carefully from the deer, so you don't frighten it.* □ *Ease off quietly.*

ease off (on someone or something**)** and **ease up (on** someone or something**)** to reduce the urgency with which one deals with someone or something; to put less pressure on someone or something. □ *Ease off on John. He has been yelled at enough today.* □ *Yes, please ease off. I can't stand any more.* □ *Tell them to ease up on the horses. They are getting tired.*

ease (on) out (of something**) 1.** *Lit.* to continue moving out of something, slowly and carefully. □ *I was able to ease on out of the parking space, but only with difficulty.* □ *I looked both ways and eased on out.* **2.** *Fig.* to leave something, such as an office or position, quietly and without much embarrassment. □ *The bum finally eased on out of office without much public notice.* □ *He eased out while the press was concerned with some other crisis.*

ease someone **(on) out (of** something**) 1.** *Lit.* to help someone continue to get out of something. □ *We helped ease her on out of the car.* □ *With care, we eased her on out.* □ *After taking a look around, Tom eased himself out of the opening.* **2.** *Fig.* to help someone decide to leave something, such as an office or position, quietly and without much embarrassment. □ *The scandal eased her on out of office in a way that an election might not have.* □ *The scandal eased her on out.*

ease someone or something **along** to help someone or something to move along, very carefully. □ *Just ease the piano along little by little.* □ *She eased the shy child along.*

ease someone or something **down**[†] **(from** something**)** to bring someone or something downward from something gently. □ *The rescuers eased the injured hiker down from the mountain.* □ *They eased down the hiker carefully.*

ease someone **out of** something and **ease** someone **out**[†] **1.** *Lit.* to get someone out of something carefully. □ *The paramedics eased the injured man out of the wreckage.* □ *Please ease out the patient carefully.* **2.** *Fig.* to get someone out of an office or position quietly and without much embarrassment. □ *We eased the sheriff out of office without a fight.* □ *The board eased out the chairman by offering him a huge bonus.*

ease up (on someone or something**)** Go to ease off (on someone or something).

easier said than done *Cliché* said of a task that is easier to talk about than to do. □ *Yes, we must find a cure for cancer, but it's easier said than done.* □ *Finding a good job is easier said than done.*

East is East and West is West (and never the twain shall meet). *Prov.* Two things are so different that they can never come together or agree. (From Rudyard Kipling's poem, "The Ballad of East and West.") □ *I had hoped that Andrew and I could be friends in spite of our political differences. But, in our case, I'm afraid that East is East and West is West.*

East, west, home's best. and **East or west, home is best.** *Prov.* Home is the best place to be no matter where it is. □ *You may think that traveling all the time is fun, but eventually you'll discover that east or west, home is best.*

***easy as A, B, C** and ***easy as falling off a log; *easy as rolling off a log; *easy as (apple) pie; *easy as duck soup** very easy. (*Also: **as** ~.) □ *If you use a cake mix, baking a cake is easy as A, B, C.* □ *Mountain climbing is as easy as pie.* □ *Finding your way to the shopping center is easy as duck soup.* □ *Getting out of jail was easy as rolling off a log.*

easy as (apple) pie Go to previous.

easy as duck soup Go to easy as A, B, C.

easy as falling off a log Go to easy as A, B, C.

easy as rolling off a log Go to easy as A, B, C.

easy as shooting fish in a barrel Go to like shooting fish in a barrel.

easy come, easy go *Cliché* said to explain the loss of something that required only a small amount of effort to acquire in the first place. □ *Ann found twenty dollars in the morning and spent it foolishly at noon. "Easy come, easy go," she said.* □ *John spends his money as fast as he can earn it. With John it's easy come, easy go.*

Easy does it. 1. Move slowly and carefully. □ *Bill (holding one end of a large crate): It's really tight in this doorway. Bob (holding the other end): Easy does it. Take your time.* □ *Nurse (holding Sue's arm): Easy does it. These first few steps are the hardest. Sue: I didn't know I was so weak.* **2.** Calm down.; Don't lose your temper. □ *John: I'm so mad I could scream. Bob: Easy does it, John. No need to get so worked up.* □ *Sue (frantic): Where is my camera? My passport is gone too! Fred: Easy does it, Sue. I think you have someone else's purse.*

easy money Go to soft money.

easy pickings [of things] easy to get or steal; [of people] easy to get or persuade. □ *The pickpockets found lots of easy pickings at the state fair.*

Easy, there! Calm down! □ *"Easy, there!" said Arizona Slim, patting his horse's neck.* □ *Easy, there! Before you start yellin', tell me what you're yellin' about.*

easy to come by easily found; easily purchased; readily available. □ *Please be careful with that phonograph record. It was not easy to come by.* □ *A good dictionary is very easy to come by.*

eat (a meal) out and **dine out** to eat a meal at a restaurant. □ *I like to eat a meal out every now and then.* □ *Yes, it's good to eat out and try different kinds of food.* □ *It costs a lot of money to dine out often.*

eat an animal **up**[†] Go to eat something up[†].

eat and run *Fig.* to eat a meal or a snack quickly and then leave. □ *Well, I hate to eat and run but I have to take care of some errands.* □ *I don't invite John to dinner anymore because he always has some excuse to eat and run.*

eat (away) at someone *Fig.* [for a problem] to trouble someone constantly. □ *The nasty situation at work began to eat away at me.* □ *Nagging worries ate at me day and night.*

eat (away) at something *Fig.* to erode something. □ *The acid ate away at the metal floor.* □ *Fingers have a mild acid that eats at the metal of the door handle.*

eat crow 1. *Fig.* to display total humility, especially when shown to be wrong. □ *Well, it looks like I was wrong, and I'm going to have to eat crow.* □ *I'll be eating crow if I'm not shown to be right.* **2.** *Fig.* to be shamed; to admit that one was wrong. □ *When it became clear that they had arrested the wrong person, the police had to eat crow.* □ *Mary talked to Joe as if he was an uneducated idiot, till she found out he was a college professor. That made her eat crow.*

Eat, drink, and be merry, for tomorrow we die. *Prov.* Enjoy yourself whenever you can, because you may die soon. ("Eat, drink, and be merry" by itself is simply a way of encouraging people to enjoy themselves.) □ *Fred: No cake for me, thank you. I'm on a diet. Jane: But, Fred, this is a birthday party. Eat, drink, and be merry.* □ *Natasha encouraged all her guests to eat, drink, and be merry, for tomorrow we die.*

eat high on the hog Go to live high off the hog.

eat humble pie to act very humble when one is shown to be wrong. □ *I think I'm right, but if I'm wrong, I'll eat humble pie.* □ *You think you're so smart. I hope you have to eat humble pie.*

eat in to eat a meal at home. □ *I really don't want to eat in tonight.* □ *Let's eat in. I'm tired.*

eat in(to something**)** to erode into something; to etch something. □ *The acidic water ate into the rocks on the shore.* □ *The acid ate in and weakened the structure.*

eat like a bird *Fig.* to eat only small amounts of food; to peck at one's food. □ *Jane is very slim because she eats like a bird.* □ *Bill is trying to lose weight by eating like a bird.*

eat like a horse *Fig.* to eat large amounts of food. □ *No wonder he's so fat. He eats like a horse.* □ *John works like a horse and eats like a horse, so he never gets fat.*

Eat my shorts! *Sl.* Leave me alone!; Nonsense!; Drop dead! □ *You're nuts! Eat my shorts!* □ *You think I'm going to clean up after you? Eat my shorts!*

eat one's **cake and have it too** Go to have one's cake and eat it too.

eat one's **fill** to eat as much as one can hold; to eat as much as one wants. □ *Please eat your fill. There's plenty for everyone.*

eat one's **hat** *Fig.* a phrase telling the kind of thing that one would do if a very unlikely event really happens. □ *If we get there on time, I'll eat my hat.* □ *I'll eat my hat if you get a raise.* □ *He said he'd eat his hat if she got elected.*

eat one's **heart out 1.** *Fig.* to grieve; to be sorrowful. (Fixed order.) □ *She has been eating her heart out over that jerk ever since he ran away with Sally.* □ *Don't eat your heart out. You really didn't like him that much, did you?* **2.** *Fig.* to suffer from envy or jealousy. (Usually a command.) □ *Yeah, the reward money is all mine. Eat your heart out!* □ *Eat your heart out! I won it fair and square.*

eat one's **words** *Fig.* to have to take back one's statements; to confess that one's predictions were wrong. □ *You shouldn't say that to me. I'll make you eat your words.* □ *John was wrong about the election and had to eat his words.*

eat out to eat a meal away from home, as at a restaurant. □ *I just love to eat out every now and then.* □ *Let's eat out tonight. I'm tired.*

eat out of someone's **hand** *Fig.* to do exactly as someone says; to grovel to someone. □ *I've got her eating out of my hand. She'll do anything I ask.* □ *He will be eating out of your hand before you are finished with him.*

eat someone **out**[†] Go to chew someone out[†].

eat someone **out of house and home** *Fig.* to eat everything that someone has in the house. □ *That huge dog is eating us out of house and home.* □ *The entire football team came over and ate poor Sally out of house and home.*

eat someone's **lunch** *Sl.* to best someone; to defeat, outwit, or win against someone. (Like a school bully taking away children's lunches and eating them.) □ *The upstart ABC Computer Company is eating IBM's lunch.*

eat someone's **salt** *Rur.* to be someone's guest. □ *The least you can do when you're eating someone's salt is to help them out around the house.* □ *That good-for-nothing Jim was flirting with Bill's wife at the same time he was eating Bill's salt.*

eat someone **up**[†] **1.** *Lit.* to consume the flesh of someone. □ *The big bad wolf said he was going to eat you up!* □ *The bear ate up the fish.* **2.** *Fig.* [for an idea] to consume a person. □ *The whole idea of visiting Australia was just eating her up.* □ *The obsession to own a car was eating up my brother and his friends.* **3.** *Fig.* [for insects] to bite a person all over. □ *These mosquitoes are just eating me up!* □ *The bugs literally ate up all the hikers.* **4.** *Fig.* [for someone] to overwhelm and devastate someone. □ *The guy is a devil! He just eats up people!* □ *Fred will just eat you up. He is a vicious administrator.*

eat something **away**[†] to erode something; to consume something bit by bit. □ *The acid ate the finish away.* □ *It ate away the finish.*

eat something **off**[†] Go to next.

eat something **off (of)** something and **eat** something **off**[†] to erode something off a larger part. (*Of* is usually retained before pronouns.) □ *The acidic rain ate the finish off the steeple.* □ *The acid ate off the finish.*

eat something **out**[†] **1.** to eat some kind of meal or a particular food away from home, as at a restaurant. □ *We eat fish out, but we don't cook it at home.* □ *We may eat out a meal or two, but certainly not every meal.* **2.** [for something or an animal] to consume the inside of something. □ *The ants ate the inside of the pumpkin out.* □ *The ants ate out the pumpkin.*

eat (something**) out of** something to eat food directly from a container, such as a bag, box, can, etc. □ *You shouldn't eat out of the can.* □ *Maria was eating potato chips right out of the bag.*

eat something **up**[†] **1.** and **eat an animal up**[†] *Lit.* to devour all of some food or an animal. □ *They ate the turkey up, and no one had to eat leftovers.* □ *The lion ate up the zebra very quickly.* **2.** *Fig.* to consume something rapidly, such as money. □ *Running this household eats my income up.* □ *The car really eats up gas.* **3.** *Fig.* to believe something. □ *Those people really eat that stuff up about tax reduction.* □ *They'll eat up almost anything you tell them.* **4.** *Fig.* to appreciate something. □ *The audience liked my singing; they really ate it up.* □ *The stuff about the federal budget went over well. They really ate up the whole story.*

eat through (something**)** to erode all the way through something. □ *The acid ate through the countertop and ruined everything in the drawers below.* □ *The vinegar ate through the top of the pickle jar.*

Eat to live, not live to eat. *Prov.* Do not be gluttonous.; Eating should not be your favorite activity, but something you do to maintain your health. □ *"Eat to live, not live to eat," was the doctor's advice to Gene, who was dangerously overweight.*

Eat up! to eat everything; to eat eagerly. (Usually a command to begin eating. Compare this with **Drink up!**) □ *Come on, let's eat up and get going.* □ *Eat up, you guys, and get back to work!*

eat(en) up with something *Fig.* consumed with something, such as jealousy. □ *Jed was so eaten up with hatred that he couldn't see straight.* □ *Effie was eaten up with jealously.*

eavesdrop on someone to listen in on people having a private conversation. □ *I saw her eavesdropping on them.* □ *Please don't eavesdrop on me.*

eavesdrop on something to listen in on a private conversation. □ *She was eavesdropping on their conversation.* □ *Maria was eavesdropping on the telephone call.*

Eavesdroppers never hear any good of themselves. and **Listeners never hear any good of themselves.** *Prov.* If you eavesdrop on people who are talking about you, chances are that you will hear them say unfavorable things about you. (This implies that you should not eavesdrop.) □ *Child: Mommy, I heard Suzy and Lisa talking about me, and they said I was a crybaby! Mother: That just goes to show you, dear, that eavesdroppers never hear any good of themselves.* □ *I knew that Mother and Dad had gone into the other room to discuss my situation, and I was tempted to put my ear to the door and* listen to them, but I remembered that listeners never hear any good of themselves.

ebb and flow to decrease and then increase, as with tides; a decrease followed by an increase, as with tides. □ *The fortunes of the major political parties tend to ebb and flow over time.* □ *The ebb and flow of democracy through history is a fascinating subject.*

ebb away to recede; to subside; to flow back. □ *His life ebbed away little by little.* □ *As the sunlight ebbed away, the sky took on a grayish color.*

echo back to something [for something] to recall something similar in the past. □ *This idea echoes back to the end of the last century, when people thought this way.*

echo with something **1.** *Lit.* [for a large space] to resound with the echoing sounds of a loud noise. □ *The cathedral echoed with the sounds of the organ.* □ *The valley echoed with the sound of horses' hooves.* **2.** *Fig.* [for something] to have reminders of something. (Literary and very limited.) □ *My thoughts echoed with the sounds of spring.* □ *The room echoed with happier days.*

economical with the truth *Euph.* untruthful. □ *The mayor was known to be economical with the truth.* □ *I discovered that my boss had been economical with the truth when she said that the company was making money.*

economize on something to save money by cutting the cost of something. □ *We will have to economize on our food budget.* □ *We can only economize on a few things.*

edge away (from someone or something**)** to move cautiously away from someone or something. □ *We edged away from the dirty man in the ragged clothes.* □ *As others saw the gun, they edged away.*

edge by (someone or something**)** to move carefully past someone or something. □ *Try to edge by the portly gentleman carefully. He is very grumpy about being bumped.* □ *Edge by as carefully as you can.*

the **edge on** someone Go to the **advantage of** someone.

edge (one's **way) across (**something**)** to make one's way across something carefully. □ *The hikers edged their way across the narrow ledge.* □ *Now, edge your way across and don't look down.*

edge (one's **way) around** something to make one's way around something carefully. □ *I edged my way around the table, trying not to disturb anyone.* □ *Sam edged around the perimeter of the room.*

the **edge over** someone Go to the **advantage of** someone.

edge someone **out of** something to pressure someone gradually to leave something; to put gradual pressure on someone to retire from a job. □ *We grasped the child's hand and edged her out of the stable without frightening the horses.* □ *The board tried to edge him out of the job by limiting his staff and budget.*

edge something **out**† Go to next.

edge something **out of** something and **edge** something **out**† to move something out of something very carefully, bit by bit. □ *Sam edged the control rod out of the reactor, using the remote control device.* □ *Mary edged the car out of the parking place.* □ *Carefully, she edged out the car.*

edge something **with** something to put an edging or border of something onto something. □ *The tailor edged the hem*

with lace, making the skirt appear longer. □ *The hem was edged with lace.*

edit something **out of** something and **edit** something **out**† to strike out words or sentences from something that is going to be published; to cut out textual material in the editing process. □ *She edited the foul language out of the essay.* □ *Frank edited out the misspelled words.*

educate someone **for** something to train someone for something or to do something. □ *I wasn't educated for doing this kind of thing.* □ *He had spent many years educating himself for just this kind of job.*

educate someone **in** something to train someone about something; to school someone in something. □ *Her parents educated her in the ways of the old country.* □ *She had educated herself in the ways of big business.*

egg someone **on** to encourage, urge, or dare someone to continue doing something, usually something unwise. □ *John wouldn't have done the dangerous experiment if his brother hadn't egged him on.* □ *The two boys kept throwing stones because the other children were egging them on.*

eighty-six something *Sl.* to throw something away. □ *Let's eighty-six this stew and go out and get some decent pizza.*

(either) feast or famine *Fig.* either too much (of something) or not enough (of something). (*Typically: **be ~; have ~**.) □ *This month is very dry, and last month it rained almost every day. Our weather is either feast or famine.* □ *Sometimes we are busy, and sometimes we have nothing to do. It's feast or famine.*

eject someone **from** some place to use force to make someone leave a place; to throw someone out of some place. □ *The management ejected Sam from the theater.* □ *He was ejected from the theater.*

eke something **out**† to extend something; to add to something. □ *He worked at two jobs in order to eke his income out.* □ *He managed to eke out a living.*

elaborate on someone or something to give additional details about someone or something. □ *Would you care to elaborate on that?* □ *I want to know more about Kelly. Could you elaborate on her?*

elbow grease *Fig.* hard scrubbing. □ *Tom: What did you use to get your car so shiny? Mary: Just regular wax and some elbow grease.* □ *Joe put a lot of elbow grease into cleaning the kitchen.*

elbow (one's **way) through (**something**)** to push or drive oneself through something, such as a crowd, perhaps using one's elbows or arms to move people out of the way. □ *She elbowed her way through the crowd.* □ *Jerry elbowed through the people gathered at the door.*

elbow someone **aside**† to push someone aside with one's elbow or arm. □ *She elbowed the other woman aside and there was almost a fight.* □ *The rude woman elbowed aside all the other people.*

elbow someone **out of** something and **elbow** someone **out**† *Fig.* to force or pressure someone out of something, such as an office, post, or status. □ *The board managed to elbow out the old head of the company.* □ *They tried to elbow me out, but I held on to what was mine.*

elect someone **(as)** something to select someone to be something by ballot. ☐ *We elected her as our representative.* ☐ *She was elected as our president.*

elect someone **to** something to select someone to be a member of something by ballot; to select someone to be an officer in something by ballot. ☐ *We elected you to office, so do your job.* ☐ *Tom was elected to the congress.*

an **elegant sufficiency** Go to a gracious plenty.

elevate someone or something **to** something to raise the status of someone to something; to promote someone to something higher, such as a job, a better status, etc. ☐ *The success elevated her to a new rank and higher pay.* ☐ *The boss's attention elevated the policy question to the highest priority.* ☐ *She sought to elevate herself to some sort of social goddess.*

eleventh-hour decision *Fig.* a decision made very late in a process, or at the last possible moment. ☐ *Eleventh-hour decisions are seldom satisfactory.* ☐ *The president's eleventh-hour decision was made in a great hurry, but it turned out to be correct.*

elicit something **from** someone to obtain information from someone. ☐ *I hoped to elicit a statement from the mayor, but I could not reach her.* ☐ *Larry was not able to elicit anything new from Jane.*

eliminate someone or something **from** something to remove someone or something from something. ☐ *We had to eliminate Jeff from the list.* ☐ *The cook eliminated veal from the menu.* ☐ *She sought to eliminate herself from consideration.*

elope with someone to sneak away with someone and get married without much ceremony. ☐ *Sally eloped with Tom, and everyone was surprised.* ☐ *I don't want to elope with Juan. I want a church wedding.*

emanate from someone or something to arise from or come out of someone or something. ☐ *A strange smell emanated from the basement.* ☐ *Some kind of eerie light emanated from the eyes of the statue.*

emancipate someone **from** someone or something to free someone from someone or something. ☐ *The president emancipated the slaves from their bondage.* ☐ *The planter emancipated Fred from slavery long before the law was written.*

embark for some place to leave for some place, usually in a ship or an airplane. ☐ *We are embarking for Denver tomorrow morning.* ☐ *Maria is embarking for Honolulu in just a few minutes.*

embark on something **1.** *Lit.* to begin a journey by boarding a ship, airplane, etc. ☐ *They embarked on their journey from San Juan.* **2.** *Fig.* to begin a project; to begin any process. ☐ *When will you embark on your new project?*

embarrass someone **about** someone or something to make someone feel bad or ashamed about someone or something. ☐ *Please don't embarrass me by mentioning my mistake again.* ☐ *There is no need to embarrass her about her unfortunate sister.*

embarrass someone **into** doing something to shame someone into doing something. ☐ *They tried to embarrass me into doing it, but I resisted.* ☐ *Juan tried to embarrass Fred into going home early.*

embarrass someone **with** something to use something to make someone feel bad or ashamed. ☐ *Please don't embarrass me with that old story again.* ☐ *Maria embarrassed Henry with a reminder of what had happened.*

embed someone or something **in** something to insert someone or something in something. ☐ *The team of oxen embedded their legs in the muddy river bottom.* ☐ *Laura embedded sequins in the candles and turned them into clever gifts.*

embed something **in** something to stick something into something. ☐ *The mugger only embedded his knife in the cloth of the victim's coat.* ☐ *A ring was embedded in the bread dough by accident.*

embellish something **with** something **1.** *Lit.* to ornament something with something. ☐ *He embellished the painting with too many little decorations.* ☐ *The room has been embellished with too many baroque sconces.* **2.** *Fig.* to add to a story with detail. ☐ *The storyteller embellished the tale with the names of people in the audience.* ☐ *I always try to embellish my tales with a little local color.* **3.** *Fig.* to add untrue things to a story. ☐ *He tends to embellish the truth with a few imaginative details.* ☐ *There is no need to embellish this story with anything untrue.*

embezzle something **from** someone or something to steal something from someone or a group. ☐ *They caught her embezzling funds from the bank.* ☐ *Jerry's business partner embezzled a large sum from their checking account.*

emblazon something **on(to)** something **1.** to decorate something with something. ☐ *The workers emblazoned wild decorations on the door.* ☐ *They emblazoned their name on the side of the building.* **2.** to put some writing or symbols that proclaim something onto something. ☐ *The knight emblazoned his crest onto his shield.* ☐ *The craftsman emblazoned the knight's crest on his shield.*

emblazon something **with** something to decorate something with writing or symbols. ☐ *They emblazoned the wall with pictures of past triumphs.* ☐ *His shield was emblazoned with the family crest.*

embody something **in** something to actualize something in something; to make something represent something else in actuality. ☐ *I tried to embody both good and evil in my painting.* ☐ *A strong sense of morality is embodied in her writing.*

embroil someone **in** something *Fig.* to entangle someone in something; to get someone involved in something. ☐ *Please do not embroil me in your squabbles.* ☐ *I wish I could keep from embroiling myself in this kind of mess.*

emerge (from something**) (as** something**)** to come out of something as something. ☐ *The caterpillar would emerge as a butterfly in a short time.* ☐ *A new man emerged from prison.*

emigrate (from some place**) (to** some place**)** to move away from a foreign land to a new land. ☐ *My family emigrated from England to this country over two centuries ago.* ☐ *They emigrated to this country from England.*

emit something **(from** something**) (into** something**)** to discharge something from something into something else. ☐ *The snake emitted poison from its fangs into the cup the man held.* ☐ *It emitted venom into the cup from its fangs.*

empathize with someone or something to have an understanding about the way someone feels; to feel emotional pain with someone. □ *I can really empathize with what you must be going through. I've been through the same thing.* □ *I empathize with people who have the same family problems that I have.*

employ someone **as** something to pay someone to work in some capacity. □ *I employed Fred as a personal secretary for about three months.* □ *Can you employ me as a stock clerk?*

employ someone **for** something to hire someone for a particular purpose. □ *I employ him for special chores around the factory.* □ *Kelly employed Walter for emergency repairs on the night shift.*

employ someone **in** something to pay someone to work in a particular type of work. □ *I employ Tom in machine maintenance.* □ *Laura is employed in accounting.*

empower someone **to** do something to authorize someone to do something; to grant someone the power to do something. □ *I will empower you to collect the dues of the members.* □ *The prime minister empowered a special office to oversee tax collection.*

emptier than a banker's heart *Rur.* completely empty. □ *My wallet was emptier than a banker's heart.* □ *His pockets were emptier than a banker's heart.*

empty into something [for a river, stream, or man-made conduit] to pour its contents into something. □ *The Amazon River empties into the Atlantic Ocean.* □ *The drainage pipe empties into the river.*

An **empty sack cannot stand upright.** *Prov.* A poor or hungry person cannot function properly. □ *Sit down and have something to eat before you go back to work. An empty sack can't stand upright.*

empty someone **out**† to cause someone to empty the bowels, stomach, or bladder. □ *This medication will empty you out.* □ *This stuff could empty out an army!* □ *He fasted for two days to empty himself out.*

empty something **into** something and **empty** something **in**† to pour something into something else. □ *Now, empty the can of soup into the pan.* □ *Open the can and empty in the contents.*

empty something **out**† to remove or pour all of the contents from something. □ *Please empty this drawer out and clean it.* □ *She emptied out the aquarium and cleaned it well.*

Empty vessels make the most sound. *Prov.* Foolish people make the most noise. □ *I suspect Amy is not very smart. She chatters constantly, and as they say, empty vessels make the most sound.*

enable someone **to** do something to make it possible for someone to do something. □ *This money will enable me to open my own business.* □ *My uncle enabled me to open my own candy shop.*

***enamored of** someone or something to feel love for someone or something. (Often an exaggeration. *Typically: **be** ~; **become** ~.) □ *She is hopelessly enamored of Tom.* □ *Tom is enamored of chocolate ice cream.*

encase someone or something **in** something to contain someone or something in something. □ *We encased her broken leg in a splint and raced to the hospital.* □ *Sammy encased the butterfly in a glass display box.*

enchant someone **with** something **1.** *Lit.* to bewitch someone or something with a magic spell. □ *The children were enchanted with a spell that made them forget.* **2.** *Fig.* to fascinate someone with some object. □ *She enchanted the children with the little drawings she made of them.* □ *We were enchanted with her drawings.*

enclose someone or something **(with)in** something to contain someone, something, or some space inside of something. □ *The police enclosed the people in a safe area while the accident was being cleaned up.* □ *The farmer enclosed the pig within a new pen.*

encompass someone or something **(with)in** something to surround or include someone or something within the domain or span of something. □ *We encompassed the group within our administrative area.* □ *They could not encompass our neighborhood in the new school district.*

encourage someone **in** something to give support to someone about something in particular. □ *We want to encourage her in her musical career.* □ *Ted encouraged me in my efforts to become a baseball player.*

encourage someone **to** do something to inspire or stimulate someone to do something; to give someone the courage to do something. □ *We encouraged her to develop her musical talents.* □ *He encouraged himself to study hard so he could make it into medical school.*

encroach (up)on someone or something to infringe or trespass on someone or something; to move into the space belonging to someone or something. (*Upon* is formal and less commonly used than *on*.) □ *I did not mean to encroach upon your property.* □ *I need lots of space. Don't encroach on me.*

encumber someone or something **with** someone or something to burden someone or something with someone or something. □ *Please do not try to encumber me with your debts.* □ *She encumbered the marriage with a number of children from a previous marriage.* □ *She encumbered herself with the weight of both children and her purse.*

***an end in itself** existing for its own sake; existing for no clear purpose. (*Typically: **be** ~; **become** ~.) □ *For Bob, art is an end in itself. He doesn't hope to make any money from it.* □ *Learning is an end in itself. Knowledge does not have to have a practical application.*

end in something [for something, such as a play, film, opera, etc.] to end in a particular way. □ *The opera ended in a lengthy duet before the death of the heroine.* □ *The party ended in a champagne toast.*

end it (all) *Euph.* to kill oneself. □ *He had been depressed for months. He decided to end it all.* □ *I'm no good to anybody. I'm going to end it. Don't try to talk me out of it.*

The **end justifies the means.** *Prov.* You can use bad or immoral methods as long as you accomplish something good by using them. (Not everyone agrees with this idea.) □ *Lucy got money for the orphanage by embezzling it from the firm where she worked. "The end justifies the means," she told herself.* □ *The politician clearly believed that the end justifies the means, since he used all kinds of nefarious means to get elected.*

End of story. *Inf.* That completes the story, and I will say no more. □ *I did it because I wanted to. End of story.*

the **end of the ball game** *Fig.* the end of some process; the end of life. □ *Well, the car broke down. I guess that's the end of the ball game.* □ *It looked like the end of the ball game as we sped too fast around the curve.*

the **end of the line** Go to next.

the **end of the road** and the **end of the line 1.** *Lit.* the place where the road stops; the end of the route, such as a bus, train, or subway route. □ *Our house is at the end of the road.* □ *We drove to the end of the road and began our hike into the mountains.* **2.** *Fig.* the end of the whole process. □ *When we reach the end of the road on this project, we'll get paid.* □ *You've come to the end of the line. I'll not lend you another penny.* **3.** *Euph.* death. □ *When I reach the end of the road, I wish to be buried in a quiet place, near some trees.* □ *She was nearly ninety when she came to the end of the line.*

end something **up**† to terminate something; to bring something to an end. □ *He ended his vacation up by going to the beach.* □ *She ended up her speech with a poem.*

end up to come to an end. □ *When will all this end up?* □ *I think that the party will have to end up about midnight.*

end up (as) (something) to become something at the end of everything. □ *I always knew I would end up as a doctor.* □ *If I don't get a job, I will end up a beggar.*

end up at something to be at something or some place at the end. □ *The plane ended up at Denver airport because of a storm in Colorado Springs.* □ *We ended up at home for the evening because the car broke down.*

end up (by) doing something and **wind up (by)** doing something **1.** to conclude something by doing something. □ *We ended up by going back to my house.* □ *They danced until midnight and wound up by having pizza in the front room.* **2.** to end by doing something [anyway]. □ *I wound up by going home early.*

end up in the poorhouse Go to in the poorhouse.

end up (somehow) to end something at a particular place, in a particular state, or by having to do something. □ *I ended up having to pay for everyone's dinner.* □ *After paying for dinner, I ended up broke.* □ *We all ended up at my house.* □ *After playing in the rain, we all ended up with colds.*

end up (somewhere) and **wind up (somewhere)** to finish at a certain place. □ *If you don't get straightened out, you'll end up in jail.* □ *I fell and hurt myself, and I wound up in the hospital.*

end up with all the marbles Go to all the marbles.

end up with someone or something to finish with the possession of someone or something or in the company of someone or something. □ *Careful or you will end up with Johnny for the weekend.* □ *Do you want to end up with the bill?* □ *I thought my date was with Sally, but I ended up with her twin sister.*

end up with the short end of the stick Go to the short end of the stick.

end with something to make something the final element, just before the end. □ *We will end with the singing of the school song.* □ *The concert ended with a vigorous march.*

endear someone **to** someone or something to cause someone to be cherished by someone else or a group. □ *Her good humor endears her to all of us.* □ *Sally endears herself to everyone because she is so funny.* □ *She failed to endear herself to her husband's parents.*

endeavor to do something to try to do something. □ *Whenever I endeavor to console her, she breaks down again.* □ *Maria endeavored to comfort Henry.*

endow someone or something **with** something **1.** to give something to someone or something. □ *We endowed her with the courage she needed to do the job.* □ *Gerald endowed the proceedings with a distinctive atmosphere.* **2.** to provide someone or something with a large sum of money that will provide income. □ *I will endow my alma mater with some of my fortune.* □ *The family endowed a chair in the humanities at the university.*

enfold someone **in** something to wrap or contain someone in something. □ *He enfolded the tiny baby in a soft blanket.* □ *Sarah enfolded herself in the silk sheets and giggled with glee.*

enforce something **on** someone to make a law effective with regard to someone. □ *I can't enforce this on her if I don't enforce it on you.* □ *This law can't be enforced on anyone.*

engage in small talk to talk only about minor matters rather than important matters or personal matters. □ *All the people at the party were engaging in small talk.* □ *They chatted about the weather and otherwise engaged in small talk.*

engage someone **as** something to hire someone to serve as something. □ *Yes, I engaged her as a secretary just last month.* □ *Will you engage me as a general troubleshooter?*

engage someone or something **in** something **1.** to make someone or a group busy doing something. □ *She knew how to engage the boys in useful activity.* □ *The den mother engaged the scouts in a woodworking project.* **2.** to draw someone or something into something. □ *The enemy sought to engage our troops in battle but failed.* □ *I tried to engage Gerald in conversation.*

engage someone **to** someone to betroth someone to someone. □ *Her parents engaged her to the man she ended up marrying.* □ *She engaged herself to some guy she met at a singles bar.*

engorge (itself) on someone or something and **engorge (itself) with** something [for an animal] to drink its fill of blood. □ *The vampire bat engorged itself on a number of creatures last night.* □ *Mosquitoes engorge on human victims.* □ *The mosquitoes engorged themselves with my blood all night long.*

engorge (itself) with something Go to previous.

engrave something **into** something to cut symbols into something. □ *She engraves a lovely design into the soap that she puts out for guests.* □ *Todd engraved his initials into the bark of the tree.*

engrave something **on(to)** something to cut symbols into the surface of something. □ *She engraved her initials onto the side of the tree.* □ *Ted engraved her name on the bracelet.*

engrave something **(up)on** something **1.** *Lit.* to cut letters or a design into the surface of something; to **engrave** something **on(to)** something. □ *Todd engraved his initials* into the bark of the tree. □ *Their names were engraved onto each of their wedding rings.* □ *He asked them to engrave his initials upon the back of his watch.* □ *He engraved his name on the desktop.* **2.** *Fig.* to imprint something firmly on someone's mind. □ *I engraved the combination to the safe upon my brain.* □ *The teacher engraved the definition of a noun into my memory.*

engrave something **with** something **1.** to carve something, such as letters, into something. □ *He engraved the soft pewter with an old motto.* □ *Can you engrave my watch with a date?* **2.** to carve on something, using some tool or device. □ *The worker engraved the watch with a sharp stylus.* □ *Can I engrave this bracelet with this tool? Is it sharp enough?*

engraved in stone Go to carved in stone.

engross someone **in** something to occupy someone's time or thinking with something. □ *You can't expect me to engross Tom in my work.* □ *We were all engrossed in what the speaker had to say.*

engulf someone or something **in** something [for the fog, a flood, or waves] to swallow up someone or something. □ *The fog engulfed the small town in heavy mist.* □ *The waves engulfed the small boat in thousands of gallons of water.*

enjoin someone or something **from** something [for a court] to order someone or something not to do something. □ *The judge enjoined her from further action in this matter.* □ *The company was enjoined from further dumping of waste.*

enjoin someone **to** do something to order someone to do something. □ *We sought to enjoin her to remain in office.* □ *Sally wants to enjoin the committee to finish its work on time.*

enjoy the best of both worlds Go to the best of both worlds.

Enjoy your meal. an expression used by food servers after the food has been served. □ *The waiter set the plates on the table, smiled, and said, "Enjoy your meal."* □ *Waiter: Here's your dinner. Jane: Oh, this lobster looks lovely! Tom: My steak looks just perfect. Waiter: Enjoy your meal.*

enlarge (up)on something Go to expand (up)on something.

enlighten someone **(about** someone or something**)** and **enlighten** someone **(on** someone or something**)** to tell someone the facts about someone or something. □ *Please enlighten me about this trip you are planning.* □ *Would you enlighten me on the current state of things?* □ *Enlighten me about Sarah.* □ *She enlightened herself about automobile engines.*

enlist (oneself) **for** something to sign up for something; to enroll for something. □ *Sam wouldn't enlist for service.* □ *Todd enlisted himself for the army last week.*

enlist (oneself) **in** something to join something; to join the armed services. □ *She decided not to enlist herself in the air force.* □ *Bill enlisted in the army.*

enlist someone **for** something to enroll someone for something; to seek help for something from someone. □ *I enlisted all of them for the understudy parts.* □ *Can I enlist you for the committee?*

enlist someone **in** something to recruit someone into something; to recruit someone into the armed services. □ *They tried to enlist me in the army, but I decided against it.* □ *David enlisted his brother in an organization that gave assistance to peasants in South America.*

enmesh someone or something **in** something **1.** *Lit.* to entangle someone or a group in something. □ *Don't enmesh yourself in these ropes and chains.* □ *I didn't mean to enmesh you in this net. I should have kept it out of the way.* □ *Jane enmeshed herself in the net that had been set out to dry.* **2.** *Fig.* to get someone or a group involved in some problem. □ *They enmeshed us in their problems even though we tried to avoid it.* □ *We enmeshed the entire committee in the lawsuit.* □ *Why do I always enmesh myself in someone else's business?*

enough and some to spare *Fig.* plenty. □ *Would you like some more pie? We've got enough and some to spare.* □ *Mary: Can I borrow a cup of milk? Tom: Don't worry about borrowing. Take it. I have enough and some to spare.*

Enough is as good as a feast. *Prov.* You do not need more than enough of anything. □ *We don't have much of a surplus of food for dinner tonight, but enough is as good as a feast.* □ *Jane: I wish I could offer you more lavish hospitality. Jane: Don't be silly. Enough is as good as a feast.*

Enough is enough. *Prov.* That is enough, and there should be no more.; Stop! □ *Stop asking for money! Enough is enough!* □ *I've heard all the complaining from you that I can take. Enough is enough!*

enough something **to plague a saint** and something **is enough to plague a saint** *Rur.* enough of something to annoy even a patient person. □ *That little boy has enough curiosity to plague a saint!* □ *Sally's a well-meaning woman, but her endless gossiping is enough to plague a saint.*

enough (something) to go (a)round enough to serve a need; enough to serve all who have a need. □ *There's not enough coffee to go around.* □ *Will there be enough chocolates to go around?*

enough to keep body and soul together *Fig.* very little; only enough to survive. (Usually refers to money.) □ *When he worked for the library, Marshall only made enough to keep body and soul together.* □ *Maria's savings were just enough to keep body and soul together while she looked for another job.*

enrich someone or something **with** something to improve or enhance someone or something with something. □ *You might want to enrich this soup with a little milk or cream.* □ *The teacher enriched her students with field trips and films.*

enroll (someone**) for** something to sign someone up for something; to allow someone to join something. □ *I intend to enroll myself for physics next year.* □ *Todd enrolled himself for a refresher course in algebra.*

enroll (someone**) in** something to sign someone up to be in something. □ *They enrolled me in calculus against my wishes.* □ *I want to enroll myself in the history class offered at the latest hour.*

ensconce oneself **in** something *Fig.* to establish oneself in something; to settle oneself into something; to place oneself firmly into something. □ *He ensconced himself in the* *most comfortable chair.* □ *Sally ensconced herself in the huge throne and pretended she was a queen.*

enshrine someone **in** one's **heart** and **enshrine** someone's **memory in** one's **heart** *Fig.* to keep the memory of someone in a special place in one's heart or mind. □ *Bob enshrined Jill's memory in his heart.*

enshrine someone's **memory in** one's **heart** Go to previous.

enshrine something **in** something to honor someone or something by placement in a shrine. □ *Bill enshrined his grandfather's watch in a glass dome.*

ensnare someone or something **in** something 1. *Lit.* to capture someone or something in something. □ *Dave ensnared the rabbit in his trap.* □ *Henry ensnared himself in the trap they had laid for deer.* 2. *Fig.* to catch or "trap" someone in an act or pattern of deception. □ *She sought to ensnare him in his own framework of lies.* □ *He ensnared himself in his many lies.*

ensue from something to result from someone or something. □ *What ensued from the change in policy was not anticipated at all.* □ *A very serious problem ensued from the events of the day.*

entangle someone or something **in** something 1. and **entangle an animal in** something *Lit.* to catch or tangle up someone, a group, or an animal in something. □ *Careful! Don't entangle your foot in the anchor chain.* □ *Somehow I entangled the dog in the fishing net.* 2. *Fig.* to get someone or a group involved in something. □ *She was trying to entangle us in her latest cause.* □ *They entangled us in their lawsuit.*

entangle someone or something **with** something to get someone or something tangled up with something. □ *He sought to entangle the pursuing mugger with a mass of ropes and boards.* □ *Sam entangled the rabid dog with a net and got away.* □ *He entangled himself with the ropes on the deck.*

enter in something to enroll as a participant in something, such as a contest, competition, etc. □ *She was not ready to enter in the competition.* □ *I can't enter in that contest. I'm not prepared.*

enter into something 1. *Lit.* to get into something. □ *She entered into the house and immediately went to work.* □ *As the people entered into the cathedral, they became quiet.* 2. *Fig.* to join in something; to participate in something. □ *I couldn't get him to enter into the spirit of the party.* □ *She just loves to enter into things and have a good time with people.*

enter one's **mind** *Fig.* [for an idea or memory] to come into one's consciousness; to be thought of. □ *Leave you behind? The thought never even entered my mind.* □ *A very interesting idea just entered my mind. What if I ran for Congress?*

enter someone or something **in(to)** something to enroll someone or something in something; to make someone or something a competitor in something. □ *I will enter you into the contest whether you like it or not.* □ *The trainer entered his fastest horse in the race.*

enter (something) **by** something and **enter** (something) **through** something to enter something or some place by way of a certain entrance. □ *We entered the building by*

the west door. □ *You should enter through the revolving door only.*

enter the fray Go to join the fray.

enter the lists *Fig.* to begin to take part in a contest or argument. □ *He had decided not to stand for Parliament, but entered the lists at the last minute.* □ *The family disagreement had almost been resolved when the grandfather entered the lists.*

enter (up)on something 1. to come in at a particular point as marked by something. □ *We entered the theater upon the most delicate point of the story.* □ *We entered on the tail end of a live scene.* 2. to begin something. □ *Todd entered upon a new phase of his life.* □ *He entered on the management of a new project.*

entertain someone **with** something to provide something for amusement or refreshment to someone. □ *Will you try to entertain the children with a game or two, please?* □ *She entertained herself with the puzzle.*

enthrall someone **with** something to charm or captivate someone with something. □ *They enthralled us with the beauty of their singing.* □ *The children enthralled us with their rustic dances.*

entice someone or an animal **into** doing something to lure or cajole someone or an animal into doing something. □ *We finally enticed him into running for office.* □ *Donna enticed the cat into coming down from the tree.*

entice someone or an animal **into** something to lure someone or an animal into something. □ *Can I entice you into the house for some cold lemonade?* □ *We were able to entice the squirrel into the box with nuts.*

entice someone or an animal **with** something to lure someone or an animal with something. □ *We tried to entice him with a description of the cake, but he was not interested in coming.* □ *If the cat won't come in, try enticing it with a bit of fish.*

entitle someone **to** do something [for something] to qualify someone to do something. □ *This ticket entitles you to go in and take a seat.* □ *Does this paper entitle me to get a discount?*

entomb someone or an animal **in** something to imprison someone or an animal in a tomblike enclosure. □ *Please don't entomb me in that huge, cold office.* □ *Unknowingly, when they closed the door, they had entombed a tiny mouse in the church.*

entrap someone **(in** something) **(with** something) *Fig.* to use something to deceive someone into involvement in something. □ *The investigators entrapped Max into breaking the law with promises to buy the goods he stole.* □ *They entrapped Max into breaking the law.*

entreat someone **to** do something to beg someone to do something. □ *They entreated us to come back as soon as we could.* □ *I entreat you to think it over again.*

entrust someone or something **to** someone to place someone or something into the protection of someone. □ *Can I entrust Johnny to you while I shop?* □ *I entrusted my share of the money to Fred until I returned to town.*

entrust someone **with** someone or something to trust someone to provide protection and care for someone or something. □ *Can I entrust you with Johnny while I go in and*

189

vote? □ *I entrusted Fred with my share of the money until I returned.* □ *I would not even entrust myself with the care of this priceless vase!*

entwine around someone or something to weave or wind around someone or something. □ *The snake entwined around the limb of the tree.* □ *The huge python entwined around the horrified farmer.*

entwine something **around** someone or something to weave or wind something around someone or something. □ *They entwined their arms around each other.* □ *Jack entwined the garland of flowers around Jill.*

enunciate something **to** someone to say something to someone very clearly and distinctly. □ *Now, enunciate it to everyone, because they probably did not understand you the first time.* □ *I will enunciate it to you one more time, slowly.*

envelop someone or something **in** someone or something to wrap someone or something in someone or something. □ *The fog enveloped us in its grasp.* □ *Mountains of fog rolled in and enveloped the house in dense vapor.*

envisage someone or something **as** someone or something to imagine or visualize someone or something as someone or something. □ *I envisaged you as a more graceful person than you are.* □ *We envisaged the living room as sort of a gathering place for the entire family.*

envision someone **as** someone else and **envision** something **as** something else to imagine or fantasize someone as someone else; to imagine or fantasize something as something else. □ *I envision her as the next company president.* □ *We envisioned this as larger than it turned out to be.*

envy someone **for** someone or something to regard one with jealousy or resentment because of someone or something one has. □ *I envy you for your lovely car.* □ *We all envy you for your beautiful children.*

equal someone or something **in** something to be even or identical with someone or something in something. □ *John equals Bill in strength and size, I think.* □ *This cake equals that one in texture but not in richness.*

equal to someone as good or as accomplished as someone else. □ *I certainly feel equal to Randy. He's nothing special.* □ *I don't think that Bill feels equal to Bob, even though they are twins.*

equal to someone or something able to handle or deal with someone or something. □ *I'm afraid that I'm not equal to Mrs. Smith's problem right now. Please ask her to come back later.* □ *That's a very difficult task, but I'm sure Bill is equal to it.*

equate someone or something **with** someone or something to compare people and things, in any combination. □ *I tend to equate Tom with trouble.* □ *I equate the Johnsons with a long boring evening.*

equate someone **to** someone else and **equate** something **to** something else to claim that someone is in some manner the same as someone else; to claim that something is in some manner the same as something else. □ *I would equate Tom to Wally when it comes to native ability.* □ *You cannot equate my car to that jalopy you drive!*

equip someone or something **(with** something**) (for** something**)** to outfit someone or something with something for something; to provide equipment for someone or some-

thing for some purpose. □ *We equipped everyone with a spade for digging.* □ *They equipped the rescuers with equipment for any conceivable occurrence.*

equip something **with** something to add a piece of equipment to something. □ *We will equip our truck with a plow blade and plow snow this winter.* □ *This car is equipped with air-conditioning.*

erase something **from** something **1.** *Lit.* to delete or wipe something from something. □ *Please erase the writing from the blackboard.* □ *I will erase the incorrectly spelled word from my paper.* **2.** *Fig.* to remove something from something. □ *Erase that smile from your face!* □ *I hope you will erase that thought from your mind.*

erupt from something to burst out of something or some place. □ *A billow of smoke erupted from the chimney.* □ *A mass of ashes and gasses erupted from the volcano.*

erupt into something [for something] to become a serious problem suddenly. □ *The argument erupted into a terrible fight.* □ *They were afraid the fight would erupt into a riot.*

escalate into something to intensify into something; to increase gradually into something. □ *This argument is going to escalate into something serious very soon.* □ *These cases of the flu could escalate into a real epidemic.*

escalate something **into** something to cause something to intensify. □ *He escalated the argument into a vicious fight.* □ *The dictator tried to escalate the disagreement into a cause for war.*

escape by the skin of one's **teeth** Go to by the skin of one's teeth.

escape (from someone or something**) (to** some place**)** to get away from someone, something, or some place to another place. □ *Max escaped from prison to a hideout in Alabama.* □ *He escaped to Alabama from one of the worst-run prisons in the land.*

escape someone's **notice** *Fig.* to go unnoticed; not to have been noticed. (Usually a way to point out that someone has failed to see or respond to something.) □ *I suppose my earlier request escaped your notice, so I'm writing again. I'm sorry. Your letter escaped my notice.*

escort someone or something **from** something to accompany or lead someone or something away from something or some place. □ *A police officer escorted them from the auditorium.* □ *A band of honorary pallbearers escorted the coffin from the chapel.*

escort someone or something **to** something to accompany or lead someone or something to something or some place. □ *We escorted the women to their seats.* □ *Claude escorted Harry to the exit and bade him farewell.*

establish someone or something **as** someone or something to validate or confirm someone or something as someone or something. □ *As soon as we establish her as a viable candidate, we will launch the publicity campaign.* □ *She established herself as an authority on rare books.*

establish someone or something **in** something to set someone or something up in something or some place; to install someone or something in something or some place. □ *We established a restaurant in the middle of downtown.* □ *My uncle established me in the candy business.*

estimate the cost at some amount to approximate the cost of something at a particular amount. □ *I estimate the cost at about one hundred dollars.* □ *The cost of repairing the car was estimated at over four thousand dollars!*

*estranged from someone to be alienated from someone. (*Typically: **be ~; become ~**.) □ *Toward the end, they were estranged from each other, so a separation was perfectly natural.* □ *She had been estranged from her husband for a number of years.*

etch something **in(to)** something and **etch** something **in**[†] to erode a design or message into something, usually with acid. □ *They etched their family crest into their good crystal.* □ *He etched in his initials.*

eternal life *Euph.* life after death. □ *He passed on into eternal life, leaving us behind to mourn.* □ *She is now at rest in eternal life.*

the **eternal triangle** a sexual or emotional relationship involving two women and one man or two men and one woman. (Typically, a couple [man and woman] and another man or woman.) □ *Henry can't choose between his wife and his mistress. It's the eternal triangle.* □ *I'm surprised Jane doesn't get tired of the eternal triangle. She goes out with Peter at the weekend and Jim during the week.*

evacuate one's **bowels** *Euph.* to defecate. □ *After taking a jog around the block, Jill felt the need to evacuate her bowels.* □ *I am afraid my little boy is sick. He has not evacuated his bowels for several days.*

evacuate someone **(from** something**) (to** something**)** to remove someone from something or some place to another thing or place, as in an emergency. □ *They had to evacuate everyone from the subway station to a nearby building.* □ *The rescuers evacuated the people from the flames.*

evaluate someone **as** something to judge someone's performance as something. □ *I will have to evaluate you as a new student.* □ *We must evaluate ourselves as teachers and leaders.*

Even a worm will turn. *Prov.* Even a meek person will become angry if you abuse him or her too much. □ *You'd better stop maltreating Amy. She's a mild-mannered woman, but even a worm will turn.*

even as we speak Go to **as we speak**.

*an even break a fair chance; a fair judgment. (*Typically: **get ~; have ~; give** someone **~**.) □ *Please give me an even break! I need some help here!*

even if it kills me *Fig.* [pledging to do something] even if [doing it] is very difficult. □ *Don't worry. I will get it done even if it kills me.*

even in the best of times even when things are good; even when things are going well. □ *It is hard to get high-quality leather even in the best of times.* □ *John had difficulty getting a loan even in the best of times because of his poor credit record.*

even something **out**[†] to make something even or level. □ *Please even the gravel out.* □ *They evened out the surface of the road.*

even something **up**[†] to make something even, square, level, equal, balanced, etc. □ *I'll even the table up.* □ *See if you can even up the legs of this table. It wobbles.*

even steven to be even (with someone or something) by having repaid a debt, replied in kind, etc. □ *Bill hit Tom; then Tom hit Bill. Now they are even steven.* □ *Mary paid Ann the $100 she owed her. Ann said, "Good, we are even steven."*

(Even) the best of friends must part. *Prov.* Even very good friends cannot stay together forever. □ *Child: I don't want Debby to move away. She's my best friend. Mother: Sometimes the best of friends must part, honey, even if they don't want to.*

*even (with someone**)** not being indebted to someone for money; no longer needing to retaliate against someone. (*Typically: **be ~; get ~**.) □ *I will get even with you for breaking my baseball bat!* □ *Jimmy got even with Bill by punching him in the nose.*

the **evening of life** *Euph.* old age. □ *As she approached the evening of life, Sarah looked back on her accomplishments with satisfaction.* □ *The residents of this rest home are all in the evening of life.*

ever and anon now and then; occasionally. (Literary and archaic.) □ *Ever and anon the princess would pay a visit to the sorcerer in the small walled garden directly behind the castle.*

Every cloud has a silver lining. *Prov.* You can derive some benefit from every bad thing that happens to you. (You can also refer to the silver lining of a particular cloud, the benefit you can derive from a particular misfortune.) □ *I'm sorry your business is going badly, but don't despair. Every cloud has a silver lining.* □ *When Mary's friends visited her in the hospital, they tried to cheer her up, but Mary never could find the silver lining in the cloud of her illness.*

Every dog has its day. and **Every dog has his day.** *Prov.* Everyone gets a chance eventually. □ *Don't worry, you'll get chosen for the team. Every dog has its day.* □ *You may become famous someday. Every dog has his day.*

every fool thing every ridiculous or insignificant thing. □ *Every fool thing seems to go wrong with this car.* □ *I don't want to hear about every fool thing you did on your vacation.*

Every horse thinks its own pack heaviest. *Prov.* Everyone thinks he or she has the hardest work to do or the most difficult problems to overcome. □ *When we were growing up, my sister and I each thought our own chores were harder than the other's. Every horse thinks its own pack heaviest.*

every inch a something and **every inch the** something completely; in every way. (Usually strengthening a following adjective.) □ *Mary is every inch the schoolteacher.* □ *Her father is every inch a gentleman.*

Every Jack has his Jill. *Prov.* Every man will eventually find a woman to be his romantic partner. □ *Bill: I'll never have a girlfriend. None of the girls I take out will agree to a second date. Fred: Cheer up; every Jack has his Jill.*

every last one every one; every single one. □ *You must eat all your peas! Every last one!* □ *Each of you—every last one—has to take some medicine.*

Every little bit helps. *Prov.* Even the smallest amount is helpful. □ *Tom: I can only give a dollar to your charity. Mary: That's OK. Every little bit helps.* □ *Jane gave me a* pair of booties for my new baby. It's not much, but every little bit helps.

every living soul *Fig.* every person. □ *I expect every living soul to be there and be there on time.* □ *This is the kind of problem that affects every living soul.*

Every man for himself (and the devil take the hindmost). and **Devil take the hindmost** *Prov.* Everyone has to fight for his or her own survival. (You can use this to describe an extremely competitive situation.) □ *At first we tried to help each other study for the exam, but soon it was every man for himself, and the devil take the hindmost.* □ *The inventors tried to collaborate, agreeing to share the profits from their invention, but they grew so suspicious of each other that each began to work separately, and devil take the hindmost.* □ *When the ship began to sink, it was every man for himself.*

Every man has his price. *Prov.* It is possible to bribe anyone as long as you know how much or what to bribe him or her with. □ *Henchman: I've offered the judge half a million dollars to give you a light sentence, but he says he can't be bought. Gangster: Keep trying. Every man has his price.* □ *Every man has his price, and the townsfolk were shocked to discover just how low their mayor's price had been.*

Every man is the architect of his own fortune. *Prov.* Your own decisions and your own actions determine what your life will be like. □ *The teacher told us, "If you work hard, you can become whatever you want. Every man is the architect of his own fortune."* □ *You shouldn't blame other people for your problems. Every man is the architect of his own fortune.*

Every man to his taste. *Prov.* Everyone likes something different, and you should not condemn people because of what they like. (Can be used to remark that someone's tastes are different from yours, as in the first example.) □ *Jill: Why don't you get some decent neckties, Fred? Fred: What do you mean, decent? My ties are perfectly fine! Jill: Oh, well. Every man to his taste.* □ *Ellen: People who like cats are much more discerning than people who like dogs, don't you think? Jane: Not necessarily. Everyone to his taste.*

Every minute counts. and **Every moment counts.** *Fig.* time is very important. (Used especially in situations where time is very limited.) □ *Doctor, please try to get here quickly. Every minute counts.* □ *When you take a test, you must work rapidly because every minute counts.* □ *When you're trying to meet a deadline, every moment counts.*

Every moment counts. Go to previous.

every mother's son (of them) *Fig.* every one of them. □ *The scout leader said that unless the scouts told him who had stolen the money, he would punish every mother's son of them.* □ *When the football team won the championship, they were all crying, every mother's son of them.*

every nook and cranny *Fig.* every small, out-of-the-way place or places where something can be hidden. □ *We looked for the tickets in every nook and cranny. They were lost. There was no doubt.* □ *The decorator had placed flowers in every nook and cranny.*

(every) now and again Go to next.

(every) now and then and **(every) now and again; (every) once in a while** occasionally; infrequently. □ *We eat lamb every now and then.* □ *We eat pork now and then.* □ *I read a novel every now and again.*

every other person or thing every second or alternate person or thing. □ *The magician turned every other card over.* □ *Every other table had an ashtray on it.*

every time one **turns around** *Fig.* frequently; at every turn; with annoying frequency. □ *Somebody asks me for money every time I turn around.* □ *Something goes wrong with Bill's car every time he turns around.*

(every) Tom, Dick, and Harry and **any Tom, Dick, and Harry** *Fig.* everyone, without discrimination; ordinary people. (Not necessarily males.) □ *The golf club is very exclusive. They don't let any Tom, Dick, or Harry join.* □ *Mary's sending out very few invitations. She doesn't want every Tom, Dick, and Harry turning up.*

Every tub must stand on its own bottom. and **Let every tub stand on its own bottom.** *Prov.* People should be independent. □ *Emily did not want to join the other students, who were helping each other study for the exam. "Every tub must stand on its own bottom," she said.* □ *Don't ask me for help. Let every tub stand on its own bottom.*

every walk of life every status and occupation. □ *We invited people from every walk of life, but only those who could afford the long drive could possibly come.*

ever(y) which way *Rur.* in all directions. □ *When they heard me yell, the kittens ran off every which way.* □ *That mountain road kind of turns you ever which way before it finally gets you to the top.*

everybody and his brother and **everybody and his uncle** *Fig.* everybody; lots of people. □ *The state fair was packed. Everybody and his brother was there.* □ *Everybody and his uncle was asking me where you was today.*

everybody and his uncle Go to previous.

Everybody loves a lord. *Prov.* People are attracted to the wealthy and powerful. □ *Although the prince was vulgar and unpleasant, he always received plenty of invitations to social gatherings; everybody loves a lord.*

everything an' all *Rur.* everything. □ *The thieves broke into Mary's house and took the television, the silver, her jewelry, everything an' all.* □ *I had to write a report about my trip to Memphis, what I did, what I ate, what I saw, and everything an' all.*

everything but the kitchen sink *Cliché* almost everything one can think of. □ *When Sally went off to college, she took everything but the kitchen sink.* □ *John orders everything but the kitchen sink when he goes out to dinner, especially if someone else is paying for it.*

Everything comes to him who waits. Go to Good things come to him who waits.

everything from A to Z Go to next.

everything from soup to nuts and **everything from A to Z** *Cliché* almost everything one can think of. □ *For dinner we had everything from soup to nuts.* □ *In college I studied everything from soup to nuts.*

everything humanly possible everything that is in the range of human powers. □ *The rescuers did everything humanly possible to find the lost campers.* □ *The doctor tried everything humanly possible to save the patient.*

Everything's coming up roses. *Fig.* Everything is really just excellent. Life is prosperous. □ *Life is wonderful. Everything is coming up roses.* □ *Q: How are things going? A: Everything's coming up roses.*

Everything's going to be all right. and **Everything will be all right.; Everything will be okay.; Everything will be just fine.; Everything will be great.** Do not worry, everything will be okay. □ *"Don't worry, Fred," comforted Bill. "Everything will be all right."* □ *Mary: I just don't know if I can go on! Bob: Now, now. Everything will be just fine.*

Everything will be all right. Go to previous.

Everything will be great. Go to Everything's going to be all right.

Everything will be just fine. Go to Everything's going to be all right.

Everything will be okay. Go to Everything's going to be all right.

Everything will work out (all right). Go to Things will work out all right.

Everything will work out for the best. Go to Things will work out all right.

evict someone **from** some place to force someone to move out of something or some place. □ *They evicted the squatters from the building.* □ *They were evicted from their home for not paying their mortgage.*

Evil be to him who evil thinks. *Prov.* May bad things happen to anyone who thinks evil things. (A curse against those who wish you harm. This is the English version of the French *Honi soit qui mal y pense,* the motto of the Most Noble Order of the Garter, a British order of knighthood.) □ *The secret brotherhood took an oath of loyalty and finished their meeting by declaring, "Evil be to him who evil thinks."*

evolve (from something**) (into** something**)** and **evolve out of** something **(into** something**)** to develop from something to something else; to develop from a more primitive form to the present form. □ *This creature evolved from a smaller, horselike creature into what we know as a horse.* □ *The human brain evolved out of a smaller and less complex form into the brain of today.*

exact something **from** someone to demand something from someone; to take something from someone. □ *The bill collector sought to exact payment from them for a debt that had been paid off long ago.* □ *You cannot exact a single cent from me.*

examine someone **in** something to give someone an examination in a particular subject or covering certain material. □ *The committee examined her in her knowledge of history.* □ *I was examined in math.*

examine someone **on** something to give someone an examination covering certain material. □ *I will have to examine you on this chapter myself.* □ *The teacher examined Larry on his understanding of phonetics.*

examine someone or something **for** something to inspect someone or something for the presence of something. □ *I examined the child for signs of abuse.* □ *You had better examine this dog for ticks.* □ *Don't forget to examine yourself for ticks after you return from the hike.*

Example is better than precept. *Prov.* You will teach people more effectively by being a good example than you will by telling them what to do. □ *Mother never lectured us; she just tried her best to be a good person, and we tried hard to be like her. She was living proof that example is better than precept.*

exceed someone or something **by** something to surpass someone or something by some amount. □ *Wally exceeded his quota by two hundred.* □ *He exceeded Larry by a large amount.*

exceed someone or something **in** something to surpass someone or something in something. □ *Tom exceeds Walter in athletic ability.* □ *Ralph exceeded the Rock of Gibraltar in hardheadedness.*

excel at something and **excel in** something to do something in a superior fashion. □ *She really excels at running.* □ *Wally does not excel at anything.* □ *Frank always hoped he would excel in math.*

excel in something Go to previous.

The **exception proves the rule.** *Prov.* Something that does not follow a rule shows that the rule exists. (Often used facetiously, to justify some rule you have proposed but which someone else has listed exceptions to. From a Latin phrase meaning that an exception *tests* a rule.) □ *Ellen: Men are always rude. Jane: But Alan's always polite. And Larry and Ted are polite, too. Ellen: They're just the exceptions that prove the rule.* □ *Bill: All the shows on TV are aimed at people with low intelligence. Alan: What about that news program you like to watch? Bill: The exception proves the rule.*

excerpt something **from** something to select a part of something from the whole. □ *We excerpted a few short scenes from the play and performed them for the class.* □ *A few paragraphs had been excerpted from the film as an example.*

exchange no more than some number of **words with** someone and **not exchange more than** some number of **words with** someone; **hardly exchange more than** some number of **words with** someone; **scarcely exchange more than** some number of **words with** someone to say hardly anything to someone. (Always negative.) □ *I know Tom was there, but I am sure that I didn't exchange more than three words with him before he left.* □ *We hardly exchanged more than two words the whole evening.* □ *Sally and Liz didn't have enough time to exchange more than five words.*

exchange something **for** something to trade something for something else. □ *I will exchange this one for a larger size.* □ *Can this be exchanged for something more suitable?*

exchange something **with** someone to trade something with someone. □ *I exchange Christmas presents with him, but I never see him otherwise.* □ *Let's exchange coats with each other.*

excite someone **about** something to stimulate someone about something. □ *I thought our vacation stories would excite her about going, but they did not.* □ *She was excited about the trip to Moscow.*

excite something **in** someone to arouse something in someone; to arouse someone with something. □ *The horror*

E

movie excited a lot of fear in Mike. □ *The smell of jasmine in the warm air excited a romantic streak in me.*

*exciting as watching (the) paint dry very, very dull. (Sarcastic. *Also: **about as ~; as ~.**) □ *This book is about as exciting as watching paint dry.* □ *Listening to you is exciting as watching the paint dry.*

exclude someone or something **from** something to leave someone or something out of something; to leave someone or something off a list. □ *Did you mean to exclude me from the party?* □ *I excluded chocolate cake from the shopping list.*

Excuse me. and **Excuse, please.; Pardon (me).; 'Scuse (me).; 'Scuse, please. 1.** an expression asking forgiveness for some minor social violation, such as belching or bumping into someone. (*'Scuse* is colloquial, and the apostrophe is not always used.) □ *John: Ouch! Bob: Excuse me. I didn't see you there.* □ *Mary: Oh! Ow! Sue: Pardon me. I didn't mean to bump into you.* □ *Tom: Ouch! Mary: Oh, dear! What happened? Tom: You stepped on my toe. Mary: Excuse me. I'm sorry.* **2.** Please let me through.; Please let me by. □ *Tom: Excuse me. I need to get past. Bob: Oh, sorry. I didn't know I was in the way.* □ *Mary: Pardon me. Sue: What? Mary: Pardon me. I want to get past you.*

Excuse my French. Go to Pardon my French.

excuse someone **1.** to forgive someone. (Usually with *me.* Said when interrupting or when some other minor offense has been committed. There are many mannerly uses of this expression.) □ *John came in late and said, "Excuse me, please."* □ *John said "excuse me" when he interrupted our conversation.* □ *When John made a strange noise at the table, he said quietly, "Excuse me."* □ *John suddenly left the room saying, "Excuse me. I'll be right back."* **2.** to permit someone to leave; to permit someone to remain away from an event. □ *The coach excused John from practice yesterday.* □ *The teacher excused John, and he ran quickly from the room.*

excuse someone **for** something to pardon someone for something or for (doing) something. □ *Please excuse me for this mess. I've not been able to clean the house.* □ *I can't excuse myself for not doing it.*

excuse someone **from** something to permit a person not to do something; to exempt someone from something. □ *Please excuse me from attending the meeting.* □ *I must excuse myself from the discussion.*

exemplify something **by** something to use something to explain or illustrate something. □ *He exemplifies wisdom by his decisions.* □ *Roger exemplifies virtue by the way he treats his employees.*

exempt someone **from** something to release someone from the obligation to do something; to allow a person not to be affected by a rule or law. □ *I cannot exempt anyone from this rule.* □ *The members of Congress exempted themselves from the wage freeze.*

exercise a firm hand Go to a firm hand.

exercise control over someone or something Go to next.

exercise power over someone or something and **exercise control over** someone or something; **exercise influence over** someone or something to have someone or something under one's control or influence. □ *The dicta-*

tor exercised power over the island for many years. □ *See if you can exercise some control over your appetite.* □ *I wish I could exercise some influence over the committee.*

exercise someone or an animal **in** something to give someone or an animal practice in doing something; to drill someone or an animal at something. □ *Please exercise the dog in obedience routines.* □ *I hope you will exercise me in my Spanish irregular verbs.*

exercised about something *Fig.* upset about something. □ *Mary: You lost a hundred dollars playing poker!? Bill: Now don't get exercised about it.* □ *I can't tell Ma I'm failing English class. She gets exercised about every dumb thing I do.*

exhort someone **to** do something to urge or pressure someone to do something. □ *She exhorted us to do better, but we only did worse.* □ *The boss exhorted the workers to increase productivity.*

exile someone **(from** something**) (to** something**)** to force someone to leave something or some place and go to something or some place, often as a punishment for political reasons. □ *The government exiled him from his hometown to an island off the coast of South America.* □ *They exiled Gerald to another country.*

exit (from something**) (to** something**)** to go out of something or some place to another. □ *The children exited from the school to the parking lot when the fire alarm rang.* □ *We exited to the main street from the parking lot.*

exorcise something **out of** someone and **exorcise** something **out** to remove or cast out evil from someone. □ *We saw a movie about a priest who exorcised a demon out of a young girl.*

expand into something to grow into something; to enlarge into something. □ *The little problem expanded into a big one in no time at all.* □ *In no time at all, the vegetable garden had expanded into a small farm.*

expand one's **horizons** *Fig.* to experience and learn new things. □ *Read more! Travel! Go out and expand your horizons!*

expand something **into** something to enlarge something into something; to make something grow into something. □ *She expanded her business into a national company.* □ *I would like to build on an addition to expand this room into a more usable space.*

expand (up)on something and **enlarge (up)on** something *Fig.* to add detail to a report about something; to say more about something. □ *Would you please expand upon that last remark?* □ *Would you care to enlarge upon your remarks?*

expatiate on someone or something to say or write many words about someone or something. □ *She expatiated endlessly on the evils of tobacco.* □ *I have heard you expatiate on Harry quite enough, thank you.*

expect someone or something **for** something to anticipate someone or a group to attend something. □ *I expect you for dinner on Thursday.* □ *We expected all of the board of directors for the meeting.*

expect something **from** someone or something **1.** to anticipate receiving something from someone or a group. □ *I expect a letter from you at least once a week while you are gone.* □ *We expect at least a postcard out of you.* **2.** and

expect something **(out) of** someone or something to demand something from someone or something. □ *I expect more effort from you. Get to work.* **3.** and **expect** something **(out) of** someone or something to anticipate a certain kind of behavior from someone or something. □ *We expected better from you. I'm very disappointed in your behavior.* □ *We really expected better behavior of you.*

expectant mother a pregnant woman. □ *The doctor's waiting room was filled with expectant mothers.* □ *The magazine has articles of interest to young parents and expectant mothers.*

expecting (a child) to be pregnant. □ *Tommy's mother is expecting a child.* □ *Oh, I didn't know she was expecting.*

expel someone **from** something to force someone to leave something or some place; to eject someone from something or some place. □ *The two men expelled the fighters from the tavern.* □ *Ken was expelled from school for disciplinary reasons.*

expel something **from** something to force or eject something out of something. □ *The machine expelled cup after cup from its opening.* □ *The volcano expelled huge globs of molten lava.*

expend something **for** something to pay a certain amount for something. □ *I expended an enormous amount for skin creams.* □ *How much money did you expend for this gaudy tie?*

expend something **in** something to use or consume something in some activity. □ *You expend too much energy in talking.* □ *Harry expended a lot of time in the preparation of his speech.*

expend something **on** someone or something to use something on someone or something. □ *Don't expend too much energy on him. He isn't worth it.* □ *There is no point in expending any more money on this car.*

Expense is no object. Go to Money is no object.

Experience is the best teacher. *Prov.* You will learn more from things that happen to you in real life than you will from hearing about or studying things that happen to other people. □ *I don't care how many books you read about how to run a business; experience is the best teacher.* □ *The nurse believed that experience was the best teacher when it came to developing a bedside manner, so she made sure that all her students spent a lot of time with patients.*

Experience is the father of wisdom. and **Experience is the mother of wisdom.** *Prov.* The more that happens to you, the more you will learn. □ *I never understood why supervisors got so frustrated with me until I became a supervisor and got frustrated with my subordinates. Experience was definitely the mother of wisdom, in my case.*

Experience is the mother of wisdom. Go to previous.

Experience is the teacher of fools. *Prov.* Only fools do not learn after seeing other people's mistakes and insist on repeating them. □ *Father: You should spend more time studying and less time having fun with your friends. If I had been a better student when I was your age, I'd have a better job now. Son: Oh, come on, Dad. School's worthless. Father: Don't make the same mistake I did! Experience is the teacher of fools.*

experiment in something to conduct research or experiments about something. □ *The research group is experimenting in the field of biomechanics.* □ *We want to experiment in thermodynamics.*

experiment (up)on someone or something to use someone or something as the subject of an experiment. (*Upon* is formal and less commonly used than *on*.) □ *Do you think we should experiment upon people?* □ *The researchers were experimenting on a new drug that might cure rabies.*

experiment with someone or something to try different experiments on someone or something; to use different people or things as key variables in an experiment. □ *They are supposed to be experimenting with new drugs.* □ *We no longer experiment with animals.*

explain at great length Go to at great length.

explain oneself **1.** to explain what one has said or done or what one thinks or feels. (Formal and polite.) □ *Please take a moment to explain yourself. I'm sure we are interested in your ideas.* □ *Yes, if you will let me explain myself, I think you'll agree with my idea.* **2.** to give an explanation or excuse for something wrong that one may have done. (Usually said in anger.) □ *Young man! Come in here and explain yourself this instant.* □ *Why did you do that, Tom Smith? You had better explain yourself, and it had better be good.*

explain someone or something **to** someone to give information or instruction about someone or something to someone. □ *Please explain it to me.* □ *Can you explain Andrew to me?*

explain something **away**† to explain something so that it is no longer a problem. □ *You can try to explain it away if you want, but that won't solve the problem.* □ *You can't just explain away all your problems.*

explode a bombshell Go to drop a bomb(shell).

explode with something **1.** *Lit.* to make a loud noise upon exploding or releasing energy. □ *The bomb exploded with a thunderous roar.* □ *When the joke was finished, the audience exploded with laughter.* **2.** *Fig.* to burst out saying something; to be about to burst with eagerness to say something. □ *The children exploded with protests when their parents told them it was bedtime.* □ *Hanna was exploding with questions.* **3.** *Fig.* to produce a sudden abundance of something. (Alludes to buds bursting or a sudden blooming or sprouting of vegetation.) □ *The fields exploded with an enormous crop of wildflowers.* □ *The cherry trees exploded with blossoms.*

export something **to** some place to sell something abroad to a particular country. □ *They are now exporting their products to Hungary.* □ *We are exporting all our product line to Eastern Europe.*

export something **to** someone or something to sell something abroad to someone or some country. □ *The company exported alcohol to Brazil.* □ *We only export books to our agents abroad.*

expose someone or an animal **to a disease** to place someone or an animal near a source of a disease. □ *Try to expose your children to chicken pox while they are young. It's horrible when you are an adult.* □ *He accidentally exposed his sheep to an infected animal.*

expose someone or something **to** someone or something to show someone or something to someone or something. □ *You should not expose the children to violent movies at their age.* □ *Do not expose the film to the light.*

expose something **or** oneself **to** someone or something to disclose someone's or something's secrets to someone or a group. □ *He exposed his inner thoughts to everyone there.* □ *She refused to expose herself to the ears of the curious and ceased talking.* □ *He exposed himself to the public when he revealed his involvement in the arms sale.*

expostulate about someone or something and **expostulate on** someone or something to comment or argue intensely about someone or something. □ *He always seems to be expostulating on something. Why can't he simply say "Yes" or "No"?* □ *Sam is expostulating on Bill's many shortcomings again.*

expound ((up)on someone or something**) (to** someone**)** to speak at length about someone or something to someone. (*Upon* is formal and less commonly used than *on*.) □ *Let me expound upon Tom to you for a while. I think you need all the details on his qualifications.* □ *Please do not expound on Bill anymore.*

express one's **anger** to allow a release or expression of anger, such as through angry words, violence, or talking out a problem. □ *Don't keep your emotions inside of you. You have to learn to express your anger.* □ *Bob expresses his anger by yelling at people.*

express oneself **(to** someone**) (on** something**)** to say what one thinks about something. □ *I will express myself to Karen on that matter at another time.* □ *She expressed herself on Karen to the entire group.*

express something **in round figures** Go to in round figures.

express something **in round numbers** Go to in round numbers.

expropriate something **(from** someone or something**) (for** someone or something**)** to seize something from someone or something for someone or something. □ *The government expropriated the land from the peasants for an airfield.* □ *They expropriated land for a highway.* □ *They expropriated land from the farmers.*

expunge something **from** something to erase something from something. □ *The judge ordered the clerk to expunge the comment from the record.* □ *Please expunge the lawyer's remark from the transcript.*

expurgate something **from** something to cleanse something by removing something. (Often refers to editing objectionable material from written or broadcast material.) □ *They expurgated the most graphic passages from the novel.* □ *We will expurgate the offensive matter from the article.*

extend across something to spread across something. □ *The shadows extended across the whole land.* □ *The fog extended across the low-lying land.*

extend credit (to someone or a company**)** and **extend** someone or a company **credit** to allow someone to purchase something on credit. □ *I'm sorry, Mr. Smith, but because of your poor record of payment, we are no longer able to extend credit to you.* □ *Look at this letter, Jane. The store won't extend credit anymore.*

extend (from something**) (to** something**)** to spread from one point to another point. □ *The cloud of smoke extended from one end of town to the other.* □ *It extended to the end of the road from our front gate.*

extend one's **sympathy (to** someone**)** to express sympathy to someone. (A very polite and formal way to tell someone that you are sorry about a misfortune.) □ *Please permit me to extend my sympathy to you and your children. I'm very sorry to hear of the death of your husband.* □ *Let's extend our sympathy to Bill Jones, who is in the hospital with a broken leg. We should send him some flowers.*

extend over someone or something to spread over someone or something. □ *The smoke extended over Tom and his friends, who were having a picnic.* □ *The cloud extended over the entire valley.*

extend someone or a company **credit** Go to extend credit **(to** someone or a company**)**.

extend something **to** something **1.** to lengthen something to reach something. □ *We extended the antenna to its full length.* □ *Extend your arm to the wall and see how straight you can make it.* **2.** to push a stated deadline further into the future. □ *I will extend the deadline to Friday.* □ *We cannot extend the due date to next month.*

extend to someone or something to reach all the way to someone or something. □ *This policy extends to you also.* □ *The road extends to Los Angeles.*

extenuating circumstances special (but otherwise unspecified) circumstances that account for an irregular or improper way of doing something. □ *Mary was permitted to arrive late because of extenuating circumstances.* □ *Due to extenuating circumstances, the teacher will not meet with the class today.*

extol someone or something **as** something to praise someone or something as something. □ *We extolled her as a heroine.* □ *The salesman extolled the medicine as a cure-all.*

extort something **from** someone or something to steal something from someone by coercion; to force someone to give something by making threats. □ *The crook was trying to extort a lot of money from the widow by selling her a worthless insurance policy.* □ *The authorities caught the accounting firm trying to extort a great deal of money from the bank.*

extract something **from** someone or something to remove something from someone or something; to make someone or a group give something. □ *We extracted the juice from the oranges.* □ *The police questioning Maggie extracted the truth from her.*

extradite someone **from** some place **(to** some place**)** to have someone sent from one place to face criminal prosecution. □ *The state's attorney sought to extradite Max from Missouri.* □ *The gang leader was extradited from Indiana to New York to face assault charges.*

extrapolate something **from** something to reason out the answer from the known facts. □ *I cannot extrapolate what he meant from these notes.* □ *Can you extrapolate the annual total from the company's sales so far this year?*

extricate someone or something **from** someone or something to disentangle someone or something from someone or something; to free someone or something from someone or something. □ *I tried to extricate myself from her, but* *she made it hard for me to get away politely.* □ *I managed to extricate the ring from the vacuum cleaner bag.*

exult at something and **exult over** something to rejoice because of something; to rejoice about something. □ *We exulted at the end of the hostilities.* □ *The citizens exulted over the downfall of the dictator.*

exult in something to take great pleasure in something; to enjoy something immensely. □ *I exult in the beauty of a spring day.* □ *We exulted in the glory of summer.*

exult over something Go to exult at something.

An **eye for an eye (and a tooth for a tooth).** *Prov.* If someone hurts you, you should punish the offender by hurting him or her in the same way. (An ancient principle of justice going back to biblical times.) □ *When they were children, the two brothers operated on the principle of an eye for an eye, so that if the older one hit the younger one, the younger one was entitled to hit him back just as hard.*

the **eye of the hurricane** and the **eye of the storm 1.** *Lit.* the area of calm in the center of a tornado, hurricane, or cyclone. □ *It is calm and peaceful in the eye of the storm.* **2.** *Fig.* a temporary peaceful time amidst more trouble

and strife yet to come. □ *Don't relax. This is the eye of the storm. The lunch hour rush is over, but the dinner rush will start soon.*

the **eye of the storm** Go to previous.

eyeball-to-eyeball *Fig.* face-to-face and often very close; in person. □ *They approached each other eyeball-to-eyeball and frowned.* □ *Let's talk more when we are eyeball-to-eyeball.*

*an **eyeful (of** someone or something) *Fig.* a shocking or surprising sight. (*Typically: **get** ~; **have** ~; **give** someone ~.) □ *The office door opened for a minute and I got an eyeful of the interior.* □ *Mary got an eyeful of the company's extravagant spending when she saw the bill for the executive board's catered lunch.*

eyes like saucers *Fig.* eyes opened widely as in amazement. □ *Our eyes were like saucers as we witnessed another display of the manager's temper.*

eyes like two burnt holes in a blanket *Rur.* eyes with dark circles around them. □ *I can tell you ain't slept. You got eyes like two burnt holes in a blanket.*

E

poor baby has a face only a mother could love. □ *Look at that guy. That's a face that could stop a clock.*

face (the) facts to confront the truth about someone or something; to confront and accept the consequences of something. □ *Eventually, you will have to face the facts. Times are hard.*

face the music *Fig.* to receive punishment; to accept the unpleasant results of one's actions. □ *Mary broke a dining-room window and had to face the music when her father got home.* □ *After failing a math test, Tom had to go home and face the music.*

face up (to someone or something**)** to confront with courage someone or something representing a threat or unpleasantness. □ *You are simply going to have to admit your mistake and face up to the boss.* □ *You must face up to the authorities if you have done something wrong.*

face-to-face 1. *Fig.* in person; in the same location. (Said only of people. An adverb.) □ *Let's talk about this face-to-face. I don't like talking over the telephone.* □ *Many people prefer to talk face-to-face.* **2.** *Fig.* facing one another; in the same location. (Used as an attributive.) □ *I prefer to have a face-to-face meeting.* □ *They work better on a face-to-face basis.*

Fact is stranger than fiction. and **Truth is stranger than fiction.** *Prov.* Things that really happen are harder to believe or more amazing than stories that people invent. □ *Did you see the story in the newspaper about the criminal who attacks people with a toenail clipper? Fact is stranger than fiction!* □ *Jill: I can't believe someone's paying 900 dollars for Tom's broken-down old car—it doesn't even run. Jane: Truth is stranger than fiction.*

the **facts of life 1.** *Euph.* the facts of sex and reproduction, especially human reproduction. (See also the **birds and the bees**.) □ *My parents told me the facts of life when I was nine years old.* □ *Bill learned the facts of life from his classmates.* **2.** *Fig.* the truth about the unpleasant ways that the world works. □ *Mary really learned the facts of life when she got her first job.* □ *Tom couldn't accept the facts of life in business, so he quit.*

fade away (into something**) 1.** to diminish into something. □ *The light faded away into nothing.* □ *The sound of the drums faded away into the distance.* **2.** Go to **fade out.**

fade back (into something**)** to move back into a particular area. □ *He faded back to throw a pass.* □ *Quickly and unnoticed, he faded back.*

fade down [for sound] to diminish. □ *The roar of the train faded down as it passed and fled into the night.* □ *As the thunder faded down, the sun began to break through the clouds.*

fade from something [for something] to leave something gradually, such as one's consciousness, memory, view, etc. (See also **fade from view**.) □ *The image faded from her memory at last.*

fade from view [for a sight] to fade away, typically owing to loss of light or distance. □ *The scene faded from view as the stage lights dimmed.* □ *My house faded from view as we drove down the long road to town.*

---

face away (from someone or something**)** to turn away from someone or something. □ *Please face away from me while I change clothes.* □ *I'll face away. You go right ahead.*

face off 1. to begin a hockey game with two players facing one another. □ *They faced off and the match was on.* **2.** to prepare for a confrontation. □ *The opposing candidates faced off and the debate began.* □ *They faced off and I knew there was going to be a fight.*

face on(to) something [for something] to have a view out onto something. □ *The house faced onto the sea and provided a beautiful view of the incoming ships.* □ *Our office building does not face onto the street.* □ *We asked for a room that faces on the main square.*

face someone **down**† to make a face-to-face stand with someone who eventually backs down. □ *Chuck succeeded in facing Tom down.* □ *Facing down Tom wasn't difficult for Chuck.*

face someone or something **forward** to turn someone or something to the front. (Also with many other directions—*backward, to the right, to the left,* etc.) □ *Please face your brother forward now.* □ *Face the book forward so we can read the title.*

face (someone or something**) into** something to turn (the face or front of) someone or something directly toward something. □ *Face the sail into the wind.* □ *Please face into the camera.*

face someone **with** something to present evidence of something to someone. □ *When I faced him with the evidence, he confessed immediately.* □ *The police faced Max with the witness's story.* □ *The CEO was faced with the problem of bringing the bankrupt firm back to profitability.*

face something **down** to turn something face downward. □ *Ted drew a card and faced it down.* □ *Face your cards down when you leave the card table.*

face something **head-on** *Fig.* to confront a problem directly and openly. □ *Let's face this problem head-on and try to solve it quickly and painlessly.*

face something **with** something to install something on the surface of something. □ *We faced the kitchen walls with yellow tile.* □ *The wall was faced with tile.*

a **face that could stop a clock** Go to next.

a **face (that) only a mother could love** and a **face that could stop a clock** *Fig.* a very ugly face. (Usually jocular. See also **homely enough to stop a clock**.) □ *The*

fade into something to diminish or change into something. □ *The light of dusk faded into blackness.* □ *In the corner of the painting, the deep reds faded into lavender.*

fade out and **fade away** to diminish and go away altogether. □ *The light in the distance faded out as the sun began to set.* □ *The light faded out as the candles burned themselves out, one by one.* □ *As it got farther into the distance, the car faded away.*

fade something **down**[†] to turn down a sound. (Broadcasting.) □ *The radio engineer faded the music down and the announcer's voice began.* □ *She faded down the music.*

fade something **in**[†] to bring a picture, sound, or both into prominence. (Broadcasting.) □ *The technician faded the picture in and the program began.* □ *Fade in the picture a little faster next time.*

fade something **out**[†] to diminish something altogether. (Broadcasting.) □ *At the end, you should fade the music out completely.* □ *Fade out the music earlier.*

fade something **up**[†] to increase the sound gradually. (Broadcasting.) □ *The director faded the music up and then down again before the announcer spoke.* □ *Fade up the music when the announcer stops talking.*

fag someone **out** *Sl.* to tire someone out. □ *All that work really fagged me out.* □ *The hard climb fagged the hikers out.*

fagged out *Sl.* exhausted. □ *I'm really fagged out after all that running.* □ *John, you sure look fagged out.*

fail in something to have not earned passing or satisfactory grades in some school subject. □ *George is failing in geometry.* □ *I hope I do not fail in math.*

fail someone **on** something to give someone an unsatisfactory grade on an assignment or test. □ *She failed us all on the math assignment.* □ *The teacher failed half the class on the assignment.*

faint dead away *Fig.* to faint and fall unconscious. □ *I almost fainted dead away.* □ *David will faint dead away when he reads this.*

faint from something to faint because of something. □ *I nearly fainted from fear!* □ *Three people along the parade route fainted from the heat.*

Faint heart never won fair lady. *Prov.* A timid suitor never won his lady. (Used to encourage boys or men to be bold in courting women.) □ *Bill: I'd really like to go out with Alice, but what if she says no? You won't know till you ask her. Faint heart never won fair lady.* □ *Don't be so shy about talking to Edith. Faint heart never won fair lady.*

the **faint of heart** *Fig.* people who are squeamish; someone who is sickened or disturbed by unpleasantness or challenge. □ *The pathway around the top of the volcano, near the crater, is not for the faint of heart.*

fair and impartial just and unbiased. (Usually referring to some aspect of the legal system, such as a jury, a hearing, or a judge.) □ *Gary felt that he had not received a fair and impartial hearing.* □ *We demand that all of our judges be fair and impartial in every instance.*

fair and square completely fair(ly); justly; within the rules. □ *She won the game fair and square.* □ *The division of the money should be fair and square.*

fair game (for something**)** someone or something that it is considered permissible to attack or abuse in some way. □ *I don't like seeing articles exposing people's private lives, but politicians are fair game for that kind of criticism.* □ *Journalists always regard movie stars as fair game.*

*a **fair shake** an instance of fair treatment. (*Typically: **get** ~; **have** ~; **give** someone ~.) □ *He's unpleasant, but we have to give him a fair shake.* □ *He got a fair shake from us. Don't worry!*

fair something **out**[†] *Rur.* to distribute something fairly. □ *She faired the meager stew out the best she could.* □ *Walter faired out the pie.*

fair to middlin' *Rur.* mediocre; not bad but not good. (*Middling* means 'of average quality.') □ *Tom: How are you feeling today? Bill: Fair to middlin'.* □ *My sewing is excellent, but my cooking is only fair to middlin'.*

fair-haired boy *Fig.* a favored person. (Not necessarily young or a boy.) □ *The teacher's fair-haired boy always does well on tests.* □ *The supervisor's son was the fair-haired boy on the construction site.*

fair-weather friend *Fig.* someone who is your friend only when things are pleasant or going well for you. □ *Bill stayed for lunch but he wouldn't help me with the yard work. He's just a fair-weather friend.* □ *A fair-weather friend isn't much help in an emergency.*

Faith will move mountains. *Prov.* If you believe in what you are doing, you can overcome any obstacle. (Sometimes refers to faith in God.) □ *Jane's faith in her cause could move mountains.* □ *You may feel disheartened sometimes, but remember that faith will move mountains.*

fake it to pretend (to do something). □ *If you don't know the right notes, just fake it.* □ *I can't fake it anymore. I've got to be honest with you.*

fake off *Sl.* to waste time; to **goof off**. □ *Hey, you guys, quit faking off!* □ *All you clowns do is fake off. Now, get busy!*

fake someone **out**[†] to deceive someone; to fool someone. □ *You really faked me out. I never would have guessed it was you.* □ *The student tried to fake out the teacher.*

fake someone **out of** something *Sl.* to get something from someone by deception. □ *He faked Tom out of his place in line.* □ *She faked me out of a lot of money.*

fall (a)foul of someone or something and **run (a)foul of** someone or something to get into a situation where one is opposed to someone or something; to get into trouble with someone or something. □ *Dan fell afoul of the law at an early age.* □ *I hope that you will avoid falling afoul of the district manager. She can be a formidable enemy.* □ *I hope I don't run afoul of your sister. She doesn't like me.*

fall (all) over oneself **(to** do something**)** *Fig.* to rush eagerly and awkwardly to do something. □ *The boys fell all over themselves to open the door for Sarah.* □ *Larry fell over himself trying to help Sarah on with her coat.*

fall all over someone *Fig.* to give a lot of attention, affection, or praise to someone. □ *My aunt falls all over me whenever she comes to visit.* □ *I hate for someone to fall all over me. It embarrasses me.*

fall apart (at the seams) and **come apart at the seams 1.** *Lit.* [for something] to break apart where its parts are joined. □ *The dress fell apart at the seams.* □ *I wouldn't have thought that a coat that cost that much money would just come apart at the seams.* **2.** *Fig.* to break down mentally. □ *Tom works too much and finally fell apart.* □ *Poor Ralph simply fell apart at the seams.*

fall asleep *Fig.* to go to sleep. □ *I fell asleep while reading the very dull book.* □ *I got in bed and fell asleep at once.*

fall asleep at the switch Go to asleep at the switch.

fall away (from someone or something**) 1.** *Lit.* [for something] to drop away from someone or something. □ *The paint is falling away from the sides of the house.* □ *Over the years, all the paint fell away.* **2.** *Fig.* [for someone] to move back or retreat from someone or something. □ *The soldiers fell away from the line of battle.* **3.** *Fig.* to distance oneself from someone; to end an association with someone. □ *The candidate's supporters fell away from her when they heard about the scandal.*

fall away toward something to slant downward toward something. □ *The yard fell away toward the shore of the lake.* □ *The broad expanse of prairie land fell away toward the river bottomland, and beyond that, the river itself.*

fall back to move back from something; to retreat from something. □ *The gang members fell back, and I took that opportunity to get away.* □ *The troops fell back to regroup.*

fall back on(to) someone or something **1.** *Lit.* to fall backwards onto someone or something. □ *She stumbled and fell back onto the lady behind her.* □ *She fell back on the couch.* **2.** *Fig.* to begin to use someone or something held in reserve. □ *We fell back on our savings to get us through the hard times.* □ *We had to fall back on our emergency generator.*

fall behind (in something**)** and **fall behind (on** something**); fall behind (with** something**); get behind (in** something**); get behind (on** something**); get behind (with** something**)** to lag behind schedule in some kind of work or some other scheduled activity. □ *You are falling behind in your car payments.* □ *I tried not to get behind on them.* □ *Please don't fall behind with your payments.* □ *I won't fall behind again.*

fall behind schedule Go to behind schedule.

fall behind (someone or something**)** to lag behind someone or something. □ *You have fallen behind everyone else in class.* □ *Our production fell behind that of the other production line.*

fall behind (with something**)** Go to fall behind (in something**).

fall below something to drop to a lower level than something. □ *The temperature has fallen below freezing again.* □ *When the audience fell below two hundred a night, they closed the play.*

fall beneath something to drop under something. □ *The thimble fell beneath the sofa.* □ *The gift that Bob had purchased for Maggie fell beneath the wheels of a truck.*

fall between something **and** something else to drop between things. □ *My loose change fell between the cushions of the sofa.* □ *I hope that my wallet doesn't fall between the table and the wall. I would never be able to move the table to get it.*

fall between two stools *Fig.* to come somewhere between two possibilities and so fail to meet the requirements of either. □ *The material is not suitable for an academic book or for a popular one. It falls between two stools.* □ *He tries to be both teacher and friend, but falls between two stools.*

fall by some amount [for an asset] to drop in value by a certain amount. □ *The gas stocks fell by nearly 10 percent today.* □ *If the stock market falls by four hundred points, I'm going to jump off a cliff.*

fall by the wayside Go to drop by the wayside.

fall down to drop or topple. □ *The baby fell down.* □ *Walk carefully on this ice or you will fall down.*

fall (down) at something to prostrate oneself before or at the feet of someone or something. □ *She fell down at the feet of the horrid man who held her child.* □ *She fell at his feet.*

fall down on someone or something to fall and drop onto someone or something. □ *Bits of the ceiling paint fell down on us and into our food.* □ *The leaves fell down on the lawn.*

fall down on the job *Fig.* to fail to do something properly; to fail to do one's job adequately. □ *The team kept losing because the coach was falling down on the job.* □ *Tom was fired because he fell down on the job.*

fall (flat) on one's **face 1.** *Lit.* to fall down, face first. □ *Bobby fell flat on his face and skinned his nose.* □ *Down he went—he fell on his face.* **2.** *Fig.* to fail miserably, usually in a performance. □ *She was terrible in the play. She fell flat on her face.* □ *The whole play fell on its face.*

fall for someone *Fig.* to fall in love with someone. □ *I fell for her in a big way. She's gorgeous!* □ *Ted fell for Alice and they decided to get married.*

fall for something *Fig.* to believe something without reservation. □ *Surely, you don't expect me to fall for that!* □ *She fell for the excuse I gave her about getting stuck in traffic.*

fall from grace 1. *Lit.* to sin and get on the wrong side of God. (A Christian concept.) □ *It was either fall from grace or starve from lack of money. That's how thieves are made.* □ *Given the choice between falling from grace and starving, few people choose to starve.* **2.** *Fig.* to do something wrong and get in trouble with someone other than God. □ *I hear that Ted lost the Wilson contract and has fallen from grace with the boss.* □ *The accounting firm has fallen from grace and the board is looking for a new one.*

fall from power *Fig.* to go out of power; to go out of office. □ *The dictator fell from power after the riots.* □ *Every ruler will fall from power sooner or later.*

fall from someone or something to fall off of someone or something. □ *The books fell from the top shelf in the earthquake.* □ *The eggs rolled and fell from the counter and broke on the floor.*

fall head over heels *Fig.* to fall down, perhaps turning over or rolling. □ *Fred tripped on the rug and fell head over heels into the center of the room.* □ *Slow down or you will fall down—head over heels.*

fall head over heels in love (with someone**)** *Fig.* to fall deeply in love with someone, especially suddenly. □ *Roger fell head over heels in love with Maggie, and they were married within the month.* □ *Very few people actually fall head*

F

over heels in love with each other. □ *She fell head over heels in love and thought she was dreaming.*

fall heir to something **1.** *Lit.* to inherit something; to end up with certain possessions of someone who has died. □ *I fell heir to all my grandmother's old photographs.* **2.** *Fig.* to end up with having to take care of something that no one else wants; to be placed in charge of something unexpectedly. □ *Bob fell heir to the Wilson project and has to complete what Jane failed to do.*

fall ill *Fig.* to become ill. □ *Tom fell ill just before he was to perform.* □ *We both fell ill after eating the baked fish.*

fall in to line up in a row, standing shoulder to shoulder. □ *The Boy Scouts were told to fall in behind the leader.* □ *The soldiers fell in quickly.*

fall in love (with each other) [for two people] to become enamored of each other. □ *They met in school and fell in love.* □ *When they fell in love, they thought it would last forever.*

fall in love (with someone**)** to develop the emotion of love for someone. □ *Tom fell in love with Mary, but she only wanted to be friends.* □ *John is too young to really fall in love.*

fall in love (with something**)** to become enamored of something. □ *I simply fell in love with the dress. I had to have it.* □ *I fell in love with the red car and bought it at once.*

fall in on someone or something to cave in on someone or something; to collapse on someone or something. □ *The roof of the mine fell in on the workers.* □ *The ceiling fell in on the diners.*

fall in the drink Go to in the drink.

fall in with someone or something to become involved with someone or a group. □ *I'm afraid that he fell in with the wrong kind of friends.* □ *John fell in with Max, who had served time in prison.*

fall in with something to concur with something; to harmonize with something. □ *We had to fall in with her wishes.* □ *The statement falls in exactly with my view.*

fall into a trap 1. *Lit.* to get caught in a trap. □ *The tiger fell into a trap and leapt out again immediately.* □ *The boys tried to get a squirrel to fall into a trap, but squirrels are too clever.* **2.** and **fall into the trap; fall into** someone's **trap** *Fig.* to become caught in someone's scheme; to be deceived into doing or thinking something. □ *We fell into a trap by asking for an explanation.* □ *I fell into his trap when I agreed to drive him home.*

fall into decay to degenerate; to rot. □ *The house was very old and had fallen into decay.* □ *The small town fell into decay, and people moved out.*

fall into disfavor to lose one's influence; to be preferred less and less. □ *This style of government fell into disfavor some years ago.* □ *Poor Lee fell into disfavor with the boss and lost all his special privileges.*

fall into disgrace to become without honor. □ *The mayor fell into disgrace because of his financial dealings.* □ *We fell into disgrace because of our criminal affiliations.*

fall into disuse to be used less and less. □ *The pump had fallen into disuse and the joints had rusted solid.* □ *Since my books had fallen into disuse, I sold them to a used-book dealer.*

fall in(to) line 1. *Lit.* to line up so that each person (except the first person) stands behind someone. □ *The teacher told the students to fall in line for lunch.* □ *Hungry students fall into line very quickly.* **2.** *Fig.* to conform; to **fall in(to) place.** □ *All the parts of the problem finally fell into line.* □ *Bill's behavior began to fall in line.* **3.** *Fig.* to behave in a manner similar to someone or something. □ *You are expected to fall into line with the other people.* □ *We want you to fall in line.*

fall into one's **lap** *Fig.* [for something of great value or usefulness] to be given or granted to someone without having been requested. □ *Some valuable antique jewelry just fell into his lap. His late mother had kept it hidden for years.*

fall in(to) place to fit together; to become organized; to make sense. □ *After we heard the whole story, things began to fall in place.* □ *When you get older, the different parts of your life begin to fall into place.*

fall into someone's **trap** Go to **fall into a trap.**

fall in(to something**)** to drop into something. □ *The rabbit fell into the hole and was trapped.* □ *It went right up to the hole and fell in.*

fall in(to step) to get into the same marching pattern as everyone else as regards which foot moves forward. (Everyone should be moving the same foot forward at the same time.) □ *I just can't seem to fall into step. I am very uncoordinated.* □ *Fall in! March with the others!*

fall into the gutter Go to in the gutter.

fall into the trap Go to **fall into a trap.**

fall into the wrong hands *Fig.* to become associated with the wrong person; to become the possession of the wrong person. □ *I don't want these plans to fall into the wrong hands.* □ *This could be dangerous if it fell into the wrong hands.*

fall like a ton of bricks Go to like a ton of bricks.

fall off to decline or diminish. □ *Business falls off during the summer months.* □ *My interest in school fell off when I became twenty.*

fall off (of something**)** to drop off something. (*Of* is usually retained before pronouns.) □ *A button fell off my shirt.* □ *I fell off the log.* □ *The twigs fell off of him as he stood up.*

fall off the wagon Go to off the wagon.

fall on deaf ears *Fig.* [for talk or ideas] to be ignored by the persons they were intended for. □ *Her pleas for mercy fell on deaf ears; the judge gave her the maximum sentence.* □ *All of Sally's good advice fell on deaf ears. Walter had made up his own mind.*

fall on hard times *Fig.* to experience difficult times, especially financially. □ *Since the war, her family had fallen on hard times.* □ *We fell on hard times during the recession.*

fall on one's **knees** and **fall to** one's **knees** to kneel down, usually in respect. □ *The people fell on their knees and prayed in gratitude for their salvation from the flood.* □ *They fell to their knees in awe.*

fall on one's **sword 1.** *Lit.* to fall down and be penetrated by one's own sword, accidentally or on purpose. □ *He tripped and fell on his sword.* **2.** *Fig.* to accept defeat; to go to extremes to indicate one's defeat. (From the ancient practice of a military commander committing suicide this way rather than being captured.) □ *So, because I lost the contract, I am supposed to fall on my sword or something?*

fall on someone's **shoulders** Go to **on** someone's **shoulders.**

fall on(to) someone or something to collapse toward or onto someone or something. □ *The fence fell onto the car, denting it severely.* □ *The branch fell on David.*

fall out 1. to happen; to result. □ *As things fell out, we had a wonderful trip.* □ *What fell out of our discussion was a decision to continue.* **2.** to leave one's place in a formation when dismissed. (Usually in scouting or the military. The opposite of **fall in.**) □ *The scouts fell out and ran to the campfire.* □ *All the soldiers fell out and talked among themselves.* **3.** to depart. □ *It's late, George. I have to fall out.* □ *Let's fall out. I have to get up early in the morning.*

fall out of bed 1. *Lit.* to roll out of one's bed onto the floor. □ *I fell out of bed and broke my arm.* □ *Billy fell out of bed and started to cry.* **2.** *Fig.* [for a measurement] to drop very low very fast. □ *The major stock averages fell out of bed today as the market suffered its second severe crash in two months.* □ *The temperature fell out of bed last night.*

fall out of favor (with someone**)** and **lose favor (with** someone**)** to lose someone's approval or acceptance. □ *This style of house has fallen out of favor with most people lately.* □ *Saving money has lost favor with most people.*

fall out of love (with someone**)** to stop being in love with someone. □ *She claimed she had fallen out of love with him.* □ *He also had fallen out of love.*

fall out (of something**)** to topple out of something. □ *Mary fell out of the tree and hurt herself.*

fall out (with someone**) (about** someone or something**)** Go to next.

fall out (with someone**) (over** something**)** and **fall out (with** someone**) (about** someone or something**)** to quarrel or disagree with someone about something. □ *Tony fell out with Nick about the video game.* □ *Bill fell out with Sally over the question of buying a new car.* □ *Bill fell out with John about who would sleep on the bottom bunk.*

fall outside something to be beyond someone's power, responsibility, or jurisdiction. □ *This matter falls outside my bailiwick.* □ *Her offense fell outside of the manager's jurisdiction.*

fall over to topple over and fall down. □ *The fence fell over and dented the car.* □ *I felt faint and almost fell over.*

fall over backwards (to do something**)** and **bend over backwards (to** do something**); lean over backwards (to** do something**)** *Fig.* to do everything possible to please someone. □ *The taxi driver fell over backwards to be helpful.* □ *The teacher bent over backwards to help the students understand.* □ *You don't have to lean over backwards to get me to help. Just ask.*

fall over someone or something to stumble over someone or something. □ *Sam came into the house and fell over a kitchen chair.* □ *Walter fell over Roger, who was napping on the floor.*

fall overboard to fall from a boat or a ship into the water. (See also **go overboard.**) □ *Someone fell overboard and* they had to stop the boat and go back. □ *The lady's sunglasses fell overboard.*

fall short to lack something; to lack enough of something, such as money, time, etc. □ *We fell short of money at the end of the month.* □ *Tom fell short of cash and had to borrow from me.*

fall short of one's **goal(s)** and **fall short of the goal(s); fall short of the record** to fail to achieve a goal. □ *We fell short of our goal of collecting a thousand dollars.* □ *Ann ran a fast race, but fell short of the record.*

fall through [for something, such as plans] to fail. □ *Our party for next Saturday fell through.* □ *I hope our plans don't fall through.*

fall through something to fall and break through something. □ *One of the skaters fell through the thin ice.* □ *A number of hailstones fell through the roof of the greenhouse.*

fall through the cracks Go to **through the cracks.**

fall to to begin doing something; to prepare to do something and go to work on it. □ *She asked for help, and everyone fell to.* □ *Fall to, you guys!*

fall to one's **knees** Go to **fall on** one's **knees.**

fall to pieces 1. *Lit.* to break into pieces. □ *The road was so rough the car almost fell to pieces.* □ *I was afraid that my bicycle would fall to pieces before I got there.* **2.** *Fig.* to become emotionally upset. □ *I was so nervous, I fell to pieces and couldn't give my speech.* □ *Roger fell to pieces when his mother died.*

fall to someone *Fig.* to become the responsibility of someone. □ *It always falls to me to apologize first.* □ *Why does it fall to me to answer the telephone every time it rings?*

fall toward something to drop or fall in the direction of something. □ *She fell toward the curb rather than toward the traffic.* □ *The tree fell toward the garage rather than toward the house.*

fall under someone or something to drop down and end up beneath someone or something. □ *The old man fell under the wheels of the truck, but he suffered only minor injuries.* □ *The child tripped and fell under Mrs. Rogers, who almost did not see her.*

fall under someone's **spell 1.** *Lit.* to come under the magical control of a magician or similar person. □ *The damsel fell under the wizard's spell and sat there speechless.* □ *As the children fell under the witch's spell, they went to sleep.* **2.** *Fig.* to be fascinated by someone; to be enchanted by someone. □ *She was so beautiful. I fell under her spell at once.* □ *Wally fell under Donna's spell and became helpless in her presence.*

fall (up)on someone [for a task] to become the duty of someone. □ *The task of telling Mother about the broken vase fell upon Jane.* □ *The job of cleaning up the spill fell upon Tom.*

fall (up)on someone or something **1.** to collapse on top of someone or something. (*Upon* is formal and less commonly used than *on.*) □ *The bridge fell upon a boat passing beneath it.* □ *A small branch fell on Jerry as he passed beneath the tree.* **2.** to attack someone or something. □ *The cat fell upon the mouse and killed it.* □ *The children fell on the birthday cake and ate it all.*

fall wide of the mark Go to **wide of the mark.**

fall within something to belong to a specific category or classification. □ *This falls within the realm of the medical profession. There's no more I can do for you.* □ *Does this fall within your area of expertise?*

a **false move** and **one false move** *Fig.* [even] a single movement that indicates that one is disobeying an order to remain still or in a nonthreatening posture. □ *The robber threatened to shoot us if we made one false move.*

falter in something to fail in doing something; to exhibit a lack of something, such as faith, loyalty, perseverance, etc. □ *He did not falter in his effort to see the project through to the end.* □ *I promised not to falter in my loyalty.*

***familiar with** someone or something to have a good knowledge of someone or something. (*Typically: **be** ~; **become** ~; **get** ~.) □ *Are you familiar with changing a flat tire?* □ *I can't speak German fluently, but I'm somewhat familiar with the language.*

Familiarity breeds contempt. *Prov.* People do not respect someone they know well enough to know his or her faults. □ *The movie star doesn't let anyone get to know him, because he knows that familiarity breeds contempt.*

familiarize someone **with** something to help someone get to know or understand someone or something. □ *I hope you will take the time to familiarize yourself with the instructions before you set out to operate this device.* □ *Let me take a moment to familiarize myself with the facts of the case.*

The **family that prays together stays together.** *Prov.* Families who practice religion together will not break apart through divorce or estrangement. □ *Mother believed that the family that prays together stays together and insisted that we all say prayers every night.*

famous last words *Fig.* assertions that are almost immediately countered. (Sarcastic.) □ *A: I said I would never speak to her again in my entire life! B: Famous last words! You just said hello to her.*

***a **fan of** someone to be a follower of someone; to idolize someone. (*Typically: **be** ~; **become** ~.) □ *My mother is still a fan of the Beatles.* □ *I'm a great fan of the mayor of the town.*

fan out *Fig.* to spread out over a wide area. □ *The searchers fanned out, looking for the child lost in the woods.* □ *Let's fan out and search a wider area.*

fan out (from some place**)** to spread outward from a particular area. □ *The paths seem to fan out from the wide trail that starts at the house.* □ *The trails fanned out and soon we were all separated.*

fan something **out**† to spread something out so that all parts can be seen better. (As one opens a wood and paper fan.) □ *Todd fanned the cards out so we could see which ones he held.* □ *He fanned out the cards.*

fan the breeze *Fig.* to chat or gossip. □ *We're just fanning the breeze, so you didn't interrupt anything.* □ *Stop fanning the breeze and get to work.*

fan the flames (of something**)** *Fig.* to make something more intense; to make a situation worse. □ *The riot fanned the flames of racial hatred even more.* □ *The hostility in the school is bad enough without anyone fanning the flames.*

fancy footwork 1. *Lit.* clever and intricate dance steps. □ *The old man was known for his fancy footwork when he was on Broadway.* **2.** *Lit.* adroit movements of the feet that help someone retain balance or move through treacherous territory. □ *It took some fancy footwork to get down the mountain carrying the injured child.* **3.** *Fig.* a clever and intricate strategy that helps someone get out of trouble. □ *The governor did some fancy footwork to keep from getting blamed for the scandal.*

Fancy meeting you here! I am very surprised to meet you here! □ *Tom: Hi, Sue! Fancy meeting you here! Sue: Hi, Tom. I was thinking the same thing about you.* □ *"Fancy meeting you here," said Mr. Franklin when he bumped into the company president at the racetrack.*

fancy someone **as** someone or something to imagine that someone were someone else or some particular type of person. □ *Can you fancy her as a zookeeper?* □ *I can fancy him as a tall, dark stranger.* □ *I really don't fancy myself as a farmer.*

fancy someone's **chances** to have confidence in someone's [including one's own] ability to be successful. □ *We all think she will refuse to go out with him, but he certainly fancies his own chances.* □ *The other contestants are so talented that I don't fancy his chances at all.*

Fancy that! and **Imagine that!** I am very surprised to hear that.; That is hard to imagine or believe. □ *Mary: My father was elected president of the board. Sally: Fancy that!* □ *Sue: This computer is ten times faster than the one we had before. Jane: Imagine that! Is it easy to operate? Sue: Of course not.*

far and away the best unquestionably the best. □ *This soap is far and away the best I've ever used.* □ *Sally is good, but Ann is far and away the best artist in our school.*

far be it from me to do something it is not really my place to do something. (Always followed by *but*, as in the example.) □ *Far be it from me to tell you what to do, but I think you should buy the book.*

a **far cry from** something a thing that is very different from something else. □ *What you did was a far cry from what you said you were going to do.* □ *The song they played was a far cry from what I call music.*

far from it not it at all; not at all. □ *Do I think you need a new car? Far from it. The old one is fine.* □ *Bill: Does this hat look strange? Tom: Far from it. It looks good on you.*

far from the madding crowd in a quiet, restful place. (From Thomas Gray's poem, "Elegy Written in a Country Churchyard.") □ *Julia sat daydreaming at her desk, wishing she were far from the madding crowd.* □ *Jane: Where shall we go this weekend? Alan: Anywhere, as long as it's far from the madding crowd.*

far gone 1. in an extreme state, usually an irrational or intoxicated state. □ *Wow, that chick is far gone. Listen to her rave.* □ *He was too far gone to make any sense.* **2.** intoxicated. □ *Larry's far gone and looking sick.* □ *Wow, is she ever far gone!*

far into the night late into the night; until very late. □ *She sat up and read far into the night.* □ *The party went on far into the night.*

far out 1. *Lit.* far from the center of things; far from town. □ *The Smiths live sort of far out.* □ *The restaurant is nice,* but too far out. **2.** *Sl.* great; extraordinary. □ *This jazz is really far out!* □ *You want to hear some far out heavy metal?* **3.** very hard to understand; arcane; highly theoretical. □ *This physics chapter is too far out for me.* □ *I can't follow your far out line of reasoning.* **4.** intoxicated. □ *Three beers and Wally was really far out.*

faraway look and **far-off look** *Fig.* an appearance on one's face of having one's mind in another place. □ *Dave had a faraway look in his eyes, so I elbowed him to get his attention.* □ *Lisa's face had a far-off look indicating that she was daydreaming.*

farm someone **out**[†] **1.** [for someone in control] to send someone to work for someone else. □ *I have farmed my electrician out for a week, so your work will have to wait.* □ *We farmed out the office staff.* **2.** to send a child away to be cared for by someone; to send a child to boarding school. □ *We farmed the kids out to my sister for the summer.* □ *We farmed out the kids.*

farm something **out**[†] **1.** to deplete the fertility of land by farming too intensely. □ *They farmed their land out through careless land management.* □ *They farmed out their land.* **2.** to send work to someone to be done away from one's normal place of business; to subcontract work. □ *We farmed the assembly work out.* □ *We always farm out the actual final assembly of the finished units.*

far-off look Go to **faraway look**.

fart around *Fig.* to waste time playing around. (Caution with *fart*, which is considered coarse.) □ *Stop farting around and get the job started.*

fashion something **into** something to make, form, or convert something into something else. □ *He fashioned the newspaper into a temporary rain hat.* □ *Sarah fashioned the clay into a little bowl.*

fashion something **on** something to model something on something else; to pattern something after something else. □ *She fashioned her dress on something she had seen in a history book.* □ *Donna fashioned the plan on the one Robert had used.*

fashion something **out of** something to make something from something; to convert something into something else. □ *He tried to fashion a dog out of balloons.* □ *Elaine was expert at fashioning a bow out of chocolate.*

fast and furious *Cliché* very rapidly and with unrestrained energy. □ *Her work in the kitchen was fast and furious, and it looked lovely when she finished.* □ *Everything was going so fast and furious at the store during the Christmas rush that we never had time to eat lunch.*

fast friends good, loyal friends. □ *The two of them had been fast friends since college.*

a **fast one** a clever and devious trick. (Compare this with **pull a fast one**.) □ *That was a fast one. I didn't know you were so devious.* □ *This was the last fast one like that you'll ever catch me with.*

fasten someone or something **(on)to** someone or something to attach people or things together. □ *He fastened himself onto the mast of the boat with a length of rope.* □ *I fastened a note onto Jimmy, so his kindergarten teacher would read it and remind him to wear his gloves home.*

fasten something **down**[†] **(to** something**)** to attach something down to something else. □ *Fasten this board down to the top of the workbench.* □ *Please fasten down the board.*

fasten something **up**[†] to close something up, using buttons, a zipper, snaps, hooks, a clasp, or other things meant to hold something closed. □ *Please fasten this up for me. I can't reach the zipper.* □ *Please fasten up my buttons in back.*

fasten (up)on someone or something **1.** *Lit.* to take firm hold of someone or something. □ *She fastened upon me and would not let me go until she finished speaking.* □ *I don't like people who fasten on me and ask a lot of questions.* **2.** *Fig.* to fix one's attention on someone or something. □ *He fastened upon the picture for a brief moment and then turned away.* □ *The baby fastened on the television screen and watched it for many minutes.*

faster and faster at an increasing rate of speed; fast and then even faster. □ *The car went faster and faster and I was afraid we would crash.* □ *The cost of education goes up faster and faster every year.*

fast-talk someone **into** something to use deceitful talk to get someone to do something. □ *You can't fast-talk me into giving you money. How dumb do you think I am?* □ *Max tried to fast-talk Lefty into robbing a bank with him.*

fast-talk someone **out of** something to use deceitful talk to get someone not to do something or to give something up. □ *Don't try to fast-talk me out of my share.*

fat and happy *Fig.* content, as if from being well-fed. □ *Since all the employees were fat and happy, there was little incentive to improve productivity.* □ *You look fat and happy. Has life been treating you well?*

fat and sassy *Fig.* in good health and spirits. □ *She came back from her vacation all fat and sassy.* □ *Under Joe's care, the runt of the litter grew up fat and sassy.*

*****fat as a pig** exceptionally fat; grotesquely fat. (*****Also: as ~.**) □ *If I don't stop eating this cake, I'll be fat as a pig!* □ *You really ought to go on a diet; you're as fat as a pig.*

fat cat *Fig.* someone who is ostentatiously and smugly wealthy. □ *I like to watch the fat cats go by in their BMWs.* □ *I'm no fat cat. I can't even pay my normal bills!*

fat chance *Fig.* very little likelihood. □ *Fat chance he has of getting a promotion.* □ *You think she'll lend you the money? Fat chance!*

*****the **fat hit the fire** *Fig.* a situation that suddenly becomes frantic and unpleasant. (*****Typically: suddenly ~; then ~; when ~.**) □ *Things were looking bad in the stock market, then the fat hit the fire and I lost everything.*

The **fat is in the fire.** *Prov.* Matters have come to a crisis; trouble is about to start. □ *Brother: Mom found out that we broke the clock. Sister: Uh-oh. The fat's in the fire now.* □ *The fat is in the fire at work; we're nowhere near finishing the project, but the deadline is in two days.*

a **fate worse than death** *Fig.* a terrible fate. (Usually an exaggeration.) □ *Having to sit through one of his lectures is a fate worse than death.*

father something **on** someone *Fig.* to regard someone as the author or originator of something. □ *Do not attempt to father that stupid idea on me!* □ *We fathered the whole plan* *on the president. And we learned later she had nothing to do with it.*

fatten someone or an animal **up**† (**with** something) to use something to make someone or an animal fat. □ *We will fatten the calf up with corn.* □ *I don't know why they keep fattening up their children with so much food.*

fatten up (**on** something) **1.** *Lit.* to get fat by eating something. □ *The cattle fattened up on the succulent grass.* □ *The bears have to fatten up on food before they hibernate for the winter.* **2.** *Fig.* to become prosperous because of something. □ *The corporations fattened up on easy profits and low taxes.* □ *The directors of the company fattened up even during the recession when the workers were laid off.*

fault someone (**for** something) to blame or criticize someone for something. □ *I can't fault you for that. I would have done the same thing.* □ *He tended to fault himself for the failure of the project.*

faunch around *Rur.* to fuss and complain. □ *Stop faunching around about your problems and go to sleep.* □ *Aunt Bess is always faunching around about something.*

favor someone or something **with** something to provide someone or something with something beneficial or special. □ *Mary favored us with a song.* □ *Nature favored Bill with curly hair.*

fawn (all) over someone *Fig.* to flatter someone or attend to someone excessively; to **curry favor with** someone. □ *Please stop fawning all over the guests. You are embarrassing me.* □ *She always fawns over us when we visit.*

fawn (up)on someone *Fig.* to praise and flatter someone. □ *Aunt Mabel fawned on the new baby till the poor child was rescued by her mother.* □ *I hate the way our aunts fawn on us at family gatherings.*

fear for someone or something to be afraid for the safety of someone or something; to worry about someone or something. □ *I fear for Tom. He has gone to a very dangerous place.* □ *I don't want to go down that rocky trail. I fear for my car.*

feast one's **eyes** ((**up)on** someone or something) *Fig.* to enjoy the sight of someone or something. (*Upon* is formal and less commonly used than *on.*) □ *Just feast your eyes on that beautiful beach.* □ *Jane feasted her eyes on Roger for a while and then went on with her studying.*

feast (up)on something to eat a great deal of something; to eat a feast built around something in particular. □ *We will feast upon turkey for weeks.* □ *We feasted on the fish Harry had caught.*

a **feather in** one's **cap** *Fig.* an honor; a reward for something. □ *Getting a new client was really a feather in my cap.* □ *John earned a feather in his cap by getting an A in physics.*

feather one's (**own**) **nest 1.** *Fig.* to decorate and furnish one's home in style and comfort. (Alludes to birds lining their nests with feathers to make them warm and comfortable.) □ *With the new family room and expanded kitchen, they seem to have feathered their nest quite comfortably.* **2.** *Fig.* to use power and prestige to provide for oneself selfishly. (Said especially of politicians who use their offices to make money for themselves.) □ *The mayor seemed to be helping people, but she was really feathering her own nest.* □ *The building contractor used a lot of public money to feather his nest.*

feature someone **as** something **1.** to imagine someone to be something or a particular type of person. □ *I really can't feature you as a ship's captain.* □ *Alice had always featured Fred as a fairly even-tempered person.* **2.** to give special prominence to someone in a particular part in a play, film, opera, etc. □ *They featured Laura as the lead singer in the group.* □ *The director refused to feature Roger as a lead.*

feature someone **in** something **1.** to imagine someone wearing something. □ *I can't feature you in that ridiculous dress.* □ *Can you feature Fran in that hat?* **2.** to imagine someone being in something or some place. □ *I can't feature you in Paris. You are too rural to enjoy a place like Paris.* □ *Can you feature David in New York City?*

*****fed up** (**to** some degree) (**with** someone or something) bored or disgusted with someone or something. (*Typically: be ~; become ~.*) □ *I am fed up to my eyeballs with your complaining.* □ *I am just fed up to here!*

Feed a cold and starve a fever. *Prov.* You should feed someone who has a cold, and withhold food from someone who has a fever.; (or, interpreted differently) If you feed someone who has a cold, that will ward off a fever. □ *Jill: I don't feel like going out to lunch with you. I have a cold. Jane: All the more reason you should get something to eat. Feed a cold and starve a fever, you know.*

feed off (**of**) something to eat something in particular customarily. (*Of* is usually retained before pronouns.) □ *This creature feeds off fallen fruit.* □ *Mosquitoes seem to want to feed off of me!*

feed one's **face** *Inf.* to put food in one's mouth; to eat (something). □ *You're always feeding your face. You're going to get fat.* □ *Stop feeding your face and listen to me.*

feed someone **a line** Go to **give** someone **a line**.

feed someone, something, or an animal **with** something **1.** to feed something to someone, a group, or an animal. □ *The camp cook fed them with hot dogs and beans.* □ *We fed the dogs with the leftovers.* **2.** to use a tool or utensil to feed someone, a group, or an animal. □ *He fed the baby with a spoon.* □ *We fed the entire group with paper plates.*

feed something **back into** something to return something back to where it came. □ *I tried to feed the stamps back into the machine, but, of course, they wouldn't go.* □ *The machine made too many boxes, but you can't feed them back into it!*

feed something **back**† **to** someone to give or hand something back to someone. □ *We fed the rope back to those in line behind us.* □ *Feed back the papers to the clerk.*

feed something **into** something to put something into something; to push a supply of something into something. □ *I fed all the coins into the telephone and waited to be connected.* □ *I will feed every coin I have into the phone and see what it does for me.* □ *Did you feed the data into the computer?*

feed something **to** someone *Fig.* to tell someone lies. □ *Don't try to feed that nonsense to me! I know it isn't so.* □ *Please don't feed any of those lies to Mark.*

feed something **to** someone or an animal to give someone or an animal food. □ *Don't feed pizza to the baby.* □ *I fed the leftover turkey to the dog.*

F

feed the kitty *Fig.* to contribute money. (A *kitty* here is a small collection of money.) □ *Please feed the kitty. Make a contribution to help sick children.* □ *Come on, Bill. Feed the kitty. You can afford a dollar for a good cause.*

feed (up)on someone or something to eat someone or something. (*Upon* is formal and less commonly used than *on*.) □ *They say that some Bengal tigers feed upon people.* □ *They feed on anything that moves.*

a **feeding frenzy 1.** *Lit.* [of sharks] a vicious, competitive feeding attack on prey animals. □ *One of the sharks was fatally bitten during a feeding frenzy amongst his own kind.* **2.** *Fig.* a vicious attack on someone or something. □ *It wasn't an office argument, it was a feeding frenzy led by the head accountant!*

feel a draft to sense that one is being rejected; to sense that someone is cool toward one, possibly for racial reasons. □ *Oh, man, I feel a draft in here. Let's leave.* □ *What a reception! I sure felt a draft.*

feel a glow of contentment Go to next.

feel a glow of happiness and **feel a glow of contentment; feel a glow of satisfaction; feel a glow of peacefulness** *Fig.* to have a good feeling of some kind. □ *Anne felt a glow of happiness as she held her new baby.* □ *Sitting by the lake, the lovers felt a warm glow of contentment.*

feel around (for someone or something**)** and **feel about (for** someone or something**)** to try to find someone or something by feel [rather than sight]. □ *He felt around for the soap in the bathtub.* □ *She felt about for the dog at the foot of the bed, but it wasn't there.* □ *Gerald felt about for a pencil.*

feel at home to feel as if one belongs; to feel as if one were in one's home; to feel accepted. □ *I liked my dormitory room. I really felt at home there.* □ *We will do whatever we can to make you feel at home.*

feel blue *Fig.* to feel sad. □ *You look like you feel blue. What's wrong?*

feel fit to feel well and healthy. □ *If you want to feel fit, you must eat the proper food and get enough rest.* □ *I hope I still feel fit when I get old.*

feel for someone to feel the emotional pain that someone else is feeling; to empathize or sympathize with someone. □ *I really feel for you. I'm so sorry it turned out this way.* □ *Fred felt for Dave, but there was nothing he could do for him.*

*a **feel for** something a natural or learned ability to do something. (*Typically: **get** ~; **have** ~.) □ *I will do better with this work as soon as I get a feel for it.* □ *He doesn't have a feel for this kind of careful work.*

feel free (to do something**)** to feel like one is permitted to do something or take something. □ *Please feel free to stay for dinner.* □ *If you see something you want in the refrigerator, please feel free.*

feel guilty (about something**)** to feel that one is to blame for something; to feel intense regret for something that one has done. □ *I feel guilty for forgetting about your birthday.* □ *You shouldn't feel guilty about the accident. It's not your fault.*

feel it beneath one **(to** do something**)** to feel that one would be lowering oneself to do something. □ *Tom feels it beneath him to scrub the floor.* □ *Ann feels it beneath her to carry her own luggage.* □ *I would do it, but I feel it beneath me.*

feel like a million (dollars) *Fig.* to feel well and healthy, both physically and mentally. □ *A quick swim in the morning makes me feel like a million dollars.* □ *What a beautiful day! It makes you feel like a million.*

feel like a new person *Fig.* to feel refreshed and renewed, especially after getting well or getting dressed up. □ *I bought a new suit, and now I feel like a new person.* □ *Bob felt like a new person when he got out of the hospital.*

feel like death warmed over Go to like death warmed over.

feel like doing something to want to do something; to be in the mood to do something; to feel well enough to do something. □ *Do you feel like stopping work to eat something?* □ *I feel like going on a vacation.*

feel like oneself **again** Go to oneself again.

feel like someone or something to have the feel of someone or something; to seem to be someone or something according to feel or touch. □ *Whoever this is feels like Tom. Sort of soft and pudgy.* □ *This thing feels like a rubber hose, not a hot dog.*

*the **feel of** something *Fig.* a sense for how something feels when it is being used correctly. (*Typically: **get** ~; **have** ~; **give** someone ~.) □ *I haven't yet got the feel of this bat. I hope I don't strike out.* □ *I can drive better now that I have the feel of this car's steering.*

feel on top of the world *Fig.* to feel very good, as if one were ruling the world. □ *I feel on top of the world this morning.* □ *I do not actually feel on top of the world, but I have felt worse.*

feel one's **gorge rise** *Fig.* to sense that one is getting very angry. □ *I felt my gorge rise and I knew I was going to lose my temper.* □ *Bob could feel his gorge rise as he read his tax bill.*

feel one's **oats** *Fig.* to be very lively. □ *Careful with that horse. He's feeling his oats today.* □ *Mary was feeling her oats and decided to go out dancing.*

feel out of place Go to out of place.

feel out of sorts Go to out of sorts.

feel out of things to feel alienated from something. □ *I feel out of things lately. Are people ignoring me?* □ *I feel a little out of things at this party, but I will try to join in the fun.*

feel pinched and **feel the pinch** *Fig.* experiencing hardship because of having too little money. □ *The Smiths used to go abroad every year, but now that he's retired, they're really feeling pinched.* □ *You're bound to feel the pinch a little when you're a student.*

feel somehow about someone or something to have ideas, opinions, or reactions regarding someone or something. □ *I feel good about him.* □ *Do you feel good about how you did on the test?* □ *How do you feel about Sally?*

feel someone **out**† **(about** someone or something**)** *Fig.* to find out what someone thinks about someone or something. (This does not involve touching anyone.) □ *I will feel him out about what he thinks about going to Florida.* □ *Let me feel out the boss about this matter.*

feel someone **up**[†] to feel someone sexually. (Use discretion with topic.) □ *I heard him say he really wanted to feel her up.* □ *He wanted to feel up the girl.*

feel something **in** one's **bones** and **know** something **in** one's **bones** *Fig.* to sense something; to have an intuition about something. □ *The train will be late. I feel it in my bones.* □ *I failed the test. I know it in my bones.*

feel something **with** something to touch and explore something with something. □ *I felt the soft little creature with my hand.* □ *Don't feel that thing with your bare hands.*

feel the pinch Go to feel pinched.

feel up to something to feel well enough or prepared enough to do something. (Often in the negative.) □ *I don't feel up to jogging today.* □ *Aunt Mary didn't feel up to making the visit.*

a **feeling about** something Go to a feeling (that something is the case).

feeling (kinda) puny feeling ill. □ *I'm feeling puny. Think I might be coming down with a cold.* □ *Bill had to skip football practice on account of he was feeling puny.*

feeling no pain numbed by alcohol and feeling nothing; intoxicated. □ *She fell off the wagon and is feeling no pain.* □ *He drank the whole thing, and he's feeling no pain.*

*a **feeling (that** something is the case) and *a **feeling about** something a premonition that [something might happen or be the case]; an intuition about something. (*Typically: **get** ~; **have** ~; **give** someone ~.) □ *I had a feeling that you might be dropping by this afternoon.* □ *I didn't have any facts to support it. I just had a feeling.*

The **female of the species is more deadly than the male.** *Prov.* In many animal species, the female is poisonous and the male is not, and, by analogy, women are more dangerous than men. □ *Bill: My old girlfriend's been threatening me ever since I broke up with her, but she's too small and weak to do me any harm. Fred: I'd be careful if I were you. The female of the species is more deadly than the male.*

fence an animal **in**[†] to enclose an animal and its area within a fence or barrier. □ *We fenced the dog in to keep it at home.* □ *We had to fence in the dog.*

fence someone **in**[†] to restrict someone in some way. □ *I don't want to fence you in, but you have to get home earlier at night.* □ *Don't try to fence me in. I need a lot of freedom.* □ *Your last stupid move fenced in the department, making us less effective.*

fence someone or an animal **out**[†] to keep someone or an animal out with a fence or barrier. □ *We decided that living in the woods was satisfactory only if we fenced the wildlife out.* □ *We had to fence out the deer.* □ *We hoped we had fenced prowlers out with the tall electric fence.*

fence someone or something **off**[†] **(from** something) to separate someone or something from something else with a fence or barrier. □ *We fenced the children's play area off from the rest of the yard.* □ *Dave fenced off the play area.* □ *We fenced off the children from the rest of the yard.*

fence something **in**[†] to enclose an area within a fence. □ *When they fenced the garden in, they thought the deer wouldn't be able to destroy the flowers.* □ *We fenced in the yard to make a safe place for the children.*

fend for oneself Go to shift for oneself.

fend someone or something **off**[†] to hold someone or something off; to fight someone or something off. □ *We knew we could fend them off only a little while longer.* □ *They could not fend off the attackers.*

fender bender *Fig.* a minor car accident. □ *A small fender bender tied up traffic on the expressway for hours!*

ferret something **out**[†] Go to ferret something out of someone or something.

ferret something **out**[†] **(from** something) *Fig.* to fetch something out from something. □ *We will have to ferret the mouse out from behind the stove.* □ *We can ferret out the mouse with the aid of the cat.*

ferret something **out of** someone or something and **ferret** something **out**[†] *Fig.* to get, remove, or retrieve something from someone or something, usually with cunning and persistence. □ *I tried very hard, but I couldn't ferret the information out of the clerk.* □ *I had to ferret out the answers one by one.*

ferry someone **around**[†] to transport people here and there in small groups. □ *I really don't want to spend all my days ferrying children around.* □ *Why am I ferrying around a bunch of kids all day?*

ferry someone or something **across** something and **ferry** someone or something **across**[†] to transport someone or something across a river on a ferryboat. □ *Can we get someone to ferry us across the lake to the island?* □ *After they ferried across all the cars, they closed the ferryboat down for the night.*

fess up (to something) to confess to having done something. (Short form of *confess.*) □ *I tried to get the boy to fess up to doing it, but he wouldn't do it.* □ *Come on, fess up.*

festoon someone or something **with** something to drape or garland someone or something with something. □ *Karen festooned her daughter with flowers for the party.* □ *The kids festooned the gymnasium with crepe paper and garlands of plastic flowers.*

fetch something **in**[†] to bring or pull something in. □ *Would you please fetch some more firewood in?* □ *Can you fetch in the paper?*

fetch something **out of** something and **fetch** something **out**[†] to pull something out of something. □ *Could you fetch me another hot dog out of the pot?* □ *I'll fetch out a hot dog for you.*

fetch up *Sl.* to empty one's stomach; to vomit. □ *I really felt like I was going to fetch up.* □ *Somebody fetched up in here and didn't clean it up.*

fetch up at some place to reach a place; to end up at a place. □ *We fetched up at Sam's house at about midnight.* □ *The car fetched up at the cabin and everyone got out.*

feud (with someone) **(over** someone or something) and **feud (with** someone) **about (**someone or something) to fight with someone over someone or something; to have an ongoing battle with someone about someone or some-

F

thing. □ *Some of the neighbors are feuding with each other over the parking places on the street.* □ *Don't feud over her with me!*

few and far between very few; few and widely scattered. □ *Get some gasoline now. Service stations on this highway are few and far between.* □ *Some people think that good movies are few and far between.*

a **few bricks short of a load** and a **few cards shy of a full deck**; a **few cards short of a deck**; **not playing with a full deck**; **two bricks shy of a load** *Fig.* lacking in intellectual ability. (Many other variants.) □ *Tom: Joe thinks he can build a car out of old milk jugs. Mary: I think Joe's a few bricks short of a load.* □ *Ever since she fell and hit her head, Jane's been a few bricks short of a load, if you know what I'm saying.* □ *Bob's nice, but he's not playing with a full deck.* □ *You twit! You're two bricks shy of a load.*

a **few cards shy of a full deck** Go to previous.

a **few cards short of a deck** Go to a few bricks short of a load.

fiddle around (with someone**)** and **fiddle about (with** someone**)** to tease, annoy, or play with someone; to waste someone's time. □ *All right, stop fiddling around with me and tell me how much you will give me for my car.* □ *Now it's time for all of you to quit fiddling around and get to work.* □ *Tom, you have to stop spending your time fiddling about with your friends. It's time to get serious with your studies.*

fiddle around (with something**)** and **fiddle about (with** something**)** to play with something; to tinker with something ineptly. □ *My brother is outside fiddling around with his car engine.* □ *He should stop fiddling around and go out and get a job.*

fiddle something **away**† to waste something. □ *She fiddled the afternoon away.* □ *Don't fiddle away the afternoon. Get to work.*

fiddle while Rome burns *Fig.* to do nothing or something trivial while knowing that something disastrous is happening. (From a legend that the Roman emperor Nero played the lyre while Rome was burning.) □ *The lobbyists don't seem to be doing anything to stop this tax bill. They're fiddling while Rome burns.*

fiddle with someone or something to tinker or play with someone or something. □ *Please don't fiddle with the stereo controls.* □ *Leave your brother alone. Don't fiddle with him. He's cranky.*

fidget around to wiggle and twitch nervously. □ *The child sat there, fidgeting around for over ten minutes.* □ *Please don't fidget around so.*

fidget with something to play with something nervously. □ *Please don't fidget with your zipper.* □ *Carl is always fidgeting with his left ear.*

field questions and **field a question** to answer a series of questions, especially from reporters. □ *After her speech, Jane fielded questions from reporters.* □ *The president's press agents field questions from the newspaper.*

Fields have eyes, and woods have ears. *Prov.* Even though you are outside in an apparently empty landscape, someone may be eavesdropping on you. □ *Jill: You said you had a secret. Tell me. Jane: Not here. Jill: But there's* nobody else in the park. Jane: Fields have eyes, and woods have ears.

a **fifth wheel** *Fig.* an unwelcome or extra person. □ *I don't like living with my son and daughter-in-law. I feel like a fifth wheel.* □ *Bill always begs to come on camping trips with us, but really, he's a fifth wheel.*

fifty-fifty even or equal. (See also go fifty-fifty (on something.) □ *The chances of success are about fifty-fifty.* □ *Even at fifty-fifty, it's probably worth it, you know.*

fight about someone or something to have a battle or argue about someone or something. □ *Why do we always have to fight about money?* □ *Let's not fight about Ed.*

fight against someone or something to battle against someone or something. □ *The general refused to fight against the enemy, which was much stronger.* □ *He fought against the disease to the very end.*

fight against time *Fig.* to hurry to meet a deadline or to do something quickly. □ *The ambulance sped through the city to reach the accident, fighting against time.* □ *All the students fought against time to complete the test.*

fight back (at someone or something**)** to defend oneself against someone or something; to retaliate against someone or something. □ *You are going to have to fight back at them. You can't expect us to defend you.* □ *It's hard for me to fight back against three of them by myself.*

Fight fire with fire. *Prov.* Use against your opponent the same methods he or she is using against you. □ *After her opponent had spent several weeks slandering her, the candidate decided to fight fire with fire.* □ *When evangelists would come to our house and try to convert us, Mother would fight fire with fire and try to convert them to her religion.*

fight for someone or something to go to battle for the benefit of someone or something; to go to battle in the name of someone or something. □ *They all went off to fight for their country.* □ *The soldiers fought for the queen and the survival of the empire.* □ *I guess I will have to learn to fight for my rights.*

fight like hell Go to like the devil.

fight like the devil Go to like the devil.

fight like the dickens Go to like the devil.

fight on to continue to fight. □ *The boys fought on until one of them was down.* □ *They fought on until they were exhausted.*

fight (one's way) back (to something**)** to struggle to return to something or some place. □ *She fought her way back to the head of the line.* □ *Jan fought back to good health.*

fight one's **way out (of** something**)** and **fight** one's **way out** to struggle to get out of something or some place. □ *He fought his way out of the crowded room and out through the door.* □ *He couldn't fight his way out of a paper bag.*

fight (one's way) through (something**) 1.** to struggle to get through something; to struggle to penetrate something. □ *I'll have to fight my way through all this crepe paper in order to reach the punch bowl.* □ *The room was filled with trash, and I had to fight through it to get to the other door.* **2.** to struggle to work through all of something. □ *I have to fight my way through this stack of papers by noon.* □ *I am tired of fighting through red tape.*

fight over someone or something to fight a battle that decides who gets someone or something. □ *Well, let's not fight over Tom. You can have him. I can make a better team without him.* □ *The children were fighting over who would get the largest piece of cake.*

fight someone or something **down**† to fight against and defeat someone or something. □ *We fought the opposition down and got our bill through the committee.* □ *We had to fight down Fred, who wanted something entirely different.*

fight someone or something **hammer and tongs** and **fight** someone or something **tooth and nail; go at it hammer and tongs; go at it tooth and nail** *Fig.* to fight against someone or something energetically and with great determination. □ *They fought against the robber tooth and nail.* □ *The dogs were fighting each other hammer and tongs.*

fight someone or something **off**† to repel an attack from someone or something. □ *We fought the enemy attack off, but they returned almost immediately.* □ *She fought off the mosquitoes all evening.* □ *Jed fought the attacker off.*

fight someone or something **with** something to attack or battle someone or something with something. □ *We can't fight the enemy with clubs and pitchforks!* □ *I fought him with my bare fists.*

fight something **down**† **1.** to struggle to hold something back; to struggle to keep from being overwhelmed by something. □ *She fought her anger down and managed to stay calm.* □ *She fought down the urge.* **2.** to struggle to swallow something; to fight to get something down one's throat. □ *It tasted terrible, but I managed to fight it down.* □ *She fought down the nasty-tasting medicine.*

fight something **out**† to settle something by fighting. □ *Do we have to fight this out? Can't we use reason?* □ *I prefer to fight out this matter once and for all.*

fight something **through**† **(**something**)** to force something through some sort of procedure or process; to railroad something **through** (something). □ *The governor fought the bill through the legislature successfully.* □ *She fought through the bill successfully.*

fight the good fight to fight a noble and well-intentioned battle. □ *He fought the good fight and left the meeting with a clear conscience.*

fight to the death to engage in a battle that isn't finished until one opponent is dead. □ *The two men looked as though they were going to fight to the death.* □ *These evil-tempered dogs will fight to the death.*

fight (with) someone or some creature **(over** someone or something**)** to fight with someone or an animal over who gets or keeps someone or something. □ *The terrier fought with the collie over the piece of meat.* □ *I don't want to fight you over Harry.*

fight (with) someone or something **(about** someone or something**)** to do battle or argue with someone or something about someone or something. □ *Let's not fight with each other about this simple matter.* □ *I don't want to fight with you about this!*

a **fighting chance** a good possibility of success, especially if every effort is made. □ *They have at least a fighting*

chance of winning the race. □ *The patient could die, but he has a fighting chance since the operation.*

figure in something [for someone or something] to play a role in something. □ *Tom figures in our plans for future office management.* □ *I don't wish to figure in your future.*

figure on doing something to plan on something. □ *I figured on arriving at the party around eight o'clock.* □ *Jane figured on spending $25 on dinner.*

figure on someone or something to count on someone or something; to assume something about someone or something. □ *I am figuring on twelve people for dinner next Friday.* □ *We are figuring on you and your wife for dinner next weekend.*

figure out the root of the problem Go to the root of the problem.

figure someone **as** something to think of a person as a particular type of person. □ *I figured her as a reliable worker.* □ *We figured them all as good credit risks.*

figure someone or something **in**† Go to **figure** someone or something in((to) something).

figure someone or something **in**† **(on** something**)** to plan on having someone or something included in something. □ *Please figure another ten people in on the picnic.* □ *I will figure in those people.*

figure someone or something **in((to)** something**)** and **figure** someone or something **in**† to reckon someone or something into the total. □ *I will figure the electric bill into the total.* □ *We can figure in one more person.*

figure someone or something **out**† to begin to comprehend someone or something; to come to understand someone or something better. □ *I just can't figure you out.* □ *I can't figure out quiet people readily.*

figure something **up**† to add up the amount of something. □ *Please figure the bill up. We have to go now.* □ *I will figure up the bill right away.*

filch something **(from** someone**)** *Sl.* to grab or steal something from someone. □ *The young boy filched a candy bar from the store.* □ *Who filched my wallet from me?*

file charges (against someone**)** Go to **press charges** (against someone).

file for something to submit an application or document for something. □ *The company filed for bankruptcy.* □ *Let's file for reorganization.*

file in((to) something**)** [for a line of people] to move into something or some place. □ *The people filed into the hall quietly.* □ *Everyone filed in quietly.*

file out (of something**)** [for a line of people] to move out of something or some place. □ *The people filed quietly out of the theater.* □ *They filed out at the end.*

file past (someone or something**)** [for a line or procession] to move past someone or something. □ *The people filed past the coffin, looking sadly at the still figure inside.* □ *As they filed past, some wept openly.*

file something **against** someone to lodge a criminal charge against someone. □ *Sally filed a charge of assault against Max.* □ *The old man filed charges against the attacker.*

file something **(away**†**)** to put something away, usually in a file folder or file cabinet. □ *She filed the letter away for*

F

future reference. □ *Please file away this report. You will need it some day.*

file something **away**† **(from** something) and **file** something **off ((of)** something)**; file** something off† to remove something from something else by filing. (*Of* is usually retained before pronouns.) □ *The dentist filed the sharp point away from the tooth.* □ *The dentist filed away the sharp point from the tooth.* □ *The dentist filed the point off.*

file something **down**† to level off a protrusion by filing. □ *File this edge down so no one gets cut on it.* □ *Please file down this edge.*

file something **off ((of)** something) Go to **file** something **away**† **(from** something).

file something **with** someone or something to submit an application or a document to someone or a group. □ *You must file this copy with the state office.* □ *I will file this with my boss.*

file something off† Go to **file** something **away**† **(from** something).

fill in [for an indentation, hole, etc.] to become full. □ *The scar filled in after a few months.* □ *Will this hole in the ground fill in by itself, or should I put some dirt in?*

fill in (for someone or something) *Fig.* to substitute for someone or something; to take the place of someone or something. □ *I will have to fill in for Wally until he gets back.* □ *I don't mind filling in.*

Fill in the blanks. You can figure out the rest.; You can draw a conclusion from that. (Fixed order. See also **fill** something **in**.) □ *Mary: What happened at Fred's house last night? Bill: There was a big fight, then the neighbors called the police. Mary: Then what happened? Bill: Fill in the blanks. What do you think?* □ *John: They had been lost for two days, then the wolves came, and the rest is history. Jane: Yes, I think I can fill in the blanks.*

fill one's **face** and **stuff** one's **face** *Sl.* to eat food fast; to stuff food into one's face. □ *Everytime I see you, you are stuffing your face. No wonder you're overweight!*

fill out to become full; to gain weight. □ *About a month after her debilitating illness, Maggie began to fill out again.* □ *The fruit on the trees began to fill out, and we knew it was going to ripen soon.*

fill someone **full of lead** *Sl.* to shoot someone. □ *The shopkeeper bought a gun and swore the next time someone broke into the shop, he'd fill him full of lead.* □ *Don't move, or I'll fill you full of lead.*

fill someone **in† (on** someone or something) to tell someone the details about someone or something. □ *Please fill me in on what happened last night.* □ *Please fill in the committee on the details.*

fill someone or something **up**† **(with** something) to put as much as possible into someone or something. □ *We filled him up with chili and crackers.* □ *We will fill up the basket with leaves.* □ *I will fill the basket up with flowers.*

fill someone's **head with** something *Fig.* to put some kind of ideas into someone's head. □ *Who's been filling your head with ideas like that?* □ *Mary has been filling my head with ideas about how to get rich.*

fill someone's **shoes** *Fig.* to take the place of some other person and do that person's work satisfactorily. (As if you were wearing the other person's shoes.) □ *I don't know how we'll be able to do without you. No one can fill your shoes.* □ *It'll be difficult to fill Jane's shoes. She did her job very well.*

fill something **in**† **1.** to add material to an indentation, hole, etc., to make it full. □ *You had better fill the crack in with something before you paint the wall.* □ *You should fill in the cracks first.* **2.** *Fig.* to write in the blank spaces on a paper; to write on a form. (See also **Fill in the blanks.**) □ *Please fill this form in.* □ *I will fill in the form for you.*

fill something **out**† *Fig.* to complete a form by writing in the blank spaces. □ *Please fill this form out and send it back to us in the mail.* □ *I will fill out the form as you asked.*

fill something **to** something to add material to something up to a certain point. □ *Fill the barrel up to here and no higher.* □ *Please fill the glass to the top.*

fill the bill and **fit the bill** to be acceptable. □ *Jane: I need some string. Tom: Here's some twine. Will it fill the bill?* □ *I need cloth to make a shirt. This muslin ought to fit the bill.*

fill the gap to serve temporarily. □ *I think that the temp will fill the gap until a new person can be hired.*

fill up 1. to become full. □ *The creek filled up after the heavy rain yesterday.* □ *The rain barrel began to fill up during the storm.* **2.** to fill one's gas tank. □ *I've got to stop and fill up. The gas tank is running low.* □ *We will fill up at the next little town.*

filled to the brim filled all the way full; filled up to the top edge. □ *I like my coffee cup filled to the brim.* □ *If the glass is filled to the brim, I can't drink without spilling the contents.*

film over [for something] to develop a film on its surface. □ *The windows had filmed over because of all the humidity.* □ *Her eyes filmed over with the cold.*

filter in(to some place) **1.** *Lit.* to leak or seep into some place. □ *The smell of bacon cooking filtered into his room and made him wake up.* □ *The smoke filtered in and burned our eyes.* **2.** *Fig.* [for people] to come into a place, a few at a time, over a period of time. □ *One by one, the guests filtered into the room.* □ *They filtered in and started on the snacks.*

filter something **out of** something and **filter** something **out**† to remove something from a fluid by running it through a filter. □ *We filtered the odors out of the water and made it fit to drink.* □ *I'm glad you filtered out the odor.*

filter through (something) to pass or seep through something. □ *The water filtered through the coffee grounds and dripped into the pot.* □ *The clear water filtered through and left the sand behind.*

filthy lucre money. □ *I sure could use a little of that filthy lucre.* □ *I don't want to touch any of your filthy lucre.*

filthy rich 1. *Fig.* very wealthy. □ *I wouldn't mind being filthy rich.* □ *There are too many filthy rich people now.* **2.** *Fig.* people who are very wealthy. □ *The filthy rich can afford that kind of thing, but I can't.* □ *I sort of feel sorry for the filthy rich.*

a **final fling** *Fig.* the last act or period of enjoyment before a change in one's circumstances or lifestyle. □ *You might as well have a final fling before the baby's born.* □ *Mary's* *going out with her girlfriends for a final fling. She's getting married next week.*

the **final say** Go to the last word.

the **final word** Go to the last word.

financially embarrassed *Euph.* broke. □ *I'm a bit financially embarrassed at the moment.* □ *Gary found himself financially embarrassed when the time came to pay the bill.*

find a way around someone or something **1.** *Lit.* to find a way to pass around someone or something to get to the other side. □ *I could hardly find a way around the tables in the crowded restaurant to get to the restroom.* **2.** *Fig.* to find a way to evade the rules, or someone's restrictions. □ *The students are always trying to find a way around the regulations.*

find against someone or something [for a jury or a judge] to announce a decision against one side of a lawsuit. □ *The jury found against the defendant, who was a horrible witness.* □ *The court found against the corporation and levied a fine.*

find fault (with someone or something**)** to find things wrong with someone or something. □ *We were unable to find fault with his arguments.* □ *Sally's father was always finding fault with her.*

find favor with someone to win the praise of someone. □ *The maid found favor with the family and was given a large salary increase.* □ *Mary found favor with her employer because of her good ideas.*

find for someone or something [for a jury or a judge] to announce a decision in favor of one side of a lawsuit. □ *The judge found for Mrs. Franklin, and that made her family quite happy.* □ *The court found for the plaintiff and admonished the defense lawyer.*

find it in one's **heart (to** do something**)** and **find it in** oneself **(to** do something**)** *Fig.* to have the courage or compassion to do something. □ *She couldn't find it in herself to refuse to come home to him.* □ *I can't do it! I can't find it in my heart.*

find it in oneself **(to** do something**)** Go to previous.

find its way somewhere [for something] to end up in a place. (This expression avoids accusing someone of moving the thing to the place.) □ *The money found its way into the mayor's pocket.* □ *The secret plans found their way into the enemy's hands.*

find (neither) hide nor hair Go to (neither) hide nor hair.

find one's **feet** *Fig.* to become used to a new situation or experience. □ *She was lonely when she first left home, but she is finding her feet now.* □ *It takes time to learn the office routine, but you will gradually find your feet.*

find one's **own level** *Fig.* to find the position or rank to which one is best suited. □ *You cannot force new clerks to be ambitious. They will all find their own level.* □ *The new student is happier in the beginning class. It was just a question of letting her find her own level.*

find one's **tongue** *Fig.* to be able to talk; to figure out what to say. □ *Tom was speechless for a moment. Then he found his tongue.* □ *Ann was unable to find her tongue. She sat there in silence.*

find one's **way (around)** *Fig.* to be able to move about an area satifactorily without getting lost. □ *I can go downtown by myself. I can find my way around.* □ *I know the area well enough to find my way.*

find one's **way around (**something**)** to discover a way to move around something or some place without getting lost. □ *Can you find your way around or shall I have someone take you?* □ *Don't worry. I can find my way around.*

find one's **way (somewhere)** [for someone] to discover the route to a place. □ *Mr. Smith found his way to the museum.* □ *Can you find your way home?*

find oneself *Fig.* to discover what one's talents and preferences are. □ *Bill did better in school after he found himself.* □ *John tried a number of different jobs. He finally found himself when he became a cook.*

find oneself **in a bind** Go to in a bind.

find oneself **in a jam** Go to in a jam.

find oneself **in the doghouse** Go to in the doghouse.

find oneself **in the market (for** something**)** Go to in the market (for something).

find oneself **in the public eye** Go to in the public eye.

find oneself **with** someone or something to discover that one has a disease or a problem. □ *I found myself with a terrible case of sunburn after the first day of my vacation.*

find oneself **without** someone or something to discover that one no longer has someone or something. □ *When I got to the head of the line, I found myself without a cent!*

find out a thing or two (about someone or something**)** Go to a thing or two (about someone or something).

find someone **a bit off** Go to a bit off.

find someone **a little off** Go to a little off.

find someone **guilty** and **find** someone **innocent; find** someone **not guilty** to decide guilt or innocence and deliver a verdict in a court of law. □ *The judge found the defendant not guilty by reason of insanity.* □ *The jury found the defendant innocent.*

find someone **in** to learn or discover that one is at home; to learn or discover that one is in one's office. □ *I never expected to find you in at this time of night.* □ *Did you really expect to find me in on a Friday night?*

find someone **innocent** Go to find someone guilty.

find someone **not guilty** Go to find someone guilty.

find someone **out 1.** to discover that someone is not at home. □ *We knocked on their door and found them out.* □ *Sam found Frank out when he arrived to collect the debt.* **2.** to discover something surprising or shocking about someone. □ *I don't want them to find me out.* □ *We found her out despite her deviousness.*

find something **in mint condition** Go to in mint condition.

find something **out**† to discover facts about someone or something; to learn a fact. □ *I found something out that you might be interested in.* □ *We found out that the Smiths are going to sell their house.*

find (something**) out**† **(about** someone or something**) (from** someone or something**)** to learn something about someone or something from someone or something. □

What did you find out about Terry from Mr. Franklin? □ I didn't find anything out about Roger from the newspaper stories. □ I found out what I wanted to know about solar flares from the encyclopedia. □ What did you find out about Bill?

find (something) out the hard way Go to learn (something) the hard way.

find the root of the problem Go to the root of the problem.

find time for someone or something Go to time for someone or something.

Finders keepers(, losers weepers). *Prov.* If you find something, you are entitled to keep it. (This is a children's rhyme and sounds childish when used by adults.) □ *Bill: Hey! How come you're using my fountain pen? Fred: It's mine now. I found it on the floor—finders keepers, losers weepers.* □ *Child: That's my hat. You can't have it. Playmate: I found it. Finders keepers.*

fine and dandy nice; good; well. □ *Well, that's just fine and dandy. Couldn't be better.* □ *I feel fine and dandy, and I'm going to have a good time here.*

Fine feathers make fine birds. *Prov.* If you dress elegantly, people will think you are elegant. (Can be used ironically, to suggest that even though someone dresses well, he or she is not a high-class person.) □ *Bill: I don't see why I should have to wear a necktie for a job interview. Jane: Fine feathers make fine birds.*

a **fine how do you do** an unpleasant situation. (Said with surprise.) □ *This is a fine how do you do! Someone left a big puddle of motor oil in my driveway.* □ *John saw his girlfriend out with another young man. He walked up to her and said, "Well, isn't this a fine how do you do!"*

a **fine kettle of fish** *Fig.* a troublesome situation; a vexing problem. (Usually appears in the expression, *This is a fine kettle of fish!*) □ *This is a fine kettle of fish. My husband is not here to meet me at the train station, and there's no phone here for me to call him.* □ *Alan: Oh, no! I've burned the roast. We don't have anything to serve our guests as a main dish. Jane: But they'll be here any minute! This is a fine kettle of fish.*

fine print Go to small print.

fine someone **for** something to demand a monetary penalty from someone for having done something. □ *The judge fined her for speeding.* □ *The agency fined our company for having the wrong kind of tank to store waste oil.*

a **fine state of affairs** Go to a pretty state of affairs.

Fine weather for ducks. Go to Lovely weather for ducks.

Fine words butter no parsnips. *Prov.* Just because someone promises something does not guarantee that he or she will do it. (Can be used as a rebuke, implying that the person you are addressing is promising something he or she will not do, as in the second example.) □ *Sue: Tom promised he would buy me any house I want if I marry him! Jane: Fine words butter no parsnips.* □ *Fred: Sweetheart, I'm very sorry I've been so short-tempered. I'll never, never be like that anymore. Ellen: Fine words butter no parsnips.*

fine-tune something **1.** *Lit.* to make delicate adjustments in some electronic or mechanical device. □ *It took a while to fine-tune the flute, but it was worth it.* **2.** *Fig.* to make small alterations in a plan or procedure. □ *We need to spend some time fine-tuning the scheme, then we will seek approval.*

finger someone **as** someone *Sl.* to identify someone as a certain person. (As if one were pointing a finger at someone.) □ *Max fingered his partner as the gunman.* □ *The accountant fingered the bookkeeper as the one who fixed the books.*

Fingers were made before forks. *Prov.* It is all right to eat with one's fingers because people had to eat somehow before there were forks. (Used to justify eating something with your fingers.) □ *Mother: Put that chicken wing back on your plate and eat it properly, with a knife and fork. Child: But Mom, fingers were made before forks.* □ *I don't see why it's considered bad manners to eat with your fingers. Fingers were made before forks.*

finish ahead of schedule Go to ahead of schedule.

finish someone or an animal **off**† to kill someone or an animal that is already injured or wounded. □ *They had to finish the wounded bear off with a revolver.* □ *The hunter finished off the bear.*

finish someone or something **off**† *Fig.* to complete some activity being performed on someone or something. □ *Let's finish this one off and go home.* □ *Yes, let's finish off this one.* □ *Nancy is cutting Elaine's hair. When she finishes her off, she will be ready to leave.*

finish someone or something **up**† *Fig.* to finish doing something to someone or something. □ *I will finish this typing up in a few minutes.* □ *She finished up Fred in a short time.*

finish (something) by doing something to bring something to a conclusion by doing something. □ *She finished the lecture by naming her sources.* □ *Sharon finished by reading a poem.*

finish something **off**† *Fig.* to eat or drink up all of something; to eat or drink up the last portion of something. □ *Let's finish the turkey off.* □ *You finish off the turkey. I've had enough.*

finish (something) off† **with** something to bring something to a conclusion with something. □ *She finished the dinner off with fancy cheeses and fruit.* □ *She finished off the dinner with pie.*

finish something **with a lick and a promise** Go to a lick and a promise.

finish with something to complete something; to become done with something. □ *I will finish with fixing this soon, and then you can have it.* □ *When will this be finished with?*

finishing touch(es) a final adjustment of something; some effort or action that completes something. □ *Norm is in his workshop putting the finishing touches on his latest project.*

fink on someone *Sl.* to inform parents, the authorities, etc. on someone. □ *You're not going to fink on me, are you?* □ *Chuck finked on all of us.*

fink out (on someone or something**)** *Sl.* to decide not to cooperate with someone or something (after all). □ *Come on, don't fink out on us now.* □ *Bob finked out on the plan.*

fire away (at someone**)** *Fig.* to ask many questions of someone; to criticize someone severely. □ *When it came time for questions, the reporters began firing away at the*

F

mayor. □ *Members of the opposite party are always firing away at the president.*

Fire is a good servant but a bad master. *Prov.* You must be careful to use fire wisely and under control so that it will not hurt you. □ *Don't play with the candle flames, children. Fire is a good servant but a bad master.* □ *At camp, we learned how to build and extinguish fires safely, since fire is a good servant but a bad master.*

fire over something to shoot over something with a weapon, usually people's heads. □ *We fired over their heads to warn them to stay away.* □ *Wally fired over the target.*

fire someone **up**† *Fig.* to motivate someone; to make someone enthusiastic. □ *See if you can fire John up and get him to rake the leaves.* □ *I have to fire up the electorate if I want them to vote for me.*

fire someone **with anger** and **fire** someone **with enthusiasm; fire** someone **with hope; fire** someone **with expectations** *Fig.* [for someone's words] to fill someone with eagerness or the desire to do something. □ *The speech fired the audience with enthusiasm for change.* □ *We were fired with anger to protest against the government.*

fire someone **with enthusiasm** Go to previous.

fire someone **with expectations** Go to fire someone with anger.

fire (something**) at** someone or something and **fire (**something**) away at** someone or something to shoot at someone or something with a weapon. □ *Someone fired a gun at my car!* □ *The cowboy fired at the rattlesnake.* □ *The hunters fired away at the ducks.* □ *On television, somebody is always firing away at somebody else.*

fire (something**) away at** someone or something Go to previous.

fire (something**) back (at** someone or something**)** to shoot back at someone or something. □ *We fired about ten rounds back at them.* □ *The soldiers in the fort did not fire back at the attackers.*

fire something **back**† **(to** someone or something**)** *Fig.* to send something back to someone or a group immediately. □ *Look this over and fire it back to me immediately.* □ *Fire back all this stuff to the printer as soon as you have proofed it.*

fire something **into** someone or something to shoot something, as a weapon, into someone or something. □ *She fired the gun into a special box that stopped the bullet. She would then examine it under a special microscope.* □ *Max fired two shots into Lefty, but even that did not stop him.*

fire something **off**† **(to** someone**)** *Fig.* to send something to someone immediately, by a very rapid means. □ *Fire a letter off to Fred, ordering him to return home at once.* □ *I fired off a letter to Fred as you asked.* □ *I finished the e-mail and fired it off.*

fire something **up**† **1.** *Lit.* to light something, such as a pipe, cigarette, etc. □ *If you fire that pipe up, I will leave the room.* □ *Please don't fire up that cigar in here!* **2.** *Fig.* to start something such as an engine. □ *Fire this thing up, and let's get going.* □ *Andy fired up the snowblower and started to clear a path.*

*a **fire under** someone *Fig.* something that makes someone start doing something. (*Typically: **build** ~; **light**

~; **start** ~.) □ *The teacher built a fire under the students, and they really started working.* □ *You had better light a fire under your staff. Either that or we will lay off some of them.*

fire up to light a cigarette, cigar, or pipe. □ *One by one, the guests went outside and fired up.* □ *I have to get out of here and fire up.*

fire (up)on someone or something to shoot at someone or something with a weapon; to shoot in the direction of someone or something. (*Upon* is formal and less commonly used than *on*.) □ *The troops fired upon the advancing army.* □ *The cops fired on Max.*

fired up *Fig.* excited; enthusiastic. □ *How can you be so fired up at this time of the morning?* □ *It's impossible to get Martin fired up at all.*

firing on all cylinders and **hitting on all cylinders 1.** *Lit.* [of an internal combustion engine] having all its cylinders working and thus providing the maximum amount of power. □ *The old car is firing on all cylinders despite its age.* □ *This thing's not hitting on all cylinders.* **2.** *Fig.* working at full strength; making every possible effort. □ *The team is firing on all cylinders under the new coach.* □ *The factory is hitting on all cylinders to finish the orders on time.*

*a **firm hand** *Fig.* [someone's] strong sense of management; a high degree of discipline and direction. (*Typically: **exercise** ~; **have** ~; **need** ~; **take** ~; **use** ~.) □ *I had to use a firm hand with Perry when he was a child. He had a problem with discipline.*

firm something **up**† **1.** *Lit.* to make something more stable or firm. □ *We need to firm this table up. It is very wobbly.* □ *You need to use a whisk to firm up the egg whites.* **2.** *Fig.* to make a monetary offer for something more appealing and attractive and therefore more "solid" and likely to be accepted. □ *You will have to firm the offer up with cash today, if you really want the house.* □ *Please firm up this offer if you still want the house.*

firm up 1. *Lit.* to develop better muscle tone; to become less flabby. □ *I need to do some exercises so I can firm up.* □ *You really ought to firm up.* **2.** *Fig.* to become more stable or viable; to recover from or stop a decline. □ *The economy will probably firm up soon.* □ *I hope that cattle prices firm up next spring.*

first and foremost *Cliché* first to be dealt with and most important. □ *First and foremost, I think you should work harder on your biology.* □ *Have this in mind first and foremost: Keep smiling!*

First catch your hare. *Prov.* Do not make plans about what you will do when you have something until you actually have it. □ *Fred: When I buy my house on the beach, you can spend summers with me there. Ellen: First catch your hare.*

First come, first served. *Prov.* The first people to arrive will be able to get the best choices. □ *You can't reserve a seat at the movie theater; it's strictly first come, first served.* □ *We should get to the book sale as soon as they open; it's first come, first served.*

*a **first crack at** something *Fig.* the first opportunity at doing, fixing, or having something. (*Typically: **get** ~;

F

have ~; give someone **~; take ~; want ~.**) □ *I'll take the first crack at it, and if I can't do it, you can try.*

The **first hundred years are the hardest.** *Prov.* The first hundred years of your life are the hardest, and after that, you can expect things to get easier; in other words, your whole life will probably be difficult. (A jocular, ironic way to console someone who is having difficulties.) □ *Don't worry; things are bound to improve for you. The first hundred years are the hardest.*

First impressions are the most lasting. *Prov.* People will remember the way you appear when you first meet them, so it is important to look and act your best when you meet someone for the first time. □ *George spent two hours picking just the right clothes to wear when he met the head of the law firm, since he knew that first impressions are the most lasting.*

the **first leg (of** a journey**)** and the **first leg (of** the journey**)** the first segment of a journey; the first flight of a multiflight trip. □ *The first leg of the journey got me to London.*

first of all as the very first thing; before anything else. □ *First of all, put your name on this piece of paper.* □ *First of all, we'll try to find a place to live.*

first off first; the first thing. (Almost the same as **first of all.**) □ *He ordered soup first off.* □ *First off, we'll find a place to live.*

first see the light of day 1. *Fig.* to be born. □ *My grandfather has taken care of me since I first saw the light of day.* **2.** *Fig.* to come into being. □ *Bob's collection of short stories first saw the light of day in a privately printed edition three years ago.*

The **first step is always the hardest.** *Prov.* Starting a new endeavor is the hardest part of it. □ *Fred: I want to quit smoking, but I can't convince myself to sign up for the "stop smoking" program. Jill: The first step is always the hardest.* □ *If I can just start this project, I know the rest will be easy. The first step is always the hardest.*

first thing (in the morning) before anything else is done in the morning. □ *Please call me first thing in the morning. I can't help you now.* □ *I'll do that first thing.*

First things first. *Prov.* Do things in the proper order; do not skip things that you should do first. □ *Jill: Should we go to the museum first, or should we go shopping? Jane: I'm hungry. Let's eat lunch before we discuss it. First things first.* □ *First things first: read the directions carefully before you try to assemble the bookcase.*

the **firstest with the mostest** the earliest and in the largest numbers; the earliest with more of what's needed. □ *Pete got the prize for being the firstest with the mostest.* □ *I always like to be there early—the firstest with the mostest.*

fish for a compliment *Fig.* to try to get someone to pay oneself a compliment. □ *When she showed me her new dress, I could tell that she was fishing for a compliment.* □ *Tom was certainly fishing for a compliment when he modeled his fancy haircut for his friends.*

fish for something **1.** *Lit.* to try to catch a particular kind of fish. □ *We are fishing for cod today, but we'll take whatever we get.* □ *We will fish for perch from the riverbank.* **2.** *Fig.* to seek some kind of information. □ *You could tell the lawyer was fishing for something from the vague way she asked the questions.* □ *The telephone caller was fishing for too much information, so I hung up.*

fish in troubled waters *Fig.* to involve oneself in a difficult, confused, or dangerous situation, especially with a view to gaining an advantage. □ *Frank is fishing in troubled waters by buying more shares of that company. They are supposed to be in financial difficulties.* □ *The company could make more money by selling armaments abroad, but they would be fishing in troubled waters.*

Fish or cut bait. *Fig.* Do something or get out of the way. □ *Fish or cut bait, Chuck. There's work to be done here.* □ *Decide whether you're going to watch or help. Fish or cut bait.*

fish someone or something **out of** something and **fish** someone or something **out†** to pull someone or something out of something or some place. □ *She is down at the riverbank, fishing driftwood out of the water.* □ *She fished out a lot of wood.*

fish something **up†** Go to next.

fish something **up out of** something and **fish** something **up†** to pull or hoist something out of something, especially after searching or reaching for it. □ *The old shopkeeper fished a huge pickle up out of the barrel.* □ *He fished up a huge pickle.*

fish story and **fish tale** *Fig.* a great big lie. (Like a fisherman who exaggerates the size of the fish that got away.) □ *That's just a fish story. Don't try to fool me.* □ *He's a master at the fish tale. Maybe he should be a politician.*

fish tale Go to previous.

a **fishing expedition** a search for information without knowledge of whether such information exists. (This involves asking questions with no preconceived notion of what the answers might reveal.) □ *The lawyer was on a fishing expedition. There was no real wrong committed to justify a lawsuit.* □ *Your honor, the prosecutor is just on a clumsy fishing expedition. I move for dismissal.* □ *We are going to have to go on a fishing expedition to try to find the facts.*

fit and trim slim and in good physical shape. □ *Jean tried to keep herself fit and trim at all times.* □ *For some people, keeping fit and trim requires time, effort, and self-discipline.*

fit around something to wrap around something. □ *This part fits around the top and keeps the water out.* □ *Will this wrench fit around the bolt?*

*****fit as a fiddle** *Cliché* in very good health. (*Also: **as ~.**) □ *You may feel sick now, but after a few days of rest and plenty of liquids, you'll be fit as a fiddle.* □ *Grandson: Are you sure you'll be able to climb all these stairs? Grandmother: Of course! I feel as fit as a fiddle today.*

fit for a king and **fit for the gods** *Fig.* very nice; luxurious. □ *What a delicious meal. It was fit for a king.* □ *Our room at the hotel was fit for a king.*

fit for the gods Go to previous.

fit in (somehow) (with something**)** to match up or harmonize with something in some fashion. □ *Your itinerary fits in well with my plans.* □ *This fits in very poorly with what I had planned.*

fit in (with someone or something**)** to be comfortable with someone or something; to be in accord or harmony with someone or something. □ *I really feel as if I fit in with that group of people.* □ *It's good that you fit in.* □ *This chair doesn't fit in with the style of furniture in my house.*

fit in((to) something**)** [for something] to be a suitable size to go into something. □ *This peg does not fit into this hole.* □ *That huge sofa simply doesn't fit in through the door.*

fit like a glove *Fig.* to fit very well; to fit snugly. □ *My new shoes fit like a glove.* □ *My new coat is a little tight. It fits like a glove.*

fit someone **for** something **1.** to measure someone for something. □ *I have to fit him for his tuxedo. I'll take his measurements and get to work on it.* □ *She was fitted for her gown in only one afternoon.* **2.** to prepare someone for something; to make someone suitable for some purpose or activity. □ *His education did not fit him for working with children.* □ *Her temperament does not fit her for this kind of work.*

fit someone or something **in((to)** something**)** and **fit** someone or something **in†** to manage to place someone or something into something. □ *I think I can fit you into my schedule.* □ *I have fit in three people already today.* □ *The shelf is tight, but I think I can fit one more book in.*

fit someone or something **out† (for** something**)** to equip someone or something for something; to outfit someone or something for something. □ *We are going to fit our boat out so we can live on it during a long cruise.* □ *We fit out the children in funny costumes for Halloween.*

fit someone or something **out† (with** something**)** to provide or furnish someone or something with something. □ *They fit out the campers with everything they needed.* □ *They fit them out for only $140.*

fit someone or something **up† (with** something**)** and **fit** someone or something **(up†) with** something to provide someone or something with something for a particular purpose. □ *We fit the couple up with fins, masks, and snorkels for skin diving.* □ *The clerk fitted up the couple with diving gear for their vacation.* □ *She fit them with tanks and weights.*

fit someone **to a T** Go to **suit** someone **to a T.**

fit something **on(to)** something and **fit** something **on†** to manage to place something onto something. □ *See if you can fit this lid onto that jar over there.* □ *Sorry, I can't fit on this lid, because it's too big.*

fit something **to** something to make something suit something else. □ *Please try to fit your remarks to the audience.* □ *Can you fit the main course to the needs of all the people who are coming to dinner?*

fit something **together†** to put the parts of something together. □ *First you have to fit the pieces together to see if they are all there.* □ *I think I can fit the parts of the model airplane together.* □ *Do you think you can fit together all the parts of the puzzle?*

fit the bill Go to **fill the bill.**

fit to be tied angry and agitated. (As if needing to be restrained.) □ *Joe was fit to be tied when his wife told him she was leaving.* □ *I was fit to be tied when Mary tried to be friendly, after three years of not speaking to me.*

fit to kill *Rur.* a great deal; to the highest possible degree. □ *We laughed fit to kill when we saw the expression on Jim's face.* □ *I had my car gussied up fit to kill.*

fit together [for things] to conform in shape to one another. □ *All the pieces of the puzzle fit together. They really do.* □ *This nut and bolt just don't fit together.*

fit with something to harmonize with something; to go well with something. □ *Do you think that your behavior fits with the occasion?* □ *This coat doesn't fit with these slacks.*

***fits and starts** with irregular movement; with much stopping and starting. (*Typically: **by** ~; **in** ~; **with** ~.) □ *Somehow, they got the job done in fits and starts.* □ *By fits and starts, the old car finally got us to town.*

five-finger discount *Sl.* shoplifting. □ *Sam used his five-finger discount to get the kind of ring Jane wanted.* □ *I got this necklace by five-finger discount.*

***a fix 1.** *Sl.* a dose of a drug or narcotic. (*Typically: **get** ~; **have** ~; **give** someone ~; **need** ~.) □ *The addict badly needed a fix and was very fidgety.* **2.** an appropriate repair. □ *Do you have a good fix for a leaky faucet?*

fix an animal *Euph.* to remove the uterus or testicles of a pet animal. □ *We took Fluffy to the veterinarian to have her fixed.* □ *The animal shelter fixes all animals that come there, to prevent overpopulation.*

***a fix on** something **1.** the exact location of something distant. (*Typically: **get** ~; **have** ~; **give** someone ~.) □ *I can't get a fix on your location. Where are you?* □ *We are trying to get a fix on your radio transmission.* **2.** *Fig.* an understanding of the direction of a discussion. (*Typically: **get** ~; **have** ~; **give** someone ~.) □ *I can't quite get a fix on what you're trying to say.* □ *I can't get a fix on where you're going with this argument.*

fix someone or something **up†** to rehabilitate someone or something. □ *The doctor said he could fix me up with a few pills.* □ *The doctor fixed up the injured hunter and sent him home.*

fix someone's **wagon** *Fig.* to punish someone; to get even with someone; to plot against someone. □ *If you ever do that again, I'll fix your wagon!* □ *Tommy! You clean up your room this instant, or I'll fix your wagon!* □ *He reported me to the boss, but I fixed his wagon. I knocked his lunch on the floor.*

fix someone **up† (with** someone**)** and **line** someone **up† (with** someone**)** to arrange for someone to have a date or a companion. □ *They lined John up with my cousin, Jane.* □ *John didn't want us to fix him up.* □ *We fixed up Bob with a date.*

fix someone **up† (with** something**)** to supply someone with something. □ *I will fix you up with some alcohol and bandages.* □ *The clerk fixed up the lady with what she needed.* □ *Larry wanted some film and the clerk fixed him up with the best.*

fix something *Sl.* to pay money in secret to have something turn out the way you want. □ *The Boss fixed all the horse races in the county.* □ *After the gun-control bill failed to pass, there were rumors that the gun lobby had fixed the legislature.*

fix something **for (a meal)** to prepare something for a specific meal. □ *I will fix some chili for lunch.* □ *Will you fix something good for dinner tonight?*

F

fix something **on(to)** something to attach something onto something. □ *We fixed a notice onto the broken door so people wouldn't use it.* □ *Please fix a label on this package.*

fix something **over**† to redo something; to **do** something over; to redecorate something. □ *I want to fix this room over next spring.* □ *I really want to fix over this room.*

fix something **with** someone **1.** to get someone's agreement or permission for something. □ *Don't worry, I'll fix it with your boss.* □ *Can you fix things with my brother? He doesn't want me to do this.* **2.** to apologize or make amends to someone for something. □ *She is upset at you, but you can fix it with her, I'm sure.* □ *I will fix it with her. Don't worry.*

fix (up)on someone or something to become preoccupied with someone or something. (*Upon* is formal and less commonly used than *on*.) □ *She seems to have fixed upon becoming a pilot.* □ *James is quite fixed on Janet.*

fixed up provided with a date. □ *Sam got fixed up with Martha.* □ *Okay, Sam is fixed up with a date for Saturday.*

fixin(g) to do something *Rur.* getting ready to do something; getting ready to start something. □ *I'm fixin' to go to the store. Need anything?*

fizz up [for a liquid] to sparkle and bubble with many tiny bubbles; [for a liquid] to effervesce. □ *The cola drink fizzed up and spilled over.* □ *As she poured the root beer, it fizzed up over the glass.*

fizzle out 1. *Lit.* [for a liquid] to lose its effervescence. □ *This seltzer has fizzled out. I need a fresh glass of it.* **2.** *Fig.* [for an item in a fireworks display] to fail to operate properly, often producing only a hiss. □ *That last rocket fizzled out. Set off another one.* □ *A lot of the fireworks fizzled out because it was raining.* **3.** *Fig.* to fade or become ineffectual gradually. □ *The party began to fizzle out about midnight.* □ *The last clerk I hired fizzled out after the first week.*

flack out and **flake out** *Sl.* to collapse with exhaustion; to lie down because of exhaustion. □ *All the hikers flacked out when they reached the campsite.* □ *After a few hours, the hikers all flaked out.*

flag someone or something **down**† to signal or wave, indicating that someone should stop. □ *Please go out and flag a taxi down. I'll be right out.* □ *She went to flag down a taxi.*

flake away (from something**)** [for bits of something] to break away from the whole gradually or from natural causes. □ *Bits of stone flaked away from the surface of the statue year after year.* □ *Bits of the steps flaked away from years of constant use.*

flake down *Sl.* to go to bed and go to sleep. □ *I've got to go home and flake down for a while.* □ *Tom is flaked down for the night.*

flake off ((of) something**)** [for bits of something] to break away from the whole, perhaps under pressure or because of damage. (*Of* is usually retained before pronouns.) □ *Little bits of marble began to flake off the marble steps.* □ *Bits flaked off from the whole.*

flake out Go to flack out.

flake something **off**† Go to next.

flake something **off of** something and **flake** something **off**† to make bits or flakes break off from the whole. □ *The sculptor flaked bits of stone off the block, but you could not yet see what the block was going to become.* □ *She flaked off a little more.*

flame up 1. [for something] to catch fire and burst into flames. □ *The trees flamed up one by one in the forest fire.* □ *Suddenly the car flamed up and exploded.* **2.** [for a fire] to expand and send out larger flames. □ *The raging fire flamed up and jumped to even more trees.* □ *As firemen opened the door and came in, the fire flamed up and filled the room.*

flame with anger and **flame with resentment; flame with lust; flame with vengeance** *Fig.* [for someone's eyes] to "blaze" or seem to communicate a particular quality or excitement, usually a negative feeling. □ *His eyes flamed with resentment when he heard Sally's good news.* □ *Her eyes flamed with hatred.*

flame with lust Go to previous.

flame with resentment Go to flame with anger.

flame with vengeance Go to flame with anger.

flank (up)on someone or something to be at the side of someone or something. (*Upon* is formal and less commonly used than *on*.) □ *The Victorian mansion flanked on the tall, modern apartment building.* □ *It flanked on a broad expanse of fir trees.*

flap around [for a sheet of something] to blow, flop, or slap around, perhaps in the wind. □ *The sails flapped around, making a lot of noise.* □ *The awning flapped around during the night.*

flap one's **gums** and **flap** one's **jaws** *Rur.* to talk aimlessly. □ *They're still out on the porch, flapping their gums.* □ *Well, I can't sit here flapping my jaws all day. Gotta get back to work.*

flap one's **jaws** Go to previous.

flare out to spread out; to widen. (Said especially of one opening of a tube or round-topped vessel.) □ *The end of the pipe flared out to a larger diameter.* □ *The top of the vase flared out, and was decorated with little blobs of colored glass.*

flare something **out**† to spread something out; to make something wider. (Said especially of one end of a tube or round-topped vessel.) □ *Can you flare the end of this pipe out a little?* □ *Flare out the end of this pipe.*

flare up 1. *Lit.* [for something] to ignite and burn. □ *The firewood flared up at last—four matches having been used.* **2.** *Lit.* [for a fire] to burn brightly again and expand rapidly. □ *After burning quietly for a while, the fire suddenly flared up and made the room very bright.* **3.** *Fig.* [for a pain or medical condition] to get worse suddenly. □ *My arthritis flares up during the damp weather.* **4.** *Fig.* [for a dispute] to break out or escalate into a battle. □ *A war flared up in the Middle East.* □ *We can't send the whole army every time a dispute flares up.* **5.** and **flare up at** someone or something *Fig.* to lose one's temper at someone or something. □ *I could tell by the way he flared up at me that he was not happy with what I had done.* □ *I didn't mean to flare up.*

flash a smile (at someone**)** *Fig.* to smile quickly and perhaps briefly at someone. □ *She flashed a smile at me as if she recognized me.*

flash across something **1.** *Lit.* [for something bright] to move quickly across something. □ *The telephone number flashed across the television screen too fast for me to copy it down.* □ *The spotlight flashed across the audience, blinding me as it went by.* **2.** *Fig.* [for an idea or image] to move quickly through one's mind. □ *A solution to the problem suddenly flashed across my mind.* □ *Thoughts of food flashed across my mind, and I began to be very hungry.*

flash back (on someone or something**)** *Fig.* to provide a glimpse of someone or something in the past. (In films, literature, and television.) □ *The next scene flashed back on Fred's murder.* □ *The story then flashed back, giving us information out of the past.*

flash back (to someone or something**)** to return briefly to a view of someone or something in the past. (In films, literature, and television.) □ *The story suddenly flashed back to Tom when he was a child.* □ *The story flashed back to Tom's childhood.*

a **flash in the pan** *Fig.* someone or something that draws a lot of attention for a very brief time. □ *I'm afraid that my success as a painter was just a flash in the pan.* □ *Tom had hoped to be a major film star, but his career was only a flash in the pan.*

flash into one's **mind** *Fig.* [for an idea or image] to enter one's mind for an instant. (See also **flash through** one's **mind**.) □ *A brilliant idea flashed into her mind, and she wrote it down.* □ *When the idea flashed into my mind, I closed my eyes and tried to forget it.*

flash into view *Fig.* to move quickly into view. □ *Suddenly, a doe and her fawn flashed into view.* □ *A bright parrot flashed into view and squawked raucously.*

flash off [for a light] to go off suddenly. (See also **flash on**.) □ *The light flashed off and it was dark for a few minutes.* □ *When the lights flashed off, I was setting my watch.*

flash on [for a light] to turn on suddenly. □ *The light flashed on and woke us up.* □ *When the light flashed on, I had just been getting to sleep.*

flash on someone or something [for a light] to shine on someone or something suddenly or in bursts. □ *The orange neon light flashed on John's face, making him look quite strange.* □ *The light flashed on the window shade, startling the occupants of the room.*

flash on something *Sl.* to remember something suddenly and vividly. □ *Then I flashed on a great idea.* □ *I was trying to flash on her name, but I couldn't bring it to mind.*

flash out [for a light] to shine out of something suddenly or in bursts. □ *The light flashed out, signaling us to stay away from the rocks.* □ *Under the door, we saw a light flashing out. Someone was watching television in that room.*

flash something **around**[†] to display something so everyone can see it. (Usually something one would hold in one's hand.) □ *Don't flash your money around on the streets.* □ *She flashed around the pictures of her grandchildren every chance she got.*

flash something **at** someone or something **1.** *Lit.* to shine a light quickly on someone or something. □ *Larry flashed a light at Frank to verify his identity.* □ *We flashed the light at each doorway, looking for the address we had been sent to.* **2.** *Fig.* to show something, such as a badge, to someone or a group quickly. □ *The cop flashed his badge at the suspect.* □ *The security officer came in and flashed his badge at the board of directors.*

flash something **up**[†] (some place) to shine a light upwards toward something. □ *Flash your light up into the tree.* □ *She flashed up her light at the cat in the tree.* □ *Gloria flashed the light up.*

flash through one's **mind** *Fig.* [for an idea or image] to move quickly through one's mind. (See also **flash into** one's **mind**.) □ *Suddenly, a great idea flashed through my mind.* □ *The same idea flashed through all of our minds at once.*

flash with anger and **flash with recognition; flash with eagerness** [for someone's eyes] to "glimmer" or seem to communicate a particular quality or excitement. □ *Her green eyes flashed with anger.* □ *Ellen's eyes flashed with recognition when she saw me.*

flash with recognition Go to previous.

*****flat as a board** and *****flat as a pancake** *Cliché* very flat. (Also used to describe someone's chest or abdomen, referring to well-developed abdominal muscles or small or nearly absent breasts or pectoral muscles—in either sex. *Also: **as** ~*.) □ *Jane was flat as a board until she was sixteen, when she suddenly blossomed.* □ *Lucy can mash an aluminum can flat as a pancake with one blow from her heel.*

flat as a pancake Go to previous.

flat broke and **flat busted** *Fig.* having no money at all. □ *Sorry, I'm flat broke. Not a cent on me.* □ *You may be flat broke, but you will find a way to pay your electricity bill or you will live in the dark.* □ *Mary was flat busted, and it was two more weeks before she was due to get paid.*

flat busted Go to previous.

flat on one's **ass 1.** *Fig. Inf.* completely exhausted. (Potentially offensive. Use only with discretion.) □ *I'm just flat on my ass. I need some rest.* □ *After the day of the marathon, Pete was flat on his ass for a week.* **2.** *Fig. Inf.* broke; financially destroyed. (Potentially offensive. Use only with discretion. An elaboration of **flat broke**.) □ *Sorry, I can't help you. I'm broke—flat on my ass.* □ *The guy's flat on his ass. Can you help him out with a loan?*

(flat) on one's **back** ill in bed. □ *I've been on my back with the flu for two weeks.* □ *She was flat on her back during her illness.*

flat out 1. clearly and definitely; holding nothing back. □ *I told her flat out that I didn't like her.* □ *They reported flat out that the operation was a failure.* **2.** at top speed. □ *How fast will this car go flat out?* □ *This car will hit about 110 miles per hour flat out.*

flatten someone or something **out**[†] to make someone or something flat. □ *If you fall under the steamroller, it will flatten you out.* □ *Flatten out that dough a little more.* □ *Please flatten it out.*

flatter one's **figure** *Fig.* [for clothing] to make one look thin or to make one's figure look better than it is. □ *The lines of this dress really flatter your figure.* □ *The trousers had a full cut that flattered Maria's figure.*

Flattery will get you nowhere. Flattering me will not increase your chances of success. □ *A: Gee, you can do*

F

217

almost anything, can't you? B: Probably, but flattery will get you nowhere.

flavor food with something to season a food with something. □ *He flavors his gravy with a little sage.* □ *Can you flavor the soup with a little less pepper next time?*

fleck something **with** something to put little specks of something on something. □ *They flecked the little figures with some kind of powder that made them sparkle.* □ *His hair was flecked with gray.*

flee from someone or something to run away from someone or something. □ *The robber fled from the scene of the crime.* □ *The children fled from the wrath of the old man.*

flee to something to escape to something or some place. □ *We fled to our little place on the coast. They never found us.* □ *The little mouse fled to its hole in the wall when the cat came around.*

fleet of foot *Fig.* able to run fast. □ *Frederick, who was notably fleet of foot, outran all the other boys and won the prize.*

a **fleeting glance** *Fig.* a quick glance; a very brief look. □ *I had a fleeting glance at the car as it sped by, but I couldn't read the license place number.*

flesh and blood 1. *Lit.* a living human body, especially with reference to its natural limitations; a human being. □ *This cold weather is more than flesh and blood can stand.* □ *Carrying 300 pounds is beyond mere flesh and blood.* **2.** *Fig.* the quality of being alive. □ *The paintings of this artist are lifeless. They lack flesh and blood.* □ *This play needs flesh and blood, not the mumbling of intensely dull actors.* **3.** and **own flesh and blood** *Fig.* one's own relatives; one's own kin. □ *That's no way to treat one's own flesh and blood.* □ *I want to leave my money to my own flesh and blood.*

flesh out to become more fleshy. □ *She began to flesh out at the age of thirteen.* □ *After his illness, Tom fleshed out and regained his strength.*

flesh something **out†** **(with** something) *Fig.* to make something more detailed, bigger, or fuller. □ *This is basically a good outline. Now you'll have to flesh it out.* □ *The play was good, except that the author needed to flesh out the third act. It was too short.*

flex something **out of shape** to bend something out of its normal shape. □ *Don't flex all the hangers out of shape. We need a few in the closet.* □ *Who flexed the gate out of shape?*

flexed out of shape *Sl.* very angry; **bent out of shape.** □ *The boss was completely flexed out of shape.* □ *I am truly flexed out of shape.*

flick out 1. [for the ends of a flame] to reach out as the flame burns. □ *The flames of the campfire flicked out and threatened the cold fingers that were too close.* □ *The flames flicked out from the burning house and set a nearby tree on fire.* **2.** [for the tongue of a reptile] to come out suddenly. □ *The snake's tongue flicked out regularly.* □ *The lizard's tongue flicked out, grabbed the insect and ate it.*

flick something **off†** **1.** to turn something off, using a toggle switch. □ *Mary flicked the light off and went out of the room.* □ *Please flick the light off as you go out the door.* □ *Please flick off the light.* **2.** Go to next.

flick something **off** someone or something and **flick** something **off†** to brush or knock a speck of something off of someone or something with a quick movement. □ *She flicked a speck of lint off his collar.* □ *She flicked off the lint.*

flick something **on†** to turn something on, using a toggle switch. □ *Mary came into the room and flicked the light on.* □ *Please flick on the light.*

flick something **out†** [for a reptile] to push out its tongue quickly. □ *The lizard flicked its tongue out repeatedly.* □ *The lizard kept flicking out its tongue at regular intervals.*

flick something **with** something to brush or knock something with something quickly or lightly. □ *She flicked her finger at the fly that had lighted nearby.* □ *Tom flicked the vase with his sleeve and knocked it over.*

flick through something to turn quickly through the pages of something. □ *Colleen flicked through the magazine, looking only at the advertisements.* □ *I have only had time to flick through the manuscript, but it looks okay.*

flicker out [for a flame] to dwindle, little by little, until it goes out. □ *The candle flickered out, leaving us in total darkness.* □ *When the last flame flickered out, the room began to get cold.*

flight of fancy an idea or suggestion that is out of touch with reality or possibility. □ *What is the point in indulging in flights of fancy about exotic vacations when you cannot even afford the rent?*

flinch from someone or something to move back suddenly from someone or something; to **shrink (back) (from** someone or something) suddenly. □ *She struck at him and he flinched from her.* □ *At the last minute the center fielder flinched from the ball.*

fling one's **head back†** to tilt one's head back quickly. □ *She flung her head back and laughed heartily.* □ *She flung back her head and laughed.*

fling oneself **at** someone Go to **throw** oneself **at** someone.

fling someone or something **around†** to sling or throw someone or something around. □ *Don't fling your wet clothing around. You are messing up the whole room.* □ *Don't fling around all your clothes.*

fling someone or something **aside†** to toss or sling someone or something aside or out of the way. □ *She flung aside the covers and leaped out of bed.* □ *She flung the covers aside.*

fling someone or something **away†** to throw or sling someone or something away or out of the way. □ *You can't just fling me away! I am your eldest son!* □ *You can't just fling away the things you don't want!*

fling someone or something **back†** **1.** to sling or throw someone or something backwards. □ *I had to fling the child back, away from the fire.* □ *I flung back the door and ran out.* □ *Walt grabbed at the door and flung it back.* **2.** to return someone or something by slinging or throwing. □ *She took the little fish and flung it back into the water.* □ *Did you fling back the ball to Roger?*

fling someone or something **down†** to throw or push someone or something down. □ *He flung the book down in great anger.* □ *He flung down the book and ran from the room.*

fling someone or something **out of** something and **fling** someone or something **out†** to sling or throw someone or something out of something or some place. □ *In anger, she flung the cat out of the window.* □ *She flung out the cat and closed the window.*

fling something **at** someone or something to throw something roughly or carelessly at someone or something. □ *Don't fling that towel at me!* □ *Don't just fling that paper at the wastebasket, hoping it will get there!*

fling something **in(to)** something and **fling** something **in**† to throw something into something. □ *I will fling this thing in the trash. It is junk!* □ *Liz opened the laundry chute and flung in her clothes.* □ *She flung them in.*

fling something **off of** oneself and **fling** something **off**† **1.** to pull or throw something off of oneself hastily. □ *She flung the blanket off herself.* □ *She flung off the blanket.* **2.** to pull or take off an article of clothing. □ *Larry flung his jacket off and went straight to the kitchen.* □ *He flung off his jacket.*

fling something **off (of)** something and **fling** something **off**† to yank or pull something off something. (*Of* is usually retained before pronouns.) □ *He flung the bedspread off the bed and dived in.* □ *He flung off the covers and dived into bed.*

fling something **on** oneself and **fling** something **on**† to put an article of clothing onto oneself hastily. □ *She got up and flung on her robe.* □ *She flung her robe on and went to answer the door.*

fling something **up**† **in** someone's **face** *Fig.* to bring a problem up and confront someone with it. □ *Don't fling it up in my face! It's not my fault!* □ *I don't like anyone to fling up my past in my face.*

fling something **up**† **(in something)** to throw one's arms or hands up in an expression of some emotion, such as despair, horror, disgust, resignation. □ *She flung her hands up in despair.* □ *She flung up her hands and cried out for help.*

fling up *Sl.* to empty one's stomach; to vomit. □ *I was afraid I was going to fling up.* □ *Who flung up on the sidewalk?*

flip around to turn end for end, all the way around, quickly. □ *The alligator flipped around and hissed at us.* □ *The kitten flipped around and pounced on my hand.*

flip one's **lid** Go to next.

flip one's **wig** and **flip** one's **lid** *Sl.* to suddenly become angry, crazy, or enthusiastic. □ *Whenever anyone mentions taxes, Mr. Jones absolutely flips his wig.* □ *Stop whistling. You're going to make me flip my lid.*

flip out *Sl.* to lose control of oneself. □ *After a sleepless night, Wally simply flipped out.* □ *I felt like I was going to flip out from the steady dripping of the faucet.*

flip over to turn over quickly. □ *The fish flipped over and flipped back over again.* □ *The cat flipped over and ran away.*

flip over someone or something *Sl.* to become very excited about someone or something; to lose control because of someone or something. □ *I flipped over her the first time I ever saw her.* □ *The guests really flipped over the Beef Wellington!*

the **flip side 1.** *Lit.* the "other" side of a phonograph record. □ *On the flip side, we have another version of "Love Me Tender" sung by Sandy Softly.* □ *You really should listen to the flip side sometime.* **2.** *Fig.* another aspect of a situation. □ *On the flip side, if we lower the taxes it may stimulate consumer spending.*

flip someone **for** something to flip [a coin] with someone to determine the posession of something or the right to do something. □ *Maybe it's yours; maybe it's mine. I'll flip you for it.*

flip someone **off**† and **flip** someone **out**†; **flip** someone **the bird** *Sl.* to give someone the finger, that is raise the middle finger, a rude sign. (The *digitus impudicus*.) □ *The youth flipped the police officer off. Not a good idea.* □ *He flipped off the cop.* □ *You better not flip a cop out!* □ *The little kid flipped the cop the bird and didn't even know what it meant.*

flip someone **out**† Go to previous.

flip someone **the bird** Go to flip someone off.

flip someone or something **over**† to turn someone or something over quickly. □ *He flipped over the fish and removed the scales from its other side.* □ *Billy flipped Bobby over and started hitting him on the other side.*

flip someone **out**† Go to flip someone off†.

flip through something to go quickly through the leaves of a book, etc., page by page. □ *She flipped through the book, looking at the pictures.* □ *Don't just flip through it. Read it.*

flirt with someone to tease or trifle with someone alluringly. □ *Are you flirting with me?* □ *Everyone knows that married men aren't supposed to flirt with anyone.*

flirt with the idea of doing something *Fig.* to think about doing something; to toy with an idea; to consider something, but not too seriously. (See also **flirt with** someone.) □ *I flirted with the idea of going to Europe for two weeks.* □ *Jane flirted with the idea of quitting her job.*

flit about to move about quickly; to **dart about.** □ *A large number of hummingbirds were flitting about.* □ *Butterflies and moths flitted about among the trees and flowers.*

flit from person to person *Fig.* to move quickly from person to person or thing to thing. (See also **flit from** something **to** something else.) □ *Tom flitted quickly from person to person, handing out snacks and beverages.* □ *The singer flitted from table to table, working the crowd for tips.*

flit from something **to** something else **1.** *Lit.* [for an insect] to fly quickly from one thing to another. □ *The butterfly flitted from flower to flower.* **2.** *Fig.* [for someone] to go quickly from task to task, spending little time on each one. □ *The housekeeper only flits from room to room without ever getting anything completely clean.*

float a loan *Fig.* to get a loan of money; to arrange for a loan of money. □ *I couldn't afford to pay cash for the car, so I floated a loan.* □ *They needed money, so they had to float a loan.*

float around to float from here to there freely. □ *All sorts of paper and trash were floating around on the surface of the pond.* □ *Water hyacinths floated around, making a very tropical scene.*

float into something **1.** *Lit.* to move on water or in air into something. □ *The huge cruise ship floated majestically into the harbor.* □ *The kite floated into a tree and was ruined.*

F

2. *Fig.* to move into something gently, as if floating. □ *She floated into the room, looking like Cinderella before midnight.* □ *Tom and Gloria floated into the theater like a king and queen. They must have rehearsed it.*

float on air *Fig.* [for someone] to feel free and euphoric. □ *I was so happy, I was floating on air.* □ *Mary was floating on air after she won first prize.*

float through something **1.** *Lit.* to move slowly through water or air, gently. □ *The boats floated through the water slowly and gracefully.* □ *As the clouds floated through the sky, they cast blotchy shadows on the ground.* **2.** *Fig.* [for someone] to move aimlessly through something. (As if semiconscious.) □ *She has no ambition. She's just floating through life.* □ *He floated through his work that day. It is probably done all wrong.*

float (up)on something to drift as if on the surface of something; to drift along through the air. (*Upon* is formal and less commonly used than *on.*) □ *The little tufts of dandelion seeds floated upon the breeze.* □ *The fluff floated on the breeze.*

flock after someone or something to follow someone or something in a group. □ *The children flocked after the man playing the flute.* □ *Fans flocked after the movie star as he went from his limo into the hotel.*

flock around someone or something to crowd around someone or something. □ *All the children will flock around the magician to see how the tricks are performed.* □ *The guests flocked around the birthday cake.*

flock in((to) some place) *Fig.* [for people] to move into some place in crowds. □ *People were flocking into the store where everything was on sale.*

flock to someone or something *Fig.* [for people] to come to someone or something in great numbers. □ *Many people flocked to the shopping mall for the postholiday discounts.* □ *The kids flocked to the movie theater on Saturday afternoon.*

flock together to gather together in great numbers. (Typically said of birds and sheep.) □ *A large number of blackbirds flocked together, making a lot of noise.* □ *Do sheep really flock together in a storm?*

flog a dead horse and **beat a dead horse** *Fig.* to insist on talking about something that no one is interested in, or that has already been thoroughly discussed. □ *The history teacher lectured us every day about the importance of studying history, until we begged him to stop flogging a dead horse.* □ *Jill: I think I'll write the company president another letter asking him to prohibit smoking. Jane: There's no use beating a dead horse, Jill; he's already decided to let people smoke.*

flog someone **to death** *Lit.* to beat someone to death with a whip. □ *In the movie, the captain ordered the first mate to flog the sailor to death.*

flog something **to death** *Fig.* to dwell on something so much that it no longer has any interest. □ *Stop talking about this! You've flogged it to death.* □ *Walter almost flogged the whole matter to death before we stopped him.*

flood in(to something**) 1.** *Lit.* [for a fluid] to flow quickly into something in great volume. □ *The water flooded in and soaked the carpets.* **2.** *Fig.* [for large amounts or numbers of people or things] to pour or rush into something.

□ *The people flooded into the hall.* □ *We opened the door, and the dogs and cats flooded in.*

flood out (of something**) 1.** *Lit.* [for water or something that flows] to rush out of something. □ *The water flooded out of the break in the dam.* **2.** *Fig.* [for people] to rush out of something or some place. □ *The people flooded out of the theater, totally disgusted with the performance.*

flood someone or something **out of** something and **flood** someone or something **out**† [for too much water] to force someone or something to leave something or some place. □ *The high waters flooded them out of their home.* □ *The high waters flooded out a lot of people.*

flood someone or something **with** something to cover or inundate someone or something with something. □ *We flooded them with praise and carried them on our shoulders.* □ *The rains flooded the fields with standing water.*

***the floor** *Fig.* the exclusive right to address the audience. (*Typically: **get** ~; **have** ~; **hold** ~; **grant** someone ~.) □ *When I get the floor, I'll make a short speech.* □ *The last time you had the floor, you talked for an hour.*

floor it *Fig.* to press down hard and fast on the accelerator of a vehicle. □ *She floored it and sped off over the hill.*

floor someone to surprise and astound someone. □ *His brashness simply floored me!*

flop around [for something] to turn around awkwardly; [for a fish out of water] to squirm and flap. □ *The hose flopped around, throwing water first this way and then that, knocking down plants as it flopped.* □ *A number of fish flopped around in the bottom of the boat.*

flop as something to be a failure in a particular aspect of something in one's life or career. □ *He flopped as an actor.* □ *I don't want to flop as a public speaker.*

flop down to sit down heavily or awkwardly. □ *Be graceful. Don't just flop down!* □ *When I reached the chair, all I could do was flop down.*

flop into something [for someone] to fall or drop into something, such as bed, a chair, a bathtub, etc. □ *Maggie flopped into the chair and slipped off her shoes.* □ *Tom flopped into bed and fell fast asleep.*

flop someone or something **over**† to turn someone or something over, awkwardly or carelessly. □ *They flopped the unconscious man over, searching for his identification.* □ *They flopped over the injured man.*

flop something **down on(to)** something and **flop** something **down**† to drop or slap something down on something. □ *She flopped the liver down on the cutting board.* □ *She flopped down the raw meat.*

flora and fauna plants and animals. □ *The magazine story described the flora and fauna of Panama.* □ *We went for a hike in the Finnish wilderness hoping to learn all about the local flora and fauna.*

floral tribute *Euph.* flowers sent to a funeral. □ *The church was filled with floral tributes.* □ *Did you wish to make any arrangements for floral tributes at your grandmother's funeral?*

flotsam and jetsam 1. *Lit.* the floating wreckage of a ship and its cargo, or floating cargo deliberately cast overboard to stabilize a ship in a rough sea. □ *All sorts of flotsam and jetsam washed up on the beach.* **2.** *Fig.* worthless matter; worthless encumbrances. □ *His mind is burdened with the flotsam and jetsam of many years of poor instruction and lax study habits.* □ *Your report would be better if you could get rid of a lot of the flotsam and jetsam and clean up the grammar a bit.*

flounce in(to some place**)** to move into a place with exaggerated or jerky motions. □ *A couple of teenagers flounced into the store and started examining the most expensive merchandise.* □ *They flounced in and caught the eye of the security guard.*

flounce out (of some place**)** to bounce or bound out of some place. □ *She turned up her nose and flounced out of the shop.* □ *She flounced out in anger.*

flounder around to struggle or wallow around. □ *The whole company is just floundering around and getting nowhere.* □ *The horse floundered around, trying to get across the soggy pasture.*

flounder through something **1.** *Lit.* to struggle through something, such as a mire, swamp, etc. □ *The Jeep floundered through the swamp without getting stuck.* □ *The horse floundered through the muddy field.* **2.** *Fig.* to struggle awkwardly through a difficult situation. □ *We floundered through the performance. I don't know how we did it, but we did it.* □ *We just floundered through our presentation, hoping for a lot of questions.*

flow across something to stream or glide across something. □ *A mass of cold air flowed across the city and froze us all.* □ *The floodwaters flowed across the fields and ruined the spring planting.*

flow along to move along evenly, as a liquid flows. □ *At the base of the dam, the river began to flow along at a slower pace.* □ *The project flowed along quite nicely.*

flow away to course or move away. □ *The floodwaters flowed away as fast as they had come.* □ *All the spilled water flowed away.*

flow from something to run out from something. □ *The blood flowed from the wound on his hand and stained his shirt.* □ *The oil flowed from the cracked engine and made a mess on the floor.*

flow (from something**) (to** something**)** to course from one thing to another. □ *This water flows all the way from Minnesota to the Gulf of Mexico.* □ *Rain flows to the river from this very drain.*

flow in(to something**)** to course into something; to pour into something. □ *The words flowed into my head, and I felt like I could write again.* □ *The water flowed in when I opened the door on the flood.*

flow out (of something**) 1.** *Lit.* to course out of something. □ *The apple juice flowed out of the press as we turned the crank.* □ *It stopped flowing out when we had crushed the apples totally.* **2.** *Fig.* [for people] to issue forth from something. □ *The people flowed out of the stadium exits.* □ *At the end of the game, the people flowed out in a steady stream.*

flow over someone or something **1.** *Lit.* [for a liquid or something that flows] to move over someone or something. □ *The water flowed over the land, covering everything.* □ *She slipped and fell into the icy creek and the water flowed over her, freezing her almost to death.* **2.** *Fig.* [for some kind of feeling] to envelop someone. □ *A sense of peace flowed over her.* □ *Patriotic feelings flowed over the crowd as they listened to the national anthem.*

flow with something to have some liquid coursing on the surface or within someone or something. □ *The sewers were flowing with the floodwaters.* □ *Her veins must flow with ice water. She is so cold.*

flub something **up†** to mess something up; to ruin something. □ *I saw you play in the tournament last Friday. You really flubbed it up, if you don't mind me saying so.* □ *You really flubbed up the tournament.*

flub the dub *Inf.* to fail to do the right thing. □ *Martin is flubbing the dub with the fund-raising campaign.* □ *Please don't flub the dub this time.*

flub up to make an error. □ *I flubbed up again!*

fluctuate between someone **and** someone else to waver between choosing one person and another. □ *I am fluctuating between Sam and Tony as my choice.* □ *The manager fluctuated between Mary and Sarah as the new assistant.*

fluctuate between something **and** something else to move between one thing and another; to change from one thing to another. □ *Things seemed to fluctuate between the very good and the very bad.* □ *The temperature in here fluctuates between too hot and too cold.*

fluctuate with something to vary in accord with something. □ *The tides fluctuate with the phase of the moon.* □ *Frank's blood pressure fluctuates with his mood.*

fluff one's **lines** and **blow** one's **lines; muff** one's **lines** to speak one's speech badly or forget one's lines when one is in a play. □ *The actress fluffed her lines badly in the last act.* □ *I was in a play once, and I muffed my lines over and over.* □ *It's okay to blow your lines in rehearsal.*

fluff something **out†** [for a bird] to move its feathers outward. □ *The parrot said good night, fluffed its feathers out, and went to sleep.* □ *The bird fluffed out its feathers.*

fluff something **up†** to make something soft appear fuller or higher. □ *Fluff your pillow up before you go to bed.* □ *She fluffed up her pillow before retiring.*

flunk out (of something**)** to leave school or a course because of failure. □ *Fred flunked out of school and never tried to go back.* □ *That's it. All F's. I've flunked out.*

flunk someone **out†** to give one a grade that forces one to leave school or a course. □ *The math professor flunked me out. He expects too much.* □ *She flunked out half the class!*

flush someone or something **out of** some place and **flush** someone or something **out†** to cause someone or something to leave a hiding place. (Originally from hunting.) □ *The police flushed the gunman out from his hiding place.* □ *They flushed out the crooks.*

flush something **away†** to wash something unwanted away. □ *Flush all this mess away!* □ *Fred flushed away all the leaves on the sidewalk.*

flush something **out†** to clean something out with a flow of liquid. □ *Flush the fuel line out to clean it.* □ *Please flush out the fuel line and clean it.*

flush with something **1.** *Lit.* even with something; sharing a surface with something. □ *The edge of the sink is flush with the counter.* □ *The wood flooring is flush with the carpet so people won't trip.* **2.** *Fig.* [of a face] red with *anger, embarrassment, rage, etc.* □ *He faced the woman he had dreamed about all his life. His face flushed with recognition and his heart pounded.* □ *Ellen's face flushed with embarrassment.*

flutter about and **flutter around 1.** *Lit.* to fly about with quick, flapping motions of the wings. □ *The moths fluttered about aimlessly.* □ *A few birds fluttered around.* **2.** *Fig.* [for someone] to move about quickly and busily. □ *Aunt Margaret fluttered about, picking up after everyone.* □ *Stop fluttering around and sit down!*

flutter about something and **flutter around** something **1.** *Lit.* to fly around something or some place. □ *The moths were fluttering about the lightbulb.* □ *The butterflies fluttered around the bright flowers.* **2.** *Fig.* to keep moving busily within a particular place. □ *The maid fluttered about the house, dusting and arranging.* □ *She fluttered around the house from room to room.*

flutter down [for flying or falling things] to flap or float downward. □ *The butterflies fluttered down onto the flowers.* □ *The leaves fluttered down from the trees when the breeze blew.*

flutter over someone or something to fly or flap above someone or something. (Also said of a person being fussy about someone or something.) □ *The little moths fluttered over us while we were in the garden.* □ *The birds flutter over the fountain, eager for a bath.*

fly across something [for a bird or a plane] to move in the air across something. □ *A bird flew across the open area in the forest.* □ *A large jet flew across the clear blue sky.*

fly apart to break apart, throwing pieces around. □ *Don't run the engine too fast or it will fly apart!* □ *Mary's bicycle wheel flew apart during the race.*

fly around to soar or float aloft randomly. □ *There were insects flying around everywhere.* □ *Planes flew around all day and all night, making it hard to sleep.*

fly around someone or something to soar or float in the air near someone or something. □ *We saw seven helicopters flying around the stadium.* □ *A bunch of mosquitoes flew around me.*

fly at someone or something to attack someone or something suddenly and violently. □ *The angry bird flew at its attacker.* □ *She flew at him, threatening to scratch his eyes out.*

fly away to take flight and depart. □ *The owl hooted one last hoot and flew away.* □ *All the birds flew away when the cat came around.*

fly by 1. *Lit.* to soar past, flying. □ *Three jet fighters flew by.* □ *A huge hawk flew by, frightening all the smaller birds.* **2.** *Fig.* [for time] to go quickly. □ *The hours just flew by, because we were having fun.* □ *Time flew by so fast that it was dark before we knew it.*

fly by the seat of one's **pants** Go to **by the seat of** one's **pants.**

fly from someone or something **(to** something**)** to escape from something or some place to a place of safety. □ *The family had to fly from their pursuers to a place of safety outside the country.* □ *They flew from the people chasing them.*

fly from something **(to** something**)** to go from something or some place to some other place by air. □ *We had to fly from Miami to Raleigh to get a flight to Chicago.* □ *We were able to fly from Miami at the last minute.*

fly in Go to **fly into** something.

fly in the face of someone or something and **fly in the teeth of** someone or something *Fig.* to challenge someone or something; to go against someone or something. □ *This idea flies in the face of everything we know about matter and energy.* □ *You had better not fly in the face of the committee.*

a **fly in the ointment** *Fig.* a small, unpleasant matter that spoils something; a drawback. □ *We enjoyed the play, but the fly in the ointment was not being able to find my hat afterward.* □ *It sounds like a good idea, but there must be a fly in the ointment somewhere.*

fly in the teeth of someone or something Go to **fly in the face of** someone or something.

fly into a rage *Fig.* to become enraged suddenly. □ *When he heard the report, he flew into a rage.* □ *We were afraid that she would fly into a rage.*

fly into something **1.** and **fly in** to go to something or some place by air; to arrive by air. □ *When are you going to fly into the airport?* □ *We will fly into Detroit tomorrow.* **2.** to crash into something while flying. □ *Birds sometimes fly into tall buildings.* **3.** to pass into something, such as fog, clouds, wind, etc., while flying. □ *We flew into some clouds, but the flight was not rough.* □ *The plane flew into some fog as it was landing.*

fly into the face of danger *Fig.* to take great risks; to threaten or challenge danger, as if danger were a person. (This may refer to flying, as in an airplane, but not necessarily.) □ *John plans to go bungee jumping this weekend. He really likes flying into the face of danger.* □ *Willard was not exactly the type to fly into the face of danger, but tonight was an exception, and he ordered extra-hot enchiladas.*

fly off 1. *Lit.* to take to flight quickly. □ *The stork flew off before we got a good look at it.* □ *The little birds flew off and things were quiet again.* **2.** *Fig.* to leave in a hurry. □ *Well, it's late. I must fly off.* □ *She flew off a while ago.*

fly off the handle *Fig.* to lose one's temper. □ *Every time anyone mentions taxes, Mrs. Brown flies off the handle.* □ *If she keeps flying off the handle like that, she'll have a heart attack.*

fly off with someone or something **1.** *Lit.* to depart with someone or something by air. □ *The eagle flew off with the kitten.* □ *The pilot flew off with the eight passengers.* **2.** *Fig.* to leave in a hurry with someone or something. □ *She flew off with her packages before she got her change.* □ *Dave flew off with his brother because they had to meet a train.*

fly out (of something**) 1.** *Lit.* to leave a place by air. □ *We are going to fly out of Manaus on a charter.* □ *We flew out on time.* **2.** *Fig.* to leave a place quickly. □ *We flew out of there as fast as we could.* □ *She opened the door and flew out.*

fly over someone or something to soar or glide over someone or something. □ *We saw an eagle fly over us.* □ *The plane flew over the desert.*

fly past (someone or something**)** to soar or glide past someone or something. □ *The stone flew past Mike's left ear, and he ducked.* □ *The plane flew past the cloud bank.*

fly someone or something **in(to** some place) **(from** some place) and **fly** someone or something **in**† to transport someone or something to some place from some place. □ *We flew the documents into Adamsville from Springfield.* □ *We flew in the documents to Chicago from Springfield.*

fly someone or something **out of** something and **fly** someone or something **out**† to transport someone or something out of something by air. □ *They flew the tourists out of the troubled area on chartered flights.* □ *The tourists flew out to any destination that was available.*

fly the coop *Fig.* to escape; to get out or get away. (Alludes to a chicken escaping from a chicken coop.) □ *I couldn't stand the party, so I flew the coop.* □ *The prisoner flew the coop at the first opportunity.*

fly to someone or something to go to someone or something quickly and eagerly; to flee to someone or something. □ *She flew to his arms as he got off the boat.* □ *Harry flew to Gloria and hugged her tight.*

fly to something to go to something or some place by air. □ *After Miami, we fly to Chicago.* □ *Let's fly to Paris for lunch.*

fly up to something to go by air to a place at a higher elevation or to a place in the north. □ *We will fly up to St. Paul for the holidays.* □ *I want to fly up to Alberta, Canada, for the summer.*

fly-by-night *Fig.* irresponsible; untrustworthy. (Alludes to a person who sneaks away secretly in the night.) □ *The carpenter we hired was a fly-by-night worker who did a very bad job.* □ *You shouldn't deal with a fly-by-night merchant.*

flying high 1. *Fig.* very successful in one's ambitions; in an important or powerful position. (Often with the implication that this is not the usual situation or will change.) □ *The government is flying high just now, but wait until the budget is announced.* □ *He's flying high these days, but he comes from a very poor family.* **2.** *Fig.* in a state of euphoria. (From good news, success, or drugs.) □ *Wow! Todd is really flying high. Did he discover a gold mine?* □ *Sally is flying high. What's she on?*

foam at the mouth 1. *Lit.* to create froth or foam around the mouth, as with some diseases. □ *The poor dog was foaming at the mouth and looked quite dangerous.* □ *What does it mean when a cow foams at the mouth?* **2.** *Fig.* to be extraordinarily angry. □ *She was almost foaming at the mouth when she heard about the cost of the car repairs.* □ *Walter was foaming at the mouth with rage.*

foam up [for something, such as soap or milk] to make foam or lather. □ *Milk will foam up when it is boiled.* □ *The boiling soup foamed up and slopped over the pot.*

fob someone or something **off**† **(on(to)** someone) to get rid of someone or something by transferring someone or something to someone. □ *Don't try to fob your girlfriend off on me!* □ *He also fobbed off a bad car on Jane.* □ *Some car dealers are always trying to fob something off.*

focus on someone or something **1.** *Lit.* to aim and adjust a lens (including the lens in the eye) onto someone or something. □ *I focused on the flower and pressed the shutter release.* □ *I focused on Fred and snapped just as he moved.* **2.** *Fig.* to dwell on the subject of someone or something. □ *Let's focus on the question of the electric bill, if you don't mind.* □ *Let us focus on Fred and discuss his progress.*

focus something **on** someone or something **1.** *Lit.* to aim a lens at someone or something and adjust the lens for clarity. □ *I focused the binoculars on the bird and stood there in awe at its beauty.* □ *He focused the camera on Jane and snapped the shutter.* **2.** *Fig.* to direct attention to someone or something. □ *Could we please focus the discussion on the matter at hand for a few moments?* □ *Let's focus our attention on Tom and discuss his achievements so far.*

fog over [for something made of glass] to become covered over with water vapor. □ *The windshield fogged over because I forgot to turn on the defroster.* □ *The mirror fogged over, and I couldn't see to shave.*

fog something **up**† to make something made of glass become covered with a film of water vapor. □ *The moisture fogged the windshield up, and we had to stop to clean it off.* □ *The moisture fogged up the glass.*

fog up [for something made of glass] to become partially or completely obscured by a film of water vapor. □ *The glass fogged up, and we couldn't see out.*

the foggiest (idea) *Fig.* (even) a hazy idea. (Usually in the negative.) □ *I'm sorry I don't know. I haven't the foggiest.* □ *I don't have the foggiest idea of how to do this.*

foist someone or something **off**† **(on** someone or something) to cast someone or something unwanted off on someone or a group. □ *Please don't try to foist cheap merchandise off on me.* □ *Don't foist off your brother on me!* □ *You can't foist that stuff off! It's worthless! People won't buy it!*

fold back [for a sheet of something] to bend back. □ *The cloth folded back, revealing the faded upholstery below.* □ *The top page folded back, revealing a neatly typed manuscript.*

fold one's **hands** to bring one's hands together, palm to palm, with the fingers interlocking; to grasp one's hands together, palm to palm, perpendicular to one another. □ *Please fold your hands and put them on the table while the teacher reads you a story.* □ *Please fold your hands and be quiet.*

fold something **away**† to fold something up and put it away. □ *Please fold the maps away.* □ *Please fold away the maps neatly.*

fold something **back**† to bend a sheet or flap of something back. □ *She very carefully folded the page back to mark her place in the book.* □ *She folded back the page to mark her place in the book.* □ *The surgeon folded the flap of skin back, revealing the torn ligament.*

fold something **into** something **1.** and **fold** something **in**† to blend something, such as eggs, into batter. (See also cut something **into** something.) □ *Carefully, the chef folded the eggs into the other ingredients.* □ *The chef folded in the eggs.* **2.** to make an object by folding something, such as paper or cloth. □ *He folded the paper into a little bird.* □ *Wally can fold a sheet of paper into an airplane that flies.*

fold something **over**† to double something over on itself; to make a fold in something. □ *I folded the paper over twice to make something I could fan myself with.* □ *Fold over each sheet, and then place it on the stack.*

fold something **up**† **1.** *Lit.* to double something over into its original folded position. □ *Please fold the paper up when you are finished.* □ *Please fold up the paper.* **2.** *Fig.* to put an end to something; to close a money-losing enterprise. □ *Mr. Jones was going broke, so he folded his business up.* □ *The producer decided to fold up the play early. It was losing money.*

fold, spindle, or mutilate to harm or disfigure. Referring to a once-standard line printed on machine-readable documents, such as computer punch cards. (Such a document, if folded, placed on a bill spike, or otherwise punctured, would no longer be machine-readable.) □ *At the bottom of the bill, it said "do not fold, spindle, or mutilate," and Jane, in her anger, did all three.* □ *Look here, chum, if you don't want to get folded, spindled, or mutilated, you had better do what you are told!*

fold up 1. *Lit.* [for something] to close by folding. □ *The table just folded up with no warning, trapping my leg.* **2.** *Fig.* [for someone] to faint. □ *She folded up when she heard the news.* □ *I was so weak that I was afraid I was going to fold up.* **3.** *Fig.* [for a business] to cease operating. □ *Our shop finally folded up because of the recession.* □ *Tom's little candy shop folded up.*

folding money bills of various dollar denominations. □ *I don't want a check. Give me folding money!* □ *You got any folding money with you?*

follow after the style of someone or something Go to after the style of someone or something.

follow in someone's **tracks** and **follow in** someone's **footsteps** to follow someone's example; to assume someone else's role or occupation. □ *The vice president was following in the president's footsteps when he called for budget cuts.* □ *She followed in her father's footsteps and went into medicine.*

follow on (after someone or something**) 1.** *Lit.* to depart and arrive after someone or something. □ *I can't leave now. I will have to follow on after the others.* □ *I will follow on later.* **2.** *Fig.* to die at a date later than someone or a group. □ *She followed on after her husband a few years later.* □ *He died in June and she followed on in August.*

follow one's **heart** *Fig.* to act according to one's feelings; to obey one's sympathetic or compassionate inclinations. □ *I couldn't decide what to do, so I just followed my heart.* □ *I trust that you will follow your heart in this matter.*

follow one's **nose 1.** *Lit.* to go straight ahead, the direction that one's nose is pointing. □ *The town that you want is straight ahead on this highway. Just follow your nose.* □ *The chief's office is right around the corner. Turn left and follow your nose.* **2.** *Fig.* to follow an odor to its source. □ *The kitchen is at the back of the building. Just follow your nose.* □ *There was a bad smell in the basement—probably a dead mouse. I followed my nose until I found it.*

follow orders to do as one has been instructed. □ *You have to learn to follow orders if you want to be a Marine.* □ *I didn't do anything wrong. I was only following orders.*

follow someone or something **about** and **follow** someone or something **around** to go the same route as someone or something all the time; to trail someone or something. □ *Why are you always following me about?* □ *Stop following me around.*

follow someone or something **out** to go out right after someone or something. □ *I followed her out and asked her if I could take her home.* □ *The dog followed Billy out and went to school with him.*

follow someone's **lead** to do as someone else does; to accept someone's guidance; to follow someone's direction. □ *Just follow my lead and you will not get lost.* □ *John followed his father's lead and became a lawyer.*

follow someone **up**[†] and **follow up (on** someone**)** to check on the work that someone has done. □ *I have to follow Sally up and make sure she did everything right.* □ *I follow up Sally, checking on her work.* □ *I'll follow up on her.*

follow something **through** Go to follow through (with something).

follow something **up**[†] and **follow up (on** something**) 1.** to check something out; to find out more about something. □ *Would you please follow this lead up? It might be important.* □ *Please follow up this lead.* □ *I'll follow up on it.* □ *Yes, please follow up.* **2.** to make sure that something was done the way it was intended. □ *Please follow this up. I want it done right.* □ *Please follow up this business.* □ *I'll follow up on it.*

follow suit to follow in the same pattern; to follow someone else's example. (From card games.) □ *Mary went to work for a bank, and Jane followed suit. Now they are both head cashiers.* □ *The Smiths went out to dinner, but the Browns didn't follow suit. They stayed home.*

follow the crowd to do what everyone else is doing. □ *I am an independent thinker. I could never just follow the crowd.* □ *When in doubt, I follow the crowd. At least I don't stand out like a fool.*

follow through (on something**)** and **carry through (on** something**)** to complete a task; to see a task through to its completion. □ *You must follow through on the things that you start.* □ *Don't start the job if you can't follow through.* □ *Ask Sally to carry through on her project.*

follow through (with something**)** and **follow** something **through** to complete an activity, doing what was promised. □ *I wish you would follow through with the project we talked about.* □ *You never follow through!*

follow up (on someone**)** Go to follow someone up[†].

follow up (on someone or something**)** to find out more about someone or something. □ *Please follow up on Mr. Brown and his activities.* □ *Bill, Mr. Smith has a complaint. Would you please follow up on it?*

follow up (on something**)** Go to follow something up[†].

foment trouble to cause trouble. □ *Leave it to Bob to foment trouble.* □ *I wasn't fomenting trouble, just expressing my opinion!*

***fond of** someone or something liking someone or something. (*Typically: **be ~; become ~**.) □ *I'm fond of chocolate.* □ *Mary isn't fond of me, but I'm fond of her.*

food for thought *Fig.* something for someone to think about; issues to be considered. □ *Your essay has provided me with some interesting food for thought.* □ *My adviser gave me some food for thought about job opportunities.*

A **fool and his money are soon parted.** *Prov.* Foolish people spend money, without thinking. (Perceived as a rebuke if you say it about the person you are addressing.) □ *Go ahead and buy a diamond collar for your dog if you really want to. A fool and his money are soon parted.* □ *Bill sends a check to every organization that asks him for money. A fool and his money are soon parted.*

fool around to waste time doing something unnecessary or doing something amateurishly. □ *Stop fooling around and clean your room as I told you.* □ *I wish you didn't spend so much time fooling around.*

fool (around) with someone or something **1.** to waste time in the company of someone or a group. □ *Stop fooling around with those guys. They're up to no good most of the time.* □ *Better not fool around with part-time work. Go get a good job if you can.* **2.** to have dealings with or tamper with someone or something. □ *You had better not fool around with my little sister.* □ *Don't fool with that thing!* **3.** to challenge or threaten someone or something. □ *You had better not fool around with me, if you know what's good for you.* □ *Don't fool with the police force!*

Fool me once, shame on you; fool me twice, shame on me. *Prov.* After being tricked once, one should be wary, so that the person cannot trick you again. □ *Fred: Would you like a can of peanuts? Jane: The last can of peanuts you gave me had a toy snake in it. Fred: This one really is peanuts. Jane: Fool me once, shame on you; fool me twice, shame on me.*

a **fool's paradise** *Fig.* a state of being happy for foolish or unfounded reasons. □ *I'm afraid that Sue's marital happiness is a fool's paradise; there are rumors that her husband is unfaithful.* □ *Fred is confident that he'll get a big raise this year, but I think he's living in a fool's paradise.*

fool someone **into** something to deceive someone or oneself into doing something. □ *You'll never fool me into believing you.* □ *We fooled the boss into giving us all the day off.*

Fools rush in where angels fear to tread. *Prov.* Foolish people usually do not understand when a situation is dangerous, so they are not afraid to do things that would frighten more sensible people. □ *Alan: Bob is too scared to go in and confront the boss, so I'm going to. Jane: Fools rush in where angels fear to tread.*

*a **foot in both camps** *Fig.* an interest in or to support each of two opposing groups of people. (*Typically: **get** ~; **have** ~; **give** someone ~.) □ *The shop steward had been promised a promotion and so had a foot in both camps during the strike—workers and management.* □ *Mr. Smith has a foot in both camps in the parent-teacher dispute. He teaches math, but he has a son at the school.*

foot the bill (for something**)** *Fig.* to pay for something; to pay for a bill. □ *My boss took me out for lunch and the company footed the bill.* □ *You paid for dinner last time. Let me foot the bill for lunch today.*

*a **foothold (**somewhere**)** *Fig.* an initial position of support; a starting point. (*Typically: **get** ~; **have** ~; **help** someone **get** ~.) □ *It's difficult to get a foothold in the education market when schools are laying off teachers.* □ *Max's father helped him get a foothold in the textile industry.*

foot-in-mouth disease the tendency to say the wrong thing at the wrong time. □ *I suffer a lot from foot-in-mouth disease.* □ *Well, Ralph has foot-in-mouth disease again.*

footloose and fancy-free *Fig.* without long-term responsibilities or commitments. □ *All the rest of them have wives, but John is footloose and fancy-free.* □ *Mary never stays long in any job. She likes being footloose and fancy-free.*

for a drive Go to for a spin.

for a lark and **on a lark** for a joke; as something done for fun. □ *For a lark, I wore a clown's wig to school.* □ *On a lark, I skipped school and drove to the beach.*

for a living [of work] done to earn enough money to live. □ *John paints houses for a living.* □ *What do you do for a living?*

for a ride Go to for a spin.

*for a song** *Fig.* cheaply. (As if the singing of a song were payment. *Typically: **buy** something ~; **get** something ~; **pick up** someone ~.) □ *No one else wanted it, so I picked it up for a song.* □ *I could buy this house for a song, because it's so ugly.*

*for a spin** and *for a ride; *for a drive** to take a ride in a vehicle or on a bicycle. (*Typically: **go** ~; **go out** ~; **take** something ~.) □ *Let's get out our bikes and go for a spin.*

for a split second Go to a split second.

for all I care I don't care if (something happens). □ *For all I care, the whole city council can go to the devil.* □ *They can all starve for all I care.*

for all I know according to the information I have; I think; probably. (Usually implies uncertainty.) □ *For all I know, the mayor has resigned already.* □ *She may have gone to town for all I know.*

for all intents and purposes *Cliché* seeming as if; looking as if. □ *Tom stood there, looking, for all intents and purposes, as if he could strangle Sally, but, being the gentleman that he is, he just glowered.* □ *Mary: Is the car washed now? John: For all intents and purposes, yes, but I didn't dry it yet.*

for all it's worth and **for what(ever) it's worth** if it has any value. (Usually implies lack of confidence.) □ *My idea—for all it's worth—is to offer them only $300.* □ *Here is my thinking, for whatever it's worth.* □ *Ask her to give us her opinion, for what it's worth.*

for (all) one's **trouble** in spite of one's efforts; in return for one's efforts. (Implies that the "trouble" was not worth taking, or was harmful.) □ *He got a punch in the jaw for all his trouble.* □ *For her trouble, she got only honorable mention.*

for all practical purposes as might be reasonably expected; essentially. □ *For all practical purposes, this is simply a matter of right and wrong.* □ *This should be considered final, for all practical purposes.*

for all someone's **problems** in spite of a person's problems (as specified). □ *For all her complaining, she still seems to be a happy person.* □ *For all my aches and pains, I'm still rather healthy.*

for all the world 1. exactly; precisely. (Especially with look.) □ *She sat there looking for all the world as if she was going to cry.* □ *It started out seeming for all the world like a beautiful day. Then a storm came up.* **2.** everything. (Usually in the negative.) □ *I wouldn't give up my baby for all the world.* □ *They wouldn't sell their property for all the world.*

for better or for worse under any conditions; no matter what happens. □ *I married you for better or for worse.* □ *For better or for worse, I'm going to quit my job.*

for chicken feed and **for peanuts** *Fig.* for nearly nothing; for very little money. (Also used without *for*.) □ *Bob doesn't get paid much. He works for chicken feed.* □ *You can buy an old car for chicken feed.* □ *I won't do that kind of work for peanuts!*

For crying in a bucket! Go to next.

For crying out loud! and **For crying in a bucket!** *Inf.* an exclamation of shock, anger, or surprise. □ *Fred: For crying out loud! Answer the telephone! Bob: But it's always for you!* □ *John: Good grief! What am I going to do? This is the end! Sue: For crying in a bucket! What's wrong?*

for days on end *Fig.* for many days. □ *We kept on traveling for days on end.* □ *Doctor, I've had this pain for days on end.*

for fear of something out of fear for something; because of fear of something. □ *He doesn't drive for fear of an accident.* □ *They lock their car doors for fear of being attacked.*

for free for no charge or cost; free of any cost. □ *They let us into the movie for free.* □ *I will let you have a sample of the candy for free.*

for giggles Go to for kicks.

for good forever; permanently. □ *I finally left home for good.* □ *They tried to repair it many times before they fixed it for good.*

for good measure as extra; (adding) a little more to make sure there is enough. □ *When I bought a pound of nails, the clerk threw in a few extra nails for good measure.* □ *I always put a little extra salt in the soup for good measure.*

For goodness sake! Go to For Pete's sake!

For gosh sake! Go to For Pete's sake!

For heaven('s) sake Go to For Pete's sake!

for hours on end *Fig.* for many hours. □ *We sat and waited in the emergency room for hours on end.* □ *The children were happy to play video games for hours on end.*

for instance for example. □ *I've lived in many cities, for instance, Boston, Chicago, and Detroit.* □ *Jane is very generous. For instance, she volunteers at the hospital and gives money to charities.*

for keeps forever. □ *Does that mean I'm going to have this scar for keeps?* □ *This is yours for keeps. Enjoy it.*

for kicks and **for laughs; for giggles** *Fig.* for fun; just for entertainment; for no good reason. □ *They didn't mean any harm. They just did it for kicks.* □ *We drove over to the next town for laughs.*

for life for the remainder of one's life. □ *The accident caused me to become blind for life.* □ *She will stay in prison for life.*

for miles *Fig.* to or in a distance extending two or more miles. □ *The huge field of wheat extends for miles.* □ *We traveled for miles without stopping.*

for my money in my opinion (as regards value or worth). □ *That's the best brand of tools there is, for my money.* □ *For my money, you can't go wrong with a pure wool sweater.*

for one's (own) part as far as one is concerned; from one's point of view. □ *For my own part, I wish to stay here.* □ *For her part, she prefers chocolate.*

for one's (own) sake for one's good or benefit; in honor of someone. □ *I have to earn a living for my family's sake.* □ *I did it for my mother's sake.*

for openers and **for starters** to start with. □ *For openers, they played a song everyone knows.* □ *For starters, I'll serve a delicious soup.*

for peanuts Go to for chicken feed.

For Pete's sake! and **For pity's sake!; For the love of Mike!; For goodness sake!; For gosh sake!; For heaven('s) sake!** a mild exclamation of surprise or shock. □ *For Pete's sake! How've ya been?* □ *For pity's sake! Ask the man in out of the cold!*

For pity's sake! Go to previous.

for real *Inf.* genuine; not imaginary. □ *Ken is really strange. Is he for real?* □ *This whole day has been weird, it just isn't for real.*

for safekeeping for the purpose of keeping someone or something safe. □ *I put my jewelry in the vault for safekeeping.* □ *I checked my fur coat at the entrance to the bar for safekeeping.*

for sale available for purchase; buyable. □ *Is this item for sale?* □ *How long has this house been for sale?* □ *My car is for sale. Are you interested?*

For shame! That is shameful! □ *Sue: Did you hear that Tom was in jail? Fred: For shame! What did he do? Sue: Nobody knows.* □ *Mary: I've decided not to go to the conference. John: For shame! Who will represent us?*

for short as an abbreviation. □ *The Internal Revenue Service is known as the IRS for short.* □ *David goes by Dave for short.*

for (some) days running and **for (some) weeks running; for (some) months running; for (some) years running** days in a series; months in a series; etc. (The *some* can be any number.) □ *I had a bad cold for five days running.* □ *For two years running, I brought work home from the office every night.*

for (some) months running Go to previous.

for (some) years running Go to for (some) days running.

for someone or something's sake and **for the sake of** someone or something for the purpose or benefit of someone or something; to satisfy the demands of someone or something. □ *I made a meatless dinner for John's sake; he's a vegetarian.* □ *The teacher repeated the assignment for the sake of the slower students.*

for starters Go to for openers.

for sure for certain. □ *I will be there for sure.* □ *Sally: Are you ready to go? Bob: For sure. Sally: Then, let's go.*

for that matter besides; in addition. □ *If you're hungry, take one of my doughnuts. For that matter, take two.* □ *I don't like this house. The roof leaks. For that matter, the whole place is falling apart.* □ *Tom is quite arrogant. So is his sister, for that matter.*

for the asking if one just asks (for something); simply by asking; on request. □ *Do you want to use my car? It's yours for the asking.* □ *I have an extra winter coat that's yours for the asking.*

*for the better to be an improvement. (*Typically: **be ~; be a change ~**.) □ *A change of government would* *be for the better.* □ *A new winter coat would certainly be for the better.*

for the birds worthless; undesirable. □ *This television program is for the birds.* □ *Winter weather is for the birds.*

for the devil of it and **for the heck of it; for the hell of it** because it is slightly evil; for no good reason. (Use caution with **hell**.) □ *The kids broke the window just for the devil of it.* □ *We just drove over for the heck of it.*

for the duration for the whole time that something continues; for the entire period of time required for something to be completed; for as long as something takes. □ *We are in this war for the duration.* □ *However long it takes, we'll wait. We are here for the duration.*

for the fun of it just for the entertainment value of doing it. □ *We went on a picnic just for the fun of it.*

for the good of someone or something for the benefit, profit, or advantage of someone or something. □ *The president said the strict drug laws were for the good of the country.* □ *David took a second job for the good of his family.*

for the heck of it Go to for the devil of it.

for the hell of it Go to for the devil of it.

for the life of me at all; even one little bit. (Used with a negative.) □ *For the life of me, I can't figure this out.* □ *I can't for the life of me climb up a mountain.*

For the love of Mike! Go to For Pete's sake!

for the moment and **for the time being** for the present; for now; temporarily. □ *This quick fix will have to do for the moment.* □ *This is all right for the time being. It'll have to be improved next week, however.* □ *This good feeling will last only for the time being.*

for the most part mostly; in general. □ *For the most part, the class is enjoying geometry.* □ *I like working here for the most part.*

for the record so that (one's own version of) the facts will be known; for open, public knowledge. (This often is said when there are reporters present.) □ *I'd like to say—for the record—that at no time have I ever accepted a bribe from anyone.* □ *For the record, I've never been able to get anything done around city hall without bribing someone.*

for the sake of someone or something Go to for someone or something's sake.

for the time being Go to for the moment.

For want of a nail the shoe was lost; for want of a shoe the horse was lost; and for want of a horse the man was lost. *Prov.* Overlooking small details can have disastrous consequences. (You can quote any of the sentences in this proverb by themselves.) □ *Jill: I don't think we need to check our bicycle tires before we go for our ride. Jane: I disagree. For want of a nail the shoe was lost.* □ *Before we began the hike into the mountains, we checked our equipment painstakingly, remembering that for want of a horse the man was lost.*

for what(ever) it's worth Go to for all it's worth.

for your information a phrase that introduces or follows a piece of information. (Can be spoken with considerable impatience.) □ *Mary: What is this one? Sue: For your information, it is exactly the same as the one you just asked about.* □ *Bob: How long do I have to wait here? Bill: For your information, we will be here until the bus driver feels that it is safe to travel.*

forage (around) (for something**)** to search for something, especially something to eat. □ *I will go to the kitchen and forage around for some cereal or something.* □ *The rabbits got into the garden and were foraging for a good meal.*

forbidden fruit *Fig.* someone or something that one finds attractive or desirable partly because having the person or thing is immoral or illegal. (Biblical; from the apple in the Garden of Eden that was forbidden to Adam by God.) □ *Jim flirts with his sister-in-law only because she's forbidden fruit.* □ *The boy watches that program only when his parents are out. It's forbidden fruit.*

force someone or an animal **from** something to drive someone or an animal away from something. □ *We forced the horses from the corral, putting them back into the pasture.* □ *I forced Tom from the room and locked the door.*

force someone or something **down**† to press or push someone or something downward. □ *I forced him down and slipped the handcuffs on him.* □ *The cop forced down the thug and handcuffed him.* □ *I forced the dog down and held it there.*

force someone or something **down** someone's **throat** Go to shove someone or something **down** someone's **throat**.

force someone or something **in(to)** something and **force** someone or something **in**† 1. to make someone or something go into something. □ *Please don't force me into that little room!* □ *They forced in many people.* 2. to make someone or something fit into something. □ *Don't try to force the plug into the socket.* □ *Don't force in the plug.* □ *Sam forced his buddy into the cabinet, and left him well hidden there.*

force someone or something **off (of)** something and **force** someone or something **off**† 1. *Lit.* to get someone, something, or an animal off something. (*Of* is usually retained before pronouns.) □ *I had to force the cat off the sofa. She just wouldn't be coaxed off.* □ *I had to force off the cat. She is so stubborn.* 2. *Fig.* to make someone or a group resign from a board, committee, panel, etc. □ *They forced her off the board before she could change any of their policies.* □ *They forced off the dissenters as well as the CEO.*

force someone or something **(off) on** someone to make someone take someone or something. □ *I didn't want it, but she forced it off on me.* □ *She forced her nephew on me and went out shopping.*

force someone or something **out of** something and **force** someone or something **out**† to drive someone or something out of something or some place. □ *The citizen's group forced the governor out of office.* □ *They forced out the governor.*

force someone or something **through** something to push someone or something through an opening. □ *First, you must force the others through the opening and then go through yourself.* □ *We forced the sofa through the door and scarred up the doorjamb.*

force someone **out of office** and **drive** someone **out of office; drive** someone **out**†; **force** someone **out**† to drive someone out of an elective office. □ *The city coun-*

cil forced out the mayor, who resigned under pressure. □ *Please resign immediately, or I'll have to drive you out.*

force someone's **hand** to force a person to reveal plans, strategies, or secrets. (Alludes to a handful of cards in card playing.) □ *We didn't know what she was doing until Tom forced her hand.* □ *We changed our game plan after we forced the other team's hand in the first period.*

force someone **to the wall** and **drive** someone **to the wall** *Fig.* to push someone to an extreme position; to put someone into an awkward position. □ *He wouldn't tell the truth until we forced him to the wall.* □ *They don't pay their bills until you drive them to the wall.*

force something **down**† to force oneself to swallow something. □ *I can't stand sweet potatoes, but I manage to force them down just to keep from making a scene.* □ *She forced down the sweet potatoes.*

force something **through** something to press or drive something through something that resists. □ *They forced the bill through the legislature.* □ *We were not able to force the matter through the board of directors.*

force something **up**† Go to **drive** something **up**.

a **force to be reckoned with** *Fig.* someone or something that is important and powerful and must not be ignored. □ *Walter is a force to be reckoned with. Be prepared to deal with him.* □ *The growing discontent with the political system is a powerful force to be reckoned with.*

fore and aft at the front and the back, usually of a boat or ship. □ *They had to attach new lights fore and aft because the old ones were not bright enough to meet the new regulations.* □ *The captain ordered a watch stationed fore and aft.*

foreclose on something to take the property on which a mortgage is held; to satisfy an unpaid loan by taking ownership of the property put up for security on the loan. □ *If you don't pay, we will be forced to foreclose on your house.* □ *The bank foreclosed on our property.*

a **foregone conclusion** *Cliché* a conclusion already reached; an inevitable result. □ *That the company was moving to California was a foregone conclusion.* □ *That the mayor will win reelection is a foregone conclusion.*

forever and a day Go to next.

forever and ever and **forever and a day** forever. □ *I will love you forever and ever.* □ *This car won't keep running forever and ever. We'll have to get a new one sometime upcoming.* □ *We have enough money to last forever and a day.*

forewarn someone **about** something and **forewarn** someone **of** something to warn someone about someone or something. □ *They forewarned us of your strange behavior.* □ *Didn't we forewarn you about Max's problem?*

Forewarned is forearmed. *Prov.* If you know about something beforehand, you can prepare for it. □ *Before you meet Lily, I should tell you that she's a little eccentric. Forewarned is forearmed, right?* □ *Check the temperature before you go outside. Forewarned is forearmed.*

Forget (about) it! 1. *Inf.* Drop the subject!; Never mind!; Don't bother me with it. □ *Jane: Then, there's this matter of the unpaid bills. Bill: Forget it! You'll have to pay them all!* □ *Sally: What's this I hear about you and Tom?*

Sue: Forget about it! I don't want to talk to you about it. **2.** *Inf.* Nothing. □ *Sue: What did you say? Mary: Forget it!* □ *Tom: Now I'm ready to go. Sue: Excuse me? Tom: Oh, nothing. Just forget it.* **3.** *Inf.* You're welcome.; It was nothing. □ *John: Thank you so much for helping me! Bill: Oh, forget it!* □ *Bob: We're all very grateful to you for coming into work today on your day off. Mary: Forget about it! No problem!*

forget about someone or something **1.** to put someone or something out of one's mind. □ *Don't forget about me!* □ *You ought to forget about all that.* **2.** to fail to remember something at the appropriate time. □ *She forgot about paying the electric bill until the lights were turned off.* □ *She forgot about the children and they were left standing on the corner.*

forget one's **manners** to do something ill-mannered. □ *Jimmy! Have we forgotten our manners?*

forget oneself to forget one's manners or training. (Said in formal situations in reference to belching, bad table manners, and, in the case of very young children, pants-wetting.) □ *Sorry, Mother, I forgot myself.* □ *John, we are going out to dinner tonight. Please don't forget yourself.*

Forget you! *Sl.* Drop dead!; Beat it! □ *Oh, yeah! Forget you!* □ *Forget you! Get a life!*

Forgive and forget. *Prov.* You should not only forgive people for hurting you, you should also forget that they ever hurt you. □ *When my sister lost my favorite book, I was angry at her for weeks, but my mother finally convinced me to forgive and forget.* □ *Jane: Are you going to invite Sam to your party? Sue: No way. Last year he laughed at my new skirt. Jane: Come on, Sue, forgive and forget.*

forgive someone **for** something to pardon someone for something. □ *Please forgive me for being late.* □ *He never forgave himself for harming her.*

fork some money **out**† **(for** something) *Fig.* to pay (perhaps unwillingly) for something. (Often mention is made of the amount of money. See the examples.) □ *Do you think I'm going to fork twenty dollars out for that book?* □ *Forking out lots of money for taxes is part of life.*

fork something **out**† **(to** someone) **1.** *Inf. Lit.* to serve food to someone, using a fork. □ *He forked out the chicken to everyone.* □ *He brought up a big dish of fried chicken and forked it out.* **2.** *Fig.* to give out something to someone. □ *We forked the coupons out to everyone who asked for them.* □ *We forked out the coupons.*

fork something **over**† **(to** someone) *Inf.* to give something to someone. (Usually refers to money.) □ *Come on! Fork the money over to me!* □ *Fork over the cash you owe me!*

form an opinion to think up or decide on an opinion. (Note the variations in the examples.) □ *I don't know enough about the issue to form an opinion.* □ *Don't tell me how to think! I can form my own opinion.* □ *I don't form opinions without careful consideration.*

form and substance structure and meaningful content. □ *The first act of the play was one screaming match after another. It lacked form and substance throughout.* □ *Jane's report was good. The teacher commented on the excellent form and substance of the paper.*

form from something [for something] to develop from something; [for something] to assume a shape, using something else as raw material. □ *Suddenly, an idea began to form from the things that you had said.* □ *It seemed that a figure was forming from the mists arising from the swamps.*

form someone or something **into** something to shape someone or something into something. □ *We formed the people into a line.* □ *Kathy formed the clay into a small elephant.*

form something **out of** something to shape something from something. □ *He formed a tiny elephant out of the clay.* □ *Wally formed a mound out of the sand.*

form (up) into something [for a group of people] to assume the shape of something. □ *The boys formed up into a jagged line.* □ *We'll form into a line.*

fortify someone or an animal **(against** something**) (with** something**)** to strengthen someone or an animal against something with something. □ *I'll need a cup of hot chocolate to fortify me against the storm.* □ *We have to fortify the dogs against the cold with extra food.*

Fortune favors the bold. Go to next.

Fortune favors the brave. and **Fortune favors the bold.** *Prov.* You will have good luck if you carry out your plans boldly. (Used to encourage people to have the courage to carry out their plans.) □ *Fortune favors the bold, Bob. Quit your day job and work on your novel full-time.* □ *Jill: Let's wait till next year before trying to start our own business. Jane: No. We'll do it this year. Fortune favors the brave.*

forty winks *Fig.* a nap; some sleep. □ *I could use forty winks before I have to get to work.* □ *I need forty winks before I get started again.*

forward something **from** some place **(to** someone or some place**)** to send something onward to someone from the place it was originally received. □ *We forwarded the letter from Chicago to Springfield.* □ *Kelly forwarded the letter to her brother.*

foul one's **own nest** *Fig.* to harm one's own interests; to bring disadvantage upon oneself. (Alludes to a bird excreting into its own nest. See also **It's an ill bird that fouls its own nest.**) □ *He tried to discredit a fellow senator with the president, but just succeeded in fouling his own nest.* □ *The boss really dislikes Mary. She certainly fouled her own nest when she spread those rumors about him.*

foul out (of something**)** [for a basketball player] to be forced out of a game because of having too many fouls. □ *The center fouled out in the first fifteen minutes.* □ *Two other players fouled out soon after.*

foul play illegal activity; bad practices. □ *The police investigating the death suspect foul play.* □ *Each student got an A on the test, and the teacher imagined it was the result of foul play.*

foul someone or something **up**[†] to cause disorder and confusion for someone or something; to tangle up someone or something; to **mess** someone or something **up.** □ *Go away! Don't foul me up any more.* □ *You've fouled up my whole day.* □ *Watch out! You're going to foul up my kite strings.*

foul up to blunder; to **mess up.** □ *Please don't foul up this time.* □ *The quarterback fouled up in the first quarter, and that lost us the game.*

fouled up messed up; ruined; tangled up. (Usually as *fouled-up* when attributive.) □ *This is sure a fouled-up mess.* □ *You sure are fouled up, you know.*

found money money that has come to someone with such ease or surprise that one might have just as well found it by accident. □ *The money he got from his uncle's estate is all found money except for the taxes. He did nothing to earn it.*

found something **(up)on** something to establish something on some kind of basis or justification. (*Upon* is formal and less commonly used than *on.*) □ *The owners founded this company upon prompt service.* □ *We founded our business on practically no money.*

four sheets in the wind and **four sheets (to the wind)** intoxicated. (See comments at **three sheets in the wind.**) □ *She's not just tipsy. She's four sheets!* □ *After only three beers, Gary was four sheets to the wind.*

'Fraid not. Go to **(I'm) afraid not.**

'Fraid so. Go to **(I'm) afraid so.**

fraidy cat *Fig.* a coward; a person who is frightened of everything. (Used in children's taunts.) □ *Don't be a fraidy cat. Go ahead, jump!* □ *Carl is such a fraidy cat. He runs inside when it starts to rain.*

frame something **in** something **1.** *Lit.* to place a frame of something around something. □ *Let us frame the photograph in a wood frame rather than a metal one.* □ *Alice chose to frame the painting in a simple, unmatted frame.* **2.** *Fig.* to express something in a particular way. □ *He framed his comments in very simple language.* □ *I hope you frame your remarks more clearly next time.*

frame something **out**[†] to build the basic wood structure of a building, such as a house. □ *The carpenters, working fast, framed the whole house out in a day.* □ *They framed out the house.*

frankly speaking Go to **(speaking) (quite) frankly.**

fraternize with someone or something to associate with someone or a group; to consort with someone or a group. □ *They were instructed not to fraternize with the opposing team before the game.* □ *Don't fraternize with Lefty "Fingers" Moran.*

fraught with danger *Cliché* [of something] full of something dangerous or unpleasant. □ *The spy's trip to Russia was fraught with danger.* □ *My escape from the kidnappers was fraught with danger.*

freak out (at someone or something**)** Go to **freak out (over** someone or something**).**

freak out (on something**)** to lose control of one's mind because of something, usually a drug. □ *She freaked out on the stuff she was smoking.* □ *She took some funny little pills and freaked out immediately.*

freak out (over someone or something**)** and **freak out (at** someone or something**)** to become very angry or lose control of one's mind because of someone or something that has happened. □ *I absolutely freaked out over the whole business!* □ *Don't freak out at me!*

freak someone **out**[†] to shock or disorient someone. □ *The whole business freaked me out.* □ *I didn't mean to freak out everybody with the bad news.*

F

229

freaked (out) 1. shocked; disoriented. (Sometimes used of the effects of drugs or alcohol.) □ *I was too freaked out to reply.* □ *Man, was I freaked.* **2.** tired out; exhausted. □ *I'm too freaked out to go on without some rest.* □ *The chick is really freaked. Let her rest.*

free and clear without encumbrance, particularly in regard to the ownership of something. □ *After the last payment, Jane owned the car free and clear.* □ *If you can't prove that you own the house and the land it stands on free and clear, you can't sell it.*

free and easy casual. □ *John is so free and easy. How can anyone be so relaxed?* □ *Now, take it easy. Just act free and easy. No one will know you're nervous.*

***free as a bird** and ***free as (the) air** *Cliché* carefree; completely free and unhindered. (*Also: **as** ~.) □ *Jane is always happy and free as a bird.* □ *The convict escaped from jail and was as free as a bird for two days.* □ *No, I'm not married. I don't even have a girlfriend. I'm free as the air.*

free as (the) air Go to previous.

free gift something extra given to you when you buy something else. □ *When you order your magazine subscription, this book is yours to keep as our free gift.* □ *This canvas tote is a free gift for everyone who opens an account at our bank today!*

***a **free hand (with** someone or something**)** *Fig.* freedom to exercise complete control over something. (*Typically: **get** ~; **have** ~; **give** someone ~.) □ *I didn't get a free hand with the last project.* □ *John was in charge then, but he didn't get a free hand either.*

free lunch *Fig.* something of value that is free. (Often negative. See also **There's no such thing as a free lunch.**) □ *There's always somebody who'll do anything to get a free lunch.*

a **free ride 1.** *Lit.* a ride to somewhere for which no payment is demanded. □ *I got a free ride from a truck driver who was headed for town.* □ *I won't call a taxi when I can get a free ride.* **2.** *Fig.* an easy time; participation without contributing anything. □ *You've had a free ride long enough. You have to do your share of the work now.* □ *No more free rides around here. Get off your duff and get a job!*

free someone or something **from** someone or something to release or unburden someone or something from someone or something. □ *We freed the raccoon from the trap.* □ *Max tried to free himself from the police officer.* □ *The dog tried to free itself from the dogcatcher.*

a **free translation** and a **loose translation** a translation or restatement that is not completely accurate and not well thought out; a translation or restatement done casually. □ *John gave a free translation of what our Japanese client asked for, and we missed the main issue.* □ *Anne gave a very free translation of the ancient Chinese poem.*

a **freeze on** doing something *Fig.* a policy that put a temporary end to something. □ *The company put a freeze on hiring as soon as they took us over.*

freeze one's **tail off** *Fig. Inf.* to freeze; to get very cold. □ *Don't stand out there in the cold wind! You'll freeze your tail off!* □ *It's as cold as a welldigger's nose today. I about froze my tail off walking to work.*

freeze (on)to something [for something] to touch something very cold and freeze hard and fast to it. □ *My hand froze to the railing.* □ *The branch froze onto the side of the house.*

freeze over [for a body of water] to get cold and form a layer of ice on top. □ *The pond froze over, so we went skating.*

freeze someone or something **in** one's **memory** *Fig.* to preserve the image of someone or something in one's memory. □ *I tried to freeze her in my memory so I would have her with me always.* □ *I froze the scene in my memory.*

freeze someone or something **to death 1.** *Lit.* [for cold weather] to kill someone or something. □ *I was afraid that the cold snap would freeze the dog to death.* **2.** *Fig.* to make someone or something very cold. □ *This weather is going to freeze us all to death.*

freeze someone **out**[†] **1.** *Lit.* to make it too cold for someone, usually by opening windows or through the use of air-conditioning. □ *Turn up the heat unless you're trying to freeze us out.* □ *Are you trying to freeze out everybody? Close the door.* **2.** *Fig.* to lock someone out socially; to isolate someone from something or a group. □ *We didn't want to freeze you out. You failed to pay your dues, however.* □ *They froze out the newcomers.*

freeze someone's **wages** *Fig.* to hold someone's pay at its current level. □ *The company froze everyone's wages as soon as the economy went sour.*

freeze something **into** something **1.** to use cold to solidify something into a different state, usually water into ice. □ *The extreme cold froze the water of the river into solid ice.* □ *The cold snap froze the water in the puddles into hard sheets of ice.* **2.** to use cold to solidify something into a particular shape. □ *We froze the ice cream into the shape of a penguin.* □ *This ice tray will freeze water into little round balls of ice.*

freeze up 1. *Lit.* [for something] to freeze and stop functioning. □ *The joint froze up and wouldn't move anymore.* **2.** *Fig.* [for someone] to become frightened and anxious, and be unable to move, speak, or continue with something. □ *I froze up and couldn't say anything more.*

fresh and sweet 1. very clean and fresh smelling. □ *Now the baby is changed and she is all fresh and sweet.* **2.** *Inf.* just out of jail. □ *Mary is fresh and sweet and back on the street.*

***fresh as a daisy** *Cliché* very fresh; [of a person] always alert and ready to go. (*Also: **as** ~.) □ *How can you be fresh as a daisy so early in the morning?* □ *I always feel fresh as a daisy after a shower.*

fresh blood Go to **(some) new blood.**

fresh out (of something**)** and **clean out (of** something**)** just now having sold or used up the last of something. □ *Sorry, I can't serve you scrambled eggs. We are fresh out of eggs.* □ *We are fresh out of nails. I sold the last box just ten minutes ago.* □ *Lettuce? Sorry. I'm clean out.*

a **fresh pair of eyes** Go to **another pair of eyes.**

***a **fresh start** a new start; an act of starting over. (*Typically: **get** ~; **get off to** ~; **give** someone ~; **have** ~; **make** ~.) □ *After our apologies and a little discussion, we decided to make a fresh start.*

*fresh (with someone**)** overly bold or impertinent with someone. (*Typically: **be** ~; **get** ~.) □ *When I tried to kiss Mary, she slapped me and shouted, "Don't get fresh with me!"* □ *I can't stand people who get fresh.*

freshen someone or something **up**[†] to revive or restore the appearance or vitality of someone or something. □ *What can we do to freshen this room up?* □ *A cold shower freshened up the runner.*

freshen up to get cleaned up, rested up, or restored. □ *I need a few minutes to freshen up before dinner.*

fret about someone or something and **fret over** someone or something to worry about someone or something. □ *Please don't fret about being a few minutes late.* □ *There is no need to fret over Larry.*

Fret not! *Inf.* Don't worry!; Do not fret about it! □ *Mary: Oh, look at the clock! I'm going to be late for my appointment! Bob: Fret not! I'll drive you.* □ *"Fret not!" said Sally. "We're almost there!"*

fret over someone or something Go to **fret about** someone or something.

A friend in need is a friend indeed. A true friend is a person who will help you when you really need help. □ *When Bill helped me with geometry, I really learned the meaning of "A friend in need is a friend indeed."*

friend or foe a friend or an enemy. □ *I can't tell whether Jim is friend or foe.* □ *"Who goes there? Friend or foe?" asked the sentry.*

*friends with someone a friend of someone. (*Typically: **be** ~; **become** ~.) □ *Sally is friends with Bill.* □ *Mary and Bill are friends with one another.*

frighten one **out of** one's **wits** and **scare** one **out of** one's **wits; frighten** someone **out of a year's growth; scare** someone **out of a year's growth; frighten** one **out of** one's **mind; scare** one **out of** one's **mind** *Fig.* to frighten one very badly. □ *Oh! That loud noise scared me out of my wits.* □ *I'll give him a good scolding and frighten him out of his wits.* □ *Oh, you frightened me out of a year's growth!* □ *You frightened Bob out of his mind.*

frighten someone or an animal **in**[†] Go to **frighten** someone or an animal **into** something.

frighten someone or an animal **into** doing something to threaten someone or an animal into doing something. □ *You can't frighten me into leaving!* □ *Let's try to frighten the coyotes into running away.*

frighten someone or an animal **into** something **1.** and **frighten** someone or an animal **in**[†] to scare someone or an animal into entering something or some place. □ *The trouble in the neighborhood frightened most of the residents into their houses.* □ *The mouse was out of its hole, but we came in and frightened the little mouse back in.* **2.** to scare someone or an animal into a particular state. □ *They frightened me into a quivering mass.* □ *The mouse was frightened into a state of confusion.*

frighten someone or an animal **to death** and **scare** someone or an animal **to death 1.** *Lit.* to frighten a living creature badly enough to cause death. □ *The roar of the plane engine seems to have frightened the little dog to death.* **2.** *Fig.* to frighten someone severely. □ *The dentist always frightens me to death.* □ *She scared me to death when she screamed.*

frighten someone or something **away**[†] and **frighten** someone or something **off**[†] to scare someone or something off. □ *The noise frightened the burglar away.* □ *Something frightened away the prowlers.* □ *The high prices frightened the shoppers off.*

frighten someone **out of a year's growth** Go to **frighten** one **out of** one's **wits.**

frighten the hell out of someone and **frighten the pants off** someone; **frighten the living daylights out of** someone; **scare the living daylights out of** someone; **scare the shit out of** someone; **scare the wits out of** someone to frighten someone badly, suddenly or both. (Use of *hell* and *shit* are crude.) □ *These figures frighten the hell out of me.* □ *The door blew shut and scared the shit out of me.* □ *It takes a lot to scare the pants off a hardened criminal.*

frighten the pants off someone Go to previous.

frightened to death and **scared to death 1.** *Lit.* frightened to the point of dying. □ *This poor animal has been frightened to death by the attacking dogs.* **2.** *Fig.* frightened or anxious. □ *I don't want to go to the dentist today. I'm frightened to death.* □ *I'm frightened to death of spiders.*

fritter something **away**[†] **(on** someone or something**)** to waste something, such as money, on someone or something, foolishly. □ *Did you fritter good money away on that old car?* □ *You frittered away one hundred dollars on that piece of junk?*

*a frog in one's **throat** *Fig.* a feeling of hoarseness or a lump in one's throat. (Often regarded as a sign of fear. *Typically: **get** ~; **have** ~.) □ *I feel like I'm getting a frog in my throat when I have to speak in public.* □ *She says she gets a frog in her throat when she is nervous.*

from A to Z *Fig.* of a complete and wide variety. □ *We have just about everything from A to Z.* □ *She ordered everything on the menu from A to Z.*

from all corners of the world and **from the four corners of the earth** *Fig.* from all places in the world. □ *People came from all corners of the world to attend the conference.*

from dawn to dusk *Fig.* during the period of the day when there is light; from the rising of the sun to the setting of the sun. □ *I have to work from dawn to dusk on the farm.* □ *The factory runs from dawn to dusk to produce hats and gloves.*

from day one Go to **day one.**

from day to day on a daily basis; one day at a time; occasionally. □ *We face this kind of problem from day to day.* □ *I'll have to check into this matter from day to day.*

from door to door moving from one door to another—typically, from one house to another. □ *The candidate went from door to door, campaigning for town council.* □ *The children went from door to door, saying "Trick or treat!" at each one.*

from far and near and **from near and far** from all around, both close by and farther away. (In either order.) □ *All the young people from far and near gathered at the high school for the game.* □ *The eagles gathered from near and far at the river where the salmon were spawning.*

F

from giddy-up to whoa *Rur.* all the way from the beginning to the end. □ *The road is paved from giddy-up to whoa.* □ *The play stinks. It is dull from giddy-up to whoa.*

from hand to hand *Fig.* from one person to a series of other persons. □ *The book traveled from hand to hand until it got back to its owner.* □ *By the time the baby had been passed from hand to hand, it was crying.*

from head to toe *Fig.* from the top of one's head to one's feet. □ *She was decked out in flowers from head to toe.* □ *The huge parka covered the small child from head to toe, assuring that she would be well-protected against the cold.*

from hell to breakfast *Rur.* from one end of the earth to the other; all over; everywhere. (Use with caution.) □ *We searched from hell to breakfast, but never did find the runaway kid.* □ *I tracked that deer from hell to breakfast, but never got a shot at it.*

from here on (in) and **from here on (out)** from this point forward. □ *From here on in we do it my way.* □ *I want everything clear from here on out.*

from here till next Tuesday *Rur.* for a great distance; for a long time. □ *If you try that again, I'll knock you from here till next Tuesday.* □ *You can lecture him from here till next Tuesday, but he won't listen.*

from Missouri requiring proof; needing to be shown something in order to believe it. (From the nickname for the state of Missouri, the Show Me State.) □ *You'll have to prove it to me. I'm from Missouri.* □ *She's from Missouri and has to be shown.*

from my perspective and **from where I stand; from my point of view; the way I see it** *Fig.* in my own opinion. □ *Mary: What do you think of all this? Tom: From my perspective, it is just terrible.* □ *Bob: From my point of view, this looks like a very good deal. Bill: That's good for you. I stand to lose money on it.* □ *Alice: From where I stand, it appears that you're going to have to pay a lot of money to get this matter settled. Sue: I'll pay anything. I just want to get all this behind me.*

from near and far Go to from far and near.

from overseas from a location on the other side of the Atlantic or Pacific Ocean, according to the point of view of someone located in the U.S. □ *The latest word from overseas is that the treaty has been signed.* □ *Is there any news from overseas about the war?*

from pillar to post *Fig.* from one place to a series of other places; (figuratively) from person to person, as with gossip. □ *My father was in the army, and we moved from pillar to post year after year.* □ *After I told one person my secret, it went quickly from pillar to post.*

from rags to riches *Fig.* from poverty to wealth; from modesty to elegance. □ *The princess used to be quite poor. She certainly moved from rags to riches.* □ *After I inherited the money, I went from rags to riches.*

***from scratch** *Fig.* [making something] by starting from the beginning with the basic ingredients. (*Typically: **bake** something ~; **do** something ~; **make** something ~; **start** (something) ~.) □ *We made the cake from scratch, using no prepared ingredients.* □ *I didn't have a ladder, so I made one from scratch.*

from sea to shining sea *Fig.* from coast to coast. (Taken from the lyrics of the song "America the Beautiful".) □ *The new insect pest spread from sea to shining sea in a matter of months.*

from side to side moving first to one side and then to the other, repeatedly. □ *The pendulum of the clock swings from side to side.* □ *The singers swayed from side to side as they sang.*

from start to finish *Fig.* entirely; throughout. □ *I disliked the whole business from start to finish.* □ *Mary caused problems from start to finish.*

from stem to stern 1. *Lit.* from the front of a boat or ship to the back. □ *He inspected the boat from stem to stern and decided he wanted to buy it.* **2.** *Fig.* from one end to another. □ *Now, I have to clean the house from stem to stern.* □ *I polished my car carefully from stem to stern.*

from the bottom of one's **heart** *Fig.* sincerely. □ *When I returned the lost kitten to Mrs. Brown, she thanked me from the bottom of her heart.* □ *Oh, thank you! I'm grateful from the bottom of my heart.*

from the cradle to the grave *Fig.* from birth to death. □ *The government promised to take care of us from the cradle to the grave.* □ *You can feel secure and well-protected from the cradle to the grave.*

from the four corners of the earth Go to from all corners of the world.

from (the) git-go *Sl.* from the very start. □ *This kind of thing has been a problem from the git-go.* □ *I warned you about this from git-go.*

from the ground up *Fig.* from the very beginning. □ *We must plan our sales campaign carefully from the ground up.* □ *Sorry, but you'll have to start all over again from the ground up.*

from the heart *Fig.* from a deep and sincere emotional source. □ *I know that your kind words come from the heart.* □ *We don't want your gift unless it comes from the heart.*

from the old school and **of the old school** *Fig.* holding attitudes or ideas that were popular and important in the past, but which are no longer considered relevant or in line with modern trends. (See also of the old school.) □ *Grammar is not taught much now, but fortunately my son has a teacher from the old school.* □ *Aunt Jane is from the old school. She never goes out without wearing a hat and gloves.*

from the outset throughout, from the very beginning. □ *I felt from the outset that Lisa was the wrong one for the job.* □ *From the outset, I felt unwelcome in the group.*

from the sublime to the ridiculous *Fig.* from something fine and uplifting to something ridiculous or mundane. □ *After Mr. Jones had introduced my wife to his wife, he jokingly turned to introduce me and said, "From the sublime to the ridiculous."* □ *After the opera singer finished, the master of ceremonies introduced the comic juggler saying, "From the sublime to the ridiculous...."*

From the sublime to the ridiculous is only a step. *Prov.* Something grand can easily become very funny. □ *Bob, I don't think you should include a bowl of breakfast cereal in your still-life painting. From the sublime to the ridiculous is only a step.* □ *The production of* Macbeth *went from the sublime to the ridiculous when Lady Macbeth came onstage in an old army uniform.*

from the top *Fig.* from the beginning of something, such as a song or a script. □ *Okay, let's try it again from the top.* □ *Play it from the top one more time.*

from the word go *Cliché* from the very beginning. □ *I knew about the problem from the word go.* □ *She was failing the class from the word go.*

from this day forward Go to next.

from this day on and **from this day forward** from today into the future. □ *We'll live in love and peace from this day on.* □ *I'll treasure your gift from this day forward.*

from time to time irregularly; now and then; occasionally; sometimes; not predictably. □ *From time to time, I like to go fishing instead of going to work.* □ *Bob visits us at our house from time to time.*

from tip to toe *Fig.* from the top to the bottom. □ *She is wearing all new clothes from tip to toe.* □ *The house needs to be cleaned thoroughly from tip to toe.*

from top to bottom *Fig.* from the highest point to the lowest point; throughout. □ *I have to clean the house from top to bottom today.* □ *We need to replace our elected officials from top to bottom.*

from way back from far in the past; from a much earlier time. □ *Grandfather comes from way back.* □ *This antique clock is from way back.*

from where I stand Go to from my perspective.

front for someone or something to serve as the public contact or public "face" for someone or something. □ *Her publicity agent fronted for her most of the time.* □ *Max fronted for a gang of thieves.*

front off (about something**)** *Sl.* to be brash and resentful about something. □ *Todd was fronting off about his assignment and got a detention for it.* □ *You will wish you hadn't fronted off about your supervisor.*

front on something [for a building or a piece of land] to face out on something. □ *The property fronts on a lovely boulevard that has very little traffic.* □ *Our house fronts on a lake.*

front someone some amount of money to provide an advance payment of some amount to someone. □ *The buyer fronted me half the purchase price as a favor.*

the **front-runner** the person or thing thought most likely to win or succeed. □ *The press found out some juicy secrets about the front-runner and made them all public.* □ *Who is the front-runner in the race to be governor?*

frost over to become covered with frost. □ *The windows had all frosted over in the night.* □ *The car windows frosted over.*

frosted (over) *Sl.* angry; annoyed. □ *The clerk was really frosted over when I asked for a better one.* □ *Why was he so frosted?*

froth something **up**[†] to whip or aerate something until it is frothy. □ *Froth the milk up before you add it to the sauce.* □ *Froth up the milk before you pour it in.*

froth up [for something] to build up a froth when whipped, aerated, or boiled. □ *The mixture began to froth up as Dan beat it.* □ *The milk frothed up as the steam went through it.*

frown at someone or something to scowl at someone or something. □ *Please don't frown at me. I didn't do anything.* □ *Frank frowned at the dog and gave it a kick.*

frown on someone or something to disapprove of someone or something; to show displeasure or disapproval of someone or something. □ *The Internal Revenue Service frowns on tax cheaters.* □ *Aunt Clara always seemed to frown on my cousin for some reason.*

the **fruits of** one's **labor(s)** *Fig.* the results of one's work. □ *We displayed the fruits of our labor at the county fair.* □ *What have you accomplished? Where is the fruit of your labors?*

fry something **up**[†] to cook something by frying. □ *Let's fry some chicken up for dinner.* □ *We fried up some chicken.*

Fuck you! a strong condemnation. (Taboo.) □ *Fuck you! Why did you have to do that?* □ *Fuck you! I don't care any more!*

fudge factor *Fig.* a margin of error. □ *I never use a fudge factor. I measure correctly, and I cut the material exactly the way I measured it.* □ *I built in a fudge factor of three percent.*

fuel something **(up**[†]**)** to put fuel into something. □ *I have to fuel this car up before I go any farther.* □ *I need to fuel up the car.*

fuel up to fill one's tank with fuel. □ *Let's stop here and fuel up.* □ *I need to fuel up at the next little town.*

*****full as a tick** very full of food or drink. (Alludes to a tick that has filled itself full of blood. See also **tight as a tick**. *Also: **as** ~.) □ *Little Billy ate and ate until he was as full as a tick.* □ *Our cat drank the cream until he became full as a tick.*

full of beans Go to full of hot air.

full of bull Go to full of hot air.

full of holes *Fig.* [of an argument or plan] that cannot stand up to challenge or scrutiny. (See also **not hold water**; **pick holes in something**.) □ *Your argument is full of holes.* □ *This plan is full of holes and won't work.*

full of hot air and **full of beans; full of bull; full of it; full of prunes** *Fig.* full of nonsense; talking nonsense. □ *Oh, shut up, Mary. You're full of hot air.* □ *Don't pay any attention to Bill. He's full of beans.* □ *My English professor is full of bull.* □ *You're full of it.*

full of Old Nick Go to full of the devil.

*****full of** oneself *Fig.* conceited; self-important. (*Typically: **act** ~; **be** ~.) □ *Mary is very unpopular because she's so full of herself.* □ *She doesn't care about other people's feelings. She's too full of herself.*

full of prunes Go to full of hot air.

full of the devil and **full of Old Nick** always making mischief. □ *Little Chuckie is sure full of the devil.* □ *Toward the end of the school year, the kids are always full of Old Nick.*

a **full plate** *Fig.* a full schedule; a lot to do. □ *I'm very busy at work, and I've got a full plate at home too.*

full steam ahead *Fig.* onward with determination. □ *We started moving full steam ahead on the project.* □ *Full steam ahead! Let's see how fast this will go!*

full up *Rur.* full. □ *I ate till I was full up.* □ *I can't get any more gas in the tank. It's full up.*

fulminate against someone or something to denounce someone or something. □ *The workers were fulminating against their employer.* □ *They are fulminating against the president of the union.*

fumble for something to try to grasp awkwardly for something. □ *He fumbled for his wallet, hoping Wally would pay the bill.* □ *Tex was shot while fumbling for his gun.*

fume about someone or something and **fume over** someone or something to be very angry about someone or something. □ *She was just fuming over her broken vase.* □ *She was still fuming about Larry the next morning.*

fume at someone *Fig.* to rage at someone. □ *She was really fuming at Sam, who had broken her table leg.*

fume over someone or something Go to fume about someone or something.

fun and games *Fig.* playing around; doing worthless things. □ *All right, Bill, the fun and games are over. It's time to get down to work.* □ *This isn't a serious course. It's nothing but fun and games.*

funked out *Sl.* intoxicated. □ *Do you think you can go through life funked out all the time?* □ *Are you funked out again?*

***funny as a barrel of monkeys** Cliché very funny. (*Also: as ~.) □ *Ron was as funny as a barrel of monkeys.* □ *The entire evening was funny as a barrel of monkeys.*

***funny as a crutch** not funny at all. (Sarcastic. *Also: **as** ~.) □ *Your trick is about as funny as a crutch. Nobody thought it was funny.* □ *The lame joke Ron told was as funny as a crutch, and we all yawned.*

funny bone and **crazy bone** a spot near the elbow bone that is very sensitive to the touch. □ *Ouch, I hit my funny bone.* □ *Effie bumped her crazy bone and made a horrendous face.*

funny business Go to monkey business.

funny ha-ha amusing; comical. (As opposed to funny peculiar.) □ *I didn't mean that Mrs. Peters is funny ha-ha. She's weird—funny peculiar in fact.* □ *Mike thinks his jokes are funny ha-ha, but we laugh because they are so silly.*

funny money 1. *Sl.* counterfeit money. □ *The bank teller spotted the funny money in the man's deposit almost immediately.* **2.** *Fig.* temporary or substitute money, good only in certain places. □ *What am I going to do with all this funny money when I leave here? It's no good anywhere else.* **3.** *Fig.* foreign currency. (Jocular.) □ *We had better buy some gifts and get rid of some of this funny money before our flight.*

funny peculiar odd; eccentric. (As opposed to funny ha-ha.) □ *I didn't mean that Mrs. Peters is funny ha-ha. She's weird—funny peculiar in fact.* □ *His face is sort of funny—funny peculiar, that is.*

a **fur piece** *Rur.* a long distance. (*Fur* = far.) □ *It's a fur piece to the library. You'd best take the bus instead of walking.* □ *It's a pretty fur piece to the nearest big town.*

furnish something **for** someone or something and **furnish** someone or something **with** something to provide something for someone or a group. □ *I would be happy to furnish dinner for the visitors.* □ *I furnished the board of directors with the information.*

furnish something **for** something to provide something to be used as something. □ *Could you furnish the salad for our picnic?* □ *We can't furnish enough glassware for the whole party.*

a **furtive glance** a secret or quick glance, quickly averted. □ *He made a furtive glance in the direction of the closet when the robbers asked where the jewelery was hidden.*

fuse something **with** something to bond something together with something. □ *You have to fuse the upper layer to the lower layer with heat.* □ *He used heat and pressure to fuse the patch with the soft rubber of the raft.*

fuse with something to bond with something. □ *The metal has fused with the glass coating on the tank.* □ *I didn't know that metal could fuse with glass.*

fuss about and **fuss around** to go about complaining; to move about in a busy manner. □ *Don't fuss about so much. Things will take care of themselves.* □ *Now, stop fussing around and sit down.*

fuss about someone or something to complain about someone or something. □ *What are you fussing about now?* □ *Are you still fussing about Tony?*

fuss and feathers *Rur.* fancy addictions that are overdone or troublesome. □ *A truly elegant dress doesn't have a lot of fuss and feathers.* □ *They ruined a nice room with all that fuss and feathers.*

fuss around Go to fuss about.

fuss (around) with someone or something to keep bothering with someone or something; to **fiddle with** someone or something. □ *Don't fuss around with it. We'll have to get a new one.* □ *Don't fuss with your children. They will get along just fine without all that attention.*

fuss at someone or something to complain at someone. □ *Stop fussing at me!* □ *The squirrel is fussing at the dog.*

fuss over someone or something to go to a lot of bother about someone or something. □ *My aunt always fusses over me and my sister.* □ *You spend a lot of time fussing over your hair.*

futz around *Sl.* to waste time. □ *Stop futzing around and get the job done.* □ *I wish you would stop futzing around!*

futz something **up**† *Sl.* to mess something up. □ *Who futzed the computer up?* □ *I don't want to futz up the deal, so I will be quiet.*

gab up a storm Go to up a storm.

gad around and **gad about** to go from place to place, having fun. □ *I'm too old to gad around like that.* □ *She wasted too much time gadding about with her friends.*

gag on something to choke on something; to retch on something. □ *The dog is gagging on whatever you gave her.* □ *This fish is good, but I hope I don't gag on a bone.*

gain dominion over someone or something to achieve total authority over someone or something. □ *The dictator sought to gain dominion over the entire country.* □ *Harry was not happy until he had gained dominion over the people who worked for him.*

gain from something to benefit from something. □ *I hope you gain from this experience.* □ *What do you think I will gain from this?*

gain ground to make progress; to advance; to become more important or popular. □ *Our new product is gaining ground against that of our competitor.* □ *Since the government announced its new policies, the opposition has been gaining ground.*

gain in something to advance in a particular quality. □ *Todd grew in stature and gained in wisdom.* □ *Mary gained in experience as the weeks went on.*

gain on someone or something to begin to catch up or move ahead of someone or something. □ *We were gaining on them when they suddenly sped up.* □ *Our horse was gaining on the horse in front.*

gain something **by** doing something to achieve some benefit by doing something. □ *What did he gain by dropping out of school?* □ *I will gain some degree of security by investing in U.S. Treasury bonds.*

gain something **from** something to earn or achieve something from something. □ *I hope you gain something worthwhile from all this.* □ *I know I will gain some valuable experience from this job.*

gallivant around to travel around aimlessly. □ *Why don't you stop gallivanting around and come home for a while?* □ *Mary is off gallivanting around with her boyfriend.*

gallop through something **1.** *Lit.* [for a horse] to pass through something at a gallop. □ *Her horse galloped through the garden and dumped her in the cabbages.* □ *A few horses galloped through the meadow.* **2.** *Fig.* to go through something quickly; to do or perform something rapidly and perhaps carelessly. □ *Mike galloped through his song and left the stage in a hurry.* □ *Don't just gallop through your homework!*

galumph around to move around looking for someone or something or transporting someone or something. □ *I am so tired of galumphing around, dropping off and picking up kids.* □ *I have to stop galumphing around day after day.*

galvanize someone **into action** *Fig.* to stimulate someone into some activity. □ *The explosion galvanized Martha into action.* □ *We were galvanized into action by the storm.*

gamble on someone or something **1.** *Lit.* to make a wager on something concerning someone or something. □ *I wouldn't gamble on it happening.* □ *Don't gamble on that horse. You'll be sorry.* **2.** *Fig.* to run a risk by choosing or depending on someone or something. □ *I wouldn't gam-*

ble on Ted's being able to come. I don't think he can. □ *Don't gamble on Ted. I'm almost sure he won't come.*

gamble something **away**† to lose all of something by gambling. □ *He gambled all his money away.* □ *He gambled away all his money.*

The game is up. and **The jig is up.** *Fig.* The illegal activity has been found out or has come to an end. □ *When the police were waiting for them inside the bank vault, the would-be robbers knew that the game was up.* □ *"The jig is up!" said the cop as he grabbed the shoulder of the pickpocket.*

a **game that two can play** *Fig.* a manner of competing that two competitors can use; a strategy that competing sides can both use. (Said when about to use the same ploy that an opponent has used.) □ *The mayor shouted at the city council, "Politics is a game that two can play."* □ *"Flattery is a game that two can play," said John as he returned Mary's compliment.*

gang up (on someone**)** to form into a group and attack someone. (Usually a physical attack, but it can also be a verbal attack.) □ *We can't win against the robber unless we gang up on him.* □ *All right, you guys, don't gang up on me. Play fair!*

gape at someone or something to stare at someone or something in wonder. □ *Don't just stand there, gaping at me. Come in.* □ *Stop gaping at the storm clouds and get in here.*

garb someone **in** something to dress someone in something. □ *He hoped that someday he wouldn't have to garb his children in rags.* □ *She garbed herself in her finest clothes and got ready to meet her husband's family.*

Garbage in, garbage out. *Prov.* If you give nonsensical instructions to people or computers, those instructions will produce nonsensical results. □ *Jill: Why is my computer generating all this gibberish? Jane: You must have made a mistake in the program. Garbage in, garbage out.* □ *Ed insists that children are so ignorant nowadays because their teachers are incompetent. "Garbage in, garbage out," he says.*

garbage something **down**† *Sl.* to gobble something up; to quickly swallow something down. □ *Don't garbage your food down!* □ *That guy will garbage down almost anything.*

garner something **in**† and **garner** something **up**† to take something in and store it; to harvest something in and store it. (Originally referred to grain stored in a granary.)

□ *Will they garner the crop in on time this year?* □ *They had garnered in the entire crop by late October.*

garnish something **with** something to embellish or decorate something, such as food, with something. □ *For the final presentation, I will garnish the dish with a sprig of parsley.* □ *The roast was garnished with slices of apple.*

gas something **up**† to put gasoline into a vehicle. □ *I have to gas this car up soon.* □ *I will stop and gas up the car at the next little town.*

gas up to fill up one's gasoline tank with gasoline. □ *I have to stop at the next service station and gas up.* □ *The next time you gas up, try some of the gasoline with alcohol in it.*

gasp at someone or something to inhale sharply in surprise or shock at someone or something. □ *I gasped at the sight that lay before me.* □ *I saw how weary Denise looked and I gasped at her.*

gasp for air to fight for a breath of air. (After one has been deprived of air.) □ *Walter popped to the surface of the water and gasped for air.* □ *The injured dog appeared to be gasping for air.*

gasp for breath to labor for one's breath. (Usually because of physical exertion.) □ *She ran and ran until she was gasping for breath.* □ *The diver finally came to the surface, gasping for breath.*

gasp something **out**† to utter something, gasping. □ *She gasped the words out haltingly.* □ *Dan was just able to gasp out the instructions before he passed out.*

gassed (up) *Sl.* intoxicated. □ *Fred is gassed up and very wobbly.* □ *He was too gassed up to drive home.*

gather a case (against someone**)** Go to **build a case (against** someone**)**.

gather around someone or something to collect around someone or something. □ *Let's all gather around her and hear her out.* □ *Please gather around the table for dinner.*

gather dust *Fig.* [for something] to sit unused for a long time. □ *Most of my talent is just gathering dust because I don't really have an opportunity to perform.*

gather someone **into** something and **gather** someone **in**† to assemble or bring people into something or some place. □ *The hostess gathered the children into the house just as the storm hit.* □ *She gathered in the children.* □ *Harry gathered them in before the storm.*

gather someone or something **around (**oneself**)** to collect people or things around oneself; to draw someone or something to oneself. □ *He gathered a lot of arty people around himself.* □ *She liked to gather exotic plants around herself.* □ *Grandpa gathered all the kids around and read them a story.*

gather someone or something **to** oneself to draw someone or something to oneself. □ *The hen gathered her chicks to herself.* □ *Harry gathered the poker chips to himself.*

gather someone or something **together**† to assemble people or things together in one place. □ *Gather everyone together in the drawing room for a meeting.* □ *Please gather together all the suspects so that they can be questioned again.* □ *Would you gather all your papers together and put them away?*

gather something **from** someone to collect something from someone. □ *I will gather the papers from Wally, and you*

go get those that Ted is working on. □ *Would you gather the pictures from everyone? We have to leave now and take them with us.*

gather something **from** someone or something to learn something from someone or something; to infer something from someone or someone's remarks. (The *something* is often a clause shifted to another position in the sentence.) □ *I gather from your brother that you do not approve of her.* □ *We gathered that from your remarks.*

gather something **from** something to collect something from something. □ *Kristine gathered the honey from the beehives.* □ *I gathered my money from the cashier.*

gather something **in**† 1. *Lit.* to collect something and bring it in; to harvest something. □ *We gathered the pumpkins in just before Halloween.* □ *We gathered in the pumpkins just in time.* 2. *Fig.* to fold or bunch cloth together when sewing or fitting clothing. □ *Try gathering it in on each side to make it seem smaller.* □ *I will have to gather in this skirt.*

gather something **up**† to collect something; to pick something up. □ *Let's gather our things up and go.* □ *Please gather up your things.*

gather together to assemble together. □ *We will gather together on the main deck for a meeting.* □ *Let's all gather together this evening and sing.*

Gather ye rosebuds while ye may. *Prov.* Enjoy yourself while you can, before you lose the opportunity or before you become too old. (From Robert Herrick's poem, "To the Virgins, to Make Much of Time.") □ *Sue: Should I go out on a date with Robbie on Saturday, or should I stay home and study? Ellen: Gather ye rosebuds while ye may.* □ *You ought to travel abroad now, while you're young, before you have responsibilities that might keep you from going. Gather ye rosebuds while ye may.*

*gaudy as a butterfly fancy; colorful. (*Also: **as** ~.) □ *Marie looked as gaudy as a butterfly in her new dress.* □ *Michael's scarf is gaudy as a butterfly.*

gawk at someone or something to stare at someone or something, obviously and awkwardly. □ *Why are you standing there, gawking at me?* □ *The tourists stood at the foot of the mountain and gawked at the top.*

gaze around (at someone or something**)** to look all around at someone or something. □ *The manager gazed around at each of us, and finally spoke.* □ *Tourists gazed around at the scenery for a while and got back in the bus.* □ *We just stood there, gazing around.*

gaze at someone or something to stare at someone or something. □ *I stood for an hour, gazing at the sea.* □ *She gazed at me for a moment and then smiled.*

gaze on someone or something to look at someone or something; to survey someone or something. □ *She gazed sullenly on the ruin that had been her home.* □ *The teacher gazed on the student and frightened her.*

gaze out on something to look out on something, such as a lovely view, from inside a building or from a particular spot. □ *She gazed out on the flowering trees and knew that life would go on.* □ *Henry sat for hours, gazing out on the lake.*

gear someone or something **up**† **(for** someone or something**)** to prepare someone or something for someone or something. □ *We have to gear up the workers for the arrival of the new manager.* □ *We geared ourselves up for Frank, who was coming to lecture to us.*

gear something **to** someone or something to cause something to match something else; to create or adapt something for a specific purpose. □ *Tim geared his speech to his audience.* □ *The newspaper geared its language to a fourth-grade reading level.*

gear up for someone or something to get ready for something. □ *We are busy gearing up for Joan's visit next week.*

generalize about someone or something and **generalize on** someone or something to interpret someone or something in very general terms. □ *Sometimes it isn't wise to generalize about a complicated issue.* □ *She is very complex and it is difficult to generalize on her.*

generalize from something to assume a general pattern in something from specific observances of something. □ *You can hardly generalize from only two instances.* □ *You can't generalize anything from the testimony of a single witness!*

generalize on someone or something Go to **generalize about** someone or something.

Generation X and **Generation X'er** people reaching puberty during the 1970s and 1980s. □ *Three or four generation X'ers were in the antique store looking eagerly at some of those horrible old dinette chairs from the 1950s.*

generous to a fault *Cliché* too generous; overly generous. □ *My favorite uncle is generous to a fault.* □ *Sally—always generous to a fault—gave away her lunch to a homeless man.*

Genius is an infinite capacity for taking pains. *Prov.* Genius is the quality of being exceedingly careful about everything you do. □ *If genius is an infinite capacity for taking pains, Marilyn certainly has it. She never overlooks a single detail that needs attention.*

Genius is ten percent inspiration and ninety percent perspiration. *Prov.* People get brilliant results primarily by working hard, not because they have special inborn powers. □ *Child: Betty always does the best drawings in art class. She must be a genius. Father: If you worked hard, you could do just as well. Remember, genius is ten percent inspiration and ninety percent perspiration.*

*****gentle as a lamb** *Cliché* [of someone] very gentle. (*Also: **as** ~.) □ *Don't be afraid of Mr. Schaeffer. He may look fierce, but he's as gentle as a lamb.* □ *Lisa was gentle as a lamb when dealing with children.*

the **genuine article** the real thing rather than a substitute. □ *Is this the genuine article or some cheap imitation substitute?* □ *I'll take the genuine article, thanks.*

get a bang out of someone or something Go to **get a charge out of** someone or something.

get a bead on someone or something Go to **draw a bead on** someone or something.

get a buzz out of someone or something *Fig.* to get some humor from someone or something. □ *I thought you'd get a buzz out of that gag.* □ *I hope you get a buzz out of Ted. He's a funny guy.*

get a charge out of someone or something and **get a bang out of** someone or something; **get a kick out of** someone or something to receive special pleasure from someone

or something. □ *I really got a charge out of that comedian's routine.* □ *Tom is really funny. I always get a kick out of his jokes.* □ *Bill really got a bang out of the present we gave him.*

get a hurry on and **get a move on** to start to hurry. □ *We are going to leave in five minutes, Jane. Get a hurry on!* □ *Mary! Get a move on! We can't wait all day.*

get a kick out of someone or something Go to **get a charge out of** someone or something.

get a laugh to do something that will create laughter. □ *John will do almost anything to get a laugh.*

Get a life! *Inf.* Change your life radically! Find something interesting to do or say! □ *You are such a twit! Get a life!* □ *Get a life, you clown!*

get a load of someone or something to get a good look at someone or something. □ *Wow! Get a load of that car!* □ *Get a load of Mary!*

get a lot of mileage out of something *Fig.* to get a lot of use from something, as if it were a car. □ *Bob always got a lot of mileage out of one joke.* □ *I got a lot of mileage out of my TV before it broke down.*

get a move on Go to **get a hurry on.**

get a rise from someone and **get a rise out of** someone *Fig.* to make someone react, usually angrily. □ *Tease Joe about his girlfriend. That generally gets a rise from him.* □ *I pestered Mary for half the afternoon, but didn't get a rise out of her.*

get a say (in something**)** Go to a **voice (in** something**).**

get a (sound) grasp of something Go to a **(solid) grasp of** something.

get a ticket to receive a traffic ticket. □ *If you keep racing along at this speed, you will get a ticket!*

get a weight off one's **mind** Go to a **load off** one's **mind.**

get a word in edgewise and **get a word in edgeways** *Fig.* to manage to say something when other people are talking and ignoring you. (Often in the negative. Alludes to trying to "squeeze" a word into a running conversation.) □ *It was such an exciting conversation that I could hardly get a word in edgewise.* □ *Mary talks so fast that nobody can get a word in edgeways.*

get aboard something to get onto a ship, a train, or an airplane. □ *What time should we get aboard the ship?* □ *Everyone can get aboard at noon.*

get about and **get around** to manage to move around. □ *I broke my hip last year, but I can still get about.* □ *Dad can't get around too much anymore, so I go over to help him.*

get across (something**)** to manage to cross something. (See also **put** something **across (to** someone**).**) □ *We finally got across the river where it was very shallow.* □ *Where the water was low, it was easy to get across.*

get after someone **1.** *Lit.* to begin to chase someone. □ *The other boys got after him and almost caught him.* □ *Henry got after Bill and almost caught up with him.* **2.** *Fig.* to bother someone about doing something; to scold someone about something. □ *I will get after Fred about his behavior.* □ *Please don't get after me all the time.*

get ahead (in something**)** to advance in one's employment, school, or life in general. □ *I work hard every day, but I* *can't seem to get ahead in my job.* □ *I want to get ahead in life.*

get ahead of oneself *Fig.* [for someone] to do or say something sooner than it ought to be done so that the proper explanation or preparations have not been made. □ *I have to stick to my notes or I will get ahead of myself in my lecture.* □ *When he bought a new little bicycle before the baby was born, he was getting ahead of himself.*

get along 1. [for people or animals] to be amiable with one another. □ *Those two just don't get along.* □ *They seem to get along just fine.* **2.** to leave; to be on one's way. □ *I've got to get along. It's getting late.* □ *It's time for me to get along. See you later.*

get along (on a shoestring) and **get by (on a shoestring)** *Fig.* to be able to afford to live on very little money. □ *For the last two years, we have had to get along on a shoestring.* □ *With so many expenses, it's hard to get by on a shoestring.*

get along on something *Fig.* to manage to survive with just something. □ *I think we can get along on what I earn.* □ *I can't get along on what they pay me.*

Get along with you! *Rur.* to go on; to depart; to go and "take oneself along." (Only with *you.*) □ *Get along with you, now. Get going!* □ *Get along with you, Sally!*

get along without (someone or something**)** to manage without someone or something; to do without someone or something. □ *I don't think I can get along without my secretary.* □ *My secretary just quit, and I don't think I will be able to get along without.*

get an amount of money **for** something to receive an amount of money in exchange for something; to sell something for a specific price. (See also **get** something **for** an amount of money.) □ *I got nearly two thousand dollars for my car.* □ *How much did they get for their house?*

get around Go to **get about**.

get around someone or something **1.** *Lit.* to cluster around someone or something. □ *Tell everyone to get around the cat so she won't run away.* □ *Let's get around Mary and sing "Happy Birthday" to her.* **2.** to manage to go around someone or something. □ *We couldn't get around the fallen tree, so we turned back.* □ *Mary couldn't get around the people standing in the hallway.* **3.** *Fig.* to avoid or elude an authority or regulation that constitutes a barrier; to circumvent someone or something in order to get one's way. □ *We knew she would oppose us, so we got around her and got it approved by someone else.* □ *I know I can find a way to get around the rule.*

get around to doing something to find time to do something; to do something after a long delay. (See also **get (around) to** someone or something.) □ *I finally got around to buying a new coat.* □ *It took Sally years to get around to visiting her aunt.*

get (around) to someone or something to be able to deal with someone or something eventually. (See also **get around to** doing something.) □ *I will get around to you in a moment. Please be patient.* □ *The mechanic will get around to your car when possible.*

get at someone *Fig.* to find a way to irritate someone; to manage to wound someone, physically or emotionally. (See also **get at** someone or an animal.) □ *Mr. Smith found*

a way to get at his wife. □ *John kept trying to get at his teacher.*

get at someone or an animal *Fig.* to attack or strike someone or an animal. □ *The cat jumped over the wall to get at the mouse.* □ *Ok, you guys. There he is. Get at him!*

get at something **1.** *Fig.* to explain or understand something. □ *We spent a long time trying to get at the answer.* □ *I can't understand what you're trying to get at.* **2.** *Fig.* begin doing something. (See also **Have at it!**) □ *I won't be able to get at it until the weekend.* □ *I'll get at it first thing in the morning.*

get away to move away. (Often a command.) □ *Get away! Don't bother me!* □ *I tried to get away, but he wouldn't let me.*

get away (from someone or something**) 1.** to escape from someone, something, or some place. □ *Max did get away from the prison guard but was caught soon after.* □ *Mary couldn't get away from the telephone all morning.* **2.** Go to **away (from** someone or something**)**.

get away with murder 1. *Lit.* to commit murder and not get punished for it. (See also **get away with** something.) □ *Don't kill me! You can't get away with murder!* **2.** *Fig.* to do something very bad and not get punished for it. □ *That guy always gets away with murder—just because he's cute.* □ *You will spoil your son if you let him get away with murder. You should punish him for his backtalk.*

get away with someone or something to escape, taking someone or something with one. □ *The kidnapper got away with little Brian.* □ *The burglars got away with a lot of cash and some diamonds.*

get away with something and **get by with** something to do something and not get punished for it. (See also **get away with murder.**) □ *You can't get away with that!* □ *Larry got by with the lie.*

get axed *Fig.* to get fired. □ *Betty and two of her friends got axed today.*

get back (to someone**) (on** something**)** *Fig.* to continue talking with someone (at a later time); to find out information and tell it to a person (at a later time). □ *I don't have the answer to that question right now. Let me find out and get back to you.* □ *Okay. Please try to get back early tomorrow.*

get back to something to return to dealing with something. □ *I will have to get back to my work now.* □ *I want to get back to my knitting.*

get better to improve. □ *I had a bad cold, but it's getting better.* □ *Business was bad last year, but it's getting better.* □ *I'm sorry you're ill. I hope you get better.*

get between someone or something **and** someone or something else to position oneself between people and things, in any combination. □ *She got between Dan and his career.* □ *The dog got between the archer and the target.*

get busy to start working; to work or appear to work harder or faster. □ *The boss is coming. You'd better get busy.* □ *I've got to get busy and clean this house up.*

get by (on a shoestring) Go to **get along (on a shoestring)**.

get by (on a small amount of money**)** to survive with only a small amount of money. □ *I can't get by on that much money.* □ *That is a very small amount of money to live on. No one could get by.*

get by (someone or something**)** to move past someone or something. □ *I need to get by this intersection, and then I will stop and look at the tires.* □ *Please let me get by.*

get by (with something**) 1.** to satisfy the minimum requirements. □ *I was failing geometry, but managed to get by with a D.* □ *I took the bar exam and just barely got by.* **2.** Go to **get away with** something.

get by (without someone or something**)** to survive without someone or something. □ *I can't get by without you.* □ *We can probably get by without two cars.*

get carried away *Fig.* to be overcome by emotion or enthusiasm (in one's thinking or actions). □ *Calm down, Jane. Don't get carried away.* □ *Here, Bill. Take this money and go to the candy store, but don't get carried away.*

get cracking *Rur.* to get to work. □ *If you want to finish that quilt by Labor Day, you best get cracking.* □ *Sit down to your homework and get cracking!*

get down 1. *Sl.* to lay one's money on the table. (Gambling.) □ *Okay, everybody get down.* □ *Get down, and let's get going!* **2.** *Sl.* to concentrate; to do something well. □ *I'm flunking two subjects, man. I gotta get down.* □ *Come on, Sam, pay attention. Get down and learn this stuff.* **3.** *Sl.* to copulate. □ *Hey, let's get down!* □ *All Steve wants to do is get down all the time.*

get down (from something**)** to get off something; to climb down from something. □ *Please get down from there this instant!* □ *Get down before you fall!*

get (down) off one's **high horse** *Fig.* to become humble; to be less haughty. □ *It's about time that you got down off your high horse.* □ *Would you get off your high horse and talk to me?*

get down (on all fours) to position oneself on one's hands and knees. □ *He got down on all fours and played with the children.* □ *Mary got down and walked around like a dog.*

get down to brass tacks *Fig.* to begin to talk about important things; to get down to business. □ *Let's get down to brass tacks. We've wasted too much time chatting.* □ *Don't you think that it's about time to get down to brass tacks?*

get down to business and **get down to work** to begin to get serious; to begin to negotiate or conduct business. □ *All right, everyone. Let's get down to business. There has been enough chitchat.* □ *When the president and vice president arrive, we can get down to business.*

get down to cases to begin to discuss specific matters; to get down to business. □ *When we've finished the general discussion, we'll get down to cases.* □ *Now that everyone is here, we can get down to cases.*

get down to (doing) something to begin doing some kind of work in earnest. □ *I have to get down to my typing.* □ *John, you get in here this minute and get down to that homework!*

get down to the facts to begin to talk about things that matter; to get to the truth. □ *The judge told the lawyer that the time had come to get down to the facts.* □ *Let's get down to the facts, Mrs. Brown. Where were you on the night of January 16?*

get down to the nitty-gritty to get down to the basic facts. □ *Stop messing around and get down to the nitty-gritty.* □ *If we could only get down to the nitty-gritty and stop wasting time.*

get down to the nuts and bolts *Fig.* to get down to the basic facts. (See also **nuts and bolts**.) □ *Stop fooling around. Get down to the nuts and bolts.* □ *Let's stop wasting time. We have to get down to the nuts and bolts.*

get down to work Go to **get down to business**.

get enough courage up[†] **(to** do something**)** Go to **get enough nerve up**[†] **(to** do something**)**.

get enough guts up[†] **(to** do something**)** Go to next.

get enough nerve up[†] **(to** do something**)** and **get enough courage up**[†] **(to** do something**)**; **get enough guts up**[†] **(to** do something**)**; **get enough pluck up**[†] **(to** do something**)**; **get enough spunk up**[†] **(to** do something**)**; **get the nerve up**[†] **(to** do something**)**; **get the courage up**[†] **(to** do something**)**; **get the guts up**[†] **(to** do something**)**; **get the pluck up**[†] **(to** do something**)**; **get the spunk up**[†] **(to** do something**)** *Fig.* to work up enough courage to do something. □ *I hope I can get enough nerve up to ask her for her autograph.* □ *I wanted to do it, but I couldn't get up enough nerve.* □ *I thought he would never get up the courage to ask me for a date.*

get euchred out of something to get cheated out of something. (Alludes to losing in the card game euchre.) □ *Joe's dad left him a farm, but he got euchred out of it by some city slicker real estate agent.* □ *I got euchred out of ten bucks by a con artist with a hard-luck story.*

get free of someone or something and **get free from** someone or something **1.** to rid oneself of the burden of someone or something. □ *Can't I get free of this problem?* □ *I can't seem to get free of Randy.* **2.** to liberate oneself from someone or something. □ *I tried to get free of Mr. Franklin, but he kept talking and wouldn't let me interrupt.* □ *Is there any way that somebody can get free of Tom?* □ *I couldn't get free of the nail that had snagged my sleeve.*

get going 1. to start moving. □ *Let's get going! We can't stand here all day.* **2.** to depart. □ *What time should we get going in the morning?*

get hell (about someone or something**)** Go to **catch hell** **(about** someone or something**)**.

get hip to someone or something Go to **hip to** someone or something.

get home to someone or something to manage to return home to someone or something there. □ *The infantryman wants to get home to his wife.* □ *I like to get home to a nice warm house.*

get in deeper *Fig.* to get in more and more trouble; to get more deeply involved with someone or something. □ *Everytime he opened his mouth to complain, he just got in deeper.*

get inside something **1.** *Lit.* to go inside of something or some place. □ *Get inside the house and wait for me.* □ *Get inside the car so you won't get wet.* **2.** *Fig.* to learn about the inner workings of something or some organization. □

G

I can't wait to get inside that company and see what makes it tick. □ *Someone needs to get inside the boardroom and straighten things out.*

get into a mess 1. *Lit.* to get some part of one into a sloppy or messy substance. □ *Look at your shoes! You really got into a mess.* □ *Please don't get into a mess in the park.* **2.** and **get into a jam** *Fig.* to get into difficulty; to get into trouble. □ *Now you have really gotten into a mess.* □ *I got into a real mess at work.*

get into an argument (with someone**) (about** someone or something**)** and **get into an argument (with** someone**) (over** someone or something**)** to enter a quarrel with someone about someone or something. □ *I don't want to get into an argument with you about Dan.* □ *Mary got into an argument about money with Fred.* □ *I really don't want to get into an argument.*

get into bed with someone *Fig.* to work closely as business partners; to merge businesses. □ *Have you heard? The company's getting into bed with Acme Industries.* □ *I want you to get into bed with the other department supervisors and sort this problem out.*

get into one's **stride 1.** *Lit.* [for a runner] to reach a comfortable and efficient pace. □ *I got into my stride right away, and that helped win the race.* □ *She never got into her stride, and that's why she lost.* **2.** *Fig.* to reach one's most efficient and productive rate of doing something. □ *When I get into my stride, I'll be more efficient.* □ *Amy will be more efficient when she gets into her stride.*

get into something **1.** to tamper with something; to open something and disturb the contents. □ *Who got into my desk?* □ *Someone has been getting into my work after the office closes.* **2.** to put oneself into clothing. □ *As soon as I get into this coat, I will help you load the car.* □ *Let me get into my boots, and then I'll be with you.* **3.** to enter something or some place. □ *I got into the theater just before the rain started.* □ *Let's get into the car and go.* **4.** *Sl.* to become involved in something; to develop an interest in something. □ *I can really get into sailing, I think.* □ *No matter how hard I try, I can't get into basketball.* **5.** to enter a particular type of business; to deal in a particular product in business. □ *Yes, I used to work for the government, but now have gotten into private industry.*

get in(to) the act *Fig.* to participate in something; to try to be part of whatever is going on. (As if someone were trying to get on stage and participate in a performance.) □ *Everybody wants to get into the act! There is not room here for everyone.* □ *I want to get in the act.*

get in(to) the swing of things *Fig.* to join in with people and their activities; to become more social and up-to-date. □ *Come on, Bill. Try to get into the swing of things.* □ *John just couldn't seem to get in the swing of things.*

get it Go to **get** something.

get it (all) together *Fig.* to become fit or organized; to organize one's thinking; to become relaxed and rational. □ *Bill seems to be acting more normal now. I think he's getting it all together.* □ *I hope he gets it together soon. His life is a mess.*

get it in the neck *Sl.* to receive trouble or punishment. □ *You are going to get it in the neck if you are not home on time.* □ *I got it in the neck for being late.*

get it off *Sl.* to achieve sexual release; to copulate. (Potentially offensive. Use only with discretion. Compare this with **get it off with** someone.) □ *Harry kept saying he had to get it off or die. What's wrong with Harry?* □ *The entire crew of the yacht came ashore to get it off.*

get it off with someone *Sl.* to have sexual intercourse with someone. □ *She said she wanted to get it off with him.* □ *She said all he wanted was to get it off with just anybody.*

get it on 1. *Sl.* to begin something. □ *Time to go back to work. Let's get it on!* □ *Get it on, you guys! Time to start your engines.* **2.** *Sl.* to begin dancing. □ *Let's go out there and get it on!* □ *He wanted to get it on, but my feet hurt.* **3.** *Sl.* [for people] to copulate. (Potentially offensive. Use only with discretion.) □ *Come on, baby, let's get it on.* □ *I don't want to get it on with you or any other creep.* **4.** *Sl.* to undertake to enjoy oneself. □ *I can really get it on with that slow jazz.* □ *Let's go listen to some new age and get it on.*

get it out *Fig.* to tell someone about a problem; to pour out one's grief. (Fixed order.) □ *Come on, get it out. You'll feel better.* □ *He would feel better if he could get it out.*

get it wrong to misunderstand someone or something. □ *Oh, Otto, you've got it wrong again!* □ *Why do you have to get it wrong every time?*

get laid to have sexual intercourse. (Use caution.) □ *Tommy wanted nothing more out of life than to get laid.*

get lost 1. to become lost; to lose one's way. □ *We got lost on the way home.* □ *Follow the path, or you might get lost.* **2.** *Inf.* Go away!; Stop being an annoyance! (Always a command.) □ *Stop bothering me. Get lost!* □ *Get lost! I don't need your help.*

get mad (at something**)** to muster all one's physical and mental resources in order to do something difficult. □ *Come on, Bill. If you're going to lift your end of the piano, you're going to have to get mad at it.* □ *The sergeant keeps yelling, "Work, work! Push, push! Come on, you guys, get mad!"*

get married to become united as husband and wife. □ *Bill and Sally got married when they were in college.* □ *We got married in Texas just after we graduated from college.*

get moving to get busy; to get started; to work harder or faster. □ *Come on, everybody. Get moving!* □ *The director is coming. You had better get moving.*

get nowhere fast *Fig.* not to make progress; to get nowhere. □ *I can't seem to make any progress. No matter what I do, I'm just getting nowhere fast.* □ *Come on. Speed up this car. We're getting nowhere fast.*

get off 1. to start off (on a friendship). □ *Tom and Bill had never met before. They seemed to get off all right, though.* □ *I'm glad they got off so well.* **2.** to leave; to depart. □ *What time did they get off?* □ *We have to get off early in the morning before the traffic gets heavy.* **3.** Go to **get off (easy)**; **get off (of)** someone or something; **get off (of)** something; **get off** something; **get off to** something; **get off with** something.

get off a few good ones *Fig.* to tell a few good jokes; to land a few good punches; to manage to make a few strong criticisms. □ *The comedian managed to get off a few good ones, but most of his material was old or obscene.*

get off (easy) and **get off (lightly)** to receive very little punishment (for doing something wrong). □ *It was a seri-*

ous crime, but Mary got off easy. □ *Billy's punishment was very light. Considering what he did, he got off lightly.*

Get off it! 1. *Inf.* Stop acting so arrogant! □ *Get off it, you jerk!* □ *Get off it! That's too much!* **2.** *Inf.* You're lying! □ *Get off it, you liar!* □ *Get off it! That can't be true.*

get off kilter Go to out of kilter.

get off (lightly) Go to get off (easy).

Get off my back! *Inf.* Stop harassing me!; Leave me alone about this matter! □ *Tom: You'd better get your paper written. Bill: I'll do it when I'm good and ready. Get off my back!* □ *Alice: I'm tired of your constant criticism! Get off my back! Jane: I was just trying to help.*

get off (of) someone or something and **get off** to get down from someone or something. (*Of* is usually retained before pronouns.) □ *Please get off of me. I can't play piggyback anymore.* □ *Get off of the sofa!*

get off (of) something and **get off** *Inf.* to stop discussing the topic that one is supposed to be discussing [and start discussing something else]; to stray from the topic at hand. (*Of* is usually retained before pronouns.) □ *I wish you wouldn't get off the subject so much.* □ *This writer gets off of his topic all the time.*

get off one's **ass** and **get off** one's **rear; get off** one's **butt** *Sl.* to get up and get busy; to stop loafing and get to work. (Caution with *ass*. *Butt* is also offensive to some people.) □ *Get off your ass and get busy!* □ *It's time you got off your butt and started to work.*

get off one's **butt** Go to previous.

get off one's **rear** Go to get off one's ass.

get off scot-free Go to go scot-free.

Get off someone's **back!** Go to next.

Get off someone's **case!** and **Get off** someone's **back!** *Fig. Inf.* Leave someone alone!; Stop picking on someone! (Usually a command.) □ *I'm tired of your criticism, Bill. Get off my case!* □ *Quit picking on her. Get off her back!*

get off someone's **tail 1.** *Fig.* to stop following someone closely, usually in an automobile. □ *Get off my tail! Keep your distance!* □ *I wish that car behind me would get off my tail.* **2.** *Fig.* to stop bothering someone; to stop monitoring someone's actions. □ *Get off my tail! I can manage without you.* □ *Who needs your help? Get off my tail!*

get off (something) to climb down from something. □ *Please get off the stairs. You know you shouldn't play on the stairs.* □ *I wish that the children would get off that ladder before they fall off.*

get off the dime *Sl.* to start moving; to get out of a stopped position. □ *Why don't you get off the dime and complete some of these projects that you started?* □ *As soon as the board of directors gets off the dime on this proposal, we will have some action.*

get off to sleep to manage to get to sleep finally. □ *About midnight everyone finally got off to sleep.* □ *I wasn't able to get off to sleep until dawn.*

get off (to something) to leave for something. □ *I've got to get off to my violin lesson.* □ *We have to get off to the hospital immediately!*

get off (with something**)** to receive only a light punishment for something. □ *Let's hope John gets off with a light sentence.* □ *Max got off with only a few years in prison.*

get on 1. to get along; to thrive. □ *Well, how are you two getting on?* □ *We are getting on okay.* **2.** Go to get on something and get on (with someone).

get on (in years) to grow older; to be aged. □ *Aunt Mattie is getting on in years.* □ *They were both getting on in years.*

get on one's **horse** *Sl.* to prepare to leave. (Usually fig., with no horse present.) □ *It's time to get on my horse and get out of here.* □ *I've got to get on my horse and go.*

get on someone *Fig.* to pester someone (about something); to pressure someone. □ *John is supposed to empty the trash every day. He didn't do it, so I will have to get on him.* □ *It's time to get on Bill about his homework. He's falling behind.*

get on (something) to enter a conveyance; to get aboard something; to climb onto something. □ *They just announced that it's time to get on the airplane.* □ *The bus stopped, and I got on.* □ *The child was afraid to get on the train.* □ *Where did you get on?*

get on the phone Go to on the telephone.

get on the track of someone or something Go to on the trail of someone or something.

get on (with someone**)** and **get along (with** someone**)** to be friends with someone; to have a good relationship with someone. (The friendship is always assumed to be good unless it is stated to be otherwise.) □ *How do you get on with John?* □ *I get along with John just fine.* □ *We get along.*

get on with something to continue doing something. □ *Let's get on with the game!* □ *We need to get on with our lives.*

get on (without someone or something**)** to survive and carry on without someone or something. □ *I think we can get on without bread for a day or two.* □ *Can you get on without your secretary for a while?*

get one **on** one's **feet** and **put** one **on** one's **feet 1.** *Lit.* to help someone stand up after a fall or prolonged bed rest. □ *We had to get him on his feet, but he was able to walk without much help.* □ *We put the child on his feet and he took off running again.* **2.** *Fig.* to get someone back to normal, financially, medically, mentally, etc. □ *When he gets himself on his feet, Tom will buy a new car.* □ *We will put him on his feet and help him along.* □ *When I get myself on my feet, things will be better.*

get one **right here** *Fig.* to affect one deeply in a specific way. (Usually accompanied with a hand gesture showing exactly where one is affected: the heart = lovingly, the stomach or bowels = sickeningly.) □ *That sort of thing gets me right here.* □ *Pete clasped his hand to his chest and said, "That sort of thing gets me right here."*

get one's **act together** to get oneself organized and on schedule. □ *I've got to get my act together and start getting my work done.* □ *When I have my act together, I'll get a job.*

get one's **ass in gear** and **get** one's **tail in gear** *Sl.* to get moving; to get organized and get started. (Use cau-

241

tion.) □ *Come on, you guys. Get moving. Get your ass in gear!*

get one's **bowels in an uproar** *Sl.* to get oneself anxious or excited. (Normally fig.) □ *Cool it! Don't get your bowels in an uproar.* □ *Fred's always getting his bowels in an uproar about nothing.*

get one's **comeuppance** to get a deserved punishment. □ *I can't wait till that snobbish girl gets her comeuppance.* □ *Joe got his comeuppance when the teacher caught him making fun of her.*

get one's **ducks in a row** *Fig.* to get one's affairs in order or organized. □ *Jane is organized. She really gets all her ducks in a row right away.* □ *You can't hope to go into a company and sell something until you get your ducks in a row.*

get one's **ears pinned back** *Fig.* to experience a severe scolding. □ *Jimmy was ordered to report to the principal's office and got his ears pinned back.*

get one's **ears set out** and **get** one's **ears lowered** *Fig.* to get one's ears made more visible by getting a haircut. □ *Well, I see you got your ears set out!* □ *Better get my ears lowered because I'm getting a little shaggy.*

get one's **feet wet** *Fig.* to get a little first-time experience with something. (Obvious literal possibilities.) □ *Of course he can't do the job right. He's hardly got his feet wet yet.* □ *I'm looking forward to learning to drive. I can't wait to get behind the steering wheel and get my feet wet.*

get one's **fingers burned** *Fig.* to receive harm or punishment for one's actions. (Normally fig.) □ *I had my fingers burned the last time I questioned the company policy.* □ *I tried that once before and got my fingers burned. I won't try it again.*

get one's **foot in the door** *Fig.* to complete the first step in a process. (Alludes to people selling things from door-to-door and blocking the door with a foot so it cannot be closed on them.) □ *I think I could get the job if I could only get my foot in the door.* □ *It pays to get your foot in the door. Try to get an appointment with the boss.*

get one's **hands dirty** and **dirty** one's **hands; soil** one's **hands 1.** *Fig.* to get closely involved in a difficult task. □ *You have to get your hands dirty if you expect to get the gutters cleaned out.* **2.** *Fig.* to become involved with something illegal; to do a shameful thing; to do something that is beneath one. □ *The mayor would never get his hands dirty by giving away political favors.* □ *I will not dirty my hands by breaking the law.*

get one's **head above water** and **have** one's **head above water 1.** *Lit.* to get one's head above the surface of the water while swimming. (See also keep one's head above water.) □ *He finally got his head above water and was able to get a good breath.* **2.** *Fig.* to manage to get oneself caught up with one's work or responsibilities. □ *I can't seem to get my head above water. Work just keeps piling up.* □ *I'll be glad when I have my head above water.*

get one's **head together** to get one's thoughts or attitude properly organized. □ *I've got to get my head together and get going.* □ *I need to take some time off and get my head together.*

get one's **hooks in(to)** someone or something and **get** one's **hooks in†** *Fig.* to obtain a strong and possessive hold on

someone or something. □ *She just can't wait to get her hooks into him.* □ *He finally got in his hooks and guarded her jealously.*

get one's **just deserts** and **get** one's **just reward(s); get** one's **[specified by context]** to get what one deserves. □ *I feel better now that Jane got her just deserts. She really insulted me.* □ *The criminal who was sent to prison got his just rewards.* □ *You'll get yours!*

get one's **just reward(s)** Go to previous.

get one's **kicks (from** someone or something**)** *Fig. Inf.* to get pleasure from someone or something. □ *Do you get your kicks from this sort of thing?* □ *I get my kicks from Billy Simpson. What a great entertainer!*

get one's **knuckles rapped 1.** *Lit.* to get one's knuckles struck with a ruler as a punishment. □ *I got my knuckles rapped for whispering too much.* □ *You will have your knuckles rapped if you are not careful.* **2.** *Fig.* to receive a minor punishment. □ *The lawyer got his knuckles rapped for talking back to the judge.* □ *Better watch your tongue if you don't want to get your knuckles rapped.*

get one's **lumps** *Inf.* to get the result or punishment one deserves. (See also take one's lumps.) □ *If she keeps acting that way, she'll get her lumps.* □ *We will see that Dave gets his lumps.*

get one's **nose out of joint** and **have** one's **nose out of joint; put** one's **nose out of joint** *Fig.* to resent that one has been slighted, neglected, or insulted. □ *You get your nose out of joint too easily about stuff like that.* □ *Now, don't get your nose out of joint. She didn't mean it.*

get one's **nose out of** someone's **business** *Fig.* to stop interfering in someone else's business; to mind one's own business. □ *Go away! Get your nose out of my business!* □ *Bob just can't seem to get his nose out of other people's business.*

get one's **rocks off (on** something**) 1.** *Sl.* [for a male] to ejaculate. (Considered coarse.) *Boys normally don't talk about getting their rocks off.* **2.** *Sl.* to enjoy something. (Fixed order.) □ *I really get my rocks off on heavy metal.* □ *I've listened to the stuff, but I sure don't get my rocks off on it.*

get one's **shit together** and **get** one's **stuff together 1.** *Fig.* to get one's possessions organized. (*Shit* is usually taboo.) □ *Let me get my shit together, and I'll be right with you.* □ *I'll get my shit together and be right with you.* □ *Will you all please get your stuff together so we can get going?* **2.** *Fig.* to get oneself mentally organized. (*Shit* is usually taboo.) □ *As soon as I get my shit together, I can be of more help.* □ *When you have your shit together you can start living independently again.*

get one's **stuff together** Go to previous.

get one's **tail in gear** Go to get one's ass in gear.

get one's **teeth into** something and **sink** one's **teeth into** something; **get** one's **teeth in†; sink** one's **teeth in†** *Fig.* to begin to do something; to get completely involved in something. □ *I can't wait to get my teeth into that Wallace job.* □ *Here, sink your teeth into this and see if you can't manage this project.* □ *He'll find it easier when he sinks his teeth.*

get one's **ticket punched** *Sl.* to die; to be killed. (Literally, to be cancelled.) □ *Poor Chuck got his ticket punched* *while he was waiting for a bus.* □ *Watch out there, or you'll get your ticket punched.*

get one's **wits about** one and **have** one's **wits about** one *Fig.* to keep one's thinking in order or make one's mind work smoothly, especially in a time of stress. (See also **keep** one's **wits about** one.) □ *Let me get my wits about me so I can figure this out.* □ *I don't have my wits about me at this time of the morning.*

get (oneself) **into a stew (over** someone or something**)** *Fig.* to be worried or upset about someone or something. □ *Please don't get yourself into a stew over Walter.* □ *Liz is the kind of person who gets into a stew over little problems.*

get oneself **up 1.** to arise from bed; to rise to one's feet. □ *I've got to get myself up and get going.* □ *Get yourself up and get going.* **2.** *Rur.* to dress oneself up. □ *I got myself up in my Sunday best.* □ *Jane got herself up as if she were a movie star.*

get on(to) someone **(about** something**)** *Fig.* to remind someone about something. □ *I'll have to get onto Sarah about the deadline.* □ *I'll get on Gerald right away.*

get on(to) the (tele)phone and **get on(to) the (telephone) extension** to pick up a telephone receiver to talk to someone or make a telephone call. □ *I'll get onto the extension and talk with Fred.* □ *I'll get on the phone and call Fran right away.*

get out 1. [for someone or an animal] to depart to the outside or to escape. □ *When did your dog get out and run away?* □ *When did he get out of jail?* **2.** [for information or a secret] to become publicly known. □ *We don't want the secret to get out.* □ *The word soon got out that he had a prison record.*

get out of a jam *Fig.* to get free from a problem or a bad situation. □ *Would you lend me five hundred dollars? I need it to get out of a jam.* □ *I need some help getting out of a jam.*

get out of a mess *Fig.* to get free of a bad situation. (Also with *this, such a,* etc.) □ *How can anyone get out of a mess like this?* □ *Please help me get out of this mess!*

get out of (doing) something to manage not to have to do something. □ *I was supposed to go to a wedding, but I got out of it.* □ *Jane had an appointment, but she got out of it.*

Get out (of here)! Go away!; Leave this place! □ *John: I've heard enough of this! Get out of here! Bill: I'm going! I'm going!* □ *Where have you been? You smell like a sewer! Get out of here!*

Get out of my sight! Go away immediately! (Usually said in anger.) □ *Get out of my sight!* □ *Please get out of my sight forever!*

get out of one's **face** *Lit. Inf.* to stop bothering or intimidating someone. □ *Look, get out of my face, or I'll poke you in yours!* □ *He told you to get out of his face, you creep!*

get out of someone's **hair** *Fig. Inf.* to stop annoying someone. □ *Will you get out of my hair! You are a real pain!*

get out of the road Go to **out of the way.**

get out of time (with someone or something**)** Go to **out of step (with** someone or something**).**

Get out of town! Beat it!; Get out of here! □ *Go away, you bother me! Get out of town!* □ *You'd better get out of town, my friend. You are a pest.*

get out of wind Go to **out of breath.**

get (out) while the getting(g)'s good and **get (out) while the going(g)'s good** to leave while it is still safe or possible to do so. □ *I could tell that it was time for me to get while the gettin's good.* □ *I told her she should get out while the goin's good.*

Get out with it! Get it said! □ *Stop stuttering around! Get out with it!* □ *Get out with it! I don't have all day to wait for you!*

get out with one's **life** *Fig.* to survive a serious or life-threatening incident or an accident without dying. □ *We were lucky to get out with our lives.*

Get over it! Forget about it and be done with it! (Said to someone who is fretting and stewing over some kind of problem.) □ *Forget about her. She's gone. Get over it!*

get over someone or something **1.** *Lit.* to move or climb over someone or something. □ *I managed to get over the sand dunes and moved on toward the shoreline.* □ *I couldn't get over the huge rock in the path, so I went around it.* **2.** *Fig.* to recover from difficulties regarding someone or something. (See also **Get over it!**.) □ *I almost never got over the shock.* □ *Sharon finally got over Tom. He had been such a pest.*

get over something to recover from a disease. (See also **get over** someone or something.) □ *It took a long time to get over the flu.* □ *I thought I would never get over the mumps.*

get over (to some place**) 1.** to go to some place. □ *I have to get over to Molly's place and pick up some papers.* □ *Go ahead and start without me. I'll get over as soon as I can.* **2.** to cross over something to get somewhere. □ *I want to get over to the other side.* □ *I can't find a way to get over!*

get past (someone or something**) 1.** to move around or ahead of someone or something that is in the way. □ *We have to get past the cart that is blocking the hallway.* □ *We just couldn't get past.* **2.** to pass ahead of someone or something that is moving. □ *I want to get past this truck, then we can get into the right lane.* □ *When we get past, I'll stop and let you drive.*

Get real! *Inf.* Start acting realistically! □ *Hey, chum! You are way off base! Get real!* □ *Get real! Wake up to reality!*

get religion *Fig.* to become serious (about something), usually after a powerful experience. (Sometimes literal.) □ *When I had an automobile accident, I really got religion. Now I'm a very safe driver.*

get right on something to do something immediately. □ *I know it has to be done today. I'll get right on it.* □ *Please get right on these reports as soon as possible.*

get rolling *Fig.* to get started. □ *Come on. It's time to leave. Let's get rolling!* □ *Bill, it's 6:30. Time to get up and get rolling!*

get screwed 1. *Sl.* to have sexual intercourse. (Considered a crude usage.) □ *A lot of the college kids on spring break in Florida do nothing but get drunk and get screwed.* **2.** *Sl.* to get cheated. □ *I really got screwed on that last deal.*

Get serious! *Inf.* Get realistic!; Stop horsing around! □ *Oh, come on! Get serious! You don't really mean that!*

get shed of someone or something Go to next.

get shut of someone or something and **get shed of** someone or something; **get shet of** someone or something *Rur.* to get rid of someone or something. □ *I can't wait to get shut of that old refrigerator.* □ *Tom followed me around for months, but I finally got shed of him.*

get smart (with someone**)** *Fig.* to become fresh with someone; to talk back to someone. □ *Don't you get smart with me!* □ *If you get smart again, I'll bop you.*

get some kind of **mileage out of** something **1.** *Lit.* to achieve some level of efficiency with a vehicle. (*Some kind of* typically includes *more, better, good,* etc.) □ *Do you get good mileage out of a vehicle like this.* **2.** *Fig.* to get [sufficient] use or service from something. □ *I wish I could get better mileage out of this car.* □ *He knows how to get a lot of mileage out of a pair of shoes.*

get (some) steam up[†] **1.** *Lit.* [for a steam engine] to build up steam pressure and become more powerful. □ *As the engine got up steam, it began to move faster.* **2.** *Fig.* to begin to be stronger and more powerful. □ *The movement to cut taxes is getting up some steam.* □ *Our little organization just couldn't get up enough steam to become effective.*

get some weight off one's **feet** *Fig.* to sit down. □ *Come in and get some weight off your feet.* □ *I need to sit down and get some weight off my feet.*

get someone **across (in a good way)** Go to put someone across (in a good way).

get someone **(all) wrong** to misunderstand someone's intentions or character. □ *I think you've got me all wrong. I want to be your friend, not your enemy.*

get someone **around the table** *Fig.* to collect people together for discussion or bargaining. □ *We have to get everyone around the table on this matter.* □ *If I can get them around the table, I'm sure I can make them agree.*

get someone **down** to depress a person; to make a person very sad. □ *My dog ran away, and it really got me down.* □ *Oh, that's too bad. Don't let it get you down.*

get someone **going** to get someone excited; to get someone talking excitedly. □ *I guess I really got him going on the subject of politics.* □ *The whole business really makes me mad. Don't get me going.*

get someone **in a family way** Go to in a family way.

get someone **in(to)** something **1.** *Lit.* to manage to put someone into a confining area or into clothing. □ *I couldn't get Billy into his boots!* **2.** *Fig.* to manage to get someone enrolled into a school, club, organization, class, etc.; to manage to get someone accepted into something. □ *Somehow, we managed to get Jody into a fine private school.* □ *We got her in the group at last!* □ *Well, I managed to get myself into the class I wanted.*

get someone **off 1.** to get someone cleared of a criminal charge. □ *Ted's lawyer got him off, although we all knew he was guilty.* □ *I hope someone can get her off. She is innocent no matter how it looks.* **2.** to get someone freed from a responsibility. (See also get off the hook.) □ *I think I can get you off.* □ *What do I need to do to get myself off?*

get someone **on(to)** someone or something to assign someone to attend to someone or something. □ *Get someone*

onto the injured man in the hall right now. □ *Get someone on the telephone switchboard at once!*

get someone or something **across** something and **get** someone or something **across** to transport someone or something across something. □ *We have to get everyone across the bridge before the floodwaters rise any more.* □ *Let's get the truck across also.* □ *It's foolhardy to try to get your car across the desert without a few gallons of water with you.*

get someone or something **away from** someone or something to take someone or something away from someone or something, in any combination. □ *Please get that cigar away from me!* □ *See if you can get Timmy away from the horse.*

get someone or something **back**[†] to receive someone or something back; to recover someone who had been taken away; to recover something that had been taken away. □ *Beth finally got her car back from the service station.* □ *She got back her car.*

get someone or something **by** someone or something and **get** someone or something **by** to get someone or something past an inspection. □ *Do you think I can get my cousin by the border guards?* □ *I don't think I can get this sausage by the customs desk.*

get someone or something **down**[†] **(from** something**)** to bring someone or something down from a higher place. □ *See if you can get my cat down from the tree.* □ *Please get down the sugar from the top shelf.*

get someone or something **down** something and **get** someone or something **down** to manage to put or force something downward. □ *We finally got her down the stairs, but it was a struggle.* □ *Don had to push and push to get his laundry down the chute.*

get someone or something **free (from** someone or something**)** to liberate someone or something from someone or something. □ *We finally got cousin George free from the talkative old man.* □ *We managed to get the animal's paw free from the trap.*

get someone or something **in(to)** something and **get** someone or something **in**[†] to manage to fit someone or something into something. □ *I will try to get you into the beginning of the line.* □ *The key is bent, but I think I can get it in.* □ *He struggled to get in the key.*

get someone or something **off** someone or something and **get** someone or something **off** to remove someone or something from someone, oneself, or something. □ *Come in and get those wet clothes off.* □ *Get him off of me!*

get someone or something **out of** one's **mind** and **get** someone or something **out of** one's **head** to manage to forget someone or something; to stop thinking about or wanting someone or something. (Almost the same as put someone or something out of one's mind.) □ *I can't get him out of my mind.* □ *Mary couldn't get the song out of her mind.*

get someone or something **out of** one's **sight** *Fig.* to remove someone or something from one's presence. (Often said in anger.) □ *Get that child out of my sight!* □ *Please get that cake out of my sight.*

get someone or something **out of** someone or something and **get** someone or something **out**[†] to release or extricate someone or something from someone, something, or some place. □ *See if you can get the cat out of this cabinet.*

□ *I can't get the nail out of the board.* □ *I can get out almost anything with my pry bar.*

get someone or something **through (to** someone or something**)** to manage to get someone or something transported or connected to someone or something. □ *I hope I can get her through to her hometown in Italy.* □ *Do you think I can get this parcel through to Istanbul?*

get someone or something **together** to gather people or things together. □ *Let's see if we can get both sides together and discuss this.* □ *I want to get Tom and Sharon together for a conference.*

get someone **out of a jam** *Fig.* to get someone out of trouble. □ *Thanks for getting my brother out of that jam.* □ *How am I going to get myself out of this jam?*

get someone **out of** one's **hair** *Fig. Inf.* to cause someone to stop annoying oneself. □ *What do I have to do to get this guy out of my hair.*

get someone's **attention** Go to grab someone's attention.

get someone's **back up** Go to get someone's dander up.

get someone's **blood up** *Fig.* to get someone or oneself angry. (Fixed order.) □ *That kind of language really gets my blood up.* □ *That will really get his blood up!*

get someone's **dander up** and **get** someone's **back up; get** someone's **hackles up; get** someone's **Irish up; put** someone's **back up** *Fig.* to make someone get angry. (Fixed order.) □ *Now, don't get your dander up. Calm down.* □ *I insulted him and really got his hackles up.* □ *Bob had his Irish up all day yesterday. I don't know what was wrong.* □ *Now, now, don't get your back up. I didn't mean any harm.*

get someone's **drift** *Fig.* to understand what someone is saying or implying. (Akin to **if you get my drift**.) □ *I don't want to hear anymore about her or you. Do you get my drift?*

get someone's **eye** Go to catch someone's eye.

get someone's **goat** *Fig.* to irritate someone; to annoy and arouse someone to anger. □ *I'm sorry. I didn't mean to get your goat.* □ *Jean got Sally's goat and Sally made quite a fuss about it.*

get someone's **hackles up** Go to get someone's dander up.

get someone's **Irish up** Go to get someone's dander up.

get someone **through** something and **get** someone **through** **1.** *Lit.* to manage to help someone move through some kind of barrier or tight opening. □ *I will do what I can to get you through the front office. From then on, it's up to you.* □ *The first opening is tight. I can help you get through, but not beyond that.* **2.** *Fig.* to help someone survive some ordeal. □ *The medication got her through the pain of the surgery.* □ *We will get you through while you recover. Don't worry.*

get someone **through (to** someone or something**)** to manage to get something to someone or some place. □ *Can I get a message through to Rome?* □ *I hope Bob can get word through to his cousin.*

get someone **up** to wake someone up; to get someone out of bed. □ *I've got to get John up, or he will be late for work.* □ *Can you get yourself up, or should I call you?*

get someone **up (for** something**)** to get someone into peak condition for something; to prepare someone for some-

thing. □ *I hope we can get Walter up for the race.* □ *Sharon was not quite prepared for the race, and the trainer did everything possible to get her up.*

get something and **get it 1.** to receive punishment. □ *Bill broke the window, and he's really going to get it.* □ *John got it for arriving late at school.* **2.** to receive the meaning of a joke; to understand a joke. □ *John told a joke, but I didn't get it.* □ *Bob laughed very hard, but Mary didn't get it.*

get something **across (to** someone**)** Go to put something across (to someone).

get something **down†** **1.** to manage to swallow something, especially something large or unpleasant. □ *The pill was huge, but I got it down.* □ *I get down all the pills despite their size.* □ *It was the worst food I have ever had, but I got it down somehow.* **2.** Go to next.

get something **down (in black and white)** and **get** something **down (on paper); get** something **down†** *Fig.* to record some important information in writing. (Alludes to the black of ink and the white of paper.) □ *Be sure to get his statement down in black and white.* □ *I'm glad we have agreed on a price. I want to get it down in black and white.* □ *Get down every word of it!* □ *This is important. Please get it down on paper.*

get something **down (on paper)** Go to previous.

get something **for** an amount of money to buy something for a certain amount of money. (See also **get** an amount of money **for** something.) □ *I got my car for only $1500.* □ *She got her dinner for a song.*

get something **for** someone to obtain something for the use or benefit of someone. □ *I will get a new book for you. Sorry I messed the old one up.* □ *Would you get a glass of water for me?*

get something **for** something to obtain a part or attachment for an object. □ *I need to get a part for the vacuum cleaner.* □ *Would you please get a bulb for my flashlight?*

get something **from** someone or something **1.** to receive something from someone or something. □ *I got this belt from my aunt for my birthday.* □ *I got a letter from the bank about the loan we applied for.* **2.** to contract a disease from someone or something. □ *I got chicken pox from my son.* □ *I probably got my cold from walking in the rain.*

get something **going with** someone to start a romance or affair with someone. □ *Todd got something going with Amy, and they both look pretty happy.* □ *I want to get something going with Chuck.*

get something **home to** someone or something to carry something home [quickly] to someone or something. □ *I have to get this pizza home to my parents before it gets cold.* □ *Please get this ice cream home to the refrigerator.*

get something **into a mess** to cause something to become messy or untidy; to cause something to become unmanageable. □ *When he made the spaghetti sauce, he got the kitchen into a real mess.* □ *You have got these accounts into a mess!*

get something **in(to)** someone to make something enter someone or something. □ *Get that morphine into her before she goes into shock.* □ *Let's get some food into him. He looks starved.*

get something **into** someone's **thick head** Go to get something through someone's thick skull.

get something **in(to)** something to manage to put something into something. □ *I got the notice into tomorrow's newspaper.* □ *I will get the replacement battery into the car right away.*

get something **off**† Go to get something off (to someone or something).

get something **off** one's **chest** to unburden oneself; to confess something; to criticize or make a personal complaint to someone. □ *You will feel better if you get it off your chest.* □ *I have to get this off my chest. I'm tired of your rudeness to me!*

get something **off the ground 1.** *Lit.* to get something into the air. □ *I'll announce the weather to the passengers as soon as we get the plane off the ground.* □ *I hope they get this plane off the ground soon.* **2.** *Fig.* to get something started. (Alludes to an airplane beginning a flight.) □ *When we get this event off the ground we can relax.* □ *It is my job to get the celebration plans off the ground.*

get something **off (to** someone or something) and **get** something **off**† to send something to someone or something. □ *I have to get a letter off to Aunt Mary.* □ *Did you get off all your packages?*

get something **out**† **1.** *Lit.* to remove or extricate something. □ *Please help me get this splinter out.* □ *Would you help me get out this splinter?* □ *The tooth was gotten out without much difficulty.* **2.** *Fig.* to manage to get something said. □ *He tried to say it before he died, but he couldn't get it out.* □ *I had my mouth full and couldn't get out the words.*

get something **out of** one's **system 1.** *Lit.* to get something like food or medicine out of one's body, usually through natural elimination. □ *He'll be more active once he gets the medicine out of his system.* □ *My baby, Mary, ate applesauce and has been crying for three hours. She'll stop when she gets the applesauce out of her system.* **2.** *Fig.* to be rid of the desire to do something; to do something that you have been wanting to do so that you aren't bothered by wanting to do it anymore. □ *I bought a new car. I've been wanting to for a long time. I'm glad I finally got that out of my system.* □ *I can't get it out of my system! I want to go back to school and earn a degree.* **3.** *Fig.* to do so much of something that one does not want or need to do it anymore. □ *I got riding roller coasters out of my system when I was young.*

get something **out of** someone to cause or force someone to give specific information. □ *We will get the truth out of her yet.* □ *The detective couldn't get anything out of the suspect.* □ *They got a confession out of him by beating him.*

get something **out (of** someone or something) to remove something from someone or something. (See also get something out of someone; get something out of something.) □ *He probably will be okay when they get the tumor out of him.* □ *Please get that dog out of the living room.*

get something **out of** something to get some kind of benefit from something. □ *I didn't get anything out of the lecture.* □ *I'm always able to get something helpful out of our conversations.*

get something **over (to** someone) **1.** to deliver something to someone. □ *Get these papers over to Mr. Wilson's office*

right away. □ *He needs it now, so try to get it over as soon as you can.* **2.** to make someone understand something; to succeed in explaining something to someone. □ *I finally got the basic concepts of trigonometry over to him.* □ *He tries to understand what I'm talking about, but I can't get it over.*

get something **past (**someone or something**) 1.** *Lit.* to move something around or ahead of someone or something that is in the way. □ *Let's get the piano past the bump in the floor, then we'll figure out how to move it farther.* □ *See if you can get the ball past their goalie by shooting high.* **2.** *Fig.* to get someone or a group to approve something; to work something through a bureaucracy. □ *Do you think we can get this past the censors?* □ *I will never get this size increase past the board.*

get something **straight** *Fig.* to understand something clearly. □ *Now get this straight. You're going to fail history.* □ *Let me get this straight. I'm supposed to go there in the morning?*

get something **straight from the horse's mouth** *Prov.* to get information from the person most directly involved or best informed. □ *Jill: Sue is going to have a baby. Jane: Who told you that? Jill: I got it straight from the horse's mouth.* □ *There's a rumor that Randolph is moving to Alaska, but I won't believe it until I get it straight from the horse's mouth.*

get something **through** someone's **thick skull** and **get** something **into** someone's **thick head** *Fig.* to manage to get someone, including oneself, to understand something. □ *He can't seem to get it through his thick skull that he has to study to pass the exam.* □ *If I could get this into my thick head once, I'd remember it.*

get something **to** someone to have something delivered or transported to someone. □ *Will you please get this to Joe Wilson today?* □ *I'll try to get it to you by the end of the day.*

get something **together (for a** particular time**)** to arrange a party or other gathering for a certain time. (Fixed order.) □ *I'll try to get a meeting together for Friday afternoon.* □ *I'm sure we can get something together.*

get something **up**† to organize, plan, and assemble something. □ *Let's get a team up and enter the tournament.* □ *I think we can get up a team quite easily.*

get something **wrapped up** Go to sewed up.

get started on something to begin doing something; to take the first steps to do something. □ *When do we get started on this project?* □ *I want to get started on this right away.*

get the ball rolling and **set the ball rolling; start the ball rolling** *Fig.* to get a process started. (See also keep the ball rolling.) □ *If I could just get the ball rolling, then other people would help.* □ *Who else would start the ball rolling?* □ *I had the ball rolling, but no one helped me with the project.*

get the courage up† **(to** do something**)** Go to get enough nerve up† **(to** do something**)**.

get the draw on someone *Fig.* to be faster than one's opponent in a fight. (Alludes originally to an Old West gunfight.) □ *The sheriff got the draw on Arizona Slim and shot him in the arm.* □ *Bill's competitor got the draw on* *him. She was the first one in town to start selling those popular new shoes.*

get the drift of something *Fig.* to understand the general idea of something. □ *I knew enough German to get the drift of this article.* □ *I don't get the drift of what you're trying to tell me.*

get the drop on someone **1.** *Sl.* [for person A] to manage to get a gun aimed at person B before person B can aim back at person A. (The gun is then "dropped" by person B.) □ *Fred got the drop on Wilbur in a flash.* □ *Wilbur was too stoned to get the drop on Fred.* **2.** *Sl.* to succeed in getting an advantage over someone. □ *I guess I got the drop on you because I was early.* □ *I got the drop on almost everybody by sending in my registration by e-mail.*

get the facts straight and **have the facts straight** *Fig.* to have an understanding of the real facts. □ *Ask a lot of questions and get all of your facts straight.* □ *Please be sure you have the facts straight before you make a decision.*

get the final word Go to the last word.

get the gate *Inf.* to be sent away; to be rejected. □ *I thought he liked me, but I got the gate.* □ *I was afraid I'd get the gate, and I was right.*

get the go-by *Inf.* to be ignored or passed by. □ *It was my turn, but I got the go-by.* □ *Tom stood on the road for fifteen minutes trying to get a ride, but all he could get was the go-by.*

get the hell out (of here) *Inf.* to depart as rapidly as possible. □ *Time for us all to get the hell out of here, I think. The cafe is closing now.* □ *He got the hell out before he was fired.*

get the kinks (ironed) out *Fig.* to fix a problem associated with something. □ *The actors had to get the kinks out before they were ready to present the play to an audience.* □ *That'll be a right nice car, when you get the kinks ironed out in the engine.*

get the lead out and **shake the lead out** *Inf.* to hurry; to move faster. (This originally refers to getting lead weights (used in exercise) off so you can move faster.) □ *Come on, you guys. Get the lead out!* □ *If you're going to sell cars, you're going to have to shake the lead out.*

Get the message? and **Get the picture?** *Inf.* Do you understand?; Are you able to figure out what is meant? (See also **(Do you) get my drift?**) □ *Things are tough around here, and we need everyone's cooperation. Get the picture?* □ *We don't need lazy people around here. Get the message?*

Get the picture? Go to Get the message?

get the point (of something**)** to understand the purpose, intention, or central idea of something. □ *I wish he would stop telling jokes and get to the point of his speech.*

get the shaft *Sl.* to be cheated; to be taken advantage of; to be mistreated. (See also **give** someone **the shaft**.) □ *Why do I get the shaft when I did nothing wrong?*

get the show on the road and **get this show on the road** *Fig.* to get (something) started. □ *Let's get started!*

Get the show on the road! □ *Get this show on the road. We don't have all day.*

get the spunk up[†] **(to** do something**)** Go to **get enough nerve up**[†] **(to** do something**)**.

get the word *Fig.* to receive an explanation; to receive the final and authoritative explanation. □ *I'm sorry, I didn't get the word. I didn't know the matter had been settled.* □ *Now that I have gotten the word, I can be more effective in answering questions.*

get the wrinkles out (of something**) 1.** *Lit.* to remove the wrinkles from fabric by ironing or flattening in some way. □ *This has been packed in my suitcase for a week, and I know I'll never be able to get the wrinkles out of it.* **2.** *Fig.* to eliminate some initial, minor problems with an invention, a procedure, a computer program, or a mechanical device. □ *I need more time working with this system to get the wrinkles out.*

get through (something**) 1.** *Lit.* to penetrate something. □ *We couldn't get through the hard concrete with a drill, so we will have to blast.* □ *The hardest drill bit we have couldn't get through.* **2.** *Fig.* to complete something; to manage to finish something. □ *I can't wait till I get through school.* □ *I'll get through college in five years instead of four.* **3.** *Fig.* to survive something; to **go through** something. □ *This is a busy day. I don't know how I'll get through it.* □ *Sally hopes to get through college while still working full-time and being a mother.*

get through (to someone**) 1.** *Lit.* to reach someone; to manage to communicate to someone. □ *I called her on the telephone time after time, but I couldn't get through to her.* □ *I tried every kind of communication, but I couldn't get through.* **2.** *Lit.* to pass through (something) to reach someone. □ *The crowd was so thick that I couldn't get through to him.* □ *I couldn't get through security without taking off my shoes and being searched.* **3.** *Fig.* to make someone understand something; to **get** something **through** someone's **thick skull.** □ *Why don't you try to understand me? What do I have to do to get through to you?* □ *Can anybody get through, or are you just stubborn?*

get through (to something**)** to make contact by radio or telephone with a company, organization, or group. □ *I could not get through to the police because the telephone line was down.* □ *Harry couldn't get through to his office.*

get through (with someone or something**) 1.** to manage to transport someone or something through difficulties or barriers. □ *Customs was a mess, but we got through with all our baggage in only twenty minutes.* □ *I got through with my aged father without any trouble.* **2.** Go to **through with** someone or something.

get to first base (with someone or something**)** and **reach first base (with** someone or something**)** *Fig.* to make a major advance with someone or something. □ *I wish I could get to first base with this business deal.* □ *John adores Sally, but he can't even reach first base with her. She won't even speak to him.*

get to one's **feet** *Fig.* to stand up. □ *On a signal from the teacher, the students got to their feet.* □ *I was so weak, I could hardly get to my feet.*

get to someone **1.** *Lit.* to manage to locate and meet someone; to manage to communicate with someone. (See also get to something.) □ *I got to her on the telephone and told her what to do.* **2.** *Fig.* [for someone or something] to annoy someone. □ *The whole business began to get to me after a while.* □ *Her high-pitched voice got to me after a while.* **3.** *Fig.* [for someone or something] to please or entice someone. □ *Lovely flowers and things like that get to me.* □ *Sad music gets to me and makes me cry.*

get to something 1. *Lit.* to reach something physically. (See also **get to someone.**) □ *I couldn't get to the telephone in time.* □ *I got to him just in time to help him.* **2.** *Fig.* to arrive at a topic of discussion. □ *Money? We will get to that in a minute.* □ *We will get to the question of where your office will be after we discuss whether you are hired or not.* **3.** *Fig.* to start on [doing] something; to begin doing something. □ *I'll get to it as soon as possible.* □ *Have you managed to get to my repair job yet?* □ *Your complaining is getting to bother me.*

get to the bottom of something *Fig.* to get an understanding of the causes of something. □ *We must get to the bottom of this problem immediately.* □ *There is clearly something wrong here, and I want to get to the bottom of it.*

get to the point (of something) *Fig.* to arrive at a discussion or explanation of the purpose of something. □ *Please get to the point of all this.* □ *Will you kindly get to the point?*

get to the top (of something) **1.** *Lit.* to get to the highest point of something. □ *We finally got to the top of the mountain and planted the flag.* □ *We had tried twice before to get to the top.* **2.** *Fig.* to work up to the highest status in something. □ *She got to the top of her field in a very short time.* □ *It takes hard work to get to the top.*

get together (with someone) **(on** someone or something) **1.** and **get together (with** someone) **(about** someone or something) *Lit.* to meet with someone about someone or something. □ *I would like to get together with you on this Wilson matter. What would be a good time for you?* □ *Let's get together on Fred and his department at our next meeting.* **2.** *Fig.* to agree with someone about someone or something. □ *I would like to get together with you on this, but we are still nowhere near agreement.* □ *I want to get together on price with the suppliers.*

get tough (with someone) to become firm with someone; to use physical force against someone. □ *The teacher had to get tough with the class because the students were acting badly.* □ *I've tried nicely to get you to behave, but it looks like I'll have to get tough and really punish you.*

get under someone's **skin** *Fig.* to bother or irritate someone. □ *John is so annoying. He really gets under my skin.* □ *I know he's bothersome, but don't let him get under your skin.*

get under something to get beneath something. □ *The cat came in and got under the sofa where she couldn't be seen.* □ *Why don't you get under the table where Billy won't find you?*

get up to wake up and get out of bed. □ *What time do you usually get up?* □ *I get up when I have to.*

get up a (full) head of steam 1. *Lit.* [for a steam engine] to build steam pressure in order to start operating. □ *It took nearly thirty minutes to get up a full head of steam so that the locomotive could start moving.* **2.** *Fig.* to develop sufficient energy, enthusiasm, commitment, or determination to undertake something. □ *It's nearly noon before I can get up a full head of steam and accomplish something.*

get up a thirst and **work up a thirst** *Fig.* to do something that will make one thirsty. (Fixed order.) □ *Jogging makes me work up a thirst.* □ *Doing this kind of work always gets up a thirst with me.*

get up against someone or something to press close against someone or something. □ *I got up against the wall, out of the way.* □ *The child got up against his father to stay warm.*

get up an appetite *Fig.* to do something to make one very hungry. (Usually in this order.) □ *He can't seem to get up an appetite these days.* □ *Whenever I jog, I really get up an appetite.*

get up (from something) to go to a standing position from a lower position. □ *She got up from the chair and walked to the door.* □ *I don't want to get up from this hammock unless I just have to.*

get up (off (of) something) to rise up and get off something. (*Of* is usually retained before pronouns.) □ *Please get up off the sofa. I have to turn the cushions over.* □ *Get up off of it!*

get up on one's **hind legs** *Fig.* to get angry and assertive. (Alludes to the action of a horse when it is excited or frightened.) □ *She got up on her hind legs and told them all to go to blazes.* □ *She has a tendency to get up on her hind legs and tell people off.*

get up on the wrong side of bed and **get out of the wrong side of bed** *Fig.* to seem grouchy on a particular day. □ *Did you get out of the wrong side of bed this morning? You are a real grouch.*

get up something to manage to climb something. □ *I was so tired I couldn't get up the stairs.* □ *The entire group was able to get up the side of the mountain.*

get up to something **1.** *Lit.* to climb up to something, at a certain height or level. □ *We finally got up to the top.* □ *How long will it take to get up to the tenth floor?* **2.** *Fig.* to arrive as far as something. □ *We got up to the halfway point and stopped.* □ *Will I ever get up to the finish line? I'm so tired of running!*

get well to become healthy again. □ *Ann had a cold for a week, and then she got well.* □ *Hurry up and get well!*

get wet to become moist or soaked with water. □ *Get out of the rain or you'll get wet.* □ *Don't get wet, or you'll catch a cold.*

get wind of something and **catch wind of** something *Fig.* to learn of something; to hear about something. □ *The police got wind of the illegal drug deal.* □ *John caught wind of the gossip being spread about him.*

get with it 1. *Inf.* to modernize one's attitudes and behavior. □ *Get with it, Martin. Go out and buy some new clothes!* □ *You really have to get with it, Ernie.* **2.** *Inf.* to hurry up and get busy; to be more industrious with something. □ *Get with it; we've got a lot to do.* □ *Let's get with it. There's a lot of work to be done.*

get with something to become alert. (Often with *it.*) □ *Hey, stupid. Get with it!* □ *Wake up, Bill. Get with what's going on!*

get with the program *Fig.* follow the rules; do what you are supposed to do. (Implies that there is a clearly known method or "program" that is usually followed.) □ *Come on, Mark. Get with the program. Do what you are told.* □ *Jane just can't seem to get with the program. She has to do everything her way, right or wrong.*

Get your ass over here! and **Get your buns over here!; Get your butt over here!** *Sl.* Get yourself over here, now! □ *Get your butt over here and help me move this trunk.*

Get your buns over here! Go to previous.

Get your head out of the clouds! *Inf.* Stop daydreaming! □ *Get your head out of the clouds and watch where you are driving! You're going to kill us all.*

Get your nose out of my business. Go to Mind your own business.

a **ghost of a chance** even the slightest chance. (Usually negative.) □ *She can't do it. She doesn't have a ghost of a chance.* □ *There is just a ghost of a chance that I'll be there on time.*

giggle at someone or something to snicker or chuckle at someone or something. □ *Are you giggling at me?* □ *Fran giggled at the antics of the clown.*

gild the lily *Fig.* to add ornament or decoration to something that is pleasing in its original state; to attempt to improve something that is already fine the way it is. (Often refers to flattery or exaggeration.) □ *Your house has lovely brickwork. Don't paint it. That would be gilding the lily.* □ *Oh, Sally. You're beautiful the way you are. You don't need makeup. You would be gilding the lily.*

Gimme a break! Go to Give me a break!

gird up one's **loins** *Fig.* to get ready, especially for hard work; to prepare oneself (for something). □ *Well, I guess I had better gird up my loins and go to work.* □ *Somebody has to do something about the problem. Why don't you gird up your loins and do something?*

give a good account of oneself *Fig.* to do (something) well or thoroughly. □ *John gave a good account of himself when he gave his speech last night.* □ *Mary was not feeling well, and she didn't give a good account of herself in last night's game.*

give a little 1. *Lit.* to give a small amount of something, probably money. □ *If everyone will just give a little, we can have enough money to provide a nice Thanksgiving dinner for the needy.* **2.** *Fig.* to move a slight amount. □ *When he pressed on the wall, it gave a little where the water had soaked in.* **3.** *Fig.* to yield a little bit on a point to someone. □ *She is so stubborn. If she would just give a little, she could get more cooperation from other people.*

give an account of someone or something **(to** someone**)** and **give someone an account of** someone or something to tell a narrative about someone or something to someone. □ *You are going to have to give an account of yourself to your parole officer.* □ *Please give an account of your day to my secretary.* □ *Give me an account of every minute.*

give (an) ear to someone or something and **give** one's **ear to** someone or something *Fig.* to listen to someone or to what someone is saying. (Compare this with **get** someone's ear.) □ *I gave an ear to Mary so she could tell me her prob-lems.* □ *She wouldn't give her ear to my story.* □ *He gave ear to the man's request.*

give as good as one **gets** *Fig.* to give as much as one receives; to pay someone back in kind. (Usually in the present tense.) □ *John can take care of himself in a fight. He can give as good as he gets.* □ *Sally usually wins a formal debate. She gives as good as she gets.*

give birth to someone or something **1.** *Lit.* to have a child; [for an animal] to bring forth young. □ *She gave birth to a baby girl.* □ *The cat gave birth to a large number of adorable kittens.* **2.** *Fig.* to bring forth a new idea, an invention, a nation, etc. □ *The company gave birth to a new technology.* □ *The basic idea of participatory democracy gave birth to a new nation.*

give cause for something to serve as a just cause for something; to warrant something. □ *Your comments give cause for further investigation.* □ *I didn't give cause for you to worry so much.*

give chase (to someone or something**)** to chase someone or something. □ *The dogs gave chase to the fox.* □ *A mouse ran by, but the cat was too tired to give chase.*

give credence to someone or something to consider someone or something as believable or trustworthy. □ *How can you give credence to a person like Henry?* □ *I can't give any credence to Donald.* □ *He tells lies. Don't give credence to what he says.* □ *Please don't give credence to that newspaper article.*

Give credit where credit is due. *Prov.* Acknowledge someone's contribution or ability. □ *Jill: Jane, that was a wonderful meal. Jane: I must give credit where credit is due; Alan helped with all of the cooking.* □ *Ellen: Roger is pompous, petty, and immature. I think he's completely worthless. Jane: Now, Ellen, give credit where credit is due; he's also extremely smart.*

give currency to something to spread a story around. (With a negative if there is doubt about what is said.) □ *I can't give any currency to anything Ralph Jones says.* □ *We give no currency to those stories.* □ *His actions gave currency to the rumor that he was about to leave.*

give evidence of something to show signs of something; to give proof of something. □ *You are going to have to give evidence of your good faith in this matter. A nominal deposit would be fine.* □ *She gave evidence of being prepared to go to trial, so we settled the case.*

give forth with something and **give out with** something to say or shout something. □ *The kids in the street gave forth with cries of excitement.* □ *Walter gave out with a loud whoop when he heard the good news.*

give free rein to someone and **give someone free rein** *Fig.* to allow someone to be completely in charge (of something). (Alludes to loosening the reins of a horse and therefore control.) □ *The boss gave the manager free rein with the new project.* □ *The principal gave free rein to Mrs. Brown in her classes.*

give ground 1. *Lit.* to retreat, yielding land or territory. □ *I approached the barking dog, but it wouldn't give ground.* **2.** *Fig.* to "retreat" from an idea or assertion that one has made. □ *When I argue with Mary, she never gives ground.*

Give her the gun. Go to Give it the gun.

give in cave in; to push in. □ *The rotting door gave in when we pushed, and we went inside.* □ *The wall gave in where I kicked it.*

give in (to someone or something**)** to yield to someone or something; to give up to someone or something. □ *He argued and argued and finally gave in to my demands.* □ *I thought he'd never give in.*

Give it a rest! *Inf.* Stop talking so much. Give your mouth a rest. (Familiar or rude. Compare this with **Give me a rest!**) □ *Mary: So, I really think we need to discuss things more and go over all our differences in detail. Bill: Stop! I've heard enough. Give it a rest! Mary: Oh, am I disturbing you?* □ *Tom: Now, I would also like to say something else. Alice: Give it a rest, Tom. We're tired of listening to you.*

Give it all you've got! *Inf.* Do your very best! □ *Go out there and try. Give it all you've got!*

Give it the gun. and **Give her the gun.** *Fig.* to make a motor or engine run faster; to rev up an engine. (The *her* is often pronounced "er.") □ *Bill: How fast will this thing go? Bob: I'll give it the gun and see.* □ *Hurry up, driver. Give 'er the gun. I've got to get there immediately.*

Give it time. Be patient.; In time, things will change. (Usually said to encourage someone to wait or be patient.) □ *Things will get better. Don't worry. Give it time.* □ *Of course, things will improve. Give it time.*

give it to someone **(straight)** to tell something to someone clearly and directly. □ *Come on, give it to me straight. I want to know exactly what happened.* □ *Quit wasting time, and tell me. Give it to me straight.*

Give it up! *Inf.* Stop trying!; You are wasting your time! (Fixed order.) □ *Bob: I just can't understand calculus! Bill: Give it up! Get out of that course and get into something less cruel.* □ *Tom: I'm just not a very good singer, I guess. Sue: It's no good, Tom. Give it up! Tom: Don't you think I'm doing better, though? Sue: Give it up, Tom!*

Give me a break! and **Gimme a break! 1.** *Inf.* Don't be so harsh to me!; Give me another chance! □ *I'm sorry! I'll do better! Give me a break!* □ *I was only late once! Give me a break!* **2.** *Inf.* That is enough, you're bothering me!; Stop it! □ *Do you have to go on and on? Give me a break!* □ *Give me a break, you guys! That's enough of your bickering!* **3.** *Inf.* I don't believe you!; You don't expect anyone to believe that! □ *You say a gorilla is loose in the city? Gimme a break!* □ *Tom said he was late again because the back stairs caved in. His boss said, "Gimme a break!"*

Give me a call. and **Give me a ring.** Please call me (later) on the telephone. □ *Mary: See you later, Fred. Fred: Give me a call if you get a chance.* □ *"When you're in town again, Sue, give me a call," said John.* □ *Bob: When should we talk about this again? Bill: Next week is soon enough. Give me a ring.*

Give me a chance! 1. Please give me an opportunity to do something! □ *Mary: I just know I can do it. Oh, please give me a chance! Sue: All right. Just one more chance.* □ *Bob: Do you think you can do it? Jane: Oh, I know I can. Just give me a chance!* **2.** Please give me a fair chance and enough time to complete the task. □ *Alice: Come on! I need more time to finish the test. Give me a chance! Teacher: Would another ten minutes help?* □ *Bob: You missed that one! Bill: You moved it! There was no way I could hit it. Give me a chance! Hold it still!*

Give me a rest! *Inf.* Stop being such a pest!; Stop bothering me with this problem! (Compare this with **Give it a rest!**) □ *"Go away and stop bothering me!" moaned Bob. "Give me a rest!"* □ *Bob: I need an answer to this right away! Bill: I just gave you an answer! Bob: That was something different. This is a new question. Bill: Give me a rest! Can't it wait?*

Give me a ring. Go to Give me a call.

Give me five! and **Give me (some) skin!; Skin me!; Slip me five!; Slip me some skin!** *Sl.* Slap my hand! (As a greeting or to show joy, etc.) □ *"Yo, Tom! Give me five!" shouted Henry, raising his hand.* □ *Bob: Hey, man! Skin me! Bill: How you doing, Bob?*

Give my best to someone. and **All the best to** someone. Please convey my good wishes to a particular person. (The *someone* can be a person's name or a pronoun. See also **Say hello to** someone **(for me).**) □ *Alice: Good-bye, Fred. Give my best to your mother. Fred: Sure, Alice. Good-bye.* □ *Tom: See you, Bob. Bob: Give my best to Jane. Tom: I sure will. Bye.* □ *Bill: Bye, Rachel. All the best to your family. Rachel: Thanks. Bye.*

give of oneself to be generous with one's time and concern. □ *Tom is very good with children because he gives of himself.* □ *If you want to have more friends, you have to learn to give of yourself.*

give one one's **freedom** to set someone free; to divorce someone. □ *Mrs. Brown wanted to give her husband his freedom.* □ *Well, Tom, I hate to break it to you this way, but I have decided to give you your freedom.*

give one's **best** Go to give something one's **best shot.**

give one's **eyeteeth (for** someone or something**)** Go to **give** one's **right arm (for** someone or something**).**

give (one's**) notice** to formally tell one's employer that one is quitting one's job. □ *Did you hear that James is leaving? He gave his notice yesterday.* □ *Lisa gave notice today. She got a job offer from another company.*

give one's **right arm (for** someone or something**)** and **give** one's **eyeteeth (for** someone or something**)** *Fig.* to be willing to give something of great value for someone or something. □ *I'd give my right arm for a nice cool drink.* □ *I'd give my eyeteeth to be there.*

give oneself **airs** Go to **put on airs.**

give oneself **over to** someone or something **1.** *Lit.* to surrender to someone or something. □ *He went to the station and gave himself over to the police.* □ *Max gave himself over to the officer.* **2.** *Fig.* to devote oneself to someone or something. □ *Laurie gave herself over to her work and soon forgot her pain.* □ *David gave himself over to the religious order.*

give oneself **up (to** someone or something**) 1.** *Lit.* to surrender to someone or something. □ *Fran gave herself up to the disease.* □ *Walter gave himself up to the police.* **2.** *Fig.* to devote oneself to someone or something; to **give** oneself **over to** someone or something. □ *She gave herself up to her children and their care.* □ *Fran gave herself up to tennis.* □ *Jane refused to give herself up to weight lifting, which is a full-time hobby.*

give out 1. to wear out and stop; to quit operating. □ *My old bicycle finally gave out.* □ *I think that your shoes are about ready to give out.* **2.** to be depleted. □ *The paper napkins gave out, and we had to use paper towels.* □ *The eggs gave out, and we had to eat cereal for breakfast for the rest of the camping trip.*

give (out) with something **1.** *Inf.* to give out information. □ *Come on, give out with the facts, man.* □ *Give with the info. We're in a hurry.* **2.** Go to **give forth with** something.

give rise to something to cause something; to instigate something. □ *The attack gave rise to endless arguments.* □ *Her ludicrous living gave rise to further speculation as to the source of her money.*

give some thought to something to think about something; to devote some time to thinking about something. □ *After I have had time to give some thought to the matter, I will call you.*

give someone **a bang** and **give** someone **a charge; give** someone **a kick** *Fig. Inf.* to give someone a bit of excitement. □ *John always gives me a bang.* □ *The whole afternoon, with all its silliness, gave me a charge anyway.*

give someone **a blank check** and **give a blank check to** someone **1.** *Lit.* to give someone a signed check that lacks only the amount or payment which can be filled in by anyone. □ *Sally sent a blank check to school with Billy to pay for his books.* **2.** *Fig.* to give someone freedom or permission to act as one wishes or thinks necessary. (See also **carte blanche.**) □ *He's been given a blank check with regard to reorganizing the workforce.* □ *The manager has been given no instructions about how to train the staff. The owner just gave him a blank check.* □ *Jean gave the decorator a blank check and said she wanted the whole house done.*

give someone **a blank look** and **give** someone **a blank stare** to look back at someone with a neutral look on one's face. □ *After I told her to stop smoking, she just gave me a blank look and kept puffing.*

give someone **a blank stare** Go to previous.

give someone **a buzz** Go to **give** someone **a ring.**

give someone **a call** Go to **give** someone **a ring.**

give someone **a charge** Go to **give** someone **a bang.**

give someone **a crack at** something Go to a **try at** something.

give someone **a dig** *Sl.* to insult someone; to say something which will irritate a person. □ *Jane gave Bob a dig about his carelessness with money.* □ *The headmaster's daughter gets tired of people giving her digs about favoritism.*

give someone **a (good) bawling out** to bawl someone out; to chastise someone. □ *When the teacher caught Billie, he gave him a good bawling out.*

give someone **a kick** Go to **give** someone **a bang.**

give someone **a lift 1.** and **give** someone **a ride** *Fig.* to provide transportation for someone. □ *I've got to get into town. Can you give me a lift?* **2.** *Fig.* to raise someone's spirits; to make a person feel better. □ *It was a good conversation, and her kind words really gave me a lift.*

give someone **a line** and **feed** someone **a line** to lead someone on; to deceive someone with false talk. □ *Don't*

pay any attention to John. He gives everybody a line. □ *He's always feeding us a line.*

give someone **a pain** *Fig.* to annoy or bother someone. □ *Please don't give me a pain. I've had a hard day.* □ *You give me a pain!* □ *She's such a pest. She really gives me a pain.*

give someone **a pat on the back** Go to **pat** someone **on the back.**

give someone **a piece of** one's **mind** *Fig.* to bawl someone out; to **tell** someone **off.** □ *I've had enough from John. I'm going to give him a piece of my mind.* □ *Sally, stop it, or I'll give you a piece of my mind.*

give someone **a red face** *Fig.* to make someone visibly embarrassed. □ *We really gave him a red face when we caught him eavesdropping.* □ *His error gave him a very red face.*

give someone **a ride** Go to **give** someone **a lift.**

give someone **a ring** and **give** someone **a buzz; give** someone **a call** *Fig.* to call someone on the telephone. □ *Nice talking to you. Give me a ring sometime.* □ *Give me a buzz when you're in town.*

give someone **a whack at** something Go to a **try at** something.

Give someone **an inch and** he'll **take a mile.** and **Give** someone **an inch and** he'll **take a yard.** *Prov.* Be generous to someone and the person will demand even more. (Describes someone who will take advantage of you if you are even a little kind to him or her.) □ *If you let Mark borrow your tools for this weekend, he'll wind up keeping them for years. Give him an inch and he'll take a mile.*

Give someone **an inch and** he'll **take a yard.** Go to previous.

give someone **away (to** someone**) 1.** *Fig.* [for the bride's father] to give the bride away to the groom. (Customarily done just prior to the actual marriage ceremony.) □ *Mr. Franklin gave Amy away to Terry just as he had done in the rehearsal.* □ *He was reluctant to give his daughter away.* **2.** *Fig.* to reveal something secret about someone to someone else. □ *Please don't give me away. I don't want anyone to know my plans.* □ *Alice did everything she could to keep from giving herself away.*

Give someone **enough rope and** he'll **hang** himself. *Prov.* If you give someone that you suspect of bad behavior the freedom to behave badly, eventually he or she will be caught and punished. □ *Jill: I think Matilda's been stealing things out of my desk. Should I tell the boss? Jane: No; give her enough rope and she'll hang herself. One of these days she'll steal something important, the boss will find out for himself, and he'll fire her.*

give someone **Hail Columbia** *Inf.* to scold someone severely. □ *The teacher gave her students Hail Columbia over their poor test scores.* □ *If Miss Ellen finds out I broke her window, she'll give me Hail Columbia for sure!*

give someone **no quarter** Go to **grant** someone **no quarter.**

give someone **odds that...** to propose a sham bet to someone, the implication being that even at favorable odds the outcome will defy the odds. (Often with a negative.) □ *I'll give you odds that you won't be able to order a decent steak at this restaurant.*

give someone or something **a wide berth** *Fig.* to keep a reasonable distance from someone or something; to **steer clear (of** someone or something**).** (Originally referred to sailing ships.) □ *The dog we are approaching is very mean. Better give it a wide berth.* □ *Give Mary a wide berth. She's in a very bad mood.*

give someone or something **away**† to reveal a secret about someone or something. □ *I thought no one knew where I was, but my loud breathing gave me away.* □ *We know that Billy ate the cherry pie. The cherry juice on his shirt gave him away.* □ *I had planned a surprise, but John gave away my secret.*

give someone or something **back**† **(to** someone or something**)** to return someone or something to someone or something. □ *Please give it back to me.* □ *You took my lunch away from me. You had better give it back.* □ *Give back the book right now!*

give someone or something **up**† **(for lost)** to abandon someone or something as being lost; to quit looking for someone or something that is lost. □ *After a week we had given the cat up for lost when suddenly she appeared.* □ *We gave up the cat for lost.*

give someone or something **up**† **(to** someone**)** to hand someone or something over to someone; to relinquish claims on someone or something in favor of someone else. □ *We had to give the money we found up to the police.* □ *We gave up the money to the police.*

give someone **pause (for thought)** *Fig.* to cause someone to stop and think. □ *When I see a golden sunrise, it gives me pause for thought.* □ *Witnessing an accident is likely to give all of us pause.*

give someone **some lip** *Inf.* to speak rudely or disrespectfully to someone; to sass someone. □ *Billy gave me some lip, so I whupped him.* □ *Jane is always giving the teacher some lip.*

give someone **some skin** *Sl.* [for two people] to touch two hands together in a special greeting, like a handshake. (One hand may be slapped down on top of the other, or they may be slapped together palm to palm with the arms held vertically. Usually said as a command.) □ *Hey, Bob, give me some skin!* □ *Come over here, you guys. I want you to meet my brother and give him some skin!*

give someone **some sugar** *Rur.* to give someone a kiss. □ *Come here, honey, and give me some sugar.* □ *"Give me some sugar!" Grandma said when she saw me.*

give someone **static** *Fig.* to argue with someone; to give someone back talk. □ *I want you to do it and do it now! Don't give me any static!*

give someone **the eye** *Fig.* to look at someone in a way that communicates romantic interest. □ *Ann gave John the eye. It really surprised him.* □ *Tom kept giving Sally the eye. She finally got disgusted and left.*

give someone **the finger 1.** *Fig.* to display the middle finger upright as a sign of derision. (The gesture is derisive and offensive. See also **flip** someone **off, flip** someone **the bird.**) □ *Did one of you guys give Ted the finger?* □ *Somebody gave the cop the finger.* **2.** *Fig. Inf.* to mistreat someone; to insult someone. □ *You've been giving me the finger ever since I started working here. What's wrong?* □ *I'm*

tired of everybody giving me the finger around here just because I'm new.

give someone **the gate** *Sl.* to get rid of someone. □ *The chick was a pest, so I gave her the gate.* □ *He threatened to give me the gate, so I left.*

give someone **the go-by** to bypass someone; to ignore someone. □ *Gert gave us all the go-by when she took up with that rich boyfriend.* □ *I didn't mean to give you the go-by. I'm preoccupied, that's all.*

give someone **the raspberry** *Inf.* to make a rude noise with the lips at someone. □ *The audience gave him the raspberry, which gave him some second thoughts about his choice of career.* □ *Even after his grandstand play, they gave him the raspberry.*

give someone **the shaft** *Sl.* to cheat or deceive someone; to mistreat someone. (See also **get the shaft.**) □ *The boss really gave Wally the shaft.* □ *Somebody always gives me the shaft.*

give someone **the shirt off** one's **back** *Fig.* to give anything that is asked for, no matter the sacrifice required. □ *Tom would give any of his old army buddies the shirt off his back.* □ *You can always count on Mark when you're in trouble; he'd give you the shirt off his back.*

give someone **the slip** *Sl.* to escape from a pursuer. □ *We were on his tail until he gave us the slip.* □ *I can give her the slip in no time at all.*

give someone **tit for tat** *Fig.* to give someone something equal to what was given you; to exchange a series of very similar things, one by one, with someone. □ *They gave me the same kind of difficulty that I gave them. They gave me tit for tat.* □ *He punched me, so I punched him. Every time he hit me, I hit him. I just gave him tit for tat.*

give someone **to understand** something to explain something to someone; to imply something to someone. (Possibly misleading someone, accidentally or intentionally. See also **given to understand.**) □ *Mr. Smith gave Sally to understand that she should be home by midnight.* □ *The mayor gave the citizens to understand that there would be no tax increase. He didn't promise, though.*

give someone **up**† **for dead 1.** *Lit.* to give up hope for someone who is dying; to abandon a dying person as already dead. □ *The cowboys gave up the poor old man for dead and rode off.* □ *We gave up the poor old man for dead and went to telephone the police.* **2.** *Fig.* to abandon hope for someone to appear or arrive. □ *We were delighted to see you. We had almost given you up for dead.* □ *After an hour, they gave up their guest for dead.*

give something **a go** Go to **give** something **a try.**

give something **a shot** Go to next.

give something **a try** and **give** something **a go; give** something **a whirl; give** something **a shot** to make a try at something. □ *Why don't you give it a go and see if you like it?*

give something **a whirl** Go to previous.

give something **away**† **(to** someone**) 1.** to donate to, or bestow something upon, someone. □ *I gave the old clothing away to Tom.* □ *I gave away my coat to Tom.* **2.** to tell a secret to someone. □ *Please don't give the surprise away to anyone.* □ *Don't give away my secret.* **3.** to reveal the answer to a question, riddle, or problem to someone. □ *Don't give the answer away to them!* □ *Don't give away the answer!*

give something **back†** (**to** someone) (**with interest**) **1.** *Lit.* to return money to someone with an additional amount for interest. □ *You are going to have to give that money back to me with interest.* □ *Please give back the proper amount...with interest!* **2.** *Fig.* to return something to someone in excess of what was received. □ *We will give back all your kindness to you with interest.* □ *We will give it all back with interest.*

give something **for** something to exchange something for something. □ *I will give two brownies for that piece of cake in your lunch box.* □ *Jed gave two pigs for an old motorcycle.*

give something **off†** to release something, such as smoke, a noise, an odor, fragrance, etc. □ *The little animal gave a foul smell off.* □ *The flower gave off its heavy perfume at dusk.*

give something one's **best shot** and **give** one's **best** *Fig.* to give a task one's best effort. □ *I gave the project my best shot.* □ *Sure, try it. Give it your best!*

give something **out†** **1.** *Lit.* to distribute something; to pass something out. □ *The teacher gave the test papers out.* □ *The teacher gave out the papers.* **2.** *Fig.* to make something known to the public. □ *When will you give the announcement out?* □ *The president gave out the news that the hostages had been released.*

give something **over (to** someone or something**)** to hand something over to someone or something. □ *Please give the money over to Sherri, who handles the accounts.* □ *She is waiting at the front office. Just go there and give it over.*

give something **to** someone to bestow something, such as a gift, on someone. □ *Please give this to Sally Wilson.* □ *Who gave this book to me? I want to thank whoever it was.*

give something **under (the) threat of** something to give something only because one is threatened. □ *He gave the money under threat of exposure. I think that is blackmail.* □ *You are asked to give your testimony under the threat of being jailed if you don't.*

give something **up†** **1.** to forsake something; to stop using or eating something. □ *I gave coffee up because of the caffeine.* □ *They advised me to give up sugar in all forms.* **2.** to quit doing something. □ *Oh, give it up! You're not getting anywhere.* □ *You should give up smoking.*

give teeth to something and **put teeth in(to)** something *Fig.* to make something powerful; to give something a real effect. □ *The severe penalty really gives teeth to the law.* □ *Strong enforcement puts teeth in the regulation.*

give the bride away Go to **give** someone **away (to** someone**)**.

give the devil her due Go to next.

give the devil his due and **give the devil her due** *Fig.* to give your foe proper credit (for something). (This usually refers to a person who has been evil—like the devil.) □ *She's very messy in the kitchen, but I have to give the devil her due. She bakes a terrific cherry pie.* □ *John is a bit too nosy, but he keeps his yard clean and is a kind neighbor. I'll give the devil his due.*

give the game away *Fig.* to reveal a plan or strategy. □ *Now, all of you have to keep quiet. Please don't give the game away.* □ *If you keep giving out hints, you'll give the game away.*

give the lie to something *Fig.* to show that something is a lie. □ *The evidence gives the lie to your testimony.* □ *Your own admission of your part in the conspiracy gives the lie to your earlier testimony.*

give up to quit; to quit trying. □ *I give up! I won't press this further.* □ *Are you going to give up or keep fighting?*

give up (all) hope to stop hoping for something. (Fixed order.) □ *Don't give up hope. There's always a chance.* □ *We had given up all hope when a miracle happened.*

give up (on someone or something**)** to give up trying to do something with someone or something, such as being friendly, giving advice, managing, etc. □ *I gave up on jogging. My knees went bad.* □ *Gloria tried to be friendly with Kelly, but finally gave up.*

give up the fight and **give up the struggle** **1.** *Lit.* to quit fighting; to stop trying to do something. □ *Don't give up the fight. Keep trying.* □ *Mary refused to give up the struggle.* **2.** *Fig.* to give up and die. □ *At the end of months of pain, she gave up the fight.* □ *In the end, he lost interest in life and just gave up the struggle.*

give up the ghost *Euph.* to die. (Fixed order. Often used to describe machines breaking down.) □ *The old man gave up the ghost.* □ *My poor old car finally gave up the ghost.*

give up the struggle Go to **give up the fight**.

Give us the tools, and we will finish the job. *Prov.* A reply to someone who wants you to do a task for which you lack the equipment. □ *How am I supposed to wash the upstairs windows without a ladder? Give us the tools, and we will finish the job!*

give vent to something *Fig.* to express anger. (The *something* is usually anger, ire, irritation, etc.) □ *John gave vent to his anger by yelling at Sally.* □ *Bill couldn't give vent to his frustration because he had been warned to keep quiet.*

give voice to something *Fig.* to express a feeling or an opinion in words; to speak out about something. □ *The bird gave voice to its joy in the golden sunshine.* □ *The protestors gave voice to their anger at Congress.*

give way to someone or something to yield to someone or something; to give preference to someone or something. □ *The cars gave way to the pedestrians.* □ *The motorboats have to give way to the sailboats.*

give weight to something *Fig.* to attach importance to something. □ *I give a lot of weight to your opinion.* □ *Kelly gave no weight at all to the comments by Betty.*

give with something *Inf.* to give something to someone; to tell something to someone. □ *Come on! Give with the money!* □ *You had better give with the information if you know what's good for you.*

given to doing something likely to do something; inclined to do something habitually. □ *Mary is given to singing in the shower.* □ *Bob is given to shouting when things don't go his way.*

given to understand [of someone] made to believe [something]. (See also **give** someone **to understand.**) □ *They were given to understand that there would be no tax* increase, but after the election taxes went up. □ *She was given to understand that she had to be home by midnight.*

*the **glad hand** *Fig.* an overly friendly welcome; a symbol of insincere attention. (*Typically: **get** ~; **give** someone ~.) □ *Whenever I go into that store, I get the glad hand.* □ *I hate to go to a party and get the glad hand.*

glance around (some place) to look quickly around some place. □ *He glanced around the room, looking for his favorite cap.* □ *Mary glanced around, looking for her friend.*

glance at someone or something to look quickly at someone or something. □ *Sharon glanced at Todd to see if he looked as if he was ready to go.* □ *I glanced at my watch and realized how long all this had taken.*

glance back (at someone) **1.** to look quickly at someone who is looking at you. □ *He glanced back at Mary, so he could remember her smile.* □ *She hoped he would notice her but he never even glanced back.* **2.** to look quickly at someone who is behind you. □ *Dan glanced back at the man chasing him and ran on even faster.* □ *He glanced back and ran faster.*

glance down (at something) to look quickly downward at something. □ *Sherri glanced down at her watch and then pressed on the accelerator.* □ *She glanced down and hurried off.*

glance off (someone or something) to bounce off someone or something. □ *The bullet glanced off the huge boulder.* □ *The baseball glanced off of Tom and left a bruise on his side where it had touched.*

glance over someone or something to examine someone or something very quickly. □ *I only glanced over the papers. They look okay to me.* □ *The doctor glanced over the injured woman and called for an ambulance.*

glance through something to look quickly at the contents of something. □ *I glanced through the manuscript, and I don't think it is ready yet.* □ *Would you glance through this report when you have a moment?*

glare at someone or something to scowl at someone or something. □ *Don't glare at me!* □ *I glared at the cat and thought mean thoughts.*

glare down on someone or something **1.** [for someone] to scowl down at someone or something. □ *The judge glared down on the accused.* □ *I glared down on the cat, which ignored me, as usual.* **2.** [for the sun] to burn down brightly on someone or something. □ *The sun glared down on the beach and made the sand hot to the touch.* □ *The bright sun glared down on the desert rocks.*

glass something **in**† to enclose something, such as a porch, in glass. □ *I want to glass this porch in, so we can use it in the winter.* □ *We glassed in our porch last year.*

glaze over 1. *Lit.* [for something] to be covered over with a coat of something cloudy or ice. □ *The roads glazed over and became very dangerous.* □ *The street is glazed over badly.* **2.** *Fig.* [for one's eyes] to assume a dull, bored appearance, signifying an inability to concentrate or a lack of sleep. □ *My eyes glaze over when I hear all those statistics.*

gleam with something to sparkle or shine with something. □ *The crystal goblets gleamed with the sparkling candlelight.* □ *The glass gleamed with a bright reflection.*

glean something **from** something **1.** *Lit.* to gather the leftovers of something from something; to gather the ears of grain left in a field after a harvest. □ *The poor people gleaned their entire living from what was left in the fields.* □ *We will have to go out and glean something from the fields.* **2.** and **glean something from** someone *Fig.* to figure something out from bits of gossip. □ *I was able to glean some important news from Tommy.* □ *Tell me the news you gleaned from the people in town.*

glide across something to float or slide across something. □ *The skaters glided across the frozen expanse of the river.* □ *The small plane glided across the sky.*

glide away (from someone or something) to slide or float away from someone or something. □ *The skaters glided away from the center of the rink.* □ *The canoes glided away from the judge who had started off the canoe race.*

glint with something to sparkle or shine with something. □ *Her bright eyes glinted with the sunlight.* □ *The crystal goblet glinted with the orange firelight.*

glisten with something to sparkle or shimmer with something. □ *The trees glistened with a thin coating of ice from the freezing rain.* □ *Fran's eyes glistened with a few tears.*

glitter with something **1.** to sparkle with something. □ *Her earrings glittered with many tiny diamonds.* □ *The tree glittered with tiny ice crystals.* **2.** [for eyes] to shine with a strong emotion. □ *Her eyes glittered with anger.* □ *The eyes of the great beast glittered with ravenous hunger.*

gloat over something to rejoice smugly over something; to be glad that something unfortunate has happened to someone else. □ *He gloated over his good luck in a way that made all of us angry.* □ *Please don't gloat over my misfortune.*

Glory be! *Inf.* an exclamation expressing surprise or shock. (A bit old-fashioned.) □ *Mary: Glory be! Is that what I think it is? Sue: Well, it's a kitten, if that's what you thought.* □ *Sally: First a car just missed hitting her, then she fell down on the ice. Mary: Glory be!*

glory in something *Fig.* to take great pleasure in something; to revel in something. □ *He just glories in all the attention he is getting.* □ *Martha tends to glory in doing things just exactly right.*

gloss over something to cover up, minimize, or play down something bad. □ *Don't gloss over your own role in this fiasco!* □ *I don't want to gloss this matter over, but it really isn't very important, is it?*

The **gloves are off.** *Fig.* There is going to be a serious dispute. (As if boxers had removed their gloves in order to inflict more damage. See also **take the gloves off.**) □ *Bob got mad and yelled, "Ok, the gloves are off!" and started cussing and pounding the table.*

glow with something **1.** *Lit.* [for something] to put out light, usually because of high heat. □ *The embers glowed with the remains of the fire.* □ *The last of the coals still glowed with fire.* **2.** *Fig.* [for someone's face, eyes, etc.] to display some quality, such as pride, pleasure, rage, health. □ *Her healthy face glowed with pride.* □ *Her eyes glowed with a towering rage.*

glower at someone or something to scowl intently at someone or something. □ *The judge glowered at the irate wit-*

ness until order was restored. □ *Fred glowered at the painting of his uncle, hating the subject of the picture.*

glue something **down†** to fix something down onto something with cement. □ *Glue the edge of the rug down before someone trips over it.* □ *You should glue down the rug.*

glue something **on(to)** something and **glue** something **to** something; **glue** something **on†** to attach something to something else with cement. □ *Please glue the binding onto this book. Someone pulled it off.* □ *Please glue on the binding.*

glue something **together†** to attach the pieces of something together with glue. □ *She glued the pieces of the model plane together.* □ *She glued together all the loose pieces.*

glued to someone or something *Fig.* following someone everywhere; very close to or touching something. □ *His little sister was glued to him all afternoon. Finally he sent her home.*

a **glut on the market** Go to a drug on the market.

glut someone or something **with** something to overfill someone or something with something. □ *The hungry lions glutted themselves with the meat of their recent kill.* □ *Sally would glut herself with doughnuts, given the chance.*

a **glutton for punishment** *Fig.* someone who is eager for a burden or some sort of difficulty; someone willing to accept a difficult task. □ *Tom works too hard. He is a glutton for punishment.* □ *I enjoy managing difficult projects, but I am a glutton for punishment.*

gnash one's **teeth** *Fig.* to grind or bite noisily with one's teeth. □ *Bill clenched his fists and gnashed his teeth in anger.* □ *The wolf gnashed its teeth and chased after the deer.*

a **gnashing of teeth** *Fig.* a show of anger or dismay. (Biblical: "weeping, wailing, and gnashing of teeth.") □ *After a little gnashing of teeth and a few threats, the boss calmed down and become almost reasonable.*

gnaw (away) at someone *Fig.* to worry someone; to create constant anxiety in someone. □ *The thought of catching some horrible disease gnawed away at her.* □ *A lot of guilt gnawed at him day and night.*

gnaw (away) at someone or something *Lit.* to chew at someone or something. □ *I hear a mouse gnawing away at the wall.* □ *The mosquitoes are gnawing at me something awful.*

gnaw on something to chew on something. (Usually said of an animal.) □ *The puppy has been gnawing on my slippers!* □ *This slipper has been gnawed on!*

go a long way toward doing something and **go a long way in** doing something *Fig.* almost to satisfy specific conditions; to be almost right. □ *This machine goes a long way toward meeting our needs.* □ *Your plan went a long way in helping us with our problem.*

go a mile a minute Go to a mile a minute.

go aboard Go to come aboard.

go about and **go around 1.** [for a rumor] to go from person to person. □ *What is this story about you that I hear going about?* □ *There was a nasty rumor about Gerald going around.* **2.** [for a disease] to spread. □ *There is a lot of* this flu going about these days. □ *There is a bad cough going around.* **3.** Go to go around someone or something.

go about one's **business** Go to about one's business.

go about something to approach the doing of something in a particular way. □ *How should I go about researching this topic?* □ *Would you tell me how to go about it?*

go about with someone or something and **go around with** someone or something to go around in the company of someone or something. □ *I always go about with my friends.* □ *Fran has been going around with James.*

go above and beyond one's **duty** and **go above and beyond the call of duty** *Fig.* to exceed what is required of one. □ *Doing what you ask goes above and beyond my duty.* □ *My job requires me to go above and beyond the call of duty almost every day.*

go above and beyond (something**)** Go to above and beyond (something).

go above and beyond the call of duty Go to go above and beyond one's duty.

go above someone Go to above someone.

go above someone or something to travel over someone or something. □ *The model airplane swooped low right at us but went above us at the last minute.*

go absent without leave Go to absent without leave.

go across (something**)** to cross something, such as water, a bridge, land, the ocean, etc. □ *We went across the ocean in just three hours.* □ *How long did it take you to go across?*

go across something **to** someone or something to cross something to someone, something, or some place on the other side. □ *We went across the bridge to the island.* □ *We came upon a little footbridge and went across to the other side.* □ *Timmy went across the street to his mother.*

go after someone to investigate someone or something for possible criminal prosecution. □ *The prosecutor went after Max first, knowing that Max was the gang leader.* □ *The police detectives went after the whole gang.*

go after someone, something, or an animal **1.** *Lit.* to pursue someone, something, or an animal. (See also go after someone.) □ *The dogs went after the burglar.* □ *I went after the gang that took my wallet.* **2.** *Fig.* to charge or attack someone or an animal. □ *The bear went after the hunters and scared them off.* □ *Then the bear went after the hunting dogs and killed two.*

go against someone or something Go to against someone or something.

go against the grain Go to against the grain.

Go ahead. Please do it.; You have my permission and encouragement to do it. □ *Alice: I'm leaving. John: Go ahead. See if I care.* □ *Jane: Can I put this one in the refrigerator? Sue: Sure. Go ahead.*

(Go ahead,) make my day! 1. Just try to do me harm or disobey me. I will enjoy punishing you. (From a phrase said in a movie where the person saying the phrase is holding a gun on a villain and would really like the villain to do something that would justify firing the gun. Compare this with **Keep it up!**) □ *The crook reached into his jacket for his wallet. The cop, thinking the crook was about to draw a gun, said, "Go ahead, make my day!"* □ *As Bill pulled back*

G

his clenched fist to strike Tom, who is much bigger and stronger than Bill, Tom said, "Make my day!" **2.** Go ahead, ruin my day!; Go ahead, give me the bad news. (A sarcastic version of ①.) □ Tom (standing in the doorway): Hello, I'm with the Internal Revenue Service. Could I come in? Mary: Go ahead, make my day! □ Sally: I've got some bad news for you. John: Go ahead, make my day!

go ahead (of someone or something) to get in front of and proceed someone or something. □ Please let me go ahead of you. □ The car carrying the parade marshall went ahead of the others.

go ahead (with something) 1. to continue with something; to continue with plans to do something. □ Can we go ahead with our party plans? □ Let's go ahead with it. **2.** to carry something ahead. □ Please go ahead with the baggage. I will meet you at the ticket counter. □ Will you please go ahead with the cake? I will bring the ice cream in a minute.

go all out (for someone or something) to do everything possible for someone or something. □ We went all out for George and threw a big party on his return. □ We went all out and it was not appreciated at all.

go all the way (with someone) and **go to bed (with someone)** Euph. to have sexual intercourse with someone. □ If you go all the way, you stand a chance of getting pregnant. □ I've heard that they go to bed all the time.

go along 1. to continue; to progress. □ Things are going along quite nicely in my new job. □ I hope everything is going along well. **2.** to accompany [someone]. □ Can I go along? □ If you're going to the party, can I go along?

go along (with someone) for the ride 1. Lit. to accompany someone just to be taking a ride. □ Why don't you go along with us for the ride? □ I am going to the store. Do you want to go along for the ride? **2.** Fig. to accompany someone, whether or not riding. □ I'll just go along for the ride to the beach. I don't want to bask in the sun all day. □ He wasn't actually invited to the party. He just went along for the ride.

go along with someone or something 1. Lit. to travel along with someone or something. □ Dorothy went along with the scarecrow for a while until they met a lion. **2.** Fig. to agree with someone or agree to something. □ I will go along with you on that matter. □ I will go along with Sharon's decision, of course. **3.** Fig. to consent on the choice of someone or something. □ I go along with Jane. Tom would be a good treasurer. □ Sharon will probably go along with chocolate. Everyone likes chocolate! **4.** Fig. to play along with someone or something; to pretend that you are party to someone's scheme. □ I went along with the gag for a while.

go ape (over someone or something) Sl. to become very excited over something. □ I just go ape over chocolate. □ Sam went ape over Mary.

go arm in arm Go to arm in arm.

go around Go to go about.

go around doing something to move around doing something. □ She keeps going around telling lies about me. □ Please stop going around knocking things over. □ She goes around helping whomever she can.

go (a)round in circles 1. Lit. to move over and over on a circular path. □ The model plane went around in circles until it ran out of fuel. □ The oxen went around in circles, pulling along a beam that was connected to the millstone. **2.** Fig. to act in a confused and disoriented manner. □ I've been going around in circles all day. □ The children have been going around in circles, waiting for you to arrive. **3.** Fig. to keep going over the same ideas or repeating the same actions, often resulting in confusion, without reaching a satisfactory decision or conclusion. □ We're just going round in circles discussing the problem. We need to consult someone else to get a new point of view. □ Fred's trying to find out what's happened but he's going round in circles. No one will tell him anything useful.

go around someone 1. Lit. to walk or travel in such a way as to avoid hitting or touching someone. □ I can't move from this place right now. You'll have to go around me. **2.** Idiomatic to avoid dealing with someone. □ I try to go around Steve. He can be very difficult. □ We will want to go around the boss. He will say no if asked.

go (a)round the bend Go to (a)round the bend.

go around (with someone) Go to hang around (with someone).

go around with someone or something Go to go about with someone or something.

go as someone or something to pretend to be someone or a type of person. □ There's a costume party this weekend. I'm going as Santa Claus. □ My husband and I are going as a king and queen.

go astray 1. Lit. to wander off the road or path. □ Stick to the path and try not to go astray. □ I couldn't see the trail and I almost went astray. **2.** Fig. [for something] to get lost or misplaced. □ My glasses have gone astray again. □ Mary's book went astray or maybe it was stolen. **3.** Fig. to turn bad or wander from the way of goodness; to make an error. □ I'm afraid your son has gone astray and gotten into a bit of trouble. □ I went astray with the computer program at this point.

go at a fast clip Go to at a fast clip.

go at a good clip Go to at a good clip.

go at it hammer and tongs Go to hammer and tongs.

go at it tooth and nail Go to fight someone or something hammer and tongs.

go at one another tooth and nail Fig. to fight one another like animals. (One another can also be each other.) □ The man and his wife went at one another tooth and nail. □ The children would go at one another tooth and nail almost every evening.

a **go at someone** Go to a **try at** someone.

go at someone or something to attack someone or something; to move or lunge toward someone or something. □ The dog went at the visitor and almost bit him. □ He went at the door and tried to break it down.

a **go at something** Go to a **try at** something.

go at something like a boy killing snakes Rur. to do something with a great deal of energy. □ Once Mary decided to take that test, she went at her books like a boy killing snakes. □ I hired Joe to weed my garden, and he went at it like a boy killing snakes.

Go away! Leave me!; Get away from me! □ *Mary: You're such a pest, Sue. Go away! Sue: I was just trying to help.* □ *"Go away!" yelled the child at the bee.*

go away empty-handed *Fig.* to depart with nothing. □ *I hate for you to go away empty-handed, but I cannot afford to contribute any money.* □ *They came hoping for some food, but they had to go away empty-handed.*

go away (for something**) 1.** to leave for a period of time. □ *I have to go away for a week or two.* □ *Sharon went away for a few days.* **2.** to leave in order to get something and bring it back. □ *Excuse me. I have to go away for a soft drink.* □ *He went away for a pizza. He'll be right back.*

go away with someone or something **1.** to leave in the company of someone or something. □ *I saw him go away with Margie.* □ *She went away with the others.* **2.** to take someone or a group away with one. □ *He went away with the baby in his arms.*

go AWOL to become absent without leave. (Originally military.) □ *Private Smith went AWOL last Wednesday. Now he's in a military prison.* □ *Tom went AWOL and finally we had to fire him.*

go back to return to the place of origin. □ *That's where I came from, and I'll never go back.* □ *I don't want to go back.*

go back on one's **promise** Go to next.

go back on one's **word** and **go back on** one's **promise; go back on** one's **pledge** to break a promise that one has made. □ *I hate to go back on my word, but I won't pay you $100 after all.* □ *Going back on your promise makes you a liar.*

go back to someone or something to return to someone, something, or some place. □ *She went back to her husband after a few months.* □ *Sharon had to go back to her office for a few minutes.*

go back to square one *Fig.* to return to the starting point. (Alludes to the squares of a board game.) □ *It's back to square one. We have to start over.* □ *It looks like it's back to square one for you.*

go back to the drawing board *Fig.* to return to the planning stage, so that a failed project can be planned again. □ *These plans have to go back to the drawing board.* □ *I thought these problems went back to the drawing board once already.*

go back to the salt mines *Fig.* to return to one's work. (Jocular; fig. on the image of menial labor working in salt mines.) □ *It's late. I have to go back to the salt mines.* □ *What time do you have to go back to the salt mines Monday morning?*

go bad to become rotten, undesirable, evil, etc. □ *I'm afraid that this milk has gone bad.* □ *Life used to be wonderful. Now it has gone bad.*

go badly with someone or something [for something] to proceed badly for someone or something. □ *I hope that things are not still going badly with you.* □ *Things are going very badly with the project.*

go ballistic and **go postal** *Fig.* to become irrationally enraged. (*Ballistic* refers to a missile launching; *postal* refers to an enraged post office employee attacking those at his place of work. See also **go into orbit**.) □ *The boss* went ballistic when he saw my expense report. □ *She was so mad, I thought she was going to go postal.*

go bananas *Sl.* to go mildly crazy. □ *Sorry, I just went bananas for a minute.* □ *I thought he was going to go bananas.*

go before someone Go to **before** someone.

go before someone or something **1.** to precede someone or something. □ *Do you wish to go before me?* □ *I will go before the other waiters and clear the aisles.* **2.** to appear before someone or something. □ *Sharon went before a magistrate and laid out her complaint.* □ *Mary went before the entire board of directors with her proposal.*

go begging *Fig.* to be left over, unwanted, or unused. (As if a thing were begging for an owner or a user.) □ *There is still food left. A whole lobster is going begging. Please eat some more.* □ *There are many excellent books in the library just going begging because people don't know they are there.*

go behind someone's **back 1.** *Lit.* to move behind someone; to locate oneself at someone's back. □ *The mugger went behind my back and put a gun to my spine.* □ *Bob went behind my back and pushed me through the opening.* **2.** *Fig.* to do something that is kept a secret from someone affected by it. □ *I hate to go behind her back, but she makes so much trouble about things like this.* □ *Please don't try to go behind my back again!*

go belly up Go to **turn belly up**.

go below to go beneath the main deck of a ship. (Nautical.) □ *I will have to go below and fiddle with the engine.* □ *The captain went below to escape the worst of the storm.*

go berserk to go crazy. □ *She went berserk and strangled her cat.*

go between someone or something **and** someone or something else to get in between people or things, in any combination. □ *The dog went between Mr. Franklin and the wall.* □ *The arrow went between Jed and Tex, injuring neither of them.*

go beyond someone or something to pass ahead of someone or something. □ *I went beyond the place where I should have turned off.* □ *Fred went beyond me a half block before he remembered who I was. Then he came back and said hello.*

go beyond something **1.** *Lit.* to do more of something than the expected amount; to go further with something than was required. □ *You clearly went beyond what was required of you.* □ *Sharon went beyond the basic requirements.* **2.** *Fig.* to go past something or some place. □ *We went beyond the town and lost our way.* □ *They went beyond the turnoff.*

go broke to completely run out of money and other assets. □ *This company is going to go broke if you don't stop spending money foolishly.* □ *I made some bad investments last year, and it looks as if I may go broke this year.*

go by (someone or something**)** to pass by someone or something. □ *We went by Alice without even noticing her.* □ *We went by because we were in a hurry.*

go by the board *Fig.* to get ruined or lost. (This is originally a nautical expression meaning "to fall or be washed overboard.") □ *I hate to see good food go by the board.*

Please eat up so we won't have to throw it out. □ *Your plan has gone by the board. The entire project has been canceled.*

go by the book Go to by the book.

go by the name of something to be known by a specific name. □ *She goes by the name of Gladys George.* □ *I used to go by the name of George.*

Go chase yourself! and **Go climb a tree!; Go fly a kite!; Go jump in the lake!** *Inf.* Go away and stop bothering me! □ *Bob: Get out of here. Bill! You're driving me crazy! Go chase yourself! Bill: What did I do to you? Bob: You're just in the way.* □ *Bill: Dad, can I have ten bucks? Father: Go climb a tree!* □ *Fred: Stop pestering me, John. Go jump in the lake! John: What did I do?* □ *Bob: Well, Bill, don't you owe me some money? Bill: Go fly a kite!*

go cold turkey *Inf.* to stop (doing something) without tapering off. (Originally drug slang. Now concerned with breaking any habit.) □ *I had to stop smoking, so I went cold turkey. It's awful!* □ *When heroin addicts go cold turkey, they get terribly sick.*

go crazy and **go nuts** to become crazy, disoriented, or frustrated. □ *It is so busy here that I think I will go crazy.* □ *Bob went nuts because his car got a flat tire.*

go down 1. to sink below a normal or expected level or height. □ *The plane went down in flames.* □ *The ship went down with all hands aboard.* **2.** to descend to a lower measurement. □ *Her fever went down.* □ *The price of the stock went down yesterday.* **3.** to be swallowed. □ *The medicine went down without any trouble at all.* □ *The pill I took simply would not go down.* **4.** to fall or drop down, as when struck or injured. □ *Sam went down when he was struck on the chin.* □ *The deer went down when it was hit with the arrow.* **5.** *Sl.* to happen. □ *Hey, man! What's going down?* □ *Something strange is going down around here.* **6.** *Sl.* to be accepted. □ *We'll just have to wait awhile to see how all this goes down.* □ *The proposal didn't go down very well with the manager.* **7.** *Sl.* to be arrested. (Underworld.) □ *Lefty didn't want to go down for a crime he didn't do.* □ *Mr. Big said that somebody had to go down for it, and he didn't care who.*

go down fighting *Fig.* to continue the struggle until one is completely defeated. □ *I won't give up easily. I'll go down fighting.* □ *Sally, who is very determined, went down fighting.*

go down for the count Go to down for the count.

go down for the third time *Fig.* to be just on the verge of failing. (From the notion that a boxer who is knocked down three times in one round normally loses the fight.) □ *I was going down for the third time when I thought of a plan that would save my job.*

go down in defeat and **go down to defeat** *Fig.* to submit to defeat; to be defeated. □ *The team went down in defeat again.* □ *She fears going down in defeat.*

go down in flames 1. *Lit.* [for a plane] to crash. □ *The enemy fighter planes went down in flames, ending the battle.* □ *The pilot and crew went down in flames near the airport.* **2.** *Fig.* to fail spectacularly. □ *The whole project went down in flames.* □ *Todd went down in flames in his efforts to win the heart of Marsha.*

go down (in history) (as someone or something**)** to be recorded for history as a significant person or event. □

You will go down in history as the most stubborn woman who ever lived. □ *She will go down as a very famous woman.*

go down on one's **knees** to kneel down. □ *The people went down on their knees and prayed.* □ *Larry went down on his knees and asked for forgiveness.*

go down something to descend something; to fall down something. □ *She went down the ladder very carefully.* □ *I did not want to go down those steep stairs.*

go down the chute and **go down the drain; go down the tube(s)** *Sl.* to fail; to be thrown away or wasted. □ *Everything we have accomplished has gone down the chute.* □ *The whole project went down the drain.*

go down the drain Go to previous.

go down the line to go from person to person or thing to thing in a line of people or things. □ *She went down the line, asking everyone for a dollar for a cup of coffee.* □ *Sam went down the line, passing out tickets.*

go down the tube(s) Go to go down the chute.

go down to defeat Go to go down in defeat.

go down to someone or something to travel to someone, something, or some place that is downtown, at a lower level, or in the South. □ *We went down to Amy's aunt in Memphis.* □ *Fran went down to Tiffany's place on the first floor.*

go down to something [for something] to decline or diminish to some level. □ *His temperature has gone down to normal.* □ *Will the temperature go down to freezing tonight?*

go down with something *Fig.* to be stricken with a disease. □ *Beth went down with the flu.* □ *She went down with a high fever.*

go downhill [for something] to decline and grow worse and worse. □ *This industry is going downhill. We lose money every year.* □ *As one gets older, one's health tends to go downhill.*

go Dutch [for each person in a pair or a group] to pay for himself or herself. □ *I don't want you to pay for my ticket. Let's go Dutch.* □ *Is it still considered a date if you go Dutch?*

go easy on someone or something to be gentle on someone or something; not to be too critical of someone or something; to take it easy on someone or something. (See also go easy on something.) □ *Go easy on Sherri. She's my friend.* □ *Try to go easy on criticizing their report. They did the best they could in the time allotted.*

go easy on something to use something sparingly. (See also take it easy on something; go easy on someone or something.) □ *Go easy on the mustard. That's all there is.* □ *Please go easy on the onions. I don't like them very much.*

go fifty-fifty (on something**)** to divide the cost of something in half with someone. □ *Todd and Jean decided to go fifty-fifty on dinner.* □ *The two brothers went fifty-fifty on a replacement for the broken lamp.*

Go figure. It's really strange.; Just try to figure it out. □ *She says she wants to have a conversation, but when I try, she does all the talking. Go figure.*

Go fly a kite! Go to Go chase yourself!

go for broke to risk everything; to try as hard as possible. □ *Okay, this is my last chance. I'm going for broke.* □

Look at Mary starting to move in the final hundred yards of the race! She is really going for broke.

Go for it! *Inf.* Go ahead! Give it a good try! □ *Sally: I'm going to try out for the basketball team. Do you think I'm tall enough? Bob: Sure you are! Go for it!* □ *Bob: Mary can't quit now! She's almost at the finish line! Bill: Go for it, Mary!*

go for nothing 1. *Lit.* [for something] to be done for no purpose. □ *All our work went for nothing.* □ *Our efforts at helping out went for nothing.* **2.** *Fig.* [for something] to be sold for a very low price. □ *This merchandise can go for nothing; let's just clear it out at 90 percent off.* □ *I don't want this good stuff to just go for nothing.*

go for someone or something **1.** *Lit.* to go out for someone or something; to go fetch someone or something. □ *I am going for bread—do we need anything else from the store?* □ *Roger went for his aunt, who had arrived at the station.* **2.** *Fig.* to find someone or something interesting or desirable. □ *I really go for chocolate in any form.* □ *Tom really goes for Gloria in a big way.* **3.** *Fig.* to believe or accept something or something that someone says. □ *It sounds pretty strange. Do you think they'll go for it?*

go forward with something *Fig.* to continue with something; to do something that is planned. □ *We will go forward with our plans.* □ *Let's go forward with the plan.*

go from bad to worse to progress from a bad situation to one that is worse. □ *Things went from bad to worse in a matter of days.* □ *I'm afraid that things are going from bad to worse.*

go from one extreme to the other to change from one thing to its opposite. □ *You go from one extreme to another about Tom—one day angry, the next day perfectly happy.*

Go fry an egg! Go away and stop bothering me! □ *Go away and stop bothering me. Go fry an egg!* □ *Get out of my way! Go fry an egg!*

go hand in hand Go to hand in hand.

go haywire *Rur.* to go wrong; to malfunction; to break down. □ *I was talking to Mary when suddenly the telephone went haywire. I haven't heard from her since.* □ *There we were, driving along, when the engine went haywire. It was two hours before the tow truck came.*

go hog wild *Rur.* to behave wildly. □ *Have a good time at the party, but don't go hog wild.* □ *The teacher cannot control a class that is going hog wild.*

go home in a box *Sl.* to be shipped home dead. (Often said in exaggeration.) □ *Hey, I'm too young to go home in a box.* □ *You had better be careful on this camping trip, or you'll go home in a box.*

go home to mama to give up something—such as a marriage—and return to one's mother's home. □ *I've had it. I'm going home to mama.* □ *Mary left him and went home to mama.*

go hungry to miss a meal and end up hungry. □ *The kids were late for dinner so they had to go hungry.*

go in Go to go into something.

go in a body Go to in a body.

go in and out (of something) to pass in and out of something or some place. □ *The nervous little mouse kept going*

in and out of its hole. □ *The cat kept going in and out of the back door.*

go in for something to take part in something; to enjoy (doing) something. □ *John doesn't go in for sports.* □ *None of them seems to go in for swimming.*

go in one ear and out the other *Cliché Fig.* [for something] to be heard and then soon ignored or forgotten. □ *Everything I say to you seems to go in one ear and out the other. Why don't you pay attention?* □ *I can't concentrate. Things people say to me just go in one ear and out the other.*

go in someone's **favor** [for something] to change to someone's benefit. (Alludes to very changeable things like game scores, wind direction, or chance in general.) □ *Things appear to be going in our favor—finally.* □ *The game was going in our favor during the first half.*

go in the hole Go to in the hole.

go in the right direction 1. *Lit.* to head or travel in the right direction. □ *Are you sure we are going in the right direction?* □ *We were supposed to turn back there. We are not going in the right direction.* **2.** *Fig.* [for plans or intentions] to be progressing sensibly. □ *Well, everything seems to be going in the right direction—for now anyway.* □ *Do you feel that this project is going in the right direction?*

go in with someone **(on** something) *Fig.* to join together with someone to work on a project; to pool financial resources with someone to buy something. □ *I would be happy to go in with you on the charity ball. I'll find a hall.* □ *Yes, we can pool our money. I'll go in with you.*

go into a huddle 1. *Lit.* [for team members] to get into a small circle and plan what they are going to do next. □ *They went into a huddle to plan their strategy.* □ *The players will go into a huddle and decide what to do.* **2.** *Fig.* [for people] to group together to talk and decide what to do. □ *We went into a huddle to plan our sales strategy.* □ *Top-level management needs to go into a huddle and come up with a good plan.*

go into a nosedive and **take a nosedive 1.** *Lit.* [for an airplane] suddenly to dive toward the ground, nose first. □ *It was a bad day for flying, and I was afraid we'd go into a nosedive.* □ *The small plane took a nosedive. The pilot was able to bring it out at the last minute, so the plane didn't crash.* **2.** *Fig.* [for someone] to fall to the ground face first. □ *She took a nosedive and injured her face.* **3.** *Fig.* to go into a rapid emotional or financial decline, or a decline in health. □ *Our profits took a nosedive last year.* □ *After he broke his hip, Mr. Brown's health went into a nosedive, and he never recovered.*

go into a song and dance (about something**)** and **go into the same old song and dance about** something *Fig.* to start repeating excuses or stories about something. (See also go into one's act.) □ *Please don't go into your song and dance about how you always tried to do what was right.* □ *John went into his song and dance about how he won the war all by himself.* □ *He always goes into the same old song and dance every time he makes a mistake.*

go into a tailspin 1. *Lit.* [for an airplane] to lose control and spin to the earth, nose first. □ *The plane shook and then suddenly went into a tailspin.* □ *The pilot was not able to bring the plane out of the tailspin, and it crashed into the sea.* **2.** *Fig.* [for someone] to become disoriented or panicked; [for someone's life] to fall apart. □ *Although John achieved great success, his life went into a tailspin. It took him a year to get straightened out.* □ *After her father died, Mary's world fell apart, and she went into a tailspin.*

go into action and **swing into action** to start doing something. □ *I usually get to work at 7:45, get some coffee, and I go into action at 8:00.* □ *When the ball is hit in my direction, you should see me swing into action.*

go into detail(s) to give all the details; to present and discuss the details. □ *The clerk went into detail about the product with the customer.* □ *I just want a simple answer. Don't go into details.*

go into effect and **take effect** [for a law or a rule] to become effective. □ *When does this new law go into effect?* □ *The new tax laws won't go into effect until next year.*

go into heat Go to in heat.

go into hiding to conceal oneself in a hidden place for a period of time. □ *The political dissident went into hiding.* □ *After robbing the bank, the bandits went into hiding for months.*

go into hock go into debt. □ *We will have to go into hock to buy a house.* □ *I go further into hock every time I use my credit card.*

go into one's **act** *Fig.* to begin to behave in a way typical to oneself. □ *The curtain opened and Steve went into his act.*

go into orbit 1. *Lit.* [for a rocket, satellite, etc.] to rotate around a heavenly body in a fixed path. □ *The satellite went into orbit just as planned.* □ *When did the moon go into orbit?* **2.** *Fig.* [for someone] to get very excited. (See also **go ballistic**.) □ *She was so upset, she went into orbit.* □ *Todd went into orbit when he heard the price.*

go into service to start operating. □ *When will the new elevator go into service?* □ *It has already gone into service.*

go into something **1.** and **go in** *Lit.* to enter something; to penetrate something. □ *The needle went into the vein smoothly and painlessly.* □ *It went in with no trouble.* **2.** *Fig.* to enter some line of business or a profession. □ *He went into accounting when he got out of college.* □ *I want to prepare to go into law enforcement.* **3.** *Fig.* to examine or study something; to discuss and explain something. (See also **go there**.) □ *I need to go into this more.* □ *When we have time, we need to go into this question more thoroughly.*

go into the bull pen Go to in the bull pen.

go into the red Go to in the red.

go into the same old song and dance about something Go to go into a song and dance (about something).

go into the service to enter one of the military services. □ *She went into the service when she got out of high school.* □ *I chose not to go into the service.*

go it alone to do something by oneself. □ *Do you need help, or will you go it alone?* □ *I think I need a little more experience before I go it alone.*

Go jump in the lake! Go to Go chase yourself!

go like clockwork *Fig.* to progress with regularity and dependability. □ *The building project is progressing nicely. Everything is going like clockwork.* □ *The elaborate pageant was a great success. It went like clockwork from start to finish.*

go like stink Go to like stink.

go like the wind Go to like the wind.

go near (to) someone or something to approach someone or something. □ *Don't go near Sue. She's got chicken pox.* □ *Now, don't go near the water!*

go nuts Go to go crazy.

go off 1. *Lit.* [for an explosive device] to explode. □ *The fireworks all went off as scheduled.* □ *The bomb went off and did a lot of damage.* **2.** *Lit.* [for a sound-creating device] to make its noise. □ *The alarm went off at six o'clock.* □ *The siren goes off at noon every day.* **3.** *Fig.* [for an event] to happen or take place. □ *The party went off as planned.* □ *Did your medical examination go off as well as you had hoped?*

go off (by oneself) to go into seclusion; to isolate oneself. □ *She went off by herself where no one could find her.* □ *I have to go off and think about this.*

go off half-cocked *Fig.* to go into action too early or without thinking. (Originally refers to a flintlock or matchlock gun firing prematurely, before the trigger was pulled.) □ *Don't go off half-cocked. Plan out what you're going to do.* □ *Bill went off half-cocked and told everybody he was running for the state legislature.*

go off (into something) to go away to something; to depart and go into something. □ *He went off into the army.* □ *Do you expect me just to go off into the world and make a living?*

go off kilter Go to out of kilter.

go off on a tangent *Fig.* to pursue a somewhat related or irrelevant course while neglecting the main subject. □ *Don't go off on a tangent. Stick to your job.* □ *Just as we started talking, Henry went off on a tangent about the high cost of living.*

go off on someone *Sl.* to berate someone. □ *Don't go off on me! I'm not the cause of your problems!* □ *The teacher went off on poor little Harry.*

go off the deep end and **jump off the deep end 1.** *Lit.* to jump into a swimming pool where the water is over one's head and one needs to be able to swim □ *You are still only learning to swim. Are you ready to go off the deep end?* □ *He jumped off the deep end where he would make a bigger splash.* **2.** *Fig.* to become deeply involved (with someone or something) before one is ready. (Applies especially to falling in love.) □ *Look at the way Bill is looking at Sally. I think he's about to go off the deep end.* **3.** *Fig.* to act irrationally, following one's emotions or fantasies. □ *Now, John, I know you really want to go to Australia, but don't go jumping off the deep end. It isn't all perfect there.*

go off (to the side) with someone Go to off (to the side) with someone.

go off (with someone) to go away with someone. □ *Tom just now went off with Maggie.* □ *I think that Maria went off with Fred somewhere.*

Go on. 1. *Lit.* Please continue. □ *Alice: I guess I should stop here. Tom: No. Don't stop talking. I'm very interested. Go on.* □ *Bill: Don't turn here. Go on. It's the next corner. Bob: Thanks. I didn't think that was where we should turn.* **2.** *Lit.*

to happen. □ *What went on here last night?* □ *The teacher asked what was going on.* **3.** *Fig.* That's silly!; You don't mean that! (Usually **Go on!**) □ *John: Go on! You're making that up! Bill: I am not. It's the truth!* □ *Bill: Gee, that looks like a snake there in the path. Bob: Go on! That isn't a snake. No snake is that big.*

go on a binge to do too much of something, especially to drink too much. □ *Jane went on a binge last night and is very sick this morning.* □ *Bill loves to spend money on clothes. He's out on a binge right now—buying everything in sight.*

go on a diet Go to on a diet.

go on a fishing expedition Go to on a fishing expedition.

go on a fool's errand Go to on a fool's errand.

go on a power trip Go to on a power trip.

go on a rampage to get very disturbed or angry. □ *The angry bull went on a rampage and broke the fence.* □ *My boss went on a rampage because the report wasn't finished.*

go on an errand Go to run an errand.

go on and on to (seem to) last or go forever. □ *You talk too much, Bob. You just go on and on.* □ *The road to their house is very boring. It goes on and on with nothing interesting to look at.*

go on (and on) (about someone or something**)** to talk endlessly about someone or something. □ *She just went on and on about her new car.* □ *Albert went on about the book for a long time.*

go on (at someone**)** to rave at someone. □ *He must have gone on at her for ten minutes—screaming and waving his arms.* □ *I wish you would stop going on at me.*

go on before (someone**) 1.** *Lit.* to precede someone. □ *Please go on before me. I will follow.* □ *She went on before.* **2.** *Euph.* to die before someone. □ *Uncle Herman went on before Aunt Margaret by a few years.* □ *He went before her, although we had all thought it would be the other way around.*

go on doing something Go to go on with something.

go on for an age and **go on for ages** *Fig.* to continue for a very long time. □ *The symphony seemed to go on for an age.* □ *It seemed to go on for ages.*

go on something **1.** *Lit.* to begin something, such as a diet, rampage, drunk, etc. □ *I went on a diet for the second time this month.* □ *Fred went on a rampage and broke a window.* **2.** *Fig.* to start acting on some information. □ *We can't go on this! We need more information before we can act on this matter!* □ *Can you please give us more information to go on?*

go on the block *Fig.* [for something] to go up for auction; [for something] to be placed on the auction block. □ *Our farm went on the block last week. Got a good price.* □ *When this painting goes on the block, I hope I get a lot for it.*

go on to a better land *Euph.* to die. □ *After a long illness, Reggie went on to a better land.* □ *When I finally go on to a better land, I hope there is enough money for a proper funeral.*

go on to something to advance to something or to doing something. □ *After a few years she went on to even greater heights.* □ *Larry went on to found his own company.*

go on tour [for a performing group] to go from place to place, performing. □ *Our play went on tour across the state.* □ *If we make the play a success, we will go on tour.*

go on with something and **go on** doing something to continue with something. □ *I can't go on with this. I have to rest.* □ *You simply cannot go on behaving like this!*

Go on (with you)! *Inf.* Go away! (Always a command. No tenses.) □ *It's time you left. Go on with you!* □ *Go on. Get yourself home.*

go out 1. to leave one's house. □ *Call me later. I'm going out now.* □ *Sally told her father that she was going out.* **2.** become extinguished. □ *The fire finally went out.* □ *The lights went out and left us in the dark.* **3.** Go to go out of fashion.

go out for someone or something to leave in order to bring back someone or something. □ *Albert just went out for a newspaper.* □ *Fran went out for Bob, who was on the back porch, smoking a cigarette.*

go out (for something**) 1.** *Lit.* to go outside to get something or to do something. □ *Jill just went out for a breath of fresh air.* □ *He just went out, and should be back any minute.* **2.** *Fig.* to try out for something. (Usually refers to a sport.) □ *Mary went out for the soccer team.* □ *Tom went out for baseball.*

go out for the count Go to out for the count.

go out from something Go to out from something.

go out in force Go to out in force.

go out in search of someone or something to leave to find someone or something. □ *I went out in search of someone to help me.* □ *Mary went out in search of Gloria.*

go out of bounds Go to out of bounds.

go out of business to stop doing commerce or business. □ *The new shop will probably go out of business if sales don't get better.* □ *I have to work hard to keep from going out of business.*

go out of control Go to out of control.

go out of fashion and **go out of style; go out** to become unfashionable; to become obsolete. □ *That kind of furniture went out of style years ago.* □ *I hope this kind of thing never goes out of fashion.* □ *It went out years ago.*

go out of favor (with someone**)** Go to out of favor (with someone).

go out of focus Go to out of focus.

go out of kilter Go to out of kilter.

go out of one's **head** Go to out of one's mind.

go out of one's **mind** Go to out of one's mind.

go out of one's **senses** Go to out of one's mind.

go out of one's **skull** Go to out of one's skull.

go out of one's **way (to** do something**) 1.** *Lit.* to travel an indirect route or an extra distance in order to do something. □ *I'll have to go out of my way to give you a ride home.* □ *I'll give you a ride even though I have to go out of my way.* **2.** *Fig.* to make an effort to do something; to accept the bother of doing something. □ *We went out of* *our way to please the visitor.* □ *We appreciate anything you can do, but don't go out of your way.*

go out of practice Go to out of practice.

go out of service [for something] to stop working; [for something] to have been turned off so it cannot be used. □ *This elevator went out of service last week.* □ *How long has it been since this thing went out of service?*

go out of sight Go to out of sight.

go out (of something) to leave something or some place. □ *I went out of there feeling sorry for myself.* □ *I went out with a smile on my face.*

go out of style Go to go out of fashion.

go out of the frying pan into the fire Go to out of the frying pan into the fire.

go out on a limb Go to out on a limb.

go (out) on strike and **go out (on strike)** [for a group of people] to quit working at their jobs until certain demands are met. □ *If we don't have a contract by noon tomorrow, we'll go out on strike.* □ *The entire workforce went on strike at noon today.*

go out to someone [for one's sympathy, heart, etc.] to be aimed toward someone. □ *All of my sympathy went out to her. I knew just how she felt.* □ *My thanks go out to you all.*

go out (with someone) 1. *Lit.* to go out with someone for entertainment. □ *The Smiths went out with the Franklins to a movie.* □ *Those guys don't have much time to go out.* **2.** *Fig.* to go on a date with someone; to date someone regularly. □ *Is Bob still going out with Sally?* □ *No, they've stopped going out.*

go out with something to go out of fashion at the same time as something else went out of fashion. □ *That style of dress went out with the bustle.* □ *Your thinking went out with the horse and buggy.*

go over *Euph.* to leave one's country and go to ideologically opposed or enemy country; to defect. □ *When the ballet company visited New York, two of the dancers went over.* □ *He had been spying for the Americans for many years, and he finally went over.*

go over big (with someone) to be very much appreciated by someone. □ *Your jokes did not exactly go over big with my parents.* □ *We hope that the musical will go over big with the audience.*

go over like a lead balloon *Fig.* to fail completely; to go over badly. □ *Your joke went over like a lead balloon.* □ *If that play was supposed to be a comedy, it went over like a lead balloon.* □ *Her suggestion went over like a lead balloon.*

go over someone Go to over someone.

go over someone or something to examine someone or something. □ *The doctor will go over you very carefully, I'm sure.* □ *I went over the papers and found nothing wrong.*

go over someone's head Go to over someone's head.

go over something with a fine-tooth comb and **search something with a fine-tooth comb; go through something with a fine-tooth comb** *Fig.* to search through something very carefully. □ *I can't find my calculus book. I went over the whole place with a fine-tooth comb.* □ *I searched this place with a fine-tooth comb and didn't find my ring.*

go over something (with someone) to review or explain something. □ *The teacher went over the lesson with the class.* □ *Can you please go over it again, more slowly?*

go over the hill Go to over the hill.

go over the wall Go to over the wall.

go over to some place to travel some distance or cross water to get to some place. □ *We went over to Cedar Point and spent the day having fun.* □ *John went over to the other side of the stadium for the rest of the tournament.*

go over (well) [for someone or something] to be accepted or well received. □ *The party went over very well.* □ *The play really went over with the audience.*

go over with a bang 1. *Fig.* [for something] to be funny or entertaining. □ *Our presentation was a success. It really went over with a bang.* □ *That's a great joke. It went over with a bang.* **2.** *Fig.* to succeed spectacularly. □ *The play was a success. It really went over with a bang.* □ *That's a great joke. It went over with a bang.*

go overboard 1. *Fig.* to fall out of a boat or off of a ship; to fall overboard. □ *Be careful or you will go overboard.* □ *Someone went overboard in the fog.* **2.** *Fig.* to do too much; to be extravagant. □ *Look, Sally, let's have a nice party, but don't go overboard. It doesn't need to be fancy.* □ *Okay, you can buy a big comfortable car, but don't go overboard on price.*

go past someone or something to pass by someone or something. □ *You went right past Tom. Did you mean to?* □ *Did I go past it?*

go past something Go to past something.

go places to become very successful. □ *I knew that Sally, with all her talent, would go places.* □ *I really want to go places in life.*

Go play in the traffic. Go to Take a long walk off a short pier.

go postal Go to go ballistic; go into orbit.

go public (with something) 1. to sell to the public shares of a privately owned company. (Securities markets.) □ *The company decided not to go public because the economy was so bad at the time.* □ *We'll go public at a later time.* **2.** to reveal something to the public. □ *It's too early to go public with the story.* □ *Just let me know when we can go public with this press release.*

go (right) through someone and **go through someone like a dose of the salts** *Fig.* [for something] to be excreted very soon after being eaten; [for something] to go immediately through the alimentary canal of a person. (Use with discretion.) □ *No, thanks. This stuff just goes right through me.* □ *The coffee went through me like a dose of salts.*

go scot-free and **get off scot-free** to go unpunished; to be acquitted of a crime. (This *scot* is an old word meaning "tax" or "tax burden.") □ *The thief went scot-free.* □ *Jane cheated on the test and got caught, but she got off scot-free.*

go sky-high *Fig.* to go very high. □ *Prices go sky-high whenever there is inflation.* □ *Oh, it's so hot. The temperature went sky-high about noon.*

go so far as to say something to put something into words; to risk saying something. □ *I think that Bob is dishonest, but I wouldn't go so far as to say he's a thief.* □ *Red meat may be harmful, but I can't go so far as to say it causes cancer.*

go (someone) one better and **do someone one better** to do something superior to what someone else has done; to top someone. □ *That was a great joke, but I can go you one better.* □ *Your last song was beautifully sung, but Mary can do you one better.*

go (somewhere) by shank's mare Go to by shank's mare.

go sour *Fig.* to turn bad or unpleasant. □ *It looks like all my plans are going sour.* □ *My whole life is going sour right now.*

go South and **head South 1.** *Sl.* to make an escape; to disappear. (Not necessarily in a southerly direction.) □ *Lefty went South the minute he got out of the pen.* □ *The mugger headed South just after the crime.* **2.** *Sl.* to fall; to go down. (Securities markets.) □ *All the stock market indexes went South today.* □ *The market headed South today at the opening bell.* **3.** *Sl.* to quit; to drop out of sight. □ *Fred got discouraged and went South. I think he gave up football permanently.* □ *After pulling the bank job, Wilbur went South for a few months.*

go stag to go to an event (which is meant for couples) without a member of the opposite sex. (Originally referred only to males.) □ *Is Tom going to take you, or are you going stag?* □ *Bob didn't want to go stag, so he took his sister to the party.*

go steady with someone Go to **go with** someone.

go stir-crazy Go to stir-crazy.

go straight to stop breaking the law and lead a lawful life instead. □ *The judge encouraged the thief to go straight.* □ *After Bob was arrested, he promised his mother he would go straight.*

go (straight) to the top *Fig.* to attempt to confer with the person at the top of the chain of command, bypassing the intermediate people. □ *When I want something, I always go straight to the top. I don't have time for a lot of bureaucracy.*

go the distance *Fig.* to do the whole amount; to play the entire game; to run the whole race. (Originally sports use.) □ *That horse runs fast. I hope it can go the distance.* □ *This is going to be a long, hard project. I hope I can go the distance.*

go the extra mile to try harder to please someone or to get the task done correctly; to do more than one is required to do to reach a goal. □ *I like doing business with that company. They always go the extra mile.* □ *My teacher goes the extra mile to help us.*

go the limit *Fig.* to do as much as possible; to get as much as possible. □ *Let's plan to do everything we can. Let's go the limit.* □ *We'll go the limit. To heck with the cost.*

go the way of the dodo and **go the way of the horse and buggy** *Fig.* to become extinct; to become obsolete. □ *The floppy disc has gone the way of the horse and buggy.*

go the way of the horse and buggy Go to previous.

go there to begin a discussion of something; to take up a certain topic. (Similar to **go into** something. Often in the negative. This has nothing to do with traveling or going to a place.) □ *A: How are things going at your place of business? B: Please! I don't want to go there.* □ *We don't have time to discuss your health problems, so let's not go there.*

go through to be approved; to succeed in getting through the approval process. □ *I sent the board of directors a proposal. I hope it goes through.* □ *We all hope that the new law goes through.*

go through channels Go to go through (the proper) channels.

go through someone **1.** *Lit.* to travel through someone's body; to go (right) through someone. □ *That medicine went right through me.* **2.** *Fig.* to work through someone; to use someone as an intermediary. □ *I can't give you the permission you seek. You will have to go through our main office.* □ *I have to go through the treasurer for all expenditures.*

go through someone **like a dose of the salts** Go to go (right) through someone.

go through someone or something [for something sharp] to penetrate someone or something. □ *The sword went through the knight cleanly and quickly.* □ *The nail went through all three boards.*

go through something **1.** to search through something. □ *She went through his pants pockets, looking for his wallet.* □ *He spent quite a while going through his desk, looking for the papers.* **2.** to use up all of something rapidly. □ *We have gone through all the aspirin again!* □ *How can you go through your allowance so fast?* **3.** [for something] to pass through an opening. □ *The piano wouldn't go through the door.* □ *Do you think that such a big truck can go through the tunnel under the river?* **4.** to pass through various stages or processes. □ *The pickles went through a number of processes before they were packed.* □ *Johnny is going through a phase where he wants everything his way.* **5.** to work through something, such as an explanation or story. □ *I went through my story again, carefully and in great detail.* □ *I would like to go through it again, so I can be sure to understand it.* **6.** to experience or endure something. □ *You can't believe what I've gone through.* □ *Mary has gone through a lot lately.* **7.** to rehearse something; to practice something for performance. □ *They went through the second act a number of times.* □ *We need to go through the whole play a few more times.*

go through something **with a fine-tooth comb** Go to go over something with a fine-tooth comb.

go through the changes *Fig.* to experience life's changes. □ *A good day, a bad day—it's all part of going through the changes.* □ *Nothing new with me, just going through the changes.*

go through the cracks Go to through the cracks.

go through the mill Go to through the mill.

go through the motions *Fig.* to make a feeble effort to do something; to do something insincerely or in cursory fashion. □ *Jane isn't doing her best. She's just going through the motions.* □ *Bill was supposed to be raking the yard, but he was just going through the motions.*

go through (the proper) channels to use the proper procedure, working through the correct people and offices to get something done; to cooperate with a bureaucracy. □ *I'm sorry. I can't help you. You'll have to go through the proper channels.* □ *I didn't get what I wanted because I didn't go through channels.*

go through the roof 1. *Fig. Inf.* to become very angry. □ *She saw what had happened and went through the roof.* □ *My father went through the roof when he saw what I did to the car.* **2.** *Fig. Inf.* [for prices] to become very high. □ *These days, prices for gasoline are going through the roof.* □ *The cost of coffee is going through the roof.*

go through with something to complete something the outcome of which is troubling or doubtful; to do something in spite of problems and drawbacks. □ *I have to go through with it, no matter what.* □ *I just couldn't go through with it.*

Go to! *Inf.* Go to hell! □ *Oh, you're terrible. Just go to!* □ *Go to, you creep!*

go to any length *Fig.* to do whatever is necessary. (See also **go to great lengths (to** do something**).**) □ *I'll go to any length to secure this contract.* □ *I want to get a college degree, but I won't go to any length to get one.*

go to bat against someone *Fig.* to aid someone against someone else. □ *I would be happy to go to bat against Dan.* □ *We refused to go to bat against one of our friends.*

go to bat for someone *Fig.* to support or help someone. □ *I tried to go to bat for Bill, but he said he didn't want any help.* □ *I heard them gossiping about Sally, so I went to bat for her.*

go to bed to go to where one's bed is, get into it, and go to sleep. □ *It's time for me to go to bed.* □ *I want to go to bed, but there is too much work to do.*

go to bed (with someone**)** Go to **go all the way (with** someone**).**

go to bed with the chickens *Fig.* to go to bed at sundown—at the same time that chickens go to sleep. □ *They say that farmers go to bed with the chickens.* □ *We always go to bed with the chickens and get up early too.*

go to bed with the sun *Fig.* to go to bed early, at sunset. □ *The campers went to bed with the sun.* □ *The children had to go to bed with the sun. The grown-ups stayed up a little later.*

Go to blazes! *Inf.* Go to hell! □ *Go to blazes! Stop pestering me!* □ *I'm sick of your complaining. Go to blazes!*

go to Davy Jones's locker Go to **Davy Jones's locker.**

go to extremes (to do something**)** to be excessive in one's efforts to do something. □ *Auntie Jane will go to extremes to make us all comfortable.* □ *Let's not go to extremes! We've already spent enough on gifts for the kids.*

go to great lengths (to do something**)** and **go to any lengths (to** do something**)** to work very hard to accomplish something; to expend great efforts in trying to do something. (See also **go to any length.**) □ *I went to great lengths to explain to him that he was not in any trouble.*

go to hell and **go to (the devil) 1.** *Inf.* to go to hell and suffer the agonies therein. (Often a command. Caution with *hell.*) □ *Oh, go to hell!* □ *Go to hell, you creep!* **2.** *Inf.* to become ruined; to go away and stop bothering some-

one. (Use *hell* with caution.) □ *This old house is just going to hell. It's falling apart everywhere.* □ *Leave me alone! Go to the devil!* □ *Oh, go to, yourself!*

go to hell in a bucket and **go to hell in a handbasket** *Fig.* to get rapidly worse and worse. □ *The school system in this district is going to hell in a bucket, and no mistake.* □ *His health is going to hell in a handbasket ever since he started drinking again.*

go to it 1. *Lit.* to start something actively; to do something with vigor. □ *Time to play ball. Go to it!* □ *Let's go to it, you guys!* **2.** *Inf.* to fight. □ *Come on, let's go to it! I'm gonna beat the daylights out of you!*

go to one's **(just) reward** *Euph.* to die. □ *Let us pray for our departed sister, who has gone to her just reward.* □ *Bill: How's your grandma these days? Tom: She went to her reward last winter, may she rest in peace.*

go to pieces 1. *Lit.* [for something] to fall apart into many pieces. □ *The vase—which had been repaired many times—just went to pieces when I put it down.* □ *When the window was hit by the ball, it went to pieces.* **2.** *Fig.* [for something] to become nonfunctional. □ *His plan went to pieces.* □ *All her hopes and ideas went to pieces in that one meeting.* **3.** *Fig.* [for someone] to have a mental collapse. □ *Poor Jane went to pieces after her divorce.* □ *Fred went to pieces during the trial.*

go to pot and **go to the dogs** *Fig.* to go to ruin; to deteriorate. □ *My whole life seems to be going to pot.* □ *My lawn is going to pot. I had better weed it.*

go to press [for a publication] to be sent to the printing presses. □ *The book went to press last week. We expect finished books by the first of the month.* □ *The book you want to order hasn't even gone to press yet.*

go to press with something [for someone] to cause something to be printed. □ *The columnist went to press with the rumor without checking any of her usual sources.* □ *We are going to press with a series of books on textiles.*

go to rack and ruin and **go to wrack and ruin** to become ruined. (The words *rack* and *wrack* mean "wreckage" and are found only in this expression.) □ *That lovely old house on the corner is going to go to rack and ruin.* □ *My lawn is going to wrack and ruin.*

go to sea to become a sailor. □ *I went to sea at an early age.* □ *When I get older, I'm going to go to sea too.*

go to seed 1. and **run to seed** *Lit.* [for a plant] to grow long enough to produce seed; [for a plant] to spend its energy going to seed. □ *The lettuce went to seed and we couldn't eat it.* □ *Plants like that ought not to be allowed to go to seed.* **2.** and **run to seed** *Fig.* [for a lawn or a plant] to produce seeds because it has not had proper care. □ *You've got to mow the grass. It's going to seed.* □ *Don't let the lawn go to seed. It looks so—seedy!* **3.** *Fig.* [for something] to decline in looks, status, or utility due to lack of care. (The same as **run to seed.**) □ *This old coat is going to seed. Have to get a new one.* □ *The front of the house is going to seed. Let's get it painted.*

go to someone **(about** someone or something**)** to discuss one's problems with someone or something with someone else. □ *I went to the boss about the new secretary.* □ *This is a real problem. I'll have to go to the manager.*

go to someone or something to travel to or toward someone or something. □ *We went to her as soon as she called saying she needed us.* □ *Are you going to the bank?*

go to someone's **head 1.** *Fig.* [for something, such as fame or success] to make someone conceited. □ *Don't let all this praise go to your head.* □ *Too much success will go to her head.* **2.** *Fig.* [for alcohol] to affect someone's brain. □ *That last glass of champagne went right to her head.* □ *Any kind of liquor goes to my head.*

go to the bathroom 1. *Fig. Euph.* to go into and use a restroom, bathroom, or toilet. □ *Bill: Where is Bob? Jane: He went to the bathroom.* □ *John went to the bathroom to brush his teeth.* **2.** *Fig. Euph.* to eliminate bodily wastes. □ *Mommy! The dog went to the bathroom on the carpet!* □ *Billy's in there going to the bathroom. Don't disturb him.*

go to the bother (of doing something) Go to go to the trouble (of doing something).

go to the crux of the matter Go to the crux of the matter.

go to (the devil) Go to go to hell.

go to the dogs Go to go to pot.

go to the expense (of doing something) to pay the (large) cost of doing something. □ *I hate to have to go to the expense of painting the house.* □ *It needs to be done, so you'll have to go to the expense.*

go to the heart of the matter Go to the crux of the matter.

go to the lavatory *Euph.* to go into a restroom and use a toilet. □ *Bob requested to leave the room to go to the lavatory.* □ *Please stop the car. I have to go to the lavatory.*

go to the limit to do as much as is possible to do. □ *Okay, we can't afford it, but we'll go to the limit.* □ *How far shall I go? Shall I go to the limit?*

go to the polls to go to a place to vote; to vote. □ *What day do we go to the polls?* □ *Our community goes to the polls in November.*

go to the root of the matter Go to the crux of the matter.

go to the toilet *Fig. Euph.* to use a toilet for defecation or urination. □ *Jimmy washed his hands after he went to the toilet.* □ *Excuse me, I have to go to the toilet.*

go to the trouble (of doing something) and **go to the trouble (to** do something); **go to the bother (of** doing something); **go to the bother (to** do something) to endure the effort or bother of doing something. □ *I really don't want to go to the trouble to cook.* □ *Should I go to the bother of cooking something for her to eat?* □ *Don't go to the trouble. She can eat a sandwich.*

go to the wall (on something) to take on great risk or to hold out to the very last on some issue. (See also push someone to the wall.) □ *I will go to the wall on this point.* □ *This is a very important matter and I will go to the wall if necessary.*

go to town 1. *Lit.* to travel into town or a city. □ *I have to go to town today.* **2.** *Fig.* to work hard or very effectively. □ *Look at all those ants working. They are really going to town.* □ *Come on, you guys. Let's go to town. We have to finish this job before noon.*

go to trial [for a case] to go into court to be tried. □ *When will this case go to trial?* □ *We go to trial next Monday.*

go to war (over someone or something) to wage a war over someone or something. (Often an exaggeration.) □ *We aren't going to go to war over this, are we?* □ *Do you want to go to war over Sarah? Is she that important to you?*

go to waste [for something] to be wasted; to be unused (and therefore thrown away). □ *Eat your potatoes! Don't let them go to waste.* □ *We shouldn't let all those nice herbs go to waste. Let's pick some before the first hard frost.*

go to work (on someone or something) to begin working on someone or something. □ *The masons went to work on repairing the wall.* □ *The surgeons went to work on the patient.* □ *Come on! Let's go to work!*

go to wrack and ruin Go to go to rack and ruin.

Go to your room! Go to On your bike!

go together 1. *Lit.* [for two or more things] to look, sound, or taste good together. □ *Do you think that this pink one and this purple one go together?* □ *Milk and grapefruit don't go together.* **2.** *Fig.* [for two people] to date each other regularly. □ *Bob and Ann have been going together for months.* □ *Tom and Jane want to go together, but they live too far apart.*

go too far to do more than is acceptable. □ *I didn't mind at first, but now you've gone too far.* □ *If you go too far, I'll slap you.*

go toward someone or something to move toward someone or something. □ *The child went toward the open door.* □ *The dog went toward the cat and the cat ran away.*

go under 1. to sink beneath the surface of the water. □ *After capsizing, the ship went under very slowly.* □ *I was afraid that our canoe would go under in the rapidly moving water.* **2.** *Fig.* [for something] to fail. □ *The company went under exactly one year after it opened.* □ *We tried to keep it from going under.* **3.** *Fig.* to become unconscious from anesthesia. □ *After a few minutes, she went under and the surgeon began to work.* □ *Tom went under and the operation began.*

go under (someone or something) **1.** to pass beneath someone or something. □ *The boats went under us as we stood on the bridge.* □ *The boat went under the bridge.* **2.** to belong beneath someone or something. □ *That box goes under the bed.* □ *All the Christmas presents go under the tree after the children are asleep.*

go under the hammer Go to come under the hammer.

go under the knife *Fig.* to submit to surgery; to have surgery done on oneself. □ *She goes under the knife tomorrow for her gallbladder.* □ *Frank lives in constant fear of having to go under the knife.*

go under the name of something [for someone or something] to be known under a particular name. □ *Now she goes under the name of Suzanne.* □ *The man you just met goes under the name of Walter Sampson.*

go under the wrecking ball *Fig.* to be wrecked or torn down. □ *That lovely old building finally went under the wrecking ball.* □ *I hate to see good architecture go under the wrecking ball.*

G

go up [for something] to go higher. □ *Gasoline prices are still going up.* □ *Prices keep going up and up, no matter what.*

go up a blind alley Go to *up a blind alley*.

go up against someone to compete with someone; to face someone in competition. □ *She is going up against Rodney in the spelling bee.* □ *The champ went up against the challenger in a match last Friday.*

go up against someone or something Go to *up against someone or something*.

go up for auction Go to *up for auction*.

go up in flames and **go up in smoke 1.** *Lit.* to burn up completely. □ *The entire forest went up in flames!* □ *The expensive house went up in smoke.* **2.** *Fig.* [for value or investment] to be lost suddenly and totally. □ *Everything we own has gone up in flames with the stock crash.* □ *The entire investment went up in smoke.*

go up in smoke Go to *previous*.

go up something to climb up something. □ *The monkey went up the tree in no time.* □ *How fast can you go up this rope?*

go up the wall 1. *Lit.* to climb or run up the wall. □ *Look at that silly cat go up the wall! How can its claws hold onto the brick?* **2.** *Fig.* to exhibit great frustration, as if trying to climb up a wall. □ *I was so upset, I almost went up the wall.* □ *We went up the wall waiting for you.*

go up to someone or something to approach someone or something. □ *The temperature will go up to near one hundred today.* □ *I went up to her and asked her for a match.*

go well with someone or something [for something] to proceed nicely for someone or something. □ *I hope things are going well with you.* □ *Things are going very well with the project.*

go whole hog to do everything possible; to be extravagant. □ *Let's go whole hog. Order steak and lobster.* □ *Show some restraint. Don't go whole hog all the time.*

go wild *Fig.* to get very excited. □ *At the end of the football game, the kick was good and the crowd went wild.*

go window-shopping to go about looking at goods in store windows without actually buying anything. □ *The office workers go window-shopping on their lunch hour, looking for things to buy when they get paid.* □ *Joan said she was just going window-shopping, but she bought a new coat.*

go with it Go to *go with the flow*.

go with someone and **go steady with** someone to have a romantic relationship with someone. (*Go steady* is dated.) □ *Sally has been going with Mark for two months now.* □ *He wants to go steady with her. He doesn't want her to see other guys.*

go with (someone or something) to depart in the company of someone or a group. □ *Jim's not here. He went with the last busload.* □ *I'm leaving now. Do you want to go with?*

go with something **1.** *Lit.* to accompany something agreeably. □ *Milk doesn't go with grapefruit.* □ *Pink doesn't go with orange.* **2.** *Fig.* to choose something (over something else). □ *I think I'll go with the yellow one.* □ *We decided to go with the oak table rather than the walnut one.*

go with the flow and **go with it** *Inf.* to cope with adversity; to accept one's lot. □ *No, just relax and go with the flow.* □ *Go with it. Don't fight it.*

go with the territory Go to *come with the territory*.

go with the tide *Fig.* to move along with the effect of outside forces. □ *I just go with the tide. I never fight fate.* □ *She just goes with the tide, never giving a thought to thinking for herself.*

go without and **do without** to manage while not having any of something that is needed; to not have any of something. □ *We were a poor family and usually went without.* □ *I didn't have enough money to buy a new coat so I did without.*

go without (someone or something) to manage without a particular type of person or thing. □ *I can't go without a doctor much longer.* □ *I need a doctor now. I simply can't go without.* □ *We can go without food for only so long.*

go wrong to fail; [for something bad] to happen. □ *The project failed. I don't know what went wrong.* □ *I'm afraid that everything will go wrong.*

goad someone **into** something to urge or coerce someone into doing something. □ *Don't try to goad me into it. I just won't do it!* □ *We goaded Mary into going with us.*

goad someone **on** to urge someone onward, possibly with jeers or challenges; to urge someone to continue. (Usually in this order.) □ *The cheering crowd goaded the team on to victory.* □ *I goaded Jed on to taking the risk.*

gobble someone or something **up**† to eat someone or something completely and rapidly. □ *The wolf said that he was going to gobble the little girl up.* □ *The wolf wanted to gobble up the little pig.*

gobble something **down**† to eat something very fast, swallowing large chunks. □ *The dog gobbled the meat down in seconds.* □ *The cat gobbled down the sardines.*

gobble something **up**† to use up, buy up, or occupy all of something. □ *The shoppers gobbled all the sale merchandise up in a few hours.* □ *They gobbled up everything.*

God forbid! and **Heaven forbid!** a phrase expressing the desire that God would forbid the situation that the speaker has just mentioned from ever happening. □ *Tom: It looks like taxes are going up again. Bob: God forbid!* □ *Bob: Bill was in a car wreck. I hope he wasn't hurt! Sue: God forbid!*

God helps them that help themselves. and **God helps those who help themselves.** *Prov.* You cannot depend solely on divine help, but must work yourself to get what you want. □ *You can't spend your days waiting for a good job to find you. God helps those that help themselves.* □ *If you want a better education, start studying. God helps those who help themselves.*

God only knows! *Inf.* Only God knows.; No one knows but God. □ *Tom: How long is all this going to take? Alice: God only knows!* □ *Bob: Where are we going to find one hundred thousand dollars? Mary: God only knows!*

God rest someone's **soul.** May God bless a previously mentioned person who has died. □ *I remember what my mother, God rest her soul, used to say about that.*

God's gift (to women) *Fig.* a desirable or perfect man. (Usually sarcastic.) □ *Tom thinks he's God's gift to women, but if the truth were known, they laugh at him behind his* back. □ *He acted like he was God's gift and I should be real grateful to be going out with him.*

God takes soonest those he loveth best. *Prov.* Good people often die young. □ *The minister told the boy's grieving parents that God takes soonest those he loveth best.* □ *It may seem to us that Nancy was too young to die, but God takes soonest those he loveth best.*

God willing. If God wants it to happen. (An expression indicating that there is a high certainty that something will happen, so high that only God could prevent it.) □ *John: Please try to be on time. Alice: I'll be there on time, God willing.* □ *Bob: Will I see you after your vacation? Mary: Of course, God willing.*

God willing and the creek don't rise and **Lord willing and the creek don't rise** *Rur.* If all goes well. □ *Tom: Will you be able to get the house painted before the cold weather sets in? Jane: Yes, God willing and the creek don't rise.* □ *We'll be able to visit our daughter for Christmas, Lord willing and the creek don't rise.*

God's in his heaven; all's right with the world. *Prov.* Everything is just as it should be. (Used to express satisfaction, joy, or contentment.) □ *Now that my wife has returned from her long trip, God's in his heaven; all's right with the world.*

The **gods send nuts to those who have no teeth.** *Prov.* People often get good fortune that is no use to them. □ *Soon after Melissa lost her hearing, she won season tickets to the symphony. The gods send nuts to those who have no teeth.*

goggle at someone or something to stare at someone or something with bulging eyes. □ *Don't stand there goggling at me!* □ *The child stood there and goggled at the newborn lamb.*

going, going, gone 1. [in an auction] close to being sold, almost sold, sold. □ *Going, going, gone. The new owner is the handsome gentleman in the back row.* **2.** *Fig.* disappearing and finally gone. □ *The little car is going, going, gone.*

going great guns *Fig.* going fast or energetically. □ *I'm over my cold and going great guns.* □ *Business is great. We are going great guns selling ice cream.*

going on happening; occurring. □ *What is going on here?* □ *Something is going on in the center of town. Can you hear the sirens?*

the **going rate** the current rate or the current charges for something. □ *The going interest rate for your account is 10 percent.* □ *Our babysitter charges us the going rate.*

going strong functioning well or energetically. □ *We are still well and going strong.*

going to tattle Go to next.

going to tell and **going to tattle** a threat that one is going to report someone's misdeed to someone in authority. □ *If you do that again, I'm going to tell!* □ *Sue just went to the teacher. She's going to tattle.*

gol dang Go to next.

gol dern and **gol dang** *Rur.* God damn.; God-damned. □ *Gol dern it, Mary, shut the screen door! Them bugs is gettin' in here in droves.* □ *The gol dang car's in the shop again.*

a **gold mine of information** *Fig.* someone or something that is full of information. □ *Grandfather is a gold mine of information about World War I.* □ *The new encyclopedia is a positive gold mine of useful information.*

A **golden key can open any door.** *Prov.* Sufficient money can accomplish anything. □ *Jill: I'm amazed that Sally got into a good university; her grades were so poor. Jane: Well, she comes from a wealthy family, and a golden key can open any door.* □ *Jane: How did Fred manage to get invited to the party at the country club? It's so exclusive there. Alan: Yes, but a golden key can open any door.*

a **golden opportunity** *Fig.* an excellent opportunity that is not likely to be repeated. □ *When I failed to finish college, I missed my golden opportunity to prepare myself for a good job.*

gone but not forgotten *Cliché* gone or dead and still remembered. □ *The good days we used to have together are gone, but not forgotten.* □ *Uncle Harry is gone but not forgotten. The stain where he spilled the wine is still visible in the parlor carpet.*

gone goose someone or something that has departed or run away. □ *Surely, the burglar is a gone goose by now.* □ *The child was a gone goose, and we did not know where to look for him.*

gone on *Euph.* died. □ *My husband, Tom—he's gone on, you know—was a great one for golf.* □ *Let us remember those who have gone on before.*

gone to meet one's **maker** *Euph.* died. □ *Poor old Bob has gone to meet his maker.* □ *After a long illness, Reggie went to meet his maker.*

gone with the wind *Fig.* gone as if taken away by the wind. (A phrase made famous by the Margaret Mitchell novel and subsequent film *Gone with the Wind.* The phrase is used to make *gone* have a stronger force.) □ *Everything we worked for was gone with the wind.*

a **goner** a dead or dying creature or person. □ *The boy brought the sick fish back to the pet store to get his money back. "This one is a goner," he said.* □ *John thought he was a goner when his parachute didn't open.*

(Good) afternoon. 1. the appropriate greeting for use between noon and supper time. □ *Sally: How are you today? Jane: Good afternoon. How are you? Sally: Fine, thank you.* □ *Bob: Afternoon. Nice to see you. Bill: Good afternoon. How are you? Bob: Fine, thanks.* **2.** an expression used on departure or for dismissal between noon and supper time. (Meaning "I wish you a good afternoon.") □ *Sally: See you later, Bill. Bill: Good afternoon. See you later.* □ *Mary: Nice to see you. Tom: Good afternoon. Take care.*

good and something very or completely something. (Something is a state of being.) □ *Joe never does anything till he's good and ready.* □ *Mary's good and mad, all right.*

*****good as done** the same as being done; almost done. (*Also: **as** ~. Many different words can replace *done* in this phrase, according to context: *cooked, dead, finished, painted, typed,* etc.) □ *This job is as good as done. It'll take another second.* □ *Yes, sir, if you hire me to paint your house, it's as good as painted.* □ *When I hand my secretary a package to be shipped, I know that it's as good as delivered right then and there.*

*good as gold *Cliché* very good. (Usually used to describe children. *Also:* **as ~**.) □ *Mother: Thank you for taking care of Gretchen; I hope she hasn't been too much trouble. Grandmother: Not at all; she's been as good as gold.* □ *We knew that Daddy would not read us a bedtime story unless we behaved, so we tried to be good as gold.*

*good as new *Cliché* as good as when it was new; as well or as healthy as normal. (*Also:* **as ~**.) □ *A little rest and I'll be as good as new.*

a **good bet** *Fig.* a great likelihood. □ *It's a good bet that he will be late because of the rain.*

the **Good Book** the Bible. □ *I read some in the Good Book every day.* □ *Sally's always quoting from the Good Book.*

The **good die young.** *Prov.* Good people tend to die at an early age. □ *Marshall's twenty-year-old son died in a car crash; it did not comfort Marshall to think that the good die young.* □ *Jill: It doesn't seem fair that Laurie is dead. She was such a wonderful person. Jane: They always say that the good die young.*

a **good egg** *Fig.* a good and dependable person. □ *He seems like a good egg. I'll take a chance on him.*

Good enough. That's good.; That's adequate. □ *Bill: Well, now. How's that? Bob: Good enough.* □ *Bob: I'll be there about noon. Tom: Good enough. I'll see you then.*

good enough for government work Go to close enough for government work.

good enough for someone or something adequate for someone or something. □ *This seat is good enough for me. I don't want to move.* □ *I'm happy. It's good enough for me.* □ *That table is good enough for my office.*

(Good) evening. 1. the appropriate greeting for use between supper time and the time of taking leave for the night or by midnight. (Compare this with **Good night.**) □ *Bob: Good evening, Mary. How are you? Mary: Evening, Bob. Nice to see you.* □ *"Good evening," said each of the guests as they passed by Mr. and Mrs. Franklin.* **2.** the appropriate phrase used for leave-taking between supper time and before the time of final leave-taking to go to bed. □ *Mary: Let's call it a day. See you tomorrow, Bill. Bill: Yes, it's been a long and productive day. Good evening, Mary.* □ *Bob: Nice seeing you, Mr. Wilson. Mr. Wilson: Good evening, Bob.*

Good fences make good neighbors. *Prov.* It is easier to be friendly with your neighbor if neither of you trespasses upon the other's property or privacy. □ *Jane: The guy next door is letting his party guests wander across our lawn again. Alan: I guess we'll have to build a fence there. Good fences make good neighbors, like they say.*

good for what ails you *Rur.* able to cure any problem or illness. (Usually used to describe food or liquor.) □ *Have a sip of this whiskey. It's good for what ails you.* □ *Sally's beef broth is good for what ails you.*

Good for you! a complimentary expression of encouragement for something that someone has done or received. □ *Sue: I just got a raise. Bill: Good for you!* □ *Jane: I really told him what I thought of his rotten behavior. Sue: Good for you! He needs it.*

Good going! Go to Nice going!

Good golly, Miss Molly! *Inf.* Good grief!; Wow! □ *Good golly, Miss Molly! This place is a mess!* □ *Good golly, Miss Molly, that's awful!*

a **(good) grasp of** something Go to a (solid) grasp of something.

Good grief! *Inf.* an exclamation of surprise, shock, or amazement. □ *Alice: Good grief! I'm late! Mary: That clock's fast. You're probably okay on time.* □ *Bill: There are seven newborn kittens under the sofa! Jane: Good grief!*

(Good) heavens! *Inf.* an exclamation of surprise, shock, or amazement. (See also **(My) heavens!**) □ *John: Good heavens! Look at that diamond ring she has! Bill: I bet it's not real.* □ *Jane: Ouch! John: Good heavens! What happened? Jane: I just stubbed my toe.*

A **good husband makes a good wife.** and A **good Jack makes a good Jill.** *Prov.* If a husband or man wants his wife or girlfriend to be respectful and loving to him, he should be respectful and loving to her. □ *Don't blame your wife for being short-tempered with you; you've been so unpleasant to her lately. A good husband makes a good wife.*

The **good is the enemy of the best.** *Prov.* Instead of making things the best that they can, people often settle for making them merely good. □ *Mother: Aren't you going to rewrite your paper? Child: Why? It's good enough. Mother: The good is the enemy of the best.*

A **good Jack makes a good Jill.** Go to A good husband makes a good wife.

Good job! Go to Nice going!

Good luck! 1. a wish of good luck to someone. □ *Mary: I have my recital tonight. Jane: I know you'll do well. Good luck!* □ *Sally: I hear you're leaving for your new job tomorrow morning. Bob: That's right. Sally: Well, good luck!* **2.** You will certainly need luck, but it probably will not work. (Sarcastic.) □ *Bill: I'm going to try to get this tax bill lowered. Sue: Good luck!* □ *Bill: I'm sure I can get this cheaper at another store. Clerk: Good luck!*

A **good man is hard to find.** Go to Good men are scarce.

a **good many** quite a few. □ *I have a good many kinfolk in Texas.* □ *Mary owns a good many acres of land.*

Good men are scarce. and A **good man is hard to find.** *Prov.* Men who make good husbands or workers are rare. □ *Larry is the best employee I've ever had, and I'll go to a good deal of effort to keep him, because good men are scarce.* □ *"I think you should marry John," Sue advised her daughter. "He's a good man, and a good man is hard to find."*

(Good) morning. the standard greeting phrase used any time between midnight and noon. □ *Bob: Good morning. Bill: Good morning, Bob. You sure get up early!*

(Good) night. 1. the appropriate departure phrase for leave-taking after dark. (This assumes that the speakers will not see one another until morning at the earliest. *Night* alone is familiar.) □ *John: Bye, Alice. Alice: Night. See you tomorrow.* □ *Bill: Good night, Mary. Mary: Night, Bill.* **2.** the appropriate phrase for wishing someone a good night's sleep. □ *Father: Good night, Bill. Bill: Night, Pop.* □ *Father: Good night. Mother: Good night.*

good old boy and **good ole boy** *Rur.* a good guy; a dependable companion. □ *Old Tom is a good old boy. He'll help.* □ *One of these good ole boys will give you a hand.*

the **good old days** back in an earlier time which everyone remembers as a better time, even if it really wasn't. □ *Back in the good old days, during World War I, they used real cactus needles in record players.* □ *The good old days didn't start until they had indoor bathrooms.*

good riddance (to bad rubbish) *Cliché* [It is] good to be rid (of worthless persons or things). (See also Good-bye and good riddance.) □ *She slammed the door behind me and said, "Good riddance to bad rubbish!"* □ *"Good riddance to you, madam," thought I.*

Good seed makes a good crop. *Prov.* Starting with good materials will help you get good results. □ *Jill: Elsie and Jim are going to have a baby. Jane: I'm sure it will be a good child, since they're both such good people. Good seed makes a good crop.* □ *I am sure Robert's business will flourish. He's capable and honest, and good seed makes a good crop.*

a **good sport** someone who can accept a loss in a competition or can accept being the butt of a joke. □ *Bob is usually a good sport, but this time he didn't seem to appreciate your joke.*

Good things come in small packages. Go to The best things come in small packages.

Good things come to him who waits. and **Everything comes to him who waits.** *Prov.* If you are patient you will get what you want. □ *Fred: Why is it taking you so long to get dinner ready? Can't you hurry up? Ellen: Good things come to him who waits.* □ *Jill: I wish our train would get here. Jane: Everything comes to her who waits.*

A **good time was had by all.** *Cliché* Everyone had a good time. □ *Jill: How was the party? Jane: A good time was had by all.* □ *After seeing the movie, the ten of us went out for ice cream, and a good time was had by all.*

good to go *Inf.* all ready to go; all checked and pronounced ready to go. □ *I've checked everything and we are good to go.* □ *Everything's good to go and we will start immediately.*

*a **(good) working over** a good scolding. (*Typically: **get** ~; **have** ~; **give** someone ~.) □ *The boss gave me a good working over before firing me.* □ *She got a working over about her performance on the project.*

Good-bye and good riddance. *Cliché* a phrase marking the departure of someone or something unwanted. □ *Fred: Supposing I was to just walk out of here, just like that? Mary: I'd say good-bye and good riddance.* □ *As the garbage truck drove away, carrying the drab old chair that Mary hated so much, she said, "Good-bye and good riddance."*

Good-bye for now. and **(Good-bye) until next time.; Till next time.; Bye for now.; Till we meet again.; Until we meet again.** Good-bye, I'll see you soon.; Good-bye, I'll see you next time. (Often said by the host at the end of a radio or television program.) □ *Alice: See you later. Good-bye for now. John: Bye, Alice.* □ *Mary: See you later. Bob: Good-bye for now.* □ *The host of the talk show always closed by saying, "Good-bye until next time. This is Wally Ott, signing off."*

(Good-bye) until then. and **(Good-bye) till then.; (Good-bye) till later.; (Good-bye) until later.** Good-bye until sometime in the future. □ *Sally: See you tomorrow. Good-bye until then. Sue: Sure thing. See you.* □ *Mary: See you later. Bob: Until later.* □ *The announcer always ended by saying, "Be with us again next week at this time. Good-bye until then."*

*the **goods on** someone something potentially damaging or embarrassing about someone. (*Typically: **get** ~; **have** ~; **give** someone ~.) □ *John beat me unfairly in tennis, but I'll get even. I'll get the goods on him and his cheating.* □ *The authorities are going to get the goods on Mr. Smith. He has been selling worthless land again.*

goof around to act silly. □ *The kids were all goofing around, waiting for the bus.* □ *Stop goofing around!*

goof off to waste time. □ *John is always goofing off.* □ *Quit goofing off and get to work!*

goof on someone *Inf.* to tease or kid someone. □ *I don't believe you. I think you're just goofing on me.*

goof someone or something **up**† *Inf.* to mess someone or something up; to ruin someone's plans; to make something nonfunctional. □ *Who goofed this machine up?* □ *Who goofed up the machine?*

goof up (on something) *Inf.* to make an error with something; to blunder while doing something. □ *Please don't goof up on this job.* □ *If you goof up one more time, you're finished.*

goofed (up) 1. *Inf.* messed up; out of order. □ *All my papers are goofed up.* □ *Everything on my desk is goofed. Who's been here?* **2.** *Inf.* confused; distraught. □ *I'm sort of goofed up today. I think I'm coming down with something.* □ *I was up too late last night, and now I'm all goofed up.*

***goose bumps** and ***goose pimples** *Fig.* a prickly feeling related to having bumps on one's skin due to fear, excitement, or cold. (*Typically: **get** ~; **have** ~; **give** someone ~.) □ *When I hear that old song, I get goose bumps.* □ *I never have goose pimples, but my teeth chatter when it's cold.*

goose egg 1. *Fig.* a raised bump on the skull as when one's head has been struck. □ *I walked into the edge of the door and got a terrible goose egg.* **2.** *Fig.* in a sports score, zero. □ *At the end of the game there was nothing but goose eggs next to our name.*

goose pimples Go to goose bumps.

gorge oneself **on** something and **gorge** oneself **with** something to eat something to the point of fullness. □ *Don't gorge yourself on the snacks. Dinner is in ten minutes.* □ *You have gorged yourself with cheese! No wonder you're not hungry.* □ *Claire gorged herself on the doughnuts that Fred bought.*

gorge someone or something **with** something to fill someone or something by eating something. □ *She gorged the dog with canned food.* □ *The puppy gorged itself with all the hamburger Paul had set out to thaw.*

gorked (out) *Sl.* heavily sedated; knocked out. □ *Once the patient was gorked, he was more cooperative.* □ *The guy in Room 226 is totally gorked out now.*

the **gospel truth** *Fig.* the undeniable truth. □ *The witness swore he was telling the gospel truth.* □ *I told my parents the gospel truth about how the vase broke.*

gossip about someone or something to talk maliciously about someone or something. □ *Who are you gossiping about now?* □ *They are gossiping about what happened last weekend.*

got to fly Go to I've got to fly.

gotta get up pretty early in the morning to do something *Rur.* it would be difficult to do something (specified) because of the ability or quality involved. □ *You gotta get up pretty early in the morning to cheat Bill Johnson. He's a sharp businessman for sure.* □ *You gotta get up pretty early in the morning to know your Bible better than Preacher Harris.*

gouge something **out**† Go to gouge something out of something.

gouge something **out of** someone to cheat someone out of something. (Compare this with **chisel** something **out of** someone.) □ *They gouged the money out of the old man.* □ *The crooks gouged the life savings out of the old lady.*

gouge something **out of** something and **gouge** something **out**† to scoop or chisel something out of something. □ *Tom gouged a horrible furrow out of the wood of the piano bench.* □ *He gouged out a horrible scratch.*

Governments have long arms. Go to Kings have long arms.

grab a bite (to eat) Go to a bite (to eat).

grab a chair and **grab a seat** *Fig.* to quickly sit down in a seat. □ *Grab a chair and join the group!*

grab a seat Go to previous.

grab at someone or something and **grab for** someone or something to grasp quickly at someone or something; to try to seize someone or something. □ *He grabbed at me, but I got away unscathed.* □ *I grabbed at the rope, but missed.* □ *The teacher grabbed for the little boy and held him.*

grab for someone or something Go to previous.

grab on(to someone or something**)** to grasp someone or something; to hold onto someone or something. □ *Here, grab onto this rope!* □ *Grab on and hold tight.*

grab someone or something **away**† **(from** someone or something**)** to snatch someone or something away from someone or something. □ *Harry's aunt grabbed the dirty candy away from him before he got it in his mouth.* □ *I grabbed away the meat from the dog.*

grab someone's **attention** and **get** someone's **attention; grip** someone's **attention** *Fig.* to draw or attract someone's attention. □ *The bright colors on the poster are there to grab your attention.* □ *The scary movie gripped my attention.*

grace someone or something **with** one's **presence** *Fig.* to honor someone or something with one's presence. □ *"How nice of you to grace us with your presence," Mr. Wilson told Mary sarcastically as she entered the classroom late.*

□ *The banquet was graced with the presence of the governor.*

grace something **with** something *Fig.* to adorn something or some place with something, especially a person's presence. □ *The lovely lady graced our home with her presence.* □ *The stage was graced with flowers and a few palm trees.*

graced with something made elegant by means of some ornament or decoration. □ *The altar was graced with lovely white flowers.* □ *The end of the beautiful day was graced with a beautiful sunset.*

*****graceful as a swan** very graceful. (*Also: as ~.) □ *The boat glided out onto the lake as graceful as a swan.* □ *Jane is graceful as a swan.*

a **gracious plenty** and an **elegant sufficiency** *Euph.* enough (food). □ *No more, thanks. I have a gracious plenty on my plate.* □ *At Thanksgiving, we always have an elegant sufficiency and are mighty thankful for it.*

grade someone **down (on** something**)** to give someone a low ranking, rating, or score on some performance. □ *I had to grade you down on your essay because of your spelling.* □ *Please don't grade me down for a minor mistake.*

graduate (from something**)** to earn and receive a degree from an educational institution. □ *I graduated from a large midwestern university.* □ *Bill intends to graduate in the spring.*

graduate (in something**) (with** something**)** to earn a degree in some subject with honors, etc. □ *I graduated in math with highest honors.* □ *Sharon graduated with honors in medicine.*

graft something **on(to)** something and **graft** something **on**† to splice a living part onto another living part. □ *The gardener grafted a red rose onto the stem of another species.* □ *The gardener grafted on a red rose.*

a **grain of truth** even the smallest amount of truth. □ *The attorney was unable to find a grain of truth in the defendant's testimony.* □ *If there were a grain of truth to your statement, I would trust you.*

the **granddaddy of them all** Go to the daddy of them all.

a **grandfather clause** a clause in an agreement that protects certain rights granted in the past even when conditions change in the future. □ *The contract contained a grandfather clause that protected my pension payments against claims such as might arise from a future lawsuit.*

grandfather someone or something **in**† to protect someone or a right through the use of a **grandfather clause.** □ *My payments were grandfathered in years ago.*

grant someone **no quarter** and **give** someone **no quarter** *Fig.* not to allow someone any mercy or indulgence. (Originally meant to refuse to imprison and simply to kill one's prisoner.) □ *The professor was harsh on lazy students. During class, he granted them no quarter.*

grant something **to** someone to give or award something to someone. □ *The foundation granted a large sum of money to Jane for her research.* □ *They granted an award to Kelly.*

graph something **out**† to draw a graph of something. □ *Please take this data and graph it out.* □ *Graph out this data, please.*

grapple (with someone**) (for** something**)** to fight or scuffle with someone to get hold of something. □ *The cop grappled with the thief for the gun.* □ *He grappled for the gun with Max.*

grapple with something *Fig.* to deal with a problem; to get a "good hold" on a problem. □ *I have enough to grapple with now. No more problems, please.* □ *I cannot grapple with any additional problems.*

grasp at someone or something to try to seize someone or something. □ *He grasped at the bar and held on tight.* □ *The beggar grasped at the pedestrian and lost his grip.*

grasp someone or something **by** something to hold onto someone or something by something. □ *He grasped his friend by the hand and pulled him to safety.* □ *Sharon grasped the dog by its collar and held on tight.*

grasping at straws *Fig.* to depend on something that is useless; to make a futile attempt at something. □ *John couldn't answer the teacher's question. He was just grasping at straws.* □ *There I was, grasping at straws, with no one to help me.*

The **grass is always greener on the other side (of the fence).** *Prov.* People always think they would be happier in a different set of circumstances. (Usually implies that the other circumstances really are not any better.) □ *Jill: My job is so tedious. I wish I had my own business, like Beatrice does. Jane: Beatrice probably wishes she had the security of her old job. The grass is always greener on the other side of the fence.*

grass widow a woman abandoned by her husband. (The origin of this is not clear.) □ *Jane's husband isn't dead, but she's a widow just the same—a grass widow.* □ *Bill ran off and left Mary a grass widow.*

grate on someone to annoy someone; to rub someone the wrong way. □ *Your negative attitude really grates on me.* □ *Everything you say grates on me.*

grate on someone**('s nerves)** *Fig.* to annoy someone; to bother someone. □ *My obnoxious brother is grating on my nerves.* □ *Your whining really grates on me.*

grate on something to rub, scrape, or abrade something. □ *The tree branch is grating on the side of the house.* □ *The bottom of the door is grating on the threshold. Please fix it.*

gratify someone**'s desires** *Euph.* to have sex with someone. □ *The prostitute promised to gratify her customer's desires.* □ *That night, he gratified her desires.*

gravitate to(ward) someone or something *Fig.* to move slowly toward someone or something, as if being pulled by gravity. □ *People tend to gravitate toward the kitchen at parties.* □ *Unless you correct their manners, the children will gravitate toward rude behavior.*

a **gray area** *Fig.* an area of a subject or question that is difficult to put into a particular category because it is not clearly defined and may have connections or associations with more than one category. □ *The responsibility for social studies in the college is a gray area. Several departments are involved.* □ *Publicity is a gray area in that firm. It is shared between the marketing and design divisions.*

*****gray hair(s) 1.** *Lit.* a lightening of the hair caused by aging or hereditary factors. (*Typically: **get** ~; **have** ~; **give** someone ~.) □ *I get more gray hair the older I get.* □ *I guess my genes give me gray hair.* **2.** *Fig.* a lightening of the hair caused by stress or frustration. (*Typically: **get** ~; **have** ~; **give** someone ~.) □ *I'm getting gray hairs because I have three teenage boys.* □ *I have gray hair from raising four kids.*

gray matter *Fig.* intelligence; brains; power of thought. □ *Use your gray matter and think what will happen if the committee resigns.* □ *Surely they'll come up with an acceptable solution if they use some gray matter.*

graze against someone or something to brush or scrape against someone or something. □ *The car grazed against the side of the truck.* □ *I grazed against an old man as I was jogging this morning.*

graze on something **1.** [for animals] to browse or forage in a particular location. □ *The cattle are grazing on the neighbor's land.* □ *I wish they wouldn't graze on other people's land.* **2.** [for animals] to browse or forage, eating something in particular. □ *The deer are grazing on my carrots!* □ *The cows were grazing on the meadow grasses for weeks.*

grease someone's **palm** and **oil** someone's **palm** *Fig.* to bribe someone. □ *If you want to get something done around here, you have to grease someone's palm.* □ *I'd never oil a police officer's palm. That's illegal.*

grease the skids *Fig.* to help prepare for or ease the way for the success or failure of someone or something. □ *Ray set out to grease the skids for the right things to happen.* □ *We need someone to grease the skids for the Wilson contract.*

a **greasy spoon** *Fig.* a cheap diner, where the silverware might not be too clean. □ *The corner greasy spoon is always busy at lunchtime.*

Great balls of fire! *Inf.* Good heavens!; Wow! □ *Mary got up to play the fiddle, and great balls of fire! That girl can play!* □ *Tom: Will you marry me? Jane: Yes, I will. Tom: Great balls of fire! I'm the happiest man on earth.*

the **great beyond** *Euph.* life after death. □ *The fortune-teller claimed to get messages from the great beyond.* □ *I often think of my loved ones in the great beyond, and long for the day I will see them again.*

Great day (in the morning)! *Rur.* My goodness! (An exclamation of surprise.) □ *Great day in the morning! I didn't expect to see you here.* □ *Great day! That thunder sure is loud!*

a **great deal** much; a lot. □ *You can learn a great deal about nature by watching television.* □ *This is a serious problem and it worries me a great deal.*

Great minds think alike. *Prov.* Very intelligent people tend to come up with the same ideas at the same time. (Used playfully, to commend someone for expressing the same thing you were thinking of; implies that you are congratulating that person for being as smart as you are. Also **Great minds run in the same gutters,** a casual and jocular variant.) □ *Jill: Let's ride our bikes to the store instead of walking. Jane: I was just thinking we should do that, too. Jill: Great minds think alike.*

Great oaks from little acorns grow. and **Mighty oaks from little acorns grow.** *Prov.* Immense things can come from small sources. □ *Don't tell lies, not even small ones. Great oaks from little acorns grow.*

Great Scott! *Inf.* an exclamation of shock or surprise. □ *"Great Scott! You bought a truck!" shrieked Mary.* □ *Fred:*

The water heater just exploded! Bill: Great Scott! What do we do now? Fred: Looks like cold showers for a while.

the **great unwashed** *Fig.* the general public; the lower middle class. □ *The Simpsons had a tall iron fence around their mansion—put there to discourage the great unwashed from wandering up to the door by mistake, I suppose.* □ *Maw says the great unwashed don't know enough to come in out of the rain.*

The **greater the truth, the greater the libel.** *Prov.* It is more offensive to say something damaging and true about someone than it is to tell a damaging lie. □ *Jill: Fred's really upset. Someone's started a rumor that he's unfaithful to his wife. Jane: But it's true. Jill: Yeah, but the greater the truth, the greater the libel.*

the **greatest thing since indoor plumbing** and the **greatest thing since sliced bread** *Rur.* the most wonderful invention or useful item in a long time. □ *As far as I'm concerned, this new food processor is the greatest thing since indoor plumbing.* □ *Joe thinks Sally is the greatest thing since sliced bread. You can tell just by the way he looks at her.*

the **greatest thing since sliced bread** Go to previous.

Greek to someone incomprehensible to someone; as mysterious as Greek writing. □ *I don't understand this. It's all Greek to me.* □ *She said it was Greek to her, and that it made no sense at all.*

green around the gills Go to pale around the gills.

*****green as grass** very green. (*Also: **as** ~.) □ *His face turned as green as grass just before he vomited.*

green stuff *Fig.* money; U.S. paper money. □ *I've run out of green stuff. Can you loan me a few bucks?*

*****green with envy** *Fig.* appearing jealous; appearing envious. (*Typically: **be** ~; **become** ~.) □ *My new car made my neighbor green with envy.* □ *Bill was green with envy that I won first place.*

greet someone or something **with** something to welcome someone or something with something; to accost someone or something with something upon arrival. □ *I greeted her with a large bouquet of roses.* □ *The sun greeted the day with bright rays of light.*

Greetings and felicitations! and **Greetings and salutations!** Hello and good wishes. (A bit stilted.) □ *"Greetings and felicitations! Welcome to our talent show!" said the master of ceremonies.* □ *Bill: Greetings and salutations, Bob! Bob: Come off it, Bill. Can't you just say "Hi" or something?*

grieve for someone or something to mourn for someone or something. □ *Don't grieve for me. I'm okay.* □ *She grieved for her lost chances.*

grieve over someone or something to lament and pine for someone or something. □ *Now, don't grieve over a lost cat.* □ *There is no reason to continue grieving over him.*

the **grim reaper** *Fig.* death. □ *I think I have a few years to go yet before the grim reaper pays me a call.*

grin and bear it *Fig.* to endure something unpleasant in good humor. □ *There is nothing you can do but grin and bear it.* □ *I hate having to work for rude people. I guess I have to grin and bear it.*

grin at someone or something **1.** to smile a beaming smile at someone or something. □ *The entire class grinned at the camera.* □ *I grinned at her and she turned away quickly.* **2.** to smile a beaming smile at the thought of, or mental picture of, someone or something. □ *He grinned at the thought of his coming home to his family.* □ *He grinned at her as she gazed upon the diamond ring he had given her.*

grin from ear to ear *Fig.* to smile a very wide, beaming smile. □ *She was grinning from ear to ear as she accepted the prize.* □ *We knew Timmy was happy because he was grinning from ear to ear.*

grind away (at someone**)** *Fig.* to needle, criticize, and nag someone continually. □ *Why are you always grinding away at me?* □ *Leave me alone. Stop grinding away!*

grind away (at something**)** to crush something into particles continually. □ *The machine ground away at the rocks, making tons of gravel.* □ *It ground away, making a terrible noise in the process.*

grind on *Fig.* [for something] to drag on endlessly. □ *The hours ground on without anything happening. I was so tired of waiting.* □ *The lecture ground on, minute after minute.*

grind someone **down†** *Fig.* to wear someone down by constant requests; to wear someone down by constant nagging. □ *If you think you can grind me down by bothering me all the time, you are wrong.* □ *The constant nagging ground down the employees at last.*

grind something **away†** to remove something by grinding. □ *Grind the bumps away and make the wall smooth.* □ *Please grind away the bumps.*

grind something **down†** to make something smooth or even by grinding. □ *Grind this down to make it smooth.* □ *Please grind down this rough spot.*

grind something **into** something **1.** to pulverize something into powder, grit, particles, etc. □ *The machine ground the rocks into gravel.* □ *The mill ground the grain into flour.* **2.** and **grind** something **in†** to crush or rub something into something. □ *People's feet ground the cigarette ashes into the carpet.* □ *Their feet ground in the ashes.*

grind something **out†** **1.** *Lit.* to produce something by grinding. □ *Working hard, he ground the powder out, a cup at a time.* □ *He ground out the powder, a cup at a time.* **2.** *Fig.* to produce something in a mechanical or perfunctory manner. □ *The factory just keeps grinding toys out, day after day.* □ *The machine grinds out the same part by the hundreds all day long.*

grind something **to** something to keep grinding something until it is something. □ *I ground the fennel seeds to a powder and threw them in the simmering sauce.* □ *The wheels of the cars, trucks, and buses had ground the football to a broken mass.*

grind something **together** to rub things together. □ *Stop grinding your teeth together.* □ *The stones ground together as we drove over them.*

grind something **up†** to pulverize or crush something by crushing, rubbing, or abrasion. □ *Please grind the fennel seeds up.* □ *Grind up the fennel seeds and sprinkle them on the top.*

grind to a halt *Fig.* to slow down and stop. □ *Every day about noon, traffic in town grinds to a halt.* □ *The bus ground to a halt at the corner and someone got off.*

*a grip on oneself *Fig.* control of one's emotions. (*Typically: **get** ~; **have** ~.) □ *Calm down, man! Get a grip on yourself!* □ *I encouraged him to get a grip on himself.*

*a grip on something **1.** and ***a hold on** something *Lit.* a good grasp on something. (*Typically: **get** ~; **have** ~; **give** someone ~.) □ *Try to get a grip on the ropes and pull yourself up.* □ *You should get a hold on the knob and turn it firmly.* **2.** *Fig.* a thorough knowledge of some topic. (*Typically: **get** ~; **have** ~; **give** someone ~.) □ *I need to have a grip on the basics of accounting.* □ *Try to get a hold on all the facts first.*

grip someone's **attention** Go to grab someone's **attention**.

gripe at someone to complain to someone. □ *Stop griping at me!* □ *There is no need to gripe at your little brother.*

gripe one's **soul** *Inf.* to annoy someone. □ *That kind of thing really gripes my soul!* □ *John, have I ever told you that you gripe my soul?*

gripe (to someone or something**) (about** someone or something**)** to make specific complaints to someone about someone or something. □ *Don't gripe to me about what she said to you!* □ *There is no need to gripe about the job to everyone.*

grist for the mill and **grist for** someone's **mill; grist to the mill** *Fig.* something useful or needed. □ *Bob bases the novels he writes on his own experience, so everything that happens to him is grist for the mill.* □ *Ever since I started making patchwork quilts, every scrap of cloth I find is grist for the mill.*

grit one's **teeth** *Fig.* to grind or clench one's teeth together in anger or determination. □ *I was so mad, all I could do was stand there and grit my teeth.* □ *All through the race, Sally was gritting her teeth. She was really determined.*

groan about someone or something to complain about someone or something. □ *What are you groaning about?* □ *She is groaning about her work.*

groan something **out†** to say something with a groan. □ *He groaned the name out.* □ *He groaned out the name of his assailant before he passed out.*

groan under something **1.** *Lit.* to groan while bearing a heavy burden. □ *He groaned under the weight of the trunk.* □ *The rafters groaned under the heavy weight of the pianos.* **2.** *Fig.* to suffer under a burden. □ *For years, the people had groaned under the cruel ruler.* □ *England groaned under the rule of Cromwell just as he had groaned under King Charles.*

groan with something to groan because of something, such as pain. □ *She groaned with pain, but no one helped her.* □ *I think the old man was groaning with boredom more than anything else.*

gronk (out) *Sl.* to conk out; to crash, as with a car or a computer. □ *My car gronked out on the way to work this morning.* □ *The program gronks every time I start to run it.*

groom someone **as** something to prepare someone for a job or position. □ *He was grooming his son as his successor.* □ *They groomed Charles as the next treasurer.*

groom someone **for** something to prepare someone for something; to prepare someone to be someone. □ *The boss is grooming his son for the presidency of the company.* □ *They are grooming the vice president for the top position.*

groove on someone or something to show interest in someone or something; to relate to someone or something. □ *Fred was beginning to groove on new age music when he met Phil.* □ *Sam is really grooving on Mary.*

grope (about) (for someone or something**)** and **grope (around) (for** someone or something**)** to feel around blindly for someone or something. □ *In the darkness, he groped about for his glasses.* □ *Fran groped for the light switch and found it.*

grope after someone or something to reach for a departing or fleeing person or thing awkwardly or ineffectually. □ *The feeble hand groped after the departing form.* □ *I groped after the cat as it ran under the bed.*

grope (around) (for someone or something**)** Go to grope (about) (for someone or something).

grope at someone or something to reach for someone or something blindly. □ *She groped feebly at the form she could hardly see.* □ *Sharon groped at Frank as he ran out to get the doctor.*

gross someone **out†** to disgust someone. □ *Those horrible pictures just gross me out.* □ *Jim's story totally grossed out Sally.*

ground someone **in** something *Fig.* to instruct someone in an area of knowledge. □ *We grounded all our children in the basics of home cooking.* □ *We were all grounded in basic cooking by the time we were six.*

ground something **on** something *Fig.* to build a firm basis for something on something else. □ *He grounded his thinking on his detailed research.* □ *His thinking was grounded on years of reading.*

grounded in (actual) fact *Fig.* based on facts. □ *This movie is grounded in fact.* □ *The stories in this book are all grounded in actual fact.*

*grounds for something the basis or cause for legal action such as a lawsuit. (*Typically: **be** ~; **become** ~.) □ *Your negligence is grounds for a lawsuit.* □ *Is infidelity grounds for divorce in this state?*

group someone or something **around** someone or something to gather people or things around people or things. □ *The photographer grouped the wedding party around the bride for the picture.* □ *The photographer then grouped them around the cake.*

group someone or something **together** to gather people or things together. □ *Try to group all the smokers together at one table.* □ *Steve grouped all the dictionaries together.*

group something **under** something to classify something under some category. □ *They have now grouped the fungi under their own families.* □ *We should group all the older ones under a separate category.*

grouse about someone or something to complain about someone or something. □ *What are you grousing about now?* □ *I am grousing about your carelessness!*

grouse at someone or an animal *Fig.* to criticize someone or an animal directly to the person or animal. □ *Stop grousing at me!* □ *Sharon is grousing at the cat again.*

grovel (about) in something to wallow around in the dirt, etc., while prostrating oneself. □ *The poor fellow groveled* *about in the mud, trying to keep from being beaten.* □ *Why are you there, groveling in the dust?*

grovel before someone or something to prostrate oneself before someone or something. □ *The prisoner groveled before his accusers.* □ *The peasant groveled before the lord of the manor.*

grovel to someone to kneel in deference to someone; to kowtow to someone. □ *You don't have to grovel to me!* □ *I refuse to grovel to anyone.*

grow accustomed to doing something Go to accustomed to doing something.

grow accustomed to someone or something Go to accustomed to someone or something.

grow apart (from someone or something**) 1.** *Lit.* [for things] to separate as they grow. □ *These trees tend to grow apart from each other as they get bigger.* □ *They need to grow apart so they won't be too crowded.* **2.** *Fig.* [for people] to separate from one another gradually. □ *Over the years, they grew apart from each other.* □ *Ted and Sharon grew apart and saw less and less of each other.*

grow away from someone [for someone] to become less intimate with someone; [for someone] to become independent of someone gradually. □ *She has grown away from her husband over the years.* □ *We expect our children to grow away from us.*

grow away from something [for something] to move away from something as it grows. □ *The tree grew away from the house—thank heavens.* □ *See if you can train the vine to grow away from the fence.*

grow back [for something that has come off] to grow back again. (Includes parts of plants and some animals, fingernails, toenails, etc.) □ *The lizard's tail grew back in a few months.* □ *The leaves will grow back in a month or so.*

grow disgusted at someone or something Go to disgusted at someone or something.

grow disgusted with someone or something Go to disgusted with someone or something.

grow dissatisfied with someone or something Go to dissatisfied with someone or something.

grow down (into something**)** [for roots] to penetrate downward as they grow. □ *The young roots grew down into the rich soil.* □ *The roots grew down and drew up the precious water.*

grow from something to develop and grow from a seed, bulb, corm, etc. □ *This huge tree grew from a little seed.* □ *What kind of plant grows from this bulb?*

grow in something **1.** [for someone] to increase in some quality, such as wisdom, strength, stature, etc. □ *As I got older, I was supposed to grow in wisdom and other good things.* □ *Sam grew in strength as he got over the disease.* **2.** [for a plant] to develop or flourish in something or some place. □ *These plants grow in rich soil with moderate moisture.* □ *They will grow well in this soil.*

grow into something **1.** *Lit.* [for a child] to develop into a particular type of person. □ *The child grew into a tall, powerful athlete.* □ *I hope I have grown into a person my parents can be proud of.* **2.** *Lit.* [for a plant] to develop into a mature specimen of its species. □ *This twig will grow into an oak tree.* □ *I hope this seedling grows into a fine*

mango tree. **3.** *Lit.* [for a plant, tumor, toenail] to penetrate into something as it grows. □ *The roots of the tree grew into our sewer line.* □ *Try to keep the tree roots from growing into the foundation.* **4.** *Lit.* to grow enough to fit into something. □ *The shirt is a little large, but Timmy will grow into it.* □ *My shoes are too big, but I will grow into them.* **5.** *Fig.* [for a situation or a problem] to develop into something more serious. □ *I hope this matter doesn't grow into something worse.* □ *This business is growing into a real crisis.*

grow knee-high by the 4th of July Go to knee-high by the 4th of July.

grow on someone **1.** *Lit.* [for a fungus, tumor, parasite, etc.] to live and grow on someone's skin. □ *I've got this stuff growing on me and I want to get rid of it.* □ *Is that an ink stain or is something growing on you?* **2.** *Fig.* [for something] to become familiar to and desired by someone; [for something] to become habitual for someone. □ *This kind of music grows on you after a while.* □ *Kenneth sort of grows on you after a while.*

grow out [for something that has been cut back] to regrow. □ *Don't worry, your hair will grow out again.* □ *Will the grass grow out again, do you think?*

grow out of (all) proportion Go to out of (all) proportion.

grow out of something **1.** *Lit.* to develop and grow outward from something. □ *Soft green shoots grew out of the trunk of the tree.* □ *A bush grew out of the gutter and hung down the front of the house.* **2.** *Lit.* to age out of something; to outgrow something; to abandon something as one matures. □ *Finally, Ted grew out of his bedwetting.* □ *Haven't you grown out of your fear of the dark yet?* **3.** *Lit.* to grow so much that some article of clothing does not fit. □ *Timmy's getting so tall that he's grown out of all his clothes.* □ *He grew out of his suit, and he's only worn it three times.* **4.** *Fig.* [for a problem] to develop from something less serious. □ *This whole matter grew out of your failure to let the cat out last night.* □ *A big argument has grown out of a tiny disagreement!*

grow over something [for vegetation] to cover over something as it grows. □ *The vines grew over the shed and almost hid it from view.*

grow poles apart Go to poles apart.

grow sick (and tired) of someone or something Go to sick (and tired) of someone or something.

grow soft on someone Go to soft on someone.

grow something **from** something to propagate a plant from a seed, bulb, corm, etc. □ *I grew these tomatoes from seeds.* □ *Can you grow a mango tree from a seed?*

grow thick-skinned Go to thick-skinned.

grow thin-skinned Go to thin-skinned.

grow to do something to gradually begin to do certain things, using verbs such as *feel, know, like, need, respect, sense, suspect, think, want, wonder,* etc. □ *I grew to hate Bob over a period of years.* □ *As I grew to know Bob, I began to like him.*

grow together [for things] to join together as they grow and develop. □ *Two of these trees grew together when they* were much smaller. □ *The broken ends of the bone grew together far more rapidly than Chuck had thought.*

grow up to become mature; to become adult. □ *All the children have grown up and the parents are left with a lot of debts.*

grow up into someone or something to mature into a type of person or a person who does a particular job. □ *She grew up into a fine young lady.* □ *I want to grow up into a strong and healthy person.*

grow worlds apart Go to worlds apart.

A **growing youth has a wolf in his belly.** *Prov.* Young people who are growing fast are hungry all the time. □ *If you doubt that a growing youth has a wolf in his belly, you should see how much my fourteen-year-old cousin eats.*

growl at someone or something to snarl at someone or something. □ *Don't growl at me like that.* □ *The dog growled at the cat.*

growl something **out**† to say something with a sound like growling or snarling. □ *Jane growled a few words out.* □ *She growled out a few words and the gates opened for us.*

a **growth experience** and a **growth opportunity;** a **learning experience** *Euph.* an unpleasant experience. □ *This job has been a growth experience for me. I've learned so much.* □ *Jim said that his trip to Mexico turned out to be a real learning experience.*

a **growth opportunity** Go to previous.

grub around (for someone or something**)** to search around for someone or something. □ *I went to the attic and grubbed around for my old uniform.* □ *The guys went out and grubbed around for another soccer player.*

grub around (in something**)** to wear old or "grubby" clothes around. □ *I was grubbing around in my jeans when Alice showed up.* □ *I was wearing my jeans and just sort of grubbing around when she came.*

***gruff as a bear** gruff; curt and unsociable. (*Also:* **as** ~.) □ *I hate to ask Erica questions; she's always gruff as a bear.* □ *I'm always as gruff as a bear before I've had my first cup of coffee.*

grumble about someone or something to complain about someone or something. □ *What are you grumbling about now?* □ *The students were grumbling about the teacher.*

grumble at someone to complain to someone. □ *Go grumble at someone else. I'm tired of listening.* □ *Stop grumbling at me!*

grunt something **out**† to say something with a snort or grunt. □ *Jane grunted a command out to someone.* □ *She grunted out a curt command and the gate opened.*

grunt work *Fig.* work that is menial and thankless. □ *During the summer, I earned money doing grunt work.* □ *I did all of the grunt work on the project, but my boss got all of the credit.*

guarantee against something to certify that something bad will not happen. □ *No one can guarantee against that happening.* □ *I can't guarantee against something going wrong.*

guarantee something **against** something **(for** something**)** to certify that something will not fail, break, or wear out, usually for a period of time. □ *We guarantee this radio*

against defects for one year. □ *I bought a service contract to guarantee my car against defects.*

guard against someone or something to take care to avoid someone or something. □ *Try to guard against getting a cold.* □ *You should guard against pickpockets.*

guard someone or something **from** someone or something to protect someone or something from someone or something. □ *The assistant manager will guard your valuables from thieves.* □ *She guarded the kitten from the angry dog.*

guess at something to estimate something; to give an opinion about what something might be. □ *I hate to just guess at it, but if you insist: ten feet long.* □ *Go ahead, guess at the number of pennies in this jar.*

Guess what! *Inf.* a way of starting a conversation; a way of forcing someone into a conversation. □ *Alice: Guess what! Bob: I don't know. What? Alice: I'm going to Europe this summer. Bob: That's very nice.* □ *John: Guess what! Jane: What? John: Mary is going to have a baby. Jane: Oh, that's great!*

guest of honor a guest who gets special attention from everyone; the person for whom a party, celebration, or ceremony is given. □ *Bob is the guest of honor, and many people will make speeches about him.* □ *The guest of honor sits at the front of the room on the dais.*

guffaw at someone or something to laugh at someone or something very hard and raucously. □ *The audience guffawed at the clown's antics.* □ *The old man guffawed at the clown.*

guide someone **around** something and **guide** someone **around** to lead or escort someone on a tour of something or some place. □ *Please let me guide you around the plant, so you can see how we do things here.* □ *I would be happy to guide you around.*

guide someone **away from** someone or something and **guide** someone **away**† to lead or escort someone away from someone, something, or some place. (Usually said of someone who requires help or guidance.) □ *A police officer guided the children away from the busy street.* □ *Please guide away those people before they bump into your grandmother.*

guide someone or something **across (**something**)** to lead or escort someone or something across something. □ *I had to guide him across the desert.* □ *The bridge was very narrow and Jill got out to guide the truck across.* □ *We had to guide it across.*

guide something **away**† **(from** someone or something**) 1.** to lead something away from someone or something. □ *I guided the lawn mower away from the children.* □ *Please stand there and guide away the cars.* **2.** to channel or route something away from someone or something. □ *The farmer guided the creek water away from the main channel through a narrow ditch.* □ *We had to guide away the sheep from the road.*

A **guilty conscience needs no accuser.** *Prov.* If you have done something wrong and feel guilty about it, you will be uncomfortable and want to confess even if no one accuses you of wrongdoing. □ *Even though no one noticed him eating most of the cookies, Peter felt so bad about it that he told us what he had done. A guilty conscience needs no accuser.*

G

gulp for air *Fig.* to eagerly or desperately try to get air or a breath. □ *Tom gulped for air after trying to hold his breath for three minutes.* □ *Mary came up out of the water, gulping for air.*

gulp something **back†** *Fig.* to force or hold back tears, sobs, etc. □ *He gulped his sobs back and clutched at his wound.* □ *He gulped back his sobs.*

gulp something **down†** to drink all of something, usually quickly. □ *He gulped his coffee down and left.* □ *He gulped down his coffee.*

gum something **up†** and **gum the works up†** *Fig.* to make something inoperable; to ruin someone's plans. □ *Please, Bill, be careful and don't gum up the works.* □ *Tom sure gummed up the whole plan.*

gun for someone **1.** *Lit.* to seek one out to shoot one. □ *They say that Tex is gunning for the sheriff.* **2.** *Fig.* to seek someone out in anger. □ *The boss is gunning for you.* □ *I think that Walter is gunning for me.*

gun someone or an animal **down†** *Lit.* to shoot someone or an animal. □ *Max tried to gun a policeman down.* □ *The cop tried to gun down the rabid dog.*

gung ho *Inf.* enthusiastically in favor of something. □ *Bobby is really gung ho on his plan to start his own company.*

gush (forth) (from someone or something**)** and **gush (forth) (out of** someone or something**); gush (out) (from** someone or something**)** to spout out of someone or something. (Can be words, water, blood, vomit, etc. The optional elements cannot be transposed.) □ *The blood gushed forth from his wound.* □ *Curses gushed forth from Sharon.* □ *Water gushed forth out of the broken pipe.* □ *The words gushed out from her mouth.* □ *The curses gushed from her mouth in torrents.*

gush over someone or something **1.** *Lit.* [for liquid] to flood over someone or something. □ *The floodwaters gushed over the farmland.* □ *The hot soup gushed over the cook as the huge pot tipped over.* **2.** *Fig.* [for someone] to heap praise, flattery, and compliments on someone or something. □ *Aunt Mattie always gushed over us children so much that we dreaded her coming.* □ *All the guests gushed over my beet salad.*

gush with something [for something] to flow with something. □ *The stream gushed with the sudden runoff of the storm.* □ *The faucet gushed with brownish water, so I turned it off.*

gussied up *Rur.* dressed up fancy. □ *All the girls got gussied up for the dance, but the guys wore their regular clothes.* □ *Mary really got gussied up. She even curled her hair.*

gussy someone or something **up†** *Rur.* to dress someone or something up; to make someone or something fancy. □ *She gussied the kids up for the wedding.* □ *See if you can gussy up this room a little before folks get here.*

gut feeling and **gut reaction; gut response** a personal, intuitive feeling or response. □ *I have a gut feeling that something bad is going to happen.* □ *My gut reaction is that we should hire Susan for the job.*

gut reaction Go to previous.

gut response Go to gut feeling.

guzzle something **down†** to drink something rapidly and eagerly. □ *He guzzled the beer down and called for another.* □ *He guzzled down the beer and called for another.*

gyp someone **out of** something to deceive someone in order to get something of value. □ *The salesclerk gypped me out of a dollar.* □ *The taxi driver tried to gyp me out of a fortune by driving all over the place.*

H*h*

habituate someone **to** someone or something to accustom someone to someone or something. □ *Soon she will habituate the baby to the new feeding schedule.* □ *The office staff worked hard to habituate the new employee to the schedule.*

hack around *Inf.* to waste time. □ *I'm just hacking around and doing nothing.* □ *Stop hacking around and get to work.*

hack (away) at someone or something to chop at someone or something continuously. □ *The brutal murderer hacked away at his victim.* □ *The woodchopper hacked at the tree and finally got it down.*

hack one's **way through** something *Fig.* to cut one's way through something. □ *We had to hack our way through the jungle.* □ *The surveyors hacked a pathway through the undergrowth.*

hack someone **(off)** *Inf.* to annoy someone; to embarrass someone. □ *It really hacks me when you drum your fingers like that.* □ *You really hack me off!*

hack someone or something **apart**[†] **1.** *Lit.* to chop up someone or something. □ *The murderer hacked the victim apart.* □ *He hacked apart the victim.* □ *The butcher hacked the chicken apart.* **2.** *Fig.* to criticize someone or something severely. □ *The review just hacked him apart for his poor showing in the play.* □ *The critic hacked apart all the actors in the play.*

hack something *Inf.* to endure something; to deal with something. (The *something* is usually *it.*) □ *I don't know if I can hack it.* □ *John works very hard, but he can't seem to hack it.*

hack something **down**[†] to chop something down. □ *Who hacked this cherry tree down?* □ *Who hacked down this cherry tree?*

hack something **off**[†] to chop something off. □ *I need to get up that tree and hack that big branch off before it bangs on the house.* □ *Please hack off that big branch.*

hack something **out of** something and **hack** something **out**[†] **1.** to cut or chop something out of something. □ *Jill hacked the bone out of the roast.* □ *She hacked out the big bone.* **2.** to fashion something by carving or chiseling from something. □ *He hacked a rabbit out of the chunk of wood.* □ *In no time, the carver had hacked out a rabbit.*

hack something **to** something to cut something up into something roughly or crudely, such as pieces, bits, smithereens. □ *The editor hacked my story to smithereens.* □ *Don't hack the turkey to pieces!*

hack something **up**[†] **1.** *Lit.* to chop something up into pieces. (Refers often to wood.) □ *Hack all this old furniture up, and we'll burn it in the fireplace.* □ *Hack up this stuff, and we'll burn it.* **2.** *Fig.* to damage or mangle something. □ *Who hacked my windowsill up?* □ *Who hacked up my table?*

hacked (off) *Inf.* angry; annoyed. □ *Wally was really hacked off about the accident.* □ *Oh, Wally is always hacked about something.*

(had) best do something ought to do something, had better do something. □ *Mary had best learn to mind her manners.* □ *You best listen to what I say.*

had (just) as soon do something and **would (just) as soon** do something prefer to do something else; to be con-

tent to do something. (The *would* or *had* is usually expressed as the contraction *'d.*) □ *They want me to go into town. I'd as soon stay home.* □ *If you're cooking stew tonight, we'd as soon eat somewhere else.* □ *I would just as soon stay home as pay to go to see a bad movie.*

(had) known it was coming Go to knew it was coming.

had rather do something and **had sooner** do something prefer to do something. (The *had* is usually expressed as the contraction, *'d.*) □ *I'd rather go to town than sit here all evening.* □ *They'd rather not.*

had sooner do something Go to previous.

hadn't oughta *Inf.* should not have. □ *You hadn't oughta teased me like that.* □ *I know I hadn't oughta stolen that candy.*

haggle about something to bargain or negotiate about something. □ *They are always willing to haggle about the price, so don't take the first price you're given.* □ *I wish you wouldn't try to haggle about everything when we shop.*

haggle (with someone**) over** someone or something and **haggle with** someone **(over** someone or something**)** to argue with someone over someone or something. □ *I don't want to haggle with you over Tom and whose team he's going to be on.* □ *Let's not haggle over the price.* □ *There is no point in haggling with her.*

hail a cab and **hail a taxi** to signal to a taxi that you want to be picked up. □ *See if you can hail a cab. I don't want to walk home in the rain.*

hail a taxi Go to previous.

hail from some place to come from some place as one's hometown or birthplace; to originate in some place. □ *He hails from a small town in the Midwest.* □ *Where do you hail from?*

hail someone **as** something to praise someone for being something. □ *The active members hailed him as fraternity brother of the year.* □ *Sally was hailed as an effective leader.*

hair and hide(, horns and tallow) *Rur.* every last thing; every part. (Refers orginally to using every part of slaughtered cattle for something.) □ *They took everything Mary had, hair and hide, horns and tallow.* □ *Joe never threw anything away. He found a use for everything, hair and hide.*

the **hair of the dog that bit** one *Fig.* a drink of liquor taken when one has a hangover; a drink of liquor taken when one is recovering from drinking too much liquor. (Often the same type of liquor as one got drunk on.) □ *Oh, I'm miserable. I need some of the hair of the dog that bit me.* □ *That's some hangover you've got there, Bob. Here, drink this. It's some of the hair of the dog that bit you.*

hale and hearty *Cliché* healthy. □ *The young infant was hale and hearty.* □ *The calf—hale and hearty—ran around the barnyard.*

hale-fellow-well-met *Fig.* friendly to everyone; falsely friendly to everyone. (Usually said of males.) □ *Yes, he's friendly, sort of hale-fellow-well-met.* □ *He's not a very sincere person. Hail-fellow-well-met—you know the type.* □ *What a pain he is. Good old Mr. Hail-fellow-well-met. What a phony!*

half a bubble off plumb *Fig.* giddy; crazy. □ *She is acting about half a bubble off plumb. What is wrong with her?* □ *Tom is just half a bubble off plumb, but he is all heart.*

Half a loaf is better than none. *Prov.* Getting only part of what you want is better than not getting anything. □ *Fred: How did your court case go? Alan: Not good. I asked for $500, and the judge only awarded me $200. Fred: Half a loaf is better than none.*

half in the bag intoxicated. □ *Jerry was half in the bag when we found him.* □ *They were all half in the bag by midnight.*

half the battle *Fig.* a significant part of an effort. □ *Getting through traffic to the airport was half the battle. The flight was nothing at all.*

half the time sometimes. □ *I like that TV show, but half the time I forget to watch it when it's on.* □ *She says she's my friend, but she can't remember my name, half the time.*

Half the truth is often a whole lie. *Prov.* If you do not tell the whole truth, you can mislead people just as if you tell them an outright lie. □ *Jill: You lied to me. Jane: I did not. Everything I said was true. Jill: But you didn't tell me the whole story. And half the truth is often a whole lie.*

Half the world knows not how the other half lives. *Prov.* You cannot understand what life is like for people who are different from you.; Often, rich people do not know what it is like to be poor, and poor people do not know what it is like to be rich. □ *Until he spent school vacation at his friend Richard's country home, Jim was never aware that some people do not have to work for a living. He discovered that half the world knows not how the other half lives.* □ *Bill decided to dress in secondhand clothes and spend the weekend among the homeless men in the warehouse district, to see how the other half lives.*

half under 1. *Lit.* semiconscious. □ *I was half under and could hear what the doctor was saying.* □ *I was afraid they would start cutting while I was only half under.* **2.** *Fig. Inf.* to be intoxicated; to be tipsy. □ *He was half under and could barely stand up.* □ *Only four beers and she was half under.*

halfhearted (about someone or something) unenthusiastic about someone or something. □ *Ann was halfhearted about the choice of Sally for president.* □ *She didn't look halfhearted to me. She looked angry.*

ham something up[†] *Fig.* to make a performance seem silly by showing off or exaggerating one's part. (A show-off actor is known as a *ham*.) □ *Come on, Bob. Don't ham it up!* □ *The play was going fine until Bob got out there and hammed up his part.*

hammer (away) at someone *Fig.* to interrogate someone; to ask questions endlessly of someone. □ *The cops kept hammering away at the suspect until he told them everything they wanted to know.* □ *They hammered at him for hours.*

hammer (away) at something 1. *Lit.* to continue to do a task that requires much hammering. □ *The roofers are hammering away at the job, trying to finish before night.* **2.** *Lit.* to pound at or on something, such as a door. □ *Who is hammering away at the door?* □ *The police are hammering at the door.* **3.** *Fig.* to dwell overly long on a point or a question. □ *Stop hammering away at the same thing over and over.* □ *The agents asked question after question. They would not stop hammering at the issue.*

hammer on someone or something to pound on someone or something. □ *The cop hammered on the poor man over and over.* □ *Sharon hammered on the door for a long time.*

hammer something down[†] to pound something down even with the surrounding surface. □ *Hammer all the nails down so that none of them will catch on someone's shoe.* □ *Hammer down all these nails!*

hammer something home[†] *Fig.* to try extremely hard to make someone understand or realize something. □ *The boss hopes to hammer the firm's poor financial position home to the staff.* □ *I tried to hammer home to Anne the fact that she would have to get a job.*

hammer something into someone and **pound something into someone**; **hammer someone in**[†]; **pound someone in**[†] *Fig.* to teach something to someone intensively, as if one were driving the information in by force. □ *Her parents had hammered good manners into her head since she was a child.* □ *They hammered in good manners every day.* □ *They pounded proper behavior into the children.*

hammer something into something and **pound something into something**; **hammer something in**[†]; **pound something in**[†] *Lit.* to drive something into something as with a hammer. □ *Todd hammered the spike into the beam.* □ *He hammered in the spike.* □ *He hammered it in with two hard blows.*

hammer something onto something and **hammer something on**[†] to pound something onto something. □ *I hammered the lid onto the paint can.* □ *She hammered on the lid very tightly.*

hammer something out[†] **1.** *Lit.* to hammer a dent away; to make a dent even with the surrounding surface. □ *I'm going to have to have someone hammer this dent in my fender out.* □ *It will take a while to hammer out the dent.* **2.** *Lit.* to expand something by hammering it thinner. □ *He hammered the gold out into a very thin sheet.* □ *He hammered out the gold into thin sheets.* **3.** *Fig.* to arrive at an agreement through argument and negotiation. □ *The two parties could not hammer a contract out.* □ *At last, we were able to hammer out an agreement.* **4.** *Fig.* to play something on the piano. □ *She hammered the song out loudly and without feeling.* □ *Listen to John hammer out that song on the piano.*

hand in glove (with someone**)** *Fig.* very close to someone. □ *John is really hand in glove with Sally.* □ *The teacher and the principal work hand in glove.*

***hand in hand 1.** Lit.* holding hands. (*Typically: **do** something ~; **sit** ~; **walk** ~.) □ *They walked down the street hand in hand.* □ *Bob and Mary sat there quietly, hand in hand.* **2.** *Fig.* [of two things] together, one with the other. (*Typically: **go** ~.) □ *Cookies and milk seem to go hand in hand.* □ *Teenagers and back talk go hand in hand.*

***a **hand in** something and **a **part in** something *Fig.* a part in establishing or running something. (*Typically: **get** ~; **have** ~; **give** someone ~.) □ *I would like to have a hand in the planning process.* □ *I will not let Jane have a part in this project.*

Hand it over. Give it to me. (Fixed order.) □ *It's mine. Hand it over!* □ *Come on. Give me the box of jewels. Hand it over!*

hand over fist *Fig.* [for money and merchandise to be exchanged] very rapidly. □ *What a busy day. We took in money hand over fist.* □ *They were buying things hand over fist.*

hand over hand *Fig.* [moving] one hand after the other (again and again). □ *Sally pulled in the rope hand over hand.* □ *The man climbed up the rope hand over hand.*

hand someone or something **over† (to** someone or something**)** to deliver someone or something to someone or a group; to relinquish someone or something to someone or a group. □ *The kidnappers handed the child over to the go-between.* □ *All right, hand over the hostage!*

hand someone something *Fig.* to tell someone something; to tell someone nonsense. □ *Don't hand me that stuff! That's silly!* □ *She handed me a line about being a famous author.*

hand something **around†** to pass something around. □ *Hand this around and let everyone look at it.* □ *Hand around each of these pictures so everyone gets to see them.*

hand something **back† (to** someone**)** to return something to someone by hand. □ *Would you please hand this paper back to Scott?* □ *Hand back this book to Fred, if you please.*

hand something **down† from** someone **to** someone to pass something down through many generations. □ *I hope we can make it a tradition to hand this down from generation to generation.* □ *My descendants will hand down this watch from generation to generation.*

hand something **down† (to** someone**) 1.** *Lit.* to pass something to a person on a lower level. □ *Hand this wrench down to the man under the sink.* □ *Please hand down this wrench.* **2.** *Fig.* to give something to a younger person. (Either at death or during life.) □ *John handed his old shirts down to his younger brother.* □ *I hope my uncle will hand down his golf clubs to me when he dies.* **3.** *Fig.* to announce or deliver a (legal) verdict or indictment. □ *The grand jury handed seven indictments down last week.* □ *The jury handed down a guilty verdict.*

hand something **in†** to submit something by hand. □ *Did you hand your application form in?* □ *I forgot to hand in my test paper.*

hand something **in† (to** someone**)** Go to **pass** something **in† (to** someone**).**

hand something **off† (to** someone**) 1.** *Lit.* to give a football directly to another player. □ *Roger handed the ball off to Jeff.* □ *He handed off the ball.* □ *Tim handed it off.* **2.** *Fig.* to give something to someone else to do or complete. □ *I'm going to hand this assignment off to Jeff.* □ *Don't hand off your dirty work to me—do it yourself!*

hand something **on (to** someone or something**) 1.** *Lit.* to pass something on to someone or a group. □ *Please hand this on to Walter after you've read it.* □ *Please read this and hand it on.* **2.** *Fig.* to bequeath something to someone or a group. □ *I want to hand this land on to my children.* □ *The family will hand on the business to a foundation.*

hand something **out† (to** someone**) 1.** to give something out to someone. □ *The judge was known for handing heavy fines out.* □ *She handed out large fines to everyone.* **2.** to pass something, usually papers, out to people. □ *The teacher handed the tests out to the students.* □ *Please hand out these papers.*

hand something **over** to give something (to someone); to relinquish something (to someone); to turn something over (to someone). □ *Come on, John! Hand over my wallet.* □ *Please hand this over to the guard.*

hand something **to** someone to give something to someone by hand. □ *The clerk handed her a message when she stopped at the desk.* □ *This message was just handed to me.*

hand something **up† (to** someone**)** to pass something to someone who is on a higher level. □ *Please hand this cup of coffee up to Carl.* □ *Please hand up this coffee to Carl.*

The **hand that rocks the cradle rules the world.** *Prov.* Mothers are the most powerful people, because they shape their children's personalities. □ *When Lena got pregnant, Lena's mother told her to take her responsibility seriously, because the hand that rocks the cradle rules the world.*

***a **hand with** something *Fig.* assistance with something, especially using the hands. (*Typically: **get** ~; **have** ~; **give** someone ~.) □ *Mary would really like to get a hand with that. It's too much for one person.* □ *I'd like to have a hand with this.*

***a **handful** *Fig.* someone, often a child, who is difficult to deal with. (*Typically: **be** ~; **become** ~.) □ *Bobby can be a real handful when he needs a nap.*

***a **handle on** something *Fig.* a means of understanding something; an aid to understanding something. (*Typically: **get** ~; **have** ~; **give** someone ~.) □ *Let me try to get a handle on this.* □ *Now that I have a handle on the concept, I can begin to understand it.*

handle someone **with kid gloves** *Fig.* to be very careful with a touchy person. □ *Bill has become so sensitive. You really have to handle him with kid gloves.* □ *You don't have to handle me with kid gloves. I can take it.*

hands down easily; unquestionably. □ *She won the contest hands down.* □ *They declared her the winner hands down.*

Hands off! Do not touch someone or something. □ *Careful! Don't touch that wire. Hands off!* □ *The sign says, "Hands off!" and you had better do what it says.*

Hands up! and **Stick 'em up!; Put 'em up!** Raise your hands in the air; this is a robbery! (Underworld and Old West.) □ *Hands up! Don't anybody move a muscle. This is a heist.* □ *Stick 'em up! Give me all your valuables.*

Handsome is as handsome does. *Prov.* It is more important to treat people well than to be good-looking.; Just because you are good-looking does not mean you are a good person. □ *Jill: I'd like to get to know George better. Jane: Why? Jill: He's so handsome. Jane: Handsome is as handsome does. He's a very unpleasant person.*

hang a few on† to take a few drinks; to have a few beers. □ *They went out to hang a few on.* □ *Let's hang on a few and then go on to the meeting.*

hang a huey *Sl.* to make a U-turn. □ *Hang a huey in the middle of the block.* □ *Right here! Hang a huey!*

hang a left *Inf.* to turn left. □ *He hung a left at the wrong corner.* □ *Hey, here! Hang a left here!*

hang a louie *Sl.* to turn left. □ *You have to hang a louie at the stop sign.* □ *Go another block and hang a louie.*

hang a ralph *Sl.* to turn right. □ *He skied down the easy slope and hung a ralph near a fir tree.* □ *Don't hang a ralph until you get past the traffic light.*

hang a right *Inf.* to turn right. □ *Hang a right about here.* □ *I told him to hang a right at the next corner, but he went on.*

hang around (some place) to loiter some place; to be in a place or in an area, doing nothing in particular. □ *Why are you hanging around my office?* □ *It's comfortable here. I think I'll hang around here for a while.*

hang around someone or something Go to **around** someone or something.

hang around (with someone) and **go around (with someone)** *Fig.* to spend a lot of time with someone; to waste away time with someone. □ *John hangs around with Bill a lot.* □ *They've been going around with the Smiths.*

hang back (from someone or something) to lag back behind someone or something; to stay back from someone or something, perhaps in avoidance. □ *Why are you hanging back from the rest of the group?* □ *Come on! Don't hang back!*

hang behind (someone or something) to stay behind someone or something. □ *Don't hang behind us, please. Come on up here and walk with us.* □ *Fred is hanging behind and may get lost at the next turn.*

hang by a hair and **hang by a thread 1.** *Lit.* to hang by something very thin, such as a thread or a hair. □ *The tiniest part of the mobile hung by a thread, the rest are on plastic cords.* **2.** and **hang on by a hair; hang on by a thread** *Fig.* to depend on something very insubstantial; to **hang in the balance.** □ *Your whole argument is hanging by a thread.* □ *John isn't failing geometry, but his passing grade is just hanging by a hair.*

hang by a thread Go to previous.

hang by something 1. to be suspended at the end of something, such as a rope, chain, string, etc. □ *The bag is only hanging by a string.* □ *The food hung by a rope from a tree to protect it from the bears that wandered into camp now and then.* **2.** to dangle, suspended by some body part, such as thumbs, legs, etc. □ *I was hanging by my legs on the exercise bar when the rain started.* □ *I can hang by just my middle fingers!*

hang down (from someone or something) to be suspended from someone or something. □ *Grasping vines hung down from the towering trees.* □ *Thousands of vines hung down.*

hang fire to delay or wait; to be delayed. □ *I think we should hang fire and wait for other information.* □ *Our plans have to hang fire until we get planning permission.*

hang five and **hang ten** *Sl.* to stand toward the front of a surfboard or diving board and hang the toes of one or both feet over the edge. (Surfing.) □ *The coach told her to hang ten and not to look down.* □ *Get out there and hang five. You can swim. Nothing can go wrong.*

hang from something to be suspended from something. □ *Colorful decorations hung from the branches of the tree.* □ *What is that hanging from the side of the building?*

hang in the balance Go to **in the balance.**

Hang in there. Be patient, things will work out. □ *Bob: Everything is in such a mess. I can't seem to get things done right. Jane: Hang in there, Bob. Things will work out.* □ *Mary: Sometimes I just don't think I can go on. Sue: Hang in there, Mary. Things will work out.*

Hang it all! *Inf.* Damn it all! □ *Oh, hang it all! I'm late.* □ *He's late again! Hang it all!*

hang it up *Sl.* to quit something. (Fixed order. See also **hang** something **up.**) □ *I've had it with this job. It's time to hang it up.* □ *Just hang it up. Don't bother with it.*

hang loose and **stay loose** to relax and stay calm. □ *Just hang loose, man. Everything'll be all right.* □ *Stay loose, chum. See ya later.*

*the **hang of** something the knowledge or knack of doing something correctly. (*Typically: **get** ~; **have** ~; **teach** someone ~.) □ *As soon as I get the hang of this computer, I'll be able to work faster.* □ *Now that I have the hang of starting the car in cold weather, I won't have to get up so early.*

hang off to wait quietly to one side. □ *The boys hung off a little, waiting to see what would happen next.* □ *Hang off awhile and don't do anything.*

hang on 1. to wait awhile. □ *Hang on a minute. I need to talk to you.* □ *Hang on. Let me catch up with you.* **2.** to survive for awhile. □ *I think we can hang on without electricity for a little while longer.* **3.** [for an illness] to linger or persist. □ *This cold has been hanging on for a month.* □ *This is the kind of flu that hangs on for weeks.* **4.** be prepared for fast or rough movement. (Usually a command.) □ *Hang on! The train is going very fast.* □ *Hang on! We're going to crash!* **5.** to pause in a telephone conversation. □ *Please hang on until I get a pen.* □ *If you'll hang on, I'll get her.*

hang on by a thread Go to **hang by a hair.**

hang on for dear life *Cliché* to hang on tight. □ *As the little plane bounced around over the mountains, we hung on for dear life.*

hang on someone's coattails Go to **ride on** someone's **coattails.**

hang on (someone's) every word *Cliché* to listen closely or with awe to what someone says. □ *I am hanging on your every word. Please go on.* □ *The audience hung on her every word throughout the speech.*

hang on (to someone or something) and **hold on (to** someone or something) **1.** *Lit.* to grasp someone or something. □ *She hung on to her husband to keep warm.* □ *She sat there and hung on, trying to keep warm.* **2.** *Fig.* to detain someone or something. □ *Please hang on to Tom if he's still there. I need to talk to him.*

Hang on to your hat! and **Hold on to your hat!** *Fig.* Get ready for what's coming!; Here comes a big shock! □ *There is a rough road ahead. Hang on to your hat!* □ *Here we go! Hold on to your hat!*

hang one on Go to tie one on.

hang one's **hat (up)** somewhere to take up residence somewhere. □ *George loves Dallas. He's decided to buy a house and hang his hat up there.* □ *Bill moves from place to place and never hangs his hat up anywhere.*

hang out (of something) to be visibly coming out of something. □ *Your shirttail is hanging out of your pants.* □ *My shirttail was hanging out.*

hang out (some place) **1.** to spend time in a place habitually. □ *Is this where you guys hang out all the time?* **2.** to spend time aimlessly; to waste time. □ *Bill: What are you doing this afternoon? Tom: Oh, I'll just hang out.* □ *Kids hang out too much these days.*

hang out (with someone or something) to associate with someone or a group on a regular basis. □ *She hangs out with Alice too much.* □ *I wish you would stop hanging out with that crowd of boys.*

hang over someone or something **1.** to be suspended over someone or something. □ *A fancy crystal chandelier hung over us.* □ *An ornate ceiling fan hung over the table.* **2.** [for some pervading quality] to seem to hover over someone or something. □ *An aura of gloom hung over Joe.* □ *A dismal pall hung over the gathering.*

hang over someone('s **head)** [for something unpleasant] to worry someone. □ *I have a horrible exam hanging over my head.* □ *I hate to have medical problems hanging over me.*

hang someone **by the neck** to execute someone or kill oneself by tying a noose around the neck and dropping the victim in order to break the neck or strangle the victim. □ *The executioner hanged him by the neck until he died.* □ *He hanged himself by the neck.*

hang someone **for** something **1.** *Lit.* to execute someone by hanging for doing something. □ *The state prosecutor will try to hang you for this crime.* □ *The sheriff wanted to hang Jed for murder.* **2.** *Fig.* to extract an overly severe punishment for some deed. □ *They are trying to hang me for a parking ticket.* □ *You can't hang me just for coming in late!*

hang someone **in effigy** *Fig.* to hang a dummy or some other figure of a hated person. □ *They hanged the dictator in effigy.* □ *The angry mob hanged the president in effigy.*

hang someone or something **from** something to suspend someone or something from something. □ *The captain wanted to hang him from the highest yardarm as punishment.* □ *I hung a colorful decoration from the windowsill.*

hang someone or something **with** something to suspend someone or something with something, such as a rope, chain, thread, etc. (The past tense *hanged* is usually used only with the hanging of people.) □ *The executioners*

hanged the criminal with a rope and later with a chain. □ *They hung the picture with a golden cord.*

hang someone **out to dry** *Fig.* to defeat or punish someone. □ *The boss was really angry at Billie. He yelled at him and hung him out to dry.*

hang something **on** someone *Sl.* to blame something on someone; to frame someone for something. (See also **hang** something **on** someone or something.) □ *Don't try to hang the blame on me!* □ *The sheriff tried to hang the bank robbery on Jed.*

hang something **on** someone or something to drape or hook something on someone or something. (See also **hang** something **on** someone.) □ *Hang this sign on Walter and see how he looks.* □ *Please hang this sign on the front door.*

hang something **out (of** something) to suspend something outside of something while it is attached to the inside of something. □ *He hung the rope out of the window so he could escape the burning building.* □ *She ran to the window and hung the rope out.*

hang something **over** someone or something to suspend something over someone or something. □ *Sally hung the colorful mobile over the baby's crib.* □ *Please hang these garlands over the party table.*

hang something **up**[†] to return the telephone receiver to its cradle. (See also **hang it up.**) □ *Please hang this up when I pick up the other phone.* □ *Please hang up the phone.*

hang ten Go to hang five.

hang together 1. *Fig.* [for something or a group of people] to hold together; to remain intact. □ *I hope our bridge group hangs together until we are old and gray.* □ *I don't think that this car will hang together for another minute.* **2.** *Fig.* [for a story] to flow from element to element and make sense. □ *This story simply does not hang together.* □ *Your novel hangs together quite nicely.* **3.** *Fig.* [for people] to spend time together. □ *We hung together for a few hours and then went our separate ways.* □ *The boys hung together throughout the evening.*

hang tough (on something) *Sl.* to stick to one's position (on something). □ *I decided I'd hang tough on it. I tend to give in too easy.* □ *Yes, just hang tough.*

hang up 1. [for a machine or a computer] to grind to a halt; to stop because of some internal complication. □ *Our computer hung up right in the middle of printing the report.* □ *I was afraid that my computer would hang up permanently.* **2.** to replace the telephone receiver after a call; to terminate a telephone call. □ *I said good-bye and hung up.* □ *Please hang up and place your call again.*

hang up (in someone's **ear)** Go to next.

hang up (on someone or something) **1.** and **hang up (in** someone's **ear)** to end a telephone call by returning the receiver to the cradle while the other party is still talking. □ *She hung up on me!* □ *I had to hang up on all that rude talk.* **2.** to give up on someone or something; to quit dealing with someone or something. □ *Finally, I had to hang up on Jeff. I can't depend on him for anything.* □ *We hung up on them because we knew we couldn't make a deal.*

hang with someone *Sl.* to spend or waste time with someone. □ *Dave spent the afternoon hanging with Don, and neither one got anything done.* □ *I'm going down to the corner and hang with the guys.*

hanker after someone or something and **hanker for** someone or something *Rur.* to want someone or something; to long for someone or something. □ *I hanker after a nice big beefsteak for dinner.*

happen before someone's **time** Go to before someone's time.

happen in the (very) nick of time Go to in the (very) nick of time.

happen to someone or something to befall someone or something; to occur to someone or something. □ *What is going to happen to me?* □ *Something awful happened to your car.*

happen (up)on someone or something to come upon someone or something, as if by accident. (See also come (up)on someone or something.) □ *I just happened upon a strange little man in the street who offered to sell me a watch.* □ *Andrew happened on a book that interested him, so he bought it.*

*happy as a clam (at high tide) and ***happy as a clam (in butter sauce); *happy as a lark; *happy as can be** contented; very happy. (*Also: **as** ~.) □ *I've been as happy as a clam since I moved to the country.* □ *I don't need much. Just somewhere to live, some work to do, and a TV to watch, and I'm happy as a clam at high tide.* □ *Matthew was happy as a lark throughout his whole vacation.* □ *Bob was happy as can be when he won the lottery.*

happy as a clam (in butter sauce) Go to previous.

happy as a lark Go to happy as a clam (at high tide).

happy as can be Go to happy as a clam (at high tide).

a **happy camper** a happy person. □ *The boss came in this morning and found his hard disk trashed. He was not a happy camper.*

happy hour a time to drink a cocktail, starting at about 5:00 P.M. (Often bars have lower prices during "happy hour.") □ *I think that Mary has been starting happy hour a little early. Before noon I think.*

Happy is the bride that the sun shines on. *Prov.* It is supposed to be good luck for the sun to shine on a couple on their wedding day. □ *Our wedding day was a sunny one, and most of my relatives made sure to remind me, "Happy is the bride that the sun shines on."*

Happy is the country which has no history. *Prov.* Since history tends to record only violent, unfortunate, or tumultuous events, a country with no history would be a country lucky enough to have no such unhappy events to record. □ *The history of our country is so full of greed, violence, and dishonesty; happy is the country which has no history.*

a **harbinger of things to come** and a **portent of things to come**; a **sign of things to come** a sample of the events that are to occur in the future. □ *The first cuts in our budget are a harbinger of things to come.* □ *Today's visit from the auditors is a portent of things to come.*

harbor something **against** someone or something to have and retain a bad feeling of some kind toward someone or something. □ *I harbor no ill will against you.* □ *Alice does not harbor any bad feeling against the company that let her go.*

a **hard act to follow** Go to a tough act to follow.

*hard as a rock and ***hard as stone** very hard. (*Also: **as** ~.) □ *This cake is as hard as a rock!* □ *I can't drive a nail into this wood. It's hard as stone.*

*hard as nails *Cliché* [of someone] stern and unyielding. (*Also: **as** ~.) □ *Don't try to bargain with Liz. She's as hard as nails.* □ *Bob may seem sweet and easily swayed, but in fact he's hard as nails.*

hard as stone Go to hard as a rock.

hard at something and **hard at** doing something working hard at something. □ *Tom's busy. He's hard at work on the lawn.*

*hard feelings *Fig.* feelings of resentment or anger. (*Typically: **cause** ~; **have** ~; **give** someone ~.) □ *The argument caused a lot of hard feelings, but finally we got over it.*

a **hard nut to crack** and a **tough nut to crack** *Fig.* difficult person or problem to deal with. □ *This problem is getting me down. It's a hard nut to crack.* □ *Tom sure is a hard nut to crack. I can't figure him out.*

hard of hearing [of someone] unable to hear well or partially deaf. □ *Please speak loudly. I am hard of hearing.* □ *Tom is hard of hearing, but is not totally deaf.*

hard on someone's **heels** Go to on someone's heels.

hard on someone harming someone's feelings; demanding much from someone. □ *I wish you wouldn't be so hard on me. So I make mistakes. I never said I was perfect.*

hard put (to do something**)** and **hard pressed (to** do something**)** able to do something only with great difficulty. □ *I'm hard put to come up with enough money to pay the rent.* □ *I get hard put like that about once a month.*

a **hard row to hoe** Go to a tough row to hoe.

*the hard sell high-pressure selling techniques. (*Typically: **get** ~; **give** someone ~.) □ *They gave me the hard sell, but I still wouldn't buy the car.* □ *The clerk gave the customer the hard sell.*

hard sledding and **tough sledding** *Fig.* a very difficult time. □ *They had some hard sledding when they were first married.* □ *It was tough sledding for sure when our crops failed that year.*

*a hard time and ***a bad time; *a rough time** trouble [over something]; unnecessary difficulty. (*Typically: **have** ~; **give** someone ~.) □ *Please don't give me a hard time.* □ *The clerk got a hard time from the boss, so he quit.*

hard times Go to bad times.

hard to believe and **hard to swallow** not easily believed; hardly believable. □ *Her story was hard to swallow, and it finally was proven to be a lie.*

hard to swallow Go to previous.

hard to take difficult or painful to accept. □ *The news was hard to take, but we soon realized that it was all for the best.*

hard up (for something**)** greatly in need of something, especially money. □ *Ann was hard up for cash to pay the bills.* □ *I was so hard up, I couldn't afford to buy food.*

Hard words break no bones. *Prov.* Verbal abuse does not physically hurt you, and therefore you should not be very upset by it. (Can be used to reply to someone who is verbally abusing you.) □ *Jill: I can't believe some of the* names Fred called me. Jane: Well, hard words break no bones.

harden oneself **to** something *Fig.* to make oneself capable of bearing something unpleasant. □ *You will have to learn to harden yourself to tragedies like this. They happen every day in a hospital.* □ *She had learned to harden herself to the kinds of poverty she had to work in.*

harden something **off†** to accustom a young plant to normal weather so it can be moved from a protected environment to the out-of-doors. □ *We put the plants by the open window to harden them off.* □ *We hardened off the plants.*

harden something **up†** to make something hard or strong. □ *Put the meat in the freezer awhile to harden it up before you try to slice it thin.* □ *Harden up the ice cream a little in the freezer.*

harder than the back of God's head *Rur.* very hard. □ *The soil was harder than the back of God's head. We had a hard time digging it.* □ *The wood was solid and dense and harder than the back of God's head.*

hardly dry behind the ears Go to wet behind the ears.

hardly exchange more than some number of **words with** someone Go to exchange no more than some number of **words** with someone.

hardly have time to breathe and **scarcely have time to breathe** *Fig.* to be very busy. □ *This was such a busy day. I hardly had time to breathe.* □ *They made him work so hard that he scarcely had time to breathe.*

hardly have time to think so busy that one can hardly think properly; very busy. □ *I've been so busy that I hardly have time to think.* □ *I hardly have time to think in the job that I do. We are just too busy.*

hard-nosed *Fig.* stern and unforgiving. □ *Mr. Howe was known to be very hard-nosed, but he could really be friendly if you got to know him.*

hark(en) back to something **1.** to have originated as something; to have started out as something. (Harken is an older word meaning "pay heed to.") □ *The word icebox harks back to refrigerators that were cooled by ice.* □ *Our modern breakfast cereals hark back to the porridge and gruel of our ancestors.* **2.** to remind one of something. □ *Seeing a horse and buggy in the park harks back to the time when horses drew milk wagons.* □ *Sally says it harkens back to the time when everything was delivered by horse-drawn wagons.*

harmonize with someone or something to blend with someone or something musically. □ *Please try to harmonize with the rest of the singers!* □ *Will you harmonize with the piano, please?*

harness an animal **up†** to put a harness on an animal, such as a horse. □ *You had better harness the horses up so we can go.* □ *Please harness up the mare for me.*

harness someone or an animal **to** something to attach someone, something, or an animal to something with a harness. □ *The instructor harnessed me to the hang glider, and I really began to get nervous.* □ *Andrew harnessed the horses to the little wagon.*

harp on someone or something *Fig.* to keep talking or complaining about someone or something; to refer to someone or something again and again. □ *I wish you would quit harping on Jeff all the time. He couldn't be all that bad.* □ *Stop harping on my mistakes and work on your own.*

has come and gone has already arrived and has already departed. □ *No, Joy is not here. She's come and gone.* □ *Sorry, you are too late for your appointment. The doctor has come and gone.*

(Has the) cat got your tongue? Why are you not saying anything? (Often said by adults to children.) □ *Grandpa used to terrify me, both because he was big and fierce-looking and because he usually greeted me by bellowing, "Cat got your tongue?"* □ *Hi, Lisa! How are you? How's your husband? Are you surprised to see me? What's the matter, has the cat got your tongue?*

has the world by the tail (with a downhill drag) *Rur.* has destiny under control. □ *The young businessman had the world by the tail with a downhill drag. He had made a million dollars before he was twenty-five.* □ *She's got the world by the tail now, but her fame won't last forever.*

hash something **over†** (**with** someone) *Fig.* to discuss something with someone. □ *I need to hash this matter over with you.* □ *I've hashed over this business enough.*

hash something **up† 1.** to chop something up. □ *Now, hash the onion and garlic up and put it in the skillet.* □ *Now, hash up the beef and brown it.* **2.** to mess something up. □ *Somebody hashed my manuscript up!* □ *Somebody hashed up my manuscript!*

hassle someone **about** something and **hassle** someone **with** something to harass someone about something. □ *Come on! Don't hassle me about the deadline!* □ *Stop hassling me with all the little details.*

Haste makes waste. *Prov.* You do not save any time by working too fast; hurrying will cause you to make mistakes, and you will have to take extra time to do the job over again. □ *Fred: Hurry up and get my car fixed. Alan: Don't rush me. Haste makes waste.*

hatch an animal **out†** to aid in releasing an animal from an egg. □ *They hatched lots of ducks out at the hatchery.* □ *The farmer hatched out hundreds of chicks each month.*

hatchet man a man who does the cruel or difficult things for someone else; someone who does someone else's dirty work. □ *He served as the president's hatchet man and ended up doing all the dirty work.*

hate someone or something **like sin** *Fig.* to hate someone or something a great deal. □ *She won't eat brussels sprouts. She hates 'em like sin.* □ *I don't want that man anywhere near me. I hate him like sin.*

hate someone's **guts** *Fig.* to hate someone very much. □ *Oh, Bob is terrible. I hate his guts!* □ *You may hate my guts for saying so, but I think you're getting gray hair.*

hats off to someone or something *Fig.* let us salute or honor someone or something. □ *Hat's off to Perry for planning the dinner and finding such a good band.*

haul off and do something **1.** *Inf.* to draw back and do something, such as strike a person. □ *She hauled off and slapped him hard.* □ *Max hauled off and poked Lefty in the nose.* **2.** *Rur.* to do something without a great deal of preparation. □ *The old man hauled off and bought him-*

self a house. □ *Someday, I'm going to haul off and buy me a new car.*

haul someone **in**[†] *Fig.* to arrest someone; [for a police officer] to take someone to the police station. □ *The cop hauled the drunk driver in.* □ *They hauled in the suspects.*

haul someone **on the carpet** Go to call someone on the carpet.

haul someone or something **over to** something to drag someone or something over to something. (Fixed order.) □ *She hauled the boy over to the mess he made and forced him to clean it up.* □ *Ken hauled the logs over to the fireplace and laid the fire.*

haul someone **over the coals** Go to rake someone over the coals.

haul someone **(up**[†]**) before** someone or something *Fig.* to bring someone into the presence of someone or something, usually some officer of the law. □ *The officer hauled the suspect up before the judge.* □ *She hauled up the suspect before the judge.*

haul something **down**[†] to pull something down from a higher level. □ *Terry hauled the sail down and put it away.* □ *Please haul down the mainsail.*

haul something **(from** some place**) to** some place and **haul** something **from** some place **(to** some place**)** to drag something from one place to another. □ *I don't want to have to haul this thing from home to office and back again.* □ *I hauled my suitcase to the airport from my hotel.*

haul something **up**[†] **(from** something**)** to drag or pull something up from below. □ *Jeff hauled the bucket up from the bottom of the well.* □ *He hauled up the bucket.*

haul up (somewhere**)** and **pull up (**somewhere**)** to stop somewhere; to come to rest somewhere. □ *The car hauled up in front of the house.* □ *My hat blew away just as the bus pulled up to the stop.*

have a bad attitude to have a negative outlook on things; to be uncooperative. □ *Perry has a bad attitude and has nothing positive to contribute to the conversation.*

have a bad case of the simples *Rur.* to be stupid. □ *That boy has a bad case of the simples. He can't understand anything.* □ *She acts smart enough on the playground, but get her in the classroom and she has a bad case of the simples.*

have a bad effect (on someone or something**)** to be bad for someone or something. □ *Aspirin has a bad effect on me.* □ *Cold weather has a bad effect on roses.*

have a ball to have an exciting time. □ *I plan to have a ball while I'm on vacation.* □ *Come on, everybody! Let's have a ball!*

have a bear by the tail Go to have a tiger by the tail.

have a bellyful *Inf.* to have as much as one can stand. □ *I've had a bellyful of your whining. Be quiet!*

have a big mouth to be a gossiper; to be a person who tells secrets. □ *Mary has a big mouth. She told Bob what I was getting him for his birthday.* □ *You shouldn't say things like that about people all the time. Everyone will say you have a big mouth.*

have a blast *Inf.* to have a great time; to have a lot of fun. □ *The food was good and we had a blast. Thanks for inviting us to the party.*

Have a blimp! *Sl.* Have a good year! (A reference to the Goodyear blimp, which is famous for being at notable events.) □ *Good-bye. Have a blimp!* □ *Have a blimp! See you next summer.*

have a blowout 1. [for one's car tire] to burst. □ *I had a blowout on the way here. I nearly lost control of the car.* □ *If you have a blowout in one tire, you should check the other tires.* **2.** *Sl.* to have a big, wild party; to enjoy oneself at a big party. □ *Mary and Bill had quite a blowout at their house Friday night.* □ *Fred and Tom had quite a blowout last night.*

have a bone to pick (with someone**)** to have a disagreement to discuss with someone; to have something to argue about with someone. □ *Hey, Bill. I've got a bone to pick with you. Where is the money you owe me?* □ *I had a bone to pick with her, but she was so sweet that I forgot about it.*

have a brush with something to have a brief contact with something; to have an experience with something. (Especially with the law. Sometimes a *close* brush.) □ *Ann had a close brush with the law. She was nearly arrested for speeding.* □ *When I was younger, I had a brush with scarlet fever, but I got over it.*

have a burr under one's **saddle** *Rur.* to be irritated by something. □ *Joe has a burr under his saddle because Jane's going out with Bill tonight.* □ *Mary must have a burr under her saddle. She's been snapping at me all day.*

have a buzz on *Fig.* to be intoxicated. (Fixed order.) □ *Pete has a buzz on and is giggling a lot.* □ *Both of them had a buzz on by the end of the celebration.*

have a case (against someone**)** to have much evidence that can be used against someone in court. □ *Do the police have a case against John?* □ *No, they don't have a case.*

have a change of heart *Fig.* to change one's attitude or decision, usually from a negative to a positive position. □ *I had a change of heart at the last minute and gave the beggar some money.* □ *Since I talked to you last, I have had a change of heart. I now approve of your marrying Sam.*

have a clear conscience (about someone or something**)** and **have a clean conscience (about** someone or something**)** to be free of guilt about someone or something. □ *I'm sorry that John got the blame. I have a clean conscience about the whole affair.* □ *I have a clear conscience about John and his problems.* □ *I didn't do it. I swear to that with a clean conscience.*

have a close call Go to next.

have a close shave and **have a close call** *Fig.* to have a narrow escape from something dangerous. □ *What a close shave I had! I nearly fell off the roof when I was working there.* □ *I almost got struck by a speeding car. It was a close shave.*

have a clue (about something**)** *Fig.* to know anything about something; to have even a hint about someone or something. (Usually negative.) □ *I don't have a clue about where to start looking for Jim.* □ *Why do you think I have a clue about Tom's disappearance?*

have a conniption (fit) *Rur.* to get angry or hysterical. (See also **have a fit**) □ *I got so mad I thought I was going to have a conniption.* □ *My father had a conniption fit when I got home this morning.*

have a corncob up one's **ass** and **have a poker up** one's **ass 1.** *Inf.* to be very stiff. (Use with caution.) □ *How come you're acting so high-and-mighty with me? Do you have a corncob up your ass?* □ *He was a terrible actor, stiff and wooden. He looked like he had a poker up his ass.* **2.** *Inf.* to be very touchy or irritable. □ *Wow! Old Mr. Webster really has a corncob up his ass this morning. Watch out!* □ *Tom has a poker up his ass and he's looking for you. Better make yourself scarce.*

have a death wish *Fig.* to seem to be willing to take all sorts of needless risks. □ *Look at the way that guy drives. He must have some sort of a death wish.*

have a familiar ring (to it) *Fig.* [for a story or an explanation] to sound familiar. □ *Your excuse has a familiar ring. Have you done this before?* □ *This term paper has a familiar ring to it. I think it has been copied.*

have a field day *Fig.* to experience freedom from one's usual work schedule; to have a very enjoyable time. (As with children who are released from classes to take part in sports and athletic contests.) □ *The boss was gone and we had a field day today. No one got anything done.* □ *The air was fresh and clear and everyone had a field day in the park during the lunch hour.*

have a finger in the pie and **have** one's **finger in the pie** *Fig.* to have a role in something; to be involved in something. (See also **have** one's **finger in too many pies**) □ *Tess wants to have a finger in the pie. She doesn't think we can do it by ourselves.* □ *Sally always wants to have a finger in the pie.*

have a fit and **throw a fit** to be very angry; to show great anger. (See also **have a conniption (fit).**) □ *The teacher had a fit when the dog ran through the classroom.* □ *John threw a fit when he found his car had been damaged.*

have a flair for something to have a talent for doing something; to have a special ability in some area. □ *Alice has quite a flair for designing.* □ *I have a flair for fixing clocks.*

have a gift for (doing) something *Fig.* to have a natural talent for doing something. □ *Tony has a gift for writing short stories.* □ *Sharon has a gift for dealing with animals.*

have a glass jaw *Fig.* to be susceptible to a knockout when struck on the head. (Said only of boxers who are frequently knocked down by a blow to the head.) □ *When the prizefighter was knocked out cold by a right to the chin in the first round, the newspapers said he had a glass jaw.* □ *Once a fighter has a glass jaw, he's finished as a boxer.*

have a go at something Go to a **try at** something.

have a good arm *Fig.* to have a strong and conditioned arm for sports, especially pitching in baseball. □ *Perry had a good arm, but he often pitched wide of the plate.*

have a good command of something to know something well. □ *Bill has a good command of French.* □ *Jane has a good command of economic theory.*

have a good head on one's **shoulders** *Fig.* to have common sense; to be sensible and intelligent. □ *Mary doesn't do well in school, but she's got a good head on her* shoulders. □ *John has a good head on his shoulders and can be depended on to give good advice.*

have a (good) mind to do something *Fig.* have an inclination to do something. □ *I have a good mind to tell him just what I think of him.* □ *She had a mind to go to college, but her folks talked her out of it.*

Have a good one. Go to **Have a nice day.**

have a good thing going to have something of an ongoing nature arranged for one's own benefit. □ *Sally paints pictures and sells them at art fairs. She has a good thing going, and she makes good money.* □ *John inherited a fortune and doesn't have to work for a living anymore. He's got a good thing going.*

Have a good time. Enjoy yourself in what you are about to do. (Often said when someone is about to leave for an event.) □ *Bill: I'm leaving for the party now. Father: Have a good time.* □ *Sue: Tonight is the formal dance at the Palmer House, and I'm going. Mary: Have a good time. I'm watching television right here.*

Have a good trip. and **Have a nice trip.** Have a pleasant journey. (Compare this with **Have a safe trip.** This phrase avoids references to safety.) □ *As Sue stepped onto the plane, someone in a uniform said, "Have a nice trip."* □ *"Have a good trip," said Bill, waving his good-byes.*

have a (good) working over Go to a **(good) working over.**

have a green thumb *Fig.* to have the ability to grow plants well. □ *Just look at Mr. Simpson's garden. He has a green thumb.* □ *My mother has a green thumb when it comes to houseplants.*

have a head for something *Fig.* have the mental capacity for something. □ *Jane has a good head for directions and never gets lost.* □ *Bill doesn't have a head for figures and should never become an accountant.*

have a heart *Fig.* to be compassionate; to be generous and forgiving; to have an especially compassionate heart. □ *Oh, have a heart! Give me some help!* □ *If Anne had a heart, she'd volunteer to help us on the charity drive.*

have a heart of gold *Cliché* to be generous, sincere, and friendly. □ *Mary is such a lovely person. She has a heart of gold.* □ *You think Tom stole your watch? Impossible! He has a heart of gold.*

have a heart of stone *Fig.* to be cold and unfriendly. □ *Sally has a heart of stone. She never even smiles.* □ *The villain in the play had a heart of stone. He was cruel to everyone.*

have a heart-to-heart (talk) *Fig.* to have a sincere and intimate talk. □ *I had a heart-to-heart talk with my father before I went off to college.* □ *I have a problem, John. Let's sit down and have a heart-to-heart.*

have a hidden talent and **have hidden talents** *Fig.* to have talents or skills that no one knows about. □ *Wow, Perry! I didn't know you had so many hidden talents.*

have a hitch in one's **gitalong** *Rur.* to have a permanent or temporary limp. □ *Pappy's got quite a hitch in his gitalong since he broke his hip.*

have a hunch (that something **is the case)** and **have a hunch about** something to have an idea about what did, will, or should happen; to have a feeling that something

H

will or should happen. □ *I had a hunch that you would be here when I arrived.* □ *I have a hunch about the way things will happen.*

have a keen interest in something to have a strong interest in something; to be very interested in something. □ *Tom had always had a keen interest in music, so he started a band.* □ *The children have a keen interest in having a pet, so I bought them a cat.*

have a kick to it *Fig.* to have a strong or spicy flavor; to have a high alcohol content. □ *I like that salsa. It has a kick to it.* □ *Tom's moonshine sure has a kick to it—don't drink too much of it, now!*

have a load on and **have got a load on** *Sl.* to be intoxicated. □ *Fred has a load on and is finished drinking for the evening.* □ *You have a load on every time I see you at a party.*

have a lot going (for one**)** to have many things working to one's benefit. □ *Jane is so talented. She has a lot going for her.* □ *She has a good job and a nice family. She has a lot going.*

have a lot on one's **mind** *Fig.* to have many things to worry about; to be preoccupied. □ *I'm sorry that I'm so grouchy. I have a lot of troubles on my mind.* □ *He forgot to go to his appointment because he had a lot on his mind.*

have a low boiling point *Fig.* to anger easily. □ *Be nice to John. He's upset and has a low boiling point.* □ *Mr. Jones sure has a low boiling point. I hardly said anything, and he got angry.*

have a mind as sharp as a steel trap *Fig.* to be very intelligent. □ *She's a smart kid. Has a mind as sharp as a steel trap.* □ *They say the professor has a mind as sharp as a steel trap, but then why can't he figure out which bus to take in the morning?*

have a mind of one's **own** *Fig.* to be very independent. □ *There is no point in telling her what to do. She has a mind of her own.*

have a mind to to be inclined to do something. □ *I have a mind to accept your challenge.* □ *Tom had a mind to call up Sally and ask her to dinner.*

have a near miss *Fig.* to nearly crash or collide. □ *The airplanes—flying much too close—had a near miss.* □ *I had a near miss with a bike while driving over here.*

Have a nice day. and **Have a good day.; Have a nice one.; Have a good one.** *Cliché* an expression said when parting or saying good-bye. (This is now quite hackneyed, and many people are annoyed by it.) □ *Clerk: Thank you. Tom: Thank you. Clerk: Have a nice day.* □ *Bob: See you, man! John: Bye, Bob. Have a good one!*

Have a nice flight. Please enjoy your flight. (Said when wishing someone well on an airplane trip. Often said by airline personnel to their passengers.) □ *Clerk: Here's your ticket, sir. Have a nice flight. Fred: Thanks.* □ *As Mary boarded the plane, the flight attendant said, "Have a nice flight."*

have a nose for something *Fig.* to have the ability to sense or find something, such as news, trouble, gossip, etc. □ *She really has a nose for news. She's a good reporter.* □ *Fred has a nose for gossip.*

have a one-track mind *Fig.* to think entirely or almost entirely about one subject. □ *Adolescent boys often have one-track minds. All they're interested in is the opposite sex.* □ *Bob has a one-track mind. He can only talk about football.*

have a passion for someone or something *Fig.* to have a strong feeling of need or desire for someone, something, or some activity. □ *Mary has a great passion for chocolate.* □ *John has a passion for fishing, so he fishes as often as he can.*

have a penchant for doing something to have a taste, desire, or inclination for doing something. □ *John has a penchant for eating fattening foods.* □ *Ann has a penchant for buying clothes.*

have a place in something to have a role in some plan or some activity. □ *Do I have a place in the negotiations?* □ *Mary did not have a place in any of this.*

have a rare old time a fine and enjoyable time at a party or something similar. □ *We had a rare old time at Tom's the other night.* □ *I haven't had a rare old time like that in years.*

have a rough time (of it) and **have a tough time (of it)** to experience a difficult period. □ *Since his wife died, Mr. Brown has been having a rough time of it.* □ *Be nice to Bob. He's been having a rough time at work.*

have a roving eye *Euph.* to be flirtatious; to be interested in having sexual relations outside of marriage. (Usually used to describe men.) □ *Poor Maria. Her husband has a roving eye.* □ *When they were first married, he had a roving eye.*

have a run of something *Fig.* to have a continuous series of events. (Especially *bad luck.*) □ *I had a run of bad luck at the casino.* □ *The city had a run of serious crimes that angered the citizens.* □ *The company had a run of huge sales increases over the last few years.*

have a run-in (with someone or something**)** to have trouble with someone or something. □ *I had a run-in with Mrs. Wilson. She's a hard case.* □ *We've had a run-in before.*

Have a safe journey. Go to next.

Have a safe trip. and **Have a safe journey.** I hope that your journey is safe.; Be careful and assure that your journey is safe. (Said as someone is about to leave for a trip.) □ *Bill: Well, we're off for London. Sally: Have a safe trip.* □ *Bill: You're driving all the way to San Francisco? Bob: Yes, indeed. Bill: Well, have a safe trip.*

have a score to settle (with someone**)** *Fig.* to have a problem to clear up with someone; to have to get even with someone about something. □ *I have a score to settle with John since he insulted me at our party.* □ *John and I have a score to settle.*

have a scrape (with someone or something**)** *Fig.* to come into contact with someone or something; to have a small battle with someone or something. □ *I had a scrape with the county sheriff.* □ *John and Bill had a scrape, but they are friends again now.*

have a screw loose and **have a loose screw; have got a screw loose** *Inf. Fig.* to be silly or eccentric. □ *He's sort of strange. I think he's got a loose screw.* □ *Yes, he has a screw loose somewhere. He wears a heavy jacket in the middle of summer.*

have a seat to sit down. (Often a polite invitation to sit down.) □ *Have a seat. I'll be with you in a minute.*

have a set-to (with someone**)** to have an argument or fight with someone. □ *Perry and Emmet had quite a set-to over the choice of music.*

have a soft spot (in one's **heart) for** someone or an animal *Fig.* to have a fondness for someone, something, or an animal. □ *I have a soft spot in my heart for Jeff. I'll always be his friend.* □ *Elaine has a soft spot for kittens.*

have a (sound) grasp of something Go to a **(solid) grasp of** something.

have a spaz *Sl.* to get angry or hysterical; to **have a conniption (fit).** (*Spaz* is short for a spastic attack or fit.) □ *If my dad hears about this, he'll have a spaz.* □ *The teacher had a spaz when I came in so late.*

have a stake in something *Fig.* to have something at risk in something; to have a financial or other interest in something. □ *I have a stake in that company. I want it to make a profit.* □ *I don't have a stake in it, so I don't care.*

have a stroke to experience sudden unconsciousness or paralysis due to an interruption in the blood supply to the brain. (Also used as an exaggeration. See the last example.) □ *The patient who received an artificial heart had a stroke two days after the operation.* □ *My great-uncle Bill— who is very old—had a stroke last May.* □ *Calm down, Bob. Don't have a stroke over a silly mistake.*

have a sweet tooth *Fig.* to desire to eat many sweet foods—especially candy and pastries. □ *I have a sweet tooth, and if I don't watch it, I'll really get fat.* □ *John eats candy all the time. He must have a sweet tooth.*

have a thing about someone or something **1.** to have a special fear or dislike of someone or something. □ *Kelly has a thing about Tim. She simply hates him.* □ *I have a thing about snakes.* **2.** to have a craving for someone or something. □ *I have a thing about Maggie. I guess I'm in love.* □ *Elaine has a thing about strawberry ice cream. She can't get enough of it.*

have a thing going (with someone**)** and **have something going (with** someone**)** *Fig.* to have a romance or a love affair with someone. □ *John and Mary have a thing going.* □ *Bill has something going with Ann.*

have a thirst for something **1.** *Lit.* to be thirsty for something to drink. □ *I have a thirst for a tall glass of iced tea.* **2.** *Fig.* to have a craving or desire for something. □ *The tyrant had an intense thirst for power.* □ *The actor's thirst for fame caused him to become unscrupulous.*

have a tiger by the tail and **have got a tiger by the tail; have a bear by the tail** *Fig.* to have become associated with something powerful and potentially dangerous; to have a very difficult problem to solve. □ *You have a tiger by the tail. You bit off more than you could chew.* □ *You've had a bear by the tail ever since you agreed to finish that big project.*

have (a) use for someone or something **1.** to have need for someone or something. (Often negative. Note the use of *any* and *no* in several examples.) □ *I have no use for Josh and his big fancy car.* □ *See if you have use for this hammer.* □ *Do you have any use for this?* □ *I have no use for that.* **2.** to like someone or something. (Often negative.

Note the use of *any* and *no*.) □ *I don't have any use for sweet potatoes.* □ *I have no use for Harry.*

have a way with someone or something to have a special and effective way of dealing with someone or something. □ *She has a way with Jeff. She can get him to do anything.* □ *Sarah has a way with flowers. She can arrange them beautifully.*

have a way with words to have talent in the effective or stylish use of words. (See also **have the gift of the gab.**) □ *Ask Perry to make the announcement. He has a way with words.*

have a weakness for someone or something *Fig.* to be unable to resist someone or something; to be (figuratively) powerless against someone or something. □ *I have a weakness for chocolate.* □ *John has a weakness for Mary. I think he's in love.*

have a weight problem *Euph.* to be fat; to be overweight. □ *He had a weight problem when he was a teenager, but he slimmed down once he started exercising.* □ *She has a weight problem, but she's a lovely woman.*

have a whack at something Go to a **try at** something.

have a whale of a time *Fig.* to have an exciting or fun time; to have a big time. (*Whale* is a way of saying *big*.) □ *We had a whale of a time at Sally's birthday party.* □ *Enjoy your vacation! I hope you have a whale of a time.*

have a yellow belly and **have a yellow streak down** one's **back** *Fig.* to be cowardly. □ *Tex has a yellow streak down his back a mile wide. He's afraid to cross the street!*

have a yellow streak down one's **back** Go to previous.

have all one's **marbles** *Fig.* to have all one's mental faculties; to be mentally sound. (Very often with a negative or said to convey doubt.) □ *I don't think he has all his marbles.* □ *Do you think Bob has all his marbles?*

have an accident 1. to experience something that was not foreseen or intended. □ *Traffic is very bad. I almost had an accident.* □ *Drive carefully. Try to avoid having an accident.* **2.** *Euph.* to lose control of the bowels or the bladder. (Usually said of a young child.) □ *"Oh, Ann," cried Mother. "It looks like you've had an accident!"* □ *Mother asked Billy to go to the bathroom before they left so that he wouldn't have an accident in the car.*

have an ace up one's **sleeve** Go to **have** something **up** one's **sleeve.**

have an affair (with someone**)** to have a love affair with someone. □ *When I was 20, I had an affair with a rock star, and really made a fool of myself.*

have an alcohol problem and **have a drinking problem** *Euph.* to be a drunkard. □ *He has an alcohol problem. It got so bad that he almost lost his job.* □ *If you have a drinking problem, our clinic can help.*

have an appetite for something **1.** *Lit.* to have a desire to eat something in particular. □ *I have an appetite for a nice big steak.* **2.** *Fig.* to have a desire to have, see, hear, etc., something. □ *Bobby has a big appetite for sports and activity.* □ *Bob has no appetite for violence on television.*

have an argument (with someone**)** to argue with someone. □ *Let's not have an argument with the boss.* □ *Tom and John had an argument.*

have an ax(e) to grind *Fig.* to have something to complain about. □ *Tom, I need to talk to you. I have an ax to grind.* □ *Bill and Bob went into the other room to argue. They had an axe to grind.*

have an ear for something *Fig.* to have the ability to learn music or languages. □ *Bill doesn't have an ear for music. He can't carry a tune.* □ *Mary has a good ear for languages.*

have an easy time of it to have an experience with something that is less difficult or severe than others have experienced. □ *We were given a hard assignment, but Fred had an easy time of it.*

have an effect on someone or something to cause a result in someone or something. □ *The storm had a bad effect on the baby, who cried all night.* □ *Will this have an effect on my taxes?*

have an eye for someone or something *Fig.* to have a taste or an inclination for someone or something. □ *Bob has an eye for beauty.* □ *He has an eye for color.*

have an impact on someone or something to leave an impression on someone or something. □ *The sharp change in interest rates had an impact on the housing market.* □ *Your story really had an impact on me.*

have another guess coming Go to next.

have another think coming and **have another guess coming** to have to rethink something because one was wrong the first time. (*Think* is a noun here.) □ *She's quite wrong. She has another think coming if she wants to walk in here like that.* □ *You have another guess coming if you think you can treat me like that!*

have arrived to have reached a position of power, authority, or prominence. □ *Jane saw her picture on the cover of the magazine and felt that she had finally arrived.* □ *When I got an office with a window, I knew that I had arrived.*

Have at it. Start doing it.; Start eating your food. □ *John: Here's your hamburger. Have at it. Jane: Thanks. Where's the mustard?* □ *John: Did you notice? The driveway needs sweeping. Jane: Here's the broom. Have at it.*

have at someone to go at someone; to attack someone. □ *The boys had at the gang members and gave them a beating.* □ *I just knew John was going to have at Fred.*

have at something Go to **get at** something.

have bats in one's **belfry** *Inf. Fig.* to be crazy. □ *You must really have bats in your belfry if you think I'll put up with that kind of stuff.* □ *Pay no attention to her. She has bats in her belfry.*

have been around to be experienced in life. (Use with caution since this can also be taken to mean to be promiscuous.) □ *Ask Sally about how the government works. She's been around the state capital for years.* □ *They all know a lot about life. They've been around.*

have been to hell and back *Fig.* to have survived a great deal of trouble. □ *What a terrible day! I feel like I have been to hell and back.* □ *After a day of shopping, I feel like I have been to hell and back.*

have bigger fish to fry and **have other fish to fry; have more important fish to fry** *Fig.* to have other things to do; to have more important things to do. □ *I can't take time for your problem. I have other fish to fry.* □

I won't waste time on your question. I have bigger fish to fry.

have broad shoulders 1. *Lit.* to have wide shoulders. □ *She has broad shoulders because she exercises and lifts weights.* **2.** *Fig.* to have the ability to cope with unpleasant responsibilities; to have the ability to accept criticism or rebuke. □ *No need to apologize to me. I can take it. I have broad shoulders.* □ *Karen may have broad shoulders, but she can't endure endless criticism.*

have calluses from patting one's **own back** and **break** one's **arm patting oneself on the back** *Fig.* to be a braggart. □ *If you haven't heard about Bill's latest achievement, he'd be glad to tell you. He has calluses from patting his own back.* □ *Jane: I did a really wonderful job, if I do say so myself. Tom: If you're not careful, you'll break your arm patting yourself on the back.*

have carnal knowledge of someone *Euph.* to have had sex with someone. (Formal or jocular.) □ *She had never before had carnal knowledge of a man.*

have cause to do something to have a justifiable reason to do something. □ *Do you have cause to think that Mary took your money?* □ *He had no cause to yell at me like that.*

have clean hands *Fig.* to be guiltless. (As if a guilty person would have dirty or bloody hands.) □ *Don't look at me. I have clean hands.* □ *The police took him in, but let him go after questioning because he had clean hands.*

have come a long way 1. *Lit.* to have traveled a long distance. □ *You've come a long way. You must be tired and hungry.* □ *I've come a long way. Please let me rest.* **2.** *Fig.* to have accomplished much; to have advanced much. □ *My, how famous you are. You've come a long way.* □ *Tom has come a long way in his career in a short time.*

have confidence in someone to trust someone; to know that someone will be true. □ *I have confidence in you, and I know you will do well.* □ *Randy tends not to have confidence in anyone.*

have designs on someone or something *Fig.* to have plans to exploit or somehow take advantage of someone or something. □ *Mrs. Brown has designs on my apple tree. I think she's going to cut off the part that hangs over her fence.* □ *Mary has designs on Bill. I think she'll try to date him.*

have dibs on something to reserve something for oneself; to claim something for oneself. (Often said by children.) □ *I have dibs on the last piece of cake.* □ *John has dibs on the last piece again. It isn't fair.*

have doubts about someone or something to have questions or suspicions about someone or something. □ *I have doubts about Alice and whether she can do it.* □ *We have no doubts about the usefulness of this project.*

have egg on one's **face** *Fig.* to be embarrassed by something one has done. (As if one went out in public with a dirty face.) □ *I was completely wrong, and now I have egg on my face.* □ *She's really got egg on her face!*

have eyes in the back of one's **head** *Fig.* to seem to be able to sense what is going on behind or outside of one's field of vision. □ *My teacher seems to have eyes in the back of her head.* □ *My teacher doesn't need to have eyes in the back of his head. He watches us very carefully.*

have faith in someone to believe someone; to trust someone to do or be what is claimed. □ *I have faith in you. I* *know you will try your best.* □ *We have faith in you and know you can do the job well.*

have feelings about someone or something to have preferences or notions about someone or something. (Usually in the negative.) □ *I don't have any feelings about Jeff. You can choose him if you want.* □ *I have no feelings about this matter. Do what you want.*

have feet of clay *Fig.* [for a strong person] to have a defect of character. □ *All human beings have feet of clay. No one is perfect.* □ *Sally was popular and successful. She was nearly fifty before she learned that she, too, had feet of clay.*

have fun to experience enjoyment. □ *Please forget your problems and have fun.*

have (got) a glow on *Fig.* to be intoxicated; to be tipsy. (Fixed order.) □ *Since you already have a glow on, I guess you won't want another drink.* □ *Jed had a glow on and was acting silly.*

have growing pains 1. *Fig.* [for a child] to have pains—which are attributed to growth—in the muscles and joints. □ *The doctor said that all Mary had were growing pains and that nothing was really wrong.* □ *Not everyone has growing pains.* **2.** *Fig.* [for an organization] to have difficulties in its early stages of growth. □ *The banker apologized for losing my check and said the bank was having growing pains.* □ *The new administration was having terrible growing pains.*

have had enough to have had as much of something as is needed or will be tolerated. □ *Stop yelling at me. I've had enough.* □ *No more potatoes, please. I've had enough.* □ *I'm leaving you, Bill. I've had enough!*

have had it (up to here) to have reached the end of one's endurance or tolerance. (When used with *up to here*, can be accompanied by a gesture, such as the hand held at the neck.) □ *Okay, I've had it. You kids go to bed this instant.* □ *We've all had it up to here with you, John. Get out!*

have had its day to be no longer useful or successful. □ *Streetcars have had their day in most American cities.* □ *Some people think that the fountain pen has had its day, but others prefer it to other kinds of pens.*

have half a mind to do something Go to next.

have half a notion to do something and **have half a mind to** do something *Fig.* to have almost decided to do something, especially something unpleasant. □ *I have half a mind to go off and leave you here.* □ *The cook had half a notion to serve cold chicken.*

have hell to pay Go to have the devil to pay.

have hidden talents Go to have a hidden talent.

have (high) hopes of something *Fig.* to be expecting something. □ *I have hopes of getting there early.* □ *We have high hopes that John and Mary will have a girl.*

Have I got something for you! *Inf.* I have something really exciting for you! (Said earnestly, before saying or showing something surprising or exciting.) □ *Have I got something for you! Wait'll you hear about it!* □ *Have I got something for you! You're gonna love it.*

Have I made myself clear? Do you understand exactly what I am telling you? (Indicates anger or dominance.) □ *I don't intend to warn you again. Have I made myself clear?*

□ *I do not want you to hang around with Tim ever again! Have I made myself clear?*

have intimate relations with someone *Euph.* to have sex with someone. □ *I understand that Jim once had intimate relations with Sarah.* □ *Rumor has it that she has had intimate relations with someone other than her husband.*

have it (all) over someone or something **(in** something**)** to be much better than someone or something. □ *This cake has it all over that one.* □ *My car has it all over yours.*

have it all together and **have got it all together** to be mentally and physically organized; to be of sound mind. □ *I don't have it all together today.* □ *Try me again later when I have it all together.*

have it both ways to have both of two incompatible things. □ *John wants the security of marriage and the freedom of being single. He wants to have it both ways.* □ *John thinks he can have it both ways—the wisdom of old age and the vigor of youth.*

have it in for someone to be mad at someone; to wish to harm someone. □ *Jane seems to have it in for Jerry. I don't know why.* □ *Max has it in for his old girlfriend since she broke up with him.*

have it in one **to** do something to have the motivation or inspiration to do something. □ *She just doesn't have it in her to go back home.* □ *I wanted to help out, but I just didn't have it in me.*

have it made and **have got it made** to have succeeded; to be set for life. □ *I have a good job and a nice little family. I have it made.* □ *He's really got it made since he won the lottery.*

have it made in the shade and **have got it made in the shade** *Sl.* to have succeeded; to be set for life. □ *Wow, is he lucky! He has it made in the shade.* □ *Sarah's got it made in the shade with her huge inheritance.*

Have it your way. It will be done your way.; You will get your way. (Usually shows irritation on the part of the speaker.) □ *Tom: I would like to do this room in blue. Sue: I prefer yellow. I really do. Tom: Okay. Have it your way.* □ *Jane: Let's get a pie. Apple would be good. Bob: No, if we are going to buy a whole pie, I want a cherry pie, not apple. Jane: Oh, have it your way!*

have just one oar in the water *Rur.* to not be thinking clearly. □ *Tom has some crazy plan for opening his own restaurant. If you ask me, he has just one oar in the water.* □ *She has just one oar in the water if she thinks Bill is going to pay any attention to her.*

have kittens to get extremely upset. □ *My mother pretty near had kittens when she found out I got fired.* □ *Calm down. Don't have kittens.*

have more luck than sense to be lucky but not intelligent. □ *Jane went driving out into Death Valley without any water. She survived—she has more luck than sense.* □ *Tom: I like to drive ninety miles an hour on the freeway. Nobody's ever caught me. Mary: You have more luck than sense.*

have more than one string to one's **fiddle** *Rur.* to have many talents. □ *Joe has more than one string to his fiddle. He's a good painter, and he also cooks and fixes cars.* □ *This job involves a lot of different duties. We'll need to hire someone who has more than one string to his fiddle.*

have neither rhyme nor reason Go to neither rhyme nor reason.

(have) never had it so good have never had so much good fortune. □ *No, I'm not complaining. I've never had it so good.* □ *Mary is pleased with her new job. She's never had it so good.*

have no business doing something to be wrong to do something; to be extremely unwise to do something. □ *You have no business bursting in on me like that!* □ *You have no business spending money like that!*

have no staying power to lack endurance; not to be able to last. □ *Sally can swim fast for a short distance, but she has no staying power.* □ *That horse can start fairly fast, but it has no staying power.*

have no truck with something *Rur.* to have nothing to do with something. □ *After the way Mary treated me, I'll have no truck with her.* □ *We only show good, wholesome movies at this theater. We have no truck with most of that Hollywood trash.*

have none of something to tolerate or endure no amount of something. □ *I'll have none of your talk about quitting school.* □ *We'll have none of your gossip.* □ *I wish to have none of the sweet potatoes, please.*

have nothing on someone **1.** to lack the evidence necessary to place a charge against someone. □ *The police had nothing on Bob, so they let him loose.* □ *You've got nothing on me! Let me go!* **2.** to have an advantage over someone. □ *Roger has nothing on me when it comes to basketball.*

have nothing on someone or something to have no information about someone or something. (See also **have nothing on** someone.) □ *The dictionary had nothing on the word I looked up.* □ *The librarian said that the library has nothing on the topic of my paper.*

have nothing to do with someone or something and **not have anything to do with** someone or something to prefer not to associate or be associated with someone or something. □ *I don't like Mike so I won't have anything to do with the books he writes.* □ *Bob will have nothing to do with Mary since she quit her job.*

have one foot in the grave *Fig.* to be almost dead. □ *I was so sick, I felt as if I had one foot in the grave.* □ *Poor old Uncle Herman has one foot in the grave.*

have one in the oven *Fig.* to be pregnant with a child. □ *She's got three kids now and one in the oven.*

have one's ass in a sling and **have got one's ass in a sling** *Sl.* to be dejected or hurt; to be pouting. (Potentially offensive. Use only with discretion.) □ *She's got her ass in a sling because she got stood up.* □ *So you didn't get a perfect score. Why do you have your ass in a sling?*

have one's back to the wall *Fig.* to be in a defensive position. □ *He'll have to give in. He has his back to the wall.* □ *How can I bargain when I've got my back to the wall?*

have one's brain on a leash *Sl.* to be drunk. □ *Max had his brain on a leash before he even got to the party.* □ *Some guy who had his brain on a leash ran his car off the road.*

have one's cake and eat it too and **eat one's cake and have it too** *Cliché* to have in one's possession something and be able to use or exploit it; to **have it both ways.** (Usually stated in the negative.) □ *Tom wants to have his cake and eat it too. It can't be done.* □ *Don't buy a car if you want to walk and stay healthy. You can't eat your cake and have it too.*

have one's druthers Go to have one's rathers.

have one's ear to the ground Go to keep an ear to the ground.

have one's eye on someone or something Go to keep an eye on someone or something.

have one's eye out (for someone or something**)** Go to keep an eye out (for someone or something**)**.

have one's feet on the ground Go to keep one's feet on the ground.

have one's finger in too many pies *Fig.* to be involved in too many things; to have too many tasks going to be able to do any of them well. (See also **have a finger in the pie.**) □ *I'm too busy. I have my finger in too many pies.* □ *She never gets anything done because she has her finger in too many pies.*

have one's finger(s) in the till Go to have one's hand in the till.

have one's hand in something *Fig.* to exercise control over something; to play an identifiable role in doing something. (See also **have a hand in something.**) □ *She always has to have her hand in everything.* □ *I want to have my hand in the arrangement.*

have one's hand in the till and **have one's finger(s) in the till** *Fig.* to steal money from one's employer. □ *James couldn't afford that car on just his salary. He must have his hand in the till.* □ *Sally was outraged when she found that one of her salesclerks had his fingers in the till.*

have one's hands full (with someone or something**)** *Fig.* to be busy or totally occupied with someone or something. □ *I have my hands full with my three children.* □ *You have your hands full with managing the store.*

have one's hands tied *Fig.* to be prevented from doing something. (As if one's hands were made immobile.) □ *I can't help you. I was told not to, so I have my hands tied.* □ *John can't help. He has his hands tied by his boss.*

have one's head in the clouds *Fig.* to be unaware of what is going on from fantasies or daydreams. □ *"Bob, do you have your head in the clouds?" asked the teacher.* □ *She walks around all day with her head in the clouds. She must be in love.*

have one's head in the sand Go to bury one's head in the sand.

have one's heart (dead) set against something *Fig.* to be totally against something; to be opposed to something. □ *Jane has her heart dead set against going to Australia.* □ *John has his heart set against going to college.*

have one's heart go out to someone *Fig.* to have compassion for someone. □ *I can't have my heart go out to everyone.* □ *To give generously to charity shows that one's heart goes out to those who are suffering.*

have one's heart in one's **mouth** *Fig.* to feel strongly emotional about someone or something. (See also one's **heart is in** one's **mouth.**) □ *I had my heart in my mouth when I heard the national anthem.*

H

have one's **heart in the right place** *Fig.* to have good intentions, even if there are bad results. ☐ *I don't always do what is right, but my heart is in the right place.* ☐ *Good old Tom. His gifts are always tacky, but his heart's in the right place.*

have one's **heart on** one's **sleeve** Go to **wear** one's **heart on** one's **sleeve**.

have one's **heart set on** something *Fig.* to be desiring and expecting something. ☐ *Jane has her heart set on going to London.* ☐ *Bob will be disappointed. He had his heart set on going to college this year.*

have one's **heart stand still** *Fig.* an expression said when one's heart (figuratively) stops beating because one is shocked or is feeling strong emotions. ☐ *I had my heart stand still once when I was overcome with joy.* ☐ *Lovers—at least the ones in love songs—usually say their hearts stood still.*

have one's **luck run out** *Fig.* for one's good luck to stop; for one's good fortune to come to an end. ☐ *I had my luck run out when I was in South America. I nearly starved.* ☐ *I hate to have my luck run out just when I need it.*

have one's **mind in the gutter** and **have got** one's **mind in the gutter** *Fig.* tending to think of or say things that are obscene. ☐ *Tiffany has her mind in the gutter. That's why she laughs at all that dirty stuff.* ☐ *Why do you tell so many dirty jokes? Do you always have your mind in the gutter.*

have one's **name inscribed in the book of life** *Euph.* to die. ☐ *He was a beloved father, brother, and friend, and he has his name inscribed in the book of life.* ☐ *By the time she was twenty, her parents, brothers, and sister had all had their names inscribed in the book of life.*

have one's **nose in a book** *Fig.* to be reading a book; to read books all the time. ☐ *Bob has his nose in a book every time I see him.* ☐ *His nose is always in a book. He never gets any exercise.*

have one's **nose in the air** *Fig.* to be conceited or aloof. ☐ *Mary always seems to have her nose in the air.* ☐ *I wonder if she knows that she has her nose in the air.*

have one's **nose out of joint** Go to **get** one's **nose out of joint**.

have one's **rathers** and **have** one's **druthers** (More informal with *druthers*.) to have what one prefers; to have one's way. ☐ *If I had my rathers, we'd go out every Friday night.* ☐ *I suspect that if Joe had his druthers, he'd be taking Mary to the dance instead of Jill.*

have one's **shoulder to the wheel** and **keep** one's **shoulder to the wheel; pit** one's **shoulder to the wheel** *Fig.* to do the hard work that needs to be done; to focus on getting a job done. ☐ *You won't accomplish anything unless you put your shoulder to the wheel.* ☐ *I put my shoulder to the wheel and finished the job quickly.*

have one's **way with** someone *Euph.* to have sexual relations with someone, possibly with that person being reluctant. ☐ *He invited her up to his apartment, hoping to have his way with her.* ☐ *Now that you have had your way with me, do I mean nothing to you?*

have one's **wires crossed** *Fig.* to have one's mental processes in disarray; to be confused. ☐ *You don't know what you are talking about. You've really got your wires crossed!*

☐ *Joan got her wires crossed about who arrived first. It was Bob, not Gary.*

have one's **words stick in** one's **throat** *Fig.* to be so overcome by emotion that one can hardly speak. ☐ *I sometimes have my words stick in my throat.* ☐ *John said that he never had his words stick in his throat.*

have one's **work cut out for** one *Fig.* to have a large and difficult task prepared for one. ☐ *They sure have their work cut out for them, and it's going to be hard.* ☐ *There is a lot for Bob to do. He has his work cut out for him.*

have one too many and **have a few too many** *Euph.* to be drunk. ☐ *He had one too many, and now he's throwing up.* ☐ *You'd better not drive. I think you've had a few too many.*

have oneself something to get, have, or take something. ☐ *I'll have myself some of that coconut cream pie, if you don't mind.* ☐ *You just go and have yourself a nice, long nap.*

have pity on someone or an animal to have compassion toward someone or an animal. (See also **take pity on** someone or an animal.) ☐ *Please! Have pity on us. Let us come in!*

have pull with someone to have influence with someone. (Also with *some, much, lots,* etc.) ☐ *Let's ask Ann to help us. She has pull with the mayor.* ☐ *Do you know anyone who has some pull with the bank president? I need a loan.*

have recourse to something to be able to use something for help; to be able to fall back on something. ☐ *You will always have recourse to the money your grandfather left you.* ☐ *You will not have recourse to that money until you are over 21 years of age.*

have relations with someone *Euph.* to have sexual relations with someone. ☐ *While engaged to Mary, he was having relations with at least two other women.* ☐ *She was having relations with one of her employees, which was strictly against policy.*

have rocks in one's **head** *Fig.* to be silly or crazy. ☐ *John is a real nut. He has rocks in his head.* ☐ *I don't have rocks in my head—I'm just different.*

have seen better days *Euph.* to be in bad condition. ☐ *My old car has seen better days, but at least it's still running.* ☐ *She's seen better days, it's true, but she's still lots of fun.*

have so Go to **have too**.

have (some) bearing on something to have relevance to something. (Note the use of *no* and *any* in the negative.) ☐ *I know something that has some bearing on the issue you are discussing.* ☐ *This has no bearing on anything that will happen today.* ☐ *This doesn't have any bearing on all that.* ☐ *What bearing does John's decision have on the situation?*

have some food to go Go to **to go**.

have (some) time to kill *Fig.* to have extra time; to have a period of time with nothing to do. ☐ *Whenever you have some time to kill, call me up and we'll chat.*

have someone **around (for** something**)** to have someone come for a visit, tea, dinner, etc. ☐ *We really should have the Wilsons around for an evening of bridge.* ☐ *Yes, let's have them around.*

have someone **back** to invite someone for a return visit. ☐ *We would love to have you back sometime.* ☐ *We want to have you back the next time you are in town.*

have someone **behind the eight ball** Go to behind the eight ball.

have someone **by** someone or something Go to by someone or something.

have someone **by** something to hold onto someone by something. (See also **have** someone **by** someone or something.) □ She had me by the shoulder and I couldn't get away. □ Timmy had Billy by the collar and was punching him on the shoulder.

have someone **dead to rights** *Fig.* to have caught someone red-handed; to have irrefutable evidence about someone's misdeed. □ We have you dead to rights on this one. □ The cops had him dead to rights with damning testimony of two eyewitnesses.

have someone **down** to have someone for a visit to a place that is on a lower level or in the south. (Fixed order.) □ Why don't we have Roger down for the weekend? □ They had us down to their place in Florida.

have someone **drawn and quartered** Go to drawn and quartered.

have someone **for breakfast** *Fig.* to defeat someone with ease. □ Careful, she'll have you for breakfast if you're not prepared to debate her. □ I'm afraid they had our team for breakfast again.

have someone **in** to call or invite someone into one's home. (Fixed order.) □ I'll have the plumber in to fix that leak. □ We had friends in for bridge last night.

have someone **in** one's **corner** *Fig.* to have someone supporting one's position or goals. (Originally from boxing.) □ As long as I have Mr. Howe in my corner, I feel confident about what I have to say.

have someone **in** one's **pocket** *Fig.* to have complete control over someone. □ Don't worry about the mayor. She'll cooperate. I've got her in my pocket. □ John will do just what I tell him. I've got him and his brother in my pocket.

have someone **in** one's **spell** and **have** someone **under** one's **spell** *Fig.* to have enchanted or captivated the attention of someone. □ She has him in her spell with her grace and beauty. □ Ken has Karen under his spell.

have someone **on a string** Go to on a string.

have someone **on the string** *Fig.* to have someone waiting for a decision. □ Sally has John on the string. He has asked her to marry him, but she hasn't replied yet. □ Yes, it sounds like she has him on the string.

have someone or something **about** and **have** someone or something **around** to have someone or something nearby habitually. □ I really don't want to have all those people about all the time. □ It's good to have a fire extinguisher around.

have someone or something **cornered 1.** *Lit.* to have someone or something trapped as in a corner. □ We had the wild cat cornered, but it jumped over the wall and got away. **2.** *Fig.* to have someone or something located and under control. □ I think I have the part you need cornered in a warehouse in Indiana. We'll order it.

have someone or something **in mind** *Fig.* to be thinking of someone or something as a candidate for something. □ Did you have anyone in mind for the job? □ I have something in mind for the living-room carpeting. □ He proba-

bly had himself in mind when he spoke about the need for new blood.

have someone or something **in** one's **hands 1.** *Lit.* to hold someone or something in one's hands. (*Have* can be replaced with *leave* or *put*.) □ I have the tools you need in my hands, ready to give them to you when you need them. **2.** *Fig.* to have control of or responsibility for someone or something. (*Have* can be replaced with *leave* or *put*.) □ You have the whole project in your hands. □ The boss put the whole project in your hands.

have someone or something **in** one's **sights 1.** *Lit.* to have one's gun aimed at someone or something. □ The sniper had the soldier in his sights. □ I had the deer in my sights. I fired. **2.** *Fig.* to consider someone or something one's goal or conquest. □ I have a promotion in my sights and I hope to get it before the end of the year. □ I've had Sally in my sights for years. I intend to marry her.

have someone or something **in tow** *Fig.* to lead, pull, or tow someone or something around. □ Mrs. Smith has her son by the hand and in tow. □ That car has a boat in tow.

have someone or something **on** one's **hands** to be burdened with someone or something. (*Have* can be replaced with *leave*.) □ I run a record store. I sometimes have a large number of unwanted records on my hands. □ Please don't leave the children on my hands.

have someone or something **on** one's **mind** and **have** someone or something **on the brain** (More informal with *brain*.) to think often about someone or something; to be obsessed with someone or something. □ Bill has chocolate on his mind. □ John has Mary on his mind every minute. □ Karen has Ken on the brain.

have someone or something **on the brain** Go to previous.

have someone or something **on track** Go to on track.

have someone or something **under (close) scrutiny** Go to under (close) scrutiny.

have someone or something **under control** Go to under control.

have someone or something **(well) in hand** *Fig.* to have someone or something under control. □ I have the child well in hand now. She won't cause you any more trouble. □ We have everything in hand. Don't worry.

have someone **over a barrel** Go to over a barrel.

have someone **over (for** something**)** to invite someone to come to one's home, for a meal, party, visit, cards, the evening, etc. (Fixed order.) □ We will have you over for dinner some day. □ We will have you over soon.

have someone **pegged as** something Go to peg someone as something.

have someone's **best interest(s) at heart** to make decisions based on someone's best interests. □ I know she was only doing what would benefit her, but she said she had my best interests at heart.

have someone's **blood on** one's **hands 1.** *Lit.* to have the blood of some other person on one's hands. □ He fell and got a terrible cut and now I have his blood on my hands as well as my shirt. **2.** *Fig.* to be responsible for someone's death; to be guilty of causing someone's death. □ The teenager's blood was on the policeman's hands. □ The king's blood was on the hands of the murderer who killed him.

have someone's **eye** *Fig.* [for someone] to establish and hold eye contact with someone; to attract someone's attention. □ *When Tom at last had her eye, he smiled at her.* □ *Once she had my eye, she began motioning toward the exit.*

have someone's **hide** *Fig.* to punish someone severely. □ *The sheriff swore he'd have the outlaw's hide.* □ *You lousy no-good so-and-so! I'll have your hide!*

have someone **slated for** something Go to slated for something.

have someone **slated to** do something Go to slated to do something.

have someone **under a spell** Go to under a spell.

have someone **under** one's **spell** Go to have someone in one's spell.

have someone **under** someone's **thumb** Go to under someone's thumb.

have someone **under** someone's **wing(s)** Go to under someone's wing(s).

have someone **up (for** something**)** to invite someone to a place that is on a higher level or in the north, for a meal, party, cards, etc. (Fixed order.) □ *We would like to have you up for dinner some evening.* □ *We will have you up soon.*

have something **against** someone or something to have a reason to dislike someone or something. (Note the replacement for *something* in the negative in the example.) □ *Do you have something against me?* □ *I have nothing against chocolate ice cream.*

have something **at** one's **fingertips** and **have** something **at hand** *Fig.* to have something within (one's) easy reach. (*Have* can be replaced with *keep*.) □ *I have a dictionary at my fingertips.* □ *I try to have everything I need at hand.*

have something **cinched** *Fig. Inf.* to have something settled; to have the results of some act assured. □ *Don't worry. I've got it cinched.* □ *You just think you've got it cinched.*

have something **coming (to** one**)** to deserve punishment (for something). □ *Bill broke a window, so he has a spanking coming to him.* □ *That's it, Bill. Now you've got it coming!*

have something **doing** and **have** something **on** to have plans for a particular period of time. (Note the variation with *anything* in the examples. Fixed order.) □ *Bob: Are you busy Saturday night? Bill: Yes, I've got something doing.* □ *I don't have anything doing Sunday night.* □ *I have something on almost every Saturday.*

have something **down to a T** *Fig.* to have something mastered. □ *I can do it. I have it down to a T.*

have something **for** (a meal) to serve or eat something at a particular meal, such as breakfast, lunch, dinner, supper, etc. □ *We had eggs for breakfast.* □ *What did you have for dinner?*

have something **for** someone to have a gift for someone; to have something in reserve for someone. □ *I have some cake for you in the kitchen if you want it.* □ *We have a present for you. Here. I hope you like it.*

have something **for** something to have a remedy for a problem, disease, etc.; to possess something used for some pur-

pose. □ *I have something for tight jar lids. It will open them immediately.* □ *I have some medicine for that disease.*

have something **going (for** oneself**)** [for someone] to have a beneficial scheme or operation going. □ *John really has something going for himself. He's a travel agent, and he gets to travel everywhere for free.* □ *I wish I could have something like that going.*

have something going (with someone**)** Go to have a thing going (with someone).

have something **hanging over** one's **head** *Fig.* to have something bothering or worrying one; to have a deadline worrying one. □ *I keep worrying about my old car breaking down. I hate to have something like that hanging over my head.* □ *I have a history paper that is hanging over my head.*

have something **hung up and salted** *Rur.* to know everything about something. (Often used ironically, as in the second example.) □ *The historian sure had Louisiana history hung up and salted.* □ *Jim's sixteen years old, and he thinks he has the opposite sex hung up and salted.*

have something **in common (with** someone or something**)** [for groups of people or things] to resemble one another in specific ways. □ *Bill and Bob both have red hair. They have that in common with each other.* □ *Bob and Mary have a lot in common. I can see why they like each other.*

have something **in hand 1.** Go to in hand. **2.** *Fig.* to have something under control. □ *I thought I had my destiny in hand, but then fate played a trick on me.* □ *Don't worry about me. I have everything in hand.*

have something **in stock** to have merchandise available and ready for sale. □ *Do you have extra large sizes in stock?* □ *Of course, we have all sizes and colors in stock.*

have something **in store (for** someone**)** *Fig.* to have something planned for one's future. □ *Tom has a large inheritance in store for him when his uncle dies.* □ *I wish I had something like that in store.*

have something **made** to hire someone to make something. □ *Isn't it a lovely coat? I had to have it made because I couldn't find one I liked in a store.* □ *We had the cake made at the bakery. Our oven isn't big enough for a cake that size.*

have something **on** Go to have something doing.

have something **on file** to have a written record of something in storage. □ *I'm sure I have your letter on file. I'll check again.* □ *We have your application on file somewhere.*

have something **on** one('s **person**) to carry something about with one. □ *Do you have any money on your person?* □ *I don't have any business cards on me.*

have something **on the ball** to have a particular amount of smartness or cleverness. □ *Both John and Mary have a lot on the ball. They should go far.* □ *I think I'd do better in school if I had more on the ball. I learn slowly.*

have something **out** to have something, such as a tooth, stone, tumor, removed surgically. (Fixed order.) □ *You are going to have to have that tumor out.* □ *I don't want to have my tooth out!*

have something **out (with** someone**)** to settle a disagreement or a complaint. (Fixed order.) □ *John has been mad at Mary for a week. He finally had it out with her today.* □ *I'm glad we are having this out today.*

H

have something **stick in** one's **craw** *Fig.* to have something irritate or displease someone. □ *I don't like to have someone's words stick in my craw.* □ *He meant to have the problem stick in my craw and upset me.*

have something **to burn** *Fig.* to have lots of something, such as money, power, food, space, cars, etc.; to have more of something than one needs. □ *Look at the way Tom buys things. You'd think he had money to burn.* □ *If I had all that acting talent to burn as he does, I'd have won an Oscar by now.*

have something **to do with** something and **not have anything to do with** something; **have nothing to do with** something to be associated with or related to something. □ *Does your dislike for Sally have something to do with the way she insulted you?* □ *My illness has something to do with my lungs.*

have something **to spare** *Fig.* to have more than enough of something. □ *Ask John for some firewood. He has firewood to spare.* □ *Do you have any candy to spare?*

have something **up** one's **sleeve** and **have an ace up** one's **sleeve** *Fig.* to have a secret or surprise plan or solution (to a problem). (Alludes to cheating at cards by having a card hidden in one's sleeve.) □ *I've got something up my sleeve, and it should solve all your problems. I'll tell you what it is after I'm elected.* □ *The manager has an ace up her sleeve. She'll surprise us with it later.*

have something **wrapped up** Go to sewed up.

have sticky fingers *Fig.* to have a tendency to steal. □ *The clerk—who had sticky fingers—got fired.* □ *The little boy had sticky fingers and was always taking his father's small change.*

have the ball in one's **court 1.** *Lit.* to have a ball belonging to a game played on a court on one's side of the court. □ *You have the ball in your court, so hit it back to me!* **2.** *Fig.* to be responsible for the next move in some process; to have to make a response to something that someone else has started. □ *You have the ball in your court now. You have to answer the attorney's questions.* □ *There was no way that Liz could avoid responding. She had the ball in her court.*

have the best of someone or something to defeat someone or something. □ *I'm afraid you have the best of me.* □ *We had the best of the opposite team by the end of the first half.*

have the cards stacked against one and **have the deck stacked against** one *Fig.* to have one's chance at future success limited by factors over which one has no control; to have luck against one. □ *You can't get very far in life if you have the deck stacked against you.* □ *I can't seem to get ahead. I always have the cards stacked against me.*

have the courage of one's **convictions** to have enough courage and determination to carry out one's goals. □ *It's fine to have noble goals in life and to believe in great things. If you don't have the courage of your convictions, you'll never reach your goals.* □ *Jane was successful because she had the courage of her convictions.*

have the deck stacked against one Go to **have the cards stacked against** one.

have the devil to pay and **have hell to pay** *Inf.* to have a great deal of trouble. (Use *hell* with caution.) □ *If you* cheat on your income taxes, you'll have the devil to pay. □ *I came home after three in the morning and had hell to pay.*

have the facts straight Go to get the facts straight.

have the final say Go to the last word.

have the gall to do something *Fig.* to have sufficient arrogance to do something. □ *I bet you don't have the gall to argue with the mayor.* □ *Only Jane has the gall to ask the boss for a second raise this month.*

have the gift of gab and **have a gift for gab** *Fig.* to have a great facility with language; to be able to use language very effectively. (See also **have a way with words**.) □ *My brother really has the gift of gab. He can convince anyone of anything.* □ *I don't talk a lot. I just don't have the gift for gab.*

have the hots for someone *Sl.* to be sexually aroused by someone. □ *Perry has the hots for Earline.*

have the makings of something *Fig.* to possess the qualities that are needed for something. □ *The young boy had the makings of a fine baseball player.* □ *My boss has all the makings of a prison warden.*

have the Midas touch *Fig.* to have the ability to be successful, especially the ability to make money easily. (From the name of a legendary king whose touch turned everything to gold.) □ *Bob is a merchant banker and really has the Midas touch.* □ *The poverty-stricken boy turned out to have the Midas touch and was a millionaire by the time he was twenty-five.*

have the mullygrubs *Rur.* to feel depressed. □ *She had the mullygrubs because her husband was out of town.* □ *Joe had the mullygrubs. We tried to cheer him up.*

have the patience of a saint and **have the patience of Job** *Fig.* to have a great deal of patience. □ *Steve has the patience of Job given the way his wife nags him.* □ *Dear Martha has the patience of a saint; she raised six children by herself.*

have the patience of Job Go to previous.

have the presence of mind to do something *Fig.* to have the calmness and ability to act sensibly in an emergency or difficult situation. □ *Jane had the presence of mind to phone the police when the child disappeared.* □ *The child had the presence of mind to write down the car's license-plate number.*

have the shoe on the other foot *Fig.* to experience the opposite situation (from a previous situation). (See the proverb The **shoe is on the other foot**. □ *I used to be a student, and now I'm the teacher. Now I have the shoe on the other foot.*

have the stomach for something **1.** *Fig.* to be able to tolerate certain foods. □ *Do you have the stomach for Tex-Mex cooking?* □ *We just don't have the stomach for onions anymore.* **2.** *Fig.* to have the courage or resolution to do something. □ *I don't have the stomach for watching those horror movies.* □ *Ken doesn't have the stomach for fighting.*

have the time of one's **life** to have a very good time; to have the most exciting time in one's life. □ *What a great party! I had the time of my life.* □ *We went to Florida last winter and had the time of our lives.*

have to do something **so bad** one **can taste it** Go to so bad one can taste it.

have to do with something to be associated with or related to something. □ *Sally's unhappiness has to do with the way you insulted her.* □ *My illness has to do with my stomach.*

have to get married *Euph.* [for a couple] to get married because the woman is pregnant. □ *They didn't have a long engagement. They had to get married, you see.* □ *They had to get married, and their first baby was born seven months later.*

have to go some (to do something**)** to need to try very hard to accomplish something. □ *That's really great, Jean! I have to go some to do better than that!*

have to hand it to someone to give someone credit [for something]. (Includes an expression of obligation, such as *must, got to, have to,* etc.) □ *You've really got to hand it to Jane. She has done a fine job.* □ *We have to hand it to Fred. That wine he brought was great.*

have to live with something to have to endure something. □ *I have a slight limp in the leg that I broke last year. The doctor says I'll have to live with it.* □ *We don't like the carpeting in the living room, but since money is so tight we'll have to live with it.*

have too and **have so** to have done something (despite anything to the contrary). (This is an emphatic way of affirming that something has happened.) □ *Mother: You haven't made your bed. Bob: I have too!* □ *I have so turned in my paper! If you don't have it, you lost it!*

have too many irons in the fire *Fig.* to be doing too many things at once. □ *Tom had too many irons in the fire and missed some important deadlines.* □ *It's better if you don't have too many irons in the fire.*

have too much of a good thing *Prov.* To hurt yourself by overindulging in something good. □ *I've gained five pounds from all the holiday dinners I've eaten this month. I think I had too much of a good thing.* □ *Alan: We're having such a good time at this resort, why don't we stay another week? Jane: I think we'd get bored with it if we stayed that long. You can have too much of a good thing, you know.*

have too much on one's **plate** and **have a lot on** one's **plate** *Fig.* to be too busy. □ *I'm sorry, I just have too much on my plate right now.* □ *If you have too much on your plate, can I help?*

have (too much) time on one's **hands** *Fig.* to have extra time; to have time to spare. □ *Your problem is that you have too much time on your hands.* □ *I don't have time on my hands. I am busy all the time.*

have two left feet *Fig.* to be very awkward with one's feet. (Often refers to awkwardness at dancing.) □ *I'm sorry, I can't dance better. I have two left feet.*

have what it takes and **have got what it takes** to have the skills, power, intelligence, etc., to do something. □ *I know I've got what it takes.* □ *I guess I don't have what it takes to be a composer.*

have words *Euph.* to argue. □ *From the sound of things, Bill and his father had words last night.* □ *We had words on the subject of money.*

have words with someone **(over** someone or something**)** *Fig.* to quarrel with someone over someone or something. □ *I had words with John over Mary and her friends.* □ *Elaine had words with Tony over his driving habits.*

(Have you) been keeping busy? and **(Have you been) keeping busy?; You been keeping busy?** *Inf.* a vague greeting asking about how someone has been occupied. □ *Tom: Been keeping busy? Bill: Yeah. Too busy.* □ *Sue: Hi, Fred. Have you been keeping busy? Fred: Not really. Just doing what I have to.*

(Have you) been keeping cool? and **(Have you been) keeping cool?; You been keeping cool?** *Inf.* an inquiry about how someone is surviving very hot weather. □ *Tom: What do you think of this hot weather? Been keeping cool? Sue: No, I like this weather just as it is.* □ *Mary: Keeping cool? Bill: Yup. Run the air-conditioning all the time.*

(Have you) been keeping out of trouble? and **(Have you been) keeping out of trouble?; You been keeping out of trouble?** *Inf.* a vague greeting asking one what one has been doing. □ *Bob: Hi, Mary. Have you been keeping out of trouble? Mary: Yeah. And you? Bob: Oh, I'm getting by.* □ *Tom: Hey, man! Been keeping out of trouble? Bob: Hell, no! What are you up to? Tom: Nothing.*

(Have you) been okay? and **You been okay?** *Inf.* a vague greeting asking if one has been well. □ *Tom: Hey, man. How you doing? Bob: I'm okay. You been okay? Tom: Sure. See you!* □ *Mary: I heard you were sick. Sally: Yes, but I'm better. Have you been okay? Mary: Oh, sure. Healthy as an ox.*

(Have you) changed your mind? and **You changed your mind?** Have you decided to alter your decision? □ *Sally: As of last week, they said you are leaving. Changed your mind? Bill: No. I'm leaving for sure.* □ *Tom: Well, have you changed your mind? Sally: Absolutely not!*

Have you heard? and **Did you hear?** a question used to introduce a piece of news or gossip. □ *Sally: Hi, Mary. Mary: Hi, Mary. Have you heard about Tom and Sue? Sally: No, what happened? Mary: I'll let one of them tell you. Sally: Oh, come on! Tell me!* □ *Bob: Hi, Tom. What's new? Tom: Did you hear that they're raising taxes again? Bob: That's not new.*

Have you met someone? a question asked when introducing someone to someone else. (The question need not be answered. The *someone* is usually a person's name.) □ *Tom: Hello, Mary. Have you met Fred? Mary: Hello, Fred. Glad to meet you. Fred: Glad to meet you, Mary.* □ *Tom: Hey, Mary! Good to see you. Have you met Fred? Mary: No, I don't believe I have. Hello, Fred. Glad to meet you. Fred: Hello, Mary.*

Haven't I seen you somewhere before? and **Haven't we met before?** a polite or coy way of trying to introduce yourself to someone. □ *Bob: Hi. Haven't I seen you somewhere before? Mary: I hardly think so.* □ *Bill (moving toward Jane): Haven't we met before? Jane (moving away from Bill): No way!*

hazard a guess Go to take a guess.

hazard an opinion *Fig.* to give an opinion. □ *Anne asked the attorney to hazard an opinion about the strength of her lawsuit.* □ *Don't feel like you have to hazard an opinion on something you know nothing about.*

He gives twice who gives quickly. *Prov.* When someone asks you for something, it is more helpful to give something right away than to wait, even if you might be

295

able to give more if you waited. □ *Morris didn't have all the money his sister asked for, but he sent what he had immediately, knowing that he gives twice who gives quickly.*

He lives long who lives well. *Prov.* If you live virtuously, you will have a long life; a person who does not live virtuously is wasting his life. □ *The pastor, exhorting his congregation to live moral lives, said, "He lives long who lives well."*

He puts his pants on one leg at a time. *Prov.* The person referred to is only human.; The person referred to is an ordinary person. □ *Sue: That man is my favorite movie star. Don't you think he's just divine? Jane: Oh, I don't know. I imagine he puts his pants on one leg at a time.*

He that cannot obey cannot command. *Prov.* If you want to become a leader, you should first learn how to follow someone else. □ *Jones can't seem to do anything I ask him to. He'll never get anywhere; he that cannot obey cannot command.*

He that hath a full purse never wanted a friend. *Prov.* A rich person always has plenty of friends. □ *Jill: Ever since Joe won the lottery, he's been getting congratulations from friends and relatives he hasn't heard from in years. Jane: You know how it is. He that hath a full purse never wanted a friend.*

He that is down need fear no fall. *Prov.* If you have nothing, you cannot lose anything by taking a risk. □ *Jim spent his last ten dollars on lottery tickets, figuring that he who is down need fear no fall.*

He that would eat the kernel must crack the nut. *Prov.* You have to work if you want to get anything good. □ *If you want to be a good pianist, you have to practice every day. He that would eat the kernel must crack the nut.*

He that would go to sea for pleasure, would go to hell for a pastime. *Prov.* Being a sailor is so unpleasant that anyone who would do it for fun must be crazy. □ *Old Sailor: Why did you decide to go to sea? Young Sailor: I thought it would be fun. Old Sailor: He that would go to sea for pleasure, would go to hell for a pastime.*

He that would have eggs must endure the cackling of hens. *Prov.* You must be willing to endure unpleasant, irritating things in order to get what you want. □ *Sue: I'm tired of working after school. All the customers at the store are so rude. Mother: But you wanted money to buy a car. He that would have eggs must endure the cackling of hens, dear.*

He that would the daughter win, must with the mother first begin. *Prov.* If you want to marry a woman, you should find a way to impress her mother, so that the mother will favor her marrying you. □ *Harry: I think I want to marry Gina. Bill: Don't propose to her until you're sure her mother is on your side. He that would the daughter win, must with the mother first begin.*

He travels fastest who travels alone. *Prov.* It is easier to achieve your goals if you do not have a spouse, children, or other connections to consider. □ *Jill: Don't go yet! Wait for me to get ready. Jane: But you always take at least half an hour. No wonder they always say that he travels fastest who travels alone.*

He wears a ten-dollar hat on a five-cent head. *Rur.* He is stupid but rich. □ *He got the job because he's the boss's son, not because he's smart. He wears a ten-dollar hat on a five-cent head.*

He who begins many things, finishes but few. *Prov.* If you start a lot of projects, you will not have time and energy to complete them all. (Can be used to warn someone against starting too many projects.) □ *Sarah's room is littered with sweaters and mittens she started to knit but never finished, a testament to the fact that she who begins many things, finishes but few.*

He who excuses himself accuses himself. *Prov.* By apologizing for something, you admit that you did it. □ *Maybe I should tell my boss I'm sorry for breaking the copy machine. On the other hand, he who excuses himself accuses himself.*

He who fights and runs away, may live to fight another day. *Prov.* It may be cowardly to run away from a fight, but running away gives you a better chance of surviving. □ *The school bully told Phillip to meet him in the playground after school, but Phillip didn't keep the appointment. When his friends called him a coward, Phillip shrugged and said, "He who fights and runs away, may live to fight another day."*

He who hesitates is lost. *Prov.* People should act decisively. □ *Jill: Should I apply for that job? At first I thought I definitely should, but now I don't know. . . . Jane: She who hesitates is lost. □ Call that girl and ask her out. Call her right now. He who hesitates is lost.*

He who laughs last, laughs best. Go to next.

He who laughs last, laughs longest. and **He who laughs last, laughs best.** *Prov.* If someone does something nasty to you, that person may feel satisfaction, but you will feel even more satisfaction if you get revenge on that person. □ *Joe pulled a dirty trick on me, but I'll get him back. He who laughs last, laughs best.*

He who pays the piper calls the tune. *Prov.* If you are paying for someone's services, you can dictate exactly what you want that person to do. □ *When Mrs. Dalton told the artist what she wanted her portrait to look like, the artist cringed to think that anyone could have such bad taste. Still, he who pays the piper calls the tune, and Mrs. Dalton got what she wanted.*

He who rides a tiger is afraid to dismount. *Prov.* Sometimes it is more dangerous to stop doing a dangerous thing than it is to continue doing it. □ *Jill: You shouldn't take out another loan. Jane: If I don't take out a loan, I can't make the payments on the loans I already have. You know how it is—she who rides a tiger is afraid to dismount.*

He who sups with the devil should have a long spoon. *Prov.* If you have dealings with dangerous people, you must be careful that they do not harm you. □ *If you're going to hang out with that disreputable bunch of people, keep in mind that he who sups with the devil should have a long spoon.*

He who would climb the ladder must begin at the bottom. *Prov.* If you want to gain high status, you must start with low status and slowly work upwards. □ *Although Thomas hoped to become a famous journalist, he didn't mind working for a small-town newspaper at first.*

"He who would climb the ladder must begin at the bottom," he said.

He will get his. and **She will get hers.** One will be punished for one's misdeeds. □ *Jill: It seems like Fred can do any evil thing he wants. Jane: Don't worry. He'll get his.* □ *You may think you will always profit by your life of crime, but you'll get yours.*

a **head** and **per head** [for] a person; [for] an individual. □ *How much do you charge per head for dinner?* □ *It costs four dollars a head.*

head and shoulders above someone or something *Fig.* clearly superior to someone or something. (Often with *stand,* as in the example.) □ *This wine is head and shoulders above that one.* □ *John stands head and shoulders above Bob.*

head away from someone or something to turn and move away from someone or something. □ *The car headed away from Andrew and he knew he was stranded for at least an hour.* □ *We headed away from the store, not knowing that my purse was riding on the roof of the car.*

head back (some place**)** to start moving back to some place. □ *I walked to the end of the street and then headed back home.* □ *This is far enough. Let's head back.*

head for someone or something to aim for or move toward someone or something. □ *She waved good-bye as she headed for the door.* □ *Ann came in and headed for her mother.*

head for the hills and **take to the hills; run for the hills 1.** *Lit.* to flee to higher ground. □ *The river's rising. Head for the hills!* □ *Head for the hills! Here comes the flood!* **2.** *Fig.* to depart quickly. □ *Here comes crazy Joe. Run for the hills.* □ *Everyone is heading for the hills because that boring Mr. Simpson is coming here again.*

head for the last roundup *Euph.* to reach the end of usefulness or of life. (Originally said of a dying cowboy.) □ *This ballpoint pen is headed for the last roundup. I have to get another one.* □ *I am so weak. I think I'm headed for the last roundup.*

head for (the) tall timber *Rur.* to run away and hide. □ *When we heard Pa's angry bellow, we headed for the tall timber.* □ *The bank robbers headed for tall timber with their loot.*

head in(to something**)** to move into something head or front end first. □ *Head into that parking space slowly. It is quite narrow.* □ *I turned the boat toward shore and headed in.*

head on directly; head to head. □ *I think we need to face this threat head on. Let's be proactive not reactive!*

head out after someone, something, or an animal to start pursuing someone, something, or an animal. □ *The sheriff and his men headed out after the bank robbers.* □ *We headed out after the runaway boat.*

head out (for something**)** to set out for something or some place; to begin a journey to something or some place. □ *We headed out for Denver very early in the morning.* □ *What time do we head out tomorrow morning?*

head over heels in debt *Fig.* deeply in debt. □ *Finally, when she was head over heels in debt, she cut up her credit cards.* □ *I couldn't stand being head over heels in debt, so I always pay off my bills immediately.*

head over heels in love (with someone**)** *Fig.* very much in love with someone. □ *John is head over heels in love with Mary.* □ *They are head over heels in love with each other.*

head someone **off at the pass** *Fig.* to intercept someone. (From Old West movies. Fixed order.) □ *I need to talk to John before he gets into the boss's office. I'll head him off at the pass.* □ *The sheriff set out in a hurry to head Jed off at the pass.*

head someone or something **at** someone or something to point or aim someone or something toward someone or something. □ *He headed the boat at the island and sped off.* □ *I headed Rachel at her brother, whom she hadn't seen for thirty years.*

head someone or something **into** someone or something to direct someone or something into someone or something. □ *Jill headed the car into the parking place.* □ *I headed Rachel into the ice cream store and left her on her own.*

head someone or something **off**† *Fig.* to intercept and divert someone or something. □ *I think I can head her off before she reaches the police station.* □ *I hope we can head off trouble.* □ *We can head it off. Have no fear.*

head something **out**† to aim something outward; to move something on its way, head or front first. □ *Head the boat out and pull out the throttle.* □ *I headed out the car and we were on our way.*

head something **up**† **1.** *Lit.* to get something pointed in the right direction. (Especially a herd of cattle or a group of covered wagons.) □ *Head those wagons up—we're moving out.* □ *Head up the wagons!* **2.** *Fig.* to be in charge of something; to be the head of some organization. □ *I was asked to head the new committee up for the first year.* □ *Will you head up the committee for me?*

head South Go to to go South.

*a **head start (on** someone**)** an early start [at something], before someone else starts. (*Typically: **get** ~; **have** ~; **give** someone ~.) □ *Bill always gets there first because he gets a head start on everybody else.* □ *I'm doing well in my class because I have a head start; I learned some of this last year.*

*a **head start (on** something**)** an early start on something, [before someone else starts]. (*Typically: **get** ~; **have** ~; **give** someone ~.) □ *I was able to get a head start on my reading during the holidays.* □ *If I hadn't had a head start, I'd be behind in my reading.*

head toward someone or something **1.** *Lit.* to point at and move toward someone, something, or some place. □ *Head toward Mary and don't stop to talk to anyone else.* □ *Sharon headed toward the parking lot, hoping to get home soon.* **2.** *Fig.* to be developing into something; to be moving toward a specific result. □ *The problem will head toward a solution when you stop making the situation worse than it is.* □ *I believe that you are heading toward severe health problems if you don't stop smoking.*

headed for something destined for something. □ *Harry is headed for real trouble.* □ *She is headed for a breakdown.*

heads or tails the face of a coin or the other side of a coin. (Often used in an act of coin tossing, where one circumstance is valid if the front of a coin appears and another circumstance is valid if the other side appears.) □ *Jim looked at Jane as he flipped the coin into the air. "Heads or tails?" he asked.* □ *It doesn't matter whether the result of the toss is heads or tails. I won't like the outcome in any case.*

Heads up! Raise your head and look around you carefully for information or something that you need to see or avoid. □ *Heads up! Watch out for that door!* □ *Heads up! There is a car coming.*

heads will roll *Fig.* people will get into severe trouble. □ *When the company's year-end results are known, heads will roll.* □ *Heads will roll when the principal sees the damaged classroom.*

heal over [for the surface of a wound] to heal. □ *The wound healed over very quickly, and there was very little scarring.* □ *I hope it will heal over without having to be stitched.*

heal someone **of** something to cure someone's ailments. □ *Are you the doctor who healed me of my wounds?* □ *Can any doctor heal us of a common cold?*

heal up [for an injury] to heal. □ *The cut healed up in no time at all.*

a **heap of** something a great deal of something. □ *Tom's got a heap of money, but no one to spend it on.* □ *A teacher has to have a heap of patience as well as a lot of smarts.*

a **heap sight** *Rur.* a lot; very much. □ *This chair is a heap sight better than that one.* □ *You got a heap sight more taters than I did.*

heap something **up**† to make something into a pile. □ *He heaped the mashed potatoes up on my plate, because he thought I wanted lots.* □ *Heap up the leaves in the corner of the yard.*

heap something **(up)on** someone or something **1.** *Lit.* to pile something up on someone or something. (*Upon* is formal and less commonly used than *on*.) □ *Please don't heap so much trouble upon me!* □ *Wally heaped leaves on the flower bed.* **2.** *Fig.* to give someone too much of something, such as homework, praise, criticism, etc. (*Upon* is formal and less commonly used than *on*.) □ *Don't heap too much praise on her. She will get conceited.* □ *The manager heaped criticism on the workers.*

heap something **with** something to pile something onto something. □ *Karen heaped Jeff's plate with way too much food.* □ *We heaped the driveway with leaves and then put them into bags.*

hear a peep out of someone *Fig.* to get some sort of a response from someone; to hear the smallest word from someone. (Usually in the negative.) □ *I don't want to hear another peep out of you.* □ *I didn't know they were there. I didn't hear a peep out of them.*

hear about someone or something to learn about someone or something. (Not necessarily by hearing.) □ *Have you heard about Tom and what happened to him?* □ *I heard about the accident.*

hear from someone or something to get a message from someone or a group. □ *I want to hear from you every now and then.* □ *We hear from the court every year or so about jury duty.*

hear of someone or something to learn of the existence of someone or something. □ *Did you ever hear of such a*

thing? □ *I have heard of Sharon Wallace and I would like to meet her.*

hear someone **out**† **1.** *Lit.* to hear all of what someone has to say. (Fixed order.) □ *Please hear me out. I have more to say.* □ *Hear out the witness. Don't jump to conclusions.* **2.** *Fig.* to hear someone's side of the story. (Fixed order.) □ *Let him talk! Hear him out! Listen to his side!* □ *We have to hear everyone out in this matter.*

hear something **through** to listen to all of something. □ *I would like you to hear this explanation through before making your decision.* □ *I won't have an opinion until I hear this through.*

hear word (from someone or something**)** Go to **word (from** someone or something**).**

hearing impaired *Euph.* deaf or nearly deaf. □ *This program is closed-captioned for our hearing-impaired viewers.* □ *His mother happens to be hearing impaired, so he learned to sign at an early age.*

hearken to someone or something *Formal or stilted* to listen to someone or something; to pay attention to someone or something. □ *Please hearken to me. I speak the truth.* □ *Hearken to the call of the nightingale.*

heart and soul *Fig.* the central core [of someone or something]. □ *Now we are getting to the heart and soul of the matter.* □ *This feature is the heart and soul of my invention.*

the **heart of the matter** Go to the **crux of the matter.**

a **heartbeat away from being** something *Cliché* set to be the next ruler upon the final heartbeat of the current ruler. (The decisive heartbeat would be the current ruler's last heartbeat.) □ *The vice president is just a heartbeat away from being president.* □ *The prince was only a heartbeat away from being king.*

heat someone **up**† *Fig.* to make someone angry. (One old [now folksy] past tense is *het*.) □ *This kind of nonsense really heats me up.* □ *Mean talk heats up the kids.*

heat something **up**† **(to** something**)** to raise the temperature of something to a certain level. □ *Please heat this room up to about seventy degrees.* □ *Can you heat up the room a little more?*

heat up 1. *Lit.* to get warmer or hot. □ *It really heats up in the afternoon around here.* □ *How soon will dinner be heated up?* **2.** *Fig.* to grow more animated or combative. □ *The debate began to heat up near the end.* □ *Their argument was heating up, and I was afraid there would be fighting.*

heave in(to) sight *Fig.* to move into sight in the distance. □ *As the fog cleared, a huge ship heaved into sight.* □ *After many days of sailing, land finally heaved in sight.*

heave something **at** someone or something to throw something at someone or something. □ *Fred heaved a huge snowball at Roger.* □ *The thug heaved the rock at the window and broke it to pieces.*

heave something **up**† **1.** *Lit.* to lift something up. □ *With a lot of effort, they heaved the heavy lid up.* □ *The workers heaved up the huge boulder.* **2.** *Fig.* to vomit something up. □ *The dog heaved most of the cake up on the kitchen floor.* □ *It heaved up the cake it had eaten.*

heave to to stop a sailing ship by facing it directly into the wind. □ *The captain gave the order to heave to.* □ *The ship hove to and everyone had a swim.*

Heaven forbid! Go to God forbid!

Heaven help us! *Fig.* Good grief!; That's awful. □ *He fell and broke his hip! Heaven help us! What's next?*

Heaven protects children(, sailors,) and drunken men. *Prov.* Children(, sailors,) and drunk(ard)s often escape being injured in dangerous situations. (Often used to express amazement that a child, sailor, or drunk person has escaped injury.) □ *Jill: Did you hear? A little girl fell out of a second-floor window in our apartment building. Jane: Was she killed? Jill: She wasn't even hurt. Jane: Heaven protects children, sailors, and drunken men.* □ *Mike was so drunk he shouldn't even have been conscious, but he managed to drive home without hurting himself or anyone else; heaven protects children and drunkards.*

Heavens to Betsy! *Inf.* My goodness! (A mild oath.) □ *Heavens to Betsy! What was that noise?* □ *Heavens to Betsy! It's good to hear your voice!*

heavy going difficult to do, understand, or make progress with. □ *Jim finds math heavy going.* □ *Talking to Mary is heavy going. She has nothing interesting to say.*

heavy into someone or something *Inf.* much concerned with someone or something; obsessed with someone or something. □ *Freddie was heavy into auto racing and always went to the races.* □ *Sam is heavy into Mary. He's been out with her every night this week.*

A **heavy purse makes a light heart.** *Prov.* If you have plenty of money, you will feel happy and secure. □ *Everyone in the office is especially cheerful on payday, since a heavy purse makes a light heart.*

hedge against something to do something to lessen the risk of something happening; to bet against something bad happening. □ *I want to hedge against something going wrong in the stock market, so I have bonds in my portfolio, too.* □ *We will hedge against any risk we can detect.*

A **hedge between keeps friendship green.** *Prov.* Your friendship will flourish if you and your friend respect each other's privacy. □ *Lynne and I are the best of friends, but we often like to spend time apart. A hedge between keeps friendship green.*

hedge one's **bets** *Fig.* to reduce one's loss on a bet or on an investment by counterbalancing the loss in some way. □ *Bob bet Ann that the plane would be late. He usually hedges his bets. This time he called the airline and asked about the plane before he made the bet.* □ *John bought some stock and then bet Mary that the stock would go down in value in one year. He has hedged his bets perfectly. If the stock goes up, he sells it, pays off Mary, and still makes a profit. If it goes down, he reduces his loss by winning the bet he made with Mary.*

hedge someone **in†** *Fig.* to restrict someone. (See also **hedge** someone or something **in.**) □ *Our decision hedged in the children so they could not have any flexibility.* □ *She hedged herself in by her own behavior.*

hedge someone or something **in†** to enclose someone or something in a hedge. (See also **hedge** someone **in.**) □ *Their overgrown yard has almost hedged us in.* □ *Their bushes hedged in our yard.*

hedge something **against** something *Fig.* to protect investments against a decline in value by making counterbalancing bets or investments. □ *The investor hedged his portfolio against a drop in stock prices by buying some bonds.* □ *I have to hedge my bets against losing.*

heist someone or something **(up†)** *Rur.* to lift someone or something. □ *See if you can heist that box onto the top shelf.* □ *Dad heisted me up so I could see over the fence.* □ *John groaned and heisted up the bale of hay.*

***hell** and ***the** **devil 1.** *Inf.* a severe scolding. (*Typically: **get** ~; **catch** ~; **give** someone ~. Use caution with *hell.*) □ *The boss just gave me hell about it.* □ *I'm really going to give Tom hell when he gets home.* **2.** *Inf.* trouble; pain. (*Typically: **give** someone ~. Use caution with *hell.*) □ *My arthritis is giving me hell in this weather.* □ *This problem is giving us hell at the office.*

hell around *Sl.* to go around making trouble or noise. □ *Who are those kids who are out there helling around every night?* □ *They hell around because it's fun.*

Hell hath no fury like a woman scorned. *Prov.* There is nothing as unpleasant as a woman who has been offended or whose love has not been returned. □ *When Mary Ann discovered that George was not in love with her, George discovered that hell hath no fury like a woman scorned.* □ *Bill: I'm getting tired of going out with Mary; I think I'll tell her we're through. Fred: Be careful. Hell hath no fury like a woman scorned, you know.*

a **hell of a mess** *Inf.* a terrible mess. (Use caution with *hell.*) □ *This is really a hell of a mess you've gotten us into.* □ *I never dreamed I'd come back to such a hell of a mess.*

a **hell of a note** *Inf.* a surprising or amazing piece of news. (Use caution with *hell.*) □ *So you're just going to leave me like that? Well, that's a hell of a note!* □ *You forgot what I asked you to bring? That's a hell of a note.*

a **hell of a** someone or something and a **helluva** someone or something **1.** *Inf.* a very bad person or thing. (Use caution with *hell.*) □ *That's a hell of a way to treat someone.* □ *He's a hell of a driver! Watch out!* **2.** *Inf.* a very good person or thing. (Use caution with *hell.*) □ *He is one hell of a guy. We really like him.* □ *We had a helluva good time.*

hell on a holiday *Rur.* a big commotion. (Use caution with *hell.*) □ *It was hell on a holiday outside the stadium when the team won the big game.* □ *What's going on down on Main Street? Sounds like hell on a holiday!*

hell on earth *Fig.* a very unpleasant situation, as if one were in hell. □ *That man made my life hell on earth!* □ *The whole time I was there was just hell on earth.*

hell-bent for leather *Inf.* moving or behaving recklessly; riding a horse fast and recklessly. □ *They took off after the horse thief, riding hell-bent for leather.* □ *Here comes the boss. She's not just angry; she's hell-bent for leather.*

hell-bent for somewhere or something *Fig.* riding or drive somewhere very fast or recklessly. □ *Fred sped along, hell-bent for home, barely missing another car.*

Hellfire and damnation! *Inf.* Damn it! (An oath used to express anger or irritation.) □ *Hellfire and damnation! Turn that radio down!* □ *Hellfire and damnation! This is the second time our picnic's been rained out.*

Hell's bells (and buckets of blood)! *Inf.* an exclamation of anger or surprise. (Use caution with *hell.*) □ *Alice:*

299

Your pants are torn in back. John: *Oh, hell's bells! What will happen next?* □ Bill: *Well, Jane, looks like you just flunked calculus.* Jane: *Hell's bells and buckets of blood! What do I do now?*

a **helluva** someone or something Go to a **hell of a** someone or something.

help oneself **(to** something) to take something oneself without asking permission. □ *The thief helped himself to the money in the safe.* □ *Help yourself to more dessert.*

help out some place to help [with the chores] in a particular place. □ *Would you be able to help out in the kitchen?* □ *Sally is downtown, helping out at the shop.*

help out (with something) to help with a particular chore. □ *Would you please help out with the dishes?* □ *I have to help out at home on the weekends.*

help someone **along 1.** to help someone move along. □ *I helped the old man along.* □ *Please help her along. She has a hurt leg.* **2.** to help someone advance. □ *I am more than pleased to help you along with your math.* □ *She helped herself along by studying hard.*

help someone **back (to** something) to help someone return to something or some place. □ *The ushers helped him back to his seat.* □ *When she returned, I helped her back.*

help someone **down (from** something) to help someone climb down from something. □ *Sharon helped the boy down from the horse.* □ *Elaine helped the children down.*

help someone **get a foothold (somewhere)** Go to a **foothold (somewhere).**

help someone **in** something to help someone with some task; to help someone in the doing of something. □ *Please help me in my efforts to win the contest.* □ *Will you help me in my reelection?*

help someone **in(to** something) to help someone get into something. □ *I will help my grandfather into the car.* □ *We all had to help him in.*

help someone **off (of)** something to help someone get off something. (*Of* is usually retained before pronouns.) □ *Please help me off this horse!* □ *Do help him off of it!*

help someone **off with** something to help someone take off an article of clothing. □ *Would you please help me off with my coat?* □ *We helped the children off with their boots and put their coats in the hall.*

help someone **on with** something to help someone put on an article of clothing. □ *Would you help me on with my coat?* □ *Please help her on with her coat.*

help someone or an animal **(get) over** something **1.** *Lit.* to aid someone or an animal climb over something. □ *I helped him get over the wall.* □ *I helped the puppy over the barrier.* **2.** *Fig.* to aid someone or an animal recover from something. □ *Sharon wanted to help Roger get over his illness.* □ *We try to help the families get over the loss of their loved ones.*

help someone or an animal **out (of** something) **1.** to help someone or an animal get out of something or some place. □ *Please help your grandmother out of the car.* □ *Please help the cat out of the carton.* **2.** to help someone or an animal get out of a garment. □ *She helped the dog out of its sweater.* □ *I helped her out of her coat when we got inside.* **3.** to help someone or an animal get out of trouble. □ *Can*

you please help me out of this mess that I got myself into? □ *You are in a real mess. We will help you out.*

help someone or something **out† with** someone or something **1.** *Lit.* to assist someone or something with a person or a thing. □ *Can you help me out with my geometry?* □ *Please help out my son with his geometry.* **2.** *Fig.* to help someone or a group by providing someone or something. □ *I need some salt. Would you help me out with a little bit of salt?* □ *Can you help out our department with a secretary?*

help someone or something **with** someone or something to give aid to someone or something in dealing with someone or something. □ *Please help your father with your little sister.* □ *I helped the committee with the problem.*

help (someone) out† to help someone do something; to help someone with a problem. □ *I am trying to raise this window. Can you help me out?* □ *I'm always happy to help out a friend.*

help someone **up† (from** something) to help someone rise up from something; to help someone get up from something. □ *She offered to help him up from the chair.* □ *Elaine helped up her grandmother who was stuck in the chair.*

Help yourself. Please take what you want without asking permission. □ *Sally: Can I have one of these doughnuts?* Bill: *Help yourself.* □ *Mother led the little troop of my friends to the kitchen table, which was covered with cups of juice and plates of cookies. "Help yourself," she said.*

***a **helping hand** *Fig.* help; physical help, especially with the hands. (*Typically: **get** ~; **need** ~; **give** someone ~; **offer** ~; **offer** someone ~.) □ *When you feel like you need a helping hand making dinner, just let me know.*

hem and haw (around) *Inf.* to be uncertain about something; to be evasive; to say "ah" and "eh" when speaking—avoiding saying something meaningful. □ *Stop hemming and hawing around. I want an answer.* □ *Don't just hem and haw around. Speak up. We want to hear what you think.*

hem someone or something **in†** *Fig.* to trap or enclose someone or something. □ *The large city buildings hem me in.* □ *Don't hem in the bird. Let it have a way to escape.*

***hepped (up)** *Sl.* to be intoxicated. (*Typically: **be** ~; **get** ~.) □ *Wally is a little too hepped up to drive home.* □ *Harry's too hepped to stand up.*

herd someone or something **together** to bunch people or animals together. □ *Let's herd all the kids together and take them in the house for ice cream and cake.* □ *I herded all the puppies together and put them in a box while I cleaned their play area.*

the **here and now** the present, as opposed to the past or the future. □ *I don't care what's happening tomorrow or next week! I care about the here and now.* □ *The past is dead. Let's worry about the here and now.*

here and there at this place and that; from place to place. □ *We find rare books in used-book stores here and there.* □ *She didn't make a systematic search. She just looked here and there.*

Here goes nothing. *Inf.* I am beginning to do something that will fail or be poorly done. □ *Sally stood on the diving board and said, "Here goes nothing."* □ *As Ann walked onto the stage, she whispered, "Here goes nothing."*

Here (it) goes. Something is going to start.; I will start now.; I will do it now. □ *I'm ready to start now. Here goes.* □ *Okay, it's my turn to kick the ball. Here it goes!*

Here's looking at you. Go to Bottoms up!

Here's mud in your eye. Go to Bottoms up!

Here's to someone or something. an expression used as a toast to someone or something to wish someone or something well. □ *Here's to Jim and Mary! May they be very happy!* □ *Here's to your new job!*

Here's to you. Go to Bottoms up!

Here's your hat, what's your hurry? *Rur.* It is time for you to go. (Jocular.) □ *I hate to rush you out the door, but here's your hat, what's your hurry?* □ *Jane: I suppose I'd better be on my way. Charlie: Here's your hat, what's your hurry?*

here, there, and everywhere *Fig.* everywhere; at all points. □ *Fred searched here, there, and everywhere, frantically looking for the lost check.* □ *She did not rest until she had been here, there, and everywhere, shopping for just the right gift.*

Here today, (and) gone tomorrow. *Prov.* Available now, but soon to be gone. (Used to describe something that does not last—often an opportunity). □ *The stores near my house don't stay in business very long—here today, and gone tomorrow.* □ *If you want this carpet, buy it now. This sale price is here today, gone tomorrow.*

Here we go again. We are going to experience the same thing again.; We are going to hear about or discuss the same thing again. □ *John: Now, I would like to discuss your behavior in class yesterday. Bill (to himself): Here we go again.* □ *Fred: We must continue our discussion of the Wilson project. Sue: Here we go again. Fred: What's that? Sue: Nothing.*

Here you go. *Inf.* Here is what you asked for. (See also **There you go.**) □ *"Here you go," said the waiter as he put the plate on the table.* □ *Here you go. Here is your hamburger and your drink.*

hesitate over something to pause before acting on something; to suspend action about someone or something. □ *We are hesitating over the final decision because we have some doubts about the competitors.* □ *Do not hesitate too long over this matter.*

hew something **down**† to fell something wooden, usually a tree. □ *We will have to hew most of this forest down.* □ *They hewed down the tree.*

hew something **out of** something and **hew** something **out**† to carve the shape of something out of something wooden. □ *Dan hewed each of the posts out of a tree trunk.* □ *He hewed out a number of posts.*

hew to something to conform to a rule or principle. □ *I wish you would hew to the rules a little better.* □ *Sarah refuses to hew to the company policies.*

a **hidden agenda** *Fig.* a secret plan; a concealed plan; a plan disguised as a plan with another purpose. □ *I am sure that the chairman has a hidden agenda. I never did trust him anyway.*

hide behind someone or something to conceal oneself behind someone or something. □ *The child hid behind his father.* □ *Rachel hid behind a tree.*

hide from someone or an animal to conceal oneself from someone or an animal. □ *Are you hiding from me?* □ *The rabbit was trying to hide from the fox.*

hide one's **face in shame** *Fig.* to cover one's face because of shame or embarrassment. □ *Mary was so embarrassed. She could only hide her face in shame.* □ *When Tom broke Ann's crystal vase, he wanted to hide his face in shame.*

hide one's **head in the sand** Go to bury one's **head in the sand.**

hide one's **light under a bushel** *Fig.* to conceal one's good ideas or talents. (A biblical theme.) □ *Jane has some good ideas, but she doesn't speak very often. She hides her light under a bushel.* □ *Don't hide your light under a bushel. Share your thoughts with other people.*

hide out (from someone or something**)** to hide oneself so that one cannot be found by someone or something. □ *Max was hiding out from the police in Detroit.* □ *Lefty is hiding out too.*

hide someone or something **away**† **(**some place**)** to conceal someone or something somewhere. □ *Please hide Randy away where no one can find him.* □ *Rachel hid the cake away, hoping to save it for dessert.* □ *Mary hid away the candy so the kids wouldn't eat it all.*

hide someone or something **behind** something to use something to conceal someone or something. □ *We hid the guests for the surprise party behind a large Oriental screen.* □ *I will hide the cake behind the screen too.*

hide something **in** something to conceal something inside something. □ *She hid her money in a book.* □ *Let's hide the cake in this closet.*

high and dry *Fig.* safe; unbothered by difficulties; unscathed. (As if someone or something were safe from a flood. See also **leave** someone **high and dry.)** □ *While the riot was going on down on the streets, I was high and dry in my apartment.* □ *Liz came out of the argument high and dry.*

***high as a kite** and ***high as the sky 1.** *Lit.* very high. (*Also: **as** ~.) □ *The tree grew as high as a kite.* □ *Our pet bird got outside and flew up high as the sky.* **2.** *Fig.* drunk or drugged. (*Also: **as** ~.) □ *Bill drank beer until he got as high as a kite.* □ *The thieves were high as the sky on drugs.*

high as the sky Go to previous.

high man on the totem pole *Fig.* the person at the top of the hierarchy; the person in charge of an organization. □ *I don't want to talk to a vice president. I demand to talk to the high man on the totem pole.* □ *Who's in charge around here? Who's high man on the totem pole?*

high on something *Sl.* **1.** excited or enthusiastic about something. □ *Tom is really high on the idea of going to Yellowstone this summer.* □ *I'm not high on going, but I will.* **2.** intoxicated. □ *John is acting as if he is high on something. Has he been doing drugs again?*

a **high roller** *Fig.* a gambler who bets heavily. □ *They welcomed me at the casino because I had the same name as one of their high rollers.*

*the **high sign** *Fig.* a prearranged signal for going ahead with something. (Often refers to a hand signal or some other visual signal. *Typically: **get** ~; **give** someone ~.)

☐ *When I got the high sign, I pulled cautiously out into the roadway.* ☐ *The train's engineer got the high sign and began to move the train out of the station.*

high-and-mighty *Fig.* self-important and arrogant. ☐ *I don't know why William is so high-and-mighty. He's no better than the rest of us.* ☐ *The boss acts high-and-mighty because he can fire us all.*

high-pressure someone **into** something *Fig.* to urge someone forcefully to do something. ☐ *Here comes Jill. Watch out. She will try to high-pressure you into working on her committee.* ☐ *You can't high-pressure me into doing anything! I'm too busy!*

hightail it out of somewhere *Rur.* to run or ride a horse away from somewhere fast; to leave in a hurry. (Typically heard in western movies.) ☐ *Here comes the sheriff. We'd better hightail it out of here.* ☐ *Look at that guy go. He really hightailed it out of town.*

highway robbery outrageous overpricing; a bill that is much higher than normally acceptable but must be paid. (As if one had been accosted and robbed on the open road or in broad daylight.) ☐ *Four thousand dollars! That's highway robbery for one piece of furniture!* ☐ *I won't pay it! It's highway robbery!*

highways and byways 1. major and minor roads. ☐ *The city council voted to plant new trees along all the highways and byways of the town.* **2.** *Cliché* routes and pathways, both major and minor. ☐ *I hope I meet you again some day on life's highways and byways.*

hike something **up** to raise something, such as prices, interest rates, a skirt, pants legs, etc. ☐ *The grocery store is always hiking prices up.* ☐ *She hiked up her skirt so she could wade across the creek.*

hind end *Rur.* the rump of someone or an animal. ☐ *If you say that again, I'll swat you right across the hind end.* ☐ *The mule slipped and came down right on her hind end.*

the **hind end of creation** *Rur.* a very remote place. ☐ *I wish I lived in the city. I'm tired of living here in the hind end of creation.* ☐ *Joe moved out to a little shack at the hind end of creation.*

hinder someone **from** something to prevent someone from doing something. ☐ *Please don't hinder me from my appointed tasks.* ☐ *You can't hinder me from doing what I want!*

hindside first *Rur.* backwards. ☐ *You've got your shirt on hindside first.* ☐ *The horse came out of the trailer hindside first.*

hinge (up)on someone or something *Fig.* to depend on someone or something; to depend on what someone or something does. (*Upon* is formal and less commonly used than *on.*) ☐ *The success of the project hinges upon you and how well you do your job.* ☐ *How well the corn crop does all hinges on the weather.*

hint at something to refer to something; to insinuate something. ☐ *What are you hinting at?* ☐ *I am not hinting at anything. I am telling you to do it!*

hint for something to give a hint that something is wanted. ☐ *I could tell she was hinting for an invitation.* ☐ *Are you hinting for a second helping of fried chicken?*

hint something **to** someone to give a hint or clue to someone. ☐ *I thought she was leaving. She hinted that to me.* ☐ *She wasn't hinting anything to you! You made it all up!*

***hip to** someone or something *Inf.* knowing about someone or something; adapting to someone or something. (*Typically: **be** ~; **get** ~; **become** ~.*) ☐ *The boss began to get hip to Mary and her deviousness.* ☐ *She finally began to get hip to what was going on.*

hire someone **away** **(from** someone or something**)** [for one] to get someone to quit working for some other employer and begin working for one. ☐ *We hired Elaine away from her previous employer, and now she wants to go back.* ☐ *The new bank hired away all the tellers from the old bank.*

hire someone or something **out** to grant someone the use or efforts of someone or something for pay. ☐ *I hired my son out as a lawn-care specialist.* ☐ *I hire out my son to mow lawns.*

hiss at someone or something **1.** [for a reptile] to make a hissing sound as a warning. ☐ *The snake hissed at me. Otherwise I wouldn't have known it was there.* ☐ *The lizard hissed at the snake.* **2.** [for someone] to make a hissing sound at someone to show disapproval. ☐ *The audience hissed at the performer, who was not all that bad.* ☐ *They hissed at all three acts.*

hiss someone **off ((of) the stage)** *Fig.* [for the audience] to hiss and drive a performer off the stage. ☐ *The boys in the front row tried to hiss her off the stage.* ☐ *The audience, angry with the quality of the singers, tried to hiss them all off.*

hiss something **out** *Fig.* to say something with a hissing voice, usually in anger or disgust. ☐ *The disgusted manager hissed his appraisal out.* ☐ *He hissed out his criticism.*

hissy (fit) *Rur.* a tantrum. (Often with *throw.* Probably refers to an angry, hissing cat.) ☐ *Jane practically has a hissy fit every time she gets a run in her nylons.* ☐ *The boss is really mad today. It's just one hissy fit after another.*

History repeats itself. *Prov.* The same kinds of events seem to happen over and over. ☐ *It seems that history is about to repeat itself for that poor country; it is about to be invaded again.* ☐ *Alan: The country is headed for an economic depression. Jane: How do you know? Alan: History repeats itself. The conditions now are just like the conditions before the last major depression.*

hit a happy medium Go to **strike a happy medium.**

hit a plateau *Fig.* to reach a higher level of activity, sales, production, output, etc., and then stop and remain unchanged for a time. ☐ *When my sales hit a plateau, my boss gave me a pep talk.* ☐ *When production hit a plateau, the company built a new factory.*

hit a snag *Fig.* to run into an unexpected problem. ☐ *We've hit a snag with the building project.* ☐ *I stopped working on the roof when I hit a snag.*

hit a sour note Go to **strike a sour note.**

hit against someone or something to strike against someone or something. ☐ *The door hit against me as I went through.* ☐ *The door hit against my foot as I went out.*

hit and miss and **hit or miss** carelessly; aimlessly; without plan or direction. ☐ *There was no planning. It was just* *hit and miss.* □ *We handed out the free tickets hit or miss. Some people got one. Others got five or six.*

hit at someone or something to strike at someone or something. □ *The injured man hit at the nurses who were trying to help him.* □ *I hit at the wall to see how solid it was.*

hit back (at someone or something**)** to strike someone or something back. □ *Tom hit Fred, and Fred hit back at Tom.* □ *I have to hit back when someone hits me.*

hit bottom *Fig.* to reach the lowest or worst point. □ *Our profits have hit bottom. This is our worst year ever.* □ *When my life hit bottom, I began to feel much better. I knew that if there was going to be any change, it would be for the better.*

hit home and **strike home** *Fig.* to really make sense; [for a comment] to make a very good point. □ *Mary's criticism of my clothes hit home, so I changed.* □ *The teacher's comment struck home and the student vowed to work harder.*

hit it off (with someone**)** *Fig.* to quickly become good friends with someone. □ *Look how John hit it off with Mary.* □ *Yes, they really hit it off.*

hit like a ton of bricks Go to like a ton of bricks.

hit on someone *Inf.* to flirt with someone; to make a pass at someone. □ *The women were all hitting on George, but he didn't complain.* □ *I thought he was going to hit on me—but he didn't.*

hit on something to discover something. □ *She hit on a new scheme for removing the impurities from drinking water.* □ *I hit on it when I wasn't able to sleep one night.*

hit one's **stride** Go to reach one's stride.

hit one **where** one **lives** and **hit** one **close to home** *Fig.* to affect one personally and intimately. □ *Her comments really hit me where I live. Her words seemed to apply directly to me.* □ *I listened carefully and didn't think she hit close to home at all.*

hit or miss Go to hit and miss.

hit out (at someone or something**) (in** something**)** to strike at someone or something in some state, such as anger, revenge, etc. □ *The frightened child hit out at the teacher in sheer terror.* □ *He hit out in terror.* □ *Andy hit out at the threat.*

hit out (for something or some place**)** *Rur.* to start out for something or some place. □ *We hit out for the top of the hill early in the morning, and it was noon before we got there.* □ *We'll hit out about noon.*

hit pay dirt 1. *Fig.* to discover something of value. (Alludes to discovering valuable ore.) □ *Sally tried a number of different jobs until she hit pay dirt.* □ *I tried to borrow money from a lot of different people. They all said no. Then when I went to the bank, I hit pay dirt.* **2.** *Fig.* to get great riches. □ *After years of poverty, the writer hit pay dirt with his third novel.* □ *Jane's doing well. She really hit pay dirt with her new business.*

hit (rock) bottom Go to (rock) bottom.

hit someone *Fig.* [of a meaning] being understood by someone. □ *I didn't understand what she was getting at until it suddenly hit me. She was asking for a ride home.*

hit someone **below the belt 1.** *Lit.* [for a boxer] to strike an opponent below the belt. (An unfair blow.) □ *The champ hit the contender below the belt and the crowd began to boo like fury.* □ *Fred was hit below the belt and suffered considerably.* **2.** *Fig.* to deal someone an unfair blow. □ *That's not fair! You told them I was the one who ordered the wrong-size carpet. That's hitting below the belt.* □ *Todd hit below the belt when he said it was all her fault because she had become ill during the trip.*

hit someone **hard** *Fig.* to affect someone's emotions strongly. □ *The death of his friend hit John hard.* □ *The investor was hit hard by the falling stock prices.*

hit someone **in** something to strike someone on a particular part of the body. □ *She hit him in the face by accident.* □ *Watch out or you'll hit yourself in the arm with the hammer.*

hit someone **like a ton of bricks** Go to like a ton of bricks.

hit someone or an animal **on** something to strike someone or an animal in a particular place. □ *The stone hit me on the leg.* □ *I hit the beaver on its side and it didn't seem to feel it.* □ *She hit herself on her left cheek.*

hit someone **(right) between the eyes 1.** *Lit.* to strike someone between the eyes. □ *The baseball hit her right between the eyes.* **2.** *Fig.* to become completely apparent; to surprise or impress someone. □ *Suddenly, it hit me right between the eyes. John and Mary were in love.* □ *Then—as he was talking—the exact nature of the evil plan hit me right between the eyes.* □ *The realization of what had happened hit me between the eyes.*

hit someone **up†** **(for** something**)** to ask someone for a loan of money or for some other favor. □ *The tramp hit up each tourist for a dollar.* □ *My brother hit up Harry for a couple of hundred bucks.*

hit someone **with** something **1.** *Fig.* to charge someone with an amount of money. □ *The government hit us with a big fine.* □ *The tax people hit us with a huge tax bill.* **2.** *Fig.* to present someone with shocking or surprising news. □ *He was shocked when she hit him with the news that she was leaving.* □ *Don't hit me with another piece of bad news!*

hit something **off†** to begin something; to launch an event. □ *She hit off the fair with a speech.* □ *The mayor hit the fair off by giving a brief address.*

hit speeds of some amount Go to speeds of some amount.

hit the books and **pound the books** *Inf. Fig.* to study hard. □ *I spent the weekend pounding the books.* □ *I gotta go home and hit the books. I have finals next week.*

hit the booze Go to next.

hit the bottle and **hit the booze** *Fig. Inf.* to go on a drinking bout; to get drunk. □ *Jed's hitting the bottle again.* □ *He's been hitting the booze for a week now.*

hit the brakes 1. *Lit.* to step on a vehicle's brakes hard and fast. □ *I came around the curve too fast and had to hit the brakes immediately.* **2.** *Fig.* to stop [something]. □ *The project seemed to be getting nowhere so we hit the brakes before too much more money was spent.*

hit the bricks and **hit the pavement 1.** *Fig. Inf.* to start walking; to go into the streets. □ *I have a long way to go. I'd better hit the bricks.* □ *Go on! Hit the pavement! Get* going! **2.** *Inf. Fig.* to go out on strike. □ *The workers hit the pavement on Friday and haven't been back on the job since.* □ *Agree to our demands, or we hit the bricks.*

hit the (broad) side of a barn *Fig.* to hit an easy target. (Usually negative.) □ *He can't park that car! He can't hit the broad side of a barn, let alone that parking place.* □ *He's a lousy shot. He can't hit the side of a barn.*

hit the bull's-eye 1. *Lit.* to hit the very center of a circular target. □ *The archer hit the bull's-eye three times in a row.* □ *I didn't hit the bull's-eye even once.* **2.** *Fig.* to achieve the goal perfectly. □ *Your idea really hit the bull's-eye. Thank you!* □ *Jill has a lot of insight. She knows how to hit the bull's-eye.*

hit the ceiling and **hit the roof** *Fig.* to get very angry. □ *She really hit the ceiling when she found out what happened.* □ *My dad'll hit the roof when he finds out that I wrecked his car.*

hit the deck 1. *Fig.* to fall down; to drop down to the floor or ground. □ *Hit the deck. Don't let them see you.* □ *I hit the deck the minute I heard the shots.* **2.** *Fig.* to get out of bed. □ *Come on, hit the deck! It's morning.* □ *Hit the deck! Time to rise and shine!*

hit the fan *Inf. Fig.* to become publicly known; to become a scandal. (From the phrase *when the shit hit the fan.*) □ *I wasn't even in the country when it hit the fan.* □ *It hit the fan, and within ten minutes the press had spread it all over the world.*

hit the ground running *Fig.* to start the day very energetically. □ *A decade ago I had a lot more energy. I would wake up, hit the ground running, and never stop until I went to bed again.*

hit the hay and **hit the sack** *Fig.* to go to bed. □ *I have to go home and hit the hay pretty soon.* □ *Let's hit the sack. We have to get an early start in the morning.*

hit the high spots *Fig.* to do only the important, obvious, or good things. □ *I won't discuss the entire report. I'll just hit the high spots.* □ *First, let me hit the high spots; then I'll tell you the details.*

hit the jackpot 1. *Lit.* to win a large amount of money gambling or in a lottery. □ *I hit the jackpot in the big contest.* □ *Sally hit the jackpot in the lottery.* **2.** *Fig.* to be exactly right; to find exactly what was sought. □ *I hit the jackpot when I found this little cafe on Fourth Street.* □ *I wanted a small house with a fireplace, and I really hit the jackpot with this one.*

hit the nail (right) on the head 1. *Lit.* to strike a nail precisely on the head with a hammer. □ *If you expect to drive a nail straight, you have to hit the nail on the head.* **2.** *Fig.* to do exactly the right thing; to do something in the most effective and efficient way. □ *You've spotted the flaw, Sally. You hit the nail on the head.* □ *Bob doesn't say much, but every now and then he hits the nail right on the head.*

hit the panic button and **press the panic button; push the panic button** *Fig.* to panic suddenly. □ *She hit the panic button and just went to pieces.* □ *Don't press the panic button. Relax and keep your eyes open.*

hit the pavement Go to hit the bricks.

hit the road *Fig.* to depart; to begin one's journey, especially on a road trip; to leave for home. □ *It's time to hit the road. I'll see you.* □ *We have to hit the road very early in the morning.*

hit the roof Go to hit the ceiling.

hit the sack Go to hit the hay.

hit the skids *Fig.* to decline; to decrease in value or status. □ *Jed hit the skids when he started drinking.* □ *The firm hit the skids when the dollar collapsed.*

hit the spot *Inf.* to be exactly right; to be refreshing. □ *This cool drink really hits the spot.* □ *That was a delicious meal, dear. It hit the spot.*

hit the trail *Inf.* to leave. (As if one were hiking or riding a horse.) □ *I have to hit the trail before sunset.* □ *Let's hit the trail. It's late.*

hit town *Fig.* to arrive in town. □ *The minute he hit town, he checked into a hotel and took a long nap.*

hit (up)on *someone* or *something* **1.** *Lit.* to strike or pound on someone or something. (*Upon* is formal and less commonly used than *on.*) □ *Jeff hit upon the mugger over and over.* □ *I hit on the radio until it started working again.* **2.** *Fig.* to discover someone or something. □ *I think I have hit upon something. There is a lever you have to press in order to open this cabinet.* □ *I hit on Tom in an amateur play production. I offered him a job in my nightclub immediately.* **3.** Go to hit on *someone;* hit on *something.*

hitch a ride Go to thumb a ride.

hitch *someone* or *something* **(up†) (to** *something***)** to attach someone or something to something. □ *Please hitch the horse up to the wagon, and let's get going.* □ *Please hitch up the horse.*

Hitch your wagon to a star. *Prov.* Always aspire to do great things.; Do not set pessimistic goals. (From Ralph Waldo Emerson's essay, "Civilization.") □ *The speaker who delivered the high school commencement address challenged the graduating students to hitch their wagons to a star.* □ *Bob: What do you want to be when you grow up? Child: I used to want to be a great actor, but my dad told me hardly anybody gets to be an actor, so now I have to pick something else. Bob: Nonsense. If you want to be an actor, then do your best to be an actor. Hitch your wagon to a star!*

hither, thither, and yon and **hither and thither** everywhere; here, there, and everywhere. (Formal and archaic.) □ *The prince looked hither, thither, and yon for the beautiful woman who had lost the glass slipper.* □ *The terrible wizard had sown the seeds of his evil vine hither, thither, and yon. Soon the evil, twisted plants began to sprout in all the land.*

hitting on all cylinders Go to firing on all cylinders.

a hive of activity *Fig.* a location where things are very busy. □ *The hotel lobby was a hive of activity each morning.* □ *During the holidays, the shopping center is a hive of activity.*

hoard *something* **up†** to accumulate a large store of something against bad times. □ *Scott was hoarding canned goods up for the hard times ahead.* □ *He hoarded up many pounds of canned tuna.*

*hoarse as a crow very hoarse. (*Also: **as** ~.*) □ *After shouting at the team all afternoon, the coach was as hoarse as a crow.* □ *Jill: Has Bob got a cold? Jane: No, he's always hoarse as a crow.*

hobnob with someone or something to associate with someone or a group, especially with those more wealthy, famous, etc. □ *I'm not used to hobnobbing with such luminaries.* □ *Walter is spending a lot of time hobnobbing with the very rich.*

Hobson's choice the choice between taking what is offered and getting nothing at all. (From the name of a stable owner in the seventeenth century who always hired out the horse nearest the door.) □ *We didn't really want that particular hotel, but it was a case of Hobson's choice. We booked very late and there was nothing else left.* □ *If you want a yellow car, it's Hobson's choice. The garage has only one.*

hoe one's **own row** *Rur.* to mind one's own business. □ *Tom: You're cutting up those carrots awful small. Jane: Hoe your own row!* □ *He didn't get involved in other people's fights. He just hoed his own row.*

hog wild wild; out of control. □ *I went hog wild at the sale and bought six new pairs of shoes.* □ *There were a dozen different desserts at the picnic. A person who liked sweets could go hog wild.*

hoist with one's **own petard** *Fig.* to be harmed or disadvantaged by an action of one's own which was meant to harm someone else. (From a line in Shakespeare's *Hamlet*.) □ *She intended to murder her brother but was hoist with her own petard when she ate the poisoned food intended for him.* □ *The vandals were hoist with their own petard when they tried to make an emergency call from the pay phone they had broken.*

Hoist your sail when the wind is fair. *Prov.* Begin a project when circumstances are the most favorable. □ *Don't ask your mother for permission now; she's in a bad mood. Hoist your sail when the wind is fair.* □ *Wait until the economy has stabilized before trying to start your own business. Hoist your sail when the wind is fair.*

hold a grudge (against someone**)** Go to bear a grudge (against someone).

hold a meeting to meet; to have a meeting (of an organization). □ *We'll have to hold a meeting to make a decision.* □ *Our club held a meeting to talk about future projects.*

hold all the aces and **hold all the cards** to be in a favorable position; to be in a controlling position. (Alludes to having possession of all four aces or all the high cards in a card game.) □ *How can I advance in my career when my competitor holds all the aces?* □ *If I held all the aces, I'd be able to do great things.* □ *I tried to get my points across, but Joan held all the cards and the board voted for her plan.*

hold all the cards Go to previous.

hold back (on something**)** to withhold something; to give or take only a limited amount. □ *Hold back on the gravy. I'm on a diet.* □ *That's enough. Hold back. Save some for the others.*

hold by something to stick by a promise. □ *I hope that you will hold by our agreement.* □ *I will hold by everything I said.*

Hold everything! *Inf.* Stop everything!; Everyone, stop! □ *"Hold everything!" cried Mary. "There's a squirrel loose in the kitchen!"* □ *Bill: Hold everything! Let's try this part again. Bob: But we've already rehearsed it four times.*

hold forth (on someone or something**)** to speak at great length about someone or something. □ *Sadie held forth on the virtues of home cooking.* □ *Sharon is holding forth, and everyone is paying close attention.*

hold good for someone or something [for an offer] to remain open to someone or a group. □ *Does your offer of help still hold good for us?* □ *Does it hold good for the entire membership?*

Hold it! *Inf.* Stop right there. □ *Tom: Hold it! Mary: What's wrong? Tom: You almost stepped on my contact lens.* □ *Bill: Hold it! Bob: What is it? Bill: Sorry. For a minute, that stick looked like a snake.*

hold no brief for someone or something not to tolerate someone or something; to be opposed to someone or something. □ *I hold no brief for Wally and his friends.* □ *Rachel holds no brief for that kind of thing.*

hold off (from) doing something to avoid doing something; to postpone doing something. □ *Can you hold off from buying a new car for another few months?* □ *I will hold off firing him until next week.*

hold off (on someone or something**)** to delay doing something concerning someone or something. □ *Please hold off on Tom until we interview the other candidates.* □ *I will hold off on this job for a while.*

hold on to be patient. □ *Just hold on. Everything will work out in good time.* □ *If you will just hold on, everything will probably be all right.*

Hold on (a minute)! and **Hold on for a minute!** Stop right there!; Wait a minute! (*Minute* can be replaced by *moment, second,* or other time periods.) □ *Bob: Hold on, Tom. Tom: What? Bob: I want to talk to you.* □ *"Hold on!" hollered Tom. "You're running off with my shopping cart!"*

***a **hold on** someone a strong and secure influence on someone. (*Typically: **get** ~; **have** ~; **give** someone ~.) □ *The strange religion seemed to have a strong hold on its followers.* □ *The drug has a hold on the minds of those who use it.*

a hold on something Go to a **grip on** something.

hold (on) tight to grasp (someone or something) tightly. □ *Here we go on the merry-go-round! Hold on tight!* □ *The children were told to hold tight on the swings.*

hold on (to someone or something**)** Go to hang on (to someone or something).

Hold on to your hat! Go to Hang on to your hat!

hold one's **breath 1.** *Lit.* to stop breathing for a short period, on purpose. □ *Do you hold your breath when you dive into the water?* □ *I can't hold my breath for very long.* **2.** *Fig.* to wait or delay until something special happens. (Usually in the negative. See also **Don't hold your breath.**) □ *I expect the mail to be delivered soon, but I'm not holding my breath. It's often late.*

hold one's **end of the bargain up**[†] and **keep** one's **end of the bargain up**[†] *Fig.* to do one's part as agreed; to attend to one's responsibilities as agreed. □ *If you don't hold your end up, the whole project will fail.* □ *Tom has to learn to cooperate. He must keep up his end of the bargain.*

hold one's **end up**[†] to carry one's share of the burden; to do one's share of the work. □ *You're not holding your end*

305

up. We're having to do your share of the work. □ *Get busy. You have to hold up your end.*

hold one's **fire 1.** *Lit.* to refrain from shooting (a gun, etc.). □ *The sergeant told the soldiers to hold their fire.* □ *Please hold your fire until I get out of the way.* **2.** *Fig.* to postpone one's criticism or commentary. □ *Now, now, hold your fire until I've had a chance to explain.* □ *Hold your fire, Bill. You're too quick to complain.*

hold one's **ground** Go to stand one's ground.

hold one's **head up**† *Fig.* to be confident of the respect of other people; to hold up one's head with pride rather than bowing one's head. (A bowed head would indicate a lack of confidence.) □ *I am so embarrassed. I will never be able to hold my head up again.* □ *Now I can hold up my head with pride.*

hold one's **liquor** *Fig.* to be able to drink alcohol in quantity without ill effects. □ *Old Jed can sure hold his liquor— and a lot of it, too.* □ *I asked him to leave because he can't hold his liquor.*

hold one's **mouth the right way** *Fig.* do something very carefully under optimal conditions. □ *It was a tedious task. If I didn't hold my mouth just the right way, I wouldn't be able to do it.*

hold one's **nose 1.** *Lit.* to use one's fingers to keep one's nose closed to avoid a bad smell or to keep water out. □ *The kid held his nose and jumped off the dock into the lake.* **2.** *Fig.* to attempt to ignore something unpleasant, illegal, or "rotten." □ *He hated doing it, but he held his nose and made the announcement everyone dreaded.*

hold one's **own** to do as well as anyone else. □ *I can hold my own in a footrace any day.* □ *She was unable to hold her own, and she had to quit.*

hold one's **peace** to remain silent. □ *Bill was unable to hold his peace any longer. "Don't do it!" he cried.* □ *Quiet, John. Hold your peace for a little while longer.*

hold one's **temper** Go to keep one's temper.

hold one's **tongue** *Fig.* to refrain from speaking; to refrain from saying something unpleasant. □ *I felt like scolding her, but I held my tongue.* □ *Hold your tongue, John. You can't talk to me that way!*

hold oneself **together** *Fig.* to maintain one's calmness or sanity. □ *I don't know if I can hold myself together through another horrible day like this one.* □ *I don't know how she held herself together through all her troubles.*

hold out (against someone or something**)** to continue one's defense against someone or something. □ *We can hold out against them only a little while longer.* □ *Dave can hold out forever.*

hold out (for someone or something**)** to strive to wait for someone or something. □ *I will hold out for someone who can do the job better than the last person we interviewed.* □ *I want to hold out for a better offer.*

hold out the olive branch *Fig.* to offer to end a dispute and be friendly; to offer reconciliation. (The olive branch is a symbol of peace and reconciliation. A biblical reference.) □ *Jill was the first to hold out the olive branch after our argument.* □ *I always try to hold out the olive branch to someone I have offended. Life is too short for a person to bear grudges for very long.*

Hold, please. Go to Hold the phone.

hold someone **accountable (for** something**)** and **hold** someone **responsible (for** something**)** to consider someone responsible for something; to blame something on someone. □ *I hold you accountable for John's well-being.* □ *I must hold you responsible for the missing money.*

hold someone **back** Go to keep someone back.

hold someone **for ransom** to demand money for the return of a person who has been kidnapped. □ *The kidnappers held me for ransom, but no one would pay.* □ *We will hold Timmy for ransom and hope that the police don't find us.*

hold someone **hostage** to keep someone as a hostage. □ *The terrorists planned to hold everyone hostage in the airplane.* □ *My neighbor was held hostage in his own home by a robber.*

hold someone or an animal **down**† **1.** *Lit.* to keep someone, something, or an animal down. □ *The heavy beam held him down, and he could not rise.* □ *The owner held down his pet while the vet treated the injured paw.* **2.** *Fig.* to prevent someone or something from advancing. □ *I had a disability that held me down in life.* □ *Too much debt held down the company while others profited.*

hold someone or something **at bay** *Fig.* to make someone, a group, or an animal stay at a safe distance. (Originally referred only to animals.) □ *I held the attacker at bay while Mary got away and called the police.* □ *The dogs held the bear at bay while I got my gun loaded.*

hold someone or something **at** something to keep someone or something at some distance, such as an arm's length, respectful distance, comfortable distance, etc. □ *I held the child at an arm's length until he could be calmed.* □ *The police held the crowd at a distance from the injured man.*

hold someone or something **by** something to grasp someone or something by a particular part. □ *I held him by the shoulder while I talked to him.* □ *Donna held the dog by the collar.*

hold someone or something **in check** Go to keep someone or something in check.

hold someone or something **in high regard** *Fig.* to think well of someone or something. □ *All of us hold the vice president in high regard.* □ *We hold these policies in high regard.*

hold someone or something **in low regard** *Fig.* to think poorly of someone or something. □ *I'm afraid that Hazel holds you in low regard.* □ *I'm afraid we hold this establishment in low regard.*

hold someone or something **in reserve** and **keep** someone or something **in reserve** *Fig.* to hold back someone or something for future needs. □ *I am holding the frozen desserts in reserve, in case we run out of cake.* □ *We are holding Sharon in reserve.* □ *Keep a few good players in reserve.*

hold someone or something **off**† **1.** and **keep** someone or something **off**† *Lit.* to do something physical to keep someone or something away; to stave someone or something off. □ *Tom was trying to rob us, but we managed to hold him off.* □ *We held off the attackers.* □ *I couldn't keep off the reporters any longer.* **2.** *Fig.* to make someone or something wait. □ *I know a lot of people are waiting to see me.*

Hold them off for a while longer. □ *See what you can do to hold off the reporters.*

hold someone or something **out (of** something) and **hold** someone or something **out**[†] to set someone or something aside from the rest; to prevent someone or a group from participating. □ *Her parents held her out of sports because of her health.* □ *They held out every player who had an injury.*

hold someone or something **over**[†] to retain someone or something (for a period of time). □ *The storm held John over for another day.* □ *The manager held over the hit movie for another week.*

hold someone or something **still** Go to **keep** someone or something **still.**

hold someone or something **together** to keep a group of people or things together. □ *She worked at two jobs in order to hold her family together.* □ *Our club was failing despite our efforts to hold it together.*

hold someone or something **up**[†] **1.** *Lit.* to keep someone or something upright. □ *Johnny is falling asleep. Please hold him up until I prepare the bed for him.* □ *Hold up the window sash while I prop it open.* **2.** *Fig.* to rob someone or a group. □ *Some punk tried to hold me up.* □ *The mild-looking man held up the bank and shot a teller.* **3.** *Fig.* to delay someone or something. □ *Driving the kids to school held me up.* □ *An accident on Main Street held up traffic for thirty minutes.*

hold someone or something **up**[†] **as an example** *Fig.* to single out someone or something as a person or thing worthy of imitation. □ *No one has ever held me up as an example.* □ *Jane held up Doris as an example.* □ *I hate to hold myself up as an example, but if you would do what I do, at least I wouldn't criticize you.*

hold someone or something **up**[†] **to ridicule** *Fig.* to ridicule someone or something. □ *They must stop holding Matt up to ridicule! Who do they think they are?* □ *She held up Donald to ridicule.*

hold someone or something **up to scorn**[†] *Fig.* to single out someone or something for repudiation. □ *The entire crowd held Randy up to scorn for his part in the riot.* □ *The disappointed fans held up the losing team to scorn.*

hold someone **responsible (for** something) Go to **hold** someone **accountable (for** something).

hold someone's **attention** *Fig.* to keep someone's attention; to keep someone interested. □ *The boring teacher could not hold the students' attention.* □ *The mystery novel held my attention and I couldn't put it down.*

hold someone's **hand 1.** *Lit.* to hold the hand of someone who is frightened, especially a child. □ *Please hold Jimmy's hand when you cross the street.* **2.** *Fig.* to comfort someone who is anxious or frightened. □ *You'll be all right, won't you? You don't need anyone to hold your hand, do you?*

hold someone, something, or an animal **back**[†] **(from** someone or something) to restrain someone, something, or an animal from getting at or getting to someone or something. □ *The parents held the children back from the cake and ice cream until the hostess said she was ready.* □ *Please hold back your dog.*

hold someone **to** something *Fig.* to make someone adhere to an agreement. □ *You promised me that you would buy*

six of them, and I'm going to hold you to your promise. □ *It was difficult, but he held himself to the terms of the contract.*

hold someone **under** someone's **thumb** Go to **under** someone's **thumb.**

hold someone **up**[†] **to** something to lift someone up to the level of something. □ *I held up little Mary to the window so she could see out.* □ *She was held up to the window so she could see better.*

hold something **against** someone *Fig.* to blame something on someone; to bear a grudge against someone; to resent someone. □ *Your brother is mean to me, but I can't hold it against you.* □ *You're holding something against me. What is it?*

hold something **against** someone or something **1.** *Lit.* to press something against someone, a group, or something. □ *Max held the gun against the bank guard's head and threatened to pull the trigger.* □ *Fred held the drill against the wall and turned it on.* **2.** *Fig.* to think badly of someone, a group, or something because of something. □ *I am the one who dented your fender. I'm sorry. I hope you don't hold it against me.* □ *I hold all this mess against the government.*

hold something **back for a rainy day** Go to **save** (something) **for a rainy day.**

hold something **for** someone **1.** to keep something safe for someone. □ *I will hold your money for you.* □ *Do you want me to hold your wallet for you while you swim?* **2.** [for a merchant] to set something aside for a purchaser who will pay for it and take delivery at a later date. □ *I will hold it for you until you can pay for it.* □ *We can hold it for you right here and give it to you when you have the money.*

hold something **in**[†] and **keep** something **in**[†] **1.** and **hold** something **inside ((of)** one(self)); **keep** something **inside ((of)** one(self)) *Fig.* to keep one's emotions inside oneself. □ *You really shouldn't hold those feelings inside of you.* □ *I have kept all this inside myself too long.* □ *You shouldn't hold in all that anger.* **2.** *Lit.* to hold in one's stomach, gut, belly, etc. □ *Hold your belly in so you don't look like a blimp.* □ *Hold in your stomach.*

hold something **in abeyance** to stall or postpone something. □ *This is a good plan but not at this time. Let's just hold it in abeyance until things get better.* □ *We will hold the matter in abeyance until we hear from you.*

hold something **in store (for** someone) Go to **in store (for** someone).

hold something **inside ((of)** one(self)) Go to **hold** something **in**[†].

hold (something) **out on** someone or something to keep news or something of value from someone or a group. □ *What's going on? Are you holding something out on me?* □ *Don't hold out on the city council. They have ways of finding out everything.*

hold something **out**[†] **(to** someone) to offer something to someone. □ *I held a bouquet of roses out to her.* □ *I held out an offer of immunity from prosecution to her, but she would not cooperate.*

hold something **over** someone('s **head)** *Fig.* to have knowledge of something about a person and to use that knowledge to control the person. □ *So I made a mistake when I* was young. Are you going to hold that over my head all my life? □ Please don't hold that over me anymore.

hold something **together** to keep the parts of an object together. □ Hold this broken vase together until I get back with the glue. □ What can I use to hold this together?

hold still Go to keep still.

hold still (for someone or something) and **keep still (for** someone or something); **stand still (for** someone or something) to remain motionless for someone or something. □ Hold still for the doctor and the shot won't hurt. □ Please keep still for the doctor.

hold still for something and **stand still for** something Fig. to tolerate or endure something. (Often in the negative.) □ I won't stand still for that kind of behavior! □ She won't hold still for that kind of talk.

hold terror for someone [for something] to be frightening to a person. □ The thought of flying to Rio by myself held great terror for me. □ Nothing holds terror for me. I am a daredevil.

hold the fort Fig. to take care of a place while someone who is usually there is gone, such as a store or one's home. (From western movies.) □ I'm going next door to visit Mrs. Jones. You stay here and hold the fort. □ You should open the store at eight o'clock and hold the fort until I get there at ten.

hold the line (at someone or something) Fig. not to exceed a certain limit regarding someone or something. □ Having your wife on the payroll is one thing, but no one else from the family—I will hold the line at her. □ We have to hold the line at this kind of expenditure. □ Okay, we'll hold the line.

Hold the phone. 1. and **Hold the wire(, please).; Hold, please.; Hold the line(, please).; Hold the phone(, please).; Please hold.** Fig. Please wait on the telephone and do not hang up. (A phrase in use before telephone "hold" circuitry was in wide use.) □ Bill: Hold the wire, please. (Turning to Tom) Tom, the phone's for you. Tom: Be right there. □ Rachel: Do you wish to speak to Mr. Jones or Mr. Franklin? Henry: Jones. Rachel: Thank you. Hold the line, please. □ Sue: Good afternoon, Acme Motors, hold please. Bill (hanging up): That makes me so mad! **2.** Fig. Wait just a minute.; Don't rush into something. □ Hold the phone! Let's think about it a little longer. □ Hold the phone. I just had another idea.

hold the purse strings Go to control the purse strings.

Hold the wire(, please). Go to Hold the phone.

hold together [for something] to keep from falling apart. □ Don't run the engine too fast because it won't hold together. □ Do you think that this book will hold together much longer?

hold true [for something] to be true; [for something] to remain true. □ Does this rule hold true all the time? □ Yes, it holds true no matter what.

hold under wraps Go to under wraps.

hold up 1. Lit. to endure; to last a long time. □ How long will this cloth hold up? □ I want my money back for this chair. It isn't holding up well. **2.** and **hold up (for** someone or something) to wait; to stop and wait for someone or

something. □ Hold up for Wallace. He's running hard to catch up to us. □ Hold up a minute.

hold up (for someone or something) Go to hold up; wait up (for someone or something).

hold up (on someone or something) to delay or postpone further action on someone or something. □ I know you are getting ready to choose someone, but hold up on Tom. There may be someone better. □ Hold up on the project, would you? □ We need to hold up for a while longer.

Hold your horses! and **Hold your tater!** Fig. Inf. Wait! □ Tom: Let's go! Let's go! Mary: Hold your horses. □ Hold your tater, now. Where did you say you are going?

Hold your tater! Go to previous.

Hold your tongue! Inf. You have said enough!; You have said enough rude things. (See also hold one's tongue.) □ Bill: You're seeing Tom a lot, aren't you? You must be in love. Jane: Hold your tongue, Bill Franklin! □ After listening to the tirade against him for nearly four minutes, Tom cried out, "Hold your tongue!"

hole in one 1. Lit. an instance of hitting a golf ball from the tee to the hole in only one try. (From the game of golf.) □ John made a hole in one yesterday. □ I've never gotten a hole in one. **2.** Fig. an instance of succeeding the first time. □ It worked the first time I tried it—a hole in one. □ Bob got a hole in one on that sale. A lady walked in the door, and he sold her a car in five minutes.

a **hole in the wall** Fig. a tiny shop, room, etc., not much wider than its doorway. □ I went into this little hole in the wall where they had the nicest little gifts. □ His office is just a hole in the wall.

hole up (somewhere) 1. to take shelter somewhere. □ During the blizzard, we holed up in a lean-to made of branches. □ Looks like bad weather coming. We'd better find a place to hole up. **2.** to hide somewhere. □ The police are looking for me. I need somewhere to hole up. □ The outlaw holed up in a cave.

holler something **out**† to yell something out. □ The guard hollered a warning out. □ They hollered out a warning.

holler uncle and **cry uncle; say uncle** Fig. to admit defeat. □ Joe kept pounding on Jim, trying to get him to holler uncle. □ He twisted my arm until I cried uncle.

hollow something **out**† to make the inside of something hollow. □ Martha hollowed the book out and put her money inside. □ She hollowed out a book.

Holy cow! Inf. Wow! □ Holy cow! I never expected such a nice gift! □ Give me a chance! Holy cow, don't rush me!

holy Joe 1. a chaplain; a cleric; a clergyman. □ I went to see the holy Joe, and he was a lot of help. □ Old holy Joe wants to see all of us at services. **2.** a very pious person. □ Martin looks stuffy, but he's no holy Joe. □ Don't let that holy Joe hear about what you've done.

Holy mackerel! Inf. Wow! □ Holy mackerel! What a beautiful day! □ Holy mackerel! What's this? A new car?

Holy moley! Inf. Wow! □ Holy moley! A whole quarter! □ Look, here's another one! Holy moley!

(home) folks Rur. one's family, especially one's parents. □ It sure is good to see the home folks again. □ Sally went to visit her folks.

H

*home free safe and without problems. (Not necessarily about home or about money. *Typically: **be ~; get ~.**) □ *Everyone else had a lot of trouble with the bureaucrats, but we got home free.*

home in (on someone or something) *Fig.* to aim directly at someone or something. □ *She came into the room and homed in on the chocolate cake.* □ *She saw the cake and homed in.*

Home is where the heart is. *Prov.* People long to be at home.; Your home is whatever place you long to be. □ *I've had a lovely time visiting you, but home is where the heart is, and I think it's time I went back.* □ *If home is where the heart is, then my home is my parents' old house. I've never loved my own apartment the way I love their place.*

home on(to something) *Fig.* to aim directly at something; to fix some type of receiver on a signal source. □ *The navigator homed onto the radio beam from the airport.* □ *The navigator located the beam and homed on.*

homely enough to stop a clock *Rur.* ugly. □ *She's a sweet girl, but homely enough to stop a clock.* □ *No one asks Mary out, and no wonder. She's homely enough to stop a clock.*

hone for someone or something *Rur.* to long for someone or something. □ *Tom: What's wrong with Jane? Mary: She's honing for her sweetheart.* □ *Jimmy was honing for the red bicycle in the toy store window.*

honest and aboveboard and **open and aboveboard** *Fig.* in the open; visible to the public; honest. □ *Don't keep it a secret. Let's make sure that everything is honest and aboveboard.* □ *You can do whatever you wish, as long as you keep it honest and aboveboard.* □ *The inspector had to make sure that everything was open and aboveboard.*

Honest to God. Go to next.

Honest to goodness. and **Honest to God.; Honest to Pete.** I speak the truth. (Some people may object to the use of *God* in this phrase.) □ *Did he really say that? Honest to goodness?* □ *Honest to Pete, I've been to the South Pole.*

Honest to Pete. Go to previous.

Honesty is the best policy. *Prov.* You should always tell the truth, even when it seems as if it would be useful to tell a lie. □ *Jill: I borrowed Jane's white blouse without asking her, and then I spilled tomato sauce on it. Should I tell her what happened, or should I just put the blouse back in her closet and hope she won't notice? Jane: Honesty is the best policy.*

The **honeymoon is over.** The early pleasant beginning (as at the start of a marriage) has ended. □ *Okay, the honeymoon is over. It's time to settle down and do some hard work.* □ *I knew the honeymoon was over at my new job when they started yelling at me to work faster.*

honk at someone or something to sound a horn at someone or something. □ *Is someone honking at me?* □ *The motorists honked at the sheep that were clogging the roadway.*

honor someone **as** something to praise someone as something; to praise someone for being something. □ *Aren't you going to honor Kevin as a hero?* □ *We will honor Henry as the most promising scholar of the year.*

honor someone **for** something to praise someone for doing something. □ *The committee agreed to honor Laurel for her role in the benefit dance.* □ *I want to honor you for your efforts on behalf of our cause.*

honor someone's **check** to accept someone's personal check in payment of an obligation. □ *The clerk at the store wouldn't honor my check. I had to pay cash.* □ *The bank didn't honor your check when I tried to deposit it. Please give me cash.*

honor someone **with** something to show one's respect for someone with something, such as a gift, party, ceremony, a response, etc. □ *We would like to honor you with a little reception.* □ *We chose to honor you with a little gift.*

hooched (up) *Sl.* intoxicated. □ *Sally is too hooched to drive.* □ *She got herself hooched up and couldn't give her talk.*

hoodwink someone **into** something *Fig.* to deceive someone into doing something. □ *She will try to hoodwink you into driving her to the airport. Watch out.* □ *You can't hoodwink me into doing that!*

hoodwink someone **out of** something *Fig.* to get something away from someone by deception. □ *Are you trying to hoodwink me out of my money?* □ *Max tried to hoodwink the old lady out of all her money.*

hoof it *Inf.* to walk. □ *If nobody gives us a ride, we'll have to hoof it.* □ *She hoofed it home from the dance in her high-heeled shoes.*

hook in(to something) to connect into something. □ *We will hook into the water main tomorrow morning.* □ *We dug the pipes up and hooked in.*

hook, line, and sinker *Fig.* totally. □ *She fell for our story hook, line, and sinker.* □ *They believed every word hook, line, and sinker.*

hook oneself **on** someone or something *Fig.* to become enamored of someone or something. □ *I'm afraid I've hooked myself on Alice.* □ *He hooked himself on Bach organ music.*

hook someone **on** something *Fig.* to addict someone to a drug or alcohol. □ *Careful, or you'll hook yourself on those tranquilizers.* □ *Some friend at school hooked Roger on dope.* □ *Sharon has hooked herself on cocaine.*

hook someone or something **up**[†] **(to** someone or something) and **hook** someone or something **up**[†] **(with** someone or something) **1.** *Lit.* to attach someone or something to someone or something. □ *The nurse hooked the patient up to the oxygen tubes.* □ *They hooked up the patient with the tubes.*

hook someone **up (with** someone) *Fig.* to arrange for someone to go out with someone. □ *I hooked Alice up with Tom last year, and now they're getting married.*

hook something **down**[†] **1.** *Lit.* to attach something and hold it down with a hook. □ *Please hook the lid down so it doesn't fall off.* □ *Please hook down the lid.* **2.** *Sl.* to toss something down to someone. □ *Hook another can of beer down to me, will you?* □ *Hook down another can of beer.* **3.** *Sl.* to eat something quickly; to gobble something up. □ *Wally hooked the first hamburger down and ordered another.* □ *He hooked down two more burgers in a few minutes.*

hook something **into** something to connect something to something. □ *I want to hook another communication line into the system.* □ *Is it possible to hook my computer into your network?*

hook something **on(to** someone or something**)** and **hook** something **on**† to attach something to someone or something by a hook. □ *Hook this sign on her and let her walk around advertising our play.* □ *Hook on the sign and hope that it stays.* □ *Hook it onto the tree carefully.*

hook something **up**† to set something up and get it working. (The object is to be connected to a power supply, electronic network, telephone lines, etc.) □ *Will it take long to hook the telephone up?* □ *As soon as they hook up the computer to the network, I can e-mail my friends.*

hook up with someone **1.** *Fig. Inf.* to meet with someone. □ *Fancy hooking up with you here, Bill. How have you been?* □ *Well, hello, Tom. I didn't think I'd hook up with you again so soon.* **2.** *Fig.* to join forces with someone. □ *If we hook up with each other it'll be easier to defeat the others.* □ *These two competitors have hooked up together and we now have a real problem.*

hooked on something **1.** *Fig.* addicted to a drug or something similar. □ *Jenny is hooked on cocaine.* □ *She was not hooked on anything before that.* **2.** *Fig.* enthusiastic about something; supportive of something. □ *Mary is hooked on football. She never misses a game.* □ *Jane is so happy! She's hooked on life.*

hoot and holler to shout in disapproval; to call and shout one's displeasure. □ *After the umpire rendered his decision, the spectators hooted and hollered their thoughts on the matter.* □ *It's hard to play a good game of basketball when the fans are hooting and hollering at everything you do.*

hoot at someone or something Go to **howl at** someone or something.

hoot someone **down**† Go to **howl** someone **down**†.

hoot someone **off the stage** [for an audience] to boo and hiss until a performer leaves the stage. □ *The rude audience hooted Carl off the stage.* □ *Carl was hooted off the stage.*

hop in(to something**)** to jump into something; to get into something. □ *Hop into your car and drive over to my house.* □ *I hopped in and drove off.*

hop off ((of) something**)** to jump off something. (*Of* is usually retained before pronouns.) □ *She hopped off her bike and came into the house.* □ *The bird on the branch hopped off.*

hop on the bandwagon Go to **on the bandwagon**.

hop on(to something**)** to jump or get onto something that is moving. □ *Sometimes you have to hop onto the cable car after it has started to move.* □ *I ran to the cable car and hopped on.*

a **hop, skip, and a jump** *Fig.* a short distance. □ *Bill lives just a hop, skip, and a jump from here. We can be there in two minutes.* □ *My car is parked just a hop, skip, and a jump away.*

hop something **up**† *Sl.* to make a machine, especially a car, run extra fast or give it extra power. □ *He will take that junk heap home and hop it up.* □ *He spent nearly every evening hopping up his old car.*

Hop to it! *Inf.* Get started right now! □ *Bill: I have to get these things stacked up before I go home. Bob: Then hop to it! You won't get it done standing around here talking.* □ *"Hurry up! Hop to it!" urged Bill. "We've got to get this done!"*

hop up (to someone or something**)** [for an animal] to come close to someone or something by hopping. □ *The bunny hopped up to me and just sat there.* □ *It hopped up and stared.*

hope against (all) hope to have hope even when the situation appears to be hopeless. □ *We hope against all hope that she'll see the right thing to do and do it.* □ *There is little point in hoping against hope, except that it makes you feel better.*

Hope deferred makes the heart sick. and **Hope deferred maketh the heart sick.** *Prov.* If you have to wait a long time for something you want, you will become despairing. (Biblical.) □ *Charlie waited so long for the woman he loved that he decided he didn't want to love anybody. Hope deferred makes the heart sick.*

Hope deferred maketh the heart sick. Go to previous.

hope for something to be optimistic that one's wish for something will come true. □ *I still hope for her return.* □ *We hope for good weather on Friday.*

hope for the best to desire the best to happen. □ *Good luck. You know we all hope for the best.* □ *Mary is worried, but she hopes for the best.*

Hope for the best and prepare for the worst. and **Hope for the best but expect the worst.** *Prov.* You should have a positive attitude, but make sure you are ready for disaster. □ *While my father was in the hospital after his heart attack, we hoped for the best and prepared for the worst.* □ *When you study for a major exam, hope for the best but expect the worst. Don't make yourself anxious worrying that it will be too difficult, but review as if you expect the exam to be extremely hard.*

Hope for the best but expect the worst. Go to previous.

Hope is a good breakfast but a bad supper. *Prov.* It is good to start the day feeling hopeful, but if none of the things you hope for come to pass by the end of the day, you will feel disappointed. (Can be used to warn someone against hoping for something that is unlikely to happen.) □ *Lisa began the day hoping that she would find work, and by the end of the day she had learned that hope is a good breakfast but a bad supper.*

Hope springs eternal (in the human breast). *Prov.* People will continue to hope even though they have evidence that things cannot possibly turn out the way they want. (From Alexander Pope's poem, "Essay on Man." Sometimes used to remark that you believe someone's situation is hopeless, as in the first example.) □ *Jill: The boss may have turned me down the first twelve times I asked for a raise, but this time I really think she'll give it to me. Jane: Hope springs eternal in the human breast.* □ *Alan: You're not still trying to teach the dog to shake hands! Jane: Hope springs eternal.*

hopeless at doing something incapable of doing something. □ *Tom is hopeless at cooking.* □ *Sally is hopeless at keeping her room clean, and it shows.*

hopped up 1. *Sl.* intoxicated with drugs or alcohol; stimulated by drugs or alcohol. □ *The old man was hopped up again. He was addicted to opium.* □ *John usually gets hopped up on the weekends.* **2.** *Inf.* excited; enthusiastic. □ *What are you hopped up about now? You're certainly cheery.* □ *I always get hopped up when I think of mountain climbing.*

hopping mad *Fig.* very angry. □ *Joe got hopping mad when the salesclerk was rude to him.* □ *The student's practical jokes made the teacher hopping mad.*

horn in (on someone**)** *Fig.* to attempt to displace someone; to interfere with someone, especially with someone's romantic interests. □ *I'm going to ask Sally to the party. Don't you dare try to horn in on me!* □ *I wouldn't think of horning in.*

horn in (on something**)** *Fig.* to attempt to participate in something without invitation or consent. □ *Are you trying to horn in on my conversation with Sally?* □ *I hope you are not trying to horn in on our party.*

horse and buggy and **horse and carriage; buggy whip** *Fig.* a carriage pulled by a horse, as opposed to a modern automobile; the horse was urged on with a whip. (A symbol of old-fashionedness or out-of-dateness. Particularly with *go out with*, as in the examples.) □ *That kind of clothing went out with the horse and buggy.* □ *I thought suspenders went out with the horse and carriage, but I see them everywhere now.*

horse and carriage Go to previous.

horse around (with someone or something**) 1.** *Fig.* to play around roughly with someone or something, possibly abusing someone or something. □ *Stop horsing around with your little brother. Leave him alone.* □ *Will you kids stop horsing around?* **2.** *Fig.* to join someone in boisterous play; to participate in rough play with someone. □ *He's horsing around with his little brother. They are really having a good time.* □ *We spent the entire afternoon just horsing around.*

a **horse of a different color** Go to next.

a **horse of another color** and a **horse of a different color** *Fig.* another matter altogether. □ *I was talking about trees, not bushes. Bushes are a horse of another color.* □ *Gambling is not the same as investing in the stock market. It's a horse of a different color.*

horse sense *Fig.* common sense; practical thinking. □ *Bob is no scholar but he has a lot of horse sense.* □ *Horse sense tells me I should not be involved in that project.*

hose someone **down**† *Sl.* to kill someone. (Underworld. From the image of spraying someone with bullets.) □ *Mr. Big told Sam to hose Wilbur down.* □ *The thugs tried to hose down the witness.*

hose someone or something **down**† to wash something down with water from a hose. □ *Hose her down to cool her off and maybe she will do the same for you.* □ *Please hose down the driveway.* □ *Hose it down.*

hot and bothered 1. *Fig.* excited; anxious. □ *Now don't get hot and bothered. Take it easy.* □ *John is hot and bothered about the tax increase.* **2.** *Fig.* amorous; interested in romance or sex. □ *John gets hot and bothered whenever Mary comes into the room.* □ *The dog seems hot and bothered. I think it's that time of the year again.*

hot and heavy *Fig.* referring to serious passion or emotions. □ *Things were getting a little hot and heavy so Ellen asked to be taken home.* □ *The movie had one hot and heavy scene after another. Pretty soon it got to be a joke.*

*****hot as fire** and *****hot as hell** very hot; burning hot. (*Also: as ~. Use *hell* with caution.) □ *I'm afraid Betsy has a high fever. Her forehead is hot as fire.* □ *It's as hot as hell outside. It must be near 100 degrees.*

hot as hell Go to previous.

Hot damn! *Inf.* Wow!; Hooray! (An exclamation of surprise and delight.) □ *Hot damn! I just won a vacation trip to Florida!*

Hot diggety (dog)! and **Hot dog!; Hot ziggety!** *Inf.* an expression of excitement and delight. (These expressions have no meaning and no relationship to dogs or to wieners.) □ *Rachel: I got an A! Hot diggety dog! Henry: Good for you!* □ *Tom: You won first place! Mary: Hot ziggety!*

hot enough to burn a polar bear's butt *Rur.* very hot. (Used to describe weather.) □ *Every day in August was hot enough to burn a polar bear's butt.* □ *Even in October, it was hot enough to burn a polar bear's butt.*

hot off the press *Fig.* freshly printed; just released by a publisher. □ *Here is a copy of the new Perry Hodder novel. It's hot off the press.*

hot on someone's **heels** Go to on someone's heels.

hot on something *Fig.* enthusiastic about something; very much interested in something; knowledgeable about something. □ *Meg's hot on animal rights.* □ *Jean is hot on modern ballet just now.*

hot on the trail (of someone, some creature, or something**)** *Fig.* very close to finding or catching up with someone, some creature, or something. □ *I am hot on the trail of the book that I have been seeking for months.*

a **hot ticket** *Fig.* something that is really popular and attractive at the moment. □ *Singers who can dance are a hot ticket right now. Who knows what folks will like next month?*

hot under the collar *Fig.* very angry. □ *The boss was really hot under the collar when you told him you lost the contract.* □ *I get hot under the collar every time I think about it.*

Hot ziggety! Go to Hot diggety (dog)!

a **hotbed of** something *Fig.* a nest of something; a gathering place of something. □ *This office is a hotbed of lazy people.* □ *My class is a hotbed of nerds.*

hotfoot it (off to) somewhere to go somewhere as fast as possible. □ *I've got to hotfoot it off to school.* □ *When they heard the police sirens, the thieves hotfooted home.*

hotfoot it out of somewhere to run away from a place. □ *Did you see Tom hotfoot it out of the office when the boss came in?* □ *Things are looking bad. I think we had better hotfoot it out of here.*

hound someone **from** some place and **hound** someone **out (of** something or some place**)** to chase someone out of some

311

place; to force someone out of something or some place. □ *They hounded Joel and his friends from the town.* □ *The sheriff hounded Tex out of town.*

hound someone or an animal **down**† to pursue and capture someone or an animal. □ *I will hound the killer down if it takes me the rest of my life.* □ *I will hound down that killer if it takes years.*

hound someone **out (of** something or some place**)** Go to hound someone **from** some place.

hound something **out of** someone *Fig.* to force someone to give information. □ *We are going to have to hound the information out of her.* □ *We hounded the combination to the safe out of them.*

A house divided against itself cannot stand. *Prov.* If the members of a group fight each other, the group will disintegrate. (Often the group under discussion is a family.) □ *The leader of the newly formed union tried hard to reconcile the different factions within his organization, because he knew that a house divided against itself cannot stand.*

house moss Go to curly dirt.

house of correction *Euph.* a prison. □ *He was sentenced to five years in the county's house of correction.* □ *The Jones House of Correction was built in the 1950s, when violent crime was much less common here.*

a **house of ill fame** Go to next.

a **house of ill repute** and a **house of ill fame** *Euph.* a house of prostitution. □ *The sign says "Health Club," but everyone knows it's a house of ill repute.* □ *He made a lot of money by running a house of ill fame.*

*a **household name** and *a **household word** *Fig.* well known by everyone; commonly and widely known. (*Typically: **be** ~; **become** ~; **make** something ~.) □ *I want my invention to become a household word.* □ *Some kid named Perry Hodder has become a household name!*

a **household word** Go to previous.

hover around (someone or something**)** to hang or wait around someone or something. □ *The mugger hovered around the side door to the theater, waiting for a victim.* □ *The birds hovered around the bird feeder.*

hover between something **and** something else **1.** *Lit.* to float or hang between things. □ *The helicopter hovered between the buildings and lowered a rescue chair.* □ *The hummingbird hovered between the blossoms, sipping from one and then the other.* **2.** *Fig.* to waver between choosing one thing and another. □ *I hovered between chocolate and vanilla.* □ *Uncle Jed hovered between life and death for days.*

hover over someone or something **1.** *Lit.* to remain suspended over someone or something. □ *The rescue helicopter hovered over the floating sailor.* □ *A huge blimp hovered over the football stadium.* **2.** *Fig.* [for someone] to stay close to someone or something, waiting, ready to advise or interfere. □ *Please don't hover over me, watching what I am doing.* □ *I have to hover over this project or someone will mess it up.*

How about a lift? Go to Could I have a lift?

How about that! Isn't that surprising! □ *A: My husband and I just celebrated our sixtieth anniversary. B: How about that!*

How about you? What do you think?; What is your choice?; **What about you?** □ *Bob: How are you, Bill? Bill: I'm okay. How about you? Bob: Fine, fine. Let's do lunch sometime.* □ *Waiter: Can I take your order? Bill: I'll have the chef's salad and ice tea. Waiter (turning to Sue): How about you? Sue: I'll have the same.*

[how are] See also the entries beginning with *How're.*

How (are) you doing? a standard greeting inquiry. (The entry without *are* is informal and usually pronounced "How ya doin'?".) □ *Jane: How are you doing? Mary: I'm okay. What about you? Jane: Likewise.* □ *Sally: Sue, this is my little brother, Bill. Sue: How are you, Bill? Bill: Okay. How you doing?*

How (are) you feeling? an inquiry into the state of someone's health. □ *Sally: How are you feeling? Bill: Oh, better, thanks. Sally: That's good.* □ *Bill: Hey, Jane! You been sick? Jane: Yeah. Bill: How you feeling? Jane: Not very well.*

How are you getting on? How are you managing?; How are you doing? □ *Jane: Well, Mary, how are you getting on? Mary: Things couldn't be better.* □ *Sue: Hey, John! How are you getting on? What's it like with all the kids out of the house? John: Things are great, Sue!*

How bout them apples? and **How do you like them apples?** *Rur.* What do you think of that? (Often used to express admiration, as in the first example; *bout* is short for *about*.) □ *Tom: I got first prize! Mary: Well! How bout them apples?* □ *Joe got a job as a newspaper reporter. How do you like them apples?*

How can I serve you? Go to How may I help you?

How come? How did that come about?; Why? □ *Sally: I have to go to the doctor. Mary: How come? Sally: I'm sick, silly.* □ *John: I have to leave now. Bill: How come? John: I just have to, that's all.* □ *Henry: How come you always put your right shoe on first? Rachel: Do I have to have a reason for something like that?*

How could you (do something**)?** How could you bring yourself to do a thing like that? (No answer is expected.) □ *Looking first at the broken lamp and then at the cat, Mary shouted, "How could you do that?"* □ *Tom: Then I punched him in the nose. Rachel: Oh, how could you?*

How do you do. a standard inquiry and response on greeting or meeting someone. (This expression never has rising question intonation, but the first instance of its use calls for a response. Sometimes the response does, in fact, explain how one is.) □ *Sally: Hello. How do you do. Bob: How do you do.* □ *Mary: How do you do. So glad to meet you, Tom. Tom: Thank you. How are you? Mary: Just fine. Your brother tells me you like camping. Tom: Yes. Are you a camper? Mary: Sort of.*

How do you know? 1. How did you get that information? (A straightforward question. The stress in on *know*.) □ *Bill: The train is about to pull into the station. Sue: How do you know? Bill: I hear it.* □ *Fred: I have to apologize for the coffee. It probably isn't very good. Jane: How do you know? Fred: Well, I made it.* **2.** *Inf.* What makes you think you are correct?; Why do you think you have enough information to make this judgment? (Contentious. The heaviest stress is on *you*.) □ *Bill: This is the best recording made all year. Bob: How do you know? Bill: Well, I guess it's just my opinion.* □ *Tom: Having a baby can be quite an ordeal. Mary: How do you know? Tom: I read a lot.*

How do you like school? a phrase used to start a conversation with a school-age person. □ *Bob: Well, Billy, how do you like school? Billy: I hate it. Bob: Too bad.* □ *Mary: How do you like school? Bob: It's okay. Almost everything else is better, though.*

How do you like that? 1. *Lit.* Do you like that?; Is that to your liking? □ *Tom: There's a bigger one over there. How do you like that? Bill: It's better, but not quite what I want.* □ *Clerk: Here's one without pleats. How do you like that? Fred: That's perfect!* **2.** *Fig.* an expression said when administering punishment. □ *"How do you like that?" growled Tom as he punched John in the stomach.* □ *Bill (being spanked): Ouch! Ow! No! Mother (spanking): How do you like that? Bill: Not much. Mother: It hurts me more than it hurts you.* **3.** *Fig.* an expression said to show surprise at someone's bad or strange behavior or at some surprising event. □ *Tom (shouting at Sue): Can it! Go away! Sue (looking at Mary, aghast): Well, how do you like that! Mary: Let's get out of here!* □ *Fred: How do you like that? Sue: What's the matter? Fred: My wallet's gone.*

How do you like them apples? Go to **How bout them apples?**

How do you like this weather? something said when greeting someone. (A direct answer is expected.) □ *Henry: Hi, Bill. How do you like this weather? Bill: Lovely weather for ducks. Not too good for me, though.* □ *Alice: Gee, it's hot! How do you like this weather? Rachel: You can have it!*

How does that grab you? *Inf.* What do you think of that? (Pronounced more like *HowZAT grab ya?*.) □ *Looks good, okay? How does that grab you?* □ *How does that grab you? Enough salt?*

How dumb do you think I am? *Inf.* Your question is insulting. I am not stupid. (Shows agitation. An answer is not expected or desired.) □ *Mary: Are you really going to sell your new car? Sally: Come on! How dumb do you think I am?* □ *Tom: Do you think you could sneak into that theater without paying? Bob: Good grief! How dumb do you think I am?*

How goes it? *Inf.* How are you?; How are things going? □ *Nice to see you. How goes it?* □ *How goes it? Everything okay?*

How goes it (with you)? and **How's it going?** *Inf.* Hello, how are you? □ *Hi, Mary. How goes it with you?*

How (have) you been? a standard greeting inquiry. (See also **How you is?**) □ *Bob: Hi, Fred! How have you been? Fred: Great! What about you? Bob: Fine.* □ *Bob: How you been? Sue: Okay, I guess. You okay? Bob: Yup.*

[how is] See the entries beginning with *how's*.

How is someone **fixed for** something? Is there enough of something? □ *How are you fixed for ketchup? Do you have enough for the picnic?*

How is someone **getting along?** How is someone feeling or progressing? □ *How is your father getting along? Is he any better?*

How is someone **making out?** How is someone doing?; How is someone surviving or getting along? □ *How are you making out since your retirement?*

How many times do I have to tell you? *Inf.* a phrase admonishing someone who has forgotten instructions. □ *Mother: How many times do I have to tell you? Do your homework! Bill: Mom! I hate school!* □ *Mary: Clean this place up! How many times do I have to tell you? Bill: I'll do it! I'll do it!*

How may I help you? and **How can I help you?; How can I serve you?; May I help you?; What can I do for you?** In what way can I serve you? (Usually said by store clerks and food service personnel. The first question is the most polite, and the last is the least polite.) □ *Waiter: How can I help you? Sue: I'm not ready to order yet.* □ *Clerk: May I help you? Jane: I'm looking for a gift for my aunt.*

How's business? *Inf.* a question asked in a conversation about the state of someone's business or job. □ *Tom: Hello, Sally. How's business? Sally: Okay, I suppose.* □ *Bob: Good to see you, Fred. Fred: Hello, Bob. How's business? Bob: Just okay.*

How's by you? *Inf.* a greeting inquiry. □ *Fred: Hey, man! How's by you? John: Just fine, Fred.* □ *Bob: Hello. What's cooking? Bill: Nothing. How's by you?*

How's every little thing? *Inf.* How are you?; **How are things with you?** □ *Bill: Hello, Tom. Tom: Hi, Bill. How's every little thing? Bill: Couldn't be better.* □ *Bill: Hi, Mary. How's every little thing? Mary: Things are fine. How are you? Bill: Fine, thanks.*

How's it going? Go to **How goes it (with you)?**

How's (it) with you? *Inf.* a greeting inquiry. □ *Tom: Hey, man. How's with you? Bob: Great! And you? Tom: Okay.* □ *Bill: How's with you, old buddy? John: Can't complain. And you? Bill: Couldn't be better.*

How's my boy? and **How's the boy?** *Inf.* How are you? (Male to male and familiar. The speaker may outrank the person addressed.) □ *Bob: How's my boy? Bill: Hi, Tom. How are you?* □ *Fred: Hello, old buddy. How's the boy? Bob: Hi, there! What's cooking? Fred: Nothing much.*

How's that again? *Inf.* Please say that again.; I did not hear it all. □ *Sue: Would you like some coffee? Mary: How's that again? Sue: I said, would you like some coffee?* □ *Tom: The car door is frozen closed. Bob: How's that again? Tom: The car door is frozen closed.*

How's the boy? Go to **How's my boy?**

How's the family? and **How's your family?** an expression used on greeting to ask about the state of the person's immediate family. □ *Bob: Hello, Fred. How are you? Fred: Fine, thanks. Bob: How's the family? Fred: Great! How's yours? Bob: Couldn't be better.* □ *"How's the family?" asked Bill, greeting his boss.*

How's the wife? *Inf.* a phrase used by a man when inquiring about a male friend's wife. □ *Tom: Hi, Fred, how are you? Fred: Good. And you? Tom: Great! How's the wife? Fred: Okay, and yours? Tom: Couldn't be better.* □ *Bill: Hi, Bob. How's the wife? Bob: Doing fine. How's every little thing? Bill: Great!*

H

313

How's the world (been) treating you? *Inf.* How are you? □ *Hi, Jane. How's the world treating you?* □ *How's the world been treating you, Bill?*

How's tricks? *Inf.* a greeting inquiry. □ *Bob: Fred! How's tricks? Fred: How are you doing, Bob? Bob: Doing great!* □ *Bill: What's up? How's tricks? Bob: I can't complain. How are things going for you? Bill: Can't complain.*

How's your family? Go to How's the family?

How should I know? and **Don't ask me.** *Inf.* I do not know.; Why should I be expected to know? (Shows impatience or rudeness.) □ *Bill: Why is the orca called the killer whale? Mary: How should I know?* □ *Sally: Where did I leave my glasses? Tom: Don't ask me.*

How so? Please explain your remark. □ *A: You have to bring all the lawn furniture in. B: How so?*

How the mighty have fallen. *Prov.* a jovial or mocking way of remarking that someone is doing something that he or she used to consider very demeaning. □ *Jill: Ever since Fred's wife left him, he has had to cook his own meals. Jane: Well! How the mighty have fallen!* □ *When Dan lost his money, he had to sell his expensive sports car. Now he drives an ugly old sedan. How the mighty have fallen.*

how the other half lives *Fig.* how poorer people live; how richer people live. □ *Now that I am bankrupt I am beginning to understand how the other half lives.* □ *Most people don't care how the other half lives.*

How will I know you? Go to next.

How will I recognize you? and **How will I know you?** a question asked by one of two people who have agreed to meet for the first time in a large busy place. □ *Tom: Okay, I'll meet you at the west door of the station. Mary: Fine. How will I recognize you? Tom: I'll be wearing dark glasses.* □ *Bill: I'll meet you at six. How will I recognize you? Mary: I'll be carrying a brown umbrella.*

a **howdy and a half** *Rur.* a short distance. □ *Tom: Is it far to the dime store? Jane: Just a howdy and a half.* □ *Her house was a howdy and a half from the place where I grew up.*

howl at *someone or something* **1.** *Lit.* [for a canine] to bay at someone or something. □ *The dog howls at me when I play the trumpet.* □ *The wolves howled at the moon and created a terrible uproar.* **2.** and **hoot at** *someone or something Fig.* to yell out at someone or something. □ *The audience howled at the actors and upset them greatly.* □ *We hooted at the singer until he stopped.* **3.** *Fig.* to laugh very hard at someone or something. □ *Everyone just howled at Tom's joke.* □ *I howled at the story Alice told.*

howl *someone* **down**† and **hoot** *someone* **down**† *Fig.* to yell at or boo someone's performance; to force someone to stop talking by yelling or booing. □ *The audience howled the inept magician down.* □ *They howled down the musician.*

howl with *something* to yell or holler because of something, such as pain. □ *Roger howled with pain as the needle went into his arm.* □ *Mary howled with grief when she saw what had happened to her roses.*

How're things going? *Inf.* a standard greeting inquiry. □ *Bob: Hi, Fred! How're things going? Fred: Could be better. How's by you?* □ *Bill: How are things going? Mary: Fine, but I need to talk to you.*

How're things (with you)? *Inf.* a greeting inquiry. □ *Sally: How are you? Bill: Fine. How are things?* □ *Bill: How are things going? Mary: Fine. How are things with you?*

huddle around *someone or something* to gather or bunch around someone or something. □ *The girls huddled around Mary to hear what she had to say.* □ *The kids huddled around the cake and consumed it almost instantaneously.*

huddle *someone* **together** to bunch people together. □ *The scoutmaster huddled the boys together to give them a pep talk.* □ *Let's huddle everyone together to keep warm.*

huddle (up) (together) to bunch up together. □ *The children huddled up together to keep warm.* □ *They huddled up to keep warm.* □ *The newborn rabbits huddled together and squirmed hungrily.*

a **hue and cry** *Fig.* a loud public protest or opposition. (See also **raise a hue and cry**.) □ *There was a hue and cry when the city government tried to build houses on the playing field.* □ *The decision to close the local school started a real hue and cry.*

huff and puff *Fig.* to breathe very hard; to pant as one exerts effort. □ *John came up the stairs huffing and puffing.* □ *He huffed and puffed and finally got up the steep hill.*

hum with activity *Fig.* [for a place] to be busy with activity. □ *The kitchen hummed with activity as usual.* □ *Our main office was humming with activity during the busy season.*

hunch over [for someone] to bend over. □ *The wounded man hunched over and staggered to the window.* □ *He was hunched over with pain.*

hunch *something* **up**† to raise up or lift up some body part, usually the shoulders. □ *He hunched his shoulders up in his effort to get warm.* □ *He hunched up his shoulders to keep warm.*

hunch up to squeeze or pull the parts of one's body together. □ *He hunched up in a corner to keep warm.* □ *Why is that child hunched up in the corner?*

hung up (on *someone or something***)** obsessed with someone or something; devoted to someone or something. □ *John is really hung up on Mary.* □ *She's hung up, too. See how she smiles at him.*

hunger after *something Fig.* to crave for something, not necessarily food. □ *I hunger after some old-fashioned gospel music.* □ *Mary hungered after something fattening, such as ice cream or even a baked potato with sour cream.*

hunger for *someone or something* to desire someone or something; to yearn for someone or something. □ *I hunger for you. I want you madly.* □ *He looked at the cake and you could see he was hungering for it.* □ *The prisoner was consumed with a hunger for freedom.*

Hunger is the best sauce. *Prov.* Everything tastes especially good when you are hungry, because you are so eager to eat it. □ *After our twenty-mile hike, we stopped at a little roadside restaurant. It may have been that they made the most delicious food in the world there, or it may have been that hunger was the best sauce.*

*hungry as a bear and ***hungry as a hunter** *Cliché* very hungry. (*Also: **as** ~.) □ *I'm as hungry as a bear. I could eat anything!* □ *We'd better have a big meal ready by* the time Tommy gets home; he's always hungry as a hunter after soccer practice.

hungry as a hunter Go to previous.

hungry for something *Fig.* desiring something, often something other than food. □ *The orphan was hungry for the warmth of a family.* □ *Bill has become hungry for knowledge and is always studying.*

hunker down (on something) *Fig.* to squat down on one's heels, a stool, a stone, etc. □ *Jeff hunkered down on the pavement and watched the world go by.* □ *He hunkered down to take a rest.*

hunker down to something *Fig.* to apply oneself to something, to get started working at something. □ *I hunkered down to my chores, hoping to get them done before noon.* □ *If you want to get a good grade on that report, you'd better hunker down to it.*

hunt after someone or something to seek or pursue someone or something. □ *I'm hunting after a tall man with straight black hair.* □ *Elaine is hunting after a place to store her bicycle.*

hunt for someone or something **1.** to chase someone or something for sport. □ *The hunter hunted for grouse on the game preserve.* □ *Frank likes to hunt for deer.* **2.** to look for someone or something. □ *I am hunting for someone to help me with the piano.* □ *I am hunting for a new piano.*

hunt high and low (for someone or something) and **look high and low (for** someone or something); **search high and low (for** someone or something) *Fig.* to look carefully in every possible place for someone or something. □ *We looked high and low for the right teacher.* □ *The Smiths are searching high and low for the home of their dreams.*

hunt someone or something **down**[†] **1.** to chase and catch someone or something. □ *I don't know where Amy is, but I'll hunt her down. I'll find her.* □ *I will hunt down the villain.* **2.** to locate someone or something. □ *I don't have a big enough gasket. I'll have to hunt one down.* □ *I have to hunt down a good dentist.*

hunt someone or something **out**[†] to find someone or something even if concealed. □ *We will hunt them all out and find every last one of those guys.* □ *We will hunt out all of them.* □ *They hunted out the murderer.*

hunt someone or something **up**[†] Go to **look** someone or something **up**[†].

hunt through something to search through the contents of something; to search among things. □ *Joel hunted through his wallet for a dollar bill.* □ *I will have to hunt through my drawers for a pair of socks that match.*

hurl insults (at someone) and **throw insults (at** someone) *Fig.* to direct insults at someone; to say something insulting directly to someone. □ *Anne hurled an insult at Bob that made him very angry.* □ *If you two would stop throwing insults, we could have a serious discussion.*

hurl someone or something **at** someone or something to throw someone or something at someone or something. □ *The huge man actually hurled me at the tree.* □ *Larry hurled his shoe at me.*

hurl someone or something **down**[†] to throw or push someone or something downward to the ground. □ *Roger hurled the football down and it bounced away wildly.* □ *He*

hurled down the football in anger. □ *The angry player hurled the ball down.*

hurl someone or something **into** something to throw someone or something into something. □ *She hurled the little boys into the storm cellar and went back to the house for the dog.* □ *Sharon hurled her belongings into the suitcase and jammed it closed.*

hurl someone or something **out (of** some place) and **hurl** someone or something **out**[†] to throw someone or something out of some place. □ *The manager hurled them out of the tavern.* □ *The manager hurled out the annoying people.*

hurl something **around**[†] to throw something, such as words, around carelessly. □ *Don't just go hurling foul words around like they didn't mean anything.* □ *You are just hurling around words!*

hurl something **away**[†] **(from** someone or something) to throw or push something away from someone or something. □ *She hurled the bricks away from the partially buried child.* □ *Hurl away the bricks as fast as you can.*

hurry away and **hurry off** to leave in a hurry. □ *I have to hurry away. Excuse me, please. It's an emergency.* □ *Don't hurry off. I need to talk to you.*

hurry back (to someone or something) to return to someone or something immediately or as fast as possible. □ *Oh, please hurry back to me as soon as you can.* □ *Hurry back!*

hurry down (to somewhere) to descend rapidly. □ *We need you down here in the basement. Hurry down.* □ *Please hurry down to the kitchen and help us.*

hurry off Go to **hurry away**.

hurry on Go to **hurry up**.

hurry one **on** one's **way** to help someone to hasten on. □ *Mary hurried Joel on his way so he could catch his train.* □ *There is no need to hurry me on my way. I am leaving.*

hurry someone or something **along** to make someone or something go faster. □ *Go hurry your mother along. We're almost late.* □ *Why don't you hurry the meeting along?*

hurry someone or something **in(to** something) to make someone or something go into something fast. □ *She hurried the chickens into the coop and closed the door on them for the night.* □ *It was beginning to rain, so Jerry hurried the children in.*

hurry someone or something **up** to make someone or something go or work faster. □ *Please hurry them all up. We are expecting to have dinner very soon.* □ *See if you can hurry this project up a little.*

hurry up and **hurry on** to move faster. □ *Hurry up! You're going to be late.* □ *Please hurry on. We have a lot to do today.*

hurry up and wait *Fig.* to do some things in a series fast and then have to wait a long time to do the next things in the series. (Originally military.) □ *That's all we ever do. Rush to stand in line somewhere. We just hurry up and wait all day long.* □ *Hurry up and wait! That's the army for you.*

hurt for someone or something Go to **ache for** someone or something.

hurt someone's **feelings** to cause someone emotional pain. □ *It hurts my feelings when you talk that way.* □ *I'm sorry. I didn't mean to hurt your feelings.*

hurtin' for something *Rur.* in need of something. □ *I went to fetch a bottle of cough syrup. My sick child was hurtin' for it.* □ *Jim was hurting for a new set of tools.*

hurtle through something to travel through something at great speed or with great force, possibly causing breakage. □ *A brick hurtled through the window and fell on the floor.* □ *The rocket hurtled through space toward Mars.*

a **hush fell over** someone or something *Fig.* a sudden silence enveloped something or a group. □ *As the conductor raised his arms, a hush fell over the audience.* □ *The coach shouted and a hush fell over the locker room.*

hush money *Fig.* money paid as a bribe to persuade someone to remain silent and not reveal certain information. □ *Bob gave his younger sister hush money so that she wouldn't tell Jane that he had gone to the movies with Sue.* □ *The crooks paid Fred hush money to keep their whereabouts secret.*

hush someone **up**† **1.** to make someone quiet. □ *Please hush the children up. I have a telephone call.* □ *Hush up those kids!* **2.** *Sl.* to kill someone. □ *The gang was afraid the witness would testify and wanted to hush him up.* □ *Mr. Big told Sam to hush up Richard.*

hush something **up**† *Fig.* to keep something a secret; to try to stop a rumor from spreading. □ *We just couldn't hush it up.* □ *We wanted to hush up the story, but there was no way to do it.*

hush up to be quiet; to get quiet; to stop talking. □ *You talk too much. Hush up!* □ *I want you to hush up and sit down!*

Hush your mouth! *Inf.* Please be quiet. (Not very polite.) □ *I've heard enough of that talk. Hush your mouth!* □ *Now, hush your mouth! You shouldn't talk like that!*

hustle and bustle *Fig.* confusion and business. □ *I can't stand the hustle and bustle of big cities.* □ *There is a lot of hustle and bustle in this office at the end of the fiscal year.*

hustle up to hurry up. □ *Hustle up, you guys. We have to get moving.* □ *Hustle up. We are almost late.*

hygienically challenged *Euph.* [of a person] dirty. (Jocular.) □ *Bill always smells terrible. He must be hygienically challenged.* □ *A couple of the kids in my class are, let us say, hygienically challenged.*

hype someone or something **(up)** to promote, advertise, or boost someone or something, often excessively. □ *No matter how much they hyped it up, it was still a very dull movie.* □ *Her agent hyped her up as a great actress.*

hypothesize about something to speculate about something; to make guesses about something. □ *Don't waste time hypothesizing about what happened.* □ *There is no point in hypothesizing about what happened when we don't know the actual truth.*

hypothesize on something to conjecture on the origin or nature of something. □ *We sat around hypothesizing on the origin of life.*

[I am] See the entries beginning with *I'm*.

I am not my brother's keeper. and **Am I my brother's keeper?** *Prov.* You are not responsible for another person's doings or whereabouts. (Biblical.) □ *Fred: Where's Robert? Jane: Am I my brother's keeper?* □ *Jill: How could you let Jane run off like that? Alan: I'm not my brother's keeper.*

I am so sure! *Inf.* I am right! □ *You are way rad! I am so sure!* □ *This is too much. I am so sure!*

(I) beg your pardon, but... and **Begging your pardon, but...** Please excuse me, but. (A very polite and formal way of interrupting, bringing something to someone's attention, or asking a question of a stranger.) □ *Rachel: Beg your pardon, but I think your right front tire is a little low. Henry: Well, I guess it is. Thank you.* □ *John: Begging your pardon, ma'am, but weren't we on the same cruise ship in Alaska last July? Rachel: Couldn't have been me.*

I believe so. Go to **I guess (so)**.

I believe we've met. a phrase suggesting that one has already met a person to whom one is being introduced. □ *John: Alice, have you met Fred? Alice: Oh, yes, I believe we've met. How are you, Fred? Fred: Hello, Alice. Good to see you again.* □ *Alice: Tom, this is my cousin, Mary. Tom: I believe we've met. Nice to see you again, Mary. Mary: Hello, Tom. Good to see you again.*

I can accept that. *Inf.* I accept your evaluation as valid. □ *Bob: Now, you'll probably like doing the other job much better. It doesn't call for you to do the things you don't do well. Tom: I can accept that.* □ *Sue: On your evaluation this time, I noted that you need to work on telephone manners a little bit. Bill: I can accept that.*

I can live with that. *Inf.* That is something I can get used to.; That is all right as far as I'm concerned. □ *Sue: I want to do this room in green. Bill: I can live with that.* □ *Clerk: This one will cost twelve dollars more. Bob: I can live with that. I'll take it.*

(I) can too. You are wrong, I can.; Don't say I can't, because I can! (The response to *(You) cannot!*) □ *Sue: I'm going to the party. Mother: You can't. Sue: I can too. Mother: Cannot! Sue: Can too!* □ *"Can too!" protested Fred. "I can, if you can!"*

I can't accept that. *Inf.* I do not believe what you said.; I reject what you said. □ *Sue: The mechanic says we need a whole new engine. John: What? I can't accept that!* □ *Tom: You're now going to work on the night shift. You don't seem to be able to get along with some of the people on the day shift. Bob: I can't accept that. It's them, not me.*

(I) can't argue with that. *Inf.* I agree with what you said.; It sounds like a good idea. □ *Tom: This sure is good cake. Bob: Can't argue with that.* □ *Sue: What do you say we go for a swim? Fred: I can't argue with that.*

(I) can't beat that. and **(I) can't top that.** *Inf.* I cannot do better than that.; I cannot exceed that. □ *Henry: That was really great. I can't beat that. Rachel: Yes, that was really good.* □ *"What a great joke! I can't top that," said Kate, still laughing.*

I can't believe (that)! That is unbelievable! □ *Tom: What a terrible earthquake! All the houses collapsed, one by one. Jane: I can't believe that!* □ *Bill: This lake is nearly two hun-*

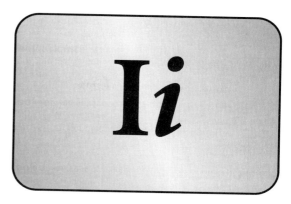

dred feet deep. Sue: I can't believe that! Bill: Take my word for it.

(I) can't complain. and **(I have) nothing to complain about.** *Inf.* a response to a greeting inquiry asking how one is or how things are going for one. □ *Sue: How are things going? Mary: I can't complain.* □ *Mary: Hi, Fred! How are you doing? Fred: Nothing to complain about.*

I can't get over something! *Fig.* I am just so amazed! (The *something* can be a fact or a pronoun, such as *that* or *it*. Also with *just*, as in the examples.) □ *"I just can't get over the way everybody pitched in and helped," said Alice.* □ *Bob: The very idea, Sue and Tom doing something like that! Bill: I can't get over it!*

(I) can't help it. There is nothing I can do to help the situation.; That is the way it is.; There is nothing I can do. (Often in answer to a criticism.) □ *Mary: Your hair is a mess. Sue: It's windy. I can't help it.* □ *Fred: I wish you'd quit coughing all the time. Sally: I can't help it. I wish I could too.*

(I) can't rightly say. *Rur.* I do not know with any certainty. □ *Fred: When do you think we'll get there? Bill: Can't rightly say.* □ *Bob: Okay, how does this look to you? Bill: I can't rightly say. I've never seen anything like it before.*

(I) can't say (as) I do. Go to **(I) can't say that I do.**

(I) can't say (as) I have. Go to **(I) can't say that I have.**

(I) can't say for sure. *Inf.* I do not know with any certainty. □ *Tom: When will the next train come through? Jane: I can't say for sure.* □ *Bob: How can the driver hit so many potholes? Bill: Can't say for sure. I know he doesn't see too well, though.*

(I) can't say's I do. Go to **(I) can't say that I do.**

(I) can't say's I have. Go to **(I) can't say that I have.**

(I) can't say that I do. and **(I) can't say's I do.; (I) can't say (as) I do.** *Fig.* a vague response to a question about whether one remembers, knows about, likes, etc., something or someone. (The *say as* and *say's* are not standard English.) □ *Jane: You remember Fred, don't you? John: Can't say as I do.* □ *Bob: This is a fine looking car. Do you like it? Bill: I can't say I do.*

(I) can't say that I have. and **(I) can't say's I have.; (I) can't say (as) I have.** *Fig.* a vague response to a question about whether one has ever done something or been somewhere. (A polite way of saying no.) □ *Bill: Have you ever been to a real opera? Bob: I can't say as I have.* □

317

Mary: Well, have you thought about going with me to Fairbanks? Fred: I can't say I have, actually.

(I) can't thank you enough. *Fig.* a polite expression of gratitude. □ *Bill: Here's the book I promised you. Sue: Oh, good. I can't thank you enough.* □ *Tom: Well, here we are. Bill: Well, Tom. I can't thank you enough. I really appreciate the ride.*

(I) can't top that. Go to **(I) can't beat that.**

(I) changed my mind. I have reversed my previous decision or statement. □ *Tom: I thought you were going to Atlanta today. Bill: I changed my mind. I'm leaving tomorrow.* □ *Mary: I thought that this room was going to be done in red. Sue: I changed my mind.*

(I) could be better. Go to **(Things) could be better.**

(I) could be worse. Go to **(Things) could be worse.**

I could eat a horse! *Fig.* I am very hungry! □ *Where's dinner? I could eat a horse!*

(I) couldn't ask for more. *Inf.* Everything is fine, and there is no more that I could want. □ *Bill: Are you happy? Sue: Oh, Bill. I couldn't ask for more.* □ *Waiter: Is everything all right? Bill: Oh, yes, indeed. Couldn't ask for more.*

I couldn't ask you to do that. That is a very kind offer, but I would not ask you to do it. (This is not a refusal of the offer.) □ *Sally: Look, if you want, I'll drive you to the airport. Mary: Oh, Sally. I couldn't ask you to do that.* □ *Bill: I'll lend you enough money to get you through the week. Sally: I couldn't ask you to do that.*

(I) couldn't be better. *Inf.* I am fine. □ *John: How are you? Jane: Couldn't be better.* □ *Bill: I hope you're completely well now. Mary: I couldn't be better.*

(I) could(n't) care less. *Inf.* It doesn't matter to me. (The *less* bears the heaviest stress in both versions. Despite the apparent contradiction, either reading of this—both the affirmative and negative—usually have the same meaning. The exception would be in a sentence where the *could* bears the heaviest stress: I COULD care less, [but I don't.].) □ *Tom: The rain is coming! The carpet will get wet! Mary: I couldn't care less.* □ *Bill: I'm going to go in there and tell off the boss! John: I could care less.*

(I) couldn't help it. There was no way I could prevent it.; I was unable to prevent something from happening.; I was unable to control myself. □ *Sally: You let the paint dry with brush marks in it. Mary: I couldn't help it. The telephone rang.* □ *Fred: You got fingerprints all over the window. Mary: Sorry. Couldn't help it.*

I declare (to goodness)! *Rur.* What a surprise! □ *I declare to goodness! You certainly have grown since I saw you.* □ *Tom: Jim and Sally are going to get married. Mary: Well, I declare!*

I didn't catch the name. and **I didn't catch your name.** I don't remember your name.; I didn't hear your name when we were introduced. □ *Bill: How do you like this weather? Bob: It's not too good. By the way, I didn't catch your name. I'm Bob Wilson. Bill: I'm Bill Franklin. Bob: Nice to meet you, Bill.* □ *Bob: Sorry, I didn't catch the name. Bill: It's Bill, Bill Franklin. And you? Bob: I'm Bob Wilson.*

I didn't hear you. Go to next.

I didn't (quite) catch that (last) remark. and **I didn't get that.; I didn't hear you.** I didn't hear what you said, so would you please repeat it. □ *John: What did you say? I didn't quite catch that last remark. Jane: I said it's really a hot day.* □ *Bill: Have a nice time, if you can. Sally: I didn't get that. Bill: Have a nice time! Enjoy!*

I do believe. a way of affirming or reaffirming one's opinion. □ *Jim's in love with that gal, I do believe.* □ *Jane's store will do well, I do believe.*

I (do) declare! *Inf.* I am surprised to hear that! (Old-fashioned.) □ *Mary: I'm the new president of my sorority! Grandmother: I declare! That's very nice.* □ *A plane had landed right in the middle of the cornfield. The old farmer shook his head in disbelief. "I do declare!" he said over and over as he walked toward the plane.*

I don't believe it! an expression of amazement and disbelief. □ *Bob: Tom was just elected president of the trade association! Mary: I don't believe it!* □ *Bob: They're going to build a Disney World in Moscow. Sally: I don't believe it!*

(I) don't believe I've had the pleasure. *Fig.* an expression meaning *I haven't met you yet.* □ *Tom: I'm Tom Thomas. I don't believe I've had the pleasure. Bill: Hello. I'm Bill Franklin. Tom: Nice to meet you, Bill. Bill: Likewise.* □ *Bob: Looks like rain. Fred: Sure does. Oh, I don't believe I've had the pleasure. Bob: I'm Bob, Bob Jones. Fred: My name is Fred Wilson. Glad to meet you.*

I don't believe this! *Inf.* What is happening right now is unbelievable! □ *It's snowing in July! I don't believe this!* □ *I don't believe this! It can't be happening.*

I don't care. It doesn't matter to me. □ *Mary: Can I take these papers away? Tom: I don't care. Do what you want.* □ *Bill: Should this room be white or yellow? Sally: I don't care.*

(I) don't care if I do. *Rur.* Thank you.; I will. (See also **(I) don't mind if I do.**) □ *Tom: Have some more grits? Jane: Don't care if I do.* □ *Charlie: Come on in and set a spell. Mary: Don't care if I do.*

I don't have time to breathe. Go to next.

I don't have time to catch my breath. and **I don't have time to breathe.** *Fig.* I am very busy.; I have been very busy. □ *Henry: I'm so busy these days. I don't have time to catch my breath. Rachel: Oh, I know what you mean.* □ *Sue: Would you mind finishing this for me? Bill: Sorry, Sue. I'm busy. I don't have time to breathe.*

I don't know. a common expression of ignorance or of lacking an answer. □ *Father: Why can't you do better in school? Bill: I don't know.* □ *Bill: Well, what are we going to do now? Sue: I don't know.*

I don't mean maybe! *Inf.* I am very serious about my demand or order. □ *Bob: Do I have to do this? Sue: Do it now, and I don't mean maybe!* □ *Father: Get this place cleaned up! And I don't mean maybe! John: All right! I'll do it!*

(I) don't mind if I do. Yes, I would like to. □ *Sally: Have some more coffee? Bob: Don't mind if I do.* □ *Jane: Here are some lovely roses. Would you like to take a few blossoms with you? John: I don't mind if I do.*

I don't mind telling you (something). I want you to know something. □ *Tom: You have a beautiful garden. Mary: Thank you. But I don't mind telling you, it's an awful lot of work.* □ *I don't mind telling you, I was as pleased as Punch when my daughter won the race.*

I don't rightly know. *Rur.* I do not know. □ *Tom: When will Joe be getting back? Charlie: I don't rightly know.* □ *Jane: What's the difference between a first cousin and a first cousin once removed? Mary: I don't rightly know.*

(I) don't think so. Go to I guess not.

I don't understand (it). and **I can't understand (it).** I am confused and bewildered (by what has happened). □ *Bill: Everyone is leaving the party. Mary: I don't understand. It's still so early.* □ *Bob: The very idea, Sue and Tom doing something like that! Alice: It's very strange. I can't understand it.*

I don't want to alarm you, but and **I don't want to upset you, but** an expression used to introduce bad or shocking news or gossip. □ *Bill: I don't want to alarm you, but I see someone prowling around your car. Mary: Oh, goodness! I'll call the police!* □ *Bob: I don't want to upset you, but I have some bad news. Tom: Let me have it.*

I don't want to sound like a busybody, but *Fig.* an expression used to introduce an opinion or suggestion. □ *Bob: I don't want to sound like a busybody, but didn't you intend to have your house painted? Bill: Well, I guess I did.* □ *Bob: I don't want to sound like a busybody, but some of your neighbors wonder if you could stop parking your car on your lawn. Sally: I'll thank you to mind your own business!*

I don't want to upset you, but Go to I don't want to alarm you, but.

I don't want to wear out my welcome. *Fig.* a phrase said by a guest who doesn't want to be a burden to the host or hostess or to visit too often. □ *Mary: Good night, Tom. You must come back again soon. Tom: Thank you. I'd love to. I don't want to wear out my welcome, though.* □ *Bob: We had a fine time. Glad you could come to our little gathering. Hope you can come again next week. Fred: I don't want to wear out my welcome, but I'd like to come again. Bob: Good. See you next week. Bye. Fred: Bye.*

I don't wonder. Go to I'm not surprised.

I doubt it. I do not think so. □ *Tom: Think it will rain today? Sue: I doubt it.* □ *Sally: Think you'll go to New York? Mary: I doubt it.*

I doubt that. I do not believe that something is so. □ *Bob: I'll be there exactly on time. Sue: I doubt that.* □ *John: Fred says he can't come to work because he's sick. Jane: I doubt that.*

I expect Go to I guess.

I expect not. Go to I guess not.

I expect (so). Go to I guess (so).

I felt like a penny waiting for change. *Rur.* I felt worthless or helpless. □ *When I lost the race, I felt like a penny waiting for change.* □ *My best girl went off with someone else. I felt like a penny waiting for change.*

I guess and **I expect; I suppose; I suspect 1.** a phrase that introduces a supposition. (Frequently, in speech, *suppose* is reduced to *'spose*, and *expect* and *suspect* are reduced to *'spect*. The apostrophe is not always shown.) □ *Bob: I guess it's going to rain. Bill: Oh, I don't know. Maybe so, maybe not.* □ *Alice: I expect you'll be wanting to leave pretty soon. John: Why? It's early yet.* **2.** a vague way

of answering 'yes'. □ *John: You want some more coffee? Jane: I 'spose. □ Alice: Ready to go? John: I spect.*

I guess not. and **(I) don't think so.; I expect not.; I suppose not.; I suspect not.; I think not.** a vague statement of negation. (More polite or gentle than simply saying *no*. Frequently, in speech, *suppose* is reduced to *'spose*, and *expect* and *suspect* are reduced to *'spect*. The apostrophe is not always shown.) □ *Bill: It's almost too late to go to the movie. Shall we try anyway? Mary: I guess not.* □ *Tom: Will it rain? Mary: I 'spect not.*

I guess (so). and **I believe so.; I expect (so).; I suppose (so).; I suspect (so).; I think so.** a vague expression of assent. (Frequently, in speech, *suppose* is reduced to *'spose*, and *expect* and *suspect* are reduced to *'spect*. The apostrophe is not always shown.) □ *Tom: Will it rain today? Bob: I suppose so.* □ *Sue: Happy? Bill: I 'spect. Sue: You don't sound happy. Bill: I guess not.*

(I) had a good time. Go to (I) had a nice time.

I had a lovely time. and **We had a lovely time.** a polite expression of thanks to the host or hostess. □ *Fred: Good-bye. I had a lovely time. Bill: Nice to have you. Do come again.* □ *Jane: We had a lovely time. Mary: Thank you and thanks for coming.*

(I) had a nice time. and **(I) had a good time.** the standard *good-bye and thank you* said to a host or hostess by a departing guest. □ *John: Thank you. I had a nice time. Sally: Don't stay away so long next time. Bye.* □ *Mary: Had a nice time. Bye. Got to run. Sue: Bye. Drive safely.*

(I) hate to eat and run. *Cliché* an apology made by someone who must leave a social event soon after eating. □ *Bill: Well, I hate to eat and run, but it's getting late. Sue: Oh, you don't have to leave, do you? Bill: I think I really must.* □ *Mary: Oh, my goodness! I hate to eat and run, but I have to catch an early plane tomorrow. Bob: Do you have to go? Mary: Afraid so.*

[I have] See also the entries beginning with *I've*.

(I have) no problem with that. That is okay with me. (See also No problem.) □ *Bob: Is it okay if I sign us up to play mixed doubles? Sally: I have no problem with that.* □ *Bill: It looks as though we will have to come back later. They're not open yet. Is that all right? Jane: No problem with that. When do they open?*

(I have) nothing to complain about. Go to (I) can't complain.

(I) have to be moving along. and **(I) have to move along.** It is time for me to leave. □ *Bill: Bye, now. Have to be moving along. Sally: See you later.* □ *Rachel: I have to be moving along. See you later. Andrew: Bye, now.* □ *Sally: It's late. I have to move along. Mary: If you must. Good-bye. See you tomorrow.*

(I) have to go now. an expression announcing the need to leave. □ *Fred: Bye, have to go now. Mary: See you later. Take it easy.* □ *Sue: Would you help me with this box? John: Sorry. I have to go now.*

(I) have to move along. Go to (I) have to be moving along.

(I) have to push off. Go to (I) have to shove off.

(I) have to run along. an expression announcing the need to leave. □ *Jane: It's late. I have to run along. Tom:*

Okay, Jane. Bye. Take care. □ *John: Leaving so soon? Sally: Yes, I have to run along.*

(I) have to shove off. and **(I've) got to be shoving off.; (I've) got to shove off.; (I) have to push off.; (It's) time to shove off.** a phrase announcing one's need to depart. □ *John: Look at the time! I have to shove off! Jane: Bye, John.* □ *Jane: Time to shove off. I have to feed the cats. John: Bye, Jane.* □ *Fred: I have to push off. Bye. Jane: See you around. Bye.*

I have to wash a few things out†. 1. *Lit.* I have to wash things by hand, such as socks and underwear. □ *I have to wash a few things out before I go to bed.* □ *She has to wash out a few things.* **2.** *Fig.* I have to do something (that keeps me from spending time with you). □ *Jane: Time to shove off. I have to wash a few things out. John: Bye, Jane.* □ *Bill: I have to wash out a few things. Bob: Why don't you use a machine? Bill: Oh, I'll see you later.*

(I) haven't got all day. *Fig.* Please hurry.; I'm in a hurry. □ *Rachel: Make it snappy! I haven't got all day. Alice: Just take it easy. There's no rush.* □ *Henry: I haven't got all day. When are you going to finish with my car? Bob: As soon as I can.*

(I) haven't seen you in a long time. *Fig.* an expression of greeting, often said as part of a series. □ *Mary: Hi, Fred! Haven't seen you in a long time. Fred: Yeah. Long time no see.* □ *Tom: Well, John. Is that you? I haven't seen you in a long time. John: Good to see you, Tom!*

(I) haven't seen you in a month of Sundays. *Rur.* I haven't seen you in a long time. □ *Tom: Hi, Bill. Haven't seen you in a month of Sundays! Bill: Hi, Tom. Long time no see.* □ *Bob: Well, Fred! Come right in! Haven't seen you in a month of Sundays! Fred: Good to see you, Uncle Bob.*

I hear what you're saying. and **I hear you. 1.** I know exactly what you mean! □ *John: The prices in this place are a bit steep. Jane: Man, I hear you!* □ *Bill: I think it's about time for the whole management team to resign! Andrew: I hear what you're saying.* **2.** an expression indicating that the speaker has been heard, but implying that there is no agreement. □ *Tom: Time has come to do something about that ailing dog of yours. Mary: I hear what you're saying.* □ *Jane: It would be a good idea to have the house painted. John: I hear what you're saying.*

I hear you. Go to previous.

I hope all goes well. I hope there is success. □ *Good luck on your operation tomorrow. I hope all goes well.*

(I) hope not. a phrase expressing the desire and wish that something is not so. □ *John: It looks like it's going to rain. Jane: Hope not.* □ *John: The Wilsons said they might come over this evening. Jane: I hope not. I've got things to do.*

(I) hope so. a phrase expressing the desire and wish that something is so. □ *Bill: Is this the right house? Bob: Hope so.* □ *John: Will you be coming to dinner Friday? Sue: Yes, I hope so.*

(I) hope to see you again (sometime). an expression said when taking leave of a person one has just met. □ *Bill: Nice to meet you, Tom. Tom: Bye, Bill. Nice to meet you. Hope to see you again sometime.* □ *Bill: Good talking to you. See you around. Bob: Yes, I hope to see you again. Goodbye.*

I just have this feeling. I have a premonition about this; I have a feeling about this. □ *I really don't know that something is wrong. I just have this feeling.* □ *I just have this feeling that she is not telling us the truth.*

(I) just want(ed) to mention something. Go to next.

(I) just want(ed) to say something. and **(I) just want(ed) to mention** something.; **(I) just want(ed) to tell you** something. a sentence opener that eases into a statement or question. (Can be followed by words like *say, ask, tell you, be,* and *come.*) □ *Rachel: I just wanted to say that we all loved your letter. Thank you so much. Andrew: Thanks. Glad you liked it.* □ *Rachel: I just wanted to tell you how sorry I am about your sister. Alice: Thanks. I appreciate it.* □ *Andrew: Just wanted to come by for a minute and say hello. Tom: Well, hello. Glad you dropped by.*

I kid you not. *Inf.* I am not kidding you.; I am not trying to fool you. □ *Bill: Whose car is this? Sally: It's mine. It really is. I kid you not.* □ *"I kid you not," said Tom, glowing. "I outran the whole lot of them."*

I know (just) what you mean. I know exactly what you are talking about, and I feel the same way about it. □ *John: These final exams are just terrible. Bob: I know just what you mean. John: Why do we have to go through this?* □ *Mary: What a pain! I hate annual inventories. John: I know what you mean. It's really boring.*

(I) love it! *Inf.* It is just wonderful. □ *Mary: What do you think of this car? Bill: Love it! It's really cool!* □ *Bob: What a joke, Tom! Jane: Yes, love it! Tom: Gee, thanks.*

I must be off. an expression announcing the speaker's intention of leaving. □ *Bill: It's late. I must be off. Bob: Me, too. I'm out of here.* □ *Sue: I must be off. John: The game's not over yet. Sue: I've seen enough.*

I must say good night. an expression announcing the speaker's intention of leaving for the night. □ *Jane: It's late. I must say good night. Bob: Can I see you again? Jane: Call me. Good night, Bob. Bob: Good night, Jane.* □ *Sue: I must say good night. Mary: Good night, then. See you tomorrow.*

I need it yesterday. *Inf.* an answer to the question "When do you need this?" (Indicates that the need is urgent.) □ *Bob: When do you need that urgent survey? Bill: I need it yesterday.* □ *Mary: Where's the Wilson contract? Sue: Do you need it now? Mary: I need it yesterday! Where is it?*

(I) never heard of such a thing! an expression of amazement and disbelief. (Compare this with **Well, I never!**) □ *Bill: The company sent out a representative the same day I called to examine the new sofa and see what the problem was with the wobbly leg. Jane: I've never heard of such a thing! That's very unusual.* □ *Bill: The tax office is now open on Sunday! Sue: Never heard of such a thing!*

(I) never thought I'd see you here! I am surprised to see you here. □ *Tom: Hi, Sue! I never thought I'd see you here! Sue: Hi, Tom. I was thinking the same thing about you.* □ *Bill: Well, Tom Thomas. I never thought I'd see you here! Tom: Likewise. I didn't know you liked opera.*

I owe you one. *Inf.* Thank you, now I owe you a favor.; I owe you something similar in return. □ *Bob: I put the extra copy of the book on your desk. Sue: Thanks, I owe you* one. □ *Bill: Let me pay for your drink. Bob: Thanks a lot, I owe you one.*

I promise you! *Inf.* I am telling you the truth! (Compare this with **Trust me!**) □ *John: Things will work out, I promise you! Jane: Okay, but when?* □ *Sue: I'll be there exactly when I said. Bob: Are you sure? Sue: I promise you, I'm telling the truth!*

(I) read you loud and clear. 1. *Lit.* a response used by someone communicating by radio stating that the hearer understands the transmission clearly. (See also **Do you read me?**) □ *Controller: This is Aurora Center, do you read me? Pilot: Yes, I read you loud and clear.* □ *Controller: Left two degrees. Do you read me? Pilot: Roger. Read you loud and clear.* **2.** *Fig.* I understand what you are telling me. (Used in general conversation, not in radio communication.) □ *Bob: Okay. Now, do you understand exactly what I said? Mary: I read you loud and clear.* □ *Mother: I don't want to have to tell you again. Do you understand? Bill: I read you loud and clear.*

(I) really must go. an expression announcing or repeating one's intention to depart. □ *Bob: It's getting late. I really must go. Jane: Good night, then. See you tomorrow.* □ *Sally: I really must go. John: Do you really have to? It's early yet.*

I rest my case. 1. *Lit.* I have completed the presentation of my argument. (Said by a lawyer.) □ *Clearly the defendant is guilty. I rest my case.* **2.** *Fig.* What you just heard sums up my point of view. □ *Your remark just supported my position! I rest my case.*

I spoke out of turn. *Fig.* I said the wrong thing.; I should not have said what I did. (An apology.) □ *Bill: You said I was the one who did it. Mary: I'm sorry. I spoke out of turn. I was mistaken.* □ *Bill: I seem to have said the wrong thing. Bob: You certainly did. Bill: I spoke out of turn, and I'm sorry.*

I spoke too soon. 1. *Fig.* I am wrong.; I spoke before I knew the facts. □ *Bill: I know I said I would, but I spoke too soon. Sue: I thought so.* □ *John: You said that everything would be all right. Jane: I spoke too soon. That was before I learned that you had been arrested.* **2.** *Fig.* What I had said was just now contradicted. □ *Bob: It's beginning to brighten up. I guess it won't rain after all. John: I'm glad to hear that. Bob: Whoops! I spoke too soon. I just felt a raindrop on my cheek.* □ *Bill: Thank heavens! Here's John now. Bob: No, that's Fred. Bill: I spoke too soon. He sure looked like John.*

I suppose Go to **I guess.**

I suppose not. Go to **I guess not.**

I suppose (so). Go to **I guess (so).**

I suspect Go to **I guess.**

I suspect not. Go to **I guess not.**

I suspect (so). Go to **I guess (so).**

I swan! *Rur.* What a surprise! □ *Well, I swan! I didn't expect to see you here!* □ *Tom: I hear Charlie just won a thousand dollars! Jane: I swan!*

I think not. Go to **I guess not.**

I think so. Go to **I guess (so).**

(I was) just wondering. a comment made after hearing a response to a previous question. (See examples for typical patterns.) □ *John: Do you always keep your film in the refrigerator? Mary: Yes, why? John: I was just wondering.* □ *Bob: Did this cost a lot? Sue: I really don't think you need to know that. Bob: Sorry. Just wondering.*

I was up all night with a sick friend. an unlikely, but popular excuse for not being where one was supposed to be the night before. □ *Bill: Where in the world were you last night? Mary: Well, I was up all night with a sick friend.* □ *Mr. Franklin said rather sheepishly, "Would you believe I was up with a sick friend?"*

I wasn't brought up in the woods to be scared by owls. *Rur.* I am not foolish or easily frightened. □ *His threats don't scare me. I wasn't brought up in the woods to be scared by owls.* □ *Mary: You'll be sorry you ever crossed me. Jane: I wasn't brought up in the woods to be scared by owls.*

[I will] See the entries beginning with *I'll.*

I wish I'd said that. a comment of praise or admiration for someone's clever remark. □ *Mary: The weed of crime bears bitter fruit. Sue: I wish I'd said that. Mary: I wish I'd said it first.* □ *John: Tom is simply not able to see through the airy persiflage of Mary's prolix declamation. Jane: I wish I'd said that. John: I'm sorry I did.*

(I) wonder if a phrase introducing a hypothesis. □ *Henry: I wonder if I could have another piece of cake. Sue: Sure. Help yourself.* □ *Andy: Wonder if it's stopped raining yet. Rachel: Why don't you look out the window?* □ *Andy: I wonder if I'll pass algebra. Father: That thought is on all our minds.*

(I) won't breathe a word (of it). and **(I) won't tell a soul.** *Fig.* I will not tell anyone your secret. □ *Bill: Don't tell anybody, but Sally is getting married. Mary: I won't breathe a word of it.* □ *Alice: The Jacksons are going to have to sell their house. Don't spread it around. Mary: I won't tell a soul.*

I won't give up without a fight. *Fig.* I will not give in easily. (Compare this with **Don't give up too eas(il)y.**) □ *Sue: Stick by your principles, Fred. Fred: Don't worry, I won't give up without a fight.* □ *Bob: The boss wants me to turn the Wilson project over to Tom. Sue: How can he do that? Bob: I don't know. All I know is that I won't give up without a fight.*

(I) won't tell a soul. Go to **(I) won't breathe a word (of it).**

[I would] See also the entries beginning with *I'd.*

(I) would if I could(, but I can't). I simply can't do it. □ *Jane: Can't you fix this yourself? John: I would if I could, but I can't.* □ *Bob: Can you go to the dance? Hardly anyone is going. Alice: Would if I could.*

I would like you to meet someone. and **I would like to introduce you to** someone. an expression used to introduce one person to another. (The word *someone* can be used as the **someone**.) □ *Mary: I would like you to meet my Uncle Bill. Sally: Hello, Uncle Bill. Nice to meet you.* □ *Tom: I would like to introduce you to Bill Franklin. John: Hello, Bill. Glad to meet you. Bill: Glad to meet you, John.*

(I) wouldn't bet on it. and **(I) wouldn't count on it.** *Fig.* I do not believe that something will happen. (Also with *that* or some specific happening. See examples.) □ *John: I'll be a vice president in a year or two. Mary: I wouldn't bet on that.* □ *John: I'll pick up a turkey on the* *day before Thanksgiving. Mary: Did you order one ahead of time? John: No. Mary: Then I wouldn't count on it.*

(I) wouldn't count on it. Go to previous.

(I) wouldn't if I were you. *Fig.* a polite way to advise someone not to do something. □ *Mary: Do you think I should trade this car in on a new one? Sally: I wouldn't if I were you.* □ *Bob: I'm going to plant nothing but corn this year. Sue: I wouldn't if I were you. Bob: Why? Sue: It's better to diversify.*

(I) wouldn't know. There is no way that I would know the answer to that question. □ *John: When will the flight from Miami get in? Jane: Sorry, I wouldn't know.* □ *Bob: Are there many fish in the Amazon River? Mary: Gee, I wouldn't know.*

I wouldn't touch it with a ten-foot pole. *Cliché* I would not have anything to do with it under any circumstances. (Said about something you think is untrustworthy, as in the first example, or in response to a remark that seems to invite a nasty reply, as in the second example. The British version is "I would not touch it with a bargepole.") □ *Jill: This advertisement says I can buy land in Florida for a small investment. Do you think I should? Jane: I wouldn't touch it with a ten-foot pole.* □ *Jane: Can you believe this? Jill said she thinks I'm bossy. You don't think I'm bossy, do you? Mary: I wouldn't touch that with a ten-foot pole.*

I wouldn't wish that on a dog. Go to next.

I wouldn't wish that on my worst enemy. and **I wouldn't wish that on a dog.** *Fig.* I would not wish that to happen to even the worst or lowliest person. □ *A skunk sprayed him! I wouldn't wish that on my worst enemy.* □ *What a hideous disease! I wouldn't wish that on a dog.*

ice over [for water] to freeze and develop a covering of ice. □ *I can't wait for the river to ice over so we can do some ice fishing.*

ice something **down**† to cool something with ice. □ *They are icing the champagne down now.* □ *They are icing down the champagne now.*

ice something **up**† to cause something to become icy. □ *I hope the cold doesn't ice the roads up.* □ *The wind and rain iced up the roads.*

ice up to become icy. □ *Are the roads icing up?*

the **icing on the cake** *Fig.* an extra enhancement. □ *Oh, wow! A tank full of gas in my new car. That's icing on the cake!* □ *Your coming home for a few days was the icing on the cake.*

(I'd be) happy to (do something). and **Be happy to (do something).** I would do it with pleasure. (The *something* is often replaced with a description of an activity.) □ *John: I tried to get the book you wanted, but they didn't have it. Shall I try another store? Mary: No, never mind. John: I'd be happy to give it a try.* □ *Alice: Would you fix this, please? John: Be happy to.*

I'd bet money (on it). *Fig.* I am certain. □ *Charlie: Do you think Joe's planning to sell his house? Tom: I'd bet money on it.* □ *I'd bet money that Jane will get that job.*

(I'd) better be going. and **(I'd) better be off.** an expression announcing the need to depart. □ *Bob: Better be going. Got to get home. Bill: Well, if you must, you must.*

Bye. □ *Fred: It's midnight. I'd better be off. Henry: Okay. Bye, Fred.* □ *Henry: Better be off. It's starting to snow. John: Yes, it looks bad out.*

(I'd) better get moving. *Inf.* an expression announcing the need to depart. □ *Jane: It's nearly dark. Better get moving. Mary: Okay. See you later.* □ *Bob: I'm off. Good night. Bill: Look at the time! I'd better get moving too.*

(I'd) better get on my horse. *Inf.* an expression indicating that it is time that one departed. □ *John: It's getting late. Better get on my horse. Rachel: Have a safe trip. See you tomorrow.* □ *"I'd better get on my horse. The sun'll be down in an hour," said Sue, sounding like a cowboy.*

(I'd) better hit the road. Go to (It's) time to hit the road.

I'd (just) as leave do something I would rather do something. □ *Tom: Do you want to go to Joe's party? Jane: We can if you want to, but I'd as leave not.* □ *I'd just as leave eat dinner at home tonight.*

I'd (just) as soon (as) do something I would prefer to do something. □ *Tom: Why don't you give Joe a call? Jane: I'd as soon as you did it.* □ *I'd just as soon we didn't stay here long.*

I'd like (for) you to meet someone. an expression used to introduce someone to someone else. (The *someone* can be a person's name, the name of a relationship, or the word *someone*.) □ *Tom: Sue, I'd like you to meet my brother, Bill. Sue: Hi, Bill. How are you? Bill: Great! How are you?* □ *Bob: Hello, Fred. I'd like for you to meet someone. This is Bill. Fred: Hello, Bill. I'm glad to meet you. Bill: Hello, Fred. My pleasure.*

I'd like (to have) a word with you. and **Could I have a word with you?** I need to speak to you briefly in private. (The alternate entry is also used with *can* or *may* in place of *could*.) □ *Bob: Can I have a word with you? Sally: Sure. I'll be with you in a minute.* □ *Sally: Tom? Tom: Yes. Sally: I'd like to have a word with you. Tom: Okay. What's it about?*

I'd like to speak to someone, **please.** the standard way of requesting to speak with a specific person on the telephone or in an office. □ *Sue (answering the phone): Hello? Bill: Hello, this is Bill Franklin. I'd like to speak to Mary Gray. Sue: I'll see if she's in.* □ *"I'd like to speak to Tom," said the voice at the other end of the line.*

I'd rather face a firing squad than do something *Fig.* I would prefer to stand and be executed by gunfire than to do something. □ *I'd rather face a firing squad than go shopping the day after Christmas.*

identify (oneself) with someone or something to classify oneself with someone or something; to relate to someone or something; to see part of oneself represented in someone or something. □ *I identify myself with the others.* □ *I identify with the birds and animals of the forest.*

identify someone **as** someone **1.** to determine that someone is a certain person. □ *Can you identify Fred as the perpetrator?* □ *Fred was identified as the thief.* **2.** to reveal one's identity or name. □ *Will you identify the man as Tom?* □ *The stranger identified himself as a meter reader from the gas company.*

identify someone or something **by** something to recognize someone or something because of something. □ *Can you* *identify your baggage by any special marks?* □ *You can identify me by the red carnation in my lapel.*

identify someone or something **with** someone or something to associate people and things, in any combination. □ *I tend to identify Wally with big cars.* □ *We usually identify green with grass.* □ *We tend to identify big cars with greedy people.*

idle about to loiter around, doing nothing. □ *Please don't idle about. Get busy!* □ *Andy is idling about today.*

An **idle brain is the devil's workshop.** *Prov.* People who have nothing worthwhile to think about will usually think of something bad to do. □ *We need to figure out something constructive for Tom to do in the afternoons after school. An idle brain is the devil's workshop.*

Idle folk have the least leisure. Go to next.

Idle people have the least leisure. and **Idle folk have the least leisure.** *Prov.* If you are not energetic and hardworking, you will never have any free time, since you will have to spend all your time finishing your work. □ *My grandmother always told me not to dawdle, since idle people have the least leisure.*

idle something **away**† *Fig.* to waste one's time in idleness; to waste a period of time, such as an afternoon, evening, one's life. □ *She idled the afternoon away and then went to a party.* □ *Don't idle away the afternoon.*

Idleness is the root of all evil. *Prov.* If you have no useful work to do, you will think of harmful things to do in order to amuse yourself. (Compare this with **Money is the root of all evil.**) □ *Child: Why do you make me do so many chores? Father: Idleness is the root of all evil.*

idolize someone or something **as** something to worship or adore someone or something as being something. □ *We all idolized Jim as our hero.* □ *They idolized wealth as a cure for all their ills.*

If a thing is worth doing, it's worth doing well. *Prov.* If you decide to do something, do it as well as you possibly can. □ *Jill: Do we have to wash the walls before we paint them? It seems like such a lot of extra work. Fred: Yes, we have to. The paint won't stick properly otherwise. If a thing is worth doing, it's worth doing well.* □ *Bruce never did sloppy work. He believed that if something is worth doing, it's worth doing well.*

If a toady frog had wings, he wouldn't bump his ass. Go to If frogs had wheels, they wouldn't bump their butts.

If anything can go wrong, it will. *Prov.* Every possible disaster will occur, whether you have prepared for it or not. (This saying is also referred to as "Murphy's Law.") □ *Fred: Your car should be fine now, as long as the battery doesn't die. Alan: Then we'd better put a new battery in. If anything can go wrong, it will; so let's make sure it can't go wrong.*

if anything should happen and **if anything happens** *Euph.* If a disaster or emergency happens. □ *I'll give you the phone number of my hotel, so that you can reach me if anything happens.* □ *If anything should happen, I want you to look after my children.*

If at first you don't succeed, try, try again. *Prov.* You have to keep trying until you get what you want. □ *Jill: I spent all morning trying to fix the computer, and it still won't work. Jane: If at first you don't succeed, try, try again.* □ *You'll learn that dance step eventually. If at first you don't succeed, try, try again.*

If frogs had wheels, they wouldn't bump their butts. and **If a toady frog had wings, he wouldn't bump his ass.** *Rur.* It is useless to wish for impossible things. (Use caution with *ass*.) □ *Tom: If I had two hundred thousand dollars, I could buy that farm. Jane: Yeah, and if frogs had wheels, they wouldn't bump their butts.* □ *Charlie: If I were rich and famous, I'd make people listen to me. Bill: If a toady frog had wings, he wouldn't bump his ass.*

If God did not exist, it would be necessary to invent Him. *Prov.* People need a deity to worship. (This is an English translation of a quote from Voltaire. It is often parodied, using a person's name instead of *God* and implying that the person is somehow necessary.) □ *The atheist tried to convince Jerry that God does not exist, and that people should not waste their time worshiping Him. "But you can't stop people from worshiping God," Jerry replied. "If God did not exist, it would be necessary to invent Him."* □ *The unscrupulous mayor was such a convenient scapegoat for the city's problems that if she had not existed, it would have been necessary to invent her.*

if I were you an expression introducing a piece of advice. □ *John: If I were you, I'd get rid of that old car. Alice: Gee, I was just getting to like it.* □ *Henry: I'd keep my thoughts to myself, if I were you. Bob: I guess I should be careful about what I say.*

If ifs and ands were pots and pans (there'd be no work for tinkers' hands). *Prov.* Wishing for things is useless. (Often said in reply to someone who says something beginning with "If only. . . .") □ *Daughter: If only we didn't have to move out of town, I'd be the happiest girl in the world. Grandmother: If ifs and ands were pots and pans, there'd be no work for tinkers' hands.*

If it ain't chickens, it's feathers. *Rur.* There are always problems.; That is life. □ *Now that I'm finally done with school, I've got to worry about getting a job. If it ain't chickens, it's feathers.* □ *He's got plenty of money now, but he's in such bad health he can't enjoy it. If it ain't chickens, it's feathers.*

If it was a snake it woulda bit you. *Rur.* It was very close to you. □ *Jane: Where's the phone book? Tom: Right there! If it was a snake it woulda bit you.* □ *Bill: I can't find my other shoe. I've looked all over the house. Mary: It's right behind you. If it was a snake it would have bit you.*

if I've told you once, I've told you a thousand times *Fig.* an expression that introduces a scolding, usually to a child. □ *Mother: If I've told you once, I've told you a thousand times, don't leave your clothes in a pile on the floor! Bill: Sorry.* □ *"If I've told you once, I've told you a thousand times, keep out of my study!" yelled Bob.*

if looks could kill a catchphrase said when someone makes a frown at someone or when someone casts a dirty look. □ *Did you see the way she looked at me? If looks could kill....* □ *If looks could kill.... What a nasty glare she gave me.*

if my memory serves me correctly *Fig.* if I have remembered it correctly... □ *If my memory serves me correctly, you are the cousin of my closest friend.*

if not if that is not [the case]; if that is not so. □ *If not cleaned, the clock will stop running.* □ *He should be here at noon. If not, we will eat without him.*

if one **knows what's good for** one *Fig.* one had better do what is expected of one. □ *You'd better be on time if you know what's good for you.* □ *If you know what's good for you, you'll call and apologize.*

if one's **a day** *Fig.* a phrase attached to an expression of someone's age. □ *She's fifty if she's a day!* □ *I'm sure he's forty-five if he's a day.*

if push comes to shove Go to when push comes to shove.

if so if that is [the case]; if that is so. □ *She might be late. If so, we will eat without her.* □ *She is supposed to be all right. If so, we have nothing to worry about.*

If that don't beat a pig a-pecking! *Rur.* That's amazing! □ *Tom: A Republican won the Senate seat! Jane: If that don't beat a pig a-pecking!* □ *Mary: Jim lost twenty pounds in one month. Charlie: If that don't beat a pig a-pecking!*

If that don't beat all! and **That beats everything!; Don't that (just) beat all!** *Rur.* That surpasses everything!; That is amazing!; That takes the cake! (The grammar error, *that don't* is built into this catchphrase.) □ *Tom: The mayor is kicking the baseball team out of the city. Bill: If that don't beat all!* □ *John: Now, here's a funny thing. South America used to be attached to Africa. Fred: That beats everything! John: Yeah.*

if the going gets tough Go to when the going gets tough.

If the mountain will not come to Mahomet, Mahomet must go to the mountain. *Prov.* If things do not change the way you want them to, you must adjust to the way they are. (*Mohammed* is often used instead of *Mahomet.* Also *the mountain has come to Mahomet,* something or someone that you would not expect to travel has arrived. There are many variations of this proverb. See the examples.) □ *The president won't see me so I will have to go to his office. If the mountain will not come to Mahomet, Mahomet must go to the mountain.* □ *If Caroline can't leave the hospital on her birthday, we'll have to take her birthday party to the hospital. If the mountain won't come to Mahomet, Mahomet will have to go to the mountain.* □ *It's true I don't usually leave my home, but if you can't come to see me, I'll have to come see you. The mountain will come to Mohammed.*

If the shoe fits(, wear it). *Prov.* An unflattering remark applies to you, so you should accept it. (Slightly rude.) □ *Fred: Hey, Jill, how's your love life? Jill: I don't like busybodies, Fred. Fred: Are you calling me a busybody? Jane: If the shoe fits, wear it.* □ *Ellen: The professor told me I don't write well! Bill: If the shoe fits, Ellen.*

if the truth were known *Prov.* if people knew how something really was, instead of how it appears to be. □ *If the truth were known, people wouldn't shop at that store. Its owners aren't as honest as they seem.* □ *Sam: You're always polite to Fred, but you don't really like him, do you? Alan: Well, no, if the truth were known.*

if (the) worst comes to (the) worst *Prov.* in the worst possible circumstances; if the worst possible thing should happen. □ *We should be able to catch the four-thirty train, but if the worst comes to the worst, we could get a taxi and still get into town on time.* □ *Of course, I hope that your wife's health recovers, but if worst comes to worst, I want you to know that we'd be happy to have you stay with us.*

If there's anything you need, don't hesitate to ask. a polite phrase offering help in finding something or by providing something. (Often said by a host or by someone helping someone settle into something. See also **If you don't see what you want, please ask (for it).**) □ *Mary: This looks very nice. I'll be quite comfortable here. Jane: If there's anything you need, don't hesitate to ask.* □ *"If there is anything you need, don't hesitate to ask," said the room clerk.*

If two ride on a horse, one must ride behind. *Prov.* When two people do something together, one of them will be the leader and the other will have to be subordinate. □ *Jane: How come every time we get together, we always do what you want to do, and never do what I want to do? Ellen: Well, dear, if two ride on a horse, one must ride behind.*

If wishes were horses, then beggars would ride. *Prov.* People make a lot of wishes, but wishing is useless. □ *Jill: If I were Queen of the World, I would make sure that everyone had enough to eat. Jane: And if wishes were horses, then beggars would ride.* □ *Alan: I sure wish I had one of those expensive cameras. Jane: If wishes were horses, then beggars would ride.*

If you can't be good, be careful. *Prov.* If you are going to do immoral things, make sure they are not dangerous.; If you are going to do something immoral, make sure to keep it secret. (Sometimes used as a flippant way of saying good-bye.) □ *Be a good girl on your vacation trip. Or if you can't be good, be careful.* □ *Ernest likes to close his letters with, "If you can't be good, be careful."*

If you can't beat them, join them. and **If you can't lick 'em, join 'em.** *Prov.* If you have to give up fighting some group because you can't win, band together with them. (The version with *lick* is informal.) □ *Jill: I just got a kitten. Jane: I can't believe it! You used to hate people who owned cats. Jill: If you can't beat them, join them.* □ *Alan: I hear you're a Republican now. Fred: Yeah, I figured, if you can't lick 'em, join 'em.*

If you can't lick 'em, join 'em. Go to previous.

If you can't stand the heat, get out of the kitchen. *Prov.* If the pressures of some situation are too much for you, you should leave that situation. (Somewhat insulting; implies that the person addressed cannot tolerate pressure.) □ *Alan: I didn't think being a stockbroker could be so stressful. Fred: If you can't stand the heat, get out of the kitchen.* □ *Jill: This exercise class is too tough; the teacher should let us slow down. Jane: If you can't stand the heat, get out of the kitchen.*

If you don't like it, (you can) lump it. *Prov.* Things cannot be changed to suit your preferences. □ *We're having fish for dinner tonight. And if you don't like it, you can lump it.* □ *We're going to go visit Aunt Sally this weekend. If you don't like it, lump it.*

If you don't make mistakes, you don't make anything. *Prov.* If you try to do something, you will likely make mistakes.; The only way to make no mistakes is to avoid trying to do anything. (Can be used to console someone who has made a mistake.) □ *Alan: I'm sorry* there's no dessert. I tried to make a cake, but I messed it up. Jane: That's OK, dear; if you don't make mistakes, you don't make anything. □ It's a shame that you ruined the sweater you were making, but if you don't make mistakes, you don't make anything.

If you don't mind! 1. an expression that rebukes someone for some minor social violation. □ *When Bill accidentally sat on Mary's purse, which she had placed in the seat next to her, she said, somewhat angrily, "If you don't mind!"* □ *Bill (pushing his way in front of Mary in the checkout line): Excuse me. Mary: If you don't mind! I was here first! Bill: I'm in a hurry. Mary: So am I!* **2.** a polite way of introducing a request. □ *Bill: If you don't mind, could you move a little to the left? Sally: No problem. (moving) Is that all right? Bill: Yeah. Great! Thanks!* □ *Jane: If you don't mind, could I have your broccoli? John: Help yourself.* **3.** a vague phrase answering yes to a question that asks whether one should do something. □ *Tom: Do you want me to take these dirty dishes away? Mary: If you don't mind.* □ *Bill: Shall I close the door? Sally: If you don't mind.*

If you don't see what you want, please ask (for it). and If you don't see what you want, just ask (for it). a polite phrase intended to help people get what they want. (See also **If there's anything you need, don't hesitate to ask.**) □ *Clerk: May I help you? Sue: I'm just looking. Clerk: If you don't see what you want, please ask.* □ *Clerk: I hope you enjoy your stay at our resort. If you don't see what you want, just ask for it. Sally: Great! Thanks.*

if you get my drift *Fig.* if you understand what I am saying or implying. (Akin to **get** someone's **drift.**) □ *I've heard enough talk and seen enough inaction—if you get my drift.*

if you know what's good for you *Fig.* if you know what will be to your benefit; if you know what will keep you out of trouble. □ *Mary: I see that Jane has put a big dent in her car. Sue: You'll keep quiet about that if you know what's good for you.* □ *Sally: My teacher told me I had better improve my spelling. Bill: If you know what's good for you, you'd better do it too.*

If you lie down with dogs, you will get up with fleas. *Prov.* If you associate with bad people, you will acquire their faults. □ *Granddaughter: It's not fair. I'm starting to get a bad reputation just because I'm friends with Suzy and she has a bad reputation. Grandmother: It's only natural. People think that if you lie down with dogs, you will get up with fleas.*

if you must All right, if you have to. □ *Sally: It's late. I have to move along. Mary: If you must. Good-bye. See you tomorrow.* □ *Alice: I'm taking these things with me. Jane: If you must, all right. They can stay here, though.*

If you play with fire, you get burned. *Prov.* If you do something dangerous, you will get hurt. □ *Joe said, "I have no sympathy for race-car drivers who get injured. They should know that if you play with fire, you get burned."* □ *My mother always told us that experimenting with hard drugs was playing with fire.*

if you please and **if you would(, please) 1.** a polite phrase indicating assent to a suggestion. □ *Bill: Shall I unload the car? Jane: If you please.* □ *Sue: Do you want me to take you to the station? Bob: If you would, please.* **2.** a polite phrase introducing or following a request. □ *John: If you please, the driveway needs sweeping. Jane: Here's the*

broom. Have at it. □ *Jane: Take these down to the basement, if you would, please. John: Can't think of anything I'd rather do, sweetie.*

If you run after two hares, you will catch neither. *Prov.* You cannot do two things successfully at the same time. □ *Vanessa: If I want to pursue my acting career, I'll have to take more days off to go to auditions. But I want to get ahead in the office, too. Jane: If you run after two hares, you will catch neither.*

If you want a thing done well, do it yourself. *Prov.* You cannot rely on other people to do things properly for you. (Sometimes *right* is used instead of *well*.) □ *I asked my son to chop the vegetables for me, but he's cut them into chunks too small to use. I should have known: if you want a thing done well, do it yourself.* □ *Laura wouldn't trust professional auto mechanics, and so did all her own car repair. "If you want something done right, do it yourself," she said.*

If you want peace, (you must) prepare for war. *Prov.* If a country is well armed, its opponents will be less likely to attack it. □ *Wilbur was always arguing with those of his friends who believed in disarmament. "Getting rid of our weapons won't promote peace," he would say. "If you want peace, you must prepare for war."*

If you would be well served, serve yourself. *Prov.* You should do things for yourself, since you cannot trust other people to do them exactly the way you want. □ *I would never hire a maid, because a maid wouldn't clean things the way I want them cleaned. Like they say: if you would be well served, serve yourself.*

if you would(, please) Go to **if you please.**

if you'll pardon the expression *Fig.* excuse the expression I am about to say or just said. □ *This thing is—if you'll pardon the expression—loused up.* □ *I'm really jacked, if you'll pardon the expression.*

If you're born to be hanged, then you'll never be drowned. *Prov.* If you escape one disaster, it must be because you are destined for a different kind of disaster. (Sometimes used to warn someone who has escaped drowning against gloating over good luck.) □ *When their ship was trapped in a terrible storm, Ellen told her husband that she feared they would die. "Don't worry," he replied with a yawn, "if you're born to be hanged, then you'll never be drowned."*

if you've a mind to do something *Rur.* if you really want to do something. □ *If you've a mind to run for class president, you'd best start making campaign posters.* □ *You can do just about anything if you've a mind to.*

Ignorance is bliss. *Prov.* Not knowing is better than knowing and worrying. □ *A: I never knew that the kid who mows our lawn has been in trouble with the police. B: Ignorance is bliss!*

Ignorance (of the law) is no excuse (for breaking it). *Prov.* Even if you do not know that something is against the law, you can still be punished for doing it. (An ancient legal principle.) □ *Police officer: I'm giving you a speeding ticket. Motorist: But I didn't know I was exceeding the speed limit! Police officer: Ignorance of the law is no excuse for breaking it.* □ *Terry protested that he didn't know it was illegal to break the windows of an abandoned build-*

ing, but the judge informed him that ignorance of the law was no excuse.

ill at ease uneasy; anxious. □ *I feel ill at ease about the interview.* □ *You look ill at ease. Please relax.*

I'll be a monkey's uncle! *Fig.* I am amazed! □ *A: I just won $500,000 in the lottery! B: Well, I'll be a monkey's uncle!*

(I'll) be right there. I'm coming. □ *Bill: Tom! Come here. Tom: Be right there.* □ *Mother: Can you come down here a minute? Child: I'll be right there, Mom.*

(I'll) be right with you. Please be patient, I will attend to you soon. (Often said by someone attending a sales counter or by an office receptionist.) □ *Mary: Oh, Miss? Clerk: I'll be right with you.* □ *Bob: Sally, can you come here for a minute? Sally: Be right with you.*

(I'll) be seeing you. Good-bye, I will see you sometime in the (near) future. □ *Bob: Bye. Be seeing you. Sally: Yeah. See you later.* □ *John: Have a good time on your vacation. I'll be seeing you. Sally: See you next week. Bye.*

I('ll) bet 1. *Inf.* I'm pretty sure that something is so or that something will happen. □ *Bob: You're late. I bet you miss your plane. Rachel: No, I won't.* □ *Sue: I'll bet it rains today. Alice: No way! There's not a cloud in the sky.* **2.** *Inf.* I agree. (Often sarcastic.) □ *Tom: They're probably going to raise taxes again next year. Henry: I bet.* □ *Fred: If we do that again, we'll really be in trouble. Andrew: I'll bet.*

I'll bite. *Inf.* Okay, I will answer your question.; Okay, I will listen to your joke or play your little guessing game. □ *Bob: Guess what is in this box? Bill: I'll bite. Bob: A new toaster!* □ *John: Did you hear the joke about the used car salesman? Jane: No, I'll bite.*

I'll call back later. a standard phrase indicating that a telephone caller will call again at a later time. □ *Sally: Is Bill there? Mary (speaking into the telephone): Sorry, he's not here right now. Sally: I'll call back later.* □ *John (speaking into the telephone): Hello. Is Fred there? Jane: No. Can I take a message? John: No, thanks. I'll call back later.*

(I'll) catch you later. *Inf.* I will talk to you later. □ *Mary: Got to fly. See you around. Sally: Bye. Catch you later.* □ *John: I have to go to class now. Bill: Okay, catch you later.*

I'll drink to that! *Inf.* I agree with that! (Originally used as a reply to a proposed toast.) □ *Great idea! I'll drink to that.* □ *That's a fine suggestion. I'll drink to that.*

I'll eat my hat. *Fig.* I will be very surprised. (Used to express strong disbelief in something.) □ *If Joe really joins the Army, I'll eat my hat.* □ *If this car gives you any trouble, I'll eat my hat.*

I'll get back to you (on that). and **Let me get back to you (on that).** I will report back later with my decision. (More likely said by a boss to an employee than vice versa.) □ *Bob: I have a question about the Wilson project. Mary: I have to go to a meeting now. I'll get back to you on that. Bob: It's sort of urgent. Mary: It can wait.* □ *Sue: Shall I close the Wilson account? Jane: Let me get back to you on that.*

I'll get right on it. I will begin work on that immediately. □ *Bob: Please do this report immediately. Fred: I'll get right on it.* □ *Jane: Please call Tom and ask him to rethink this proposal. John: I'll get right on it.*

I'll have the same. and The **same for me.** I would like the same thing that the last person chose. □ *Waitress: What would you like? Tom: Hamburger, fries, and coffee. Jane: I'll have the same.* □ *John: For dessert, I'll have strawberry ice cream. Bill: I'll have the same.*

I'll have to beg off. *Fig.* a polite expression used to turn down an informal invitation. □ *Andrew: Thank you for inviting me, but I'll have to beg off. I have a conflict. Henry: I'm sorry to hear that. Maybe some other time.* □ *Bill: Do you think you can come to the party? Bob: I'll have to beg off. I have another engagement. Bill: Maybe some other time.*

I'll (have to) let you go. *Fig.* It is time to end this phone conversation. □ *Well, I'll let you go. It's getting late.* □ *I have to go to work early tomorrow, so I'll let you go.*

I'll look you up when I'm in town. *Fig.* I will try to visit you or contact you the next time I am in town. □ *Bill: I hope to see you again sometime. Mary: I'll look you up when I'm in town.* □ *Andrew: Good-bye, Fred. It's been nice talking to you. I'll look you up when I'm in town. Fred: See you around, dude.*

I'll put a stop to that. I'll see that the just-mentioned undesirable activity is stopped. □ *Fred: There are two boys fighting in the hall. Bob: I'll put a stop to that.* □ *Sue: The sales force is ignoring almost every customer in the older neighborhoods. Mary: I'll put a stop to that!*

(I'll) see you in a little while. a phrase indicating that the speaker will see the person spoken to within a few hours at the most. □ *John: I'll see you in a little while. Jane: Okay. Bye till later.* □ *Sally: I have to get dressed for tonight. Fred: I'll pick you up about nine. See you in a little while. Sally: See you.*

I'll see you later. and **(See you) later.** Good-bye until I see you again. □ *John: Good-bye, Sally. I'll see you later. Sally: Until later, then.* □ *Bob: Time to go. Later. Mary: Later.*

(I'll) see you next year. a good-bye expression said toward the end of one year. □ *Bob: Happy New Year! Sue: You, too! See you next year.* □ *John: Bye. See you tomorrow. Mary: It's New Year's Eve. See you next year! John: Right! I'll see you next year!*

(I'll) see you (real) soon. Good-bye. I will meet you again soon. □ *Bill: Bye, Sue. See you. Sue: See you real soon, Bill.* □ *John: Bye, you two. Sally: See you soon. Jane: See you, John.*

(I'll) see you then. I will see you at the time we've just agreed upon. □ *John: Can we meet at noon? Bill: Sure. See you then. Bye. John: Bye.* □ *John: I'll pick you up just after midnight. Sally: See you then.*

(I'll) see you tomorrow. I will see you when we meet again tomorrow. (Typically said to someone whose daily schedule is the same as one's own.) □ *Bob: Bye, Jane. Jane: Good night, Bob. See you tomorrow.* □ *Sue: See you tomorrow. Jane: Until tomorrow. Bye.*

(I'll) talk to you soon. I will talk to you on the telephone again soon. □ *Sally: Bye now. Talk to you soon. John: Bye now.* □ *Bill: Nice talking to you. Bye. Mary: Talk to you soon. Bye.*

I'll thank you to keep your opinions to yourself. *Fig.* I do not care about your opinion of this matter. □

Jane: This place is sort of drab. John: I'll thank you to keep your opinions to yourself. □ *Bill: Your whole family is sort of loud. John: I'll thank you to keep your opinions to yourself.*

I'll thank you to mind your own business. *Fig.* a version of **Mind your own business.** (Shows a little anger.) □ *Tom: How much did this cost? Jane: I'll thank you to mind your own business.* □ *Bob: Is your house in your name or your brother's? John: I'll thank you to mind your own business.*

(I'll) try to catch you later. Go to next.

(I'll) try to catch you some other time. and **(I'll) try to catch you later.; I'll try to see you later.** *Fig.* We do not have time to talk now, so I'll try to talk to you or meet with you later. (An expression said when it is inconvenient for one or both parties to meet or converse.) □ *Bill: I need to get your signature on this contract. Sue: I really don't have a second to spare right now. Bill: Okay, I'll try to catch you some other time. Sue: Later this afternoon would be fine.* □ *Bill: I'm sorry for the interruptions, Tom. Things are very busy right now. Tom: I'll try to see you later.*

ill will hostile feelings or intentions. □ *I hope you do not have any ill will toward me because of our argument.* □ *Dave felt such ill will toward his family that he left his fortune to his best friend.*

ill-disposed to doing something not friendly; not favorable; opposed. □ *I am ill-disposed to doing hard labor.* □ *The police chief was ill-disposed to discussing the details of the case to the news reporters.*

ill-gotten gains money or other possessions acquired in a dishonest or illegal fashion. □ *Bill cheated at cards and is now living on his ill-gotten gains.* □ *Mary is enjoying her ill-gotten gains. She deceived an old lady into leaving her $5,000 in her will.*

illuminate something **with** something **1.** *Lit.* to light up something with something. □ *The lights illuminated the monument with a bright glow.* □ *The monument was illuminated with mercury vapor lamps.* **2.** *Fig.* to clarify or elucidate something with explanation. □ *Please try to illuminate this matter with an explanation.* □ *Could you illuminate your answer with a little more detail?* **3.** to decorate a manuscript with pictures or designs, as done in medieval monasteries. □ *The monks spent all their days illuminating manuscripts with pictures.* □ *No one has the patience to illuminate books with tiny designs.*

illustrate something **with** something **1.** to provide pictorial examples for a book or other document. □ *She illustrated her book with clever line drawings.* □ *We need someone to illustrate this book with drawings.* **2.** *Fig.* to use something to show how something works, how something is meant to be, or how to do something. □ *Would you please illustrate how to do it with a drawing or two?* □ *I think I can illustrate what I mean with a little more explanation.*

(I'm) afraid not. and **'Fraid not.** I believe, regrettably, that the answer is no. (The apostrophe is not always shown.) □ *Rachel: Can I expect any help with this problem? Henry: I'm afraid not.* □ *Andrew: Will you be there when I get there? Bill: Afraid not.*

(I'm) afraid so. and **'Fraid so.** I believe, regrettably, that the answer is yes. (The apostrophe is not always shown.) □ *Alice: Do you have to go? John: Afraid so.* □ *Rachel: Can I expect some difficulty with Mr. Franklin? Bob: I'm afraid so.*

I'm all ears. Go to I'm listening.

I'm awful at names. Go to I'm terrible at names.

I'm busy. Do not bother me now.; I cannot attend to your needs now. □ *Bob: Can I talk to you? Bill: I'm busy. Bob: It's important. Bill: Sorry, I'm busy!* □ *Fred: Can you help me with this? Bill: I'm busy. Can it wait a minute? Fred: Sure. No rush.*

I'm cool. *Inf.* I'm fine. □ *Bob: How you been? Fred: I'm cool, man. Yourself? Bob: The same.* □ *Father: How are you, son? Bill: I'm cool, Dad. Father (joking): So should I turn up the heat?*

I'm damned if I do and damned if I don't. *Fig.* There are problems if I do something and problems if I don't do it. □ *I can't win. I'm damned if I do and damned if I don't.* □ *No matter whether I go or stay, I am in trouble. I'm damned if I do and damned if I don't.*

(I'm) delighted to have you (here). and **(We're) delighted to have you (here).** You're welcome here any time.; Glad you could come. (See also **(It's) good to have you here.**) □ *Bill: Thank you for inviting me for dinner, Mr. Franklin. Bill: I'm delighted to have you.* □ *"We're delighted to see you," said Tom's grandparents. "It's so nice to have you here for a visit."*

(I'm) delighted to make your acquaintance. *Fig.* I am very glad to meet you. □ *Tom: My name is Tom. I work in the advertising department. Mary: I'm Mary. I work in accounting. Delighted to make your acquaintance. Tom: Yeah. Good to meet you.* □ *Fred: Sue, this is Bob. He'll be working with us on the Wilson project. Sue: I'm delighted to make your acquaintance, Bob. Bob: My pleasure.*

(I'm) doing okay. 1. *Inf.* I'm just fine. □ *Bob: How you doing? Bill: Doing okay. And you? Bob: Things could be worse.* □ *Mary: How are things going? Sue: I'm doing fine, thanks. And you? Mary: Doing okay.* **2.** *Inf.* I'm doing as well as can be expected.; I'm feeling better. □ *Mary: How are you feeling? Sue: I'm doing okay—as well as can be expected.* □ *Tom: I hope you're feeling better. Sally: I'm doing okay, thanks.*

I'm easy (to please). I accept that because I am not particular.; That's okay with me. □ *Tom: Hey, man! Do you care if we get a sausage pizza rather than mushroom? Bob: Fine with me. I'm easy.* □ *Mary: How do you like this music? Bob: It's great, but I'm easy to please.*

(I'm) feeling okay. I am doing well.; I am feeling well. □ *Alice: How are you feeling? Jane: I'm feeling okay.* □ *John: How are things going? Fred: Feeling okay.*

(I'm) glad to hear it. a phrase expressing pleasure at what the speaker has just said. □ *Sally: We have a new car, finally. Mary: I'm glad to hear it.* □ *Tom: Is your sister feeling better? Bill: Oh, yes, thanks. Tom: Glad to hear it.*

(I'm) glad you could come. and **(We're) glad you could come.** a phrase said by the host or hostess [or both] to a guest. □ *Tom: Thank you so much for having me. Sally: We're glad you could come. John: Yes, we are. Bye.* □ *Bill: Bye. Sally: Bye, Bill. Glad you could come.*

(I'm) glad you could drop by. and **(We're) glad you could drop by.; (I'm) glad you could stop by.; (We're) glad you could stop by.** a phrase said by the host or hostess (or both) to a guest who has appeared suddenly or has come for only a short visit. □ *Tom: Good-bye. Had a nice time. Mary: Thank you for coming, Tom. Glad you could drop by.* □ *Tom: Thank you so much for having me. Sally: We're glad you could drop by.*

I'm gone. *Inf.* an expression said just before leaving. (See also **I'm out of here.**) □ *Bob: Well, that's all. I'm gone. Bill: See ya!* □ *Jane: I'm gone. See you guys. John: See you, Jane. Fred: Bye, Jane.*

(I'm) having a wonderful time; wish you were here. *Cliché* a catchphrase that is thought to be written onto postcards by people who are away on vacation. □ *John wrote on all his cards, "Having a wonderful time; wish you were here." And he really meant it too.* □ *"I'm having a wonderful time; wish you were here," said Tom, speaking on the phone to Mary, suddenly feeling very insincere.*

I'm having quite a time. 1. *Lit.* I am having a very enjoyable time. □ *John: Having fun? Jane: Oh, yes. I'm having quite a time.* □ *Bob: Do you like the seashore? Sally: Yes, I'm having quite a time.* **2.** *Fig.* I am having a very difficult time. □ *Doctor: Well, what seems to be the problem? Mary: I'm having quite a time. It's my back. Doctor: Let's take a look at it.* □ *Father: How's school? Bill: Pretty tough. I'm having quite a time. Calculus is killing me.*

(I'm) having the time of my life. *Fig.* I am having the best time ever. □ *Bill: Are you having a good time, Mary? Mary: Don't worry about me. I'm having the time of my life.* □ *Mary: What do you think about this theme park? Bill: Having the time of my life. I don't want to leave.*

I'm history. *Inf.* Good-bye, I am leaving. □ *I'm history. See you tomorrow.* □ *Later. I'm history.*

(I'm) just getting by. an expression indicating that one is just surviving financially or otherwise. □ *Bob: How you doing, Tom? Tom: Just getting by, Bob.* □ *"I wish I could get a better job," remarked Tom. "I'm just getting by as it is."*

I'm just looking. Go to **I'm only looking.**

(I'm just) minding my own business. *Fig.* an answer to a greeting inquiry asking what one is doing. (This answer also can carry the implication "Since I am minding my own business, why aren't you minding your own business?") □ *Tom: Hey, man, what are you doing? Bill: Minding my own business. See you around.* □ *Sue: Hi, Mary. What have you been doing? Mary: I'm just minding my own business and trying to keep out of trouble.*

(I'm) (just) plugging along. *Inf.* I am doing satisfactorily.; I am just managing to function. □ *Bill: How are things going? Bob: I'm just plugging along.* □ *Sue: How are you doing, Fred? Fred: Just plugging along, thanks. And you? Sue: About the same.*

(I'm) (just) thinking out loud. *Fig.* I'm saying things that might better remain as private thoughts. (A way of characterizing or introducing one's opinions or thoughts. Also past tense.) □ *Sue: What are you saying, anyway? Sounds like you're scolding someone. Bob: Oh, sorry. I was just thinking out loud.* □ *Bob: Now, this goes over here. Bill:*

You want me to move that? Bob: Oh, no. Just thinking out loud.

I'm like you an expression introducing a statement of a similarity that the speaker shares with the person spoken to. □ *Mary: And what do you think about this pair? Jane: I'm like you, I like the ones with lower heels.* □ *"I'm like you," confided Fred. "I think everyone ought to pay the same amount."*

I'm listening. and **I'm all ears.** *Inf.* You have my attention, so you should talk. □ *Bob: Look, old pal. I want to talk to you about something. Tom: I'm listening.* □ *Bill: I guess I owe you an apology. Jane: I'm all ears.*

I'm not finished with you. I still have more to say to you. □ *Bill started to turn away when he thought the scolding was finished. "I'm not finished with you," bellowed his father.* □ *When the angry teacher paused briefly to catch his breath, Bob turned as if to go. "I'm not finished with you," screamed the teacher, "Don't leave here until I say you can!"*

I'm not kidding. I am telling the truth.; I am not trying to fool you. □ *Mary: Those guys are all suspects in the robbery. Sue: No! They can't be! Mary: I'm not kidding!* □ *John (gesturing): The fish I caught was this big! Jane: I don't believe it! John: I'm not kidding!*

I'm not surprised. and **I don't wonder.** It is not surprising.; It should not surprise anyone. □ *Mary: All this talk about war has my cousin very worried. Sue: No doubt. At his age, I don't wonder.* □ *John: All of the better-looking ones sold out right away. Jane: I'm not surprised.*

I'm off. an expression said by someone who is just leaving. □ *Bob: Time to go. I'm off. Mary: Bye.* □ *Sue: Well, it's been a great party. Good-bye. Got to go. Mary: I'm off too. Bye.*

I'm only looking. and **I'm just looking.** I am not a buyer, I am only examining your merchandise. (A phrase said to a shopkeeper or clerk who asks **May I help you?**) □ *Clerk: May I help you? Mary: No, thanks. I'm only looking.* □ *Clerk: May I help you? Jane: I'm just looking, thank you.*

I'm out of here. and **I'm outa here.** *Inf.* I am leaving this minute. □ *In three minutes I'm outa here.* □ *I'm out of here. Bye.*

(I'm) pleased to meet you. an expression said when introduced to someone. (See also **(I'm) (very) glad to meet you.**) □ *Tom: I'm Tom Thomas. Bill: Pleased to meet you. I'm Bill Franklin.* □ *John: Have you met Sally Hill? Bill: I don't believe I've had the pleasure. I'm pleased to meet you, Sally. Sally: My pleasure, Bill.*

I'm (really) fed up (with someone or something). *Fig.* I have had enough of someone or something. Something must be done. □ *Tom: This place is really dull. John: Yeah. I'm fed up with it. I'm out of here!* □ *Sally: Can't you do anything right? Bill: I'm really fed up with your complaining! You're always picking on me!*

(I'm) sorry. an expression used to excuse oneself politely or apologize, especially when one has collided with someone, when one has offended someone, or to ask someone to repeat what has been said. □ *"I'm sorry," I said to the woman I bumped into.* □ *I'm sorry, what did you say? I couldn't hear you.*

(I'm) sorry to hear that. an expression of consolation or regret. □ *John: My cat died last week. Jane: I'm sorry to hear that.* □ *Bill: I'm afraid I won't be able to continue here as head teller. Bank manager: Sorry to hear that.*

(I'm) sorry you asked (that). I regret that you asked about something I wanted to forget. □ *Tom: What on earth is this hole in your suit jacket? Bill: I'm sorry you asked. I was feeding a squirrel and it bit through my pocket where the food was.* □ *Sally: Why is there only canned soup in the cupboard? John: Sorry you asked that. I just haven't been to the grocery store in awhile. Sally: Want some soup?*

I'm speechless. *Fig.* I am so surprised that I cannot think of anything to say. □ *Mary: Fred and I eloped last week. Sally: I'm speechless.* □ *Tom: The mayor just died! Jane: What? I'm speechless!*

I'm terrible at names. and **I'm awful at names.** I can't seem to remember anyone's name. (Said as an apology to someone whose name you have forgotten.) □ *I'm terrible at names. Please tell me yours again.* □ *Haven't we met already? I'm awful at names.*

(I'm) (very) glad to meet you. a polite expression said to a person to whom one has just been introduced. (See also **(I'm) pleased to meet you.**) □ *Mary: I'd like you to meet my brother, Tom. Bill: I'm very glad to meet you, Tom.* □ *Jane: Hi! I'm Jane. Bob: Glad to meet you. I'm Bob.*

I'm with you. I agree with you.; I will join with you in doing what you suggest. (With a stress on both *I* and *you*.) □ *Sally: I think this old bridge is sort of dangerous. Jane: I'm with you. Let's go back another way.* □ *Bob: This restaurant looks horrible. Bill: I'm with you. Want to go somewhere else?*

imagine someone or something **as** someone or something to think of someone or something as another person or another type of thing. □ *I really can't imagine you as a sailor.* □ *When I imagine John as our new president, I really worry about our future as a company.*

Imagine that! Go to **Fancy that!**

imbue someone **with** something to indoctrinate someone with something; to build something into someone. □ *I tried to imbue my children with a strong sense of justice.* □ *Her thinking and attitudes had been imbued with childhood fears.*

Imitation is the sincerest form of flattery. *Prov.* Copying someone is flattering because it shows you want to be like that person. □ *Child: Susie's doing everything I do. Make her stop. Mother: Don't be cross with her. Imitation is the sincerest form of flattery.* □ *Imitation may be the sincerest form of flattery, but I don't feel flattered when Mary copies my answers to the homework.*

immediate occupancy [of an apartment or house] ready to be moved into at this moment. □ *This house is for immediate occupancy. You can move in today if you want.* □ *The apartment is empty, so that means immediate occupancy.*

immerse someone or something **in** something **1.** *Lit.* to submerge someone or something beneath the surface of a liquid; to soak someone or something in a liquid. □ *The preacher immersed the baptism candidate in the water.* □ *We immersed all the dirty plates in the soapy water and left them to soak.* □ *She immersed herself in the bathwater.*

2. *Fig.* to saturate or steep someone or a group in information or some type of instruction. □ *The trainers immersed us in details day after day.* □ *The teachers will immerse the entire class in nothing but the Spanish language, day after day.*

immigrate (in)to some place **(from** some place**)** to migrate into a place from some other place. □ *Many of them immigrated into Minnesota from northern Europe.* □ *My family immigrated to Chicago.*

immunize someone **against** something to vaccinate someone against some disease; to do a medical procedure that causes a resistance or immunity to a disease to develop in a person. □ *They wanted to immunize all the children against the measles.* □ *Have you been immunized against polio?*

impact (up)on someone or something [for something] to have an effect on someone or something. (*Upon* is formal and less commonly used than *on.*) □ *This plant closing will impact upon the local economy for years to come.* □ *The day's troubles impacted on Rachel quite seriously.*

impale someone or something **on** something to put someone or something on a pointed object and press down. □ *The crowd had impaled an effigy of the dictator on a sharpened stick.* □ *The waves almost impaled me on a submerged tree branch.*

impart something **to** someone or something **1.** to bestow a quality on someone or a group. □ *That hat imparts an aura of grandeur to her presence.* □ *Walnut paneling imparts an expensive seriousness to a law office.* **2.** to tell something to someone or a group. □ *My professor tried to impart her knowledge to us.* □ *The speaker imparted a great deal of wisdom to the group.*

impeach someone **for** something **1.** to charge someone with doing something illegal. □ *You can't impeach her for just disagreeing!* □ *We tried to impeach Gus for failing to attend sessions.* **2.** to criticize or discredit someone for something. □ *The opposition impeached him for his position in no uncertain terms.* □ *Liz was impeached by the press for her views.*

impinge (up)on someone or something to affect or interfere with someone or something. (*Upon* is formal and less commonly used than *on.*) □ *This will not impinge upon me at all.* □ *Will this matter impinge on my policies in any way?*

implant something **in(to)** someone or something to embed something into someone or something. □ *The surgeon implanted a pacemaker into Fred.* □ *They implanted the device in Fred's chest.*

implicate someone **(in** something**)** to suggest that someone is involved in something. □ *The mayor was implicated in the bribery scandal.* □ *Jane's essay implicated her teacher in the cheating scandal.*

import something **(from** something**) ((in)to** something**)** to buy and transport something from a foreign place into a country. □ *We imported the carpets from the Orient into this country.* □ *They imported wine into this country from France.* □ *I imported this from Germany.*

an **important milestone in** someone's **life** Go to a **milestone in** someone's **life.**

impose something **(up)on** someone to force something on someone. (*Upon* is formal and less commonly used than *on*.) ☐ *Don't try to impose your ideas upon me!* ☐ *The colonists tried to impose their values on the indigenous peoples.*

impose (up)on someone to be a bother to someone; to make a request of something to someone. (Often refers to being an overnight guest or having a meal at someone's house. *Upon* is formal and less commonly used than *on*.) ☐ *I don't mean to impose upon you, but could you put me up for the night?* ☐ *Don't worry, I won't let you impose on me.*

impregnate something **with** something **1.** *Lit.* to saturate something with something; to penetrate something with some fluid. ☐ *They impregnated the boards with a wood preservative.* ☐ *The process impregnated the fibers with a bright yellow dye.* **2.** *Fig.* to put something negative into something. ☐ *You have impregnated the entire matter with unpleasantness.* ☐ *The whole scheme has been impregnated with needless flaws.*

impress someone **as** something to be memorable to someone as a particular type of person. ☐ *She didn't impress me as a particularly wise individual.* ☐ *Liz impressed us all as a skilled artisan.*

impress someone **by** something to make someone notice one's good qualities. ☐ *You impress me by your willingness to serve.* ☐ *We were all impressed by your candor.*

impress someone **with** someone or something to awe someone with someone or something. ☐ *Are you trying to impress me with your wisdom?* ☐ *She impressed him with her friend, who was very tall.*

impress something **into** something to press something into something. ☐ *I impressed the key into the wax, making a perfect copy.* ☐ *Andy impressed his thumb into the pie.*

impress something **(up)on** someone to make someone fully aware of something. (*Upon* is formal and less commonly used than *on*.) ☐ *You must impress these facts upon everyone you meet.* ☐ *She impressed its importance on me.*

impress something **(up)on** something to press something into the surface of something, leaving a mark. ☐ *The ribbing of my socks impressed a pattern upon my calves.* ☐ *The heavy vase impressed its outline on the pine tabletop.*

imprint something **into** something Go to next.

imprint something **on(to)** something **1.** to print something onto something. ☐ *We imprinted your name onto your stationery and your business cards.* ☐ *Please imprint my initials on this label.* **2.** and **imprint** something **into** something to record something firmly in the memory of someone. ☐ *The severe accident imprinted a sense of fear onto Lucy's mind.* ☐ *Imprint the numbers into your brain and never forget them!* **3.** and **imprint** something **into** something to make a permanent record of something in an animal's brain. (As with newly hatched fowl, which imprint the image of the first moving creature they see into their brains.) ☐ *The sight of its mother imprinted itself on the little gosling's brain.* ☐ *Nature imprints this information into the bird's memory.*

imprint something **with** something to print something with a message. ☐ *Amy imprinted each bookmark with her name.* ☐ *Each bookmark was imprinted with her name.*

imprison someone **in** something to lock someone up in something. ☐ *The authorities imprisoned him in a separate cell.* ☐ *Bob imprisoned Timmy in the closet for an hour.*

improve (up)on something to make something better. (*Upon* is formal and less commonly used than *on*.) ☐ *Do you really think you can improve upon this song?* ☐ *No one can improve on my favorite melody.*

improvise on something [for a musician] to create a new piece of music on an existing musical theme. ☐ *For an encore, the organist improvised on "Mary Had a Little Lamb."* ☐ *She chose to improvise on an old folk theme.*

impute something **to** someone or something to ascribe something to someone or something; to attribute something to someone or something. ☐ *I didn't mean to impute a bad intention to your company.* ☐ *The lawyer imputed perjury to the witness.*

*in a bad mood sad; depressed; grouchy; with low spirits. (*Typically: **be** ~; **get** ~; **put** someone ~.) ☐ *He's in a bad mood. He may yell at you.* ☐ *Please try to cheer me up. I'm in a bad mood.*

in a bad way Go to in bad shape.

in a big way very much; intensely. ☐ *I'm really interested in her in a big way.* ☐ *He plays to win—in a big way.*

*in a bind and ***in a jam** *Fig.* in a tight or difficult situation; stuck on a problem. (*Typically: **be** ~; **get [into]** ~; **find** oneself ~.) ☐ *I'm in a bind. I owe a lot of money.* ☐ *Whenever I get into a jam, I ask my supervisor for help.* ☐ *When things get busy around here, we get in a bind. We could use another helper.*

in a (blue) funk sad; depressed. ☐ *I've been in a blue funk all week.* ☐ *Don't get in a funk about your job. Things'll get better.*

*in a body *Fig.* as a group of people; as a group; in a group. (*Typically: **arrive** some place ~; **go** ~; **leave** ~; **reach** some place ~; **travel** ~.) ☐ *The tour members always traveled in a body.*

in a cold sweat in a state of fear. ☐ *He stood there in a cold sweat, waiting for something bad to happen.* ☐ *I was in a cold sweat while they counted the ballots.*

in a (constant) state of flux Go to in flux.

in a coon's age and **in a month of Sundays** *Rur.* in a very long time. (The *coon* is a *raccoon*.) ☐ *How are you? I haven't seen you in a coon's age.* ☐ *I haven't had a piece of apple pie this good in a coon's age.*

in a dead heat *Fig.* [finishing a race] at exactly the same time; tied. ☐ *The two horses finished the race in a dead heat.* ☐ *They ended the contest in a dead heat.*

in a delicate condition *Euph.* pregnant. (Old fashioned.) ☐ *Are you sure you're up for this hike? I know you're in a delicate condition.* ☐ *She shouldn't be lifting those boxes. She's in a delicate condition.*

in a dither confused; nervous; bothered. ☐ *Mary is sort of in a dither lately.* ☐ *Don't get yourself in a dither.*

*in a family way and ***in the family way** *Fig.* pregnant. (*Typically: **be** ~; **get** someone ~.) ☐ *I've heard that Mrs. Smith is in a family way.* ☐ *Our dog is in the family way.*

*in a fix *Fig.* in a bad situation. (*Typically: **be ~; get [into]** ~.) □ *I really got myself into a fix. I owe a lot of money on my taxes.* □ *John is in a fix because he lost his wallet.* □ *John got into a fix.*

in a flash *Fig.* quickly; immediately. □ *I'll be there in a flash.* □ *It happened in a flash. Suddenly my wallet was gone.*

in a fog and **in a haze** *Fig.* dazed; not paying attention to what is going on around one; not alert. □ *Jane always seems to be in a fog.* □ *When I get up, I'm in a fog for an hour.* □ *After surgery, I was in a haze until the anesthetic wore off.*

in a heartbeat *Fig.* almost immediately. □ *If I had the money, I would go back to college in a heartbeat.* □ *Just tell me that you need me and I'll come there in a heartbeat.*

*in a huff *Fig.* in an angry or offended manner. (*Typically: **be ~; get [into]** ~.) □ *He heard what we had to say, then left in a huff.* □ *She came in a huff and ordered us to bring her something to eat.*

in a jam Go to in a bind.

in a jiffy *Fig.* very fast; very soon. □ *Just wait a minute. I'll be there in a jiffy.* □ *I'll be finished in a jiffy.*

*in a lather *Fig.* flustered; excited and agitated. (*Typically: **be ~; get [into]** ~.) □ *Now, calm down. Don't be in a lather.* □ *I always get in a lather when I'm late.* □ *I get into a lather easily.*

in a little bit *Fig.* in a small amount of time. □ *I will be there in a little bit. Please wait.* □ *In a little bit, we can go outside and play.*

in a mad rush *Fig.* in a hurry. □ *I ran around all day today in a mad rush, looking for a present for Bill.* □ *Why are you always in a mad rush?*

in a month of Sundays Go to in a coon's age.

in a nutshell *Fig.* [of news or information] in a (figurative) capsule; in summary. □ *This cable channel provides the latest news in a nutshell.* □ *In a nutshell, what happened at work today?*

In a pig's ass! Go to In a pig's eye!

In a pig's ear! Go to next.

In a pig's eye! and **In a pig's ass!; In a pig's ear!** *Rur.* Nonsense! (Use caution with *ass.*) □ *Tom: I wasn't going to steal it. I was just looking at it. Jane: In a pig's eye! I saw you put it in your pocket!* □ *Mary: Bill says he's sorry and he'll never yell at me again if I take him back. Jane: In a pig's ass! He's made those promises a hundred times before.* □ *Tom: I thought you said I could keep this. Charlie: In a pig's ear! I said you could borrow it.*

in a pinch as a substitute. □ *A piece of clothing can be used as a bandage in a pinch.* □ *In a pinch, you can use folded paper to prop up the table leg so the table won't rock.*

in a pique *Fig.* having a feeling of resentment; feeling that one's pride has been hurt. □ *In a real pique, Anne insulted all of her friends.* □ *John's found himself in a pique over Bob's harsh criticism.*

*in a (pretty) pickle *Fig.* in a mess; in trouble. (*Typically: **be ~; get [into]** ~.) □ *John has gotten himself into a pickle. He has two dates for the party.* □ *Now we are in a pretty pickle. We are out of gas.*

*in a quandary uncertain about what to do; perplexed. (*Typically: **be ~; get [into]** ~.) □ *Mary was in a quandary about what college to go to.* □ *I couldn't decide what to do. I was in such a quandary.*

*in a rut *Fig.* in a type of boring habitual behavior. (As when the wheels of a buggy travel in the ruts worn into the ground by other buggies making it easiest to go exactly the way all the other buggies have gone before. *Typically: **be ~; get** ~.) □ *My life has gotten into a rut.* □ *I try not to get into a rut.*

in a sense in a way; in one way of looking at it. □ *In a sense, cars make life better.* □ *But, in a sense, they also make life worse.*

in (a) shambles *Fig.* in a messy state; destroyed. □ *After the earthquake, the town lay in shambles.* □ *The TV set was in a shambles after John tried to fix it.*

*in (a) single file *Fig.* lined up, one behind the other; in a line, one person or one thing wide. (*Typically: **be ~; get [into]** ~; **march** ~; **walk** ~.) □ *Have you ever seen ducks walking in single file?* □ *Please get into single file.* □ *Please march in single file.*

in a snit *Fig.* in a fit of anger or irritation. □ *Don't get in a snit. It was an accident.* □ *Mary is in a snit because they didn't ask her to come to the shindig.*

in a split second Go to a split second.

in a stage whisper *Fig.* in a loud whisper that everyone can hear. □ *John said in a stage whisper, "This play is boring."* □ *"When do we eat?" asked Billy in a stage whisper.*

*in a stew (about someone or something**)** *Fig.* upset or bothered about someone or something. (*Typically: **be ~; get [into]** ~.) □ *I'm in such a stew about my dog. She ran away last night.* □ *Now, now. Don't get in a stew. She'll be back when she gets hungry.*

in a stupor in a dazed condition; in a condition in which one cannot concentrate or think. □ *The drunk driver walked away from the car accident in a stupor.* □ *In the morning, Mary remains in a stupor until she drinks coffee.*

*in a (tight) spot *Fig.* caught in a problem; in a jam. (*Typically: **be ~; get [into]** ~. See also in a bind and the examples.) □ *Look, John, I'm in a tight spot. Can you lend me twenty dollars?* □ *I'm in a spot too. I need $300.*

*in a tizzy *Fig.* in an excited and confused condition. (*Typically: **be ~; get [into]** ~.) □ *John is in a tizzy because we're an hour late.* □ *Mary was in a tizzy when she couldn't find her keys.*

in a twit upset; frantic. □ *She's all in a twit because she lost her keys.* □ *Pete was in a twit and was quite rude to us.*

in a twitter in a giddy state; silly. □ *Don't get yourself in a twitter.* □ *We were all in a twitter over the upcoming event.*

*in a vicious circle *Fig.* in a situation in which the solution of one problem leads to a second problem, and the solution of the second problem brings back the first problem, etc. (*Typically: **be ~; get [into]** ~.) □ *Life is so strange. I seem to be in a vicious circle most of the time.* □ *I put lemon in my tea to make it sour, then sugar to make it sweet. I'm in a vicious circle.* □ *Don't let your life get into a vicious circle.*

in a word *Fig.* said simply; concisely said. □ *Mrs. Smith is—in a word—haughty.* □ *In a word, the play flopped.*

*in a world of one's **own** *Fig.* aloof; detached; self-centered. (*Typically: **be ~; get [into] ~; live ~.**) □ *John lives in a world of his own. He has very few friends.* □ *Mary walks around in a world of her own, but she's very intelligent.*

in abeyance in reserve. □ *Until the judge determined that the evidence could be used in the trial, it was held in abeyance.* □ *I kept my opinion in abeyance.*

in accord (with someone or something**) (about** someone or something**)** agreeing with someone or something. □ *I am in complete accord with you about the policy changes.* □ *We are in accord about the proposal.*

in accordance with something in agreement with something; in conformity with something. □ *In accordance with our discussion, I have prepared a contract.* □ *I did this in accordance with your request.*

in addition (to something**)** additionally; further; more-over; as an additional thing or person. □ *In addition, I would like for you to sweep the kitchen floor.* □ *I put the books away, and in addition to that, I cleaned up my desk.*

in advance [of something given, paid, or provided] before it is due. □ *The bill isn't due for a month, but I paid it in advance.* □ *I want my pay in advance.*

in agreement (with someone or something**)** in conformity with someone or something; agreeing with someone or something. □ *We are in total agreement.* □ *I am in agreement with your proposal.*

in (all) good conscience *Fig.* having good motives; displaying motives that will not result in a guilty conscience. □ *In all good conscience, I could not recommend that you buy this car.* □ *In good conscience, she could not accept the reward. She had only been acting as a good citizen should.*

in all my born days *Rur.* in my entire life. □ *I've never seen such fireworks in all my born days.* □ *That's the best party I was ever at in all my born days.*

in all probability very likely; almost certainly. □ *He'll be here on time in all probability.* □ *In all probability, they'll finish the work today.*

in an age of years *Rur.* in a long time. □ *How have you been? I haven't talked to you in an age of years.* □ *Jane hasn't ridden a horse in an age of years.*

*in an interesting condition *Euph.* pregnant. (*Typically: **be ~; get ~.**) □ *Young Mrs. Lutin is in an interesting condition.* □ *The bride appeared to be in an interesting condition.*

*in an ivory tower *Fig.* in a place, such as a university, where one can be aloof from the realities of living. (*Typically: **be ~; dwell ~; live ~; work ~.**) □ *If you didn't spend so much time in your ivory tower, you'd know what people really think!* □ *Many professors are said to live in ivory towers. They don't know what the real world is like.*

in and of itself considering it alone. □ *The idea in and of itself is not bad, but the side issues introduce many difficulties.* □ *Her action, in and of itself, caused us no problem.*

in any case and **in any event** no matter what happens. □ *I intend to be home by supper time, but in any case by eight o'clock.* □ *In any event, I'll see you this evening.*

in any event Go to previous.

in any way, shape, or form *Fig.* in any manner. □ *I refuse to tell a lie in any way, shape, or form!*

*in apple-pie order *Fig.* in very good order; very well organized. (*Typically: **be ~; get** something **~; put** something **~.**) □ *Please put everything in apple-pie order before you leave.* □ *I always put my desk in apple-pie order every evening.* □ *I've put my entire life into apple-pie order.*

*in arrears [of debts; of an account] overdue. (*Typically: **be ~; get ~.**) □ *Jane's student-loan payments are in arrears.* □ *The accounts of the bankrupt company were in arrears.*

in (at) one ear and out (of) the other *Prov.* heard but not remembered. (Used to describe something that some-one does not listen to.) □ *Ellen: Did you tell Junior to be careful with the car when he drives it? Fred: Yes, but I think it went in one ear and out the other.* □ *The teacher felt that everything she told her students was in one ear and out the other.*

in at the kill and **in on the kill 1.** *Lit.* present and participating in the killing of prey. □ *The baby cheetah wanted to be in on the kill.* **2.** *Fig.* involved at the final moment of something in order to share in the spoils. □ *At the end of the battle, everyone wanted to be in at the kill.* □ *The press packed the room, wanting to be in on the kill of the governor's resignation.*

in awe (of someone or something**)** fearful and respectful of someone or something. □ *Everyone in the country was in awe of the king and queen.* □ *I love my new car. In fact, I'm in awe of it.*

in bad faith *Fig.* without sincerity; with bad or dishonest intent; with duplicity. □ *It appears that you acted in bad faith and didn't live up to the terms of our agreement.* □ *If you do things in bad faith, you'll get a bad reputation.*

in bad shape and **in a bad way 1.** *Lit.* injured or debilitated in any manner. □ *Fred had a little accident, and he's in bad shape.* □ *Tom needs exercise. He's in bad shape.* **2.** pregnant. □ *Jill's in bad shape again, I hear.* □ *Yup, she's in bad shape all right—about three months in bad shape.* **3.** *Fig. Inf.* intoxicated. □ *Two glasses of that stuff and I'm in really bad shape.* □ *Fred is in bad shape. I think he's going to toss his cookies.*

in bad sorts in a bad humor. □ *Bill is in bad sorts today. He's very grouchy.* □ *I try to be extra nice to people when I'm in bad sorts.*

in bad taste and **in poor taste** rude; vulgar; obscene. □ *Mrs. Franklin felt that your joke was in bad taste.* □ *We found the play to be in poor taste, so we walked out in the middle of the second act.*

*in bad (with someone**)** in trouble with someone. (*Typically: **be ~; get ~.**) □ *I tried not to get in bad with Wally.* □ *We got in bad with each other from the start.*

in behalf of someone and **in** someone's **behalf; on behalf of** someone; **on** someone's **behalf; in** someone's **name** [doing something] as someone's agent; [doing something] in place of someone; for the benefit of some-one. □ *I'm writing in behalf of Mr. Smith, who has applied* *for a job with your company.* □ *I'm calling on behalf of my client, who wishes to complain about your actions.* □ *I'm calling in her behalf.* □ *I'm acting on your behalf.*

in between located in the middle of two things, states, or possibilities. □ *The bath water is not hot or cold. It's in between.* □ *A sandwich consists of two slices of bread with some other food in between.*

*in black and white *Fig.* [of an agreement, contract, or statement] official, in writing or printing. (*Typically: **be** ~; **get** something ~.) □ *I have it in black and white that I'm entitled to three weeks of vacation each year.*

in bloom Go to next.

in blossom and **in bloom** blooming; covered with blossoms. □ *All the apple trees are in blossom now.* □ *When are the fruit trees in bloom in this part of the country?*

in brief briefly; concisely. □ *The whole story, in brief, is that Bob failed algebra because he did not study.* □ *Please tell me in brief why you want this job.*

in broad daylight in the open light of day; clearly visible. □ *The crime was committed in broad daylight.* □ *Bill stood there in broad daylight, but we never saw him.*

in bulk in large quantities or amounts, rather than smaller, more convenient quantities or amounts. □ *Jane always bought office supplies in bulk to save money.* □ *Dave purchased cereal in bulk because his family used so much of it.*

in business operating; equipped or ready to operate. □ *We're in business now, and things are running smoothly.* □ *Now it works. Now we're in business.*

in cahoots (with someone**)** *Rur.* in conspiracy with someone; in league with someone. □ *The mayor is in cahoots with the construction company that got the contract for the new building.* □ *Those two have been in cahoots before.*

in care of someone [to be delivered to someone] through someone or by way of someone. (Indicates that mail is to be delivered to a person at some other person's address.) □ *Bill Jones is living at his father's house. Address the letter to Bill in care of Mr. John Jones.* □ *Bill said, "Please send me my mail in care of my father at his address."*

in case of something if a problem occurs; if something happens; in the event that something happens. □ *What do we do in case of fire?* □ *In case of an accident, call the police.*

in case (something happens**)** in the event that something takes place. □ *She carries an umbrella in case it rains.* □ *I have some aspirin in my office in case I get a headache.* □ *He keeps a fire extinguisher in his car, just in case.*

in character *Fig.* typical of someone's behavior. □ *For Tom to shout that way wasn't at all in character. He's usually quite pleasant.* □ *It was quite in character for Sally to walk away angry.*

in charge (of someone or something**)** in control of someone or something; having the responsibility for someone or something. □ *Who is in charge of this office?* □ *Do you like being in charge?*

in clover *Fig.* having good fortune; in a very good situation, especially financially. □ *If I get this contract, I'll be in clover for the rest of my life.* □ *I have very little money saved, so when I retire I won't exactly be in clover.*

in cold blood *Fig.* without feeling; with cruel intent. (Frequently said of a crime, especially murder.) □ *The killer* walked up and shot the woman in cold blood. □ *How insulting! For a person to say something like that in cold blood is just horrible.*

in cold storage dead; in a state of death. (Alludes to the actual storage of certain things, such as fur coats, in cold storerooms.) □ *Tom gets paid for putting his subjects in cold storage.* □ *Poor old Jed is in cold storage.*

in concert (with someone**)** *Fig.* in cooperation with someone; with the aid of someone. □ *Mrs. Smith planned the party in concert with her sister.* □ *In concert they planned a lovely event.*

in condition and **in(to) shape** in good health; strong and healthy; fit. □ *Bob exercises frequently, so he's in condition.* □ *If I were in shape, I could run faster and farther.* □ *I'm really overweight. I have to try to get into shape.*

in consequence (of something**)** as a result of something; because of something. □ *In consequence of the storm, there was no electricity.* □ *The wind blew down the wires. In consequence, we had no electricity.*

in consideration of something in return for something; as a result of something. □ *In consideration of your many years of service, we are pleased to present you with this gold watch.* □ *In consideration of your efforts, here is a check for $3,000.*

in contact (with someone or something**)** communicating with someone or a group; to share information with someone or a group. □ *I have been in contact with our supplier, who will deliver the part next week.* □ *I am in contact with the Senate committee now.*

in contempt (of court) showing disrespect for a judge or courtroom procedures. □ *The bailiff ejected the lawyer who was held in contempt.* □ *The judge found the juror in contempt of court when she screamed at the attorney.*

in control of someone or something **1.** in charge of someone or something. □ *Who is in control of this place?* □ *I am not in control of her. She works for another department.* **2.** to have someone or something mastered or subdued; to have achieved management of someone or something. □ *You should be in control of your dog at all times.* □ *The attendant was instructed to be in control of his patient at all times.*

in creation Go to on earth.

in custody (of someone or something**)** and **in** someone's or something's **custody** being kept guarded by legal authorities. □ *The suspect was in the sheriff's custody awaiting a trial.* □ *The prisoner is in the custody of the state.* □ *The police have two suspects in custody.*

in debt having debts; having much debt; owing money. □ *Mary is deeply in debt.* □ *I am in debt to the bank for my car loan.*

in deep 1. *Fig.* deeply involved (with someone or something). □ *Mary and Sam are in deep.* □ *Wilbur got in deep with the mob.* **2.** *Fig.* deeply in debt. (Often with *with* or *to.*) □ *Willie is in deep with his bookie.* □ *I'm in deep to the department store.*

in deep water *Fig.* in a dangerous or vulnerable situation; in a serious situation, especially one that is too difficult or is beyond the level of one's abilities; in trouble. □ *John is having trouble with back taxes. He's in deep water.* □ *Bill* *got in deep water in algebra class. The class is too difficult for him, and he's almost failing.*

in defiance (of someone or something**)** against someone's will or against instructions; in bold resistance to someone or someone's orders. □ *Jane spent the afternoon in the park in defiance of her mother's instructions.* □ *She did it in defiance of her mother.* □ *She has done a number of things in defiance lately.*

in denial in a state of refusing to believe something that is true. □ *Mary was in denial about her illness and refused treatment.* □ *Tom doesn't think he's an alcoholic because he's still in denial.*

in detail with lots of details; giving all the details. (Often used with an adjective showing the level of detail, such as *great, enormous,* etc., as in the second example.) □ *I explained the policy to the customer in detail.* □ *We planned the entire project in great detail.*

in dire straits *Fig.* in a very serious, bad circumstance. □ *We are nearly broke and need money for medicine. We are in dire straits.*

in disguise hidden behind a disguise; looking like something else. □ *Santa Claus was really the little child's father in disguise.* □ *What I thought was terrible turned out to be a blessing in disguise!*

in drag wearing the clothing of the opposite sex. (Usually refers to a man wearing women's clothing.) □ *Two actors in drag did a skit about life on the farm.* □ *Gary looks better in drag than he does in a suit.*

in dribs and drabs in small portions; bit by bit. □ *I'll have to pay you what I owe you in dribs and drabs.* □ *The whole story is being revealed in dribs and drabs.*

in droves *Fig.* in large numbers. (See also **be out in droves.**) □ *The settlers arrived on the prairie in droves.*

in due course and **in due time; in good time; in the course of time; in time** in a normal or expected amount of time. □ *The roses will bloom in due course.* □ *The vice president will become president in due course.* □ *I'll retire in due time.* □ *Just wait, my dear. All in good time.* □ *It'll all work out in the course of time.* □ *In time, things will improve.*

in due time Go to previous.

***in Dutch (with** someone**)** in trouble with someone. (*Typically: **be** ~; **get** ~.) □ *I'm in Dutch with my parents for my low grades.* □ *You're in Dutch quite often, it seems.*

***in earnest** with sincerity. (*Typically: **act** ~; **be** ~; **speak** ~.) □ *I've done all the research I need. I spent the day writing the paper in earnest.* □ *Mary's comments were in earnest. She really meant them.*

in effect producing a particular effect; effectively. □ *In effect, this new law will raise taxes for most people.* □ *This policy harms domestic manufacturers. In effect, all our clothing will be made in foreign countries.*

in essence basically; essentially. □ *I have lots of detailed advice for you, but in essence, I want you to do the best you can.* □ *In essence, lightning is just a giant spark of electricity.*

in exchange (for someone or something**)** in return for someone or something. □ *They gave us two of our prisoners in exchange for two of theirs.* □ *I gave him chocolate in exchange for some licorice.* □ *John gave Mary a book and got a sweater in exchange.*

in existence now existing; currently and actually being. □ *The tiger may not be in existence in a few decades.* □ *All the oil in existence will not last the world for another century.*

in fact in reality; really; actually. □ *I'm over forty. In fact, I'm forty-six.* □ *This is a very good computer. In fact, it's the best.*

in fashion in style; current and socially acceptable. □ *Is that kind of thing still in fashion?* □ *It won't be in fashion very long.*

in favor of someone to someone, as when writing a check. □ *Please make out a check for $300 in Tom's favor.* □ *I'm making out the check in favor of Mr. Brown.*

in favor (of someone or something**)** approving, supporting, or endorsing someone or something. □ *Are you in favor of lower taxes?* □ *Of course, I'm in favor.*

in fear and trembling *Cliché* with anxiety or fear; with dread. □ *In fear and trembling, I went into the room to take the test.* □ *The witness left the courtroom in fear and trembling.*

in fine feather 1. *Fig.* well dressed; of an excellent appearance. (Alludes to a bird that has clean, bright, and flawless feathers.) □ *Well, you are certainly in fine feather today.* □ *I like to be in fine feather when I have to give a speech.* **2.** *Fig.* in good form; in good spirits. □ *Mary was really in fine feather tonight. Her concert was great!* □ *I feel in fine feather and ready to go!*

in fits and starts Go to **fits and starts.**

in flight while flying. □ *A passenger became ill in flight and the pilot had to return to the airport.* □ *I really don't care to eat in flight. I am too nervous.*

in flux and **in a (constant) state of flux** in constant change; ever-changing. □ *I can't describe my job because it's in a constant state of flux.* □ *The price of gold is in flux.*

***in focus 1.** *Lit.* [of an image] seen clearly and sharply. (*Typically: **be** ~; **come [into]** ~; **get [into]** ~; **get** something **[into]** ~.) □ *I have the slide in focus and can see the bacteria clearly.* **2.** *Lit.* [for optics, such as lenses, or an optical device, such as a microscope] to be aligned to allow something to be seen clearly and sharply. □ *I've adjusted the telescope; Mars is now in focus.* **3.** *Fig.* [of problems, solutions, appraisals of people or things] perceived or understood clearly. (*Typically: **be** ~; **get [into]** ~; **get** something **[into]** ~.) □ *Now that things are in focus, I feel better about the world.*

in for something due to receive a surprise; due to receive punishment. (When the *something* is *it,* the *it* usually means punishment.) □ *I hope I'm not in for any surprises when I get home.* □ *Tommy, you broke my baseball bat. You're really in for it!* □ *If I ever catch that chicken thief, he'll be in for it for sure.*

***in force 1.** [of a rule or law] currently valid or in effect. (*Typically: **be** ~.) □ *Is this rule in force now?* □ *The constitution is still in force.* **2.** *Fig.* in a very large group. (*Typically: **arrive** ~; **attack** ~.) □ *The entire group arrived in force.* □ *The mosquitoes will attack in force this evening.*

in full flight fleeing at great speed; escaping rapidly. □ *The robbers were in full flight before the bank manager even called the sheriff.*

***in full swing** and ***in high gear** *Fig.* at the peak of activity; moving fast or efficiently. (*Typically: **be** ~; **move [into]** ~; **get [into]** ~.) □ *In the summer months, things really get into full swing around here.* □ *We go skiing in the mountains each winter. Things are in high gear there in November.*

in general referring to the entire class being discussed; speaking of the entire range of possibilities; in most situations or circumstances. □ *I like vegetables in general, but not beets.* □ *In general, I prefer a hotel room on a lower floor, but will take a higher room if it's special.*

in glowing terms *Fig.* using words of praise; using complimentary expressions. □ *The college president described his accomplishments in glowing terms and awarded him with an honorary degree.*

in good condition Go to **in good shape**.

in good faith *Fig.* with good and honest intent; with sincerity. □ *We are convinced you were acting in good faith, even though you made a serious error.* □ *I think you didn't sign the contract in good faith. You never intended to carry out our agreement.*

in good hands *Fig.* in the safe, competent care of someone. □ *Don't worry. Your children are in good hands. Sally is an experienced baby-sitter.* □ *Your car is in good hands. My mechanics are factory-trained.*

in good repair *Fig.* operating well; well taken care of. (Usually said of a thing rather than a person.) □ *The house is in good repair and ought to attract a number of potential buyers.* □ *If the car were in good repair, it would run more smoothly.*

***in good shape** and ***in good condition** physically and functionally sound and sturdy. (Used for both people and things. *Typically: **be** ~; **get** ~; **keep** ~.) □ *This car isn't in good shape. I'd like to have one that's in better condition.* □ *Mary is in good condition. She exercises and eats right to stay healthy.* □ *You have to make an effort to get into good shape.*

in good spirits *Fig.* happy and cheerful; positive and looking toward the future, despite unhappy circumstances. □ *The patient is in good spirits and that will speed her recovery.* □ *Tom wasn't in very good spirits after he heard the bad news.*

in good time Go to **in due course**.

***in (good) (with** someone**)** in someone's favor. (*Typically: **be** ~; **get** ~.) □ *I hope I can get in good with the teacher. I need an A in the course.* □ *Mary is always trying to get in with the people who are in charge.*

in great demand wanted by many people. □ *Liz is in great demand as a singer.* □ *Mary's paintings are in great demand.*

in great haste very fast; in a big hurry. □ *John always did his homework in great haste.* □ *Why not take time and do it right? Don't do everything in great haste.*

***in hand** in one's possession or control. (*Typically: **be** ~; **have** something ~.) □ *It's in hand. I have it right here.* □ *The papers are in hand. Have no fear.*

***in harm's way** *Fig.* liable to be harmed; subject to potential causes of harm. (*Typically: **be** ~; **get** ~; **put** someone ~.) □ *Soldiers are expected to know what to do when they are in harm's way.*

***in harmony (with** someone or something**) 1.** *Lit.* in musical concord with someone or something. (*Typically: **be** ~; **get** ~.) □ *This part is in harmony with the tenor's solo.* □ *The tenor part is not in harmony with the accompaniment.* **2.** *Fig.* agreeable or compatible with someone or something. (*Typically: **be** ~; **get** ~.) □ *This is in complete harmony with our earlier discussions.* □ *Fred's position is quite clear. What you have said is not in harmony with Fred.*

***in heat** in a period of sexual excitement; in estrus. (Estrus is the period of time in which females are most willing to breed. This expression is usually used for animals. It has been used for humans in a joking sense. *Typically: **be** ~; **get [into]** ~; **go [into]** ~.) □ *Our dog is in heat.* □ *She goes into heat every year at this time.*

in heaven *Fig.* in a state of absolute bliss or happiness. □ *Lisa was in heaven after winning the lottery.* □ *Resting in his hammock, John was simply in heaven.*

in high cotton and **in tall cotton** *Rur.* to be doing very well; successful. □ *Jim's in high cotton ever since he got that raise.* □ *Tom: How's your sister? Mary: She's in high cotton. Just bought a nice new house.* □ *We were in tall cotton until the IRS caught up with us.*

in high dudgeon *Fig.* feeling or exhibiting great resentment; taking great offense at something. (Often with *leave*.) □ *After the rude remarks, the person who was insulted left in high dudgeon.* □ *Dennis strode from the room in high dudgeon, and we knew he would get his revenge eventually.*

***in high gear 1.** [of a machine, such as a car] set in its highest gear, giving the greatest speed. (*Typically: **be** ~; **get [into]** ~; **move [into]** ~.) □ *When my car is in high gear, it goes very fast.* □ *You can't start out in high gear. You must work up through the low ones.* **2.** Go to **in full swing**.

in (high) hopes of something *Fig.* expecting something. □ *I was in hopes of getting there early.* □ *We are in high hopes that John and Mary will have a girl.*

in hindsight Go to **in retrospect**.

in hock in debt. □ *After buying the luxury car, Bob was in hock for years.*

in hog heaven *Fig.* very happy; having a wonderful time. □ *Bill's a fan of Clark Gable, so when the movie theater had a Clark Gable movie festival, Bill was in hog heaven.* □ *Jane loves to quilt, so she was in hog heaven when they opened that new store for quilters.*

in honor of someone or something showing respect or admiration for someone or something. □ *Our club gave a party in honor of the club's president.* □ *I wrote a poem in honor of John and Mary's marriage.*

in horror with intense shock or disgust. □ *Mike stepped back from the rattlesnake in horror.* □ *The jogger recoiled in horror when she came upon a body in the park.*

***in hot water (with** someone**) (about** someone or something**)** *Fig.* in trouble. (*Typically: **be** ~; **get [into]** ~.) □ *You are going to get into hot water with Rebecca about* that. □ *Amy got into hot water about Todd with Rebecca.* □ *John got himself into hot water by being late.*

in ink written or signed with a pen that uses ink, not with a pencil. □ *You should write your report in ink.* □ *You must sign your checks in ink.*

in its entirety and **in their entirety** completely; until completely done or gone. □ *I watched the basketball game in its entirety.* □ *My friends and I ate the two large pizzas in their entirety.*

in its prime Go to **in** one's **prime**.

in jeopardy to be at risk; to be at peril. □ *John puts himself in jeopardy every time he goes skydiving.* □ *I was in jeopardy when my car broke down on the deserted road.*

in (just) a minute Go to next.

in (just) a second and **in (just) a minute** in a very short period of time. □ *I'll be there in a second.* □ *I'll be with you in just a minute. I'm on the phone.*

in keeping (with something**)** and **in line with** something in accord or harmony with something; following the rules of something. □ *In keeping with your instructions, I've canceled your order.* □ *I'm disappointed with your behavior. It really wasn't in line with what it should be.*

in kind 1. in goods rather than in money. □ *The country doctor was usually paid in kind. He accepted two pigs as payment for an operation.* □ *Do you have to pay tax on payments made in kind?* **2.** similarly; [giving] something similar to what was received. □ *John punched Bill, and Bill gave it back in kind.* □ *She spoke rudely to me, so I spoke to her in kind.*

in labor [of a woman] experiencing the pains and exertion of childbirth. □ *Susan was in labor for nearly eight hours.* □ *As soon as she had been in labor for an hour, she went to the hospital.*

in league (with someone**)** *Fig.* [of people] secretly cooperating, often to do something bad or illegal. □ *The county sheriff is in league with criminals.* □ *The car thieves and some crooked police are in league to make money from stolen cars.*

in less than no time *Fig.* very quickly. (See also in no time (at all).) □ *I'll be there in less than no time.* □ *Don't worry. This won't take long. It'll be over with in less than no time.*

in lieu of something *Fig.* in place of something; instead of something. (The word *lieu* occurs only in this phrase.) □ *They gave me roast beef in lieu of ham.* □ *We gave money to charity in lieu of sending flowers to the funeral.*

In like a lion, out like a lamb. Go to **March comes in like a lion, and goes out like a lamb.**

***in limbo 1.** Lit.* a region of the afterlife on the border of hell. (In some Christian religions, there is a *limbo* set aside for souls that do not go to either heaven or hell. This sense is used only in this religious context. *Typically: be ~; remain ~; stay ~.) □ *The baby's soul was in limbo because she had not been baptized.* **2.** *Fig.* in a state of neglect; in a state of oblivion; in an indefinite state; on hold. (*Typically: be ~; leave something ~; put something ~.) □ *We'll have to leave the project in limbo for a month or two.* □ *After I got hit on the head, I was in limbo for about ten minutes.*

in line and **on line** standing and waiting in a line of people. (*On line* is used especially in the New York City area.) □ *I've been in line for an hour.* □ *Get in line if you want to buy a ticket.* □ *We waited on line to see the movie.*

in line with something Go to **in keeping (with** something**)**.

in love (with someone or something**)** feeling love for someone or something; experiencing a strong affectionate emotion for someone or something. □ *Mary was in love with her new car! It was perfect for her.* □ *John is deeply in love with Mary.*

in low cotton *Rur.* depressed. □ *She was in low cotton because her dress got torn.* □ *Jed is in low cotton because his favorite hound is dead.*

in luck fortunate; lucky. □ *You want a red one? You're in luck. There is one red one left.* □ *I had an accident, but I was in luck. It was not serious.*

in many respects Go to **in some respects**.

in marching order organized and equipped; ready to go. (Originally military.) □ *Is our luggage all packed and in marching order?* □ *We're in marching order and eager to go, sir.*

in memory of someone to continue the good memories of someone; for the honor of a deceased person. □ *Many streets were renamed in memory of John F. Kennedy.* □ *We planted roses in memory of my deceased father.*

in midair in a point high in the air. □ *The planes crashed in midair.* □ *Extra fuel was released from the plane in midair.*

***in mint condition** Fig.* in perfect condition. (*Typically: be ~; find something ~.) □ *This is a fine car. It runs well and is in mint condition.* □ *We saw a house in mint condition and decided to buy it.*

in my humble opinion *Cliché* a phrase introducing the speaker's opinion. □ *"In my humble opinion," began Fred, arrogantly, "I have achieved what no one else ever could."* □ *Bob: What are we going to do about the poor condition of the house next door? Bill: In my humble opinion, we will mind our own business.*

in my opinion Go to **as I see it**.

in my view Go to **as I see it**.

in name only nominally; not actual, only by terminology. □ *The president is head of the country in name only. Congress makes the laws.* □ *Mr. Smith is the boss of the Smith Company in name only. Mrs. Smith handles all the business affairs.*

in need (of something**)** [of someone or an animal] to require something. □ *We are in need of a new car.* □ *The company is in need of a larger building to hold all its employees.*

in neutral with the shift lever of a vehicle in the position where the motor is running but is not powering the wheels or other moving parts. □ *The car rolled down the hill because I'd left it in neutral and did not put on the brake.* □ *If you are moving and in neutral, you do not have control of your vehicle.*

in no mood to do something not feeling like doing something; not wishing to do something. □ *I'm in no mood to cook dinner tonight.* □ *Mother is in no mood to put up with our arguing.*

in no time (at all) very quickly. (Compare this with **in less than no time**.) □ *I'll be there in no time.* □ *It won't take long. I'll be finished in no time at all.*

in no time flat Go to **in nothing flat**.

in no uncertain terms *Cliché* in very specific and direct language. □ *I was so mad. I told her in no uncertain terms to leave and never come back.* □ *I told him in no uncertain terms to stop calling me.*

in nothing flat and **in no time flat** *Fig.* very quickly; in much less time than expected. □ *Of course I can get there in a hurry. I'll be there in nothing flat.* □ *We covered the distance between New York and Philadelphia in nothing flat.* □ *The waiter brought our food in no time flat.*

*__in on__ *something* **1.** involved with something, such as an organization or an idea; informed about special plans. (*Typically: **be ~; come ~; get ~; let** someone **~**.) □ *There is a party upstairs, and I want to get in on it.* □ *I want to get in on your club's activities.* □ *Mary and Jane know a secret, but they won't let me in on it.* **2.** receiving a share of something. (*Typically: **be ~; come ~; get ~; let** someone **~**.) □ *I want to get in on the new European business that is supposed to develop.* □ *We will all want to get in on the scheme.*

*__in on the act__ *Fig.* involved in something with someone else. (Often refers to an unwelcome attempt to join someone's performance. *Typically: **be ~; get ~; let** someone **~**.) □ *Everybody wants to get in on the act.* □ *Why are you trying to get in on the act?*

*__in on the ground floor__ *Fig.* involved at the very beginning of something. (Alludes to riding in an elevator that will become increasingly crowded as it ascends. You will be able to get in most easily at the lowest level. *Typically: **be ~; get ~; let** someone **~**.) □ *If you are starting a new project, I want to get in on the ground floor.* □ *Invest now so you can get in on the ground floor.*

in on the kill Go to **in at the kill**.

in one fell swoop Go to **at one fell swoop**.

*__in one's birthday suit__ *Fig.* naked; nude. (In the "clothes" in which one was born. *Typically: **be ~; get [into] ~**.) □ *I've heard that John sleeps in his birthday suit.* □ *We used to go down to the river and swim in our birthday suits.*

in one's blood Go to **in the blood**.

in one's book *Fig.* according to one's own opinion. □ *He's okay in my book.* □ *In my book, this is the best that money can buy.*

in one's cups *Euph.* drunk. □ *She doesn't make much sense when she's in her cups.* □ *The speaker—who was in his cups—could hardly be understood.*

in one's element *Fig.* in a natural or comfortable situation or environment. □ *Sally is in her element when she's working with algebra or calculus.* □ *Bob loves to work with color and texture. When he's painting, he's in his element.*

in one's glory *Fig.* at one's happiest or best. □ *When I go to the beach on vacation, I'm in my glory.* □ *Sally is a good teacher. She's in her glory in the classroom.*

in one's mind's eye *Fig.* in one's mind or imagination. (Alludes to visualizing something in one's mind.) □ *In my mind's eye, I can see trouble ahead.* □ *In her mind's eye,*

she could see a beautiful building beside the river. She decided to design such a building.

in one's opinion according to one's belief or judgment. □ *In my opinion, that is a very ugly picture.* □ *That isn't a good idea in my opinion.*

in one's or its prime *Fig.* at one's or its peak or best time. □ *Our dog—which is in its prime—is very active.* □ *The building was in its prime back in the Fifties, but it has not been well maintained.* □ *I could work long hours when I was in my prime.*

in one's (own) backyard *Fig.* very close to one, where one lives, or where one is. □ *That kind of thing is quite rare. Imagine it happening right in your backyard.* □ *You always think of something like that happening to someone else. You never expect to find it in your own backyard.*

in one's (own) (best) interest(s) to one's advantage; as a benefit to oneself. □ *It is not in your own interests to share your ideas with Jack. He will say that they are his.* □ *Jane thought it was in the best interest of her friend to tell his mother about his illness.*

in one's own way 1. as the best one can do; using a personal and individual strategy. □ *I don't know the answer to the problem, but perhaps I can help in my own way.* □ *She couldn't go to war and carry a gun, but she helped the war effort in her own way.* **2.** in the special way that one wishes or demands. □ *I don't like doing it your way. I want to do it in my own way.* □ *I prefer to do it in my own way.*

in one's right mind *Fig.* sane; rational and sensible. (Often in the negative.) □ *That was a stupid thing to do. You're not in your right mind.* □ *You can't be in your right mind! That sounds crazy!*

in one's salad days *Fig.* in one's youth. (Usually formal or literary. Comparing the greenness of a salad with the greenness, or freshness and inexperience, of youth.) □ *I recall the joys I experienced on school vacations in my salad days.* □ *In our salad days, we were apt to get into all sorts of mischief on the weekends.*

in one's second childhood *Fig.* [of an adult] interested in things or people that normally interest children. □ *My father bought himself a toy train, and my mother said he was in his second childhood.* □ *Whenever I go to the river and throw stones, I feel as if I'm in my second childhood.*

in one's spare time in one's extra time; in the time not reserved for work or doing something else. □ *I write novels in my spare time.* □ *I'll try to paint the house in my spare time.*

*__in one's Sunday best__ *Rur.* in one's best clothes; in the clothes one wears to church. (*Typically: **be ~; get [into] ~**.) □ *All the children were dressed up in their Sunday best.* □ *I like to be in my Sunday best whenever I go out.* □ *Let's get into our Sunday best and go out for dinner.*

in opposition (to someone or something**)** against someone or something; opposing someone or something. □ *You'll find that I'm firmly in opposition to any further expenditures.* □ *The council and the mayor are usually in opposition.*

*__in orbit 1.__ *Lit.* [of something] circling a heavenly body. (*Typically: **be ~; put** something **[into] ~**.) □ *The moon is in orbit around the earth.* □ *They put the satellite into orbit.* **2.** *Fig.* ecstatic; thrilled; emotionally high.

(*Typically: **be** ~.) □ *Jane is in orbit about her new job.* □ *John went into orbit when he got the check in the mail.* **3.** *Inf.* intoxicated. □ *After having six drinks all to herself, Julie was in orbit.*

***in order** properly arranged. (*Typically: **get** something ~; **have** something ~; **put** something ~.) □ *Please get your desk in order.* □ *I wish you would put things in order!*

in order to do something for the purpose of doing something; as a means of doing something. □ *I went to college in order to further my education.* □ *I gave John three dollars in order to buy lunch.*

in other words a phrase introducing a restatement of what has just been said. □ *Henry: Sure I want to do it, but how much do I get paid? Andrew: In other words, you're just doing it for the money.* □ *Bill: Well, I suppose I really should prepare my entourage for departure. Bob: In other words, you're leaving? Bill: One could say that, I suppose. Bob: Why didn't one?*

***in over** one's **head (with** someone or something**) 1.** *Lit.* in water that is deeper than one is tall. (*Typically: **be** ~; **get** ~.) □ *Johnny! Don't go out too far! You are in over your head.* **2.** *Fig.* too deeply involved with someone or something, beyond what one can deal with. (*Typically: **be** ~; **get** ~.) □ *They are all in over their heads with this money business.* **3.** *Fig.* having more difficulties than one can manage. □ *Calculus is very hard for me. I'm in over my head.*

in park [of an automobile transmission] having the gears locked so the automobile cannot move. □ *The driver stopped the car and placed it in park.* □ *You have to be in park in order to start this car.*

in part partly; to a lesser degree or extent. □ *I was not there, in part because of my disagreement about the purpose of the meeting. I also had a previous appointment.* □ *I hope to win, in part because I want the prize money.*

in particular specifically; especially. □ *I'm not going anywhere in particular.* □ *Of the three ideas, there is one I like in particular.*

in passing casually; said or mentioned as an aside. □ *I just heard your name in passing. I didn't hear more than that.* □ *The lecturer referred to George Washington in passing.*

in pencil written or signed with a pencil. □ *Why did you write your report in pencil?* □ *You can't sign a check in pencil!*

in perpetuity for an indefinitely long period of time; eternally. □ *My trust fund generates income in perpetuity.* □ *The right for the road to cross my land was granted in perpetuity to the county.*

in person [of someone] actually physically present in a place rather than appearing in a film, on a television or computer screen, on a telephone, or through a radio broadcast. □ *All the famous movie stars were there in person.* □ *You must appear in our office in person to collect the money that is due to you.*

***in perspective** within a reasonable view or appraisal. (*Typically: **be** ~; **get** something ~; **have** something ~; **put** something **[into]** ~.) □ *Let's try to keep everything in perspective.* □ *If we put the matter into perspective, I think we can discuss it reasonably.*

***in place** in (someone's or something's) proper place or location. (*Typically: **be** ~; **put** something **[into]** ~.) □ *The maid came into the room and put everything into place.* □ *It's good to see everything in place again.*

in place of someone or something instead of someone or something; as a substitute for someone or something. □ *I changed my mind. I want a red one in place of the blue one.* □ *John came to help in place of Max, who was sick.*

in plain English Go to next.

***in plain language** and ***in plain English** *Fig.* in simple, clear, and straightforward language. (*Typically: **be** ~; **put** something **[into]** ~; **say** something ~; **write** something ~.) □ *That's too confusing. Please say it again in plain English.* □ *Tell me again in plain language.*

***in play 1.** *Lit.* [of a ball, in a game] under the effect of the rules of the game. (*Typically: **be** ~; **get back** ~; **put** something **back** ~.) □ *The ball is in play again and the activity is furious.* □ *The ball is not in play yet.* **2.** *Fig.* [of a company or its stock] in the process of being bought out by another company. (*Typically: **be** ~; **put** something ~.) □ *The company I bought stock in is now in play.* □ *This stock is in play.*

in point of fact just to point out a fact; in fact. □ *In point of fact, I am not late. You are simply way too early.*

in poor taste Go to in bad taste.

***in power** in control; in charge. (*Typically: **be** ~; **come [into]** ~; **get [into]** ~.) □ *Who is in power now?* □ *No one is in power.* □ *The provisional government came into power six months ago.*

in practice 1. in the actual doing of something; in reality. □ *Our policy is to be very particular, but in practice we don't care that much.* □ *The instructions say not to set it too high. In practice I always set it as high as possible.* **2.** well-rehearsed; well-practiced; well-exercised. □ *The swimmer was not in practice and almost drowned.* □ *I play the piano for a living, and I have to keep in practice.*

in press [of a book or other document] in the process of being printed. □ *This book is in press. It won't be available for at least two months.* □ *This book has been in press for a long time.*

in print [of a book, magazine, newspaper, or other written material] to be available from the publisher. □ *Ten thousand copies of the first edition remain in print.* □ *The publisher listed all of its books in print.*

in private privately; without others present. □ *I'd like to speak to you in private.* □ *I enjoy spending the evening in private.*

in progress under way; happening; developing or moving right now. □ *Don't enter the studio. There's a show in progress.* □ *We now return you to the regularly scheduled show in progress.*

in proportion showing the correct size or proportion relative to something else. □ *That man's large head is not in proportion to his small body.* □ *The cartoonist drew the dog in proportion to its surroundings.*

in public in a place or way so that other people can see or know about something. □ *It's illegal to walk naked in public.* □ *John always tries to embarrass me whenever we're in public.*

in pursuit of something chasing after something. □ *Bill spends most of his time in pursuit of money.* □ *Every year Bob goes into the countryside in pursuit of butterflies.*

in quest of someone or something and **in search of** someone or something seeking or hunting something; trying to find something. □ *They went into town in quest of a reasonably priced restaurant.* □ *Monday morning I'll go out in search of a job.*

in rags *Fig.* in worn-out and torn clothing. □ *Oh, look at my clothing. I can't go to the party in rags!* □ *I think the new casual fashions make you look as if you're in rags.*

in rare form 1. *Fig.* well prepared for a good performance; at one's best. □ *The goalie is in rare form today; that's his third great save already.* □ *We are not exactly in rare form on Monday mornings.* **2.** *Inf.* intoxicated. □ *Gert is in rare form, but she'll have time to sleep it off.* □ *When Harry was finally in rare form, he slid beneath the table.*

in reality viewing things realistically; really. □ *Jane dreamed it was snowing, but in reality, it was very warm.* □ *John looks happy, but in reality, he is miserable.*

in receipt of something in a state of having received something. (Used in business correspondence.) □ *We are in receipt of your letter of request.* □ *When we are in receipt of your check for the full balance, we will mark your bill as paid.*

in recent memory *Fig.* the period of time in which things are still remembered and discussed. □ *Never in recent memory has there been this much snow!* □ *I haven't been this happy in recent memory!*

in reduced circumstances *Euph.* in poverty. □ *After Frederick lost his position, we lived in reduced circumstances while waiting for my inheritance.*

in reference to someone or something and **with reference to** someone or something concerning or about someone or something; in connection with someone or something. □ *What shall we do in reference to Bill and his problem?* □ *With reference to what problem?*

in regard to someone or something Go to **with regard to** someone or something.

in rehearsal a stage of development in the production of a play, opera, or concert, involving many rehearsals. □ *The play is in rehearsal now and will open next month.* □ *While the opera was still in rehearsal, the star developed a hatred for the director.*

in relation to someone or something relating to someone or something; in connection with someone or something. □ *I mention this fact in relation to your proposed trip.* □ *Let's discuss Bill in relation to his future with this company.*

in remission [of a serious disease] not worsening or progressing. □ *While the disease was in remission, John got to leave the hospital.* □ *The doctor said my cancer was in remission.*

in retrospect and **in hindsight** reconsidering the past with the knowledge one now has. □ *In retrospect, I would have gone to a better college.* □ *David realized, in hindsight, that he should have finished school.*

in return for (someone or something) by way of giving something back; as a way of paying someone back for something; as part of an exchange. □ *I helped Tom yes-*

terday, and he helped me in return for my efforts. □ *I paid $20 and received four tickets in return.*

in round figures Go to next.

***in round numbers** and ***in round figures** *Fig.* as an estimated number; a figure that has been rounded off. (*Typically: **be** ~; **express** something ~; **write** something ~.) □ *Please tell me in round numbers what it'll cost.* □ *I don't need the exact amount. Just give it to me in round figures.*

***in ruins** in a state of destruction. (*Typically: **be** ~; **lay** ~; **leave** something ~.) □ *The enemy army left the cities they attacked in ruins.* □ *The crops laid in ruins after the flood.*

in search of someone or something Go to **in quest of** someone or something.

in season 1. [of a game animal] subject to legal hunting. □ *You cannot shoot ducks. They are not in season.* **2.** [of a female animal] ready to breed; in heat. □ *The cat's in season again.* **3.** to be currently available for selling. (Some foods and other things are available only at certain seasons. *Typically: **be** ~; **come [into]** ~.) □ *Oysters are available in season.* □ *Strawberries aren't in season in January.*

in secret secretly. □ *They planned in secret to blow up the bridge.* □ *I will tell her in secret so no one else will hear.*

in service [of something] operating or operable. (See also **put** something **in(to) service**.) □ *Is this elevator in service?*

in session [of a court, congress, or other organization] operating or functioning. □ *Use of cameras is forbidden while the meeting is in session.* □ *The spectators must remain quiet while court is in session.*

in seventh heaven *Fig.* in a very happy state. □ *Ann was really in seventh heaven when she got a car of her own.* □ *I'd be in seventh heaven if I had a million dollars.*

in shape Go to **in condition**.

in short stated briefly. □ *At the end of the financial report, the board president said, "In short, we are okay."* □ *My remarks, in short, indicate that we are in good financial shape.*

in short order very quickly. □ *I can straighten out this mess in short order.* □ *The maids came in and cleaned the place up in short order.*

in short supply *Fig.* scarce. □ *Fresh vegetables are in short supply in the winter.* □ *Yellow cars are in short supply because everyone likes them and buys them.* □ *At this time of the year, fresh vegetables go into short supply.*

in sight 1. *Lit.* within the range of vision; visible. □ *The goal is in sight.* □ *The end of the road is in sight.* **2.** *Fig.* known; expected. □ *The end of the project is finally in sight.*

in so many words *Fig.* exactly; explicitly; in plain, clear language. □ *I told her in so many words to leave me alone.* □ *He said yes, but not in so many words.*

in some neck of the woods *Rur.* in some vicinity or neighborhood; in some remote place. (The *some* is usually *this, that, your, their*, etc. Can be used to refer to some specific section of a forest.) □ *I think that the Smiths live in your neck of the woods.* □ *What's happening over in that neck of the woods?*

in some respects and **in many respects** with regard to some or many details. □ *In some respects, Anne's comments are similar to yours.* □ *The three proposals are quite different in many respects.*

in some transaction **for** someone having value for someone; having a benefit for someone. (Usually a question: **What's in it for me?**) □ *What is in this deal for me?* □ *There is a lot of money in it for you.*

in someone else's **place** Go to next.

in someone else's **shoes** and **in** someone else's **place** *Fig.* seeing or experiencing something from someone else's point of view. (See also **in a bind** and the examples.) □ *You might feel different if you were in her shoes.* □ *Pretend you're in Tom's place, and then try to figure out why he acts the way he does.*

in someone's **behalf** Go to **in behalf of** someone.

in someone's **care** Go to **in the care of** someone.

*in someone's **face** *Sl.* in a provocative attitude, as if ready to fight or argue. (*Typically: **be ~; get ~.**) □ *Ted's a real pain. He likes to get in your face. He'll argue about anything.* □ *I know you are angry, but don't get in my face. I had nothing to do with it.*

in someone's **favor 1.** to someone's advantage or credit. (Especially in sports scores, as in the examples.) □ *The score was ten to twelve in our favor.* □ *At the end of the second half, the score was forty to three in the other team's favor.* **2. *in** someone's **favor** liked by someone; approved of by someone. (*Typically: **be ~; get [into] ~.**) □ *John might be able to help me. I hope I'm currently in his favor.* □ *My mother is mad at me. I'm certainly not in her favor.* □ *I'll try to get into her favor.*

*in someone's **good graces** *Fig.* in good with someone; in someone's favor. (*Typically: **be ~; get ~.**) □ *I'm not in her good graces so I shouldn't be the one to ask her.*

*in someone's **hair 1.** *Lit.* tangled in someone's hair. (*Typically: **be ~; get [into] ~.**) □ *My bubble gum got in my hair and I had to cut it out.* **2.** *Fig.* annoying someone. (*Typically: **be ~; get [into] ~.**) □ *You can watch what I am doing, but don't get in my hair.* □ *I wish you wouldn't get in my hair when I'm trying to do something.*

in someone's **name 1.** in someone's ownership; as someone's property. □ *The house is in my name. I own all of it.* □ *The car is in our names.* **2.** Go to **in behalf of** someone.

in someone's or something's **way** and **in the way of** someone or something *Fig.* in the pathway or movement of someone or something. □ *Don't get in my way.* □ *That car is in the way of the bus and all the other traffic.*

*in someone's **possession** held by someone; owned by someone. (*Typically: **be ~; come [into] ~.**) □ *The book is now in my possession.* □ *How long has this object been in your possession?*

in someone's **prayers** [of someone] remembered and called by name when someone prays. □ *I am sorry to hear of your sickness. You will be in our prayers.* □ *The whole family is in my prayers because they have suffered so much.*

*in someone's **way 1.** *Lit.* in the pathway of someone. (*Typically: **be ~; get [into] ~; stand ~.**) □ *Don't get in Bob's way while he is bringing groceries in from the car.* **2.** and **in the way of** someone('s **plans**) *Fig.* inter-

fering with a person in the pursuit of plans or intentions; hindering someone's plans. (*Typically: **be ~; get ~; stand ~.**) □ *I am going to leave home. Please don't get in my way.* □ *She intends to become a lawyer and no one had better get in her way.* □ *I would never get into the way of her plans.*

in spades in the best or most extreme way possible; extravagantly. □ *He flunked the test in spades.* □ *He succeeded at life in spades—honors degree, great career, rich wife, lovely children, and early retirement.*

in spite of someone or something without regard to someone or something; even though another course had been prescribed; ignoring a warning. □ *In spite of her orders to stay, I left.* □ *In spite of the bad weather, I had fun on vacation.*

*in step (with someone) *Fig.* [marching or dancing] in cadence with another person. (*Typically: **be ~; get [into] ~; march ~; keep ~.**) □ *Please keep in step with Jane.* □ *You two, back there. You aren't in step.*

in step (with someone or something) *Fig.* as up-to-date as someone or something. □ *Bob is not in step with the times.* □ *We try to keep in step with the fashion of the day.*

in step (with something) and **in time (with** something) *Fig.* keeping in cadence with music. □ *John, your violin isn't in step with the beat. Sit up straight and try it again.* □ *I'm trying to play in time.*

in stitches *Fig.* laughing very hard. □ *Charlie had us in stitches with all his jokes.* □ *The movie sure was funny. I was in stitches!*

in stock to have merchandise available and ready for sale. □ *Do you have extra-large sizes in stock?* □ *Of course, we have all sizes and colors in stock.*

in storage in a place where things are stored or kept. □ *Mary placed her winter clothes in storage during the summer.* □ *John's furniture is in storage while he is in the army.*

*in store (for someone) awaiting someone in the future. (*Typically: **be ~; hold** something **~; lie ~.**) □ *None of us knows what lies in store for us tomorrow.* □ *Some good lies in store for me, I think.*

in style 1. *Lit.* in fashion; fashionable. □ *This old coat isn't in style anymore.* □ *I don't care if it's not in style. It's warm.* □ *I hope this coat comes into style again.* **2.** *Fig.* in elegance; in luxury. □ *If I had a million dollars, I could really live in style.* □ *If he saves his money, someday he'll be able to live in style.*

in surgery to be involved in surgery. (Can refer to a doctor, nurse, or patients.) □ *Dr. Smith is in surgery now.* □ *The patient is still in surgery.*

in tall cotton Go to **in high cotton.**

in tandem [of two or more things] in single file. □ *We marched to the door in tandem.* □ *They rode along in tandem.*

in tatters *Fig.* in torn pieces of cloth. □ *The poor man's clothes hung in tatters.* □ *The flag was in tatters after the storm.*

in terms of something regarding something; concerning something. □ *I don't know what to do in terms of John's problem.* □ *Now, in terms of your proposal, don't you think you're asking for too much?*

in the absence of someone or something while someone or something isn't here; without someone or something. □ *In the absence of the cook, I'll prepare dinner.* □ *In the absence of opposition, she won easily.*

in the act (of doing something**)** while doing something. □ *There he was, in the act of opening the door.* □ *I tripped while in the act of climbing.*

in the affirmative in the form of an answer that means yes. □ *The soldier answered in the affirmative by nodding his head "yes."* □ *My manager's response was in the affirmative.*

in the air *Fig.* everywhere; all about. □ *There is such a feeling of joy in the air.* □ *We felt a sense of tension in the air.*

***in the altogether** and ***in the buff**; ***in the nude**; ***in the raw** *Fig.* naked; nude. (*Typically: **be** ~; **get** [**into**] ~; **sleep** ~.) □ *The museum has a painting of some ladies in the buff.* □ *Mary felt a little shy about getting into the altogether.* □ *Bill says he sleeps in the raw.*

in the back in the back part of a building; in the back room of a building. □ *I don't have your size here, but perhaps I can find it in the back.* □ *He's not in the shop right now. I'll see if he's in the back.*

***in the back of** someone's **mind** *Fig.* remembered by someone, but not very important; vaguely remembered by someone. (*Typically: **have** something ~; **keep** something ~; **leave** something ~; **put** something ~; **remain** ~; **stay** ~.) □ *You should put this problem in the back of your mind and concentrate on other things.*

***in the bag 1.** *Fig.* cinched; achieved. (*Typically: **be** ~; **have** something ~.) □ *It's in the bag—as good as done.* □ *The election is in the bag unless the voters find out about my past.* **2.** *Fig. Inf.* intoxicated. (*Typically: **be** ~.) □ *Kelly looks like he is in the bag.* □ *John is in the bag and mean as hell.*

***in the balance** in an undecided state; at risk. (*Typically: **be** ~; **hang** ~.) □ *He stood on the edge of the cliff, his life in the balance.* □ *With his fortune in the balance, John rolled the dice.*

in the ballpark *Fig.* within certain boundaries; [of an estimate] close to what is expected. □ *Your estimate is not even in the ballpark. Please try again.*

***in the best of health** very healthy. (*Typically: **be** ~; **get** oneself ~.) □ *Bill is in the best of health. He eats well and exercises.* □ *I haven't been in the best of health. I think I have the flu.*

in the black *Fig.* not in debt; in a financially profitable condition. (As opposed to **in the red**.) □ *I wish my accounts were in the black.* □ *Sally moved the company into the black.*

in the blood and **in** one's **blood** *Fig.* built into one's personality or character. □ *John's a great runner. It's in his blood.* □ *The whole family is very athletic. It's in the blood.*

***in the boondocks** and ***in the boonies** in a rural area; far away from a city or population. (*Typically: **be** ~; **camp** ~; **live** ~; **stay** ~.) □ *Perry lives out in the boonies with his parents.*

in the boonies Go to previous.

in the buff Go to in the altogether.

***in the bull pen 1.** *Lit.* [of a baseball pitcher to be] in a special place near the playing field, warming up to pitch. (*Typically: **be** ~; **go** [**into**] ~.) □ *You can tell who is pitching next by seeing who is in the bull pen.* □ *Our best pitcher just went into the bull pen. He'll be pitching soon.* **2.** *Fig.* in reserve, ready if needed. □ *I'm willing to be in the bull pen. Just call me if you need me.*

***in the cards** *Fig.* in the future. (*Typically: **be** ~; **see** something ~.) □ *Well, what do you think is in the cards for tomorrow?* □ *I asked the boss if there was a raise in the cards for me.*

***in the care of** someone and ***in the charge of** someone; ***in** someone's **care**; ***under** someone's **care** in the keeping of someone. (*Typically: **be** ~; **leave** someone or something ~; **place** someone or something [**into**] ~.) □ *I left the baby in the care of my mother.* □ *I placed the house into the care of my friend.*

in the case of someone or something in the matter of someone or something; in the instance of someone or something. □ *In the case of John, I think we had better allow his request.* □ *In the case of this woman, we'll not grant permission.*

in the catbird seat *Sl.* in a dominant or controlling position. □ *Sally's in the catbird seat—telling everybody where to go.* □ *I hold all the aces. I'm in the catbird seat.*

in the C.E. Go to in the Common Era.

in the charge of someone Go to in the care of someone.

in the chips *Fig.* wealthy; having lots of money. (Having lots of gambling chips.) □ *I'm in the chips this month. Let's go squander it.* □ *If I were in the chips, I'd buy a Rolls Royce.*

***in the clear 1.** *Lit.* not obstructed; not enclosed. (*Typically: **be** ~; **get** [**into**] ~; **get** someone or something [**into**] ~.) □ *You're in the clear. Go ahead and back up.* □ *Once the deer got into the clear, it ran away.* **2.** *Fig.* to be innocent; not to be guilty. (*Typically: **be** ~; **get** [**into**] ~; **get** someone or something [**into**] ~.) □ *Don't worry, Tom. I'm sure you're in the clear.* □ *I'll feel better when I get into the clear.*

in the Common Era and **in the C.E.** [of dates] a year after the year 1 according to the Western calendar. (Offered as a replacement for *Anno Domini* and A.D.) □ *The comet was last seen in the year 1986 in the Common Era.* □ *The Huns invaded Gaul in 451 C.E.*

in the context of something in the circumstances under which something happens or has happened. □ *In the context of a funeral, laughing loudly is inappropriate.* □ *In the context of an argument, it is fine to speak firmly.*

In the country of the blind, the one-eyed man is king. *Prov.* A person who is not particularly capable can attain a powerful position if the people around him or her are even less capable. □ *Jill: How on earth did Joe get promoted to be head of his department? He's such a blunderer! Jane: In the country of the blind, the one-eyed man is king.*

in the course of time Go to in due course.

***in the dark (about** someone or something**)** *Fig.* uninformed about someone or something; ignorant about someone or something. (*Typically: **be** ~; **keep** someone ~; **stay** ~.) □ *I'm in the dark about who is in charge around here.* □ *I can't imagine why they are keeping me in the dark.* □ *She's in the dark about how this machine works.*

341

*in the doghouse *Fig.* in trouble; in (someone's) disfavor. (*Typically: **be ~; get ~; find** oneself **~; put** someone **[into] ~.**) □ *I'm really in the doghouse with my boss. I was late for an appointment.* □ *I hate being in the doghouse all the time. I don't know why I can't stay out of trouble.*

*in the doldrums *Fig.* sluggish; inactive; in low spirits. (*Typically: **be ~; put** someone **[into] ~.**) □ *He's usually in the doldrums in the winter.* □ *I had some bad news yesterday, which put me into the doldrums.*

*in the drink *Fig.* in the water; in the ocean. (*Typically: **be ~; fall ~; throw** someone **~.**) □ *He fell in the drink and had to be rescued.*

in the driver's seat *Fig.* in control; in charge of things. (As if one were driving and controlling the vehicle.) □ *Now that Fred is in the driver's seat, there is a lot less criticism about how things are being done.* □ *Joan can't wait to get into the driver's seat and do what she can to turn things around.*

in the event of something if something happens; on the chance that something happens. □ *In the event of his late arrival, please call me.* □ *In the event of rain, the parade is canceled.*

in the family way Go to in a family way.

*in the fast lane *Fig.* in a very active or possible risky manner. (See also life in the fast lane. *Typically: **be ~; live ~; move~; stay ~.**) □ *Fred lives in the fast lane. It's lucky he's still alive.*

in the final analysis and **in the last analysis** in truth; when all the facts are known; when the truth becomes known. (Usually used when someone is speculating about what the final outcome will be.) □ *In the final analysis, it is usually the children who suffer most in a situation like this.* □ *In the last analysis, you simply do not want to do as you are told!*

in the first instance Go to next.

in the first place and **in the first instance** initially; to begin with. □ *In the first place, you don't have enough money to buy one. In the second place, you don't need one.* □ *In the first instance, I don't have the time. In the second place, I'm not interested.*

in the flesh *Fig.* bodily present; in person; totally real. □ *I've heard that the queen is coming here in the flesh.* □ *I've wanted a flat-screen TV for years, and now I've got one right here in the flesh.*

in the forefront (of something**)** Go to at the forefront (of something).

*in the groove *Sl.* attuned to something. (*Typically: **be ~; get ~.**) □ *I was uncomfortable at first, but now I'm beginning to get in the groove.* □ *Fred began to get in the groove, and things went more smoothly.*

*in the gutter *Fig.* [of a person] in a low state; poor and homeless. (*Typically: **be ~; fall [into] ~; put** someone **[into] ~.**) □ *You had better straighten out your life, or you'll end in the gutter.* □ *His bad habits put him into the gutter.*

*in the hole *Fig.* in debt. (*Typically: **be ~; get ~; go ~; put** someone **~.**) □ *I'm $200 in the hole.* □ *We went into the hole on that deal.*

*in the (home)stretch *Fig.* in the last stage of a process. (From horse racing. *Typically: **be ~; get ~.**) □ *We're in the homestretch with this project and can't change it now.* □ *We're in the stretch. Only three more days till we graduate.*

in the hopper *Fig.* in process; in line to be processed. (A hopper is a chute for incoming work or material to be processed.) □ *It's in the hopper. I'll get to it.* □ *Your job is in the hopper, and your turn is next.*

in the hot seat Go to on the hot seat.

in the interest of saving time in order to hurry things along; in order to save time. □ *Mary: In the interest of saving time, I'd like to save questions for the end of my talk. Bill: But I have an important question now!* □ *"In the interest of saving time," said Jane, "I'll give you the first three answers."*

in the interest of someone or something as an advantage or benefit to someone or something; in order to advance or improve someone or something. □ *In the interest of health, people are asked not to smoke.* □ *The police imprisoned the suspects in the interest of the safety of the public.*

in the interim (between things**)** in the meantime; in the time between the ending of something and the beginning of something else. □ *In the interim between her morning and afternoon classes, Susan rushed home to get a book she had forgotten.* □ *My favorite show starts in five minutes, but I'll talk to you in the interim.*

in the know knowledgeable. □ *Let's ask Bob. He's in the know.* □ *I have no knowledge of how to work this machine. I think I can get myself in the know very quickly though.*

in the lap of luxury *Cliché* in luxurious surroundings. □ *John lives in the lap of luxury because his family is very wealthy.* □ *When I retire, I'd like to live in the lap of luxury.*

in the last analysis Go to in the final analysis.

in the laundry with the clothes that are waiting to be washed. □ *Is my blue shirt clean or is it in the laundry?* □ *All my socks are in the laundry. What shall I do?*

in (the) light of something *Fig.* because of certain knowledge now in hand; considering something. (As if knowledge or information shed light on something.) □ *In light of what you have told us, I think we must abandon the project.* □ *In light of the clerk's rudeness, we didn't return to that shop.*

in the limelight Go to in the spotlight.

in the line of duty *Fig.* as part of one's expected duties. □ *When soldiers fight people in a war, it's in the line of duty.* □ *Police officers have to do things they may not like in the line of duty.*

in the long haul Go to over the long haul.

in the long run Go to over the long haul.

in the loop *Fig.* in the group of persons communicating regularly about a specific plan or project. □ *I don't know what's going on with the Jones deal since I'm not in the loop.* □ *Bob and Jean are in the loop. They can tell you what's happening.*

in the main basically; generally. □ *Mary: Everything looks all right—in the main. Sally: What details need attention? Mary: Just a few things here and there. Like on page 27.* □

John: Are you all ready? Sue: I think we're ready, in the main. John: Then, we shall go.

*in the mainstream (of something) following the current trends or styles that are popular or are considered normal. (*Typically: **be ~; get [into] ~.**) □ *Bob is too old-fashioned to be in the mainstream of modern living.*

in the making in development; in the process of developing. □ *This is a real problem in the making. Let's try to keep it from getting any worse.*

*in the market (for something) *Fig.* wanting to buy something. (*Typically: **be ~; find** oneself **~.**) □ *I'm in the market for a new camera.* □ *If you have a boat for sale, we're in the market.*

in the meantime the period of time between two things; the period of time between now and when something is supposed to happen. □ *The movie starts at 6:00. In the meantime, let's eat dinner.* □ *My flight was at 8:00. In the meantime, I played solitaire.*

*in the middle of nowhere *Fig.* in a very remote place. (*Typically: **be ~; drive [into] ~; put** someone or something **[into] ~.**) □ *To get to my house, you have to drive into the middle of nowhere.* □ *We found a nice place to eat, but it's out in the middle of nowhere.*

in the money 1. *Fig.* wealthy. □ *John is really in the money. He's worth millions.* □ *If I am ever in the money, I'll be generous.* **2.** *Fig.* in the winning position in a race or contest. (As if one had won the prize money; in horse racing the top three finishers can pay off on bets.) □ *I knew when Jane came around the final turn that she was in the money.* □ *The horses coming in first, second, and third are said to be in the money.*

in the mood (for something) and **in the mood (to do something)** having the proper state of mind for a particular situation or for doing something. □ *I'm not in the mood to see a movie tonight.* □ *Are you in the mood for pizza?*

in the near future *Cliché* in the time immediately ahead. □ *I don't plan to go to Florida in the near future.* □ *Today's prices won't be around in the near future.*

in the nude Go to **in the altogether**.

in the offing happening at some time in the future. □ *There is a big investigation in the offing, but I don't know when.* □ *It's hard to tell what's in the offing if you don't keep track of things.*

*in the open in the outdoors; in an area that is not closed in. (*Typically: **be ~; put** something **~.**) □ *John's bike was stolen because he left it out in the open.* □ *Mary loves gardening because she loves to be in the open.*

*in the picture *Fig.* well-informed; aware of what is going on. (*Typically: **be ~; keep** someone **~; put** someone **~.**) □ *Please, keep me fully in the picture.* □ *John found out about the plan. He's in the picture, so take care.*

*in the pink (of condition) and ***in the pink (of health)** *Fig.* in very good health; in very good condition, physically and emotionally. (*Typically: **be ~; get [into] ~.**) □ *He recovered completely from his surgery and has been in the pink ever since.* □ *She was lively and active and in the pink of condition.*

in the pink (of health) Go to previous.

in the pipeline *Fig.* backed up somewhere in a process; in process; in a queue. □ *There's a lot of goods still in the pipeline. That means no more new orders will be shipped for a while.* □ *Your papers are in the pipeline somewhere. You'll just have to wait.*

*in the poorhouse 1. *Lit.* in a (historical) communal dwelling for impoverished persons. (*Typically: **live ~; end up ~.**) □ *He couldn't pay his debts and had to live in the poorhouse.* **2.** *Fig.* in a state of poverty. (*Typically: **live ~; end up ~.**) □ *If I lose my job, we'll end up in the poorhouse.*

in the prime of life *Fig.* in the best and most productive and healthy period of life. □ *The good health of one's youth can carry over into the prime of life.* □ *He was struck down by a heart attack in the prime of life.*

*in the public eye *Fig.* publicly; visible to all; conspicuous. (*Typically: **be ~; find** oneself **~; get [into] ~.**) □ *Elected officials find themselves constantly in the public eye.* □ *The mayor made it a practice to get into the public eye as much as possible.*

in the raw Go to **in the altogether**.

in the rear located in the space or area behind someone or something. □ *The waiter told me that the bathrooms were in the rear.* □ *All deliveries must be made in the rear.*

*in the red *Fig.* losing money. (*Typically: **be ~; go [into] ~;** as opposed to **in the black**.) □ *State government has been operating in the red for five straight years.* □ *What with all those car repairs, we're going to be in the red this month.*

in the right correct; morally or legally correct. □ *I know I'm in the right.* □ *You are not in the right on this point.*

in the right place at the right time in the location where something good is to happen exactly when it happens. □ *I got a good deal on a car because I was in the right place at the right time.* □ *Unless you are in the right place at the right time, you won't get a chance to meet a movie star.*

in the road 1. *Lit.* on the roadway. □ *What's that in the road ahead?* **2.** *Fig.* in the way; obstructing the way. □ *You are always in the road. Move aside.*

in the running *Fig.* in competition; competing and having a chance to win. (See also **in a bind** and the examples.) □ *Is Tom still in the running? Does he still have a chance to be elected?* □ *I don't know about Tom, but Gladys is definitely still in the running.*

*in the same boat (as someone) in the same situation; having the same problem. (*Typically: **be ~; get [into] ~.**) □ *Tom: I'm broke. Can you lend me twenty dollars? Bill: Sorry. I'm in the same boat.* □ *Jane and Mary are both in the same boat. They have been called for jury duty.*

in the same breath *Fig.* [stated or said] almost at the same time. □ *He told me I was lazy, but then in the same breath he said I was doing a good job.* □ *The teacher said that the students were working hard and, in the same breath, that they were not working hard enough.*

in the second place secondly; in addition. (Usually said after one has said **in the first place**.) □ *In the first place, you don't have enough money to buy one. In the second place, you don't need one.* □ *In the first place, I don't have the time. In the second place, I'm not interested.*

in the short haul Go to over the short haul.

in the short run Go to over the short haul.

*in the soup *Fig.* in a bad situation. (*Typically: **be ~; get [into]** ~.) □ *Now I'm really in the soup. I broke Mrs. Franklin's window.* □ *I make a lot of mistakes. It's easy for me to get into the soup.*

in the spotlight 1. *Fig.* in the beam of a spotlight, as on a stage. □ *The singer was in the spotlight but the band was almost in the dark.* **2.** and **in the limelight** *Fig.* at the center of attention. (*Limelight* refers to an obsolete type of spotlight, and the word occurs only in this phrase.) □ *John will do almost anything to get himself into the limelight.* □ *I love being in the spotlight.* □ *All elected officials spend a lot of time in the limelight.*

*in the swim of things *Fig.* involved in or participating in events or happenings. (*Typically: **be ~; get [into]** ~.) □ *I've been ill, but soon I'll be back in the swim of things.* □ *I can't wait to settle down and get into the swim of things.*

*in the trust of someone under the responsibility or in the care of someone. (*Typically: **be ~; leave** someone or something ~; **place** someone or something ~.) □ *The state placed the orphan in the trust of the foster parents.* □ *Our bonds are left in the trust of our broker.*

in the twinkling of an eye and **in the wink of an eye** *Fig.* very quickly. □ *In the twinkling of an eye, the deer had disappeared into the forest.* □ *I gave Bill ten dollars and, in the twinkling of an eye, he spent it.*

in the unlikely event of something and **in the unlikely event that** something happens if something—which probably will not happen—actually happens. □ *In the unlikely event of my getting the job, I'll have to buy a car to get there every day.* □ *In the unlikely event of a fire, please walk quickly to an exit.*

*in the (very) nick of time *Fig.* just in time; at the last possible instant; just before it's too late. (*Typically: **arrive ~; get there ~; happen ~; reach** something ~; **save** someone ~.) □ *The doctor arrived in the nick of time. The patient's life was saved.* □ *I reached the airport in the very nick of time and made my flight.*

in the wake of something *Fig.* after something; as a result of some event. (Alludes to a ship's wake.) □ *We had no place to live in the wake of the fire.* □ *In the wake of the storm, there were many broken tree limbs.*

in the way of someone('s **plans**) Go to in someone's way.

in the way of someone or something Go to in someone's or something's way.

in the way of something as a kind of something; as a style of something. □ *What do you have in the way of dress shoes?* □ *We have nothing in the way of raincoats.*

in the wind *Fig.* about to happen. □ *There are some major changes in the wind. Expect these changes to happen soon.* □ *There is something in the wind. We'll find out what it is soon.*

in the wink of an eye Go to in the twinkling of an eye.

in the works *Fig.* being prepared; being planned; being done. □ *There are some new laws in the works that will*

affect all of us. □ *I have some ideas in the works that you might be interested in.*

in the world Go to on earth.

in the worst way *Fig.* very much. □ *I want a new car in the worst way.* □ *Bob wants to retire in the worst way.*

in the wrong wrong; morally or legally incorrect. □ *I am not in the wrong, you are.* □ *No, you are in the wrong.*

in the wrong place at the wrong time in the location where something bad is to happen exactly when it happens. □ *I always get into trouble. I'm just in the wrong place at the wrong time.* □ *It's isn't my fault. I was just in the wrong place at the wrong time.*

in their entirety Go to in its entirety.

in theory according to a theory; theoretically. □ *In theory, if I take my medicine regularly, I will get well.* □ *How things work in theory doesn't always match with how things work in reality.*

in there *Sl.* sincere; likeable. □ *Martha is really in there. Everybody likes her.* □ *I like a guy who's in there—who thinks about other people.*

in there pitching *Fig.* trying very hard. □ *Bob is always in there pitching.* □ *Just stay in there pitching. You'll make some progress eventually.*

in these parts *Rur.* around here; in this area. □ *There aren't any big hospitals in these parts.* □ *Joe's the richest man in these parts.*

the in thing (to do) the fashionable thing to do. □ *Eating low-fat food is the in thing to do.* □ *Bob is very old-fashioned. He never does the in thing.*

in this day and age *Fig.* now; in these modern times. □ *Bill: Ted flunked out of school. Mother: Imagine that! Especially in this day and age.* □ *Bill: Taxes keep going up and up. Bob: What do you expect in this day and age?*

in those parts *Rur.* around there; in that area. □ *I've got a cousin who lives in those parts.* □ *We used to spend our vacations in those parts.*

in time Go to in due course.

in time (with something) Go to in step (with something).

in times past *Fig.* long ago; in previous times. □ *In times past, you would not have been able to wear casual clothing to work.* □ *In times past, the air always seemed fresher and cleaner.*

in top form 1. [of someone or some creature] in very good physical condition. □ *The runners are in top form, so this should be a good race.* □ *I'm not in top form, but I'm not completely out of shape either.* **2.** able to make witty remarks and clever statements quickly and easily. □ *That was really funny, Bob. You are in top form tonight.* □ *The president was in top form and entertained the audience with her speech.*

*in touch (with someone) **1.** *Fig.* in contact with someone by letter or telephone. (*Typically: **be ~; get ~; keep ~.**) □ *I tried to get in touch with her, but she never answered her phone.* □ *I just couldn't seem to get in touch.* **2.** *Fig.* [of oneself] having self-knowledge. (*Typically: **be ~; get ~.**) □ *I need to get in touch with myself and the way I really feel about things.* □ *She needs to try more to be in touch with herself and her feelings.*

*in touch with someone or something **1.** *Fig.* in communication with someone or a group. (*Typically: **be** ~; **get** ~.) □ *Are you in touch with your brother, or have you two grown apart?* □ *I am in touch with the person whom you asked about.* **2.** *Fig.* sympathetic or sensitive to someone or something; having good contact or rapport with someone or something. (*Typically: **be** ~; **get** ~.) □ *We talk to each other, but we're not really in touch with each other.*

in tow closely following; under someone's control. □ *The nanny walked into the park with three children in tow.* □ *The manager went to the meeting with her staff in tow.*

in transit while in the process of being transported. □ *Dave is in transit from London to Chicago.* □ *The new stereo is now in transit from the manufacturer.*

in triplicate [of a document] produced in three copies. □ *Mr. Smith asked me to copy his notes in triplicate.* □ *I completed each form in triplicate.*

*in trouble 1. in danger; in difficulty; due for punishment. (*Typically: **be** ~; **get [into]** ~.) □ *If you don't be quiet, you're going to be in trouble.* □ *The company was in trouble for months, and then went bankrupt.* **2.** *Euph.* pregnant and unmarried. (*Typically: **be** ~; **get [into]** ~.) □ *They had to get married. She was in trouble.* □ *She'll be in trouble before long, if she doesn't quit running around like that.*

in tune in a state where musical notes are at their proper intervals so that none are flat or sharp. □ *Your piano is in tune.* □ *The choir members all sang in tune.*

*in tune with someone or something **1.** *Lit.* in musical harmony with someone or something. (*Typically: **be** ~; **get** ~.) □ *The violin is in tune with the piano.* □ *The tenor is not in tune with the bass.* **2.** *Fig.* in agreement with someone or something. (*Typically: **be** ~; **get** ~.) □ *Bill is just not in tune with the company's policies.*

*in tune with the times *Fig.* up-to-date; in fashion. (*Typically: **be** ~; **get** ~.) □ *Look at that old jacket, Bill. You're not in tune with the times.*

in turn in the appropriate point in the series or order; when one's turn comes. □ *Someone has to wash the dishes after every meal. All of us will have to do it in turn.* □ *All three of them shared the task of carrying water in turn.*

in two shakes of a lamb's tail *Fig.* in a very short time; very quickly. □ *Jane returned in two shakes of a lamb's tail.* □ *Mike was able to solve the problem in two shakes of a lamb's tail.*

in unison [of musical notes, instruments, or voices] having the same pitch. □ *This part of the piece is performed in unison.* □ *The twins sang in unison.*

in use [of some facility or device] occupied or busy. □ *Sorry, this room is in use.* □ *How long will it be in use?*

in vain for no purpose; [done] as a failure. □ *They rushed her to the hospital, but they did it in vain.* □ *We tried in vain to get her there on time.*

in view of something in consideration of something; because of something. □ *In view of the high cost of gasoline, I sold my car.* □ *I won't invite John to the meeting in view of his attitude.*

*in vogue fashionable; faddish. (*Typically: **be** ~; **get** ~.) □ *This style of coat is no longer in vogue.* □ *That word isn't in vogue any longer.*

*an in (with someone**)** a way to request a special favor from someone; an amount of influence with someone. (The *in* is a noun. *Typically: **get** ~; **have** ~; **give** someone ~.) □ *Did you get an in with the mayor? I have to ask him a favor.* □ *Sorry, I don't have an in, but I know someone who does.*

*in with someone favored by someone; experiencing someone's goodwill. (*Typically: **be** ~; **get** ~.) □ *I'm really in with my Spanish professor.* □ *I am trying to get in with the bank manager so I can get a loan.* □ *Are you in with John? I need to ask him for a favor.*

*in writing in written form rather that spoken. (*Typically: **get** something ~; **have** something ~; **put** something ~.) □ *Be sure to get their salary offer in writing.*

inaugurate someone **as** something to install or introduce someone as something. □ *The club inaugurated Amy as the new president.* □ *We will inaugurate Ken as vice president.*

incapacitate someone **(for** something**) (for** a period of time**)** to make someone physically unfit for [doing] something for a period of time. □ *The accident incapacitated Rick for further work for a year.* □ *Sam's carelessness incapacitated Frank for a month.*

incarcerate someone **in** something to imprison someone in something. □ *The sheriff incarcerated Lefty in the county jail.* □ *He had wanted to incarcerate Max in the jail too.*

inch along (something**)** to move slowly along something little by little. □ *The cat inched along the carpet toward the mouse.* □ *Traffic was inching along.*

inch back to move back very slowly. □ *The trainer inched back from the angry tiger.* □ *The tiger inched back and sprang.*

inch by inch *Fig.* one inch at a time; little by little. □ *Traffic moved along inch by inch.* □ *Inch by inch, the snail moved across the stone.*

inch forward to move forward very slowly. □ *Inch forward very slowly, and try not to make any noise.* □ *The cat inched forward, taking care not to alert the bird to its presence.*

inch one's **way across** something and **inch** oneself **across** something to creep slowly across something. □ *The little green worm inched its way across the branch.* □ *It inched itself across the leaf.*

inch one's **way along** something and **inch** oneself **along** something to creep slowly on or along something. □ *I inched my way along the ledge and almost fell off.* □ *Sharon inched herself along the side of the bridge.*

inch oneself **across** something Go to **inch** one's **way across** something.

inch oneself **along** something Go to **inch** one's **way along** something.

inch over to move over a tiny bit. □ *Could you inch over a little? I need just a little more room.* □ *Please inch over a little.*

incite someone **to** something to excite or provoke someone to something. □ *The radicals tried to incite the students to* *violence.* □ *The students were incited to violent behavior by the lecturer.*

incline away (from someone or something**)** to lean or slope away from someone or something. □ *I inclined away from her to avoid her alcohol breath.* □ *The land inclined away from the house.*

incline forward to lean forward; to slant forward. □ *The earthquake-ravaged building inclined forward a little bit more and looked as if it was going to fall.* □ *My chair inclined forward and I kept feeling as if I were going to fall off.*

incline something **forward** to lean something forward; to make something slant forward. □ *Incline the light forward a little bit, so you can see better.* □ *The fence had been inclined slightly forward to make it harder to climb.*

incline toward someone or something **1.** to lean or slant toward someone or something. □ *The piece of scenery inclined toward Roger very slowly and he jumped out of the way just in time.* □ *The tree inclined toward the direction of the wind.* **2.** to favor or "lean" toward choosing someone or something. □ *I don't know which to choose. I incline toward Terri but I also favor Amy.* □ *I'm inclining toward chocolate.*

inclined to do something to tend to do something; to lean toward doing something. □ *Tom is inclined to tell jokes when he is with a group of people.* □ *I'm inclined to go to the beach tomorrow if it doesn't rain.*

include someone **in (**something**)** to invite someone to participate in something. □ *Let's include Terri in the planning session.* □ *Without asking, Henry included himself in the group going on a picnic.*

include someone or something **among** something to count someone or something as a member of a group or collection. □ *I am happy to include you among my friends.* □ *Do you include chocolate among your favorite flavors?*

include someone **out (of** something**)** *Fig.* to exclude someone from something. (Jocular.) □ *I'm not interested in your games. Include me out of them.* □ *Include me out too.*

include something **in the bargain** Go to **throw** something into the bargain.

incorporate someone or something **in(to)** something to build someone or something into something; to combine someone or something into something. □ *We want to incorporate you into our sales force very soon.* □ *The prince had incorporated himself into the main governing body.*

increase by leaps and bounds *Fig.* to increase or grow by large increments. (See also **gain by leaps and bounds.**) □ *The price of our stock is increasing by leaps and bounds.*

increase in something to grow or expand in some quality. □ *He increased in stature and wisdom.* □ *The tree increased in size every year.*

increase something **by** something to enlarge something by an amount or degree. □ *They increased the size of the house by two hundred square feet.* □ *The engine size on the new model has been increased by a small amount.*

increase something **(from** something**) (to** something**)** to enlarge something from something to something bigger; to enlarge something from one size to a larger size. □ *We*

plan to increase sales from four million to six million dollars. □ *I increased my bid to two thousand from one thousand.*

increment something **by** something to increase a sum by a supplement [of a certain figure]. □ *Increment the numbering by ten so that 1, 2, 3 becomes 10, 20, 30.* □ *The base number was incremented by 4.*

inculcate someone **with** something to touch or impress someone with some specific knowledge. □ *The teacher sought to inculcate the students with the knowledge they needed.* □ *Her parents inculcated her with good manners.*

inculcate something **in(to)** someone to instill specific knowledge into someone; to teach something to someone so that it will be remembered. □ *They inculcated good manners into their children all their lives.* □ *We tried to inculcate good morals into our students.*

incumbent (up)on someone **to** do something obligatory for someone to do something. □ *It is incumbent upon me to inform you that you are up for review.* □ *It was incumbent on Mary to mail her application before June 1st.*

indemnify someone or something **against** something to agree to protect someone or something against something, such as damage or a lawsuit. □ *Their employer indemnified them against legal action.* □ *We indemnified the publisher against legal trouble.*

indicate something **to** someone to signify something to someone. (By speech, writing, or some other sign.) □ *Karen indicated her agreement to the lawyer.* □ *Fred indicated his assent to me.*

indict someone **for** something [for a legal body] to arraign someone for a crime or name someone formally as the one accused of a crime. □ *The grand jury indicted her for murder.* □ *Then they indicted Max for grand larceny.*

indoctrinate someone **into** something to teach someone the ways of a group or some activity. □ *The staff sought to indoctrinate Walter into the ways of office procedure.* □ *Todd indoctrinated Ken into camp life.*

indoctrinate someone **with** something to teach someone the official or fundamental knowledge about something. □ *They indoctrinated all their spies with the importance of being loyal to the death.* □ *Ken indoctrinated Todd with revolutionary thinking.*

induce labor in someone to cause the onset of childbirth in a mother-to-be. □ *They decided to induce labor in the mother-to-be.* □ *They decided not to induce labor in Alice.*

induct someone **into** something **1.** to conscript someone into the armed services; to bring a nonvolunteer into the armed services. □ *They inducted Wally into the army in a little ceremony.* **2.** to draft someone into something. □ *They inducted a number of new members into the group.* **3.** to install someone in an office or position. □ *They inducted her into the presidency.* □ *The college inducted a new president into office last week.*

indulge in something **1.** to take pleasure in doing something; to do something habitually. □ *No, I don't indulge in contact sports anymore.* □ *We don't indulge in strenuous activity.* **2.** to choose to eat a certain food or drink something, usually alcohol. □ *I don't usually indulge in hard spirits, but just this once.* □ *I indulge in chocolate until I can't hold any more.*

indulge someone **with** something to grant someone the favor or privilege of something. □ *Please indulge me with this one favor.* □ *He always indulged himself with dinner at a nice restaurant when he went into town.*

***infatuated with** someone or something to be in love with someone or something. (*Typically: **be** ~; **become** ~.*) □ *She is infatuated with John.* □ *John is infatuated with chocolate ice cream.*

infect someone **with** something **1.** to transmit disease-causing organisms to someone. (*Someone includes oneself.*) □ *Please don't infect me with your cold germs.* □ *Somehow, she infected herself with the virus she was studying.* **2.** to affect someone with something, such as excitement, joy, desires, etc. □ *Her explosive laughter infected everyone with good spirits.*

infer something **from** something to reach a conclusion from something; to deduce facts from something, such as someone's words, a situation, etc. □ *What can we infer from the experience we have just had?* □ *You should not infer anything from Sue's remarks.*

***infested with** something to be contaminated with a swarm or throng of some pest. (*Typically: **be** ~; **get** ~.*) □ *All the campers are infested with lice.* □ *The dog is infested with ticks.*

infiltrate into something **1.** to permeate something; to filter into something. □ *The sour smell infiltrated into everything in the refrigerator.* □ *The paint smell infiltrated into every room in the house.* **2.** and **infiltrate** something to penetrate a group, secretly, for the purposes of spying or influencing the activities of the group. □ *The spy infiltrated into the enemy headquarters.* □ *They infiltrated into the government.*

inflate something **with** something **1.** *Lit.* to fill up something with air or some other gas. □ *Jerry has to inflate all the balloons with helium.* □ *Ken inflated the balloons with gas.* **2.** *Fig.* to make a sum appear larger by including additional irrelevant amounts. □ *I think that she has inflated her expense report with too many miles of travel.* □ *Don't inflate your expense report with extra costs.*

inflict someone **(up)on** someone to burden someone with the care or keeping of someone else. (*Upon* is formal and less commonly used than *on*.) □ *Please don't inflict Bob upon me.* □ *My brother inflicted his children on us for the weekend.* □ *Well, I certainly don't want to inflict myself on you for the weekend, but I do need a place to stay.*

inflict something **(up)on** someone or something to impose something, such as pain, a burden, a problem, etc., on someone or something. (*Upon* is formal and less commonly used than *on*.) □ *I hate to inflict an additional burden upon you, but someone has to clean the oven.* □ *Please don't inflict that on me.*

inform on someone to tell the authorities about someone; to tattle on someone. □ *I am going to have to inform on you.* □ *Liz informed on Ken to their mother.*

inform someone **about** someone or something to tell someone about someone or something. □ *How is my friend Tom getting on? I asked you to inform me about him from time to time.* □ *Please inform me about the state of the contract for the book.*

inform someone **of** something to tell someone a fact. □ *Please inform Sally of my decision.* □ *Sally has been informed of your decision.*

inform someone **on** someone to tattle (on someone) (to someone). □ *I will inform the teacher on you!* □ *Billy informed his mother on Bobby.*

infringe (up)on something to interfere with the rights of someone or with someone's property rights; to encroach on something. (*Upon* is formal and less commonly used than *on*.) □ *You are infringing upon my right to free speech.* □ *I am not infringing on your property. I'm in my own yard.*

infuse someone **with** something to teach someone a body of knowledge or a perspective on a body of knowledge. □ *The schools sought to infuse the children with a sense of history.* □ *Children should be infused with a respect for the rights of others.*

infuse something **into** someone to instill specific knowledge into a person; to teach someone something very well. □ *The boss infused a lot of company information into the new assistant before she took another job.* □ *The teacher infused a lot of knowledge into the students in a short time.*

infuse something **into** something to mix something into something. □ *You should infuse this mixture into the tea.* □ *The tea was infused into the water very slowly.*

infuse something **with** something to make something mix into some liquid. □ *He infused the mixture with a strong solution of soap.* □ *The chemical mixture was infused with the other solution.*

ingratiate oneself **into** something to work hard to bring oneself into the favor of someone. □ *Oh, how he fawns over the guests! Isn't it terrible the way he tries to ingratiate himself into their favor?* □ *You will never succeed in ingratiating yourself into my good graces.*

ingratiate oneself **with** someone to work oneself into someone's favor. □ *Why do you have to ingratiate yourself with everyone? Don't you know how to be just plain friends?* □ *She was very obvious in her effort to ingratiate herself with the boss.*

inherit something **from** someone **1.** to receive something from the estate of a person who has died. □ *I inherited this silver bowl from my aunt.* □ *Liz inherited her house from her parents.* **2.** to receive a genetic or behavioral trait from a relative. □ *I inherited my stubbornness from my father's side of the family.* □ *My dark hair was inherited from my father.*

inhibit someone **from** doing something to keep someone from doing something. □ *We will attempt to inhibit Karen from doing it, but we have no control over her.* □ *A serious case of shyness inhibited Harry from participating in things.*

inhibit something **from** doing something to keep something from happening. □ *We need to inhibit the weeds from further growth.* □ *The weeds were inhibited from spreading by the application of a pesticide.*

initiate someone **into** something **1.** to induct someone into an organization or activity, usually in a ceremony. □ *They will initiate me into the fraternity next week.* □ *They initiated all their new members into the club at once.* **2.** to introduce someone to the activities associated with a job or other situation. □ *The personnel department will initiate you into our office routines.* □ *Our procedures are com-*

plicated and it takes weeks to initiate a new employee into all our procedures.

inject something **into** someone, something, or some creature and **inject** someone, something, or some creature **with** something to give a hypodermic injection of something to someone or an animal. □ *The nurse injected the medicine into my arm.* □ *He injected a very large dose into the patient.*

inject something **into** something 1. *Lit.* to squirt something, such as oil, water, etc., into something. □ *The pump injected the oil into the wheel bearings when I squeezed the lever.* □ *The mechanic injected a solvent into the lock.* **2.** *Fig.* to put something, such as humor, excitement, etc., into a situation. □ *Let's inject a little humor into this dismal affair.* □ *She likes to inject a lot of excitement into her books.*

ink something **in**† **1.** to fill in an outline with ink. □ *Please ink the drawing in with care.* □ *Ink in the drawing carefully.* **2.** to write something in ink. □ *Please ink your name in on the dotted line.* □ *Now, ink in your signature on this line right here.*

*an **inkling (about** someone or something**)** an idea about someone or something; a hint about the nature of someone or something. (*Typically: **get** ~; **have** ~; **give** someone ~.) □ *I had an inkling about the problems that you were going to run into.*

*an **inkling (of** something**)** a hint about something that is to happen. (*Typically: **get** ~; **have** ~; **give** someone ~.) □ *The speeches gave us an inkling of what we could expect from the new president.*

inlay something **with** something to decorate something by cutting in a design and filling the cut with some decorative substance. □ *The workers inlaid the tabletop with bits of polished seashell.* □ *The tabletop was inlaid with a lovely design.*

*innocent as a lamb** and *innocent as a newborn babe 1.** guiltless. (*Also: **as** ~.) □ *"Hey! You can't throw me in jail," cried the robber. "I'm innocent as a lamb."* **2.** naive; inexperienced. (*Also: **as** ~.) □ *She's eighteen years old, but innocent as a newborn babe.*

innocent as a newborn babe Go to previous.

inoculate someone **against** something to immunize someone against a disease. □ *We need to inoculate all the children against whooping cough.* □ *Have you been inoculated against measles?*

inoculate someone **with** something to use a particular substance in immunizing someone against a disease. □ *Donna inoculated Richard and Nancy with yellow fever vaccine for their trip.* □ *She also inoculated Sam with something to prevent malaria.*

inquire about someone or something to ask about someone or something. □ *I inquired about Tom and was told that he doesn't live here anymore.* □ *You will have to inquire about that at the front desk.*

inquire after someone to ask about the well-being of someone. □ *Jerry inquired after you when I saw him at the store today.* □ *I will inquire after his wife the next time I see him.*

inquire for someone to ask to see someone. □ *Mr. Franklin, there is a man out here inquiring for you. What shall I tell him?* □ *Who is inquiring for me?*

inquire into something to look into something; to investigate something by asking questions. □ *I will inquire into your complaint. It sounds as if something is wrong.* □ *We have not inquired into it yet.*

inquire something **of** someone to ask some information of someone. □ *I need to inquire something of you.* □ *May I inquire something personal of you?*

inquire within to ask questions of a person inside [some place, such as a store or office]. (Formula. On a sign posted outside.) □ *"Help wanted. Inquire within," read the sign on the door.* □ *If you want to apply, you must inquire within.*

the **ins and outs (of** something**)** the correct and successful way to do something; the special things that one needs to know to do something. □ *I don't understand the ins and outs of politics.* □ *Jane knows the ins and outs of repairing computers.*

inscribe something **into** something to write or engrave a dedication on a gift to someone. (Emphasis is on the act of inscribing.) □ *It was a lovely watch. I asked them to inscribe something into the back, so I could remember the occasion.* □ *My initials were inscribed into the wristband.*

inscribe something **on(to)** something to write or engrave certain information on something. (Emphasis is on the message that is inscribed.) □ *The jeweler inscribed Amy's good wishes onto the watch.* □ *I inscribed my name on my tools.*

inscribe something **with** something to engrave something with a message. □ *Could you please inscribe this trophy with the information on this sheet of paper?* □ *I inscribed the bracelet with her name.*

insert something **between** something **and** something else to put something in between things. □ *Insert this marker between pages ten and eleven.* □ *A marker was inserted between the pages.*

insert something **in(to)** something to push or stick something into something. □ *Insert the card into the slot and pull the lever.* □ *Insert the coins in the machine.* □ *I need to insert another paragraph into this article.*

inside a week in less than a week. □ *We must get all this sorted out inside a week; all right?* □ *We've got inside a week to get it right.*

inside information information known only by those most involved with the issue; secret information relating to an organization. □ *I have some inside information about the Smith Company.*

an **inside job** a crime committed by someone working or living at the scene of the crime. □ *There was little doubt that it was an inside job, thought the inspector.* □ *It's a particularly cunning way to carry out an inside job.*

an **inside joke** a joke that only certain people understand; a joke understood only by people who know certain facts and context. □ *What you said must be an inside joke. It makes no sense to me.*

the **inside story** an explanation known only by those most involved with the issue. □ *Well, I've heard the inside story, and it isn't what you were told at all!*

*the **inside track** *Fig.* an advantage (over someone) gained through special connections, special knowledge, or favoritism. (*Typically: **get** ~; **have** ~; **give** someone ~.) □ *If I could get the inside track, I could win the contract.* □ *The boss likes me. Since I've got the inside track, I'll probably be the new office manager.*

insinuate oneself **into** something to work oneself into a group or situation. □ *She had sought for years to insinuate herself into Terry's organization.* □ *Must you always insinuate yourself into my set of friends?*

insinuate something **to** someone to hint at something to someone; to imply something to someone. □ *You think I am interested in you for your money! Is that what you are insinuating to me?* □ *I did not insinuate anything to you!*

insist (up)on something to demand something. (*Upon* is formal and less commonly used than *on.*) □ *I want you here now! We all insist upon it!* □ *I insist on it too.*

inspire someone **with** something to use something to inspire someone; to stimulate or encourage someone with something. □ *The president inspired us all with patriotic speeches.* □ *She inspired us all with her story of heroism.*

inspire something **in** someone to stimulate a particular quality in someone. □ *You do not particularly inspire trust in me.* □ *She inspires fear in me.*

install someone **as** something to inaugurate or launch someone into the role of something. □ *The board installed Jerry as the new parliamentarian.* □ *She installed herself as the boss of the kitchen and wouldn't allow anyone else in.*

install something **in** someone or something to insert or build something into someone or something. □ *We are going to install a trash compactor in our kitchen.* □ *The doctors installed a pacemaker in Donald.*

instigate someone **to** do something to prompt someone to do something; to urge or cause someone to do something. □ *Are you the one who instigated Terry to start all this trouble?* □ *Did you instigate the children to do this?*

instill someone **with** something to imbue or impress someone with something. □ *Her story instilled us all with courage.* □ *She instilled us with courage.*

instill something **in(to)** someone to impress something into someone's mind. □ *You need to remember your manners. I want to instill that into you.* □ *Good manners were instilled in me at home.*

instill something **in(to)** something to add something to a situation. □ *The presence of the mayor instilled a legitimacy into the proceedings.* □ *Sharon sought to instill a little levity in the meeting.*

institute something **against** someone or something to initiate something against someone or something. □ *The hospital decided to institute proceedings against her for failing to pay her bill.* □ *The prosecutor instituted a case against the county board.*

instruct someone **in** something to teach someone about something. □ *Amy will instruct you in the way to hang paper.* □ *The manager instructed Ken in the best method of entering data into the computer.*

instrumental in doing something playing an important part in doing something. □ *John was instrumental in getting the contract to build the new building.* □ *Our senator was instrumental in defeating the bill.*

insulate someone or something **against** someone or something and **insulate** someone or something **from** someone or something to protect someone or something against the effect of someone or something. □ *Use an extra blanket to insulate the baby against the cold.* □ *John is a bad influence on the children, and I've taken care to insulate them against him.* □ *We insulated the children from the effects of John and his bad habits.*

insure against something to guard or protect against something. □ *You must insure against theft and fire.* □ *I will insure against all risks.*

insure someone or something **(against** something) **(for** something) to provide insurance for someone or something against certain perils up to a certain amount of money. □ *I insured my wife against accidental death for $100,000.* □ *We insured the car for its current value against all losses.*

insure someone or something **with** something to provide insurance for someone or something from a specific company. □ *I insured Amy with a fine old insurance company.* □ *We insured the car with Acme Insurance in Adamsville.*

integrate someone or something **into** something to combine someone or something into something; to work someone or something into something. □ *We sought to integrate Amy into the everyday affairs of the company.* □ *We sought to integrate the new family into the ways of the community.*

integrate someone **with** someone to mix people together; to unify people into one group. □ *The new regional YMCA will help Hispanics integrate with others in our community.* □ *They integrated themselves with the people already in attendance.*

integrate something **with** something to merge things together; to join things into one. □ *I want to integrate the accounting department with the auditing department to save a little money.* □ *They integrated your department with mine.*

intend something **as** something to mean something to serve as something. □ *We intend this money as a gift. Do not even think about paying it back.* □ *This money is intended as a gift.*

intend something **for** someone or something to mean for someone or something to get something. □ *I intended this one for you. I'm sorry I failed to give it to you in time.* □ *Aunt Em intended this cake for the county fair, but you can have it instead.*

intent on doing something determined to do something. □ *The children were intent on making a snowman.* □ *The prisoner was intent on escaping.*

inter someone **in** something to bury someone in something or in some place. □ *They chose to inter her in the family burial plot.* □ *She was interred in the vault with the rest of the family.*

interact with someone to converse with and exchange ideas with someone. □ *In act two, I want Terri to interact with Amy a little more. They act as if they never even met each other.* □ *The students will interact with one another in their study projects.*

interact with something to have a reciprocal action with something; to react with something. (Often refers to the negative consequences of interaction.) □ *Will this drug interact with coffee?* □ *This drug will not interact with your current medication.*

intercede (for someone**) (with** someone or something**)** to intervene on behalf of someone with someone or a group; to plead someone's case with someone or a group. □ *I will intercede for Charlotte with the council.* □ *Tom interceded with Fred for Sharon, who was too shy to speak for herself.*

interchange someone **with** someone else to exchange one person for another. □ *I interchanged Sally with Roger for the honor of being first speaker.* □ *Roger has been interchanged with Sally.*

interchange something **with** something to exchange one thing for another. □ *Please interchange the orange one with the purple one.* □ *The orange one has been interchanged with the red one.*

interest someone **in** someone or something to arouse the interest of someone in someone or something. □ *Yes, I can recommend someone for you to hire. Could I interest you in Tom? He's one of our best workers.* □ *Can I interest you in checking out a book from the library?*

interest someone **in** something to cause someone to wish to purchase something. □ *Could I interest you in something with a little more style to it?* □ *Can I interest you in some additional insurance on your life?*

interface someone or something **with** someone or something to bring about a complex connection of people and things, in any combination. (Originally having to do with computers.) □ *Let's interface Walter with the staff from the main office.* □ *I want to interface my data with Sam, who has some relevant statistics from prior years.*

interface with someone or something to develop a connection or interaction with someone or something. □ *Call Walter and set up a meeting so we can interface with him.* □ *This computer is meant to interface with as many as five others just like it.*

interfere in something to meddle in something; to become involved in someone else's business. □ *Don't interfere in my business!* □ *Are you interfering in this matter again?*

interfere with someone or something to meddle with something or someone's affairs. □ *Please do not interfere with us.* □ *Are you interfering with my project?*

interject someone **into** something to force someone into something, usually into someone else's business. □ *I am going to have to interject Fred into this matter before it gets out of hand.* □ *I hate to interject myself into your affairs, but I have something to say.*

interject something **into** something to volunteer information or a comment into a conversation. □ *We can always count on Liz to interject something sensible into our discussions.* □ *At last, something sensible has been interjected into our discussions.*

interlace something **with** something to weave something into something else. □ *I will interlace some silver thread with the white yarn.* □ *The manufacturer had interlaced a silver thread into the yarn.*

intermarry with someone [for members of a group] to marry into another group, race, or clan. □ *Our people*

don't intermarry with people of that clan. □ *They do not intermarry with other groups on purpose.*

intermingle something **with** something to mingle or merge things with things. □ *Don't intermingle the U.S. mail with the interoffice mail.* □ *The office mail had been intermingled with the regular mail!*

intermingle with someone to mingle or merge with people. □ *The mugger intermingled with the people on the street and could not be recognized.* □ *Let's intermingle with the guests.*

intern someone **in** something to detain or imprison a person in something. □ *The government interned the enemy prisoners in the camps for a few months.* □ *He was interned in a prison camp during the war.*

interpose someone or something **between** people or things to put someone or something between people or things, in any combination. □ *I do not wish to interpose Randy between the twins.* □ *We will not interpose our own standards between these two warring factions.*

interpose something **in(to)** something to introduce something into something; to put a question into a conversation. □ *The chairman interposed a question into the discussion.* □ *May I interpose an observation in the proceedings?*

interpret for someone to translate speech in a foreign language for someone. (Interpreting is done in real time.) □ *Nina interpreted for Michael, since he understood very little Russian.* □ *Is there someone who can interpret for me?*

interpret something **as** something to assume that something means something. □ *Don't interpret what I just said as criticism.* □ *It will be interpreted as criticism no matter what you say.*

interpret something **for** someone **1.** to translate a foreign language for someone. (Interpreting is done in real time.) □ *Could you interpret the ambassador's address for me?* □ *Nina interpreted the director's greetings for the visitors.* **2.** to explain something unclear to someone. □ *Let me interpret the instructions for you.* □ *The instructions have been interpreted for me by the manager.*

intersperse something **among** something to place something among things at random. □ *We interspersed a few chocolate doughnuts among all the plain ones.* □ *Some chocolate ones had been interspersed among the plain ones.*

intersperse something **between** something to place things between other things, perhaps regularly or in a pattern. □ *We interspersed an onion plant between each pair of plants.* □ *Onions had been interspersed between every two marigold plants.*

intersperse something **throughout** something to put things throughout something. □ *He interspersed recommendations for a better life throughout the book.* □ *Good advice had been interspersed throughout the book.*

intersperse something **with** something to provide or bestow something with something. □ *You should intersperse some red flowers with the orange ones.* □ *The book was interspersed with good advice.*

intertwine something **with** something to mingle or twist something together with something else. □ *She intertwined the flowers with the sprigs of greenery, making a* lovely wreath. □ *The flowers were intertwined with sprigs of greenery.*

intertwine with something to twist together with something else. □ *The vines intertwined with the ropes and cables that had once held the beached raft together.* □ *The cables from the two cranes intertwined with each other, causing a serious accident.*

intervene between someone **and** someone else to intercede between someone and someone else. □ *I decided to intervene between Ralph and his brother, who were arguing endlessly.* □ *There was no point in intervening between Bill and Bob.*

intervene in something to get involved in something. □ *I will have to intervene in this matter. It's getting out of hand.* □ *I want to intervene in this before it becomes a major problem.*

intervene with someone or something to step into a matter concerning someone or something. □ *Megan said she would intervene with the bank manager on our behalf.* □ *Do I need to intervene with this process?*

interview someone **for** something [for an employer] to discuss employment in a particular job with a person seeking employment. □ *We will interview her for the manager's job.* □ *We will interview the rest of them for the position tomorrow.*

interview with someone **for** something [for a person seeking employment] to discuss employment in a particular job with an employer. □ *She interviewed with the civic opera company for a job in the business department.* □ *I interviewed with Roger for the job.*

intimate apparel *Euph.* women's underwear. □ *"You'll find bras and body shapers in the intimate apparel," said the salesclerk at the department store.* □ *The catalog features intimate apparel for the grande dame.*

intimate something **to** someone to suggest or imply something to someone. □ *What are you intimating to me?* □ *I intimated nothing at all to you.*

*intimate with someone *Euph.* having sexual intercourse with someone. (*Typically: **be** ~; **get** ~.) □ *He had never been intimate with a woman before.* □ *They were intimate with each other for the first time that night.*

intimidate someone **into** something to threaten or frighten someone into doing something. □ *Do you think you can intimidate me into working for you?* □ *We weren't intimidated into doing it.*

intimidate someone **with** something to threaten or frighten someone with something. □ *Please don't try to intimidate me with your silly threats!* □ *We hadn't been intimidated with their threats.*

in(to) a jam *Fig.* in(to) a difficult situation. □ *Mary cannot keep track of the many times Dave got himself into a jam.* □ *I found myself in a jam when my car overheated on the highway.*

into being into existence. □ *The new law brought more problems into being.* □ *That idea came into being centuries ago.*

in(to) someone's **clutches** *Fig.* in the control of someone who has power or authority over someone else. □ *Snow White fell into the clutches of the evil witch.* □ *Once you're in my clutches, I'll ruin you.*

intoxicate someone **with** someone or something *Fig.* to enthrall or entrance someone with someone or something. (See also **intoxicate** someone **with** something.) □ *She intoxicated him with her smiling eyes.* □ *The king intoxicated the dignitaries with his beautiful daughter, whom he offered in marriage to the bravest of them all.*

intoxicate someone **with** something to make someone drunk with alcohol. □ *I think that the plaintiff set out to intoxicate the defendant with liquor and then fake a crime.* □ *Jed set out to intoxicate Max with gin and then rob him.* □ *Alice intoxicated herself with too much whiskey.*

intrigue someone **with** someone or something to fascinate someone with someone or something. □ *Walter intrigued the baby with his keys and funny faces.* □ *The king intrigued the guests with a seductive dancer who had trained in the Far East.*

intrigue (with someone**) (against** someone**)** to conspire with someone against someone. □ *You are guilty of intriguing with an enemy against the government.* □ *I did not intrigue against anyone.*

introduce someone **into** something to bring someone into something; to launch someone into something. □ *Tony introduced Wally into his club.* □ *You do not wish me to introduce myself into local social life, do you?*

introduce someone **to** someone to make someone acquainted with someone else. □ *I would like to introduce you to my cousin, Rudolph.* □ *Allow me to introduce myself to you.*

introduce something **into** something to bring something into something or some place; to bring something into something as an innovation. □ *The decorator introduced a little bit of bright red into the conference room.* □ *After I introduced the new procedures into the factory, production increased enormously.*

intrude into something to get involved in something that is someone else's business. □ *I don't want to intrude into your affairs, but I see that you're short of money.* □ *Please don't intrude into this matter.*

intrude oneself **into** something to work oneself into some matter that is someone else's business. □ *I hate to intrude myself into your conversation, but don't I know you?* □ *Please do not intrude yourself into this matter.*

intrude (up)on someone or something to encroach on someone or something or matters that concern only someone or something. (*Upon* is formal and less commonly used than *on*.) □ *I didn't mean to intrude upon you.* □ *Please don't intrude on our meeting. Please wait outside.*

inundate someone or something **with** something **1.** *Lit.* to flood someone or something with fluid. □ *The river inundated the fields with three feet of water.* □ *The storm inundated us with heavy rain.* **2.** *Fig.* to overwhelm someone with someone or something. □ *They inundated us with mail.* □ *The children inundated us with requests for their favorite songs.* □ *The citizens inundated the legislature with demands for jobs.*

inure someone or something **to** something to accustom someone to someone or something. □ *We wanted to inure you to this kind of problem, but here it is and you must face it.*

□ *The coach inured the team to the thought of losing.* □ *She had long ago inured herself to criticism of this type.*

invasion of (someone's**) privacy** *Fig.* an intrusion that results in the loss of someone's privacy. □ *Your invasion of my privacy is not welcome!* □ *The athlete complained about the invasion of his privacy by the press.*

inveigh against someone or something to attack someone or something verbally. □ *Why must you always inveigh against Dan whenever I mention his name?* □ *Stop inveighing against the government all the time.*

inveigle someone **into** something to coax or trick someone into doing something. □ *We tried to inveigle her into attending, but she caught on to us.* □ *I was inveigled into doing it.*

inveigle someone **out of** something to deceive someone into giving something up. □ *Are you trying to inveigle me out of my money?* □ *I was inveigled out of my money by a common thief.*

inveigle something **out of** someone to get something away from someone, usually by deception or persuasion. □ *They inveigled a large donation out of Mrs. Smith.* □ *The crooks tried to inveigle a fortune out of the old lady.*

invest in someone or something to put resources into someone or something in hopes of increasing the value of the person or thing. (The emphasis is on the act of investing.) □ *We invested in Tom, and we have every right to expect a lot from him.* □ *She invested in junk bonds heavily.*

invest someone's **time in** something *Fig.* to put one's time, effort, or energy into a project. □ *Mary invests her time in charity work.* □ *I invested five weeks of my time building this model ship.*

invest someone **with** something to endow someone with something, such as power or privilege. □ *The constitution invests the vice president with the authority to act on the president's behalf in certain conditions.* □ *The state has invested me with the authority to unite this couple in marriage.*

invest something **in** someone or something **1.** to put money, time, effort, etc., into someone or something, hoping for a return. □ *We will invest time and effort in Fred and make him into a recording star.* □ *Sharon invested a lot of money in the stock market.* **2.** to place power or authority under control of someone or something. □ *The constitution has invested certain powers in the federal government and left the rest to the states.* □ *The law invests the power to arrest criminals in the sheriff's department.*

invite someone **into** some place and **invite** someone **in**† to bid or request someone to enter a place. □ *Don't leave Dan out there in the rain. Invite him into the house!* □ *Oh, do invite in the children!*

invite someone **out**† to ask someone out on a date. □ *I would love to invite you out sometime. If I did, would you go?* □ *Has he ever invited out a girl on a date?*

invite someone **over**† **(for** something**)** to bid or request someone to come to one's house for something, such as a meal, party, chat, cards, etc. □ *Let's invite Tony and Nick over for dinner.* □ *Let's invite over some new people.*

invite someone **to** something to bid or request someone to come to an event. □ *Shall we invite Sally to the party?* □ *I didn't invite her. She invited herself to this affair.*

invoke something **(up)on** someone or something to call something, such as judgment, power, wrath of God, etc., to deal with someone or something. (*Upon* is formal and less commonly used than *on*.) □ *The duke invoked the wrath of God upon his enemies—to no avail.* □ *Walter invoked divine assistance on the proceedings, which weren't going very well.*

involve someone **in** something to draw someone into a matter or problem. □ *Please don't involve me in this mess.* □ *I do not wish to involve myself in Alice's business.* □ *I didn't want to involve you in the problem we are having with the police.*

involve someone **with** someone or something **1.** to cause someone to associate with someone or something. □ *Don't try to involve me with John. I can't stand him.* □ *We will try to involve all the teachers with the new association.* □ *I will not involve myself with such goings-on.* **2.** to connect someone or someone's name to activity (often wrongdoing) associated with someone or something. □ *Don't try to involve Amy with the crime. She is innocent.* □ *We involved the committee with the intense lobbying effort, and everyone began to see the extent of its influence.*

*involved (with someone**) 1.** associated with someone romantically. (*Typically: **be ~; get ~.**) □ *Sally is getting involved with Bill. They've been seeing a lot of each other.* □ *I hope they don't get too involved with each other.* **2.** having established a romantic association with something. (*Typically: **be ~; get ~.**) □ *Bill is involved with Jane, and it's looking serious.* □ *Mary is very much involved with Tom.*

*involved with something established in an association with something or some organization. (*Typically: **be ~; get ~; become ~.**) □ *Bill got involved with a volunteer organization.* □ *Mary is very much involved with her club activities.*

iron something **out**† **1.** *Lit.* to use a flatiron to make cloth flat or smooth. □ *I will iron the drapes out, so they will hang together.* □ *I ironed out the drapes.* **2.** *Fig.* to ease a problem; to smooth out a problem. (Here *problem* is synonymous with *wrinkle.*) □ *It's only a little problem. I can iron it out very quickly.* □ *We will iron out all these little matters first.*

is all *Rur.* That is all [and nothing more].; That is all I meant to say and there are no further implications. (Often used to end a sentence.) □ *I'm not mad at you. I'm just disappointed, is all.* □ *Jane's not a bad kid. She's headstrong, is all.*

(Is) anything going on? *Inf.* Is there anything exciting or interesting happening here? □ *Andrew: Hey, man! Anything going on? Henry: No. This place is dull as can be.* □ *Bob: Come in, Tom. Tom: Is anything going on? Bob: No. You've come on a very ordinary day.*

(Is) everything okay? *Inf.* How are you?; How are things? □ *John: Hi, Mary. Is everything okay? Mary: Sure. What about you? John: I'm okay.* □ *Waiter: Is everything okay? Bill: Yes, it's fine.*

(Is it) cold enough for you? *Inf.* a greeting inquiry made during very cold weather. □ *Bob: Hi, Bill! Is it cold enough for you? Bill: It's unbelievable!* □ *John: Glad to see you. Is it cold enough for you? Bill: Oh, yes! This is awful!*

(Is it) hot enough for you? *Inf.* a greeting inquiry made during very hot weather. □ *Bob: Hi, Bill! Is it hot enough for you? Bill: Yup.* □ *John: Nice to see you here! Is it hot enough for you? Bill: Good grief, yes! This is awful!*

Is someone there? a way of requesting to talk to someone in particular over the telephone. (This is not just a request to find out where *someone* is. The *someone* is usually a person's name.) □ *Tom: Hello? Mary: Hello. Is Bill there? Tom: No. Can I take a message?* □ *Tom: Hello? Mary: Hello. Is Tom there? Tom: Speaking.*

Is that everything? Go to (Will there be) anything else?

Is that right? Go to next.

Is that so? and **Is that right? 1.** Is what you said correct? (With rising question intonation.) □ *Henry: These are the ones we need. Andrew: Is that right? They don't look so good to me.* □ *Fred: Tom is the one who came in late. Rachel: Is that so? It looked like Bill to me.* **2.** That is what you say, but I do not believe you. (No rising question intonation. Slightly rude.) □ *Mary: You are making a mess of this. Alice: Is that so? And I suppose that you're perfect?* □ *Bob: I found your performance to be weak in a number of places. Henry: Is that right? I suppose you could have done better?*

Is there any truth to something? Is something true?; Is what I have heard true? (*no truth to* in the negative.) □ *Is there any truth to the gossip that Harry is leaving school?* □ *No, there is no truth to that at all.*

Is there anything else? Go to (Will there be) anything else?

Is there some place I can wash up? Go to Where can I wash up?

(Is) this (seat) taken? an inquiry made by a person in a theater, auditorium, etc., asking someone already seated whether an adjacent seat is available or already taken. □ *Finally, Bill came to a row where there was an empty seat. Bill leaned over to the person sitting beside the empty seat and whispered, "Is this seat taken?"* □ *Fred: 'Scuse me. This taken? Alice: No. Help yourself.*

isolate someone or something **from** someone or something to keep people or things separated from one another, in any combination. □ *They isolated everyone from Sam, who was ill with malaria.* □ *We isolated the children from the source of the disease.*

issue a call for something to make a public invitation or request for something. □ *The prime minister issued a call for peace.* □ *The person who organized the writing contest issued a call for entries.*

issue (forth) from some place to go out or come out of a place. □ *The news releases issued forth from the pressroom on a regular basis.* □ *Clear water issued from the side of the hill.*

issue from something to come out or flow out of something. □ *A delicious perfume issued from Sally's hair as she passed.* □ *A wonderful aroma issued from the kitchen as the bread baked.*

issue someone **with** something to provide someone with something; to distribute something to someone. □ *We issued them with the clothes they needed for the trip.* □ *Everyone was issued with supplies.*

issue something **as** something to release or send out something as something. □ *They issued this month's magazine as a special double issue.* □ *The publisher issued this month's magazine as the very last one.*

issue something **to** someone to distribute or dispense something to someone. □ *The front office issued new assignments to everyone today.* □ *New keys were issued to everyone.*

It ain't fittin'. *Rur.* It is not right; It is inappropriate. □ *It ain't fittin' for the bridegroom to see his bride before the ceremony.* □ *Young folks shouldn't talk back to their elders. It ain't fittin'.*

(It) beats me. and **(It's) got me beat.; You got me beat.** *Inf.* I do not know the answer.; I cannot figure it out. The question has me stumped. (The stress is on *me*.) □ *Bill: When are we supposed to go over to Tom's? Bill: Beats me.* □ *Sally: What's the largest river in the world? Bob: You got me beat.*

it behooves one **to** do something *Cliché* it is necessary for one to do something; it is **incumbent (up)on** someone **to do** something. □ *It behooves me to report the crime.* □ *It behooves you to pay for the window that you broke.*

It blows my mind! *Sl.* It really amazes and shocks me. □ *Bill: Did you hear about Tom's winning the lottery? Sue: Yes, it blows my mind!* □ *John: Look at all that paper! What a waste of trees! Jane: It blows my mind!*

(It) can't be helped. and **(It) couldn't be helped.** Nothing can be done to help the situation.; The situation could not have been avoided. □ *John: The accident has blocked traffic in two directions. Jane: It can't be helped. They have to get the people out of the cars and send them to the hospital.* □ *Bill: My goodness, the lawn looks dead! Sue: It can't be helped. There's no rain and water is rationed.* □ *John: I'm sorry I broke your figurine. Sue: It couldn't be helped. John: I'll replace it. Sue: That would be nice.* □ *Bill: I'm sorry I'm late. I hope it didn't mess things up. Bob: It can't be helped.*

(It) couldn't be better. and **(Things) couldn't be better.** Everything is fine. □ *John: How are things going? Jane: Couldn't be better.* □ *Bill: I hope everything is okay with your new job. Mary: Things couldn't be better.*

(It) couldn't be helped. Go to (It) can't be helped.

It cuts two ways. *Inf.* There are two sides to the situation. □ *You have to help, too. It cuts two ways.* □ *It cuts two ways, you know. It can't always all be my fault.*

(It) doesn't bother me any. and **(It) doesn't bother me at all.** It does not trouble me at all.; I have no objection. (Compare this with **(It) don't bother me none.** Not very polite or cordial. See also **(It) won't bother me any.** for the future tense of this expression.) □ *John: Do you mind if I sit here? Jane: Doesn't bother me any.* □ *Sally (smoking a cigarette): Do you mind if I smoke? Bill: It doesn't bother me any.*

(It) doesn't bother me at all. Go to previous.

(It) doesn't hurt to ask. and **(It) never hurts to ask.** a phrase said when one asks a question, even when the answer is known to be no. □ *John: Can I take some of these papers home with me? Jane: No, you can't. You know that. John: Well, it doesn't hurt to ask.* □ *Sue: Can I have two of* *these? Sally: Certainly not! Sue: Well, it never hurts to ask. Sally: Well, it just may!*

It doesn't quite suit me. Go to **This doesn't quite suit me.**

(It) don't bother me none. *Inf.* It does not affect me one way or the other.; **It doesn't bother me any.** (Familiar and ungrammatical. Sometimes used for effect.) □ *John: Mind if I sit here? Bob: It don't bother me none.* □ *Mary: Can I smoke? Bill: Don't bother me none.*

(It) don't cut no ice (with someone**).** and **(It) don't cut no squares (with** someone**).** *Rur.* (It) doesn't influence me. □ *That excuse don't cut no ice with me.* □ *I'm tired of you coming home drunk. Your fancy apologies don't cut no squares.*

(It) don't cut no squares (with someone**)** Go to previous.

(It) don't make me no nevermind. Go to **(It) makes no difference to me.**

It figures. It makes sense.; It confirms what one might have guessed.; I'm not surprised. □ *Bob: Tom was the one who broke the window. Bill: It figures. He's very careless.* □ *Ann: Mary was the last one to arrive. Sally: It figures. She's always late.*

It has someone's **name on it.** *Fig.* It belongs to someone.; It is meant for someone. □ *A: Is that an extra piece of cake? B: Yes, and it has your name on it.*

(It) hasn't been easy. and **Things haven't been easy.** Things have been difficult, but I have gotten through. □ *Bill: I'm so sorry about all your troubles. I hope things are all right now. Bob: It hasn't been easy, but things are okay now.* □ *John: How are you getting on after your dog died? Bill: Things haven't been easy.*

[it is] See also the entries beginning with *it's.*

It is a long lane that has no turning. *Prov.* Bad times cannot continue forever.; Things will soon improve. □ *Nancy: It's been six months, and neither one of us can find work. I'm afraid we're going to lose everything. Bill: Don't despair, honey. It is a long lane that has no turning.* □ *Your luck has been bad for a long time, but it is a long lane that has no turning. I'm sure things will change soon.*

It is a poor heart that never rejoices. and **It is a sad heart that never rejoices.** *Prov.* Even a habitually sad person cannot be sad all the time. (Sometimes used to indicate that a habitually sad person is happy about something.) □ *Jill: I've never seen Sam smile before, but today, at his retirement party, he smiled. Jane: It is a poor heart that never rejoices.*

It is a wise child that knows its own father. *Prov.* You can never have certain proof that a certain man is your father. (Implies that the child in question might be illegitimate.) □ *It is a wise child that knows its own father, but Emily is so much like her dad that there's very little uncertainty.*

It is all over with someone. and **It is all over for** someone. *Euph.* Someone is about to die.; Someone has just died. □ *I am afraid it is all over with Aunt Sarah. Her last surgery did not go well at all.* □ *The doctor told us that it was all over for Daddy. We sat for a moment in shock.*

It is better to be born lucky than rich. *Prov.* If you are born rich, you may lose your money, but if you are born lucky, you will always get what you need or want just by chance. □ *Maybe your family doesn't have a lot of money, but you are lucky, you know. And it's better to be born lucky than rich.*

It is better to give than to receive. and **It is more blessed to give than to receive.** *Prov.* It is more virtuous to give things than to get them. (Biblical.) □ *Susan told her children, "Instead of thinking so much about what you want for your birthday, think about what to give your brothers and sisters for their birthdays. Remember, it is better to give than to receive."* □ *Our charity encourages you to share the good things you have. It is more blessed to give than to receive.*

It is better to travel hopefully than to arrive. *Prov.* You should enjoy the process of doing something, rather than anticipate the result of doing it. □ *Bill: I can't wait till I get my high school diploma. Fred: You should concentrate on enjoying high school instead. It is better to travel hopefully than to arrive.*

It is better to wear out than to rust out. *Prov.* It is better to work until you die than to be idle just because you are old. □ *Nancy: Grandma, you shouldn't work so hard. You're not young anymore, you know. Grandmother: Thanks for your concern, dear, but I plan to keep working. It's better to wear out than to rust out.* □ *Bill: You really ought to relax. I'm afraid you'll kill yourself with too much work. Nancy: So what? It's better to wear out than to rust out.*

It is easier to tear down than to build up. *Prov.* Destroying things is easier than building them. □ *Jill: That poor politician—he served honestly and well for all those years and now his career is ruined by one little scandal. Jane: It is easier to tear down than to build up.*

It is easy to be wise after the event. *Prov.* After you see the consequences of a decision, it is easy to tell if the decision was good, but it is also too late, since the consequences have already happened. □ *Jill: I should never have invited Aunt Betsy to stay with me; I haven't had a peaceful moment since she got here. Jane: Well, it's easy to be wise after the event.*

It is more blessed to give than to receive. Go to **It is better to give than to receive.**

It is never too late to learn. and **You are never too old to learn.** *Prov.* You can always learn something new. □ *Alan: Help me make the salad dressing. Jane: But I don't know anything about making salad dressing. Alan: You are never too old to learn.* □ *Grandma decided to take a course in using computers. "It's never too late to learn," she said.*

It is never too late to mend. *Prov.* It is never too late to apologize for something you have done or try to repair something you have done wrong. □ *Sue: I still miss Tony, but it's been a year since our big fight and we haven't spoken to each other since. Mother: Well, it's never too late to mend; why don't you call him up and apologize?*

It is not work that kills, but worry. *Prov.* Working hard will not hurt you, but worrying too much is bad for your health. □ *Nancy: You've been working so many hours every day, I'm afraid you'll get sick. Bill: It's not work that kills, but worry.*

It is the pace that kills. *Prov.* Trying to do too much too fast is bad for you. □ *Nancy: I hate college. Bill: Why? Is the subject material too difficult? Nancy: No, they just expect me to learn too much of it too fast. It is the pace that kills.*

It isn't worth it. 1. Its value does not justify the action you propose. □ *Mary: Should I write a letter in support of your request? Sue: No, don't bother. It isn't worth it.* □ *John: Do you suppose we should report that man to the police? Jane: No, it isn't worth it.* **2.** Its importance does not justify the concern you are showing. □ *Tom: I'm so sorry about your roses all dying. Mary: Not to worry. It isn't worth it. They were sort of sickly anyway.* □ *John: Should I have this coat cleaned? The stain isn't coming out. Sue: It isn't worth it. I only wear it when I shovel snow anyway.*

It isn't worth the trouble. Don't bother. It isn't worth it. □ *Tom: Shall I wrap all this stuff back up? Mary: No. It's not worth the trouble. Just stuff it in a paper bag.* □ *Jane: Do you want me to try to save this little bit of cake? John: Oh, no! It's not worth the trouble. I'll just eat it.*

(It) just goes to show (you) (something). That incident or story has an important moral or message. □ *Tom: The tax people finally caught up with Henry. Sally: See! It just goes to show.* □ *Angry at the young grocery clerk, Sally muttered, "Young people. They expect too much. It just goes to show you how society has broken down."*

(It) (just) goes without saying. *Cliché* [something] is so obvious that it need not be said. □ *It goes without saying that you are to wear formal clothing to the White House dinner.* □ *Of course you must be on time. That goes without saying.*

(It) makes me no difference. Go to next.

(It) makes no difference to me. and **(It) makes me no difference.; (It) makes me no nevermind.; (It) don't make me no nevermind.** *Inf.* I really do not care, one way or the other. (The first one is standard, the others are colloquial.) □ *Bill: Mind if I sit here? Tom: Makes no difference to me.* □ *Bill: What would you say if I ate the last piece of cake? Bob: Don't make me no nevermind.*

(It) never hurts to ask. Go to (It) doesn't hurt to ask.

It never rains but it pours. *Prov.* Good (or bad) things do not just happen a few at a time, but in large numbers all at once. □ *Fred: I can't believe this. This morning I had a flat tire. When I went to the garage to get the tire patched, I discovered I didn't have any money, and I couldn't even charge it because my credit card's expired. Jane: It never rains but it pours.*

It (only) stands to reason. It is only reasonable to hold a certain opinion. □ *It stands to reason that most people will not buy a new car if they don't think they can pay for it.* □ *I think he will come back to pick up his check. It only stands to reason.*

(It) (really) doesn't matter to me. I do not care. □ *Andrew: What shall I do? What shall I do? Alice: Do whatever you like. Jump off a bridge. Go live in the jungle. It really doesn't matter to me.* □ *Tom: I'm leaving you. Mary and I have decided that we're in love. Sue: So, go ahead. It doesn't matter to me. I don't care what you do.*

It's a (dead) cinch. *Fig.* It's a very easy task. (*Dead* means absolutely.) □ *Tom: Did you figure out how to change the tire? Jane: Yep! It was a cinch.* □ *Altering clothes patterns is difficult for me, but for Mary, it's a dead cinch.*

It's a deal. Okay.; It is agreed. □ *You want to sell me your stereo for $100? It's a deal.* □ *Bill: Let's go to dinner together tonight. Mary: It's a deal.*

It's a jungle out there. The real world is severe.; It's hard to get by in everyday life. □ *A: Gee, people are so rude in this town. B: Yup, it's a jungle out there.*

It's a snap. *Inf.* It's really easy to do. □ *Nothing to it. It's a snap. A baby could do it.*

It's a toss-up. *Inf.* It's hard to tell the winner, and it could be won by either player or either team. □ *The game's almost over, and it's a toss-up.*

It's about time! *Inf.* It is almost too late!; I've been waiting a long time! (Said with impatience.) □ *So you finally got here! It's about time!* □ *They finally paid me my money. It's about time!*

It's (all) Greek to me. Go to Greek to someone.

It's all over but the shouting. *Fig. Cliché* It is decided and concluded.; It is essentially decided and finished. (Meaning that though there may be more to some process, the outcome is clear. An elaboration of **all over,** which means "finished.") □ *The last goal was made with only 4 seconds to go in the game. "Well, it's all over but the shouting," said the coach.* □ *Tom worked hard in college and passed his last test with an A. When he saw the grade, he said, "It's all over but the shouting."*

It's all someone **needs.** Go to That's all someone needs.

It's always darkest just before the dawn. See The darkest hour is just before the dawn.

It's an ill bird that fouls its own nest. *Prov.* Only a foolish or dishonorable person would bring dishonor to his or her self or his or her surroundings.; Only a bad person would ruin the place where he or she lives. (See also foul one's own nest.) □ *I don't like my new neighbor. Not only does he never mow his lawn, he covers it with all kinds of trash. It's an ill bird that fouls its own nest.*

It's an ill wind that blows nobody (any) good. *Prov.* Even misfortune can benefit someone or something.; A calamity for one person usually benefits somebody else. □ *The tremendous hailstorm left gaping holes in most of the roofs in town, so many families were homeless. The roofing companies, however, made plenty of money fixing those holes. It's an ill wind that blows nobody any good.*

It's anybody's guess No one knows, so anyone's guess is as good as anyone else's. □ *A: When will the messenger be here? B: It's anybody's guess.*

It's been. *Inf.* a phrase said on leaving a party or other gathering. (A shortening of **It's been lovely** or some similar expression.) □ *Mary: Well, it's been. We really have to go, though. Andy: So glad you could come over. Bye.* □ *Fred: Bye, you guys. See you. Sally: It's been. Really it has. Toodle-oo.*

It's been a slice! *Sl.* It's been good. □ *Good-bye and thank you. It's been a slice!* □ *It's been a slice. I hope to see you again some day.*

(It's been) good talking to you. and **(It's) been good to talk to you.; (It's been) nice talking to you.** a polite phrase said upon departure, at the end of a conversation. □ *Mary (as the elevator stops): Well, this is my floor. I've got to get off. John: Bye, Mary. It's been good talking to you.* □ *John: It's been good talking to you, Fred. See you around. Fred: Yeah. See you.*

(It's) better than nothing. Having something that is not satisfactory is better than having nothing at all. □ *John: How do you like your dinner? Jane: It's better than nothing. John: That bad, huh?* □ *John: Did you see your room? How do you like it? Jane: Well, I guess it's better than nothing.*

It's for a fact. *Rur.* It is true. □ *Charlie: I can't believe that Bill's selling his house. Tom: It's for a fact!* □ *It's for a fact that chocolate is poison to cats.*

It's for you. This telephone call is for you. □ *Henry: Hello? Fred: Hello. Is Bill there? Henry: Hey, Bill! It's for you. Bill: Thanks. Hello?* □ *"It's for you," said Mary, handing the telephone receiver to Sally.*

(It's) good to be here. and **(It's) nice to be here.** I feel welcome in this place.; It is good to be here. □ *John: I'm so glad you could come. Jane: Thank you. It's good to be here.* □ *Alice: Welcome to our house! John: Thank you, it's nice to be here.*

(It's) good to have you here. and **(It's) nice to have you here.** Welcome to this place.; It is good that you are here. □ *John: It's a pleasure to have you here. Jane: Thank you for asking me.* □ *Alice: Oh, I'm so glad I came! Fred: Nice to have you here.*

(It's) good to hear your voice. a polite phrase said upon beginning or ending a telephone conversation. □ *Bob: Hello? Bill: Hello, it's Bill. Bob: Hello, Bill. It's good to hear your voice.* □ *Bill: Hello, Tom. This is Bill. Tom: Hi, Bill. It's good to hear your voice. What's cooking?*

(It's) good to see you (again). a polite phrase said when greeting someone whom one has met before. □ *Bill: Hi, Bob. Remember me? I met you last week at the Wilsons'. Bob: Oh, hello, Bill. Good to see you again.* □ *Fred: Hi. Good to see you again! Bob: Nice to see you, Fred.*

(It's) got me beat. Go to **(It) beats me.**

it's high time *Rur.* it is about the right time for something. □ *It's high time we were leaving.* □ *It's high time you started thinking about saving for your old age.*

It's ill waiting for dead men's shoes. *Prov.* You should not be eager for someone to die so that you inherit something. □ *Phil: Why should I bother to learn some kind of trade? I'll be rich when Grandpa dies and leaves me all his money. Alan: It's ill waiting for dead men's shoes.*

It's just one of those things. It is something that couldn't have been prevented.; It is an unfortunate thing caused by fate. □ *I'm sorry, too. It's not your fault. It's just one of those things.* □ *I feel terrible that I didn't pass the bar exam. I guess it was just one of those things.*

(It's) just what you need. Go to **That's all** someone needs.

(It's) nice to be here. Go to **(It's) good to be here.**

(It's) nice to have you here. Go to **(It's) good to have you here.**

(It's) nice to meet you. an expression said just after being introduced to someone. □ *Tom: Sue, this is my sister, Mary. Sue: It's nice to meet you, Mary. Mary: How are*

you, Sue? □ *Bob: I'm Bob. Nice to see you here. Jane: Nice to meet you, Bob.*

(It's) nice to see you. an expression said when greeting or saying good-bye to someone. □ *Mary: Hi, Bill. It's nice to see you. Bill: Nice to see you, Mary. How are things?* □ *John: Come on in, Jane. Nice to see you. Jane: Thanks, and thank you for inviting me.*

It's no picnic! *Inf.* There is nothing easy or pleasant about it. □ *I was on welfare for a year, and it's no picnic.*

(It's) no trouble (at all). Do not worry, this is not a problem. □ *Mary: Do you mind carrying all this up to my apartment? Tom: It's no trouble.* □ *Bob: Would it be possible for you to get this back to me today? Bill: Sure. No trouble at all.*

It's no use crying over spilled milk. and **Don't cry over spilled milk.** *Prov.* Do not be upset about making a mistake, since you cannot change that now. □ *I know you don't like your new haircut, but you can't change it now. It's no use crying over spilled milk.* □ *OK, so you broke the drill I lent you. Don't cry over spilled milk.*

(It's) none of your business! It is nothing that you need to know. It is none of your concern. (Not very polite.) □ *Alice: How much does a little diamond like that cost? Mary: None of your business!* □ *John: Do you want to go out with me Friday night? Mary: Sorry, I don't think so. John: Well, what are you doing then? Mary: None of your business!*

It's not cricket. and **It's not kosher.** It's not done.; It's not acceptable. □ *You can't do that! It's not cricket!*

(It's) not half bad. It's not as bad as one might have thought. □ *Mary: How do you like this play? Jane: Not half bad.* □ *Jane: Well, how do you like college? Fred: It's not half bad.*

It's not kosher. Go to **It's not cricket.**

(It's) not over till it's over. *Inf.* It is not over yet and will not be until the event has completely played out. □ *It looks like we have won, but it's not over 'til it's over!* □ *They haven't won the game yet. It's not over 'til it's over.*

(It's) not supposed to. and **(Someone's) not supposed to.** a phrase indicating that someone or something is not meant to do something. (Often with a person's name or a pronoun as a subject. See the examples.) □ *Fred: This little piece keeps falling off. Clerk: It's not supposed to.* □ *Bill: Tom just called from Detroit and says he's coming back tomorrow. Mary: That's funny. He's not supposed to.*

It's not the heat, it's the humidity. *Prov.* When the air is damp, hot days feel even hotter and more miserable. □ *Jill: I hope the air-conditioning is fixed soon; the heat is unbearable in here. Jane: It's not the heat, it's the humidity.* □ *Alan: I thought the summers were hot when I was growing up in New Mexico, but they're even hotter here in Iowa. Jane: The climate is moister here; it's not the heat, it's the humidity.*

It's on me. I will pay this bill. (Usually a bill for a meal or drinks. Compare this with **This one's on me.**) □ *As the waiter set down the glasses, Fred said, "It's on me," and grabbed the check.* □ *John: Check, please. Bill: No, it's on me this time.*

It's raining cats and dogs. Go to next.

It's raining pitchforks (and hammer handles). and **It's raining cats and dogs.** *Rur.* It is raining very hard. □ *Take an umbrella. It's raining pitchforks and hammer handles out there!* □ *Charlie: Have you looked outside? How's the weather? Mary: It's raining cats and dogs.*

It's six of one, half a dozen of another. *Cliché* Two options are equivalent. □ *To get downtown, we can either take the highway or the side streets. It's six of one, half a dozen of another, since both routes take the same amount of time.* □ *Jill: Would you rather peel the carrots or wash the lettuce? Jane: It's six of one, half a dozen of the other.*

(It's) time for a change. an expression announcing a decision to make a change. □ *Bill: Are you really going to take a new job? Mary: Yes, it's time for a change.* □ *Jane: Are you going to Florida for your vacation again? Fred: No. It's time for a change. We're going skiing.*

(It's) time to go. It is now time to leave. (Usually said by guests, but can be said by an adult to children who are guests.) □ *Jane: Look at the clock! Time to go! John: Yup! I'm out of here too.* □ *Mother: It's four o'clock. The party's over. Time to go. Bill: I had a good time. Thank you.*

(It's) time to hit the road. and **(I'd) better hit the road.; (I've) got to hit the road.** *Inf. Fig.* a phrase indicating that it is time that one departed. (See also **(I) have to shove off** and **(It's) time to run** for other possible variations.) □ *Henry: Look at the clock. It's past midnight. It's time to hit the road. Andy: Yeah. We've got to go. Sue: Okay, good night.* □ *Bill: I've got to hit the road. I have a long day tomorrow. Mary: Okay, good night. Bill: Bye, Mary.*

(It's) time to run. and **(It's) time to move along.; (It's) time to push along.; (It's) time to push off.; (It's) time to split.** *Inf.* an announcement of one's desire or need to depart. (See also **(I) have to shove off** and **(It's) time to hit the road** for an illustration of other possible variations.) □ *Andy: Time to push off. I've got to get home. Henry: See you, dude.* □ *John: It's time to split. I've got to go. Sue: Okay. See you tomorrow.*

(It's) time to shove off. Go to **(I) have to shove off**.

(It's) time to split. Go to **(It's) time to run**.

It's time we should be going. a statement made by one member of a pair (or group) of guests to the other member(s), indicating a desire to leave. (Typically, a way for one person in a couple to signal the other, indicating a desire to leave.) □ *Mr. Franklin looked at his wife and said softly, "It's time we should be going."* □ *Tom: Well, I suppose it's time we should be going. Mary: Yes, we really should. Alice: So early?*

It's written all over one's **face.** *Fig.* It is very evident and can easily be detected when looking at someone's face. □ *I know she's guilty. It's written all over her face.*

It's you! It suits you perfectly.; It is just your style. □ *John (trying on jacket): How does this look? Sally: It's you!* □ *Sue: I'm taking a job with the candy company. I'll be managing a store on Maple Street. Mary: It's you! That's a nice step up, and that store is so close by.*

It's your funeral. *Fig.* If that is what you are going to do, you will have to endure the dire consequences. □ *Tom: I'm going to call in sick and go to the ball game instead of to work today. Mary: Go ahead. It's your funeral.* □ *Bill:*

I'm going to go into the boss and tell what I really think of him. Sue: It's your funeral.

It's your move. 1. and **It's your turn.** *Lit.* [in a game] It's your time to play. □ *It's your move, and I think I have you trapped.* **2.** *Fig.* It is time for you to do something. □ *I've done everything I could do. Now, it's your move.*

It's your turn. Go to previous.

it strikes me that *Fig.* it seems to me that. □ *Henry: It strikes me that you are losing a little weight. Mary: Oh, I'm so glad you noticed!* □ *"It strikes me that all this money we are spending is accomplishing very little," said Bill.*

It sucks. Go to **That sucks**.

(It) suits me (fine). It is fine with me. □ *John: Is this one okay? Mary: Suits me.* □ *John: I'd like to sit up front where I can hear better. Mary: Suits me fine.*

It takes all kinds (to make a world). *Fig.* There are many different kinds of people, and you should not condemn them for being different. □ *Jill: Eleanor's trying another fad diet. This week she's sprinkling dried algae on all her food. Jane: It takes all kinds.* □ *Child: Mommy, I saw a weird man today. He was walking down the street singing real loud. I wish they'd put weird people like that away. Mother: Now, now, honey, it takes all kinds to make a world.*

It takes money to make money. *Prov.* In order to make money, you must first have some money to invest. □ *I've been reading a lot of books about how to become wealthy, and they all make it depressingly clear that it takes money to make money.*

(It) takes one to know one. *Inf.* You are one also. □ *A: You are a stupid oaf. B: So are you. It takes one to know one.*

It takes (some) getting used to. It is very unpleasant at first, but after a time it will not be so bothersome. (Said in recognition of the unpleasantness of something.) □ *I never ate raw oysters before. It takes some getting used to.* □ *These hot Mexican dishes seem impossible at first. They take some getting used to, I agree. But it's worth it.*

It takes two to make a bargain. *Prov.* Both parties in a negotiation must agree in order for the negotiation to be successful. □ *Jill: You'll give me a ride to work every day this week, like we agreed, won't you? Jane: Wait a minute. I only said I'd give you a ride to work today. It takes two to make a bargain.* □ *Ellen: We decided you should make dinner tonight, right? Fred: No, we didn't decide that; you decided that. It takes two to make a bargain.*

It takes two to make a quarrel. *Prov.* An argument is never only one person's fault.; If the other person refuses to participate, there cannot be an argument. □ *Sue: I think Mimi ought to apologize for arguing with me. Mother: It takes two to make a quarrel, dear. Maybe you ought to apologize to her.* □ *Jill: Why are you always so quarrelsome? Jane: Hey, it's not just my fault. It takes two to make a quarrel.*

(It) takes two to tango. *Prov.* Some things cannot happen by one person acting alone. □ *Alan: You're always arguing! Stop arguing all the time. Jane: I can't argue all by myself. It takes two to tango.* □ *Fred: Did you hear? Janice got herself pregnant. Jill: Well, she didn't do it all by herself. Takes two to tango, you know.*

I

It will be your ass! *Sl.* You will pay dearly!; You will suffer the consequences. (Potentially offensive. Use only with discretion.) □ *If you do that again, it will be your ass!* □ *It will be your ass if it isn't done right this time.*

It will take some doing. It will require considerable effort and care. □ *It'll take some doing, but it'll get done.* □ *It's not impossible. It'll just take some doing.*

(It) won't bother me any. and **(It) won't bother me at all.** *Inf.* It will not trouble me at all.; I have no objection if you wish to do that. (Not very polite or cordial. For the present tense of this expression, see also **(It) doesn't bother me any.**) □ *John: Will you mind if I sit here? Jane: Won't bother me any.* □ *Sally (lighting a cigarette): Do you mind if I smoke? Bill: It won't bother me at all.*

(It) won't bother me at all. Go to previous.

It won't wash! *Fig.* Nobody will believe it! □ *Sorry, it won't wash. Try another approach.* □ *Don't expect me to believe that! It won't wash.*

(It) works for me. *Inf.* It is fine with me. (With stress on *works* and *me*. The answer to a question implying **Does it work for you?**) □ *Bob: Is it okay if I sign us up for the party? Sally: It works for me.* □ *Tom: Is Friday all right for the party? Bill: Works for me. Bob: It works for me too.*

It would take an act of Congress to *do something.* It is almost impossible to do something. □ *It would take an act of Congress to get Bill to wear a necktie.* □ *She's a sour woman. It would take an act of Congress to get her to put a smile on her face.*

*****an **itch for** *something* a desire for something. (*Typically: **get** ~; **have** ~; **give** someone ~.) □ *I have an itch for some ice cream.* □ *We had an itch for a good movie, so we went.*

itch for *something Fig.* to desire something. □ *I'm just itching for a visit from Amy.* □ *We are itching for some chocolate.*

*****an **itch to** *do something Fig.* a desire to do something. (*Typically: **get** ~; **have** ~; **give** someone ~.) □ *I have an itch to see a movie tonight.* □ *Tom has an itch to go swimming.*

an **itching palm** Go to an **itchy palm.**

*****itchy feet** *Fig.* the need to leave; a feeling of a need to travel. (*Typically: **get** ~; **have** ~; **give** someone ~.) □ *Hearing the train whistle at night gives me itchy feet.*

*****an **itchy palm** and *****an **itching palm** *Fig.* [of a hand] in need of a tip. (As if placing money in the palm would stop the itching. *Typically: **get** ~; **have** ~; **give** someone ~.) □ *All the waiters at that restaurant have itchy palms.* □ *The cabdriver was troubled by an itching palm. Since he refused to carry my bags, I gave him nothing.* □ *Whenever he sees expensive luggage, the hotel doorman gets an itching palm.*

It'll all come out in the wash. *Fig.* It does not matter.; No lasting damage has been done. □ *Tom: I feel so bad about what I said to Bill. I don't think he'll ever forgive me. Mary: Oh, don't worry. It'll all come out in the wash.* □ *Jane: I'll never forgive myself for losing Mary's book. Charlie: Just tell her you're sorry, and offer to pay for the book. It'll all come out in the wash.*

It'll be a cold day in hell when *something happens. Rur.* Something will never happen or is highly unlikely. □ *It'll be a cold day in Hell when the city council agrees on where to build that bridge.* □ *It'll be a cold day in Hell when I forgive you.*

It'll be a long day in January when *something happens. Rur.* Something will never happen. (There are fewer hours of daylight in January.) □ *Tom: Maybe this will be the year that Mama treats herself to a nice vacation. Jane: Are you kidding? It'll be a long day in January when she does that!* □ *It'll be a long day in January when that car dealer gives an honest price.*

It'll never fly. *Fig.* It will never work!; It will never be approved! (Refers originally to an evaluation of an unlikely-looking aircraft of some type.) □ *I have read your report and studied your proposal. It'll never fly.* □ *Your design for a new electric automobile is interesting, but it'll never fly!*

it's no use (doing something**)** it is hopeless to do something; it is pointless to do something. □ *It's no use trying to call on the telephone. The line is always busy.* □ *They tried and tried, but it was no use.*

itty-bitty and **itsy-bitsy** very small. (Childish.) □ *I remember when you was just an itty-bitty baby.* □ *Gramma sewed with itsy-bitsy stitches.*

(I've) been getting by. *Inf.* a response to a greeting inquiry into one's well-being indicating that one is having a hard time surviving or that things could be much better. (See also **(I'm) just getting by.**) □ *John: How are things? Jane: Oh, I've been getting by.* □ *Sue: How are you doing? Mary: Been getting by. Things could be better.*

(I've) been keeping cool. and **(I've been) keeping cool.** *Inf.* an answer to a question about what one has been doing during very hot weather. □ *Jane: How do you like this hot weather? Bill: I've been keeping cool.* □ *Mary: Been keeping cool? Bob: Yeah. Been keeping cool.*

(I've) been keeping myself busy. and **(I've been) keeping myself busy.** a standard response to a greeting inquiry asking what one has been doing. □ *Bill: What have you been doing? Bob: I've been keeping myself busy. What about you? Bill: About the same.* □ *John: Yo! What have you been up to? Bill: Been keeping myself busy.*

(I've) been keeping out of trouble. and **(I've been) keeping out of trouble.** *Fig.* a standard response to a greeting inquiry that asks what one has been doing. □ *John: What have you been doing, Fred? Fred: Been keeping out of trouble. John: Yeah. Me too.* □ *Mary: How are things, Tom? Tom: Oh, I've been keeping out of trouble.*

(I've) been okay. *Inf.* a standard response to a greeting inquiry that asks how one has been. □ *Bill: Well, how have you been, good buddy? John: I've been okay.* □ *Sue: How you doing? Jane: Been okay. And you? Sue: The same.*

(I've) been there(, done that). *Inf.* I know exactly what you are talking about from my own experience.; I know exactly what you are going through. □ *John: Wow! Those sales meetings really wear me out! Jane: I know what you mean. I've been there.* □ *Sue: These employment interviews are very tiring. Bob: I know it! I've been there.*

(I've) been under the weather. *Fig.* a greeting response indicating that one has been ill. □ *John: How have you* *been? Sally: I've been under the weather, but I'm better.* □ *Doctor: How are you? Mary: I've been under the weather. Doctor: Maybe we can fix that. What seems to be the trouble?*

I've done my do. *Rur.* I have done my share. □ *Tom: Aren't you going to finish cleaning the kitchen? Jane: I've done my do. You can do the rest.* □ *I feel I've done my do, and someone else should do the rest.*

(I've) (got) better things to do. There are better ways to spend my time.; I cannot waste any more time on this matter. (Either *I've got* or *I have.*) □ *Andy: Good-bye. I've got better things to do than stand around here listening to you brag. Henry: Well, good-bye and good riddance.* □ *Mary: How did things go at your meeting with the zoning board? Sally: I gave up. Can't fight city hall. Better things to do.*

(I've) got to be shoving off. Go to **(I) have to shove off.**

I've got to fly. and **I('ve) gotta fly.; (I've) got to fly.** *Fig. Inf.* I have to leave right now. □ *Time's up. I've got to fly.* □ *I've gotta fly. See you later.*

(I've) got to get moving. I have to leave right now. (See also **(I) have to shove off** for other possible variations.) □ *Tom: Time to go. Got to get moving. Sally: Bye, Tom.* □ *Mary: It's late and I've got to get moving. Sue: Well, if you must, okay. Come again sometime. Mary: Bye.*

(I've) got to go. a phrase announcing one's need to depart. (See also **(I) have to shove off** for other possible variations.) □ *Andy: Bye, I've got to go. Rachel: Bye, little brother. See you.* □ *Sally: Got to go. Sue: See ya! Take it easy.*

(I've) got to go home and get my beauty sleep. *Fig.* a phrase announcing one's need to depart because it is late. (See also **(I) have to shove off** for other possible variations.) □ *Sue: Leaving so early? John: I've got to go home and get my beauty sleep.* □ *Jane: I've got to go home and get my beauty sleep. Fred: Well, you look to me like you've had enough. Jane: Why, thank you.*

(I've) got to hit the road. Go to **(It's) time to hit the road.**

(I've) got to run. *Fig.* a phrase announcing one's need to depart. (See also **(I) have to shove off** for other possible variations.) □ *John: Got to run. It's late. Jane: Me too. See ya, bye-bye.* □ *Mary: Want to watch another movie? Bill: No, thanks. I've got to run.*

(I've) got to shove off. Go to **(I) have to shove off.**

(I've) got to split. *Inf. Fig.* I have to leave now. (See also **(I) have to shove off** for other possible variations.) □ *Jane: Look at the time! Got to split. Mary: See you later, Jane.* □ *Bill: It's getting late. I've got to split. Sue: Okay, see you tomorrow. Bill: Good night.*

(I've) got to take off. *Fig.* a phrase announcing one's need to depart. (See also **(I) have to shove off** for other

possible variations.) □ *Mary: Got to take off. Bye. Bob: Leaving so soon? Mary: Yes. Time to go. Bob: Bye.* □ *"Look at the time. I've got to take off!" shrieked Alice.*

I've got work to do. 1. *Lit.* I'm too busy to stay here any longer. □ *Jane: Time to go. I've got work to do. John: Me too. See you.* □ *Bob: I have to leave now. Bill: So soon? Bob: Yes, I've got work to do.* **2.** *Fig.* Do not bother me. I'm busy. □ *Bill: Can I ask you a question? Jane: Not right now. I've got work to do.* □ *Mary: There are some things we have to get straightened out on this Wilson contract. John: I've got work to do. It will have to wait.*

I('ve) gotta fly. Go to **I've got to fly.**

I've had a lovely time. and **We've had a lovely time.** a polite expression said to a host or hostess on departure. □ *Bob: I've had a lovely time. Thanks for asking me. Fred: We're just delighted you could come. Good night. Bob: Good night.* □ *Sue: We've had a lovely time. Good night. Bill: Next time don't stay away so long. Good night.*

I've had enough of this! I will not take any more of this situation! □ *Sally: I've had enough of this! I'm leaving! Fred: Me too!* □ *John (glaring at Tom): I've had enough of this! Tom, you're fired! Tom: You can't fire me, I quit!*

I've had it up to here (with *someone* or *something*)**.** I will not endure any more of someone or something. □ *Bill: I've had it up to here with your stupidity. Bob: Who's calling who stupid?* □ *John: I've had it up to here with Tom. Mary: Are you going to fire him? John: Yes.*

I've heard so much about you. a polite phrase said upon being introduced to someone you have heard about from a friend or the person's relatives. □ *Bill: This is my cousin Kate. Bob: Hello, Kate. I've heard so much about you.* □ *Sue: Hello, Bill. I've heard so much about you. Bill: Hello. Glad to meet you.*

(I've) never been better. and **(I've) never felt better.** a response to a greeting inquiry into one's health or state of being. □ *Mary: How are you, Sally? Sally: Never been better, Mary. How about you?* □ *Doctor: How are you, Jane? Jane: Never felt better. Doctor: Then why are you here?*

(I've) seen better. a noncommittal and not very positive judgment about something or someone. □ *Alice: How did you like the movie? John: I've seen better.* □ *Bill: What do you think about this weather? Bob: Seen better.*

I've seen better heads on nickel beers. *Rur.* This person is stupid. □ *Jim's good-looking, but I've seen better heads on nickel beers.* □ *My students this term aren't what you'd call bright. I've seen better heads on nickel beers.*

(I've) seen worse. a noncommittal and not totally negative judgment about something or someone. □ *Alice: How did you like the movie? John: I've seen worse.* □ *Bill: What do you think about this weather? Gladys: Seen worse.*

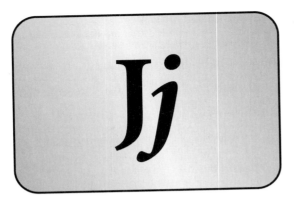

jab at someone or something to poke or punch at someone or something. □ *Tom jabbed at Fred.* □ *Don't jab at the cat!*

jab someone **in** something to poke someone in a particular location on the body. □ *Fred jabbed Tom in the side.* □ *He jabbed himself in the hand.*

jab someone **with** something to poke or stick someone with something. □ *He jabbed Henry with the rake handle on purpose.* □ *The mugger jabbed the victim with a knife.*

jab something **at** someone or something to poke someone or something with something. □ *Tom jabbed the stick at the dog.* □ *I jabbed my fist at Walter.*

jab something **into** something and **jab** something **in**† to stab something into something. □ *Billy jabbed his spoon into the gelatin.* □ *He jabbed in his spoon.* □ *He jabbed it in.*

jab something **out**† to thrust something out. □ *Molly jabbed her fist out suddenly.* □ *She jabbed out her fist.*

jabber about someone or something **1.** to talk or chat very informally about someone or something. □ *Who are they jabbering about?* □ *Those kids are jabbering about school again.* **2.** to talk unintelligibly about someone or something. □ *Is she jabbering about whatever comes to mind?* □ *She is jabbering about something, but we can't understand her.*

jack around and **jerk around** *Sl.* to waste time. □ *Stop jacking around and get some work done!* □ *The kids spend most of the day jerking around.*

jack of all trades someone who can do several different jobs instead of specializing in one. □ *John can do plumbing, carpentry, and roofing—a real jack of all trades. He isn't very good at any of them.* □ *Take your car to a certified engine mechanic, not a jack of all trades.*

a **jack of all trades is a master of none.** *Prov.* If you are able to do a lot of things fairly well, you will not have time to learn to do one thing extremely well. □ *Jill: I envy Bob; he can do so many things. He writes novels, paints pictures, makes sculptures, and even plays the dulcimer. Jane: It's true he does a lot of things, but he probably doesn't do them all terribly well. A jack of all trades is a master of none, you know.*

jack someone **around**† and **jerk** someone **around**† *Sl.* to give someone a difficult time; to harass someone. □ *Come on! Stop jacking me around!* □ *Max started jerking Lefty around, and it looked as if there was going to be trouble.* □ *You jack around everyone you know!*

jack someone **up**† **1.** *Sl.* to excite or stimulate someone, possibly with drugs. □ *Tom jacked up his buddy by talking to him.* □ *Tom jacked up Fred with a lot of encouragement.* **2.** *Sl.* to motivate someone; to stimulate someone to do something. □ *The mail is late again today. We'll have to jack those people up at the post office.* □ *I guess I'll have to jack up the carpenter again to repair my stairs.*

jack something **up**† **1.** *Lit.* to raise something up on a mechanical lifting device. □ *Now I have to jack the car up, so I can change the tire.* □ *Please jack up the car.* **2.** *Fig.* to raise the price of something. □ *The store keeps jacking prices up.* □ *The grocery store jacked up the prices again last night.*

jacked (out) *Sl.* angry; annoyed. □ *Boy was that old guy jacked out at you.* □ *Yup, he was jacked all right.*

a **jam session** an informal session where musicians play together. □ *Andy and Nick had a jam session last night and kept all the neighbors awake.*

jam someone or something **in((to)** something**)** and **jam** someone or something **in**† to force or compress someone or something into something or some place. □ *Sam jammed all his clothes into the canvas bag.* □ *The conductor jammed all the passengers into one car.* □ *Don't jam in everything!* □ *They had to jam themselves into the tiny room, because there was no other place to meet.*

jam someone or something **together** to pack people or things close together. □ *The usher jammed everybody together so more people could be seated.* □ *Don't just jam the boxes together! Sort them out first.*

jam something **together** to assemble something hastily or carelessly. □ *The fragile contents were just jammed together in one box and everything was broken.* □ *The thing was just jammed together with no care at all.*

jam something **up**† **1.** to clog up something; to impede or block the movement of or through something. □ *Rachel jammed traffic up when her car stalled.* □ *All the leaves and branches jammed up the sewer.* **2.** *Fig.* to force something upwards in haste or anger. □ *Who jammed the window up?* □ *Wally jammed up the window and nearly broke it.*

jam something **up** something to thrust something up something. □ *She poked the broom handle up the chimney, hoping to force the bird to fly out.* □ *She jammed it up a few times, but it had no effect.*

jam something **(up**†**) with** something to clog something with something. □ *Time had jammed the pipe up with rust.* □ *Time had jammed up the pipe with rust.* □ *Jam the hole with a cloth so nothing else will leak out.*

jam the brakes on† to press down hard on a vehicle's brakes. □ *Alice jammed the brakes on and the car skidded all over the place.* □ *She jammed on the brakes.*

jam with someone to play music in an improvised band with someone. □ *Andy loves to jam with the other students.* □ *Let's set up a time when we can jam with the others.*

jangle on something **1.** *Fig.* to ring a bell incessantly. □ *Will you stop jangling on that doorbell!* □ *Who is jangling on that bell?* **2.** *Fig.* to irritate someone's nerves; to make someone nervous. □ *All that noise jangles on my nerves.* □ *Too much chattering jangles on Ken's nerves.*

jar against someone or something to bump against someone or something. □ *The guest jarred against the wall,* knocking a picture askew. □ Someone jarred against Fran, almost knocking her over.

jar on someone or something to bother someone or someone's nerves. (Similar to **jangle on** something.) □ Her voice really jars on me. □ My brash manner jars on her, I guess.

jaw about someone or something Fig. to talk aimlessly about someone or something. □ Do we have to keep jawing about Tom all day? □ Stop jawing about your problems and set about fixing them.

jaw at someone Fig. to lecture at someone; to talk endlessly to someone. □ Please stop jawing at me. □ You are jawing at me too much lately.

jaw someone **down**† Sl. to talk someone down; to wear someone down talking. □ We'll try to jaw him down. If that doesn't work, I don't know what we will do. □ We will jaw down the objectors.

jazz someone or something **up**† to make someone or something more exciting or sexy; to make someone or something appeal more to contemporary tastes. □ Let's jazz this room up a little bit. □ They jazzed up Donna till she looked like a rock star.

jazzed (up) 1. alert; having a positive state of mind. □ I am jazzed up and ready to face life. □ Those guys were jazzed and ready for the game. **2.** intoxicated. □ Dave was a bit jazzed up, but not terribly. □ Gert was jazzed out of her mind. **3.** enhanced; with something added; made more enticing. □ The third act was jazzed up with livelier music. **4.** forged or altered. □ Better not try to cash a jazzed check at this bank.

jeer at someone or something to poke fun at someone; to make rude sounds at someone. □ Please stop jeering at my cousin! □ The others just jeered at my idea.

Jekyll and Hyde someone with both an evil and a good personality. (From the novel The Strange Case of Dr. Jekyll and Mr. Hyde by Robert Louis Stevenson.) □ Bill thinks Mary is so soft and gentle, but she can be very cruel—she is a real Jekyll and Hyde. □ Jane doesn't know that Fred is a Jekyll and Hyde. She sees him only when he is being kind and generous, but he can be very cruel.

jerk around Go to jack around.

jerk someone **around**† and **jerk** someone **over**† to hassle someone; to waste someone's time. □ Stop jerking me around and give me my money back. □ They sure like to jerk around people in that music shop.

jerk someone or something **out of** something and **jerk** someone or something **out**† to pull someone or something out of something sharply and quickly. □ She jerked the baby out of the crib and ran from the burning room. □ I jerked the puppy out of the mud. □ She jerked out the puppy before it got soaked.

jerk someone **over**† Go to jerk someone around†.

jerk something **away (from** someone, something, or an animal) to snatch something away or quickly pull something back from someone or an animal. □ I jerked the bone away from the dog. □ Kelly jerked the ant poison away from the child. □ Mary jerked her hand away from the fire.

jerk something **off**† Go to next.

jerk something **off (of)** someone or something and **jerk** something **off**† to snatch or quickly pull something off some-

one or something. (Of is usually retained before pronouns.) □ Alice jerked the top off the box and poured out the contents. □ She jerked off the box top.

jerk something **out of** someone or something and **jerk** something **out**† to pull something out of someone or something quickly. □ The doctor jerked the arrow out of Bill's leg. □ He jerked out the arrow.

jerk something **up**† **1.** to pull something up quickly. □ He jerked his belt up tight. □ He jerked up the zipper to his jacket. **2.** to lift up something, such as ears, quickly. □ The dog jerked its ears up. □ The dog jerked up its ears when it heard the floor creak. □ The soldier jerked his binoculars up to try to see the sniper.

jest about someone or something to make jokes about someone or something. □ There is no need to jest about Lady Bracknell. □ I wish you would not jest about that.

jest at someone or something to make fun of someone or something. □ Please don't jest at my cousin. □ Is someone jesting at my hairdo?

jest with someone to joke with someone; to try to fool someone. □ Surely you are jesting with me. □ Don't jest with me!

jet (from some place) **(to** some place) to travel from some place to some other place by jet airplane. □ They jetted from here to there. □ They jetted to here from there.

jet from something to spurt from something. □ Water jetted from the broken pipe. □ A column of water jetted from the top of the fountain.

jibe with something [for something] to agree with something. □ Your story doesn't jibe with what we heard from the arresting officer. □ Her tale jibes with yours quite well.

The **jig is up.** See The **game is up.**

jim-dandy excellent. □ This is a jim-dandy knife. Where'd you get it? □ Tom: I'll meet you at six, OK? Charlie: That'll be jim-dandy.

jimmy something **up**† pry something up. □ See if you can jimmy this window up. □ Can you jimmy up this window?

jockey around to move around as if trying to get into a special position. □ I spent most of the movie jockeying around, trying to get comfortable. □ She always has to jockey around a bit when she is getting into a parking place.

jockey for position 1. Lit. to work one's horse into a desired position in a horse race. □ Three riders were jockeying for position in the race. □ Ken was behind, but jockeying for position. **2.** Fig. to work oneself into a desired position. □ The candidates were jockeying for position, trying to get the best television exposure. □ I was jockeying for position but running out of campaign money.

jockey someone or something **into position** to manage to get someone or something into a desirable position. (See also **jockey for position.**) □ The rider jockeyed his horse into position. □ Try to jockey your bicycle into position so you can pass the others.

jockey something **around**† to maneuver something around; to manage something. □ We had to jockey our bikes around a number of stalled cars. □ We jockeyed *around a few cars to make room for the bus in the parking lot.*

jog along to trot or run along at a slow pace. □ *She was jogging along quite happily.* □ *I had been jogging along for a few minutes when my shoelaces broke.*

jog someone's **memory** *Fig.* to stimulate someone's memory to recall something. □ *Hearing the first part of the song I'd forgotten really jogged my memory.* □ *I tried to jog Bill's memory about our childhood antics.*

jog to the right and **jog to the left** [for a road, path, etc.] to turn to the right or left. □ *The road jogs to the right here. Don't run off.* □ *Keep going until the road jogs to the left. Our driveway is on the right side.*

join forces (with someone**)** *Fig.* to combine one's efforts with someone else's efforts. □ *The older boys joined forces with the younger ones to sing the school song.* □ *Let's join forces with the other faction and run our own slate of candidates.*

join hands [for people] to hold hands so that each person is holding the hands of two other people; [for two people] to hold each other's hands. □ *Let us join hands and pray together.* □ *The dancers joined hands and formed a circle that moved to the left.*

join in (with someone**)** to join someone in doing something. □ *Do you mind if we join in with you?* □ *Please join in.*

join in ((with) something**)** to participate in doing something. □ *The older boys joined in with the singing.* □ *I'm glad they joined in. We needed basses.*

join someone **with** someone else and **join** something **with** something else to connect things or people. □ *I joined Fred with the others.* □ *We joined the older puppies with the full-grown dogs.*

join something **and** something else **together**† to connect or unite things. □ *We joined the pipe and the hose together.* □ *He joined together all the blue wires and the red ones.*

join something **to** something else to connect something to something else. □ *We joined our club to the other club.* □ *We joined our chorus to the other chorus, making a huge singing group.*

join something **with** something else Go to join someone with someone else.

Join the club! *Inf.* an expression indicating that the person spoken to is in the same, or a similar, unfortunate state as the speaker. □ *You don't have anyplace to stay? Join the club! Neither do we.* □ *Did you get fired too? Join the club!*

join the fray and **jump into the fray; enter the fray** *Fig.* to join the fight or argument. □ *After listening to the argument, Mary decided to jump into the fray.* □ *Tom joined the fray and immediately got knocked down.*

join up to join some organization. □ *The club has opened its membership rolls again. Are you going to join up?* □ *I can't afford to join up.*

join (up) with someone or something to bring oneself into association with someone or something. □ *I decided to join up with the other group.* □ *Our group joined with another similar group.*

join with someone Go to **with** someone.

joined at the hip *Sl.* closely connected; always together. □ *Those two are joined at the hip. They are always together.* □ *Sam and Martha are joined at the hip.*

The **joke is on** someone. **1.** Someone is the butt of the joke. □ *The joke is on Bob, so it's good that he is a good sport.* **2.** The joke has backfired on someone. □ *Ha, ha! The joke's on you after all.*

joke (with someone**) (about** someone or something**)** to quip with someone about someone or something; to make verbal fun with someone about someone or something. □ *I was joking with Tom about the performance.* □ *I joked about Andy with Fran.*

jolt someone **out of** something to startle someone out of inertness. □ *The cold water thrown in her face was what it took to jolt Mary out of her deep sleep.* □ *At the sound of the telephone, he jolted himself out of his stupor.*

jolt to a start and **jolt to a stop** to start or stop moving suddenly, causing a jolt. □ *The truck jolted to a stop at the stop sign.* □ *The little car jolted to a quick start and threw the passenger back in his seat.*

jolt to a stop See previous.

jostle someone **around**† to push or knock someone around. □ *Please don't jostle me around.* □ *Don't jostle around everyone!*

jostle someone **aside**† to push or nudge someone aside. □ *Poor little Timmy was jostled aside by the crowd every time he got near the entrance.* □ *The big kids jostled aside all the little ones.*

jostle with someone to struggle with someone. □ *Andy jostled with Fred for access to the door.* □ *Timmy and Bobby jostled with one another while they were waiting to get in.*

jot something **down**† to make a note of something. □ *This is important. Please jot this down.* □ *Jot down this note, please.*

judge between someone or something **and** someone or something else to decide between people or things, in any combination. □ *You can't expect me to judge between apples and oranges, can you?* □ *Can you judge between the prosecution and the defense?*

Judge not, lest ye be judged. and **Judge not, that ye be not judged.** *Prov.* If you condemn other people, then they will have the right to condemn you, so it is best not to condemn them. (Biblical.) □ *Jill: I'm sure Gloria is the one who's been stealing from petty cash. She's so sloppy, nasty, and ill-mannered. Don't you think she'd be capable of theft? Jane: Judge not, lest ye be judged.*

Judge not, that ye be not judged. Go to previous.

judge one **on** one's **own merits** to evaluate one on one's own good and bad points and no one else's. □ *Please judge Janet on her own merits.* □ *I was judged on my own merits.*

judge something **on its own merits** to evaluate something on its own good and bad points and nothing else. □ *You must judge this proposal on its own merits.* □ *The proposal has not been judged on its own merits.*

judging by something and **judging from** something to make a decision or judgment based on something. □ *Judging by the amount of food eaten, everyone must have been* *very hungry.* □ *Judging from the mess that's left, the party must have been a good one.*

jugged (up) *Sl.* intoxicated. □ *I'm not jugged up. I'm not even tipsy.* □ *Fred was too jugged to drive home.*

juggle someone or something **around**† to alter the position or sequence of someone or something. □ *We will juggle everyone around so that the second round of interviews are in a different order.* □ *I think I can juggle my schedule around so I can have lunch with you.* □ *Please juggle around my appointments for this afternoon so I can have a late lunch.*

juice and cookies trivial and uninteresting snacks or refreshments. □ *The party was not much. Nothing but juice and cookies.* □ *After juice and cookies, we all went back into the meeting room for another hour of talk, talk, talk.*

juice something **back**† *Sl.* to drink all of something alcoholic, quickly. □ *He juiced a beer back.* □ *Max juiced back another beer.*

juice something **up**† **1.** *Sl.* to make something more powerful. □ *How much did it cost to juice this thing up?* □ *Wally juiced up his car.* **2.** *Sl.* to turn on the electricity to something. □ *It's time to juice the stage lights up.* □ *Juice up the stage lights.*

juice up *Sl.* to drink one or more alcoholic drinks. □ *Hey, man, let's go out and juice up tonight.* □ *Stop juicing up every night.*

jumble someone or something **together** to mix people or things together randomly into a hodgepodge. □ *They just jumbled everything together and made a real mess.* □ *The army just jumbled everybody together, no matter what their skills and talents were.*

jumble something **together** to assemble something clumsily and hastily. □ *They just jumbled some holiday decorations together. It really wasn't very well done.* □ *I hope this airplane wasn't jumbled together as badly as this meal.*

jumble something **up**† to make a hodgepodge out of things. □ *Who jumbled my papers up?* □ *Who jumbled up all my papers?*

jump across something to leap over something that is broad rather than tall. □ *The frog jumped across the puddle.* □ *Timmy tried but failed to jump across the puddle.*

jump all over someone and **jump down** someone's **throat; jump on** someone *Fig.* to scold someone severely. □ *If I don't get home on time, my parents will jump all over me.* □ *Don't jump on me! I didn't do it!* □ *Please don't jump all over John. He wasn't the one who broke the window.* □ *Why are you jumping down my throat? I wasn't even in the house when it happened.*

jump at someone or something to jump in the direction of someone or something. □ *The frog jumped at me, but I dodged it.* □ *The cat jumped at the leaf as it fell from the tree.*

jump at something *Fig.* to seize the opportunity to do something. (See also **leap at the opportunity (to do something)**.) □ *When I heard about John's chance to go to England, I knew he'd jump at it.* □ *If something you really want to do comes your way, jump at it.*

jump at the opportunity (to do something**)** Go to **leap at the opportunity (to** do something**)**.

jump bail and **skip bail** *Fig.* to fail to appear in court for trial and forfeit one's bail bond. □ *Not only was Bob arrested for theft, he skipped bail and left town. He's in a lot of trouble.* □ *The judge issued a warrant for the arrest of the man who jumped bail.*

jump clear of something *Fig.* to get out of the way of something; to leap off something before it crashes. □ *I barely had time to jump clear of the oncoming truck.* □ *I jumped clear of the ball as it came my way.*

jump (down) (from something**)** to jump downward off something. □ *A small mouse jumped down from the shelf.* □ *A tiny mouse jumped from the shelf.*

jump down someone's **throat** Go to **jump all over** someone.

jump down something to leap downward into or through something. □ *The rats jumped down the manhole.* □ *Timmy jumped down the stairs on the morning of his birthday party.*

jump for joy Go to **leap for joy**.

jump from something **to** something to leap from one place to another. □ *A frog jumped from lily pad to lily pad.* □ *The child jumped from stone to stone.*

jump in with both feet Go to **dive in with both feet**.

jump in((to) something**)** to leap into something, such as water, a bed, a problem, etc. □ *She was so cold she just jumped into bed and pulled up the covers.* □ *I jumped in and had a refreshing swim.*

jump into the fray Go to **join the fray**.

jump off ((of) something**)** to leap off something. (*Of* is usually retained before pronouns.) □ *Rachel lost her balance and jumped off the diving board instead of diving.* □ *Better to jump off than to fall off.*

jump off the deep end Go to **go off the deep end**.

jump off the deep end (over someone or something**)** *Fig.* to get deeply involved with someone or something. (Often refers to romantic involvement.) □ *Jim is about to jump off the deep end over Jane.* □ *Jane is great, but there is no need for Jim to jump off the deep end.*

the **jump on someone a chance to do something before someone else. (*Typically: **get ~; have ~; give** someone ~.) □ *Each reporter is trying to get the jump on the others with the story about the earthquake.* □ *Kelly finally got the jump on Sam.*

jump on someone Go to **jump all over** someone.

jump on someone or something to pounce on someone or something. □ *The cat jumped on the mouse.* □ *Max jumped on the unsuspecting tourist and robbed him.*

jump on the bandwagon Go to **on the bandwagon**.

jump on((to) something**) 1.** to get onto something. □ *The cat jumped onto the sofa and took a nap.* □ *I was sitting on the sofa and the cat jumped on it and scared me.* **2.** to get involved in something very quickly. □ *Jump onto that story now and get it done for tonight's edition.* □ *I'll jump on the story right now, boss.*

jump out of something to leap from something. □ *A mouse jumped out of the cupboard and scared me.* □ *I jumped out of bed and ran to answer the telephone.*

jump out of the frying pan into the fire Go to out of the frying pan into the fire.

jump over something to leap over or across something. □ *The fellow named Jack jumped over a candle placed on the floor.* □ *Puddles are to be jumped over, not waded through.*

jump over the broomstick *Rur.* to get married. □ *Jim and Jane have decided to jump over the broomstick.* □ *The happiest day of my life was when your mother said she'd jump over the broomstick with me.*

jump ship 1. *Lit.* to leave one's job on a ship and fail to be aboard it when it sails; [for a sailor] to go AWOL. □ *One of the deckhands jumped ship at the last port.* **2.** *Fig.* to leave any post or position; to quit or resign, especially when there is difficulty with the job. □ *None of the editors liked the new policies, so they all jumped ship as soon as other jobs opened up.*

jump the gun *Fig.* to start before the starting signal. (Originally used in sports contests that are started by firing a gun.) □ *We all had to start the race again because Jane jumped the gun.* □ *When we took the test, Tom jumped the gun and started early.*

jump the track 1. *Lit.* [for something] to fall or jump off the rails or guides. (Usually said about a train.) □ *The train jumped the track, causing many injuries to the passengers.* □ *The engine jumped the track, but the other cars stayed on.* **2.** *Fig.* to change suddenly from one thing, thought, plan, or activity to another. □ *The entire project jumped the track, and we finally had to give up.* □ *John's mind jumped the track while he was in the play, and he forgot his lines.*

jump through a hoop and **jump through hoops** *Fig.* to do everything possible to obey or please someone; to **bend over backwards (to** do something**).** (Trained circus animals jump through hoops.) □ *She expects us to jump through hoops for her.* □ *What do you want me to do—jump through a hoop?*

jump to conclusions and **leap to conclusions** *Fig.* to judge or decide something without having all the facts; to reach unwarranted conclusions. (See also rush to conclusions.) □ *Now don't jump to conclusions. Wait until you hear what I have to say.* □ *Please find out all the facts so you won't leap to conclusions.*

jump up (from something**)** to leap upward from something. □ *The dog jumped up from its resting place.* □ *The dog jumped up and ran to the door.*

jump up (on someone or something**)** to leap upward onto someone or something. □ *A spider jumped up on me and terrified me totally.* □ *The cat jumped up on the sofa.*

jump up (to something**)** to leap upward to the level of something. □ *The child jumped up to the next step.* □ *The dog couldn't reach the piece of meat on the edge of the table, so it jumped up and got it.*

jump with something *Fig.* to be very active with excitement or enthusiasm. □ *The crowd was jumping with enthusiasm.* □ *The bar was jumping with young people.*

jumping-off place Go to next.

jumping-off point and **jumping-off place** a point or place from which to begin something. □ *The local library is a good jumping-off point for your research.* □ *The office job in that company would be a good jumping-off place for a career in advertising.*

junk mail annoying, unsolicited mail, such as promotional letters, etc. □ *I am so incredibly tired of getting pound after pound of junk mail every day. I could just scream.*

The **jury is still out on** someone or something. *Fig.* a decision has not been reached on someone or something; the people making the decision on someone or something have not yet decided. □ *The jury is still out on Jane. We don't know what we are going to do about her.* □ *The jury is still out on the question of building a new parking lot.*

just a minute only a short time; [wait] a short period of time. □ *I'm almost done. I'll be there in just a minute!* □ *Could I have just a minute of your time?*

Just a minute (you)! Stop where you are! (Not very polite.) □ *Just a minute, you! Where are you going with my coat?*

(just) a stone's throw away (from something**)** Go to within a stone's throw (of something).

(just) a stone's throw (from something**)** Go to within a stone's throw (of something).

(just) as I expected I thought so; I knew it would be this way. □ *Just as I expected. The window was left open and it rained in.* □ *As I expected, he left work early again.*

just fell off the turnip truck *Rur.* ignorant; unsophisticated. □ *He stood there gawking at the buildings in town like he just fell off the turnip truck.* □ *My cousin acts like she just fell off the turnip truck.*

just in case in the event that (something happens). □ *All right. I'll take it just in case.* □ *I'll take along some aspirin, just in case.*

just in time at the last possible time. □ *He got to the meeting just in time. They had just started the topic he was supposed to talk about.*

just let me say Go to let me (just) say.

just like that in just the way it happened or was stated; without any [further] discussion or comment. □ *Sue: You can't walk out on me just like that. John: I can too. Just watch!* □ *Mary: And then she slapped him in the face, just like that! Sally: She can be so rude.*

just off the boat *Fig.* to be newly immigrated and perhaps gullible and naive. □ *I'm not just off the boat. I know what's going on.* □ *He may act like he's just off the boat, but he's very savvy.*

just one's **cup of tea** *Fig.* to be something that one prefers or desires. □ *This spy novel is just my cup of tea.* □ *Teaching children to read is just my cup of tea.*

just passing through just moving through an area and not stopping. □ *We didn't stop in Moose Jaw. We were just passing through.*

just so 1. in perfect order; neat and tidy. □ *Her hair is always just so.* □ *Their front yard is just so.* **2.** Precisely right!; Quite right! (Usually **Just so!**) □ *Bill: The letter should arrive tomorrow. Tom: Just so!* □ *Jane: We must always try our best. Martin: Just so!*

(just) taking care of business *Fig.* doing what I am supposed to do; an answer to the question "What are you doing lately?" (Also abbreviated **T.C.B.**) □ *Bill: Hey, man.*

What you been doing? Tom: Just taking care of business. □ *Andy: Look, officer, I'm just standing here, taking care of business, and this Tom guy comes up and tries to hit me for a loan. Tom: That's not true!*

just the same Go to all the same.

just the same (to someone) Go to all the same (to someone).

just the ticket *Fig.* to be just the perfect thing. □ *This soup is just the ticket for a quick lunch.* □ *A good, hot cup of coffee will be just the ticket.*

just what the doctor ordered *Fig.* exactly what is required, especially for health or comfort. □ *That meal was delicious, Bob. Just what the doctor ordered.* □ *Bob: Would you like something to drink? Mary: Yes, a cold glass of water would be just what the doctor ordered.*

Just (you) wait (and see)! Go to You (just) wait (and see)!

justify something **by** something to try to explain why something needs doing or why it is acceptable to do something. □ *You cannot justify violence by quoting proverbs.* □ *Your action was totally justified by the circumstances.*

justify something **to** someone to explain something to someone and show why it is necessary. □ *Please try to justify this to the voters.* □ *I can justify your action to no one.*

jut out (from something) to stick outward from something. □ *The flagpole juts out from the side of the building.* □ *His nose juts out sharply.*

jut out (into something) to stick outward into an area. □ *The back end of the truck jutted out into the street.* □ *The back end jutted out.*

jut out (over someone or something) to stick out over someone or something. □ *The roof of the house jutted out over the patio.* □ *I'm glad the roof jutted out and kept us dry during the brief storm.*

juxtapose someone or something **to** someone or something to place people or things next to each other, in any combination. (Also implies that the placing or arranging is done carefully.) □ *I went to the meeting room early so I could juxtapose myself to the head of the table.* □ *I juxtaposed the chair to the view out the window.*

J

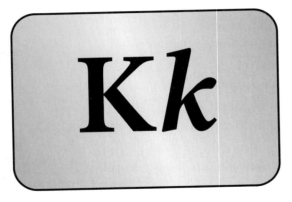

Kk

a **kangaroo court** a bogus or illegal court. □ *Is this a staff meeting or a kangaroo court?* □ *You have turned this interview into a kangaroo court.*

Katie bar the door Prepare immediately for an advancing threat. □ *Katie bar the door, the grandchildren are here and they all look hungry.*

keel over [for a person] to fall over or fall down in a faint or in death. □ *It was so hot in the room that two people just keeled over.*

keel something **over**† *Rur.* to push something over. □ *He leaned on the flimsy wall and keeled it right over.* □ *The high wind keeled over that sorry old fence.*

keen about someone or something Go to **keen on** someone or something.

keen on doing something willing or eager to do something. □ *Dave isn't very keen on going to the opera.* □ *The children are keen on swimming this afternoon. Shall I take them?*

keen on someone or something and **keen about** someone or something to be enthusiastic about someone or something. □ *I'm not too keen on going to Denver.* □ *Sally is fairly keen about getting a new job.* □ *Mary isn't keen on her new boss.*

keep a civil tongue (in one's **head)** *Fig.* to speak decently and politely. □ *Please, John. Don't talk like that. Keep a civil tongue in your head.* □ *John seems unable to keep a civil tongue.*

keep a close rein on someone or something Go to **keep a tight rein on** someone or something.

keep a close watch on someone or something to watch someone or something very carefully. □ *Let's keep a close watch on Fred and his friends.* □ *I want to keep a close watch on the house across the street.*

keep a firm grip on someone or something and **keep a tight grip on** someone or something **1.** *Lit.* to hold on to someone or something tightly. □ *As they approached the edge, Sally kept a firm grip on little Timmy.* □ *She kept a tight grip on him.* □ *Keep a firm grip on my hand as we cross the street.* **2.** *Fig.* to keep someone or something under firm control. □ *The manager keeps a firm grip on all the employees.* □ *I try to keep a firm grip on all the accounts.*

keep a lid on something Go to **a lid on** something.

keep a low profile Go to **a low profile.**

keep a promise and **keep** one's **promise** to make good on a promise; to fulfill one's promise. □ *If you can't keep your promises, you shouldn't make them in the first place.*

keep a secret to know a secret and not tell anyone. □ *Please keep our little secret private.* □ *Do you know how to keep a secret?*

Keep a stiff upper lip. *Prov.* Act as though you are not upset.; Do not let unpleasant things upset you. (English people are stereotypically supposed to be very good at keeping a stiff upper lip.) □ *Even though he was only three years old, Jonathan kept a stiff upper lip the whole time he was in the hospital recovering from his surgery.* □ *Jill: Sometimes this job frustrates me so much I could just break down in tears. Jane: Keep a stiff upper lip. Things are bound to improve.*

keep a straight face Go to **a straight face.**

Keep a thing seven years and you'll (always) find a use for it. *Prov.* If you keep a seemingly useless thing for seven years, you will supposedly have some occasion to use it during that time. □ *Jill: My mother sent me a four-foot-tall ceramic vase for my birthday. What can I possibly use it for? Jane: Keep it seven years and you'll find some use for it.*

keep a tight grip on someone or something Go to **keep a firm grip on** someone or something.

keep a tight rein on someone or something and **keep a close rein on** someone or something *Fig.* to watch and control someone or something diligently. (Alludes to controlling a horse by a tight grip on the reins.) □ *The office manager kept a tight rein on the staff.* □ *Mary keeps a close rein on her children.*

keep abreast of someone or something Go to **abreast of** someone or something.

keep after someone **(about** something**)** and **keep at** someone **(about** something**); keep on** someone **(about** something**); stay after** someone **(about** something**)** to remind or nag someone over and over to do something. □ *I'll keep after you until you do it!* □ *Mother stayed after Bill until he did the dishes.* □ *She kept at him until he dried them and put them away.* □ *We will have to keep on him about the report until he turns it in.*

keep ahead (of someone or something**)** Go to **ahead (of** someone or something**).**

keep ahead of something Go to **ahead of** something.

keep ahead of the game Go to **ahead of the game.**

keep aloof from someone or something Go to **aloof from** someone or something.

keep an act up† and **keep** one's **act up**† to maintain behavior that is a false show; to continue with one's facade. (The *an* can be replaced with *the, this, that*, etc.) □ *How long do I have to keep this act up? I am tired of fooling people.* □ *I am weary of keeping up my act.*

keep an ear to the ground and **have an ear to the ground; keep** one's **ear to the ground; have** one's **ear to the ground** *Fig.* to devote attention to watching or listening for clues as to what is going to happen. □ *John had his ear to the ground, hoping to find out about new ideas in computers.* □ *His boss told him to keep his ear to the ground so that he'd be the first to know of a new idea.*

keep an eye on someone or something and **have an eye on** someone or something; **keep** one's **eye(s) on** someone or something; **have** one's **eye on** someone or something *Fig.* to watch someone or something; to monitor someone or something closely. □ *I have my eye on the apple tree. When the apples ripen, I'll harvest them.* □ *Please keep an eye on the baby.* □ *Will you please keep your eye on my house while I'm on vacation?*

keep an eye out (for someone or something**)** and **have an eye out (for** someone or something**); keep** one's **eye out (for** someone or something**); have** one's **eye out (for** someone or something**)** *Fig.* to watch for the arrival or appearance of someone or something. (See also **keep** one's **eyes open (for** someone or something**).**) □ *Please try to have an eye out for the bus.* □ *Keep an eye out for rain.* □ *Have your eye out for a raincoat on sale.*

keep an open mind Go to an open mind.

keep at arm's length from someone or something and **keep** someone or something **at arm's length** *Fig.* to retain a degree of physical or social remoteness from someone or something. □ *I try to keep at arm's length from Larry, since our disagreement.* □ *I keep Tom at arm's length because we don't get along.*

Keep at it! Keep doing what you are doing!; Keep trying! (Said as encouragement to keep working at something.) □ *The boss told me to keep at it every time he passed my desk.* □ *Keep at it, Tom! You can do it!*

keep at someone **(about** something**)** Go to keep after someone **(about** something**).**

keep at something to persist at doing something; to continue trying to do something. □ *John kept at his painting until the whole house was done.* □ *Keep at the job if you want to get it finished.*

keep away (from someone or something**)** Go to away **(from** someone or something**).**

keep banker's hours *Fig.* to work or be open for business for less than eight hours a day. □ *The advertising agency keeps banker's hours. They are only open until four.* □ *James doesn't really work full-time. He keeps banker's hours.*

keep body and soul together *Fig.* to manage to keep existing, especially when one has very little money. (Compare this with **keep the wolf from the door.**) □ *We hardly had enough to keep body and soul together.* □ *I don't earn enough money to keep body and soul together.*

keep clear of something Go to clear of something.

keep (close) watch (on someone or something**)** to monitor someone or something; to observe someone or something. □ *Keep close watch on Bill. I think he's loafing.* □ *Okay. I'll keep watch, but I think he's a good worker.*

keep (close) watch (over someone or something**)** to guard or care for someone or something. □ *I'm keeping watch over my children to make sure they have the things they need.* □ *I think that an angel is keeping close watch over her to make sure nothing bad happens to her.*

keep company (with someone**) 1.** *Lit.* to spend much time with someone; to associate with or consort with someone. □ *Bill has been keeping company with Ann for three months.* □ *Bob has been keeping company with a tough-looking bunch of boys.* **2.** *Fig.* to be courting some-

one. □ *Mary and Bill are keeping company.* □ *I heard that Joe is keeping company with Jim Brown's daughter.*

keep cool *Inf.* to stay calm and undisturbed. □ *Relax, man, keep cool!* □ *If Sally could just keep cool before a race, she could probably win.*

keep faith with someone to be loyal to someone. □ *I intend to keep faith with my people and all they stand for.* □ *We could not keep faith with them any longer.*

keep fit to keep in good physical condition. □ *I do everything I can to keep fit.*

keep from something to avoid doing something; to refrain from doing something. □ *How could I keep from crying? It was so sad!* □ *Try to keep from falling off the ladder.*

keep (going) on about someone or something to continue to talk excessively about someone or something. □ *I wish you would not keep going on about Tom and Jill.* □ *Don't keep on about my haircut. It's perfect!*

keep (going) on at someone or something to continue to complain about or scold someone or a group. □ *Don't keep going on at him. Give him the dickens and be done with it.* □ *Please don't keep on at the committee. They did the best they could.*

keep good time [for a watch or clock] to be accurate. □ *I have to return my watch to the store because it doesn't keep good time.* □ *Mine keeps good time.*

keep harping on something to continue to talk or complain about something; to keep raising a topic of conversation. (See also **harp on something.**) □ *Why do you keep harping on the same old complaint?* □ *You keep harping on my problems and ignore your own!*

keep house to manage a household. □ *I hate to keep house. I'd rather live in a tent than keep house.* □ *My grandmother kept house for nearly sixty years.*

keep in good condition Go to in good condition.

keep in good shape Go to in good shape.

keep in good with someone to remain in someone's favor. □ *I always try to keep in good with the boss's secretary.* □ *It's also good to keep in good with the boss.*

keep in step (with someone**)** Go to in step (with someone**).**

Keep in there! *Inf.* Keep trying! □ *Andy: Don't give up, Sally. Keep in there! Sally: I'm doing my best!* □ *John: I'm not very good, but I keep trying. Fred: Just keep in there, John.*

Keep in touch. Good-bye. (Sometimes a sarcastic way of saying good-bye to someone one doesn't care about.) □ *Nice talking to you. Keep in touch.* □ *Sorry, we can't use you anymore. Keep in touch.*

keep in touch (with someone**)** Go to in touch (with someone**).**

keep in touch (with someone or something**)** and **remain in touch (with** someone or something**); stay in touch (with** someone or something**)** to maintain communications with someone; to maintain up-to-date knowledge about someone or something. (See also **get in touch (with** someone**).**) □ *After my neighbor moved, we still remained in touch.* □ *I want to stay in touch with my office over the weekend.*

K

keep in training to maintain oneself in good physical condition. □ *I try to keep in training so I will live longer.* □ *Try to keep in training.*

keep inside ((of) something) to remain inside of something, usually a shelter, house, etc. (*Of* is usually retained before pronouns.) □ *Please keep inside of the house while it's raining.* □ *I want you to keep inside.*

keep it down (to a dull roar) *Fig.* to keep quiet or as quiet as possible. □ *Keep it down, you kids!* □ *Please try to keep it down to a dull roar, could you?*

keep (it) in mind that a statement emphasizing something that the speaker wants remembered. □ *Bill: When we get there I want to take a long hot shower. Father: Keep it in mind that we are guests, and we have to fit in with the routines of the household.* □ *Sally: Keep it in mind that you don't work here anymore, and you just can't go in and out of offices like that. Fred: I guess you're right.*

Keep it up! 1. Keep up the good work!; Keep on doing it.; Keep (on) trying. □ *Jane: I think I'm doing better in calculus. John: Keep it up!* □ *Sally: I can now jog for almost three miles. Fred: Great! Keep it up!* **2.** Just keep acting that way and see what happens to you. (Compare this with **(Go ahead,) make my day!**) □ *John: You're just not doing what is expected of you. Bill: Keep it up! Just keep it up, and I'll quit right when you need me most.* □ *"Your behavior is terrible, young man! You just keep it up and see what happens," warned Alice. "Just keep it up!"*

keep late hours to stay up or stay out until very late at night. □ *I'm always tired because I keep late hours.* □ *If I didn't keep late hours, I wouldn't sleep so late in the morning.*

keep off (of) someone's back and **keep off (of) someone's case** *Inf. Fig.* to leave someone alone; to stop criticizing or scolding someone. □ *Keep off my back! Leave me alone.* □ *Keep off my case!*

keep off (of) someone's case Go to previous.

keep off ((of) something) to remain off something; to stay off of something. (*Of* is usually retained before pronouns.) □ *Please keep off the grass.* □ *This is not a public thoroughfare! Keep off!* □ *You had better keep off of my property.*

keep on Go to **keep on** something.

keep on an even keel *Fig.* to remain cool and calm. (Originally nautical.) □ *If Jane can keep on an even keel and not panic, she will be all right.* □ *Try to keep on an even keel and not get upset so easily.*

keep on (doing something) to continue to do something. □ *Are you going to keep on singing all night?* □ *Yes, I'm going to keep on.*

keep on keeping on *Inf.* keep trying; keep doing what you are doing. □ *I do my best. I just keep on keeping on.*

keep on (one's) guard (against someone or something) Go to **on (one's) guard (against someone or something)**.

keep on one's toes Go to **on one's toes**.

keep on someone (about something) Go to **keep after someone (about something)**.

keep on someone's case Go to **on someone's case**.

keep on something 1. and **keep on** *Lit.* to work to remain mounted on something, such as a horse, bicycle, etc. □ *It's really hard for me to keep on a horse.* □ *It's hard to keep on when it's moving all over the place.* **2.** *Fig.* to pay close attention to something. (See also **keep on top of someone or something**.) □ *Keep on that story until everything is settled.* □ *This is a problem. Keep on it until it's settled.*

keep on the good side of someone Go to **keep on the right side of someone**.

keep on the left(-hand) side (of something) to stay on the left-hand side of something. □ *Please don't keep on the left side all the time when everyone else is on the right!* □ *In England you keep on the left-hand side.*

keep on the right side of someone and **keep on the good side of someone**; **stay on the good side of someone**; **stay on the right side of someone** *Fig.* to remain in someone's favor. (This has nothing to do with the right-hand side.) □ *You had better keep on the right side of Mr. Franklin. He's very particular.* □ *I will keep on the good side of him.*

keep on the right(-hand) side (of something) to stay on the right-hand side of something. □ *We always keep on the right side of the road in this country.* □ *Please keep on the right-hand side.*

keep on (the) track *Fig.* to stay on the path that one is on; to continue doing the things one is doing. □ *Keep on the track and you will end up where you want to be.* □ *I know I can keep on track.*

keep on top (of someone or something) to stay well-informed about the status of someone or something. □ *I need to keep on top of the president, because I am doing a report on him.* □ *News is easy to get these days, and I do what I can to keep on top.*

keep on trucking *Inf.* to continue to do well; to continue to try. □ *Just keep on trucking, man.* □ *All I can do is keep on trucking.*

Keep (on) trying. and **Don't quit trying.** *Fig.* a phrase encouraging continued efforts. □ *Jane: I think I'm doing better in calculus. John: Keep trying! You can get an A.* □ *Sue: I really want that promotion, but I keep getting turned down. Bill: Don't quit trying! You'll get it.*

keep on with something to continue with something. □ *Just keep on with your work. Don't pay any attention to me.* □ *Can I keep on with this while you are talking?*

keep one in one's place to make someone stay in the proper rank or station. □ *I guess you want to keep me in my place, is that right?* □ *I know enough to keep myself in my place.*

keep one on one's toes Go to **on one's toes**.

keep one's act up† Go to **keep an act up†**.

keep one's cards close to one's chest Go to **play one's cards close to one's chest**.

keep one's cards close to one's vest Go to **keep one's cards close to one's chest**.

keep one's chair and **keep one's seat** *Fig.* to stay seated; to remain in one's chair or place. □ *That's all right. Keep your chair. I'll find my own way out.* □ *Please keep your seats until after the question-and-answer period.*

keep one's **chin up** *Fig.* to keep one's spirits high; to act brave and confident. □ *Keep your chin up, John. Things will get better.* □ *Just keep your chin up and tell the judge exactly what happened.*

keep one's **cool** *Inf.* to remain calm and in control. □ *Relax, man! Just keep your cool.* □ *It's hard to keep your cool when you've been cheated.*

keep one's **distance (from** someone or something**)** *Fig.* to maintain a respectful or cautious distance from someone or something. □ *Keep your distance from John. He's in a bad mood.* □ *Keep your distance from the fire.*

keep one's **ear to the ground** Go to keep an ear to the ground.

keep one's **end of the bargain up**† Go to hold one's end of the bargain up†.

keep one's **end up**† **1.** *Lit.* to hold one's end of a load so that the load is level. □ *Be sure to keep your end up while we go up the stairs.* □ *Try to keep up your end.* **2.** *Fig.* to carry through on one's part of a bargain. □ *You have to keep your end up like the rest of us.* □ *Don't worry, I'll keep up my end.*

keep one's **eye on** someone or something and **have** one's **eye on** someone or something *Fig.* to have one's attention directed to someone or something. □ *Please keep your eye on the children while I go to the store.* □ *Bill kept an eye on his expenses because he was spending too much money.*

keep one's **eye on the ball 1.** *Fig.* to watch or follow the ball carefully, especially when one is playing a ball game; to follow the details of a ball game very carefully. □ *John, if you can't keep your eye on the ball, I'll have to take you out of the game.* □ *"Keep your eye on the ball!" the coach roared at the players.* **2.** *Fig.* to remain alert to the events occurring around oneself. □ *If you want to get along in this office, you're going to have to keep your eye on the ball.* □ *Bill would do better in his classes if he would just keep his eye on the ball.*

keep one's **eyes open (for** someone or something**)** and **keep** one's **eyes peeled (for** someone or something**)** *Fig.* to remain alert and watchful for someone or something. (The entry with *peeled* is informal. *Peel* refers to moving the eyelids back. See also **keep an eye out (for** someone or something**)**.) □ *I'm keeping my eyes open for a sale on winter coats.* □ *Please keep your eyes peeled for Mary. She's due to arrive here any time.* □ *Okay. I'll keep my eyes open.*

keep one's **eye(s) out (for** someone or something**)** Go to keep an eye out (for someone or something).

keep one's **eyes peeled (for** someone or something**)** Go to keep one's eyes open (for someone or something).

keep one's **feet on the ground** and **have** one's **feet on the ground** *Fig.* to remain calm and stable. □ *You will do all right if you have your feet on the ground. Don't get carried away.* □ *Just keep your feet on the ground and you will do fine.*

keep one's **finger on the pulse of** something *Fig.* to monitor the current state of something frequently. □ *I have to keep my finger on the pulse of the city if I want to be a good reporter.* □ *It is hard to keep your finger on the pulse of Washington, D.C., but a U.S. senator must do it.*

keep one's **fingers crossed (for** someone or something**)** and **cross** one's **fingers** to wish for luck for someone or

something, sometimes by actually crossing one's fingers; to hope for a good outcome for someone or something. □ *I hope you win the race Saturday. I'm keeping my fingers crossed for you.* □ *I'm trying out for a play. Keep your fingers crossed!*

keep one's **hand in (**something**)** *Fig.* to remain involved in something, perhaps only a token involvement. □ *I want to keep my hand in things even after I retire.* □ *I always have to keep my hand in so I will feel a part of things.*

keep one's **hands off (**something**)** to refrain from touching or handling something. □ *I'm going to put these cookies here. You keep your hands off them.* □ *Get your hands off my book, and keep them off.*

keep one's **hands to** oneself *Fig.* to refrain from touching anything or anyone; to refrain from punching or poking someone. □ *Won't you keep your hands to yourself?* □ *Keep your hands to yourself while we are in the toy store.* □ *I want you boys to stop fighting and keep your hands to yourselves.*

keep one's **head** *Fig.* to remain calm and sensible when in an awkward situation that might cause a person to panic or go out of control. □ *She was very angry. We had to calm her down and encourage her to keep her head.* □ *Always try to keep your head when others are panicking.*

keep one's **head above water 1.** *Lit.* to keep from drowning when swimming or floating. (See also **get** one's **head above water**.) □ *I was so tired I could hardly keep my head above water.* **2.** *Fig.* to manage to survive, especially financially. □ *We have so little money that we can hardly keep our heads above water.* □ *It's hard to keep your head above water on this much money.* **3.** *Fig.* to keep up with one's work. □ *It's all I can do to keep my head above water with the work I have. I can't take on any more.* □ *We have so many orders that we can hardly keep our heads above water.*

keep one's **mind on** someone or something to concentrate on someone or something. □ *He is keeping his mind on Jane instead of his work.* □ *I find it hard to keep my mind on my reading.*

keep one's **mouth shut (about** someone or something**)** *Fig.* to keep quiet about someone or something; to keep a secret about someone or something. □ *They told me to keep my mouth shut about the boss or I'd be in big trouble.* □ *I think I'll keep my mouth shut.*

keep one's **nose clean** *Fig.* to keep out of trouble, especially trouble with the law. □ *I'm trying to keep my nose clean by staying away from those rough guys.* □ *John, if you don't learn how to keep your nose clean, you're going to end up in jail.*

keep one's **nose out of** someone's **business** *Fig.* to refrain from interfering in someone else's business. (See also **keep** one's **nose out of** something.) □ *Let John have his privacy, and keep your nose out of my business, too!* □ *Keep your nose out of my business!*

keep one's **nose out of** something *Fig.* to stay out of something, such as someone else's business. (See also **keep** one's **nose out of** someone's **business**.) □ *Try to keep your nose out of stuff that doesn't concern you.* □ *Keep your nose out of my personal affairs.*

keep one's **nose to the grindstone** *Fig.* to work hard and constantly. □ *Son: I'll never get good grades. I might as well not even study. Mother: Don't give up yet. I'm sure that if you just keep your nose to the grindstone, you'll get the results you want.* □ *Mary kept her nose to the grindstone while her friends were out enjoying themselves.*

keep one's **opinions to** oneself to stop mentioning one's own opinions, especially when they disagree with someone else's. □ *You ought to keep your opinions to yourself rather than upset our guests.* □ *Please keep your rude opinions to yourself!*

keep one's **own counsel** *Fig.* to keep one's thoughts and plans to oneself; to withhold from other people one's thoughts and plans. □ *Jane is very quiet. She tends to keep her own counsel.* □ *I advise you to keep your own counsel.*

keep one's **pants on** Go to keep one's **shirt on.**

keep one's **place** *Fig.* to exhibit only the behavior appropriate to one's position or status in life. □ *When I complained about the food, they told me to keep my place!* □ *I suggest you keep your place until you're in a position to change things.*

keep one's **promise** Go to keep a promise.

keep one's **seat** Go to keep one's **chair.**

keep one's **shirt on** and **keep** one's **pants on** *Fig.* to be patient. □ *Wait a minute! Keep your shirt on!* □ *Keep your pants on! I'll be with you in a minute.*

keep one's **shoulder to the wheel** Go to have one's shoulder to the wheel.

keep one's **side of the bargain** Go to live up to one's end of the bargain.

keep one's **temper** and **hold** one's **temper** to hold back an expression of anger. (The opposite of lose one's temper.) □ *She should have learned to keep her temper when she was a child.* □ *Sally got thrown off the team because she couldn't hold her temper.*

keep one's **weather eye open** *Fig.* to watch for something (to happen); to be on the alert (for something); to be on guard. □ *Some trouble is brewing. Keep your weather eye open.* □ *Try to be more alert. Learn to keep your weather eye open.*

keep one's **wits about** one *Fig.* to remain rational when threatened or under stress; to keep one's mind operating in a time of stress. □ *If Jane hadn't kept her wits about her during the fire, things would have been much worse.* □ *I could hardly keep my wits about me.*

keep one's **word** to uphold one's promise; to do as one says. (The opposite of break one's **word.**) □ *I told her I'd be there to pick her up, and I intend to keep my word.* □ *Keeping one's word is necessary in the legal profession.*

keep one **step ahead of** someone or something and **stay** one **step ahead of** someone or something *Fig.* to be or stay slightly in advance of someone or something. □ *Al kept one step ahead of Detective Rogers.* □ *Try to keep one step ahead of the investigators.*

keep oneself **above suspicion** Go to above suspicion.

keep oneself **to** oneself to remain aloof. □ *He does tend to keep himself to himself.* □ *Keep yourself to yourself, and you'll be all right there.*

keep out from under someone's **feet** *Fig.* to stay out of someone's way. □ *Please keep out from under my feet. I'm very busy.* □ *Try to keep out from under Tom's feet while he is working.*

Keep out of my way. and **Stay out of my way. 1.** *Lit.* Don't get in my pathway. □ *John: Keep out of my way! I'm carrying a heavy load. Bill: Sorry.* □ *"Keep out of my way!" shouted the piano mover.* **2.** *Fig.* Don't cause me any trouble. □ *Henry: I'm going to get even no matter what. Keep out of my way. Andy: Keep it up! You'll really get in trouble.* □ *John: I intend to work my way to the top in this business. Mary: So do I, so just keep out of my way.*

keep out of sight Go to out of sight.

keep out (of something) **1.** *Lit.* to remain outside something or some place. □ *You should keep out of the darkroom when the door is closed.* □ *The door is closed. Keep out!* **2.** *Fig.* to remain uninvolved with something. □ *Keep out of this! It's my affair.* □ *It's not your affair. Keep out!*

Keep out of this! and **Stay out of this!** This is not your business, so do not try to get involved. □ *John: Now you listen to me, Fred! Mary: That's no way to talk to Fred! John: Keep out of this, Mary! Mind your own business! Fred: Stay out of this, Mary! Mary: It's just as much my business as it is yours.*

keep pace (with someone or something) **1.** *Lit.* to move at the same speed as someone, something, or an animal; to match someone or some creature pace for pace. □ *The black horse was having a hard time keeping pace with the brown one.* □ *Tom runs very fast and I couldn't keep pace with him.* **2.** *Fig.* to manage to move, learn, change, etc., at the same rate as someone or something. □ *Bill can't keep pace with the geometry class.* □ *You've just got to keep pace.*

keep people straight (in one's **mind)** *Fig.* to correctly distinguish one person from other people. □ *The twins look exactly alike. Not even their mother can keep them straight.*

keep quiet (about someone or something) and **keep still (about** someone or something) to refrain from talking about someone or something; to keep a secret about someone or something. □ *Please keep quiet about the missing money.* □ *Please keep still about it.* □ *All right. I'll keep still.*

keep sight of someone or something to keep someone or something in view. □ *Try to keep sight of the skier.* □ *I want to keep sight of the children at all times.*

Keep smiling. a good-bye phrase encouraging someone to have good spirits. □ *John: Things are really getting tough. Sue: Well, just keep smiling. Things will get better.* □ *Bill: What a day! I'm exhausted and depressed. Bob: Not to worry. Keep smiling. Things will calm down.*

keep someone **at** something to make sure someone continues to work at something. □ *Please keep Walter at his chores.* □ *I was so sick I couldn't keep myself at my work.*

keep someone **back** and **hold** someone **back 1.** *Lit.* to restrain people from moving forward or getting in the way. □ *The police were ordered to keep people back so they wouldn't interfere with the paramedics.* **2.** *Fig.* to keep a child in the same grade for an extra year. □ *We asked them to keep John back a year.* □ *John was kept back a year in school.* **3.** *Fig.* to keep someone from advancing in life. □

I think that your limited vocabulary is keeping you back. □ *Her lack of computer skills kept her back in her career.*

keep someone **company** to sit or stay with someone, especially someone who is lonely. □ *I kept my uncle company for a few hours.* □ *He was very grateful for someone to keep him company. He gets very lonely.*

keep someone **down** to prevent someone from advancing or succeeding. □ *His lack of a degree will keep him down.* □ *I don't think that this problem will keep her down.*

keep someone **from** doing something to prevent someone from doing something. □ *I kept the child from falling in the lake by grabbing his collar.* □ *I try to keep myself from overeating, but I seem to fail frequently.*

keep someone **from** someone or something to hold someone away from someone or something; to prevent someone from getting at someone or something. □ *You must keep the child from her mother until the mother is infection-free.* □ *It is hard to keep a child from the playground, even a sick child.* □ *I could hardly keep myself from the dessert table.*

keep someone **honest** to manage to make someone behave honestly and fairly and tell the truth. □ *I love to tell about our vacations, and my wife is usually with me to keep me honest.*

keep someone **in (a state of) suspense** to make someone wait anxiously for something. □ *Tell us what happened. Don't keep us in a state of suspense.* □ *Don't keep me in suspense!*

keep someone **in ignorance (about** someone or something**)** to prevent someone from learning specific information about someone or something. □ *I think we had better keep them all in ignorance about the money for a while.* □ *I don't know about her. I have kept myself in ignorance on purpose.*

keep someone **in sight** to make sure that a person is visible at all times. □ *He looks suspicious. Keep him in sight at all times.* □ *I cannot keep him in sight day and night.*

keep someone **in stitches** *Fig.* to cause someone to laugh loud and hard, for a period of time. □ *The comedian kept us in stitches for nearly an hour.* □ *The teacher kept the class in stitches, but the students didn't learn anything.*

keep someone **in the dark (about** someone or something**)** Go to in the dark (about someone or something).

keep someone **in the picture** Go to in the picture.

keep someone **on** *Fig.* to retain someone in employment longer than is required or was planned. □ *She worked out so well that we decided to keep her on.* □ *Liz was kept on as a consultant.*

keep someone **on a string** Go to on a string.

keep someone **on (something) 1.** *Lit.* to make or help someone stay mounted on something, such as a horse, bicycle, etc. □ *Her father kept her on the bicycle as she was learning to ride it.* □ *I couldn't keep myself on the horse.* **2.** *Fig.* to retain someone as an employee. □ *We can't keep you on the payroll any longer.* □ *Ken could not be kept on any longer.*

keep someone **on tenterhooks** *Fig.* to keep someone in suspense. □ *Don't keep me on tenterhooks! Tell me your news!* □ *We were all kept on tenterhooks waiting to find out what happened.*

keep someone or an animal **in**[†] to make someone or an animal stay inside. □ *I will have to keep Billy in until his cold is better.* □ *Keep the dog in. It's too cold for her to go out.* □ *Keep in the children and the animals until it warms up.*

keep someone or an animal **in line** *Fig.* to make certain that someone behaves properly. □ *It's very hard to keep Bill in line. He's sort of rowdy.* □ *The teacher had to struggle to keep the class in line.*

keep someone or some creature **out in the cold** Go to out in the cold.

keep someone or something **about** and **keep** someone or something **around** to have someone or something nearby habitually. □ *Try to keep some spare parts about.* □ *He doesn't work very hard, but we keep him around anyway.*

keep someone or something **apart** to keep someone away from someone else; to keep something away from something else. □ *Try to keep the dogs and cats apart.* □ *Can you keep Bill and Bob apart?*

keep someone or something **around** Go to keep someone or something **about**.

keep someone or something **at a distance** to retain some amount of physical distance from someone or something. □ *Please try to keep Tom at a distance. He just gets in the way.* □ *I wanted to keep the smelly plant at a distance.*

keep someone or something **at arm's length** Go to keep at arm's length from someone or something.

keep someone or something **at bay** Go to at bay.

keep someone or something **away (from** someone or something**)** to maintain a physical distance between someone or something and someone or something, in any combination. □ *I will try to keep the smokers away from you.* □ *Try to keep the dog away from the roast.*

keep someone or something **back**[†] to hold someone or something in reserve. □ *Keep back some of the food for an emergency.* □ *We are keeping Karen back until the other players have exhausted themselves.*

keep someone or something **by** someone to make someone or something stay next to someone. □ *Try to keep the twins by you until we have taken a few more pictures.* □ *Please keep this package by you until we are ready to present it.*

keep someone or something **down** to hold someone or something in a hidden or protected position. □ *Try to keep Sam down where no one can see him.* □ *Please keep the noise down so Fred won't know it's a party when he comes in.*

keep someone or something **for** someone **1.** to retain and care for someone or something. □ *I would be happy to keep Rover for you while you are away.* □ *Would you keep my dog for me?* **2.** to keep someone or something in reserve for someone. □ *John wanted to return to the accounting department, but I will keep him here for you for last-minute changes.* □ *I am keeping some birthday cake here for you, since you will miss the party.*

keep someone or something **from** doing something to prevent someone or something from doing something. □ *Would you please keep your dog from digging in my garden?* □ *Her lack of a degree kept her from advancing.*

K

keep someone or something **going** to sustain someone or something. □ *I try to eat just enough food to keep me going. Enjoying food is just not an issue any more.*

keep someone or something **hanging (in midair)** Go to leave someone or something hanging (in midair).

keep someone or something **in check** and **hold** someone or something **in check** to keep someone or something under control; to restrain someone or something. □ *Hang on to this rope to keep the dog in check.* □ *I was so angry I could hardly hold myself in check.*

keep someone or something **in mind** and **bear** someone or something **in mind** to remember and think about someone or something. □ *When you're driving a car, you must bear this in mind at all times: Keep your eyes on the road.* □ *As you leave home, keep your family in mind.*

keep someone or something **in mind (for** someone or something**)** to remember to bring up someone or something in regard to someone or something. □ *Would you keep me in mind for the vice president job?* □ *I will keep a position in mind for John, since he is graduating soon.*

keep someone or something **in order** to keep people or things in the proper sequence. □ *Please try to keep the children in order until their turn to perform comes.* □ *Can you keep these books in order for me?*

keep someone or something **in reserve** Go to hold someone or something in reserve.

keep someone or something **in** some place to house or maintain someone or something in some place. □ *We keep the boys in an apartment just off campus. It's cheaper than three dormitory rooms.* □ *We can keep your dog in the garage until you return.*

keep someone or something **in with** someone or something to locate people or things together, in any combination. □ *I will keep Tom in with me until he gets his own room.* □ *We will keep the cat in with Tom until there is room elsewhere.*

keep someone or something **off**† Go to hold someone or something off†.

keep someone or something **off ((of)** someone or something**)** to make sure that someone or something remains off someone or something. (*Of* is usually retained before pronouns.) □ *Keep that woman off of me! She's obsessed with me!* □ *Please keep Timmy off the couch.* □ *Keep him off!*

keep someone or something **on (the) (right) track** *Fig.* to make sure that someone or some process continues to progress properly. □ *You have to watch him and keep him on the right track.* □ *I will do what I can to keep the process on the track.*

keep someone or something **on track** Go to on track.

keep someone or something **out (of** something**) 1.** to prevent someone or something from getting into something or some place. □ *Keep your kids out of my yard.* □ *She just couldn't keep herself out of the cookie jar.* **2.** to keep the subject of someone or something out of a discussion. □ *Keep the kids out of this! I don't want to talk about them.* □ *They kept Dorothy out of the discussion.*

keep someone or something **out of the way** to prevent someone or something from getting in the way. □ *Please keep your children out of the way.*

keep someone or something **quiet** Go to next.

keep someone or something **still 1.** *Lit.* and **keep** someone or something **quiet** to make someone or something silent or less noisy. □ *Can you please keep the baby still?* □ *Keep that stereo quiet!* **2.** Go to keep something quiet. **3.** and **hold** someone or something **still** *Fig.* to restrain or control someone or something so that the person or thing cannot move. □ *Please keep your foot still. It makes me nervous when you wiggle it.* □ *You have to hold the nail still if you want to hit it.*

keep someone or something **together** to keep things or a group of people together; to keep something, including a group of people, from falling apart. □ *I hope we can keep our club together for a few more years.* □ *We will keep it together for a while longer.* □ *Keep your toys together. Don't scatter them all over the house.*

keep someone or something **under (close) scrutiny** Go to under (close) scrutiny.

keep someone or something **under control** Go to under control.

keep someone or something **under** something to store, hide, or cache someone or something beneath something. □ *Keep Max under the packing crate until the police go away.* □ *I keep a box of extra sweaters under the bed.*

keep (someone or something) within bounds *Fig.* to cause someone or something to remain constrained or be reasonable; to cause someone to act or something to be in good taste. □ *I know you want artistic freedom, but if you want an audience, you are going to have to keep within bounds.* □ *Try to keep the children within bounds.* □ *Do keep your behavior within bounds.*

keep someone **posted** *Fig.* to keep someone informed (of what is happening); to keep someone up to date. □ *If the price of corn goes up, I need to know. Please keep me posted.* □ *Keep her posted about the patient's status.*

keep someone, something, or an animal **back (from** someone or something**)** to make someone, something, or an animal stay in a position away from someone or something. □ *Keep everyone back from the injured lady.* □ *Please keep the dogs back from the turtle.*

keep someone **under** someone's **thumb** Go to under someone's thumb.

keep someone **up 1.** *Lit.* to hold someone upright. □ *Try to keep him up until I can get his bed made.* □ *Keep her up for a few minutes longer.* **2.** *Fig.* to prevent someone from going to bed or going to sleep. □ *I'm sorry, was my trumpet keeping you up?* □ *The noise kept us up.*

keep someone **young at heart** Go to young at heart.

keep something **by** to keep something handy; to keep something in reserve, ready to be used. □ *Keep this extra glue by in case you need it.* □ *This money had been kept by for just such an emergency.*

keep something **down 1.** *Lit.* to make the level of noise lower and keep it lower. □ *Please keep it down. You are just too noisy.* □ *Keep the noise down, or I will call the police.* **2.** *Fig.* to retain food in one's stomach rather than throwing it up. □ *I've got the flu and I can't keep any food down.* □ *She couldn't keep the milk down.* **3.** *Fig.* to keep spending under control. □ *I work hard to keep expenses down.* □ *Please try to keep the cost of the new project down.*

keep something **for a rainy day** Go to save (something) for a rainy day.

keep something **for another occasion** Go to leave something for another occasion.

keep something **from** someone not to tell something to someone. □ *Why did you keep the news from me? I needed to know.* □ *This matter shouldn't have been kept from me.*

keep something **in**† Go to hold something in†.

keep something **in the back of** someone's **mind** Go to in the back of someone's mind.

keep something **inside ((of) one(self))** Go to hold something in†.

keep something **of** someone's or something's to retain something that belongs to or is associated with someone or something. □ *I would love to keep this handkerchief of yours.* □ *I want to keep a memento of the occasion.*

keep something **on**† to continue to wear an article of clothing. □ *I'm going to keep my coat on. It's a little chilly in here.* □ *I'll keep on my coat, thanks.*

keep something **on an even keel** *Fig.* to keep something in a steady and untroubled state. □ *The manager cannot keep the firm on an even keel any longer.* □ *When the workers are unhappy, it is difficult to keep the factory on an even keel.*

keep something **on its feet** *Fig.* to keep something stable and viable. □ *It takes a lot of effort to keep this old firm on its feet. We may have to go out of business.* □ *Can we keep this business on its feet another year?*

keep something **quiet** and **keep** something **still** *Fig.* to keep something a secret. □ *I'm quitting my job, but my boss doesn't know yet. Please keep it quiet.* □ *Okay. I'll keep it still.*

keep something **still** Go to previous.

keep something **to a minimum** to make something as small, few, or little as possible. □ *Do what you can to keep construction dust to a minimum.* □ *The dust should be kept to a minimum.*

keep something **to** oneself to keep something a secret. □ *I want you to keep this news to yourself.* □ *This should be kept to yourself.*

keep something **under** one's **hat** *Fig.* to keep something a secret; to keep something in one's mind (only). (If the secret stays under your hat, it stays in your mind. Note the use of *but* in the examples.) □ *Keep this under your hat, but I'm getting married.* □ *I'm getting married, but keep it under your hat.*

keep something **under wraps** *Fig.* to keep something concealed (until some future time). □ *We kept the plan under wraps until after the election.* □ *The automobile company kept the new model under wraps until most of the old models had been sold.*

keep something **until** some time to retain something until a certain time. □ *Can you keep this box until I call for it next week?* □ *The package will be kept until Monday.*

keep something **up**† **1.** *Lit.* to hold or prop something up. □ *Keep your side of the trunk up. Don't let it sag.* □ *Keep up your side of the trunk.* **2.** *Fig.* to continue doing something. □ *I love your singing. Don't stop. Keep it up.* □ *Please*

keep up your singing. **3.** *Fig.* to maintain something in good order. □ *I'm glad you keep the exterior of your house up.* □ *You keep up your house nicely.*

keep something **with** someone to leave something in the care of someone. □ *Can I keep my bicycle with you while I am gone?* □ *I can keep your bicycle with me.*

Keep still. 1. and **Hold still.** Do not move. □ *Quit wiggling. Keep still!* □ *"Hold still. I can't examine your ear if you're moving," said the doctor.* **2.** Go to keep quiet (about someone or something).

keep still (for someone or something**)** Go to hold still (for someone or something).

keep tab(s) (on someone or something**)** and **keep track (of** someone or something**)** *Fig.* to monitor someone or something; to follow the activities of someone or something. □ *I'm supposed to keep track of my books.* □ *Try to keep tabs on everyone who works for you.* □ *It's hard to keep tabs when you have a lot of other work to do.* □ *I can't keep track of the money I earn. Maybe someone else is spending it.*

keep the ball rolling 1. *Lit.* to keep a rolling ball moving. □ *You have to throw hard enough to keep the ball rolling all the way to the bowling pins.* **2.** *Fig.* to cause something that is in progress to continue. □ *Tom started the project, and we kept the ball rolling.* □ *Who will keep the ball rolling now that she is gone?*

keep the home fires burning *Fig.* to keep things going at one's home or other central location. (From a World War I song.) □ *My uncle kept the home fires burning when my sister and I went to school.* □ *The manager stays at the office and keeps the home fires burning while I'm out selling our products.*

keep the stork busy Go to next.

keep the stork flying and **keep the stork busy** *Rur.* to have lots of children. □ *Sally's pregnant again, with their sixth. They sure do keep the stork flying!* □ *Grandma and grandpa kept the stork flying. I've got ten aunts and uncles.*

keep the wolf from the door *Fig.* to maintain oneself at a minimal level; to keep from starving, freezing, etc. □ *I don't make a lot of money, just enough to keep the wolf from the door.* □ *We have a small amount of money saved, hardly enough to keep the wolf from the door.*

keep things straight (in one's **mind)** *Fig.* to correctly distinguish one thing from other things. □ *These two bottles look so much alike. It's hard to keep them straight.*

Keep this to yourself. a phrase introducing something that is meant to be a secret. □ *Andy: Keep this to yourself, but I'm going to Bora Bora on my vacation. Henry: Sounds great. Can I go too?* □ *John: Keep this to yourself. Mary and I are breaking up. Sue: I won't tell a soul.*

keep time 1. *Lit.* to maintain a musical rhythm. □ *Bob had to drop out of the band because he couldn't keep time.* □ *Since he can't keep time, he can't march, and he can't play the drums.* **2.** *Fig.* to keep watch over the time in a game or an athletic contest. □ *Ann kept time at all the basketball games.* □ *Whoever keeps time has to watch the referee very carefully.* **3.** *Fig.* [for a clock or a watch] to keep track of time accurately. □ *This watch doesn't keep time.* □ *My other watch kept time better.*

K

keep to oneself to be solitary; to stay away from other people. □ *Ann tends to keep to herself. She doesn't have many friends.* □ *I try to keep to myself each morning so I can get some work done.*

keep to something to adhere to an agreement; to follow a plan; to keep a promise. □ *Please keep to the agreed-upon plan.* □ *Can you keep to what we agreed on?*

keep to the straight and narrow *Fig.* to behave properly and correctly; to stay out of trouble. □ *If you keep to the straight and narrow, you can't help but win in the end.* □ *I always keep to the straight and narrow.*

keep together to remain as a group. □ *We will keep together to the very end.* □ *Our group decided to keep together.*

keep track (of someone or something**)** Go to keep tab(s) **(on** someone or something**).**

keep under something to remain beneath something. □ *Keep under the packing crate, Max.* □ *I ordered the dog to keep under the table.*

keep under wraps Go to under wraps.

keep up an act and **keep up** one's **act** *Fig.* to maintain a false front; to act in a special way that is different from one's natural behavior. □ *Most of the time John kept up an act. He was really not a friendly person.* □ *He works hard to keep up his act.*

keep up appearances to make things look all right whether they are or not. □ *We must keep up appearances even if it means little sacrifices here and there.* □ *Things may be unpleasant, but we will keep up appearances.*

keep up one's **act** Go to keep up an act.

Keep up the good work. Please keep doing the good things that you are doing now. (A general phrase of encouragement.) □ *Father: Your grades are fine, Bill. Keep up the good work. Bill: Thanks, Dad.* □ *"Nice play," said the coach. "Keep up the good work!"*

keep up (with someone or something**)** **1.** *Lit.* to advance at the same rate as someone or something; to be just as productive as someone or something. □ *Don't work so fast. I can't keep up with you.* □ *You're running so fast that I cannot keep up with you.* □ *I don't make enough money to keep up with your spending.* **2.** *Fig.* to pay attention to the news about someone or something. □ *I don't see the Smiths a lot since they moved, but I keep up with them by phone.* □ *I try to keep up with current events.*

keep up with the Joneses *Fig.* to try to match the lifestyle of one's neighbors. □ *I am tired of trying to keep up with the Joneses. Let's just move if we can't afford to live here.* □ *We never try to keep up with the Joneses.*

keep up with the times *Fig.* to work to appear contemporary and fashionable. □ *I am too old-fashioned. I have to keep up with the times better.* □ *I don't care about keeping up with the times.*

keep watch on someone or something to monitor someone or something. □ *Keep watch on the lady in the big coat. She may be a shoplifter.* □ *Try to keep watch on the committee's work.*

keep watch over someone or something to supervise someone or something; to take care of someone or some-thing. □ *Please keep watch over the project.* □ *Will you keep watch over Timmy for a minute?*

keep within something to remain within a thing or within the boundaries of something. □ *If you keep within the tourist area, you will be safe.* □ *Please keep within the yard.*

Keep your chin up. *Fig.* an expression of encouragement to someone who has to bear some emotional burdens. (Fixed order.) □ *Fred: I really can't take much more of this. Jane: Keep your chin up. Things will get better.* □ *John: Smile, Fred. Keep your chin up. Fred: I guess you're right. I just get so depressed when I think of this mess I'm in.*

Keep your head down. *Fig.* Lie low, try not to be noticed. □ *My advice to you is to keep your head down for the moment.* □ *Keep your head down. It'll blow over.*

Keep your mouth shut (about someone or something**).** *Fig.* Do not tell anyone about someone or something. □ *Bob: Are you going to see the doctor? Mary: Yes, but keep your mouth shut about it.* □ *Bob: Isn't Tom's uncle in tax trouble? Jane: Yes, but keep your mouth shut about him.*

Keep your nose out of my business. Go to Mind your own business.

Keep your opinions to yourself! *Fig.* I do not want to hear your opinions! □ *Jane: I think this room looks drab. Sue: Keep your opinions to yourself! I like it this way!* □ *Sally: You really ought to do something about your hair. It looks like it was in a hurricane. John: Keep your opinions to yourself. This is the latest style where I come from.*

Keep your pants on! Go to Keep your shirt on!

Keep your powder dry. Go to Put your trust in God, and keep your powder dry.

Keep your shirt on! and **Keep your pants on!** *Inf.* Just wait a minute! □ *I'll be right with you. Keep your shirt on!* □ *Keep your pants on! You're next.*

Keep your shop and your shop will keep you. *Prov.* If you work hard at running your business, then your business will always make enough of a profit to support you. □ *When Grandpa turned his hardware store over to me, he said, "It's hard work, but it's a good living. Keep the shop and the shop will keep you."*

key someone **up**† to cause someone to be anxious or excited. □ *The excitement of the moment really keyed me up.* □ *Thoughts of their vacation keyed up the children so much they couldn't sleep.*

the **key to success** *Fig.* the secret to someone's success. □ *Bob said that the key to his success is working hard, being on time, and being extremely lucky.*

***keyed up (about** something**)** and ***keyed up (over** something**)** to be excited or anxious. (*Typically: **be** ~; **get** ~.) □ *Why are you so keyed up about nothing?* □ *She is keyed up over her son's health.*

kick a habit and **kick the habit; shake the habit; shake a habit** to break a habit. □ *It's hard to kick a habit, but it can be done. I stopped biting my nails.* □ *I used to drink coffee every morning, but I kicked the habit.*

kick about someone or something *Fig.* to complain about someone or something. □ *Why are you kicking about your cousin? What has he done now?* □ *They kicked about our regulations, but they finally accepted them.*

K

kick against someone or something to give someone or something a blow with the foot. □ *I kicked against the side of the television set, and it came on.* □ *He kicked against the giant of a man, but it had no effect.*

kick around Go to knock around.

kick ass and **kick butt** *Sl.* to actively motivate people to do something. □ *It looks like I'm going to have to kick ass to get people moving around here.*

kick at someone or something to make kicking motions toward someone or something. □ *The horse kicked at me, but I knew it was just a threat.* □ *The boys kicked at the can aimlessly.*

kick back 1. *Inf.* to relax; to lean back and relax. (See also lie back.) □ *I really like to kick back and relax.* □ *It's time to kick back and enjoy life.* **2.** *Inf.* [for an addict] to return to an addiction or a habit, after having "kicked the habit." □ *Lefty kicked back after only a few days of being clean.* □ *A lot of addicts kick back very soon.*

kick back (at someone or something**)** to kick at someone or something in revenge. □ *She kicked at me, so I kicked back at her.* □ *If you kick me, I'll kick back.*

kick butt Go to kick ass.

kick in (on something**) (for** someone or something**)** *Fig.* to contribute to something for someone or something. □ *Would you like to kick in on a gift for Joel?* □ *I'll be happy to kick in on a gift.* □ *Sure, I would like to kick in for the gift.*

a **kick in the ass** Go to a kick in the (seat of the) pants.

a **kick in the butt** Go to a kick in the (seat of the) pants.

a **kick in the guts** *Sl.* a severe blow to one's body or spirit. □ *The news was a kick in the guts, and I haven't recovered yet.* □ *I didn't need a kick in the guts like that.*

a **kick in the (seat of the) pants** and a **kick in the ass; a kick in the butt; a kick in the teeth** *Fig. Inf.* a strong message of encouragement or demand. (Use ass and butt with discretion.) □ *All he needs is a kick in the seat of the pants to get him going.* □ *A kick in the butt will get her moving.*

a **kick in the teeth** Go to previous.

kick like a mule and **kick like a steer** to kick very hard. □ *They say that ostriches will kick like a mule if you bother them.* □ *Stay away from the back end of Tom's horse. It will kick like a steer when a stranger comes up.*

kick like a steer Go to previous.

kick off 1. *Lit.* to start play in a football game by kicking the ball. □ *Tom kicked off in the last game. Now it's my turn.* □ *John tripped when he was kicking off.* **2.** and **kick the bucket** *Fig.* to die. □ *Don't say that George Washington "kicked off." Say that he "passed away."* □ *My cat kicked off last night. She was tough as a lion.* □ *When I kick the bucket, I want a huge funeral with lots of flowers and crying.*

kick one's **heels up**[†] *Fig.* to act frisky; to be lively and have fun. (Somewhat literal when said of hoofed animals.) □ *I like to go to an old-fashioned square dance and really kick up my heels.* □ *For an old man, your uncle is really kicking his heels up.*

kick oneself **(for** doing something**)** *Fig.* to regret doing something. □ *I could just kick myself for going off and not locking the car door. Now the car has been stolen.* □ *Don't kick yourself. It's insured.*

kick out (at someone or something**)** to thrust one's foot outward at something. □ *The ostrich kicked out at the men trying to catch her.* □ *The mule kicked out and just missed me.*

kick over Go to turn over.

kick over the traces *Fig.* to do what one is meant not to do; to rebel against authority. (Alludes to a horse that steps on the wrong side of the straps that link it to whatever it is pulling.) □ *At the age of sixty, Walter kicked over the traces and ran away to Brazil.* □ *All these young kids seem to want to kick over the traces.*

kick some ass (around) *Sl.* to take over and start giving orders; to **raise hell.** (Potentially offensive. Use only with discretion.) □ *Do I have to come over there and kick some ass around?* □ *Willie is just the one to kick some ass over there.*

kick someone or an animal **out**[†] Go to **boot** someone or an animal **out**[†].

kick someone or something **around 1.** *Lit.* to strike someone, something, or some animal with the foot repeatedly. □ *Billy is out in the alley kicking a can around.* □ *Stop kicking that dog around!* **2.** *Fig.* to treat someone or something badly. □ *I finally quit my job. My boss wouldn't stop kicking me around.* □ *Stop kicking my car around. It does everything I need a car to do.*

kick someone or something **aside**[†] **1.** *Lit.* to get someone or something out of the way by kicking. □ *The bully kicked Timmy aside and grabbed our cake.* □ *I kicked aside the cats and came into the room.* **2.** *Fig.* to get rid of someone or something. □ *He simply kicked aside his wife and took up with some young chick.* □ *I kicked the old laptop aside and got a new one.*

kick someone or something **away**[†] to force someone or something away by kicking. □ *Fred kicked the intruder away from the gun he had dropped on the floor.* □ *Then he kicked away the gun.* □ *The kickboxer kicked the mugger away.*

kick something **around**[†] **1.** *Lit.* to move something around by kicking it, as in play. □ *Kick the ball around awhile and then try to make a goal.* □ *The boys kicked a can around, making a lot of noise.* □ *Don't kick around all the dirt. You'll make a mess.* **2.** *Fig.* to discuss something; to chat about an idea. □ *We got together and kicked her idea around.* □ *Fred and Bob kicked around some plots for a new movie.*

kick something **back (to** someone or something**)** to move something back to someone, something, or some place by kicking. □ *I kicked the ball back to Walter.* □ *He kicked it to me, and I kicked it back.*

kick something **down**[†] to break down something by kicking. □ *I was afraid they were going to kick the door down.* □ *Don't kick down the door!*

kick something **in**[†] **1.** to break through something by kicking. □ *Tommy kicked the door in and broke the new lamp.* □ *He kicked in the door by accident.* **2.** Go to next.

kick something **in**[†] **(on** something**) (for** someone or something**)** to contribute something, such as money, on something for someone or something. □ *I will kick a few bucks in on some flowers for the receptionist.* □ *I will kick in a few bucks on the gift for Marge.*

kick something **off**† *Fig.* to begin something; to hold a party or ceremony to mark the start of something. (Alludes to starting a football game by *kicking off* the ball for the first play.) □ *The city kicked the centennial celebration off with a parade.* □ *They kicked off the celebration with a parade.*

kick something **off (of)** someone or something and **kick** something **off**† to knock something off someone or something by kicking. (*Of* is usually retained before pronouns.) □ *The baby must have kicked her covers off of herself in the night.* □ *She kicked off her covers in the night.*

kick something **out of** something and **kick** something **out**† to move something out of something or some place by kicking. □ *The soccer player kicked the ball out of the tangle of legs.* □ *She got into the fracas and kicked out the ball.*

kick the bucket Go to kick off.

kick the habit Go to kick a habit.

kick the (natural) stuffing out of someone and **beat the (natural) stuffing out of** someone; **take the stuffing out of** someone; **knock the starch out of** someone; **knock the stuffing out of** someone *Rur.* to kick or beat someone severely. □ *Last time I was in a fight with Joe, he kicked the natural stuffing out of me.* □ *You do that again and I'll kick the stuffing out of you.* □ *Bill threatened to beat the natural stuffing out of any no-'count rascal who laid a hand on his sister.*

kick up to cause trouble or discomfort. □ *The ignition in my car is kicking up again. I will have to have it looked into.* □ *Aunt Jane's arthritis is kicking up. She needs to see the doctor again.*

kick up a fuss and **kick up a row; kick up a storm** *Fig.* to become a nuisance; to misbehave and disturb (someone). (*Row* rhymes with *cow*. Note the variations in the examples.) □ *The customer kicked up such a fuss about the food that the manager came to apologize.* □ *I kicked up such a row that they told me to leave.* □ *Oh, what pain! My arthritis is kicking up a storm.*

kick up a row Go to previous.

kick up a storm Go to kick up a fuss.

kid around (with someone**)** to tease and joke with someone. □ *I like to kid around with John. We are great friends.* □ *Yes, John and I used to kid around a lot.*

kid's stuff a very easy task. □ *Climbing that hill is kid's stuff.* □ *Driving an automatic car is kid's stuff.*

kid someone **about** someone or something to tease someone about someone or something. □ *You wouldn't kid me about Jody, would you?* □ *Please don't kid me about my long hair!*

kill for something *Sl.* to be willing to go to extremes to get something that one really wants or needs. (An exaggeration.) □ *I could kill for a cold beer.*

kill someone or an animal **off**† to kill all of a group of people or creatures. □ *Lefty set out to kill Max and his boys off.* □ *Something killed off all the dinosaurs.*

kill someone **with kindness** *Fig.* to be enormously kind to someone. □ *You are just killing me with kindness. Why?* □ *Don't kill them with kindness.*

kill the fatted calf *Fig.* to prepare an elaborate banquet (in someone's honor). (From the biblical story recounting the return of the prodigal son.) □ *When Bob got back from college, his parents killed the fatted calf and threw a great party.* □ *Sorry this meal isn't much, John. We didn't have time to kill the fatted calf.*

Kill the goose that lays the golden egg(s). *Prov.* To destroy something that is profitable to you. □ *Fred's wife knew he wasn't happy in his job, even though it paid well; still, she felt that advising him to leave it would be killing the goose that laid the golden eggs.*

kill time *Fig.* to use something up, especially time. □ *I killed time reading a novel.* □ *The employees were not encouraged to kill time.*

kill two birds with one stone *Fig.* to solve two problems at one time with a single action. □ *John learned the words to his part in the play while peeling potatoes. He was killing two birds with one stone.* □ *I have to cash a check and make a payment on my bank loan. I'll kill two birds with one stone by doing them both in one trip to the bank.*

killed outright killed immediately. □ *The driver was killed outright in the accident.* □ *Twenty people were killed outright in the explosion.*

killer instinct *Cliché* an inborn desire or ability to be ruthless. □ *Fred has a real killer instinct. He's a difficult boss to work for.*

Kind of. Go to Sort of.

a **kind of** something a variety of something that is fairly close to the real thing, even though it is not exactly the real thing. (See also kind of something.) □ *I used a folded newspaper as a kind of hat to keep the rain off.* □ *Bill is serving as a kind of helper or assistant on this project.*

kind of something Go to sort of something.

*a **king's ransom** *Fig.* a great deal of money. (To pay an amount as large as one might have to pay to get back a king held for ransom. *Typically:* **cost ~; pay ~; spend ~**.) □ *I would like to buy a nice watch, but I don't want to pay a king's ransom for it.* □ *It's a lovely house. I bet it cost a king's ransom.*

Kings have long arms. and **Governments have long arms.** *Prov.* Those who are in power can always catch and punish people who have opposed them, no matter how far away those opponents may go. □ *After his attempt to assassinate the king, the prince sailed to a distant country, although his wife warned him it would be to no avail. "Kings have long arms," she reminded him.*

kink up [for something] to develop kinks or tangles. □ *The leather parts tend to shrink and kink up in the damp weather.* □ *My hair kinks up in this weather.*

kiss and make up 1. *Lit.* [for two people who have been arguing] to kiss each other and apologize. □ *John apologized to his wife for disagreeing with her, and they finally kissed and made up.* **2.** *Fig.* to forgive someone and be friends again. □ *They were very angry, but in the end they kissed and made up.* □ *I'm sorry. Let's kiss and make up.*

kiss and tell *Fig.* to participate in something secret and private, and then tell other people about it. (In actual use, it usually refers to a person of the opposite sex even when it does not refer to actual kissing.) □ *The project was supposed to be a secret between Jane and me, but she spread it* all around. *I didn't think she was the type to kiss and tell.* □ *I am willing to discuss it with you, but only if you promise not to kiss and tell.*

the **kiss of death** *Fig.* an act that puts an end to someone or something. □ *The mayor's veto was the kiss of death for the new law.* □ *Fainting on stage was the kiss of death for my acting career.*

kiss off 1. *Sl.* to die. □ *The cat is going to have to kiss off one of these days soon.* □ *The cat kissed off after eighteen years of joy and devotion.* **2.** *Sl.* death. (Usually **kiss-off.**) □ *When the time comes for the kiss-off, I hope I'm asleep.* □ *The kiss-off came wrapped in lead, and it was instant.* **3.** *Sl.* the dismissal of someone or something. (Usually **kiss-off.**) □ *The kiss-off was when I lost the Wilson contract.* □ *Pete got the kiss-off and is now looking for a new job.*

kiss someone **off**† *Sl.* to kill someone. □ *Max kissed Lefty off with a small gun he carried in his boot.* □ *He kissed off Lefty with a small gun.*

kiss someone **on** something to kiss someone on a particular place. □ *He kissed her right on the tip of her nose.* □ *She was kissed on the tip of her nose.*

kiss someone or something **off**† *Fig.* to dismiss someone or something lightly; to abandon or write off someone or something. □ *I kissed off about $200 on that last deal.* □ *They kissed me off and that was the end of that job.*

kiss someone's **ass** *Sl.* to fawn over someone; to flatter and curry favor with someone. (Potentially offensive. Use **ass** with discretion.) □ *What does he expect me to do? Kiss his ass?* □ *I won't kiss your ass for anything.*

kiss something **away**† **(from** something) to kiss something and make something bad go away, such as tears, grief, pain, etc. □ *She kissed the tears of pain and disappointment away from her son's face.* □ *She kissed away his tears.* □ *She kissed the tears away.*

kiss something **good-bye** to anticipate or experience the loss of something. □ *If you leave your camera on a park bench, you can kiss it good-bye.* □ *You kissed your wallet good-bye when you left it in the store.*

kiss the dust *Sl.* to fall to the earth, because of death or because of being struck. □ *I'll see that you kiss the dust before sunset, cowboy!* □ *You'll kiss the dust before I will, Sheriff.*

kiss up to someone *Sl.* to flatter someone; to curry favor with someone. □ *Edgar is in kissing up to the boss again.* □ *Stop kissing up to me.*

kissing cousins relatives who know one another well enough to kiss when they meet. □ *Joe and I are kissing cousins, though we ain't seen one another since we was kids.* □ *Technically, we're second cousins once removed, but I just say we're kissing cousins.*

kith and kin friends and relatives; people known to someone. □ *I was delighted to find all my kith and kin waiting for me at the airport to welcome me home.* □ *I sent cards to my kith and kin, telling them of my arrival.*

klutz around *Inf.* to go about acting stupidly or clumsily. □ *Stop klutzing around and get your act together.* □ *Why are you klutzing around so much?*

*knee-deep in something **1.** *Fig.* heavily involved in something. (*Typically: **be** ~; **get** ~.) □ *Right now, we are knee-deep in trouble.* **2.** *Fig.* having plenty of something. (*Typically: **be** ~; **stand** ~.) □ *We are knee-deep in orders and loving it.*

*knee-high by the 4th of July *Fig.* grown as tall as it should. (Corn seedlings are proverbially supposed to be as high as someone's knee by July 4th.) (*Typically: **be** ~; **become** ~; **grow** ~.) □ *What with this drought, I don't think the crop will be knee-high by the 4th of July.* □ *It's gonna be a good year. Knee-high by the 4th of July.*

knee-high to a grasshopper Go to next.

*knee-high to a jackrabbit and ***knee-high to a grasshopper** *Rur.* very small or short. (Usually used to describe children. *Typically: **be** ~; **since** someone **was** ~.) □ *I've known you since you were knee-high to a jackrabbit.* □ *My, how you've grown! The last time I saw you, you were knee-high to a grasshopper!*

a **knee-jerk reaction** *Fig.* an automatic or reflex reaction; an immediate reaction made without examining causes or facts. □ *With one of his typical knee-jerk reactions, he said no immediately, citing some moral argument that no one understood.*

kneel down to get down on one's knees. □ *Please kneel down and fold your hands.* □ *You should at least kneel down and be quiet.*

kneel down (before someone or something**)** to show respect by getting down on one's knees in the presence of someone or something. □ *We were told to kneel down in front of the altar.* □ *Kneel down when the queen enters!*

knew it was coming and **(had) known it was coming** to have expected in advance that something was to happen. □ *I shouldn't act surprised. I knew it was coming.* □ *It's his own fault. He should have known it was coming.*

knit one's **brow** to cause one's brow to wrinkle. □ *Bob knitted his brow when he was confused.* □ *Jane knitted her brow because she was angry.*

knit something **together**† to join things together by knitting. □ *Terry knitted the parts of the sweater together.* □ *Sally knitted together the two parts of the glove.*

knit together [for broken bones] to join or grow together. □ *The bones are knitting together exactly as expected.* □ *If the bones don't knit together properly, we will have to do something a little more drastic.*

knock about (some place**) (with** someone**)** and **knock around (**some place**) (with** someone**)** to hang around some place with someone; to wander idly about some place with someone. □ *Sally was knocking about France with her friends.* □ *I knocked around town with Ken for a while.*

knock about (somewhere**)** to travel around; to act as a vagabond. □ *I'd like to take off a year and knock about Europe.* □ *If you're going to knock about, you should do it when you're young.*

knock against someone or something to bump against someone or something. □ *Mickey knocked against Mary and said he was sorry.* □ *I didn't mean to knock against your sore knee.*

knock around 1. to waste time. □ *Stop knocking around and get to work!* □ *I need a couple of days a week just for knocking around.* **2.** and **kick around** to wander around; to bum around. □ *I think I'll knock around a few months before looking for another job.* □ *We're just knocking around and keeping out of trouble.*

knock around (some place) (with someone) Go to knock about (some place) (with someone).

knock at something to knock [on something] at a particular location. □ *I could hear someone knocking at the door next to mine.* □ *Who is knocking at the door?*

knock away (at something) to continue to knock at something. □ *The loose shutter kept knocking away at the side of the house.* □ *It knocked away all night, keeping me awake.*

knock back a drink and **knock one back; knock one over** *Sl.* to swallow a drink of an alcoholic beverage. □ *Todd knocked back one drink, and then had another.* □ *Kelly knocked one back.* □ *She knocked one over and left the bar.*

Knock it off! *Inf.* Be quiet!; Stop that noise! Stop doing that! □ *John: Hey, you guys! Knock it off! Bob: Sorry. Bill: Sorry. I guess we got a little carried away.* □ *Sue: All right. Knock it off! Bill: Yeah. Let's get down to business.*

knock off (doing something) to stop doing something. (See also **knock off work.**) □ *Knock off shoveling snow now, and come in for a hot drink.* □ *I wish he would knock off practicing for a while.*

knock off (work) to quit work, for the day or for a break. □ *What time do you knock off work?* □ *I knock off about five-thirty.*

knock on something to rap or tap, often with the knuckles, on something. (See also **knock on wood.**) □ *She knocked on the door several times.* □ *Knock on it again. Maybe she didn't hear you.*

knock on wood to rap on something made of wood. (Said as a wish for good luck. Usually a phrase attached to another statement. Sometime said while knocking or rapping on real wood.) □ *I think I am well at last—knock on wood.* □ *I knock on wood when I wish something were true.*

knock one back Go to knock back a drink.

knock one off one's **feet** Go to sweep one off one's feet.

knock one over Go to knock back a drink.

knock one's **head (up) against a brick wall** *Fig.* to be totally frustrated. □ *Trying to get a raise around here is like knocking your head up against a brick wall.* □ *No need to knock your head against a brick wall over this problem.*

knock one's **knees together** *Fig.* [for one's knees] to shake together from fright. □ *I stood there freezing for ten minutes, knocking my knees together in the cold.* □ *It takes a lot of energy to knock your knees together.*

knock oneself **out (to** do something) **(for** someone or something) to make a great effort to do something for someone or some group. (As if one had worked oneself into unconsciousness.) □ *I knocked myself out to plan this party for you!* □ *She knocked herself out for us.* □ *I don't know why I knock myself out to do these things for you. You are not at all appreciative.* □ *He knocked himself out to get there on time.*

knock over something **1.** *Sl.* to steal something. (The *over* is usually before the object in this expression.) □ *The gang knocked over an armored car.* □ *Some cheap crook knocked over a load of television sets.* **2.** *Sl.* to rob a place. (The *over* is usually before the object in this expression.) □ *Max knocked over two banks in one week.* □ *He was the kind of punk who would try to knock over a filling station.*

knock some heads together *Fig.* to scold some people; to get some people to do what they are supposed to be doing. □ *If you kids don't quiet down and go to sleep, I'm going to come up there and knock some heads together.* □ *The government is in a mess. We need to go to Washington and knock some heads together.*

knock some sense into someone and **knock some sense in†** to strike one, making one smarter, or at least obedient. □ *I think his father finally knocked some sense into him.* □ *The accident finally knocked in some sense.* □ *I thought that last week's experience would knock some sense in.*

knock someone **back (an** amount of money) to cost an amount of money. □ *That trip to Spain knocked me back almost $3,500.* □ *How much did that new furniture knock us back?*

knock someone **cold 1.** *Fig.* to render someone unconscious by a violent blow. □ *One swipe, and he knocked him cold.* □ *If you touch her again, I'll knock you cold.* **2.** and **knock** someone **dead** *Fig.* to put on a stunning performance or display for someone. (*Someone* is often replaced by 'em from them.) □ *This band is going to do great tonight. We're going to knock them dead.* □ *"See how your sister is all dressed up!" said Bill. "She's going to knock 'em cold."*

knock someone **dead** Go to previous.

knock someone **down a peg (or two)** Go to take someone down a peg (or two).

knock someone **down to size** Go to beat someone down to size.

knock someone **for a loop 1.** *Fig.* to strike someone hard. □ *You really knocked me for a loop. I hope that was an accident.* □ *I was really knocked for a loop by the falling branch.* **2.** and **throw** someone **for a loop** *Fig.* to confuse or shock someone. (This is more severe and upsetting than throw someone a curve.) □ *When Bill heard the news, it threw him for a loop.* □ *The manager knocked Bob for a loop by firing him on the spot.*

knock someone **into** something to strike one, sending one into something. □ *The blow knocked him into the wall.* □ *Max knocked Lefty into a lamp post.*

knock someone **off†** Go to bump someone off†.

knock someone or something **about** and **knock** someone or something **around 1.** to jostle someone or something. □ *The bumpy road was knocking everyone in the truck about.* □ *The bumpy road knocked the old truck around a lot.* □ *Don't knock the grocery bags around. You'll break the eggs.* **2.** to strike someone or something; to beat on someone or something. □ *Max knocked his brother about.* □ *Stop knocking me around.*

knock someone or something **down†** to thrust someone or something to the ground by hitting. □ *The force of the blast knocked us down.* □ *It knocked down everyone in the room.*

knock someone or something **over**[†] to push or strike someone or something, causing the person or the thing to fall. (See also knock over something; knock someone over (with a feather); knock something over.) □ *I am sorry. I didn't mean to knock you over. Are you hurt?* □ *Who knocked over this vase?*

knock someone **out**[†] **1.** *Lit.* to knock someone unconscious. (*Someone* includes *oneself*.) □ *Fred knocked Mike out and left him there in the gutter.* □ *Fred knocked out Mike.* **2.** *Fig.* to make someone unconscious. □ *The drug knocked her out quickly.* □ *The powerful medicine knocked out the patient.* **3.** *Fig.* to surprise or please someone. □ *I have some news that will really knock you out.* **4.** *Fig.* to wear someone out; to exhaust someone. □ *All that exercise really knocked me out.* □ *The day's activities knocked the kids out and they went right to bed.*

knock someone **over (with a feather)** *Fig.* to leave someone stunned or surprised by something extraordinary. (Fixed order.) □ *I was so surprised that you could have knocked me over with a feather.* □ *Todd could have knocked me over with a feather when he told me his news.*

knock someone's **block off** *Sl.* to hit someone hard in the head. □ *Wilbur almost knocked Tom's block off by accident.* □ *He threatened to knock my block off if I didn't do as I was told.*

knock someone's **socks off** and **knock the socks off (of)** someone *Sl.* to surprise someone thoroughly. (Fixed order. *Of* is usually retained before pronouns.) □ *The exciting news just knocked my socks off!* □ *The news knocked the socks off of everyone in the office.*

knock someone **some skin** *Sl.* to slap hands with someone, a sign of friendship. □ *Hey, man, knock me some skin!* □ *Pete knocked Sam some skin, and they left the building together.*

knock someone **up**[†] *Inf.* to make a woman pregnant. (See also knocked up.) □ *They say it was Willie who knocked her up.* □ *He did not knock up Sue. I did.*

knock something **against** something to strike something against something. □ *He knocked a chair against the table and tipped both pieces of furniture over.* □ *A chair was knocked against the table, upsetting a vase.*

knock something **back**[†] *Sl.* to drink down a drink of something, especially something alcoholic. (See also knock back a drink.) □ *I don't see how he can knock that stuff back.* □ *John knocked back two beers in ten minutes.*

knock something **down**[†] **1.** *Sl.* to drink a portion of liquor. □ *Here, knock this down and let's go.* □ *He knocked down a bottle of beer and called for another.* **2.** *Sl.* to earn a certain amount of money. □ *I'm lucky to knock down twenty thousand.* □ *She must knock down about twenty thou a year.*

knock something **into a cocked hat** *Fig.* to demolish a plan, a story, etc. □ *I knocked his plans into a cocked hat.* □ *This bad weather has knocked everything into a cocked hat.*

knock something **off**[†] **1.** to manufacture or make something, especially in haste. □ *I'll see if I can knock another one off before lunch.* □ *They knocked off four window frames in an hour.* **2. to knock off some amount from the price of something, lowering its price.**

□ *The store manager knocked 30 percent off the price of the coat.* □ *Can't you knock something off on this damaged item?* **3.** to copy or reproduce a product. □ *The manufacturer knocked off a famous designer's coat.* □ *They are well known for knocking off cheap versions of expensive watches.* **4.** Go to knock something **off (of)** someone or something.

knock something **off kilter** Go to out of kilter.

knock something **off (of)** someone or something and **knock** something **off**[†] to remove something from someone or something by striking. (*Of* is usually retained before pronouns.) □ *I knocked the hard hat off of Wally when I hit him accidentally with the ladder.* □ *My elbow knocked off the book.*

knock something **out**[†] **1.** to create something hastily. □ *He knocked a few out as samples.* □ *He knocked out a few of them quickly, just so we could see what they were going to look like.* **2.** *Fig.* to put something out of order; to make something inoperable. □ *The storm knocked the telephone system out.* □ *The high winds will probably knock out electrical service all over town.*

knock something **out of kilter** Go to out of kilter.

knock something **out of place** Go to out of place.

knock something **out of** someone to beat someone until something emerges or dissipates. □ *Max knocked the truth out of the spy.* □ *Lefty knocked the story out of Max.*

knock something **out of** something to beat or knock on something until something comes out. □ *Timmy knocked the stuffing out of his pillow.* □ *Someone knocked the coins out of my piggy bank.*

knock something **over**[†] to tip something over. (See also knock over something.) □ *Someone knocked the chair over.* □ *Who knocked over the flower pot?*

knock something **to** someone to hit something, such as a ball, to someone. □ *The coach knocked the ball to each player in turn.* □ *The ball was knocked to the guy out in center field.*

knock something **together**[†] to assemble something hastily. □ *I knocked this model together so you could get a general idea of what I had in mind.* □ *See if you can knock together a quick snack.* □ *This thing has just been knocked together!*

knock the bejeebers out of someone or something *Inf.* to beat someone or something severely. □ *If I catch you doing that again, I'll knock the bejeebers out of you.* □ *He grabbed the poor dog and just knocked the bejeebers out of it.*

knock the bottom out (of something) **1.** and **knock the bottom out**[†] *Lit.* to break the bottom of a container. □ *I knocked the bottom out of the barrel and used it to store compost.* □ *Knock out the bottom and set it right on the soil.* **2.** *Fig.* [for something] to go down so low as to knock out the bottom. □ *The bad news knocked the bottom out of the stock market.* □ *The recession knocked the bottom out of our profits.*

knock the habit to stop using drugs; to break a drug addiction. □ *I just can't knock the habit.* □ *He tried to knock the habit by drinking lots of booze.*

knock the hell out of someone or something *Inf.* to strike someone or something very hard. (Use *hell* with discre-

K

tion.) □ *The bully knocked the hell out of Sam.* □ *You really knocked the hell out of my front bumper.*

knock the (living) daylights out of someone *Fig. Inf.* to beat someone severely. □ *If you do that again, I will knock the living daylights out of you.* □ *Fred wants to knock the living daylights out of his enemy, Mike "Fingers" Moran.*

knock the props out from under someone *Fig.* to destroy someone's emotional, financial, or moral underpinnings; to destroy someone's confidence. □ *When you told Sally that she was due to be fired, you really knocked the props out from under her.*

knock the stuffing out of someone Go to kick the (natural) stuffing out of someone.

knock the wind out of someone's **sails 1.** *Lit.* to bring someone to an abrupt halt by a heavy blow to the body, presumably knocking the person's wind out. (Alludes to a ship being slowed by positioning another ship to block off the wind from the first ship's sails.) □ *Fred hit Mike and really knocked the wind out of his sails.* □ *Fred ran into the side of the garage and knocked the wind out of his sails.* **2.** *Fig.* to humiliate someone. □ *The sharp rebuke from the boss knocked the wind out of his sails.* □ *That scolding really knocked the wind out of her sails.*

knock through something to break through something. □ *They knocked through the wall and put in a doorway.* □ *The wall had to be knocked through before we could install a doorway.*

knock (up) against someone or something to bump against someone or something. □ *The loose shutter knocked up against the side of the house.* □ *The large branch knocked against the garage in the storm.*

knock-down, drag-out fight a serious fight; a serious argument. □ *Boy, they really had a knock-down, drag-out fight.* □ *Stop calling each other names, or you're going to end up with a real knock-down, drag-out fight.*

knocked in *Sl.* arrested. (Underworld.) □ *Would you believe that Larry has never been knocked in?* □ *When Lefty was knocked in, they found his heat on him.*

knocked out 1. *Lit.* unconscious. □ *The losing boxer lay on the canvas, knocked out.* **2.** *Fig.* exhausted. □ *We were all knocked out at the end of the day.* □ *I'm knocked out after just a little bit of work.* **3.** *Fig.* overwhelmed. □ *We were just knocked out when we heard your news.* □ *Were we surprised? We were knocked out—elated!* **4.** *Fig.* intoxicated. □ *They were all knocked out by midnight.* □ *Gary was knocked out when we dropped by, so we tried to sober him up.*

knocked up 1. *Lit.* battered; beaten. □ *Sally was a little knocked up by the accident.* □ *This book is a little knocked up, so I'll lower the price.* **2.** *Sl.* intoxicated. □ *Bill was knocked up and didn't want to drive.* □ *Wow, was that guy knocked up!* **3.** *Inf.* pregnant; made pregnant. □ *Sue got knocked up but won't say who the father is.*

knot something **together**† to tie something together in a knot. □ *Knot these strings together and trim the strings off the knot.* □ *Are the ropes knotted together properly?* □ *Quickly knot together the two loose ends!*

know a thing or two (about someone or something**)** Go to a thing or two (about someone or something).

know a trick or two to know some special way of dealing with a problem. □ *I think I can handle all of this with no trouble. I know a trick or two.* □ *I may be a senior citizen, but I still know a trick or two. I think I can help you with this.*

know about someone or something to have information or expertise about someone or something. □ *I know about John and what he does.* □ *I know about cars, but I can't fix this one!*

know all the angles to know all the tricks and artifices of dealing with someone or something. □ *Ask my accountant about taxes. He knows all the angles.* □ *Larry knows all the angles. That's how he keeps out of the slammer.*

know as much about something **as a hog knows about Sunday** *Rur.* to have no knowledge of something. □ *Don't let Jim make dessert for the picnic. He knows as much about pies as a hog knows about Sunday.* □ *I had quite a time changing the tire, since I know as much about cars as a hog knows about Sunday.*

know at a glance that… to know [something] without much evidence; to know or understand something without a lot of observation. □ *I knew at a glance that Bobbie was severely injured and had to be gotten to a hospital as soon as possible.*

know better (than to do something**)** to be wise enough, experienced enough, or well trained enough not to have done something wrong. □ *Mary should have known better than to accept a lift from a stranger.* □ *Children should know better than to play in the road.*

know from something to know about something. (Used on the eastern seaboard.) □ *Do you know from thermostats?* □ *You don't know from anything!*

know no more about something **than a frog knows about bedsheets** *Rur.* to have no knowledge of something. □ *Don't let Bill fix your car. He knows no more about cars than a frog knows about bedsheets.* □ *When I first started studying French literature, I knew no more about it than a frog knows about bedsheets.*

know of someone or something to be aware of the existence of someone or something. □ *I think I know of someone who can help you.* □ *I didn't know of Wally's arrival.*

know one **for what** one **is** to recognize someone as some type of person or thing. □ *I know you for what you are, you devil.* □ *We know him for the thief he is.*

know one's **ABCs** *Fig.* to know the alphabet; to know the most basic things (about something). □ *Bill can't do it. He doesn't even know his ABCs.* □ *You can't expect to write a letter when you don't even know your ABCs.*

know one's **onions** Go to know one's stuff.

know one's **place** to know the behavior appropriate to one's position or status in life. □ *I know my place. I won't speak unless spoken to.* □ *People around here are expected to know their place. You have to follow all the rules.*

know one's **stuff** and **know** one's **onions** to know what one is expected to know. □ *I know my stuff. I can do my job.* □ *She can't handle the assignment. She doesn't know her onions.*

know one's **way about** Go to next.

know one's **way around 1.** and **know** one's **way about** Lit. to know how to get from place to place. □ I can find my way. I know my way around. □ I don't know my way around this city yet. **2.** Fig. to know how to deal with people and situations; to have had much experience at living. □ I can get along in the world. I know my way around. □ Do you think I don't know my way around?

know shit from Shinola and **tell shit from Shinola** Fig. Inf. to know what's what; to be intelligent and aware. (Always in the negative. Shinola is a brand of shoe polish. A person who doesn't **know shit from Shinola** is very stupid.) □ Poor Tom doesn't know shit from Shinola. □ Fred can't tell shit from Shinola, and he's been made my boss.

know someone **as** someone to know someone by a different name. □ I know her as Candy La Tour. □ She has been known as Mary Rogers since her marriage.

know someone **by sight** to recognize a person's face, but not know the name. □ I'm afraid I don't know her by sight. □ I know all my employees by sight.

know someone **from** someone to tell the difference between one person and another. □ I don't know Fred from his twin brother. □ I know Bill from Bob, but I can't tell most identical twins apart.

know someone or something **as** something to recognize someone or something as something. □ I know Mr. Franklin as a fine man. □ I know this name as a very fine brand.

know someone or something **by name** to recognize the name but not the appearance of someone or something. □ I only know her by name. I have no idea what she looks like. □ I know this brand of sausage by name, but I have never tasted it.

know someone or something **by** something to recognize someone or something by a certain characteristic. □ I know her by her perfume. □ I know this committee only by its reputation, which is not good, by the way.

know someone or something **like the back of** one's **hand** Go to next.

know someone or something **like the palm of** one's **hand** and **know** someone or something **like the back of** one's **hand; know** someone or something **like a book** to know someone or something very well. □ Of course I know John. I know him like the back of my hand. □ I know him like a book.

know something **backwards and forwards** and **know** something **forwards and backwards** Fig. to know something very well; to know a passage of language so well that one could recite it backwards as well as forwards. □ Of course I've memorized my speech. I know it backwards and forwards.

know something **by heart** Fig. to know something perfectly; to have memorized something perfectly. □ I know my speech by heart. □ I went over and over it until I knew it by heart.

know something **forwards and backwards** Go to know something backwards and forwards.

know something **from memory** to have memorized something so that one does not have to consult a written version; to know something well from seeing it very often. (Almost the same as **know** something **by heart**.) □ Mary didn't need the script because she knew the play from mem-

ory. □ The conductor went through the entire concert without sheet music. He knew it from memory.

know something **from** something to tell the difference between one thing and another. (Often with a negative.) □ You don't know a smoked herring from a squid! □ She didn't know a raven from a crow, and who does?

know something **in** one's **bones** Go to feel something in one's bones.

know something **inside out** to know something thoroughly; to know about something thoroughly. □ I know my geometry inside out. □ I studied and studied for my driver's test until I knew the rules inside out.

know something **only too well** to know something very well; to know something from unpleasant experience. (Note the variation in the examples.) □ I know the problem only too well. □ I know only too well the kind of problem you must face.

know something **through and through** to know something very well. □ I want you to know this project through and through before the staff meeting. □ I know my part in the play through and through.

know the big picture Go to the big picture.

know the ropes Go to the ropes.

know the score and **know what's what** Fig. to know the facts; to know the facts about life and its difficulties. □ Bob is so naive. He sure doesn't know the score. □ I know what you're trying to do. Oh, yes, I know what's what.

Know thyself. Prov. Be aware of your own limitations; know what you are capable of doing. (This was the motto inscribed on the temple of Apollo at Delphi.) □ The motto of the ballet corps was "Know thyself"; every dancer was expected to know how far she could stretch, and not hurt herself by trying to exceed her limits. □ "Know thyself," the high school guidance counselor admonished us, "and try to find a career that makes the most of your abilities."

know the tricks of the trade Go to the tricks of the trade.

Know what? Go to (Do you) know what?

know what's what Go to know the score.

know when one **is not wanted** to sense when one's presence is not welcome; to know when one is not among friends. (Usually said when someone feels hurt by being ignored by people.) □ I'm leaving this place! I know when I'm not wanted! □ She doesn't know when she's not wanted. Can't she tell she's out of place?

know where all the bodies are buried Fig. to know all the secrets and intrigue from the past; to know all the relevant and perhaps hidden details. □ He is a good choice for president because he knows where all the bodies are buried. □ Since he knows where all the bodies are buried, he is the only one who can advise us.

know where it's at to be alert and know how the world—or some part of it—really works. □ Man, you just don't know where it's at! □ I don't know where cool jazz is at.

know where one **is coming from** to understand someone's motivation; to understand and relate to someone's position. □ I know where you're coming from. I've been

K

there. □ *We all know where he's coming from. That's why we are so worried.*

know where someone **stands (on** someone or something**)** to know what someone thinks or feels about something. □ *I don't know where John stands on this issue.* □ *I don't even know where I stand.*

know where something **is at** to know where something is located. (Without *at,* this sense is standard English. See also **know where it's at.**) □ *Do you know where the hammer is at?* □ *I don't know where my glasses are at.*

know whereof one **speaks** to know well the subject that one is speaking about. □ *You are wrong! You do not know whereof you speak.* □ *He simply doesn't know whereof he speaks.*

know which is which and **tell which is which** to be able to distinguish one person or thing from another person or thing. □ *I have an old one and a new one, but I don't know which is which.* □ *I know that Bill and Bob are twins, but I can't tell which is which.*

know which side one's **bread is buttered on** *Prov.* to be aware of where your money comes from; to be loyal to the person or thing that will benefit you the most. □ *Wife: Please be sure not to upset Grandma. You know we can't do without the money she sends us every month. Husband: Don't worry. I know which side my bread is buttered on.*

Knowledge is power. *Prov.* The more you know, the more you can control. □ *Child: How come I have to study history? I don't care what all those dead people did hundreds of years ago. Mother: Knowledge is power. If you know something about the past, it may help you to anticipate the future.*

known fact something that is generally recognized as a fact. □ *That grass is green is a known fact.* □ *It is a known fact that John was in Chicago on the night of the murder.*

known quantity someone whose character, personality, and behavior are recognized and understood. □ *We need not worry about how John will behave. He is a known quantity.* □ *Lisa is a known quantity and I am sure she will not surprise us by voting with the opposition.*

knuckle down (to something**)** *Fig.* to get busy doing something. □ *I want you to knuckle down to your work and stop worrying about the past.* □ *Come on. Knuckle down. Get busy.*

*a knuckle sandwich *Inf.* a punch. (*Typically: **ask for** ~; **get** ~; **give** someone ~; **want** ~.) □ *A: Nyah! Your mother smokes cigars! B: You want a knuckle sandwich?*

knuckle under (to someone or something**)** to submit to someone or something; to yield or give in to someone or something. □ *You have to knuckle under to your boss if you expect to keep your job.* □ *I'm too stubborn to knuckle under.*

kowtow to someone or something to grovel to someone or something. □ *I won't kowtow to anyone!* □ *You don't expect me to go in there and kowtow to that committee, do you?*

label someone or something **as** something to designate someone or something as something. □ *She labeled him as an uncouth person.* □ *We labeled the committee as a worthless organization.*

label someone or something **with** something to mark or identify someone or something with something. □ *They labeled each person who had paid the admission fee with a symbol stamped on the hand.* □ *I labeled each book with my name.*

labor at something to work hard at something. □ *He is laboring at his gardening and won't be back in the house until dinnertime.* □ *What are you laboring at so intensely?*

labor for someone or something to work on behalf of someone or something. □ *I labored for them all day, and they didn't even thank me.* □ *I have labored for this cause for many years.*

labor for something to work in order to get something, such as money. □ *I was laboring for a pittance, so I decided to get another job.* □ *I labor for the love of it.*

a **labor of love** *Fig.* a task that is either unpaid or badly paid and that one does simply for one's own satisfaction or pleasure or to please someone whom one likes or loves. □ *Jane made no money out of the biography she wrote. She was writing about the life of a friend and the book was a labor of love.* □ *Mary hates knitting, but she made a sweater for her boyfriend. What a labor of love.*

labor over someone or something to work hard on someone or something. □ *The surgeon labored over the patient for four hours.* □ *I labored over this painting for months before I got it the way I wanted it.*

labor under an assumption *Fig.* to function or operate believing something; to go about living while assuming something [that may not be so]. □ *I was laboring under the idea that we were going to share the profits equally.* □ *Are you laboring under the notion that you are going to be promoted?*

lace into someone or something and **light into** someone or something *Fig.* to attack, devour, or scold someone or something. □ *We laced into a big meal of pork and beans.* □ *The bully punched John once, and then John really laced into him.* □ *John lit into him with both fists.*

lace someone **into** something to tighten the laces of something someone is wearing. □ *Sally helped Billy lace himself into his boots.* □ *The maid laced Gloria into her corset.*

lace someone **up**† to tie someone's laces; to help someone get dressed in a garment having laces. □ *Would you please lace me up? I can't reach the ties in the back.* □ *I laced up Sally, as she requested.*

lace something **up**† to tie the laces of something. □ *Lace your shoes up, Tommy.* □ *Lace up your shoes.*

lace something **with** something to adulterate something with something, often with something alcoholic. □ *Someone laced the punch with strong whiskey.* □ *Who laced my coffee with brandy?*

lack for something to lack something. □ *We don't lack for new ideas.* □ *We lack for nothing, thank you.*

Ladies first. an expression of courtesy indicating that women should go first, as in going through a doorway. □

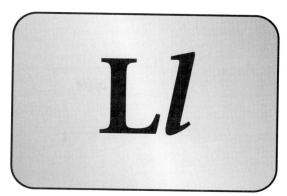

Bob stepped back and made a motion with his hand indicating that Mary should go first. "Ladies first," smiled Bob.

a **ladies' man** *Fig.* a man who likes the company of women and whose company is liked by women, the suggestion being that he likes to flirt with them. □ *John is a real ladies' man. He hates all-male parties.* □ *The new boss is always flirting with the women in the office. He's a bit of a ladies' man.*

ladle something **out of** something and **ladle** something **out**† to scoop something out of something with a spoon or ladle. □ *Marie ladled the last of the gravy out of the gravy boat and went to the kitchen for more.* □ *She ladled out the soup.*

ladle something **up**† to scoop something up in a ladle. □ *Jerry ladled a cool dipper of water up and quenched his thirst.* □ *Please ladle up the soup and serve it.*

lady of the evening *Euph.* a prostitute. □ *I saw several ladies of the evening down on Main Street.* □ *He was approached by a lady of the evening.*

lag behind in something to fall behind in something. □ *I am lagging behind in my car payments.* □ *She is lagging behind in her homework assignments.*

lag behind (someone or something) to linger behind someone or something; to fall behind someone or something. □ *Come on up here. Don't lag behind us or you'll get lost.* □ *Please don't lag behind the donkeys. Come up here with the rest of the hikers.*

laid back 1. calm and relaxed. □ *Willie is not what I would call laid back.* □ *You are really one laid-back guy!* **2.** intoxicated. □ *He's a little laid back and can't come to the phone.* □ *How can those guys work when they are laid back by noon?*

laid out 1. intoxicated. □ *Man, you got yourself laid out!* □ *I'm too laid out to go to work today.* **2.** well-dressed. □ *Look at those silks! Man are you laid out!* □ *She is all laid out in her Sunday best.*

laid up [of people or things] immobilized for recuperation or repairs. □ *I was laid up for two weeks after my accident.* □ *My car is laid up for repairs.* □ *I was laid up with the flu for a week.*

lam into someone or an animal *Fig.* to attack someone or an animal. □ *Paul was so angry that he lammed into his friend and struck him in the side.* □ *The angry coachman lammed into the poor horses.*

lame duck 1. *Fig.* someone who is in the last period of a term in an elective office and cannot run for reelection. □ *You can't expect much from a lame duck.* □ *As a lame duck, there's not a lot I can do.* **2.** *Fig.* having to do with someone in the last period of a term in an elective office. (Used as an adjective; sometimes *lame-duck.*) □ *You don't expect much from a lame-duck president.* □ *Lame-duck Congresses tend to do things they wouldn't dare do otherwise.*

lament over someone or something and **lament (for)** someone or something to sorrow over someone or something. □ *There is no need to lament over Sam. There is nothing that crying will do for him now.* □ *She is still lamenting for her cat.*

land a blow 1. *Lit.* to strike someone. □ *He kept moving, and I found it almost impossible to land a blow.* □ *The boxer landed a blow to the face of his opponent.* **2.** *Fig.* to make a point. □ *I think I really landed a blow with that remark about extortion.* □ *The point about justice landed a blow.*

land a job to find a job and be hired. □ *As soon as I land a job and start to bring in some money, I'm going to get a stereo.* □ *I managed to land a job at a factory.*

land at some place **1.** [for a ship] to come to port at a place. □ *The ship landed at the wharf and the passengers got off.* □ *We landed at the island's main city and waited for customs to clear us.* **2.** [for an airplane] to return to earth at an airport. □ *We landed at O'Hare at noon.* □ *We were to land at Denver, but there was bad weather.*

land in something **1.** *Lit.* [for an airplane] to return to earth in or near a particular city. □ *We landed in Chicago on time.* □ *They could not land in San Francisco, so they flew on to Sacramento.* **2.** *Fig.* [for someone] to end up in something, such as a mess, jail, trouble, etc. □ *If you don't mend your ways, you're going to land in jail!* □ *Andy is going to land in hot water if he doesn't start paying his bills.* **3.** [for an airplane] to make a landing in something, such as bad weather, darkness, daylight, fog, etc. □ *You can't land this plane in fog like this.* □ *The novice pilot is not capable of landing in the dark.*

Land o' Goshen! *Rur.* My goodness gracious! (A mild oath. Goshen was an agricultural region in Egypt occupied by the Israelites before the Exodus.) □ *Land o' Goshen, it's sure good to see you.* □ *Land o' Goshen! Look at that rain come down!*

the **land of Nod** a state of sleep. (Humorous. From the fact that people sometimes nod when they are falling asleep.) □ *The baby is in the land of Nod.* □ *Look at the clock! It's time we were all in the land of Nod.*

land so poor it wouldn't even raise a fuss and **land too poor to raise a racket on** *Rur.* land where nothing will grow. □ *I inherited two hundred acres from my uncle, but it's land so poor it wouldn't even raise a fuss.* □ *The soil's exhausted. That land is so poor it wouldn't even raise a fuss.* □ *Jill can grow a garden anywhere, even on land too poor to raise a racket on.*

land someone **in** something to cause someone to end up in something. □ *His criminal activity finally landed him in jail.* □ *You really landed yourself in a fine mess!*

land something **at** some place to bring a boat, ship, or airplane to rest or to port at or near a place. □ *The captain landed the boat at a small island in hopes of finding a place to make repairs.* □ *They had to land the plane at a small town because of a medical emergency.*

land too poor to raise a racket on Go to land so poor it wouldn't even raise a fuss.

land up somehow *Fig.* to end up in some way. □ *If you keep eating all those sweets, you'll land up sick.* □ *Do you want to land up without a job?*

land up somehow or somewhere to finish somehow or somewhere; to come to be in a certain state or place at the end. □ *We set out for Denver but landed up in Salt Lake City.* □ *He's so extravagant that he landed up in debt.*

land (up)on both feet and **land (up)on** one's **feet 1.** *Lit.* to end up on both feet after a jump, dive, etc. (*Upon* is formal and less commonly used than *on.*) □ *She jumped over the bicycle and landed upon both feet.* □ *Donna made the enormous leap and landed on her feet.* **2.** *Fig.* to come out of something well; to survive something satisfactorily. (*Upon* is formal and less commonly used than *on.*) □ *It was a rough period in his life, but when it was over he landed on both feet.* □ *At least, after it was over I landed on my feet.*

land (up)on one's **feet** Go to previous.

land (up)on someone or something to light on someone or something. (*Upon* is formal and less commonly used than *on.*) □ *A bee landed upon her and frightened her.* □ *The spoon I dropped landed on the cake and ruined the icing.*

land-office business *Fig.* a large amount of business done in a short period of time. □ *We always do a land-office business at this time of year.* □ *We keep going. Never do land-office business—just enough to make out.*

Land(s) sakes (alive)! and **Sakes alive!** *Rur.* My goodness! (A mild oath.) □ *Lands sakes! I sure am glad to get home!* □ *Sakes alive! Can't you even set the table without making a fuss?*

a **landslide victory** a victory by a large margin; a very substantial victory, particularly in an election. □ *The mayor won a landslide victory in the election.* □ *The younger candidate won a landslide victory in the presidential election.*

language that would fry bacon *Rur.* profanity; swearing; curse words. ("Hot" language.) □ *He carried on in language that would fry bacon.* □ *I was shocked when I heard that sweet little girl use language that would fry bacon.*

languish in some place **1.** to become dispirited in some place; to weaken and fade away in some place. □ *Claire languished in prison for her crime.* □ *I spent over three days languishing in a stuffy hotel room.* □ *We languished in the airport waiting room while they refueled the plane.* **2.** to suffer neglect in a place. □ *The bill languished in the Senate for months on end.* □ *The children languished in the squalid conditions until the court intervened.*

languish over someone or something to pine over someone or something. □ *There is no point in languishing over Tim. He'll never come back.* □ *She wasted half her life languishing over her lost opportunities.*

the **lap of luxury** *Fig.* a luxurious situation. □ *I rather enjoy living in the lap of luxury.* □ *You call this pigpen the lap of luxury?*

lap over (something) [for something] to extend or project over the edge or boundary of something. □ *The lid lapped over the edge of the barrel, forming a little table.* □ *The blanket did not lap over enough to keep me warm.*

lap something **up**† **1.** *Lit.* [for an animal] to lick something up. □ *The dog lapped the ice cream up off the floor.* □ *The dog lapped up the ice cream.* **2.** *Fig.* [for someone] to accept or believe something with enthusiasm. □ *Of course, they believed it. They just lapped it up.* □ *They lapped up the lies without questioning anything.*

lap (up) against something [for waves] to splash gently against something. □ *The waves lapped up against the shore softly.* □ *The waves lapped against the side of the boat all night long, and I couldn't sleep.*

lapse from grace 1. *Lit.* to fall out of favor with God. □ *The child was told that if he ever smoked even one cigarette, he would lapse from grace for certain.* □ *It is easy, these days, to lapse from grace.* **2.** *Fig.* to fall out of favor. □ *Ted lapsed from grace when he left the lobby door unlocked all weekend.* □ *I have to be there on time every day or I will lapse from grace for sure.*

lapse into something to weaken or slip into something, especially a coma. □ *The survivor of the crash lapsed into a coma.* □ *Aunt Mary lapsed into unconsciousness and died.*

***large as life** *Fig.* in person; actually, and sometimes surprisingly, present at a place. (*Also: **as** ~.) □ *I thought Jack was away, but there he was as large as life.* □ *Jean was not expected to appear, but she turned up large as life.*

large as life (and twice as ugly) Go to big as life (and twice as ugly).

larger than life *Fig.* [of someone] having an aura of greatness, perhaps not supported by the real person. □ *Perry seemed larger than life to those who had only read about him. To the rest of us, he was a boor.* □ *To the children, the star athlete who spoke at the school assembly seemed larger than life.*

lash against something [for something, such as wind or water] to beat or whip heavily against something. □ *The angry waves lashed against the hull of the boat, frightening the people huddled inside.* □ *The wind lashed against the house and kept us awake all night.*

lash at someone or something to thrash or beat someone or something violently. □ *The rain lashed at the windows.* □ *The mule driver lashed at his beasts with his whip.*

lash back (at someone or something**)** to strike or fight back against someone or something—physically or verbally. □ *Randy lashed back at his attackers and drove them away.* □ *If you threaten Fred, he'll lash back.*

lash down on someone or something [for rain] to beat down on someone or something. □ *The wind and rain lashed down on us.* □ *The rain lashed down on the young plants and pounded them into the soil.*

lash into someone or an animal to attack someone or an animal—physically or verbally. □ *Dad lashed into my brother, who had smashed up the car again.* □ *Walter lashed into the cat for tearing the upholstery.*

lash into something to begin to eat something with vigor. □ *Mary lashed into the huge ice cream sundae, and ate almost the whole thing.* □ *The workers lashed into their lunches and did not say a word until they had finished.*

lash out (at someone or something**)** and **lash out (against** someone or something**)** to strike out in defense or attack—physically or verbally. □ *Amy was angry with Ed and lashed out at him just to show who was boss.* □ *She was so angry with him that she just lashed out against him.* □ *Gretchen was fed up with the cat and lashed out savagely in her anger.*

lash someone or something **down**† to tie someone or something down. □ *The villain lashed Nell down to the railroad tracks.* □ *He lashed down the innocent victim.* □ *Lash that cask down so it doesn't wash overboard.*

lash someone or something **to** something to tie someone or something to something. □ *The boys lashed one of their number to a tree and danced around him like savages.* □ *Abe lashed the cask to the deck.* □ *Frank lashed himself to the mast.*

lash something **about** to whip or fling something about violently. □ *The big cat lashed its tail threateningly.* □ *The strong wind lashed the tall grass about.*

lash something **together** to tie something or things together. □ *Let's lash these logs together and make a raft.* □ *Lash two or three of the poles together to make them stronger.*

last but not least *Cliché* last in sequence, but not last in importance. (Often said when introducing people.) □ *The speaker said, "And now, last but not least, I'd like to present Bill Smith, who will give us some final words."* □ *And last but not least, here is the final graduate.*

last call (for something**)** and **last chance (for** something**)** *Fig.* the last opportunity for doing, getting, or having something. □ *This is the last call for ice cream and cake. It's almost all gone.*

last chance (for something**)** Go to previous.

last for something **1.** to exist for a period of time; to serve or function for a period of time. □ *This condition has lasted for some time.* □ *Enjoy it while you can. It won't last forever.* **2.** to hold out or survive for a period of time. □ *It's so hot in here. I don't think I can last for another minute.* □ *Can you last for another few minutes while I get this window open?*

last (from something**) until** something to endure from one point in time to another. □ *The meeting lasted from noon until midnight.* □ *The party lasted until the food ran out.*

the **last hurrah** *Fig.* a final appearance, as at the end of one's career; the last time for doing something. □ *Tom is retiring, and we are having a little party as his last hurrah right now. He won't be here the next time you visit our offices.*

*the **last laugh (on** someone**)** *Fig.* laughter or ridicule at someone who has laughed at or ridiculed you. (*Typically: **get** ~; **have** ~; **give** someone ~.) □ *John laughed when I got a D on the final exam. I got the last laugh, though. He failed the course.* □ *Mr. Smith said I was foolish when I bought an old building. I had the last laugh when I sold it a month later for twice what I paid for it.*

last out to hold out; to endure. □ *How long can you last out?* □ *I don't think we can last out much longer without food and water.*

the **last roundup** *Fig.* death. (Old West.) □ *To everyone's surprise, he clutched the wound and faced the last roundup* *with a smile.* □ *When I know I'm headed for the last roundup, I'll write a will.*

last something **out**† to endure until the end of something. □ *Ed said that he didn't think he could last the opera out and left.* □ *He couldn't last out the first act.*

the **last straw** and the **straw that broke the camel's back** the final difficulty in a series; the last little burden or problem that causes everything to collapse. (From the image of a camel being loaded down with much weight. Finally, at some point, one more straw will be too much and the camel's back will break.) □ *When our best player came down sick, that was the straw that broke the camel's back. We hoped to make the playoffs, but lost all the rest of our games.* □ *When she showed up late a third time, that was the straw that broke the camel's back. We had to fire her.*

last will and testament a will; the last edition of someone's will. □ *The lawyer read Uncle Charles's last will and testament to a group of expectant relatives.* □ *Fred dictated his last will and testament on his deathbed.*

*the **last word** and *the **final word;** *the **final say** *Fig.* the final point (in an argument); the final decision (in some matter). (*Typically: **get ~; have ~; give** someone ~.) □ *The boss gets the last word in hiring.* □ *Why do you always have to have the final word in an argument?*

***last-ditch effort** *Fig.* a final effort; the last possible attempt. (*Typically: **be ~; have ~; make ~.**) □ *I made one last-ditch effort to get her to stay.* □ *It was a last-ditch effort. I didn't expect it to work.*

latch on(to someone**)** to get hold of someone. □ *I don't know where Jane is. Let me try to latch onto her.*

latch onto something **1.** *Fig.* to obtain something. (See also latch on(to someone or something).) □ *I have to latch onto a hundred bucks by Friday night.* □ *I latched onto a good book about repairing plumbing.* **2.** *Fig.* to begin to understand something. □ *When Fred finally latched onto the principles of algebra, he began to get better grades.* □ *Sue doesn't quite latch onto the proper stance in golf.*

The **latch string is always out.** *Fig.* You are always welcome. □ *Come by anytime. The latch string is always out.* □ *No need to call before you come over. For you folks, the latch string is always out.*

a **late bloomer 1.** *Lit.* a plant that blooms later than similar plants or that blooms late in the season. □ *There are a few late bloomers in the garden, but by fall, we don't care much anymore about flowers.* **2.** *Fig.* a person who finally develops a useful or superior skill or talents later than expected or desired. □ *Joseph was a late bloomer, but turned out to be a formidable scholar in the long run.*

late in life *Fig.* when one is old. □ *Grandma injured her hip running. She's exercising rather late in life.* □ *Isn't it sort of late in life for your grandparents to buy a house?*

late in the day *Fig.* far along in a project or activity; too late in a project or activity for action, decisions, etc., to be taken. □ *It was a bit late in the day for him to apologize.* □ *It's late in the day to try to change the plans.*

the **late unpleasantness** *Euph.* the U.S. Civil War. (Old.) □ *The town courthouse was burned in the late unpleasantness.* □ *Many of my ancestors lost their lives in the late unpleasantness.*

Later, alligator. Go to See you later, alligator.

lather something **up**† to apply thick soapsuds to something, such as part of the body or all of it. □ *He lathered his face up in preparation for shaving.* □ *He lathered up his face.*

lather up 1. [for a horse] to develop a foam of sweat from working very hard. □ *The horses lathered up heavily during the race.* □ *Don't let your horse lather up!* **2.** [for soap] to develop thick suds when rubbed in water. □ *This soap won't lather up, even when I rub it hard.* □ *When the soap lathers up, spread the lather on your face and rub.* **3.** and **lather** oneself **up** [for one] to apply soap lather to one's body. □ *He will spend a few minutes lathering himself up before he rinses.* □ *He lathered up and then shaved.*

laugh about someone or something to chuckle or giggle loudly about someone or something. □ *Please don't laugh about Sue. It's not funny.* □ *They were laughing about my haircut.*

laugh all the way to the bank *Fig.* to be very happy about money that has been earned by doing something that other people might think is unfair or that they criticized. □ *He may not be in the nicest business, but he is doing well and can laugh all the way to the bank.* □ *She makes tons of money doing what no one else will do and laughs all the way to the bank.*

Laugh and the world laughs with you; weep and you weep alone. *Prov.* When you are happy, people will want to be around you and share your happiness, but when you are sad, people will avoid you. □ *Nancy: When Harry and I were dating, all our friends invited us places and called to say hello. Now that we've broken up, they treat me as if I don't exist. Jane: Laugh and the world laughs with you; weep and you weep alone.*

laugh at someone or something to chuckle or giggle loudly at someone or something, perhaps in ridicule. □ *Thank goodness, the audience laughed at all my jokes.* □ *Don't laugh at me! I'm doing my best!* □ *Everyone laughed at the love scene because it was so badly done.*

laugh away at someone or something to continue to laugh at someone or something. □ *They laughed away at Sue until she fled the room in embarrassment.* □ *All the children at the party laughed away at the magician.*

laugh in someone's **face** to laugh in derision directly to someone's face; to show displeasure or ridicule at something one has said by laughing directly into one's face. □ *It is very impolite to laugh in someone's face!* □ *After I heard what she had to say, I just laughed in her face.*

laugh one's **head off** *Fig.* to laugh very hard and loudly, as if one's head might come off. (See also **cough** one's head off. Fixed order.) □ *The movie was so funny I almost laughed my head off.* □ *I laughed my head off at Mary's joke.*

laugh oneself **out of** something to lose out on something because one has made light of it or laughed at it. □ *While you were howling with laughter about my hat, you laughed yourself out of a ride to town. The bus just pulled away.* □ *You laugh too much. You just laughed yourself out of a job.*

laugh oneself **silly** *Fig.* to laugh very, very hard. □ *I laughed myself silly when I heard that Steven was really going to give the graduation address.*

laugh out of the other side of one's **face** and **laugh out of the other side of** one's **mouth** *Fig.* to be forced to take a different or opposite view of something humbly; to sing a different tune. □ *When you get the kind of punishment you deserve, you'll laugh out of the other side of your face.* □ *Phil played a dirty trick on me, but he'll be laughing out of the other side of his mouth when I get through with him.*

laugh out of the other side of one's **mouth** Go to previous.

laugh someone **off the stage** *Fig.* to laugh rudely, forcing a person to leave a stage. □ *The rude audience laughed the politician off the stage.* □ *The children laughed the soprano off the stage. She really wasn't very good, you know.*

laugh someone or something **down**† to cause someone to quit or cause something to end by laughing in ridicule. □ *Her singing career was destroyed when the audience laughed her down as an amateur.* □ *The cruel audience laughed down the amateur singer.* □ *They laughed down the magic act also.*

laugh someone **out of** something to force someone to leave a place by laughing in ridicule. □ *The citizens laughed the speaker out of the hall.* □ *We laughed the city council out of the auditorium.*

laugh something **away**† **1.** to spend an amount of time laughing. □ *We laughed the hour away listening to the comedian.* □ *We laughed away the evening.* **2.** to get rid of something negative by laughing. □ *Kelly knows how to laugh her problems away, and it cheers up the rest of us too.* □ *She laughed away her problems.*

laugh something **off**† to treat a serious problem lightly by laughing at it. □ *Although his feelings were hurt, he just laughed the incident off as if nothing had happened.* □ *He laughed off the incident.*

laugh something **out of court** to dismiss something presented in earnest as ridiculous. □ *The committee laughed the suggestion out of court.* □ *Bob's request for a large salary increase was laughed out of court.*

laugh up one's **sleeve** to laugh secretly; to laugh quietly to oneself. □ *Jane looked very serious, but I knew she was laughing up her sleeve.* □ *I told Sally that her dress was darling, but I was laughing up my sleeve because her dress was too small.*

laugh with something to laugh in a particular manner. □ *Everyone was laughing with glee at the antics of the clown.* □ *Max laughed with malice as he saw his plan beginning to work.*

laughingstock someone or something that is the target of ridicule. □ *After he passed out at the president's dinner, he became the laughingstock of all his colleagues.*

launch forth on something Go to **set forth on** something.

launch forth ((up)on something**)** to set out on something; to begin on something, such as a journey or a long lecture or sermon. (*Upon* is formal and less commonly used than *on*.) □ *We launched forth on our trip before dawn.* □ *What time shall we launch forth tomorrow morning?*

launch into something to start in doing something. □ *Now, don't launch into lecturing me about manners again!* □ *Tim's mother launched into a sermon about how to behave at the dinner table.*

launch (one's **lunch)** *Sl.* to empty one's stomach; to vomit. □ *When I saw that mess, I almost launched my lunch.* □ *Watch out! She's going to launch!*

launch out on something to start out to do something or go somewhere. □ *When are you going to launch out on your expedition?* □ *Ted and Bill launched out on their trip through the mountains.*

launch something **against** someone or something to set something going against someone or something. □ *The general launched an attack against the town.* □ *Claire launched a gossip attack against James.*

lavish something **(up)on** someone to give something freely to someone; to squander something on someone. (*Upon* is formal and less commonly used than *on*.) □ *The manager lavished all sorts of favors upon the new employee.* □ *Susan lavished compliments on the cook.*

*a **law unto** oneself *Fig.* one who ignores laws or rules; one who sets one's own standards of behavior. (*Typically: **be** ~; **become** ~.*) □ *You can't get Bill to follow the rules. He's a law unto himself.* □ *Jane is a law unto herself. She's totally unwilling to cooperate.*

lay a finger on someone or something to touch someone or something, even slightly, as with only a finger. □ *Don't you dare lay a finger on my pencil. Go get your own!* □ *If you lay a finger on me, I'll scream.*

lay a guilt trip on someone Go to next.

lay a (heavy) trip on someone **1.** *Inf.* to criticize someone. □ *There's no need to lay a trip on you. I agree with you.* □ *When he finally does get there, I'm going to lay a heavy trip on him like he'll never forget.* **2.** *Inf.* to confuse or astonish someone. □ *After he laid a heavy trip on me about how the company is almost broke, I cleaned out my desk and left.* □ *After Mary laid a trip on John about leaving him, all he could do was cry.* **3.** and **lay a guilt trip on** someone *Inf.* to attempt to make someone feel very guilty. □ *Why do you have to lay a guilt trip on me? Why don't you go to a shrink?* □ *Of course, she just had to lay a trip on him about being bossy, self-centered, and aloof.* **4.** *Inf.* to reveal serious or devastating information to someone. □ *That's a powerful story. I didn't know you were going to lay a heavy trip like that on me.* □ *Man, you really laid a trip on me.*

lay about Go to lay around.

lay alongside something [for a ship] to rest afloat next to something. □ *The ship lay alongside a lovely island while a shore party searched for fresh water.* □ *Our ship lay alongside the narrow wooden pier.*

lay an egg 1. *Lit.* [for a hen, etc.] to deposit an egg. □ *Old Red stopped laying eggs, so we stewed her for Sunday dinner.* **2.** *Fig.* [for someone] to do something bad or poorly; to perform poorly on stage. □ *I guess I really laid an egg, huh?* □ *The cast laid an egg in both performances.*

lay around and **lay about** to lie around. (Common errors for lie about, lie around.) □ *Don't just lay around all day!* □ *I need to lay around for a few days.*

lay claim to something to place a claim on something. □ *Do you really think you can lay claim to that money after all these years?* □ *Someone came by and laid claim to the wallet you found.*

lay down to give up. □ *Do you expect me to just lay down?* □ *You really think I should just lay down and let them walk all over me?*

lay down on the job Go to **lie down on the job.**

lay down one's **arms** *Fig.* to put one's gun, sword, club, etc., down; to stop fighting; to surrender. □ *The prisoners were instructed to lay down their arms.* □ *The soldiers laid down their arms and surrendered.*

lay down one's **life (for** someone or something) *Fig.* to sacrifice one's life for someone or something. □ *Would you lay down your life for your country?* □ *There aren't many things for which I'd lay down my life.*

lay down the law (to someone) **(about** something) *Fig.* to scold someone; to make something very clear to someone in a very stern manner. □ *Wow, was she mad at Ed. She really laid down the law about drinking to him.* □ *She laid down the law to Ed.* □ *She laid down the law about drinking.*

lay emphasis on something and **lay stress on** something to place emphasis on something; to emphasize something. □ *When you present this explanation, lay emphasis on the matter of personal responsibility.* □ *I'm afraid I laid too much stress on the notion of good attendance. If you are really sick, stay home!*

lay eyes on someone or something Go to **set eyes on** someone or something.

lay for someone or something to lie in wait for someone or something. □ *The sheriff was laying for the outlaw.* □ *Bill was laying for me when I came out of the saloon.*

lay hold of someone or something to grasp someone or something with the hands. □ *Just wait till I lay hold of Bill!* □ *I can't wait to lay hold of that fishing pole. I'm ready to catch a huge fish.*

lay in ruins Go to **in ruins.**

lay into someone or something to attack, consume, or scold someone or something. □ *Bob laid into the big plate of fried chicken.* □ *The bear laid into the hunter.* □ *My father really laid into me when I got home.*

lay it on the line and **put it on the line** *Fig.* to make something very clear; to be very definite about something. □ *I am going to lay it on the line and you had better listen to me. If you eat any of these mushrooms, you will die.* □ *I've said it before, but this time I'm going to put it on the line. Don't eat the mushrooms!*

lay it on thick and **lay it on with a trowel; pour it on thick; spread it on thick** *Fig.* to exaggerate or overstate praise, excuses, or blame. □ *Sally was laying it on thick when she said that Tom was the best singer she had ever heard.* □ *After Bob finished making his excuses, Sally said that he was pouring it on thick.* □ *Bob always spreads it on thick.*

lay it on with a trowel Go to previous.

lay low Go to **lie low.**

lay low and sing small *Rur.* to hide; to make oneself inconspicuous. □ *After he robbed the bank, the outlaw decided to lay low and sing small awhile.* □ *Jane is looking for you, and she sure is angry. You'd best lay low and sing small.*

the **lay of the land 1.** *Lit.* the arrangement of features on an area of land. (Also with *lie,* especially British English.) □ *The surveyor mapped the lay of the land.* □ *The geologist studied the lay of the land, trying to determine if there was oil below.* **2.** *Fig.* the arrangement or organization of something other than land. □ *As soon as I get the lay of the land in my new job, things will go better.* □ *The company's corporate structure was complex, so understanding the lay of the land took time.*

lay off ((from) something) to cease doing something. □ *Lay off from your hammering for a minute, will you?* □ *That's enough! Please lay off.*

lay off ((of) someone or something) to stop doing something to someone or something; to stop bothering someone or something. (*Of* is usually retained before pronouns.) □ *Lay off of me! You've said enough.* □ *Please lay off the chicken. I cooked it as best I could.*

lay off (someone or something) to leave someone or something alone. □ *Lay off the booze for a while, why don't ya?* □ *Lay off me! I didn't do anything!*

lay one on Go to **tie one on.**

lay one's **cards on the table** and **put** one's **cards on the table** *Fig.* to be very candid about one's position on some issue. (Alludes to laying playing cards on the table, face up, showing the cards.) □ *All right. Let's lay our cards on the table and speak very candidly about this matter.* □ *It's time we put our cards on the table and spoke honestly.*

lay one's **hands on** someone, something, or an animal Go to **put** one's **hands on** someone, something, or an animal.

lay (oneself) down to lie down. □ *Just lay yourself down there and try to sleep.* □ *I'll lay myself down here for just a few minutes.*

lay over (some place) to pause some place during one's journey. □ *I had to lay over in San Antonio for a few hours before my plane left.* □ *I want a bus that goes straight through. I don't want to lay over.*

lay (some) rubber *Sl.* to spin one's car tires when accelerating, leaving black marks on the street. □ *At that age all they want to do is get in the car and lay some rubber.* □ *You wanna know how well I can lay some rubber in this thing?*

lay some sweet lines on someone and **put some sweet lines on** someone *Sl.* to speak kindly to someone; to **soft-soap** someone. □ *I just laid some sweet lines on her, and she let me use her car.* □ *If you put some sweet lines on him, maybe he won't ground you.*

lay someone **away**† *Euph.* to bury someone. □ *Yes, he has passed. We laid him away last week.* □ *He laid away his uncle in a simple ceremony.*

lay someone **down** to ease someone into a reclining position; to ease someone into bed. □ *The baby woke up when I tried to lay him down.* □ *The nurse laid the disturbed patient down time and time again.*

lay someone **off**† **(from** something) to put an end to someone's employment at something. □ *The automobile factory laid five hundred people off from work.* □ *They laid off a lot of people.* □ *We knew they were going to lay a lot of people off.*

lay someone or something **in(to)** something to place someone or something in something. ☐ *The women laid the king into the coffin and the funeral procession assembled.* ☐ *The cook laid the salmon in the poaching liquid.*

lay someone **out†** **1.** *Sl.* to knock someone down with a punch; to knock someone unconscious. ☐ *Tom laid out Bill with one punch to the chin.* ☐ *The policeman laid the thief out.* **2.** to prepare a corpse for burial or for a wake. ☐ *They laid out their uncle for the wake.* ☐ *The women of the community used to lay their dead out.* **3.** *Sl.* to scold someone severely. ☐ *Don't lay me out! I didn't do it!* ☐ *She really laid out the guy but good. What did he do, rob a bank?*

lay someone **out in lavender** *Fig.* to scold someone severely. ☐ *She was really mad. She laid him out in lavender and really put him in his place.* ☐ *If you ever feel like you need to lay me out in lavender again, just forget it.*

lay someone **to rest** *Euph.* to bury a dead person. ☐ *They laid her to rest by her mother and father, out in the old churchyard.* ☐ *We gather together today to lay our beloved son to rest.*

lay someone **up†** to cause someone to be ill in bed. ☐ *A broken leg laid me up for two months.* ☐ *Flu laid up everyone at work for a week or more.*

lay something **against** something to lean or place something against something. ☐ *They laid the Christmas tree against the house where they could get to it easily when the time came.* ☐ *Lay this hot cloth against the sore and hold it there.*

lay something **alongside ((of)** something**)** to place something next to something else, lengthwise. (*Of* is usually retained before pronouns.) ☐ *Please lay the spoon alongside the knife.* ☐ *Find the knife and lay the spoon alongside.*

lay something **aside†** to set something aside; to place something to one side, out of the way. ☐ *He laid his papers aside and went out to welcome the visitor.* ☐ *He laid aside his papers.*

lay something **aside†** **for** someone or something to put something aside, in reserve, for someone or something. ☐ *I laid some cake aside for Tom, but someone else got it.* ☐ *I laid aside some cake for Tom.*

lay something **at** someone's **door** and **put** something **at** someone's **door 1.** *Fig.* to blame a problem on someone; to hold someone responsible for something. (Alludes to someone laying incriminating evidence at the door of a guilty person, perhaps in the night.) ☐ *I'm laying responsibility for this mess at your door!* ☐ *Don't put this at my door!* **2.** *Fig.* to give or assign a problem to someone for solving. ☐ *I am going to lay this problem right at your door. You are the one who can settle it.* ☐ *I will put this business at your door and hope you can do something about it.*

lay something **at** someone's **feet** and **put** something **at** someone's **feet 1.** *Lit.* to place something on the ground in front of someone. ☐ *The cat came up to me and laid a mouse at my feet.* ☐ *The dog put a rabbit at my feet.* **2.** *Fig.* to hold someone responsible for something. ☐ *I am going to lay this matter at your feet. You are clearly to blame.* ☐ *I will put this matter at your feet. It is your fault.*

lay something **away†** **(for** someone**)** to put something in storage for someone to receive at a later time. (Often said of a purchase that is held until it is paid for.) ☐ *Please lay this away for me. I'll pay for it when I have the money.* ☐ *Please lay away this coat until I can get the money together.*

lay something **before** someone **1.** *Lit.* to present something to someone. ☐ *The cat laid the mouse before her mistress.* ☐ *Dave laid the present before her as a peace offering.* **2.** *Fig.* to present something for someone to judge. ☐ *All you can do is lay the matter before the teacher and hope for a favorable response.* ☐ *I want to lay this before you and let you decide.*

lay something **by** Go to put something by.

lay something **down†** **(on** something**)** to place something down on something. ☐ *Lay the plates down on the table gently.* ☐ *Please lay down your book and listen to me.*

lay something **for** someone or something to prepare something (for a meal) for the benefit of someone or a group. ☐ *She laid a lovely picnic for the two of them.* ☐ *Would you lay the table for dinner for our guests?*

lay something **in†** to get something and store it for future use. ☐ *They laid a lot of food in for the holidays.* ☐ *We always lay in a large supply of firewood each November.*

lay something **on†** to supply something in abundance. ☐ *Look at him lay that butter on! What do you suppose the insides of his arteries look like?* ☐ *They laid on a beautiful buffet lunch.*

lay something **on** someone **1.** *Sl.* to present a plan or an idea to someone. ☐ *Here is this century's greatest idea. Let me lay it on you.* ☐ *I'm going to lay a great idea on you.* **2.** *Sl.* to attempt to make someone feel guilty about something. ☐ *Don't lay that stuff on me. Face your own problem.* ☐ *Every week she calls up to lay a guilt trip on me about something or other.* **3.** Go to lay something on someone or something.

lay something **on** someone or something to place something on someone or something; to cover someone or something with something. ☐ *As soon as he breathed his last, the nurse laid a cloth on him.* ☐ *Ken laid the bundle of flowers on the coffee table.*

lay something **out†** **1.** *Lit.* to spread something out. ☐ *The nurse laid the instruments out for the operation.* ☐ *The valet laid out the clothing for his employer.* **2.** *Fig.* to explain a plan of action or a sequence of events. ☐ *Let me lay it out for you.* ☐ *Lay out the plan very carefully, and don't skip anything.* **3.** *Fig.* to spend some amount of money. ☐ *I can't lay that kind of money out every day!* ☐ *She laid out about $24,000 for that car.*

lay something **out†** **on** someone or something and **lay** something **out†** **for** someone or something *Fig.* to spend an amount of money on someone or something. ☐ *We laid out nearly ten thousand dollars on that car.* ☐ *We laid a fortune out on the children.*

lay something **over** someone or something to cover someone or something with something. ☐ *Here, lay this blanket over the baby.* ☐ *Please lay a napkin over the bread before you take it to the table.*

lay something **to rest** Go to put something to rest.

lay something **to** something to attribute something to something. ☐ *I lay all our problems to the inadequacy of our training.* ☐ *Mary laid her success to a good upbringing.*

L

lay something **to waste** and **lay waste to** something *Fig.* to destroy something; to ruin or mess up something. □ *The invaders laid the village to waste.* □ *The kids came in and laid waste to my clean house.*

lay something **together** to lay things side by side. □ *Lay all the logs together and stack them as high as you can.* □ *Lay the red ones together and put all the others over there in a pile.*

lay something **under** something to place something beneath something. □ *Please lay a cloth under your workbench to catch the sawdust.* □ *Would you mind laying a sheet of plastic over the table?*

lay something **up**[†] **1.** to acquire and store something. □ *Try to lay as much of it up as you can.* □ *I am trying to lay up some firewood for the winter.* **2.** [for something] to disable something. □ *The accident laid up the ship for repairs.* □ *A wreck laid the bus up for months.*

lay stress on something Go to **lay emphasis on** something.

lay the blame (for something) **on** someone *Fig.* to place the blame for something on someone. □ *We could not possibly lay the blame for the accident on you.* □ *Don't try to lay the blame on me!*

lay the blame on someone or something Go to **put the blame on** someone or something.

lay the finger on someone Go to **put the finger on** someone.

lay to to begin doing something, such as fighting or eating. □ *All right, you guys. Lay to. The stuff will get cold if you don't eat it.* □ *Lay to! Let's get on with it.*

lay waste to something Go to **lay** something **to waste**.

laze something **away**[†] to spend a period of time being lazy. □ *I just love to sit here and laze the day away.* □ *I will laze away the entire day.*

leach away [for something] to erode or wash away gradually by leaching. □ *The soft sandstone leached away under the constant rains.* □ *The flowerpots sat out in the rain, where all the nutrients in the soil leached away.*

leach in(to something) [for a substance] to seep or penetrate into something. □ *The salt leached into the soil and ruined it.* □ *A tremendous amount of salt leached in.*

leach out of something [for a substance] to seep or drain out of something. □ *All the nutrients leached out of the soil and nothing would grow.* □ *The phosphorus leached out of the soil after a few years.*

leach something **away**[†] **(from** something) and **leach** something **out (of** something); **leach** something **out**[†]; **leach** something **away**[†] to remove something from something by leaching. □ *The heavy rains leached nutrients away from the soil.* □ *The rains leached away the nutrients.*

lead a dog's life and **live a dog's life** *Fig.* to lead a drab or boring life. □ *Poor Jane really leads a dog's life.* □ *I've been working so hard. I'm tired of living a dog's life.*

lead back (to some place) [for a pathway] to return to a place. □ *This path leads back to the camp.* □ *I hope it leads back. It seems to be going the wrong way.*

lead down to something [for a pathway or other trail] to run downward to something. □ *The trail led down to a spring at the bottom of the hill.* □ *These stairs lead down to the furnace room.*

lead forth [for someone] to go on ahead; to precede someone. □ *You lead forth, and I will follow.* □ *Wallace led forth, but no one came after him.*

lead in(to something) **1.** to begin something; to work into something. □ *Let me lead into the first number with a little talk about the composer.* □ *I'll lead in, then you pick up the melody.* **2.** to make a transition into something; to segue into something. □ *Now, we will lead into the second scene with a little soft orchestral music.* □ *The soft music will lead in, then the curtains will open.*

lead off to be the first one to go or leave. □ *You lead off. I'll follow.* □ *Mary led off and the others followed closely behind.*

lead off (with someone or something) [for a person, process, or performance] to begin with someone or something. □ *The musical revue led off with a bassoon trio.* □ *Sharon, the singer, will lead off tonight.*

lead on to continue to lead onward. □ *The guide led on and we followed.* □ *Lead on, my friend. We are right behind you!*

lead someone **astray** to direct or guide someone in the wrong direction. □ *I am afraid that this young man has been leading you astray. I think you had better stop seeing him.* □ *No one can lead me astray. I know what I am doing.*

lead someone **by** something to guide someone by grasping a part and moving. □ *Do you expect me to lead you around by the hand, showing you everything to do in your job?* □ *The cop grabbed Max and led him around by the collar.*

lead someone **by the nose 1.** *Fig.* to force someone to go somewhere (with you); to lead someone by coercion. □ *John had to lead Tom by the nose to get him to the opera.* □ *I'll go, but you'll have to lead me by the nose.* **2.** *Fig.* to guide someone very carefully and slowly. (As if the person were not very smart.) □ *He will never find his way through the tax form unless you lead him by the nose.* □ *Don't lead me by the nose! I'm coming!*

lead someone **down (**something**)** to help someone down something, such as stairs, a steep path, a ladder, etc. □ *The usher led the couple down the aisle and seated them at the front.* □ *I am going to the cellar myself. Let me lead you down.*

lead someone **down the garden path** and **lead** someone **up the garden path** to deceive someone. □ *Now, be honest with me. Don't lead me down the garden path.* □ *That cheater really led her up the garden path.*

lead someone **down to** something to guide someone downward to something. □ *She led us down to a little room in the cellar, where the old trunk had been kept for all these years.* □ *Would you please lead me down to the wine cellar?*

lead someone **into** something and **lead** someone **in**[†] to guide someone into something or some place. □ *The usher led us into the darkened theater and showed us our seats.* □ *She led in the children.* □ *We led them in.*

lead someone **on 1.** to guide someone onward. □ *We led him on so he could see more of the gardens.* □ *Please lead Mary on. There is lots more to see here.* **2.** and **lead** someone **on**[†] to tease someone; to encourage someone's roman-

L

tic or sexual interest without sincerity. □ *You are just leading me on!* □ *It's not fair to continue leading him on.* □ *It's easy to lead on teenage boys.*

lead someone **on a merry chase** *Fig.* to lead someone in a purposeless pursuit. □ *What a waste of time. You really led me on a merry chase.* □ *Jane led Bill on a merry chase trying to find an antique lamp.*

lead someone or an animal **out of** something and **lead** someone or an animal **out**† to guide someone or an animal out of something or some place. □ *Someone finally led the hiker out of the valley or he would still be there now.* □ *She led out the striking workers.*

lead someone or an animal **to** something to guide someone or an animal to something or some place. □ *Would you lead Paul to the place where the trunks are kept?* □ *The cat is so old that we had to lead her to her food.*

lead someone or something **against** someone or something to manage someone or a group in an attack on someone or something. □ *The general led the entire company against the troops holding the city.* □ *They led two platoons against the enemy position.*

lead someone or something **(away**†**) (from** someone or something**)** to direct or guide someone or something away from someone or something. □ *The officer led the victim's wife away from the accident.* □ *The trainer led away the dog from the other animals.* □ *We led them away.*

lead someone or something **back**† **(to** someone or something**)** to guide someone or something back to someone or something. □ *Someone will have to lead me back to camp. I just know I'll get lost if I go by myself.* □ *The park ranger led back the hikers to their tent.* □ *I will lead them back.*

lead someone or something **forth**† to bring or usher someone or something forward. □ *The captain led the soldiers forth to the parade ground.* □ *They led forth the army into battle.*

lead someone or something **off**† to guide someone or something away. □ *The guide led the hikers off on the adventure of their lives.* □ *The dog owners led off their animals and they awaited the decision of the judges.*

lead someone **to believe** something *Fig.* to imply something to someone; to cause someone to believe something untrue. □ *But you led me to believe that this watch was guaranteed!* □ *Did you lead her to believe that she was hired as a clerk?*

lead someone **to** do something *Fig.* to cause someone to do something. □ *This agent led me to purchase a worthless piece of land.* □ *My illness led me to quit my job.*

lead someone **up** something to guide someone upward along some route. □ *Would you please lead Tom up the path so he can leave his things at the cabin on the hill?* □ *Mary led the visitors up the stairs to the loft, which she had recently redecorated.*

lead someone **up the garden path** Go to **lead** someone **down the garden path.**

lead the life of Riley and **live the life of Riley** *Fig.* to live in luxury. (No one knows who Riley alludes to.) □ *If I had a million dollars, I could live the life of Riley.* □ *The treasurer took our money to Mexico, where he lived the life of Riley until the police caught him.*

lead the way to lead (someone) along the proper pathway. □ *You lead the way, and we'll follow.* □ *I feel better when you're leading the way. I get lost easily.*

lead up to something **1.** *Lit.* to aim at or route movement to something. □ *A narrow path led up to the door of the cottage.* □ *This road leads up to the house at the top of the hill.* **2.** *Fig.* to prepare to say something; to lay the groundwork for making a point. (Typically with the present participle.) □ *I was just leading up to telling you what happened when you interrupted.* □ *I knew she was leading up to something, the way she was talking.*

lead with someone or something to start out with someone or something. □ *The coach led with Walter as pitcher and Sam on first base.* □ *We will lead with our best players.*

lead with something to tend to strike first with a particular fist—the right, the left, the best, etc. (Boxing.) □ *Watch that guy, Champ, he always leads with his right.* □ *Get in there and lead with your left.*

leading question a question that suggests the kind of answer that the person who asks it wants to hear. □ *The mayor was angered by the reporter's leading questions.* □ *"Don't you think that the police are failing to stop crime?" is an example of a leading question.*

a **lead-pipe cinch** *Fig.* something very easy to do; something entirely certain to happen. □ *I knew it was a lead-pie cinch that I would be selected to head the publication committee.*

leaf out [for a plant] to open its leaf buds. □ *Most of the bushes leaf out in mid-April.* □ *The trees leafed out early this year.*

leaf through something Go to **thumb through** something.

leak in(to something**)** [for a fluid] to work its way into something. □ *Some of the soapy water leaked into the soil.* □ *The rainwater is leaking in!*

leak out [for information] to become known unofficially. □ *I hope that news of the new building does not leak out before the contract is signed.* □ *When the story leaked out, my telephone would not stop ringing.*

leak out (of something**)** [for a fluid] to seep out of something or some place. □ *Some of the brake fluid leaked out of the car and made a spot on the driveway.* □ *Look under the car. Something's leaking out.*

leak something **(out)** and **let** something **(get) out** *Fig.* to disclose special information to the press so that the resulting publicity will accomplish something. (Usually said of government disclosures. Also used for accidental disclosures.) □ *Don't leak that information out.* □ *I don't want to be the one to leak it.*

leak something **to** someone *Fig.* to tell [otherwise secret] information to someone. □ *The government leaked a phony story to the press just to see how far it would travel.* □ *The government leaks things to the press occasionally, just to see the reaction.*

leak through something [for a fluid] to seep through something. □ *Rainwater leaked through the roof.* □ *I was afraid that the crushed orange would leak through the paper bag.*

lean across someone or something to incline oneself across someone or something. □ *She leaned across me to reach* the telephone and spilled my wine. □ *Laura leaned across the table and knocked my coffee over.*

lean against someone or something to prop oneself against someone or something. □ *The child leaned against her sister to keep warm.* □ *I leaned against the back of the chair and went right to sleep.*

lean and mean *Fig.* fit and ready for hard, efficient work. □ *Dave got himself lean and mean and is ready to play in Saturday's game.* □ *The management is lean and mean and looks to turn a profit next year.*

lean back [for someone] to recline backwards, usually in a chair. □ *Lean back and make yourself comfortable.* □ *Let's lean back and be comfortable.*

lean back (against someone or something**)** to recline backwards, putting weight on someone or something. □ *Just lean back against me. I will prevent you from falling.* □ *Relax and lean back. Nothing bad is going to happen.*

lean back (on someone or something**)** to recline backwards, pressing on someone or something. □ *Don't lean back on me! I'm not a chair!* □ *Lean back on the couch and tell me what you are thinking.*

lean down to bend over. □ *Lean down and tie your shoe before you trip.* □ *He leaned down and picked something up from the floor.*

lean forward to bend forward. □ *Lean forward a minute so I can put a cushion behind your back.* □ *When Betsy leaned forward, she lost her balance and fell.*

lean in(to something**)** to incline or press into something. □ *You have to lean into the wind when you walk or you will be blown over.* □ *As you walk into the wind, lean in a little bit.* □ *The north wall of the barn leans in a little. Is it going to fall?*

lean on someone *Fig.* to try to make someone do something; to coerce someone to do something. (From **lean on** someone or something.) □ *If she refuses to do it, lean on her a bit.* □ *Don't lean on me! I don't have to do it if I don't want to.*

lean on someone or something **1.** *Lit.* to incline or press on someone or something. □ *Don't lean on me. I'm not strong enough to support both of us.* □ *Lean on the wall and rest a little while.* **2.** *Fig.* to depend on someone or something. □ *You lean on your parents too much. You must be more independent.* □ *You can't lean on the government forever.*

lean out of something to hang or bend out of something or some place. □ *She leaned out of the window so she could watch what was going on.* □ *Don't lean out of the car window. You will fall.*

lean over 1. to bend over. □ *Lean over and pick the pencil up yourself! I'm not your servant!* □ *As Kelly leaned over to tie her shoes, her chair slipped out from under her.* **2.** to tilt over. □ *The fence leaned over and almost fell.* □ *As the wind blew, the tree leaned over farther and farther.*

lean over backwards (to do something**)** Go to **fall over backwards (to** do something**)**.

lean something **against** someone or something to prop something against someone or something. □ *She leaned her spade against the house and wiped the sweat from her brow.* □ *Bill leaned the mirror against his leg while he screwed the hook into the wall.*

lean something **forward** to tilt or bend something forward. □ *Lean the board forward a little bit, please.* □ *Someone leaned this panel forward a little too much.*

*lean times (ahead) *Fig.* a future period of lowered income or revenue; a future period when there will be shortages of goods and suffering. (*Typically: **be** ~; **cause** ~; **have** ~; **mean** ~.) □ *The economy is going sour which means lean times ahead.*

lean toward doing something to tend toward doing something; to favor doing something. □ *The union is leaning toward accepting the proposal.* □ *My friends leaned toward swimming instead of shopping.*

lean toward someone or something **1.** to incline toward someone or something. □ *Tom is leaning toward Randy. I think he is going to fall on him.* □ *The tree is leaning toward the edge of the cliff. It will fall eventually.* **2.** to tend to favor [choosing] someone or something. □ *I am leaning toward Sarah as the new committee head.* □ *I'm leaning toward a new committee.*

leap at someone or something **1.** to jump toward someone or something. □ *The grasshopper leapt at me and scared me to death.* □ *The cat leapt at the mouse and caught it.* **2.** to accept or choose someone or something eagerly. □ *We leapt at Carl when his department offered him to us.* □ *When we had the chance to hire Carl, we leapt at it.*

leap at the chance (to do something**)** Go to next.

leap at the opportunity (to do something**)** and **leap at the chance (to** do something**); jump at the chance (to** do something**); jump at the opportunity (to** do something**)** *Fig.* to accept an opportunity eagerly. □ *Frank leapt at the opportunity to become a commercial artist.* □ *It was a great idea and we leapt at the opportunity.* □ *I would leap at the chance to go to Moscow.* □ *His company proposed to send him to England, and John jumped at the chance.*

leap down (from something**)** to hop down from something or some place. □ *The performer leapt down from the stage and ran up the aisle.* □ *She leapt down and ran away.*

leap for joy and **jump for joy** *Fig.* to jump up because one is happy; to be very happy. □ *Tommy leapt for joy because he had won the race.* □ *We all leapt for joy when we heard the news.*

leap forward to jump or hop forward. □ *The little creature leapt forward and looked carefully at us.* □ *As the frog leapt forward, the kitten jumped straight up and fled.*

*a leap of faith *Fig.* acceptance of an idea or conclusion largely on faith. (*Typically: **be** ~; **make** ~; **require** ~.) □ *We had to make quite a leap of faith to accept his promise after the last time he let us down.*

leap out (of something**)** to jump outward from something. □ *A mouse leapt out of the cereal box and frightened everyone.* □ *I opened the box and a mouse leapt out.*

leap over something to jump over something. □ *The dog leapt over the hedge and chased the rabbit around the corner of the house.* □ *Please don't leap over my roses. You'll damage them.*

leap to conclusions Go to **jump to conclusions**.

leap up to jump upwards. □ *The dog leapt up and licked my cheek.* □ *I leapt up so I could see over the wall for just a second.*

learn a thing or two (about someone or something**)** Go to a thing or two (about someone or something).

learn about someone or something to find out about someone or something. □ *What have you learned about Mr. Franklin and his business dealings?* □ *I learned about what causes rain.*

learn by something to learn [something] from some kind of actual experience. □ *The best way to learn is to learn by doing.* □ *The best way to learn to sail is to learn by sailing.*

learn from someone or something to learn [something] from the experience of someone or something. □ *Pay attention to what Sarah does. I think you can learn from her.* □ *This was quite an experience, and we all can learn from it.*

learn of someone or something to find out about someone or something. □ *I'm not in the telephone book. How did you learn of me?* □ *How did you learn of our company?*

learn something **by heart** *Fig.* to learn something so well that it can be written or recited without thinking; to memorize something. □ *The director told me to learn my speech by heart.* □ *I had to go over it many times before I learned it by heart.*

learn something **by rote** *Fig.* to learn something by memorizing without giving any thought to what is being learned. □ *I learned history by rote; then I couldn't pass the test that required me to think.* □ *If you learn things by rote, you'll never understand them.*

learn something **from** someone or something to find out something from someone or something. □ *I don't know when the children are due to arrive. See what you can learn from Walter.* □ *I am sure we can learn something from this experience.*

learn something **from the bottom up** *Fig.* to learn something thoroughly, from the very basics; to learn all aspects of something, even the least important ones. □ *I learned my business from the bottom up.* □ *I started out sweeping the floors and learned everything from the bottom up.*

learn (something) **the hard way** and **find** (something) **out the hard way** to learn something by experience, especially by an unpleasant experience. (As opposed to learning in school, from reading, etc.) □ *She learned how to make investments the hard way.* □ *I wish I didn't have to learn things the hard way.* □ *I found out the hard way that it's difficult to work and go to school at the same time.*

learn the ropes Go to the ropes.

learn to live with something *Fig.* to learn to adapt to something unpleasant or painful. □ *Finally the doctor told Marion that she was going to have to learn to live with her arthritis.* □ *The floor plan of the house we bought is not as spacious as we had thought, but we will learn to live with it.*

learn the tricks of the trade Go to the tricks of the trade.

a **learning experience** Go to a growth experience.

lease something **back†** to sell something, then rent it from the buyer. □ *We sold the building to a real estate firm and*

then leased it back. There was some tax saving involved. □ *We leased back the building.*

lease something **from** someone to rent something from someone. □ *We decided to lease the building from the owner rather than buying it.* □ *The company always leases its cars from the dealership.*

lease something **(out†) to** someone to rent something to someone. □ *The company leases cars out to its customers.* □ *Can you lease this building to me for two years?* □ *Lease out only the first two floors.*

the **least little thing** the smallest possible thing. □ *He gets upset over the least little thing.* □ *When she was a girl, she would throw a tantrum over the least little thing.*

least of all the thing of smallest importance. (Compare this with **most of all**.) □ *There were many things wrong with the new house. Least of all, the water faucets leaked.* □ *What a bad day. Many things went wrong, but least of all, I tore my shirt.*

leave a bad taste in someone's **mouth** [for something] to leave a bad feeling or memory with someone. □ *The whole business about the missing money left a bad taste in his mouth.* □ *It was a very nice hotel, but something about it left a bad taste in my mouth.*

leave a lot to be desired *Cliché* to be lacking something important; to be inadequate. (A polite way of saying that something is bad.) □ *This report leaves a lot to be desired.* □ *I'm sorry to have to fire you, Mary, but your work leaves a lot to be desired.*

leave a paper trail Go to a paper trail.

leave a sinking ship Go to desert a sinking ship.

leave ahead of time Go to ahead of time.

leave an impression (on someone**)** and **leave** someone **with an impression** *Fig.* to provide a lasting memory for someone after one has left. (Akin to **make an impression on** someone.) □ *Her performance was less than stunning. She didn't leave a very good impression on us.*

leave for some place to depart for some place. □ *We will leave for Denver at dawn.* □ *When do we leave for Grandmother's house?*

leave go of someone or something *Inf.* to let go of someone or something. (Usually considered nonstandard.) □ *Leave go of me!* □ *Leave go of my hand!*

leave in a body Go to in a body.

leave it at that to leave a situation as it is. □ *This is the best we can do. We'll have to leave it at that.* □ *I can do no more. I will have to leave it at that.*

leave it to someone to depend on someone to behave in a certain way. □ *Leave it to Harry to mess things up.* □ *She did it wrong again. Leave it to Janet!* □ *Jane: Will you do this as soon as possible? Mary: Leave it to me.*

Leave me alone! Stop harassing me!; Don't bother me! □ *John: You did it. You're the one who always does it. Bill: Leave me alone! I never did it.* □ *Fred: Let's give Bill a dunk in the pool. Bill: Leave me alone!*

leave no stone unturned *Fig.* to search in all possible places. (As if one might search under every rock.) □ *Don't worry. We'll find your stolen car. We'll leave no stone*

L

unturned. □ *In searching for a nice place to live, we left no stone unturned.*

a **leave of absence** a period of time away from one's job, with the employer's permission. □ *Mr. Takaguchi is on leave of absence because he is going back to school.* □ *His leave of absence is expected to end next month.*

leave off something to quit something. □ *I have to leave off working for a while so I can eat.* □ *I left off reading and went downstairs for supper.*

leave one's **mark on** someone *Fig.* [for someone like a teacher] to affect the behavior and performance of another person. □ *The wise professor left her mark on her students.* □ *My father left his mark on me, and I will always remember all his good advice.*

leave one **to** one's **fate** to abandon someone to whatever may happen—possibly death or some other unpleasant event. □ *We couldn't rescue the miners and were forced to leave them to their fate.* □ *Please don't try to help. Just go away and leave me to my fate.*

leave one **to** one's **own devices** and **leave** one **to** one's **own resources** *Fig.* to make one rely on oneself. □ *I am sure that she will manage if we leave her to her own devices.* □ *I will leave her to her own resources and everything will turn out fine.*

leave one **to** one's **own resources** Go to previous.

leave oneself **wide open for** something and **leave** oneself **wide open to** something *Fig.* to invite criticism or joking about oneself; to fail to protect oneself from criticism or ridicule. □ *Yes, that was a harsh remark, Jane, but you left yourself wide open to it.* □ *I can't complain about your joke. I left myself wide open for it.*

leave some loose ends Go to some loose ends.

leave someone **at loose ends** Go to at loose ends.

leave someone **cold** to leave someone unaffected or bored. □ *He said it was dull, and it left him cold.* □ *The music's good, but the story left the producer cold.*

leave someone **flat 1.** *Fig.* to fail to entertain or stimulate someone. □ *Your joke left me flat.* □ *We listened carefully to his lecture, but it left us flat.* **2.** *Fig.* to leave someone without any money—**flat broke.** □ *Paying all my bills left me flat.* □ *The robber took all my money and left me flat.* **3.** *Fig.* to leave someone completely and suddenly alone. □ *I was at the dance with Harry, but when he met Alice, he left me flat.* □ *They just walked off and left us flat.*

leave someone **for dead** to abandon someone as being dead. (The abandoned person may actually be alive.) □ *He looked so bad that they almost left him for dead.* □ *As the soldiers turned—leaving the enemy captain for dead—the captain fired at them.*

leave someone **high and dry 1.** *Lit.* [for water] to recede and leave someone untouched. □ *The waters receded and left us high and dry.* **2.** *Fig.* to leave someone unsupported and unable to maneuver; to leave someone helpless. □ *All my workers quit and left me high and dry.* □ *All the children ran away and left Billy high and dry to take the blame for the broken window.* **3.** *Fig.* to leave someone flat broke. □ *Mrs. Franklin took all the money out of the bank and left Mr. Franklin high and dry.* □ *Paying the bills always leaves me high and dry.*

leave someone **holding the bag** and **leave** someone **holding the baby** *Fig.* to allow someone to take all the blame; to leave someone appearing to be guilty. □ *They all ran off and left me holding the bag. It wasn't even my fault.* □ *It was all the mayor's fault, but he wasn't left holding the bag.*

leave someone **in peace** to stop bothering someone; to go away and leave someone alone. (Does not necessarily mean to go away from a person.) □ *Please go—leave me in peace.* □ *Can't you see that you're upsetting her? Leave her in peace.*

leave someone **in the lurch** *Fig.* to leave someone waiting for or anticipating your actions. □ *Where were you, John? You really left me in the lurch.* □ *I didn't mean to leave you in the lurch. I thought we had canceled our meeting.*

leave someone or some creature **out in the cold** Go to out in the cold.

leave someone or something **alone** Go to let someone or something alone.

leave someone or something **(at)** some place **1.** to abandon someone or something at some place. □ *Don't leave me here by myself!* □ *Betty left her newspaper at the table, hoping someone else would enjoy it.* **2.** to allow someone or something to remain at some place. □ *You leave me here and go on ahead.* □ *Please leave your packages at the door.* **3.** to allow someone or something to stay behind through forgetfulness. □ *I left my glasses behind on my desk.* □ *I was left at the movie theater by mistake.*

leave someone or something **be** Go to let someone or something alone.

leave someone or something **behind** to fail or forget to bring someone or something along. □ *John was sick, so we had to leave him behind.* □ *Oh, I left my money behind.*

leave someone or something **hanging (in midair)** and **keep** someone or something **hanging (in midair) 1.** *Lit.* to keep someone or something suspended in midair when support for the person or thing is removed. □ *The ladder collapsed and left me hanging in midair. Fortunately, I grabbed onto the windowsill.* **2.** *Fig.* to suspend dealing with someone or something; to leave someone or something waiting to be finished or continued. □ *She left her sentence hanging in midair.* □ *Tell me the rest of the story. Don't leave me hanging in midair.*

leave someone or something **in** one's **hands** *Fig.* to give one control of or responsibility for someone or something. □ *You left the whole project in my hands!* □ *I have to leave the care of baby in your hands while I go to the doctor.*

leave someone or something **in** someone's **care** Go to in the care of someone.

leave someone or something **in (something)** to permit someone or something to remain in something. □ *We left the children in the house while we went out to greet the guests.* □ *Did you leave the dog in the car? Poor puppy! I didn't mean to leave you in.*

leave someone or something **in the care of** someone Go to in the care of someone.

leave someone or something **in the trust of** someone Go to in the trust of someone.

L

leave someone or something **out of** something and **leave** someone or something **out†** to neglect to include someone or something in something. □ *Please leave me out of it.* □ *Can I leave John out this time?* □ *Leave out the last two eggs.*

leave someone or something **to** someone to give or abandon someone or something to someone. □ *I leave Mr. Franklin to you. Good luck in dealing with him.* □ *I leave the whole problem to you. Good luck.*

leave someone or something **under** someone's **care** Go to in the care of someone.

leave someone or something **with** someone or something to allow someone or something to remain with someone or something. □ *Can I leave Jimmy with you while I shop?* □ *Do you mind if I leave my papers with the committee, just in case they have time to look at them?*

leave someone **sitting pretty** Go to sitting pretty.

leave someone, something, or some creature **alone** and **let** someone, something, or some creature **alone; leave** someone, something, or some creature **be; let** someone, something, or some creature **be** to stop bothering someone or something. □ *Don't torment the cat. Leave it alone.* □ *I don't want your help. Let me alone.* □ *Don't argue about it. Let it be!*

leave someone **to it** to withdraw and allow someone to finish something alone. □ *I hate to leave before the job is finished, but I'll have to leave you to it.* □ *I will leave them to it. I have to go home now.*

leave someone **up in the air** *Fig.* to leave someone waiting for a decision. □ *Please don't leave me up in the air. I want to know what's going to happen to me.* □ *Nothing was decided, and they left me up in the air.*

leave someone **with an impression** Go to leave an impression (on someone).

leave something **aside†** **1.** to leave something in reserve. □ *Leave some of the sugar aside for use in the icing.* □ *Leave aside some cookies too.* **2.** to ignore something, especially a fact. □ *Let's leave the question of who will pay for it aside for a while.* □ *We will leave aside the current situation and talk about the future.*

leave something **down** to leave something in a lowered or low position. □ *Leave the window down, please. It's hot in this car.* □ *Leave the window down. This house is cold enough as it is.*

leave something **for another occasion** and **keep** something **for another occasion** to hold something back for later. (*Occasion* can be replaced with *time, day, person,* etc.) □ *Please leave some cake for another day.* □ *Don't eat all the cheese. Leave some for another occasion.* □ *I have to leave some of my earnings for next month.*

leave something **for** someone or an animal to allow something to remain for the use of someone or an animal. □ *I will leave this bread here for you, so you won't starve.* □ *Don't clean it up. Leave it for the dog.*

leave something **in limbo** Go to in limbo.

leave something **in ruins** Go to in ruins.

leave something **in the back of** someone's **mind** Go to in the back of someone's mind.

leave something **(lying) around** and **leave** something **(lying) about** to permit something to lie around unguarded; to leave something somewhere carelessly. □ *Don't leave your clothes lying around. Hang them up.* □ *Don't leave stuff lying about!*

leave something **on†** **1.** to continue to wear some article of clothing. □ *I think I will leave my coat on. It's chilly in here.* □ *I'll leave on my coat.* **2.** to allow something [that can be turned off] to remain on. □ *Who left the radio on?* □ *Please leave on the light for me.*

leave something **on** someone or something to allow something to remain on someone or something. □ *Leave the coats on the children. We are taking them out to a movie almost immediately.* □ *Who left this book on the table?*

leave something **on** someone's **shoulders** Go to on someone's **shoulders**.

leave something **open** to leave a date or time unscheduled. □ *I left something open on Friday, just in case we want to leave work early.* □ *Please leave an appointment open for Mrs. Wallace next week. She will be calling in to our office for an appointment.*

leave something **to chance** to allow something to be settled by chance. □ *Plan your day. Don't leave anything to chance.* □ *It is not a good idea to leave any of this to chance.*

leave something **to** someone **1.** *Lit.* to will something to someone. □ *My grandfather left his house to my mother.* □ *I will leave this watch to one of my grandchildren.* **2.** to assign work to or reserve a task for someone. □ *I will leave this last little bit of the job to you.* □ *Can I leave this last part to Carl to finish?* **3.** Go to **leave it to** someone.

leave something **up†** to leave something in a raised or high position. □ *It's still warm in here. Please leave the window up.* □ *Please leave up the window. It's so hot!*

leave something **up in the air** *Fig.* to leave a matter undecided. (Alludes to something drifting in the air, moving neither up nor down.) □ *Let's get this settled now. I don't want to leave anything up in the air over the weekend.* □ *The whole matter was left up in the air for another week.*

leave something **up to** someone or something Go to up to someone or something.

leave the door open (for something**)** *Fig.* to provide for the possibility that something might happen. □ *I think that the matter is completely settled, although we have left the door open for one or two last-minute changes.*

leave the room 1. to go out of the room. □ *I had to leave the room to get drinks for everyone.* **2.** *Euph.* to leave to go to the toilet. □ *I have to leave the room. I'll be back in a minute.*

leave them rolling in the aisles Go to rolling in the aisles.

leave well enough alone Go to let well enough alone.

leave with someone to depart in the company of someone. □ *I left with Frank early in the evening and did not see what happened to Tom and Edna.* □ *Mary is gone. She left with Gerald.*

leave word for someone **to** do something *Fig.* to leave a message or a request for someone. (See also leave word (with someone).) □ *I left word for you to come to my office.* □ *We left word for her to hurry up and come home.*

leave word (with someone**)** *Fig.* to leave a message with someone (who will pass the message on to someone else).

□ *If you decide to go to the convention, please leave word with my secretary.* □ *Leave word before you go.* □ *I left word with your brother. Didn't he give you the message?*

lecture at someone **(about** something**)** to talk to someone about something in the manner of a lecture. □ *There is no need to lecture at me about the problem. I know how serious the matter is.* □ *Don't lecture at me all the time!*

lecture someone **for** something to give someone a talking-to about something. □ *Please don't lecture me for being late. It won't help now, will it?* □ *There is no point in lecturing us for something we didn't do.*

lecture ((to) someone**) about** someone or something and **lecture ((to)** someone**) on** someone or something **1.** to give an instructional speech to someone about someone or something. □ *He always lectured his children about their duty to vote.* □ *She lectured to all her classes on employment opportunities.* **2.** to scold someone about someone or something. □ *Please don't lecture me about my behavior.* □ *I like Ted! Don't lecture about him.*

leer at someone to gaze at someone flirtatiously or with lust. □ *Why are you leering at that woman in the bikini?* □ *Stop leering at me!*

left and right Go to right and left.

The **left hand doesn't know what the right hand is doing.** *Prov.* One part of an organization does not know what another part is doing. (Biblical.) □ *It was evident that the left hand did not know what the right hand was doing when we planned our potluck dinner party, since everyone brought dessert and no one brought a main dish.*

left-handed compliment Go to backhanded compliment.

*a **leg up** *Fig.* a kind of help where someone provides a knee or crossed hand as a support for someone to place a foot on to get higher, as in mounting a horse or climbing over something. (*Typically: **get ~; have ~; give** someone ~.) □ *I gave her a leg up, and soon she was on her horse.* □ *Can I give you a leg up?* □ *Could I please have a leg up?*

*a **leg up on** someone *Fig.* an advantage that someone else does not have. (*Typically: **get ~; have ~; give** someone ~.) □ *I have a leg up on Walter when it comes to getting around town, since I have a car.* □ *I want to practice indoors all winter and get a leg up on Ken, since he thinks he can beat me at tennis.*

a **legend in** one's **own (life)time** *Fig.* someone who is very famous and widely known for doing something special. □ *The young golfer became a legend in his own lifetime.*

legislate against something to prohibit something; to pass a law against something. □ *You can't just legislate against something. You have to explain to people why they shouldn't do it.* □ *The Congress has just legislated against insolvent banks.*

legislate for something to pass a law that tries to make something happen. □ *The candidate pledged to legislate for tax relief.* □ *We support your efforts to legislate for lower taxes.*

legwork the physical work accompanying a task. □ *I don't mind making the phone calls if you do the legwork.* □ *I have a gopher to do the legwork for me.*

lend a hand (to someone**)** Go to lend (someone) a hand.

lend an ear to someone or something and **lend your ear to** someone or something *Fig.* to listen to someone or what someone has to say. □ *Lend an ear to me and I will tell you a story.* □ *Lend your ear to what I am saying.*

lend color to something *Fig.* to provide an interesting accompaniment for something. □ *Your clever comments lent a great deal of color to the slide show of your vacation.* □ *The excellent master of ceremonies will lend color to an otherwise dry panel discussion.*

lend oneself or itself **to** something *Fig.* [for someone or something] to be adaptable to something; [for someone or something] to be useful for something. □ *This room doesn't lend itself to bright colors.* □ *John doesn't lend himself to casual conversation.* □ *I don't think that this gown lends itself to outdoor occasions.*

lend (someone**) a hand** and **lend a hand (to** someone**)** *Fig.* to give someone some help, not necessarily with the hands. □ *Could you lend me a hand with this piano? I need to move it across the room.* □ *Could you lend a hand with this math assignment?* □ *I'd be happy to lend a hand.*

lend someone **a hand with** something *Fig.* to help someone with something. (This need not involve "hands.") □ *Could you please lend us a hand with this?* □ *Can I lend you a hand with that?*

lend something **out† (to** someone**)** to allow someone to borrow something. □ *I lent my tuxedo out to a friend who was going to a dance, and now I haven't anything to wear to the opera.* □ *I lent out my copy of the book.* □ *Sorry, I lent it out.*

lend something **to** someone to make a loan of something to someone. □ *Never lend money to a friend.* □ *Would you be able to lend your coat to Fred?*

lend your ear to someone or something Go to lend an ear to someone or something.

Lend your money and lose your friend. *Prov.* You should not lend money to your friends; if you do, either you will have to bother your friend to repay the loan, which will make your friend resent you, or your friend will not repay the loan, which will make you resent your friend. □ *Bill: Joe needs a hundred dollars to pay his landlord. I'm thinking about lending it to him. Alan: Lend your money and lose your friend.*

lengthen out to stretch or grow longer. □ *The days began to lengthen out and we knew summer was upon us.* □ *As we approached the end of the trail, the distance seemed to lengthen out.*

A **leopard cannot change his spots.** *Prov.* One cannot change the basic way one is. □ *Bill may say he'll stop being so jealous after Cindy marries him, but I doubt he will. A leopard can't change his spots.*

Less is more. *Cliché* fewer or small is better. □ *Simplicity now rules our lives. Less is more. Smaller houses and cars. The world will be a better place!*

The **less said (about** something**), the better.** *Prov.* A way of indicating that you think something should not be talked about any further. □ *Jane: How are things going with your divorce proceedings? Ellen: The less said, the better.* □ *The less said about my financial situation, the better.*

less than pleased displeased. □ *We were less than pleased to learn of your comments.* □ *Bill was less than pleased at the outcome of the election.*

the **lesser (of the two)** the smaller one (of two); the one having the lesser amount. □ *The last two pieces of pie were not quite the same size, and I chose the lesser of the two.* □ *Faced with a basket containing too much and one with too little, Tom chose the lesser.*

the **lesser of two evils** the less bad thing of a pair of bad things. □ *I didn't like either politician, so I voted for the lesser of two evils.* □ *Given the options of going out with someone I don't like and staying home and watching a boring television program, I chose the lesser of the two evils and watched television.*

let alone someone or something not to mention or think of someone or something; not even to take someone or something into account. (Fixed order.) □ *Do I have a dollar? I don't even have a dime, let alone a dollar.* □ *I didn't invite John, let alone the rest of his family.*

Let bygones be bygones. *Cliché* Forgive someone for something he or she did in the past. □ *Jill: Why don't you want to invite Ellen to your party? Jane: She was rude to me at the office picnic. Jill: But that was six months ago. Let bygones be bygones.* □ *Nancy held a grudge against her teacher for a long time, but she finally decided to let bygones be bygones.*

let down to relax one's efforts or vigilance. □ *Now is no time to let down. Keep on your guard.* □ *After the contest was over, Jane let down a bit so she could relax.*

Let every man skin his own skunk. *Prov.* Everyone should do his own job and not interfere with others.; Each person should do his own dirty work. □ *We weren't supposed to help each other with the homework. "Let every man skin his own skunk," the teacher said.*

Let every tub stand on its own bottom. Go to Every tub must stand on its own bottom.

let fly with something *Fig.* to throw or thrust something, such as a rock, ball, punch, etc. □ *The pitcher wound up and let fly with a strike—right over the plate.* □ *Max let fly with a blow to Lefty's chin.*

Let George do it. *Fig.* Let someone else do it: it doesn't matter who. □ *Billie always says, "Let George do it." She is unwilling to help with things that don't interest her.*

let go of someone or something to release someone or something. □ *Please let go of me!* □ *Don't let go of the steering wheel.*

let go (with something) and **cut loose (with** something); **let loose (with** something) **1.** to shout something out or expel something; to shout or express something wildly. □ *The whole team let go with a loud shout.* □ *The audience cut loose with a loud cheer.* **2.** to deliver a strong verbal reprimand. □ *Molly let loose with a tremendous scolding at Dave.* □ *Dave cut loose with a vengeful retort.*

let grass grow under one's **feet** *Fig.* to do nothing; to stand still. □ *Mary doesn't let the grass grow under her feet. She's always busy.* □ *Bob is too lazy. He's letting the grass grow under his feet.*

Let her rip! and **Let it roll!** *Inf.* Let it go!; Let it start! □ *Time to start. Let her rip!* □ *There's the signal! Let it roll!*

let it all hang out *Inf.* to be yourself, assuming that you generally are not; to become totally relaxed and unpretentious. □ *Come on. Relax! Let it all hang out.* □ *I tried to let it all hang out, but I still felt out of place.*

Let it be. Leave the situation alone as it is. □ *Alice: I can't get over the way he just left me there on the street and drove off. What an arrogant pig! Mary: Oh, Alice, let it be. You'll figure out some way to get even.* □ *John: You can't! Bill: Can too! John: Can't! Bill: Can too! Jane: Stop arguing! Let it be! That's enough!*

Let it go. Forget it.; Stop worrying about it. □ *Don't get so angry about it. Let it go.* □ *Let it go. Stop fretting.*

Let it roll! Go to Let her rip!

let loose of someone or something **1.** to loosen the grasp on someone or something. □ *Please let loose of me!* □ *Will you let loose of the doorknob?* **2.** to become independent from someone or something. □ *She is nearly forty years old and has not yet let loose of her mother.* □ *Dave can't let loose of his childhood.*

let loose (with something) Go to let go (with something).

Let me get back to you (on that). Go to I'll get back to you (on that).

Let me have it! and **Let's have it!** *Inf.* Tell me the news. □ *Bill: I'm afraid there's some bad news. Bob: Okay. Let me have it! Bill: The plans we made did away with your job. Bob: What? □ John: I didn't want to be the one to tell you this. Bob: What is it? Let's have it!*

let me (just) say and **just let me say** a phrase introducing something that the speaker thinks is important. □ *Rachel: Let me say how pleased we all are with your efforts. Henry: Why, thank you very much.* □ *Bob: Just let me say that we're extremely pleased with your activity. Bill: Thanks loads. I did what I could.*

let off (some) steam and **blow off (some) steam 1.** *Lit.* [for something] to release steam. □ *The locomotive let off some steam after it came to a halt.* □ *With a great hiss, it let off steam and frightened the children.* **2.** *Fig.* to work or play off excess energy. □ *Those boys need to get out and let off some steam.* □ *Go out and let off steam!* **3.** *Fig.* to release one's pent-up emotions, such as anger, usually verbally. □ *I'm sorry I yelled at you. I guess I needed to let off some steam.* □ *She's not that mad. She's just letting off steam.*

let on (about someone or something) **(to** someone) to confirm or reveal something about someone or something. □ *I won't let on about Kate.* □ *You promised you wouldn't let on about Sally and her new job!* □ *He was having money troubles, but he never let on about it to us.*

let on something to pretend something. □ *She let on that she was a college graduate.* □ *He looked quite tired, but that wasn't how he let on.*

let on (to someone) **(about** someone or something) to reveal knowledge about someone or something to someone. (See also let on (about someone or something).) □ *Please don't let on to anyone about what happened last night.* □ *I won't let on to anyone.*

let one's **emotions show** to be emotional, especially where it is not appropriate. □ *I'm sorry for the outburst. I didn't mean to let my emotions show.* □ *Please stop crying. You mustn't let your emotions show.*

let one's **guard down**† *Fig.* to stop guarding oneself against trouble; to relax one's vigilance. □ *He never lets his guard down because he trusts no one.*

let one's **hair down 1.** *Lit.* to undo one's hair and let it fall freely. □ *When she took off her glasses and let her hair down, she was incredibly beautiful.* **2.** *Fig.* to tell [someone] everything; to tell one's innermost feelings and secrets. □ *Let your hair down and tell me all about it.* □ *Come on. Let your hair down and tell me what you really think.*

let oneself **go 1.** *Fig.* to become less constrained; to get excited and have a good time. □ *I love to dance and just let myself go.* □ *Let yourself go, John. Learn to enjoy life.* **2.** *Fig.* to let one's appearance and health suffer. □ *When I was depressed, I let myself go and was really a mess.* □ *He let himself go and gained 30 pounds.*

let oneself **in for** something to make oneself vulnerable to some difficulty. □ *I don't want to let myself in for a lot of extra work.* □ *You really let yourself in for some problems!*

let out [for an event that includes many people] to end. (The people are then permitted to come out.) □ *What time does the movie let out? I have to meet someone in the lobby.* □ *The meeting let out at about seven o'clock.* □ *School lets out in June.*

let out some kind of sound [for a living creature] to make some kind of a noise or sound. □ *Be quiet. Don't let out a sound!* □ *Suddenly, Jane let out a shriek.*

let out (with) something **1.** to state or utter something loudly. □ *The man let out with a screaming accusation about the person whom he thought had wounded him.* □ *She let out a torrent of curses.* **2.** to give forth a scream or yell. □ *She let out with a bloodcurdling scream when she saw the snake in her chair.* □ *They let out with shouts of delight when they saw the cake.*

Let's bump this place! *Sl.* Let's get out of this place!; Let's leave! □ *Time to go. Let's bump this place!* □ *Let's bump this place! It's dead here.*

Let's call it a day. *Fig.* Let us end what we are doing for the day. □ *Mary: Well, that's the end of the reports. Nothing else to do. Sue: Let's call it a day.* □ *Bob: Let's call it a day. I'm tired. Tom: Me too. Let's get out of here.*

Let's do lunch (sometime). Go to **We('ll) have to do lunch sometime.**

Let's do this again (sometime). and **We must do this again (sometime).** an expression indicating that one member of a group or pair has enjoyed doing something and would like to do it again. □ *Bill: What a nice evening. Mary: Yes, let's do this again sometime. Bill: Bye. Mary: Bye, Bill.* □ *Sue (saying good night): So nice to see both of you. Mary: Oh, yes. We must do this again sometime.*

Let's dump. *Sl.* Let's go. □ *It's late. Let's dump.* □ *Let's dump. I've still got a lot to do at home tonight.*

Let's get down to business. *Fig.* a phrase marking a transition to a business discussion or serious talk. □ *John: Okay, enough small talk. Let's get down to business. Mary: Good idea.* □ *"All right, ladies and gentlemen, let's get down to business," said the president of the board.*

Let's get out of here. Let us leave (and go somewhere else). □ *Alice: It's really hot in this room. Let's get out of*

here. *John: I'm with you. Let's go.* □ *Bill: This crowd is getting sort of angry. Bob: I noticed that too. Let's get out of here.*

Let's get together (sometime). a vague invitation to meet again, usually said upon departing. (The *sometime* can be a particular time or the word *sometime*.) □ *Bill: Goodbye, Bob. Bob: See you, Bill. Let's get together sometime.* □ *Jane: We need to discuss this matter. John: Yes, let's get together next week.*

Let's go somewhere where it's (more) quiet. Let us continue our conversation where there is less noise or where we will not be disturbed. □ *Tom: Hi, Mary. It's sure crowded here. Mary: Yes, let's go somewhere where it's quiet.* □ *Bill: We need to talk. Sally: Yes, we do. Let's go somewhere where it's more quiet.*

Let's have it! Go to **Let me have it!**

Let's not go through all that again. We are not going to discuss that matter again. (Compare this with **Do we have to go through all that again?**) □ *Bill: Now, I still want to explain again about last night. Sally: Let's not go through all that again!* □ *Sally: I can't get over the way you spoke to me at our own dinner table. Fred: I was only kidding! I said I was sorry. Let's not go through all that again!*

Let's rock and roll! *Inf.* Let's get started!; Let's get moving! □ *A: Everybody ready? B: Yeah. A: Good. Let's rock and roll!*

let's say introduces an estimate or a speculation. □ *I need about—let's say—twenty pounds.* □ *Let's say I go over and talk to him. What do you think?*

Let's shake on it. Let us mark this agreement by shaking hands on it. □ *Bob: Do you agree? Mary: I agree. Let's shake on it. Bob: Okay.* □ *Bill: Good idea. Sounds fine. Bob (extending his hand): Okay, let's shake on it. Bill (shaking hands with Bob): Great!*

Let's talk (about it). Let us talk about the problem and try to settle things. □ *Tom: Bill! Bill! I'm sorry about our argument. Let's talk. Bill: Get lost!* □ *Sally: I've got a real problem. Bob: Let's talk about it.*

Let sleeping dogs lie. *Prov.* Do not instigate trouble.; Leave something alone if it might cause trouble. □ *Jill: Should I ask the boss if he's upset at my coming in late in the mornings? Jane: If he hasn't said anything about it, just let sleeping dogs lie.* □ *I thought I would ask Jill if she wanted to pay her back right away, but then I decided to let sleeping dogs lie.*

let someone **down** to disappoint someone; to fail someone. □ *I'm sorry I let you down. Something came up, and I couldn't meet you.* □ *I don't want to let you down, but I can't support you in the election.*

let someone **(get) by** and **let** someone **pass by** to permit someone to pass. □ *Please let me get by. I am in a hurry.* □ *Let the paramedics by, please.*

let someone **get by with** something to allow someone to do something wrong and not be punished or reprimanded. (An elaboration of **get by (with** something).) □ *She lets those kids get by with anything.* □ *They won't let you get by with that!*

let someone **(get) off** (something) to permit someone to disembark, dismount, or leave something. □ *Please move and let me get off the bus.* □ *Let her off!*

L

let someone **get on with** something to permit someone to continue something. □ *I will leave now and let you get on with your work.* □ *She had to settle the matter first. She would not let herself get on with life until the matter was settled.*

let someone **(get) past** to allow someone to pass; to get out of the way so someone can pass. □ *Please let me get past. I'm in a hurry.* □ *Do let me past.*

let someone **go** *Euph.* to fire someone. □ *They let Jane go from her job.* □ *I'm afraid we're going to have to let you go.*

let someone **have it (with both barrels)** *Fig.* to strike someone or attack someone verbally. (*With both barrels* intensifies the phrase; it alludes to firing a double-barreled shotgun.) □ *I really let Tom have it with both barrels. I told him he had better not do that again if he knows what's good for him.* □ *Bob was really angry and let John have it— with both barrels.*

let someone **in for** something to cause someone to be involved in something, usually something unpleasant. □ *Fred had no idea what his brother had let him in for when he agreed to take his place in the race.* □ *Jack didn't know what he was letting himself in for when he married that dreadful woman.*

let someone **in on** something Go to in on something.

let someone **in on the act** Go to in on the act.

let someone **in on the ground floor** Go to in on the ground floor.

let someone **know (about** something**)** to tell someone something; to inform someone of something. □ *Please let me know about it soon.* □ *Will you be coming to the picnic? Please let me know.*

let someone **off**[†] **1.** to permit someone to disembark or leave a means of transportation. □ *The driver let Mary off the bus.* □ *"I can't let you off at this corner," said the driver.* □ *He let off passengers at every stop.* **2.** Go to next.

let someone **off (easy)** and **let** someone **off**[†] to release or dismiss someone without punishment. □ *The judge didn't let me off easy.* □ *The judge let off Mary with a warning.*

let someone **off the hook** Go to off the hook.

let someone or an animal **(get) out (of** something**) 1.** to permit someone or an animal to exit or escape from something or some place. □ *Please let the president get out of the car.* □ *Don't let the snake get out!* **2.** to permit someone or an animal to evade something. □ *I will not let you get out of your responsibilities.* □ *They wouldn't let me out of the contract.*

let someone or an animal **out of** something and **let** someone or an animal **out**[†] to permit someone or an animal to exit from something or some place. □ *Would you please let Ed out of his room?* □ *Please let out Ed.*

let someone or something **alone** and **leave** someone or something **alone; leave** someone or something **be** to avoid touching, bothering, or communicating with someone or something. □ *Leave me alone. I don't want your help.* □ *Let it alone! Don't touch it! It may be hot!*

let someone or something **at** someone or something to permit someone or something to attack or get at someone or something. □ *He did that? Just let me at him!* □ *Let the committee at her, then she'll change her tune.*

let someone or something **down**[†] *Fig.* to fail someone or something; to disappoint someone or a group. □ *Please don't let me down. I am depending on you.* □ *I let down the entire cast of the play.*

let someone or something **into** something and **let** someone or something **in**[†] to permit someone or something to enter something or some place; to make it possible for someone or something to enter something or some place. □ *Would you let Ed into his room? He forgot his key.* □ *Please let in the dog.*

let someone or something **through (**something**)** to permit someone or something to move through an opening or through a congested area. □ *The usher wouldn't let me through the door.* □ *Please let the ambulance through the crowd.*

let someone **pass by** Go to let someone (get) by.

let someone **slide by** *Fig.* to permit someone to get past a barrier or a challenge too easily. □ *You let too many students slide by. You need to be more rigorous.* □ *Don't let even one unqualified person slide by!*

let someone, something, or some creature **alone** Go to leave someone, something, or some creature **alone**.

let someone, something, or some creature **be** Go to leave someone, something, or some creature **alone**.

let something **(get) out** Go to leak something (out).

let something **off**[†] to release something; to give something off. □ *The engine let some evil smelling smoke off.* □ *The flower let off a wonderful smell.*

let something **out**[†] **1.** *Fig.* to reveal something; to tell about a secret or a plan. (See also leak something out.) □ *It was supposed to be a secret. Who let it out?* □ *Who let out the secret?* **2.** *Fig.* to enlarge an article of clothing. □ *She had to let her overcoat out because she had gained some weight.* □ *I see you have had to let out your trousers.*

let something **out**[†] **(to** someone**)** to rent something to someone. □ *I let the back room out to a college boy.* □ *I let out the back room to someone.*

let something **pass** *Fig.* to let something go unnoticed or unchallenged. □ *Bob let Bill's insult pass because he didn't want to argue.* □ *Don't worry, I'll let this little incident pass.*

let something **ride** *Fig.* to allow something to continue or remain as it is. □ *It isn't the best plan, but we'll let it ride.* □ *I disagree with you, but I'll let it ride.*

let something **slide** Go to let things slide.

let something **slide by** Go to next.

let something **slip by** and **let** something **slide by 1.** *Lit.* to permit something to move quickly by oneself. □ *He let the ball slip by and he knew he had better get the next one.* □ *The careless cashier let the leaky milk carton slide by.* **2.** *Fig.* to forget or miss an important time or date. □ *I'm sorry I just let your birthday slip by.* □ *I let it slide by accidentally.* **3.** *Fig.* to waste a period of time. □ *You wasted the whole day by letting it slip by.* □ *We were having fun, and we let the time slide by.*

let something **slip (out)** *Fig.* to reveal a secret carelessly or by accident. □ *I didn't let it slip out on purpose. It was an accident.* □ *John let the plans slip when he was talking to Bill.*

L

Let the buyer beware. *Prov. Cliché* When you buy something, you must take precautions against being cheated, because you cannot trust merchants to be honest about what they sell. □ *Let the buyer beware when shopping for a used car.* □ *Several of the lamps among those Max offered for sale were broken. "If a customer isn't smart enough to try a lamp before he buys it, that's his problem," Max argued. "Let the buyer beware."*

let the cat out of the bag *Fig.* to reveal a secret or a surprise by accident. □ *When Bill glanced at the door, he let the cat out of the bag. We knew then that he was expecting someone to arrive.* □ *It's a secret. Try not to let the cat out of the bag.*

let the chance slip by *Fig.* to lose the opportunity (to do something). □ *When I was younger, I wanted to become a doctor, but I let the chance slip by.* □ *Don't let the chance slip by. Do it now!*

Let the chips fall where they may. *Prov.* Let something happen regardless of the consequences and no matter what happens. □ *I'm going to tell Ellen the truth about her husband, let the chips fall where they may.* □ *Kathy decided to risk her money on the investment, and let the chips fall where they may.*

Let the cobbler stick to his last. *Prov.* Do not advise someone in matters outside your area of expertise. □ *Whenever Ted, who is a lawyer, tried to give Bob suggestions about how to write his novel, Bob would say, "Let the cobbler stick to his last."* □ *Bill: I don't think you should put so much oregano in the spaghetti sauce. Nancy: You're a construction worker, not a chef. Let the cobbler stick to his last.*

Let the dead bury the dead. *Prov.* Do not try to revive old grievances.; Forget about past conflicts. (Biblical.) □ *The Nelson family and the Hopkins family had been feuding for decades, but when Andrew Nelson and Louise Hopkins declared that they wanted to get married, their families decided to let the dead bury the dead.*

Let them eat cake. *Prov.* A joking disclaimer of responsibility for some group of people. (Supposed to have been said by Marie Antoinette when she heard that the common people had no bread.) □ *Fred: The budget will allow each one of our managers to get a substantial holiday bonus. Jane: And what about the rest of the employees? Fred: Let them eat cake!*

let things slide and **let something slide** *Fig.* to ignore the things that one is supposed to do; to fall behind in the doing of one's work. □ *I am afraid that I let the matter slide while I was recovering from my operation.* □ *If I let things slide for even one day, I get hopelessly behind in my work.*

let up 1. to diminish. □ *I hope this rain lets up a little soon.* □ *When the snow lets up so I can see, I will drive to the store.* **2.** to stop [doing something] altogether. □ *The rain let up about noon, and the sun came out.*

let up (on someone or something**)** *Fig.* to reduce the pressure or demands on someone or something. □ *You had better let up on Tom. He can't handle any more work.* □ *Please let up on the committee. It can only do so much.* □ *Do let up. You are getting too upset.*

Let us do something**.** We will do something [together]. □ *Let us go in peace.* □ *Let us bow our heads in prayer.*

let well enough alone and **leave well enough alone** to leave things as they are (and not try to improve them). □ *There isn't much more you can accomplish here. Why don't you just let well enough alone?* □ *This is as good as I can do. I'll stop and leave well enough alone.*

level a charge against someone *Fig.* to place a charge against someone; to accuse someone of something. □ *The neighbors leveled a disturbance of the peace charge against us.* □ *The cops leveled an assault charge against Max.*

level off [for variation or fluctuation in the motion of something] to diminish; [for a rate] to stop increasing or decreasing. □ *The plane leveled off at 10,000 feet.* □ *After a while the workload will level off.* □ *Things will level off after we get through the end of the month.*

level out [for something that was going up and down] to assume a more level course or path. □ *The road leveled out after a while and driving was easier.* □ *As we got down into the valley, the land leveled out and traveling was easier.*

a **level playing field** *Fig.* a situation that is fair to all; a situation where everyone has the same opportunity. (See also **level the (playing) field.**) □ *If we started off with a level playing field, everyone would have an equal chance.*

level something **at** someone or something to direct something at someone or something; to aim a remark at someone. □ *The sheriff leveled his rifle at the fleeing bandit.* □ *Why did you think you had to level that barrage of words at me? I didn't make the problem.* □ *Sam leveled an acid comment or two at the committee.*

level something **down** to make something level or smooth. □ *The soil is very uneven in this part of the garden. Would you please level it down?* □ *The huge earth-moving machines leveled the hill down in preparation for the building of the highway.*

level something **off**† to make something level or smooth. □ *You are going to have to level the floor off before you put the carpet down.* □ *Please level off the floor.*

level something **out**† to cause something to assume a more level course or path. □ *Level this path out before you open it to the public.* □ *They have to level out this roadway.*

level something **to the ground** to crush or demolish something down to the ground. □ *They were forced to level the building to the ground, because they could not afford to maintain it.* □ *The house was leveled to the ground by the tornado.*

level something **up**† to move something into a level or plumb position. □ *Use a piece of wood under the table's leg to level it up.* □ *I will level up the table.*

level the (playing) field *Fig.* to create a state where everyone has the same opportunity. (See also a **level playing field.**) □ *Let's level the playing field and give everyone a chance.*

level with someone **(about** someone or something**)** *Fig.* to be straightforward with someone about something; to be sincere or truthful about someone or something. □ *The police encouraged the criminal to level with them about the crime.* □ *Level with me, and tell me what you thought of my cake.*

levy something **(up)on** someone or something to place a tax on someone or something. (*Upon* is formal and less commonly used than *on*.) □ *The Congress was very straight-*

L

forward. *It levied room taxes upon rich people.* □ *The city council levied a heavy tax on hotel guests.*

A liar is not believed (even) when he tells the truth. *Prov.* If people think that you are a liar, they will not believe anything you say. □ *As it turned out, Fred was right when he warned his friends that the police were planning to raid their party; but they paid no attention to him, since they knew him to be a liar, and a liar is not believed even when he tells the truth.*

liberate someone or something **from** someone or something to free someone or something from someone or something; to set someone or something free from the control of someone or something. □ *The police hoped to liberate the child from his kidnappers.* □ *We liberated the town from the enemy.* □ *I liberated the cat from the trap.*

license to do something permission, right, or justification to do something. □ *You have no license to behave in that manner!* □ *Who granted you license to enter my house without knocking?*

***a lick and a promise** *Fig.* a hasty bit of work; a quick once-over. (*Typically: **finish** something **with ~; give** something **~.**) □ *I was pressed for time, so I just gave the housework a lick and a promise.* □ *Mary spent so much time on her history paper that she had to finish her math homework with a lick and a promise.*

lick at something to draw the tongue over something repeatedly. □ *Jimmy was just licking at the ice-cream cone, and soon it began to melt and drip off his elbow.* □ *I don't just lick at the ice cream. I take big bites of it.*

a lick of work a bit of work. (Used with a negative.) □ *I couldn't get her to do a lick of work all day long!* □ *The boys didn't do a lick of work while you were away.*

lick one's **chops** *Fig.* to show one's eagerness to do something, especially to eat something. □ *We could tell from the way the boys were licking their chops that they really wanted a turn at riding the motorcycle.* □ *Fred started licking his chops when he smelled the turkey roasting in the oven.*

lick one's **lips** *Fig.* to show eagerness or pleasure about a future event. (From the habit of people licking their lips when they are about to enjoy eating something.) □ *The children licked their lips at the sight of the cake.* □ *The author's readers were licking their lips in anticipation of her new novel.*

lick one's **wounds** *Fig.* to recover from a defeat or a rebuke. (Also literal for an animal.) □ *After the terrible meeting and all the criticism, I went back to my office to lick my wounds.*

lick someone or something **into shape** to press or force someone or something into good shape or condition. □ *The drama coach will try to lick her into shape by performance time.* □ *Please try to lick this report into shape by tomorrow morning.*

lick something **into shape** and **whip** something **into shape** *Fig.* to put something into good condition, possibly with considerable effort. □ *I've got about two days more to lick this place into shape so I can sell it.* □ *I want to whip this house into shape for Saturday night.*

lick something **off (of)** something and **lick** something **off†** to remove something from something by licking with the

tongue. (*Of* is usually retained before pronouns.) □ *The dog licked the grease off of the floor where the meat had dropped.* □ *The dog licked off the grease.*

lick something **up†** to clean up all of some substance by licking with the tongue. (Usually said of an animal.) □ *Don't worry about the spilled milk. The dog will lick it up.* □ *The dog licked up the milk.*

***a licking** a spanking; a beating in a fight. (*Typically: **get ~; take ~; give** someone **~.**) □ *Billy, you had better get in here if you don't want to get a licking.* □ *Bob took a real licking in the stock market.* □ *Tom gave Harry a licking in the fight he was in.*

***a lid on** something **1.** *Lit.* a cover on something, such as a pot, pan, etc. (*Typically: **get ~; keep ~; put ~.**) □ *Keep the lid on the pot until the stew is almost done.* □ *Put the lid on the skillet for just a little while.* **2.** *Fig.* a scheme to suppress a scandalous or embarrassing situation and keep it secret. (*Typically: **get ~; keep ~; put ~.**) □ *We can't keep the lid on this any longer. The press has got wind of it.*

lie about 1. [for someone] to recline lazily somewhere. □ *She just lay about through her entire vacation.* □ *Don't lie about all the time. Get busy.* **2.** [for something] to be located somewhere casually and carelessly, perhaps for a long time. □ *This hammer has been lying about for a week. Put it away!* □ *Why are all these dirty dishes lying about?*

lie about someone or something **(to** someone**)** to say something untrue about someone or something to someone. □ *I wouldn't lie about my boss to anyone!* □ *I wouldn't lie about anything like that!*

lie ahead of someone or something and **lie before** someone or something **1.** to exist in front of someone or something. □ *A small cottage lay ahead of us near the trail.* □ *A huge mansion lay before the car at the end of the road.* **2.** to be fixed in the future of someone or something. □ *I just don't know what lies ahead of me.* □ *We don't know what lies before our country.*

lie alongside ((of) someone or an animal**)** to lie next to someone or an animal. (*Of* is usually retained before pronouns.) □ *Jimmy came in to lie alongside of his father in bed.* □ *The puppy lay alongside its mother.*

lie around (some place**)** to recline some place; to spend some time lazily in some place. □ *I think I will just lie around the house all day.* □ *I need to lie around every now and then.*

lie at anchor [for a ship] to wait or rest at anchor. □ *The ship lay at anchor throughout the day while a shore party searched for the runaway.* □ *We lay at anchor overnight, waiting for the tide.*

lie at death's door *Fig.* to be close to dying. □ *She lay at death's door for over a month.* □ *I do not want to lie at death's door suffering. I hope to pass on quickly.*

lie back to relax; to lean back in a chair and relax. (See also kick back.) □ *Just lie back and try to get comfortable.* □ *I really need to get home and lie back and relax.*

lie before someone or something Go to lie ahead of someone or something.

lie behind someone or something **1.** [for something] to be positioned to the rear of someone or something. □ *A wide expanse of water lay behind the sentry, and a narrow road-*

way lay in front. □ *A vast field lies behind the house.* **2.** [for something] to be in someone's or a group's past. □ *Now that all of our difficulties lie behind us, we can get on with our business.* □ *The busy season lay behind the company and people could take their vacations.*

lie below someone or something Go to **below** someone or something.

lie beyond someone or something **1.** to be located on the other side of someone or something. □ *The stream lies beyond those men you see working in the field.* □ *The village lies just beyond that hill there.* **2.** to be outside the grasp or the ability of someone or a group. □ *I am afraid that this matter lies beyond Dave.* □ *The solution lies beyond the power of the committee.*

lie doggo *Fig.* to remain unrecognized (for a long time). □ *This problem has lain doggo since 1967.* □ *If you don't find the typos now, they will lie doggo until the next edition.*

lie down to recline. □ *Why don't you lie down for a while?* □ *I need to lie down and have a little snooze.*

lie down on something to recline on something. □ *Don't lie down on that couch!* □ *I will just lie down on my bed for a few minutes.*

lie down on the job and **lay down on the job** *Fig.* to do one's job poorly or not at all. (*Lay* is a common error for *lie.*) □ *Tom was fired because he was laying down on the job.* □ *You mean he was lying down on the job, don't you?*

lie down under something to lie down beneath something. □ *She was tired, so she lay down under a willow tree by the brook.* □ *The dog lay down under a lawn chair and slept.*

lie fallow 1. *Lit.* [for farmland] to exist unplanted for a period of time. □ *The fields lay fallow under the burning sun. It had been too wet to plant last spring.* **2.** *Fig.* [for a skill and talent] to remain unused and neglected. □ *You should not let your talent lie fallow. Practice the piano before you forget how to play it.* □ *His writing had lain fallow for so long that he could hardly write a proper sentence.*

lie in [for a woman] to lie in bed awaiting the birth of her child. □ *The child is due soon, and the mother is lying in at the present time.* □ *She did not lie in at all. She worked right up to the onset of labor pains.*

lie in ruins to exist in a state of ruin, such as a destroyed city, building, scheme, plan, etc. □ *The entire city lay in ruins.* □ *My garden lay in ruins after the cows got in and trampled everything.*

lie in something to recline in something, such as a bed, a puddle, etc. □ *I found my wallet lying in a puddle. My money was soaked!* □ *We found Jimmy lying in a pile of leaves, napping.*

lie in state [for a dead body] to be on display for public mourning. □ *The president will lie in state in the Capitol Rotunda.* □ *Mourners filed past the leader where he lay in state.*

lie in store (for someone**)** Go to **in store (for** someone**)**.

lie in wait (for someone or something**)** *Fig.* to stay still and hidden, waiting for someone or something. □ *Bob was*

lying in wait for Anne so he could scold her about something. □ *The assassin lay in wait for his target to approach.*

lie like a rug *Sl.* to tell lies shamelessly. □ *He says he didn't take the money, but he's lying like a rug.* □ *I don't believe her. She lies like a rug.*

lie low and **lay low** *Fig.* to keep quiet and not be noticed; to avoid being conspicuous. (*Lay* is a common error for *lie.*) □ *I suggest you lie low for a few days.* □ *The robber said that he would lay low for a short time after the robbery.*

lie out (in something**)** to remain out (unenclosed or unprotected) in some area. □ *Who left my screwdriver lying out in the rain?* □ *It's not lying out. It's in the drawer.*

lie through one's **teeth** *Fig.* to lie boldly. □ *I knew she was lying through her teeth, but I didn't want to say so just then.* □ *If John denies it he's lying through his teeth, because I saw him do it.*

lie to someone **(about** someone or something**)** to tell an untruth about someone or something to someone. □ *You wouldn't lie to me about Sarah, would you?* □ *I'm not lying to you!*

lie (up)on someone Go to **(up)on** someone.

lie with someone **1.** to recline with someone. □ *Come and lie with me and we will keep warm.* □ *Jimmy and Franny were lying with each other to keep warm.* **2.** *Euph.* to recline with someone and have sex. □ *She claimed he asked her to lie with him.* □ *Do you mean to imply that she lay with him?*

lie within something to remain within a defined area or domain. □ *The boundaries of the village lie completely within the river valley.* □ *The cost you cited lies within the range I was considering.*

Life begins at forty. *Prov.* By the time you are forty years old, you have enough experience and skill to do what you want to do with your life. (Often said as an encouragement to those reaching middle age.) □ *Alan: Why are you so depressed? Jane: Tomorrow's my fortieth birthday. Alan: Cheer up! Life begins at forty.* □ *For Pete, life began at forty, because by that time he had enough financial security to enjoy himself now and then, rather than having to work all the time.*

life in the fast lane a very active or possible risky way to live. (See also **in the fast lane.**) □ *Life in the fast lane is too much for me.*

Life is just a bowl of cherries. *Prov.* Everything is going well.; Life is carefree. (Often used ironically, as in the second example.) □ *The real estate salesman tried to convince us that life in the suburbs is just a bowl of cherries.* □ *Jill: Hi, Jane. How are you? Jane: Oh, my alarm clock didn't go off this morning, and then my car wouldn't start, and I missed the bus and got to work late, and I just found out my rent's going up fifty dollars a month. Life is just a bowl of cherries.*

Life is short and time is swift. *Prov.* You should enjoy life as much as possible, because it does not last very long. □ *Jill: Want to go to the movies with me? Jane: Oh, I don't know; I should probably stay at work and finish a few things. Jill: Come on, Jane, life is short and time is swift.*

Life is too short. Life is short and there is no point in wasting it on things like worry, hatred, vengeance, etc. □ *I am not going to spend any more time trying to get even* with Wally. Life's too short. □ It's a waste of time worrying about money. Life is too short for that.

Life isn't all beer and skittles. *Prov.* Life is not pleasurable all the time; you cannot always be having fun. (Skittles is a game like bowling.) □ *I don't really mind going back to work when my vacation is over. Life isn't all beer and skittles, and I enjoy my fun that much more because I have work to compare it to.* □ *When George's parents stopped supporting him, George suddenly discovered that life isn't all beer and skittles.*

the **life of the party** *Fig.* a person who is lively and helps make a party fun and exciting. □ *Bill is always the life of the party. Be sure to invite him.* □ *Bob isn't exactly the life of the party, but he's polite.*

Life's been good (to me). I am grateful that I am doing well in life. □ *I can't complain. Life's been good to me.* □ *I am doing fine. Life's been good.*

lift a hand (against someone or something**)** and **raise a hand (against** someone or something**)** *Fig.* to threaten (to strike) someone or something. (Often in the negative. The *a hand* can be replaced with *one's hand*.) □ *She's very peaceful. She wouldn't lift a hand against a fly.* □ *Would you raise your hand against your own brother?*

lift off [for a plane or rocket] to move upward, leaving the ground. □ *The rocket lifted off exactly on time.*

lift one's elbow Go to **bend** one's **elbow.**

lift someone or something **down†** **(from** something**)** to move someone or something down (from something or some place) by lifting and carrying. □ *Would you please lift Jimmy down from the top bunk?* □ *Frank lifted down the heavy box.*

lift someone or something **up†** to raise someone or something. □ *I helped lift him up and put him on the stretcher.* □ *Please lift up Tommy.*

lift someone's **spirits** Go to someone's **spirits.**

lift something **from** someone or something to raise something off someone or something. □ *Please lift this burden from me.* □ *I lifted the glass from the tray carefully.*

lift something **off (of)** someone or something and **lift** something **off†** to raise something and uncover or release someone or something. (*Of* is usually retained before pronouns.) □ *Lift the beam off of him and see if he is still breathing.* □ *Please lift off the heavy lid.*

lift something **out of context** Go to **out of context.**

lift up to raise up. □ *Suddenly, the top of the box lifted up and a hand reached out.* □ *Bill's hand lifted up and fell back again.*

light a fire under someone Go to a **fire under** someone.

*light as a feather and ***light as air** *Cliché* light in weight; [of cakes and pastries] delicate and airy. (*Also: **as ~.**) □ *Carrying Esther from the car to the house was no problem; she was as light as a feather.* □ *What a delicious cake, Tom! And light as air, too.*

light as air Go to previous.

light into someone or something Go to **lace into** someone or something.

light out (for some place**)** Go to **cut out (for** some place**).**

light out (of some place**) (for** some place**)** *Fig.* to leave a place in a great hurry for some place. □ *I lit out of there for home as fast as I could.* □ *I lit out of there as fast as I could go.*

A **light purse makes a heavy heart.** *Prov.* If you do not have enough money, you will worry and be unhappy. □ *Nathan is a cheerful person by nature, but since he lost his job, worry has made him glum. A light purse makes a heavy heart.*

light someone or something **up†** to shine lights on someone or something. (See also **light** something **up.**) □ *We lit Fred up with the headlights of the car.* □ *Light up the stage and let's rehearse.*

light something **up†** **1.** to light a fire, a gas burner, etc. □ *I lit the kindling up and soon the fire was going.* □ *You light up the stove and get dinner going.* **2.** to light something to smoke, such as a cigarette, pipe, etc. (See also **light** someone or something **up.**) □ *She lit the cigarette up and took in a great breath of the smoke.* □ *She lit up a cigarette.*

light something **with** something **1.** to set something afire with something else. □ *Kelly lit the fire with her last match.* □ *I will light the fire with a cigarette lighter.* **2.** to illuminate something using something. □ *She lit the room with a few candles.* □ *We lit the Christmas tree with colored lights.*

light up 1. to become brighter. □ *Suddenly, the sky lit up like day.* □ *The room lit up as the fire suddenly came back to life.* **2.** [for someone] to become interested and responsive in something. □ *We could tell from the way Sally lit up that she recognized the man in the picture.* □ *She lit up when we told her about our team's success.*

light (up)on someone or something **1.** *Lit.* to land on someone or something; to settle on someone or something. (*Upon* is formal and less commonly used than *on*.) □ *Three butterflies lit on the baby, causing her to shriek with delight.* □ *The bees lit on the clover blossom and pulled it to the ground.* □ *Her glance lit upon a dress in the store window.* **2.** *Fig.* to arrive at something by chance; to happen upon something. □ *The committee lit upon a solution that pleased almost everyone.* □ *We just happened to light upon this idea as we were talking to each other.*

lighten something **up†** to make something lighter or brighter. □ *Some white paint will lighten this room up a lot.* □ *The sunlight came in and lightened up the kitchen.*

lighten up to become lighter or brighter. (See also **lighten up (on** someone or something**).**) □ *We applied a new coat of white paint to the walls, and the room lightened up considerably.* □ *The sky is beginning to lighten up a little.*

lighten up (on someone or something**)** to be less rough and demanding or rude with someone or something. (See also **lighten up.**) □ *Please lighten up on her. You are being very cruel.* □ *You are too harsh. Lighten up.*

Lightning never strikes (the same place) twice. *Prov.* The same highly unlikely thing never happens to the same person twice. □ *Jill: I'm scared to drive ever since that truck hit my car. Alan: Don't worry. Lightning never strikes the same place twice.* □ *It's strange, but I feel safer since my apartment was robbed; I figure lightning never strikes the same place twice.*

L

like a bat out of hell *Inf.* very fast or sudden. (Use caution with **hell**.) □ *The cat took off like a bat out of hell.* □ *The car pulled away from the curb like a bat out of hell.*

like a blind dog in a meat market *Rur.* out of control. □ *The drunk staggered out of the saloon like a blind dog in a meat market, stumbling all over the sidewalk.* □ *The kids tore through the museum like a blind dog in a meat market, touching everything they weren't supposed to touch.*

like a bolt from the blue Go to next.

like a bolt out of the blue and **like a bolt from the blue** *Fig.* suddenly and without warning. (Alludes to a bolt of lightning coming out of a clear blue sky.) □ *The news came to us like a bolt from the blue.* □ *Like a bolt out of the blue, the boss came and fired us all.*

like a bull in a china shop Go to a bull in a china shop.

like a bump on a log *Fig.* completely inert. (Derogatory.) □ *Don't just sit there like a bump on a log; give me a hand!* □ *You can never tell what Julia thinks of something; she just stands there like a bump on a log.*

like a can of corn *Rur.* very easy. □ *Whipping up dinner for twelve is like a can of corn, as far as Jane is concerned.* □ *The championship game was like a can of corn for our team. We won easily.*

like a fish out of water *Fig.* appearing to be completely out of place; in a very awkward manner. □ *Bob stood there in his rented tuxedo, looking like a fish out of water.* □ *Whenever I am with your friends, I feel like a fish out of water. What on earth do you see in them—or me?*

like a house on fire and **like a house afire** *Rur.* rapidly and with force. □ *The truck came roaring down the road like a house on fire.* □ *The crowd burst through the gate like a house afire.*

like a kid with a new toy *Fig.* very pleased; happily playing with something. □ *Every time Bill gets a new gadget for his kitchen, he's like a kid with a new toy.* □ *Jane is absorbed in that computer. Just like a kid with a new toy.*

like a lamb to the slaughter Go to like lambs to the slaughter.

like a million (dollars) *Fig.* very good or well. (Usually with verbs such as *feel, look, run,* etc.) □ *This old buggy runs like a million dollars.* □ *Man, I feel like a million.* □ *Your new hairdo looks like a million dollars.*

like a sitting duck Go to a sitting duck.

like a three-ring circus *Fig.* chaotic; exciting and busy. □ *Our household is like a three-ring circus on Monday mornings.* □ *This meeting is like a three-ring circus. Quiet down and listen!*

*like a ton of bricks *Inf.* like a great weight or burden. (*Typically: **fall ~; hit ~; hit** someone **~.**) □ *Suddenly, the truth hit me like a ton of bricks.* □ *The sudden tax increase hit like a ton of bricks. Everyone became angry.*

(like) an open book *Fig.* [of someone or something] easy to understand. □ *Jane's an open book. I always know what she is going to do next.* □ *The committee's intentions are an open book. They want to save money.*

Like breeds like. *Prov.* People tend to raise children who are like them; something tends to give rise to things that resemble it. □ *Jill: I think Fred's little boy is going to be just*

as disagreeable as Fred. Jane: That's no surprise. Like breeds like.

like crazy and **like mad** *Fig.* furiously; very much, fast, many, or actively. □ *People are coming in here like crazy. There isn't enough room for them all.* □ *We sold ice cream like crazy. It was a very hot day.*

*like death warmed over *Fig.* very ill; appearing very sickly. (*Typically: **feel ~; look ~.**) □ *Oh dear, I feel like death warmed over.* □ *Poor Carol said you look like death warmed over.*

like father, like son *Prov.* Fathers and sons resemble each other, and sons tend to do what their fathers did before them. □ *Jill: George's father smoked all the time, and now George is smoking excessively, too. Jane: Like father, like son, eh?* □ *I think my son will grow up tall, just like his father. Like father, like son.*

like fighting snakes *Rur.* chaotic; challenging. (As if every time one snake is subdued, another one attacks.) □ *It's like fighting snakes to get anything done at this time of year.* □ *Arguing with you is like fighting snakes.*

like flies to manure *Rur.* eagerly gathering in large numbers. (Has unpleasant connotations because of the reference to manure.) □ *Look at all them folks going to the freak show like flies to manure.* □ *The reporters hovered around the movie star like flies to manure.*

like gangbusters with great excitement and speed. (From the phrase "Come on like gangbusters," a radio show that "came on" with lots of noise and excitement.) □ *She works like gangbusters and gets the job done.* □ *They are selling tickets like gangbusters.*

like greased lightning *Rur.* very fast. □ *Once I get her tuned up, this old car will go like greased lightning.* □ *He's a fat kid, but he can run like greased lightning.*

like hell Go to like the devil.

like hell and high lightning *Rur.* very fast. □ *The snowmobiles came zooming down the trail like hell and high lightning.* □ *The powerboat sped up the river like hell and high lightning.*

like herding frogs *Rur.* chaotic; disorderly. (On the image of trying to direct frogs, which will jump any which way.) □ *Trying to get those kids to march into the auditorium is like herding frogs.* □ *Trying to get everybody to cooperate is like herding frogs.*

like I was saying Go to as I was saying.

Like it or lump it! *Inf.* There is no other choice. Take that or none. □ *John: I don't like this room. It's too small. Bill: Like it or lump it. That's all we've got.* □ *Jane: I don't want to be talked to like that. Sue: Well, like it or lump it! That's the way we talk around here.*

Like it's such a big deal! *Inf.* It really isn't all that important! (Sarcastic.) □ *So I dropped the glass. Like it's such a big deal.* □ *Like it's such a big deal. Who cares?*

like it was going out of style *Fig.* rapidly or frequently. □ *I'm worried about Sally. She's taking aspirin like it's going out of style.* □ *The kids have been eating sweet corn like it was going out of style.*

like lambs to the slaughter and **like a lamb to the slaughter** *Fig.* quietly and without seeming to realize the likely difficulties or dangers of a situation. □ *Young men* *fighting in World War I simply went like lambs to the slaughter.* □ *Our team went on the football field like lambs to the slaughter to meet the league-leaders.*

like looking for a needle in a haystack *Fig.* engaged in a hopeless search. □ *Trying to find a white glove in the snow is like looking for a needle in a haystack.* □ *I tried to find my lost contact lens on the beach, but it was like looking for a needle in a haystack.*

like mad Go to like crazy.

Like mother, like daughter. *Prov.* Daughters resemble their mothers.; Daughters tend to do what their mothers did before them. □ *My mother loved sweets, and every time my father saw me with a cookie in my hand, he would sigh, "Like mother, like daughter."* □ *Jill: Gina's beautiful. Jane: Like mother, like daughter; her mother's gorgeous, too.*

like nobody's business *Inf.* very well; very much. □ *She can sing like nobody's business. What a set of pipes!* □ *My mom can cook chocolate chip cookies like nobody's business.*

like nothing on earth 1. *Fig.* very untidy or very unattractive. □ *Joan arrived at the office looking like nothing on earth. She had fallen in the mud.* □ *Alice was like nothing on earth in that electric yellow dress.* **2.** *Fig.* very unusual; very distinctive. □ *The new car models look like nothing on earth this year.* □ *This cake is so good! It's like nothing on earth!*

like one of the family as if someone (or a pet) were a member of one's family. □ *We treat our dog like one of the family.* □ *We are very happy to have you stay with us, Bill. I hope you don't mind if we treat you like one of the family.*

like pigs to the slaughter *Rur.* obediently and in large numbers. (See also like lambs to the slaughter.) □ *Look at all the people lining up to mail their tax forms on time, like pigs to the slaughter.*

like rats abandoning a sinking ship Go to Rats abandon a sinking ship.

like shooting fish in a barrel and **as easy as shooting fish in a barrel** *Rur.* ridiculously easy. □ *Jane's a good mechanic. Changing a tire is like shooting fish in a barrel, for her.* □ *That comedian has an easy job. Making fun of politicians is like shooting fish in a barrel.*

like stealing acorns from a blind pig *Rur.* very easy. □ *Getting Mary to sign the house over to me was like stealing acorns from a blind pig.* □ *Tom: Was it hard to fool so many people? Charlie: Nope. It was like stealing acorns from a blind pig.*

***like stink** *Inf.* rapidly. (As fast as a smell spreads. *Typically:* **go ~; move ~; run ~; swim ~**.) □ *Those kids moved through the whole test like stink. Real eager-beavers.* □ *The wood chipper went through the brush like stink and turned it into a small pile in minutes.*

like taking candy from a baby and **as easy as taking candy from a baby** *Cliché* very easy. □ *Getting to the airport was easy. It was like taking candy from a baby.*

***like the devil** and ***like the dickens; *like hell** *Fig.* with a fury; in a great hurry; with a lot of activity. (*Typically:* **fight ~; run ~; scream ~; thrash around ~**.) □ *We were working like the dickens when the rain started and made us quit for the day.*

***like the dickens** Go to previous.

***like the wind** *Fig.* very fast; as fast and easy as the wind. (*Typically:* **go ~; move ~; run ~**.) □ *Emily's sleek new bicycle can really go like the wind.* □ *The racehorse ran like the wind, beating its nearest opponent by several lengths.*

like there ain't no tomorrow Go to next.

like there's no tomorrow and **like there ain't no tomorrow** *Rur.* eagerly; rapidly; without stopping. □ *You can't go on eating candy bars like there's no tomorrow.* □ *Jim's spending money like there's no tomorrow.*

like to *Rur.* almost. □ *I like to died laughing when I saw Jim come in wearing a dress.* □ *Mary like to passed out when she saw how bad her house was damaged in the storm.*

like to hear oneself **talk** [for someone] to enjoy one's own talking more than people enjoy listening to it. □ *I guess I don't really have anything to say. I just like to hear myself talk, I guess.* □ *There he goes again. He just likes to hear himself talk.*

like tryin' to scratch your ear with your elbow *Rur.* impossible. □ *Getting those kids to settle down is like tryin' to scratch your ear with your elbow.* □ *Fixing all the leaks in that old roof is like tryin' to scratch your ear with your elbow.*

like (two) peas in a pod *Cliché* very close or intimate. (Compare this with as alike as (two) peas in a pod.) □ *Yes, they're close. Like two peas in a pod.* □ *They're always together. Like peas in a pod.*

like water off a duck's back *Fig.* easily; without any apparent effect. □ *Insults rolled off John like water off a duck's back.* □ *The bullets had no effect on the steel door. They fell away like water off a duck's back.*

like, you know *Inf.* a combining of the (essentially meaningless) expressions *like* and *you know*. (Never used in formal writing.) □ *She is, well, like, you know, uncool.* □ *This is, well, like, you know, too much!*

***likely as not** *Fig.* probably; with an even chance either way. (*Also:* **as ~.**) □ *He will as likely as not arrive without warning.* □ *Likely as not, the game will be canceled.*

liken someone or something **to** someone or something to compare someone or something to someone or something, concentrating on the similarities. □ *He is strange. I can only liken him to an eccentric millionaire.* □ *The poet likened James to a living statue of Mercury.*

the likes of someone or something someone or something similar to that person or thing; the equal or equals of someone or something. □ *I never want to see the likes of you again!* □ *We admired the splendid old ships, the likes of which will never be built again.*

Likewise(, I'm sure). *Fig.* The same from my point of view. (A hackneyed phrase said in greeting someone. See examples.) □ *Alice: I'm delighted to make your acquaintance. Bob: Likewise, I'm sure.* □ *John: How nice to see you! Sue: Likewise. John: Where are you from, Sue?*

limber someone or something **up**† to make someone or something more flexible or loose. □ *Let me give you a massage; that will limber you up.* □ *I need to limber up my arms.*

limit someone **to** something **1.** to restrict someone to a certain amount or number of something. □ *I will have to limit you to two helpings of mashed potatoes.* □ *I limit* myself to cola drinks only. **2.** to restrict someone to a certain area. □ *Please try to limit your children to your own yard.* □ *They limited themselves to the north side of town.*

limit something **to** something to restrict something to a limited set, a certain amount, or a specific number of something. □ *Please limit your comments to five minutes.* □ *Can you limit your remarks to the subject at hand?*

the **line of least resistance** the course of action that will cause least trouble or effort. □ *Jane won't stand up for her rights. She always takes the line of least resistance.* □ *Joan never states her point of view. She takes the line of least resistance and agrees with everyone else.*

*a **line on** someone or something *Fig.* an idea on how to locate someone or something; an idea for finding someone who can help with someone or something. (*Typically: **get** ~; **have** ~; **give** someone ~.) □ *I got a line on a book that might help explain what you want to know.* □ *Sally has a line on someone who could help you fix up your apartment.*

line one's **own pocket(s)** *Fig.* to make money for oneself in a greedy or dishonest fashion. □ *They are interested in lining their pockets first and serving the people second.* □ *You can't blame them for wanting to line their own pockets.*

line someone or something **up†** **1.** *Lit.* to put people or things in line. □ *Line everyone up and march them onstage.* □ *Line up the kids, please.* □ *Please line these books up.* □ *Hey, you guys! Line yourselves up!* **2.** *Fig.* to schedule someone or something [for something]. □ *Please line somebody up for the entertainment.* □ *We will try to line up a magician and a clown for the party.* □ *They lined up a chorus for the last act.*

line someone or something **up†** **against** something to put people or things into a row in front of or against something. □ *We lined everyone up against the wall for the photograph.* □ *Please line up everyone against the wall.*

line someone or something **up†** **behind** someone or something to put people or things into a line behind someone or something. □ *Please line all the children up behind the tallest child.* □ *Line up everyone behind the curtain.*

line someone or something **up†** **(in** something**)** to put people or things into some kind of formation, such as a row, column, ranks, etc. □ *The teacher lined the children up in two rows.* □ *Please line up the children in a row.*

line someone or something **up†** **on** something to place people or things into a line oriented on one or more things. □ *Line them all up on the edge of the grass.* □ *Line up the children on the white line.*

line someone or something **up†** **with** someone or something **1.** *Lit.* to place people or things into a line with other people or things. □ *Line Fred up with the others.* □ *Line up these books with the others.* □ *Please line yourselves up with the others.* **2.** *Lit.* to place people or things into a line that is oriented on someone or something. □ *Line everyone up with the flagpole so we can march into the hall.* □ *Please line up everyone with the flagpole straight ahead.* **3.** *Fig.* to schedule a meeting date with someone or a group of people. □ *Will you line everyone up with us for a Monday morning meeting?* □ *See if you can line up a meeting with Todd and Frank.*

line someone or something **up†** **with** something to position someone or something (or a group) in reference to other things. □ *Please line the chairs up with the floor tiles.* □ *Line up this brick with the bricks below and at both sides. That's the way you lay bricks.*

line someone **up†** **behind** someone or something *Fig.* to organize people in support of someone or something. □ *I will see if I can line a few supporters up behind our candidate.* □ *I can line up everyone behind you.*

line someone **up†** **(for** something**)** *Fig.* to schedule someone for something; to arrange for someone to do or be something. □ *I lined gardeners up for the summer work on the gardens.* □ *I lined up four of my best friends to serve as ushers at my wedding.*

line someone **up†** **(with** someone**)** Go to **fix** someone **up† (with** someone**)**.

line something **with** something to place a layer of something over the inside surface of something. □ *You should line the drawers with clean paper before you use them.* □ *I want to line this jacket with new material.*

line up to form a line; to get into a line. □ *All right, everyone, line up!*

line up against someone or something to organize against someone or something. □ *Our people lined up against the candidate and defeated her soundly.* □ *We will line up against the opposing party as we did during the last election.*

line up alongside someone or something to form or get into a line beside someone or something. □ *Can you line up alongside the other people?* □ *Line up alongside the wall and get ready to be photographed.*

line up behind someone or something **1.** to form or get into a line behind someone or something. □ *Please line up behind Kelly.* □ *Please go and line up behind the sign.* **2.** and **get behind** someone or something to organize in support of someone or something. □ *We all got behind Todd and got him elected.* □ *We got behind the most active political party.*

line up for something to form or get into a line and wait for something. □ *Everyone lined up for a helping of birthday cake.* □ *Let's line up for dinner. The doors to the dining room will open at any minute.*

line up in(to) something to form or get into a line, row, rank, column, etc. □ *Please line up in three columns.* □ *I wish you would all line up into a nice straight line.*

line up on something to form a line oriented on something. □ *Line up on the white line painted on the pavement.* □ *Please line up on the marks on the floor.*

line up with someone to get into a line with someone. □ *Go over and line up with the others.* □ *Would you please line up with the other students?*

linger around to wait around; to be idle some place. □ *Don't linger around. Get going!* □ *All the students were lingering around, waiting until the last minute to go into the building.*

linger on to remain for a long time; to exist longer than would have been thought. □ *This cold of mine just keeps lingering on.* □ *Some of the guests lingered on for a long time after the party was over.*

linger on (after someone or something**)** and **stay on (after** someone or something**)** to outlast someone or something; to live longer than someone else or long after an event. □ *Aunt Sarah lingered on only a few months after Uncle Herman died.* □ *She lingered on and was depressed for a while.*

linger on something to delay moving on to the next thing; to remain at something and not move on. □ *Don't linger on that one problem so long.* □ *I don't want to waste a lot of time lingering on this question.*

linger over something **1.** to take too much time or idle over something, such as a meal, a cup of coffee, etc. □ *I could linger over coffee all morning, given the chance.* □ *Don't linger over your soup. It will get cold.* **2.** to dawdle over the doing of something. □ *You shouldn't linger over eating your dinner.* □ *It would be best not to linger over making up your mind.*

link someone or something **to** someone or something and **link** someone or something **and** someone or something **together; link** someone or something **together with** someone or something; **link** someone or something **with** someone or something **1.** to discover a connection between people and things, in any combination. □ *I would never have thought of linking Fred to Tom. I didn't even know they knew each other.* □ *I always sort of linked Tom with honesty.* **2.** to connect people and things, in any combination. □ *We have to link each person to one other person, using this colored yarn to tie them together.* □ *We linked each decoration together with another one.*

link someone or something **up**[†] **(to** something**)** to connect someone or something to something, usually with something that has a type of fastener or connector that constitutes a link. □ *They promised that they would link me up to the network today.* □ *They will link up my computer to the network today.*

link someone or something **with** someone or something Go to **link** someone or something **to** someone or something.

link up to someone or something and **link (up) with** someone or something to join up with someone or something. □ *I have his new e-mail address so I can link up to Bruce.* □ *Now my computer can link up with a computer bulletin board.*

the **lion's share of** something**)** *Fig.* the largest portion of something. □ *I earn a lot, but the lion's share goes for taxes.* □ *The lion's share of the surplus cheese goes to school cafeterias.*

liquor someone **up**[†] to get someone tipsy or drunk. □ *He liquored her up and tried to take her home with him.* □ *They liquored up the out-of-town visitors.*

liquor up to drink an alcoholic beverage, especially to excess. □ *Sam sat around all evening liquoring up.* □ *They seem to liquor up almost every night of the week.*

list someone **as** something to categorize someone as someone, usually in a written list. □ *I will list you as a contributor to the Preservation Fund, if you don't mind.* □ *Although she was not registered as such, she listed herself as a stockbroker.*

list someone or something **among** something to include someone or something in a particular category. □ *I list*

George among the all-time greats. □ *I have to list the budget committee as the most efficient ever.*

list someone or something **off**[†] to recite a list of people or things, one by one. □ *She listed everyone off in order without having to look at her notes.* □ *She listed off the names of the people who are always late.* □ *Dale listed each one off.*

list to a direction to lean to one side or another; to lean toward a specific direction. (Usually of ships or boats.) □ *The ship had listed to one side since being struck by the speedboat.* □ *The huge ship listed a tiny bit to starboard.*

listen for someone or something to try to hear someone or something. □ *I will have to let you in the front door if you come home late. I will listen for you.* □ *I am listening for the telephone.*

listen in (on someone or something**) 1.** to join someone or a group as a listener. □ *The band is rehearsing. Let's go listen in on them.* □ *It won't hurt to listen in, will it?* **2.** to eavesdrop on someone. □ *Please don't try to listen in on us. This is a private conversation.* □ *I am not listening in. I was here first. You are talking too loud.*

listen to reason to yield to a reasonable argument; to take the reasonable course. □ *Please listen to reason, and don't do something you'll regret.* □ *She got into trouble because she wouldn't listen to reason.*

listen to someone or something **1.** to pay attention to and hear someone or something. □ *Listen to me! Hear what I have to say!* □ *I want to listen to his speech.* **2.** to heed someone, orders, or advice. □ *Listen to me! Do what I tell you!* □ *You really should listen to his advice.*

listen up to listen carefully. (Usually a command.) □ *Now, listen up! This is important.* □ *Listen up, you guys!*

Listeners never hear any good of themselves. Go to Eavesdroppers never hear any good of themselves.

litmus test 1. *Lit.* a test used to determine the acidity or alkalinity of chemical substances. (Acid turns litmus paper red and alkaline compounds turn it blue.) □ *I used a litmus test to show that the compound was slightly acid.* **2.** *Fig.* a question or experiment that seeks to determine the state of one important factor. □ *His performance on the long exam served as a litmus test to determine whether he would go to college.* □ *The amount of white cells in my blood became the litmus test for diagnosing my disease.*

litter something **about** and **litter** something **around** to cast around something, such as trash, clothing, personal possessions, etc. □ *Don't litter all that stuff about.* □ *I wish you wouldn't litter your trash around.*

litter something **up**[†] to mess something up with litter, trash, possessions, etc. □ *Who littered this room up?* □ *Who littered up this room?*

Little and often fills the purse. *Prov.* If you get a little bit of money frequently, you will always have enough. □ *Jill: I don't think I'll ever be able to save very much; I can only afford to save such a little bit of money from every paycheck. Jane: Ah, but little and often fills the purse.*

A **little bird told me.** *Fig.* a way of indicating that you do not want to reveal who told you something. (Sometimes used playfully, when you think that the person you are addressing knows or can guess who was the source of your information.) □ *Jill: Thank you for the beautiful pre-*

sent! How did you know I wanted a green silk scarf? *Jane: A little bird told me.* □ *Bill: How did you find out it was my birthday? Jane: A little bird told me.*

a **little bit (of** something**)** a small amount; some. □ *Can I have a little bit of candy?* □ *I need a little bit of time to finish this essay.*

little bitty very little. □ *Can I have just a little bitty piece of that lemon meringue pie?* □ *He was just a little bitty boy.*

little by little gradually, a little bit at a time. □ *I earned enough money, little by little, to buy a car.* □ *Jimmy crawled, little by little, until he reached the door.*

A **little (hard) work never hurt anyone.** and A **little (hard) work never killed anyone.** *Prov.* One should expect to do hard or difficult work and not avoid doing it. □ *Go help your father with the yard work. A little hard work never hurt anyone.* □ *Go ahead. Bring me some more bricks. A little work never killed anyone.*

A **little knowledge is a dangerous thing.** and A **little learning is a dangerous thing.** *Prov. Cliché* If you only know a little about something, you may feel you are qualified to make judgments when, in fact, you are not. □ *After Bill read one book on the history of Venezuela, he felt he was an authority on the subject, but he wound up looking like a fool in discussions with people who knew a lot more about it than he did. A little learning is a dangerous thing.*

(a little) new to (all) this an apologetic way of saying that one is experiencing something new or participating in something new. □ *I'm sorry I'm slow. I'm a little new to all this.* □ *She's new to this. She needs practice.*

a **(little) nip in the air** a cold feeling; cold weather. □ *I felt a little nip in the air when I opened the window.* □ *There's more of a nip in the air as winter approaches.*

a **little off** Go to a bit off.

little old someone or something ordinary; harmless. (Said to downplay or minimize the importance of something.) □ *Aw, honey, I wasn't gambling. I just went to one little old poker game.* □ *Charlie: Did you eat that whole chocolate cake that I was saving for the party? Jane: Little old me?*

Little pitchers have big ears. *Prov.* Children like to listen to adult conversations and can understand a lot of what they hear. (Used to warn another adult not to talk about something because there is a child present.) □ *I started to tell Mary about the date I had on Saturday, but she interrupted me, saying, "Little pitchers have big ears," and looked pointedly at her six-year-old daughter, who was in the room with us.*

a **little pricey** Go to a **little steep.**

little shaver *Rur.* a child; a baby. □ *I think the little shaver needs her diaper changed.* □ *Tom thinks his grandson is the cutest little shaver there ever was.*

a **(little) short on one end** *Rur.* short. □ *You'll recognize Bill right away. He's got red hair, and he's a little short on one end.* □ *He's not small; he's just short on one end.* □ *The barber cut my hair a little short on one end.*

a **little steep** and a **little pricey** *Fig.* relatively expensive; costing more than one wants to pay. □ *The food here is a little pricey, but you get a lot of it.*

Little strokes fell great oaks. *Prov.* You can complete a large, intimidating task by steadily doing small parts of

it. □ *Jill: How can I possibly write a fifty-page report in two months? Jane: Just write a little bit every day. Little strokes fell great oaks.*

Little thieves are hanged, but great ones escape. *Prov.* Truly expert criminals are never caught. □ *Everyone's making such a fuss because they convicted that bank robber, but he must not have been a very dangerous criminal. Little thieves are hanged, but great ones escape.*

Little things please little minds. and **Small things please small minds.** *Prov.* People who are not intelligent are pleased by trivial things. (Implies that the person you are talking about is not intelligent.) □ *Jill: Nathaniel's been awfully cheerful today. Jane: Yes, his favorite TV show is on tonight. Jill: Little things please little minds, they say.*

a **little white lie** *Fig.* a small, usually harmless lie; a fib. □ *Every little white lie you tell is still a lie and it is still meant to mislead people.*

live a dog's life Go to lead a dog's life.

live a life of something to have a life of a certain quality or style. □ *The movie star lived a life of luxury.* □ *After Anne won the lottery, she lived the life of a queen.*

live above someone or something and **live over** someone or something to live in a place that is at a higher level than someone or something; to dwell directly over someone or something. □ *We used to live above a small grocery store.* □ *Now we live over a student, who often has noisy parties.*

live among someone to live in a community with someone or a community made up of certain people. □ *The anthropologist lived among the small tribe for two years.* □ *They lived among the Jivaro Indians for a brief period.*

live and learn *Cliché* to increase one's knowledge by experience. (Usually said when one is surprised to learn something.) □ *I didn't know that snakes could swim. Well, live and learn!* □ *John didn't know he should water his houseplants a little extra in the dry winter months. When they all died, he said, "Live and learn."*

live and let live *Cliché* not to interfere with other people's business or preferences. □ *I don't care what they do! Live and let live, I always say.* □ *Your parents are strict. Mine just live and let live.*

live apart (from someone**)** to live separated from a person whom one might be expected to live with. □ *John lives apart from his wife, who has a job in another city.* □ *He lives apart, but they are still married.*

live around someone or something Go to **around** someone or something.

live beyond one's **means** to spend more money than one can afford. □ *The Browns are deeply in debt because they are living beyond their means.* □ *I keep a budget so that I don't live beyond my means.*

live by one's **wits** *Fig.* to survive by being clever. □ *When you're in the kind of business I'm in, you have to live by your wits.* □ *John was orphaned at the age of ten and grew up living by his wits.*

live by something **1.** to live near something. □ *We live by a lovely park that is filled with children in the summer.* □ *I would love to live by the sea.* **2.** to survive by doing or using something in particular. (See also **live by** one's wits.) □ *She lives by her own skill and hard work.* □ *We live by the skills that we have—and hard work, of course.*

Live by the sword, die by the sword. *Prov.* If you use violence against other people, you can expect to have violence used against you.; You can expect to become a victim of whatever means you use to get what you want. (Biblical.) □ *The gang leader who organized so many murders was eventually murdered himself. Live by the sword, die by the sword.* □ *Bill liked to spread damaging gossip about other people, until he lost all his friends because of some gossip that was spread about him. Live by the sword, die by the sword.*

live for someone or something **1.** to exist for the benefit of someone or something. □ *She just lives for her children.* □ *Roger lives for his work.* **2.** to exist to enjoy someone or something. □ *She lives for her vacations in Acapulco.*

live for the moment *Fig.* to live only for the pleasures of the present time without planning for the future. □ *You need to make plans for your future. You cannot live just for the moment!* □ *He lives only for the moment.*

live from day to day *Fig.* to survive on limited means one day at a time with no plans or possibilities for the future. □ *The Simpsons just live from day to day. They never plan for the future.* □ *I can't live from day to day. I have to provide for the future.*

live from hand to mouth *Fig.* to live in poor circumstances. □ *When both my parents were out of work, we lived from hand to mouth.* □ *We lived from hand to mouth during the war. Things were very difficult.*

live happily ever after *Cliché* to live in happiness after a specific event. (A formulaic phrase at the end of fairy tales.) □ *The prince and the princess lived happily ever after.* □ *They went away from the horrible haunted castle and lived happily ever after.*

live high off the hog and **live high on the hog; eat high on the hog** *Rur.* to live well and eat good food. (Note the variation with *pretty.*) □ *After they discovered oil on their land, they lived pretty high on the hog.* □ *Looks like we're living high off the hog tonight. What's the occasion?*

live in to live at the residence at which one works. □ *In order to be here early enough to prepare breakfast, the cook has to live in.* □ *Mr. Simpson has a valet, but he doesn't live in.*

live in a world of one's **own** Go to in a world of one's own.

live in an ivory tower Go to in an ivory tower.

live in hope(s) of something to live with the hope that something will happen. □ *I have been living in hopes that you would come home safely.* □ *Greg lives in hope of winning a million dollars in the lottery.*

live in sin to live with and have sex with someone to whom one is not married. (Sometimes serious and sometimes jocular.) □ *Would you like to get married, or would you prefer that we live in sin for a few more years?* □ *Let's live in sin. There's no risk of divorce.*

live in something to dwell within something or some place. □ *They live in the village.* □ *She lives in a large house in the country.*

live in the best of both worlds Go to the best of both worlds.

live in the boonies Go to in the boondocks.

live in the fast lane Go to in the fast lane.

live in the past *Fig.* to live while dwelling on past memories without participating in the present or planning for the future. □ *You are just living in the past. Join us in the twenty-first century.* □ *Living in the past has its advantages.*

live in the poorhouse Go to in the poorhouse.

live in the present *Fig.* to deal with contemporary events and not be dominated by events of the past or planning for the future. □ *Forget the past; live in the present.* □ *It was no longer possible to get Uncle Herman to live in the present.*

live in (with someone**)** [for servants or lovers] to live in a residence that one might be expected only to visit rather than reside in. □ *Their maid lives in with them.* □ *She lived in for a few months before they were married.*

live it up to have an exciting time; to do what one pleases—regardless of cost—to please oneself. □ *At the party, John was really living it up.* □ *Come on! Have fun! Live it up!*

live large to live in luxury; to spend time in grand style. □ *George loved to live large, dining at fine French restaurants.*

live like a marked man Go to a marked man.

live next door (to someone**)** to live in the house or dwelling next to someone. □ *I live next door to John.* □ *John lives next door to me.* □ *John lives next door.*

live off campus Go to off campus.

live off (of) someone or something to obtain one's living or means of survival from someone or something. (*Of* is usually retained before pronouns.) □ *You can't live off your uncle all your life!* □ *I manage to live off of my salary.*

live off the fat of the land *Fig.* to live on stored-up resources or abundant resources. □ *If I had a million dollars, I'd invest it and live off the fat of the land.* □ *I'll be happy to retire soon and live off the fat of the land.*

live off the land to live by eating only the food that one produces from the land; to survive by gathering or stealing food, fruits, berries, eggs, etc., while traveling through the countryside. □ *We lived off the land for a few years when we first started out farming.* □ *The homeless man wandered about, living off the land.*

live on (after someone**)** to outlive someone. □ *Aunt Sarah lived on after Uncle Herman only a short time.* □ *She had hoped to live on after him and have some fun.*

live on (after someone or something**)** to be remembered long after someone or something might otherwise be forgotten or dead, in the case of persons. □ *His good works will live on long after him.* □ *Fears of war will live on after the actual conflict.* □ *I hope my memory lives on.*

live on an amount of money to live on a specific amount of money; to manage to live on a specific amount of money. □ *Can you live on only that much money?* □ *I can live on a very small amount of money.*

live on borrowed time *Fig.* to exist only because of good fortune; to live on when death was expected. □ *The doc-*

tors told him he was living on borrowed time. □ *You are living on borrowed time, so make the best of it.*

live on one's **own** to live independently, in a separate dwelling. □ *I moved out of my parents' house because I wanted to live on my own for a while.* □ *It's time you were out living on your own.*

live on something to depend on something for sustenance. (Compare this with **live off** someone or something.) □ *I can't live on bread and water.* □ *We can hardly live on $500 a week.*

live on the edge Go to on the edge.

live out of a suitcase *Fig.* to stay very briefly in several places, never unpacking one's luggage. □ *I hate living out of a suitcase. For my next vacation, I want to go to just one place and stay there the whole time.*

live out of cans *Fig.* to eat only canned food. □ *You have to have some fresh fruit and vegetables. You can't just live out of cans.* □ *We lived out of cans for the entire camping trip.*

live out one's **days** and **live out** one's **life** to live for the remainder of one's life. (Usually with some reference to a place.) □ *Where do you plan to live out your days?* □ *I will live out my life in sunny Florida.*

live over someone or something Go to **live above** someone or something.

live something **down**† to overcome the shame or embarrassment of something. □ *You'll live it down someday.* □ *Wilbur will never be able to live down what happened at the party last night.*

live something **out**† to act out something such as one's fantasies. □ *She tried to live her dreams out.* □ *He has a tendency to try to live out his fantasies.*

live something **over** to go back and live a part of one's life again in order to do things differently. □ *I wish I could go back and live those days over again. Boy, would I do things differently!* □ *I would like to live that period of my life over again.*

live the life of Riley Go to **lead the life of Riley**.

live through something to endure something; to survive an unpleasant or dangerous time of one's life. □ *I almost did not live through the operation.* □ *I know I can't live through another attack.*

live to do something **1.** to survive long enough to do something. □ *I just hope I live to see them get married and have children.* □ *Bill wants to live to see his grandchildren grow up.* **2.** to exist only to do something. □ *He lives to work.* □ *One shouldn't live to eat.*

live to the (ripe old) age of something to survive to a specific [advanced] age. □ *Sally's aunt lived to the ripe old age of one hundred.* □ *Ken lived to the age of sixty-two.*

live together 1. [for two people] to dwell in the same place. □ *I live together with my sister in the house my parents left us.* □ *Henry and Jill live together in their parents' house.* **2.** [for two people] to dwell together in a romantic relationship. □ *I heard that Sally and Sam are living together.* □ *They are living together and may get married.*

live (together) with someone [for someone] to live with someone else. □ *She lives together with her sister in a condo.* □ *He lives with his family.*

live under someone or something to dwell directly beneath someone or something. □ *We live under the Johnsons. They are fairly quiet.* □ *We lived under a law office for a few years.*

live under something (negative) to exist under some kind of worry or threat. □ *I can't continue to live under the threat of bankruptcy all the time.* □ *It is hard to live under the worry of another war.*

live under the same roof (with someone**)** *Fig.* to share a dwelling with someone. (Implies living in a close relationships, as a husband and wife.) □ *I don't think I can go on living under the same roof with her.* □ *She was quite happy to live under the same roof with him.*

live up to one's **end of the bargain** and **keep** one's **side of the bargain; live up to** one's **side of the bargain; keep** one's **end of the bargain** to carry though on a bargain; to do as was promised in a bargain. □ *You can't quit now. You have to live up to your end of the bargain.* □ *Bob isn't keeping his end of the bargain, so I am going to sue him.*

live up to something to fulfill expectations; to satisfy a goal or set of goals. (Often with one's reputation, promise, word, standards, etc.) □ *I hope I can live up to my reputation.* □ *The class lives up to its reputation of being exciting and interesting.*

live with someone *Euph.* to live together with someone; to live in a romantic relationship with someone outside of marriage. □ *I lived with my aunt when I was growing up.* □ *Is Frank living with his girlfriend?* □ *Sandy is living with her domestic partner.*

live with something to put up with something; to endure something. (Does not mean "to dwell with.") □ *That is not acceptable. I can't live with that. Please change it.* □ *Mary refused to live with the proposed changes.*

live within one's **means** to spend no more money than one has. □ *We have to struggle to live within our means, but we manage.* □ *John is unable to live within his means.*

live within something **1.** to live within certain boundaries. □ *Do you think you can live within your space, or are we going to argue over the use of square footage?* □ *Ted demanded again that Bill live within his assigned area.* **2.** to keep one's living costs within a certain amount, especially within one's budget, means, etc. □ *Please try to live within your budget.* □ *You must learn to live within your take-home pay every month.*

live without something to survive, lacking something. □ *I just know I can't live without my car.* □ *I am sure we can live without vegetables for a day or two.*

live worlds apart Go to **worlds apart**.

liven something **up**† to make something more lively or less dull. □ *Some singing might liven things up a bit.* □ *The songs livened up the evening.*

the **living end** *Fig.* the absolute best [person]. □ *We really like Ralph. He is the living end as far as his girlfriend is concerned.*

Lo and behold! *Cliché* Look here!; Thus! (An expression of surprise.) □ *Lo and behold! There is Fred! He beat us here by taking a shortcut.*

load into something [for people] to get into something. □ *Everyone loaded into the bus, and we set off for Denver.* □ *The kids all loaded into the station wagon for the trip.*

*a **load off** one's **feet** *Fig.* the weight of one's body no longer supported by one's feet, as when one sits down. (*Typically: **get** ~; **take** ~.) □ *Come in, John. Sit down and take a load off your feet.* □ *Yes, I need to get a load off my feet. I'm really tired.*

*a **load off** one's **mind** and *a **weight off** one's **mind** *Fig.* the relief from a mental burden gained by saying what one is thinking or by speaking one's mind. (*Typically: **get** ~; **take** ~.) □ *I think you'll feel better after you get a load off your mind.*

load someone or something **down**† (**with** someone or something) to burden someone or something with someone or something. □ *Don't load down my car with too many people.* □ *Tom loaded himself down with work every weekend.*

load someone or something **into** something and **load** someone or something **in**† to put someone or something into something. □ *Would you load the dishes into the dishwasher?* □ *Let's load the kids into the car and go to the zoo.* □ *Load them in, and let's go.*

load someone or something **up**† (**with** someone or something) to burden someone or something greatly or to the maximum with someone or something. □ *I loaded her up with a number of books on investments, so she could learn what to do with her money.* □ *Don't load up your shelves with books you will never look at.*

load something **onto** someone or something and **load** something **on**† to lift something onto someone or something. □ *We loaded the trunk onto Sam, and he carried it up the stairs into the house.* □ *Please help me load the boxes onto the cart.* □ *Load on the boxes, and let's go.*

load something **with** something to burden something with something; to put a lot of something onto or into something. □ *Load this box with all the clothing you can get into it.* □ *Don't load these drawers with so much stuff.*

load up (**with** something) to take or accumulate a lot of something. □ *Don't load up with cheap souvenirs. Save your money.* □ *Whenever I get into a used-book store, I load up.*

loaded for bear 1. *Inf.* angry. □ *He left here in a rage. He was really loaded for bear.* □ *When I got home from work, I was really loaded for bear. What a horrible day!* **2.** *Inf.* drunk. (An elaboration of *loaded*, which means "drunk.") □ *By the end of the party, Bill was loaded for bear.* □ *The whole gang drank for an hour until they were loaded for bear.*

loaded to the barrel Go to next.

loaded to the gills and **loaded to the barrel** *Sl.* intoxicated. □ *He's loaded to the gills.* □ *Man, he's loaded to the barrel and fighting mad.*

loaf around to waste time; to idle the time away doing almost nothing. □ *Every time I see you, you are just loafing around.* □ *I enjoy loafing around on the weekend.*

loaf something **away**† to waste away a period of time. □ *You have loafed the entire day away!* □ *He loafed away the entire day.*

loan something **to** someone to lend something to someone. (Considered to be an error for *lend*.) □ *Can you loan a few bucks to Sam and me?* □ *I will not loan anything to you.*

lob something **at** someone or something to throw or toss something at someone or something. □ *Who lobbed this thing at me?* □ *They lobbed a stone at the cat, but that only made it mad.*

lobby against something to solicit support against something, such as a piece of legislation or a government regulation. □ *We sent a lot of lawyers to the state capital to lobby against the bill, but it passed anyway.* □ *They lobbied against the tax increase.*

lobby for something to solicit support for something among the members of a voting body, such as the Congress. □ *Tom is always lobbying for some reform bill or other.* □ *The manufacturers lobbied for tax relief.*

local yokel a local resident of a rural place. (Mildly derogatory.) □ *One of the local yokels helped me change the tire.* □ *The local yokels all listen to the same radio station.*

lock horns (**with** someone) *Fig.* to get into an argument with someone. □ *Let's settle this peacefully. I don't want to lock horns with the boss.* □ *The boss doesn't want to lock horns either.*

lock in on someone or something and **lock on(to)** someone or something *Fig.* to fix some kind of electronic sensing device on someone or something. □ *The enemy pilot was flying just ahead of us. Aiming the laser, we locked in on him and shot him down.* □ *We locked onto the satellite and got an excellent TV picture.*

lock on(to someone or something) to fasten or grab onto someone or something. (See also **lock in on** someone or something.) □ *She locked onto the child and wouldn't leave his side for an instant.* □ *I saw the thing I wanted and locked on.*

lock someone or an animal (**up**) **in** (something) and **lock** someone or an animal **up**† to fasten the opening to something so someone, a group, or an animal cannot get out. □ *Take Chuck and lock him up in the cell.* □ *Lock up the killer and throw away the key!*

lock someone or something **away**† to put someone or something away in a locked container or space. □ *You will have to lock all the medications away when the grandchildren come to visit.* □ *They locked away some cash for a rainy day.* □ *They locked it away.*

lock someone or something **out of** something and **lock** someone or something **out**† to lock something to prevent someone or something from getting into it. □ *Someone locked me out of my office.* □ *Who locked out the office staff this morning?*

lock someone or something **up**† (**somewhere**) to lock someone or something within something or some place. □ *The captain ordered the sailor locked up in the brig until the ship got into port.* □ *Don't lock me up!* □ *The sheriff locked up the crook in a cell.*

lock something **in**† to make something, such as a rate of interest, permanent over a period of time. □ *You should try to lock in a high percentage rate on your bonds.* □ *We locked in a very low rate on our mortgage.*

lock something **onto** someone or something and **lock** something **on**† to attach or fix something onto someone or

411

something. □ *The cop locked the handcuffs onto the mugger and led him away.* □ *Andy locked his bicycle onto the signpost.* □ *See that bike rack? Lock your bike on and keep an eye on it.*

lock, stock, and barrel *Cliché* everything. □ *We had to move everything out of the house—lock, stock, and barrel.* □ *We lost everything—lock, stock, and barrel—in the fire.*

Lock the stable door after the horse is stolen. Go to Shut the stable door after the horse has bolted.

lodge someone **with** someone to have someone stay with someone as a guest. □ *We lodged the visitor with George for the weekend.* □ *Would it be possible for us to lodge Mary with you?*

lodge something **against** someone to place a charge against someone. □ *The neighbors lodged a complaint against us for walking on their grass.* □ *I want to lodge an assault charge against Randy.*

lodge something **against** something to place or prop something against something. □ *We lodged the chest against the door, making it difficult or impossible to open.* □ *Let's lodge the stone against the side of the barn to help support it.*

lodge something **in** something to get something stuck in something or some place. □ *She lodged her coat in the door and tore it.* □ *He lodged a screwdriver in the machine's gears by accident.*

lodge with someone to stay or reside with someone. □ *I lodged with my cousin while I was in Omaha.* □ *Tricia plans to lodge with us while she is here.*

log off and **log out** to record one's exit from a computer system. (This action may be recorded, or logged, automatically in the computer's memory.) □ *I closed my files and logged off.* □ *What time did you log out?*

log on to begin to use a computer system, as by entering a password, etc. (This action may be recorded, or logged, automatically in the computer's memory.) □ *What time did you log on to the system this morning?* □ *I always log on before I get my first cup of coffee.*

log out Go to log off.

log someone **for** something **1.** to schedule someone for something. □ *I am going to log you for sentry duty on the weekends.* □ *We will have to log Bill for service as a parking attendant.* **2.** to make a note in a log about someone's bad behavior. □ *The captain logged the first mate for the navigation error.* □ *I will have to log you for that.*

log someone **off** and **log** someone **out** [for someone] to cause someone to exit from a computer system. (This exit may be recorded, or logged, automatically in the computer's memory.) □ *Mary had to rush off to an appointment, so I logged her off.*

log someone **on**[†] **(to** something**)** to allow someone to link (electronically) to a computer system. (This action may be recorded, or logged, automatically in the computer's memory.) □ *I will log you on to the system if you forgot how to do it.* □ *I will log on Jill, who is late.*

log someone **out** Go to **log** someone **off**.

log something **up**[†] to record an amount of something. □ *The ship logged many nautical miles up on its last voyage.* □ *It logged up a lot of miles.*

loiter around to idle somewhere; to hang around. □ *Stop loitering around! Get going!* □ *The kids were loitering around for most of the summer.*

loiter over something to dawdle or linger over something. □ *Don't loiter over your meal. I want to start the dishwasher.* □ *I wish you wouldn't loiter over your chores.*

loiter something **away**[†] to idle away a period of time. □ *Those boys will loiter half their lives away.* □ *They loitered away their summer vacation.*

loll about (some place**)** to lie, lounge, or droop some place. □ *The tired travelers lolled about all over the hotel lobby until their rooms were ready.* □ *They were still lolling about at three in the afternoon.*

loll around to roll, flop, or hang around. □ *The dog's tongue lolled around as it rolled on its back, trying to keep cool.* □ *Stop lolling around and get to work.*

loll back [for a head] to fall or droop backwards. □ *As he passed out, his head lolled back and struck the corner of the table.* □ *Her head lolled back and suddenly she was fast asleep.*

loll out [for a tongue] to hang or flop out. □ *The dog's tongue lolled out as it lay sleeping.* □ *Since the dog's tongue lolled out every time it opened its mouth, it is a wonder it didn't bite it when it closed its mouth.*

lollygag (around) to loaf; to loiter. □ *How can I get my work done with you lollygagging around?* □ *I spent my vacation just lollygagging.*

the **long and the short of it** and the **short and the long of it** *Fig.* the most important point; the summary of the matter. □ *Jill: Is there some reason that you've spent the last half hour complaining about Fred? Jane: The long and the short of it is, I hate working with him so much that I'm going to resign.* □ *Dad keeps saying that he can't spend the rest of his life in mourning for Mother. I finally asked him if he was thinking of getting married again. "That's the long and the short of it," he admitted.*

the **long arm of the law** *Fig.* the police; the law. □ *The long arm of the law is going to tap you on the shoulder some day, Lefty.* □ *The long arm of the law finally caught up with Gert.*

long for someone or something to desire or pine for someone or something. □ *She is longing for her old friends.* □ *Walter longed for his hometown in the mountains.*

long gone gone a long time ago; used up a long time ago. □ *The ice cream and cake are long gone. You are simply too late for the refreshments.*

long in the tooth *Fig.* old. □ *That actor is getting a little long in the tooth to play the romantic lead.* □ *I may be long in the tooth, but I'm not stupid.*

*a **long shot** *Fig.* a risky bet; an attempt, bet, or proposition that has a low probability of success. (*Typically: **be ~; seem like ~**.) □ *Your solution is a long shot, but we'll try it and hope it works.*

long story short *Sl.* to make a long story short. □ *Okay, long story short: everything that goes up comes down, okay?* □ *Then the guy comes over, and—long story short—"You got a match?"*

Long time no see. *Cliché* I have not seen you in a long time.; We have not seen each other in a long time. □ *Tom:*

Hi, Fred. Where have you been keeping yourself? Fred: Good to see you, Tom. Long time no see. □ *John: It's Bob! Hi, Bob! Bob: Hi, John! Long time no see.*

The longest way round is the shortest way home. and **The longest way round is the nearest way home.** *Prov.* It may seem as if it will take too long to do something carefully and according to directions, but in fact it will take less time than doing something carelessly, because you will not have to fix it afterwards. □ *I would advise you to read the instructions before trying to use your new stereo. It takes some time, but the longest way round is the nearest way home.*

look a gift horse in the mouth *Fig.* to be ungrateful to someone who gives you something; to treat someone who gives you a gift badly. (Usually with a negative.) □ *Never look a gift horse in the mouth.* □ *I advise you not to look a gift horse in the mouth.*

look about (for someone or something**)** to try to locate someone or something. □ *I have to look about for someone to serve as a babysitter.* □ *I don't see it here. I'll have to look about.*

look after number one and **look out for number one** to take care of oneself first. □ *You gotta look after number one, right?* □ *It's a good idea to look out for number one. Who else will?*

look after someone or something to take care of someone or something. □ *Please look after my little boy.* □ *Will you look after my cat while I'm away?* □ *Do you want me to look after your car?*

look ahead to something to try to foresee something; to think into the future about something. □ *She looked ahead to a bright future in sales.* □ *I look ahead to a new job when I graduate.*

look alike to appear similar. □ *All these cars look alike these days.* □ *The twins look alike and not many people can tell them apart.*

Look alive! Act alert and responsive! □ *"Come on, Fred! Get moving! Look alive!" shouted the coach, who was not happy with Fred's performance.* □ *Bill: Look alive, Bob! Bob: I'm doing the best I can.*

look around (at something**)** to investigate something; to study something visually. □ *Go into the room and look around at the way they have fixed it up.* □ *I went in and looked around.*

look around for someone or something to seek someone or something out. □ *Look around for Ted and tell him to come home.* □ *I looked around for the can opener, but it's not there.*

look around (in) some place to investigate some place. □ *Look around the kitchen. You will find what you want.* □ *Tell her to look around in the attic. Maybe the camping gear is there.*

look as if butter wouldn't melt in one's **mouth** *Fig.* to appear to be cold and unfeeling (despite any information to the contrary). □ *Sally looks as if butter wouldn't melt in her mouth. She can be so cruel.* □ *What a sour face. He looks as if butter wouldn't melt in his mouth.*

look aside to look to one side; to turn one's head aside so as not to see someone or something. □ *As I approached,*

he looked aside, pretending not to recognize me. □ *She looked aside, hoping I wouldn't see her.*

look askance at someone or something *Fig.* to be surprised or shocked at someone or something. □ *The teacher looked askance at the student who had acted so rudely.* □ *Everyone had looked askance at her efforts as an artist.*

look at someone **cross-eyed** *Fig.* to merely appear to question, threaten, or mock someone. (Often in the negative.) □ *You had better be on your best behavior around Tony. Don't even look at him cross-eyed!* □ *If you so much as look at me cross-eyed, I will send you to your room.*

look at someone or something to examine someone or something. □ *The doctor needs to look at the wound before you leave.* □ *You had better have the doctor look at you. That is a nasty wound.*

look at the crux of the matter and **look at the heart of the matter; look at the root of the matter** Go to the crux of the matter.

look at the heart of the matter Go to previous.

Look (at) what the cat dragged in! *Inf.* Look who's here! (A good-humored and familiar way of showing surprise at someone's presence in a place, especially if the person looks a little rumpled. Compare this with **look like** something **the cat dragged in.**) □ *Bob and Mary were standing near the doorway talking when Tom came in. "Look what the cat dragged in!" announced Bob.* □ *Mary: Hello, everybody. I'm here! Jane: Look at what the cat dragged in!*

look away (from someone or something**)** to turn one's gaze away from someone. □ *She looked away from him, not wishing her eyes to give away her true feelings.* □ *In embarrassment, she looked away.*

look back (at someone or something**)** and **look back (on** someone or something**) 1.** *Lit.* to gaze back and try to get a view of someone or something. □ *She looked back at the city and whispered a good-bye to everything she had ever cared for.* □ *I went away and never looked back.* **2.** *Fig.* to think about someone or something in the past. □ *When I look back on Frank, I do remember his strange manner, come to think of it.* □ *When I look back, I am amazed at all I have accomplished.*

look becoming on someone Go to becoming on someone.

Look before you leap. *Prov. Cliché* Think carefully about what you are about to do before you do it. □ *I'm not saying you shouldn't sign the lease for that apartment. I'm just saying you should look before you leap.* □ *Jill: I'm thinking about going to night school. Jane: Are you sure you can spare the time and the money? Look before you leap.*

look beyond someone or something **1.** *Lit.* to try to see to a point farther than someone or something. □ *Look beyond Claire at the forest in the distance.* □ *Look beyond the house and see what you can spot in the trees behind it.* **2.** *Fig.* to try to think or plan further than someone or something. □ *Sally will be gone soon. Look beyond Sally and decide whom you want to hire.* □ *Look beyond Tom. Think about how you will deal with the next person who has Tom's job.*

look daggers at someone *Fig.* to give someone a dirty look. □ *Tom must have been mad at Ann from the way he*

L

was looking daggers at her. □ *Don't you dare look daggers at me! Don't even look cross-eyed at me!*

look down (at someone or something**) 1.** to turn one's gaze downward at someone or something. □ *She looked down at me and giggled at the awkward position I was in.* □ *She looked down and burst into laughter.* **2. and look down** one's **nose at** someone or something; **look down on** someone or something to view someone or something as lowly or unworthy. □ *She looked down at all the waiters and treated them badly.* □ *They looked down on our humble food.* □ *Don't look down your nose at my car just because it's rusty and noisy.*

look fit to kill *Fig.* [dressed up] to look very fancy or sexy. □ *Mary put on her best clothes and looked fit to kill.* □ *John looked fit to kill in his new tuxedo.*

look for someone or something to seek someone or something. □ *I am looking for Mr. William Wilson. Do you know where he lives?* □ *I am looking for the address of Bill Wilson.*

look for someone or something **high and low** and **look high and low (for** someone or something**)** to search everywhere for someone or something. □ *Where were you? I looked for you high and low.* □ *I looked high and low for my passport.*

look for trouble Go to ask for trouble.

look forward to something to anticipate something with pleasure. □ *I'm really looking forward to your visit next week.* □ *We all look forward to your new book on gardening.*

look good on paper to seem fine in theory, but not perhaps in practice; to appear to be a good plan. □ *The plan looks good on paper, but it may not work.* □ *This looks good on paper. Let's hope it works in the real world.*

look here a phrase emphasizing the point that follows. (Can show some impatience.) □ *Henry: Look here, I want to try to help you, but you're not making it easy for me. Rachel: I'm just so upset.* □ *Andy: Look here, I just asked you a simple question! Bob: As I told you in the beginning, there are no simple answers.*

look high and low (for someone or something**)** Go to look for someone or something high and low.

look in (on someone or something**)** and **check in (on** someone or something**)** to see to the welfare of someone or something; to check briefly on someone or something. □ *I'll stop by your house and look in on things while you're on vacation.* □ *Yes, just look in and make sure nothing is wrong.*

look into something **1.** *Lit.* to gaze into the inside of something. □ *Look into the box and make sure you've gotten everything out of it.* □ *Look into the camera's viewfinder at the little red light.* **2. and check into** something; **see into** something *Fig.* to investigate something. □ *I'll have to look into that matter.* □ *The police checked into her story.* □ *Don't worry about your problem. I'll see into it.*

look like a candidate for a pair of wings Go to a candidate for a pair of wings.

look like a case of something Go to a case of something.

look like a (dead) ringer (for someone**)** Go to a (dead) ringer (for someone).

look like a million dollars Go to like a million dollars.

look like a saddle on a sow *Rur.* to look ridiculous and out of place. □ *Tom: How do you like my new diamond earring? Jane: It looks like a saddle on a sow.* □ *The fancy wheels on that beat-up old car look like a saddle on a sow.*

look like death warmed over Go to like death warmed over.

look like someone or something to resemble someone or something. □ *You look like my cousin Fred.* □ *This one looks like an apple.*

look like something to give the appearance of predicting (something). □ *The sky looks like rain.* □ *No, it looks like snow.* □ *Oh, oh. This looks like trouble. Let's go.*

look like something **the cat dragged in** *Fig.* to look very shabby, worn, exhausted, or abused. (Sometimes with drug.) □ *That new sofa of theirs looks like something the cat dragged in.* □ *Poor Dave looks like something the cat drug in. He must have been out late last night.*

look like the cat that swallowed the canary *Fig.* to appear as if one had just had a great success. □ *After the meeting John looked like the cat that swallowed the canary. I knew he must have been a success.* □ *Your presentation must have gone well. You look like the cat that swallowed the canary.*

Look me up when you're in town. When you next come to my town, try to find me (and we will get together). (A vague and perhaps insincere invitation.) □ *Bob: Nice to see you, Tom. Bye now. Tom: Yes, indeed. Look me up when you're in town. Bye.* □ *Sally (on the phone): Bye. Nice talking to you. Mary: Bye, Sally. Sorry we can't talk more. Look me up when you're in town.*

look none the worse for wear Go to none the worse for wear.

look on to be a spectator and watch what is happening without participating. □ *The beating took place while a policeman looked on.* □ *While the kittens played, the mother cat looked on contentedly.*

look on someone **as** something to view or think of someone as something. □ *I look on you as a very thoughtful person.* □ *Mary looked on Jane as a good friend.*

look on the bright side *Fig.* consider the positive aspects of a negative situation. □ *Look on the bright side. Things could have been much worse than they are.*

look on (with someone**)** to share and read from someone else's notes, paper, book, music, etc. □ *I don't have a copy of the notice, but I will look on with Carlo.* □ *Carla has a copy of the music. She doesn't mind if I look on.*

look out Go to watch out for someone or something.

look out for number one Go to look after number one.

look out for someone Go to watch out for someone.

look out (of) something to gaze outward from inside something. (*Of* is usually retained before pronouns.) □ *Look out of the window and see if it is raining.* □ *I looked out of the door to see what the weather was like.*

look (out) on(to) something [for something] to face onto something or some place. □ *The balcony looks out onto the meadow.* □ *My window looks onto the street.*

look someone **in the eye** Go to next.

look someone **in the face** and **look** someone **in the eye; stare** someone **in the face** *Fig.* to face someone directly. (Facing someone this way is a sign of sincerity.) □ *I don't believe you. Look me in the eye and say that.* □ *She looked him in the face and said she never wanted to see him again.*

look someone or something **over**† to examine someone or something. □ *I think you had better have the doctor look you over.* □ *Please look over these papers.*

look someone or something **up**† and **hunt** someone or something **up**† **1.** to seek someone, a group, or something out. □ *I lost track of Sally. I'll try to look her up and get in touch with her.* □ *I am going to look up an old friend when I am in Chicago.* □ *I am going to hunt that old gang up.* □ *Ted came into town and looked up his favorite pizza place.* **2.** to seek information about someone or something in a book or listing. □ *I don't recognize his name. I'll look him up and see what I can find.* □ *I'll look up this person in a reference book.* □ *She looked herself up in the telephone book to make sure her name was spelled correctly.*

look the other way 1. *Lit.* to look in the opposite direction. □ *To make sure it's safe to cross the street, look the other way before you step off the curb.* **2.** *Fig.* to ignore something on purpose. □ *John could have prevented the problem, but he looked the other way.* □ *By looking the other way, he actually made the problem worse.*

look through something **1.** to gaze through something. □ *Look through the window at what the neighbors are doing.* □ *Look through the binoculars and see if you can get a better view.* **2.** to examine the parts, pages, samples, etc., of something. □ *Look through this report and see what you make of it.* □ *I will look through it when I have time.*

look to be a million miles away Go to a **million miles away.**

look to one's **laurels** *Fig.* to take care not to lower or diminish one's reputation or position, especially in relation to that of someone else potentially better. □ *With the arrival of the new member of the football team, James will have to look to his laurels to remain as the highest scorer.* □ *The older members of the team will have to look to their laurels when the new players arrive.*

look to someone or something **(for** something) to expect someone or something to supply something. □ *Children look to their parents for help.* □ *Tom looked to the bank for a loan.*

look to the naked eye Go to the **naked eye.**

look toward someone or something to face in the direction of someone or something. □ *Look toward Sarah and see where she is standing. Isn't that a lovely garden she's in?* □ *Look toward the sea and see what a sunset is meant to look like.*

look under the hood to examine the engine of a car; to check the oil, water, and other such routine items associated with the engine of a car. □ *I finished putting gas in. I need to look under the hood.* □ *Do you want me to look under the hood, sir?*

look up to show promise of improving. □ *My prospects for a job are looking up.* □ *Conditions are looking up.*

look up and down (for someone or something**)** to look everywhere for someone or something. □ *Where is Kelly? I looked up and down for her.* □ *I can't find her. I looked up and down, but no Kelly.*

look up and down something to gaze up and then down something, such as a street. □ *We looked up and down the street and saw no cars, no houses, and no people.* □ *Mary looked up and down the highway, but she could not find her lost hubcap.*

look up at someone or something to raise one's gaze to someone or something. □ *Would you please look up at me while I am talking to you? I hate to be ignored.* □ *Look up at the top of that building.*

look up (from something**)** to gaze upwards; to stop reading or working and lift one's gaze upward. □ *She looked up from her reading and spoke to us.* □ *Mary looked up as we came into the room.*

look up to someone *Fig.* to view someone with respect and admiration. □ *Bill really looks up to his father.* □ *Everyone in the class looked up to the teacher.*

look (up)on someone or something **as** something to view someone or something as something; to consider someone or something to be something. □ *I look upon Todd as a fine and helpful guy.* □ *I look on these requests as an annoyance.*

look (up)on someone or something **with** something to view someone or something with an attitude, such as scorn, favor, anger, disgust, etc. □ *She looked upon all of us with scorn.* □ *Bill looked on the food set before him with disgust.*

Look who's here! an expression drawing attention to someone present or who just arrived at a place. □ *Bill: Look who's here! My old friend Fred. How goes it, Fred? Fred: Hi, there, Bill! What's new? Bill: Nothing much.* □ *Bill: Look who's here! Mary: Yeah. Isn't that Fred Morgan?*

Look who's talking! *Fig.* You are guilty of doing the same thing that you have criticized someone else for doing or that you accused someone else of doing. □ *Andy: You criticize me for being late! Look who's talking! You just missed your flight! Jane: Well, nobody's perfect.* □ *Mary: You just talk and talk, you go on much too long about practically nothing, and you never give a chance for anyone else to talk, and you just don't know when to stop! Sally: Look who's talking!*

looking like a sitting duck Go to a **sitting duck.**

looking over one's **shoulder** *Fig.* keeping watch for danger or threats to oneself. □ *Bob's a little paranoid. He's always looking over his shoulder.*

*a look-see *Rur.* a look at someone or something; a peek. (*Typically: **get ~; have ~; give** someone **~; take ~.**) □ *A: Do you think they have finished painting your office yet? B: Let's go down there and take a look-see.*

loom large (on the horizon) *Cliché* to be of great importance, especially when referring to an upcoming problem, danger, or threat. □ *The exams were looming large on the horizon.* □ *Eviction was looming large when the tenants could not pay their rent.*

L

415

loom out of something to appear to come out of or penetrate something. □ *A truck suddenly loomed out of the fog and just missed hitting us.* □ *A tall building loomed out of the mists.*

loom up to appear to rise up [from somewhere]; to take form or definition, usually threatening to some degree. □ *A great city loomed up in the distance. It looked threatening in the dusky light.* □ *A ghost loomed up, but we paid no attention, since it had to be a joke.* □ *The recession loomed up, and the stock market reacted.*

a **loose cannon** a person whose actions are unpredictable and uncontrollable. □ *As it turned out, he's not just a loose cannon. He makes sense.* □ *Some loose cannon in the State Department has been leaking stories to the press.*

Loose lips sink ships. Don't talk carelessly because you don't know who is listening. (From wartime. Literally, "Don't reveal even the location of a loved one on a ship, because the location could be communicated to the enemy by a spy.") □ *You never know who is going to hear what you say and how they will use what they hear. Remember, loose lips sink ships.*

a **loose translation** Go to a free translation.

loosen someone or something **up**† to make someone's muscles and joints move more freely by exercising them. □ *The exercise loosened me up quite nicely.* □ *It loosened up my legs.* □ *I have to do some exercises to loosen myself up.*

loosen someone **up**† *Fig.* to make someone or a group more relaxed and friendly. □ *I loosened up the audience with a joke.* □ *Loosen yourself up. Relax and try to enjoy people.*

loosen up to become loose or relaxed. □ *Loosen up. Relax.* □ *We tried to get Mary to loosen up, but she did not respond.*

lop something **off (of)** something and **lop** something **off**† to chop or cut something off something. (*Of* is usually retained before pronouns.) □ *Lop that long branch off the tree before you put the saw away, will you?* □ *Please lop off that branch.*

lope along to move along, bounding. □ *The dog loped along at a very even pace, answering to his master's whistle.* □ *The horses loped along, eager to get home.*

(lord) high muck-a-muck *Rur.* a very important person. (Humorous.) □ *Jim's acting like he's some kind of lord high muck-a-muck. What's gotten into him?* □ *Mary got a promotion, so now she's a real high muck-a-muck.*

lord it over someone *Fig.* to dominate someone; to direct and control someone. □ *Mr. Smith seems to lord it over his wife.* □ *The boss lords it over everyone in the office.*

Lord knows I've tried. *Fig.* I certainly have tried very hard. □ *Alice: Why don't you get Bill to fix this fence? Mary: Lord knows I've tried. I must have asked him a dozen times—this year alone.* □ *Sue: I can't seem to get to class on time. Rachel: That's just awful. Sue: Lord knows I've tried. I just can't do it.*

Lord love a duck! *Fig.* My goodness! (An exclamation of surprise.) □ *Lord love a duck! How that rain is coming down!* □ *Lord love a duck! Did you see that cat chasing that dog?*

Lord willing and the creek don't rise Go to God willing and the creek don't rise.

lose a bundle *Sl.* to lose a lot of money. □ *Don lost a bundle on that land purchase.* □ *I know I would lose a bundle if I went to a casino and gambled.*

lose (all) one's marbles Go to lose one's marbles.

lose (all) one's marbles and **lose one's mind** *Fig.* to go crazy; to go out of one's mind. □ *What a silly thing to say! Have you lost your marbles?* □ *Look at Sally jumping up and down and screaming. Is she losing all her marbles?* □ *I can't seem to remember anything. I think I'm losing my mind.*

lose at something to be defeated at a particular game or activity. □ *We lost at basketball but we won at football this weekend.* □ *I hate to lose at checkers.*

lose by something to be defeated by a certain amount. □ *Our team lost by ten points.* □ *I only lost by a few points.*

lose contact with someone or something and **lose touch with** someone or something [for communication with someone or a group] to fail or fade away; to let one's friendship or relationship with someone or a group lapse. □ *I hope I don't lose contact with you.* □ *I don't want to lose touch with my old friends.*

lose count of someone or something to fail to be able to count someone or something, especially because there are so many. □ *I have lost count of the people who have asked that question.* □ *I am afraid I have lost count of all the times we have run out of money.*

lose face *Fig.* to lose status; to become less respectable. □ *John is more afraid of losing face than losing money.* □ *Things will go better if you can explain to him where he was wrong without making him lose face.*

lose favor (with someone**)** Go to fall out of favor (with someone).

lose ground (to someone or something**)** to fall behind someone or something. □ *I am losing ground to Wendy in the sales contest.* □ *We were losing ground to the opposite team in our quest for the trophy.*

lose heart *Fig.* to lose one's courage or confidence. □ *Now, don't lose heart. Keep trying.* □ *What a disappointment! It's enough to make one lose heart.*

lose it 1. *Sl.* to empty one's stomach; to vomit. □ *Oh, God! I think I'm going to lose it!* □ *Go lose it in the bushes.* **2.** *Sl.* to get angry; to lose one's temper. □ *It was too much for him. Ted lost it.* □ *I sat there calmly, biting my lip to keep from losing it.*

lose money on something to have a net loss on something, such as an investment. □ *I lost thousands on that deal.* □ *I don't want to lose money on any investment.*

lose one's **appetite** to lose one's desire to eat. □ *After that gory movie, I'm afraid I've lost my appetite.*

lose one's **cool** and **blow** one's **cool** to lose one's temper; to lose one's nerve. □ *Wow, he really lost his cool! What a tantrum!* □ *Whatever you do, don't blow your cool.*

lose one's **grip on** someone or something Go to lose one's hold on someone or something.

lose one's **head (over** someone or something**)** *Fig.* to become confused or overly emotional about someone or something. □ *Don't lose your head over John. He isn't worth it.* □ *I'm sorry. I got upset and lost my head.*

lose one's **hold on** someone or something and **lose** one's **grip on** someone or something **1.** *Lit.* to fail to keep one's handhold on someone or something. □ *I lost my hold on the child, and she nearly slipped away.* □ *She lost her grip on the bag of jewels and it fell overboard.* **2.** and **lose** one's **hold over** someone or something *Fig.* to give up control over someone or something. □ *The manager lost her hold on her employees and was fired.* □ *Fred is losing his grip on his workers.* □ *He is losing his hold over his empire.*

lose one's **lunch** Go to blow (one's) lunch.

lose one's **reason** *Fig.* to lose one's power of reasoning, possibly in anger. □ *I was so confused that I almost lost my reason.* □ *Bob seems to have lost his reason when he struck John.*

lose one's **shirt** *Fig.* to lose a lot of money; to lose all of one's assets (as if one had even lost one's shirt). □ *I almost lost my shirt on that deal. I have to invest more wisely.* □ *No, I can't loan you $200. I just lost my shirt at the racetrack.*

lose one's **temper (at** someone or something**)** *Fig.* to become angry at someone or something. □ *Lisa lost her temper and began shouting at Bob.* □ *I hate to lose my temper at someone. I always end up feeling guilty.*

lose one's **touch (with** someone or something**)** *Fig.* to lose one's ability to handle someone or something. □ *I seem to have lost my touch with my children. They won't listen to me anymore.* □ *We've both lost our touch as far as managing people goes.*

lose one's **train of thought** *Fig.* to forget what one was talking or thinking about. □ *Excuse me, I lost my train of thought. What was I talking about?* □ *Your question made the speaker lose her train of thought.*

lose oneself **in** someone or something to be thoroughly absorbed in someone or something; to become engrossed in someone or something. □ *Frank loses himself in his children when he is at home.* □ *When I lose myself in my work, time just rushes by.*

lose out 1. to lose in competition; to lose one's expected reward. □ *Our team lost out because our quarterback broke his leg.* □ *I ran my best race, but I still lost out.* **2. lose out (on** something**)** Go to miss out (on something).

lose out to someone or something to lose a competition to someone or something. □ *Our team lost out to the other team.* □ *Bill lost out to Sally in the contest.*

lose patience (with someone or something**)** to stop being patient with someone or something; to become impatient with someone or something. □ *Please try to be more cooperative. I'm losing patience with you.*

lose sight of someone or something **1.** *Lit.* to have one's vision of someone or something fade because of distance or an obstruction. □ *I lost sight of Alice as she walked into the distance.* □ *We lost sight of the ship as it sailed out of the harbor.* **2.** *Fig.* to forget to consider someone or something. □ *Don't lose sight of Alice and her basic contributions.* □ *Don't lose sight of the basic value of the land on which the house sits.*

lose sleep over someone or something and **lose sleep about** someone or something *Fig.* to worry about someone or something a lot, sometimes when one should be sleeping. (Often used with *any* and the negative.) □ *Yes,* Kelly is in a little bit of trouble, but I'm not going to lose any sleep over her. □ *Don't lose any sleep over the matter.* □ *I refuse to lose sleep about it.*

lose some amount of **time** [for some amount of time] to be wasted. □ *We lost a lot of time waiting for Hermione.* □ *He lost no time in getting out of there.*

lose something **at** something to lose a wager at playing something or at gambling. □ *I lost a fortune at gambling.* □ *We lost all our money at dice.*

lose something **in** something to misplace something in something. □ *I lost my wallet in the barn.* □ *Did someone lose something in the dining room?*

lose something **to** someone to yield or give up something in defeat to someone. □ *We lost the case to the opposing lawyers.* □ *Mary lost her title to last year's runner-up.*

lose the use of something to be deprived of the use of something. □ *After the accident, I lost the use of my left arm for a few days.* □ *Andy lost the use of the car for a week.*

lose to someone or something to be defeated by someone or something. □ *I lost to Wendy in the sales contest.* □ *Our team lost to the Adamsville Raiders for the seventh year in a row.*

lose touch with reality to began to think unrealistically; to become unrealistic. □ *I am so overworked that I am losing touch with reality.* □ *The psychotic criminal had lost touch with reality.*

lose touch with someone or something Go to lose contact with someone or something.

lose trace of someone or something *Rur.* to fail to maintain a way of finding someone or something. □ *I lost trace of Walter after we left high school.* □ *I lost trace of the stock certificates after about twenty years.*

lose track (of someone or something**)** to lose contact with someone; to forget where something is. □ *I lost track of all my friends from high school.* □ *Tom has lost track of his glasses again.*

*****a **losing streak** *Fig.* a series of losses [in sports, for instance]. (*Typically: **be on ~; have ~; continue** one's **~.**) □ *The team was on a losing streak that started nearly three years ago.*

lost and gone forever lost; permanently lost. □ *My poor doggy is lost and gone forever.* □ *My money fell out of my pocket and I am sure that it is lost and gone forever.*

a **lost cause** a futile attempt; a hopeless matter. □ *Our campaign to have the new party on the ballot was a lost cause.* □ *Todd gave it up as a lost cause.*

*****lost in** something enveloped in something; engrossed in something. (*Typically: **be ~; get ~.**) □ *Ed sat under the tree, lost in reverie.* □ *Excuse me. I didn't hear you. I was lost in my own thoughts.*

*****lost on** someone *Fig.* wasted on someone; not valued or appreciated by someone. (*Typically: **be ~; get ~.**) □ *My jokes are lost on him. He is too literal.* □ *The humor of the situation was lost on Mary. She was too upset to see it.*

lost without someone or something unable to function without someone or something. □ *I am just lost without you.* □ *The engineer is lost without his pocket computer.*

L

417

lost-and-found an office or department that handles items that someone has lost that have been found by someone else. □ *The lost-and-found office had an enormous collection of umbrellas and four sets of false teeth!* □ *I found a book on the seat of the bus. I turned it in to the driver, who gave it to the lost-and-found office.*

a **lot of give-and-take 1.** *Fig.* a lot of two-way discussion. □ *It was a good meeting. There was a lot of give-and-take, and we all learned.* **2.** *Fig.* a lot of negotiating and bargaining. □ *After an afternoon of give-and-take, we were finally able to put all the details into an agreement.*

*a **lot of nerve 1.** *Fig.* great rudeness; a lot of audacity or brashness. (*Typically: **have** ~; **take** ~.) □ *He walked out on her, and that took a lot of nerve!* □ *You have a lot of nerve! You took my parking place!* **2.** *Fig.* courage. (*Typically: **have** ~; **take** ~.) □ *He climbed the mountain with a bruised foot. That took a lot of nerve.* □ *He has a lot of nerve to go into business for himself.*

*a **lot of promise** much promise for the future. (*Typically: **have** ~; **show** ~.) □ *Sally is quite young, but she has a lot of promise.* □ *This bush is small, but it shows a lot of promise.*

a **lot of** someone or something and **lots of** people or things a large number of people or things; much of something. □ *I got a lot of presents for my birthday.* □ *I ate lots of cookies after dinner.*

Lots of luck! 1. Good luck! □ *I'm glad you're giving it a try. Lots of luck!* □ *Lots of luck in your new job!* **2.** You don't have a chance!; Good luck, you'll need it! (Sarcastic.) □ *Think you stand a chance? Lots of luck!* □ *You a senator? Lots of luck!*

lots of people or things Go to a **lot of** someone or something.

loud and clear clear and distinctly. (Originally said of radio reception that is heard clearly and distinctly.) □ *Tom: If I've told you once, I've told you a thousand times: Stop it! Do you hear me? Bill: Yes, loud and clear.* □ *I hear you loud and clear.*

lounge around (some place) to pass time idly some place. □ *I am going to lounge around the house this morning.* □ *Don't lounge around all day.*

louse someone or something **up**[†] *Inf.* to ruin something; to **mess** someone or something **up.** □ *You really loused me up! You got me in a real mess!* □ *Who loused up my scheme?*

lousy with someone or something *Inf.* having lots of someone or something. (Like an infestation of lice.) □ *Old Mr. Wilson is lousy with money.* □ *Tiffany is lousy with jewels and furs, but she's got bad teeth.*

love at first sight *Fig.* love established when two people first see one another. □ *Bill was standing at the door when Ann opened it. It was love at first sight.* □ *It was love at first sight when they met, but it didn't last long.*

Love begets love. *Prov.* If you behave lovingly to other people, they will behave lovingly to you. □ *Child: I hate Tammy! She's always mean to me. Father: If you're nicer to her, maybe she'll change her ways. Love begets love.*

Love is blind. *Cliché* If you love someone, you cannot see any faults in that person. □ *Jill: I don't understand why Joanna likes Tom. He's inconsiderate, he's vain, and he isn't even good-looking. Jane: Love is blind.*

Love makes the world go round. *Prov.* Life is more pleasant when people treat each other lovingly. □ *Come on, guys, stop fighting with each other all the time. Love makes the world go round.*

Love me, love my dog. *Prov.* If you love someone, you should accept everything and everyone that the person loves. □ *Jill: I wish you'd keep your dog out of the house when I come over. Jane: Love me, love my dog.* □ *Most of Alice's friends didn't like her sister, but they accepted her because Alice insisted, "Love me, love my dog."*

The **love of money is the root of all evil.** Go to Money is the root of all evil.

Love will find a way. *Prov.* People who are in love will overcome any obstacles in order to be together. (Sometimes used ironically, to suggest that someone is in love with whatever he or she is struggling to be near, as in the second example.) □ *Jill: I feel so sorry for Lily and Craig. They just got engaged, and now his job is transferring him across the country. Jane: Love will find a way, I'm sure.* □ *Alan: Fred's feeling discouraged because he didn't get the loan he needed to buy the sports car he wants. Bill: I'm sure he'll get that car eventually. Love will find a way.*

Love you! *Inf.* You are great! (Often insincere.) □ *See ya around, Martin. Let's do lunch! Love ya! Bye-bye.* □ *Nice talking to you, babe. Love you!*

a **love-hate relationship** *Fig.* a relationship of any kind that involves both devotion and hatred. □ *Tommy has a love-hate relationship with his teacher. Mostly, though, it's hate lately.*

Lovely weather for ducks. and **Fine weather for ducks.** *Cliché* a greeting meaning that this unpleasant rainy weather must be good for something. □ *Bill: Hi, Bob. How do you like this weather? Bob: Lovely weather for ducks.* □ *Sally: What a lot of rain! Tom: Yeah. Lovely weather for ducks. Don't care for it much myself.*

low man on the totem pole *Fig.* the least important or lowest-ranking person of a group. □ *I was the last to find out because I'm low man on the totem pole.* □ *I can't be of any help. I'm low man on the totem pole.*

*a **low profile** *Fig.* a persona or character that does not draw attention. (*Typically: **assume** ~; **have** ~; **keep** ~; **give** oneself ~.) □ *I try to be quiet and keep a low profile. It's hard because I just love attention.*

*the **lowdown (on** someone or something**)** the full story about someone or something. (*Typically: **get** ~; **have** ~; **give** someone ~.) □ *I need to get the lowdown on John. Is he still an accountant?* □ *Sally wants to get the lowdown on the new pension plan. Please tell her all about it.*

lower one's **sights** *Fig.* to set one's goals lower. (Alludes to pointing the barrel of a rifle lower to lower the aim of the rifle.) □ *Even though you get frustrated, don't lower your sights.* □ *I shouldn't lower my sights. If I work hard, I can do what I want.*

lower one's **voice** *Fig.* to speak more softly. □ *Please lower your voice or you'll disturb the people who are working.* □ *He wouldn't lower his voice, so everyone heard what he said.*

lower oneself **to** some level *Fig.* to bring oneself down to some lower level of behavior. □ *I refuse to lower myself to your level.* □ *Has TV news lowered itself to the level of the tabloids?*

L

lower someone's **ears** *Rur.* to cut someone's hair. □ *I asked the barber to lower my ears.* □ *Looks like somebody lowered Joe's ears!*

lower someone's **spirits** Go to someone's **spirits**.

lower the boom on someone *Fig.* to scold or punish someone severely; to crack down on someone; to **throw the book at someone.** □ *If Bob won't behave better, I'll have to lower the boom on him.* □ *The teacher lowered the boom on the whole class for misbehaving.*

low-hanging fruit *Fig.* the easiest person(s) to sell something to, to convince of something, or to fool. (From the much older **easy pickings**.) □ *People who always want to be the first to buy something, they're low-hanging fruit for this product.* □ *Don't be satisfied with the low-hanging fruit. Go after the hard-sell types.*

luck into something to find something by luck; to get involved in something by luck. □ *I lucked into this apartment on the very day I started looking.* □ *We lucked into a good deal on a used car.*

the **luck of the draw** the results of chance; the lack of any choice. □ *Why do I always end up with the luck of the draw?* □ *The team was assembled by chance. It was just the luck of the draw that we could work so well together.*

luck out to be fortunate; to strike it lucky. □ *I really lucked out when I ordered the duck. It's excellent.* □ *I didn't luck out at all. I rarely make the right choice.*

luck out of something to get out of something by luck alone. □ *I lucked out of taking a driving test. I only had to pass a vision test to get my license.* □ *Man, I really lucked out of it.*

Lucky at cards, unlucky in love. *Prov.* If you frequently win at card games, you will not have happy love affairs. (Can imply the converse, that if you do not win at card games, you will have happy love affairs.) □ *Fred: I wish I was George. He always wins tons of money at our poker games. Alan: Don't be jealous of him. Lucky at cards, unlucky in love.*

a **lucky break** and a **nice break;** a **big break** significant good fortune or opportunity. □ *I need a lucky break about now.* □ *She's never had a lucky break.* □ *Mary is going to get a big break soon.*

a **lucky dog** *Fig.* a lucky person. □ *You won the lottery? You are a lucky dog!*

lucky for you a phrase introducing a description of an event that favors the person being spoken to. □ *Andy: Lucky for you the train was delayed. Otherwise you'd have to wait till tomorrow morning for the next one. Fred: That's luck, all right. I'd hate to have to sleep in the station.* □ *Jane: I hope I'm not too late. Sue: Lucky for you, everyone else is late too.*

*a **lucky streak** and *a **streak of luck** *Fig.* a series of lucky wins in gambling or games. (*Typically: **be on ~; have ~.**) □ *Thanks to a lucky streak, I won enough in Las Vegas to pay for the trip.*

the **lull before the storm** and the **calm before the storm** a quiet period just before a period of great activity or excitement. (Literal in reference to weather.) □ *It was very quiet in the cafeteria just before the students came in for lunch. It was the lull before the storm.* □ *In the brief calm before the storm, the clerks prepared themselves for the doors to open and bring in thousands of shoppers.*

lull someone **into a false sense of security** *Cliché* to lead someone into believing that all is well before attacking or doing someone bad. □ *We lulled the enemy into a false sense of security by pretending to retreat. Then we launched an attack.* □ *The boss lulled us into a false sense of security by saying that our jobs were safe and then let half the staff go.*

lull someone or an animal **to sleep** to quiet and comfort someone or an animal to sleep. □ *The sound of the waves lulled me to sleep.* □ *The dog's heartbeat lulled her puppies to sleep.*

lumber along to lope or walk along heavily and awkwardly. □ *The horses were lumbering along very slowly because they were tired out.* □ *They were lumbering along, hoping to get there on time.*

lumber off to move or lope away heavily and awkwardly. □ *The frightened bear lumbered off, and we left in a hurry.* □ *He lumbered off, leaving us there alone.*

*a **lump in** one's **throat** the feeling of something in one's throat—as if one were going to cry. (*Typically: **get ~; have ~; give** one **~.**) □ *Whenever they play the national anthem, I get a lump in my throat.* □ *I have a lump in my throat because I'm frightened.*

Lump it! *Inf.* Forget it!; Go away! □ *Well, you can just lump it!* □ *Lump it! Drop dead!*

lump someone **and** someone else **together** and **lump** something **and** something else **together** to classify people or things as members of the same category. □ *You just can't lump Bill and Ted together. They are totally different kinds of people.* □ *I tend to lump apples and oranges together.*

the **lunatic fringe** the more extreme members of a group. □ *Most of the members of that religious sect are quite reasonable, but Lisa belongs to the lunatic fringe.* □ *Many people try to avoid eating a lot of fat, but Mary is part of the lunatic fringe and will eat anything.*

lunch off something to make a lunch by eating something or part of something. □ *We will be able to lunch off the leftover turkey for days!* □ *I can lunch off what is in the refrigerator. Don't worry about me.*

lunch out to eat lunch away from one's home or away from one's place of work. □ *I think I'll lunch out today. I'm tired of carrying lunches.* □ *I want to lunch out today.*

lunge at someone or something to jump or dive at someone or something. □ *The dog lunged at the man, but he got out of the way without getting bitten.* □ *The dog lunged at the bicycle.*

lunge for someone or something to charge or jump at someone or something; to attack someone or something. □ *The mugger lunged for her, but she dodged him.* □ *Ted lunged for the door, but Bill beat him to it.*

lurch at someone or something and **lurch toward** someone or something to sway or turn quickly toward someone or something. □ *Todd lurched at the door and got it open just as the guard saw him.* □ *Bill lurched toward the ship's rail and hung on.*

L

lurch forward to jerk or sway forward. □ *The car lurched forward and shook us around.* □ *When the train lurched forward, we were pushed back into our seats.*

lure someone or something **away**† **(from** someone or something**)** to entice or draw someone away from someone or something. □ *Do you think we could lure her away from her present employment?* □ *They were not able to lure away many of the employees of the other companies.*

lure someone or something **in to** something and **lure** someone or something **in**† to entice someone or something into something or a place. □ *The thief tried to lure the tourist into an alley to rob him.* □ *Using an old trick, the thief lured in the tourist.*

lurk around to slink or sneak around somewhere. □ *Who is that guy lurking around the building?* □ *Stop lurking around.*

lust after someone and **lust for** someone to desire someone sexually. □ *You could see that Sam was lusting after Sally.* □ *Roger claims that he does not lust for anyone.*

lust for something *Fig.* to desire something. □ *He says he lusts for a nice cold can of beer.* □ *Mary lusts for rich and fattening ice cream.*

luxuriate in something to indulge oneself in something; to enjoy the luxury of something. □ *She stood in front of the mirror, luxuriating in her lovely new coat.* □ *They were all luxuriating in the warm, bubbling waters of the hot tub.*

L

mad about someone or something Go to **crazy about** someone or something.

*mad as a hatter and ***mad as a march hare 1.** crazy. (Alludes to the crazy characters in Lewis Carroll's *Alice's Adventures in Wonderland.* *Also: **as** ~.) □ *Poor old John is as mad as a hatter.* □ *All these screaming children are driving me mad as a hatter.* **2.** angry. (This is a misunderstanding of *mad* in the first sense. *Also: **as** ~.) □ *You make me so angry! I'm as mad as a hatter.* □ *John can't control his temper. He's always mad as a hatter.*

*mad as a hornet and ***mad as a wet hen; *mad as hell** very angry. (*Also: **as** ~. Use *hell* with caution.) □ *You make me so angry. I'm as mad as a hornet.* □ *What you said made Mary mad as a wet hen.* □ *Those terrorists make me mad as hell.*

mad as a march hare Go to mad as a hatter.

mad as a wet hen Go to mad as a hornet.

mad as hell Go to mad as a hornet.

*mad (at someone or something**)** angry at someone or something. (*Typically: **be** ~; **get** ~; **make** someone ~.) □ *Don't get mad at me. I didn't do it.* □ *I got mad at my car. It won't start.*

mad enough to chew nails (and spit rivets) and **angry enough to chew nails; mad enough to spit nails** *Inf. Fig.* very angry, as if to be able to bite through metal nails. □ *I am mad enough to chew nails! Who took my checkbook?* □ *Her sudden tirade made him angry enough to chew nails.* □ *He stomped in, mad enough to chew nails and spit rivets.*

mad enough to kick a cat *Rur.* very angry. □ *Stay out of my way. I'm mad enough to kick a cat!* □ *The team lost. The coach was mad enough to kick a cat.*

mad enough to spit nails Go to mad enough to chew nails (and spit rivets).

made conspicuous by one's **absence** Go to conspicuous by one's absence.

made for each other [of two people] very well suited romantically. □ *Bill and Jane were made for each other.* □ *Mr. and Mrs. Smith were not exactly made for each other. They really don't get along.*

made for someone created to please someone or look good on someone in particular. □ *This hat was made for me.* □ *This suit was just made for me!*

made for something to have been designed or manufactured for some purpose; to be very suitable for something or some purpose. □ *This night was made for love.* □ *This wrench is manufactured from the strongest metal. It is made for jobs just like this one.*

made from the same mold Go to cut from the same cloth.

made to measure [of clothing] made especially to fit the measurements of a particular person. □ *Jack has his suits made to measure because he's rather large.* □ *Having clothes made to measure is rather expensive.*

made to order made to one's own measurements and on request. (See also **make** something **to order.**) □ *This suit fits so well because it's made to order.* □ *His feet are so big that all his shoes have to be made to order.*

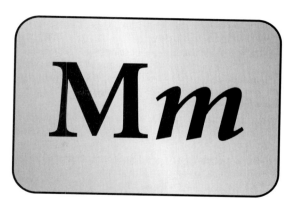

maiden voyage *Fig.* the first voyage of a ship or boat. □ *The liner sank on its maiden voyage.* □ *Jim is taking his yacht on its maiden voyage.*

mail something **from** some place to send something by mail from a particular place. □ *I mailed the check from my office.* □ *I will mail it from the main post office.*

mail something **to** someone to send something to someone by mail. □ *I mailed the check to you yesterday.* □ *I mailed a gift to my niece.*

main strength and awkwardness *Fig.* great force; brute force. □ *They finally got the piano moved in to the living room by main strength and awkwardness.* □ *Lifting the antique table must be done carefully. This is not a job requiring main strength and awkwardness.*

maintain someone **in** something to keep or provide for someone in a certain style or condition. □ *I insist that you maintain me in the style to which I have become accustomed.* □ *He had hoped to maintain himself in comfort.*

maintain something **at** something to keep something at a certain level, setting, degree, amount, etc. □ *You must maintain the temperature at 30 degrees Celsius.* □ *We have to maintain the temperature at a very high level.*

major in something to specialize in a certain subject in college. □ *I majored in history in college.* □ *I want to major in math.*

make a beeline for someone or something *Fig.* to head straight toward someone or something. (Alludes to the straight flight of a bee.) □ *Billy came into the kitchen and made a beeline for the cookies.* □ *After the game, we all made a beeline for John, who was serving cold drinks.*

make a believer (out) of someone to convince someone decisively about something. □ *The game they played made a believer out of me; from now on, I'm betting on them.* □ *It was an interesting discussion, but it did not make a believer out of me.*

make a big deal about something Go to make a federal case out of something.

make a (big) stink (about someone or something**)** and **raise a (big) stink (about** someone or something**)** *Fig.* to make trouble about someone or something. □ *Why did you raise a big stink about it?* □ *Jim is making a stink about Alice.*

make a bolt for someone or something *Fig.* to run quickly to or at someone or something. □ *The child came into the*

M

room and made a bolt for her mother. □ *The dog made a bolt for the door.*

make a break for someone or something *Fig.* to run suddenly toward someone or something; to seize an opportunity to run toward someone or something. □ *The crook made a break for the cop in order to get his gun.* □ *Max made a break for the door.*

make a bundle and **make a pile** to make a lot of money. □ *John really made a bundle on that deal.* □ *I'd like to make a pile and retire.*

make a check (out†) (to someone or something**)** *Fig.* to write a check to someone or a group. □ *Please make the check out to Bill Franklin.* □ *Make out a check to me.* □ *Please make a check out to the bank.* □ *Make a check to the phone company.*

make a check over to someone or something to endorse the back of a check, making it payable to someone or a group. □ *Please make the check over to Bill Franklin.* □ *Would you make the check over to my bank?*

make a check to someone or something to write a check to someone. (See also **make a check out (to** someone or something**).**) □ *The check should be for fifty dollars. Please make it to me.* □ *Make the check to Jim.* □ *She made the check to the bank, and sent it off in the mail.*

make a clean breast of something **(to** someone**)** *Fig.* to admit something to someone. □ *You should make a clean breast of the matter to someone.* □ *You'll feel better if you make a clean breast of the incident.*

make a clean sweep *Fig.* to do something completely or thoroughly, with no exceptions. □ *The boss decided to change the direction of the company, so he made a clean sweep and fired all the top management.* □ *They made a clean sweep through the neighborhood, repairing all the sidewalks.*

make a comeback to return to one's former (successful) career. □ *After ten years in retirement, the singer made a comeback.* □ *You're never too old to make a comeback.*

make a dash for someone or something to run quickly for someone or something. □ *Suddenly Max made a dash for Lefty and punched him in the stomach.* □ *John made a dash for the bathroom as soon as they arrived home.*

make a day of doing something and **make a day of it** to spend the whole day doing something. □ *We went to the museum to see the new exhibit and then decided to make a day of it.* □ *They made a day of cleaning the attic.*

make a day of it Go to previous.

make a deal with someone to strike a bargain with someone. □ *I want to buy your car and I think I can make a deal with you.* □ *I will make a deal with you that you will like.*

make a dent in something **1.** *Lit.* to make a depression in something. □ *I kicked the side of the car and made a dent in it.* □ *Please don't make a dent in the side of the house.* **2.** *Fig.* to use only a little of something; to make a small amount of progress with something. □ *Look at what's left on your plate! You hardly made a dent in your dinner.* □ *I've been slaving all day, and I have hardly made a dent in my work.*

make a difference in someone or something to cause a noticeable change in someone or something. □ *Getting a*

job made a big difference in my lifestyle. □ *His mother's death made a difference in his attitude toward doctors.*

make a difference to someone [for one choice or another] to matter to someone. □ *The big one or the little one—does it really make a difference to anyone?* □ *It makes quite a difference to me!*

make a face (at someone**)** and **make faces (at** someone**) 1.** to show a funny or distorted expression to someone in ridicule. □ *Mother, Billy made a face at me!* □ *The teacher sent Jane to the principal for making a face in class.* **2.** to attempt to communicate to someone through facial gestures, usually an attempt to say "no" or "stop." □ *I started to tell John where I was last night, but Bill made a face so I didn't.* □ *John made a face at me as I was testifying, so I avoided telling everything.*

make a fast buck and **make a quick buck** to make money with little effort or in a short time. □ *Tom is always ready to make a fast buck.* □ *I made a quick buck selling used cars.*

make a federal case out of something and **make a big deal about** something to exaggerate the seriousness of something. □ *Come on. It was nothing! Don't make a federal case out of it.* □ *I only stepped on your toe. Don't make a big deal about it.*

make a fool (out) of someone and **make a monkey (out) of** someone to make someone look foolish. □ *John made a monkey out of himself while trying to make a fool out of Jim.* □ *John made a fool out of himself at the party.* □ *Are you trying to make a monkey out of me?*

make a fresh start Go to a fresh start.

make a friend and **make friends** to establish a link of friendship with someone. □ *I have never found it difficult to make friends.* □ *Mary had to make new friends when she changed schools.*

make a fuss (over someone or something**) 1.** to worry about or make a bother about someone or something. □ *Why do you make a fuss over a problem like that?* □ *Please don't make a fuss. Everything will be all right.* **2.** to be very solicitous and helpful toward a person or a pet. □ *How can anyone make a fuss over a cat?* □ *Billy was embarrassed when his mother made a fuss over him.* **3.** to argue about someone or something. □ *Please don't make a fuss over who gets the last cookie.* □ *Please discuss it. Don't make a fuss over it!*

make a go of something to succeed at something. (Often with *it.*) □ *She just didn't have the energy or inclination to make a go of her marriage.* □ *I did everything I could to make a go of it.*

make a grab at someone or something to grasp at someone or something. □ *Don made a grab at Betsy, but she eluded him.* □ *Kelly made a grab at the ball, but it went on past her.*

make a great show of something *Fig.* to make something obvious; to do something in a showy fashion. □ *Ann made a great show of wiping up the drink that John spilled.* □ *Jane displayed her irritation at our late arrival by making a great show of serving the cold dinner.*

make a guess Go to take a guess.

make a habit of something to do something so often that it becomes a habit. □ *You mustn't make a habit of interrupting.* □ *I make a habit of counting my change.*

make a hit with someone to please someone; to impress someone. □ *The dessert you served really made a hit with the guests.* □ *Her talk made a hit with the audience.*

make a killing *Fig.* to have a great success, especially in making money. □ *John has got a job selling insurance. He's not exactly making a killing.* □ *Bill made a killing at the racetrack yesterday.*

make a (kind of) life for oneself to develop and live a particular kind of lifestyle for oneself. □ *She made a good life for herself in New York City, working as a freelancer.*

Make a lap! *Sl.* to sit down. □ *Hey, make a lap and get out of the way!* □ *Pull up a chair and make a lap!*

make a laughingstock of oneself **or** something and **make** oneself **or** something **a laughingstock** to make oneself a source of ridicule or laughter; to do something that invites ridicule. □ *Laura made herself a laughingstock by arriving at the fast-food restaurant in full evening dress.* □ *The board of directors made the company a laughingstock by hiring an ex-convict as president.*

make a living by doing something Go to next.

make a living from something and **make a living by** doing something to earn a living from something or by doing something. □ *John makes a living from painting houses.* □ *Can you really make a living by selling jewelry?*

make a long story short and **cut a long story short** to leave out parts of a story to make it shorter; to bring a story to an end. (A formula that introduces a summary of a story or a joke. See also **long story short**.) □ *And—to make a long story short—I never got back the money that I lent him.* □ *If I can make a long story short, let me say that everything worked out fine.*

make a man of someone *Fig.* to make a young male into an adult male. □ *The experience will make a man of Ted.* □ *Send Wally into the army. That'll make a man of him.*

make a meal of something **1.** to eat something. □ *The cat made a meal of the fish.* □ *They made a meal of the roast beef and enjoyed it very much.* **2.** to eat enough of something to consider it or have it as a full meal. □ *I really don't want to make a meal of lettuce alone.* □ *Can we make a meal of this turkey, or should we save some for sandwiches?*

make a mental note of something to remember something. □ *So, you want to be considered for a job. I'll make a mental note of that.* □ *Please make a mental note of my telephone number.*

make a mess of something *Fig.* to mess something up; to ruin something. □ *Give it a try, but don't make a mess of it.* □ *Jerry made a mess of the kitchen.*

make a mistake to commit an error; to do something wrong accidentally. □ *I made a mistake and I am really sorry about it.*

make a mockery of something to make a deliberate parody or a poor imitation of something. □ *What a mess. You made a mockery of the task.* □ *You have made a mockery of my position!*

make a monkey (out) of someone Go to **make a fool (out) of** someone.

make a mountain out of a molehill *Cliché* to make a major issue out of a minor one; to exaggerate the importance of something. □ *Come on, don't make a mountain out of a molehill. It's not that important.* □ *Mary is always making mountains out of molehills.*

make a move on someone to attempt to seduce someone. □ *Was he making a move on me? I think he was.* □ *Jed is known for making moves on young women.*

make a name (for oneself**)** *Fig.* to become famous. □ *Sally wants to work hard and make a name for herself.* □ *It's hard to make a name without a lot of talent and hard work.*

make a night of it *Fig.* to spend the entire evening or night doing something. (Especially when one had intended to devote only a little time to the outing.) □ *We went out to have a bite to eat and were having such a good time that we decided to make a night of it.* □ *I did not want to make a night of it, so I left early.*

make a note of something **1.** *Lit.* to write something down as a reminder. □ *Please make a note of it so you will remember.* □ *I will make a note of it and try to remember where I put the note.* **2.** *Fig.* to make a mental note of something. □ *You want to be considered for promotion. I'll make a note of it.* □ *Please make a note of it.*

make a nuisance of oneself to be a constant bother. □ *I'm sorry to make a nuisance of myself, but I do need an answer to my question.* □ *Stop making a nuisance of yourself and wait your turn.*

make a paper trail Go to **a paper trail**.

make a pass at someone to flirt with or suggest sexual activity with someone. □ *Can you believe it? Larry made a pass at me!* □ *No one ever makes a pass at me.*

make a pass at something to fly over or close by something. □ *The plane made a pass at the landing field and pulled up at the last minute.* □ *The bird made a pass at me because I got too close to its nest.*

make a pig of oneself *Fig.* to eat too much, too fast, or noisily; to eat more than one's share. □ *Don't make a pig of yourself!* □ *Sam is making a pig of himself and taking more than his share.*

make a pile Go to **make a bundle**.

make a pitch (for someone or something**)** *Fig.* to say something in support of someone or something; to attempt to promote, sell, or advance someone or something. □ *Bill is making a pitch for his friend's new product again.* □ *The theatrical agent came in and made a pitch for her client.* □ *Every time I turn on the television set, someone is making a pitch.*

make a play (for someone**)** to attempt to attract the romantic interest of someone. □ *Ann made a play for Bill, but he wasn't interested in her.* □ *I knew he liked me, but I never thought he'd make a play.*

make a point and **make points 1.** *Lit.* to score a point in a game. □ *Bob made a point in the last match.* □ *Karen made twenty points in the second half.* **2.** *Fig.* to state an item of importance. (See also **make a point of** someone or something; **make points (with** someone**).)** □ *You made a point that we all should remember.* □ *He spoke for an hour without making a point.*

M

make a point of doing something and **make a point of something** *Fig.* to make an effort to do something. □ *Please make a point of mailing this letter. It's very important.* □ *The hostess made a point of thanking me for bringing flowers.*

make a point of someone or something and **make an issue of** someone or something *Fig.* to turn someone or something into an important matter. □ *Please don't make a point of John's comment. It wasn't that important.* □ *I hope you make an issue of Tom's success and the reasons for it.*

make a practice of something and **make** something **a practice** to turn something into a habitual activity. □ *Jane makes a practice of planting daisies every summer.* □ *Her mother also made it a practice.*

make a quick buck Go to make a fast buck.

make a reservation and **make reservations** to reserve a seat, as in an airplane, restaurant, or theater in advance; to reserve a room, as in a hotel in advance. □ *Did you make a reservation or are we just going to chance getting a table?* □ *I made reservations for a flight at twelve noon.*

make a run for it *Fig.* to run fast to get away or get somewhere. □ *When the guard wasn't looking, the prisoner made a run for it.* □ *In the baseball game, the player on first base made a run for it, but he didn't make it to second base.*

make a scene and **create a scene** *Fig.* to make a public display or disturbance. □ *When John found a fly in his drink, he started to create a scene.* □ *Oh, John, please don't make a scene. Just forget about it.*

make a secret of something to act as if something were a secret. □ *I'm not making a secret of it. I am quitting this job.* □ *Mary made a secret of her intentions.*

make a start on something to set out to do something; to make a beginning on something. □ *See if you can make a start on the project.* □ *I will try to make a start on the cleaning before I leave today.*

make a stink (about something**)** Go to create a stink (about something).

make a virtue of necessity *Prov.* to do what you have to do cheerfully or willingly. □ *When Bill's mother became sick, there was no one but Bill to take care of her, so Bill made a virtue of necessity and resolved to enjoy their time together.*

make advances at someone Go to next.

make advances to someone and **make advances at** someone to flirt with someone; to begin to seduce someone. □ *She began making advances to me, and I left the room.* □ *Mary made advances at every male she encountered.*

make allowance(s) (for someone or something**) 1.** to allow time, space, food, etc., for someone or something. □ *When planning the party, please make allowances for John and his family.* □ *I'm making allowance for ten extra guests.* **2.** to make excuses or explanations for someone or something; to take into consideration the negative effects of someone or something. □ *You're very late even when we make allowance for the weather.* □ *We have to make allowance for the age of the house when we judge its condition.*

make amends (to someone**) (for** someone or something**)** to make up to someone for something that someone or something did. □ *Don't worry. I will make amends to her for my sister, who behaved so badly.* □ *I will try to make amends for the accident.* □ *I can make amends to Sam, I'm sure.*

make an all-out effort Go to an all-out effort.

make (an amount of) headway 1. *Lit.* to move forward. □ *Even in a light wind, the ship could not make any headway.* **2.** *Fig.* to advance toward completing a task. □ *With the help of Garret, Christopher made a lot of headway on the project.*

make an appearance to appear; to appear in a performance. □ *We waited for thirty minutes for the professor to make an appearance, then we went home.* □ *The famous singing star made an appearance in Detroit last August.*

make an appointment (with someone**)** to schedule a meeting with someone. □ *I made an appointment with the doctor for late today.* □ *The professor wouldn't see me unless I made an appointment.*

make an entrance to enter [a place], in some formal or special way, as onto the stage in a play or opera. □ *She made her entrance too early and threw everyone into confusion.*

make an example of someone to do something to someone that shows the bad results of bad behavior; to point to someone as a bad example. □ *The judge said that he would make an example of Sally and would fine her the maximum amount.* □ *The teacher made an example of me to the class, with a detention on the first day of school.*

make an exception (for someone**)** to suspend a rule or practice for someone in a single instance. □ *Please make an exception just this once.* □ *The rule is a good one, and I will not make an exception for anyone.*

make an exhibition of oneself to show off; to try to get a lot of attention for oneself. □ *She is not just dancing, she is making an exhibition of herself.* □ *Whenever Rudy drinks, he makes an exhibition of himself.*

make an honest woman of someone *Fig.* to marry a woman. (Intended as jocular.) □ *So you finally made an honest woman out of Denise.* □ *She had wanted Max to make an honest woman of her, but you can't depend on Max to do anything right.*

make an impression on someone to produce a positive memorable effect on someone while one is present. (Akin to **leave an impression (on** someone**).**) □ *Tom made quite an impression on the banker.*

make an issue of someone or something Go to **make a point of** someone or something.

make an offer one **cannot refuse** Go to an offer one cannot refuse.

make an uproar Go to create an uproar.

make application (to someone or something**) (for** something**)** to apply to a person or an office for something. □ *You must make application to the committee for admission.* □ *Can I make application to this office for a scholarship?*

make arrangements for someone to plan accommodations for someone. □ *John is coming for a visit next week.*

Please make arrangements for him at the hotel. □ *I will make arrangements for everyone when I call the hotel.*

make arrangements to do something to plan to do something; to facilitate the doing of something. □ *Please make arrangements to have all this stuff hauled away.* □ *We will make arrangements to be there on time.*

make arrangements (with someone**) (for** something**)** to make plans with someone for something. □ *I will make arrangements with Fred for the loan.* □ *We can make arrangements for a car with the manager.*

make as if to do something to act as if one were about to do something. □ *The thief made as if to run away but changed his mind.* □ *Jane made as if to smack the child.*

make away with someone or something and **make off with** someone or something to take someone or something away; to make someone or something disappear. □ *The robber made away with the jewelry.* □ *The maid quickly made off with the children. We only saw them for a moment.*

make believe that... to pretend that... □ *Make believe that you have a million dollars. What would you do with it?*

make book on something **1.** *Sl.* to make or accept bets on something. □ *Well, she might. But I wouldn't make book on it.* □ *Don't make book on my success in this game.* **2.** *Sl.* to feel confident enough about something to accept wagers on it. □ *Of course the delivery date is certain. You can make book on it!* □ *The work might be done on time, but I wouldn't make book on it.*

make (both) ends meet *Fig.* to earn and spend equal amounts of money. (Usually in reference to a meager living with little if any money after basic expenses.) □ *I have to work at two jobs to make ends meet.* □ *Through better budgeting, I am learning to make both ends meet.*

make certain of something to check something in order to be sure. □ *Please make certain of what you want to do.* □ *Would you please make certain of the number of things you want to order?*

make change (for someone**) (for** something**) 1.** to return change [coins] for someone to use for some purpose. □ *Will you please make change for me for the telephone?* □ *I will make change for the telephone for you.* **2.** to return change [coins or bills or both] to someone for paper money. □ *The clerk refused to make change for her for the dollar bill.* □ *I will be happy to make change for a ten for you.*

make chin music *Fig.* to talk or chatter. □ *We sat around all evening making chin music.* □ *You were making chin music when you should have been listening.*

make contact with someone Go to **contact with** someone.

make cracks about someone or something *Fig.* to make jokes or smart remarks about someone or something. □ *Stop making cracks about my cousin.* □ *Ken made a few cracks about the movie.*

make demands of someone or something and **make demands on** someone or something to expect someone or something to do something or act in a particular way. □ *Please don't make demands of everyone in the shop.* □ *The boss is making a lot of demands on the new machinery.*

make do (with someone or something**)** to do as well as possible with someone or something. (See also **do with** someone or something.) □ *You'll have to make do with less money next year. The economy is very weak.* □ *We'll have to make do with John even though he's a slow worker.*

make every effort to do something to try very hard to accomplish something. □ *I will make every effort to be there on time.*

make eyes at someone *Fig.* to flirt with someone. □ *Mother, he's making eyes at me!* □ *Jed tried to make eyes at all the young women.*

make faces (at someone**)** Go to **make a face (at** someone**)**.

make fast work of someone or something Go to **make short work of** someone or something.

make for somewhere to set out for somewhere; to run or travel to somewhere. □ *Wilbur made for Philadelphia when he heard the police in the Big Apple were after him.* □ *Barlowe made for the stairs, but two shots rang out, and he knew it was all over for Mary.*

make free with someone to exploit someone; to take advantage of someone. □ *You shouldn't make free with your employees. They are liable to take you to court.* □ *He was making free with his secretary, having her do his private business.*

make free with something to use something freely; to exploit something. □ *You can make free with the hot water. We have a huge tank.* □ *Sally is making free with the sugar I was saving for breakfast cereal.*

make friends Go to **make a friend**.

make friends with someone to work to become a friend of someone. □ *I want to make friends with all the people I am going to be working with.* □ *Let's try to make friends with each other.*

make fun of someone or something to ridicule someone or something. □ *Are you making fun of me?* □ *I am making fun of your hat.*

make good as something to succeed in a particular role. □ *I hope I make good as a teacher.* □ *John made good as a football player.*

make good (at something**)** to succeed at something. □ *Bob worked hard to make good at selling.* □ *Jane was determined to make good.*

make good money to earn a sizable amount of money. □ *Ann makes good money at her job.* □ *I don't know what she does, but she makes good money.*

make good on something **1.** to fulfill a promise. □ *Tom made good on his pledge to donate $1,000.* □ *Bill refused to make good on his promise.* **2.** to repay a debt. (See also **set** something **right**.) □ *I couldn't make good on my debts, and I got in a lot of trouble.* □ *If you don't make good on this bill, I'll have to take back your car.*

make good time to proceed at a fast or reasonable rate. □ *On our trip to Toledo, we made good time.* □ *I'm making good time, but I have a long way to go.*

make (good) use of something to use something well. □ *I am sure I can make good use of the gift you gave me.* □ *We will make use of this book.*

make hamburger (out) of someone Go to make mince-meat (out) of someone.

Make haste slowly. and **More haste, less speed.** *Prov.* Act quickly, but not so quickly that you make careless mistakes. □ *Jane: Why are you throwing your clothes around the room? Alan: You told me to get my things packed in a hurry. Jane: Yes, but make haste slowly; otherwise we'll have to spend an hour cleaning up the mess you make.* □ *I know you want to finish that sweater by Joe's birthday, but you're knitting so fast that you make mistakes. More haste, less speed.*

Make hay while the sun shines. *Prov.* If you have an opportunity to do something, do it before the opportunity expires. □ *Jane: While my husband's out of town, I'm going to watch all the movies he wouldn't take me to see. Jane: Why not? Make hay while the sun shines.*

make heads or tails of someone or something *Fig.* to understand someone or something that someone has said. (Usually with the negative.) □ *I can't make heads or tails of Fred.* □ *No one can make heads or tails of this problem.*

make inroads into something *Fig.* to succeed in getting something done or at least started. □ *George was unable to make inroads into solving the problem.* □ *We are making no inroads into the high-priority project.*

make it 1. to achieve one's goals. □ *I can see by looking around this room that you have really made it.* □ *I hope I make it someday. But if not, I tried.* **2.** *Sl.* to copulate (with someone). □ *There was no doubt in his mind that those bedroom eyes were telling him their owner wanted to make it.* □ *She wanted to make it, but he convinced her they should wait.*

make it big to become successful, especially financially. □ *I always knew that someday I would make it big.* □ *My brother made it big, but it has just led to tax problems.*

make it by the seat of one's **pants** Go to by the seat of one's pants.

make it hot for someone *Fig.* to make things difficult for someone; to put someone under pressure. □ *Maybe if we make it hot for them, they'll leave.* □ *John likes making it hot for people. He's sort of mean.*

make it one's **business to** do something and **take it upon** oneself **to** do something *Fig.* to do something on one's own even if it means interfering in something that does not directly concern one. (As opposed to minding one's own business.) □ *I know it doesn't concern me, but I made it my business to call city hall because someone had to.* □ *Jane took it upon herself to find out exactly what had happened to the old lady.*

Make it snappy! *Inf.* Hurry up!; Move quickly and smartly. □ *Andy: Make it snappy! I haven't got all day. Bob: Don't rush me.* □ *Mary: Do you mind if I stop here and get some film? Bob: Not if you make it snappy! Mary: Don't worry. I'll hurry.*

make it (to) some place to reach some place; to be able to attend an event at a place. □ *I couldn't make it to the party.* □ *He didn't think his car could make it to Cleveland.*

make it to something; **make it as far as** something Go to make it (until something).

Make it two. I wish to order the thing that someone else just now ordered. (Said to food or drink server.) □ *Bill (speaking to the waiter): I'll have the roast chicken. Mary: Make it two.* □ *Waiter: Would you like something to drink? Tom: Just a beer. Waiter (turning to Mary): And you? Mary: Make it two.*

make it (until something**)** and **make it to** something; **make it as far as** something to endure until something; to last until some time or until reaching some place. □ *I hope my car can make it to the next town.* □ *Do you think you can make it until we come to a hotel?*

make it worth someone's **while** *Euph.* to tip or offer special (usually extra) payment to someone. □ *I made it worth the waiter's while to give us good service.* □ *If you'll throw a few contracts my way, I'll make it worth your while.*

make last-ditch effort Go to last-ditch effort.

make life miserable for someone to give someone misery; to be a great nuisance to someone. □ *This nagging backache is making life miserable for me.* □ *I wish you would stop making life miserable for me.*

make light of something to treat something as if it were unimportant or humorous. □ *I wish you wouldn't make light of his problems. They're quite serious.* □ *I make light of my problems, and that makes me feel better.*

make like a tree and leave *Sl.* to leave; to depart. (Jocular; a pun on the *leaf* of a tree.) □ *I have to leave now. It's time to make like a tree and leave.* □ *Hey, Jane. Don't you have an appointment somewhere? Why don't you make like a tree and leave?*

make like someone or something to act like someone or something. □ *Why don't you make like a bunny and run away? Beat it!* □ *Would you please make like a butler and hold the door open for me?*

make little of someone or something to minimize someone or something; to **play** someone or something **down**; to belittle someone or something. □ *John made little of my efforts to collect money for charity.* □ *The neighbors made little of John and thought he would amount to nothing.*

make love (to someone**) 1.** to kiss and caress someone. □ *Ernest made love to Linda in the garden in the moonlight.* □ *She liked the way he made love to her—all that poetry.* **2.** *Euph.* to have sex with someone. □ *I really think that he wanted to make love to me.* □ *She did not want to make love to him.*

make mention of someone or something to mention someone or something. □ *Did you have to make mention of Sally? I'm angry with her.* □ *I will have to make mention of your failure to secure additional business.*

make merry to have fun; to have an enjoyable time. □ *The guests certainly made merry at the wedding.* □ *The children were making merry in the backyard.*

make mincemeat (out) of someone and **make hamburger (out) of** someone *Fig.* to beat or pound someone or something; to treat someone or something roughly. (As if chopping someone up.) □ *If you don't behave, I'll make mincemeat out of you.* □ *Do you want Fred to make hamburger out of you?*

Make mine something. I wish to have the thing named. (The *something* can be a particular food or drink, a flavor of a food, a size of a garment, or a type of almost anything. Most typically used for food or drink.) □ *Bill: I want some pie. Yes, I'd like apple. Tom: Make mine cherry.*

□ *Waiter: Would you care for some dessert? The ice cream is homemade. Tom: Yes, indeed. Make mine chocolate.*

make mischief to cause trouble. □ *Bob loves to make mischief and get other people into trouble.* □ *Don't believe what Mary says. She's just trying to make mischief.*

make money on something to make a certain amount of profit on something. □ *I am sure I can make something on the deal.* □ *Can I make any money on this sale?*

Make my day! *Inf.* Go ahead, do what you are going to do, and I will be very happy to do what I have to do! (A catchphrase from a movie scene of a police officer who has a gun pointed at a criminal. The police officer wants the criminal to do something that will justify pulling the trigger, which the police officer will do with pleasure. Used in real life in any context, and especially in sarcasm.) □ *Move a muscle! Go for your gun! Go ahead, make my day!* □ *Make my day. Just try it.*

Make no bones about it. to make no mistake (about it); no need to doubt it; absolutely. □ *This is the greatest cake I've ever eaten. Make no bones about it.* □ *Make no bones about it, Mary is a great singer.*

make no difference (to someone) [for a choice] not to matter to someone. (*Any* is used with negative nouns or verbs.) □ *Pick whom you like. It makes no difference to me.* □ *It doesn't make any difference to me.* □ *Nothing much makes any difference to them anymore.*

Make no mistake (about it)! *Inf.* Do not be mistaken! You can be certain. □ *Sally: I'm very angry with you! Make no mistake about it! Fred: Whatever it's about, I'm sorry.* □ *Clerk: Make no mistake, this is the finest carpet available. Sally: I'd like something a little less fine, I think.*

make nonsense of something to make something appear to be silly or nonsensical. □ *You are just making nonsense of everything I have tried to do.* □ *Your statement makes nonsense of everything you have said before.*

make nothing of something to ignore something as if it had not happened; to think no more about something. (Often with *it*.) □ *My father caught me throwing the snowball, but he made nothing of it.* □ *I made nothing of the remark, even though it seemed quite rude.* □ *I saw him leave early, but I made nothing of it.*

make off with someone or something Go to **make away with** someone or something.

make one an offer one **cannot refuse** Go to **an offer** one **cannot refuse**.

make one's **mark** to do something that allows one to receive appropriate recognition. □ *Perry made his mark by inventing a special kind of holder for a cell phone.*

make one's **mind up†** (**about** someone or something) to decide about someone or something. □ *Please make your mind up about Ralph. Will you pick him or not?* □ *Make up your mind about her!* □ *I just couldn't make my mind up.*

make one's **money stretch** Go to **stretch** one's **money**.

make one's **(own) bed 1.** *Lit.* to restore order to the bedclothes on one's own bed. □ *Jimmy, you are old enough to make your own bed.* **2.** *Fig.* to be the cause of one's own misery. □ *Well, I guess I made my own bed. Now I have to lie in it.* □ *"We all make our own beds," said the minister.*

make (one's) peace with someone to set things right with someone; to make amends with someone. □ *I will make my peace with Jane. You needn't be the one to patch things up.* □ *Let's go make peace with Karen.*

make one's **way along** something to move along something slowly or carefully. □ *Todd made his way along the slippery walk.* □ *The old man made his way along the street carefully.*

make one's **way back (to** something**)** to work one's way back to something or some place. □ *I made my way back to the little town in the densest fog I have ever seen.* □ *I went for a walk and got lost. It took hours for me to make my way back.*

make one's **way in the world** *Fig.* to succeed in the world independently. □ *I intend to prepare myself to make my way in the world by getting a college degree.* □ *I know that all my children can make their way in the world.*

make one's **way through** something Go to **pick** one's **way through** something.

make oneself at home to make oneself comfortable as if one were in one's own home. □ *Please come in and make yourself at home.* □ *I'm glad you're here. During your visit, just make yourself at home.*

make oneself conspicuous to attract attention to oneself. □ *Please don't make yourself conspicuous. It embarrasses me.* □ *Ann makes herself conspicuous by wearing brightly colored clothing.*

make oneself heard to speak loudly so that one will be heard above background noise. □ *I had to shout to make myself heard.* □ *He screamed to make himself heard over the sound of the plane's engines.*

make oneself miserable to do things which cause one to be unhappy. □ *You're just making yourself miserable by trying to do something you aren't qualified to do.* □ *I'm not making myself miserable! You're making me miserable.*

make oneself or something a laughingstock Go to **make a laughingstock of** oneself or something.

make oneself scarce *Fig.* [for someone] to become difficult to find; [for someone to] go into hiding. □ *Tom is mad and is looking for you. Better make yourself scarce.* □ *Make yourself scarce! Here comes the sheriff.*

make (oneself) up to put makeup on oneself. □ *I have to make up now. I go on stage in ten minutes.* □ *I will make myself up. I don't need your help.*

make or break someone [of a task, job, career choice] to bring success to or improve, or ruin, someone. □ *The army will either make or break him.* □ *It's a tough assignment, and it will either make or break her.*

make (out) after someone or something to run after someone or something; to start out after someone or something. □ *Paul made out after Fred, who had taken Paul's hat.* □ *The police officer made after the robber.*

make (out) for someone or something to run toward someone, something, or some place. □ *They made out for Sam as soon as they saw him coming.* □ *The boys made for the swimming pool as soon as the coach blew the whistle.*

make out like a bandit *Rur.* to make a large profit. □ *Joe's making out like a bandit, selling expensive cameras.* □

Mary made out like a bandit, playing twenty-one in Las Vegas.

make (out) like something *Rur.* to pretend something. □ *Let's make out like we're cowboys and Indians.* □ *Joe made out like he had a lot of money, and folks believed him.*

make out that... to pretend that [something is so]. □ *He made out that he hadn't seen me.* □ *We all made out that we hadn't heard the sound.*

make out (with someone**)** to kiss and pet with someone. □ *All evening long, he was trying to make out with me.* □ *Sharon was trying to make out with Bill.*

make out (with someone or something**) 1.** to manage to do something with someone or something. □ *I think I can make out with this hammer.* □ *If I can't make out with a crew of four, I'll have to ask for more help.* **2.** Go to **make out (with** someone**).**

make overtures about doing something to give hints about something; to present or suggest ideas. □ *The company made overtures about hiring me.* □ *Tom is making overtures about inviting us to his country home next month.*

make points (with someone**)** *Fig.* to gain favor with someone; to impress someone. (See also **make a point.**) □ *Tom is trying to make points with Ann. He wants to ask her out.* □ *He's trying to make points by smiling and telling her how nice she looks.*

make reservations Go to **make a reservation.**

make room (for someone or something**)** to provide space for someone or something. □ *Make room for Sam. He needs a place to sit.* □ *Can you make room for this package?*

make sense to be understandable. □ *John doesn't make sense.* □ *What John says makes sense to me.*

make short work of someone or something and **make fast work of** someone or something to finish with someone or something quickly. □ *I made short work of Tom so I could leave the office to play golf.* □ *Billy made fast work of his dinner so he could go out and play.*

make so bold as to do something Go to **be so bold as to** do something.

make (some) sense (out) of someone or something to understand someone or something. □ *I can't make sense out of Doris and what she has done!* □ *No one can make sense out of Tom's story.*

make someone *Sl.* to identify someone. (Used especially in the context of law enforcement.) □ *The cop stared at Wilbur and tried to make him, but failed to identify him and let him go.* □ *The cops took the suspect downtown where the police chief made him as a wanted criminal.*

make someone **an offer** to offer someone an amount of money for something. (Usually an invitation.) □ *Do you like it? Make me an offer.*

make someone **eat crow** *Fig.* to cause someone to retract a statement or admit an error. □ *Because Mary was completely wrong, we made her eat crow.* □ *They won't make me eat crow. They can't prove I was wrong.*

make someone **look good** to cause someone to appear successful or competent (especially when this is not the case). □ *John arranges all his affairs to make himself look*

good. □ *The manager didn't like the quarterly report because it didn't make her look good.*

make someone **look ridiculous** to make someone look foolish (not funny). □ *This hat makes me look ridiculous.* □ *Please make me look good. Don't make me look ridiculous!*

make someone **mad (at** someone or something**)** Go to **mad (at** someone or something**).**

make someone or something **available to** someone to supply someone with someone or something. □ *I made my car available to Bob.* □ *They made their maid available to us.*

make someone or something **into** something to turn someone or something into something. □ *I will make you into a Hollywood star!* □ *We made our basement into a family room.*

make someone or something **tick** *Fig.* to cause someone or something to run or function. (Usually with *what*. *Tick* refers to a watch or clock.) □ *I don't know what makes it tick.* □ *What makes John tick? I just don't understand him.* □ *I took apart the radio to find out what made it tick.*

make someone **over**[†] Go to **do** someone **over**[†].

make someone's **bed (up**[†]**)** Go to **make the bed (up**[†]**).**

make someone's **blood boil** *Fig.* to make someone very angry. □ *It just makes my blood boil to think of the amount of food that gets wasted around here.* □ *Whenever I think of that dishonest mess, it makes my blood boil.*

make someone's **blood run cold** *Fig.* to shock or horrify someone. □ *The terrible story in the newspaper made my blood run cold.* □ *I could tell you things about prisons that would make your blood run cold.*

make someone's **flesh crawl** and **make** someone's **skin crawl** to cause someone's skin to feel funny or get goose pimples through fright. □ *Just to hear the story of the killings made my flesh crawl.* □ *The horror movie made our skin crawl.*

make someone's **gorge rise** *Fig.* to cause someone to become very angry. □ *The unnecessary accident made my gorge rise.* □ *Getting his tax bill made Bob's gorge rise.*

make someone's **hair curl** Go to **curl** someone's **hair.**

make someone's **hair stand on end** *Fig.* to cause someone to be very frightened. □ *The horrible scream made my hair stand on end.* □ *The ghost story made our hair stand on end.*

make someone's **head spin** Go to next.

make someone's **head swim** and **make** someone's **head spin 1.** *Fig.* to make someone dizzy or disoriented. □ *Riding the merry-go-round makes my head swim.* □ *Breathing the gas made my head swim.* **2.** *Fig.* to confuse or overwhelm someone. □ *All these numbers make my head swim.* □ *The physics lecture made my head spin.*

make someone's **mind up**[†] to decide; to do something that decides something for someone. □ *Will you please make up your mind?* □ *I will help make up your mind.*

make someone's **mouth water** to make someone hungry (for something); to cause saliva to flow in someone's mouth. □ *That beautiful salad makes my mouth water.* □ *Talking about food makes my mouth water.*

make someone's **position clear** to clarify where someone stands on an issue. □ *I don't think you understand what I said. Let me make my position clear.* □ *I can't tell whether you are in favor of or against the proposal. Please make your position clear.*

make someone's **skin crawl** Go to make someone's flesh crawl.

make someone **sick** to disgust someone. □ *I am really tired of your vile talk. You make me sick!* □ *She screamed at him that he made her sick and then she ran out of the house.*

make someone **sick at heart** Go to sick at heart.

make someone **stir crazy** Go to stir crazy.

make someone **the scapegoat for** something to make someone take the blame for something. □ *They made Tom the scapegoat for the whole affair. It wasn't all his fault.* □ *Don't try to make me the scapegoat. I'll tell who really did it.*

make someone **up**† to put makeup on someone. □ *You have to make the clowns up before you start on the other characters in the play.* □ *Did you make up the clowns?*

make something to attend an event. □ *I hope you can make our party.* □ *I am sorry, but I won't be able to make it.*

make something **a practice** Go to make a practice of something.

make something **about** someone or something to make comments, remarks, a furor, a fuss, etc., about someone or something. □ *Why are you making such a furor about such a minor matter?* □ *You are making too many negative remarks about Sue.*

make something **against** someone or something to build a legal case, argument, speech, etc., against someone or something. □ *The prosecutor made a strong case against Tim.* □ *I made a strong speech against the proposed legislation.*

make something **at** someone to make some sign or signal at or to a person. □ *Carlo made a sign at Bill, who seemed to know just what to do.* □ *Jimmy made an obscene gesture at me!*

make something **clear to** someone to help someone understand something. □ *Let me help make the contract clear to you.* □ *I want to make it clear to you, so ask questions if you want.*

make something **for** someone or something to prepare something for someone or something. □ *I made a big bowl of fruit salad for the visitors.* □ *James made a cake for the party.*

make something **from scratch** Go to from scratch.

make something **from** something to make something from certain parts or ingredients. □ *I made this cake from fresh butter and eggs.* □ *They made the fences from the stones of a ruined Roman fort.*

make something **good** Go to set something right.

make something **in** something to make money in a particular enterprise. □ *She made a lot of money in real estate.* □ *I hope to make some money in the stock market.*

make something **of** someone or something to succeed with improving someone or something; to turn someone or something into someone or something worthwhile. □ *I*

tried to make something of you, but you had to do things the way you saw fit. □ *I think I can make something of this script.*

make something **of** something **1.** to make an interpretation of something. □ *What do you make of this letter?* □ *Look through this and see what sense you make of it.* **2.** to turn an incident into a dispute. (Usually with *it*. Often as an invitation to fight. See also **make** something **(out) of** something.) □ *Do you want to make something of it?* □ *He looks like he wants to make something of it.*

make something **off (of)** someone or something to make money from someone or something. (*Of* is usually retained before pronouns.) □ *Are you trying to make your fortune off of me?* □ *We think we can make some money off the sale of the house.*

make something **out**† to see, read, or hear something well enough to understand it. □ *What did you say? I couldn't quite make it out.* □ *Can you make out what he is saying?*

make something **out of nothing 1.** *Lit.* to create something of value from nearly worthless parts. □ *My uncle—he sells sand—made a fortune out of nothing.* □ *My model airplane won the contest even though I made it out of scrap.* **2.** *Fig.* to make an issue of something of little importance. □ *Relax, John, you're making a big problem out of nothing.* □ *You have no evidence. You're making a case out of nothing.*

make something **(out) of** something **1.** *Lit.* to make something out of parts or raw materials. □ *I will make the cake out of the very best ingredients.* □ *Can you make a salad out of these vegetables?* **2.** *Fig.* to make an interpretation of something. □ *Can you make anything out of this message? I don't understand it.* □ *I'm sorry, I can't make any sense out of it.* **3.** *Fig.* to interpret something negatively. (See also **make** something **of** something.) □ *The hostess made too much out of my absence.*

make something **out to be** something else to portray something as something else. □ *You are trying to make this tragedy out to be a minor matter.* □ *They made the disease out to be something far more serious than it really is.*

make something **over**† Go to do something over†.

make something **right** Go to set something right.

make something **to order** to custom-make an item; to make an item to fit someone's specifications. (See also **made to order**.) □ *The tailor made the jacket to order for me.* □ *The carpenter made the built-in bookcase to order for us.*

make something **up**† **1.** to redo something; to do something that one has failed to do in the past. □ *Can I make the lost time up?* □ *Can I make up the test that I missed?* **2.** to assemble something. □ *We will ship the parts to China where we will make up the computers with cheap labor.* (See also **make the bed (up)**.) □ *Have they finished making up the pages for the next edition of the magazine?* **3.** to think up something; to make and tell a lie. □ *That's not true! You just made that up!* □ *I didn't make it up!* □ *You made up that story!* **4.** to mix something up; to assemble something. □ *John: Is my prescription ready? Druggist: No, I haven't made it up yet.* □ *I'll make up your prescription in a minute.*

M

make something **up**† **from** something to create something from something. □ *I will make some stew up from the ingredients available in the fridge.* □ *I will make up a stew from the leftovers.*

make something **up**† **out of whole cloth** *Fig.* to fabricate a story or a lie. □ *That's a lie. You just made that up out of whole cloth.* □ *That's a lie. You just made up that story out of whole cloth.*

make something **up to** someone to make amends to someone. □ *I'm so sorry. I will do what I can to make it up to you.* □ *I will make it up to them. Don't worry.*

make something **with** something to make something out of something. □ *I will make the cake with margarine rather than butter.* □ *Can you make our coffee with spring water, please?*

make sure (of something**)** to check something and be certain about it. □ *Please make sure of your facts before you write the report.* □ *We made sure of the route we had to follow before we left.* □ *Please double-check and make sure.*

make the arrangements *Euph.* to arrange a funeral. □ *A funeral services practitioner will be happy to help you make the arrangements.* □ *When my father died, I was the one who made the arrangements.*

make the bed (up†**)** and **make** someone's **bed (up**†**)** to restore a bed to an unslept-in condition. □ *I make my bed every morning.* □ *The maid goes to all the rooms to make the beds.* □ *Please make up all the beds early today.*

make the best of a bad job *Prov.* to try to salvage something from a ruined situation. □ *When the dry cleaners ruined Mrs. Anderson's coat, they made the best of a bad job by offering to buy her another one.*

make the best of something to do as well as possible with something that is not too promising. □ *I don't like it, but I will try to make the best of my summer landscaping job by getting a good tan.* □ *I will make the best of it, for a while anyway.*

make the fur fly and **make the feathers fly** *Fig.* to cause a fight or an argument; to **create an uproar.** □ *When your mother gets home and sees what you've done, she'll really make the fur fly.* □ *When those two get together, they'll make the feathers fly. They hate each other.*

make the grade to be satisfactory; to be what is expected. □ *I'm sorry, but your work doesn't exactly make the grade.* □ *This meal doesn't just make the grade. It is excellent.*

make the most of something to make something appear as good as possible; to exploit something; to get as much out of something as is possible. □ *Mary knows how to make the most of her talents.* □ *They designed the advertisements to make the most of the product's features.*

make the scene 1. *Sl.* to attend an event. □ *We plan to make the scene, but we may be a bit late.* □ *I hope everybody can make the scene.* **2.** *Sl.* to understand a situation; to appreciate the situation. □ *I can't quite make the scene, but it looks like Willie punched the guy over here. Then he moved to the window over here, and that's when the woman across the street saw him.* □ *I can make the scene. It's just like you said, except Willie came in and found the guy laid out on the floor.*

make the team to have been qualified enough to be selected to play on a sports team. □ *I tried out, but I didn't make the team.*

make time for someone or something Go to **time for** someone or something.

make time (with someone**)** to flirt with, date, or hang around with someone. □ *I hear that Tom's been making time with Ann.* □ *I hear they've been making time for months.*

make (too) much of someone or something to pay too much attention to someone or something. □ *We all believe you are making much of Tom when he has done no more than anyone else.* □ *Don't make too much of it. It was really nothing.*

make tracks (for something**)** *Fig.* to move rapidly toward something or some place. □ *The cowboys all made tracks for the chuck wagon.* □ *Let's make tracks! Here comes the sheriff.*

make trouble to cause trouble or additional work. □ *I don't want to make trouble, but I have a few suggestions that could make things work more smoothly.*

make up to put on makeup. □ *I have to go make up before Joe comes to pick me up.*

make up a foursome to assemble into a team of four people. □ *We have three people now. Who can we get to make up a foursome?* □ *Let's make up a foursome and play bridge.*

make up for lost time to catch up; to go fast to balance a period of going slow or not moving. □ *We drove as fast as we could, trying to make up for lost time.* □ *Hurry. We have to make up for lost time.*

make up for someone or something **1.** to take the place of someone or something. □ *John can't play in the game Saturday, but I think I can make up for him.* □ *Do you think that this cat can make up for the one that ran away?* **2.** to compensate for someone or something someone did. □ *We all had to do extra work to make up for Harry, who was very tired from being out late the night before.* □ *We will certainly make up for what we failed to do.*

make up something to constitute something. (See also **make** something **up.**) □ *Two chapters make up this volume.* □ *Over forty freight cars made up the train.*

make up (to someone**) 1.** to apologize to someone. □ *It's too late to make up to me.* □ *I think you should go make up to Jerry.* **2.** to try to become friends with someone. □ *Look how the cat is making up to Richard!* □ *Jimmy is making up to Donna, and she doesn't even notice.*

make up (with someone**)** to reconcile with someone; to end a disagreement (with someone). □ *Bill and Max decided to make up.* □ *They made up with each other and are now very good friends.*

make use of someone or something to utilize someone or something; to do something useful with someone or something. □ *Can you make use of these papers?* □ *We were unable to make use of the items you shipped to us.*

make war (on someone or something**) 1.** *Lit.* to attack someone or something and start a war. □ *The small country's generals made war on the United States, hoping for foreign aid when they lost the war.* **2.** *Fig.* to actively oppose someone or something. □ *The police made war on violent street crime.*

make water *Euph.* to urinate. □ *She's got some kind of condition where it hurts when she makes water.* □ *Can we stop at this here gas station? I need to make water.*

make waves *Sl.* to cause difficulty. (Often in the negative.) □ *Just relax. Don't make waves.* □ *If you make waves too much around here, you won't last long.*

make way to make progress; to move ahead. (Originally nautical. See also **make way (for** someone or something**).)** □ *Is this project making way?* □ *A sailboat can't make way if there is no wind.*

make way (for someone or something**)** to clear a path for someone or something. □ *Make way for the stretcher.* □ *Here comes the doctor—make way!*

make with something *Sl.* to deliver something. □ *Come on, make with the stuff you promised!* □ *Make with the information, Max, or you will stay in jail even longer!* □ *Come on, make with the cash.* □ *I want to know. Come on, make with the answers!*

Make your mind up†. *Fig.* Please make a decision.; Please choose. □ *Henry: I don't have all day. Make up your mind. Rachel: Don't rush me.* □ *Bob: Make your mind up. We have to catch the plane. Mary: I'm not sure I want to go.*

Make yourself at home. *Fig.* Please make yourself comfortable in my home. (Also a signal that a guest can be less formal.) □ *Andy: Please come in and make yourself at home. Sue: Thank you. I'd like to.* □ *Bill: I hope I'm not too early. Bob: Not at all. Come in and make yourself at home. I've got a few little things to do. Bill: Nice place you've got here.*

man about town a fashionable man who leads a sophisticated life. □ *He prefers a nightclub to a quiet night at home—a man about town.* □ *Bob's too much of a man about town to go to a football game.*

a **man after my own heart** *Fig.* a man with similar tastes and preferences to mine. □ *You like creamed chip-beef on toast? There's a man after my own heart.*

Man does not live by bread alone. *Prov.* In order to survive, people need more than physical things like food and shelter.; People need mental or spiritual things like satisfaction and love. (Biblical.) □ *Alan: I'm so miserable. Jill: How can you be miserable? You've got a good place to live, plenty to eat, nice clothes. . . . Alan: But man does not live by bread alone.*

the **man in the street** *Fig.* the ordinary person. □ *Politicians rarely care what the man in the street thinks.* □ *The man in the street has little interest in literature.*

A **man is known by the company he keeps.** *Prov.* A person tends to associate with people who are like him or her. □ *Son, when you go away to school, spend your time with serious people; don't hang around with people who go to parties all the time. A man is known by the company he keeps.* □ *If you want to know what kind of person George is, look at his friends. A man is known by the company he keeps.*

a **man of few words** *Fig.* someone, not necessarily a man, who speaks concisely or not at all. □ *He is a man of few words, but he usually makes a lot of sense.*

a **man of the cloth** *Fig.* a clergyman. □ *Father Brown is a man of the cloth and is welcome at our table for dinner every Sunday.*

Man proposes, God disposes. *Prov.* People may make plans, but they cannot control the outcome of their plans. □ *Jill: Are you really going to be able to finish writing your novel by the end of the year? Bob: Man proposes, God disposes.*

man's best friend *Fig.* a dog; dogs in general. □ *Man's best friend just peed all over my shoes!*

A **man's home is his castle.** *Prov. Cliché* One can do whatever one wants to in one's own home. □ *Don't tell me not to go around the house in my underwear. A man's home is his castle.* □ *I'll play my radio loud if I want to. A man's home is his castle.*

man's inhumanity to man *Fig.* human cruelty toward other humans. □ *It doesn't take a war to remind us of man's inhumanity to man.*

manage with someone or something to do as well as possible with only someone or something (less than one had hoped for). □ *We wanted Kelly to help us, but we will manage with Larry.* □ *I am sure we can manage with the money that we have.*

manage without someone or something to do as well as possible without someone or something. □ *Carla said that she just can't manage without Jerry.* □ *We just can't manage without some more money.*

maneuver for something to get into position for something. □ *Sally is maneuvering for a shot at a promotion.* □ *Todd maneuvered for some attention, but they ignored him.*

maneuver someone **into** something to lure, position, or deceive someone into (doing) something. □ *I will see if I can maneuver him into accepting the offer.* □ *He was maneuvered into accepting the offer.*

maneuver someone **out of** something to trick someone out of getting or achieving something. □ *Are you trying to maneuver me out of the running for the job?* □ *The runner maneuvered her opponent out of first place.*

manna from heaven *Fig.* unexpected help or comfort. (A biblical reference.) □ *The arrival of the rescue team was like manna from heaven to the injured climber.* □ *The offer of a new job just as she had been fired was manna from heaven to Joan.*

Many a true word is spoken in jest. and **There's many a true word spoken in jest.** *Prov.* Just because something is said as a joke, it can still be true. □ *Fred: Why did you make a joke about my being stingy? Do you really think I'm cheap? Ellen: Of course not, don't be silly. It was just a joke. Fred: But many a true word is spoken in jest.*

many (and many)'s the time there have been many times. □ *Many and many's the time I warned him not to go to the swimmin' hole by himself.* □ *Many's the time she's forgiven her husband.*

Many are called but few are chosen. *Prov.* Many people may answer a call for something, but only a few people are finally selected. (Biblical.) □ *When it comes to getting into a good college, many are called but few are chosen.*

M

Many hands make light work. *Prov.* If everyone helps with a large task, it will get done easily and quickly. □ *Cleaning up the banquet room won't take long if we all help; many hands make light work.* □ *You do have a lot of dishes to wash, but you also have all of us to help you, and many hands make light work.*

map something **out**[†] to plot something out carefully, usually on paper. □ *I have a good plan. I will map it out for you.* □ *I will map out the plan for you.*

mar something **up**[†] to dent or scratch something; to harm the smooth finish of something. □ *Please don't mar the furniture up.* □ *Don't mar up my desk.*

march against someone or something to march in a demonstration against someone or something. □ *The demonstrators marched against the mayor.* □ *The citizens got together and marched against crime and injustice.*

march behind someone or something Go to **behind** someone or something.

March comes in like a lion, and goes out like a lamb. and **In like a lion, out like a lamb.** *Prov.* The month of March usually starts with cold, unpleasant weather, but ends mild and pleasant. (Either part of the proverb can be used alone.) □ *March certainly is coming in like a lion this year; there's been a snowstorm every day this week.* □ *Jill: Today is March twenty-fifth, and it's beautiful and warm outside, when just two weeks ago, everything was covered with ice. Jane: In like a lion and out like a lamb, all right.*

march (from some place**) (to** some place**)** to move along, walking with purposeful steps, from some place to some place. □ *The army marched from one town to another.* □ *They marched to the battlefield from town.*

march in (a) single file Go to **in (a) single file**.

march in step (with someone**)** Go to **in step (with** someone**)**.

march on 1. *Lit.* to continue marching. □ *Please march on. Don't stop here; there are other parts of the parade coming along behind you.* □ *Let's march on. We have a long way to go.* **2.** *Fig.* [for time] to continue. □ *Time marches on. We are all getting older.* □ *As the day marches on, try to get everything completed.*

march out of time (with someone or something**)** Go to **out of step (with** someone or something**)**.

march past someone or something to move in a file or formation past someone or something. □ *The people in the parade marched past the children standing on the curb.* □ *The soldiers marched past the general.*

march to (the beat of) a different drummer *Fig.* to believe in a different set of principles. □ *John is marching to a different drummer, and he doesn't associate with us anymore.* □ *Since Sally started marching to the beat of a different drummer, she has had a lot of great new ideas.*

mark my word(s) *Fig.* remember what I'm telling you. □ *Mark my word, you'll regret this.* □ *This whole project will fail—mark my words.*

mark someone **down**[†] [for a teacher] to give someone a low score. □ *He'll mark you down for misspelled words.* □ *I marked down Tom for bad spelling.*

mark someone **for life** *Fig.* to affect someone for life. □ *The tragedy marked her for life and she was never the same.* □ *She was marked for life by her brother's untimely death.*

mark someone or something **off**[†] and **mark** someone or something **out**[†] to cross off the name of someone or something. □ *They were late, so I marked them off.* □ *I marked off the late people.* □ *Could you mark that title out? It has been discontinued.*

mark someone or something **out**[†] Go to previous.

mark someone or something **with** something **1.** to use something with which to mark someone or something. □ *She marked one of the twins with a sticker so she could identify him later.* □ *Jill marked the ones that were sold with a wax pencil.* **2.** to place a particular kind of mark on someone or something. □ *The attendant marked the concertgoers who had paid with a rubber stamp.* □ *Frank marked the book with his initials.*

mark something **as** something to make a mark next to the name of something on a list indicating what the thing is. □ *I will mark this one as expired.* □ *This one is marked as needing repair work.*

mark something **down**[†] **1.** *Lit.* to write something down on paper. □ *She marked the number down on the paper.* □ *She marked down the number.* **2.** *Fig.* to reduce the price of something. □ *We are going to mark all this merchandise down next Monday.* □ *We marked down the merchandise.*

mark something **in**[†] to write or make a mark on something, perhaps in a box or on a line. □ *I will mark an X in the box by your name.* □ *I'll mark in the X.*

mark something **up**[†] **1.** to mess something up with marks. □ *Don't mark up your book!* □ *Who marked this book up?* **2.** to grade a paper and make lots of informative marks and comments on it. □ *The teacher really marked up my term paper.* □ *Why did you mark my test up so much? I hardly made any errors.* **3.** to raise the price of something. □ *The grocery store seems to mark the price of food up every week.* □ *They don't mark up the price of turkey at Thanksgiving.*

mark time *Fig.* to wait; to do nothing but wait. □ *I'll just mark time till things get better.* □ *Do you expect me to just stand here and mark time?*

*a **marked man** *Fig.* to be someone, usually a male, who is in danger from harm by someone else. (*Typically: **be ~; live like ~**.) □ *Bob's a marked man. His parents found out that he's skipping school.* □ *Fred's a marked man, too. Jack is looking for him to get his money back.*

maroon someone **on** an island to strand someone on something; to abandon someone on something, such as an island. □ *The pirate captain marooned his first mate on a small island in the Caribbean.* □ *Through a navigation error, I marooned myself on a tiny island east of Guam.*

a **marriage made in heaven** and a **match made in heaven** a happy or harmonious marriage or partnership. (See also **Marriages are made in heaven**.) □ *The partnership of George and Ira Gershwin was a match made in heaven; they wrote such beautiful songs.*

Marriages are made in heaven. *Prov.* You cannot foretell who will marry whom.; Two people may love each other very much but may end up not marrying each other, and two people who do not even know each other may marry each other in the end. □ *Tom and Eliza were childhood sweethearts, had a happy family, and now are celebrating their fiftieth wedding anniversary. Marriages are made in heaven.*

marry above oneself *Fig.* to marry someone in a higher social class than oneself. □ *They say she married above herself, but who cares?* □ *Scott thought it would not be possible to marry above himself.*

marry below oneself and **marry beneath** oneself *Fig.* to marry someone in a lower social class than oneself. □ *He married beneath himself, but he is happy, and what more is required of a marriage?* □ *He did not want to marry beneath himself.*

marry beneath oneself Go to previous.

Marry in haste, (and) repent at leisure. *Prov.* If you marry someone you do not know well, or decide to marry someone without first carefully considering what you are doing, you will probably regret it for a long time. □ *Sally wanted some time to consider Sam's proposal of marriage; she had heard the saying, "Marry in haste, and repent at leisure."*

marry into something to become a part of a family or a fortune by marriage. □ *She married into money, they say.* □ *I always wanted to marry into a large family until I found out what that means in terms of buying gifts.*

marry one's **way out of** something to get out of something, such as poverty, by marrying someone. □ *She was able to marry her way out of poverty but regretted it in the long run.* □ *Sally married her way out of one unhappy home into another one.*

marry someone **off**† **(to** someone**)** to manage to get someone married to someone and out of the house or family. □ *Her parents wanted nothing more than to marry her off to a doctor.* □ *They married off their children soon.*

marry up (with someone**)** *Rur.* to marry someone. □ *They married up in the spring.* □ *Jane's going to marry up with someone she met at school.*

marshal someone or something **together** to organize or gather someone or something together. □ *The leader marshaled all his people together in preparation for the parade.* □ *Let's marshal the troops together for the attack.*

marvel at someone or something *Fig.* to express wonder or surprise at someone or something. □ *I can only marvel at Valerie and all she has accomplished.* □ *We all marveled at the beauty of the new building.*

a **marvel to behold** someone or something quite exciting or wonderful to see. □ *Our new high-definition television is a marvel to behold.* □ *Mary's lovely new baby is a marvel to behold.*

mash on something to press on something, such as a button. (Southern.) □ *He kept mashing on the doorbell until someone responded.* □ *Just mash on this button if you want someone to come.*

mash something **up**† to crush something into a paste or pieces. □ *Mash the potatoes up and put them in a bowl.* □ *Mash up the potatoes and serve them to our guests.*

mash something **with** something **1.** to use something to mash something up. □ *Vernon mashed the potatoes with*

a spoon because he couldn't find the masher. □ *Gerald used the heel of his shoe to mash the wasp.* **2.** to combine ingredients while mashing. □ *Mash the turnips with the butter.* □ *She mashed the potatoes with sour cream, cream cheese, and a little garlic salt.*

mask something **out**† to conceal or cover part of something from view. □ *The trees masked the city dump out, so it could not be seen from the street.* □ *The trees masked out the dump.*

masquerade as someone or something to appear disguised as someone or something; to pretend to be someone or something. □ *We decided to masquerade as ghosts for the party.* □ *Mr. Wilson, who is a bit overweight, masqueraded as Cinderella's coach.*

a **match for** someone, something, or an animal someone, something, or an animal that is the equal of someone, something, or some other animal, especially in a contest. □ *My older brother is no match for me; he's much weaker.* □ *Your horse is no match for mine in a race. Mine will always win.*

a **match made in heaven** Go to a **marriage made in heaven**.

match someone **against** someone else or something **against** something else to challenge someone with someone else in a contest; to challenge something with something else in a contest. □ *I will match my boxer against your boxer any day.* □ *I'll match myself against you any day!*

match someone or something **in** something to equal someone or something in some quality. □ *I am sure I match her in wisdom if not in grace and beauty.* □ *You do not match her in any way.*

match someone **(up**† **) (with** someone**)** and **match** something **(up**† **) (with** something**)** to pair people or things. □ *I will match Carl up with Kelly and George with Jane.* □ *I will match up Carl with Kelly.*

match up [for things or people] to match, be equal, or complementary. □ *These match up. See how they are the same length?* □ *Sorry, but these two parts don't match up.*

match up to something [for something] to match, be equal to, or complementary to something. □ *This sock does not match up to the other one.* □ *This one matches up to all the others.*

match wits (with someone**)** *Fig.* to enter into intellectual competition with someone. □ *Whenever I try to match wits with Fred, he always ends up running circles around me with his clever repartee.*

mate someone **with** someone and **mate** an animal **with** some other animal to pair or breed people or animals. □ *The king sought to mate his daughter with the son of a magician.* □ *Harry wanted to mate his guppies with June's guppies.*

mate with an animal [for an animal] to copulate with its own kind. □ *The gander mated with the goose in the barnyard.* □ *The coyote acted as if it wanted to mate with the dog.*

mate with someone to marry with someone, and presumably, to copulate with someone. □ *Did you meet anyone you would like to mate with and spend the rest of your life with?*

materialize out of nowhere Go to out of nowhere.

a **matter of life and death** *Cliché* an issue of great urgency; an issue that will decide between living and dying. □ *We must find a doctor. It's a matter of life and death.* □ *A matter of life and death demands that I return home at once.*

a **matter of opinion** the question of how good or bad someone or something is. □ *It's a matter of opinion how strong the company is. John thinks it's great and Fred thinks it's poor.*

matter to someone to be important to someone. □ *Does money really matter to you?* □ *Yes, it matters to me a lot.*

max out to reach one's maximum in something, such as weight in weight lifting or credit on a credit card. □ *Andy finally maxed out at 300 pounds.* □ *Randy just knew when he had maxed out. Something in his body told him to stop.*

maxed out 1. *Sl.* exhausted; tired. □ *I am just maxed out. I haven't been getting enough sleep.* □ *I had to stop work because I was too maxed out.* **2.** *Sl.* intoxicated. □ *Sam was maxed out and seemed happy enough to sit under the table and whimper.* □ *I hadn't seen Barlowe so maxed out in years. He was nearly paralyzed.*

may as well Go to might as well.

May I be excused? May I leave this place, please?; May I leave to use the toilet? □ *Nature calls. May I be excused?* □ *The student raised her hand and said, "Teacher, may I be excused?"*

May I help you? Go to Could I help you?; How may I help you?

May I see you again? Go to Could I see you again?

May I speak to someone? Go to Could I speak to someone?

May I take a message? Go to Could I take a message?

May I take your order (now)? Go to Could I take your order (now)?

May I tell him who's calling? Go to Could I tell him who's calling?

May I use your powder room? Go to Could I use your powder room?

Maybe some other time. and **We'll try again some other time.** a polite phrase said by a person whose invitation has just been turned down by another person. □ *Bill: Do you think you can come to the party? Bob: I'll have to beg off. I have another engagement. Bill: Maybe some other time.* □ *John: Can you and Alice come over this Friday? Bill: Gee, sorry. We have something else on. John: We'll try again some other time.*

mean business to be very, very serious. □ *Stop laughing! I mean business.* □ *I could tell from the look on her face that she meant business.*

mean by something to intend a certain meaning by words or deeds. □ *What do you mean by that?* □ *I did not mean anything special by my remarks.*

mean (for someone) **to** do something to intend (for someone) to do something. □ *John meant to go with us to the zoo.* □ *John meant for Jane to do the dishes.*

mean lean times (ahead) Go to lean times (ahead).

mean no offense not to intend to offend. (See also take no offense.) □ *I'm really sorry. I meant no offense.* □ *It was simply a slip of the tongue. He meant no offense by it.*

mean nothing (to someone) **1.** not to make sense to someone. □ *This sentence means nothing to me. It isn't clearly written.* □ *I'm sorry. This message means nothing.* **2.** [for someone] not to have feeling for someone or something. □ *Do I mean nothing to you after all these years?* □ *Do all those years of devotion mean nothing?*

mean something **as** something to intend something to be understood as something. □ *Do you mean your remarks as criticism?* □ *I meant my comment as encouragement.*

mean something **for** someone or something **1.** *Lit.* to imply something important for someone or something; to be important or meaningful for someone or something. □ *Are your comments supposed to mean something special for me?* □ *I mean these remarks for the government.* **2.** *Fig.* to intend for someone or something to have or receive something. □ *Do you mean this gift for me?* □ *I mean this gift for the entire community.*

mean something **(to** someone) **1.** *Lit.* to make sense to someone. □ *Does this line mean anything to you?* □ *Yes, it means something.* **2.** *Fig.* [for someone] to cause positive feelings in another person. □ *You mean a lot to me.* □ *This job means a lot to Ann.*

a **mean streak** *Fig.* a tendency for a person to do things that are mean. □ *I think that Wally has a mean streak that no one ever saw before this incident.*

mean to (do something) to intend to do something. □ *Did you mean to do that?* □ *No, it was an accident. I didn't mean to.*

mean well to intend to be nice, polite, helpful, etc., but fail in the effort. □ *I know you mean well, but your comments are sort of insulting.*

meaner than a junkyard dog (with fourteen sucking pups) *Rur.* cruel; eager to fight. □ *Don't mess with her. She's meaner than a junkyard dog with fourteen sucking pups.* □ *They say Jim's meaner than a junkyard dog, but really, he's a sweetheart.*

meant to be destined to exist. □ *Our love was meant to be!* □ *It was not meant to be.*

meant to be something destined or fated to be something. □ *Jane was meant to be a chemist.* □ *I was meant to be rich, but something didn't work right!*

measure someone **against** someone else or something **against** something else to compare someone with someone else; to compare something with something else. □ *Daniel measured his brother against the boy next door.* □ *We measured the new building against the older ones and found the new one lacking in many respects.* □ *I measured myself against Tom and found him superior in almost everything.*

measure someone **up against** someone or something to place someone up against someone or something else for the purpose of comparing size or other qualities. □ *Please measure Fred up against Tom and see who has the best qualifications.* □ *Can you measure Brian up against the mark on the wall to see how tall he is growing?*

measure something **off**† to determine the length of something. □ *He measured the length of the room off and wrote*

M

down the figure in his notebook. □ *Fred measured off the width of the house.* □ *Fred measured a few feet of string off, and cut it with a knife.*

measure something **out**† to measure and distribute something as it is being taken out, unwrapped, unfolded, etc. □ *Carl measured the grain out a cup at a time.* □ *He measured out the grain little by little.*

measure up (to someone or something**)** to compare well to someone or something. □ *He just doesn't measure up to Sarah in intelligence.* □ *This meal doesn't measure up to my expectations.*

a **Mecca for** someone *Fig.* a place that is frequently visited by a particular group of people because it is important to them for some reason. (From the city of Mecca, the religious center of Islam.) □ *New York City is a Mecca for theatergoers.* □ *St. Andrews is a Mecca for golf enthusiasts because of its famous course.*

meddle in something to intrude [oneself] into something. □ *I wish you wouldn't meddle in my affairs.* □ *Go meddle in someone else's business.*

meddle with someone or something to interfere with someone or something; to mess around with someone or something. □ *Please don't meddle with me. I am in a bad mood.* □ *Would you please stop meddling with my computer?*

mediate between someone **and** someone else to negotiate an agreement between people. □ *I will have to mediate between Mary and Vernon.* □ *No one wants to mediate between them.*

meditate on someone or something to reflect on someone or something. □ *Judy was instructed to meditate on a flower.* □ *I will meditate on that happy thought.*

*****meek as a lamb** [of someone] shy, quiet, and docile. (*Also: **as** ∼.) □ *Only an hour after their argument, Joe went to Elizabeth and, meek as a lamb, asked her to forgive him.* □ *Betsy terrorizes the other children, but she's as meek as a lamb around her elders.*

meet one's **death** and **meet** one's **end** *Fig.* to die. □ *After 20 years, my dog finally met his death when he got hit by a bus.* □ *The skydiver met his end when his parachute didn't open.*

meet one's **end** Go to previous.

meet one's **match** *Fig.* to meet one's equal; to encounter someone who can match or outdo one in some activity, talent, etc. □ *John played tennis with Bill yesterday, and it looks as if John has finally met his match.* □ *Listen to Jane and Mary argue. I always thought that Jane was loud, but she has finally met her match.*

meet one's **Waterloo** *Fig.* to meet one's final and insurmountable challenge. (Alludes to the final defeat of Napoleon at Waterloo.) □ *The boss is being very hard on Bill. It seems that Bill has finally met his Waterloo.* □ *John was more than Sally could handle. She has finally met her Waterloo.*

meet someone **halfway** *Fig.* to compromise with someone. □ *No, I won't give in, but I'll meet you halfway.* □ *They settled the argument by agreeing to meet each other halfway.*

meet the requirements (for something**)** to fulfill the requirements for something. □ *Sally was unable to meet*

the requirements for the job. □ *Jane met the requirements and was told to report to work the next day.*

meet up with someone or something to meet someone or something, usually by accident. □ *I met up with Don on the street yesterday.* □ *James met up with a strange accident.*

meet with someone to have a meeting with someone. □ *I will meet with all of them on Monday.* □ *When can I meet with you?*

meet with something **1.** [for someone] to experience something, such as an accident. □ *Poor Carlo met with a serious accident.* □ *Henry always feared meeting with a horrible fate.* **2.** [for someone or something] to strike or touch something. □ *That board is supposed to meet perfectly with the surface of the wall.* □ *Her head met with the top of the car a number of times during the journey.* **3.** to encounter some kind of response. □ *The proposal met with unexpected opposition.* □ *Her speech was met with universal approval.*

a **meeting of the minds** the establishment of agreement; complete agreement. □ *After a lot of discussion we finally reached a meeting of the minds.* □ *We struggled to bring about a meeting of the minds on the issues.*

a **mell of a hess** *Inf.* a hell of a mess. (A deliberate spoonerism.) □ *What a mell of a hess you've gotten us into this time.* □ *Have you ever seen such a mell of a hess?*

mellow out 1. to become less angry. □ *When you mellow out, maybe we can talk.* □ *Come on, man, stop yelling and mellow out!* **2.** to become generally more relaxed. □ *Gary was nearly forty before he started to mellow out a little and take life less seriously.* □ *After his illness, he mellowed out and seemed more glad to be alive.*

melt away to melt into a liquid. □ *The ice cubes melted away quickly in the intense heat.* □ *When the wax candles melted away, they ruined the lace tablecloth.*

melt down 1. *Lit.* [for something frozen] to melt. □ *The glacier melted down little by little.* □ *When the ice on the streets melted down, it was safe to drive again.* **2.** *Fig.* [for a nuclear reactor] to become hot enough to melt through its container. □ *The whole system was on the verge of melting down.*

melt in one's **mouth 1.** to taste very good. (Also can be literal.) □ *This cake is so good it'll melt in your mouth.* □ *John said that the food didn't exactly melt in his mouth.* **2.** [of meat] to be very, very tender. □ *My steak is so tender it could melt in my mouth.* □ *This filet will melt in your mouth!*

melt in something **1.** [for something] to melt to a liquid at a high temperature. □ *Surely the plastic cup will melt in such heat.* □ *This tray will melt in the oven, so keep it out of there.* **2.** [for something] to dissolve in a particular liquid. □ *Sugar melts in hot water easily.* □ *Will this substance melt in heated water?*

melt into something to melt and change into a different state. □ *All the ice cream melted into a sticky soup.* □ *The candles melted into a pool of colored wax in all the heat we had last summer.*

melt something **away**† to cause something to melt into a liquid. □ *The sun melted the ice away.* □ *The sun melted away the ice.*

melt something **down**[†] to cause something frozen to melt; to cause something solid to melt. □ *The rays of the sun melted the candle down to a puddle of wax.* □ *The heat melted down the ice.*

melt something **into** something to cause something to change its state when melting. □ *The ice melted into a cold liquid that we could drink.* □ *We melted the fat into a liquid that we could deep-fry in.*

Men are blind in their own cause. *Prov.* If you believe in something very fervently, you will not recognize the flaws in what you believe or the dangers associated with it. □ *Jill: Lyle is so intent on converting people to his religion, that he doesn't see that his constant preaching is alienating his friends. Jane: Men are blind in their own cause.*

Men make houses, women make homes. *Prov.* Men are often the ones who build or acquire houses for their families, but women provide the things that make a house into a home. □ *When William moved into his own apartment, his mother insisted on choosing and arranging the furniture and decorations for him. "Men make houses, women make homes," she said, "and I want you to have a home as nice as the one you grew up in."*

mend (one's**) fences 1.** *Lit.* to repair fences as part of one's chores. □ *Tom is mending fences today at the south end of the ranch.* **2.** *Fig.* to restore good relations (with someone). □ *I think I had better get home and mend my fences. I had an argument with my daughter this morning.* □ *Sally called up her uncle to apologize and try to mend fences.*

mend one's **ways** *Fig.* to improve one's behavior. □ *John used to be very wild, but he's mended his ways.* □ *You'll have to mend your ways if you go out with Mary. She hates people to be late.*

*a mental block (against something**)** *Fig.* to have some psychological barrier that prevents one from doing something. (*Typically: **get** ~; **have** ~; **give** someone ~.) □ *Perry has a mental block against speaking in public.*

mention someone or something **in passing** to mention someone or something casually; to mention someone or something while talking about someone or something else. □ *He just happened to mention in passing that the mayor had resigned.* □ *John mentioned in passing that he was nearly eighty years old.*

mention someone or something **in** something **1.** to name someone or something in a particular context. □ *We mentioned you in regard to nominations for the congress.* □ *Everyone mentioned your book in the discussions.* **2.** to name someone or something in a will, lecture, story, article, etc. □ *They mentioned your name in the discussion.* □ *Uncle Herman mentioned you in his will.*

mention something **to** someone to refer to something while talking to someone. □ *Please mention it to your father.* □ *You had better not mention that to anyone.*

a **mere trifle** *Fig.* a tiny bit; a small, unimportant matter; a small amount of money. □ *But this isn't expensive! It costs a mere trifle!*

merge in(to something**)** to join into something. □ *The stream merged into the main channel of the river.*

merge someone or something **into** something and **merge** someone or something **in**[†] to route someone or something into something else. □ *They merged the marchers into the parade and no one ever knew they were late.* □ *We merged in the latecomers to the parade at an intersection.*

merge something **with** something else to join two things together. □ *The management merged the sales division with the marketing division.* □ *We merged the accounting department with the auditing department.*

merge with someone or something to join with someone or something. □ *Ted merged with Fred and they created a very profitable partnership.* □ *Our company merged with a larger one, and we all kept our jobs.* □ *This stream merges with a larger stream about two miles to the west.*

*merry as a cricket and ***merry as the day is long** very happy and carefree. (*Also: **as** ~.) □ *Mary is as merry as a cricket whenever she has company come to call.* □ *The little children are as merry as the day is long.*

merry as the day is long Go to previous.

mesh together to fit together. □ *Their interests and personalities mesh together perfectly.* □ *Their ideas don't mesh together too well.*

mesh with something to fit with something. □ *Your idea just doesn't mesh with my plans.* □ *Currently, your proposed project doesn't mesh at all well with our long-range planning.*

mess about Go to mess around.

mess about (with something**)** Go to mess around (with something).

mess around and **mess about 1.** to waste time; to do something ineffectually. □ *Stop messing around and get busy.* □ *I wish you wouldn't mess about so much. You waste a lot of time that way.* **2.** to play [with someone] sexually. □ *Those two have been messing around.* □ *Pete was messing around with Maria during the summer.*

mess around (with something**)** and **mess about (with** something**); monkey around (with** something**) 1.** to play with or fiddle with something idly and with no good purpose. □ *Don't mess around with the ashtray.* □ *You'll break it if you don't stop messing about with it.* **2.** to experiment with something; to use and learn about something. □ *We had been messing about with some new video techniques when we made our discovery.* □ *The people in this lab are messing around with all kinds of polymers.*

mess someone **over**[†] *Sl.* to treat someone badly; to beat or harm someone. □ *Max messed Lefty over and sent him to the hospital.* □ *Max messed over Lefty.*

mess someone's **face up**[†] *Sl.* to beat someone about the face. □ *The champ threatened to mess the challenger's face up.* □ *The champ broke the challenger's nose and really did mess up his face.*

mess someone **up**[†] *Sl.* to rough someone up; to beat someone up. □ *The robbers threatened to mess Bob up if he didn't cooperate.* □ *John messed up Bill a little, but no real harm was done.*

mess something **up**[†] to make something disorderly; to create disorder in something; to throw someone's plans awry. □ *You really messed this place up!* □ *Who messed up my bed?*

mess up to make an error; to do something wrong; to flub up. □ *I hope I don't mess up on the quiz.* □ *You really messed up and now you're in big trouble!*

mess with someone or something and **monkey with** someone or something to bother or interfere with someone or something. □ *Come on, don't monkey with my new camera.* □ *Don't mess with me unless you want trouble.*

messed up 1. confused. □ *I'm sort of messed up since my divorce.* □ *Most kids are sort of messed up at this age.* **2.** intoxicated. □ *Somehow I must have got messed up. What caused it, do you think?* □ *Everybody at the party was too messed up to drive home.*

metamorphose into something to transform into something. □ *This ugly caterpillar will surely metamorphose into something beautiful.* □ *At about eighteen, Wally metamorphosed into a reasonably handsome young man.*

mete something **out**† to measure something out. □ *She meted the solution out carefully into a row of test tubes.* □ *She meted out the cookies to each of them.*

*****method in** one's **madness** *Fig.* a purpose in what one is doing, even though it seems to be crazy. (*Typically: **be** ~; **have** ~.) □ *What I'm doing may look strange, but there is method in my madness.* □ *Wait until she finishes; then you'll see that she has method in her madness.*

a **middle ground** a position of compromise; a state of thinking where two opposing parties can discuss an issue politely and productively. □ *If we could only reach a middle ground on this issue, things wouldn't be so confrontational.*

the **middle of nowhere** a very isolated place. □ *I don't want to stay out here in the middle of nowhere.* □ *I was stranded in the middle of nowhere for an hour with a flat tire.*

might and main *Cliché* great physical strength; great force. □ *The huge warrior, with all his might and main, could not break his way through the castle gates.* □ *The incredible might and main of the sea crushed the ship against the cliff.*

might as well and **may as well** a phrase indicating that it is probably better to do something than not to do it. □ *Bill: Should we try to get there for the first showing of the film? Jane: Might as well. Nothing else to do.* □ *Andy: May as well leave now. It doesn't matter if we arrive a little bit early. Jane: Why do we always have to be the first to arrive?*

might as well be hung for a sheep as (for) a lamb *Rur.* might as well commit a large fault as a small one, since the same punishment will result. □ *I'll take the expensive fishing rod. My wife will be mad at me no matter how much I spend, so I might as well be hung for a sheep as for a lamb.*

might could *Rur.* might be able to. □ *Charlie: Can you come out with me after work? Tom: I might could. I'll have to see if my wife has other plans.* □ *I might could help you, if you'll tell me what's the matter.*

Might makes right. *Prov. Cliché* The stronger of two opponents will always control the situation. □ *Child: How come the country with the biggest army always tells the other countries what to do? Father: Might makes right.*

might(y) nigh *Rur.* very nearly. □ *We mighty nigh lost Mary that time she fell through the ice in the river.* □ *That was might nigh the worst night of my life.*

Mighty oaks from little acorns grow. Go to Great oaks from little acorns grow.

migrate between some place **and** some place else to change residence from one place to another, perhaps repeatedly. □ *These birds migrate between the north and the south.* □ *They migrate between their cottage in the North in the summer and their condo in Florida in the winter.*

migrate (from some place**) (to** some place**)** [for a population] to move from some place to another. □ *The birds all migrate from Europe to Africa.* □ *They migrate to Canada from South America.*

*****a mile a minute** *Fig.* very fast. (*Typically: **go** ~; **move** ~; **talk** ~; **travel** ~.) □ *She talks a mile a minute and is very hard to keep up with.*

a **milestone in** someone's **life** and an **important milestone in** someone's **life** a very important event or point in one's life. (From the [former] stone markers at the side of a road showing the distance to or from a place.) □ *Joan's wedding was a milestone in her mother's life.* □ *The birth of a child is a milestone in every parent's life.*

militate against something [for something] to work against something. □ *Everything you have said today militates against an early settlement to our disagreement.* □ *This really militates against my going to college.*

the **milk of human kindness** *Fig.* natural kindness and sympathy shown to others. (From Shakespeare's play *Macbeth, I. v.*) □ *Mary is completely hard and selfish—she doesn't have the milk of human kindness in her.* □ *Roger is too full of the milk of human kindness and people take advantage of him.*

milk someone **for** something *Fig.* to pressure someone into giving information or money. □ *The reporter milked the mayor's aide for information.* □ *The thief milked me for $20.*

mill around and **mill about** to wander or move around aimlessly within a small area. □ *Everyone was milling around, looking for something to do.* □ *The students milled about between classes.*

The mill cannot grind with water that is past. *Prov.* Do not waste the opportunities you now have.; Do not waste time wishing for what you had in the past. □ *If you want to go abroad, do it now, while you're young and have the money. The mill cannot grind with water that is past.*

*****a million miles away** *Fig.* lost in thought; [of someone] daydreaming and not paying attention. (Only one's mind is far away. *Typically: **be** ~; **look to be** ~; **seem** ~.) □ *He was a million miles away during the entire lecture.* □ *Look at her. She is a million miles away, not paying any attention to what she is doing.*

The mills of God grind slowly, yet they grind exceeding small. *Prov.* It may take a long time, but evil will always be punished. □ *Jill: It really doesn't seem right that Fred can be so horrible and dishonest, but he always gets everything he wants. Jane: Be patient. The mills of God grind slowly, yet they grind exceeding small.*

a **millstone about** one's **neck** a continual burden or handicap. ☐ *This huge and expensive house is a millstone about my neck.* ☐ *Bill's inability to control his temper is a millstone about his neck.*

mince (one's**) words** to soften the effect of one's words. ☐ *Tell me what you think, and don't mince your words.* ☐ *A frank person never minces words.*

Mind if...? Go to (Do you) mind if...?

mind one's **own business** *Fig.* to attend only to the things that concern one. ☐ *Leave me alone, Bill. Mind your own business.* ☐ *I'd be fine if John would mind his own business.*

mind one's **p's and q's.** *Prov.* to behave properly; to display good manners. ☐ *When you children go to visit Aunt Muriel, you'll have to mind your p's and q's; not like at home, where I let you do as you please.* ☐ *We'd better mind our p's and q's for this new teacher; I hear he's very strict.*

mind over matter *Fig.* [an instance where there are] intellectual powers overriding threats, difficulties, or problems. ☐ *You need to concentrate harder. Pay no attention to your surroundings. This is a case of mind over matter.*

mind the store and **watch the store** *Fig.* to take care of local matters. ☐ *Please stay here in the office and mind the store while I go to the conference.* ☐ *I had to stay home and watch the store when Ann went to Boston.*

mind you a phrase introducing something that should be taken into consideration. ☐ *He's very well dressed, but mind you, he's got plenty of money to buy clothes.* ☐ *Lisa is unfriendly to me, but mind you, she's never very nice to anyone.*

Mind your own beeswax. to mind one's own business. (Juvenile.) ☐ *You just mind your own beeswax!* ☐ *Lay off! Mind your own beeswax!*

Mind your own business. and **Get your nose out of my business.; Keep your nose out of my business.** *Fig.* Stop prying into my affairs. (Not at all polite. The expressions with *get* and *keep* can have the literal meanings of removing and keeping removed.) ☐ *Andy: This is none of your affair. Mind your own business. Sue: I was only trying to help.* ☐ *Bob: How much did you pay in federal taxes last year? Jane: Good grief, Bob! Keep your nose out of my business!* ☐ *Tom: How much did it cost? Sue: Tom! Get your nose out of my business!* ☐ *"Hey!" shrieked Sally, jerking the checkbook out of Sue's grasp. "Get your nose out of my business!"*

mine for something to dig into the ground in search of a mineral, a metal, or an ore. ☐ *The prospectors ended up mining for coal.* ☐ *What are they mining for in those hills?*

a **mine of information** *Fig.* someone or something that is full of information. ☐ *Grandfather is a mine of information about World War II.* ☐ *The new search engine is a positive mine of useful information.*

mingle in (with someone**)** to join in with someone; to mix with people. ☐ *I am going to go into the hall and mingle in with the rest of the guests.* ☐ *Ken came into the room and mingled in at once.*

mingle someone **with** someone else and **mingle** something **with** something else to mix people together; to mix things together. ☐ *Try to mingle your friends with mine.* ☐ *You*

had better not mingle your money with that of the corporation.

mingle with someone to mix with people. ☐ *Try to mingle with the guests.* ☐ *I would like to get out and mingle with people more.*

minister to someone or something to take care of someone or someone's needs. ☐ *Sarah tried to minister to the people of the village.* ☐ *He sought to minister to the grief of the widow.*

minor in something to study a secondary subject in college. (Compare this with **major in something.**) ☐ *I minored in math in college.* ☐ *I decided to minor in history.*

the **minute** something **happens** the point in time at which an event happens. ☐ *I'll be inside the minute it rains.* ☐ *Call me the minute you get to town.*

a **miscarriage of justice** a wrong or mistaken decision, especially one made in a court of law. ☐ *Sentencing the old man on a charge of murder proved to be a miscarriage of justice.* ☐ *Punishing the student for cheating was a miscarriage of justice. He was innocent.*

Misery loves company. *Prov.* Unhappy people like other people to be unhappy too. ☐ *Jill: Why is Linda criticizing everybody today? Jane: Her boss criticized her this morning, and misery loves company.* ☐ *I should probably feel bad because my sister is so depressed, but I'm pretty depressed myself. Misery loves company.*

Misfortunes never come singly. *Prov.* Bad things tend to happen in groups. ☐ *I already told you that my wife lost her job. Well, misfortunes never come singly; our house was robbed last night.*

mislead someone **about** something to misrepresent something to someone. ☐ *I hope you are not trying to mislead me about the price.* ☐ *I'm afraid I misled you on this matter.*

misplace one's **trust (in** someone**)** to put trust in the wrong person; to put trust in someone who does not deserve it. ☐ *The writer misplaced his trust in his editor.* ☐ *The voters misplaced their trust in the corrupt politician.*

miss a trick *Fig.* to miss an opportunity or chance. (Typically with the negative.) ☐ *She hardly ever misses a trick.* ☐ *Mr. Big never misses a trick.* ☐ *How did a smart guy like you miss a trick like that?*

A **miss is as good as a mile.** *Prov.* Almost having done something is the same as not having done it at all, since in both cases the thing does not get done. ☐ *We only missed the train by one minute? Well, a miss is as good as a mile.*

miss out (on something**)** and **lose out (on** something**)** to fail to participate in something; to fail to take part in something. ☐ *I'm sorry I missed out on the ice cream.* ☐ *I lost out on getting in the class photo because I was sick that day.*

miss (something**) by a mile** *Fig.* to fail to hit something by a great distance; to land **wide of the mark**. ☐ *Ann shot the arrow and missed the target by a mile.* ☐ *"Good grief, you missed by a mile," shouted Sally.*

miss the boat 1. *Lit.* to miss out (on something); to be ignorant (of something). ☐ *Pay attention, John, or you'll miss the boat and not learn algebra.* ☐ *Tom really missed* *the boat when it came to making friends.* **2.** *Fig.* to have made an error; to be wrong. □ *If you think you can do that, you have just missed the boat.* □ *The guy's missed the boat. He's a lunkhead.*

miss the point to fail to understand the important part of something. □ *I'm afraid you missed the point. Let me explain it again.* □ *You keep explaining, and I keep missing the point.*

mission in life one's purpose in life; the reason for which one lives. □ *Bob's mission in life is to make money.* □ *My mission in life is to help people live in peace.*

mist over and **mist up** [for glass] to fog up; [for glass] to develop a coating of water vapor so that one cannot see. □ *The windshield misted over and we could hardly see out.* □ *The glass misted up and we had to wipe it off.*

mist up Go to previous.

mistake someone **for** someone else and **mix** someone **up with** someone else to confuse someone with someone else; to think that one person is another person. □ *I'm sorry. I mistook you for John.* □ *Tom is always mistaking Bill for me. We don't look a thing alike, though.* □ *Try not to mix Bill up with Bob, his twin.*

mistake something **for** something else and **mix** something **up with** something else to confuse two things with each other. □ *Please don't mix this idea up with that one.* □ *I mistook my book for yours.*

mix and match 1. to assemble a limited number of items, usually clothing, in a number of different ways. □ *Alice learned to mix and match her skirts, blouses, and sweaters so that she always could be attractively dressed on a limited budget.* □ *Gary always bought black, blue, and gray trousers and shirts so he could mix and match without too many bad combinations.* **2.** to select a number of items from an assortment, often in order to get a quantity discount. (As opposed to getting a quantity discount for buying a lot of only one item.) □ *The candles were 25 percent off, and you could mix and match colors, sizes, and length.* □ *I found a good sale on shirts. They were four for fifty dollars, and the store would let you mix and match.*

mix in (with someone or something**)** to mix or combine with people or substances. □ *The band came down from the stage and mixed in with the guests during the break.* □ *The eggs won't mix in with the shortening!*

mix it up (with someone**)** to fight with someone; to quarrel with someone. □ *Wilbur and Walt mixed it up for a while, and then things calmed down.* □ *Richard came out of the shop and began to mix it up with Walt.*

mix someone or something **into** something and **mix** someone or something **in†** to combine someone or something into something. □ *We will try to mix the new people into the group.* □ *We will mix in the new people a few at a time.*

mix someone **up†** to confuse someone. □ *Please don't ask questions now; you'll mix me up!* □ *You mixed up the speaker with your question.*

mix someone **up† in** something to get someone involved in something. □ *Please don't mix me up in this problem.* □ *Walter mixed up his daughter in the sordid affair.*

mix someone **up with** someone else Go to **mistake** someone **for** someone else.

mix something **up†** to bring something into disorder; to throw something into a state of confusion. □ *Don't mix up the papers on my desk.* □ *He mixes up things in his eagerness to speak.*

mix something **up† (with** something**) 1.** to mix or stir something using a mixing or stirring device. □ *He mixed the batter up with a spoon.* □ *First, mix up the batter.* **2.** to combine substances and mix them together. □ *Please mix the egg up with the sugar first.* □ *Please mix up the egg with the sugar.*

mix something **up with** something else Go to **mistake** something **for** something else.

mix with someone or something to mix socially with someone or a group. □ *Tom dislikes Bill and Ted so much that he could never mix with them socially.* □ *She finds it difficult to mix with friends.*

mix with something [for a substance] to combine with a substance. □ *Will this pigment mix with water?* □ *Water will not mix with oil.*

a **mixed bag** a varied collection of people or things. (Refers originally to a bag of game brought home after a day's hunting.) □ *The new students in my class are a mixed bag—some bright, some positively stupid.* □ *The furniture I bought is a mixed bag. Some of it is antique and the rest is quite contemporary.*

***mixed feelings (about** someone or something**)** uncertainty about someone or something. (*Typically: **get** ~; **have** ~; **give** someone ~.) □ *I have mixed feelings about Bob. Sometimes I think he likes me; other times I don't.* □ *I have mixed feelings about my trip to England. I love the people, but the climate upsets me.*

***mixed up in** something involved in something, especially something wrong or illegal. (*Typically: **be** ~; **get** ~.) □ *The youth has had problems ever since he got mixed up in a group of boys that stole a car.*

***mixed up with** someone else involved with another person, possibly romantically. (*Typically: **be** ~; **get** ~.) □ *I hear that Sam is mixed up with Sally.* □ *Who is Jerry mixed up with now?*

moan about something to complain about something. □ *What are you moaning about?* □ *I am not moaning about anything.*

moan something **out†** to say something in a moan. □ *The injured woman moaned the name of her assailant out.* □ *She moaned out the name.*

moan with something to groan because of pain or pleasure. □ *The patient moaned with pain and fear.* □ *Ken moaned with pleasure.*

mock something **up†** to make a model or simulation of something. □ *The engineers mocked the new car design up for the managers to see.* □ *They mocked up the new car design.*

model someone **on** someone and **model** something **on** something to use something as a pattern for something; to use someone as a pattern for someone. □ *I will model my house on the house we saw in the Mediterranean.* □ *She tried to model herself on her mother.*

M

model something **in** something to make a model of something in a particular substance. □ *She modeled the figure in clay.* □ *I modeled a bear in modeling clay.*

model something **on** something Go to **model** someone **on** someone.

Moderation in all things. *Prov.* Do not do anything too much or too little. □ *Felicia always ate sparingly. "Moderation in all things," she told herself.* □ *Jane: I think you watch too much TV. Jill: So you think I shouldn't watch any? Jane: No, just watch a reasonable amount. Moderation in all things.*

modulate to a (different) key to change from one musical key to another by means of a musical transition. □ *Suddenly, the organist modulated to a key that was too high for most of the singers.* □ *I will have to modulate to a lower key before I start the next hymn.*

moist around the edges intoxicated. □ *Charlie is more than moist around the edges. He is soused.* □ *Didn't that guy seem a little moist around the edges?*

mold something **out of** something and **mold** something **from** something to form something, using a pliable substance, such as clay, plastic, wet concrete, etc. □ *She molded a small turtle out of the moist clay.* □ *Elaine molded a turtle from the clay.*

the **moment everyone has been waiting for** Go to the **big moment.**

the **moment of truth** *Fig.* the point at which someone has to face the reality of a situation. □ *The moment of truth is here. Turn over your exam papers and begin.* □ *Now for the moment of truth when we find out whether we have got planning permission or not.*

Monday's child is fair of face. *Prov.* A child born on Monday will be good-looking. (This comes from a rhyme that tells what children will be like, according to which day they are born: "Monday's child is fair of face, / Tuesday's child is full of grace, / Wednesday's child is full of woe, / Thursday's child has far to go, / Friday's child is loving and giving, / Saturday's child works hard for a living, / But a child that is born on the Sabbath day / Is blithe and bonny, good and gay.") □ *Joan is so pretty, she must be a Monday's child. Monday's child is fair of face.*

Money burns a hole in someone's **pocket.** An expression decribing someone who spends money as soon as it is earned. □ *Sally can't seem to save anything. Money burns a hole in her pocket.* □ *If money burns a hole in your pocket, you never have any for emergencies.*

Money does not grow on trees. *Prov.* It is not easy to get money. (Implies that the person you are addressing spends money too easily.) □ *Child: Can I have ten dollars to go to the movies? Father: Ten dollars?! Money doesn't grow on trees.*

money from home 1. easily gotten money. (Underworld.) □ *There is nothing to a simple con job like this. It's money from home.* □ *This job is like taking candy from a kid. It's money from home.* **2.** something as welcome as long-awaited money from home. □ *This cool drink is money from home right now.* □ *Having you visit like this is like getting money from home, Mary.*

Money is no object. and **Expense is no object.** *Fig.* It does not matter how much something costs. □ *Please show me your finest automobile. Money is no object.* □ *I want the finest earrings you have. Don't worry about how much they cost because expense is no object.*

Money is power. *Prov.* If you have money, you can get things and do things. □ *Emily wanted a career that would make her a lot of money, since money is power.*

Money is the root of all evil. and The **love of money is the root of all evil.** *Prov.* People do many evil things in order to get rich. (Biblical. Compare this with **Idleness is the root of all evil.**) □ *Fred: I know I could make more money if I just knew the right things to invest in. Ellen: Don't worry so much about money. It's the root of all evil, after all.* □ *As the newspapers continued to report the dastardly things the wealthy young banker had done to become even wealthier, people shook their heads and remarked, "The love of money is the root of all evil."*

Money talks. *Fig.* Money gives one power and influence to help get things done or get one's own way. □ *Don't worry. I have a way of getting things done. Money talks.* □ *I can't compete against rich old Mrs. Jones. She'll get her way because money talks.*

monkey business and **funny business** silliness; dishonest tricks. □ *That's enough monkey business. Now, settle down.* □ *Stop the funny business. This is serious!*

Monkey see, monkey do. *Prov.* Children imitate what they see other people doing. □ *I don't let my children watch TV programs that show kids being disrespectful to their elders. I know what would happen if I did: monkey see, monkey do.*

monkey suit a tuxedo. (Jocular. Possibly in reference to the fancy suit worn by an organ-grinder's monkey.) □ *Do I have to wear a monkey suit to dinner?* □ *All the men except me wore monkey suits at dinner on the cruise.*

monkey with someone or something Go to **mess with** someone or something.

months running Go to **days running.**

mooch (something) from someone to beg something from someone. □ *Can I mooch a match from you?* □ *Go mooch some money from Fred.* □ *Why do you always mooch from people?*

moon about someone or something and **moon over** someone or something *Fig.* to pine or grieve about someone or something. □ *Stop mooning about your cat. Cats always come back eventually.* □ *Jill is still mooning over Robert.*

moon something **away**† *Fig.* to waste time pining or grieving. □ *Don't moon the whole year away!* □ *You have mooned away half the year. Now pull yourself together!*

mop something **down**† to clean a surface with a mop. □ *Please mop this floor down now.* □ *Please mop down this floor.*

mop something **off**† to wipe the liquid off something. □ *Please mop the counter off with paper towels.* □ *Mop off the counter.*

mop something **up**† to clean up something, such as a spill, with a mop or with a mopping motion. □ *Please mop this mess up.* □ *I will mop up this mess.*

mop something **up**† **with** something to clean or remove something from something else using a mop, rag, towel,

M

etc. □ *I can mop the mess up with this old rag mop.* □ *She will mop up the mess with the rag.*

mop the floor up† **with** someone to overwhelm and physically subdue someone; to beat someone. □ *Stop talking like that, or I'll mop the floor up with you!* □ *Did you hear that? He threatened to mop up the floor with me!*

mop up (after someone or something**) 1.** *Lit.* to clean up with a mop a sloppy mess made by someone or something. □ *I am the one who has to mop up after the mess you made!* **2.** *Fig.* to rectify a problem that someone or something has created. □ *You made a fuss in the conference and upset everyone. I spent hours mopping up after you in private meetings with all in attendance.*

mope around to go about in a depressed state. □ *Since her dog ran away, Sally mopes around all day.* □ *Don't mope around. Cheer up!*

a **mopping-up operation** a clean-up operation; the final stages in a project where the loose ends are taken care of. □ *It's all over except a small mopping-up operation.* □ *The mopping-up operation from the hurricane should cost just under twenty million.*

moralize about someone or something to utter moral platitudes about someone or something. □ *There is no point in moralizing about Carlo. He can't be changed.* □ *Why are you moralizing about the election? The people are always right.*

more and more an increasing amount; additional amounts. □ *As I learn more and more, I see how little I really know.* □ *Dad seems to be smoking more and more lately.*

more dead than alive *Fig.* exhausted; in very bad condition; near death. (Almost always an exaggeration.) □ *We arrived at the top of the mountain more dead than alive.* □ *The marathon runners stumbled one by one over the finish line, more dead than alive.*

more fun than a barrel of monkeys and **as much fun as a barrel of monkeys** *Cliché* a great deal of fun. (Compare this with **as funny as a barrel of monkeys.**) □ *Roger always makes me laugh! He is as much fun as a barrel of monkeys.* □ *The circus was more fun than a barrel of monkeys.*

More haste, less speed. Go to Make haste slowly.

more often than not *Fig.* usually. □ *These flowers will live through the winter more often than not.* □ *This kind of dog will grow up to be a good watchdog more often than not.*

more or less somewhat; approximately; a phrase used to express vagueness or uncertainty. □ *Henry: I think this one is what I want, more or less. Clerk: A very wise choice, sir.* □ *I spent more or less a half hour waiting for my flight to depart.*

More power to you! Well done!; You really stood up for yourself!; You really did something for your own benefit! (The stress is on *to,* and the *you* is usually "ya.") □ *Bill: I finally told her off, but good. Bob: More power to you!* □ *Sue: I spent years getting ready for that job, and I finally got it. Mary: More power to you!*

more's the pity *Fig.* it is a great pity or shame; it is sad. (Sometimes with *the.*) □ *Jack can't come, more's the pity.* □ *Jane had to leave early, more's the pity.*

more someone or something **than** one **can shake a stick at** *Rur.* a lot; too many to count. □ *There were more snakes than you could shake a stick at.* □ *There are lots of flowers in the field—more than one can shake a stick at.*

more something **than Carter has (liver) pills** *Fig.* a great deal of something. (Older; refers to a product called *Carter's Little Liver Pills.*) □ *Why he's got more problems than Carter has pills!* □ *Bobby has more marbles than Carter has liver pills!*

more than one **bargained for** more than one thought one would get. (Usually in reference to trouble or difficulty.) □ *When Betsy brought home the sweet little puppy for a companion, she got more than she bargained for. That animal has cost her hundreds of dollars in bills.* □ *I got more than I bargained for when I took this job.*

more than one **can bear** and **more than** one **can take; more than** one **can stand** more of something, such as trouble or something bad, than a person can endure. □ *This tragic news is more than I can bear!* □ *I've heard enough of this horrid music. It's more than I can stand.*

more than you('ll ever) know a great deal, more than you suspect. □ *Bob: Why did you do it? Bill: I regret doing it. I regret it more than you know.* □ *John: Oh, Mary, I love you. Mary: Oh, John, I love you more than you'll ever know.*

the **more the merrier** *Cliché* the more people there are, the happier the situation will be. □ *Of course you can have a ride with us! The more the merrier.* □ *The manager hired a new employee even though there's not enough work for all of us now. Oh, well, the more the merrier.*

more (to something**) than meets the eye** *Fig.* [there are] hidden values or facts regarding something. □ *There is more to that problem than meets the eye.* □ *What makes you think that there is more than meets the eye?*

The **more you get, the more you want.** and The **more you have, the more you want.** *Prov.* People are never satisfied with what they have. □ *You may think that you'll be content being department supervisor, but power is like anything else—the more you have, the more you want.*

The **more you have, the more you want.** Go to previous.

the **morning after (the night before)** a hangover; the feelings associated with having drunk too much alcohol. □ *Do worries about the morning after keep you from having a good time at parties?* □ *She's suffering from the morning after the night before.*

Morning dreams come true. *Prov.* If you dream something in the morning, it will really happen. (According to a superstition.) □ *As I was sleeping through the sound of my alarm clock this morning, I dreamed I was late to work. That morning dream definitely came true.*

most of all of greatest importance; more than any other. (Compare this with **least of all.**) □ *I wanted to go to that museum most of all. Why can't I go?* □ *There are many reasons why I didn't use my car today. Most of all, it's a lovely day for walking.*

motherhood and apple pie *Fig.* an often parodied sentiment expressed about allegedly quintessential elements of American home life. □ *Fred is so old-fashioned. Everything about old times is good to him. He's all motherhood and apple pie.*

M

motion (for) someone **to** do something to give someone a hand signal to do something. □ *The minister motioned the organist to begin playing.* □ *I motioned Ken to raise the curtain so the play could begin.* □ *Sally motioned for the waiter to bring the check.* □ *I will motion to the usher and try to get him to come over here and help us.*

motion someone **aside**[†] to give a hand signal to someone to move aside. (See also **motion** someone **to one side.**) □ *He motioned her aside and had a word with her.* □ *I motioned aside the guard and asked him a question.*

motion someone **away from** someone or something to give a hand signal to someone to move away from someone or something. □ *She motioned me away from Susan.* □ *The police officer motioned the boys away from the wrecked car.*

motion someone **to one side** and **motion** someone **to the side** to give someone a hand signal to move to the side of something, such as the road. (Very similar to **motion** someone **aside.**) □ *The cop motioned her to the side of the road.* □ *Claire motioned Fred to one side, where she spoke to him.*

motion to someone to make some sort of hand signal to a person. □ *Did you motion to me? What do you want?* □ *I did not motion to you.*

mound something **up**[†] to form something into a mound. □ *Mound the dirt up around the base of the shrub.* □ *Please mound up the leaves around the rosebushes.*

mount something **against** someone or something to create or instigate something against someone or something. □ *The prosecutor mounted a questionable case against Robert.* □ *The state mounted a very complex case against the company.*

mount something **on** something to place or attach something onto something. □ *Mount the butterflies on plain white paper.* □ *Sue mounted her favorite stamps on a display board.*

mount up 1. to get up on a horse. □ *Mount up and let's get out of here!* □ *Please mount up so we can leave.* **2.** [for something] to increase in amount or extent. □ *Expenses really mount up when you travel.* □ *Medical expenses mount up very fast when you're in the hospital.*

mourn for someone or something and **mourn over** someone or something to grieve for someone or something. □ *Everyone will mourn for you when you go.* □ *We all mourned over the end of the holiday.* □ *There is no point in mourning over your cat. It won't come back.*

The **mouse that has but one hole is quickly taken.** *Prov.* It is dangerous to always depend on just one thing, because if it fails you, you will not have any alternatives. □ *Don't put all your money in a single bank account. The mouse that has but one hole is quickly taken.*

a **mouth full of South** *Sl.* a southern accent. □ *You sure do have a mouth full of South.* □ *I just love to hear a man with a mouth full of South.*

mouth off to speak out of turn; to backtalk. □ *If you mouth off, I will ground you for three weeks.* □ *Don't mouth off at me, buster!*

mouth on someone to inform the authorities on someone; to tattle on someone. □ *Max mouthed on his accomplice and got him arrested.* □ *You had better not mouth on me!*

a **movable feast 1.** *Lit.* a religious holiday that is on a different date from year to year. □ *Easter is the best known movable feast.* **2.** *Fig.* a meal that is served in motion or with different portions of the meal served at different locations. (Jocular or a complete misunderstanding of ① but in wide use.) □ *We enjoyed a real movable feast on the train from Washington to Maimi.*

move a mile a minute Go to a mile a minute.

move about Go to move around.

move ahead of someone or something to advance beyond someone or something. □ *All my coworkers are moving ahead of me in salary. What am I doing wrong?* □ *The police moved ahead of the parade, pushing back the crowd.*

move along to continue to move; to start moving out of the way. (Often a command.) □ *The crowd moved along slowly.* □ *Please just move along. There is nothing to see here.*

move around and **move about** to move here and there a bit; to stir; to walk around a bit. □ *Stay where you are. Don't move around at all!* □ *I wish you would stop moving about.*

move as one Go to as one.

move aside to step or move out of the way. □ *Please move aside.* □ *Could you please move aside so we can get this cart through?*

move at a fast clip Go to at a fast clip.

move at a good clip Go to at a good clip.

move away (from someone or something**) 1.** to withdraw from someone or something. □ *Please don't move away from me. I like you close by.* □ *I have to move away from the smoking section.* □ *There was too much smoke there, so I moved away.* **2.** to move, with one's entire household, to another residence. □ *Timmy was upset because his best friend had moved away.* □ *They moved away just as we were getting to know them.*

move back (from someone or something**)** to move back and away. (Often a command.) □ *Please move back from the edge.* □ *Please move back!*

move beyond someone or something Go to **beyond** someone or something.

move clear of something Go to clear of something.

move close to someone or something Go to **close to** someone or something.

move down to move oneself farther down a line of things. □ *Someone else needs to sit on this bench. Please move down.* □ *Could you move down a little so we can have some more room?*

move for something to make a parliamentary or legal motion in favor of something. □ *I move for dismissal of the case against my client.* □ *My lawyer moved for a recess of the trial.*

move forward with something to advance with something; to make progress with something. □ *Let us try to move forward with this matter at once.* □ *I want to move forward with the project at a fast pace.*

move (from some place**) (to** some place**)** to travel from one place to another. □ *The whole family moved from Denver to Chicago.* □ *We moved to the country.*

M

move heaven and earth to do something *Fig.* to make a major effort to do something. □ *"I'll move heaven and earth to be with you, Mary," said Bill.* □ *I had to move heaven and earth to get there on time.*

move in for the kill Go to close in for the kill.

move in (on someone**)** to come to live with someone. □ *My brother moved in on me without even asking.* □ *I don't mean to move in on you. I just need a place for a few days.*

move in (on someone or something**) 1.** *Lit.* to move closer to someone or something; to make advances or aggressive movements toward someone or something. (See also **move in (on** someone**).**) □ *The crowd moved in on the frightened guard.* □ *They moved in slowly.* **2.** *Fig.* to attempt to take over or dominate someone or something. □ *The police moved in on the drug dealers.* □ *Max tried to move in on the rival gang's territory.*

move in the fast lane Go to in the fast lane.

move in with someone to take up residence with someone. □ *Sally moved in with Sam.* □ *Jimmy moved in with his brother and shared expenses.*

move into full swing Go to in full swing.

move into high gear Go to in full swing; in high gear.

move in(to something**) 1.** *Lit.* [for someone] to come to reside in something or some place. □ *I moved into a new apartment last week.* □ *When did the new family move in?* **2.** *Lit.* to enter something or some place. □ *The whole party moved into the house when it started raining.* □ *All the children just moved in and brought the party with them.* **3.** *Fig.* to begin a new line of activity. □ *After failing at real estate, he moved into house painting.* □ *It looked like he could make some money, so he moved into the stock market with his assets.*

move like stink Go to like stink.

move like the wind Go to like the wind.

move off campus Go to off campus.

move off (from someone or something**)** to move away from someone or something. □ *The doctor moved off from the patient, satisfied with her work.* □ *The officer stopped for a minute, looked around, and then moved off.*

move off (to the side) with someone Go to off (to the side) with someone.

move on to continue moving; to travel on; to move along and not stop or tarry. □ *Move on! Don't stop here!* □ *Please move on!*

move on someone to attempt to pick up someone; to attempt to seduce someone. □ *Don't try to move on my date, old chum.* □ *Harry is trying to move on Tiffany. They deserve each another.*

move on something to do something about something. □ *I will move on this matter only when I get some time.* □ *I have been instructed to move on this and give it the highest priority.*

move on (to something**)** to change to a different subject or activity. □ *Now, I will move on to a new question.* □ *That is enough discussion on that point. Let's move on.*

move out (from under someone or something**)** Go to out (from under someone or something).

move out (of some place**) 1.** to leave a place; to leave; to begin to depart. (Especially in reference to a large number of persons or things.) □ *The crowd started to move out of the area about midnight.* □ *They had moved out by one o'clock.* **2.** to leave a place of residence permanently. □ *We didn't like the neighborhood, so we moved out of it.* □ *We moved out because we were unhappy.*

move over to move a bit [away from the speaker]. □ *Move over. I need some space.* □ *Please move over. Part of this space is mine.*

move someone or something **around** to move someone or something from place to place. □ *I wish that the army would stop moving me around. I have moved ten times in eight years.* □ *Let's move the furniture around and see how this room looks.*

move someone or something **away (from** someone or something**)** to cause someone or something to withdraw from someone or something. □ *Move Billy away from Tommy so they will stop fighting.* □ *Move the cake away from Billy.*

move someone or something **back (from** someone or something**)** to cause someone or something to move back and away from someone or something. □ *Please move your child back from the lawn mower.* □ *Move everyone back from the street.*

move someone or something **down**† to cause someone or something to move farther down or along [something]. □ *Move Tom down a few seats. We need more space here.* □ *Move down all these chairs. We need more space.*

move someone or something **forward** to cause someone or something to advance. □ *Move her forward. She is too far back.* □ *Please move the chair forward.*

move someone or something **into** something and **move** someone or something **in**† to cause someone or something to enter something or some place. □ *We moved Carla into the spare room.* □ *We found a vacant room and moved in the piano.*

move someone or something **off ((from)** someone or something**)** and **move** someone or something **off ((of)** someone or something**)** to remove someone or something from on top of someone or something. (*Of* is usually retained before pronouns.) □ *The referee moved the wrestler off from his fallen opponent.* □ *I moved the beam off of the leg of the man.*

move someone or something **on** to cause someone or something to move onward or out of the way. □ *Please move those people on. They are in the way.* □ *The officers worked hard to move the crowd on.*

move someone or something **out (of** some place**)** to cause someone to depart or leave; to carry someone or something out of a place. □ *Move those people out of here. They are crowding up the room.* □ *Please move all that stuff out.*

move someone or something **out of the way** Go to out of the way.

move someone or something **over** to cause someone or something to move a little way away. □ *Move Tom over a little bit. He is taking too much space.* □ *Would you move your foot over a little?*

move someone or something **to** something to make someone or something shift toward something. □ *Can you move* *your foot to the right a little?* □ *Would you move yourself to the right?*

move someone or something **up** to cause someone or something to go higher or more forward. □ *She is too far down. Move her up one step.* □ *Would you move the sofa up a little? It is too far back.*

move someone **to tears** to bring someone to the point of crying. □ *The story moved me to tears.* □ *As she recounted the accident, she moved herself to tears.*

move someone **up**[†] to advance or promote someone. □ *We are ready to move you up. You have been doing quite well.* □ *It will be years before they move up the new people.*

move to some place to move one's household to some place, perhaps permanently. □ *When we retired, we moved to Arizona.* □ *I hope we can move to a larger house.*

move toward someone or something **1.** *Lit.* to move in the direction of someone or something. □ *The car is moving toward Roger!* **2.** *Fig.* to tend to favor a particular conclusion. □ *We are moving toward making the final decision.*

move up to advance; to go higher. □ *Isn't it about time that I move up? I've been an office clerk for over a year.* □ *I had hoped that I would move up faster than this.*

move up in the world and **come up in the world** *Fig.* to advance (oneself) and become successful. □ *The harder I work, the more I move up in the world.* □ *Keep your eye on John. He's really coming up in the world.*

move up into something to advance into something. □ *I moved up into administration and I like it fine.* □ *When I move up into management, I will get a bigger office.*

move up through something to advance through something. □ *He moved up through the ranks at a very rapid pace.* □ *He moved up through every level of management to become CEO.*

move up (to something**)** to advance to something; to purchase a better quality of something. □ *We are moving up to a larger car.* □ *There are too many of us now for a small house. We are moving up.*

move within earshot (of something**)** Go to **within earshot (of** something**).**

move within range Go to **within range.**

move within range (of something**)** Go to **within range (of** something**).**

movers and shakers people who get things done; organizers and managers. □ *The movers and shakers in this firm haven't exactly been working overtime.* □ *Who are the movers and shakers around here?*

Moving three times is as bad as a fire. *Prov.* If you move your household three times, you will lose or damage as many things as a fire in your house would have destroyed or damaged. □ *Fred: The company is transferring me again. Ellen: But we can't make another move! Moving three times is as bad as a fire.*

mow someone or something **down**[†] to cut, knock, or shoot someone or something down. □ *The speeding car almost mowed us down.* □ *The car mowed down the pedestrian.*

Mr. Nice Guy a friendly, forgiving fellow. □ *You'll find that I am Mr. Nice Guy as long as you play fair with me.* □ *Oh, my boss is Mr. Nice Guy. He'll give me the day off, I'm sure.*

Mr. Right the one man who is right for a woman to marry. □ *Some day Mr. Right will come along and sweep you off your feet.* □ *I'm tired of waiting for Mr. Right. Where is Mr. Maybe?*

much ado about nothing *Cliché* a furor over something unimportant. (The name of a Shakespeare play.) □ *All this arguing is much ado about nothing.*

much in evidence *Cliché* very visible or evident. □ *John was much in evidence during the conference.* □ *Your influence is much in evidence. I appreciate your efforts.*

Much obliged. *Rur.* Thankful and owing a debt of gratitude. □ *A: Sit down, Elmer, and have a drink on me. B: Much obliged.*

much of a muchness too much of something that there is generally a lot of. □ *All this talk about e-commerce and business-2-business is too much of a muchness.*

***much sought after** *Cliché* wanted or desired very much. (*Typically: be ~; become ~.)* □ *This kind of crystal is much sought after. It's very rare.* □ *Sally is a great singer. She's much sought after.*

muck something **up**[†] to ruin something. □ *I should never have trusted Jim with the repair work. He was bound to muck it up.* □ *I asked her to take over for me while I was gone, and she really mucked it up.* □ *She mucked up the whole deal.*

muddle along to progress in confusion; to continue awkwardly. □ *I will just have to muddle along as best I can until things get straightened out.* □ *The project muddled along until the new manager got hold of it.*

muddle around to work inefficiently. □ *I can't get anything done today. I'm just muddling around.* □ *Jed is not doing his job well. He is muddling around and getting nothing done.*

muddle something **up**[†] to mix something up; to make something confusing. □ *You really muddled the language of this contract up.* □ *Who muddled up the wording?*

muddle through (something**)** to manage to get through something awkwardly. □ *We hadn't practiced the song enough, so we just muddled through it.* □ *We didn't know what we were meant to do, so we muddled through.*

muddled (up) intoxicated. □ *I've had a little too much muddler, I think. Anyway, I'm muddled.* □ *Larry is too muddled up to drive.*

muddy something **up**[†] *Lit.* **1.** to make water muddy; to stir up the mud in water, as at the bottom of a pond or river. □ *Don't muddy the water up. It will clog our filters.* □ *Don't muddy up the water.* **2.** *Fig.* to make something unclear. □ *You have really muddied this issue up. I thought I understood it.* □ *You sure muddied up this issue.*

muddy the water *Fig.* to make something less clear; to make matters confusing; to create difficulty where there was none before. □ *Things were going along quite smoothly until you came along and muddied the water.* □ *The events of the past month have muddied the water as far as our proposed joint venture is concerned.*

muff one's **lines** Go to **fluff** one's **lines.**

muffle something **up**[†] to deaden or stifle a sound. □ *Betty tried to muffle the sounds up, but everyone heard what was going on.* □ *She muffled up the sounds.*

mulct something **out of** someone to cheat something away from someone. □ *Are you trying to mulct my inheritance out of me?* □ *Max tried to mulct every last cent out of his victim.*

mull something **over**[†] to think about something; to ponder or worry about something. □ *That's an interesting idea, but I'll have to mull it over.* □ *I'll mull over your suggestions and reply to you next week.*

multiply by something to use the arithmetic process of multiplication to expand numerically a certain number of times. □ *To get the amount of your taxes, multiply by .025.* □ *Can you multiply by sixteens?*

multiply something **by** something to use the arithmetic process of multiplication to expand numerically a particular number a certain number of times. □ *Multiply the number of dependents you are claiming by one thousand dollars.* □ *Multiply 12 by 16 and tell me what you get.*

a **multitude of sins** *Fig.* many kinds of sins or errors. □ *The term* offensive *covers a multitude of sins.*

Mum's the word. *Fig.* a pledge not to reveal a secret or to tell about something or someone. □ *"Mum's the word,"* said Jane to ease Mary's mind about her secret.

munch out *Sl.* to overeat. □ *I can't help it. Whenever I see french fries, I just have to munch out.* □ *I try not to munch out more than once a week.*

mung something **up**[†] *Sl.* to mess something up. □ *Don't mung it up this time.* □ *The team munged up the play, and the coach blasted them but good.*

murder on something very destructive or harmful to something. □ *Running a marathon is murder on your knees.* □ *This dry weather is murder on my crops.*

Murder will out. *Prov.* Murder will always be discovered.; A bad deed will be found out. □ *Horace thought he had disposed of his victim in such a way that no one would ever discover his crime, but murder will out.*

murmur against someone or something to grumble about someone or something. □ *Everyone was murmuring against the manager.* □ *The citizens will begin murmuring about the government soon.*

murmur at someone or an animal to say something softly or indistinctly to someone or an animal. □ *Stop murmuring at me. Speak up!* □ *Gene sat alone, murmuring at his favorite cat for over an hour.*

muscle in (on someone or something**)** to try forcefully to displace someone or take over someone's property, interests, or relationships. □ *Are you trying to muscle in on my scheme?* □ *If you try to muscle in, you'll be facing big trouble.*

muscle someone **out of** something and **muscle** someone **out**[†] to force someone out of something; to push someone out of something. (Can be physical or by coercion.) □ *Are you trying to muscle me out of my job?* □ *The younger people are muscling out the older ones.*

muse over someone or something to reflect or meditate on someone or something. □ *We were just now musing over Sarah and the way she has changed.* □ *Tom is so strange. I was musing over his behavior just yesterday.*

mushroom into something *Fig.* to grow suddenly into something large or important. □ *The question of pay sud-* denly mushroomed into a major matter. □ *The unpaid bill mushroomed into a nasty argument and, finally, a court battle.*

music to someone's **ears** *Fig.* a welcome sound to someone; news that someone is pleased to hear. □ *A: Here's your paycheck for this month. B: Ah, that's music to my ears!*

muss someone or something **up**[†] to put someone or something into disarray. □ *Don't muss me up!* □ *You mussed up my hair.* □ *I'm afraid I mussed myself up a little.*

muster out of something to be discharged from military service. □ *He mustered out of the service before his time was up.* □ *I want to know how I can muster out too.*

muster something **up**[†] to call up some quality, such as courage. □ *Do you think you can muster enough courage up to do the job?* □ *Can you muster up enough strength to do the job?*

mutiny against someone or something **1.** to rebel against a ship's captain or the captain's authority. □ *The crew mutinied against the officers.* □ *They know better than to mutiny against an authority as great as that held by Captain Bligh.* **2.** to rebel against someone or something. □ *It does no good to mutiny against the professor.* □ *The students mutinied against the school's administration.*

mutter about someone or something to grumble or complain about someone or something. □ *Are you muttering about me? What is your complaint?* □ *Why is everyone muttering about the food here? It is excellent.*

mutter something **about** someone or something to say something softly and indistinctly about someone or something. □ *I heard him mutter something about being late.* □ *Sharon is muttering something about Dave. What does she mean?*

mutter something **under** one's **breath** Go to **under** one's **breath.**

My cup runneth over. *Prov.* I have received so many benefits that I cannot contain them all. (Said when you feel overcome because many good things have happened to you.) □ *This week, I finished paying off my mortgage, my arthritis improved, and my first grandchild was born. My cup runneth over.* □ *Janet was speechless with happiness when she saw how many of her friends and relatives had joined together to give her a surprise party. "My cup runneth over," she finally said.*

My foot! *Inf.* I do not believe it!; Like hell! (An exclamation of contradiction.) □ *Your prices are the best in town, my foot! I know two places cheaper.* □ *She's going to marry you? My foot!*

(My) goodness (gracious)! a general expression of interest or mild amazement. □ *Bill: My goodness! The window is broken! Andy: I didn't do it! Bill: Who did, then?* □ *"Goodness! I'm late!" said Kate, glancing at her watch.* □ *"Goodness gracious! Are you hurt?" asked Sue as she helped the fallen student to his feet.*

my gut tells me (that) my instincts tell me that. (This refers to one's *gut reaction* or *gut response*.) □ *My gut tells me that her idea is a sound one.* □ *This looks good on paper, but my gut tells me that it is all wrong.*

(My) heavens! *Inf.* a mild exclamation of surprise or amazement. □ *Bill: Heavens! The clock has stopped. Bob: Don't you have a watch?* □ *Sally: The police are parked in*

M

445

our driveway, and one of them is getting out! Mary: My heavens!

My house is your house. and **Our house is your house.** *Fig.* a polite expression said to make a guest feel at home. (From the Spanish phrase *Mi casa, su casa.*) □ *Bill: Hello, Tom. Tom (entering): So nice you can put me up for the night. Bill: My house is your house, make yourself at home.* □ *Mary: Come in, you two. Bill: Thanks. Sue: Yes, thank you. Mary: Well, what can I get you? My house is your house.*

(My,) how time flies. 1. Time has gone by quickly, it is time for me to go. □ *Bill: Look at the clock! Mary: How time flies! I guess you'll be going. Bill: Yes, I have to get up early.* □ *John: My watch says it's nearly midnight. How time flies! Jane: Yes, it's late. We really must go.* **2.** Time passes quickly. (Said especially when talking about how children grow and develop.) □ *"Look at how big Billy is getting,"* said Uncle Michael. *"My, how time flies."* □ *Tom: It seems it was just yesterday that I graduated from high school. Now I'm a grandfather. Mary: My, how time flies.*

My lips are sealed. *Fig.* I will tell no one this secret or this gossip. □ *Mary: I hope you don't tell anyone about this. Alice: Don't worry. My lips are sealed.* □ *Bob: Don't you dare tell her I told you. Bill: My lips are sealed.*

My(, my). an expression of mild surprise or interest. □ *Fred: My, my! How you've grown, Bill. Bill: Of course! I'm a growing boy. Did you think I would shrink?* □ *Doctor: My, my, this is interesting. Jane: What's wrong? Doctor: Nothing that a little exercise won't fix.*

my one and only one's spouse or lover. (See also the **one and only**.) □ *Look at the time. I've got to get home to my one and only.* □ *You're my one and only. There is no one else for me.*

My pleasure. 1. You're welcome.; It is my pleasure to do so. (From *It's my pleasure.* There is a stress on both words.) □ *Mary: Thank you for bringing this up here. Bill: My pleasure.* □ *Jane: Oh, Doctor, you've really helped Tom. Thank you so much! Doctor: My pleasure.* **2.** Happy to meet you.; Happy to see you. □ *Sally: Bill, meet Mary, my cousin. Bill: My pleasure.*

M

nag at someone **(about** someone or something**)** to pester someone about someone or something. □ *Don't keep nagging at me about her.* □ *Stop nagging at me!*

nail someone **down**[†] **(on** something**)** Go to **pin** someone **down**[†] **(on** something**).**

nail someone's **ears back**[†] *Fig.* to scold someone severely. □ *I'm going to nail your ears back for doing that!* □ *Who's going to nail back my ears?*

nail someone**('s hide) to the wall** Go to next.

nail someone **to a cross** and **nail** someone**('s hide) to the wall** *Fig.* to punish or scold someone severely. (Literally, to crucify someone or to nail someone's skin to the wall like that of a captured animal.) □ *That guy was really mad. He really nailed you to a cross.* □ *She must hate your guts. She sure nailed your hide to the wall.*

nail something **back**[†] to secure something back out of the way by nailing it. □ *Please nail the shutters back so they won't bang against the house.* □ *I'll nail back the shutters.*

nail something **down**[†] **1.** to secure something down by nailing it. □ *Please nail the floorboard down or someone will trip over it.* □ *I'll nail down these floorboards.* **2.** Go to **pin** something **down.**

nail something **into** something to drive a nail or something similar into something. □ *She nailed the hanger into the wall to hold the picture up.* □ *Please nail in this tack.*

nail something **onto** something and **nail** something **to** something; **nail** something **on**[†] to attach something onto something by nailing. □ *Suzy nailed the hose bracket onto the side of the house.* □ *She nailed on the bracket.* □ *Laura nailed the bracket to the wall.*

nail something **up**[†] **1.** to put something up, as on a wall, by nailing. □ *Please nail this up.* □ *I'll nail up this picture for you.* **2.** to nail something closed; to use nails to secure something from intruders. □ *Sam nailed the door up so no one could use it.* □ *Who nailed up the door? I can't get in!*

***naked as a jaybird** *Cliché* naked; bare. (*Also: **as** ~.) □ *Two-year-old Matilda escaped from her nurse, who was bathing her, and ran out naked as a jaybird into the dining room.* □ *Uncle John sometimes spends a whole day walking around his house as naked as a jaybird.*

***the **naked eye** the human eye, unassisted by optics, such as a telescope, microscope, or spectacles. (*Typically: **appear to** ~; **look to** ~; **see with** ~; **visible to** ~.) □ *I can't see the bird's markings with the naked eye.* □ *The scientist could see nothing in the liquid with the naked eye, but with the aid of a microscope, she identified the bacteria.* □ *That's how it appears to the naked eye.*

the **naked truth** the complete, unembellished truth. □ *Sorry to put it to you like this, but it's the naked truth.* □ *I can take it. Just tell me the naked truth.*

the **name of the game** *Inf.* the way things are; the way things can be expected to be. □ *The name of the game is money, money, money.* □ *I can't help it. That's the name of the game.*

name someone **after** someone else and **name** someone **for** someone else to give someone (usually a baby) the name of another person. □ *We named our baby after my aunt.* □ *My parents named me for my grandfather.*

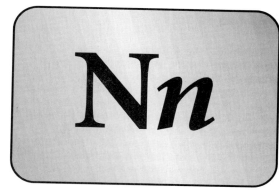

name someone **as** something to select someone as something. □ *The mayor named Karen as corporate council.* □ *The president named himself as chairman of the new committee.*

name someone **for** someone else Go to **name** someone **after** someone else.

name someone or something **for** someone or something to name someone or something, using the name of someone or something, in any combination. □ *I named her for the beauty of the rising sun.* □ *They named the mountain for the first person to see it.*

Name your poison. Go to **What'll it be?**

narrow something **down**[†] **(to** people or things**)** to reduce a list of possibilities from many to a selected few. □ *We can narrow the choice down to green or red.* □ *We narrowed down the choice to you or Paul.*

narrow squeak *Fig.* a success almost not achieved; a lucky or marginal success; a problem almost not surmounted. □ *That was a narrow squeak. I don't know how I survived.* □ *Another narrow squeak like that and I'll give up.*

Nature abhors a vacuum. *Prov.* If there is a gap, something will fill it. □ *Jill: As soon as the beggar who used to work that corner left, another one showed up. Jane: Nature abhors a vacuum.*

a **nature stop** *Fig.* a stop to use the toilet, especially during road travel. □ *I think I need a nature stop when it's convenient.* □ *I left my comb back at the last nature stop.*

nause someone **out**[†] *Sl.* to make someone ill; to disgust someone. (From *nauseate.*) □ *That's awful. I bet it nauses Jennifer out.* □ *This day naused out everybody I know.* □ *He naused himself out just thinking of the accident.*

near at hand close or handy (to someone). □ *Do you have a pencil near at hand?* □ *My dictionary isn't near at hand.*

The **nearer the church, the farther from God.** *Prov.* Church officials, or people who live near the church, are not truly pious. □ *Jill: I think our pastor is an evil man. Jane: I didn't think evil men could be pastors. Jill: Of course they can! The nearer the church, the farther from God.*

nearly jump out of one's **skin** Go to **(almost) jump out of** one's **skin.**

***neat as a pin** *Cliché* neat and orderly. (*Also: **as** ~.) □ *Brad is such a good housekeeper; his apartment is always as neat as a pin.* □ *Joanne certainly is well-organized. Her desk is neat as a pin.*

Necessity is the mother of invention. *Prov.* When people really need to do something, they will figure out a way to do it. □ *When the fan belt on Linda's car broke in the middle of the desert, Linda used her stockings as a replacement. Necessity is the mother of invention.*

Necessity knows no law. *Prov.* If you are desperate, you may have to do illegal things. □ *I'm an honest person by nature, but I lost my job, and my kids needed food and clothes, and it seemed like the best way to get money was to deal in illegal drugs. Necessity knows no law.*

neck and neck *Fig.* exactly even, especially in a race or a contest. □ *John and Tom finished the race neck and neck.* □ *Mary and Ann were neck and neck in the spelling contest. Their scores were tied.*

neck with someone to engage in amorous kissing and caressing with someone. □ *Ted is over there necking with Molly.* □ *Molly is necking with Ted and thinking of Ken.*

need a firm hand Go to a firm hand.

need a helping hand Go to a helping hand.

need a pick-me-up Go to a pick-me-up.

need doing and **need (to be)** done [is] required to be done. (The second form, although widespread, is considered by some to be less standard than the first.) □ *This chair needs fixing.* □ *This chair needs fixed.*

need I remind you that... and **need I remind you of...** a phrase that introduces a reminder. (A little haughty or parental.) □ *Bill: Need I remind you that today is Friday? Bob (sarcastically): Gee, how else would I have known?* □ *John: Need I remind you of our policy against smoking in the office? Jane: Sorry, I forgot.*

Need I say more? Is it necessary for me to say any more? □ *Mary: There's grass to be mowed, weeds to be pulled, dishes to be done, carpets to be vacuumed, and there you sit! Need I say more? Tom: I'll get right on it.* □ *"This project needs to be finished before anyone leaves tonight," said Alice, hovering over the office staff. "Need I say more?"*

need so bad one **can taste it** Go to so bad one can taste it.

need some elbow room Go to some elbow room.

need some shut-eye Go to some shut-eye.

need something **like a hole in the head** not to need something at all. □ *I need a house cat like I need a hole in the head!* □ *She needs another car like she needs a hole in the head.*

need something **yesterday** *Inf.* to require something in a very big hurry. □ *Yes, I'm in a hurry! I need it yesterday!* □ *When do I need it? Now! Now! No, I need it yesterday!*

need (to be) done Go to need doing.

needle someone **about** someone or something to pester or bother someone about someone or something. □ *Please don't needle me about Jane.* □ *Stop needling me about eating out.*

needless to say It is so obvious that it doesn't need to be said, but.... □ *Needless to say, I should have spent more time on the report, but I just didn't have it.*

Needs must when the devil drives. *Prov.* When you are desperate, you must do things you ordinarily would not do. □ *We're going to have to get an enormous loan to pay for your mother's surgery. I hate to go into debt, but needs must when the devil drives.*

neglect to do something to fail to do something. □ *I hope you do not neglect to lock the door.* □ *He neglected to water the plants.*

negotiate (with someone or something) **(over** someone or something) and **negotiate (with** someone or something) **(about** someone or something) to bargain with someone or a group about someone or something. □ *We decided to negotiate with them over the terms of the contract.* □ *We want to negotiate with them about the cost of the goods.* □ *They refused to negotiate with our purchasing agent.*

neighbor on something to be directly adjacent to something. □ *Our house neighbors on a park.* □ *The park neighbors on a stretch of beach.*

Neither a borrower nor a lender be. *Prov.* It is difficult to be friends with someone who owes you money or with someone to whom you owe something, so it is better not to borrow or lend in the first place. □ *After losing several of my favorite books because I didn't have the nerve to insist that my friends return them, I learned that it is best to neither a borrower nor a lender be.*

Neither can I. I cannot do that either. (Any subject pronoun can be used in place of I.) □ *Bill: No matter what they do to them, I just can't stand sweet potatoes! Bob: Neither can I.* □ *John: Let's go. I cannot tolerate the smoke in here. Jane: Neither can I.*

neither does someone [does] not either. □ *Susan does not own a cat, and neither does Mary.* □ *Bill doesn't want to see a movie tonight, and neither do I.*

neither fish nor fowl *Cliché* not any recognizable thing. □ *The car that they drove up in was neither fish nor fowl. It must have been made out of spare parts.* □ *This proposal is neither fish nor fowl. I can't tell what you're proposing.*

neither here nor there *Cliché* of no consequence or meaning; irrelevant and immaterial. □ *Whether you go to the movie or stay at home is neither here nor there.* □ *Your comment—though interesting—is neither here nor there.*

***(neither) hide nor hair** *Cliché* no sign or indication of someone or something. (*Typically: **find** ~; **see** ~.) □ *We could find neither hide nor hair of him. I don't know where he is.* □ *There has been no one here. We found neither hide nor hair.*

***neither rhyme nor reason** *Cliché* without logic, order, or planning. (Describes something disorganized. *Typically: **be** ~; **have** ~.) □ *There seems to be neither rhyme nor reason to Gerald's filing system.* □ *The novel's plot had neither rhyme nor reason.*

nerves of steel *Fig.* very steady nerves; great patience and courage. □ *I was scared to death, but Fred, who has nerves of steel, faced the thugs bravely.*

a (nervous) breakdown *Fig.* a physical and mental collapse brought on by great anxiety over a period of time. □ *After month after month of stress and strain, Sally had a nervous breakdown.*

nest in something to build a nest in something and live in it. □ *Some mice nested in a corner of the garage.* □ *The birds nested in the eaves.*

N

nest together to fit together or within one another compactly. □ *These mixing bowls nest together.* □ *I want some of those Russian wooden dolls that nest together.*

nestle down (in something**)** to settle down in something; to snuggle into something, such as a bed. □ *They nestled down in their warm bed.* □ *Please nestle down and go to sleep.*

nestle (up) against someone or something and **nestle up (to** someone or something**)** to lie close to someone or something; to cuddle up to someone or something. □ *The kitten nestled up against its mother.* □ *The shivering puppy nestled up to Kathy.*

never a dull moment [it's] always exciting around here. (Describes an exciting or hectic situation.) □ *Every time I visit Jean, she has dozens of things planned for us to do: parties and theaters to attend, restaurants to try, scenic places to see. Never a dull moment.* □ *Alan: How was work today? Jane: First of all, my boss called me in to yell at me. Then I had to fire one of my subordinates. And then my desk chair broke when I sat down on it. Never a dull moment.*

Never ask pardon before you are accused. *Prov.* Do not apologize for something if nobody knows that you did it, because by apologizing, you are admitting that you did it. □ *Alan: Should I apologize to Jane for losing the necktie she gave me? Jane: Wait and see if she asks you what happened to the necktie. Never ask pardon before you are accused.*

never fear do not worry; have confidence. □ *I'll be there on time—never fear.* □ *I'll help you, never fear.*

Never halloo till you are out of the woods. *Prov.* Do not rejoice until you are certain that your problems are over. □ *Jill: Now that I have a full-time job, I'm certain to be able to pay all my debts. Jane: But it's just a temporary job; it may not last long. Never halloo till you are out of the woods.*

Never in a thousand years! Go to Not in a thousand years!

never in my life an emphatic expression showing the depth of the speaker's feelings. □ *Sally: Never in my life have I seen such a mess! John: Well, it's always this way. Where have you been all this time? Sally: I just never noticed before, I suppose.* □ *Sue: Never will I go to that hotel again! Never in my life! Bob: That bad, huh? Sue: Yes! That bad and worse!*

Never make a threat you cannot carry out. *Prov.* You should not threaten to do something you cannot do; otherwise, people will not believe you are serious when you threaten. □ *Bill: If you don't stop being rude to me, I'll have you fired! Jane: You're not my boss. Never make a threat you cannot carry out.*

Never mind! Forget it!; It's not important! □ *Sally: What did you say? Jane: Never mind! It wasn't important.* □ *John: I tried to get the book you wanted, but they didn't have it. Shall I try another store? Mary: No, never mind.*

Never say die. *Prov.* Do not give up. □ *Jill: I don't think I can finish this project in time. Jane: Never say die.* □ *Alan: It's no use. I can't make my checkbook balance. Jane: Never say die!*

Never speak ill of the dead. *Prov.* You should not say bad things about dead people. □ *Your Uncle Phil had a lot of faults, but there's no reason to talk about them now that he's gone. Never speak ill of the dead.* □ *I hate to speak ill of the dead, but Amy was a mean woman, God rest her soul.*

Never tell tales out of school. *Prov.* Do not tell secrets; do not gossip. □ *Fred: I just learned something really scandalous about the president of our company. Ellen: Well, I don't want to hear it. You shouldn't tell tales out of school.*

Never trouble trouble till trouble troubles you. *Prov.* If you think something might cause trouble, leave it alone and wait until it actually causes trouble. □ *Ellen: My daughter's teacher is going to be troublesome, I can tell. Maybe I should go to the school and talk to her. Jane: Why not wait till she actually does something? Never trouble trouble till trouble troubles you.*

never would have guessed 1. never would have thought something to be the case. (Not used in other tenses.) □ *He was the one who did it? I never would have guessed.* □ *I never would have guessed that he wanted the job. He kept it a very good secret.* **2.** knew it all the time because it was so obvious. (Sarcastic. Not used in other tenses.) □ *I never would have guessed that he wanted the job. He only begged and begged for it.* □ *Now she wants to go back home? I never would have guessed! She has been homesick for days.*

New brooms sweep clean. and A **new broom sweeps clean.** *Prov.* Someone who is new in a particular job will do a very good job at first, to prove how competent he or she is. □ *Jill: That new supervisor is awfully strict. Jane: New brooms sweep clean.* □ *The new teacher immediately flunked three of the laziest students. "A new broom sweeps clean," one of the students shrugged.*

new kid on the block 1. *Lit.* a child who has just moved to a certain neighborhood. □ *The new kid on the block turned out to be a really good baseball player.* **2.** *Fig.* the newest person in a group. □ *I'm just the new kid on the block. I've only been working here for a month.*

a **new lease on life** *Cliché* a renewed and revitalized outlook on life. □ *Getting the job offer was a new lease on life.* □ *When I got out of the hospital, I felt as if I had a new lease on life.*

new one on someone something that one has not heard before and that one is not ready to believe. □ *Bob's talk of poverty is a new one on me. He always seems to have plenty of money.* □ *The firm's difficulties are a new one on me. I thought that it was doing very well.*

Next question. *Inf.* That is settled, let's move on to something else. (Usually a way of evading further discussion.) □ *Mary: When can I expect this construction noise to stop? Bob: In about a month. Next question.* □ *Bill: When will the board of directors raise the dividend again? Mary: Oh, quite soon. Next question.*

next to nothing *Fig.* hardly anything; almost nothing. □ *This car's worth next to nothing. It's full of rust.* □ *I bought this antique chair for next to nothing.*

next to someone or something near to someone or something; adjacent to someone or something. □ *I live next to a bank.* □ *Please sit next to me.*

the **next world** *Euph.* life after death. □ *We will meet in the next world.* □ *He believed he had made contact with spirits from the next world.*

nibble at something to take tiny bites of some kind of food. □ *The children nibbled at their dinner because they had eaten too much candy.* □ *Stop nibbling at that candy.*

nibble away at something to eat at something in tiny bits; to erode away tiny bits of something. □ *The waves nibbled away at the base of the cliff, year after year.* □ *The mice nibbled away at the huge wheel of cheese.*

nice and some quality [being or having] enough of some quality; adequately; sufficiently. □ *It is nice and cool this evening.* □ *I think your steak is nice and done now, just the way you like it.*

a **nice break** Go to a **lucky break**.

Nice going! and **Good job!; Good going!; Nice job! 1.** *Inf.* That was done well. □ *John: Well, I'm glad that's over. Sally: Nice going, John! You did a good job.* □ *Tom: Nice job, Bill! Bill: Thanks, Tom!* **2.** *Fig.* That was done poorly. (Sarcastic.) □ *Fred: I guess I really messed it up. Bill: Nice job, Fred! You've now messed us all up! Fred: Well, I'm sorry.* □ *"Nice going," frowned Jane, as Tom upset the bowl of potato chips.*

Nice guys finish last. *Prov.* You will never be able to get what you want by being kind and considerate. □ *The unscrupulous salesman advised his trainees, "Don't worry if you have to lie about the product to get the customer to buy it. Nice guys finish last."*

Nice job! Go to **Nice going!**

Nice meeting you. It is nice to have met you. (Said when leaving someone whose acquaintance you have just made.) □ *I must go now, Fred. Nice meeting you.* □ *Well, nice meeting you. I must get home now.*

Nice place you have here. Your home is nice. (A compliment paid by a guest. The word *place* might be replaced with *home, house, room, apartment,* etc.) □ *Jane came in and looked around. "Nice place you have here," she said.* □ *Bob: Come in. Welcome. Mary: Nice place you have here. Bob: Thanks. We like it.*

Nice weather we're having. 1. *Lit.* Isn't the weather nice? (Sometimes used to start a conversation with a stranger.) □ *Bill: Nice weather we're having. Bob: Yeah. It's great.* □ *Mary glanced out the window and said to the lady sitting next to her, "Nice weather we're having." 2. Fig.* Isn't this weather bad? (Sarcastic.) □ *Bill: Hi, Tom. Nice weather we're having, huh? Tom: Yeah. Gee, it's hot!* □ *Mary: Nice weather we're having! Sally: Sure. Lovely weather for ducks.*

nick something **up**† to make little dents or nicks in something, ruining the finish. □ *Someone nicked the kitchen counter up.* □ *Who nicked up the coffeepot?*

nickel-and-dime someone **(to death)** *Fig.* to make numerous small monetary charges that add up to a substantial sum. □ *Those contractors nickel-and-dimed me to death.* □ *Just give me the whole bill at one time. Don't nickel-and-dime me for days on end.*

niggle about something to make constant petty complaints about something. □ *Please don't niggle about little things like this. This is just not important.* □ *Let's not niggle about it.*

niggle (over something**) (with** someone**)** to have a petty disagreement over some minor thing. □ *Stop niggling over this with me!* □ *I don't want to niggle with you over this.*

night and day Go to **day and night**.

a **night on the town** a night of celebrating (at one or more places in a town). □ *Did you enjoy your night on the town?* □ *After we got the contract signed, we celebrated with a night on the town.*

night owl *Fig.* someone who stays up at night; someone who works at night. □ *My roommate is a night owl and usually reads until 5:00 A.M.* □ *A few night owls stayed at the café all night long.*

a **night person** *Fig.* someone who is more alert and active at night than in the daytime. (Compare this with a **day person**.) □ *I'm really not efficient until after supper. I am the quintessential night person.*

a **nine days' wonder** *Fig.* something that is of interest to people only for a short time. □ *Don't worry about the story about you in the newspaper. It'll be a nine days' wonder and then people will forget.* □ *The elopement of Bob and Anne was a nine days' wonder. Now people never mention it.*

nine times out of ten *Fig.* usually; almost always. □ *Nine times out of ten people will choose coffee rather than tea.*

nineteen to the dozen *Prov.* very rapidly or energetically. □ *Whenever I get together with my cousins, we always gossip away nineteen to the dozen.* □ *While Alan got the other ingredients, Jane was chopping up potatoes nineteen to the dozen.*

nine-to-five job a job with normal daytime hours. □ *I wouldn't want a nine-to-five job. I like the freedom I have as my own boss.* □ *I used to work nights, but now I have a nine-to-five job.*

nip and tuck *Fig.* almost even; almost tied. □ *The horses ran nip and tuck for the first half of the race. Then my horse pulled ahead.* □ *In the football game last Saturday, both teams were nip and tuck throughout the game.*

nip at someone or something to bite at someone or something. □ *The dog nipped at the visitor, but didn't cause any real harm.* □ *A small dog nipped at my heels.*

nip something **in the bud** *Fig.* to put an end to something before it develops into something larger. (Alludes to destroying a flower bud before it blooms.) □ *I wanted to nip that little romance in the bud.* □ *The whole idea was nipped in the bud.*

nip something **off (of)** something and **nip** something **off**† to clip or cut something off something. (*Of* is usually retained before pronouns.) □ *Let me nip a few blossoms off the rosebush.* □ *I nipped off a few blossoms and made a bouquet.*

no big deal and **no biggie** *Inf.* [of something] not difficult or troublesome. □ *Don't worry. It's no big deal to wash the car.* □ *No problem. It's no biggie.*

no biggie Go to **previous**.

no buts about it Go to **no ifs, ands, or buts (about it)**.

No can do. *Inf.* It can't be done.; I can't do it. □ *Sorry, John. No can do. I can't sell you this one. I've promised it to Mrs. Smith.* □ *Bill: Please fix this clock today. Bob: No can do. It'll take a week to get the parts.*

No comment. I have nothing to say on this matter. □ *Q: When did you stop beating your dog? A: No comment.* □

Q: Georgie, did you chop down the cherry tree? A: No comment.

no contest 1. *Lit.* [in games] a situation where one team fails to appear for a competition. □ *It was declared no contest because the opposing team was stuck in traffic out on the expressway.* **2.** *Fig.* a situation where the winner-to-be of a contest is obvious even before holding the contest. □ *It was no contest. The wrestler was so big and strong that no one could have defeated him.*

no dice *Inf.* no; not possible. □ *When I asked about a loan, he said, "No dice."* □ *No. It can't be done, no dice.*

no doubt a transitional or interpretative phrase strengthening the rest of a previous sentence. □ *Sue: Mary is giving this party for herself? Rachel: Yes. She'll expect us to bring gifts, no doubt.* □ *Mary: All this talk about war has my cousin very worried. Sue: No doubt. At his age, I don't wonder.*

no earthly reason no conceivable reason. □ *There is no earthly reason for your rude behavior.* □ *I can think of no earthly reason why the repairs should cost so much.*

no end of something an endless supply of something. □ *Have some candy. I have no end of chocolate drops.* □ *I've had no end of trouble ever since I bought this car.*

No fair! *Inf.* That isn't fair! □ *Bill: No fair! You cheated! Bob: I did not!* □ *"No fair," shouted Tom. "You stepped over the line!"*

no flies on someone *Fig.* someone is not slow; someone is not wasting time. (On the image of flies not being able to land on someone moving fast.) □ *Of course I work fast. I go as fast as I can. There are no flies on me.* □ *There are no flies on Robert. He does his work very fast and very well.*

no go *Inf.* negative; inopportune. (This is hyphenated before a nominal.) □ *We're in a no-go situation.* □ *Is it go or no go?*

no great shakes *Inf.* someone or something that is not very good. (There is no affirmative version of this.) □ *Your idea is no great shakes, but we'll try it anyway.* □ *Ted is no great shakes when it comes to brains.*

no hard feelings and **not any hard feelings** *Fig.* no anger or resentment. □ *I hope you don't have any hard feelings.* □ *No, I have no hard feelings.*

No harm done. It is all right. No one or nothing has been harmed. □ *It's okay. No harm done.* □ *A: I am sorry I stepped on your toe. B: No harm done.*

no holds barred *Fig.* with no restraints. (Alludes to a wrestling match in which all holds are legal.) □ *I intend to argue it out with Mary, no holds barred.* □ *When Ann negotiates a contract, she goes in with no holds barred and comes out with a good contract.*

no ifs, ands, or buts (about it) and **no buts about it** *Fig.* absolutely no discussion, dissension, or doubt about something. □ *I want you there exactly at eight, no ifs, ands, or buts about it.* □ *This is the best television set available for the money, no buts about it.*

no joke a serious matter. □ *It's no joke when you miss the last train.* □ *It's certainly no joke when you have to walk home.*

No kidding! 1. *Inf.* You are not kidding me, are you? (An expression of mild surprise.) □ *Jane: I got elected vice pres-*ident. Bill: No kidding! That's great! **2.** *Inf.* Everyone already knows that! Did you just find that out? (Sarcastic.) □ *Sue: It looks like taxes will be increasing. Tom: No kidding! What do you expect?* □ *Alice: I'm afraid I'm putting on a little weight. Jane: No kidding!*

no laughing matter a serious issue or problem. □ *Be serious. This is no laughing matter.* □ *This disease is no laughing matter. It's quite deadly if not treated immediately.*

No lie? *Inf.* You are not lying, are you? □ *Bill: A plane just landed on the interstate highway outside of town! Tom: No lie? Come on! It didn't really, did it? Bill: It did too! Tom: Let's go see it!* □ *Bob: I'm going to take a trip up the Amazon. Sue: No lie?*

No man can serve two masters. *Prov.* You cannot work for two different people, organizations, or purposes in good faith, because you will end up favoring one over the other. (Biblical.) □ *Al tried going to school and working, both full-time, but soon discovered that he could not serve two masters.*

no matter how you slice it *Fig.* no matter what your perspective is; no matter how you try to portray something. □ *No matter how you slice it, the results of the meeting present all sorts of problems for the office staff.*

no matter what (happens) in any event; without regard to what happens (in the future). □ *We'll be there on time, no matter what.* □ *No matter what happens, we'll still be friends.*

No more than I have to. an answer to the greeting question "What are you doing?" □ *Bob: Hey, Fred. What you been doing? Fred: No more than I have to.* □ *Sue: Hi, Bill. How are you? Bill: Okay. What have you been doing? Sue: No more than I have to.*

No news is good news. Not hearing any news signifies that nothing is wrong. □ *Fred: I wonder if Jill is doing all right in her new job. Jane: No news is good news.* □ *Jane: I'm worried about my sister. She hasn't called me for months. Alan: No news is good news, right?*

No, no, a thousand times no! *Fig.* Very definitely, no! (Jocular.) □ *Bob: Here, have some sweet potatoes. Bill: No, thanks. Bob: Oh, come on! Bill: No, no, a thousand times no!* □ *Sue: The water is a little cold, but it's invigorating. Come on in. Bill: How cold? Sue: Well, just above freezing, I guess. Come on in! Bill: No, no, a thousand times no!*

no nonsense without any tricks, deceit, or wasting of time. (Hyphenated before nominals.) □ *Let's have no nonsense while we are rehearsing the presentation!* □ *Elton is a no-nonsense kind of guy.*

No offense meant. I did not mean to offend [you]. (See also **No offense taken.**) □ *Mary: Excuse that last remark. No offense meant. Susan: It's okay. I was not offended.*

No offense taken. I am not offended [by what you said]. (See also **No offense meant.**) □ *Pete: Excuse that last remark. I did not want to offend you. Tom: It's okay. No offense taken.*

No one is indispensable. *Prov.* Anyone may become unnecessary; anyone may lose his or her job. □ *Fred: You can't fire me. I'm absolutely necessary to this company. Nancy: No one is indispensable, Fred.* □ *The housekeeper was sure that her employer would always need her, but she discovered when she was let go that no one is indispensable.*

N

451

No pain, no gain. *Fig.* If you want to improve, you must work so hard that it hurts. (Associated with sports and physical exercise.) □ *Player: I can't do any more push-ups. My muscles hurt. Coach: No pain, no gain.* □ *Come on, everybody! Run one more lap! No pain, no gain!*

no point in something no purpose in doing something. □ *There is no point in locking the barn door now that the horse has been stolen.* □ *There's no point is crying over spilled milk.*

no problem Go to no sweat.

no questions asked no inquiries [to be] made to find out who did something. □ *Fines at the library will be suspended, no questions asked, for all late books returned during the first week of July.*

No rest for the wicked. *Fig.* It's because you are wicked that you have to work hard. (Usually jocular.) □ *A: I can't seem to ever get all my work done. B: No rest for the wicked.*

no sale no. □ *I wanted to go to Florida for the holidays, but my father said, "No sale."* □ *No sale. You can't do it.*

no salesman will call a phrase indicating that no salesman will visit or contact you if you make an inquiry about a product. □ *All inquiries are confidential and no salesman will call.*

no shortage of something lots of something; plenty of something. □ *Oh, don't worry about that. I have no shortage of money!* □ *We've no shortage of fried chicken, so help yourself.*

No siree(, Bob)! *Inf.* Absolutely no! (Not necessarily said to a male, and rarely to any Bob.) □ *Bill: Do you want to sell this old rocking chair? Jane: No siree, Bob!* □ *Bill: You don't want sweet potatoes, do you? Fred: No siree!*

no skin off someone's **nose** Go to next.

no skin off someone's **teeth** and **no skin off** someone's **nose** *Fig.* no difficulty for someone; no cause for concern to someone. □ *It's no skin off my nose if she wants to act that way.* □ *She said it was no skin off her teeth if we wanted to sell the house.*

no soap *Inf.* no. □ *I can't do it. No soap.* □ *No soap, I don't lend anyone money.*

no sooner said than done an expression indicating that something has been done quickly and obediently. □ *Jill: Can I help you out? Jane: Yes! Put these files in alphabetical order. Jill: No sooner said than done.* □ *The service at the hotel was really remarkable. Everything we asked for was no sooner said than done.*

no spring chicken *Fig.* a person well past youth; an old person. □ *That actress is no spring chicken, but she does a pretty good job of playing a twenty-year-old girl.* □ *Jane: How old do you think Robert is? Jill: Well, he's certainly no spring chicken.*

no stress *Inf.* no problem; no bother. □ *Don't worry, man, no stress.* □ *Relax. No stress. It doesn't bother me at all.*

no sweat and **no problem** *Inf.* no difficulty; do not worry. □ *Of course I can have your car repaired by noon. No sweat.* □ *You'd like a red one? No problem.*

No, thank you. and **No, thanks.** a phrase used to decline something. □ *Bob: Would you care for some more coffee? Mary: No, thank you.* □ *John: Do you want to go downtown tonight? Jane: No, thanks.*

no thanks to you I cannot thank you for what happened, because you did not cause it.; I cannot thank you for your help, because you did not give it. □ *Bob: Well, despite our previous disagreement, he seemed to agree to all our demands. Alice: Yes, no thanks to you. I wish you'd learn to keep your big mouth shut!* □ *Jane: It looks like the picnic wasn't ruined despite the fact that I forgot the potato salad. Mary: Yes, it was okay. No thanks to you, of course.*

no trespassing do not enter. (Usually seen on a sign. Not usually spoken.) □ *The sign on the tree said, "No Trespassing." So we didn't go in.* □ *The angry farmer chased us out of the field shouting, "Get out! Don't you see the 'No Trespassing' sign?"*

no two ways about it no choice about it; no other interpretation of it. (Note the form *there's* rather than *there are*.) □ *You have to go to the doctor whether you like it or not. There's no two ways about it.* □ *This letter means you're in trouble with the tax people. There's no two ways about it.*

No way! *Inf.* No! □ *Me join the Army? No way!* □ *She can't do that. No way!*

No way, José! *Inf.* No! (An elaboration of *No. José* is pronounced with an initial *H*.) □ *Bob: Can I borrow a hundred bucks? Bill: No way, José!* □ *Sally: Can I get you to take this nightgown back to the store for me and get me the same thing in a slightly smaller size? Bob: No way, José!*

no wonder [something is] not surprising. □ *No wonder the baby is crying. She's wet.* □ *It's no wonder that plant died. You watered it too much.*

nobody's fool *Fig.* a sensible and wise person who is not easily deceived. □ *Mary is nobody's fool. She watches out for people who might try to cheat her.* □ *Anne may seem as though she's not very bright, but she's nobody's fool.*

***the nod** *Fig.* someone's choice for a position or task. (*Typically: **get ~; have ~; give** someone **~.**) □ *The manager is going to pick the new sales manager. I think Ann will get the nod.* □ *I had the nod for captain of the team, but I decided not to do it.*

nod at someone to make a motion to someone with one's head indicating a greeting, agreement, or something else. □ *I nodded at Fred, but I really didn't agree.* □ *Molly nodded at Fred, and Fred, knowing she wanted to leave the party, went for their coats.* □ *When she offered him some ice cream, he only nodded. She thought he was rude and decided not to give him any.*

A nod is as good as a wink to a blind horse. *Prov.* You cannot get people to take a hint if they are determined not to. □ *Jill: I keep hinting to the boss that I deserve a raise, but he doesn't seem to get the point. Jane: I'm not surprised. A nod's as good as a wink to a blind horse.*

nod off to fall asleep, usually while sitting up. □ *Jack nodded off during the minister's sermon.* □ *Father always nods off after Sunday lunch.*

noise something **about** and **noise** something **abroad; noise** something **around** to spread around a secret; to gossip something around. □ *Now don't noise it about, but I am going to Houston next week to see my girl.* □ *Please don't noise this abroad.* □ *Stop noising that gossip around.*

nominate someone **as** something to suggest someone to be the candidate to serve as something. □ *I would like to* nominate Karen as our representative. □ She nominated herself as the one most likely to do the job.

nominate someone **for** something to suggest someone as a candidate for a particular office. □ I will nominate Carolyn for president. □ You cannot nominate yourself for this office.

nominate someone **to** something to suggest someone to become a member of a group. □ I am the one who nominated her to the board. □ The president nominated herself to the position of chairman of the board.

None but the brave deserve the fair. Prov. Only a courageous and gallant man deserves a beautiful woman.; Only the best deserves the best. □ Stop making excuses and just call Gina. None but the brave deserve the fair.

none of someone's **beeswax** Inf. none of someone's business. (Jocular.) □ It's none of your beeswax. I'm not telling. □ You'll never know. The answer is none of your beeswax.

none of someone's **business** not of someone's concern. (A gentle rebuke.) □ Q: When are you going to leave for home? A: None of your business. □ How I managed to afford all this is none of your business.

None of your lip! Fig. Shut up!; I don't want to hear anything from you about anything! □ A: You are being a real nuisance about the broken window. B: None of your lip! Just help me clean it up.

none other than Cliché the very [person]. (Expresses surprise.) □ The new building was opened by none other than the president. □ Bob's wife turned out to be none other than my cousin.

none the wiser not knowing any more in spite of events or exposure to facts. □ I was none the wiser about black holes after the lecture. It was a complete waste of time. □ Anne tried to explain the situation tactfully to Bob, but in the end, he was none the wiser.

***none the worse for wear** Fig. no worse because of use or effort. (See also the **worse for wear**. *Typically: **be ~; become ~; look ~**.) □ I lent my car to John. When I got it back, it was none the worse for wear. □ I had a hard day today, but I'm none the worse for wear.

none too something not very something; not at all something. □ The towels in the bathroom were none too clean. □ It was none too warm in their house.

noodle around to wander around; to fiddle around with something. □ I couldn't find the instructions so I spent the afternoon noodling around, trying to find out how it worked. □ I noodled around until I found the right address.

noodle over something Inf. to think about something. □ Let's noodle over this problem for a bit and discuss it at our next meeting.

nose about (for someone or something) and **nose around (for** someone or something) to search here and there to find someone or something. □ We spent an hour nosing about for a newspaper. □ I will nose around for someone to help you. □ We nosed about for a while, but found no one.

nose around (something) to pry into something; to snoop around something. □ I caught her nosing around my desk. □ Wally is always nosing around.

nose in(to something) [for a boat or other vehicle] to move or be moved into something or some place carefully, nose first. □ The captain nosed into the channel, and our journey had begun. □ He nosed in and we sailed on.

nose out (of something) to move cautiously out of something or some place, nose first. □ She nosed out of the little room, hoping she hadn't been observed. □ She nosed out quickly and stealthily.

nose someone or a group **out**† to defeat someone or something by a narrow margin. (Alludes to a horse winning a race "by a nose.") □ Karen nosed Bobby out in the election for class president by one vote. □ Our team nosed out the opposing team in last Friday's game.

nose something **out of** something and **nose** something **out**† 1. Lit. [for an animal] to force something out of something gently and cautiously. (As if pushing with the nose.) □ The cat nosed her kitten out of the corner. □ The cat nosed out her kittens where we could see them. □ She nosed them out. 2. Fig. to move something cautiously out of something or some place, nose first. □ Todd nosed the car out of the parking place carefully. □ He nosed out the car with skill. □ Ted nosed it out.

nose something **(out**†**) (onto** something) to drive or push something carefully out onto the surface of something, nose first. □ I nosed the car out onto the highway, looking both ways. □ She nosed out the car.

nosh on something to make a snack of something. □ After Thanksgiving, we noshed on turkey for three days. □ Who's been noshing on the chocolate cake?

not a bit none at all; not at all. □ Am I unhappy? Not a bit. □ I don't want any mashed potatoes. Not a bit!

Not a chance! Inf. There is no chance at all that something will happen. (A variation of **(There is) no chance.**) □ Sally: Do you think our team will win today? Mary: Not a chance! Jane: Can I have this delivered by Saturday? Clerk: Not a chance!

not a clue Go to next.

not a glimmer (of an idea) and **not a clue** Fig. no idea. □ A: Where's the subway? B: Sorry. Not a glimmer of an idea. □ How long till we're there? Not a clue.

not a hope in hell Go to not have a snowball's chance in hell.

not a kid anymore Fig. no longer in one's youth. □ You can't keep partying all weekend, every weekend. You're not a kid anymore. □ Kathy: Bill is just as wild as ever, I hear. Jane: Bill needs to realize that he's not a kid anymore.

not a living soul Fig. nobody. (See some of the possible variations in the examples.) □ I won't tell anybody—not a living soul. □ I won't tell a living soul.

not a moment to spare and **without a moment to spare** just in time; with no extra time. □ Hurry, hurry! There's not a moment to spare! □ I arrived without a moment to spare.

not able See the expressions listed at **can't** as well as those listed below.

not able to call one's **time** one's **own** too busy; so busy as not to be in charge of one's own schedule. □ It's been so busy around here that I haven't been able to call my time my own. □ She can't call her time her own these days.

N

not able to get something **for love or money** *Fig.* not able to get something at any price; completely unable to get something. □ *Oranges were so scarce last winter that you couldn't get them for love or money.* □ *I wanted to go to the concert, but I was not able to get a ticket for love or money.*

not able to go on unable to continue (doing something—even living). (*Not able to* is often expressed as *can't.*) □ *I just can't go on this way.* □ *Before her death, she left a note saying she was not able to go on.*

not able to help something unable to prevent or control something. (*Not able to* is often expressed as *can't.*) □ *I'm sorry about being late. I wasn't able to help it.* □ *Bob can't help being boring.*

not able to make anything out of someone or something unable to understand someone or something. (*Not able to* is often expressed as *can't.* The *anything* may refer to something specific, as in the first example.) □ *I can't make sense out of what you just said.* □ *We were not able to make anything out of the message.*

not able to make head or tail of something *Fig.* not able to understand something at all. □ *I couldn't make head or tail of the professor's geology lecture this morning.* □ *Can you help me fill out my tax forms? I can't make head or tail of the instructions.*

not able to see the forest for the trees *Cliché* allowing many details of a situation to obscure the situation as a whole. (*Not able to* is often expressed as *can't.*) □ *The solution is obvious. You missed it because you can't see the forest for the trees.* □ *She suddenly realized that she hadn't been able to see the forest for the trees.*

not able to stomach someone or something and **cannot stomach** someone or something *Fig.* not to be able to put up with someone or something; not to be able to tolerate or endure someone or something. □ *Jane cannot stomach violent movies.* □ *The sensitive student could not stomach a lot of ridicule.*

not able to wait to have to go to the bathroom urgently. (Also more broadly literal.) □ *Mom, I can't wait.* □ *Driver, stop the bus! My little boy can't wait.*

Not again! *Inf.* I cannot believe that it happened again! □ *Mary: The sink is leaking again. Sally: Not again! Mary: Yes, again.* □ *Fred: Here comes Tom with a new girlfriend. Sue: Not again!*

not agree with someone [for food] to make someone ill; [for something that one has eaten] to give one stomach distress. □ *Fried foods don't agree with Tom.* □ *I always have onions in my garden, but I never eat them. They just don't agree with me.*

not all something **is cracked up to be** and **not what** something **is cracked up to be** *Fig.* not as good as something is said to be. (Not always in the negative.) □ *This isn't a very good pen. It's not all it's cracked up to be.* □ *Is this one all it's cracked up to be?*

not all there *Fig.* not mentally adequate; crazy or silly. □ *Sometimes I think you're not all there.* □ *Be nice to Sally. She's not all there.*

Not always. a conditional negative response. (See examples.) □ *John: Do you come here every day? Jane: No, not*

always. □ *John: Do you find that this condition usually clears up by itself? Doctor: Not always.*

not amount to a hill of beans Go to not worth a hill of beans.

not any hard feelings Go to no hard feelings.

Not anymore. The facts you mentioned are no longer true.; A previous situation no longer exists. □ *Mary: This cup of coffee you asked me to bring you looks cold. Do you still want it? Sally: Not anymore.* □ *Tom: Do the Wilsons live on Maple Street? Bob: Not anymore.*

not as young as one **used to be** *Fig.* getting old. □ *Aunt Lila isn't as young as she used to be. She can't take a lot of trips anymore.* □ *Don't walk so fast! I'm not as young as I used to be. It takes me awhile to catch up.*

not at all and **not in the least** certainly not; absolutely not. □ *No, it doesn't bother me—not at all.* □ *I'm not complaining. Not me. Not in the least.*

Not bad (at all). 1. [Someone or something is] quite satisfactory. □ *Bill: How do you like your new teacher? Jane: Not bad.* □ *Bob: Is this pen okay? Bill: I guess. Yeah. Not bad.* **2.** [Someone or something is] really quite good. (The person or thing can be named, as in the examples.) □ *John: How do you like that new car of yours? Mary: Not bad. Not bad at all.* □ *Tom: This one looks great to me. What do you think? Sue: It's not bad.*

not bat an eye Go to next.

not bat an eyelid and **not bat an eye** *Fig.* to show no signs of distress even when something bad happens or something shocking is said. □ *Sam didn't bat an eyelid when the mechanic told him how much the car repairs would cost.* □ *The pain of the broken arm must have hurt Sally terribly, but she did not bat an eyelid.*

not believe one's **ears** *Fig.* not believe the news that one has heard. □ *I couldn't believe my ears when Mary said I won the first prize.*

not believe one's **eyes** *Fig.* not to believe what one is seeing; to be shocked or dumbfounded at what one is seeing. □ *I walked into the room and I couldn't believe my eyes. All the furniture had been stolen!* □ *When Jimmy opened his birthday present, he could hardly believe his eyes. Just what he wanted!*

not born yesterday *Fig.* experienced; knowledgeable in the ways of the world. □ *I know what's going on. I wasn't born yesterday.* □ *Sally knows the score. She wasn't born yesterday.*

not breathe a word (about someone or something**)** and **not breathe a word of it** *Fig.* to keep a secret about someone or something. □ *Don't worry. I won't breathe a word about this matter.* □ *Please don't breathe a word about Bob and his problems.* □ *Don't worry. I won't breathe a word of it.*

not breathe a word of it Go to previous.

not buy something *Fig.* not accept something (to be true). □ *You may think so, but I don't buy it.* □ *The police wouldn't buy his story.*

not by a long shot *Fig.* not by a great amount; not at all. □ *Did I win the race? Not by a long shot.* □ *Not by a long shot did she complete the assignment.*

not care two hoots about someone or something and **not give two hoots about** someone or something; **not give a hang about** someone or something; **not give a hoot about** someone or something *Inf.* not to care at all about someone or something. □ *I don't care two hoots about whether you go to the picnic or not.* □ *She doesn't give a hoot about me. Why should I care?* □ *I don't give a hang about it.*

not dry behind the ears Go to wet behind the ears.

not enough room to swing a cat *Rur.* not very much space. □ *Their living room was very small. There wasn't enough room to swing a cat.* □ *How can you work in a small room like this? There's not enough room to swing a cat.*

not exchange more than some number of **words with** someone Go to exchange no more than some number of words with someone.

not feel like oneself Go to next.

not feeling oneself and **not feel like** oneself *Fig.* to feel upset, troubled, or disturbed in some way. □ *I'm sorry I said what I said. I'm not feeling myself today.*

not for a moment not at all; not even for a short amount of time; never. □ *I don't want you to leave. Not for a moment!* □ *I could not wish such a horrible punishment on anyone. Not for a moment!*

not for all the tea in China *Fig.* not even if you rewarded me with all the tea in China; not for anything at all. □ *No I won't do it—not for all the tea in China.*

not for (anything in) the world and **not for love nor money; not on your life** *Fig.* not for anything (no matter what its value). (Note the variation in the examples. The order of *love nor money* is fixed.) □ *I won't do it for love nor money.* □ *He said he wouldn't do it—not for the world.*

not for hire [of a taxi] not available to take new passengers. □ *The taxi was going to pick someone up at a nearby hotel and was not for hire.* □ *The taxi had a lighted sign that said it was not for hire.*

not for love nor money Go to not for (anything in) the world.

Not for my money. Not as far as I'm concerned. (Has nothing to do with money or finance.) □ *Sue: Do you think it's a good idea to build all these office buildings in this part of the city? Mary: Not for my money. That's a real gamble.* □ *John: We think that Fred is the best choice for the job. Do you think he is? Mary: Not for my money, he's not.*

not for publication not to be talked about openly; secret. □ *Please tell no one about this. It's not for publication.* □ *This report is not for publication, so keep it to yourself.*

not get one's **hopes up** *Fig.* [one] should not expect something to happen; [one] should not start hoping that something will happen. □ *The rain could stop so we can go to the beach, but you should not get your hopes up.*

not give a hang about someone or something Go to not care two hoots about someone or something.

not give a tinker's damn *Fig.* not to care at all. (A tinker's damn or dam may be a worthless curse from a tinker or a small dam or barrier used to contain molten metal.) □ *I don't give a tinker's damn whether you go or not!*

not give anyone the time of day *Fig.* to ignore someone (usually out of dislike). □ *Mary won't speak to Sally. She won't give her the time of day.* □ *I couldn't get an appointment with Mr. Smith. He wouldn't even give me the time of day.*

not give it another thought not to worry about something anymore. (A polite way of accepting someone's apology.) □ *It's okay. Please don't give it another thought.* □ *You should not give it another thought. No one was bothered at all.*

not give two hoots about someone or something Go to not care two hoots about someone or something.

not going to win any beauty contests *Fig.* homely; ugly. □ *Fred isn't going to win any beauty contests, but he's smart and considerate and he does well at his job.* □ *This old truck of mine is not going to win any beauty contests, but I wouldn't trade it for anything.*

not grow on trees *Fig.* not to be abundant; not to be expendable. (Usually said about money.) □ *I can't afford that. Money doesn't grow on trees, you know.* □ *Don't waste the glue. That stuff doesn't grow on trees, you know.*

not have a care in the world *Fig.* free and casual; unworried and carefree. □ *I really feel good today—as if I didn't have a care in the world.* □ *Ann always acts as if she doesn't have a care in the world.*

not have a leg to stand on *Fig.* [for an argument or a case] to have no support. □ *You may think you're in the right, but you don't have a leg to stand on.* □ *My lawyer said I didn't have a leg to stand on, so I shouldn't sue the company.*

not have a snowball's chance in hell and **not a hope in hell** *Inf.* a very poor chance. (Usually in the negative.) □ *She doesn't have a snowball's chance in hell of getting it done on time.* □ *I know I don't have a hope in hell, but I'll try anyway.*

not have a stitch of clothes (on) *Fig.* naked. □ *He walked through the house and didn't have a stitch of clothes on.*

not have all one's **marbles** *Fig.* not to have all one's mental capacities. □ *John acts as if he doesn't have all his marbles.* □ *I'm afraid that I don't have all my marbles all the time.*

not have anything to do with someone or something Go to have nothing to do with someone or something.

not have anything to do with something Go to have something to do with something.

not have the heart to do something *Fig.* to be too compassionate to do something. □ *I just don't have the heart to tell him the bad news.*

not hold a candle to someone or something Go to next.

not hold a stick to someone or something and **not hold a candle to** someone or something *Fig.* not to be nearly as good as someone or something. □ *Sally is much faster than Bob. Bob doesn't hold a stick to Sally.* □ *This TV doesn't hold a candle to that one. That one is much better.*

not hold water 1. *Lit.* [of a container] not able to contain water without leaking. □ *This old wading pool won't hold water any longer.* **2.** *Fig.* not able to be proved; not correct or true. □ *Jack's story won't hold water. It sounds*

N

too unlikely. □ *The police's theory will not hold water. The suspect has an ironclad alibi.*

not hold with something *Rur.* to disagree with something; to not tolerate something. □ *I don't hold with what you are saying.* □ *We don't hold with that kind of thing around here.*

not hurt a flea *Fig.* not to harm anything or anyone, even a tiny insect. (Also with other forms of negation.) □ *Ted would not even hurt a flea. He could not have struck Bill.* □ *Ted would never hurt a flea, and he would not hit anyone as you claim.*

Not if I see you first. Go to next.

Not if I see you sooner. and **Not if I see you first.** *Inf.* a response to **I'll see you later.** (This means you will not see me if I see you first, because I will avoid you.) □ *Tom: See you later. Mary: Not if I see you sooner.* □ *John: Okay. If you want to argue, I'll just leave. See you later. Mary: Not if I see you first.*

Not in a thousand years! and **Never in a thousand years!** *Fig.* No, never! □ *John: Will you ever approve of her marriage to Tom? Sue: No, not in a thousand years!* □ *Mary: Will all this trouble ever subside? John: Never in a thousand years!*

Not in my book. *Fig.* Not according to my views. (Compare this with **Not for my money.**) □ *John: Is Fred okay for the job, do you think? Mary: No, not in my book.* □ *Sue: My meal is great! Is yours good, too? Bob: Not in my book.*

not in the least Go to **not at all.**

not in the same league with someone or something not nearly as good as someone or something. □ *John isn't in the same league with Bob at tennis.* □ *This house isn't in the same league with our old one.*

not just whistling Dixie *Rur.* not talking nonsense. (Alludes to a song titled "Dixie.") □ *Man, you are right! You're not just whistling Dixie.* □ *When you say she is wrong, you're not just whistling Dixie.*

not know beans (about someone or something**)** *Inf.* to know nothing about someone or something. □ *Bill doesn't know beans about flying an airplane.* □ *When it comes to flying, I don't know beans.*

not know enough to come in out of the rain *Fig.* to be very stupid. □ *Bob is so stupid he doesn't know enough to come in out of the rain.* □ *You can't expect very much from somebody who doesn't know enough to come in out of the rain.*

not know from nothing *Inf.* to be stupid, innocent, and naive. (This *nothing* is not replaced with *something.* Usually used with *don't,* as in the examples.) □ *Old John—he don't know from nothing.* □ *What do you expect from somebody who don't know from nothing?*

not know if one **is coming or going** Go to **not know whether** one **is coming or going.**

not know one's **own strength** not to realize how destructive or harmful one's strength can be. □ *I didn't mean to hurt you. I guess I don't know my own strength.* □ *He might break the door down by accident. He doesn't know his own strength and could end up pushing too hard against the door.*

not know someone **from Adam** *Fig.* not to know someone by sight at all. □ *I wouldn't recognize John if I saw him* up close. *I don't know him from Adam.* □ *What does she look like? I don't know her from Adam.*

not know the first thing about someone or something *Fig.* not to know anything about someone or something. □ *I don't know the first thing about flying an airplane.* □ *She doesn't know the first thing about John.*

not know what to make of someone or something not to understand someone or something; not to be able to interpret something or the actions of someone. □ *We really don't know what to make of his request.*

not know where to turn and **not know which way to turn** to have no idea about what to do (about something). □ *I was so confused I didn't know where to turn.* □ *We needed help, but we didn't know which way to turn.*

not know whether one **is coming or going** and **not know if** one **is coming or going** *Fig.* to be very confused. □ *I'm so busy that I don't know if I'm coming or going.* □ *You look as if you don't know whether you're coming or going.*

not know which end is up *Inf.* not to be alert and knowledgeable. □ *Don't try to hustle me, sister. You think I don't know which end is up?* □ *Poor Jed doesn't even know which end is up.*

not know which way to turn Go to **not know where to turn.**

not let someone **catch** someone doing something and **not want to catch** someone doing something an expression that scolds someone who has done something wrong. (The idea is that the person ought not to do the wrong thing again, not that the person simply avoid getting caught.) □ *How many times have I told you not to play ball in the house? Don't let me catch you doing that again.* □ *If I've told you once, I've told you a thousand times: Don't do that! I don't want to catch you doing it again!*

not let the grass grow under one's **feet** *Fig.* not to stay in one place for a long time; to be always on the move. □ *He is always doing something. He never lets the grass grow under his feet.* □ *I have always thought that I ought not to let the grass grow under my feet.* □ *Jane: Last night I told Alan that we needed a new bookshelf, and he had built one by the time I got home today. Jill: Boy, he doesn't let the grass grow under his feet.*

not lift a finger (to help someone**)** and **not lift a hand (to help** someone**)** *Fig.* to do nothing to help someone. (The *someone* is *anyone* with the negative.) □ *They wouldn't lift a finger to help us.* □ *Can you imagine that they wouldn't lift a finger?* □ *Sally refused to lift a hand to help her own sister.*

not lift a hand (to help someone**)** Go to previous.

Not likely. *Inf.* That is probably not so; that probably will not happen. □ *Mary: Is it possible that you'll be able to fix this watch? Sue: Not likely, but we can always try.* □ *Sally: Will John show up on time, do you think? Bob: Not likely.*

not long for this world *Fig.* about to die. □ *Our dog is nearly twelve years old and not long for this world.* □ *I'm so tired. I think I'm not long for this world.*

not made of money *Fig.* [of a person] not having a lot of money; not having an unlimited supply of money. □ *I can't afford a car like that. I'm not made of money you know.*

□ *There is only so much they can pay. They're not made of money.*

not miss a thing Go to next.

not miss much 1. and **not miss a thing** *Inf.* not to miss observing any part of what is going on. (Usually with *do* as in the examples.) □ *Ted doesn't miss much. He is very alert.* □ *The puppy doesn't miss a thing. He sees every move you make.* **2.** *Inf.* not to miss experiencing something that really was not worth experiencing anyway. (Usually with *do* as in the examples.) □ *I missed the big sales meeting last week, but I understand I didn't miss much.* □ *Bill: I didn't see that new movie that is showing at the theater. Tom: You didn't miss much; it was pretty bad.*

not miss something **for love nor money** Go to next.

not miss something **for the world** and **not miss** something **for love nor money** *Fig.* would not miss something for any reason at all. □ *Of course I'll be at your wedding. I wouldn't miss it for the world.*

not move a muscle to remain perfectly motionless. □ *Be quiet. Sit there and don't move a muscle.* □ *I was so tired I couldn't move a muscle.*

not on any account Go to on no account.

not one iota not even a tiny bit. □ *I won't give you any at all! Not one iota!* □ *I did not get one iota of encouragement from any of those people.*

not one's **cup of tea** *Fig.* not one's choice or preference. (Used to describe an activity you do not enjoy. Can sound somewhat affected.) □ *You three visit the museum without me. Looking at fussy old paintings is not my cup of tea.* □ *Going to church, Mary said, was not her cup of tea.*

not one's **place** not one's role to do something. □ *It was not my place to criticize my boss.* □ *It was not Bill's place to ask the questions; it's my project.*

not open one's **mouth** and **not utter a word** *Fig.* not to say anything at all; not to tell something (to anyone). □ *Don't worry, I'll keep your secret. I won't even open my mouth.* □ *Have no fear. I won't utter a word.*

not playing with a full deck Go to a few cards shy of a full deck.

not put (a lot) of stock in something Go to take no stock in something.

not put it past someone to think that someone would not dare to do something. □ *He might run away from school. I wouldn't put it past him.* □ *I wouldn't put it past Roger to arrive unannounced.*

Not right now, thanks. No for the present. (It is hoped that one will be asked again later. Usually used for a [temporary] refusal of a serving of food or drink. There is an implication that more will be wanted later.) □ *Waiter: Do you want some more coffee? Mary: Not right now, thanks.* □ *John: Can I take your coat? Sue: Not right now, thanks. I'm still a little chilly.*

not see any objection (to something**)** Go to see no objection (to something).

not set foot somewhere not to go somewhere. □ *I wouldn't set foot in John's room. I'm very angry at him.* □ *He never set foot here.*

not shed a tear *Fig.* not to show any emotion even when something is very sad. □ *At his uncle's funeral, he didn't shed a tear. They never got along.*

not show one's **face** not to appear somewhere; not to go to some place. □ *After what she said, she had better not show her face around here again.* □ *If I don't say I'm sorry, I'll never be able to show my face again.*

not sleep a wink not to sleep at all. □ *I couldn't sleep a wink last night.* □ *Ann hasn't been able to sleep a wink for a week.*

not so hot *Inf.* not very good. □ *The service here is not so hot. This restaurant is highly overrated.*

not take no for an answer *Fig.* not to accept someone's refusal. (A polite way of being insistent.) □ *Now, you must drop over and see us tomorrow. We won't take no for an answer.* □ *I had to go to their party. They just wouldn't take no for an answer.*

not take stock in something Go to take no stock in something.

not tell a (living) soul not to reveal something to anyone. □ *You secret is safe with me. I won't tell a living soul.* □ *Promise you won't tell a soul, but I'm engaged.*

not to put too fine a point on it *Fig.* a phrase introducing a fine or important point, apologetically. □ *Rachel: Not to put too fine a point on it, Mary, but you're still acting a little rude to Tom. Mary: I'm sorry, but that's the way I feel.* □ *John: I think, not to put too fine a point on it, you ought to do exactly as you are told. Andy: And I think you ought to mind your own business.*

not to touch a drop *Fig.* not to drink any of something, usually alcohol. □ *He pledged not to touch a drop all weekend, but he broke his pledge on Friday night.*

Not to worry. *Inf.* Please do not worry. □ *Bill: The rain is going to soak all our clothes. Tom: Not to worry, I put them all in plastic bags.* □ *Sue: I think we're about to run out of money. Bill: Not to worry. I have some more travelers checks.*

Not (too) much. a response to greeting inquiries into what one has been doing. □ *John: What have you been doing? Mary: Not much.* □ *Sue: Been keeping busy? What are you up to? Bob: Not too much. Sue: Yeah. Me too.*

not too shabby 1. *Inf.* nice; well done. (With emphasis on *shabby*.) □ *Is that your car? Not too shabby!* □ *That play was not too shabby.* **2.** *Inf.* very shabby; very poor indeed. (With emphasis on *too*. Sarcastic.) □ *Did you see that shot she missed? Not too shabby!* □ *What a way to treat someone. Not too shabby!*

not touch someone or something **with a ten-foot pole** *Cliché* not to have anything to do with someone or something. (Always negative.) □ *No, I won't hire Fred. I wouldn't touch him with a ten-foot pole.* □ *I wouldn't touch that job with a ten-foot pole.*

not trouble one's **(pretty) (little) head about** something *Rur.* not to worry about something. (Considered demeaning by many.) □ *Don't you trouble your little head about that. I'll take care of it.* □ *You shouldn't trouble your head about it. Everything will turn out fine.*

not under any circumstances Go to under no circumstances.

N

not up to scratch and **not up to snuff** *Fig.* not adequate. □ *Sorry, your paper isn't up to scratch. Please do it over again.* □ *The performance was not up to snuff.*

not up to snuff Go to previous.

not utter a word Go to **not open** one's **mouth.**

not want to catch someone doing something Go to **not let** someone **catch** someone doing something.

not what something **is cracked up to be** Go to **not all** something **is cracked up to be.**

not with it not able to think clearly; not able to understand things. □ *Lisa's mother is not really with it anymore. She's going senile.* □ *Tom's not with it yet. He's only just come around from the anesthetic.*

not worth a damn *Inf.* worthless. □ *This pen is not worth a damn.* □ *When it comes to keeping score, she's not worth a damn.*

not worth a dime and **not worth a red cent** worthless. □ *This land is all swampy. It's not worth a dime.* □ *This pen I bought isn't worth a dime. It has no ink.*

not worth a hill of beans and **not amount to a hill of beans; not worth a plugged nickel; not worth beans** *Fig.* worthless. □ *Your advice isn't worth a hill of beans.* □ *This old cow isn't worth a plugged nickel.*

not worth a red cent Go to **not worth a dime.**

not worth mentioning 1. not important enough to require a comment. □ *There are others, but they are not worth mentioning.* □ *A small number of books hint at the phenomenon, but they aren't worth mentioning.* **2.** [of an error or wrong] not worth apologizing for. □ *This isn't a problem at all. It's not worth mentioning.* □ *No need to apologize to me. No harm done. It's not worth mentioning.*

not worth one's **while** not worth bothering with; not worth spending time on. □ *It's not worth my while to discuss it with you.* □ *Don't bother trying to collect money from them. It isn't worth your while.*

not worth the paper it's printed on Go to next.

not worth the paper it's written on and **not worth the paper it's printed on** *Fig.* [of a document] meaningless or without authority; of no value. □ *That contract isn't worth the paper it's written on. All the signatures are forged.* □ *Don't take a check from that guy. It's not worth the paper it's written on.*

not worth the trouble not important enough to require a comment or any effort. □ *Don't bother with it. It isn't worth the trouble.* □ *There is no point in trying to get the spot out of the carpet. It isn't worth the trouble.*

a **notch above** (someone or something) and a **notch better than** (someone or something) *Fig.* a little higher in quality than someone or something. □ *This latest candidate we interviewed seems a notch above the rest, so let's hire her.* □ *That telescope is a notch better than the others in terms of magnification.*

a **notch below** (someone or something) *Fig.* a little lower in quality than someone or something. □ *I believe that this wine is a notch below the one we had with the fish.*

notch something **up†** to count up something; to add up or score something. □ *We notched yet another victory up in* our efforts to regain the trophy. □ *Well, it looks like we notched up another victory.*

note something **down†** to write down a note about something. □ *Please note these words down.* □ *Note down the following facts.*

*****noted for** something *Fig.* famed for something; memorable for something. (*Typically: **be** ~; **become** ~.) □ *We were all noted for our polite manners.* □ *The restaurant was noted for its traditional fare.* □ *Tom was noted far and wide for his excellent pies and cakes.*

nothing but only; just. □ *Jane drinks nothing but milk.* □ *Dave buys nothing but expensive clothes.*

nothing but skin and bones and **(all) skin and bones** *Fig.* very thin or emaciated. □ *Bill has lost so much weight. He's nothing but skin and bones.* □ *Look at Bill. He's just skin and bones.* □ *That old horse is all skin and bones. I won't ride it.*

Nothing comes of nothing. *Prov.* If you contribute nothing, you will get nothing. □ *Jill: Why are you so depressed today? Jane: No reason. Jill: There has to be a reason. Nothing comes of nothing.* □ *I'm not surprised you did so poorly in school; you haven't been putting in any effort. Nothing comes of nothing.*

Nothing doing! *Inf.* I will not permit it!; I will not participate in it! □ *John: Can I put this box in your suitcase? Bill: Nothing doing! It's too heavy now.* □ *Sue: We decided that you should drive us to the airport. Do you mind? Jane: Nothing doing! I've got work to do.*

nothing down requiring no down payment. □ *You can have this car for nothing down and $140 a month.* □ *I bought a winter coat for nothing down and no payments due until February.*

Nothing for me, thanks. I do not want any of what was offered. (Typically to decline a serving of food or drink.) □ *Waiter: Would you care for dessert? Bob: Nothing for me, thanks.* □ *Bob: We have beer and wine. Which would you like? Mary: Nothing for me, thanks.*

Nothing is certain but death and taxes. *Prov.* Everything in life is unpredictable, except that you can be sure you will die and you will have to pay taxes. (You can also refer to *death and taxes* as the only certain things in life.) □ *Son: I can't believe how much tax money is being withheld from my paycheck! Father: Welcome to adult life, where nothing is certain but death and taxes.*

Nothing is certain but the unforeseen. *Prov.* You cannot foresee what will happen. □ *Jill: Now that we've got a new boss, this is certain to be a nicer place to work. Jane: Nothing is certain but the unforeseen.*

Nothing is given so freely as advice. *Prov.* People will give you advice more willingly than they give you anything else. □ *Although no one in my family was willing to give me a loan, they all had suggestions about how I could get the money from elsewhere. Nothing is given so freely as advice.* □ *Don't hesitate to ask people what they think you ought to do. Nothing is given so freely as advice.*

Nothing much. *Inf.* not much; hardly anything; nothing of importance. (Often a reply to a greeting asking what one has been doing.) □ *John: Hey, man! How's by you? Bob: Hiya! Nothing much.* □ *Bill: What have you been doing? Tom: Nothing much.*

nothing of the kind 1. no; absolutely not. □ *I didn't tear your jacket—nothing of the kind!* □ *Did I break your vase? Nothing of the kind!* **2.** nothing like that. □ *That's not true. We did nothing of the kind!* □ *She did nothing of the kind! She wasn't even there!*

nothing short of something more or less the same as something bad; as bad as something. □ *His behavior was nothing short of criminal.* □ *Climbing those mountains alone is nothing short of suicide.*

Nothing so bad but (it) might have been worse. *Prov.* Although bad things do happen, they are not as bad as other things you can imagine that might have happened. □ *Joan: This is like a nightmare! My house burned down—I lost everything! Nancy: At least you and your family are safe. Nothing so bad but might have been worse.* □ *My bicycle tire blew out, but at least it blew out within walking distance of a repair shop. Nothing so bad but it might have been worse.*

Nothing succeeds like success. *Prov.* If you have succeeded in the past, you will continue to be successful in the future. □ *After Alan's brilliant courtroom victory, everyone wanted to be his client. Nothing succeeds like success.*

nothing to be sneezed at Go to nothing to sneeze at.

nothing to boast about not worth bragging about; mediocre. □ *In high school, my grades were acceptable, but they were nothing to boast about.* □ *Jill: Does this town have a good library? Nancy: It's nothing to boast about.*

nothing to choose from no choice; no choice in the selection; not enough of something to make a choice. □ *I went to the store looking for new shoes, but there was nothing to choose from.* □ *By the time I got around to selecting a team of helpers, there was nothing to choose from.*

Nothing to it! It is very easy! □ *Look, anybody can do it! Nothing to it!* □ *Changing a lightbulb is easy. Nothing to it!*

nothing to sneeze at and **nothing to be sneezed at** *Fig.* nothing small or unimportant. □ *It's not a lot of money, but it's nothing to sneeze at.* □ *Our house isn't a mansion, but it's nothing to sneeze at.* □ *A few thousand dollars is nothing to be sneezed at!*

nothing to speak of not many; not much. □ *John: What's happening around here? Bill: Nothing to speak of.* □ *Mary: Has there been any rain in the last week? Sally: Nothing to speak of.*

nothing to write home about *Fig.* mediocre; not as good as you expected. □ *I went to that new restaurant last night. It's nothing to write home about.* □ *Jill: I went to see a movie last night. Jane: How was it? Jill: Nothing to write home about.*

nothing upstairs *Fig.* no brains; stupid. □ *Tom is sort of stupid. You know—nothing upstairs.* □ *I know what's wrong with you. Nothing upstairs.*

Nothing ventured, nothing gained. If you do not take risks, you will never accomplish anything. □ *Bill: Should I ask my boss for a promotion? Jane: Nothing ventured, nothing gained.* □ *I think I'll audition for a part in that play. Nothing ventured, nothing gained.*

notify someone **about** someone or something to inform someone about someone or something. □ *Please notify the insurance company about the accident.* □ *I have to notify the doctor about Ed, who is ill.*

notify someone **of** something to inform someone about something. □ *Can you notify my parents of my arrival at the airport?* □ *We were notified of it last night.*

now and then sometimes; occasionally. (See also **(every) now and then.**) □ *I like to go to a movie now and then.* □ *We visit my parents now and then, but we rarely see our other relatives.*

Now hear this! Pay attention to what is going to be said! (In the manner of an announcement over a public address system, especially in the military.) □ *Now hear this! You have to turn off the television and go to bed!* □ *Now hear this! Now hear this! Everyone is ordered to abandon ship.*

now, now *Inf.* a calming and consoling phrase that introduces good advice. □ *"Now, now, don't cry," said the mother to the tiny baby.* □ *Jane: I'm so upset! Andy: Now, now, everything will work out all right.*

*now or never at this time and no other. (*Typically: **be ~; become ~.**) □ *This is your only chance, John. It's now or never.* □ *I decided that it was now or never, and jumped.*

now then a sentence opener indicating that a new topic is being opened or that the speaker is getting down to business. (Expressions such as this often use intonation to convey the connotation of the sentence that is to follow. The brief intonation pattern accompanying the expression may indicate sarcasm, disagreement, caution, consolation, sternness, etc.) □ *"Now then, where's the pain?" asked the doctor.* □ *Mary: Now then, let's talk about you and your interests. Bob: Oh, good. My favorite subject.* □ *Sue: Now then, what are your plans for the future? Alice: I want to become a pilot.* □ *"Now then, what did you have in mind when you took this money?" asked the police investigator.*

Now what? and **What now?** *Inf.* What is going to happen now?; What kind of new problem has arisen? □ *The phone rang again, and Tom said, rising from the chair, "Now what?"* □ *Bob: There's a serious problem—sort of an emergency—in the mail room. Sue: What now? Bob: They're out of stamps or something silly like that.*

(Now,) where was I? I was interrupted, so please help me remember what I was talking about. (The emphasis is on *was*.) □ *Now, where was I! I think I lost my place.* □ *Q: Where was I? A: You had just described the War of 1812.*

Now you're cooking (with gas)! *Inf. Fig.* Now you are doing what you should be doing! □ *As Bob came to the end of the piece, the piano teacher said, "Now you're cooking with gas!"* □ *Tom (painting a fence): How am I doing with this painting? Any better? Jane: Now you're cooking. Tom: Want to try it?*

Now you're talking! *Inf.* Now you are saying the right things. □ *Tom: I won't put up with her behavior any longer. I'll tell her exactly what I think of it. Bill: Now you're talking!* □ *John: When I get back to school, I'm going to study harder than ever. Mother: Now you're talking!*

nowhere near not nearly. □ *We have nowhere near enough wood for the winter.* □ *They're nowhere near ready for the game.*

no-win situation a situation where there is no correct or satisfactory solution. □ *The general was too weak to fight and too proud to surrender. It was a no-win situation.* □ *The huge dog my father gave us as a gift eats too much. If we get rid of the dog, my father will be insulted. If we keep it, we will go broke buying food for it. This is a classic no-win situation.*

nudge someone or something **aside**† to push or bump someone or something out of the way. □ *We nudged the old man aside and went on ahead.* □ *She nudged aside the cat to make room on the sofa.*

null and void *Cliché* without legal force; having no legal effect. □ *The court declared the law to be null and void.* □ *The millionaire's will was null and void because it was unsigned.*

number in something to total up to a certain figure. □ *The birds numbered in the thousands.* □ *These pesky ants number in the hundreds. Let's move to another picnic table.*

a **number of** things or people some things or people, in an indefinite amount. □ *I subscribe to a number of different magazines.* □ *A number of people are here now.*

number off (by something) to say a number in a specified sequence when it is one's turn. □ *Please number off by tens.* □ *Come on, number off!*

number someone or something **among** something to include someone or something in a group of something. □ *I number her among my best friends.* □ *I number this product among the most popular developed during the past year.*

number someone **with** something to include someone in a list of people. □ *I number Clara Wilson with the all-time greats.* □ *Todd numbered himself with the top athletes at the school.*

nurse a grudge (against someone) *Fig.* to keep resenting and disliking someone over a period of time. (Usually implies that it has been an unreasonably long time.) □ *Sally is still nursing a grudge against Mary.* □ *How long can anyone nurse a grudge?*

nurse someone **back to health** to care for a sick person until good health returns. □ *Sally was glad to help nurse her mother back to health.* □ *She nursed her children back to health when they all had the flu.*

nurse someone or an animal **along**† to aid or encourage the well-being or return to health of someone or an animal. (See also **nurse** something **along**.) □ *She nursed the old man along for a few years until he died.* □ *She nursed along the invalid.* □ *The vet nursed the horse along for the rest of the night.* □ *He nursed himself along with chicken noodle soup and hot baths until the virus ran its course.*

nurse someone **through** (something) to care for a sick person during the worst part of a sickness or recovery. □ *There was no one there to nurse him through the worst part of his illness.* □ *It was a horrible ordeal, but John nursed her through.*

nurse something **along**† *Fig.* to manage something with care and thrift. (See also **nurse** someone or an animal **along**.) □ *The board of directors agreed to nurse the firm along for a while and then sell it.* □ *She nursed along the failing business until it was showing a profit.*

a **nut case** *Fig.* a crazy person; an irrational person. □ *Bob is acting stranger and stranger. He is turning into a real nut case.*

nut up *Sl.* to go crazy. (See also **crack up**.) □ *I knew I would nut up if I didn't quit that job.* □ *I almost nutted up at the last place I worked.*

nuts about someone or something Go to **crazy about** someone or something.

nuts and bolts 1. *Fig.* the mundane workings of something; the basics of something. (See also **get down to the nuts and bolts**.) □ *I want you to learn how to write well. You have to know the nuts and bolts of writing.* □ *She's got a lot of good, general ideas, but when it comes to the nuts and bolts of getting something done, she's no good.* **2.** *Sl.* the subject of psychology in college. □ *I took a class in nuts and bolts and didn't learn anything at all about what makes me tick.* □ *Tom is flunking nuts and bolts because he won't participate in the required "experiments."*

Nuts to you! *Inf.* Go away!; Drop dead! □ *Well, nuts to you! You are just plain rude!* □ *Nuts to you! I will NOT lend you money!*

nuttier than a fruitcake Go to next.

***nutty as a fruitcake** and **nuttier than a fruitcake** crazy. (*Also: **as** ~.) □ *Don't pay any attention to John; he's nutty as a fruitcake.* □ *Mary's schemes for making money are nuttier than a fruitcake.*

nuzzle up against someone or something and **nuzzle up (to** someone or something) [for an animal] to rub its nose against someone or something; to rub against someone or something, softly, in the manner of rubbing the nose against someone or something; to snuggle up to someone or something. (*Nuzzle* is related to *nose*.) □ *The dog nuzzled up against my leg, wanting to be friends.* □ *The dog nuzzled up to me and licked my hand.*

object to someone or something to disapprove of someone or something. □ *I object to him as your choice.* □ *I object to your opinion.*

obligate someone **to** someone or something to force someone to do something for someone or something. □ *This contract obligates you to the company for five years!* □ *I don't wish to obligate myself to anyone.*

oblige someone **by** something to accommodate someone by doing something. □ *Please oblige me by closing the window.* □ *Would you oblige me by accompanying me to the dance?*

oblige someone **to** do something to require someone to do something. □ *You are obliged to arrive on time and enter by the side door.* □ *The lateness of the hour obliged Tony to enter by the back door.*

oblige someone **with** something to accommodate someone with something. □ *He obliged her with a willing attitude.* □ *Please oblige me with a big piece of cake.*

obliterate someone or something **from** something to destroy or wipe out someone or something from something. □ *Karen obliterated the writing from the wall.* □ *Max set out to obliterate Lefty "Fingers" Moran from the face of the earth.*

*****obsessed with** someone or something preoccupied with someone or something. (*Typically: **be** ~; **become** ~.) □ *Kathy was obsessed with the kitten.* □ *Roger was obsessed with Kathy.*

obstinate as a mule Go to stubborn as a mule.

obtain something **for** someone or something to get or receive something for someone or something. □ *I promised I would obtain a pet for Becky.* □ *I obtained a new part for the vacuum cleaner.*

occupy oneself **by** something to keep busy by doing something. □ *Don't worry. I can occupy myself by knitting or sewing.* □ *While waiting, I occupied myself by knitting a scarf.*

occupy someone **with** something to keep someone busy with something. □ *Can you occupy the child with this toy?* □ *Here, occupy yourself with this crossword puzzle.*

occur before someone's **time** Go to before someone's time.

occur to someone [for an idea or thought] to come into someone's mind. □ *It occurred to me that you might be hungry after your long journey.* □ *Would it ever occur to you that I want to be left alone?*

oceans of someone or something and an **ocean of** someone or something a very large amount of something. □ *The naughty student was in oceans of trouble.* □ *After a week of vacation, there was an ocean of work to do.*

odd man out an unusual or atypical person or thing. □ *I'm odd man out because I'm not wearing a tie.* □ *You had better learn to use the new system software unless you want to be odd man out.*

the **odd** something an extra or spare something; a chance something. □ *The tailor repaired the odd loose button on my shirt.* □ *When I travel, I might buy the odd trinket or two, but I never spend much money.*

odds and ends miscellaneous things. □ *There were lots of odds and ends in the attic, but nothing of real value.* □

Oo

I had the whole house cleaned out except for a few odds and ends that you might want to keep.

the **odds are against** one [for fate] to be against one generally. □ *You can give it a try, but the odds are against you.* □ *I know the odds are against me, but I wish to run in the race anyway.*

the **odds-on favorite** the most popular choice of a wager. □ *Fred is the odds-on favorite for president of the board of trustees.*

odor of sanctity *Fig.* an atmosphere of excessive holiness or piety. □ *I hate their house. There's such an odor of sanctity with Bibles and holy pictures everywhere.* □ *The huge, medieval Gothic cathedral had a distinct odor of sanctity.*

of a single mind (about someone or something) Go to of one mind (about someone or something).

*****of age** old enough to marry, buy alcohol, or to sign legal agreements. (*Typically: **be** ~; **come** ~.) □ *Now that Mary is of age, she can buy her own car.* □ *When I'm of age, I'm going to get married and move to the city.*

Of all things! Can you imagine?; Imagine that! (Usually said about something very strange.) □ *She wore jeans to the dance. Of all things!* □ *Billy, stop eating the houseplant! Of all things!*

of benefit (to someone) serving someone well; to the good of someone. □ *I can't believe that this proposal is of benefit to anyone.* □ *Oh, I'm sure you'll find the new health plan to be of benefit.*

of course yes; certainly; for sure. □ *Sally: Are you ready to go? Bob: Of course. Sally: Then let's go.* □ *Jane: Are you coming with us? John: Of course. I wouldn't miss this for the world.* □ *"And you'll be there, of course?" asked Alice.* □ *"I would be happy to help, of course," confided Tom, a little insincerely.*

of interest (to someone) interesting to someone. □ *These archived files are no longer of any interest.* □ *This is of little interest to me.*

of late lately. □ *Have you seen Sally of late?* □ *We haven't had an opportunity to eat out of late.*

of mature years *Euph.* old. □ *My employer is a man of mature years.* □ *The professor, a woman of mature years, is planning to retire at the end of the school term.*

of no avail Go to to no avail.

of one mind (about someone or something) and **of a single mind (about** someone or something) in agreement

461

about someone or something. □ *You will have to attend one of the state universities. Your father and I are of a single mind about this.*

of one's **own accord** and **of** one's **own free will** by one's own choice, without coercion. □ *I wish that Sally would choose to do it of her own accord.* □ *I'll have to order her to do it because she won't do it of her own free will.*

of service (to someone**)** helping someone; serving someone. □ *Good morning, madam. May I be of service to you?* □ *Welcome to the Warwick Hotel. May I be of service?*

of the first water *Fig.* of the finest quality. □ *This is a very fine pearl—a pearl of the first water.* □ *Tom is of the first water—a true gentleman.*

of the old school Go to from the old school.

of the persuasion that... holding a belief that something is true or is in existence. □ *Anne is of the persuasion that supports that candidate for mayor.* □ *The paranoid was of the persuasion that aliens lived among us.*

of two minds (about someone or something**)** *Fig.* holding conflicting opinions about someone or something; being undecided about someone or something. □ *I am of two minds about whether I should go to the convention.*

off again, on again Go to on again, off again.

off and on Go to on and off.

off and running 1. *Lit.* [of horses, dogs, or people] having started racing. □ *It's a beautiful day at the races, and, yes, they're off and running!* **2.** *Fig.* started up and going. □ *The car was finally loaded by 9:30, and we were off and running.* □ *The construction of the building was going to take two years, but we were off and running, and it appeared we would finish on schedule.*

off artist Go to (rip-)off artist.

*off base 1. *Lit.* [of a runner in baseball] not having a foot touching the base. (*Typically: **be** ~; **get** ~.) □ *The runner was off base but the first baseman didn't tag him out.* **2.** *Fig.* unrealistic; inexact; wrong. *Typically: **be** ~; **get** ~.) □ *I'm afraid you're off base when you state that this problem will take care of itself.* □ *You're way off base if you think I was to blame!*

*off campus not located or present on the grounds of a college or university. (*Typically: **be** ~; **live** ~; **move** ~.) □ *Tom has an apartment off campus.* □ *The dean is off campus and cannot be reached.*

off center not exactly in the center or middle. □ *The arrow hit the target a little off center.* □ *The picture hanging over the chair is a little off center.*

off chance slight possibility. □ *I need your phone number on the off chance I need more help.* □ *There's an off chance that we might be hiring next month.*

*off course 1. *Lit.* not going in the right direction. (*Typically: **be** ~; **drift** ~; **get** ~.) □ *The ship is off course and may strike the reef!* **2.** *Fig.* not following the plan correctly. (*Typically: **be** ~; **get** ~.) □ *The project is off course and won't be finished on time.* □ *I am off course and doing poorly.*

off duty not working at one's job. (The opposite of **on duty**.) □ *I'm sorry, I can't talk to you until I'm off duty.* □ *The police officer couldn't help me because he was off duty.*

off like a shot away [from a place] very quickly. □ *He finished his dinner and was off like a shot.* □ *The thief grabbed the lady's purse and was off like a shot.*

*off on a sidetrack *Fig.* on a digression; discussing a topic that is not the main topic. (Alludes to a train waiting on a siding. *Typically: **be** ~; **get** ~; **get** someone ~.) □ *Anne got off on a sidetrack and never returned to her topic.* □ *The ineffective committee got off on one sidetrack after another.*

off on someone or something in a rage about someone or something; on a tirade about someone or something. □ *Are you off on Sally again? Why can't you leave her alone?*

*off (on something**) 1.** incorrect in one's planning or prediction. (*Typically: **be** ~; **get** ~.) □ *I was off on my estimates a little bit.* □ *I guess I was off too much.* **2.** to have started on something, such as a task or a journey. (*Typically: **be** ~; **get** ~.) □ *What time should we be off on our trip?* □ *We should be off by dawn.* □ *I'm off on my diet again.* **3.** *Sl.* to get high on some kind of drug. □ *Max likes to get off on marijuana.*

*off on the right foot (with someone or something**)** and ***off to a good start (with** someone or something**)** *Fig.* starting out correctly; beginning something carefully and cautiously. (*Typically: **be** ~; **get** ~.) □ *This time, I want to get off on the right foot with him.* □ *I tried to get off to a good start with my new job.*

*off on the wrong foot and ***off to a bad start** *Fig.* starting something (such as a friendship) with negative factors. (*Typically: **be** ~; **get** ~.) □ *Bill and Tom got off on the wrong foot. They had a minor car accident just before they were introduced.* □ *Let's work hard to be friends. I hate to get off on the wrong foot.*

*off one's **game** *Fig.* not able to play a sport as well as normal. (*Typically: **be** ~; **put** one ~; **throw** one ~.) □ *I'm a little tired, and that generally puts me off my game.*

off one's **nut** Go to next.

*off one's **rocker** and ***off** one's **nut**; ***off** one's **trolley** *Fig.* crazy; silly. (*Typically: **be** ~; **go** ~.) □ *Sometimes, Bob, I think you're off your rocker.* □ *Good grief, John. You're off your nut.*

off one's **trolley** Go to previous.

off season not in the busy time of the year. □ *We don't have much to do off season.* □ *Things are very quiet around here off season.*

off someone or something **goes** someone or something is leaving. (Said on the departure of someone or something.) □ *It's time to leave. Off I go.* □ *Sally looked at the airplane taking off and said, "Off it goes."*

off the air not broadcasting (a radio or television program). □ *The radio audience won't hear what you say when you're off the air.* □ *When the performers were off the air, the director told them how well they had done.*

off the beaten path Go to next.

*off the beaten track and ***off the beaten path** *Fig.* away from the frequently traveled routes. (*Typically: **be** ~; **go** ~; **travel** ~.) □ *We found a nice little Italian restaurant off the beaten track.*

*off the hook *Fig.* freed from an obligation. (Alludes to a fish freeing itself from a fishhook. *Typically: **be** ~;

get ~; get someone **~; let** someone **~.**) □ *Thanks for getting me off the hook. I didn't want to attend that meeting.* □ *I couldn't get myself off the hook no matter what I tried.*

off the mark *Fig.* not quite exactly right. □ *Her answer was a little off the mark.* □ *You were off the mark when you said we would be a little late to the party. It was yesterday, in fact!*

off the record *Fig.* unofficial; informal. (Of comments to the press that one does not want reported.) □ *This is off the record, but I disagree with the mayor on this matter.* □ *Although her comments were off the record, the newspaper published them anyway.*

off the shelf *Fig.* ready made for purchase; not custommade. (Hyphenated when prenominal.) □ *I generally buy off-the-shelf clothing. I am a perfect size eight.*

off the subject not concerned with the subject being discussed. □ *I got off the subject and forgot what I was supposed to be talking about.* □ *The speaker was off the subject, telling about his vacation in Hawaii.*

off the track 1. Go to off the (beaten) track. **2.** *Fig.* [of comments] irrelevant and immaterial. □ *I'm afraid you're off the track, John. Try again.* □ *I'm sorry. I was thinking about dinner, and I got off the track.*

*off the wagon 1. *Fig.* drinking liquor after a period of abstinence. (*Typically: **be ~; fall ~; get ~.**) □ *Poor John fell off the wagon again. Drunk as a skunk.* □ *He was off the wagon for a year the last time before he sobered up.* **2.** *Fig.* back on drugs after a period of abstinence. (*Typically: **be ~; fall ~; get ~.**) □ *Wilbur is off the wagon and shooting up again.* □ *He can't be off the wagon, because he has never stopped using, even for a day.*

off to a bad start Go to off on the wrong foot.

*off (to a flying start) *Fig.* having a very successful beginning to something. (*Typically: **be ~; get ~.**) □ *The new business got off to a flying start with those export orders.* □ *We shall need a large donation from the local citizens if the charity is to get off to a flying start.*

off to a good start (with someone or something**)** Go to off on the right foot (with someone or something).

off to a running start with a good, fast beginning, possibly a head start. □ *I got off to a running start in math this year.* □ *The horses got off to a running start.*

off to one side beside something; (moved) slightly away from something. □ *Our garden has roses in the middle and a spruce tree off to one side.* □ *He took me off to one side to tell me the bad news.*

off to the races *Fig.* an expression characterizing the activity or excitement that is just beginning; [we are] leaving for something interesting or exciting. □ *The tour bus is out in front waiting and we've said goodbye to everyone. Looks like we're off to the races.*

*off (to the side) with someone moving aside with someone to discuss something. (*Typically: **get ~; go ~; move ~; step ~.**) □ *I got off with Charles and we discussed the contract.* □ *I moved off to the side with the client and explained the offer a little better.*

*off topic not on the topic of discussion; far from the general subject of a discussion; not part of the purpose of a particular communication channel, such as an Internet newsgroup. (*Typically: **be ~; get ~; get** someone **~.**) □ *The boys in the back of the room just love to get the teacher off topic.*

Off with you! Go away!; Get going! (Formal or pompous.) □ *Off with you! We've had enough of your banter!*

*off (work) and **off from work; off of work 1.** having left one's work at the end of the day. (*Typically: **be ~; get ~.**) □ *What time do you get off from work?* □ *I get off work about five o'clock.* □ *She gets off from work later than I do.* **2.** absent from one's work with permission. (*Typically: **be ~; get ~.**) □ *I think I can get off of work so I can go to the doctor.* □ *Sorry, I can't join you. Things are busy at the office, and I can't get off.*

offend against someone or something to anger or affront someone or something. □ *We do not wish to offend against anyone.* □ *He didn't realize that he offended against their cultural values.*

offend someone **with** something to anger or affront someone with something. □ *Don't offend us with your bad jokes.* □ *I offended Ralph with my constant niggling.*

offer a helping hand Go to a helping hand.

*an offer one **cannot refuse** *Cliché* a very attractive offer. (*Typically: **give** one **~; make ~; make** one **~.**) □ *He made me an offer I could not refuse, so I sold him my car.*

offer something **for** something to suggest a certain amount of money as a purchase price for something. □ *I'll offer you ten bucks for that watch.* □ *They offered me very little for my car.*

offer something **to** someone **(as** something**)** to propose giving something to someone as a gift, peace offering, payment, etc. □ *They offered us a bunch of flowers as a peace offering.* □ *As an apology, I offered a gift to the hostess.*

offer something **up†** **(to** someone or something**)** to give something to someone or something as a mark of devotion, thanks, etc. □ *We offered our gratitude up to the ruler.* □ *We offered up our gratitude to the queen.*

officiate (as something**) (at** something**)** to serve as an official or moderator at some event. □ *They asked me to officiate as a judge at the contest.* □ *Laura will officiate as parade marshal.*

off-key [of music or singing] off pitch; out of tune. □ *She always sings off-key and makes the rest of the choir sound like baying hounds.*

off-kilter Go to out of kilter.

off-limits Go to out-of-bounds.

off-line not connected to a computer, by direct connection or via the telephone system, etc. (Compare this with online.) □ *When he's off-line he's sort of lost.* □ *The system was off-line all day, so we could get nothing done.*

off-the-cuff *Fig.* spontaneous; without preparation or rehearsal. □ *Her remarks were off-the-cuff, but very sensible.* □ *I'm not very good at making speeches off-the-cuff.*

off-the-wall *Fig.* odd; silly; unusual. □ *Why are you so off-the-wall today?* □ *This book is strange. It's really off-the-wall.*

ogle (at) someone or something to stare at someone or something, usually with amorous or erotic relish. □ *Don't just stand there and ogle at me!* □ *Stop ogling at those magazines.*

Oh, boy. 1. *Inf.* Wow! (Usually **Oh, boy!** An exclamation. It has nothing to do with boys.) □ *Bill: Oh, boy! An old-fashioned circus!* □ *"Oh, boy!" shouted John. "Dinner smells great! When do we eat?"* **2.** *Inf.* I dread this!; This is going to be awful! □ *"Oh, boy!" moaned Fred, as his old car stalled out, "Here we go again."* □ *Doctor: It looks like something fairly serious. Jane: Oh, boy. Doctor: But nothing modern medicine can't handle.*

Oh, sure (someone or something **will)!** *Inf.* a sarcastic expression claiming that someone or something will do something or that something will happen. □ *Andy: Don't worry. I'll do it. Rachel: Oh, sure you will. That's what you always say.* □ *Bob: I'll fix this fence the first chance I get. Mary: Oh, sure. When will that be? Next year?*

Oh, ye of little faith. *Fig.* You who trust no one. (Jocular; the word *ye* is an old form of *you* used in the Bible.) □ *You thought I wouldn't show up on time? Oh, ye of little faith.*

Oh, yeah? *Inf.* Is that what you think? (Rude and hostile.) □ *Tom: You're getting to be sort of a pest. Bill: Oh, yeah? Tom: Yeah.* □ *Bob: This sauce tastes bad. I think you ruined it. Bill: Oh, yeah? What makes you think so? Bob: My tongue tells me!*

oil someone's **palm** Go to **grease** someone's **palm.**

oink out *Sl.* to overeat. □ *I oink out every time we have chocolate cake.* □ *This Thursday starts a four-day weekend, and I plan to oink out every day.*

*****old as Methuselah** very old. (Of a person; refers to a biblical figure held to have lived to be 969. *Also: **as** ~.) □ *Old Professor Stone is as old as Methusehah but still gets around with a cane.*

*****old as the hills** very old; ancient. (*Also: **as** ~.) □ *That's not a new joke; it's as old as the hills!* □ *Our family custom of eating black-eyed peas on New Year's Day is old as the hills.*

old battle-axe a bossy old woman. □ *She is such an old battle-axe. I'll bet she's hell to live with.*

old college try a valiant effort. □ *Will made the old college try, but that wasn't enough to get the job done.*

old enough to be someone's **father** Go to next.

old enough to be someone's **mother** and **old enough to be** someone's **father** as old as someone's parents. (Usually a way of saying that a person is too old.) □ *You can't go out with Bill. He's old enough to be your father!* □ *He married a woman who is old enough to be his mother.*

Old habits die hard. *Prov.* People find it difficult to change their accustomed behavior. □ *Joan retired last year, but she still gets up as early as she used to when she had to go to work. Old habits die hard.*

an **old hand at** doing something someone who is experienced at doing something. □ *The maid was an old hand at polishing silver.* □ *Bob is an old hand at training dogs.*

old hat *Fig.* old-fashioned; outmoded. □ *That's a silly idea. It's old hat.* □ *Hardly anybody uses typewriters anymore. That's just old hat.*

*****the (old) heave-ho** the act of throwing someone out; the act of firing someone. (From nautical use, where sailors used *heave-ho* to coordinate hard physical labor. One sailor called "Heave-ho," and all the sailors would pull at the same time on the *ho*. *Typically: **get** ~; **give** someone ~.) □ *I wanted to complain to the management, but they called a security guard and I got the old heave-ho. That's right. They threw me out!* □ *They fired a number of people today, but I didn't get the heave-ho.*

the **old one-two** a series of two punches delivered quickly, one after another. □ *Tom gave Bill the old one-two, and the argument was ended right there.* □ *Watch out for Tom. He's a master of the old one-two.*

An **old poacher makes the best gamekeeper.** *Prov.* The best person to guard something is someone who knows all about how to steal it, so he or she can anticipate what thieves might do. □ *We should hire the computer hacker to design computer security systems. An old poacher makes the best gamekeeper.*

*****an old warhorse** a performance piece that is performed often. (*Typically: **be** ~; **become** ~; **perform** ~; **play** ~.) □ *The symphony orchestra played a few old warhorses and then some ghastly contemporary stuff that will never again see the light of day.*

an **old wives' tale** *Fig.* a myth or superstition. □ *You really don't believe that stuff about starving a cold do you? It's just an old wives' tale.*

omit someone or something **from** something to leave someone or something out of something. □ *You omitted Carol from the list.* □ *I think that you omitted our company from the bidding.* □ *She omitted herself from the list of participants.*

*****on a diet** trying to lose weight by eating less food or specific foods. (*Typically: **be** ~; **go** ~; **put** someone ~; **stay** ~.) □ *I didn't eat any cake because I'm on a diet.* □ *I'm getting too heavy. I'll have to go on a diet.* □ *I have a lot of trouble staying on a diet.*

*****on a first-name basis (with** someone**)** knowing someone very well; good friends with someone. (*Typically: **be** ~; **get** ~.) □ *I'm on a first-name basis with John.* □ *John and I are on a first-name basis.*

*****on a fool's errand** *Fig.* involved in a useless journey or task. (*Typically: **be** ~; **go** ~.) □ *Bill went for an interview, but he was on a fool's errand. The job had already been filled.* □ *I was sent on a fool's errand to buy some flowers. I knew the shop would be closed by then.*

on a lark Go to **for a lark.**

on a moment's notice Go to **at a moment's notice.**

*****on a pedestal** *Fig.* elevated to a position of honor or reverence. (Alludes to honoring someone on display on a pedestal like a statue. *Typically: **place** someone ~; **put** someone ~.) □ *He puts his wife on a pedestal. She can do no wrong in his opinion.* □ *I was just doing my job. There is no point in placing me on a pedestal!*

*****on a power trip** exercising power and authority, especially unduly. (*Typically: **be** ~; **be off** ~; **go** ~; **have** ~.) □ *Old Molly is off on a power trip again. She loves ordering everyone about.*

on a roll in the midst of a series of successes. □ *Don't stop me now. I'm on a roll.* □ *Things are going great for Larry. He's on a roll now.*

on a shoestring *Fig.* with a very small amount of money. □ *We lived on a shoestring for years before I got a good-paying job.* □ *John traveled to Florida on a shoestring.*

*on a silver platter *Fig.* using a presentation [of something] that is appropriate for a very formal setting. (*Typically: **give** something **to** someone ~; **present** something ~; **serve** something ~; **want** something ~.) □ *Aren't paper plates good enough for you? You want dinner maybe on a silver platter?*

*on a string *Fig.* under control, as one would control a marionette. (*Typically: **get** someone ~; **have** someone ~; **keep** someone ~.) □ *She keeps him on a string so he won't get involved with other women.*

on a tight leash 1. *Lit.* [of an animal] on a leash, held tightly and close to its owner. □ *I keep my dog on a tight leash so it won't bother people.* **2.** *Fig.* under very careful control. □ *My father keeps my brother on a tight leash.* □ *We can't do much around here. The boss has us all on a tight leash.* **3.** *Sl.* addicted to some drug. □ *Wilbur is on a tight leash. He has to have the stuff regularly.* □ *Gert is kept on a tight leash by her habit.*

*on a wing and a prayer *Fig.* to arrive or fly in with one's plane in very bad condition. (Sometimes used fig. of other vehicles. *Typically: **come (in)** ~; **arrive** ~.) □ *Finally we could see the plane through the smoke, coming in on a wing and a prayer.*

on account [money paid or owed] on a debt. □ *I paid twelve dollars on account last month. Wasn't that enough?* □ *I still have $100 due on account.*

on active duty in battle or ready to go into battle. (Military.) □ *The soldier was on active duty for ten months.* □ *That was a long time to be on active duty.*

on advance notice Go to **with advance notice.**

on again, off again and **off again, on again** uncertain; indecisive. □ *I don't know about the picnic. It's on again, off again. It depends on the weather.* □ *Jane doesn't know if she's going to look for a new job. She's off again, on again about it.*

on all fours on one's hands and knees. □ *I dropped a contact lens and spent an hour on all fours looking for it.* □ *The baby can walk, but is on all fours most of the time anyway.*

on and off and **off and on** occasionally; erratically; now and again. □ *I feel better off and on, but I'm not well yet.* □ *He only came to class on and off.*

on any account for any purpose; for any reason; no matter what. □ *On any account, I'll be there on time.* □ *This doesn't make sense on any account.*

on approval for examination, with the privilege of return. □ *I ordered the merchandise on approval so I could send it back if I didn't like it.* □ *Sorry, you can't buy this on approval. All sales are final.*

on average Go to **on the average.**

on behalf of someone Go to **in behalf of** someone.

on bended knee kneeling, as in supplication. (The verb form is obsolescent and occurs now only in this phrase.) □ *Do you expect me to come to you on bended knee and*

ask *you for forgiveness?* □ *The suitors came on bended knee and begged the attention of the princess.*

on board 1. *Lit.* aboard (on or in) a ship, bus, airplane, etc. □ *Is there a doctor on board? We have a sick passenger.* □ *When everyone is on board, we will leave.* **2.** *Fig.* employed by someone; working with someone. □ *Our company has a computer specialist on board to advise us about the latest technology.* □ *Welcome to the company, Tom. We're all glad you're on board now.*

on Broadway *Fig.* located in the Broadway theater district in New York City; performed in the Broadway theater district. (Regarded as having the best of American stage productions.) □ *Our musical is the best thing on Broadway!* □ *I want to be a star on Broadway someday.*

on call ready to serve when called. □ *I live a very hard life. I'm on call twenty hours a day.* □ *I'm sorry, but I can't go out tonight. I'm on call at the hospital.*

on campus located or being on the grounds of a college or university. □ *Do you live on campus or off campus?* □ *I don't think that Lisa is on campus right now.*

on cloud nine *Fig.* very happy. □ *When I got my promotion, I was on cloud nine.* □ *When the check came, I was on cloud nine for days.*

on consignment [of goods] having been placed in a store for sale, with payments made for the goods by the operator of the store only if they are sold. □ *The artist placed his work in a gallery on consignment.* □ *I will attempt to sell your clothing on consignment.*

*on course 1. *Lit.* going in the right direction or on the right route. (*Typically: **be** ~; **get** ~; **stay** ~.) □ *We are on course and should arrive at our port about noon.* **2.** *Fig.* following the plan correctly. (*Typically: **be** ~; **get** ~; **stay** ~.) □ *Is the project on course?* □ *Nothing I am doing is exactly on course right now.*

on credit using credit; buying something using credit. □ *I tried to buy a new suit on credit, but I was refused.* □ *The Smiths buy everything on credit and are very much in debt.*

on dangerous ground Go to **on shaky ground.**

on dead center 1. *Lit.* at the exact center of something. □ *The arrow hit the target on dead center.* □ *When you put the flowers on the table, put them on dead center.* **2.** *Fig.* exactly correct. □ *Mary is quite observant. Her analysis is on dead center.* □ *My estimate wasn't on dead center, but it was very close to the final cost.*

on deck 1. *Lit.* on the deck of a boat or a ship. □ *Everyone except the cook was on deck when the storm hit.* □ *Just pull up the anchor and leave it on deck.* **2.** *Fig.* ready (to do something); ready to be next (at something). □ *Ann, get on deck. You're next.* □ *Who's on deck now?*

on duty at work; currently doing one's work. (The opposite of **off duty.**) □ *I can't help you now, but I'll be on duty in about an hour.* □ *Who is on duty here? I need some help.*

on earth and **in creation; in the world** *Fig.* really; indeed; in fact. (Used as an intensifier after *who, what, when, where, how.*) □ *What on earth do you mean?* □ *How in creation do you expect me to do that?* □ *Who in the world do you think you are?*

on easy street *Fig.* in a state of financial independence and comfort. □ *I want to live on easy street when I grow up.* □ *When I get this contract signed, I'll be on easy street.*

on edge 1. *Lit.* on something's own edge. □ *Can you stand a dime on edge?* □ *You should store these crates on edge, not lying flat.* **2.** *Fig.* nervous. (As if one were balanced as in ①. See also **on the edge**.) □ *I have really been on edge lately.* □ *Why are you so on edge?*

on fire 1. *Lit.* burning; being burned with flames. □ *Help! My car is on fire!* □ *That house on the corner is on fire!* **2.** *Sl.* very attractive or sexy. □ *She is really on fire!* □ *Look at those jet-set people! Each one of them is just on fire.* **3.** *Fig. Inf.* doing very well; very enthusiastic. □ *Jill's new book is really on fire. Everyone is buying it.* □ *Fred is on fire in his new job. He'll get promoted in no time.*

on foot [running or walking] using the feet. □ *My car won't work so I have to travel on foot.* □ *We go everywhere around the campus on foot.*

on good terms (with someone**)** friendly with someone; able to interact well and be friends with someone. □ *Bill is on good terms with the people he works with.* □ *We are not on very good terms and don't speak to each other much.*

on hold 1. *Lit.* waiting; temporarily halted. □ *The building project is on hold while we try to find money to complete it.* □ *We put our wedding plans on hold until we finished school.* **2.** *Fig.* left waiting on a telephone line. □ *I hate to call up someone and then end up on hold.* □ *I waited on hold for ten minutes when I called city hall.*

on horseback on the back of a horse. □ *Anne rode on horseback across the field.* □ *Because they loved horses, the couple decided to marry on horseback.*

on ice 1. *Lit.* stored or preserved on ice or under refrigeration. □ *I have a lot of root beer on ice for the picnic.* □ *All the soft drinks are on ice.* **2.** *Fig.* [action on someone or something] suspended or left hanging. □ *I was on ice for over a month while the matter was being debated.* □ *This matter should be on ice for a while.*

on impulse after having had an impulse or sudden thought. □ *On impulse, Bob decided to buy a car.* □ *I didn't need a cellular telephone. I just bought it on impulse.*

on in years Go to **up in years**.

*on its feet *Fig.* organized and functioning; started up and functioning. (*Typically: **get** something **~; have** something **~; put** something **~**.) □ *Trying to get this company on its feet is harder than I thought.* □ *What will it take to put this company on its feet again?*

on land on the ground; on the land and not at sea or in the air. □ *The flight was rough and I feel better now that I am back on land.* □ *When I am at sea, I feel more relaxed than when I am on land.*

on loan (from someone or something**)** [of possession] temporarily granted by someone or some group. □ *This lovely painting is on loan from the Kimble Museum for the rest of the year.*

on location [of a movie] being filmed in a place distant from the studio. □ *This movie was shot on location in Ontario.* □ *The actress went on location in Spain for her latest film.*

on medication taking medicine for a current medical problem. □ *I can't drive the car since I am on medication.* □ *He is on medication and hopes to be well soon.*

on moral grounds considering reasons of morality. □ *He complained about the television program on moral gounds. There was too much ridicule of his religion.*

on no account and **not on any account** for no reason; absolutely not. □ *On no account will I lend you the money.* □ *Will I say I'm sorry? Not on any account.*

on occasion occasionally. □ *I like to go to the movies on occasion.* □ *On occasion, Mary would walk her dog through the park.*

on one's **best behavior** being as polite as possible. □ *When we went out, the children were on their best behavior.* □ *I try to be on my best behavior all the time.*

on one's **deathbed** while one is in bed and dying. □ *While he lay on his deathbed, he told his lawyer that he wanted to give all his money to charity.*

on one's **feet 1.** *Lit.* standing up. □ *Get on your feet. They are playing the national anthem.* □ *I've been on my feet all day, and they hurt.* **2.** *Fig.* well and healthy, especially after an illness. □ *I hope to be back on my feet next week.* □ *I can help out as soon as I'm back on my feet.*

*on (one's**) guard (against** someone or something**)** alert against someone or something. (*Typically: **be ~; keep ~; remain ~; stay ~**.) □ *Try to stay on guard against pickpockets.* □ *I am always on my guard when you go into the city.* □ *Be on guard when you go into the city.*

on one's **high horse** *Fig.* in a haughty manner or mood. □ *Larry is on his high horse again, bossing people around.* □ *The boss is on her high horse about the cost of office supplies.*

on one's **honor** *Fig.* on one's solemn oath; sincerely. □ *On my honor, I'll be there on time.* □ *He promised on his honor that he'd pay me back next week.*

on one's **mind** *Fig.* occupying one's thoughts; currently being thought about. □ *You've been on my mind all day.* □ *Do you have something on your mind? You look so serious.*

on one's **own** independently. □ *Our baby can now walk on his own.* □ *I have lived on my own since I was 18.*

on one's **own hook** all by oneself. □ *I don't need any help. I can do it on my own hook.* □ *She did it on her own hook without having to call on anyone.*

on one's **own time** not while one is at work. □ *The boss made me write the report on my own time. That's not fair.* □ *Please make your personal telephone calls on your own time.*

on one's **person** [of something] carried with one. □ *Always carry identification on your person.* □ *I'm sorry, I don't have any money on my person.*

*on one's **toes** *Fig.* alert. (*Typically: **be ~; keep ~; keep** one **~; stay ~**.) □ *You have to be on your toes if you want to be in this business.* □ *I have to stay on my toes to keep from getting fired.*

*on one's **way ((to)** some place**)** leaving one place for another; en route to a place. (*Typically: **be ~; get ~**.) □ *I have to leave. I am on my way to the bank.* □ *I will be there soon. I'm on my way now.*

on one's **way (to** something or some place) Go to **on the way (to** something or some place).

on order ordered with delivery expected. □ *Your car is on order. It'll be here in a few weeks.* □ *I don't have the part in stock, but it's on order.*

on par (with someone or something) equal to someone or something. □ *Your effort is simply not on par with what's expected from you.* □ *These two departments are right on par in productivity.*

on pins and needles *Fig.* anxious; in suspense. □ *I've been on pins and needles all day, waiting for you to call with the news.* □ *We were on pins and needles until we heard that your plane had landed safely.*

on probation 1. *Lit.* serving a period of probation, typically after conviction for a crime. □ *While Anne was on probation, she reported to the police regularly.* □ *John was on probation for a year.* **2.** *Fig.* serving a trial period. □ *All new members are on probation for a year.* □ *I was on probation in my job for a full year before it became permanent.*

on purpose intentionally; in a way that is meant or intended; not an accident. □ *The bully stepped on my foot on purpose.* □ *Jealously, Jimmy destroyed Billy's sand castle on purpose.*

on record and **on the books** recorded for future reference. □ *We had the coldest winter on record last year.* □ *This is the fastest race on record.*

on sale available for sale at a reduced price. (Always implies lower than usual sale price.) □ *These pots are on sale for $20.* □ *I bought these pants on sale for half price.*

on schedule at the expected or desired time. □ *The plane came in right on schedule.* □ *Things have to happen on schedule in a theatrical performance.*

on second thought *Fig.* having given something more thought; having reconsidered something. □ *On second thought, maybe you should sell your house and move into an apartment.* □ *On second thought, let's not go to a movie.*

on shaky ground and **on dangerous ground** *Fig.* [of an idea or proposal] on an unstable or questionable foundation; [of an idea or proposal] founded on a risky premise. □ *When you suggest that we are to blame, you are on shaky ground. There is no evidence that we are at fault.* □ *The case for relying solely on nuclear energy seems to be on dangerous ground.*

on short notice quickly and without a timely notification of other people; with very little lead time. □ *She called the meeting on such short notice that we had no time to prepare.*

***on** someone or something [incriminating or harmful information] about someone or something. (*Typically: **get** something ~; **have** something ~; **give** someone something ~.) □ *I've gotten something on Albert that would really shock you.* □ *She is trying to get something on her husband so she can divorce him.*

on someone's **account** because of someone. □ *Don't do it on my account.* □ *They were late on Jane's account.*

on someone's **back** Go to **on** someone's **case.**

on someone's **behalf** Go to **in behalf of** someone.

***on** someone's **case** and ***on** someone's **back** *Inf.* harassing someone about a personal problem; annoying someone. (*Typically: **be** ~; **get** ~; **keep** ~.) □ *I'll get on Tom's case about being late so much.* □ *I'm sorry, I won't get on your case anymore.*

on someone's **doorstep** Go to **at** someone's **doorstep.**

on someone's **good side** Go to **on the good side of** someone.

on someone's **head** *Fig.* [for something negative] belonging only to one person or group. □ *All the blame fell on their heads.* □ *I don't think that all the criticism should be on my head.*

***on** someone's **heels** *Fig.* following someone very closely; following very closely at someone's heels. (*Typically: **hard** ~; **hot** ~; **right** ~. See also **on** someone's **tail.**) □ *I ran as fast as I could, but the dog was still hard on my heels.* □ *Here comes Sally, and John is hot on her heels.*

***on** someone's **nerves** *Fig.* annoying someone. (*Typically: **be** ~; **get** ~.) □ *Our noisy neighbors are beginning to get on my nerves.* □ *That radio is getting on my nerves.*

on someone's or something's **last legs** *Fig.* for someone or something to be almost worn out or finished. □ *This building is on its last legs. It should be torn down.* □ *I feel as if I'm on my last legs. I'm really tired.*

on someone's **say-so** on someone's authority; with someone's permission. □ *I can't do it on your say-so. I'll have to get a written request.* □ *Bill: I canceled the contract with the A.B.C. Company. Bob: On whose say-so?*

***on** someone's **shoulders** *Fig.* on someone's own self. (*Typically: **be** ~; **carry** something ~; **fall** ~; **have** something ~; **leave** something ~; **put** something ~.) □ *Why should all the responsibility fall on my shoulders?* □ *She carries a tremendous amount of responsibility on her shoulders.*

on someone's **tail** *Inf. Fig.* following someone closely. (See also **on** someone's **heels.**) □ *There is a huge truck on my tail. What should I do?* □ *Keep on her tail and don't let her out of your sight.*

on someone's **watch** while someone is on duty; while someone is supposed to be in charge of a situation. □ *I am not responsible since it didn't happen on my watch.* □ *I guess I have to bear the blame since it happened on my watch.*

on someone's **wrong side** Go to **on the wrong side of** someone.

on something 1. taking a medication. □ *I am on an antibiotic for my chest cold.* □ *I want you to be on this drug for another week.* **2.** taking an illegal drug or controlled substance and acting strangely. □ *What is the matter with that kid? Is he on something?* □ *She acted as if she were on barbiturates or something.*

on speaking terms (with someone) on friendly terms with someone. (Often with the negative.) □ *I'm not on speaking terms with Mary. We had a serious disagreement.* □ *We're not on speaking terms.*

on spec 1. using money risked in the hope of profit; on speculation. □ *He lives by buying and selling houses on spec.* □ *I think it might be an idea to build a few yachts on spec just now.* **2.** as specified; right on specifications. □ *This* *has been built exactly on spec—just as you asked.* □ *It's important to make sure the design is on spec or the customer will not pay.*

on standby waiting for one's turn, especially describing the status of travelers who wait at a soon-to-depart train, plane, or bus, hoping that a seat will become available. □ *The passenger waited on standby for an available seat.* □ *The agent was able to seat all of the passengers on standby.*

on tap 1. *Lit.* having to do with beer served from a barrel or keg. □ *Do you have any imported beers on tap here?* □ *I like beer on tap. The canned stuff tastes funny to me.* **2.** *Fig.* immediately available. □ *I have just the kind of person you're talking about on tap.* □ *The cook has any kind of food you might want on tap.*

on target on schedule; exactly as predicted. □ *Your estimate of the cost was right on target.* □ *My prediction was not on target.*

on the air broadcasting (a radio or television program). □ *The radio station came back on the air shortly after the storm.* □ *We were on the air for two hours.*

on the alert (for someone or something**)** watchful and attentive for someone or something. □ *Be on the alert for pickpockets.* □ *You should be on the alert when you cross the street in heavy traffic.*

on the average and **on average** generally; usually. □ *On the average, you can expect about a 10 percent failure rate.* □ *This report looks OK, on average.*

*on the back burner *Fig.* [of something] on hold or suspended temporarily. (Alludes to putting a pot that needs less active attention on a back burner of a stove, leaving space for pots that need to be stirred. Compare this with **on the front burner**. *Typically: **be** ~; **put** something ~.) □ *The building project is on the back burner for now.* □ *This matter was on the back burner for a long time.*

on the ball *Inf.* knowledgeable; competent; attentive. (See also **have** something **on the ball**.) □ *This guy is really on the ball.* □ *If you were on the ball, this wouldn't have happened.*

*on the bandwagon *Fig.* on the popular side (of an issue); taking a popular position. (*Typically: **be** ~; **climb** ~; **get** ~; **hop** ~; **jump** ~.) □ *You really should get on the bandwagon. Everyone else is.* □ *Jane has always had her own ideas about things. She's not the kind of person to jump on the bandwagon.*

on the beam *Fig.* exactly right; thinking along the correct lines. □ *That's the right idea. Now you're on the beam!* □ *She's not on the beam yet. Explain it to her again.*

on the bench 1. [of a judge] directing a session of court. □ *I have to go to court tomorrow. Who's on the bench?* □ *It doesn't matter who's on the bench. You'll get a fair hearing.* **2.** sitting, waiting for a chance to play in a game. (In sports, such as basketball, football, soccer, etc.) □ *Bill is on the bench now. I hope he gets to play.* □ *John played during the first quarter, but now he's on the bench.*

on the bias on a diagonal line; on a diagonal pathway or direction. □ *The panels of the dress were cut on the bias.* □ *The seamstress sewed the fabric on the bias.*

on the bird available on satellite television. □ *There is a whole lot of good stuff on the bird, but you need a receiving*

dish to get it. □ *I get a huge book every month listing what programs are on the bird.*

on the bleeding edge and **on the leading edge** having the most advanced technology; knowing about the most advanced technology. (Alludes to the *cutting edge* of a sword.) □ *This gadget is brand new. It's really on the bleeding edge.* □ *Tom is on the leading edge when it comes to optical storage technology.*

on the blink Go to **on the fritz**.

on the block 1. *Lit.* on a city or suburban block. □ *John is the biggest kid on the block.* □ *We had a party on the block last weekend.* **2.** on sale at auction; on the auction block. □ *We couldn't afford to keep up the house, so it was put on the block to pay the taxes.* □ *That's the finest painting I've ever seen on the block.*

on the books Go to **on record**.

on the borderline in an uncertain position between two statuses; undecided. □ *Bill was on the borderline between an A and a B in biology.* □ *Jane was on the borderline of joining the navy.*

on the bottom rung (of the ladder) Go to **at the bottom of the ladder**.

on the bright side *Fig.* [ignoring the bad for a moment] considering the positive aspects of a situation. (See also **look on the bright side**.) □ *On the bright side, the car you wrecked was covered by insurance.*

on the brink (of doing something**)** *Fig.* on the verge of doing something; almost to the point of doing something. □ *I was on the brink of selling my car to make ends meet when the tax refund came in the mail.*

on the button exactly right; in exactly the right place; at exactly the right time. □ *That's it! You're right on the button.* □ *He got here at one o'clock on the button.*

on the contrary Go to **to the contrary**.

on the cusp (of something**)** *Fig.* at the point in time that marks the beginning of something. □ *The transistor was on the cusp of a new age in electronics.*

on the cutting edge *Fig.* [for someone] to be trendy and very up-to-date; [for something] to be of the latest design. (Akin to **on the bleeding edge**.) □ *This technology is right on the cutting edge. It's so new, it's not available to the public yet.*

on the defensive weary and ready to defend oneself. □ *John goes on the defensive when his athletic ability is questioned.* □ *The child was on the defensive when questioned about cheating.*

on the dole receiving welfare money. □ *I spent six months on the dole, and believe me, it's no picnic.*

*on the dot *Fig.* at exactly the right time. (*Typically: **be** somewhere ~; **arrive (**somewhere**)** ~; **get** somewhere ~; **see** someone ~; **show up** ~.) □ *I'll be there at noon on the dot.* □ *I expect to see you here at eight o'clock on the dot.*

on the double very fast; twice as fast as normal. (Originally military. Alludes to "double time" in marching.) □ *Get over here right now—on the double!* □ *She wants to see you in her office on the double.*

*on the edge *Fig.* very anxious and about to become distraught; on the verge of becoming irrational. (*Typically: **be ~; live ~**. See also **on edge**.) □ *After the horrible events of the last week, we are all on the edge.*

on the edge of one's **seat** *Fig.* [of a member of an audience] closely following the action and excitement of a performance. □ *We sat on the edge of our seats during the entire play.*

on the eve of something *Fig.* just before something, possibly the evening before something. □ *John decided to leave school on the eve of his graduation.* □ *The team held a party on the eve of the tournament.*

on the face of it *Fig.* superficially; from the way it looks. □ *This looks like a serious problem on the face of it. It probably is minor, however.* □ *On the face of it, it seems worthless.*

on the fast track *Fig.* following an expedited procedure; being acted upon sooner or more quickly than is typical. □ *Let's put this project on the fast track and maybe we'll see results sooner.*

*on the fence (about something**)** *Fig.* undecided about something. (*Typically: **be ~; sit ~**.) □ *Ann is on the fence about going to Mexico.* □ *I wouldn't be on the fence. I'd love to go.*

on the fly [done] while something or someone is operating or moving. □ *I'll try to capture the data on the fly.* □ *Please try to buy some aspirin somewhere on the fly today.*

on the fringe 1. *Lit.* at the outer boundary or edge of something. □ *He doesn't live in the city, just on the fringe.* **2.** *Fig.* at the extremes of something, typically political thought. □ *He is way out. His political ideas are really on the fringe.*

on the fritz and **on the blink** not operating; not operating correctly. □ *This vacuum cleaner is on the fritz. Let's get it fixed.* □ *How long has it been on the blink?*

*on the front burner *Fig.* receiving particular attention or consideration. (Compare this with **on the back burner**. *Typically: **be ~; put** something **~**.) □ *So, what's on the front burner for us this week?* □ *Move this project to the front burner so it will get some attention.*

on the go busy; moving about busily. □ *I'm usually on the go all day long.* □ *I hate being on the go all the time.*

*on the good side of someone and ***on** someone's **good side** *Fig.* in someone's favor. (*Typically: **be ~; get ~**.) □ *I tried to get on the good side of the teacher, but that teacher has no good side.* □ *First of all, don't try to get on the boss's good side.*

on the heels of something *Fig.* soon after something. □ *There was a rainstorm on the heels of the windstorm.* □ *The team held a victory celebration on the heels of their winning season.*

on the horizon 1. *Lit.* appearing at the boundary between the earth and the sky. □ *There is a storm on the horizon.* **2.** *Fig.* soon to happen. □ *Do you know what's on the horizon?* □ *There is some excitement on the horizon, but I can't tell you about it.*

on the horns of a dilemma *Fig.* having to decide between two things, people, etc. □ *Mary found herself on the horns of a dilemma. She didn't know which to choose.*

□ *I make up my mind easily. I'm not on the horns of a dilemma very often.*

on the hot seat and **in the hot seat** *Fig.* in a difficult position; subject to much attention or criticism. □ *I was really in the hot seat for a while.* □ *Now that John is on the hot seat, no one is paying any attention to what I do.*

on the hour at each hour on the hour mark. □ *I have to take this medicine every hour on the hour.* □ *I expect to see you there on the hour, not one minute before and not one minute after.*

on the house [of something] given away free by a merchant. □ *"Here," said the waiter, "have a cup of coffee on the house."* □ *I went to a restaurant last night. I was the ten thousandth customer, so my dinner was on the house.*

on the job working; doing what one is expected to do. □ *I'm always on the job when I should be.* □ *I can depend on my furnace to be on the job day and night.*

on the lam running from the police. (Underworld.) □ *Richard has been on the lam for a week now.* □ *The gang leader broke out of prison and is still on the lam.*

on the leading edge Go to **on the bleeding edge**.

on the level honest; straightforward. □ *Come on now, on the level, tell me the truth.* □ *Is the ad on the level?*

on the lookout (for someone or something**)** watchful for someone or something. □ *Be on the lookout for signs of a storm.* □ *I'm on the lookout for John, who is due here any minute.*

on the loose running around free. □ *Look out! There is a bear on the loose from the zoo.* □ *Most kids enjoy being on the loose when they go to college.*

on the make 1. building or developing; being made. □ *There is a company that is on the make.* □ *That was a very good sales strategy, John. You're a real-estate agent on the make.* **2.** making sexual advances; seeking sexual activities. □ *It seems like Bill is always on the make.* □ *He should meet Sally, who is also on the make.*

on the mark *Fig.* right on the measurement point; showing just the right amount. □ *It's exactly one quart, right on the mark.*

*on the market openly available for sale. (*Typically: **be ~; get** something **~; put** something **~**.) □ *We put our house on the market last year and it still hasn't sold.*

on the mend getting better; becoming healthy again. □ *I cared for my father while he was on the mend.* □ *I took a leave of absence from work while I was on the mend.*

on the money and **on the nose** exactly right; in exactly the right place; in exactly the right amount (of money). □ *That's a good answer, Bob. You're right on the money.* □ *This project is going to be finished right on the nose.*

on the move 1. moving from place to place. □ *Are the cattle on the move now, or are they still grazing?* **2.** progressing; advancing. □ *Finally the market has turned around now and is really on the move.* □ *At last, we are on the move!*

on the nose Go to **on the money**.

on the off chance because of a slight possibility that something may happen or might be the case; just in case. □ *I went to the theater on the off chance that there were* *tickets for the show left.* □ *We didn't think we would get into the football game, but we went on the off chance.*

on (the) one hand *Fig.* from one point of view; as one side (of an issue). □ *On one hand, I really ought to support my team. On the other hand, I don't have the time to attend all the games.* □ *On the one hand, I really could use Ann's help. On the other hand, she and I don't get along very well.*

on the other hand *Fig.* a phrase introducing an alternate view. □ *John: I'm ready to go; on the other hand, I'm perfectly comfortable here. Sally: I'll let you know when I'm ready, then.* □ *Mary: I like this one. On the other hand, this is nice too. Sue: Why not get both?*

on the outs (with someone**)** *Inf.* in a mild dispute with someone; sharing ill will with someone. □ *Tom and Bill are on the outs again.* □ *Tom has been on the outs with Bill before. They'll work it out.*

on the phone Go to on the telephone.

on the pill taking birth control pills. □ *Is it true that Mary is on the pill?* □ *She was on the pill, but she isn't now.*

on the point of doing something and **at the point of** doing something *Fig.* ready to start doing something. □ *I was just on the point of going out the door.* □ *We were almost at the point of buying a new car.*

on the prowl looking for someone for sexual purposes. (Alludes to a prowling cat.) □ *Tom looks like he is on the prowl again tonight.* □ *That whole gang of boys is on the prowl. Watch out.*

on the QT quietly; secretly. (An abbreviation of *quiet*.) □ *The company president was making payments to his wife on the QT.* □ *The mayor accepted a bribe on the QT.*

on the rag 1. *Sl.* menstruating. (Potentially offensive. Use with caution.) □ *Kim's on the rag and in a bad mood.* □ *Sue doesn't go swimming when she's on the rag.* **2.** *Sl.* ill-tempered. □ *Bill is on the rag and making trouble for everyone.* □ *Wow, Bob, you are on the rag. What's eating you?*

on the right track 1. *Lit.* following the right track or trail; riding on the correct track, as with a train. □ *The train was on the right track when it left the station. I can't imagine how it got lost.* **2.** *Fig.* following the right set of assumptions. □ *Tom is on the right track and will solve the mystery soon.* □ *You are on the right track to find the answer.*

on the rise *Fig.* increasing in frequency or intensity. □ *The number of auto thefts in Cook County is on the rise again.*

on the road *Fig.* traveling from place to place, not necessarily on the highways; working away from one's home or office. □ *I was on the road with the circus for six months.* □ *I don't work in the main office anymore. Now I'm on the road.*

on the road to recovery *Cliché* recovering; getting better; improving. □ *It's been two weeks since her surgery, and she is on the road to recovery.*

on the rocks 1. *Lit.* [of a ship] broken and marooned on rocks in the sea. □ *The ship crashed and was on the rocks until the next high tide.* **2.** *Fig.* [of an alcoholic drink] served with ice cubes. □ *I'd like mine on the rocks, please.* □ *Give me a scotch on the rocks, please.* **3.** *Fig.* in a state of

ruin or bankruptcy. □ *That bank is on the rocks. Don't put your money in it.* □ *My finances are on the rocks just now.*

on the run 1. *Fig.* while one is moving from place to place. □ *I will try to pick up some aspirin today on the run.* □ *I will think about it on the run.* **2.** *Fig.* running from the police. □ *Richard is on the run from the cops.* □ *The gang of crooks is on the run.*

on the safe side *Fig.* taking the risk-free path. □ *Let's be on the safe side and call first.* □ *I think you should stay on the safe side and call the doctor about this fever.*

on the same wavelength *Fig.* thinking in the same pattern. □ *We're not on the same wavelength. Let's try again.* □ *We kept talking until we got on the same wavelength.*

on the sauce drinking regularly; intoxicated. □ *Poor old Ron is on the sauce again.* □ *He is on the sauce most of the time.*

on the scene *Fig.* available or present where something is happening or where something has happened. □ *The ambulance was on the scene almost immediately.* □ *I wasn't on the scene when it happened.*

on the shelf 1. *Fig.* not active socially; left to oneself in social matters. (Alludes to being left or stored on a shelf.) □ *I've been on the shelf long enough. I'm going to make some friends.* □ *She likes being on the shelf.* **2.** *Fig.* postponed. □ *We'll have to put this matter on the shelf for a while.* □ *I have a plan on the shelf just waiting for an opportunity like this.*

on the side 1. *Lit.* extra, such as with a job or an additional order of food. □ *I would like an order of eggs with toast on the side, please.* □ *She is a bank teller and works as a waitress on the side.* **2.** *Fig.* in addition to one's spouse. □ *He is married, but also has a woman on the side.* □ *She has boyfriends on the side, but her husband knows about them.*

on the skids *Sl.* on the decline. □ *My newly started business is on the skids.* □ *Her health is really on the skids, but she stays cheery anyway.*

on the sly *Fig.* secretly and deceptively. □ *She was stealing little bits of money on the sly.* □ *Martin was having an affair with the maid on the sly.*

on the spot 1. *Lit.* at exactly the right place; at exactly the right time. □ *It's noon, and I'm glad you're all here on the spot. Now we can begin.* □ *I expect you to be on the spot when and where trouble arises.* **2.** *Fig.* in trouble; in a difficult situation. □ *There is a problem in the department I manage, and I'm really on the spot.* □ *I hate to be on the spot when it's not my fault.*

on the spur of the moment *Fig.* suddenly; spontaneously. □ *We decided to go on the spur of the moment.* □ *I had to leave town on the spur of the moment.*

***on the stick** *Inf.* organized and busy. (*Typically: **be ~; get ~**.) □ *Get on the stick and get this job done!* □ *Come on, you guys. Let's get on the stick!*

on the street 1. *Fig.* widely known. □ *Sue put it on the street, and now everyone knows.* □ *It's on the street. There isn't anyone who hasn't heard it.* **2.** *Fig.* on Wall Street or elsewhere in the New York City financial districts. (Similar to ③, except that it refers to a specific street. Usually with a capital *s*.) □ *I heard on the Street today that bank stocks are headed up.* □ *It's on the Street that the market is*

O

due to crash again. **3.** *Fig.* at discount prices; as available at its lowest retail price. (As if some item were being sold on the street by a peddler.) □ *It lists at $2200 and can be got for about $1650 on the street.* □ *On the street it goes for about $400.*

on the strength of something *Fig.* because of the support of something, such as a promise or evidence; due to something. □ *On the strength of your comment, I decided to give John another chance.* □ *On the strength of my testimony, my case was dismissed.*

on the table *Fig.* subject to discussion by the group; submitted as a point of discussion. □ *The chairman said we could not discuss salaries since the topic was no longer on the table.*

on the take taking bribes. (Underworld.) □ *I heard that the mayor is on the take.* □ *Everyone in city hall is on the take.*

*on the telephone and ***on the phone** *Fig.* speaking on the telephone. (*Typically: **be** ~; **get** ~.) □ *She's on the phone but won't be long.* □ *Please take a seat while I'm on the phone.* □ *Get on the phone and call him back immediately!*

on the throne 1. *Lit.* [of royalty] currently reigning. □ *King Samuel was on the throne for two decades.* **2.** *Fig. Sl.* seated on the toilet. □ *I can't come to the phone. I'm on the throne.*

*on the tip of one's **tongue** *Fig.* [of a thought or idea] about to be said or almost remembered. (*Typically: **be** ~; **have** something ~.) □ *I have his name right on the tip of my tongue. I'll think of it in a second.* □ *John had the answer on the tip of his tongue, but Anne said it first.*

*on the track of someone or something Go to next.

*on the trail of someone or something and ***on the track of** someone or something seeking someone or something; about to find someone or something. (*Typically: **be** ~; **get** ~.) □ *I'm on the trail of a new can opener that is supposed to be easier to use.* □ *I spent all morning on the track of a vendor who can meet our requirements.*

on the up-and-up legitimate; open and aboveboard. □ *Is this deal on the up-and-up? What's the catch?* □ *Everything I do is on the up-and-up. I am totally honest.*

on the verge of doing something and **on the verge of** something at the very beginning of doing something; just about to do something. □ *Bill was on the verge of leaving town when he found a job.* □ *Susan was on the verge of laughter, so she left the lecture hall.*

on the wagon *Fig.* not drinking alcohol. □ *No, I don't care for a cocktail. I'm on the wagon.* □ *Bob's old drinking buddies complained that he was no fun when he went on the wagon.*

on the waiting list and **on the wait list** [for someone's name to be] on a list of people waiting for an opportunity to do something. □ *I couldn't get a seat on the plane, but I got on the waiting list.* □ *There is no room for you, but we can put your name on the waiting list.*

on the wane becoming less; fading away. □ *Her influence in on the wane, but she is still the boss.*

on the warpath very angry. □ *The boss is on the warpath again. Watch out!* □ *I am on the warpath about setting goals and standards again.*

on the watch for someone or something alert and watching for someone or something. □ *Please stay on the watch for trouble.* □ *I'm always on the watch for Ann. I want to know when she's around.*

*on the way (to something or some place) and ***on** one's **way (to** something or some place) moving toward a place; advancing toward a new status or condition. (*Typically: **be** ~; **get** ~.) □ *Is he here yet or is he on the way?* □ *Mary is better now and on the way to recovery.* □ *She's now on the way to San Francisco.* □ *Yes, she's on her way.*

on the whole generally; considering everything. □ *On the whole, this was a very good day.* □ *Your work—on the whole—is quite good.*

on the wing *Fig.* while flying; while in flight. (Usually refers to birds, fowl, etc., not people or planes.) □ *There is nothing as pretty as a bird on the wing.* □ *The hawk caught the sparrow on the wing.*

on the (witness) stand [of a witness] giving testimony in court, seated in place in view of the court. □ *I was on the witness stand, answering questions, when the judge declared a recess.*

*on the wrong side of someone and ***on** someone's **wrong side** *Fig.* out of favor with someone. (*Typically: **be** ~; **get** ~.) □ *Don't get on the wrong side of her.* □ *I do what I can not to get on the wrong side of people.*

on the wrong track 1. *Lit.* [of a train] following the wrong set of tracks. □ *We had to back up, because somehow we got on the wrong track.* **2.** *Fig.* going the wrong way; following the wrong set of assumptions. □ *You'll never get the right answer. You're on the wrong track.* □ *They won't get it figured out because they are on the wrong track.*

on thin ice 1. *Lit.* on ice that is too thin to support one. (See also **skate on thin ice; walk on thin ice.**) □ *Billy is on thin ice and is in great danger.* **2.** *Fig.* in a risky situation. □ *If you try that you'll really be on thin ice. That's too risky.* □ *If you don't want to find yourself on thin ice, you must be sure of your facts.*

on time before the deadline; by the stated time. □ *Please make sure that your essays are completed on time.* □ *My taxes were not done on time, so I had to pay a penalty.*

on tiptoe standing or walking on the front part of the feet (the balls of the feet) with no weight put on the heels. (This is done to gain height or to walk quietly.) □ *I had to stand on tiptoe in order to see over the fence.* □ *I came in late and walked on tiptoe so I wouldn't wake anybody up.*

on top of something **1.** *Fig.* up-to-date on something; knowing about the current state of something. □ *Ask Mary. She's on top of this issue.* □ *This issue is constantly changing. She has to pay attention to it to stay on top of things.* **2.** *Fig.* in addition to something. □ *Jane told Bill he was dull. On top of that, she said he was unfriendly.* □ *On top of being dull, he's unfriendly.* **3.** *Fig.* victorious over something; famous or notorious for something. □ *It was a close game, but the home team came out on top.* □ *Bill is on top in his field.*

O

on top of the world *Fig.* feeling wonderful; glorious; ecstatic. □ *Wow, I feel on top of the world.* □ *Since he got a new job, he's on top of the world.*

*****on track** on schedule; progressing as planned. (*Typically: **be** ~; **get** someone or something ~; **have** someone or something ~; **keep** someone or something ~; **put** someone or something ~; **set** someone or something ~.) □ *Try to keep these procedures on track this time.* □ *Please get this discussion on track. Time is limited.*

on trial 1. [of someone] in a legal case before a judge. □ *The criminal was on trial for over three months.* □ *I am not on trial. Don't treat me like that!* **2.** being tested; being examined or experimented with. □ *The new strain of wheat is on trial in Kansas at the present time.* □ *The teaching method is on trial in the school system.*

on vacation away, taking time off work; on holiday. □ *Where are you going on vacation this year?* □ *I'll be away on vacation for three weeks.*

on view visible; on public display. □ *The painting will be on view at the museum.* □ *I'll pull the shades so that we won't be on view.*

on with someone [of a date or appointment] agreed to and confirmed with someone. □ *Is the Friday date still on with you?* □ *It's on with me.*

On your bike! and **Go to your room!** *Sl. imperative.* Get out of here!; Get on your bike and get out! □ *What a bad joke! No puns allowed here! On your bike!* □ *That was a ridiculous remark. Go to your room!*

on your mark, get set, go and **ready, set, go** [in preparing to start a race involving speed] move to the starting point, get set to move, go. □ *Runners on your mark, get set, go.*

Once a priest, always a priest. and **Once a whore, always a whore.** *Prov.* A person who has done a certain kind of job will always have the characteristics of people who do that job, even after he or she no longer does that kind of work. (This can be applied to many different occupations.) □ *Alan: My cousin left the clergy, but boy! He still preaches at me all the time. Jane: Once a priest, always a priest, huh?*

Once a whore, always a whore. Go to previous.

once and for all finally; permanently. □ *Sue: I'm going to get this place organized once and for all! Alice: That'll be the day!* □ *"We need to get this straightened out once and for all," said Bob, for the fourth time today.*

Once bitten, twice shy. *Prov.* When something or someone has hurt you once, you tend to avoid that thing or person. □ *Jill: Let's go ride the roller coaster. Jane: No, thanks. I got really sick on one of those once—once bitten, twice shy.* □ *I once sent in money for something I saw advertised in the back of a magazine, but the merchandise was of such poor quality I was sorry I'd bought it. I'll never buy anything that way again; once bitten, twice shy.*

once in a blue moon *Cliché* very seldom. □ *Jill: Does your husband ever bring you flowers? Ellen: Once in a blue moon.* □ *Once in a blue moon, I buy a fashion magazine, just to see what people are wearing.*

once more and **one more time** Please do it one more time. □ *Mary: You sang that line beautifully, Fred. Now, once more. Fred: I'm really tired of all this rehearsing.* □

John (finishing practicing his speech): How was that? Sue: Good! One more time, though. John: I'm getting bored with it.

once upon a time *Cliché* once in the past. (A formula used to begin a fairy tale.) □ *Once upon a time, there were three bears.* □ *Once upon a time, I had a puppy of my own.*

once-in-a-lifetime chance and **once-in-a-lifetime opportunity** a chance that will never occur again in one's lifetime. □ *This is a once-in-a-lifetime chance. Don't miss it.* □ *She offered me a once-in-a-lifetime opportunity, but I turned it down.*

once-in-a-lifetime opportunity Go to previous.

*****the once-over** a quick, visual examination. (*Typically: **get** ~; **give** someone ~.) □ *Every time John walks by I get the once-over. Does he like me?* □ *I went to the doctor yesterday, but I only had a once-over.*

once-over-lightly 1. *Fig.* a quick and careless treatment. (A noun. Said of an act of cleaning, studying, examination, or appraisal.) □ *Bill gave his geometry the once-over-lightly and then quit studying.* □ *Ann, you didn't wash the dishes properly. They only got a once-over-lightly.* **2.** *Fig.* cursory; in a quick and careless manner. (An adverb.) □ *Tom studied geometry once-over-lightly.* □ *Ann washed the dishes once-over-lightly.*

one and all everyone. □ *"Good morning to one and all," said Jane as she walked through the outer office.* □ *Let's hope that this turns out to be a wonderful party for one and all.*

the one and only the famous and talented (person). (Used in theatrical introductions. See also **my one and only**.) □ *And now—the one and only—Jane Smith!* □ *Let's have a big hand for the one and only Bob Jones!*

one and the same *Cliché* the very same person or thing. □ *John Jones and J. Jones are one and the same.* □ *Men's socks and men's stockings are almost one and the same.*

one brick shy of a load *Inf.* stupid; dense. □ *Joyce has done some stupid things. Sometimes I think she is one brick shy of a load.* □ *Ted is one brick shy of a load. He can't seem to do what he is told without messing up.*

one by one and **one at a time** the first one, then the next one, then the next one, etc.; each in turn. □ *I have to deal with problems one by one. I can't handle them all at once.* □ *Okay, just take things one at a time.* □ *The children came into the room one by one.*

One cannot be in two places at once. *Prov.* You cannot be in more than one place or do more than one thing at the same time. □ *Child: Mom! Mom! Come help me wash my hair! Mother: Just a minute! I'm putting clean sheets on your bed right now, and I can't be in two places at once.*

One cannot love and be wise. *Prov.* People often fall in love with someone with whom they are not compatible or behave foolishly when they are in love. □ *My son and his girlfriend have decided to get married in the spring. I don't think that's wise, since they won't have enough money saved by then to set up house. But then, one cannot love and be wise.*

*****one eye on** someone or something *Fig.* [get/have] a small amount of attention devoted to someone or something. (*Typically: **keep** ~; **have** ~.) □ *I have to have one eye on you at all times or you will get into trouble.* □ *I* *have one eye on the speedometer of my car whenever I am driving.*

one false move Go to a false move.

one final thing Go to next.

one final word and **one final thing** *Fig.* a phrase introducing a parting comment or the last item in a list. □ *John: One final word—keep your chin up. Mary: Good advice!* □ *And one final thing, don't haul around a lot of expensive camera stuff. It just tells the thieves who to rob.*

one for the (record) books a record-breaking or very remarkable act. □ *What a dive! That's one for the record books.* □ *I've never heard such a funny joke. That's really one for the books.*

*one for the road a drink; a drink before a journey or before leaving a bar. (*Typically: **down ~; drink ~; have ~; take ~.**) □ *Let's have one for the road.* □ *Don't down one for the road if you are going to be the driver.*

One good turn deserves another. *Prov.* If someone does you a favor, you should do a favor for that person in return. □ *Jill: Thanks for the ride. Jane: It's the least I can do after you helped me wash the car last week. One good turn deserves another.* □ *Child: I don't want to help Grandma go shopping. Father: But she helped you with your homework yesterday. And one good turn deserves another.*

One hand for oneself **and one for the ship.** *Prov.* When you are on a ship, always use one hand to steady yourself, and one to work; likewise, always put some effort into safeguarding yourself as well as into working. □ *The old sailor chastised us for forgetting to hold onto something during the rough weather. "One hand for yourself and one for the ship," he bellowed.* □ *This company expects you to work hard, but not so hard that you hurt yourself. One hand for yourself and one for the ship.*

One has to draw the line somewhere. *Prov.* It is necessary to set limits and enforce them. □ *Ellen: This is the fifth night this week that my son has stayed out too late. Jane: Why not punish him, then? You have to draw the line somewhere.* □ *I am a fairly easygoing employer, but I cannot allow my employees to take two hours for lunch. I have to draw the line somewhere.*

one in a hundred Go to next.

one in a thousand and **one in a hundred; one in a million** *Fig.* nearly unique; one of a very few. □ *He's a great guy. He's one in million.* □ *Mary's one in a hundred—such a hard worker.*

one jump ahead (of someone or something**)** and **one move ahead (of** someone or something**)** *Fig.* one step in advance of someone or something. □ *Try to stay one jump ahead of the competition.* □ *If you're one move ahead, you're well prepared to deal with problems. Then, nothing is a surprise.*

one law for the rich and another for the poor *Prov.* Rich people are sometimes able to escape without punishment when they commit crimes, while poor people are usually punished. □ *It doesn't seem fair—rich people can avoid paying their taxes and not get in trouble, but poor people are always punished if they don't pay. We shouldn't have one law for the rich and another for the poor.*

one little bit any at all; at all. □ *Jean could not be persuaded to change her mind one little bit.* □ *I don't want to hear anything more about it. Not even one little bit.*

One man's loss is another man's gain. *Prov.* When one person loses something, another person gets it. (You can substitute appropriate names or pronouns for the phrases *one man's* and *another man's*, as in the second example.) □ *Mike found a five-dollar bill on the sidewalk. "One man's loss is another man's gain," he thought to himself, as he took the money.* □ *Jane: Andy just got fired. Jill: I know. And Andy's loss is my gain; I'm getting promoted to his job!*

One man's meat is another man's poison. *Prov.* Something that one person likes may be distasteful to someone else. □ *Fred: What do you mean you don't like French fries? They're the best food in the world! Alan: One man's meat is another man's poison.* □ *Jill: I don't understand why Don doesn't like to read science fiction. It's the most interesting thing to read. Jane: One man's meat is another man's poison.*

One man's trash is another man's treasure. *Prov.* Something that one person considers worthless may be considered valuable by someone else. □ *Q: Why would anyone want to hang a picture like that on the wall? A: One man's trash is another man's treasure.* □ *A: Bob's uncle is always going through people's garbage, looking for old stuff. B: One man's trash is another man's treasure.*

One moment, please. Please wait briefly. (A polite way of acknowledging that you noticed someone's request.) □ *John: Can you help me? Clerk: One moment, please. I will be with you shortly.* □ *Bill (answering the phone): Hello? Bob: Hello. Can I speak to Tom? Bill: One moment, please. (handing phone to Tom) It's for you. Tom: Hello, this is Tom.*

one more time Go to once more.

one move ahead (of someone or something**)** Go to one jump ahead (of someone or something).

one of these days someday; in some situation like this one. □ *One of these days, someone is going to steal your purse if you don't take better care of it.* □ *You're going to get in trouble one of these days.*

One of these days is none of these days. *Prov.* If you say you will do something "one of these days," you probably do not seriously intend to do it, and therefore it will not get done. □ *Alan: When are you going to fix the garage door? Jane: One of these days. Alan: One of these days is none of these days.* □ *Jill: One of these days, I'll pay you the money I owe you. Jane: One of these days is none of these days.*

One's bark is worse than one's **bite.** *Prov.* Someone makes a lot of harsh-sounding threats but never carries them out. □ *Don't get upset at anything my father says. His bark is worse than his bite.* □ *Jill: Lisa says she's going to sue me for letting my dog dig up her rosebushes. John: Don't pay any attention. Her bark is worse than her bite.*

*one's bearings the knowledge of where one is; the knowledge of how one is oriented to one's immediate environment. (*Typically: **get ~; find ~; have ~; lose ~; tell** one **~.**) □ *After he fell, it took Ted a few minutes to get his bearings.* □ *Jean found her compass and got her bearings almost immediately.*

one's best bib and tucker *Rur.* one's best clothing. □ *I always put on my best bib and tucker on Sundays.* □ *Put on your best bib and tucker, and let's go to the city.*

one's best shot *Fig.* one's best attempt (at something). □ *That was his best shot, but it wasn't good enough.* □ *I always try to give something my best shot.*

one's better half *Fig.* one's spouse. (Usually refers to a wife.) □ *I think we'd like to come for dinner, but I'll have to ask my better half.* □ *I have to go home now to my better half. We are going out tonight.*

one's (butter and) egg money *Fig.* money that a farm woman earns. (Farm women would often sell butter and eggs for extra money that would be stashed away for an emergency.) □ *Jane was saving her butter and egg money for a new TV.* □ *I've got my egg money. Let's go shopping.*

one's claws are showing one is acting catty; one is saying spiteful and cruel things. □ *Gloria: Did you see what she was wearing? I wouldn't be caught dead in it! Sally: Gloria, my dear, your claws are showing.*

one's days are numbered *Fig.* one is facing death or dismissal. □ *If I don't get this contract, my days are numbered at this company.* □ *Uncle Bill has a terminal disease. His days are numbered.*

one's deepest sympathy one's very sincere sympathy. □ *I am so sorry about the death of your father. You have my deepest sympathy.* □ *She sent her deepest sympathy to the family.*

one's ears are red *Fig.* [for someone's ears] to be red from embarrassment. □ *I'm so embarrassed. Wow, are my ears red!* □ *My ears are red! I can't believe I said that.*

one's ears are ringing *Fig.* [for someone's ears] to have a ringing sound because of an illness or other condition; very loud music, or some other very loud sound. □ *After the explosion, my ears were ringing for hours.* □ *My ears are ringing because I have a sinus infection.*

one's eyes are bigger than one's stomach *Fig.* one has taken more food than one can eat. □ *I can't eat all this. I'm afraid that my eyes were bigger than my stomach.* □ *Try to take less food. Your eyes are bigger than your stomach at every meal.*

one's fair share the amount of something that one is due relative to what other people are receiving. □ *Let him take more. He didn't get his fair share.* □ *I want my fair share. You cheated me! Give me some more!*

***one's fill of** someone or something *Fig.* [get/have] as much of someone or something as one needs or can tolerate. (*Typically: **get** ~; **have** ~.) □ *You'll soon get your fill of Tom. He can be quite a pest.* □ *I can never get my fill of shrimp. I love it.*

one's for the asking *Fig.* [can become] one's property if one asks for it. □ *I have a cherry pie here. A slice is yours for the asking if you want it.* □ *Uncle Mac said we could have his old car if we wanted it. It was ours for the asking.*

one's frame of mind *Fig.* one's mood or mental state. □ *My frame of mind is sort of low at the moment. I've had a very bad day.*

One's future looks bright. *Fig.* One has a promising future. □ *Tom's future looks bright and he will do well if he keeps working hard.*

one's goose is cooked one is finished; one has been found out and is in trouble. □ *It's over. His goose is cooked!* □ *If I get caught, my goose is cooked.*

one's heart goes out to someone *Fig.* one feels great sympathy for someone. □ *My heart goes out to the grieving family.* □ *Let your heart go out to those who are suffering, and pray for their improvement.*

one's heart is (dead) set against something *Fig.* one is totally against something. □ *Jane's heart is set against going to that restaurant ever again.*

one's heart is in one's mouth *Fig.* one feels strongly emotional (about someone or something). (See also have one's heart in one's mouth.) □ *"Gosh, Mary," said John, "My heart is in my mouth whenever I see you."* □ *It was a touching scene. My heart was in my mouth the whole time.*

one's heart is in the right place *Fig.* one has good intentions, even if the results are bad. □ *She gave it a good try. Her heart was in the right place.* □ *He is awkward, but his heart is in the right place.*

one's heart is set on something *Fig.* one desires and expects something. □ *Jane's heart is set on going to London.* □ *My heart is set on returning home.*

one's heart misses a beat and **one's heart skips a beat** *Fig.* one's heart flutters or palpitates; one has a strong emotional reaction. □ *Whenever I'm near you, my heart skips a beat.* □ *When the racehorse fell, my heart missed a beat.*

one's heart skips a beat Go to previous.

one's heart stands still *Fig.* one's heart (figuratively) stops beating because of strong emotions. □ *When I first saw you, my heart stood still.* □ *My heart will stand still until you answer.*

one's home away from home a place, other than one's home, where one can feel at home. □ *Please make our house your home away from home when you are in town.*

one's John Hancock Go to next.

one's John Henry and **one's John Hancock** one's signature. □ *Just put your John Henry on this line, and we'll bring your new car around.*

one's last resting place *Euph.* one's grave. □ *Daddy has gone to his last resting place.* □ *I want to be beside her in her last resting place.*

one's luck runs out *Fig.* one's good luck stops. □ *My luck ran out, so I had to come home.* □ *She will quit gambling when her luck runs out.*

one's mind went blank *Fig.* someone's mind has experienced total forgetfulness. □ *He knew all his lines in rehearsal, but his mind went blank when he went before an audience.*

***one's money's worth** *Fig.* everything that one has paid for; the best quality for the money paid. (*Typically: **get** ~; **have** ~.) □ *Weigh that package of meat before you buy it. Be sure you're getting your money's worth.* □ *I didn't get my money's worth with my new camera, so I took it back.*

one's name is mud *Fig.* one is in trouble or humiliated. □ *If I can't get this contract signed, my name will be mud.* □ *His name is mud ever since he broke the crystal vase.*

one's next of kin one's closest living relative or relatives. □ *The police notified the dead man's next of kin.* □ *My next of kin lives 800 miles away.*

one's next-door neighbor the person living in the house or apartment closest to one's own. □ *My next-door neighbor came over to borrow a shovel.* □ *I will be visiting our next-door neighbor if you need me.*

one's nose is in the air *Fig.* one is acting conceited or aloof. □ *Mary's nose is always in the air since she got into that exclusive boarding school.* □ *Her mother's nose was always in the air, too.*

one's number is up *Fig.* one's time to die—or to suffer some other unpleasantness—has come. □ *John is worried. He thinks his number is up.* □ *When my number is up, I hope it all goes fast.*

one's old stamping ground *Fig.* the place where one was raised or where one has spent a lot of time. (There are variants with *stomping* and *grounds*.) □ *Ann should know about that place. It's near her old stamping ground.* □ *I can't wait to get back to my old stomping grounds.*

*__one's (own) way__ one's way of doing something; one's will or desire. (*Typically: **get** ~; **have** ~.) □ *She always has to have her own way. She thinks no one else can do it right.*

*__one's (own) way (with someone or something)__ [get/have] one's control over someone or something. (*Typically: **get** ~; **have** ~.) □ *The mayor got his way with the city council.* □ *He seldom gets his own way.* □ *How often do you have your way with your own money?* □ *Parents usually have their way with their children.*

*__one's own worst enemy__ *Fig.* consistently causing oneself to fail; more harmful to oneself than other people are. (*Typically: **be** ~; **become** ~.) □ *Ellen: My boss is my enemy. She never says anything good about me. Jane: Ellen, you're your own worst enemy. If you did your job responsibly, your boss would be nicer.*

*__one's say__ one's stance or position; what one thinks. (*Typically: **get** ~; **have** ~.) □ *I want to have my say on this matter.* □ *He got his say, and then he was happy.*

*__one's sea legs__ *Fig.* one's ability to tolerate the movement of a ship at sea. (*Typically: **get** ~; **have** ~.) □ *Jean was a little awkward on the cruise at first, but in a few days she got her sea legs and was fine.* □ *You may feel a little sick until you get your sea legs.*

*__one's second wind 1.__ *Lit.* one's stabilized breathing after exerting oneself for a short time. (*Typically: **get** ~; **have** ~.) □ *John was having a hard time running until he got his second wind.* □ *Bill had to quit the race because he never got his second wind.* **2.** *Fig.* one's greater or renewed energy and productivity, gained at some time after starting. (*Typically: **get** ~; **have** ~.) □ *I usually get my second wind early in the afternoon.* □ *Mary is a better worker after she has her second wind.*

*__one's start__ one's first career opportunity. (*Typically: **get** ~; **have** ~; **give** one ~.) □ *I had my start in painting when I was thirty.* □ *She helped me get my start by recommending me to the manager.*

one's sunset years *Euph.* one's old age. □ *Many people in their sunset years love to travel.* □ *Now is the time to think about financial planning for your sunset years.*

*__one's walking papers__ *Fig.* a notice that one is fired from one's job. (*Typically: **get** ~; **have** ~; **give** one ~.) □ *Well, I'm through. I got my walking papers today.* □ *They are closing down my department. I guess I'll get my walking papers soon.*

one's way of life one's lifestyle; one's pattern of living. □ *That kind of thing just doesn't fit into my way of life.* □ *Our way of life includes contributing to worthy causes.*

one's word is one's bond *Fig.* one's statement of agreement is as sound as a posting of a performance bond. □ *Of course, you can trust anything I agree to verbally. My word is my bond. There's no need to get it in writing.*

one's work is cut out for one *Fig.* one's task is prepared for one; one has a lot of work to do. □ *This is a big job. My work is cut out for me.* □ *The new president's work is cut out for him.*

one sandwich short of a picnic *Inf.* not very smart; lacking intelligence. (Jocular.) □ *Poor Bob just isn't too bright. He's one sandwich short of a picnic.* □ *She's not stupid. Just one sandwich short of a picnic.*

One swallow does not make a summer. and **One swallow does not a summer make.** *Prov.* You should not assume that something is true just because you have seen one piece of evidence for it. □ *Amanda: I got a good grade on this quiz! My troubles in school are over. Nancy: One swallow does not a summer make.*

the **one that got away** *Fig.* the big fish that got away, especially as the subject of a fisherman's story. □ *The one that got away is always bigger than the one that got caught.*

One thing leads to another. One event sets things up for another event, and so on. (As an explanation of how little things lead to big problems.) □ *I kept spending more and more money until I was broke. You know how one thing leads to another.* □ *He bought a car, then a house, then a boat. One thing leads to another.*

one thing or person after another a series of things or people that seems without limit. □ *It's just one problem after another.* □ *One customer after another has been buying shoes today!*

one to a customer *Fig.* each person can have or receive only one. (As in sales restrictions where each customer is permitted to buy only one.) □ *"Only one to a customer!" said the chef as he handed out the hamburgers.* □ *Is it one to a customer, or can I take two now?*

one too many *Euph.* one drink of liquor too many, implying drunkenness. □ *I think I've had one too many. It's time to stop drinking.* □ *Don't drive if you've had one too many.*

*__one up (on someone)__ ahead of someone; having an advantage over someone. (*Typically: **be** ~; **get** ~.) □ *Tom is one up on Sally because he got a job and she didn't.* □ *Yes, it sounds like Tom is one up.*

one way or another somehow. □ *Tom: Can we fix this radio, or do I have to buy a new one? Mary: Don't fret! We'll get it repaired one way or another.* □ *John: I think we're lost. Alice: Don't worry. We'll get there one way or another.*

one-horse town *Fig.* a very small town; a small and backward town. □ *I refuse to spend a whole week in that one-horse town!* □ *I grew up in a one-horse town, and I liked it very much.*

one-man show 1. *Lit.* a performance put on by one person. □ *It was a one-man show, but it was very entertaining.* □ *For a one-man show, it was very long.* **2.** *Fig.* an exhibition of the artistic works of one person. □ *She is having a one-man show at the Northside Gallery.* □ *I'm having a one-man show next weekend. Come and see what I have done.*

one-night stand 1. *Lit.* a performance lasting only one night. □ *The band did a series of one-night stands down the East Coast.* □ *You can't make a living doing one-night stands.* **2.** *Fig.* a romance or sexual relationship that lasts only one night. □ *It was not a romance, just a one-night stand.* □ *It looked like something that would last longer than a one-night stand.*

*oneself again showing signs of being healthy again or restored. (*Typically: **act like ~; be ~; feel like ~; seem like ~**.) □ *After such a long illness, it's good to be myself again.* □ *I'm sorry that I lost my temper. I think I feel like myself again now.*

one-track mind *Fig.* a mind that thinks entirely or almost entirely about one subject. □ *Adolescent boys often have one-track minds. All they're interested in is the opposite sex.* □ *Bob has a one-track mind. He can only talk about football.*

online 1. Go to in line. **2.** *Fig.* connected to a computer or network. □ *As soon as I get online, I can check the balance of your account.* □ *I was online for an hour before I found out what I wanted to know.*

only have eyes for someone *Fig.* [to be] loyal to only one person, in the context of romance. □ *Oh, Jane! I only have eyes for you!* □ *Don't waste any time on Tom. He only has eyes for Ann.*

(Only) time will tell. *Prov.* You will only know the outcome after time has passed. □ *Jill: Do you think Bill and Nancy will have a happy marriage? John: Only time will tell.* □ *I'm not sure yet if our advertising campaign was a success. Time will tell.*

the **only way to go** the best way to do something; the best choice to make. □ *Get a four-wheel drive car. It's the only way to go.* □ *That's it! A new house. It's the only way to go.*

*onto a good thing having found something useful, promising, or profitable. (*Typically: **be ~; get ~**.) □ *This is a great scheme. I know I'm onto a good thing.* □ *I'm onto a good thing. I'm sure I am.*

*onto someone seeing through someone's deception. (*Typically: **be ~; get ~; catch ~**.) □ *By the time we got on to the con artists, they were out of town.* □ *The sheriff got on to Jed, and Jed wanted to get out of town fast.*

*onto something **1.** *Fig.* alerted to or aware of a deceitful plan. (*Typically: **be ~; catch ~**.) □ *The cops are onto your little game here.* *Fig.* having found something useful or promising; on the verge of discovering something. (*Typically: **be ~; get ~**.) □ *I think we are really onto something this time.* □ *I am onto a new discovery.*

ooze (out) (from someone or something**)** and **ooze out (of** someone or something**)** to seep out of someone or something. □ *The heavy oil oozed out from the hole in the barrel.* □ *Some blood was oozing out of his nose.*

ooze with something **1.** *Lit.* to flow or seep with something; to be covered with some oozing substance. □ *The*

wound oozed with blood. □ *The roast beef oozed with juices.* **2.** *Fig.* [for someone] to exude an ingratiating or insincere manner. □ *The used-car salesman oozed with insincerity.* □ *The young woman oozed with charm.*

open a can of worms Go to a can of worms.

open a conversation to start a conversation. (See also strike up a conversation.) □ *I tried to open a conversation with him, but he had nothing to say.* □ *She opened a conversation with an inquiry into my health, which got me talking about my favorite subject.*

open a few doors (for someone**)** Go to open some doors (for someone).

open and aboveboard Go to honest and aboveboard.

(Open) confession is good for the soul. *Prov.* If you have done something wrong, you will feel better if you confess that you did it. □ *You ought to tell Dad that you broke his radio. Open confession is good for the soul.* □ *Sue: I've been so upset about cheating on the exam that I haven't been sleeping nights. Sam: You can do something about it; confession is good for the soul.*

open fire (on someone**)** *Fig.* to start (doing something, such as asking questions or criticizing). (Based on open fire on someone or something.) □ *The reporters opened fire on the mayor.* □ *When the reporters opened fire, the mayor was smiling, but not for long.*

open fire (on someone or something**)** to begin shooting at someone or something. □ *The troops opened fire on the enemy.* □ *The trainees opened fire on the target.*

open for business [of a shop, store, restaurant, etc.] operating and ready to do business. □ *The store is now open for business and invites you to come in.* □ *The construction will be finished in March, and we will be open for business in April.*

open into something to open inward to something. □ *The passageway opened into a dining room.* □ *Our kitchen opens into a bright breakfast nook.*

*an open mind a mind or attitude that is open to new ideas and opinions. (*Typically: **get ~; have ~; keep ~**.) □ *Please try to be nice and keep an open mind. It's all not as bad as you think.*

open one's **heart to** someone or something **1.** *Fig.* to tell all of one's private thoughts to someone. □ *I didn't mean to open my heart to you.* □ *She opened her heart to the wrong magazine, and it published a scandalous story.* **2.** *Fig.* to become loving and solicitous toward someone; to donate money generously to someone or some cause. □ *We opened our hearts to Fred, who was soliciting for a good cause.* □ *We hope you will all open your hearts to our plea.*

open oneself **to criticism** to do something that makes one vulnerable to criticism. □ *By saying something so stupid in public, you really opened yourself to criticism.*

open (out) on(to) something [for a building's doors] to exit toward something. □ *The French doors opened out onto the terrace.* □ *The doors opened on a lovely patio.*

open Pandora's box *Fig.* to uncover a lot of unsuspected problems. □ *When I asked Jane about her problems, I didn't know I had opened Pandora's box.* □ *You should be cautious with people who are upset. You don't want to open Pandora's box.*

open season (on some creature**)** a time of unrestricted hunting of a particular game animal. □ *It's always open season on rabbits around here.*

open season (on someone**)** *Fig.* a period of time when everyone is criticizing someone. (Based on **open season (on** some creature**).**) □ *It seems as if it's always open season on politicians.* □ *At the news conference, it was open season on the mayor.*

an **open secret** something that is supposed to be known only by a few people but is known in fact to a great many people. □ *Their engagement is an open secret. Only their friends are supposed to know, but in fact, the whole town knows.* □ *It's an open secret that Max is looking for a new job.*

open some doors (for someone**)** and **open a few doors (for** someone**)** *Fig.* to gain access to opportunity or influence (for someone). □ *Morris was able to open a few doors for Mary and get her an interview with the president.*

open someone's **eyes to** someone or something *Fig.* to cause someone, including oneself, to become aware of someone or something. □ *We finally opened our eyes to what was going on around us.* □ *The events of last night opened my eyes to Tom.*

open someone **up†** *Fig.* to perform a surgical operation requiring a major incision on someone. □ *The doctor had to open George up to find out what was wrong.* □ *They opened up George, seeking the cause of his illness.*

open something **out†** to unfold or expand something; to open and spread something out. □ *When she opened the fan out, she saw it was made of plastic.* □ *The peacock opened out its tail feathers and delighted the children.*

open something **up† 1.** *Lit.* to unwrap something; to open something. □ *Yes, I want to open my presents up.* □ *I can't wait to open up my presents.* □ *Open up this door!* **2.** *Fig.* to begin examining or discussing something. □ *Do you really want to open it up now?* □ *Now is the time to open up the question of taxes.* **3.** *Fig.* to reveal the possibilities of something; to reveal an opportunity. □ *Your letter opened new possibilities up.* □ *Your comments opened up a whole new train of thought.* **4.** *Fig.* to start the use of something, such as land, a building, a business, etc. □ *They opened the coastal lands up to resort development.* □ *We opened up a new store last March.* **5.** *Fig.* to make a vehicle go as fast as possible. (As in opening up the throttle.) □ *We took the new car out on the highway and opened it up.* □ *I've never really opened up this truck. I don't know how fast it'll go.* **6.** to make something less congested. □ *They opened the yard up by cutting out a lot of old shrubbery.* □ *We opened up the room by taking the piano out.*

open something **up† (to** someone**)** to make something available to someone; to permit someone to join something or participate in something. □ *We intend to open the club up to everyone.* □ *We will open up our books to the auditors.*

open the door to someone **1.** *Lit.* to permit someone to enter a room, building, etc. □ *The butler opened the door to the guests and they all entered.* □ *I opened the door to Mr. Wilson.* **2.** to make a move or passage easier for a person. □ *Ann opened the door to Fred, who wanted to start a new career in writing.* □ *Mark opened the door to her, and she was always grateful to him.*

open the door to something *Fig.* to invite something to happen. □ *The armistice opened the door to peace talks.* □ *The door was opened to further discussion.*

open to criticism vulnerable to criticism. □ *Anything the president does is open to criticism.*

open to question [an action or opinion] inviting question, examination, or refutation. □ *Everything he told you is open to question and you should look into it.*

open to something *Fig.* agreeable to hear or learn about new ideas and suggestions. □ *The store owner was open to suggestions from her employees.* □ *We are always open to new ideas.*

open up 1. *Lit.* open your door; open your mouth. (Usually **Open up!**) □ *I want in. Open up!* □ *Open up! This is the police.* **2.** *Fig.* to become available. □ *A new job is opening up at my office.* □ *Let me know if any other opportunities open up.* **3.** *Fig.* to go as fast as possible. (As in opening up the throttle.) □ *I can't get this car to open up. Must be something wrong with the engine.* □ *Faster, Tom! Open up! Let's go!* **4.** to become clear, uncluttered, or open. □ *As we drove along, the forest opened up, and we entered into a grassy plain.* □ *The sky opened up, and the sun shone.*

open up (about someone or something**) (with** someone**)** and **open up (on** someone or something**) (with** someone**)** to speak freely about someone or something; to speak a great deal about someone or something. □ *After a while, he began to open up about his disagreements.* □ *He opened up with us about the accident.* □ *She opened up on Fred with Alice.*

open up (on someone, something, or an animal**)** to fire a gun or other weapon at someone, something, or an animal. □ *The sergeant told the soldiers to open up on the enemy position.* □ *"Okay, you guys," shouted the sergeant. "Open up!"*

open (up) one's kimono *Sl.* to reveal what one is planning. (From the computer industry, referring especially to the involvement of the Japanese in this field.) □ *Sam isn't one to open his kimono much when it comes to new products.* □ *Even if Tom appears to open up his kimono on this deal, don't put much stock in what he says.*

open up (to someone**)** and **open up (with** someone**)** to tell [everything] to someone; to confess to someone. □ *If she would only open up to me, perhaps I could help her.* □ *She just won't open up. Everything is "private."*

open up to something to become more accepting of someone or something. □ *Finally, he opened up to the suggestion that he should leave.* □ *Finally the boss opened up to the notion of Tom as a manager.*

open up (with someone**)** Go to **open up (to** someone**).**

open with someone or something to begin a season, session, series, or performance with someone or something. □ *The conference will open with a series of invited speakers.* □ *The performance opened with Donna, who played the flute.*

an **open-and-shut case** a simple and straightforward situation without complications. (Often said of criminal cases where the evidence is convincing.) □ *The murder trial was an open-and-shut case. The defendant was caught with the murder weapon.* □ *Bob's death was an open-and-shut case of suicide. He left a suicide note.*

opening gambit *Fig.* an opening movement, tactic, or statement which is made to secure a position that is to one's advantage. □ *The rebel army's opening gambit was to bomb the city's business district.* □ *The prosecution's opening gambit was to call a witness who linked the defendant to the scene of the crime.*

operate against someone or something to work against someone or something; to have a negative effect on someone or something. □ *All of this operates against our idea of fixing the garage up as a family room.* □ *The new vacation policy operates against my plan to take all of July off.*

operate from something to work out of something or some place. □ *I'm in business for myself. I operate from my home.* □ *We operate from a garage in the back of City Hall.*

operate on someone to perform a surgical operation on someone. □ *They decided not to operate on her.* □ *She wasn't operated on after all.*

operate on something **1.** to work on something; to work with the insides of something. (As a surgeon might operate.) □ *He tried to operate on his watch and ruined it.* **2.** to function or conduct business on a certain principle or assumption. □ *The company has always operated on the theory that the customer is always right.* □ *Sam operates on the assumption that everyone is out to get him.*

Opportunity knocks but once. *Prov.* You will only have one chance to do something important or profitable. (You can say *opportunity knocks* to signal that someone's chance to do something important is here right now.) □ *When Nancy got a scholarship offer from a college far away, her parents encouraged her to go, even though they didn't like the thought of her moving so far from home. "Opportunity knocks but once," they said, "and this may be your only chance to get a good education."*

Opportunity makes a thief. *Prov.* Anyone would steal, given a chance to do so without being punished. □ *Mr. Cooper thought of himself as a moral man. But opportunity makes a thief, and with the safe unguarded he had the opportunity to steal thousands of dollars undetected.*

opposed to something in opposition to something. □ *I am strongly opposed to your suggestion.* □ *He is morally opposed to war.*

the **opposite sex** the other sex; (from the point of view of a female) males; (from the point of view of a male) females. (Also with *member of,* as in the example.) □ *Ann is crazy about the opposite sex.* □ *Bill is very shy when he's introduced to the opposite sex.* □ *Do members of the opposite sex make you nervous?*

opt for something to choose a particular option. □ *I opted for the orange one.* □ *I opt for not going out at all.*

opt in favor of someone or something to choose a particular person; to choose a particular thing. □ *Do you think she will opt in favor of this one or that?* □ *We will opt in favor of David.*

opt in(to something**)** to choose to join in. □ *She opted into our plans.* □ *She opted in almost immediately.*

opt out (of something**)** to choose not to be in something. □ *If you do that, I'm going to have to opt out of the club.* □ *Then go ahead and opt out.*

or else or suffer the consequences. (An inspecific threat of bad consequences.) □ *Do what I tell you, or else.* □ *Don't be late for work, or else!*

or what? a way of adding emphasis to a yes-or-no question the speaker has asked. (In effect, if it wasn't what I said, what is it?) □ *Bob: Now, is this a fine day or what? John: Looks okay to me.* □ *Tom: Look at Bill and Mary. Do they make a fine couple or what? Bob: Sure, they look great.*

or words to that effect *Fig.* or similar words meaning the same thing. □ *John: It says right here in the contract, "You are expected to attend without fail," or words to that effect. Mary: That means I have to be there, huh? John: You got it!* □ *Sally: She said that I wasn't doing my job well, or words to that effect. Jane: Well, you ought to find out exactly what she means. Sally: I'm afraid I know.*

orbit (around) someone or something to circle around something in an orbit. □ *The flies orbited around Fred and his ice-cream cone.* □ *Many satellites orbit around our planet.*

ordain someone **(as)** something **1.** *Lit.* to establish someone as a priest or minister. □ *In a lovely ceremony, they ordained David as a priest.* □ *He was ordained as a priest by a bishop.* **2.** *Fig.* to establish someone as something. □ *They ordained the poor old man as a deputy sheriff.* □ *Was he duly ordained as a Mercedes mechanic?*

the **order of the day** something necessary or usual at a certain time. □ *Warm clothes are the order of the day when camping in the winter.* □ *Going to bed early was the order of the day when we were young.*

order some food **to go** Go to to go.

order someone **about** and **order** someone **around** to give commands to someone. □ *I don't like for someone to order me about.* □ *Don't order me around!*

order someone **in(to** something**)** to command someone to get into something. □ *The officer ordered Ann into the wagon.* □ *She didn't want to go, but the cop ordered her in.*

order someone **off ((of)** something**)** to command someone to get off something. (*Of* is usually retained before pronouns.) □ *The teacher ordered Tom off the steps.* □ *He ordered him off.*

order someone **off the field** [for a game official] to command a player to leave the playing area. □ *The referee will order you off the field.* □ *He ordered us off the field.*

order someone **out of** some place and **order** someone **out**† to command that someone leave a place. □ *The cook ordered Judy out of the kitchen.* □ *The teacher ordered out all the kids.*

order something **from** someone or something to agree to purchase something from someone or a group. □ *We ordered some plants from the mail-order company.* □ *I will order some of those clever little things from you as soon as I can.*

order something **in**† to have something, usually food, brought into one's house or place of business. □ *Do you want to order pizza in?* □ *Shall I order in pizza?*

orient someone **to** something **1.** *Lit.* to help someone locate a compass direction or other similar location. □ *Try to orient Karen to the light so I can photograph her.* □ *It took time, but I oriented myself to north at last.* **2.** *Fig.* to help someone adjust to something, a position, or a relationship.

□ *Will you please orient Bill to our routine?* □ *She found it difficult to orient herself to the new procedures.*

originate from something to come from something or some place. □ *Did you originate from around here?* □ *I originated from a different area of the country.* □ *Some of our customs originate from old beliefs.*

originate in something to have had a beginning in something or some place. □ *The river originates in the Andes Mountains.* □ *All your troubles originate in your lungs.*

originate with someone or something to have been started by someone, something, or during a time period or event. □ *Did this policy originate with you?* □ *This idea originated with the committee.*

ornament something **with** something to decorate something with something. □ *The driver ornamented his truck with lots of chrome.* □ *The room was ornamented with velvet drapes, wood paneling, family portraits—a den of Victorian virtue.*

oscillate between someone or something **and** someone or something else to swing between (choosing) someone and someone else; to swing between (choosing) something and something else. □ *Fred oscillated between going to college and getting a job.* □ *The boss oscillated between John and Roger.*

the **other place** *Euph.* hell. □ *If you're good, you'll go to heaven, and if you're bad, you'll go to the other place.* □ *If she keeps up her drinking and gambling, she's headed to the other place for sure.*

the **other side of the tracks** and the **wrong side of the tracks** the poor part of a town or city. □ *He was a rich boy, and she was a girl from the other side of the tracks.* □ *You don't want to buy a house in that neighborhood. It's on the wrong side of the tracks.*

other things being equal and **all things being equal** *Cliché* if things stay the way they are now; if there are no complications from other factors. □ *Other things being equal, we should have no trouble getting your order to you on time.* □ *I anticipate no problems, all things being equal.*

Other times, other manners. *Prov.* Different generations or eras have different customs. □ *Amy thought her grandchildren addressed their friends in startlingly rude terms. "But then," she reflected, "other times, other manners."* □ *Jane: The young folks today are so shocking. Why, when I was their age, you wouldn't kiss your husband in public, let alone some of the things these children do! Alan: Other times, other manners.*

the **other way (a)round** the reverse; the opposite. □ *No, it won't fit that way. Try it the other way round.* □ *It doesn't make any sense like that. It belongs the other way around.*

An **ounce of common sense is worth a pound of theory.** *Prov.* Common sense will help you solve problems more than theory will. □ *The psychologist had many elaborate theories about how to raise her child, but often forgot that an ounce of common sense is worth a pound of theory.*

An **ounce of discretion is worth a pound of wit.** *Prov.* Knowing when to refrain from making jokes is better than being able to make jokes all the time. □ *Mabel makes fun of everybody, regardless of whether or not she*

hurts their feelings. *Someone should tell her that an ounce of discretion is worth a pound of wit.*

An **ounce of prevention is worth a pound of cure.** *Prov.* If you put in a little effort to prevent a problem, you will not have to put in a lot of effort to solve the problem. □ *Brush your teeth every day; that way you won't have to go to the dentist to have cavities filled. An ounce of prevention is worth a pound of cure.* □ *If you get in the habit of being careful with your new stereo, chances are you won't break it and have to have it fixed later. An ounce of prevention is worth a pound of cure.*

Our house is your house. Go to My house is your house.

oust someone **from** something to force someone to leave something or some place; to throw someone out of something or some place. □ *They ousted the boys from the bar.* □ *The underage kids were ousted from the tavern quickly.*

*an **out** an excuse; means of avoiding something. (*Typically: **have** ~; **give** someone ~.) □ *He's very clever. No matter what happens, he always has an out.*

out an amount of money lacking something; having lost or wasted something. □ *I'm out ten bucks because of your miscalculation.* □ *I'm out the price of a meal.*

*out and about outside the house; outdoors. (*Typically: **be** ~; **get** ~.) □ *Beth has been ill, but now she's out and about.* □ *As soon as I feel better, I'll be able to get out and about.*

out at some place located at a distant place. □ *Tom's out at the farm and there's no phone there, so you can't talk to him.* □ *Jed is out at the cabin on a hunting trip.*

out cold and **out like a light 1.** *Fig.* unconscious. □ *I fell and hit my head. I was out cold for about a minute.* □ *Tom fainted! He's out like a light!* **2.** *Fig.* intoxicated. □ *Four beers and he was out cold.* □ *He sat in his chair at the table, out cold.* **3.** *Fig.* sound asleep. □ *After a few minutes of tossing and turning, she was out like a light.*

out for blood *Fig.* aggressively seeking to harm or get revenge; angry and looking for the cause of one's distress. □ *The opposite team is out for blood, but we have a good defense.*

out for the count Go to down for the count.

*out from something some distance away from something. (*Typically: **be** ~; **get** ~; **go** ~.) □ *I would like to be farther out from the city.* □ *I need to get out from the town.*

*out (from under someone or something) 1.** *Lit.* out from beneath someone or something. (*Typically: **be** ~; **get** ~; **crawl** ~; **creep** ~; **move** ~.) □ *Will you please get out from under my bed?* □ *The dog got out from under her just before she sat down.* **2.** *Fig.* free of someone's control or the burden of a problem. (*Typically: **be** ~; **get** ~; **crawl** ~; **move** ~.) □ *Mary wanted to get out from under her mother.* □ *There is so much work to do! I don't know when I'll ever get out from under it.*

out front 1. in the front of one's house. □ *Our mailbox is out front.* □ *We have a spruce tree out front and a maple tree in the back.* **2.** leading, as in a race. □ *My horse was out front by two lengths until the final turn.* □ *The other candidate is out front in the polls.*

out (in bloom) Go to next.

*out (in blossom) and ***out (in bloom)** [of a plant or tree] blooming; [of flowers] open in blooms. (*Typically: **be** ~; **come** ~.) □ *All the trees were out in blossom.* □ *The daffodils won't be out until next week.*

out in droves Go to out in large numbers.

*out in force *Fig.* appearing in great strength. (*Typically: **be** ~; **come** ~; **go** ~. See also out in large numbers.) □ *What a night! The mosquitoes are out in force.* □ *The police went out in force over the holiday weekend.*

*out in large numbers and ***out in droves** *Fig.* in evidence in some large amount. (*Typically: **be** ~; **come** ~.) □ *The sidewalk salesmen are out in droves today.* □ *The ants were out in large numbers at the picnic.*

out in left field *Fig.* offbeat; unusual and eccentric. (See also out of left field.) □ *Sally is a lot of fun, but she's sort of out in left field.* □ *What a strange idea. It's really out in left field.*

*out in the cold 1. *Lit.* outdoors where it is cold. (*Typically: **be** ~; **keep** someone or some creature ~; **leave** someone or some creature ~; **put** someone or some creature ~.) □ *Open the door! Let me in! Don't keep me out in the cold!* □ *Who left the dog out in the cold all night?* **2.** *Fig.* not informed about what is happening or has happened. (*Typically: **be** ~; **keep** someone ~; **leave** someone ~.) □ *Don't keep your supervisor out in the cold. Tell her what's going on.* □ *Please don't leave me out in the cold. Share the news with me!* **3.** *Fig.* excluded. (*Typically: **be** ~; **keep** someone ~; **leave** someone ~.) □ *There was a party last night, but my friends left me out in the cold.* □ *When it came to the final prizes in the dog show, they left our animals out in the cold.*

*out in the open 1. *Lit.* visible in an open space; exposed in an open area. (*Typically: **be** ~; **bring** something ~; **come** ~; **get** ~; **get** something ~.) □ *The trucks are out in the open where we can see them.* □ *They came out in the open.* **2.** *Fig.* [for something] to be public knowledge. (*Typically: **be** ~; **bring** something ~; **get** ~; **get** something ~.) □ *Is this matter out in the open, or is it still secret?* □ *Let's get this out in the open and discuss it.*

out like a light Go to out cold.

out of action not operating temporarily; not functioning normally. □ *The pitcher was out of action for a month because of an injury.* □ *I will be out of action for a while.*

*out of (all) proportion of exaggerated importance; of an unrealistic importance or size compared to something else. (*Typically: **be** ~; **blow** something ~; **grow** ~.) □ *This problem has grown out of all proportion.* □ *Yes, this figure is way out of proportion to the others in the painting.*

*out of breath and ***out of wind** breathing fast and hard; gasping for breath. (*Typically: **be** ~; **get** ~.) □ *I ran so much that I got out of breath.* □ *Mary gets out of wind when she climbs stairs.*

out of character 1. unlike one's usual behavior. □ *Ann's remark was quite out of character.* □ *It was out of character for Ann to act so stubborn.* **2.** inappropriate for the character that an actor is playing. □ *Bill went out of character when the audience started giggling.* □ *Bill played the part so well that it was hard for him to get out of character after the performance.*

out of circulation 1. *Lit.* no longer available for use or lending. (Usually said of library materials, certain kinds of currency, etc.) □ *I'm sorry, but the book you want is temporarily out of circulation.* □ *How long will it be out of circulation?* **2.** *Fig.* not interacting socially with other people. □ *I don't know what's happening because I've been out of circulation for a while.* □ *My cold has kept me out of circulation for a few weeks.*

out of commission 1. *Lit.* [for a ship] to be not currently in use or under command. □ *This vessel will remain out of commission for another month.* □ *The ship has been out of commission since repairs began.* **2.** *Fig.* broken, unserviceable, or inoperable; not currently in use. □ *My watch is out of commission and needs a new battery.* □ *I can't run in the marathon because my knees are out of commission.*

out of condition Go to out of shape.

out of consideration (for someone or something**)** with consideration for someone or something; with kind regard for someone or something. □ *Out of consideration for your past efforts, I will do what you ask.* □ *They let me do it out of consideration. It was very thoughtful of them.*

*out of context [of an utterance or the report of an action] removed from the surrounding context of the event, thereby misrepresenting the intent of the utterance or report. (*Typically: **be** ~; **lift** something ~; **quote** someone or something ~; **take** something ~.) □ *You took her remarks out of context! You're the dishonest person, not her!*

*out of control 1. *Lit.* [of something, such as a machine] not responding to direction or instructions. (*Typically: **be** ~; **go** ~.) □ *The computer is out of control and making funny-looking characters all over the screen.* □ *My CD player is out of control and only makes screeching noises.* **2.** and ***out of hand** *Fig.* acting wildly or violently. (*Typically: **be** ~; **get** ~.) □ *Watch out, that dog is out of control.* □ *The kids got out of hand again.*

out of courtesy (to someone**)** in order to be polite to someone; out of consideration for someone. □ *We invited Mary's brother out of courtesy to her.* □ *They invited me out of courtesy.*

*out of debt no longer owing a debt. (*Typically: **be** ~; **get** ~; **get** oneself ~.) □ *I've taken a second job so I can get myself out of debt.*

out of earshot *Fig.* too far from the source of a sound to hear the sound. □ *I was out of earshot and could not hear the conversation.* □ *Mary waited until her children were out of earshot before mentioning the presents she got them.*

out of fashion Go to out of style.

*out of favor (with someone**)** no longer desirable or preferred by someone. (*Typically: **be** ~; **go** ~.) □ *I can't ask John to help. I'm out of favor with him.* □ *That kind of thing has been out of favor for years.*

*out of focus blurred or fuzzy; seen indistinctly. (*Typically: **be** ~; **get** ~; **go** ~.) □ *What I saw through the binoculars was sort of out of focus.* □ *The scene was out of focus.*

*out of gas 1. *Lit.* without gasoline (in a car, truck, etc.). (*Typically: **be** ~; **run** ~.) □ *We can't go any farther. We're out of gas.* □ *This car will be completely out of gas in a few more miles.* **2.** *Fig.* tired; exhausted; worn out. (*Typ-

O

ically: **be** ~; **run** ~.) □ *What a day! I've been working since morning, and I'm really out of gas.* □ *I think the old washing machine has finally run out of gas. I'll have to get a new one.*

out of hand Go to out of control.

*out of harm's way *Fig.* not liable to be harmed; away from any causes of harm. (*Typically: **be** ~; **get** ~; **get** someone ~.) □ *We should try to get all the civilians out of harm's way.*

out of hock 1. *Lit.* [of something] bought back from a pawn shop. □ *When I get my watch out of hock, I will always be on time.* **2.** *Fig.* out of debt; having one's debts paid. □ *When I pay off my credit cards, I'll be out of hock for the first time in years.*

out of it 1. Go to out to lunch. **2.** intoxicated. □ *Two drinks and she was totally out of it.* □ *When they are out of it, they are quite dangerous.*

out of keeping (with something**)** [of something said or some behavior] failing to fit in with something. □ *This kind of thing is completely out of keeping with our standards of behavior.* □ *That is quite out of keeping with your statement of yesterday.*

*out of kilter and ***off-kilter 1.** *Lit.* out of balance; crooked or tilted. (*Typically: **be** ~; **get** ~; **knock** something ~.) □ *John, your tie is sort of off-kilter. Let me fix it.* □ *Please straighten the picture on the wall. It's out of kilter.* **2.** *Fig.* malfunctioning; on the fritz. (*Typically: **be** ~; **go** ~.) □ *My furnace is out of kilter. I have to call someone to fix it.* □ *This computer is out of kilter. It doesn't let me log on.*

out of left field suddenly; from an unexpected source or direction. (See also out in left field.) □ *Most of your ideas are out of left field.* □ *All of his paintings are right out of left field.*

out of line (with something**) 1.** *Lit.* not properly lined up in a line of things. □ *I told you not to get out of line. Now, get back in line.* □ *One of those books on the shelf is out of line with the others. Please fix it.* **2.** *Fig.* beyond certain set or assumed limits. □ *Your bid on this project is completely out of line with our expectations.* □ *The cost of this meal is out of line with what other restaurants charge.* □ *Your asking price is quite out of line!* **3.** *Fig.* [of something said or behavior] improper. □ *I'm afraid that your behavior was quite out of line. I do not wish to speak further about this matter.* □ *Bill, that remark was out of line. Please be more respectful.* □ *Your request is out of line.*

out of luck without good luck; having bad fortune. □ *If you wanted some ice cream, you're out of luck.* □ *I was out of luck. I got there too late to get a seat.*

out of necessity because of necessity; due to need. □ *I bought this hat out of necessity. I needed one, and this was all there was.* □ *We sold our car out of necessity.*

*out of nowhere appearing suddenly, without warning. (*Typically: **appear** ~; **come** ~; **materialize** ~.) □ *A huge bear appeared out of nowhere and roared and threatened us.* □ *Suddenly, a truck came out of nowhere.* □ *Without warning, the storm came out of nowhere.*

*out of one's **depth** *Fig.* involved in something that is beyond one's capabilities. (*Typically: **be** ~; **get** ~.) □

You know, you are really out of your depth in this project. □ *I am sure I am out of my depth in organic chemistry.*

*out of one's **element** *Fig.* not in a natural or comfortable situation. (*Typically: **be** ~; **get** ~.) □ *When it comes to computers, I'm out of my element.* □ *Sally's out of her element in math.*

out of one's **head** Go to next.

*out of one's **mind** and ***out of** one's **head; *out of** one's **senses** *Fig.* to be silly and senseless; to be crazy and irrational. (*Typically: **be** ~; **go** ~.) □ *Why did you do that? You must be out of your mind!* □ *Don't drive so fast, Tom! You have to be out of your head!*

*out of one's **skull** *Sl.* intoxicated. (*Typically: **be** ~; **go** ~.) □ *Oh, man, I drank till I was out of my skull.* □ *Two beers and he went out of his skull.*

out of one's **way** Go to out of the way.

out of order 1. *Lit.* [of something or things] out of the proper sequence. □ *She noticed that the books on the shelf were out of order.* □ *All these cards were alphabetized, and now they're out of order.* **2.** *Fig.* [of something] incapable of operating; [of something] broken. □ *The elevator is out of order again.* □ *My stereo is out of order.* **3.** *Fig.* not following correct parliamentary procedure. □ *I was declared out of order by the chair.* □ *Anne inquired, "Isn't a motion to table the question out of order at this time?"*

*out of patience annoyed and impatient after being patient for a while. (*Typically: **be** ~; **run** ~.) □ *I finally ran out of patience and lost my temper.* □ *The boss is finally out of patience with me.*

*out of place 1. *Lit.* not in the proper place. (*Typically: **be** ~; **get** ~; **knock** something ~.) □ *The book I wanted was out of place, and I almost did not find it.* □ *How did the furniture in this room get out of place?* **2.** *Fig.* inappropriate. (*Typically: **be** ~; **seem** ~.) □ *That kind of behavior is out of place at a party.* □ *Your crude language is out of place.* **3.** *Fig.* [of someone] awkward and unwelcome. (*Typically: **be** ~; **feel** ~; **seem** ~.) □ *I feel out of place at formal dances.* □ *Bob and Ann felt out of place at the picnic, so they went home.*

*out of practice performing poorly due to a lack of practice. (*Typically: **be** ~; **get** ~; **go** ~.) □ *I used to be able to play the piano extremely well, but now I'm out of practice.* □ *The baseball players lost the game because they were out of practice.*

out of print [for a book] to be no longer available from the publisher. □ *The book you want just went out of print, but perhaps I can find a used copy for you.* □ *It was published nearly ten years ago, so it's probably out of print.*

out of proportion Go to out of (all) proportion.

out of reach 1. *Lit.* not near enough to be reached or touched. □ *Place the cookies out of reach, or the children will eat them all.* □ *The mouse ran behind the piano, out of reach. The cat just sat and waited for it.* **2.** *Fig.* unattainable. □ *I wanted to be president, but I'm afraid that such a goal is out of reach.* □ *I shall choose a goal that is not out of reach.*

out of season 1. not now available for sale. □ *Sorry, oysters are out of season. We don't have any.* □ *Watermelon is out of season in the winter.* **2.** *Fig.* not now legally able to be hunted or caught. □ *Are salmon out of season?* □ *I caught a trout out of season and had to pay a fine.*

out of service inoperable; not currently operating. □ *Both elevators had been put out of service, so I had to use the stairs.* □ *The washroom is temporarily out of service.*

out of shape and **out of condition** not in good physical condition. □ *I get out of breath when I run because I'm out of shape.* □ *Keep exercising regularly, or you'll get out of condition.*

*__out of sight__ 1.** not visible; too far away to be seen. (*Typically: **be** ~; **get** ~; **go** ~; **keep** ~; **stay** ~.) □ *The cat kept out of sight until the mouse came out.* □ *"Get out of sight, or they'll see you!" called John.* **2.** figuratively stunning, unbelievable, or awesome. (*Typically: **be** ~; **get** ~.) □ *Wow, this music is out of sight!* □ *What a wild party. It's out of sight!* **3.** *Fig.* very expensive; high in price. (*Typically: **be** ~; **get** ~; **go** ~.) □ *Prices at that restaurant are out of sight.* □ *The cost of medical care has gone out of sight.* **4.** *Sl.* heavily intoxicated. (*Typically: **be** ~.) □ *They've been drinking since noon, and they're out of sight.* □ *Man, is she ever out of sight!*

Out of sight, out of mind. *Prov.* If you do not see someone or something frequently, you will forget about it. (Sometimes used to imply that you will forget about people who have moved away.) □ *Ever since I moved, none of my old friends have gotten in touch with me. It's out of sight, out of mind with them, evidently.* □ *My electric bill somehow got moved to the bottom of the stack on my desk, and I forgot all about paying it. Out of sight, out of mind.*

*__out of someone's hands__ 1.** *Lit.* no longer in someone's grasp. (*Typically: **get** ~; **pull** something ~; **take** something ~.) □ *The police officer took the gun out of Fred's hands.* □ *The heavy tray was pulled out of my hands just in time.* **2.** *Fig.* no longer in someone's control. (*Typically: **get** ~; **pull** something ~; **take** something ~.) □ *The boss decided to take the project out of Roger's hands.* □ *The contract had to be gotten out of Alice's hands because she announced that she was leaving.*

out of someone's **way** Go to out of the way.

*__out (of something)__ 1.** gone; having left some place; absent from a place; escaped. (*Typically: **be** ~; **get** ~.) □ *The monkey is out of its cage.* □ *Sam is out of the building at present.* **2.** having no more of something. (*Typically: **be** ~; **run** ~.) □ *Sorry, we are fresh out of cucumbers.* □ *We ran out of catsup and mustard halfway through the picnic.* **3.** free of the responsibility of doing something. (*Typically: **get** ~.) □ *Are you trying to get out of this job?* □ *You agreed to do it, and you can't get out of it!*

*__out of sorts__ not feeling well; grumpy and irritable. (*Typically: **be** ~; **feel** ~; **get** ~.) □ *I've been out of sorts for a day or two. I think I'm coming down with something.* □ *The baby is out of sorts. Maybe she's getting a new tooth.*

out of spite with the desire to harm someone or something. □ *Jane told some evil gossip about Bill out of spite.* □ *That was not an accident! You did it out of spite.*

*__out of step (with__ someone or something**) 1.** and *__out of time (with__ someone or something**)** *Lit.* out of cadence with someone else. (*Typically: **be** ~; **dance** ~; **get** ~; **march** ~.) □ *You've gotten out of step with the music.*

□ *Pay attention, Ann. You're out of time.* **2.** *Fig.* not as up-to-date as someone or something. (*Typically: **be** ~; **get** ~.) □ *John is out of step with the times.* □ *Billy missed three days and now is out of step with the rest of the class.*

out of stock not immediately available in a store; [for goods] to be temporarily unavailable. □ *Those items are out of stock, but a new supply will be delivered on Thursday.* □ *I'm sorry, but the red ones are out of stock. Would a blue one do?*

out of style and **out of fashion** not fashionable; old-fashioned; obsolete. (See also go out of fashion.) □ *John's clothes are really out of style.* □ *He doesn't care if his clothes are out of fashion.*

*__out of sync__ uncoordinated; unsynchronized. (An abbreviation for *synchronization.* *Typically: **be** ~; **get** ~.) □ *Our efforts are out of sync.* □ *My watch and your watch are out of sync.*

out of the ballpark *Fig.* beyond the amount of money suggested or available. □ *Your estimate is completely out of the ballpark. Just forget it.*

*__out of the closet__ 1.** *Fig.* revealing one's secret interests. (*Typically: **be** ~; **come** ~; **get** ~.) □ *Tom Brown came out of the closet and admitted that he likes to knit.* □ *It's time that all of you lovers of chamber music came out of the closet and attended our concerts.* **2.** *Fig.* revealing that one is homosexual. (*Typically: **be** ~; **come** ~; **bring** someone ~.) □ *Tom surprised his parents when he came out of the closet.* □ *It was difficult for him to be out of the closet.*

out of the corner of one's **eye** *Fig.* [seeing something] at a glance; glimpsing something, as with peripheral vision. □ *I saw someone do it out of the corner of my eye. It might have been Jane who did it.* □ *I only saw the accident out of the corner of my eye. I don't know who is at fault.*

*__out of the frying pan (and) into the fire__ *Fig.* from a bad situation to a worse situation. (*Typically: **get** ~; **go** ~; **jump** ~.) □ *When I tried to argue about my fine for a traffic violation, the judge charged me with contempt of court. I really went out of the frying pan into the fire.* □ *I got deeply in debt. Then I really got out of the frying pan into the fire when I lost my job.*

*__out of the goodness of__ one's **heart** *Fig.* simply because one is kind. (*Typically: **be** something ~; **do** something ~.) □ *What are you going to pay me? You don't expect me to do this out of the goodness of my heart, do you?*

out of the hole *Fig.* out of debt. □ *I get paid next week, and then I can get out of the hole.* □ *I can't seem to get out of the hole. I keep spending more money than I earn.*

Out of the mouths of babes (oft times come gems). *Prov.* Children occasionally say remarkable or insightful things. □ *Mr. and Mrs. Doyle were quietly bickering in the kitchen when their seven-year-old daughter came in and said, "You guys should get counseling." After a surprised pause, Mrs. Doyle remarked, "Out of the mouths of babes."* □ *Child: Don't eat so much candy, Mommy. Candy is bad for your teeth. Mother: Out of the mouths of babes oft times come gems.*

out of the ordinary unusual. □ *It was a good meal, but not out of the ordinary.* □ *Your report was nicely done, but nothing out of the ordinary.*

out of the picture *Fig.* no longer relevant to a situation; departed; dead. □ *Now that Tom is out of the picture, we needn't concern ourselves about his objections.* □ *With her husband out of the picture, she can begin living as she pleases.*

out of the question *Fig.* not allowed; not permitted. □ *I'm sorry, but your taking my car is out of the question.* □ *You can't go to Florida this spring. We can't afford it. It's out of the question.*

out of the red *Fig.* out of debt; into profitability. □ *This year our company is likely to get out of the red before fall.* □ *If we can cut down on expenses, we can get out of the red fairly soon.*

out of the running *Fig.* no longer being considered; eliminated from a contest. □ *After the first part of the diving meet, three members of our team were out of the running.* □ *After the scandal was made public, I was out of the running. I pulled out of the election.*

out of the swim of things *Fig.* not in the middle of activity; not involved in things. (The opposite of **in the swim of things**.) □ *While I had my cold, I got out of the swim of things.* □ *I've been out of the swim of things for a few weeks. Please bring me up-to-date.*

*out of the way 1. and ***out of** someone's **way; *out of the road** *Lit.* not blocking or impeding the way. (*Typically: **get** ~; **get** someone or something ~; **move** someone or something ~.) □ *Please get out of my way.* □ *Would you please get your foot out of the way?* **2.** and ***out of** one's **way** *Fig.* not along the way; not included in the proposed route. (*Typically: **be** ~.) □ *I'm sorry, but I can't give you a ride home. It's out of my way.* □ *That route is out of our way.* **3.** *Fig.* completed; finished. (*Typically: **be** ~; **get** something ~; **have** something ~.) □ *I'm sure glad to have that test out of the way.* □ *I'll be happy to have all this medical stuff out of the way.*

out (of) the window *Fig.* gone; wasted. □ *All that work gone out the window because my computer crashed.* □ *My forty dollars—out the window! Why didn't I save my money?*

out of the woods *Fig.* past a critical phase; out of the unknown. □ *When the patient got out of the woods, everyone relaxed.* □ *I can give you a better prediction for your future health when you are out of the woods.*

*out of the woodwork *Fig.* out into the open from other places or a place of concealment. (*Typically: **bring** someone or something ~; **come** ~; **creep** ~.) □ *When the cake appeared, all the office people suddenly came out of the woodwork.*

out of thin air *Fig.* out of nowhere; out of nothing. □ *Suddenly—out of thin air—the messenger appeared.* □ *You just made that excuse up out of thin air.*

out of this world 1. *Fig.* wonderful and exciting. □ *This pie is out of this world.* □ *My boyfriend is just out of this world.* **2.** intoxicated. □ *Man, is she ever out of this world! What did she drink?* □ *He drank until he was out of this world.*

out of time (with someone or something**)** Go to **out of step (with** someone or something**)**.

out of touch (with someone or something**)** *Fig.* knowing no news of someone or something; not keeping informed of the developments relating to someone or something. □ *I've been out of touch with my brother for many years.* □ *I couldn't go back into mechanics because I've been out of touch for too long.*

out of town temporarily not in one's own town. □ *I'll go out of town next week. I'm going to be at a conference.* □ *I take care of Mary's cat when she's out of town.*

*out of tune (with someone or something**) 1.** *Lit.* not in musical harmony with someone or something. (*Typically: **be** ~; **get** ~.) □ *The oboe is out of tune with the flute.* □ *The flute is out of tune with John.* □ *They are all out of tune.* **2.** *Fig.* not in agreement with someone or something. (*Typically: **be** ~.) □ *Your proposal is out of tune with my ideas of what we should be doing.* □ *Your ideas are out of tune with company policy.*

out of turn not at the proper time; not in the proper or expected order. □ *We were permitted to be served out of turn because we had to leave early.* □ *Bill tried to register out of turn and was sent away.*

*out of w(h)ack 1. crazy, silly, or irrational. (*Typically: **be** ~.) □ *Why do you always act as if you're out of whack?* □ *I'm not out of wack. I'm eccentric.* **2.** *Fig.* out of adjustment; to be out of order. (*Typically: **be** ~; **get** ~.) □ *I'm afraid that my watch is out of whack.* □ *The elevator is out of wack. We'll have to walk up.*

out of wind Go to **out of breath**.

out of work unemployed; having lost one's job. □ *Todd was out of work for almost a year.* □ *Too many people were out of work, and the economy got into trouble.*

*out on a limb 1. *Lit.* out on a limb of a tree where it is dangerous. (*Typically: **be** ~; **go** ~.) □ *It's okay to climb the tree, but don't go out on a limb and fall off.* **2.** *Fig.* in a dangerous position to do something; at risk. (*Typically: **be** ~; **go** ~; **put** someone ~.) □ *I don't want to go out on a limb, but I think we can afford to do it.* □ *If I had to go out on a limb, I would say that it will be a month before your merchandise will be delivered.*

out on bail out of jail after a court appearance and pending trial because bail bond money has been paid. (The money will be forfeited if the person who is **out on bail** does not appear for trial at the proper time.) □ *Bob got out on bail waiting for his trial.* □ *The robber committed another crime while out on bail.*

(out) on parole out of prison, conditionally, before one's total sentence is served. □ *Bob was caught using drugs while out on parole and was sent back to prison.* □ *He has to be careful and obey the law because he is out on parole.*

(out) on patrol away from a central location, watching over a distant or assigned area. (Said especially of police and soldiers.) □ *Officer Smith is out on patrol and cannot see you now.* □ *The soldiers who are on patrol on this snowy night must be very cold.*

out (on strike) to be away from one's job in a strike or protest. □ *The workers went out on strike.* □ *We can't do anything while the workers are out.*

out on the town *Fig.* celebrating at one or more places in a town. □ *I'm really tired. I was out on the town until dawn.* □ *We went out on the town to celebrate our wedding anniversary.*

Out, please. Please let me get out. (Said by someone trying to get out of an elevator. Compare this with **Coming through(, please).**) □ *The elevator stopped again, and someone at the back said, "Out, please."* □ *Jane: Out, please. This is my floor. John: I'll get out of your way. Jane: Thanks.*

out to (a meal) to be away, eating a meal. □ *Mary is out to lunch right now.* □ *Fred went out to dinner for the evening.*

out to get someone *Fig.* intending to harm someone in particular. □ *I know they are out to get me! They hate me!*

out to lunch 1. *Lit.* eating lunch away from one's place of work or activity. □ *I'm sorry, but Sally Jones is out to lunch. May I take a message?* □ *She's been out to lunch for nearly two hours. When will she be back?* **2.** and **out of it** *Fig.* not alert; giddy; uninformed. □ *Bill is really out of it. Why can't he pay attention?* □ *Don't be out of it, John. Wake up!* □ *Ann is really out to lunch these days.*

out to win determined to win. □ *Bobby is out to win at all costs! He can't face losing.*

out West in the western part of the United States. □ *We lived out West for nearly ten years.* □ *Do they really ride horses out West?*

***out-of-bounds 1.** *Lit.* outside the boundaries of the playing area. (*Typically: **be** ~; **get** ~; **go** ~.) □ *The ball went out-of-bounds just at the end of the game.* □ *The whistle blew when Juan went out-of-bounds.* **2.** and ***off-limits** *Fig.* forbidden. (*Typically: **be** ~.) □ *This area is off-limits. You can't go in there.* □ *Don't go there. It's out-of-bounds.* □ *That kind of behavior is off-limits. Stop it!*

out-of-pocket expenses *Fig.* the actual amount of money spent. (Alludes to the money one person pays while doing something on someone else's behalf. One is usually paid back this money.) □ *My out-of-pocket expenses for the party were nearly $175.* □ *My employer usually reimburses all out-of-pocket expenses for a business trip.*

outside of something except for something; besides something. □ *Outside of the cost of my laundry, I have practically no expenses.* □ *Outside of some new shoes, I don't need any new clothing.*

***over a barrel** *Fig.* out of one's control; in a dilemma. (*Typically: **get** someone ~; **have** someone ~; **put** someone ~.) □ *He got me over a barrel, and I had to do what he said.* □ *Ann will do exactly what I say. I've got her over a barrel.*

over and above something *Fig.* more than something; in addition to something. □ *I'll need another twenty dollars over and above the amount you have already given me.* □ *You've been eating too much food over and above what is required for good nutrition. That's why you're gaining weight.*

***over (and done) with** finished. (*Typically: **be** ~; **get** something ~; **have** something ~.) □ *I'm glad that's over and done with.* □ *Now that I have college over and done with, I can get a job.*

Over and out. I am finished talking. (From two-way radio communications.) □ *That's all. Good day. Over and out.*

over and over (again) repeatedly. □ *She stamped her foot over and over again.* □ *Bill whistled the same song over and over.*

over easy *Fig.* [of eggs] turned carefully during cooking. □ *I want mine cooked over easy.* □ *Over easy eggs are better than scrambled.*

Over my dead body! *Inf. Fig.* a defiant phrase indicating the strength of one's opposition to something. (A joking response is "That can be arranged.") □ *Sally: Alice says she'll join the circus no matter what anybody says. Father: Over my dead body! Sally: Now, now. You know how she is.* □ *Bill: I think I'll rent out our spare bedroom. Sue: Over my dead body! Bill (smiling): That can be arranged.*

***over** someone's **head 1.** *Fig.* [of the intellectual content of something] too difficult for someone to understand. (*Typically: **be** ~; **go** ~; **pass** ~.) □ *All that talk about computers went over my head.* □ *I hope my lecture didn't go over the students' heads.* **2.** and ***over** someone; ***above** someone *Fig.* to an authority higher than someone. (*Typically: **be** ~; **go** ~.) □ *I don't want to have to go over your head, but I will if necessary.* □ *I had to go over Fran to get it done.* □ *My boss wouldn't listen to my complaint, so I went above her.*

over the counter *Fig.* [of medication bought or sold] without a prescription. (Hyphenated when prenominal. See also **under the counter**.) □ *This is a good product. You can buy it over the counter.* □ *I don't put much trust in over-the-counter medications.*

over the edge *Fig.* excessive; out of control. □ *His performance was over the edge. Too long, too dirty, and too loud!*

***over the hill 1.** *Fig. Inf.* escaped from prison or the military. (*Typically: **be** ~; **go** ~.) □ *Two privates went over the hill last night.* □ *They broke out of jail and went over the hill.* **2.** *Fig.* too old (for something). (*Typically: **be** ~; **go** ~.) □ *You're only fifty! You're not over-the-hill yet.* □ *Some people seem over-the-hill at thirty.*

over the hump 1. *Fig.* over the hard part; past the midpoint. □ *Things should be easy from now on. We finally got over the hump.* □ *When you get over the hump, life is much better.* **2.** intoxicated on drugs. □ *Harry is over the hump now. He is stoned.* □ *This stuff makes you sick at first. Then suddenly you are over the hump and floating.*

over the long haul and **in the long haul; in the long run** *Fig.* long term; over a long period of time. □ *Over the long haul, this model will prove best.* □ *This will last in the long haul.*

over the short haul and **in the short haul; in the short run** *Fig.* for the immediate future. □ *Over the short haul, you'd be better off to put your money in the bank.* □ *Over the short haul, you may wish you had done something different. But things will work out all right.*

over the top 1. *Fig.* having gained more than one's goal. □ *Our fund-raising campaign went over the top by $3,000.* □ *We didn't go over the top. We didn't even get half of what we set out to collect.* **2.** *Fig.* outrageously overdone. □ *The comedy sketch was so over-the-top that most of the audience was embarrassed.*

***over the wall** reaching freedom from a prison. (*Typically: **be** ~; **go** ~.) □ *Max tried to go over the wall, but they caught him.* □ *Lefty was over the wall for a week before that caught him.*

*over (with) finished; concluded. (*Typically: **be** ~; **get** ~.) □ *I hope this thing gets over with pretty soon.* □ *When will the lecture get over?*

overdose (someone) on something and **overdose** someone **with** something to give someone too much of some substance, usually a drug. □ *The police say he overdosed on heroine.* □ *Sam overdosed his sister on the cough medicine.* □ *She overdosed herself with aspirin.*

overflow into something to spill over into something. □ *The river overflowed into the surrounding farmland.* □ *The water in the bowl overflowed into the sink.*

overflow with someone or something to have so much or so many people or things that they spill over. □ *The kitchen overflowed with the guests.* □ *My cup overflowed with coffee and spilled on the counter.*

owe someone **a debt of gratitude** a large amount of thanks owed to someone who deserves gratitude. (Actually payment of the debt is owed.) □ *We owe you a debt of gratitude for all you have done for us.*

owe someone **a pound of flesh** Go to a pound of flesh.

owe something **(to** someone**) (for** something**)** to be under obligation to pay or repay someone for something. □ *I owe forty dollars to Ann for the dinner.* □ *I owe money for the gift to Ann.* □ *I still owe money for the gift.* □ *Do you still owe money to Ann?*

owing to because of something; due to the fact of something. □ *Owing to the lateness of the evening, I must go home.* □ *We were late owing to the heavy traffic.*

own flesh and blood Go to flesh and blood.

own up to someone to confess or admit something to someone. □ *Finally, he owned up to his mother about breaking the vase.* □ *We had hoped he would own up to us sooner.*

own up (to something**)** to admit something; to confess to something. □ *I know you broke the window. Come on and own up to it.*

O

pace around and **pace about** to walk around nervously or anxiously. □ *Stop pacing around and sit down.* □ *There is no need to pace about.*

pace back and forth and **pace up and down** to walk over and over the same short route nervously or anxiously. □ *The leopard paced back and forth in its cage.* □ *I paced up and down, worrying about a variety of things.*

pace something **off**† to mark off a distance by counting the number of even strides taken while walking. □ *The farmer paced a few yards off and pounded a stake into the soil.* □ *He paced off a few yards.*

pace something **out**† **1.** *Lit.* to measure a distance by counting the number of even strides taken while walking. □ *He paced the distance out and wrote it down.* □ *He paced out the distance from the door to the mailbox.* **2.** *Fig.* to deal with a problem by pacing around. □ *When she was upset, she walked and walked while she thought through her problem. When Ed came into the room, she was pacing a new crisis out.* □ *She usually paced out her anxiety.*

pace up and down Go to **pace back and forth**.

pack a punch Go to next.

pack a wallop and **pack a punch** *Fig.* to provide a burst of energy, power, or excitement. □ *Wow, this spicy food really packs a wallop.* □ *I put a special kind of gasoline in my car because I thought it would pack a punch. It didn't.*

pack down [for something] to settle down in a container. □ *The cereal has packed down in the box so that it seems that the box is only half full.* □ *Everything was packed down carefully inside.*

pack it in 1. *Fig.* to quit trying to do something; to give up trying something and quit. □ *I was so distressed that I almost packed it in.* □ *I've had enough! I'm going to pack it in.* **2.** *Fig.* to go to bed. □ *Good night. It's time for me to pack it in.* □ *We drove to a hotel and packed it in.*

a **pack of lies** a series of lies. □ *The thief told a pack of lies to cover up the crime.* □ *John listened to Bill's pack of lies about the fight and became very angry.*

pack someone **off**† **(to** someone or something**)** to send someone away to someone or some place. □ *Laura just packed all the kids off to summer camp.* □ *She packed off the kids to their camp.* □ *After a lot of planning and a few tears, she packed them all off.*

pack someone or something **in**† Go to **pack** someone or something **into** something.

pack someone or something **(in**†**) like sardines** *Fig.* to squeeze in as many people or things as possible. (From the way that many sardines are packed into a can.) □ *They packed us in like sardines. There was no room to breathe.* □ *They packed in the people like sardines.* □ *Dave got a box and packed old negatives in like sardines.*

pack someone or something **into** something and **pack** someone or something **in**† to press or push someone or something into something; to manage to get a lot of things or people into a place. □ *The boys packed a lot of kids into a telephone booth as a gag.* □ *They packed in a lot of kids.*

pack someone or something **together**† to press or squeeze people or things together. □ *The ushers packed the people together as much as they dared.* □ *They packed together all the people standing in the room.* □ *They packed the cups together too tightly and some broke.*

pack something **away**† to pack something up and put it away. □ *Pack this mirror away where it will be safe.* □ *Please pack away this mirror carefully.*

pack something **down**† to make something more compact; to press something in a container down so it takes less space. □ *The traffic packed down the snow.* □ *Pack the grass down in the basket so the basket will hold more.*

pack something **in** something to surround or enclose something in something. □ *They packed his wounded hand in ice, then took him to the hospital.* □ *Pack the vase in shredded paper before you close the box.*

pack something **off**† **(to** someone or something**)** to send something to someone or something. □ *I will pack the books off to you immediately.* □ *She packed off the books to my home address.* □ *Harry found the books I wanted and packed them off.*

pack something **up**† **(in** something**)** to prepare something to be transported by placing it into a container. □ *Gerry will pack the dishes up in a strong box, using lots of crumpled paper.* □ *Please pack up the dishes carefully.*

pack them in *Fig.* to draw a lot of people. □ *It was a good night at the theater. The play really packed them in.* □ *The circus manager knew he could pack them in if he advertised the lion tamer.*

pack up to prepare one's belongings to be transported by placing them into a container; to gather one's things together for one's departure. □ *If we are going to leave in the morning, we should pack up now.* □ *I think you should pack up and be ready to leave at a moment's notice.* □ *He didn't say good-bye. He just packed up and left.*

a **package deal** *Fig.* a collection or group of related goods or services sold as a unit. □ *I got all these tools in a package deal for only $39.95.* □ *What about giving me all three shirts as a package deal?*

packed (in) like sardines *Fig.* packed very tightly. □ *It was terribly crowded there. We were packed in like sardines.* □ *The bus was full. The passengers were packed like sardines.*

pad down (some place**)** *Sl.* to make one's bed somewhere, usually a casual or temporary bed. □ *Do you mind if I pad down at your place for the night?* □ *Can I pad down tonight?*

pad out *Sl.* to go to bed or to sleep. □ *Man, if I don't pad out by midnight, I'm a zombie.* □ *Why don't you people go home so I can pad out?*

pad something **out**† *Fig.* to make something appear to be larger or longer by adding unnecessary material. □ *If we pad the costume out here, it will make the person who wears it look much plumper.* □ *Let's pad out this paragraph a little.*

pad the bill *Fig.* to put unnecessary or additional items on a bill to make the total cost higher. □ *The plumber had padded the bill with things we didn't need.* □ *I was falsely accused of padding the bill.*

paddle one's **own canoe** *Fig.* to do something by oneself; to be alone. □ *I've been left to paddle my own canoe too many times.* □ *Sally isn't with us. She's off paddling her own canoe.*

a **pain in the ass** and a **pain in the butt**; a **pain in the rear** *Fig.* a very annoying thing or person. (Crude. Potentially offensive. Use only with discretion. An elaboration of *pain.* Use caution with *ass. Butt* is less offensive. *Rear* is euphemistic.) □ *That guy is a real pain in the ass.* □ *Things like that give me a pain in the butt.*

a **pain in the neck** *Fig.* a bother; an annoyance. □ *This assignment is a pain in the neck.* □ *Your little brother is a pain in the neck.*

a **pain in the rear** Go to a **pain in the ass.**

paint on something to apply paint to the surface of something. □ *He painted on the fence a while and then went inside to rest.* □ *Please don't paint on the area that is not sanded down.*

paint over something to cover something up with a layer of paint. □ *Sam painted over the rusty part of the fence.* □ *The work crew was told to paint over the graffiti.*

paint something **in**† to paint something extra onto a painted area. □ *I know that there is supposed to be a big white spot here. We will have to paint it in.* □ *We will have to paint in the spot.*

paint something **onto** something and **paint** something **on**† to apply a design or picture to something, using paint. □ *Joel painted the portrait onto a large sheet of plywood.* □ *He painted on some leaves and flowers too.*

paint something **out**† to cover something up or obliterate something by applying a layer of paint. □ *The worker painted the graffiti out.* □ *They had to paint out the graffiti.*

paint the town (red) *Sl.* to go out and celebrate; to go on a drinking bout; to get drunk. □ *I feel like celebrating my promotion. Let's go out and paint the town.* □ *They were out painting the town red last night.*

pair off [for two people or other creatures] to form a couple or pair. □ *All of them paired off and worked as teams to solve the puzzle.* □ *Everyone should pair off and discuss the issue for a while.*

pair up (with someone**)** to join with someone to make a pair. □ *Sally decided to pair up with Jason for the dance contest.* □ *Sally and Jason paired up with each other.*

pal around (with someone**)** to associate with someone as a good friend. □ *I like to pal around with my friends on the weekends.* □ *They like to pal around.* □ *They often palled around with each other.*

pal up (with someone**)** to join with someone as a friend. □ *I palled up with Henry and we had a fine time together.*

□ *We palled up and had a fine time together.* □ *They palled up with each other.*

pale around the gills and **blue around the gills; green around the gills** *Fig.* looking sick. (The *around* can be replaced with *about.*) □ *John is looking a little pale around the gills. What's wrong?* □ *Oh, I feel a little green about the gills.*

***pale as a ghost** and ***pale as death** very pale. (*Also: **as** ~ .) □ *Laura came into the room, as pale as a ghost. "What happened?" her friends gasped.* □ *What's the matter? You're pale as death!*

pale as death Go to previous.

pale at something to become weak, frightened, or pale from fear of something or the thought of something. □ *Bob paled at the thought of having to drive all the way back to get the forgotten suitcase.* □ *We paled at the notion that we would always be poor.*

pale beside someone or something *Fig.* to appear to be weak or unimportant when compared to someone or something. □ *He is competent, but he pales beside Fran.* □ *My meager effort pales beside your masterpiece.*

pale by comparison and **pale in comparison** *Fig.* to appear to be deficient in comparison to something else. □ *My work pales by comparison with yours. You are a real pro.*

pally (with someone**)** friendly or overly friendly with someone, as a pal would be. □ *I don't know why Sue acts so pally. I hardly know her.* □ *She doesn't seem pally with me.*

palm someone or something **off**† **(on** someone**) (as** someone or something**)** and **pass** someone or something **off**† **(on** someone**) (as** someone or something**); pawn** someone or something **off**† **(on** someone**) (as** someone or something**)** *Fig.* to give someone or something to someone as a gift that appears to be someone or something desirable. (As if the gift had been concealed in one's palm until it was gotten rid of.) □ *Are you trying to palm that annoying client off on me as a hot prospect?* □ *Don't palm off that pest on me.* □ *Please don't pass that problem off on me as a challenge.* □ *Don't pass it off on me!* □ *Don't pawn it off on me as something of value.*

pan across to someone or something to turn or rotate a film or television camera so that the picture follows movement or moves to and settles on someone or something. □ *The camera panned across to Mary, who was sitting, looking out the window.* □ *The camera operator panned across to the window on the opposite side of the room.*

pan for something to search for a precious metal, usually gold, by using a pan to locate the bits of metal in sand and gravel in a stream bed. □ *When I was in Alaska, I panned for gold in a little stream set aside for tourists.* □ *The old prospector spent many hours panning for gold.*

pan in (on someone or something**)** Go to **zoom in (on** someone or something**).**

pan out 1. and **zoom out** to move back to a wider angle picture using a zoom lens. □ *The camera zoomed out.* □ *Pan out at this point in the script and give a wider view of the scene.* **2.** Go to **turn out (all right).**

pan over someone or something to turn or rotate a film or television camera so that the picture moves across a view

P

of someone or something. □ *The camera panned over the skyline, picking up interesting cloud formations.* □ *It panned over Roger as if he weren't there—which is exactly the effect the director wanted.*

pander to someone or something to cater toward undesirable tastes or people with undesirable tastes. □ *All your writing seems to pander to persons with poor taste.* □ *You are pandering to the moral dregs of society.*

panic at something to lose control in a frightening or shocking situation. □ *Try not to panic at what you see. It will be a shock.* □ *Don't panic at the price of food. It will be worse next week.*

panic someone **by** something to make someone lose control by doing something. □ *She panicked Denise by describing the event too vividly.* □ *She panicked her horse by jerking the reins too tightly.*

pant for air to breathe fast and hard in need of air. □ *The dog was panting for air.* □ *I was panting for air after my long climb.*

pant for someone or something *Fig.* to desire or long for someone or something. □ *My heart is panting for you!* □ *I am just panting for some interesting news.*

pant something **out**† to tell something while panting for breath. □ *Laura had been running but she was able to pant the name of the injured person out.* □ *She panted out the name.*

paper over something **1.** *Lit.* to put a layer of wallpaper on a wall. □ *We papered over the wall, giving the room a bright, new look.* □ *We papered over the old plaster on the wall.* **2.** to cover up some sort of blemish on a wall with wallpaper. □ *We papered over a lot of little cracks.* □ *Sam papered over all the flaws in the plaster wall.* **3.** *Fig.* to conceal something; to cover something up. □ *Don't try to paper over the mess you have made.* □ *George tried to paper over all his mistakes.*

paper over the cracks (in something**)** *Fig.* to try to hide faults or difficulties, often in a hasty or not very successful way. (Based on **paper over** something ②.) □ *The politician tried to paper over the cracks in his party's economic policy.* □ *Tom tried to paper over the cracks in his relationship with the boss, but it was not possible.* □ *She didn't explain it. She just papered over the cracks.*

*a **paper trail** *Fig.* a series of records that is possible to examine to find out the sequence of things that happen. (*Typically: **have** ~; **leave** ~; **make** ~.) □ *The legal department requires all these forms so that there is a paper trail of all activity.*

par for the course typical; about what one could expect. (This refers to golf courses, not school courses.) □ *So he went off and left you? Well that's about par for the course. He's no friend.* □ *I worked for days on this proposal, but it was rejected. That's par for the course around here.*

parade by (someone**)** to march past someone in a parade or as if in a parade. □ *The soldiers paraded by the commander in chief.* □ *Looking quite sharp, they paraded by.*

parade someone or an animal **out**† to bring or march someone or an animal out in public. □ *He parades his children out every Sunday as they go to church.* □ *He paraded out all his children.*

parade someone or something **in front of** someone or something to exhibit someone or something in front of someone or something, as if in a parade. □ *One by one, the teacher paraded the honor students in front of the parents.* □ *The sheriff paraded the suspects in front of the camera.* □ *The sheriff paraded the suspects in front of the victim.*

a **paradise (on earth)** *Fig.* a place on earth that is as lovely as paradise. □ *The retirement home was simply a paradise on earth.* □ *The beach where we went for our vacation was a paradise.*

parcel someone or something **out**† *Fig.* to divide up and send or give away people or things. □ *Carla parceled all the uniforms out so everyone would have one to wear for the parade.* □ *We will parcel out the children for the summer.*

parcel something **up**† to wrap something up in a package. □ *Would you parcel the papers up and set them in the corner?* □ *Parcel up the files and place them on top of the file cabinet.*

Pardon (me). Go to Excuse me.

Pardon me for living! *Inf.* a very indignant response to a criticism or rebuke. □ *Fred: Oh, I thought you had already taken yourself out of here! Sue: Well, pardon me for living!* □ *Tom: Butt out, Mary! Bill and I are talking. Mary: Pardon me for living!*

Pardon my French. and **Excuse my French.** *Inf.* Excuse my use of swear words or taboo words. (Does not refer to real French.) □ *Pardon my French, but this is a hell of a day.* □ *What she needs is a kick in the ass, if you'll excuse my French.*

pardon someone **for** something **1.** to excuse someone for doing something. □ *Will you please pardon me for what I did?* □ *I can't pardon her for that.* **2.** to excuse and release a convicted criminal. □ *The governor pardoned Max for his crime.* □ *The governor did not pardon any drug dealers for their crimes.*

pare something **down**† **(to** something**)** to cut someone down to something or a smaller size. □ *I will have to pare the budget down to the minimum.* □ *I hope we can pare down the budget.* □ *After much arguing, we pared it down.*

pare something **off (of)** something and **pare** something **off**† to cut something off something. (*Of* is usually retained before pronouns.) □ *See if you can pare a bit of this extra wood off the edge of the base of this pillar.* □ *Pare off some of the wood.*

park it (somewhere**)** *Inf.* sit down somewhere; sit down and get out of the way. □ *Hey, park it! You're in the way.* □ *Richard, park it over there in the corner. Stop pacing around. You make me nervous.*

parlay something **into** something *Fig.* to exploit an asset in such a way as to increase its value to some higher amount. □ *She is trying to parlay her temporary job into a full-time position.* □ *Alice parlayed her inheritance into a small fortune by investing in the stock market.*

parley with someone *Fig.* to talk with someone. □ *I need to parley with my brother before making a financial commitment.* □ *We need to parley with each other sometime soon.*

part and parcel Go to bag and baggage.

P

part company (with someone) *Fig.* to leave someone; to depart from someone. □ *Tom finally parted company with his brother.* □ *They parted company, and Tom got in his car and drove away.*

part from someone to leave someone. □ *I just hate parting from you.* □ *I must part from her now.*

a **part in** something Go to a **hand in** something.

part over something [for people] to separate because of something. □ *We had to part over our disagreement.* □ *They parted over a very small matter.*

part someone or an animal **from** someone or an animal to take someone or an animal away from someone or some other animal. □ *It was difficult to part the mother dog from her puppies.* □ *I hated to part the mother from her child.*

part someone's **hair 1.** *Lit.* to divide someone's hair into separate sections while combing it. □ *The barber asked me where I parted my hair.* **2.** *Fig.* to come very close to someone. (Usually an exaggeration.) □ *That plane flew so low that it nearly parted my hair.* □ *He punched at me and missed. He only parted my hair.*

part with someone or something to give up or let go of someone or something. □ *She did not want to part with her friend.* □ *I could never part with my books.*

partake in something to participate in something. □ *Valerie does not care to partake in those childish games.* □ *I would like to partake in the fun.*

partake of something **1.** to have a portion of something, such as food or drink. □ *Would you care to partake of this apple pie with me?* □ *I would like to partake of that fine dinner I see set out on the table.* **2.** to take part in or experience something. □ *Sarah had always wanted to partake of the good life.* □ *Roger had no intention of partaking of the events offered at the fair.*

*partial to someone or something favoring or preferring someone or something. (*Typically: **be** ~; **get** ~.) □ *The boys think their teacher is partial to female students.* □ *I am partial to vanilla ice cream.*

partially sighted *Euph.* not able to see well. □ *Carrie is partially sighted, but she is not able to see well enough to read.* □ *I am not blind. I am partially sighted.*

participate (in something) **(with** someone or something**)** to take part in something with someone or a group. □ *I will not participate in this activity with you.* □ *They don't participate with our team in this contest.*

the **particulars of** something specific details about something. □ *My boss stressed the important particulars of the project.* □ *What are the particulars of your request?*

a **parting of the ways** a point at which people separate and go their own ways. (Often with *come to a, arrive at a, reach a,* etc.) □ *Jane and Bob finally came to a parting of the ways.* □ *Bill and his parents reached a parting of the ways.*

partition something **into** something to divide or separate something into something [smaller]. □ *I will partition this room into two separate spaces.* □ *Do you think you can partition this box into four compartments so we can store files by quarter?*

partition something **off**[†] to divide off a section of something. □ *They planned to partition the basement off.* □ *We will partition off a larger area.*

partners in crime 1. *Fig.* persons who cooperate in committing a crime or a deception. (Usually an exaggeration.) □ *The sales manager and the used-car salesmen are nothing but partners in crime.* **2.** persons who cooperate in some legal task. □ *The legal department and payroll are partners in crime as far as the average worker is concerned.*

the **party line** *Fig.* the official ideas and attitudes that are adopted by the leaders of a particular group and that the other members are expected to accept. □ *Tom has left the club. He refused to follow the party line.* □ *Many politicians agree with the party line without thinking.*

The **party's over.** *Fig.* A happy or fortunate time has come to an end. □ *We go back to school tomorrow. The party's over.* □ *The staff hardly worked at all under the old management, but they'll find the party's over now.*

a **party to** something a participant in something; someone who is involved in something. □ *I refuse to be a party to your dishonest plan!*

pass as someone or something to succeed in being accepted as someone or something. □ *The spy was able to pass as a regular citizen.* □ *The thief was arrested when he tried to pass as a priest.*

pass away and **pass on** *Euph.* to die. □ *My aunt passed away last month.* □ *When I pass on, I won't care about the funeral.*

pass by (someone or something**)** to move or travel past someone, something, or some place. □ *Please don't pass by me so fast.* □ *If you pass by a large white house with a red roof, you have gone too far.*

pass for someone or something to be accepted as someone, some type of person, or something. □ *You could pass for your twin brother.* □ *This painting could almost pass for the original.*

pass for something to pay for something; to treat someone by paying for something. □ *Come on. Let's go out. I'll pass for dinner.* □ *I'll pass for drinks if you want.*

pass from something to fade away from something; to go away gradually. □ *The larger trees had passed from the scene years ago.* □ *The exact details passed from Harry's memory some time ago.*

pass gas *Euph.* to release intestinal gas through the anus. □ *Someone on the bus had passed gas. It smelled awful.* □ *Something I ate at lunch made me pass gas all afternoon.*

pass in review [for marchers] to move past an important person for a visual examination. □ *All the soldiers passed in review on the Fourth of July.* □ *As they passed in review, each of them saluted the officers on the reviewing stand.*

pass into something to move into something; to fade away into something. □ *Thoughts about the accident, little by little, passed into oblivion.* □ *All her old school chums passed into oblivion.*

pass judgment (on someone or something**)** to make a judgment about someone or something. □ *I should not pass judgment on you, but I certainly could give you some good advice about how to be more pleasant.* □ *The judge*

P

passed judgment on the defendant, who was then taken away to prison.

pass muster *Fig.* to measure up to the required standards. ☐ *I tried, but my efforts didn't pass muster.* ☐ *If you don't wear a jacket and tie, you won't pass muster at that fancy restaurant. They won't let you in.*

pass on Go to **pass away.**

pass on someone or something to accept or approve someone or something. ☐ *She refused to pass on Ted, so he will not be appointed.* ☐ *The committee passed on the proposal, so work can now begin.*

pass out to faint; to lose consciousness. ☐ *Oh, look! Tom has passed out.* ☐ *When he got the news, he passed out.*

pass over (someone or something) **1.** to skip over someone or something; to fail to select someone or something. ☐ *I was next in line for a promotion, but they passed over me.* ☐ *I passed over the bruised apples and picked out the nicest ones.* **2.** to pass above someone or something. ☐ *A cloud passed over our little group, cooling us a little.* ☐ *The huge blimp passed over the little community.*

pass over someone's **head** Go to **over** someone's **head.**

pass sentence on someone **1.** *Lit.* [for a judge] to read out the sentence of punishment for a convicted criminal. ☐ *It is my job as judge to pass sentence on you.* ☐ *The judge was about to pass sentence on Max—ten years in prison.* **2.** *Fig.* [for someone] to render a judgment on another person in the manner of a judge. ☐ *You have no right to pass judgment on me!* ☐ *I wish you wouldn't pass judgment on everyone around you.*

pass someone **on**† **(to** someone**)** to send, hand, or conduct a person to someone else. ☐ *I passed the baby on to the next admiring relative.* ☐ *She passed on the baby to her aunt.*

pass someone or something **by**† to miss someone or something; to overlook someone or something. ☐ *The storm passed by the town leaving it unharmed.* ☐ *The teacher passed me by and chose the next person in line.*

pass someone or something **off**† **(on** someone**) (as** someone or something**)** Go to **palm** someone or something **off**† **(on** someone**) (as** someone or something**).**

pass someone or something **up**† **1.** to fail to select someone or something. ☐ *The committee passed Jill up and chose Kelly.* ☐ *They passed up Jill.* **2.** to travel past someone or something. ☐ *We had to pass the museum up, thinking we could visit the next time we were in town.* ☐ *We passed up a hitchhiker.*

pass something **along**† **(to** someone**) 1.** to give or hand something to someone. ☐ *Would you kindly pass this along to Hillary?* ☐ *Please pass along my advice to Wally over there.* **2.** to relay some information to someone. ☐ *I hope you don't pass this along to anyone, but I am taking a new job next month.* ☐ *Could you pass along my message to Fred?*

pass something **around**† **(to** someone**)** to offer something to everyone. ☐ *Please pass the snacks around to everyone.* ☐ *Would you pass around the snacks?*

pass something **back (to** someone**)** to return something by hand to someone. ☐ *Kelly passed the pictures back to Betty.* ☐ *They weren't Betty's and she passed them back to Beth.*

pass something **down**† **(to** someone**)** and **pass** something **on (to** someone**) 1.** to send something down a line of people to someone. (Each person hands it to the next.) ☐ *Please pass this down to Mary at the end of the row.* ☐ *Pass down this box to Mary.* **2.** to will something to someone. ☐ *My grandfather passed this watch down to me.* ☐ *He passed on the watch to me.*

pass something **forward** to send something toward the front of a group of people. (Each person hands it to the next.) ☐ *Please pass this forward to the front of the room.* ☐ *Would you pass this book forward, please?*

pass something **in**† **(to** someone**)** and **hand** something **in**† **(to** someone**)** to turn in or hand in something, such as a school assignment, paper, etc., to someone. ☐ *They were told to pass their papers in to the teacher.* ☐ *Hand in your papers to me.*

pass something **off**† Go to **pass** something **off (on** someone**) (as** something**).**

pass something **off (as** something**)** Go to **shrug** something **off (as** something**).**

pass something **off (on** someone**) (as** something**)** and **pass** something **off**† to get rid of something deceptively by giving or selling it to someone as something else. ☐ *I passed the rhinestone off on John as a diamond.* ☐ *Don't try to pass that fake off on me!* ☐ *He couldn't pass off the stone on the clever jeweler.*

pass something **on**† **1.** *Lit.* to hand or give something (to another person). ☐ *Have a piece of toffee and pass the box on.* ☐ *Please pass on this book to the next person on the list.* **2.** *Fig.* to tell someone something; to spread news or gossip. ☐ *Don't pass this on, but Bill isn't living at home any more.* ☐ *I refuse to pass on rumors.*

pass something **on (to** someone**)** Go to **pass** something **down**† **(to** someone**).**

pass something **out**† **(to** someone**)** to distribute something to someone. ☐ *Please pass these out to everyone.* ☐ *Pass out these papers to everyone.*

pass something **over (to** someone**)** to send something to someone farther down in a line of people. (Each person hands it to the next.) ☐ *Please pass this paper over to Jane.* ☐ *Would you pass this paper over to Jane?*

pass something **to** someone to hand or send something to someone, usually by way of a number of other people. ☐ *Please pass this paper to Betty.* ☐ *Who passed this to me?*

pass the buck *Fig.* to pass the blame (to someone else); to give the responsibility (to someone else). (See also **The buck stops here.**) ☐ *Don't try to pass the buck! It's your fault, and everybody knows it.* ☐ *Some people try to pass the buck whenever they can.*

pass the hat (around†**) (to** someone**)** *Fig.* to collect donations of money from people. (Could also be literal.) ☐ *Jerry passed the hat around to all the other workers.* ☐ *He passed around the hat to everyone.* ☐ *I'll pass the hat around.*

pass the time (of day) to spend time doing something; to consume or use spare time by doing something. ☐ *I read to pass the time while waiting in the doctor's office.* ☐ *I passed the time of day by talking to Dave.*

pass the time of day (with someone**)** to chat or talk informally with someone. □ *I saw Mr. Brown in town yesterday. I stopped and passed the time of day with him.* □ *No, we didn't have a serious talk; we just passed the time of day.*

pass through someone to be digested through the bowels of someone. □ *This fruit should pass through you in no time at all.* □ *He will be better when the offending food passes through him.*

pass through someone's **mind** and **cross** someone's **mind** *Fig.* [for a thought] to come to mind briefly; [for an idea] to occur to someone. □ *Let me tell you what just crossed my mind.* □ *As you were speaking, something passed through my mind that I'd like to discuss.*

pass through something to travel through something or some place. □ *I passed through the countryside and breathed the good clean air.* □ *Perhaps I will stop and visit Joe the next time I pass through Adamsville.*

pass under something to move or travel beneath something. □ *The ship slowly passed under the bridge.* □ *Harry counted the cars as they passed under the bridge.*

passport to something *Fig.* something that allows something good to happen. □ *John's new girlfriend is his passport to happiness.* □ *Anne's new job is a passport to financial security.*

past caring *Fig.* [of someone] beyond caring about someone or something that is hopeless. □ *I don't care what you do! I'm past caring!*

***a** **past master at** something *Fig.* someone proven extremely good or skillful at an activity. (*Typically: **be ~; become ~**.) □ *Mary is a past master at cooking omelets.* □ *Pam is a past master at the art of complaining.*

past someone's or something's **prime** *Fig.* beyond the most useful or productive period. □ *Joan was a wonderful singer, but she's past her prime now.* □ *This old car's past its prime. I'll need to get a new one.*

paste someone **one** *Sl.* to land a blow on someone. □ *I pasted him one right on the nose.* □ *Next time you do that, I'll paste you one!*

paste something **down**[†] to secure something down [onto something] with paste or glue. □ *The poster will look better if you will paste the loose edges down.* □ *Please paste down the edges.*

paste something **on** someone **1.** *Lit.* to affix something to someone with paste or glue. □ *We had to paste a mustache on her for the last scene of the play.* □ *They pasted beards on themselves too.* **2.** *Sl.* to charge someone with a crime. □ *You can't paste that charge on me! Max did it!* □ *The cops pasted a robbery charge on Lefty "Fingers" Moran.* **3.** *Sl.* to land a blow on someone. (See also **paste** someone **one**.) □ *If you do that again, I'll paste one on you.* □ *Max pasted a nasty blow on Lefty's chin.*

paste something **up**[†] **1.** to repair something with paste. □ *See if you can paste this book up so it will hold together.* □ *Paste up the book and hope it holds together for a while.* **2.** to assemble a complicated page of material by pasting the parts together. □ *There is no way a typesetter can get this page just the way you want it. You'll have to paste it up yourself.* □ *Paste up this page again and let me see it.*

a **pat answer** a quick, easy answer; a simplified or evasive answer. □ *Don't just give them a pat answer. Give some more explanation and justification. Otherwise you will just end up answering a lot more questions.*

pat someone **on the back** and **give** someone **a pat on the back 1.** *Lit.* to pat someone's back to show praise. □ *The coach patted each player on the back after the game.* **2.** *Fig.* to praise someone for something. □ *The teacher patted all the students on the back for their good work.* □ *They were patting themselves on the back for winning when the final whistle blew.*

pat someone or something **on** something to tap someone or something on a particular place with the open hand. □ *She patted the child on the bottom.* □ *I patted the car on its hood to show how proud I was of it.*

pat something **down**[†] to tap something down with the open hand. □ *I heaped some soil over the seeds and patted it down.* □ *I patted down the soil.*

patch a quarrel up[†] *Fig.* to put an end to a quarrel; to reconcile quarreling parties. □ *Tom and Fred were able to patch their quarrel up.* □ *I hope we can patch up this quarrel.*

patch someone **up**[†] to give medical care to someone. □ *That cut looks bad, but the doc over there can patch you up.* □ *The doc patched up my friend.*

patch something **together (with** something**)** to use something to repair something hastily or temporarily. □ *I think I can patch the exhaust pipe together with some wire.* □ *See if you can patch this engine together well enough to run for a few more hours.*

patch something **up**[†] **1.** *Lit.* to repair something in a hurry; to make something temporarily serviceable again. □ *Can you patch this up so I can use it again?* □ *I'll patch up the hose for you.* **2.** *Fig.* to "repair" the damage done by an argument or disagreement. □ *Mr. and Mrs. Smith are trying to patch things up.* □ *We patched up our argument, then kissed and made up.*

the **path of least resistance** *Fig.* the easiest course to follow; the easiest route. (Often with *follow the* or *take the*.) □ *John will follow the path of least resistance.* □ *I like challenges. I won't usually take the path of least resistance.*

Patience is a virtue. *Prov.* It is good to be patient. □ *Jill: I wish Mary would hurry up and call me back! Jane: Patience is a virtue.* □ *Fred: The doctor has kept us waiting for half an hour! If he doesn't call us into his office pretty soon, I may do something violent. Ellen: Calm down, dear. Patience is a virtue.*

***patient as Job** very patient. (Alludes to the biblical figure Job. *Also: **as ~**.) □ *If you want to teach young children, you must be as patient as Job.* □ *The director who is working with that temperamental actor must have the patience of Job.*

the **patter of tiny feet** the sound of young children; having children in the household. □ *I really liked having the patter of tiny feet in the house.* □ *Darling, I think we're going to be hearing the patter of tiny feet soon.*

pattern something **after** something to use something as an example or model when making something. □ *I patterned my house after one I saw in England.* □ *She wanted to pattern her coat after her mother's.*

P

pattern something **on** something to use something as a model for something else. □ *Try to pattern your sales speech on Jane's. She's got it just right.* □ *We patterned our approach on Bob's.*

pave the way (for someone or something**) (with** something**)** *Fig.* to prepare the way with something for someone to come or something to happen. (Alludes to paving a road.) □ *I will pave the way for her with an introduction.* □ *I am sure I can pave the way for your success.* □ *I will pave the way with an introduction.*

pawn someone or something **off**[†] **(on** someone**) (as** someone or something**)** Go to palm someone or something off[†] **(on** someone**) (as** someone or something**).**

pay a call *Euph.* to go to the toilet; to leave to go to the toilet. (See also **pay a call on** someone.) □ *Excuse me. I have to pay a call.* □ *Tom left to pay a call. He should be back soon.*

pay a call on someone to visit someone. □ *Grandmother always paid us a call on Sundays.* □ *Let's pay a call on Mary at the hospital.*

pay a king's ransom Go to a king's ransom.

pay a visit to someone or something Go to pay (someone or something) a visit.

pay an arm and a leg (for something**)** and **pay through the nose (for** something**)** *Fig.* to pay too much [money] for something. □ *I hate to have to pay an arm and a leg for a tank of gas.* □ *If you shop around, you won't have to pay an arm and a leg.* □ *Why should you pay through the nose?*

pay as you go to pay costs as they occur; to pay for goods as they are bought (rather than charging them). □ *You ought to pay as you go. Then you won't be in debt.* □ *If you pay as you go, you'll never spend too much money.*

pay attention (to someone or something**)** to give attention (to someone or something). □ *Please pay attention to the teacher.* □ *Max always pays careful attention to what is being told to him.*

pay by something **1.** *Lit.* to use something as a medium of payment. □ *Will you pay by cash or check?* □ *The bill was paid by check.* **2.** *Fig.* to pay by a certain time. □ *You will have to pay by the end of the month or we will cancel your lease.* □ *I promise I will pay by the end of the month.*

pay court to someone *Fig.* to solicit someone's attention; to woo someone. □ *The lawyer was thought to be paying court to too many politicians.* □ *The lobbyist paid court to all the influential members of Congress.*

pay for something **1.** *Lit.* to pay out money for something. □ *Did you pay for the magazine, or shall I?* □ *No, I'll pay for it.* **2.** *Fig.* to suffer punishment for something. □ *The criminal will pay for his crimes.* □ *I don't like what you did to me, and I'm going to see that you pay for it.* □ *Max paid for his wicked ways.*

pay heed to someone to listen to and accommodate someone. □ *You had better pay heed to your father!* □ *They are not paying heed to what I told them.*

pay homage to someone or something to openly honor or worship someone or something. □ *Do you expect me to pay homage to your hero?* □ *I refuse to pay homage to your principles.*

pay in advance to pay (for something) before it is received or delivered. □ *I want to make a special order. Will I have to pay in advance?* □ *Yes, please pay in advance.*

pay into something to pay money into an account. □ *I intend to pay into my vacation account until I have enough for a nice vacation.* □ *We paid a lot into our savings account this month.*

pay lip service (to something**)** *Fig.* to express loyalty, respect, or support for something insincerely. □ *You don't really care about politics. You're just paying lip service to the candidate.* □ *Don't sit here and pay lip service. Get busy!*

pay off to yield profits; to result in benefits. □ *My investment in those stocks has really paid off.* □ *The time I spent in school paid off in later years.*

pay on something to make a payment against a bill. □ *You have to pay on this every month or we will repossess it.* □ *How much do you plan to pay on the car per month?*

pay one's **debt (to society)** *Cliché* to serve a sentence for a crime, usually in prison. □ *The judge said that Mr. Simpson had to pay his debt to society.* □ *Mr. Brown paid his debt in state prison.*

pay one's **dues 1.** *Lit.* to pay the fees required to belong to an organization. □ *If you haven't paid your dues, you can't come to the club picnic.* □ *How many people have paid their dues?* **2.** *Fig.* to have earned one's right to something through hard work or suffering. □ *He worked hard to get to where he is today. He paid his dues and did what he was told.* □ *I have every right to be here. I paid my dues!*

pay one's **last respects (to** someone**)** to go to someone's funeral. □ *I paid my last respects to Mr. Kantor yesterday.* □ *Scores of people came to pay their last respects.*

pay one's **own way** to pay for one's own transportation, entrance fees, tickets, room, board, etc. □ *I wanted to go to Florida this spring, but my parents say I have to pay my own way.*

pay someone **a backhanded compliment** and **pay** someone **a left-handed compliment** *Fig.* to give someone a false compliment that is really an insult or criticism. □ *John said that he had never seen me looking better. I think he was paying me a left-handed compliment.* □ *I'd prefer that someone insulted me directly. I hate it when someone pays me a backhanded compliment—unless it's a joke.*

pay someone **a compliment** *Fig.* to give someone a compliment. □ *Tom paid Bill a compliment when he told him he was intelligent.* □ *Mary was very gracious when Anne paid her a compliment.*

pay someone **a left-handed compliment** Go to pay someone a backhanded compliment.

pay someone **a pound of flesh** Go to a pound of flesh.

pay someone **back**[†] **1.** *Lit.* to return money that was borrowed from a person. □ *You owe me money. When are you going to pay me back?* □ *You must pay John back. You have owed him money for a long time.* □ *You have to pay back everyone you owe money to.* **2.** *Fig.* to get even with someone [for doing something]. □ *I will pay her back for what she said about me.* □ *Fred eventually will pay Mike back. He bears grudges for a long time.* □ *He intends to pay back everyone who has wronged him!*

pay someone **(for** something**) (with** something**)** to make payment with something to someone for something or for doing something. ☐ *I will pay you for the loan you made me with the money I get from selling my car.* ☐ *I will pay you with a check.*

pay someone **off**[†] **1.** *Lit.* to pay what is owed to a person. ☐ *I can't pay you off until Wednesday when I get my paycheck.* ☐ *I have to use this money to pay off Sarah.* **2.** *Fig.* to bribe someone. ☐ *Max asked Lefty if he had paid the cops off yet.* ☐ *Lefty paid off the cops on time.*

pay (someone or something**) a visit** and **pay a visit to** someone or something to visit someone or something. ☐ *Bill paid a visit to his aunt in Seattle.* ☐ *Please pay a visit to our house whenever you are in town.*

pay someone **respect** to honor someone; to have and show respect for someone. ☐ *You really should pay your boss more respect.* ☐ *We have to pay our parents a lot of respect.*

pay someone's **way** to pay the costs (of something) for a person. ☐ *My aunt is going to pay my way to Florida—only if I take her with me!*

pay something **back**[†] **(to** someone**)** to repay someone. ☐ *I paid the money back to Jerry.* ☐ *Can I pay back the money to George now?* ☐ *Please pay the money back now.*

pay something **down**[†] **1.** *Lit.* to make a deposit of money on a purchase. ☐ *You will have to pay a lot of money down on a car that expensive.* ☐ *I only paid down a few thousand dollars.* **2.** *Fig.* to reduce a bill by paying part of it, usually periodically. ☐ *I think I can pay the balance down by half in a few months.* ☐ *I will pay down the balance a little next month.*

pay something **into** something and **pay** something **in**[†] to pay an amount of money into an account. ☐ *Mary paid forty dollars into my account by mistake.* ☐ *She paid in a lot of money.* ☐ *I have an account here and I want to pay something in.*

pay something **off**[†] to pay all of a debt; to pay the final payment for something bought on credit. ☐ *This month I'll pay the car off.* ☐ *Did you pay off the gas bill yet?*

pay something **out**[†] to unravel or unwind wire or rope as it is needed. (See also **play** something **out.**) ☐ *One worker paid the cable out, and another worker guided it into the conduit.* ☐ *The worker paid out the cable.*

pay something **out**[†] **(for** someone or something**)** to disburse or spend money for someone or something. ☐ *We have already paid too much money out for your education.* ☐ *We paid out too much money.*

pay something **out**[†] **(to** someone**)** to pay money to someone. ☐ *The utility paid one hundred dollars out to everyone who had been overcharged.* ☐ *They paid out money to every customer.*

pay something **up**[†] to pay all of whatever is due; to complete all the payments on something. ☐ *Would you pay up your bills, please?* ☐ *Your dues are all paid up.*

pay the penalty 1. *Lit.* to pay a fine for doing something wrong. ☐ *You ran the red light and now you will have to pay the penalty.* **2.** *Fig.* to suffer the consequences for doing something wrong. ☐ *My head really hurts. I am paying the penalty for getting drunk last night.*

pay the piper *Fig.* to face the results of one's actions; to receive punishment for something. ☐ *You can put off paying your debts only so long. Eventually you'll have to pay the piper.* ☐ *You can't get away with that forever. You'll have to pay the piper someday.*

pay the price 1. *Lit.* to pay the price that is asked for goods or services. (Usually implying that the price is high.) ☐ *If this is the quality of goods that you require, you will have to pay the price.* **2.** *Fig.* to suffer the consequences for doing something or risking something. ☐ *Oh, my head! I am paying the price for drinking too much last night.*

pay through something to make payment through an intermediary, such as a bank. ☐ *I will pay the bill through my bank in New York.* ☐ *Sam had to pay through his brokerage account.*

pay through the nose (for something**)** Go to **pay an arm and a leg (for** something**).**

pay to do something to be beneficial to do something; to be profitable. ☐ *It doesn't pay to drive downtown when you can take the train.* ☐ *It pays to take an umbrella with you if it's supposed to rain.*

pay tribute to someone or something *Fig.* to salute someone or something; to give public recognition to someone or something. ☐ *Many of Judy's friends gathered to pay tribute to her.* ☐ *We will have a reception to pay tribute to the work of the committee.*

pay up to pay what is owed. (Often a command: **Pay up!**) ☐ *I want my money now. Pay up!* ☐ *If you don't pay up, I'll take you to court.*

peace of mind *Fig.* a tranquility that results from not having worries, guilt, or problems. ☐ *If peace of mind is more important to you than earning a lot of money, maybe you should consider teaching.*

peal out [for bells or voices] to sound forth musically. ☐ *The bells pealed out to announce that the wedding had taken place.* ☐ *All six of the bells seemed to peal out at once.*

peck at something **1.** *Lit.* [for a bird] to poke someone or something with its beak. ☐ *The bird pecked at the ground, snatching up the ants.* ☐ *I tried to hold on to the bird but it pecked at me hard.* **2.** *Fig.* [for someone] to eat just a little bit of something, being as picky as a bird. ☐ *Are you well, Betty? You are just pecking at your food.* ☐ *Please don't peck at your food. You should eat everything.*

peck something **up**[†] [for a bird] to eat something up by pecking at it. ☐ *The chickens pecked all the grain up.* ☐ *The birds pecked up the grain.*

peek at someone or something to sneak a glimpse at someone or something. ☐ *Now, don't peek at me while I am changing my shirt.* ☐ *I peeked at the dessert you made. It looks delicious.*

peek in (on someone or something**)** to glance quickly into a place to see someone or something. ☐ *Would you please peek in on the baby?*

peek in(to something**)** to steal a quick glimpse into something. ☐ *Sam peeked into the oven to see what was cooking.* ☐ *Laura opened the oven door and peeked in.*

peek out (from behind someone or something**) 1.** to look outward from behind someone or something. ☐ *A shy kitten peeked out from behind the sofa.* ☐ *I looked toward the* back of the sofa just as a little cat face peeked out. **2.** to show just a little bit with the rest concealed behind someone or something. □ *A bit of yellow peeked out from behind the tree, so we knew Frank was hiding there.* □ *We saw a flash of Frank's yellow shirt peek out.*

peek out (from underneath someone or something**)** **1.** to look outward from beneath someone or something. □ *A small furry face peeked out from underneath the sofa.* □ *At the base of the sofa, a cat peeked out.* **2.** to show just a little bit with the rest concealed under someone or something. □ *Her petticoat peeked out from underneath her skirt.* □ *Her skirt was a tad too short and a little bit of her slip peeked out.*

peek out of something **(at** someone or something**)** **1.** to be inside of something and take a look out. □ *A pair of glimmering eyes peeked out of the darkened room at the two people standing at the door.* □ *I peeked out of my room at the eerie shadows in the hallway.* □ *Jerry peeked out of the bathroom to see if anyone was looking.* **2.** [for a little bit of something] to be revealed with the rest concealed within. □ *A bit of white skin peeked out beneath his pants cuff.*

peek over something **1.** to examine something with a quick glance. □ *I really can't say how good the story was. I only peeked over it.* □ *I peeked over your manuscript, and it looks good.* **2.** to raise up and look over some barrier. □ *I peeked over the wall and saw the lovely garden.* □ *Don't peek over the sofa and let Roger see you. It will ruin the surprise.*

peek through (something**)** **1.** to peer or glimpse through something. □ *I'll just peek through your picture album. I'll study it more carefully later.* □ *I only have time to peek through. I would like to spend more time with it later.* **2.** [for something] to become slightly visible through something. □ *Mary, the lace of your slip is peeking through your blouse!* □ *Some lace is peeking through.*

peek under something to sneak a little glance beneath something. □ *I peeked under the table, hoping to see the dog waiting there for the part of my dinner I wasn't going to eat.* □ *Peek under the chair and see if the cat is there.*

peel off (from something**)** [for one or more airplanes] to separate from a group of airplanes. □ *The lead plane peeled off from the others, and soon the rest followed.* □ *The lead plane peeled off and dived into the clouds.*

peel off ((of) something**)** [for a surface layer] to come loose and fall away from something. (*Of* is usually retained before pronouns.) □ *The paint is beginning to peel off the garage.* □ *The paint is peeling off.*

peel out [for a driver] to speed off in a car with a screeching of tires. □ *Dave got in his car and peeled out, waking the neighbors.* □ *I wish he would stop peeling out!*

peel something **away**[†] **(from** something**)** to peel something from the surface of something. □ *Peel the label away from the envelope and place it on the order form.* □ *Peel away the label carefully.*

peel something **back**[†] **(from** something**)** to lift something away from the surface of something. □ *He peeled the sheets back from the bed and got in.* □ *He peeled back the sheets and got into the bed.*

peel something **off**[†] **((of)** something**)** and **peel** something **off**[†] **from** something to remove the outside surface layer from something. (*Of* is usually retained before pronouns.)

□ *She carefully peeled the skin off the apple.* □ *She peeled off the apple's skin.*

*****a **peep** a quick look at someone or something. (*Typically:* **have ~; take ~.**) □ *Have a peep into the refrigerator and see if we need any milk.* □ *I took a peep at the comet through the telescope.*

peep at someone or something to get a glimpse of someone or something, as if looking through a hole. □ *I peeped at Tom through the venetian blinds.* □ *Look in the microscope and peep at this bacterium.*

peep in(to something**)** to get a quick look into something, as through a hole in the wall or something similar. □ *I peeped into the oven to see what was cooking for dinner.* □ *She opened the oven door and peeped in.*

peep out (of something**) (at** someone or something**)** to sneak a glimpse of someone or something out of something, as through a hole. □ *A little mouse peeped out of its hole at the bright lights in the room.* □ *Johnny, hiding in the closet, peeped out at the guests through the partly opened door.*

peep over something to raise up and sneak a glance over some barrier; to look over the top of something. □ *The child peeped over the wall to get a look at the yard next door.* □ *Grandfather peeped over his glasses to look at the television set for a moment.*

peep through something to take a quick glance through something, such as a hole, telescope, etc. □ *Sam peeped through the keyhole and saw that the room was dark.* □ *Peep through the telescope and have a look at the moon!*

peep under something to take a quick little glance under something. □ *Would you please peep under the table and see if my shoes are there?* □ *Dave peeped under the bed, looking for the cat.*

peer about to stare around; to look at everything about. □ *She came into the room and peered about.* □ *Mary peered about, looking for a place to sit.*

peer at someone or something to look at someone or something closely; to stare at and examine someone or something. □ *The child peered at me for a while in a strange way.* □ *The owl peered at the snake for a moment before grabbing it.*

peer in(to something**)** to stare into something; to look deep into something. □ *I peered into the room, hoping to get a glimpse of the lovely furnishings.* □ *I only had time to peer in and then I walked on by.*

peer out at someone or something to stare out at someone or something. □ *A little puppy peered out at them from the cage.* □ *When I looked under the box, Timmy peered out at me with a big smile.*

peer over something to stare out or look over something, such as one's glasses. □ *The old man peered over his glasses and looked off into the distance.* □ *She peered over the wall to see what she could see.*

peer through something **1.** to view or look through glasses, spectacles, binoculars, etc. □ *From the way she peered through her glasses at me, I knew I was in trouble.* □ *Claire stood on the balcony, peering through her binoculars.* **2.** to stare through a partial barrier, such as a window, drapes, the haze, the fog, etc. □ *George peered through the drapes and spied on the party next door.* □ *Sally*

P

peered through the haze as best she could, trying to see if the way was clear.

peer under something to look underneath something. □ *She peered under the bed, hoping to find her slippers.* □ *When she peered under the bed, she found nothing but lint.*

peg away (at something) Go to **plug away (at** something).

peg out *Sl.* to die. □ *I was so scared, I thought I would peg out for sure.* □ *Uncle Herman almost pegged out last week.*

peg someone **as** something and **have** someone **pegged as** something to think of someone in a certain way. □ *Susan pegged the new employee as a lazy worker.* □ *I had you pegged as an angry rebel before I got to know you.*

peg something **down**† to fasten something to the ground with pegs. □ *After he had finished pegging the tent down, he built a fire.* □ *He pegged down the tent before building a fire.*

pelt down (on someone or something) [for something] to fall down on someone or something hard or in quantity. (Typically rain, hail, sleet, stones, etc.) □ *The rain pelted down on the children as they ran to their school bus.* □ *The ashes from the volcanic eruption pelted down on the town, covering the houses in a gray shroud.*

pelt someone or something **with** something to hit or strike someone or something with something. □ *The citizens pelted Max with rocks.* □ *The boys pelted the mad dog with a hail of stones.*

The **pen is mightier than the sword.** *Prov.* Eloquent writing persuades people better than military force. □ *Believing that the pen is mightier than the sword, the rebels began publishing an underground newspaper.* □ *Alan: Why do you want to become a journalist? Bill: The pen is mightier than the sword.*

pen someone or an animal **in**† **(some place)** to confine someone or an animal in a pen. □ *We penned all the kids in out in the backyard while we got the party things ready in the house.* □ *We had to pen in the kids to keep them away from the traffic.* □ *Alice penned her dog in.*

pen someone or an animal **up**† to confine someone to a confined space or an animal to a pen. □ *He said he didn't want them to pen him up in an office all day.* □ *They penned up the dog during the day.*

penalize someone **for** something to punish someone for something. □ *It's not fair to penalize her for being late.* □ *You needn't penalize yourself for the failure. It wasn't all your fault.*

pencil someone or something **in**† to write in something with a pencil. (Implies that the writing is not final.) □ *This isn't a firm appointment yet, so I will just pencil it in.* □ *I penciled in a tentative answer.*

penetrate into someone or something to pierce into someone or something; to stick deep into someone or something. □ *The lance penetrated into the knight, right through his armor.* □ *The bullet penetrated into the wall.*

penetrate something **with** something to pierce something with something. □ *I could not even penetrate the steel door with a cold chisel.* □ *It was easy to penetrate the lid with a can opener.*

penetrate through something to pierce all the way through something. (Some people will view the *through*

as redundant.) □ *The bullet could not penetrate through the metal plating.* □ *It did not have enough force to penetrate through the steel.*

A **penny for your thoughts!** *Prov.* What are you thinking about?; I would give you a penny if you tell me your thoughts. □ *Noticing that Janet looked pensive, Bill said, "A penny for your thoughts!"* □ *You seem very pleased with yourself today. A penny for your thoughts!*

A **penny saved is a penny earned.** *Prov.* Money that you save is more valuable than money that you spend right away.; It is good to save money. □ *Now that you have your first job, you ought to open a savings account. A penny saved is a penny earned.* □ *Mary worked hard to save money; she knew that a penny saved is a penny earned.*

penny-wise and pound-foolish *Prov.* thrifty with small sums and foolish with large sums. (Describes someone who will go to a lot of trouble to save a little money, but overlooks large expenses to save a little money. Even in the United States, the reference is to British pounds sterling.) □ *Sam: If we drive to six different grocery stores, we'll get the best bargains on everything we buy. Alan: But with gasoline so expensive, that's penny-wise and pound-foolish.*

pension someone **off**† to retire someone with a pension. □ *The company tried to pension me off before I was ready to retire.* □ *They pensioned off the long-time workers.*

people something **with** someone to provide population for something or some place, using someone or some kind of people. □ *The government decided to people the frontier with a variety of races.* □ *The island had been peopled with marooned sailors.*

People who live in glass houses shouldn't throw stones. *Prov.* You should not criticize other people for having the same faults that you yourself have. □ *Jill: Richard sure was drinking a lot at the office party. Jane: I noticed you had quite a few cocktails yourself. People who live in glass houses shouldn't throw stones.*

pep someone or something **up**† to make someone or something more vigorous. □ *Nancy needs to take some vitamins to pep her up.* □ *The coffee break pepped up the tired workers.* □ *Better food might pep your cat up.*

pepper someone or something **with** something to shower someone or something with something, such as stones, bullets, etc. □ *The angry crowd peppered the police with stones.* □ *The sheriff's posse peppered the bandit's hideout with bullets.*

perceive someone or something **as** something to think of someone or something as something or as displaying certain characteristics. □ *I perceive Randy as sort of hot-headed.* □ *We all perceive this problem as solvable.*

perch on something **1.** [for a bird] to stand at rest on something. □ *A robin perched on the branch by my window.* □ *We saw a parrot perched on some kind of flowering tree.* **2.** to sit or balance on something. □ *I can't perch on this fence forever. Let's go.* □ *Sam was perched on the bicycle and he looked very uncomfortable.*

perch someone or something **on** something to place, seat, or stand someone or something in a place. □ *She perched the little girl on the edge of the tub.* □ *Walter perched his hat on the top shelf.*

P

percolate through something [for a liquid] to seep down through something. □ *The water percolated through the coffee grounds too slowly for Fred, who was just dying for a hot cup of the stuff.* □ *The water percolated through the subsoil and appeared again at the bottom of the hill.*

a **perfect stranger** and a **total stranger** *Fig.* a person who is completely unknown [to oneself]. □ *I was stopped on the street by a perfect stranger who wanted to know my name.* □ *If a total stranger asked me such a personal question, I am sure I would not answer!*

perform an old warhorse Go to an **old warhorse.**

perform something **on** someone or something to do something to someone or something; to carry out a procedure on someone or something. □ *The surgeon performed a simple office procedure on the patient.* □ *Do you expect me to perform magic on this problem?*

Perhaps a little later. Not now, but possibly later. □ *Waiter: Would you like your coffee now? Bob: Perhaps a little later. Waiter: All right.* □ *Sally: Hey, Bill, how about a swim? Bob: Sounds good, but not now. Perhaps a little later. Sally: Okay. See you later.*

perish from something to die from a particular cause, such as a disease. □ *Nearly all the fish perished from the cold.* □ *I was afraid that I would perish from hunger.*

perish in something to die because of involvement in something. □ *Four people perished in the flames.* □ *Our cat perished in an accident.*

Perish the thought. *Fig.* Do not even consider thinking of such a (negative) thing. □ *If you should become ill—perish the thought—I'd take care of you.* □ *I'm afraid that we need a new car. Perish the thought.*

perish with something to feel bad enough to die because of something, such as heat, hunger, etc. (Often an exaggeration.) □ *I was just perishing with hunger when we arrived at the restaurant.* □ *Mary felt as if she would perish with the intense heat of the stuffy little room.*

perk someone **up**† to make someone more cheery or refreshed. □ *A nice cup of coffee would really perk me up.* □ *A cup of coffee will perk up the sleepiest person.*

perk something **up**† to refresh or brighten something; to make something more lively. □ *A bit of bright yellow here and there will perk this room up a lot.* □ *We need something to perk up the second act of the play.*

perk up to become invigorated; to become more active. □ *After a bit of water, the plants perked up nicely.* □ *About noon, Andy perked up and looked wide-awake.*

permeate something **with** something to saturate something with something. □ *The comedian permeated his act with smutty jokes.* □ *The evening air was permeated with the smell of jasmine.*

permeate through something to seep in and saturate something. □ *The coffee spilled on the desk and permeated through all the papers and stuff.* □ *The strong odor permeated through the walls and nearly suffocated us.*

Permit me. Go to **Allow me.**

permit someone **into** something and **permit** someone **in**† to allow someone to enter something or some place. □ *They would not permit me in the dining room since I had*

no tie. □ *They would not permit in that bunch of rowdy brats or any other of her friends.*

permit someone **out (of** something**)** to allow someone to go out of something or some place. □ *His mother won't permit him out of his room all weekend.* □ *I didn't do anything, but she won't permit me out!*

permit someone **through (**something**)** to allow someone to pass through something. □ *Would you permit me through the door? I have to get into this building.* □ *Janet said she was in a hurry, but they wouldn't permit her through.*

permit someone **up (**something**)** to allow someone to come up something. □ *She would not permit me up the ladder.* □ *I wanted to climb the ladder to be with Walter, but he wouldn't permit me up.*

permit someone **up to** something to allow someone to come up to something or some place. □ *The teacher would not permit the smallest children up to the edge.* □ *They would not permit us up to the gate before our turn came.*

persecute someone **for** something to harass or repress someone for something. □ *They were persecuting the native people for being underdeveloped.* □ *They were persecuted for being simple and unsuspecting.*

persevere at something to keep trying to do something. □ *I will persevere at my studies and I'm sure I will succeed.* □ *Todd persevered at his job and got promoted in no time.*

persevere in something to persist in [doing] something. □ *I will persevere in my efforts to win election.* □ *Kelly persevered in her studies and graduated with honors.*

persevere with something to continue to try to accomplish something. □ *Do you really think it is wise to persevere with your plan?* □ *Sally persevered with her scheme to earn a million dollars.*

persist in doing something to continue doing something. □ *John persists in thinking that he's always right.* □ *Tom persists in demanding that I agree to his terms.*

persist with something to continue the state of something; to extend an action or state. □ *Please do not persist with your demands that I agree to your terms.* □ *If you persist with this intrusion, I'm going to call the police.*

person of color a person of an African, Asian, or Native American race. (The plural is *people of color*.) □ *The apartment manager clearly discriminated against people of color. He would only rent to whites.* □ *As a person of color, I felt threatened by the racist jokes that my coworker told.*

*a **perspective on** something a way of looking at a situation and determining what is important. (*Typically: **get** ~; **have** ~; **gain** ~; **give** someone ~.) □ *The jury did not have a good perspective on the crime since some of the evidence had to be ignored.* □ *Studying history gives one a perspective on the past.*

persuade someone **of** something to convince someone of something. □ *Laura was unable to persuade me of the truth of her statement.* □ *We were all persuaded of the need for higher taxes.*

persuade someone **to** do something to convince someone to do something. □ *Are you sure I can't persuade you to have another piece of cake?* □ *Richard was easily persuaded to have another piece of his favorite cake.*

P

pertain to someone or something to relate to someone or something; to have something to do with someone or something. □ *I don't think that anything discussed in this meeting pertained to me.* □ *It really doesn't pertain to the matter at hand.*

pester someone **about** someone or something to bother someone about someone or something. □ *Please don't pester me about Frank.* □ *Stop pestering me about money.*

pester someone **into** something to annoy someone into doing something. □ *We are trying to pester her into accepting the position.* □ *I don't want to be pestered into losing my temper!*

pester someone **out of** something **1.** to annoy someone out of doing something. □ *Dave pestered Mary out of going away for the weekend.* □ *He pestered her out of leaving without him.* **2.** to annoy one out of one's mind, senses, good manners, etc. □ *I was pestered out of my mind by a series of silly questions.*

pester someone **with** something to annoy someone with something. □ *Don't pester me with your constant questions!* □ *I was pestered with phone call after phone call.*

pester the life out of someone *Fig.* to annoy someone excessively. □ *Leave me alone. You are pestering the life out of me.* □ *Stop pestering the life out of me!*

pet hate *Fig.* something that is disliked intensely and is a constant or repeated annoyance. □ *My pet hate is being put on hold on the telephone.* □ *Another pet hate of mine is having to stand in line.*

pet peeve *Fig.* a frequent annoyance; one's "favorite" or most often encountered annoyance. □ *My pet peeve is someone who always comes into the theater after the show has started.* □ *Drivers who don't signal are John's pet peeve.*

peter out [for something] to die or dwindle away; [for something] to become exhausted gradually. □ *When the fire petered out, I went to bed.* □ *My money finally petered out, and I had to come home.*

petition someone or something **for** something to make a formal request of someone or a group for something. □ *They petitioned us for an end to the stringent dress code.* □ *We had to petition the upper administration for a revision in the policy.*

phase someone or something **into** something and **phase** someone or something **in**† to work someone or something into use or service gradually. □ *They decided to phase Ruth into the job little by little.* □ *They phased in Ruth over a long period of time.*

phase someone or something **out of** something and **phase** someone or something **out**† to work someone or something out of use or service or out of a group gradually. □ *We are going to have to phase you out of the job of treasurer.* □ *They phased out the unneeded workers.*

phone in (to someone or something**)** to call in by telephone to a central person or central point. □ *I will phone in to my secretary and report the change in schedule.* □ *I have to phone in and report the changes.*

phone someone **up**† to call someone on the telephone. □ *I don't know what he will do. I will phone him up and ask him.* □ *Phone up your brother and ask his advice.*

phone something **in**† **(to** someone or something**)** to transmit information to a central person or central point by telephone. □ *I will phone this order in to the plant right away.* □ *I will phone the order in to my secretary right now.* □ *Don't worry. I'll phone it in.*

***phony as a three-dollar bill** and ***queer as a three-dollar bill** phony; bogus. (*Also: **as** ~.) □ *This guy's as phony as a three-dollar bill.* □ *The whole deal stinks. It's as queer as a three-dollar bill.*

a **photo op(portunity)** a time or event designed for taking pictures of a celebrity. □ *All the photographers raced toward a photo op with the president.*

***physical (with** someone**) 1.** *Lit.* physical in the use of force against someone. (*Typically: **be** ~; **get** ~.) □ *The coach got in trouble for getting physical with some members of the team.* □ *When the suspect wouldn't cooperate, the police were forced to get physical.* **2.** *Fig.* physical in touching someone in lovemaking. (*Typically: **be** ~; **get** ~.) □ *I've heard that Bill tends to get physical with his dates.* □ *I don't care if he gets physical—within reason.*

Physician, heal thyself. *Prov.* Do not rebuke someone for a fault or problem you have yourself. (Biblical.) □ *Ellen: You're such a spendthrift. You should go on a strict budget. Fred: But you manage money even worse than I do! Physician, heal thyself.* □ *Jane: You look like you're gaining weight. You should probably get more exercise. Alan: Physician, heal thyself. You're getting a little pudgy, too.*

pick a fight (with someone**)** and **pick a quarrel (with** someone**)** to start a fight or argument with someone on purpose. □ *Are you trying to pick a fight with me?* □ *Max intended to pick a quarrel with Lefty.*

pick a lock to open a lock without using a key. □ *The robber picked the lock with a nail file.* □ *The thief picked the lock on the safe and stole the money.*

pick a quarrel (with someone**)** Go to **pick a fight (with** someone**).**

pick and choose to choose very carefully from a number of possibilities; to be selective. □ *You must take what you are given. You cannot pick and choose.* □ *Meg is so beautiful. She can pick and choose from a whole range of boyfriends.*

pick at someone or something to be very critical of someone or something; to **pick on** someone or something. □ *Why are you always picking at me?* □ *The critics picked at the little things, missing the serious problems.*

pick at something **1.** *Lit.* to try to pull away bits of something. □ *Don't pick at the bookbinding. It will fall apart.* **2.** *Fig.* to eat just a tiny bit of a meal or some kind of food. □ *You are just picking at your food!*

pick holes in something **1.** and **pick** something **to pieces** to criticize something severely; to point out the flaws or fallacies in an argument. □ *The lawyer picked holes in the witness's story.* □ *They will pick holes in your argument.* □ *Stop picking holes in everything I say!* **2.** to poke or pinch little holes in something. □ *Look! You've picked holes in the bread! How can I make sandwiches?* □ *Who picked holes in the blanket?*

the **pick of** something the best of the group. □ *This playful puppy is the pick of the whole lot.* □ *These potatoes are the pick of the crop.*

pick on somebody your own size Go to pick on someone your own size.

pick on someone or something to harass or bother someone or something, usually unfairly. □ *Please stop picking on me! I'm tired of it.* □ *You shouldn't pick on the cat.*

pick on someone your own size and **pick on somebody your own size** to abuse someone who is big enough to fight back. □ *Go pick on somebody your own size!* □ *Wilbur should leave his little brother alone and pick on someone his own size.*

pick one's **way through** something and **make** one's **way through** something **1.** to move along a route full of obstacles; to travel, usually on foot, through an area of heavy vegetation or through a crowd of people or things. □ *When the grandchildren visit, I have to pick my way through the toys on the floor.* □ *We slowly picked our way through the thorny bushes to get to the ripe raspberries.* **2.** to work slowly and meticulously through something. □ *My teacher said he couldn't even pick his way through my report. It was just too confusing.* □ *I spent an hour picking my way through the state tax forms.*

pick someone or something **apart**[†] **1.** *Lit.* to pick at and pull someone or something to pieces. □ *The vultures attacked the hunger-weakened man and tried to pick him apart.* □ *They tried to pick apart the body.* □ *Harry picked his piece of cake apart, looking to get all the nuts out.* **2.** *Fig.* to analyze and criticize someone or something negatively. □ *You didn't review her performance; you just picked her apart.* □ *The critics picked apart the performers.*

pick someone or something **from** someone or something to choose someone from a group of people; to choose something from a group of things. □ *I picked Joe from all the other boys.* □ *Tony picked this one from the collection.*

pick someone or something **off**[†] **1.** *Fig.* to kill someone or something with a carefully aimed gunshot. □ *The hunter picked the deer off with great skill.* □ *The killer tried to pick off the police officer.* **2.** Go to next.

pick someone or something **off (of)** someone or something and **pick** someone or something **off**[†] to pull or gather someone or something off something. (*Of* is usually retained before pronouns.) □ *The teacher picked the little boys off the jungle gym and hurried them back into the school building before the storm hit.* □ *Pick off the ripe tomatoes and leave the rest.*

pick someone or something **out**[†] Go to pick someone or something out of something.

pick someone or something **out**[†] **(for** someone or something**)** to choose someone or something to serve as someone or something. □ *I picked one of the new people out for Santa Claus this year.* □ *I picked out several large potatoes for the stew.*

pick someone or something **out of** something and **pick** someone or something **out**[†] **1.** to lift or pull someone or something out of something. □ *The mother picked her child out of the fray and took him home.* □ *I picked out the mushrooms before eating the soup.* **2.** to select someone or something out of an offering of selections. □ *I picked Jerry out of all the boys in the class.* □ *I picked out Jerry.*

pick someone or something **to pieces 1.** *Lit.* to pull or pinch at someone or something until only pieces are left.

□ *The savage birds picked the carcass to pieces.* □ *The mice seem to have picked the stuffed doll to pieces.* **2.** *Fig.* to criticize someone or something harshly or unduly. □ *You have just picked her to pieces. Leave her alone!* □ *The critic picked the play to pieces.*

pick someone's **brain(s)** *Fig.* to talk with someone to find out information about something. □ *I spent the afternoon with Donna, picking her brain for ideas to use in our celebration.* □ *Do you mind if I pick your brains? I need some fresh ideas.*

pick someone **up**[†] **1.** to attempt to become acquainted with someone for romantic or sexual purposes. □ *Who are you anyway? Are you trying to pick me up?* □ *No, I never picked up anybody in my life!* **2.** [for the police] to find and bring someone to the police station for questioning or arrest. □ *The cop tried to pick her up, but she heard him coming and got away.* □ *Sergeant Jones, go pick up Sally Franklin and bring her in to be questioned about the jewel robbery.* **3.** to stop one's car, bus, etc., and offer someone a ride. □ *Don't ever pick a stranger up when you're out driving!* □ *I picked up a hitchhiker today, and we had a nice chat.* **4.** to go to a place in a car, bus, etc., and take on a person as a passenger. □ *Please come to my office and pick me up at noon.* □ *I have to pick up Billy at school.*

pick something **away**[†] to pull or pinch something loose from something. □ *Mary picked the meat away from the bones.* □ *He picked away the burrs.*

pick something **over**[†] *Fig.* to look through something carefully, looking for something special. □ *The shoppers who got here first picked everything over, and there is not much left.* □ *They picked over all the merchandise.*

pick something **to pieces** Go to pick holes in something.

pick something **up**[†] **1.** *Lit.* to lift up or raise something from a lower place. □ *Please help me pick this stuff up off the pavement.* □ *Pick up every bit of it!* **2.** *Fig.* to tidy up or clean up a room or some other place. □ *Let's pick this room up in a hurry.* □ *I want you to pick up the entire house.* **3.** *Fig.* to find, purchase, or acquire something. □ *Where did you pick that up?* □ *I picked up this tool at the hardware store.* **4.** *Fig.* to learn something. □ *I pick languages up easily.* □ *I picked up a lot of knowledge about music from my brother.* **5.** *Fig.* to cause something to go faster, especially music. □ *All right, let's pick up the tempo and get it moving faster.* □ *Okay, get moving. Pick it up!* **6.** *Fig.* to resume something. □ *Pick it up right where you stopped.* □ *I'll have to pick up my work where I left off.* **7.** *Fig.* to receive radio signals; to bring something into view. □ *I can just pick it up with a powerful telescope.* □ *I can hardly pick up a signal.* **8.** *Fig.* to find a trail or route. □ *The dogs finally picked the scent up.* □ *You should pick up highway 80 in a few miles.*

pick up 1. to tidy up. (See also pick up (after someone or something).) □ *When you finish playing, you have to pick up.* □ *Please pick up after yourself.* **2.** to get busy; to go faster. □ *Things usually pick up around here about 8:00.* □ *I hope business picks up a little later. It's boring here.*

pick up after someone or something to tidy up after someone or a group. □ *I refuse to pick up after you all the time.* □ *I refuse to pick up after your rowdy friends.*

pick up on something to become alert to something; to take notice of something; to learn or catch on to something. □

She's real sharp. She picks up on everything. □ *The cop picked up on the car with the expired license plates.*

pick up someone **for a song** Go to **for a song**.

pick up speed to increase speed. □ *The train began to pick up speed as it went downhill.* □ *The car picked up speed as we moved into the left lane.*

pick up the check Go to **pick up the tab**.

pick up the pace to speed up the tempo; to increase the rate that something is being done. □ *We are going to have to pick up the pace of activity around here if we are to get the job done.*

pick up the pieces (of something**) 1.** *Lit.* to gather up each piece or part. □ *Norma picked up the pieces of the broken lamp.* □ *She stooped down to pick up the pieces.* **2.** *Fig.* to try to repair emotional, financial, or other damage done to one's life. □ *I need some time to pick up the pieces of my life after the accident.* □ *After a while, Fred was able to pick up the pieces and carry on.*

pick up the tab and **pick up the check** to pay the bill. □ *Whenever we go out, my father picks up the tab.* □ *Order whatever you want. The company is picking up the check.*

picked over rejected; worn, dirty, or undesirable. □ *This merchandise looks worn and picked over. I don't want any of it.* □ *Everything in the store is picked over by the end of the month.*

A **picture is worth a thousand words.** *Prov.* Pictures convey information more efficiently and effectively than words do. □ *It's much easier to learn how machines work by looking at pictures, rather than by hearing someone describe them. A picture is worth a thousand words.* □ *The newspaper editor decided to devote more space to photographs of the disaster than to text, since a picture is worth a thousand words.*

the **picture of (good) health** in a very healthy condition. □ *The doctor says I am the picture of good health.* □ *Each of the children is the picture of health.*

picture perfect *Fig.* looking exactly correct or right. (Hyphenated as a modifier.) □ *At last, everything was picture perfect.* □ *Nothing less than a picture-perfect party table will do.*

picture someone **as** someone or something to imagine someone as someone or a type of person; to form a mental picture of someone as someone or a type of person. □ *Just picture me as Santa Claus!* □ *I can't picture you as a doctor.*

picture someone **in** something **1.** to form a mental picture of someone wearing something. □ *I can just picture Tony in that baseball uniform.* □ *Can you picture yourself in a dress like this?* **2.** to form a mental picture of someone inside something or some place. □ *I can just picture you in that car!* □ *Can you picture yourself in jail?*

piddle around *Fig.* to waste time doing little or nothing. □ *Stop piddling around and get busy.* □ *I'm not piddling around. I am experimenting.*

piddle something **away**† *Fig.* to waste away money or a period of time. □ *Please don't piddle all your money away.* □ *Jane piddled away most of the day.*

pie in the sky 1. *Fig.* a future reward after death, considered as a replacement for a reward not received on earth. □ *Don't hold out for pie in the sky. Get realistic.* □ *If he didn't hope for some heavenly pie in the sky, he would probably be a real crook.* **2.** *Fig.* having to do with a hope for a special reward. (This is hyphenated before a nominal.) □ *Get rid of your pie-in-the-sky ideas!* □ *What these pie-in-the-sky people really want is money.*

piece of cake *Fig.* something easy to do. □ *No problem. When you know what you're doing, it's a piece of cake.* □ *Glad to help. It was a piece of cake.* □ *Rescuing frightened cats is my specialty. Piece of cake!*

a **piece (of the action)** and a **bit of the action**; a **slice of the action** *Sl.* a share in the activity or the profits. (Especially of a business scheme or gambling activity.) □ *If you get in on that real estate deal, I want a piece, too.* □ *Deal Tom in. He wants a piece of the action.*

piece something **out**† **1.** *Lit.* to add patches or pieces to something to make it complete. □ *There is not quite enough cloth to make a shirt, but I think I can piece it out with some scraps of a complementary color for the collar.* □ *We managed to piece out the material that we needed.* **2.** *Fig.* to add missing parts to a story, explanation, or narrative to make it make sense. □ *Before she passed out, she muttered a few things and we were able to piece the whole story out from that.* □ *We pieced out the story from the few bits we heard from her.*

piece something **together**† to fit something together; to assemble the pieces of something, such as a puzzle or something puzzling, and make sense of it. □ *The police were unable to piece the story together.* □ *The detective tried to piece together the events leading up to the crime.*

pierce through something to poke through something; to penetrate something. □ *He pierced through the meat with a fork and put it in a spicy marinade.* □ *Mary pierced the yarn through with the knitting needles.*

a **piercing scream** *Fig.* a very loud and shrill scream. □ *Suddenly, there was a piercing scream from the next room.* □ *Bob heard Susan's piercing scream and ran to help her.*

pig out (on something**)** *Inf.* to eat too much of something; to make a pig of oneself. □ *I intend to really pig out on pizza.* □ *I love to pig out on ice cream.*

pile in(to something**)** to climb in or get in roughly. □ *Okay, kids, pile in!* □ *The children piled into the car and slammed the door.*

pile off (something**)** to get down off something; to clamber down off something. □ *All the kids piled off the wagon and ran into the barn.* □ *She stopped the wagon, and they piled off.*

pile on((to) someone or something**)** to make a heap of people on someone or something. □ *The football players piled onto the poor guy holding the ball.* □ *They ran up to the ballcarrier and piled on.*

pile out (of something**)** [for many people] to get out of something roughly. □ *Okay, kids, pile out!* □ *The car door burst open, and the children piled out.*

pile someone **into** something and **pile** someone **in**† to bunch people into something in a disorderly fashion. □ *She piled the kids into the van and headed off for school.* □ *She piled in the kids and closed the doors.* □ *Pile them in and let's go.* □ *They piled themselves into the car and sped off.*

pile someone or something **on(to)** someone or something and **pile** someone or something **on**† to heap people or things onto someone or something. □ *The wrestler piled the referee onto his unconscious opponent.* □ *We piled the kids on the heap of leaves we had raked up.* □ *Pile on the chili! What's a hot dog without chili?*

pile something **up**† **1.** to crash or wreck something. □ *Drive carefully if you don't want to pile the car up.* □ *The driver piled up the car against a tree.* **2.** to make something into a heap. □ *Carl piled all the leaves up and set them afire.* □ *Please pile up the leaves.*

pile the work on (someone) *Fig.* to give someone a lot of work to do. □ *The boss really piled the work on me this week.* □ *The boss piled on the work this week.*

pile up 1. *Lit.* [for things] to gather or accumulate. □ *The newspapers began to pile up after a few days.* □ *Work is really piling up around here.* **2.** *Fig.* [for a number of vehicles] to crash together. □ *Nearly twenty cars piled up on the bridge this morning.*

pilfer from someone or something to steal from someone or a group. □ *The petty thief had pilfered from several merchants in town.* □ *Someone has pilfered from the petty-cash drawer.*

pilfer something **from** someone or something to steal something from someone or something. □ *Did you pilfer this money from your parents?* □ *Who pilfered some money from the cash box?*

pillar of strength and **pillar of support** someone or something that consistently provides moral, emotional, or financial support as does a pillar. □ *My parents are my pillars of support.* □ *John looked to God as his pillar of strength.*

pillar of support Go to previous.

pilot someone or something **through** (something) to guide or steer someone or something through something, especially through a waterway. □ *We hired someone to pilot us through the harbor entrance.* □ *The channel was treacherous, and we hired someone to pilot the ship through.*

pilot something **into** something and **pilot** something **in**† to steer or guide something into something. (Usually refers to steering a ship.) □ *We need to signal for a pilot to pilot our ship into the harbor.* □ *Fred piloted in the freighter.*

pilot something **out of** something and **pilot** something **out**† to steer or guide something out of something. (Usually refers to steering a ship.) □ *The chubby little man with a pipe piloted the huge ship out of the harbor.* □ *The storm made it very difficult to pilot the ship out.* □ *Help me pilot out this old tub.*

pin one's **faith on** someone or something and **pin** one's **hopes on** someone or something *Fig.* to fasten one's faith or hope to someone or something. □ *Don't pin your faith on Tom. He can't always do exactly what you want.* □ *He pinned his hopes on being rescued soon.*

pin one's **hopes on** someone or something Go to previous.

pin someone **down**† **(on** something) and **nail** someone **down**† **(on** something) *Fig.* to demand and receive a firm answer from someone to some question. (Alludes to shifting from answer to answer; commit to one answer or another.) □ *I tried to pin him down on a time and place,* but he was very evasive. □ *Don't try to pin down the mayor on anything!* □ *I want to nail her down on a meeting time.*

pin someone or something **against** something to press and hold someone or something against something. □ *The police pinned the mugger against the wall and put handcuffs on him.* □ *The wildlife veterinarian pinned the rhino against the walls of the enclosure and subdued it so it could be treated.*

pin someone or something **beneath** someone, something or an animal to trap someone or something beneath someone, an animal, or something. □ *The mine cave-in pinned four miners beneath a beam.* □ *I held the alligator's mouth closed and pinned it beneath me.*

pin someone or something **under** someone or something to trap someone or something under someone or something. □ *Someone knocked Gerry down and pinned Randy under him.* □ *The accident pinned Maggie under the car.*

pin someone's **ears back**† **1.** *Fig.* to beat someone, especially about the head. □ *Don't talk to me like that or I will pin your ears back!* □ *Max wanted to pin back Lefty's ears for making fun of him.* **2.** *Fig.* to give someone a good scolding. □ *Did you hear him? He really pinned Chuck's ears back.* □ *He pinned back Chuck's ears.*

pin something **back**† to hold something back by pinning. □ *I will pin the curtains back to let a little more light in.* □ *Jane pinned back the curtains.*

pin something **down**† and **nail** something **down**† **1.** *Lit.* to attach or affix something with nails or pins. □ *Pin the pattern down temporarily.* □ *Nail down this piece of flooring every 12 inches.* **2.** *Fig.* to determine or fix something, such as a date, an agreement, an amount of money, a decision, etc. □ *It will be ready sometime next month. I can't pin the date down just yet, however.* □ *I can't pin down the exact date just now.*

pin something **on** someone *Fig. Inf.* to blame something on someone; to frame someone for a crime; to make it appear that an innocent person has actually committed a crime. (See also **pin** something **on** someone or something.) □ *Don't try to pin that crime on me! I didn't do it.* □ *The gang member tried to pin the crime on a rival gang.*

pin something **on** someone or something to hang something on someone or something by pinning. (See also **pin** something **on** someone.) □ *The mayor pinned the medal on the boy who had rescued the swimmer.* □ *I pinned a yellow ribbon on my lapel.*

pin something **(on)to** something to attach or fix something to someone or something by pinning. □ *The mayor pinned the medal onto the lapel of the brave young hero.* □ *She pinned a medal to his lapel.*

pin something **up**† **1.** to raise something and hold it up with pins. □ *I will pin this hem up and then sew it later.* □ *Please pin up the hem so I can see where to sew it.* **2.** Go to next.

pin something **up on(to)** something and **pin** something **up**† to attach something to something, for display, with pins. □ *I pinned the picture up onto the bulletin board where everyone could see it.* □ *I pinned up the picture.*

pinch and scrape Go to scrimp and save.

pinch someone **for** something *Sl.* to arrest someone for something. □ *The cops pinched Max for driving without a license.* □ *Max was pinched for speeding.*

pinch something **back**† to pinch off a bit of the top of a plant so it will branch and grow more fully. □ *You should pinch this back so it will branch.* □ *Pinch back the new leaves at the top.*

pinch something **from** someone or something *Sl.* to steal something from someone or something. □ *Sam pinched an apple from the produce stand.* □ *We saw a pickpocket pinch a wallet from an old man.*

pinch something **off**† Go to next.

pinch something **off (of)** something and **pinch** something **off**† to sever something from something by pinching. (*Of* is usually retained before pronouns.) □ *Pinch the buds off the lower branches so the one at the top will bloom.* □ *Pinch off the lower buds.*

pinch-hit for someone **1.** *Fig.* to bat for someone else in a baseball game. □ *Wally Wilson will pinch-hit for Gary Franklin.* □ *Rodney Jones is pinch-hitting for Babe DiMaggio.* **2.** *Fig.* to substitute for someone in any situation. □ *Bart will pinch-hit for Fred, who is at another meeting today.* □ *Who will pinch-hit for me while I am on vacation?*

pine after someone or something and **pine for** someone or something; **pine over** someone or something to long for or grieve for someone or something. □ *Bob pined after Doris for weeks after she left.* □ *Dan is still pining for his lost dog.* □ *There is no point in pining over Claire.*

pine away (after someone or something**)** to waste away in melancholy and longing for someone or something. □ *A year later, he was still pining away after Claire.* □ *Still, he is pining away.*

pine for someone or something Go to **pine after** someone or something.

pine over someone or something Go to **pine after** someone or something.

pins and needles *Fig.* a tingling feeling in some part of one's body, especially the arms and legs. (See also **on pins and needles.**) □ *I've got pins and needles in my legs.* □ *Mary gets pins and needles if she crosses her arms for long.*

pipe down to become quiet; to cease making noise; to shut up. (Especially as a rude command.) □ *Pipe down! I'm trying to sleep.* □ *Come on! Pipe down and get back to work!*

a **pipe dream** *Fig.* a wish or an idea that is impossible to achieve or carry out. (From the dreams or visions induced by the smoking of an opium pipe.) □ *Going to the West Indies is a pipe dream. We'll never have enough money.* □ *Your hopes of winning a lot of money are just a silly pipe dream.*

pipe something **away**† to conduct a liquid or a gas away through a pipe. □ *We will have to pipe the excess water away.* □ *They piped away the water.*

pipe something **from** some place **(to** some place**)** to conduct a liquid or a gas from one place to another place through a pipe. □ *One oil company wanted to pipe oil all the way from northern Alaska to a southern port on the Pacific.* □ *The company pipes gas from the storage tanks in the middle of the state.*

pipe something **into** some place and **pipe** something **in**† **1.** *Lit.* to conduct a liquid or a gas into some place through a pipe. □ *An excellent delivery system piped oxygen into* every hospital room. □ *They piped in oxygen to every room.* □ *They piped it in.* **2.** *Fig.* to bring music or other sound into a place over wires. □ *They piped music into the stairways and elevators.* □ *The elevators were nice except that the management had piped in music.*

pipe up (with something**)** *Fig.* to interject a comment; to interrupt with a comment. □ *Nick piped up with an interesting thought.* □ *You can always count on Alice to pipe up.*

piping hot [of food] extremely hot. □ *On a cold day, I like to eat piping hot soup.* □ *Be careful! This coffee is piping hot!*

pipped (up) *Sl.* intoxicated. □ *I'm not drunk. Just a little pipped up.* □ *She's pipped and ready to get sick.*

pique someone's **curiosity** and **pique** someone's **interest** to arouse interest; to arouse curiosity. □ *The advertisement piqued my curiosity about the product.* □ *The professor tried to pique the students' interest in French literature.*

pique someone's **interest** Go to previous.

piss someone **off**† *Inf.* to make someone angry. (Crude. Potentially offensive, even though it is widely used. Use with discretion.) □ *She really pissed me off!* □ *That's enough to piss off anybody.*

pissed (off) *Inf.* angry. (Crude. Potentially offensive, even though it is heard widely. Use with discretion.) □ *I was so pissed off I could have screamed.* □ *He's come back, and he's sure pissed.*

the **pit of** one's **stomach** *Fig.* the middle of one's stomach; the location of a "visceral response." □ *I got a strange feeling in the pit of my stomach when they told me the bad news.*

pit one's **shoulder to the wheel** Go to **have** one's **shoulder to the wheel.**

pit someone or something **against** someone or something to set someone or something in opposition to someone or something. □ *The rules of the tournament pit their team against ours.* □ *John pitted Mary against Sally in the tennis match.*

pitch a tent to erect a tent at a campsite. □ *The campers pitched their tent in a clearing in the woods.* □ *I pitched my tent next to a large oak tree.*

pitch black very black; as black as pitch. □ *The hearse was pitch black.* □ *The bandit rode on a pitch black horse and wore black clothing.*

pitch camp to set up or arrange a campsite. □ *We pitched camp near the stream.* □ *Two campers went ahead of us to pitch camp while it was still light.*

pitch dark very dark; as dark as pitch. □ *I couldn't see anything outside because it was pitch dark.* □ *The room was pitch dark, and I couldn't find the light switch!*

pitch forward to jerk or thrust forward. □ *Suddenly the car pitched forward, jerking the passengers around.* □ *We pitched forward inside the car as we went over the bumpy road.*

pitch in (and help) (with something**)** *Fig.* to join in and help someone with something. □ *Would you please pitch in and help with the party?* □ *Come on! Pitch in!*

P

pitch someone **a curve(ball)** *Fig.* to surprise someone with an unexpected act or event. (Referring to a curve-ball in baseball. It is the route of the ball that is curved, not the ball itself. See also **throw** someone **a curve(ball)**.) □ *You really pitched me a curveball when you said I had done a poor job. I did my best.* □ *You asked Tom a trick question. You certainly pitched him a curve.*

pitch someone or something **out (of)** something and **pitch** someone or something **out**† to throw someone or something out of something or some place. (*Of* is usually retained before pronouns.) □ *The usher pitched the drunk out of the theater.* □ *The usher pitched out the annoying person.*

pitch someone or something **over** something to toss someone or something over something. □ *Then Max tried to pitch Lefty over the railing onto the tracks.* □ *Billy pitched the stone over the wall.*

pitch something **at** someone or something **1.** to throw something at someone or something. □ *The boys pitched cans at the tree.* □ *We all pitched rocks at the big boulder.* **2.** to aim advertising at a particular group. □ *They pitched the ad campaign at teenagers.* □ *These comedy programs are pitched at the lowest level of mentality.*

pitch something **away**† to toss or throw something away. □ *He pitched the broken stick away, and looked around for something stronger.* □ *He pitched away the stick.*

pitch something **into** something and **pitch** something **in**† to toss or throw something into something. □ *Please pitch your aluminum cans into this container.* □ *She pitched in the can.*

pitch something **out**† to throw something away; to discard something. □ *This cottage cheese is so old, I'm going to pitch it out.* □ *They pitched out the bad food.*

pitch (the) woo *Inf.* to kiss and caress; to woo someone. (Old but still heard.) □ *They were out by the barn pitching woo.* □ *Old Ted can hardly see any more, but he can still pitch the woo.*

pivot on something to rotate on something; to spin around, centered on something. □ *This part spins around and pivots on this little red spot, which is what they call a jewel.* □ *If the lever will not pivot on the bar, it needs some lubrication.*

place a price on one's **head** Go to a **price on** one's **head**.

place a strain on someone or something **1.** *Lit.* to burden and nearly overwhelm someone or something. □ *The weight of all the trucks placed a strain on the bridge.* **2.** *Fig.* to tax the resources or strength of someone, a group, or something to the utmost. □ *All of the trouble at work placed a strain on Kelly.* □ *The recession placed a strain on the economy.*

place an order to submit an order. □ *My secretary placed an order for a new computer.* □ *I placed my order only yesterday.*

A **place for everything, and everything in its place.** *Prov.* Everything in order and put away where it belongs. (Used to describe a very orderly thing or place.) □ *I like to put my books in alphabetical order by author. She has a place for everything, and everything in its place.* □ *Barbara's room is so tidy. A place for everything, and everything in its place.*

place of business a place where business is done; a factory or office. □ *Our place of business opens at 9:00 A.M. each day.* □ *You will have to come to our place of business to make a purchase.*

a **place of concealment** a hiding place. □ *She brought her little safe out of a place of concealment where it had been for decades.*

place one's **trust in** someone or something to trust someone or something. □ *If you place your trust in me, everything will work out all right.* □ *You should place your trust in your own proven talent.*

place someone to recall someone's name; to recall the details about a person that would help you identify the person. □ *I am sorry, I can't seem to place you. Could you tell me your name again?* □ *I can't place her. Did I meet her once before?*

place someone **by** someone or something Go to **by** someone or something.

place someone **in an awkward position** *Fig.* to put someone in an embarrassing or delicate situation. □ *Your decision places me in an awkward position.* □ *I'm afraid I have put myself in sort of an awkward position.*

place someone **on a pedestal** Go to **on a pedestal**.

place someone or something **above** someone or something **1.** *Lit.* to put someone or something in a place that is higher than someone or something else. □ *I placed Sally above everyone else in a place where she could see everything.* □ *I placed the book above Sally on a shelf.* □ *Who placed the mirror above the fireplace?* **2.** *Fig.* to hold someone or something in higher regard than someone or something else. □ *I place her above all others in honesty.* □ *She seems to place money above her family.* □ *She placed herself above almost everyone else.*

place someone or something **at** something **1.** to put someone or something somewhere. □ *The king placed extra guards at the door for the night.* □ *I placed the wine bottle at the left of the host.* **2.** to figure that someone or something was in a certain place. □ *The detective placed Randy at the scene of the crime about midnight.* □ *I place the getaway car at the first tollbooth at dawn.*

place someone or something **before** someone or something and **put** someone or something **before** someone or something **1.** to put someone or something in front of someone or something, especially in a line. □ *The teacher placed George before Bob, because Bob was a little taller.* □ *Tom placed himself before the group and began to speak.* **2.** to consider someone or something more important than someone or something. □ *I am sorry, but I place my wife and her welfare before yours!* □ *He places his job before his family!*

place someone or something **behind** someone or something **1.** to move someone or something to a place behind or to the rear of someone or something else. □ *Place the taller boy behind John in the second row.* □ *Place the iris behind the nasturtium.* **2.** to rank or estimate someone or something behind someone or something else. □ *I would place George behind Fred in this contest.* □ *Frank placed the white horse well behind the black one in the race.*

place someone or something **in jeopardy** to put someone or something at risk. □ *Do you realize that what you just* said places all of us in jeopardy? □ *She has placed the entire project in jeopardy.*

place someone or something **in** someone's **care** Go to in the care of someone.

place someone or something **in the trust of** someone Go to in the trust of someone.

place someone or something **into the care of** someone Go to in the care of someone.

place someone or something **next to** someone or something to put someone or something immediately adjacent to someone or something. □ *Please don't place Donna next to Betty for the class photograph. They are wearing identical dresses.* □ *Please don't place the flowers next to me. I have hay fever.*

place someone or something **on** someone or something to put or lay someone or something on someone or something. □ *The archbishop placed the crown on the new queen.* □ *The police officer placed Timmy on the sergeant's desk and gave him an ice-cream cone.*

place someone or something **under** someone's **care** Go to in the care of someone.

place someone **with** someone or something to get someone a job with someone or some company. □ *The agency was able to place me with Dave, who runs a small candy store on Maple Street.* □ *They placed me with a firm that makes doghouses.*

place something **aside**† to set something aside or out of the way. □ *Place this one aside and we'll keep it for ourselves.* □ *Place aside some of the smaller ones for later.*

place something **at a premium** to force up the value of something so that its price is higher. □ *The rapid changes in the market placed all the medical stocks at a premium.* □ *The goods had been placed at a premium by the changing market conditions.*

place something **back 1.** to move something backwards. □ *Place this chair back a little. It is in the walkway.* □ *Would you please place the boxes back so there is more room to get through?* **2.** to return something to where it was. □ *You found it on the table. Place it back when you finish.* □ *When you finish examining the book from the shelf, place it back.*

place something **down**† **(on something)** to put something down on something. □ *Place the book down on the top of the table.* □ *Please place down the book on the table.*

place something **in** something to put something inside something. □ *Place the rabbit in the pen with the others.* □ *Please place your dishes in the sink when you finish.*

place something **under** someone or something to put something beneath someone or something. □ *Bill was in the tree trying to get down, so we placed a ladder under him.* □ *I placed my wallet under my pillow.*

place something **up against** something Go to up against something.

place something **with** someone or something to leave something in the care of someone or something. □ *We placed the trunk with Fred and his wife.* □ *Mary placed the problem with the committee, hoping a solution could be found.*

place the blame on someone or something **(for something)** to blame someone or something for something. □ *Please*

don't try to place the blame on me for the accident. □ *The insurance company placed the blame on the weather.*

a **place to call** one's **own** a home of one's very own. □ *I am tired of living with my parents. I want a place to call my own.*

plague someone or something **with** something to bother or annoy someone or something with something. □ *Stop plaguing me with your requests.* □ *We plagued the committee with ideas.*

plain and simple Go to pure and simple.

plain as a pikestaff Go to next.

***plain as day** and ***plain as a pikestaff 1.** *Cliché* very plain and simple. (*Also:* **as** ~.) □ *Although his face was as plain as day, his smile made him look interesting and friendly.* □ *Fred: I have a suspicion that Marcia is upset with me. Alan: A suspicion? Come on, Fred, that's been plain as a pikestaff for quite some time!* **2.** and ***plain as the nose on** one's **face** *Cliché* clear and understandable. (*Also:* **as** ~.) □ *The lecture was as plain as day. No one had to ask questions.* □ *Jane: I don't understand why Professor Potter has been so friendly this week. Alan: It's plain as the nose on your face. He wants to be nominated for Professor of the Year.*

plan for someone to prepare enough [of something] for someone. □ *Fred just called and said he can show up for dinner after all. Please plan for him.* □ *Tony wasn't planned for, and there is no place for him to sit.*

plan for something **1.** to prepare for something. □ *I need to take some time and plan for my retirement.* □ *We carefully planned for almost every possibility.* **2.** to prepare or estimate for a certain number [of people or things]. □ *I am planning for twelve. I hope everyone can come.*

plan on someone to be ready for someone; to anticipate someone's arrival. □ *Don't plan on Sam. He has a cold and probably won't come.* □ *We are planning on Ted and Bill.*

plan on something to prepare for something; to be ready for something; to anticipate something. □ *If I were you, I would plan on a big crowd at your open house.* □ *This was not planned on.*

plan something **out**† to make thorough plans for something. □ *Let us sit down and plan our strategy out.* □ *We sat down and planned out our strategy.*

plane something **away**† to smooth off bumps or irregularities with a plane. □ *Please plane the bumps away so that the board is perfectly smooth.* □ *Sam planed away the bumps.*

plane something **down**† to smooth something down with a plane; to remove some material from something with a plane. □ *I will have to plane the door down before I hang it again.* □ *I planed down the edge of the door for you.*

plane something **off**† to remove bumps, nicks, or scrapes by planing. □ *Plane the rough places off so the surface will be as smooth as possible.* □ *Sam planed off the bumps.*

plank over something to cover something over with planking. □ *The county planked over the old bridge so bicyclists could use it.*

plant something **in** something **1.** *Lit.* to set out a plant in something; to sow seeds in something. □ *Are you going to plant tomatoes in these pots?* □ *What have you planted in* *the garden?* **2.** *Fig.* to put an idea in someone's brain, head, or thinking. □ *Who planted that silly idea in your head?* □ *I want to plant this concept in her thinking.* **3.** *Fig. Inf.* to conceal something in something. □ *The crook planted the money in the back of the refrigerator.* □ *What did the cops plant in your pockets?*

plant something **on** someone **1.** to hide incriminating evidence on a person for later discovery and use in prosecution. (Drugs. Allegedly a police practice used to entrap drug offenders.) □ *The cops planted crack on Richard and then arrested him for carrying it.* □ *Don't touch me! You'll plant something on me!* **2.** to conceal narcotics or other contraband on an unsuspecting person for the purpose of smuggling. (This person will bear the risk of discovery and arrest.) □ *The crooks planted the stuff on a passenger, but couldn't find him when the plane landed.* □ *Someone had planted coke on me, and the airport security officer found it.*

plaster one's **hair down**† *Fig.* to use water, oil, or cream to dress the hair for combing. (The result looks plastered to the head.) □ *Tony used some strange substance to plaster his hair down.* □ *He plastered down his hair with something that smells good.*

plaster over something to cover over something with plaster. □ *I think that we will just plaster over the cracks in the wall.*

plaster something **onto** something and **plaster** something **on**† to spread a substance onto something. □ *She plastered great globs of the jam onto the toast.* □ *She plastered on lots of butter.*

plaster something **up**† to close something up with plaster; to cover over holes or cracks in a wall with plaster. □ *He plastered the cracks up and then painted over them.* □ *You have to plaster up the cracks.*

plaster something **with** something to spread some substance onto something. □ *Jane plastered each slice of bread with butter and then heaped on a glob of jam.* □ *She plastered the wall with a thin coat of fine white plaster.*

play a big part (in something**)** and **play a large part (in** something**)** *Fig.* to serve as a major part of some situation or event. □ *The incredible amount of duplicative paperwork played a large part in my decision to find employment elsewhere.*

play a bit part to perform a small part in a play or a movie. □ *She played a few bit parts in minor Broadway plays, and then got the lead in an exciting new musical.*

play a joke on someone to make a joke that tricks someone. □ *The children played a joke on their teacher.* □ *I don't like it when you play jokes on me.*

play a large part (in something**)** Go to play a big part (in something).

play a part in something and **play a role in** something **1.** to participate in something in a specific way. □ *I hope to play a part in the development of the new product.* □ *I want to play a role in this procedure.* **2.** to portray a character in a performance. □ *He played a part in The Mikado, but it was not a major role.* □ *Larry wanted to play a role in the next play.*

play a prank on someone Go to play a trick on someone.

play a role in something Go to play a part in something.

play a trick on someone and **play a prank on** someone to do a trick that affects someone. □ *Somebody played a trick on me by hiding my shoes.* □ *The little boys planned to play a trick on their teacher by turning up the heat in the classroom.*

play about (with someone or something**)** Go to play around (with someone or something).

play against someone or something to compete against someone or something in a team sport. □ *We won't be ready to play against the other team this weekend.* □ *We refuse to play against you until the field is in better condition.*

play along (with someone or something**) 1.** *Lit.* to play a musical instrument with someone or a group. □ *The trombonist sat down and began to play along with the others.* □ *Do you mind if I play along?* **2.** *Fig.* to pretend to cooperate with someone or something in a joke, scam, etc. □ *I decided that I would play along with Larry for a while and see what would happen.* □ *I don't think I want to play along.*

play an old warhorse Go to an old warhorse.

play around (with someone or something**) 1.** and **play about (with** someone or something**)** to play and frolic with someone or something. □ *Kelly likes to play around with the other kids.* □ *The boys are out in the yard, playing about with the neighbor girls.* □ *Will you kids stop playing about and get busy?* □ *Stop playing around and get busy!* **2.** *Euph.* to have a romantic or sexual affair with someone or persons in general. □ *Kelly found out that her husband had been playing around with Susan.* □ *I can't believe that Roger is playing around!*

play at full blast Go to at full blast.

play at something to pretend to be doing something. □ *You are not fixing the car, you are just playing at repair work!* □ *Stop playing at doing the dishes and get the job done.*

play ball with someone **1.** *Lit.* to toss a ball back and forth with someone. □ *Carla is out playing ball with the little kids.* □ *Will you play ball with us?* **2.** *Lit.* to play baseball or some other team sport with someone. □ *Do you want to play ball with our team?* □ *I decided I wouldn't play ball with the school team anymore.* **3.** *Fig.* to cooperate with someone. □ *Why can't you guys play ball with us?* □ *Max won't play ball with the gang anymore.*

play both ends (against the middle) *Fig.* [for one] to scheme in a way that pits two sides against each other (for one's own gain). □ *I told my brother that Mary doesn't like him. Then I told Mary that my brother doesn't like her. They broke up, so now I can have the car this weekend. I succeeded in playing both ends against the middle.* □ *If you try to play both ends, you're likely to get in trouble with both sides.*

play by ear Go to play something by ear.

play by the book Go to by the book.

play cat and mouse with someone *Fig.* to be coy and evasive with someone. □ *I know what you are up to. Don't play cat and mouse with me!* □ *I wish that they wouldn't play cat and mouse with me!*

play dead to pretend to be dead. □ *When the bear attacked me, I just dropped down and played dead.*

play down to someone to condescend to one's audience. □ *Why are you playing down to the audience? They will walk out on you!* □ *Don't play down to the people who have paid their money to see you.*

play dumb Go to play ignorant.

play fair to do something by the rules; to play something in a fair and just manner. □ *John won't play with Bill anymore because Bill doesn't play fair.* □ *You moved the golf ball with your foot! That's not playing fair!*

play fast and loose (with someone or something**)** *Fig.* to act carelessly, thoughtlessly, and irresponsibly. □ *I'm tired of your playing fast and loose with me. Leave me alone.* □ *Bob got fired for playing fast and loose with the company's money.*

play first chair 1. to be the leader of a section of instruments in an orchestra or a band. (More literal than the following sense.) □ *Sally learned to play the violin so well that she now plays first chair in the orchestra.* □ *I'm going to practice my flute so I can play first chair.* **2.** *Fig.* to act as a leader. □ *I need to get this job done. Who plays first chair around here?* □ *You're not the boss! You don't play first chair.*

play footsie with someone **1.** to get romantically or sexually involved with someone. (Refers literally to secretly pushing or rubbing feet with someone under the table.) □ *Someone said that Ruth is playing footsie with Henry.* □ *Henry and Ruth are playing footsie with each other.* **2.** to get involved in a scheme with someone; to cooperate with someone. □ *The guy who runs the butcher shop was playing footsie with the city meat inspector.* □ *Henry was playing footsie with the mayor in order to get the contract.*

play for keeps to do things with permanent effect; to be serious in one's actions. (From the game of marbles, where the winner actually keeps all the marbles won.) □ *Are we playing for keeps or can we give everything back at the end of the game?* □ *We are playing for keeps, so be careful of what you do.*

play for something **1.** to gamble for something; to use something as the medium of exchange for gaming or gambling. □ *Let's just play for nickels, okay?* □ *We will play for dollar bills.* **2.** to play for a particular reason, other than winning. □ *We are just playing for fun.* □ *They are not competing. They are playing for practice.*

play for time *Fig.* to stall; to act in such a way as to gain time. □ *I'll play for time while you sneak out the window.* □ *The lawyers for the defense were playing for time while they looked for a witness.*

play freeze-out to open windows and doors, or turn down a thermostat, making someone cold. □ *Wow, it's cold in here! Who's playing freeze-out?* □ *Is someone trying to play freeze-out?*

play games (with someone**)** *Fig.* to use clever strategies against someone. □ *Come on! Stop playing games with me. Let's talk this over.*

play hard to get *Fig.* to be coy, intentionally shy, and fickle. (Usually refers to someone of the opposite sex.) □ *Why can't we go out? Why do you play hard to get?* □ *Sally annoys all the boys because she plays hard to get.*

play hardball (with someone**)** *Fig.* to act strong and aggressive about an issue with someone. □ *Things are getting a little tough. The president has decided to play hard-ball on this issue.* □ *If he wants to play hardball with us, we can play that way, too.*

play havoc with someone or something Go to **raise havoc with** someone or something.

play hell with someone or something *Fig.* to cause enormous disruptions with someone or something. (Use discretion with *hell*.) □ *Your proposal would play hell with Gerry and his plans.* □ *This new event really plays hell with my schedule.*

play hob with someone or something Go to **raise hob with** someone or something.

play hooky to fail to attend school or some other event. □ *Why aren't you in school? Are you playing hooky?* □ *I don't have time for the sales meeting today, so I think I'll just play hooky.*

play ignorant and **play dumb** to pretend to be ignorant [of something]. □ *I played ignorant even though I knew about the surprise party.* □ *John played dumb when I asked him if he knew who had been on the telephone.*

play in something **1.** to play a musical instrument in some musical organization. □ *I used to play in a band.* □ *I wanted to play in the orchestra but I wasn't good enough.* **2.** [for someone] to play the action of a game in a particular position or location. □ *Fred played in left field for the rest of the game.* □ *I will play in the backfield for the rest of the game.* **3.** to perform in a specific production. □ *She played in the Broadway production of* Major Barbara. □ *Once, I played in* The Mikado.

play in the big leagues *Fig.* to be involved in something of large or important proportions. (Alludes to playing a professional sport at the highest level.) □ *You had better shape up if you want to play in the big leagues.* □ *The conductor shouted at the oboist, "You're playing in the big leagues now. Tune up or ship out."*

play innocent to pretend to be innocent and not concerned. □ *There is no need to play innocent! I know you broke the lamp!* □ *John is playing innocent, and he knows more than he is telling us.*

play into someone's **hands** *Fig.* [for a person one is scheming against] to assist one in one's scheming without realizing it. □ *John is doing exactly what I hoped he would. He's playing into my hands.* □ *John played into my hands by taking the cash he found in my desk. I caught him and had him arrested.*

play it cool 1. *Inf.* to do something while not revealing insecurities or incompetence; to act blasé. □ *Play it cool, man. Look like you belong there.* □ *If the boss walks in, just play it cool.* **2.** *Inf.* to hold one's temper. □ *Come on now. Let it pass. Play it cool.* □ *Don't let them get you mad. Play it cool.*

play it for all it's worth *Fig.* to exploit a problem, disability, or injury to get as much sympathy or compensation as possible. □ *He injured his hand before the examination and he played it for all it was worth in order to get the exam delayed.*

play it safe to be or act safe; to avoid taking a risk. □ *You should play it safe and take your umbrella.* □ *If you have a cold or the flu, play it safe and go to bed.*

play like someone or something to pretend to be someone or a type of a person. □ *Sam is playing like Mr. Watson,*

P

the teacher. □ *He is playing like a teacher and helping Mary with her homework.*

play on to continue to play. □ *The band played on and the dance continued until the wee hours of the morning.* □ *We played on and on until the last guests left the party.*

play on someone's **heartstrings** *Fig.* to attempt to get sympathy from someone. □ *She is crying so she can play on your heartstrings and try to get you to take her home.*

play on something to have an effect on something; to manage something for a desired effect. (The *on* can be replaced by *upon.*) □ *The clerk played on my sense of responsibility in trying to get me to buy the book.* □ *See if you can get her to confess by playing on her sense of guilt.*

play one's **cards close to** one's **chest** and **play** one's **cards close to** one's **vest; keep** one's **cards close to** one's **chest; keep** one's **cards close to** one's **vest** *Fig.* to keep to oneself or be very cautious in one's dealing with people. (As if one were playing cards and not permitting anyone to see any of the cards.) □ *He is very cautious. He plays his cards close to his chest.* □ *You seem to be playing your cards close to your vest.*

play one's **cards right** and **play** one's **cards well** *Fig.* to work or negotiate correctly and skillfully. □ *If you play your cards right, you can get whatever you want.* □ *She didn't play her cards well, and she ended up with something less than what she wanted.*

play one's **cards well** Go to previous.

play one's **heart out** Go to cry one's heart out.

play one's **trump card 1.** *Lit.* [in certain card games] to play a card that, according to the rules of the game, outranks certain other cards and is thus able to take any card of another suit. □ *Bob played his trump card and ended the game as the winner.* **2.** *Fig.* to use a special trick; to use one's most powerful or effective strategy or device. □ *I won't play my trump card until I have tried everything else.* □ *I thought that the whole situation was hopeless until Mary played her trump card and solved the whole problem.*

play out [for a process] to run out; to finish. □ *The whole incident is about to play out. Then it all will be forgotten.* □ *When the event plays out, everything will return to normal.*

play politics 1. *Lit.* to negotiate politically. □ *Everybody at city hall is playing politics as usual.* □ *If you're elected as a member of a political party, you'll have to play politics.* **2.** to allow politics to dominate in matters where principle should prevail. □ *Look, I came here to discuss the legal issues of this trial, not play politics.* □ *They're not making reasonable decisions. They're playing politics.*

play possum *Fig.* to pretend to be inactive, unobservant, asleep, or dead. (The *possum* refers to an opossum.) □ *I knew that Bob wasn't asleep. He was just playing possum.* □ *I can't tell if this animal is dead or just playing possum.*

play second fiddle (to someone) *Fig.* to be in a subordinate position to someone. □ *I'm tired of playing second fiddle to John.* □ *I'm better trained than he, and I have more experience. I shouldn't always play second fiddle.*

play someone **against** someone else to cause someone to dispute with someone else. □ *Don tried to play George against David, but they figured out what he was up to.* □ *Alice never managed to play Tom against Fred.*

play someone **for a fool** *Fig.* to treat someone like a fool; to assume someone is naive or stupid. □ *Don't play me for a fool. I won't have it.* □ *You are playing me for a fool! Stop it!*

play someone **off against** someone else to scheme in a manner that pits two of your adversaries against one another. □ *Bill wanted to beat me up and so did Bob. I did some fast talking, and they ended up fighting with each other. I really played Bill off against Bob.* □ *The president played the House off against the Senate and ended up getting his own way.*

play someone or something **down**† to lessen the effect or importance of someone or something. □ *John is a famous actor, but the director tried to play him down as just another member of the cast.* □ *Her lawyer tried to play down her earlier arrest.*

play someone or something **up**† to make someone or something seem to be more important. □ *The director tried to play Ann up, but she was not really a star.* □ *Try to play up the good qualities of our product.*

play something **as** something to deal with something as if it were something else. □ *I will play this matter as a simple case of mistaken identity.* □ *We will play this lapse as an instance of forgetfulness and not make too much of it.*

play something **at full blast** Go to at full blast.

play something **back**† **(to** someone) to play a recording to someone. □ *Can you play the speech back to me?* □ *Please play back the speech to me, so I can hear how I sound.*

play something **by ear 1.** to be able to play a piece of music after just listening to it a few times, without looking at the notes. □ *I can play "Stardust" by ear.* □ *Some people can play Chopin's music by ear.* **2.** and **play by ear** to play a musical instrument well, without formal training. □ *John can play the piano by ear.* □ *If I could play by ear, I wouldn't have to take lessons—or practice!* **3.** to improvise; to decide one's next steps after one is already involved in a situation. □ *If we go into the meeting unprepared, we'll have to play everything by ear.* □ *He never prepared his presentations. He always played things by ear.*

play something **off**† to play a game to break a tied score. □ *They decided not to play the tie off because it had grown so late.* □ *They went ahead and played off the tie after all.*

play something **on** someone or something to aim a light or a hose on someone or something. □ *The fireman played water on the burning building.* □ *The stagehand played a spotlight on the singer.*

play something **out**† **1.** to play something, such as a game, to the very end. □ *I was bored with the game, but I felt I had to play it out.* □ *She played out the rest of the game.* **2.** to unwind, unfold, or unreel something. (See also pay something **out.**) □ *Please play some more rope out.* □ *They played out many feet of cable.*

play something **over** to replay something, such as a game, a videotape, an audio recording, etc. □ *There was an objection to the way the referee handled the game, so they played it over.* □ *Let's play that song over again.*

play something **through**† to play something, such as a piece of recorded music, all the way through. □ *I played the album through, hoping to find even one song I liked.* □ *As I played through the album, I didn't hear anything I liked.*

play something **up**† to emphasize something; to be a booster of something. □ *The press played the scandal up so much that everyone became bored with it.* □ *They really played up the scandal.*

play something **with** someone or something **1.** to play a game with someone or a group. □ *Do you want to play checkers with me?* □ *Fran played ball with the dog for a while.* **2.** to assume a particular role with someone or some group. □ *Don't play the fool with me!* □ *Don always tried to play the successful entrepreneur with the board of directors.*

play (the) devil's advocate *Fig.* to put forward arguments against or objections to a proposition—which one may actually agree with—purely to test the validity of the proposition. (The devil's advocate opposes the canonization of a saint in order to prove that the grounds for canonization are sound.) □ *I agree with your plan. I'm just playing the devil's advocate so you'll know what the opposition will say.* □ *Mary offered to play devil's advocate and argue against our case so that we would find out any flaws in it.*

play the devil with something *Fig.* to cause disruption with something; to foul something up. □ *Your being late really played the devil with my plans for the day.* □ *This weather is really playing the devil with my arthritis.*

play the field to date many different people rather than just one. □ *When Tom told Ann good-bye, he said he wanted to play the field.* □ *He said he wanted to play the field while he was still young.*

play the fool *Fig.* to act in a silly manner in order to amuse other people. □ *The teacher told Tom to stop playing the fool and sit down.* □ *Fred likes playing the fool, but we didn't find him funny last night.*

play the heavy *Fig.* to act the part of a mean person; to do the unpleasant tasks that no one else wants to do. (Refers originally to playing the role of someone evil in a movie, etc.) □ *I'm a nice guy, but at work, I am required to play the heavy. The boss makes me do all the cruel things.*

play the horses Go to next.

play the ponies and **play the horses** to wager on horse races. □ *I used to play the ponies every afteroon during the summer. Then I ran out of money.*

play the race card Go to the the race card.

play the (stock) market to invest in the stock market. (As if it were a game or as if it were gambling.) □ *Would you rather put your money in the bank or play the market?* □ *I've learned my lesson playing the market. I lost a fortune.*

play through [for golfers] to pass someone on the golf course. □ *Do you mind if we play through? We have to get back to the courtroom by two o'clock.* □ *We let them play through because they were moving so fast.*

play to someone or something **1.** to perform something for someone or a group. □ *The cast played to one of their classmates who was confined to the hospital.* □ *Gerald Watson will play to a small gathering of wealthy socialites this Saturday evening.* **2.** to aim one's performance only toward a particular person, group, or a particular taste. □ *The comedian was playing only to the juveniles in the audience.* □ *It was clear that she was playing to the people in the cheaper seats.*

play to the crowd Go to next.

play to the gallery and **play to the crowd** to perform in a manner that will get the strong approval of the audience; to perform in a manner that will get the approval of the lower elements in the audience. □ *John is a competent actor, but he has a tendency to play to the crowd.* □ *When he made the rude remark, he was just playing to the gallery.*

play tricks on someone **1.** *Lit.* to pull pranks on someone. □ *You had better not play any tricks on me!* □ *Stop playing tricks on people!* **2.** *Fig.* [for something, such as the eyes] to deceive someone. □ *Did I see him fall down or are my eyes playing tricks on me?* □ *My brain is playing tricks on me. I can't remember a word you said.*

play up to someone to flatter someone; to try to gain influence with someone. □ *It won't do any good to play up to me. I refuse to agree to your proposal.* □ *I played up to him and he still wouldn't give in to me.*

play (up)on something **1.** *Lit.* to make music on a musical instrument. (*Upon* is formal and less commonly used than *on.*) □ *Can you play upon this instrument, or only the one you are holding?* □ *I can't play on this! It's broken.* **2.** *Lit.* to play a game on a field or court. □ *Shall we play on the floor or on the table?* □ *Let's play on the field. It's dry enough now.* **3.** *Fig.* to exploit something—including a word—for some purpose; to develop something for some purpose. (*Upon* is formal and less commonly used than *on.*) □ *You are just playing on words!* □ *You are playing on a misunderstanding.* **4.** *Fig.* [for light] to sparkle on something. □ *The reflections of the candles played on the surface of the wall.* □ *The lights played on the crystal goblets.*

play with a full deck 1. *Lit.* to play cards with a complete deck, containing all the cards. □ *Are we playing with a full deck or did some card drop on the floor? I haven't seen the three of hearts all evening!* **2.** *Fig.* to operate as if one were mentally sound. (Usually in the negative. One cannot play cards properly with a partial deck.) □ *That guy's not playing with a full deck.* □ *Look sharp, you dummies! Pretend you are playing with a full deck.*

play with fire 1. *Lit.* to use fire as a toy; to experiment with flames and fire. □ *Jimmy! I've told you never to play with fire!* **2.** *Fig.* to do something dangerous or risky. (Usually *playing with fire.*) □ *Be careful with that knife! You are playing with fire!* □ *If you mess with Max, you are playing with fire.*

play with someone or something **1.** to play games with someone or a group. □ *I love to play Ping-Pong. Will you play with me?* □ *They won't play with our team. We are too good.* **2.** to toy with someone or something. □ *You are just playing with me. Can't you take me seriously?* □ *Please don't play with that crystal vase.*

play-by-play description a description of an event given as the event is taking place. (Usually in reference to a sporting event.) □ *And now here is Bill Jones with a play-by-play description of the baseball game.* □ *John was giving me a play-by-play description of the argument going on next door.*

played out too exhausted to continue. □ *At the end of the race, Donna was played out.* □ *After the race, we were played out for the rest of the day.*

plead for someone to beg for someone to be spared. □ *Tom pleaded for Dave, but it was no use. Dave was found guilty.* □ *She pleaded for her husband, but the judge sentenced him to ten years in prison.*

plead for something to beg for something. □ *I don't want to have to plead for what's already mine.* □ *The children were pleading for ice cream, so we got some for them.*

plead guilty to something to state that one is guilty of a crime before a court of law. □ *Gerald refused to plead guilty to the crime and had to stand trial.* □ *Max pleaded guilty to the charge and then fled town.*

plead to something to enter an admission of guilt to a specific crime. □ *Max pleaded to the lesser charge of larceny.* □ *Lefty pleaded to the grand larceny charge.*

plead with someone to beg something of someone; to make an emotional appeal to someone. □ *Do I have to plead with you to get you to do it?* □ *You can plead with me as much as you want. I won't permit you to go.*

(Please) don't get up. Please, there is no need to rise to greet me or in deference to me. □ *Mary approached the table to speak to Bill. Bill started to push his chair back as if to rise. Mary said, "Don't get up. I just want to say hello."* □ *Tom (rising): Hello, Fred. Good to see you. Fred (standing): Don't get up. How are you?*

Please hold. Go to **Hold the phone.**

please oneself to do what one wishes. □ *We don't mind whether you stay or not. Please yourself!* □ *The boss preferred me to work late, but he told me to please myself.*

***pleased as Punch** delighted; very pleased. (*Also: **as ~**.) (This refers to Punch from the "Punch and Judy" shows.) □ *Child: Do you think Grandma will like the picture I'm making for her? Father: I think she'll be as pleased as Punch.* □ *Fred was pleased as Punch to discover that Ellen was making lemon pie, his favorite, for dessert.*

pleased for someone or something happy for someone or a group. □ *I am very pleased for you.* □ *We were all pleased for the committee. The members got all the praise they deserved.* □ *Everyone could see how pleased Sam was for himself and his whole family.*

***pleased with** someone or something happy and satisfied with someone or something. (*Typically: **be ~; become ~**.) □ *I am quite pleased with you. You did a fine job.* □ *We are pleased with your work.*

pledge something **to** someone to promise something to someone. □ *I pledged one hundred dollars to Ralph for his cause.* □ *We pledged a lot of money to our favorite charity.*

plenty of something lots of something; an abundance of something; enough of something. □ *I have plenty of candy. Do you want some?* □ *This project is giving me plenty of trouble.*

plight one's **troth to** someone to become engaged to be married to someone. (Literary or jocular.) □ *I chose not to plight my troth to anyone who acts so unpleasant to my dear aunt.* □ *Alice plighted her troth to Scott.*

plod along to move along slowly but deliberately. □ *I'm just plodding along, but I am getting the job done.* □ *The old man plodded along, hardly able to stand.* □ *The movie plodded along putting most of the audience to sleep.*

plod away at something to keep trying to do something. □ *He continues to plod away at writing his novel. It's been three years now.* □ *How long have you been plodding away at that book?*

plod through something to work one's way through something laboriously. □ *I just plodded through my work today. I had no energy at all.* □ *This is certainly a lot of papers to have to plod through.*

plonk something **down**[†] to slap something down; to plop something down. □ *He plonked a dollar down and demanded a newspaper.* □ *He plonked down his beer mug on the bar.*

plot against someone or something to make a scheme against someone or something. □ *All the counselors plotted against the czar.* □ *We plotted against the opposing party.*

plot something **on** something to draw a route or outline on something. □ *He plotted the course they would be taking on a map of the area.* □ *The captain plotted the course on a chart of the upper reaches of the Nile.*

plot something **out**[†] to map something out; to outline a plan for something. □ *I have an idea about how to remodel this room. Let me plot it out for you.* □ *I plotted out my ideas for the room.*

The **plot thickens.** Things are becoming more complicated or interesting. □ *The police assumed that the woman was murdered by her ex-husband, but he has an alibi. The plot thickens.* □ *John is supposed to be going out with Mary, but I saw him last night with Sally. The plot thickens.*

plot with someone to scheme with someone. □ *Mary looks as though she is plotting with Jerry to make some sort of mischief.* □ *I am not plotting with anyone. I am planning everything myself.*

plow into someone or something to crash into someone or something; to bump hard into someone or something. □ *The car plowed into the ditch.* □ *The runner plowed into another player.*

plow something **back into** something and **plow** something **back**[†] to put something, such as a profit, back into an investment. □ *We plowed all the profits back into the expansion of the business.* □ *Bill and Ted plowed back everything they earned into the company.*

plow something **in**[†] to work something into soil by plowing. □ *Lay the fertilizer down and plow it in.* □ *Plow in the fertilizer as soon as you can.*

plow something **under** (something) to turn something under the surface of soil by plowing. □ *The farmer plowed the wheat stubble under the surface of the soil.* □ *The farmer plowed the stubble under.*

plow something **up**[†] to uncover something by plowing. □ *The farmer plowed some old coins up and took them to the museum to find out what they were.* □ *He plowed up some valuable coins.*

plow through something **1.** *Lit.* to move through something such as snow or mud with a plow. □ *The huge truck plowed through the snow-covered streets so traffic could move again.* **2.** *Fig.* to work through something with determination. □ *She plowed through the book to learn everything she could.* □ *Billy plowed through dinner and ran outside to play.*

pluck at someone or something to pull or pick at someone or something. □ *Kelly plucked at Ed, picking off the burrs that had caught on his clothing.* □ *Kelly plucked at the strings of the guitar.*

pluck something **from** someone or something to pick, grab, or snatch something from someone. □ *Sally plucked a chocolate from the box and popped it into her mouth.* □ *He stooped over and plucked a rose from the bush.*

pluck something **off (of)** someone or something and **pluck** something **off**† to pick something off someone or something. (*Of* is usually retained before pronouns.) □ *She plucked the mosquito off his back before it could bite him.* □ *She plucked off the bud.*

pluck something **out of** something and **pluck** something **out**† to snatch something out of something. □ *She plucked the coin out of his hand and put it in her pocket.* □ *Reaching into the fountain, Jane plucked out the coin.*

pluck up someone's **courage** to bolster someone's, including one's own, courage. □ *I hope you are able to pluck up your courage so that you can do what has to be done.* □ *Some good advice from a friend helped pluck up my courage.*

plug away (at something**)** and **peg away (at** something**)** to keep trying something; to keep working at something. □ *John kept pegging away at the trumpet until he became pretty good at it.* □ *I'm not very good at it, but I keep plugging away.*

plug (oneself) **in(to** something**)** to become attached to something; to become attached to some sort of network or system. □ *As soon as I have plugged my laptop into the local network, I will have access to the Internet.* □ *I plugged myself into the computer network and began to communicate quickly and efficiently.*

plug something **into** something and **plug** something **in**† to connect something to something else, usually by connecting wires together with a plug and socket. □ *Plug this end of the wire into the wall.* □ *Plug in the lamp and turn it on.*

plug something **up**† to stop or fill up a hole, crack, or gap. □ *Take out the nail and plug the hole up with something.* □ *You have to plug up the cracks to keep out the cold.*

plumb loco *Rur.* completely crazy. (*Loco* is from a Spanish word meaning "mad.") □ *You're plumb loco if you think I'll go along with that.* □ *All those people were running around like they were plumb loco.*

plummet to earth to fall rapidly to earth from a great height. □ *The rocket plummeted to earth and exploded as it struck.* □ *As the plane plummeted to earth, all the people on the ground were screaming.*

plummet to something to drop or fall to some level or low point. □ *Stock prices plummeted to record low levels.* □ *The rock plummeted to the river at the base of the cliff.*

plump for someone or something to support or promote someone or something. □ *Henry spent a lot of energy plumping for Bill, who was running for vice president.* □ *She spent a lot of time plumping for our candidate.*

plump something **down**† **1.** to drop a heavy load of something. □ *She plumped the load of groceries onto the bench and looked through her purse for the keys.* □ *Jill plumped down her packages.* **2.** to drop something as if it were a heavy load. □ *He plumped the potatoes down on each plate,* making a loud noise each time. □ *Dave plumped down a huge slab of meat onto the grill.*

plump something **up**† to pat or shake something like a pillow into a fuller shape. □ *Todd plumped his pillow up and finished making the bed.* □ *He plumped up his pillow.*

plunge down something to run or fall down something. □ *The car plunged down the hill and ran into a tree at the bottom.* □ *The bicyclist plunged down the side of the hill at a great speed.*

plunge from something to fall or flee from something or some place. □ *The eagle plunged from the sky to the lake to capture its prey.* □ *Lily plunged from the room in embarrassment.*

plunge in(to something**)** to dive or rush into something; to immerse oneself in something. □ *Ned took off his shoes and plunged into the river, hoping to rescue Frank.* □ *He plunged into his work and lost track of time.*

plunge something **into** someone or something and **plunge** something **in**† to drive or stab something into someone or something. □ *The murderer plunged the knife into his victim.* □ *She plunged in the dagger.*

plunge to something **1.** to fall or drop down to something. □ *The temperature plunged to zero last night.* □ *The burning car plunged to the floor of the canyon.* **2.** to dive or fall to one's death. □ *She walked straight to the edge of the cliff and plunged to her death.* □ *The burro slipped and plunged to an untimely end.*

plunk (oneself) **down** to sit or fall down hard. □ *Nancy pulled up a chair and plunked herself down.* □ *She pulled the chair up and plunked down.* □ *She plunked herself down in the middle of the kids and began to sing.*

plunk someone or something **down**† to place, drop, or plop someone or something down hard. □ *He picked her up and plunked her down in a chair and began to shout at her.* □ *Sally plunked down the book in anger.*

ply between something **and** something else to travel between things or places regularly or constantly. □ *There are a number of small craft that ply between Santerem and Manaus on a regular basis.* □ *Our little ship was unable to ply the entire distance between the two islands.*

ply someone **with** something else to try to supply or give something to someone. (Implies an attempt to influence or fawn upon someone.) □ *We plied the mayor with gifts and favors, but it got us nowhere.* □ *Don't try to ply the police officer with gifts. That is considered a bribe.*

pock something **with** something to cause dents or small craters by shooting or throwing something at something. □ *The hail pocked the roof of the car with dents.* □ *The side of the house was pocked with tiny dents where the hail had struck.*

a pocket of resistance *Fig.* a small group of people who resist change or domination. □ *The accounting department seems to be a pocket of resistance when it comes to automating.*

poetic justice appropriate, ideal, or ironic punishment. □ *It was poetic justice that Jane won the race after Mary tried to get her banned from the race.* □ *The car thieves tried to steal a car with no gas. That's poetic justice.*

poetic license liberties or license of the type taken by artists, especially poets, to violate patterns of rhyme, harmony, structure, etc. □ *I couldn't tell whether he kept making spelling mistakes or if it was just poetic license.*

point at someone or something **1.** [for someone] to direct an extended finger at someone or something; to point one's finger at someone or something. □ *You should not point at people.* □ *Harry pointed at the mess Jerry had made and scowled.* **2.** [for something] to aim at someone or something. □ *The gun pointed directly at him. He was frightened.* □ *The sign pointed at a small roadside cafe, populated by truck drivers.*

point down to something to aim downward to something. □ *The sign pointed down to the little bell sitting on the counter.* □ *The room clerk pointed down the stairs to a little cafe on the lower level.*

the **point of no return** the halfway point; the point at which it is too late to turn back. (Often with *past*.) □ *The flight was past the point of no return, so we had to continue to our destination.* □ *The entire project is past the point of no return; we will have to continue with it.*

point of view a way of thinking about something; [someone's] viewpoint; an attitude or expression of self-interest. □ *From my point of view, all this talk is a waste of time.* □ *I can understand her point of view. She has made some good observations about the problem.*

point someone or something **out**† to select or indicate someone or something (from a group). □ *Everyone pointed the error out.* □ *She pointed out the boy who took her purse.*

point something **at** someone or something to aim or direct something at someone or something. □ *Don't ever point a gun at anyone!* □ *Point the rifle at the target and pull the trigger.*

point something **up**† **1.** *Fig.* to emphasize something; to emphasize one aspect of something. □ *This is a very important thing to learn. Let me point it up one more time by drawing this diagram on the board.* □ *This points up what I've been telling you.* **2.** *Fig.* to tuck-point something; to repair the joints in masonry. □ *I hired someone to point the chimney up.* □ *Carl pointed up the brick wall.*

point the finger at someone *Fig.* to blame someone; to identify someone as the guilty person. □ *Don't point the finger at me! I didn't take the money.* □ *The manager refused to point the finger at anyone in particular and said that everyone was sometimes guilty of being late.*

point to someone or something to aim at someone or something. □ *Who is she pointing to?* □ *He pointed to the door.*

point to something to indicate, reveal, or suggest something. □ *All the evidence seems to point to his guilt.* □ *The signs point to a very cold winter.*

point to something **as** something to identify something as something. □ *All the indications pointed to Jill as the next president.*

point toward someone or something to direct an extended finger toward someone or something. □ *The teacher pointed toward Laura and asked her to come to the front of the room.* □ *Randy pointed toward the door and frowned at the dog.*

poise oneself **for** something to get ready for something. □ *She poised herself for her dive.* □ *Fred poised himself for a fall, but everything worked out all right.*

poise over someone or something to hover or hang over someone or something. □ *She spent the entire afternoon poised over her desk, pouting.* □ *The dog poised over the downed duck, waiting for the hunter.*

poised for something ready for something; in the right position and waiting for something. □ *The cat stared at the mouse, poised for action.* □ *The army was poised for battle.*

poised to do something ready to do something; in the right position to do something. □ *The cat is poised to jump on the mouse.* □ *The army is poised to attack at dawn.*

poison someone **against** someone or something to cause someone to have negative or hateful thoughts about someone, a group, or something. □ *You have done nothing more than poison Gerald against all of us! Stop talking to him!* □ *Your negative comments poisoned everyone against the proposal.*

poison someone or an animal **with** something to render someone or an animal sick or dead with a poison. □ *He intended to poison his wife with arsenic.* □ *Barry wanted to poison the cat with something that left no trace.* □ *He poisoned himself with the cleaning compound.*

poison something **with** something to render something poisonous with something. □ *She poisoned the soup with arsenic.* □ *They are poisoning our water supply with pollutants.*

poke a hole in something and **poke a hole through** something to make a hole by pushing something through something; to push something through a hole. □ *The carpenter poked a hole in the wall with a nail.* □ *The fisherman poked a hole through the ice with a pick.*

poke about Go to poke around.

poke about (in something**)** and **poke around (in** something**)** to rummage around in something or some place; to look through things in something or some place. □ *I'll have to go up and poke about in the attic to see if I can find it.* □ *Janet went to the attic and spent the rest of the afternoon poking around.*

poke along to move along slowly; to lag or tarry. □ *Get moving. Stop poking along.* □ *I was just poking along, taking my time, not paying attention to what was going on around me.*

poke around 1. and **poke about** to look or search around. □ *I've been poking around in the library looking for some statistics.* □ *I don't mind if you look in my drawer for a paper clip, but please don't poke about.* **2.** to waste time while moving about. □ *I just poked around all afternoon and didn't accomplish much.* □ *Stop poking around and get moving.*

poke around (in something**)** Go to poke about (in something).

poke at someone or something to thrust or jab at someone or something. □ *Stop poking at me!* □ *Don't poke at the turtle. It might bite you.*

poke fun at someone or something to make fun of someone or something. □ *You shouldn't poke fun at me for my* mistakes. □ *They are just poking fun at the strange architecture.*

poke one's **nose in(to** something) and **stick** one's **nose in(to** something) *Fig.* to interfere with something; to be nosy about something. □ *I wish you'd stop poking your nose into my business.* □ *She was too upset for me to stick my nose in and ask what was wrong.*

poke out (of something) to stick out of something; to extend out of something. □ *The bean sprouts were beginning to poke out of the soil of the garden.* □ *I knew there were little birds in the birdhouse, because a little head poked out now and then.*

poke someone **in** something to strike or jab someone in some body part. □ *Billy poked Bobby in the tummy and made him cry.* □ *She poked herself in the eye accidentally.*

poke something **at** someone or something to jab or thrust something at someone or something. □ *Don't poke that thing at me!* □ *The hunter poked his spear at the pig one more time and decided it was dead.*

poke something **into** something and **poke** something **in**† to stick or cram something into something. □ *He poked his finger into the jam, pulled it out again, and licked it.* □ *Jeff poked in his finger.*

poke something **out of** something and **poke** something **out**† to thrust something out of something. □ *The lobster poked its antennae out of the little cave and wiggled them around.* □ *It poked out its antennae.*

poke something **through** someone or something to jab or stab something through someone or something. □ *The evil knight poked his weapon through Arthur and withdrew it again.* □ *Danny poked his finger through the plastic pool liner by mistake.*

poke through (something) to stick through something; to extend through something. □ *The tips of Tommy's toes poked through his sneakers and looked very cold.* □ *The end of the lost spoon poked through the piecrust on the freshly baked pie. Now we knew where it had disappeared to.*

polarize something **into** something to divide a group into two segments. □ *Your actions have just polarized the students into two opposing groups!* □ *We polarized the entire population into two factions.*

*****poles apart** very different; far from coming to an agreement. (Alludes to the distance between the north and south poles. *Typically: **be** ~; **become** ~; **grow** ~.)* □ *Mr. and Mrs. Jones don't get along well. They are poles apart.* □ *They'll never sign the contract because they are poles apart.*

polish something **off**† to eat, consume, exhaust, or complete all of something. □ *Who polished the cake off?* □ *Who polished off the cake?*

polish something **up**† to rub something until it shines. □ *Polish the silver up and make it look nice and shiny.* □ *If you will polish up the silver, I will put it away.*

a **political football** *Fig.* an issue that becomes politically divisive; a problem that doesn't get solved because the politics of the issue get in the way. □ *The question of campaign contributions has become a political football. All the politicians who accept questionable money are pointing fingers at each other.*

Politics makes strange bedfellows. *Prov.* People who would normally dislike and avoid one another will work together if they think it is politically useful to do so. □ *Jill: I never would have thought that genteel, aristocratic candidate would pick such a rabble-rousing, rough-mannered running mate. Jane: Politics makes strange bedfellows.*

pollute something **with** something to adulterate something with something; to dirty something with something. □ *You should not pollute the stream with chemicals.* □ *Someone polluted the sewer with automotive oil.*

ponder (up)on something to think on something; to consider something. (*Upon* is formal and less commonly used than *on*.) □ *Ponder upon this awhile. See what you come up with.* □ *I need to ponder on this.*

pontificate on something to speak and act dogmatically and pompously. □ *Must you pontificate on your own virtues so much?* □ *The speaker was pontificating on the virtues of a fat-free diet.*

pooch out to stick or bulge out, as with a belly. □ *His chubby tummy pooched out when he relaxed.*

poop out *Inf.* to quit; to wear out and stop. □ *He pooped out after about an hour of hard work.* □ *I think I'm going to poop out pretty soon.*

poop someone or something **out** *Inf.* to cause someone to become exhausted or give out. □ *All that exercise really pooped everyone out.* □ *A full day of play at the beach had pooped the dog out.* □ *The activity pooped out the dog.*

pooped (out) 1. *Inf.* [of a person or an animal] exhausted; worn out. □ *I'm really pooped out.* □ *The horse looked sort of pooped in the final stretch.* **2.** *Inf.* intoxicated. □ *How much of that stuff does it take to get pooped?* □ *He's been drinking all night and is totally pooped out.*

*****poor as a church mouse** and *****poor as church mice** very poor. (*Also: **as** ~.)* □ *My aunt is as poor as a church mouse.* □ *The Browns are poor as church mice.*

poor but clean *Cliché* having little money but clean and of good habits, nonetheless. (Either extremely condescending or jocular. Some people would consider it offensive.) □ *My salary isn't very high, and I only have one old car. Anyway, I'm poor but clean.* □ *When Fred uttered the phrase "poor but clean" in reference to some of the people working in the yard, Ellen went into a rage.*

pop around (for a visit) and **pop by (for a visit); pop in (for a visit); pop over (for a visit)** to come by [someone's residence] for a visit. □ *You simply must pop around for a visit sometime.* □ *I will pop by about noon.* □ *I can pop in for only a minute.*

pop back (for something) to come back to a place for just a moment. □ *Okay, I think I can pop back for a minute.* □ *I have to pop back for something I forgot.*

pop by (for a visit) Go to pop around (for a visit).

pop down (for a visit) to come or go to someone's home that is downstairs or in a place on a lower level. □ *You simply must pop down for a visit whenever you get a chance.* □ *I'll try to pop down tomorrow evening after dinner.*

pop for something *Inf.* to pay for a treat (for someone). □ *Let's have some ice cream. I'll pop for it.* □ *It's about time you popped for coffee.*

pop in (for a visit) Go to pop around (for a visit).

pop in(to something**) 1.** *Lit. Inf.* to come or go into some place, such as a store, shop, etc., for a moment. □ *Let me pop into the bakery for a minute.* □ *I have to pop into the drugstore for some shampoo.* **2.** *Fig.* to snap into place in something. □ *The little plastic thing popped into its slot, and the model plane was finished.* □ *It pops in and holds tight if you do it right.*

pop off 1. *Sl.* to make an unnecessary remark; to interrupt with a remark; to sound off. □ *Please don't pop off all the time.* □ *Bob keeps popping off when he should be listening.* **2.** *Sl.* to lose one's temper. □ *Now, don't pop off. Keep your cool.* □ *I don't know why she popped off at me. All I did was say hello.* **3.** *Sl.* to die. □ *My uncle popped off last week.* □ *I hope I'm asleep when I pop off.* **4.** *Sl.* to leave; to depart in haste. □ *Bye, I must pop off.* □ *Got to pop off. I'm late.*

pop one's **cork 1.** *Fig.* to suddenly become mentally disturbed; to go crazy. □ *I was so upset that I nearly popped my cork.* □ *They put him away because he popped his cork.* **2.** *Fig.* to become very angry. □ *My mother popped her cork when she heard about my low grades.* □ *Calm down! Don't pop your cork.*

pop out (of something**)** to jump out of something; to burst out of something. □ *Suddenly, a little mouse popped out of the drawer.* □ *I opened the drawer and a mouse popped out.*

pop over (for a visit) Go to pop around (for a visit).

pop (some) tops *Sl.* to drink beer. □ *Wanna go out tonight and pop some tops?* □ *We are going to pop tops and watch the B-ball game.*

pop someone **off**[†] *Inf.* to kill someone. □ *Max was told to pop Lefty off because he was trying to muscle in on the gang's turf.* □ *Max intended to pop off Lefty.*

pop someone **on** something *Inf.* to strike someone on some body part. □ *If you don't sit down, I'll pop you on the chin!* □ *Max popped Lefty on the nose.*

pop something **into** something and **pop** something **in**[†] to fit, snap, or press something into place in something. □ *Lee popped the lever into place, and the machine began to function.* □ *Lee popped in the plastic part, and the toy ran beautifully.*

pop something **on(to)** something and **pop** something **on**[†] to snap something onto something. □ *Denise took one more sip of the medicine and popped the lid onto the bottle.*

pop something **out of** something and **pop** something **out**[†] to release something from something so that it jumps or bursts out, possibly with a popping sound. □ *Sue popped the cork out of the champagne bottle.* □ *It took a little effort to pop the cork out.* □ *She popped out the cork with a quick tug.*

pop something **up**[†] to remove something by making it jump or burst upwards. □ *Henry popped the lid up and helped himself to the strawberry preserves.* □ *He popped up the lid and cleaned out the jam jar.*

pop the question [for a man] to ask a woman to marry him. (Could also be used by a woman asking a man.) □ *She waited for years for him to pop the question.* □ *Finally she popped the question.*

pop up 1. [for a baseball batter] to hit a baseball that goes high upward rather than outward. □ *The catcher came to*

bat and popped up. □ *I hope I don't pop up this time.* **2.** [for a baseball] to fly high upward rather than outward. □ *The ball popped up and went foul.* □ *The ball will always pop up if you hit it in a certain way.* **3.** to arise suddenly; to appear without warning. □ *New problems keep popping up all the time.* □ *Billy popped up out of nowhere and scared his mother.*

pop up (some place) to appear suddenly and unexpectedly some place. □ *I never know where Henry is going to pop up next.* □ *A new problem has popped up.*

pore over something to look over something carefully. □ *She pored over the reports, looking for errors.* □ *I need to take a few hours to pore over these contracts and see if they are ready to be signed.*

pork out (on something**)** *Inf.* to overeat on something; to become fat as a pig from eating something. (A play on pig out.) □ *I pork out on french fries whenever I get the chance.* □ *I wish I didn't pork out all the time.*

portent of things to come Go to a harbinger of things to come.

portion something **out**[†] to give out shares of something. □ *Who will portion the cake out?* □ *She portioned out the chocolate carefully, making sure everyone got an equal share.*

portray someone **as** someone or something to represent or describe someone as someone or a type of person. □ *Fred portrayed his political opponent as an evil man.* □ *She tried to portray herself as a grand lady, but she fooled no one.*

portray someone or something **as** someone to develop a character that one is playing in a dramatic production as a kind of person or someone having certain characteristics or a particular personality. □ *Tom portrayed Scrooge as an evil old man.* □ *Randy hopes to portray his character as a sympathetic friend.*

pose a question to ask a question; to imply the need for asking a question. □ *Genetic research poses many ethical questions.* □ *My interviewer posed a hypothetical question.*

pose as someone to pretend to be someone else. □ *The impostor posed as the president of the company.* □ *My twin posed as me while I went on vacation.*

pose as someone or something to pretend to be someone or a type of person. □ *I posed as Gerald and got the job.* □ *I posed as a nurse and got a job at a summer camp.*

pose for someone or something to assume a posture appropriate to the subject of a photograph or painting. □ *Paul wanted me to pose for him, but I declined.* □ *Will you pose for my painting?*

***possessed by** something obsessed or driven by something. (*Typically: **be** ~; **become** ~.) □ *Ned was possessed by a desire to become the best at everything he did.* □ *Jan acts as if she is possessed by the need to be right all the time.*

***possessed of** something having something; possessing something. (*Typically: **be** ~; **become** ~.) □ *She is possessed of a large amount of money.* □ *Todd wishes he were possessed of a large car and a fine house.*

Possession is nine-tenths of the law. *Prov.* If you actually possess something, you have a stronger legal claim to owning it than someone who merely says it belongs to him or her. □ *Dana may say he owns this house, but we actually live in it, and possession is nine-tenths of the law.*

post someone **somewhere** to place someone, as if on guard, at something or some place. □ *The police chief posted a guard at the hospital door.* □ *The boss posted himself at the water cooler to catch up on the gossip.*

post something **on** something to fasten a notice onto something. □ *Please post this notice on the door where everyone will see it.* □ *I will post this photo on the bulletin board.*

post something **to** someone to mail something to someone. □ *I posted it to him over a month ago. I can't imagine where it is now.* □ *The letter was posted last week.*

post something **up**† to record a transaction in an account. □ *I'll post this charge up right away, and then you can check out.* □ *Please post up the charges a little later.*

postage and handling charges for shipping [something] and for wrapping and handling the item. □ *The cost of the book was quite reasonable, but the postage and handling was outrageous.* □ *They did not charge postage and handling because I prepaid the order.*

a **poster child (for** something) *Fig.* someone who is a classic example of a state or type of person. □ *She is a poster child for soccer moms.*

postpone something **until** something to delay something until something happens or until a later time. □ *Can we postpone our meeting until tomorrow?* □ *The picnic was postponed until Saturday.*

posture as someone or something to pretend to be someone or a particular type of person. □ *Why is the secretary posturing as the manager and giving out assignments?* □ *Carla entered the ballroom, posturing as a grand duchess of somewhere or another.*

The **pot is calling the kettle black.** and **That's the pot calling the kettle black.** *Prov.* You should not criticize someone for a fault that you have too. (Not polite to say about the person you are addressing.) □ *Bill told Barbara she was sloppy, but Bill never cleans up after himself, either. That's the pot calling the kettle black.* □ *My sister says I dress funny, but if you've seen some of the clothes she wears, you know it's a case of the pot calling the kettle black.*

a **pot of gold 1.** *Lit.* a container filled with gold, as in myth guarded by a leprechaun. □ *I was hoping to find a pot of gold in the cellar, but there were only cobwebs.* **2.** *Fig.* an imaginary reward. □ *Whoever gets to the porch first wins a pot of gold.*

pot something **up**† to put plants into pots. □ *If you would like one of these tomato plants, I'll pot one up for you.* □ *Jan potted up a plant for me.*

pounce (up)on someone or something to spring or swoop upon someone or something; to seize someone or something. (*Upon* is formal and less commonly used than *on*.) □ *As Gerald came into the room, his friend Daniel pounced on him and frightened him to death.* □ *The cat pounced upon a mouse.*

pound a beat *Fig.* to walk a regular route. □ *The cop pounded the same beat for years and years.* □ *Pounding a beat will wreck your feet.*

pound along something **1.** *Fig.* to walk or run along something awkwardly or heavily. □ *As the horse pounded along the street, the rider tried hard to get it to slow down.* □ *Tom pounded along the pavement, looking a bit angry.* **2.** *Fig.* to tap or hammer along something. □ *The worker pounded along the edge of the roof, looking for rotten places.* □ *I pounded along the wall, looking for a stud to nail into.*

pound away (at someone or something**)** to hammer or batter constantly on someone or something. □ *The cops pounded away at the poor guy, and then they put him in handcuffs.* □ *The jackhammer kept pounding away at the pavement.*

pound for pound [Usually of value, quality, strength, etc.] considering the amount of weight involved. □ *Pound for pound, a dog fed properly is much stronger than a dog that has to fend for itself.* □ *Pound for pound, there is more food value in beef than in chicken.*

*a **pound of flesh** *Fig.* a payment or punishment that involves suffering and sacrifice on the part of the person being punished. (*Typically: **give** someone ~; **owe** someone ~; **pay** someone ~; **take** ~.) □ *He wants revenge. He won't be satisfied until he takes his pound of flesh.*

pound on someone or something to beat or hammer on someone or something. □ *She kept pounding on him until he released her.* □ *Will you please stop pounding on that drum?*

pound one's **ear** *Sl.* to sleep. □ *I've got to spend more time pounding my ear.* □ *She went home to pound her ear an hour or two before work.*

pound someone's **head in**† *Fig.* to beat someone, especially about the head. □ *Fred looked like he wanted to pound Mike's head in; he was so mad!* □ *You want me to pound in your head?*

pound something **down**† to hammer, flatten, or batter something. □ *Please pound that nail down so that no one gets hurt on it.* □ *Yes, please pound down that nail!*

pound something **in**† Go to **hammer** something **into** something.

pound something **into** someone Go to **hammer** something **into** someone.

pound something **on** someone or something to hit or strike someone or something with something. □ *Sarah pounded the vase on the robber until it broke.* □ *Betty stood pounding her shoe on the radiator, hoping the racket would magically bring heat.*

pound something **out**† **1.** *Lit.* to flatten something by pounding. □ *He pounded the gold leaf out very thin.* □ *He pounded out the gold leaf.* **2.** *Fig.* to play something loudly on the piano, perhaps with difficulty or clumsily. □ *Here, pound this one out. A little softer, please.* □ *She was pounding out a nice little tune.* **3.** *Fig.* to type something on a keyboard. □ *I have finished writing it. Can I borrow your laptop so I can pound it out?* □ *All the reporters were pounding out stories for the next edition of the paper.*

pound something **up**† to break something up by pounding. □ *Pound the crackers up into crumbs and use them to coat the chicken before you fry it.* □ *Pound up the crackers and put the crumbs in a jar.*

pound the books Go to **hit the books.**

pound the pavement *Fig.* to walk through the streets looking for a job. □ *I spent two months pounding the pavement after the factory I worked for closed.* □ *Hey, Bob. You'd better get busy pounding those nails unless you want to be out pounding the pavement.*

pour (all) over someone or something to flood over someone or something. (Compare this with **pore over something**.) □ *The water from the broken dam poured all over the rocks standing at its base.* □ *The spilled milk poured over my lap.*

pour along something to rush along something in great numbers or in a great amount. □ *Hundreds of people poured along the street during the lunch hour.* □ *The rainwater poured along the gutter, heading toward the sewer basin.*

pour cold water on something **1.** *Lit.* to douse something with cold water. □ *Pour cold water on the vegetables to freshen them.* □ *I poured cold water on my head to cool myself off.* **2.** and **dash cold water on** something; **throw cold water on** something *Fig.* to discourage doing something; to reduce enthusiasm for something. (Alludes to cooling passion with cold water.) □ *When my father said I couldn't have the car, he poured cold water on my plans.* □ *John threw cold water on the whole project by refusing to participate.*

pour down (on someone or something**) 1.** *Lit.* [for water, as with rain] to shower down on someone. □ *The rain poured down on us, soaking us to the bone.* **2.** *Fig.* [for blessings, criticism, praise, kudos, etc.] to flow down on someone or something. □ *Criticism poured down on the mayor until he resigned.* □ *Blessings poured down on the early settlers in the form of good harvests and plentiful game.*

pour forth to gush out; to gush forth. □ *The milk gushed out of the hole in the container.* □ *A tremendous amount of water poured forth when the fire hydrant was knocked over.*

pour in(to something**) 1.** *Lit.* to flow or flood into something. □ *The rain poured into the open window.* □ *I left the window open and the rain just poured in.* **2.** *Fig.* [for people or things] to continue to arrive in great numbers. □ *Complaints poured into the television station after the scandalous broadcast.* □ *Cards and letters are still pouring in.*

pour it on thick Go to **lay it on thick**.

pour money down the drain *Fig.* to waste money; to throw money away. □ *What a waste! Buying that old car is just pouring money down the drain.* □ *Don't buy any more of that low-quality merchandise. That's just throwing money down the drain.*

pour oil on troubled water(s) *Fig.* to calm someone or something down. (A thin layer of oil will actually calm a small area of a rough sea.) □ *Don can calm things down. He's good at pouring oil on troubled waters.* □ *Alice is very good at pouring oil on troubled water.*

pour one's **heart out to** someone and **pour** one's **heart out** *Fig.* to tell one's personal feelings to someone else. □ *I didn't mean to pour my heart out to you, but I guess I just had to talk to someone.* □ *She poured out her heart to her friend.*

pour oneself **into** something **1.** *Fig.* to get deeply involved with something. □ *He distracted himself from his grief by*
pouring himself into his work. □ *She poured herself into the project and got it done on time.* **2.** *Fig.* to fit oneself into clothing that is very tight. (Usually jocular.) □ *Marilyn didn't put that dress on, she poured herself in!* □ *She looks as if she poured herself into those jeans.*

pour out (of something**) 1.** *Lit.* [for something] to stream, fall, or gush out of something or some place. □ *The water poured out of the broken pipe and flooded the basement.* □ *The pipe split and the water just poured out.* **2.** *Fig.* [for people] to come out of a place in great numbers. □ *At the end of the game, people poured out of the stadium for an hour.*

pour out one's **soul** *Fig.* to confess something [to someone]; to reveal one's deepest concerns. □ *Every time she calls me up, she takes an hour or more to pour out her soul.*

pour something **back† (in(to** something**))** to replace a liquid into something. □ *Larry poured the extra glass of orange juice back into the pitcher.* □ *Lily took too much and poured some back.* □ *Pour back the extra juice into the pitcher.*

pour something **into** something and **pour** something **in†** to guide a flow of liquid into something. □ *She poured the lemonade into the pitcher and carried it to the porch.* □ *She held the glass and poured in the lemonade.*

pour something **off (of)** something and **pour** something **off†** to drain liquid off the top of something. (*Of* is usually retained before pronouns.) □ *Valerie poured the cream off the milk.* □ *Valerie poured off the cream.*

pour something **on(to)** something to discharge a vessel of something onto something. □ *Don broke open the piggy bank and poured the money onto the kitchen table.* □ *Don spread out a towel on the table and poured the money on it.*

pour something **out on(to)** someone or something and **pour** something **out†** to empty something onto someone or something. □ *She poured the pitcher of ice water out onto Dave, making him scream.* □ *Sarah poured out the pitcher on the floor by accident.*

pour something **over** someone or something to cover or douse someone or something with something. □ *As I poured the cooling water over myself, I felt relaxed for the first time since I began the long hike.* □ *Mary poured some milk over her cereal.*

pour something **through** something to cause something to flow through something, such as a filter. □ *The chemist poured the mixture through the filter or opening.* □ *I can't get the syrup into the bottle without pouring it through a funnel.*

pour through something to flow freely through something. □ *The water poured through the leak in the window frame.* □ *The rain poured through the hole in the roof.*

pour with rain to rain heavily. (Said of the sky, day, morning, night, the weather, etc.) □ *The sky was pouring with rain and the sun never shone from dawn to dusk.* □ *It poured with rain the entire night.*

pouring rain very heavy rain. □ *The children's clothes were soaked after they played out in the pouring rain.* □ *I waited in the pouring rain for the next bus.*

pout about someone or something to be sullen about someone or something. □ *There is no need to pout about the cat. She'll come back.* □ *Sally is pouting about her lost dog.*

Poverty is no sin. Go to next.

Poverty is not a crime. and **Poverty is no sin.** *Prov.* You should not condemn someone for being poor. □ *Ellen: I wish there were a law to make all those poor people move out of our neighborhood. Jim: Poverty is not a crime, Ellen.*

powder one's **face** Go to next.

powder one's **nose** and **powder** one's **face** to depart to the bathroom. (Usually said by women, or jocularly by men.) □ *Excuse me, I have to powder my nose.* □ *She just went out to powder her face.*

powder up *Sl.* to drink heavily; to get drunk. □ *Let's go out and powder up.* □ *He's at the tavern powdering up.*

the **power behind the throne** *Fig.* the person who actually controls the person who is apparently in charge. □ *Mr. Smith appears to run the shop, but his brother is the power behind the throne.* □ *They say that the vice president is the power behind the throne.*

a **power play** *Fig.* a strategy using one's power or authority to carry out a plan or to get one's way. □ *In a blatant power play, the manager claimed he had initiated the sales campaign.*

power something **up**† to start something, such as an engine. □ *You should power the engine up and let it run awhile before you drive away.* □ *Power up the engine and mow the grass.*

power something **with** something to provide something as the source of energy for something to operate. □ *The government decided to power its vans with natural gas engines.* □ *We will power the generators with coal as long as it is cheap.*

power up to start an engine. □ *Well, let's power up so we will be ready to leave with the others.* □ *It's time to power up and get going.*

the **powers that be** the people who are in authority. □ *The powers that be have decided to send back the immigrants.* □ *I have applied for a license, and the powers that be are considering my application.*

A **pox on** someone or something! *Fig.* A curse on someone or something! (Old. Now usually jocular.) □ *A pox on you, you creep!* □ *I've been trying to make this computer work all day. A pox on it!*

Practice makes perfect. *Prov. Cliché* Doing something over and over again is the only way to learn to do it well. □ *Jill: I'm not going to try to play the piano anymore. I always make so many mistakes. Jane: Don't give up. Practice makes perfect.* □ *Child: How come you're so good at peeling potatoes? Father: I did it a lot in the army, and practice makes perfect.*

practice (up)on someone or something to train or drill on someone or something. (In preparation for the real thing. *Upon* is formal and less commonly used than *on.*) □ *I do not want a dental student practicing upon me.* □ *I want to learn how to braid hair. Can I practice on you?*

Practice what you preach. *Prov. Cliché* You yourself should do the things you advise other people to do. □ *Dad always told us we should only watch an hour of television every day, but we all knew he didn't practice what he preached.*

praise someone or something **to the skies** *Fig.* to give someone or something much praise. □ *He wasn't very good, but his friends praised him to the skies.* □ *They liked your pie. Everyone praised it to the skies.*

prance around to dance, jump, or strut around. □ *The little deer were prancing around, enjoying the spring air.* □ *Stop prancing around and get to work.*

prance around something to dance or jump in celebration around something or throughout some place. (Compare this with **waltz around something.**) □ *The kids pranced around the room, celebrating.* □ *They pranced around the table that held the ice cream and cake.*

prattle (away) about someone or something to chatter idly and endlessly about someone or something. □ *The little girl prattled away for an hour about her school, her friends, and her toys.* □ *I wish you would stop prattling about your friends.*

pray for someone or something **1.** to beseech God, or some other deity, on behalf of someone or something. □ *I will pray for you to recover from your illness quickly.* □ *As the fire spread throughout the old church, the congregation prayed for its preservation.* **2.** to ask God, or some other deity, to grant something. □ *The family prayed for David's safety.* □ *All the people prayed for peace.*

pray over something **1.** to say grace over a meal. □ *Do you pray over your meals?* □ *We prayed over dinner just after we sat down to eat.* **2.** to seek divine guidance about something through prayer. □ *I will have to think about it and pray over it awhile. I'll have an answer next week.* □ *She prayed over the problem for a while and felt she had a solution.*

pray to someone or something to utter prayers of praise or supplication to some divine or supernatural being or something. □ *I pray to God that all this works out.* □ *The high priest prayed to the spirits of his ancestors that the rains would come.*

pray to the porcelain god *Sl.* to kneel at the toilet bowl and vomit from drunkenness. □ *Wally spent a while praying to the porcelain god last night.* □ *I think I have to go pray to the porcelain god.*

preach about something to give a moral or stern discourse on something. □ *Please don't preach about the evils of fried food. I like the stuff, and people eat it all the time and don't die!* □ *She was preaching about the value of a fat-free diet.*

preach against someone or something to exhort against someone or something. □ *The evangelist preached against the operator of the town's only saloon.* □ *The principal kept preaching against drinking and drugs.*

preach at someone to lecture or moralize at someone. □ *Don't preach at me! I don't need any of your moralizing.* □ *I really don't wish to be preached at.*

preach to someone to give a moral discourse to someone. □ *Please don't preach to me. I know that I did wrong.* □ *When you preach to us like that, we don't pay any attention to you.*

preach to the choir and **preach to the converted** *Fig.* to make one's case primarily to one's supporters; to make one's case only to those people who are present or who are already friendly to the issues. □ *There is no need to convince us of the value of hard work. We already know* *that. You are just preaching to the choir.* □ *Don't waste your time telling us about the problem. That's preaching to the choir.* □ *Bob found himself preaching to the converted when he was telling Jane the advantages of living in the suburbs. She already hates city life.*

preach to the converted Go to previous.

*precedence over someone or something the right to come before someone or something else; greater importance than someone or something else. (*Typically: **take** ~; **have** ~; **be given** ~.) □ *Ambulances have precedence over regular cars at intersections.* □ *My manager's concerns take precedence over mine.*

precious few and **precious little** very few; very little. (*Few* for people or things that can be counted, and *little* for amounts.) □ *We get precious few tourists here in the winter.* □ *There's precious little food in the house and there is no money.*

precious little Go to previous.

precipitate into something **1.** *Lit.* [for a chemical] to go out of solution into solid form. □ *The sodium chloride precipitated into a salt.* □ *Will this compound precipitate into anything if I cool it?* **2.** *Fig.* [for something] to become a more serious matter. □ *By then, the street fight had precipitated into a riot.* □ *We were afraid that the argument would precipitate into a fight.*

precipitate something **into** something **1.** *Lit.* to cause a chemical to go out of a solution into a solid form. □ *Adding just one salt grain at the right time will precipitate the salt dissolved into the water into large crystals.* □ *One grain precipitated the dissolved salt into crystals.* **2.** *Fig.* to cause something to become more serious. □ *The gunshot precipitated the incident into a riot.* □ *The rally was precipitated into a serious brawl.*

preclude someone or something **from** something to prevent someone or something from being included in something; to eliminate someone from something in advance. □ *Your remarks do not preclude me from trying again, do they?* □ *These facts do not preclude my company from consideration, do they?*

predicate something **(up)on** something to base something on something. □ *There is no need to predicate my promotion upon the effectiveness of my secretary!* □ *You can hardly predicate the picnic on the weather, can you?*

predispose someone or something **to(ward)** something to make someone or something susceptible to something. □ *Your comments will not predispose me toward a favorable treatment of your case.* □ *Do you think that this weather will predispose me to catching a cold?*

preface something **by** something to begin something by saying, writing, or reading something. □ *I would like to preface my prepared remarks by making a personal observation.* □ *Her remarks were prefaced by the reading of a poem.*

preface something **with** something to begin something with a particular message. □ *She prefaced her speech with a recitation of one of her favorite poems.* □ *Alice prefaced her remarks with a few personal comments.*

prefer someone or something **to** someone or something else to rank the desirability of someone or something over someone or something else. □ *For the post of treasurer, I prefer Don to Jill.* □ *I prefer missing a meal to Jill's cooking.*

prefer something **against** someone to file legal charges against someone [with the police]; to file a complaint or a charge against someone. □ *The neighbors preferred charges against the driver of the car who ruined their lawns.* □ *I will not prefer charges against the driver, since it was partly my fault.*

prefix something **to** something to place something at the beginning of a word or part of a word. □ *If you prefix a re- to some verbs, you get an entirely different meaning.* □ *You can't prefix anything to some verbs.*

prejudice someone or something **against** someone or something to turn someone or a group against someone or something. □ *I believe that the lawyer was trying to prejudice the jury against the defendant.* □ *The discussion about how calves are raised prejudiced me against eating veal.*

a **prelude to** something an act or event that comes before and signals another act or event. □ *Her rudeness to her boss was a prelude to her resignation.* □ *The Munich Pact was a prelude to World War II.*

prepare someone **for** something to build someone up for shocking news. □ *I went in and had a talk with her to prepare her for the report.* □ *You should prepare yourself for the worst.*

prepare someone or something **for** something to get someone or something ready for something. □ *I prepared her for her trip by going over her itinerary.* □ *I prepared the garden for planting.*

prescribe something **for** someone to order a medication to be given to or sold to someone. □ *I asked the doctor to prescribe a painkiller for me.* □ *What can you prescribe for me for this illness?*

prescribe something **for** something to suggest or recommend something for a particular disease. □ *Could you prescribe something for my cold?* □ *What can you prescribe for this illness?*

present someone **(to** someone) **(at** something) to introduce someone to someone at some event. □ *They presented him to the queen at her birthday party.* □ *I will present you to the rest of the committee.*

present someone **with** something Go to **present** something to someone.

present something **on a silver platter** Go to on a silver platter.

present something **to** someone and **present** someone **with** something to give something to someone, especially if done ceremoniously. □ *They presented a watch to me when I retired.* □ *They presented me with a watch when I retired.*

preserve someone or something **against** something to guard or protect someone or something against something. (Stilted or old-fashioned in reference to people.) □ *I hope that the vaccine will preserve us against influenza.* □ *There is nothing in the jam to preserve it against spoilage.*

preserve someone or something **from** someone or something to protect or guard someone or something from someone or something. □ *Please help preserve our people from the attacks of our enemies.* □ *Is there any way to preserve my skin against the harmful rays of the sun?*

preserve something **for** someone or something to save, maintain, or protect something for someone or something. □ *Try to preserve some of these memories for your grandchildren.* □ *We learned how to preserve leaves for future reference.*

preside at something to manage or act as chair at a meeting or a ceremony. □ *The mayor presided at the meeting, assuring that the speeches would be very short.* □ *She presided at the ceremony.*

preside over something to be in control of the order and procedures of a meeting or ceremony. □ *The vice president will have to preside over the next meeting.* □ *I will be glad to preside over the discussion.*

press against someone or something to push or bear upon someone or something. □ *I pressed against Henry, trying gently to get him to move out of the way.* □ *Don't press against the glass door!*

press charges (against someone**)** and **file charges (against** someone**)** *Fig.* to make a formal charge of wrongdoing against someone. □ *They agreed not to press charges against me if I agreed to pay for the damages.*

press down on someone or something to push down on someone or something. □ *The weight of all the covers was pressing down on me, and I couldn't sleep.* □ *Press down on this lever and the recorder will start.*

press for something **1.** to urge for something to be done; to request something. □ *The mayor is pressing for an early settlement to the strike.* □ *I will press her for an answer.* □ *The citizens are pressing for an investigation of the incident.* **2.** to press a button for service. □ *If you need any help, just press for service.* □ *Here is the steward's button. Just press for immediate service.*

press forward to move forward; to struggle forward; to continue. □ *Do not be discouraged. Let us press forward.* □ *We must press forward and complete this work on time.*

press on something to push or depress something, such as a button, catch, snap, etc. □ *Press on this button if you require room service.* □ *Don't press on this because it rings a loud bell.*

press one's **luck** Go to push one's luck.

press on(ward) to continue; to continue to try. □ *Don't give up! Press onward!* □ *I have lots to do. I must press on.*

press someone or something **into service** to force someone or something to serve or function. □ *I don't think you can press him into service just yet. He isn't trained.* □ *I think that in an emergency, we could press this machine into service.*

press someone **to the wall** Go to push someone to the wall.

press something **against** someone or something to push or force something against someone or something. □ *The person in line behind Betty kept pressing his elbow against her.* □ *I pressed my hand against the door and it opened.*

press something **into** something and **press** something **in**[†] **1.** to force something into something, such as a mold. □ *Now, you need to press the clay into the mold carefully.* □ *Now, hold the mold with one hand and press in the clay.* **2.** to force or drive something into the surface of something. □ *You are standing on my chewing gum, and you have pressed it into the carpet!* □ *Don't press in the gum by standing on it.*

press something **on**[†] Go to next.

press something **onto** something and **press** something **on**[†] to put pressure on something and cause it to stick to the surface of something. □ *I pressed the label onto the envelope and took it to the post office.* □ *I pressed on the label.*

press something **out of** something and **press** something **out**[†] to squeeze something out of something by applying pressure. □ *The Indians press the acid out of the manioc before they use it as food.* □ *Gene used an iron to press the wrinkles out of his suit coat.* □ *Go back and press out all the wrinkles!*

press something **together** to use pressure to close or unite things. □ *He pressed his lips together and would say no more.* □ *Why are his lips pressed together so tightly?*

press something **(up)on** someone to urge or force something on someone; to try to get someone to accept something. (*Upon* is formal and less commonly used than *on*.) □ *He always presses second helpings upon his guests.* □ *She pressed a gift on us that we could not refuse.*

press (the) flesh *Sl.* to shake hands. □ *Hey, chum! Glad to press flesh with you!* □ *He wanted to press the flesh, but I refused even to touch him.*

press the panic button Go to hit the panic button.

press (up)on someone or something to put pressure on someone or something. (*Upon* is formal and less commonly used than *on*.) □ *The crowd pressed upon the child, squeezing out all his breath.* □ *The load presses on your car's springs very heavily.*

pressed for cash Go to next.

*pressed for money and ***pressed for cash; *pushed for cash; *pushed for money** *Fig.* needful of money; short of money. (*Typically: **be ~; become ~; get ~.**) □ *We are usually pushed for money at this time of year.* □ *I'm a little pressed for money just now.*

*pressed for time and ***pushed for time** *Fig.* needing time; in a hurry. (*Typically: **be ~; become ~; get ~; seem ~.**) □ *If I weren't so pressed for time, I could help you.* □ *I can't talk to you. I'm too pushed for time.* □ *Can't talk to you now. I'm pressed for time.*

pressure someone **into** something to force someone into doing something. □ *Please don't try to pressure me into taking that promotion.* □ *You can't pressure me into it. I won't do it!*

presume (up)on someone or something to take unwelcome advantage of someone or something. □ *I didn't mean to seem to presume upon you. I apologize.* □ *I did not feel that you presumed on me.*

pretend to something to claim to have a skill or quality. □ *I can hardly pretend to the artistry that Wally has, but I can play the piano a bit.* □ *I can't pretend to that level of skill.*

*pretty as a picture very pretty. (*Also: **as ~.**) □ *Sweet little Mary is as pretty as a picture.* □ *Their new house is pretty as a picture.*

Pretty is as pretty does. *Prov.* It is more important to treat people well than to be good-looking; just because you are good-looking does not mean you are a good person. (Said only of girls and women.) □ *Janice may have a*

P

pretty face, but pretty is as pretty does; the way she behaves isn't pretty at all.

pretty oneself or something **up**† *Rur.* to make oneself or something more attractive; to tidy oneself or something up. □ *I tried to pretty myself up for him, but he didn't notice.* □ *Let's try to pretty up this room.*

a **pretty pickle** *Fig.* a difficult situation. (*Pickle* = a bad situation.) □ *Well, this is a pretty pickle you've gotten us into.*

Pretty please? an emphasised form of *please?* □ *Pretty please? I need an answer!* □ *Can I have my book back? Pretty please?*

a **pretty state of affairs** and a **fine state of affairs** an unpleasant state of affairs. □ *This is a pretty state of affairs, and it's all your fault.* □ *What a fine state of affairs you've got us into.*

prevail against someone or something to win out over someone or something; to dominate someone or something. □ *You will not prevail against me!* □ *I am sure that our team will prevail against the challengers.*

prevail (up)on someone or something **(to** do something**)** to appeal to someone or a group to do something. (*Upon* is formal and less commonly used than *on*.) □ *I will prevail upon her to attend the meeting.* □ *I prevailed on the committee to no avail.*

prevent someone **from** doing something to keep someone from doing something. □ *You can't prevent me from doing it!* □ *We must try to prevent her from going back there.*

Prevention is better than cure. *Prov.* It is better to try to keep a bad thing from happening than it is to fix the bad thing once it has happened. (See also An **ounce of prevention is better than a pound of cure.**) □ *If we spend more money on education, so that children learn to be responsible citizens, we won't have to spend so much money on prisons. Prevention is better than cure.*

prey on something [for an animal] to feed on another animal as a matter of habit or preference. □ *Owls prey on mice.* □ *Many birds prey on snakes.*

prey (up)on someone or something *Fig.* to take advantage of someone or something. (See also **prey on something.** *Upon* is formal and less commonly used than *on*.) □ *The people of that island prey on tourists and do not give them good treatment.* □ *I really don't want to seem to prey upon your kindness.*

*a **price on** one's **head** a reward for one's capture. (*Typically: **get** ~; **have** ~; **put** ~; **place** ~.) □ *We captured a thief who had a price on his head, and the sheriff gave us the reward.* □ *The crook was so mean, he turned in his own brother, who had a price on his head.*

the **price** one **has to pay** the sacrifice that one has to make; the unpleasantness that one has to suffer. □ *Being away from home a lot is the price one has to pay for success.*

price someone or something **out of the market** to raise or lower a price and drive someone or something out of the marketplace. □ *You are a very good singer, but your agent has priced you out of the market.* □ *The discount prices posted by the chain store were meant to price us out of the market.*

price something **down**† to lower the price of something. □ *When they start pricing this stuff down at the end of the season, I'll come in and buy something.* □ *I hope to price down the merchandise soon.*

price something **out** to list and total all the component prices of goods and services for a complex project. □ *I have finished listing all the materials required for the project, and now I have to price it out so that we can decide if we can afford it.*

price something **up**† to raise the price of something. □ *They have priced oranges up so high that I can't afford any.* □ *Why do they price up these common foods so high?*

prick up its ears† and **prick up** one's **ears**† *Fig.* [for an animal or a person] to become attentive. (The animal will adjust its ears toward the sound.) □ *The sound made the dog prick its ears up.* □ *When Fred heard his name, he pricked up his ears.* □ *She pricked her ears up when she heard her name.*

pride and joy *Fig.* something or someone that one is very proud of. (Often in reference to a baby, a car, a house, etc. Fixed order.) □ *And this is our little pride and joy, Roger.* □ *Fred pulled up in his pride and joy and asked if I wanted a ride.*

Pride goes before a fall. and **Pride goeth before a fall.** *Prov.* If you are too proud and overconfident, you will make mistakes leading to your defeat. (Biblical.) □ *Sue: I'm the best student in my history class. I'm sure I can pass the exam without studying very hard. Sam: Be careful. Pride goes before a fall, you know.*

pride oneself **in** something and **pride** oneself **on** something to take pride in one of one's qualities or accomplishments. □ *She prides herself in her ability to spot a shoplifter.* □ *I pride myself on my ability to find compromises.*

prime mover *Fig.* the force that sets something going; someone or something that starts something off. □ *The assistant manager was the prime mover in getting the manager sacked.* □ *Discontent with his job was the prime mover in John's deciding to retire early.*

prime something **with** something to enable something to start working or functioning with something. □ *Larry primed the pump with a little water, and it began to do its work.* □ *We will prime the market for our new product with a free coupon offer.*

primp (oneself) up to get dressed up; to fix oneself up by combing, brushing, adjusting, etc. □ *Let me stop in the powder room and primp myself up a bit.* □ *I have to go in here and primp up.*

the **primrose path** *Fig.* earthly delights that come to an end. □ *She led him down the primrose path until she got tired of him.*

print something **in** something **1.** to make block letters in a specific location on a paper. □ *Please print your name in the box.* □ *Would you please print the information in the space provided?* **2.** to publish something in a publication. □ *They printed my letter in today's paper.* □ *Her stories have been printed in several magazines.*

print something **out**† **1.** to write something out by using block letters. □ *Please print it out. I can't read your handwriting.* □ *Print out your name, please.* **2.** to use a computer printer to print something. □ *I will print a copy out and send it to you.* □ *Please print out another copy.*

print something **up**† to set something in type and print it; to print something by any process. □ *This looks okay to me. Let's print it up now.* □ *Print up the final version.*

privy to something *Fig.* knowledgeable about something secret or private. □ *The reporter became privy to the senator's evil plan.* □ *Why are you privy to this secret information?*

prize someone or something **above** someone or something to value someone or something more than anyone or anything else. □ *He prized his only daughter above everyone else in the world.* □ *Scott seemed to prize his sports car above all the members of his family.*

probe into something to investigate something. □ *The police will probe into the matter and report to the commissioner.* □ *We will take some time and probe into that for you.*

probe something **for** something to poke around in something for something. □ *He probed his memory for some clue as to where he had been on that date.* □ *Sam probed the darkened space for the tool that he had mislaid.*

proceed against someone or something **1.** to begin to move against someone or something. □ *The entire platoon proceeded against the single enemy soldier who refused to surrender.* □ *The army proceeded against the fortress as planned.* **2.** to start legal action against someone or something. □ *The district attorney will proceed against the suspect next week.* □ *The state prosecutor will proceed against the company as soon as one of the witnesses is located.*

proceed (from something**) (to** something**)** to go from something or some place to something or some place. □ *Next, we will proceed from Vienna to Budapest.* □ *We proceeded from Detroit, passing through rural Michigan.*

proceed with something to move ahead with something; to continue something. □ *Now, we will proceed with the reading of the minutes of the last meeting.* □ *When will you proceed with the needed action?*

Procrastination is the thief of time. *Prov.* If you put off doing what you ought to do, you will end up not having enough time to do it properly. □ *Jim: Have you started looking for a job yet? Jane: Oh, that can wait till tomorrow. Jim: Procrastination is the thief of time.*

procure something **(from** someone or something**) (for** someone or something**)** to get something from someone or something for someone or some purpose. □ *I will procure a copy of the paper from Kelly for you.* □ *I have to procure a book for my sister.*

prod at someone or something to poke at someone or something. □ *The boys prodded at the prone body of the man to see if he was dead or sleeping.* □ *If you prod at the turtle, it will never come out of its shell.*

prod someone **into** something to motivate someone into doing something; to provoke someone into action. □ *Do I have to prod you into going? Can't you volunteer for once?* □ *We will prod her into getting it done on time.*

produce an attack (of an illness**)** Go to an **attack (of** an illness**).**

produce something **for** something **1.** to make something for some purpose. □ *This production line produces brackets for the installation of the circuit boards in the next production line.* □ *We produce the seats for the trucks that they assemble on the other side of town.* **2.** to bring something out for some purpose. □ *Lee quickly produced a penknife for cutting the string on the package.* □ *Ruth can always produce the right tool for the job.*

produce something **from** something to create something from something; to make something out of something. □ *We are able to produce a high-quality writing paper from the scraps we trim off the edges of the books as we bind them.* □ *Jane produces an excellent jelly from the grapes she grows in her backyard.*

profit by something and **profit from** something **1.** *Lit.* to gain money from something. □ *You will surely profit by investing in this stock.* □ *I know I will profit from this investment.* **2.** *Fig.* to learn from something. □ *I am sure you will profit by your unpleasant experience.* □ *Yes, I will profit from my failure.*

progress to something to reach all the way to something or some place. □ *The crisis has progressed to its final stage.* □ *Things had progressed to a serious stage where nothing more could be done for him.*

progress toward something to move partway toward some goal. □ *Nancy is progressing toward her degree quite nicely.* □ *We are progressing toward the end of the project.*

progress with something to continue to move toward something or completing something. □ *I can't seem to progress with this project.* □ *How are you progressing with the building of your model ship?*

prohibit someone **from** something **1.** to prevent someone from doing something. □ *The committee voted to prohibit people from leaving before the meeting was over.* □ *They prohibit anyone from being seated after the first act has started.* **2.** to keep someone out of some place. □ *Our policy is to prohibit people from the beach area after dark.* □ *State law prohibits children from this dangerous area while the machines are running.*

prohibit something **from** something **1.** to prevent something from happening or from doing something. □ *My mother prohibits me from going out with friends on school nights.* □ *Why do you want to prohibit the cars from traveling on this street during rush hour?* **2.** to keep something out of or away from something or some place. □ *The law prohibited bicycles from the sidewalks.* □ *The city council prohibits unleashed dogs from the public parks.*

project into something to extend into something. □ *The end of the grand piano projected into the next room, but she had to have a grand, nonetheless.* □ *The front of the car projected into the flower bed when it was parked, but that was all right.*

project something **onto** someone to imagine that someone else experiences one's feelings, especially one's guilt or anger. □ *Since you project your anger onto your best friends, you imagine you have gathered a number of angry people around you.* □ *You should not project your feelings onto other people.*

project something **on(to)** someone or something and **project** something **upon** someone or something to show a pic-

519

ture, such as from a film, transparency, etc., onto something, such as a screen, wall, etc., or even onto a person. □ *Henry projected the pictures onto the screen as he discussed each one.* □ *The teacher had to project the slides upon the wall.*

promise someone **the moon** Go to **promise the moon (to** someone**).**

promise something **to** someone to pledge something to someone. □ *I promised this vase to my niece.* □ *Is this book promised to anyone?*

promise the moon (to someone**)** and **promise** someone **the moon** to make extravagant promises to someone. □ *Bill will promise you the moon, but he won't live up to his promises.* □ *My boss promised the moon, but never gave me a raise.*

Promises are like piecrust, made to be broken. *Prov.* It is useless to make promises, because people always break their promises. □ *Lisa made Andrew promise not to drink anymore, but promises are like piecrust, made to be broken.*

promote someone **(from** something**) (to** something**)** to raise someone's rank from something to something. □ *They promoted her from teller to vice president.* □ *Carl promoted his daughter to supervisor.*

prone to something likely to [do] something; apt to have something. □ *My boss is prone to anger when my work isn't done on schedule.* □ *My sister is prone to sneezing because of her allergies.*

pronounce something **on** someone or something to make a statement, usually a judgment, about someone or something. □ *The judge pronounced final judgment on the prisoner.* □ *The family all pronounced a positive opinion on the cake.*

The **proof is in the pudding.** *Prov.* You cannot be sure that you have succeeded until you have examined the result of your efforts. □ *Jill: I think we've done a good job of fixing the lawn mower. Jane: Well, the proof is in the pudding. We haven't tried to mow the lawn with it yet.*

prop someone or something **up**† **(against** someone or something**)** to stand or lean someone or something against someone or something. □ *He was so tired I had to prop him up against the wall while I looked for the door key.* □ *I propped up the man against the wall.* □ *I propped the mop up against the wall.*

A **prophet is not without honor save in his own country.** *Prov.* Everyone recognizes that a wise person is wise, except for the people close to him or her. (Biblical.) □ *No one in the novelist's country would publish her books, but last year she won the Nobel Prize. A prophet is not without honor save in his own country.*

propose a toast to make a toast before a celebratory drink. □ *I'd like to propose a toast in honor of your birthday.* □ *At the wedding reception, the bride's father proposed a toast to the new couple.*

propose something **to** someone to suggest something to someone. □ *I have an idea I would like to propose to you.* □ *Sam wanted to propose a new plan to Sarah.*

propose to someone to suggest marriage to someone, usually a male to a female. □ *Guess who proposed to me last night?* □ *Do you think that Sam will propose to Mary?*

prospect for something to search for something, especially for metals or minerals. □ *The old men said they were prospecting for gold.* □ *What are they prospecting for out in the desert?*

prosper from something to gain wealth from something. □ *Carla prospered from trading on the options exchange.* □ *I hope you prosper from your new enterprise.*

prostrate oneself **before** someone or something **1.** *Lit.* to lay oneself out in respect or obedience in front of someone or something. □ *The members of the cult prostrated themselves before their leader.* □ *They prostrated themselves before the altar.* **2.** *Fig.* to submit to someone's dominance. □ *If you think I'm going to prostrate myself before you and do as you ask, you are wrong.* □ *I will not prostrate myself before the high council!*

protect someone or something **against** someone or something and **protect** someone or something **from** someone or something to shield or preserve someone or something against someone or something. □ *Please come along and protect us against muggers as we walk home.* □ *What will protect my car against thieves?*

protest about someone or something and **protest against** someone or something **1.** to complain about someone or something. □ *Valerie is always protesting about some problem at work.* □ *She filed a complaint that protested against her supervisor.* **2.** to rally or demonstrate against someone or something. □ *A number of people protested about the war.* □ *They were mainly protesting against the draft.*

protrude from someone or something to stick out from someone or something. □ *Even in the dark, I knew he was hurt because I could see the knife protruding from him.* □ *A knife protruded from the victim's back.*

***proud as a peacock** and ***vain as a peacock** overly proud; vain. (*Also: **as** ~.) □ *Mike's been strutting around proud as a peacock since he won that award.* □ *I sometimes think Elizabeth must spend all day admiring herself in a mirror. She's as vain as a peacock.*

prove oneself **as** something to demonstrate that one can serve in a certain office or capacity. □ *It's time to promote her. She has proved herself as a teller.* □ *I proved myself as an investor by making a lot of money in the stock market.*

prove something **to** someone to substantiate a claim about something to someone; to make someone believe or accept a statement about something. □ *What do I have to do to prove my innocence to you?* □ *Nothing you say will prove it to me.*

prove to be something to be shown to be someone or something; to be found to be someone or something. □ *Susan proved to be a good friend when she lent me some money.* □ *The food proved to be spoiled when I smelled it.*

provide against something to plan against something happening. □ *Have you provided against the possible collapse of the agreement?* □ *We have not provided against financial disaster.*

provide for someone or something to supply the needs of someone or something. □ *Don't worry, we will provide for you.* □ *We will provide for the committee in the budget.*

provide someone **with** something to supply something to someone. □ *I will provide you with an escort to your car.*

□ *Jane provided herself with just enough food to get through the weekend.*

provide something **for** someone or something to supply something for someone or something. □ *I will provide salad for the guests.* □ *Ted provided food for his dog.*

provide something **under** something to supply something in keeping with a contract, rule, guideline, agreement, etc. □ *We have agreed to provide two tons of coal per month under our contract. Do you want more?* □ *We will agree to provide ample insurance for our employees under union guidelines.*

provided that on the condition that. □ *I will come, provided that I am invited.* □ *I will help you, provided that you pay me.*

provoke someone **into** something to incite someone into doing something. □ *The soldiers sought to provoke the demonstrators into starting a riot.* □ *They provoked us into leaving.*

prowl about and **prowl around** to sneak around, looking for someone or something. □ *Something is prowling about out there in the yard.* □ *There is someone outside prowling around.*

prune something **away**† to cut away something unwanted or unneeded. □ *Please prune the lower branches of the trees away. They are starting to annoy pedestrians.* □ *We pruned away the dead branches.*

prune something **of** something to clear, clean, or groom something of something by pruning. □ *Sally was out in the orchard pruning the apple trees of dead branches.* □ *They pruned the roses of their unneeded branches.*

prune something **off (of)** something and **prune** something **off**† to cut something off something. (*Of* is usually retained before pronouns.) □ *Claire pruned the dead branch off the apple tree.* □ *She pruned off the dead branch.*

pry around to sneak or prowl around looking for something. □ *Why are you prying around? Mind your own business!* □ *Please don't pry around. You might find out something you don't want to know.*

pry into something to snoop into something; to get into someone else's business. □ *Why are you prying into my affairs all the time?* □ *I wish you wouldn't pry into my personal life.*

pry something **from** someone and **pry** something **out of** someone to work information out of someone; to force someone to reveal information. □ *I couldn't even pry her name from her.* □ *The police tried to pry the name of the killer out of Max.*

pry something **from** something and **pry** something **out (of** something) to remove something from something with or as if with a lever. □ *See if you can pry this wedge from its slot.* □ *I pried the rotted board out of the side of the house.*

pry something **off (of)** something and **pry** something **off**† to use a lever to get something off something. (*Of* is usually retained before pronouns.) □ *Tom pried the top off the jelly jar.* □ *He pried off the jar top.*

pry something **out of** someone Go to **pry** something **from** someone.

pry something **out (of** something) Go to **pry** something **from** something.

pry something **up**† to raise something with or as with a lever. □ *See if you can pry that trapdoor up.* □ *Pry up that lid.*

psych out 1. *Inf.* to have a nervous or emotional trauma; to go mad for a brief time. □ *Another day like this one and I'll psych out for sure.* □ *He looked at the bill and psyched out.* **2.** *Inf.* to become very excited; to lose mental control. □ *I was so angry, I almost psyched out.* □ *The kids were psyching out over the rock star.*

psych someone **out**† **1.** *Inf.* to get someone very excited; to cause someone to lose mental control. □ *Wow! What you just said really psyched me out!* □ *He psyched out his friends.* **2.** *Inf.* to figure someone out; to know how someone thinks. □ *It took me a while to psych out Fred, but I have him figured out now.* □ *Don't waste time trying to psych me out. I am an enigma.*

psych someone **up**† *Inf.* to get someone excited or mentally prepared for something. □ *I psyched myself up to sing in front of all those people.* □ *The coach psyched up the team for the game.*

psych up *Inf.* to get mentally ready for something. □ *I have to psych up before the big game tonight.* □ *We want to psych up so we can play a good game.*

psyched (out) 1. *Inf.* excited; overwhelmed; thrilled. □ *She's really psyched out.* □ *That's great. I'm really psyched about my new job!* **2.** *Inf.* intoxicated. □ *She's just lying there psyched out.* □ *Two beers and a shot of whiskey and he was psyched out.*

psyched (up) *Inf.* completely mentally ready (for something). □ *I'm really psyched for this test.* □ *The team isn't psyched up enough to do a good job.*

psyched up (for something) *Inf.* excited and enthusiastic. □ *I can play a great tennis game if I'm psyched up.* □ *She is really psyched up for the game.*

publish or perish *Fig.* [for a professor] to try to publish scholarly books or articles to prevent getting released from a university or falling into disfavor in a university. (Also occurs as other parts of speech. See the examples.) □ *Alice knew she would have to publish or perish if she took the teaching job.* □ *This is a major research university and publish or perish is the order of the day.*

pucker something **up**† to cause something to wrinkle up, especially the edges of the mouth, as when tasting something very sour. □ *She puckered her lips up and pouted for a while.* □ *She puckered up her lips when she tasted the lemon juice.*

pucker up 1. *Lit.* to tighten one's lips together into a circle as if to kiss. □ *He puckered up and kissed her once, and then again.* **2.** *Fig.* [for something] to shrink up and get wrinkled. □ *The material puckered up when I washed it.* □ *The top edge of the drapes puckered up and I don't know how to straighten it out.*

puff along 1. [for someone] to run along, puffing to breathe. □ *Sam puffed along, jogging on his morning route.* □ *As Wally puffed along, he thought again about going on a diet.* **2.** [for an engine] to move along, putting out puffs of smoke or steam. □ *The old engine puffed along, driving the small boat slowly up the river.* □ *The locomotive puffed along, not making very much headway up the hill.*

puff (away) at something **1.** to blow at or into something in puffs. □ *She puffed away at the beach ball, blowing it up as fast as she could.* □ *Todd puffed at the fire until it grew larger.* **2.** and **puff (away) on** something to smoke something, such as a cigar, cigarette, or pipe. □ *Scott was puffing away at his pipe.* □ *She is always puffing on a cigarette.*

puff out to swell out. □ *The frog's throat puffed out, and we expected to hear a croak.* □ *The sail puffed out, and the boat began to move.*

puff someone or something **up**† to boost or promote someone or something. □ *Judy puffed Nell up so much that Nell could not begin to live up to her reputation.* □ *Don't puff up your own accomplishments so much.*

puff something **out**† to cause something to swell out or expand outward. □ *The frog puffed its throat out and croaked.* □ *The frog puffed out its throat and croaked a mighty croak.*

puff up to swell up. □ *Her finger puffed up and she thought she might have an infection.* □ *His eyelids had puffed up during the night.*

puff up (into something**)** to assume a larger shape by filling up with air or water; to swell up into something. □ *The strange-looking fish puffed up into a round ball.* □ *The fish puffed up and stuck out its spines.*

pull a boner *Inf.* to do something stupid or silly. □ *Boy, I really pulled a boner! I'm so dumb.* □ *If you pull a boner like that again, you're fired!*

pull a fast one *Inf.* to succeed in an act of deception. □ *She was pulling a fast one when she said she had a headache and went home.* □ *Don't try to pull a fast one with me! I know what you're doing.*

pull a few strings Go to pull (some) strings.

pull a gun (on someone**)** and **pull a knife (on** someone**)** to bring out a gun or knife suddenly so that it is ready for use against someone. □ *I screamed when the mugger pulled a knife on me.* □ *The police shot the thief when he pulled a gun.*

pull a job *Sl.* to carry out a crime, especially a robbery. (Police and underworld. Note the variations in the examples.) □ *Richard decided that it was not a good time to pull a bank job.* □ *Willie and Richard left town after they pulled the job.*

pull a knife (on someone**)** Go to pull a gun (on someone).

pull a muscle to strain a muscle and suffer the attendant pain. □ *I pulled a muscle in my back and can't play golf today.*

pull a stunt (on someone**)** and **pull a trick (on** someone**)** to deceive someone; to play a trick on someone. □ *Let's pull a trick on the teacher.* □ *Don't you dare pull a stunt like that!*

pull a trick (on someone**)** Go to previous.

pull ahead (of someone or something**)** to pass someone or something and continue moving. □ *The runner pulled ahead of the rest of the field.* □ *Our car pulled ahead of theirs.*

pull all the stops out† *Fig.* to use everything available; to not hold back. (Alludes to pulling out all of the stops on an organ so that it will sound as loud as possible.) □

The mayor decided to pull out all the stops and campaign in every district. □ *Todd pulled all the stops out for his exhibition and impressed everyone with his painting artistry.*

pull around to something to drive around to something or some place. □ *Please pull around to the back and deliver the furniture there.* □ *We told the driver to pull around to the service entrance.*

pull at someone to vie for someone's attention or concern. (See also pull at someone or something.) □ *There are too many demands pulling at me. I need to cut down on my responsibilities.* □ *I don't see how I can function with so many different things pulling at me.*

pull at someone or something to tug at someone or something. (See also **pull at someone**.) □ *The child kept pulling at her mother to get her attention.* □ *Don't keep pulling at your hair. It will come out.*

pull away from someone or something to jerk away or draw away from someone or something. □ *Suddenly, she pulled away from me and fled.* □ *The car pulled away from the curb and drove off.*

pull back (from someone or something**)** to move back from someone or something. □ *When I saw how sick he looked, I pulled back from him in shock.* □ *I took one look at the snake and pulled back.*

pull down (an amount of money**)** *Fig. Inf.* to earn a stated amount of money. ("An amount of money" is expressed as a figure or other indication of an actual amount.) □ *She pulls down about $40,000 a year.* □ *They pull down pretty good salaries.*

pull for someone or something to support and cheer for someone, a group, or something. □ *We're pulling for you. We know you can do it!* □ *All the students were pulling for the team.*

pull in one's **ears** *Fig.* to stop listening in on someone or something. (The opposite of prick up one's ears.) □ *Now, pull in your ears. This is none of your business.* □ *Pull in your ears and mind your own business.*

pull in one's **horns** Go to draw in one's horns.

pull in some place [for a wheeled vehicle] to steer or drive to a point off the main route. □ *Let's pull in at the next motel and get some rest.* □ *I want to pull in at a service station and have my tires checked.*

pull in(to some place**)** to drive into some place. □ *A strange car just pulled into our driveway.* □ *Some stranger just pulled in.*

pull off (something**)** to steer or turn a vehicle off the road. □ *I pulled off the road and rested for a while.* □ *I had to pull off and rest.*

pull on something to tug something. □ *I pulled on the rope, hoping to get it loose.* □ *Please help me pull on the anchor chain so we can raise the anchor.*

pull one over on someone to deceive someone. □ *Don't try to trick me! You can't pull one over on me.*

pull one's **belt in**† **(a notch)** Go to take one's belt in† **(a notch).**

pull one's **(own) weight** Go to carry one's (own) weight.

pull one's **punches 1.** [for a boxer] to strike with light blows to enable the other boxer to win. □ *Bill has been* *barred from the boxing ring for pulling his punches.* □ *"I never pulled punches in my life!" cried Tom.* **2.** *Fig.* to hold back in one's criticism. (Usually in the negative. The *one's* can be replaced with *any* in the negative.) □ *I didn't pull any punches. I told her exactly what I thought of her.* □ *The teacher doesn't pull any punches when it comes to discipline.*

pull oneself **together 1.** *Fig.* to compose oneself; to gather one's wits about one. □ *I have to pull myself together and try it again.* □ *Now try to pull yourself together and get through this crisis.* **2.** *Fig.* to gather up one's things; to pull one's things together. □ *I'll be ready to leave as soon as I pull myself together.* □ *I want to pull myself together and leave.*

pull oneself **up by** one's **(own) bootstraps** *Fig.* to improve or become a success by one's own efforts. □ *If Sam had a little encouragement, he could pull himself up by his bootstraps.* □ *Given a chance, I'm sure I can pull myself up by my own bootstraps.*

pull (out) in front of someone or something to drive out into the road in front of someone or some vehicle. □ *A car pulled out in front of me, and I almost hit it.* □ *The car pulled in front of a truck and there was a terrible wreck.*

pull out (of something**) 1.** to withdraw from something. □ *For some reason, he pulled out of the coalition and went his own way.* □ *The other side got impatient with the negotiations and pulled out.* **2.** to drive out of something, such as a driveway, parking space, garage, etc. □ *The car pulled out of the driveway and nearly hit a truck.* □ *Look out! A car is about to pull out!*

pull over (to something**)** to steer over to something, such as the side of the road. □ *Betty pulled over to the side of the road and waited for the traffic to thin.* □ *The police officer ordered her to pull over.*

pull rank (on someone**)** *Fig.* to assert one's rank, authority, or position over someone when making a request or giving an order. □ *Don't pull rank on me! I don't have to do what you say!* □ *When she couldn't get her way politely, she pulled rank and really got some action.*

pull (some) strings and **pull a few strings** to use influence (with someone to get something done). □ *I can get it done easily by pulling a few strings.* □ *Is it possible to get anything done around here without pulling some strings?*

pull someone **about 1.** *Lit.* to drag someone around. □ *The boys were pulling one another about and playing very rough.* □ *Don't pull your little brother about so!* **2.** *Fig.* to give someone a hard time. □ *I'm tired of your double-talk! Stop pulling me about!* □ *You can't believe what she tells people. She is always pulling people about.*

pull someone **apart 1.** *Lit.* to separate people who are entangled. □ *The teacher pulled the fighting boys apart and sent them home.* □ *They hugged each other so tightly that no one could have pulled them apart.* **2.** *Fig.* to upset someone very much; to cause someone grief and torment. □ *This whole terrible affair has just pulled me apart.* □ *Don't let this matter pull you apart. Things won't always be this bad.*

pull someone **aside**[†] to grasp and pull a person to one side. □ *I pulled the child aside and scolded him for trying to sneak into the theater.* □ *I pulled aside the child to say something to him.*

pull someone **down**[†] *Fig.* to degrade someone; to humiliate someone. (See also **pull** someone or something **down.**) □ *I'm afraid that your so-called friends are pulling you down behind your back.* □ *There is no need to pull down everyone.*

pull someone **in**[†] Go to **pull** someone **into** something; **pull** someone **into** a place.

pull someone **into** a place and **pull** someone **in**[†] *Lit.* to bring someone into a place; to draw someone into a place. □ *Advertising will pull hundreds of customers in.* □ *The sale pulled in a lot of customers.*

pull someone **into** something and **pull** someone **in**[†] *Fig.* to get someone involved in something. □ *Please don't pull me into this argument.* □ *Don't pull in anyone else.*

pull someone or an animal **down**[†] to drag or force someone or an animal down. □ *The wolves pulled the hunter down and set upon him.* □ *They pulled down the hunter.*

pull someone or an animal **through (**something**) 1.** *Lit.* to manage to get someone or an animal through an opening. □ *Do you think you can pull the cow through this narrow door to the shed?* **2.** *Fig.* to help someone or an animal survive a difficult time or situation. □ *All her friends worked hard to pull her through the crisis.* □ *The vet worked hard to pull the cat through the illness.*

pull someone or something **apart**[†] to separate or dismember someone or something. □ *The murderer pulled his victim apart and sought to dispose of the parts.* □ *He pulled apart his victim.* □ *Nick pulled the parts of the box apart.*

pull someone or something **around**[†] to drag or haul someone or something around. □ *The woman had pulled her children around all day while she did the shopping. All of them were glad to get home.* □ *Nick pulled around his wagon and collected discarded aluminum cans.*

pull someone or something **away from** someone or something and **pull** someone or something **away**[†] to grasp and haul someone or something away from someone or something. □ *The lady pulled the child away from the edge of the well.* □ *Please pull your dog away from my hedge.* □ *Pull away that dog, or I will call the police!*

pull someone or something **back**[†] **(from** someone or something**)** to grasp and haul someone or something away from someone or something. □ *The cop pulled the kid away from the other kid and made them stop fighting.* □ *I pulled back the child from the dangerous hole.*

pull someone or something **by** something to grasp someone or something by something and tug or haul. □ *I pulled him by the hand, trying to get him to follow me.* □ *Timmy pulled the toy duck by its string and it quacked as it waddled along.*

pull someone or something **into** something and **pull** someone or something **in**[†] to haul or drag someone or something into something or some place. □ *She pulled him into the room and closed the door.* □ *Lisa pulled in her friend and closed the door.*

pull someone or something **over (to** something**)** [for someone] to cause someone or a vehicle to drive over to something, such as the side of the road. □ *The cop pulled Betty over to the side of the road.* □ *I pulled the car over to the side.*

pull someone or something **to pieces** to pull someone or something apart; to separate someone or something into pieces. □ *The machine almost pulled him to pieces when he got his arm caught in it.*

pull someone or something **under 1.** *Lit.* to drag someone or something beneath the surface of something. □ *The strong undertow pulled John under the surface.* □ *The whirlpool nearly pulled the boat under.* **2.** *Fig.* to cause someone or something to fail. □ *The heavy debt load pulled Don under. He went out of business.* □ *The recession pulled his candy shop under.*

pull someone or something **up**[†] to drag or haul someone or something upward or to an upright position. □ *Bob had slipped down into the creek, so I reached down and pulled him up.* □ *I pulled up Bob and nearly fell in myself.* □ *Nick pulled the cushion up and propped it against the back of the sofa.*

pull someone's **leg** *Fig.* to kid, fool, or trick someone. □ *You don't mean that. You're just pulling my leg.* □ *Don't believe him. He's just pulling your leg.*

pull someone's or something's **teeth** *Fig.* to reduce the power or efficacy of someone or something. □ *The mayor tried to pull the teeth of the new law.* □ *The city council pulled the teeth of the new mayor.*

pull someone **through** (something) to help someone survive or get through something difficult. □ *With the help of the doctor, we pulled her through her illness.* □ *With lots of encouragement, we pulled her through.*

pull someone **up short** to cause someone to stop short. □ *My scream pulled him up short.* □ *The sudden thought that everything might not be all right pulled Tom up short.*

pull something **down**[†] **1.** to demolish something; to raze something. □ *Why do they want to pull the building down? Why not remodel it?* □ *They are going to pull down the old building today.* **2.** to lower or reduce the amount of something. □ *That last test pulled my grade down.* □ *Let's see if we can pull down your temperature with aspirin.*

pull something **down over** someone or something to draw something down over someone or something. □ *Lucy's mother pulled the dress down over Lucy and buttoned it up in back.* □ *Sarah pulled the cover down over the birdcage and turned out the lights.*

pull something **off**[†] **1.** *Inf.* to manage to make something happen. □ *Yes, I can pull it off.* □ *Do you think you can pull off this deal?* **2.** and **pull** something **off (of)** someone or something *Lit.* to tug or drag something off someone or something else. (*Of* is usually retained before pronouns.) □ *Sam pulled the covers off the bed and fell into it, dead tired.* □ *He pulled off his clothes and stepped into the shower.*

pull something **on**[†] to draw on an article of clothing. □ *He pulled his pants on.* □ *He pulled on his pants quickly and ran outside while putting on his shirt.*

pull something **on** someone to play a trick on someone; to deceive someone with a trick. (The word *something* is often used.) □ *You wouldn't pull a trick on me, would you?* □ *Who would pull something like that on an old lady?*

pull something **out**[†] Go to **pull** something **out of** someone or something.

pull something **out of a hat** and **pull** something **out of thin air 1.** *Lit.* [for a magician] to make something, such as a live rabbit, seem to appear by pulling it out of a top hat or out of the air. □ *He pulled a rabbit out of a hat and then pulled a chicken out of thin air.* **2.** *Fig.* to produce something seemingly out of nowhere. □ *Where am I going to get the money? I can't just pull it out of a hat!* □ *I don't know where she found the book. She pulled it out of thin air, I guess.*

pull something **out of** someone to draw or force information out of someone. □ *The cops finally pulled a confession out of Max.* □ *I thought I would never pull her name out of her.*

pull something **out of** someone or something and **pull** something **out**[†] to withdraw something from someone or something. □ *I pulled the arrow out of the injured soldier and tried to stop the bleeding.* □ *I pulled out the arrow.*

pull something **out of** someone's **hands** Go to **out of** someone's **hands**.

pull something **out of the fire 1.** *Lit.* to drag or take something out of a fire before it is consumed. □ *The fire was too big, so he pulled a few logs out of the fire.* **2.** *Fig.* to rescue something; to save something just before it's too late. □ *Can we rescue this project? Is there time to pull it out of the fire?* □ *There is no way we can pull this one out of the fire.*

pull something **out of thin air** Go to **pull** something **out of a hat**.

pull something **over** someone or something to draw something over someone or something. □ *The doctor pulled a sheet over Gerald and left the room.* □ *Sharon pulled the cover over the birdcage for the night.*

pull something **to** to close something, usually a door of some type. □ *The door is open a little. Pull it to so no one will hear us.* □ *Please pull the door to.*

pull something **together 1.** *Lit.* to close something, such as a pair of drapes or sliding doors. □ *Please pull the doors together when you finish in the closet.* □ *Would you pull the drapes together before you turn on the lights?* **2.** *Fig.* to assemble something, such as a meal. □ *I will hardly have time to pull a snack together.* □ *I will pull a nice dinner together for the two of us.* **3.** *Fig.* to organize something; to arrange something. □ *How about a party? I'll see if I can pull something together for Friday night.* **4.** *Fig.* to tidy things up; to straighten things up and make them orderly. □ *This place is a mess. Please pull things together.*

pull something **toward** oneself to draw something closer to oneself. □ *He pulled his plate toward himself and began eating like a starving man.* □ *Mary pulled the basket of fruit toward herself and chose a nice juicy peach.*

pull something **up**[†] Go to **pull** something **up to** something.

pull something **up**[†] **(out of** something) to draw something upward out of something. □ *The worker pulled a cold wet dog up out of the pond.* □ *He pulled up the dog out of the pond.*

pull something **up to** something and **pull** something **up**[†] to draw something close to something else. □ *She pulled the chair up to the table and began to examine the papers.* □ *She pulled up a chair.*

pull the plug (on someone) **1.** *Lit.* to turn off someone's life-support system in a hospital. (Based on **pull the plug (on** something) ①. This results in the death of the person whose life support has been terminated.) □ *They had to get a court order to pull the plug on their father.* □ *Fred signed a living will making it possible to pull the plug on him without a court order.* **2.** *Fig.* to put an end to someone's activities or plans. (Based on **pull the plug (on** something) ②.) □ *The mayor was doing a fine job until the treasurer pulled the plug on him.* □ *David pulled the plug on Fred, who was taking too long with the project.*

pull the plug (on something) **1.** *Lit.* to terminate the functions of something by pulling a connector from a socket. □ *While she was working at the computer, I accidentally pulled the plug.* □ *I pulled the plug on the vacuum because the switch was broken.* **2.** *Fig.* to reduce the power or effectiveness of something; to disable something. □ *Jane pulled the plug on the whole project.* □ *The treasurer pulled the plug because there was no more money in the budget.*

pull the rug out† **(from under** someone) *Fig.* to make someone or someone's plans fall through; to upset someone's plans. □ *Don pulled the rug out from under me in my deal with Bill Franklin.* □ *I was close to getting the contract until Don came along and pulled out the rug.*

pull the wool over someone's **eyes** *Fig.* to deceive someone. □ *You can't pull the wool over my eyes. I know what's going on.* □ *Don't try to pull the wool over her eyes. She's too smart.*

pull through (something) to survive something. □ *I am sure that your uncle will pull through the illness.* □ *I'm glad he pulled through.*

pull together (as a team) to cooperate; to work well together. □ *Let's all pull together and get this done.* □ *If we pull together as a team, we can get this job done on time.*

Pull up a chair. Please get a chair and sit down and join us. (Assumes that there is seating available. The speaker does not necessarily mean that the person spoken to actually has to move a chair.) □ *Tom: Well, hello, Bob! Bob: Hi, Tom. Pull up a chair.* □ *The three men were sitting at a table for four. Bob came up and said hello. Bill said, "Pull up a chair." Bob sat in the fourth chair at the table.*

pull (up) alongside ((of) someone or something) to move to a point beside someone or something. (*Of* is usually retained before pronouns.) □ *The car pulled up alongside the truck and honked and the people inside waved and waved.* □ *Please pull alongside the curb.*

pull up (somewhere) Go to **haul up** (somewhere).

pull up stakes 1. *Lit.* to pull up tent stakes to take down a tent in preparation to leaving. □ *Let's pull up stakes and head home before the storm hits.* **2.** *Fig.* to end one's ties to a particular place; to get ready to move away from a place where one has lived or worked for a long time. □ *Even after all these years, pulling up stakes is easier than you think.* □ *It's time to pull up stakes and move on.*

pull up to something to drive up close to something. □ *I pulled up to the drive-in window and placed my order.* □ *When the taxi pulls up to the curb, open the door and get in.*

pulse through someone or something to flow or surge through someone or something. □ *A jolt of electricity*

pulsed through Sam, causing him to jerk his hand away from the wire. □ *They repaired the power lines and electricity began to pulse through the wires again.*

pump (some) iron *Sl.* to lift weights for exercise. □ *Andy went down to the gym to pump some iron.* □ *Mary's hobbies are pumping iron and running.*

pump someone **for** something *Inf.* to try to get information about something out of someone. □ *The representative of the other company pumped Harry for information, but he refused to say anything.* □ *Are you trying to pump me for company secrets?*

pump someone **up (for** something) *Inf.* to get someone, including oneself, mentally ready for something. □ *The coach tried to pump the team up so they would win.* □ *The coach talked and talked to pump them up.*

pump something **into** someone or something and **pump** something **in†** to try to force something, such as a gas, liquid, information, or money into someone or something. □ *First you have to pump some air into the ball to make it hard.* □ *I pumped in the air.* □ *The hospital oxygen system pumped life-giving oxygen into Karen's lungs.*

pump something **out of** someone or something and **pump** something **out†** to remove something from someone or something by force or suction. □ *The doctors pumped the poison out of her stomach.* □ *They pumped out the poison.*

pump something **through** something to force something, such as a gas or fluid, through something. □ *They pumped crude oil through this pipeline, all the way to the south shore.* □ *They pumped fresh air through the sewers while the workers were working inside.*

pump something **up† 1.** to inflate something. □ *Do you have something with which I can pump my basketball up?* □ *I pumped up the ball just an hour ago.* **2.** *Sl.* to exercise to make muscles get bigger and stronger. □ *The bodybuilder pumped her muscles up in preparation for the competition.* □ *She pumped up her muscles.*

pumped (up) *Sl.* excited; physically and mentally ready. □ *The team is really pumped up for Friday's game.* □ *She really plays well when she's pumped!*

punch a hole in something to make a hole in something with something. □ *John punched a hole in the wall with his fist.* □ *Mary punched a hole in the paper with her pencil.*

punch in to record one's arrival at one's workplace at a certain time. □ *What time did you punch in?* □ *I punched in at the regular time.*

punch out to record that one has left one's workplace at a certain time. □ *Why didn't you punch out when you left last night?* □ *I punched out at the regular time.*

punch someone **in** something to strike someone in some body part. □ *Tony punched Nick in the side.* □ *Why didn't you punch that mean guy in the nose?*

punch someone **on** something to strike someone on some body part, typically the shoulder. (Not with the intention of causing harm.) □ *Sally punched Frank on the shoulder just to show they were still friends.* □ *Tom punched Fred on the shoulder in a friendly way.*

punch someone **out†** *Sl.* to overcome or beat someone by punching. □ *He threatened to punch me out.* □ *The thug punched out the cop and ran down an alley.*

P

punch someone's **lights out** *Sl.* to knock someone out with a fist. □ *You had better stop that, or I will punch your lights out!* □ *Do you want me to punch your lights out?*

punch something **down**† to press something down. □ *Punch this lever down and then try to place your telephone call.* □ *Punch down this lever and push this button.*

punch something **in**† to crush or smash something in. □ *Who punched the cereal box in?* □ *Who punched in the cereal box?*

punch something **into** something to stick or press something into something. □ *She punched her finger into the cake and ruined my lovely icing job.* □ *He finally punched a spoon into the cereal box to get it open.*

punch something **out of** something and **punch** something **out**† to press on something and make it pop out of something. □ *She punched the perforated stickers out of the page and stuck them onto her schoolbooks.* □ *Jane punched out the stickers.*

punch something **up**† to register a figure on a cash register or calculator. □ *Jake punched the total up, and the register drawer opened.* □ *He punched up the total too carelessly.*

Punctuality is the soul of business. *Prov.* You should be on time for all your business appointments. □ *The office manager insisted on everyone's coming to work on time, not a minute late. "Punctuality is the soul of business," she said.*

punctuate something **with** something **1.** to add a particular punctuation mark to a piece of writing. □ *You have punctuated this ad with too many exclamation points.* □ *This letter is punctuated with dashes to emphasize the key points.* **2.** to add emphasis to one's speaking by adding phrases, exclamations, or other devices. □ *Her comments were punctuated with a few choice swear words.* □ *Tom punctuated his address with a few choice comments about politicians.*

punish someone **by** something to discipline someone by doing something. □ *The headmaster punished the children by forcing them to go to bed early.* □ *She punished herself by not eating.*

punish someone **for** something to discipline someone for [doing] something. □ *Someone will punish you for what you did.* □ *Please don't punish me for doing it. I'm sorry.*

punish someone **with** something to use something to discipline someone. □ *The captain punished the sailor with the lash.* □ *Sally threatened to punish Timmy with a spanking.*

punk out *Sl.* to chicken out (of something); to withdraw from something in cowardice. □ *He was supposed to ask her out, but he punked out at the last minute.* □ *Come on! Stick with it! Don't punk out!*

puppy love *Fig.* mild infatuation; infatuation as in a crush. (Used especially of adolescent relationships.) □ *Is it really love or just puppy love?* □ *Look at them together. It may be puppy love, but it looks wonderful.*

purchase something **for** someone to buy something for someone else; to buy something to give to someone. □ *Tony purchased a number of toys for the children in the orphanage.* □ *Who did you purchase this gift for?*

pure and simple and **plain and simple** absolutely; without further complication or elaboration. □ *I told you what you must do, and you must do it, pure and simple.* □ *Will you kindly explain to me what it is, pure and simple, that I am expected to do?* □ *Just tell me plain and simple, do you intend to go or don't you?*

***pure as the driven snow** pure and chaste. (Often used ironically. *Also: **as** ~.) □ *Jill: Sue must have gone to bed with every man in town. Jane: And I always thought she was as pure as the driven snow.* □ *Robert was notoriously promiscuous, but tried to convince all his girlfriends that he was pure as the driven snow.*

pure luck and **blind luck** complete luck; nothing but plain luck. □ *I have no skill. I won by pure luck.*

purge someone or something **from** something to rid something of someone or something. □ *We are going to purge the delinquent members from the list.* □ *The court purged her arrest from the records.*

purge someone or something **of** someone or something to rid someone or something of someone or something. □ *The medicine is designed to purge the patient of the deadly toxin.* □ *We purged the list of the delinquent members.*

purge something **away**† to wash or flush something away. □ *We will purge the rusty water away and then start up the pump again. We will have fresh, clean water again in no time.* □ *Laura purged away the rusty water.*

purr like a cat and **purr like a kitten 1.** *Fig.* [for an engine] to run well and smoothly. □ *My car really purred after I got it tuned up.* □ *New spark plugs and this old heap will really purr like a cat.* **2.** *Fig.* [for a person] to be very pleased, and perhaps moan or purr with pleasure. □ *She was so pleased that she purred like a cat.* □ *Sarah really purrs like a kitten when she is happy.*

purr like a kitten Go to previous.

purse something **up**† to bunch or pucker something up. (Usually the lips.) □ *When he tasted the lemon juice, he pursed his lips up and spat it out.* □ *Don pursed up his lips as if to spit it out.*

push ahead (with something) **1.** *Lit.* to go on ahead, pushing with something. □ *The worker pushed ahead with the plow, moving the snow to the side of the road.* □ *Our car followed the snowplow, which was pushing ahead at a fast clip.* **2.** and **push ahead (on** something) *Fig.* to continue to progress with something. □ *Let's push ahead with this project immediately.* □ *I want to push ahead on this project.*

push along to move along; to travel along as with a purpose. □ *We must push along. We have a long way to travel before morning.* □ *They pushed along at a steady clip until they arrived at their destination.*

push at someone or something to apply pressure to and try to move someone or something. □ *She pushed at him, trying to get him to get out of the way, but he wouldn't budge.* □ *Mary pushed at the door, trying to open it against the wind.* □ *There is no need for you to push at me so hard.*

push down on something to press down on something, such as a button, stamp, lever, etc. □ *Push down on this button if you want room service.* □ *Don't push down on the door handle too hard. It will break.*

push for something to request or demand something. □ *The citizens are pushing for an investigation of the police department.* □ *My secretary is pushing for a raise.*

push forward to move forward; to move onward toward a goal. □ *We have lots to do. We must push forward!* □ *They are pushing forward, hoping to complete the project on time.*

push off and **shove off** to leave. (As if one were pushing a boat away from a dock.) □ *Well, it looks like it's time to push off.* □ *It's time to go. Let's shove off.*

push on someone or something to put pressure on someone or something. □ *Don't push on me! I can't move any faster than the person in front of me!* □ *Push on this button if you want the steward to come.* □ *Push on the door a little. It will open.*

push on (to something) **1.** to move on to another topic; to stop doing one thing and move on to another. □ *Okay. Let's push on to the next topic.* □ *Let us push on. We are nearly finished with the list.* **2.** to travel onward to something or some place. □ *We left Denver and pushed on to Omaha.* □ *Let us push on. We are nearly there.*

push on (with something) to continue to try to make progress with something. □ *Let's push on with this project. We must finish it soon.* □ *Yes, let's push on and finish.*

push one's **luck** and **press** one's **luck** to expect continued good fortune; to expect to continue to escape bad luck. (Often implies unreasonable expectation.) □ *You're okay so far, but don't push your luck.* □ *Bob pressed his luck too much and got into a lot of trouble.*

push (oneself**) away (from** something) to move oneself back and away from something. □ *The skater pushed herself away from the wall.* □ *Tom pushed himself away from the table when he had eaten enough.*

push (oneself**) by (**someone or something**)** to shove or thrust oneself past someone or something. □ *In a hurry, I pushed myself by the security guard, and almost got arrested for doing so.* □ *I pushed by Jane and went in first.*

push (oneself**) off (on** something) [for someone in a boat] to apply pressure to something on the shore, thus propelling the boat and oneself away. □ *The weekend sailor pushed himself off on the boat he had been moored to.* □ *We pushed off on the dock.*

push out to spread out; to expand outward. □ *The sides of the box pushed out, and I was afraid it would break.* □ *His little tummy pushed out when he was full.*

push past (someone or something**)** to force one's way past someone or something. (Considered a rude act.) □ *Nick pushed past the others and made himself first in line.* □ *I pushed past the gate and went right in.*

push someone **around** Fig. to harass someone physically; to jostle someone. (See also **push** someone or something **about**.) □ *I wish you would stop pushing me around all the time.* □ *Stop pushing Max around if you know what's good for you.*

push someone **into** something and **push** someone **in†** to force someone into a situation; to force someone to do something. □ *They are trying to push me into signing the contract.* □ *Please don't push me into it!* □ *You pushed me in!*

push someone or something **about** and **push** someone or something **around** to jostle someone or something around. □ *The crowd pushed the visitors around and made them feel unwelcome.* □ *People on the sidewalk pushed the delegation about during the noon rush hour.*

push someone or something **about in** something and **push** someone or something **around in** something; **push** someone or something **around†** to propel someone or something about on wheels. □ *Freddie pushed his brother about in the wagon.* □ *The nurse pushed around Aunt Mary in her wheelchair.*

push someone or something **across (**something**)** to move or propel someone or something across something. □ *Jill pushed Fred across the ice. He simply could not skate at all.* □ *The old car stalled just before the bridge, so we pushed it across.*

push someone or something **ahead of** someone to push someone or something forward from behind. □ *I pushed Gerald ahead of me so he could get a better view.* □ *Sally pushed the cart ahead of her and filled it from the supermarket shelves.*

push someone or something **along** to apply pressure to move someone or something along. □ *The mother tried to push her child along, but he wouldn't go.* □ *Jane pushed the cart along, down the supermarket aisle.*

push someone or something **around** Go to **push** someone or something **about**.

push someone or something **around in** something Go to **push** someone or something **about in** something.

push someone or something **aside†** to shove someone or something to one side. □ *Martha pushed Bill aside and went in ahead of him.* □ *He pushed aside the papers and laid his books on the desk.*

push someone or something **(away) (from** someone or something**)** to move or force someone or something away from someone or something. □ *The police pushed the crowd away from the movie star.* □ *They pushed away the hecklers from the stage.*

push someone or something **back† (from** someone or something**)** to move or force someone or something back from someone or something. □ *I quickly pushed her back from the edge. She almost fell over.* □ *There wasn't enough room, so we pushed back the furniture.* □ *Tony pushed Jane back from the edge.*

push someone or something **down†** to force someone or something downward. □ *Every time he tried to get up, the other boys pushed him down again.* □ *I pushed down the button and the machine began to operate.*

push someone or something **forward** to shove or move someone or something to the front. □ *Mary's mother pushed her forward where she would be seen.* □ *Let me push the piano bench forward for you.*

push someone or something **into** someone or something to cause someone or something to bump into someone or something. □ *Todd accidentally pushed Marlene into Bill.* □ *I pushed the lawn mower into the tree by accident.*

push someone or something **off (of)** someone or something and **push** someone or something **off†** to apply pressure to and force someone or something off someone or something. (*Of* is usually retained before pronouns.) □ *He con-*

tinued to come at me, but I managed to push him off me and escape. □ *I pushed off the attacker.*

push someone or something **on (ahead) (of** someone or something**)** to move or propel someone or something ahead. □ *He did not want to go in with me, but I pushed him on forward or ahead of me.* □ *I went into each room to clean it, pushing the laundry cart on ahead.* □ *She paused for a moment to rest, and then pushed the baby stroller on.*

push someone or something **out of** something and **push** someone or something **out†** to force someone or something out of something. □ *Nick pushed the intruder out of the house.* □ *Tony pushed out the intruder.*

push someone or something **over†** to make someone or something fall over or fall down. □ *When you ran into me, you nearly pushed me over.* □ *You nearly pushed over your friend.*

push someone or something **over (**something**)** to cause someone or something to move over something. □ *The convict pushed his buddy over the wall and followed after him.* □ *He climbed up to the top of the fence and I pushed him over.*

push someone or something **to** someone or something to propel someone or something to or as far as someone or something. □ *Max pushed Lefty to the window and made him look out.* □ *I pushed the chair to the window.*

push someone or something **toward** someone or something to propel someone or something to someone or something. □ *The drama coach got behind the shy young actor playing Romeo and pushed him toward Juliet.* □ *Clyde pushed his victim toward the edge of the cliff.*

push someone or something **up†** to raise or lift someone or something. □ *Jake is sliding down again. Push him up.* □ *Push up the window, please.*

push someone, something, or an animal **into** something to guide, shove, or press someone, something, or an animal inside of something. □ *I pushed the lawn mower into the garage and closed the door.* □ *I opened the garage door and pushed the dog in.*

push someone **to** something to try to drive or force a person to do something. □ *After the bankruptcy the board pushed the president to resign.* □ *We pushed her to reconsider, but her mind was made up.*

push someone **to the wall** and **press** someone **to the wall** to force someone into a position where there is only one choice to make; to put someone in a defensive position. □ *There was little else I could do. They pushed me to the wall.*

push someone **too far** *Fig.* to antagonize someone too much; to be too confrontational with someone. □ *I guess I pushed him too far, because he began shouting at me and threatening to hit me.*

push someone **up against the wall** Go to up against the wall.

push something **in†** to crush something in; to make something cave in. □ *He ran at the door and pushed it in.* □ *He pushed in the door.*

push something **off on(to)** someone to place one's task onto another person; to make someone else do an unwanted job. □ *Don't push the dirty work off onto me.* □ *Kelly pushed some of her workload off on me.*

push something **through (**something**) 1.** *Lit.* to force something to penetrate something. □ *Tony pushed the needle through the cloth, and drew the thread tight.* □ *He pushed the needle through just like a tailor.* **2.** *Fig.* to force passage of a motion or law. □ *The committee chairman managed to push the bill through the committee.* □ *With a little lobbying, they pushed it through.*

push something **to** to close or nearly close something, such as a door. □ *The door is open a little. Please push it to.* □ *Todd came in and pushed the door to.*

push something **(up) against** someone or something to press something against someone or something. □ *I pushed the chair up against the door to prevent the robber from getting in.* □ *Accidentally, I pushed the door against Donna and hurt her sore elbow.*

push the envelope *Fig.* to expand the definition, categorization, dimensions, or perimeters of something. □ *The engineers wanted to completely redesign the product, but couldn't push the envelope because of a very restricted budget.*

push the panic button Go to hit the panic button.

push through (something**)** to work through or force one's way through something. □ *I pushed through the snow, trying to get to the post office on time.* □ *The snow was very deep, but I pushed through.*

push toward someone or something to move or struggle toward someone or something. □ *The crowd pushed toward the convicted man, but the police held them back.* □ *The horses pushed toward the corral gate.*

push (up) against someone or something to put pressure on someone or something. □ *The small dog pushed up against me, wagging its tail.* □ *Push up against the ceiling tile while I try to tack it back in place.*

push up on something to raise something upward; to push something up from below. □ *Larry pushed up on the trapdoor and lifted it so he could climb out.* □ *Push up on this lever if you want the lights to get brighter.*

pushed for money Go to pressed for money.

pushed for time Go to pressed for time.

pushing up (the) daisies *Fig.* dead and buried. (Usually in the future tense.) □ *I'll be pushing up daisies before this problem is solved.* □ *If you talk to me like that again, you'll be pushing up the daisies.*

pussyfoot around *Fig.* to go about timidly and cautiously. (Alludes to a cat walking carefully.) □ *Stop pussyfooting around! Get on with it!* □ *I wish that they would not pussyfoot around when there are tough decisions to be made.*

put a bee in someone's **bonnet (about** someone or something**)** *Fig.* to give someone an idea about someone or something; to urge someone to do something. □ *Julie put a bee in my bonnet about a way to solve our money problems.* □ *Sam put a bee in my bonnet about having a party for Jane.* □ *He put a bee in my bonnet about Jane.* □ *I'm glad he put a bee in my bonnet.*

put a cap on something *Fig.* to put a limit on something. □ *We need to put a cap on spending in every department.* □ *The city put a cap on the amount each landlord could charge.*

put a contract out on someone [for an underworld character] to order someone to kill someone else. □ *The mob put out a contract on some crook from Detroit.*

put a damper on something *Fig.* to have a dulling or numbing influence on something. □ *The bad news really put a damper on everything.* □ *The rainy weather put a damper on our picnic.*

put a dog off the scent to distract a dog from trailing the scent of someone or an animal. □ *The odor of a skunk put the dogs off the scent.*

put a hold on something to place restriction on something so that it is reserved, delayed, or inactivated. □ *The bank put a hold on my credit card until I paid my bill.* □ *The committee agreed to put a hold on the troublesome piece of business.*

put a horse out to pasture to retire a horse by allowing it to live out its days in a pasture with no work. (See also **put** someone **out to pasture**.) □ *The horse could no longer work, so we put it out to pasture.*

put a lid on something Go to a **lid on** something.

put a plug in† (**for** someone or something) to say something favoring someone or something; to advertise someone or something. □ *I hope that when you are in talking to the manager, you put a plug in for me.* □ *I could use some help. While you're there, put in a plug.*

put a premium on something to make something harder or more expensive to obtain or do. □ *The recent action of the bank directors put a premium on new home loans.* □ *The scarcity of steel put a premium on the cost of new cars.*

put a price on one's **head** Go to a **price on** one's **head**.

put a smile on someone's **face** *Fig.* to please someone; to make someone happy. □ *We are going to give Andy a pretty good raise, and I know that'll put a smile on his face.* □ *The surprise birthday party really put a smile on my dad's face.*

Put a sock in it! Go to **Stuff a sock in it!**

put a spin on something to twist a report or story to one's advantage; to interpret an event to make it seem favorable or beneficial to oneself or one's cause. □ *The mayor tried to put a positive spin on the damaging polls.* □ *The pundit's spin on the new legislation was highly critical.*

put a stop to something and **put an end to** something to bring something to an end. □ *I want you to put a stop to all this bad behavior.* □ *Please put an end to this conversation.*

put a strain on someone or something to burden or overload someone or something. □ *All this bad economic news puts a strain on everyone's nerves.* □ *The epidemic put a strain on the resources of the hospital.*

put all one's **eggs in one basket** *Fig.* to make everything dependent on only one thing; to place all one's resources in one place, account, etc. (If the basket is dropped, all is lost.) □ *Don't invest all your money in one company. Never put all your eggs in one basket.* □ *I advise you to diversify and not to put all your eggs in one basket.*

put an amount of time **in on** something to spend an amount of time (doing something). □ *You put how much time in?* □ *I put in four months on that project.*

put an animal **down†** *Euph.* to take the life of an animal mercifully. □ *We put down our old dog last year.* □ *It's kind to put fatally ill animals down.*

put an animal **out†** to send an animal, such as a pet, outdoors. □ *Did you put the cat out?* □ *Yes, I put out the cat.*

put an end to something Go to **put a stop to** something.

put another way Go to **to put it another way.**

put balls on something *Sl.* to make something more masculine or powerful; to give something authority and strength. (Potentially offensive. Use only with discretion.) □ *Come on, sing louder. Put some balls on it.* □ *This story is too namby-pamby. Put some balls on it.*

Put 'em up! Go to **Hands up!**

Put 'er there(, pal). *Inf.* Please shake hands with me. □ *Glad to meet you. Put 'er there, pal.*

put hair on someone's **chest** *Fig.* to do or take something to invigorate or energize someone, always a male, except in jest. □ *Here, have a drink of this stuff! It'll put hair on your chest.* □ *That stuff is powerful. It will really put hair on your chest.*

put ideas into someone's **head** *Fig.* to suggest something—usually something bad—to someone (who would not have thought of it otherwise). □ *Bill keeps getting into trouble. Please don't put ideas into his head.* □ *Bob would get along all right if other kids didn't put ideas into his head.*

put in a good word (for someone) *Fig.* to say something (to someone) in support of someone else. □ *I hope you get the job. I'll put in a good word for you.* □ *Yes, I want the job. If you see the boss, please put in a good word.*

put in a hard day at work and **put in a hard day's work** *Fig.* to work very hard at one's job. □ *I put in a hard day at work at the office, and now I want to be left alone to rest.*

put in an appearance (at something) to appear briefly at some place or at some event. □ *I only wanted to put in an appearance at the reception, but I ended up staying for two hours.* □ *Do we have to stay a long time, or can we just put in an appearance?*

put in for something to apply for something; to make a request for something. □ *I put in for a transfer, but I bet I don't get it.* □ *She put in for a new file cabinet, but she never got one.*

put in some place to dock [a vessel] temporarily some place. □ *The ship put in at Bridgetown, Barbados, for repairs.* □ *We will put in at Honolulu for a few hours.*

put it on the line Go to **lay it on the line.**

put money up† (**for** something) to provide the funding for something. □ *The government put the money up for the cost of construction.* □ *Who will put up the money for my education?*

put off by someone or something distressed or repelled by someone or something. □ *I was really put off by your behavior.* □ *We were all put off by the unfairness of the rules.*

put on to pretend; to act as if something were true. □ *Ann wasn't really angry. She was just putting on.* □ *I can't believe she was just putting on. She really looked mad.*

put on a (brave) front Go to **put up a (brave) front.**

put on airs and **give** oneself **airs** *Fig.* to act better than one really is; to pretend to be good or to be superior. □ *Pay no attention to her. She is just putting on airs.* □ *Stop giving yourself airs and act like the rest of us.*

put on an act to pretend that one is something other than what one is. □ *Be yourself, Ann. Stop putting on an act.* □ *You don't have to put on an act. We accept you the way you are.*

put on the dog and **put on the ritz** to make things extra special or dress formally for a special event. □ *Frank's really putting on the dog for the big party Friday night.* □ *They really put on the ritz for us.*

put on the ritz Go to previous.

put on weight to gain weight; to get fat. □ *I think I am putting on a little weight. I had better go on a diet.* □ *He has put on a lot of weight since last year.*

put one **at (**one's**) ease** *Fig.* to cause someone to relax or feel welcome. □ *She usually tells a little joke to put you at your ease.* □ *Please do something to put me at ease.*

put one foot in front of the other 1. *Lit.* to walk deliberately. □ *I was so tired that I could hardly even put one foot in front of the other.* □ *She was putting one foot in front of the other so carefully that I thought she must be ill.* **2.** *Fig.* to do things carefully and in their proper order. □ *Let's do it right now. Just put one foot in front of the other. One thing at a time.* □ *All I need to do is put one foot in front of the other. Everything else will take care of itself.*

put one **in** one's **place** to rebuke someone; to remind one of one's (lower) rank or station. □ *The boss put me in my place for criticizing her.* □ *Then her boss put her in her place for being rude.*

put one **in over** one's **head** Go to in over one's head.

put one **off** one's **game** Go to off one's game.

put one **off** one's **stride 1.** *Lit.* to cause one to deviate from a rhythmic stride while walking, running, or marching. □ *A rabbit ran across the path and put me off my stride.* **2.** *Fig.* to interfere with one's normal and natural progress or rate of progress. □ *Your startling comments put Larry off his stride for a moment.* □ *He was put off his stride by an interruption from the audience.*

put one **on** one's **feet** Go to get one on one's feet.

put one **on** one's **guard** to make one wary or cautious. □ *The menacing growl by the watchdog put me on my guard.* □ *Every time the boss comes around, it puts me on my guard.*

put one **on** one's **honor** *Fig.* to inform one that one is trusted to act honorably, legally, and fairly without supervision. □ *I'll put you on your honor when I have to leave the room during the test.* □ *They put us on our honor to take no more than we had paid for.*

put one **out of (**one's**) misery 1.** *Euph. Fig.* to kill someone as an act of mercy. (See also **put** some creature **out of its misery.**) □ *Why doesn't the doctor simply put her out of her misery?* □ *He took pills to put himself out of his misery.* **2.** *Fig.* to end a suspenseful situation for someone. □ *Please, put me out of misery; what happened?* □ *I put her out of her misery and told her how the movie ended.*

put one over on someone Go to put something over on someone.

put one's **back (in)to** something **1.** *Fig.* to apply great physical effort to lift or move something. □ *All right, you guys. Put your backs into moving this piano.* □ *You can lift it if you put your back to it.* **2.** *Fig.* to apply a lot of mental or creative effort to doing something. (From ①.) □ *If we put our backs to it, we can bake twelve dozen cookies today.* □ *The artist put his back into finishing the picture on time.*

put one's **best foot forward** *Fig.* to act or appear at one's best; to try to make a good impression. □ *When you apply for a job, you should always put your best foot forward.* □ *I try to put my best foot forward whenever I meet someone for the first time.*

put one's **cards on the table** Go to lay one's cards on the table.

put one's **dibs on** something to lay a claim to something; to announce one's claim to something. □ *She put her dibs on the last piece of cake.* □ *I put my dibs on the seat by the window.*

put one's **face on** *Fig.* [for a woman] to apply cosmetics. □ *Martha's gone to put her face on.* □ *We'll be on our way once my wife has put her face on.*

put one's **feet up**[†] to sit down, lean back, and rest; to lie down. □ *He was really exhausted and had to go put his feet up.* □ *Time to put up my feet and get some rest.*

put one's **finger on** something **1.** *Lit.* to touch something with one's finger. □ *I put my finger on the button and pressed.* □ *Put your finger on this spot and push hard.* **2.** *Fig.* to identify and state the essence of something. □ *That is correct! You have certainly put your finger on the problem.* □ *When she mentioned money, she really put her finger on the problem.*

put one's **foot down (about** someone or something**)** *Fig.* to assert something strongly. □ *The boss put her foot down and refused to accept any more changes to the plan.*

put one's **foot in it** Go to next.

put one's **foot in** one's **mouth** and **put** one's **foot in it; stick** one's **foot in** one's **mouth** *Fig.* to say something that you regret; to say something stupid, insulting, or hurtful. □ *When I told Ann that her hair was more beautiful than I had ever seen it, I really put my foot in my mouth. It was a wig.* □ *I put my foot in it by telling John's secret; he found out.*

put one's **hair up**[†] to arrange one's hair into a ponytail, bun, etc. (with curlers, hairpins, etc.). □ *I can't go out because I just put my hair up.* □ *I put up my hair every night.*

put one's **hand to the plow** *Fig.* to get busy; to help out; to start working. (Alludes to grasping a plow, ready to work the fields.) □ *You should start work now. It's time to put your hand to the plow.* □ *Put your hand to the plow and get the job done!*

put one's **hand up**[†] to raise one's hand to get attention from whomever is in charge. □ *The student put his hand up to ask a question of the teacher.* □ *She put up her hand to ask a question.*

put one's **hands on** someone, something, or an animal and **lay** one's **hands on** someone, something, or an animal **1.** *Lit.* to place one's hands on someone or an animal. □ *He put his hands on the sick woman and proclaimed her cured. This act of faith healing failed, alas.* □ *He laid his* *hands on the dog and gently felt for broken bones.* **2.** *Fig.* to locate and get hold of someone or something. □ *As soon as I can lay my hands on him, I'll get him right over here.* □ *I am trying to put my hands on the book you suggested.* **3.** *Fig.* to get hold of someone or an animal with punishment or harm as a goal.* □ *Just wait till I put my hands on you!* □ *When I lay my hands on Ken, he will be sorry he ever lied to me.*

put one's **head on the block (for** someone or something**)** *Fig.* to take great risks for someone or something; to go to a lot of trouble or difficulty for someone or something; to attempt to gain favor for someone or something. □ *I don't know why I should put my head on the block for Joan. What has she ever done for me?* □ *Sally tried to get me to put in a good word about her with the boss. But the last time I put my head on the block for anyone, it all backfired, and when the person goofed up, I looked like an idiot!*

put one's **heart (and soul) into** something *Fig.* to put all of one's sincere efforts into something. □ *She put her heart and soul into the singing of the national anthem.* □ *Come on, choir. You can sing better than that. Put your heart into it!*

put one's **house in order** *Fig.* to put one's business or personal affairs into good order. (As if one were cleaning one's house. See also **put** one's **own house in order.**) □ *There was some trouble in the department office and the manager was told to put his house in order.* □ *Every now and then, I have to put my house in order. Then life becomes more manageable.*

put one's **mind to** something and **set** one's **mind to** something *Fig.* to concentrate on doing something; to give the doing of something one's full attention. □ *I know I can do it if I put my mind to it.* □ *I will set my mind to it and finish by noon.*

put one's **money on** someone or something **(to** do something**) 1.** *Fig.* to bet money that someone or something will accomplish something. □ *I put my money on the favorite to win the race.* □ *Donna put her money on the winning horse.* **2.** *Fig.* to predict the outcome of an event involving someone or something. (This is not a wager.) □ *I put my money on Bob to get elected this time.* □ *Alice put her money on the most popular candidate.*

put one's **neck on the line** *Fig.* to put oneself at great risk. □ *I put my neck on the line and recommended you for the job, and now look what you've done! I'm ruined!*

put one's **nose in (where it's not wanted)** and **stick** one's **nose in (where it's not wanted)** *Fig.* to interfere in someone else's business. □ *Why do you always have to stick your nose in?* □ *Please don't put your nose in where it's not wanted!*

put one's **nose out of joint** Go to **get** one's **nose out of joint.**

put one's **nose to the grindstone** *Fig.* to keep busy doing one's work. (Also with *have* and *get*, as in the examples.) □ *The boss told me to put my nose to the grindstone.* □ *I've had my nose to the grindstone ever since I started working here.* □ *If the other people in this office would get their noses to the grindstone, more work would get done.*

put one's **oar in**[†] and **stick** one's **oar in**[†]; **put** one's **two cents(' worth) in**[†] *Fig.* to add one's comments or opin-

ion, even if unwanted or unasked for. □ *You don't need to put your oar in. I don't need your advice.* □ *I'm sorry. I shouldn't have stuck my oar in when you were arguing with your wife.* □ *Do you mind if I put in my oar? I have a suggestion.* □ *There is no need for you to put in your two cents' worth.*

put one's **own house in order** to make one's own affairs right, before or instead of criticizing someone else. (See also **put** one's **house in order.**) □ *You should put your own house in order before criticizing someone else.* □ *I have to put my own house in order before I criticize others.*

put one's **thinking cap on**[†] *Fig.* to start thinking in a serious manner. (Usually used with children.) □ *It's time to put our thinking caps on, children.* □ *All right now, let's put on our thinking caps and do some arithmetic.*

put one's **trust in** someone or something to trust someone or something. □ *Will I never be able to put my trust in you?* □ *You can put your trust in the bank. Its deposits are insured.*

put one's **two cents(' worth) in**[†] Go to **put** one's **oar in**[†].

put one **through** one's **paces** and **put** something **through its paces** *Fig.* to give someone or something a thorough test; to show what someone or something can do. □ *I brought the young gymnast out and put her through her paces.*

put oneself **in** someone else's **place** and **put** oneself **in** someone else's **shoes** to allow oneself to see or experience something from someone else's point of view. □ *Put yourself in someone else's place, and see how it feels.* □ *I put myself in Tom's shoes and realized that I would have made exactly the same choice.*

put oneself **out** to inconvenience oneself. □ *I just don't know why I put myself out for you!* □ *No, I did not put myself out at all. It was no trouble, in fact.*

put out to generate [lots of something]. □ *What a great machine. It really puts out!* □ *The new laser printer really puts out!*

put out a warrant (on someone**)** and **send out a warrant (on** someone**)** to issue a warrant for the arrest of someone. □ *The police put out a warrant on Max.* □ *We sent out a warrant on Lefty "Fingers" Moran at the same time.*

put out (about someone or something**)** irritated; bothered. □ *John behaved rudely at the party, and the hostess was quite put out.* □ *Liz was quite put out about the question.*

put out (some) feelers (on someone or something**)** to arrange to find out about something in an indirect manner. □ *I put out some feelers on Betty to try and find out what is going on.* □ *I will put out feelers on what's going on with June.*

put paid to something to consider something closed or completed; to mark or indicate that something is no longer important or pending. (As if one were stamping a bill "paid".) □ *At last, we were able to put paid to the matter of who is to manage the accounts.*

put people or things together to join or combine people or things. □ *We will put Sam and Trudy together at the dinner table.* □ *Let's put all the crystal goblets together.*

put people's **heads together** to join together with someone to confer. □ *Let's put our heads together and come up with a solution to this problem.* □ *Mary and Ted put their heads together, but failed to provide anything new.*

put pressure on something to apply weight or pressure to something. (See also **put (the) pressure on** someone **(to** do something).) □ *Put pressure on the wound to stop the bleeding.* □ *Put some pressure on the papers to flatten them out.*

put roots down† **(some place)** to settle down somewhere; to make a place one's permanent home. □ *I'm not ready to put roots down anywhere yet.* □ *I'm ready to put down roots some place.* □ *I want to settle down. I want to put roots down and buy a house.*

put some creature **out of its misery** to kill an animal in a humane manner. (See also **put** one **out of** one's **misery.**) □ *The vet put that dog with cancer out of its misery.* □ *Please, put my sick goldfish out of its misery.*

put some distance between someone **and** oneself or something to move or travel away from someone or something. □ *Jill and I aren't getting along. I need to put some distance between her and me.* □ *I drove fast to put some distance between Max and me.*

put some sweet lines on someone Go to **lay some sweet lines on** someone.

put some teeth into something *Fig.* to increase the power or efficacy of something. □ *The mayor tried to put some teeth into the new law.* □ *The delivery clause in the contract is too weak. Put some teeth into it.*

put (some) years on someone or something *Fig.* to cause someone or something to age prematurely; to cause deterioration in the state of someone or something. (The *some* may be replaced with a specific number or period of time.) □ *The events of the last week have really put a lot of years on Gerald.* □ *The severe weather put many years on the roof of the house.*

put someone **across (in a good way)** and **get** someone **across (in a good way)** to present someone in a good way or a good light. □ *I don't want Tom to make the speech. He doesn't put himself across well.* □ *I get myself across in situations like this. I'll do it.*

put someone **away**† **1.** *Sl.* to kill someone. (Underworld.) □ *The gangster threatened to put me away if I told the police.* □ *They've put away witnesses in the past.* **2.** *Euph.* to bury someone. □ *My uncle died last week. They put him away on Saturday.* □ *They put away my uncle in the cold ground.* **3.** and **send** someone **away** *Euph.* to have someone put into a mental institution. □ *My uncle became irrational, and they put him away.* □ *They put away my aunt the year before.* **4.** and **send** someone **away** *Euph.* to sentence someone to prison for a length of time. (Underworld.) □ *They put Richard away for fifteen years.* □ *The judge put away the whole gang.*

put someone **behind bars** Go to **behind bars.**

put someone **behind the eight ball** Go to **behind the eight ball.**

put someone **by** someone or something Go to **by** someone or something.

put someone **down as** something bad to judge that someone is bad or undesirable in some way. (See also **put** someone or something **down as** something.) □ *He was so rude that I put him down as someone to be avoided.* □ *If you act silly all the time, people will put you down as a fool.*

put someone **down (for** something) to put someone's name on a list of people who volunteer to do something or give an amount of money. □ *Can I put you down for ten dollars?* □ *We're having a picnic, and you're invited. Everyone is bringing something. Can I put you down for potato salad?*

put someone **in**† Go to **put** someone **into power.**

put someone **in a bad mood** Go to **in a bad mood.**

put someone **in an awkward position** to make a situation difficult for someone; to make it difficult for someone to evade or avoid acting. □ *Your demands have put me in an awkward position. I don't know what to do.* □ *I'm afraid I've put myself in sort of an awkward position.*

put someone **in harm's way** Go to **in harm's way.**

put someone **in mind of** someone or something to remind someone of someone or something. □ *Mary puts me in mind of her mother when she was that age.* □ *This place puts me in mind of the village where I was brought up.*

put someone **in the hole** Go to **in the hole.**

put someone **in the picture** Go to **in the picture.**

put someone **in touch with** someone or something to cause or help someone to communicate with someone or something. □ *Can you put me in touch with Liz?* □ *Would you please put me in touch with the main office?*

put someone **in(side) (something)** to place or insert someone inside something. □ *The sheriff put Roger inside the cell and locked the door.* □ *He opened the cell door and put Roger in.*

put someone **into power** and **put** someone **in**† to elect or appoint someone to office or a position of power. □ *The board decided to put an unknown from another company into the presidency.* □ *They put in a complete unknown.*

put someone **into the doghouse** Go to **in the doghouse.**

put someone **into the doldrums** Go to **in the doldrums.**

put someone **into the gutter** Go to **in the gutter.**

put someone **off**† **1.** to delay dealing with someone until a later time. □ *I hate to keep putting you off, but we are not ready to deal with you yet.* □ *I had to put off the plumber again. He really wants his money.* **2.** to repel someone; to distress someone. □ *You really put people off with your scowling face.* □ *You put off people with your arrogance.* **3.** to avoid or evade someone. □ *I don't wish to see Mr. Brown now. Please put him off.* □ *I won't talk to reporters. Tell them something that will put them off.* □ *Put off those annoying people!*

put someone **off (of)** something and **put** someone **off**† to remove someone from a form of transportation, such as a train, ship, or airplane, owing to illness or misbehavior. (See also **put** someone **off.** *Of* is usually retained before pronouns.) □ *The captain ordered that the unruly passengers be put off the ship at the next port.* □ *We put the thief off at the dock.*

put someone **off the scent** *Fig.* to distract someone or a group from following a scent or trail. (From **put a dog off the scent;** the scent or trail can be purely figurative.

(See also **put** someone **off the track**.) □ *The clever maneuvers of the bandits put the sheriff's posse off the scent.* □ *The mob laundered the drug money to try to put investigators off the trail.*

put someone **off the track** and **put** someone **off the trail** to cause someone to lose a trail that is being followed. (See also **put** someone **off the scent; throw** someone **off the track**.) □ *A distraction put me off the track and I almost got lost in the jungle.* □ *I was following an escaped convict and something put me off the trail.*

put someone **off the trail** Go to previous.

put someone **on** to tease or deceive someone innocently and in fun. □ *Come on! You're just putting me on!* □ *He got real mad even though they were only putting him on.*

put someone **on a diet** Go to **on a diet**.

put someone **on a pedestal** Go to **on a pedestal**.

put someone **on hold** *Fig.* to stop all activity or communication with someone. (See also **put** someone or something **on hold**.) □ *John put Ann on hold and started dating Mary.* □ *"You can't just put me on hold!" cried Ann.*

put someone **on the spot** *Fig.* to ask someone forthright questions; to demand that someone produce as expected. □ *Don't put me on the spot. I can't give you an instant answer.* □ *The boss put Bob on the spot and demanded that he do everything he had promised.*

put someone **onto** someone or something to alert someone to the existence of someone or something; to lead someone to someone or something. □ *Nancy put Elaine onto George, who knew of a job that Elaine might be interested in.* □ *Nancy put Elaine onto a good job lead.*

put someone or an animal **out of** something and **put** someone or an animal **out†** to get rid of someone or an animal; to eliminate someone or an animal from something or some place. □ *The usher put the noisy boys out of the theater.* □ *He put out the boys.* □ *Please put out the cat after dinner.*

put someone or an animal **to sleep 1.** to cause someone or an animal to sleep, perhaps through drugs or anesthesia. □ *The doctor put the patient to sleep before the operation.* □ *I put the cat to sleep by stroking its tummy.* **2.** *Euph.* to kill someone or an animal. □ *We had to put our dog to sleep.* □ *The robber said he'd put us to sleep forever if we didn't cooperate.*

put someone or some creature **to death** to kill someone or some creature. □ *The killer was put to death right at midnight.*

put someone or some creature **out in the cold** Go to **out in the cold**.

put someone or something **above** someone or something to place someone or something at a higher level than someone or something. □ *The captain put one soldier above the wall so he could see trouble coming.* □ *In the painting, the artist put an angel above the small shed.*

put someone or something **ahead (of** someone or something**) 1.** to move or place someone or something in front of someone or something. □ *The teacher put Freddie ahead of Mike, because Mike had been disrespectful.* □ *Don't put him ahead! I didn't do anything.* **2.** to think of someone or something as more important than someone or something. □ *I put Gerry ahead of Betty as far as strength is concerned.* □ *Yes, I would put Gary ahead.* □ *She put herself ahead of everyone else and expected special treatment.*

put someone or something **among** someone or something to place someone or something in the midst of people or things. □ *The martial arts instructor put Fred among the strongest students to see what he would do.* □ *The shopkeeper put the green pears among the ripe ones and tried to sell them.*

put someone or something **at loose ends** Go to **at loose ends**.

put someone or something **at** someone's **disposal** to make someone or something available to someone; to offer someone or something to someone. □ *I'd be glad to help you if you need me. I put myself at your disposal.* □ *I put my car at my neighbor's disposal.*

put someone or something **before** someone or something Go to **place** someone or something **before** someone or something.

put someone or something **down† 1.** Go to **set** someone or something **down. 2.** *Fig.* to belittle or degrade someone or something. □ *It's an old car, but that's no reason to put it down.* □ *You put down everything you don't understand!*

put someone or something **down† as** something to write down the name of someone or a group as something. (See also **put** someone **down as** something.) □ *I will put you down as cook for the benefit luncheon.* □ *I put down John as a likely prospect.*

put someone or something **forward 1.** *Lit.* to move someone or something forward. □ *The director put all the players forward during the last scene, leaving more room for the chorus to come on for the finale.* □ *Could you put your left foot forward a little?* **2.** *Fig.* to suggest someone or something; to advance the name of someone or something. □ *I put Henry forward as a possible nominee.* □ *I would like to put forward a plan.*

put someone or something **in†** Go to **put** someone or something **into** something.

put someone or something **in(to) jeopardy** to put someone or something into danger. □ *What you just said puts Bill into jeopardy.* □ *It puts his plans in jeopardy.*

put someone or something **into order** to put people or things into a proper sequence. □ *Would you please put these people into order by height so we can march into the auditorium?* □ *Could you put these magazines into order?*

put someone or something **into** something and **put** someone or something **in†** to insert or install someone or something into something. □ *The magician put the woman into the cabinet and locked the door.* □ *She put in the woman and locked the cabinet.*

put someone or something **into the middle of nowhere** Go to **in the middle of nowhere**.

put someone or something **on hold** to put someone or someone's telephone call on an electronic hold. (See also **put** someone **on hold**.) □ *Please don't put me on hold! I'm in a hurry!* □ *I am going to have to put your call on hold.*

put someone or something **on ice 1.** *Lit.* to put a body part or corpse on ice or under refrigeration to preserve it; to put a foodstuff on ice or under refrigeration to cool it. □ *The surgeon transplanted a heart that had been put on ice*

P

for two hours. □ *Please put the soda pop on ice.* **2.** *Fig.* to postpone acting on someone or something. □ *I know he keeps pestering you for an answer, but we'll just have to put him on ice until we have more facts to go on.* □ *Let's put this project on ice till we find out how well it's financed.*

put someone or something **on** something to place someone or something on top of something. □ *The man put the child on the pony and led it about.* □ *June put the lid on the pickle jar and put it in the fridge.*

put someone or something **on track** Go to on track.

put someone or something **out of** one's **mind** to forget someone or something; to make an effort to stop thinking about someone or something. (Almost the same as **get** someone or something **out of** one's **mind.**) □ *Try to put it out of your mind.* □ *I can't seem to put him out of my mind.*

put someone or something **out of the way** to move someone or something out of a pathway. (See also put someone out of the way.) □ *Please put that chair out of the way before someone trips on it.* □ *Put the baby out of the way so the noise doesn't bother her.*

put someone or something **over** to succeed in making someone or something be accepted. □ *The public relations expert helped put John over to the public.* □ *Do you think we can put this new product over?*

put someone or something **through (to** someone**)** to put someone's telephone call through to someone. □ *Will you please put me through to the international operator?* □ *Please put my call through.*

put someone or something **to the test** *Fig.* to see what someone or something can achieve. □ *I think I can jump that far, but no one has ever put me to the test.* □ *I'm going to put my car to the test right now, and see how fast it will go.*

put someone or something **under** something to place someone or something beneath something. □ *Dave put Sam under the loft in the barn, hoping no one would find him there.* □ *Alice put the birthday present under the couch, where she could get to it in a hurry.*

put someone or something **with** someone to place someone or something with someone; to assign someone or something to someone. □ *I will put David with you and let you two work together for a while.* □ *I will put this project with you for the time being.*

put someone **out** to distress or inconvenience someone. □ *I'd like to have a ride home, but not if it puts you out.* □ *Don't worry. It won't put out anybody.*

put someone **out of the way** *Euph.* to kill someone. □ *The police suspected that she had put her uncle out of the way in order to inherit his property.*

put someone **out on a limb** Go to out on a limb.

put someone **out to pasture** *Fig.* to retire someone. (Based on put a horse out to pasture.) □ *Please don't put me out to pasture. I have lots of good years left.* □ *This vice president has reached retirement age. It's time to put him out to pasture.*

put someone **over a barrel** Go to over a barrel.

put someone's **back up** Go to get someone's dander up.

put someone's **eye out** to puncture or harm someone's eye and destroy its ability to see. □ *Careful with that stick*

or you'll put your eye out. □ *He fell on a stick and almost put out his eye!*

put someone's **nose out of joint** *Fig.* to make someone resentful. □ *What's wrong with Jill? What put her nose out of joint?* □ *Don't put your nose out of joint. I didn't mean anything by what I said.*

put someone **through** something to cause someone to have to endure something. □ *The doctor said he hated to put me through all these tests, but that it was medically necessary.*

put someone **through the mill** Go to through the mill.

put someone **through the wringer** *Fig.* to give someone a difficult time; to interrogate someone thoroughly. (Alludes to putting something through an old-fashioned clothes wringer.) □ *The lawyer really put the witness through the wringer!* □ *The teacher put the students through the wringer.*

put someone **to bed** and **send** someone **to bed** to make someone go to bed. □ *Mother put Jimmy to bed and kissed him.* □ *Sally was naughty and was sent to bed.*

put someone **to bed with a shovel** *Sl.* to bury someone; to kill and bury someone. □ *Shut up! You want me to put you to bed with a shovel?* □ *The leader of the gang was getting sort of tired and old, so one of the younger thugs put him to bed with a shovel.*

put someone **to shame 1.** to embarrass someone; to make someone ashamed. □ *I put him to shame by telling everyone about his bad behavior.* **2.** to show someone up. □ *Your excellent efforts put us all to shame.*

put someone **to sleep 1.** to bore someone. □ *That dull lecture put me to sleep.* □ *Her long story just put me to sleep.* **2.** Go to put someone or an animal to sleep.

put someone **under** *Fig.* to anesthetize someone. □ *They put him under with ether.* □ *After you put her under, we will begin the operation.*

put someone **under a spell** Go to under a spell.

put someone **under arrest** Go to under arrest.

put someone **up** to provide lodging for someone. □ *I hope I can find someone to put me up.* □ *They were able to put up John for the night.*

put someone **up against** someone to place someone into competition with someone else. □ *The coach put his best wrestler up against the champ from the other team.* □ *The varsity put themselves up against the alumni team in a game to benefit charity.*

put someone **up (for** something**)** to nominate or offer someone for some office or task. □ *I put Henry up for club president.* □ *We put up Shannon for treasurer.*

put someone **up to** something to cause someone to do something; to give someone the idea of doing something. □ *Who put you up to throwing the party?* □ *Nobody put me up to it. I thought it up myself.*

put someone **up with** someone to house someone with someone. □ *I will put her up with my cousin, who has an extra bedroom.* □ *We will put up the lady with us.*

put someone **wise to** someone or something Go to wise to someone or something.

put something **across (to** someone**)** and **get** something **across (to** someone**)** *Fig.* to make something clear to someone; to convince someone of something; to get a plan accepted. □ *I don't know how to put this point across to my class. Can you help?* □ *Can you help me get this across?*

put something **aside†** to set or place something to the side. □ *I put the magazine aside and began reading a book.* □ *Put aside your work for a minute and listen to what I have to tell you.*

put something **aside for a rainy day** Go to save (something) for a rainy day.

put something **aside† (for** something**)** to hold something in reserve for some purpose. □ *You should put a little of the sugar aside for your coffee in the morning.* □ *Please put aside some money for me.* □ *I can put a little aside.*

put something **at a premium** to make something available only at an extra cost or through extra effort. □ *The scarcity of fresh vegetables at this time of year puts broccoli at a premium.* □ *The high demand for apples puts them at a premium.*

put something **at** an amount to price something at a certain amount of money; to estimate something at a certain figure. □ *I would put the charges at about two hundred dollars.* □ *She put the damages at nearly two hundred thousand dollars.*

put something **at** someone's **door** Go to lay something at someone's door.

put something **away†** **1.** *Lit.* to return something to its proper storage place. □ *When you are finished with the hammer, please put it away. Don't leave it out.* □ *Put away this mess!* **2.** *Fig.* to eat something. □ *Are you going to put this last piece of cake away?* □ *Did you put away that whole pizza?*

put something **back†** **1.** to return something to where it was before. □ *Please put the book back when you finish it.* □ *Put back the book when you finish.* **2.** Go to set something back.

put something **back in play** Go to in play.

put something **back on track** Go to back on track.

put something **behind** one *Fig.* to try to forget about something. □ *I look forward to putting all my problems behind me.* □ *She will be happier when all this can be put behind her.*

put something **behind** someone or something to place something in back of someone or something. □ *I put the box behind Mary, and she didn't even know it was there.* □ *Please put the present behind the couch where Janet will not see it.*

put something **by** and **lay** something **by** to reserve a portion of something; to preserve and store something, such as food. □ *I put some money by for a rainy day.* □ *I laid some eggs by for our use tomorrow.*

put something **down†** **1.** *Fig.* to repress or put a stop to something such as a riot or rebellion. □ *The army was called to put down the rebellion.* □ *The police used tear gas to put the riot down.* **2.** Go to set something down.

put something **down† in black and white** and **set** something **down† in black and white** *Fig.* to write down the terms of an agreement; to draw up a written contract; to put the details of something down on paper. (Alludes to black ink and white paper.) □ *We agree on all the major*

points. Now, let's set it down in black and white. □ *I think I understand what you are talking about, but we need to put down the details in black and white.*

put something **down to** something and **set** something **down to** something to explain something as being caused by something else. □ *I put his bad humor down to his illness.* □ *We set your failure down to your emotional upset.*

put (something**) forth** to exert effort. □ *You are going to have to put more effort forth if you want to succeed.* □ *You need to put forth. You are not carrying your load.*

put something **forward†** to state an idea; to advance an idea. □ *Toward the end of the meeting, Sally put an idea forward.* □ *He put several suggestions forward.*

put something **in†** to submit something, such as an order, request, or demand. □ *In fact, I put the order in some time ago.* □ *I put in a request for a new monitor.*

put something **in a nutshell** *Fig.* to state something very concisely. (Alludes to the small size of a nutshell and the amount that it would hold.) □ *The explanation is long and involved, but let me put it in a nutshell for you.* □ *To put it in a nutshell: you are fired!*

put something **in apple-pie order** Go to in apple-pie order.

put something **in layaway** and **put** something **in will-call** to purchase something by paying part of the price initially, and not receiving the goods until all the money has been paid. □ *I couldn't afford a winter coat right now, so I picked one out and put it in layaway.* □ *Please put this in will-call. I'll pay for it next month.*

put something **in limbo** Go to in limbo.

put something **in mothballs 1.** *Lit.* to put something into storage in mothballs. □ *He put his winter coat in storage with mothballs each fall and had to air it out for a week each spring.* **2.** *Fig.* to put something into storage or reserve. (Often said of warships.) □ *The navy put the old cruiser in mothballs and no one ever expected to see it again.* □ *Let's just put this small bicycle in mothballs until we hear of a child who can use it.*

put something **in order** Go to in order.

put something **in play** Go to in play.

put something **in quotes** to put quotation marks around writing or printing. □ *Please put this word in quotes, since it means something special the way you have used it here.* □ *They put it in quotes so people would know it means something different.*

put something **in the back of** someone's **mind** Go to in the back of someone's mind.

put something **in the open** Go to in the open.

put something **in the way of** someone or something to place a barrier in the way of someone or something. □ *You know I don't want to put anything in the way of your happiness.* □ *I would never put anything in the way of you and Donna.*

put something **in will-call** Go to put something in layaway.

put something **in writing** Go to in writing.

put something **in((side)** someone or something**)** to place or insert something inside someone or something. □ *The surgeon put a tube inside Chuck and left it there to drain* *fluid.* □ *While you have the closet door open, will you put this in?*

put something **into effect** and **put** something **into force** to make something take effect; to begin using or enforcing a policy or procedure. □ *When will the city council put this law into effect?* □ *We will put it into force tomorrow.*

put something **into orbit** Go to in orbit.

put something **in(to) order** to make something tidy. □ *Please put this room into order.* □ *I will put it in order as soon as I have a minute.*

put something **into perspective** Go to in perspective.

put something **into place** Go to in place.

put something **into practice** to make a suggested procedure the actual procedure. □ *That is a good policy. I suggest you put it into practice immediately.* □ *I plan to put the new technique into practice as soon as I can.*

put something **in(to) print** to publish something; to record something spoken in printed letters. □ *The article looks good. We will put it into print as soon as possible.* □ *We'll put it in print as soon as we can.*

put something **in(to) service** and **put** something **into use** to start to use a thing; to make a device operate and function. □ *I hope that they are able to put the elevator into service again soon. I am tired of climbing stairs.* □ *We will put it in service within an hour.* □ *When can we put the new copier into use?*

put something **in(to) someone's head** *Fig.* to give ideas to someone who might not have thought of them without help. □ *Who put that idea into your head?* □ *No one put it in my head. I thought of it all by myself.*

put something **into use** Go to put something in(to) service.

put something **into words** *Fig.* to form an idea into sentences that can be spoken or written. □ *I find it hard to put my thoughts into words.* □ *She put it into words quite nicely.*

put something **off†** to postpone something; to schedule something for a later time. □ *I have to put off our meeting until a later time.* □ *I put off a visit to the dentist as long as I could.*

put something **on†** to place clothing onto one's body; to get into a piece of clothing. □ *I put a heavy coat on to go outside in the cold.* □ *Please put on this one and see if it fits.*

put something **on hold** to postpone something; to stop the progress of something. (See also put someone on hold; put someone or something on hold.) □ *They put the project on hold until they got enough money to finish it.* □ *Sorry, but we must put your plan on hold.*

put something **on its feet** Go to on its feet.

put something **on paper** *Fig.* to write something down. □ *You have a great idea for a novel. Now put it on paper.* □ *I'm sorry, I can't discuss your offer until I see something in writing. Put it on paper, and then we'll talk.*

put something **on** someone or an animal to clothe someone or an animal in something. □ *The mother put a little jacket on her child.* □ *Alice puts a silly little coat on her poodle during the winter.*

put something **on** someone or something to place or set something on someone or something. □ *She put sand on Tom as he lay napping on the beach.* □ *Please put the paper on the coffee table.*

put something **on** someone's **shoulders** Go to on someone's shoulders.

put something **on the back burner** Go to on the back burner.

put something **on the cuff** *Fig.* to buy something on credit; to add to one's credit balance. □ *I'll take two of those, and please put them on the cuff.* □ *I'm sorry, Tom. We can't put anything more on the cuff.*

put something **on the front burner** Go to on the front burner.

put something **on the map** *Fig.* to make some place famous or popular. □ *The good food you serve here will really put this place on the map.* □ *Nothing like a little scandal to put an otherwise sleepy town on the map.*

put something **on the market** Go to on the market.

put something **on the street** *Sl.* to tell something openly; to spread news. □ *There is no need to put all this gossip on the street. Keep it to yourself.* □ *Now, please don't put this on the street, but I am going to get married.*

put something **out†** **1.** to emit something. □ *The factory put a lot of fumes out.* □ *It put out nasty fumes.* **2.** to extinguish something on fire. □ *He used flour to put the grease fire out.* □ *He put out the fire with flour.* **3.** to manufacture or produce something. □ *That factory puts electrical supplies out.* □ *We put out some very fine products.* **4.** to publish something. □ *When was this book put out?* □ *We put out both books last year.*

put something **over†** to accomplish something; to put something across. (See also put someone or something over.) □ *This is a very hard thing to explain to a large audience. I hope I can put over the main points.* □ *This is a big request for money. I go before the board of directors this afternoon, and I hope I can put it over.*

put something **over on** someone and **put one over on** someone to play a trick on someone; to deceive someone with something. □ *We really put one over on the teacher and boy, was he mad.* □ *I'm too observant. You can't put anything over on me.*

put something **plainly** to state something firmly and explicitly. □ *To put it plainly, I want you out of this house immediately.* □ *Thank you. I think you've put your feelings quite plainly.*

put something **right** Go to set something right.

put something **straight** Go to set something straight.

put something **through its paces** Go to put one through one's paces.

put something **to bed** *Fig.* to complete work on something and send it on to the next step in production, especially in publishing. (From put someone to bed.) □ *This week's edition is finished. Let's put it to bed.* □ *Finish the editing of this book and put it to bed.*

put something **to (good) use** to apply a skill or ability; to use a skill or ability. □ *The lawyer put her training to good use for the charity.* □ *The pianist put his talents to use at the party.*

put something **to rest** and **lay** something **to rest** *Fig.* to put an end to a rumor; to finish dealing with something and forget about it. □ *I've heard enough about Ann and her illness. I'd like to put the whole matter to rest.* □ *I'll be happy to lay it to rest, but will Jane?*

put something **together 1.** *Lit.* to assemble something. □ *How long will it take to put dinner together?* □ *This model was put together incorrectly.* **2.** *Fig.* to consider some facts and arrive at a conclusion. □ *I couldn't put everything together to figure out the answer in time.* □ *When I put together all the facts, I found the answer.*

put something **under pressure** Go to under pressure.

put something **up†1.** to build a building, a sign, a fence, a wall, etc. □ *We'll put a garage up next month.* □ *The city put up a fence next to our house.* **2.** to store and preserve food by canning or freezing. □ *This year we'll put some strawberries up.* □ *We put up a lot of tomatoes every year.*

put something **up for auction** Go to up for auction.

put something **up for sale** Go to up for sale.

put teeth in(to) something Go to give teeth to something.

Put that in your pipe and smoke it! *Fig. Inf.* See how you like that!; It is final, and you have to live with it. □ *Well, I'm not going to do what you want, so put that in your pipe and smoke it!* □ *I'm sick of you, and I'm leaving. Put that in your pipe and smoke it!*

put the arm on someone *Fig.* to apply pressure to someone. □ *John's been putting the arm on Mary to get her to go out with him.* □ *John has been putting the arm on Bill to get him to cooperate.*

put the bite on someone and **put the touch on** someone *Sl.* to try to get money from someone. □ *Tom put the bite on me for ten dollars.* □ *Bill put the touch on me, but I told him to forget about it.*

put the blame on someone or something and **lay the blame on** someone or something; **place the blame on** someone or something to blame someone or something; to assign a bad outcome to someone or something. □ *Don't put the blame on me. I didn't do it.* □ *We'll have to place the blame for the damage on the storm.*

put the brakes on someone *Fig.* to block someone's activities; to cause someone to stop doing something. (Based on **put the brakes on something.**) □ *The boss put the brakes on Gerald, who was trying too aggressively to get promoted.* □ *We are going to have to put the brakes on you if you make any more difficulties.*

put the brakes on something to halt or impede some process. □ *The manager had to put the brakes on the Wilson project due to lack of funds.* □ *We will put the brakes on this project because it is costing too much money.*

put the cart before the horse *Fig.* to have things in the wrong order; to have things confused and mixed up. (Also with have.) □ *You're eating your dessert first! You've put the cart before the horse.* □ *John has the cart before the horse in most of his projects.*

put the chill on someone and **put the freeze on** someone *Sl.* to ignore someone; to end social contact with someone. □ *Max put the chill on the guys who threatened him.* □ *Max put the freeze on Lefty.*

put the clamps on someone or something and **put the clamps on†** *Sl.* to impede or block someone or something; to restrain or restrict someone. □ *Fred had to put the clamps on Tony, who was rushing his work too much.* □ *Tony is getting a little anxious. Time to put on the clamps.*

put the fear of God in(to) someone *Fig.* to frighten someone severely; [for something] to shock someone into contrite behavior. □ *A near miss like that really puts the fear of God into you.* □ *Yes, it puts the fear of God in you.*

put the feed bag on† and **put the nose-bag on†** *Fig.* to eat a meal. (Both refer to a method of feeding a horse by attaching a bag of food at its nose and mouth.) □ *It's time to put the feed bag on! I'm starved!* □ *When do we put on the nose-bag?*

put the finger on someone and **lay the finger on** someone *Sl.* to accuse someone; to identify someone as the one who did something. □ *Tom put the finger on John, and John is really mad.* □ *He'd better not lay the finger on me. I didn't do it.*

put the freeze on someone Go to put the chill on someone.

put the hard word on someone Go to put the make on someone.

put the heat on†1. to turn on central heating; to increase the amount of heat in a room or house. □ *It's going to get cold tonight. I'd better put the heat on.* □ *Let's put on the heat to take off the chill.* **2.** Go to next.

put the heat on (someone) and **put the screws on** (someone); **put the squeeze on** (someone); **put the heat on**; **put the screws on**; **put the squeeze on** *Sl.* to put pressure on someone (to do something); to coerce someone. □ *John wouldn't talk, so the police were putting the heat on him to confess.* □ *When my boss puts the screws on, he can be very unpleasant.* □ *The police know how to put the squeeze on.*

put the kibosh on someone or something *Fig.* to squelch someone or something; to veto someone or someone's plans. □ *I hate to put the kibosh on Randy, but he isn't doing what he is supposed to.* □ *Your comments put the kibosh on the whole project.*

put the make on someone and **put the moves on** someone; **put the hard word on** someone *Sl.* to attempt to seduce or proposition someone. □ *I think he was beginning to put the make on me. I'm glad I left.* □ *James tried to put the hard word on Martha.* □ *Are you putting the moves on me?*

put the moves on someone Go to previous.

put the nose-bag on† Go to put the feed bag on†.

put the pedal to the metal *Sl.* to press a car's accelerator to the floor; to drive very fast. □ *Let's go, man. Put the pedal to the metal.* □ *Put the pedal to the metal, and we'll make up some lost time.*

put (the) pressure on someone **(to do something)** to make demands on someone; to try to get someone to do something. □ *Please don't put pressure on me to go there!* □ *We put the pressure on him to get him to come, but he refused.*

put the screws on (someone) Go to put the heat on (someone).

P

537

put the skids on (something) *Sl.* to cause something to fail. □ *They put the skids on the project when they refused to give us any more money.* □ *That's the end of our great idea! Somebody put the skids on.*

put the skids under someone or something *Sl.* to cause someone or something to fail. □ *Her lateness put the skids under our presentation to the board of directors.* □ *He thought he could get promoted if he put the skids under the vice president.*

put the squeeze on someone **1.** *Inf.* to attempt to get money out of someone. □ *The mob put the squeeze on all the merchants, threatening to break their windows if they didn't pay.* □ *Are you trying to put the squeeze on me for more money?* **2.** Go to put the heat on (someone).

put the touch on someone Go to put the bite on someone.

put to bed with a shovel 1. *Sl.* dead and buried. (Alludes to burying someone.) □ *You wanna be put to bed with a shovel? Just keep talking that way.* □ *Poor old Jake. He was put to bed with a shovel last March.* **2.** *Sl.* intoxicated. □ *He wasn't just tipsy. He was put to bed with a shovel!* □ *Dead drunk? Yes, he was put to bed with a shovel.*

put to it strained or exhausted. □ *Man, I'm really put to it! What a day!* □ *John was put to it to get there on time.*

put too fine a point on something *Fig.* to make too much out of something; to dwell overly long on a small detail of a complaint or argument. (Usually with *not*. Formal or stilted.) □ *Not to put too fine a point on it, but did you really mean to say that Paul was the former secretary of the organization? Wasn't he the corresponding secretary?* □ *When he said that everyone was angry, he put too fine a point on it.*

put two and two together to figure something out from the information available. □ *Well, I put two and two together and came up with an idea of who did it.* □ *Don't worry. John won't figure it out. He can't put two and two together.*

put up a (brave) front and **put on a (brave) front** *Fig.* to appear to be brave (even if one is not). □ *Mary is frightened, but she's putting up a brave front.* □ *If she weren't putting on a front, I'd be more frightened than I am.*

put up a fight and **put up a struggle** to make a struggle, a fight, etc. (Fixed order.) □ *Did he put up a fight?* □ *No, he only put up a bit of a struggle.*

put up a struggle Go to previous.

put up one's **dukes** *Fig.* to be prepared to fight. □ *He's telling you to put up your dukes.* □ *Put up your dukes and be a man!*

Put up or shut up! 1. *Inf.* a command to prove something or stop talking about it; Do something or stop promising to do it! □ *I'm tired of your telling everyone how fast you can run. Now, do it! Put up or shut up!* □ *Now's your chance to show us that you can run as fast as you can talk. Put up or shut up!* **2.** *Inf.* a command to bet money in support of what one advocates. □ *If you think that your horse is faster than mine, then make a bet. Put up or shut up!* □ *You think you can beat me at cards? Twenty bucks says you're wrong. Put up or shut up!*

put up with someone or something to tolerate or endure someone or something; to be able to stand someone or something. □ *I cannot put up with your constant whining any longer!* □ *We can put up with John's living here until he finds a place of his own.*

put upon by someone to be made use of to an unreasonable degree. (Typically passive.) □ *My mother was always put upon by her neighbors. She was too nice to refuse their requests for help.* □ *Jane feels put upon by her live-in mother-in-law.*

put wear (and tear) on something to cause deterioration in the state of something. (There can be various amounts of wear and tear. See the examples.) □ *This road salt puts a lot of wear on cars.* □ *All this wave action puts too much wear and tear on the boat dock.*

put weight on[†] *Fig.* to gain weight; to grow fat. □ *The doctor says I need to put some weight on.* □ *I have to go on a diet because I've been putting on a little weight lately.*

put weight on some part of the body to subject an injured body part, as a foot or knee, to the weight of standing, to test its strength. □ *My doctor told me I can put weight on my broken leg next week.*

put words in(to) someone's **mouth** *Fig.* to interpret what someone said so that the words mean what you want and not what the speaker wanted. □ *I didn't say that! You are putting words into my mouth.* □ *Stop putting words in my mouth!*

Put your money where your mouth is! *Inf.* Stop just talking and stake your own money! (From gambling. Can also be said to someone giving investment advice.) □ *You want me to bet on that horse? Did you? Why don't you put your money where your mouth is?* □ *If this is such a good stock, you buy it. Put your money where your mouth is!*

Put your trust in God, and keep your powder dry. and **Keep your powder dry.** *Prov.* Have faith that God will make sure that you win a conflict, but be prepared to fight well and vigorously. (Supposed to have been said by Oliver Cromwell; *powder* means gunpowder.) □ *Bill: Am I going to win my lawsuit? Alan: All you can do is put your trust in God, and keep your powder dry.*

putt along to move along rapidly, usually in a motorized vehicle. ("Putt-putt" is the sound made to mimic engines, especially small engines.) □ *The little car was putting along down the highway, when one of the tires went flat.* □ *We were putting along very smoothly all the way into town.*

putter about Go to putter around.

putter around and **putter about** to do little things of little consequence; to do small tasks as found around the house. □ *I spent all of Saturday just puttering around, not really getting anything done.* □ *I stayed home and puttered about during my vacation.*

*putty in someone's **hands** *Fig.* [of someone] easily influenced by someone else; excessively willing to do what someone else wishes. (Putty is soft and malleable. *Typically: **be ~; seem like ~**.) □ *Bob's wife is putty in his hands. She never thinks for herself.* □ *Jane is putty in her mother's hands. She always does exactly what her mother says.*

a **put-up job** *Inf.* a deception; a deceptive event. □ *That's really phony; a put-up job if I ever saw one.* □ *No put-up job is clever enough to fool me.*

putz around *Inf.* to fiddle around; to mess around. □ *Stop putzing around and get to work.* □ *Those guys spend most of their time just putzing around.*

puzzle over someone or something to consider or ponder someone or something. □ *Anne is a bit strange. I've spent some time puzzling over her.* □ *While I was puzzling over why she had slapped me, she did it again.*

puzzle something **out**† to figure something out. □ *It took me a while to puzzle it out.* □ *I can't puzzle out the meaning of this argument.*

P

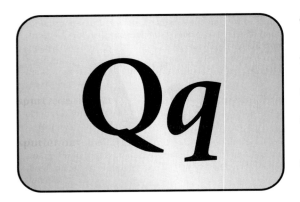

quail at someone or something to show fear at someone or something; to shrink from someone or something. □ *Todd quailed at the thought of what he had to do.* □ *The students quailed at the teacher who had been so hard on them in the past.*

quail before someone or something to cower before or at the threat of someone or something. □ *The students quailed before the angry principal.* □ *They quailed before the thought of punishment.*

quake in one's **boots** Go to shake in one's boots.

quake with something to shake as with fear, terror, etc. □ *Alice was quaking with fear as the door slowly opened.* □ *Todd quaked with terror when he saw the vicious dog at the door.*

qualify as something to fulfill the requirements to be something. □ *Tom qualified as a mechanic.* □ *I have been qualified as a mechanic since I was twenty.*

qualify for something to meet the requirements for something. □ *I'm sorry, you do not qualify for this job.* □ *I don't qualify for it.*

qualify someone **as** something to cause someone to fulfill the requirements for something. □ *Does this course qualify me as a stockbroker?* □ *She qualified herself as a realtor.*

qualify someone **for** something to enable someone to meet the requirements for something. □ *His years with the company qualified him for pension.* □ *Does this ticket qualify me for the drawing?*

quality time time spent with someone allowing interaction and closeness. □ *He was able to spend a few minutes of quality time with his son, Buxton, at least once every two weeks.*

***qualms (about** someone or something**)** an uneasy feeling of one's conscience about someone or something. (*Typically: **cause** ~; **have** ~; **have no** ~; **give** someone ~.) □ *Do you have any qualms about telling a little white lie to Mary about her not getting an invitation to the party?*

quarrel (with someone**) (about** someone or something**)** to have an argument with someone about the subject of someone or something. □ *Please don't quarrel with me about money.* □ *You are always quarreling with Claire.*

quarrel (with someone**) (over** someone or something**)** to have an argument with someone about someone or something. □ *Todd quarreled with Carl over who was going to get the new secretary.* □ *They are quarreling over Sally.*

quarrel with something to argue against something; to have a complaint about something. □ *I can't quarrel with that.* □ *Does anyone want to quarrel with that last remark?*

The **Queen's English** "Official" British English. □ *He can't even speak The Queen's English! Despicable!*

queer as a three-dollar bill Go to phony as a three-dollar bill.

queer for something *Inf.* in the mood for something; desiring something. (Old.) □ *I'm queer for a beer right now.* □ *She's queer for him because of his money.*

quest for someone or something to seek after someone or something. □ *Martin is off questing for a book on baroque organ building.* □ *She is questing for a better way to do it.*

a **question of** something a matter of something; a problem of something. □ *It's not a matter of not wanting to go to the opera. It's a question of money.*

question someone **about** someone or something to ask someone about someone or something. □ *The police questioned Roger about the crime.* □ *Then they questioned Claire about Roger.*

question someone **at great length** Go to at great length.

queue up (for something**)** to line up for something. (Typically British.) □ *We had to queue up for tickets to the play.* □ *You must queue up here to get in.*

quibble (about someone or something**) (with** someone**)** and **quibble (over** someone or something**) (with** someone**)** to be argumentative or contentious with someone about someone or something. □ *Let's not quibble about it.* □ *Please don't quibble with your sister.* □ *No need to quibble over it.*

quick and dirty *Fig.* [done] fast and carelessly; [done] fast and cheaply. □ *I am not interested in a quick and dirty job. I want it done right.* □ *The contractor made a lot of money on quick and dirty projects that would never last very long.*

quick as a flash Go to next.

***quick as a wink** and ***quick as a flash**; ***quick as (greased) lightning**; ***swift as lightning** very quickly. (*Also: **as** ~.) □ *As quick as a wink, the thief took the lady's purse.* □ *I'll finish this work quick as a flash.* □ *Quick as greased lightning, the thief stole my wallet.*

quick as (greased) lightning Go to previous.

quick like a bunny really quick. □ *Now's your chance. Do it! Quick like a bunny!*

quick off the mark quick starting or reacting. (Compare this with slow off the mark.) □ *Boy, you were quick off the mark there!* □ *If you can be really quick off the mark, you can soon find the answer.*

quick on the draw Go to next.

quick on the trigger and **quick on the draw 1.** *Lit.* quick to draw a gun and shoot. □ *Some of the old cowboys were known to be quick on the trigger.* □ *Wyatt Earp was particularly quick on the draw.* **2.** *Fig.* quick to respond to anything. □ *John gets the right answer before anyone else. He's really quick on the trigger.* □ *Sally will probably win the quiz game. She's really quick on the draw.*

quick on the uptake quick to understand or learn something. □ *Just because I'm not quick on the uptake, it doesn't mean I'm stupid.* □ *Mary understands jokes before anyone else because she's so quick on the uptake.*

a **quick study** a person who is quick to learn things. (Compare this to a **slow study**.) □ *Jane, who is a quick study, caught the joke immediately and laughed before everyone else.*

a **quick temper** and a **short temper**; a **short fuse** a bad temper that can be easily aroused. □ *Tyler has a quick temper and doesn't mind letting everyone see it.*

quicker than hell *Inf.* very fast. □ *You got over here quicker than hell.* □ *Be careful in the stock market. You can lose all your money quicker than hell.*

quicker than you can say Jack Robinson Go to before you can say Jack Robinson.

*quiet as a (church) mouse and ***quiet as the grave** very quiet. (*Also:* **as ~**.) □ *You'd better be as quiet as a mouse while Grandma takes her nap so you won't wake her up.* □ *This town is quiet as the grave now that the factories have closed.*

quiet as the grave Go to previous.

quiet down to become quiet; to become less noisy. □ *Please quiet down.* □ *Ask them to quiet down.*

quiet someone or an animal **down**† to make someone or an animal more quiet. □ *Please go and quiet the children down.* □ *Try to quiet down the children.* □ *Please quiet that dog down.*

quip about someone or something to joke about someone or something. □ *The kids were quipping about the principal's hairpiece.* □ *It is rude to quip about an elderly person.*

quit a place to leave a place. □ *In the autumn, Melinda quit Paris and traveled south to warmer climes.*

quit on someone **1.** [for something] to quit while someone is using it. □ *This stupid car quit on me.* □ *I hope this thing doesn't quit on me.* **2.** [for one] to leave one's job, usually suddenly or unannounced. □ *Wally, the park supervisor, quit on us at the last minute.* □ *My assistant quit on me.*

quit over someone or something to stop working or doing something because of someone or something; to quit because of a dispute over someone or something. □ *Please don't quit over a silly thing like that.* □ *She quit over one of her fellow workers.*

quit while one **is ahead** to stop doing something while one is still successful. □ *When will I learn to quit while I'm ahead?* □ *Get into the market. Make some money and get out. Quit while you're ahead.*

quite a bit Go to next.

quite a few and **quite a lot**; **quite a bit**; **quite a number** much or many. □ *Do you need one? I have quite a few.* □ *I have quite a bit—enough to spare some.* □ *How many? Oh, quite a number.*

quite a lot Go to previous.

quite a number Go to quite a few.

quite a something definitely something; a good example of something. □ *The captain of the swim team is quite a swimmer.* □ *That's quite a bruise you have there.*

quite something something very good or remarkable. □ *You should see their new house. It's quite something.* □ *Meg's mother has bought a new hat for the wedding and it's quite something.*

quiver with something **1.** *Lit.* to shake or shiver from something, such as cold, fear, anticipation, etc. □ *On seeing the bear, the dogs quivered with fear.* □ *Todd quivered with the cold.* **2.** *Fig.* to experience eagerness or joy. □ *I quivered with delight when I saw the dessert.* □ *Tom quivered with eagerness as the door opened.*

quiz out (of something**)** to earn permission to waive a college course by successful completion of a quiz or exam. □ *Andrew was able to quiz out of calculus.* □ *After studying very hard, he quizzed out.*

quiz someone **about** someone or something to ask someone many questions about someone or something. □ *The general quizzed the soldier about the incident.* □ *The officer quizzed her about Randy.*

quiz someone **on** someone or something to give someone a quiz or test over the subject of someone or something. □ *The teacher quizzed the students on the chapter she had assigned for homework.* □ *I hope they quiz me on George Washington. I am prepared.*

quote a price to name or state in advance the charge for doing or supplying something. □ *The mechanic quoted a price of $100 to repair my car.* □ *The carpenter quoted a price for fixing the stairs.*

quote someone or something **out of context** Go to out of context.

quote (something**) from** someone or something to recite something verbatim that someone else has said; to recite something verbatim from a printed source. □ *May I quote from your letter of the tenth?* □ *Do you mind if I quote a line from Keats?*

quote, unquote a parenthetical expression said before a word or short phrase indicating that the word or phrase would be in quotation marks if used in writing. □ *So I said to her, quote, unquote, it's time we had a little talk.*

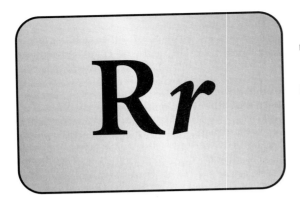

Rr

race against someone or something to attempt to win a trial of speed against someone or something. □ *I don't want to race against Kelly. She is too fast.* □ *I had to race against time to get there before the baby got worse.*

race against time 1. a rush; a rush to beat a deadline. □ *We were in a race against time to beat the deadline.* □ *It was a race against time, but we made it.* **2.** to hurry to beat a deadline. □ *We had to race against time to finish before the deadline.* □ *You don't need to race against time. Take all the time you want.*

race around to run or move around in a great hurry. □ *Stop racing around and calm down!* □ *I have been racing around all morning, trying to get some things done.*

race around (after someone or something**)** to rush here and there to find or fetch someone or something. □ *I had to race around after Tom. I couldn't seem to catch up to him.* □ *I wish I could find the dog without having to race around all over the neighborhood.*

race for something to run or drive fast to get to something in a hurry. □ *I raced for the door to see who was there.* □ *The children raced for the best seats in front of the television set.*

race into someone or something to bump or crash into someone or something. □ *The boys raced into the side of the car, and one of them was hurt.* □ *We raced into Mary and knocked her over.*

race into something to run into a place. □ *The children raced into the room and headed straight for their presents.* □ *Please don't race into the garden. You will trample the flowers.*

race someone **for** something to compete against someone for a prize; to try to outrun someone to get to something first. □ *I will race you for the grand prize.* □ *Ned raced his sister for the breakfast table every morning.*

race someone **to** some place to compete against someone to see who gets to a place first. □ *I will race you to the door.* □ *Tim wanted to race me to the corner.*

race through someone or something to run or chase through a group of people or a place. □ *The children raced through the group of ladies standing by the door.* □ *The dogs raced through the room, upsetting a lamp.*

race through something to perform some task very rapidly. □ *They raced through their prayers and jumped into bed.*

□ *The children raced through dinner, in a hurry to get outside to play.*

race to someone or something to run to someone or something. □ *The girls raced to the front room.* □ *We all raced to Mary, who had the candy.*

race up to someone or something to run to someone or something. □ *Molly raced up to Paul and kissed him on the cheek.* □ *We raced up to the door and opened it cautiously.*

race with someone or something to enter a speed contest with someone or something. □ *I refuse to race with Carla. She is much too fast for me.* □ *I can't race with a horse!*

rack one's **brain(s)** *Fig.* to try very hard to think of something. □ *I racked my brains all afternoon, but couldn't remember where I put the book.* □ *Don't waste any more time racking your brain. Go borrow the book from the library.*

rack out *Sl.* to go to bed and to sleep. □ *I'm really tired. I've got to go rack out for a while.* □ *I racked out until nearly noon.*

rack something **up**[†] **1.** *Lit.* to place something onto or into its rack. □ *You had better rack the billiard balls up when you finish this game.* □ *Please rack up the balls.* **2.** *Fig.* to accumulate something; to collect or acquire something. □ *They all racked a lot of profits up.* □ *We racked up twenty points in the game last Saturday.* **3.** *Sl.* to wreck or damage something. □ *Fred racked his new car up.* □ *He racked up his arm in the football game.*

racked with pain suffering from severe pain. □ *My body was racked with pain, and I nearly passed out.* □ *My head was racked with pain.*

radiate from someone or something to spread out from someone or something, as with rays. □ *Happiness radiated from Mary. She was so proud!* □ *The heat radiated from the wall next to the furnace room.*

raffle something **off**[†] to give something away by a drawing or raffle. □ *They will raffle a television set off.* □ *They are going to raffle off a television set this weekend at the school.*

rag on someone and **rake on** someone *Sl.* to bother someone; to irritate someone; to criticize and humiliate someone. □ *I wish you would stop ragging on me. I don't know why you are so annoyed at me.* □ *Stop raking on me!*

rag out *Sl.* to dress up. □ *I like to rag out and go to parties.* □ *I hate to rag out. I like comfortable clothes.*

rag someone **about** someone or something **1.** to complain to someone about someone or something. □ *Why are you always ragging me about Mary?* □ *Stop ragging me about being late.* **2.** to tease someone about someone or something. □ *I wish you would stop ragging me about my hat.* □ *Why do you always rag me about my funny walk? I can't help it.*

rage against someone or something to vent one's anger about someone or something; to criticize someone or something severely. □ *She exhausted herself raging against Judy.* □ *Mary is raging about the office politics again.*

rage at someone or something to direct one's anger at someone or something. □ *Why are you raging at me? What on earth did I do?* □ *Nothing can be solved by raging at the police department.*

rage out of control to become uncontrollable. □ *The fire raged out of control and threatened the residential area.* □ *If we didn't do something quickly, the fire would be raging out of control.*

rage over someone or something to fight furiously over someone or something. □ *The two managers both wanted to hire the same prospective employee. They raged over her for nearly an hour.* □ *The bears raged over that one fish for a long time.*

rage through something **1.** *Lit.* [for a fire] to burn rapidly through an area or a building. □ *The fire raged through the unoccupied building.* □ *When the fire began to rage through the forest, we knew we had better head for the river.* **2.** *Fig.* [for someone] to move rapidly through some sequence or process, as if in a rage. □ *Harry raged through the contract, looking for more errors.* □ *She raged through the book, angry with everything she read.*

rail against someone or something to complain vehemently about someone or something. □ *Why are you railing against me? What did I do?* □ *Leonard is railing against the tax increase again.*

rail at someone **(about** something**)** to complain loudly or violently to someone about something. □ *Jane railed at the payroll clerk about not having received her check.* □ *I am not responsible for your problems. Don't rail at me!*

railroad someone **into** something to force someone into doing something in great haste. □ *The salesman tried to railroad me into signing the contract.* □ *You can't railroad me into doing anything!*

railroad something **through (**something**)** to force something through some legislative body without due consideration. □ *The committee railroaded the new constitution through the ratification process.* □ *Mary felt she could railroad the legislation through.*

rain cats and dogs *Fig.* to rain very hard. □ *It's raining cats and dogs. Look at it pour!* □ *I'm not going out in that storm. It's raining cats and dogs.*

a **rain check (on** something**) 1.** a piece of paper allowing one to see an event—which has been canceled—at a later time. (Originally said of sporting events that had to be canceled because of rain. *Typically: **get ~; have ~; take ~; give** someone **~.**) □ *The game was canceled because of the storm, but we all got rain checks on it.* □ *I can't use a rain check because I'm leaving town for a month.* **2.** a reissuance of an invitation at a later date. (Said to someone who has invited you to something that you cannot attend now, but would like to attend at a later time. *Typically: **get ~; have ~; take ~; give** someone **~.**) □ *We would love to come to your house, but we are busy next Saturday. Could we take a rain check on your kind invitation?* □ *Oh, yes. You have a rain check that's good anytime you can come by and visit.* **3.** a piece of paper that allows one to purchase an item on sale at a later date. (Stores issue these pieces of paper when they run out of specially priced sale merchandise. *Typically: **get ~; have ~; take ~; give** someone **~.**) □ *The store was all out of the shampoo they advertised, but I got a rain check.* □ *Yes, you should always take a rain check so you can get it at the sale price later when they have more.*

rain down on someone or something to fall or drop down on someone or something like rain. □ *The ashes from the*

incinerator rained down on us, getting our clothes dirty. □ *The hail rained down on us—some of it quite large.*

rain in on someone or something [for rain] to enter a window or other opening and get someone or something wet. □ *Carol left the window open, and it rained in on her in the night.* □ *The storm rained in on my carpet!*

rain on someone's **parade** and **rain on** someone or something *Fig.* to spoil something for someone. □ *I hate to rain on your parade, but your plans are all wrong.* □ *She really rained on our plans.*

rain or shine no matter whether it rains or the sun shines. (See also **come rain or shine**.) □ *Don't worry. I'll be there rain or shine.* □ *We'll hold the picnic—rain or shine.*

rain something **down†** (**on** someone or something**)** to pour something, such as criticism or praise, onto someone or something. (Based on **rain down on** someone or something.) □ *The employees rained criticism down on the personnel manager for the new policy on sick leave.* □ *The audience rained down compliments on the performers.*

rain something **out†** [for the weather] to spoil something by raining. □ *Oh, the weather looks awful. I hope it doesn't rain the picnic out.* □ *It's starting to sprinkle now. Do you think it will rain out the ball game?*

rain (up)on someone or something [for rain, or something similar] to fall on someone or something. (*Upon* is formal and less commonly used than *on*.) □ *The ashes from the erupting volcano rained on all the people fleeing the village.* □ *It rained on the fields until they were flooded.*

raise a (big) stink (about someone or something**)** Go to **make a (big) stink (about** someone or something**)**.

raise a few eyebrows Go to **raise some eyebrows**.

raise a hand (against someone or something**)** Go to **lift a hand (against** someone or something**)**.

raise a hue and cry (about something**)** *Fig.* to make an issue about something; to alert people to a problem or difficulty. (See also **hue and cry**.) □ *The city council raised a hue and cry about the mayor's proposed budget.*

raise a stink (about something**)** Go to **create a stink (about** something**)**.

raise (an) objection (to someone or something**)** to mention an objection about someone or something. □ *I hope your family won't raise an objection to my staying for dinner.* □ *I'm certain no one will raise an objection. We are delighted to have you.*

raise Cain to make a lot of trouble; to **raise hell**. (A Biblical reference, from Genesis 4.) □ *Fred was really raising Cain about the whole matter.* □ *Let's stop raising Cain.*

raise havoc with someone or something and **play havoc with** someone or something to create confusion or disruption for or among someone or something. □ *Your announcement raised havoc with the students.* □ *I didn't mean to play havoc with them.*

raise hell (with something**)** Go to **raise the devil (with** something**)**.

raise hob with someone or something and **play hob with** someone or something to do something devilish to someone or something; to cause trouble for someone or something. (A *hob* is a hobgoblin, a wicked little elf.) □ *Your sudden* *arrival is going to play hob with my dinner plans.* □ *Sorry, I didn't mean to raise hob with you.*

raise money for someone or something and **raise money to** do something to work to earn money or encourage donations for the benefit of someone, something, or doing something. □ *I worked hard to raise money for college, and then decided not to go.*

raise one's **glass to** someone or something to propose a drinking toast in salute to someone or something. □ *Let us all raise our glasses to George Wilson!* □ *They raised their glasses to the successful campaign.*

raise one's **sights** *Fig.* to set higher goals for oneself. (Alludes to someone lifting the sights of a gun in order to fire farther.) □ *When you're young, you tend to raise your sights too high.* □ *On the other hand, some people need to raise their sights.*

raise one's **voice against** someone or something *Fig.* to speak out loudly or angrily against someone or something; to complain about someone or something. □ *Tony was very polite and did not raise his voice against Roger.* □ *I was too timid to raise my voice against the injustices of the day.*

raise one's **voice (to** someone) *Fig.* to speak loudly or shout at someone in anger. □ *Don't you dare raise your voice to me!* □ *I'm sorry. I didn't mean to raise my voice.*

raise some **eyebrows** and **raise a few eyebrows** *Fig.* to shock or surprise people mildly (by doing or saying something). (*Some* can be replaced with *a few, someone's, a lot of,* etc.) □ *What you just said may raise some eyebrows, but it shouldn't make anyone really angry.* □ *John's sudden marriage to Ann raised a few eyebrows.*

raise someone **from** something to help someone up from a lowly state. □ *They hoped for some windfall to raise them from their poverty.* □ *They raised me from the depressed state I was in.*

raise someone **from the dead** *Fig.* to bring a dead person back to life. (When used figuratively, usually refers to something very bad or offensive.) □ *How great are your magic powers? Can you raise people from the dead?* □ *They say her singing could raise people from the dead.*

raise someone or an animal **from** something *Fig.* to bring up someone or an animal from a young state. □ *My grandmother raised me from a baby.* □ *We raised all these rabbits from babies.*

raise someone or something **to** something to elevate someone or something to something at a higher level. □ *Dan raised Alice up to the window.* □ *I helped raise the ladder to the top of the roof.*

raise someone or something **to the surface (of** something) to bring someone or something up to the surface of a body of water. □ *The pull of the inflatable life vest raised Tom to the surface of the water.* □ *The divers were able to raise the sunken ship to the surface.*

raise someone or something **up†** to lift someone or something up. □ *The aides raised the patient up while the nurse spread clean linen beneath him.* □ *Jane raised up the lid.*

raise someone's **spirits** Go to someone's **spirits.**

raise someone **to** something to promote or advance someone to a higher rank. □ *The boss raised her to vice president after one year.* □ *I hope she raises me to head clerk.*

raise something **with** someone to bring up a matter with someone. □ *I will raise that question with Mary when she comes in.* □ *Please raise the question with the boss.*

raise the ante Go to up the ante.

raise the bar *Fig.* to make a task a little more difficult. (As with raising the bar in high jumping or pole vaulting.) □ *Just as I was getting accustomed to my job, the manager raised the bar and I had to perform even better.*

raise the devil (with someone) to severely chastise someone or a group. □ *The coach came in and raised the devil with Sally for her error in the first quarter of the game.* □ *I'm going to raise the devil with him!*

raise the devil (with something) and **raise hell (with** something) to cause trouble with something. □ *That idea raises hell with my plan.* □ *The onions raised the devil with my stomach.*

raise the dickens (with someone or something) to act in some extreme manner; to make trouble; to behave wildly; to be very angry. □ *John was out all night raising the dickens.* □ *That cheap gas I bought really raised the dickens with my car's engine.*

raise up to lift oneself up; to get up or begin to get up. □ *She raised up and then fell back onto her bed. She was too weak to get up.* □ *I could not raise up enough to see out the window.*

raised in a barn brought up to behave like a barnyard animal; having crude behavior. □ *Close the door behind you! Were you raised in a barn?* □ *Don't wipe your nose on your sleeve. Were you raised in a barn?*

rake on someone Go to **rag on** someone.

rake someone **over the coals** and **haul** someone **over the coals** *Fig.* to give someone a severe scolding. □ *My mother hauled me over the coals for coming in late last night.* □ *The manager raked me over the coals for being late again.*

rake something **around†** to spread something around with a rake. □ *She raked the leaves around, spreading them over the flower beds as natural fertilizer.* □ *I need to rake around the soil and stir it up.*

rake something **in†** **1.** *Lit.* to draw or pull something inward with a rake. □ *Jane is raking in the leaves into a big pile.* **2.** *Fig.* to take in a lot of something, usually money. □ *Our candidate will rake votes in by the thousand.* □ *They were raking in money by the bushel.*

rake something **off†** **1.** to steal or embezzle a portion of a payment or an account. □ *They claimed that no one was raking anything off and that the money was only mislaid.* □ *The county treasurer was caught raking off some of the tax money.* **2.** Go to next.

rake something **off (of)** something and **rake** something **off†** to remove something from something by raking. (*Of* is usually retained before pronouns.) □ *Please rake the leaves off the lawn.* □ *Rake off the leaves.*

rake something **out of** something and **rake** something **out†** to clean something out of something by raking. □ *You ought to rake the leaves out of the gutter so the water will flow.* □ *Please rake out the leaves.*

rake something **up†** **1.** *Lit.* to gather and clean up something with a rake. □ *Would you please rake these leaves up before it rains?* □ *Please rake up the leaves.* **2.** to clean something up by raking. □ *Would you rake the yard up?* □ *I will rake up the yard.* **3.** *Fig.* to find some unpleasant information. □ *His opposition raked an old scandal up and made it public.* □ *That is ancient history. Why did you have to rake up that old story?*

rake through something *Fig.* [for someone] to rummage through something, as if with a rake. □ *She quickly raked through the mass of loose papers, looking for the right one.* □ *I will have to rake through everything in this drawer to find a red pencil.*

rally around someone or something *Fig.* to unite or assemble in support of someone or something. □ *All the other workers rallied around Fred in his fight with management.* □ *They rallied around the principle that Fred stood for.*

rally to someone or something to unite in support of someone or something. □ *The students rallied to Betty, their elected president.* □ *We all rallied to the cause.*

ralph something **up†** *Sl.* to vomit something. (Teens and collegiate.) □ *The doctor gave him some stuff that made him ralph it up.* □ *He ralphed up his dinner.*

ram into someone or something to crash into someone or something. □ *Mary accidentally rammed into a fence as she rode along.* □ *The car rammed into the tree and was totally wrecked.*

ram someone or something **down** someone's **throat** Go to **shove** someone or something **down** someone's **throat**.

ram something **down†** to pack something down by pounding, as with a ram. □ *The worker used a pole to ram the earth down and pack it tight.* □ *The worker rammed down the earth.*

ram something **into** someone or something and **ram** something **in†** to pound something into someone or something. □ *He rammed his fist into Bill's side and shouted something angry at him.* □ *He rammed in his fist.*

ram something **through** (something) **1.** to force something through something. □ *He rammed his fist through the window, cutting himself in the process.* □ *Harry put the brick up to the window glass and rammed it through. Next time he would remember his key.* **2.** to force something through a deliberative body, usually not allowing due consideration. □ *They rammed the bill through the city council.* □ *The President was unable to ram the measure through Congress.*

ram through something to crash or pound through something. □ *The car rammed through the back of the garage.* □ *I was afraid that the truck would ram through the fence.*

ramble on 1. to wander about aimlessly. (As with a traveler or a winding path.) □ *The road rambled on through mile after mile of wilderness.* **2.** [for a structure] to spread out over a large area, perhaps in a random way. □ *This old house rambles on, way back into the woods.*

ramble on (about someone or something**)** *Fig.* [for someone] to talk endlessly and aimlessly about someone or something. (Based on **ramble on.**) □ *I wish you wouldn't ramble on about your first husband all the time.* □ *Must you ramble on so?*

range from something **to** something to vary from one thing to another. □ *The winter weather ranges from bad to ter-*

rible in this part of the north. □ *The appraisals of the property ranged from high to low.*

range over something to cover an area; to travel about in one area. □ *The buffalo ranged over vast areas of prairie, grazing and breeding.* □ *These animals range over a very large territory.*

rank above someone to outrank someone; to rank higher than someone. □ *I think that I rank above you, so I will sit by the window.* □ *The boss ranks above everyone and demands that everyone recognize the fact.*

rank among something to be included in a particular group. □ *In my opinion, Kelly ranks among the very best.* □ *Tom ranks among the most widely known of the contemporary writers.*

rank and file 1. *Lit.* regular soldiers, not the officers. □ *I think there is low morale among the rank and file, sir.* □ *The rank and file usually do exactly as they are told.* **2.** *Fig.* the ordinary members of a group, not the leaders. □ *The rank and file will vote on the proposed contract tomorrow.* □ *The last contract was turned down by the rank and file last year.*

rank as something to have a particular rank; to serve in a particular rank. □ *She ranks as a fine pianist in my book.* □ *Don ranks as the top economist of the day.*

rank on someone *Sl.* to attack someone verbally; to gossip about someone. □ *Please stop ranking on my family!* □ *Tom keeps ranking on Jennifer, and she is really mad about it.*

rank someone **among** something to judge someone to be essentially equal to a specific group of people. □ *I don't rank Kelly among the best drivers in the world.* □ *Our committee ranked Fred among the best of the current applicants.*

rank someone or something **as** something to assign a particular rank to someone or something. □ *I have to rank Sally as number one. She's the best.* □ *Mary ranked the chocolate as the best she had ever eaten.*

rank someone **(out†) 1.** *Sl.* to annoy someone. □ *He really ranks me out. What a pest!* **2.** *Sl.* to chastise someone. □ *She ranked him out for being a coward.* □ *I ranked out the whole gang, but good!*

rank someone **with** someone to judge someone to be equal with someone. □ *Would you rank Tom with Donna?* □ *Fred ranked himself with Tom when it came to diving.*

rank with someone or something to be equal to someone or something. □ *Do you think Sarah ranks with Albert?* □ *No one ranks with Albert.* □ *The food at that restaurant ranks with that of the best places in New York.*

rant against someone or something to rave and yell against someone or something. □ *She spent most of the morning ranting against her mother-in-law.* □ *Leonard spent the entire morning ranting against the government.*

rant and rave (about someone or something**)** to shout angrily and wildly about someone or something. □ *Barbara rants and raves when her children don't obey her.* □ *Bob rants and raves about anything that displeases him.*

rant (at someone**) about** someone or something to talk in a loud, violent way, about someone or something. □ *Anne ranted about the bad service she had received at the store.*

R

□ *On the bus, someone was ranting at me about the end of the world.*

rant at someone or something to rave and yell at someone or something. □ *Stop ranting at me!* □ *The boss would never rant at the office staff.*

rap at something and **rap on** something to tap on something to attract someone's attention. □ *Who is that rapping at my door?* □ *Someone is rapping at the window, trying to get my attention.* □ *I will rap on her window and try to wake her.*

rap on something Go to previous.

rap someone **across the knuckles** and **rap** someone **on the knuckles; rap** someone's **knuckles** to strike someone on the knuckles. □ *As punishment, she rapped him across the knuckles.* □ *The teacher rapped the student on the knuckles.*

rap something **out†** (**on** something) to tap out the rhythm of something on something. □ *Try to rap the rhythm out on the table.* □ *He rapped out the rhythm on the table.*

rap with someone *Sl.* to have a chat with someone or a group of people. (Old.) □ *Come in, sit down, and rap with me for a while.* □ *Let's get together and rap with one another sometime.*

rarin' to go extremely keen to act or do something. □ *Jane can't wait to start her job. She's rarin' to go.* □ *Mary is rarin' to go and can't wait for her university term to start.*

rasp something **out†** to carve or smooth something out with a rasp. □ *You should use this tool to rasp the inside of the bowl out. Use sandpaper to make the inside smoother.* □ *Rasp out the inside carefully.*

rat around *Sl.* to waste time loafing around; to **kick around**. (Collegiate.) □ *I didn't do anything but rat around all summer.* □ *If kids don't have jobs, they just rat around.*

rat on someone *Inf.* to report someone's bad behavior to someone in authority; to tattle on someone. □ *John ratted on me, and I got in trouble.* □ *If he rats on me, I'll hit him!*

rat out *Sl.* to quit; to **fink out (on** someone or something). □ *It's too late to rat out.* □ *He tried to rat out at the last minute.*

rat race *Fig.* a fierce struggle for success, especially in one's career or business. □ *Bob got tired of the rat race. He's retired and gone to the country.* □ *The money market is a rat race, and many people who work in it get out quickly because of the stress.*

rate someone or something **above** someone or something else to judge someone to rank higher than someone else; to judge something to rank higher than something else. □ *Do you rate Alice above Valerie?* □ *I rate chocolate ice cream above vanilla.*

rate someone or something **among** something to judge someone or something to be essentially equal to something. □ *I rate Polly among the best of this year's class.* □ *We rate these contestants among the best ever.*

rate someone or something **as** something to assign a particular rating to someone or something. □ *I rate her as a number four.* □ *The judge rated my cake as second place.*

rate someone or something **below** someone or something else to judge someone to rank lower than someone else; to judge something to rank lower than something else. □ *I have to rate Carol below Donna in this regard.* □ *We all rate plain chocolate ice cream below rocky road ice cream.*

rate someone or something **with** someone or something else to judge someone or something to be equal to someone or something else. □ *I rate Fred with Don. They are equally good.* □ *Vanilla is very nice, but I don't rate it with chocolate ice cream.*

rate something **at** something to assign a particular level of rating to something. □ *I rate this brand at about a B-.* □ *The broker rated this stock at a buy.*

rate something **below** something else Go to **rate** someone or something **below** someone or something else.

rate with someone to be in someone's favor; to be thought of highly by someone. □ *Ann is great. She really rates with me.* □ *She doesn't rate with me at all.*

ration something **out†** (**among** someone) to give people limited shares of something, attempting to make it last as long as possible. □ *The captain rationed the water out among all the crew, trying to make it last as long as possible.* □ *Jane rationed out the cookies among the kids.*

Rats abandon a sinking ship. and **like rats abandoning a sinking ship** *Prov.* You can tell when something is about to fail because large numbers of people begin to leave it. (Can imply that the people who leave are "rats," that is, selfish and disloyal.) □ *Jill: The company next door must be going bankrupt. Jane: How do you know? Jill: All its employees are resigning. Rats abandon a sinking ship.*

rattle around in something **1.** *Lit.* to make a rattling noise inside something. □ *What is rattling around in this package?* □ *There is something rattling around in my glove compartment.* **2.** *Fig.* to ride about in a vehicle with a rattle. □ *I am perfectly happy to rattle around in my ten-year-old car.* □ *Todd rattles around in his grandfather's old car.* **3.** *Fig.* to live in a place that is much too big. □ *We have been rattling around in this big old house for long enough. Let's move to a smaller place.* □ *I can't afford to rattle around in a three-story house any longer.*

rattle away to chatter endlessly and aimlessly. □ *The two old men sat there and rattled away at one another.* □ *Tom rattled away at Jane for a few minutes and then left the house.*

rattle its saber Go to **rattle** one's **saber**.

rattle on (about someone or something**)** *Fig.* to talk endlessly about someone or something. □ *Martin talked incessantly. He would rattle on about any topic whenever he could trap an unfortunate listener.*

rattle one's **saber** and **rattle its saber** *Fig.* to make threatening statements or actions. □ *The president is just rattling his saber. He would never attack such a small country!*

rattle something **off†** and **reel** something **off†** to recite something quickly and accurately. □ *She can really reel song lyrics off.* □ *Listen to Mary rattle off those numbers.*

raunch someone **out**† *Sl.* to disgust someone. □ *These dirty socks absolutely raunch me out!* □ *Sam and Beavis enjoy raunching out everyone in the room.*

rave about someone or something **1.** to rage in anger about someone or something. □ *Gale was raving about Sarah and what she did.* □ *Sarah raved and raved about Gale's insufferable rudeness.* **2.** to sing the praises of someone or something. □ *Even the harshest critic raved about Larry's stage success.* □ *Everyone was raving about your excellent performance.*

rave over someone or something to recite praises for someone or something. □ *The students were just raving over the new professor.* □ *Donald raved over the cake I baked. But he'll eat anything.*

ravished with delight *Fig.* happy or delighted; overcome with happiness or delight. □ *Mary was ravished with delight by the dozen roses.* □ *My parents were ravished with delight when I graduated from college.*

***a **raw deal** an instance of unfair or bad treatment. (*Typically: **get** ~; **have** ~; **give** someone ~.) □ *Mary got a raw deal on her traffic ticket. She was innocent, but she had to pay a big fine.* □ *I bought a used TV that worked for two days and then quit. I sure got a raw deal.* □ *You sure had a raw deal.*

raw recruit a new, inexperienced, or fresh recruit, such as someone just entering the army, navy, police, etc. □ *These boys are nothing but raw recruits. They've never seen a gun up close!*

raze something **to the ground** to tear down something, usually a building, to ground level. □ *The council decided to raze the old city hall to the ground.* □ *This building is to be razed to the ground.*

reach a compromise to achieve a compromise; to negotiate an agreement. □ *After many hours of discussion, we finally reached a compromise.* □ *We were unable to reach a compromise and quit trying.*

reach a conclusion to complete discussion and decide an issue. □ *It took three days of talks to reach a conclusion.* □ *When we reach a conclusion, we will notify you of the results.*

reach a dead end Go to come to a dead end.

reach a decision Go to arrive at a decision.

reach a turning point Go to a turning point.

reach an accord (with someone) and **reach an agreement (with** someone) to come to an agreement with someone. □ *I hope that we can reach an accord with the union so work can start again.* □ *We will try one more time to reach an agreement with you.* □ *We reached an agreement and signed a contract.*

reach an agreement (with someone) Go to previous.

reach an impasse to progress to the point that a barrier stops further progress. □ *When negotiations with management reached an impasse, the union went on strike.* □ *The discussion reached an impasse and no one was able to propose a compromise.*

reach an understanding with someone and **come to an understanding (with** someone) to achieve a settlement or an agreement with someone. □ *I hope we are able to reach an understanding with the commissioners.* □ *We were able to reach an understanding with Tony.*

reach back (in)to something to extend back into a particular period in time. □ *This policy reaches back into the last century.* □ *Our way of making fine candies reaches back to the recipes used by the founder of the company.*

reach down to extend downward. □ *The stems of the plant reached down almost to the floor.* □ *The drapes don't quite reach down to the floor.*

reach first base (with someone or something) Go to get to first base (with someone or something).

reach for someone or something to extend one's grasp to someone or something. □ *I reached for my father, but he wasn't there.* □ *I reached for a pen, but I only had a pencil.*

reach for the sky 1. and **aim for the sky; shoot for the sky** *Fig.* to set one's sights high. □ *Reach for the sky! Go for it!* □ *You should always reach for the sky, but be prepared for not attaining your goals every time.* **2.** *Fig. Inf.* to put one's hands up, as in a burglary. □ *The gunman told the bank teller to reach for the sky.* □ *Reach for the sky and give me all your money!*

Reach for the stars! Go to Aim for the stars!

reach in(to something) to stick one's hand into something to grasp something. □ *Bob reached into the cookie jar and found it empty.* □ *Bob went to the cookie jar and reached in.*

reach one's **stride** and **hit** one's **stride** to do something at one's best level of ability. □ *When I reach my stride, things will go faster, and I'll be more efficient.* □ *Now that I've hit my stride, I can work more efficiently.*

reach out 1. *Lit.* to extend one's grasp outward. □ *He reached out, but there was no one to take hold of.* □ *I reached out and grabbed onto the first thing I could get hold of.* **2.** *Fig.* to enlarge one's circle of friends and experiences. □ *If you are that lonely, you ought to reach out. Get to know some new friends.* □ *I need to reach out more and meet people.*

reach out (after someone or something) and **reach out (for** something) to extend one's grasp to someone or something. □ *Don reached out after Doris, but she slipped away before he could get a good hold on her.* □ *Doris reached out for the door, but it slammed closed.*

reach out into something to extend one's grasp out into something, such as the darkness. □ *Laura reached out into the darkness, looking for the light switch.* □ *Jane reached out into the unlit room, hoping to find a lamp or even a candle.*

reach out to someone **1.** *Fig.* to offer someone a helping hand. □ *You reached out to me just when I needed help the most.* □ *I reach out to other people in trouble because I would want someone to do that for me.* **2.** *Fig.* to seek someone's help and support. □ *When I reached out to Don for help, he turned me down.* □ *Jane reached out to her friends for the help and support that she needed.*

reach (rock) bottom Go to (rock) bottom.

reach someone **1.** *Lit.* to travel up to or as far as someone. □ *I ran until I reached her just in time to save her from going over the cliff.* **2.** *Fig.* to manage to be understood by someone; to have one's message appreciated by someone. □ *If* we could only reach them with our message, we might be able to convince them to stay in school.

reach some place **in a body** Go to in a body.

reach something **down†** *Inf.* to hand something down. □ *Please reach the hammer down to me.* □ *Would you reach down the hammer to Jane?*

reach something **in the (very) nick of time** Go to in the (very) nick of time.

reach something **up to** someone *Inf.* to hand something up to someone. □ *I reached the hammer up to Jack, who was fixing a loose shingle on the roof.* □ *Please reach this cold drink up to your brother.*

reach speeds of some amount Go to **speeds of** some amount.

reach to something to extend all the way to something. □ *Our property reaches to the bank of the river.* □ *The grounds reach all the way to the banks of the river.*

reach toward someone or something to aim one's reach to someone or something. □ *Sam reached toward Walter and took hold of his shoulder.* □ *He reached toward the apple but withdrew his hand when he saw it was rotten.*

react against someone or something to respond negatively to someone or something. □ *Why did she react against me so strongly?* □ *There is no need to react against the plan with such force.*

react to someone or something to act in response to someone or something. □ *You made some very good points. I would like to take some time to react to you.* □ *How did Mary react to the news?*

read about someone or something to read information concerning someone or something. □ *Did you read about John in the newspaper?* □ *I read about bonds, and learned a lot about finance.*

read between the lines *Fig.* to infer something (from something else); to try to understand what is meant by something that is not written explicitly or openly. □ *After listening to what she said, if you read between the lines, you can begin to see what she really means.* □ *Don't believe everything you read literally. Learn to read between the lines.*

read for something to read, looking especially for something, such as errors, clarity, etc. □ *Please read this manuscript for spelling and grammar errors.* □ *Read this book for entertainment and nothing more.*

read from something to read [aloud] from something in particular. □ *I will now read from a book of poetry that I like very much.* □ *I like that poem very much. What are you reading from?*

read from the same page and **sing from the same hymnbook** *Cliché* share the same understanding of something. □ *Okay, I think we are reading from the same page now. We can discuss the future of this project more productively.*

read it and weep *Fig.* read the bad news; hear the bad news. □ *I'm sorry to bring you the bad news. Read it and weep.*

Read my lips! Go to Watch my lips!

read of someone or something **(somewhere)** to read news about someone or something in something. □ *I think I have read of you in the papers.* □ *Mary read of the job opening in the newspaper.*

read on to continue to read. □ *Please read on. Don't stop.* □ *She read on until she had come to the end of the story.*

read one one's **rights** to make the required statement of legal rights to a person who has been arrested. □ *All right, read this guy his rights and book him on a charge of theft.* □ *You have to read them their rights before questioning them.*

read oneself to sleep to read something in preparation for falling asleep. □ *I need a really dull book so I can read myself to sleep.* □ *That's the kind of book I use to read myself to sleep.*

read someone **like a book** *Fig.* to understand someone very well. □ *I've got John figured out. I can read him like a book.* □ *Of course I understand you. I read you like a book.*

read someone or something **as** something to interpret someone or something as something. □ *I read you as a quiet guy who wants to settle down and have kids.* □ *Mary read the problem as one that did not require a lot of understanding.*

read someone **out†** **(for** something**)** to chastise someone verbally for doing something wrong. □ *The coach read the player out for making a silly error.* □ *She really read out the lazy players.*

read someone **out of** something to expel someone from an organization, such as a political party. □ *Because of her statement, they read her out of the party.* □ *The officers tried to read me out of the society, but they didn't succeed.*

read someone's **lips** to manage to understand speech by watching and interpreting the movements of the speaker's lips. □ *I couldn't hear her but I could read her lips.*

read someone's **mind** *Fig.* to guess what someone is thinking. □ *You'll have to tell me what you want. I can't read your mind, you know.* □ *If I could read your mind, I'd know what you expect of me.*

read (someone**)** something **out of** something to read something [aloud] from something. □ *He read us a story out of the book.* □ *Mary read the story out of the magazine.*

read someone **the riot act** *Fig.* to give someone a severe scolding. □ *The manager read me the riot act for coming in late.* □ *The teacher read the students the riot act for their failure to do their assignments.*

read something **back†** **(to** someone**)** to read back some information to the person who has just given it. □ *Yes, I have written the telephone number down. Let me read it back to you to make sure I have it right.* □ *Please read back the letter to me.*

read something **in** something to read something in particular in a some publication or document. □ *I read an interesting article about moose in today's newspaper.* □ *Did you read that in today's newspaper?*

read something **into** something *Fig.* to attach or attribute a new or different meaning to something; to presume inferences as one reads something. □ *This statement means exactly what it says. Don't try to read anything else into it.* □ *Am I reading too much into your comments?*

R

548

read something **off**† to read aloud from a list. □ *Nick read the list of the names off, and I wasn't on the list.* □ *Jane read off the names.*

read something **out**† to read something aloud. □ *Please read it out so everyone can hear you.* □ *Read out the names loudly.*

read something **over**† to read something. □ *When you have a chance, read this over.* □ *Also, read over this report.*

read something **through**† to read all of something. □ *Take this home and read it through.* □ *Read through this report and see if you can find any errors.*

read (something) **to** someone to read something aloud to someone. □ *Please read a story to me.* □ *Grandpa read to Timmy all afternoon.*

read the handwriting on the wall *Fig.* to anticipate what is going to happen by observing small hints and clues. (See also **see the (hand)writing on the wall.**) □ *I know I am going to be fired. I can read the handwriting on the wall.* □ *Can't you read the handwriting on the wall? Can't you see what they are planning?*

read up (**on** someone or something) to find and read some information about someone or something. □ *Please go to the library and read up on George Washington.* □ *I don't know anything about that. I guess I need to read up.*

readjust to someone or something to make a new adjustment to someone or something. □ *Please make an attempt to readjust your work schedule for the next two weeks.* □ *I don't think I can readjust to this climate.*

ready, set, go Go to **on your mark, get set, go.**

***ready** (**to** do something) prepared to do something. (*Typically: **be** ~; **get** ~.) □ *Get ready to jump!* □ *It's time to get ready to go to work.*

ready, willing, and able *Cliché* eager or at least willing [to do something]. □ *If you need someone to help you move furniture, I'm ready, willing, and able.* □ *Fred is ready, willing, and able to do anything you ask him.*

a (**real**) **go-getter** an active, energetic, and aggressive person. □ *Mary is very aggressive in business. A real go-getter.*

the **real McCoy** an authentic thing or person. □ *Of course it's authentic. It's the real McCoy.*

the **real thing** something that is genuine and not an imitation. □ *I don't want frozen yogurt, I want the real thing! Yes, ice cream!* □ *She hates plastic that looks like wood. She wants the real thing.*

the **reality of the situation** the truth or actuality of the situation; the way the situation really is. □ *The reality of the situation is that we must act right now.* □ *Let's face the reality of the situation and go out and get jobs so we can pay our bills.*

realize one's **potential** to fulfill one's potential; to do as well as one possibly can. □ *I hope I can get a good education so I can realize my potential.*

realize something **from** something **1.** to perceive something from some kind of evidence. □ *I just now realized something from what you've been saying.* □ *Tom realized how wrong he had been from what Mary told him.* **2.** to reap a profit by selling an asset that has increased in value. □

He realized a large profit from the sale of the house. □ *We hoped to realize a lot of money from the sale of stock.*

ream someone **out**† *Sl.* to scold someone severely. □ *The teacher really reamed him out.* □ *The coach reamed out the whole team.*

ream something **out**† to widen or clean an interior cavity or channel by scraping, grinding, or drilling. □ *Ream the opening out so the flow will be faster.* □ *We had to ream out the pipes so the fuel would flow to the engine.*

reap something **from** something **1.** *Lit.* to harvest something from something. □ *We reaped a fine harvest from our cornfields this year.* □ *They will reap nothing from their flooded fields.* **2.** *Fig.* to gain something from something. □ *The students reaped a lot of information from their interview with the police chief.* □ *I hope to reap some good advice from the discussion.*

reappoint someone **as** something to select or appoint someone to serve again in the same office. □ *Are they going to reappoint Alan as the chairman again?* □ *Alan was reappointed as the head of the committee.*

rear back 1. *Lit.* [for a horse] to pull back and up onto its hind legs in an effort to move backwards rapidly or throw a rider. (See also **rear up.**) □ *The animal reared back in terror.* □ *The horse reared back and almost threw its rider.* **2.** *Fig.* [for a person] to pull back and stand up or sit up straighter. □ *He reared back in his chair and looked perturbed.* □ *Tom reared back in his chair, waiting for something else to happen.*

rear its ugly head *Fig.* [for something unpleasant] to appear or become obvious after lying hidden. □ *Jealousy reared its ugly head and destroyed their marriage.* □ *The question of money always rears its ugly head in matters of business.*

rear up 1. *Lit.* [for a horse] to lean back on its hind legs and raise its front legs, assuming a threatening posture or avoiding something on the ground such as a snake. (See also **rear back.**) □ *The horse reared up suddenly, throwing the rider onto the ground.* □ *When the horse reared up, I almost fell off.* **2.** *Fig.* [for something, especially a problem] to raise up suddenly. □ *A new problem reared up and cost us a lot of time.* □ *A lot of new costs reared up toward the end of the month.*

reason against something to argue against something, using reason. □ *I can hardly be expected to reason against a silly argument like that!* □ *I reasoned against it, but they paid no attention to me.*

reason something **out**† to figure something out; to plan a reasonable course of action. □ *Now let's be calm and try to reason this out.* □ *Let us reason out our difficulties.*

reason with someone to discuss something with someone, seeking a reasonable solution to a problem. □ *Try to reason with Jill. If she won't listen, forget her.* □ *You cannot reason with someone who is so narrow-minded.*

reassign someone **to** something to change someone's assignment to something else. □ *I will reassign Jill to a different department.* □ *I was reassigned to the accounting department.*

reassure someone **about** something to give someone confidence about something. □ *Nancy reassured Betty about her promotion.* □ *Betty was reassured about her promotion.*

reassure someone **of** something to promise or guarantee someone something. □ *Kelly reassured her friend of her support in the election.* □ *Please reassure Tom of our continued support.*

rebel against someone or something to resist and revolt against someone or something. □ *Barbara rebelled against the teachers at the school.* □ *Most young people have to rebel against authority for a while.*

rebel at someone or something to resist and defy someone or something. □ *It is natural for teenagers to rebel at their parents.* □ *I feel as if I have to rebel at all these rules.*

rebound from something **1.** *Lit.* to bounce back from something. □ *The ball rebounded from the wall and hit Randy hard on the elbow.* □ *When the ball rebounded from the backboard, it bounced onto the court and Tom tripped on it.* **2.** *Fig.* to recover quickly from something. □ *Barbara rebounded from her illness in less than a week.* □ *I hope I can rebound from this cold quickly.*

rebuke someone **for** something to reprimand someone for something. □ *There is no need to rebuke me for a simple mistake like that.* □ *Sally was rebuked for overspending her budget.*

recall someone **from** something to call someone back from something or some place. □ *The president recalled our ambassador from the war-torn country.* □ *I was recalled from retirement to help out at the office.*

recall someone or something **from** something to remember someone or something from some event or some place. □ *I recall someone by that name from my days at the university.* □ *Mary recalled the appropriate fact from her history studies.*

recall something **to mind** to cause [someone] to remember something. □ *The events of the day recall similar days in the past to mind.* □ *This book recalls a similar book published some years ago to mind.*

recall something **to** someone to bring something to the mind of someone. □ *Your comments recall another event to me—something that happened years ago.* □ *What you just said recalled an old saying to me.*

recast something **in** something to rebuild or redevelop something in a different form. □ *She recast the sentence in the negative, hoping to make it less blunt.* □ *I will recast my request in different language.*

recede from something to pull back from something. □ *The river receded from its banks during the dry season.* □ *I think that my hair is receding from my forehead.*

receive someone **as** someone or something to welcome and accept someone as someone or something. □ *The king received the ambassador as an honored guest.* □ *They said they would receive their former guest as a welcome visitor.*

receive someone **into** something to welcome someone into something, some place, or some organization. □ *Everyone received the new member into the club with eager congratulations.* □ *We received them into our homes and fed them well.*

receive someone or something **back** to get someone or something back. □ *Martha received her husband back after his escapade.* □ *I sent a letter off with the wrong postage and received it back two weeks later.*

receive someone **with open arms** and **welcome** someone **with open arms 1.** *Lit.* to greet someone with arms spread wide to hug someone. □ *His mother greeted him with open arms at the door.* **2.** *Fig.* to greet someone eagerly. □ *I'm sure they wanted us to stay for dinner. They received us with open arms.* □ *When I came home from college, the whole family welcomed me with open arms.*

receive something **from** some place to get and accept something from some place. □ *I just received a letter from Budapest!* □ *Mary received a package from Japan.*

receive something **from** someone to get and accept something from someone. □ *Tony received a sweater from his grandfather for his birthday.* □ *Who did you receive this from?*

receive word (from someone or something**)** Go to **word (from** someone or something**).**

reckon someone **as** someone or something to perceive someone as someone or something. □ *I reckoned her as a more thoughtful individual than she turned out to be.* □ *Mary reckoned Scott as a constant irritation, and she was right on the button.*

reckon someone or something **among** something to judge someone or something to belong among a select group. □ *I reckon Donna among the best tennis pros in the country.* □ *We reckon this automobile among the most advanced in the world.*

reckon someone or something **into** something and **reckon** someone or something **in**† to figure someone or something in; to include someone or something in one's calculations. □ *I will reckon Jane into the total number of guests.* □ *I reckoned in a few too many people.*

reckon with someone or something to deal with someone or something; to cope with someone or something. □ *I have to reckon with the troublesome Mr. Johnson this afternoon.* □ *Mary knew just exactly how she had to reckon with the bill collector.*

reckon without someone to fail to think about someone. □ *He thought he'd get away with his crime, but he reckoned without the FBI agents.* □ *He had thought he was gone for sure, but he had reckoned without the paramedics.*

reclaim someone or something **from** someone or something to bring someone or something back from someone or something. □ *The mother reclaimed Sally from her father, who had abducted her contrary to the divorce decree.* □ *Mary reclaimed the book from her brother's desk.*

recognize one **for what** one **is** Go to **recognize** something **for what it is.**

recognize someone **as** someone or something to accept and acknowledge someone to be someone; to accept and acknowledge something to be something. □ *Mary didn't recognize the lawyer as her legal representative.* □ *Lizzy didn't recognize the car as her car.*

recognize someone or something **by** something to know someone or something by some distinguishing sign. □ *You will be able to recognize me by my long mustache.* □ *Mary recognized her car by the ribbon tied to the antenna.*

recognize someone or something **for** something **1.** to identify someone or something as something. □ *I recognized the deal for a scam as soon as I heard about it.* □ *Anyone*

R

could recognize Max for a common thief. **2.** to show appreciation to someone or something for something. □ *The organization recognized Laura for her excellent contributions to the philanthropy committee.* □ *The officers recognized the committee for its outstanding efforts.*

recognize something **for what it is** and **recognize** one **for what** one **is** to see and understand exactly what someone or something is or represents. □ *The disease represented a serious threat to all peoples, and Dr. Smith recognized it for what it was.* □ *I recognize you for what you are, you scoundrel!*

recoil at the sight (of someone or something**)** and **recoil at the thought (of** someone or something**)** *Fig.* to flinch or cringe at the sight or thought of someone or something. □ *Sally recoiled at the sight of Gerry, who had said something unspeakable.* □ *Mary recoiled at the very thought.*

recoil at the thought (of someone or something**)** Go to previous.

recoil from someone or something to draw back from someone or something. □ *I recoiled from Sally when she told me what she had done.* □ *I recoiled from the horror and slammed the door.*

recommend someone **as** something to suggest someone as something. □ *Could you recommend Frank as a good carpenter?* □ *I can recommend Jane Smith as a good artist.*

recommend someone **for** something to suggest someone for something. □ *I would be very glad to recommend you for promotion.* □ *She recommended herself as the best choice.*

recommend someone or something **to** someone to suggest that someone choose someone or something. □ *I would like to recommend Sally to you as a good prospect for membership on the committee.* □ *Could you recommend a good mechanic to me?*

recompense someone **for** something to (re)pay someone for something. □ *I am required to recompense Mrs. Wilson for her broken window.* □ *Can I recompense you for your expenses?*

reconcile oneself **to** something to grow to feel comfortable with an undesirable or challenging situation. □ *John reconciled himself to living alone.* □ *Anne reconciled herself to having to wear glasses.*

reconcile something **with** something to bring something into harmony, accord, or balance with something. □ *The accountants were not able to reconcile the expense claims with the receipts that had been turned in.* □ *I can't reconcile your story with those of the other witnesses.*

reconstruct something **from** something **1.** to rebuild something from something. □ *I was not able to reconstruct the puzzle from the pieces that were left on the floor.* □ *Can you reconstruct the damaged part of the house from these materials?* **2.** to recall and restate a story or the details of an event from something. □ *Can you reconstruct the story from the fragments you have just heard?* □ *I cannot reconstruct the chain of events from memory.*

record something **from** something to make an audio or video recording of something from some source. □ *Listen to this. I recorded it from a radio broadcast.* □ *From what TV show did you record this?*

record something **in** something to enter a record of something into something. □ *I will record your appointment in my notebook.* □ *Jane recorded the memo in her computer.*

record something **on** something to make a record of something on the surface of something. □ *Nancy recorded the appointment on the calendar that served as a blotter on the top of her desk.* □ *Please record this on your calendar.*

recount something **to** someone to tell something to someone; to narrate a series of events, in order. □ *Carl recounted the events of the day to his wife.* □ *The strange events were recounted by a number of people.*

recoup something **from** someone or something to salvage something from someone or something. □ *I hope I can recoup my expenses from the company this week.* □ *Mary intended to recoup her money from the investment.*

recover from someone or something to get over an experience with someone or something. □ *My great-uncle just left, and it will take a day or two to recover from him.* □ *I hope I recover from his visit soon.*

recover from something to recuperate from a disease. □ *I hope I recover from this cough soon.* □ *She recovered from her cold soon enough to go on the trip.*

recover something **from** someone or something to retrieve or salvage something from someone, something, or some place. □ *The police recovered my purse from the thief who had taken it.* □ *Mary recovered her deposit from the failed bank.*

recruit someone **for** something to seek and engage someone for something. □ *Harry had to recruit a few people for the new jobs that opened up.* □ *We recruited three more people for the project.*

recruit someone **from** something to convince someone to leave something and join one's own group. □ *Phyllis recruited a new work team from the company she used to work for.* □ *We recruited a number of people from private industry.*

recruit someone **into** something to seek out and induct someone into something. □ *The recruitment office tried to recruit ten people a week into the army.* □ *The army recruited almost no one during the month of December.*

recuperate from something to recover from something; to be cured or to heal after something. □ *I hope that you recuperate from your illness soon.* □ *Has she recuperated from her surgery yet?*

***red as a cherry** and ***red as a poppy**; ***red as a rose**; ***red as a ruby**; ***red as blood** bright red. (*Also: **as** ~.) □ *When she came in from ice-skating, Clara's nose was as red as a cherry.* □ *When her boss praised her in front of the whole office, Emily turned red as a poppy.* □ *I would like to make a dress out of that beautiful velvet that is red as a rose.* □ *Jane painted her fingernails with polish as red as a ruby.* □ *I want to have my car painted red as blood.*

red as a poppy Go to previous.

red as a rose Go to red as a cherry.

red as a ruby Go to red as a cherry.

red as blood Go to red as a cherry.

a **red herring** a piece of information or suggestion introduced to draw attention away from the real facts of a situation. (A red herring is a type of strong-smelling smoked fish that was once drawn across the trail of a scent to mislead hunting dogs and put them off the scent.) □ *The detectives were following a red herring, but they're on the right track now.* □ *The mystery novel has a couple of red herrings that keep readers off guard.*

red in the face *Fig.* embarrassed. □ *After we found Ann hiding in the closet, she became red in the face.* □ *The speaker kept making errors and became red in the face.*

red ink *Fig.* debt; indebtedness as shown in red ink on a financial statement. □ *There is too much red ink in my financial statement.* □ *Too much red ink and the company will collapse.*

red tape *Fig.* over-strict attention to the wording and details of rules and regulations, especially by government workers. (From the color of the tape used by government departments in England to tie up bundles of documents.) □ *Because of red tape, Frank took weeks to get a visa.* □ *Red tape prevented Jack's wife from joining him abroad.*

*the **red-carpet treatment** *Fig.* very special treatment; royal treatment. (*Typically: **get** ~; **have** ~; **give** someone ~.*) □ *I love to go to fancy stores where I get the red-carpet treatment.* □ *The queen expects to get the red-carpet treatment wherever she goes.*

rededicate oneself or something **to** someone or something to reaffirm the dedication of oneself or something to someone or something. □ *I must ask you to rededicate yourself to our high purposes.* □ *They rededicated their church to God.*

a **red-letter day** *Fig.* an important or significant day. (From the practice of printing holidays in red on the calendar.) □ *Today was a red-letter day in our history.* □ *It was a red-letter day for our club.*

redound on someone to have an effect on someone. □ *The hot weather has redounded on all of us in a bad way.* □ *The problems created by your mistake have redounded on the entire company.*

reduce someone **to silence** to cause someone to be silent. □ *The rebuke reduced him to silence—at last.* □ *Mary was reduced to silence by Jane's comments.*

reduce someone **to tears** to cause a person to cry through insults, frustration, and belittling. □ *He scolded her so much that she was reduced to tears by the end of the meeting.*

reduce something **by** something to diminish something by a certain amount. □ *I have to reduce your allowance by two dollars per week until you pay me back for the broken window.* □ *I will reduce the bill by a few dollars.*

reduce something **from** something **to** something to diminish something from one degree to a lower degree. □ *I will reduce the fine from two hundred dollars to one hundred dollars.* □ *Mary reduced her demands from a large sum to a smaller one.*

reduced to doing something brought into a certain humble condition or state. □ *The poor man was reduced to begging for food.*

A **reed before the wind lives on, while mighty oaks do fall.** *Prov.* An insignificant, flexible person is more likely not to get hurt in a crisis than a prominent or rigid person. □ *Our office has new managers now; I plan to be as inconspicuous as possible while they reorganize everyone. A reed before the wind lives on, while mighty oaks do fall.*

reef a sail **in**† to reduce the area of a ship's sail, by folding the sail. □ *The first mate ordered the sailors to reef the sails in.* □ *They had to reef in the sails.*

reek of something **1.** *Lit.* to have the stench or smell of something. □ *This whole house reeks of onions! What did you cook?* □ *She reeks of a very strong perfume. She must have spilled it on herself.* **2.** *Fig.* to give a strong impression of something. □ *The neighborhood reeks of poverty.* □ *The deal reeked of dishonesty.*

reek with something to stink with some smell. □ *This place reeks with some horrible odor.* □ *Jane reeks with too much perfume.*

reel back (from something**)** to fall or stagger backwards, as from a blow. □ *The boxer reeled back from the blow, stunned.* □ *Another blow to the midsection and he reeled back and fell.*

reel something **in**† to bring in something, such as a fish, by winding up the line on a reel. □ *With great effort, she reeled the huge fish in.* □ *Hurry and reel in the fish!*

reel something **off**† Go to **rattle** something **off**†.

reel under something **1.** *Lit.* to stagger under the weight of something. □ *Tony reeled under the weight of the books.* □ *She knew she would reel under the heavy load.* **2.** *Fig.* to stagger because of a blow. □ *The boxer reeled under the blow to his chin.* □ *Fred reeled under the beating that Mike gave him.* **3.** *Fig.* to suffer because of a burden. □ *Gary reeled under the responsibilities he had been given.* □ *I was just reeling under the burdens of my new job.*

refer someone **back to** someone or something to suggest that someone go back to someone or something, such as the source. □ *I referred the client back to the lawyer she had originally consulted.* □ *Tom referred the customer back to the manufacturer who had made the shoddy product.*

refer someone **to** someone or something to direct someone to someone or something; to send someone to someone or something. □ *The front office referred me to you, and you are now referring me to someone else!* □ *They should have referred you to the personnel department.*

refer something **back to** someone or something and **refer** something **back**† to send something back to someone or a group for action. □ *Dr. Smith knows more about this kind of case, so I referred it back to him.* □ *They referred back all the bills.*

refer to someone or something to mention someone or something. □ *Are you referring to me when you speak about a kind and helpful person?* □ *I was referring to the personnel department.*

refill a prescription sell a second or subsequent set of doses of a medicine upon a doctor's orders. □ *The pharmacy refused to refill my prescription because it has expired.* □ *If you want the drugstore to refill your prescription, just give them the prescription number over the telephone.*

reflect (back) (up)on someone or something to remember or think about someone or something. (*Upon* is formal and less commonly used than *on*.) □ *When I reflect back on the years I spent with my parents, I think I had a good childhood.* □ *I like to reflect on my great-grandmother.*

reflect credit (up)on someone or something [for some act] to bring credit to someone or something. (*Upon* is formal and less commonly used than *on*.) □ *Your efforts really reflect credit upon you.* □ *Mary's success really reflected credit on the quality of her education.*

reflected in something **1.** *Lit.* [of something] mirrored in something, such as a mirror, water, ice, etc. □ *His image was reflected in the mirror, giving him a good view of his sunburn.* □ *When the hermit's image was reflected in the pool, he was amazed.* **2.** *Fig.* [of something] shown in a result. □ *The extra charges will be reflected in next month's bill.* □ *I do not understand all the charges that are reflected in my statement.*

refrain from something to hold back from doing something; to choose not to do something as planned. □ *I wish you would refrain from shouting.* □ *Please refrain from hollering.*

refresh someone **with** something to renew or revive someone with something. □ *Here, let me refresh you with a cool glass of lemonade.* □ *After the game, Wally will probably refresh himself with a bottle of iced tea.*

refresh something **with** something to restore or brighten up something. □ *I think we can refresh this drab old room with a coat of fresh paint.* □ *The old house was refreshed with new siding and some landscaping.*

refund something **to** someone to return payment for something to someone. □ *I insist that you refund the money to me at once.* □ *Her money was refunded to her by the store as soon as she asked for it.*

refuse something **to** someone to deny someone permission to receive or use something. □ *You wouldn't refuse water to me, would you?* □ *Nothing at all was refused to the new employee.*

refuse to do something to reject doing something; to reject a request to do something. □ *I absolutely refuse to go there!* □ *We all refused to break the law.*

regain one's **composure** *Cliché* to become calm and composed after being angry or agitated. □ *I found it difficult to regain my composure after the argument.* □ *Here, sit down and relax so that you can regain your composure.*

regain one's **feet 1.** *Lit.* to stand up again after falling or stumbling. □ *I fell on the ice and almost couldn't regain my feet.* □ *I helped my uncle regain his feet as he tried to get up from the floor.* **2.** *Fig.* to become independent after financial difficulties. □ *I lent Bill $400 to help him regain his feet.* □ *I'll be able to pay my bills when I regain my feet.*

regain something **from** someone or something to take back possession of one's property or right from someone or something. □ *I intend to regain my money from Herb.* □ *The finance company regained the car from the delinquent buyer.*

regale someone **with** something to present a great deal of something, such as lavish entertainment or fine food, to someone. □ *They regaled their guests with food and music*

well into the night. □ *The committee was regaled with tales of wrongdoing by the government.*

regard someone or something **as** someone or something to look upon someone or something as someone or something; to consider someone or something to be someone or something. □ *I have always regarded you as my friend.* □ *The cult members regarded the stone idol as their dead leader.*

regard someone or something **with** something to look upon someone or something with a certain attitude or with certain expectations. □ *The child regarded the teacher with a questioning expression.* □ *The kitten regarded the fishbowl with great curiosity.*

regardless of something without considering something; at any rate; whatever is done; whatever option is chosen. □ *Regardless of what you say, I'm still going to the club tonight.* □ *I still have to pay the bill, regardless of the facts.*

register for something to sign up to participate in something. □ *Have you registered for the class yet?* □ *She is registered for the same classes as I am.*

register in something to enter one's name on a list for something; to sign oneself up to belong to something. □ *Are you going to register in the pie-eating contest?* □ *We registered in the drawing for a new car.*

register on something [for an effect] to show on something, such as someone's face. □ *Recognition registered on her face when she saw the photograph of Walter.* □ *The total of the votes registered on the large scoreboard at the front of the hall.*

register someone **as** something to record someone's name on a list of a category of people. □ *I will register you as an independent voter.* □ *I am registered as a qualified financial advisor.*

register someone **for** something to sign someone up to participate in something. □ *Would you please register me for the workshop when you sign up?* □ *Excuse me. I have to go register myself for the contest.*

register someone **in** something **1.** to enter someone's name on a list in something. □ *I will register you in the competition.* **2.** to sign someone up to belong to something. □ *I registered my cousin in the club.*

register something **with** someone or something to record the existence of something with someone or something. □ *Did you register your new stereo with the manufacturer?* □ *If you bring any packages into this store, please register them with the manager.*

register with someone **1.** *Lit.* to sign up with someone. □ *You will have to register with the lady at the front desk.* □ *I registered with the attendant when I came in.* **2.** *Fig.* [for something] to be realized or understood by someone. □ *Suddenly, the import of what she had said registered with me.* □ *My name did not register with her, and I had to explain who I was.*

regress to something to go back to an earlier, probably simpler, state; to go back to a more primitive state. □ *Bob claimed that Gerald's behavior was regressing to that of a three-year-old.* □ *I tend to regress to my college ways when I am out with the guys.*

R

*regular as clockwork *Cliché* very regular; completely predictable. (*Also: as ~.*) □ *George goes down to the bus stop at 7:45 every morning, as regular as clockwork.* □ *You can always depend on Nancy to complain about the office for fifteen minutes every afternoon, regular as clockwork.*

a **regular fixture** someone who is found so frequently in a place as to be considered a fixture of, or part of the place. □ *The manager attached himself to the luncheon club and became a regular fixture there.*

a **regular guy** a normal and dependable guy. □ *Don't worry about Tom. He's a regular guy. He won't give you any trouble.*

rehearse for something to practice for something. □ *We will rehearse for the graduation exercises on Saturday morning.* □ *We rehearsed for the play all weekend.*

reign over someone or something to rule over someone or something. □ *The king reigned over his subjects for over thirty years.* □ *The queen reigned over the country for a long time.*

reimburse someone **for** something to repay someone for making a purchase, such as a business expense. □ *I will reimburse you for whatever it cost you.* □ *The treasurer reimbursed himself for his expenses.*

reimburse something **to** someone to repay money to someone, such as a business expense. □ *I will reimburse the money to you. Don't worry.* □ *The full cost was reimbursed to me.*

rein back on someone or something to control or diminish the intensity of someone or something. □ *The manager was urged to rein back on her assigning overtime.* □ *She reined back on expenses and demanded that others do likewise.*

rein someone or something **in**† to bring someone or something under control; to slow down someone or something. □ *Fred is getting out of hand. The boss undertook to rein him in a bit.* □ *The boss is trying to rein in Jane's enthusiasm.*

rein something **up**† to bring something, usually a horse, to a stop. □ *She reined her horse up and stopped for a chat.* □ *Rein up your horse and stop for a while.*

rein up [for a horse rider] to stop. □ *The equestrian reined up and dismounted.* □ *We all reined up and waited for the cars to pass by.*

reinforce someone or something **with** something to strengthen someone or something with something. □ *The general reinforced his troops with volunteers fresh from basic training.* □ *I had to reinforce the garage roof with new boards.*

reinstate someone **as** something to put someone back as a certain officeholder. □ *The city council agreed to reinstate Mr. Wilson as alderman.* □ *Fred was reinstated as the court clerk.*

reinstate someone **in** something to put someone back into a certain office or position. □ *If you will pay your dues, we will reinstate you in the organization.* □ *Fred was reinstated in office.*

reinvent the wheel *Fig.* to make unnecessary or redundant preparations. □ *You don't need to reinvent the wheel.*

Read up on what others have done. □ *I don't have to reinvent the wheel, but I will be cautious before I act.*

reissue something **to** someone to release or distribute to someone something that has been distributed before. □ *I plan to reissue the check to you next week.* □ *The check was reissued to Mary the very next day.*

reject someone or something **out of hand** to reject someone or something without any thought or study. □ *Fred is so contrary that they rejected him out of hand when his name came up for a committee position.*

rejoice at something to celebrate or revel about something. □ *Everyone rejoiced at the lucky events that had saved them.* □ *We all rejoiced at the outcome of the election.*

rejoice in someone or something to take great joy at someone or something. □ *I am in love and I rejoice in my beloved!* □ *Roger rejoices in a good night's sleep.*

rejoice over something to celebrate because of something. □ *Everyone rejoiced over their good fortune.* □ *What happened to us next was nothing to rejoice over.*

relapse into something to experience a return to a worse condition. □ *Valerie relapsed into a coma in the afternoon.* □ *Mary relapsed into her depression after a brief period of normalcy.*

relate something **to** someone to tell something to someone; to narrate something to someone. □ *Very slowly, she related the events of the past week to her parents.* □ *I have an interesting story to relate to you.*

relate something **to** something to associate something to something. □ *I relate this particular problem to the failure of the company to provide proper training.* □ *This point is related to what I just told you.*

relate to someone or something to understand, accept, or feel kinship with someone or something. □ *He relates to people well.* □ *I really don't relate to your thinking at all.*

*related to someone connected through blood kinship or through marriage to someone. (**Typically: be ~; become ~.*) □ *I wonder if he is related to you, because he looks a little like you.* □ *I am not related to anyone here.*

relative to someone or something **1.** concerning someone or something. □ *I have something to say relative to Bill.* □ *Do you have any information relative to the situation in South America?* **2.** in proportion to someone or something. □ *My happiness is relative to yours.* □ *I can spend an amount of money relative to the amount of money I earn.*

relax into something **1.** to sit or lie down in something, relaxing. □ *I want to go home and relax into my easy chair.* □ *I relaxed into the reclining chair and was asleep in a few moments.* **2.** [for something that is tense] to assume a more relaxed shape or condition. □ *His cramped muscle finally relaxed into a soft mass of tissue.* □ *As her tight neck relaxed into softness, her face brightened.*

relax one's **hold on** someone or something to lessen one's grasp on someone or something. □ *When she relaxed her hold on me, I got away.* □ *Never relax your hold on an alligator.*

relay something **to** someone to pass something on to someone. □ *Can you relay this to Frank, who is way down the line?* □ *The message was relayed to Frank, who was at the end of the line.*

R

release someone or something **from** something to liberate or let someone or something go from something. □ *The police officer released George from the handcuffs.* □ *I released all the dogs from the city dog pound.*

release someone **to** someone to discharge or distribute someone to someone. □ *The judge released the defendant to his mother.* □ *Don was released by the police to his father, who was more than a little bit angry.*

relegate someone **to** someone or something to assign someone to someone or something. (Often refers to something unimportant or demeaning.) □ *They relegated the old man to a bed in the corner.* □ *The former vice president was relegated to the position of manager of special projects.*

reliance on someone or something trust and dependence on someone or something. □ *John's reliance on his family is holding him back.* □ *Reliance on sleeping pills is dangerous.*

relieve one **of** one's **duties** *Euph.* to fire someone; to dismiss someone from employment. □ *I am afraid I must relieve you of your duties.* □ *After the scandal, she was relieved of her duties at the embassy.*

relieve oneself *Euph.* to urinate or defecate. □ *He stopped by the side of the road to relieve himself.* □ *She needed badly to relieve herself, but there was no bathroom in sight.*

relieve someone **of** something **1.** *Lit.* to unburden someone of something. □ *Here, let me relieve you of that heavy box.* □ *At last, he could relieve himself of the problem.* **2.** *Fig.* to lessen someone's responsibilities. □ *I will relieve you of some of the responsibility you have carried for so long.* □ *Let me relieve you of that job. You have enough to do.*

religious about doing something *Fig.* strict about something; conscientious about something. □ *Bob is religious about paying his bills on time.* □ *Max tries to be religious about being polite to everyone.*

relinquish something **over** someone to release the hold on or control of someone. □ *She refused to relinquish control over the operations of the front office.* □ *Mary was ordered to relinquish her hold over the children for a month each year.*

relinquish something **to** someone or something to surrender something to someone or something. □ *Todd refused to relinquish his authority to anyone.* □ *I finally relinquished the car to the bank.*

relocate someone or something **in** something to reposition or move someone or something in or at something. □ *I will have to relocate you in a different office.* □ *Can I relocate the copy machine in the other room?*

reluctant to do something unwilling to do something; not wanting to do something. □ *David was reluctant to admit his mistakes.* □ *Although reluctant to appear in court, the witness was ordered to by subpoena.*

rely (up)on someone or something to depend on someone or something; to trust in someone or something. (*Upon* is formal and less commonly used than *on*.) □ *I know I can rely upon you to do a good job.* □ *Can we rely on this old car to get us there?*

remain ahead (of someone or something**)** Go to ahead (of someone or something).

remain ahead of something Go to ahead of something.

remain ahead of the game Go to ahead of the game.

remain aloof from someone or something Go to aloof from someone or something.

remain at bay Go to at bay.

remain at some place to stay at some place; to stay behind at some place. □ *I will remain at the office until supper time.* □ *Please remain at home until I call you.*

remain away (from someone or something**)** to stay away from someone or something. □ *I must ask you to remain away from my daughter.* □ *I cannot remain away any longer. I must be with her.*

remain behind to stay at a place even when others have left. □ *Can't I go too? Do I have to remain behind?* □ *I will remain behind for a day or two.*

remain behind someone or something Go to behind someone or something.

remain clear of something Go to clear of something.

remain down to stay down; to keep down. □ *I asked them to remain down until the shooting stopped.* □ *Please remain down with me so no one will see us.*

remain in limbo Go to in limbo.

remain in (something**) 1.** to stay within something. □ *Please remain in the house today. It is too cold to go out.* □ *You should remain in because the weather is bad.* **2.** to stay in an organization as a member. □ *He remained in the Boy Scouts until he was sixteen.* □ *I will remain in the teacher's union for many years.*

remain in the back of someone's **mind** Go to in the back of someone's mind.

remain in touch (with someone or something**)** Go to keep in touch (with someone or something).

remain on 1. to continue to stay in one place. (The *on* is an adverb, not a preposition.) □ *Everyone else left, but I decided to remain on there.* □ *I remained on for a while during the time they were training my replacement.* **2.** and **remain on** something to continue to be on something; to continue to serve on a body. □ *Will you remain on the board of directors for another year?* □ *I will remain on this committee as long as I am needed.* **3.** to continue to take a particular medicine. □ *How long should I stay on these pills?* □ *I want you to remain on this medication until you run out.*

remain on (one's**) guard (against** someone or something**)** Go to on (one's) guard (against someone or something).

remain on something Go to remain on.

remain together to stay close together; to stay in association. □ *We will have to remain together while we are on this tour. It is very easy to get lost in this town.* □ *The two boys remained together throughout college.*

remain under something to continue to stay beneath the surface of something. □ *Please remain under the umbrella so you don't get wet.* □ *A lot of people decided to leave the shelter, but I remained under it.*

remain up to stay awake and out of bed. □ *I remained up throughout most of the night.* □ *I cannot remain up much longer.*

R

remain within (something) to stay inside something or some place. □ *Please try to remain within the boundaries of the campus.* □ *Everyone else went out, but I decided to remain within.*

remand someone **(in)to the custody of** someone and **remand** someone **over to** someone to order someone placed into the custody of someone. □ *The court remanded the prisoner into the custody of the sheriff.* □ *The judge remanded Mary to the custody of the sheriff.* □ *The judge remanded Gerald over to his father.*

remand someone **over to** someone Go to previous.

remark (up)on someone or something to comment on someone or something. (*Upon* is formal and less commonly used than *on*.) □ *She remarked upon his tardiness and then continued the lesson.* □ *There is no need to remark on me or anything I do or don't do.*

Remember me to someone. Please carry my good wishes to someone. (The *someone* can be a person's name or a pronoun.) □ *Tom: My brother says hello. Bill: Oh, good. Please remember me to him. Tom: I will.* □ *Fred: Bye. John: Good-bye, Fred. Remember me to your Uncle Tom.*

remember someone **as** something to recall someone as being a particular type of person. □ *I remember Terri as a rather cheerful girl, always willing to help out.* □ *William will be remembered as a grouchy person.*

remember someone **in** one's **will** to bequeath something to someone in one's will. □ *My uncle always said he would remember me in his will.* □ *He failed to remember me in his will.*

remember someone **to** someone to carry the greetings of someone to someone else. □ *Please remember all of us to your uncle.* □ *I will remember you to my brother, who asks of you often.*

Remember to write. and **Don't forget to write.**
1. *Lit.* a final parting comment made to remind someone going on a journey to write to those remaining at home. □ *Alice: Bye. Mary: Good-bye, Alice. Remember to write. Alice: I will. Bye.* □ *Sally: Remember to write! Fred: I will!* **2.** *Fig.* a parting comment made to someone in place of a regular good-bye. (Jocular.) □ *John: See you tomorrow. Bye. Jane: See you. Remember to write.* □ *John: Okay. See you after lunch. Jane: Yeah. Bye. Remember to write.*

remind someone **about** someone or something to cause someone to remember someone or something. □ *Will you please remind me about Fred? He's coming to visit next week.* □ *I will remind you about your appointments for today.*

remind someone **of** someone or something to bring a memory of someone or something into someone's mind. □ *You remind me of my brother.* □ *The happy song reminded us of our cabin on the lake.*

reminisce about someone or something to think about one's memories of someone or something; to discuss or share memories of someone or something. □ *They were reminiscing about their old friends.* □ *The old men sat and reminisced about the good old days.*

reminisce with someone to share memories with someone. □ *I love to reminisce with my sister about old times.* □ *Todd was reminiscing with Alice about the good old days.*

reminiscent of someone or something reminding someone about someone or something; seeming like or suggesting someone or something. □ *This fragrance is reminiscent of fresh flowers.* □ *Jane's dress seems reminiscent of the style worn in the 1920s.*

remit something **to** someone or something to send something, especially money, to someone or a group. □ *Please remit your rent to your landlady immediately.* □ *You are requested to remit your loan payment to the bank on time this month.*

remonstrate (with someone**) (about** someone or something**)** to protest to someone about someone or something. □ *After remonstrating with the manager about the price for a while, Vernon left quietly.* □ *I spent an hour remonstrating about Ted with Alice.*

remove someone **from** something to take someone out of an office or position. □ *The county board removed the sheriff from office.* □ *She removed herself from office voluntarily.*

remove someone or something **from** someone or something to take someone or something away from someone or something. □ *The authorities removed the child from his mother.* □ *They removed the dog from the kennel.*

remunerate someone **for** something **1.** to pay someone for something. □ *Of course, I will remunerate you for your time.* □ *She was promptly remunerated for the hours she spent working on the project.* **2.** to repay someone for money spent. □ *I will remunerate you for the cost of the book if you will give me the receipt.* □ *Please remunerate me for the charges as soon as possible.*

rend something **from** someone or something to tear something from someone or something. (The past tense and past participle are *rent*.) □ *Harry rent the burning clothing from the man who had just fled from the burning building.* □ *I will rend these dirty old clothes from my body and shower.*

rend something **into** something to rip or tear something into something. (The past tense and past participle are *rent*.) □ *The tailor rent the garment into shreds in his anger.* □ *The garment was rent into bits and pieces by the machine.*

render something **down**† **1.** *Lit.* to cook the fat out of something. □ *Polly rendered the chicken fat down to a bit of golden grease that she would use in cooking a special dish.* □ *Jane rendered down the fat for use later.* □ *The cook rendered it down.* **2.** *Fig.* to reduce or simplify something to its essentials. □ *Let's render this problem down to the considerations that are important to us.* □ *Can't we render down this matter into its essentials?* □ *Not all of this is important. Let's render it down.*

render something **in(to)** something to translate something into something. □ *Now, see if you can render this passage in French.* □ *Are you able to render this into German?*

render something **to** someone or something and **render** something **up (to** someone or something**)** to give something to someone or a group. □ *You must render your taxes to the government.* □ *I will render my money to the tax collector.* □ *I had to render up all my earnings.*

renege on something to go back on one's promise or commitment. □ *I am mad at you because you reneged on your promise!* □ *I did not renege on what I promised.*

renounce someone **for** something to repudiate someone for doing something. □ *She renounced her brother for his political orientation.* □ *Jane was renounced for her illegal activities.*

rent something **from** someone to pay someone for the use of something. □ *We rented a small car from one of the rental agencies.* □ *They rented a house from a local realtor.*

rent something **(out†) (to** someone) to sell temporary rights for the use of something to someone. □ *I rented the back room out to a nice young student.* □ *We rented the back room to someone.* □ *For how long did you rent it out?* □ *Let's rent out the garage.*

repair to some place to move oneself to some place. □ *I will repair to my room until the crisis is over.* □ *She repaired to a safe place for the duration of the storm.*

repatriate someone **to** some place to restore one to one's country of origin. □ *He asked that they repatriate him to the land of his birth.* □ *She was repatriated to her homeland.*

repay someone **by** something to recompense someone by doing something; to settle a debt with someone by doing something. □ *I will repay you by cutting your lawn free for a year. How's that?* □ *Can I repay you by taking you to dinner?*

repay someone **for** something to remunerate someone for doing something. □ *I refused to repay him for his excessive expenses.* □ *She was repaid for her kindness many times over.*

repay someone **with** something to remunerate someone with something. □ *The farmer's wife repaid the plumbers with fresh eggs and cream.* □ *We were repaid with fresh eggs from the farm.*

repel someone **from** something to push someone back from something; to fight someone off from something. □ *The army repelled the attackers from the entrance to the city.* □ *The attacking army was repelled from the city.*

replace someone or something **by** someone or something and **replace** someone or something **with** someone or something to remove someone or something and add someone or something in place of the first. □ *The manager replaced two workers by a machine.* □ *Walter replaced his old lawn mower with a newer one.*

replenish something **with** something to rebuild the supply of something with more of it. □ *I will replenish the checking account with more money at the end of the month.* □ *Can I replenish your glass with more iced tea?*

reply to someone or something to give a response to someone or something. □ *I replied to her already. There is no reason to do it again.* □ *I will reply to her letter as soon as I can.*

report about someone or something to deliver information about someone or something. □ *Isn't it time to report about Frank and how well he is doing?* □ *I want to report about the accident.*

report back (on someone or something) to return with information or an explanation from someone or something. □ *I need you to report back on Walter by noon.* □ *I'll report back as soon as I can.*

report back (to someone or something) **1.** to go back to someone or something and present oneself. □ *Report back to me at once!* □ *I'll report back immediately.* **2.** to present information or an explanation to someone or some group. □ *Please report back to me when you have the proper information.* □ *I'll report back as soon as I have all the information.*

report for something to present oneself for something. □ *Please report for duty on Monday morning at eight o'clock sharp.* □ *I can't report for my examination at the time we agreed upon.*

report in to present oneself; to make one's presence known. □ *Please report in when you get back in town.* □ *He reported in and his name was taken off the absentee list.*

report in sick to call one's office to say that one will not come to work because one is sick; to show up for work ill. (See also **call in sick.** Normally, one must be present to report in.) □ *I don't feel well today. I will report in sick.* □ *The phone was busy, so I reported in sick by e-mail.*

report something **to** someone to present a body of information to someone. □ *Please report the results to the supervisor.* □ *The event was reported to the proper person.*

report to someone or something **1.** to present oneself to someone or an office. □ *You must report to me for duty at noon.* □ *They told me to report to this office at this time.* **2.** to be supervised by someone or an office. □ *When you start work here, you will report to Mrs. Franklin.* □ *I report directly to the home office.* **3.** to return to someone or an office and make a report. □ *Please report to me when you have the results.* □ *If you have any more to say, please report to headquarters and tell the whole story.*

report (up)on someone or something to present an explanation on someone or something. (*Upon* is formal and less commonly used than *on.*) □ *The detective visited Mrs. Jones to report upon Mr. Jones.* □ *I want to report on the events of the day. Do you have time to listen?*

repose in something **1.** to lie stretched out in something, such as a bed. □ *I think I would like to repose in my own bed for an hour or two before I begin my journey.* □ *Tom reposed in a comfortable chair for the rest of the evening.* **2.** to lie stretched out in a particular state, such as death or slumber. □ *She lay on the cot, reposed in slumber, waiting for Prince Charming to arrive.* □ *The ruler reposed in death on public view for two days.* **3.** [for something] to exist in something or be part of the essence of something. □ *Much of our cultural heritage reposes in our literature.* □ *Considerable important thinking reposes in folktales and myths.*

repose (up)on something to lie on something. (*Upon* is formal and less commonly used than *on.*) □ *I will repose upon these cushions until my bathwater has been drawn.* □ *Dawn reposed on the sofa for over an hour.*

represent someone **in** something to act as one's advocate or agent in business or legal proceedings. □ *My lawyer represented me in court.* □ *His attorney will represent him in all his dealings with the publishing company.*

represent someone or something **as** something to depict or portray someone or something as something; to think of someone or something as something. □ *I don't think you* *should represent me as so perfect. After all, I'm human.* □ *The artist represented my puppy as a playful animal.*

represent something **to** someone **1.** to exemplify something to someone. □ *What does this behavior represent to you?* □ *This represents a lapse in manners to me.* **2.** to explain a matter to someone. □ *He represented the matter to me in a much more charitable light.* □ *I did not represent it properly to you.*

reprimand someone **for** something to scold someone for something; to admonish someone for something. □ *There is no need to reprimand me for a simple accident!* □ *Mary was reprimanded for being late.*

reproach someone **for** something to rebuke or censure someone for something. □ *She reproached Jerry for gambling away all their money.* □ *She reproached herself mercilessly for her failure.*

reproach someone **with** something to rebuke someone with reference to something. □ *I wish you wouldn't continue to reproach me with things that happened long ago.* □ *She was reproached with something out of the past.*

reproduce something **from** something to make a copy of something from something else. □ *I think we can reproduce the picture from the copy that you have there. We don't need the negative.* □ *Can you reproduce a good copy from this old print?*

reprove someone **for** something to criticize or censure someone for something. □ *The boss reproved all the employees for their use of the telephones for personal calls.* □ *We were all reproved for being late too often.*

repulse someone or something **from** something to resist or repel someone or something from something. □ *The royal guard repulsed the rebels from the palace grounds.* □ *Only the use of guns could repulse the starving wolves from the area around the cabin.*

a **reputation (as a something) a state of having a particular kind of reputation for being something. (Can be a good or a bad reputation. *Typically: **get ~; have ~; give** someone ~.) □ *She once had a reputation as a singer.* □ *Unfortunately, Tom's got a reputation as a cheat.*

a **reputation (for doing something) a state of having a particular kind of reputation for doing something. (Often a bad reputation, as in the examples. *Typically: **get ~; have ~; give** someone ~.) □ *You'll get a reputation for cheating.* □ *I don't want to get a reputation for being late.*

reputed to thought to do, be, or have someone or something. □ *My boss is reputed to have cancer.* □ *My neighbor was reputed to have been a spy during the war.*

request someone **to** do something to ask someone to do something. □ *I am going to request you to turn your radio down.* □ *Mary was requested to arrive a few minutes early.*

request something **from** someone to call for something from someone. □ *I will request an explanation from the employee in question.* □ *A full report was requested from each person present.*

request something **of** someone to call for someone to give or do something. □ *I have to request a favor of you.* □ *Can I request anything more of him?*

require a leap of faith Go to a leap of faith.

require something **from** someone to demand something from someone. □ *The telephone company required a deposit from John and Martha before they would install a telephone.* □ *They required some help from us.*

require something **of** someone to expect or demand someone to give or do something. □ *I require absolute loyalty of my employees.* □ *What is required of me in this job?*

requisition something **for** someone or something to present an order or formal request for something for someone or some purpose. □ *I will have to requisition a desk for you. You can't work an eight-hour day at a table.* □ *We will requisition catering for the office party.*

requisition something **from** someone or something to send an order or formal request to someone or something for something. □ *The general requisitioned food and bedding from the supply depot.* □ *We requisitioned a new bookcase from central supply.*

rescue someone or something **from** someone or something to save or liberate someone or something from someone or something. □ *I hoped that someone would come and rescue me from this boring person.* □ *Nothing can rescue us from the ravages of time.*

research into someone or something to study about someone or something thoroughly. □ *I decided that I would research into Queen Elizabeth.* □ *We researched into the period in which she lived.*

resemble someone or something **in** something to look or seem like someone or something. □ *You resemble my Uncle Herman in the way you walk.* □ *This resembles vanilla ice cream in flavor, but not in consistency.*

reserve something **for** someone or something to save or set aside something for someone or something. □ *I am reserving this seat for Claire.* □ *We are reserving some of the cake for tomorrow.*

reside in some place to dwell in some place. □ *I reside in a small apartment in the center of town.* □ *The Wilsons resided in a large house on a hill.*

reside in someone or something to be a property or characteristic of someone or something. □ *I never knew such anger could reside in such a calm person.* □ *The finest acoustics that can be found in the world reside in this hall.*

resign from something to make a written statement that removes one from an office or position of employment. □ *Andy resigned from the fraternity.* □ *I will not resign from my job. You will have to fire me.*

resign oneself **to** something to accept something reluctantly. □ *I finally resigned myself to going to Mexico even though I didn't want to.* □ *Mary resigned herself to her fate.*

resign under fire Go to under fire.

resonate with someone *Fig.* [for an idea, issue, or concept] to appeal to someone or cause someone to relate to it. □ *The concept of wearing worn-looking clothing seems to resonate with young people.* □ *Your notion just doesn't resonate with the public in general.*

resort to something to turn to something that is not the first choice. □ *I hope they don't resort to a lawsuit to accomplish their goals.* □ *She will resort to anything to get her way.*

resound through(out) something to roar, noisily, through a space or an enclosed area. □ *An explosion*

R

resounded through the busy train station. □ An explosion resounded throughout the busy train station.

resound with something [for something, such as the air or a place] to be filled with sound or sounds. □ The hall resounded with the sounds of the orchestra. □ The house resounded with the laughter of children.

respect someone **as** something to admire someone as something. □ I respect you as a friend and supervisor. □ We respected them all as colleagues and coworkers.

respect someone **for** something to admire someone for something. □ I really respect George for his courage. □ Mary respected the company for its fine products.

respond to someone or something **1.** to answer someone or something. □ Would you please respond to me? □ When are you going to respond to my letter? **2.** to react to someone or something. □ You have heard his presentation. How would you respond to him? □ I need you to respond to the points in the report by the end of the day. □ The police responded right away to the riot call.

the **responsible party** the person or organization responsible or liable for something. □ I intend to find the responsible party and get some answers to my questions. □ Mary sued the responsible party in the car crash.

rest against someone or something to lean against someone or something; to take a rest period positioned against someone or something. □ The child rested against his father until it was time to board the train. □ A fishing pole rested against the side of the garage, ready to go to work.

rest assured to be assured; to be certain. □ Rest assured that you'll receive the best of care. □ Please rest assured that we will do everything possible to help.

rest from something to take it easy and recover from something. □ I need to take a few minutes and rest from all that exertion. □ When you have rested from your running, please come in here and help me.

rest in peace to lie dead peacefully for eternity. (A solemn entreaty used in funeral prayers, eulogies, etc.) □ We prayed that the deceased would rest in peace. □ The bodies of the soldiers will rest in peace.

rest in something **1.** to be comfortable in something, such as a chair or a bed. □ I rested in the chair for a while and then got up and made supper. □ I will rest in bed until I feel better. **2.** to be at ease in a particular condition or status, such as comfort or comfortable surroundings. □ I hope that you can rest in comfort for the rest of the night. □ We rested in the plush surroundings and then went back out into the hot sun to work. **3.** [for something] to have its source in something. □ The source of her magnetism rests in the way she uses her eyes. □ His skill rests in his thorough training.

The **rest is gravy.** Fig. Any additional money received is just an easily acquired bonus. □ There is some cost involved in buying the raw materials, and the cost of manufacturing is negligible. When we pay off the costs, the rest is gravy.

The **rest is history.** Fig. Everyone knows the rest of the story that I am referring to. □ Bill: Then they arrested all the officers of the corporation, and the rest is history. □ Bob: Hey, what happened between you and Sue? Bill: Finally we realized that we could never get along, and the rest is history.

rest on one's **laurels** Fig. to stop trying because one is satisfied with one's past achievements. □ Despite our success, this is no time to rest on our laurels. □ We rested on our laurels too long. Our competitors took away a lot of our business.

rest something **against** something to lean or position something against something, allowing it to bear part of the weight of the thing being rested. □ Rest the heavy end of the box against the wall and we'll slide it down the stairs. □ Please rest the board against something solid while you paint it.

rest something **in** someone or something to place or vest something in someone or something. □ The board of directors saw fit to rest the power to hire and fire in the office of the vice president. □ The president rested the power to hire and fire in the hands of his son, who promptly fired all the top managers.

rest up (for something) to take it easy in advance of something tiring. □ Excuse me, but I have to go rest up for the concert tonight. □ I really need to rest up a while.

rest up (from something) to recover or recuperate from something tiring. □ I need about a week to rest up from my long travels. □ I'll need a few days to rest up.

rest (up)on something to lie on something; to take it easy on something. (Upon is formal and less commonly used than on.) □ Here, rest upon this mat. □ I'll just rest on this chair, thanks.

rest with someone or something to remain with someone or something; to be vested with someone or something. □ The final decision rests with you. □ The power rests with the board of directors.

restore someone's **trust in** something and **restore** someone's **belief in** something; **restore** someone's **faith in** something to reinstate someone's belief, faith, trust, etc., in something. □ I knew that a good performance on the test would restore my parents' belief in me. □ Her faith was restored in the government.

restore something **to** someone to give something back to someone; to cause something to be returned to someone. □ I will restore the man's wallet to him after we lock the thief up. □ His wallet was restored to him by a police officer.

restore something **to** something to bring something to its original state. □ The state restored the park to its original condition. □ The government forced the mining company to restore the area to its original state.

restrain someone **from** something to prevent someone from doing something. □ I had to restrain her from hurting herself. □ I was unable to restrain myself from giggling at the wisecrack.

restrict someone or something **to** someone or something to limit someone or something to someone or something; to confine someone or something to someone or something. (The first something may typically refer to a choice or selection.) □ When choosing team members, we are restricting them to people they already know. □ We restricted the choices to Bill, Bob, or Ted.

result from something to emerge from something; to be the outcome of something. □ It will be interesting to see

R

what results from your efforts. □ *Nothing resulted from all that work.*

result in something to achieve something; to bring about something; to cause something to happen. □ *I hope that this will result in the police finding your car.* □ *All my effort resulted in nothing at all.*

resurrect someone or something **from** something to restore someone or something from some state to its formal state. □ *We decided to resurrect Toby from the ranks of the retired.* □ *I resurrected my old uniform from its tattered and wrinkled state.*

retail at something to sell at a retail price of something. □ *This model normally retails at a much higher price.* □ *What does a product like this usually retail at?*

retail for something to sell for a retail price of an amount of money. □ *This item retails for less than ten dollars.* □ *How much does this retail for?*

retail something **to** someone to sell something to someone at a retail price. □ *I can retail this merchandise at ninety percent of the price of my competitor.* □ *We are not allowed to retail this to anyone in the state of Maine.*

retain something **over** someone or something to keep or maintain something, such as power or control, over someone or something. □ *Tony found a way to retain control over Fred.* □ *I wish to retain veto power over the committee.*

retaliate against someone or something to take revenge against someone or something. □ *The striking workers will retaliate against the company with a protest march.* □ *The students retaliated against the administration.*

retire from something to withdraw from something. (Usually to terminate a working career permanently.) □ *I retired from the company early.* □ *When do you intend to retire from your job?*

retire (in)to something to quit working and move into something or some place. □ *Sam and Ella retired into a Florida condo.* □ *Joe did not want to retire to Florida.*

retire on something to quit working and live on something or a particular amount of money. □ *I already have enough money to retire on.* □ *I cannot retire on a sum like that!*

retire someone or something **from** something to take someone or something out of service permanently. □ *The company retired the vice president from the job and gave it to someone else.* □ *It is time to retire my automobile from service.*

retire to some place to quit working permanently and move to a particular location. □ *When I quit working, I want to retire to Florida.* □ *We will retire to our place in the country.*

retool for something **1.** *Lit.* to set up with new or altered tools for a different kind of production. □ *The factory was closed down so they could retool for next year's model.* □ *How soon can we retool for this new line of products?* **2.** *Fig.* to prepare oneself for a different kind of work. □ *He decided to retool for a new job in the computer industry.* □ *I am too old to retool for a job like this.*

retool something **for** something to set up a factory with new or altered tools for a different kind of production. □ *The*

manager decided to retool the factory for greater efficiency. □ *We will retool the plant for next year's models.*

retreat (from something) **(to** some place) to withdraw from something to some place. □ *The army retreated from the battlefield to the safety of the forest.* □ *They retreated to the other side of the river.*

retrieve someone or something **from** some place to recover and bring back someone or something from some place. □ *The mother hurried to the school and retrieved her child from the classroom.* □ *I retrieved my cat from the well into which she had fallen.*

retrieve something **from** someone to get something back from someone. □ *I hope I can retrieve my book from the person who borrowed it.* □ *We were not able to retrieve the lawn mower from Fred before he moved away and took it with him.*

return from some place to come back from some place. □ *I just returned from a research trip in the Amazon basin.* □ *When will they return from their vacation?*

return someone or something **to** someone to give someone or something back to someone. □ *Please return my tools to me.* □ *Would you return my book to me soon?*

return someone's **compliment** Go to return the compliment.

return something **for** something to give or pay back something for something. □ *The clerk returned the correct change for a twenty-dollar bill.* □ *I hope that the product returns good value for my money.*

return the compliment and **return** someone's **compliment** to pay a compliment to someone who has paid you a compliment. □ *Mary told me that my hair looked nice, so I returned her compliment and told her that her hair was lovely.* □ *When someone says something nice, it is polite to return the compliment.*

return the favor to do a good deed for someone who has done a good deed for you. □ *You helped me last week, so I'll return the favor and help you this week.* □ *There is no point in helping Bill. He'll never return the favor.*

return to haunt one Go to come back to haunt one.

return to some place to go or come back to some place. □ *When do you plan to return to your home?* □ *I will return there when I have finished here.*

return with something to come back with something. □ *He went to town and returned with the doctor just in time.* □ *She returned with the material they had requested.*

reunite someone or something **with** someone or something to bring someone or something together with someone or something. □ *Mary was pleased to reunite Sally with her sister.* □ *I reunited the lost cat with its owner.*

rev something **up**† to make an idling engine run very fast, in short bursts of power. □ *Hey! Stop revving it up!* □ *I wish that Tom wouldn't sit out in front of our house in his car and rev up his engine.*

rev up to increase in amount or activity. □ *Production revved up after the strike.* □ *We're hoping business will rev up soon.*

reveal someone or something **to** someone to show or disclose someone or something to someone. □ *The magician* opened the door of the cabinet and revealed his assistant to the audience. □ *I revealed my secret to no one.* □ *She stepped out from behind the tree and revealed herself to the hostess.*

revel in something to rejoice or celebrate about something. □ *All the children reveled in the fresh, warm, spring air.* □ *Tony reveled in his success.*

Revenge is a dish best served cold. *Prov.* It is very satisfying to get revenge a long time after the event for which you want revenge. □ *I don't mind waiting to get revenge on Greg; I'll wait ten years if I have to. Revenge is a dish best served cold.*

Revenge is sweet. *Prov.* It is very pleasurable to revenge yourself on someone. □ *Jill: Remember when Tom left me for another woman? Well, she just left him, and he asked me out on a date. I told him I had better things to do. Jane: Revenge is sweet, huh?*

revenge oneself **(up)on** someone or something to retaliate against someone or something. (*Upon* is formal and less commonly used than *on*.) □ *There is no need for you to revenge yourself upon Walter. It was an accident.* □ *She did not know how she would revenge herself on Joe, but she knew she would.*

reverberate through something [for sound] to roll through or pass through a space. □ *The thunder reverberated through the valley.* □ *The sound of the organ reverberated through the church.*

reverberate throughout something [for sound] to roll about and fill a space. □ *The thunder reverberated throughout the valley.* □ *The noise of chairs scraping the floor reverberated throughout the room.*

reverberate with something to echo or resound with something. □ *The hall reverberated with the rich basso voice of Walter Rogers.* □ *The church reverberated with the roar of the pipe organ.*

revere someone or something **for** something to admire or venerate someone or something for something. □ *I will always revere my dear aunt for her devotion to all of us.* □ *We have always revered his lovely gift for our little kindness.*

revert to someone or something **1.** to return to some type of person or a former state. □ *After he was out of prison, he reverted to a life of crime.* □ *She quickly reverted to her childhood dialect after a few weeks at home.* **2.** to become the property of someone, a group, or an institution. □ *At the end of ten years, this house and the land it sits on reverts to the youngest living child.* □ *Then the property reverts to the state.*

review for something to study material again for something, such as an examination. □ *I need some time to review for the examination.* □ *Have you had enough time to review for your speech?*

revolt against someone or something to rebel or rise against someone or something. □ *The citizens were gathering arms, preparing to revolt against the government.*

revolted at someone or something sickened by someone or something. □ *I was revolted at Frank and his behavior.* □ *We were all revolted at the scene of the bloody highway accident.*

revolve around someone or something and **revolve about** someone or something **1.** *Lit.* to spin or move around someone or something. □ *Do you think that the whole world revolves around you?* □ *The moon revolves about the earth.* **2.** *Fig.* [for people or things] to center upon someone or something or to be primarily concerned with someone or something. □ *The way all of this is going to turn out revolves around Bob.* □ *The success of the picnic revolves around the weather.*

reward someone **for** something to give someone a prize or a bonus for doing something. □ *I would like to reward you for your honesty.* □ *She wanted to reward herself for her hard work, so she treated herself to a massage.*

reward someone **with** something to honor someone with a gift of something. □ *She rewarded the helpful child with a chocolate chip cookie.* □ *He rewarded himself with a night on the town.*

rhapsodize over someone or something to go on and on about the virtues of someone or something. □ *Young Thomas likes to rhapsodize over Francine, his girlfriend.* □ *Please do not rhapsodize over this poem anymore.*

rhyme something **with** something [for someone] to make one word rhyme with another word. □ *I need to rhyme* tree *with some other word. Any suggestions?* □ *Can I rhyme* good *with* food?

rhyme with something [for a word] to rhyme with another word. □ *You can't use* house *in that line of the poem, because it doesn't rhyme with* mice. □ *The last word in your poem doesn't rhyme with any other word in the poem!*

rich in something having valuable resources, characteristics, traditions, or history. □ *The entire region is rich in historical churches.* □ *Our soil is rich in important nutrients.*

A **rich man's joke is always funny.** *Prov.* Everyone wants to curry favor with rich people and so will always laugh at their jokes. (From a poem by Thomas Edward Brown.) □ *We all thought that Mr. Lisle was a narrow-minded, unpleasant old man, but we were careful to act otherwise, because he was wealthy. A rich man's joke is always funny.*

rich with something having a lot of something; abundant in something. □ *The beautiful book was rich with color illustrations.* □ *The old town was rich with elegant Victorian houses.*

ricochet off something [for some rapidly moving object, such as a bullet] to bounce off something at an angle. □ *The bullet ricocheted off the wall and struck the gunman.* □ *Bullets were ricocheting off the walls from all angles.*

__*rid of__ someone or something free of someone or something. (*Typically: **be** ~; **get** ~.) □ *I'm trying to get rid of Mr. Smith. He's bothering me.* □ *I'll be happy when I get rid of my old car.*

rid oneself or something **of** someone or something to free oneself or something of someone or something; to deliver oneself or something from someone or something. □ *The boys were not clever enough to rid themselves of Tom's little sister.* □ *Will we ever be able to rid this house of spiders?*

riddle someone or something **with** something to fill someone or something with small holes, such as bullet holes. □ *Max pulled the trigger of the machine gun and riddled*

R

Lefty with holes. □ *The police riddled the wall with holes trying to shoot the escaped convict in the house.*

ride away to depart, riding a bike or a horse or similar animal. □ *She got on her horse and rode away.* □ *They rode away without even saying good-bye.*

ride by someone or something to pass by someone or something, riding. (As on a horse or bicycle, or as a passenger in a car.) □ *She rode by me without saying anything.* □ *I rode by the store and forget to stop and go in.*

ride herd on someone or something *Fig.* to supervise someone or something. (Alludes to a cowboy supervising cattle.) □ *I'm tired of having to ride herd on my kids all the time.* □ *My job is to ride herd on this project and make sure everything is done right.*

ride off to depart, riding something such as a horse or a bicycle. □ *Betty said good-bye and rode off.* □ *We rode off, each one in a different direction.*

ride off in all directions 1. *Fig.* [for people] to scatter, riding something, such as a horse or a bicycle. (See also **run off in all directions.**) □ *The boys hopped on their bikes and rode off in all directions.* □ *The sheriff got the posse together and they rode off in all directions, looking for the bank robber.* **2.** *Fig.* to behave in a totally confused manner; to try to do everything at once. □ *Bill has a tendency to ride off in all directions. He's not organized enough.* □ *Now, calm down. There is no sense in riding off in all directions.*

ride on to continue to ride, traveling onward. □ *We rode on for at least an hour before finding a rest stop.* □ *They rode on for a while.*

ride on someone's **coattails** and **hang on** someone's **coattails** *Fig.* to make one's good fortune or success on the strength of someone else's. (Also with *else*, as in the examples.) □ *Bill isn't very creative, so he rides on John's coattails.* □ *Some people just have to hang on somebody else's coattails.*

ride on something **1.** *Lit.* to travel on something. □ *Do you like to ride on the train?* □ *I have never ridden on a horse.* **2.** *Fig.* to be borne on something and carried along. (On something other than a means of transportation.) □ *She rode on a wave of popularity to reelection.* □ *He rode on his past laurels as long as he could.*

ride out (of some place**)** to travel out of a place on something such as a horse or bicycle. □ *All the racers rode out of the starting area and began the bicycle marathon.* □ *At the sound of the starting gun, all the contestants rode out.*

ride over someone or something to pass over someone or something, riding something such as a horse or a bicycle. □ *Bobby fell down and Susan rode over him with her bicycle, but he wasn't hurt at all.* □ *Tom almost rode over my toe!*

ride roughshod over someone or something and **run roughshod over** someone or something *Fig.* to treat someone or something with disdain or scorn. □ *Tom seems to ride roughshod over his friends.* □ *You shouldn't have come into our town to ride roughshod over our laws and our traditions.*

ride someone **about** something to continue to bother someone about something. □ *Stop riding me about my weight!*

This is how I'm supposed to be! □ *It's not fair to ride someone about being bald.*

ride someone or an animal **down**[†] to chase down someone or an animal while riding on horseback. □ *The mounted policeman rode the mugger down and captured him.* □ *The rider rode down the thief.* □ *We had to ride down the runaway horse.*

ride something **down** to ride on something that is going down, such as an elevator. □ *You take the stairs, and I will ride the elevator down.* □ *I don't want to ride the cable car down. I will walk.*

ride something **out**[†] to endure something unpleasant. (Originally referred to ships lasting out a storm.) □ *It was a nasty situation, but the mayor tried to ride it out.* □ *The mayor decided to ride out the scandal.*

ride the gravy train *Fig.* to live in ease or luxury. □ *If I had a million dollars, I sure could ride the gravy train.* □ *I wouldn't like loafing if I were rich. I don't want to ride the gravy train.*

ride to some place to travel to a place, riding something such as a horse or a bicycle, or a vehicle one does not drive. □ *I will ride to town and get the doctor.* □ *Tom will ride to the store on his bike to get a loaf of bread.*

ride up (on someone**) 1.** *Lit.* [for someone on a horse] to approach someone, riding. □ *I rode up on him and frightened him.* □ *I guess I was in the house when you rode up.* **2.** *Fig.* [for clothing, especially underpants] to keep moving higher on one's body. □ *I don't like it when my pants ride up on me.* □ *I hate it when my underpants ride up.*

ride (up)on someone or something to use someone or something as a beast of burden. (*Upon* is formal and less commonly used than *on*.) □ *As a game, the children used to ride on their father.* □ *We rode upon burros along the narrow mountain trails.*

ride with someone to travel with someone on or in a vehicle or a beast of burden. □ *I'm going to the store for some milk. Do you want to ride with me?* □ *Can I ride with you to the store?*

riding for a fall *Fig.* risking failure or an accident, usually due to overconfidence. □ *Tom drives too fast, and he seems too sure of himself. He's riding for a fall.* □ *Bill needs to eat better and get more sleep. He's riding for a fall.*

rifle through something to ransack something; to search quickly or roughly through something looking for something. □ *The teenager quickly rifled through the cabinets, looking for something worth eating.* □ *The soldiers rifled through every house they could break into.*

rig someone or something **out**[†] **(in** something**)** to outfit someone or something in something; to decorate or dress someone or something in something. (Alludes to the rigging of a sailing ship.) □ *Joan rigged her daughter out in a witch's costume for the Halloween party.* □ *He rigged out his car with lights for the parade.*

rig something **up**[†] to prepare something, perhaps on short notice or without the proper materials. □ *We don't have what's needed to make the kind of circuit you have described, but I think we can rig something up anyway.* □ *We will rig up whatever you need.*

R

right and left and **left and right** to both sides; on all sides; everywhere. □ *I dropped the tennis balls, and they rolled right and left.* □ *There were children everywhere—running right and left.*

*right as rain *Cliché* perfectly fine; all right. (Based on the alliteration with *r*. *Also: **as** ~.) □ *Lily has sprained her ankle, but after a few weeks of rest she should be as right as rain.* □ *All we need to do is tidy the house up; then it will be right as rain.*

right at a certain time exactly or precisely at a specific place or time. □ *Meet me at this corner right at 3:00 P.M.* □ *The restaurant is right at First and Main Streets.*

right away and **right now** immediately. □ *John: Take this over to Sue. Bill: Right away.* □ *John: How soon can you do this? Sue: Right away.*

right down someone's **alley** and **right up** someone's **alley** *Fig.* ideally suited to one's interests or abilities. □ *Skiing is right down my alley. I love it.* □ *This kind of thing is right up John's alley.*

right in the kisser *Inf.* right in the mouth or face. □ *Wilbur poked the cop right in the kisser.* □ *He caught a punch right in the kisser.*

right now Go to right away.

right off the bat and **straight off the bat** *Fig.* immediately; first thing. □ *When he was learning to ride a bicycle, he fell on his head right off the bat.* □ *The new manager demanded new office furniture right off the bat.*

(right) off the top of one's **head** *Fig.* without giving it too much thought or without precise knowledge. □ *Mary: How much do you think this car would be worth on a trade? Fred: Well, right off the top of my head, I'd say about a thousand.* □ *Tom: What time does the morning train come in? Bill: Off the top of my head, I don't know.*

Right on! *Sl.* Exactly!; That is exactly right! □ *After the speaker finished, many people in the audience shouted, "Right on!"* □ *One member of the crowd called out, "Right on!"*

right on someone's **heels** Go to on someone's heels.

right on time at the correct time; no later than the specified time. □ *Bill always shows up right on time.* □ *If you get there right on time, you'll get one of the free tickets.*

right side up with the correct (top) side upwards, as with a box or some other container. □ *Keep this box right side up, or the contents will be crushed.* □ *Please set your coffee cup right side up so I can fill it.*

the **right stuff** the right or correct character or set of skills to do something well. □ *She's got the right stuff to be a winner.*

*a right to do something and ***the right to** do something the freedom to do something; the legal or moral permission or license to do something. (*Typically: **get** ~; **have** ~; **give** someone ~.) □ *You don't have the right to enter my home without my permission.* □ *I have a right to grow anything I want on my farmland.*

*a right to something and ***the right to** something a privilege or license to have something. (*Typically: **get** ~; **have** ~; **give** someone ~.) □ *I have the right to have the kind of house I want.* □ *You have a right to any house you can afford.*

(right) under someone's **(very) nose 1.** *Fig.* right in front of someone. □ *I thought I'd lost my purse, but it was sitting on the table under my very nose.* □ *How did Mary fail to see the book? It was right under her nose.* **2.** *Fig.* in someone's presence. □ *The thief stole Jim's wallet right under his nose.* □ *The jewels were stolen from under the very noses of the security guards.*

right up someone's **alley** Go to right down someone's alley.

*the right-of-way the legal right to occupy a particular space on a public roadway. (*Typically: **get** ~; **have** ~; **give** someone ~; **yield** ~.) □ *I had a traffic accident yesterday, but it wasn't my fault. I had the right-of-way.* □ *Don't pull out onto a highway if you haven't yielded the right-of-way.*

rile someone **up**† to get someone excited and angry. □ *He yelled at them and riled them up. They left quite angry.* □ *He riles up everyone he talks to.*

ring a bell *Fig.* [for something] to cause someone to remember something or for it to seem familiar. □ *I've never met John Franklin, but his name rings a bell.* □ *Whenever I see a bee, it rings a bell. I remember when I was stung by one.*

ring around something to circle something. □ *The children ringed around the maypole, dancing and singing.* □ *The mourners had ringed around the coffin for the final ceremony.*

ring back to call back on the telephone. □ *No, there's no message. I'll ring back later.* □ *She's not here now. I suggest you ring back after dinner.*

ring in someone's **ears** and **ring in** someone's **mind** *Fig.* [for words or a sound] to linger in one's consciousness. □ *Her words rang in my ears for days.* □ *The sound of the choir rang in their minds long after they had finished their anthem.*

ring in someone's **mind** Go to previous.

ring in the new year *Fig.* to celebrate the beginning of the new year at midnight on December 31. □ *We are planning a big party to ring in the new year.* □ *How did you ring in the new year?*

ring off the hook *Fig.* [for a telephone] to ring incessantly and repeatedly. □ *What a busy day! The telephone has been ringing off the hook all day long.* □ *The telephone has been ringing off the hook ever since the ad appeared in the paper.*

ring out [for a loud sound] to go out. □ *The bells rang out at the end of the wedding ceremony.* □ *Loud cheers rang out at the end of the game.* □ *A shot rang out and started all the dogs barking.*

ring out the old *Fig.* to celebrate the end of a year while celebrating the beginning of a new one. (See also ring in the new year.) □ *I don't plan to ring out the old this year. I'm just going to go to bed.* □ *We never ring out the old because it's too dismal.*

ring someone **back**† to call someone back on the telephone. □ *I will have to ring back the store at a later time.* □ *Please ring me back when you have a moment.*

ring someone **up**† to call someone on the telephone. □ *I will ring her up when I get a chance.* □ *I have to ring up a whole list of people.*

R

ring something **up**[†] to record the cost of an item on a cash register. □ *Please ring this chewing gum up first, and I'll put it in my purse.* □ *The cashier rang up each item and told me how much money I owed.*

ring the bell *Inf.* to be just what is needed; to **hit the spot.** □ *This cold water really rings the bell.* □ *A good hot bowl of soup would ring the bell about now.*

ring the curtain down[†] **(on** something) and **bring the curtain down**[†] **(on** something) **1.** *Fig.* to lower a theater curtain, usually at the end of an act or a play. (More literal than ②.) □ *After one hundred performances, it's time to ring the curtain down on our show for the last time.* □ *As we bring down the curtain on another successful performance, let's be thankful nothing serious went wrong.* **2.** *Fig.* to bring something to an end; to declare something to be at an end. □ *It's time to ring the curtain down on our relationship. We have nothing in common anymore.* □ *We've tried our best to make this company a success, but it's time to ring down the curtain.*

ring the curtain up[†] **1.** *Fig.* to raise the curtain in a theater. (Alludes to sending the signal to raise the curtain.) □ *The stagehand rang the curtain up precisely on time.* □ *Let's ring up the curtain. It's time to start the show.* **2.** *Fig.* to start a series of activities or events. □ *I am set to ring up the curtain on a new lifestyle.* □ *It's a little late to ring up the curtain for a new career.*

ring true *Fig.* to sound or seem true or likely. (From testing the quality of metal or glass by striking it and evaluating the sound made.) □ *The student's excuse for being late doesn't ring true.* □ *Do you think that Mary's explanation for her absence rang true?*

ring with something **1.** *Lit.* to resound with something. □ *The morning air rang with the sound of church bells.* □ *The canyon rang with the sound of gunfire.* **2.** [for a bell] to ring in some characteristic way. □ *The bells seemed to ring with unusual clarity on this fine Sunday morning.* □ *The doorbell rang with an urgency that could not be ignored.*

rinse someone or something **down**[†] to wash or clean someone or something with water or other fluid. □ *I rinsed him down for an hour and still didn't get the smell of skunk off him.* □ *I had to rinse down the driveway.*

rinse someone or something **off**[†] to wash or clean someone or something by flushing with water or other fluid. □ *Mother rinsed the baby off and dried him with a soft towel.* □ *She rinsed off the baby.*

rinse someone's **mouth out**[†] **(with soap)** and **wash** someone's **mouth out**[†] **(with soap)** *Fig.* to punish one by washing one's mouth out with soap, especially for using foul language. (Usually a jocular threat.) □ *If you say that again, I'll rinse your mouth out with soap.* □ *I will wash out your mouth if you swear.*

rinse something **down**[†] **(with** something**)** to wash something down one's throat with a liquid; to follow something that one has eaten with a drink to aid its going down. □ *Alice rinsed the cheeseburger down with a milkshake.* □ *She rinsed down the sandwich with a drink.*

rinse something **out**[†] **1.** to clean cloth or clothing partially by immersing it in water and squeezing it out. □ *Can you please rinse this rag out? It's all dirty.* □ *Please rinse out your clothes to make sure there is no soap left in them.* **2.** to laun-

der something delicate, such as feminine underwear, using a mild soap. □ *I have to go rinse a few things out.* □ *After I rinse out some things, I will be right with you.* **3.** to clean the inside of a container partially by flushing it out with water. □ *Rinse the bottle out and throw it away.* □ *Rinse out the bottle and throw it away.*

rinse something **out of** something to remove something from something by flushing it with water. □ *See if you can rinse the dirt out of this jacket.* □ *I can't rinse out the dirt.*

rinse something **with** something to flush something with some fluid. □ *You should rinse your clothes in milk or tomato juice to remove the smell of the skunk.* □ *Please rinse the stain with cold water.*

a **riot of color** *Cliché* a selection of many bright colors. □ *The landscape was a riot of color each autumn.*

rip into someone or something **1.** *Lit.* to attack someone or something by ripping. □ *The raccoons ripped into the trash bags, scattering papers and stuff all over the street.* □ *The horrid murderer ripped into the helpless victim.* **2.** *Fig.* to criticize or censure someone or something severely. □ *The drama critic ripped into Larry.* □ *The critics really ripped into Larry's poor performance.*

rip off [for something] to tear or peel off. □ *My pocket ripped off, and my money is gone now!* □ *A piece of the bumper ripped off my car.*

rip on someone *Sl.* to give someone a hard time; to hassle someone. □ *Stop ripping on me! What did I do to you?* □ *Tim is ripping on Mary and she is getting really mad.*

ripsnorter *Rur.* a remarkable person or thing; a hilarious joke. □ *Old Fred is a real ripsnorter.* □ *Her new car is a ripsnorter, I tell you.* □ *Let me tell you a ripsnorter about a farmer and his cow.*

rip someone **off**[†] *Inf.* to steal [something] from someone; to cheat someone. □ *That merchant ripped me off!* □ *She rips off everyone.*

rip someone or something **apart**[†] to tear someone or something apart into pieces. □ *The automobile accident ripped the car apart.* □ *Don't rip apart the newspaper!*

rip someone or something **to** something **1.** *Lit.* to tear someone or something into small pieces, expressed as bits, pieces, shreds, etc. □ *If you fall into that lawn mower, it will rip you to pieces.* □ *The lawn mower ripped the newspaper to tiny bits.* **2.** *Fig.* to criticize someone or something mercilessly. □ *The critics ripped Gerald to pieces even though the audience just loved his show.* □ *They ripped the whole production to pieces.*

rip someone or something **up**[†] to tear someone or something into bits; to mutilate someone or something. □ *Careful! That machine will rip you up if you fall in.* □ *I ripped up the contract and threw the pieces in the trash.*

rip something **away**[†] **(from** someone**)** to grab or snatch something away from someone. □ *Betty ripped the box away from Frank and walked away with it.* □ *She ripped away the box and opened it.*

rip something **away**[†] **(from** something**)** to tear or strip something away. □ *Billy ripped the wrapping paper away from the box.* □ *He ripped away the paper.*

rip something **down**[†] to tear something down. (Alludes to something that has been posted or mounted.) □ *The cus-*

todian ripped all the posters down at the end of the day. □ *He ripped down the posters.*

rip something **in half** and **rip** something **in two** to tear something into two parts. □ *Did you know that Ed can rip a telephone book in half?* □ *I can rip a newspaper in two.*

rip something **in two** Go to previous.

rip something **off†** *Inf.* to steal something [from someone]. □ *The mugger ripped my purse off of me.* □ *Jane ripped off a lot of money.* □ *Somebody ripped my wallet off.*

rip something **off (of)** someone or something and **rip** something **off†** to tear something away from someone or something. (*Of* is usually retained before pronouns.) □ *I ripped the cover off of the book accidentally.* □ *I ripped off the book cover.*

rip something **out of** someone or something and **rip** something **out†** to tear something out of someone or something. □ *The high priest ripped the beating heart out of the sacrificial victim.* □ *The priest ripped out the victim's heart.*

rip something **up†** to take something up by force and remove it. (Usually refers to something on the floor or ground, such as carpeting or pavement.) □ *They are going to rip all the broken sidewalk up.* □ *The workers ripped up the pavement and loaded the pieces into a truck.*

a **ripe old age** a very old age. □ *Mr. Smith died last night, but he lived to a ripe old age—99.* □ *All the Smiths seem to reach a ripe old age.*

ripen into something **1.** *Lit.* to ripen and become something recognizable. □ *This little green ball will ripen into an apple.* **2.** *Fig.* to mature into something. □ *This problem is going to ripen into a real crisis if we don't do something about it right now.* □ *The small matter ripened into a large problem in a short time.*

(rip-)off artist *Inf.* a con artist. □ *Fred is such an off artist.* □ *Beware of the rip-off artist who runs that shop.*

a **ripple of excitement** a series of quiet but excited murmurs. □ *A ripple of excitement spread through the crowd.* □ *As the president came near, a ripple of excitement indicated that people could really see him.*

a **ripple of protest** quiet remarks protesting something; a small amount of subdued protest. □ *There was only a ripple of protest about the new tax law.* □ *The rude comedian hardly drew a ripple of protest.*

ripple through something **1.** *Lit.* to move through a liquid so as to cause ripples or tiny waves. □ *The canoe rippled through the still water.* □ *A tiny snake rippled through the water of the swamp.* **2.** *Fig.* to move through something or a group of people in a ripple or wave motion. □ *A murmur of excitement rippled through the crowd.* □ *Some giggling rippled through the group of children sitting by the door.*

rise above something **1.** *Lit.* to move up above something. □ *The huge sun rose above the horizon and spread its red glow across the sea.* **2.** *Fig.* [for one] to ignore petty matters and do what one is meant to do in spite of them. □ *He was able to rise above the squabbling and bring some sense to the proceedings.* □ *Jane was never able to rise above her petty dislikes.*

Rise and shine! *Fig.* Get out of bed and be lively and energetic! (Often a command.) □ *Come on, children! Rise and shine! We're going to the beach.* □ *Father always calls "Rise and shine!" in the morning when we want to go on sleeping.*

rise from someone or something to emanate from someone or something in the manner of a cloud of dust or a cheer. □ *After the singer finished, a loud cheer rose from the crowd.* □ *A cloud of smoke rose from the burning barn.*

rise from the ashes *Fig.* [for a structure] to be rebuilt after destruction. □ *The entire west section of the city was destroyed and a group of new buildings rose from the ashes in only a few months.* □ *Will the city rise again from the ashes? No one knows.*

rise from the dead and **rise from the grave** *Fig.* to come back to life after being dead. □ *Albert didn't rise from the dead. He wasn't dead in the first place.* □ *The movie was about a teenager who rose from the grave and haunted his high school friends.*

rise from the grave Go to previous.

rise from the ranks *Fig.* to achieve position or office, having worked up from the masses. □ *He rose from the ranks to become president of the company.* □ *Most of the officers of the company have risen from the ranks.*

rise in something to increase in something. □ *I hope that this land rises in value over the next few years.* □ *Her expensive antique car actually rose in value during the first year.*

rise to one's **feet** to stand up. □ *The entire audience rose to its feet, applauding wildly.* □ *We rose to our feet when the bride came down the aisle.*

rise to the bait *Fig.* to respond to an allurement; to fall for an enticement or fall into a trap. (Alludes to a fish coming up from deep water to seize bait.) □ *You can get him here easily. Tell him that there will be lots of food and he will rise to the bait.* □ *He rose to the bait and did just as he was expected to do.*

rise to the challenge *Fig.* to accept a challenge. (Usually in reference to success with the challenge.) □ *You can depend on Kelly to rise to the challenge.* □ *We were not able to rise to the challenge and we lost the contract.*

rise to the occasion *Fig.* to meet the challenge of an event; to try extra hard to do a task. □ *John was able to rise to the occasion and make the conference a success.* □ *It was a big challenge, but he rose to the occasion.*

rise to the top to move or float to something, such as the top, surface, etc. □ *The cream will rise to the top.* □ *The lighter oil rose to the top and we scooped it up and saved it.*

rise up 1. to come up; to ascend. □ *The water is rising up fast. You had better get to higher ground.* □ *As the water rose up, it covered the fields and streets.* **2.** to get up from lying down. □ *The deer rose up and darted off into the woods.* □ *I rose up and brushed my clothing.*

rise (up) against someone or something to challenge someone or something; to rebel against someone or something. □ *The citizens rose up against their elected officials.* □ *They rose up against the abusive power of the government.*

risk of rain and **risk of showers; risk of thunder-(storms)** a chance of precipitation. (Used only in

R

weather forecasting. There is no "risk" of hazard or injury involved.) □ *And for tomorrow, there is a slight risk of showers in the morning.* □ *There is a 50 percent risk of rain tonight.*

risk of showers Go to previous.

risk of thunder(storms) Go to risk of rain.

risk one's **neck (to** do something) *Fig.* to accept the risk of physical harm in order to accomplish something. □ *Look at that traffic! I refuse to risk my neck just to cross the street to buy a paper.* □ *I refuse to risk my neck at all.*

risk something **on** someone or something to chance losing something on someone or something. □ *I wouldn't risk any money on him. He's a poor credit risk.* □ *Don't risk your life on his being there to help you.*

rival someone **in** something to have a quality or status that is comparable to that of someone else. □ *I would say that Jane rivals Dave in the ability to find the essential elements of a problem and deal with them swiftly.* □ *No one rivals Ted in pitching a baseball.*

rivet one's **gaze on** someone or something and **rivet** one's **glare on** someone or something *Fig.* to fasten one's gaze onto someone or something. (As if it were attached by rivets.) □ *He riveted his gaze on the surly young man.* □ *Walter riveted his hateful glare on the last page of the contract and sneered.*

rivet one's **glare on** someone or something Go to previous.

rivet someone's **attention** *Fig.* to keep someone's attention fixed [on something]. □ *The movie riveted the audience's attention.* □ *Professor Jones's lecture riveted the students' attention.*

rivet something **on(to)** something and **rivet** something **on†** to attach something to something with rivets. □ *The pockets of these jeans are riveted onto the body of the pants.* □ *You should rivet on this part of the frame to the wall.*

riveted to the ground *Fig.* [of someone or someone's feet] unable to move. □ *I was riveted to the ground out of fear.* □ *My feet were riveted to the ground and I could not move an inch.*

road hog *Fig.* someone who drives carelessly and selfishly. □ *Look at that road hog driving in the middle of the road and stopping other drivers from passing him.* □ *That road hog nearly knocked the children over. He was driving too fast.*

The **road to hell is paved with good intentions.** *Prov.* People often mean well but do bad things. (Can be a strong rebuke, implying that the person you are addressing did something bad and his or her good intentions do not matter.) □ *Jane: I'm sorry. I didn't mean to hurt your feelings; I only wanted to help you. Jane: Oh, yeah? The road to hell is paved with good intentions.*

roam about and **roam around** to wander or range about freely. □ *Stay where you are and don't roam about.* □ *I'm too tired to roam around very much.*

roar at someone or something **1.** *Lit.* to bellow or bawl at someone or something. □ *Don't roar at me! Control your temper.* □ *The lion roared at the hyena, who ran off.* **2.** *Fig.* to laugh very hard at someone or something. □ *The audience roared at the clown.* □ *The children roared at Dad's jokes.*

roar away to speed away, making a loud clamor. □ *The car roared away into the night with tires screeching.* □ *The train roared away, carrying Andy to Canada.*

roar something **out†** to bellow something out loudly. □ *Walter roared his protest out so everyone knew how he felt.* □ *Jane roared out her criticism.*

rob Peter to pay Paul *Fig.* to take or borrow from one in order to give or pay something owed to another. □ *Why borrow money to pay your bills? That's just robbing Peter to pay Paul.* □ *There's no point in robbing Peter to pay Paul. You will still be in debt.*

rob someone **blind 1.** *Fig.* to steal freely from someone. □ *Her maid was robbing her blind.* □ *I don't want them to rob me blind. Keep an eye on them.* **2.** *Fig.* to overcharge someone. □ *You are trying to rob me blind. I won't pay it!* □ *Those auto repair shops can rob you blind if you don't watch out.*

rob someone **of** something to deprive someone of something, not necessarily by theft. □ *What you have done has robbed me of my dignity!* □ *If you do that, you will rob yourself of your future.*

rob the cradle *Fig.* to marry or date someone who is much younger than oneself. □ *I hear that Bill is dating Ann. Isn't that sort of robbing the cradle? She's much younger than he is.* □ *Uncle Bill—who is nearly eighty—married a thirty-year-old woman. That is really robbing the cradle.*

rock around to tilt or totter about. □ *The boat rocked around, tossing the passengers to and fro.* □ *The road was bumpy and the huge car rocked around.*

*(rock) bottom the lowest point or level. (*Typically: **be at ~; hit ~; reach ~.**) □ *The value of the goods is at rock bottom right now.* □ *Prices have reached rock bottom.* □ *When my life hit bottom, I gradually began to feel much better.*

rock someone **to** something to help someone, usually an infant, get to sleep by rocking in a rocking chair, cradle, or carriage. □ *It is best to rock the baby to sleep after you feed her.* □ *Somehow she learned to rock herself to sleep.*

rock the boat 1. *Lit.* to do something to move a boat from side to side, causing it to rock. (Often in a negative sense.) □ *Sit down and stop rocking the boat. You'll turn it over!* **2.** *Fig.* to cause trouble where none is welcome; to disturb a situation that is otherwise stable and satisfactory. (Often negative.) □ *Look, Tom, everything is going fine here. Don't rock the boat!* □ *You can depend on Tom to mess things up by rocking the boat.*

rocket (in)to something **1.** *Lit.* [for a projectile] to ascend into the sky or into space; [for something] to shoot rapidly into something. □ *The space shuttle rocketed into space.* □ *The locomotive rocketed into the darkness.* **2.** *Fig.* [for someone] to ascend rapidly into something, such as fame or prominence. □ *Jill rocketed into prominence after her spectacular performance on the guitar.* □ *She will undoubtedly rocket to success.*

rocket something **into** something to send something somewhere—usually into space—by rocket. □ *The government rocketed the satellite into space.* □ *Someone suggested rocketing our waste into space.*

a **rocky road** a difficult period of time. □ *Bob's been going down quite a rocky road since his divorce.*

Roger (wilco). Yes. (From aircraft radio communication. *Wilco* = "will comply.") □ *John: Can you do this right now? Bob: Roger.* □ *Mary: I want you to take this over to the mayor's office. Bill: Roger wilco.*

roll about to move about, turning or rotating, as a wheel or a ball. □ *The ball rolled about awhile and then came to rest.* □ *His eyes rolled about in amazement before he spoke.*

roll along 1. *Lit.* [for wheels or something on wheels] to move along, smoothly and rapidly. □ *The wheels of the cart rolled along, making a grinding noise as they went.* □ *Our car rolled along rapidly toward our destination.* **2.** *Fig.* [for something] to progress smoothly. □ *The project is rolling along nicely.* □ *I hope that your career is rolling along quite well.*

roll around to move about, rotating, turning over, turning, or moving on wheels. □ *The baby rolled around on the floor, giggling and cooing.* □ *The toy truck won't roll around anymore.*

roll away to move away, rotating, turning over, turning, or moving on wheels. □ *The ball rolled away and fell down a storm sewer.* □ *The cart rolled away, and we had to chase it down the hill.*

roll back [for something] to return, rotating or turning or moving on wheels. □ *I rolled the ball away, thinking it would roll back. It didn't.* □ *I struck the golf ball out of the sand trap, but it rolled back.*

roll by 1. *Lit.* to pass by, rotating, as a wheel or a ball; to move past, rolling on wheels. □ *The wheel of a car rolled by, all by itself. It must have come off a car somewhere down the road.* □ *The traffic rolled by relentlessly.* **2.** *Fig.* to move (past), as if rolling. □ *The years rolled by, and soon the two people were old and gray.* □ *The clouds were rolling by, spreading patterns of light and dark across the land.*

roll down to move downward, rotating, as a wheel or a ball, or to move downward on wheels. □ *I pushed the wagon up the driveway, and it rolled down again.* □ *Don't place the cart at the top of the hill. It will roll down.*

roll down something to move downward, along something, rotating, as a wheel or a ball, or moving downward on wheels. □ *The ball rolled down the hall to the end.* □ *The cart went rolling down the hill all by itself.*

roll in *Fig.* to come in large numbers or amounts, easily, as if rolling. (Alludes to the arrival of many wheeled conveyances.) □ *We didn't expect many people at the party, but they just kept rolling in.* □ *Money is simply rolling in for our charity.*

roll in something 1. *Lit.* to rotate about in something. □ *What is that dog rolling in?* □ *We had fun rolling in the leaves.* **2.** *Fig.* to have lots of something, such as money—enough to roll in. □ *She is just rolling in cash.* □ *Mary is rolling in money because she won the lottery.*

roll in(to some place) to arrive at a place; to come into some place. □ *The two cars rolled into the parking lot at about the same time.* □ *What time did they roll in?*

roll off (someone or something) to flow or fall off someone or something. □ *The ball rolled off the shelf and bounced across the room.* □ *The ball rolled off and struck the lampshade.*

roll on 1. *Lit.* [for something] to continue rolling. □ *The ball rolled on and on.* □ *The cart came rolling down the hill and rolled on for a few yards at the bottom.* **2.** *Lit.* [for something] to be applied by rolling. □ *This kind of deodorant just rolls on.* □ *She rolled on too much paint and it dripped from the ceiling.* **3.** *Fig.* [for something, such as time] to move on slowly and evenly, as if rolling. □ *The years rolled on, one by one.* □ *As the hours rolled on, I learned just how bored I could get without going to sleep.*

roll one's sleeves up† **1.** *Lit.* to turn one's sleeves upward, exposing the arms. □ *He rolled his sleeves up and began to wash the dishes.* □ *Don rolled up his sleeves so he would be cooler.* **2.** *Fig.* to prepare to get to work. □ *Let's roll our sleeves up and get this job done!* □ *Jane rolled up her sleeves and got to work.*

roll (oneself) up in something to spin or swivel oneself so as to be contained in a coil of something. □ *Roll yourself up in some cloth and go to the costume party as a mummy.* □ *The caterpillar rolled up in a leaf.*

roll out the red carpet (for someone) 1. *Lit.* to unwind a roll of red carpet for someone important to walk on. □ *The city council decided to roll out the red carpet for the visit of the foreign prince.* **2.** *Fig.* to give someone treatment befitting royalty. □ *The citizens of the small community enjoyed rolling out the red carpet for important visitors.*

roll over to turn over; to rotate one half turn. □ *The old man rolled over and started snoring again.* □ *Please roll over and give me some more space in the bed.*

roll over and play dead *Fig.* to just give up and be unable to cope with life or a problem. □ *Why can't I complain about this? Am I supposed to roll over and play dead?*

roll (over) in one's grave Go to turn (over) in one's grave.

roll over something [for something that rolls] to pass over something. (See also **roll something over**.) □ *The wheelbarrow rolled over the hose, making the water squirt off and on.* □ *After all the traffic had rolled over Timmy's ball, there was very little left to it.*

roll prices back† *Fig.* to reduce prices. □ *The store rolled all its prices back for the sale.* □ *The protesters demanded that the big oil companies roll back their prices.*

roll someone or something over to turn someone or something over. □ *Bobby rolled Billy over and began tickling him ruthlessly in the tummy.* □ *Mary rolled the stone over, hoping to find a snake underneath.*

roll someone or something (up) in something to turn or wrap someone or something so as to contain someone or something in something. □ *Roll this painting up in a sheet of heavy wrapping paper.* □ *They rolled the burning man up in a blanket to put out the flames.*

roll something away† to cause something to move away, rotating, turning over, turning, or moving on wheels. □ *Jane rolled the ball away and it was lost.* □ *Jane rolled away the ball.*

roll something back† to return something to someone by rotating it, as with a wheel or a ball, or moving it back on wheels. □ *I intercepted the ball and rolled it back.* □ *Jane rolled back the ball.*

R

roll something **down†** **1.** to move something down, making it rotate like a wheel or a ball, or moving it on wheels. □ *Don't carry the ball down; roll it down!* □ *I rolled down the ball as you asked.* **2.** to crank down something, such as a car window. □ *Please roll the window down and get some air in this car.* □ *Please roll down the car window.*

roll something **down** something to cause something to move down along something, rotating it like a wheel or a ball. □ *Claire rolled the bowling ball down the alley for a strike.* □ *Roll the barrel down the ramp carefully. It is heavy.*

roll something **in†** to bring something in by rotating it like a wheel or a ball or by moving it on wheels. □ *She put the round table on its edge and rolled it in. Then she went out and got the chairs before the rain started.* □ *The waiters rolled in the table with the wedding cake on it.*

roll something **in** something to turn something over and over in something, as if to coat the thing being rolled. □ *Tony rolled each of the meatballs in flour and popped them into the hot oil.* □ *Roll each of these cookies in powdered sugar.*

roll something **off (of)** someone or something and **roll** something **off†** to cause something to roll away, off someone or something. (*Of* is usually retained before pronouns.) □ *The other workers quickly rolled the wheel off of the injured man.* □ *Please roll off the wheel quickly!*

roll something **onto** something and **roll** something **on†** to apply something or a coat of a substance by rolling something saturated with the substance on the thing to be coated. □ *You should roll another coat of paint onto this wall over here.* □ *Roll on another coat.*

roll something **out†** **1.** to bring or take something out by rolling it; to push something out on wheels. □ *Jane rolled her bike out to show it off.* □ *Alice rolled out her bicycle for us to see.* **2.** to flatten something by rolling it. □ *You should roll the pastry out first.* □ *They rolled out the steel in a huge mill.*

roll something **over†** *Fig.* to renew a financial instrument as it expires. (See also **roll over** something.) □ *Do you plan to roll this certificate of deposit over?* □ *Are you going to roll over your certificates of deposit?*

roll something **to** someone or something to send something revolving toward someone or something or moving toward someone or something on wheels. □ *I rolled the ball to the baby, who just sat and looked at it.* □ *The blow with the mallet rolled the croquet ball to the wicket.*

roll something **up†** to coil or rotate something into a coil or roll of something. □ *I rolled the poster up and put it back in its mailing tube.* □ *I have to roll up this paper.*

roll something **up†** **(into** something**) 1.** to include something into something that is being rotated into a coil. □ *I guess I accidentally rolled the letter up into the poster that was lying on my desk.* □ *I rolled up the letter into the poster.* **2.** to make something into a round shape by rolling it. □ *He rolled the gum up into a ball and tossed it away.* □ *Jane rolled up the dough into a ball.*

roll with the punches *Fig.* to absorb the force of a blow, as in boxing. □ *You have to learn to roll with the punches. Accept what is dealt to you.* □ *Paul could never roll with the punches. He always had to get even.*

rolling in it Go to **rolling in** something.

rolling in money Go to next.

rolling in something and **rolling in money; rolling in it** *Fig.* having large amounts of something, usually money. □ *That family is rolling in money.* □ *Bob doesn't need to earn money. He's rolling in it.*

*rolling in the aisles *Fig.* [of an audience] wild with laughter. (*Typically: **get them ~; have them ~; leave them ~**.) □ *I have the best jokes you've ever heard. I'll have them rolling in the aisles.* □ *What a great performance. We had them rolling in the aisles.*

A **rolling stone gathers no moss.** *Prov.* A person who does not settle down is not attached to anything or anyone. (Can be said in admiration or in censure, depending on whether or not the speaker feels it is good to be attached to something or someone.) □ *I worry about Tom. He's never lived in the same place for two years in a row, and he keeps changing jobs. A rolling stone gathers no moss.*

Rome was not built in a day. *Prov.* It takes a lot of time to achieve something important. □ *Professor: When will you finish your research project? Student: It'll take me a while. Rome wasn't built in a day, you know.*

romp all over someone Go to **romp on** someone.

romp around to run and bounce around playfully. □ *The horses were in the meadow, romping around in the crisp autumn air.* □ *The children need to get out and romp around.*

romp on someone and **romp all over** someone **1.** *Fig. Inf.* to beat or win over, as in a sports contest. □ *Our team romped on our opponents and beat them 10 to 1.* □ *We romped all over them.* **2.** *Fig. Inf.* to scold someone. □ *The teacher romped on the students for their behavior.* □ *He romped all over all of them.*

romp through something to run through something fast and playfully. □ *The conductor romped through the slow movement of the symphony as if it were a march.* □ *The cast romped through the last act, knowing that the play would be closed that very night.*

roof something **over†** to build a roof over something; to provide something with a roof. □ *After the destructive storm they had to roof the shed over so that the cow would have some shelter.* □ *We will roof over the patio and turn the area into a porch.*

room and board food to eat and a place to live; the cost of food and lodging. □ *That college charges too much for room and board.* □ *How much is your room and board?*

room together [for two or more people] to share a room, as in a college dormitory. □ *Sarah and I roomed together in college.* □ *We don't want to room together anymore.*

room with someone to share a room with someone, as in college. □ *I need someone to room with me next year.* □ *No one wants to room with Kelly.*

root around (for something**)** to dig or shuffle in or through something, looking for something. □ *Alice rooted around in her desk drawer for a pen.* □ *I'll root around here and see if I can find it.*

root for someone or something to cheer and encourage someone or something. □ *Are you rooting for anyone in particular, or are you just shouting because you're excited?* □ *I'm rooting for the home team.*

the **root of the matter** Go to the crux of the matter.

*the **root of the problem** an understanding of the causes or basis of a problem. (*Typically: **determine ~; figure out ~; find ~; get to ~; get at ~**.) □ *It will take a little more study to get to the root of the problem.* □ *Let's stop avoiding the issue and get at the root of the problem.*

root someone or something **out of** something and **root** someone or something **out**[†] to seek and remove someone or something from something or some place; to seek to discover or bring something to light. □ *The committee wanted to root all the lazy people out of the club.* □ *The manager rooted out all the deadwood.*

root something **in** something to start a plant growing roots in something. □ *I tried to root the plants in sand, but they died.* □ *You have to root this kind of tree in very rich soil.*

root something **out**[†] to get rid of something completely; to destroy something to its roots or core. □ *No government will ever root out crime completely.* □ *The principal wants to root out troublemakers at the local school.*

root something **up**[†] [for a pig] to find something in the ground by digging with its nose. □ *The pigs will root your plants up if they get out of their pen.* □ *The pigs will root up your plants if they get out of their pen.*

rooted in something based on something; connected to a source or cause. □ *The civil war was rooted in old cultural hatred.* □ *This fictional book was rooted in actual events.*

***rooted to** something [of someone] firmly attached to something. (*Typically: **be ~; become ~**.) □ *She is firmly rooted to her homeland and has no intention of emigrating.* □ *The farmer is rooted to the land and will not leave.*

***rooted to the spot** *Fig.* unable to move because of fear or surprise. (*Typically: **appear to be ~; be ~; become ~**.) □ *Jane stood rooted to the spot when she saw the ghostly figure.* □ *Mary stood rooted to the spot when the thief snatched her bag.*

rope someone **in**[†] Go to rope someone into something.

rope someone **into** doing something *Fig.* to persuade or trick someone into doing something. □ *I don't know who roped me into doing this, but I don't want to do it.* □ *See if you can rope somebody into taking this to the post office.*

rope someone **into** something and **rope** someone **in**[†] *Fig.* to cause someone to get involved in some project. □ *She's always trying to rope me into her club.* □ *Let's rope in someone to help with cleaning up.*

rope someone or an animal **up**[†] to tie someone or an animal up with a rope. □ *Rope this guy up tight so he won't get away.* □ *The cowboy roped up the steer.*

rope something **off**[†] to isolate something with a rope barrier. □ *The police roped the scene of the accident off.* □ *The police roped off the scene of the accident.*

rope something **together**[†] to tie or bind up a thing or things with rope. □ *Rope this carton together and put it in the trunk of the car.* □ *Rope together these two packages and take them to the truck.*

*the **ropes** *Fig.* knowledge of how to do something; how to work something. (*Typically: **know ~; learn ~; show** someone **~; teach** someone **~**.) □ *I'll be able to do my job very well when I know the ropes.* □ *John is very slow to learn the ropes.*

A **rose by any other name would smell as sweet.** *Prov.* The nature of a thing is more important than what it is called. (From Shakespeare's play, *Romeo and Juliet*.) □ *Bob was upset when his job title was changed from "administrative assistant" to "secretary." We tried to convince him that a rose by any other name would smell as sweet.*

rot away to decompose; to decompose and fall away. □ *The fallen trees rotted away and surrendered their nutrients to the soil.* □ *As the wood rotted away, it became rich humus.*

rot off to decompose. □ *If you don't clean and repaint that old windowsill, it will rot off.* □ *A few old branches finally rotted off, but the ancient tree looked as if it would survive the wet spell.*

rot out to decompose and fall out. □ *If you don't clean your teeth regularly, they'll rot out!* □ *Some of the rafters in the shed rotted out, but we replaced them easily.*

rotate on something to spin on something; to pivot on something. □ *This wheel rotates on this little red jewel on the main frame of the watch.* □ *The record rotates on this device, which is called a turntable.*

a **rotten apple** a single bad person or thing. □ *There always is a rotten apple to spoil it for the rest of us.* □ *Tom sure has turned out to be the rotten apple.*

The **rotten apple spoils the barrel.** *Prov.* A bad person influences everyone he or she comes into contact with, making them bad too. □ *Helen is the rotten apple that spoils the barrel in our office. Everyone sees her come in late to work and take long coffee breaks, and they think, "Why can't I do the same?"*

a **rotten egg** and a **bad egg** a bad or despised person; an evil influence. □ *That guy is a real rotten egg.* □ *She sure has turned out to be a rotten egg.*

rotten luck *Fig.* bad luck. □ *Of all the rotten luck!* □ *I've had nothing but rotten luck all day.*

rotten to the core *Fig.* really bad; corrupt. □ *That lousy punk is rotten to the core.* □ *The entire administration is rotten to the core.*

*a **rough idea (about** something) and *a **rough idea (of** something) a general idea; an estimate. (*Typically: **get ~; have ~; give** someone **~**.) □ *I need to get a rough idea of how many people will be there.* □ *I'll manage to get a rough idea. That's good enough.*

rough it to live without luxury; to live simply; to camp out. □ *During the blackout, we roughed it without electricity.* □ *The campers roughed it in the remote cabin for a week.*

rough someone **up**[†] to beat someone up; to maltreat someone. □ *Am I going to have to rough you up, or will you cooperate?* □ *The crooks roughed up the old lady before taking her purse.*

rough something **in**[†] to construct or draw something initially, temporarily, or crudely. □ *The carpenter roughed the doorways in without consulting the plans.* □ *The carpenter roughed in the doorways without consulting the plans.*

R

rough something **out**[†] to make a rough sketch of something. □ *I will rough it out and have one of the staff artists attend to the details.* □ *Jane roughed out a picture of the proposed building.*

rough something **up**[†] to scrape or rub something in a way that makes it rough. □ *All you have to do is rough the ground up, sow the seeds, and then water them.* □ *Rough up the surface a little before you paint it.*

rough stuff unnecessary roughness; physical violence or threats of violence. □ *Okay, let's cut out the rough stuff!* □ *There was too much rough stuff in the football game.*

a **rough time** Go to a **hard time**.

rough-and-ready 1. strong, active, and ready for anything. □ *John is not exactly rough-and-ready, but he is a moderately good athlete.* □ *Ralph is very rough-and-ready, but his table manners are very bad.* **2.** Go to **rough-and-tumble**.

rough-and-tumble and **rough-and-ready** disorderly; aggressive. □ *That was a rough-and-tumble football game.* □ *George is too rough-and-ready for me. He doesn't know how to act around civilized people.*

round off to something and **round up to** something; **round down to** something to express a number in the nearest whole amount or nearest group of 1, 10, 100, 1,000, 1/10, 1/100, 1/1,000, etc. □ *When doing taxes, Anne rounded her figures off to the nearest dollar.* □ *These census population figures are rounded up to the nearest million.*

round someone or something **up**[†] to locate and gather someone or something. □ *Please round the suspects up for questioning.* □ *The police rounded up the two possible suspects.*

round something **down**[†] to reduce a fractional part of a number to the next lowest whole number. (See also **round off to** something.) □ *You can round this figure down if you want. It won't affect the total all that much.* □ *Please round down all figures having fractions less than one-half.*

round something **off**[†] to change a number to the next higher or lower whole number. (See also **round off to** something.) □ *You should round 8.122 off.* □ *I rounded off 8.789 to 9.*

round something **off**[†] **(with** something**)** to finish something with something; to complement something with something. (See also **round** something **off**.) □ *We rounded the meal off with a fine cognac.* □ *We rounded off the meal with a sinful dessert.*

round something **out**[†] to complete or enhance something. □ *We will round the evening out with dessert at a nice restaurant.* □ *They rounded out the meal with dessert.*

round something **up**[†] **1.** to collect a group of people or things; to organize people or things into a group. □ *The cowboys rounded up the cattle for market.* □ *See if you can round some helpers up.* **2.** to change a number to the next higher whole number. (See also **round off to** something.) □ *I rounded up 8.789 to 9.* □ *You should round $65.99 up to $66.*

round up to something Go to **round off to** something.

a **rounding error** a large amount of money that is relatively small in comparison to a much larger sum. □ *To a large company like Smith & Co., a few thousand dollars is just a rounding error. It's not a lot at all.*

round-trip ticket a ticket (for a plane, train, bus, etc.) that allows one to go to a destination and return. □ *A round-trip ticket is usually cheaper than two one-way tickets.* □ *How much is a round-trip ticket to San Francisco?*

rouse someone **from** something to awaken someone from something; to cause someone to come out of something. □ *I roused Tom from his nap and sent him on his way.* □ *We could not rouse her from her deep sleep.*

rouse someone **out of** something to awaken someone out of a state, such as sleep. □ *It was almost impossible to rouse George out of his sleep.* □ *They could not rouse us out of our drowsy state.*

rouse someone **to** something to stir someone to something. □ *I will rouse the workers to action. They will work or have to find other jobs.* □ *The speech by the president roused the citizens to action.*

roust someone **out of** something and **roust** someone **out**[†] to force someone out of something. □ *Bob's brother rousted him out of bed just in time for the school bus.* □ *He rousted out his brother.*

rout someone or something **out of** some place and **rout** someone or something **out**[†] to remove someone or something from some place by force. □ *The soldiers routed the snipers out of the deserted buildings.* □ *They routed out the snipers.*

route someone or something **around** something to send someone or something on a path that avoids something. □ *The travel agent routed us around the congestion of the big city.* □ *Due to the storm, they routed the trains around the fallen bridge.*

route something **to** someone to send something along a particular path to someone. □ *Try to route this to Walter, who is on a ship at sea. I'll get the name of the ship for you.* □ *I will route a copy of the invoice to you.*

row (someone or something**) out**[†] **to** something to carry someone or something in a rowboat from the shore out to something. □ *Will you row me out to the island?* □ *I rowed out all the visitors to the little island.*

a **royal pain** a great annoyance. □ *This guy's a royal pain, but we have to put up with him because he's the boss.*

the **royal treatment** very good treatment; very good and thoughtful care of a person. □ *I was well cared for. They gave me the royal treatment.* □ *I got the royal treatment when I stayed at that expensive hotel.*

rub (away) at something to chafe or scrape something, repeatedly. □ *The side of his shoe rubbed away at the side of his desk until the paint wore off.* □ *Don't rub at your sore. It will get worse.*

rub elbows (with someone**)** and **rub shoulders with** someone *Fig.* to associate with someone; to work closely with someone. (No physical contact is involved.) □ *I don't care to rub elbows with someone who acts like that!* □ *I rub shoulders with John at work. We are good friends.*

rub off ((of) something**)** [for something] to become detached from something because of incidental rubbing or scraping. (*Of* is usually retained before pronouns.) □

The label rubbed off this can. What do you think it is? □ *I can't tell what it is. The label rubbed off.*

rub off (on someone**)** [for a characteristic of one person] to seem to transfer to someone else. □ *I'll sit by Ann. She has been lucky all evening. Maybe it'll rub off on me.* □ *Sorry. I don't think that luck rubs off.*

rub off on(to) someone or something [for something, such as a coating] to become transferred to someone or something through the contact of rubbing. □ *Look what rubbed off on me!* □ *The wet paint rubbed off onto my pants leg.*

rub salt in a wound *Fig.* to deliberately make someone's unhappiness, shame, or misfortune worse. □ *Don't rub salt in the wound by telling me how enjoyable the party was.* □ *Bill is feeling miserable about losing his job and Bob is rubbing salt into the wound by saying how good his replacement is.*

rub shoulders with someone Go to **rub elbows (with** someone**)**.

rub someone or an animal **down** to stroke or massage someone or an animal, for muscular well-being. □ *Sam rubbed his horse down after his ride.* □ *He rubbed down his horse.*

rub someone or something **with** something to wipe someone or something with something. □ *The mother rubbed the baby gently with a soft cloth.* □ *Todd rubbed the surface of the car with a rag to polish it.*

rub someone **out** *Sl.* to kill someone. (Underworld.) □ *The gunman was eager to rub somebody out.* □ *The crooks tried to rub out the witness.*

rub someone**('s** **fur) the wrong way** *Fig.* to irritate someone. □ *I'm sorry I rubbed your fur the wrong way. I didn't mean to upset you.* □ *Don't rub her the wrong way!*

rub someone's **nose in it** *Fig.* to remind one of something one has done wrong; to remind one of something bad or unfortunate that has happened. (Alludes to a method of housebreaking pets.) □ *When Bob failed his exam, his brother rubbed his nose in it.* □ *Mary knows she shouldn't have broken off her engagement. Don't rub her nose in it.*

rub something **against** someone or something to scrape or chafe something against someone or something repeatedly. □ *The cat kept rubbing its tail against me.* □ *I wish John would stop rubbing his hand against my leg.*

rub something **away** to remove something by chafing or rubbing. □ *See if you can rub some of the dirt away.* □ *Rub away the dirt if you can.*

rub something **in** *Fig.* to keep reminding one of one's failures; to nag someone about something. □ *I like to rub it in. You deserve it!* □ *Why do you have to rub in everything I do wrong?*

rub something **into** something and **rub** something **in** to cause something to penetrate a surface by rubbing it against the surface. □ *Rub this lotion into your muscles. It will stop the aching.* □ *Try rubbing in this lotion.*

rub something **off (of)** something and **rub** something **off** to remove something from something by rubbing. (*Of* is usually retained before pronouns.) □ *The butler rubbed the tarnish off the pitcher.* □ *The butler rubbed off the dark tarnish.*

rub something **onto** something and **rub** something **on** to apply something onto the surface of something by rubbing. □ *Alice rubbed suntan lotion onto her arms and legs.* □ *Rub on some of this lotion.*

rub something **out** to obliterate something by rubbing. □ *See if you can rub those stains out.* □ *Rub out the graffiti on the side of the car if you can.*

rub something **over** something to cover something with something, spreading it by rubbing. □ *The chef rubbed the herbal butter over the skin of the turkey.* □ *Please rub the lotion over my back.*

rub something **together** to press two things together and move them back and forth. □ *Sam rubbed his fingers together, indicating that he needed some money before he could continue.* □ *Mary rubbed her hands together to get them warmed up.*

rub something **up** to raise something, such as the nap of a rug, by rubbing. □ *When you run the vacuum cleaner across the floor, you rub the nap of the rug up and get the dirt out.* □ *Don't rub up the nap.*

rub (up) against someone or something to bump or scrape against someone or something. □ *The cat rubbed up against me and seemed friendly.* □ *The side of the car rubbed against the fence.*

ruffle its feathers [for a bird] to point its feathers outward. □ *The bird ruffled its feathers when it was annoyed.* □ *My parrot ruffles its feathers whenever it is ready to preen itself.*

ruffle someone's **feathers** *Fig.* to irritate or annoy someone. □ *I didn't mean to ruffle his feathers. I just thought that I would remind him of what he promised us.*

ruffle something **up** to raise something, such as feathers, up or outward. □ *The bird ruffled its feathers up and started to preen.* □ *It ruffled up its feathers.*

rug rat *Sl.* a small child, especially an infant or toddler. (Also a term of address.) □ *You got any rug rats at your house?* □ *Hey, you cute little rug rat, come over here.*

the ruin of someone or something the cause of destruction; a failure. □ *Your bad judgment will be the ruin of this company!* □ *The greedy politicians were the ruin of the old empire.*

rule against someone or something to give a judgment against someone or something. □ *The judge ruled against the prosecutor.* □ *The judge ruled against my motion.*

rule in favor of someone or something and **rule for** someone or something [for a judge or deliberating body] to award a decision to someone or something or to render a decision favoring someone or something. □ *The judge ruled for the defendant.* □ *The examining board ruled in favor of dismissing George.*

a rule of thumb a general principle developed through experiential rather than scientific means. □ *As a rule of thumb, I move my houseplants outside in May.* □ *Going by a rule of thumb, we stop for gas every 200 miles when we are traveling.*

rule on something to give a decision or judgment about something. □ *How long will it be before the court rules on your petition?* □ *The boss will rule on your request tomorrow.*

rule over someone or something to serve as the boss or chief over someone or something. □ *I guess you could say that the boss rules over me.* □ *The president of a democracy doesn't really rule over the country.*

rule someone or something **out**† to prevent, disqualify, over-rule, or cancel someone or something. □ *John's bad temper rules him out for the job.* □ *The rainy weather ruled out a picnic for the weekend.*

rule the roost *Fig.* to be the boss or manager, especially at home. □ *Who rules the roost at your house?* □ *Our new office manager really rules the roost.*

rule with a velvet glove *Fig.* to rule in a very gentle way. □ *She rules with a velvet glove, but she gets things done, nonetheless.* □ *He may appear to rule with a velvet glove, but he is really quite cruel.*

rule with an iron fist *Fig.* to rule in a very stern manner. □ *The dictator ruled with an iron fist and terrified the citizens.* □ *My boss rules with an iron fist. I'm looking for a new job.*

ruminate about something and **ruminate on** something to ponder and think about something. (Alludes to a cow, relaxing and chewing its cud, as if it is thinking.) □ *He sat, ruminating about the events of the day, humming and eating peanuts.* □ *Let me ruminate on this a little bit.*

ruminate on something Go to previous.

rummage around (somewhere) (for something) to move things about haphazardly while looking for something somewhere. □ *Alice rummaged around in the drawer for a candy bar she had been saving.* □ *After she rummaged around for the candy bar, she found it.* □ *She rummaged around in the old trunk.*

rummage through something to move things about haphazardly while searching through something. □ *I rummaged through my top drawer, looking for any two socks that matched.* □ *Mary spent some time rummaging through the toolbox before she found what she was looking for.*

rumor has it that... there is a rumor that.... □ *Rumor has it that Fred is seeing Mary and that they are engaged.*

rump session a meeting held after a larger meeting. □ *A rump session continued after the meeting was adjourned.* □ *A lot of business was conducted in the rump session.*

rumple someone or something **up**† to bring disorder to someone['s clothing] or something; to wrinkle someone or something. □ *One of the little boys knocked another boy down and rumpled him up.* □ *He rumpled up Dan's shirt.*

run a comb through something to comb one's hair quickly. □ *Run a comb through your hair after you come back in the house.* □ *She ran a comb through Timmy's hair, and tried to make him look presentable.*

run a fever and **run a temperature** to have a body temperature higher than normal; to have a fever. □ *I ran a fever when I had the flu.* □ *The baby is running a temperature and is grouchy.*

run a make on someone to perform an identity check on someone. □ *The cops ran a make on Lefty and learned about his prison record.* □ *We tried to run a make on him and came up with nothing.*

run a red light to pass through an intersection having a red traffic light without stopping. □ *Sam got a ticket for running a red light.*

run a risk (of something**)** and **run the risk (of** something**)** to take a chance that something (bad) will happen. □ *I don't want to run the risk of losing my job.* □ *Don't worry. You won't have to run a risk.*

run a tab to accumulate charges on a bill at a bar or tavern. □ *They won't let me run a tab here. I have to pay for each drink as I order it.*

run a taut ship Go to **run a tight ship**.

run a temperature Go to **run a fever**.

run a tight ship and **run a taut ship** to run a ship or an organization in an orderly and disciplined manner. (*Taut* and *tight* mean the same thing. *Taut* is correct nautical use.) □ *The new office manager really runs a tight ship.* □ *Captain Jones is known for running a taut ship.*

run across someone or something Go to **come across** someone or something.

run across something to cross something while running. □ *The joggers all ran across the bridge together.* □ *The mice ran across the floor, not knowing that a cat was watching them.*

run (a)foul of someone or something Go to **fall (a)foul of** someone or something.

run after someone to chase someone of the opposite sex hoping for a date or some attention. □ *Is John still running after Ann?* □ *No, Ann is running after John.*

run after someone or something Go to **after** someone or something.

run against someone to compete against someone for elective office. □ *Eisenhower ran against Adlai Stevenson in 1952.* □ *Not many people run against an incumbent.*

run against someone or something Go to **against** someone or something.

run against the grain Go to **against the grain**.

run aground (on something**)** [for a ship] to ram its hull into something beneath the water and get stuck. □ *The ship ran aground on a reef and had to wait for high tide to get free.* □ *I was afraid we would run aground in the storm.*

run along to leave. □ *Please run along and leave me alone.* □ *I have to run along now. Good-bye.*

run amok and **run amuck** to go awry; to go bad; to turn bad; to go into a frenzy. (From a Malay word meaning to run wild in a violent frenzy.) □ *Our plan ran amok.* □ *He ran amuck early in the school year and never quite got back on the track.*

run amuck Go to previous.

run an errand and **do an errand; go on an errand** to take a short trip to do a specific thing; to complete an errand. □ *I've got to run an errand. I'll be back in a minute.* □ *John has gone on an errand. He'll be back shortly.*

run around 1. to run here and there. □ *Why are you running around? Sit down and be quiet.* □ *Please stop running around. You are making me nervous.* **2.** to go here and there having meetings or doing errands. □ *I've been running*

R

around all day, shopping for the party tonight. □ *I am so tired of running around, carting children to various places.*

run around after someone or something to chase after someone or something; to seek after someone or something. □ *Where have you been? I've run around after you all over town!* □ *I have been running around after the right-sized shoes all morning.*

run around like a chicken with its head cut off and **run (around) in circles** *Fig.* to run around frantically and aimlessly; to be in a state of chaos. (Alludes to a chicken that continues to run around aimlessly after its head has been chopped off.) □ *I spent all afternoon running around like a chicken with its head cut off.* □ *If you run around in circles, you'll never get anything done.*

run around with someone to be friends with someone; to go places with regular friends. □ *John and I were great friends. We used to run around with each other all the time.* □ *Mary ran around with Jane for about a year.*

run as something to run for office in a certain party. □ *Do you suppose I can run as an independent?* □ *Fred ran as a Democrat and won a seat in the legislature.*

run at a fast clip Go to at a fast clip.

run at a good clip Go to at a good clip.

run at full blast Go to at full blast.

run at someone or something to run toward someone or something; to charge someone or something. □ *The bull started to run at us, but changed its mind—thank heavens.* □ *The huge crocodile ran at the goat, but the goat leapt away.*

run away (from someone or something**)** to flee someone or something. □ *Please don't run away from me. I mean you no harm.* □ *Our dog ran away from the lawn mower.*

run away with someone 1. to flee in the company of someone. □ *Frank arrived on the scene, saw what had happened, and ran away with the other boys.* □ *Tom ran away with Bill to a place where they could hide.* 2. [for two people] to elope. □ *Jill ran away with Jack, much to her father's relief.* □ *Jill and Jack ran away with each other.*

run away with something 1. to flee with something in one's possession. □ *The crook ran away with the watch.* □ *Someone ran away with that lady's purse.* 2. to capture or steal a performance by being the best performer. □ *Henry ran away with the show, and everyone loved him.* □ *The dog ran away with the whole performance.*

run back to come back, running. □ *She ran to the barn and then ran back.* □ *Tom ran back, very much afraid.*

run back over something to review something. □ *Would you please run back over that last part again?* □ *Let me run back over the hard part for you.*

run back to someone or something to return to someone or something in a hurry. □ *The child ran back to her mother.* □ *We all ran back to the house.*

run behind to be late; to run late. □ *We are running behind. You had better hurry.* □ *Things are running behind, and we will not finish on time.*

run behind someone or something to travel along behind someone or something, running. □ *I will run behind you*

in the race. □ *Mary ran behind the bicycle until she could not run anymore.*

run between something **and** something else 1. to travel between someone or something, running. □ *I spent all afternoon running between my office and the conference room.* □ *We ran between the two quarreling people all day long, trying to settle the argument.* 2. to pass between someone or something, running. □ *The child ran between the two ladies, giving them quite a start.* □ *Please don't run between the bushes. You will wear a path there.*

run circles around someone and **run rings around** someone *Fig.* to outrun or outdo someone. (Alludes to someone who runs fast enough to run in circles around a competitor and still win the race.) □ *John is a much better racer than Mary. He can run circles around her.* □ *Mary can run rings around Sally.*

run counter to something to be in opposition to something; to run against something. (This has nothing to do with running.) □ *Your proposal runs counter to what is required by the manager.* □ *His idea runs counter to good sense.*

run down 1. to come down, running or very quickly; to go down, running or very quickly. □ *I need to talk to you down here. Can you run down?* □ *I will run down and talk to you.* **2.** [for something] to lose power and stop working. □ *The clock ran down because no one was there to wind it.* □ *The toy ran down and wouldn't go again until it had been wound.* **3.** to become worn or dilapidated. □ *The property was allowed to run down, and it took a lot of money to fix it up.* □ *The old neighborhood has certainly run down since we moved away.*

run down some lines 1. *Sl.* to converse (with someone). □ *I was running down some lines with Fred when the bell rang.* □ *Hey, man, let's run down some lines.* **2.** *Sl.* to try to seduce someone; to go through a talk leading to seduction. □ *Go run down some lines with someone else.* □ *I was just standing there running down some lines with Mary when those guys broke in.*

run down to some place to travel to a place. (By running or any other means.) □ *I have to run down to the store and get some bread.* □ *I want to run down to the bank, but my car is out of gas.*

run down to someone or something to come or go down to someone or something, rapidly. □ *Sally ran down the slope to Bob, who stood waiting for her with outstretched arms.* □ *I ran down to the well to get some water for Ed, who had the hiccups.*

run for it to escape by running. (See also **swim for it**.) □ *The dogs were coming after me fast. There was nothing I could do but run for it.* □ *I ran for it when I saw the police coming.*

run for one's **life** to run away to save one's life. □ *The dam has burst! Run for your life!* □ *The captain told us all to run for our lives.*

*a **run for** one's **money 1.** *Fig.* the results or rewards one deserves, expects, or wants. (*Typically: **get** ~; **have** ~; **give** someone ~.) □ *I get a run for my money at the club tennis tournament.* □ *I had a run for my money in the stock market.* **2.** *Fig.* a challenge. (*Typically: **get** ~; **have** ~; **give** someone ~.) □ *Bob got a run for his money when he* *tried to beat Mary at pool.* □ *Bill got a run for his money playing cards with John.*

run for something **1.** to travel quickly by running to a place of safety. □ *The picnickers ran for the shelter when the rain started to fall.* □ *Tom and Jane ran for the house as soon as they heard your call.* **2.** to try to be elected to a particular office. □ *Who's going to run for president?* □ *I am running for mayor.*

run for the hills Go to head for the hills.

run from someone or something to flee someone or something, usually on foot. □ *She ran from the mugger who had accosted her.* □ *Mary ran from the dog and jumped over a fence to safety.*

run from something **to** something to travel on foot from one thing or place to another, running. □ *Do you think you can run from the bank downtown to the post office on Maple Street?* □ *I ran from door to door, telling people what had happened.*

run in circles 1. *Lit.* to run in a circular path. □ *The horses ran in circles around the corral for their daily exercise.* □ *The children ran in circles around the tree.* **2.** and **run around in circles** *Fig.* to waste one's time in aimless activity. □ *Stop running in circles and try to organize yourself so that you are more productive.* □ *I have been running around in circles over this matter for days.*

run in something to compete in something, such as a race or an election. □ *I will run in the one-hundred-yard dash.* □ *I will not run in a race this time.* □ *Who will run in this year's election?*

run in the family [for a characteristic] to appear in many (or all) members of a family. □ *My grandparents lived well into their nineties, and it runs in the family.* □ *My brothers and I have red hair. It runs in the family.*

run into a stone wall *Fig.* to come to a barrier against further progress. □ *We've run into a stone wall in our investigation.* □ *Algebra was hard for Tom, but he really ran into a stone wall with geometry.*

run into someone Go to bump into someone.

run into someone or something to bump into someone or something. □ *I didn't mean to run into you. I'm sorry.* □ *Mary ran into the fence and scraped her elbow.*

run in(to something) **1.** [for a liquid] to flow into something or a place. □ *The water is running into the basement!* □ *It's running in very fast.* **2.** to enter something or a place on foot, running. □ *The boys ran into the room and out again.* □ *They ran in and knocked over a lamp.* **3.** to stop by a place for a quick visit or to make a purchase quickly. □ *I have to run in the drugstore for a minute.* □ *I ran into the store for a loaf of bread.* □ *I want to visit Mrs. Potter. I can't stay long. I can only run in for a minute.*

Run it by (me) again. Go to Run that by (me) again.

run it down *Sl.* to tell the whole story; to tell the truth. □ *Come on! What happened? Run it down for me!* □ *I don't care what happened. Run it down. I can take it.*

run its course [for something] to continue through its cycle of existence, especially a disease. □ *Sorry. There is no medicine for it. It will just have to run its course.*

run like clockwork to run very well; to progress very well. □ *I want this office to run like clockwork—with every-* thing on time and everything done right. □ *The plans for the party were made and we knew that we could depend on Alice to make sure that everything ran like clockwork.*

run like stink Go to like stink.

run like the wind Go to like the wind.

run low (on something) to near the end of a supply of something. □ *We are running low on salt. It's time to buy more.* □ *The car is running low on gas.*

run off 1. to flee. □ *The children rang our doorbell and then ran off.* □ *They ran off as fast as they could.* **2.** to have diarrhea. □ *He said he was running off all night.* □ *One of the children was running off and had to stay home from school.* **3.** [for a fluid] to drain away from a flat area. □ *By noon, all the rainwater had run off the playground.*

run off at the mouth *Sl.* to talk too much. □ *I wish you would stop running off at the mouth.* □ *Tom runs off at the mouth too much. I wish he would temper his remarks.*

run off in all directions *Fig.* [for people] to set out to do something or go somewhere in an aimless and disorganized fashion. (Can also apply to one person. See also ride off in all directions.) □ *The people in the marketing department need some organization. They are always running off in all directions.* □ *Stop running off in all directions and focus your energy.*

run off something to drive or travel off something, such as rails, tracks, a road, etc. □ *The train ran off its rails and piled up in a cornfield.* □ *We almost ran off the road during the storm.*

run off (with someone) to run away with someone, as in an elopement. □ *Tom ran off with Ann.* □ *Tom and Ann ran off and got married.*

run off with someone or something **1.** to take someone or something away, possibly running. (See also run off (with someone).) □ *Fred ran off with Ken. They'll be back in a minute.* □ *Who ran off with my dictionary?* **2.** to capture and take away someone or something; to steal someone or something. □ *The kidnappers ran off with little Valerie.* □ *The kids ran off with a whole box of candy, and the storekeeper is going to press charges.*

run on 1. to continue running. □ *I wanted to stop her and ask her something, but she just ran on.* □ *The joggers had a chance to stop and rest, but they just ran on.* **2.** to continue on for a long time. □ *The lecture ran on and bored everyone to tears.* □ *How long is this symphony likely to run on?*

run on all cylinders 1. *Lit.* [for an engine] to run well and smoothly. □ *This car is now running on all cylinders, thanks to the tune-up.* □ *You can hear if an engine is not running on all cylinders.* **2.** *Fig.* to function well or energetically. □ *Our department seems to be running on all cylinders. Congratulations.* □ *I am back at my desk after my illness—running on all cylinders.*

a **run on** something Go to a rush on something.

run one's **eye over** something *Fig.* to gaze at the whole of something; to glance at all of something. □ *She ran her eyes over the lines of the automobile and nodded her approval.* □ *He ran his eyes over the drawing and decided that he had to have it.*

run one's **feet off** *Fig.* to run very hard and fast. □ *I ran my feet off and I'm really tired now that the race is over.* □ *I almost ran my feet off getting over here to see you!*

run one's **fingers through** one's **hair** and **run** one's **hand through** one's **hair** to comb one's hair with one's fingers. □ *I came in out of the wind and ran my fingers through my hair to straighten it out a bit.* □ *He ran his hand through his hair and tried to make himself presentable.*

run one's **hand through** one's **hair** Go to previous.

run one's **head against a brick wall** *Fig.* to be frustrated by coming up against an insurmountable obstacle. □ *There is no point in running your head against a brick wall. If you can't succeed in this case, don't even try.* □ *I have been running my head against a brick wall about this problem long enough.*

run one's **rhymes** *Sl.* to say what you have to say; to give one's speech or make one's plea. □ *Go run your rhymes with somebody else!* □ *I told him to run his rhymes elsewhere.*

run out at someone or something to come out of a place and charge or attack someone or something. □ *The badger ran out at us and then went back to its den.* □ *The dogs ran out at the speeding car.*

run out of gas Go to out of gas.

run out of patience Go to out of patience.

run out of some place to leave a place quickly, on foot; to flee a place. □ *He ran out of the room as fast as he could.* □ *We ran out of the building as soon as we felt the first signs of the earthquake.*

run out (of something) Go to out (of something).

run out of steam *Fig.* to lose momentum and fail. □ *Toward the end of the lecture, he seemed to run out of steam, leaving us with no summary or conclusion.*

run out of time to have used up most of the allotted time; to have no time left. □ *You have just about run out of time.* □ *I ran out of time before I could finish the test.*

run out (on someone) to depart and leave someone behind. □ *My date ran out on me at the restaurant, and I had to pay the bill.* □ *Her boyfriend ran out when she needed him the most.*

run over 1. to come by for a quick visit. □ *Can you run over for a minute after work?* □ *I will run over for a minute as soon as I can.* **2.** to overflow. □ *The bathtub ran over and there was water all over the floor.* □ *She poured the coffee until the cup ran over.*

run over someone or something to drive, steer, or travel so as to pass over someone or something. □ *The bus ran over the fallen man.* □ *That car almost ran over my toe.*

run over (something) to exceed a limit. □ *The lecture ran over the allotted time.* □ *Bob ran over the amount he was budgeted to spend.*

run over something **with** someone to review something with someone. □ *I would like to run over this with you one more time.* □ *I want to run over the proposal with Carl again.*

run over to something to go to something or some place, running or by any independent mode of transportation.

□ *Would you run over to the store and get me some eggs?* □ *I have to run over to the bank to cash a check.*

run over with something to drop over for a visit, bringing something. □ *Do you mind if I run over with the cup of sugar I borrowed last week?* □ *Mary ran over with the papers you requested.*

run rampant to run, develop, or grow out of control. □ *The children ran rampant through the house.* □ *Weeds have run rampant around the abandoned house.*

run rings around someone Go to **run circles around** someone.

run riot and **run wild** *Fig.* to get out of control. □ *The dandelions have run riot in our lawn.* □ *The children ran wild at the birthday party and had to be taken home.*

run roughshod over someone or something Go to **ride roughshod over** someone or something.

run scared to behave as if one were going to fail. □ *The mayor was running scared, but won anyway.* □ *When we lost that big contract, everyone in the office was running scared. We thought we'd be fired.*

run short (of something) to begin to run out of something. □ *We are running short of eggs.* □ *I always keep enough so I will never run short.*

run someone **in**[†] to arrest one and take one to the police station. □ *The cop ran George in so they could question him extensively.* □ *They ran in George to protect him from the rioters.*

run someone or something **down**[†] **1.** to collide with and knock down someone or something. □ *The drunken driver ran three pedestrians down.* □ *Mary ran down a stop sign.* **2.** to criticize or deride someone or something. □ *Please stop running me down all the time. I can't be that bad!* □ *You run down everybody who takes your old job!* **3.** to hunt for and locate someone or something. □ *Could you run some information down for me?* □ *I was finally able to run down my old friend.*

run someone or something **into** something and **run** someone or something **in**[†] to take or drive someone or something into something or some place. □ *Let me run you into the city this morning. I need the car today.* □ *Do you want to go to town? I have to run in George and you can come along.*

run someone or something **off (of)** something and **run** someone or something **off**[†] to drive someone or something off something. (*Of* is usually retained before pronouns.) □ *Go out and run those dogs off the lawn.* □ *Go run off the dogs from the lawn.*

run someone or something **out of** something and **run** someone or something **out**[†] to chase someone or something out of something or some place. □ *The old man ran the kids out of his orchard.* □ *He ran out the kids.*

run someone or something **to earth** to find something after a search. □ *Lisa finally ran her long-lost cousin to earth in Paris.* □ *After months of searching, I ran a copy of Jim's book to earth.*

run someone or something **to** something **1.** to run someone or something to some extreme extent, such as death. □ *The villain's idea was to run his victim to death by chasing him.* □ *He nearly ran his horse to death.* **2.** to drive someone or something to some place. □ *Could you run me to the store?* □ *Please run these clothes to the cleaners.*

run someone **ragged** *Fig.* to keep someone or something very busy. □ *This busy season is running us all ragged at the store.* □ *What a busy day. I ran myself ragged.*

run someone **through** something **1.** to make or guide someone though an area while running. □ *They ran us through a maze as part of our training.* □ *We ran the little boys through the park so they could get some exercise.* **2.** to guide a person through a process. □ *Let me run you through the process so you will know what is happening to you.* □ *Can I run you through this procedure again?* **3.** to rehearse someone. □ *The director ran the cast through the last act three times.* □ *She ran herself through the part at home between rehearsals.*

run someone **through (with** something**)** to stab a person all the way through with something, such as a sword. □ *The knight ran the attacker through with his own sword.* □ *He ran him through and stole his horse.*

run something **at full blast** Go to at full blast.

run something **back**† to wind something back to the beginning. □ *Run the tape back and listen to it again.* □ *Run back the tape and listen again.*

run something **by (**someone**) (again)** to explain something to someone again; to say something to someone again. □ *I didn't hear you. Please run that by me again.* □ *Please run it by so we can all hear it.*

run something **by the book** Go to by the book.

run something **down**† to use something having batteries, a motor, or an engine until it has no more power and it stops. □ *Who ran my electric toothbrush down?* □ *Someone ran down my batteries.*

run something **in**† Go to run something into something.

run something **in**† **(for** something**)** to bring or drive something quickly into a place for some purpose. □ *I have to run my car in for an oil change.* □ *I will run in the truck for the mechanic to take a look at it.*

run something **into** something and **run** something **in**† **1.** to guide or route something, such as a wire or a pipe, into something or a place. □ *The worker ran the circuit into each room.* □ *He ran in the circuit as specified.* **2.** to guide something into something; to drive or steer something into something else. □ *Bobby ran his bicycle into the wall, bending the front wheel.* □ *Please don't run your car into the wall!*

run something **into the ground** and **drive** something **into the ground 1.** *Lit.* to pound or force something into the ground. □ *Use a heavy mallet to drive the stakes into the ground.* □ *Run this post into the ground and nail this sign to it.* **2.** *Fig.* to carry something too far. □ *It was a good joke at first, Tom, but you've run it into the ground.* □ *Just because everyone laughed once, you don't have to drive it into the ground.*

run something **off**† **1.** to get rid of something, such as fat or energy, by running. □ *The little boys are very excited. Send them outside to run it off.* □ *They need to run off their energy.* **2.** to duplicate something, using a mechanical duplicating machine. □ *If the master copy is ready, I will run some other copies off.* □ *I'll run off some more copies.*

run something **onto** something to drive or guide something onto the surface of something. □ *He ran the car onto the grass and washed it.* □ *Please run your bicycle onto the porch and I will try to fix it for you.*

run something **out of** something and **run** something **out**† to drive or steer something out of something or some place. □ *The cowboys ran the cattle out of the corral.* □ *They ran out the cattle.*

run something **over to** someone or something and **run** something **over**† to carry something to someone or something. □ *Would you please run this package over to Mrs. Franklin?* □ *Do you know where Bill lives? Please run over this package.*

run something **through** something **1.** to drive or propel something through the midst of something or a group. □ *The cowboys ran the cattle right through the crowd of people standing at the station.* □ *He ran his truck through the bushes at the end of the driveway.* **2.** to process something by going through a procedure, a deliberative body, or a department. □ *I will have to run this through the board of directors.* □ *She ran the invoice through the accounting department.*

run something **up**† **1.** *Lit.* to raise or hoist something, such as a flag. □ *Harry ran the flag up the flagpole each morning.* □ *Will you please run up the flag today?* **2.** *Fig.* to cause something to go higher, such as the price of stocks or commodities. □ *A rumor about higher earnings ran the price of the computer stocks up early in the afternoon.* □ *They ran up the price too high.* **3.** *Fig.* to accumulate indebtedness. □ *I ran up a huge phone bill last month.* □ *Walter ran up a bar bill at the hotel that made his boss angry.* **4.** to stitch something together quickly. □ *She's very clever. I'm sure she can run up a costume for you.* □ *The seamstress ran up a party dress in one afternoon.*

Run that by (me) again. and **Run it by (me) again.** *Inf.* Please repeat what you just said.; Please go over that one more time. □ *Alice: Do you understand? Sue: No. I really didn't understand what you said. Run that by me again, if you don't mind.* □ *John: Put this piece into the longer slot and the remaining piece into the slot on the bottom. Sue: Run that by again. I got lost just after* put. □ *Mary: Keep to the right, past the fork in the road, then turn right at the crossroads. Do you follow? Jane: No. Run it by me again.*

run the gamut to cover a wide range [from one thing to another]. □ *She wants to buy the house, but her requests run the gamut from expensive new carpeting to completely new landscaping.* □ *His hobbies run the gamut from piano repair to portrait painting.*

run the gauntlet 1. *Lit.* to race, as a punishment, between parallel lines of men who thrash one as one runs. □ *The knight was forced to doff his clothes and run the gauntlet.* **2.** and **run the gauntlet of** something *Fig.* to endure a series of problems, threats, or criticism. □ *After the play, the director found himself running the gauntlet of questions and doubts about his ability.*

run the good race to do the best that one could; to live life as well and as fully as possible. □ *He didn't get what he wanted, but he ran the good race.* □ *Joan ran the good race, and she will be remembered by all of us.*

run the risk (of something**)** Go to **run a risk (of** something**)**.

run the show to be in charge; to be in command. □ *Who's running this show?* □ *No, I don't want to have to run the show again.*

run through something **1.** to pass through an area, running. □ *Stop running through the living room!* □ *We ran through the park as part of our exercise.* **2.** to go through a procedure or sequence; to rehearse a procedure or sequence. □ *I want to run through act two again before we end this rehearsal.* **3.** to read or examine something quickly. □ *I ran through your report this afternoon.* □ *Sally ran through the list, checking off the names of the people who had already paid for tickets.* **4.** to spend or use a supply of something wastefully and rapidly. □ *He ran through his inheritance in two years.* □ *Have we run through all the peanut butter already?*

run to seed Go to **go to seed**.

run to someone or something to travel quickly on foot to someone or something; to go to someone or something with some urgency. □ *Mary ran to Alice and greeted her.* □ *I ran to the door and fled.*

run to something to amount to a certain amount of money. □ *In the end, the bill ran to thousands of dollars.* □ *His account ran to more than I expected.*

run up against someone or something Go to **up against** someone or something.

run up to some place to travel to a place quickly or for a brief time. □ *Let's run up to the lake for the weekend.*

run up (to someone or something**)** to run as far as someone or something and stop; to run to the front of someone or something. □ *I ran up to the mailman and said hello to him.* □ *I ran up and said hello.*

run wild Go to **run riot**.

run with someone or something to stay in the company of someone or some group. □ *Fred was out running with Larry when they met Vernon.* □ *Let's go out and run with the other guys this morning.*

run with something **1.** Lit. to run, showing a particular characteristic. □ *Sally runs with speed and grace.* □ *Fred runs with tremendous speed.* **2.** Fig. to take over something and handle it aggressively and independently. □ *I know that Alice can handle the job. She will take it on and run with it.* □ *I hope she runs with this next project.*

run with the hare and hunt with the hounds Fig. to support both sides of a dispute. □ *In our office politics, Sally always tries to run with the hare and hunt with the hounds, telling both the clerical workers and the management that she thinks they should prevail.*

*the runaround a series of excuses, delays, and referrals. (*Typically: **get ~; have ~; give** someone **~**.) □ *You'll get the runaround if you ask to see the manager.* □ *I hate it when they give me the runaround.*

running high [for feelings] to be in a state of excitement or anger. □ *Feelings were running high as the general election approached.* □ *The mood of the crowd was running high when they saw the mother slap her child.*

run-of-the-mill common or average; typical. □ *The restaurant we went to was nothing special—just run-of-the-*

mill. □ *The service was good, but the food was run-of-the-mill or worse.*

the **runt of the litter 1.** Lit. the smallest animal born in a litter; the animal in a litter least likely to survive. □ *No one wanted to buy the runt of the litter, so we kept it.* **2.** and the **runt of the family** Fig. the smallest child in the family. □ *I was the runt of the litter and the butt of all the jokes.*

rush at someone or something to run at or charge toward someone or something. □ *The dog rushed at us and scared us to death.* □ *Mary rushed at the door, but it slammed shut before she got there.*

rush for something to hurry to something. □ *All the people rushed for the exits when the game was over.* □ *We rushed for the picnic tables as soon as they said that lunch was ready.*

rush hour the period of time when heavy traffic is moving into or out of a city. □ *This is the slowest rush hour I have ever been in. Traffic is almost in gridlock.*

rush in(to something**) 1.** to run or hurry into a thing or a place. □ *Everyone rushed into the shelter when the rain started.* □ *They all rushed in at once.* **2.** to begin doing something without the proper preparation. □ *Don't rush into this job without thinking it through.* □ *Mary rushed in without thinking.*

rush off (from some place**)** to hurry away from some place. □ *I'm sorry, but I will have to rush off from this meeting before it's over.* □ *Mary had to rush off before the party was over.*

a **rush on** something and a **run on** something a large demand for something. □ *There was a rush on bottled water during the drought.* □ *During the hot summer, there was a run on air conditioners.*

rush out (of something**)** to exit in a hurry. □ *Everyone rushed out of the room at the same time.* □ *They rushed out because they smelled smoke.*

rush someone **into** something to hurry someone into doing something. □ *We rushed Harry into taking the job.* □ *Sally has always hated that dress. Sam rushed her into buying it.*

rush someone or something **into** something and **rush** someone or something **in**† to lead or carry someone or something into something or some place hurriedly. □ *I rushed her into the hospital emergency room, and everything was soon all right.* □ *The nurse rushed in the emergency medical equipment.*

rush someone or something **out of** something and **rush** someone or something **out**† to lead or guide someone or something out of something or some place hurriedly. □ *The ushers rushed everyone out of the church so they could clean the place before the next wedding.* □ *They rushed out another edition of the newspaper that afternoon.*

rush someone **to the hospital** to take someone to the hospital very quickly. □ *They had to rush her to the hospital because she had stopped breathing.* □ *We rushed Uncle Harry to the hospital after he complained of chest pains.*

rush something **into print** to print up something hastily. □ *The story was so timely that the newspaper editor rushed it into print without checking all the details.* □ *We will rush the book into print as soon as the author finishes.*

rush something **off**[†] **(to** someone or something) to send something quickly to someone or something. □ *I will rush your order off to you immediately.* □ *I need to rush off this package to Walter.*

rush something **through (**something**) 1.** *Lit.* to pass something through a physical area rapidly. □ *He rushed the ambulance through the gate to the stadium.* □ *Strong blowers rushed many cubic feet of air through the ductwork into all the rooms.* **2.** *Fig.* to move something through some process or office in a hurry. □ *He was in a hurry so we rushed his order through the shipping department.* □ *He asked us to rush it through.*

rush through something to hurry to get something finished; to race through something. □ *Please don't rush through this business. Get it right.* □ *Timmy rushed through dinner so he could go out and play.*

rush to conclusions to try to reach a conclusion too fast, probably with insufficient evidence; to **jump to conclusions.** □ *I hope that you don't rush to any conclusions. I can explain this.* □ *I'm afraid you are rushing to conclusions when you speak of canceling the performance.*

rush to someone or something to hurry to get to someone, something, or some event. □ *I rushed to the injured man to try to help him.* □ *We all rushed to the office to see what had happened.*

rust away to dissolve away into rust. □ *In a few years, this car will rust away if you don't take care of it.* □ *The bridge is rusting away, little by little.*

rust belt *Fig.* the industrial north of the United States. (Patterned on **sun belt.**) □ *The economy in the rust belt is slowing down.* □ *The salt they put on the roads in the winter made my car all rusty. I guess that's why they call this area the rust belt.*

rust out to develop holes or weak places owing to rust. □ *Our hot water heater rusted out and flooded the basement.*

rustle something **up**[†] *Rur.* to manage to prepare a meal, perhaps on short notice. □ *I think I can rustle something up for dinner.* □ *Please rustle up something to eat.*

R

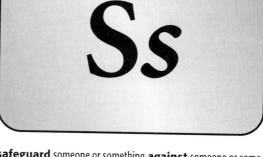

*the sack and ***the ax** dismissal from one's employment. (*Typically: **get ~; give** someone **~**.) □ *Poor Tom got the sack today. He's always late.* □ *I was afraid that Sally was going to get the ax.*

sack out to go to bed or go to sleep. □ *It's time for me to sack out.* □ *Let's sack out early tonight.*

sack something **up**† to put something into bags or sacks. □ *Please sack the groceries up and put them in the cart.* □ *I will sack up your groceries.*

sacked out asleep. □ *Mary is sacked out in her room.* □ *Here it is ten o'clock, and you are still sacked out!*

sacred cow *Fig.* something that is regarded by some people with such respect and veneration that they do not like it being criticized by anyone in any way. (From the fact that the cow is regarded as sacred in India and is not eaten or mistreated.) □ *A university education is a sacred cow in the Smith family. Fred is regarded as a failure because he quit school at 16.* □ *Don't talk about eating meat to Pam. Vegetarianism is one of her sacred cows.*

sacrifice someone or something **for** someone or something to forfeit someone or something for the sake of someone or something. □ *Surely you won't sacrifice your dear wife for a silly twit like Francine!* □ *Would you sacrifice your bank account for a chance to go to Europe?*

sacrifice someone or something **to** someone or something to make an offering of or give up someone or something to someone or some power. □ *The high priest prepared to sacrifice the prisoner to the gods.* □ *I sacrificed a lot of money to a fancy lifestyle.*

a **sad sight** Go to a **sorry sight**.

sadder but wiser *Cliché* unhappy but knowledgeable [about someone or something—after an unpleasant event]. □ *After the accident, I was sadder but wiser, and would never make the same mistake again.* □ *We left the meeting sadder but wiser, knowing that we could not ever come to an agreement with Becky's aunt.*

saddle an animal **up**† to put a saddle on a horse or some other beast of burden. □ *Please saddle my horse up. I have to leave.* □ *Would you saddle up my horse for me?*

saddle someone **with** someone or something *Fig.* to burden someone with someone or something undesirable, annoying, or difficult to deal with. □ *I apologize for saddling you with my young cousin all day.* □ *I didn't mean to saddle you with my problems.*

saddle up 1. *Lit.* to prepare one's horse for riding by putting a saddle on it. □ *Let's saddle up and go for a ride.* **2.** *Fig.* to mount one's horse and sit in the saddle. □ *The cowboys saddled up and took off after the rustlers.*

saddled with someone or something *Fig.* burdened with someone or something. □ *I've been saddled with the children all day. Let's go out tonight.* □ *I don't want to be saddled with your work.*

safe and sound unharmed and whole or healthy. □ *It was a rough trip, but we got there safe and sound.* □ *I'm glad to see you here safe and sound.*

safeguard against someone or something to protect against someone or something. □ *We will try to safeguard against accidents.* □ *How can I safeguard against prowlers?*

safeguard someone or something **against** someone or something to protect someone or something against someone or something. □ *We will take action that will safeguard you against a recurrence of the unpleasantness.* □ *I will safeguard my family against the prowler.*

safety in numbers safety achieved by being concealed in or united with large numbers of people or other creatures. □ *We stayed close together, thinking that there was safety in numbers.* □ *The elderly people went out together for a walk, knowing that there was safety in numbers.*

sag away (from something**)** to settle or droop down or away. □ *The cloth sagged away from the edge of the table.*

sag down to droop downward. □ *The branch sagged down and nearly touched the ground.* □ *When the rain got the drapes wet, they sagged down and touched the floor.*

sag under something to droop under the burden of something. □ *The porch roof sagged under the weight of the snow.* □ *The springs of the car sagged under the weight of all the passengers.*

sage advice very good and wise advice. □ *My parents gave me some sage advice when I turned 18.* □ *I asked my uncle for some of his sage advice.*

sail against something to operate a boat or ship, so as to move against the wind. □ *It takes skill and training to sail against the wind.* □ *The huge cruise ship sailed against the wind all the way to St. Thomas.*

sail along (something**)** to travel on a course in a boat or plane. □ *The huge white ship sailed along the Amazon River slowly and peacefully.* □ *The boat sailed along peacefully.*

sail around to travel by water in a boat or ship. □ *We sailed around for about an hour and then went back to the shore.* □ *Let's go out and sail around before dinner.*

sail for some place to depart in a boat or ship for some place. □ *This ship sails for Bridgetown, Barbados, at noon today.* □ *We will sail for home early in the morning.*

sail from some place **to** some place else to move or travel from one place to another in a boat or ship. □ *We sailed from San Juan to Acapulco.* □ *The ship sailed from its home port to Baltimore overnight.*

sail into someone *Fig.* to attack someone; to chastise someone. (Based on **sail into** someone **or something**.) □ *The angry coach sailed into the players.* □ *The teacher sailed into Timmy for breaking the window.*

S

sail into someone or something **1.** to crash into someone or something with a boat or ship. □ *The boat sailed into the dock, causing considerable damage.* □ *I was in my skiff when a larger boat sailed into me.* **2.** to crash into someone or something. □ *The missile sailed into the soldiers, injuring a few.* □ *The car sailed into the lamppost.*

sail in(to something**) 1.** *Lit.* to travel into something or some place in a boat or ship. □ *We sailed into the harbor nearly an hour late.* □ *We sailed in at noon.* **2.** *Fig.* to move or proceed into something or some place gracefully or without resistance. □ *She sailed into the room wearing a flowing gown.* □ *Three young maidens sailed into the room before the door closed.*

sail (right) through something **1.** *Lit.* to travel through something in a boat or ship. □ *The line of boats sailed right through the Grenadines in the daylight hours.* □ *We sailed through the narrows without a pilot.* **2.** *Fig.* to go through something very quickly and easily. □ *The kids just sailed right through the ice cream and cake. There was not a bit left.* □ *You have sailed through your allowance already.* **3.** *Fig.* to get through a procedure, evaluation, or vote quickly and easily. □ *The proposal sailed through the committee with no debate.* □ *I hope that this matter sails through quickly.*

sail under false colors 1. *Lit.* to sail with false identification. (Pirates often sailed under the national flag of the ship they planned on attacking.) □ *The ship, sailing under false colors, suddenly started to pursue our ship.* □ *Bluebeard the pirate was known for sailing under false colors.* **2.** *Fig.* to function deceptively. □ *You are not who you seem to be. You are sailing under false colors.* □ *Tom was sailing under false colors and finally got found out.*

sail up a river to travel upstream on a river in a boat or ship. □ *We sailed up the Amazon River in a large, seagoing ship.* □ *It was not possible to sail up the Mississippi as far as we wanted.*

Sakes alive! Go to Land(s) sakes (alive)!

sally forth to go forth; to leave and go out. □ *The soldiers sallied forth from behind the stone wall.* □ *Well, it's time to sally forth and drive to work.*

the **salt of the earth** *Fig.* the most worthy of people; a very good or worthy person. (A biblical reference, Matthew 5:13.) □ *Mrs. Jones is the salt of the earth. She is the first to help anyone in trouble.* □ *Frank's mother is the salt of the earth. She has five children of her own and yet fosters three others.*

salt something **away**[†] **1.** *Lit.* to store and preserve a foodstuff by salting it. □ *The farmer's wife salted a lot of fish and hams away for the winter.* □ *She salted away a lot of food.* **2.** *Fig.* to store something; to place something in reserve. □ *I need to salt some money away for my retirement.* □ *I will salt away some money for emergencies.*

salt something **down**[†] to place salt on something, such as icy roads. □ *I won't go out until midmorning, after they have salted the roads down.* □ *I hope they salt down the roads soon.*

salt something **with** something **1.** *Lit.* to put a variety of salt or a salt substitute onto some food. □ *Oscar salts his food with a salt substitute.* □ *Did you salt your meat with salt or something else?* **2.** *Fig.* to put something into something

as a lure. (Refers to putting a bit of gold dust into a mine in order to deceive someone into buying the mine.) □ *The land agent salted the bank of the stream with a little gold dust hoping for a land rush to start.* □ *Someone salted the mine to fool the prospectors.*

salute someone **with** something **1.** *Lit.* to greet someone with a formal hand salute. □ *He failed to salute the officer with the proper salute and was reprimanded.* □ *David saluted the captain with the appropriate salute and passed on by.* **2.** *Fig.* to greet or honor someone with the firing of guns or an overflight of airplanes. (Military or government.) □ *The government saluted the visiting dignitary with a twenty-one gun salute.* □ *They saluted the prime minister with a flight of acrobatic jets.*

salvage something **from** someone or something to rescue or save something from someone or something. □ *The baby got into the eggs, but I was able to salvage about six of them from him before they were broken all over the place.* □ *I salvaged a good pair of shoes from the trash.*

the **same as** someone or something identical to someone or something. □ *Can you build me a birdhouse the same as yours?* □ *Have you noticed that Mary looks the same as her mother?*

same difference the same; no difference at all. □ *Pink, fuchsia, what does it matter? Same difference.* □ *Whether you go or I go, it's the same difference.*

The **same for me.** Go to I'll have the same.

Same here. Me too!; I agree! □ *Bob: I'll have chocolate ice cream! Bill: Same here.* □ *Mary: I'll vote for the best candidate. Tom: Same here!*

same o(l)' same o(l)' *Sl.* the same old thing as one has had before or is used to. □ *I'm getting tired of the same ol' same ol'.* □ *Why not something different? Do you like the same o' same o'?*

the **same old story** something that occurs or has occurred in the same way often. □ *Jim's got no money. It's the same old story. He's spent it all on clothing.* □ *The company is getting rid of workers. It's the same old story—a shortage of orders.*

The **same to you.** The same comment applies to you. (This can be a polite or a rude comment.) □ *Bill: Have a pleasant evening. Bob: Thank you. The same to you.* □ *Mary: You're the most horrible person I've ever met! John: The same to you!*

sand something **down**[†] **1.** to make something smooth by rubbing it with sandpaper. (To act on the main body of the object, not the imperfections.) □ *You should sand the board down before you paint it.* □ *Please sand down the board.* **2.** to remove bumps or imperfections on the surface of something by rubbing them with sandpaper. (To act on the imperfections, not the main body of the object.) □ *Sand these bumps down, will you?* □ *Sand down these bumps, please.*

the **sands of time** *Fig.* the accumulated tiny amounts of time; time represented by the sand in an hourglass. □ *The sands of time will make you grow old like everyone else.* □ *My only enemy is the sands of time.*

sandwich someone or something **between** people or things *Fig.* to enclose someone or something on both sides between people or things in any combination. □ *We had* to sandwich the children between us because there were no other seats close by. □ We had to sandwich the package between Ed and the side of the bus.

satiate someone or an animal **with** something to provide enough of something for someone or an animal. □ *The waiters set out to satiate the guests with whatever sinful desserts they desired.* □ *The zookeeper satiated the tigress with a huge leg of beef.*

satisfy someone or an animal **with** something to use something to please or content someone or an animal. □ *Do you think I can satisfy Mrs. Franklin with payment for her broken window?* □ *A dog biscuit will satisfy the dog until its regular feeding time.*

satisfy something **by** something and **satisfy** something **with** something to fulfill a requirement, using a particular thing, such as a school or college course. □ *Can I satisfy the requirements by taking a course in art?* □ *Will I satisfy the requirement with this course?*

saturate someone or something **with** something to drench someone or something thoroughly with something. □ *The rain saturated them all with cooling water.* □ *Irrigation saturated the field with the moisture they needed.*

Saturday night special a small, easily obtainable pistol. □ *There was another killing last night with a Saturday night special.* □ *That's the tenth shooting done with a Saturday night special this week.*

saunter along to walk along slowly; to ramble along. □ *Bob sauntered along, looking as if he didn't have a care in the world.* □ *I was just sauntering along, minding my own business, when all of a sudden a mugger jumped out and swiped my purse.*

save a bundle (on something) *Fig.* to save a lot of money on the purchase of something. □ *I managed to save a bundle on a car by buying a used one.*

Save it! *Inf.* Stop talking.; Shut up!; Tell it to me later. □ *I've heard enough. Save it!* □ *Save it! You talk too much!*

save (money) on something to save money or some amount of money on the purchase of something. □ *I can save a lot of money on this purchase by buying it somewhere else.* □ *I am sure you can save on a new car if you shop wisely.*

save (money) toward something to accumulate money toward the purchase of something. □ *I am saving my money toward the purchase of a big-screen TV.* □ *I'm saving toward a new car.*

save money up† **(for** something) to accumulate an amount of money for the purchase of something. □ *I'm saving my money up for a car.* □ *Save up your money for a car.*

save one's **bacon** Go to **save** someone's **skin.**

save one's **breath** *Fig.* to refrain from talking, explaining, or arguing. □ *There is no sense in trying to convince her. Save your breath.* □ *Tell her to save her breath. He won't listen to her.*

save (one's**) face** *Fig.* to preserve one's good standing, pride, or high position (after a failure). □ *The ambassador was more interested in saving his face than winning the argument.* □ *Most diplomats are concerned with saving face.*

save oneself **(for marriage)** *Euph.* to remain a virgin until marriage. □ *No, I can't. I love you, but I'm saving myself for marriage.* □ *His buddies teased him, asking if he was saving himself.*

save someone **in the (very) nick of time** Go to **in the (very) nick of time.**

save someone or something **from** someone or something to rescue someone or something from someone or something. □ *The cop was able to save the kid from his attackers.* □ *I managed to save some old photographs from the fire.*

save someone's **neck** Go to next.

save someone's **skin** and **save** someone's **neck; save** one's **bacon** *Fig.* to save someone from injury, embarrassment, or punishment. □ *I saved my skin by getting the job done on time.* □ *Thanks for saving my neck! I would have fallen down the stairs if you hadn't held my arm.*

save (something**) for a rainy day** and **put** something **aside for a rainy day; hold** something **back for a rainy day; keep** something **for a rainy day** *Fig.* to reserve something—usually money—for some future need. □ *I've saved a little money for a rainy day.* □ *Keep some extra allowance for a rainy day.*

save something **for** someone or something to reserve something for someone or something. □ *Please save some cake for me.* □ *I am saving this cake for tomorrow.*

save something **up**† to save something; to accumulate something. □ *I'm saving up cans for recycling.* □ *If you'd only save your money up, you could buy anything you want.*

save the day to produce a good result when a bad result was expected. □ *The team was expected to lose, but Sally made three points and saved the day.* □ *Your excellent speech calmed the crowd and saved the day.*

save (up) (for something) to accumulate money in order to buy something. □ *I can't buy a car because I am saving up for college.* □ *I don't have the money now, but I am saving up.*

saved by the bell *Cliché* saved by the timely intervention of someone or something. (Alludes to a boxer who is saved from being counted out by the bell that ends a round.) □ *I was going to have to do my part, but someone knocked on the door and I didn't have to do it. I was saved by the bell.* □ *I wish I had been saved by the bell.*

saving grace *Cliché* the one thing that saves or redeems someone or something that would otherwise be a total disaster. □ *Her saving grace is that she has a lot of money.* □ *The saving grace for the whole evening was the good music played by the band.*

savor of something to taste like something. □ *This casserole savors of nutmeg.* □ *The meat savors of too much garlic.*

saw against the grain Go to **against the grain.**

saw into something to cut into something with a saw. □ *The carpenter sawed into the beam and had it cut in two in no time at all.* □ *Be careful not to saw into the table.*

saw something **down**† to cut something down with a saw. □ *We are going to have to saw that dead tree down before it falls on the house.* □ *I'll saw down the tree.*

saw something **off (of)** something and **saw** something **off**† to cut something off something with a saw. (*Of* is usually retained before pronouns.) □ *He sawed the branch off of the tree.* □ *Sam sawed the dead branch off.* □ *Saw off another branch on the other side.*

saw something **(up†) (in(to)** something**)** to cut something up into pieces with a saw. □ *Jake sawed the logs up into pieces the right size for the fireplace.* □ *Would you saw up the logs into smaller pieces?*

saw through something to cut through something with a saw. □ *I can't saw through this wood. It's too hard!* □ *I can saw through it!*

say a mouthful *Fig.* to say a lot; to say something very important or meaningful. □ *When you said things were busy around here, you said a mouthful. It is terribly busy.* □ *You sure said a mouthful, Bob. Things are really busy.*

Say cheese! *Inf.* an expression used by photographers to get people to smile, which they must do while saying the word *cheese.* □ *"All of you please stand still and say cheese!" said the photographer.* □ *"Is everybody ready? Say cheese!" asked Mary, aiming the camera.*

say grace to say a prayer of gratitude before or after a meal. □ *Grandfather always says grace at Thanksgiving.* □ *A local preacher said grace at the banquet.*

Say hello to someone **(for me).** Please convey my good wishes to someone. (The *someone* can be a person's name or a pronoun. See also **Give my best to someone.; Remember me to someone.**) □ *Andy: Good-bye, Tom. Say hello to your brother for me. Tom: Sure. Bye, Andy.* □ *Sally: Well, good-bye. Mary: Bye, Sally. And say hello to Jane. Mary: Sure. Bye-bye.*

a **say (in** something**)** Go to a **voice (in** something**).**

Say no more. *Inf.* I agree.; I will do it.; I concede, no need to continue talking. □ *John: Someone ought to take this stuff outside. Bill: Say no more. Consider it done.* □ *Mary: Shouldn't we turn here if we plan to visit Jane? Alice: Say no more. Here we go.*

say one's **piece** and **speak** one's **piece** to say what one must say; to recite what one has planned to say. □ *Look, just say your piece and get out of here.* □ *I said my piece and left.*

say something **about** someone or something **1.** to make remarks about someone or something. □ *What did you say about me?* □ *I think that Fran must have said something about me to you.* **2.** to indicate or reveal something about someone or something. □ *They all cheered. That really says something about Tom's popularity.* □ *The fact that almost no one came to his party says something about Walter, I think.*

say something **against** someone or something to speak out against someone or something; to make a case against someone or something. □ *I would never say anything against you!* □ *No one would say anything against your work.*

say something **for** something [for something] to imply something good about something. □ *The speed with which we were able to sell the house says something for the state of the real estate market.* □ *The number of new cars on the road says something for the state of the nation's economy.*

say something **in a roundabout way** to imply something without saying it; to say something indirectly; to speak using circumlocution. □ *Why don't you say what you*

mean? Why do you always say something in a roundabout way? □ *What did she mean? Why did she say it in a roundabout way?*

say something **in plain English** Go to **in plain English.**

say something **in plain language** Go to **in plain language.**

say something **out loud** to say something so it can be heard; to say something that others might be thinking, but not saying. □ *Yes, I said it, but I didn't mean to say it out loud.* □ *If you know the answer, please say it out loud.*

say something **over (and over (again))** to repeat something, perhaps many times. □ *I have said it over and over again! Why don't you listen?* □ *Why do you keep saying it over?*

say something **(right) to** someone's **face** to say something (unpleasant) directly to someone. □ *She knew I thought she was rude because I said it right to her face.* □ *I thought she felt that way about me, but I never thought she'd say it to my face.*

say something **to oneself 1.** *Lit.* to mutter something to oneself so that no one else can hear. □ *He said something to himself, but I didn't catch what it was.* □ *I said the answer to myself and no one else was supposed to hear it.* **2.** *Fig.* to think something to oneself. □ *When I thought of him as a basketball player, I said to myself that he really isn't tall enough.* □ *I said a few choice critical remarks to myself when she presented her talk.*

say something **to** someone to tell something to someone. □ *He didn't say anything to me.* □ *Did someone say something to you?*

say something **to** something to say yes or no to a proposal, request, etc. □ *I hope you will say yes to my proposal.* □ *Nothing was said to your request at the last meeting.*

say something **under** one's **breath** Go to **under** one's **breath.**

say that... to assume [something]; to suppose [that something were so]. □ *Say that x is equal to a whole number greater than 10.* □ *Say that two trains leave two different cities at the same time.*

say the word to give a signal to begin; to say yes or okay. □ *I'm ready to start any time you say the word.* □ *We'll all shout "Happy Birthday!" when I say the word.*

say uncle Go to **holler uncle.**

Say what? *Inf.* What did you say?; Please repeat what you said. □ *Sally: Would you like some more salad? Fred: Say what? Sally: Salad? Would you like some more salad?* □ *John: Put this one over there. Sue: Say what? John: Never mind, I'll do it.*

Say when. *Inf.* Tell me when I have given you enough of something, usually a liquid. (Sometimes answered simply with *When.*) □ *Tom (pouring milk into Fred's glass): Say when, Fred. Fred: When.* □ *John: Do you want some more juice? Mary: Yes. John: Okay. Say when.*

Says me! and **Sez me!** *Inf.* a formulaic answer to *Says who?* □ *Tom: Says who? Fred: Says me, that's who!* □ *Tom: You? Fred: You got it, buster. Says me!*

Says who? and **Sez who?** *Inf.* a formulaic challenge indicating disagreement with someone who has said something. □ *Tom: Says who? Fred: Says me, that's who!* □ *She*

S

drew herself up to her full height, looked him straight in the eye, and said, "Says who?"

Says you! *Inf.* That's just what you say!; You don't know what you are talking about! □ *Fred: You are fat and ugly. Tom: Says you!* □ *Mary: People who go around correcting other people were found to be very annoying in a recent survey. Bill: Says you!*

scab over [for a wound] to form a scab. □ *The wound soon scabbed over and the injury was well on its way to healing.* □ *I hope this shaving cut scabs over before I have to leave for work.*

scale something down† to reduce the size or cost of something. □ *The bad economy forced us to scale the project down.* □ *Liz scaled down the project.*

scale something to something to design or adjust the size of one thing to match or complement the size of another thing. □ *The architect sought to scale the office building to the buildings surrounding it.* □ *The playhouse will have to be scaled to the main house.*

scamper along [for a child or small animal] to run along nimbly. □ *The rabbit scampered along, unaware that a fox was following it.* □ *It is time for Timmy to scamper along home.*

scamper away [for a child or small animal] to run away nimbly. □ *The rabbit scampered away across the lawn.* □ *The children scampered away when they heard the teacher coming.*

scar over [for an injury] to form and leave a scar. □ *The wound will scar over, but your arm will never be the same as it was before the accident.*

*scarce as hen's teeth and **scarcer than hen's teeth** *Cliché* scarce; seldom found. (*Also: **as ~.**) □ *I do declare, decent people are as scarce as hen's teeth in these chaotic times.* □ *Handmade lace is scarcer than hen's teeth; most lace is made by machine.*

scarcely exchange more than some number of **words with** someone Go to exchange no more than some number of words with someone.

scarcely have time to breathe Go to hardly have time to breathe.

scarcer than hen's teeth Go to scarce as hen's teeth.

scare one out of one's mind Go to frighten one out of one's wits.

scare one out of one's wits Go to frighten one out of one's wits.

scare someone or an animal off† to frighten someone or an animal away. □ *The dog's barking scared the burglar off.* □ *The barking scared off the prowler.*

scare someone or an animal out† Go to scare someone or an animal out of something.

scare someone or an animal out of something and **scare someone or an animal out†** to frighten someone or an animal out of something or some place. □ *The old man tried to scare the kids out of his orchard by shouting at them.* □ *Karen scared out the intruder.*

scare someone or an animal to death Go to frighten someone or an animal to death.

scare someone or something away† (**from** someone or something) to frighten someone or something away from someone or something. □ *He put on a gruff exterior to scare everyone away from him.* □ *The bear scared away a lot of people from the campground.*

scare someone or something up† *Rur.* to search for and find someone or something. □ *Go out in the kitchen and scare some food up.* □ *I'll see if I can scare up somebody to fix the broken chair.*

scare someone out of something to startle someone; to frighten someone into losing something, such as a year's worth of growth, ten years of life, etc. □ *You nearly scared me out of my skin!* □ *The bad news scared Roger out of ten years' growth.*

scare someone stiff *Fig.* to frighten someone severely. (*Stiff = dead.*) □ *That loud noise scared me stiff.* □ *The robber jumped out and scared us stiff.*

scare something out of someone to frighten someone very badly. (The *something* can be *the living daylights, the wits, the hell, the shit,* etc. Use discretion with *shit.*) □ *Gee, you scared the living daylights out of me!* □ *The police tried to scare the truth out of her.* □ *The door blew shut and scared the hell out of me.*

scare the living daylights out of someone Go to frighten the hell out of someone.

scare the pants off (of) someone to frighten someone very badly. (*Of* is usually retained before pronouns.) □ *Wow! You nearly scared the pants off me!* □ *The explosion scared the pants off of everyone.*

scare the wits out of someone Go to frighten the hell out of someone.

scared silly frightened very much. □ *I was scared silly by the loud explosion.* □ *We were scared silly to go into the park after dark.*

scared stiff *Fig.* badly frightened. □ *We were scared stiff by the robber.* □ *I was scared stiff when the dog growled at me.*

scared to death Go to frightened to death.

scarf out *Sl.* to overeat. □ *I scarf out whenever we have pizza.* □ *My brother scarfs out every day—around the clock!*

scarf something down† *Sl.* to eat something, perhaps in a hurry; to swallow something, perhaps in a hurry. □ *Are you going to scarf this whole thing down?* □ *Here, scarf down this sandwich.*

scatter something about† and **scatter something around†** to throw or distribute something about. □ *The children scattered the books about and left the room in a general mess.* □ *They scattered about all the books and papers.*

scavenge (around) for someone or something to search everywhere for someone or something. □ *We had to scavenge for a person who would agree to run for president in my place.* □ *Sam scavenged around for a socket wrench.*

scheme against someone or something to plot or conspire against someone or something. □ *A group of generals was plotting against the government.* □ *They schemed against the king until he caught them and put an end to it.*

scheme for something to plot and plan for something, perhaps using deception. □ *She is scheming for a raise.* □ *Ted is always scheming for a way to miss work.*

schiz(z) out *Sl.* to freak out; to lose mental control. □ *What a day! I nearly schizzed out.* □ *I schizzed out during the test. Got an F.*

the school of hard knocks *Fig.* the school of life's experiences, as opposed to a formal, classroom education. □ *I didn't go to college, but I went to the school of hard knocks. I learned everything by experience.*

school of thought a particular philosophy or way of thinking about something. □ *One school of thought holds that cats cause allergic reactions.* □ *I come from the school of thought that believes people should always be polite.*

school someone **in** something to train, discipline, or coach someone in something. □ *The voice coach schooled the singer in excellent breathing techniques.* □ *We were schooled in oratory and debate.* □ *She schooled herself in patience.*

scoff at someone or something to show ridicule or scorn for someone or something. □ *The directors scoffed at her when she presented her plan.* □ *They scoffed at my new hat, not realizing how stylish it was.*

scold someone **about** something to rebuke or chastise someone about something. □ *How many times have I scolded you about that?* □ *Please don't scold me about something I didn't do.*

scold someone **for** something to rebuke or chastise someone for doing something. □ *The manager scolded the worker for misplacing the door key.* □ *The teacher scolded all the students for their bad behavior.*

scoop something **out of** something and **scoop** something **out**† to remove something from something by dipping or scooping. □ *She scooped the water out of the bottom of the rowboat.* □ *Karen scooped out the water.*

scoop something **up**† to gather and remove something by scooping, dipping, or bailing. □ *Karen scooped the nuts up and put them in a bag.* □ *Jill scooped up all the money she had won and left the poker table.*

scoot down (to some place**)** to go (down) somewhere in a hurry. □ *I want you to scoot down to the store and get me a dozen eggs. Okay?* □ *I'll scoot down as soon as I finish reading the newspaper.*

scoot over to slide sideways while seated. □ *Scoot over and let me sit down.* □ *If you scoot over, we can get another person in this row.*

scoot over to someone or something to travel or move over to someone or something or some place in a hurry. □ *Scoot over to Don and ask him to come here for a minute.* □ *We all scooted over to the stadium for the football game.*

scope (on) someone *Sl.* to evaluate a member of the opposite sex visually. □ *He scoped every girl who came in the door.* □ *He wouldn't like it if somebody scoped on him. Or would he?*

scope someone or something **out**† *Sl.* to look someone or something over; to check someone or something out. □ *Hey, scope the new car out!* □ *Dave was scoping out all the girls.*

score against someone or something to make a point or goal against someone or some team. □ *Because of his bad ankle, Fred was unable to score against his defender.* □ *We never scored against the visiting team.*

score something **for** something **1.** to arrange music for one or more musical instruments; to arrange music for a particular type of voice or voices. □ *The arranger scored the music for two pianos.* □ *The arranger scored the song for a four-part chorus.* **2.** to scratch something, such as glass, for breaking. □ *Valerie scored the piece of glass for breaking and then snapped it off.* □ *The worker scored the pane of glass for snapping off.*

score something **(up**†**) against** someone or something to tally up a score against someone or some team. □ *Tara scored a few points against Sally.* □ *The Bears scored up thirteen points against the Giants.*

score with someone or a group *Inf.* to please someone or a group. □ *Her rendition of "Old Kentucky Home" really scored with the audience.* □ *You really score with me.*

scour something **for** someone or something to look carefully and thoroughly in something for someone or something. □ *I scoured the entire roster of members for a person who would agree to run for president.* □ *The police scoured the entire area for any sign of the suspects.*

scour something **off (of)** something and **scour** something **off**† to clean something off something else by scouring. (*Of* is usually retained before pronouns.) □ *See if you can scour the rust off the cookie sheet.* □ *I will scour off the rust with steel wool.*

scour something **out**† to clean something out by scouring. □ *Would you scour the pans out?* □ *Please scour out the pans—don't just wash them.*

scour something **out of** something to clean something out of something by scouring. □ *Did you scour the rust out of the pan?* □ *Please scour the burned material out of the bowl.*

scout around (for someone or something**)** to look around for someone or something. □ *I don't know who would do a good job for you, but I'll scout around for a likely candidate.* □ *You stay here. I'll scout around.*

scout someone or something **out**† to search for and discover someone or something. □ *I will scout a new salesclerk out for you if you want.* □ *I'll scout out a new clerk for you.*

scout someone or something **up**† to search for and find someone or something. □ *I'll scout up a costume for the Halloween party.* □ *Can you scout a date up for Friday night?*

scowl at someone or something to make a frown of disapproval or displeasure at someone or something. □ *Why are you scowling at me? I didn't do anything wrong!* □ *Mary scowled at her noisy cat.*

scramble for someone or something to push and struggle to get to someone or something. □ *All the teenagers scrambled for the rock star but couldn't catch him.* □ *The children scrambled for the candy as it fell from the piñata.*

scrape along (on something**)** and **scrape along (with** something**)** to manage just to get along with a minimum amount of something. □ *We can just scrape along on the money I earn from my sewing.* □ *Do you think you can scrape along with just $400 per month?*

scrape by (on something**)** and **scrape by (with** something**)** to manage just to get by with something. (Usually applies to a more specific period or time or a more specific event than **scrape along (on** something**).**) □ *There is not really enough money to live on, and we just have to* scrape by on what we can earn. □ We can't scrape by with only that amount of money.

scrape by (something) to manage just to get by something. □ I scraped by the man standing at the gate and got into the theater without a ticket. □ Mary scraped by the cart that was blocking the crowded hallway.

scrape by (with something) Go to scrape by (on something).

scrape someone or something **together**[†] and **scrape** someone or something **up**[†] Fig. to find and collect something; to locate and assemble a group of people or things. (Based on **scrape** something **up**.) □ I'm sure we can scrape up someone for the job. □ Mary scraped a few dollars together for some new books. □ John barely scraped up enough money to pay his rent.

scrape something **away**[†] **(from** something) to scratch or rasp something off something. □ Ted scraped the rough places away from the fender he was repairing. □ Ted scraped away the rough places.

scrape something **off (of)** someone or something and **scrape** something **off**[†] to rub or stroke something off someone or something. (Of is usually retained before pronouns.) □ I sat down and scraped the caked mud off of me. It was everywhere! □ Jake scraped off the rust.

scrape something **out**[†] to empty something by scraping. □ Scrape the pan out. Don't leave any of that good sauce inside. □ Please scrape out the pan.

scrape something **out of** something and **scrape** something **out**[†] to remove something by scraping. □ Scrape all the peanut butter out of the jar before you discard it. □ Scrape out the peanut butter.

scrape something **together**[†] to gather things together by scraping. □ The waiter scraped all the crumbs together and removed them from the table with a little gadget. □ Karen scraped together all the trimmings and set them aside.

scrape the bottom of the barrel to select from among the worst; to choose from what is left over. □ You've bought a bad-looking car. You really scraped the bottom of the barrel to get that one. □ The worker you sent over was the worst I've ever seen. Send me another—and don't scrape the bottom of the barrel.

scrape through (something**) 1.** Lit. to move through something, scraping or rubbing the sides. □ The car, going at a very high speed, scraped through the tunnel. □ It just managed to scrape through. **2.** Fig. to get by something just barely; to pass a test just barely. □ Alice passed the test, but she just scraped through it. □ I just scraped through my calculus test.

scratch about (for something) and **scratch around (for** something) **1.** Lit. to hunt for something in dirt, gravel, rocks, etc. □ The prospector spent the day scratching about for signs of gold. □ The chickens were scratching around for something to eat. **2.** Fig. to look very hard for something. □ The children were scratching about the kitchen for something to eat. □ I've been scratching around for a new assistant for months now.

scratch at something to scratch something. □ You shouldn't scratch at a chigger bite because it might get infected. □ Don't scratch at it!

scratch someone or something **from** something to mark the name of someone or something off a list. □ We were obliged to scratch Dave from the list. □ The judges scratched the large collie from the eligibility list.

scratch someone or something **out**[†] to mark out the name of someone or something. □ I scratched John out and wrote in George instead. □ I scratched out John and forgot about him.

scratch someone or something **up**[†] to damage or mar someone or something by scratching. □ Being thrown clear of the car in the accident didn't break any bones, but it scratched her up a lot. □ Who scratched up my coffee table?

scratch someone's **back 1.** Lit. to scratch, usually with the fingers, the parts of someone's back that they cannot reach. □ Please scratch my back between my shoulder blades. **2.** Fig. to do a favor for someone in return for a favor done for you. □ You scratch my back, and I'll scratch yours. □ We believe that the mayor has been scratching the treasurer's back.

scratch something **away**[†] to rub or scrape something off by scratching. □ Look at the finish on this furniture. The cat has almost scratched it away! □ That cat scratched away the finish on the table!

scratch the surface 1. Lit. to scratch something just on the surface, not extending the mark below the finish into the wood, stone, marble, below. □ There is no serious damage done to the bench. You only scratched the surface. **2.** Fig. to just begin to find out about something; to examine only the superficial aspects of something. □ The investigation of the governor's staff revealed some suspicious dealing. It is thought that the investigators have just scratched the surface. □ We don't know how bad the problem is. We've only scratched the surface.

scream at someone or something to yell or screech at someone or something. □ Why are you screaming at me? □ Go scream at the dog, not me!

scream bloody murder and **yell bloody murder** Fig. to complain bitterly; to complain unduly. □ When we put him in an office without a window, he screamed bloody murder. □ There is something wrong next door. Everyone is yelling bloody murder.

scream down (on someone or something) Fig. [for something, such as birds or bombs] to dive down on someone or something, with a loud noise or very swiftly. □ The bombs screamed down on the helpless peasants. □ As the bombs screamed down, some people ran and some prayed.

scream for something to yell or shriek for something. □ The teenage audience applauded and screamed for more. □ The children said they were screaming for ice cream.

scream someone **down**[†] to scream loudly at someone; to outscream someone. (Compare this with **shout** someone **down**.) □ The angry crowd screamed down the politician. □ They screamed her down and drove her from the platform.

scream something **out**[†] to say something in a very loud voice. □ She screamed his name out for everyone to hear. □ Liz screamed out the winner's name.

scream with something to scream because of something, such as pain, anger, rage, etc. □ Frank screamed with pain *when the car door closed on his fingers.* □ *The teacher screamed with rage when the student talked back.*

screeching (drunk) *Sl.* intoxicated; very drunk. □ *How can anybody be so screeching drunk on four beers?* □ *She's not just drunk; she's screeching.*

screen someone or something **(off†) (from** someone or something**)** to make someone or something out of sight or blocked off to someone or something by erecting a screen. □ *We screened her off from the patient in the next bed.* □ *We screened off the yard from the street.*

screen someone or something **out of** something and **screen** someone or something **out†** to filter someone or something out of something. □ *The test screened all the unqualified candidates out of the group.* □ *We screened out the suppliers who were not financially sound.*

screw around 1. *Inf.* to mess around; to waste time. □ *Stop screwing around and get to work!* □ *I'm not screwing around, I'm thinking.* **2.** *Inf.* to play sexually; to indulge in sexual intercourse. □ *A few couples were screwing around at the party.* □ *They say that Ted and Alice are screwing around a lot.*

screw around with someone or something *Inf.* to fiddle with or mess around with someone or something. □ *Andy screwed around with his clock until he broke it.* □ *Look, chum! Don't screw around with me!*

screw off *Inf.* to waste time. □ *Stop screwing off and get busy!* □ *I'm not screwing off. This is my lunch hour.*

screw someone **around** *Inf.* to harass or bother someone. □ *Don't screw me around, man! I bite back!* □ *Max got tired of being screwed around by Lefty.*

screw someone or something **up†** *Inf.* to interfere with someone or something; to mess up someone or something. □ *Try again and don't screw it up this time.* □ *You really screwed up my brother by not being on time.*

screw someone **out of** something *Inf.* to cheat someone out of something. □ *I think you screwed me out of ten bucks on that deal.* □ *Max screwed me out of what was due me.*

screw someone **over†** *Sl.* to give someone a very bad time; to scold someone severely. □ *Those guys really screwed you over. What started it?* □ *Don't think you can screw over me and my friends. I won't let you.*

screw someone **up†** *Inf.* to confuse someone mentally. □ *Please don't screw me up again!* □ *You screwed up my train of thought.*

screw something **down†** to secure something to the floor or a base by the use of screws. □ *You had better screw these seats down or someone will knock them over.* □ *Please screw down the shelf.*

screw something **into** something to twist something that is threaded into something. □ *I screwed all the screws into the back of the computer and turned it on.* □ *Please screw this bracket into the wall.*

screw something **(on)(to** something**)** to attach something to something by the use of screws or other threaded fasteners. □ *Screw the bracket onto the wall, will you?* □ *Screw on the bracket to the wall.*

screw something **up†** to attach something to a higher place by the use of screws. □ *The bracket holding the shelf up*

has come loose. Will you please screw it up again? □ *Please screw up this loose bracket.*

screw up 1. *Inf.* to mess up. □ *I hope I don't screw up this time.* □ *The waiter screwed up again.* **2.** *Inf.* a mess; a blunder; utter confusion. (Usually **screw-up.**) □ *This is the chef's screw-up, not mine.* □ *One more screw-up like that and you're fired.*

screw up one's **courage** *Fig.* to build up one's courage. □ *I guess I have to screw up my courage and go to the dentist.* □ *I spent all morning screwing up my courage to take my driver's test.*

screwed, blued, and tattooed 1. *Sl.* taken advantage of □ *I got a bad deal. I got screwed, blued, and tattooed.* □ *When John bought his wreck of a car, he got screwed, blued, and tattooed.* **2.** *Sl.* intoxicated. □ *Who wants to go out and get screwed, blued, and tattooed?* □ *All four of them went out and got screwed, blued, and tattooed.*

screwed up *Inf.* ruined; messed up. □ *This is a really screwed up schedule. Let's start over again.* □ *Your schedule is completely screwed up.*

scribble away (at something**)** to write hard and fast at some task. □ *He scribbled away at his notes as the lecturer droned on.* □ *Jane sat in the library scribbling away.*

scribble something **down†** to write something down fast and not too neatly. □ *He scribbled the figure down and raced for the telephone.* □ *Liz scribbled down the telephone number.*

scrimp and save and **pinch and scrape** to be very thrifty; to live on very little money, often in order to save up for something. □ *We had to scrimp and save in order to send the children to college.* □ *The Smiths pinched and scraped all year in order to go on a Caribbean cruise.*

scrimp on something to try to economize on the use of something; to fail to use enough of something. □ *Please don't scrimp on the quality of the food.* □ *There is enough money. You don't have to scrimp on anything.*

scrounge around (for someone or something**)** *Fig.* to look around all over for someone or something. □ *I scrounged around for Jamie, but she was nowhere to be found.* □ *I will try to scrounge around for a replacement part that will do the job.*

scrounge someone or something **up†** *Fig.* to find someone or something somewhere; to dig someone or something up. □ *I can't think of anyone just now, but I will scrounge someone up.* □ *They scrounged up an escort for Liz.*

scrub someone or something **down†** to clean someone or something thoroughly by rubbing. □ *The mother scrubbed the baby down gently and put lotion on her.* □ *Please scrub down this floor.*

scrub someone or something **off†** to clean someone or something by rubbing. □ *Mother scrubbed Timmy off.* □ *Liz scrubbed off the countertop.*

scrub something **away†** to clean something away by rubbing. □ *See if you can scrub that rust away.* □ *Scrub away that rust if you can.*

scrub something **off (of)** something and **scrub** something **off†** to clean something off something by scrubbing. (*Of* is usually retained before pronouns.) □ *I have to scrub the mud off the porch steps.* □ *Did you scrub off all the grease?*

scrub something **out**† to clean out the inside of something by rubbing or brushing. □ *Please scrub these pots out and put them away.* □ *Jim will scrub out the pots.*

scrub something **out of** something and **scrub** something **out**† to clean something out of something by scrubbing. □ *Please scrub the gravy out of the pot.* □ *Are you going to scrub out the burned material?*

scrub up 1. *Lit.* to clean oneself up. □ *You have to scrub up before dinner.* □ *Please go scrub up before you come to the table.* **2.** *Fig.* to clean oneself, especially one's hands and arms, as a preparation for performing a surgical procedure. □ *The surgeon scrubbed up thoroughly before the operation.* □ *When you finish scrubbing up, someone will help you on with sterile clothing.*

scrunch down to squeeze or huddle down into a smaller shape. □ *Mary scrunched down, trying to hide behind the chair.* □ *The children scrunched down so they wouldn't be seen.*

scrunch down into something to squeeze down into a small area or container. □ *Fred scrunched down into his seat, hoping no one would see him there.* □ *Don't scrunch down into your seat. It's bad for your posture.*

scrunch something **down**† **(into** something) **1.** to squeeze something into a smaller size or shape. □ *He scrunched the wad of paper down into a hard ball.* □ *Liz scrunched down the cloth into a pad for the hot pan.* □ *Scrunch the boxes down before you throw them away.* **2.** to pack something tightly into something. □ *Dave scrunched his clothing down into the drawer and closed it.* □ *Dave scrunched down his clothing into the suitcase.*

scrunch something **up**† to crush or crunch up. □ *I pounded the biscuits and scrunched them up into crumbs.* □ *He scrunched up the note and threw it upon the fire.*

scuff something **up**† to scrape or scratch something. □ *Who scuffed my floor up?* □ *Please don't scuff up my freshly polished floors!*

scuffle with someone to struggle or have a fight with someone. □ *The two prisoners scuffled with each other a little till a guard came along and saw them.* □ *The cowboys scuffled with the deputies when they came out of the saloon.*

scurry along to run or scamper along fast. □ *The children scurried along, trotting to school.* □ *We scurried along the trail, keeping watch out for things that might trip us up.*

scuttle across something to hurry across something. (Said especially of a small animal.) □ *A tiny mouse scuttled across the kitchen floor and startled me.* □ *A rabbit scuttled across my path.*

scuttle away [for a small animal] to run away. □ *The otters scuttled away as we approached.* □ *A skunk scuttled away quickly—thank heavens.*

scuzz someone **out**† *Sl.* to nauseate someone. □ *He had this unreal face that almost scuzzed me out!* □ *It's not nice to scuzz out people like that, especially when you hardly know them.*

a **sea change** *Fig.* a major change or transformation. □ *This is not the time for a sea change in our manufacturing division. There are too many orders at the moment.*

seal a bargain and **seal the bargain** *Fig.* to signify or celebrate the reaching of an agreement or bargain. □ *They*

signed the papers and sealed the bargain by drinking champagne.

seal someone's **fate** *Fig.* to determine finally the fate of someone. □ *His lying and cheating sealed his fate. He was convicted and sent to prison.*

seal something **off from** someone or something and **seal** something **off**† to make something inaccessible to someone or something. □ *The police sealed the building off from everyone.* □ *They sealed off the building from all the reporters.*

seal something **(up**†**) (with** something**)** to fasten something closed with something. □ *Please seal this box up with twine.* □ *Would you seal up this box with tape?*

seal the bargain Go to seal a bargain.

sealed (up) *Sl.* settled; secured; cinched. □ *The matter was sealed by Monday morning.* □ *The contract was sealed up just in time.*

sealed with a kiss and **SWAK** written and sent with love and care. (The initialism is sometimes written on love letters. Also an acronym.) □ *All her letters come SWAK.* □ *I know they are sealed with a kiss, because she says so.*

seam something **with** something to join the edges of something together with something. □ *The worker seamed the two parts of the carpet with a special tool.* □ *She seamed the material with a strip of cloth to strengthen the seam.*

the **seamy side of life** *Fig.* the most unpleasant or roughest aspect of life. (A reference to the inside of a garment where the seams show.) □ *Doctors in that area really see the seamy side of life.* □ *Mary saw the seamy side of life when she worked as a volunteer in the homeless shelter.*

search after someone or something to look for someone or something. (Perhaps over a long period of time.) □ *We searched after a suitable candidate for weeks.* □ *I am searching after a part for my '57 Chevy.*

search for someone or something to look very hard for someone or something. □ *I searched for Ted everywhere, but he was already gone.* □ *I have searched for my glasses high and low.*

search high and low (for someone or something**)** Go to hunt high and low (for someone or something).

Search me. *Inf.* I do not know.; You can search my clothing and my person, but you won't find the answer to your question anywhere near me. (The two words have equal stress.) □ *Jane: What time does Mary's flight get in? Sally: Search me.* □ *John: What kind of paint should I use on this fence? Bill: Search me.*

search someone **for** something to feel, touch, pat, frisk, or examine electronically a person's body, looking for something hidden underneath the clothes. □ *The police searched the suspect for hidden weapons.* □ *The airport guard used an electronic instrument to search the passengers for weapons.*

search someone or something **out**† to seek and find someone or something. □ *I will search Fred out. I know he's here somewhere.* □ *We have to search out the key to the safe-deposit box.*

search something **for** someone or something to examine something, looking for someone or something. □ *Everyone searched the house for little Wally, but he was not to be* *found.* □ *I searched all my coat pockets for the note, but I didn't find it.*

search something **with a fine-tooth comb** Go to go over something with a fine-tooth comb.

search through something to examine all the things found in something. □ *I searched through my books for the answer.* □ *My drawers were searched through thoroughly.*

season something **with** something to make something more flavorful with specific spices and herbs. □ *I always season my stews with lots of freshly ground black pepper.* □ *The chili was seasoned with cumin and allspice, among other things.*

seat someone **by** someone or something Go to **by** someone or something.

secede from something to withdraw from something. □ *Which was the first state to secede from the Union?* □ *We do not want to secede from the organization, but we will if we must.*

second-guess someone to try to predict what some person will do before it is known to anyone, including the person. □ *There is no point in trying to second-guess Bob. He is completely unpredictable.*

second hand from another person or source, not directly from personal experience or observation. □ *I wasn't present at the meeting. I heard about it at second hand.* □ *Frank tells stories about the Gulf War, but he got them second hand. He wasn't actually in the desert with the troops.*

***second nature to** someone easy and natural for someone. (*Typically: be ~; become ~.)* □ *Swimming is second nature to Jane.* □ *Flying a helicopter is no problem for Bob. It's become second nature to him.*

***second thoughts (about** someone or something**)** new doubts about someone or something. (*Typically: get ~; have ~; give someone ~.)* □ *I'm beginning to get second thoughts about Tom.* □ *You're giving me second thoughts about going there.* □ *I'm having second thoughts also.*

second to none better than everything else. □ *This is an excellent car—second to none.* □ *Her suggestion was second to none, and the manager accepted it eagerly.*

secure something **against** someone, something, or an animal **1.** to fasten something against the entry of someone, an animal, or something. □ *Jane secured the doors and windows against the prowler who was roving around the neighborhood.* □ *You had better secure the henhouse against coyotes.* **2.** to obtain a legal order involving someone or something. □ *I secured an injunction against Harry. If he bothers you again, he'll have to go into court to explain himself.* □ *We can't secure an injunction against this ruling.*

security against something something that keeps something safe; something that protects; a protection. □ *Insurance provides security against the financial losses owing to theft, loss, or damage.* □ *A good education is a security against unemployment.*

seduce someone **from** something to lure someone away from something. □ *The crooked agent seduced Jerry from his usual honest behavior.* □ *Frank was seduced from his proper ways by the offer of money.*

see a man about a dog *Fig.* to leave for some unmentioned purpose. (Often refers to going to the rest room.) □ *I don't know where Tom went. He said he had to see a man about a dog.* □ *When John said he was going to see a man about a dog, I thought he would be gone for only a minute.*

see about someone or something to investigate someone or something; to check on something that someone has said. □ *I don't know who is going on the trip. You ask Jill, and I'll see about Jerry.* □ *I will see about your request.*

see after someone or something to take care of someone or something. (The same as but less common than **look after** someone or something.) □ *Would you please see after Walter? He looks a little pale.* □ *I will see after the committee while they are meeting.*

see ahead (of someone or something**)** to be able to see into the distance in front of someone or something. □ *The fog was so thick I couldn't see ahead of the car.* □ *I can't see ahead, so I will have to stop.*

see around something **1.** *Lit.* to see what is on the other side of or partially concealed by something. □ *I could not see around the truck in front of me.* □ *Do you think I can see around corners?* **2.** *Fig.* to perceive someone's deception. □ *I see around your trickery!* □ *We all see around your stated purpose!*

see beyond something **1.** *Lit.* to be able to perceive into the distance beyond something. □ *Can you see beyond the big tree there, where the barn is on the horizon?* □ *I can't see beyond the end of the road. I think I need glasses.* **2.** *Fig.* to be able to imagine the future beyond a certain time or event. □ *He can't see beyond the next day—no sense of the future.* □ *Todd is usually able to see beyond his immediate situation. I do not know what happened this time.*

see double to see two of everything instead of one, owing to a medical disorder. □ *When I was driving, I saw two people on the road instead of one. I'm seeing double. There's something wrong with my eyes.* □ *Mike at first thought he was seeing double when he saw Mary with her sister. He didn't know she had a twin.*

see eye to eye (about someone or something**) (with** someone**)** and **see eye to eye (on** someone or something**) (with** someone**)** *Fig.* [for someone] to agree about someone or something with someone else. □ *I'm glad we see eye to eye about Todd with Mary.* □ *I see eye to eye with Mary.* □ *Will labor and management ever see eye to eye on the new contract?*

see fit (to do something**)** to decide to do something. □ *If I see fit to return, I'll bring Bill with me.* □ *She'll do it if she sees fit.*

See if I care! *Inf.* I do not care if you do it! □ *Mary: That does it! I'm going home to Mother! John: See if I care!* □ *Sue: I'm putting the sofa here, whether you like it or not. Bill: Go ahead! See if I care!*

see (neither) hide nor hair Go to **(neither) hide nor hair.**

See no evil, hear no evil, speak no evil. *Prov.* Ignore any evil that you come in contact with; be virtuous even though there is evil around you. (Often represented by three monkeys, one of which is covering his eyes, one his ears, and one his mouth.) □ *Jill: Do you have any idea why*

S

Fred is staying in the office so late every night? Jane: Not me. Like the three little monkeys, I see no evil, hear no evil, speak no evil.

see no further than the end of one's **nose** and **cannot see (any) further than the end of** one's **nose; can't see beyond the end of** one's **nose** *Fig.* to be narrow-minded; to lack understanding and perception. □ *She is so selfish she can see no further than the end of her nose.* □ *You don't care about anyone but yourself. You can't see any further than the end of your nose.*

see no objection (to something) and **not see any objection (to** something) not to think of any objection to something. □ *I see no objection to your idea.* □ *Do you see any objection?* □ *I do not see any objection to anything you have done.*

see one's **way (clear) (to** do something) to find it possible to do something. □ *I'd be happy if you could see your way clear to attend our meeting.* □ *I wanted to be there, but I couldn't see my way clear.*

see over something to be able to have a view over something such as a wall, fence, etc. □ *I couldn't see over the fence, but I could hear what was going on.* □ *We could not see over the wall.*

see red to be angry. □ *Whenever I think of the needless destruction of trees, I see red.* □ *Bill really saw red when the tax bill arrived.*

see someone **about** someone or something to confer with someone about someone or something. □ *Jill has to see the boss about one of her office staff members.* □ *I will have to see Jill about getting permission to go.*

see someone **across** something to accompany someone across a dangerous area. □ *Paul saw his mother across the field, which contained a number of hazards.* □ *Timmy offered to see the elderly lady across the street.*

see someone **as** someone or something to visualize someone as some other person or type of person. □ *I see you as a perfect candidate for the job.* □ *I don't see you as mayor.*

see someone **as** something to consider someone or something; to deem someone or something as something. □ *The manager saw the skilled employee as a godsend.* □ *John saw the new salesman as a threat to his territory.*

see someone **back (to** something) to accompany someone back to something or some place. □ *I saw her back to her apartment.* □ *I will see her back safely.*

see someone **down to** something to accompany or escort someone to a lower level. □ *I will see you down to the front door.* □ *Would you please see Mrs. Bracknell down to the door?*

see someone **home** to accompany someone home. □ *Bill agreed to see his aunt home after the movie.* □ *You don't need to see me home. It's perfectly safe, and I can get there on my own.*

see someone **into** something and **see** someone **in**† to usher or accompany someone into something or some place. □ *Please see her into the room and make sure she is seated where she can hear the speaker.* □ *Please see in the speaker and make sure she finds her seat on the stage.*

see someone **off**† to accompany one to the point of departure for a trip and say good-bye upon departure. □ *We*

went to the train station to see Andy off. □ *We saw off all the scouts going to camp.*

see someone **off** something to accompany someone who is leaving something; to escort someone away from something. □ *I saw the elderly lady off the station platform safely.* □ *The emcee saw the contestants off the stage.*

see someone **on the dot** Go to on the dot.

see someone or something **around** something to notice someone or something in the vicinity of something or near something. □ *I saw the boys around the swings on the playground.* □ *Did you see my cat around the neighborhood anywhere?*

see someone or something **in a new light** *Fig.* to understand someone or something in a different way [than before]. □ *After we had a little discussion, I began to see Fred in a new light.* □ *I can now see the problem in a new light.*

see someone **out (of** something) and **show** someone **out (of** something) to accompany or escort someone out of something or some place. □ *Please see our guest out of the factory.* □ *Please show our guest out.*

see someone **to** some place to escort someone to a place; to make sure that someone gets some place safely; to accompany someone to a place. □ *I saw Mary to her apartment, and then got back in my car and left.* □ *Bill saw his cousin to the train station, and then they parted.*

see someone **to** something to accompany or escort someone to something or some place. (See also **see** someone **to** the door.) □ *Let me see you to the station.* □ *Would you please see your aunt to her car?*

see someone **to the door** Go to show someone (to) the door.

see someone **up to** something to accompany or escort someone to a higher level. □ *That is the end of the tour of the wine cellar. I will see you up to the exit.* □ *Ted saw Mary up to her apartment.*

see something **against** something **1.** *Lit.* to view something against something else. □ *I can't see the cars against the evening sky if their lights aren't on.* □ *The cars can't be seen against the evening sky.* **2.** *Fig.* to view or consider something within the context of something else. □ *If you can see this issue against the background of a long series of problems, perhaps you will understand how concerned we are.* □ *You really need to see this matter against the background of what has happened before.*

see something **as** something else to visualize or fantasize something as something else. □ *I see this as a wonderful way to interest some new people in our organization.* □ *We all see this as a golden opportunity to get to know one another better.*

see something **in** someone or something to appreciate a certain quality in someone or something. □ *I see a strong sense of dignity in Fred. That's good.* □ *I now see the strong points in your proposal.*

see something **in the cards** Go to in the cards.

see something **of** someone or something to know, experience, or visit with someone or some group for some amount of time. □ *I hope we are able to see something of you while you* are in town. □ We don't see enough of the town council. What does it do?

see something **through** to follow through on something until it is completed. □ *Mary is prepared to see the project through.* □ *It's going to be an unpleasant experience, but I hope you'll see it through.*

see stars *Fig.* to seem to see flashing lights after receiving a blow to the head. □ *I saw stars when I bumped my head on the attic ceiling.* □ *The little boy saw stars when he fell headfirst onto the concrete.*

see the big picture Go to the big picture.

see the color of someone's **money** *Fig.* to verify that someone has money or has enough money. □ *So, you want to make a bet? Not until I see the color of your money.* □ *I want to see the color of your money before we go any further with this business deal.*

see the (hand)writing on the wall *Fig.* to know that something is about to happen. □ *If you don't improve your performance, they'll fire you. Can't you see the writing on the wall?* □ *I know I'll get fired. I can see the handwriting on the wall.*

see the last of someone or something to have experienced the last visit, episode, adventure, etc., with someone or something. □ *I hope I have seen the last of Robert Ellis!* □ *We have seen the last of grandma's homemade strawberry jam.*

see the light *Fig.* to understand something clearly at last. □ *After a lot of studying and asking many questions, I finally saw the light.* □ *I know that geometry is difficult. Keep working at it. You'll see the light pretty soon.*

see the light (at the end of the tunnel) *Fig.* to foresee an end to one's problems after a long period of time. (See also begin to see the light.) □ *I had been horribly ill for two months before I began to see the light at the end of the tunnel.* □ *I began to see the light one day in early spring. At that moment, I knew I'd get well.*

see the light (of day) *Fig.* to come to the end of a very busy time. □ *Finally, when the holiday season was over, we could see the light of day. We had been so busy!* □ *When business lets up for a while, we'll be able to see the light.*

see the sights to see the important things in a place; to see what tourists usually see. □ *We plan to visit Paris and see the sights.* □ *Everyone left the hotel early in the morning to see the sights.*

see through someone or something **1.** *Lit.* [for one's vision] to penetrate something clear or opaque or a person. □ *Of course, I can see through the window!* □ *With x-rays, they can see through your body!* **2.** *Fig.* to understand or detect the true nature of someone or something. □ *You can't fool me anymore. I can see through you and all your tricks.* □ *This plan is designed to make money for you, not to help people. I can see through it! I'm not a fool!*

see (to it) that something is done to make sure of something; to make certain of something; to be certain to do something. □ *The manager saw to it that everyone began working on time.* □ *The mayor should see that the potholes are repaired.*

see to someone or something to take care of someone or something. □ *Tom will see to the horses. Come to the house*

and freshen up. □ *I hear the doorbell. Will someone please see to answering the door?*

see which way the wind is blowing to determine what is the most expedient thing to do under the conditions at hand. □ *We studied the whole situation to see which way the wind was blowing and decided to avoid any conflict at that time.* □ *Sam failed to see which way the wind was blowing and got himself caught up in an argument.*

see with the naked eye Go to the naked eye.

See ya. Go to See you.

See ya, bye-bye. *Inf.* Bye. □ *Bill: I have to be off. Bob: See ya, bye-bye.* □ *Mary: See ya, bye-bye. Sue: Toodle-oo.*

See you. and **See ya.** *Inf.* Good-bye. (See also I'll see you later.) □ *Good game, Tom. See ya.* □ *See you, old chum. Give me a ring.*

See you around. *Inf.* I will see you again somewhere. □ *Bob: Bye for now. Jane: See you around.* □ *Tom: See you around, Fred. Fred: Sure, Tom. See you.*

(See you) later. Go to I'll see you later.

See you later, alligator. and **Later, alligator.** *Inf.* Good-bye. (Sometimes the reply is After while(, crocodile.)) □ *Bob: See you later, alligator. Jane: After while, crocodile.* □ *Bob: Bye, Tom. Tom: See you later, alligator. Bob: Later.*

Seeing is believing. *Prov.* It is hard to believe something you have not seen. (Implies that you will not believe the thing under discussion until you have actually seen it.) □ *Jill: They say Melissa has become a wonderful housekeeper now that she has her own apartment. Jane: Seeing is believing.* □ *I really didn't think that Jerry's girlfriend could be as pretty as he said she was, but seeing is believing.*

seeing pink elephants and **seeing pink spiders; seeing snakes** intoxicated; recovering from a drinking bout; having the delirium tremens. □ *When I got to the point of seeing pink elephants, I knew that something had to be done.* □ *The old one who's shaking—he's probably seeing snakes.*

seeing pink spiders Go to previous.

seeing snakes Go to seeing pink elephants.

seeing that... considering...; since... □ *Seeing that she has no money, Sally won't be going shopping.* □ *Seeing that it's raining, we won't go to the beach.*

seeing things imagining that one sees someone or something that is not there. □ *Lisa says that she saw a ghost, but she was just seeing things.* □ *I thought I was seeing things when Bill walked into the room. Someone had told me he was dead.*

seek after someone or something to keep looking for someone or something. □ *I will continue to seek after the thief who stole my car.* □ *The thief was seeking after a late-model sedan.*

Seek and ye shall find. *Prov.* If you search hard enough for something, you will find it. (Biblical. Can imply that the only thing you need to do to get something is look for it.) □ *The bookstore on the corner is an excellent one. Any book you want, just seek and ye shall find.*

seek professional help *Euph.* to get psychiatric or psychological treatment. □ *If you are seriously thinking of sui-*

S

cide, now is the time to seek professional help. □ His friends suggested that he seek professional help.

seek revenge (against someone**)** Go to **take revenge (against** someone**)**.

seek someone or something **out†** to search for and find someone or something. □ We will seek someone out to do the work for us. □ Liz sought out a helper for Karen.

seek something **from** someone or something to pursue something from someone or something. □ We will seek an injunction from the judge. □ My lawyer sought an injunction from the court to try to stop the building project.

seem high-and-mighty Go to **high-and-mighty**.

seem like a long shot Go to **a long shot**.

seem like oneself **again** Go to **oneself again**.

seem like putty in someone's **hands** Go to **putty in** someone's **hands**.

seem like someone or something to appear to be like some kind of person or something. □ You seemed like such a nice person when I met you. □ This seems like a nice day.

seem like the last person Go to **the last person**.

seem out of place Go to **out of place**.

seem pushed for time Go to **pressed for time**.

seep away [for a fluid] to escape little by little, as through a leak. □ All the oil seeped away, leaving none in the engine. □ The water seeped away after a while.

seep in(to something**)** [for a fluid] to trickle or leak out of something. □ Water is seeping into the basement. □ Water is seeping in very slowly.

seep out (of something**)** [for a fluid] to trickle or leak out of something. □ A lot of oil has seeped out of the car onto the driveway. □ There is oil seeping out. There must be a leak.

seep through something [for a fluid] to permeate something and escape. □ The oil seeped through the gasket onto the ground. □ Some water seeped through the ceiling, ruining our carpet as well as the ceiling.

seethe with someone or something to swarm or seem to "boil" with someone or something. □ The wedding reception was seething with guests and well-wishers. □ The room was just seething with flies and other flying creatures.

seethe with something [for someone] to be agitated with anger, hatred, scorn, disgust, etc. □ Laura was seething with rage as she entered the tax office. □ We were seething with disgust at the rude way they treated the people who had just moved in.

segregate someone **from** someone else and **segregate** something **from** something else to separate someone from someone else or something from something else. □ I was asked to segregate the swimmers from the nonswimmers. □ Let's segregate the larger fish from the smaller ones.

segregate someone, something, or an animal **into** something to isolate someone, an animal, or something into something or a special place. □ We segregated the infected people into a separate room. □ Let's segregate the white pigs into a different pen.

segregate something **from** something else Go to **segregate** someone **from** someone else.

segue into something to make a smooth transition into something. (From filmmaking and broadcasting. Rhymes with egg - day.) □ At this point in the script, you should segue into the next scene. □ Don't segue here, this is where a commercial goes.

seize onto someone or something to grab onto someone or something. □ The beggar seized onto the well-dressed gentleman and demanded money. □ Tony seized onto the doorknob and gave it a hard jerk.

seize someone or something **with** something to grab someone or something with something. □ The robot seized Roger with its mechanical claws. □ The dockworker seized the cable with a long hook.

seize something **up†** to grab or take something. □ The crow seized the freshly hatched chick up and flew away. □ The huge bird seized up the tiny chick.

seize the opportunity to take advantage of an opportunity when offered. □ My uncle offered me a trip to Europe, so I seized the opportunity. □ Whenever you have a chance, you should seize the opportunity.

seize up to freeze or halt; to grind suddenly to a stop. □ The engine seized up, and the car coasted to a stop. □ My knee seized up in the middle of a football game.

seize (up)on something **1.** Lit. to grasp something tightly. (Upon is formal and less commonly used than on.) □ Dave seized upon the knob of the door and yanked hard. □ I seized on the railing and held on tight. **2.** Fig. to accept or adopt something, such as a plan, idea, etc. □ I heard her ideas and seized upon them immediately. □ The committee seized on my plan at once.

seized with something Fig. affected suddenly by something, such as laughter, coughing, sneezing, fits of rage, etc. □ Suddenly, I was seized with a fit of coughing. □ Mary was seized with laughter at the sight of Ted in a clown suit.

select from someone or something to make a choice from a group of people or things. □ You will have to select from the people we have asked to interview with you today. □ They told me that I had to select from what you have in stock.

select someone **from** something to choose someone from a group of people. □ You will have to select a new secretary from the available pool of workers. □ I selected Ted from the applicants I had at the time.

select someone or something **as** something to choose someone or something to be something. □ The voters selected Alice as the county treasurer. □ We selected Acme as our main distributor.

select someone or something **for** someone or something to choose someone or something for the benefit of someone or something. □ You need a helper, so I will select someone for you. □ Jane selected a car for her husband.

Self-praise is no recommendation. Prov. If you praise yourself, people will think that you are boastful and will not respect you. □ After listening to the lawyer brag about his achievements for a solid half hour, I decided I would find someone else to handle my case. Self-praise is no recommendation.

Self-preservation is the first law of nature. Prov. Every living thing will fight to survive.; It is natural to think of yourself first. □ When Joe's best friend was *arrested, Joe pretended not to know him. "Perhaps it wasn't very loyal of me," he thought, "but self-preservation is the first law of nature."*

sell at something [for something] to be marketed at a particular price. □ *This coat formerly sold at twice this price.* □ *Next month, this will sell at a 60 percent markup.*

sell like hotcakes *Fig.* [for something] to be sold very fast. □ *The delicious candy sold like hotcakes.* □ *The fancy new cars were selling like hotcakes.*

sell out [for an item] to be sold until there is no more. □ *All the plastic hangers have sold out.*

sell out (to someone**) 1.** to sell everything, such as all one's property or one's company, to someone. □ *The farmer finally gave up and sold out to a large corporation.* □ *I refuse to sell out no matter what they offer me.* **2.** to betray someone or something to someone. □ *I think that you have sold out to the enemy!*

sell someone **a bill of goods** *Fig.* to get someone to believe something that isn't true; to deceive someone. □ *Don't pay any attention to what John says. He's just trying to sell you a bill of goods.* □ *I'm not selling you a bill of goods. What I say is true.*

sell someone **down the river** Go to **sell** someone **out**[†].

sell someone **on** something to convince someone to do something; to convince someone to accept an idea. □ *Mary sold me on ordering pizza for dinner.* □ *John sold Anne on switching long-distance phone companies.*

sell someone or something **as** something to put someone or something up for consideration as something. □ *The political party tried to sell the candidate as a responsible administrator.* □ *The sales force was told to sell the paint as the best available anywhere.*

sell someone or something **short** *Fig.* to underestimate someone or something; to fail to see the good qualities of someone or something. □ *This is a very good restaurant. Don't sell it short.* □ *When you say that John isn't interested in music, you're selling him short. Did you know he plays the violin quite well?*

sell someone **out**[†] and **sell** someone **down the river** to betray someone; to reveal damaging information about someone. □ *Bill told everything he knew about Bob, and that sold Bob down the river.* □ *You'll be sorry if you sell me out.* □ *Lefty sold out his friends, and we'll all soon be arrested.*

sell something **at** something **1.** to market something at a particular price. □ *Do you think we can sell these things at four dollars each?* □ *We cannot sell these at ten times what we paid for them!* **2.** to market something at something or some place. □ *We will try to sell our old kitchen sink at the flea market in Adamsville.* □ *He sold all his watermelons at the farmers market in town.*

sell something **for** a certain price to market something at a certain price. □ *I think I can sell this for twice what I paid for it.* □ *This is selling for twice the price at the shop down the street.*

sell something **for a song** *Fig.* to sell something for very little money. (As in trading something of value for the singing of a song.) □ *I had to sell my car for a song because I needed the money in a hurry.* □ *I have two geometry books and I would sell one of them for a song.*

sell something **off**[†] to sell all of something. □ *We ended up with a large stock of out-of-style coats and we had to sell them all off at a loss.* □ *We sold off all the excess stock.*

sell something **on credit** to sell something now and let the purchaser pay for it later. □ *I'm sorry, we don't sell groceries on credit. It's strictly cash-and-carry.* □ *There is a shop around the corner that sells clothing on credit.*

sell something **out**[†] to sell all of something. □ *Have they sold their supply out yet?* □ *The stores sold out their stocks of that game long before Christmas.*

sell the farm and **bet the farm** *Fig.* to liquidate all one's assets in order to raise money to invest in something. □ *It's a risky proposition. I wouldn't bet the farm on it.*

a **selling point** a feature of a product or idea that is worth mentioning when trying to sell the product or idea. □ *The fact that the book had large type is an important selling point.*

send after someone or something to request that someone or something be brought; to **send for** someone or something. □ *You really ought to send after a doctor.* □ *Let's send after a taxi to take us to the airport.*

send ahead for something to send a message for something to be ready or available when one arrives. □ *I will send ahead for a taxi to meet us at the station.* □ *We sent ahead for room reservations at the hotel.*

send away (for something**)** to order something to be brought or sent from some distance. □ *I sent away for a new part to replace the one that was broken.* □ *I couldn't find the part locally. I had to send away for it.*

send for someone or something to make a request that someone or something be brought. □ *Mr. Franklin sent for his secretary.* □ *I think we should send for an ambulance.*

send in for something and **send off for** something to dispatch an order for something to a company or other body making a public offer of goods. □ *I sent in for a new product that is supposed to make my hair grow back.* □ *Did you send in for that country-and-western CD as you said you would?* □ *I sent off for the proper contest entry forms.*

send off for something Go to previous.

send one about one's business to send someone away, usually in an unfriendly way. □ *Is that annoying man on the telephone again? Please send him about his business.* □ *Ann, I can't clean up the house with you hanging around. I'm going to have to send you about your business.*

send one to one's death to order one to go on a mission or journey that will result in one's death. □ *The general sent many fine young men to their deaths that day.* □ *They were sent to their death by the act of a madman.*

send out (for someone or something**)** to send an order by messenger, telephone, cable, or fax that someone or something is to come or be delivered. □ *We sent out for a public stenographer to record the will as Uncle Herman dictated it.* □ *There was no food in the refrigerator, so we decided to send out.*

send someone **after** someone or something to send someone to get someone or something. □ *Please send John after the doctor. This is an emergency.* □ *The telephone was out so we sent someone after an ambulance.*

send someone **away** Go to **put** someone **away**.

send someone **away with** something to make someone leave and carry something away. □ *I sent him away with a message for his mother.* □ *She sent Ted away with a little booklet about manners.*

send someone **back for** something to cause someone to return to get something. □ *He came without it, so I sent him back for it.* □ *Ted sent Roger back for the rest of the groceries.*

send someone **before** someone or something to cause someone to appear before someone or a group. □ *I sent my lawyer before the mayor to plead my cause.* □ *Donna sent a friend before the committee.*

send someone **below** to send someone to one of the lower decks of a ship. □ *The first mate sent the sailor below to shovel coal into the boiler.* □ *The captain sent Mr. Wallace below, where he would be out of the way during the storm.*

send someone **down for** something to request someone to go to a place on a lower level to get something. □ *I sent the butler down for another bottle of wine.* □ *I sent the butler down for more of this vintage.*

send someone **for** someone or something to cause someone to go and get someone or something. □ *Please send Jerry for the doctor. This is an emergency.* □ *Could you send someone for pizza?*

send someone **from pillar to post** *Fig.* to send someone to many different places, none of which is the correct place. (Compare this with **send** someone **on a wild-goose chase.**) □ *Jill sent Roger from pillar to post to look for a special kind of paper.* □ *Roger was sent from pillar to post with his problem.*

send someone **in**[†] Go to **send** someone **into** something.

send someone **in for** someone to send someone into a game as a replacement for someone else. □ *The coach sent Jill in for Alice, who was beginning to tire.* □ *Ted sent Bill in for Wally.*

send someone **into** a state or condition to cause someone to be in a certain state or condition. □ *The horrifying news sent our family into hysterics.* □ *The clerk's rude behavior sent the customer into a fit of anger.*

send someone **into** something and **send** someone **in**[†] to make someone go into something or some place. □ *George sent me into the house for a hammer.* □ *The boys know where it is. He should have sent in the boys.* □ *George sent me in.*

send someone **off** to participate in saying good-bye to someone who is leaving. □ *We had a party to send Tom off on his retirement.* □ *Bob's parents sent him off from the airport.*

send someone **off (to** something**)** to send someone away to something or some place, especially away on a journey; to be present when someone sets out on a journey to something or some place. □ *We sent both kids off to camp this summer and had peace in the house for the first time in years.* □ *Liz sent Karen off to the store.*

send someone **on a wild-goose chase** *Fig.* to send someone on a pointless or futile search. □ *You sent me on a wild-goose chase! There are no straw hats for sale anywhere in town!* □ *Fred was sent on a wild-goose chase while his friends prepared a surprise party for him.*

send someone or something **across (**something**)** to cause someone or something to cross something. □ *The coach sent the player across the field to give a message to someone on the other side.* □ *We sent the taxi across the river to pick up Gerald on the other side.*

send someone or something **along**[†] to help someone or something continue along; to send someone. □ *I knew it was time for Johnny to go home, so I sent him along.* □ *I will send along the baggage later.*

send someone or something **around**[†] to cause someone or something to go from place to place. □ *I sent my secretary around to look for the missing book.* □ *I will send around some papers for you to sign.*

send someone or something **around for** someone or something to make someone or something go somewhere to pick up someone or something. □ *I will send my driver around for you at about six.* □ *We sent a taxi around for Jane.*

send someone or something **away**[†] to cause someone, a group, or something to leave. □ *I sent the salesman away.* □ *The store sent away all late deliveries.*

send someone or something **back**[†] to cause someone or something to return. □ *He came to apologize, but I sent him back.* □ *Send back these goods. They are defective.*

send someone or something **down**[†] to dispatch someone or something to some place on a lower level. □ *They wanted someone downstairs to help with the moving, so I sent John down.* □ *I sent down John to help.*

send someone or something **on**[†] **(ahead) (of** someone or something**)** to dispatch someone or something to arrive before someone or something else. □ *I sent my personal assistant on ahead of me to get the rooms ready.* □ *Jeff sent on his luggage.*

send someone or something **under** something to force someone or something under something. □ *The accident sent poor Roger under the wheels of a truck.* □ *Mary kicked the ball and sent it under a bush.*

send someone or something **up**[†] **1.** *Lit.* to order someone to go upward to a higher level; to arrange for something to be taken upward to a higher level. □ *I'll send up Gary.* □ *They are hungry on the tenth floor. Let's send some sandwiches up.* **2.** *Fig.* to parody or ridicule someone or something. □ *Comedians love to send the president or some other famous person up.* □ *The comedian sent up the vice president.*

send someone **out**[†] Go to **send** someone **out of** something.

send someone **out**[†] **(for** someone or something**)** to send someone out to search for someone or something. □ *We sent Gerald out for Walter, who was supposed to have been here already.* □ *Karen sent out Liz for some medicine.*

send someone **out of** something and **send** someone **out**[†] to order someone to leave something or some place. □ *The teacher sent the student out of the room.* □ *The teacher sent out the troublesome students.*

send someone **(out) on an errand** to dispatch someone to perform an errand. □ *Jerry will be back in a minute. I sent him out on an errand.* □ *Who sent you on an errand?*

send someone **over (to)** some place and **send** someone **over**[†] to order someone to go to some place. □ *I sent Dave over to the main office.* □ *Please send over someone else.*

send someone **packing** *Fig.* to send someone away; to dismiss someone, possibly rudely. □ *I couldn't stand him anymore, so I sent him packing.* □ *The maid proved to be so incompetent that I had to send her packing.*

send someone **through the mill** Go to through the mill.

send someone **to bed** Go to put someone to bed.

send someone **to glory 1.** *Fig.* to kill someone. □ *One shot sent him to glory.* □ *You want me to send you to glory or something?* **2.** *Fig.* to officiate at the burial services for someone. □ *The preacher sent him to glory amidst the sobs of his relatives.* □ *The preacher probably gets fifty bucks for every stiff he sends to glory.*

send someone **to the locker room** Go to next.

send someone **to the showers** and **send** someone **to the locker room** *Fig.* to order a player from the playing field, thus ending the player's participation for the day. □ *The coach had sent four players to the showers before the end of the game.* □ *He was angry enough to send them all to the locker room.*

send someone **up**[†] *Fig.* to mock or ridicule, particularly by imitation. □ *Last week, he sent the prime minister up.* □ *In his act, he sends up famous people.*

send someone **up (the river)** *Fig.* to send someone to prison. (Underworld. As done by a judge or indirectly by the police.) □ *They tried to send me up the river, but my testimony got me off.* □ *I'm gonna send you up the river if it's the last thing I do.*

send someone **up the wall** *Fig.* to annoy and irritate someone; to drive someone crazy. □ *Don't scratch your fingers on the blackboard. It sends me up the wall!* □ *That noise sends me up the wall!*

send something **by** something to dispatch something by a particular carrier. □ *I will send it to you by special messenger.* □ *We sent the package by air freight.*

send something **C.O.D.** to send merchandise to someone who will pay for it when it is delivered. (*C.O.D.* means "cash on delivery" or "collect on delivery.") □ *I asked them to send the book C.O.D.* □ *This person has ordered a copy of our upcoming release. Send it C.O.D.*

send something **from** something to dispatch something from something or some place. □ *Ted sent the package from the downtown post office.* □ *The gifts were sent off in a large box from the company's shipping dock.*

send something **into** something and **send** something **in**[†] to dispatch something, such as an order, to a company or other body making a public offer of goods. □ *I sent the order in to the home office.* □ *I sent in the order.*

send something **off**[†] **(to** someone or something**)** to dispatch something to someone, something, or some place. □ *I will send the package off to you in tomorrow's mail.* □ *Karen sent off a letter to her aunt.*

send something **over**[†] **((to)** some place**)** to cause something to be taken to some place. □ *I sent the package over to your home.* □ *Please send over the rest of the mail.*

send something **to** someone or something to dispatch something to someone, something, or some place. □ *I will send the books to my parents.* □ *I sent the order to Detroit.*

send up a trial balloon to suggest something and see how people respond to it; to test public opinion. □ *Mary had an excellent idea, but when we sent up a trial balloon, the response was very negative.* □ *Don't start the whole project without sending up a trial balloon.*

send word to someone to get a message to someone by any means. □ *I will send word to her as soon as I have something to report.* □ *Tom sent word to Bill just in time.*

a **sense of humor** the ability to appreciate good humor and jokes; the ability to create jokes and say funny things. □ *Does he have a sense of humor? He looks like he has never laughed in his life.*

sensitize someone **to** something **1.** to make a person have an allergic reaction to something. □ *Frequent exposure to the chemical sensitized Harry to it and made him get a rash.* □ *He became sensitized to pet dander.* **2.** to make someone more thoughtful and receptive to something. □ *We want to sensitize you to the feelings of other people.* □ *He never became sensitized to the needs of others.*

sentence someone **to** something **(for** something**)** [for a judge] to order someone to suffer confinement, death, or labor for committing a crime. □ *The judge sentenced Roger to three years in prison for the crime.* □ *The judge sentenced him to hard labor.*

separate but equal segregated but of equal value or quality. (A doctrine once sanctioned by the U.S. Supreme Court regarding racial segregation.) □ *The separate but equal doctrine was abandoned years ago.* □ *They were provided with facilities that were said to be separate but equal—but were really of a lower standard.*

separate off (from something**)** to move or head away from something. □ *The road to the cabin separates off from the main road and goes along for a mile or two.* □ *It separates off about a mile from here.*

separate someone **from** someone else and **separate** something **from** something else to segregate people or things. □ *The nurse separated the infected people from the healthy ones.* □ *Please separate the spoiled apples from the good ones.*

separate someone or something **into** something to divide people or things into subdivisions. □ *We had to separate the kids into smaller groups.* □ *Jane separated the apples into three groups by size.*

separate something **from** something else Go to separate someone from someone else.

separate something **off from** something and **separate** something **off**[†] to remove something from something. □ *Frank separated the cream off from the milk.* □ *Separate off the hens from the rooster.*

separate something **out of** something and **separate** something **out**[†] to remove something out from something. □ *She used a filter to separate the dirt particles out of the water.* □ *A filter separated out the impurities.*

separate the men from the boys and **separate the sheep from the goats** *Fig.* to separate the competent from those who are less competent. (Not necessarily just about males.) □ *This is the kind of task that separates the*

S

men from the boys. □ Working in a challenging place like this really separates the sheep from the goats.

separate the wheat from the chaff *Prov.* to separate what is useful or valuable from what is worthless. □ *When it comes to books, time will separate the wheat from the chaff. Good books will have lasting appeal, and the rest will be forgotten.* □ *The managers hoped that the new procedure for evaluating employees would separate the wheat from the chaff.*

serious about someone in love with someone; romantically interested in someone. □ *I'm afraid I'm getting serious about Bill.* □ *Bill, unfortunately, is pretty serious about Mary.*

serve a (useful) purpose to be useful in accomplishing some purpose. □ *This large book should serve a useful purpose. We can use it for a doorstop.*

serve as a guinea pig *Fig.* [for someone] to be experimented on; to allow some sort of test to be performed on one. (Alludes to the use of guinea pigs for biological experiments.) □ *Try it on someone else! I don't want to serve as a guinea pig!* □ *Jane agreed to serve as a guinea pig. She'll be the one to try out the new flavor of ice cream.*

serve as someone or something to act in the capacity of someone or something. □ *I served as the mayor's assistant for a number of years.* □ *This brick will not serve as a doorstop.*

serve as the driving force (behind someone or something**)** Go to the driving force (behind someone or something).

serve notice (on someone**)** to formally or clearly announce something to someone. □ *John served notice that he wouldn't prepare the coffee anymore.* □ *I'm serving notice that I'll resign as secretary next month.*

serve on something to carry out one's duty or responsibility on something, such as a committee or a board. □ *Will you be able to serve on this committee next year also?* □ *Sarah refused to serve on the committee again.*

serve someone **right** [for an act or event] to punish someone fairly (for doing something). □ *John copied off my test paper. It would serve him right if he fails the test.* □ *It'd serve John right if he got arrested.*

serve someone's **purpose** Go to answer someone's purpose.

serve someone **with** something to officially deliver something, such as a subpoena, to someone. □ *He served her with papers from the circuit court.* □ *Has Tom been served with the subpoena?*

serve something **around**† to distribute something to eat or drink to everyone present. □ *Please serve the snacks around so that everyone gets some.* □ *Serve around the birthday cakes, would you?*

serve something **for** something to distribute something to eat or drink for a particular purpose. □ *We served smoked salmon for an appetizer.* □ *What will you serve for a main course?*

serve something **in** something to present something to eat or drink in a particular container. □ *Kelly served the lemonade in paper cups.* □ *What will you serve the soup in?*

serve something **on a silver platter** Go to on a silver platter.

serve something **on** someone to officially deliver something, such as a subpoena, to someone. □ *A prosecuting attorney served the subpoena on Max.* □ *The document was served on the plaintiff by a sheriff's deputy.*

serve something **out**† to carry out one's duty or responsibility for the whole time, all the way to the end. □ *She was unable to serve her term out.* □ *The convict served out his sentence in solitary confinement.*

serve something **to** someone† **1.** to present someone with something to eat or drink. □ *The host served the snacks to everyone and left the room to work on the salad.* □ *The snacks were served to everyone in attendance.* **2.** to officially deliver something, such as a subpoena, to someone. □ *The sheriff at the door was there to serve a subpoena to Fred.* □ *She served the papers to the person who lived there.*

serve something **up**† to distribute or deliver food for people to eat. □ *The cook served the stew up and then passed around the bread.* □ *Can you serve up the food now?*

serve time to spend a certain amount of time in jail. □ *The criminal served ten years in jail.* □ *After the felon served his time, he was released from prison.*

serve under someone or something to carry out one's responsibility under the direction or in the employment of someone. □ *I served under the president of the company as special assistant.* □ *Jane served under the previous administration as an investigator.*

serve with someone to perform military service alongside or with someone. □ *I served with Harry when we were both in the army.* □ *At the reunion, I met a lot of the guys I served with in the navy.*

Set a beggar on horseback, and he'll ride to the devil. *Prov.* If a poor person becomes wealthy, he or she will quickly become corrupt. □ *Jill: Since Phil inherited all that money, all he does is go to parties and take drugs. Jane: Yep. Set a beggar on horseback, and he'll ride to the devil.*

set a precedent to establish a pattern; to set a policy that must be followed in future cases. □ *I'll do what you ask this time, but it doesn't set a precedent.* □ *We've already set a precedent in matters such as these.*

Set a thief to catch a thief. *Prov.* The best person to catch a thief is another thief, because he or she knows how thieves think. □ *The government set a thief to catch a thief, hiring a stockbroker convicted of fraudulent practices to entrap the stockbroker they were investigating for fraud.*

set a trap to adjust and prepare a trap to catch an animal. □ *Bill set a mousetrap and baited it with cheese.* □ *The old man set a trap to catch an annoying squirrel.*

set about doing something to begin to do something. □ *When are you going to set about fixing the roof?* □ *We will set about painting the house when the weather gets a little cooler.*

set eyes on someone or something and **lay eyes on** someone or something *Fig.* to see someone or something for the first time. □ *I knew when I set eyes on that car that it was the car for me.* □ *Have you ever laid eyes on such a beautiful flower?*

S

set fire to someone or something and **set** someone or something **on fire** to ignite someone or something; to put someone or something to flames. □ *The thief set fire to the building.* □ *The poor man accidentally set himself on fire.*

set foot in some place to enter into some place; to begin to enter some place. □ *The judge ordered him never to set foot in her house again.* □ *I would never set foot in a place like that.*

set for life prepared to exist for the rest of one's life; having adequate supplies for the rest of one's life. □ *As soon as I win the lottery, I will be set for life. I'll never have to work again!*

set forth on something and **launch forth on** something **1.** *Lit.* to start out on something, such as a journey. □ *We intend to set forth on our journey very early in the morning.* □ *What time will you launch forth on your trip?* **2.** *Fig.* to begin presenting a speech or an explanation. □ *As soon as John set forth on his speech, three people walked out.* □ *Every time he launches forth on a presentation, it's a half hour before he shuts up.*

set great store by someone or something to have positive expectations for someone or something; to have high hopes for someone or something. □ *I set great store by my computer and its ability to help me in my work.* □ *Bill sets great store by his expensive tools.*

set in to begin; to become fixed for a period of time. □ *A severe cold spell set in early in November.* □ *When high temperatures set in, the use of electricity went up considerably.*

set in one's **ways** leading a fixed lifestyle; living according to one's own established patterns. □ *At her age, she's getting sort of set in her ways.* □ *If you weren't so set in your ways, you'd be able to understand young people better.*

a **set of pipes** *Fig.* a very loud voice; a good singing voice. □ *She has a nice set of pipes.* □ *With a set of pipes like that, she's a winner.*

a **set of wheels** *Fig.* a car. □ *I need a new set of wheels.* □ *Man, look at that set of wheels that chick has!*

set off (for something**)** to leave for something or some place. □ *We set off for Springfield three hours late.* □ *It was afternoon before we could set off.*

set off on something to begin on a journey or expedition. □ *When do you plan to set off on your journey?* □ *We will set off on our adventure tomorrow morning.*

set one **(back) on** one's **feet** and **set** one **on** one's **feet again** *Fig.* to reestablish someone; to help someone become active and productive again. □ *Gary's uncle helped set him back on his feet.* □ *We will all help set you on your feet again.*

set one **back on** one's **heels** *Fig.* to surprise or shock someone. □ *I'll bet that news really set her back on her heels!* □ *The bill for the repairs set me back on my heels.*

set one **on** one's **feet again** Go to set one (back) on one's feet.

set one's **heart against** something *Fig.* to turn against something; to become totally against something. □ *Jane set her heart against going to Australia.* □ *I set my heart against her departure.*

set one's **heart on** someone or something *Fig.* to be determined to get or do someone or something. □ *I am sorry you didn't get to pick the one you wanted. I know you had set your heart on Fred.* □ *Jane set her heart on going to London.*

set one's **hopes on** someone or something *Fig.* to have one's hopes or expectations dependent on someone or something. □ *Please don't set your hopes on me in the race. I can't run as fast as I used to.* □ *I have set my hopes on the effectiveness of the new law.*

set one's **house in order** *Fig.* to make certain that one's affairs are in proper legal order. □ *Before we can ask for a bank loan, we have to set our house in order.* □ *I found an accountant who would help me set my house in order.*

set one's **mind on** someone or something *Fig.* to be determined to get or have someone or something. □ *I've set my mind on Dave. I have to have him on my team.* □ *Jamie set her mind on the red sports car.*

set one's **mind to** something Go to put one's mind to something.

set one's **(own) price** to name the (relatively high) price at which one is willing to sell something. □ *If you have a first edition of Milton, you can almost set your own price. They are in great demand by collectors.*

set one's **sights on** someone or something *Fig.* to regard having someone or something as one's goal. □ *He wanted a wife and he had set his sights on Alice.* □ *James set his sights on a law degree.*

set out (for some place**) (from** some place**)** to leave from some place on a journey for some place. □ *We set out for home from the cabin on the very next morning.* □ *We set out from the cabin at dawn.*

set out on one's **own** Go to strike out on one's own.

set out (on something**)** to begin a journey; to begin a project. □ *We set out on our trip exactly as planned.* □ *We set out at noon.*

set out to do something to begin to do something; to intend to do something. □ *Jill set out to weed the garden, but pulled up a few valuable plants in the process.* □ *I set out to repair the door, not rebuild the whole porch.*

set sail for some place to leave in a ship or boat for some place. (Not limited to ships having sails.) □ *We set sail for Grenada at noon.* □ *When do we set sail for Nantucket?*

set someone **about** something to make someone begin doing something. □ *I set the boys about raking up the leaves.* □ *She set herself about repairing the damaged machine.*

set someone **apart from** someone else to make someone stand out when compared to someone else. □ *Her flaming red hair sets her apart from all the others in her class.* □ *They set themselves apart from the rest due to their superb accomplishments.*

set someone **back (**some amount of money**)** to cost someone (an amount of money). □ *This coat set me back about $250.* □ *That fancy dinner at the restaurant last night really set us back.*

set someone **down (on(to)** something**)** to place a person one is carrying or lifting onto something. □ *I set the small*

S

boy down onto the desk and gave him a piece of candy. □ *Set the baby down and come over here.*

set someone **off**[†] **1.** *Fig.* to cause someone to become very angry; to ignite someone's anger. (Based on **set** something **off** ①.) □ *That kind of thing really sets me off!* □ *Your rude behavior set off Mrs. Franklin.* **2.** *Fig.* to cause someone to start talking or lecturing about a particular subject. (Based on **set** something **off** ②.) □ *When I mentioned high taxes it really set Walter off. He talked and talked.* □ *The subject set off my uncle, and he talked on endlessly.*

set someone **on fire** *Fig.* to excite someone; to make someone passionate. (Based on **set fire to** someone or something.) □ *Her oratory set everyone on fire.* □ *Ted's presentation didn't exactly set me on fire, but it was a good summary of the project.*

set someone or an animal **on** someone or an animal to command someone or an animal to attack someone or an animal. □ *The gang leader set his thugs on the unwary tourists.* □ *Scott set his hounds on the raccoon.*

set someone or something **above** someone or something **1.** to place someone or something in a physical location higher than someone or something. □ *Timmy's dad set him above the others so he could see better.* □ *I set the trophy above the television on a little shelf.* **2.** to regard someone or something as better than someone or something else. □ *Fred set his wife and children above everyone else.* □ *Gene set his job above his family.*

set someone or something **down**[†] and **put** someone or something **down**[†] to lower or set down someone or something. (See also **set** something **down**; **put** someone or something **down**.) □ *Put me down!* □ *Please set that vase down. It cost a fortune.* □ *Put down that gun!*

set someone or something **free (from** something**)** to release someone or something from something. □ *The commando set the secret agent free from the prison.* □ *Who set the chickens free from their pens?* □ *At last, he set himself free from the inhibitions that held him back.*

set someone or something **on fire** Go to **set fire to** someone or something.

set someone or something **on track** Go to **on track.**

set someone or something **to work** to start someone or something working; to cause someone or something to begin functioning. □ *The captain set everyone to work repairing the tears in the fabric of the sails.* □ *We will set the machines to work at the regular time.*

set someone or something **up**[†] **against** someone or something to put someone or something into competition against someone or something. □ *The coach set his team up against the Lions.* □ *He set up Will against a very fast runner.*

set someone or something **up**[†] **as** something to arrange for or equip someone or something to be or work as something. □ *His uncle set him up as a tax consultant.* □ *Lee set up his nephew as a tax consultant.* □ *Ken set the company up as a partnership.*

set someone's **mind at ease (about** someone or something**)** to make someone feel mentally comfortable about someone or something. □ *Alice is upset. I will have to do something to set her mind at ease about the accident.* □ *Please set your mind at ease. Everything will be all right.*

set someone's **teeth on edge 1.** *Fig.* [for a scraping sound] to irritate someone's nerves. □ *That noise sets my teeth on edge!* □ *Tom's teeth were set on edge by the incessant screaming of the children.* **2.** *Fig.* [for a person or an idea] to upset someone very much. □ *Her overbearing manner usually sets my teeth on edge.* □ *The very thought of doing that set her teeth on edge.*

set someone **straight** to make certain that someone understands something exactly. (Often said in anger or domination.) □ *Please set me straight on this matter. Do you or do you not accept the responsibility for the accident?* □ *I set her straight about who she had to ask for permission to leave early.*

set someone **up**[†] to lead—by deception—a person to play a particular role in an event; to arrange an event—usually by deception—so that a specific person suffers the consequences for the event; to frame someone. (See also **set** someone **up (as** something**).**) □ *I had nothing to do with the robbery! I was just standing there. Somebody must have set me up!* □ *John isn't the one who started the fight. Somebody set up the poor guy.*

set someone **up (in business)** to help establish someone in business; to provide the money someone needs to start a business. □ *My father set my sisters up in business.* □ *He helped set them up so he could keep the business in the family.*

set something **against** someone or something **1.** to place or lean something against someone or something. □ *Dave set the chair against Fred and had to move it away.* □ *I set the rake against the side of the house.* **2.** to make someone hate or oppose someone or something. □ *His second wife set him against his former in-laws.* □ *The Civil War set brother against brother.*

set something **apart from** something else **1.** to move something so it is away from something else. □ *Set the old ones apart from the others so we can sell them first.* □ *The stale loaves were set apart from the fresh ones.* **2.** to make something stand out when compared to something else. □ *The bright green really sets this plant apart from the others.* □ *Her golden hair sets her apart from all the others.*

set something **aside**[†] to place something in a place that is to one side or out of the way. □ *Betty set the manuscript aside until she had more time to work on it.* □ *Liz set aside her book for a while.*

set something **aside**[†] **(for** someone or something**)** to reserve something for someone or some purpose. □ *I will set a piece of cake aside for you.* □ *Liz set aside some cake for Karen.*

set something **at** something to fix something at a particular value or amount. □ *Please set the thermostat at a lower temperature.* □ *Who set the refrigerator at freezing?*

set something **back**[†] and **put** something **back**[†] to set something, like a timepiece, to a lower number. (*Put* is less common.) □ *It's that time of year when you must set your clocks and watches back!* □ *Set back your clock tonight.* □ *I have to put all the clocks back.*

set something **back from** something else and **set** something **back**[†] to place something at some distance from something else. □ *Set the glasses back from the edge or they will* get knocked off. □ *You should set back the crystal vase a little. It's too close to the edge.*

set something **before** someone, something, or some creature to place something in front of someone, an animal, a group, or something. □ *I set the plate of sandwiches before the children and they were gone in a few minutes.* □ *Jane set the bowl of food before the cats.*

set something **beside** something to place something near or next to something. □ *Please set the chair beside the window.* □ *I set the suitcase beside the door so I would not forget it.*

set something **down**† and **put** something **down**† **1.** to place something on the surface of something. □ *Andy set the hot skillet down on the dishcloth and burned a hole in it.* □ *He set down the skillet here and burned the counter.* **2.** to write something on paper. □ *Let me put this down on paper so we will have a record of what was said.* □ *I will set down this note on paper.* **3.** to land an aircraft. □ *The pilot put the plane down exactly on time.* □ *I can't set down this plane in the fog.*

set something **down as** something to regard something as something. (See also put something **down to** something.) □ *I set his behavior down as an event that would not repeat itself.* □ *Please just set the whole afternoon down as an exercise in patience.*

set something **down**† **in black and white** Go to put something down† **in black and white.**

set something **down to** something Go to put something **down to** something.

set something **for** something to adjust something for a particular setting. □ *I set the thermostat for a lower temperature.* □ *Please set the air conditioning for about 75 degrees.*

set something **forth**† to explain something; to present some information. □ *She set her ideas forth in an organized and interesting manner.* □ *Please set forth your thoughts quickly and concisely.*

set something **forward 1.** to move something to a more forward position. □ *Please set the chair forward a little bit. It is in the walkway.* □ *If you set the vase forward, it will show up better against the dark background.* **2.** to reset a timepiece to a later time. □ *You are supposed to set your clock forward at this time of year.* □ *Did you set your watch forward?*

set something **in**† Go to set something into something.

set something **in** a place to locate the action of a play or movie in a place. □ *The author set the second act in a wooded glade.* □ *The opera was set in a forest outside Moscow.*

set something **in** a type face to set something in type, a particular style of type, or a particular font. □ *Why not set this section in italics to make it stand out from the rest?* □ *Why was this paragraph set in bold type?*

set something **in motion** to start something moving. □ *The mayor set the project in motion by digging the first shovelful of soil.* □ *I cannot set the procedure in motion until I receive a purchase order.*

set something **into** something and **set** something **in**† to install something into its place. □ *The movers set the stove into*

its proper place, and the plumber hooked it up two days later. □ *They set in the stove carefully.*

set something **off**† **1.** *Lit.* to ignite something, such as fireworks. □ *The boys were setting firecrackers off all afternoon.* □ *They set off rocket after rocket.* **2.** *Fig.* to cause something to begin. □ *The coach set the race off with a shot from the starting pistol.* □ *She set off the race with a whistle.* **3.** *Fig.* to make something distinct or outstanding. □ *The lovely stonework sets the fireplace off quite nicely.* □ *The white hat really sets off Betsy's eyes.*

set something **out**† **(for** someone or something**)** to remove something and place it so that it is available for someone or some purpose. □ *I set a piece of cake out for you to eat whenever you get home.* □ *Liz set out some cake for Karen.*

set something **over** something to place something in a position above something else. □ *Toby set the plate over the hole in the tablecloth.* □ *Please place the kettle over the fire.*

set something **right** and **make** something **right; make** something **good; put** something **right** to correct something; to alter a situation to make it more fair. □ *This is a very unfortunate situation. I'll ask the people responsible to set this matter right.* □ *I'm sorry that we overcharged you. We'll try to put it right.* □ *I know I owe you some money, but don't worry, I'll make it good.*

set something **straight** and **put** something **straight** to figure out and correct something; to straighten out a mess. □ *I am sorry for the error. I am sure we can set it straight.* □ *We'll put this matter straight in a short time.*

set something **to music** to write a piece of music to accompany a set of words. □ *The musician set my lyrics to music.* □ *The rock band set the poem to music.*

set something **up**† **1.** *Lit.* to put something together; to erect something. □ *My parents bought me a dollhouse, but I had to set it up myself.* □ *It took nearly an hour to set up the tent.* **2.** *Fig.* to establish or found something. □ *We set up a fund to buy food for the needy.* □ *The business owners set a bank up in the small town.*

set something **up**† **(with** someone**)** to make plans for something. □ *John is hard at work setting something up with Bill and Mary.* □ *Sally and Tom set up a party for Saturday night.*

set something **(up)on** something to place something on the surface of something. □ *Mrs. Franklin set a bowl of fruit upon the table.* □ *I set my empty glass on the counter.*

set the ball rolling Go to get the ball rolling.

set the record straight *Fig.* to put right a mistake or misunderstanding; to make sure that an account, etc., is correct. □ *The manager thought Jean was to blame, but she soon set the record straight.* □ *Jane's mother heard that Tom is a married man, but he set the record straight. He's divorced.*

set the stage for something **1.** *Lit.* to arrange for a stage for an act or scene of a production. □ *The stage crew set the stage for the first act.* □ *They set the stage for the second scene while the orchestra played.* **2.** *Fig.* to prepare something for some activity. □ *The initial meeting set the stage for further negotiations.* □ *Your negative comments set the stage for another big argument.*

set the table to place plates, glasses, napkins, etc., on the table before a meal. (The opposite of **clear the table.**) □

Jane, would you please set the table? □ I'm tired of setting the table. Ask someone else to do it.

set the world on fire *Fig.* to do exciting things that bring fame and glory. (Frequently with the negative.) □ *I'm not very ambitious. I don't want to set the world on fire.* □ *You don't have to set the world on fire. Just do a good job.*

set to to begin to fight; to attack or commence someone or something. □ *The two boys set to almost as soon as they met each other.* □ *They set to and fought for about ten minutes, cursing and screaming.*

***set to** do something ready to do something. (*Typically: **be** ~; **get** ~.) □ *I'm all set to go. Are you ready?* □ *We are set to leave at a moment's notice.*

set to work (on someone or something**)** to begin working on someone or something. □ *We have finished questioning Tom, so we will set to work on Fred.* □ *We set to work on dinner at noon.*

set tongues (a)wagging *Fig.* to cause people to start gossiping. □ *The affair between the boss and her accountant set tongues awagging.* □ *If you don't get the lawn mowed soon, you will set tongues wagging in the neighborhood.*

set type to arrange type for printing; to prepare finished pages for printing. □ *Have you finished setting the type for page one yet?* □ *John sets type for a living.*

set up shop somewhere to establish one's place of work somewhere. □ *Mary set up shop in a small office building on Oak Street.* □ *The police officer said, "You can't set up shop right here on the sidewalk!"*

set upon someone or something to attack someone or something violently. □ *The dogs set upon the bear and chased it up a tree.* □ *Bill set upon Tom and struck him hard in the face.*

settle a score with someone and **settle the score (with** someone**)** *Fig.* to clear up a problem with someone; to get even with someone. □ *John wants to settle a score with his neighbor.* □ *Tom, it's time you and I settled the score.*

settle down 1. to calm down. □ *Now, children, it's time to settle down and start class.* □ *If you don't settle down, I'll send you all home.* **2.** to settle into a stable way of life; to get married and settle into a stable way of life. □ *Tom, don't you think it's about time you settled down and stopped all of this running around?* □ *Bill and Ann decided to settle down and start a family.*

settle for something to agree to accept something (even though something else would be better). □ *We wanted a red one, but settled for a blue one.* □ *Ask your grocer for Wilson's canned corn—the best corn in cans. Don't settle for less.*

settle in to become accustomed to one's new surroundings; to get used to living in a place or a new dwelling. □ *I need a little time to settle in, then I can think about buying a car.*

settle on something to decide on something. □ *We've discussed the merits of all of them, and we've settled on this one.* □ *I can't settle on one or the other, so I'll buy both.*

settle someone's **affairs** to deal with one's business matters; to manage the business affairs of someone who can't.

□ *When my uncle died, I had to settle his affairs.* □ *I have to settle my affairs before going to Mexico for a year.*

settle someone's **hash** *Sl.* to calm someone down, perhaps by threats or by violence. □ *If he comes in here, I'll settle his hash.* □ *Now, that ought to settle your hash.*

settle (something**) (out of court)** to end a disagreement and reach an agreement without having to go through trial in a court of justice. □ *The plaintiff and defendant decided to settle before the trial.* □ *Mary and Sue settled out of court before the trial.*

settle the score (with someone**)** Go to settle a score with someone.

settle up with someone to pay someone what one owes; to pay one's share of something. □ *I must settle up with Jim for the bike I bought for him.* □ *Bob paid the whole restaurant bill and we all settled up with him later.*

a **seven-day wonder** *Fig.* a person or a process supposedly perfected in only seven days. (Sarcastic.) □ *Tommy is no seven-day wonder. It took him 6 years to get through high school!*

the **seven-year itch** a real or imagined longing for other women in a man's seventh year of marriage. □ *Looks like Jack has the seven-year itch.* □ *The seven-year itch is just a rumor.*

sever ties with someone *Fig.* to end a relationship or agreement suddenly or completely. □ *The company severed its ties with the dishonest employee.* □ *John has severed all ties with his parents.*

sew someone or something **up**† **1.** *Lit.* to stitch together an opening in someone or something. □ *The surgeon sewed the patient up and pronounced the operation a success.* □ *This is torn. Can you sew up this rip?* **2.** *Fig.* to complete one's dealings with or discussion of someone or something. □ *It's time to sew this up and go home.* □ *I think we can sew up the shipping contract this afternoon and get on to someone else.* □ *Let's sew up this last matter and go.*

***sewed up 1.** *Lit.* [the sewing of a gap in cloth] completed. (*Typically: **get** something ~; **have** something ~.) □ *Have you got that tear sewed up yet?* **2.** and ***wrapped up** *Fig.* settled or finished. (*Typically: **get** something ~; **have** something ~.) □ *I'll take the contract to the mayor tomorrow morning. I'll get the whole deal sewed up by noon.* □ *Don't worry about the car loan. I'll have it wrapped up in time to make the purchase.*

Sez me! Go to Says me!

Sez who? Go to Says who?

shack up (with someone**)** *Inf.* to sleep or live with someone temporarily in a sexual relationship. □ *They shacked up for over a year until her parents found out and stopped sending her money.*

shackle someone **with** something to fetter or hobble someone with something, such as chains, etc. □ *The sheriff shackled the prisoner with handcuffs and leg irons.* □ *The prisoners were shackled with leg irons.*

shades of someone or something *Fig.* reminders of someone or something; a thing that is reminiscent of someone or something. □ *When I met Jim's mother, I thought "shades of Aunt Mary."* □ *"Shades of grade school," said Jack as the university lecturer rebuked him for being late.*

S

*a shadow of oneself and ***a shadow of itself; *a shadow of** one's **former self** *Fig.* someone or something that is not as strong, healthy, full, or lively as before. (*Typically: **be ~; become ~**.) □ *The sick man was a shadow of his former self.* □ *The abandoned mansion was merely a shadow of its old self.*

a **shady character** and a **suspicious character** *Fig.* an untrustworthy person; a person who makes people suspicious. □ *There is a suspicious character lurking about in the hallway. Please call the police.*

a **shady deal** *Fig.* a questionable and possibly dishonest deal or transaction. □ *The lawyer got caught making a shady deal with a convicted felon.*

shag (off) *Sl.* to depart. □ *I gotta shag. It's late.* □ *Go on! Shag off!* □ *I gotta shag. Somebody's calling my name.*

shagged out *Sl.* exhausted. □ *What a day! I'm shagged out!* □ *You guys look sort of shagged out.*

a **shaggy-dog story** a kind of funny story that relies for its humor on its length and its sudden ridiculous ending. □ *Don't let John tell a shaggy-dog story. It'll go on for hours.* □ *Mary didn't get the point of Fred's shaggy-dog story.*

shake a disease or illness **off**† *Fig.* [for the body] to fight off a disease or illness. □ *I thought I was catching a cold, but I guess I shook it off.* □ *I hope I can shake off this flu pretty soon.*

shake a habit Go to kick a habit.

shake a leg 1. to hurry; to move faster. (Often as a command.) □ *Let's shake a leg, you guys. We gotta be there in twenty minutes.* □ *She told me to shake a leg, so I hurried the best I could.* **2.** to dance. □ *Let's shake a leg. The music's great.* □ *Hey, Jill! You wanna shake a leg with me?*

shake hands and **shake** someone's **hand** to take someone's hand and move it up and down to greet someone or mark an agreement with someone. (See also shake hands (with someone).) □ *David shook my hand when he greeted me.* □ *Anne and John shook hands before their business appointment.*

shake (hands) on something to clasp and shake the hand of someone as a sign of agreement about something. □ *The two people didn't sign a contract; they just shook hands on the terms of the agreement.* □ *I think it would be better to sign an agreement than just shake on it.*

shake hands (with someone**)** to clasp and shake the hand of someone as a greeting. □ *His hands were full, and I didn't know whether to try to shake hands with him or not.* □ *He put down his packages, and we shook hands.*

shake in one's **boots** and **quake in** one's **boots** *Fig.* to be afraid; to shake from fear. □ *I was shaking in my boots because I had to go see the manager for being late.* □ *Stop quaking in your boots, Bob. I'm not going to fire you.*

Shake it (up)! *Inf.* Hurry!; Move faster! □ *Get going, chum! Shake it up!* □ *We're late. Shake it!*

shake someone **down**† **1.** to blackmail someone. (Underworld.) □ *Fred was trying to shake Jane down, but she got the cops in on it.* □ *The police chief was trying to shake down just about everybody in town.* **2.** to put pressure on someone to lend one money. □ *We tried to shake down Max for a few hundred, but no deal.* □ *If you're trying to shake me down, forget it. I have no cash.*

shake someone or something **off**† *Fig.* to get rid of someone; to get free of someone who is bothering you. □ *Stop bothering me! What do I have to do to shake you off?* □ *I wish I could shake off John. He's such a pest!*

shake someone or something **up**† to jostle or knock someone or something around; to toss someone or something back and forth. □ *We rode over a rough road, and that shook us up.* □ *The accident shook up John quite a bit.*

shake someone's **hand** Go to shake hands.

shake someone **up**† to shock or upset someone. □ *The sight of the injured man shook me up.* □ *Your rude remark really shook up Tom.*

shake something **down**† Go to shake something out†.

shake something **off**† to get rid of something that is on one by shaking. (See also shake a disease or illness off.) □ *I tried to shake the spider off.* □ *The dog shook off the blanket Billy had put on him.*

shake something **out**† **1.** *Lit.* to clean something of dirt or crumbs by shaking. □ *Please shake the tablecloth out.* □ *Can you shake out your coat? It's really dusty.* **2.** and **shake** something **down**† *Fig.* to test something to find out how it works or what the problems are. □ *I need to spend some time driving my new car to shake it out.* □ *We need to shake down this car before I buy it.*

shake something **up**† **1.** *Lit.* to shake a container to mix its contents together well. □ *Please shake this up before using it.* □ *I shook up the medicine bottle like it says on the label.* **2.** *Fig.* to reorganize a group or organization, not always in a gentle way. □ *The new manager shook the office up and made things run a lot better.* □ *The coach shook the team up before the last game and made them better organized.*

shake the habit Go to kick a habit.

shake the lead out Go to get the lead out.

The **shame of it (all)!** That is so shameful!; I am so embarrassed; I am shocked. (Considerable use jocularly or as a parody. Compare this with For shame!) □ *John: Good grief! I have a pimple! Always, just before a date. Andy: The shame of it all!* □ *Tom: John claims that he cheated on his taxes. Bill: Golly! The shame of it!*

Shame on you! a phrase scolding someone for being naughty. (Typically said to a child or to an adult for a childish infraction.) □ *John: I think I broke one of your figurines. Mary: Shame on you! John: I'll replace it, of course. Mary: Thanks, I sort of liked it.* □ *"Shame on you!" said Mary. "You should have known better!"*

shank it *Sl.* to use one's legs to get somewhere; to walk. □ *My car needs fixing so I had to shank it to work today.* □ *I like to shank it every now and then.*

shank's mare *Fig.* travel on foot. □ *You'll find that shank's mare is the quickest way to get across town.* □ *Is there a bus, or do I have to use shank's mare?*

shape someone **up**† to get someone into good physical shape; to make someone behave or perform better. □ *I've got to shape myself up to improve my health.* □ *The trainer was told that he'd have to shape up the boxer before the fight.*

shape up 1. to improve; to reform. □ *I want to get things shaped up around here.* □ *I guess I'd better shape up if I want to stay in school.* **2.** to assume a final form or structure. □ *The game plan for the election was beginning to*

S

shape up. □ *Her objectives began to shape up in her senior year.*

Shape up or ship out. *Fig.* Either improve one's performance (or behavior) or leave. (Used as a command.) □ *Okay, Tom. That's the end. Shape up or ship out!* □ *John was late again, so I told him to shape up or ship out.*

share and share alike *Cliché* having or taking equal shares. □ *I kept five and gave the other five to Mary—share and share alike.* □ *The two roommates agreed that they would divide expenses—share and share alike.*

share someone's **pain** to understand and sympathize with someone's pain or emotional discomfort. (Said in order to sound sympathetic.) □ *I am sorry about the loss of your home. I share your pain.* □ *We sympathize about the loss of your mother. We share your pain.*

share someone's **sorrow** to grieve as someone else grieves. □ *We all share your sorrow on this sad, sad day.* □ *I am sorry to hear about the death in your family. I share your sorrow.*

*****sharp as a razor 1.** very sharp. (*Also: **as** ~.) □ *The penknife is sharp as a razor.* □ *The carving knife will have to be as sharp as a razor to cut through this gristle.* **2.** and *****sharp as a tack** very sharp-witted or intelligent. (*Also: **as** ~.) □ *The old man's senile, but his wife is as sharp as a razor.* □ *Sue can figure things out from even the slightest hint. She's as sharp as a tack.*

*****sharp as a tack** Go to previous.

a **sharp tongue** *Fig.* an outspoken or harsh manner; a critical manner of speaking. □ *He has quite a sharp tongue. Don't be totally unnerved by what he says or the way he says it.*

a **sharp wit** *Fig.* a good and fast ability to make jokes and funny comments. □ *Terry has a sharp wit and often makes cracks that force people to laugh aloud at inappropriate times.*

She will get hers. Go to He will get his.

shed crocodile tears and **cry crocodile tears** *Fig.* to shed false tears; to pretend that one is weeping. □ *The child wasn't really hurt, but she shed crocodile tears anyway.* □ *He thought he could get his way if he cried crocodile tears.*

shed (some) light on something and **throw (some) light on** something *Fig.* to reveal something about something; to clarify something. (Also with *any.*) □ *This discussion has shed some light on the problem.* □ *Let's see if Ann can throw any light on this question.*

shell out (an amount of money) to spend a certain amount of money. □ *I'm not going to shell out $400 for that!* □ *Come on. You owe me. Shell out!*

*****a **shellacking 1.** *Fig.* a physical beating. (*Typically: **get** ~; **take** ~; **give** someone ~.) □ *The boxer took a shellacking and lost the fight.* □ *I got a shellacking when I broke the window.* **2.** *Fig.* a beating—as in sports. (*Typically: **get** ~; **take** ~; **give** someone ~.) □ *Our team played well, but got a shellacking anyway.* □ *I practiced my tennis game so I wouldn't take a shellacking in the tournament.*

shift for oneself and **fend for** oneself to get along by oneself; to support oneself. □ *I'm sorry, I can't pay your rent anymore. You'll just have to shift for yourself.* □ *When I became twenty years old, I left home and began to fend for myself.*

shift one's **ground** *Fig.* to change one's opinions or arguments, often without being challenged or opposed. □ *At first Jack and I were on opposite sides, but he suddenly shifted ground and started agreeing with me.* □ *Jim has very fixed views. You won't find him shifting his ground.*

shine up to someone *Fig.* to try to gain someone's favor by being extra nice. □ *John is a nice guy, except that he's always trying to shine up to the professor.* □ *Mary never tries to shine up to the manager.*

shipping and handling the costs of handling a product and transporting it to a customer. □ *Shipping and handling charges were included in the price.* □ *The cost of the goods is low and shipping and handling added only a few dollars.*

ships that pass in the night *Cliché* people who meet each other briefly by chance, sometimes having a sexual liaison, and who are unlikely to meet again or have an ongoing relationship. □ *Mary wanted to see Jim again, but to him, they were ships that passed in the night.* □ *We will never be friends. We are just ships that passed in the night.*

shirk one's **duty** to neglect one's job or task. □ *The guard was fired for shirking his duty.* □ *You cannot expect to continue shirking your duty without someone noticing.*

Shit happens. *Sl.* Bad things just happen and are unavoidable. (Potentially offensive. Use only with discretion.) □ *Too bad that your new car got dented, but shit happens.* □ *Shit happens. There's nothing that can be done about it.*

*****the **shock of** one's **life** *Fig.* a serious (emotional) shock. (*Typically: **get** ~; **have** ~; **give** one ~.) □ *I opened the telegram and got the shock of my life.* □ *I had the shock of my life when I won $5,000.*

The **shoe is on the other foot.** *Prov.* One is experiencing the same (often bad) things that one caused another person to experience. (Note the variations in the examples.) □ *The teacher is taking a course in summer school and is finding out what it's like when the shoe is on the other foot.* □ *When the policeman was arrested, he learned what it was like to have the shoe on the other foot.*

shook up upset; shocked. (See also **all shook up.**) □ *Relax, man! Don't get shook up!* □ *I always get shook up when I see a bad accident.*

shoot a place up† and **shoot the place up**† *Fig.* to fire a gun in or at a place, usually at people. □ *The cowboy walked into the saloon and began to shoot the place up.* □ *They shot up the place.*

Shoot first, ask questions later. *Prov.* Assume that everyone you encounter is hostile to you.; Take action, even though you do not know enough to be sure if it is the right action. □ *If the foreman saw that one of the workers was working slowly, he didn't stop to find out if the worker was sick or unhappy; he just fired him. He believed in shooting first and asking questions later.*

shoot for something **1.** *Lit.* to aim for or at something. (Usually in reference to basketball.) □ *The center shot for the basket just before the end of the game.* □ *Wally shot for the basket but missed.* **2.** *Fig.* to aim for something; to set something as one's goal. □ *You have to shoot for the very* best. Don't be satisfied with less. □ She shot for the highest attainable goal.

shoot for the sky Go to **reach for the sky**.

shoot from the hip 1. *Lit.* to fire a gun that is held at one's side, beside one's hip. (This increases one's speed in firing a gun but is much less accurate.) □ *When I lived at home on the farm, my father taught me to shoot from the hip.* □ *I quickly shot the snake before it bit my horse. I'm glad I learned to shoot from the hip.* **2.** *Fig.* to speak directly and frankly. (Alluding to the rapidity of firing a gun from the hip.) □ *John has a tendency to shoot from the hip, but he generally speaks the truth.* □ *Don't pay any attention to John. He means no harm. It's just his nature to shoot from the hip.*

shoot one's **breakfast** Go to next.

shoot one's **cookies** and **shoot** one's **breakfast; shoot** one's **supper** *Sl.* to empty one's stomach; to vomit. □ *I think I'm gonna shoot my cookies.* □ *I shot my supper, and I was glad to get rid of it.*

shoot one's **mouth off**† *Inf.* to boast or talk too much; to tell secrets. □ *Don't pay any attention to Bob. He's always shooting his mouth off.* □ *Oh, Sally! Stop shooting off your mouth! You don't know what you're talking about.*

shoot one's **supper** Go to **shoot** one's **cookies**.

shoot one's **wad** *Sl.* to spend all or nearly all one's cash on hand. □ *I shot my wad on junk food.* □ *I can't afford a cab. I shot my wad at the restaurant.*

shoot oneself **in the foot** *Fig.* to cause oneself difficulty; to be the author of one's own misfortune. □ *I am a master at shooting myself in the foot.* □ *Again, he shot himself in the foot by saying too much to the press.*

shoot someone **down in flames** *Fig.* to ruin someone; to bring about someone's downfall. (See also **go down in flames**.) □ *It was a bad idea, okay, but you didn't have to shoot me down in flames at the meeting.* □ *I didn't mean to shoot you down in flames.*

shoot someone or something **(all) to hell 1.** *Lit.* to destroy someone or something with gunfire. (Use discretion with hell.) □ *Fred shot the crook to hell with his machine gun.* □ *The farm boys had shot the stop sign all to hell.* **2.** *Fig.* to destroy, exhaust, or damage someone or something. □ *The hard work in the morning shot me all to hell for the rest of the day.* □ *You shot my ideas to hell.*

shoot someone, something, or an animal **down**† to bring down someone, something, or an animal by gunfire. □ *Fred shot Mike down in the street.* □ *They shot down the plane.*

shoot something **down**† *Fig.* to foil a plan through criticism; to counter an idea with criticism. (Based on **shoot** someone, something, or an animal **down**.) □ *He raised a good point, but the others shot him down almost immediately.* □ *Liz shot down Jeff's best idea.*

shoot something **out**† **1.** to stick, throw, or thrust something outward. □ *The diamond shot bright shafts of light out when the sun fell on it.* □ *The little girl shot out her tongue at the teacher.* **2.** to settle a matter by the use of guns. □ *Bill and the cowboy—with whom he had been arguing—went out in the street and shot it out.*

shoot the breeze *Fig.* to chat casually and without purpose. □ *We spent the entire afternoon just shooting the breeze.* □ *It was good to shoot the breeze with you, Mary.*

shoot the bull and **shoot the crap; shoot the shit** *Inf.* to chat and gossip. (The same as **throw the bull**. Use caution with *crap, shit*.) □ *Let's get together sometime and shoot the bull.* □ *You spend too much time shooting the crap.*

shoot the cat *Sl.* to empty one's stomach; to vomit. □ *I must have shot the cat a dozen times during the night.* □ *Shooting the cat is no fun when you're weak and dizzy.*

shoot the crap Go to **shoot the bull**.

shoot the shit Go to **shoot the bull**.

shoot the works 1. to do everything; to use everything; to bet all one's money. □ *Okay, let's go out to dinner and shoot the works.* □ *Don't shoot the works! Save some for a cab.* **2.** *Sl.* to empty one's stomach; to vomit. □ *Suddenly she turned sort of green, and I knew she was going to shoot the works.* □ *After she shot the works, she looked fine—but I was sort of pale.*

shoot up *Sl.* to take drugs by injection. □ *Wallace was caught by the cops shooting up in the high school rest room.*

shop around (for something**)** to shop at different stores to find what you want at the best price. □ *I've been shopping around for a new car, but they are all priced too high.* □ *You can find a bargain, but you'll have to shop around.*

shopping list 1. *Lit.* a list of things one needs to buy. □ *I made up a shopping list for groceries that we are out of.* □ *Don't forget to take the shopping list with you to the store.* **2.** *Fig.* a list of things, especially questions or things one wants. □ *I have a shopping list of absolute musts.* □ *He showed up for the interview with a shopping list so long that it took two pages.*

shore someone **up**† *Fig.* to (figuratively) prop up or support someone. □ *Mary's solid character and personality helped shore her up during her recent problems with the law.* □ *Everyone co-operated to shore up John when his mother died.*

shore something **up**† to prop up or support something. □ *The fence fell over, so we shored it up with more posts.* □ *The storm weakened the foundation of our house, and we had to have workers shore up the house.*

short and sweet *Cliché* brief (and pleasant because of briefness). □ *That was a good sermon—short and sweet.* □ *I don't care what you say, as long as you make it short and sweet.*

the **short and the long of it** Go to the **long and the short of it**.

*the **short end of the stick** *Fig.* the smaller or less desirable part, rank, task, or amount. (*Typically: **get** ~; **have** ~; **give** someone ~; **end up with** ~.) □ *Why do I always get the short end of the stick? I want my fair share!* □ *She's unhappy because she has the short end of the stick again.*

short for something [of a form] being a shortened form of a word or phrase. □ *Photo is short for photograph.* □ *Dave is short for David.*

short of something not having enough of something. □ *I wanted to bake a cake, but I was short of eggs.* □ *Usually at the end of the month, I'm short of money.*

Short reckonings make long friends. *Prov.* If you borrow something from a friend, pay it back as soon as possible so that the two of you remain friendly. □ *Now that you've finished using Bert's saw, take it right back to him. Short reckonings make long friends.*

(a) **short shrift** a brief period of consideration of a person's ideas or explanations. □ *They gave the reporter short shrift and got him out of the office.* □ *My plan got short shrift from the board—a ten-minute presentation; they then voted it down.*

a **short temper** Go to a quick temper.

*****short with** someone abrupt and a little bit rude in speaking to a person. (*Typically: **be ~; become ~; get ~.**) □ *Please don't be short with me. I am doing the best that I can.*

a **shot at** someone Go to a try at someone.

shot full of holes and **shot to ribbons; shot to hell; shot to pieces 1.** *Fig.* [of an argument that is] demolished or comprehensively destroyed. □ *Come on, that theory was shot full of holes ages ago.* □ *Your argument is all shot to hell.* **2.** to be very intoxicated due to drink or drugs. □ *Tipsy? Shot to ribbons, more like!* □ *Boy, I really felt shot full of holes. I'll never drink another drop.* **3.** totally ruined. (Use *hell* with caution.) □ *My car is all shot to hell and can't be depended on.* □ *This rusty old knife is shot to hell. I need a sharper one.*

a **shot in the arm 1.** *Lit.* an injection of medicine. □ *The doctor administered the antidote to the poison by a shot in the arm.* **2.** *Fig.* a boost or act of encouragement. □ *The pep talk was a real shot in the arm for all the guys.* □ *The good test grade was a shot in the arm for Gary.* **3.** *Fig.* a drink of liquor. □ *I could use a little shot in the arm.* □ *How about a little shot in the arm, bartender?*

a **shot in the dark** *Fig.* a very general attempt; a wild guess. □ *It was just a shot in the dark. I had no idea I was exactly correct.* □ *Come on, try it. Even a shot in the dark may win.*

shot through with something *Fig.* containing something; interwoven, intermixed, or filled with something. □ *The rose was a lovely pink shot through with streaks of white.* □ *John's comments are often shot through with sarcasm.*

a **shotgun wedding** *Fig.* a forced wedding. (From imagery of the bride's father having threatened the bridegroom with a shotgun to force him to marry the bride because he made her pregnant.) □ *Mary was six months pregnant when she married Bill. It was a real shotgun wedding.* □ *Bob would never have married Jane if she hadn't been pregnant. Jane's father saw to it that it was a shotgun wedding.*

should have stood in bed *Fig.* an expression used on a bad day, when one should have stayed in one's bed. □ *What a horrible day! I should have stood in bed.* □ *The minute I got up and heard the news this morning, I knew I should have stood in bed.*

shoulder the blame for something Go to the blame for something.

shoulder to shoulder *Fig.* side by side; with a shared purpose. □ *The two armies fought shoulder to shoulder against the joint enemy.* □ *The strikers said they would stand shoulder to shoulder against the management.*

shouldn't happen to a dog *Fig.* an expression of something that is so bad that no creature deserves it. □ *Poor guy. That shouldn't happen to a dog.* □ *This cold I got shouldn't happen to a dog.*

shout about someone or something **1.** to yell about someone or something. □ *Alice is shouting about Tom, the guy who stood her up.* □ *What are you shouting about?* **2.** to show one's pride or enthusiasm about someone or something. (Usually with the object shifted to the front of the sentence.) □ *That's really something to shout about.* □ *She's something to shout about.*

shout someone or something **down†** to overwhelm someone or something by shouting. □ *Mary was trying to speak, but Sally shouted her down.* □ *Ann brought up a very important suggestion, but Bob shouted it down.* □ *The lecturer had to shout down the entire audience to be heard.*

shove off Go to push off.

shove one's **way** somewhere to make a path through a crowd by pushing. □ *The impatient man shoved his way through the crowd.* □ *The reporter shoved her way to the front of the crowd.*

shove someone **around†** **1.** *Lit.* to push someone around. □ *The bigger boys shoved him around easily because he is so small.* □ *Karen shoved around the little kids until they got mad at her.* **2.** *Fig.* to harass someone. □ *Stop shoving me around! Who do you think you are? □ Do you think you can shove around just anybody?*

shove someone or something **down** someone's **throat** and **ram** someone or something **down** someone's **throat**; **force** someone or something **down** someone's **throat 1.** *Lit.* to force someone to swallow something. □ *The harsh nurse forced the medicine down the patient's throat.* □ *The zookeepers rammed the food down the python's throat.* **2.** *Fig.* to force someone to accept something. □ *Don't try to force that car down my throat! I don't want it!* □ *You can't force that nonsense down my throat!* □ *I don't want any more insurance, and I don't want anyone to shove any insurance down my throat.* □ *Mary isn't invited to my party, and I don't wish for anyone to ram her down my throat!*

show a lot of promise Go to a lot of promise.

show and tell a session where objects are presented and described. (Essentially a kindergarten or grade school activity, but often used figuratively.) □ *It was a short lecture with lots of show and tell.* □ *I can't take another show and tell session.*

show good faith to demonstrate good intentions or good will. □ *I'm certain that you showed good faith when you signed the contract.* □ *Do you doubt that she is showing good faith?*

a **show of hands** a display of raised hands [in a group of people] that can be counted for the purpose of votes or surveys. □ *We were asked to vote for the candidates for captain by a show of hands.* □ *Jack wanted us to vote on paper, not by a show of hands, so that we could have a secret ballot.*

show off to do things in a way that is meant to attract attention. □ *Please stop showing off! You embarrass me.* □ *John is always showing off to his girlfriend.*

S

show one's **hand** *Fig.* to reveal one's intentions to someone. (From card games.) □ *I don't know whether Jim is intending to marry Jane or not. He's not one to show his hand.* □ *If you want to get a raise, don't show the boss your hand too soon.*

show one's **teeth** and **bare** one's **teeth** *Fig.* to act in an angry or threatening manner. (Alludes to what an angry wolf or dog does.) □ *We thought Bob was meek and mild, but he really showed his teeth when Jack insulted his girlfriend.* □ *The enemy forces didn't expect the country they invaded to bare its teeth.*

show one's **(true) colors** *Fig.* to show what one is really like or what one is really thinking. □ *Whose side are you on, John? Come on. Show your colors.* □ *It's hard to tell what Mary is thinking. She never shows her true colors.*

show one to one's **seat** Go to **show** someone **to a seat**.

show signs of something to show hints or indications of something. □ *I let the horse run at full speed until it began to show signs of tiring.* □ *Sally is showing signs of going to sleep.*

show someone **around** (some place) to give someone a tour of a place. □ *I'm very glad you've come to work here. Let me show you around so you'll know where things are.* □ *Welcome to our town. As soon as you unpack, I'll get someone to show you around.*

show someone **into** somewhere and **show** someone **in**[†] to lead or usher someone into somewhere. □ *The butler showed me into the sitting room and asked me to wait.* □ *The car dealer showed me into the sales office and asked me to sign some papers.* □ *The butler showed in the guests one by one.*

show someone one's **stuff** *Fig.* to show someone how well one can do something. □ *We'll audition Kate now. Okay, Kate, show us your stuff.*

show someone or something **off**[†] to display someone or something so that the best features are apparent. □ *Bill drove around all afternoon showing his new car off.* □ *Mrs. Williams was showing off her baby to the neighbors.*

show someone **out** (of something) Go to **see** someone **out** (of something).

show someone **the big picture** Go to **the big picture**.

show someone **the ropes** Go to **the ropes**.

show someone **to a seat** and **show** one **to** one's **seat** to lead or direct someone to a place to sit. □ *May I show you to your seat, sir?* □ *The ushers showed us to our seats politely and efficiently.*

show someone **(to) the door** and **see** someone **to the door** to lead or take someone to the door or exit. □ *After we finished our talk, she showed me to the door.* □ *Bill and I finished our chat as he saw me to the door.*

show someone **the tricks of the trade** Go to **the tricks of the trade**.

show someone **up**[†] to make someone's faults or shortcomings apparent. □ *John is always trying to show someone up to make himself look better.* □ *John's excellent effort really showed up Bill, who didn't try very hard at all.*

show someone **up**[†] **as** something to reveal that someone is really something (else). □ *The investigation showed her up*

as a fraud. □ *The test showed up the candidate as unqualified.*

show something **to good advantage** to display the best features of something; to display something so that its best features are apparent. □ *Put the vase in the center of the table and show it to good advantage.* □ *Having and using a large vocabulary shows your intelligence to good advantage.*

show up to appear; to arrive. □ *Where is John? I hope he shows up soon.* □ *When will the bus show up?* □ *Weeds began to show up in the garden.*

show up ahead of time Go to **ahead of time**.

show up on the dot Go to **on the dot**.

shower someone or something **with** something to cover someone or something with cascades of something. □ *Mary's friends showered her with gifts on her twenty-first birthday.* □ *The guests showered the bride and groom with confetti and rice.*

a **shrinking violet** *Fig.* someone who is very shy and not assertive. □ *I am not exactly a shrinking violet, but I don't have the guts to say what you said to her.*

shroud someone or something **in** something to wrap or conceal someone or something in something. □ *They shrouded Mr. Carlson in sailcloth and prepared him for burial at sea.* □ *They shrouded the decision in a series of formalities.*

Shrouds have no pockets. *Prov.* You cannot take any material goods with you when you die. □ *You should use your money to enjoy yourself while you're alive. Shrouds have no pockets.*

shrug something **off (as** something**)** and **pass** something **off (as** something**)** to ignore something unpleasant or offensive as if it meant something else. □ *She shrugged off the criticism as harmless.* □ *I passed off the remark as misinformed.* □ *Bill scolded me, but I just passed it off.*

shuck something **off**[†] **1.** to take something off. □ *Tom shucked his jacket off and sat on the arm of the easy chair.* □ *He shucked off his jacket.* **2.** to get rid of someone or something. □ *She shucked all her bad habits off.* □ *Tom shucked off one girlfriend after another.*

shuffle off this mortal coil *Euph.* to die. (Often jocular or formal euphemism. Not often used in consoling someone.) □ *Cousin Fred shuffled off this mortal coil after suffering a heart attack.* □ *When I shuffle off this mortal coil, I want to go out in style—bells, flowers, and a long, boring funeral.*

shush (up) to be quiet. □ *Shush! I want to hear the weather.* □ *Shush up and listen to the lecture.*

shut down Go to **close down**.

shut one's **eyes to** something Go to **close** one's **eyes to** something.

shut someone or something **out**[†] to exclude someone or something; to refuse entrance to someone or something. □ *We tried to get into the stadium, but they shut us out because there was no more room.* □ *My parents shut out their children when they made important decisions.*

shut someone **up**[†] to silence someone. □ *Oh, shut yourself up!* □ *Will you please shut up that crying baby!*

shut something **down**† Go to close something down†.

shut the door (up)on someone or something and **close the door on** someone or something; **close the door to** someone or something **1.** *Lit.* to close a door, preventing someone or something from passing through. (*Upon* is formal and less commonly used than *on*.) □ *They shut the door upon me, and I couldn't get in!* □ *We quickly closed the door on the smoke.* **2.** *Fig.* to eliminate an opportunity for someone or something. □ *The board of directors shut the door on me, and there was no further opportunity for me to pursue.* □ *They closed the door on further discussions.*

Shut the stable door after the horse has bolted. and **Lock the stable door after the horse is stolen.** *Prov.* To try to prevent something that has already happened; to act too late. □ *When Ray heard that the bank had failed, he tried to withdraw his money, but there was no money to withdraw. He was shutting the stable door after the horse had bolted.* □ *Jenny has stopped smoking since the doctor told her that her lungs were in bad shape, but I'm afraid she's locking the stable door after the horse is stolen.*

Shut up! *Inf.* Be quiet! (Impolite.) □ *Bob: And another thing. Bill: Oh, shut up, Bob!* □ *Andy: Shut up! I've heard enough! Bob: But I have more to say!* □ *"Shut up! I can't hear anything because of all your noise!" shouted the director.*

Shut up about it. *Inf.* Do not tell anyone about it. □ *Bill: I heard that you had a little trouble with the police. Tom: Just shut up about it! Do you hear?* □ *Andy: Didn't you once appear in a movie? Alice: Shut up about it. No one has to know.*

Shut your cake hole! and **Shut your pie hole! Shut your face!** *Inf.* Shut up!; Shut your mouth! □ *I've heard enough! Shut your cake hole!*

shuttle someone or something **from person to person** and **shuttle** someone or something **from place to place** (Specific persons or places are sometimes expressed.) to move or pass someone or something from person to person; to move or pass someone or something from place to place. □ *My phone call was shuttled from person to person.* □ *Mary shuttled her children from home to school to practice.*

shy away (from someone or something**)** to avoid someone or something. □ *The dog shies away from John since he kicked it.* □ *I can understand why the dog would shy away.*

*__sick (and tired) of__ someone or something *Fig.* tired of someone or something, especially something that one must do again and again or someone or something that one must deal with repeatedly. (*Typically: **be ~; become ~; get ~; grow ~.**) □ *I am sick and tired of cleaning up after you.* □ *Mary was sick of being stuck in traffic.*

*__sick as a dog__ *Cliché* very sick; sick and vomiting. (*Also: **as ~.**) □ *We've never been so ill. The whole family was sick as dogs.* □ *Sally was as sick as a dog and couldn't go to the party.*

*__sick at heart__ *Fig.* distressed and depressed. (*Typically: **be ~; become ~; make** someone **~.**) □ *I became sick at heart just looking at all the homeless children.*

sick in bed remaining in bed while (one is) ill. □ *Tom is sick in bed with the flu.* □ *He's been sick in bed for nearly a week.*

sick to death (of someone or something**)** totally disgusted with someone or something. □ *I am sick to death of your constant bickering.* □ *This reporting about the scandals in the government just has me sick to death.*

sick (up) *Sl.* to empty one's stomach; to vomit. □ *I think I'm going to sick up. Isn't there supposed to be a barf bag in one of these seat pockets?* □ *He's got to sick, and there's no air sickness bag. Help!*

side against someone to be against someone; to take sides against someone. □ *I thought you were my friend! I never thought you would side against me!* □ *The two brothers were always siding against their sister.*

side by side (of two or more people or things) lined up so their sides are adjacent. □ *We walked side by side across the lawn.*

side with someone to join with someone; to take someone else's part; to be on someone's side. □ *Why is it that you always side with him when he and I argue?* □ *I never side with anybody. I form my own opinions.*

sidle away (from someone or something**)** to avoid someone or something by moving to the side; to ease away from someone or something. □ *The cowboy sidled away from the bar and drew his gun.* □ *He sidled away and snuck out the door.*

sidle up (to someone or something**)** to move close to someone or something cautiously or furtively; to move closer to someone or something gradually. □ *Tex sidled up to Dolly and said howdy in a soft, shy voice.* □ *Dolly sidled up and picked the cowboy's pocket.*

sift something **from** something to remove something from something by sifting. □ *Fran sifted all the impurities from the flour before using it.* □ *Timmy sifted all the leaves from the sand in his sandbox.*

sift something **out of** something and **sift** something **out**† to get rid of something in something else by sifting. □ *Dan sifted the impurities out of the flour.* □ *Walter sifted out the foreign matter.*

sift something **through** something to make something pass through something such as a sieve. □ *She sifted the powdered sugar through a strainer.* □ *Please sift the soil through this screen and watch for bits of pottery.*

sift through something to examine all parts of something. □ *The fire inspector sifted through the rubble, looking for clues to the start of the fire.* □ *We sifted through all the papers in the old trunk, but we did not find what we were looking for.*

sigh about something to release a deep breath, indicating anxiety, distress, or relief about something. □ *What are you sighing about?* □ *She sighed about her illness and then shifted her thoughts to something else.*

sigh for someone to release a deep breath, indicating anxiety about one's emotional attachment for someone. □ *Dave spent a lot of his time sighing for Laura, on whom he had a crush.* □ *Laura has been sighing for some as-yet-unnamed young man.*

S

a **sight for sore eyes** *Fig.* a welcome sight. □ *Oh, am I glad to see you here! You're a sight for sore eyes.* □ *I'm sure hungry. This meal is a sight for sore eyes.*

sign for someone to sign something, using one's own signature in place of someone else's signature; to sign something, using another person's name, adding the phrase "by [one's own name]." □ *He's not here. I will sign for him. Where do I sign?* □ *Who will sign for Mr. Wilson?*

sign for something to sign a piece of paper indicating that one has received something. □ *Would you sign for this, please?* □ *Ted signed for the package and opened it up.*

sign in to indicate that one has arrived somewhere and at what time by signing a piece of paper or a list. □ *Please sign in so we will know you are here.* □ *Did you remember to sign in this time?*

a **sign of the times** something that signifies the situation evident in the current times. □ *Your neighbor's unmowed grass is just a sign of the times. Nobody really cares any longer.*

a **sign of things to come** Go to a **harbinger of things to come**.

sign off 1. *Lit.* [for a broadcaster] to announce the end of programming for the day; [for an amateur radio operator] to announce the end of a transmission. □ *Wally signed off and turned the transmitter off.* □ *Channel 43 failed to sign off at the scheduled time last night.* **2.** *Fig.* to quit doing what one has been doing and leave, go to bed, quit trying to do something, etc. □ *I have to sign off and get to bed. See you all.* □ *When you finally sign off tonight, please turn out all the lights.*

sign off on something to sign a paper, indicating that one has finished with something or agrees with the state of something. □ *The publisher signed off on the book and sent it to be printed.* □ *I refuse to sign off on this project until it is done correctly.*

sign on to announce the beginning of a broadcast transmission. □ *The announcer signed on and then played "The Star-Spangled Banner."* □ *We usually sign on at six in the morning.*

sign on the dotted line 1. *Lit.* to indicate one's agreement or assent by placing one's signature on a special line provided for that purpose. (The line may be solid or dotted.) □ *I agreed to the contract, but I haven't signed on the dotted line yet.* □ *When you have signed on the dotted line, please give me a call.* **2.** *Fig.* to indicate one's agreement to something. □ *Okay. I agree to your terms. I'll sign on the dotted line.* □ *He is thinking favorably about going with us to Canada, but he hasn't signed on the bottom line.*

sign on (with someone or something**) (as** something**)** to join up with someone or something in a particular capacity by signing a contract or agreement. □ *I signed on with the captain of the Felicity Anne as first mate.* □ *Roger signed on as manager for the new store.*

sign one's **own death warrant** *Fig.* to do something (knowingly) that will most likely result in severe trouble. (As if one were ordering one's own execution.) □ *I wouldn't ever gamble a large sum of money. That would be signing my own death warrant.* □ *The killer signed his own death warrant when he walked into the police station and gave himself up.*

sign out to indicate that one is leaving a place or going out temporarily by signing a piece of paper or a list. □ *I forgot to sign out when I left.* □ *Please sign out every time you leave.*

sign someone **in**† to record that someone has arrived somewhere and at what time by recording the information on a paper or a list. □ *I will sign you in. What is your name?* □ *Do I have to sign in everyone?*

sign someone **on**† to employ someone; to recruit someone as an employee. □ *How many workers did the manager sign on?* □ *The construction company signed on ten new workers.*

sign someone **out of** some place and **sign** someone **out**† to make a record of someone's departure from some place. □ *Did someone sign you out of the factory, or did you just open the door and leave?* □ *I signed out those two who just left.*

sign someone **up**† **(for** something**)** to record the agreement of someone, including oneself, to participate in something. □ *Has anyone signed you up for the office picnic?* □ *Can you sign up Liz for the party?*

sign someone **up**† **(with** someone or something**)** to record the agreement of someone to join someone, a group of people, or an organization. □ *I want to sign George up with our softball team.* □ *Tom signed up his friends with the agency.*

sign something **away**† to sign a paper in which one gives away one's rights to something. □ *Valerie signed her rights away.* □ *She signed away her claim to the money.*

sign something **for** someone **1.** to sign one's signature on a paper in place of someone else's signature. □ *Would you please sign this for me?* □ *I can't sign it right now. Would you sign it for me?* **2.** to sign a paper for another person, using that person's name, adding the phrase "by [one's own name]." □ *When the delivery comes, will you please sign my name for me?* □ *I signed Ted's name for him.*

sign something **in**† to record that something has been received at a particular time by recording the information on a paper or a list. □ *I have to sign this package in, then I will be right with you.* □ *Should I sign in this shipment now?*

sign something **out of** some place and **sign** something **out**† to make a record of the borrowing of something from some place. □ *Dave signed the tape recorder out of the library.* □ *Dave signed out the tape recorder as well as some blank tapes.*

sign something **over**† **(to** someone**)** to sign a paper granting the rights to or ownership of something to a specific person. □ *Larry signed all the rights to his book over to the publisher.* □ *He signed over all the rights to the publisher.*

sign up (for something**)** to record one's agreement to participate in something. □ *I want to sign up for guitar lessons.* □ *We will sign up as soon as possible.*

sign (up) with someone or something to enter into an agreement with someone or a group. □ *I signed up with Tom and John to crew their ship in the regatta.* □ *Did you sign with the office equipment supplier yet?*

signal for someone to make a sign for someone to come. □ *I signaled for the waiter and got the check.* □ *Ted signaled for the parking lot attendant.*

signal for something to make a sign that something should be done. □ *I caught the waiter's eye and signaled for the check.* □ *The director signaled for applause.*

signal (to) someone **(to do something)** [for someone] to give someone a command or instruction using a signal. □ *The traffic cop signaled me to stop.* □ *The state trooper signaled the driver to pull over to the side of the road.*

signed, sealed, and delivered *Fig.* formally and officially signed; [for a formal document to be] executed. □ *Here is the deed to the property—signed, sealed, and delivered.* □ *I can't begin work on this project until I have the contract signed, sealed, and delivered.*

Silence gives consent. *Prov.* If you do not object to what someone says or does, you can be assumed to agree with or condone it. □ *Jill: What did Fred say when you told him we were thinking about leaving the office early? Jane: He didn't say anything. Jill: Then he must not mind if we go. Silence gives consent.*

Silence is golden. *Prov.* Silence is often good or desirable. □ *Jerry has two teenage children who listen to music using their headphones all day. He knows that silence is golden.* □ *Hush! Silence is golden.*

*****silent as the dead** and *****silent as the grave** completely silent. (Has ominous connotations because of the reference to death. Usually used to promise someone that you will be silent and therefore not betray a secret. *Also: **as ~**.) □ *I knew something was wrong as soon as I entered the classroom; everyone was silent as the dead.* □ *Jessica is as silent as the grave on the subject of her first marriage.* □ *If you tell me what Katy said about me, I promise to be as silent as the grave.*

silent as the grave Go to previous.

*****silly as a goose** very foolish. (*Also: **as ~**.) □ *Edith is as silly as a goose. She thinks that reading aloud to her houseplants will help them grow.* □ *The ad in the newspaper said this lotion would make my hair grow back, but I've been using it for a whole month and my hair is still the same. Jane: You're as silly as a goose! Do you believe everything you read in newspaper ads?*

silt up [for a body of water] to become filled with silt. □ *The river moved too fast to silt up.* □ *The lake silted up in a very few years.*

simmer down 1. *Lit.* to decrease in intensity. (As boiling dies down when the heat is lowered or removed.) □ *The hectic activity of the day finally simmered down.* □ *When things simmer down in the fall, this is a much nicer place.* **2.** *Fig.* [for someone] to become calm or less agitated. □ *I wish you would simmer down.* □ *Please simmer down, you guys!*

sin against someone or something to offend or desecrate someone or something sacred or revered. □ *The critic said that Walter sinned against the poet when he read the poem in a sarcastic manner.* □ *I would say that Walter sinned against poetry, not just one poet.*

since day one Go to day one.

since someone **was knee-high to a grasshopper** Go to knee-high to a jackrabbit.

since time immemorial since a very long time ago. (Literally, since time before recorded history.) □ *My hometown has had a big parade on the Fourth of July since time immemorial.* □ *Since time immemorial, the trees have blossomed each spring.*

Since when? *Inf.* When was that decided?; **That's news to me.**; When was that done? □ *Tom: You've been assigned to the night shift. John: Since when?* □ *Jane: Fred is now the assistant manager. Pete: Since when? Jane: Since I appointed him, that's when.*

sing a different tune and **sing another tune** *Fig.* to change one's manner, usually from bad to good. (Almost the same as **dance to another tune**.) □ *When she learned that I was a bank director, she began to sing a different tune.* □ *You will sing another tune as soon as you find out how right I am!*

sing along (with someone or something**)** to sing with someone or with the accompaniment of some instrument(s). □ *Harry played all the old songs and everybody sang along.* □ *Let's sing along with Mary. She knows some good songs.*

sing another tune Go to sing a different tune.

Sing before breakfast, you'll cry before night. and **Sing before breakfast, you'll cry before supper.** *Prov.* If you wake up feeling very happy, your mood will change before the end of the day. □ *Jill: I woke up in such a good mood today. I don't even know why, but everything seems good. Jane: Sing before breakfast, you'll cry before night.* □ *Alan: Good morning, dear! Isn't it a wonderful day? I feel great. Jane: Sing before breakfast, you'll cry before supper.*

sing from the same hymnbook Go to read from the same page.

sing of someone or something to tell about or sing a song about someone or something. □ *The folksinger sang of Paul Bunyan.* □ *They all sang of happier times in the past.*

sing one's **heart out** Go to cry one's heart out.

sing out to sing louder. □ *Sing out, please. This is a very large hall.* □ *The sopranos will have to sing out more.*

sing someone's or something's **praises** and **sing the praises of** someone or something *Fig.* to praise someone highly and enthusiastically. □ *The boss is singing his new secretary's praises.* □ *The theater critics are singing the praises of the young actor.*

sing someone **to sleep** to sing softly and sweetly to someone until sleep comes. □ *The mother sang her baby to sleep.* □ *Please sing Timmy to sleep. He is very restless.*

sing something **out**† to sing or announce something loudly. □ *The teacher sang the names out loud and clear.* □ *She sang out "The Star-Spangled Banner" in a loud voice.*

sing the praises of someone or something Go to sing someone's or something's **praises**.

sing to someone or something to sing a song and direct it at someone or something. □ *The singer sang to a man in the front row, and he was very embarrassed by it.* □ *Claire sang to an older audience and put many of them to sleep.*

sing together [for people] to coordinate their singing. □ *Let's sing together now. Everyone should watch the conductor and follow the beat.* □ *You have to sing together if you want your words to be understood.*

sing up a storm Go to up a storm.

S

single file a line of things or people, one person or one thing wide. (See also **in single file.**) □ *Please get into single file.* □ *You have to march single file.*

single someone or something **out†** (**for** something) to choose or pick someone or something for something; to select an eligible person or thing for something. □ *The committee singled her out for a special award.* □ *We singled out Liz for special honors.*

sink back (**into** something) to lean back and relax in something, such as a soft chair. □ *I can't wait to get home and sink back into my easy chair.* □ *He sank back and went to sleep almost immediately.*

sink below someone or something Go to **below** someone or something.

sink below something to descend below a certain level. □ *The boat sank below the surface of the water and was gone.* □ *The temperature sank below the freezing mark again today.*

sink down to sink or submerge. □ *The sun sank down and darkness spread across the land.* □ *She sat in the chair and sank down, enjoying her moment of relaxation.*

sink in 1. *Lit.* to sink, submerge, or descend into something. □ *How long will it take the water to sink in?* □ *It might take days for the oil to sink in, so you have time to clean it up.* **2.** *Fig.* [for knowledge] to be understood. □ *I heard what you said, but it took a while for it to sink in.* □ *I pay careful attention to everything I hear in calculus class, but it usually doesn't sink in.*

sink into despair to become depressed; to become completely discouraged. □ *After facing the hopelessness of the future, Jean Paul sank into despair.* □ *Mary sank into despair upon learning of the death of her grandmother.*

sink into oblivion *Fig.* to fade into obscurity. □ *She may be famous now, but in no time she will sink into oblivion.* □ *In his final years, Wally Wilson sank into oblivion and just faded away.*

sink one's **teeth into** something Go to **get** one's **teeth into** something.

sink or swim *Fig.* to fail or succeed. (Alludes to the choices available to someone who has fallen into the water.) □ *After I've studied and learned all I can, I have to take the test and sink or swim.* □ *It's too late to help John now. It's sink or swim for him.*

sink something **in(to)** someone or something and **sink** something **in† 1.** *Lit.* to drive or push something into someone or something. □ *The brave hero sank the wooden stake into the vampire.* □ *The hero sank in the stake.* **2.** *Fig.* to invest time or money in someone or something. (Sometimes implying that it was wasted.) □ *You would not believe how much money I've sunk into that company!* □ *She sank in a lot of money, but it was all wasted.*

sink to (**doing**) something *Fig.* to lower oneself to doing something bad or mean. □ *I never thought he would sink to doing that.* □ *There is nothing that Max wouldn't sink to.*

sink under (**something**) to submerge. □ *The small boat turned over and sank under the surface.* □ *It sank under and went straight to the bottom.*

*a sinking feeling the feeling that everything is going wrong; a bad feeling in the base of one's stomach. (*Typically: **get** ~; **have** ~; **give** someone ~.) □ I get a sinking feeling whenever I think of the night of the accident.*

siphon something **off†** (**from** something) **1.** *Lit.* to suck or draw a liquid off from something. □ *Harry siphoned the cream off the milk.* □ *He siphoned off the cream.* **2.** *Fig.* to embezzle or steal something a little at a time. *The teller had been siphoning money off for years.* □ *She siphoned off a few dollars from the collection every week or so.*

sit around to relax sitting; to waste time sitting. □ *Don't just sit around! Get moving!* □ *I need to sit around every now and then and reorganize my thoughts.*

sit around something to be seated at the edge or perimeter of something. □ *They sat around the campfire for hours.* □ *We used to sit around the big kitchen table and talk.*

sit around (**somewhere**) to sit somewhere and relax or do nothing; to sit idly somewhere. □ *Tom likes to sit around the house in shorts and a T-shirt on hot days.* □ *Too many people are just sitting around doing nothing at my office.*

sit at something to be seated in front of something, such as a table. □ *He sat at the table, taking his tea.* □ *Please sit at your desk and finish your work before taking a break.*

sit at the feet of someone *Fig.* to pay homage to someone; to pay worshipful attention to someone. □ *The graduate student sat at the feet of the famous professor for years.* □ *I do not intend to sit at the feet of an incompetent for years and years.*

sit back to push oneself back in one's seat; to lean against the back of one's seat. □ *Please sit back. I can't see around you.* □ *I sat back and made myself comfortable, assuming that the movie would bore me to sleep.*

sit back and let something happen *Fig.* to relax and not interfere with something; to let something happen without playing a part in it. □ *I can't just sit back and let you waste all our money!* □ *Don't worry. Just sit back and let things take care of themselves.*

sit behind someone or something Go to **behind** someone or something.

sit below someone or something Go to **below** someone or something.

sit beneath something Go to **beneath** something.

sit bolt upright to sit up straight. □ *Tony sat bolt upright and listened to what the teacher was saying to him.* □ *After sitting bolt upright for almost an hour in that crowded airplane, I swore I would never fly again.*

sit by someone to sit next to someone. □ *May I sit by you?* □ *Come over here and sit by me.*

sit close to someone or something Go to **close to** someone or something.

sit down to be seated; to sit on something, such as a chair. □ *Please sit down and make yourself comfortable.* □ *Can I sit down here?*

sit down on something to be seated on something. □ *Please sit down on this chair and wait until you are called.* □ *I don't want to sit down on this hard bench.*

sit down to something to sit down at a table to do something, such as eat a meal or attend to some business. □ *I* look forward to going home and sitting down to a quiet supper. □ Ted looked forward to sitting down to a big Thanksgiving dinner.

sit for an exam to take an exam to qualify for a license, such as a bar exam. □ *When do you sit for the bar exam?* □ *I will sit for the exam next week.*

sit for one's **portrait** to serve as the subject of a portrait being done by a painter or photographer. □ *I sat for the picture for two hours.* □ *Do you mind sitting for the painter all day? It will be easier if you get it over with all at once.*

sit for someone **1.** to care for someone in the role of babysitter. □ *I sit for Timmy sometimes. I like him. He's a good little kid.* □ *Mary doesn't sit for anyone anymore. It leaves no time for a social life.* **2.** to serve as a babysitter in someone's employ. □ *I sit for Mrs. Franklin every now and then.* □ *Ted used to sit for the Wilsons.* **3.** to serve as a model or subject for someone, such as an artist. □ *She sat for the portrait painter every day for a week.* □ *She is looking for someone to sit for her so she can develop her skills.*

sit hand in hand Go to hand in hand.

sit idly by and **stand idly by** to remain close, doing nothing to help. □ *I do not intend to stand idly by while my children need my help.* □ *The wealthy man sat idly by while the poor people starved.*

sit in (for someone**)** to act as a substitute for someone. (Usually involves actual sitting, such as at a meeting.) □ *I am not a regular member of this committee. I am sitting in for Larry Smith.* □ *Do you mind if I sit in? My representative can't be here.*

sit in judgment (up)on someone or something to make a judgment about someone or something. (*Upon* is formal and less commonly used than *on*.) □ *I don't want to sit in judgment upon you or anyone else, but I do have some suggestions.* □ *There is no need to sit in judgment on the proposal at this time.*

sit in (on something**)** to attend something as a visitor; to act as a temporary participant in something. □ *Do you mind if I sit in on your discussion?* □ *Please do sit in.*

sit on its hands and **sit on their hands** *Fig.* [for an audience] to refuse to applaud. (See also **sit on** one's **hands**.) □ *The performance was really quite good, but the audience sat on its hands.* □ *They sat on their hands during the first act.*

sit on one's **ass** *Inf.* to sit idle; to sit around doing nothing. (Use *ass* with discretion.) □ *Don't just sit on your ass! Get busy!* □ *He just sat on his ass, watching what was going on.*

sit on one's **hands** *Fig.* to do nothing; to fail to help. (See also **sit on its hands.**) □ *When we needed help from Mary, she just sat on her hands.* □ *We need the cooperation of everyone. You can't sit on your hands!*

sit on someone or something **1.** *Lit.* to place oneself in a sitting position on someone or something. □ *The enormous woman knocked the crook out and sat on him until the police came.* □ *I need to sit on this chair for a minute and catch my breath.* **2.** *Fig.* to hold someone or something back; to delay someone or something. □ *The project cannot be finished because the city council is sitting on the final approval.* □ *Ann deserves to be promoted, but the manager is sitting on her because of a disagreement.* □ *It's hard to do your best*

when you know that someone is sitting on you, and no matter what you do, it won't help your advancement.

sit on the fence *Fig.* not to take sides in a dispute; not to make a clear choice between two possibilities. (Fig. on the image of someone straddling a fence, representing indecision.) □ *When Jane and Tom argue, it is best to sit on the fence and not make either of them angry.* □ *No one knows which of the candidates Joan will vote for. She's sitting on the fence.*

sit on the fence (about something**)** Go to on the fence (about something).

sit on their hands Go to sit on its hands.

sit out to elect not to participate in something. □ *I think I will not join in this game. I'll sit it out.* □ *I'll sit out for this round.*

sit right with someone *Fig.* [for something] to be acceptable or understandable to someone. (Very close to **sit well with someone.**) □ *What you just said doesn't really sit right with me. Let's talk about it.* □ *It didn't sit right with the boss.*

sit something **out**† not to participate in something; to wait until something is over before participating. □ *Oh, please play with us. Don't sit it out.* □ *I'm tired of playing cards, so I think I'll sit out this game.*

sit still for something **1.** *Lit.* to remain seated without fidgeting during something. □ *The child could hardly be expected to sit still for the opera.* □ *Timmy would not sit still for his haircut.* **2.** *Fig.* to remain idle rather than act to prevent something; to endure or tolerate something. □ *I won't sit still for that kind of treatment.* □ *She would not sit still for an insult like that.*

sit through something to remain seated and in attendance for all of something, even though it is boring or poorly done. □ *I can't stand to sit through that class one more time!* □ *Do I have to sit through the whole lecture?*

sit tight to wait; to wait patiently. (This does not necessarily refer to sitting.) □ *Just relax and sit tight. I'll be right with you.* □ *We were waiting in line for the gates to open when someone came out and told us to sit tight because it wouldn't be much longer before we could go in.*

sit up 1. to rise from a lying to a sitting position. □ *When the alarm went off, he sat up and put his feet on the floor.* □ *She couldn't sleep, so she sat up and read a book.* **2.** to sit more straight in one's seat; to hold one's posture more upright while seated. □ *Please sit up. Don't slouch!* □ *You wouldn't get backaches if you would sit up.*

sit up and take notice to become alert and pay attention. □ *A loud noise from the front of the room caused everyone to sit up and take notice.* □ *The company wouldn't pay any attention to my complaints. When I had my lawyer write them a letter, they sat up and took notice.*

sit up with someone to stay with someone through the night, especially with a sick or troubled person or with someone who is waiting for something. □ *I had to sit up with my younger sister when she was ill.* □ *I sat up with Bill while he waited for an overseas telephone call.*

sit well with someone to be acceptable to someone. □ *Your explanation of your absence doesn't sit well with the president.* □ *The whole affair didn't sit well with the manager.*

S

sit with someone **1.** to stay with someone; to **sit up with** someone. □ *My uncle sat with me my first day in the hospital.* **2.** to stay with and care for one or more children; to babysit for someone. □ *I hired Mrs. Wilson to sit with the children.* □ *We couldn't go out for dinner because we couldn't find anyone to sit with the kids.*

*a **sitting duck** *Fig.* someone or something vulnerable to attack, physical or verbal. (Alludes to a duck floating on the water, not suspecting that it is the object of a hunter or predator. *Typically: **be** ~; **like** ~; **looking like** ~.) □ *You look like a sitting duck out there. Get in here where the enemy cannot fire at you.* □ *The senator was a sitting duck because of his unpopular position on school reform.*

sitting on a gold mine *Fig.* in control of something very valuable; in control of something potentially very valuable. □ *When I found out how much the old book was worth, I realized that I was sitting on a gold mine.* □ *Mary's land is valuable. She is sitting on a gold mine.*

sitting on a powder keg *Fig.* in a risky or explosive situation; in a situation where something serious or dangerous may happen at any time. (A powder keg is a keg of gunpowder.) □ *Things are very tense at work. The whole office is sitting on a powder keg.* □ *The fire at the oil field seems to be under control for now, but all the workers there are sitting on a powder keg.*

(sitting) on top of the world *Fig.* feeling wonderful; glorious; ecstatic. □ *Wow, I feel on top of the world.* □ *Since he got a new job, he's on top of the world.*

*****sitting pretty** living in comfort or luxury; living in a good situation. (*Typically: **be** ~; **leave** someone ~.) □ *My uncle died and left enough money for me to be sitting pretty for the rest of my life.* □ *Now that I have a good-paying job, I'm sitting pretty.*

six feet under *Fig.* dead and buried. □ *Fred died and is six feet under.* □ *They put him six feet under two days after he died.*

six of one and half a dozen of the other *Fig.* about the same one way or another. □ *It doesn't matter to me which way you do it. It's six of one and half a dozen of the other.* □ *What difference does it make? They're both the same—six of one and half a dozen of the other.*

a **sixth sense** a supposed power to know or feel things that are not perceptible by the five senses of sight, hearing, smell, taste, and touch. □ *My sixth sense told me to avoid going home by my usual route. Later I discovered there had been a fatal accident on it.* □ *Jane's sixth sense demanded that she not trust Tom, even though he seemed honest enough.*

the **sixty-four-dollar question** *Fig.* the most important question; the question that everyone wants to know the answer to. □ *Who will win? Now, that is the sixty-four-dollar question.* □ *Now for the sixty-four-dollar question. What's the stock market going to do this year?*

size someone or something **up**† to observe someone or something to get information; to **check** someone or something **out.** □ *The comedian sized the audience up and decided not to use his new material.* □ *I like to size up a situation before I act.*

skate around to skate here and there in no particular direction. □ *Let's go over to the pond and skate around.* □ *We will skate around for a while until we get too cold.*

skate around someone or something **1.** to skate to one side or the other of someone or something. □ *Somehow I managed to skate around the child without knocking her down.* □ *I skated around the tree limb and avoided an accident.* **2.** to circle someone or something while skating. □ *The children skated around their instructor until she was satisfied with their form.* □ *We skated around the post in a circle.*

skate on something to skate on a particular surface. □ *You can't skate on that ice! It's too thin.* □ *Don't skate on the ice until it has been scraped smooth.*

skate on thin ice *Fig.* to be in a risky situation. (Fig. on the image of someone taking the risk of ice skating on thin ice.) □ *I try to stay well informed so I don't end up skating on thin ice when the teacher asks me a question.* □ *You are skating on thin ice when you ask me that!*

skate over something **1.** *Lit.* to move over something, skating. □ *I love to be the first one to skate over newly frozen ice.* □ *I skated over the pond too soon and the ice cracked while I was on it.* **2.** *Fig.* to move over or deal with something quickly. □ *The speaker skated over the touchy issues with discretion.* □ *I will skate over the things that I am not sure about.*

skeleton(s) in the closet a hidden and shocking secret. □ *You can ask anyone about how reliable I am. I don't mind. I don't have any skeletons in the closet.* □ *My uncle was in jail for a day once. That's our family's skeleton in the closet.*

sketch something **in**† to draw in the image of someone or something. □ *I sketched a figure of a woman in so that she appears to be standing beneath the tree.* □ *I'll sketch in the house in the upper left corner.*

sketch something **out**† to create a rough idea or image of something by sketching or some other means. (Does not necessarily require an actual sketch.) □ *Sally sketched the furniture arrangement out so we could get an idea of what it was to look like.* □ *Would you sketch out your ideas, please?*

skid across something to slip or glide across something, such as ice or wet pavement. □ *The car skidded across the pavement and crashed into a tree.* □ *Our bus skidded across the icy bridge and ran into a ditch on the other side.*

skid into someone or something to slip or glide into someone or something. □ *The bicycle skidded into a pedestrian.* □ *The car skidded into a guard rail.*

skim over something **1.** *Lit.* to glide across something. □ *The sailboat skimmed over the waves like a bird.* □ *The bird skimmed over the treetops, darting and dodging.* **2.** *Fig.* to go over or review something hastily. □ *I just skimmed over the material and still got an A on the test!* □ *Please skim over chapter four for Thursday.*

skim something **off (of)** something and **skim** something **off**† **1.** *Lit.* to scoop something off the surface of something. (*Of* is usually retained before pronouns.) □ *The cook skimmed the fat off the stew.* □ *The cook skimmed off the fat.* **2.** *Fig.* to remove a portion of something of value, such as money, from an account. (*Of* is usually retained before pronouns.) □ *The auditor was skimming a few dol-*

lars a day off the bank's cash flow. □ *Kelly skimmed off a few dollars each day.*

skim through something to go through something hastily; to read through something hastily. □ *She skimmed through the catalogs, looking for a nice gift for Gary.* □ *I will skim through your manuscript and see whether it looks promising.*

skimp on something to use too little of something; to save something by using less of it than needed for something. □ *Please don't skimp on the gravy. I like my potatoes swimming in it.* □ *They skimped on quality a little when they furnished the lobby.*

Skin me! Go to Give me five!

skin someone **alive** *Fig.* to be very angry with someone; to scold someone severely. (*Fig.* on being angry enough to do this kind of bodily harm to someone.) □ *I was so mad at Jane that I could have skinned her alive.* □ *If I don't get home on time, my parents will skin me alive.*

***skinny as a beanpole** very thin; very skinny. (*Also: as ~.*) □ *I exercised and dieted until I was skinny as a beanpole.*

skinny-dip to swim naked. □ *The boys were skinny-dipping in the creek when Bob's mother drove up.*

skip bail Go to jump bail.

Skip it! *Inf.* Never mind!; Forget it! (Shows impatience or disappointment.) □ *John: I need some help on this project. Mary: What? John: Oh, skip it!* □ *Jane: Will you be able to do this, or should I get someone with more experience? Bob: What did you say? Jane: Oh, skip it!*

skip off (with something) *Fig.* to leave and take something with one. □ *The little kid with the freckles skipped off with a candy bar.* □ *He took the candy bar I offered him and skipped off.*

skip (out) *Inf.* to leave; to run away without doing something, such as paying a bill. □ *The guy skipped when the waitress wasn't looking.* □ *Fred skipped out, leaving me with the bill.*

skip out (on someone or something) *Fig.* to sneak away from someone or some event; to leave someone or an event suddenly or in secret. □ *I heard that Bill skipped out on his wife.* □ *I'm not surprised. I thought he should have skipped out long ago.*

skip out with something *Fig.* to leave and take something with one; to steal something. □ *The hotel guest skipped out with the towels.* □ *Someone skipped out with the petty cash box.*

skip over someone or something not to choose someone or something next in line. □ *She skipped over me and chose the next one in line.* □ *I skipped over the red ones and took a blue one.*

skip rope to jump over an arc of rope that is swung beneath one's feet then over one's head, repeatedly. □ *The children skipped rope on the playground.* □ *The boxer skipped rope while training.*

skip through something to go through a book or a stack of papers without dealing with every page. □ *I skipped through the book, just looking at the pictures.* □ *Ted skipped through the report, not bothering to read it.*

skirmish with someone or something to have a minor fight with someone, a group, or something. □ *Tim skirmished a bit with his brother and then ran into the house.* □ *I don't want to skirmish with the committee.*

skirt around someone or something *Fig.* to move around and avoid someone or something. (*Something* can be a topic of conversation.) □ *We talked the whole evening and managed to skirt around Fred.* □ *We had to skirt around the subject.*

The **sky's the limit.** *Inf.* there is no upper limit. □ *I can afford it. The sky's the limit.* □ *You can do anything you set your mind to, Billy. The sky's the limit.*

slack off 1. to taper off; to reduce gradually. □ *Business tends to slack off during the winter months.* □ *The storms begin to slack off in April.* **2.** [for someone] to become lazy or inefficient. □ *Near the end of the school year, Sally began to slack off, and her grades showed it.* □ *John got fired for slacking off during the busy season.*

slack up (on something) and **slack off (on** something) to release the pressure or tension on something. (See also slack off!) □ *Slack up on the rope a bit, will you?* □ *Please slack off!*

slam dunk 1. *Lit.* [in basketball] a goal scored by shooting the ball down from above the rim. □ *He was wide open and scored on an easy slam dunk.* **2.** *Fig.* an action or accomplishment that is easily done. □ *Finishing that project with all his experience should be a slam dunk for George.*

slam into someone or something to crash into someone or something. □ *The race car—out of control—slammed into the stands.* □ *The bus slammed into a truck.*

slam someone or something **down**† to drive or strike someone or something downward. □ *The wrestler slammed his opponent down hard.* □ *He slammed down his opponent and injured him.*

slam something **down**† **(on(to)** something) to bang something down onto something. □ *She slammed her fist down on the table in anger.* □ *Karen slammed down her fist onto the table.*

slam the brakes on† to push on a vehicle's brakes suddenly and hard. (*The* can be replaced by a possessive pronoun.) □ *The driver in front of me slammed her brakes on and I nearly ran into her.* □ *Don't slam on your brakes when the road is wet.*

slam the door in someone's **face 1.** *Lit.* to swing a door closed with force while someone is standing in the doorway. □ *I didn't know Todd was behind me and I accidentally slammed the door in his face.* □ *Please don't slam the door in my face!* **2.** *Fig.* suddenly to withdraw an opportunity from someone. □ *The events of the last week effectively slammed the door in my face for future employment.* □ *We slammed the door in Bill's face since he was so rude when we interviewed him.*

slant against something to rest obliquely against something. □ *The bookcase slants against the wall, and it should be straight.* □ *The lumber was left slanted against the garage.*

slant something **against** someone or something to bias something against someone or something; to twist information so it is against someone or something. □ *The writer slanted the story against the innocent people of the*

S

town. □ *The reporter slanted her story against one political party.*

slant something **toward** someone or something and **slant** something **in favor of** someone or something to bias something toward someone or something; to twist information so it favors someone or something. □ *The writer slanted the story toward the plaintiff's charges.* □ *The reporter slanted her story in favor of one political party.*

slant toward someone or something to incline toward someone or something. □ *The scenery slanted toward the actors and looked as if it would fall.* □ *Everything in your sketch slants toward the right.*

slap against someone or something [for something] to flap or strike against someone or something. □ *The flag kept slapping against Ed, making it hard for him to remain at attention.* □ *The awning slapped against the side of the house.*

a **slap in the face** an insult; an act that causes disappointment or discouragement. □ *Losing the election was a slap in the face for the club president.* □ *Failing to get into a good college was a slap in the face to Tim after his years of study.*

*a **slap on the wrist 1.** *Lit.* a hit on the wrist as a mild punishment for putting one's hands where they shouldn't be or taking something. (*Typically: **get** ~; **give** someone ~.) □ *When Billy tried to grab another cookie, he got a slap on the wrist.* **2.** *Fig.* to get a light punishment (for doing something wrong). (*Typically: **get** ~; **give** someone ~.) □ *He created quite a disturbance, but he only got a slap on the wrist from the judge.* □ *I thought I'd get a slap on the wrist for speeding, but I got fined $500.*

slap someone **down**[†] **1.** *Lit.* to cause someone to fall by striking with the open hand. □ *She became enraged and slapped him down when he approached her again.* □ *Liz slapped down the insulting wretch.* **2.** *Fig.* to squelch someone; to rebuke or rebuff someone. □ *I had a great idea, but the boss slapped me down.* □ *Don't slap down people without hearing what they have to say.*

slap someone **in** something *Fig. Inf.* to put or throw someone in jail or prison. □ *The sheriff slapped the crooks in jail.* □ *Do you want me to slap you in jail?*

slap someone **on** something to slap a particular part of someone. □ *Gerald was always slapping his friends on the back.* □ *He slapped himself on the knee and laughed very loudly.*

slap someone **on the wrist** and **slap** someone's **wrist 1.** *Lit.* to strike someone's wrist with the open hand, as a punishment. □ *Aunt Maude slapped Tony on the wrist when he grabbed a couple of her freshly baked cookies.* □ *Tony was slapped on the wrist when he tried to swipe some cookies.* **2.** *Fig.* to administer only the mildest of punishments to someone. □ *The judge did nothing but slap the mugger on the wrist.*

slap something **against** someone or something to flap or strike something onto someone or something. □ *The wind slapped the branch against Walter.* □ *The gusts from the storm slapped the shutters against the side of the house.*

slap something **down**[†] to strike downward with something flat in one's hand. □ *She slapped the dollar bill down in great anger and took her paper cup full of water away with*

her. □ *Karen slapped down the money that the bailiff demanded.*

slap something **on**[†] **1.** *Inf.* to dress in something hastily. □ *Henry slapped a shirt on and went out to say something to the garbage hauler.* □ *He slapped on a shirt and ran to the bus stop.* **2.** Go to slap something **onto** someone or something.

slap something **on** someone *Inf.* to serve someone with a legal paper or citation. □ *The strange man came into the office and slapped a subpoena on Mary.* □ *I will slap a citation on you for speeding if you don't stop arguing.*

slap something **onto** someone or something and **slap** something **on**[†] to place something onto someone or something by slapping. □ *Tim slapped a sign onto Gary that said "kick me."* □ *Tim came up to Gary's back and slapped on a sign.*

slap something **together**[†] Go to throw something together[†].

slash and burn 1. *Lit.* of a farming technique where vegetation is cut down and burned before crops are planted. (Hyphenated before nominals.) □ *The small farmers' slash-and-burn technique destroyed thousands of acres of forest.* **2.** *Fig.* of a crude and brash way of doing something. (Hyphenated before nominals.) □ *The new manager's method was strictly slash and burn. He looks decisive to his boss and merciless to the people he fires.*

slash (out) at someone to thrust out at someone with a knife or something similar, with the intent of cutting. □ *The attacker slashed out at his victim and then ran away.* □ *Max slashed at the cop with a pocketknife.*

slate someone or something **for** something to schedule someone or something for some thing or a particular time. □ *They slated me for a trip to Columbia, Missouri, in August.* □ *Wally slated the meeting room for his presentation.*

*****slated for** something scheduled for something. (As if a schedule had been written on a slate. *Typically: **be** ~; **have** someone ~.) □ *John was slated for Friday's game, but he couldn't play with the team.* □ *Ann is slated for promotion next year.*

*****slated to** do something scheduled to do something. (*Typically: **be** ~; **have** someone ~.) □ *Mary is slated to go to Washington in the fall.* □ *We are slated to leave in November.*

slave away (at something) *Fig.* to work very hard (doing something). □ *I'm tired of slaving away at this and getting nowhere.* □ *I'm slaving away for $7.00 an hour and have no prospects for the future.*

slave over something *Fig.* to stand over something, working at it very hard, typically cooking over a hot stove. □ *I've been slaving over this hot stove for hours to cook this meal!* □ *Ted slaved over his special dessert for hours.*

*a **slave to** something *Fig.* someone who is under the control of something; someone whose time or attention is controlled or "owned by" by something. (Fig. on being a slave to a person. *Typically: **be** ~; **become** ~.) □ *Mary is a slave to her job.* □ *Bill is a slave to his drug addiction.*

sled down something to ride down something on a sled. □ *I love to sled down the hill in the winter.* □ *This hill is too steep to sled down safely.*

sled over something to travel over something, such as snow, in a sled. □ *We sledded rapidly over the fresh snow, scooting down the hill.* □ *We wanted to sled over the new snow, but we had to wait until Uncle Herman had taken a picture of it for his scrapbook.*

sleep around the clock to sleep for a full twenty-four hours; to sleep for a very long time. □ *I was so tired I could have slept around the clock.* □ *When I got home, I lay down and slept around the clock.*

sleep around (with someone) *Inf.* to have sex with several partners over time; to be promiscuous. □ *They say she sleeps around with just anybody all the time.* □ *Yes, she sleeps around.*

sleep in to oversleep; to sleep late in the morning. □ *If you sleep in again, you'll get fired.* □ *I really felt like sleeping in this morning.*

sleep in the buff Go to in the altogether.

sleep like a log and **sleep like a baby** to sleep very soundly. □ *Everyone in our family sleeps like a log, so no one heard the thunderstorm in the middle of the night.* □ *Nothing can wake me up. I usually sleep like a baby.*

sleep on something **1.** *Lit.* to recline on something and slumber. □ *I like to sleep on a firm bed.* □ *Mary had to sleep on the floor because her sister was visiting.* **2.** *Fig.* to postpone a decision until one has slept through the night. (As if one were going to think through the decision while sleeping.) □ *It sounds like a good idea, but I'd like to sleep on it before giving you my response.* □ *You go home and sleep on it and give me your answer in the morning.*

sleep out to sleep outside or away from one's home. □ *Can I sleep out tonight?* □ *Didn't you sleep out last night?*

sleep over (with someone) (some place) to spend the night sleeping at someone else's home. (Typically said by teenagers or younger children who spend the night with a friend.) □ *Mom, can I sleep over with Tony?* □ *Can I sleep over at Tony's house?*

sleep something **away**† to spend or waste a specific period of time sleeping. □ *You can't sleep the whole day away!* □ *Jim slept away his whole vacation.*

sleep something **off**† to sleep while the effects of liquor or drugs pass away. □ *John drank too much and went home to sleep it off.* □ *Bill is at home sleeping off the effects of the drug they gave him.*

sleep through something to remain sleeping through some event. □ *I didn't hear the storm. I guess I slept through it.* □ *Wally slept through the entire opera—even the loud part.*

sleep tight to sleep warm and safe. (Usually said with good night to someone going to bed.) □ *Sleep tight, Bobby. See you in the morning.*

sleep together 1. [for two or more people] to share a bed. □ *Do you mean that Fred and Dave have to sleep together?* □ *My brother and I used to have to sleep together.* **2.** *Euph.* [for two people] to copulate. □ *Do you think they slept together?* □ *Ted and Alice slept together a lot when they were in college.*

sleep with someone **1.** to share a bed with someone. □ *Do I have to sleep with my little brother?* □ *Many little boys have to sleep with their brothers.* **2.** *Euph.* to copulate with

someone. □ *I hear Sam's sleeping with Sally now.* □ *Whom did you say he slept with?*

a **sleeping giant** a great power that is still and waiting. □ *The huge country to the south is a sleeping giant, waiting for its chance to become sufficiently industrialized to have real prosperity.* □ *The U.S. was a sleeping giant at the outbreak of both world wars.*

slice in(to something**)** to cut into something, usually with a knife or something similar. □ *Betty sliced into the cake and discovered it was chocolate all the way through.* □ *It wasn't until she sliced in that she found out what kind of cake it was.*

a **slice of the action** Go to a piece (of the action).

a **slice of the cake** a share of something. □ *There's not much work around and so everyone must be content with a slice of the cake.* □ *The company makes huge profits and the workers want a slice of the cake.*

slice someone or something **up**† to cut someone or something up into slices. □ *The blades of the lawn mower can slice you up if you get too close.* □ *The sharp blades sliced up Bobby's rubber ball.*

slice something **off**† to cut something off with slicing motions. □ *Sue sliced the dead branches off with a tree saw.* □ *Karen sliced off a nice piece of turkey.*

slice through something to cut through something with slicing motions. □ *The chef sliced through the ham as if it were butter.* □ *The knife was too dull to slice through the tomato.*

*****slick as a whistle** quickly and cleanly; quickly and skillfully. (*Also: **as** ~.) □ *Tom took a broom and a mop and cleaned the place up as slick as a whistle.* □ *Slick as a whistle, Sally pulled off the bandage.*

slick something **down**† to brush or comb down hair, usually with some sort of dressing or water. □ *He used something gooey—grease or something—to slick his hair down.* □ *Please slick down your hair. You look a mess.*

slick something **up**† to tidy up something or some place. □ *I have to slick this house up a little.* □ *Please slick up this room before company gets here.*

slide along to slip or glide along. □ *The sled slid along at a good clip down the gently sloping hill.* □ *We slid along on the icy roads and had a hard time stopping and turning.*

slide around to slip or skid around. □ *Many cars slide around on the roads when they are icy.* □ *The pedestrians were sliding around on the icy pavement.*

slide by to get along with a minimum of effort. □ *She didn't do a lot of work—she just slid by.* □ *Don't just slide by. Put in some effort.*

slide down from something to slip down on something from a higher place. □ *Beth slid down from the top of the mound.* □ *The boys slid down from the roof of the shed and got their pants all dirty.*

slide down something to slip down something, such as a pole. □ *The fire captain slid down the pole and ran to the engine.* □ *Please don't slide down the stairs. You'll ruin the carpet.*

slide into something to slip or glide into something, as a car going into a ditch. □ *It was raining hard, and car after* car slid into the ditch at the sharp turn near Wagner Road. □ Mary's car slid right into the side of a bus.

slide out of something to slip or glide out of something without much effort. □ Mary slid out of the car and ran to the front door. □ The CD-ROM slid out of the computer.

slide over something to slip or glide over something. □ The car almost slid over the edge of the cliff. □ We almost slid over the edge.

slide something **around** to push, twist, or turn something around. (The thing must be movable, but not often on wheels.) □ Please slide the carton around and look at the address on the other side. □ Can you slide the refrigerator around so I can clean the back of it?

slide something **into** something and **slide** something **in**[†] to insert something into something effortlessly. □ Henry slid the end of the seat-belt buckle into its holder and started the car. □ Slide in the buckle and make sure it's tight.

slide something **out of** something and **slide** something **out**[†] to cause something to slip or glide out of something without much effort. □ The hunter slid his knife out of its sheath and got ready to skin the deer. □ He slid out the heavy box.

slightly rattled 1. Inf. upset; confused. □ Tom was slightly rattled by the policeman at the door. □ I'm slightly rattled. I'll get over it. **2.** Inf. tipsy; intoxicated. □ He's only slightly rattled. He'll recover by morning. □ She can be really drunk and still seem only slightly rattled.

a **slim chance** a slight chance; a small chance. □ There is a slim chance that I will arrive on Monday, but Tuesday is more likely.

slim down to become thinner; to lose weight. □ You have really slimmed down a lot since I last saw you. □ I need to eat less so I can slim down. □ He slimmed down quite a bit after he had his health problem.

slim someone **down**[†] to cause someone to lose weight. □ They started to slim her down in the hospital, but she gained the weight back as soon as she got out. □ The dietitian slimmed down all the patients under his care.

sling something **at** someone or something to heave or toss something at someone or something. □ The child slung a handful of mud at his playmate. □ Who slung this muddy mess at the side of the house?

sling something **out**[†] **1.** to toss or heave something outward. □ The fishermen slung their nets out into the water. □ They slung out their nets. **2.** to throw something away. □ Just sling all that old junk out, if you will. □ Sling out that stuff into the trash!

sling the cat Sl. to empty one's stomach; to vomit. □ Suddenly Ralph left the room to sling the cat, I guess. □ That stuff will make you sling the cat.

slink around to creep or slither around furtively. □ The cat slunk around, waiting for a chance to get at the bird. □ Don't slink around like that. Someone is likely to take you for a robber.

slink away to creep or slither away furtively. □ The fox slunk away, leaving the henhouse as quietly as such a thing is possible. □ I hope that the skunk will slink away as quietly as it came.

slink in(to something) to creep into something. □ The cat slunk into the hallway and lay down in the middle of the floor. □ I left the door ajar and a cat slunk in.

slink off to creep away furtively. □ Carl was embarrassed and tried to slink off, but the ushers spotted him. □ The boys slunk off from the picnic and smoked some cigarettes.

slink out (of some place) to creep out of some place furtively. □ The fox slunk out of the henhouse just as the farmer came out. □ It slunk out and got away.

slip around to slide or skid around. □ The pedestrian slipped around and finally fell on the ice. □ The dog slipped around on the ice and finally made it to shore.

slip away 1. and **slip off** to go away or escape quietly or in secret; to slip out. □ I slipped away when no one was looking. □ Let's slip off somewhere and have a little talk. □ I'll try to slip out for an hour or two when Tom is asleep. **2.** Euph. to die. □ Uncle Charles slipped away in his sleep last night.

slip back (to someone or something) to move quietly and cautiously back to someone or something. □ Walter slipped back to Sally when her parents weren't looking. □ He slipped back and then Mary's parents slipped back, and there was quite a scene.

slip between the cracks Fig. [for someone or something] to be forgotten or neglected. (Fig. on something being lost by falling between floorboards.) □ Where is Alice? I guess we neglected her and she slipped between the cracks. □ This issue seems to have slipped between the cracks and become forgotten.

slip by 1. and **slip by** someone or something to move by someone or something quickly or unnoticed; to move through a tight area or past someone or something in a tight area. □ The hall was narrow, and I could hardly have slipped by. **2.** [for time] to pass quickly or unnoticed. □ Goodness, almost an hour has slipped by! How time flies. □ The entire workday slipped by before I knew it.

slip down to slide or glide downward. □ His socks kept slipping down. □ He lost so much weight that his pants almost slipped down.

slip from something to fall away from something; to lose one's step or grasp and fall from something. □ He slipped from the top step and fell down the other three. □ Ted slipped from the stool and fell on the floor.

slip in (some place) to sneak or go into a place quietly and unnoticed. □ I think we can slip in the rear door unnoticed. □ We slipped in and crept up the stairs.

slip in(to something) to slide or glide into something, such as clothing, a sleeping bag, a tight place, etc. □ I don't want to slip into a cold sleeping bag. How can I warm it up? □ I opened the bag and slipped in.

Slip me five! Go to Give me five!

a **slip of the tongue** an error in speaking in which a word is pronounced incorrectly, or in which the speaker says something unintentionally. □ I didn't mean to tell her that. It was a slip of the tongue. □ I failed to understand the instructions because the speaker made a slip of the tongue at an important point.

slip off Go to slip away.

slip off ((of) someone or something) to fall away from or off someone or something. (*Of* is usually retained before pronouns.) □ *The jacket slipped off of Sally, but she grabbed it before it hit the floor.* □ *She hung the jacket on the back of the chair, but it slipped off.*

slip off (to some place) to sneak away to some place. □ *Judy and Jeff slipped off to the movies unnoticed.* □ *They slipped off and no one saw them leave.*

slip on something to step on and slide on something. □ *Valerie slipped on a banana peel and hurt her back.* □ *Don't slip on that wet spot on the floor!*

slip one over on someone or something Go to **slip** something **over on** someone or something.

slip one's mind [for something that was to be remembered] to be forgotten. □ *I meant to go to the grocery store on the way home, but it slipped my mind.* □ *My birthday slipped my mind. I guess I wanted to forget it.*

slip one's trolley *Sl.* to become a little crazy; to lose one's composure. □ *I was afraid I would slip my trolley.* □ *He slipped his trolley and went totally bonkers.*

slip out 1. [for someone] to exit quietly without bothering anyone. □ *I slipped out during intermission.* **2.** [for information] to be spoken without realizing that it is secret or privileged. □ *The secret about her divorce slipped out when we were discussing old friends.*

slip out (of something) 1. to sneak out of a place unnoticed. □ *Gloria slipped out of the theater at intermission.* □ *She slipped out and went home.* **2.** to slide out of an article of clothing. □ *She slipped out of her dress and hung it neatly in the closet.* □ *Ted slipped out of his T-shirt and left it on the floor where it fell.*

slip past someone or something to sneak or move past someone or something unnoticed. □ *It is impossible to slip past the armed guards and metal detectors.* □ *Do you think I can slip past the doorway without being seen?*

slip someone **a Mickey** to secretly put a *Mickey Finn* in someone's alcoholic drink. (This drug either makes the victim ill or causes immediate diarrhea.) □ *Somebody slipped Barlowe a Mickey and sent him into action.* □ *For a ten-spot, the bartender slipped Slim a Mickey.*

slip someone **five** *Sl.* to shake someone's hand. □ *Billy slipped me five, and we sat down to discuss old times.* □ *Come on, man, slip me five!*

slip someone or something **past** someone or something to cause someone or something to move past someone or something unnoticed; to manage to get something past the scrutiny of someone. □ *I slipped another one of my friends past the usher into the theater.* □ *Do you think I can slip this sausage past the customs officers?* □ *I slipped a note past the guard.*

slip something **back**† **1.** to pull or place something back. □ *Alice slipped the gearshift lever back and away they went.* □ *She slipped back the gearshift and sped away.* **2.** to return something secretively. □ *Someone took my wallet away and slipped it back later.* □ *The thief slipped back my wallet, but the money was gone.*

slip something **down**† to slide something downward. □ *I slipped my pants down a little so the doctor could give me a shot in what they call your "hip."* □ *He slipped down his pants a little.*

slip something **in(to)** something and **slip** something **in**† to cause something to slide or glide into something. □ *Max slipped the bullets into their chambers and got ready to fire.* □ *He slipped the bullets in silently.*

slip something **off**† to let an item of clothing slide off one's body; to remove an item of clothing easily or casually. □ *He slipped his coat off and put it on a chair.* □ *She slipped off her shoes and relaxed.*

slip something **on**† to put on an article of clothing, possibly in haste or casually. □ *I will go in and slip my bathing suit on and join you in a minute.* □ *She slipped on her shoes and we left.*

slip something **over on** someone or something and **slip one over on** someone or something; **slip** something **over; slip one over** to deceive someone. □ *Are you trying to slip something over on me?* □ *I think he tried to slip one over on me.*

slip something **over** someone or something to cause something to slide or glide over and onto someone or something. □ *Mother slipped the covers over Timmy and kissed him good night.* □ *Jane slipped the cover over the birdcage for the night.*

slip something **through** (something) **1.** *Lit.* to cause something to slide or glide through something. □ *The nickel I dropped slipped through the crack in the floor.* □ *It rolled toward a crack in the floor and slipped through.* **2.** *Fig.* to get something approved without much fuss by a group of people, perhaps by deception. □ *I will try to slip this through the committee.* □ *I can slip it through for you.*

slip through someone's **fingers 1.** *Lit.* to slide through and out of one's grasp. □ *The glass slipped through his fingers and crashed to the ground.* □ *The rope slipped through his fingers and followed the anchor to the bottom of the lake.* **2.** *Fig.* to escape from someone; to elude someone's capture or control. □ *The prisoner slipped through the sheriff's fingers.* □ *Don't let Max slip through your fingers again this time!*

slip through something to slide or slither through something narrow or crowded. □ *Gerald slipped through the narrow opening and got away.* □ *The dog slipped through the door and ran out into the street.*

slip through the cracks Go to **through the cracks**.

slip up to make an error. □ *I hope you don't slip up again. Try to be more careful.*

slip up on someone, something, or an animal to sneak up on someone, something, or an animal quietly. (See also **slip up**.) □ *I slipped up on Harry and scared him to death.* □ *The cat slipped up on a mouse and grabbed it.*

slip up on something to make an error in something. □ *I guess I slipped up on that last job.* □ *Fred slipped up on compiling that list—there are a lot of names missing.*

slip up something to climb something, slipping along the way. □ *The hikers slipped up the wet slope.* □ *Ted slipped up the stairs, tracking mud and water as he went along.*

*slippery as an eel devious and untrustworthy, but impossible to catch. (*Also: **as ~**.) □ *Don't sign a lease with that landlord; I think he's as slippery as an eel.* □ *The con artist was slippery as an eel. Although he defrauded many people, he never went to prison.*

a **slippery customer 1.** *Fig.* a clever and deceitful customer. □ *Watch out for that guy with the big padded coat. He may snatch something. He's a real slippery customer.* **2.** *Fig.* a slippery creature. □ *This little fish is a slippery customer. Get me something to scoop it back into its bowl.*

a **slippery slope** a dangerous pathway or route to follow; a route that leads to trouble. □ *The matter of euthanasia is a slippery slope with both legal and moral considerations.*

slither along to slink or crawl along. □ *The snake slithered along, unmindful of our presence.* □ *A pair of otters slithered along playfully.*

slither away to sneak or crawl away, like a snake. □ *The little lizards slithered away soundlessly.* □ *The snake slithered away while Maggie was still screaming.*

slob up *Sl.* to eat. □ *What time do you people slob up around here?* □ *Fred stopped slobbing up long enough to change the channel on the TV set.*

slobber (all) over someone or something to drool on someone or something. (See also **slobber over** something.) □ *The dog slobbered over the child. It was just being friendly.* □ *Jenny has slobbered all over her dress.*

slobber over someone or something *Fig.* to drool with delight or eagerness at the thought of someone or something. (Based on **slobber over** something. See also **slobber (all) over** someone or something.) □ *Fred was slobbering over Donna as she lay sunbathing in a tiny bikini.* □ *Jamie was slobbering over Mary's new car.*

slobber over something to drool with delight or eagerness before or while eating something. (See also **slobber over** someone or something.) □ *The dog was slobbering over a chunk of meat when the cat came in and hissed at the dog.*

slog through something to wade or trudge through something, such as mud or snow. □ *Do I have to slog through the snow to go to school? Can't you drive me?* □ *When I was your age, I slogged through snow twice this deep to get to school.*

slop around 1. [for someone] to splash around in a body of liquid, such as a bath. □ *Timmy was in his bath, slopping around and singing.* □ *Bob is out in the pool, slopping around.* **2.** [for a liquid] to splash or rush around in a container. □ *The water was slopping around in the bottom of the boat even though the lake we were traveling on was calm.* □ *There is some coffee left. I hear it slopping around in the bottom of the pot.*

slop out (of something) [for a liquid] to spill or splash out of a container. □ *Some of the orange juice slopped out of the container, making a mess on the table.* □ *Some milk slopped out. Please clean it up.*

slop over [for a liquid] to splash out of or overflow a container. □ *The milk slopped over and messed up the carpet.* □ *Her cup slopped over and spilled its contents on the kitchen table.*

slop something **around**† to spill portions of a liquid here and there. □ *Don't slop the milk around as you pour it.* □ *Please don't slop around the paint while you work.*

slop something **on(to)** someone or something to spill or splash a liquid onto someone or something. □ *Don't slop the pancake batter onto yourself.* □ *Who slopped paint on the floor?*

slop something **over** something to spill or splash some liquid onto something. □ *He slopped the starting fluid over the charcoal and lit it.* □ *The artist slopped some grape juice over the canvas and proceeded to spread it around in an artistic fashion.*

slope away from something to slant downward and away from something. □ *The lawn sloped away from the patio toward the riverbank.* □ *The porch sloped away from the house at a very slight angle.*

slope down (to something or some place**)** to slant downward toward something or some place from a higher level. □ *The wide white beach sloped down to the azure water.* □ *The yard sloped down, making a lovely view from the living room.*

slope (down) toward something to slant downward toward something. □ *The backyard slopes down toward the river.* □ *It slopes toward the water.*

slope up (to something**)** to slant upward in the direction of something. □ *The ramp sloped up to the door, allowing wheelchairs to enter.* □ *It sloped up rather steeply.*

slosh around (in something**) 1.** [for a liquid] to rush or splash around in an enclosure or container. □ *The milk sloshed around in the pitcher and splashed over a little bit.* □ *The fluid sloshed around, making a splashing sound.* **2.** to move or splash through a liquid, usually standing on one's feet. □ *Billy sloshed around in the wading pool.* □ *The kids have been sloshing around in puddles again.*

slosh over [for a liquid] to splash over its container. □ *The water in the wading pool sloshed over and made the grass slippery.* □ *Don't fill the glass too full. It will slosh over.*

slosh something **(all) over** someone or something to spill or splash a liquid over someone or something. □ *Laura tripped and sloshed the grape juice all over Martha.* □ *Martin sloshed pancake batter over the side of the stove.*

slosh something **around**† to cause a liquid to rush or splash in a container. □ *The chef sloshed the dressing around a few times and poured it on the salad.* □ *The chef sloshed around the dressing and poured it on the salad.*

slosh something **on(to)** someone or something and **slosh** something **on**† to splash or spill a liquid onto someone or something. □ *Betty sloshed the charcoal lighter fluid on Fred, and he went in to wash it off.* □ *Then she sloshed the fluid onto the charcoal.* □ *Slosh on some more.*

slosh through something [for a person] to wade or splash through something. □ *The little kids sloshed through every puddle on their way home.* □ *We sloshed through the stream, ruining our shoes and soaking our cuffs.*

slouch around to move around with a stooped or bent body. (One may slouch because of age, illness, fatigue, depression, fear, or with the intention of not being observed.) □ *She is slouching around because she is tired.* □ *Don't you slouch around when you are tired?*

slouch behind something to remain behind something, slouching with depression, fear, or the intent of not being observed. □ *Jim slouched behind a chair where no one could see him.* □ *A weary clerk slouched behind the counter, wanting a nap more than anything else.*

slouch down to slump or droop down. □ *Don't always slouch down, Timmy! Stand up straight.* □ *I slouch down because I am tired.*

slouch down (in something) to sink or snuggle down into something, trying to become less visible or more comfortable. □ *Please don't slouch down in your chair, Tim.* □ *He can't sit in anything without slouching down.*

slouch over to lean or crumple and fall to one side; [for someone] to collapse in a sitting position. □ *He slouched over and went to sleep in his chair.* □ *When he slouched over, I thought something was wrong.*

slough something **off**† **1.** *Lit.* to brush or rub something off. □ *The snake sloughed its old skin off.* □ *It sloughed off its skin.* **2.** *Fig.* to ignore or disregard a negative remark or incident. □ *I could see that the remark had hurt her feelings, but she just pretended to slough it off.* □ *Liz sloughed off the remark.*

Slow and steady wins the race. *Prov.* If you work slowly but constantly, you will succeed better than if you work fast for a short while and do not continue. (Associated with Aesop's fable of "The Tortoise and the Hare.") □ *Joy only had a little bit of time to spend sewing every day, but she worked steadily and soon had finished a beautiful quilt. Slow and steady wins the race.*

***slow as molasses in January** and **slower than molasses in January** very slow-moving. (*Also: as ~.) □ *Can't you get dressed any faster? I declare, you're as slow as molasses in January.* □ *The traffic on the way to the concert was slower than molasses in January.*

slow but sure and **slowly but surely** slow but unstoppable. □ *Bob's progress on his novel was slow but sure.* □ *Nancy is finishing the paint job on her house, slowly but surely.*

slow down to decrease speed; to go slower. □ *Please slow down. You are going too fast.*

slow going the rate of speed when one is making slow progress. □ *It was slow going at first, but I was able to finish the project by the weekend.* □ *Getting the heavy rocks out of the field is slow going.*

slow off the mark 1. *Lit.* slow in starting or reacting. (Compare this with **quick off the mark**.) □ *If you are always that slow off the mark you will never win the race.* □ *Boy, you were slow off the mark there!* **2.** *Fig.* slow-witted. □ *The guy's slow off the mark but very friendly.* □ *Yes, I'm afraid Tony is a bit slow off the mark when it comes to trigonometry.*

slow on the draw 1. *Lit.* slow in drawing a gun. (Cowboy and gangster talk.) □ *Bill got shot because he's so slow on the draw.* □ *The gunslinger said, "I have to be fast. If I'm slow on the draw, I'm dead."* **2.** and **slow on the uptake** *Fig.* slow to figure something out; slow-thinking. □ *Sally didn't get the joke because she's sort of slow on the draw.* □ *Bill—who's slow on the uptake—didn't get the joke until it was explained to him.*

slow on the uptake Go to previous.

slow someone or something **up**† and **slow** someone or something **down**† to cause someone or something to reduce speed. □ *I'm in a hurry. Don't try to slow me down.* □ *Please slow up the train. There are sheep near the track.*

a **slow study** a person who is slow to learn things. (Compare this to a **slow study**.) □ *Fred, who is a slow study, never caught on to the joke.*

slow up to go slower; to reduce speed in order for someone or something to catch up. □ *Slow up a little! I can't keep up with you!* □ *Please slow up. I can't follow your lecture when you talk so fast.*

slower and slower at a decreasing rate of speed; slow and then even slower. □ *The car is going slower and slower and will stop soon.* □ *The dog's breathing got slower and slower as it went to sleep.*

slower than molasses in January Go to slow as molasses in January.

slowly but surely Go to slow but sure.

sluff (off) *Sl.* to waste time; to goof off. □ *Watch him. He will sluff off if you don't keep after him.* □ *He won't sluff. I know I can trust him.*

slug it out to fight something out; to argue intensely about something. □ *They finally went outside to slug it out.* □ *We'll just have to sit down in the conference room and slug it out.*

sluice something **down**† to rinse something down; to flood the surface of something with water or other liquid to clean it. □ *John sluiced the driveway down.* □ *Karen sluiced down the garage floor.*

sluice something **out**† to rinse something out; to flood the inside of something to clean it. □ *Sluice the wheelbarrow out, will you?* □ *Please sluice out the wheelbarrow.*

slump down [for someone] to collapse and fall down; [for someone] to crumple. □ *The shot hit Max and he slumped down.* □ *Suddenly, Mr. Wilson slumped down in pain.*

slump down in(to) something [for someone] to bend down or collapse into something, such as a chair or bed. □ *Gary grabbed at his chest and slumped down into the bed.* □ *He slumped down into the chair and draped himself over the arm.*

slump over [for someone] to collapse and fall over forward in a sitting position. □ *Just after the gunshot, Bruno slumped over and slid from his chair.*

slur over something **1.** *Lit.* to avoid saying difficult or crucial words by mumbling them; to speak over words unclearly. □ *The speaker slurred over so many words that we didn't know what she was saying.* □ *Unfortunately, Ted slurred over many of the important parts of his speech.* **2.** *Fig.* to avoid talking about or mentioning an issue. □ *The mayor slurred over the major issue of the day.* □ *She slurred over the major problems.*

slush up to become messy with slush. □ *As the winter storm increases in intensity, the roads will slush up and become impassable.* □ *After an hour of snow and rain, the roads were so slushed up that we could not travel.*

slut's wool Go to curly dirt.

***sly as a fox** and ***cunning as a fox** *Cliché* smart and clever. (*Also: as ~.) □ *My nephew is as sly as a fox.* □ *You have to be cunning as a fox to outwit me.*

smack (dab) in the middle exactly in the middle. □ *I came in smack dab in the middle of the play.* □ *I want a piece that is not too big and not too small—just smack in the middle.*

a **smack in the face** *Fig.* something that will humiliate someone, often when it is considered deserved; an insult. □ *Being rejected by Jane was a real smack in the face for*

S

617

Tom, who thought she was fond of him. □ *Meg thought she was the best-qualified candidate for the job, and not getting it was a smack in the face.*

smack of something to be reminiscent of something; to imply something. □ *The whole scheme smacked of dishonesty and deception.* □ *All of this story smacks of illegal practices.*

smack someone **down**† **1.** *Lit.* to knock a person down or cause a person to retreat with a slap or a blow. □ *He tried to touch her again and she smacked him down.* □ *She smacked down the rude fellow.* **2.** *Fig.* to rebuke someone. □ *She smacked him down by telling him that he didn't fit in there anymore.* □ *He has a way of smacking down people who ask stupid questions.*

smack something **down**† **(on(to)** something) to slap something down onto something. □ *He smacked his bet down onto the table, angry with his mounting losses.* □ *Todd smacked down his hand on the table.* □ *She smacked her dollar down and grabbed the newspaper.*

smack the road *Sl.* to leave; to **hit the road.** □ *Time to smack the road! Let's go!* □ *Let's smack the road. I have to get up early.*

small change *Fig.* an insignificant person. (Also a rude term of address.) □ *Look, small change, why don't you just move along?* □ *The guy you think is small change happens to own this building you seem to be guarding so well.*

a **small fortune** a rather sizeable amount of money. □ *This set of wheels cost me a small fortune.* □ *I've got a small fortune tied up in test equipment.*

small fry 1. *Lit.* newly hatched fish; small, juvenile fish. □ *The catch was bad today. Nothing but small fry.* **2.** *Fig.* unimportant people. □ *The police have only caught the small fry. The leader of the gang is still free.* □ *You people are just small fry! I want to talk to the boss.* **3.** *Fig.* children. □ *Peter's taking the small fry to the zoo.* □ *We should take the small fry to the pantomime.*

the **small hours (of the night)** and the **wee hours (of the night)** the hours immediately after midnight. □ *The dance went on into the small hours of the night.* □ *Jim goes to bed in the wee hours and gets up at lunchtime.*

small potatoes something or someone insignificant; small fry. □ *This contract is small potatoes, but it keeps us in business till we get into the real money.* □ *Small potatoes are better than no potatoes at all.*

small print and **fine print** an important part of a document that is not easily noticed because of the smallness of the printing. □ *You should have read the small print before signing the contract.* □ *You should always read the fine print of an insurance policy.*

Small things please small minds. Go to **Little things please little minds.**

smart ass someone who makes wisecracks and acts cocky. (Potentially offensive. Use only with discretion.) □ *Some smart ass came in here and asked for a sky hook.* □ *Don't be such a smart ass!*

smart at something to suffer the pains of something. □ *Over an hour later she was still smarting at his cruel remarks.* □ *For many days Ted smarted at the scolding he got.*

smart from something **1.** *Lit.* to get a stinging pain from something. □ *His arm smarted from many mosquito bites.* □ *Her legs smarted from the scratches she got from walking through the briars.* **2.** *Fig.* to suffer mental distress from something. □ *She smarted from wounded vanity.* □ *He smarted for hours from the rude rebuff.*

smart guy someone who acts cocky or rude. □ *All right, smart guy, see if you like this one.* □ *Some smart guy put chewing gum on this bench.*

smart money money belonging to smart or clever people. □ *Most of the smart money is going into utility stocks right now.* □ *Watch and see what the smart money is doing.*

smart mouth someone who makes wisecracks; a cocky person who speaks out of turn. □ *Don't be a smart mouth with me!* □ *Mr. Atkins is going to get a reputation as a smart mouth.*

smart under something to suffer stinging pain under something. □ *The sailor's back smarted under the blows of the lash.* □ *Ted smarted under the lash for his wrongdoings.*

smarten up to get smarter; to become more alert and knowing. □ *You had better smarten up if you want to survive around here.* □ *I knew he would smarten up sooner or later.*

a **smash hit** a play, movie, musical, etc., that is a big success. □ *Her first book was a smash hit. The second was a disaster.* □ *A smash hit doesn't always make people rich.*

smash into something to crash into something; to bump or crash into something. □ *Judy smashed into the coffee table and hurt her leg.* □ *The car smashed into the side of a bus and caused a lot of damage.*

smash out of something to break [one's way] out of something. □ *The prisoner smashed out of his cell and ran.* □ *The horse smashed out of its stable.*

smash someone's **face in**† **1.** *Fig.* to crush someone's face. □ *The accident smashed Harry's face in, and he had to have extensive surgery.* □ *The accident smashed in his face.* **2.** *Inf.* to strike someone in the face. □ *You had better stop that or I will smash your face in.* □ *Max tried to smash in Lefty's face.*

smash something **in**† to crush something inward; to make something collapse inward by striking it. □ *Andy gave one good kick and smashed the box in.* □ *Liz smashed in the window.*

smash something **up**† to break something up; to destroy something. □ *I hope the children don't smash any of the good china up if we use it tonight.* □ *The driver fell asleep and smashed up the car.*

smash through something to break [one's way] through some sort of barrier. □ *The fleeing car smashed through the police barrier.* □ *Max got angry and smashed through the office door.*

a **smear campaign (against** someone**)** a campaign aimed at damaging someone's reputation by making accusations and spreading rumors. □ *The politician's opponents are engaging in a smear campaign against him.* □ *Jack started a smear campaign against Tom so that Tom wouldn't get the manager's job.*

S

smear someone or something **with** something **1.** to spread or rub someone or something with some substance. □ Billy smeared Bobby with mud and made him very angry. □ You should smear that burn with lotion. □ He smeared himself with grease and ruined his shirt. **2.** to damage the reputation of someone or something by spreading serious charges or rumors. □ He smeared his opponent with all sorts of charges. □ The speaker smeared the entire city with his criticism.

smear something **on(to)** someone or something and **smear** something **on†** to spread or rub something onto someone or something. □ Judy asked Jeff to smear the sun lotion onto her, and he was very happy to do so. □ She smeared on the lotion. □ Jane smeared a little on.

smell a rat to suspect that something is wrong; to sense that someone has caused something wrong. □ I don't think this was an accident. I smell a rat. Bob had something to do with this. □ The minute I came in, I smelled a rat. Sure enough, I had been robbed.

smell blood Fig. to be ready for a fight; to be ready to attack; to be ready to act. (Like sharks, which are sent into a frenzy by the smell of blood.) □ Lefty was surrounded, and you could tell that the guys from the other gang smelled blood. □ The lawyer heard the crash and came running— smelling blood and bucks.

smell fishy to seem suspicious. □ Barlowe squinted a bit. Something smells fishy here, he thought. □ Something about the deal smelled fishy—too good to be true.

smell like a rose Fig. to seem innocent. □ I came out of the whole mess smelling like a rose, even though I caused all the trouble. □ The politician survived the scandal smelling like a rose, but I knew different.

smell of something to have the smell of something; to smell like something. □ This house smells of onions. □ Her cooking always smells of entirely too much garlic.

smell someone, something, or an animal **out** to locate someone, something, or an animal by smelling or as if by smelling. □ The dog smelled the crook out from the place in the alley where he was hiding. □ The dog smelled out the raccoon.

smell something **up†** to cause a bad or strong odor in a place or on something. □ Your cooking sure smelled this place up! □ The spoiled meat really smelled up the house!

smell to (high) heaven 1. Go to stink to high heaven. **2.** Fig. to give signals that cause suspicion. □ This deal is messed up. It smells to high heaven. □ Something's wrong here. Somebody blabbed. This setup smells to high heaven.

smile at someone to make a smiling face at someone. □ I love the way you smile at me. □ I am glad you smile at me occasionally.

smile on someone or something to be favorable to someone or something. □ Fate smiled on me and I got the job. □ Lady luck smiled on our venture and we made a profit.

smile (up)on someone or something to bestow approval on someone or something. (Upon is formal and less commonly used than on.) □ Fate has smiled upon me at last! □ I wish good luck would smile on me.

Smile when you say that. Inf. I will interpret that remark as a joke or as kidding. □ John: You're a real pain in the neck. Bob: Smile when you say that. □ Sue: I'm going to bop you on the head! John: Smile when you say that!

smiling like a Cheshire cat Fig. smiling very broadly. (Alludes to a grinning cat in Alice's Adventures in Wonderland.) □ There he stood, smiling like a Cheshire cat, waiting for his weekly pay.

smirk at someone or something to smile in a smug or sneering way at someone or something. □ Why are you smirking at me like that? □ Jane looked at the report and smirked at it.

smite someone **with** something to strike someone with something. (Literary or biblical.) □ The silver knight approached the black knight and smote him with his sword. □ Please go and smite the dragon with your sword.

smoke and mirrors deception and confusion. (Said of statements or more complicated rhetoric used to mislead people rather than inform. Alludes to the way a magician uses optical illusion to create believability while performing a trick. Fixed order.) □ Most people know that the politician was just using smoke and mirrors to make things look better than they really were. □ Her report was little more than smoke and mirrors. No one will believe any of it.

smoke like a chimney to smoke a great deal of tobacco or other smokable substances. □ My uncle smoked like a chimney when he was living. □ Somebody who smokes like a chimney in a restaurant ought to be thrown out.

smoke someone, something, or an animal **out of** something and **smoke** someone, something, or an animal **out† 1.** Lit. to force someone, something, or an animal out of something or a place, using smoke. □ The police used tear gas to smoke the kidnappers out of the house. □ They smoked out the crooks. **2.** Fig. to drive someone or something out into public view, as if using smoke or something similar. □ What will it take to smoke these crooks out of government? □ We will smoke out the corrupt officials yet.

smoke something **up†** to cause something or a place to become smoky. □ Get out of here with that cigarette! I don't want you smoking my house up! □ The burning beans sure smoked up the house.

smoke-filled room a room where a small group of people make important decisions. (Usually used in reference to political parties.) □ The smoke-filled rooms are still producing the candidates for most offices, despite all the political reforms. □ The deal was cut in a smoke-filled room.

the **smoking gun** Fig. the indisputable sign of guilt. (Fig. on a murderer being caught just after shooting the victim.) □ Mr. South was left holding the smoking gun. □ The chief of staff decided that the the aide should be found with the smoking gun.

*****smooth as glass** and *****smooth as silk** Cliché smooth and shiny. (Often used to describe calm bodies of water. *Also: **as ~**.) □ The bay is as smooth as glass, so we should have a pleasant boat trip. □ This custard is smooth as silk.

smooth as silk Go to previous.

smooth sailing Go to clear sailing.

smooth something **away†** to remove something, such as wrinkles or other unevenness, by pressing or smoothing. □ Jeff put the cloth on the table and smoothed the wrinkles away with his hand. □ Jeff smoothed away the wrinkles.

S

smooth something **back**† to flatten and position something by pressing or smoothing. ☐ *He smoothed his hair back out of his eyes.* ☐ *Jeff smoothed back his hair.*

smooth something **down**† to make something flat or smooth by pressing. ☐ *She smoothed her skirt down, fluffed her hair, and went into the boardroom.* ☐ *Karen smoothed down the bedclothes.*

smooth something **onto** someone or something and **smooth** something **on**† to spread or flatten something onto someone or something. ☐ *Ted smoothed the suntan lotion onto Alice, who lay on a towel in the sand.* ☐ *He smoothed on some lotion.*

smooth something **out**† **1.** *Lit.* to flatten or even something by smoothing or pressing. ☐ *Wally smoothed the bedspread out.* ☐ *Wally finished making the bed by smoothing out the spread.* **2.** *Fig.* to polish and refine something. ☐ *The editor smoothed John's style out.* ☐ *You need to smooth out your delivery when you are speaking.* **3.** and **smooth** something **over**† *Fig.* to reduce the intensity of an argument or a misunderstanding; to try to make people feel better about something disagreeable that has happened. (Fig. on ①.) ☐ *Mary and John had a terrible argument, and they are both trying to smooth it over.* ☐ *Let's get everyone together and try to smooth things out. We can't keep on arguing with one another.* ☐ *We can smooth over the whole affair.*

smother someone or something **with** something **1.** *Lit.* to suffocate someone or something with something. ☐ *The villain tried to smother his victim with a pillow.* ☐ *Fred tried to smother the cat with a plastic bag.* **2.** *Fig.* to cover someone or something with something. (An exaggeration.) ☐ *She smothered him with kisses.* ☐ *Aunt Margaret smothered us with the ruffles on the front of her dress when she hugged us.*

smuggle someone or something **across** something to move someone or something across a border illegally and in secret. ☐ *The terrorists smuggled one of their number across the border last night.* ☐ *Larry helped smuggle contraband across the border.*

smuggle someone or something **into** some place and **smuggle** someone or something **in**† to move someone or something across a border into a place illegally and in secret. ☐ *The secret agent smuggled his family into the country and then defected.* ☐ *He smuggled in his family.*

smuggle someone or something **out of** some place and **smuggle** someone or something **out**† to move someone or something across a border out of a place illegally and in secret. ☐ *Judy smuggled her cousin out of the country in a van.* ☐ *She smuggled out her cousin.*

smuggle someone or something **past** (someone or something) to move something past a guard or monitor illegally and in secret. ☐ *We failed in our attempt to smuggle Mary past the border.* ☐ *It is easy to smuggle wine past the border guards.*

smuggle someone or something **through** (something) to move something through a guard post or other barrier illegally and in secret. ☐ *The officers smuggled the child through the barrier so he could be with his mother.* ☐ *We smuggled some other goods through, too.*

snack off (of) something to eat food, bit by bit, in little snacks. (*Of* is usually retained before pronouns.) ☐ *Please*

don't snack off the turkey so we can get another meal out of it. ☐ *Who has been snacking off of last night's roast beef?*

snake along to move along in a curving line, looking like a snake; to move along in a line, moving as a snake moves. ☐ *The train snaked along, gaining speed as it went downhill.* ☐ *The line of people waiting to buy tickets snaked along slowly.*

snake in the grass a sneaky and despised person. ☐ *How could I ever have trusted that snake in the grass?* ☐ *John is such a snake in the grass.*

snakebite medicine *Inf.* inferior whiskey; strong whiskey; homemade whiskey. ☐ *That old-time snakebite medicine is good for what ails you.* ☐ *Snakebite medicine is a tremendous protection against snakebites if you can get the snake to drink the stuff before it bites you.*

snap at someone to speak sharply or angrily to someone. (Based on **snap at** someone or something.) ☐ *Don't snap at me. What did I do?* ☐ *Why did you snap at me? I did nothing wrong.*

snap at someone or something to bite at someone or something. (See also **snap at** someone; **snap at** something.) ☐ *The dog snapped at my pants leg, but I escaped the attack unharmed.* ☐ *The fox snapped at the chicken and finally caught hold of it.* ☐ *The dog snapped at the judge and was disqualified.*

snap at something *Fig.* to seize an opportunity. (See also **snap at** someone or something.) ☐ *It is such a good deal, I knew you would snap at it.* ☐ *Just as I thought, Ted snapped at my final offer.*

snap back (after something**)** to return to normal after an accident or similar event. ☐ *He is upset now, but he will snap back after things settle down.* ☐ *Things will snap back in no time at all.*

snap back (at someone**)** to give a sharp or angry response to someone. ☐ *The telephone operator, unlike in the good old days, snapped back at the caller.* ☐ *Please don't snap back. I've had a bad day.*

snap back (on someone or something**)** [for something] to be jerked back onto someone or something. ☐ *The branch snapped back on Tim and left a welt on his arm.* ☐ *The whip snapped back and stung Tex's hand.*

snap into something [for something] to be put or fit into an opening with an audible snap. ☐ *The larger edge of the card snaps into the slot at the base.* ☐ *This part snaps right into the other part.*

Snap it up! *Inf.* Hurry up! ☐ *John: Come on, Fred. Snap it up! Fred: I'm hurrying! I'm hurrying!* ☐ *Sally: Snap it up! You're going to make us late. John: That's exactly what I had in mind.*

snap one's cookies *Sl.* to vomit; to regurgitate. ☐ *I think I'm gonna snap my cookies.* ☐ *Some jerk snapped his cookies on the sidewalk.*

snap out of something *Fig.* to become suddenly freed from a condition. (The condition can be a depression, an illness, unconsciousness, etc.) ☐ *I was very depressed for a week, but this morning I snapped out of it.* ☐ *It isn't often that a cold gets me down. Usually I can snap out of it quickly.*

snap someone's **head off** *Fig.* to speak very sharply to someone. (Based on **snap at** someone.) ☐ *How rude! Don't* snap my head off! □ *Mary snapped Ted's head off because he had come in late.*

snap something **back**† to cause something to jerk back. □ *The force of the crash snapped his head back and injured his neck.* □ *The crash snapped back his head.*

snap something **into** something and **snap** something **in**† to put or press something into something with an audible snap. □ *Next, you snap this little part into this slot here.* □ *Snap in these legs then tighten the screws.*

snap something **off**† to break off something brittle. □ *Liz snapped a bit of the rock off and put it in her bag.* □ *Carl snapped off a piece of the candy and gave it to Timmy.*

snap something **on**† to attach something to something else, causing an audible snap. □ *Dawn took two pills from the bottle and snapped the lid on.* □ *She snapped on the lid.*

snap something **out of** something and **snap** something **out**† to remove something from something, causing an audible snap. □ *Jeff snapped the plastic plug out of the socket.* □ *He snapped out the plug.*

snap something **up**† **1.** *Lit.* to grasp something quickly. □ *Karen snapped her pencil up and strode out of the room.* □ *Harry walked through the kitchen and snapped up two cookies on the way.* **2.** *Fig.* to purchase something quickly, because the price is low or because the item is so hard to find. (Fig. on ①.) □ *We put the cheap shirts out for sale this morning and people snapped them up in only a few minutes.* □ *They snapped up the bargains quickly.* **3.** *Fig.* to believe something eagerly; to believe a lie readily. □ *They are so gullible that you can say anything and they'll snap it up.* □ *They will snap up anything that sounds good.*

snap to (attention) *Fig.* to move quickly to military attention. □ *The troops snapped to attention when they saw the general appear.* □ *Snap to when I tell you!*

Snap to it! *Inf.* Move faster!; Look alert! □ *Bill: Snap to it! Mary: Don't rush me!* □ *John: Get in line there. Snap to it! Sally: What is this, the army? You just wait till I'm ready!*

snarl at someone, something, or an animal to growl at someone, something, or an animal angrily and threateningly. □ *The dog snarled at everyone who passed by.* □ *Our dog used to sit in front of the washing machine and snarl at it.*

snarl someone or something **up**† to tangle someone or something; to mess something up. □ *The wind snarled my hair up terribly.* □ *The wind snarled up my hair.*

snarl something **out**† to utter something by snarling or growling. □ *Lefty snarled a naughty word out at the police.* □ *Walt the pickpocket snarled out a curse as the cop grabbed his coat collar.*

snatch at someone or something to grasp at someone or something. □ *The mugger snatched at Jane just as she sprayed Mace on him.* □ *He snatched at the Mace, but it was too late.*

snatch someone **from the jaws of death** Go to snatch someone **out of the jaws of death.**

snatch someone or something **(away) from** someone or something to grab and take someone or something from someone or something. □ *The mother snatched her child away from the doctor and fled.* □ *She snatched the candy from the child.*

snatch someone **out of the jaws of death** and **snatch** someone **from the jaws of death** *Fig.* to save someone from almost certain or imminent death. □ *The soldier snatched the tiny child from the jaws of death.*

snatch something **out of** something to grab something out of something. □ *The police officer snatched the gun out of Don's hand.* □ *Mary snatched the piece of chicken out of the fire as soon as it fell in.*

snatch something **up**† **1.** *Lit.* to grasp something and lift it up. □ *Tom snatched the last cookie up and popped it into his mouth.* □ *He snatched up the last piece of cake.* **2.** *Fig.* to collect or acquire as many of something as possible. □ *The shoppers snatched the sale merchandise up very quickly.* □ *The shoppers snatched up the sale merchandise very quickly.*

snatch victory from the jaws of defeat *Cliché* to win at the last moment. □ *At the last moment, the team snatched victory from the jaws of defeat with a last-second full-court basket.*

snazz something **up**† *Sl.* to make something classy or exciting. □ *Come on, let's try to snazz this up.* □ *What can I do to snazz up my face?*

sneak around (some place**)** to move about a place in a sneaky or stealthy fashion. □ *Please don't sneak around the house. It makes me nervous.* □ *Please stop sneaking around!*

sneak around someone or something **1.** *Lit.* to creep around or past someone or something. □ *The cat sneaked around Molly and ran out the door.* □ *We had to sneak around the corner so we wouldn't be seen.* **2.** *Fig.* to circumvent the control or censorship of someone or some group. □ *I think we can sneak around the board of directors and authorize this project ourselves.* □ *Yes, let's sneak around the board.*

sneak away (from some place**)** to go away from a place quietly and in secret. □ *Jeff tried to sneak away from the party, but Judy saw him.* □ *They sneaked away together.*

sneak in(to some place**)** to enter a place quietly and in secret, perhaps without a ticket or permission. □ *The kids tried to sneak into the rock concert, but they were stopped by the guards.* □ *Never try to sneak in. Sometimes they arrest you for trespassing.*

sneak out (of some place**)** to go out of a place quietly and in secret. □ *I sneaked out of the meeting, hoping no one would notice.* □ *Jamie saw me and sneaked out with me.*

sneak up on someone or something to approach someone or something quietly and in secret. □ *Please don't sneak up on me like that.* □ *I sneaked up on the cake, hoping no one would see me. Someone did.*

sneak up to someone or something to move close to someone or something quietly and in secret. □ *I sneaked up to Don and scared him to death.* □ *Don sneaked up to the punch bowl and helped himself before the party began.*

sneer at someone or something to make a haughty or deprecating face at someone or something; to show one's contempt for someone or something. □ *I asked her politely to give me some more room, and she just sneered at me.* □ *Jamie sneered at the report that Ken had submitted.*

sneeze at someone to sneeze in someone's direction. □ *Please don't sneeze at me! Cover your nose and mouth!* □ *You should never sneeze at anyone. It is very bad manners.*

S

sneeze at something *Fig.* to indicate one's disapproval of something; to belittle someone or something. □ *I wouldn't sneeze at that amount of money if I were you. It's better than nothing.* □ *I though it was a good offer, but the customer just sneezed at it.*

sneeze into something to aim a sneeze into something. □ *You should always sneeze into a handkerchief.* □ *Please sneeze into a tissue or something.*

sneeze on someone or something to aim a sneeze onto someone or something, probably by accident. □ *Don't sneeze on me!* □ *Don't sneeze on anything. Cover your nose and mouth!*

sniff at someone or something **1.** *Lit.* to try to get the smell of someone or something by smelling. □ *The dog sniffed at the visitor.* □ *The cat sniffed at almost every inch of the rug that the dog had walked on.* **2.** *Fig.* to show one's disapproval of someone or something by sniffing. (Sometimes this is figurative, the "sniffing" being expressed by tone of voice or gesture.) □ *I made one suggestion, but Claire just sniffed at me.* □ *Gale just sniffed at the idea and would say nothing.*

sniff someone or something **out**[†] to locate someone or something by sniffing or as if by sniffing. □ *The dog sniffed the intruder out and the police captured him.* □ *The dog sniffed out the mole in the lawn.*

snip something **off**[†] Go to snip something off (of) something.

snip something **off (of)** something and **snip** something **off**[†] to cut something off something. (*Of* is usually retained before pronouns.) □ *She snipped a dead blossom off the rosebush.* □ *Jane snipped off a bud.*

snipe at someone or something **1.** *Lit.* to fire a weapon at someone or something from a concealed position. □ *Someone with a rifle sniped at the troops as they went through the jungle.* □ *A rifleman was busy sniping at the platoon.* **2.** *Fig.* to make petty complaints attacking someone or something. □ *Stop sniping at me and everything I do.* □ *Ken is always sniping at my reports.*

snitch on someone to tattle on someone. □ *You wouldn't snitch on me, would you?* □ *Timmy snitched on his older brother.*

snoop around (something**)** to look around in a place, trying to find out something secret or about someone else's affairs. □ *Why are you snooping around my house?* □ *I am not snooping around.*

snoop into something to pry into something or someone else's affairs. □ *I wish you would stop snooping into my business!* □ *Whose affairs are they snooping into now?*

snort at someone or something to show one's displeasure with someone or something by snorting. □ *The customer snorted at the waiter for his surliness.* □ *The customer snorted at the prices and walked out.*

snotnose(d) (kid) *Inf.* a young child; a relatively young person. (Derogatory. Potentially offensive. Use only with discretion.) □ *Some little snotnose swiped my wallet.* □ *A little snotnosed kid came in and asked for money.*

snow bunny 1. someone learning to ski. □ *This little slope is for snow bunnies.* □ *Most of the snow bunnies come here to socialize.* **2.** a young, attractive female at a skiing lodge. □ *Some cute little snow bunny came over and sat beside me.*

□ *This place is swarming with snow bunnies who have never even seen a ski.*

a **snow job** a systematic deception; a deceptive story that tries to hide the truth. □ *You can generally tell when a student is trying to do a snow job.* □ *This snow job you call an explanation just won't do.*

snow someone or something **in**[†] [for heavy snowfall] to block someone or something in a place. □ *The sudden storm snowed us in.* □ *The storm snowed in most of the people in town.*

snow someone or something **under with** something and **snow** someone or something **under**[†] to burden someone or something with something. (Usually too much work.) □ *The busy season snowed us all under with too much work.* □ *The heavy workload snowed under the office staff.*

snowball into something *Fig.* [for something] to become larger or more serious by growing like a snowball being rolled. □ *This whole problem is snowballing into a crisis very rapidly.* □ *The argument soon snowballed into a full-blown riot.*

snowed in trapped (somewhere) because of too much snow. □ *The snow was so deep that we were snowed in for three days.* □ *Being snowed in is no problem if you have enough food.*

snowed under overworked; exceptionally busy. □ *Look, I'm really snowed under at the moment. Can this wait?* □ *He really has been snowed under with work.*

snuff someone **out**[†] *Sl.* to kill someone. □ *Max really wanted to snuff the eyewitness out, once and for all.* □ *Lefty wanted to snuff out his partner.*

snuff something **out**[†] to extinguish something, such as a flame. □ *She snuffed all the candles out and went to bed.* □ *Karen snuffed out the flames one by one.*

***snug as a bug in a rug** *Cliché* wrapped up tight, warm, and comfortable. (Playful; often used when addressing a child. *Also: as ~.) □ *The bedroom in Aunt Jane's house was cold, but after she wrapped me up in four or five quilts and put a stocking cap on my head, I was snug as a bug in a rug and ready to go to sleep.* □ *Alan: Are you warm enough? Jane: Yes, I'm as snug as a bug in a rug.*

snug down (some place**)** to become comfortable and warm in a place. □ *The cat snugged down at the foot of the bed.* □ *Finally the children snugged down and we could go to sleep.*

snuggle down (into something**)** to nestle into something, such as a warm bed. □ *Toby snuggled down into his nice warm bed.* □ *He got into bed and snuggled down.*

snuggle down (with someone**)** to nestle [into something] with someone else. □ *Billy snuggled down with his sister in the big feather bed.* □ *They snuggled down and went to sleep.*

snuggle down (with something**)** to nestle [into something] with something, such as a blanket, doll, book, etc. □ *The baby snuggled down with her blanket and was asleep in no time.* □ *Sally grabbed onto her favorite doll and snuggled down for the night.*

snuggle (up) against someone or something to press or cuddle against someone or something, as if to keep warm. □ *Tiffany snuggled up against Tad and asked him to give*

S

her some chewing gum. □ *He snuggled against the warm wall on the other side of the fireplace.*

snuggle up (to someone or something**)** to cuddle up close to someone or something. □ *Kelly snuggled up to Jeff.* □ *She snuggled up and said she wanted him to go pick up a pizza.*

*so bad one **can taste it** *Fig.* very much, indeed. (*Typically: **need** ~; **want** ~; **have to** do something ~.) □ *I want that car so bad I can taste it.* □ *He had to get to Philadelphia so bad he could taste it.*

So be it. This is the way it will be. □ *If you insist on running off and marrying her, so be it. Only don't say I didn't warn you!* □ *Mary has decided that this is what she wants. So be it.*

so clean you could eat off the floor [of a room or a house] very clean. □ *Her kitchen is so clean you could eat off the floor!* □ *It's so clean here you could eat off the floor. I prefer a little mess, myself.*

so cold you could hang meat *Fig.* very cold; as cold as a meat storage locker. □ *Lord it was cold there! So cold you could hang meat.* □ *A: How cold was it? B: So cold you could hang meat.*

So do I. I do too. □ *Mary: I want some more cake. Sally: So do I.* □ *Bob: I have to go home now. Tom: So do I. Bob: Bye.*

so far as anyone **knows** Go to as far as anyone knows.

so far as possible Go to as far as possible.

so far as someone **is concerned** Go to as far as someone is concerned.

so far as something **is concerned** Go to as far as something is concerned.

So far, so good. All is going well so far. □ *We are half finished with our project. So far, so good.* □ *The operation is proceeding quite nicely—so far, so good.*

So gross! *Sl.* How disgusting! □ *He put chocolate syrup on his pie! So gross!* □ *He's barfing! So gross!*

So help me(, God)! I so pledge and vow in God's name. □ *I will do it. I really will, so help me, God!*

So it goes. *Inf.* That is the kind of thing that happens.; That is life. □ *Too bad about John and his problems. So it goes.* □ *I just lost a twenty-dollar bill, and I can't find it anywhere. So it goes.*

So long. Good-bye. □ *So long, see ya later.* □ *It's been good talking to you. So long.*

so long as Go to as long as.

so mad I could scream very mad. □ *I am just so mad I could scream! Why is he such a jerk?* □ *She makes me so mad I could scream.*

So many countries, so many customs. *Prov.* People in different countries have different ways of behaving. □ *In the last place I visited, it was considered rude to put your hands on the table at dinner, but here, it's rude to keep them under the table. So many countries, so many customs.*

so much for someone or something that is the last of someone or something; there is no need to consider someone or something anymore. □ *It just started raining. So much for our picnic this afternoon.* □ *So much for John. He just called in sick and can't come to work today.*

So much for that. That is the end of that.; We will not be dealing with that anymore. □ *John tossed the stub of a pencil into the trash. "So much for that," he muttered, fishing through his drawer for another.* □ *Mother: Here, try some carrots. Child (brushing the spoon aside): No! No! Mother: Well, so much for that.*

so much the better even better; all to the better. □ *Please come to the picnic. If you can bring a salad, so much the better.* □ *The flowers look lovely on the shelf. It would be so much the better if you put them on the table.*

so quiet you could hear a pin drop Go to so still you could hear a pin drop.

So's your old man! *Inf.* The same to you!; Drop dead! (Old. A catch phrase indicating basic disagreement or hostility.) □ *Bill: You're acting like an idiot! Tom: So's your old man!* □ *I don't know what you said, but so's your old man!*

so soon early; before the regular time; ahead of schedule. □ *I got there early because my bus arrived so soon.* □ *Because the meeting ended so soon, I had some extra time.*

so still you could hear a pin drop and **so quiet you could hear a pin drop** *Fig.* very quiet. (Also with *can*.) □ *When I came into the room, it was so still you could hear a pin drop. Then everyone shouted, "Happy birthday!"* □ *Please be quiet. Be so quiet you can hear a pin drop.*

So, sue me. If you are so angry, why don't go ahead and sue me. (A rude way of brushing off an angry person.) □ *A: You ran into my car! You didn't even look where you were going! B: So, sue me.*

so to speak as one might say; said a certain way, even though the words are not exactly accurate. □ *John helps me with my taxes. He's my accountant, so to speak.* □ *I just love my little poodle. She's my baby, so to speak.*

So (what)? *Inf.* Why does that matter? (Can be considered rude.) □ *Bob: Your attitude always seems to lack sincerity. Mary: So what?* □ *John: Your car sure is dusty. Sue: So?*

(So) what else is new? *Inf.* This isn't new. It has happened before; Not this again. □ *Mary: Taxes are going up again. Bob: So what else is new?* □ *John: Gee, my pants are getting tight. Maybe I'm putting on a little weight. Sally: What else is new?*

soak in(to something**)** [for moisture] to penetrate something. □ *The rain soaked into the parched ground as fast as it fell.* □ *I'm glad it soaked in. I was afraid it would run off.*

soak one's **face** *Sl.* to drink heavily. □ *They're down at the tavern soaking their faces.* □ *Well, I guess I'll go soak my face in a few beers.*

soak someone or something **with** something to get someone or something thoroughly wet with some liquid. □ *The rain soaked us all with icy cold drops of water.* □ *The storm soaked the land with much-needed moisture.*

soak someone **to the skin** [for water, rain, or other liquid] to work its way through someone's clothing to the skin. □ *The storm soaked us all to the skin.* □ *She soaked herself to the skin in the storm.*

soak something **in** something to leave something immersed in a liquid, intending for it to be absorbed. □ *Soak your feet in Epsom salts to make them feel better.* □ *I had to soak my elbow in ice water to take down the swelling.*

S

soak something **off (of)** something and **soak** something **off**[†] to remove something, such as a label or surface soil, from something by soaking in a liquid. (*Of* is usually retained before pronouns.) □ *She soaked the labels off the bottles and jars.* □ *Please soak off the label.*

soak something **out of** something and **soak** something **out**[†] to remove something, such as a stain, from something by soaking in a liquid. □ *Dan soaked the stain out of his shirt and then washed it.* □ *Dan soaked out the stain.*

soak something **up**[†] **1.** *Lit.* to gather up moisture or a liquid, using an absorbent cloth, paper, etc. □ *Alice soaked the spill up with a sponge.* □ *She soaked up the spilled milk.* **2.** *Lit.* [for cloth, paper, or other absorbent material] to absorb moisture or a liquid. □ *Please get some paper towels to soak the spill up.* □ *The sponge soaked up the orange juice.* **3.** *Fig.* to learn or absorb some information; to learn much information. □ *I can't soak information up as fast as I used to be able to.* □ *The tourists will soak up anything you tell them.*

soak through something [for liquid] to work its way through something, such as cloth or paper. □ *Please wipe up that mess before it soaks through the tablecloth.* □ *It's too late. The grape juice has soaked through the carpet into the mat.*

soaked to the skin wet clear through one's clothing to the skin. □ *I was caught in the rain and got soaked to the skin.* □ *Oh, come in and dry off! You must be soaked to the skin.*

so-and-so a despised person. (This expression is used in place of other very insulting terms. Often modified, as in the examples.) □ *You dirty so-and-so! I can't stand you!* □ *Don't you call me a so-and-so, you creep!*

soap someone or something **down**[†] to cover someone or something thoroughly with soap or suds. □ *Mother soaped Timmy down and rinsed him off in warm water.* □ *She soaped down the floor.*

sob one's **heart out** Go to cry one's **heart out**.

sob oneself **to sleep** to cry until one falls asleep. □ *He sobbed himself to sleep for days after his grandpa died.* □ *The child sobbed himself to sleep night after night.*

sob something **out**[†] to speak something out while sobbing. □ *Wally sobbed his story out while the police made notes.* □ *He sobbed out his sad tale.*

sob something **to** someone to cry and tell one's troubles to someone. □ *He is always sobbing his sad tale to anyone who will listen.* □ *Timmy sobbed his story to the teacher.*

sob story *Fig.* a sad story that is likely to draw tears. □ *I've heard nothing but sob stories today. Isn't anybody happy?* □ *She had quite a sob story, and I listened to the whole thing.*

***sober as a judge 1.** Cliché* very formal, somber, or stuffy. (*Also: **as** ~.*) □ *You certainly look gloomy, Bill. You're sober as a judge.* □ *Tom's as sober as a judge. I think he's angry.* **2.** *Cliché* not drunk; alert and completely sober. (*Also: **as** ~.*) □ *John's drunk? No, he's as sober as a judge.* □ *You should be sober as a judge when you drive a car.*

sober someone **up**[†] **1.** *Lit.* to take actions that will cause a drunken person to become sober. □ *Some coffee ought to sober him up.* □ *He tried to sober himself up because he had to drive home.* □ *They tried to sober up the guys who had been out all night.* **2.** *Fig.* to cause someone to face reality.

□ *The harsh reality of what had happened sobered him up immediately.* □ *The arrival of the police sobered up all the revelers.*

sober up to recover from alcohol or drug intoxication. □ *Barlowe had one hour to sober up and get to the station.* □ *It took him a while to sober up.*

sock it to someone **1.** to punch someone; to punch one's fist at someone. □ *Max really socked it to Lefty!* □ *Lefty socked it to Roger and knocked him down.* **2.** to tell bad news to someone in a straightforward manner. □ *I can take it. Sock it to me!* □ *I don't care how bad it seems. Sock it to me!*

sock someone or something **in**[†] [for fog] to cause someone or something to remain in place. □ *The heavy fog socked us in for six hours.* □ *The fog socked in the airport for an hour.*

sock something **away**[†] to place something, such as money, into reserve; to store something in a secure place. □ *I try to sock a little money away each month for my vacation.* □ *I will sock away some money.*

socked in fogged in. □ *The airport was completely socked in.* □ *We couldn't take off because we were socked in.*

A **soft answer turneth away wrath.** *Prov.* If you speak softly and meekly to someone who is angry with you, that person will calm down. (Biblical.) □ *It won't do any good for you to yell at John because he yelled at you. Remember that a soft answer turneth away wrath.*

soft as a baby's backside Go to next.

***soft as a baby's bottom** and **soft as a baby's backside**; ***soft as down**; ***soft as silk**; ***soft as velvet** *Cliché* very soft and smooth to the touch. (*Also: **as** ~.*) □ *This cloth is as soft as a baby's bottom.* □ *The kitten's fur was as soft as down.* □ *Your touch is soft as silk.* □ *This lotion will make your skin soft as velvet.*

soft as down Go to previous.

soft as silk Go to soft as a baby's bottom.

soft as velvet Go to soft as a baby's bottom.

soft in the head *Fig.* stupid; witless. □ *George is just soft in the head. He'll never get away with his little plan.* □ *You're soft in the head if you think I'll go along with that.*

soft money and **easy money** money obtained without much effort. □ *Don't become dependent on soft money.* □ *In college he got spoiled by soft money—a check from his parents every week.*

***soft on** someone **1.** *Fig.* romantically attracted to someone. (*Typically: **be** ~; **get** ~.*) □ *Fred is soft on Martha, I've heard.* □ *He looked like he was getting a little soft on Sally.* **2.** *Fig.* not severe enough on someone; too easy on someone or a class of people. (*Typically: **be** ~; **get** ~; **grow** ~.*) □ *The judge was viewed as being too soft on drug pushers.* □ *The cops are soft on speeders in this town.*

soft sell a polite attempt to sell something; a very gentle sales pitch. □ *Some people won't bother listening to a soft sell. You gotta let them know you believe in what you are selling.* □ *I tried the soft sell, but that didn't work.*

soft soap 1. flattering talk; sweet talk. □ *I don't mind a little soft soap. It won't affect what I decide, though.* □ *Don't waste my time with soft soap. I know you don't mean it.* **2.** (Usually **soft-soap.**) to attempt to convince someone (of something) by gentle persuasion. □ *We couldn't soft-soap her into it.* □ *Don't try to soft-soap her. She's an old battle-ax.*

soft touch 1. a gentle way of handling someone or something. □ *Bess has a soft touch and can bring both sides together.* □ *Kelly lacks the kind of soft touch needed for this kind of negotiation.* **2.** a gullible person; a likely victim of a scheme. □ *John is a soft touch. You can always ask him for a few bucks.* □ *Here comes the perfect soft touch—a nerd with a gleam in his eye.*

soften one's **stance (on** someone or something**)** *Fig.* to reduce the severity of one's position regarding someone or something. □ *If he would soften his stance on the matter, I could easily become more cooperative.*

soften someone **up**[†] *Fig.* to prepare to persuade someone of something. □ *I will talk to Fred and soften him up for your request.* □ *I will soften up your father before you ask him about it.*

soften something **up**[†] to take actions that will make something softer. □ *Soften the butter up before you add it to the batter.* □ *Please soften up the ice cream before you try to serve it.*

soften up 1. *Lit.* [for something] to become softer. □ *The butter softened up in the heat of the day.* □ *The candles will probably soften up and bend over in this hot weather.* **2.** *Fig.* [for someone] to adopt a more gentle manner. □ *After a while, she softened up and was more friendly.* □ *It was weeks before Ted softened up and treated us more kindly.*

soft-pedal something to play something down; to de-emphasize something. (Alludes to the soft pedal on the piano, which reduces the volume.) □ *Try to soft-pedal the problems we have with the cooling system.* □ *I won't soft-pedal anything. Everyone must know the truth.*

soil one's **diaper(s)** [for a baby] to excrete waste into its diaper. □ *The baby soiled his diapers.* □ *I detect that someone has soiled his diaper.*

soil one's **hands** Go to get one's hands dirty.

sold on someone or something convinced of the value of someone or something. □ *I'm not yet sold on your idea.* □ *The crowd was sold on Gary. Nothing he had done or could do would cool their enthusiasm.*

sold out [of a product] completely sold with no more items remaining; [of a store] having no more of a particular product. □ *The tickets were sold out so we couldn't go to the concert.* □ *I wanted new shoes like yours, but they were sold out.*

solicit for someone or something to seek money or other contributions for someone or something, such as a charitable cause. □ *I am soliciting for crippled children. Would you care to contribute?* □ *Are you soliciting for a local cause?*

solicit someone **for** something to attempt to persuade someone to give something, such as money, for a specific purpose. □ *The school band solicited the owners of the business for a contribution.* □ *Fred solicited everyone in his department for at least a dollar.*

*solid as a rock *Cliché* very solid; dependable. (*Also: as ~.)* □ *Jean has been lifting weights every day, and her arm muscles are solid as a rock.* □ *This company has always built power tools that are as solid as a rock.*

*a (solid) grasp of something and ***a (sound) grasp of** something; ***a (good) grasp of** something *Fig.* a firm understanding of something. (*Typically: **get ~; have ~; give** someone ~.)* □ *Try to get a grasp of the basic rules.* □ *You don't have a good grasp of the principles yet.* □ *John was unable to get a solid grasp of the methods used in his work, and we had to let him go.*

some creature's time has come Go to someone's time has come.

*some elbow room *Fig.* room to move about in; extra space to move about in. (*Typically: **allow ~; get ~; have ~; give** someone ~; **need ~.)* □ *This table is too crowded. We all need some elbow room.*

*some loose ends *Fig.* some things that are not yet finished; some problems not yet solved. (*Typically: **are ~; have ~; leave ~; tie ~ up**[†]; **take care of ~.)* □ *I have to stay in town this weekend and tie up some loose ends.*

(some) new blood and **fresh blood** *Fig.* new personnel; new members brought into a group to revive it. □ *This company needs some new blood on its board to bring in new ideas.* □ *We're trying to get some new blood in the club. Our membership is falling.*

Some people (just) don't know when to quit. and **Some people (just) don't know when to give up.; Some people (just) don't know when to stop. 1.** You, or someone being talked about, should stop doing something, such as talking, arguing, scolding, etc. (Often directed toward the person being addressed.) □ *Bill: I hate to say it again, but that lipstick is all wrong for you. It brings out the wrong color in your eyes, and it makes your mouth larger than it really is. Jane: Oh, stop, stop! That's enough! Some people just don't know when to quit.* □ *John: Those bushes out in the backyard need trimming. Sally: You keep criticizing! Is there no end to it? Some people don't know when to stop!* **2.** Some people do not know when to slow down and stop working so hard. □ *Jane: He just kept on gambling. Finally, he had no money left. Sally: Some people don't know when to quit.*

some pumpkins and **some punkins** someone or something great or special. (Old.) □ *That chick is some punkins!* □ *Isn't this little gadget really some pumpkins?*

*some shut-eye some sleep. (*Typically: **get ~; have ~; use ~; need ~.)* □ *I need to get home and get some shut-eye before I do anything else.* □ *We all could use some shut-eye.*

Someone had better keep still about it. Go to Better keep still about it.

someone of note a person who is famous. □ *We invited a speaker of note to lecture at the next meeting.* □ *The baseball player of note was inducted into the Hall of Fame.*

the someone or something from hell *Fig.* someone or something that is terrible or unbearable. □ *I just attended the meeting from hell! It was quite a strain on all of us.* □ *We live next to the neighbors from hell. They are constantly fighting and their vicious dog terrorizes our kids.*

Someone or something is supposed to. Go to Supposed to.

someone's ace in the hole Go to ace in the hole.

someone's bread and butter *Fig.* someone's basic income; someone's livelihood—the source of one's food. □ *I can't* miss another day of work. That's my bread and butter. □ I worked as a bartender for a year, and it was the tips that were my bread and butter.

someone's claim to fame someone's reason for being well-known or famous. □ *Her claim to fame is that she can recite the entire works of Shakespeare.*

someone's dirty laundry *Fig.* someone's unpleasant secrets. □ *I don't want to hear about her dirty laundry. Why do you feel it necessary to gossip about things like this?*

someone's fate is sealed *Fig.* the destiny of somene has been determined. □ *When the driver finally saw that the bridge was out, he knew his fate was sealed.*

someone's hands are tied *Fig.* someone is not able to help or intervene. (See also have one's hands tied.) □ *I'm sorry. There's nothing I can do. My hands are tied.*

someone's level best one's very best effort. □ *I will do my level best to find your husband.* □ *Don't go to a whole lot of trouble. Your level best is good enough.*

(Someone's) not supposed to. Go to (It's) not supposed to.

someone's point is well taken someone's idea or opinion is accepted and appreciated. □ *Your point is well taken and I will see that it is not forgotten.*

someone's time has come and **some creature's time has come** *Euph.* someone or some creature is about to die. □ *The poor old dog's time has come.* □ *My time has come. I'm ready to go.*

someone's train of thought *Fig.* someone's pattern of thinking or sequence of ideas; what one was just thinking about. (See also lose one's train of thought.) □ *My train of thought is probably not as clear as it should be.* □ *I cannot seem to follow your train of thought on this matter. Will you explain it a little more carefully, please?*

someone's true colors *Fig.* a person's true attitude, opinions, and biases. □ *When he lost his temper at his wife, I began to see his true colors.*

(someone's) ups and downs a person's good fortune and bad fortune. □ *I've had my ups and downs, but in general life has been good to me.* □ *All people have their ups and downs.*

someone's word is good someone can be believed and trusted. □ *You can believe her. Her word is good.*

someone's word of honor someone's trustworthy pledge or promise. □ *He gave me his word of honor that he would bring the car back by noon today.*

Someone will be with you in a minute. Go to With you in a minute.

something about someone or something something alluring or curious about someone or something. □ *There is something about Jane. I just can't figure her out.* □ *I love Mexican food. There's just something about it.*

something else (again) something entirely different. □ *Borrowing is one thing, but stealing is something else.* □ *Skindiving is easy and fun, but scuba diving is something else again.*

Something is better than nothing. *Prov.* It is better to get only some of what you want than to get nothing at all. (See also (It's) better than nothing.) □ *Fred: I only got*

$50 for all those books I sold. Jane: Something is better than nothing. □ Jill: Is your camera very good? Jane: It's better than nothing.

something is killing someone *Fig.* something is causing someone pain. □ *Wow, my feet are killing me!*

Something is rotten in (the state of) Denmark. *Prov.* Something suspicious is going on. (From Shakespeare's play *Hamlet.*) □ *Jim: Look, there's a light on in the office, even though it's way past the time everyone should have left. John: Something is rotten in the state of Denmark.* □ *Jane: I wonder why Fred is coming in so late every morning. Jane: Something is rotten in Denmark.*

something never fails a particular thing always works. □ *My old folk remedy for hiccups never fails.*

something of sorts an inferior example of a kind of something. □ *Well, it's a solution of sorts, I suppose.* □ *It was a novel of sorts, but not what I'd ever have chosen.*

something of the sort something of the kind just mentioned. □ *The tree isn't exactly a spruce tree, just something of the sort.* □ *Jane has a cold or something of the sort.*

something or other something unspecified; one thing or another. □ *I can't remember what Ann said—something or other.* □ *A messenger came by and dropped off something or other at the front desk.*

Something's got to give. Emotions or tempers are strained, and there is going to be an outburst. □ *Alice: There are serious problems with Mary and Tom. They fight and fight. Sue: Yes, something's got to give. It can't go on like this.* □ *Bill: Things are getting difficult at the office. Something's got to give. Mary: Just stay clear of all the bickering.*

something's up something is going to happen; something is going on. □ *Everybody looks very nervous. I think something's up.* □ *From the looks of all the activity around here, I think something's up.*

***something to shout about** *Fig.* something that causes one to show pride or enthusiasm about someone or something. (*Typically: be ~; have ~.) □ *Getting into med school is really something to shout about.* □ *She's something to shout about.*

something to that effect something like that just mentioned. □ *She said she wouldn't be available until after three, or something to that effect.* □ *I was told to keep out of the house—or something to that effect.*

(somewhere) in the neighborhood of something *Fig.* approximately a particular amount or measurement. □ *I take somewhere in the neighborhood of ten pills a day for my various ailments.* □ *My rent is in the neighborhood of $700 per month.*

somewhere to hang (up) one's **hat** *Fig.* a place to live; a place to call one's home. □ *What I need is somewhere to hang up my hat. I just can't stand all this traveling.* □ *A home is a lot more than a place to hang your hat.*

son of a bachelor Go to son of a gun.

son of a bitch 1. *Inf.* a very horrible person. (Use with caution. Usually intended as a strong insult. Never used casually.) □ *Bill called Bob a son of a bitch, and Bob punched Bill in the face.* □ *This guy's a son of a bitch. He treats everybody rotten.* **2.** *Inf.* a useless thing. □ *This car is a son of a bitch. It won't ever start when it's cold.* □ *This*

S

bumpy old road needs paving. It's a real son of a bitch. **3.** *Inf.* a difficult task. □ *This job is a son of a bitch.* □ *I can't do this kind of thing. It's too hard—a real son of a bitch.*

son of a gun and **son of a bachelor** a worthless person. (A substitute for **son of a bitch**.) □ *That tightfisted son of a gun won't buy me a beer.* □ *He can be a real son of a bachelor when he's in a bad mood.*

son of a sea biscuit *Euph.* a person, usually a male. (Sometimes a substitute for **son of a bitch**.) □ *Why, good to see you, you old son of a sea biscuit.* □ *You son of a sea biscuit! You make me so mad I could slug you.*

*soon as possible at the earliest time. (**Also:* **as ~**.) □ *I'm leaving now. I'll be there as soon as possible.* □ *Please pay me soon as possible.*

Soon ripe, soon rotten. Go to Early ripe, early rotten.

sooner or later eventually; in the short term or in the long term. □ *He'll have to pay the bill sooner or later.* □ *She'll get what she deserves sooner or later.*

Sooner than you think. an expression stating that something will happen sooner than a time expected or just mentioned. □ *Sally: I'm going to have to stop pretty soon for a rest. Mary: Sooner than you think, I'd say. I think one of our tires is low.* □ *Tom: The stock market is bound to run out of steam pretty soon. Bob: Sooner than you think from the look of today's news.*

The **sooner the better.** The sooner something [referred to] gets done, the better things will be. □ *Bob: When do you need this? Mary: The sooner the better.* □ *Bob: Please get the oil changed in the station wagon. The sooner the better. Alice: I'll do it today.*

sop something **up†** to mop or soak up a liquid. □ *Use this rag to sop the spilled milk up.* □ *The rag will sop up the mess a little at a time.*

sopping (wet) intoxicated. □ *He's soused—you know, sopping wet.*

*sore (at someone**)** *Fig.* angry at someone. (**Typically:* **be ~; get ~; make** someone **~**.) □ *When Mary hears what you said about her, she'll get sore for sure.* □ *Please don't get sore at me.*

sorrow over someone or something to grieve or feel sad about someone or something. □ *There is no need to sorrow over Tom. He will come back.* □ *He is sorrowing over the business he has lost because of the weather.*

sorry about that and **sorry 'bout that** sorry; whoops. (A gross understatement, said more as a self-deprecating joke than as an apology.) □ *You spill hot cocoa on my coat, and all you can say is "Sorry 'bout that"?* □ *When the passenger stepped on my toe, she said, "Sorry about that."*

a **sorry sight** and a **sad sight** a sight that one regrets seeing; someone or something that is unpleasant to look at. □ *Well, aren't you a sorry sight! Go get cleaned up and put on some fresh clothes.*

Sorry (that) I asked. Now that I have heard the answer, I regret asking the question. □ *Alice: Can we get a new car soon? The old one is a wreck. John: Are you kidding? There's no way that we could ever afford a new car! Alice: Sorry I asked.* □ *After he heard the long list of all the reasons he*

wouldn't be allowed to go to the concert, Fred just shrugged and said, "Sorry that I asked."

Sort of. and **Kind of.** Yes, but only to a small degree. □ *Bob: Do you like what you're doing in school? Alice: Kind of.* □ *Henry: What do you think about all these new laws? Do they worry you? John: Sort of.*

sort of something and **kind of** something almost something; somewhat; somehow. □ *Isn't it sort of cold out?* □ *That was kind of a stupid thing to do, wasn't it?*

sort oneself **out** to pull oneself together; to figure out what to do about one's problems. (*Fig. on* **sort** something **out** ②.) □ *I need a few days to sort myself out.* □ *I need some time to sort myself out.*

sort something **out†** **1.** *Lit.* to sort something; to arrange according to class or category. □ *Let's sort these cards out.* □ *Would you please sort out your socks?* **2.** *Fig.* to study a problem and figure it out. □ *I can't sort this out without some more time.* □ *Let's sort out this mess and settle it once and for all.*

(soul) brother a black person's male, black friend. □ *Another brother took a fall last night.* □ *Terry's a soul brother, and I'll do anything for him.*

(soul) sister a black person's female, black friend. □ *Many of the top singing groups of the '60s featured soul sisters.*

sound as a barrel Go to all oak and iron bound.

*sound as a bell in perfect condition or health; undamaged. (**Also:* **as ~**.) □ *The doctor says that the old man's heart's as sound as a bell.* □ *I thought the vase was broken when it fell, but it was sound as a bell.*

*sound as a dollar 1. *Cliché* very secure and dependable. (**Also:* **as ~**.) □ *This investment is as sound as a dollar.* □ *I wouldn't put my money in a bank that isn't sound as a dollar.* **2.** *Cliché* sturdy and well-constructed. (**Also:* **as ~**.) □ *This house is as sound as a dollar.* □ *The garage is still sound as a dollar. Why tear it down?*

sound as if and **sound like** to seem, from what has been said, as if something were so. (*Sound like* is colloquial.) □ *It sounds as if you had a good vacation.* □ *You sound like you are angry.*

sound asleep completely asleep; in a deep sleep. □ *I was sound asleep when the fire broke out.*

a **(sound) grasp of** something Go to a (solid) grasp of something.

sound like Go to sound as if.

sound like a broken record to say the same thing over and over again. (*Fig. on* a scratch in a phonograph record causing the needle [or stylus] to stay in the same groove and play it over and over.) □ *He's always complaining about the way she treats him. He sounds like a broken record!* □ *I hate to sound like a broken record, but we just don't have enough people on the payroll to work efficiently.*

sound off to speak something loudly; to call out one's name or one's place in a numerical sequence. □ *All right, sound off, you guys!* □ *Each one sounded off.*

sound off (about something**) 1.** to complain about something; to gripe about something. □ *You are always sounding off about something that gripes your soul.* □ *Just sound off if you've got a beef.* **2.** to speak out of turn about something. □ *Who asked you to sound off about this?* □ *Don't just sound off without raising your hand.*

sound someone **out**[†] to try to find out what someone thinks (about something). □ *I don't know what Jane thinks about your suggestion, but I'll sound her out.* □ *Please sound out everyone in your department.*

sound something **out**[†] to pronounce the letters or syllables of a word as a means of figuring out what the word is. (Usually said to a child.) □ *This word is easy, Bobby. Try to sound it out.*

Soup's on! *Rur.* The meal is ready to eat. (Said for any food, not just soup.) □ *Tom: Soup's on! Bill: The camp chef has dished up another disaster.* □ *John: Soup's on! Come and get it! Mary: Well, I guess it's time to eat again.*

soup something **up**[†] to increase the power of something. □ *He souped his car up so it will do nearly 120 miles per hour.* □ *If only I could soup up this computer to run just a little faster.*

souped up made more powerful. □ *That souped-up car of John's sure makes a lot of noise.* □ *Why do all cars driven by males under the age of twenty have to be souped up?*

***sour as vinegar 1.** [of something] very sour. (*Also: **as** ~.) □ *This milk is as sour as vinegar.* □ *The juice they gave us is sour as vinegar.* **2.** [of someone] ill-natured and disagreeable. (*Fig.* on ①. *Also: **as** ~.) □ *The old man greeted us ill-naturedly, his face as sour as vinegar.* □ *Jill: Is Mary in a bad mood today? Jane: Yes, sour as vinegar.*

sour grapes *Fig.* something that one cannot have and so disparages as if it were never desirable. □ *Of course you want to buy this expensive jacket. Criticizing it is just sour grapes, but you still really want it.*

sow one's **wild oats** to do wild and foolish things in one's youth. (Often assumed to have some sort of sexual meaning.) □ *Jack was out sowing his wild oats last night, and he's in jail this morning.* □ *Mrs. Smith told Mr. Smith that he was too old to be sowing his wild oats.*

Sow the wind and reap the whirlwind *Prov.* to start some kind of trouble that grows much larger than you planned. (Biblical.) □ *Our enemy has sown the wind by provoking this war, and they will reap the whirlwind when we vanquish them.*

space out to become giddy or disoriented. □ *Judy spaced out during the meeting and I didn't understand a word she said.* □ *I have a tendency to space out at the end of a hard day.*

space someone **out**[†] to cause someone to become giddy. □ *The circus clowns just spaced me out.* □ *The hilarious spectacle spaced out the entire audience.*

spaced (out) silly; giddy. □ *I have such spaced-out parents!* □ *He's so spaced!*

spade something **up**[†] to turn over the soil in a garden plot with a spade. □ *Please go out and spade the garden up so I can plant the potatoes and onions.* □ *I will spade up the garden when I have time.*

spar with someone **1.** *Lit.* to box with someone for practice. □ *The champ needs someone to spar with every day.* □ *Ted was sparring with his brother when the phone rang and saved him from further exertion.* **2.** *Fig.* to argue or quibble with someone. □ *I think you really enjoy sparring*

with people just to irritate them. □ *Stop sparring with me! I am not here to argue.*

spare someone something to exempt someone from having to listen to or experience something. □ *I'll spare you the details and get to the point.* □ *Please, spare me the story and tell me what you want.*

Spare the rod and spoil the child. *Prov.* You should punish a child when he or she misbehaves, because if you do not, the child will grow up expecting everyone to indulge him or her. □ *Jane: How can you allow your little boy to be so rude? Ellen: It distresses me to punish him. Jane: I can understand that, but spare the rod and spoil the child.*

spare tire 1. a thickness in the waist; a roll of fat around one's waist. □ *I've got to get rid of this spare tire.* □ *The spare tire started when I was twenty-six.* **2.** an unneeded person; an unproductive person. □ *Gary is a spare tire. Send him home.* □ *You spare tires over there! Get to work.*

spark something **off**[†] **1.** *Lit.* to ignite something flammable or explosive. □ *The lightning sparked a fire off.* □ *The match sparked off a raging inferno.* **2.** *Fig.* to cause or start some violent or energetic activity. □ *We were afraid there would be a riot and the speaker nearly sparked it off.* □ *The speaker sparked off quite a discussion.*

sparkle with something to glitter or twinkle because of something. □ *The crystal goblets sparkled with the light from the flickering candles.* □ *Her eyes sparkled with the reflection of the candles.*

spatter on someone or something [for a liquid or something moist] to splash onto someone or something. □ *When Kelly painted the hallway, a lot of paint spattered on the floor.* □ *The hot fat spattered on me.*

spatter someone or something **up**[†] to get drops of a liquid or bits of something moist onto someone or something. □ *The painter spattered his partner up when he dropped the paint bucket accidentally.* □ *The falling paint bucket spattered up the wall.*

spatter someone or something **with** something to splash someone or something with drops of a liquid or bits of something moist. □ *Frank spattered us with grapefruit juice as he was eating a half of grapefruit.* □ *He even spattered the wall with juice.*

spatter something **around**[†] to scatter bits or drops of a liquid or something moist here and there. □ *Ted spattered paint around everywhere when he redecorated his kitchen.* □ *Don't spatter around the paint.*

spatter something **on(to)** someone or something to scatter or splash bits or drops of a liquid or something moist onto someone or something. □ *Who spattered barbecue sauce onto the wall?* □ *The paint can fell and spattered paint on everyone.*

spaz around *Sl.* to waste time; to mess around. □ *You kids are always spazzing around. Why don't you do something useful?* □ *We're just spazzing around. Leave us alone.*

spaz down *Sl.* to relax. □ *Spaz down, man! Chill out!* □ *We tried to get the crowd to spaz down, but they were very excited.*

spaz out 1. *Sl.* to overreact to something; to become overly excited about something. □ *I knew you would spaz out! But my grades are not that bad!* □ *Come on, don't spaz out!* **2.** *Sl.* an emotional display. (Usually **spaz-out.**) □

There's no need for a spaz-out! □ *She threw a hell of a spaz-out.*

speak about someone or something to mention or discuss someone or something. □ *And now I will speak about Abraham Lincoln.* □ *Let us speak about what happened yesterday.*

speak against someone or something **1.** to criticize someone or something. □ *Many people are speaking against the mayor. She will not be reelected.* □ *Please don't speak against cats in my presence.* **2.** to testify or argue against someone or something. □ *Judy spoke against the candidate at length.* □ *The next speaker spoke against nuclear waste.*

speak as one Go to as one.

speak at great length Go to at great length.

speak down to someone to address someone in simpler terms than necessary; to speak condescendingly to someone. □ *There is no need to speak down to me. I can understand anything you are likely to say.* □ *Sorry. Sometimes I tend to speak down to people over the telephone.*

speak for itself and **speak for themselves** [for something] not to need explaining; to have an obvious meaning. □ *The facts speak for themselves. Tom is guilty.* □ *Your results speak for themselves. You need to work harder.*

speak for oneself to speak on one's own behalf. □ *I can speak for myself. I don't need you to speak for me.* □ *Speak for yourself. What you say does not represent my thinking.*

speak for someone or something **1.** to testify or argue for someone or something. □ *I would be happy to speak for you in court. Just tell me when.* □ *My attorney will speak for our position.* **2.** to lay claim to someone or something. □ *Fred is spoken for.* □ *I want to speak for the red one.*

speak for themselves Go to speak for itself.

speak from something to draw authority or credibility in one's speaking from something such as knowledge or experience. □ *Believe me, I speak from experience.* □ *Listen to her. She speaks from a lot of knowledge and training.*

speak highly of someone or something **1.** [for someone] to say good things about someone or something. □ *She always speaks highly of you.* □ *Everyone spoke highly of this movie, but it is not good.* **2.** [for a fact] to reflect well on someone or something. □ *The success of your project speaks highly of you.* □ *All of this good news speaks highly of your ability to influence people.*

speak ill of someone to say something bad about someone. □ *I refuse to speak ill of any of my friends.* □ *Max speaks ill of no one and refuses to repeat gossip.*

speak in earnest Go to in earnest.

speak of someone or something **1.** to mention or discuss someone or something. □ *Were we speaking of Judy? I don't recall.* □ *We were speaking of the new law.* **2.** [for a type of behavior or action] to reflect a particular quality. □ *Jeff's behavior spoke of a good upbringing.* □ *Her good singing voice speaks of years of training.*

Speak of the devil (and in he walks). and **Talk of the devil (and he is sure to appear).** *Prov.* Talk about a certain person, and that person appears. (Used when someone appears whom you have just been talking about.) □ *Alan: I haven't seen Bob for weeks. Jane: Look, here comes Bob right now. Alan: Well, talk of the devil.* □

Hi, there. We were just talking about you. Speak of the devil and in he walks.

speak off-the-cuff *Fig.* to speak without preparing a speech; to speak extemporaneously; to render a spoken opinion or estimate. (As if one's notes had been written hastily on one's cuff.) □ *She is capable of making sense and being convincing even when she speaks off-the-cuff.* □ *I find it very difficult to speak off-the-cuff.*

speak one's **mind** *Fig.* to say frankly what one thinks (about something). □ *Please let me speak my mind, and then you can do whatever you wish.* □ *You can always depend on John to speak his mind. He'll let you know what he really thinks.*

speak one's **piece** Go to say one's piece.

speak out to speak loudly; to speak to be heard. (See also speak out (about someone or something).) □ *Please speak out. We need to hear you.* □ *They won't hear you in the back row if you don't speak out.*

speak out (about someone or something) to express oneself about someone or something; to tell what one knows about someone or something. (See also speak out.) □ *I could keep silent no longer. I had to speak out about the alleged accident.* □ *I had to speak out!*

speak out (against someone or something) to speak negatively and publicly about someone or something; to reveal something negative, in speech, about someone or something. □ *I don't want to speak out against my friends, but I am afraid I have to.* □ *The citizens spoke out against corruption in government.*

speak out of turn *Fig.* to say something unwise or imprudent; to say something at the wrong time. □ *Excuse me if I'm speaking out of turn, but what you are proposing is quite wrong.* □ *Bob was quite honest, even if he was speaking out of turn.*

speak out (on something) to say something frankly and directly; to speak one's mind. □ *This law is wrong, and I intend to speak out on it until it is repealed.* □ *You must speak out. People need to know what you think.*

speak someone's **language** *Fig.* to say something that one agrees with or understands. □ *I gotcha. Now you're speaking my language.* □ *Mary speaks Fred's language. They get along fine.*

speak the same language 1. *Lit.* [for two or more people] to communicate in a shared language. □ *These two people don't speak the same language and need an interpreter.* **2.** *Fig.* [for people] to have similar ideas, tastes, etc. □ *Jane and Jack get along very well. They really speak the same language about almost everything.* □ *Bob and his father didn't speak the same language when it comes to politics.*

speak to someone to talk to someone. □ *I am angry with him and I refuse to speak to him.* □ *Were you speaking to me?*

speak to something [for something] to address, indicate, or signal something. □ *This event speaks to the need for good communication.* □ *Your present state of employment speaks to your need for a better education.*

speak up 1. *Lit.* to speak more loudly. □ *They can't hear you in the back of the room. Please speak up.* □ *What? Speak up, please. I'm hard of hearing.* **2.** *Fig.* to speak out (on something). □ *If you think that this is wrong, you must speak up and say so.* □ *I'm too shy to speak up.*

speak up (against someone or something**)** to end one's silence and speak negatively and publicly about someone or something. □ *She finally spoke up against her cruel boss.* □ *We all felt like we had to speak up and denounce this tyrant.*

speak up for someone or something to speak in favor of someone or something. □ *If anybody says bad things about me, I hope you speak up for me.* □ *I want to speak up for the rights of students.*

speak (up)on something to talk about a particular topic. (*Upon* is formal and less commonly used than *on*.) □ *This evening, I will speak upon the subject of Plato's thoughts on the universe.* □ *What will you speak on today?*

speak volumes *Fig.* [for something that is seen] to reveal a great deal of information. □ *The unsightly yard and unpainted house speaks volumes about what kind of people live there.*

speak with a forked tongue *Fig.* to tell lies; to try to deceive someone. □ *Jean's mother sounds very charming, but she speaks with a forked tongue.* □ *People tend to believe Fred because he seems plausible, but we know he speaks with a forked tongue.*

speak with someone (**about** someone or something**) 1.** to talk with someone about someone or something; to discuss someone or something with someone. □ *I was speaking with Fred about Don, who is a mutual friend.* □ *I need to know something about Don. I will speak with his friend Fred.* **2.** to reprimand one about one's dealing with someone or something. □ *He should not have insulted Kelly. I will speak with him about her.* □ *He did what? I will speak with him!*

speaking for oneself an expression indicating that one is expressing only one's own opinion. □ *Speaking for myself, I am ready to cancel the contract.* □ *Sally is speaking for herself. She is not expressing our opinions.*

speaking (quite) candidly an expression introducing a frank or forthright statement. □ *"Speaking quite candidly, I find your behavior a bit offensive," stated Frank, obviously offended.* □ *Mary: Tell me what you really think about this skirt. Sally: Speaking candidly, I think you should get your money back.*

(speaking) (quite) frankly and **frankly speaking** a transitional phrase announcing that the speaker is going to talk in a more familiar and totally forthright manner. □ *Tom: Speaking quite frankly, I'm not certain she's the one for the job. Mary: I agree.* □ *Bob: We ought to be looking at housing in a lower price bracket. Bill: Quite frankly, I agree.* □ *"Frankly speaking," said John, "I think you're out of your mind!"*

spear something **out** (**of** something) to bring something forth from something by sticking it with something sharp and pulling. □ *Richard spears pickles right out of the jar with a fork.* □ *He speared out a pickle.*

specialize in something to limit oneself to or be specially trained to practice one particular thing. □ *I specialize in tropical medicine.* □ *What do you specialize in?*

speculate about someone or something to make guesses about someone or something; to hypothesize about some-

one or something. □ *I refuse to speculate about Sally. I don't presume to guess what she will do.* □ *We don't speculate about the future.*

speculate in something to make risky business deals in the buying and selling of something. □ *Jeff made a fortune speculating in cotton.* □ *I do not wish to speculate in anything. It is too risky.*

speculate on something to make a hypothesis about something. □ *I really don't want to speculate on what might happen next.* □ *Would you care to speculate on what might happen if you quit your job?*

speed away (from someone or something**)** to move or drive away very fast from someone or something. □ *The taxi sped away from the passenger who had just alighted.* □ *The car sped away from the accident.* □ *The motorcycle sped away.*

speed someone or something **up**† to cause someone or something to move faster. □ *We tried to speed him up, but he is just a very slow person.* □ *We sped up the process, but it still took too long.*

speed up to go faster. □ *Please speed up. We are late.*

***speeds of** some amount a variety of speeds (of movement) of a certain level. (*Typically: **clock** someone **at** ~; **have** ~; **hit** ~; **reach** ~.) □ *The cops clocked him at speeds of up to one hundred miles per hour.*

spell disaster *Fig.* to indicate or predict disaster. □ *What a horrible plan! It would spell disaster for all of us!*

spell someone (**at** something) to take a turn at doing something while the person who was doing it can take a rest. □ *I will spell you at selling tickets while you go and grab a bite to eat.*

spell someone **down**† to win over someone in a spelling match. □ *Frank spelled everyone else down and won the spelling bee.* □ *He spelled down almost everyone.*

spell something **for** someone to spell a word or name for someone's benefit. □ *I don't recognize that word. Would you please spell it for me?* □ *It is a difficult name. I will have to spell it for you.*

spell something **out**† **1.** *Lit.* to spell something (with letters). □ *I can't understand your name. Can you spell it out?* □ *Please spell out all the strange words so I can write them down correctly.* **2.** *Fig.* to give all the details of something. □ *I want you to understand this completely, so I'm going to spell it out very carefully.* □ *The instruction book for my computer spells out everything very carefully.*

spell trouble to signify future trouble; to mean trouble. □ *This letter that came today spells trouble.* □ *The sky looks angry and dark. That spells trouble.*

spend a king's ransom Go to a king's ransom.

spend money like it's going out of style and **spend money like there's no tomorrow** *Fig.* to spend money recklessly; to spend money as if it were worthless or will soon be worthless. □ *Extravagant? She spends money like it's going out of style! I can't control it. I spend money like there is no tomorrow.*

spend money like there's no tomorrow Go to previous.

spend something **for** something to pay out an amount of money for something. □ *I spent nearly forty dollars for that* *vase!* □ *How much did you spend for this house—if I may ask?*

spend something **on** someone or something to pay out an amount of money for the benefit of someone or something. □ *How much did you spend on him for his birthday?* □ *I spent a lot on Mary's gift.*

spend time in something to stay in something or some place for a period of time. □ *I spent time in Barbados when I was younger.* □ *I am afraid that you will have to spend some time in the hospital until the infection is cleared up.*

spending money cash, as opposed to money in the bank. □ *I'm a little short of spending money at the present. Could I borrow ten dollars?* □ *I don't have any spending money either.*

spew one's **guts (out) 1.** *Sl.* to empty one's stomach; to vomit. □ *Fred is spewing his guts out because of that lousy fish you served.* □ *He's spewing his guts because he has the flu.* **2.** *Sl.* to tell everything that one knows; to confess everything. (Underworld.) □ *Lefty was sitting there in the police station spewing his guts out about the bank job.* □ *If he really is spewing his guts, the mob will cancel his Christmas.*

spew something **out**† to have something gush forth. □ *The faucet spewed a little yellowish water out and stopped altogether.* □ *The faucet spewed out some yellowish water.*

spew something **up**† to gush something upward. □ *The geyser spewed hot water and steam up every hour on the hour.* □ *The fountain spewed up a thin stream of cool, clear water.*

spice something **up**† **1.** *Lit.* to make some food or drink more spicy. □ *Judy spiced the cider up by adding cinnamon and nutmeg.* □ *She spiced up the chili too much.* **2.** *Fig.* to make something more interesting, lively, or sexy. □ *I'm afraid that the nude scenes spiced the musical up too much. Some people walked out.* □ *Judy liked to spice her lectures up by telling jokes.* □ *She spiced up each lecture with a joke.* □ *They spiced up the play too much.*

spiel something **off**† to recite a list of things very rapidly; to recite something very rapidly. □ *I used to be able to spiel the names of the presidents off.* □ *Liz spieled off her gift list to the clerk.*

spiff something **up**† to polish and groom something very well; to make something clean and tidy. □ *See if you can spiff this place up a little.* □ *I will spiff up the room a little.*

spiffed out *Sl.* to be dressed in one's finest clothes and well-groomed. □ *He got himself all spiffed out for the wedding reception.* □ *Man, are you ever spiffed out!*

spiffed up dressed up, groomed, and polished up nicely; clean and tidy. □ *See if you can get yourself a little spiffed up before we go out to dinner. We wouldn't want the Wilmington-Thorpes to think you only have one suit.* □ *The house doesn't have to be too spiffed up for the Franklins. They are used to clutter.*

spill one's **guts** *Sl.* to tell all; to confess. □ *I had to spill my guts about the broken window. I didn't want you to take the blame.* □ *Mary spilled her guts about the window. She confessed that she was trying to shield Bob.*

spill (out) into something and **spill (over) into** something to be so great in number or volume as to expand into

another area. □ *The crowd spilled out into the street.* □ *The well-wishers spilled over into the neighbor's yard.*

spill out (of something**)** to scatter, flow, or drop out of something. □ *All the rice spilled out of the box onto the floor.* □ *The rice spilled out on the floor.*

spill over 1. [for a container] to overflow. □ *I hope your bucket of water doesn't spill over.* □ *The milk glass spilled over because it was filled too full.* **2.** [for the contents of a container] to overflow. □ *The bucket is too full. I don't know why the water doesn't spill over.* □ *The milk spilled over because you overfilled the glass.*

spill (over) into something Go to **spill (out) into** something.

spill over on(to) someone or something [for something] to scatter, flow, or drop (out of something) onto someone or something. □ *The bowl of milk spilled over onto the children when they jarred the table.* □ *The bowl spilled over on the floor.*

spill the beans and **spill the works** *Fig.* to give away a secret or a surprise. □ *There is a surprise party for Heidi on Wednesday. Please don't spill the beans.* □ *Paul spilled the works about Heidi's party.*

spill the works Go to previous.

spin a yarn *Fig.* to tell a tale. □ *Grandpa spun an unbelievable yarn for us.* □ *My uncle is always spinning yarns about his childhood.*

spin around 1. to turn around to face a different direction. □ *Jill spun around to face her accuser.* □ *Todd spun around in his chair so he could see who was talking to him.* **2.** to rotate, possibly a number of times. □ *The propellers spun around and soon the old plane began to taxi down the runway.* □ *The merry-go-round spun around at a moderate speed.*

spin doctor someone who gives a twisted or deviously deceptive version of an event. (Usually in the context of manipulating the news for political reasons.) □ *Things were going bad for the candidate, so he got himself a new spin doctor.* □ *A good spin doctor could have made the incident appear far less damaging.*

spin off [for something] to part and fly away from something that is spinning; [for something] to detach or break loose from something. □ *The blade of the lawn mower spun off, but fortunately no one was injured.* □ *The rusted-on nut spun off easily after I got it loosened.*

spin one's **wheels** to waste time; to remain in a neutral position, neither advancing nor falling back. (Fig. on a car that is running but is not moving because its wheels are spinning in mud, etc.) □ *I'm just spinning my wheels in this job. I need more training to get ahead.* □ *The whole project was just spinning its wheels until spring.*

spin out [for a vehicle] to go out of control, spinning. □ *You nearly spun out on that last turn!* □ *Cars were spinning out all over the highway when the ice storm hit.*

spin something **off**† **1.** *Lit.* [for something rotating] to release a part that flies away. □ *The propeller spun one of its blades off and then fell apart all together.* □ *It spun off one of its blades.* **2.** *Fig.* [for a business] to divest itself of one of its subparts. □ *The large company spun one of its smaller divisions off.* □ *It spun off a subsidiary and used the cash to pay down its debt.* **3.** *Fig.* [for an enterprise] to pro-

631

duce useful or profitable side effects or products. □ *We will be able to spin off a number of additional products.* □ *The development of this product will allow us to spin off dozens of smaller, innovative products for years to come.*

spin something **out**† to prolong something. □ *Was there really any need to spin the whole process out so long?* □ *Why did they spin out the graduation ceremony for such a long time?*

spin something **out of** something and **spin** something **out**† to remove liquid from something by spinning. □ *The washer spun the water out of the load of clothing.* □ *The washer spun out all the water in the clothes.*

spiral down to descend in a spiral path. □ *The ancient trail spiraled down the mountain peak.* □ *A path spiraled down and at the bottom was a small refreshment stand.*

spiral up to ascend in a spiral path. □ *The smoke spiraled up to the sky.* □ *The trail spiraled up the slope to the top.*

The **spirit is willing, but the flesh is weak.** *Prov.* People cannot always do what they know they ought to do.; People are not always physically capable of doing what they are willing to do. (Biblical.) □ *Alan: Have you started the diet your doctor recommended? Fred: The spirit is willing, but the flesh is weak.*

spirit someone or something **away**† **(somewhere)** to sneak someone or something away to another place. □ *The police spirited the prisoner away before the crowd assembled in front of the jail.* □ *They spirited away the celebrity.*

spirit someone or something **off**† **(to** some place**)** to hurry someone or something away, presumably unnoticed, to another place. □ *Aunt Jane spirited the children off to bed at half-past eight.* □ *She spirited off the leftover roast beef.*

*the **spit and image of** someone and *the **spitting image of** someone the very likeness of someone; a very close resemblence to someone. (*The second version is a frequent error. *Typically: **be** ~; **look like** ~.) □ *John is the spit and image of his father.* □ *At first, I thought you were saying spitting image.*

spit and polish orderliness; ceremonial precision and orderliness. □ *I like spit and polish. It comes from being in the military.* □ *There is no such thing as too much spit and polish.*

spit at someone or something to expectorate on someone or something or in the direction of someone or something. □ *The angry crowd cursed and spit at the prisoner as he was being taken back to jail.* □ *Max actually spit at the police station door as he was dragged in.*

spit something **in(to)** something and **spit** something **in**† to expel something from the mouth into something. □ *He spit his gum into the toilet.* □ *He opened the toilet and spit in his gum.*

spit something **on(to)** something to expel something from the mouth onto something. □ *You shouldn't spit your gum onto the sidewalk!* □ *Don't spit your gum on the pavement.*

spit something **out**† **1.** *Lit.* to cast something from the mouth. □ *The food was so terrible that I spit it out.* □ *I spit out the sweet potatoes.* **2.** *Fig.* to manage to say something. □ *Come on! Say it! Spit it out!* □ *Spit it out! Get it said!* **3.** *Fig.* to say something scornfully. □ *He spit out his words in utter derision.* □ *She spit out the most unpleasant string of curse words I have ever heard from anyone.*

spit something **up**† *Euph.* to vomit something. □ *She almost spit her dinner up.* □ *Sally was afraid she was going to spit up her dinner.*

spit up *Euph.* to vomit. □ *The food was so bad, she was afraid she would spit up.* □ *Mommy, I have to spit up!*

spit (up)on someone or something **1.** to eject spit onto someone or something. (*Upon* is formal and less commonly used than *on*.) □ *The angry crowd spit on the convict.* □ *Don't spit on the sidewalk.* **2.** to spew spittle onto someone or something while talking. (*Upon* is formal and less commonly used than *on*.) □ *I always have a fear of accidentally spitting on someone in the first row while I am talking.* □ *I regret spitting on you, but it was an accident.*

the **spitting image of** someone Go to the **spit and image of** someone.

splash about and **splash around 1.** to move about in a volume of a liquid, splashing. □ *The children splashed about in the pool.* □ *They splashed around for an hour.* **2.** [for a liquid] to move about, splashing. □ *The water splashed about in the bucket.* □ *It splashed around as I carried the bucket.*

splash down [for a space capsule] to land in the water. □ *The capsule splashed down very close to the pickup ship.*

splash on someone or something to scatter [a liquid] on someone or something. □ *Try to keep from splashing on anybody.* □ *Don't splash on the wall!*

splash over [for a volume of liquid] to overflow its container. □ *A lot of the coffee splashed over before I got to the table with the cup.* □ *Don't fill it so full and it won't splash over.*

splash someone or something **up**† to scatter a liquid onto someone or something. □ *Don't get that stuff all over. Don't splash the place up!* □ *She splashed up the kitchen when she washed the dishes.*

splash someone or something **with** something to scatter or slosh someone or something with a liquid. □ *The whales at Sea World splashed everyone in the audience with water.* □ *I splashed the side of the stove with pancake batter when I dropped the bowl.*

splash something **about** to scatter or slosh a liquid about. □ *Please don't splash that about. It will stain anything you spill it on.* □ *Don't splash that stuff about!*

splash something **(all) over** someone or something to cause a liquid to overflow or engulf someone or something. □ *Tony splashed water all over Nick.* □ *Who splashed milk all over the table?*

splash something **on(to)** someone or something to make a liquid scatter onto someone or something. □ *Accidentally, the lab assistant splashed acid onto his arm.* □ *He splashed something on the counter.*

splatter someone or something **up**† to cover someone or something with drops of a liquid. □ *The painter splattered his coworker up with both red and blue.* □ *Don't splatter up the wall!*

splay out to spread out; to extend out at an angle. □ *His feet splayed out so much that it was hard to see how he could stand up.* □ *The legs of the table splayed out and gave it sturdy support.*

splice something **(in)to** something to connect something to something; to cut and join something into something to connect the two. ☐ *The workers spliced the small wires into the main cable.* ☐ *Let's splice this rope into the larger one at the halfway point.*

splice something **together**† to connect things together, usually by twisting or tying a joint between the two. ☐ *I spent over an hour splicing the two ends of the ropes together, and it didn't hold for even a minute.* ☐ *He carefully spliced together the two ropes.*

splinter off ((of) something) and **splinter off (from** something) [for a bit of something] to tear off or separate from something. (*Of* is usually retained before pronouns.) ☐ *A piece of wood splintered off of the oar and dropped into the water.* ☐ *A tiny bit splintered off and stuck in my hand.*

split a gut and **bust a gut 1.** *Fig. Inf.* to laugh very hard. ☐ *He laughed until he nearly split a gut.* ☐ *The clown made me bust a gut laughing.* **2.** *Fig. Inf.* to work very hard. ☐ *I split a gut to get this place fixed up in a week.* ☐ *Don't bust a gut cleaning up for me. I love things that are a bit messy.*

split hairs *Fig.* to quibble; to try to make petty distinctions. ☐ *They don't have any serious differences. They are just splitting hairs.* ☐ *Don't waste time splitting hairs. Accept it the way it is.*

split in something to divide into a certain number of groups. (The *something* can be *half, thirds, two, quarters,* etc.) ☐ *Lightning struck the big tree and the trunk split in half.* ☐ *The vase dropped and split in quarters.*

split off (from something) to separate away from something; to sever connection with and separate from something. ☐ *A large iceberg split off from the glacier and made an enormous splash.* ☐ *A giant chunk of ice split off and floated away.*

split one's **sides (with laughter)** *Fig.* to laugh so hard that one's sides almost split. (Always an exaggeration.) ☐ *The members of the audience almost split their sides with laughter.* ☐ *When I heard what happened to Patricia, I almost split my sides.*

split people up† to separate two or more people (from one another). ☐ *If you two don't stop chattering, I'll have to split you up.* ☐ *I will have to split up that twosome in the corner.*

*a **split second** an instant; a tiny period of time. (*Typically: **for** ~; **in** ~.) ☐ *The lightning struck, and in a split second the house burst into flames.* ☐ *For a split second, it looked like she would fall.*

split someone or something **up**† **(into** something) to divide people or things up into something, such as groups. ☐ *I had to split the group up into two sections—there were so many who showed up.* ☐ *I split up the class into two discussion sections.*

split someone or something **with** someone or something to divide someone or something with someone or a group of people. ☐ *I will split the campers with you. You lead your half on the hike, and I will lead my half.* ☐ *Will you split your candy bar with me?*

split something **between (**someone **and** someone else) and **split** something **between (**something **and** something else) to divide something between two people or things. ☐ *The cook split the last of the pie between Jane and Carla.* ☐ *We*

have to split the copies of the reports between the two committees.

split something **fifty-fifty** Go to **divide** something **fifty-fifty.**

split something **into** something to divide or sever something into something. ☐ *Jeff split the log into four parts.* ☐ *Please split this log in half so it will burn better.*

split something **off (of)** something and **split** something **off**† to sever connection with something; to separate from something. (*Of* is usually retained before pronouns.) ☐ *Dave split a piece of wood off the log to use for kindling.* ☐ *He split off a stick of wood.*

split the difference to divide the difference evenly (with someone else). ☐ *You want to sell for $120, and I want to buy for $100. Let's split the difference and close the deal at $110.* ☐ *I don't want to split the difference. I want $120.*

split up (with someone) [for someone] to separate from someone; to break up a marriage or love affair. ☐ *Jeff split up with Judy.* ☐ *I had heard that they had split up with each other.*

a **splitting headache** *Fig.* a severe headache, as if one's head were splitting open. ☐ *I'm sorry, I can't. I have a splitting headache. Maybe Fred will play bridge with you.* ☐ *This splitting headache has been going on for hours.*

splurge on someone or something to spend a lot of money on someone or something. ☐ *I really splurged on my wife for her birthday.* ☐ *Mary really splurged on that dinner!*

spoiled rotten *Fig.* indulged in; greatly spoiled. ☐ *This kid is spoiled rotten!* ☐ *I was spoiled rotten when I was a child, so I'm used to this kind of wasteful luxury.*

spoiling for a fight argumentative; asking for a fight. ☐ *They were just spoiling for a fight, and they went outside to settle the matter.* ☐ *She was grouchy, and you could tell she had been spoiling for a fight all day.*

spoken for taken; reserved (for someone). ☐ *I'm sorry, but this piece of cake is already spoken for.* ☐ *Pardon me. Can I sit here, or is this seat spoken for?*

sponge someone or something **down**† to remove the [excess] moisture from someone or something; to wipe someone or something with a sponge. ☐ *The fight manager sponged his boxer down.* ☐ *I will sponge down the countertop.*

sponge something **away**† to absorb, wipe up, and wipe away something, as with a sponge. ☐ *Try sponging the stain away with some soda water.* ☐ *I will sponge away the mess.*

sponge something **from** someone to beg or borrow money or food from someone. ☐ *Gary tried to sponge a few bucks from me.* ☐ *I can't continue sponging food from my relatives.*

sponge something **from** something to remove moisture from something, as with a sponge. ☐ *Liz sponged the sauce from her blouse.* ☐ *We gently sponged the splattered paint from the carpet.*

sponge something **off of** someone or something and **sponge** something **off**† to beg or borrow money or food from someone or a group. ☐ *Please stop sponging food and money off your relatives!* ☐ *Stop sponging off food and money all the time!*

S

sponge something **up**† to absorb or take up moisture, as with a sponge. □ *I had to sponge the spilled milk up from the floor, the chair, the table, and the baby. What a mess!* □ *Liz sponged up the water.*

spook someone or something to startle or disorient someone or something. □ *A snake spooked my horse, and I nearly fell off.* □ *Your warning spooked me, and I was upset for the rest of the day.*

spoon something **out**† to serve something out, as with a spoon; to give something out, as with a spoon. □ *The cook spooned the beans out, giving plenty to each camper.* □ *The cook spooned out the beans.*

spoon something **up**† to serve something that requires finding and bringing up out of a pot with a spoon. □ *The cook spooned the hard-cooked eggs up one by one.* □ *The cook spooned up chunks of meat from the stew.*

spoon-feed someone *Fig.* to treat someone with too much care or help; to teach someone with methods that are too easy and do not stimulate the learner to independent thinking. □ *The teacher spoon-feeds the students by dictating notes on the novel instead of getting the children to read the books.* □ *You mustn't spoon-feed the new recruits by telling them what to do all the time. They must use their initiative.*

the **sport of kings** horse racing. □ *The sport of kings has sure impoverished a lot of commoners.*

sport with someone or something to tease or play with someone or something. □ *What a tease you are! You are just sporting with me!* □ *The dog was sporting with a turtle down by the stream.*

a **sporting chance** a reasonably good chance. □ *If you hurry, you have a sporting chance of catching the bus.* □ *The firm has only a sporting chance of getting the export order.*

spot someone **as** something to recognize someone to be something; to realize that someone is something. □ *I spotted you as a troublemaker from the very beginning.* □ *The guard spotted Max as a potential thief the moment he saw him.*

spot someone **(something) 1.** *Sl.* to give an advantage to someone. □ *I'll spot you twenty points.* □ *No need to spot me. I'm the greatest!* **2.** *Sl.* to lend someone something. □ *Can you spot me a few bucks?* □ *I can spot you a whole hundred!*

spout from something [for a liquid] to gush from something. □ *A plume of water vapor spouted from the blowhole of the whale.* □ *Water spouted from the top of the fountain and flowed down the sides.*

spout off (about someone or something**) 1.** to brag or boast about someone or something. □ *Stop spouting off about Tom. Nobody could be that good!* □ *Alice is spouting off about her new car.* **2.** to speak out publicly about someone or something; to reveal information publicly about someone or something. □ *I wish you wouldn't spout off about my family affairs in public.* □ *There is no point in spouting off about this problem.*

spout something **out**† **1.** *Lit.* to exude a liquid. □ *The hose spouted the cooling water out all over the children.* □ *It spouted out cooling water.* **2.** *Fig.* to blurt something out; to speak out suddenly, revealing some important piece of information. □ *She spouted the name of the secret agent out under the effects of the drug.* □ *She spouted out everything we wanted to know.*

sprain one's **ankle** to become pregnant. □ *She has, ah, sprained her ankle.* □ *From the looks of her, she must have sprained her ankle some months ago.*

sprawl about and **sprawl around** to slouch or lounge somewhere; to spread oneself out casually while lounging. (Usually refers to habitual action, perhaps in a number of places.) □ *He sprawled about, loafing the afternoon away.* □ *When I came into the room, four teenage boys were sprawled around the furniture, watching television.*

sprawl out to spread oneself out casually while lounging. (Usually done one time, not habitually. Compare this with **sprawl about.**) □ *He sprawled out and took up most of the space.* □ *I need more room so I can sprawl out.*

spray someone or something **with** something to coat someone or something with a mist or stream of liquid. □ *The elephant sprayed us with water.* □ *I sprayed the fence with white paint.* □ *He sprayed himself with some of the cologne.*

spray something **onto** someone or something and **spray** something **on**† to direct a mist or stream of a liquid onto someone or something. □ *Danny sprayed cold water onto the boys and cooled them off.* □ *Dan sprayed on some cold water.* □ *I sprayed the paint on and it dried almost immediately.*

spread all over (some place) Go to **all over** (some place).

spread it on thick Go to **lay it on thick.**

spread like wildfire *Fig.* [for something] to spread rapidly. □ *Rumors spread like wildfire when people are excited.* □ *This disease will spread like wildfire when it gets going.*

spread oneself **too thin** *Fig.* to do so many things at one time that you can do none of them well. □ *It's a good idea to get involved in a lot of activities, but don't spread yourself too thin.* □ *I'm too busy these days. I'm afraid I've spread myself too thin.*

spread out to separate and distribute over a wide area. □ *The sheriff told the members of the posse to spread out and continue their search.* □ *The wine spread out and stained a large area of the carpet.*

spread over someone or something† [for something] to cover someone or something gradually. □ *The shade slowly spread over the picnickers.* □ *Dusk spread its final shadows over the land.*

spread someone or something **around**† to distribute people or things over an area. □ *Spread the good singers around so they can help the others in the choir.* □ *Liz spread around the seeds so they would dry.*

spread something **around**† to distribute news or gossip. □ *Please don't spread this around, but Don ran away from home!* □ *Don't spread around that story!*

spread something **on**† Go to **spread** something **onto** something.

spread something **on thick 1.** to distribute a thick layer of something. □ *This paint will cover well if you spread it on thick.* □ *If you spread the paint on thick, you will only need one coat.* **2.** Go to **lay it on thick.**

spread something **onto** something and **spread** something **on**[†] to distribute a coating of something onto something. □ *Spread the butter onto the bread evenly.* □ *Spread on the butter evenly.* □ *Donna spread the paint on with a roller.*

spread something **out**[†] to open, unfold, or lay something over a wider area. □ *Spread the wet papers out so they will dry.* □ *She spread out the papers to dry them.*

spread something **over** someone or something to cause something to cover or be distributed over someone or something. □ *The cloud spread its shadow over everyone at the picnic.* □ *We spread fertilizer over the prepared ground.* □ *He spread the work over a few weeks.*

spread something **under** someone or something to extend or unfold something, such as a tarpaulin, beneath someone or something. □ *Please spread some newspapers under Jimmy while he is working this clay.* □ *Would you spread some newspapers under your work, please?*

spread something **with** something to cover something with a coat of something. □ *Using the roller, Judy spread the wall with a thick coat of pink paint.* □ *Spread the lasagna with a layer of cheese mixture and cover that with another layer of lasagna.*

spread the word to tell many people some kind of information. □ *I need to spread the word that the meeting is canceled for this afternoon.*

spread to someone or something to expand or extend to reach someone or something. □ *The epidemic finally spread to me and my family.* □ *The business slowdown spread to the West Coast.*

spring at someone or something to jump at someone or something. □ *The cat sprang at me but could not sink in its claws.* □ *The spider sprang at the moth and captured it.*

spring back (to some place**)** to jump, bounce, or recoil back to a place. □ *The cat sprang back to its original place on the top of the table.* □ *The lid sprang back to a closed position.*

spring for something and **bounce for** something *Sl.* to treat someone by buying something. □ *I'm bouncing for pizza. Any takers?* □ *Ralph sprang for drinks, and we all had a great time.*

spring (forth) from someone or something to come forth from someone or something; to gush out of someone or something, as with a spring of water; to jump from or out of someone or something. □ *The best ideas spring forth from the mind of Mary!* □ *What new example of pure genius can we expect to spring from Mary today?*

spring into action *Fig.* to suddenly begin moving or doing something. □ *As soon as the boss came in the door, everyone sprang into action.* □ *Every morning, I jump out of bed and spring into action.*

spring out at someone to jump out at someone. □ *A grasshopper sprang out at me when I peered into the hollow log.* □ *I was afraid that something would spring out at me, so I opened the cellar door carefully.*

spring out of something to jump out of something. □ *The cat sprang out of the closet when I opened the door.* □ *The boys sprang out of the cold water as fast as they could.*

spring something **on** someone **1.** to surprise someone with something. □ *I hate to spring this on you at the last*

moment, but I will need some money to travel on. □ *Please don't spring any other demands on me.* **2.** to pull a trick on someone. □ *Let me tell you about the trick I sprang on Sally.* □ *What are you going to spring on her this time?*

spring to attention to move quickly to assume the military posture of attention. □ *The recruit sprang to attention.*

spring to life *Fig.* to become suddenly alive or more alive. □ *The party sprang to life after midnight.* □ *The city sprang to life at dawn.*

spring to one's **feet** *Fig.* to stand up quickly. □ *He sprang to his feet and demanded that the chair recognize him.* □ *The audience sprang to its feet and cheered madly when the soprano finished.*

spring to someone's **defense** *Fig.* to go quickly to defend someone. (Can be against physical or verbal attack.) □ *Fred was attacked and Ralph sprang to his defense.* □ *We sprang to Mary's defense when she was accused of doing wrong.*

spring up to appear or develop suddenly; to sprout, as with a seedling. □ *We knew it was really spring when all the flowers sprang up.* □ *It seems as if the tulips sprang up overnight.* □ *The dog's ears sprang up when the refrigerator opened.*

spring (up)on someone, something, or an animal to jump on someone, something, or an animal; to pounce on someone, something, or an animal. (*Upon* is formal and less commonly used than *on.*) □ *The lion sprang upon him and knocked him down.* □ *The cat sprang on the mouse and captured it.*

sprinkle someone or something **with** something to lightly cover someone or something with something by scattering or sprinkling. □ *The storm sprinkled us with a few droplets of water and then blew over.* □ *Larry sprinkled his grapefruit with powdered sugar.*

sprinkle something **on(to)** someone or something and **sprinkle** something **on**[†] to scatter or dribble something onto someone or something. □ *The minister sprinkled the water onto the baby.* □ *The cook sprinkled on a dusting of powdered sugar.*

sprout up to grow upward quickly, as do newly sprouted seedlings. □ *The seeds sprouted up in the warm rains.* □ *Many of the newly planted seeds failed to sprout up on time.*

sprout wings *Fig.* to behave so well as to resemble an angel. □ *The kid is not about to sprout wings, but he probably won't get into jail again.* □ *He was so good and helpful, I thought he would sprout wings.*

spruce someone or something **up**[†] **1.** *Lit.* to tidy up and groom someone or something. □ *Laura's mother took a few minutes to spruce her daughter up for the party.* □ *She spruced up her room each day.* **2.** *Fig.* to refurbish or renew someone or something. □ *Do you think we should spruce this room up a little?* □ *Yes, let's spruce up this room with new furniture and drapes.*

spur someone **on**[†] to urge someone onward; to egg someone on. (*Fig.* on applying spurs to a horse.) □ *The crowd spurred the runners on throughout the race.* □ *The cheering spurred on the runners.*

spurt out (of someone or something**)** and **spurt (out) (from** someone or something**)** to squirt out of someone or

S

something; to erupt in a stream out of someone or something. □ *Hot lava spurted out of the volcano.* □ *Hot lava spurted out from the volcano.* □ *The blood spurted out from Walter where he had been slashed.* □ *Blood spurted from the wound.* □ *The fountain had a carved fish with water spurting from its mouth.*

spurt something **out**† to eject something in a stream. □ *The octopus spurted its ink out as the scuba diver approached it.* □ *It spurted out all its ink.*

sputter out [for a flame] to go out in little puffs. □ *The candle flame flickered and sputtered out.* □ *The fire sputtered out after midnight and we all got very cold before down.*

sputter something **out**† to utter something while stuttering or faltering. (As when one is physically or mentally disoriented.) □ *She was so excited she could hardly sputter her name out.* □ *He could only sputter out a few words.*

spy (up)on someone or something to watch someone or something to learn secret or concealed information. (*Upon* is formal and less commonly used than *on*.) □ *Are you spying upon me?* □ *I wasn't spying on you! I was just trying to see who you were.*

squabble about someone or something to quarrel and disagree about someone or something. □ *Please stop squabbling about Jeff, or I'll put him on my team so neither of you can have him.* □ *There is no need to squabble about the last piece of pie. There's more in the kitchen.*

squabble over someone or something to fight over someone or something. □ *Please don't squabble over me. I don't want to be chosen by any of you!* □ *Stop squabbling over money and go out and get a job.*

squabble with someone to argue with someone. □ *Please don't squabble with your sister!* □ *I wish that everyone would stop squabbling with me!*

squabble with something to argue about something. □ *I won't squabble with what you said, but you are wrong.* □ *One political party will squabble with any issue the other party brings up.*

squander something **away**† to waste something; to use up something valuable wastefully. □ *Where is all the money I gave you last month? Did you squander it all away?* □ *Frank squandered away all his assets.*

squander something **on** someone or something to waste all of something on someone or something. □ *I am tired of squandering money on this rickety old house.* □ *I squandered a fortune on Roger and what did it get me?*

square accounts (with someone**) 1.** *Lit.* to settle one's financial accounts with someone. □ *I have to square accounts with the bank this week, or it'll take back my car.* □ *I called the bank and said I needed to come in and square accounts.* **2.** *Fig.* to get even with someone; to straighten out a misunderstanding with someone. □ *I'm going to square accounts with Tom. He insulted me in public, and he owes me an apology.* □ *Tom, you and I are going to have to square accounts.*

a **square deal** a fair and honest transaction; fair treatment. □ *All the workers want is a square deal, but their boss underpays them.* □ *You always get a square deal with that travel company.*

square (meal) a good and nutritious meal. (Always with quantifier when *square* is used without *meal*.) □ *I need three squares a day—at least.* □ *The old beggar looks like he could use a square meal.*

square off (for something**)** to get ready for an argument or a fight. □ *John was angry and appeared to be squaring off for a fight.* □ *When those two square off, everyone gets out of the way.*

a **square peg in a round hole** *Fig.* someone who is uncomfortable or who does not belong in a particular situation. (Also the cliché: **trying to fit a square peg into a round hole,** trying to combine two things that do not belong or fit together.) □ *I feel like a square peg in a round hole at my office. Everyone else there seems so ambitious, competitive, and dedicated to the work, but I just want to make a living.* □ *Trying to teach me math is like trying to fit a square peg into a round hole. I'm convinced my brain is not built right to understand algebra.*

square someone **away**† to get someone or something arranged or properly taken care of. □ *See if you can square Bob away in his new office.* □ *When you are squared away, come back and we'll talk.*

square something **off**† to make something square; to trim something until it is square. □ *You will have to square this corner off a bit so it will match the part it will be attached to.* □ *Please square off this corner.*

square something **up**† to cause something to have right angles. □ *Please square the door frames up better before you nail them in.* □ *Can you square up this box a little better?*

square something **with** someone to make certain that something is approved by a particular person. □ *I am sure I can square this matter with Sally.* □ *Sam intended to square everything with Henry when he had time.*

square up (for fighting**)** to get ready for an argument or a fight. □ *John was angry and appeared to be squaring up for a fight.* □ *When those two square up, everyone gets out of the way.*

square up to someone or something to face someone or something bravely; to tackle someone or something. □ *You'll have to square up to the bully or he'll make your life miserable.* □ *It's time to square up to your financial problems. You can't just ignore them.*

square up with someone to pay someone what one owes; to pay one's share of something to someone. □ *I'll square up with you later if you pay the whole bill now.* □ *Bob said he would square up with Tom for his share of the gas.*

square with someone **1.** *Lit.* to settle a disagreement with someone. □ *I will try to square with Fred before the end of the school year.* □ *Max refused to square with Lefty and they are still feuding.* **2.** *Fig.* to apologize to someone. □ *I will try to square with Harold. I really am sorry, you know.* □ *Finally, Mary squared with Alice and they forgave each other.*

square with something *Fig.* [for a statement] to agree, match, or correspond to something. □ *Your answer doesn't square with mine.* □ *The figures I have don't square with those the government has.*

squared away arranged or properly taken care of. □ *Is Ann squared away in her dorm room yet?* □ *I will talk to you when I am squared away.*

squash someone or something **up**† to grind someone or something up; to mash someone or something up. □ *You had better stay out of the traffic, or some big truck will squash you up!* □ *The truck squashed up the tiny car.*

squash something **down**† to crush something down; to pack something down. □ *Squash the ice cream down so the air will be pushed out.* □ *Who squashed down my hat?*

squash something **in**† to crush or make something concave by squashing or mashing. □ *The children squashed the Halloween jack-o'-lantern in and ruined it.* □ *Someone squashed in the lampshade.*

squash something **into** something and **squash** something **in**† to press or mash something into something. □ *She squashed the clay into the mold.* □ *She squashed in the clay and started to make a bowl.*

squash up against someone or something to press hard up against someone or something. (Usually said of something soft.) □ *The egg squashed up against the window and splattered all over.* □ *The pumpkin squashed up against the side of the truck.*

squawk about something to complain about something. □ *Stop squawking about how much money you lost. I lost twice as much.* □ *What are you squawking about now?*

squeak by (someone or something) **1.** *Fig.* to manage just to squeeze past someone or something. □ *I squeaked by the fat man in the hallway only to find myself blocked by another.* □ *I just barely squeaked by.* **2.** *Fig.* to manage just to get past a barrier represented by a person or thing, such as a difficult teacher or an examination. □ *Judy just squeaked by Professor Smith, who has a reputation for flunking students.* □ *I took the test and just squeaked by.*

squeak something **through** *Fig.* to manage just to get something accepted or approved. □ *I just managed to squeak the proposal through.* □ *Tom squeaked the application through at the last minute.*

squeak through (something) **1.** *Fig.* to manage just to squeeze through an opening. □ *The child squeaked through the opening and escaped.* □ *Sally squeaked through and got away.* **2.** *Fig.* to manage just to get past a barrier, such as an examination or interview. (Fig. on ①.) □ *Sally just barely squeaked through the interview, but she got the job.* □ *I wasn't too alert and I just squeaked through.*

The **squeaking wheel gets the oil.** and The **squeaky wheel gets the oil.** *Prov.* People who complain the most will get attention or what they want. □ *If you don't get good service at the hotel, make sure to tell the manager that you're dissatisfied. The squeaking wheel gets the oil.*

squeal (on someone**) (to** someone**)** *Fig.* to report someone to someone. □ *Max was afraid that the witness would squeal on him to the cops.* □ *Sally threatened to squeal to the boss.* □ *Please promise you won't squeal on me!*

squeal with something *Fig.* to shriek or squeak, exhibiting some characteristic emotion or experience, such as delight, pain, glee, etc. □ *The baby saw the bright picture and squealed with delight.* □ *Timmy squealed with excitement when he saw the presents and the birthday cake.*

squeeze by (someone or something**)** to manage just to press oneself past someone or something. □ *The hall was crowded and I had to squeeze by a number of rotund gen-*

tlemen. □ *I squeezed by the crowd and ran on to my appointment.*

squeeze someone or something **into** something and **squeeze** someone or something **in**† to press or push someone or something into something small. □ *Let's see if we can squeeze everyone into the car.* □ *Let's squeeze in one more.*

squeeze someone or something **through** (something**)** to push and compress until someone or something passes through something. □ *John's cellmate managed to squeeze John through the window just before the guards walked by.* □ *I squeezed some food through the crack and the trapped miner was glad to get it.*

squeeze someone or something **together** to press people or things together. □ *The driver squeezed us together so he could get more people in the taxi.* □ *See if you can squeeze the vegetables together a little so we can get more in the basket.*

squeeze someone or something **up**† to press people or things close together. □ *The usher tried to squeeze us up so she could seat more people.* □ *Don't squeeze up the cars too tight in the parking area.*

squeeze something **from** something **1.** *Lit.* to press something out of something; to press on something until something comes out. □ *Betty squeezed some toothpaste from the tube.* □ *Don't squeeze so much mustard from the bottle.* **2.** *Fig.* to get a little more of something from something. □ *Let's see if we can squeeze a few more miles from this tank of gas before we fill up again.* □ *I think I can squeeze another few minutes from this candle before I have to light a new one.*

squeeze something **out of** something and **squeeze** something **out**† to press something until something is expelled from something. □ *Claire squeezed some toothpaste out of the tube.* □ *She squeezed out some toothpaste.*

squeeze (themselves) together [for creatures] to press close together. □ *The little pigs squeezed themselves together to get a better chance at some food.* □ *They squeezed together and gobbled their dinner.* □ *They squeezed themselves together to keep warm.*

squeeze (themselves) up [for people] to press themselves closely together. □ *Everyone squeezed themselves up in the tiny car so there would be room for one more.* □ *Let's squeeze up so Jamie can sit down.* □ *They squeezed themselves up so they would take less space.*

squeeze through something to manage to press oneself through an opening. □ *I think I can squeeze through the window and get out of this place.* □ *The cat squeezed through a hole in the fence and got away.*

squeeze up against someone or something to press close up against someone or something. □ *He squeezed up against me, trying to keep warm.* □ *The puppies squeezed up against their mother.*

squiff out *Sl.* to collapse from drink. □ *Hank squiffed out at midnight, right on the dot.* □ *She kept from squiffing out and barely made it home.*

squint at someone or something to look at someone or something with the eyes partly closed. (When squinting, the eyes are partly closed by pressing the upper and lower

S

eyelids toward one another.) □ *Why are you squinting at me?* □ *I had to squint at the small print in order to read it.*

squint out of something **1.** to cast one's gaze from something, such as a place of concealment, with one's eyes partly closed. □ *The prisoner squinted out of the little hatch in the door to his cell.* □ *You could see that many people were squinting out of the windows, trying to get a good view of the movie star who was visiting.* **2.** to cast one's gaze through something, such as glasses, one eye, etc., with one's eyes partly closed. □ *She squinted out of one eye in the bright sun.* □ *Tony squinted out of his glasses and his mother decided that he needed to have his eyes checked again.*

squirm in(to something**)** to press into something that is tight; to crawl or wiggle into something tight. (For people, this is often clothing that is too tight. For other creatures, it is more variable.) □ *Dave squirmed into his jeans and pledged to himself that he would lose some weight.* □ *He squirmed in and knew he could never close the zipper.*

squirm out (of something**) 1.** *Lit.* to crawl or wiggle out of something. □ *The worm squirmed out of its hole and was gobbled up by a bird.* □ *The worm squirmed out.* **2.** *Fig.* to escape doing something; to escape the responsibility for having done something. □ *He agreed to go but squirmed out at the last minute.* □ *You did it and you can't squirm out of it by denying it!*

squirm with something to fidget or move around restlessly, showing irritation of some type. □ *The children squirmed with impatience, but they kept quiet.* □ *I squirmed with discomfort, hoping that the time on the aircraft would pass rapidly.*

squirrel something **away**[†] *Fig.* to hide something or store something in the way that a squirrel stores nuts for use in the winter. □ *I squirreled a little money away for an occasion such as this.* □ *Liz squirreled away a lot of money while she was working.*

squirt from something [for a liquid] to be ejected in a spurt from something. □ *The water squirted from the hose.* □ *Juice squirted from the orange when I squeezed it.*

squirt out (of someone or something**)** [for something, especially a liquid] to gush or spurt forth from someone or something. □ *In the horror movie, black stuff squirted out of this guy whenever he got angry.* □ *A lot of blood squirted out of the gash and I closed my eyes.*

squirt something **at** someone or something **1.** to direct a narrow stream of liquid onto someone or something. □ *They squirted the water at the cat and it ran away.* □ *Who is squirting catsup at people?* **2.** to direct a device for squirting liquid at someone or something. □ *Tom squirted the hose at the cat.* □ *Who is squirting the firehose at the front of the house?*

squirt something **out of** something and **squirt** something **out**[†] to cause something to spurt out of something. □ *He squirted a bit of the vaccine out of the syringe, making sure the needle was not clogged.* □ *He squirted out a bit of the vaccine.*

a **stab at** someone Go to a **try at** someone.

stab at someone or something to thrust at someone or something with something sharp, such as a knife. □ *The hor-*

rid man stabbed at me and missed. □ *The stork stabbed at the frog with its beak.*

a **stab at** something Go to a **try at** something.

stab someone **in** something to stab someone in a particular place. □ *Max stabbed a prison guard in the belly and left him to die.* □ *Tom stabbed himself in the thigh by accident.*

stab someone **in the back 1.** *Lit.* to thrust a knife into someone's back. □ *Max planned to stab his hostage in the back if he screamed.* □ *The murderer stabbed his victim in the back and fled.* **2.** *Fig.* to betray someone. □ *I wish you would not gossip about me. There is no need to stab me in the back.*

stab something **at** someone or something to thrust something at someone or something. □ *The hunter stabbed a stick at the bear to see if there was any life at all left in it.* □ *The stork tried to stab its beak at me as I held it, but I held tight while the vet examined it.*

stack something **against** someone or something to make a pile of something that leans against someone or something. (See also **stack the deck (against** someone or something**).**) □ *Watch what you are doing! Why are you stacking the books against me? They will fall when I move.* □ *Stack the books against the wall.*

stack something **up**[†] to make a stack of things. (Also without the *up*.) □ *Where should I stack them up?* □ *Please stack up these boxes.*

stack the cards (against someone or something**)** Go to next.

stack the deck (against someone or something**)** and **stack the cards (against** someone or something**)** to arrange things against someone or something. (Originally from card playing; stacking the deck is to cheat by arranging the cards to be dealt out to one's advantage.) □ *I can't get ahead at my office. Someone has stacked the cards against me.* □ *Do you really think that someone has stacked the deck? Isn't it just fate?*

stack up [for something] to accumulate, as in stacks. □ *Your work is stacking up. You will have to work late to finish it.* □ *I hate to let my work stack up. I have to do it sooner or later.*

stack up to someone or something [for someone or something] to measure up favorably when compared to someone or something. □ *How do you think I stack up to Liz?* □ *My car stacks up pretty well to yours.*

stagger around to go about tottering or wobbling, especially as if drunk. □ *The wounded man staggered around and then fell.* □ *A lot of people came out of the party and staggered around.*

stagger from something to move out of a place, tottering. □ *The drunk staggered from the tavern and fell into the gutter.* □ *The wounded man staggered from the door and called for help.*

stagger in(to some place**)** to walk into some place, tottering. □ *The old man staggered into the room and collapsed.* □ *He staggered in and fell down.*

stagger out (of some place**)** to walk out of some place, tottering. □ *The drunk staggered out of the tavern and fell down.* □ *She staggered out and sat on the curb.*

stagger under something to struggle or totter under a serious burden, either a heavy object or a serious problem or responsibility. □ *The welfare budget is staggering under the burden of having to care for many people.* □ *Sam staggered under the heavy load and finally fell.*

stain something **with** something **1.** to cause a blemish or blotch on something with something. (Usually an accident.) □ *Judy stained the carpet with some grape juice.* □ *You will stain your clothing with that food if you drop any of it.* **2.** to affect the coloring of something through the use of a chemical stain. (A purposeful act, much the same as painting.) □ *Walter stained the house with a long-lasting reddish stain.* □ *We decided to stain the doors with a special varnish rather than paint them.* **3.** *Fig.* to injure or blemish someone's reputation. □ *They stained his reputation with their charges.* □ *I don't want to do anything that would stain my reputation.*

stake a claim to someone or something *Fig.* to state or record one's claim on someone or something. (Alludes to marking off an area by pounding in wooden stakes.) □ *She staked a claim to Jeff and told all her rivals to stay away.* □ *The prospector staked a claim to the gold-rich area.*

stake one's **reputation on** someone or something to risk harming one's reputation on someone or something. □ *Of course Denise is great. I will stake my reputation on her!* □ *It may be so, but I wouldn't stake my reputation on it.*

stake out a claim to something and **stake out a claim on** something to lay claim to something. □ *The prospector staked out a claim to the promising piece of land.* □ *We staked out a claim on two seats at the side of the auditorium.*

stake someone or something **out**† **1.** to position a person so that someone or something can be observed or followed. □ *The cops staked the car out and made the arrest.* □ *Barlowe staked out the apartment building and watched patiently for an hour.* **2.** to position a person to observe someone or something. □ *He staked his best operative out in front of the building.* □ *We staked out two men to keep watch.*

stake someone **to** something to make a loan of something to someone. □ *I will stake you to a hundred bucks if that will help.* □ *Jed refused to stake Tex to a loan.*

stake something **off**† to mark out the boundaries of an area of land with stakes. □ *The prospectors staked an area off for themselves.* □ *The prospectors staked off an area in which they would look for gold.*

stalk in(to some place) to stride into a place, perhaps indignantly. □ *Carl stalked into the manager's office and began his tirade.* □ *He stalked in and began to complain.*

stalk out of some place to stride out of a place indignantly. □ *Jeff stalked out of the store and went straight to the police.* □ *Mary got angry and stalked out of the meeting.*

stall for time to cause a delay intentionally. □ *You are just stalling for time. Please hurry.* □ *She is stalling for time, hoping someone will rescue her.*

stall someone or something **for** something to delay someone or something for a period of time. □ *I stalled him for as long as I could.* □ *I could not stall the proceedings for another second.*

stall someone or something **off**† to put off or delay someone or something. □ *The sheriff is at the door. I'll stall him*

off while you get out the back door. □ *You can stall off the sheriff, but you can't stall off justice.*

stammer something **out**† to manage to say something, but only haltingly. □ *Fred stammered the words out haltingly.* □ *He stammered out the name of the winner.*

stamp a fire out† to extinguish a fire by stamping on it. □ *Quick, stamp that fire out before it spreads.* □ *Tom stamped out the sparks before they started a fire.*

stamp on someone or something to strike down hard on someone or something with the bottom of the foot. □ *The attacker stamped on his victim after he had knocked him down.* □ *Walter stamped on a spider.*

stamp someone or something **as** something to label someone or something as something; to mark someone or something as something. □ *His manner stamped him as a fool.* □ *The committee stamped the proposal as wasteful.*

stamp someone or something **with** something to affix a label onto someone or something with something; to apply a particular message or symbol onto someone or something, as with a rubber stamp. □ *Judy stamped everyone who went into the dance with a symbol that showed that each had paid admission.* □ *Mary stamped the bill with the PAID symbol.*

stamp someone **out**† *Sl.* to get rid of or kill someone. (Fig. on **stamp** something **out.**) □ *You just can't stamp somebody out on your own!* □ *The victim wanted to stamp out the robbers without a trial.*

stamp something **onto** something to affix an informative label onto something, as with a rubber stamp. □ *She stamped her name and address onto all her books.* □ *Tom stamped his identification onto all his papers and books.*

stamp something **out**† *Fig.* to eliminate something. □ *The doctors hope they can stamp cancer out.* □ *Many people think that they can stamp out evil.*

stamp something **out of** someone or something and **stamp** something **out**† *Fig.* to eliminate a characteristic of someone or something; to destroy a characteristic of someone or something. □ *I would really like to stamp that mean streak out of you.* □ *We were not able to stamp the excess costs out of the proposal and had to reject it.* □ *We couldn't stamp out their bad behavior.*

stamp something **(up)on** someone or something to affix an informative label onto someone or something, as with a rubber stamp. (*Upon* is formal and less commonly used than *on.*) □ *The attendant stamped a date upon each person who entered the dance hall.* □ *The person at the door stamped something on my hand when I came in.*

stampede in(to some place) [for a crowd of people or other creatures] to move rapidly into a place, as if in panic. □ *The shoppers stampeded into the store the minute the doors opened.* □ *The doors opened and the shoppers stampeded in.*

stampede out of some place [for a crowd of people or other creatures] to move rapidly out of a place, as if in panic. □ *The patrons stampeded out of the smoky theater.* □ *The cattle stampeded out of the corral.*

stampede someone or something **into** something to cause people or other creatures to move rapidly into a place, in panic or as if in panic. □ *The loud noises stampeded the crowd into the parking lot across from the stadium.* □ *The cowboys stampeded the cattle into the corral.*

S

639

stand a chance (of doing something**)** to have a chance of doing something. □ *Do you think I stand a chance of winning first place?* □ *Everyone stands a chance of catching the disease.*

stand against someone or something Go to **against** someone or something.

stand and deliver to give up something to someone who demands it. (Originally used by highway robbers asking for passengers' valuables.) □ *And when the tax agent says "Stand and deliver" you have to be prepared to pay what is demanded.* □ *The robber stopped the coach and demanded of Lady Ellen, "Stand and deliver!"*

stand apart (from someone or something**)** **1.** *Lit.* to stand, separated from someone or something. □ *Please stand apart from the person next to you. We want to see the table between you.* □ *Stand apart. Leave some space between you.* **2.** *Fig.* to appear clearly different from other things or people. □ *Alice really stands apart from her peers.* □ *This book really stands apart. It is much better than the others.*

stand around to wait around, standing; to loiter. □ *Please don't stand around. Get busy!* □ *Why are all these people standing around doing nothing?*

stand aside 1. *Lit.* to step aside; to get out of the way. □ *Please stand aside while the bridal party passes by.* □ *The guests stood aside while the bride and groom left.* **2.** *Fig.* to withdraw and ignore something; to remain passive while something happens. □ *He just stood aside and let his kids behave as they pleased.* □ *She stood aside and did not try to come between them.*

stand at something **1.** to stand in front of something; to stand in the vicinity of something. □ *I stood at the window, watching the traffic.* □ *Tom stood at the door, counting people as they came in.* **2.** to stand or remain in a particular state, such as attention or readiness. □ *The troops stood at attention for a very long time.* □ *The entire platoon is standing at readiness, awaiting further orders.*

stand back (from someone or something**)** to stand or move well away and to the rear of someone or something. □ *Stand back from Sam. He is really angry.* □ *Would you please stand back from the edge?*

stand behind someone or something Go to **stand (in) back of** someone or something.

stand between someone or something **and** someone or something else to position oneself between things and people, so as to act as a barrier. □ *I don't want to stand between you and your family.* □ *We won't stand between you and your goals.*

stand by to wait and remain ready. (Generally heard in communication, such as broadcasting, telephones, etc.) □ *Your transatlantic telephone call is almost ready. Please stand by.* □ *Is everyone ready for the telecast? Only ten seconds—stand by.*

stand by someone to support someone; to continue supporting someone even when things are bad. □ *Don't worry. I'll stand by you no matter what.* □ *I feel as though I have to stand by my brother even if he goes to jail.*

stand by someone or something to stand next to someone or something. □ *Jeff, please stand by Judy. I want to take your picture.* □ *Can I stand by the window and watch the birds?*

stand clear of something Go to **clear of** something.

stand close to someone or something Go to **close to** someone or something.

stand corrected to admit that one has been wrong. □ *I realize that I accused him wrongly. I stand corrected.* □ *We appreciate now that our conclusions were wrong. We stand corrected.*

stand down 1. to step down, particularly from the witness stand in a courtroom. □ *The bailiff told the witness to stand down.* □ *Please stand down and take your seat.* **2.** [for military forces] to move away from readiness for war. □ *After the peace treaty was signed, troops on both sides stood down.*

stand for something **1.** to permit something; to endure something. □ *The teacher won't stand for any whispering in class.* □ *We just can't stand for that kind of behavior.* **2.** to signify something. □ *In a traffic signal, the red light stands for "stop."* □ *The abbreviation Dr. stands for "doctor."* **3.** to endorse or support an ideal. □ *The mayor claims to stand for honesty in government and jobs for everyone.* □ *Every candidate for public office stands for all the good things in life.*

stand head and shoulders above someone or something *Fig.* [for someone or something] to be considerably superior to someone or something. □ *Alice stands head and shoulders above all the rest of the people we interviewed.* □ *Your proposal stands head and shoulders above the rest.*

stand idly by Go to **sit idly by.**

stand in awe (of someone or something**)** *Fig.* to be overwhelmed with respect for someone or something. □ *Many people stand in awe of the president.* □ *Bob says he stands in awe of a big juicy steak. I think he's exaggerating.*

stand (in) back of someone or something and **stand behind** someone or something **1.** *Lit.* to place oneself at the rear of someone or something. □ *Please stand behind your friends.* □ *The police told them to stand behind the fence.* **2.** *Fig.* to guarantee someone or something; to guarantee the performance or worth of someone or something. □ *I will stand back of Elaine. I trust her totally.* □ *The manufacturer stands behind this product.*

stand in (for someone**)** to substitute for someone; to serve in someone's place. □ *The famous opera singer was ill, and an inexperienced singer had to stand in for her.* □ *The new singer was grateful for the opportunity to stand in.*

stand in someone's **way** Go to **in** someone's **way.**

stand knee-deep in something Go to **knee-deep in** something.

stand off from someone or something to be or remain at some distance from someone or something. □ *Charles stood off from the group.* □ *Mary stood off from the fireside, where all the excitement was taking place.*

stand off some place [for a ship] to wait some distance from a point on shore. □ *The ship stood off at some distance, waiting for its berth.* □ *We stood off about a mile from shore and went to land in small boats called tenders.*

stand on ceremony to hold rigidly to protocol or formal manners. (Often in the negative.) □ *Please help yourself to more. Don't stand on ceremony.* □ *We are very informal around here. Hardly anyone stands on ceremony.*

S

stand on one's **dignity** to remain dignified in spite of difficulties. □ *I will stand on my dignity to the very end.* □ *She stood on her dignity and ignored all the nonsense going on around her.*

stand on one's **head 1.** *Lit.* to stand or balance vertically with one's head and hands—rather than one's feet—touching the floor. □ *Can you stand on your head?* □ *Todd stood on his head as a form of exercise.* **2.** *Fig.* to attempt to impress someone by hard work or difficult feats. □ *You don't have to stand on your head to succeed in this office. Just do your assigned work on time.*

stand on one's **(own) two feet** to act in an independent and forthright manner. □ *I can stand on my own two feet without any help from you!* □ *Dave will be better off when he gets a job and can stand on his own feet.*

stand on something **1.** to step or tread on something, perhaps by accident. □ *I didn't mean to stand on the cat's tail.* □ *Please don't stand on the nice carpet with muddy shoes.* **2.** to elevate oneself by standing on something, such as a chair or stool. □ *Tony stood on a stool so he could reach the cookie jar.* □ *Don't stand on that box. It won't hold you and it's not tall enough.*

stand one's **ground** and **hold** one's **ground** to stand up for one's rights; to resist an attack. □ *The lawyer tried to confuse me when I was giving testimony, but I managed to stand my ground.* □ *Some people were trying to crowd us out of the line for tickets, but we held our ground.*

stand out (against someone or something**)** to be prominent or conspicuous against a background of someone or something. □ *Your red coat really stands out against all those dull brown ones.* □ *With that deep tan, you really stand out against the others.*

stand out (from someone or something**)** to be prominent when compared to someone or something. □ *As a programmer, she stands out from all the others.* □ *This entry stands out from all the rest in this show.*

stand out (from something**)** to protrude from something. □ *One very straight branch in particular stood out from the tree and looked suitable for a post.* □ *The branch stood out and made a perfect place to hang my shirt while I worked.*

stand outside ((of) something**)** to remain outside of a place, standing. (*Of* is usually retained before pronouns.) □ *Judy stood outside the shop, waiting for it to open.* □ *How long have you been standing outside the door in this cold wind?*

stand over someone or something to hover over someone or something; to monitor or keep close watch on someone or something. □ *Please don't stand over me while I work!* □ *Dave stood over the machine, making sure it did what it was supposed to do.*

stand pat (on something**)** to stick firmly to one's position or opinions. □ *I am going to stand pat on this issue.* □ *I thought you would stand pat in the absence of new information.*

stand someone **in good stead** [for something] to be of great use and benefit to someone. □ *I know that my large vocabulary will always stand me in good stead at college.* □ *Any experience you can get in dealing with the public will stand you in good stead no matter what line of work you go into.*

stand someone or something **off** to repel the attack of someone or something; to defend against someone or something; to stave someone or something off. □ *It was all we could do to stand them off.* □ *The soldiers stood off the attackers as long as they could.*

stand someone **to a treat** to pay for a treat for someone. □ *Come on. Let's go out and eat. I'll stand you to a treat.* □ *It seems as if I am always standing someone to a treat.*

stand someone **up†** **1.** to place someone into a standing position. □ *I tried to stand him up, but he was just too tired.* □ *Let's try to stand up Timmy and get him awake.* **2.** to fail to show up for a meeting or a date. □ *He stood her up once too often, so she broke up with him.* □ *Tom stood up Mary once, and she never forgave him.*

stand something **on its head** *Fig.* to stir up, baffle, or surprise a group or organization. □ *The new owners came into the company and stood it on its head. Nothing will ever be the same.* □ *The mayor set out to stand the town on its head, but after one month, it was business as usual.*

stand still for something Go to **hold still for** something.

stand tall to be brave and proud. □ *I can still stand tall. I'm innocent.* □ *Our athletes stand tall in the knowledge that they did their best.*

stand the test of time *Prov.* to be well regarded; to last for a long time. □ *Bill and Nancy just celebrated their fiftieth wedding anniversary. Their marriage has stood the test of time.* □ *The singer's work was not popular while she was alive, but it has stood the test of time.*

stand there with one's **bare face hanging out** *Rur.* to stand some place looking helpless and stupid. □ *Say something. Don't just stand there with your bare face hanging out.* □ *She just stood there with her bare face hanging out while they took away everything she owned.*

stand to lose something to be likely to lose something or have it taken away. □ *I stand to lose hundreds of dollars if I am not there on time.*

stand to reason to seem reasonable. □ *It stands to reason that it'll be colder in January than it is in November.* □ *It stands to reason that Bill left in a hurry, although no one saw him go.*

stand together 1. to stand in a group. □ *All the members of the family stood together for a photograph.* □ *Please stand together so I can count you.* **2.** to remain united. □ *We must stand together if we want to defeat this enemy.* □ *If we don't stand together, we will be defeated one by one.*

stand trial to be the accused person in a trial before a judge; to be on trial. □ *He had to stand trial for perjury and obstruction of justice.*

stand up 1. to arise from a sitting or reclining position. □ *He stood up and looked across the valley.* □ *She had been sitting for so long that it was a pleasure to stand up.* **2.** to be in a standing position. □ *I've been standing up all day and I'm exhausted.* □ *I stood up throughout the whole trip because there were no more seats on the train.* **3.** to wear well; to remain sound and intact. □ *This material just doesn't stand up well when it's washed.* □ *Her work doesn't stand up under close scrutiny.* **4.** [for an assertion] to remain believable. □ *His testimony will not stand up in court.* □ *When the police checked the story, it did not stand up.*

S

stand up against someone or something to withstand or hold one's own against someone or something. □ *He's good, but he can't stand up against Jill.* □ *Can this tent stand up against the wind?*

stand up and be counted to state one's support (for someone or something). □ *If you believe in more government help for farmers, write your representative—stand up and be counted.* □ *I'm generally in favor of what you propose, but not enough to stand up and be counted.*

stand up before someone Go to **up before** someone.

stand up for someone or something to take the side of someone or something; to defend someone or something. □ *I hope you will stand up for me if the going gets rough.* □ *We will have to stand up for our rights someday.*

stand up in court [for a case] to survive a test in a court of law. □ *Do you think that this case will stand up in court?* □ *These charges will never stand up in court. They are too vague.*

stand up to someone or something to take a stand against someone or something; to hold one's ground or principles in the face of a challenge by someone or something. □ *He is a tough customer, and you have to learn to stand up to him.* □ *Can the witness stand up to questioning by the prosecution?*

stand up with someone to attend someone who is being married. (Usually refers to males.) □ *I agreed to stand up with my buddy at his wedding.* □ *Tom stood up with Harry when the latter got married.*

stand (up)on someone or something to be on someone or something, standing. (*Upon* is formal and less commonly used than *on.*) □ *To help his back pain, he lay down on his tummy and Jill stood upon him, digging her toes into his back.* □ *Please don't stand on the bed.*

stand well with someone to be acceptable or agreeable to someone. □ *That idea doesn't stand well with the management.* □ *I hope my suggestions stand well with you.*

stand with someone to unite with someone, as in defense. □ *Don't worry. I'll stand with you to the end.* □ *He stood with her and they faced the threat together.*

a **standing joke** a subject that regularly and over a period of time causes amusement whenever it is mentioned. □ *Uncle Jim's driving was a standing joke. He used to drive incredibly slowly.* □ *Their mother's inability to make a decision was a standing joke in the Smith family all their lives.*

star as someone or something [for someone] to be a featured performer, representing a particular person, or play in a particular role. □ *Judy starred as Evita in the broadway production of the same name.* □ *Mary starred as an aging countess.*

star in something to be a featured actor in a play, movie, opera, etc. □ *Roger starred in an off-Broadway play last season.* □ *Mary always wanted to star in her own movie, but it was not to be.*

star-crossed lovers ill-fated lovers. □ *I suppose that Romeo and Juilet are star-crossed lovers.*

stare at someone or something to look fixedly at someone or something. □ *Why are you staring at me?* □ *I was staring at the scenery behind you.*

stare into something to gaze fixedly into something. □ *She just sat there, staring into space.* □ *Tom stared into the water, hoping to see a fish or maybe a turtle.*

stare out at someone or something **1.** to be in a place staring outward at someone or something. □ *I stayed in my little room and stared out at the others having fun in the crisp fall air.* □ *We stared out at the deep snow.* **2.** [for a face or eyes visible in a place] to be seen staring outward from that place. □ *Two bright little cat eyes stared out at me from the basket.* □ *Her faced stared out of the tiny window.*

stare someone **down**† to pressure someone to capitulate, back down, or yield by staring. □ *Don't try to stare me down. I have nerves of steel.* □ *I tried to stare down my opponent, but it didn't work.*

stare someone **in the face 1.** Go to **look** someone **in the face. 2.** [for evidence] to confront someone directly. (Fig. on **stare** someone **in the face; look** someone **in the face.**) □ *Finally, the truth stared me in the face, and I had to admit to myself what had really happened.* □ *When the facts in the case stared the jury in the face, there was nothing they could do but acquit.*

stark raving mad *Cliché* totally insane; completely crazy; out of control. (Often an exaggeration.) □ *When she heard about what happened at the office, she went stark raving mad.* □ *You must be start raving mad if you think I would trust you with my car!*

***stars in** one's **eyes** *Fig.* an obsession with celebrities, movies, and the theater. (Alludes to movie stars. *Typically: **get** ~; **have** ~; **give** one ~.) □ *Many young people have stars in their eyes at this age.* □ *Anne has stars in her eyes. She wants to go to Hollywood.*

***a start 1.** and ***a jump(start)** battery power to help start someone's car, etc. (*Typically: **get** ~; **have** ~; **give** someone ~.) □ *My car is stalled. I need to get a start.* □ *I got my car going. I got a jump from John.* **2.** help in beginning one's career; a first opportunity in the beginning of one's career. (*Typically: **get** ~; **have** ~; **give** someone ~.) □ *She got a start in show business in Cincinnati.* □ *She had a start when she was only four.*

start a fire under someone Go to **a fire under** someone.

start an all-out effort Go to **an all-out effort.**

start as something to begin in some original condition or status. □ *Every forest fire starts as a small spark.* □ *The argument started as a small disagreement.*

start back (to some place**)** to begin the journey back to a place. □ *When do we start back to Chicago?* □ *It's time to start back.*

start for some place to begin a journey to some place. □ *When shall we start for Springfield?* □ *We will start for Detroit before dawn.*

start from scratch to start from the very beginning; to start from nothing. □ *Whenever I bake a cake, I start from scratch. I never use a cake mix in a box.* □ *I built every bit of my own house. I started from scratch and did everything with my own hands.*

start from some place **1.** [for someone] to begin a journey at some place. (The emphasis is on the location of the start of the journey.) □ *We started from California.* □ *Where will you start from?* **2.** [for a journey] to begin from a particular point. □ *The journey started from Chicago.* □ *Our trip started from the airport in New York.*

start in on someone or something to begin dealing with, discussing, or chastising someone or something. □ *Please don't start in on me again! You said enough the previous three times.* □ *When will you be ready to start in on painting the house?*

start off to begin; to set out on a journey. □ *When do you want to start off?* □ *We will start off as soon as we can get everything packed.*

start off as someone or something to begin in a particular status, character, rank, etc. □ *I started off as a waiter and ended up as the owner of the restaurant.* □ *This tree started off as a tiny seedling only a few years ago.*

start off (by doing something) to begin a process by doing a particular thing first. □ *Can I start off by singing the school song?* □ *That's a good way to start off.*

start off from some place to begin a journey from some place. (The emphasis is on the inception of the journey.) □ *We will start off from Detroit and drive to Chicago.* □ *He started off from work rather than home.*

start off (on something) **1.** to begin a series or sequence. □ *Today I start off on the first volume of my trilogy.* □ *I am ready to start off now.* **2.** to begin a journey. □ *When do we start off on our trip?* □ *I'm ready to start off. What about you?*

start off on the wrong foot and **step off on the wrong foot** *Fig.* to begin things incorrectly. (As if one were beginning to march and began on the right rather than the left foot.) □ *Give me some advice. I don't want to start off on the wrong foot.* □ *Tim stepped off on the wrong foot in his new job.*

start (off) with a bang *Fig.* to begin with considerable excitement. □ *The program started off with a bang and the whole show was great.* □ *The day started off with a bang and kept going that way.*

start (off) with a clean slate and **start (over) with a clean slate** *Fig.* to start out again afresh; to ignore the past and start over again. □ *I plowed under all last year's flowers so I could start with a clean slate next spring.* □ *If I start off with a clean slate, then I'll know exactly what each plant is.* □ *When Bob got out of jail, he started over with a clean slate.*

start (off) with someone or something to begin a task or a process with someone or something. □ *I will start off with one volunteer and then add others as we go along.* □ *I will start off with one hot dog and get another later if I want it.*

start on someone or something **1.** to begin dealing with someone or something. □ *We have finished talking about Gary, and now we will start on Bob.* □ *We will start on dessert after you have finished your broccoli.* **2.** to begin to castigate someone or something □ *Don't start on me! I didn't do anything wrong!* □ *The politician started on the opposing party, and everyone in the audience cheered.*

start out to begin. □ *Whenever you are ready, we will start out.* □ *We can't start out until Tom is here.*

start out as something to begin one's career as something. □ *I started out as a clerk and two years later I'm still a clerk!* □ *I wanted to start out as an assistant manager.*

start out (on something) to begin something, such as a trip, a career, an investigation, etc. □ *When we started out on this investigation, I never dreamed we would uncover so much.* □ *What time did you start out this morning?*

start out with someone or something to begin something in association with someone or something. □ *I started out the project with Jeff, but he had to be replaced.* □ *We started out with the Acme Corp., but they could not handle all our work.*

start over to begin again. □ *I have messed this up so much that there is nothing to do now but start over.* □ *When you start over, try to do it right this time.*

start (over) with a clean slate Go to start (off) with a clean slate.

start someone **in (as** something) and **start** someone **out (as** something) to start someone on a job as a certain kind of worker. □ *I got a job in a restaurant today. They started me in as a dishwasher.* □ *I now work for the telephone company. They started me out as a local operator.*

start someone **off**[†] **(on** something) to cause someone to begin on a task or job. □ *I have to start Jeff off on this task, then I will talk to you.* □ *I will start off my workers on the job tomorrow.*

start someone **out (as** something) Go to start someone in (as something).

start someone **out at** an amount of money to start someone working at a particular salary. □ *We will start you out at $30,000.* □ *I wanted to be started out at $35,000.*

start someone **over** to cause someone to begin again; to lead someone to begin again. □ *The orchestra messed up the first few bars, so the conductor started them over again.* □ *I hope the conductor doesn't start us over again. This is getting boring to play.*

start someone **up**[†] **(in** something) to help someone get a start in some enterprise. □ *My uncle started me up in business.* □ *I started up my niece in the candy business.*

start something to start a fight or an argument. (*Something* can be replaced by *anything* or *nothing* with the negative.) □ *Hey, you! Better be careful unless you want to start something.* □ *I don't want to start anything. I'm just leaving.*

start something **up**[†] to start something, such as a car or some procedure. (Also without *up.*) □ *It was cold, but I managed to start up the car without any difficulty.* □ *We can't start the project up until we have more money.*

start something **up**[†] **with** something to use something in the process of starting something else. □ *Do you have to start this old car up with a crank?* □ *Do you start up this car with a crank?*

start the ball rolling Go to get the ball rolling.

start up to begin; to begin running, as with an engine. □ *The car started up without a problem.* □ *The engines of the plane started up one by one.*

start up with someone or something to begin by using someone or something. □ *We will start up with two clerks and add more as we grow.* □ *We started up with one old cash register, and now we have six.*

startle someone **out of** something to frighten someone very badly. (The *something* that may be lost may be expressed as *wits, senses, ten years' growth,* etc.) □ *The explosion star-*

S

tled Polly out of her senses. □ I frightened myself out of ten years' growth.

starve for some food to be very hungry for something. □ I am just starved for some fresh peaches. □ We were starved for dinner by the time we finally got to eat.

starve for someone or something *Fig.* to have a strong desire or need for someone or something. (Based on **starved for** some food.) □ I am starved for Jane. I miss her so! □ Claire was starved for affection.

starve someone or an animal **into** something to force someone or an animal to do something by starvation. □ The torturers finally starved the prisoner into telling the battle plans. □ They starved the water buffalo into a state of weakness.

starve someone or an animal **out of** some place and **starve** someone or an animal **out**† to force a living creature to come out of a hiding place or a place of security by starvation. □ The attackers tried to starve the people out of the walled city. □ We tried to starve out the mice.

stash something **away**† to hide something; to set something aside for use at a later time. □ Please stash this away somewhere. You may need it someday. □ You should stash away some money for later.

stash something **in** something to put or shove something into something; to store or hide something in something. □ You should stash your food in a place that is safe from bears when you go camping. □ I stashed my clothes in my suitcase and called a taxi.

state of mind basic attitude or outlook at a point in time. □ She was in a terrible state of mind when she was interviewed for a job.

state of the art using the most recent technology. (Hyphenated before nouns.) □ Our company's computer setup is strictly state of the art. □ This state-of-the-art radio is capable of filling the whole room with sound.

station someone **at** something to position or place someone near something. □ The manager stationed a receptionist at the door. □ Would you station a guard at the back door to keep people out?

stave someone or something **off**† to hold someone or something off; to defend against the attack of someone or something. (See also **stave** something **off**.) □ The citizen was not able to stave the mugger off. □ The army staved off the attackers for three hours without letup.

stave something **in**† to crush something in. (The past tense is usually *stove* with ships, and otherwise, *staved*.) □ The rocks on the reef staved the hull of the ship in. □ The angry sailor staved in the cask of rum.

stave something **off**† to delay or postpone something unwanted, such as hunger, foreclosure, death, etc. (See also **stave** someone or something **off**.) □ He could stave his thirst off no longer. Despite the enemy sentries, he made a dash for the stream. □ The lost hiker could not stave off her hunger any longer.

stay abreast of someone or something Go to **abreast of** someone or something.

stay after someone **(about** something**)** Go to **keep after** someone **(about** something**)**.

stay after (someone or something**)** to remain behind later than someone or something. □ I will stay after the others and clean up. □ I would be happy to stay after school.

stay ahead of something Go to **ahead of** something.

stay ahead of the game Go to **ahead of the game**.

stay aloof from someone or something Go to **aloof from** someone or something.

stay at some place **1.** to remain at a place. □ Have you ever tried to make a cat stay at one place? □ Please stay at home until I call you. **2.** to live at a place temporarily. □ I am staying at the Statler Hotel. □ At what hotel are you staying while you are in town?

stay at something to keep working at something. □ You should stay at something until you finish it. □ She couldn't seem to stay at her place of work for a whole day.

stay away (from someone or something**)** Go to **away (from** someone or something**)**.

stay back (from something**)** to keep one's distance from someone or something. □ Stay back from the lawn mower! □ This is dangerous. Stay back!

stay behind [for someone] to remain in a place when others have left. □ I will stay behind and tell the late arrivers where you have gone. □ Fred always stayed behind to clean up.

stay behind someone or something Go to **behind** someone or something.

stay by someone or something to remain close to someone or something. □ Please stay by me until we get through this crowd of rough-looking people. □ Stay by the wall and move along slowly.

stay clear of someone or something to keep one's distance from something, usually something dangerous. □ Please stay clear of me. I have the flu. □ Stay clear of that machine. It is dangerous.

stay down to remain in a prone, squatting, or sitting position. □ Stay down until the danger is over. □ Stay down so they won't see you.

stay for something to remain in a place to participate in something. □ Would you please stay for dinner? □ I am sorry, but we cannot stay for dinner.

stay in limbo Go to **in limbo**.

stay in (something**)** to remain inside a place or thing; to stay indoors. □ Please stay in the house. It's too cold to go outside. □ You should stay in when it's this cold.

stay in the back of someone's **mind** Go to **in the back of** someone's **mind**.

stay in the boonies Go to **in the boondocks**.

stay in the dark (about someone or something**)** Go to **in the dark (about** someone or something**)**.

stay in the fast lane Go to **in the fast lane**.

stay in touch (with someone or something**)** Go to **keep in touch (with** someone or something**)**.

stay loose Go to **hang loose**.

stay off (something**)** to keep off of something. □ Please stay off my lawn! □ Stay off!

stay on a diet Go to *on a diet*.

stay on (after someone or something**)** Go to *linger on (after* someone or something**)**.

stay on course Go to *on course*.

stay on (one's) guard (against someone or something**)** Go to *on (one's) guard (against* someone or something**)**.

stay on one's **toes** Go to *on one's toes*.

stay on (some place) to remain at a place longer than had been planned. □ *I stayed on in Paris for nearly two years.* □ *Mary liked it there and decided to stay on.*

stay on something **1.** to remain on something, such as a horse, road, stool, etc. □ *The first time I rode, I could hardly stay on the horse.* □ *It was so slippery that I had trouble staying on the road.* **2.** to continue to pursue something. □ *I will stay on this problem until it is settled.* □ *She stayed on the matter for weeks until it had been dealt with.*

stay on the good side of someone Go to *keep on the right side of* someone.

stay on top of someone or something **1.** *Lit.* to remain positioned on the top of someone or something. □ *Please stay on top of the hill until we call you.* □ *The wind is blowing and this sheet of plastic will not stay on top of me, so I am getting soaked!* **2.** *Fig.* to keep well-informed about someone or something; to keep watch over someone or something. □ *You have to stay on top of her if you want her to do it right.* □ *I will stay on top of this project.*

stay one **step ahead of** someone or something Go to *keep one step ahead of* someone or something.

Stay out of my way. Go to *Keep out of my way.*

stay out of sight Go to *out of sight*.

stay out (of something**) 1.** *Lit.* to keep out of something or some place. □ *Stay out of here!* □ *Please stay out until we are ready.* **2.** *Fig.* to remain uninvolved in some piece of business. □ *I decided to stay out of it and let someone else handle it.* □ *My help wasn't needed there, so I just stayed out.*

Stay out of this! Go to *Keep out of this!*

stay over (somewhere) to stay overnight in a dwelling other than one's own. □ *Can I stay over at Jimmy's tonight?* □ *No, you can't stay over.*

stay put not to move; to stay where one is. □ *We've decided to stay put and not to move to Florida.* □ *If the children just stay put, their parents will come for them soon.*

stay to something to remain in a place for something, such as dinner. □ *I hope you will stay to dinner.* □ *I stayed to lunch because they were having fried shrimp.*

stay under (something) to remain concealed or protected beneath something. □ *You had better stay under the blankets until I get the fire started in the fireplace.* □ *Stay under and keep warm.*

stay up (for something**)** to remain awake and out of bed for some nighttime event. □ *I will stay up for her arrival.* □ *I can't stay up that late.*

stay up late to remain awake and out of bed later than usual. □ *I am in the practice of staying up late.* □ *I can't stay up late three nights in a row.*

stay up until a particular time to remain awake and out of bed until a particular time. □ *I stayed up until long past midnight last night.* □ *Do you think Susie should stay up until midnight?*

stay with someone or something to remain in the company of someone or something. □ *Please stay with me for a little while.* □ *How long did you stay with the company?*

stay within something to remain inside something. □ *You will have to stay within the immediate area until things return to normal in the town.* □ *Our dog just can't seem to stay within our yard.*

stay young at heart Go to *young at heart*.

***steady as a rock** Cliché very steady and unmovable; very stable. (*Also: **as** ~.) □ *His hand was steady as a rock as he made each incision.* □ *You must remain as steady as a rock when you are arguing with your supervisor.*

steal a base *Fig.* to sneak from one base to another in baseball. □ *The runner stole second base, but he nearly got put out on the way.* □ *Tom runs so slowly that he never tries to steal a base.*

steal a glance at someone or something *Fig.* to sneak a peek at someone or something. □ *He stole a glance at his brother, who appeared to be as frightened as he was.* □ *Karen stole a glance at her watch and yawned.*

steal a march on someone or something to precede someone who has the same goal; to accomplish something before someone else does. □ *Jeff stole a march on all of us when he had his story published.* □ *Our competitor stole a march on us and got the big contract.*

steal away (from someone or something**)** to sneak away from someone or something. □ *The thief stole away from the policeman.* □ *We stole away from the boring lecture.*

steal from someone or something to rob someone or something. □ *You wouldn't steal from a poor man, would you?* □ *Max didn't feel bad about stealing from a bank.*

steal out of some place to sneak quietly out of some place. □ *The critic stole out of the theater, unable to endure any more of the abysmal play.* □ *I stole out of the lecture and went back to my room.*

steal over someone or something **1.** [for a covering of some sort] to move slowly over someone or something. (As with the sun or the shade of a cloud.) □ *The shade stole over the sunbathers and ended their day.* □ *Darkness stole over the land.* **2.** [for a feeling] to spread through someone gradually. □ *A feeling of gloom stole over the crowd.* □ *A sense of high excitement stole over the boys as they waited.*

steal someone's **heart** *Fig.* to capture someone's affections; to cause someone to fall in love with oneself. □ *When I first met him, I knew he would steal my heart away. And he did.*

steal someone's **thunder** *Fig.* to lessen someone's force or authority. □ *What do you mean by coming in here and stealing my thunder? I'm in charge here!* □ *Someone stole my thunder by leaking my announcement to the press.*

steal something **from** someone or something to take the property belonging to someone or something without permission; to commit the theft of something from someone or something. □ *Max stole $50 from Henry.* □ *Lefty stole an apple from the fruit stand.*

S

steal something **off** someone to rob something from someone. □ *I think that guy who walked past me stole my wallet off me!* □ *Max stole a lot of money off tourists last season.*

steal the show Go to next.

steal the spotlight and **steal the show** *Fig.* to give the best performance in a show, play, or some other event; to get attention for oneself. □ *The lead in the play was very good, but the butler stole the show.* □ *Ann always tries to steal the spotlight when she and I make a presentation.*

steal up on someone or something to sneak up on someone or something. □ *We will steal up on Tony and give him a scare.* □ *The fox stole up on the hen and grabbed it.*

steam across something [for a ship] to cross a body of water under power. (Originally referred to steam engines, but now can be any sort of engine.) □ *How long does it take to steam across the Atlantic these days?* □ *We steamed across the bay in less than an hour.*

steam in((to) something**)** [for a vehicle, usually a ship] to enter something under power. (Originally referred to steam engines, but now can be any sort of engine.) □ *The ship steamed into the harbor and headed for the pier.* □ *Right on time, the ship steamed in.*

steam out (of some place**)** [for a conveyance, usually a ship] to exit something under power. (Originally referred to steam engines, but now can be any sort of engine.) □ *The huge diesel engines began to labor, and the ship steamed out of its berth.* □ *It shuddered a couple of times and steamed out.*

steam someone's **beam** *Sl.* to make someone angry. □ *Being stood up really steams my beam!* □ *Come on, don't steam your beam. Remember how hard times are now.*

steam someone **up†** **1.** *Sl.* to get someone excited. □ *Steam yourselves up and get in there and win this game!* □ *The coach can really steam up those guys.* **2.** *Sl.* to get someone angry. □ *This whole mess steamed me up but good.* □ *The long critical statement simply steamed up my opponent in the debate.*

steam something **off (of)** something and **steam** something† to loosen and remove something by an application of steam. (*Of* is usually retained before pronouns.) □ *Toby steamed the old paper off the wall.* □ *Toby steamed off the old wallpaper.*

steam something **out of** something and **steam** something **out†** to remove something embedded, through an application of steam. □ *The cleaner was not able to steam the wrinkles out of my jacket.* □ *I tried to steam out the gum.*

steam something **up†** to cause something to be covered with water vapor due to the presence of steam. □ *Our breaths steamed the windows up.* □ *The hot shower steamed up the mirror.*

steam up 1. *Lit.* to become covered with a film of steam or water vapor. □ *The windows steamed up and we had to wipe them so we could see out.* □ *The window has steamed up, and I can't see.* **2.** to drink heavily; to get drunk. □ *Fred and Mike were steaming up in the back room.*

steamed (up) angry. □ *Now, now, don't get so steamed up!* □ *She is really massively steamed.* **2.** *Sl.* intoxicated and fighting. □ *He was really steamed—and could hardly stand up.* □ *By midnight, Larry was too steamed to drive home, and he had to spend the night.*

steaming (mad) *Fig.* very angry; very mad; very upset. □ *The steaming coach yelled at the clumsy players.* □ *The principal was steaming mad when he found that his office had been vandalized.*

steel oneself **for** someone or something to prepare oneself for someone or something difficult or unpleasant; to get ready to face someone or something. □ *Aunt Helen is coming for a visit. We should steel ourselves for her.* □ *I think something is going wrong. We had better steel ourselves for a shock.*

steel someone **against** someone or something to fortify someone against someone or something; to prepare someone to endure someone or something. □ *I tried to steel Liz against Carl, who was bringing her some very bad news.* □ *We steeled her against the bad news.*

a **steely gaze** *Cliché* an intense, staring gaze. □ *The principal turned a steely gaze toward the frightened student and suddenly smiled.*

steep someone **in** something *Fig.* to immerse someone in some kind of knowledge or other experience; to saturate someone with some kind of experience or training. (Fig. on **steep** something **in** something.) □ *Her parents steeped her in good literature and music.* □ *She steeped herself in the legends of her people.*

steep something **in** something to soak something in a liquid. □ *I steeped the shirt in red dye.* □ *You have to steep these herbs in steamy hot water for five minutes.*

steer away from someone or something to move or turn away from someone or something. □ *You had better steer away from Jeff. He is in a terrible mood.* □ *Try to steer away from the potholes. The road is full of them.*

steer clear (of someone or something**)** to avoid someone or something. □ *John is mad at me, so I've been steering clear of him.* □ *Steer clear of that book. It has many errors in it.*

steer into something to turn or drive into something. □ *Try to steer into the right parking space this time.* □ *Poor Wally steered into the curb.*

steer someone or something **through** something to guide someone or something through something that is confusing or treacherous. □ *I tried to steer Judy through the registration procedure, but I really didn't know what I was doing.* □ *Should I try to steer my car through all this foot traffic or take a different route?*

steer something **for** something to aim oneself or one's vehicle toward something. □ *Jeff steered the car for the entrance to the tunnel and stepped on the gas.* □ *The driver steered the bus for the center lane just in time.*

steer something **toward** someone or something to guide something in the direction of someone or something. □ *The farmer steered the tractor toward the sheriff, who had come to talk to the farmer.* □ *Please steer the car toward the right side.*

steer through something to maneuver through something that is confusing or treacherous. □ *Do you think you can steer through this flooded tunnel?* □ *I can't steer through this mess of leaves and mud on the road.*

steer toward someone or something to turn or drive toward someone or something. □ *He steered toward the empty* *parking space, but someone got there before he did.* □ *Steer toward the house with the red door.*

stem from something [for an event] to result from something. □ *These problems all stem from your mismanagement.* □ *Our difficulties stem from the bad weather we have been having.*

step aside (for someone**) 1.** *Lit.* to move out of someone's way. □ *Would you step aside for my uncle and his walker?* □ *We had to step aside for the people in wheelchairs to get by.* **2.** *Fig.* to retire from an office so someone else can take over. □ *The president retired and stepped aside for someone else.* □ *Walter stepped aside for a younger person to take over.*

step away from one's **desk** Go to away from one's desk.

step back (from someone or something**)** to move away from someone or something; to move back so as to provide space around someone or something. □ *Please step back from the injured woman. Give her some air.* □ *Step back and give her some air.*

step back on someone or something to move back and tread on someone or something in the process. □ *Jeff stepped back on Judy and made her yelp with pain.* □ *Jeff stepped back on the cat.*

step between someone or something **and** someone or something else to move between things or people. □ *Jeff stepped between Judy and the gunman.* □ *He stepped between Judy and the wall.*

step down (from something**) 1.** *Lit.* to come down from something; to alight from something. □ *Please step down from the platform.* □ *She stepped down and went back to her chair.* **2.** *Fig.* to resign a job or a responsibility. □ *The mayor stepped down from office last week.* □ *It's unusual for a mayor to step down.*

step forward 1. *Lit.* to move forward one step or several steps. □ *The volunteer stepped forward.* □ *I stepped forward and someone moved up behind me immediately.* **2.** *Fig.* to volunteer to present important information. □ *When I go into court, I will have to step forward and present evidence. It is my civic duty.* □ *If you have information to present, you should step forward and seek recognition to do so.*

step in something Go to step into something.

step inside (some place**)** to walk into a place. □ *Please step inside my office, and we will discuss this matter.* □ *Please step inside.*

step in(to some place**)** to walk into a place. □ *Tiffany stepped into the room and said hello to everyone.* □ *She stepped in to say hello.*

step into someone's **shoes** *Fig.* to take over a job or some role from someone. □ *I was prepared to step into the boss's shoes, so there was no disruption when he left for another job.* □ *There was no one who could step into Alice's shoes when she left, so everything came to a stop.*

step into something **1.** *Lit.* and **step in** something to step into something wet, messy, or dirty. □ *Don't step in the mud!* □ *What is that stinky stuff you stepped into?* **2.** *Fig.* to involve oneself in some matter; to intervene in an affair or dispute. □ *I will have to step into the business and settle the problem.* □ *Please don't step into something that does not concern you.*

step in(to the breach) *Fig.* [for someone] to assume a position or take on a responsibility when there is a need or an opportunity to do so. □ *The person who was supposed to help didn't show up, so I stepped into the breach.* □ *The manager stepped into the breach when Jane got sick.*

step off to come off something by taking a step. □ *She came to the bottom step and stepped off.* □ *Ed was afraid to dive in from the side of the pool, so he just stepped off.*

step off (of) something to leave something elevated with one's first step. (*Of* is usually retained before pronouns.) □ *She stepped off the bottom step and walked down the street.* □ *Tony stepped off of the bank and waded across the stream.*

step off on the wrong foot Go to start off on the wrong foot.

step off (to the side) with someone Go to off (to the side) with someone.

step on it Go to step on the gas.

step on someone or something to tread on someone or something. □ *Ouch! You stepped on me!* □ *Don't step on the flooring in that spot. It's weak.*

step on someone's **toes** and **tread on** someone's **toes 1.** *Lit.* to step down onto someone's toes, causing pain. □ *Please don't step on my toes as you walk by.* **2.** *Fig.* to offend or insult someone, as if causing physical pain. □ *You're sure I won't be stepping on her toes if I talk directly to her supervisor?* □ *I didn't mean to tread on your toes.*

step on the gas and **step on it** to hurry up; to make a vehicle go faster. (As if stepping on an automobile's accelerator. □ *Step on the gas. We are going to be late!* □ *Step on it! Let's go!*

step out into something to go out from a place into a different set of conditions. □ *Julie stepped out of her previous job into a whole new world.* □ *Wally stepped out into the bright sunlight.*

step out of line 1. *Lit.* to move out of a line of people. □ *If you step out of line, you will lose your place in it.* □ *I had to step out of line to sit down on the curb and rest for a minute.* **2.** *Fig.* to misbehave; to deviate from normal, expected, or demanded behavior. □ *If you step out of line again, I'll slap you.* □ *Tom stepped out of line once too often and got yelled at.*

step out (of something**) 1.** to go out of a place. □ *She stepped out of the house without a coat and nearly froze to death.* □ *Jamie stepped out and got wet in the rain.* **2.** to take one step to get out of pants of some type that have been dropped. □ *He stepped out of his pants and pulled off his shirt.* □ *He dropped his pants and stepped out.*

step out (on someone**)** to be unfaithful to a spouse or lover. □ *Jeff has been stepping out on Judy.* □ *I was not stepping out!*

step outside 1. to go outside, as if to get some fresh air. □ *I need to step outside for a minute to get a breath of air.* □ *Tom and Harry stepped outside for a moment.* **2.** to go outside to fight or settle an argument. □ *I find that insulting. Would you care to step outside?* □ *Max invited Lefty to step outside.*

step over someone or something to walk so as to avoid stepping on someone or something. □ *I stepped over Tom, who* was napping on the floor. □ *Please step over the things on the floor. We are doing the spring cleaning.*

step over (to) some place to move to a place a few steps away. □ *Please step over here and I'll show you some other merchandise.* □ *If you will step over to the display case, I will show you some earrings.*

step right up to come right to where the speaker is; to come forward to the person speaking. (Used by people selling things, as at carnival sideshows.) □ *Please step right up and buy a ticket to see the show.* □ *Don't be shy! Step right up and buy one of these.*

step something **down**† to reduce the intensity or amount of something by one step or grade. □ *See if you can step the lights down a little.* □ *Step down the lights just a little more.*

step something **off**† to measure a distance by counting the paces required to cover it. □ *She stepped the distance off and noted it on her pad.* □ *Liz stepped off the number of feet from the window to the opposite wall.*

step something **up**† **1.** to make something more active. □ *I hope we can step the pace of business up in the next few days.* □ *We can step up business considerably by putting out a larger sign.* **2.** to make something go or run faster. □ *The engineer stepped the motors up and the production line moved even faster.* □ *Please step up the speed of your activity.*

step up to increase. □ *Industrial production stepped up a large amount this last quarter.* □ *Traffic has stepped up since the road was paved.*

step up to something to walk to something, especially a counter or a bar. □ *Jake stepped up to the ticket counter and bought a single ticket for the balcony.* □ *When Wally stepped up to the ticket window, he learned that the show was sold out.*

step up to the plate 1. *Lit.* [for a batter in baseball] to move near home plate in preparation for striking the ball when it is pitched. □ *The batter stepped up to the plate and glared at the pitcher.* **2.** *Fig.* to move into a position where one is ready to do a task. □ *It's time for Tom to step up to the plate and take on his share of work.*

step-by-step 1. *Lit.* [walking] one step at a time. □ *The old man slowly moved across the lawn step-by-step.* **2.** *Fig.* little by little. □ *Just follow the instructions step-by-step, and everything will be fine.*

stew in one's **own juice** *Fig.* to be left alone to suffer one's anger or disappointment. □ *John has such a terrible temper. When he got mad at us, we just let him go away and stew in his own juice.* □ *After John stewed in his own juice for a while, he decided to come back and apologize to us.*

stick around [for a person] to remain in a place. □ *The kids stuck around for a time after the party was over.* □ *Oh, Ann. Please stick around for a while. I want to talk to you later.*

stick at something to keep trying to do something; to stay on a task or job. □ *I hope he can stick at this job.* □ *He doesn't seem to be able to stick at anything for very long.*

stick by someone or something and **stick with** someone or something to support someone or something; to continue supporting or committing to someone or something when things are bad. □ *Don't worry. I'll stick by you no matter*

what. □ *I feel as if I have to stick by my brother even if he goes to jail.*

Stick 'em up! Go to Hands up!

stick in someone's **mind** to remain in someone's thinking. □ *The events of that day stuck in my mind for a very long time.* □ *The image of her smiling face stuck in Henry's mind for a long time.*

stick in something to remain embedded in something; to remain held in something. □ *Do you think this will stick in the hole, or is it too small?* □ *A fish bone stuck in his throat for a while.*

stick it to someone *Inf.* to give someone a problem; to confront someone. □ *They stuck it to me about the stopped-up drain.* □ *He was late, and the boss really stuck it to him.*

stick man *Sl.* a police patrol officer (who carries a stick). □ *The stick man is due here in about three minutes. Hurry.* □ *I was a stick man for a few years till my feet went bad.*

stick one's **foot in** one's **mouth** Go to put one's foot in one's mouth.

stick one's **neck out (for** someone or something**)** *Fig.* to take a risk. □ *Why should I stick my neck out to do something for her? What's she ever done for me?* □ *He made a risky investment. He stuck his neck out for the deal because he thought he could make some big money.*

stick one's **nose in (where it's not wanted)** Go to put one's nose in (where it's not wanted).

stick one's **nose in(to** something**)** Go to poke one's nose in(to something).

stick one's **nose up in the air** *Fig.* to behave in a haughty manner. □ *Jeff stuck his nose up in the air and walked out.* □ *Don't stick your nose up in the air. Come down to earth with the rest of us.*

stick one's **oar in**† Go to put one's oar in†.

stick one's **tongue out**† *Fig.* to cause one's tongue to project outward. (A gesture of contempt.) □ *Don't stick your tongue out at me!* □ *She stuck out her tongue at me!*

stick out to project outward. □ *You can't lock your suitcase because there is a bit of cloth sticking out.* □ *Some cloth stuck out of the top of the drawer.*

stick out a mile *Fig.* to project outward very obviously. □ *My nose sticks out a mile! I hate it!* □ *His stomach sticks out a mile. What do you suppose is in there?*

stick out against something to be highly visible against a background of something. □ *Your cold, red nose sticks out against your white, frozen face.* □ *The red vase sticks out against the pale blue wallpaper.*

stick out (from someone or something**)** to project outward from someone or something. □ *His right arm, which was in a cast, stuck out from him like a crane.* □ *His arm stuck out.*

stick out like a sore thumb *Fig.* to be very obvious. □ *That pimple really sticks out like a sore thumb.* □ *Do you think I would stick out like a sore thumb at the party if I wear this coat?*

stick out (of someone or something**)** to protrude from someone or something. □ *The arrow stuck out of him, wobbling as he staggered.* □ *A dollar bill stuck out of the book. What a strange bookmark.*

S

stick shift 1. having to do with a nonautomatic transmission or a car that has one. □ *I prefer a stick shift car—I don't know why.* □ *The stick shift models are cheaper—that's why.* **2.** a nonautomatic transmission. □ *I can't drive a stick shift!* □ *My husband took the other car and stuck me with the stick shift.*

stick someone or something **up**† to rob someone or a business establishment. (Presumably with the aid of a gun.) □ *Max tried to stick the drugstore up.* □ *Max stuck up the store.*

stick someone **with** someone or something to burden someone with someone or something. □ *The dishonest merchant stuck me with a faulty television set.* □ *John stuck me with his talkative uncle and went off with his friends.*

stick something **down**† to fasten something down, as with glue or paste. □ *Get some glue and stick down this wallpaper, please.* □ *Stick this wallpaper down, would you?*

stick something **into** someone or something and **stick** something **in**† to insert something into someone or something. □ *The technician stuck a needle into my arm and took some blood out.* □ *She stuck in the needle.*

stick something **on(to)** someone or something and **stick** something **on**† to affix something onto someone or something. □ *The baggage clerk stuck a label onto Jimmy as a joke.* □ *Jimmy stuck on the label.*

stick something **out**† to endure something; to stay with something. (The *something* can be vaguely expressed using *it*.) □ *I will stick it out as long as I can.* □ *She stuck out the abuse as long as she could; then she started looking for another job.*

stick something **out**† **to** someone to hold something, such as one's hand, out where someone can grasp it. □ *She stuck her hand out to him, intending that he shake it.* □ *Ted stuck out his hand to Bill, but withdrew it suddenly.*

stick something **through** someone or something to push something so that it penetrates someone or something. □ *The good knight stuck his lance through the bad knight.* □ *I stuck my fist through the flimsy wall.*

stick something **together 1.** to glue or paste something together. □ *Use glue to stick these pieces together.* □ *Please stick the pieces of the broken vase together with glue.* **2.** to assemble something, perhaps in haste. □ *He just stuck the model plane together, making a mess of it.* □ *Don't stick the parts together so fast. It won't look good.*

stick something **up**† **1.** to fasten something to a place where it can be seen; to put something on display, especially by gluing, tacking, or stapling. □ *Stick this notice up. Put a copy on every bulletin board.* □ *Please stick up this notice.* **2.** to raise something; to hold something up. □ *She stuck her hand up because she knew the answer.* □ *The elephant stuck up its trunk and trumpeted.*

stick to one's **guns** *Fig.* to remain firm in one's convictions; to stand up for one's rights. (Fig. on a soldier remaining in place to fire a gun even when all appears to be lost.) □ *I'll stick to my guns on this matter. I'm sure I'm right.* □ *Bob can be persuaded to do it our way. He probably won't stick to his guns on this point.*

stick to one's **ribs** *Fig.* [for food] to last long and fortify one well; [for food] to sustain one even in the coldest weather. □ *This oatmeal ought to stick to your ribs. You need something hearty on a cold day like this.* □ *I don't want just a salad! I want something that will stick to my ribs.*

stick to someone or something **1.** *Lit.* to adhere to someone or something; to remain affixed to someone or something. □ *The tape stuck to me and I couldn't get it off.* □ *This stamp won't stick to the envelope.* **2.** *Fig.* to continue to accompany someone or something. □ *Stick to me and I'll lead you out of here.* □ *Stick to the group of us, and you'll be okay.* **3.** *Fig.* to continue to use or employ someone or something. □ *I'll stick to Jill. She does a good job and she's my friend.* □ *We decided to stick to our present supplier.*

stick to someone's **fingers** *Fig.* to remain in someone's possession; to be stolen by someone. □ *Other people's watches tend to stick to Max's fingers.* □ *Watch that clerk. Your change tends to stick to his fingers.*

stick together 1. *Lit.* to adhere to one another. □ *The noodles are sticking together. What shall I do?* □ *You need to keep the pieces separate while you fry them or else they will stick together.* **2.** *Fig.* to remain in one another's company. □ *Let us stick together so we don't get lost.* □ *They stuck together through thick and thin.*

stick up to stand upright or on end; to thrust upward. □ *The ugly red flower stuck up from the bouquet.* □ *Why is the worst-looking flower sticking up above all the rest?*

stick up for someone or something to support someone or something; to speak in favor of someone or something. □ *Everyone was making unpleasant remarks about John, but I stuck up for him.* □ *Our team was losing, but I stuck up for it anyway.*

Stick with it. Do not give up. Stay with your task. □ *Bill: I'm really tired of calculus. Father: Stick with it. You'll be a better person for it.* □ *Bill: This job is getting to be such a pain. Sue: True, but it pays well, doesn't it? Stick with it.*

stick with someone or something Go to **stick by** someone or something.

stick-in-the-mud *Fig.* a dull and old-fashioned person. □ *Don't be such an old stick-in-the-mud.* □ *Some stick-in-the-mud objected to the kind of music we wanted to play in church.*

Sticks and stones may break my bones, but words will never hurt me. *Prov.* You do not hurt me by calling me names. (A reply to someone who has called you names. Primarily used by children; sounds childish when used by adults.) □ *Brother: You're stupid and mean, and everybody hates you! Sister: Sticks and stones may break my bones, but words will never hurt me.*

***stiff as a poker** rigid and inflexible; stiff and awkward. (Usually used to describe people. *Also: **as** ~.) □ *This guy's dead. He's cold and as stiff as a poker.* □ *John is not a very good dancer; he's stiff as a poker.*

stiffen something **up**† to make something rigid or tense. □ *He added a little starch to the rinse water to stiffen his collars up a bit.* □ *The cold draft has stiffened up my neck.*

stiffen up to become stiff. □ *The bread dough stiffened up as it got cold.* □ *My knees began to stiffen up after I sat still for an hour.*

stigmatize someone **as** something to brand or label someone as something. □ *The opposition will try to stigmatize you as a spendthrift.* □ *Tony was stigmatized as a poor loser.*

S

*still as death *Cliché* immobile; completely still. (The reference to death gives this expression ominous connotations. *Also: **as** ~.) □ *George sat as still as death all afternoon.* □ *When the storm was over, everything was suddenly still as death.*

A still tongue makes a wise head. *Prov.* If you are wise, you do not talk very much.; You should only speak when you have judged that it is appropriate to do so. □ *Don't chatter about whatever comes to your mind. A still tongue makes a wise head.* □ *Kathy really offended Mr. Parker by talking so much about his ex-wife. She needs to learn that a still tongue makes a wise head.*

Still waters run deep. *Prov.* Quiet people are often very thoughtful. □ *Jill: I get the impression that Nathan is not very smart. He never says anything. Jane: Don't be so sure. Still waters run deep, you know.*

stimulate someone or an animal **into** something to excite or cause someone or an animal to do something. □ *The promises of bonuses stimulated the workers into higher productivity for the week.* □ *The morning light stimulates the birds into singing.*

sting someone **for** something *Sl.* to cheat someone of a particular amount; to make someone pay for something. □ *That guy stung me for twenty bucks!* □ *Toby was stung for the lunch bill.*

sting someone **with** something to use something to sting someone. □ *The bee stung me with its stinger.* □ *The wasp can sting you with its poisonous barb.*

stink on ice *Sl.* to be really rotten. (So rotten as to reek even when frozen.) □ *This show stinks on ice.* □ *The whole idea stank on ice.*

stink something **up** to make something or some place smell very bad. □ *Your cooking really stunk the place up!* □ *The rotten eggs will stink up the whole house.*

stink to high heaven and **smell to high heaven** *Fig.* to smell very bad. □ *What happened? This place stinks to high heaven.* □ *This meat smells to high heaven. Throw it away!*

stink with something to smell very bad with the smell of something. □ *The room stinks with a garlicky smell.* □ *Our garden stinks with the smell of something rotting.*

stinking rich *Fig.* very rich. □ *I'd like to be stinking rich for the rest of my life.* □ *Tiffany is stinking rich, and she acts like it.*

stinking with something *Fig.* having lots of something. □ *Mr. Wilson is just stinking with cash.* □ *Those guys are stinking with jewelry.*

stir someone **(in)to** something to excite someone into doing something. □ *The events of the day stirred everyone into action.* □ *The danger stirred them to action.*

stir someone **up** *Fig.* to get someone excited; to get someone angry. (Fig. on **stir** something **up**.) □ *The march music really stirred the audience up.* □ *The march stirred up the audience.*

stir something **around** to agitate or mix a liquid substance by moving it in a circular motion. □ *Stir the mixture around to mix it up.* □ *You should stir the dressing around a bit before you serve it.*

stir something **in** Go to next.

stir something **into** something and **stir** something **in** to mix something into something. □ *The painter stirred too much red pigment into the paint.* □ *The painter stirred in the pigment.*

stir something **up** **1.** *Lit.* to mix something by stirring. □ *Please stir the pancake batter up before you use it.* □ *Please stir up the batter.* **2.** *Fig.* to cause trouble. □ *Why are you always trying to stir trouble up?* □ *Are you stirring up trouble again?*

stir up a hornet's nest *Fig.* to create a lot of trouble. (Fig. on **stir** something **up** ②.) □ *If you say that to her, you will be stirring up a hornet's nest.* □ *There is no need to stir up a hornet's nest.*

*stir-crazy crazy from being confined. (*Typically: **be** ~; **become** ~; **go** ~; **get** ~; **make** someone ~. Stir is a slang word for prison.) □ *I am going to go stir-crazy if I don't get out of this office.*

A stitch in time saves nine. *Prov.* If you fix a small problem right away, it will not become a bigger problem later. □ *Let's patch the roof before that hole gets bigger. A stitch in time saves nine.*

stitch something **onto** something and **stitch** something **on** to sew something onto the surface of something else. □ *Fred stitched the badge onto his jacket.* □ *Fred stitched on the badge.*

stitch something **up** to sew something together; to mend a tear or ripped seam. □ *I tore my shirt. Would you stitch it up, please?* □ *Please stitch up my shirt.*

stock in trade whatever goods, skills, etc., are necessary to undertake an activity of some kind. □ *Of course I am glad to help. Packing household goods is my stock in trade.*

stock something **(up)** **with** something to load something with a supply of something. □ *Let's stock the wine cellar with good vintages this year.* □ *We will stock up our wine cellar with whatever is on sale.*

stock up (on something**)** to build up a supply of something in particular. □ *I need to stock up on food for the party.* □ *We need fresh vegetables. We will have to stock up before the weekend.*

stock up (with something**)** to build up a supply of something. □ *You had better stock up with firewood before the first snowstorm.* □ *Yes, I will stock up today.*

stoke something **up** **1.** to poke or add fuel to a fire to make it burn hotter. □ *Grandpa had to go down each winter morning to stoke the fire up.* □ *He stoked up the furnace every morning during the winter.* **2.** *Sl.* to start something, such as an engine. □ *Stoke this old car up so we can leave.* □ *Stoke up your motorcycle and let's get going.*

*stoked on someone or something *Sl.* excited by someone or something. (*Typically: **be** ~; **get** ~.) □ *I am really stoked on that movie.* □ *She was really stoked on Tom.*

stoked out *Sl.* exhausted. □ *I ran all the way and got stoked out.* □ *Alex is totally stoked out from working in the hot sun.*

Stolen fruit is sweetest. and **Stolen pleasures are sweetest.** *Prov.* People often enjoy illicit things just because they are illicit. □ *To judge from the number of his extramarital affairs, John must believe that stolen pleasures are sweetest.*

Stolen pleasures are sweetest. Go to previous.

stomp on someone **1.** *Lit.* to stamp someone down. □ *The angry crowd knocked him down and stomped on him.* □ *The crowd stomped on the mugger.* **2.** *Fig.* to repress someone. □ *Every time I get a good idea, the boss stomps on me.* □ *Don't stomp on her every time she says something.*

stone dead *Rur.* dead; unquestionably dead; long dead. □ *The cat was stone dead and stiff as a board by the time we got to him.* □ *Old Tom is stone dead and in the ground.*

stone(-cold) sober and **cold sober** absolutely sober. □ *I am stone-cold sober, or I will be by morning anyway.* □ *I found the secret to waking up cold sober. Don't drink.*

a **stone's throw away** *Fig.* a short distance; a relatively short distance. □ *John saw Mary across the street, just a stone's throw away.* □ *Philadelphia is just a stone's throw away from Camden, New Jersey.*

stool (on someone**)** *Sl.* to inform (on someone). □ *Jane would stool on anybody, even her own mother.* □ *Somebody stooled and ruined the whole layout.*

stool (pigeon) and **stoolie** an informer. (Originally underworld.) □ *Some stool pigeon spilled the works to the boys in blue.* □ *There's nothing I hate worse than a stoolie.*

stoop down to dip, duck, or squat down. □ *I had to stoop down to enter the tiny door.* □ *Stoop down so you don't bump your head.*

stoop over to bend over. □ *Carl stooped over to pick up his napkin and lost his balance.* □ *As he stooped over, he lost his balance and fell.*

stoop to doing something to degrade oneself or condescend to doing something; to do something that is beneath one. □ *Whoever thought that the manager of the department would stoop to sweeping up?* □ *I never dreamed that Bill would stoop to stealing.*

stop at something **1.** to go as far as something and then stop. □ *I will stop at the end of the road.* □ *The road stopped at the base of a mountain.* **2.** to stop briefly at something and then continue. □ *I have to stop at the store for a minute.* □ *Do you mind if I stop at a drug store?* **3.** to spend the night at some place. (Typically with *motel, inn, bed and breakfast,* and *hotel.*) □ *We stopped at a nice little inn for the night.* □ *When we travel, we like to stop at hotels that are run by one of the national chains.*

stop behind someone or something to bring oneself or one's vehicle to a stop behind someone or something. □ *I stopped behind Fred at the red light.* □ *Fred stopped behind a minivan.*

stop by (some place**)** and **stop in (**some place**)** to visit some place, usually briefly. □ *I was coming home, but I decided to stop by my aunt's on the way.* □ *She was very glad that I stopped in.*

stop dead in one's **tracks** *Fig.* to stop completely still suddenly because of fear, a noise, etc. □ *I stopped dead in my tracks when I heard the scream.* □ *The deer stopped dead in its tracks when it heard the hunter step on a fallen branch.*

stop for someone to halt one's vehicle to allow someone to get in. □ *I stopped for Jeff, but he didn't want a ride.* □ *I didn't have time to stop for you. I hope you will forgive me.*

stop for something to halt one's vehicle because of something or the need of something. □ *I had to stop for a red light.* □ *We stopped for some gas.*

stop in (some place**)** Go to **stop by (**some place**)**.

stop, look, and listen to exercise caution, especially at street corners and railroad crossings, by stopping, looking to the left and to the right, and listening for approaching vehicles or a train. □ *Sally's mother trained her to stop, look, and listen at every street corner.* □ *It is a good practice to stop, look, and listen at a railroad crossing.*

stop off (some place**) (for** a period of time**)** to halt or pause for a certain period of time. □ *I need to stop off for a rest.* □ *Let's find a little town and stop off.* □ *I have to stop off at the store for a minute.* □ *We stopped off for a while at the park.*

stop on a dime *Fig.* to come to a stop in a very short distance. □ *This thing will stop on a dime.* □ *Imagine a bus that could stop on a dime.*

stop on something to go as far as something [on the floor or the ground] and then stop. □ *Please stop on the line.* □ *You are supposed to stop on the white line or behind it.*

stop one or something **dead in** one's or something's **tracks** *Fig.* to stop someone or something suddenly and completely. □ *The gunshot stopped the killer dead in her tracks.* □ *The arrow stopped the deer dead in its tracks.*

stop over (some place**)** to break one's journey, usually overnight or even longer. □ *On our way to New York, we stopped over in Philadelphia for the night.* □ *That's a good place to stop over. There are some nice hotels in Philadelphia.*

stop short of a place not to go as far as something. □ *The bus stopped short of the end of the road.* □ *The speeding car stopped short of the sidewalk where children were playing.*

stop short of doing something not to go as far as doing something. □ *Fortunately Bob stopped short of hitting Tom.* □ *The boss criticized Jane's work but stopped short of firing her.* □ *Jack was furious but stopped short of hitting Tom.*

stop someone **cold** to halt someone immediately. □ *When you told us the bad news, it stopped me cold.*

stop someone **from** doing something to prevent someone from doing something. □ *I can't stop her from running away.* □ *They couldn't stop themselves from eating.*

stop something **up**† **(with** something**)** to plug or clog something with something. □ *Gary stopped the sink up with bacon grease.* □ *He stopped up the sink with bacon grease.* □ *Try not to stop the sink up.*

Stop the music! and **Stop the presses!** *Inf.* Stop everything!; Hold it! (*Presses* refers to the printing presses used to print newspapers. This means that there is recent news of such magnitude that the presses must be stopped so a new edition can be printed immediately.) □ *John (entering the room): Stop the music! There's a fire in the kitchen! Mary: Good grief! Let's get out of here!* □ *"Stop the presses!" shouted Jane. "I have an announcement."*

Stop the presses! Go to previous.

stop up [for something] to become clogged. □ *The sink stopped up again!*

store something **away**† to put something away for future use; to set something aside. □ *Store the extra rice away for use next week.* □ *Please store away the extra food.*

store something **in** something to set something aside in something. □ *Can I store my bicycle in your garage?* □ *Do you mind if I store my coat in your locker?*

store something **up**† to build up and lay away a supply of something. □ *The bears will store fat up for the long winter.* □ *They store up fat for the winter.*

storm around *Fig.* to go about in a fury. □ *What is he storming around about?* □ *Martin was storming around all morning because he lost his car keys.*

storm at someone or something *Fig.* to direct one's anger at someone or something. □ *She stormed at him because he was late again.* □ *Richard was storming at the cat again.*

storm in(to some place**)** *Fig.* to burst into something or some place angrily. □ *The army stormed into the town and took many of the citizens as prisoners.* □ *Leonard stormed in, shouting at everyone.*

A **storm is brewing. 1.** There is going to be a storm. □ *Look at the clouds. A storm is brewing.* □ *A storm is brewing in the west.* **2.** There is going to be trouble or emotional upset. □ *He looks angry. A storm is brewing.*

storm out (of some place**)** *Fig.* to burst out of some place angrily. □ *Carol stormed out of the office in a rage.* □ *She got mad and stormed out.*

stow away to conceal oneself in a vehicle, originally a ship, in order to travel without paying. □ *Don got to this country by stowing away on a cargo ship.*

stow something **away**† to pack something away. □ *I have to stow my clothes away before I go to bed.* □ *Please stow away your things and get right to work.*

straddle the fence *Fig.* to support both sides of an issue. (As if one were partly on either side of a fence.) □ *The mayor is straddling the fence on this issue, hoping the public will forget it.* □ *The legislator wanted to straddle the fence until the last minute, and that alone cost her a lot of votes.*

the **straight and narrow** *Fig.* a straight and law-abiding route through life. (Referring to a morally rigid and correct course of behavior. Fixed order.) □ *You should have no trouble with the police if you stick to the straight and narrow.* □ *Roger was the kind who followed the straight and narrow every day of his life.*

*****straight as an arrow 1.** *Cliché* [of something] very straight. (*Also: **as** ~.) □ *The road to my house is as straight as an arrow, so it should be very easy to follow.* **2.** *Cliché* [of someone] honest or forthright. (*Straight* here means honest. *Also: **as** ~.) □ *Tom is straight as an arrow. I'd trust him with anything.*

straightaway and **straight off** right away; immediately; without thinking or considering. □ *We'll have to depart straight off.* □ *Straightaway I knew something was wrong.*

the **straight dope** the true information; the full story. □ *He gave us the straight dope.* □ *I want the straight dope. I can take it.*

*****a **straight face** *Fig.* a face free from smiles or laughter. (*Typically: **have** ~; **keep** ~.) □ *It's hard to keep a straight face when someone tells a funny joke.*

(straight) from the horse's mouth *Fig.* from an authoritative or dependable source. (See also **get** something straight from the horse's mouth.) □ *I know it's true! I heard it straight from the horse's mouth!* □ *This comes straight from the horse's mouth, so it has to be believed.*

straight from the shoulder *Fig.* very direct, without attenuation or embellishment. □ *Okay, I'll give it to you straight from the shoulder.* □ *Right straight from the shoulder: clean out your desk; you're through.*

straight low *Sl.* the absolute truth. (From *lowdown* = the story; the truth.) □ *Can you give me the straight low on this mess?* □ *Nobody ain't gonna tell no warden the straight low; you can be sure of that.*

straight man someone who sets up jokes or gags so that someone else can say the punch line. □ *I need a straight man to set up all my jokes.* □ *I'm tired of being a straight man for a has-been comic.*

straight off Go to straightaway.

straight off the bat Go to right off the bat.

straight out frankly; directly. □ *Bob told Pam straight out that he didn't want to marry her.* □ *Jim was told straight out to start working harder.*

straight shooter *Fig.* an honest person. □ *I trust Mike; he's a straight shooter.* □ *We need a straight shooter in office who will work for the people rather than some lobbyists.*

straight talk direct and honest talk. □ *It's about time for a little straight talk around here.* □ *If they want straight talk and can handle straight talk, give 'em straight talk.*

straight up 1. *Sl.* upright. □ *A fine guy—really straight up.* □ *She is one of the most straight up brokers in town.* **2.** *Sl.* [of a drink] served without ice; neat. □ *I'll have a bourbon, straight up, please.* □ *No, not straight up. Just a little ice.* **3.** *Sl.* [of eggs] cooked sunny-side up; having to do with eggs cooked with the yolks facing up. □ *Two eggs, straight up, and a cup of coffee.* □ *I like my eggs straight up, but the white part has to be cooked solid.*

straighten out 1. to become straight. □ *The road finally straightened out.* □ *The train tracks straightened out on the plain.* **2.** to improve one's behavior or attitude. □ *I hope he straightens out before he gets himself into real trouble.* □ *Fred had better straighten out soon if he wants to get a job.*

straighten someone or something **up**† **1.** to put someone or something into an upright position. □ *The fence is tilted. Please straighten that post up when you get a chance.* □ *Bill, you're slouching again. Straighten up your back.* **2.** to tidy up someone or something. □ *John straightened himself up a little before going out for dinner.* □ *This room is a mess. Let's straighten up this place, right now!*

straighten someone **out**† **1.** to make someone's body straight or orderly. □ *The undertaker straightened Sam out in his coffin.* □ *Straighten out your body so I can massage your back.* **2.** to cause someone to behave better or to have a better attitude; to reform someone. □ *You are terrible. Someone is going to have to straighten you out!* □ *The principal straightened out the troublesome boys.* **3.** to help someone become less confused about something. □ *Can you straighten me out on this matter?* □ *I will do what I can to straighten out the office staff on this question.*

straighten something **out**† **1.** to make something straighter. □ *I can't straighten these heavy boxes out.* □ *Please straighten out this line of people.* **2.** to bring order to something that is disorderly. □ *See if you can straighten this mess out.* □ *Will you straighten out your room, please?*

straighten up 1. to sit or stand more straight. □ *Billy's mother told him to straighten up or he'd fall out of his chair.* □ *John straightened up so he'd look taller.* **2.** to behave better. □ *Bill was acting badly for a while; then he straightened up.* □ *Sally, straighten up, or I will punish you!*

straighten up and fly right *Fig.* to improve one's behavior or attitude and perform better. (Originally referred to an airplane.) □ *If you want to keep out of trouble, you had better straighten up and fly right.* □ *Straighten up and fly right or I will send you to the principal.*

strain after something [for a singer] to work very hard to reach a very high or a very low note. □ *Don't strain after the note. Let it come naturally, like a cooling breeze.* □ *She was straining after each note as if it hurt her to sing, which it probably did.*

strain at gnats and swallow camels *Prov.* to criticize other people for minor offenses while ignoring major offenses. (Biblical.) □ *Jill: Look at that. Edward is combing his hair at his desk. How unprofessional. Jane: Don't strain at gnats and swallow camels. There are worse problems than that around here.*

strain at the leash 1. *Lit.* [for a dog] to pull very hard on its leash. □ *It's hard to walk Fido, because he is always straining at the leash.* □ *I wish that this dog would not strain at the leash. It's very hard on me.* **2.** *Fig.* [for a person] to want to move ahead with things, aggressively and independently. □ *She wants to fix things right away. She is straining at the leash to get started.* □ *Paul is straining at the leash to get on the job.*

strain away (at something**)** to work very hard, continuously, at doing something. □ *She strained away at her weights, getting stronger every day.* □ *She was straining away on the rowing machine when we came in.*

strain for an effect to work very hard to try to achieve some effect. □ *The actors were straining so hard for an effect that they forgot their lines.* □ *Don't strain for effect so much. The authors of this drama knew what they were doing, and it's in the lines already.*

strain something **off** of something and **strain** something **off**† to remove the excess or unwanted liquid from something. □ *The cook strained the grease off the cooking juices.* □ *The cook strained off the grease.*

strain something **through** something to filter a liquid or a watery substance by pouring it through something. □ *Tony strained the strawberry jelly through cheesecloth.* □ *We will have to strain the clabber to take out the curds.*

strand someone **on** something to abandon someone on something from which there is no escape. □ *The shipwreck stranded our little group on a deserted beach.* □ *We were stranded on the little island by a storm.*

stranger to something or some place someone who is new to an area or place. □ *Although John was a stranger to big cities, he enjoyed visiting New York.* □ *You are a stranger to our town, and I hope you feel welcome.*

strap someone or something **down**† to tie or bind someone or something down to something. □ *The nurses strapped Gary down in preparation for the operation.* □ *They strapped down the patient and gave him a sedative.*

strap someone or something **in(to)** something and **strap** someone or something **in**† to tie or bind someone or something into something. □ *Mother strapped little Jimmy into his seat.* □ *She strapped in Jimmy.*

strap something **onto** someone or something and **strap** something **on**† to tie or bind something onto someone or something. □ *The hiker strapped the load onto her partner.* □ *She strapped on the backpack.*

***strapped for** something needing something, usually money. (*Typically: **be** ~; **get** ~.) □ *I am really strapped for cash. Can you lend me some?* □ *Ted is strapped for money and cannot pay his bills.*

a **straw man** a weak proposition posited only to be demolished by a simple countering argument. □ *So you can knock down your own straw man! Big deal. The question is how can you deal with real problems.*

the **straw that broke the camel's back** Go to the last straw.

stray (away) (from something**)** to drift away from or wander away from a particular topic or location. (The option elements cannot be transposed.) □ *Please don't stray from the general area of discussion.* □ *Sally strayed away from her topic a number of times.*

stray in(to something**)** to wander into something. □ *The deer strayed into the town and ruined almost everyone's garden.* □ *We left the gate open, and the cows strayed in and drank from the pond.*

stray onto something to wander onto an area, such as a parcel of land. □ *Your cows strayed onto my land and ate my marigolds!* □ *If your horse strays onto my land one more time, it's my horse!*

streak across something to move across something very fast. □ *A comet streaked across the night sky.* □ *Tom streaked across the street to get a cup of coffee.*

a **streak of bad luck** and a **string of bad luck** a series of events that are only bad luck. □ *After a long string of bad luck, we finally got a lucky break.*

a **streak of good luck** and a **string of good luck** a series of fortunate events. □ *After a series of failures, we started out on a streak of good luck.*

a **streak of luck** Go to a lucky streak.

stream down (on someone or something**)** [for a liquid or light] to flow downward onto someone or something. □ *The water streamed down on all of them.* □ *The light broke through the clouds and streamed down on all of them.* □ *The waterfall streamed down and soaked them all.*

stream in(to something**)** to flow or rush into something. □ *The people streamed into the hall, each seeking the best possible seat.* □ *Water streamed into the room from the broken pipe.* □ *Complaints about the bawdy performance streamed in.*

stretch a point and **stretch the point** *Fig.* to interpret a point flexibly and with great latitude. □ *Would it be stretching a point to suggest that everyone is invited to your*

S

picnic? □ *To say that everyone is invited is stretching the point.*

stretch away (from something**)** to extend away from something. □ *A vast plain stretched away from the river-bank.* □ *The plain stretched away as far as we could see.*

stretch away to some place to extend as far as some place. □ *The forest stretched away to the horizon.* □ *The river stretched away to the sea.*

stretch forth (from something**)** to extend out or forth from something. □ *A path stretched forth from the cabin, leading deep into the woods.* □ *Outside the cabin door, a path stretched forth.*

stretch it Go to stretch the truth.

stretch one's **legs** *Fig.* to walk around and loosen one's leg muscles after sitting down or lying down for a time. □ *We wanted to stretch our legs during intermission.* □ *After sitting in the car all day, the travelers decided to stretch their legs.*

stretch one's **money** and **make** one's **money stretch** *Fig.* to economize so that one's money lasts longer. □ *We have to stretch our money in order to be able to buy groceries at the end of the month.*

stretch out [for one] to extend and stretch one's body to its full length. □ *She lay down, stretched out, and relaxed for the first time in days.* □ *I need a bigger bed. I can't stretch out in this one.*

stretch out to someone or something to extend as far as someone or something. □ *His arm stretched out to the guy next to him and established the correct amount of separation in the ranks.* □ *The beach stretched out to the horizon.*

stretch someone or something **out**† to extend or draw out someone or something. □ *Molly stretched the baby out to change his clothes.* □ *She stretched out the baby, who had rolled into a ball.*

stretch something **out**† **(to** someone or something**)** to reach something out to someone or something. □ *Jeff stretched his hand out to Tiffany.* □ *He stretched out his hand to the visitor.*

stretch the point Go to next.

stretch the truth and **stretch the point; stretch it** *Fig.* to exaggerate. □ *When he claimed to have a Ph.D., he was stretching the truth.* □ *Sally tends to stretch the point when telling tales about her wild teenage years.*

Stretch your arm no further than your sleeve will reach. *Prov.* Do not spend more money than you have. □ *Sue: I can get enough money for college if I take out several loans. Bill: I'd advise against it. Stretch your arm no further than your sleeve will reach.*

strew something **(all) over** something to sow or spread something over an area. □ *Clean this place up! You have strewn your clothing all over the place.* □ *The wind strewed the leaves over the lawns.*

strew something **on** someone or something to sow or spread something on someone or something. □ *The wind strewed the dandelion seeds on Fred and his friends.* □ *A child went down the aisle, strewing flowers on the white walkway ahead of the bride.*

strew something **over** someone or something to spread or scatter something over someone or something. □ *The silo*

explosion strewed the grain over everyone in the vicinity. □ *The explosion strewed wreckage over a two-block area.*

strew something **with** something to cover something with bits of something. □ *Who strewed the sidewalk with rice and confetti?* □ *The yards were strewn with leaves and branches after the storm.*

*stricken with something afflicted or overwhelmed with something. (*Typically: **be** ~; **become** ~; **get** ~.) □ *Albert was stricken with a strange disease.* □ *Fred was stricken with remorse because of his rude remarks.* □ *Tom was stricken with the flu after his trip to Russia.*

strictly business 1. a matter or issue that is all business and no pleasure. □ *This meeting is strictly business. We don't have time for any leisure activity.* **2.** a person who is very businesslike and does not waste time with nonbusiness matters. □ *Joe is strictly business. I don't think he has a sense of humor. At least I have never seen it.*

(strictly) from hunger *Sl.* very mediocre; acceptable only when nothing else is available. □ *This kind of entertainment is from hunger.* □ *The singer was strictly from hunger.*

(strictly) on the level honest; dependably open and fair. □ *How can I be sure you're on the level?* □ *You can trust Sally. She's strictly on the level.*

(strictly) on the up-and-up honest; fair and straight. □ *Do you think that the mayor is on the up-and-up?* □ *Yes, the mayor is strictly on the up-and-up.*

stride in(to some place**)** to walk with long steps into some place. □ *Jeff strode into the restaurant and demanded the best table.* □ *He strode in and ordered roast chicken.*

stride out of some place to walk with long steps out of some place. □ *The angry customer strode out of the shop without purchasing anything.* □ *We strode out of the restaurant, pledging never to go there again.*

strike a balance (between two things**)** to find a satisfactory compromise between two extremes. □ *The political party must strike a balance between the right wing and the left wing.* □ *Jane is overdressed for the party and Sally is underdressed. What a pity they didn't strike a balance between them.*

strike a bargain and **strike a deal** to reach an agreement on a price or negotiation (for something). □ *They argued for a while and finally struck a bargain.* □ *They were unable to strike a bargain, so they ended their meeting.*

strike a chord (with someone**)** *Fig.* to cause someone to remember something; to remind someone of something; to be familiar. □ *The woman in the portrait struck a chord with me, and I realized that it was my grandmother.* □ *His name strikes a chord, but I don't know why.*

strike a deal Go to strike a bargain.

strike a happy medium and **hit a happy medium; find a happy medium** to find a compromise position; to arrive at a position halfway between two unacceptable extremes. □ *Ann likes very spicy food, but Bob doesn't care for spicy food at all. We are trying to find a restaurant that strikes a happy medium.* □ *Tom is either very happy or very sad. He can't seem to hit a happy medium.*

strike a match to light a match by rubbing it on a rough surface. □ *Mary struck a match and lit a candle.* □ *When*

S

Sally struck a match to light a cigarette, Jane said quickly, "No smoking, please."

strike a pose to position oneself in a certain posture. □ *Bob struck a pose in front of the mirror to see how much he had bulked up.* □ *Lisa walked into the room and struck a pose, hoping she would be noticed.*

strike a sour note and **hit a sour note** *Fig.* to signify something unpleasant. □ *Jane's sad announcement struck a sour note at the annual banquet.* □ *News of the accident hit a sour note in our holiday celebration.*

strike at someone or something to hit at or toward someone or something. □ *She struck at him, but he parried the blows.* □ *The bear struck at the branch, hoping to break it and get at the honey.*

strike back (at someone or something**)** to return the blows of someone or something; to return the attack of someone or something. □ *The victim struck back at the mugger and scared him away.* □ *The victim struck back in the courts.*

strike for something to conduct a work stoppage in order to gain something. □ *The workers were striking for longer vacations.* □ *We are striking for higher pay.*

strike home Go to hit home.

strike home with someone [for something] to awaken recognition and acceptance in a person. □ *What you said really strikes home with me.* □ *Her comments struck home with her audience.*

strike it rich to acquire wealth suddenly. □ *If I could strike it rich, I wouldn't have to work anymore.* □ *Sally ordered a dozen oysters and found a huge pearl in one of them. She struck it rich!*

strike out 1. *Lit.* [for a baseball batter] to be declared out after making three strikes. (Baseball.) □ *And so Drew Wilson strikes out for his second time in this game!* □ *He struck out in the second inning, and the manager took him out then.* **2.** *Fig.* to fail. □ *Well, we struck out again, but we'll keep trying.* □ *I hear you struck out on that Acme proposal. Better luck next time.*

strike out (at someone or something**)** to hit at someone or something with the intention of threatening or harming. □ *Dave would strike out at anyone who came near him, but it was all bluff.* □ *He was mad, and when anyone came close, he struck out.*

strike out for some place to begin a journey to some place; to set out on a journey for some place. □ *We struck out for Denver, hoping to get there in a few hours.* □ *The hikers struck out for the cabin but were delayed by a sudden storm.*

strike out on one's **own** and **set out on** one's **own** to start out to live, work, or travel by oneself. □ *I couldn't get along with my business partner, so I decided to strike out on my own.*

strike over something to mark out printed words by putting x's over them or a line through them. □ *Please don't strike over your errors. Erase them altogether.* □ *Betty struck over most of the misspellings.*

strike someone **as** something **1.** [for a thought or behavior] to affect someone a certain way. □ *John's rude behavior struck me as surprising.* □ *Mary's attitude struck me as*

childish. **2.** [for a person] to impress someone as something or a particular type of person. □ *You strike me as thoughtful.* □ *You don't strike me as the type of person to do something like that.*

strike someone **funny** *Fig.* to seem funny to someone. □ *Sally has a great sense of humor. Everything she says strikes me funny.* □ *Why are you laughing? Did something I said strike you funny?*

strike someone or something **down**† to knock someone or something down by striking. □ *Max struck Lefty down with one blow.* □ *He struck down the weeds with a scythe.*

strike someone or something **from** something to remove someone or something from something, such as a list. □ *I will have to strike David from our rolls. He never shows up.* □ *We struck the red car from the list of eligible racers.*

strike someone or something **on** something to hit someone or something on a particular place or part. □ *The ball struck me on my elbow, causing a great deal of pain.* □ *I struck the bear on the paw, and that only made it madder.*

strike someone or something **with** something to hit someone or something with something. □ *Max struck Lefty with his fist.* □ *The mayor struck the table with his fist.*

strike someone's **fancy** to appeal to someone. □ *I'll have some ice cream, please. Chocolate strikes my fancy right now.* □ *Why don't you go to the store and buy a CD that strikes your fancy?*

strike something **down**† [for a court] to invalidate a ruling or law. □ *The higher court struck the ruling of the lower court down.* □ *The court struck down the ruling.*

strike something **into** something to knock something, such as a ball, into something. □ *Johnny struck the ball into the vacant lot.* □ *Ted struck golf ball after golf ball into the water.*

strike something **off (of)** someone or something and **strike** something **off**† to knock something off someone or something. (*Of* is usually retained before pronouns.) □ *She accidentally struck John's hat off of him.* □ *She struck off a chunk of ice.*

strike something **out**† to cross something out of a section of printing or writing. □ *This is wrong. Please strike it out.* □ *Strike out this sentence.*

strike something **up**† to begin something; to cause something to begin. (Typically, the playing of a band, a conversation, or a friendship.) □ *We tried to strike a conversation up—to no avail.* □ *I struck up a conversation with Molly.*

strike something **(up)on** something to hit or bang something on something else. □ *She struck her head upon the side of the bed.* □ *Mary struck her elbow on the doorjamb.*

strike the right note *Fig.* to achieve the desired effect; to do something suitable or pleasing. □ *Meg struck the right note when she wore a dark suit to the interview.* □ *The politician's speech failed to strike the right note with the crowd.*

strike up a conversation to start a conversation (with someone). □ *I struck up an interesting conversation with someone on the bus yesterday.* □ *It's easy to strike up a conversation with someone when you're traveling.*

S

655

strike up a friendship to become friends (with someone). □ *I struck up a friendship with John while we were on a business trip together.* □ *If you're lonely, you should go out and try to strike up a friendship with someone you like.*

strike up the band 1. *Lit.* to cause a (dance) band to start playing. □ *Strike up the band, maestro, so we all can dance the night away.* **2.** *Fig.* to cause something to start. □ *Strike up the band! Let's get this show on the road.*

Strike while the iron is hot. *Prov.* When you have an opportunity to do something, do it before you lose your chance. □ *This is the best time in the last ten years to buy a house. Strike while the iron is hot.* □ *Ask Lisa for a favor now, while she's in a good mood. Strike while the iron is hot.*

string along (with someone**) 1.** to follow with someone. □ *Do you mind if I string along with you?* □ *I don't mind if you string along.* **2.** to agree with someone's policies and actions. □ *Okay. I will string along with you this time, but I don't know about the future.* □ *I would appreciate it if you would string along just this one time.*

a **string of bad luck** Go to a **streak of bad luck**.

a **string of good luck** Go to a **streak of good luck**.

string someone **along** to maintain someone's attention or interest, probably insincerely. □ *You are just stringing me along because you like to borrow my car. You are not a real friend.* □ *Rachel strung her along for the sake of old times.*

string someone **up**[†] to hang someone. □ *The sheriff swore he would string Tex up whenever he caught him.* □ *He never strung up Tex.*

string something **out**[†] **1.** *Lit.* to unwind, stretch, or straighten something, such as wire, and extend it. □ *The workers strung the wires out before installing them.* □ *They strung out the wires first.* **2.** *Fig.* to cause something to take more time than it ought to. □ *Is there any good reason to string this meeting out any longer?* □ *Don't string out the meetings so long.*

string something **together** to connect things, such as beads, together, as with string. □ *I spent all afternoon stringing beads together.* □ *My pearls broke and I had to take them to a jeweler to have them strung together again.*

strip down to remove one's clothing. □ *The doctor told Joe to strip down for his examination.* □ *Joe stripped down for the examination.*

strip for something to take off one's clothing for something. □ *Todd went into the locker room and stripped for his shower.* □ *All the recruits stripped for their medical examination.*

strip someone or something **down to** something and **strip** someone or something **down**[†] to remove the covering of someone or something down to the lowest level. □ *The emergency room nurse stripped the unconscious patient down to his shorts.* □ *He stripped down the patient to his underwear.* □ *He stripped the patient down.*

strip someone or something **of** something to take something, such as status or property, away from someone or something. □ *The court stripped him of all his property.* □ *We stripped him of his rights when we put him in jail.*

strip something **away**[†] **(from** someone or something**)** to remove or peel something from someone or something. □ *The emergency room nurse stripped the clothing away from the burn victim.* □ *He stripped away the victim's clothing.* □ *Jamie stripped away the old paint from the bathroom wall.*

strip something **in**[†] to insert something into a line of print by gluing or a strip of paper. □ *You will have to strip the accent in.* □ *Strip in a grave accent right here.*

strip something **off (of)** someone or something and **strip** something **off**[†] to tear something from someone or something. (*Of* is usually retained before pronouns.) □ *The paramedic stripped the shirt off the burn victim and began to treat her burns.* □ *The medic stripped off the patient's shirt.*

strip to something to take off one's clothing down to a particular level, usually to one's skin, the waist, or some euphemistic way of expressing nudity or near nudity. □ *Tom stripped to the waist and continued to labor in the hot sun.* □ *Tom stripped to the bare essentials and got ready to be examined by the doctor.*

strive after something to try very hard to obtain something. □ *I am always striving after perfection.* □ *Ted was striving after a promotion and finally got it.*

strive against something to work against something. □ *He worked hard, striving against failure at every turn.* □ *Things were difficult. I had to strive against quitting almost every day.*

strive for something to try to obtain or bring about something. □ *I am striving for the best possible result.* □ *Mary strives for perfection in everything she does.*

strive to do something to try hard to do something. □ *She strove very hard to do what she had set out to do.* □ *Please strive to do it as best you can.*

strive toward something to work toward a goal. □ *I always strive toward perfection.* □ *Mary strove toward doing her best at all times.*

a **stroke of genius** an act of genius; a very clever and innovative idea or task. □ *Your idea of painting the rock wall red was a stroke of genius.*

a **stroke of luck** *Fig.* a bit of luck; a lucky happening. □ *I had a stroke of luck and found Tom at home when I called. He's not usually there.* □ *Unless I have a stroke of luck, I'm not going to finish this report by tomorrow.*

stroke someone's **ego** *Fig.* to flatter and praise someone. □ *If you have trouble with him, just take a few minutes and stroke his ego. You'll soon have him eating out of your hand.*

stroll arm in arm Go to **arm in arm**.

stroll around to walk around casually. □ *I think I will stroll around a bit this evening.* □ *Would you like to stroll around a little and see the sights?*

stroll through something to walk casually through something or some place. □ *Would you like to stroll through the park with me?* □ *Let's stroll through a few shops and see what the prices are like here.*

*****strong as a horse** and *****strong as an ox**; *****strong as a lion** *Cliché* [of a living creature] very strong. (*Also: **as** ~.) □ *Jill: My car broke down; it's sitting out on the street. Jane: Get Linda to help you push it; she's as strong as a horse.* □ *The athlete was strong as an ox; he could lift his own weight with just one hand.* □ *The football player was strong as a lion.*

S

strong as a lion Go to previous.

strong as an ox Go to strong as a horse.

the **strong, silent type** a strong, quiet man. □ *Clark looks like the strong, silent type. Actually he is slightly deaf and that's fat, not muscle.*

strong-arm tactics force; the use of force. □ *No more strong-arm tactics. You need to be more subtle.* □ *Strong-arm tactics are out. The boss says be gentle and don't hurt anybody.*

struggle against someone or something to strive or battle against someone or something. □ *There is no point in struggling against me. I will win out.* □ *He struggled against the disease for a year before he died.*

struggle along under something to make do as well as one can under a particular burden. □ *I will have to struggle along under these poor conditions for quite a while.* □ *I am sorry you have to struggle along under such burdens.*

struggle along (with someone or something**)** to make do as well as one can with someone or something. □ *I really need someone who can work faster, but I'll struggle along with Walter.* □ *We struggled along the best we could.*

struggle for something to strive to obtain something. □ *I was struggling for a law degree when I won the lottery.* □ *I had to struggle for everything that came my way.*

struggle on with something to make do as well as one can with something. □ *I will have to struggle on with the car that I have.* □ *We will struggle on with what we have, hoping for better someday.*

struggle through (something**)** to get through something in the best way possible. □ *I am going to struggle through this dull book to the very end.* □ *The course was dull, but I struggled through.*

struggle to do something to strive or battle to do something. □ *She struggled hard to meet her deadlines.* □ *We had to struggle to make ends meet.*

struggle to the death 1. *Lit.* a bitter struggle ending in death. □ *The wolf and the elk fought in a struggle to the death.* **2.** *Fig.* a serious problem with someone or something; a difficult challenge. □ *I had a terrible time getting my car started. It was a struggle to the death, but it finally started.*

struggle with someone **for** something to fight with someone to obtain something. □ *Max struggled with Lefty for the gun, and it went off.* □ *Timmy struggled with Bobby for the bicycle, and finally David took it away from both of them.*

struggle with someone or something to fight or battle with someone or something. □ *Fred struggled with Tom for a while and finally gave in.* □ *Tom struggled with the disease for a while and finally succumbed to it.*

strum something **on** something to brush or play with the fingers some stringed instrument, such as a guitar. □ *She strummed a nice little melody on her guitar.* □ *He strummed the accompaniment on the guitar.*

strung out 1. extended in time; overly long. □ *Why was that lecture so strung out? She talked and talked.* □ *It was strung out because there was very little to be said.* **2.** *Sl.* doped or drugged. □ *Bob acted very strangely—as if he*

were strung out or something. □ *I've never seen Bob or any of his friends strung out.*

strut around to stride around pompously. □ *Stop strutting around in your new jeans and get to work!* □ *Tex was strutting around, showing off his new boots.*

strut in(to some place**)** to stride pompously into a place. □ *He strutted into the house as if he owned the place.* □ *Betty strutted in and sat down.*

strut one's **stuff** *Sl.* to walk proudly and show off one's best features or talents. □ *Get out there on that stage and strut your stuff!* □ *I'm going to strut my stuff and become a star.*

strut out of some place to stride pompously or showily out of some place. □ *The clowns strutted out of the tent and joined the parade through the big top.* □ *Tex strutted out of the saloon and got on his horse.*

stub one's **toe against** something and **stub** one's **toe on** something to ram one's toe accidentally against some hard object. □ *Don't stub your toe against that brick in the path.* □ *Claire stubbed her toe against one of the legs of the sofa.* □ *I stubbed my toe on the bottom step.*

stub something **out**† to put out something, such as a cigarette or cigar, by crushing the burning end against a hard object. □ *Max stubbed his cigar out and tossed it into the street.* □ *He stubbed out his cigar.*

***stubborn as a mule** and ***obstinate as a mule** *Cliché* very stubborn. (*Also: as ~.) □ *I tried to convince Jake to go to the doctor, but he's as stubborn as a mule.* □ *For four years, Henry pestered his parents to let him learn the trumpet. They tried to talk him into some other, quieter instrument, but he was stubborn as a mule, and now he has a trumpet.*

(stuck) in a rut *Fig.* kept in an established way of living or working that never changes. □ *David felt like he was stuck in a rut, so he went back to school.* □ *Anne was tired of being in a rut, so she moved to Los Angeles.*

stuck in traffic to be caught in a traffic jam. □ *I am sorry I am late. I was stuck in traffic.* □ *Our taxi was stuck in traffic and I thought I would never get to the airport on time.*

***stuck on** someone or something **1.** *Lit.* attached, as if by glue, to someone or something. (*Typically: **be** ~; **become** ~; **get** ~.) □ *The gum is stuck on me. How do I get it off?* □ *The gum is stuck on the floor.* **2.** *Fig.* in love with someone or something; entranced with someone or something. (*Typically: **be** ~; **become** ~; **get** ~.) □ *Judy is really stuck on Jeff.* □ *She is stuck on herself.*

stuck on something **1.** *Fig.* to be locked into an idea, cause, or purpose. □ *Mary is really stuck on the idea of going to France this spring.* □ *You've proposed a good plan, Jane, but you're stuck on it. We may have to make some changes.* **3.** *Fig.* to be confused by something, such as a puzzle or a task. (Typically: **be** ~; **become** ~; **get** ~.) □ *I'm stuck on this question about the tax rates.*

stuck with someone or something burdened with someone or something; left having to care for or deal with someone or something. □ *Please don't leave me stuck with your aunt. She talks too much.* □ *My roommate quit school and left me stuck with the telephone bill.*

S

study for something to try to learn in preparation for an examination. □ *I have to study for my calculus exam.* □ *Have you studied for your exam yet?*

study up on someone or something to learn all one can about someone or something. □ *I have to study up on Abraham Lincoln in preparation for my speech.* □ *John studied up on seashells.*

Stuff a sock in it! and **Put a sock in it!** *Inf.* Shut up! □ *I've heard enough. Stuff a sock in it!* □ *Stuff a sock in it! You are a pain.*

stuff and nonsense foolishness; foolish talk. □ *Come on! Don't give me all that stuff and nonsense!* □ *I don't understand this book. It's all stuff and nonsense as far as I am concerned.*

stuff one's **face** Go to **fill** one's **face.**

stuff someone or something **into** someone or something and **stuff** someone or something **in**† to force someone or something into someone or something. □ *The sheriff stuffed Tex into the tiny cell.* □ *He stuffed in some other prisoners, too.* □ *Donna got down her suitcase and stuffed her clothes in.* □ *The nurse stuffed the oatmeal into the old man faster than he could swallow it.*

stuff someone or something **with** something to fill up someone or something with something. □ *She stuffed the kids with pancakes and sent them to school.* □ *Dale stuffed the doll with fluffy material and gave it back to Timmy.* □ *He was afraid he would stuff himself with food as he usually did.*

stuff someone's **head with** something to fill someone's brain with certain kinds of thoughts. □ *Who has been stuffing your head with that nonsense?* □ *Tex thought that the government was stuffing peoples' heads with all sorts of propaganda.*

stuff something **down** someone's **throat** *Fig.* to force someone to hear, learn, endure, etc., some kind of information. □ *I don't like the nonsense they are stuffing down our throats.* □ *Please don't try to stuff those lies down our throats.*

stuff something **down** something to force something down inside of something. □ *Don stuffed the cauliflower leaves down the garbage disposal and turned it on.* □ *Timmy stuffed the leaves down the hole and covered them with dirt.*

stuff something **up**† to plug something by stuffing something in its opening. □ *He stuffed the hole up with old newspapers.* □ *Liz stuffed up the hole with paper.*

stuff something **up** something to force something upward or up into something. □ *He tried to hide the book by stuffing it up the chimney.* □ *Sam stuffed the money he found up the downspout, where he thought no one would find it.*

stuff the ballot box to fill a ballot box with illegal votes or with more votes than the number of actual voters. □ *The politician was charged with stuffing the ballot box.* □ *The ballot box was stuffed with lots of votes for the crooked politician.*

stumble across someone or something and **stumble (up)on** someone or something; **stumble into** someone or something to find someone or something, usually by accident. (See also **stumble into** someone or something.) □ *I stumbled across an interesting book yesterday when I was* shopping. □ *Guess who I stumbled into at the library yesterday?* □ *I got lucky and stumbled on the right answer.*

stumble into someone or something to trip and lurch into someone or something. **1.** □ *Not seeing the brick in the path, Carl tripped and stumbled into Alice.* □ *Jamie stumbled into the wall.* **2.** Go to **stumble across** someone or something.

stumble on someone or something **1.** Go to **stumble across** someone or something. **2.** to trip over someone or something. □ *There were three of us sleeping in the small tent. Each of us would stumble on the others whenever we went out or came in.* □ *I stumbled on the curb and twisted my ankle.*

stumble over someone or something to trip over someone or something. □ *Tom stumbled over Bill, who was napping on the floor.* □ *Don't stumble over the laundry basket.*

stumble through something to get through a sequence of something awkwardly and falteringly. □ *The cast stumbled through the first act and barely finished the second.* □ *Mary stumbled through her speech and fled from the stage.*

stumble (up)on someone or something Go to **stumble across** someone or something.

a **stumbling block** *Fig.* something that prevents or obstructs progress. □ *We'd like to buy that house, but the high price is a stumbling block.* □ *Jim's age is a stumbling block to getting another job. He's over sixty.*

stump for someone to go about making political speeches in support of someone. □ *The vice president was out stumping for members of Congress who were running this term.* □ *Since all the politicians were out stumping for one another, there was no one in the capital to vote on important legislation.*

stump someone to confuse or puzzle someone. □ *I have a question that will really stump you. When was the Achaean League established?*

sub for someone or something to substitute for someone or something. □ *I have to sub for Roger at work this weekend.* □ *Will pliers sub for the wrench you wanted?*

sub someone **for** someone else and **sub** something **for** something else to substitute someone for someone else or something for something else. □ *I will sub Chuck for Roger for this next play only.* □ *We will sub the red ones for the blue ones.*

subdivide something **into** something to divide something into parts. □ *They subdivided the land into several valuable parcels.* □ *Sam tried to subdivide his large lot into three smaller lots, but the zoning commission wouldn't let him do it.*

subject someone or something **to** something to cause someone to endure someone or something. □ *I didn't mean to subject you to Uncle Harry.* □ *I am sorry I have to subject you to all this questioning.*

subject to something likely to have something, such as a physical disorder. □ *The sick man was subject to dizzy spells.* □ *I am subject to frequent headaches.*

subjugate someone **to** someone to suppress someone in someone else's favor. □ *The army sought to subjugate everyone to the king.*

submerge someone or something **in** something to immerse someone or something in a liquid. □ *The preacher submerged Jeff in the water of the river as part of the baptism ceremony.* □ *Submerge the fish in the marinade for at least two hours.*

submerge someone or something **under** something to put someone or something below the surface of a liquid. □ *The maid submerged her mistress under the surface of the water for a moment and brought her up and dried her off.* □ *They submerged themselves under the surface of the water and had a look around.*

submit someone or something **to** something to allow someone or something to undergo the effects of something. □ *I hate to submit you to all this questioning, but that is the way we do things here.* □ *Don't submit your car to a lot of misuse.*

submit to something to surrender to something; to agree to something. □ *He submitted to the cross-examination.* □ *She will probably refuse to submit to surgery.*

subordinate someone or something **to** someone or something else to put someone in an inferior position to someone else; to put something in an inferior position to something else. □ *I am going to have to subordinate you to the other manager, because she has more experience.* □ *The first thing you learn is that you must subordinate yourself to your boss.*

subpoena someone **to** do something to formally deliver a document forcing someone to do something for a legal process. □ *The attorney subpoenaed a number of witnesses to testify.* □ *I subpoenaed four witnesses to appear but none of them showed up.*

subscribe to something **1.** to agree with a policy. □ *I don't subscribe to the scheme you have just described.* □ *You don't have to subscribe to the policy to accept it.* **2.** to hold a standing order for a magazine or other periodical, or for a computer service. □ *I subscribe to three magazines, and I enjoy them all.* □ *I don't subscribe to any of them anymore.*

subsist on something to exist on something; to stay alive on something. □ *We can barely subsist on this amount of money. We need more!* □ *They are able to do no more than subsist on what Mrs. Harris is paid.*

substitute for someone or something to serve as a replacement for someone or something. □ *I have to substitute for Roger at work this weekend.* □ *Do you think that this will substitute for the one you wanted?*

substitute someone **for** someone else and **substitute** something **for** something else to exchange someone or something for someone or something else; to replace someone or something with someone or something else. □ *Shall I substitute Fred for Mary in the front office?* □ *Please substitute fish for beef on my dinner order.*

subtract something **from** something else to deduct or take away something from something else. □ *Please subtract the cost of the meal from my fee.* □ *I demanded that they subtract the extra charge from my bill.*

succeed as something to flourish or prosper as a type of person. □ *I hope I succeed as a bank teller.* □ *Jamie succeeded as an investigator.*

succeed at something to prosper or flourish in some task. □ *I hope I can succeed at the task you have assigned me.* □ *I am sure you will succeed at it.*

succeed in something to prosper or flourish in some position or office. □ *I hope you succeed in your new job.* □ *We knew you would succeed in doing what you wanted to do.*

succeed someone **as** something to take the place of someone as something; to supplant someone in something. □ *Jeff will succeed Claude as president of the organization.* □ *You are not allowed to succeed yourself as president.*

succeed to something to fall heir to something; to take something over. □ *Carl will succeed to the throne when he is of age.* □ *Mary succeeded to the throne at the age of three months.*

succumb to something to yield to something, especially a temptation, fatal disease, a human weakness, etc. □ *He finally succumbed to his pneumonia.* □ *She did not succumb to the disease until she was very old.*

such and such someone or something whose name has been forgotten or should not be said. □ *Mary said that such and such was coming to her party, but I forgot their names.* □ *If you walk into a store and ask for such and such and they don't have it, you go to a different store.*

such as... for example. □ *Bill enjoys many kinds of fruit, such as apples, pears, and plums.* □ *Mary has many hobbies, such as swimming, bowling, and running.*

such as it is *Cliché* in the imperfect state that one sees it; in the less-than-perfect condition in which one sees it. □ *This is where I live. This is my glorious home—such as it is.* □ *I've worked for days on this report, and I've done the best that I can do. It's my supreme effort—such as it is.*

Such is life! That is the way things happen! (Usually in reference to an unfortunate outcome.) □ *Oh, well. Everything can't be perfect. Such is life!* □ *So I failed my test. Such is life! I can take it again some time.*

suck (some) brew and **suck (some) suds** *Sl.* to drink beer. □ *Wanna go suck some brew?* □ *I'm tired of sucking suds. Got any whisky?*

suck (some) suds Go to previous.

suck someone **in**[†] and **take** someone **in**[†] to deceive someone. □ *I try to shop carefully so that no one can take me in.* □ *I think that someone sucked in both of them. I don't know why they bought this car.*

suck someone or something **down**[†] [for a vacuum or water currents] to pull someone or something downward. □ *The savage currents sucked the swimmers down to their death.* □ *The current sucked down the floating trees.*

suck someone or something **into** something and **suck** someone or something **in**[†] [for a vacuum] to draw someone or something into something. □ *The whirlpool sucked the swimmers into the depths of the river.* □ *The whirlpool sucked in a swimmer.* □ *A whirlpool nearly sucked our canoe in.*

suck someone or something **under** [for a current or waves] to pull someone or something beneath the surface of the water. □ *The strong rip tide almost sucked me under!* □ *It almost sucked our boat under.*

suck someone's **hind tit** *Sl.* to be forced to do someone's bidding no matter how unpleasant or impossible. (Fig. on

659

the idea of the last of a litter of animals to get its mother's milk. Potentially offensive. Use only with discretion.) □ *What am I supposed to do—suck his hind tit?* □ *She acts like everybody has to suck her hind tit to keep their jobs.*

suck something **from** something to draw something out of something by the application of a vacuum. □ *Freddie used his straw to suck the last of the cola from the can.* □ *The machine sucked the water from the bottom of the barrel.*

suck something **in**† **1.** *Lit.* to draw something into one's mouth by sucking. □ *She sucked the milk shake in so hard she nearly collapsed the straw.* □ *Liz sucked in the fresh air.* **2.** *Fig.* to draw in one's belly, gut, or stomach. □ *Suck that belly in!* □ *Suck in that gut!*

suck something **up**† to pick something up by suction, as with a vacuum cleaner, or through a straw. □ *Will this vacuum suck all this dirt up?* □ *The vacuum cleaner sucked up all the dirt.*

suck up to someone *Sl.* to attempt to gain influence with or favor from someone. □ *In school, Richard was always sucking up to the teacher.* □ *Don't suck up to me. It won't do any good.*

a **sucker for** someone or something someone who is prejudiced in favor of someone or something; someone who is drawn to someone or something. □ *I'm a sucker for a pretty face.* □ *Ted is a sucker for any dessert with whipped cream on it.* □ *I don't know why I volunteered for this job. I'm a sucker for punishment I guess.*

sucker list *Fig.* a list of potential dupes; a list of people who might be taken in by deception. □ *I'm sure on their sucker list. They are trying to get me to give a lecture and receive a free clock or something.* □ *Here's the sucker list. Call them all and try to get them interested.*

sucker someone **into** something and **sucker** someone **in**† *Sl.* to deceive someone into some sort of scam or confidence game; to play someone for a fool. □ *Surely you don't think you can sucker me into doing something as stupid as that, do you?* □ *The con artist suckered in an unsuspecting tourist.*

suddenly the fat hit the fire Go to the fat hit the fire.

sue for something to file a lawsuit in order to get something. □ *If you so much as harm a hair on my head, I will sue for damages.* □ *Ted sued for back pay in his dispute with a former employer.*

sue someone **for** something to file a lawsuit against someone in order to get something. □ *I will sue you for damages if you do anything else to my car!* □ *She sued her employer for failure to provide a safe workplace.*

sue the pants off (of) someone *Sl.* to sue someone for a lot of money. (*Of* is usually retained before pronouns.) □ *If they harm me in any way, I'll sue the pants off of them.* □ *He sued the pants off his landlord.*

suffer a setback to have a minor or temporary failure. □ *We suffered a setback when much of our vineyard was damaged by a fungus.*

suffer an attack (of an illness) Go to an attack (of an illness).

suffer from something to endure or experience unpleasantness, a disease, or a health condition. □ *Jeff is suffering from the flu.* □ *I'm afraid that you must suffer from*

the disease until it has run its course. □ *Toby is really suffering from the cold.*

suffer under someone to endure the punishments or bad treatment of someone. □ *The citizens suffered badly under the rule of the cruel king.* □ *We suffered under Carlos and we will suffer under his successor.*

suffice for someone or something to be sufficient for someone or something. □ *This serving will suffice for me. Did you get enough?* □ *Will this suffice for you?*

Sufficient unto the day is the evil thereof. *Prov.* You should not worry about things that might happen in the future.; It is enough to worry about things that are happening today. (Biblical.) □ *Jane: I can't get to sleep; I keep thinking about the interview I have to do tomorrow. Alan: If the interview is tomorrow, worry about it tomorrow. Sufficient unto the day is the evil thereof.*

suffix something **onto** something to add an inflection or other part of a word onto another word. □ *The students were told to suffix the correct plural marker onto all the nouns in the list.* □ *What do you get when you suffix -ed onto a verb like talk?*

suffuse something **with** something to saturate something with something, usually a color. □ *The sun suffused the afternoon sky with orange and yellow.* □ *The bright light suffused the leaves with a golden glow.*

suggest itself to someone [for an idea] to seem to present itself to someone. □ *A new scheme suggested itself to Alice as she looked at the records of the last attempt.* □ *As you read this, does anything suggest itself to you?*

suggest something **to** someone to make a suggestion of something to someone. □ *The waiter suggested the roast beef to all his customers.* □ *What did you suggest to the people at the other table? They look quite pleased with their meal.*

*****suggestive of** something reminiscent of something; suggesting something. (*Typically: **be** ~; **become** ~.) □ *Bill's homemade soup is suggestive of his mother's.* □ *The new movie was suggestive of an old one I had seen on TV.*

suit one's **actions to** one's **words** to behave in accordance with what one has said; to do what one has promised or threatened to do. □ *Mr. Smith suited his actions to his words and punished the children.* □ *John threatened to quit, and when he didn't get his way, he suited his actions to his words.*

suit oneself to do something one's own way; to do something to please oneself. □ *If he doesn't want to do it my way, he can suit himself.*

suit (oneself) **up** to get into one's uniform, especially an athletic uniform. □ *The coach told the team to suit up for the game by three o'clock.* □ *It's time to suit up!* □ *She suited herself up and went out on the court.*

suit someone or something **to** something to match someone or something to something. □ *I am sorry, but we don't suit the worker to the job. We find a job that suits the worker.* □ *Let's try to suit a new sports jacket to the slacks you have on.*

suit someone's **fancy** to appeal to someone's imagination, fantasy, or preferences. □ *Does this handbag suit your fancy, or would you prefer something larger?* □ *I think a big bowl of ice cream would suit my fancy quite nicely.*

S

suit someone **to a T** and **fit** someone **to a T** to be very appropriate for someone. □ *This kind of job suits me to a T.* □ *This is Sally's kind of house. It fits her to a T.*

Suit yourself. *Inf.* You decide the way you want it.; **Have it your way.** □ *Mary: I think I want the red one. Tom: Suit yourself.* □ *John (reading the menu): The steak sounds good, but it's hard to pass up the fried chicken. Sally: Suit yourself. I'll have the steak.*

*suited for something appropriate for something. (*Typically: **be ~; become ~**.) □ *Do you think I am suited for this kind of work?* □ *Those clothes are not suited for outdoor work.*

sulk about someone or something and **sulk over** someone or something to pout or be sullen about someone or something. □ *What are you sulking about now?* □ *There is no need to sulk over Mary.*

sum and substance a summary; the gist. □ *Can you quickly tell me the sum and substance of your proposal?* □ *In trying to explain the sum and substance of the essay, Thomas failed to mention the middle name of the hero.*

sum (something) **up**† to give a summary of something. □ *I would like to sum this lecture up by listing the main points I have covered.* □ *It is time for me to sum up.* □ *She summed up the president's speech in three sentences.*

summon someone **before** someone or something to request or order someone to appear before someone or a group. □ *The president summoned the committee before her.* □ *The judge summoned Donna before the court.*

summon someone **to** someone or something to order or request someone to come to someone or something. □ *Uncle Fred summoned the waitress to him.* □ *He summoned her to our table.*

summon something **up**† to call forth particular qualities, such as strength, courage, wisdom, etc. □ *She summoned her courage up and went into the room.* □ *Liz summoned up all her courage.*

the **sun belt** *Fig.* the southern U.S. states, where it is generally warm and sunny. □ *I want to retire to the sun belt.* □ *The population of the sun belt is exploding.*

Sunday best one's best clothing, which one would wear to church. (See also **Sunday-go-to-meeting clothes**.) □ *We are in our Sunday best, ready to go.* □ *I got mud on my Sunday best.*

Sunday driver a slow and leisurely driver who appears to be sightseeing and enjoying the view, holding up traffic in the process. (Also a term of address.) □ *I'm a Sunday driver, and I'm sorry. I just can't bear to go faster.* □ *Move over, you Sunday driver!*

Sunday-go-to-meeting clothes *Rur.* one's best clothes. (See also **Sunday best**.) □ *John was all dressed up in his Sunday-go-to-meeting clothes.* □ *I hate to be wearing my Sunday-go-to-meeting clothes when everyone else is casually dressed.*

sunny-side up *Fig.* [of eggs] with yolks facing up and not turned over or cooked through; **straight up.** □ *I'll have my eggs sunny-side up, with toast and coffee.* □ *People who like sunny-side up eggs wouldn't dream of eating a whole raw egg.*

superimpose something **on(to)** someone or something to cover an image of someone or something with an image of something. □ *We superimposed a mustache onto Toby's face, and he looked just like the suspect.* □ *When we superimposed the mustache on him, we knew he was guilty.*

supply and demand the availability of things or people as compared to the need to utilize the things or people; the availability of goods compared to the number of willing customers for the goods. □ *Sometimes you can find what you want by shopping around and other times almost no store carries the items you are looking for. It depends entirely on supply and demand. (Alludes to a principle of market economics.)* □ *Sometimes customers ask for things we do not carry in stock and other times we have things in abundance that no one wants to buy. Whether or not we can make money off of a product depends entirely on supply and demand.*

supply someone or something **with** something to provide something to someone or something. □ *We will supply you with all the pencils you need.* □ *We supplied the committee with ice water.*

supply something **(to** someone or something**) (from** something**)** to provide someone or something with something from some source. □ *I supplied ice cream to the new restaurant from a very expensive source.* □ *We supplied nuts from a pushcart.* □ *Frank supplied nothing at all to them.*

Suppose I do? and **Supposing I do?** *Inf.* And what does it matter if I do? What are you going to do about it? □ *Alice: Do you really think it's right to do something like that? Sue: Suppose I do?* □ *Fred: Are you going to drive up into the mountains as you said you would? Sally: Supposing I do? Fred: I'm just asking.*

Suppose I don't? and **Supposing I don't?** *Inf.* And what will happen if I don't? (Said as a sort of threat. Not usually with question intonation.) □ *Bill: You'd better get yourself over to the main office. Tom: Suppose I don't?* □ *Father: You simply must do better in school. Tom: Supposing I don't? Father: Your clothing and personal belongings will be placed on the curb for the garbage pickup, and we will have the locks changed. Next question.*

Supposed to. and Someone or something **is supposed to.** Someone or something is meant to do something. (Frequently, in speech, *supposed* is reduced to *s'posed*. The words *someone* or *something* can be replaced with nouns or pronouns, or used themselves.) □ *Mary: They didn't deliver the flowers we ordered. Sue: Supposed to. Give them a call.* □ *Sally: This screw doesn't fit into hole number seven in the way the instructions say it should. Bill: It's supposed to. Something's wrong.*

supposed to do something expected or intended to do something; obliged or allowed to do something. □ *You're supposed to say "excuse me" when you burp.* □ *Mom says you're supposed to come inside for dinner now.*

Supposing I do? Go to Suppose I do?

Supposing I don't? Go to Suppose I don't?

sure as eggs is eggs Go to sure as God made little green apples.

sure as fate Go to next.

*sure as God made little green apples and ***sure as eggs is eggs; *sure as fate; *sure as I'm stand-**

ing here; *sure as you live** *Rur.* absolutely certain. (*Also: **as** ~.) □ *I'm as sure as God made little green apples that he's the one.* □ *I'm right, as sure as you live!*

***sure as hell** *Inf.* very sure. (Use discretion with *hell*. *Also: **as** ~.) □ *As sure as hell, Ill be there on time.* □ *As sure as hell he did it!*

sure as I'm standing here Go to sure as God made little green apples.

Sure as shooting! *Inf.* Absolutely yes! (An elaboration of *Sure*.) □ *Bill: Are you going to be there Monday night? Bob: Sure as shooting!* □ *Bob: Will you take this over to the main office? Bill: Sure as shooting!*

sure as you live Go to sure as God made little green apples.

a **sure bet** and a **sure thing** a certainty; something that is sure to take place. □ *Of course, this land will become valuable in a few years. It's a sure thing!*

Sure thing. *Inf.* I certainly will. □ *Sue: Will you be at the reception? Bob: Sure thing.* □ *Bill: You remember my cousin, Tom, don't you? Bob: Sure thing. Hi, Tom.*

surf and turf fish and beef; lobster and beef. (A dinner serving incorporating both expensive seafood and an expensive cut of beef. Alludes to the sea and to the pasture. Fixed order.) □ *Walter ordered the surf and turf, but Alice ordered only a tiny salad.* □ *No surf and turf for me. I want fish and fish alone.*

surf the Net to browse around in the contents of the Internet. □ *I spend an hour a day or more surfing the Net.*

surge in(to something) to burst or gush into something or some place. □ *The water surged into the valley after the dam broke.* □ *The doors opened and the people surged in.*

surge out (of something) to burst forth or gush out of something or some place. □ *The water surged out of the huge crack in the dam.* □ *We saw the crack where the water surged out.*

surge up to rush or gush upwards. □ *A spring of fresh water surged up under the stone and flowed out on the ground.* □ *The oil surged up and blew out into the open air in a tall black column.*

surpass someone or something in something to exceed someone or something in some deed or quality. □ *I will never be able to surpass Jill in speed or agility.* □ *My car surpasses yours in almost every respect.*

surprise someone by something to astonish someone by doing or being something. □ *You surprised me by your forthrightness.* □ *No one was surprised by the way it happened.*

surprise someone with something to astonish someone by presenting or showing something. □ *I surprised her with a bouquet of roses.* □ *He surprised Roger with a new car.*

surrender someone or something to someone or something to give up someone or something to someone or something. □ *You must surrender your child to the nurse for the child's own good. She will give her right back.* □ *He surrendered his car to the bank.*

surrender to someone or something to give in to someone or something; to yield to someone or something. □ *The robber surrendered to the cops.* □ *I will never surrender to my baser passions.*

surround someone or something with someone or something to encircle or enclose someone or something with people, something, or things. □ *We surrounded him with his friends as he lay in the hospital bed.* □ *We surrounded the tree with wire netting to protect it against rabbits.* □ *They surrounded the display of jewels with guards.*

the **survival of the fittest** the idea that the most able or fit will survive (while the less able and less fit will perish). (This is used literally as a principle of the theory of evolution.) □ *In college, it's the survival of the fittest. You have to keep working in order to survive and graduate.* □ *I don't give my houseplants very good care, but the ones I have are really flourishing. It's the survival of the fittest, I guess.*

susceptible to something 1. easily persuaded; easily influenced. □ *The students were susceptible to the allure of drugs.* □ *The young revolutionaries were susceptible to propaganda.* **2.** likely to contract a sickness; likely to become sick. □ *People with AIDS are susceptible to pneumonia.* □ *Infants and the elderly are more susceptible to illness than other people.*

suspect someone of something to think or believe that someone has done something. □ *I suspect the clerk of stealing.* □ *Ted was suspected of leaving the door unlocked when he left last Friday.*

suspend someone from something to prevent someone from participating in something. (Usually as a form of discipline.) □ *The principal suspended the student from classes for a week.* □ *Ted was suspended from school for three days.*

suspend someone or something from something to hang someone or something from something. □ *The hangman suspended the thief from a gibbet as a warning to others.* □ *Jill suspended each decoration from a different branch.*

suspend something by something to hang something by something. □ *The workers carefully positioned the stone that was suspended by a steel cable.* □ *Will suspended the decoration by a fine thread.*

a **suspicious character** Go to a shady character.

suss someone out† *Sl.* to try to figure someone out. □ *I can't seem to suss Tom out. What a strange guy.* □ *I don't have any luck sussing out people I don't know well.*

sustain someone in something to stand by or support someone through some problem. □ *She knew she could count on her friends to sustain her in times of trouble.* □ *We will sustain you in the difficult times the best we can.*

swab something down† to wash or scrub something, such as the deck of a ship. □ *The sailors were told to swab the deck down each day.* □ *Swab down the deck!*

swab something out† to wash or wipe something out in order to make it clean. □ *The doctor swabbed my ear out carefully.* □ *The doctor swabbed out my ear carefully.*

swab something out of something and **swab something out†** to wipe or mop something out of something. □ *The doctor swabbed the wax out of my ear.* □ *I swabbed out the last of the mud on the floor.*

SWAK Go to sealed with a kiss.

swallow one's pride *Fig.* to forget one's pride and accept something humiliating. □ *I had to swallow my pride and admit that I was wrong.* □ *When you're trying to master a* *new skill, you find yourself swallowing your pride quite often.*

swallow someone or something **up**† **1.** *Lit.* to eat or gobble up someone or something. □ *The fairy-tale wolf threatened to swallow the pig up in one bite.* □ *The wolf swallowed up the meat in one bite.* **2.** *Fig.* to engulf or contain something. □ *The vast garage seemed to swallow the cars up.* □ *The huge sweater swallowed up the tiny child.*

swallow something **down**† to swallow something. □ *Here, take this pill and swallow it down.* □ *Liz swallowed down the pill.*

swallow something **hook, line, and sinker** *Fig.* to believe something completely. (These terms refer to fishing and fooling a fish into being caught.) □ *I made up a story about why I was so late. The boss swallowed it hook, line, and sinker.* □ *I feel like a fool. I swallowed her lies hook, line, and sinker.*

swamp someone or something **with** something to cover or deluge someone or something with something. □ *The flood swamped our property with river water.* □ *The many orders for their product swamped the small business with too much to do.*

swan song *Fig.* the last work or performance of a playwright, musician, actor, etc., before death or retirement. □ *His portrayal of Lear was the actor's swan song.* □ *We didn't know that her performance last night was the singer's swan song.*

swap notes (on someone or something**)** to share information on someone or something. □ *The two girls sat around swapping notes on guys they knew.* □ *The mechanics were swapping notes on rude customers they had dealt with in the last month.*

swap someone or something **for** someone or something else to trade someone or something for someone or something else. □ *I will swap my shortstop for your second baseman.* □ *There are times when I would gladly swap you for a new car—even an old car!*

swap someone or something **with** someone to exchange a person or thing for someone else's person or thing. □ *The representatives of the two countries swapped spies with each other.* □ *Can I swap jackets with you?*

swap with someone to exchange someone or something with someone. □ *I like yours better. I'll swap with you.* □ *If you don't want the sandwich you have, I will swap with you.*

swarm (all) over someone or something to gather and move all about on someone or throughout something or some place. □ *The ants swarmed all over our picnic table.* □ *The children swarmed over the furniture.*

swarm around someone or something to gather or crowd around someone or something, in the manner of a swarm of bees. □ *The little children swarmed around the lady with the candy.* □ *The bees swarmed around the flowers.*

swarm in(to something**)** [for a throng] to crowd into something or some place. □ *People were swarming into the auditorium to hear the guitarist.* □ *They swarmed in and ran for the best seats.*

swarm out of something to move out of something in great numbers. □ *The bees swarmed out of the hive.* □ *People swarmed out of the park at the end of the game.*

swarm through something to gather in a crowd and move through something or some place. □ *The shoppers swarmed through the store, buying everything in sight.* □ *The locusts swarmed through the field, eating the entire harvest.*

swarm with someone or something to be abundant or crowded with moving people or things. □ *The playground was swarming with children, and I couldn't find my own.* □ *The picnic blanket swarmed with ants.*

swathe someone or something **in** something to wrap or drape someone or something in something. □ *Molly swathed her children in sheets to turn them into ghosts on Halloween.* □ *She swathed the statue in black velvet for the unveiling ceremony.*

swathe someone or something **with** something to wrap or drape someone or something with something. □ *The sculptor swathed his unfinished pieces with heavy drapes.* □ *The designer swathed the window with billows of taffeta.*

sway back and forth to swing or bend from one direction to another. □ *The pendulum swayed back and forth, counting off the seconds.* □ *Mary was swaying back and forth, keeping time to the music.*

sway from side to side to swing or bend from one side to the other. □ *The car swayed from side to side as we started out, indicating that something was seriously wrong.* □ *He swayed from side to side with the rhythm of the music.*

sway someone **to** something to convince someone to do something. □ *I think I can sway her to join our side.* □ *We could not sway Ted to our position.*

swear at someone or something to curse someone or something. □ *Please don't swear at the children.* □ *Scott swore at the police station as he drove by.*

swear by someone or something **1.** *Lit.* to utter an oath on someone or something. □ *I swear by Jupiter that I will be there on time.* □ *She swore by her sainted mother that she would never do it again.* □ *The sheriff swore by his badge that he would lock her up if she ever did it again.* **2.** *Fig.* to announce one's full faith and trust in someone or something. □ *I would swear by Roger any time. He is a great guy, and he tells the truth.* □ *I swear by this computer. It has always served me well.*

swear like a trooper to curse and swear with great facility. (The trooper here refers to a soldier.) □ *Mrs. Wilson was known to swear like a trooper on occasion.* □ *The clerk started swearing like a trooper, and the customer started crying.*

swear off (something**)** to pledge to avoid or abstain from something. □ *I've sworn off desserts. I am on a diet.* □ *No dessert for me. I've sworn off.*

swear on a stack of Bibles and **swear on** one's **mother's grave** to state something very earnestly, pledging to tell the truth. (**~ a stack of Bibles** refers in an exaggerated way to swearing to tell the truth in court by placing one's hand on a Bible.) □ *I swear on a stack of Bibles that I am telling the truth.* □ *Of course, I'm telling the truth. I swear on my mother's grave!*

swear on one's **mother's grave** Go to previous.

swear someone **in**† **(as** something**)** to administer an oath to someone who then officially begins in office. □ *The* judge swore Alice in as street commissioner. □ *The judge swore in Alice as the new director.*

swear someone **to** something to cause someone to take an oath pledging something, such as silence or secrecy, about something. □ *I swore Larry to secrecy, but he told anyway.* □ *We were sworn to silence about the new product.*

swear something **out**† **against** someone to file a criminal complaint against someone. □ *Walter swore a warrant out against Jeff.* □ *He swore out a warrant against Tony.*

swear something **to** someone to pledge or promise something to someone. □ *I had to swear my allegiance to the general before I could become one of his bodyguards.* □ *We swore our loyalty to our country.*

swear to something to claim that what one says is absolutely true. □ *It is true. I swear to it.* □ *I think I have remembered it all, but I couldn't swear to it.*

swear (up)on someone or something to take an oath on someone or something. (*Upon* is formal and less commonly used than *on*.) □ *He swore upon the Bible to tell the truth.* □ *I swear on the memory of my sainted mother that I am telling the truth.*

sweat blood and **sweat bullets** *Fig.* to be very anxious and tense. □ *What a terrible test! I was really sweating blood at the last.* □ *Bob is such a bad driver. I sweat bullets every time I ride with him.*

sweat bullets Go to previous.

sweat for something *Fig.* to work very hard for something. □ *I sweat for every dollar I bring in.* □ *Ted really sweats for his salary.*

sweat something **off**† *Fig.* to get rid of excess fat or weight by exercising or taking a steam bath to produce sweat. □ *I think I can sweat a lot of this fat off.* □ *Tony tried to sweat off some of his excess weight.*

sweat something **out**† **1.** *Lit.* to get rid of something in one's body by sweating. □ *I have a bit of a cold, and I am going to try to sweat it out.* □ *I took a steamy shower, trying to sweat out my cold.* **2.** *Fig.* to endure something unpleasant. □ *It was an ordeal, but I sweated it out.* □ *I managed to sweat out the exam.* **3.** *Fig.* to endure suspense about something. □ *She sweated the two-hour wait out until she heard the results of her bar exams.* □ *Karen sweated out the long wait peacefully.*

sweat something **out of** someone and **sweat** something **out**† **1.** *Lit.* to apply enough heat to cause someone to sweat, with the goal of removing bodily poisons or the cause of a disease. □ *They used the ancient treatment of sweating the disease out of me. It worked!* □ *They used steam to sweat out the flu.* **2.** *Fig.* to force someone to reveal information under pressure. □ *The cops couldn't sweat the information out of Max.* □ *They couldn't sweat out the information.*

sweep along to glide along smoothly, as if flying. □ *The sailboat swept along, pushed by the strong wind.* □ *The fallen leaves blew up against the fence, swept along by a strong wind.*

sweep down on someone or something to flow or rush down onto someone or something. □ *The storm swept down on the campers.* □ *A flash flood swept down on the streambed.*

sweep in (from some place**)** and **breeze in (from** some place**)** to arrive suddenly from some place. □ *Tom just swept in from his vacation to face a pile of work on his desk.* □ *Max breezed in from Vegas and asked about Lefty.*

sweep in(to some place**)** to dash or run into some place. □ *The kids swept into the candy store and bought little bits of things.* □ *They swept in and spent all of a dollar before they left.*

sweep off to exit quickly. □ *He stopped only briefly, then swept off again.* □ *Mary swept off, leaving Ted standing there confused.*

sweep one **off** one's **feet** and **knock** one **off** one's **feet 1.** *Lit.* to knock someone down. □ *The wind swept me off my feet.* □ *Bill punched Bob playfully, and knocked him off his feet.* **2.** *Fig.* to overwhelm someone (figuratively). □ *Mary is madly in love with Bill. He swept her off her feet.* □ *The news was so exciting that it knocked me off my feet.*

sweep out of some place to exit from some place quickly with style or grace. □ *The famous actress swept out of the room in a grand fashion.* □ *She swept out of her dressing room and walked on stage just as her cue was uttered.*

sweep over someone **1.** *Lit.* to pass over and cover someone. □ *The waves swept over us and nearly drowned us.* □ *The flood swept over the farmers who would not leave their homes.* **2.** *Fig.* [for something] to overwhelm someone. □ *A wave of nausea swept over me and I guess I slumped to the floor.* □ *The need for fresh air swept over all of us trapped in that room.*

sweep someone **into** something and **sweep** someone **in**† to place someone into an elective position decisively. □ *The decisive victory swept all the candidates of the reform party into office.* □ *The victory swept in the candidates.*

sweep someone or something **aside**† to push or brush someone or something aside. □ *The guards swept the spectators aside as the king's coach approached.* □ *They swept aside the spectators.*

sweep someone or something **away**† to dispose of someone or something by pushing or brushing away. □ *The waves nearly swept us away.* □ *The waves caused by the storm swept away all the debris on the beach.*

sweep someone or something **out of** something and **sweep** someone or something **out**† to remove or brush someone or something from something or some place. □ *The voters swept the crooks out of office.* □ *We swept out the dirt.*

sweep something **back**† to push or move something backward in the shape of a curve. □ *He took the brush and swept his hair back in a huge wave.* □ *She swept back her hair in a striking arrangement.*

sweep something **down**† to clean something by sweeping. □ *Please sweep this floor down whenever you make a mess here.* □ *Jeff will sweep down the floor before he goes home.*

sweep something **into** something and **sweep** something **in**† to move something into something or some place by sweeping. □ *Liz swept the crumbs into the dish.* □ *Liz held the dish and swept in the crumbs.*

sweep something **off (of)** something and **sweep** something **off**† to remove something by sweeping. (*Of* is usually retained before pronouns.) □ *The waiter swept the crumbs off the tablecloth.* □ *He swept off the crumbs.*

sweep something **out**† to clean something out by sweeping. □ *Someone has to sweep the garage out.* □ *Don't sweep out this room. I'll do it.*

sweep something **under the carpet 1.** *Lit.* to hide dirt by brushing it away under the edge of a carpet. □ *He was in such a hurry with the cleaning that he just swept the dirt under the carpet.* □ *She swept the dirt under the carpet, hoping no one would find it.* **2.** *Fig.* to hide or ignore something. □ *You made a mistake that you can't sweep under the carpet.* □ *Don't try to sweep it under the carpet. You are wrong!*

sweep something **up**† **1.** *Lit.* to clean up and remove something, such as dirt, by sweeping. □ *Please sweep these crumbs up.* □ *Can you sweep up these crumbs?* **2.** *Lit.* to clean up some place by sweeping. □ *Please sweep this room up.* □ *Can you sweep up this room, please?* **3.** *Fig.* to arrange something, such as hair, into a curve or wave. □ *The hairstylist swept her hair up over the top. No one liked it.* □ *Sweep up my hair the way it looks in this picture.*

sweep through (something) **1.** *Lit.* to move through something or some place quickly and with grand flourishes. □ *She swept through the room, speaking to no one.* □ *She swept through in a great hurry.* **2.** *Fig.* to perform some task quickly. □ *She swept through the musical number and ran offstage.* □ *It required a slower tempo, but she just swept through.*

sweep up to clean up by sweeping. □ *Would you sweep up this time?* □ *Please give me a few minutes to sweep up before you come to visit.*

sweep up after someone to clean up the dirt left on the floor by someone. □ *Do you mind sweeping up after the kids?* □ *I had to sweep up after your party and I am not happy about it!*

sweet and sour a combination of fruity sweet and sour, but not necessarily salty, flavors. (Typically referring to certain Chinese-American foods.) □ *I prefer sweet-and-sour pork to anything else on the menu.* □ *Alice does not care for sweet-and-sour dishes, but she will usually eat whatever we serve her.*

***sweet as honey** and **sweeter than honey; sweet as sugar** very sweet; charming. (*Also: **as** ~.) □ *Larry's words were sweeter than honey as he tried to convince Alice to forgive him.* □ *Jill: Is Mary Ann nice? Jane: Yes, indeed. She's as sweet as honey.* □ *Your little girl is darling! Just as sweet as sugar.*

sweet nothings affectionate but unimportant or meaningless words spoken to a loved one. □ *Jack was whispering sweet nothings in Joan's ear when they were dancing.* □ *The two lovers sat in the cinema exchanging sweet nothings.*

***sweet on** someone *Rur.* fond of someone. (*Typically: **be** ~; **become** ~.) □ *Tom is sweet on Mary. He may ask her to marry him.* □ *Mary's sweet on him, too.*

sweeten someone **up**† to make someone more pleasant. □ *I had hoped that a week in the Caribbean would sweeten him up.* □ *The trip sweetened him up, but not for long.*

sweeten something **up**† to make something taste sweeter. □ *Where is the sugar? I need to sweeten this up a little.* □ *A little sugar will sweeten up the coffee.*

sweeten the pot *Fig.* to increase the amount of money bet in a card game with hopes of encouraging other players to bet more enthusiastically. □ *John sweetened the pot hoping others would follow.*

sweeten (up) the deal *Fig.* to make a bargain or a business transaction more appealing by adding value to the transaction. □ *The dealer sweetened the deal by throwing in free car washes.* □ *He wasn't willing to do anything to sweeten the deal, so I left.* □ *She sweetened up the deal with a little extra money.*

sweeter than honey Go to sweet as honey.

sweetheart agreement and **sweetheart deal** a private agreement reached between a public agency or government official and a private company that includes illicit payments or special favors. □ *They found that the mayor was involved in a number of sweetheart agreements.* □ *Most of the building contractors in town would be out of business if they didn't have sweetheart deals with the local politicians.*

sweetheart deal Go to previous.

sweet-talk someone *Rur.* to talk convincingly to someone with much flattery. □ *I didn't want to help her, but she sweet-talked me into it.* □ *He sweet-talked her for a while, and she finally agreed to go to the dance with him.*

swell out to bulge outward; to expand outward. □ *The sides of the box swelled out because it was too full.* □ *The west wall of the garage swelled out just before the building collapsed.*

swell up to enlarge; to inflate; to bulge out. □ *I struck my thumb with a hammer and it swelled up something awful.*

swell with something **1.** *Lit.* to expand from a particular cause. □ *My knee joints swelled with arthritis.* □ *His nose swelled after it was struck by the door.* **2.** *Fig.* to seem to swell with a feeling such as pride. □ *His chest swelled with pride at the thought of his good performance.* □ *Ted swelled with pride at the announcement.*

***a swelled head** *Fig.* a state of being conceited. (*Typically: **get** ~; **have** ~; **give** someone ~.) □ *John got a swelled head after he won the prize.* □ *Don't get a swelled head from all this success.*

swerve (away) (from someone or something**)** to turn sharply away from someone or something. □ *The car swerved away from Carla just in time.* □ *It swerved away just in time.*

swerve into someone or something to turn sharply and directly into someone or something. (Usually an accident.) □ *The car almost swerved into a pedestrian.* □ *The bus swerved into a truck.*

swift and sure fast and certain. (As with the flight of a well-aimed arrow.) □ *The response of the governor to the criticism by the opposing party was swift and sure.* □ *The boxer's punch was swift and sure and resulted in a quick knockout and a very short match.*

***swift as an arrow** and ***swift as the wind; *swift as thought** very fast. (*Also: **as** ~.) □ *The new intercity train is swift as an arrow.* □ *You won't have to wait for me long; I'll be there, swift as thought.*

swift as lightning Go to quick as a wink.

swift as the wind Go to swift as an arrow.

swift as thought Go to swift as an arrow.

swill something **down**† to drink something, especially an alcoholic drink, in great gulps. □ *The guy took a quart of beer and swilled it down in a few seconds.* □ *He swilled down a quart of beer.*

swim against the current Go to next.

swim against the tide and **swim against the current 1.** *Lit.* to swim in a direction opposite to the flow of the water. □ *She became exhausted, swimming against the tide.* □ *If you really want strenuous exercise, go out in the stream and swim against the current.* **2.** *Fig.* to do something that is in opposition to the general movement of things. □ *Why can't you cooperate? Do you always have to swim against the tide?* □ *You always seem to waste your energy swimming against the current.*

swim around to swim here and there. □ *I just like to get into the pool and swim around.* □ *I saw only one fish swimming around in your aquarium.*

swim before someone's **eyes** *Fig.* [for something, such as spots or visions] to appear in one's field of vision. □ *I was getting feverish and spots swam before my eyes.* □ *Visions of total destruction swam before my eyes as the bus skidded in the snow.*

swim for it to escape by swimming. (See also **run for it.**) □ *I escaped from the guard, dived into the river, and swam for it.* □ *Max swam for it, but he didn't get away.*

swim for someone or something to travel toward someone or something by swimming. □ *I swam for George, who was farther out, holding onto a float.* □ *I am going to swim for the island.*

swim in something **1.** *Lit.* to swim in a body of water. □ *Is it safe to swim in this water?* □ *Can we swim in your pool?* **2.** *Fig.* to experience an overabundance of something. (Not directly related to ①.) □ *We are just swimming in orders right now. Business is good.* □ *Mr. Wilson is swimming in money.*

swim into something to enter something swimming. □ *They swam into a lovely grotto.* □ *Ted swam into the cove and got out on the beach.*

swim like stink Go to **like stink.**

swim toward someone or something to swim in the direction of someone or something. □ *Jeff swam toward the drowning man and helped him.* □ *I swam toward the boat.*

swim with something to swim in the same direction as the movement of water. □ *Fred had no trouble swimming with the current.* □ *Please swim with the current and not against it.*

swimming in something *Fig.* having lots of something. □ *Right now we are swimming in merchandise. In a month it will be gone.* □ *The Wilmington-Thorpes are just swimming in money.*

swimming with someone or something *Fig.* engulfed with someone or something. □ *The scene of the crime was swimming with cops and reporters.* □ *The hotel was swimming with out-of-town visitors.*

swindle someone **out of** something and **swindle** something **out of** someone to cheat someone out of something. □ *The crooks tried to swindle her out of her inheritance.* □ *The crooks swindled $3,000 out of the old woman.*

swing around (to something**)** to move one's body or view around to another position. □ *She swung around to the left, where she could see better.* □ *The bear suddenly swung around and charged.*

swing at someone or something to strike at someone or something. □ *Max swung at the cop—a serious mistake.* □ *The batter swung at the ball and missed.*

swing for something *Fig.* [for someone] to die by hanging for committing a crime. □ *The sheriff swore that Tex would swing for the killing.* □ *Max said he would not swing for something that Lefty had done.*

swing from something to hang or dangle from something. □ *The child was swinging from an exercise bar on her swing set.* □ *Ted was swinging from the edge of the cliff, waiting to be rescued.*

swing into action Go to **go into action.**

swing into high gear to begin operating at a fast pace; to increase the rate of activity. □ *During the winter season we swing into high gear around here.* □ *The chef swings into high gear around six o'clock in preparation for the theater crowd.*

swing into something to enter something by swinging. □ *The monkey swung into its cage, and I quickly locked the cage door.* □ *I grabbed a rope and swung into the cave, where my pursuer couldn't see me.*

swing something *Fig.* to make something happen. □ *I hope I can swing a deal that will make us all a lot of money.* □ *We all hope you can swing it.*

swing to something to change to a different position or attitude. □ *The mood of the country is swinging to conservatism.* □ *Soon the attitudes of the people will swing to the opposite side.*

swing with someone or something *Sl.* to appreciate someone or something. □ *Man, I can really swing with that color. Glorious!* □ *I can really swing with John. He and I are real close.*

swirl about someone or something [for something, such as dust or a fluid] to circle and wind about someone or something. □ *The snow swirled about me as I walked along.* □ *The smoke swirled about the tiny campfire.*

swirl around [for dust or a fluid] to circle around. □ *The liquid swirled around in the flask as Toby shook it up.* □ *Dust swirled around the room in the sunlight.*

swish around [for a fluid] to slosh or rush around. □ *All that water I drank is swishing around in my stomach.* □ *I can hear the water swishing around in the pipes.*

swish something **off (of)** someone or something and **swish** something **off**† to brush something off someone or something. (*Of* is usually retained before pronouns.) □ *The barber swished the loose hairs off of Paul's collar.* □ *The barber swished off the loose hairs.*

switch around to change, swing, or turn around. □ *The horse switched around and ran the other way.* □ *I switched around and sat looking the other way for a while.*

switch (around) (with someone or something**)** to exchange or trade with someone or something. (The optional elements cannot be transposed.) □ *I liked Jill's lunch, and she liked mine, so I switched around with her.*

□ *I liked Jill's, and she liked mine, so we switched around with each other.*

switch back (to something**) 1.** to return to using or doing something. □ *I decided to switch back to my old shampoo.* □ *I switched back and was glad I did.* **2.** [for a road] to reverse upon itself. □ *The mountain road switched back twenty times in three miles.* □ *It switched back every now and then.*

switch from someone **to** someone else to change one's choice from one person to another. □ *I had chosen Jeff, but I will switch from him to Judy.* □ *Tom wanted to try a new barber, so he switched from Nick to Bruno.*

switch from something **to** something else to change one's choice from one thing to another. □ *We switched from oil to gas heat in our house.* □ *I don't like to switch from one brand to another.*

switch into something to change [one's clothes] into something else. □ *Let me switch into something a little more dressy if we are going to a nice restaurant.* □ *I have to switch into something more comfortable.*

switch off 1. *Lit.* [for something] to turn itself off. □ *At midnight, all the lights switched off automatically.* □ *The television switched off after I went to sleep.* **2.** *Fig.* [for someone] to stop paying attention; to become oblivious to everything. □ *I got tired of listening and switched off.* □ *You could see that the audience was switching off.*

switch on 1. [for something] to turn itself on. □ *Exactly at midnight, the lights switched on.* □ *The radio switched on early in the morning to wake us up.* **2.** *Sl.* [for someone] to become alert or excited. □ *The wild music made all the kids switch on and start to dance.* □ *About midnight, Ed switches on and becomes a real devil.*

switch over (to someone or something**)** to change to or choose someone or something else. □ *That newscaster is too contentious. Switch over to another station.* □ *Okay, I'll switch over.*

switch someone or something **around**[†] to change, swing, or turn someone or something. □ *I was prepared for a late flight out of Miami, but they switched me around at the last minute.* □ *They switched around my flights.*

switch someone or something **off**[†] to cause someone or something to be quiet or stop doing something. □ *I got tired of listening to her, so I punched the button and switched her off.* □ *I switched off the television set.*

switch someone or something **over to** something to reassign, change, or convert someone or something to something. □ *They switched me over to a later flight.* □ *I want to switch my furnace over to gas.*

switch someone or something **over to** someone or something to transfer electronically a signal from someone or something to someone or something else. □ *Tom is on the line. Shall I switch him over to Jeff?* □ *Please switch the call over to my other line.*

switch someone or something **through** to connect someone or something with something else. □ *I will switch you through the priority network.* □ *The operator switched the call through.*

switch something **back**[†] **(to** something**)** to return something to the way it was. □ *I switched the television back to the previous channel.* □ *I switched back the channel to what I was watching before.*

switch something **(from** something**) (in)to** something to change something from one thing into another. □ *The magician switched the silk scarf from red into green.* □ *I would love to be able to switch lead into gold.*

switch something **on**[†] to close an electrical circuit that causes something to start functioning or operating. □ *Please switch the fan on.* □ *I switched on the fan.*

switch something **out**[†] to remove something from an electrical circuit to turn it off. □ *Please switch the light out.* □ *I switched out the light.*

switch something **over**[†] **(to** something**)** to convert something to something else. □ *We are switching our furnace over to gas.* □ *We switched over our furnace to gas.*

switch something **to** something else to change something to something else. □ *It was hot so I switched the thermostat from heating to cooling.* □ *Mary switched the controls to automatic so she wouldn't have to worry about them constantly.*

switch to something to change to something. □ *I am going to switch to a cheaper brand of tissues.* □ *We switched to a different long-distance telephone company to save some money.*

switched on 1. *Sl.* alert and up-to-date; with it. □ *My brother is switched on and has lots of friends.* □ *I'm not switched on. In fact, I am pretty dull.* **2.** *Sl.* excited. □ *I get switched on by that kind of music.* □ *I am never switched on by raucous music.*

swoon over someone or something to seem to faint or pass out about someone or something. □ *The kids swooned over the rock star like the kids of thirty years ago.* □ *Evangeline swooned over the frightful news.*

swoop down (up)on someone or something **1.** *Lit.* to dive or plunge downward on someone or something. □ *The eagle swooped down upon the lamb.* **2.** *Fig.* [for someone] to pounce on and consume something. □ *The children swooped down on the ice cream and cake.*

sympathize with someone **(about** someone or something**)** to share someone else's sorrow or anger about someone or something; to comfort someone who is sad or angry (about someone or something). □ *I sympathize with you about what you are going through.* □ *I really sympathize with you.*

synchronize something **with** something else to set or adjust something to coordinate its timing with something else. □ *Would you please synchronize your watch with mine?* □ *We could never synchronize our schedules so that we could get together.*

S

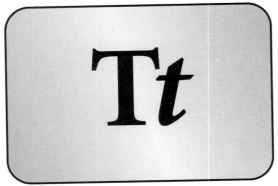

Tt

tab someone **for** something to choose someone for something. □ *The director tabbed Sam for a walk-on part.* □ *I wanted her to tab me for a part.*

table a motion to postpone the discussion of something during a meeting. □ *Mary suggested that they should table the motion.* □ *The motion for a new policy was tabled until the next meeting.*

tack something **down**† to fasten something down with small nails. □ *Someone had better tack this carpet down.* □ *Please tack down this carpet.*

tack something **onto** something and **tack** something **on**† to add something onto something. □ *The waiter kept tacking charges onto my bill.* □ *He tacked on charge after charge.*

tack something **up**† to fasten something onto something with tacks. □ *The drapes started to fall, so we tacked them up again.* □ *Please tack up these posters.*

tag along (after someone**)** and **tag along (behind** someone**)** to follow along after someone; to go along with someone. □ *The family dog tagged along after the children wherever they went.* □ *Can I tag along?* □ *Do you mind if I tag along behind you?*

tag someone **out**† [in baseball] to touch with the ball, and thereby put someone out. □ *The shortstop tagged the runner out and retired the side.* □ *He tagged out the runner.*

tail after someone *Fig.* to follow after someone. □ *Why do you always have to tail after me?* □ *There is someone tailing after you.*

tail off to dwindle to nothing. □ *The number of people filing for unemployment insurance is beginning to tail off.* □ *As the storms tailed off, we began to realize how much damage had been done.*

the **tail wagging the dog** a situation where a small part is controlling the whole of something. □ *John was just hired yesterday, and today he's bossing everyone around. It's a case of the tail wagging the dog.* □ *Why is this small matter taking so much time? Now it's the tail wagging the dog!*

tailor someone or something **to** someone or something to fit or revise someone or something to fit someone or something. □ *The coach tailored his defensive team to the opposition.* □ *We can tailor service to your company very easily.* □ *I will tailor this suit to your specifications for no extra charge.*

taint something **with** something to spoil or debase something with something. □ *The flood tainted the drinking water with disease germs.* □ *The food had been tainted with germs.*

take a backseat (to someone or something**)** *Fig.* to become less important than someone or something else. □ *My homework had to take a backseat to football during the play-offs.* □ *Jimmy always took a backseat to his older brother, Bill, until Bill went away to college.*

take a bath Go to **take a shower.**

take a bath (on something**)** *Sl.* to accumulate large losses on a business transaction or an investment. (Alludes to *getting soaked,* a slang expression meaning "being heavily charged for something.") □ *Sally took a bath on that stock that she bought. Its price went down to nothing.* □ *I'm afraid that I will take a bath on any investment I make.*

take a beating to be beaten, bested, or defeated. □ *The candidate took a beating in the primaries.* □ *The team took quite a beating.*

take a bow to bow and acknowledge credit for a good performance. □ *At the end of the concerto, the pianist rose and took a bow.* □ *The audience applauded wildly and demanded that the conductor come out and take a bow again.*

take a break and **take** one's **break** to have a short rest period in one's work. □ *It's ten o'clock—time to take a break.* □ *I don't usually take my break until 10:30.*

take a chance and **take a risk** to try something where failure or bad fortune is likely. □ *Come on, take a chance. You may lose, but it's worth trying.* □ *I'm not reckless, but I don't mind taking a risk now and then.*

take a chance on someone or something to gamble that something good might happen or that someone might do well; to take a risk that something would go wrong or that someone would do badly. □ *I just couldn't take a chance on Walter, so I picked David.* □ *I would never take a chance on that horse!*

take a collection up† **(from** someone**) (for** someone or something**)** to collect money from people for someone or something. □ *Karen took a collection up from everyone in the office for Bill.* □ *Karen took up a collection for Bill from everyone in the office.*

take a course (in something**)** to enroll in a course and do the required work. □ *I decided to take a course in history.* □ *Bob drives into the city where he is taking a course.*

take a crack at someone Go to **a crack at** someone.

take a crack at something Go to **a try at** something.

take a dig at someone and **take a jab at** someone; **take digs at** someone *Fig.* to insult or pester someone. □ *Why did you take a jab at Sam?* □ *You're always taking digs at people who think they're your friends.* □ *Jane is always taking digs at Bob, but she never really means any harm.*

take a dim view of someone or something to disapprove of someone or something. □ *Of all the boys, the teacher likes Dave the least. She takes a dim view of him.* □ *I take a dim view of that law.*

take a dirt nap *Sl.* to die and be buried. □ *I don't want to end up taking a dirt nap during this operation.* □ *Isn't Tom a little young to take a dirt nap?*

take a dive Go to **take a fall.**

take a drag (on something**)** Go to a drag (on something).

take a fall and **take a dive** to fake being knocked out in a boxing match. □ *Wilbur wouldn't take a fall. He doesn't have it in him.* □ *The boxer took a dive in the second round and made everyone suspicious.*

take a fancy to someone or something and **take a liking to** someone or something; **take a shine to** someone or something to develop a fondness or a preference for someone or something. □ *John began to take a fancy to Sally late last August at the picnic.* □ *I've never taken a liking to cooked carrots.* □ *I think my teacher has taken a shine to me.*

take a firm grip on someone or something **1.** *Lit.* to grasp someone or something tightly. □ *The police officer took a firm grip on Fred and led him to the squad car.* □ *Mary took a firm grip on the handle and pulled hard.* **2.** *Fig.* to gain control of someone or something. □ *You will have to take a firm grip on Andrew. He has a mind of his own.* □ *Someone needs to take a firm grip on this department and get it organized.*

take a (firm) stand on something to express and maintain a strong opinion of something. □ *I hope you take a firm stand on the need for more office security.* □ *Yes, I will take a stand on it.*

take a gander (at someone or something**)** to look at someone or something. □ *Wow, take a gander at that new car!* □ *I wanted to take a gander at the new computer before they started using it.*

take a go at someone Go to a go at someone.

take a go at something Go to a try at something.

take a guess and **hazard a guess; make a guess** to guess. □ *Even if you don't know, please take a guess.* □ *If you don't know the answer, hazard a guess.*

take a hand in something to help with something; to participate in something. □ *Would you take a hand in this work? We need your efforts.* □ *Ted refused to take a hand in the preparations for the evening meal.*

take a hard line (with someone**)** *Fig.* to be firm with someone; to have a firm policy for dealing with someone. □ *The manager takes a hard line with people who show up late.* □ *This is a serious matter. The police are likely to take a hard line.*

take a hike and **take a walk 1.** *Fig.* to go on a hike; to do hiking. □ *It's a beautiful day. Let's take a hike in the woods.* □ *We took a hike through the forest to visit John's cabin.* **2.** *Fig.* to leave; to beat it. □ *Okay, I've had it with you. Take a hike! Beat it!* □ *I had enough of the boss and the whole place, so I cleaned out my desk and took a walk.* **3.** Go to take a walk.

take a hint to understand a hint and behave accordingly. □ *I said I didn't want to see you anymore. Can't you take a hint? I don't like you.* □ *Sure I can take a hint, but I'd rather be told directly.*

take a jab at someone **1.** and **take a punch at** someone to hit at someone; to poke someone. □ *Max took a jab at Lefty and missed.* □ *Lefty took a punch at Max.* **2.** Go to take a dig at someone.

take a leaf out of someone's **book** and **take a page from** someone's **book** *Fig.* to behave or to do something in a way that someone else would. □ *When you act like that, you're taking a leaf out of your sister's book, and I don't like it!* □ *You had better do it your way. Don't take a leaf out of my book. I don't do it well.*

take a leak *Inf.* to urinate. (Crude. Use caution with the topic. Usually in reference to a male.) □ *I gotta go take a leak. Back in a minute.* □ *He just went out to take a leak.*

take a licking Go to a licking.

take a liking to someone or something Go to take a fancy to someone or something.

take a load off (of) someone's **mind** and **take a lot off (of)** someone's **mind** *Fig.* to relieve one's mind of a problem or a worry. (*Of* is usually retained before pronouns.) □ *I'm glad to hear that. It sure takes a load off of my mind.* □ *This will take a load off her mind.*

take a load off one's **feet** Go to a load off one's feet.

Take a long walk off a short pier. and **Go play in the traffic.** *Inf.* Get out of here!; Go do something that will get you permanently out of here! □ *Get out of here! Take a long walk off a short pier!* □ *You bother me. Go play in the traffic.*

take a look at someone or something and **have a look at** someone or something to observe or examine someone or something. □ *I asked the doctor to take a look at my cut.* □ *Would you please have another look at your work? It is not complete.*

take a look for someone or something and **have a look for** someone or something to make a visual search for someone or something; to look for someone or something. □ *Please go to the library and have a look for a book about snakes.* □ *Take a look for a man in a black suit. He is your guide.*

take a lot of nerve Go to a lot of nerve.

take a lot off (of) someone's **mind** Go to take a load off (of) someone's mind.

take a lot out of someone to drain a lot of energy from someone. □ *This kind of workout takes a lot out of the team.* □ *Hot days like this take a lot out of me.*

take a nap to have a brief period of sleep. □ *I took a short nap just after lunch.* □ *The baby takes a long nap each afternoon.*

take a new turn [for something] to begin a new course or direction. □ *When I received the telegram with the exciting news, my life took a new turn.* □ *I began taking the medicine at noon, and by evening the disease had begun to take a new turn. I was getting better!*

take a nosedive Go to go into a nosedive.

take a page from someone's **book** Go to take a leaf out of someone's book.

take a poke at someone Go to next.

take a pop at someone and **take a poke at** someone to punch at someone. □ *Willie took a pop at me, but I ducked.* □ *The drunk took a poke at the cop—which was the wrong thing to do.*

take a potshot at someone or something **1.** *Lit.* to shoot at someone or something, as with a shotgun. (*A potshot* refers to the type of shooting done to provide meat for the cooking pot.) □ *The hunters were taking potshots at each* other in the woods. □ *Someone has been taking potshots at my mailbox!* **2.** *Fig.* to criticize or censure someone or something, often just to be mean. □ *Why are you taking potshots at me? What did I do to you?* □ *Everyone in the audience was taking potshots at the comedian's toupee.*

take a pound of flesh Go to **a pound of flesh.**

take a powder *Sl.* to leave; to leave town. (Underworld.) □ *Why don't you take a powder? Go on! Beat it!* □ *Willie took a powder and will lie low for a while.*

take a punch at someone Go to **take a jab at** someone.

take a rain check (on something**)** Go to **a rain check (on** something**).**

take a risk Go to **take a chance.**

Take a running jump (in the lake)! *Sl.* Go away!; Get away from me! □ *You know what you can do? You can take a running jump. Beat it!* □ *You can just take a running jump in the lake, you creep!*

take a shine to someone or something Go to **take a fancy to** someone or something.

take a shot at someone or something **1.** to fire a shot at someone or something. □ *The hunter took a shot at the deer.* □ *Who took a shot at my mailbox?* **2.** Go to **a try at** something.

take a shower and **take a bath** to bathe. □ *I take a shower every morning.* □ *John takes a hot bath to relax.*

take a spill to have a fall; to tip over. (Also with *bad, nasty, quite,* etc. Also with *have.*) □ *Ann tripped on the curb and took a nasty spill.* □ *John had quite a spill when he fell off his bicycle.*

take a stab at someone Go to **a stab at** someone.

take a stab at something Go to **a try at** something.

take a stand (against someone or something**)** to take a position in opposition to someone or something; to oppose or resist someone or something. □ *The treasurer was forced to take a stand against the board because of its wasteful spending.* □ *The treasurer took a stand, and others agreed.*

take a swing at someone to attempt to punch someone. □ *He took a swing at me!* □ *Tom took a swing at Bob, but Bob ducked out of the way.*

take a swipe at someone or something **1.** *Sl.* to hit at someone or something. □ *Max took a swipe at the cop by mistake.* □ *Lefty took a swipe at the punching bag—and missed.* **2.** *Sl.* to have a try at someone or something. □ *I think I can persuade him. I'll take a swipe at him and see.* □ *I will probably fail, but I'll take a swipe at it.*

take a try at someone Go to **a try at** someone.

take a try at something Go to **a try at** something.

take a turn for the better to start to improve; to start to get well. □ *She was very sick for a month; then suddenly she took a turn for the better.* □ *Things are taking a turn for the better at my store. I may make a profit this year.*

take a turn for the worse to start to get worse. □ *It appeared that she was going to get well; then, unfortunately, she took a turn for the worse.* □ *My job was going quite well; then last week things took a turn for the worse.*

take a vacation to go somewhere for a vacation; to stop work to have a vacation. □ *Sue took a vacation at the Grand Canyon last year.* □ *I need to take a vacation and relax.*

take a walk Go to **take a hike.**

take a weight off one's **mind** Go to **a load off** one's **mind.**

take a whack at something Go to **a try at** something.

take a whiff of something Go to **a whiff of** something.

take account of someone or something to pay attention to someone or something. □ *You should take account of Tom. He has some good advice.* □ *Do I have to take account of the new policies?*

take action against someone or something to begin activity against someone or something. □ *The city council vowed to take action against the mayor.* □ *I will take action against the company for its negligence.*

take action on someone or something to act on someone or something; to do what has to be done on someone or something. □ *We still have to discuss what to do with Sam. I hope we can take action on him today.* □ *Do we still have time to take action on this proposal?*

take advantage of someone **1.** to deceive someone. □ *I knew that you wouldn't take advantage of me! I trusted you.* □ *Please don't take advantage of me the way you took advantage of Carl.* **2.** to impose on someone. □ *I am glad to have your help. I hope I am not taking advantage of you.* □ *I am glad to do it. You are not taking advantage of me.*

take advantage of someone or something to utilize someone or something to the fullest extent. □ *Try to take advantage of every opportunity that comes your way.* □ *Please take advantage of the consultant while she is here in the office.*

take after someone to resemble a close, older relative. □ *Don't you think that Sally takes after her mother?* □ *No, Sally takes after her Aunt Ann.*

take (a)hold of someone or something Go to **(a)hold of** someone or something.

take aim at someone or something *Fig.* to prepare to deal with someone or something; to focus on someone or something. (Based on **take aim (at** someone, something, or an animal**).**) □ *Now we have to take aim at the problem and try to get it solved.* □ *The critics took aim at the star of the musical and tore her to pieces.*

take aim (at someone, something, or an animal**)** to aim [something] at someone, something, or an animal. □ *The hunter took aim at the deer and pulled the trigger.* □ *You must take aim carefully before you shoot.*

take an amount of money **for** something to charge a certain amount for something. □ *I'll take four thousand for that car there.* □ *How much will you take for a big bag of flour?*

take an interest in someone or something to become concerned or interested in someone or something. □ *Do you take an interest in your children?* □ *You should take an interest in everything your child does.*

take an oath to make an oath; to swear to something. □ *You must take an oath that you will never tell anyone about this.* □ *When I was a witness in court, I had to take an oath that I would tell the truth.*

take attendance to make a record of persons attending something. □ *The teacher took attendance before starting the class.* □ *I will take attendance each day.*

take away from someone or something to lessen the value or esteem of someone or something; to detract from someone or something. □ *The fact that she is quiet does not take away from her one bit.* □ *The huge orange spot in the center of the painting takes away from the intense green of the rest of the work.*

Take care. Go to Take care (of yourself).

take care of number one and **take care of numero uno** to take care of oneself. □ *Mike, like everybody else, is most concerned with taking care of number one.* □ *If you don't take care of numero uno, who will?*

take care of numero uno Go to previous.

take care of someone **1.** to tip someone. □ *I took care of the doorman as we left.* □ *Did you remember to take care of the waiter?* **2.** *Euph.* to kill or dispose of someone. □ *Max said he was going to take care of Lefty once and for all.* □ *The crime king ordered Max to take care of a certain private detective.*

take care of someone or something to oversee and protect someone or something; to care for someone or something. □ *Please take care of my child while I am away.* □ *I will take care of everything for you.*

take care of something to deal with something; to handle or manage a problem or detail. □ *Would you please take care of this little problem?* □ *This is an easy thing to take care of. I will fix it immediately.*

Take care (of yourself). 1. Good-bye and keep yourself healthy. □ *John: I'll see you next month. Good-bye. Bob: Good-bye, John. Take care of yourself.* □ *Mary: Take care. Sue: Okay. See you later.* **2.** Take care of your health and get well. □ *Mary: Don't worry. I'll get better soon. Sue: Well, take care of yourself. Bye.* □ *Jane: I'm sorry you're ill. Bob: Oh, it's nothing. Jane: Well, take care of yourself.*

take charge (of someone or something**)** to take (over) control of someone or something. □ *The president came in late and took charge of the meeting.* □ *When the new manager took charge, things really began to happen.*

take cold Go to catch cold.

take control of someone or something to get the power and right to direct someone or something. □ *I will take control of him and see that he does what I want.* □ *Will you take control of the Wilson project?*

take cover to seek shelter from gunfire or other projectiles. □ *As soon as the firing started, we took cover behind a huge boulder.*

take credit for something to allow people to believe that one has done something praiseworthy, whether or not one has actually done it. □ *I can't take credit for the entire success. Toby helped a lot.* □ *Mary took credit for everything that Dave did.*

take digs at someone Go to take a dig at someone.

take effect Go to go into effect.

take exception (to something**) 1.** to take offense at something. □ *I must take exception to your remark.* □ *Sue took exception to Fred's characterization of Bill as a cheapskate.*

2. to disagree with something. □ *I have to take exception to the figure you quoted.* □ *The manager took exception to the statement about having only three employees.*

take first crack at something Go to first crack at something.

take five *Sl.* to take a five-minute rest period; to take a short break. □ *Okay, everybody. Take five!* □ *Hey, Bob. I'm tired. Can we take five?*

take forty winks Go to catch forty winks.

take fuel on† to refuel; to be refueled. (Usually said of a large conveyance, such as a ship or a plane.) □ *We need to land at the next major airport to take fuel on.* □ *We will land somewhere to take on fuel.*

take (great) pains (to do something**)** *Fig.* to make a great effort to do something. □ *Tom took pains to decorate the room exactly right.* □ *We took great pains to get there on time.*

take heart (from something**)** to receive courage or comfort from some fact. □ *I hope that you will take heart from what we told you today.* □ *Even though you did not win the race, take heart from the fact that you did your best.* □ *I told her to take heart and try again next time.*

take heed (of someone or something**)** to be cautious with someone or something; to pay attention to someone or something. □ *We will have to take heed of Wendy and see what she will do next.* □ *You will learn to take heed of these little signs that things are not going well.*

take hold of someone or something to grasp someone or something. □ *He took hold of the child, which frightened her very much.* □ *Terry took hold of the doorknob and turned it.*

take ill Go to take sick.

take into account someone or something Go to take someone or something into account.

take inventory to make an inventory list. □ *They are taking inventory in the warehouse, counting each item and writing the number on a list.* □ *The hardware store closed once a year in order to take inventory.*

take issue with someone to argue with someone. □ *I heard your last statement and I have to take issue with you.* □ *Tom took issue with Maggie about the cost of the house.*

take issue with something to disagree with or argue about something. □ *I have to take issue with that statement.* □ *I want to take issue with the last statement you made.*

take it to endure something, physically or mentally. (Often negative.) □ *I just can't take it anymore.* □ *If you can't take it, quit.*

Take it away! *Inf.* Start up the performance!; Let the show begin! (Typically a public announcement of the beginning of a musical performance.) □ *And now, here is the band playing "Song of Songs." Take it away!* □ *Sally will now sing us a song. Take it away, Sally!*

Take it easy. 1. *Inf.* Good-bye and be careful. □ *Mary: Bye-bye. Bill: See you, Mary. Take it easy.* □ *Sue: Take it easy, Tom. Tom: Bye, Sue. See you soon.* **2.** *Inf.* Be gentle.; Treat someone carefully. □ *Sue: Then I want you to move the piano and turn all the mattresses. Andy: Come on. Take it easy! I'm not made of steel, you know.* □ *Henry: Oh, I'm* pooped. *Alice: You just need a little rest and you'll feel as good as new. Just take it easy.* **3.** *Inf.* Calm down.; Relax.; Do not get excited. □ *Andy: I am so mad I could blow my top! Rachel: Now, now. Take it easy. What's wrong?* □ *Mary could see that Sally was very upset at the news. "Now, just take it easy," said Mary. "It can't be all that bad."*

take it easy on someone, something, or an animal to be gentle on someone, something, or an animal. (See also **Take it easy!; take it easy on something.**) □ *Take it easy on Mary. She's been sick.* □ *Please take it easy on the furniture. It has to last us many years.*

take it easy on something *Fig.* to use less of something (rather than more). □ *Take it easy on the soup. There's just enough for one serving for each person.* □ *Please take it easy! There are hardly any left.*

Take it from me! *Inf.* Believe me! □ *It's true! Take it from me!* □ *Take it from me. This is a very good day for this part of the country.*

take it from the top *Fig.* to begin [again] at the beginning, especially the beginning of a piece of music. (Originally in reference to the top of a sheet of music.) □ *The conductor stopped the band and had the players take it from the top again.* □ *Let's take it from the top and play it a bit softer this time.*

take it like a man [for a male] to suffer misfortune stoically. (Compare this with **take it.**) □ *She said some really cutting things to him, but he took it like a man.* □ *I knew he could take it like a man.*

take it on the chin and **take it on the nose 1.** *Lit.* to stand up to something adverse, such as criticism. (Fig. on taking a direct punch to the head in boxing.) □ *They laid some blunt criticism on him, but he took it on the chin.* □ *I knew he could take it on the nose.* **2.** *Fig.* to receive the full brunt of something. □ *Why do I have to take it on the chin for something I didn't do?* □ *If you did it, you have to learn to take it on the chin.*

take it on the lam *Sl.* to get out of town; to run away. (Underworld.) □ *Both crooks took it on the lam when things got hot.* □ *Walt knew that the time had come to take it on the lam.*

take it on the nose Go to **take it on the chin.**

Take it or leave it. *Inf.* Take this one or none; you have no choice. □ *Bill: That's my final offer. Take it or leave it. Bob: Aw, come on! Take off a few bucks.* □ *Bill: Aw, I want eggs for breakfast, Mom. Mother: There's only cornflakes left. Take it or leave it.*

take it out on someone or something to punish or harm someone or something because one is angry or disturbed about something. □ *I'm sorry about your difficulty, but don't take it out on me.* □ *Don't take it out on the cat.*

take it slow to go slowly and carefully. □ *Just relax and take it slow. You've got a good chance.* □ *You'll make it. Take it slow and keep your spirits up.*

take it that... to understand it to be thus... □ *Am I to take it that you think this is the end of our relationship?*

take it to one's **grave** to carry a secret with one until one dies. □ *I will never tell anyone. I'll take your secret to my grave.* □ *She took the answer to the mystery to her grave.*

take it to the street *Sl.* to tell everyone about your problems. □ *If there's something bothering her, she's gonna take it to the street, first thing.* □ *Come on, don't take it to the street.*

take it upon oneself **to** do something Go to **make it** one's **business to** do something.

take it with one *Fig.* to take possessions with you when you die. (Usually negative.) □ *Spend a little on yourself. You can't take it with you, you know.* □ *He knew he couldn't take it with him, so he spent it all.*

take its course to continue along its way; [for a disease] to progress the way it normally progresses until it is cured naturally. □ *There is really no good medicine for this. This disease simply has to take its course.*

take kindly to something to be agreeable to something. □ *My father doesn't take kindly to anyone using his tools.* □ *I hope they'll take kindly to our request.*

take leave of one's **senses** *Fig.* to become irrational. (Often verbatim with one's.) □ *What are you doing? Have you taken leave of your senses?* □ *What a terrible situation! It's enough to make one take leave of one's senses.*

take leave of someone or something to go away from someone or something. □ *It is time for me to take leave of all of you.* □ *It saddened me to take leave of the city I grew up in.*

take liberties with someone or something and **make free with** someone or something to freely use or abuse someone or something. □ *You are overly familiar with me, Mr. Jones. One might think you were taking liberties with me.* □ *I don't like it when you make free with my lawn mower. You should at least ask when you want to borrow it.*

Take my word for it. Believe me.; **Trust me,** I am telling you the truth. □ *Bill: Take my word for it. These are the best power tools you can buy. Bob: But I don't need any power tools.* □ *Rachel: No one can cook better than Fred. Take my word for it. Bill: Really? Fred: Oh, yes. It's true.*

take names *Sl.* to make a list of wrongdoers. (Often figuratively, referring to a schoolteacher making a list of the names of misbehaving students to be sent to the principal.) □ *The boss is madder than hell, and he's taking names.* □ *Gary is coming by to talk about the little riot last night, and I think he's taking names.*

take no prisoners 1. *Lit.* to kill the enemy rather than seize the enemy as prisoners. □ *The soldiers' orders were to take no prisoners.* **2.** *Fig.* to be extremely ruthless with the opposition. □ *The new manager takes no prisoners. He is ruthless and stern.*

take no stock in something and **not take stock in** something; **not put (a lot) of stock in** something to pay no attention to someone; not to believe or accept something. □ *I take no stock in anything John has to say.* □ *He doesn't take stock in your opinions either.*

take note of someone or something *Fig.* to notice someone or something; to commit something about someone or something to one's memory, possibly by making a note on paper. □ *I took note of her when she came in. I thought she had left the company.* □ *Please take note of the hour. It is late.*

take notice of someone or something *Fig.* to notice the presence or existence of someone or something. □ *They* *didn't take notice of me, so I left.* □ *I took notice of the amount of the bill.*

take off 1. *Fig.* to leave the ground and begin to fly. (As with a bird or an airplane.) □ *When do we take off?* □ *The eagle took off and headed toward the mountains.* **2.** *Fig.* [for someone] to leave in a hurry. □ *She really took off from there quickly.* □ *I've got to take off—I'm late.* **3.** *Fig.* [for something] to start selling well. □ *The fluffy dog dolls began to take off, and we sold out the lot.* □ *Ticket sales really took off after the first performance.* **4.** *Fig.* to become active and exciting. □ *Did the party ever take off, or was it dull all night?* □ *Things began to take off about midnight.*

take off (after someone or something**)** and **take out (after** someone or something**)** to begin to chase someone or something. □ *The bank guard took off after the robber.* □ *Did you see that police car take off?* □ *It took out after the bank robber's car.*

take off (for some place**) 1.** *Lit.* to take flight, heading for some place. □ *We took off for Moscow early in the evening.* □ *We took off at dawn.* **2.** *Fig.* to leave for some place. □ *The girls took off for home when they heard the dinner bell.* □ *It's late. I have to take off.*

take off from something to take flight from something or some place. □ *The plane took off from the busy airport right on schedule.* □ *We will take off from the airport on one side of town, fly across the city, and land at our destination within 15 minutes.*

take off from work and **take ((some) time) off from work; take off (from work)** not to appear at one's place of work for a period of time, hours or days. (Often used of an excused or planned absence.) □ *I will have to take off from work to go to the doctor.* □ *I want to take some time off from work and paint the house.* □ *Ken took off from work when he was ill.*

take off (on something**)** to start out speaking on something; to begin a discussion of something. □ *My father took off on the subject of taxes and talked for an hour.* □ *My uncle is always taking off on the state of the economy.*

take off one's **hat (to** someone**)** *Fig.* to offer praise for someone's good accomplishments. □ *I have to take off my hat to Mayor Johnson. She has done an excellent job.* □ *Yes, we all ought to take off our hats. She is our best mayor ever.*

take offense (at someone or something**)** to be insulted by someone or something. □ *Bill took offense at Mary for her thoughtless remarks.* □ *Almost everyone took offense at Bill's new book.* □ *I'm sorry you took offense. I meant no harm.*

take office to begin serving as an elected or appointed official. □ *When did the mayor take office?* □ *All the elected officials took office just after the election.*

take on a new meaning Go to next.

take on a new significance and **take on a new meaning** [for an event] to acquire a new interpretation; [for something] to become more meaningful or more significant. □ *All these monuments take on a new meaning when you realize the amount of human artistry and skill it took to design and build them.*

take on (so) to behave very emotionally. (Usually negative.) □ *Stop crying. Please don't take on so.* □ *I wish you wouldn't take on about this matter.*

take one **at** one's **word** to believe what someone says and act accordingly. □ *She told me to go jump in the lake, and I took her at her word.* □ *You shouldn't take her at her word. She frequently says things she doesn't really mean.*

take one **back (to** some time**)** *Fig.* to cause one to think of a time in the past. □ *This takes me back to the time I spent the summer in Paris.* □ *What you said really takes me back.*

take one for the road Go to one for the road.

take one's **belt in**[†] **(a notch)** and **pull** one's **belt in**[†] **(a notch) 1.** *Lit.* to tighten one's belt a bit. (Probably because one has not eaten recently or because one has lost weight.) □ *He pulled his belt in a notch and smiled at his success at losing weight.* □ *He took in his belt a notch and wished he had something to eat.* **2.** *Fig.* to reduce expenditures; to live or operate a business more economically. (As if one were going to have to eat less.) □ *They had to take their belts in a notch budgetarily speaking.* □ *The people at city hall will have to pull in their belts a notch unless they want to raise taxes.*

take one's **break** Go to take a break.

take one's **cue from** someone to use someone else's behavior or reactions as a guide to one's own. (From the theatrical cue as a signal to speak, etc.) □ *If you don't know which spoons to use at the dinner, just take your cue from John.* □ *The other children took their cue from Tommy and ignored the new boy.*

take one's **death (of cold)** Go to catch one's death (of cold).

take one's **eyes off (of)** someone or something to cease looking at someone or something. (Usually negative. *Of* is usually retained before pronouns.) □ *I couldn't take my eyes off of the usher.* □ *Ken couldn't take his eyes off Judy.*

take one's **gloves off**[†] *Fig.* to stop being calm or civil and show an intention of winning a dispute by any means. (As if boxers were to remove their gloves in order to inflict more damage. See also The gloves are off.) □ *Both of them took their gloves off and really began arguing.*

take one's **hands off (of)** someone or something and **get** one's **hands off (of)** someone or something to let go of someone or something. (*Of* is usually retained before pronouns.) □ *Get your hands off of me!* □ *Please take your hands off the cake plate.*

take one's **hat**[†] **off to** someone *Fig.* to salute or pay an honor to someone. □ *Good work. I take my hat off to you.* □ *I take off my hat to you! What an excellent job!*

take (one's) leave (of someone**)** to say good-bye to someone and leave. □ *I took leave of the hostess at an early hour.* □ *One by one, the guests took their leave.*

take one's **lumps** *Inf.* to accept the result or punishment one deserves. (See also get one's lumps.) □ *You've got to learn to take your lumps if you're going to be in politics.* □ *I hate taking my lumps. I'd rather pretend nothing had happened.*

take one's **medicine** *Fig.* to accept the consequences or the bad fortune that one deserves. (Alludes to having to take unpleasant-tasting medicine.) □ *I know I did wrong, and I know I have to take my medicine.* □ *Billy knew he was going to get spanked, and he didn't want to take his medicine.*

take one's **own life** to kill oneself; to commit suicide. □ *Bob tried to take his own life, but he was stopped in time.* □ *Later, he was sorry that he had tried to take his own life.*

take one's **pick of** someone or something to be able to have one's choice of someone or something. □ *Can I take my pick of anyone in the group?* □ *Please take your pick of desserts.*

take one's **time** to go as slow as one wants or needs to; to use as much time as is required. □ *There is no hurry. Please take your time.* □ *Bill is very careful and takes his time so he won't make any mistakes.*

take one's **turn** [when playing a game] to make one's move or play one's cards; [when alternating with someone, waiting for one's opportunity or place in a sequence] to perform one's task. □ *Somebody please wake Max up so he can take his turn.*

take oneself **off** some place to go away to some place more private. □ *I need to take myself off someplace and think all this over.* □ *She kept her sanity by taking herself off to her bedroom for a few hours each day.*

take out a loan to get a loan of money, especially from a bank. □ *Mary took out a loan to buy a car.* □ *We will have to take out a loan to remodel the kitchen.*

take out (after someone or something**)** Go to take off (after someone or something).

take over (from someone**)** to assume the role or job of someone. □ *I take over for the manager next month.* □ *Liz takes over and will be in charge.*

take pains over something *Fig.* to deal with something with great care. (See also **take pains with** someone or something.) □ *She certainly takes pains over her work.* □ *You will have to take pains over this if you want it to be done right.*

take pains with someone or something *Fig.* to deal with someone or something with great care. □ *He really took pains with me to make sure I understood it all.* □ *Ken took pains with the model plane.*

take part (in something**)** to participate in something. □ *Bill refused to take part in the game.* □ *Everyone is asked to take part in the celebration.*

take pity (on someone or an animal**)** to feel sorry for someone or an animal. □ *We took pity on the hungry people and gave them some hot food.* □ *She took pity on the little dog and brought it in to get warm.*

take place to happen. □ *When will this party take place?* □ *It's taking place right now.*

take possession (of something**)** to assume ownership of something. □ *I am to take possession of the house as soon as we sign the papers.*

take precedence over someone or something Go to precedence over someone or something.

take pride in someone or something to be proud of someone or something. □ *I take a great deal of pride in my children.* □ *She takes pride in her work and it shows in her products.*

take (quite) a toll (on someone or something**)** to cause damage or wear by using something or by hard living. □ *Years of sunbathing took a toll on Mary's skin.* □ *Drug abuse takes quite a toll on the lives of people.*

take refuge in something to hide in something; to seek safety or the comfort of being safe in something. □ *The rabbits took refuge in a hole in the ground.* □ *The children took refuge in the house as soon as the storm began.*

take revenge (against someone**)** and **seek revenge (against** someone**); get revenge against** someone; **take revenge (on** someone**) (for** something**)** to get even with someone. □ *Linda planned to take revenge against Ellen.* □ *I intend to take revenge on Paul for what he did.* □ *I will not seek revenge.*

take root 1. *Lit.* [for a plant] to develop roots in soil or some other growing medium. □ *The new plants should take root in a few weeks and start growing.* **2.** *Fig.* to begin to take hold or have effect. □ *Things will begin to change when my new policies take root.* □ *My ideas began to take root and influence other people.*

take shape [for something, such as plans, writing, ideas, arguments, etc.] to begin to be organized and specific. □ *My plans are beginning to take shape.* □ *As my manuscript took shape, I started showing it to publishers.*

take sick and **take ill** to become ill. □ *I took sick with a bad cold last week.* □ *I hope I don't take ill before final exams.*

take sides to choose one side of an argument. □ *They were arguing, but I didn't want to take sides, so I left.* □ *I don't mind taking sides on important issues.*

take sides against someone or something to join a faction opposing someone or something; to establish a faction against someone or something. □ *Both of them took sides against me. It wasn't fair.* □ *We took sides against the bank.*

take solace (in something**)** to console oneself with some fact. □ *I am inordinately impoverished, but I take solace in the fact that I have a splendiferous vocabulary.*

take some doing to require considerable effort and care. □ *It'll take some doing, but it'll get done.* □ *It's not impossible. It'll just take some doing.*

take some heat Go to take the heat.

take (some) time off Go to time off.

take ((some) time) off from work Go to take off from work.

take someone **apart**† **1.** *Sl.* to beat someone up. (See also **take** something **apart**.) □ *Don't talk to me that way, or I'll take you apart.* □ *He was so mad that I thought he was going to take apart all of us.* **2.** *Inf.* to criticize or defame someone or something. □ *They really took me apart, but I just ignore bad reviews.* □ *The editorial took apart the entire city government.*

take someone **around**† to show someone the premises; to introduce someone to the people on the premises. □ *Mr. Franklin needs a plant tour. Would you take him around?* □ *Would you kindly take around our guests?*

take someone **as** someone to assume that someone is someone or a type of person. □ *I took her as some sort of crank.* □ *She didn't want to be taken as some sort of busybody.*

take someone **aside**† to remove someone temporarily from the group for the purposes of discussing something privately. □ *I'm sorry he insulted you. I'll take him aside and* talk to him about it. □ I took aside my secretary and explained the procedure.

take someone **below** to guide someone to a lower deck on a ship. □ *The captain told the first mate to take the passengers below.* □ *Please take Mr. Wilson below, where he will not be in the way.*

take someone **by surprise** and **catch** someone **by surprise** to startle someone; to surprise someone with something unexpected. □ *Oh! You took me by surprise because I didn't hear you come in.* □ *Bill caught his mother by surprise by coming to the door and pretending to be selling something.*

take someone **down a notch (or two)** Go to next.

take someone **down a peg (or two)** and **take** someone **down a notch (or two); knock** someone **down a peg (or two); knock** someone **down a notch (or two)** *Fig.* to reprimand someone who is acting too arrogant. □ *The teacher's scolding took Bob down a notch or two.* □ *He was so rude that someone was bound to knock him down a peg or two.*

take someone **down (to size)** Go to cut someone down (to size).

take someone **for a fool** Go to take someone for an idiot.

take someone **for a ride 1.** *Lit.* to carry someone about, usually for recreation, in a car, plane, boat, etc. □ *Would you take us for a ride in your boat?* □ *Please take me for a ride in your new car.* **2.** *Fig.* to deceive someone. □ *You really took those people for a ride. They really believed you.* □ *I was taken for a ride on this matter.* **3.** *Fig.* to take away and murder a person. (Underworld.) □ *Mr. Big told Mike to take Fred for a ride.* □ *The gang leader had said he thought Mike had better take Walter for a ride.*

take someone **for an idiot** and **take** someone **for a fool** to assume that someone is stupid. □ *I wouldn't do anything like that! Do you take me for an idiot?* □ *I don't take you for a fool. I think you're very clever.*

take someone **for dead** to assume that someone who is still alive is dead. □ *When we found her, we took her for dead, but the paramedics were able to revive her.* □ *He was taken for dead and abandoned.*

take someone **for** someone or something to perceive someone as someone or something. □ *I took you for a fairly even-tempered person. You aren't.* □ *Alice took Jim for a gentleman—which he was.*

take someone **for** something **1.** *Lit.* to escort someone to and through some activities, such as a walk, a swim, a ride, etc. □ *Can I take you for a ride?* □ *He took me for a walk in the park, and then we came home.* **2.** *Inf.* to cheat someone by a certain amount of money. □ *That crook took me for a hundred bucks.* □ *How much did he take you for?*

take someone **hostage** to kidnap or seize someone to be a hostage. □ *The terrorists planned to take the ambassador hostage.* □ *The entire family was taken hostage by the robber.*

take someone **in**[†] **1.** to give someone shelter. (See also take something in.) □ *Do you think you could take me in for the night?* □ *I don't take in strangers.* **2.** Go to suck someone in.

take someone **in**[†] **as** something to make someone a member of an organization. □ *We took her in as an associate at first.* □ *I took in Karen as an associate.*

take someone **in hand** *Fig.* to take control of someone; to assume the responsibility of guiding someone. □ *Someone is going to have to take Tim in hand and help him out.* □ *Alice decided that she would take the new worker in hand.*

take someone **into** one's **confidence** to trust someone with confidential information; to tell a secret to someone and trust the person to keep the secret. □ *We are good friends, but I didn't feel I could take her into my confidence.* □ *I know something very important about Jean. Can I take you into my confidence?*

take someone **off**[†] *Sl.* to kill someone. (Underworld.) □ *The mob took the witness off a week before the trial.* □ *Barlowe didn't want to have to take off Lefty, but he was afraid he might talk.*

take someone **on 1.** to enter into a fight or argument with someone. □ *I pretended to agree because I really didn't want to take him on.* **2.** to employ someone. □ *I think we could take you on as an assistant editor, but it doesn't pay very well.*

take someone or an animal **in**[†] to provide shelter for someone or an animal. □ *When I needed a place to live, my uncle took me in.* □ *Mrs. Wilson took in the lonely little dog and gave it a loving home.*

take someone or an animal **into** one's **heart** *Fig.* to grow to love and trust someone or an animal; to receive a newcomer graciously and lovingly. □ *He was such a cute little boy. We took him into our hearts immediately.* □ *We loved the puppy instantly and took her into our hearts at once.*

take someone or something **aboard** to load someone or something onto a ship. □ *The ship was in its berth, taking passengers aboard.* □ *The ship took many tons of cargo aboard.*

take someone or something **across (something)** to carry or lead someone or something across something. □ *Tim took Liz across the bridge.* □ *We took a lot of food and medicine across before the flooded river washed the bridge out.*

take someone or something **along**[†] to bring someone or something along with one. □ *Can I take my friend along on the hike?* □ *You should take along your own drinking water.*

take someone or something **at face value** to accept someone or something just as it appears; to believe that the way things appear is the way they really are. □ *He means what he says. You have to take him at face value.* □ *I take everything he says at face value.*

take someone or something **away**[†] **(from** someone or something**)** to remove someone or something to some distance away from someone or something else; to remove someone or something from the possession of someone or something else. □ *Take her away from me!* □ *Take away that horrible food.*

take someone or something **before** someone or something to bring someone or something in front of someone or a group for judgment. □ *I will have to take Tom before the manager and let Tom tell his story.* □ *I took the invention before the committee.*

take someone or something **by** something to grasp someone or something by holding on to some part. □ *She took him by the hand and helped him up.* □ *Tom took the dog by the collar and led it out.*

take someone or something **by storm 1.** *Fig.* to conquer someone or something in a fury. □ *The army took city after city by storm.* □ *They crashed in and took the general by storm.* **2.** *Fig.* to succeed overwhelmingly with someone, some place, or a group. □ *The singing star took the audience in each town by storm.* □ *The star took the critics by storm.*

take someone or something **by surprise** to startle or surprise someone or something. □ *She bolted into the room and took them by surprise.* □ *I took the little bird by surprise, and it flew away.*

take someone or something **down**† to move someone or something to a lower position or level. □ *The boss is downstairs and wants to meet our visitor. Will you take her down?* □ *The way down to the lobby is confusing. Let me take down our visitor.* □ *Let me take the sandwiches down.*

take someone or something **for granted** to expect someone or something to be always available to serve in some way without thanks or recognition; to value someone or something too lightly. □ *I wish you didn't take me for granted.* □ *I guess that I take a lot of things for granted.*

take someone or something **into account** and **take into account** someone or something to remember to consider someone or something. □ *I hope you'll take Bill and Bob into account when you plan the party.* □ *I'll try to take into account all the things that are important in a situation like this.*

take someone or something **off**† *Sl.* to rob someone or something. (Underworld.) □ *Weren't you in that bunch that took the bank off in Philly?* □ *No, we never took off no bank, did we, Lefty?*

take someone or something **off** someone's **hands** *Fig.* to relieve someone of the burden or bother of someone or something. □ *I would be happy to take your uncle off your hands for a few hours.* □ *Will you please take some of this food off my hands?*

take someone or something **off** (something) to remove someone or something from the surface of something. □ *Bob helped take his children off the merry-go-round.* □ *Please take your books off the table.*

take someone or something **on**† to accept the task of handling a difficult person or thing. □ *I'll take it on if nobody else will do it.* □ *Nobody wanted to take on Mrs. Franklin, but it had to be done.*

take someone or something **out of** something and **take** someone or something **out**† to carry, lead, or guide someone or something out of something or some place. (See also take something out.) □ *He was becoming quite ill from the smoke, and I had to take him out of the room.* □ *They took out the injured people.*

take someone or something **over**† to take charge (of someone or something); to assume control of someone or something. □ *The new manager will take the office over next week.* □ *Will you please take over your children? I can't seem to control them.*

take someone or something **over** (**to** someone or something) to deliver someone or something to someone or something. □ *Would you take this over to Tiffany?* □ *Would you take Tiffany over to the office?*

take someone or something **with** one to take away someone or something when one leaves. □ *When you go, take Liz with you.* □ *Please take your dog with you.*

take someone or something **wrong** to misunderstand someone or something. □ *Please don't take me wrong, but I believe that your socks don't match.* □ *You'll probably take this wrong, but I have to say that I've never seen you looking better.*

take someone **out**† **1.** to date someone. □ *I hope he'll take me out soon.* □ *She wanted to take out her guest for the evening.* **2.** to block out a player in football. □ *You take Joe out and I'll carry the ball.* □ *Who was supposed to take out that huge guy?* **3.** *Sl.* to kill someone. (Underworld.) □ *Mr. Gutman told Lefty to take Max out.* □ *One more word out of you, and I'm going to take you out.*

take someone **out**† **to dinner** to take someone as one's guest to a meal at a restaurant. □ *Can I take you out to dinner sometime?* □ *We will take out the visitors to dinner tonight.*

take someone's **blood pressure** to measure a person's blood pressure. □ *The doctor takes my blood pressure every time I am in the office.* □ *Bob takes his blood pressure at home every day.*

take someone's **breath away 1.** *Lit.* to cause someone to be out of breath due to a shock or hard exercise. □ *Running this fast takes my breath away.* □ *Mary frightened me and took my breath away.* **2.** *Fig.* to overwhelm someone with beauty or grandeur; to surprise or astound someone. □ *The magnificent painting took my breath away.* □ *Ann looked so beautiful that she took my breath away.*

take someone's **head off** *Fig.* to scold or berate someone severely. □ *There is no need to take his head off about such a simple matter.*

take someone's **life** to kill someone. (Can include onself.) □ *It's the executioner's job to take people's lives.*

take someone's **life in** one's **hands** *Fig.* to risk someone's life. □ *If you go into the war zone, you will be taking your life in your hands.* □ *Ted didn't want to take his life in his hands by going there alone.*

take someone's **part** *Fig.* to take a side in an argument; to support someone in an argument. □ *My sister took my mother's part in the family argument.* □ *You are always taking the part of the underdog!*

take someone's **pulse** to measure the frequency of the beats of a person's pulse. □ *I can take my own pulse.* □ *The nurse took my pulse and said I was fine.*

take someone's **temperature** to measure a person's body temperature with a thermometer. □ *I took my temperature and I found that I am running a fever.* □ *The nurse took my temperature and said I was okay.*

take someone's **word for** something and **take** someone's **word on** something to believe what someone says about something without seeking further information or proof. □ *It's true! Take my word for it.* □ *I can't prove it. You will have to take my word on it.*

take someone's **word on** something Go to previous.

take someone, something, or an animal **in(side)** to transport someone, something, or an animal to shelter or inside something. □ *Please take your little brother in. It's starting to rain.* □ *Take the dog inside when you go.*

take someone **through** (something) to escort someone through something or some place. □ *Would you mind taking Jerry through the factory?* □ *I would be happy to take him through.*

take someone **to court** to sue someone; to force someone to appear in court. □ *I will take you to court if you persist in pestering my client.* □ *Don was taken to court in a negligence suit.*

take someone **to one side** *Fig.* to lead someone to a relatively private place, to say something private or give private instructions. (See also **take** someone **aside**.) □ *Gary took Fran to one side to talk to her.* □ *I will take Sue to one side and have a word with her about this matter.*

take someone **to task** to scold or reprimand someone. □ *The teacher took John to task for his bad behavior.* □ *I lost a big contract, and the boss took me to task in front of everyone.*

take someone **to the cleaners 1.** *Sl.* to take a lot of someone's money; to swindle someone. □ *The lawyers took the insurance company to the cleaners, but I still didn't get enough to pay for my losses.* □ *The con artists took the old man to the cleaners.* **2.** *Sl.* to defeat or best someone. □ *We took the other team to the cleaners.* □ *Look at the height they've got! They'll take us to the cleaners!*

take someone **under** someone's **wing(s)** Go to **under** someone's **wing(s)**.

take someone **up** to discuss or deal with someone. (See also **take** something **up**.) □ *What are we going to do about Bill? Are we going to take Bill up today at the board meeting?* □ *Let's take up the applicants in our next meeting.*

take someone **up on** something to accept an offer that someone has made. □ *That's a good offer. I'll take you up on it.* □ *Tom took Sue up on her offer of dinner.*

take something to endure something; to survive something. □ *I don't think I can take any more scolding today. I've been in trouble since I got up this morning.* □ *Mary was very insulting to Tom, but he can take it.*

take something **aloft** to take an aircraft into the air. □ *The pilot took the plane aloft and tested it out.* □ *When will you take this aloft for a test flight?*

take something **amiss** and **take** something **the wrong way** to understand something as wrong or insulting. □ *Would you take it amiss if I told you I thought you look lovely?* □ *I was afraid you'd take it the wrong way.*

take something **apart** **1.** *Lit.* to disassemble something. (See also **take** someone **apart**.) □ *Bobby took his bicycle apart.* □ *You take apart everything that is mechanical.* **2.** *Fig.* to damage or ruin something. □ *The wreck took both cars apart.* □ *The high wind took apart the roof and the fence.* **3.** *Fig.* to criticize something severely. □ *The critic took the play apart.* □ *The teacher took apart John's essay in front of the class.*

take something **around** to take something from various people or places. □ *Would you take the pictures around and show them to everyone?* □ *I will take around this stack of pictures and show them to each person.*

take something **as** something *Fig.* to assume that something is intended a certain way. □ *I took your comments as a severe criticism.* □ *Sam's actions were taken as constructive.*

take something **at face value** to accept something exactly the way it appears to be. □ *I don't know whether I can take her story at face value, but I will assume that she is not lying.* □ *The committee took the report at face value and approved the suggested changes.*

take something **away** **(from** someone or something**)** to detract from someone or something. □ *The bright costume on the soprano takes a lot away from the tenor, who is just as important.* □ *The main subject of the picture is good, but the busy background takes away a lot.*

take something **back** to retract a statement; to rescind one's remark. □ *You had better take back what you said about my sister.* □ *I won't take what I said back! She's a twit!*

take something **back** **(from** someone**)** to take possession of something that one had previously given away. □ *I took my sweater back from Tim, since he never wore it.* □ *I took back my money from the child.*

take something **back** **to** someone or something to carry or transport something from someone or something. □ *Please take this report back to Liz.* □ *Take back this book to Karen.*

take something **down** **1.** to take some large or complicated things apart. □ *They plan to take all these buildings down and turn the land into a park.* □ *Do they plan to take down the television broadcasting tower?* **2.** to write something down in something. □ *Please take these figures down in your notebook.* □ *Take down these figures in your record of this meeting.*

take something **for a drive** Go to **for a spin**.

take something **from** someone **1.** *Lit.* to remove something from someone's possession. □ *Jimmy took Tim's cookie from him.* □ *Please don't take my money from me.* **2.** *Fig.* to endure abuse from someone. □ *I cannot take any more from you!* □ *Tom could not take any more bad treatment from Alice.*

take something **from** something to subtract something from something; to remove something from something. □ *Take ten from twenty and see what you have left.* □ *If you take the lettuce out of the salad, what do you have left?*

take something **home (with** oneself**)** **1.** *Lit.* to carry something to one's home. □ *We took a lot of souvenirs home with us.* **2.** *Fig.* to take a thought, idea, or concept away [to one's home] from a meeting or conference. □ *Take this idea home with you—diversify your investments.*

take something **in** **1.** to reduce the size of a garment. □ *This is too big. I'll have to take it in around the waist.* □ *I'll have to take in these pants.* **2.** to view and study something; to attend something involving viewing. □ *The mountains are so beautiful! I need an hour or so to take it all in.* □ *I want to sit here a minute and take in the view.* □ *Would you like to take in a movie?* **3.** to receive money as payment or proceeds. □ *How much did we take in today?* □ *The box office took nearly a thousand dollars in within just the last hour.* **4.** to receive something into the mind, usually visually. □ *Could you take those explanations in? I couldn't.* □ *I could hardly take in everything she said.* **5.** to inhale, drink, or eat something. □ *I think I'll go for a walk and take some fresh air in.* □ *Jane was very ill, but she managed to take in some fresh air from the open window.* **6.** Go to **take** something **into** some place.

take something **in (one's) stride** *Fig.* to accept advances or setbacks as the normal course of events. □ *She faced a serious problem, but she was able to take it in her stride.* □ *I'll just take it in stride.* □ *We were afraid that success would spoil her, but she just took it in stride.*

take something **into account** and **take** something **into consideration** to consider something to be an important factor in some decision. □ *We will take your long years of service into account when we make our final decision.* □ *You can be certain that we will take it into consideration.*

take something **into** one's **head** *Fig.* to get an obsession or overpowering idea into one's thinking. □ *George took this strange idea into his head about fixing the car himself.* □ *I don't know why she took that strange idea into her head.*

take something **into** some place and **take** something **in†** to carry something into a place. □ *Fred took the birthday cake into the dining room.* □ *Liz took in the cake for us.*

take something **lying down** *Fig.* to endure something unpleasant without fighting back. □ *He insulted me publicly. You don't expect me to take that lying down, do you?* □ *I'm not the kind of person who'll take something like that lying down.*

take something **off†** to remove something, such as an article of clothing. □ *Please take your coat off and stay awhile.* □ *Please take off your coat.*

take something **on faith** to accept or believe something on the basis of little or no evidence. □ *Please try to believe what I'm telling you. Just take it on faith.* □ *Surely you can't expect me to take a story like that on faith.*

take something **on the chin 1.** *Lit.* to absorb a blow on the chin. □ *The boxer tried to duck but took the blow on the chin.* **2.** *Fig.* to experience and endure bad news or other trouble. □ *The bad news was a real shock, but John took it on the chin.* □ *The worst luck comes my way, and I always end up taking it on the chin.*

take something **on trust** to accept that something is true through trust. □ *I don't know if it's so, but I'll take it on trust.* □ *You will have to take it on trust because I can't prove it.*

take something **out† 1.** *Lit.* to carry something outside. □ *Please take the trash out.* □ *I'll take out the trash.* **2.** *Inf.* to bomb or destroy something. □ *The enemy took out one of the trucks, but not the one carrying the medicine.* □ *The last mission took two enemy bunkers out.* **3.** Go to **take** something **out of** someone or something.

take something **out in trade** *Fig.* to accept someone's goods or services in payment of a bill. □ *The grocer told the plumber that he would pay the plumber by allowing him to take his bill out in trade.* □ *I don't have any cash right now. Can you take what I owe you out in trade?*

take something **out of context** Go to **out of context.**

take something **out of** someone or something and **take** something **out†** to remove something from the inside of some-

one or something. □ *The doctors took a large intestinal tumor out of Wally.* □ *She took out a sheet of paper.*

take something **out of** someone's **hands** Go to **out of** someone's **hands.**

take something **out† on** someone or something to punish someone or something because of something, such as anger, hurt feelings, frustration, etc. □ *I know you're angry, but don't take it out on me!* □ *Don't take out your anger on me.*

take something **over† 1.** to assume responsibility for a task. □ *It looks as if I'm going to have to take the project over.* □ *I will take over the project.* **2.** to acquire all of an asset; [for a company] to acquire another company. □ *Carl set out to take the failing airline over.* □ *He took over the failing company with the help of a number of investment bankers.* **3.** to take control of something. □ *The dictator hoped to take over the world little by little.* □ *He just might take it over.*

take something **personally** to interpret a remark as if it were mean or critical about oneself. □ *Don't take it personally, but you really need a haircut.* □ *I want to tell you something, but please don't take it personally.*

take something **public 1.** to make something known to the public. □ *You gotta take it public—put it on the street—even when it's none of your business.* □ *Don't take it public. You'll just get talked about.* **2.** to sell shares in a company to the general public. (Securities markets.) □ *The board decided not to take the company public.* □ *We're going to take it public whenever the market looks good.*

take something **the wrong way** Go to **take** something **amiss.**

take something **to heart** *Fig.* to consider that some comment is significant to oneself. □ *Mary listened to Bob's advice and took it all to heart.* □ *All Sue's advice was taken to heart by the show committee.*

take something **to pieces** *Inf.* to disassemble something. □ *I will have to take the vacuum cleaner to pieces to find out what's wrong with it.* □ *The machine was taken to pieces again in an effort to find where the leftover part belonged.*

take something **to** someone or something to carry something to someone or something. □ *Should I take this package to Carol?* □ *Would you take this to the post office?*

take something **under advisement** to hear an idea and think about it carefully. □ *It's a good idea, but I'll have to take it under advisement.* □ *The suggestion was taken under advisement, and a reply was not expected for at least a month.*

take something **up† 1.** [for someone or a group] to deliberate something. □ *When will the board of directors take this up?* □ *Let's take up that matter now.* **2.** to raise something, such as the height of a hem. □ *The skirt is too long. I'll have to take it up.* □ *Can you take up this skirt for me?* **3.** to continue with something after an interruption. □ *They took it up where they left off.* □ *Let's take up this matter at the point we were at when we were interrupted.* □ *We must take up our work again.* **4.** to begin something; to start to acquire a skill in something. (See also **take** something **up† (with** someone).) □ *When did you take this hobby up?* □ *I took up skiing last fall.* **5.** to absorb something. □ *This old sponge doesn't take much water up.* □ *It used to* *take up more.* **6.** to adopt something new. □ *I see you've taken a new lifestyle up.* □ *Toby took up the life of a farmer.*

take something **up to** someone to deliver something to a person on a higher level. □ *I will take this up to the boss and try to get it approved.* □ *Please take this up to Sue on the next floor and see what she thinks about it.*

take something **up†** (**with** someone) to raise and discuss a matter with someone. □ *This is a very complicated problem. I'll have to take it up with the office manager.* □ *She'll take up this problem with the owner in the morning.*

take something (**up**)**on** oneself to accept the entire burden of something on oneself. (*Upon* is formal and less commonly used than *on.*) □ *You didn't need to take it all upon yourself. There are others here who can help, you know.* □ *Jan takes too much on herself.*

take something **with a pinch of salt** and **take something with a grain of salt** *Fig.* to listen to a story or an explanation with considerable doubt. □ *You must take anything she says with a grain of salt. She doesn't always tell the truth.* □ *They took my explanation with a pinch of salt. I was sure they didn't believe me.*

take something **with** one to take something [away] with one. □ *I am going to take this food with me.* □ *Can I take one of these catalogs with me?*

take something **with** something to eat or swallow something, such as medicine, with something. □ *You have to take this medicine with milk or soda water.* □ *I will take this pill with milk.*

take steps (to prevent something) *Fig.* to do what is necessary to prevent something. □ *I took steps to prevent John from learning what we were talking about.* □ *I have to keep John from knowing what I've been doing. I can prevent it if I take steps.*

take stock (of something) to make an appraisal of resources and potentialities. □ *I spent some time yesterday taking stock of my good and bad qualities.* □ *We all need to take stock now and then.*

take the bit between the teeth Go to next.

take the bit in one's **teeth** and **take the bit between the teeth** to put oneself in charge; to take charge. □ *Someone needed to direct the project, so I took the bit in my teeth.* □ *If you want to get something done, you've got to take the bit between your teeth and get to work.*

Take the bitter with the sweet. *Prov.* Accept the bad things as well as the good things that happen. (Implies that the bad and good things you are talking about are very serious or important.) □ *If you intend to get married, you must be prepared to take the bitter with the sweet.*

take the blame (for doing something) to acknowledge that one is to blame for doing something. □ *Do you really expect for me to take the blame for something I didn't do?*

take the bull by the horns *Fig.* to confront a problem head-on and deal with it openly. □ *It's time to take the bull by the horns and get this job done.*

take the chill off ((of) a place) to do something that warms a place up slightly. □ *Let's build a fire and take the chill off this place.* □ *I turned up the heat to take the chill off of the apartment.*

take the coward's way out *Euph.* to kill oneself. □ *When faced with financial disaster, Sarah took the coward's way out.* □ *I can't believe that Bill would take the coward's way out. His death must have been an accident.*

take the cure to enter into any treatment program or treatment center. (Especially those dealing with drugs and alcohol.) □ *I wanted to take the cure, but I just couldn't bring myself to do it.* □ *It's hard to get those addicted to realize that they are the ones who have to decide to take the cure.*

take the day off Go to the day off.

take the easy way out to get free of something by taking the path of least resistance. □ *You can depend on Kelly to take the easy way out of a tough situation.* □ *I'm not the type that takes the easy way out.*

take the edge off ((of) something**) 1.** *Lit.* to dull a blade. (*Of* is usually retained before pronouns.) □ *Cutting hard stuff like that will take the edge off your knife blade.* **2.** *Fig.* to decrease the effect of something; to make something less blunt, critical, etc. (*Of* is usually retained before pronouns.) □ *He did not mean to insult the guest, and he quickly thought of something to say that would take the edge off his remark.* □ *Her comments were quite cruel, and nothing could be said to take the edge off of them.*

take the fall *Sl.* to get arrested for a particular crime. (Especially when others are going unpunished for the same crime.) □ *Walt and Tony pulled the job off together, but Tony took the fall.* □ *You did it, and I won't take the fall!*

take the floor 1. *Fig.* to stand up and address the audience. □ *When I take the floor, I'll make a short speech.* □ *The last time you had the floor, you talked for an hour.* **2.** *Fig.* to go to the dance floor in order to dance. □ *They took the floor for the foxtrot.* □ *When the band played, everyone took the floor.*

Take the goods the gods provide. *Prov.* If you have good fortune, enjoy it and use it to your advantage. □ *Frances: I feel I have an unfair advantage over other people in the violin contest. After all, my parents were able to give me lessons with the very best teachers when I was young. Alan: Frances, take the goods the gods provide.*

take the heat and **take some heat** *Sl.* to receive or put up with criticism (for something). □ *The cops have been taking some heat about the Quincy killing.* □ *If you can't take the heat, stay out of the kitchen.*

take the heat off (of) someone or something *Fig. to* relieve the pressure on someone or something. (*Of* is usually retained before pronouns.) □ *That really takes the heat off of all of us.* □ *The change in the deadline takes the heat off the office staff.*

take the initiative (to do something) to activate oneself to do something even if one has not been asked to do it. □ *The door hinges squeak because no one will take the initiative to oil them.* □ *Sometimes, in order to get things done, you have to take the initiative.*

take the law into one's **own hands** *Fig.* to attempt to administer the law; to pass judgment on someone who has done something wrong. □ *Citizens don't have the right to take the law into their own hands.* □ *The shopkeeper took the law into his own hands when he tried to arrest the thief.*

T

take the liberty of doing something to do something for someone voluntarily; to do something slightly personal for someone that would be more appropriate if one knew the person better. (Often used as an overly polite exaggeration in a request.) □ *Do you mind if I take the liberty of flicking a bit of lint off your collar?* □ *May I take the liberty of removing your coat?* □ *I took the liberty of ordering an entree for you. I hope you don't mind.*

take the lid off (of) something and **take the lid off†** **1.** *Lit.* to remove the lid from something. (*Of* is usually retained before pronouns.) □ *I took the lid off the box and set it aside.* □ *Karen took off the lid.* **2.** *Fig.* to reveal a set of previously concealed problems. (*Of* is usually retained before pronouns.) □ *You took the lid off this mess. You straighten it out!* □ *You took off the lid, so you have to settle it.*

take the (long) count *Sl.* to die. (*Fig.* on a boxer being counted out and losing a fight.) □ *The poor cat took the long count at last.* □ *I'm too young to take the count.*

take the pledge *Fig.* to promise to abstain from drinking alcohol. □ *I'm not ready to take the pledge yet, but I will cut down.* □ *My aunt tried to get me to take the pledge.*

take the plunge to marry someone. □ *I'm not ready to take the plunge yet.* □ *Sam and Mary took the plunge.*

take the pulse of something *Fig.* to sample or survey something to learn about its progress or state. □ *Two executives came in to take the pulse of the local business unit.*

take the rap (for someone**)** *Inf.* to take the blame [for doing something] for someone else. □ *I don't want to take the rap for you.* □ *John robbed the bank, but Tom took the rap for him.*

take the rap (for something**)** *Inf.* to take the blame for (doing) something. □ *I won't take the rap for the crime. I wasn't even in town.* □ *Who'll take the rap for it? Who did it?*

take (the) roll Go to call (the) roll.

Take the rough with the smooth. *Prov.* Accept difficult as well as easy times. □ *Don't give up on your business just because you lost money this month. You have to take the rough with the smooth.*

take the slack up† **1.** *Lit.* to tighten a rope that is holding something loosely. □ *Take the slack up if you can.* □ *This clothesline is too loose. Do something to take up the slack.* **2.** *Fig.* to do what needs to be done; to do what has been left undone. □ *Do I have to take the slack up?* □ *Jill did her job poorly and I have to take up the slack.*

take the spear (in one's **chest)** *Sl.* to accept full blame for something; to accept the full brunt of the punishment for something. □ *The CFO got the short straw and had to take the spear in his chest.* □ *I sure didn't want to take the spear.*

take the stage *Fig.* to become the center of attention; to become the focus of everyone's attention. □ *Later in the day, the problems in the warehouse took the stage, and we discussed them until dinnertime.*

take the stand to go to and sit in the witness chair in a courtroom. □ *I was in court all day, waiting to take the stand.* □ *The lawyer asked the witness to take the stand.*

take the starch out of someone **1.** *Fig.* to make someone less arrogant or stiff. □ *I told a joke that made Mr. Jones laugh very hard. It really took the starch out of him.* □ *John is so arrogant. I'd really like to take the starch out of him!* **2.** *Fig.* to make someone tired and weak. □ *This hot weather really takes the starch out of me.* □ *What a long day! It sure took the starch out of me.*

take the stuffing out of someone Go to kick the (natural) stuffing out of someone.

take the trouble (to do something**)** to make an effort to do something (that one might not otherwise do). □ *I wish I had taken the trouble to study this matter more carefully.* □ *I just didn't have enough time to take the trouble.*

take the wind out of someone's **sails** *Fig.* to challenge someone's boasting or arrogance. □ *John was bragging about how much money he earned until he learned that most of us make more. That took the wind out of his sails.* □ *Learning that one has been totally wrong about something can really take the wind out of one's sails.*

take the words out of someone's **mouth** *Fig.* to say something just before someone else was going to say the same thing; to say something that someone who agrees with you might have said. □ *That is exactly right! You took the words right out of my mouth!* □ *When you said "expensive," you took the words right out of my mouth!*

take things easy 1. to live well and comfortably. □ *I'll be glad when I can make enough money to take things easy.* □ *I make enough to take things easy.* **2.** to relax temporarily and recuperate. □ *The doctor says I'm supposed to take things easy for a while.* □ *I want you to take it easy until the stitches heal.*

take time out to spend time away from studying or working. □ *He's taking time out between high school and starting at the university.* □ *Mary's taking time out from her job to work abroad for a year.*

take to one's **bed** to go to bed, as with an illness. □ *I feel a little ill, so I'll take to my bed for a day or so.* □ *Sam took to his bed with a fever.*

take to one's **heels** *Fig.* to run away. □ *The little boy said hello and then took to his heels.* □ *The man took to his heels to try to get to the bus stop before the bus left.*

take to someone or something to become fond of or attracted to someone or something. □ *Mary didn't take to her new job, and she quit after two weeks.* □ *The puppy seems to take to this new food just fine.*

take to the hills Go to head for the hills.

take too much on† to undertake to do too much work or too many tasks at one time. □ *Don't take too much on, or you won't be able to do any of it well.* □ *Ann tends to take on too much and get exhausted.*

take turns ((at) doing something**)** and **take turns (at** something**); take turns (with** something**)** [for two or more people] to alternate in doing something. □ *Let's take turns with mowing the lawn.* □ *Do you want to take turns at answering the telephone?*

take turns with someone to alternate [doing something] with someone. □ *We both can't be there at the same time. I'll take turns with you.* □ *You have to take turns with your brother.*

T

take turns (with something**)** Go to take turns ((at) doing something).

take umbrage at something to feel that one has been insulted by something. □ *The employee took umbrage at not getting a raise.* □ *Mary took umbrage at the suggestion that she was being unreasonable.*

take up arms (against someone or something**)** to prepare to fight against someone or something. □ *Everyone in the town took up arms against the enemy.* □ *They were all so angry that the leader convinced them to take up arms.*

take up one's **abode** some place to make some place one's home. □ *I am going to take up my abode in a different city.* □ *I will take up my abode in this place and hope to find a job close by.*

take up residence some place to make a residence of a place. □ *Ed took up residence in a small efficiency apartment.* □ *It looks as if a family of mice has taken up residence in the cupboard.*

take up room Go to take up space.

take up (someone's**) time** to require too much of someone else's time; to waste someone's time. (Also with *so much of* or *too much of,* as in the examples.) □ *You're taking up my time. Please go away.* □ *This problem is taking up too much of my time.*

take up space and **take up room** to fill or occupy space. (Note the variations in the examples.) □ *The piano is taking up too much room in our living room.* □ *John, you're not being any help at all. You're just taking up space.*

take up the challenge to respond to a challenge and do what the challenge asks. □ *I am not prepared to take the challenge up.* □ *Dave took up the challenge without much urging.*

take up where one **left off** to start up again in the very place that one has stopped. □ *I had to leave the room for a minute, but when I got back, I took up where I left off.* □ *It's time to stop for lunch. After lunch, we will take up where we left off.*

take up with someone to become close with someone; to become friends with someone. □ *I think that Albert may have taken up with the wrong people.* □ *I did not want Lefty to take up with Max, but he did, and look where it's gotten him.*

take years off (of) someone or something to make someone seem or look younger. (*Of* is usually retained before pronouns.) □ *My exciting vacation took years off of me.* □ *Your shorter haircut has taken years off your face.*

Take your seat. Please sit down. (Often plural.) □ *Please take your seats so we can begin.*

taken aback *Cliché* surprised and confused. □ *When Mary told me the news, I was taken aback for a moment.* □ *When I told my parents I was married, they were completely taken aback.*

taken for dead appearing to be dead; assumed to be dead. □ *I was so ill with the flu that I was almost taken for dead.* □ *The accident victims were so seriously injured that they were taken for dead at first.*

taken with someone or something highly attracted to someone or something. □ *She was really quite taken with the* young man who escorted her to the ball. □ *The audience was taken with the stage setting.*

take-off artist *Sl.* a thief. (Underworld.) □ *A take-off artist known as the Cat is cleaning out closets and jewelry boxes all over town.* □ *He's not a sales agent. He's a take-off artist, pure and simple.*

taking calls willing to receive telephone calls. □ *I'm sorry, but she's not taking calls at the moment. Can I have her call you later?*

A **tale never loses in the telling.** *Prov.* When people tell stories, they tend to exaggerate. □ *Johnny's bicycle accident tale never loses in the telling; he convinced his friends that four semitrucks had been involved, when in fact he only ran into one parked car.*

tale of woe a sad story; a list of personal problems; an excuse for failing to do something. □ *I listened to her tale of woe without saying anything.* □ *This tale of woe that we have all been getting from Kelly is just too much.*

talk a blue streak *Fig.* to talk very much and very rapidly. □ *Billy didn't talk until he was two, and then he started talking a blue streak.* □ *I can't understand anything Bob says. He talks a blue streak, and I can't follow his thinking.*

talk a mile a minute Go to a mile a minute.

talk about someone or something to discuss someone or something. □ *I don't want to talk about Jerry anymore.* □ *Let's not talk about it now.*

Talk about someone or something**!** If you think that thing or person is remarkable, then... □ *Talk about ugly buildings! This one is horrendous.*

talk around something to talk, but avoid talking directly about the subject. □ *You are just talking around the matter! I want a straight answer!* □ *He never really said anything. He just talked around the issue.*

talk at someone to say words at someone; to talk to someone in a desultory manner. □ *You are just talking at her and she isn't paying attention.* □ *Talk to me, not at me. I want to communicate with you.*

talk back (to someone**)** to challenge verbally a parent, an older person, or one's superior. □ *Please don't talk back to me!* □ *I've told you before not to talk back!*

talk big to brag; to make grandiose statements. □ *She talks big but can't produce anything.* □ *He has some deep need to talk big, but it's just talk—no action.*

talk down to someone to speak to someone in a patronizing manner; to speak to someone in the simplest way. □ *The manager insulted everyone in the office by talking down to them.* □ *Please don't talk down to me. I can understand anything you have to say.*

talk in circles *Fig.* to talk in a confusing or roundabout manner. □ *I couldn't understand a thing he said. All he did was talk in circles.* □ *We argued for a long time and finally decided that we were talking in circles.*

Talk is cheap. *Prov.* It is easier to say you will do something than to actually do it. (Saying this in response to someone who promises you something implies that you do not believe that person will keep the promise.) □ *My boss keeps saying she'll give me a raise, but talk is cheap.* □ *You've been promising me a new dishwasher for five years now. Talk is cheap.*

T

talk like a nut to say stupid things. □ *You're talking like a nut! You don't know what you are saying.* □ *Don't talk like a nut! We can't afford a trip to Florida!*

the **talk of** a place someone or something who is the subject of a conversation somewhere, such as the town, the office, the community, etc. □ *The handsome new teacher was the talk of the town.* □ *John's new car is the talk of the office.*

talk of someone or something to speak about someone or something. □ *Weren't we talking of old Mrs. Watson just now?* □ *We were just talking of old times—happier times.*

Talk of the devil (and he is sure to appear). Go to Speak of the devil (and in he walks).

talk on to continue to talk. □ *The lecturer talked on for hours.* □ *How can anyone talk on so long without saying anything useful?*

talk on someone or something to speak on the subject of someone or something. □ *Today, I will talk on Abraham Lincoln.* □ *Ann is going to talk on the subject of manners.*

talk one's **head off** *Fig. Inf.* to talk endlessly; to argue vigorously. □ *I talked my head off trying to convince them.* □ *Don't waste time talking your head off to them.*

talk one's **way out of** something to get out of something by verbal persuasion. □ *You are in a mess and you can't talk your way out of it.* □ *If I get into some sort of problem, I will try to talk my way out of it.*

talk oneself **out** to talk until one can talk no more. □ *She talked herself out and was silent for the rest of the day.* □ *I talked until I talked myself out.*

talk over someone's **head** *Fig.* to say things that someone cannot understand; to speak on too high a level for one's audience. □ *The speaker talked over our heads and we learned nothing.* □ *It is not a good idea to talk over your audience's heads.*

talk over something to use something, such as a microphone, intercom, or telephone, to talk. □ *I don't mind talking over the telephone.* □ *I will talk to Jeff over the intercom and see what he thinks about the idea.*

talk shop to talk about business or work matters at a social event (where such talk is out of place). □ *All right, everyone, we're not here to talk shop. Let's have a good time.* □ *Mary and Jane stood by the punch bowl, talking shop.*

talk someone **down†** **1.** to win at debating someone. □ *Liz was able to talk her opponent down.* □ *She talked down her opponent.* **2.** to direct a novice pilot to make a safe landing by giving spoken instructions over the airplane's radio. □ *The people on the ground talked down the amateur pilot successfully.* □ *I wonder how many movies have been made about someone talking a pilot down.* **3.** to convince someone to lower the price of something. □ *The price tag said $2,000 for the car, but I talked down the salesman by threatening to go elsewhere.* □ *This is my final offer. Don't try to talk me down.*

talk someone **into (doing)** something to overcome someone's objections to doing something; to convince someone to do something. □ *They talked me into going to the meeting, even though I didn't really have the time.* □ *No one can talk me into doing something illegal.* □ *She finally talked herself into making the dive.*

talk someone or something **over† (with** someone) to discuss someone or something with someone. □ *I want to talk John over with my staff.* □ *I will talk over this matter with Sam.*

talk someone or something **up†** to promote or speak in support of someone or something. □ *I've been talking the party up all day, trying to get people to come.* □ *They keep talking up the candidate as if he represented a real change.*

talk someone **out of** doing something to convince someone not to do something. □ *I tried to talk her out of going, but she insisted.* □ *Don't try to talk me out of quitting school. My mind is made up.*

talk someone **out of** something to convince someone to give up or change something. □ *They were trying to talk me out of my decision.* □ *Timmy tried to talk Mary out of her ice cream cone.*

talk someone **ragged** *Fig.* to talk to someone too much; to bore someone. □ *That was not an interview. She talked me ragged.* □ *He always talks me ragged, but I always listen.*

talk someone's **ear off** *Fig.* to talk to someone endlessly; to bore someone with too much talk. □ *My aunt always talks my ear off when she comes to visit.* □ *Stay away from Mr. Jones. He will talk your ear off if he gets a chance.*

talk someone's **head off 1.** *Fig.* [for someone] to speak too much. □ *Why does John always talk his head off? Doesn't he know he bores people?* □ *She talks her head off and doesn't seem to know what she's saying.* **2.** *Fig.* to talk to and bore someone. □ *John is very friendly, but watch out or he'll talk your head off.* □ *My uncle always talked my head off whenever I went to visit him.*

talk something **out†** to settle something by discussion. □ *Let's not get mad. Let's just talk it out.* □ *Please, let's talk out this matter calmly.*

talk something **over†** to discuss something. □ *Come into my office so we can talk this over.* □ *We talked over the plans for nearly an hour.*

talk something **through† 1.** to discuss something in detail. □ *Let's talk the issue through and get it decided.* **2.** to get something approved by talking convincingly. □ *The board was reluctant to approve it, but I talked it through.* □ *We will talk through this matter in the board meeting.*

talk something **up†** to promote or advertise something by saying good things about it to as many people as possible. □ *Let's talk the play up around campus so we can get a good audience.* □ *I will talk up the play all I can.*

talk through one's **hat** *Fig.* to brag or exaggerate; to talk nonsense. □ *That can't be so! You are just talking through your hat!* □ *Pay no attention to Mary. She is just talking through her hat.*

talk to hear one's **own voice** *Fig.* to talk far more than is necessary; to talk much, in an egotistical manner. □ *Oh, he's just talking to hear his own voice.* □ *Am I just talking to hear my own voice, or are you listening to me?*

talk to someone **1.** *Lit.* to speak to someone; to confer with someone. □ *Talk to me! I really want your opinion.* □ *I will have to talk to Mark to see what he thinks.* **2.** *Fig.* to lecture to someone; to reprimand someone. □ *I wish you would talk to your son. He is creating havoc in the classroom.*

☐ *I am going to have to talk to Roberta. She is not getting things clean.*

talk turkey *Fig.* to talk business; to talk frankly. ☐ *Okay, Bob, we have business to discuss. Let's talk turkey.* ☐ *John wanted to talk turkey, but Jane just wanted to joke around.*

talk until one **is blue in the face** *Fig.* to talk until one is exhausted. ☐ *I talked until I was blue in the face, but I couldn't change her mind.* ☐ *She had to talk until she was blue in the face in order to convince him.*

talk up a storm Go to up a storm.

talk with someone (**about** someone or something) to hold a discussion with someone or a group. ☐ *Could I talk with you about Alice?* ☐ *Can I talk with you about my salary?*

talked out tired of talking; unable to talk more. ☐ *I can't go on. I'm all talked out.* ☐ *She was talked out in the first hour of discussion.*

a **tall drink of water** Go to a big drink of water.

*a **tall order** a request that is difficult to fulfill. (*Typically: **be** ~; **give** someone ~.) ☐ *That's a tall order. Do you think anyone can do it?* ☐ *Well, it's a tall order, but I'll do it.*

tall timber(s) some remote place in the country or the woods. ☐ *Oh, Chuck lives out in the tall timbers somewhere. He only has a post office box number.* ☐ *You're not going to move me out into the tall timber somewhere!*

tally something **up**† to add something up. ☐ *Please tally everything up and tell me the total.* ☐ *Let's tally up everything and ask for donations.*

tally with something **1.** *Lit.* [for one set of figures] to match another set of figures. ☐ *Your figures don't tally with mine. Let's add them up again.* ☐ *The total Sam got didn't tally with what the tax agent had come up with.* **2.** *Fig.* [for one thing] to agree or correlate with another. ☐ *What you just said doesn't tally with what you told me before.* ☐ *His story doesn't tally with what I already know.*

tamp something **down**† to pat or pack something down. ☐ *Tamp the soil down over the seeds after you plant them.* ☐ *Please tamp down the soil firmly.*

tamper with someone or something to fiddle with someone or something; to meddle with someone or something. ☐ *I've got him believing just what I want him to believe. Don't tamper with him.* ☐ *Please don't tamper with the thermostat.*

tan someone's **hide** to spank someone. ☐ *Billy's mother said she'd tan Billy's hide if he ever did that again.* ☐ *"I'll tan your hide if you're late!" said Tom's father.*

tangle someone or something **up**† to entangle someone or something. ☐ *Please don't tangle me up in your ropes.* ☐ *I tangled up my feet in the cords on the floor.*

tangle with someone or something (**over** someone or something) to battle against someone or something about someone or something. ☐ *Tim tangled with Karen over the children.* ☐ *I hope I don't have to tangle with the bank over this loan.* ☐ *I don't want to tangle with city hall.*

tank up (on something) and **tank up with** something **1.** *Lit.* to fill one's fuel tank with something. ☐ *I need to tank up on premium gas to stop this engine knock.* ☐ *It's time to stop and tank up.* ☐ *We need to tank up with gas.*

2. *Sl.* to drink some kind of alcoholic beverage. ☐ *Toby spent the evening tanking up on bourbon.* ☐ *Jerry tanked up with gin and went to sleep.*

tap at something to make one or more light blows on something. ☐ *Fred tapped at the door, but no one heard him.* ☐ *Who is tapping at my window?*

tap on something to make one or more light blows on something. ☐ *Who is that tapping on my windowpane?* ☐ *I wish you would stop tapping on the tabletop.*

tap out 1. *Sl.* to lose one's money in gambling or in the securities markets. ☐ *I'm gonna tap out in about three more rolls—just watch.* ☐ *I really tapped out on that gold-mining stock.* **2.** *Sl.* to die; to expire. ☐ *My dog tapped out after being hit by a car.* ☐ *Mary was so tired that she thought she was going to tap out.*

tap someone (**for** something) to select someone for some purpose or position. ☐ *The committee tapped John to run for Congress.* ☐ *I had thought they were going to tap Sally.*

tap someone or something **on** something to make one or more light blows on some part of someone or something. ☐ *Someone tapped me on the shoulder, and I turned around to see who it was.* ☐ *I tapped the drum on the top to find its pitch.*

tap something **down**† to pound something down with light blows. ☐ *Please tap that nail down so no one gets hurt on it.* ☐ *Tap down the tack, if you would.*

tap something **into** something and **tap** something **in**† to move something in with light blows. ☐ *The mechanic tapped the bracket into place.* ☐ *The worker tapped in the bracket.*

tap something **out**† **1.** *Lit.* to clean something, as the ashes out of a pipe, by tapping. ☐ *He took the pipe out of his mouth and tapped the ashes out.* ☐ *He tapped out the soil from the flower pot.* **2.** *Fig.* to send a message in Morse code, as on a telegraph. ☐ *The telegraph operator tapped a message out and waited for a reply.* ☐ *The operator tapped out a message.* **3.** *Fig.* to thump the rhythm of a piece of music [on something]. ☐ *Tap the rhythm out until you get it right.* ☐ *Let's tap out the rhythm together.*

tap something **with** something to make light blows on something with something. ☐ *Alice tapped the table with her keys in an annoying fashion.* ☐ *Just tap the nail lightly with your hammer.*

tap-dance like mad *Sl.* to appear busy continuously; to have to move fast or talk cleverly to distract someone. ☐ *When things get tough, the whole Congress tap-dances like mad.* ☐ *Any public official knows how to tap-dance like mad when the press gets too nosy.*

taper off (doing something) gradually to stop doing something; to do less and less of something until there is no more to do. ☐ *Bob tried to taper off smoking again.* ☐ *I can't taper off overeating. I have to stop all at once by going on a strict diet.*

tar and feather someone to punish or humiliate someone by coating them with tar and feathers. ☐ *The people of the village tarred and feathered the bank robber and chased him out of town.* ☐ *They threatened to tar and feather me if I ever came back into their town.*

target someone or something **as** something to aim at someone or something as something; to choose someone or

T

683

something as someone or something. □ *The board targeted Alice as a potential candidate.* □ *We targeted the first of August as the starting date.*

tarred with the same brush *Fig.* sharing the same characteristic(s); having the same good or bad points as someone else. □ *Jack and his brother are tarred with the same brush. They're both crooks.* □ *The Smith children are tarred with the same brush. They're all lazy.*

taste blood *Fig.* to experience something exciting, and perhaps dangerous, for the first time. □ *She had tasted blood once, and she knew that the life of a race-car driver was for her.* □ *Once you taste blood, you're hooked.*

*a **taste for** something a desire for a particular food, drink, or experience. (*Typically: **get** ~; **have** ~; **give** someone ~; **acquire** ~.) □ *The Smiths have a taste for adventure and take exotic vacations.* □ *When she was pregnant, Mary often had a taste for pickles.*

taste like more to taste very good; to taste so good as to make one want to eat more. □ *This pie is great. It tastes like more.* □ *Mom's cooking always tastes like more.*

taste like something to have the same taste as something. □ *This stuff tastes like watermelon.* □ *What do you think this tastes like?*

*a **taste of** one's **own medicine** and *a **dose of** one's **own medicine** *Fig.* a sample of the unpleasantness that one has been giving other people. (*Typically: **get** ~; **have** ~; **give** someone ~.) □ *Now you see how it feels to have someone call you names! You are getting a taste of your own medicine!* □ *John, who is often rude and abrupt with people, was devastated when the teacher treated him rudely. He doesn't like having a dose of his own medicine.*

taste of something **1.** to have a taste similar to something; to have the hint of a certain flavor. □ *This ice cream tastes of apricots.* □ *Why does this wine taste of vinegar?* **2.** to take a taste of something. (Typically southern.) □ *Here, taste of this pie.* □ *Can I taste of your apple?*

a **taste of** something an experience; an example. □ *Bill gave Sue a taste of her own rudeness.* □ *My friend used a parachute and got a taste of what it's like to be a bird.*

Tastes differ. *Prov.* Different people like different things. □ *Fred: Bill always goes out with such stupid girls. I can't understand why. Alan: Tastes differ.*

tattle (on someone**) (to** someone**)** to tell on someone to someone. □ *Are you going to tattle on me to my mother?* □ *Please don't tattle on me.*

taunt someone **about** something to mock, tease, or torment someone about something. □ *Stop taunting me about something that happened years ago!* □ *Terry was being taunted about his gaudy tie, so he took it off.*

taunt someone **into** something to mock, tease, or torment someone into doing something. □ *The gang taunted Liz into taking unnecessary chances.* □ *Don was taunted into leaving the room.*

taunt someone **with** something to tease or tantalize someone with something. □ *Jerry taunted Fran with the plate of fudge.* □ *Please don't taunt me with food I shouldn't eat.*

tax someone or something **with** something to burden or tire someone or something with something. □ *Please don't tax me with any more requests for my immediate attention.* □

You are continuing to tax this committee with your constant complaints.

tax-and-spend spending freely and taxing heavily. (Referring to a legislative body that repeatedly passes expensive new laws and keeps raising taxes to pay for the cost. Fixed order.) □ *I hope that people do not elect another tax-and-spend Congress this time.* □ *The only thing worse than a tax-and-spend legislature is one that spends and runs up a worsening deficit.*

teach one's **grandmother to suck eggs** *Fig.* to try to tell or show someone more knowledgeable or experienced than oneself how to do something. □ *Don't suggest showing Mary how to knit. It will be like teaching your grandmother to suck eggs.* □ *Don't teach your grandmother to suck eggs. Bob has been playing tennis for years.*

teach someone **a lesson** to get even with someone for bad behavior. □ *John tripped me, so I punched him. That ought to teach him a lesson.* □ *That taught me a lesson. I won't do it again.*

teach someone **the hang of** something Go to the **hang of** something.

teach someone **the tricks of the trade** Go to the **tricks of the trade.**

*the **teacher's pet** the teacher's favorite student. (*Typically: **be** ~; **become** ~.) □ *Sally is the teacher's pet. She always gets special treatment.* □ *The other students don't like the teacher's pet.*

a **team player** someone who works well with the group; someone who is loyal to the group. □ *Ted is a team player. I am sure that he will cooperate with us.*

team up against someone or something Go to **up against** someone or something.

team up (with someone**)** to join with someone. □ *I teamed up with Jane to write the report.* □ *I had never teamed up with anyone else before. I had always worked alone.*

tear a place **apart**† *Fig.* to search somewhere to the point of destruction. □ *The cops came with a search warrant and tore your room apart.* □ *If you don't come up with the money you kept for us, we'll tear apart your house!*

tear across something to move rapidly across some area. □ *The boys tore across the lawn to the swimming pool.* □ *As the plane tore across the sky it made a horrendous roar.*

tear along to go along very fast, as in running, driving, cycling, etc. □ *The cars tore along the road, raising dust and making noise.* □ *Andy tore along on his bicycle, trying to see how fast he could go.*

tear around (some place**)** to move or run around rapidly and perhaps recklessly. □ *The kids were tearing around through the house all day. They've made a real mess.* □ *Please don't tear around the house.*

tear at someone or something to rip at someone or something; to try to tear someone or something up. □ *The badger tore at me, but I dodged it and ran away fast.* □ *Timmy tore at the package, struggling to get the paper off.*

tear away (from someone or something**)** to leave someone or something, running. □ *Dave tore away from Jill, leaving her to find her own way home.* □ *Roger tore away from the meeting, trying to make his train.*

tear down something to race down something very fast. (See also **tear** something **down**.) □ *The girls tore down the hallway as fast as they could run.* □ *They tore down the stairs and ran out the door.*

tear into some place to run or race into a place. □ *The kids tore into the house and knocked over a lamp.* □ *Kelly tore into the boss's office and put the papers on the desk.*

tear into someone *Fig.* to scold someone severely; to attack someone with criticism. □ *I was late, and the boss tore into me like a mad dog.* □ *I don't know why she tore into me. I was at work when the window was broken.*

tear into someone or something to attack someone or something; to attack someone or something with the intent of eating someone or something. □ *The wolves tore into the hunter and injured him severely.* □ *The kids tore into the cake and ate it all.*

tear into something *Fig.* to begin eating food with gusto. □ *The family tore into the mountain of food like they hadn't eaten since breakfast—which was true, in fact.* □ *Jimmy tore into the turkey leg and cleaned it off in no time.*

tear loose (from someone or something**)** to manage to break away from someone or something. □ *The quarterback tore loose and took twenty yards for a first down.* □ *Barlowe tore loose from Bill and made for the door.*

tear off (from someone or something**)** to leave someone or something in a great hurry. □ *I hate to tear off from you guys, but I'm late for dinner.* □ *It's time for me to go. I have to tear off.*

tear one's **hair (out)** *Fig.* to be anxious, frustrated, or angry. □ *I was so nervous, I was about to tear my hair.* □ *I had better get home. My parents will be tearing their hair out.*

tear (oneself**) away (from** someone or something**)** *Fig.* to force oneself to leave someone or something. □ *Do you think you can tear yourself away from your friends for dinner?* □ *I could hardly tear myself away from the concert.*

tear out (of some place**)** to leave a place in a great hurry. □ *The kids tore out of the house after they broke the window.* □ *They saw what they had done and tore out.*

tear someone **apart**† **1.** *Lit.* to rip someone apart savagely. (See also **tear** something **apart**.) □ *Max threatened to tear Tom apart.* □ *The bear tore apart the hiker.* **2.** *Fig.* to cause two people, presumably lovers, to separate unwillingly. □ *The enormous disruption of the accident tore them apart and they separated.* □ *The bickering between their parents finally tore apart the engaged couple.* **3.** *Fig.* to cause someone enormous grief or emotional pain. □ *The death of her dog tore her apart.* □ *It was the dog's death that tore apart Barbara.* **4.** *Fig.* to criticize someone mercilessly. □ *The critic tore apart the entire cast of the play.* □ *Why do you have to tear yourself apart for making a little error?*

tear someone or some animal **limb from limb** to rip someone or an animal to bits. □ *The explosion tore the workers limb from limb.* □ *The crocodiles attacked the wading zebras and tore them limb from limb.*

tear someone or something **down**† to criticize or degrade someone or something. □ *Tom is always tearing Jane down. I guess he doesn't like her.* □ *It's not nice to tear down the people who work in your office.* □ *Why are you always tearing my projects down?*

tear someone or something **to pieces** and **tear** someone or something **to shreds** to rip or shred someone or something into bits. □ *Careful of that dog. It will tear you to pieces!* □ *The dog tore the newspaper to pieces.* □ *It tore my shoes to shreds.*

tear someone **up**† *Fig.* to cause someone much grief. (See also **tear** someone **apart**.) □ *The news of Tom's death really tore Bill up.* □ *Bad news tears up some people. Other people can take it calmly.*

tear something **apart**† **1.** to pull or rip something apart. (See also **tear** someone **apart**.) □ *The bear tore the tent apart.* □ *The lions tore apart the wildebeest in minutes, and began eating it.* **2.** to criticize something mercilessly. □ *The critic tore apart the entire cast of the play.* **3.** to divide something or the members of a group, citizens of a country, etc. □ *The financial crisis tore the club apart.* □ *The crisis tore apart the organization.*

tear something **away**† **(from** someone or something**) 1.** to peel something away from someone or something. □ *The paramedic tore the clothing away from the burn victim and began to treat the wounds immediately.* □ *She tore away the clothing from the victim.* □ *She tore the clothing away.* **2.** to quickly take something away from someone or something. □ *I tore the firecracker away from the child and threw it in the lake.* □ *Liz tore away the cover from the book.* □ *She tore the wrapping paper away.*

tear something **down**† to dismantle or destroy something. □ *They plan to tear the old building down and build a new one there.* □ *They'll tear down the building in about two weeks.*

tear something **from** something to rip or peel something from something. □ *He tore the wrapping from the gift.* □ *The monkey tore the peel from the banana and took a bite of it.*

tear something **off (of)** someone or something and **tear** something **off**† to peel or rip something off someone or something. (*Of* is usually retained before pronouns.) □ *Max tore the necklace off his victim and ran away with it.* □ *He tore off the necklace.*

tear something **on** something to rip something on something sharp or jagged. □ *I tore my pants on the corner of the desk.* □ *Mary tore her new skirt on something sharp on the side of the car.*

tear something **out of** something and **tear** something **out**† to remove something from something by ripping or tearing. □ *Tear the coupons out of the magazine and save them.* □ *Please tear out the coupons.*

tear something **up**† to rip someone or something to pieces. □ *The two drunks tore the bar up in their brawling.* □ *The dog tore up the newspaper.*

tease someone **about** someone or something to make fun of someone about someone or something; to poke fun at someone about someone or something. □ *The boys teased Don about his girlfriend.* □ *Stop teasing me about it!*

tease someone **into** doing something to force someone to do something through teasing or tormenting. □ *Sam teased her into doing what he wanted.* □ *Perhaps you can tease him into leaving, but he won't go if you ask him.*

tease something **out**† *Fig.* to separate threads or hairs by combing. □ *The hairdresser teased Jill's hair out carefully.* □ *The hairdresser teased out Jill's hair.*

tease something **out of** something and **tease** something **out**† to lure something out of something by teasing or tempting. □ *I managed to tease the cat out of the tree with a bit of fish.* □ *I teased out the cat.*

tee off 1. *Lit.* to start the first hole in a game of golf. □ *It's time to tee off. Let's get on the course.* □ *What time do we tee off?* **2.** *Fig.* to begin [doing anything]; to be the first one to start something. □ *The master of ceremonies teed off with a few jokes and then introduced the first act.* □ *Everyone is seated and ready to begin. Why don't you tee off?*

tee someone **off**† *Sl.* to make someone angry. (See also **teed off.**) □ *That really teed me off!* □ *Well, you sure managed to tee off everybody!*

teed off *Inf.* angry. □ *I'm not teed off! I'm enraged.* □ *I was so teed off I could have spit!*

teed (up) *Sl.* intoxicated. □ *She was totally teed up by midnight.* □ *Tom was too teed to drive.*

teem with someone or something to swarm with someone or something; to be abundant with someone or something. □ *The porch was teeming with flies, so we couldn't eat there.* □ *The beach teemed with people enjoying the sunny weather.*

teething troubles 1. *Lit.* pain and crying on the part of a baby whose teeth are growing in. □ *Billy has been whining because of teething troubles.* **2.** *Fig.* difficulties and problems experienced in the early stages of a project, activity, etc. □ *There have been a lot of teething troubles with the new computer system.* □ *We have finally gotten over the teething troubles connected with the new building complex.*

telegraph one's **punches 1.** *Fig.* to signal, unintentionally, what blows one is about to strike. (Boxing.) □ *Wilbur used to telegraph his punches until his trainer worked with him.* □ *Don't telegraph your punches, kid! You'll be flat on your back in twenty seconds.* **2.** *Fig.* to signal, unintentionally, one's intentions. □ *When you go in there to negotiate, don't telegraph your punches. Don't let them see that we're in need of this contract.* □ *The mediator telegraphed his punches, and we were prepared with a strong counterargument.*

telephone something **in**† **(to** someone**)** to call someone on the telephone, usually to give particular information. (The person called is in a special location, such as one's workplace or headquarters.) □ *I will telephone my report in to my secretary.* □ *I telephoned in my report.* □ *I will telephone it in tomorrow.*

telescope into something [for one cylindrical part of something] to fit down inside another part, thereby reducing the length of the whole. □ *This part telescopes into this part.* □ *The tent poles telescoped into a small, compact unit.*

tell all to tell everything, even the secrets. □ *Some reporter got hold of the actress's maid who offered to tell all for a fee.*

Tell it like it is. *Inf.* Speak frankly.; Tell the truth no matter who is criticized or how much it hurts. □ *Come on man, tell it like it is!* □ *Well, I've got to tell it like it is.*

Tell it to the marines! *Inf.* I do not believe you (maybe the marines will)! □ *Your excuse is preposterous. Tell it to the marines.* □ *I don't care how good you think your reason is. Tell it to the marines!*

tell its own story and **tell its own tale** *Fig.* [for the state of something] to indicate clearly what has happened. □ *The upturned boat told its own tale. The fisherman had drowned.* □ *The girl's tear-stained face told its own story.*

tell its own tale Go to previous.

Tell me another (one)! *Inf.* What you just told me was a lie, so go ahead and tell me another lie! (Indicates incredulity.) □ *Bill: Did you know that the football coach was once a dancer in a movie? Tom: Go on! Tell me another one!* □ *"Tell me another one!" laughed Bill at Tom's latest exaggeration.*

tell of someone or something to speak of someone or something. □ *The messenger told of great destruction, hunger, and disease in the northern part of the country.* □ *I want you to tell of Jane and how she is doing.*

tell on someone to report someone's bad behavior; to tattle on someone. □ *If you do that again, I'll tell on you!* □ *Please don't tell on me. I'm in enough trouble as it is.*

tell one one's **bearings** Go to one's **bearings.**

tell one **to** one's **face** to tell [something] to someone directly. □ *I'm sorry that Sally feels that way about me. I wish she had told me to my face.* □ *I won't tell Tom that you're mad at him. You should tell him to his face.*

tell people or things **apart**† to distinguish one from another. □ *I can't tell Bob and Bill apart.* □ *I find it easy to tell apart Bill and Bob.* □ *The two cakes look different, but in taste, I can't tell this one and that one apart.*

tell shit from Shinola Go to know shit from Shinola.

tell someone **a thing or two (about** someone or something**)** Go to a thing or two (about someone or something).

tell someone **about** someone or something to give information to someone about someone or something. □ *Please tell me about Wallace.* □ *You were going to tell me about the old neighborhood.*

tell someone **from** someone else and **tell** something **from** something else to distinguish one from another. □ *I can't tell Chuck from Roger. They look so much alike.* □ *I can't tell orange from yellow.*

tell someone **off**† to scold someone; to attack someone verbally. (This has a sense of finality about it.) □ *I was so mad at Bob that I told him off.* □ *By the end of the day, I had told off everyone else, too.*

tell someone **on** someone to tattle to someone about someone. □ *I'm going to tell your mother on you!* □ *I'll tell the teacher on you!*

tell someone or something **by** something to identify someone or something by something. □ *You can tell Jim by the old-fashioned shoes he wears.* □ *I can tell the new season's fashions by how short the skirts are.*

tell someone **what to do with** something to reject someone's idea by suggesting that someone do something rude with something. (With the unspoken notion that one should stick it up one's ass.) □ *I'll tell you what you can do*

T

with it. □ *If that's the way he wants to be, you can just tell him what to do with it.*

tell someone **where to get off** to scold someone; to express one's anger to someone; to **tell** someone **off.** □ *Wait till I see Sally. I'll tell her where to get off!* □ *She told me where to get off and then started in scolding Tom.*

tell something **from** something to know something because of something, such as evidence, signs, experience, etc. □ *I can tell that she's lying from the way she holds her eyebrows.* □ *I can't tell anything from what you told me.*

tell something **from** something else Go to **tell** someone **from** someone else.

tell something **to** someone to say something to someone. □ *Please tell the whole truth to me.* □ *Please tell your explanation to Mary.*

tell tales out of school to tell secrets or spread rumors. □ *I wish that John would keep quiet. He's telling tales out of school again.* □ *If you tell tales out of school a lot, people won't know when to believe you.*

tell the difference between someone **and** someone else **or** something **and** something else to recognize the things that distinguish people or things. □ *I can't tell the difference between Billy and Bobby.* □ *Sam can't tell the difference between Granny Smith and Royal Gala apples.*

Tell the truth and shame the devil. *Prov.* To tell the truth even though you have strong reasons for concealing it. □ *Jill: Have you been using my computer without asking permission? Jane: Uh . . . no. . . . Jill: Come on, Jane, tell the truth and shame the devil.*

tell the (whole) world *Fig.* to spread around someone's private business. □ *Well, you don't have to tell the whole world.* □ *Go ahead, tell the world!*

tell things **apart** to distinguish one thing or a group of things from another thing or group of things. □ *This one is gold, and the others are brass. Can you tell them apart?* □ *Without their labels, I can't tell them apart.*

tell time 1. *Lit.* to keep or report the correct time. □ *This clock doesn't tell time very accurately.* □ *My watch stopped telling time, so I had to have it repaired.* **2.** *Fig.* to be able to read time from a clock or watch. □ *Billy is only four. He can't tell time yet.* □ *They are teaching the children to tell time at school.*

tell which is which Go to **know which is which.**

temper something **with** something **1.** *Fig.* to harden something, such as metal, with something. □ *You have to temper the metal pieces with very high heat.* □ *The sheet of metal was tempered by the application of great pressure.* **2.** *Fig.* to soften the impact of something, such as news, with something. □ *We can temper this disaster story a bit with a picture of the happy survivors.* □ *The news story was tempered with a paragraph of explanation and justification.*

a **tempest in a teacup** and a **tempest in a teapot** an argument or disagreement over a very minor matter. □ *The entire issue of who was to present the report was just a tempest in a teapot.* □ *The argument at the office turned into a tempest in a teacup. No one really cared about the outcome.*

a **tempest in a teapot** Go to previous.

tempt someone **into** something to lure or seduce someone into something. □ *Could I tempt you into going swimming?* □ *She would not be tempted into eating the rich and fattening cake.*

tempt someone **to** do something to entice someone to do something. □ *You can't tempt me to eat any of that cake!* □ *I wasn't even tempted to go into town with the others.*

tempt someone **with** something to entice someone with something. □ *Can I tempt you with a bit of chocolate cake?* □ *I was tempted with a free book if I sent in my name, but I decided against it.*

tend to do something to have a tendency to do something. □ *Jill tends to play with her hair while she works.* □ *Sam tends to say things like that when he is upset.*

tend toward something to have a tendency to display a certain characteristic. □ *Roger tends toward the dramatic.* □ *We all tend toward bad humor during bad weather.*

the **tender age of...** the young age of... □ *She left home at the tender age of 17 and got married to a rock singer.*

tender something **for** something to offer something (of value) for something. □ *The shareholders were asked to tender one of their shares for two of the offering company's.* □ *I decided not to tender my shares.*

tender something **(to** someone**) (for** something**)** to offer or present something to someone for something. □ *Laura tendered payment to Gary for the tickets.* □ *Walter tendered the old shares to the company for new shares.*

tense up (for something**)** to become tense, anxious, and ready for something. □ *Liz tensed up for the game and was very nervous.* □ *He tensed up and that made it hard to give him the injection he needed.*

terrify someone **into** something and **terrorize** someone **into** something to threaten or frighten someone into doing something. □ *The salesman is just trying to terrify you into buying a new car by saying the one you have is dangerous.* □ *They tried to terrorize people into staying off the streets.*

terrify someone **or an animal out of** something **1.** to terrify someone or an animal to leave something or some place. □ *The attackers terrified the farmers out of their homes.* □ *The snake terrified the gophers out of their burrow.* **2.** to cause someone or an animal to lose something through fear. □ *They tried to terrify the old lady out of her money, but she refused to tell where it was.* □ *The eagle terrified the hawk out of the food it was holding.*

terrorize someone **into** something Go to **terrify** someone **into** something.

test for something to try to find out about something by testing. □ *We are testing for weak places in your roof. That's the noise you hear up there.* □ *They are testing for some sort of infection.*

test out (of something**)** to score high enough on a placement test that one does not need to take a particular course. □ *I tested out of calculus.* □ *I don't know enough Spanish to test out.*

test someone **in** something to test someone in a particular subject. □ *The committee decided to test her in her knowledge of the laws of the state.* □ *We were all tested in math and English.*

test someone or something **for** something to apply a test to someone or something to try to determine something or identify something. □ *They tested me for all sorts of diseases.* □ *Ken tested the roof for weak spots.*

test something **out**† to try something out; to test something to see if it works. □ *I can't wait to test my new laptop out.* □ *I will test out the new brakes on the car.*

testify against someone or something to be a witness against someone or something. □ *Who will testify against him in court?* □ *I cannot testify against the company I work for.*

testify for someone to present evidence in favor of someone; to testify on someone's behalf. □ *I agreed to testify for her at the trial.* □ *Max testified for Lefty, but they were both convicted.*

testify to something to swear to something. □ *I will testify to your whereabouts if you wish.* □ *I think I know what happened, but I would not testify to it.*

Thank God for small favors. *Rur.* Be thankful that something good has happened in a bad situation. □ *Charlie: We're out of gas, but I think I see a gas station up ahead. Tom: Thank God for small favors.* □ *He had a heart attack, but it was right there in the doctor's office, so they could take care of him right away. Thank God for small favors.*

Thank goodness! and **Thank heavens!** Oh, I am so thankful! □ *John: Well, we finally got here. Sorry we're so late. Mother: Thank goodness! We were all so worried.* □ *Jane: There was a fire on Maple Street, but no one was hurt. Bill: Thank heavens!*

Thank heavens! Go to previous.

thank one's **lucky stars** *Fig.* to be thankful for one's luck. □ *You can thank your lucky stars that I was there to help you.* □ *I thank my lucky stars that I studied the right things for the test.*

thank someone **for** something to show or state one's gratitude to someone for something. □ *We would all like to thank you for coming tonight.* □ *Thank you for inviting me.*

Thank you. I am grateful to you and offer you my thanks. □ *Bill: Here, have some more cake. Bob: Thank you.* □ *John: Your hair looks nice. Mary: Thank you.*

Thank you a lot. Go to Thanks (a lot).

Thank you for a lovely evening. an expression said by a departing guest to the host or hostess at the end of an evening. (Other adjectives, such as *nice*, can be used in place of *lovely*.) □ *Mary: Thank you for a lovely evening. John: Will I see you again?* □ *Bill: Thank you for a nice evening. Mary: Thank you so much for coming. Good night.*

Thank you for a lovely time. an expression said by a departing guest to the host or hostess. (Other adjectives, such as *nice*, can be used in place of *lovely*.) □ *Bill: Thank you for a nice time. Mary: Thank you so much for coming. Bye now.* □ *John: Thank you so much for coming. Jane: Well, thank you for a lovely time. John: Don't stay away so long next time.*

Thank you for calling. Thank you for calling on the telephone. (Said when the call is helpful or a bother to the caller.) □ *Mary: Good-bye. Sue: Good-bye, thanks for calling.* □ *John: Okay. Well, I have to get off the phone. I just* wanted you to know what was happening with your order. *Jane: Okay. Bye. Thanks for calling.*

Thank you for having me. Go to next.

Thank you for inviting me. and **Thank you for inviting us.; Thank you for having me.; Thank you for having us.** a polite expression said to a host or hostess on departure. □ *Mary: Good-bye, glad you could come. Bill: I had a great time. Thank you for inviting me.* □ *John: I had a good time. Thank you for inviting me. Sally: Come back again, John. It was good talking to you.*

Thank you for sharing. *Inf.* a sarcastic remark made when someone tells something that is unpleasant, overly personal, disgusting, or otherwise annoying. □ *Thank you for sharing. I really need to hear about your operation.* □ *Thank you for sharing, Bob. I hope your parents' divorce goes well.*

Thank you kindly. Thank you very much. □ *Tom: May I give you a lift? Jane: Why, yes. Thank you kindly.* □ *Mary: That's a nice suit, and you wear it well. Charlie: Thank you kindly, ma'am.*

Thank you so much. Go to next.

Thank you very much. and **Thank you so much.** a more polite and emphatic way of saying **Thank you.** □ *Tom: Welcome. Come in. Bob: Thank you very much.* □ *Bill: Here's the book I promised you. Sue: Thank you so much.*

*thankful for small blessings grateful for any small benefits or advantages one has, especially in a generally difficult situation. (*Typically: **be** ~; **become** ~.) □ *We have very little money, but we must be thankful for small blessings. At least we have enough food.* □ *Bob was badly injured in the accident, but at least he's still alive. Let's be thankful for small blessings.*

thanks a bunch *Inf.* thanks. □ *Thanks a bunch for your help.* □ *He said "thanks a bunch" and walked out.*

Thanks (a lot). and **Thank you a lot. 1.** *Inf.* Thank you, I am grateful. □ *Bill: Here, take mine. Bob: Thanks a lot.* □ *Mary: Well, here's your pizza. Bill: Thanks.* **2.** That is not worth much.; That is nothing to be grateful for. (Sarcasm is indicated by the tone of voice used with this expression.) □ *John: I'm afraid that you're going to have to work the night shift. Bob: Thanks a lot.* □ *Fred: Here's your share of the money. We had to take out nearly half to make up for the damage you did to the car. Bill: Thanks a lot.*

Thanks a million. *Inf.* Thank you a lot. □ *Bill: Oh, thanks a million. You were very helpful. Bob: Just glad I could help.* □ *John: Here's your book. Jane: Thanks a million. Sorry I needed it back in such a rush.*

Thanks awfully. Thank you very much. □ *John: Here's one for you. Jane: Thanks awfully.* □ *Mary: Here, let me help you with all that stuff. Sue: Thanks awfully.*

Thanks, but no thanks. *Inf.* Thank you, but I am not interested. (A way of turning down something that is not very desirable.) □ *Alice: How would you like to buy my old car? Jane: Thanks, but no thanks.* □ *John: What do you think about a trip over to see the Wilsons? Sally: Thanks, but no thanks. We don't get along.*

Thanks for the lift. Go to next.

Thanks for the ride. and **Thanks for the lift.** Thank you for giving me a ride in your car. □ *John (stopping the* *car): Here we are. Bob: Thanks for the ride. Bye. John: Later.* □ *As Fred got out of the car, he said, "Thanks for the lift."*

Thanks loads. *Inf.* Thanks a lot. □ *Mary: Here, you can have these. And take these too. Sally: Thanks loads.* □ *John: Wow! You look great! Sally: Thanks loads. I try.*

thanks to someone or something due to someone or something; because of someone or something. (This does not necessarily suggest gratitude.) □ *Thanks to the storm, we have no electricity.* □ *Thanks to Mary, we have tickets to the game. She bought them early before they were sold out.*

That ain't hay. *Inf.* That is not a small amount of money. (The highly informal word *ain't* is built into the expression.) □ *I paid forty dollars for it, and that ain't hay!* □ *Bob lost his wallet with $200 in it—and that ain't hay.*

That ain't no lie. *Rur.* What was said is true. (The highly informal word *ain't* is built into the expression.) □ *Tom: Sure is hot today. Jane: That ain't no lie.* □ *I'm plumb exhausted, and that ain't no lie.*

That ain't the way I heard it. *Rur.* That is not the way I heard the story told. (The highly informal word *ain't* is built into the expression.) □ *John: It seemed like a real riot, then Sally called the police and things calmed down. Sue: That ain't the way I heard it. John: What? Sue: Somebody said the neighbors called the police.* □ *Fred: Four of us went fishing and were staying in this cabin. These women stopped and said they were having car trouble. What could we do? Sally: That ain't the way I heard it.*

That (all) depends. My answer depends on factors that have yet to be discussed. □ *Tom: Will you be able to come to the meeting on Thursday night? Mary: That all depends.* □ *Bob: Can I see you again? Sally: That depends.*

That beats everything! Go to If that don't beat all!

that beats something **all to pieces** *Rur.* that is much better than the person or thing named. □ *Mary's layer cake beats mine all to pieces.* □ *I say the book beats the movie all to pieces.*

That brings me to the (main) point. a transitional expression that introduces the main point of a conversation. (See also which brings me to the (main) point.) □ *Father: It's true. All of us had to go through something like this when we were young, and that brings me to the point. Aren't you old enough to be living on your own and making your own decisions and supporting yourself? Tom: Well, yes, I guess so.* □ *Fred: Yes, things are very expensive these days, and that brings me to the main point. You simply have to cut back on spending. Bill: You're right. I'll do it!*

(That causes) no problem. That will not cause a problem for me or anyone else. (No problem is informal.) □ *Mary: Do you mind waiting for just a little while? Bob: No problem.* □ *Sue: Does this block your light? Can you still read? Jane: That causes no problem.*

That does it! 1. *Inf.* That completes it!; It is now done just right! □ *When Jane got the last piece put into the puzzle, she said, "That does it!"* □ *John (signing a paper): Well, that's the last one! That does it! Bill: I thought we'd never finish.* **2.** and **That tears it!** *Inf.* That's the last straw!; Enough is enough! □ *Bill: We're still not totally pleased with your work. Bob: That does it! I quit!* □ *Sally: That tears*

it! I never want to see you again! Fred: I only put my arm around you!

[that is] See the entries beginning with *that's.*

That makes two of us. *Inf.* The same is true for me. □ *So you're going to the football game? That makes two of us.* □ *Bill: I just passed my biology test. Bob: That makes two of us!*

That (really) burns me (up)! *Inf.* That makes me very angry! □ *Bob: Did you hear that interest rates are going back up? Mary: That really burns me up!* □ *Sue: Fred is telling everyone that you are the one who lost the party money. Mary: That burns me! It was John who had the money in the first place.*

That's a fine how-do-you-do. *Inf.* That is a terrible situation. □ *Well, that's a fine how-do-you-do! I tried to call Mary, and her number is disconnected!* □ *That's a fine how-do-you-do. I come home and find the kids are playing catch with my best crystal bowl.*

That's a new one on me! *Inf.* I had not heard that before. □ *Bob: Did you hear? They're building a new highway that will bypass the town. Fred: That's a new one on me! That's terrible!* □ *Sue: All of us will have to pay our taxes monthly from now on. Mary: That's a new one on me!*

That's about the size of it. *Inf.* That is the way it is. (Often a response to someone who has acknowledged bad news.) □ *Bob: We only have a few hundred dollars left in the bank. Sally: That means that there isn't enough money for us to go on vacation? Bob: That's about the size of it.* □ *Bob: I'm supposed to take this bill to the county clerk's office and pay them four hundred dollars? Sally: That's about the size of it.*

That's all for someone. *Inf.* Someone will get no more chances to do things correctly. □ *That's all for you, Tom. I've had all I can take from you. One disappointment after another.* □ *You've gone too far, Mary. That's all for you. Good-bye!*

That's all she wrote. and **That's what she wrote.** *Inf.* That is all of it.; That is the last of it. □ *Here's the last one we have to fix. There, that's all she wrote.* □ *That's what she wrote. There ain't no more.*

That's all someone **needs.** and **It's all** someone **needs.; (It's) just what you need.; That's just what you need.** Someone does not need that at all.; That's the last straw! (Always sarcastic. The *someone* can be a person's name or a pronoun.) □ *Jane: The dog died and the basement is just starting to flood. Fred: That's all we need.* □ *Sally: Bill, the check you wrote to the Internal Revenue Service was returned. There's no more money in the bank. Bill: That's all we need.* □ *Bob: On top of having too many bills to pay, now I have car trouble! Mary: That's just what you need!*

That's easy for you to say. You can say that easily because it really does not affect you the way it affects others. □ *Waiter: Here's your check. Mary: Thanks. (turning to others) I'm willing to just split the check evenly. Bob: That's easy for you to say. You had lobster!* □ *Sally: Let's each chip in ten bucks and buy him a sweater. Sue: That's easy for you to say. You make twice what I do.*

That's enough! *Inf.* No more!; Stop that! □ *Sue: Here, I'll stack another one on top. Mary: That's enough! It will fall.*

□ *John: I could go on with complaint after complaint. I could talk all week, in fact. Bob: That's enough!*

That's enough for now. No more of that for now.; Please stop for a while. □ *Mary: Here, have some more cake. Do you want a larger piece? Bill: Oh, no. That's enough for now.* □ *Bill: Shall I cut a little more off this tree, lady, or save the rest till spring? Jane: No, that's enough for now.*

(That's) enough (of this) foolishness! 1. Stop this foolish behavior. □ *Bill: Enough of this foolishness. Stop it! Sally: Sorry.* □ *Father: That's enough of this foolishness. You two stop fighting over nothing. Bob: Okay. Bill: Sorry.* **2.** I have had enough of this. (Does not refer to something that is actual foolishness.) □ *Andy: Enough of this foolishness. I hate ballet. I'm leaving. Sue: Well, please leave quietly.* □ *Sally: That's enough foolishness. I'm leaving and I never want to see you again! Bob: Come on! I was only teasing.*

(That's) fine with me. and **(That's) fine by me.; (That's) okay by me.; (That's) okay with me.** That is agreeable as far as I am concerned. (The expressions with *by* are colloquial.) □ *Sue: I'm giving away your old coat. Bob: That's fine with me.* □ *Sally: Can I take twenty dollars out of your wallet? Fred: That's okay by me—if you can find it, of course.*

That's for dang sure! *Rur.* That is quite certain! (The formulaic response to *That's for sure!*. The accent is always on the *dang*.) □ *Tom: That's for sure! Jane: That's for dang sure!* □ *Sally: We'll be there and that's for sure! Bill: Yup! That's for dang sure!*

That's funny. That is strange or peculiar. □ *Bill: Tom just called from Detroit and says he's coming back tomorrow. Mary: That's funny. He's not supposed to.* □ *Sue: The sky is turning very gray. Mary: That's funny. There's no bad weather forecast.*

That's it! 1. *Inf.* That does it!; That's the **last straw!** □ *That's it! I'm leaving! I've had enough!* □ *Okay. That's it! I'm going to report you to human resources!* **2.** That is the answer! □ *That's it! You are right.* □ *That's it! You got the right answer.*

That's (just) the way it goes. and **That's (just) how it goes.; That's (just) the way it is.** *Inf.* That is the normal way of things.; That is fate. □ *Mary: All my roses died in the cold weather. Sue: That's the way it goes.* □ *Sally: Someone stole all the candy we left out in the front office. Jane: That's just how it goes.*

That's (just) too much! 1. *Inf.* That is unpleasant and unacceptable!; That is more than I can bear! □ *"That's just too much!" exclaimed Sue, and she walked out.* □ *Bill: I'm afraid this movie isn't what we thought it was going to be. Sue: Did you see that? That's too much! Let's go!* **2.** *Inf.* That is just too funny. (Compare this with **You're too much.**) □ *After Fred finished the joke, and Bill had stopped howling with laughter, Bill said, "That's too much! Your jokes are so hilarious."* □ *When Tom stopped laughing, his sides ached and he had tears in his eyes. "Oh, that's too much!" he moaned.*

That's just what you need. Go to **That's all** someone needs.

That's more like it. That is better.; That is a better response this time. □ *Waiter: Here is your order, sir. Roast chicken as you requested. Sorry about the mix-up. John: That's more like it.* □ *Clerk: Now, here's one that you might like. Sally: Now, that's more like it!*

That's my boy. and **That's my girl.** That is my child of whom I am proud.; I'm proud of this young person. □ *After the game, Tom's dad said, "That's my boy!"* □ *That's my girl! Always a winner!*

That's my girl. Go to previous.

That's news to me. I did not know that.; I had not been informed of that. □ *Bill: They've blocked off Maple Street for some repairs. Tom: That's news to me.* □ *Sally: The telephones are out. None of them work. Bill: That's news to me.*

That's show business (for you). That is the way that life really is. (Also with *biz* and *show biz*.) □ *And now the car won't start. That's show business for you.* □ *Too bad about the bad investment. That's show biz.*

That's that! *Inf.* That is the end of that! Nothing more can be done. □ *Tom: Well, that's that! I can do no more. Sally: That's the way it goes.* □ *Doctor (finishing an operation): That's that! Would you close for me, Sue? Sue: Nice job, Doctor. Yes, I'll close.*

That's the pot calling the kettle black. Go to The pot is calling the kettle black.

That's the spirit! That is the right attitude and preferred evidence of high motivation. □ *A: I am sure I can do it! B: That's the spirit!*

That's the stuff! *Inf.* That is the right attitude or action. □ *Bob: I'm sure I can do it! Fred: That's the stuff!* □ *"That's the stuff!" cried the coach as Mary crossed the finish line.*

That's the ticket! *Inf.* That is what is required! □ *Mary: I'll just get ready and drive the package directly to the airport! Sue: That's the ticket. Take it right to the airport post office.* □ *Bob: I've got it! I'll buy a new computer! Bill: That's the ticket!*

That's the way the ball bounces. and **That's the way the cookie crumbles.; That's the way the mop flops.** *Prov.* You cannot control everything that happens to you.; You should accept the bad things that happen. □ *Bill: I bought a hundred lottery tickets this week, but I still didn't win! Alan: That's the way the ball bounces.* □ *I was planning to have fun on my vacation, but I've been sick the whole time. I guess that's just the way the cookie crumbles.* □ *That's tough, but that's the way the mop flops.*

That's the way the cookie crumbles. Go to previous.

That's the way the mop flops. Go to **That's the way** the ball bounces.

(That's the) way to go! *Inf.* a phrase encouraging someone to continue the good work. □ *As John ran over the finish line, everyone cried, "That's the way to go!"* □ *"Way to go!" said Mary when Bob finally got the car started.*

(That's) too bad. It is unfortunate.; **I'm sorry to hear** that. □ *Tom: I hurt my foot on our little hike. Fred: That's too bad. Can I get you something for it? Tom: No, I'll live.* □ *Bob: My uncle just passed away. Tom: That's too bad. I'm sorry to hear that. Bob: Thanks.*

That's what I say. *Inf.* I agree with what was just said. □ *Tom: We've got to get in there and stand up for our rights! Mary: That's what I say.* □ *Bob: They shouldn't do that! They should be put in jail! Mary: That's what I say!*

That's what she wrote. Go to That's all she wrote.

that's why! a tag on the end of a statement that is an answer to a question beginning with *why*. (Shows a little impatience.) □ *Sue: Why do you always put your right shoe on first? Bob: Because, when I get ready to put on my shoes, I always pick up the right one first, that's why!* □ *Mary: Why do you eat that awful peppermint candy? Tom: Because I like it, that's why!*

That sucks. and **It sucks.** *Sl.* That is worthless. □ *Yuck! That sucks!* □ *This meat loaf is terrible. It sucks.*

That takes care of that. *Inf.* That is settled. □ *That takes care of that, and I'm glad it's over.* □ *I spent all morning dealing with this matter, and that takes care of that.*

That takes the cake! 1. *Inf.* That is good, and it wins the prize! (Assuming that the prize is a cake.) □ *"What a performance!" cheered John. "That takes the cake!"* □ *Sue: Wow! That takes the cake! What a dive! Rachel: She sure can dive!* **2.** *Inf.* That is too much; That does it! □ *Bob: What a dumb thing to do, Fred! Erik: Yeah, Fred. That takes the cake!* □ *Bob: Wow! That takes the cake! Bill: What is it? Bob: That stupid driver in front of me just hit the car on the left and then swung over and hit the car on the right.*

That tears it! Go to That does it!

that there *Rur.* that. □ *Gimme that there can of nails.* □ *That there car is an old Pontiac.*

that very thing exactly that. □ *Why, I was just looking for that very thing!* □ *You know, I was just about to say that very thing.*

[that will] See the entries beginning with *that'll*.

That will do. That is enough.; Do no more. □ *That'll do, Billy. Stop your crying.* □ *"That will do," said Mr. Jones when he had heard enough of our arguing.*

That'll be the day! *Inf.* It will be an unusually amazing day when that happens! □ *Bill: I think I'll fix that lamp now. Andy: When you finally get around to fixing that lamp, that'll be the day!* □ *Sue: I'm going to get this place organized once and for all! Alice: That'll be the day!*

That'll teach someone! *Inf.* What happened to *someone* is a suitable punishment! (The *someone* is usually a pronoun.) □ *Bill: Tom, who has cheated on his taxes for years, finally got caught. Sue: That'll teach him.* □ *Bill: Gee, I got a ticket for speeding. Fred: That'll teach you!*

thaw out to warm up from being frozen. □ *How long will it take for the chicken to thaw out?* □ *I can't wait for the cake to thaw out. I want some now!*

thaw someone or something **out**† to raise the temperature of someone or something above freezing; to warm someone up. □ *We need to get inside so I can thaw my brother out. His toes are almost frozen.* □ *Did you thaw out the chicken?*

the American dream the idealistic notion that Americans are preoccupied with obtaining certain materialistic goals. □ *The American dream of home ownership, a car in the garage, and a chicken in every pot started in the early thirties.*

(the) be-all and (the) end-all *Cliché* something that is the very best or most important; something so good that it will end the search for something better. □ *Finishing the building of his boat became the be-all and end-all of Roger's existence.* □ *Sally is the be-all and the end-all of Don's life.*

(The) best of luck (to someone**).** I wish good luck to someone. □ *Alice: Good-bye, Bill. Bill: Goodbye, Alice. Best of luck. Alice: Thanks. Bye.* □ *"Good-bye, and the best of luck to you," shouted Mary, waving and crying at the same time.*

The butler did it. 1. *Lit.* The butler performed the crime. (A catchphrase.) □ *I know who killed Lord Drax. The butler did it! I saw him!* **2.** *Fig.* It happened just the way it always happens. □ *Of course, that's it. The butler did it. The butler always does it.*

the heavens opened *Fig.* It started to rain heavily. □ *The heavens opened, and we had to run for cover.* □ *We were waiting at the bus stop when the heavens opened.*

The hell you say! Nonsense!; I don't believe it! □ *A: I won the lottery! B: The hell you say!*

(the) Lord only knows no one but God knows. □ *The Lord only knows if John's marriage will be a happy one.* □ *How Mary can stay so cheerful through her terrible illness, the Lord only knows.*

the luck of the Irish luck associated with the Irish people. (Also said as a catch phrase for any kind of luck.) □ *Bill: How did you manage to do it, Jeff. Jeff: It's the luck of the Irish, I guess.*

The proof of the pudding is in the eating. *Prov.* You don't know the quality of something until you have tried it or experienced it. □ *Theory says that this material will produce a superior widget, but the proof of the pudding is in the eating.*

*the race card *Cliché* the issue of race magnified and injected into a situation which might otherwise be nonracial. (*Typically: **deal ~; play ~; use ~.**) □ *At the last minute, the opposition candidate played the race card and lost the election for himself.*

The very idea! I do not approve!; That is outrageous! □ *Resignation? The very idea!* □ *The very idea! Absolutely not!*

The wages of sin is death. *Prov.* Doing bad things can get you in a lot of trouble. □ *Serves him right. I always said, "The wages of sin is death."*

the way I see it Go to from my perspective.

The wolf is at the door. *Fig.* The threat of poverty is upon us. □ *I lost my job, my savings are gone, and now the wolf is at the door.*

Them as has, gits. *Rur.* Rich people can always get more. □ *The millionaire keeps making more and more money, because he has lots of money to invest. Them as has, gits.* □ *Tom: Bill already owns half the property in town, and here the court went and awarded him that vacant lot. Jane: You know how it is—them as has, gits.*

Them's fighting words! *Rur.* What you just said will lead to a fight. (Said as a threat.) □ *I heard what you said about my brother, and them's fighting words.* □ *Put up your dukes. Them's fighting words!*

then and there *Cliché* right at that time and place. □ *I asked him right then and there exactly what he meant.* □ *I decided to settle the matter then and there and not wait until Monday.*

T

then the fat hit the fire Go to the fat hit the fire.

theorize about someone or something to hypothesize about someone or something; to conjecture about someone or something. □ *Let's not waste time theorizing about Ted. He won't change.* □ *I can only theorize about what happened.*

theorize on something to make a theory about something. □ *There is no point in theorizing on something when you have all the empirical evidence you need to draw a conclusion.* □ *He spent the afternoon theorizing on the origin of the universe.*

There ain't no such thing as a free lunch. Go to There's no such thing as a free lunch.

(There ain't) nothin' to it. *Rur.* It is easy. □ *Mary: How do you keep your car so shiny? Tom: There ain't nothin' to it. I just wax it once a week.* □ *It took Jane just two minutes to sew up the hole in my shirt. "See?" she said. "Nothin' to it!"*

There are plenty of (other) fish in the sea. *Fig.* There are other choices. (Used to refer to persons.) □ *When John broke up with Ann, I told her not to worry. There are plenty of other fish in the sea.* □ *It's too bad that your secretary quit, but there are plenty of other fish in the sea.*

There are tricks in every trade. *Prov.* In every occupation, there are established ways of doing things. (See also the **tricks of the trade**.) □ *John thought that he wouldn't have to learn much in order to wait tables. But there are tricks in every trade, and the experienced waiters were able to teach him a lot.*

There are two sides to every question. and **There are two sides to every story.** *Prov.* There are valid reasons for holding opposing opinions. □ *Jim: I can't see why anyone would object to building a city park on the corner. John: There are two sides to every question. Maybe the people who own the buildings on the corner don't want them knocked down.* □ *Fred: Only an idiot would want to go hang gliding. It's too dangerous. Ellen: There are two sides to every question. Maybe some people think it's enjoyable enough to be worth the risk.*

There are two sides to every story. Go to previous.

There aren't enough hours in the day. There are too many things to do and not enough time. □ *I am behind in all my work. There aren't enough hours in the day!* □ *We can't handle all the problems that come our way. There aren't enough hours in the day.*

There but for the grace of God (go I). *Prov.* I would likely have experienced or done the same bad thing if God had not been watching over me. (You can say this to refer to someone who has had bad luck; implies that the person is no less virtuous than you are but is now miserable purely because of bad luck, which might happen to you as well.) □ *Jill: Ever since Julia's house burned down, she's been drinking heavily; she'll probably lose her job because of it. Jane: There but for the grace of God. . . .* □ *Whenever Sally saw a beggar, she thought, "There but for the grace of God go I."*

There is a fine line between something **and** something **else.** There is little difference between something and something else. □ *There is a fine line between a frown and a grimace.*

There is a remedy for everything except death. *Prov.* Everything but death can be cured.; As long as you are alive, your problems can somehow be solved. □ *Bill: I'll never recover from losing Nancy. Fred: Nonsense. There is a remedy for everything except death.* □ *Whenever Linda despaired, she sternly reminded herself that there is a remedy for everything except death.*

There is a tide in the affairs of men. *Prov.* If you have a favorable opportunity to do something, do it, or you will lose your chance. (From Shakespeare's play, *Julius Caesar.*) □ *I think that this is the best possible time to start our own business. We shouldn't hesitate. There is a tide in the affairs of men.*

There is a time and a place for everything. *Prov.* Different things are appropriate on different occasions. □ *There is a time and a place for everything, but this formal dinner is not the time or the place to eat with your fingers.*

There is honor among thieves. *Prov.* Criminals do not commit crimes against each other. □ *The gangster was loyal to his associates and did not tell their names to the police, demonstrating that there is honor among thieves.*

There is no accounting for taste(s). *Prov.* You cannot blame different people because they like different things, even if you do not understand why they like what they like. □ *Jill: I can't believe so many people are going to see that idiotic movie. Jane: There's no accounting for tastes.*

(There is) no chance. There is no chance that something will happen. (*No chance* is informal.) □ *Tom: Do you think that some little country like that will actually attack England? John: There's no chance.* □ *Bill: No chance you can lend me a few bucks, is there? Bill: Nope. No chance.*

there is no doing something one is not permitted to do something (as specified). □ *There is no arguing with Bill.* □ *There is no cigarette smoking here.*

(There is) no doubt about it. It cannot be doubted.; It is obvious. □ *Jane: It's really cold today. Fred: No doubt about it!* □ *Sue: Things seems to be getting more and more expensive. Tom: There's no doubt about that. Look at the price of oranges!*

There is no love lost (between someone **and** someone else**).** There is no friendship wasted between someone and someone else (because they are enemies). □ *Ever since their big argument, there has been no love lost between Tom and Bill.* □ *You can tell by the way that Jane is acting toward Ann that there is no love lost.*

(There is) no need (to). You do not have to.; It is not necessary. □ *Mary: Shall I try to save all this wrapping paper? Sue: No need. It's all torn.* □ *Bob: Would you like me to have it repaired? I'm so sorry I broke it. Bill: There is no need to. I can just glue it, thanks.*

There is no pleasure without pain. *Prov.* For every pleasure you enjoy, you must suffer some pain. □ *We had a fabulous vacation, but it's going to take us years to pay for it. Oh, well, there's no pleasure without pain.* □ *Yesterday I basked in the warm sunshine all afternoon; today I'm badly sunburned. There is no pleasure without pain.*

There is no rest for the weary. *Prov.* Even people who are worn-out must continue to work. (Describes a situation in which a tired person has to do more work.) □ *By the time I finished doing the laundry, it was so late I had to* *begin cooking supper for the family. There is no rest for the weary.*

There is no royal road to learning. *Prov.* Learning things requires work. □ *Sue: I don't see why we have to do homework every night. Why can't we just listen to the lectures? Nancy: There is no royal road to learning.*

There is nothing new under the sun. *Prov.* Everything that is happening now has happened before. (Biblical.) □ *Jill: The newspaper today is shocking. Three prominent politicians have been convicted of fraud. Jane: That's not shocking. It only proves that there's nothing new under the sun.*

There is safety in numbers. *Prov.* A group of people is less likely to be attacked than a single person. □ *Gail never went out after dark without at least three friends, since she knew that there is safety in numbers.* □ *We should gather together a group of people to make our complaint to the boss. There's safety in numbers.*

There is trouble brewing. Go to Trouble is brewing.

There's many a good tune played on an old fiddle. *Prov.* Old people can be very capable. □ *Just because Nigel is old doesn't mean he's useless. There's many a good tune played on an old fiddle.*

There's many a slip 'twixt the cup and the lip. *Prov.* Many things may happen to prevent you from carrying out what you intend to do. □ *Bob: Now that I have a contract with a publisher, nothing in the world can stop me from writing this book. Alan: Don't be so sure. There's many a slip 'twixt the cup and the lip.*

There's many a true word spoken in jest. Go to Many a true word is spoken in jest.

There's more than one way to skin a cat. *Prov.* You can always find more than one way to do something. □ *Jill: How will we fix the sink without a wrench? Jane: There's more than one way to skin a cat.* □ *Our first approach didn't work, but we'll figure out some other way. There's more than one way to skin a cat.*

There's no accounting for taste. *Prov. Cliché* There is no explanation for people's preferences. □ *Look at that purple and orange car! There's no accounting for taste.* □ *Some people seemed to like the music, although I thought it was worse than noise. There's no accounting for taste.*

There's no flies on someone. *Rur.* Someone is full of energy and drive. □ *There's no flies on Jane. She's up at five every morning, training for the big race.*

There's no fool like an old fool. *Prov. Cliché* Old people are supposed to be wise, so if an old person behaves foolishly, it is worse than a young person behaving foolishly. □ *As old Mrs. Fleischman watched her husband try to dance the way their grandchildren danced, she muttered, "There's no fool like an old fool."*

There's no place like home. *Prov. Cliché* Home is the most satisfying place to be. □ *After his long trip, Bob came into his house, sat down in his favorite chair, and happily sighed, "There's no place like home."* □ *Jane: Are you glad to be home from school? Jenny: There's no place like home.*

There's no rose without a thorn. *Prov.* To enjoy any beautiful or pleasant thing, you must endure something difficult or painful. □ *Mike: My bride is lovely and gra-cious, but I'm discovering that she has a terrible temper. Bill: There's no rose without a thorn.*

(There's) no smoke without fire. and **Where there's smoke there's fire.** *Prov.* There is usually some truth behind every rumor. □ *I'm going to withdraw all my money from that bank. I read an article that the bank was in financial trouble, and where there's smoke there's fire.*

There's no such thing as a free lunch. and **There ain't no such thing as a free lunch.** *Prov. Cliché* Everything costs something. (Can imply that you should be suspicious of anything that appears to be free.) □ *Fred: This advertisement says I can get an expensive camera for free! Jane: Don't be so gullible. There's no such thing as a free lunch.* □ *Mary gave me her sewing machine, but I had to give it $100 worth of repairs before I could even use it. There's no such thing as a free lunch.*

(There's) no time like the present. *Prov. Cliché* Do what you are supposed to do now. (You can use this to suggest that something be done right away.) □ *Jill: When should we start cleaning up the house? Jane: No time like the present.* □ *Start studying for the big exam now, instead of waiting till the night before. There's no time like the present.*

(There's) no way to tell. No one can find out the answer. □ *Tom: How long are we likely to have to wait before the plane takes off? Clerk: Sorry, sir. There's no way to tell.*

There's nobody home. There are no brains in someone's head. □ *There's lots of goodwill in that head, but there's nobody home.* □ *What a fool! There's nobody home—that's for sure.*

There's none so blind as those who will not see. *Prov.* You cannot make someone pay attention to something that he or she does not want to notice. (Used often to upbraid someone for being unwilling to notice what you are trying call attention to.) □ *Mother: This is the fifth time our daughter has been arrested for shoplifting. Don't you think we ought to seek some kind of help for her? Father: Our girl would never shoplift. I'm sure all those arrests were just some kind of mistake. Mother: There's none so blind as those who will not see.* □ *By October, it was obvious to everyone that Richard was coming in drunk every morning. Obvious, that is, except to his devoted secretary; there's none so blind as those who will not see.*

There's none so deaf as those who will not hear. *Prov.* If you tell someone something that he or she does not want to know, he or she will not pay attention to you. □ *I tried repeatedly to tell my supervisor about the low morale in our department, but there's none so deaf as those who will not hear.*

(There's) nothing to it! **1.** *Inf.* It is easy! □ *John: Is it hard to learn to fly a small plane? Sue: There's nothing to it!* □ *Bill: Me? I can't dive off a board that high! I can hardly dive off the side of the pool! Bob: Aw, come on! Nothing to it!* **2.** *Inf.* The rumor you heard is not true. □ *Pay no attention to all that talk. There's nothing to it.*

There, there. and **There, now.** an expression used to comfort someone. □ *There, there. You'll feel better after you take a nap.* □ *There, now. Everything will be all right.*

There will be hell to pay. and **There will be the devil to pay.** *Inf.* There will be a lot of trouble if something is done or if something is not done. (See also **have**

the devil to pay.) □ *Fred: If you break another window, Andy, there will be hell to pay. Andy: I didn't do it! I didn't.* □ *Bill: I'm afraid there's no time to do this one. I'm going to skip it. Bob: There will be hell to pay if you do.* □ *Bill broke a window, and now there will be the devil to pay.*

There will be the devil to pay. Go to previous.

There you are. That's the way things are.; This is the way things have worked out. (A fatalistic dismissal.) □ *"There's nothing more that can be done. We've done what we could. So there you are," said Fred, dejected.* □ *Andy: Then what happened? Bob: Then they put me in a cell until they found I was innocent. Somebody stole my watch in there. All because of mistaken identity. So there you are.*

There you go. 1. Hooray! You did it right! (Usually **There you go!**) □ *There you go! That's the way!* □ *Good shot, Chuck! There you go!* **2.** That is the way things are, just like I told you.; Isn't this just what you would expect? □ *There you go. Isn't that just like a man!* □ *There you go, acting rude and ugly!* **3.** You are doing it again. □ *There you go! You said it again.* □ *I just told you not to put that junk on the table, and there you go.* **4.** Here is what you wanted. (As might be said by a food server in a restaurant when placing your food in front of you.) □ *"There you go," said the waiter.* □ *Who ordered the fried shrimp? There you go.*

thereby hangs a tale there is an interesting story connected with this matter. □ *Yes, she comes in late most mornings, and thereby hangs a tale. She has a drinking problem.*

They also serve who only stand and wait. *Prov.* Sometimes you must be patient and do nothing, even though you would like to be actively helping. (From John Milton's poem, "On His Blindness.") □ *Jill: Can I help? Jane: No, we've got enough people helping. Jill: But I want to help. Jane: They also serve who only stand and wait.*

They don't make them like they used to. *Cliché* Goods are not as well made now as they were in the past. (Often used as a catchphrase. Them is often 'em.) □ *Look at this flimsy door! They don't make 'em like they used to.* □ *Why don't cars last longer? They just don't make 'em like they used to.*

They must have seen you coming. You were really cheated. They saw you coming and decided they could cheat you easily. □ *Andy: It cost two hundred dollars. Rachel: You paid two hundred dollars for that thing? Boy, they must have seen you coming.* □ *Bob: Do you think I paid too much for this car? It's not as good as I thought it was. Tom: It's almost a wreck. They must have seen you coming.*

They went that a'way. *Cliché* The villains went in that direction. (From Western movies.) □ *Those guys aren't here. They went that a'way.*

thick and fast in large numbers or amounts and at a rapid rate. □ *The enemy soldiers came thick and fast.* □ *New problems seem to come thick and fast.*

*thick as a short plank and ***thick as two short planks** exceptionally dim-witted. (*Also: **as ~.**) □ *Dumb? He's as thick as a short plank, more like.* □ *Oh, I'd not say she was stupid. As thick as two short planks, yes, but stupid? Never!*

*thick as pea soup [of fog] very thick. (*Also: **as ~.**) □ *This fog is as thick as pea soup. You can't see ten feet in front of you.*

*thick as thieves *Cliché* very close-knit; friendly; allied. (*Thick* = close and loyal. *Also: **as ~.**) □ *Mary, Tom, and Sally are as thick as thieves. They go everywhere together.* □ *Those two families are thick as thieves.*

thick as two short planks Go to **thick as a short plank**.

thicken something **up**[†] **1.** to make something, such as a fluid, thicker. □ *I have to thicken this gravy up before we can serve dinner.* □ *Please thicken up the gravy before you serve it.* **2.** to make something wider. □ *See this line here? You need to thicken it up so that it shows more clearly.* □ *Try to thicken up the line a little.*

*thick-skinned *Fig.* not easily upset or hurt; insensitive. (The opposite of **thin-skinned**. *Typically: **be ~; become ~; grow ~.**) □ *Tom won't worry about your insults. He's completely thick-skinned.* □ *Jane's so thick-skinned she didn't realize Fred was being rude to her.*

thin down to become thinner or slimmer. □ *He stopped eating desserts and fatty foods so he could thin down.* □ *I have to thin down so I can get into my winter coat.*

thin on top *Fig.* balding. □ *James is wearing a hat because he's getting thin on top.* □ *Father got a little thin on top as he got older.*

thin out to spread out; to become less dense. □ *The trees began to thin out as we got higher up the mountain.* □ *The crowd began to thin out as we got a little farther from the theater.*

thin someone **down**[†] to make someone thinner or slimmer. □ *What you need to thin you down is less, not more.* □ *The hospital dietitian tried to thin down the obese man.*

thin something **down**[†] to dilute a fluid. □ *You should thin this down with a little water.* □ *Try to thin down this paint a little.*

thin something **out**[†] to make something less dense; to scatter something. □ *You will have to thin the young plants out, because there is not room for all of them.* □ *Can you thin out these young plants?*

A **thing of beauty is a joy forever.** *Prov.* Beautiful things give pleasure that lasts even longer than the beautiful things themselves. (This is a line from John Keats's poem "Endymion." Also **a thing of beauty and a joy forever,** used to describe something beautiful in lofty terms, often ironically.) □ *Jill: I don't understand why someone would pay millions of dollars to have some old painting. Jane: Because a thing of beauty is a joy forever.*

*a thing or two (about someone or something**) 1.** bits of information or criticism about someone or something; a few facts about someone or something. (*Typically: **find out ~; know ~; learn ~; tell** someone **~.**) □ *I told Bob a thing or two about cars.* □ *I know a thing or two about Mary that would really shock you.* **2.** a few points of criticism about someone or something. (*Typically: **tell** someone **~.**) □ *I told her a thing or two about her precious little boy!* □ *Let me tell you a thing or two about your messy yard!*

A thing you don't want is dear at any price. *Prov.* You should not buy something just because it is cheap. □ *Jill: There's a sale on black-and-white film; we should get some. Jane: We never use black-and-white film. Jill: But it's so cheap. Jane: A thing you don't want is dear at any price.*

Things are looking up. Conditions are looking better. □ *Since I got a salary increase, things are looking up.* □ *Things are looking up at school. I'm doing better in all my classes.*

Things are seldom what they seem. *Prov.* Things often appear different from what they really are. □ *Emily seems to be a fine young lady, but be careful. Things are seldom what they seem.* □ *To judge from his elegant clothing and luxurious car, William was a wealthy man. But things are seldom what they seem; in fact, he was in desperate need of money.*

(Things) could be better. and **(I) could be better.; (Things) might be better.** a response to a greeting meaning "My state is not as good as it might be." (Not necessarily a direct answer.) □ *John: How are things going, Fred? Fred: Things could be better. And you? John: About the same.* □ *Bob: Hi, Bill! How are you? Bill: I could be better. What's new with you? Bob: Nothing much.*

(Things) could be worse. and **(I) could be worse.** a response to a greeting meaning "My state is not as bad as it might be." (Not necessarily a direct answer.) □ *John: How are you, Fred? Fred: Things could be worse. And you? John: Okay, I guess.* □ *Bob: Hi, Bob! What's happening? Bob: I could be worse. What's new with you?*

(Things) couldn't be better. Go to (It) couldn't be better.

Things haven't been easy. Go to (It) hasn't been easy.

(Things) might be better. Go to (Things) could be better.

Things will work out (all right). and **Everything will work out (all right).; Everything will work out for the best.; Things will work out for the best.** The situation will reach a satisfactory conclusion.; The problem(s) will be resolved. □ *"Cheer up!" Mary said to a gloomy Fred. "Things will work out all right."* □ *Mary: Oh, I'm so miserable! Bill: Don't worry. Everything will work out for the best.* □ *"Now, now, don't cry. Things will work out," consoled Sally, hoping that what she was saying was really true.*

think a great deal of someone or something Go to next.

think a lot of someone or something and **think a great deal of** someone or something; **think highly of** someone or something; **think much of** someone or something to think well of someone or something. □ *The teacher thinks a lot of Mary and her talents.* □ *No one really thinks a great deal of the new policies.* □ *I think highly of John.* □ *The manager doesn't think much of John and says so to everyone.*

think about someone or something to contemplate someone or something. □ *Whenever I think about him, I get goose bumps.* □ *I don't want to think about it.*

think ahead of one's **time** Go to ahead of one's time.

think ahead (to something**)** to have thoughts about something that is to happen in the future. □ *I began to think ahead to next year when the same thing might happen.* □ *You must learn to think ahead if you want to get ahead.*

think back (on someone or something**)** to remember and think about someone or something. □ *When I think back on Sally and the good times we had together, I get very sad.* □ *I like to think back on my childhood and try to remember what it was like.*

think back (to something**)** to remember back to something in the past. □ *Now, try and think back to the night of January 16.* □ *I can't think back. My mind is preoccupied with other things.*

think before doing something to consider the consequences before doing something. □ *You really ought to think before you take on a job like that.* □ *I finally learned to think carefully before accepting jobs like the one I just took on.*

think better of someone or something to raise one's opinion of someone or something. □ *I think better of him since I saw how well he does in the sales meetings.* □ *I hope that you will think better of the plan now.*

think better of something to reconsider doing something and end up not doing it. □ *I hope that you will think better of what you are doing and how many people you are hurting.* □ *I will think better of making such a careless remark next time.*

think for oneself to do one's own thinking; to think independently. □ *I think for myself. I don't need anyone to tell me what to do, do I?* □ *Sam has to learn to think for himself. He can't let other people make his decisions for him all his life.*

think highly of someone or something Go to think a lot of someone or something.

think inside the box *Fig.* to think in traditional fashion, bound by old, nonfunctional, or limiting structures, rules, or practices. (As if thinking or creativity were confined or limited by a figurative box. Compare this with think outside the box.) □ *You won't come up with good ideas if you think only inside the box.* □ *You guys only think inside the box and will never find a better solution.*

think little of someone or something and **think nothing of** someone or something to have a low opinion of someone or something. □ *Most experts think little of Jane's theory.* □ *People may think nothing of it now, but in a few years everyone will praise it.* □ *The critics thought little of her latest book.*

think much of someone or something Go to think a lot of someone or something.

think nothing of doing something to give no thought or hesitation to doing something. □ *She thinks nothing of helping other people at any time of day or night.* □ *Toby thinks nothing of driving one block to the store.*

Think nothing of it. and **Don't give it another thought.; Don't give it a (second) thought. 1.** You're welcome.; It was nothing.; I was glad to do it. □ *Mary: Thank you so much for driving me home. John: Think nothing of it.* □ *Sue: It was very kind of you to bring the kids back all the way out here. Alice: Think nothing of it. I was delighted to do it.* **2.** You did no harm at all. (A very polite way of reassuring someone that an action has not harmed or hurt the speaker.) □ *Sue: Oh, sorry. I didn't mean to bump you! Bob: Think nothing of it.* □ *Jane: I hope I didn't hurt your feelings when I said you were too loud. Bill: Don't give it a second thought. I was too loud.*

think nothing of someone or something Go to **think little of** someone or something.

think of someone or something to contemplate someone or something. □ *I think of you whenever I go to the restaurant where we used to eat.* □ *Whenever I see a rainbow, I think of Susan.*

think on one's **feet** *Fig.* to be able to speak and reason well while (standing and talking) in front of an audience, especially extemporaneously. □ *She really thinks on her feet well.* □ *I am not able to think on my feet too well before a bunch of people.*

think out loud *Fig.* to say one's thoughts aloud. □ *Excuse me. I didn't really mean to say that. I was just thinking out loud.* □ *Mr. Johnson didn't prepare a speech. He just stood there and thought out loud. It was a terrible presentation.*

think outside the box *Fig.* to think freely, not bound by old, nonfunctional, or limiting structures, rules, or practices. (As if thinking or creativity were confined in or limited by a figurative box. Compare this with **think inside the box**.) □ *You won't come up with good ideas until you think outside the box.* □ *Let's think outside the box for a minute and try to find a better solution.*

think someone **fit for** something to judge someone to be in condition or healthy enough for something. □ *Do you think me fit for the race?* □ *She is not fit for the game Friday night.*

think someone **hung the moon (and stars)** and **think** someone **is God's own cousin** *Rur.* to think someone is perfect. □ *Joe won't listen to any complaints about Mary. He thinks she hung the moon and stars.* □ *Jim is awful stuck-up. He thinks he's God's own cousin.*

think someone **is God's own cousin** Go to previous.

think someone or something **fit for** someone or something to judge someone or something to be suitable for someone or something. □ *I do not think this book fit for young readers.* □ *You are not fit for the office of mayor!* □ *This plate is not fit for further use.* □ *I don't think John fit for the job.*

think something **of** someone or something to hold a particular kind of opinion of someone or something; to hold someone or something in a particular kind of regard. (Such as ill, good, highly, bad, much, a lot, a great deal.) □ *Please don't think ill of me. It was a silly mistake. That's all.* □ *We think quite highly of your plan.*

think something **out**† to think through something; to prepare a plan or scheme. □ *This is an interesting problem. I'll have to take some time and think it out.* □ *We spent all morning thinking out our plan.*

think something **over**† to think about something and whether one will choose to do it. □ *I need a few minutes to think it over.* □ *Let me think over your request for a day or so.*

think something **through**† to run over and try to settle something in one's mind. □ *Let me think this through and call you in the morning.* □ *I will think through this matter and get back to you.*

think something **up**† to contrive or invent something. □ *Don't worry. I'll find a way to do it. I can think something up in time to get it done.* □ *John thought up a way to solve our problem.*

think straight to think clearly. (Often negative.) □ *I'm so tired I can't think straight.*

think the sun rises and sets on someone *Fig.* to think someone is the most important person in the world. □ *Her daddy just thinks the sun rises and sets on her.* □ *She worships that boyfriend of hers. She thinks the sun rises and sets on him.*

think the world of someone or something *Fig.* to be very fond of someone or something. □ *Mary thinks the world of her little sister.* □ *The old lady thinks the world of her cats.*

think to do something to remember to do something. □ *Sorry. I didn't think to call you in time.* □ *I will try to think to bring everything with me next time.*

think twice about someone or something to give careful consideration to someone or something. □ *Ed may be a good choice, but I suggest that you think twice about him.* □ *You will want to think twice about it.*

think twice (before doing something**)** to consider carefully whether one should do something; to be cautious about doing something. □ *You should think twice before quitting your job.* □ *That's a serious decision, and you should certainly think twice.*

think under fire Go to **under fire**.

think (up)on someone or something to contemplate someone or something; to muse or reflect on someone or something. (*Upon* is formal and less commonly used than *on*.) □ *I thought upon Abraham Lincoln and how much we all owe him.* □ *I thought on all the fine things we used to do.*

think worlds apart Go to **worlds apart**.

*****thin-skinned** *Fig.* easily upset or hurt; sensitive. (The opposite of **thick-skinned**. *Typically: **be** ~; **become** ~; **grow** ~.) □ *You'll have to handle Mary's mother carefully. She's very thin-skinned.* □ *Jane weeps easily when people tease her. She's too thin-skinned.*

*****the **third degree** *Fig.* a long and detailed period of questioning. (*Typically: **get** ~; **give** someone ~.) □ *Why is it I get the third degree from you every time I come home late?* □ *Poor Sally spent all night at the police station getting the third degree.*

The **third time's the charm.** *Prov.* The third time you try to do something, it will work. □ *Jill: I've called Miriam twice, but she doesn't answer her phone. Jane: Try again. The third time's the charm.*

thirst for something **1.** *Lit.* to desire something to drink. (Somewhat formal.) □ *"I thirst for something cooling and refreshing." said the preacher.* □ *You could see that everyone there was thirsting for water, or even coffee, but there was no refreshment in sight.* **2.** *Fig.* to have a strong desire for something. (See also **have a thirst for something**.) □ *In the old days, students were said to thirst for knowledge.* □ *The generals thirsted for new battles to be fought.*

thirsty for something **1.** *Lit.* needing to drink something. □ *I'm thirsty for a glass of cold water.* **2.** *Fig.* craving or desiring something. □ *The students were thirsty for knowledge.* □ *That evil tyrant is thirsty for power.*

this a-way and that a-way *Rur.* first one way and then the other. □ *She was craning her neck this a-way and that a-way, looking for him.* □ *The dogs were running this a-way and that a-way.*

This doesn't quite suit me. and **It doesn't quite suit me.** This is not quite what I want.; This does not please me. (Compare this with (It) suits me (fine).) □ *Clerk: How do you like this one? Mary: It doesn't quite suit me.* □ *Bob: This doesn't quite suit me. Let me see something a little darker. Clerk: How's this? Bob: Better.*

this here *Rur.* this. □ *Just let me fix this here chair leg.* □ *This here picture was painted by my Aunt Lena.*

This is it. This is the time, place, or thing that we have been looking or waiting for. □ *This is it. This is the chance you've been waiting for!* □ *This is it. This is my stop. I have to get off the bus.*

This is my floor. a phrase said by someone at the back of an elevator suggesting that people make way for that person to exit at a particular floor. □ *Mary said, "This is my floor," and everyone made room for her to get out of the elevator.* □ *"Out, please," said Tom loudly. "This is my floor!"*

This is where I came in. *Fig.* I have heard all this before. (Said when a situation begins to seem repetitive, as when a film one has seen part of before reaches familiar scenes.) □ *John sat through a few minutes of the argument, and when Tom and Alice kept saying the same thing over and over John said, "This is where I came in," and left the room.* □ *The speaker stood up and asked again for a new vote on the proposal. "This is where I came in," muttered Jane as she headed for the door.*

This one is on someone the cost of this drink or meal will be paid by the person named or designated. □ *A: Should we ask for separate checks or what? B: No, no, this one's on the boss!* □ *As the waiter set down the glasses, Fred said, "This one's on me."*

(this) vale of tears *Fig.* the earth; mortal life on earth. (A *vale* is a literary word for *valley*.) □ *When it comes time for me to leave this vale of tears, I hope I can leave some worthwhile memories behind.* □ *Uncle Fred left this vale of tears early this morning.*

thither and yon there and everywhere. (Stilted or jocular.) □ *I sent my résumé thither and yon, but no one responded.* □ *The children are all scattered thither and yon, and it is difficult for them to get home for the holidays.*

*a **thorn in** someone's **flesh** Go to next.

*a **thorn in** someone's **side** and *a **thorn in** someone's **flesh** *Fig.* a constant bother or annoyance to someone. (*Typically: **be** ~; **become** ~.*) □ *This problem is a thorn in my side. I wish I had a solution for it.* □ *John was a thorn in my flesh for years before I finally got rid of him.*

Those were the days. *Cliché* The days we have been referring to were the greatest of times. □ *Ah, yes. The eighties. Those were the days!* □ *Those were the days. Back when people knew right from wrong.*

Those who can, do; those who can't, teach. *Prov.* People who are able to do something well can do that thing for a living, while people who are not able to do anything that well make a living by teaching. (Used to disparage teachers. From George Bernard Shaw's *Man and Superman*.) □ *Bob: I'm so discouraged. My writing teacher told me my novel is hopeless. Jane: Don't listen to her, Bob. Remember: those who can, do; those who can't, teach.*

thoughts to live by Go to words to live by.

thrash around to move about restlessly or violently. □ *Settle down and stop thrashing around.* □ *Timmy thrashed around all night when he had the high fever.*

thrash something **out**† *Fig.* to discuss something thoroughly and solve any problems. □ *The committee took hours to thrash the whole matter out.* □ *John and Anne thrashed out the reasons for their constant disagreements.*

thrash something **out of** someone *Lit.* to beat something out of someone. □ *The sheriff really wanted to thrash the truth out of Tex, but that is illegal.* □ *Max wanted to know where the money was hidden and he tried to thrash it out of Lefty.*

thread one's **way through** something *Fig.* to make a path for oneself through a crowded area; to make one's way carefully through a crowded area. □ *The spy threaded his way through the crowd.* □ *The bicyclists threaded their way through the cars stopped in traffic.*

thread through something *Fig.* to travel through a crowded area; to move carefully through an area where there are many obstacles. □ *The spy threaded through the crowd at the palace.* □ *The joggers threaded through the shoppers on the sidewalks.*

threaten someone **with** someone or something to warn someone that there will be punishment in the form of someone or something if conditions are not met. □ *No, no! Your Uncle Herman is not coming here! Please don't threaten me with Uncle Herman!* □ *Are you threatening me with bodily harm?*

three bricks shy of a load stupid; dense; shortchanged on intelligence. □ *I would never say she was dense. Just three bricks shy of a load.* □ *Why do you act like you're three bricks shy of a load?*

three sheets in the wind and **three sheets (to the wind); two sheets to the wind** *Inf.* intoxicated and unsteady. (Sheets are the ropes used to manage a ship's sails. It is assumed that if these ropes were blowing in the wind, the ship would be out of control.) □ *He had gotten three sheets to the wind and didn't pay attention to my warning.* □ *By midnight, he was three sheets.*

three squares (a day) three nourishing meals a day. (With breakfast, lunch, and dinner considered the usual three meals.) □ *I was glad to get back home to three squares.* □ *If I could limit myself to three squares, I could lose some weight.*

Three strikes and you are out. *Fig.* Three chances and you are finished. (From baseball.) □ *One more arrest for speeding and you lose your license. You know, three strikes and you're out.*

thrill at someone or something to become excited by someone or something. □ *The opera was mystically intoxicating, and the audience thrilled at the tenor lead.* □ *We thrilled at the agility of the dancers.*

thrill someone **to pieces** and **thrill** someone **to death; thrill** someone **to bits** *Fig.* to please or excite someone very much. □ *John sent flowers to Ann and thrilled her to pieces.* □ *Your wonderful comments thrilled me to death.*

thrill someone **with** something to create or use something to cause someone much joy. □ *The famous singer thrilled us with a lovely song.* □ *Sally was thrilled with the praise heaped upon her daughter.*

thrill to something to become excited by something; to experience great joy while experiencing something. □ *I always thrill to the sound of a marching band.* □ *The crowd thrilled to the sight of the winning team parading down Main Street.*

thrilled to death and **thrilled to pieces** *Fig.* very excited; to be very pleased. □ *She was thrilled to death to get the flowers.* □ *I'm just thrilled to pieces to have you visit me.*

thrilled to pieces Go to previous.

thrive (up)on something to grow vigorously because of something. (*Upon* is formal and less commonly used than *on*.) □ *These plants thrive upon wet soil.* □ *Children thrive on love.*

throng around someone or something to crowd around someone or something. □ *The children thronged around the lady with the bags of candy.* □ *Everyone thronged around the piano for the group sing.*

throng in(to something**)** [for a crowd] to swarm into some place. □ *The eager crowd thronged into the department store to partake in the advertised sale.* □ *The doors opened and they thronged in.*

throng out (of something**)** [for a crowd] to swarm out of something or some place. □ *The people thronged out of the concert hall at the end of the program.* □ *At half past ten, the crowd thronged out.*

throttle something **down**[†] to reduce the speed of an engine by adjusting the throttle. □ *She throttled her engine down and came to a stop.* □ *She throttled down her engine.*

through and through thoroughly; completely. □ *I've studied this report through and through trying to find the facts you've mentioned.* □ *I was angry through and through, and I had to sit and recover before I could talk to anyone.*

through hell and high water *Fig.* through all sorts of severe difficulties. (Use *hell* with caution.) □ *I came through hell and high water to get to this meeting on time. Why don't you start on time?* □ *You'll have to go through hell and high water to accomplish your goal, but it'll be worth it.*

*through the cracks *Fig.* [moving] past the elements that are intended to catch or detect such things. (*Typically: **fall** ~; **drop** ~; **go** ~; **slip** ~.*) □ *I am afraid that some of these issues will slip through the cracks unless we make a note about each one.*

*through the mill *Fig.* badly treated; abused and exhausted. (Fig. on a grain mill. *Typically: **be** ~; **go** ~; **put** someone ~; **send** someone ~.*) □ *This has been a rough day. I've really been through the mill.* □ *This old car is banged up, and it hardly runs. We really put it through the mill.*

through thick and thin *Cliché* through good times and bad times. □ *We've been together through thick and thin, and we won't desert each other now.* □ *Over the years, we went through thick and thin and enjoyed every minute of it.*

*through with someone or something finished with someone or something. (*Typically: **be** ~; **get** ~.*) □ *I'm all through with course requirements. Now I can learn something I really enjoy.* □ *Lily is through with Max.*

throw a fight *Fig.* to lose a boxing match on purpose. (Boxing. Other words can replace *a*.) □ *I just know that Wilbur didn't throw that fight.* □ *The guy would never throw a fight.*

throw a fit Go to **have a fit.**

throw a game *Fig.* to lose a game on purpose. □ *I know Wilbur. He could never throw a game.* □ *There's a couple of those guys who would throw a game if they got enough money to do it.*

throw a glance at someone or something to take a quick peek at someone or something. □ *Liz threw a glance at her brother to see what he was going to do.* □ *I threw a glance at my watch and got ready to go.*

throw a monkey wrench in the works *Fig.* to cause problems for someone's plans. □ *I don't want to throw a monkey wrench in the works, but have you checked your plans with a lawyer?* □ *When John suddenly refused to help us, he really threw a monkey wrench in the works.*

throw a party (for someone**)** *Fig.* to have a party; to hold a party; to arrange a party. □ *Bill threw a party for his sister before she went away to college.* □ *Things seem sort of dull. Let's throw a party.*

throw a punch to jab; to punch. □ *She tried to throw a punch at me, but I blocked it.* □ *Wilbur threw a punch at the thug.*

throw a tantrum to have a temper tantrum; to put on an active display of childish temper. □ *I never dreamed that Bob would throw a tantrum right there in the department store. You must be so embarrassed!*

throw an amount of **light on** someone or something to present some revealing information about someone or something. □ *What you have just told me throws a lot of light on George and his motivation.* □ *Will you please throw some light on the problem?*

throw caution to the wind *Cliché* to become very careless. □ *Jane, who is usually cautious, threw caution to the wind and went swimming in the ocean.* □ *I don't mind taking a little chance now and then, but I'm not the type of person who throws caution to the wind.*

throw cold water on something Go to **pour cold water on** something.

Throw dirt enough, and some will stick. *Prov.* If you persistently say bad things about someone, people will begin to believe your accusations, even if they are not true. (Sometimes *mud* is used instead of *dirt*.) □ *One of the candidates in the election kept accusing the other one of having cheated on his income tax, and eventually the voters believed it. As they say, throw dirt enough, and some will stick.*

throw down the gauntlet *Fig.* to challenge someone to an argument or to (figurative) combat. □ *When Bob chal-*

lenged my conclusions, he threw down the gauntlet. I was ready for an argument. □ Frowning at Bob is the same as throwing down the gauntlet. He loves to get into a fight about something.

throw good money after bad *Fig.* to waste additional money after wasting money once. □ *I bought a used car and then had to spend $300 on repairs. That was throwing good money after bad.* □ *The Browns are always throwing good money after bad. They bought an acre of land that turned out to be swamp, and then had to pay to have it filled in.*

throw in the sponge Go to next.

throw in the towel and **throw in the sponge; toss in the sponge** *Fig.* (From boxing, where this is done by a boxer's trainer to stop the fight.) to signal that one is going to quit; to quit. □ *When John could stand no more of Mary's bad temper, he threw in the towel and left.* □ *Don't give up now! It's too soon to throw in the sponge.*

throw in with someone to join with someone; to join someone's enterprise. □ *I will throw in with you and we can all go hunting together.* □ *Do you mind if I throw in with you?*

throw insults (at someone**)** Go to hurl insults (at someone).

throw money at something *Fig.* to try to solve a problem by indiscriminately spending money on it. □ *This agency has thrown money at the housing problem, but it has been nothing but a long-term disaster.* □ *Don't just throw money at it.*

throw one off one's **game** Go to off one's game.

throw one out on one's **ear** *Fig.* to remove someone from a place forcibly. □ *Straighten up, or I'll throw you out on your ear.* □ *The caretaker caught us and threw us out on our ear.*

throw one's **hands up**[†] **(in despair) 1.** *Lit.* to make a gesture of throwing up one's hands indicating futility, despair, finality, etc. □ *He threw his hands up in despair and walked away.* □ *She threw up her hands and fled.* **2.** *Fig.* to give up in despair. □ *John threw his hands up in despair because they wouldn't let him see his brother in the hospital.* □ *Don't give up! Don't just throw up your hands!*

throw one's **hands up**[†] **in horror** *Fig.* to be shocked and horrified. □ *When Bill heard the bad news, he threw his hands up in horror.* □ *I could do no more. I had seen more than I could stand. I just threw up my hands in horror and screamed.*

throw one's **hat in the ring** Go to toss one's hat into the ring.

throw one's **voice** to project one's voice so that it seems to be coming from some other place. □ *The ventriloquist threw his voice.* □ *Jane can throw her voice, so I thought she was standing behind me.*

throw one's **weight around** *Fig.* to attempt to boss people around; to give orders. □ *The district manager came to our office and tried to throw his weight around, but no one paid any attention to him.* □ *Don't try to throw your weight around in this office. We know who our boss is.*

throw oneself **at** someone and **fling** oneself **at** someone *Fig.* to give oneself willingly to someone else for romance. □

I guess that Mary really likes John. She practically threw herself at him when he came into the room. □ *Everyone could see by the way Tom flung himself at Jane that he was going to ask her for a date.*

throw oneself **at** someone's **feet 1.** *Lit.* to bow down humbly at someone's feet; to prostrate oneself before someone. □ *In his guilt and horror, he threw himself at the feet of his master and begged forgiveness.* **2.** *Fig.* to beg someone's mercy, forgiveness, blessing, etc. □ *I throw myself at your feet and beg for your blessing.* □ *I love you sincerely, Jane. I throw myself at your feet and await your command. I'm your slave!*

throw oneself **at the mercy of** some authority and **throw** oneself **on the mercy of** some authority; **throw** oneself **(up)on** someone's **mercy** *Fig.* to seek mercy from a court of law, especially at one's sentencing for a crime; to seek help from an official or institution. □ *He pleaded guilty and threw himself at the mercy of the court.* □ *It did no good to throw myself on the mercy of the State Department.* □ *Please don't! I throw myself upon your mercy!*

throw oneself **into** something **1.** *Lit.* to jump into something, such as a body of water. □ *He stood on the bridge and threw himself into the river because he was unhappy with life.* **2.** *Fig.* to dress in something hurriedly. □ *She threw herself into the dress.* □ *He just threw himself into his tux and ran on stage.* **3.** *Fig.* to enter into or join something eagerly and wholeheartedly. □ *Todd always threw himself into a project from start to finish.* □ *She threw herself into the project and helped immensely.*

throw oneself **on the mercy of** some authority Go to throw oneself at the mercy of some authority.

throw people together to bring or put two or more people together. □ *The crisis threw complete strangers together, and they became fast friends before it was over.* □ *They were thrown together by fate.*

throw (some) light on something Go to shed (some) light on something.

throw someone *Fig.* to confuse someone. □ *You threw me for a minute when you asked for my identification. I thought you recognized me.* □ *The question the teacher asked was so hard that it threw me, and I became very nervous.*

throw someone **a curve 1.** *Lit.* to pitch a curveball to someone in baseball. (See pitch someone a curve(ball).) □ *The pitcher threw John a curve, and John swung wildly against thin air.* □ *During that game, the pitcher threw everyone a curve at least once.* **2.** *Fig.* to confuse someone by doing something tricky or unexpected. □ *When you said "house" you threw me a curve. The password was supposed to be "home."* □ *John threw me a curve when we were making our presentation, and I forgot my speech.*

throw someone **for a loop** Go to knock someone for a loop.

throw someone **for a loss** to cause someone to be uncertain or confused. (Often passive.) □ *The stress of being in front of so many people threw Ann for a loss. She forgot her speech.* □ *It was a difficult problem. I was thrown for a loss for an answer.*

throw someone **in the drink** Go to in the drink.

throw someone **off** to interrupt and confuse someone; to mislead someone. □ *The interruption threw me off, and I*

T

lost my place in the speech. □ *Little noises throw me off. Please try to be quiet.* □ *Your comment threw me off.*

throw someone **off balance 1.** *Lit.* to cause someone to falter (and probably fall). □ *The cyclist bumped into me and threw me off balance.* □ *I was thrown off balance by the gust of wind.* **2.** *Fig.* to confuse or disorient one. □ *Your last question sort of threw me off balance.* □ *The teacher was thrown off balance by the students' difficult questions.*

throw someone **off the track 1.** and **throw** someone **off the trail** *Lit.* to cause someone to lose the trail (when following someone or something. See also put someone off the track). □ *The raccoon threw us off the track by running through the creek.* □ *The robber threw the police off the trail by leaving town.* **2.** *Fig.* to cause one to lose one's place in the sequence of things. □ *The interruption threw me off the track for a moment, but I soon got started again with my presentation.* □ *Don't let little things throw you off the track. Concentrate on what you're doing.*

throw someone **off the trail** Go to previous.

throw someone or an animal **off (of)** something and **throw** someone or an animal **off**[†] to divert or confuse someone or an animal away from something, such as the scent, track, or trail. (*Of* is usually retained before pronouns.) □ *She put a little detail in her story to throw the cops off her trail.* □ *The diversion threw off the investigation.*

throw someone or something **around**[†] to toss or cast someone or something around. □ *The belligerent fellow at the bar threatened to throw me around a little if I didn't get out of his way.* □ *Don't throw around your empty cans.*

throw someone or something **aside**[†] **1.** *Lit.* to cast someone or something to the side. □ *He threw his child aside just as the car was about to run him down.* □ *Don't just throw aside the wrapper!* **2.** *Fig.* to get rid of someone or something. □ *He threw his wife aside and took up with a younger woman.* □ *Don't throw aside material that might still be useful.*

throw someone or something **back**[†] to return someone or something by tossing. □ *The sailor climbed out of the water into the boat, and his mates grabbed him and threw him back. That was their idea of fun.* □ *Karen threw back the undersize fish.*

throw someone or something **in**[†] Go to **throw** someone or something **into** something.

throw someone or something **into confusion** to cause people or a process to become confused, aimless, or disorderly. □ *She made her entrance early and threw eveyone onstage into confusion.* □ *The judge's surprise ruling threw the courtroom into confusion.*

throw someone or something **into** something and **throw** someone or something **in**[†] to cast or hurl someone or something into something. □ *The cops threw Max into jail again.* □ *The warden opened the cell door and threw in the prisoner.* □ *We threw the aluminum cans in the bin.*

throw someone or something **off (of)** something and **throw** someone or something **off**[†] to cast someone or something off something. (*Of* is usually retained before pronouns.) □ *The character in the movie wanted to throw the heroine off a cliff.* □ *He went to the middle of the bridge and threw off the gun used in the shooting.*

throw someone or something **on(to)** something to hurl someone or something onto something. □ *The intruder threw Jason onto the floor and began to kick him.* □ *He threw the book on the floor and stalked out.*

throw someone or something **out of** something and **throw** someone or something **out**[†] to eject someone or something from something or a place. □ *The intruder tried to throw Walter out of the window.* □ *He went to the window and threw out Walter.*

throw someone or something **over** someone or something to toss someone or something over someone or something; to lay someone or something across someone or something. □ *The wrestler picked his opponent up and threw him over the referee.* □ *He threw his opponent over the ropes.*

throw someone **out of** something and **throw** someone **out**[†] to force a person to leave a place or an organization. □ *John behaved so badly that they threw him out of the party.* □ *I was very loud, but they didn't throw me out.*

throw someone **over** to end a romance with someone. □ *Jane threw Bill over. I think she met someone she likes better.* □ *Bill was about ready to throw her over, so it's just as well.*

throw someone **over**[†] **for** someone else to break up with a lover in order to take another lover. □ *Sarah threw Jason over for Larry.* □ *She threw over Jason for Walter.*

throw someone's **name around** *Fig.* to impress people by saying you know a famous or influential person. □ *You won't get anywhere around here by throwing the mayor's name around.* □ *When you get to the meeting, just throw my name around a bit, and people will pay attention to you.*

throw someone **to the dogs** *Fig.* to abandon someone to enemies or evil. □ *He served the evil empire well, but in the end, they threw him to the dogs.*

throw someone **to the wolves** *Fig.* to sacrifice someone to save the rest; to abandon someone to harm. (*Fig.* on the image of giving one person to the wolves to eat so the rest can get away.) □ *Don't try to throw me to the wolves. I'll tell the truth about the whole affair!* □ *The investigation was going to be rigorous and unpleasant, and I could see they were going to throw someone to the wolves.*

throw something **across** someone or something to toss or spread something, such as a blanket, over someone or something. □ *Tom threw a blanket across Martha.* □ *Tom threw a blanket across his knees.*

throw something **across** something to toss something over something, from one side of it to the other. □ *Can you throw this stone across the river?* □ *Walter threw the ball across the court to Michael.*

throw something **at** someone or something to toss or cast something at someone or something. □ *The boy threw a rock at his sister.* □ *He threw the stone at the target.*

throw something **away**[†] to toss something out; to dispose of something. □ *Should I throw this away?* □ *Don't throw away anything that might be useful.*

throw something **away**[†] **on** someone or something to waste something on someone or something. □ *I won't throw any more money away on your brother-in-law.* □ *I've thrown away too much money on that project.*

throw something **back**[†] *Sl.* to eat or drink something quickly. □ *He threw a beer back and got up and left.* □ *She threw back a beer.*

throw something **back**[†] **at** someone *Fig.* to return a problem or difficulty to the person from whom it came. □ *He said that the problem was mine alone, and he threw it back at me.* □ *I tried to get someone else to take care of it, but it was thrown back at me.*

throw something **back**[†] **to** someone **1.** *Lit.* to return something to someone by throwing. □ *Liz threw the ball back to Kelly.* □ *She threw back the ball.* **2.** *Fig.* to return a problem to someone. □ *I can't do anything about this. I'll throw it back to Roger.* □ *Karen threw back the problem to Roger, who had caused it.*

throw something **down**[†] to cast something down onto the ground; to cast something to a lower level. □ *Dave took one look at the box and threw it down.* □ *He threw down the box.*

throw something **down** something to hurl something downward through something, such as a stairway, a duct, a drain, a hole. □ *Max threw the weapon down the storm sewer.* □ *Someone threw the bucket down the well.*

throw something **in**[†] Go to **throw** something **into** the bargain.

throw something **into sharp relief** *Fig.* [for something] to make something plainly evident or clearly visible. □ *The dull, plain background threw the ornate settee into sharp relief.* □ *The red vase was thrown into sharp relief against the black background.*

throw something **in(to)** someone's **face 1.** *Lit.* to hurl or splash something into someone's face. □ *Jerry got mad at Bob and threw his drink into Bob's face.* □ *He threw the pie in Ken's face.* **2.** *Fig.* to confront someone with a problem or criticism. □ *Jerry caused this mess. I'll just throw the whole problem into his face and tell him to fix it.* □ *It's her fault. Just throw this problem in her face and make her deal with it.*

throw something **into the bargain** and **include** something **in the bargain; throw** something **in**[†] to include something extra in a deal. □ *To encourage me to buy a new car, the car dealer threw a free radio into the bargain.* □ *If you purchase three pounds of chocolates, I'll throw one pound of salted nuts into the bargain.* □ *She threw in a free calendar.*

throw something **off**[†] **1.** *Lit.* to cast something, such as a coat, off one's body. □ *He threw his jacket off and dived into the icy water.* □ *He threw off his jacket.* **2.** *Fig.* to resist or recover from a disease. □ *It was a bad cold, but I managed to throw it off in a few days.* □ *I can't seem to throw off my cold. I've had it for weeks.* **3.** *Fig.* to emit or give off an odor. □ *The small animal threw a strong odor off.* □ *The flowers threw off a heavy perfume.*

throw something **on** someone or something to toss or sling something over or onto someone or something. (*Upon* is formal and less commonly used than *on.*) □ *Mommy, Jimmy threw some mud on me!* □ *Throw a cloth on the sofa to protect it from paint spatters.*

throw something **to** someone or something to toss something to someone or something. □ *Throw the ball to me!* □ *Gary threw a bit of meat to the dog to quiet it.*

throw something **together**[†] and **slap** something **together**[†] to assemble or arrange something in haste. □ *Don't just slap something together! Use care and do it right.* □ *You assembled this device very badly. It seems that you just slapped it together.* □ *John went into the kitchen to throw together something for dinner.*

throw something **up**[†] **1.** to build or erect something in a hurry. □ *They sure threw that building up in a hurry.* □ *They threw up the building in only a few weeks.* **2.** to vomit something. □ *Poor Wally threw his dinner up.* □ *He threw up his dinner.*

throw something **up to** someone to confront someone with something. □ *I threw the whole matter up to her, but she had nothing to say about it.* □ *I can't figure out what to do. I will just throw the whole business up to the boss.*

throw something **up to** someone or something to cast something upward to someone or something. □ *Gary threw a hammer up to the top of the porch roof where Ted could get it.* □ *Please throw a can of lemonade up to me.*

throw the baby out[†] **with the bath(water)** *Fig.* to dispose of the good while eagerly trying to get rid of the bad. (*Fig.* on the image of carelessly emptying a tub of both the water inside as well as the baby that was being washed.) □ *In her haste to talk down a project that had only a few disagreeable points, she has thrown the baby out with the bathwater.* □ *Hasty action on this major spending bill will result in throwing out the baby with the bath.*

throw the book at someone *Fig.* to charge or convict someone with as many crimes as is possible. □ *I made the police officer angry, so he took me to the station and threw the book at me.* □ *The judge threatened to throw the book at me if I didn't stop insulting the police officer.*

throw the bull and **throw the crap** *Sl. Fig.* to chat; to boast. (Use caution with *crap*.) □ *Tom could really throw the bull and sound right as rain.* □ *You're just throwing the crap. Can it!*

throw the crap See previous.

throw up to vomit. □ *I was afraid I would throw up, the food was so horrible.* □ *This food is bad enough to make you throw up.*

throw up one's **toenails** *Sl.* to vomit heavily. □ *I was so sick. I nearly threw up my toenails.* □ *Frank was in the bathroom, throwing up his toenails.*

thrust and parry *Fig.* to enter into verbal combat [with someone]; to compete actively [with someone]. (*Fig.* on the sport of fencing.) □ *I spent the entire afternoon thrusting and parrying with a committee of so-called experts in the field of insurance.* □ *I do not intend to stand here and thrust and parry with you over a simple matter like this. Let's get someone else's opinion.*

thrust out to stick out; to stab outward; to protrude outward. □ *A deck thrust out from the back of the house, offering a lovely view of the stream far below.* □ *As he grew angrier, his chin thrust out farther and farther.*

thrust someone or something **against** someone or something to drive or shove someone or something against someone or something. □ *The force of the crash thrust Liz against Tiffany.* □ *The crash thrust Liz against the car door.*

thrust someone or something **aside**[†] to push someone or something out of the way or to one side. □ *Walter thrust Fred aside and dashed by him into the room.* □ *He thrust aside Fred and came into the room.*

thrust someone or something **away**[†] **from** someone or something to push or throw someone or something away from someone or something. □ *The guards thrust the spectators away from the path the rock star was taking.* □ *They thrust away the spectators from the star.*

thrust someone or something **back**[†] to push someone or something backward and away. □ *Tom moved forward, but the guard thrust him back.* □ *He thrust back the door, which had closed on his foot.*

thrust someone or something **through** something to drive or push someone or something through something. □ *I thrust Larry through the open door and followed along quickly.* □ *Ann thrust the wad of papers through the opening.*

thrust something **at** someone or something to stab at someone or something with something. □ *The goat thrust its head at the dog.* □ *Ann thrust the pencil at the balloon and popped it.*

thrust something **down**[†] to jab something downward. □ *Max thrust the knife down and speared a piece of chicken.* □ *He thrust down the fork like a spear.*

thrust something **down** something to jab or stab something down into something. □ *The keeper quickly thrust the medicine down the lion's throat.* □ *The chimney sweep thrust his brush down the chimney.*

thrust something **forward** to jab something forward. □ *She thrust her jaw forward and walked into the room.* □ *Roger thrust his hand forward just in time to stop the child from crossing the street.*

thrust something **into** someone or something and **thrust** something **in**[†] to stab or run something into someone or something. □ *The knight thrust his lance into the villain.* □ *He thrust in his knife.*

thrust through something to drive or push through something forcefully. □ *The front end of the car thrust through the side of the house.* □ *The stock clerk's knife thrust through the box, ruining the packages of noodles inside.*

thrust up through something to stick or stab upward through something. □ *The tallest of the trees thrust up through the canopy of leaves far overhead.* □ *We heard a ripping sound and saw the tent pole thrust up through the top of the tent.*

thud against someone or something to thump against someone or something, making a dull noise on impact. □ *The pumpkin thudded against Jerry, breaking open and messing up his clothes.* □ *The ball thudded against the wall and bounced back.*

thud into someone or something to bump into someone or something, making a dull noise on impact. □ *The door blew open and thudded into Marie, giving her a bump on the knee.* □ *The ball thudded into the side of the house.*

thumb a ride and **hitch a ride** to get a ride from a passing motorist; to make a sign with one's thumb that indicates to passing drivers that one is asking for a ride. □ *My car broke down on the highway, and I had to thumb a ride to get back to town.* □ *Sometimes it's dangerous to hitch a ride with a stranger.*

thumb one's **nose at** someone or something **1.** *Lit.* to show a sign of derision at someone or something by placing the thumb to the side of the nose. (Often while wiggling the other fingers of the hand.) □ *Don't thumb your nose at me unless you want a fight.* □ *Fred thumbed his nose at the car as it drove off.* **2.** *Fig.* to dismiss someone or something as worthless, verbally. □ *Walter thumbed his nose at Fred and asked the gang to send someone else to do the job.* □ *She thumbed her nose at the whole idea.*

thumb through something and **leaf through** something to look through a book, magazine, or newspaper, without reading it carefully. □ *I've only thumbed through this book, but it looks very interesting.* □ *I leafed through a magazine while waiting to see the doctor.*

a **thumbnail sketch** a brief or small picture or description. □ *The manager gave a thumbnail sketch of her plans.* □ *The student wrote a thumbnail sketch of his project.*

thumbs down 1. a sign of disapproval. □ *The board gave our proposal a thumbs down.* □ *The administration's tax bill got a thumbs down in Congress.* **2.** disapproving; negative. □ *It was thumbs down, and I was disappointed.* □ *The thumbs-down decision was a victory for good sense.*

thumbs up 1. a sign of approval. □ *It was a thumbs up on the new filtration plant at Thursday's village board meeting.* □ *There was no thumbs up for the mayor as she faced certain defeat in today's balloting.* **2.** approving; positive. □ *The new filtration plant got a thumbs-up decision at the board meeting.* □ *A thumbs-up vote assured another three years of financial assistance.*

thump on someone or something to pound on someone or something. □ *Tim was angry with Roger and thumped on him a little, but decided to forgive him.* □ *Andy thumped on the bass drum for an hour.*

thump something **down**[†] to throw something down so it makes a pounding noise. □ *Nancy thumped the parcel down and caught her breath.* □ *She thumped down the parcel.*

thump something **out**[†] **(on the piano)** to pound out music on a piano. □ *Joel thumped a happy tune out on the piano.* □ *He thumped out a well-known tune.*

thunder across something *Fig.* to move across something, making a rumbling sound. □ *The jets thundered across the sky, heading for their home base.* □ *As the race car thundered across the track, people strained to get a better view.*

thunder past someone or something *Fig.* to move past someone or something, rumbling. □ *As the traffic thundered past, I wondered why there was so much of it.* □ *The train thundered past the sleeping town.*

thunder something **out**[†] *Fig.* to respond with words spoken in a voice like thunder. □ *He thundered the words out so everyone could hear them.* □ *He thundered out the words.*

tick away [for seconds or minutes] to go by as the clock ticks. □ *The seconds ticked away as the fateful time got closer.* □ *As time ticked away, the surgeons worked feverishly to repair the walls of Roger's heart.*

tick someone **off**[†] to make someone angry. □ *That really ticks me off!* □ *Doesn't that tick off everyone?*

ticked (off) angry. □ *Wow, was she ticked off!* □ *Kelly was totally ticked.*

ticket someone **for** some place to supply a ticket for someone to go to some place. □ *The airlines clerk ticketed me for Houston and checked in my baggage.* □ *I was ticketed for both flights, saving me some time.*

tickle someone **pink** *Fig.* to please or entertain someone very much. □ *Bill told a joke that really tickled us all pink.* □ *I know that these flowers will tickle her pink.*

tickle someone's **fancy** to interest someone; to make someone curious. □ *I have an interesting problem here that I think will tickle your fancy.* □ *This doesn't tickle my fancy at all. This is dull and boring.*

tickle someone **to death 1.** *Fig.* to tickle someone a great deal. □ *Bobby nearly tickled Tim to death. Tim was left breathless.* □ *We got him down and tickled him to death.* **2.** and **tickle** someone **to pieces** *Fig.* to please someone a great deal. (See also tickle someone **pink**.) □ *What you told her just tickled her to death!* □ *That story just tickles me to pieces.*

tickle someone **to pieces** Go to previous.

tickle the ivories to play the piano. □ *I used to be able to tickle the ivories real nice.* □ *She sat down to tickle the ivories for a while.*

tickled pink *Fig.* very much pleased or entertained. □ *I was tickled pink to have you visit us.* □ *We were tickled pink when your flowers arrived.*

tide someone **over†** (**until** something) to supply someone until a certain time or until something happens. □ *Will this amount tide us over until next week?* □ *There is enough food here to tide over the entire camp until next month.* □ *Yes, this will tide us over.*

the **tide turned 1.** *Lit.* the tide changed from high tide to low tide or vice versa. □ *The tide turned before the ship had sailed out of the harbor.* **2.** *Fig.* the trend changed from one thing to another. □ *We planned our investments to take advantage of the growth of the stock market. Then the tide turned and we lost buckets of money.*

tidy something **up†** to clean something up; to make something more orderly. □ *Please tidy this room up.* □ *I'll tidy up the kitchen later.*

tidy up to clean up [oneself or a place]. □ *Please tidy up. This place is a mess.* □ *Please tidy up. You are a mess.*

tie in (with someone or something**)** to join with someone or something; to connect with someone or something. (See also tie in with something.) □ *I would like to tie in with you and see if we can solve this together.* □ *We would like for you to tie in and share your expertise.*

tie in with something [for a piece of information] to complement other information. □ *These figures tie in with what I just said.* □ *The crime lab report ties in with our current theory.*

tie in(to something**)** to fasten or connect to something. □ *Can you fix it so my computer can tie into Rachel's?* □ *This one will not tie into her computer.*

tie it on Go to tie one on.

tie on the nose-bag Go to put the feed bag on.

tie one on and **hang one on; lay one on; tie it on** *Sl.* to get drunk. □ *The boys went out to tie one on.* □ *They laid one on, but good.*

tie someone **down (to** someone or something**)** *Fig.* to encumber something with someone or something; to make someone responsible to or for someone or something. □ *Please don't tie me down to your uncle. Let your sister help out.* □ *Yes, don't tie me down all week.*

tie someone or something **down†** to fasten someone or something down by tying or binding. □ *The robbers tied Gary down so he couldn't get up and get away.* □ *They tied down Gary.*

tie someone or something **into** something and **tie** someone or something **in†** to seek to establish a connection between someone or something and something. □ *The police tried to tie Sarah into the crime.* □ *They tried to tie in Liz, too.*

tie someone or something **to** something to bind someone or something to something. □ *The robber tied the clerk to a chair.* □ *I tied colored yarn to the birthday present.*

tie someone or something **up†** **1.** *Lit.* to bind someone or something securely. □ *The sheriff tied the crooks up and took them to a cell.* □ *He tied up the bandit.* □ *I tied the package up and put a label on it.* **2.** *Fig.* to keep someone or something busy or occupied. □ *Sally tied up the photocopy machine all afternoon.* □ *The meeting tied me up all afternoon.*

tie someone's **hands 1.** *Lit.* to use rope or string to tie someone's hands together. □ *The robber tied my hands and I couldn't call the police.* **2.** *Fig.* to prevent someone from doing something. □ *I'd like to help you, but my boss has tied my hands.* □ *Please don't tie my hands with unnecessary restrictions. I'd like the freedom to do whatever is necessary.*

tie someone **to** something *Fig.* to associate someone with something; to make a connection between someone and something. □ *The police are trying to tie Lefty to the burglary.* □ *They'll never tie me to that bunch of crooks!*

tie someone (**up) in knots** *Fig.* to become anxious or upset. □ *John tied himself in knots worrying about his wife during her operation.* □ *This waiting and worrying really ties me up in knots.*

tie something **back†** to bind or fasten something back out of the way. □ *George tied the curtains back to let a little more light in.* □ *Let me tie back the vines out of the way.*

tie something **in a knot** to bend something, such as a rope, upon itself to make a knot. □ *I ended up tying the rope in a knot.* □ *The rope was tied in a knot and no one could get it undone.*

tie something **off†** to tie the ends of something losing fluid, as blood vessels to prevent bleeding. □ *The surgeons tied all the blood vessels off—one by one—as they were exposed.* □ *They tied off all the vessels very quickly.*

tie something **onto** someone or something and **tie** something **on†** to attach something to someone or something by tying or binding. □ *I tied his house key onto him so he wouldn't lose it.* □ *I tied on his gloves so he would not lose them.*

tie something **up†** **1.** *Lit.* to tie strings or cords on something in order to close or contain it. □ *Please tie this pack-*

age up securely so I can mail it. □ *Tie up your shoes!* **2.** *Fig.* to conclude and finalize something. (See also **tie** someone or something **up**.) □ *Let's try to tie up this deal by Thursday.* □ *We'll manage to tie our business up by Wednesday at the latest.* **3.** *Fig.* to block or impede something, such as traffic or progress. □ *The stalled bus tied traffic up for over an hour.* □ *The stalled bus tied up traffic.*

tie the knot 1. *Fig.* to marry a mate. □ *We tied the knot in a little chapel on the Arkansas border.* □ *They finally tied the knot.* **2.** *Fig.* [for a cleric or other authorized person] to unite a couple in marriage. □ *It was hard to find somebody to tie the knot at that hour.* □ *It only took a few minutes for the ship's captain to tie the knot.*

tie traffic up[†] *Fig.* to cause road traffic to stop. □ *If you tie traffic up for too long, you'll get a traffic ticket.* □ *Please don't stop on the roadway. It'll tie up traffic.*

tie up (some place**)** [for a skipper] to moor a ship or boat some place. □ *We need to tie up some place for the night.* □ *The captain tied up at the dock and sent the first mate for fuel.*

tie (with someone**) (for** something**)** to have the same score as someone for the prize in some contest. □ *I tied with Joel for first place.* □ *I tied for the trophy with Joel.*

tied down *Fig.* restricted by responsibilities. □ *I love my home, but sometimes I don't like being tied down.* □ *I don't feel tied down, even though I have a lot of responsibility.*

tied to one's **mother's apron strings** *Fig.* dominated by one's mother; dependent on one's mother. □ *Tom is still tied to his mother's apron strings.* □ *Isn't he a little old to be tied to his mother's apron strings?*

tied up *Fig.* busy. □ *How long will you be tied up?* □ *I will be tied up in a meeting for an hour.*

*tight as a drum 1. stretched tight. (*Also: **as ~**.) □ *Julia stretched the upholstery fabric over the seat of the chair until it was as tight as a drum.* □ *The skin on his scalp is tight as a drum.* **2.** sealed tight. (*Also: **as ~**.) □ *Now that I've caulked all the windows, the house should be tight as a drum.* □ *Your butterfly died because the jar is as tight as a drum.* **3.** and ***tight as Midas's fist** very stingy. (*Also: **as ~**.) □ *He won't contribute a cent. He's as tight as a drum.* □ *Old Mr. Robinson is tight as Midas's fist. Won't spend money on anything.*

*tight as a tick 1. very tight. (*Fig.* on the image of a tick swollen tight with blood or of a tick stuck tightly in someone's skin. *Also: **as ~**.) □ *This lid is screwed on tight as a tick.* □ *The windows were closed—tight as a tick—to keep the cold out.* **2.** intoxicated. (*Fig.* on **full as a tick**. *Also: **as ~**.) □ *The old man was tight as a tick but still lucid.* □ *The host got tight as a tick and fell in the pool.* **3.** [of a race] close, as if the racers are moving very closely together. (*Also: **as ~**.) □ *This election is as tight as a tick.* **4.** very friendly and close; as thick as thieves. (*Also: **as ~**.) □ *Those two are tight as a tick. They are always together.*

*tight as Dick's hatband *Fig.* very tight. (*Also: **as ~**.) □ *I've got to lose some weight. My belt is as tight as Dick's hatband.* □ *This window is stuck tight as Dick's hatband.*

tight as Midas's fist Go to **tight as a drum**.

a **tight race** a close race. □ *It was a tight race right up to the final turn when my horse pulled ahead and won easily.*

tighten one's **belt** *Fig.* to manage to spend less money; to use less of something. (See also **take** one's **belt in (a notch)**.) □ *Things are beginning to cost more and more. It looks like we'll all have to tighten our belts.* □ *Times are hard, and prices are high. I can tighten my belt for only so long.*

tighten something **on(to)** something to make something more tightly attached to something. □ *Will you please tighten this nut onto the bolt?* □ *I tightened the lid on the pickle jar.*

tighten something **up**[†] to make something tighter. □ *Tighten your seat belt up. It looks loose.* □ *Can you tighten up all the bolts?*

tighten up 1. *Lit.* [for something] to get tighter. □ *The door hinges began to tighten up, making the door hard to open and close.* □ *His grip around the handle tightened up and he refused to let go.* **2.** *Fig.* [for someone or a group] to become miserly. □ *The government tightened up and our budget was slashed.* □ *We almost went out of business when we couldn't get credit because the bank tightened up.* **3.** *Fig.* [for someone or something] to become more restrictive. □ *The boss is tightening up on new hiring.* □ *There are more rules and the people who enforce them are tightening up.*

tightfisted (with money) and **closefisted (with money)** *Fig.* very stingy with money. □ *The manager is very closefisted with expenditures.* □ *My parents are very tightfisted with money.*

till all hours (of the day and night) Go to **all hours (of the day and night)**.

till hell freezes over *Inf.* forever. (Use caution with *hell*.) □ *That's all right, boss; I can wait till hell freezes over for your answer.* □ *I'll be here till hell freezes over.*

till kingdom come *Fig.* until the end of the world; forever. □ *Do I have to keep assembling these units till kingdom come?* □ *I'll hate her guts till kingdom come.*

Till next time. Go to **Good-bye for now**.

till the bitter end Go to **to the bitter end**.

till the fat lady sings and **when the fat lady sings** *Fig.* at the end; a long time from now. (Supposedly from a tale about a child—sitting through an opera—who asks a parent when it will be over. "Not until the fat lady sings" is the answer.) □ *Relax. It won't be over till the fat lady sings.* □ *We can leave with everybody else when the fat lady sings.*

Till we meet again. Go to **Good-bye for now**.

tilt at windmills *Fig.* to fight battles with imaginary enemies; to fight against unimportant enemies or issues. (As with the fictional character, Don Quixote, who attacked windmills.) □ *Aren't you too smart to go around tilting at windmills?* □ *I'm not going to fight this issue. I've wasted too much of my life tilting at windmills.*

tilt something **back**[†] to move something so it leans back. □ *Alice tilted her chair back and nearly fell over.* □ *She tilted back her chair and relaxed.*

tilt to something to lean or slant toward something or in a particular direction. □ *The picture tilts to the left.* □ *Her head was tilted to the left because she was trying to see around the corner.*

T

tilt toward someone or something **1.** *Lit* to lean toward someone or something. □ *The table is tilting toward Roger.* □ *The old shed tilted toward the west.* **2.** *Fig.* to favor choosing someone or something; to **lean toward** doing something. □ *I am tilting toward Roger for my assistant.* □ *I am tilting toward the red car, not the black one.*

time after time and **time and (time) again** repeatedly; over and over (again). □ *You've made the same error time after time! Please try to be more careful!* □ *I've told you time and again not to do that.* □ *You keep saying the same thing over and over, time and time again. Stop it!*

Time and tide wait for no man. *Prov.* Things will not wait for you when you are late. □ *Hurry up or we'll miss the bus! Time and tide wait for no man.* □ *Ellen: It's time to leave. Aren't you finished dressing yet? Fred: I can't decide which necktie looks best with this shirt. Ellen: Time and tide wait for no man, dear.*

time and (time) again Go to time after time.

time flies (when you're having fun) *Fig.* time passes very quickly. (From the Latin *tempus fugit.*) □ *I didn't really think it was so late when the party ended. Doesn't time fly?* □ *Time simply flew while the old friends exchanged news.*

***time for** someone or something the time to deal with someone or something. (Often with the negative. *Typically: **get** ~; **have** ~; **give** someone ~; **make** ~; **find** ~.) □ *I'm sorry, I don't have time for you today.* □ *I don't think I have time for a game of chess.* □ *I have time for one short game.*

Time hangs heavy on someone's **hands.** *Prov.* Time seems to go slowly when one has nothing to do. (Note the variations in the examples.) □ *I don't like it when time hangs so heavily on my hands.* □ *John looks so bored. Time hangs heavy on his hands.*

time in to record one's arrival time. □ *Did you remember to time in this morning?* □ *When did she time in?*

Time is a great healer. *Prov.* Emotional pain will grow less as time passes. □ *You may think your heart is broken and you can never possibly love again, but time is a great healer.*

Time is money. (My) time is valuable, so don't waste it. □ *I can't afford to spend a lot of time standing here talking. Time is money, you know!* □ *People who keep saying time is money may be working too hard.*

Time is of the essence. Timing and meeting all the deadlines are essential and required. (Often seen in contractual agreements.) □ *The final payment is due on the first day of December, by midnight. Time is of the essence.*

The **time is ripe.** *Prov.* It is the most favorable time to do something. □ *You ought to buy a house this year. Prices are so low, and you have enough money saved for a down payment. The time is ripe.* □ *Since Joe was in a good mood, I judged that the time was ripe to ask him for the favor I needed.*

Time is up. *Fig.* The allotted time has run out. □ *You must stop now. Your time is up.* □ *Time's up! Turn in your tests whether you're finished or not.*

***time off** a period of time that is free from employment. (*Typically: **get** ~; **have** ~; **give** someone ~; **take**

(some) ~.) □ *I'll have to get time off for jury duty.* □ *I have time off to go downtown and shop.*

***time off for good behavior 1.** *Lit.* a reduction in one's prison sentence because of good behavior. (*Typically: **get** ~; **have** ~; **give** someone ~.) □ *Bob will get out of jail tomorrow rather than next week. He got time off for good behavior.* **2.** *Fig.* a shortened time period—such a meeting, period of punishment, school class, etc. (Jocular. *Typically: **get** ~; **have** ~; **give** someone ~.) □ *They let me out of the meeting early. They said I got time off for good behavior.*

Time (out)! Stop everything for just a minute! □ *"Hey, stop a minute! Time out!" yelled Mary as the argument grew in intensity.* □ *Right in the middle of the discussion, Alice said, "Time!" Then she announced that dinner was ready.*

time out 1. to record one's departure time. □ *Did you remember to time out when you left work?* □ *I timed out at the regular time.* **2.** a call for officially stopping the clock in a game. □ *Time out! Wally is injured!*

time's a-wastin' *Rur.* Time is running out.; It is getting late. □ *Hurry up! Time's a-wastin'!* □ *How come you're still in bed? Time's a-wastin'!*

time someone **in**† to record someone's arrival time. □ *I timed you in at noon. Where were you?* □ *My job is to time in people.*

time someone **out**† to record someone's departure time. □ *Harry had to time everyone out because the time clock was broken.* □ *I had to time out everyone.*

Time to call it a day. It's time to quit for the day. □ *Jane: Well, I'm done. Time to call it a day. Sue: Yes, let's get out of here.* □ *Jane: Well, I've finished all my work. Sue: Yes, it's late. Time to call it a day.*

Time to call it a night. It's time to quit one's activities for the night. (Can refer to work or partying.) □ *Bob: Wow, it's late! Time to call it a night. Mary: Yes, it's really dark! Good night.* □ *Fred: Gee, I'm tired. Look at the time! Jane: Yes, it's time to call it a night.*

***time to catch** one's **breath** *Fig.* enough time to relax or behave normally. (*Typically: **get** ~; **have** ~; **give** one ~.) □ *When things slow down around here, I'll get time to catch my breath.* □ *Sally was so busy she didn't even have time to catch her breath.*

time was (when) there was a time when; at a time in the past. □ *Time was when old people were taken care of at home.* □ *Time was when people didn't travel around so much.*

Time will tell. Something will become known in the course of time. □ *I don't know if things will improve. Time will tell.* □ *Who knows what the future will bring? Only time will tell.*

Time works wonders. *Prov.* The passing of time can resolve many problems. □ *I thought I would never forgive my ex-husband for leaving me, but now, ten years later, I feel pretty well disposed toward him. Time works wonders.* □ *You'll change your mind eventually. Time works wonders.*

Times are changing. a response to a surprising piece of news from someone. □ *Sue: They paid nearly five hundred thousand for their first house! Rachel: Well, I shouldn't be so surprised. Times are changing, I guess.* □ *"Times are*

T

changing," warned Mary. "You can't expect the world to stand still."

Times change and we with time. *Prov.* As time passes, people and situations change. □ *Jill: Linda was such a conservative when we were in school; I don't understand how she can be so liberal now. Jane: Times change and we with time.*

Times change(, people change). *Prov.* As time passes, different things become acceptable. □ *Grandmother: In my day, no decent young woman would wear anything as immodest as what you've got on. Granddaughter: Times change, Grandma.* □ *Alan: When I was in business school, the practices you call good business were called dishonest. Fred: Yeah, well, times change, people change.*

a **tin ear** *Fig.* a poor ear for music; a poor hearing ability when it comes to music and distinguishing pitches. □ *I think I had better not try to sing along with you. I have a tin ear and would ruin your performance.*

tinge something **with** something to give something a bit of the character, color, state of mind, light, etc., of something. □ *The dust in the air had tinged the sunset with orange.* □ *The evening air was tinged with the smell of jasmine.*

tinker (around) (with something**)** to meddle with something; to play with something, trying to get it to work or work better. □ *Let me tinker around with it for a while and see if I can get it to work.* □ *Please don't tinker with the controls.*

the **tip of the iceberg** *Fig.* only the part of something that can be easily observed, but not the rest of it, which is hidden. (Referring to the fact that the majority of an iceberg is below the surface of the water.) □ *The problems that you see here now are just the tip of the iceberg. There are numerous disasters waiting to happen.*

tip one's **hand** to reveal what one is going to do; to reveal one's secrets. (From card playing.) □ *I didn't tip my hand at all. I left them guessing.* □ *They tried to get me to tip my hand.*

tip over to topple over and fall. □ *Roger shook the table slightly, and the vase tipped over.* □ *The truck was overloaded and looked so heavy that I thought it would tip over.*

tip someone **off**[†] **(about** someone or something**)** and **tip** someone **off (on** someone or something**)** to give someone a valuable piece of news about someone or something. □ *I tipped the cops off about Max and where he was going to be that night.* □ *I tipped off the mayor about the financial crisis.*

tip someone **over** to cause someone to fall. □ *Oh! You almost tipped me over!* □ *Todd fell against Maggie and tipped her over.*

tip someone **with** something to pay a tip of a certain amount to someone. □ *I tipped the headwaiter with a twenty or we would still be waiting.* □ *How much did you tip the waitress with?*

tip something **over**[†] to cause something to fall over. □ *Did you tip this chair over?* □ *Who tipped over the chair?*

tip something **up**[†] to tilt something so it dumps. □ *Jason tipped the wheelbarrow up and dumped the dirt out.* □ *He tipped up the glass, dumping the orange juice on the table.*

tip the scales at something to weigh a particular weight. □ *Albert tips the scales at nearly 200 pounds.* □ *The champ weighed in and tipped the scales at 180.*

tire of someone or something to grow weary of someone or something. □ *She tired of him and left him.* □ *I am beginning to tire of the furniture in the living room.*

tire out to become exhausted. □ *I tire out easily.* □ *When I had the flu, I found that I tired out easily.*

tire someone **out**[†] to exhaust someone. □ *The extra work tired him out a lot.* □ *Too much work will tire out the horses.*

'Tis better to have loved and lost than never to have loved at all. *Prov.* Love is such an important experience that even the pain of losing someone you love is better than not having loved that person. (A line from Alfred Lord Tennyson's poem, "In Memoriam A. H. H.") □ *Tom: I've been so miserable since Nancy and I broke up. I wish I'd never met her. Fred: Come on, now—'tis better to have loved and lost than never to have loved at all.*

tits and ass a public display of [the human female] breasts and buttocks. (Referring to television, film, and stage performances in which women breasts and buttocks or in which these body parts are emphasized or made prominent. Use caution with the expression. Fixed order.) □ *We have a really fine choice on television tonight. There is brutal violence on channel 2, bloody horror on channel 5, and tits and ass on channel 10.* □ *Without tits and ass, many Broadway musicals would flop.*

to a great extent *Cliché* mainly; largely. □ *To a great extent, Mary is the cause of her own problems.* □ *I've finished my work to a great extent. There is nothing important left to do.*

to and fro [of movement] toward and away from something. □ *The puppy was very active—running to and fro—wagging its tail.* □ *The lion in the cage moved to and fro, watching the people in front of the cage.*

to be on the safe side to be safe; to be cautious; [to do something just] in case it is necessary; to be very well prepared. □ *To be on the safe side, carry some extra money in your shoe.* □ *I like to be on the safe side and stay in my hotel room at night.*

to be safe to be cautious; to be careful; [to do something just] in case it is necessary; to be very well prepared. □ *Just to be safe, you should take some extra water with you.* □ *Other people like to drive over the speed limit, but I prefer to be safe.*

to beat the band very briskly; very fast. □ *He's selling computers to beat the band since he started advertising.* □ *She worked to beat the band to get ready for this.*

to boot in addition. □ *For graduation, I got a new suit and a coat to boot.* □ *She got an F on her term paper and flunked the final to boot.*

to date up to the present time. □ *How much have you accomplished to date?* □ *I've done everything I'm supposed to have done to date.*

to die for *Sl.* important or desirable enough to die for; worth dying for. □ *This chocolate cake is to die for!* □ *We had a beautiful room at the hotel and the service was to die for.*

T

To each his own. *Prov.* Each person has the right to make choices. □ *A: Bob likes chopped prunes on ice cream! B: To each his own.*

To err is human(, to forgive divine). *Prov.* You should not be too harsh with someone who makes a mistake, because all human beings make mistakes. (Often used as a roundabout way to ask someone to forgive you for making a mistake.) □ *Jill: How could you let my dog get out when I told you a hundred times that he should stay in the house! Ellen: To err is human, to forgive divine.*

*to go 1. [of a purchase of cooked food] to be taken elsewhere to be eaten. (*Typically: **buy** some food ~; **get** some food ~; **have** some food ~; **order** some food ~.) □ *Let's stop here and buy six hamburgers to go.* □ *I didn't thaw anything for dinner. Let's stop off on the way home and get something to go.* **2.** [of a number or an amount] remaining; yet to be dealt with. □ *I finished with two of them and have four to go.*

to have a hollow leg *Fig.* to have a great capacity or need for food or drink. □ *Bobby can drink more beer than I can afford. I think he has a hollow leg!*

to hell and gone 1. *Inf.* very much gone; lost completely. (Use *hell* with caution.) □ *All my hard work is to hell and gone.* □ *When you see everything you've planned to hell and gone, you get kind of angry.* **2.** Go to **all over creation.**

(To) hell with that! *Inf.* I reject that! (Very stern or angry. Use *hell* with caution.) □ *Mary: I think we ought to go to the dance Friday night. Tom: To hell with that!* □ *Fred: Don't you want to drive me down to school? John: To hell with that!*

to no avail and **of no avail** *Cliché* with no effect; unsuccessful. □ *All of my efforts were to no avail.* □ *Everything I did to help was of no avail. Nothing worked.*

to one's **heart's content** *Fig.* as much as one wants. □ *John wanted a week's vacation so he could go to the lake and fish to his heart's content.* □ *I just sat there, eating chocolate to my heart's content.*

to put it another way and **put another way** a phrase introducing a restatement of what someone, usually the speaker, has just said. □ *Father: You're still very young, Tom. To put it another way, you don't have any idea about what you're getting into.* □ *John: Could you go back to your own room now, Tom? I have to study. Put another way, get out of here! Tom: Okay, okay. Don't get your bowels in an uproar!*

to put it mildly and **put it mildly** to understate something; to say something politely. (Note the variation in the examples.) □ *She was angry at almost everyone—to put it mildly.* □ *To say she was angry is putting it mildly.* □ *To put it mildly, she was enraged.*

to say nothing of someone or something not to even mention the importance of someone or something. □ *John and Mary had to be taken care of, to say nothing of Bill, who would require even more attention.* □ *I'm having enough difficulty painting the house, to say nothing of the garage that is very much in need of paint.*

to say the least at the very least; without overemphasizing the subject; **to put it mildly.** □ *We were not at all pleased with her work—to say the least.* □ *When they had an accident, they were upset to say the least.*

to some extent to some degree; in some amount; partly. □ *I've solved this problem to some extent.* □ *I can help you understand this to some extent.*

to someone's **liking** fitting someone's personal preferences. □ *I had my house painted, but the job was not to my liking.* □ *Large meals with lots of fat are not to Bob's liking.*

to someone's **way of thinking** in someone's opinion. □ *This isn't satisfactory to my way of thinking.* □ *To my way of thinking, this is the perfect kind of vacation.*

to the best of one's **ability** as well as one is able. □ *I did the work to the best of my ability.* □ *You should always work to the best of your ability.*

to the best of one's **knowledge** Go to **as far as** anyone **knows.**

to the bitter end and **till the bitter end** *Fig.* to the very end. (Originally nautical. This originally had nothing to do with bitterness.) □ *I'll stay till the bitter end.* □ *It took me a long time to get through school, but I worked hard at it all the way to the bitter end.*

to the contrary and **on the contrary** as the opposite of what has been stated; contrary to what has been stated. □ *The brown horse didn't beat the black horse. To the contrary, the black one won.* □ *Among spiders, the male is not the larger one. On the contrary, the female is larger.*

to the core all the way through; basically and essentially. (Usually with some negative sense, such as *evil, rotten*, etc.) □ *Bill said that John is evil to the core.* □ *This organization is rotten to the core.*

to the ends of the earth *Fig.* to the remotest and most inaccessible points on the earth. □ *I'll pursue him to the ends of the earth.* □ *We've explored almost the whole world. We've traveled to the ends of the earth trying to learn about our world.*

to the last to the very end; to the conclusion. □ *All of us kept trying to the last.* □ *It was a very boring play, but I sat through it to the last.*

to the letter exactly as instructed; exactly as written. □ *I didn't make an error. I followed your instruction to the letter.* □ *We didn't prepare the recipe to the letter, but the cake still turned out very well.*

to the max *Sl.* as much as possible, maximally. □ *She is happy to the max.* □ *They worked to the max their whole shift.*

to the nth degree to the maximum amount. □ *Jane is a perfectionist and tries to be careful to the nth degree.* □ *This scientific instrument is accurate to the nth degree.*

to the tune of some amount of money *Fig.* to a certain amount of money. □ *My checking account is overdrawn to the tune of $340.* □ *My wallet was stolen, and I'm out to the tune of $70.*

To the victors belong the spoils. *Prov.* The winners achieve power over people and property. □ *The mayor took office and immediately fired many workers and hired new ones. Everyone said, "To the victors belong the spoils."*

to whom it may concern *Cliché* to the person to whom this applies. (A form of address used when you do not know the name of the person who handles the kind of business you are writing about.) □ *The letter started out,*

T

"To whom it may concern." □ *When you don't know who to write to, just say, "To whom it may concern."*

to wit namely; that is; that is to say. □ *The criminal was punished; to wit, he received a 20-year sentence.* □ *Many students, to wit Mary, Bill, Sue, and Anne, complained about their teacher.*

toady (up) to someone to fawn over someone; to try to flatter and impress someone. □ *Carl is always toadying up to people.* □ *He has never toadied to me!*

Today here, tomorrow the world. *Prov.* Successful in this location now, with later recognition in the rest of the world. (Describes something whose influence seems certain to spread. The name of an appropriate locality is usually substituted for *here.*) □ *I thought that silly fashion in clothes was unique to California, but it seems to be spreading. Today Los Angeles, tomorrow the world.*

toddle along 1. to walk along in an unconcerned manner. □ *Kathleen was just toddling along, minding her own business.* **2.** to walk away. □ *Why don't you toddle along now and let me get some work done?*

toddle away and **toddle off** to walk away. □ *Not even noticing what had happened, the old lady got up and toddled away.* □ *Sam toddled away, leaving us behind to explain things to the boss.* □ *Wally toddled off, leaving his dinner untouched.* □ *Don't just toddle off when I'm talking to you!*

toddle off Go to previous.

toe the line Go to next.

toe the mark and **toe the line** *Fig.* to do what one is expected to do; to follow the rules. □ *You'll get ahead, Sally. Don't worry. Just toe the mark, and everything will be okay.* □ *John finally got fired. He just couldn't learn to toe the line.*

toil for someone **1.** to work on behalf of someone or for someone's benefit. □ *I don't mind toiling for her as long as she thanks me.* □ *I don't know why I toil for you. You are totally ungrateful.* **2.** to do someone else's work. □ *I don't know why I should have to toil for you. Do your own work!* □ *I won't toil for him. He can do his own work.*

toil for something **1.** to work toward a particular goal or ideal. □ *I am willing to toil for something I believe in.* □ *She spent the afternoon toiling for her favorite charity.* **2.** to work for a certain rate of pay. □ *It's hard to toil for slave's wages.* □ *Do you expect me to toil endlessly for such low pay?*

toil over someone or something to work hard on someone or something. □ *The doctors toiled over the patient for hours.* □ *Ken toiled over his model plane well into the night.*

toil up something to work hard to climb something steep. □ *The hikers toiled up the slope slowly.* □ *As the bus toiled up the hill, we worried that the engine might be overheating.*

toing and froing (on something**)** moving back and forth on an issue, first deciding one way and then changing to another. □ *The boss spent most of the afternoon toing and froing on the question of who was to handle the Wilson account.* □ *I wish you would stop toing and froing and make up your mind.*

a **token gesture** an action or a decision that is so small or inconsequential as to be only symbolic. □ *Offering to pay for my dinner was only a token gesture. That does little to make up for my inconvenience.*

tol(er)able (well) *Rur.* pretty well; okay. □ *Tom: How are you feeling? Jane: Tolerable well.* □ *Charlie: How's the work coming? Tom: Tolable well.* □ *Mary: How's your aunt after her surgery? Jane: She's getting along tolable.*

toll for someone [for a bell] to ring for someone. □ *Who are the bells tolling for?* □ *The bells are tolling for Mr. Green, who died last night.*

Tomorrow is another day. *Prov.* Things may improve tomorrow; tomorrow you will have a chance to solve the problems that are upsetting you today. (Often used to encourage someone to relax and wait until tomorrow to do or worry about something.) □ *Child: This math homework is horrible! I can't do it! Mother: Put it away for tonight and go to bed. You'll be able to think more clearly when you've had some sleep, and tomorrow is another day.*

Tomorrow never comes. *Prov.* When the day arrives that you are now calling "tomorrow," you will call that day "today" and a different day will be called "tomorrow." (Therefore, you should not resolve to do something tomorrow, since that day will never arrive.) □ *Jill: When are you going to go to lunch with me? Jane: Tomorrow. Jill: Tomorrow never comes.*

tone someone or something **up**[†] to make someone or something stronger or more fit, muscularly. □ *I suggested an exercise that would tone him up and make him feel better.* □ *The exercises toned up his tummy muscles.* □ *I need to get busy and tone myself up.*

tone something **down**[†] to cause something to have less of an impact on the senses of sight or sound; to lessen the impact of something prepared for public performance or consumption. □ *This is rather shocking. You had better tone it down a bit.* □ *Tone down this paragraph.*

tongue-in-cheek *Fig.* insincere; joking. □ *Ann made a tongue-in-cheek remark to John, and he got mad because he thought she was serious.* □ *The play seemed very serious at first, but then everyone saw that it was tongue-in-cheek, and they began laughing.*

*a **tongue-lashing** *Fig.* a severe scolding. (*Typically: **get** ~; **have** ~; **give** someone ~.) □ *I really got a tongue-lashing when I got home.* □ *Ted will have a tongue-lashing at home.*

tons of something lots of something. □ *We got tons of fried chicken, so help yourself.* □ *You are in tons of trouble.*

too big for one's **britches** *Rur.* too haughty for one's status or age. □ *Bill's getting a little too big for his britches, and somebody's going to straighten him out.* □ *You're too big for your britches, young man! You had better be more respectful.*

too close for comfort *Cliché* [for a misfortune or a threat] to be dangerously close. □ *That car nearly hit me! That was too close for comfort.* □ *When I was in the hospital, I nearly died from pneumonia. Believe me, that was too close for comfort.*

*too funny for words** extremely funny. (*Typically: **be** ~; **get** ~.) □ *Tom is usually too funny for words at parties.* □ *The joke Tom told was really too funny for words.*

*too good to be true almost unbelievable; so good as to be unbelievable. (*Typically: **be ~; become ~; get ~**.) □ *The news was too good to be true.* □ *When I finally got a big raise, it was too good to be true.*

too little, too late *Prov.* Not enough help to save the situation, and arriving too late. □ *After a lifetime of bad diet and no exercise, Lorna tried to save her health by improving her habits, but it was too little, too late.* □ *Fred: I know how to keep my business from going bankrupt. I'll invest all my savings in it. Bill: I'm sorry, Fred; even that much would be too little, too late.*

Too many chiefs and not enough Indians. *Prov.* Too many people want to be the leader, and not enough people are willing to follow to do the detail work. □ *Everyone on that committee wants to be in charge. Too many chiefs and not enough Indians.* □ *We'll never finish this project if everyone keeps trying to give orders. There are too many chiefs and not enough Indians.*

Too many cooks spoil the broth. Go to next.

Too many cooks spoil the stew. and **Too many cooks spoil the broth.** *Prov. Cliché* Too many people trying to manage something simply spoil it. □ *Let's decide who is in charge around here. Too many cooks spoil the stew.* □ *Everyone is giving orders, but no one is following them! Too many cooks spoil the broth.*

*too much overwhelming; excellent. (*Typically: **be ~; get to be ~**.) □ *It's wonderful. It's just too much!* □ *You are so kind. This is too much.*

too much of a good thing more of a thing than is good or useful. □ *I usually take short vacations. I can't stand too much of a good thing.* □ *Too much of a good thing can make you sick, especially if the good thing is chocolate.*

too rich for someone's **blood 1.** too expensive for one's budget. □ *This hotel is too rich for my blood.* □ *Europe is getting too rich for our blood.* **2.** too high in fat content for one's diet. □ *This dessert is too rich for my blood.* □ *Most ice cream is too rich for my blood.*

tool around (in something**)** to go around in a car; to speed around in a car. □ *Who is that kid tooling around in that souped-up car?* □ *Ann spends a lot of time tooling around in her new car.*

tool something **up**† to equip a factory or production line with particular tools and machines, as for new products. □ *The manager closed down the factory so she could tool it up for the new models.* □ *She tooled up the factory in record time.*

tool up to become equipped with tools. □ *I need some money so I can tool up to do the job.* □ *The factory tooled up to make the new cars in only two weeks.*

toot one's **own horn** Go to blow one's own horn.

top brass the highest leader(s); the boss(es). (Originally military.) □ *The top brass turned thumbs down on the proposal.* □ *You'll have to check it out with the top brass. She'll be home around five.*

top notch the absolute best. (Hyphenated before a nominal.) □ *Julie's singing in the musical is top notch.* □ *He prepared a top-notch meal before the movie and dessert for afterward.*

the **top of the heap** *Fig.* a position superior to everyone else. □ *For some reason, Jerry has to be at the top of the heap.* □ *She fought her way to the top of the heap and means to stay there.*

top someone or something to do or be better than someone or something. □ *Ann has done very well, but I don't think she can top Jane.* □ *Do you think your car tops mine when it comes to gas mileage?*

top something **off** to add to the difficulty of something. □ *Jane lost her job, and to top that off, she caught the flu.* □ *I had a bad day, and to top it off, I have to go to a meeting tonight.*

top something **off**† **(with** something**) 1.** to end or terminate something with something; to put something on the top of something. □ *They topped the building off with a tall flagpole.* □ *He topped off each piece of pie with a heap of whipped cream.* **2.** to celebrate an end to something with something. □ *They topped the evening off with a bottle of champagne.* □ *They topped off the evening with a bottle of champagne.*

top something **up**† to add a bit of something to replenish the amount that was used. □ *Let me top your drink up.* □ *Can I top up your glass?*

top something **with** something to decorate or finish something by adding something. □ *They topped the new garage with a weather vane.* □ *Molly-Jo topped each sundae with a big red cherry.*

top story and **upper story** *Sl.* the brain; one's mind and intellect. □ *A little weak in the upper story, but other than that, a great guy.* □ *He has nothing for a top story.*

topple down [for a stack of something] to crumple and fall down. □ *The chimney toppled down in the earthquake.* □ *The woodpile toppled down during the night and scared us all to death.*

topple off (of) something and **topple from** something to fall off the top of something very tall. (*Of* is usually retained before pronouns.) □ *Careful there! You might topple off of that wall.* □ *I didn't get too close to the edge, because I was afraid of toppling off.* □ *She toppled off the wall.* □ *The vase toppled from its shelf in the quake.*

topple over [for something very tall] to fall over. □ *I was afraid that Jimmy's stack of blocks would topple over.* □ *The stack of books toppled over and ended up as a jumbled mess on the floor.*

topple something **down**† to cause a stack of something to crumple and fall down. □ *The earthquake toppled the chimney down.* □ *The hurricane toppled down the weakest buildings.*

tore (up) and **torn (up) 1.** *Sl.* distraught; emotionally upset. □ *I knew you'd be tore up.* □ *Fred's really torn up about the accident.* **2.** *Sl.* intoxicated. □ *He wasn't just drunk—he was massively tore up.* □ *Boy, was she torn.*

torment someone **into** doing something to force someone to agree to do something through threats or maltreatment. □ *You can't torment me into doing something I don't want to do!* □ *Alice was tormented into going on the picnic.*

torn between someone **and** someone else and **torn between** something **and** something else *Fig.* uncertain whether to choose one or the other. □ *I don't know which*

709

to take. *I'm torn between Fred and Alice.* □ *I'm torn between red and green.*

torn (up) Go to **tore (up).**

torture someone **into** something to force someone to do something through the use of torture. (More severe than **torment** someone **into** something.) □ *The agents threatened to torture me into telling the secrets, so I gave in immediately, of course.* □ *Max tried to torture the old prospector into telling where the gold was hidden.*

toss a salad to mix various salad ingredients together. □ *The chef tossed the salad.* □ *I tossed the salad just before my guests arrived.*

toss in the sponge Go to **throw in the towel.**

toss one's **cookies** *Sl.* to vomit. □ *Don't run too fast after you eat or you'll toss your cookies.* □ *Oh, I feel terrible. I think I'm going to toss my cookies.*

toss one's **hat into the ring** and **throw** one's **hat in the ring** *Fig.* to announce that one is running for an elective office. □ *Jane wanted to run for treasurer, so she tossed her hat in the ring.* □ *I won't throw my hat into the ring until the last minute.*

toss (someone) **for** something *Fig.* to decide with someone, by tossing a coin, who will get or do something. □ *Let's see who gets to go first. I'll toss you for it.* □ *I'll toss for it.* □ *Let's toss for it.*

toss someone or something **around**† to throw someone or something around. □ *The waves tossed him around and almost dashed him on the rocks.* □ *The waves tossed around all the little boats.*

toss someone or something **aside**† to throw someone or something aside or out of the way. □ *The kidnapper tossed the child aside and reached for his gun.* □ *The soldier tossed aside the helpless civilian and ran into the house.* □ *Fred tossed the can aside and Alice picked it up.*

toss someone or something **away**† to throw someone or something away; to discard someone or something. □ *You can't just toss me away! I'm your husband!* □ *She tossed away her husband of twenty years.* □ *She tossed the cigarette away.*

toss someone or something **back**† **1.** to throw or force someone or something backward. □ *The blast tossed me back into the room.* □ *The blast tossed back the emergency personnel.* **2.** to throw someone or something back to where someone or something came from. □ *My father always threatened to toss me back where I came from, the way a fish is returned to the water.* □ *I will toss back all the undersize fish.*

toss someone or something **off (of)** something and **toss** someone or something **off**† to hurl someone or something from something. (*Of* is usually retained before pronouns.) □ *The gigantic ape was going to toss the woman off of the Empire State Building.* □ *The ape did not toss off the woman.*

toss someone or something **out of** something and **toss** someone or something **out**† to discard someone or something; to throw someone or something out of something or some place. □ *The bartender tossed Walter out of the bar.* □ *The litterbug tossed out the empty can.*

toss something† Go to **toss** something **into** something.

toss something **around**† *Fig.* to discuss something. □ *I have a few things to discuss. Can we meet later and toss them around?* □ *We tossed around a few ideas after dinner.*

toss something **at** someone or something to throw something at someone or something. □ *Jimmy tossed an apple at Sarah to see what she would do.* □ *John tossed a stone at the wall.*

toss something **back and forth 1.** *Lit.* [for two or more people] to toss something to each other alternately. □ *Carol and Kelly tossed the ball back and forth for a few minutes.* □ *We will toss the ball back and forth until we get tired.* **2.** *Fig.* to trade remarks, quips, insults, etc. □ *They tossed insulting remarks back and forth.* □ *Walter and David spent the evening tossing quips back and forth.*

toss something **down**† *Fig.* to drink down a drink quickly. □ *He tossed a beer down and left the bar.* □ *Sam tossed down a couple of shots.*

toss something **into** something and **toss** something† to cast or throw something into something. □ *Frank tossed the wood into the fire.* □ *He tossed in the wood.*

toss something **off**† **1.** *Lit.* to throw something off (of oneself). □ *Bob coughed so hard he tossed his blanket off.* □ *Tom tossed off his jacket and sat down to watch television.* **2.** *Fig.* to ignore or resist the bad effects of something. □ *John insulted Bob, but Bob just tossed it off.* □ *If I couldn't toss off insults, I'd be miserable.* **3.** *Fig.* to produce something easily or quickly. □ *I tossed that article off in only an hour.* □ *Joe just tossed off a few words and left the room.* **4.** *Fig.* to drink a drink very quickly. □ *He tossed a few beers off and left.* □ *He tossed off a beer.*

toss something **together** to assemble something hastily. (See also **throw** something **together.**) □ *This report is useless. You just tossed it together!* □ *This meal was just tossed together, but it was delicious.*

toss something **up**† to throw something upward to a higher place or up into the air. □ *He tossed the coin up, calling "heads" and hoping for the best.* □ *He tossed up the coin.*

total something **up**† to add up the total of something. □ *Please total the bill up and let me see the cost.* □ *Total up the bill and give it to me.*

a **total stranger** Go to a **perfect stranger.**

totally awesome *Sl.* very, very impressive. □ *His motorcycle is totally awesome. It must have cost a fortune.*

tote something **up**† to add something up. □ *The clerk toted the bill up and asked for an enormous sum.* □ *Tote up your expense report quickly and submit it to accounts payable.*

touch a sore point Go to next.

touch a sore spot and **touch a sore point** *Fig.* to refer to a sensitive matter that will upset someone. (*Fig.* on the notion of touching an injury and causing pain.) □ *I seem to have touched a sore spot. I'm sorry. I didn't mean to upset you.* □ *When you talk to him, avoid talking about money. It's best not to touch a sore point if possible.*

touch at some place *Fig.* [for a ship or an airplane] to visit or call at a port. □ *We touched at Aruba for about an hour.* □ *Our little boat touched at a number of different islands during the two-week cruise.*

touch base (with someone**)** to talk to someone; to confer with someone briefly. □ *I need to touch base with John* *on this matter.* □ *John and I touched base on this question yesterday, and we are in agreement.*

touch down [for an airplane] to come in contact with the ground; to land. □ *Flight twelve is due to touch down at midnight.* □ *When will this plane touch down?*

a **touch of** something **1.** a mild case of some illness. □ *I have a touch of the flu and need some more bed rest.* **2.** a little bit of something, particularly a small helping of food or drink. □ *A: How about some more? What do you need? B: I'll have just a touch of that meatloaf if there's enough to go around.*

touch on something *Fig.* to mention something; to talk about something briefly. □ *In tomorrow's lecture I'd like to touch on the matter of taxation.* □ *The teacher only touched on the subject. There wasn't time to do more than that.*

touch someone or something **off**† *Fig.* to ignite or excite someone or something; to excite anger or chaos. □ *She is very excitable. The slightest thing will touch her off.* □ *The appearance of the fox touched off a furor in the henhouse.*

touch someone or something **with** something to bring something into contact with someone or something. □ *Don't touch me with that filthy stick!* □ *I touched the snake with a stick to make sure it was dead.* □ *Wherever he touched himself with the leaf, his skin blistered.*

touch someone **(up) for** something *Fig.* to approach someone and ask for something; to beg or borrow something from someone. □ *Jerry tried to touch me for twenty bucks, but I didn't have it.* □ *It won't do any good to touch me up for money. I don't have any.*

touch something **to** something to bring something into contact with something. □ *She touched her hand to her ear to indicate to the speaker to talk louder.* □ *The magician touched his wand to the hat and a rabbit jumped out.*

touch something **up**† to fix up the minor flaws in something; to repair a paint job on something. □ *It's only a little scratch in the finish. We can touch it up easily.* □ *Tom touched up the scrape with a little paint.*

touch (up)on something *Fig.* to mention something; to talk about something briefly. □ *In tomorrow's lecture I'd like to touch on the matter of taxation.* □ *The teacher only touched upon the subject. There wasn't time to do more than that.*

touch-and-go very uncertain or critical. □ *Things were touch-and-go at the office until a new manager was hired.* □ *Jane had a serious operation, and everything was touch-and-go for two days after her surgery.*

touched by someone or something *Fig.* emotionally affected or moved by someone or something. □ *Sally was very nice to me. I was very touched by her.* □ *I was really touched by your kind letter.*

touched (in the head) *Rur.* crazy. □ *Sometimes Bob acts like he's touched in the head.* □ *In fact, I thought he was touched.*

a **tough act to follow** and a **hard act to follow** *Fig.* a difficult presentation or performance to follow or improve upon with one's own performance. □ *Bill's speech was excellent. It was a tough act to follow, but my speech was*

good also. □ *In spite of the fact that I had a tough act to follow, I did my best.*

***tough as an old boot** and ***tough as old (shoe) leather 1.** [of meat] very tough. (*Also:* **as** ∼.) □ *This meat is tough as an old boot.* □ *Bob couldn't eat the steak. It was as tough as an old boot.* **2.** [of someone] very strong willed. (*Also:* **as** ∼.) □ *When Brian was lost in the mountains, his friends did not fear for him; they knew he was tough as leather.* □ *My English teacher was as tough as an old boot.* **3.** [of someone] not easily moved by feelings such as pity. (*Also:* **as** ∼.) □ *She doesn't care. She's as tough as old shoe leather.* □ *He was born tough as an old boot and has only grown more rigid.*

tough as old (shoe) leather Go to previous.

a **tough break** a bit of bad fortune. □ *I'm sorry to hear about your accident. Tough break.* □ *John had a lot of tough breaks when he was a kid, but he's doing okay now.*

a **tough call** a difficult judgment to make. □ *It's a tough call, but I choose Fred and Mary. Sorry Tom and Carole.* □ *We're still undecided on whether to buy a place or rent— it's a tough call.*

a **tough cookie** a person who is difficult to deal with. □ *He's a tough cookie, but I can handle him.* □ *There was a tough cookie in here this morning who demanded to see the manager.*

tough cookies Go to tough luck.

a **tough customer** someone who is difficult to deal with. □ *Some of those bikers are really tough customers.* □ *Walt is a tough customer. Just keep away from him.*

tough going progress that is difficult. □ *It was tough going for the first few miles, but the trail became much easier as we got farther into the forest.*

tough guy a strong and severe man; a man who might be part of the underworld. □ *He was your typical tough guy— jutting chin, gruff voice—but he was just our decorator checking up on the drapes.* □ *So, you want to be a tough guy, huh?*

tough luck and **tough cookies** That is too bad. (Said as a reply to someone relating an unfortunate situation.) □ *Tough luck, but that's the way the cookie crumbles.* □ *That's too bad, tough cookies.*

a **tough nut to crack** Go to a hard nut to crack.

***tough on** someone severe and demanding in dealing with someone. (*Typically:* **act** ∼; **be** ∼; **become** ∼; **get** ∼.) □ *My boss is very tough on me, but I need the structure and discipline.*

a **tough row to hoe** and a **hard row to hoe** *Fig.* a difficult task to carry out; a heavy set of burdens. □ *It's a tough row to hoe, but hoe it you will.* □ *This is not an easy task. This is a hard row to hoe.*

tough sledding Go to hard sledding.

tough something **out** to carry on with something despite difficulties or setbacks. □ *Sorry, you'll just have to tough it out.* □ *I think I can tough this job out for another month.*

tough times Go to bad times.

toughen someone or something **up**† to cause someone or something to be stronger, more uncompromising, or more severe. □ *A few days behind the service counter at the dis-*

count store will toughen her up quickly. □ Having to deal with complaints toughened up the clerk quickly. □ She tried to toughen the skin on her palms up.

toughen up to become tougher, stronger, or more severe. □ She will toughen up after a while. You have to be tough around here to survive. □ You are going to have to toughen up if you want to play on the team.

tout someone or something **around** to promote and boost someone or something publicly. □ He is touting his favorite candidate around, hoping to get a few votes for her. □ Roger is touting his book around, trying to boost sales.

tout someone or something **as** something to present someone or something as a beneficial type of person or something. □ Joel touted his candidate as the best of all. □ Ann touted her medicine as a cure-all.

tout suite! right away; with all haste. (Pronounced "toot sweet." From French *toute de suite*.) □ John: Come on, get this finished! Bob: I'm trying. John: Tout suite! Get moving! □ "I want this mess cleaned up, tout suite!" shouted Sally, hands on her hips and steaming with rage.

tow someone or something **away**† to pull something, such as a car or a boat, away with another car, boat, etc. (The *someone* refers to the property of someone, not the person.) □ If I don't get back to my car, they will tow me away. □ The truck towed away my car. □ A big truck came and towed the illegally parked car away.

tow someone or something **into** something and **tow** someone or something **in**† to pull something, such as a car or a truck, into something, such as a garage. (The *someone* refers to the property of someone, not the person.) □ They had to tow my car into the garage to be repaired. □ They towed in my car.

tow someone or something **out (of** some place**)** to pull something, such as a car, out of something, such as a ditch. (The *someone* refers to the property of someone, not the person.) □ The farmer used his tractor to tow Andrew out of the ditch. □ He towed the car out of the ditch.

tow someone or something **out (to** something**)** to pull something, such as a boat, or someone in or on something out in the water, to something. (The *someone* refers to the property of someone, not the person.) □ Frank, who was on his surfboard, asked Tony to tow him out to the little island. □ We towed the raft out where the water is deep.

towel someone or something **down**† to rub someone or something dry with a towel. □ The mother toweled her child down and dressed her in clean clothes. □ She toweled down the child gently. □ Towel down the dog. He's wet and shaking.

towel someone or something **off**† to dry someone or something with a towel. □ The young mother toweled the baby off with a soft, warm towel. □ She toweled off the baby.

tower above someone or something to stand or be much taller than someone or something. (Often used in exaggeration.) □ The basketball player towered above everyone else in the room. □ The new building towered above all the others in town.

tower head and shoulders above someone or something **1.** *Lit.* [for someone] to stand much taller than someone or something. (Often used in exaggeration.) □ Bob towers head and shoulders above both his parents. □ The

boys towered head and shoulders above the walls of the maze. They found their way around easily. **2.** *Fig.* to be far superior to someone or a group. □ The new vice president towers head and shoulders above the old one. □ The chairman towered head and shoulders above the rest of the committee.

a **tower of strength** *Fig.* a person who can always be depended on to provide support and encouragement, especially in times of trouble. □ Mary was a tower of strength when Jean was in the hospital. She looked after her whole family. □ Jack was a tower of strength during the time that his father was unemployed.

tower over someone or something to stand much taller than someone or something. □ Tom towers over his older brother, Stan. □ Tom towered over the little desk he had been assigned to.

town-and-gown the relations between a town and the university located within the town; the relations between university students and the nonstudents who live in a university town. (Usually in reference to a disagreement. Fixed order.) □ There is another town-and-gown dispute in Adamsville over the amount the university costs the city for police services. □ There was more town-and-gown strife reported at Larry's Bar and Grill last Saturday night.

toy with someone to tease someone; to deal lightly with someone's emotions. □ Ann broke up with Tom because he was just toying with her. He was not serious at all. □ Don't toy with me! I won't have it!

toy with something to play with something; to fiddle with something. □ You are just toying with me! □ Please don't toy with the stereo controls.

trace around something to press something against paper and draw a line around the edges that are in contact with the paper. □ Trace around this piece of material and cut out a new pattern. □ If you trace around the edges carefully, you will end up with a good drawing of the outline.

trace over something **1.** to draw over something lightly. □ Trace over the drawing to make it a little darker. □ I had to trace over it twice to make it visible. **2.** to copy something by placing a thin sheet of paper over it and drawing an outline of the thing to be copied. □ Trace over this picture and then photocopy about ten copies for us all. □ This needs to be traced over again.

trace someone or something **(back**†**) (to** someone or something**)** to trail or track the origin of someone or something back to someone or something. □ We traced her back to the car she had ridden in, but lost her trail at that point. □ We traced the letter back to her. □ See if you can trace back the check to its writer.

track someone or something **down**† to search out where someone or something is. □ I don't know where Anne is. I'll try to track her down. □ I'll track down Anne for you.

track something **(all) over** something to spread something everywhere in a place from the bottom of one's shoes or feet. □ You're tracking mud all over my house! □ Who tracked stuff over my carpet?

track something **into** some place and **track** something **in**† to bring something, such as mud, into a place on the bottom of one's shoes or feet. □ Please don't track mud into the office. □ Don't track in any mud!

T

track something **up**† to mess something up by spreading around something dirty or messy with one's shoes or feet. □ *Please don't track the floor up!* □ *Claire tracked up the floor.*

trade at some place to buy and sell at some place; to shop at someplace. □ *Do you trade at that store anymore?* □ *We don't trade there because their prices are too high.*

trade insults (with someone**)** to take turns with someone in mutual insulting. □ *We traded insults with each other for a while and then settled down to some serious discussions of our differences.*

trade on something to use a fact or a situation to one's advantage. □ *Tom was able to trade on the fact that he had once been in the army.* □ *John traded on his poor eyesight to get a seat closer to the stage.*

a **trade secret 1.** *Lit.* a secret way of making or selling a product; a business secret. □ *The exact formula of the soft drink is a trade secret.* **2.** *Fig.* any secret method. (Jocular.) □ *A: How do you manage to sell so many of these each month? B: It's a trade secret.*

trade someone or something **for** someone or something to exchange someone or something for someone or something. □ *I will trade you our shortstop for your catcher and two additional promising ball players.* □ *I will trade you my office desk for a conference table.*

trade something **in**† **(for** something**)** and **trade something in**† **(on** something**)** to return something, such as a car, to a place where cars are sold as partial payment on a new car. □ *I traded my old car in on a new one.* □ *I traded in my old jalopy for a newer car.*

trade something **off**† **1.** *Lit.* to get rid of something in an exchange. □ *I traded my car off.* □ *I traded off my old car for a new one.* **2.** *Fig.* to sacrifice something in an exchange. □ *You may end up trading job security off for more money.* □ *Don't trade off your job security.*

trade something **with** someone to exchange something with someone. □ *Would you trade seats with me? I want to sit there.* □ *Can I trade books with you? This one is dull.*

trade up from something to exchange a specific lower-level product for a higher-level product. □ *I decided to trade up from my little car to a much larger one.* □ *I can't afford what I have, let alone be able to trade up to anything.*

trade up (to something**)** to exchange a lower-level product for a specific higher-level product. □ *I would like to trade up to a more luxurious model.* □ *I would like to trade up.*

trade with someone or something to do business with someone or something. □ *I don't like the owner of that shop. I won't trade with him anymore.* □ *Thank you for trading with us all these years.* □ *We don't trade with that company because their prices are too high.*

traffic in something to deal in something; to trade in something, usually something illegal. □ *Max had been trafficking in guns for years before they caught him.* □ *The president of the country was trafficking in drugs for years.*

a **traffic jam** vehicle traffic that is so heavy and slow that it can no longer move. □ *Going to the airport, we got stuck in a traffic jam for nearly and hour and missed our plane.*

trail (along) (after someone or something**) 1.** to drag along after someone or something. □ *His pants were torn, and a piece of his trouser leg trailed along after him.* □ *His trouser leg trailed after him.* **2.** to follow along after someone or something. □ *A little dog trailed along after Mary and Karen.* □ *Is that your dog trailing along?*

trail away Go to **trail off.**

trail behind (someone or something**) 1.** to follow or drag along behind someone or something. □ *A long satin train trailed behind the bride.* □ *A long train trailed behind.* **2.** to move along behind someone or a group in a competition. □ *Sally trailed behind the rest of the marathon runners.* □ *Roger trailed behind Dave during most of the race.*

trail off and **trail away** to fade away, as with speech, words, singing, etc. □ *Her voice trailed off as she saw who was waiting at the door.* □ *Ken's words trailed away as he passed out.*

trail over something to lie behind, flowing out over something. □ *Her long gown trailed over the marble floor.* □ *The flowering vine trailed over the wall, making a lovely little garden area.*

trail someone or something **by** something to have a smaller score than someone or something by a specific number of points. □ *Our team trails the visiting team by only six points.* □ *I trailed her by only a few points.*

train for something to practice or drill for some task. □ *I am training for the marathon.* □ *We all have to train for the upcoming football season.*

train one's **sights on** something and **have** one's **sights trained on** something *Fig.* to have something as a goal; to direct something or oneself toward a goal. (Alludes to someone using the sights of a gun to aim it. Note plural use of *sights*.) □ *You should train your sights on getting a promotion in the next year.* □ *Lisa has her sights trained on a new car.*

train someone **in** something to drill and practice someone in a particular skill or body of knowledge. □ *Her mentor trained her in the art of argumentation.* □ *I will try to train you in the skills needed to perform this task.*

train someone **on** something to educate someone in the use of something. □ *We trained him on the high diving board, but he isn't ready for competition yet.* □ *She trained herself on the computer so she could write a book.*

train someone or an animal **as** something to educate someone or an animal to serve in a particular way. □ *We trained him as a first-rate mechanic.* □ *I trained my cocker spaniel as a moderately effective watchdog.*

train someone or an animal **for** something to educate someone or an animal for some purpose. □ *His parents trained him for work in the family business.* □ *He was trained for factory work.*

train something **on** someone, something, or an animal to aim something at someone, something, or an animal. □ *Dave trained the spotlight on Fred, who was just coming out of the building.* □ *Train your lens on that bush. There is a deer back there.*

train up to something to practice or drill up to a certain level of proficiency. □ *I don't have enough stamina for the*

T

marathon now, but I am training up to it. □ *Alice trained up to the long-distance swim for years.*

traipse around (some place) to walk or travel around some place. □ *I spent all afternoon traipsing around town looking for just the right gift for Roger.* □ *She has been traipsing around all day.*

traipse over and **traipse in** to go or arrive carelessly or thoughtlessly. □ *He traipsed over and invited himself in.* □ *She came traipsing in at about midnight.*

tramp across something to march or stamp across an area. □ *The kids tramped across the yard and wore a path.* □ *Please don't tramp across my garden.*

tramp through something to march or stamp a passage through something. □ *The kids tramped through every puddle in town on their way to school.* □ *Don't tramp through every mud puddle you see.*

trample someone or something **down**† to crush down someone or something with the feet. □ *Stay out of crowds at rock concerts. Those kids will trample you down if they get excited.* □ *The cows trampled down the stalks of corn.*

trample someone or something **to** something to stomp or crush someone or something underfoot to the point of death or destruction. □ *The elephant trampled the photographer to death.* □ *All the joggers trampled the grass to a muddy mess.*

trample something **out**† to create a pathway by marching or stamping the same trail over and over. □ *The mail carriers have trampled a path out through my marigolds!* □ *Jim trampled out a path in my garden.*

trample (up)on someone or something to crush someone or something underfoot. (*Upon* is formal and less commonly used than *on.*) □ *Please don't trample upon the flowers!* □ *The bulls running through the streets trampled on some of the bystanders.*

transcribe something **from** someone or something to write something down from an audible source. □ *We transcribed the folktales from authentic storytellers.* □ *I transcribed the tale from an old phonograph recording.*

transcribe something **in** something **1.** to transliterate one alphabet into another. □ *Can you translate these romanized Korean words into the Korean script?* □ *We had to transcribe the entire novel into Cyrillic.* **2.** to represent speech sounds in a phonetic transcription. □ *The editor wanted the pronunciation transcribed in dictionary-style phonetics.* □ *It is much easier to transcribe the material in the International Phonetic Alphabet.* **3.** to write something down in something. □ *Please transcribe this list of names in your notebook.* □ *I can't read what is transcribed in my book.*

transfer someone or something **(from** some place**) (to** some place**)** to move or relocate someone or something from one place to another. □ *Her company transferred her from Houston to Los Angeles.* □ *We transferred the boxes from one place to another.*

transfer someone or something **to** someone to reassign someone or something to someone. □ *I transferred my secretary to Joel, who can get along with almost anyone.* □ *Ann transferred her car registration to her sister.*

transfer something **(from** someone**) (to** someone else**)** to reassign something from one person to another. □ *I have to transfer ownership of this car to my daughter.* □ *The title of the car was transferred from me to someone else.*

transfer to something to have oneself reassigned to something. □ *I am transferring to the accounting department.* □ *Andy wanted to transfer to a different school.*

transform someone or something **(from** someone or something**) (in)to** someone or something to change someone or something from someone or something into someone or something else. □ *Time had transformed gangly little Rachel into a lovely young woman.* □ *Manners transformed Tom from a pest into a prince.*

transgress against someone or something to make an offense against someone or something. (Stilted and formal.) □ *I did not mean to transgress against you.* □ *We did not transgress against the rules of the college.*

translate something **(from** something**) ((in)to** something**)** to decode something from something, such as a language, to another. □ *Will you please translate this from Russian into English?* □ *I can translate it into Russian from any Romance language.*

transliterate something **(from** something**) ((in)to** something**)** to decode something from one set of symbols to another. □ *Donald transliterated the tale from Cyrillic script into Roman letters and still couldn't read it aloud.* □ *Can you transliterate this from the original Bengali script into the Roman alphabet?* □ *I will transliterate this into Cyrillic.*

transmit something **(from** some place**) (to** some place**)** to send or dispatch something from one place to another. □ *Can you transmit a fax from your hotel to your office?* □ *I can transmit it to any place in the world.*

transmit something **to** someone or something to send or dispatch something to someone or something. □ *Please transmit this message to Rachel.* □ *I will transmit the message to my office.*

transmute something **(from** something**) ((in)to** something**)** to change something from one thing into another. □ *Do you believe that it is possible to transmute gold into lead?* □ *No, you cannot transmute one metal into another.*

transport someone or something **(from** some place**) (to** some place**)** to move or convey someone or something from one place to another. □ *In his car, he transported us from our home to the airport.* □ *Please see that this box gets transported from here to the loading dock.*

transpose something **(from** something**) ((in)to** something**)** to change something, usually in music, from one musical key to another. □ *Can you transpose this from F-sharp to a higher key?* □ *It would be easy to transpose it into a higher key.*

trap someone **in** something to catch someone in an inconsistency or contradiction. □ *The lawyer trapped the witness in his inconsistencies.* □ *She trapped herself in her own argument.*

trap someone **into** something to get one into such a position that one has little choice but to do something unwanted. □ *You'll never trap me into going out with Roger!* □ *I was trapped into going there.*

trap someone or something **in** something to catch someone or something in a trap. □ *Jed accidentally trapped Tex in his bear trap.* □ *Jerry trapped a rabbit in his trap.*

travel a mile a minute Go to a mile a minute.

travel across something to make a journey across something or some place. □ *We have to travel across the desert to get there.* □ *I do not want to travel across that rickety bridge on the way back.*

travel at a fast clip Go to at a fast clip.

travel at a good clip Go to at a good clip.

Travel broadens the mind. *Prov.* When you travel, you learn things about the people and places you see. □ *Marie: I never realized how well-off most Americans are until I visited India. Jane: So it's true that travel broadens the mind, huh?* □ *Everyone who gets the chance should go abroad. Travel broadens the mind.*

travel by something **1.** to make a journey, using a particular conveyance. □ *I will go by train, since I don't like to travel by plane.* □ *We traveled by car, since that is the cheapest.* **2.** to make a journey under particular conditions. □ *I don't ever travel by night.* □ *We like to travel by day so we can see the scenery.*

travel for someone or something to go from place to place selling for someone or a company. □ *Walter travels for his uncle, who runs a toy factory.* □ *She travels for a company that makes men's clothing.*

travel in a body Go to in a body.

travel off the beaten path Go to off the beaten track.

travel on something **1.** to make a journey on a particular conveyance. □ *Do you like to travel on the train?* □ *I do not care to travel on the bus.* **2.** to travel having certain bodily states, such as on an empty stomach, on a full stomach. □ *I hate traveling on a full stomach.* □ *I can't stand to travel on a full stomach.*

travel over something **1.** to go over something as part of a journey. □ *We had to travel over an old bridge over the Mississippi to get to my sister's house.* □ *We will travel over a long narrow strip of land to get to the marina.* **2.** to travel widely over a great area. □ *She spent the summer traveling over Europe.* □ *I have traveled over the entire country and never failed to find someone I could talk to.*

travel through something **1.** to make a journey through some area or country. □ *We will have to travel through Germany to get there.* □ *Do you want to travel through the desert or through the mountains?* **2.** to make a journey through some kind of weather condition. □ *I hate to travel through the rain.* □ *I refuse to travel through a snowstorm.*

travel with someone **1.** to associate with someone; to move about in association with someone. □ *She travels with a sophisticated crowd.* □ *I am afraid that Walter is traveling with the wrong group of friends.* **2.** to make a journey with someone. □ *Do you mind if I travel with you?* □ *Who are you going to travel with?*

travel with something to have something with one as one travels. □ *I always travel with extra money.* □ *I hate to travel with three suitcases. That is more than I can handle.*

a **travesty of justice** a miscarriage of justice; an act of the legal system that is an insult to the system of justice.

□ *The jury's verdict was a travesty of justice.* □ *The lawyer complained that the judge's ruling was a travesty of justice.*

tread on someone's **toes** Go to **step on** someone's toes.

tread (up)on someone or something to walk or step on someone or something. (*Upon* is formal and less commonly used than *on*. *Step* is more common than *tread*.) □ *Don't tread on Sam, who is napping under the tree.* □ *Please don't tread on the freshly shampooed carpeting on the stairs.*

treat a case of something Go to a **case of** something.

treat someone **(for** something**) (with** something**)** to attempt to cure someone's illness, injury, or disease with something. □ *The doctor treated me for the flu with aspirin. It didn't work, but it was cheap.* □ *They treated him for his broken bones.* □ *Ann treated him with the appropriate therapy.*

treat someone or something **as** something to deal with someone or something as something. □ *Please don't treat me as a guest.* □ *You treat the editorial board as a needless barrier.*

treat someone or something **like** someone or something to deal with someone or something as if the person or thing were really someone, a type of a person, or something. □ *I like him. He treats me like a king.* □ *He treats Jane like Mary—he ignores them both.*

treat someone **to** something to provide and pay for something for someone as a gift or as entertainment. □ *I will be delighted to treat you to dinner.* □ *After the play, they treated themselves to pie and coffee.*

The **tree is known by its fruit.** *Prov.* People judge your character by what you do. (Biblical.) □ *The politician may say she believes in more spending on child care, but the tree is known by its fruit; she hasn't voted for a single measure that would help.*

trek across something to hike or march across something. □ *The scouts trekked across the fields of the small farming community.* □ *I don't look forward to trekking across the desert.*

trek to some place to hike or march to some place. □ *I have to trek all the way to the store because my car is in the shop.* □ *We trekked to the cabin and made that our base camp for the whole two weeks.*

tremble at something to shake with fear or anticipation at the thought of something. □ *David trembled at the thought of having to go to Russia by himself.* □ *Carl trembled at the idea of winning first place.*

tremble from something to shake or vibrate in response to something like an explosion or an earthquake. □ *The house trembled from the blast.* □ *I could feel the bridge trembling from the minor earthquake that I was hearing about on the radio.*

tremble with something to tremble because of something. □ *The children trembled with fear during the storm.* □ *David trembled with rage when he saw his slashed tires.*

trend toward something to move gradually toward something. □ *Fashions are trending toward the gaudy and flamboyant.* □ *Attitudes are trending toward the more conservative.*

trespass (up)on something to intrude or encroach onto a restricted or private area. (*Upon* is formal and less commonly used than *on*.) □ *You had better not trespass upon Mr. Green's land.* □ *I wouldn't trespass on that fenced-off land!*

trial and error trying repeatedly for success. □ *I finally found the right key after lots of trial and error.* □ *Sometimes trial and error is the only way to get something done.*

trial balloon a test of someone's or the public's reaction. □ *It was just a trial balloon, and it didn't work.* □ *The trial balloon was a great success.*

trials and tribulations *Cliché* problems and tests of one's courage or perseverance. □ *I suppose I have the normal trials and tribulations for a person of my background, but some days are just a little too much for me.* □ *I promise not to tell you of the trials and tribulations of my day if you promise not to tell me yours!*

Trick or treat! Give me a treat of some kind or I will play a trick on you! (The formulaic expression said by children after they ring someone's doorbell and the door is answered on Halloween. It is now understood to mean simply that the child is requesting a treat of some kind—candy, fruit, popcorn, etc.) □ *"Trick or treat!" cried Jimmy when the door opened.* □ *Mr. Franklin opened the door to find four very small children dressed like flowers standing silently on his doorstep. After a moment, he said, "Isn't anyone going to say 'Trick or treat'?"*

trick someone **into** (doing) something to fool someone; to deceive someone; to cheat someone. □ *The thief tricked John into giving him $10.* □ *Mary tricked her friends into paying for her dinner.*

trick someone **out of** something and **trick** something **out of** someone to get something from someone by trickery. □ *You can't trick me out of my money. I'm not that dumb!* □ *Stay alert so that no one tricks you out of your money.* □ *They tricked the information out of Bob.*

trickle away [for a liquid] to seep or dribble away. □ *All the water trickled away down the drain.* □ *After the last of the spilled milk had trickled away, Timmy began to cry.*

trickle down (to someone or something) **1.** *Lit.* [for a liquid] to seep or dribble downward to reach someone or something. □ *The water trickled down the wall to the floor.* □ *It trickled down very slowly.* **2.** *Fig.* [for something] to be distributed to someone or something in little bits at a time. □ *The results of the improved economy trickled down to people at lower-income levels.* □ *Information about what happened finally trickled down to me.*

trickle in(to something) **1.** *Lit.* [for a liquid] to seep or dribble into something or a place. □ *Some of the rainwater trickled into my car through a leak.* □ *It trickled in during the night.* **2.** *Fig.* [for someone or something] to come into something or a place, a few at a time. □ *The audience trickled into the hall little by little.* □ *They trickled in over a period of an hour or more.*

trickle out (of something) **1.** *Lit.* [for a liquid] to leak or dribble out of something or a place. □ *The oil trickled out of the engine little by little.* □ *It trickled out and made a puddle on the floor.* **2.** *Fig.* [for someone or something] to go out of something or a place, a few at a time. □ *The dissatisfied members of the audience trickled out of the theater*

three and four at a time. □ *They trickled out as the evening wore on.*

trickle through (something**) 1.** *Lit.* [for a liquid] to seep through something. □ *The water trickled through the cracked windowpane.* □ *They taped the glass, but the water trickled through anyway.* **2.** *Fig.* [for someone or something] to move through something little by little. □ *The people trickled through the door into the store in far smaller numbers than we had expected.* □ *They trickled through very slowly.*

*****the **tricks of the trade** special skills and knowledge associated with any trade or profession. (*Typically: **know** ~; **learn** ~; **show** someone ~; **teach** someone ~.) □ *I know a few tricks of the trade that make things easier.* □ *I learned the tricks of the trade from my uncle.*

tried and true trustworthy; dependable. (Hyphenated before nominals.) □ *The method I use to cure the hiccups is tried and true.* □ *Finally, her old tried-and-true methods failed because she hadn't fine-tuned them to the times.*

trifle something **away**[†] (**on** someone or something) to waste something, such as money, on someone or something, little by little. □ *Don't trifle all your money away on your friends.* □ *Don't trifle away any more money on silly purchases.*

trifle with someone or something to act without seriousness or respect toward someone or something. □ *Don't talk that way to me! I am not to be trifled with.* □ *I wish that Ann wouldn't trifle with our efforts at reform.*

trigger someone **off**[†] to cause someone to become angry. (Fig. on **trigger** something **off**.) □ *Your rude comments triggered her off.* □ *Your comments triggered off Bob's temper.*

trigger something **off**[†] to set something off, such as an explosion. □ *We were afraid that the sparks from the engine would trigger an explosion off.* □ *The sparks triggered off an explosion.*

trim (oneself**) down** to take action to become slimmer or lose weight. □ *I need to trim myself down before I go on vacation.* □ *I decided to trim down, but I never got around to it.* □ *You really need to trim down and stay at a lower weight.*

trim something **away**[†] (**from** something) to cut something away (from something). □ *The butcher trimmed the fat away from the steak.* □ *Please trim away the fat from the meat.*

trim something **down**[†] to reduce the size of something. □ *You will have to trim the picture down to get it into the frame.* □ *Trim down the picture before you frame it.*

trim something **from** something to cut something away from something. □ *I trimmed the fat from the steaks.* □ *We had to trim a lot of the fat from the meat after we got it home.*

trim something **off (of)** someone or something and **trim** something **off**[†] to cut something off someone or something. (*Of* is usually retained before pronouns.) □ *I asked the barber to trim the beard off of Ralph.* □ *The barber trimmed off Ralph's beard.*

trim something **with** something to decorate something with something. □ *She trimmed the dress with lace.* □ *Bobby and Timmy trimmed the tree with colorful ornaments.*

T

trip along to move along happily. □ *The kids tripped along on their way to school.* □ *We were just tripping along, not having any notion of what was about to happen.*

trip on someone or something and **trip over** someone or something to stumble on someone or something. □ *The place was filled with sleeping people. I tripped over perfect strangers on my way to the door.* □ *I tripped on a brick and fell into the wall.*

trip someone **up**[†] **1.** *Lit.* to cause someone to trip; to entangle someone's feet. (*Someone* includes *oneself.*) □ *The rope strewn about the deck tripped him up.* □ *The lines tripped up the crew.* **2.** *Fig.* to cause someone to falter while speaking, thinking, etc. □ *Mary came in while the speaker was talking and the distraction tripped him up.* □ *The noise in the audience tripped up the speaker.*

trip the light fantastic *Jocular* to dance. □ *Shall we go trip the light fantastic?*

triumph over someone or something to achieve victory over someone or something. □ *Our team triumphed over all the others.* □ *Our army triumphed over theirs.*

troop across someone or something [for a mass of creatures] to move across someone or something. □ *The huge herds of wildebeest began to troop across the plain in search of food.* □ *The ants trooped across Karen as she lay in the sand.*

troop in(to something**)** to flock or march into something or some place in numbers. □ *The scouts trooped into the mess hall and sat down.* □ *They trooped in and sat down.*

trot after someone to follow along after someone, as done by a small dog. □ *The puppy trotted along after the kids wherever they went.* □ *My little brother would always come trotting after us, annoying us a lot.*

trot along to step along in a lively fashion. □ *The horses trotted along in time with the music.* □ *The horses were trotting along, going exactly where we led them.*

trot someone or something **out**[†] to bring out and display someone or something. □ *The boss trotted the new vice president out for us to meet.* □ *The boss trotted out his daughter and introduced her as a new vice president.* □ *Fred trotted out his favorite project for everyone to see.*

trot something **out**[†] *Fig.* to mention something regularly or habitually, without giving it much thought. (*Fig.* on the image of trotting out a pony for display.) □ *When James disagreed with Mary, she simply trotted her same old political arguments out.* □ *Bob always trots out the same excuses for being late.*

Trouble is brewing. and **There is trouble brewing.** *Fig.* Trouble is developing. □ *Trouble's brewing at the office. I have to get there early tomorrow.* □ *There is trouble brewing in the government. The prime minister may resign.*

trouble one's **head about** someone or something to worry about someone or something. □ *Please don't trouble your head about me. I'll get along.* □ *I wish you wouldn't trouble your head about the problem. We can solve it.*

trouble oneself **about** someone or something to worry oneself about someone or something. (Usually in the negative.) □ *Please don't trouble yourself about me. I'm doing fine.* □ *I can't take time to trouble myself about this matter. Do it yourself.*

trouble oneself **(to** do something**)** to bother oneself to do something. □ *He didn't even trouble himself to turn off the light when he left.* □ *No, thank you. I don't need any help. Please don't trouble yourself.*

A **trouble shared is a trouble halved.** *Prov.* If you tell someone about a problem you are having, or request someone's help with a problem, the problem will not seem so daunting. (Can be used to encourage someone to confide in you or ask for your help.) □ *Jill: Is something wrong? You've seemed so depressed lately. Jane: Oh, I wouldn't want to bother you with it. Jill: Don't be silly. A trouble shared is a trouble halved, remember.*

trouble someone **about** someone or something to bother someone by asking about someone or something. □ *Please don't trouble me about Larry.* □ *Can I trouble you about a billing problem?*

trouble someone **for** something to ask someone to pass something or give something. (Usually a question.) □ *Could I trouble you for the salt?* □ *Could I trouble you for some advice?*

trouble someone **to** do something to ask someone to do something. (Usually a question.) □ *Could I trouble you to pass the salt?* □ *Could I trouble you to give me some advice?*

trouble someone **with** something to bother someone with something, such as a question or a problem. □ *I hate to trouble you with this, but could you help me adjust my binoculars?* □ *Don't trouble yourself with this matter.*

trudge along to plod along on foot. □ *It seemed as if we trudged along for miles.* □ *As we trudged along, we forgot how cold it was.*

trudge through something **1.** *Lit.* to walk through snow, sand, or something similar. □ *We trudged through the hot sand all the way down the beach.* □ *I used to have to trudge through snow like this all winter to get to school.* **2.** *Fig.* to work one's way through something difficult. □ *I hate to have to trudge through these reports on the weekend.* □ *I have to trudge through a lot of work before I can go home.*

***true as steel** very loyal and dependable. (*Also: **as ~**.*) □ *Through all my troubles, my husband has been as true as steel.* □ *Pedro was a staunch friend, true as steel.*

true something **up**[†] to straighten something up; to put something into true plumb. □ *Please true this door frame up better before you hang the door.* □ *Can you true up this wall a little?*

true to form exactly as expected; following the usual pattern. (Often with *running*, as in the example.) □ *As usual, John is late. At least he's running true to form.* □ *And true to form, Mary left before the meeting was adjourned.*

true to one's **word** keeping one's promise. □ *True to his word, Tom showed up at exactly eight o'clock.* □ *We'll soon know if Jane is true to her word. We'll see if she does what she promised.*

trump something **up**[†] **1.** to promote or boost something. □ *They think they have to trump something up to get people to see it.* □ *They trumped up the movie so much that many people were disappointed when it finally came out.* **2.** to think something up; to contrive something. □ *Do you just sit around trumping charges up against innocent people?* □ *They trumped up the charges in an effort to disgrace me.*

trumped up 1. heavily promoted; overly praised. (Hyphenated before nominal.) □ *I don't care for trumped-up stuff like that movie.* □ *That movie was so trumped up. I expected to see something much better than it turned out to be.* **2.** made-up; contrived. □ *They put Larry in the slammer on some trumped-up charge.* □ *It was a silly, trumped-up idea. Just forget it.*

truss someone or something **up**† to bind, tie, or bundle someone or something up. □ *The attendants trussed Walter up and took him to a padded cell.* □ *They trussed up Walter tightly.* □ *Ann trussed the bundle up and sent it off.*

trust in someone or something to believe in someone or something. □ *Trust in me. I know what I am saying.* □ *Can I trust in the figures in this report?*

Trust me! I am telling you the truth. Please believe me. □ *Tom said with great conviction, "Trust me! I know exactly what to do!"* □ *Mary: Do you really think we can keep this party a secret until Thursday? Sally: Trust me! I know how to plan a surprise party.*

trust someone **for** something to depend on someone for payment for something. □ *I will lend you one hundred dollars. I know I can trust you for it.* □ *I loaned Ted a lot of money. It's all right. I can trust him for it.*

trust someone or something **to** someone to leave someone or something in the possession of someone whom you assume will take good care of someone or something. □ *Can I trust my little Jimmy to you?* □ *I am perfectly comfortable trusting this money to you.*

trust someone **to** do something to believe that someone can be relied on to do something. □ *You can trust her to be here on time.* □ *I can't trust myself to eat wisely.*

trust someone **with** someone or something to leave someone in the care of someone or something. □ *Can I trust you with my uncle? He needs to have his medicine right on time.* □ *I am sure I can trust you with the money.* □ *Don't leave that cake with me. I can't trust myself with it.*

Truth is stranger than fiction. Go to Fact is stranger than fiction.

The truth will out. *Prov.* The truth will always be discovered. (Can be used to remark that someone who had been concealing the truth is now revealing it, as in the second example.) □ *The embezzler may think that someone else will be blamed for his crime, but the truth will out.* □ *Ellen: Remember last week, when I told you I bought some shoes? Fred: Yes. . . . Ellen: Well, before you look at the bill from the shoe store, I ought to tell you that I bought ten pairs. Fred: Aha. The truth will out.*

try as I may and **try as I might** *Cliché* a phrase that introduces an expression of regret or failure. □ *Bill: Try as I may, I cannot get this thing put together right. Andy: Did you read the instructions?* □ *Rachel: Wow! This place is a mess! Mother: Try as I might, I can't get Andrew to clean up after himself.*

try as I might Go to previous.

*a **try at** someone and *a **shot at** someone; *a **crack at** someone; *a **go at** someone *a **stab at** someone an attempt to convince someone of something; an attempt to try to get information out of someone; an attempt to try to train someone to do something. (The expressions with *shot* and *crack* are more informal than the main entry phrase. (*Typically:* **take** ~; **have** ~; **give** someone ~.) □ *Let me have a crack at him. I can make him talk.* □ *Let the new teacher have a try at Billy. She can do marvels with unwilling learners.* □ *Give me a crack at him. I know how to make these bums talk.*

*a **try at** something and *a **shot at** something; *a **crack at** something; *a **go at** something; *a **stab at** something; *a **whack at** something to take a turn at trying to do something. (*Typically:* **take** ~; **have** ~; **give** someone ~.) □ *All of us wanted to have a try at the prize-winning shot.* □ *Let Sally have a shot at it.* □ *If you let me have a crack at it, maybe I can be successful.*

try for something to try to win or achieve something. □ *I am going to try for the silver trophy in this year's race.* □ *Will you try for a place on the team?*

Try me. Ask me.; Give me a chance. □ *A: I don't suppose you know what the Achaean League is. B: Try me.*

try one's **hand (at** something**)** to take a try at something. □ *Someday I'd like to try my hand at flying a plane.* □ *Give me a chance. Let me try my hand!*

try one's **luck (at** something**)** to attempt to do something (where success requires luck). □ *My great-grandfather came to California to try his luck at finding gold.* □ *I went into a gambling casino to try my luck.*

try one's **wings (out**†**)** *Fig.* to try to do something one has recently become qualified to do. (Fig. on the image of a young bird trying to fly.) □ *I recently learned to snorkel, and I want to go to the seaside to try my wings.* □ *You've read about it enough. It's time to try out your wings.*

try out (for something**)** to audition for a part in some performance or other activity requiring skill. □ *I intend to try out for the play.* □ *I'm going to try out, too.*

try someone **back (again)** to try to return someone's telephone call again. □ *She's not in, so I'll try her back later.* □ *Jan will try her back.*

try someone **for** something to put someone through a court trial for some crime or wrongdoing. □ *The prosecutor wanted to try Harry for fraud.* □ *Anne was tried for shoplifting.*

try someone or something **out**† to test someone or something for a while; to sample the performance of someone or something. □ *We will try her out in the editorial department and see how she does.* □ *We will try out this employee in another department for a while.*

try someone's **patience** to strain someone's patience; to bother someone as if testing the person's patience. (*Try* means *test* here.) □ *My loud neighbors are trying my patience today.* □ *You really try my patience with all your questions!*

try something **(on**†**) (for size) 1.** *Lit.* to put on an article of clothing to see if it fits. □ *Here, try this on for size and see if it fits any better.* □ *Please try on this shirt for size.* **2.** *Fig.* to evaluate an idea or proposition. □ *Now, try on this idea.* □ *Try this plan for size. I think you'll like it.*

try something **on with** someone to get someone's opinion about an idea or plan. □ *Let me try this idea on with you.* □ *She tried the new idea on with the boss, but the response was not good.*

try something **out**† **on** someone to see how someone responds to something or some idea. □ *Let me try this idea out on you and see what you think.* □ *Let me try out this new medicine on her.*

trying times Go to bad times.

tub of lard a fat person. (Insulting.) □ *Who's that tub of lard who just came in?* □ *That tub of lard can hardly get through the door.*

tuck into something to begin eating something vigorously. □ *The kids really tucked into the stew.* □ *I could see from the way that they tucked into their meal that they were really hungry.*

tuck someone **in(to)** something and **tuck** someone **in**† to place someone into something carefully; to wrap someone in blankets or something similar. □ *Father tucked Jimmy into bed an hour later than he should have.* □ *Please tuck in Jimmy.*

tuck something **around** someone or something to wrap something snugly around someone or something. □ *I tucked crumpled newspapers around the cups in the box to keep them from breaking.* □ *Molly-Jo tucked the covers around the baby.*

tuck something **away**† **1.** *Lit.* to hide or store something away. □ *Tuck this away where you can find it later.* □ *Can you tuck away this money somewhere?* **2.** *Fig.* to eat something. □ *The boys tucked away three pizzas and an apple pie.* □ *When I was younger, I could tuck away my dinner in no time at all.*

tuck something **in(to)** something and **tuck** something **in**† to fold or stuff something into something. □ *Please tuck your shirttail into your pants.* □ *Tuck in your shirttail.* □ *When you make the bed, you have to tuck the sheets in.*

tuck something **up**† to raise up some part of one's clothing and attach it temporarily. □ *She tucked her skirt up and waded through the flooded basement.* □ *She tucked up her skirt.*

tuck something **up**† **(under** something**)** to place or push something, such as cloth, up under something. □ *Tuck the sheet up under the mattress when you make the bed.* □ *Tuck up the sheet under the mattress when you make the bed.*

tucker someone **out** to tire someone out. □ *All this work has tuckered me out.* □ *The heavy work tuckered the staff out early in the day.*

tug at someone or something to pull at someone or something. □ *Stop tugging at me! I'll talk to you in a minute.* □ *The dog tugged at my pants cuff.*

tug away (at something**)** to pull hard at something; to haul something. □ *She tugged away at the rope, but the anchor would not budge.* □ *No matter how much she tugged away, it didn't move.*

tumble along to roll or bounce along. □ *The ball tumbled along, across the lawn and into the street.* □ *As the boulder tumbled along, it crushed everything in its path.*

tumble down to fall down; to topple. □ *The old barn was so rickety that it almost tumbled down on its own.* □ *The pile of books tumbled down all over the floor.*

tumble from something to fall from something. □ *The food tumbled from the tray and fell to the floor.* □ *The books tumbled from the shelf during the earthquake.*

tumble into bed to get into or fall into bed. □ *Liz went home and tumbled into bed.*

tumble into someone or something to fall down and roll into someone or something. (Either accidentally or on purpose.) □ *Liz tripped and tumbled into the table.* □ *She tumbled into Ken.*

tumble out of something to fall, topple, or drop out of something. □ *Don't let the baby tumble out of the chair!* □ *The children tumbled out of the car and ran for the school building.*

tumble over to fall over. □ *The vase tumbled over and broke.* □ *I held Timmy up to keep him from tumbling over.*

tumble over someone or something to trip or stumble over someone or something and fall down. □ *I tumbled over Fred, who was napping under the tree.* □ *I tumbled over a chair and fell down.*

tumble over (something**)** to fall over the edge of something. □ *Stay away from the edge. I don't want any of you tumbling over it.* □ *Don't go too close. You'll tumble over.*

tumble someone or something **down** something to tip or push someone or something down something. □ *Timmy tumbled his brother down the hill.* □ *Ann tumbled her laundry down the chute.*

tune in (on someone or something**)** and **tune in (to** someone or something**) 1.** *Lit.* to adjust a radio or television set to receive a broadcast of someone or something. □ *Let's tune in on the late news.* □ *I don't want to tune in tonight.* **2.** and **tune in (to** something**)** *Fig.* to pay attention to someone or something. □ *I just can't tune in on these professors.* □ *I listen and I try, but I just can't tune in.*

tune in (to something**)** Go to tune in (on someone or something).

tune out *Fig.* to cease paying attention to anything at all. □ *I wasn't interested, so I just tuned out.* □ *I think that most of the audience tuned out during the last part of the lecture.*

tune someone or something **out**† to put someone or something out of one's consciousness; to cease paying attention to someone or something. □ *I had to tune the radio out in order to concentrate.* □ *I tuned out what the speaker was saying and daydreamed for a while.*

tune something **in**† to adjust a radio or television set so that something can be received. □ *Could you tune the newscast in?* □ *Please tune in the station a little better.*

tune something **up**† *Fig.* to adjust an engine to run the best and most efficiently. □ *You need to tune this engine up.* □ *Please tune up this engine so it will run more economically.*

tune up [for one or more musicians] to bring their instruments into tune. □ *You could hear the orchestra behind the curtain, tuning up.* □ *We have to tune up before the concert.*

tuned in aware; up-to-date. □ *Jan is tuned in and alert to what is going on around her.* □ *Hey, Jill! Get tuned in, why don't you?*

tunnel through something to make a tunnel or passageway through something or a group of people. □ *Roger had to tunnel through the crowd to get to the rest room.* □ *The workers tunneled through the soft soil to reach the buried cable.*

tunnel under someone or something to dig a tunnel under someone or something. □ *All the time she was standing in the yard talking about the moles, they were tunneling under her.* □ *They took many months to tunnel under the English Channel.*

tunnel vision 1. *Lit.* a visual impairment wherein one can only see what is directly ahead of oneself. □ *I have tunnel vision, so I have to keep looking from side to side.* **2.** *Fig.* an inability to recognize other ways of doing things or thinking about things. □ *The boss really has tunnel vision about sales and marketing. He sees no reason to change anything.*

a **turkey's nest** Go to a dust bunny.

turn a blind eye (to someone or something**)** *Fig.* to ignore something and pretend you do not see it. □ *The usher turned a blind eye to the little boy who sneaked into the theater.* □ *How can you turn a blind eye to all those starving children?*

turn a deaf ear (to someone or something**)** to ignore what someone says; to ignore a cry for help. □ *How can you just turn a deaf ear to their cries for food and shelter?* □ *Jack turned a deaf ear to our pleading.*

turn a place **upside down** *Fig.* to search a place thoroughly. □ *The cops turned the whole house upside down but never found the gun.* □ *I had to turn the place upside down to find my car keys.*

turn a profit to earn a profit. □ *The company plans to turn a profit two years from now.*

turn a trick *Sl.* to perform an act of prostitution. (Use caution with the topic.) □ *She can turn a trick and be on the streets again in six minutes flat.* □ *She's upstairs, turning a trick.*

turn about Go to turn around.

turn against someone or something Go to **against** someone or something.

turn around and **turn about** to reverse direction; to face the opposite direction or turn completely. □ *The bus turned around and went the other way.* □ *Please turn around so I can see who you are.*

turn (away) (from someone or something**)** to turn oneself to avoid someone or something. □ *She turned away from me as I walked past, pretending not to see me.* □ *She turned from Ken and ran.*

turn back (from some place**)** to stop one's journey and return. □ *We turned back from the amusement park so we could go home and get the tickets we had forgotten.* □ *We turned back at the last minute.*

turn back the clock and **turn the clock back**

turn belly up and **go belly up 1.** *Sl.* to fail. (See also turn turtle.) □ *I sort of felt that the whole thing would go belly up, and I was right.* □ *The computer—on its last legs anyway—turned belly up right in the middle of an important job.* **2.** *Sl.* to die. (As a fish does when it dies.) □ *The cat was acting strangely for a while before she turned belly up.* □ *Every fish in Greg's tank went belly up last night.*

turn in 1. [for something] to fold or point inward. □ *Do my toes turn in too much?* □ *The legs of the table turned in at the bottom, giving a quaint appearance to the piece of furniture.* **2.** [for someone] to go to bed. □ *It's time to turn in. Good night.* □ *I want to turn in early tonight.*

turn in (up)on oneself to become introverted. □ *Over the years, she had turned in upon herself and was quiet and alone.* □ *The death of his wife caused Jed to turn in on himself.*

turn in((to) some place**)** to walk or steer one's vehicle into a place. □ *Turn into the next service station for some gas.* □ *I'll turn in for gas now.* □ *She walked down the street and turned into the drugstore.*

turn into someone or something to change into someone or something. □ *After work is over, he turns into a fairly nice person.* □ *The room turned into a very pleasant place when the lights were dimmed.*

a **turn of fate** Go to a twist of fate.

the **turn of the century** the time when the year changes to one with two final zeros, such as from 1899 to 1900. (Although technically incorrect—a new century begins with the year ending in 01—most people ignore this.) □ *My family moved to America at the turn of the century.* □ *My uncle was born before the turn of the last century.*

turn off [for something] to go off; to switch off. □ *All the lights turn off automatically.*

turn off something to walk or turn a vehicle one way or another so that one leaves the road or route to another. □ *You are supposed to turn off the highway at the yellow mailbox.*

turn off (something**) onto** something to walk or steer one's vehicle from one route to another. □ *I turned off the main highway onto a side road.* □ *Ann turned off onto the shoulder.*

turn off (something**) (**some place**)** to walk or steer one's vehicle off a route at a particular place. □ *Turn off the highway at the first exit after the city.* □ *Let's turn off here.* □ *We turned off the path just past the big oak tree.*

turn on 1. *Lit.* [for something] to switch on and start running. □ *The lights turned on right at dusk.* □ *At what time do the street lights turn on?* **2.** *Fig.* to become interested or excited. □ *He turns on when he sees the mountains.* □ *Ann will turn on if she hears this song.*

turn on a dime *Fig.* [for a vehicle] to turn in a very tight turn. □ *This car can turn on a dime.* □ *I need a vehicle that can turn on a dime.*

turn on someone to attack someone. □ *I thought the strange dog was friendly, but suddenly it turned on me and bit me.* □ *Bob knows a lot about lions, and he says that no matter how well they are trained, there is always the danger that they'll turn on you.*

turn on the waterworks *Fig.* to begin to cry. □ *Every time Billy got homesick, he turned on the waterworks.* □ *Sally hurt her knee and turned on the waterworks for about twenty minutes.*

Turn on, tune in, drop out. A slogan (popularized by Dr. Timothy Leary) promoting the use of LSD among young people. □ *The key phrase in the heyday of acid was "turn on, tune in, drop out."* □ *Millions heard "turn on, tune in, drop out" and did just that.*

turn one's **back (on** someone or something**) 1.** *Lit.* to turn one's body so that one's back faces someone or something. □ *I turned my back on the dead horse and walked slowly away.* □ *I turned my back on the shouting man and left the* room. **2.** *Fig.* to abandon or ignore someone or something. □ *Don't turn your back on your old friends.* □ *Bob has a tendency to turn his back on serious problems.* □ *This matter needs your attention. Please don't just turn your back.*

turn one's **hand to** something to begin to or to be able to do something. □ *I would like to turn my hand to Chinese cooking.* □ *He gave up accounting and turned his hand to writing poetry.*

turn one's **nose up†** **at** someone or something **1.** *Lit.* to raise one's head and therefore one's nose slightly as a sign of rejection. □ *I never turn my nose up at food.* □ *I never turn up my nose at dessert, no matter what it is.* **2.** *Fig.* to sneer at someone or something; to reject someone or something. □ *John turned his nose up at Ann, and that hurt her feelings.* □ *He turned up his nose.*

turn one hundred and eighty degrees Go to do a one-eighty.

turn onto something **1.** *Lit.* to walk or steer one's vehicle onto a road, highway, or path. □ *Turn onto the main road and go west about a mile.* □ *As she turned onto the familiar highway, she realized that she had left her purse in the store.* **2. turn onto** someone or something *Inf. Fig.* to become interested in someone or something. □ *Jeff turned onto electronics at the age of fourteen.* □ *I tried to get her to turn onto me, but she could only think of John.*

turn out [for something] to aim outward. □ *Her toes turned out just right for a ballet dancer.* □ *The legs of the chair turned out just a little, adding a bit of stability.*

turn out (all right) and **pan out; work out (all right)** to end satisfactorily. □ *I hope everything turns out all right.* □ *Oh, yes. It'll all pan out.* □ *Things usually work out, no matter how bad they seem.*

turn out (for something) [for people, especially an audience] to [leave home to] attend some event. □ *A lot of people turned out for our meeting.* □ *Almost all the residents turned out for the meeting.*

turn out somehow to end in a particular way, such as well, badly, all right, etc. □ *I hope everything turns out all right.* □ *The party did not turn out well.*

turn out (that) to happen; to end up; to result. □ *After it was all over, it turned out that both of us were pleased with the bargain.* □ *Have you heard how the game turned out?*

turn out to be someone or something to develop or become someone or something in the end. □ *In the end, he turned out to be a handsome prince in disguise.* □ *The previous prince turned out to be a frog.*

turn over 1. *Lit.* to rotate so that the side that was on the bottom is now on top. □ *The turtle turned over and crawled away.* □ *She turned over to get some sun on her back.* **2.** and **kick over** *Fig.* [for an engine] to start or to rotate. □ *My car engine was so cold that it wouldn't even turn over.* □ *The engine kicked over a few times and then stopped for good.* **3.** *Fig.* to undergo exchange; to be replaced. □ *The employees turn over pretty regularly in this department.*

turn over a new leaf *Fig.* to begin again, fresh; to reform and begin again. (*Fig.* on turning to a fresh page. The leaf is a page—a fresh, clean page.) □ *I have made a mess of my life. I'll turn over a new leaf and hope to do better.* □

Why don't you turn over a new leaf and surprise everyone with your good characteristics?

turn (over) in one's **grave** and **roll (over) in** one's **grave** *Fig.* to show enormous disfavor for something that has happened after one's death. □ *If our late father heard you say that, he'd turn over in his grave.* □ *Please don't change the place around too much when I'm dead. I do not wish to be rolling in my grave all the time.*

turn some place **inside out** *Fig.* to search some place thoroughly. □ *I will find that book if I have to turn this place inside out!* □ *I turned the room inside out and still didn't find it.*

turn someone **aside†** to divert someone from the flow of people. □ *The attendant turned the poorly dressed man aside.* □ *The attendant turned aside all the persons who arrived late.*

turn someone **down†** to issue a refusal to someone. □ *We had to turn Joan down, even though her proposal was okay.* □ *We turned down Joan, even though her credentials were good.*

turn someone **off†** to dull someone's interest in someone or something. □ *The boring prof turned me off to the subject.* □ *The preacher set out to turn off the congregation to sin.*

turn someone **on†** to excite or interest someone. □ *Fast music with a good beat turns me on.* □ *That stuff doesn't turn on anyone.*

turn someone or an animal **(away) (from** something) to cause someone or an animal to avoid moving toward something; to cause someone or an animal to avoid moving toward harm. □ *The police officer turned the pedestrians away from the scene of the accident.* □ *He turned the horses away from the gate.*

turn someone or an animal **out of** something and **turn** someone or an animal **out†** to eject someone or an animal from a place. □ *She turned her own son out of the house.* □ *You wouldn't turn a cat out on a night like this, would you?* □ *She actually turned out her own brother!*

turn someone or something **against** someone or something to cause someone to defy or revolt against someone or something; to make someone antagonistic toward someone or something. □ *He turned the whole board against Molly.* □ *She turned the city council against the proposed law.*

turn someone or something **back†** to cause someone or something to stop and go back; to cause someone or something to retreat. □ *The border guards turned us back because we had no passports.* □ *They turned back the bus because the bridge was down.*

turn someone or something **in†** **(to** someone or something) to submit or refer someone or something to someone or a group, especially in some official capacity. □ *The good citizen turned his neighbor in for watering his lawn during the wrong hours.* □ *I turned in the report to the treasurer.*

turn someone or something **inside out** to evert someone or something; to pull the inside of someone or something out to become the outside. (With people, this refers to mutilation.) □ *I felt like the explosion was going to turn me inside out.* □ *Ken turned his pockets inside out.*

turn someone or something **into** someone or something to change someone or something into someone or something else. ☐ *The magician tried to turn Ginny into a robin.* ☐ *She turned the parrot into a dove.*

turn someone or something **over**† to rotate someone or something so that the side that was on the bottom is now on the top. ☐ *The nurses turned the patient over so they could give her some medicine.* ☐ *They turned over the unconscious patient.*

turn someone or something **over**† **to** someone or something to release or assign someone or something to someone or something; to transfer or deliver someone or something to someone or something. ☐ *The deputy turned the bank robber over to the sheriff.* ☐ *I turned over the money I found to the police.*

turn someone or something **to** something to aim someone or something to face something. ☐ *The nurse turned the old man to the sun so he could get warm.* ☐ *Ken turned the plant to the light.*

turn someone or something **toward** someone or something to turn someone or something to face someone or something. ☐ *The nurse turned the old man toward his daughter, who had come to visit him.* ☐ *Ken turned the microphone toward the speaker.*

turn someone or something **up**† **1.** *Lit.* to increase the volume of a device emitting the sound of someone or something. ☐ *I can't hear the lecturer. Turn her up.* ☐ *Turn up the radio, please.* **2.** *Fig.* to discover or locate someone or something. ☐ *See if you can turn up any evidence for his presence on the night of January 16.* ☐ *Have you been able to turn up a date for Friday night?*

turn someone or something **upside down 1.** *Lit.* to invert someone or something. ☐ *The wrestler turned his opponent upside down and dropped him on his head.* ☐ *I turned the bottle upside down, trying to get the last drop out.* **2.** *Fig.* to upset someone or something; to thoroughly confuse someone or something. ☐ *The whole business turned me upside down. It'll take days to recover.*

turn someone **out**† **1.** *Lit.* to send someone out of somewhere. ☐ *I didn't pay my rent, so the manager turned me out.* ☐ *I'm glad it's not winter. I'd hate to turn out someone in the snow.* **2.** *Fig.* to train or produce someone with certain skills or talents. ☐ *The state law school turns lawyers out by the dozen.* ☐ *A committee accused the state university of turning out too many veterinarians.*

turn someone's **head** *Fig.* [for flattery or success] to distract someone; to cause someone not to be sensible. ☐ *Don't let our praise turn your head. You're not perfect!* ☐ *Her successes had turned her head. She was now quite arrogant.*

turn someone's **stomach** *Fig.* to upset one's stomach. ☐ *The violent movie turned my stomach.* ☐ *The rich, creamy food turned John's stomach.*

turn someone's **water off**† *Sl.* to deflate someone; to silence someone. ☐ *He said you were stupid, huh? Well, I guess that turns your water off!* ☐ *That really turned off her water.*

turn something **around** and **turn** something **about** to reverse the direction of something; to cause something to face the opposite direction. ☐ *Turn the car around and*

head it in the other direction. ☐ *If you turn the chair around, we can see one another while we talk.*

turn something **aside**† to evade something. ☐ *Ann turned the awkward questions aside.* ☐ *She turned aside the questions she didn't want to answer.*

turn something **down**† **1.** to bend or fold something down. ☐ *He turned his coat collar down when he got inside the house.* ☐ *Timmy had turned down his cuffs and caught one of them in his bicycle chain.* **2.** to decrease the volume of something. ☐ *Please turn the radio down.* ☐ *Can't you turn down that stereo?* **3.** to reject something; to deny someone's request. ☐ *The board turned our request down.* ☐ *She had turned down John's offer of help, too.*

turn something **off**† to switch something off so that it stops running or operating. ☐ *Please turn the light off.* ☐ *Turn off the lights as you leave.*

turn something **on**† to switch on something to make it run. ☐ *I turned the microwave oven on and cooked dinner.* ☐ *I turned on the lights when the sun went down.*

turn something **out**† **1.** to manufacture or produce something in numbers. ☐ *The factory turns too few cars out.* ☐ *The factory turns out about seventy-five cars a day.* **2.** to turn off a light. ☐ *Please turn the hall light out.* ☐ *Turn out the light.*

turn something **over**† **in** one's **mind** *Fig.* to think about something. ☐ *I have to turn your suggestion over in my mind a bit before I decide what to do.* ☐ *After Alice had turned the matter over in her mind, she gave us her verdict.* ☐ *Please take some time to turn over this matter in your mind.*

turn something **to good account** to use something in such a way that it is to one's advantage; to make good use of a situation, experience, etc. ☐ *Pam turned her illness to good account and did a lot of reading.* ☐ *Many people turn their retirement time to good account and take up interesting hobbies.*

turn something **to** one's **advantage** to make an advantage for oneself out of something (which might otherwise be a disadvantage). ☐ *Sally found a way to turn the problem to her advantage.* ☐ *The ice cream store manager was able to turn the hot weather to her advantage.*

turn something **under** (something) to fold something underneath something. ☐ *Please turn the frayed edge of the sheet under so that it does not show.* ☐ *Please turn the edge under.*

turn something **up**† **1.** to bend or fold something up. (See also **turn up.**) ☐ *Please turn your cuffs up. They are getting muddy.* ☐ *He turned up his coat collar to keep the rain off his neck.* **2.** to turn playing cards face up. ☐ *Please turn all the cards up.* ☐ *Sally turned up the cards one at a time.*

turn something **upside down** *Fig.* to throw things all about in a thorough search for someone or something. ☐ *We turned this place upside down, looking for the lost ring.* ☐ *Please don't turn everything upside down, looking for your book.*

turn tail (and run) *Fig.* to flee; to run away in fright. ☐ *I couldn't just turn tail and run, but I wasn't going to fight that monster, either.* ☐ *Sometimes turning tail is the only sensible thing to do.*

turn the clock back and **turn back the clock 1.** *Lit.* to set a clock to an earlier time. □ *I have to turn the clocks back each fall.* □ *Please turn back the clock.* **2.** *Fig.* to try to return to the past. □ *You are not facing up to the future. You are trying to turn the clock back to a time when you were more comfortable.* □ *Let us turn back the clock and pretend we are living at the turn of the century—the time that our story takes place.*

turn the corner *Fig.* to pass a critical point in a process. □ *The patient turned the corner last night. She should begin to show improvement now.* □ *The project has turned the corner. The rest should be easy.*

turn the heat up† (**on** someone) *Fig.* to use force to persuade someone to do something; to increase the pressure on someone to do something. □ *Management is turning the heat up to increase production.* □ *The teacher really turned up the heat on the students by saying that everyone would be punished if the real culprit was not found.*

turn the other cheek *Fig.* to ignore abuse or an insult. □ *When Bob got mad at Mary and yelled at her, she just turned the other cheek.* □ *Usually I turn the other cheek when someone is rude to me.*

turn the other way *Fig.* to look away and ignore someone or something. □ *When I tried to talk to her, she turned the other way and made it clear that she was angry.*

turn the tables (**on** someone) *Fig.* to cause a reversal in someone's plans; to make one's plans turn back on one. □ *I went to Jane's house to help get ready for a surprise party for Bob. It turned out that the surprise party was for me! Jane really turned the tables on me!* □ *Turning the tables like that requires a lot of planning and a lot of secrecy.*

turn the tide *Fig.* to cause a reversal in the direction of events; to cause a reversal in public opinion. □ *It looked as if the team were going to lose, but near the end of the game, our star player turned the tide.* □ *At first, people were opposed to our plan. After a lot of discussion, we were able to turn the tide.*

turn three hundred and sixty degrees Go to **do a three-sixty.**

turn thumbs down (**on** someone or something) *Fig.* to reject someone or something; to grow to reject someone or something. □ *The boss turned thumbs down on Tom. They would have to find someone else.* □ *The minute I saw it, I turned thumbs down.*

turn thumbs up (**on** someone or something) *Fig.* to accept someone or something; to approve someone or something. □ *The board of directors turned thumbs up on my proposal and voted to fund the project.* □ *The committee turned thumbs up on Carl as the new manager.* □ *When the boss turned thumbs up, I knew everything was okay.*

turn to *Fig.* to begin to get busy. □ *Come on, you guys! Turn to! Let's get to work.* □ *If you people will turn to, we can finish this work in no time at all.*

turn to someone or something (**for** something) to seek or expect something from someone or something. □ *I turned to Sally for advice.* □ *I turn to my dictionary for help two or three times a day.*

turn turtle *Fig.* to turn upside down. (See also **turn belly up.**) □ *The sailboat turned turtle, but the sailors only got wet.* □ *The car ran off the road and turned turtle in the ditch.*

turn up 1. [for part of something] to point upward. □ *The ends of the elf's funny little shoes turned up.* **2.** *Fig.* to happen. □ *Something always turns up to prevent their meeting.* □ *I am sorry I was late. Something turned up at the last minute.* **3.** *Fig.* to appear; to arrive and attend. □ *We'll send out invitations and see who turns up.* □ *Guess who turned up at my door last night?*

turn up one's **toes** *Sl.* to die. □ *When I turn up my toes, I want a big funeral with lots of flowers.* □ *Our cat turned up his toes during the night. He was nearly ten years old.*

turn up (somewhere) *Fig.* [for someone or something] to appear in a place. □ *Her name is always turning up in the gossip columns.* □ *He turned up an hour late.*

turn up† **the heat** (**on** someone or something) *Fig.* to put pressure on someone or something; apply additional pressure to someone or something. □ *The FBI turned the heat up on the gang.* □ *The police turned up the heat on the people who park illegally every day.*

turn (up)on someone or something to attack or oppose someone or something, especially the person or group in charge. (*Upon* is formal and less commonly used than *on*.) □ *I never thought that my own dog would turn on me!* □ *The treasurer turned on the entire board of directors.*

Turnabout is fair play. *Prov.* It is fair for one to suffer whatever one has caused others to suffer. □ *So, you don't like being made fun of! Well, turnabout is fair play.*

turned off uninterested. □ *I'm sort of turned off to stuff like that these days. Part of getting older, I guess.* □ *I can't pay attention if I'm turned off, now can I?*

*a turning point *Fig.* a time when things may change; a point at which a change of course is possible or desirable. (Originally nautical. Fig. on the image of a ship approaching a point where a change of course has been planned. (*Typically:* **be at ~; come to ~; reach ~.**) □ *Things are at to a turning point. Bob can no longer afford the payments on his car.* □ *I think we have come to a turning point and there ought to be some improvement henceforth.*

tussle with someone or something **1.** to struggle or battle with someone or something. □ *Tim tussled with Roger for a while, and then they made peace.* □ *I tussled with the trunk, trying to get it into the attic.* **2.** *Fig.* to argue or contend with someone, a group, or something. (Fig. on ①.) □ *I tussled with my conscience all night.* □ *We tussled with the committee and won our point.*

tweak something **off** (**of**) someone or something and **tweak** something **off†** to flick something off someone or something; to remove something from someone or something by pinching. (*Of* is usually retained before pronouns.) □ *Sarah tweaked a little beetle off of Fred.* □ *Sarah tweaked off a little bug.*

twelve good men and true *Fig.* a jury composed of trustworthy men. □ *He was convicted by a jury of twelve good men and true. Not a wino in the lot.*

twiddle one's **thumbs** *Fig.* to pass the time by twirling one's thumbs. □ *What am I supposed to do while waiting for you? Sit here and twiddle my thumbs?* □ *Don't sit around twiddling your thumbs. Get busy!*

twiddle with something to play with something; to play with something, using one's fingers; to fiddle with something. □ *I asked Jason to stop twiddling with the pencils.* □ *Someone is twiddling with the stereo controls.*

twilight years *Fig.* the last years before death. □ *In his twilight years, he became more mellow and stopped yelling at people.*

twine around something to weave or coil around something. □ *The snake twined around the branch.* □ *As the vine grew, it twined around the lamppost.*

twinkle with something [for someone's eyes] to sparkle because of something. □ *Her eyes twinkled with laughter.* □ *Tom's eyes twinkled with recognition when he saw Gwen again.*

twist around to turn around part way at the waist, without moving one's feet or legs. □ *Nancy twisted around to get a better look at who was sitting behind her.* □ *I had to twist around to see who was there.*

a **twist of fate** and a **turn of fate** *Fig.* a fateful event; an unanticipated change in a sequence of events. □ *A strange turn of fate brought Fred and his ex-wife together at a New Year's Eve party in Queens.*

twist (slowly) in the wind *Fig.* to suffer the agony of some humiliation or punishment. (Alludes to an execution by hanging.) □ *I'll see you twist in the wind for trying to frustrate this investigation.* □ *The prosecutor was determined that Richard would twist slowly in the wind for the crime.*

twist someone **around** one's **little finger** and **wind** someone **around** one's **little finger** *Fig.* to manipulate and control someone. □ *Bob really fell for Jane. She can twist him around her little finger.* □ *Billy's mother has wound him around her little finger. He's very dependent on her.*

twist someone's **arm** *Fig.* to pressure someone. (Fig. on the image of hurting someone until they agree to cooperate.) □ *I had to twist her arm a little, but she agreed.* □ *Do I have to twist your arm, or will you cooperate?*

twist someone's **words (around)** to restate someone's words inaccurately; to misrepresent what someone has said. □ *Stop twisting my words around! Listen to what I am telling you!* □ *You are twisting my words again. That is not what I said!*

twist something **around** someone or something to wrap something around someone or something. □ *Max twisted the wire around Lefty, and totally immobilized him.* □ *I twisted the rope around the post and tied a knot.*

twist something **into** something to change or distort something into something else, as if by twisting. □ *Kelly twisted the balloons into the shape of a dog.* □ *Ann twisted the silver wires into an earring.*

twist something **off (of)** something and **twist** something **off**† to take something off something by twisting. (*Of* is usually retained before pronouns.) □ *Fran twisted the top off of the bottle of mineral water and poured it.* □ *She twisted off the top.*

twist something **out of** something to remove something from something by twisting. □ *Flo twisted the cork out of*

the bottle and smelled the wine. □ *Roger twisted the bulb out of its socket and replaced it with a good one.*

twist up 1. to move upward in a twisting path. □ *The smoke twisted up into the sky.* □ *As the car twisted up the narrow path, we got a good view of the valley.* **2.** to become twisted. □ *The rope twisted up and had to be unwound.*

two bricks shy of a load Go to a **few cards shy of a full deck.**

Two can play (at) this game (as well as one). *Fig.* Both competitors—not just one—can compete in this manner or with this strategy. (See also a **game that two can play.**) □ *You are not the only one who knows how to cheat and lie. Two can play this game.*

Two heads are better than one. *Prov.* Two people working together have a better chance of solving a problem than one person working alone. □ *Come over here and help me balance my checkbook. Two heads are better than one.* □ *Jane: Can you figure out what this insurance document means? Alan: Why ask me? I don't know anything about insurance. Jane: Neither do I, but two heads are better than one.*

Two is company, (but) three's a crowd. and **Two's company(, three's a crowd).** *Prov.* A way of asking a third person to leave because you want to be alone with someone. (Often implies that you want to be alone with the person because you are romantically interested in him or her.) □ *When Lucy followed Mark and Nora into the drawing room, Nora turned to her and said, "Two's company, but three's a crowd."* □ *Bill: Can I go to lunch with you and Tom? Jane: Two's company, three's a crowd, Bill.*

two jumps ahead of someone *Fig.* a good way ahead of someone. □ *Her market research kept her two jumps ahead of her competitors.* □ *I was just starting to think of vacation plans, not realizing that my wife was two jumps ahead of me. She had already made hotel reservations.*

two of a kind *Fig.* people or things of the same type or that are similar in character, attitude, etc. □ *Jack and Tom are two of a kind. They're both ambitious.* □ *The companies are two of a kind. They both pay their employees badly.*

two shakes of a lamb's tail *Fig.* quickly; rapidly. □ *I'll be there in two shakes of a lamb's tail.* □ *In two shakes of a lamb's tail, the entire pile of bricks had collapsed.*

two sheets to the wind Go to **three sheets in the wind.**

***two strikes against** one **1.** two strikes on a baseball batter, three being the number that will put the batter "out." (Such a player is in a vulnerable position. *Typically:* **get ~; have ~.**) □ *Sammy has two strikes against him and might just strike out.* **2.** *Fig.* a critical number of things against one; a position wherein success is unlikely or where the success of the next move is crucial. (Fig. on ①. *Typically:* **get ~; have ~.**) □ *Poor Bob had two strikes against him when he tried to explain where he was last night.* □ *I can't win. I've got two strikes against me before I start.*

two (w)hoops and a holler *Rur.* a short distance. □ *Lexington? That's just two whoops and a holler from here.* □ *We're just two hoops and a holler from the downtown.*

Two wrongs do not make a right. *Prov.* Someone else may do something bad and not be punished, but that does not mean you are allowed to do bad things. □ *Jill: I'd really like to humiliate Fred, after he made fun of me in front of everyone at lunch. Jane: Now, now, Jill. Two wrongs don't make a right.*

a **two-edged sword** and a **double-edged sword** *Fig.* something that offers both a good and bad consequence. □ *The ability to get your insurance to pay for it is a double-edged sword. They may raise your rates.* □ *Her authority in the company is a two-edged sword. She makes more enemies than allies.*

two-fisted *Fig.* [of a male] aggressive and feisty. □ *Perry is a real, two-fisted cowboy, always ready for a fight or a drunken brawl.*

a **two-time loser** a confirmed **loser**. □ *Poor Richard is a two-time loser.* □ *Martin is a two-time loser, or at least he looks like one.*

two-time someone *Sl.* to cheat on or betray one's spouse or lover by dating or seeing someone else. □ *When Mrs. Franklin learned that Mr. Franklin was two-timing her, she* left him. □ *Ann told Bob that if he ever two-timed her, she would cause him a lot of trouble.*

a **two-way street** a reciprocal situation. □ *This is a two-way street, you know. You will have to help me someday in return.* □ *Friendship is a two-way street.*

type over something to type one letter over another. □ *Just type over the o with an e. No one will notice.*

type something **into** something and **type** something **in**† to insert information into a form or a place on a form by typing or keying it. □ *Please type your name and address into this box.* □ *Please type in your name.*

type something **out**† to make some information presentable by typing or keying it. □ *Please type this out before you submit it to the board for approval.* □ *Can you type out this report before quitting time?*

type something **up**† to type a handwritten document; to type a document, perhaps using a computer. □ *I will give this to you as soon as I type it up.* □ *Please type up this document.*

T

Uu

*ugly as a toad [of a living creature] very ugly. (*Also: **as ~.**) □ *Maria may be a beautiful woman, but when she was a child she was as ugly as a toad.* □ *The shopkeeper was ugly as a toad, but he was kind and generous, and everyone loved him.*

*ugly as sin *Cliché* extremely ugly. (*Also: **as ~.**) □ *Why would anyone want to buy that dress? It's as ugly as sin!* □ *Harold is ugly as sin, but his personality is very charming.*

unaccustomed to someone or something not used to someone or something. □ *The poor family was unaccustomed to going to fancy restaurants.* □ *Bill was unaccustomed to mailing his own letters.*

unbosom oneself **to** someone *Fig.* to reveal one's inner thoughts and secrets to someone. □ *He unbosomed himself to his best friend.* □ *Todd unbosomed himself to almost everyone he met.*

unburden oneself **to** someone *Fig.* to tell someone about one's trouble or anxiety. □ *I didn't mean to unburden myself to you. I'm just so upset.* □ *She unburdened herself to her mother.*

under a cloud (of suspicion) *Fig.* suspected of something. □ *Someone stole some money at work, and now everyone is under a cloud of suspicion.* □ *Even the manager is under a cloud.*

under a deadline Go to under pressure.

*under a spell *Fig.* enchanted; under the control of magic. (*Typically: **be ~; have** someone **~; put** someone **~.**) □ *Her soft voice and faint perfume put Buxton under a spell. Then enchantment was broken when he found his wallet missing.*

*under arrest arrested and in the custody of the police in preparation for the filing of a charge. (*Typically: **be ~; put** someone **~.**) □ *Stop where you are! You are under arrest!* □ *Am I under arrest, officer? What did I do?*

under certain **circumstances** and **under** certain **conditions** *Fig.* depending on or influenced by something; because of something. □ *Under certain conditions, you can see across the lake to the other side.* □ *Under certain circumstances, what you propose to do is all right.*

under certain **conditions** Go to previous.

*under (close) scrutiny *Fig.* being watched or examined closely. (*Typically: **be ~; have** someone or something **~; keep** someone or something **~.**) □ *The suspect was kept under scrutiny throughout the investigation.*

under construction *Fig.* being built or repaired. □ *We cannot travel on this road because it's under construction.* □ *Our new home has been under construction all summer. We hope to move in next month.*

*under control *Fig.* manageable; restrained and controlled; not out of control. (*Typically: **be ~; bring** someone or something **~; get** someone or something **~; have** someone or something **~; keep** someone or something **~.**) □ *We finally got things under control and functioning smoothly.* □ *The doctor felt she had the disease under control and that I would get well soon.*

*under fire *Fig.* during an attack; being attacked. (*Typically: **be ~; resign ~; think ~.**) □ *There was a scandal in city hall, and the mayor was forced to resign under fire.* □ *John is a good lawyer because he can think under fire.*

under no circumstances and **not under any circumstances** *Fig.* absolutely never. □ *Andy: Under no circumstances will I ever go back there again! Rachel: Why? What happened?* □ *Sue: Can I talk you into serving as a referee again? Mary: Heavens, no! Not under any circumstances!*

under normal circumstances *Fig.* normally; usually; typically. □ *"We'd be able to keep the dog at home under normal circumstances," said Mary to the vet.* □ *"Under normal circumstances you'd be able to return to work in a week," explained the doctor.*

under oath *Fig.* bound by an oath; having taken an oath. □ *You must tell the truth because you are under oath.* □ *I was placed under oath before I could testify in the trial.*

*under one's **belt 1.** *Fig.* eaten or drunk and in one's stomach. (*Fig.* on the image of swallowed food ending up under one's belt. *Typically: **get** something **~; have** something **~.**) □ *I need to have something filling under my belt. I've had it with just soup.* □ *I want to get a nice juicy steak under my belt.* **2.** *Fig.* achieved; counted or scored. (*Fig.* on ①. *Typically: **have** something **~.**) □ *Minnie has over four hundred wins under his belt.* □ *This fighter pilot has over 20 kills under his belt.* **3.** *Fig.* learned; mastered. (*Fig.* on ①. *Typically: **get** something **~.**) □ *Finally, she got good painting techniques under her belt.* □ *When I get the right procedures under my belt, I will be more efficient.*

*under one's **breath** *Fig.* [spoken] so softly that almost no one can hear it. (*Typically: **curse ~; curse** someone or something **~; mutter ~; mutter** something **~; say** something **~.**) □ *John was muttering something under his breath, and I don't think it was very pleasant.* □ *I'm glad he said it under his breath. If he had said it out loud, it would have caused an argument.*

under one's **own steam** *Fig.* by one's own power or effort. □ *I missed my ride to class, so I had to get there under my own steam.* □ *John will need some help with this project. He can't do it under his own steam.*

*under pressure 1. and ***under a deadline; *under the gun (about** something**)** *Fig.* facing or enduring something such as pressure or a deadline. (*Typically: **be ~; get ~.**) □ *I have to get back to work. I am under a deadline.* □ *I am under a lot of pressure lately.* □ *The management is under the gun for the mistakes made last year.* **2.** [of a gas or liquid] being forced, squeezed, or compressed. (*Typically: **be ~; deliver** something **~; put**

726

something ~.) □ *The gas in the pipes leading to the oven are under pressure.*

under someone's **care** Go to in the care of someone.

***under** someone's **thumb** *Fig.* under someone's control and management. (*Typically: **get** someone ~; **have** someone ~; **hold** someone ~; **keep** someone ~.) □ *You can't keep your kids under your thumb all their lives.* □ *I don't want to have these people under my thumb. I'm not the manager type.*

***under** someone's **wing(s)** *Fig.* receiving someone's care and nurturing. (*Typically: **get** someone ~; **have** someone ~; **take** someone ~.) □ *John wasn't doing well in geometry until the teacher took him under her wing.* □ *I had a number of the new workers under my wing for a few weeks.*

under the aegis of someone and **under the auspices of** someone *Fig.* under the sponsorship or protection of someone or some group; under the control or monitoring of someone or some group. □ *The entire project fell under the aegis of Thomas.* □ *The entire program is under the auspices of Acme-Global Paper Co., Inc.*

under the auspices of someone Go to previous.

under the circumstances *Fig.* in a particular situation; because of the circumstances. □ *I'm sorry to hear that you're ill. Under the circumstances, you may take the day off.* □ *We won't expect you to come to work for a few days, under the circumstances.*

under the counter *Fig.* [bought or sold] in secret or illegally. (Compare this to **over the counter**.) □ *The drugstore owner was arrested for selling liquor under the counter.* □ *The clerk sold dirty books under the counter.*

under the gun (about something**)** Go to **under pressure.**

under the influence (of alcohol) *Euph.* drunk; nearly drunk; affected by alcohol. □ *She behaves quite rudely when under the influence of alcohol.* □ *Ed was stopped by a police officer for driving while under the influence.*

under the sun *Fig.* anywhere on earth at all. □ *This is the largest cattle ranch under the sun.* □ *Isn't there anyone under the sun who can help me with this problem?*

under the table 1. *Sl.* intoxicated. □ *Jed was under the table by midnight.* □ *By 3:00 in the morning, everyone was under the table.* **2.** *Fig.* secret; clandestine. (This is hyphenated before a nominal.) □ *It was strictly an under-the-table deal.* □ *The mayor made a few bucks under the table, too.*

under the weather 1. ill. □ *I feel sort of under the weather today.* □ *Whatever I ate for lunch is making me feel a bit under the weather.* **2.** intoxicated. □ *Daddy's had a few beers and is under the weather again.* □ *Wally's just a tad under the weather.*

under the wire *Fig.* just barely in time or on time. □ *I turned in my report just under the wire.* □ *Bill was the last person to get in the door. He got in under the wire.*

***under way** *Fig.* moving; running; started. (*Typically: **be** ~; **get** something ~; **have** something ~.) □ *The time has come to get this game under way.* □ *Now that the president has the meeting under way, I can relax.*

***under wraps** *Fig.* concealed; suppressed. (*Typically: **be** ~; **have** ~; **hold** ~; **keep** ~.) □ *We kept the candidate's conviction under wraps until after the election.* □ *The plan we had under wraps had to be scrapped anyway.*

undertake to do something to try to do something; to take the responsibility of doing something. □ *The carpenter undertook to repair the door frame.* □ *I will undertake to fix it.*

Uneasy lies the head that wears a crown. *Prov.* A person who has a lot of power and prestige also has a lot of responsibilities, and therefore worries more than other people. (From Shakespeare's play, *Henry IV, Part II.*) □ *Susan began to have trouble sleeping shortly after she was promoted to head of her department. "Uneasy lies the head that wears a crown," her friends teased.*

The **unexpected always happens.** *Prov.* The things you do not foresee will happen to you; when you plan, you cannot think of everything that might happen. □ *It took us an hour to drive to the restaurant, and when we got there, it was closed. I would never have expected a restaurant to be closed on a Friday night, but the unexpected always happens. Especially to me.*

unfamiliar territory an area of knowledge unknown to the speaker. □ *We are in unfamiliar territory and I don't know the answer.* □ *Astronomy is unfamiliar territory for me, and I cannot answer any questions about the stars.*

unfold into something **1.** [for something folded up] to unfold into something. □ *The greeting card unfolded into a little paper house.* □ *It unfolded into a cute scene.* **2.** *Fig.* [for a story] to develop into something interesting. (Fig. on ①.) □ *The story unfolded into a real mystery.* □ *The tale unfolded into a farce.*

unfold something **into** something to spread something out into something. □ *The child unfolded the page into a model village.* □ *I unfolded the brochure into a large colorful sheet of advertising.*

unify someone or something **into** something to combine people or things into a united whole. □ *The mayor unified his party into a powerful force.* □ *I unified the committee into a strong body.*

Union is strength. *Prov.* If people join together, they are more powerful than if they work by themselves. □ *The students decided to join together in order to present their grievances to the faculty, since union is strength.* □ *We cannot allow our opponents to divide us. Union is strength.*

unite against someone or something to join against someone or something. □ *We will unite against the opposing forces.* □ *We must unite against the incumbent legislators.*

unite for something to join together for some purpose. □ *All the forces united for the attack.* □ *We will unite for a great party.*

unite in something to come together in something. □ *Let us unite in our efforts.* □ *We will unite in song.*

unite someone **against** someone or something to cause people to join together against someone or something. □ *The mayor united his staff against the federal investigators.* □ *Ted united us against John.* □ *They united themselves against the enemy.*

unite someone **in** something to join two or more people in something, usually marriage. □ *The preacher united the couple in matrimony.* □ *A judge united them in marriage.*

unite someone or something **into** something to form something by merging people together; to form something by merging things together. □ *Let us unite the party into a powerful political force.* □ *We will unite ourselves into a powerful force.*

unite someone or something **(together†)** to join people or groups of people together. □ *They united all the workers together for the strike.* □ *The event united together the people who cared about the quality of life.*

unite someone or something **with** someone or something to join people or things, in any combination. □ *We united Tom with his brother Arnold during the evening.* □ *We united our committee with the president in an effort to expand our influence.*

unite with someone to join with someone; to go or come together with someone. □ *I was pleased to unite with my family for the holidays.* □ *The brothers united with their sister after many years of separation.*

United we stand, divided we fall. *Prov.* People who join together as a group are much harder to defeat than they would be separately. □ *The tenants of this building must band together if we are to make the landlord agree to our demands. United we stand, divided we fall!* □ *We had better all agree on what we are going to say to the boss before we go in there and say it. United we stand, divided we fall.*

***an **unknown quantity** *Fig.* a person or thing about which no one is certain. (*Typically: **be** ~; **become** ~.) □ *John is an unknown quantity. We don't know how he's going to act.* □ *The new clerk is an unknown quantity. Things may not turn out all right.*

unleash someone or something **against** someone or something to turn someone or something loose against someone or something. □ *The army unleashed a horrible attack against the enemy.* □ *Max unleashed his bullies against the helpless merchants.*

unleash someone or something **(up)on** someone or something to turn someone or something loose on someone or something. (*Upon* is formal and less commonly used than *on.*) □ *The air force unleashed a bombing attack upon the enemy.* □ *The mob chief unleashed his tough guys on Lefty.*

unload someone or something **on(to)** someone to get rid of a burdensome person or thing on someone else. □ *I unloaded my obnoxious little cousin onto his aunt.* □ *I didn't mean to unload my problems onto you.*

unload something **from** something to take things off of something; to remove the burden from something. □ *Please unload the groceries from the car.* □ *I unloaded the groceries from the bags.*

unsung hero *Fig.* a hero who has gotten no praise or recognition. □ *The time has come to recognize all the unsung heroes of the battle for low-cost housing.*

until all hours *Fig.* until very late. □ *Mary is out until all hours, night after night.* □ *If I'm up until all hours two nights in a row, I'm just exhausted.*

until all hours (of the day and night) Go to all hours (of the day and night).

until hell freezes over Go to when hell freezes over.

(un)til the cows come home *Rur.* until the last; until very late. (Referring to the end of the day, when the cows come home to be fed and milked.) □ *We were having so much fun that we decided to stay at the party until the cows came home.* □ *Where've you been? Who said you could stay out till the cows come home?*

Until we meet again. Go to Good-bye for now.

***up a blind alley** *Fig.* at a dead end; on a route that leads nowhere. (*Typically: **be** ~; **go** ~.) □ *I have been trying to find out something about my ancestors, but I'm up a blind alley. I can't find anything.* □ *The police are up a blind alley in their investigation of the crime.*

up a creek Go to up the creek (without a paddle).

***up a storm** *Fig.* [doing or making] a great amount with fury or intensity. (*Typically: **cook** ~; **gab** ~; **sing** ~; **kick** ~; **talk** ~.) □ *Whenever we get together, we always talk up a storm.* □ *Everyone was gabbing up a storm and didn't hear the chairman come in.*

up a tree 1. confused; without an answer to a problem; in difficulty. □ *This whole business has me up a tree.* □ *I'm up a tree, and I need some help.* **2.** intoxicated. □ *Only two glasses of booze and he was up a tree for sure.* □ *My buddy here is up a tree and needs a place to crash for the night.*

***up against** someone or something in opposition to someone or something, as in a contest. (*Typically: **be** ~; **come** ~; **go** ~; **run** ~; **team** ~.) □ *Let's team up against Paul and Tony in the footrace.* □ *We came up against a very strong team.*

***up against** something **1.** *Fig.* resting firmly against something. (*Typically: **be** ~; **place** something ~.) □ *The car is up against the back of the garage! Back out a little!* **2.** *Fig.* in conflict with something; facing something as a barrier. (Fig. on ①. *Typically: **be** ~; **go** ~.) □ *I am up against some serious problems.*

***up against the wall** *Fig.* in serious difficulties. (*Typically: **be** ~; **get** ~; **push** someone ~.) □ *Let's face it, we're up against the wall this time.* □ *It's when you're up against the wall that your true character shows.*

***(up and) about** and ***up and around** out of bed and moving about. (*Typically: **be** ~; **get** ~.) □ *I'm up and about, but I'm not really well yet.* □ *The flu put Alice into bed for three days, but she was up and around on the fourth.*

up and at 'em *Fig.* up and taking action. □ *Dad woke me at seven, saying, "Up and at 'em!"* □ *It's six-thirty. Time for us to be up and at 'em.*

up and away *Fig.* [of a bird or an airplane] up into the air and into flight. □ *After a few seconds of speeding down the runway, our flight to Tucson was up and away.* □ *Just before the cat pounced on the sparrows, they were up and away and the cat was left with empty paws and jaws.*

up and did something *Rur.* did something suddenly. □ *That summer, she up and died.* □ *He had lived here for twenty years, and then one day, he up and left for good.*

up and running *Fig.* [of a machine] functioning. □ *As soon as we can get the tractor up and running, we will plant the corn crop.*

***up before** someone *Fig.* standing in front of someone to receive something. (Especially in front of a judge. *Typically: **be** ~; **come** ~; **stand** ~.) □ *Have you been up before me before?* □ *I have never been up before any judge.*

*up for auction *Fig.* to be sold at an auction. (*Typically: **be ~; come ~; go ~; put** something **~**.) □ *The old farm where I lived as a child is up for auction.*

up for grabs 1. *Fig.* available for anyone; not yet claimed. □ *The election is up for grabs. Everything is still very chancy.* □ *I don't know who will get the promotion. It's up for grabs.* **2.** *Fig.* in total chaos. □ *This is a madhouse. The whole place is up for grabs.* □ *When the market crashed, the whole office was up for grabs.*

*up for reelection *Fig.* to be running for reelection to an office or position. (*Typically: **be ~; come ~**.) □ *The governor is up for reelection in the fall.* □ *Lily is up for reelection this fall.*

*up for sale *Fig.* available for purchase. (*Typically: **be ~; come ~; put** something **~**.) □ *When this lot comes up for sale, let me know.* □ *Is this property up for sale?*

*up for something **1.** *Fig.* [of someone] mentally ready for something. (*Typically: **be ~; get ~; get** oneself **~**.) □ *The team is up for the game tonight.* □ *We are all up for the contest.* **2.** *Sl.* agreeable to something. (*Typically: **be ~**.) □ *I'm up for a pizza. Anybody want to chip in?* □ *Who's up for a swim?*

up front 1. in the forefront; under fire (at the front). □ *You guys who are up front are gonna get the most fire.* □ *You two go up front and see if you can help.* **2.** *Fig.* at the beginning; in advance. □ *She wanted $200 up front.* □ *The more you pay up front, the less you'll have to finance.* **3.** *Fig.* open; honest; forthcoming. □ *She is a very up front gal—trust her.* □ *I wish the salesman had been more up front about it.*

*up in arms 1. *Fig.* in armed rebellion. (*Typically: **be ~; get ~**.) □ *The entire population is up in arms.* □ *They are up in arms, ready to fight.* **2.** *Fig.* very angry. (Fig. on ①, but without weapons. *Typically: **be ~; get ~**.) □ *Wally was up in arms about the bill for the broken window.* □ *I am really up in arms about what happened.*

up in the air (about someone or something**)** *Fig.* undecided about someone or something; uncertain about someone or something. □ *I don't know what Sally plans to do. Things were sort of up in the air the last time we talked.* □ *Let's leave this question up in the air until next week.*

up in years and **advanced in years; along in years; on in years** *Fig.* old; elderly. □ *My uncle is up in years and can't hear too well.* □ *Many people lose their hearing somewhat when they are along in years.*

up North to or at the northern part of the country or the world. □ *I don't like living up North. I want to move down South where it's warm.* □ *When you say "up North," do you mean where the polar bears live or just in the northern states?*

up on someone or something *Fig.* knowledgeable about someone or something. □ *Ask Tom about the author of this book. He's up on stuff like that.*

up one side and down the other *Rur.* thoroughly. □ *She scolded him up one side and down the other.* □ *They shopped the whole downtown up one side and down the other.*

up stakes to prepare for leaving and then leave. (*Up* has the force of a verb here. The phrase suggests pulling up tent stakes in preparation for departure.) □ *They just upped stakes and left without saying good-bye.* □ *It's that time of the year when I feel like upping stakes and moving to the country.*

up the ante and **raise the ante 1.** *Fig.* to raise the opening stakes in a betting game. □ *Pete upped the ante on that the poker game to $100 per hand.* □ *Don't up the ante any more. You're betting far too much money already.* **2.** *Fig.* to increase a price. (Fig. on ②.) □ *Sensing how keen the people looking at the house were, Jerry upped the ante another $5,000.* □ *"Don't try to up the ante on us," said the man, "We know what the asking price is."*

up the creek (without a paddle) and **up a creek; up shit creek** *Inf. Fig.* in an awkward position with no easy way out. □ *I'm sort of up the creek and don't know what to do.* □ *You are up a creek! You got yourself into it, so get yourself out.*

up the pole *Fig.* intoxicated. □ *You sound a little up the pole. Why don't you call back when you're sober?* □ *She's up the pole and shouldn't drive.*

up the river *Sl.* in prison. (Underworld.) □ *Gary was up the river for a couple of years, but that doesn't make him an outcast, does it?* □ *The judge who sent him up the river was indicted for accepting bribery. If Gary had only known sooner!*

up the wall *Fig.* in a very bad situation; very upset or anxious. □ *He's really up the wall about Mary's illness.* □ *We were all up the wall until the matter was resolved.*

up to doing something [feeling] able to do something. □ *Do you feel up to going back to work today?* □ *She just isn't up to staying up so late.*

*up to here (with something**)** having had as much as one can bear. (*Typically: **be ~; get ~**.) □ *I'm up to here with your excuses!* □ *We are all up to here with this mystery.*

up to no good *Fig.* doing something bad. □ *I could tell from the look on Tom's face that he was up to no good.* □ *There are three boys in the front yard. I don't know what they are doing, but I think they are up to no good.*

up to one's **ears (in** something**)** Go to up to one's **neck (in** something**)**.

up to one's **eyeballs (in** something**)** Go to up to one's **neck (in** something**)**.

*up to one's **knees** *Fig.* deep in something, such as paperwork or water. (The idea is that it is hard to move or make progress. *Typically: **be ~; get ~**.) □ *We're up to our knees with orders and getting more all the time.* □ *The orders are up to our knees.*

*up to one's **neck (in** something**)** and ***up to** one's **ears (in** something**); *up to** one's **eyeballs (in** something**)** having a lot of something; *Fig.* very much involved in something; immersed in something. (*Typically: **be ~; get ~**.) □ *I can't come to the meeting. I'm up to my neck in these reports.* □ *Mary is up to her ears in her work.* □ *I am up to my eyeballs in things to do! I can't do any more!*

up to par *Fig.* as good as the standard or average; up to standard. □ *I'm just not feeling up to par today. I must be coming down with something.* □ *The manager said that the report was not up to par and gave it back to Mary to do over again.*

up to snuff and **up to scratch** *Fig.* as good as is required; meeting the minimum requirements. □ *Sorry, Tom. Your performance isn't up to snuff. You'll have to improve or find another job.* □ *My paper wasn't up to scratch, so I got an F.*

*__up to__ someone or something *Fig.* decided by someone. (*Typically: **be** ~; **become** ~; **leave** something ~.) □ *If it were up to me, I would say yes.* □ *It is up to the decision of the judges!*

up to something **1.** *Fig.* [of someone] plotting something. □ *I think they are up to something.* □ *I am sure that Lily and Max are up to something evil.* **2.** *Fig.* [of someone] well enough or rested enough to do something. □ *I'm not quite up to the party.* □ *Are you up to a game of volleyball?* **3.** to be as good as something; to be good enough for something. □ *This work's not up to the standard of the class.* □ *Your last essay was not up to your best.*

*__up to speed__ **1.** *Fig.* moving, operating, or funtioning a normal or desired rate. (*Typically: **be** ~; **bring** something ~; **get** ~; **get** something ~.) □ *Terri did everything she could to bring her workers up to speed, but couldn't.* □ *Can we get this production line up to speed?* **2.** and *__up to speed on__ someone or something *Fig.* fully apprised about someone or something; up-to-date on the state of someone or something. (*Typically: **be** ~; **bring** someone ~; **get** ~; **get** someone ~.) □ *Please bring me up to speed on this matter.* □ *I'll feel better about it when I get up to speed on what's going on.*

*__up to the minute__ *Fig.* current. (*Typically: **be** ~; **bring** something ~.) □ *This report is up to the minute and fresh from the wire services.*

*__up with__ someone *Fig.* even with someone; caught up with someone. (*Typically: **be** ~; **catch** ~; **get** ~.) □ *I'm up with the best of them.* □ *Are you up with your colleagues on this one?*

up-and-coming *Fig.* enterprising and alert. □ *Jane is a hard worker—really up-and-coming.* □ *Bob is also an up-and-coming youngster who is going to become well known.*

upbraid someone **for** something to scold someone for doing something. □ *The judge upbraided David severely for his crime.* □ *Walter upbraided his son for denting the car.*

update someone **about** someone or something and **update** someone **on** someone or something to tell someone the latest news about someone or something. □ *Please update me about the current situation in France.* □ *Please update me about Tony.*

upgrade someone or something **to** something to raise someone or something to a higher grade or rank. □ *Please upgrade me to first class.* □ *They upgraded the terrorist alert status to red.*

upgrade to something to move up to a higher grade or rank. □ *I would like to upgrade to a first-class seat.* □ *Please upgrade me to a better room.*

an **uphill battle** and an **uphill struggle** *Fig.* a hard struggle. □ *Convincing the senator to see our point of view was an uphill battle, but we finally succeeded.*

upon impact *Fig.* at the place or time of an impact. □ *The car crumpled upon impact with the brick wall.* □ *The man who fell from the top of the building died on impact.*

*__(up)on__ someone *Fig.* to be someone's obligation or responsibility. (*Typically: **be** ~; **lie** ~.) □ *The obligation is upon you to settle this.* □ *The major part of the responsibility is on you.*

upper crust *Fig.* the higher levels of society; the upper class. (From the top, as opposed to the bottom, crust of a pie.) □ *Jane speaks like that because she pretends to be from the upper crust, but her father was a miner.* □ *James is from the upper crust, but he is penniless.*

*the **upper hand (on** someone**)** *Fig.* a position superior to someone; the advantage of someone. (*Typically: **get** ~; **have** ~; **give** someone ~.) □ *John is always trying to get the upper hand on someone.* □ *He never ends up having the upper hand, though.*

upper story Go to **top story.**

uproot someone **from** some place *Fig.* to cause someone to move from a well-established home or setting. □ *You should not uproot people from the land in which they were born.* □ *I just couldn't uproot myself from my home.*

uproot something **from** some place to take up a plant or tree, roots and all. □ *Wally uprooted the bush from the backyard and replanted it on the other side of the house.* □ *Who uprooted a rosebush from my garden?*

upset someone's **plans** *Fig.* to ruin someone's plans. □ *I hope it doesn't upset your plans if I'm late for the meeting.* □ *No, it won't upset my plans at all.*

upset the apple cart *Fig.* to mess up or ruin something. □ *Tom really upset the apple cart by telling Mary the truth about Jane.* □ *I always knew he'd tell secrets and upset the apple cart.*

the **upshot of** something *Fig.* the result or outcome of something. □ *The upshot of my criticism was a change in policy.* □ *The upshot of the argument was an agreement to hire a new secretary.*

*__upside-down__ *Fig.* in a financial state such that one owes more money on a car, truck, house, etc., than its resale value. (*Typically: **be** ~; **get** ~.) □ *When I tried to trade in the car, I found that I was upside-down and couldn't close the deal without more money.* □ *I took a loan period that was too long and was upside-down in two years.*

*__up-to-date__ modern or contemporary. (*Typically: **be** ~; **get** ~.) □ *Is the room up-to-date, or is it standard?* □ *Your knowledge is not really up-to-date on this matter.*

up-to-date modern; up to the current standards of fashion; having the most current information. □ *I'd like to see a more up-to-date report on Mr. Smith.* □ *This is not an up-to-date record of the construction project.*

up-to-the-minute the very latest or most recent. □ *I want to hear some up-to-the-minute news on the hostage situation.* □ *I just got an up-to-the-minute report on Tom's health.*

urban legend *Fig.* a myth or piece of folklore that is totally false. □ *That story about the rats in the sewer being as big as dogs is an urban legend. It's just not so.*

urge someone **along** to encourage someone to continue or go faster. □ *We urged them along with much encouragement.* □ *They won't do well, but we urged them along anyway.*

urge someone **forward** to encourage someone to move forward. □ *The generals urged the troops forward.* □ *Sally urged Timmy forward into the classroom.*

U

urge someone **to** do something to try to get someone to do something. □ *I urge you to give skiing a try.* □ *Ken urged Lily to finish her dinner.*

urge something **(up)on** someone to try to get someone to take something. (*Upon* is formal and less commonly used than *on*.) □ *Arnold urged the new policy on the employees.* □ *He urged restraint upon them.*

use a firm hand Go to a firm hand.

use every trick in the book *Fig.* to use every method possible. □ *I used every trick in the book, but I still couldn't manage to get a ticket to the game Saturday.* □ *Bob tried to use every trick in the book, but he still failed.*

use foul language *Euph.* to swear. □ *There's no need to use foul language.* □ *When she gets angry, she tends to use foul language.*

use one's **head** and **use** one's **noggin; use** one's **noodle** *Fig.* to use one's own intelligence. (The words *noggin* and *noodle* are slang terms for "head.") □ *You can do better in math if you'll just use your head.* □ *Jane uses her noggin and gets things done correctly and on time.* □ *Yes, she sure knows how to use her noodle.*

use one's **noggin** Go to previous.

use one's **noodle** Go to use one's head.

use some elbow grease *Fig.* use some effort, as in scrubbing something. (As if lubricating one's elbow would make one more efficient. Note the variations in the examples.) □ *Come on, Bill. You can do it. Just use some elbow grease.* □ *I tried elbow grease, but it doesn't help get the job done.*

use some shut-eye Go to some shut-eye.

use someone or something **as an excuse** to blame someone or something (for a failure). (See also **use** someone or something **as** something.) □ *John used his old car as an excuse for not going to the meeting.* □ *My husband was sick in bed, and I used him as an excuse.*

use someone or something **as** something to make someone or something function as something. (See also **use** someone or something **as an excuse.**) □ *You have used me as your tool!* □ *I don't like your using my car as your private taxi.*

use someone or something **for** something to make use of someone or something for a specific purpose. □ *Would you please use Don for your errands?* □ *You can use my car for the trip.*

use someone **up** *Fig.* to use all the effort or talent a person has. □ *His career simply used him up.* □ *I used myself up. I'm done. I can't function anymore.*

use something **before** something **1.** to consume or use something before using something else. □ *Use this jar before that one. This one is older.* □ *I used the old one before the one you just bought.* **2.** to consume or use something before a specified date. □ *I will use this bottle of catsup before May.* □ *You should use this one before the date stamped on the bottom.*

use something **by** something to consume or complete the use of something by a specified time. □ *Please use this jar of mayonnaise by the last day of the month.* □ *Use this one by next week.*

use something **over (again)** to reuse something. □ *Do I have to use this stuff over again?* □ *Yes. Please use it over.*

use something **up**[†] to consume or use all of something. □ *Use the flour up. I have more in the cupboard.* □ *Use up every bit of it. Go ahead.*

use something **with** something to use something in a particular manner. □ *Use this tool with a lot of skill and caution.* □ *Use this one with great care.*

use strong language *Euph.* to swear, threaten, or use abusive language. □ *I wish you wouldn't use strong language in front of the children.* □ *If you feel that you have to use strong language with the manager, perhaps you had better let me do the talking.*

use the bathroom and **use the toilet** *Euph.* to urinate or defecate. □ *May I be excused to use the bathroom?* □ *I have to use the toilet.*

use the race card Go to the race card.

use the toilet Go to use the bathroom.

use your head for more than a hatrack and **use your head for more than something to keep your ears apart** *Rur.* to think. □ *How are we going to solve this problem? Come on, use your head for more than a hatrack.* □ *Instead of whining about it, why don't you use your head for more than something to keep your ears apart?*

use your head for more than something to keep your ears apart Go to previous.

used to do something to have done something [customarily] in the past. □ *We used to go swimming in the lake before it became polluted.* □ *I used to eat nuts, but then I became allergic to them.*

***used to** someone or something *Fig.* accustomed to someone or something; familiar and comfortable with someone or something. (*Typically: **be** ~; **become** ~; **get** ~.) □ *I am used to eating better food than this.* □ *I am used to the doctor I have and I don't want to change.*

user friendly *Fig.* easy to use. (Hyphenated before nominals.) □ *The set-up instructions for the printer were very user friendly.* □ *I have a user-friendly computer that listens to my voice and does what I tell it.*

usher someone or something **into** some place and **usher** someone or something **in**[†] to escort or lead a person, a group, or something into a place. □ *The guard ushered the group into the palace.* □ *They ushered in the visitors.*

usher someone or something **out of** some place and **usher** someone or something **out**[†] to escort or lead someone or a group out of a place. □ *We ushered them from the room.* □ *The woman ushered out the guest.*

usher someone **to** something to escort or lead someone to something, such as a seat, the door, etc. □ *The well-dressed gentleman ushered the bride to the altar.* □ *Her father ushered her to the altar.*

utilize someone or something **for** something to use someone or something for something or for some purpose. □ *Is there any way you can utilize Peter for the project?* □ *Can you utilize this contraption for anything?*

U

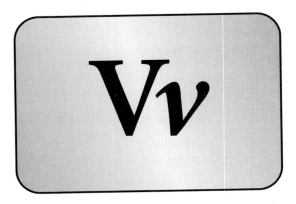

vaccinate someone or an animal **against** something to inoculate or immunize someone or an animal against some disease. □ *They had to vaccinate us against yellow fever.* □ *The vet vaccinated the horse against everything that threatened it.*

vaccinate someone or an animal **with** something to inoculate or immunize someone or an animal with some substance. □ *This time the doctor vaccinated Tom with killed virus.* □ *The vet vaccinated the cat with something that would prevent rabies.*

vacillate between someone **and** someone else or something **and** something else to waver between a choice of people or a choice of things. □ *He kept vacillating between Fred and Alice.* □ *Wayne vacillated between chocolate and vanilla.*

vacuum something **out**† to clean an enclosed area out with a vacuum cleaner. □ *Please vacuum this car out now!* □ *Can you vacuum out the car?*

vacuum something **up**† **(from** something**)** to clean something up from something with a vacuum cleaner. □ *Fred vacuumed the dirt up from the carpet.* □ *He vacuumed up the birdseed from the kitchen floor.*

vain as a peacock Go to proud as a peacock.

value someone or something **above** someone or something to hold someone or something to be more important than someone or something. □ *I value her above all things.* □ *He values his car above his family!*

value someone or something **as** something to hold someone or something in esteem as something; to find someone or something to be as good as something. □ *I value you as a close friend.* □ *I value this watch as a keepsake.*

value someone or something **for** something to hold someone or something in esteem for a particular quality. □ *I value him for his skill in negotiation.* □ *I value this car for its speed and dependability.*

value something **at** something to consider something to be worth a certain amount. □ *The museum curator valued the vase at one million dollars.* □ *I value this vase at one million dollars.*

vanish away to disappear. (The *away* is considered redundant.) □ *The pizza vanished away in no time at all.* □ *The city lights vanished away as dawn broke.*

vanish from something to disappear from something or some place. □ *The money vanished from the desk drawer.* □ *My glasses have vanished from sight again.*

vanish into something to disappear by going into something. □ *All the deer vanished into the forest.* □ *Money seems to vanish into a black hole.*

vanish into thin air *Cliché* to disappear without leaving a trace. □ *My money gets spent so fast. It seems to vanish into thin air.* □ *When I came back, my car was gone. I had locked it, and it couldn't have vanished into thin air!*

Variety is the spice of life. *Prov. Cliché* You should try many different kinds of experiences, because trying different things keeps life interesting. □ *I know we usually spend our summer vacation camping out, but I think we should try something different this year. Variety is the spice of life.*

vary between someone **and** someone else and **vary between** something **and** something else to fluctuate in choosing between people or things. □ *In choosing a bridge partner, Sam varied between Tom and Wally.* □ *I varied between chocolate and vanilla cake for dessert.*

vary between something **and** something else to fluctuate between one thing and another. □ *The daytime temperatures vary between 80 and 90 degrees.* □ *She varies between angry and happy.*

vary (from something**) (in** something**)** to differ from something. □ *This one varies from that one in many ways.* □ *It varies from the other one a little.*

vary from something **to** something to fluctuate over the range from something to something. □ *The colors vary from red to orange.* □ *It varies from warm to very hot during the summer.*

vary with something **1.** to be at variance with someone's figures or a sum or estimate. □ *My figures vary with yours considerably.* □ *Her estimate varies with yours by a few dollars.* **2.** to change according to something. □ *The rainfall in New York State varies with the season.* □ *His mood varies with the stock market average.*

vault into something to jump or dive into something. □ *The diver vaulted into the pool.* □ *He vaulted into bed and pulled up the covers.*

vault over someone or something to jump or leap over someone or something. □ *Molly vaulted over Ted and kept on running.* □ *She vaulted over the trunk.*

veer (away) (from someone or something**)** to swerve away from someone or something; to turn aside to avoid someone or something. □ *The plane veered away from the mountain.* □ *The car veered from the children who were in its path.*

veer off (from someone or something**)** to turn or steer sharply away from someone or something. □ *The bird veered off from the cluster of trees.* □ *The bird veered off and missed hitting the post.*

veer toward someone or something to turn sharply or swerve toward someone or something. □ *The car suddenly veered toward me.* □ *The horse veered toward the side of the bridle path.*

veg out to cease working and take it easy; to vegetate. □ *Someday, I just want to veg out and enjoy life.* □ *I think I'll just veg this weekend.*

vegged out debilitated by drugs or alcohol. □ *Ernie is vegged out and has quit his job and everything.* □ *Won't be long till Larry is vegged out altogether.*

vent one's **spleen** *Fig.* to get rid of one's feelings of anger caused by someone or something by attacking someone or something else. □ *Jack vented his spleen at his wife whenever things went badly at work.* □ *Peter vented his spleen on his car by kicking it when it broke down.*

vent something **(up)on** someone or something to release one's emotional tension on someone or something. (*Upon* is formal and less commonly used than *on*.) □ *Henry vented his anger on Carl.* □ *It's no use to vent your hatred on a door. Kicking it won't help.*

venture forth 1. *Fig.* to set out; to go forward; to go out cautiously. □ *George ventured forth into the night.* □ *I think I will venture forth. It looks safe.* **2.** *Fig.* to go forth bravely. □ *Let us venture forth and conquer the enemy.* □ *We will arm ourselves and venture forth against our foe.*

venture out ((of) something**)** to go out of something cautiously. (*Of* is usually retained before pronouns.) □ *Peter ventured out of his house for only a minute into the cold.* □ *He ventured out the door for only a moment.*

venture (up)on someone or something to come upon someone or something by chance. (*Upon* is formal and less commonly used than *on*. The entire expression is formal or stilted.) □ *David ventured upon Fred, who was out looking for mushrooms.* □ *I ventured on a little shop on Maple Street that deals in old model trains.*

verge into something to change gradually into something. □ *The reds verged into a violet color that seemed to glow.* □ *The cool morning verged imperceptibly into a steamy midday.*

verge (up)on something to be almost identical to something; to be similar to or almost the same as something. (*Upon* is formal and less commonly used than *on*.) □ *Your actions verge upon mutiny.* □ *What you said verges on an insult.*

verify something **with** someone to check with someone to make sure that something is the truth. □ *I will have to verify your story with the storekeeper.* □ *I verified your story with the other witness.*

Very good. 1. It is good. □ *John: How do you like your lobster? Alice: Mmm. Very good.* □ *Jane: What did you think of the movie? Fred: Very good. Jane: Is that all? Fred: Yeah.* **2.** Thank you for your instructions. (Typically said by someone in a serving role, such as a clerk, waiter, waitress, butler, maid, etc.) □ *Waiter: What are you drinking, madam? Sue: It's just soda. No more, thanks. Waiter: Very good.* □ *Mary: Would you charge this to my account? Clerk: Very good.*

the **very last** *Fig.* the end; an absolute end of something. □ *At the very last of the movie, the hero gets killed.* □ *Bill stayed at the party until the very last.*

the **(very) picture of** something *Fig.* the perfect example of something; an exact image of something. □ *The young newlyweds were the picture of happiness.* □ *My doctor told me that I was the very picture of good health.*

the **very thing** *Fig.* the exact thing that is required. □ *The vacuum cleaner is the very thing for cleaning the stairs.* □ *I have the very thing to remove that stain.*

vest someone **with** something to grant power, rights, or ownership to someone. □ *Who vested you with the power to order me around?* □ *The dictator vested himself with the power to imprison almost anyone.*

vest something **in** someone or something to grant sole power or control over something to someone or some group. □ *The king vested all the military power in his own hands.* □ *The constitution vests the power to tax in the legislature.*

*a **vested interest in** something *Fig.* a personal or biased interest, often financial, in something. (*Typically: **have** ~; **give** someone ~.) □ *Margaret has a vested interest in wanting her father to sell the family firm. She has shares in it and would make a large profit.* □ *Bob has a vested interest in keeping the village traffic-free. He has a summer home there.*

vie (with someone**) (for** someone or something**)** and **vie (with** someone**) (over** someone or something**)** to compete or contend with someone for someone or something. □ *They vied with each other for Mary's favor.* □ *I really don't want to have to vie with Randy for recognition.*

the **villain of the piece** *Fig.* someone or something that is responsible for something bad or wrong. (Fig. on the villainous role in a drama.) □ *I wonder who told the newspapers about the local scandal. I discovered that Jane was the villain of the piece.* □ *We couldn't think who had stolen the meat. The dog next door turned out to be the villain of the piece.*

vim and vigor *Cliché* energy; enthusiasm. □ *Show more vim and vigor! Let us know you're alive.* □ *She's sure got a lot of vim and vigor.*

vindicate someone **of** something to clear or acquit someone of something. □ *The police sought to vindicate Donald of the charges.* □ *They vindicated themselves of the charges with a clear alibi.*

virtual reality *Fig.* computer imaging that attempts to mimic real scenes or places. □ *The movie had so much virtual reality that the regular photographic scenes began to look funny.*

Virtue is its own reward. *Prov.* You should not be virtuous in hopes of getting a reward, but because it makes you feel good to be virtuous. □ *Bill: If I help you, will you pay me? Fred: Virtue is its own reward.*

visible to the naked eye Go to the naked eye.

a **visit from the stork** *Fig.* a birth. (According to legend, babies are brought to their parents by a stork.) □ *I hear that Maria is expecting a visit from the stork.* □ *The young couple had a visit from the stork.*

visit something **(up)on** someone *Fig.* to inflict something upon someone. (Stilted. *Upon* is formal and less commonly used than *on*.) □ *The FBI visited a plague of investigations on the mayor's staff.* □ *The storm visited disaster on the little village.*

visit the plumbing *Euph.* to go to the bathroom. □ *I think I'd better visit the plumbing before we go.* □ *I want you kids to visit the plumbing before we get in the car.*

V

visit with someone to pay a social call on someone. □ *I would like to come by and visit with you for a while.* □ *I will enjoy visiting with you.*

visualize someone or something **as** someone or something to imagine or envision someone as someone or something or something as something. □ *I can almost visualize you as the president.* □ *I visualize this room as a meeting place for everyone.*

visually impaired *Euph.* blind or partly blind. □ *I am visually impaired, but I like TV just as much as the next person.* □ *The disease left him visually impaired.*

*a **voice (in** something) and *a **say (in** something) *Fig.* a part in making a decision. (*Typically: **get** ~; **have** ~; **give** someone ~.) □ *I'd like to have a voice in choosing the carpet.* □ *John wanted to have a say in the issue also.* □ *He says he seldom gets a say.*

volunteer as something to submit oneself as a person ready or willing to do something. □ *Would you be willing to volunteer as a marcher?* □ *I will volunteer as a helper in the hospital.*

volunteer for something **1.** to submit oneself for some task without being asked. □ *I volunteered for the job.* □ *I didn't volunteer for this.* **2.** to work as an unpaid volunteer for a charity, etc. □ *On Sundays she volunteers as a receptionist at the hospital.*

vomit something **out**† *Fig.* [for something] to spill forth a great deal of something. □ *The volcano vomited the lava out for days.* □ *It vomited out hot lava for months.*

vomit something **up**† to bring up something from the stomach by vomiting. □ *The dog vomited the chocolate cake up.* □ *Fido vomited up the rabbit.*

vote a split ticket *Fig.* to cast a ballot on which one's votes are divided between two or more parties. □ *I always vote a split ticket since I detest both parties.* □ *Mary voted a split ticket for the first time in her life.*

vote a straight ticket *Fig.* to cast a ballot on which all one's votes are for members of the same political party. □ *I'm not a member of any political party, so I never vote a straight ticket.* □ *I usually vote a straight ticket because I believe in the principles of one party and not in the other's.*

vote against someone or something to cast a ballot against someone or something. □ *Are you going to vote against the provision?* □ *I plan to vote against David.*

vote for someone or something to cast a ballot in favor of someone or something. □ *Did you vote for Alice?* □ *I plan to vote for the tax freeze.* □ *Of course, I voted for myself! Wouldn't you?*

a **vote of confidence** *Fig.* a poll taken to discover whether or not a person, party, etc., still has the majority's support. □ *The government easily won the vote of confidence called for by the opposition.* □ *The president of the club resigned when one of the members called for a vote of confidence in his leadership.*

a **vote of thanks** *Fig.* a speech expressing appreciation and thanks to a speaker, lecturer, organizer, etc., and inviting the audience to applaud. □ *John gave a vote of thanks to Professor Jones for his talk.* □ *Mary was given a vote of thanks for organizing the dance.*

vote someone **into** something and **vote** someone **in**† to elect someone to office or to membership in a group. □ *The other party finally voted a candidate into office.* □ *The people voted in the new officers.*

vote someone **on(to** something) to elect someone to something, such as a board. □ *Let's vote Christine onto the board.* □ *We voted Dave on last term.*

vote someone or something **down**† to defeat someone or something in an election. □ *The community voted the proposal down.* □ *They voted down the proposal.*

vote someone **out of** something and **vote** someone **out**† to remove one from office by defeating one in an election. □ *They voted her out of office.* □ *The electorate voted out a number of incumbents.*

vote something **into law** and **vote** something **in**† to take a vote on a proposal and make it a law. □ *They voted the proposal into law.* □ *If we vote in this proposal, will that solve everything?*

vote something **through**† to get something through a set of procedures by voting in favor of it. □ *They were not able to vote the bill through.* □ *They voted through the bill.*

vote (up)on someone or something to make a decision about someone or something by ballot. (*Upon* is formal and less commonly used than *on*.) □ *The committee decided to vote on it.* □ *Are we going to vote on this?*

vote with one's **feet** *Fig.* to express one's dissatisfaction with something by leaving, especially by walking away. □ *I think that the play is a total flop. Most of the audience voted with its feet during the second act.* □ *I am prepared to vote with my feet if the meeting appears to be a waste of time.*

vouch for someone or something to support or back someone or something; to endorse someone or something. □ *I can vouch for Tom.* □ *Irene will vouch for my honesty.*

V

wade across something to walk across something covered by water. □ *Let's wade across the stream at this point.* □ *If I wade across it, I will get wet.*

wade in(to something**) 1.** to walk into an area covered by water. □ *The horse waded right into the stream.* □ *It waded right in.* **2.** *Fig.* to get quickly and directly involved in something. (Fig. on ①.) □ *Don't just wade into things. Stop and think about what you are doing.* □ *Just wade in and get started.*

wade through something **1.** to walk with effort through a substance, such as water, mud, garbage, etc. □ *The soldiers waded through the mud on the way to battle.* □ *They waded through the mess to get to where they were going.* **2.** *Fig.* to struggle through something with difficulty. (Fig. on ①.) □ *You mean I have to wade through all these applications?* □ *I have to wade through forty term papers in the next two days.*

waffle around and **waffle about** to be indecisive; to be wishy-washy about making a decision. □ *Make up your mind. Stop waffling around.* □ *Now, don't waffle about. Make up your mind.*

wag one's **chin** *Rur.* to talk. □ *She loves to visit. She'll wag her chin for hours.* □ *He was on the phone, wagging his chin to his buddy.*

wage something **against** someone or something to carry on something against someone or a group. □ *They waged war against the aggressors.* □ *Are you still waging your battle against your father?*

wager on someone or something to bet on someone or something. □ *I wouldn't want to wager on the outcome.* □ *I'll wager on Bill, the fastest runner in town.*

wager something **on** someone or something to bet a certain amount of money on someone or something. □ *I'll wager twenty bucks on you.* □ *I would never wager anything on that horse!*

wait (around) (for someone or something**)** to stay somewhere until something happens or someone or something arrives. □ *I'll wait around for you for an hour or so.* □ *I don't want to wait around.*

wait at something **(for** someone or something**)** to stay at something or some place until something happens or someone or something arrives. □ *Wait at the door for me.* □ *I waited at the office for your call.*

wait for the next wave Go to catch the next wave.

wait for the other shoe to drop *Fig.* to wait for the inevitable next step or the final conclusion. □ *He just opened his mail and moaned. Now, I'm waiting for the other shoe to drop when he finds the subpoena.*

wait on someone **hand and foot** *Fig.* to serve someone very well, attending to all personal needs. □ *I don't mind bringing you your coffee, but I don't intend to wait on you hand and foot.* □ *I don't want anyone to wait on me hand and foot. I can take care of myself.*

wait (on) tables *Fig.* to serve food and tend diners, as at a restaurant. □ *I waited on tables for years to pay my college tuition.*

wait one's **turn** *Fig.* to keep from doing something until everyone ahead of you has done it. □ *You can't cross the intersection yet. You must wait your turn.* □ *I can't wait my turn. I'm in a tremendous hurry.*

wait something **out**† to wait until something ends. □ *I will wait the summer out, and if nothing happens, I'll write again.* □ *I can wait out the storm inside.*

Wait up (a minute)! Wait for me while I catch up with you! □ *Tom, who was following Mary down the street, said, "Wait up a minute! I need to talk to you."* □ *John: Hey, Sally! Wait up! Sally: What's happening?*

wait up (for someone or something**) 1.** *Fig.* to stay up late waiting for someone to arrive or something to happen. □ *I'll be home late. Don't wait up for me.* □ *We waited up for the coming of the new year, and then we went to bed.* **2.** and **hold up (for** someone or something**)** *Fig.* to wait for someone or something to catch up. □ *Hey! Don't go so fast. Wait up for me.* □ *Hold up! You're going too fast.*

wait up (until something**)** to delay going to bed until a certain time or until something happens or someone arrives. □ *Are you going to wait up until midnight?* □ *We waited up until we heard him come in the back door.*

wait (up)on someone *Fig.* to pay homage to someone. (Stilted.) □ *Do you expect me to wait upon you like a member of some medieval court?* □ *She waited on her grown children as if they were gods and goddesses.*

wait-and-see attitude *Fig.* a skeptical attitude; an uncertain attitude in which someone will just wait to see what happens before reacting. □ *John thought that Mary couldn't do it, but he took a wait-and-see attitude.* □ *His wait-and-see attitude seemed to indicate that he didn't really care what happened.*

waiting in the wings *Fig.* ready or prepared to do something, especially to take over someone else's job or position. □ *Mr. Smith retires as manager next year, and Mr. Jones is just waiting in the wings.* □ *Jane was waiting in the wings, hoping that a member of the hockey team would drop out and she would get a place on the team.*

wake someone or an animal **up**† to cause someone or an animal to awaken. □ *Please don't wake me up until noon.* □ *Wake up your brother at noon.*

wake someone **(up**†**) from** something to awaken someone from something, such as a sound sleep, a nap, dreams, etc. □ *Henry woke Fred up from his dreams.* □ *He woke up Fred from a deep sleep.*

wake someone **up**† **(to** something**)** to cause someone to become alert and pay attention. (Does not refer to someone actually asleep.) □ *We tried to wake them up to the dangers.* □ *Try to wake up the students to their responsibilities.*

wake the dead *Fig.* to be so loud as to wake those who are "sleeping" the most soundly: the dead. □ *You are making enough noise to wake the dead.* □ *Stop hollering! You'll wake the dead!*

wake up to awaken; to become alert. □ *Wake up! We have to get on the road.* □ *It's time to wake up!*

Wake up and smell the coffee. *Prov.* Try to pay attention to what's going on. □ *Things have changed around here, Wallace J. Hodder! Wake up and smell the coffee!*

wake (up) from something to awaken from something, such as a sound sleep, sleep, dreams, etc. □ *She woke up from a deep sleep.* □ *Elaine woke from her dreams with a start.*

wake (up) to something and **waken to** something to awaken and face something, such as a problem, sunlight, music, noise, etc. □ *I love to wake up to soft music.* □ *We woke to the smell of freshly brewed coffee.*

walk a tightrope *Fig.* to be in a situation where one must be very cautious. □ *I've been walking a tightrope all day. I need to relax.* □ *Our business is about to fail. We've been walking a tightrope for three months.*

walk across something to move across something on foot. □ *We walked across the bridge carefully.* □ *Jerry walked across the field and examined the fence on the other side.*

walk ahead of someone or something to move on ahead of someone or something on foot. □ *Please walk ahead of me where I can see you.* □ *The road was so bad, I had to walk ahead of the car and look for potholes.*

walk all over someone or something **1.** *Lit.* to tread on someone or something. □ *Who walked all over the posters I had spread out on the floor?* □ *The rioters walked all over a child who had fallen in the confusion.* **2.** *Fig.* to treat someone or something very badly; to beat someone or something soundly in a competition. □ *The prosecution walked all over the witness.* □ *The attorney walked all over my case.*

walk along to move along on foot. □ *I was just walking along when my heel broke off.* □ *I'm in no hurry. I'll just walk along at my own speed.*

walk along something to move beside something on foot. □ *Let's not walk along the road. It's too dangerous.* □ *Walk along the wall where it's safer.*

walk arm in arm Go to arm in arm.

walk around to move around walking; to pace around. □ *I need to walk around and get some fresh air.* □ *Why don't we walk around for a while before we go in?*

walk around something **1.** to avoid something by passing around it. □ *Let's walk around this muddy place in the path.* **2.** to tour something or some place on foot. □ *I will walk around the park while I am waiting for you.* □ *Let me walk around the grounds and see what potential they offer.*

walk away from someone or something **1.** to depart from someone or something on foot. □ *Don't walk away from me while I am talking to you.* □ *I walked away from the concert by myself.* **2.** to abandon someone or something; to go away and leave someone or something. □ *Todd*

walked away from the problem. □ *I walked away from him and never saw him again.*

walk away with someone or an animal to lead, take, accompany, or carry someone or an animal away. □ *I walked away with my brother.* □ *The young man walked away with the heifer.*

walk away with something and **walk off with** something **1.** *Fig.* to win something easily. (With little more effort than is required to carry off the winning trophy.) □ *John won the tennis match with no difficulty. He walked away with it.* □ *Our team walked away with first place.* **2.** *Fig.* to take or steal something. □ *I think somebody just walked off with my purse!* □ *Somebody walked off with my daughter's bicycle.*

walk back ((to) something**)** to return to something or some place on foot. □ *I walked back to my office alone.* □ *She walked back home.* □ *Thanks for the offer of a ride. I'll walk back.*

walk down something to go down something on foot. □ *She walked down the path and turned to the right.* □ *Todd was walking down the road when they caught up with him.*

walk hand in hand Go to hand in hand.

walk in (a) single file Go to in (a) single file.

walk in on someone or something to interrupt someone or something by entering a place. □ *I didn't mean to walk in on you. I didn't know anyone was in here.* □ *Alice walked in on the meeting by accident.*

walk in(to something**)** to enter something on foot. □ *We walked into the parking garage and tried to find our car.* □ *He walked in and sat down.*

walk off to walk away; to leave on foot abruptly. □ *She didn't even say good-bye. She just walked off.* □ *He walked off and never looked back.*

walk off the job 1. *Fig.* to abandon a job abruptly. □ *I was so mad I almost walked off the job.* □ *Fred almost walked off the job when he saw how bad things were.* **2.** *Fig.* to go on strike at a workplace. □ *The workers walked off the job and refused to negotiate.* □ *They walked off the job and called a strike.*

walk off with something Go to walk away with something.

walk on to continue walking. □ *Walk on. Go all the way to the end.* □ *I knew I wasn't there yet, so I just walked on.*

walk on air *Fig.* to be very happy; to be euphoric. □ *Ann was walking on air when she got the job.* □ *On the last day of school, all the children are walking on air.*

walk on eggs and **walk on thin ice** *Fig.* to proceed very cautiously; to be in a very precarious position. (Fig. on the image of someone walking on something that offers little support and may collapse at any moment.) □ *I have to remember that I'm walking on eggs when I give this speech.* □ *Careful with radical ideas like that. You're walking on thin ice.*

walk on eggshells 1. *Fig.* to walk very carefully; to take steps gingerly. □ *Since he stumbled and fell against the china cabinet, Bill has been walking on eggshells.* **2.** *Fig.* to be very diplomatic and inoffensive. □ *I was walking on eggshells trying to explain the remark to her without offending her further.*

W

walk on stage and off again *Fig.* to play a very small role where one goes on stage and quickly leaves again. □ *It was a very small part. I walked on stage and right off again.*

walk on thin ice Go to walk on eggs.

walk out (of something**)** to exit something or some place. □ *We walked out of the shop when we had made our purchases.* □ *She went to the door and walked out.*

walk out (on someone**)** *Fig.* to abandon someone; to leave one's spouse. □ *Mr. Franklin walked out on Mrs. Franklin last week.* □ *Bob walked out on Jane without saying good-bye.*

walk out (on something**)** *Fig.* to leave a performance (of something by someone). □ *We didn't like the play at all, so we walked out.* □ *John was giving a very dull speech, and a few people even walked out on him.*

walk out with someone to exit something or some place with someone on foot. □ *After the play, Jane and I walked out together and had a nice talk.* □ *We walked out with Mr. Wilson, who had sat next to us during the show.*

walk over (to someone or something**)** to move to someone or something on foot. □ *I walked over to her and asked her what she thought.* □ *I just walked over.*

walk right in to enter on foot without hesitation. □ *He went up to the door, opened it, and walked right in.* □ *Please just walk right in!*

walk (right) into a trap to fall right into a trap or deception. □ *You walked right into my trap. Now I have you right where I want you.* □ *The unsuspecting agent walked into the FBI setup.*

walk (right) into someone or something to bump into someone or something. □ *Fred walked right into the edge of the door and broke his nose.* □ *Sam walked into Liz and frightened her.*

walk right up (to someone or something**)** to move up close to someone or something, on foot; not to hesitate to approach someone or something. □ *Walk right up to him and ask him what you want to know.* □ *Just walk right up.*

walk soft to be unobtrusive; to be gentle and humble. □ *I try to walk soft and not rock the boat.* □ *The guy's a tyrant. He walks soft just to mislead people.*

walk someone **out** to accompany someone out, walking. □ *I'll walk you out. The exit is hard to find.* □ *Please let me walk you out so you don't get lost.*

walk someone **over to** someone or something to accompany someone a short distance on foot to someone or something. □ *I'll walk her over to the personnel department and show her what to do.* □ *I will walk her over to Richard. I think he's in his office.* □ *She walked herself over to the window and looked out.*

walk someone's **feet off** *Fig.* to walk too much and tire out someone's feet, including one's own. □ *I've gone all over town today. I walked my feet off, looking for just the right present for Jill.* □ *I need to know where I am going before I leave so I won't walk my feet off.*

walk someone **through** something **1.** to lead or accompany someone through an opening, arch, doorway, etc. □ *Mike walked Mary through the arch into a lovely garden.* □ *Todd walked Rita through the doorway, into the ballroom.* **2.** *Fig.* to lead someone through a complex problem or thought process. □ *Mary walked Jane through the complex solution to the calculus problem.* □ *Do I have to walk you through this solution?*

walk tall *Fig.* to be brave and self-assured. □ *I know I can walk tall because I'm innocent.* □ *You go out on that stage and walk tall. There is no reason to be afraid.*

walk the floor *Fig.* to pace nervously while waiting. □ *While Bill waited for news of the operation, he walked the floor for hours on end.* □ *Walking the floor won't help. You might as well sit down and relax.*

walk the plank *Fig.* to suffer punishment at the hand of someone. (*Fig.* on the image of pirates making their blindfolded captives die by walking off the end of a plank jutting out over the open sea.) □ *Fred may think he can make the members of my department walk the plank, but we will fight back.* □ *Tom thought he could make John walk the plank, but John fought back.*

walk through something *Fig.* to rehearse something in a casual way; to go through a play or other performed piece, showing where each person is to be located during each speech or musical number. □ *Let's walk through this scene one more time.*

walk together [for two or more people] to walk as a group. □ *Let's all walk together so we can talk to one another.* □ *We walked together for a while.*

walk up something **1.** to move up an incline or stairs on foot. □ *Sally will have to walk up the stairs by herself.* **2.** to walk the length of something. □ *I walked slowly up the hall.*

walk up to someone or something to approach someone or something on foot. □ *I walked up to the manager and told him my problem.* □ *Eric walked up to the door and rang the bell.*

walk with someone to walk in the company of someone. □ *Why don't you walk with me for a while?* □ *Can I walk with you?*

walk with something **1.** to walk with the aid of something, such as a cane, crutches, etc. □ *You can recognize her easily. She walks with a cane.* □ *Dan walks with the help of a crutch.* **2.** to walk in a characteristic manner, such as with a limp, halting gait, a sprightly step, etc. □ *Martha's uncle walks with a limp.* □ *I have always walked with a halting gait.*

wall someone or something **in**[†] to contain someone or something behind or within a wall. (Implies a constriction of space, but not necessarily an inescapable area. See **wall** something **up**.) □ *The count walled his prisoner in permanently.* □ *Jane decided to wall in the little garden at the side of the house.* □ *She walled the garden in.*

wall someone or something **off**[†] to separate or segregate someone or something by building a wall. □ *She sat right across from me at her desk, listening to every phone call I made. Finally, the manager walled her off so we now can carry on our business in privacy.* □ *They walled off the south door to the building.*

wall something **off**[†] **(from** someone or something**)** to deny access to an area by building a wall as a barrier. □ *The manager was told to wall the incinerator area off from the machinery area.* □ *Please wall off the incinerator area.*

wall something **up**† **1.** to seal something up behind a wall. ☐ *We simply walled the old furnace up. It was cheaper than removing it.* ☐ *They walled up the old furnace.* **2.** to fill up an opening, such as a window or door, by building a wall. ☐ *We will have to hire someone to wall the doorway up.* ☐ *They walled up the doorway.*

wallow (around) in something to roll around in something. ☐ *Pigs enjoy wallowing around in mud.* ☐ *They wallow in mud to keep cool.*

wallow in something *Fig.* to experience an abundance of something. (Fig. on **wallow (around) in** something.) ☐ *Roger and Wilma are just wallowing in money.* ☐ *Claire spent the entire day wallowing in self-pity.* ☐ *The villagers are all wallowing in superstition.*

Walls have ears. *Prov.* Someone may be listening. (A warning that you think your conversation is being overheard.) ☐ *Jill: Did I tell you what I found out about Fred? He— Jane: Shhh! Walls have ears.* ☐ *Don't say anything about our business dealings in here. Walls have ears.*

wall-to-wall (with) something *Fig.* covered with something in all places. (From *wall-to-wall carpeting.*) ☐ *The hallway is wall-to-wall with Jimmy's toys.* ☐ *The beach was wall-to-wall tourists.*

waltz around something *Fig.* to move around or through a place happily or proudly. ☐ *She waltzed around the room, very pleased with herself.* ☐ *Who is that person waltzing around, trying to look important?*

waltz in(to some place**)** *Fig.* to step or walk into a place briskly and easily. ☐ *She waltzed into the room and showed off her ring.* ☐ *Eric waltzed in and said hello.*

waltz off *Fig.* to depart briskly and easily. ☐ *They said good-bye and waltzed off.*

waltz off (with something**)** *Fig.* to take something away easily. ☐ *The thieves waltzed off with a giant screen television in broad daylight.* ☐ *They just picked the thing up and waltzed off. Nobody asked them any questions.*

waltz through something *Fig.* to get through something easily. ☐ *I waltzed through my comps and started on my research in my second year of grad school.* ☐ *I tried to waltz through my assignment, but it was too hard.*

waltz up (to someone**)** *Fig.* to approach someone boldly. ☐ *He just waltzed up to her and introduced himself.* ☐ *He waltzed up and said hello.*

wander about and **wander around** to stroll or amble around without any purpose evident; to roam around. ☐ *We just wandered about downtown all morning, looking at the shop windows.* ☐ *It's fun to wander around in a strange town.*

wander away (from someone or something**)** and **wander off (from** someone or something**)** to roam away from someone or something. ☐ *The little boy wandered away from his mother.* ☐ *He wandered off from his sister.* ☐ *The dog wandered off.*

wander from something to stray from something, such as a path, a set of rules, etc. ☐ *Please do not wander from the path I have set for you.* ☐ *If you wander from our guidelines, your finished product may not be acceptable.*

wander in(to something**)** to stray or roam into something or some place. ☐ *A deer wandered into the parking lot and*

frightened some of the shoppers. ☐ *Someone wandered in and sat down.*

wander off (from someone or something**)** Go to **wander away (from** someone or something**)**.

wangle out of something *Fig.* to get out of having to do something; to argue or deceive one's way out of a responsibility. ☐ *Don't try to wangle out of this mess. You must stay and fix the problems you made.* ☐ *Mary managed to wangle out of staying late again.*

wangle something **from** someone and **wangle** something **out of** someone *Fig.* to obtain, through argument or deception, something from someone. ☐ *Are you trying to wangle money from me?* ☐ *You can't wangle any money out of me.*

Wanna make sumpin' of it? Go to **Want to make something of it?**

want a knuckle sandwich Go to **a knuckle sandwich**.

want a pick-me-up Go to **a pick-me-up**.

Want a piece of me? Go to **(You) want a piece of me?**

want first crack at something Go to **first crack at** something.

want for nothing *Fig.* not to lack anything; to have everything one needs or desires. ☐ *The Smiths don't have much money, but their children seem to want for nothing.* ☐ *Lisa's husband spoils her. She wants for nothing.*

want for something *Fig.* to lack something; to need something. ☐ *I certainly don't want for advice. In fact, I have had too much.* ☐ *We don't want for helpers around here.*

want in((to) something**)** to want to come into something or some place. ☐ *It's cold out here! I want into the house.* ☐ *The dog wants in.*

want off ((of) something**)** to desire to be off or get off something. (Of is usually retained before pronouns.) ☐ *I want off of this bus this very minute!* ☐ *Stop this train! I want off!*

want out (of something**) 1.** to desire to get out of something or some place. ☐ *I want out of this stuffy room.* ☐ *Where's the door? I want out.* **2.** *Fig.* to desire to be relieved of a responsibility. ☐ *I want out of this responsibility. I don't have the time to do it right.* ☐ *This job is no good for me. I want out.* **3.** *Fig.* to want to remove oneself from some association or relationship. ☐ *I want out. This relationship is stifling me.*

want so bad one **can taste it** Go to **so bad** one **can taste it**.

want someone **for** something **1.** to desire someone for some job or purpose. ☐ *I want Fred for my team.* ☐ *We all want you for a candidate.* **2.** to hunt or seek someone as a criminal suspect. ☐ *The police want Max for questioning.* ☐ *They want him for a number of crimes.*

want someone or something **back** to desire the return of someone or something. ☐ *Timmy wanted his mother back very badly.* ☐ *I want my money back!*

want someone or something **in** something to desire that someone or something be in something or some place. ☐ *I want you in my office immediately.* ☐ *I want some coffee in this room now!*

want someone or something **out of** something to desire that someone or something leave or be removed from something or some place. □ *I want you out of here immediately.* □ *I want this box out of here now!*

want something **for** someone or something to desire to have something for someone or something. □ *I want a gift for my wife. What would you suggest?* □ *I want a button for my shirt.*

want something **on a silver platter** Go to **on a silver platter**.

Want to make something of it? and **Wanna make sumpin' of it?** *Inf.* Do you want to fight about it? (See also **(Do you) want to make something of it?**) □ *So, I'm a little ugly. Wanna make sumpin' of it?* □ *I'm sitting in your usual chair, you say? Want to make something of it?*

war against someone or something to fight against someone or something; to oppose someone or something. □ *That country is always warring against its neighbors.* □ *Why do you want to war against the city council?*

war over someone or something to fight about who is to get someone or something. □ *Stop warring over Tom. He refuses to play on either team.* □ *There is no point in warring over the contract.*

war with someone to fight or dispute with someone. □ *Ruth is always warring with someone, usually about something trivial.* □ *Please don't war with me!*

ward someone or something **off**[†] to hold someone or something off; to fight **someone or something off.** □ *The army was able to ward the attackers off repeatedly.* □ *We couldn't ward off the attackers any longer.*

*****warm as toast** very warm and cozy. (*Also: **as** ~.) □ *The baby will be warm as toast in that blanket.* □ *We were as warm as toast by the side of the fire.*

warm body a person; just any person (who can be counted on to be present). □ *See if you can get a couple of warm bodies to stand at the door and hand out programs.* □ *You mean among all these warm bodies nobody knows calculus?*

warm someone or something **up**[†] to make someone or something warmer; to take the chill off someone or something. □ *I put him by the fire to warm him up a little.* □ *We warmed up our feet before the fire.* □ *Could you warm up my coffee, please?*

warm someone **up**[†] **1.** to make someone warmer. □ *Stand by the fire and warm yourself up.* □ *Warm up the kids and then give them some cookies.* **2.** *Fig.* to help someone get physically prepared to perform in an athletic event. (As if exercising or loosening up someone's muscles.) □ *The referee told the coach to warm his team up so the game could begin.* □ *You have to warm up the team before a game.* □ *Be sure to warm yourself up before playing.* **3.** *Fig.* to prepare an audience for another—more famous—performer. (Fig. on ②.) □ *A singer came out to warm us up for the main attraction.* □ *This comedian is a superb choice to warm up the audience.*

warm something **over**[†] **1.** to reheat food to serve it as leftovers. □ *I'll just warm the rest over for lunch tomorrow.* □ *Jane warmed over yesterday's turkey.* **2.** *Fig.* to bring up a matter that was thought to have been settled. (Fig. on ①.) □ *Please don't warm that business over again. It is settled*

and should remain that way. □ *Don't warm over that matter. We have discussed it enough.*

warm the bench *Fig.* [for a player] to remain out of play during a game—seated on a bench. □ *John spent the whole game warming the bench.* □ *Mary never warms the bench. She plays from the beginning to the end.*

warm the cockles of someone's **heart** *Fig.* to make someone feel warm and happy. □ *It warms the cockles of my heart to hear you say that.* □ *Hearing that old song again warmed the cockles of her heart.*

warm up 1. [for the weather or a person] to become warmer or hotter. □ *I think it is going to warm up next week.* **2.** *Fig.* [for someone] to become more friendly. (A warm person is a friendly person.) □ *Todd began to warm up halfway through the conference.* □ *After he had worked there for a while, he began to warm up.* **3.** and **warm up for** something *Fig.* to prepare for some kind of performance or competition. □ *The team had to warm up before the game.* □ *They have to warm up.*

warm up to someone or something *Fig.* to become more fervent and earnest toward someone, something, or a group; to become more responsive and receptive to someone, a group, or something. □ *After we talked, he began to warm up to us a little.* □ *I warmed up to the committee as the interview went on.*

warmed over not very original; rehashed. □ *I am not interested in reading warmed over news on a computer screen.* □ *The lecture sounded sort of warmed over, but it wasn't too dull.*

warn someone **about** someone or something to advise someone about the dangers associated with someone or something. □ *Didn't I warn you about the dangers of going there?* □ *I warned you about Alice.*

warn someone **against** someone or something to advise someone against someone, something, or doing something. □ *We warned them all against going to the region at this time.* □ *I warned her against Gerald.*

warn someone **away from** someone or something to advise someone to avoid someone or something. □ *We warned her away from the danger, but she did not heed our warning.* □ *Why didn't you warn me away from Roger?*

warn someone **of** something to advise someone that something bad is likely to happen. □ *I wish you had warned us of what was going to happen.* □ *Please warn John of the heavy traffic he may run into.*

warn someone **off**[†] to advise a person to stay away. □ *We placed a guard outside the door to warn people off until the gas leak could be fixed.* □ *The guards warned off everyone in the vicinity.*

warts and all *Cliché* even with the flaws. □ *It's a great performance—warts and all.* □ *Yes, we admire each other very much, warts and all.*

was had Go to **been had.**

wash away to be carried away by water or some other liquid. □ *The bridge washed away in the flood.* □ *All the soil washed away and left the rocks exposed.*

wash off ((of) someone or something**)** to be carried off of or away from someone or something by the action of water or another liquid. (*Of* is usually retained before pro-

W

nouns.) □ *The dirt washed off of the floor easily.* □ *The label washed off this can, and now I don't know what's in it.*

wash one's **dirty linen in public** Go to **air** one's **dirty linen in public.**

wash one's **hands of** someone or something *Fig.* to end one's association with someone or something. (*Fig.* on the notion of getting rid of a problem by removing it as if it were dirt on the hands.) □ *I washed my hands of Tom. I wanted no more to do with him.* □ *That car was a real headache. I washed my hands of it long ago.*

wash out 1. *Inf.* to fail and be removed from something, such as school. □ *I studied all I could, but I still washed out.* □ *I don't want to wash out. It's my whole future.* **2.** *Inf.* to have a serious wreck; to **wipe out.** □ *The little car washed out on the curve.* □ *The vehicles have a tendency to wash out when cornering.* **3.** *Inf.* to lose a large amount of money. □ *Fred washed out on that stock deal.* □ *Lefty and Willie washed out at the racetrack.* **4.** *Inf.* to break down or collapse from exhaustion. □ *The whole play began to wash out during the second act. It was a lost cause by the third.* □ *Finally, after a long day, I just washed out. They had to call the paramedics.*

wash over someone *Fig.* [for a powerful feeling] to flood over a person. □ *A feeling of nausea washed over me.* □ *A strong feeling of satisfaction washed over me.*

wash overboard [for someone or something] to be carried overboard (off the deck of a ship) by water. □ *Our chairs washed overboard in the storm.* □ *I was afraid that the dog would wash overboard, so I took her below.*

wash someone or something **away**[†] [for a flood of water] to carry someone or something away. □ *The flood washed the boats away.* □ *The high water washed away much of the sand along the shoreline.*

wash someone or something **off**[†] to clean someone or something by washing. □ *She washed the muddy children off with a hose and put their clothes right into the washing machine.* □ *Jane washed off the children.*

wash someone or something **overboard** [for water] to flood up and carry someone or something off the deck of a ship into the sea. □ *The high seas washed two of the sailors overboard.* □ *The storm washed our chairs overboard.*

wash someone or something **up**[†] **1.** to clean up someone or something by washing. □ *Please wash the baby up as long as you are changing the diaper.* □ *I'll wash up the baby.* □ *Sam will wash himself up before dinner.* **2.** [for water or the waves] to bring someone or something up onto the shore or beach. □ *Look what the waves washed up! A bottle with a note in it!* □ *The waves washed a bottle up.*

wash someone **out**[†] *Fig.* to deplete the strength or vitality of someone. □ *The flu really washed me out.* □ *The disease washed out the whole class.*

wash someone **out of** something and **wash** someone **out**[†] to make it necessary for a person to leave a place or program; to wash someone up. (See also **wash** someone **out.**) □ *That professor just loves to wash students out of the course.* □ *The professor washed out over half the class.*

wash someone **up**[†] to terminate someone in something. □ *This error is going to wash you up as an account execu-*

tive. □ *That washed me up.* □ *Problems like this have washed up quite a few careers.*

wash something **away**[†] to clean something by scrubbing and flushing away the dirt. □ *Fresh water will wash the seawater away.* □ *Let's wash away these muddy footprints.*

wash something **down** something to get rid of something by flooding it down the sewer, drain, sink, etc. □ *Wash all the soap suds down the drain and clean the sink, please.* □ *Please wash all that stuff down the drain.*

wash something **down**[†] **(with** something**) 1.** to clean something by flooding with water, alcohol, etc. □ *The doctor washed the area down and began to stitch up the wound.* □ *She washed down the wound with alcohol to clean it thoroughly.* □ *Todd washed the driveway down with water.* **2.** *Fig.* to use fluid to aid the swallowing of food or medicine. □ *Molly washed the pills down with a gulp of coffee.* □ *She washed down the pills with a glass of water.*

wash something **of** something to get something cleaned of something by washing. □ *I washed my hair of the smell of cigarette smoke I was saturated with in the meeting.* □ *I have to get home and wash my trousers of this stain.*

wash something **off (of)** someone or something and **wash** something **off**[†] to clean something off someone or something. (*Of* is usually retained before pronouns.) □ *I have to wash this tomato sauce off my jacket before it stains it.* □ *I will wash off the tomato stains.*

wash something **out**[†] **1.** to wash out the inside of something; to wash something made of fabric. □ *I have to wash my socks out tonight.* □ *Wash the pitcher out before you put it away.* □ *I will wash out my socks tomorrow.* **2.** *Fig.* to rain on or flood an event so that it must be canceled. (*Fig.* on ①.) □ *Rain washed the game out.* □ *The storm washed out the picnic.* **3.** to wash or erode something out or away. □ *The flood washed the new bushes out.* □ *The rains washed out the paving stones.*

wash something **out of** something and **wash** something **out**[†] to clean some kind of dirt from something. □ *You had better wash all the stains out of the clothing before you put it in the dryer.* □ *You will want to wash out the dirt.*

wash up (for something**)** to clean [oneself] up for something, such as a meal. □ *Please wash up for dinner.* □ *Go and wash up!*

washed out *Inf.* exhausted; tired. □ *I feel too washed out to go to work today.* □ *Poor Ted really looks washed out.*

washed up *Fig.* finished. □ *"You're through, Tom," said the manager, "Fired—washed up!"* □ *Wilbur is washed up as a bank teller.*

waste away to wither or dwindle away. □ *Our money just seemed to waste away.* □ *As she grew older, she just sort of wasted away.*

Waste not, want not. *Prov. Cliché* If you do not waste anything, you will always have enough. □ *Always save the fabric scraps left over from your sewing projects; you can use them to make something else. Waste not, want not.* □ *Sam never let his leftovers spoil in the refrigerator but made sure to eat them. "Waste not, want not," he said.*

a **waste of space** something that is completely without value. □ *The wrecked furniture in here is just a waste of space.* □ *This broken-down car is a waste of space!*

W

waste one's **breath** *Fig.* to waste one's time talking; to talk in vain. □ *Don't waste your breath talking to her. She won't listen.* □ *You can't persuade me. You're just wasting your breath.*

waste someone *Sl.* to kill someone. □ *The thief tried to waste the bank guard after the bank robbery.* □ *The crook said, "Try that again, and I'll waste you!"*

waste something **away**† to use something up wastefully; to dissipate something. □ *He wasted all his money away and had to live in poverty.* □ *They wasted away everything and regretted it later.*

waste something **on** someone or something to throw something away on someone or something. □ *Please don't waste any sweet potatoes on me. I don't like them.* □ *I can't waste any more money on this car.*

watch for someone or something to keep looking for someone or something to appear. □ *Watch for me. I'll be wearing a red carnation in my hair.* □ *I will watch for the bus.*

Watch it! 1. *Inf.* Be careful. □ *Rachel: Watch it! There's a broken stair there. Jane: Gee, thanks.* □ *Mary: Watch it! There's a pothole in the street. Bob: Thanks.* **2.** *Inf.* Do not act or talk that way. □ *Sally: I really hate John! Sue: Watch it! He's my brother!* □ *Bill: You girls always seem to take so long to do a simple thing like getting dressed. Mary: Watch it!*

Watch my lips! and **Read my lips!** *Inf.* I am going to say something rude to you that I will not say out loud! □ *You jerk! Watch my lips!* □ *Hey, chum! Read my lips!*

watch one's **step 1.** be careful of one's walking or stepping. □ *It's slippery here. Watch your step.* **2.** *Fig.* to act with care and caution so as not to make a mistake or offend someone. □ *John had better watch his step with the new boss. He won't put up with his lateness.* □ *Mary was told by the teacher to watch her step and stop missing classes.*

watch out for someone and **look out for** someone *Fig.* to watch over and care for someone. □ *When I was a kid, my older brother always watched out for me.* □ *I really needed someone to look out for me then.*

watch out for someone or something and **look out for** someone or something **1.** to be on guard for someone or something; to be on watch for the arrival or approach of someone or something. □ *Watch out for someone wearing a white carnation.* □ *Look out for John and his friends. They'll be coming this way very soon.* **2.** and **look out; watch out** *Fig.* to try to avoid a confrontation with someone or something. □ *Watch out! That car nearly hit you!* □ *Look out for John. He's looking for you, and he's really mad.* □ *Thanks. I'd better look out.*

watch over someone or something to keep guard over someone or something; to care for someone or something. □ *Could you please watch over my little girl while I go to the store?* □ *I will watch over your house while you are away.*

watch someone or something **like a hawk** *Fig.* to watch someone or something very carefully. □ *The teacher watched the pupils like a hawk to make sure they did not cheat on the exam.* □ *We had to watch our dog like a hawk in case he ran away.*

watch the store Go to mind the store.

Watch your mouth! and **Watch your tongue! Watch your language!** *Inf.* Pay attention to what you are say-ing!; Do not say anything rude! □ *Hey, don't talk that way! Watch your mouth!* □ *Watch your tongue, garbage mouth!*

A **watched pot never boils.** *Prov.* Something you are waiting for will not happen while you are concentrating on it. □ *Don't just sit there staring at the phone while you wait for Lucy to call. A watched pot never boils.* □ *I'd better do something besides look out the window waiting for Emily to drive up. A watched pot never boils.*

water over the dam and **water under the bridge** *Fig.* past and unchangeable events. □ *Your quarrel with Lena is water over the dam; now you ought to concentrate on getting along with her.* □ *George and I were friends once, but that's all water under the bridge now.*

water something **down**† **1.** to dilute something. □ *Who watered the orange juice down?* □ *Jim watered down the orange juice.* **2.** to water something thoroughly. □ *Will you water the lawn down tonight?* □ *Water down the lawn this evening so it will grow tomorrow.* **3.** *Fig.* to reduce the effectiveness or force of something. (Fig. on ①.) □ *Please don't water my declaration down.* □ *The new laws watered down the power of the president.*

water under the bridge Go to water over the dam.

watering hole 1. *Lit.* a place where there is water for animals (and people) to drink. □ *The elephants came down to the watering hole and chased away the lions so they could drink in peace.* **2.** *Fig.* a bar or tavern. □ *Fred is down at the local watering hole boozing it up.*

wave at someone and **wave to** someone to move an upraised hand in such a way as to signal recognition to someone. □ *The people in the boat waved at us.* □ *They waved to us after we waved at them.*

wave back (at someone**)** to return someone's hand signal of greeting. □ *I waved back at her, but she didn't see me.* □ *She didn't wave back.*

wave someone **back (from** something**)** to motion someone to move back from something. □ *The police officer waved the curious onlookers back from the scene of the crime.* □ *The students started to go onstage, but the teacher waved them back.*

wave someone or something **aside**† to make a signal with the hand for someone or something to move aside. □ *The police officer waved us aside and would not let us turn into our street.* □ *The officer waved aside the spectators.* □ *She waved all the traffic aside.*

wave someone or something **away**† **(from** someone or something**)** to make a signal with the hand for someone or something to move away from someone or something. □ *The officer waved us away from the intersection where we were about to turn left.* □ *The guard waved away the traffic from the intersection.*

wave someone or something **off**† to make a signal with the hand for someone or something to remain at a distance. □ *There was someone standing in front of the bridge, waving everyone off. The bridge must have collapsed.* □ *He waved off all the traffic.*

wave someone or something **on**† to make a signal with the hand for someone or something to move on or keep moving. □ *The traffic cop waved us on.* □ *The cop waved on the hordes of pedestrians.*

W

wave something **around**† to raise something up and move it around so that everyone can see it. □ *When Ruth found the money, she waved it around so everyone could see it.* □ *She kept waving around the dollar she found in the street.*

wave to someone Go to **wave at** someone.

waver between someone **and** someone else to vacillate between choosing one person or another. □ *I had to appoint the new manager, and I was wavering between Jane and Janet.* □ *We wavered between Bill and Bob for the position.*

waver between something **and** something else to vacillate between choosing one thing and another; to linger indecisively between doing one thing or another. □ *The captain was wavering between St. Thomas and St. Croix.* □ *We wavered between chocolate and vanilla.*

wax and wane *Fig.* to increase and then decrease, as the phases of the moon. □ *As the moon waxes and wanes, so does the height of the tide change.* □ *Voter sentiment about the tax proposal waxes and wanes with each passing day.*

wax angry and **wax wroth** *Fig.* to speak in anger and with indignity. □ *Seeing the damage done by the careless children caused the preacher to wax wroth at their parents.*

wax eloquent *Fig.* to speak with eloquence. □ *Perry never passed up a chance to wax eloquent at a banquet.*

wax poetic *Fig.* to speak poetically. □ *I hope you will pardon me if I wax poetic for a moment when I say that your lovely hands drift across the piano keys like swans on a lake.*

wax wroth Go to **wax angry.**

the **way it plays** *Sl.* the way it is; the way things are. □ *The world is a rough place, and that's the way it plays.* □ *It's tough, but it's the way it plays.*

way off (base) *Inf. Fig.* on the wrong track; completely wrong. □ *I think you're way off base. Try again.* □ *Sorry. You are way off. You should just give up.*

way out 1. extreme; arcane. □ *Some of your ideas are really way out.* □ *What a way-out hairdo.* **2.** heavily intoxicated. □ *That guy is way out—can't even walk.* □ *She was so way-out, she was almost unconscious.*

(way) over there in a place some distance away. □ *I see a house way over there in the field.* □ *My hat is over there on the table.*

The **way to a man's heart is through his stomach.** *Prov.* If you want a man to love you, you should feed him good food. □ *Sue: I want Keith to notice me, but he doesn't even know I'm alive. Mother: Invite him over and cook him a good meal. The way to a man's heart is through his stomach.*

We aim to please. *Fig.* We try hard to please you. (Usually a commercial slogan, but can be said in jest by one person, often in response to **Thank you.**) □ *Mary: This meal is absolutely delicious! Waiter: We aim to please.* □ *Tom: Well, Sue, here's the laundry detergent you wanted from the store. Sue: Oh, thanks loads. You saved me a trip. Tom: We aim to please.*

[we are] See the entries beginning with *we're.*

(We) don't see you much around here anymore. and **(We) don't see you around here much anymore.** *Fig.* We haven't seen you for a long time. (The *we* can be replaced with *I.*) □ *Bill: Hello, Tom. Long time no see. Tom: Yes, Bill. We don't see you much around here anymore.* □ *"We don't see you around here much anymore," said the old pharmacist to John, who had just come home from college.*

We had a lovely time. Go to **I had a lovely time.**

We must do this again (sometime). Go to **Let's do this again (sometime).**

We must learn to walk before we can run. *Prov.* You must master a basic skill before you are able to learn more complex things. □ *Maria wanted to make a tailored jacket as her first sewing project, but her mother convinced her that she should make something much simpler; she would have to learn to walk before she could run.*

We need to talk about something. an expression urging or ordering someone to discuss something. □ *Bill: Can I come over tonight? We need to talk about something. Mary: I guess so.* □ *"Mr. Franklin," said Bill's boss sort of sternly, "I want to see you in my office for a minute. We need to talk about something."*

We were just talking about you. a phrase said when a person being discussed appears on the scene. (Compare this with **Speak of the devil.**) □ *Tom: Speak of the devil, here comes Bill. Mary: We were just talking about you, Bill.* □ *Sally (approaching Tom and Bill): Hi, Tom. Hi, Bill. What's new? Bill: Oh, Sally! We were just talking about you.*

[we will] See the entries beginning with *we'll.*

***weak as a baby** and ***weak as a kitten** *Cliché* [of someone] physically very weak. (*Also: **as ~.**) □ *Six weeks of illness left the athlete as weak as a baby.* □ *John is as weak as a kitten because he doesn't eat well.*

weak as a kitten Go to previous.

the **weak link (in the chain)** *Fig.* the weak point or person in a system or organization. □ *Joan's hasty generalizations about the economy were definitely the weak link in her argument.*

weak sister a timid person, usually a male. □ *It looks like Dave is the weak sister on the team.* □ *We've got to pull together and stop playing like a bunch of weak sisters.*

a **wealth of** something *Fig.* a large amount of something. □ *There's a wealth of information on parrots at the library.* □ *The junkyard had a wealth of used car parts.*

wean someone **(away**†**) from** something to force someone or an animal to break a habit. (Fig. on the notion of ending the dependence of a young creature on milk alone.) □ *It was almost impossible to wean her from her high spending habits.* □ *We couldn't wean away the dog from its mother.*

wear and tear (on something**)** *Fig.* the process of wearing down or breaking down something by regular use. □ *Driving in freezing weather means lots of wear and tear on your car.* □ *I drive carefully and have my car serviced regularly to avoid wear and tear.*

wear away at someone or something to annoy or diminish someone or something. □ *Facing the same problems year after year was wearing away at the president of the company.* □ *The rain wore away at the stone through time.*

wear down *Fig.* to break down with wear; to erode. □ *The steps had worn down so much that each one was curved and slanted dangerously.*

wear more than one hat and **wear two hats** *Fig.* to have more than one set of responsibilities; to hold more than one office. □ *The mayor is also the police chief. She wears more than one hat.* □ *I have too much to do to wear more than one hat.* □ *He wears two hats; he's both CEO and chairman of the board.*

wear off [for the effects of something] to become less; to stop gradually. □ *The effects of the painkiller wore off and my tooth began to hurt.* □ *I was annoyed at first, but my anger wore off.*

wear off ((of) something) [for something] to be ground or rubbed away. (*Of* is usually retained before pronouns.) □ *The paint has worn off the porch steps.* □ *The finish is wearing off.*

wear on (for a period of time) *Fig.* [for an event] to continue for a long period of time. □ *The lecture seemed to wear on for hours.* □ *It wore on until I went to sleep.*

wear on someone *Fig.* to bother or annoy someone. □ *We stayed with them only a short time because my children seemed to wear on them.* □ *Always being short of money wears on a person after a while.*

wear one's **heart on** one's **sleeve** and **have** one's **heart on** one's **sleeve** *Fig.* to display one's feelings openly and habitually, rather than keep them private. □ *John always has his heart on his sleeve so that everyone knows how he feels.* □ *Because she wears her heart on her sleeve, it's easy to hurt her feelings.*

wear out to become worn from use; to become diminished or useless from use. □ *My car engine is about to wear out.* □ *It takes a lot of driving to wear out an engine.*

wear out one's **welcome** *Fig.* to stay too long (at an event to which one has been invited); to visit somewhere too often. □ *Tom visited the Smiths so often that he wore out his welcome.* □ *At about midnight, I decided that I had worn out my welcome, so I went home.*

wear someone **down**† 1. *Fig.* to exhaust someone. □ *This hot weather wears me down.* □ *The steamy weather wore down the tourists and made them stay in their hotels.* 2. *Fig.* to reduce someone to submission or agreement by constant badgering. □ *Finally they wore me down and I told them what they wanted to know.* □ *The interrogation wore down the suspect.*

wear someone **out**† *Fig.* to exhaust someone; to make someone tired. □ *The coach made the team practice until he wore them out.* □ *If he wears out everybody on the team, nobody will be left to play in the game.*

wear someone **to a frazzle** *Fig.* to exhaust someone. □ *Her work wears her to a frazzle.* □ *Taking care of all those kids must wear you to a frazzle.*

wear something **away**† to erode something. □ *The constant rains wore the side of the cathedral away.* □ *The flooding wore away the topsoil.*

wear something **down**† to grind something away; to erode something. □ *The constant rubbing of the door wore the carpet down.* □ *The rubbing of the door wore down the carpet.*

wear something **off (of)** something and **wear** something **off**† to grind or rub something off something. (*Of* is usually retained before pronouns.) □ *The grinding of the bot-* tom of the boat on the sandbanks wore the barnacles off the hull. □ *The sand wore off the barnacles.*

wear something **out**† to make something worthless or nonfunctional from use. □ *I wore my shoes out in no time at all.* □ *I wore out my shoes in less than a month.*

wear something **(up)on** something to have something on something as clothing or adornment. (*Upon* is formal and less commonly used than *on*.) □ *I wore a lovely diamond pin upon my blouse.* □ *I wore the flower on my lapel.*

wear the britches (in the family) and **wear the pants (in the family)** *Rur.* to be in charge in the family. □ *Jane bosses her husband around something scandalous. It's clear that she wears the britches in the family.* □ *I don't intend to let my wife wear the pants in the family.* □ *Mary's a strong-minded woman, but her husband still wears the britches.*

wear the pants (in the family) Go to previous.

wear through something to grind or rub through something. □ *My heel finally wore through the carpeting beneath the accelerator of my car.* □ *The constant rubbing of hands wore through the paint on the railing.*

wear two hats Go to **wear more than one hat**.

wear (up)on someone to diminish someone's energy and resistance; to bore or annoy someone. (*Upon* is formal and less commonly used than *on*.) □ *You could see that the lecture was beginning to wear upon the audience.* □ *This kind of thing really wears on me.*

wear (up)on something to grind or rub at something. (*Upon* is formal and less commonly used than *on*.) □ *The bottom of the door is wearing upon the carpet and leaving marks.* □ *It is wearing on the carpet.*

weary of someone or something to become tired of or bored with someone or something. □ *I am beginning to weary of you. Isn't it time you were going?* □ *We soon wearied of chicken twice a week.*

weary someone **with** something to tire or bore someone with something. □ *He wearied her with his constant requests.* □ *Please don't weary me with your complaints.*

weasel out (of something**) 1.** *Fig.* to squeeze one's way out of something. □ *Somehow, the child managed to weasel out of the hole she was stuck in.* □ *The mouse tried to weasel out.* **2.** *Fig.* to evade or avoid a job or responsibility. (Fig. on ①.) □ *Don't try to weasel out of your responsibility!* □ *You can't weasel out! You have to do it.*

weather permitting *Fig.* if the weather allows it. □ *Weather permitting, we will be there on time.* □ *The plane lands at midnight, weather permitting.*

weather the storm 1. *Fig.* to experience and survive a storm. □ *We decided to stay in the building and weather the storm there with the other visitors.* **2.** *Fig.* to experience something and survive it. (Fig. on ①.) □ *The manager went on another shouting rampage and frightened his assistants. The rest of us stayed in our offices to weather the storm.*

weave around to move about, changing directions at random. □ *The drunken driver wove around all over the road.* □ *He was weaving around everywhere.*

weave in and out (of something**)** *Fig.* to move, drive, or walk in and out of something, such as traffic, a line, etc.

743

☐ *The car was weaving in and out of traffic dangerously.* ☐ *The deer ran rapidly through the forest, weaving in and out of the trees.*

weave something **from** something **1.** to make a fabric from some type of fiber. ☐ *They weave this cloth from a fine plant fiber.* ☐ *This cloth is woven from silk threads.* **2.** *Fig.* to make a story or explanation out of a small amount of information. (Fig. on ①.) ☐ *You have woven the entire tale from something you heard me say to Ruth.* ☐ *Your explanation has been woven from supposition.*

weave something **into** something **1.** to form fibers into a fabric. ☐ *They could weave the threads into simple cloth with a primitive loom.* ☐ *We will weave this wool into a rug.* **2.** *Fig.* to turn separate episodes into a story. (Fig. on ①.) ☐ *Skillfully, the writer wove the elements into a clever story.* ☐ *Memories from her childhood were woven into a series of short stories.*

weave through something to move through something by turning and dodging. ☐ *The car wove through traffic, almost hitting a number of other cars.* ☐ *We wove through the jungle vines, trying to avoid touching the poisonous ones.*

wed someone **to** someone to marry someone to someone else. ☐ *Her parents wedded her to a young prince when she was only twelve.* ☐ *They cannot wed her to anyone if she has already married someone of her own choosing.*

wed someone **to** something *Fig.* to join someone firmly to a concept. (Fig. on **wed** someone **to** someone.) ☐ *Don't try to wed me to your way of doing things. I have my own way.* ☐ *Don't wed yourself to that idea.*

wed(ded) to someone married to someone. ☐ *The couple will have been wed to each other for fifty years next June.* ☐ *Anne is wed to one of my cousins.*

wedded to something *Fig.* mentally attached to something; firmly committed to something. (Fig. on **wed(ded) to** someone.) ☐ *The manager was wedded to the idea of getting new computers.* ☐ *The mayor was wedded to the new budget plan.*

wedge someone or something **(in†) between** people or things to work someone or something into a tiny space between people or things. ☐ *The usher wedged us in between two enormously fat people, and we were all very uncomfortable.* ☐ *They wedged in the package between Jane and the wall.* ☐ *We had to wedge Timmy between Jed and the side of the car.*

the **wee hours (of the night)** Go to the **small hours (of the night).**

weed someone or something **out†** *Fig.* to remove someone or something unwanted or undesirable from a group or collection. (Fig. on removing weeds from the soil.) ☐ *We had to weed the less productive workers out one by one.* ☐ *The auditions were held to weed out the actors with the least ability.* ☐ *I'm going through my books to weed out those that I don't need anymore.*

week in, week out *Fig.* every week, week after week. ☐ *We have the same old food, week in, week out.* ☐ *I'm tired of this job. I've done the same thing—week in, week out—for three years.*

weeks running Go to **days running.**

weep about someone or something to cry about someone or something; to mourn someone or something. ☐ *She*

was weeping about her grandfather, who had passed away in the night.* ☐ *There is no use weeping about spilled milk.*

weep for joy *Fig.* to cry out of happiness. ☐ *She was so happy, she wept for joy.* ☐ *We all wept for joy at the safe return of the child.*

weep for someone or an animal to cry out of sorrow for someone or an animal. ☐ *She wept for her puppy when it was terribly sick.* ☐ *Please don't weep for me after I'm gone.*

weep over someone or something to cry about someone or something. ☐ *No need to weep over me. I'll do all right.* ☐ *There is no point in weeping over something you can't do anything about.*

weigh against someone or something *Fig.* to count against someone or something; [for some fact] to work against someone or something. ☐ *I hope my many absences do not weigh against me on the final grade.* ☐ *This will weigh against you.*

weigh in (at something) *Fig.* to present oneself at a certain weight. (Usually said of boxers.) ☐ *The fighter weighed in at over two hundred pounds.* ☐ *The contenders weighed in yesterday.*

weigh on someone's **mind** *Fig.* [for something] to be in a person's thoughts; [for something] to be bothering someone's thinking. ☐ *This problem has been weighing on my mind for many days now.* ☐ *I hate to have things weighing on my mind. I can't sleep when I'm worried.*

weigh someone **down†** *Fig.* [for a thought] to worry or depress someone. ☐ *All these problems really weigh me down.* ☐ *Financial problems have been weighing down our entire family.*

weigh someone or something **down†** to burden someone or something. ☐ *The heavy burden weighed the poor donkey down.* ☐ *The load of bricks weighed down the truck.*

weigh someone's **words 1.** *Fig.* to consider carefully what someone says. ☐ *I listened to what he said, and I weighed his words very carefully.* ☐ *Everyone was weighing his words. None of us knew exactly what he meant.* **2.** *Fig.* to consider one's own words carefully when speaking. ☐ *I always weigh my words when I speak in public.* ☐ *John was weighing his words carefully because he didn't want to be misunderstood.*

weigh something **against** something to ponder something by balancing it against something. ☐ *I weighed going to town against staying here and sleeping and I decided to stay here.* ☐ *When I weigh your suggestion against my own ideas, I realize that I must follow my own conscience.*

weigh something **out†** to weigh something as it is distributed. ☐ *The merchant weighed the cuts of meat out for each of the waiting women.* ☐ *They weighed out the grain carefully.*

weigh something **up†** to find out the weight of something. ☐ *I can't tell you how much this will cost until I weigh it up.* ☐ *Liz weighed up the meat and jotted down the price.*

weigh (up)on someone *Fig.* to burden or worry someone. (*Upon* is formal and less commonly used than *on.*) ☐ *The problems at the office were beginning to weigh upon Mr. Franklin.* ☐ *My problems began to weigh on me.*

a **weight off** one's **mind** Go to a **load off** one's **mind.**

W

weight someone or something **down†** (**with** something) to place a heavy weight in or on someone or something; to press down or hold down someone or something with a heavy weight. □ *The inquisitors weighted the accused down with stones, but he still refused to say what they wanted.* □ *Karen weighted down the papers with an ornamental paperweight.*

weight something **against** someone or something to bias something against someone or something. □ *The prosecutor tried to weight the evidence against the defendant.* □ *The police weighted the case against the accused company.*

weird out *Sl.* to become emotionally disturbed or unnerved; to **flip out.** □ *The day was just gross. I thought I would weird out at noon.* □ *I weirded out at the news of Frankie's death.*

weirded out *Sl.* disturbed or unnerved by drugs or events. □ *I was totally weirded out and couldn't control myself.* □ *After the blowup, Fred was really weirded out.*

Welcome aboard. *Fig.* Welcome to employment at our company. (See also **on board.** Invariably said in greeting to a new employee.) □ *Glad to meet you. Welcome aboard.*

welcome someone **into** something and **welcome** someone **in†** to greet one as one is ushered into something or some place. □ *The Franklins welcomed us into their home.* □ *Please welcome in our new members.*

welcome someone or something **back†** to greet the return of someone or something. □ *We are delighted to welcome you back to our house.* □ *The students welcomed back the teacher who had been ill.*

welcome someone **to** something to greet someone who has come into something or some place. □ *I am very pleased to welcome you to Adamsville!* □ *They welcomed us to the party and showed us where to put our coats and hats.*

welcome someone **with open arms** Go to **receive** someone **with open arms.**

welcome someone **with** something to present something to someone as a sign of greeting. (See also **receive** someone **with open arms.**) □ *The natives welcomed us with garlands of flowers.* □ *I welcomed the visitors with gifts and good wishes.*

welcome to do something free to do something; allowed to do something. □ *The audience is welcome to ask questions at the end of the speech.* □ *You are welcome to help yourself to anything in the kitchen.*

Welcome to our house. an expression said by a host or hostess when greeting guests and bringing them into the house. □ *Andy: Hello, Sally. Welcome to our house. Come on in. Sally: Thanks. It's good to be here.* □ *Tom: Welcome to our house. Make yourself at home. Henry: Thanks, I'm really tired.*

weld someone **and** someone else **together** *Fig.* to bind people together. (*Fig.* on **weld** something **and** something else **together.**) □ *Their experiences in the war welded Tom and Sam together for life.* □ *They were welded together by their common goals.*

weld something **and** something else **together** to attach things to one another by welding. □ *The worker welded the ends of the rods together.* □ *See if you can weld these plates together.*

Well begun is half done. *Prov.* Beginning a project well makes it easier to do the rest.; Once you have begun a project well, you do not need to put in much more effort to finish it. □ *Jill: I'm afraid I'll never be able to finish writing this report. Jane: You've already written a good introduction. Well begun is half done.*

Well, bust my buttons! *Rur.* What a surprise! □ *Well, bust my buttons! It's good to see you!* □ *Well, bust my buttons! You did all the dishes!*

***well disposed to(ward)** someone or something *Fig.* friendly with someone or something; having a positive or favorable attitude toward someone or something. (*Typically: **be** ~; **become** ~.) □ *I am not well disposed toward Walter.* □ *We are quite well disposed to all of them.*

Well done! *Fig.* You did that nicely! □ *Sally: Well done, Tom. Excellent speech. Tom: Thanks.* □ *In the lobby after the play, Tom was met with a chorus of well-wishers saying, "Well done, Tom!"*

We('ll) have to do lunch sometime. and **Let's do lunch (sometime).** We must have lunch together sometime. (A vague statement that may lead to lunch plans.) □ *Rachel: Nice to talk to you, Tom. We have to do lunch sometime. Tom: Yes, good to see you. I'll give you a ring.* □ *Tom: Can't talk to you now. Catch you later. Mary: We'll have to do lunch sometime.* □ *John: Good to see you, Tom. Tom: Right. Let's do lunch sometime. John: Good idea. I'll call you.* □ *Mary: Catch you later. Sue: Sure. Let's do lunch. Mary: Okay. Call me. Bye.*

(Well,) I never! 1. *Inf.* I have never been so humiliated! □ *Bill: Just pack up your things and get out! Jane: Well, I never!* □ *Tom: Look, your manners with the customers are atrocious! Jane: Well, I never!* **2.** *Inf.* I never heard of such a thing. □ *Tom: Now they have machines that will do all those things at the press of a button. Sally: Well, I never! I had no idea!* □ *John: Would you believe I have a whole computer in this pocket? Alice: I never!*

(Well,) I'll be! *Rur.* I am very surprised! □ *Charlie: Joe and Sally got married last weekend. Jane: Well, I'll be!* □ *I'll be! Bill got the top score on the test!*

well in hand *Fig.* under control. □ *Is that matter well in hand?* □ *We have everything well in hand. Don't worry.*

***well into** something *Fig.* far into something or far along in something. (*Typically: **be** ~; **get** ~.) □ *It was well into the morning before she awoke.* □ *The car was well into the tunnel when it broke down.*

well out (of something) to gush out of something. □ *I opened the door and the water welled out.*

well out(side) of something far outside something. □ *We were well out of the city when the air-raid sirens went off.*

well over [for a liquid] to fill up and spill over. □ *The laundry tub finally welled over as it became too full.* □ *The milk glass began to well over, and Timmy began to cry.*

Well said. *Fig.* You said that very well, and I agree. □ *As Sally sat down, Mary complimented her, "Well said, Sally. You made your point very well."* □ *John: And I for one will never stand for this kind of encroachment on my rights again! Mary: Well said! Bob: Well said, John! Fred: Yes, well said.*

Well, shut my mouth! *Rur.* I am very surprised! □ *Well, shut my mouth! I didn't know you were in town!* □ *Tom:*

W

745

The governor's on the phone and wants to talk to you. Jane: Well, shut my mouth!

We'll try again some other time. Go to Maybe some other time.

well up (from something**)** and **well up (out of** something**)** [for a liquid] to gush or pour up and away from something. □ *The blood welled up from the wound.* □ *Clear water welled up out of the rocks.* □ *A gusher of muddy water welled up.* □ *Tears welled up out of the baby's eyes.*

well up in years *Euph.* aged; old. □ *Jane's husband is well up in years. He is nearly seventy-five.* □ *Joan's well up in years but healthy.*

well up (inside someone**)** *Fig.* [for a feeling] to seem to swell and move inside one's body. □ *A feeling of revulsion began to well up inside Fred.* □ *Burning resentment welled up, and George knew he was going to lose his temper.*

well up (out of something**)** Go to well up (from something).

well up with something to fill up or gush with something, such as water. □ *Her eyes welled up with tears.* □ *The basement drain welled up with the floodwaters.*

(Well,) what do you know! *Inf.* a way of expressing surprise at finding something that is unexpected; an expression of mild surprise at something someone has said. (No answer is expected or desired.) □ *Andy: Well, what do you know! Here's a brand new shirt in this old trunk. Bob: I wonder how it got there.* □ *Tom: These two things fit together like this. John: Well, what do you know!*

well-heeled and **well-fixed; well-off** *Fig.* wealthy; with sufficient money. □ *My uncle can afford a new car. He's well-heeled.* □ *Everyone in his family is well-off.*

well-to-do *Fig.* wealthy and of good social position. (Often with *quite,* as in the examples.) □ *The Jones family is quite well-to-do.* □ *There is a gentleman waiting for you at the door. He appears quite well-to-do.*

welsh on someone to renege on a bet or an agreement made with someone. (Also spelled *welch.*) □ *You had better not welsh on me if you know what is good for you.* □ *Max welshed on the mob boss and made a lot of trouble for himself.*

welsh on something **(with** someone**)** to renege on a bet or agreement made with someone. (Also spelled *welch.*) □ *Max welshed on his bet with Lefty. That was not a wise thing to do.* □ *It is not wise to welsh on a bet.*

welter in something **1.** to roll about or wallow in something; to be immersed in or surrounded by something. □ *Most breeds of pigs will welter happily in mud.* □ *I hate having to welter in the heat.* **2.** [for someone or something] to drip or run with liquid, such as blood, sweat, water, etc. □ *Three minutes into the jungle, we were weltering in our own sweat.* □ *The wounded man weltered in his blood.* **3.** *Fig.* to be immersed in something such as activity, work, demands, etc. (Fig. on ①.) □ *Toward the peak of the season, we welter in orders for our goods.* □ *She was weltering in work, eager to take a break.*

(We're) delighted to have you (here). Go to (I'm) delighted to have you (here).

(We're) glad you could come. Go to (I'm) glad you could come.

Were you born in a barn? *Rur.* an expression chiding someone who has left a door open or who is ill-mannered or messy. □ *Andy: Close the door! Were you born in a barn? Bob: Sorry.* □ *Fred: Can't you clean this place up a little? Were you born in a barn? Bob: I call it the messy look.*

wet behind the ears and **not dry behind the ears; hardly dry behind the ears** *Fig.* young and inexperienced. □ *John's too young to take on a job like this! He's still wet behind the ears!* □ *He may be wet behind the ears, but he's well-trained and totally competent.* □ *Tom is going into business by himself? Why, he's hardly dry behind the ears.*

a **wet blanket** *Fig.* a dull or depressing person who spoils other people's enjoyment. □ *Jack's fun at parties, but his brother's a wet blanket.* □ *I was with Anne and she was being a real wet blanket.*

wet one's **whistle** *Rur.* to take a drink. □ *He stopped at the bar to wet his whistle.* □ *I don't need a big glass of water. Just enough to wet my whistle.*

wet someone or something **down**[†] to put water onto someone or something. □ *Mother wet the children down with a hose while she was washing the car.* □ *Karen wet down the children with the hose.* □ *We wet the new concrete down to help it cure in all the heat.*

We've had a lovely time. Go to I've had a lovely time.

a **whack at** something Go to a try at something.

whack someone or something **up**[†] *Sl.* to damage someone or something. □ *Bob got mad at Greg and whacked him up.* □ *Clara whacked up her car yesterday.*

whack something **off**[†] **1.** *Sl.* to complete something easily or quickly. □ *If you want a pair of these, I can whack them off for you in a few minutes.* □ *The artisan whacked off a set of the earrings in a few minutes.* **2.** *Sl.* to cut or chop something off. □ *A tree branch is rubbing against the house. I guess I'll go out and whack that branch off.* □ *Whack off that other branch while you are at it.*

whack something **up**[†] *Sl.* to chop something up. □ *In about an hour, he had whacked the tree up into small logs.* □ *Have you whacked up the chicken for frying yet?*

whacked (out) *Sl.* intoxicated. □ *Gee, is he ever whacked!* □ *Dave was so whacked out he couldn't stand up.*

whale into someone or an animal *Fig.* to attack or punish someone or an animal □ *Jimmy's dad really whaled into him.* □ *The sailor whaled into the dog.*

whale the tar out of someone *Inf.* to spank or beat someone. (See also beat the living daylights out of someone.) □ *My father threatened to whale the tar out of me.* □ *I'll whale the tar out of you when we get home if you don't settle down.*

wham bam thank you ma'am *Rur.* a bump in the road. □ *We hit a wham bam thank you ma'am and lost one of our hubcaps.* □ *Watch out for the wham bam thank you ma'am at the corner of Third Street.*

What (a) nerve! and **Of all the nerve!** *Inf.* How rude! □ *Bob: Lady, get the devil out of my way! Mary: What a nerve!* □ *Jane: You can't have that one! I saw it first! Sue: Of all the nerve! I can too have it!*

What a pity! and **What a shame!** *Fig.* an expression of consolation meaning That's too bad. (Can also be used sarcastically.) □ *Bill: I'm sorry to tell you that the cat died* *today.* Mary: *What a pity!* □ Mary: *The cake is ruined!* Sally: *What a shame!*

What a shame! Go to previous.

What about (doing) something? Would you like to do something? □ *What about going on a picnic?* □ *What about a picnic?*

What about (having) something? *Inf.* Would you like to have something? □ *What about having another drink?* □ *What about another drink?*

What about it? *Inf.* So what?; Do you want to argue about it? (Contentious.) □ Bill: *I heard you were the one accused of breaking the window.* Tom: *Yeah? So, what about it?* □ Mary: *Your piece of cake is bigger than mine.* Sue: *What about it?*

What about you? 1. *Fig.* What is your choice? (Compare this with **How about you?**) □ Tom: *I'm having the pot roast and a cup of coffee. What about you?* Mary: *I want something fattening and unhealthy.* □ Sally: *I prefer green and purple for this room. What about you?* Mary: *Well, purple's okay, but green is not right for this room.* 2. What will happen to you? □ Mary: *My parents are taking my brothers to the circus.* Sue: *What about you?* Mary: *I have a piano lesson.* □ Mary: *All my friends have been accepted to colleges.* Sue: *What about you?* Mary: *Oh, I'm accepted too.*

What are you drinking? 1. *Fig.* a phrase inquiring what someone is already drinking so that the person who asks the question can offer another drink of the same thing. □ Bill: *Hi, Tom. Nice to see you. Can I get you something to drink?* Tom: *Sure. What are you drinking?* Bill: *Scotch and water.* □ Waiter: *What are you drinking, madam?* Sue: *It's just soda. No more, thanks.* Waiter: *Very good.* 2. *Fig.* a phrase inquiring what is being drunk at a particular gathering so that the person asking can request the same drink. (A way of finding out what drinks are available.) □ Mary: *Do you want a drink?* Sue: *Yes, thanks. Say, that looks good. What are you drinking?* Mary: *It's just ginger ale.* □ Bill: *Can I get you something to drink?* Jane: *What are you drinking?* Bill: *I'm having gin and tonic.* Jane: *I'll have that too, thanks.*

What are you driving at? *Fig.* What are you implying?; What do you mean? □ *What are you driving at? What are you trying to say?* □ *Why are you asking me all these questions? What are you driving at?*

What are you having? *Fig.* What food or drink are you planning to order? (Either part of a conversation or a request from food service personnel. In a restaurant, sometimes the host or hostess will signal to a guest to order first by saying this. Sometimes a guest will ask this of a host or hostess to determine the price range that is appropriate.) □ Waiter: *Would you care to order now?* Tom: *What are you having?* Mary: *You order. I haven't made up my mind.* □ Waiter: *May I help you?* Tom: *What are you having, Pop?* Father: *I'll have the roast chicken, I think, with fries.* Tom: *I'll have the same.*

What brings you here? *Fig.* What is your reason for being here? (A polite request for this information. More polite than "Why are you here?") □ Tom: *Hello, Mary. What brings you here?* Mary: *I was invited, just like you.* □ Doctor: *Well, John, what brings you here?* John: *I've had this cough for nearly a month, and I think it needs looking into.*

What can I do for you? Go to How may I help you?

What can I say? *Inf.* I have no explanation or excuse. What do you expect me to say? (See also **What do you want me to say?**) □ Bill: *Why on earth did you lose that big order?* Sally: *What can I say? I'm sorry!* □ Bob: *You're going to have to act more aggressive if you want to make sales. You're just too timid.* Tom: *What can I say? I am what I am.*

What can I tell you? 1. *Lit.* What kind of information do you want? □ Bill: *I have a question.* Bob: *What can I tell you?* Bill: *When do we arrive at Chicago?* □ Mary: *I would like to ask a question about the quiz tomorrow.* Bill: *What can I tell you?* Mary: *The answers, if you know them.* 2. *Inf.* I haven't any idea of what to say. (Compare this with **What can I say?**) □ John: *Why on earth did you do a dumb thing like that?* Bill: *What can I tell you? I just did it, that's all.* □ Mary: *I'm so disappointed with you, Fred.* Fred: *What can I tell you? I am, too.*

What can't be cured must be endured. *Prov.* If you cannot do anything about a problem, you will have to live with it. □ Alan: *No matter what I do, I can't make the dog stop barking in the middle of the night.* Jane: *What can't be cured must be endured, then, I guess.*

What difference does it make? Does it really matter?; Does it cause any trouble? □ *What if I choose to leave home? What difference does it make?* □ *So Jane dropped out of the club. What difference does it make?*

What do you know? *Inf.* a typical inquiry on greeting someone. (A specific answer is not expected. Often pronounced "Wha-da-ya know?") □ Bob: *Hey, Tom! What do you know?* Tom: *Look who's here! Hi, Bob!* □ John: *What do you know?* Mary: *Nothing. How are you?* John: *Okay.*

What do you know (about that)? *Inf.* That is very interesting. □ Tom: *I heard that Jim and Mary are getting married.* Jane: *Well! What do you know about that?* □ *What do you know? Bill finally sold his house!*

What do you know for sure? *Inf.* How are you?; What do you know? (Familiar. An elaboration of **What do you know?** Does not require a direct answer.) □ Tom: *Hey, man! What do you know for sure?* Bill: *Howdy, Tom. What's new?* □ John: *How are you doing, old buddy?* Bill: *Great, John! John: What do you know for sure?* Bill: *Nothing much.*

What do you say? 1. *Inf.* Hello, how are you? □ Bob: *What do you say, Tom?* Tom: *Hey, man. How are you doing?* □ Bill: *What do you say, man?* Fred: *What's the good word, you old so-and-so?* 2. *Lit.* What is your answer or decision? □ Bill: *I need an answer from you now. What do you say?* Bob: *Don't rush me!* □ Sue: *I can offer you seven hundred dollars for your old car. What do you say?* Bob: *I'll take it!* 3. *Lit.* an expression urging a child to say **Thank you** or please. □ When Aunt Sally gave Billy some candy, his mother said to Billy, "What do you say?" "Thank you," said Billy. □ Mother: *Here's a nice glass of milk.* Child: *Good.* Mother: *What do you say?* Child: *Very good.* Mother: *No. What do you say?* Child: *Thank you.*

What do you think? What is your opinion? □ Mary: *This is our new company stationery. What do you think?* Bill: *Stunning. Simply stunning.* □ Mary: *We're considering moving out into the country. What do you think?* Sue: *Sounds good to me.*

W

What do you think of that? and **What do you think about that?** Isn't that remarkable?; What is your opinion of that? □ *Bob: I'm leaving tomorrow and taking all these books with me. What do you think of that? Mary: Not much.* □ *Sue: I'm going to start taking cooking lessons. What do you think about that? Bill: I'm overjoyed! John: Thank heavens! Mary: Fortune has smiled on us, indeed!*

What do you think of this weather? a phrase used to open a conversation with someone, often someone one has just met. □ *Sue: Glad to meet you, Mary. Mary: What do you think about this weather? Sue: I've seen better.* □ *Bill: What do you think about this weather? Jane: Lovely weather for ducks.*

What do you think you are doing here? Why are you in this place? (Stern and threatening.) □ *John: Mary! Mary: John! John: What do you think you're doing here?* □ *"What do you think you're doing here?" said Fred to a frightened rabbit trapped in the garage.*

What do you want me to say? *Inf.* You caught me and I'm sorry, and I don't know what more to say. □ *What do you want me to say? I apologized. There is nothing more I can do.* □ *Okay, so I'm wrong. What do you want me to say?*

What does that prove? *Fig.* So what?; that does not mean anything. (A defensive expression. The heaviest stress is on *that*. Often with *so*, as in the examples.) □ *Tom: It seems that you were in the apartment the same night that it was robbed. Bob: So, what does that prove? Tom: Nothing, really. It's just something we need to keep in mind.* □ *Rachel: You're late again on your car payment. Jane: What does that prove? Rachel: Simply that you can't afford the car and we are going to repossess it.*

What else can I do? Go to **What more can I do?**

What else can I do for you? In what other way can I serve you? (Said by shopkeepers, clerks, and service personnel.) □ *Bill: What else can I do for you? Bob: Please check the oil.* □ *"Here's your prescription. What else can I do for you?" said the pharmacist.*

***what for 1.** *Fig.* a scolding; a stern lecture. (*Typically: **get** ~; **give** someone ~.) □ *Billy's mother gave him what for because he didn't get home on time.* □ *I will really give you what for if you don't straighten up.* **2.** Why?; For what reason? □ *Father: "I want you to clean your room." Child: "What for? It's clean enough."* □ *What did you do that for?*

What gives? *Inf.* What happened?; What went wrong?; What's the problem? □ *Bill: Hi, you guys. What gives? Bob: Nothing, just a little misunderstanding. Tom's a little angry.* □ *Bob: Where's my wallet? What gives? Tom: I think one of those roughnecks who just walked by us has borrowed it for a little while.*

What goes up must come down. *Prov.* Anything that has risen or been raised up must eventually fall down. □ *When it came time to move out of our second-floor apartment, we looked at our large, heavy sofa with dismay, not sure how we would get it down the stairs. "What goes up must come down," my husband said, "Somehow."*

What happened? What went wrong here? □ *Bob (approaching a crowd): What happened? Tom (with Bob): What's wrong? Bystander: Just a little mix-up. A car wanted to drive on the sidewalk, that's all.* □ *There was a terrible noise, an explosion that shook the house. Bob looked at Jane and said, "What happened?"*

What have you been up to? *Inf.* I haven't seen you for a long time, so tell me what you have been doing? □ *Hi, Tom. Where have you been? What have you been up to?* □ *What have you been up to? Busy, I am sure.*

What if...? What would be the result if something were true? □ *What if you had all the money you want?* □ *What if everyone thought you were great?*

What if I do? Does it matter to you if I do it?; What difference does it make if I do it? □ *Tom: Are you really going to sell your leather coat? Bob: What if I do?* □ *Jane: You're not going to go out dressed like that, are you? Sue: So what if I do?*

What if I don't? Does it matter to you if I do not do it?; What difference does it make if I do not do it? □ *Bob: You're certainly going to tidy up a bit before going out, aren't you? Tom: What if I don't?* □ *Father: You are going to get in by midnight tonight or you're grounded. Fred: So what if I don't? Father: That's enough! You're grounded as of this minute!*

What (in) the devil? and **What (in) the dickens?** *Inf.* What has happened?; What? (Often with the force of an exclamation.) □ *What in the devil? Who put sugar in the salt shaker?* □ *What the dickens? Who are you? What are you doing in my room?*

What (in) the dickens? Go to previous.

What (in) the hell? 1. *Inf.* What has happened?; What? □ *What in the hell? Who did this?* □ *What the hell happened here?* **2.** *Inf.* What does it matter? Why not? (Usually with the force of an exclamation.) □ *Give her a new one. What the hell!* □ *Don't be such a cheapskate. Get the nice one. What the hell!*

What in (the) Sam Hill? *Inf.* What has happened?; What? (An elaboration of *what. Sam Hill* is a euphemism for **hell**. Often with the force of an exclamation. See examples for variations.) □ *What in Sam Hill is going on around here?* □ *What in the Sam Hill do you think you are doing?*

[what is] See also the entries beginning with *what's*.

What is it? What do you want from me?; Why do you want to get my attention? □ *Tom: John, can I talk to you for a minute? John: What is it?* □ *Sue: Jane! Jane: What is it? Sue: Close the door, please.*

what makes someone **tick** *Fig.* something that motivates someone; something that makes someone behave in a certain way. (*Fig.* on **what makes something tick**.) □ *William is sort of strange. I don't know what makes him tick.* □ *When you get to know people, you find out what makes them tick.*

what makes something **tick** *Fig.* the sense or mechanism that makes something run or function. (With reference to the ticking of a clock representing the functioning of the clock.) □ *I don't know what makes it tick.* □ *I took apart the radio to find out what made it tick.*

What makes you think so? 1. *Lit.* Why do you think that?; What is your evidence for that conclusion? □ *Tom: This bread may be a little old. Alice: What makes you think so? Tom: The green spots on the edges.* □ *Bob: Congress is in session again. Tom: What makes you think so? Bob: My wallet's empty.* **2.** *Inf.* Is that not totally obvious? (Sarcas-

W

tic.) □ *John: I think I'm putting on a little weight. Mary: Oh, yeah? What makes you think so?* □ *Mary (shivering): Gee, I think it's going to be winter soon. Sally (also shivering): Yeah? What makes you think so?*

What more can I do? and **What else can I do?** I am at a loss to know what else to do. Is there anything else I can do? (An expression of desperation, not an inquiry.) □ *Bob: Did you hear about the death in the Wilson family. Bill: Yes, I feel so helpless. I sent flowers. What more can I do?* □ *Bill: Is your child still sick? Mary: Yes. I'm giving her the right medicine. What more can I do?*

What must be, must be. and **What(ever) will be, will be.** *Prov.* If something is fated to happen, you cannot stop it from happening.; You cannot foretell the future. □ *Harry hoped for many months that he would regain the use of his legs after the accident, but it soon became apparent that he would not. "What must be, must be," he thought resignedly.* □ *I'd like to win the contest, but I can't be sure that I will. What will be, will be.* □ *The doctors have done all they can. Whatever will be, will be.*

What now? Go to Now what?

What number are you calling? an expression used when one suspects that a telephone caller may have gotten the wrong number. □ *Bob (on the telephone): Hello? Mary: Hello, is Sally there? Bob: Uh, what number are you calling? Mary: I guess I have the wrong number. Sorry. Bob: No problem. Good-bye.* □ *When the receptionist asked, "What number are you calling?" I realized I had made a mistake.*

What of it? *Inf.* What does it matter?; Why treat it as if it were important?; Why do you think that this is any of your business? (A bit contentious.) □ *John: I hear you've been having a little trouble at the office. Bob: What of it?* □ *Sue: You missed a spot shaving. Fred: What of it?*

What one **doesn't know won't hurt** one. *Cliché* Unknown facts cannot worry or upset a person. □ *Don't tell me that I have made a mistake. What I don't know won't hurt me.* □ *Don't tell him the truth about his missing dog. What he doesn't know won't hurt him.*

What price something? What is the value of something?; What good is something? (Said when the value of the thing referred to is being diminished or ignored.) □ *Jane's best friend told us all about Jane's personal problems. What price friendship?* □ *Jack simply declared himself president of the political society. What price democracy?*

What's buzzin' (cousin)? *Sl.* What's happening? □ *Hey, chum! What's buzzin' cousin?* □ *What's buzzin' around here?*

What's coming off? and **What's going down?** *Sl.* What is happening here?; What is going to happen? (Also a greeting inquiry.) □ *Bill: Hey, man! What's coming off? Tom: Oh, nothing, just takin' it easy.* □ *Bob: Hey, we just got here! What's going down? Bill: What does it look like? This is a party, dude!*

***what's coming to** one what one deserves. (*Typically: get ~; have ~; give one ~.) □ *If you cheat, you'll get in trouble. You'll get what's coming to you.* □ *They gave Billy what was coming to him.*

What's cooking? *Inf.* What is happening?; How are you? □ *Bob: Hi, Fred! What's cooking? Fred: How are you doing,* *Bob?* □ *Bob: Hi, Fred! What's cooking? Bill: Nothing. Anything happening with you?*

What's done cannot be undone. *Prov.* You cannot change what has already happened. □ *Jill: I wish I hadn't insulted Maria. Jane: What's done cannot be undone.* □ *Jill soon regretted telling Mike that she loved him, but she knew that what's done cannot be undone.*

What's done is done. *Prov.* It is final and in the past. □ *It's too late to change it now. What's done is done.* □ *What's done is done. The past cannot be altered.*

What's eating someone? *Inf. Fig.* What is bothering someone? □ *Tom: Go away! Bob: Gee, Tom, what's eating you?* □ *Bill: Tom's so grouchy lately. What's eating him? Bob: Beats me!*

What's going down? Go to What's coming off?

What's going on (around here)? What is happening in this place?; What is the explanation for the strange things that are happening here? □ *Bill: There was an accident in the factory this morning. Bob: That's the second one this week. What's going on around here?* □ *Mary: What's all the noise? What's going on? Sue: We're just having a little party.*

What's got(ten) into someone? What is bothering someone?; What caused someone to act that way? (Past or perfect only. The *has* is contracted except for emphasis.) □ *I just don't know what's gotten into her.* □ *I don't know what got into me.*

What's happ(ening)? *Sl.* Hello, what's new? □ *Hey, dude! What's happening?* □ *What's happ? How's it goin'?*

what's his face and **what's his name** *Sl.* someone whose name has been forgotten; someone whose name is being avoided. □ *Was what's his name there? I never can remember his name.* □ *I can't remember what's his face's name either.*

what's his name Go to previous.

What's in a name? *Prov.* The name of a thing does not matter as much as the quality of the thing. (From Shakespeare's play, *Romeo and Juliet*.) □ *Sue: I want to buy this pair of jeans. Mother: This other pair is much cheaper. Sue: But it doesn't have the designer brand name. Mother: What's in a name?*

What's in it for me? *Inf.* What is the benefit for me in this scheme? □ *Bob: Now that plan is just what is needed. Bill: What's in it for me? What do I get out of it?* □ *Sue: We signed the Wilson contract yesterday. Mary: That's great! What's in it for me?*

What's it to you? *Inf.* Why does it matter to you?; It's none of your business. (A bit contentious.) □ *Tom: Where are you going? Jane: What's it to you?* □ *Mary: Bill's pants don't match his shirt. Jane: Does it matter? What's it to you?*

What's keeping someone? What is delaying someone? (The *someone* is replaced by a person's name or a pronoun.) □ *Bob: Wasn't Mary supposed to be here? Bill: I thought so. Bob: Well, what's keeping her? Bill: How should I know?* □ *Bill: I've been waiting here for an hour for Sally. Sue: What's keeping her?*

What's new? *Inf.* What things have happened since we last met? □ *Mary: Greetings, Jane. What's new? Jane: Nothing much.* □ *Bob: What's new? Tom: Not a whole lot.*

What's new with you? *Inf.* a typical greeting, often a response to **What's new?** □ *Mary: What's new with you? Sally: Oh, nothing. What's new with you? Mary: The same.* □ *Fred: Hi, John! How you doing? John: Great! What's new with you?*

What's on tap for today? *Inf.* What is on the schedule for today?; What is going to happen today? (As a beer that is on tap and ready to be served.) □ *Tom: Good morning, Fred. Fred: Morning. What's on tap for today? Tom: Trouble in the morning and difficulty in the afternoon. Fred: So nothing's new.* □ *Sally: Can we have lunch today? Sue: I'll have to look at my schedule and see what's on tap for today.*

What's poppin'? *Sl.* Hello, what is happening? □ *What's poppin'? Anything new?* □ *What's poppin', G?*

What's sauce for the goose is sauce for the gander. *Prov.* What is good for one person is good for another.; What is good for the man in a couple is good for the woman. □ *Jane: You're overweight; you should get more exercise. Alan: But I don't really have time to exercise. Jane: When I was overweight, you told me to exercise; what's sauce for the goose is sauce for the gander.*

What's shakin' (bacon)? *Sl.* How are you?; What is new? □ *What's shakin' bacon? What's going down?* □ *Hi, Jim. What's shakin'?*

What's that? What did you say? □ *Tom: We're leaving tomorrow. Jane: What's that?* □ *What's that? Did you say "Iowa" or "Idaho"?*

What's the (big) idea? *Inf.* Why did you do that? (Usually said in anger.) □ *Please don't do that! What's the idea?* □ *Why did you shove me? What's the big idea?*

What's the catch? *Sl.* What is the drawback?; It sounds good, but are there any hidden problems? □ *Sounds too good to be true. What's the catch?* □ *This looks like a good deal. What's the catch?*

What's the damage? *Sl.* What are the charges?; How much is the bill? □ *Bill: That was delicious. Waiter, what's the damage? Waiter: I'll get the check, sir.* □ *Waiter: Your check sir. Tom: Thanks. Bill: What's the damage, Tom? Let me pay my share. Tom: Nonsense, I'll get it. Bill: Okay this time, but I owe you one.*

What's the deal? Go to **What's the scam?**

What's the drill? 1. *Inf.* What is going on here? □ *Bill: I just came in. What's the drill? Tom: We have to carry all this stuff out to the truck.* □ *"What's the drill?" asked Mary. "Why are all these people sitting around like this?"* **2.** *Inf.* What are the rules and procedures for doing this? □ *Bill: I need to apply for new license plates. What's the drill? Is there a lot of paperwork? Clerk: Yes, there is.* □ *Bill: I have to get my computer repaired. Who do I talk to? What's the drill? Bob: You have to get a purchase order from Fred.*

What's the good of *something?* What is the point of something?; Why bother with something? □ *What's the good of my going at all if I'll be late?* □ *There is no need to get there early. What's the good of that?*

What's the (good) word? *Sl.* Hello, how are you? □ *Hi, Jim! What's the good word?* □ *Haven't seen you in a long time. What's the good word?*

What's the matter (with you)? 1. *Lit.* Is there something wrong with you?; Are you ill? □ *Bill: What's the matter with you? Fred: I have this funny feeling in my chest. Bill:*

Sounds serious. □ *Bob: I have to stay home again today. Bill: What's the matter with you? Have you seen a doctor?* □ *Mary: Oh, I'm so miserable! Sue: What's the matter? Mary: I lost my contact lenses and my glasses.* □ *John: Ouch! Alice: What's the matter? John: I bit my tongue.* **2.** *Inf.* How very stupid of you! How can you be so stupid? (Usually said in anger.) □ *As Fred stumbled over the step and dumped the birthday cake on the floor, Jane screamed, "What's the matter with you? The party is in fifteen minutes and now we have no cake!"* □ *Mary: I think I just lost the Wilson account. Sue: What! What's the matter with you? That account pays your salary!*

What's the problem? 1. *Lit.* What problem are you presenting to me? □ *Bill (coming in): I need to talk to you about something. Tom: What's the problem, Bill?* □ *"What's the problem?" said Mary, peering at her secretary over her glasses.* **2.** *Inf.* a question asking what the problem is and implying that there should not be a problem. □ *Child (crying): He hit me! Father: What's the problem? Child: He hit me! Father: Are you hurt? Child: No. Father: Then stop crying.* □ *Bob: Hi, Fred. Fred: What's the problem? Bob: There's no problem. Why do you ask? Fred: I've had nothing but problems today.*

What's the scam? and **What's the deal?** *Sl.* What is going on around here? (Often implies that something seems to be wrong.) □ *There's a big rumpus down the hall. What's the scam?* □ *I gave you a twenty, and you give me five back? What's the deal? Where's my other five?*

What's the scoop? *Inf.* What is the news?; **What's new with you?** □ *Bob: Did you hear about Tom? Mary: No, what's the scoop?* □ *"Hi, you guys!" beamed John's little brother. "What's the scoop?"*

What's (there) to know? *Inf.* This doesn't require any special knowledge, so what are you talking about? □ *Bill: Do you know how to wind a watch? Bob: Wind a watch? What's there to know?* □ *Sue: We must find someone who knows how to repair a broken lawnmower. Tom: What's to know? Just a little tightening here and there. That's all it needs.*

What's up? *Inf.* Hello. What is happening? □ *What's up? How're you doing?* □ *Hey, Chuck! What's up?*

What's up, doc? *Cliché* What's happening around here?; What are you doing? □ *Your bike's spread out all over the garage. What's up, Doc?*

What's with *someone or something?* Why is someone or something in that condition?; What's going on with someone or something? □ *Mary: What's with Tom? He looks depressed. Bill: He broke up with Sally.* □ *"What's with this stupid coffee maker? It won't get hot!" groused Alice.*

What's wrong? There is something wrong here. What has happened? □ *Mary: Oh, good grief! Bill: What's wrong? Mary: I forgot to feed the cat.* □ *Sue (crying): Hello, Sally? Sally: Sue, what's wrong? Sally: Oh, nothing. Tom left me.*

What's your age? *Sl.* Hello, how are you? □ *Tim: What's your age? Joe: Hey, Tim, what's going on with you?* □ *Yo, Sam! What's your age?*

What's yours? Go to **What'll it be?**

What's yours is mine, and what's mine is mine. *Prov.* A humorous way of saying, "Everything belongs to me."; (A jocular variant of "What's yours is mine, and what's mine is yours," an expression of generosity.) □ *I know you won't mind lending me your radio. After all, what's yours is mine, and what's mine is mine.* □ *The thief took his confederate's share of the money they had stolen, saying, "What's yours is mine, and what's mine is mine."*

What say? *Inf.* What did you say? (Widely used.) □ *Tom: My coat is there on the chair. Could you hand it to me? Bob: What say? Tom (pointing): Could you hand me my coat?* □ *Sue: Here's your paper. Fred: What say? Sue (louder): Here is your newspaper!*

what someone or something **is cracked up to be** what someone or something is supposed to be. □ *This pizza isn't what it's cracked up to be.* □ *I wanted to find out whether this stuff was what it is cracked up to be.*

What someone **said.** *Sl.* I agree with what someone just said, although I might not have been able to say it as well or so elegantly. □ *What John said. And I agree 100 percent.* □ *What you said. That's my feeling, too.*

What the deuce? *Sl.* What has happened?; What? (*Deuce* is an old word for *devil.*) □ *What the deuce! Who are you?* □ *What the deuce! Who did this?*

What the devil? and **What the fuck?; What the hell?; What the shit?** What has happened?; What? (Often with the force of an exclamation. **What the fuck?** and **What the shit?** are taboo.) □ *What the devil? Who put sugar in the salt shaker?* □ *What the fuck? Who are you? What are you doing in my room?* □ *What the shit are you doing here? You're supposed to be at work.*

What the eye doesn't see, the heart doesn't grieve over. *Prov.* You cannot be upset by something you do not know about. □ *When Robbie cracked his mother's favorite vase, he simply turned the cracked side toward the wall. "What the eye doesn't see, the heart doesn't grieve over," he thought.*

What the fuck? Go to What the devil?

What the heck! *Inf.* It doesn't matter! (Often with the force of an exclamation.) □ *Oh, what the heck! Come on in. It doesn't matter.* □ *Oh, what the heck! I'll have another beer. Nobody's counting.*

What the hell? Go to What the devil?

What was the name again? Please tell me your name again. (More typical of a clerk than of someone just introduced.) □ *Clerk: What was the name again? Bill: Bill.* □ *"What was the name again? I didn't write it down," confessed Fred.*

[what will] See also the entries beginning with *what'll.*

What will be, will be. Go to What must be, must be.

what with something because of something. □ *What with the children being at home and my parents coming to stay, I have too much to do.* □ *The Smiths find it difficult to manage financially, what with Mr. Smith losing his job and Mrs. Smith being too ill to work.*

What would you like to drink? an offer to prepare or serve a drink. □ *Bill: Come in and sit down. What would you like to drink? Andy: Nothing, thanks. I just need to relax a moment.* □ *Waiter: What would you like to drink? Alice: Do you have any grape soda? Waiter: I'll bring you some ginger ale, if that's all right. Alice: Well, okay. I guess.*

What would you say if...? an expression introducing a request for an opinion or a judgment. □ *Bill: What would you say if I ate the last piece of cake? Bob: Go ahead. I don't care.* □ *Mary: What would you say if we left a little early? Sally: It's okay with me.*

What you don't know won't hurt you. and **What you don't know can't hurt you.** *Prov.* If you do not know about a problem or a misdeed, you will not be able to make yourself unhappy by worrying about it. (Often used to justify not telling someone about a problem or misdeed.) □ *Ellen: What a beautiful diamond necklace! Thank you! But how on earth did you get the money to pay for it? Fred: What you don't know won't hurt you.*

What you see is what you get. The product you are looking at is exactly what you get if you buy it. □ *It comes just like this. What you see is what you get.* □ *What you see is what you get. The ones in the box are just like this one.*

What(ever) goes around, comes around. *Prov.* The results of things that one has done will someday have an effect on the person who started the events. □ *So he finally gets to see the results of his activities. What goes around, comes around.* □ *Now he is the victim of his own policies. Whatever goes around comes around.*

Whatever turns you on. 1. *Inf.* Whatever pleases or excites you is okay. □ *Mary: Do you mind if I buy some of these flowers? Bill: Whatever turns you on.* □ *Mary: I just love to hear a raucous saxophone play some smooth jazz. Bob: Whatever turns you on, baby.* **2.** *Inf.* a comment implying that it is strange to get so excited about something. (Essentially sarcastic.) □ *Bob: I just go wild whenever I see pink gloves on a woman. I don't understand it. Bill: Whatever turns you on.* □ *Jane: You see, I never told anybody this, but whenever I see snow falling, I just go sort of mushy inside. Sue: Weird, Jane, weird. But, whatever turns you on.*

Whatever will be, will be. Go to What must be, must be.

What'll it be? and **Name your poison.; What'll you have?; What's yours?** *Inf.* What do you want to drink?; What do you want?; How can I serve you? (Typically said by a bartender or bar waiter or waitress.) □ *Tom: What'll it be, friend? Bill: I'll just have a ginger ale, if you don't mind.* □ *Waitress: What'll you have? Bob: Nothing, thanks.*

wheedle someone **into** something to get someone to agree to do something by begging or flattery. □ *She is always trying to wheedle us into coming for a visit.* □ *You can't wheedle me into doing that!*

wheedle something **away from** someone and **wheedle** something **out of** someone to get something away from someone by begging or flattery. □ *The crooks wheedled the old lady's money away from her.* □ *Tim wheedled a few dollars out of his uncle.*

wheel and deal to take part in clever (but sometimes dishonest or immoral) business deals. □ *John loves to wheel and deal in the money markets.* □ *Jack got tired of all the wheeling and dealing of big business and retired to run a pub in the country.*

wheel around to turn around quickly; to change direction quickly. □ *She wheeled around quickly to face him.* □ *Suddenly, Roger wheeled around and started chasing Wally.*

W

wheel someone or something **around**† to push or steer around someone or something on wheels. □ *I had to wheel my great-uncle around all day when we visited the zoo.* □ *I wheeled around my uncle so he could enjoy the park.* □ *I wheeled the heavy shopping cart around the grocery store.*

wheel someone or something **away**† to push away someone or something on wheels. □ *The nurse wheeled the old man away, into the shelter of the porch.* □ *She wheeled away the old man.*

wheel someone or something **into** something and **wheel** someone or something **in**† to bring someone or something into something or some place on wheels. □ *The orderly wheeled the man into the operating room.* □ *The orderly wheeled in the patient.*

wheel someone or something **off**† to push or steer someone or something on wheels some distance away. □ *The nurse wheeled the old man off.* □ *Karen wheeled off the patient.*

wheel someone or something **out of** something and **wheel** someone or something **out**† to push or steer someone or something out of something on wheels. □ *The nurse wheeled the new mother out of the hospital.* □ *Liz wheeled out the new mother.*

wheeze something **out**† to say something, while wheezing; to say something, using a wheeze for a voice. (As if one is out of breath.) □ *He was out of breath from running and was only able to wheeze a few words out.* □ *Liz wheezed out a quick hello.*

when all is said and done *Cliché* when everything is finished and settled; when everything is considered. □ *When all is said and done, this isn't such a bad part of the country to live in after all.* □ *When all is said and done, I believe I had a very enjoyable time on my vacation.*

When do we eat? What time is the next meal served? (Indicates that the speaker is hungry, but considered impolite.) □ *Bill: This is a lovely view, and your apartment is great. When do we eat? Mary: We've already eaten. Weren't you just leaving? Bill: I guess I was.* □ *Andy: Wow! Something really smells good! When do we eat? Rachel: Oh, mind your manners.*

When in Rome(, do as the Romans do). *Prov.* Behave however the people around you behave. Adapt yourself to the customs of the places you visit. □ *Jill: Everyone in my new office dresses so casually. Should I dress that way, too? Jane: By all means. When in Rome, do as the Romans do.*

when it comes right down to it *Cliché* all things considered; when one really thinks about something. □ *When it comes right down to it, I'd like to find a new job.* □ *When it comes right down to it, he can't really afford a new car.*

when it comes to something as for something; speaking about something. □ *When it comes to fishing, John is an expert.* □ *When it comes to trouble, Mary really knows how to cause it.*

when least expected when one does not expect something. □ *An old car is likely to give you trouble when least expected.* □ *My pencil usually breaks when least expected.*

When one door shuts, another opens. *Prov.* When you lose one opportunity, you often find a different one. □ *Jane: I just found out I'm failing two classes. I'll never get into college with grades like this. Jill: Well, maybe you'll* find something better than college. When one door shuts, another opens.

when one is good and ready when one is completely ready. □ *I'll be there when I'm good and ready.* □ *Ann will finish the job when she's good and ready and not a minute sooner.*

when one's ship comes in *Fig.* when one becomes rich and successful. □ *When my ship comes in, we'll live in one of these huge mansions on the hill, my lass.* □ *When your ship comes in, Otto, I'll probably die of amazement!*

When poverty comes in at the door, love flies out of the window. and **When the wolf comes in at the door, love creeps out of the window.** *Prov.* If a couple gets married because they are in love, but they do not have enough money, they will stop loving each other when the money runs out. □ *You young folks may think you can live on love alone, but when poverty comes in at the door, love flies out of the window.* □ *After Susan lost her job, she and her unemployed husband had a big argument. When the wolf comes in at the door, love creeps out of the window.*

when push comes to shove and **if push comes to shove** *Fig.* when things get a little pressed; when the situation gets more active or intense. □ *When push comes to shove, you know I'll be on your side.* □ *If push comes to shove at the meeting, the front office can back you up with some statistics.*

When the cat's away, the mice will play. *Prov.* When no one in authority is present, the subordinates can do as they please. □ *When the teacher left for a few minutes, the children nearly wrecked the classroom. When the cat's away, the mice will play.* □ *Jill: You shouldn't be reading a novel at your desk. Jane: But the boss isn't here. And when the cat's away, the mice will play.*

when the chips are down *Fig.* at the final, critical moment; when things really get difficult. □ *When the chips are down, I know that I can depend on Jean to help out.* □ *I knew you would come and help when the chips were down.*

when the dust settles 1. *Lit.* when the dust falls out of the air. □ *When the dust settles, we will have to begin sweeping it up.* **2.** *Fig.* when things have calmed down. □ *When the dust settles, we can start patching up all the hurt feelings.*

when the fat hit the fire Go to the fat hit the fire.

when the fat lady sings Go to till the fat lady sings.

when the going gets tough and **if the going gets tough; when the going gets rough; if the going gets rough** as things get extremely difficult; when it becomes difficult to proceed. □ *When the going gets tough, I will be there to help you.* □ *If the going gets tough, just give me a call.*

When the going gets tough, the tough get going. *Prov.* When things are difficult, strong people take action and do not despair. (Can be used to encourage someone to take action.) □ *The football team was losing the game, so at halftime the coach reminded them that when the going gets tough, the tough get going.* □ *Jill: I don't think I can walk all the way to the top of this hill; it's so steep! Jane:*

Don't give up. When the going gets tough, the tough get going.

when the shit hits the fan *Sl.* when all the expected trouble materializes. □ *When the shit hits the fan, you had better be prepared to support those of us who are involved in this mess.*

when the time is ripe *Fig.* at exactly the right time. □ *I'll tell her the good news when the time is ripe.* □ *When the time is ripe, I'll bring up the subject again.*

When the wolf comes in at the door, love creeps out of the window. Go to When poverty comes in at the door, love flies out of the window.

when you get a chance Go to next.

when you get a minute and **when you get a chance** a phrase introducing a request, especially to talk to someone. □ *Bill: Tom? Tom: Yes. Bill: When you get a minute, I'd like to have a word with you.* □ *"Please drop over for a chat when you get a chance," said Fred to Bill.*

Where can I wash up? and **Is there some place I can wash up?** *Euph.* a way of asking where the toilet or bathroom is without referring to one's need to use it. (Of course, this is also appropriate to ask where one can wash one's hands.) □ *The minute he got to the house, he asked Fred, "Where can I wash up?"* □ *Fred: Welcome. Come in. Bill: Oh, is there some place I can wash up?*

Where do (you think) you get off? *Inf.* What do you think you are doing?; Who do you think you are? (A sharp reply to something offensive or impolite.) □ *How rude! Where do you think you get off?* □ *Where do you get off, talking to me like that?*

Where have you been all my life? *Inf.* an expression of admiration usually said to a lover. □ *Mary: I feel very happy when I'm with you. John: Oh, Mary, where have you been all my life?* □ *John grasped her hand, stared directly at her left ear, and stuttered, "Where have you been all my life?"*

Where (have) you been hiding (yourself)? Go to next.

Where (have) you been keeping yourself? and **Where (have) you been hiding (yourself)?** *Inf.* I haven't seen you for a long time. Where have you been? □ *Bill: Hi, Alice! Where you been keeping yourself? Alice: Oh, I've been around. How are you doing? Bill: Okay.* □ *John: What's up? Bill: Hi, man. Where you been keeping yourself? John: Oh, I've been busy.*

Where ignorance is bliss, 'tis folly to be wise. *Prov.* If knowing something makes you unhappy, it would be better not to know it. (Also the cliché: **ignorance is bliss**.) □ *Ellen: The doctor didn't tell Dad that Mom probably won't recover from her illness. Do you think we should tell him? Bill: No. It would only make him unhappy and ruin their last months together. Where ignorance is bliss, 'tis folly to be wise.*

Where in the world...? *Inf.* Where? (An intensive form of *where*. See examples for variations.) □ *Where in the world have you been?* □ *Where in the world did I put my glasses?*

Where is the restroom? the appropriate way of asking for the toilet in a public place. □ *Bob: 'Scuse me. Waiter: Yes, sir. Bob: Where is the restroom? Waiter: To your left, sir.*

□ *Mary: Where is the restroom, please? Clerk: Behind the elevators, ma'am.*

where it's at *Sl.* what one is aiming for; what is needed. (This does not refer to a place.) □ *Keep on trying. That's where it's at!* □ *Good strong friends. That's where it's at.*

Where on (God's green) earth? *Inf.* (Exactly) where? (An intensive form of *where*. See examples for variations.) □ *Where on God's green earth did you get that ridiculous hat?* □ *Where on earth is my book?* □ *Where on God's green earth were you?*

where one is coming from one's point of view. □ *I think I know what you mean. I know where you're coming from.* □ *Man, you don't know where I'm coming from! You don't understand a single word I say.*

Where's the beef? *Inf.* Where is the substance?; Where is the important content? □ *That's really clever and appealing, but where's the beef?* □ *Where's the beef? There's no substance in this proposal.*

Where's the fire? *Inf.* Where are you going in such a hurry? (Typically said by a police officer after stopping a speeding driver.) □ *Officer: Okay, where's the fire? Mary: Was I going a little fast?* □ *"Where's the fire?" Bob called ahead to Sue, who had gotten well ahead of him in her excitement.*

where someone is at *Sl.* what mental condition someone is in. □ *I know where you're at. I know what you are talking about.* □ *You said it! I know just where you're at!*

where someone lives *Inf.* at one's core; in one's personal situation. □ *That really hits you where you live, doesn't it?* □ *Yes, that gets me where I live.*

where someone's head is at *Inf.* the state of one's mental well-being. □ *As soon as I figure where my head is at, I'll be okay.* □ *He doesn't know where his head is at.*

where the action is where important things are happening. □ *I want to be where the action is.* □ *Right there in city hall. That's where the action is.*

where the rubber meets the road *Fig.* at the point in a process where there are challenges, issues, or problems. □ *Now we have spelled out the main area of dissent. This is where the rubber meets the road.*

where the sun don't shine *Sl.* in a dark place, namely the anus. □ *I don't care what you do with it. Just put it where the sun don't shine.* □ *For all I care you can shove it where the sun don't shine.*

Where there's a will, there's a way. *Prov. Cliché* If you truly want to do something, you will find a way to do it, in spite of obstacles. □ *We'll get this piano up the stairs somehow. Where there's a will, there's a way.* □ *I have no doubt that Bob will find a publisher for his novel. Where there's a will, there's a way.*

Where there's life there's hope. Go to While there's life there's hope.

Where there's smoke there's fire. Go to (There's) no smoke without fire.

Where will I find you? Please give me directions for finding you. (Said when people are arranging a meeting somewhere.) □ *Sue: Where will I find you? Bob: I'll be sitting in the third row somewhere.* □ *Tom: We'll get to the farm about noon. Where will we find you? Sally: Probably*

W

in the barn. If you can't find me, just go up to the house and make yourself comfortable on the porch.

*the wherewithal (to do something) the means to do something, especially energy or money. (*Typically: **get** ~; **have** ~; **give** someone ~.) □ *He has good ideas, but he doesn't have the wherewithal to carry them out.* □ *I could do a lot if only I could get the wherewithal.*

whet someone's appetite *Fig.* to cause someone to be interested in something and to be eager to have, know, learn, etc., more about it. □ *Seeing that film really whetted my sister's appetite for horror films. She now sees as many as possible.* □ *My appetite for theater was whetted when I was very young.*

whether or not either if something is the case or if something is not the case; one way or the other. □ *I'll drive to New York tomorrow whether or not it rains.* □ *I'm going to the mall whether you come with me or not.*

which brings me to the (main) point a transitional phrase that introduces the main point of a discussion. □ *Bill: Keeping safe at times like this is very important—which brings me to the main point. Does your house have an adequate burglar alarm? Sally: I knew you were trying to sell me something! Out!* □ *Lecturer: . . . which brings me to the point. John (whispering): Thank heavens! I knew there was a point to all this.*

*a whiff of something 1. *Lit.* the smell or odor of something. (*Typically: **get** ~; **catch** ~; **have** ~; **take** ~; **give** someone ~.) □ *Did you get a whiff of the turkey roasting? Yummy.* □ *I caught a whiff of something rather unpleasant in the attic. I think there is a dead mouse up there.* **2.** *Fig.* a bit of knowledge of something. (*Typically: **get** ~; **catch** ~; **give** someone ~.) □ *The boss got a whiff of the problems in the accounting department.* □ *No one will get a whiff of your trouble with the police. I'll see to that.*

while a period of time **away† (doing something)** to spend or waste time doing something. □ *I whiled an hour away just staring at the sea.* □ *Liz whiled away the entire afternoon, snoozing.* □ *I just love to while away the hours.*

While there's life there's hope. and **Where there's life there's hope.** *Prov. Cliché* As long as you are alive, you should be hopeful, because it is possible that your situation will improve. □ *Nancy: What will we do, now that our house and everything we own has burned up? Bill: While there's life there's hope.* □ *Ellen: Ever since my divorce, it seems as if I have nothing to hope for. Jane: I know things seem bleak, but where there's life there's hope.*

whine about someone or something to whimper or complain about someone or something. □ *Please don't whine about Sally. She is sorry she couldn't come to your party, but it's not the end of the world.* □ *The dog is whining about its hurt paw.*

whine something out† to say something in a whine; to say something, using a whine for a voice. □ *She whined her complaint out so everyone could hear it.* □ *Jake whined out his usual complaints.*

whip around 1. to reverse suddenly. (As with the tip of a whip.) □ *The rope suddenly whipped around and struck me in the face.* □ *A branch whipped around and tore my shirt.* **2.** to turn around very quickly and suddenly. □ *John*

whipped around when he heard the noise. □ *Claire whipped around to face her opponent.*

whip back (on someone) [for something] to snap back and strike someone. □ *The branch whipped back and struck Jill in the leg.* □ *It whipped back and slapped my side.*

whip into something *Fig.* to go quickly into something or some place. □ *They whipped into the parking space before I could get there.* □ *I whipped into the store to pick up a few things.*

whip someone **into** a state *Fig.* to excite, arouse, or foment someone into some state. (Based on **whip** someone **into** doing something.) □ *The governor's speech whipped the audience into a frenzy.* □ *The angry cries from the audience whipped the speaker into a rage.*

whip someone **into** doing something to beat someone into doing something. □ *The cruel captain whipped his men into going on with the journey.* □ *You can't whip me into betraying my friends.*

whip someone or something **around†** to cause someone or something to reverse direction quickly. □ *The roller coaster whipped around the riders, right and left, until they were almost sick.* □ *The sharp turn whipped me around, but I wasn't hurt.*

whip someone or something **into shape** to cause someone or something to be in a better condition. □ *The coach was not able to whip the players into shape before the game.* □ *I think I can whip this proposal into shape quickly.* □ *Hey, Tom, whip yourself into shape. You look a mess.*

whip someone or something **on†** to force someone or something to continue by whipping or beating. □ *The rider whipped his horse on, faster and faster.* □ *The stage coach driver whipped on the team of horses.*

whip someone **up†** to excite or stir up someone. □ *Well, you've certainly whipped them up with that speech.* □ *Harry whipped up the crowd with a few good jokes.*

whip something **away† (from** someone) to jerk something away from someone suddenly. □ *The mugger whipped Sally's purse away from her and ran.* □ *The thief whipped away the purse.*

whip something **into shape** Go to **lick** something **into shape.**

whip something **into** something to beat one soft ingredient into another. □ *Whip the butter into the egg and make a smooth paste.* □ *First, you must whip the egg whites into the cream.*

whip something **off† 1.** *Inf.* to do or create something quickly. □ *If you need another receipt, I can whip one off in a jiffy.* □ *She whipped off another set of earrings for the tourist.* **2.** *Inf.* to remove something, such as an item of clothing, quickly. □ *He whipped the coat off and dived into the water.* □ *I whipped off my cap.*

whip something **out† 1.** *Inf.* to complete making or working on something quickly. □ *I think I can whip one out for you very quickly.* □ *The factory whips out twenty of these every minute.* **2.** *Inf.* to jerk something out [of some place]. □ *Liz whipped a pencil out of her pocket.* □ *She whipped out a pencil and signed the contract.*

whip something **over (to** someone) *Fig.* to send or give something to someone with great speed. □ *I will whip this* letter over to Mr. Franklin right away. □ Sam whipped the package over to Alice immediately.

whip something **up**[†] to prepare, create, or put something together. □ *I haven't written my report yet, but I'll whip one up before the deadline.* □ *I will whip up the most beautiful arrangement you have ever seen.*

whip something written **off**[†] **to** someone *Inf.* to write and send off a letter to someone quickly. □ *After I got her letter, I whipped an answer off to her the same afternoon.* □ *Liz whipped off a letter to her grandmother.*

whip through something *Fig.* to work through something very fast. □ *Do this carefully. Don't just whip through it.* □ *She whipped through her homework and went outside to play.*

a **whipping boy** *Fig.* someone who is punished for someone else's misdeeds. □ *The president has turned out to be the whipping boy for his party.*

whirl around to turn around very quickly. □ *I tapped him on the shoulder and he whirled around to see who it was.* □ *Todd whirled around and grabbed Max by the wrists.*

whirl someone or something **around**[†] to turn someone or something around quickly. □ *I grabbed him by the shoulder and whirled him around to face me.* □ *I whirled around the book display and found what I wanted.*

whisk someone **around**[†] to move someone around rapidly from place to place. □ *I didn't get much chance to see the city. They just whisked me around.* □ *We whisked around the visitor from place to place.*

whisk someone or an animal **off**[†] to brush [something] off someone or an animal. □ *The barber quickly whisked him off and collected the fee.* □ *The barber whisked off the customer.*

whisk someone or something **away**[†] to move someone or something out of the way rapidly. □ *The firemen came and whisked the students away to a safe place.* □ *The agents whisked away a number of people.*

whisk someone or something **off**[†] **(to** something) to move someone or something to something or some place rapidly. □ *The government agents whisked the witness off to a secret place.* □ *They whisked off the suspect to a holding cell.*

whisk something **off (of)** someone or something and **whisk** something **off**[†] to brush something off someone or something. (*Of* is usually retained before pronouns.) □ *The barber whisked the loose hairs off of the customer.* □ *The barber whisked off the loose hairs.*

whisper about someone or something to speak about someone or something in a quiet, breathy voice, as if telling secrets. □ *I hope they aren't whispering about me.* □ *Everyone is whispering about the incident in the lunchroom.*

whisper something **around** to spread secrets or gossip around. □ *Now, don't whisper this around, but Sam is going to run away from home.* □ *If you whisper this around, you will spoil the surprise.*

whistle at someone or something to indicate approval or disapproval of someone or something by whistling. □ *The men whistled at the beautiful woman who walked by.* □

Everyone whistled at the enormous roast of beef the cook's assistant carried in.

whistle for someone or something to summon someone or something by whistling. □ *I stood on the corner and whistled for a cab, but they all ignored me.* □ *I whistled for the dog, but it did not appear.*

whistle in the dark *Fig.* to guess aimlessly; to speculate as to a fact. □ *Am I close, or am I just whistling in the dark?* □ *She was whistling in the dark. She has no idea of what's going on.*

white as a ghost Go to next.

***white as a sheet** and ***white as a ghost; *white as snow; *white as the driven snow** [of someone] extremely pale, as if frightened. (*Also: **as** ~.) □ *Marilyn turned as white as a sheet when the policeman told her that her son had been in a car wreck.* □ *Did something scare you? You're white as a sheet!* □ *Jane made up the bed with her best linen sheets, which are always as white as snow.* □ *We have a new kitten whose fur is white as the driven snow.*

white as snow Go to previous.

white as the driven snow Go to white as a sheet.

white elephant something that is large and unwieldy and is either a nuisance or expensive to keep up. □ *Bob's father-in-law has given him an old Rolls Royce, but it's a real white elephant. He has no place to park it and can't afford the gas for it.* □ *Those antique vases Aunt Mary gave me are white elephants. They're ugly and I have no place to put them.*

white knuckle something to survive something threatening through strained endurance, that is to say, holding on tight. □ *The flight from New York was terrible. We had to white knuckle the entire flight.*

whittle at something to cut or carve at something. □ *He just sat there, whittling at a chunk of wood.* □ *I am not carving anything, I am just whittling at some wood.*

whittle someone **down to size** *Fig.* to reduce someone's ego; to cause someone to have better, more respectful behavior. (Fig. on whittle something down (to size).) □ *After a few days at camp, the counselors had whittled young Walter down to size.* □ *It took some doing, but they whittled him down to size.*

whittle something **away**[†] to cut or carve something away. □ *The carver whittled the wood away until only a small figure was left.* □ *He whittled away the wood.*

whittle something **down (to size)** and **whittle** something **down**[†] to cut or diminish something to a more appropriate size or to the proper size. □ *I whittled the peg down to size and it fit in the hole perfectly.* □ *You are going to have to whittle down expenses.*

whittle something **out of** something to carve something out of something. □ *The young man whittled a small boat out of wood.* □ *Can you whittle an elephant out of this chunk of wood?*

whiz past someone or something to move or travel past someone or something at a high speed. □ *The train whizzed past one little town after another.* □ *I whizzed past Chuck because I did not recognize him.*

whiz (right) through something **1.** to speed through a place. □ *One car after another whizzed right through the little town.* □ *We whizzed through the kitchen, stopping just*

W

long enough for a glass of iced tea. **2.** to work one's way through something quickly. □ *She whizzed right through the test with no trouble.* □ *Jane whizzed through her interview and got the job.*

Who cares? Does anyone really care?; It is of no consequence. □ *John: I have some advice for you. It will make things easier for you. Bob: Who cares? John: You might.* □ *Sue: You missed a spot shaving. Fred: Who cares?*

Who could have thought? Go to **Who would have thought?**

Who do you think you are? *Inf.* Why do you think you can lord it over people that way?; Why are you so arrogant? (Usually in anger.) □ *Tom: Just a minute! Who do you think you are? You can't talk to me that way! Bob: Says who?* □ *"Who do you think you are, bursting in here like that?" sputtered the doorman as Fred bolted into the club lobby.*

Who do you think you're kidding? *Inf.* You aren't fooling anyone.; Surely, you do not think you can fool me, do you? □ *Bill: I must pull down about eighty thou a year. Bob: You? Who do you think you're kidding?* □ *Mary: This carpet was made in Persia centuries ago. Tom: Who do you think you're kidding?*

Who do you think you're talking to? *Inf.* Do you know the importance of the person who you are talking to? □ *Who do you think you're talking to? I'm the boss here, you know?* □ *Don't talk to me that way! Who do you think you are talking to?*

Who do you want to speak to? Go to next.

Who do you want (to talk to)? and **Who do you want to speak to?**; **Who do you wish to speak to?**; **Who do you wish to talk to?** Who do you want to speak to over the telephone? (All these questions can also begin with *whom*. Compare this with **With whom do you wish to speak?**) □ *Sue: Wilson residence. Who do you want to speak to? Bill: Hi, Sue. I want to talk to you.* □ *Tom (answering the phone): Hello? Sue: Hello, who is this? Tom: Who do you wish to speak to? Sue: Is Sally there? Tom: Just a minute.*

Who (in) the devil? Go to next.

Who (in) the hell? and **Who (in) the devil?** *Inf.* Who? (An elaboration of *who*. See examples for variations.) □ *Who in the hell was that masked man?* □ *Who the hell are you?*

Who is it? Go to **Who's there?**

Who is this? Who is making this telephone call?; Who is on the other end of this telephone line? □ *Tom (answering the phone): Hello? Fred: Hello. Do you have any fresh turkeys? Tom: Who is this? Fred: Isn't this the Harrison Poultry Shop? Tom: No. Fred: I guess I have the wrong number.* □ *Mary (answering the phone): Hello? Sue: Hello, who is this? Mary: Well, who did you want? Sue: I want Grandma. Mary: I'm sorry, I think you have the wrong number.*

Who knows? Who knows the answer to that question? □ *Tom: When will this train get in? Rachel: Who knows?* □ *Andy: Why can't someone put this stuff away? Rachel: Who knows? Why don't you put it away?*

Who's calling(, please)? Who is this making this telephone call? □ *Rachel: Yes, Tom is here. Who's calling, please? Tom: Who is it? Rachel: It's Fred.* □ *Fred (answering the phone): Hello? Tom: Hello, is Bill there? Fred: Who's calling, please? Tom: This is Tom Wilson returning his call.*

Who's on the line? Go to next.

Who's on the phone? and **Who's on the line?** Who is on the telephone line now?; Who just called on the telephone? (The caller may still be waiting.) □ *Bill was on the telephone, and Mary walked by. "Who's on the phone?" asked Mary, hoping the call was for her.* □ *Tom asked, "Who's on the line?" Mary covered the receiver and said, "None of your business!"*

Who's there? and **Who is it?** a question asking who is on the other side of a door or concealed in some other place. □ *Hearing a noise, Tom called out in the darkness, "Who's there?"* □ *Hearing a knock on the door, Mary went to the door and said, "Who is it?"*

Who's your friend? *Sl.* Who is that following along behind you? □ *John: Hi, Tom. Who's your friend? Tom: Oh, this is my little brother, Willie. John: Hi, Willie.* □ *Looking at the little dog almost glued to Bob's pants cuff, Sally asked, "Who's your friend?"*

Who was it? Who called on the telephone or who was at the door? (Assumes that the caller is not waiting on the telephone or at the door.) □ *Sue (as Mary hangs up the telephone): Who was it? Mary: None of your business.* □ *Bill (as he leaves the door): What a pest! Sue: Who was it? Bill: Some silly survey.*

Who would have thought? and **Who could have thought?** a question phrase indicating surprise or amazement; I would never have guessed that something so surprising could happen. (No answer is expected.) □ *Tom: Fred just quit his job and went to Africa. Bill: Who would have thought he could do such a thing?* □ *Andy: They say Bill is training for the Olympics in his spare time. Rachel: Who would have thought?*

Whoa, Nellie! *Rur.* Wait! Stop! □ *Tom: When I get that money, I'm gonna get me my own place, and then you and I can get married, and— Jane: Whoa, Nellie! When did I say I was going to marry you?* □ *Whoa, Nellie! Did you measure them boards before you started cuttin' 'em?*

whole bag of tricks *Fig.* everything; every possibility, argument, or technique. □ *Well now. I've used my whole bag of tricks, and we still haven't solved this.* □ *It may take my whole bag of tricks to do it, but I'll try.*

the **whole ball of wax** and the **whole shooting match** the whole thing; the whole matter or affair; the entire affair or organization. □ *John is not a good manager. Instead of delegating jobs to others, he runs the whole shooting match himself.* □ *There's not a hard worker in that whole shooting match.* □ *I will be glad to be finished with this project. I want to be done with the whole ball of wax.* □ *I am tired of this job. I am fed up with the whole ball of wax.*

the **whole enchilada** *Inf.* the whole thing; everything. (From Spanish.) □ *Nobody, but nobody, ever gets the whole enchilada.* □ *Richard wants the whole enchilada.*

a **whole heap more** and a **whole lot more** *Rur.* a great deal more. □ *I think a whole heap more of Joe than I do of his brother.* □ *Don't quit now. There's a whole heap more work to be done.*

the **whole kit and caboodle** *Inf.* a group of pieces of equipment or belongings. (The word *caboodle* is used only in this expression.) □ *When I bought Bob's motorhome, I got furniture, refrigerator, and linen—the whole kit and caboodle.* □ *The salesman managed to sell John the whole kit and caboodle.*

a **(whole) mess of** someone or something *Rur.* a lot of someone or something. □ *We went out on the lake and caught a whole mess of bluegill.* □ *I cooked up a mess of chili and had all my friends over to eat it.*

a **(whole) new ball game** *Fig.* a completely different situation; something completely different. □ *Now that you're here, it's a whole new ball game.* □ *With a faster computer, it's a whole new ball game.*

the **whole nine yards** *Sl.* the entire amount; everything, as far as possible. □ *For you I'll go the whole nine yards.* □ *You're worth the whole nine yards.*

a **whole nother thing** *Rur.* a completely different matter. (Often "corrected" to *a whole other thing*. The word *nother* is a shortening of *another*.) □ *Borrowing! That's a whole nother thing! I thought you said stealing!*

the **whole shebang** everything; the whole thing. □ *Mary's all set to give a fancy dinner party. She's got a fine tablecloth, good crystal, and silverware, the whole shebang.* □ *How much do you want for the whole shebang?*

the **whole shooting match** Go to the **whole ball of wax**.

the **whole wide world** *Fig.* everywhere; everywhere and everything. □ *It's the best in the whole wide world.* □ *I've searched the whole wide world for just the right hat.*

the **whole works** everything; the complete amount. □ *I cashed my paycheck and lost the whole works playing the ponies.*

Whom the gods love die young. *Prov.* Virtuous or gifted people die at an early age, because the gods want those people to be with them in the afterlife. □ *So many brilliant authors and artists died before the age of fifty that it's easy to believe that whom the gods love die young.*

whoop it up to celebrate, especially with cheers and whoops. □ *It was a very noisy party. Everyone was whooping it up well past midnight.* □ *The campaign workers whooped it up for their candidate.* □ *I can't get out there and whoop it up for something I don't believe in.*

Why buy a cow when milk is so cheap? Go to next.

Why buy a cow when you can get milk for free? and **Why buy a cow when milk is so cheap?** *Prov.* Why pay for something that you can get for free otherwise. (Sometimes used to describe someone who will not marry because sex without any commitment is so easy to obtain. Jocular and crude.) □ *I don't have a car because someone always gives me a ride to work. Why buy a cow when you can get milk for free?* □ *Mary told her daughter, "You may think that boy will marry you because you're willing to sleep with him, but why should he buy a cow if he can get milk for free?"*

why don't you? a question tag that is put onto the end of a command. □ *Andy: Move aside, why don't you? Bob: Okay. Sorry. I didn't know I was in the way.* □ *"Just keep bugging me, why don't you?" threatened Wally.* □ *Andy: Try it again, why don't you? Sue: I hope I get it right this time.*

Why keep a dog and bark yourself? *Prov.* You should not do something you have hired someone else to do. □ *Ellen: The cleaning lady washes my floors every Tuesday, but I always wash them over again. Jane: Don't be silly, Ellen. Why keep a dog and bark yourself?*

Why not? 1. *Lit.* Please explain your negative answer. □ *Mother: No, you can't. Mary: Why not?* □ *Sue: Could I have another piece of cake? Mary: No. Sue: Why not? Mary: I want it.* **2.** *Inf.* I cannot think of a reason not to, so yes. □ *Bob: You want to go see a movie next Friday? Jane: Why not?* □ *Fred: Do you feel like wandering over to the bowling alley? Tom: Why not?*

the **whys and wherefores of** something the reasons or causes relating to something. □ *I refuse to discuss the whys and wherefores of my decision. It's final.* □ *Bob doesn't know the whys and wherefores of his contract. He just knows that it means he will get a lot of money when he finishes the work.*

wide of the mark 1. *Lit.* far from the target. (*Typically: **be ~; fall ~.**) □ *Tom's shot was wide of the mark.* □ *The pitch was quite fast but wide of the mark.* □ *The arrow fell wide of the mark.* **2.** *Fig.* inadequate; far from what is required or expected. (*Typically: **be ~; fall ~.**) □ *Jane's efforts were sincere but wide of the mark.* □ *He failed the course because everything he did was wide of the mark.*

wide open 1. as fast as possible; at full throttle. □ *I was driving along wide open when I became aware of a flashing red light.* □ *It was wide open and still wouldn't do better than eighty.* **2.** [of a town or place] full of crime or corruption; vice-ridden. □ *This town is wide open!* □ *Because the prison is understaffed, it is wide open.*

a **wide place in the road** a very small town. □ *The town is little more than a wide place in the road.* □ *We stopped at a wide place in the road called Adamsville.*

wig out *Sl.* to become intoxicated. □ *One more drink and Wally will wig out.* □ *This guy has wigged out. Get him out of here.*

wiggle out of something **1.** *Lit* to get out of something or some place; to squirm out of something or some place. □ *The kitten was able to wiggle out of the cage in which it had been put.* □ *The squirrel wiggled out of the trap we caught it in.* **2.** *Fig.* to manage to get out of a job, the blame for something, or a responsibility. □ *Don't try to wiggle out of your job!* □ *You are to blame and don't try to wiggle out of it!*

wild about someone or something very excited about someone or something. □ *I'm just wild about comedies.* □ *John is wild about antique cars.*

wild and woolly *Inf.* exciting. □ *Things get a little wild and woolly on a Friday evening at Wally's place.* □ *The ride home was a little wild and woolly.*

Wild horses couldn't drag someone **away (from** something.**)** *Prov.* Someone is determined to remain with something. □ *Once Elaine starts playing a video game, wild horses can't drag her away from it.* □ *Jim was determined to remain fishing at the lake. Wild horses couldn't drag him away from it.*

a **wild-goose chase** a worthless hunt or chase; a futile pursuit. □ *I wasted all afternoon on a wild-goose chase.* □

W

John was angry because he was sent out on a wild-goose chase.

will be the death of someone or something **(yet)** [the thing named] will be the end or ruin of someone or something. □ *This job will be the death of me!* □ *Rough roads will be the death of these tires.*

will come of something will result from something. □ *I don't think that much will come of this.* □ *Nothing at all will come of it.*

Will do. *Inf.* I will do it. □ *Will do. I'll get right on it.* □ *Fix the stuck window? Will do.*

will eat someone **for breakfast** and **will have** someone **for breakfast** *Fig.* will defeat someone thoroughly. □ *Watch out! Those guys are incredibly aggressive. They will eat you for breakfast.*

Will I see you again? a question asked toward the end of a date implying that further dating would please the speaker. (This question leaves it open to the other party to confirm that the interest is mutual by requesting a further date. Compare this with **Can I see you again?**) □ *Tom: I had a wonderful time tonight, Mary. Good night. Mary: Will I see you again? Tom: That would be nice. Can I call you tomorrow?* □ *"Will I see you again?" asked Sally, cautiously and hopefully.*

[will not] See the entries beginning with *won't.*

will not hear of something and **won't hear of** something will refuse to tolerate or permit something. □ *You mustn't drive home alone. I will not hear of it.* □ *My parents won't hear of my staying out that late.*

will something **away**† to give something away in a will. □ *The old man simply willed all his money away. He said he wouldn't need it when he was dead.* □ *She had willed away all of her treasures to her grandchildren.*

will something **to** someone to give something to someone in a will. □ *My uncle willed this chair to me. It's an antique.* □ *This watch was willed to me by my grandfather.*

will stop at nothing *Cliché* will do everything possible (to accomplish something); will be unscrupulous. □ *Bill would stop at nothing to get his way.* □ *Bob is completely determined to get promoted. He'll stop at nothing.*

Will that be all? Go to **(Will there be) anything else?**

(Will there be) anything else? and **Is that everything?; Is there anything else?; Will that be all?** Is there anything else you want?; Is there any other matter you wish to discuss?; Is there any other request? (These phrases are used by shopkeepers, clerks, and food service personnel to find out if the customer wants anything more.) □ *Clerk: Here's the roast you ordered. Will there be anything else? Rachel: No, that's all.* □ *Waiter: Anything else? Bill: Just coffee.* □ *The clerk rang up the last item and asked, "Will that be all?"* □ *Waiter: Anything else? Jane: No, that's everything.*

Will you excuse us, please? Go to **Could you excuse us, please?**

Will you hold? Go to **Could you hold?**

wimp out (of something**)** *Sl.* to chicken out (of something); to get out of something difficult, inconvenient, or dangerous, leaving others to carry the burden. □ *Come on!*

Don't wimp out now that there's all this work to be done. □ *Ted wimped out on us.*

Win a few, lose a few. Sometimes one succeeds, and sometimes one fails. □ *Tom: Well, I lost out on that Wilson contract, but I got the Jones job. Sally: That's life. Win a few, lose a few.* □ *"Win a few, lose a few," said Fred, staring at yesterday's stock prices.*

win all the marbles Go to **all the marbles.**

win at something to triumph at some competition. □ *Will I ever be able to win at golf?* □ *She always wins at poker.*

win by a nose *Fig.* to win by the slightest amount of difference. (Can be literal in horses races.) □ *I ran the fastest race I could, but I only won by a nose.* □ *Sally won the race, but she only won by a nose.*

win (out) (over someone or something**)** to defeat someone or something. □ *I hope our team wins out over you guys.* □ *Good teamwork always wins out.*

win someone **away (from** someone or something**)** to convince someone to dissociate from someone or something. □ *We were not able to win Christine away from her strange ideas.* □ *We tried to win her away but failed.*

win someone or something **back (from** someone or something**)**† to regain someone or something from someone or something. □ *I hope to win the money I lost back from the other poker players.* □ *We were not able to win Sally back from the cult.* □ *We won back everything.* □ *We won back Sally.*

win someone **over**† **(to** something**)** to succeed in making someone favorable to something. □ *I hope I can win them all over to our side.* □ *I won over the mayor to our side.*

win someone's **heart** and **win the heart of** someone *Fig.* to gain the affection of someone; to win the love of someone exclusively. □ *I hope to win her heart and make her my bride.*

win something **at** something to win a prize in some sort of competition. □ *I won this silly doll at the ring-toss game.* □ *Did you win anything at the fair?*

win the day Go to **carry the day.**

win the heart of someone Go to **win** someone's **heart.**

win through something to succeed by a certain method or procedure. □ *Winning is no good if you have to win through dishonesty.* □ *Sally won through her own hard work.*

wince at something to shrink back because of something, such as pain. □ *She winced at the pain but did not cry out.* □ *After he had just winced at the pain for a while, he finally screamed.*

wind around [for something, such as a road] to make a turn or turns around. □ *The road wound around and ended up at the lake.* □ *The path wound around and came to a stop at the cabin door.*

wind around someone or something to twist or coil around someone or something. □ *The python wound around the rabbit, suffocating it.* □ *The vines wound around the gatepost.*

wind back [for something, such as a road] to turn so that it heads in the direction from whence it came. □ *The road we got lost on wound back and we were not able to reach*

W

the lake on time. □ When we were lost, we found a stream in the woods, but it wound back and did not lead us in the direction we wanted.

wind down to start running or operating slower. □ *Things will begin to wind down at the end of the summer.* □ *As things wind down, life will be a lot easier.* □ *The clock wound down and finally stopped.*

wind into something to coil up into something. □ *The snake wound into a tight coil.* □ *The rubber bands wound into a knot and were worthless.*

wind someone **around** one's **little finger** Go to twist someone **around** one's **little finger**.

wind someone **up 1.** *Inf. Fig.* to get someone excited. □ *That kind of music really winds me up!* **2.** *Inf. Fig.* to get someone set to do a lot of talking. (Fig. on winding up a clock.) □ *The excitement of the day wound Kelly up and she talked almost all night.* □ *A good movie tends to wind me up for a while.*

wind something **around** something to twist or coil something around something. □ *Wind this cloth around your hand to stop the bleeding.* □ *Wind the string around this stick so it won't get all tangled up.*

wind something **down**[†] to slow something down; to make something less hectic. □ *Let's wind this party down and try to get people to go home. It's really late.* □ *We tried to wind down the party, but it kept running.*

wind something **in**[†] to reel something in. □ *She wound in the rope that was tied to the anchor.* □ *Liz wound in the cable that raised the awning.*

wind something **off**[†] to unreel or unwind something. □ *He wound the rope off, little by little, until he had as much as he needed.* □ *Karen wound off as much as she needed.*

wind something **onto** something and **wind** something **on**[†] to coil or wrap something onto something. □ *Wind this string onto the ball and save it.* □ *If you find the ball of string, please wind on this string.*

wind something **up**[†] **1.** *Lit.* to tighten the spring in something, such as a watch or a clock. □ *Please wind your watch up now—before it runs down.* □ *Wind up your watch before you forget.* **2.** *Fig.* to conclude something. □ *Today we'll wind that deal up with the bank.* □ *I have a few items of business to wind up. Then I'll be with you.*

wind something **(up**[†]**) (into** something**)** to coil something up into a ball or similar shape. □ *Tony wound all the string up into a ball.* □ *Wind up the string into a ball.* □ *Please wind this into a ball.*

wind through something [for a pathway] to twist or turn through an area. □ *The trail wound through the jungle, avoiding the densest places.* □ *A path wound through the woods, leading us to the main road.*

wind up (as) something to end up as something. □ *Roger wound up as a millionaire.* □ *He thought he would wind up a pauper.*

wind up (by) doing something Go to **end up (by)** doing something.

wind up somehow to end up in some fashion. □ *I don't want to wind up broke and depressed.* □ *You don't want to wind up like Ted, do you?*

wind up (somewhere) Go to **end up (somewhere)**.

wind up with someone or something to end up having someone or something. □ *I don't want to wind up with all the kids for the weekend.* □ *We wound up with Thanksgiving at our house again.*

a **window of opportunity** *Fig.* a brief time period in which an opportunity exists. □ *This afternoon, I had a brief window of opportunity when I could discuss this with the boss, but she wasn't receptive.*

wine and dine someone to treat someone to an expensive meal of the type that includes fine wines; to entertain someone lavishly. □ *The lobbyists wined and dined the senators one by one in order to influence them.* □ *We were wined and dined every night and given the best hotel accommodations in town.*

wing it to improvise; to do something extemporaneously. □ *I lost my lecture notes, so I had to wing it.* □ *Don't worry. Just go out there and wing it.*

wink at someone to close one eye at a person as a sign of friendliness or flirtation. □ *She winked at him and he was shocked.* □ *I hope she winks at me again.*

wink at something to pretend not to see something; to condone something wrong. (See also **blink at** something ②.) □ *The police officer winked at my failure to make a complete stop.* □ *I cannot wink at blatant infractions of the law!*

wink something **away**[†] to blink the eyes to try to clear them of tears, dirt, etc. □ *He looked up at me and tried to wink away his tears, but he was just too upset.* □ *Jane winked away her tears.*

winner take all a situation where the one who defeats others takes all the spoils of the conflict. □ *The contest was a case of winner take all. There was no second place or runner-up.*

winter over (some place**)** to spend the winter at some place. □ *The bears all winter over in their dens.* □ *All the animals are getting ready either to migrate or to winter over.* □ *My parents winter over in Florida.*

Wipe it off! *Inf.* Wipe that smile off your face! □ *It's not funny. Wipe it off!* □ *Wipe it off! Nothing funny here, soldier.*

wipe out 1. *Inf.* to crash. □ *I wiped out on the curve.* □ *The car wiped out on the curve.* **2.** *Inf.* to fall off or away from something, such as a bicycle, skates, a surfboard, a skateboard, etc. □ *I wiped out and skinned my knee.* □ *If I wipe out again, my mother says I'm through.* **3.** *Inf.* to fail badly. □ *The test was terrible! I'm sure I wiped out.* □ *It was a bad test. I wiped out for sure.*

wipe someone or something **off**[†] to clean something off someone or something by wiping. □ *She wiped the baby off and put clean clothes on him.* □ *Please wipe off your shoes.* □ *John fell in the mud and Sam wiped him off.*

wipe someone or something **off the face of the earth** *Fig.* to demolish every trace of someone or something. □ *A great storm will come and wipe all the people off the face of the earth.* □ *The wind blew my old barn off the face of the earth! Nothing was left.*

wipe someone or something **(off**[†]**) (with** something**)** to clean someone or something by wiping with something. □ *Tony wiped the baby off with a soft cloth.* □ *Jane wiped off the counter with a rag.* □ *Tom fell in the mud and asked Ralph to wipe him off.*

W

wipe someone **out**† **1.** *Sl.* to kill someone. □ *Max intended to wipe Lefty's gang out.* □ *Lefty wiped out Max's gang.* **2.** *Sl.* to exhaust or debilitate someone. □ *The long walk wiped me out.* □ *The trip wiped out the hikers.* **3.** *Inf.* to ruin someone financially. □ *The loss of my job wiped us out.* □ *The storm ruined the corn crop and wiped out everyone in the county.*

wipe someone's **slate clean** and **wipe the slate clean** *Fig.* to get rid of or erase someone's (bad) record. (As if erasing information recorded on a slate.) □ *I'd like to wipe my slate clean and start all over again.* □ *Bob did badly in high school, but he wiped his slate clean and did a good job in college.*

wipe something **away**† to clean or mop something away. □ *Wipe all this mud away and scrub the floor clean.* □ *Jake wiped away the mud.*

wipe something **down**† to rub or mop something down. □ *Wipe the counter down and keep it clean!* □ *Don will wipe down the counter.*

wipe something **off**† **1.** to remove something (from something else) by wiping or rubbing. □ *There is mud on your shirt. Please wipe it off.* □ *I must wipe off the ketchup from my shirt.* **2.** to tidy or clean something by wiping (something else) off. □ *Please wipe the table off. There's water on it.* □ *Wipe off your shirt. There's ketchup on it.*

wipe something **(off**†**) (on** something**)** to remove something by wiping it on something else. □ *Don't wipe your feet off on the carpet.* □ *Don't wipe off your feet on the carpet.* □ *Wipe them on the mat.*

wipe something **off** (one's **face**) **1.** *Lit.* to remove something, such as food or dirt, from one's own face. □ *Wipe that peanut butter off your face!* **2.** *Fig.* to remove a smile, grin, silly look, etc., from one's face. □ *Wipe that silly grin off your face, private!* □ *Wipe that smile off!*

wipe something **out**† *Sl.* to use up all of something. □ *I wiped the cookies out—not all at once, of course.* □ *Who wiped out the strawberry preserves?*

wipe something **up**† **1.** to clean something up by wiping. □ *Please wipe that spilled milk up.* □ *Jim wiped up the spill.* **2.** to clean something dirty by wiping. □ *The floor was sticky so I wiped it up.* □ *Please wipe up the countertop.*

wipe the floor up† **with** someone *Inf.* to beat or physically abuse someone. (Usually said as a threat.) □ *You say that to me one more time, and I'll wipe the floor up with you.* □ *Oh, yeah! You're not big enough to wipe up the floor with anybody!*

wipe the slate clean Go to **wipe** someone's **slate clean.**

wire ahead (for something**)** to send a telegram to one's destination, requesting something to be available upon one's arrival. □ *I wired ahead for a room. I hope that they still have one by the time we get to the hotel.* □ *We wired ahead for reservations.*

wire for something to send for something by telegram. □ *I wired for money, but it hasn't come yet.* □ *I will have to wire for further advice.*

wire someone or something **for** something to send a telegram to someone or something requesting something. □ *I wired my father for some money. I'm sure he'll send it, officer.* □ *Sarah wired the supplier for a replacement part.*

wire something **back to** someone to send something, such as a reply or money, back to someone by telegram. □ *Please wire your answer back to me by tomorrow.* □ *The reply wasn't wired back in time.*

wire something **in**† to send something into a central point by telegram. □ *I can't mail my story to my editor in time, so I will have to wire it in.* □ *I've got to wire in this story.*

wire something **together** to bind the pieces of something together with wire; to bind things together with wire. □ *I wired the car's exhaust pipe together, hoping to get a few more miles out of it.* □ *I will wire it together to keep it from dragging on the roadway.*

wire something **up**† **1.** to repair or reattach something with wire, especially something electrical. □ *I will wire this light fixture up and it will work like new.* □ *As soon as I wire up this again, it will work very well.* **2.** to attach something to a high place with wire. □ *We wired the satellite dish up to the side of the chimney.* □ *We wired up the antenna to the chimney.*

wired into someone or something *Sl.* closely concerned with someone or something; really involved with someone or something. □ *Mary is really wired into classical music.* □ *Sam and Martha are totally wired into one another.*

wise as an owl Go to next.

***wise as Solomon** and ***wise as an owl** very wise. (*Also: as ~.) □ *If you are in trouble, get Chris to advise you. He's as wise as Solomon.* □ *This is a difficult problem. You'd need to be as wise as an owl to be able to solve it.*

wise someone **up (about** someone or something**)** *Inf.* to instruct someone about something; to give someone important information. □ *Let me wise you up about the way we do things around here.* □ *I will do what I can to wise her up.*

***wise to** someone or something fully aware of someone or something. (*Typically: **be ~; get ~; put** someone **~**.) □ *The cops are wise to the plan.*

wise up (to someone or something**)** to (finally) begin to understand someone or something; to realize and accept the facts about someone or something. (Also as a command.) □ *Sally finally wised up to Richard.* □ *Come on, Sally! Wise up!*

wish for someone or something to wish to have someone or something. □ *She spent most of her life wishing for Prince Charming, who would come along and sweep her off her feet.* □ *She still wishes for escape.*

The **wish is father to the thought.** *Prov.* People sometimes come to believe something that they wish were true. □ *Jane hoped that her boss would resign, and the wish was father to the thought. Soon she had told everyone in the office that she was sure her boss was leaving.*

wish list a list of things one wishes to have. □ *I put a new car at the top of my wish list.* □ *I have a DVD player on my wish list.*

wish someone or something **away**† to wish that someone or something would go away. □ *You can't just wish him away. You'll have to ask him to leave!* □ *Don't try to wish away the difficulties of your life.*

wish someone or something **(off**†**) on** someone to foist someone or something off on someone else. □ *I would* never wish my uncle off on you, even for an hour. □ I wouldn't wish off my cousin Roger on anyone. □ I wouldn't wish this matter on you.

wishful thinking believing that something is true or that something will happen just because one wishes that it were true or would happen. □ Hoping for a car as a birthday present is just wishful thinking. Your parents can't afford it. □ Mary thinks that she is going to get a big raise, but that's wishful thinking. Her boss is so tight with money.

with a heavy heart Cliché sadly. □ With a heavy heart, she said good-bye. □ We left our summer cottage on the last day with a heavy heart.

with a vengeance Cliché with determination and eagerness. □ The angry soldier attacked the enemy with a vengeance. □ Bill ate all his dinner and gobbled up his dessert with a vengeance.

with a view to doing something and **with an eye to** doing something with the intention of doing something. □ I came to this school with a view to getting a degree. □ The mayor took office with an eye to improving the town.

with a will with determination and enthusiasm. □ The children worked with a will to finish the project on time. □ The workers set about manufacturing the new products with a will.

with advance notice and **on advance notice** with some kind of notification or indication that something is going to happen or is expected before it actually happens. □ We are happy to provide special meals for anyone with advance notice.

with all one's **heart (and soul)** Cliché very sincerely. □ Oh, Bill, I love you with all my heart and soul, and I always will! □ She thanked us with all her heart and soul for the gift.

with all the fixin(g)s Rur. with all the condiments or other dishes that accompany a certain kind of food. □ For $12.99 you get a turkey dinner with all the fixings. □ Max likes his hamburgers with all the fixin's.

with all the trimmings with all the extra things, especially with food. □ We had a lovely Thanksgiving dinner with all the trimmings. □ I look forward to roast turkey with all the trimmings.

with an eye to doing something Go to **with a view to** doing something.

with bated breath Cliché while holding one's breath. □ We stood there with bated breath while the man hung on the side of the bridge. □ They listened with bated breath for the announcement about the winner.

with bells on (one's **toes)** Fig. eagerly, willingly, and on time. □ Oh, yes! I'll meet you at the restaurant. I'll be there with bells on. □ All the smiling children were there waiting for me with bells on their toes.

with both hands tied behind one's **back** Go to **with one hand tied behind** one's **back**.

***with child** Euph. pregnant. (Biblical. *Typically: **be** ~; **get** a woman ~.) □ The first thing he did after he got married was to get his wife with child. □ She deliberately set out to get herself with child, as they say.

with each passing day as days pass, one by one; day by day. □ Things grow more expensive with each passing day. □ We are all growing older with each passing day.

with ease without effort. □ The smart student passed the test with ease. □ The gymnast did a back flip with ease.

with every (other) breath Fig. [saying something] repeatedly or continually. □ Bob was out in the yard, raking leaves and cursing with every other breath. □ The child was so grateful that she was thanking me with every breath.

with everything (on it) [of a sandwich] ordered with everything available on it, such as ketchup, mustard, onions, cheese, peppers, chili, lettuce, tomato, etc., as appropriate. □ Do you want it with everything? □ Give me a cheeseburger with everything on it.

with fits and starts Go to **fits and starts**.

with flying colors Cliché easily and excellently. □ John passed his geometry test with flying colors. □ Sally qualified for the race with flying colors.

(with) hat in hand Fig. with humility. (Fig. on the image of someone standing, respectfully, in front of a powerful person, asking for a favor.) □ She stormed off but came back with hat in hand when she ran out of money. □ We had to go hat in hand to the committee to get a grant for our proposal.

with impunity without risk of punishment; with immunity from the negative consequences of an act; while being exempt from punishment. □ The diplomat parked in illegal parking spaces with impunity. □ Bob used his brother's property with impunity.

with it 1. Inf. alert and knowledgeable. □ Jane isn't making any sense. She's not really with it tonight. □ Jean's mother is not really with it anymore. She's going senile. □ Peter's not with it yet. He's only just come round from the anesthetic. **2.** Inf. up-to-date. □ My parents are so old-fashioned. I'm sure they were never with it. □ Why do you wear those baggy old clothes? Why aren't you with it?

with my blessing a phrase expressing consent or agreement; yes. □ Bob: Can I take this old coat down to the rummage sale? Sue: With my blessing. □ Mary: Shall I drive Uncle Tom to the airport a few hours early? Sue: Oh, yes! With my blessing!

with no strings attached and **without any strings attached** Fig. unconditionally; with no obligations or conditions attached. □ My parents gave me use of their car without any strings attached. □ I will accept this job only if there are no strings attached.

with one hand tied behind one's **back** and **with both hands tied behind** one's **back** Fig. even if under a handicap; easily. □ I could put an end to this argument with one hand tied behind my back. □ John could do this job with both hands tied behind his back.

with (one's**) eyes (wide) open** Fig. totally aware of what is going on. □ I went into this with my eyes open. □ We all started with eyes open but didn't realize what could happen to us.

with one's **tail between** one's **legs** Fig. appearing frightened or cowardly. (Fig. on the image of a frightened or defeated dog going off threatened or humiliated.) □ John seems to lack courage. When people criticize him unjustly, he just goes away with his tail between his legs and doesn't

W

tell them that they're wrong. □ *The frightened dog ran away with its tail between its legs when the bigger dog growled.*

With or without? Do you wish your tea or coffee to be with or without sugar or with or without milk? □ *How do you like your tea? With or without?* □ *Do you drink your coffee with or without?*

With pleasure. a phrase indicating eager consent to do something. □ *Fred: Would you please take this note over to the woman in the red dress? Waiter: With pleasure, sir.* □ *Sue: Would you kindly bring in the champagne now? Jane: With pleasure.*

with reference to someone or something Go to **in reference to** someone or something.

with regard to someone or something and **in regard to** someone or something concerning someone or something. □ *What shall we do in regard to planning dinner?* □ *With regard to Bill, I think he is working too hard.*

with relish with pleasure or enjoyment. □ *John put on this new coat with great relish.* □ *We accepted the offer to use their beach house with relish.*

with respect to someone or something of or about someone or something. □ *With respect to radiation, this power plant is very safe.* □ *This article examines experiments with respect to ethical issues.*

with someone or something **for** some time employed by or associated with someone or something for a period of time. □ *I've been with the company for nearly ten years.* □ *Lily has been with Max for years.*

with something **to spare** Go to **and** something **to spare.**

with the best will in the world however much one wishes to do something or however hard one tries to do something. □ *With the best will in the world, Jack won't be able to help Mary get the job.* □ *With the best will in the world, they won't finish the job in time.*

with the naked eye with eyes that are not aided by telescopes, microscopes, or binoculars. □ *The moon is quite visible with the naked eye.* □ *Bacteria are too small to be seen with the naked eye.*

With whom do you wish to speak? a polite phrase used by people who answer the telephone to find out whom the caller wants to speak to. (Compare this with **Who do you want to talk to?**) □ *John answered the telephone and then said, "With whom do you wish to speak?"* □ *Tom (answering the phone): Good morning, Acme Air Products. With whom do you wish to speak? Sue: Sorry, I have the wrong number. Tom: That's perfectly all right. Have a nice day.*

With you in a minute. and Someone **will be with you in a minute.** Please be patient, someone will attend to you very soon. (The *someone* can be any person's name or a pronoun, typically *I*. If there is no one mentioned, *I* is implied. The *minute* can be replaced by *moment* or *second*.) □ *Sue: Oh, Miss? Clerk: Someone will be with you in a minute.* □ *Bill: Please wait here. I'll be with you in a minute. Bob: Please hurry.*

withdraw from something **1.** to depart from something physically. □ *I withdrew from the smoky room and ran to the open window to get some air.* □ *I withdrew from the unpleasant-looking cafe and looked for something more to my liking.* **2.** to end one's association with someone or

something. □ *I decided to withdraw from all my professional organizations.* □ *I had to withdraw from the association because the dues had become too high.*

withdraw into oneself to become introverted; to concern oneself with one's inner thoughts. □ *After a few years of being ignored, she withdrew into herself.* □ *I have to struggle to keep from withdrawing into myself.*

withdraw into something to pull back into something. □ *The turtle withdrew into its shell.* □ *The mouse withdrew into its hole.*

withdraw someone **from** something **1.** to pull someone out of something physically. □ *She withdrew the child from the water just in time.* □ *I had to withdraw my child from the kindergarten room. He was having such a good time, he wouldn't leave on his own.* **2.** to remove someone from an organization or a nomination. □ *The committee withdrew John from nomination and put up someone else.* □ *I withdrew my son from kindergarten.*

withdraw something **from** someone or something to pull something out of someone or something. □ *She withdrew the book from the stack.* □ *I withdrew the splinter from Dave carefully.*

withdraw something **into** something to pull something back into something. □ *The turtle withdrew its head into its shell.* □ *It then withdrew its feet into the shell also.*

wither away to shrivel up; to shrink up. □ *Soon, the wart withered away.* □ *Many of our roses withered away in the hot sun.*

wither on the vine and **die on the vine 1.** *Lit.* [for fruit] to shrivel on the vine or stem, unharvested. □ *If we don't get out there into the field, the grapes will wither on the vine.* □ *The apples will die on the vine if not picked soon.* **2.** *Fig.* [for someone or something] to be ignored or neglected and thereby be wasted. □ *I hope I get a part in the play. I don't want to just die on the vine.* □ *Fred thinks he is withering on the vine because no one has chosen him.*

wither up to shrivel up. □ *It was so hot that the leaves of the trees withered up.*

withhold something **from** someone or an animal to hold something back or in reserve from someone or an animal. □ *We withheld some of the food from the guests.* □ *I had to withhold some food from the dog so there would be enough for tomorrow.*

within a hair('s breadth) of something Go to **within an ace of (doing)** something.

within a stone's throw (of something**)** and **(just) a stone's throw away (from** something**); (just) a stone's throw (from** something**)** *Fig.* very close (to something). (Possibly as close as the distance one could throw a stone. It usually refers to a distance much greater than one could throw a stone.) □ *The police department was located within a stone's throw of our house.* □ *We live in Carbondale, and that's just a stone's throw away from the Mississippi River.* □ *Come visit. We live just a stone's throw away.*

within an ace of (doing) something and **within a hair('s breadth) of** something very close to doing something. □ *I came within an ace of getting into an accident.* □ *We were* within an ace of beating the all-time record. □ We were within a hair's breadth of beating the all-time record.

within an inch of one's **life** *Fig.* very close to losing one's life; almost to death. □ *The accident frightened me within an inch of my life.* □ *When Mary was seriously ill in the hospital, she came within an inch of her life.*

within bounds Go to within limits.

within calling distance Go to within hailing distance.

***within earshot (of** something**)** close enough to something to hear it. (*Typically: **be** ~; **come** ~; **get** ~; **move** ~.) □ *As soon as I got within earshot of the music, I decided that I really didn't belong there.*

within hailing distance and **within calling distance; within shouting distance** close enough to hear someone call out. □ *When the boat came within hailing distance, I asked if I could borrow some gasoline.* □ *We weren't within shouting distance, so I couldn't hear what you said to me.*

within limits and **within bounds** up to a certain point; with certain restrictions. □ *You're free to do what you want—within limits, of course.* □ *You must try to keep behavior at the party within bounds.*

***within** one's **grasp 1.** *Lit.* where one can grasp something with one's hand. (*Typically: **be** ~; **get** ~; **get** something ~.) □ *The rope was within his grasp, but he was too weak to reach for it.* **2.** *Fig.* [for something] to be obtainable; [for a goal] to be almost won. (Does not involve grabbing or grasping. *Typically: **be** ~; **get** ~; **get** something ~.) □ *Victory is within our grasp, so we must keep playing the game to win.* □ *Her goal is within her grasp at last.*

***within** one's **rights** acting legally in one's own interest. (*Typically: **be** ~; **act** ~.) □ *I know I am within my rights when I make this request.* □ *You are not within your rights!*

***within range (of** something**)** inside an area that can be covered by something, such as a gun, camera lens, measuring device, etc. (*Typically: **be** ~; **come** ~; **get** ~; **move** ~.) □ *The sick elephant was within range, so we shot it with tranquilizer darts so we could treat it.* □ *When the ducks were within range of my gun, I sneezed and frightened them away.* □ *You won't be able to hear what they are saying until you get within range of the P.A. system.*

within reason reasonable; reasonably. □ *You can do anything you want within reason.* □ *I'll pay any sum you ask—within reason.*

within shouting distance Go to within hailing distance.

within someone's **grasp** Go to next.

within someone's **reach** and **within** someone's **grasp 1.** *Lit.* close enough to be grasped. □ *The ball was almost within his reach!* **2.** *Fig.* almost in the possession of someone. □ *My goals are almost within my reach, so I know I'll succeed.* □ *We almost had the contract within our grasp, but the deal fell through at the last minute.*

within walking distance close enough to walk to. □ *Is the train station within walking distance?* □ *My office is within walking distance from here.*

without a doubt a phrase expressing certainty or agreement; yes. □ *John: This cheese is as hard as a rock. It must have been in the fridge for weeks. Fred: Without a doubt.* □ *Mary: Taxes will surely go up before I retire. Jane: Without a doubt!*

without a hitch *Fig.* with no problem(s). □ *Everything went off without a hitch.* □ *We hoped the job would go off without a hitch.*

without a moment to spare Go to not a moment to spare.

without a shadow of a doubt and **beyond the shadow of a doubt** without the smallest amount of doubt. □ *I am certain that I am right, without a shadow of a doubt.* □ *I felt the man was guilty beyond the shadow of a doubt.*

without any strings attached Go to with no strings attached.

without batting an eye *Lit. Fig.* without showing alarm or response; without blinking an eye. □ *I knew I had insulted her, and she turned to me and asked me to leave without batting an eye.* □ *Right in the middle of the speech—without batting an eye—the speaker walked off the stage.*

without fail for certain; absolutely. □ *I'll be there at noon without fail.* □ *The plane leaves on time every day without fail.*

without further ado *Cliché* without further talk. (An overworked phrase usually heard in public announcements.) □ *And without further ado, I would like to introduce Mr. Bill Franklin!* □ *The time has come to leave, so without further ado, good evening and good-bye.*

without half trying *Rur.* effortlessly. □ *He was so strong, he could bend an iron bar without half trying.* □ *I wish I had his ability to cook. He makes the most delicious dishes without half trying.*

without missing a beat *Lit. Fig.* without pausing for any potential interruption. □ *He kept right on giving his speech without missing a beat, despite the interruptions.* □ *She went right on drumming without missing a beat.*

without question absolutely; certainly. □ *She agreed to help without question.* □ *She said, "I stand ready to support you without question."*

without rhyme or reason *Cliché* without purpose, order, or reason. (See variations in the examples. Fixed order.) □ *The teacher said my report was disorganized. My paragraphs seemed to be without rhyme or reason.* □ *Everything you do seems to be without rhyme or reason.*

without (so much as) a (for or) by your leave without (the least hint of) asking for permission. □ *Without so much as a for or by your leave, they just walked into our house.* □ *He left, without a by your leave.*

without so much as doing something without even doing something, such as a simple courtesy. □ *Jane borrowed Bob's car without so much as asking his permission.* □ *Mary's husband walked out without so much as saying good-bye.*

witness for someone or something to serve as a witness for some person or some deed. □ *They could find no one to*

W

witness for the accused person. □ *The police found someone to witness for the hour of the crime.*

witness to something to serve as a witness to some act or deed. □ *I was witness to the beating.* □ *We were not witness to any of the activities you have described.*

wobble about and **wobble around** to rock, quiver, or flounder around. □ *The little baby wobbled about and finally fell.* □ *The vase wobbled around a little and fell over.*

Woe is me! I am unfortunate.; I am unhappy. (Usually humorous.) □ *Woe is me! I have to work when the rest of the office staff is off.* □ *Woe is me. I have the flu and my friends have gone to a party.*

a **wolf in sheep's clothing** *Fig.* a dangerous person pretending to be harmless. □ *Carla thought the handsome stranger was gentle and kind, but Susan suspected he was a wolf in sheep's clothing.* □ *Mimi: Why shouldn't I go out with David? He's the nicest man I've ever met. Alan: He's a wolf in sheep's clothing, Mimi. Can't you tell?*

wolf something **down**† *Fig.* to eat something very rapidly and in very large pieces. (As a wolf might eat.) □ *Don't wolf your food down!* □ *Liz would never wolf down her food.*

woman of ill repute *Euph.* a prostitute. □ *His favorite companion was a woman of ill repute.* □ *If you can't be faithful to your husband, you're no better than a woman of ill repute.*

A **woman's place is in the home.** *Prov.* Women should remain in the home, doing housework and raising children. (This notion is generally regarded as old-fashioned.) □ *As soon as our child is old enough to go to school, I'm going to go back to my job at the newspaper. And don't give me any of that nonsense about a woman's place being in the home.*

A **woman's work is never done.** *Prov.* Housework and raising children are jobs that have no end. (Typically said by a woman to indicate how busy she is.) □ *"As soon as I finish washing the breakfast dishes, it's time to start fixing lunch," Elizabeth observed. "A woman's work is never done."* □ *After a difficult day at the office, Greta came home and began cooking dinner. "A woman's work is never done," she sighed.*

woman to woman Go to man to man.

wonder about someone or something to be curious or in doubt about someone or something. □ *I wonder about Carl and what he is up to.* □ *Sometimes I wonder about life on other planets.* □ *Jenny's performance record made me wonder about her chances for success.*

wonder at someone or something to be amazed at or in awe of someone or something. (Stilted.) □ *We all wondered at Lee and the way he kept his spirits up.* □ *The people wondered at the bright light that lit up the sky.*

Wonders never cease! and **Will wonders never cease!** *Prov.* What an amazing thing has happened! (Said when something very surprising happens. Somewhat ironic; can imply that the surprising thing should have happened before, but did not.) □ *Fred: Hi, honey. I cleaned the kitchen for you. Ellen: Wonders never cease!* □ *Jill: Did you hear? The company is allowing us to take a holiday tomorrow. Jane: Wonders never cease!* □ *Not only was my*

plane on time, the airline also delivered my luggage safely. Will wonders never cease?

won't hold water to be inadequate, insubstantial, or ill-conceived. □ *Sorry, your ideas won't hold water. Nice try, though.* □ *The prosecution's case wouldn't hold water, so the defendant was released.*

Won't you come in? the standard phrase used to invite someone into one's home or office. □ *Bill: Won't you come in? Mary: I hope I'm not early.* □ *Tom stood in the doorway of Mr. Franklin's office for a moment. "Won't you come in?" said Mr. Franklin without looking up.*

woo someone **away**† **(from** someone or something**)** to lure someone away from someone or something; to seduce someone away from someone or something. □ *The manager of the new bank wooed all the tellers away from the old bank.* □ *They wooed away all the experienced people.*

the **woods are full of** someone or something *Fig.* there are lots and lots of people or things. □ *The woods are full of cheap, compatible computer clones.* □ *The woods are full of nice-looking guys who'll scam you if you aren't careful.*

word by word one word at a time. □ *We examined the contract word by word to make sure everything was the way we wanted.* □ *We compared the stories word by word to see what made them different.*

word for word in the exact words; verbatim. □ *I memorized the speech, word for word.* □ *I can't recall word for word what she told us.*

***word (from** someone or something**)** messages or communication from someone or something. (*Typically: get ~; have ~; hear ~; receive ~.*) □ *We have just received word from Perry that the contract has been signed.*

A **word (once) spoken is past recalling.** *Prov.* Once you have said something, you cannot undo the result of having said it. □ *Hilary apologized for having called Mark's suit cheap, but Mark was still offended. A word once spoken is past recalling.*

a **word to the wise** a good piece of advice; a word of wisdom. (See also A word to the wise (is enough).) □ *If I can give you a word to the wise, I would suggest going to the courthouse about an hour before your trial.* □ *Here is a word to the wise. Keep your eyes open and your mouth shut.*

A **word to the wise (is enough).** and A **word to the wise is sufficient.** *Prov.* You only have to hint something to wise people in order to get them to understand it.; Wise people do not need long explanations. (Often used to signal that you are hinting something.) □ *John's a pleasant man, but I wouldn't trust him with money. A word to the wise, eh?* □ *Donna hinted about Lisa's drinking problem to Lisa's fiancé, hoping that a word to the wise would be enough.*

*a **word with** someone **(about** something**)** a chance to talk to someone about something, usually briefly. (*Typically: get ~; get in ~; have ~.*) □ *Can I have a word with you about your report?*

words to live by and **thoughts to live by** useful philosophical or spiritual expressions. □ *Thank you for your expression of gratitude. You gave us words to live by.*

work against someone or something **1.** [for someone] to struggle against someone or something. □ *She worked hard against the passage of the law.* □ *Dave worked against*

Betty. **2.** [for something] to militate against someone or something. □ *This sort of works against your plan, does it not?* □ *Everything you said works against your client.*

work among someone or something to do one's work among some people or things. □ *I wanted to work among the Indians, but I set up my medical practice in the inner city.* □ *I want to get a job in forestry and work among the trees.*

work around someone or something to manage to do one's work while avoiding someone or something. □ *He is being a problem, but he will have to leave pretty soon. You'll just have to work around him for now.* □ *You have to work around the piano. It is too heavy to move.*

work around to someone or something to get around to dealing with someone or something. □ *You're not next in line. We will have to work around to you.* □ *I can't take care of it now. I'll have to work around to it.*

work as something to work in the capacity of something. □ *I worked as a waiter for a year when I was in college.* □ *I will work as a stockbroker for a while, and then move on to something else.*

work at something **1.** to work in a particular trade or craft. □ *He works at carpentry when he has the time.* □ *Julie works at editing for a living.* **2.** to work on a specific task, machine, device, etc. □ *She was working at repairing the cabinet when I came home.* □ *Todd is working at his computer.*

work away (at something**)** to continue to work industriously at something. □ *All the weavers were working away at their looms.* □ *They just kept working away.*

work down (the line) (to someone or something**)** to progress through a series until someone or something is reached. □ *I will work down to the papers on the bottom gradually. You can't hurry this kind of work.* □ *We will work down the line to Katie.* □ *We have to work down to the last one.* □ *They are working down the line as fast as they can, but everyone has to be taken in order.*

work for someone **1.** to be employed by someone. □ *She works for Scott Wallace.* □ *Who do you work for?* **2.** to work as a substitute for someone. □ *I will work for you while you are having your baby.* □ *Right now, I am working for Julie, who is out sick.*

work for something **1.** to work for a group, company, etc. □ *Everyone at the picnic works for the same employer.* □ *We work for the telephone company.* **2.** to work for a certain amount of money. □ *She says she works for a very good wage.* □ *I won't work for that kind of pay.* **3.** to work for an intangible benefit, such as satisfaction, glory, honor, etc. □ *The pay isn't very good. I just work for the fun of it.* □ *Sam says he works for the joy of working.*

work in an ivory tower Go to in an ivory tower.

work itself out [for a problem] to solve itself. □ *Eventually, all the problems worked themselves out without any help from us.* □ *This will work itself out. Don't worry.*

work like a beaver and **work like a mule; work like a horse; work like a slave** *Fig.* to work very hard. □ *She has an important deadline coming up, so she's been working like a beaver.* □ *You need a vacation. You work like a slave in that kitchen.* □ *I'm too old to work like a horse. I'd prefer to relax more.*

work of art 1. *Lit.* a piece of art. □ *She purchased a lovely work of art for her living room.* **2.** *Fig.* a good result of one's efforts. □ *Your report was a real work of art. Very well done.*

work on someone **1.** *Lit.* [for a physician] to treat someone; [for a surgeon] to operate on someone. □ *The doctor is still working on your uncle. There is no news yet.* □ *They are still working on the accident victims.* **2.** *Fig.* [for someone] to try to convince someone of something. □ *I'll work on her, and I am sure she will agree.* □ *They worked on Max for quite a while, but he still didn't agree to testify.* **3.** *Fig.* [for something, such as medication] to have the desired effect on someone. □ *This medicine just doesn't work on me.* □ *Your good advice doesn't seem to work on Sam.*

work on something to repair, build, or adjust something. □ *The carpenter worked on the fence for three hours.* □ *Bill is out working on his car engine.*

work one's **ass off** and **work** one's **buns off** and **work** one's **butt off** Go to work one's tail off.

work one's **fingers to the bone** *Cliché* to work very hard. □ *I worked my fingers to the bone so you children could have everything you needed. Now look at the way you treat me!* □ *I spent the day working my fingers to the bone, and now I want to relax.*

work one's **tail off** and **work** one's **buns off; work** one's **ass off; work** one's **butt off** *Inf. Fig.* to work very hard. (Use caution with *butt*.) □ *I worked my tail off to get done on time.* □ *You spend half your life working your butt off—and for what?*

work one's **way along** something to move or labor alongside something or a route. □ *She worked her way along the ledge and finally came to a wide space where she could relax.* □ *They worked themselves along the jungle path, chopping and cutting as they went.*

work (one's **way) into** something **1.** to get into something tight or small gradually and with effort. □ *He worked himself into the dark corner and hid there for a while.* □ *The mouse worked into the crack and got stuck.* **2.** to get more deeply involved in something gradually. □ *I don't quite understand my job. I'll work my way into it gradually.* □ *Fred worked into the daily routine gradually.*

work (one's **way) through** something **1.** *Lit.* to work to earn money to pay the bills while one is in college, medical school, law school, etc. □ *I worked my way through college as a waiter.* **2.** *Fig.* to progress through something complicated. □ *I spent hours working my way through the tax forms.* □ *I worked through the forms very slowly.* **3.** *Fig.* to struggle through an emotional trauma. □ *When she had finally worked through her grief, she was able to function normally again.* □ *Larry worked through the pain.*

work one's **way up (to** something**)** Go to work oneself up (to something).

work oneself up to allow oneself to become emotionally upset. □ *Todd worked himself up, and I thought he would scream.* □ *Don't work yourself up over Sally. She's not worth it.*

work oneself (up) into a lather and **work oneself (up) into a sweat 1.** and **work up a sweat** *Lit.* to work very hard and sweat very much. (In the way that a horse works up a lather.) □ *Don't work yourself up into a lather.*

We don't need to finish this today. □ *I worked myself into a sweat getting this stuff ready.* **2.** *Fig.* to get excited or angry. (An elaboration of **work oneself up to something**.) □ *Now, now, don't work yourself up into a lather.* □ *He had worked himself into such a sweat, I was afraid he would have a stroke.*

work oneself **up into** something **1.** *Lit.* to struggle to raise oneself upward into something or some place. □ *I worked myself up into the top of the tree.* □ *I worked myself up into the rafters of the barn and couldn't get down.* **2.** *Fig.* to bring oneself into an extreme emotional state. □ *I worked myself up into a state of hysteria.* □ *Don't work yourself up into hysteria.*

work oneself **up (to** something) **1.** to prepare oneself with sufficient energy or courage to do something. □ *I can't just walk in there and ask for a raise. I have to work myself up to it.* □ *I worked myself up and went into the boss's office.* **2.** and **work** one's **way up (to** something) to progress in one's work to a particular rank or status. □ *I worked myself up to sergeant in no time at all.* □ *Claude worked his way up to master sergeant.*

work out 1. [for something] to turn out all right in the end. (See also **turn out (all right); work out (as** something).) □ *Don't worry. Everything will work out.* □ *This will work out. Don't worry.* **2.** [for someone] to do a program of exercise. □ *I work out at least twice a week.* □ *I need to work out more often.*

work out (all right) Go to **turn out (all right)**.

work out (as something) to perform satisfactorily in a particular role. □ *We all hope she works out as a security monitor.* □ *I'm sure she will work out.*

work out (at something) **1.** [for someone] to perform satisfactorily doing something in particular. □ *I hope I work out at my new job.* □ *I'm sure you'll work out.* **2.** to perform satisfactorily working in a particular location. □ *I hope I work out at the factory. I really need that job.* □ *Things will work out at home in time.*

work out for the best [for a bad situation] to turn out all right in the end. □ *Don't worry. Everything will work out for the best.* □ *I think that nothing ever works out for the best.*

work out (somehow) to result in a good conclusion; to finish positively. □ *Don't worry. I am sure that everything will work out all right.* □ *Things always work out in the end.*

work some fat off† and **work some weight off**† to get rid of body fat by doing strenuous work. □ *I was able to work a lot of weight off by jogging.* □ *I need to work off some fat.*

work some weight off† Go to previous.

work someone or something **into** something and **work** someone or something **in**† **1.** to manage to fit someone or something into something physically. □ *The magician worked the lady into the tiny cabinet from which she was to disappear.* □ *The magician opened the little box and worked in the lady and two small dogs.* **2.** to fit someone or something into a sequence or series. □ *I don't have an appointment open this afternoon, but I'll see if I can work you into the sequence.* □ *I can't work in all of you.*

work someone or something **over**† to give someone or something a thorough examination or treatment. □ *The doc-*

tor really worked me over but couldn't find anything wrong. □ *They worked over the patient but found nothing.*

work someone or something **to** someone or something to struggle to manipulate someone or something to someone or something. □ *The quarterback worked the ball to the fullback so that the opposition didn't know what was going on.* □ *The rescuers worked the trapped child to the top of the tunnel.*

work someone **over**† **1.** to threaten, intimidate, or beat someone. □ *Walt threatened to work Sam over.* □ *Max had worked over Sam, and Sam knew that this was no idle threat.* **2.** to give someone's body a thorough examination or treatment. □ *The doctors worked her over to the tune of $1,500, but couldn't find anything wrong with her.* □ *The dermatologist worked over her entire body looking for moles.*

work someone **up**† to get someone ready for something, especially medical treatment. (See also **work oneself up.**) □ *The staff worked up three patients for surgery that morning.* □ *The doctor told the nurse to work Mr. Franklin up for surgery.*

work something **down**† to lower or reduce something, especially an amount of money. □ *Over a few months, they worked the price down, and the house soon was sold.* □ *They worked down the price so much that the house was a steal.*

work something **down (into** something) to manipulate something downward into something. □ *The crane operator worked the load down into the ship's hold.* □ *The operator worked it down carefully.*

work something **down (over** something) to manipulate something downward over something. □ *Now, you work this part down over this little tube, and then it won't leak.* □ *Liz worked the lid down and tightened it on.*

work something **into** something and **work** something **in**† to press, mix, or force a substance into something. □ *You should work the butter into the dough carefully.* □ *Work in the butter carefully.*

work something **off**† **1.** *Lit.* to get rid of anger, anxiety, or energy by doing physical activity. □ *I was so mad! I went out and played basketball to work my anger off.* □ *He works off nervousness by knitting.* **2.** *Fig.* to pay off a debt through work rather than by money. □ *I had no money so I had to work the bill off by washing dishes.* □ *I have to work off my debt.*

work something **out of** something and **work** something **out**† to manipulate something to get it out of something. □ *You have to work the bubbles out of the paint before you use it.* □ *You have to stir the batter to work out the lumps.*

work something **out**† **(with** someone) to come to an agreement with someone; to figure out with someone a way to do something. □ *I think we can work this out with you so that all of us are satisfied.* □ *I will work out something with Karen.* □ *I'm sure we can work it out.*

work something **over**† to rework something. □ *He saved the play by working the second act over.* □ *Would you work over this report and see if you can improve it?*

work something **through** (something) **1.** to guide or push something through a physical barrier. □ *I could hardly work the needle through the tightly woven cloth.* □ *I worked the needle through.* **2.** to guide or maneuver a law, proposal, motion, through a governing body. □ *The lobbyist*

W

was unable to work the law through the legislature. □ *The usual party hacks worked the law through.*

work something **under** something to manipulate something beneath something. □ *She worked the knife blade under the window and tried to pry the window up.* □ *Work the envelope under the office door. She will find it when she opens the door in the morning.*

work something **up**[†] to prepare something, perhaps on short notice. □ *There are some special clients coming in this weekend. We need to make a presentation. Do you think you can work something up by then?* □ *I will work up something for this weekend.*

work something **up**[†] **into** something to develop something into something. □ *I will work this story up into a screenplay in a few months.* □ *I can work up this idea into a good novel.*

work things out to improve one's state gradually by solving a series of problems. □ *If we sit down and talk this over, I am sure we can work things out.*

work through channels *Fig.* to try to get something done by going through the proper procedures and persons. □ *You can't accomplish anything around here if you don't work through channels.* □ *I tried working through channels, but it takes too long. This is an emergency.*

work together [for people or things] to cooperate or function together. □ *Come now! Let's all work together and get this done on time!* □ *We will work together on this and enjoy it more.*

work toward something **1.** to progress toward a goal, such as a promotion. □ *He was working toward a position with the new company.* □ *She was working toward a law degree when the accident happened.* **2.** to struggle physically to move toward something or some place. □ *The turtle worked toward the water despite the hot sun.* □ *I worked toward the cabin in the forest, fighting mosquitoes all the way.*

work under someone to have one's work supervised by someone. □ *I work under Michael, who is head of the department.* □ *Who do you work under?*

work under something to work underneath something. □ *I have to work under the car for a while. Please don't start it.* □ *The plumber had to work under the house to fix the pipes.*

work up a sweat Go to **work** oneself **(up) into a lather.**

work up a thirst Go to **get up a thirst.**

work up to something **1.** *Lit.* [for something] to build or progress to something. (Usually concerning the weather.) □ *The sky is working up to some kind of storm.* □ *The weather is working up to something severe.* **2.** *Fig.* [for someone] to lead up to something. □ *You are working up to telling me something unpleasant, aren't you?* □ *I think I am working up to a good cry.*

work (up)on something **1.** to repair or tinker with something. (*Upon* is formal and less commonly used than *on*.) □ *He's out in the kitchen, working upon his tax forms.* □ *He's working on his car.* **2.** [for something] to have the desired effect on something. (*Upon* is formal and less commonly used than *on*.) □ *This medicine should work well upon your cold.* □ *I hope it will work on your cold.*

work with someone or something to manipulate or work on someone or something. □ *Let me work with him for a while. I'll convince him.* □ *I want to work with this engine and see if I can get it started.*

work with something to do work with some tool or instrument. □ *She is working with a chisel now. In a minute she will switch to a tiny knife.* □ *Do you know how to work with a voltmeter?*

work wonders (with someone or something**)** to be surprisingly beneficial to someone or something; to be very helpful with someone or something. □ *This new medicine works wonders with my headaches.* □ *Jean was able to work wonders with the office staff. They improved their efficiency as soon as she took over.*

*****worked up (over** something**)** and *****worked up (about** something**)** excited and agitated about something. (*Typically: **be** ~; **get** ~; **get** oneself ~.) □ *Tom is all worked up over the tax increase.* □ *Don't get so worked up about something that you can't do anything about.*

a **working stiff** *Fig.* someone who works, especially in a nonmanagement position. (Originally and typically referring to males.) □ *But does the working stiff really care about all this economic stuff?* □ *All the working stiffs want is a raise.*

*****the works** a lot of something; everything possible. (*The works* can be a lot of food, good treatment, bad treatment, etc. *Typically: **get** ~; **have** ~; **give** someone ~.) □ *Bill: Shall we order a snack or a big meal? Jane: I'm hungry. Let's get the works.* □ *But, your honor. I shouldn't get the works. I only drove too fast!*

The **world is** one's **oyster.** *Fig.* One rules the world.; One is in charge of everything. □ *I feel like the world is my oyster today.* □ *The world is my oyster! I'm in love!*

*****worlds apart** *Fig.* greatly separated by differing attitudes, needs, opinions, or temperaments. (*Typically: **be** ~; **grow** ~; **live** ~; **think** ~.) □ *They are worlds apart. I can't imagine how they ever decided to get married.*

The **worm (has) turned.** *Fig.* Someone who is usually patient and humble has decided to stop being so. □ *Jane used to be treated badly by her husband and she just accepted it, but one day she hit him. The worm turned all right.* □ *Tom used to let the other boys bully him on the playground, but one day the worm turned and he's now leader of their gang.*

worm (one's **way) in(to** something**) 1.** *Fig.* to wiggle into something or some place. (Fig. on the image of a worm working its way into a very small space.) □ *The little cat wormed her way into the box and got stuck.* □ *The cat wormed into the opening.* **2.** *Fig.* to manipulate one's way into participation in something. □ *She tried to worm her way into the play, but the director refused.* □ *You can't have a part, so don't try to worm in.*

worm (one's **way) out (of** something**) 1.** *Fig.* to wiggle out of something or some place. (Fig. on the image of a worm working its way out of a very small space.) □ *Somehow she managed to worm her way out of the handcuffs.* □ *Frank wormed out of the opening.* □ *He struggled and struggled and wormed out.* **2.** *Fig.* to manipulate oneself out of a job or responsibility. □ *Don't try to worm your-*

self out of this affair. It is your fault! □ You can't worm out of this.

worm something **out of** someone to draw or manipulate information out of someone. □ I managed to worm the name of the doctor out of her before she ran off. □ You can't worm the names out of me!

worried sick (about someone or something**)** very worried or anxious about someone or something. □ Oh, thank heavens you are all right. We were worried sick about you!

worry about someone or something to fret or be anxious about the welfare of someone or something. □ Please don't worry about me. I'll be all right. □ Don't worry about the bill. I'll pay it.

worry an animal **out of** something to pester an animal until it leaves something or some place. □ The cat finally worried the mouse out of its hole and caught it. □ We worried the squirrel out of the attic by making lots of noise.

worry oneself **about** someone or something to allow oneself to fret or become anxious about someone or something. □ Please don't worry yourself about me. I'll be all right. □ There is no need for Karen to worry herself about this.

worry over someone or something to fret or be anxious about someone or something. □ She worried over dinner, but it came out all right. □ Jerry is worried over his daughter, Alice.

worry something **out of** someone to annoy some information out of someone. □ They finally worried the correct number out of me. □ You can't worry the information out of her. It will require force.

worry through something to think and fret through a problem. □ I can't talk to you now. I have to worry through this tax problem. □ We worried through the financial problem over a three-day period.

worrywart someone who worries all the time. □ Don't be such a worrywart. □ I'm sorry I'm such a worrywart.

the **worse for wear 1.** Euph. intoxicated. □ You were the worse for wear last night. □ The three came stumbling in, the worse for wear again. **2.** damaged or worn through use. □ Eventually, every machine becomes worse for wear, you know. □ The truth is it's the worse for wear; you will just have to get a new one. **3.** injured. □ Tom fell into the street and he's much the worse for wear. □ Fred had a little accident with his bike and he's the worse for wear.

worship someone **as** something to revere or honor one as if one were something divine or special. □ He worships her as a goddess. □ She worships her father as a god.

worship the ground someone **walks on** Fig. to honor someone to a great extent. □ She always admired the professor. In fact, she worshiped the ground he walked on.

*the **worst of** something the poorest share of something; the worst part of something. (*Typically: **get** ~; **have** ~; **give** someone ~.) □ I knew I would get the worst of the deal because I was absent when the goods were divided up. □ I'm sorry that you got the worst of it.

the **worst-case scenario** Cliché the worse possible future outcome. □ Now, let's look at the worst-case scenario. □ In the worst-case scenario, we're all dead.

worth its weight in gold Fig. very valuable. □ This book is worth its weight in gold. □ Oh, Bill. You're wonderful. You're worth your weight in gold.

The **worth of a thing is what it will bring.** Prov. A thing is worth whatever someone will pay for it. □ Ellen: I'm thinking about selling my grandmother's silver tea set. What do you suppose it's worth? Fred: The worth of a thing is what it will bring.

worth one's **salt** Fig. worth (in productivity) what it costs to keep or support one. □ We decided that you are worth your salt, and you can stay on as office clerk. □ You're not worth your salt. Pack up!

worth someone's **while** worth one's time and trouble. □ The job pays so badly it's not worth your while even going for an interview. □ It's not worth Mary's while going all that way just for a one-hour meeting.

worthy of the name deserving to be so called; good enough to enjoy a specific designation. □ There was not an actor worthy of the name in that play. □ Any art critic worthy of the name would know that painting to be a fake.

would as soon do something **as look at you** Rur. would be eager to do something harmful as simply look at you. □ He was a mean so-and-so who would as soon shoot you as look at you. □ He'd as soon pick a fight as look at you.

would (just) as soon do something Go to **had (just) as soon** do something.

would like (to have) someone or something to want someone or something; to prefer someone or something. □ I would like to have three cookies. □ I would like a piece of cake.

would not be caught dead (doing something) Go to next.

would not be seen dead (doing something) and **would not be caught dead** (doing something) would not do something under any circumstances. □ I wouldn't be seen dead going out with Bruno! □ Martha would not be caught dead going into a place like that.

would rather would more willingly; would more readily. □ I would rather have an apple than a pear. I don't like pears. □ I'd rather live in the north than the south, because I like snow.

Would you believe! Inf. Isn't that unbelievable?; How shocking! □ Tom: Jane has run off and married Fred! Sally: Would you believe! □ Jane: Then the manager came out and asked us to leave. Would you believe? Mary: It sounds just awful. I'd send them a letter of complaint.

(Would you) care for another (one)? Do you want another drink or serving? □ Tom stood there with an almost empty glass. Bill said, "Would you care for another one?" □ Waiter: Care for another one, madam? Sue: No, thank you.

(Would you) care to...? a polite phrase introducing an inquiry as to whether someone wishes to do something. □ John: Would you care to step out for some air? Jane: Oh, I'd love it. □ Sue: Care to go for a swim? Mary: Not now, thanks.

(Would you) care to dance? Do you want to dance with me?; Would you please dance with me? □ John:

Would you care to dance? Mary: I don't dance, but thank you for asking. □ *"Care to dance?" asked Bill, politely.*

(Would you) care to join us? Do you want to join us? □ *Tom and Mary saw Fred and Sally sitting at another table in the restaurant. Tom went over to them and said, "Would you care to join us?" □ Mary: Isn't that Bill and Sue over there? John: Yes, it is. Shall I ask them to join us? Mary: Why not? John (after reaching the other table): Hi, you guys! Care to join us? Bill: Love to, but Sue's mom is going to be along any minute. Thanks anyway.*

Would you excuse me? 1. a polite question that essentially announces one's departure. (Compare this with Could I be excused?; Excuse me.) □ *Jane: Would you excuse me? I have to get home now. Andy: Oh, sure. I'll see you to the door.* □ *Rising to leave, Jane said, "Would you excuse me?" and left by the rear door.* **2.** a polite way to request passage through or by a group of people; a way to request space to exit an elevator. □ *There were two people talking in the corridor, blocking it. Tom said, "Would you excuse me?" They stepped aside.* □ *Fred: Would you excuse me? This is my floor. Sally: Sure. It's mine, too.*

Would you excuse us, please? Go to Could you excuse us, please?

Would you please? a polite phrase that agrees that what was offered to be done should be done. □ *Bill: Do you want me to take this over to the bank? Mary: Would you please?* □ *Tom: Can I take your coat? Sally: Would you please?*

wouldn't dream of doing something would not even consider doing something. □ *I wouldn't dream of taking your money!* □ *I'm sure that John wouldn't dream of complaining to the manager.*

wouldn't touch someone or something **with a ten-foot pole** *Cliché* would not be involved with something under any circumstances. □ *I know about the piece of vacant land for sale on Maple Street. I wouldn't touch it with a ten-foot pole because there used to be a gas station there and the soil is polluted.* □ *Tom said he wouldn't touch Sally with a ten-foot pole.*

wouldn't want to be in someone's **shoes** *Fig.* would not trade places with someone who is in a bad situation. □ *Now Jim has to explain to his wife how he wrecked their car. I wouldn't want to be in his shoes.* □ *She may be rich, but I wouldn't want to be in her shoes. Everyone in her family hates her.*

wrack and ruin *Cliché* complete destruction or ruin. □ *They went back after the fire and saw the wrack and ruin that used to be their house.* □ *Drinking brought him nothing but wrack and ruin.*

wrangle (with someone) **(about** someone or something) to bicker or argue with someone about someone or something. □ *Stop wrangling with everyone about Tom. He can take care of himself and does not need any special treatment.* □ *Stop wrangling with everyone you meet.*

wrangle (with someone) **(over** someone or something) to bicker or argue with someone over who will end up with someone or something. □ *I don't want to wrangle with Kelly over the contract.* □ *I see no need to wrangle over Dolly.*

wrap around someone or something to enclose or fold about someone or something. □ *The snake wrapped around the helpless man and it was soon all over.* □ *The flames wrapped around the barn and swallowed it up.*

wrap one's **car around** something to drive one's car into something at fairly high speed. □ *She wrapped her car around a light pole.* □ *If he hadn't wrapped his car around a tree, he'd be here with us tonight.*

wrap someone or something **around** something to bend or coil someone or something around something. □ *I'll wrap you around that lamppost unless you cooperate!* □ *Don wrapped the rope around the tree and tied it tight.*

wrap someone or something **(up†) (in** something) to enclose or enfold someone or something inside of something. □ *I will have to wrap the baby up in a heavy blanket if we are going out in this cold.* □ *We wrapped up the children in their warmest clothing.* □ *Please wrap the package up in pretty paper.* □ *Would you wrap this in yellow paper?*

wrap someone or something **(up†) (with** something) to enclose or enfold someone or something, using something. □ *Try to wrap the baby up with something warmer.* □ *We will have to wrap up the baby with extra blankets tonight.*

wrap something **around** someone to fold or drape something onto someone. □ *He wrapped a towel around himself and went to answer the telephone.* □ *She wrapped a blanket around her little boy to keep him warm.*

wrap something **up†** to complete work on something; to bring something to an end. □ *I will wrap the job up this morning. I'll call you when I finish.* □ *I can wrap up this little project in a week.*

wrapped up Go to sewed up.

wrapped up (in someone or something**)** concerned or obsessed with someone or something. □ *Sally is pretty wrapped up in herself.* □ *I'm too wrapped up in my charity work to get a job.*

***wrapped up (with** someone or something**)** involved with someone or something. (*Typically:* **be ~; get ~.**) □ *She is all wrapped up with her husband and his problems.* □ *She is just too wrapped up.*

wreak havoc (with something) to cause a lot of trouble with something; to ruin or damage something. □ *Your bad attitude will wreak havoc with my project.* □ *The rainy weather wreaked havoc with our picnic plans.*

wreak something **(up)on** someone or something to cause damage, havoc, or destruction to someone or something. (*Upon* is formal and less commonly used than *on.*) □ *The storm wreaked destruction upon the little village.* □ *It wreaked much havoc on us.*

wreak vengeance (up)on someone or something *Cliché* to seek and get revenge on someone by harming someone or something. □ *The gangster wreaked his vengeance by destroying his rival's house.* □ *The general wanted to wreak vengeance on the opposing army for their recent successful attack.*

wreathe (itself) around someone or something [for something] to form itself into a wreath or circle around someone or something. □ *The smoke wreathed around the smokers' heads, almost obliterating sight of them.* □ *The smoke wreathed around the green tree near the fire.*

W

wreathe someone or something **in** something to enclose someone or something in a wreath or a wreath-shaped area. □ *The trees wreathed them in a lovely frame. It made a beautiful photograph.* □ *The vines wreathed the campers in a gentle bower.*

wreathe something **around** someone or something to form something into a wreath around someone or something. □ *The smoke wreathed a ring around the old man holding a pipe.* □ *The cloud wreathed a huge halo around the tip of the mountain.*

wrench something **from** someone to grab or twist something out of someone's grasp. □ *The policeman wrenched the gun from Lefty's hand and called for his partner.* □ *Max wrenched the wallet from Jed's hand and fled with it.*

wrench something **off (of)** someone or something and **wrench** something **off**† to yank or twist something off someone or something. (*Of* is usually retained before pronouns.) □ *He wrenched the shoes off the sleeping man and ran away.* □ *He wrenched off the catsup bottle cap.*

wrench something **out of** something to yank or twist something out of something. □ *The policeman wrenched the gun out of Lefty's hand and told Lefty to put his hands up.* □ *Tom wrenched the bone out of the dog's mouth and threw it away.*

wrest someone or something **(away) from** someone or something to struggle to get someone or something from the grip of someone or something. □ *The kidnappers wrested the baby from his mother and ran away with him.* □ *The policeman wrested the gun away from Lefty.*

wrest something **off (of)** something and **wrest** something **off**† to struggle to get something off something. (*Of* is usually retained before pronouns.) □ *Somehow he wrested the hubcap off the wheel.* □ *He wrested off the hubcap.*

wrestle something **from** someone to get something away from someone after a physical struggle. □ *Wally wrestled the gun away from Max and threw it out the window.* □ *I could not wrestle my wallet from the thief.*

wrestle something **into** something to struggle with something large to get it into something or some place. □ *She wrestled the packages into the backseat of the car.* □ *I wrestled the suitcases into the rack over my seat.*

wrestle with someone to contend with someone in a physical wrestling match. □ *You are too big to wrestle with him!* □ *I want to wrestle with someone my own size.*

wrestle with something **1.** to struggle with something large to move it about. □ *He wrestled with the piano and finally got it to move.* □ *The two men were wrestling with the heavy trunk for nearly ten minutes, trying to get it up the stairs.* **2.** to grapple or struggle with some large animal. □ *The man wrestled with the tiger for a while but was seriously mauled in a short time.* □ *Sam liked to wrestle with the family dog.* **3.** to struggle with a difficult problem; to struggle with a moral decision. □ *We wrestled with the problem and finally decided to go ahead.* □ *Let me wrestle with this matter for a while longer.*

wriggle in(to something**)** to wiggle and squeeze into something or some place. □ *You will never be able to wriggle into that swimming suit.* □ *I can just wriggle in!*

wriggle out (of something**) 1.** *Lit.* to wiggle and squeeze out of something or some place. □ *She wriggled out of her*

tight skirt and changed into something more comfortable. □ *The skirt was so tight, she had to wriggle out. She couldn't pull it off.* **2.** *Fig.* to get out of having to do something; to evade a responsibility. □ *Don't try to wriggle out of this.* □ *I won't let you wriggle out this time.*

wring something **from** something and **wring** something **out of** something to remove liquid from something by squeezing or twisting. □ *She wrung the water from the cloth and wiped up the rest of the spill.* □ *Alice wrung the water out of the washcloth.*

wring something **out**† to squeeze or twist something dry of liquid. □ *He wrung the rag out and wiped up more of the spilled milk.* □ *Liz wrung out the rag and wiped up more of the spilled milk.*

wring something **out of** someone to pressure someone into telling something. □ *The police will wring the truth out of her.* □ *After a lot of questioning, they wrung the information out of Fred.*

wring something **out of** something Go to **wring** something **from** something.

wrinkle something **up**† to make something get wrinkles and creases. □ *I love the way you wrinkle your nose up.* □ *Don't wrinkle up your jacket.*

wrinkle up [for something] to draw up in wrinkles; [for something] to become wrinkled. □ *His nose wrinkled up as he smelled the burning pie.* □ *The cloth wrinkled up in the intense heat.*

write about someone or something to write a narrative or description of someone or something. □ *I wanted to write about wild canaries, but there is not much to say.* □ *Sally writes about famous people.*

write against someone or something to oppose someone or something in writing. □ *John writes against the current administration too harshly.* □ *Almost everyone enjoys writing against the CIA.*

write away to write a lot; to continue writing. □ *There he was, writing away, not paying attention to anything else.* □ *I spent the entire afternoon writing away, having a fine, productive time.*

write away for something to send for something in writing, from a distant place. □ *I wrote away for a book on the rivers of the world.* □ *You will have to write away for another copy of the instruction manual.*

write back to someone to write a letter to someone in return for a letter received from someone. □ *I wrote back to her at once, but I have heard no more from her.* □ *Please write back to me when you have a chance.*

write down to someone to write to someone condescendingly. □ *You should never write down to your audience if you want to be convincing.* □ *I have to write down to them, because they are very young.*

write for something **1.** to write and request something. □ *I wrote for clarification but received none.* □ *Julie wrote for another copy of the instruction book.* **2.** to produce writing for a particular kind of publication. □ *I write for science magazines.* □ *Sam writes for the local newspaper.*

write in(to something**) (for** something**)** to send a written request to something for something in particular. □ *Please* *write in for a detailed recipe of all the dishes on today's program.* □ *I am going to write in for a clarification.*

write of someone or something to write about the general topic of someone or something. □ *He wrote of the beauty of nature and the way we are destroying it.* □ *She wrote of Henry, her ancient house cat.*

write off (to someone**) (for** something**)** to send a written request for something away to someone. □ *I wrote off to my parents for some money, but I think they are ignoring me.* □ *I wrote off for money.* □ *I need money so I wrote off to my parents.*

write on and on to write too much; to write endlessly. □ *You tend to write on and on. Try to focus on one point and leave it at that.* □ *I think you write on and on just to fill up space.*

write someone **down as** something to list someone's name, noting something. □ *I'll write you down as a contributor.* □ *Can I write you down as a charter member?*

write someone **for** something to send a written request to someone for something. □ *Henry wrote Harry for a firm quote, but Harry never responded.* □ *Did you write me for permission?*

write someone **in**† **(on** something**)** to write the name of someone in a special place on a ballot, indicating a vote for the person. (Done when the person's name is not already printed on the ballot.) □ *Please write my name in on the ballot.* □ *I wrote in your name on the ballot.*

write someone or something **about** something to send an inquiry or statement to someone in writing about someone or something. □ *I will write her about what you just told me.* □ *Sarah wrote the company about the faulty merchandise.*

write someone or something **off**† to drop someone or something from consideration. □ *The manager wrote Tom off for a promotion.* □ *I wrote off that piece of swampy land as worthless. It can't be used for anything.*

write someone or something **off**† **(as a** something**) 1.** to give up on turning someone or something into something. □ *I had to write Jill off as a future executive.* □ *The company wrote off the electric automobile as a dependable means of transportation. He would never work out. We wrote him off.* **2.** to give up on someone or something as a dead loss, waste of time, hopeless case, etc. □ *Don't write me off as a has-been.* □ *We almost wrote off the investment as a dead loss.* **3.** to take a charge against one's taxes. □ *Can I write this off as a deduction, or is it a dead loss?* □ *Can I write off this expense as a tax deduction?*

write someone or something **up**† to write an article about someone or something. □ *A reporter wrote me up for the Sunday paper.* □ *I wrote up a local business and sent the story to a magazine, but they didn't buy the story.*

write something **against** someone or something to write something in opposition to someone or something. □ *I wrote an article against her proposal, but they refused to print it.* □ *Sarah wrote an essay against the president.*

write something **back to** someone to write a letter answering someone. □ *I wrote an answer back to her the same day that I received the letter.* □ *Will you please write something back to Julie? She complains that you are ignoring her.* □ *I wrote a letter back to Harry, explaining what had happened.*

write something **down**† to make a note of something; to record something in writing. □ *Please write this down.* □ *Please write down what I tell you.*

write something **in**† Go to write something into something.

write something **in plain English** Go to in plain English.

write something **in round figures** Go to in round figures.

write something **into** something and **write** something **in**† **1.** to write information into something. □ *I wrote her telephone number into my notebook.* □ *I wrote in her number.* □ *I took out my notebook and wrote it in.* **2.** to include a specific statement or provision in a document, such as a contract or agreement. □ *I want you to write a stronger security clause into my contract.* □ *I will write in a stronger clause.*

write something **off**† to absorb a debt or a loss in accounting. □ *The bill couldn't be collected, so we had to write it off.* □ *The bill was too large, and we couldn't write off the amount. We decided to sue.*

write something **off**† **(on** one's **taxes)** to deduct something from one's income taxes. □ *Can I write this off on my income taxes?* □ *I'll write off this trip on my taxes.* □ *Oh, yes! Write it off!*

write something **out**† **1.** to spell or write a number or an abbreviation. □ *Don't just write "7," write it out.* □ *Please write out all abbreviations, such as Doctor for Dr.* **2.** to put thoughts into writing, rather than keeping them in memory. □ *Let me write it out. Then I won't forget it.* □ *Karen wrote out her objections.*

write something **to** someone **1.** to send specific information to someone in writing. □ *I wrote the facts to John, and he thanked me for the information.* □ *They wrote all the details to me, and I filed them.* **2.** to compose a letter or e-mail and send it to someone. □ *Sam wrote a letter to his father.* □ *Did you write that memo to Mark yet?*

write something **to** something to write something that is supplementary to something else. □ *Molly wrote an epilogue to her story covering the time up till now.* □ *I will write the introduction to the book this afternoon.*

write something **up**† to prepare a bill, order, or statement. □ *Please write the order up and send me a copy.* □ *As soon as I finish writing up your check, I'll bring you some more coffee.*

write to someone to compose a letter or e-mail and send it to someone. □ *I will write to her again, but I don't expect to hear anything.* □ *Please write to me as soon as you can.*

write (up)on someone or something **1.** to write about someone or something. (*Upon* is very formal here and much less commonly used than *on.*) □ *I had to write an essay, so I wrote on my uncle.* □ *What are you going to write upon?* **2.** to write on someone's skin or something. (*Upon* is formal and much less commonly used than *on.*) □ *Don't write on Billy. After all, he's your brother.* □ *Who wrote on this page of the book?* **3.** to use someone [such as someone's back] or something as a flat base to support something that is being written upon. □ *I have to sign this check. Here, let me write on you.* □ *Do you mind if I write on your desk? I just need to sign this.*

W

771

writer's block the temporary inability for a writer to think of what to write. □ *I have writer's block at the moment and can't seem to get a sensible sentence on paper.*

writhe in something Go to **writhe with** something.

writhe under something **1.** *Lit.* to squirm with pain from being beaten with something. □ *The sailor writhed under the sting of the lash.* □ *The child writhed under the pain of his spanking.* **2.** *Fig.* to suffer under a mental burden. □ *I writhed under her constant verbal assault and finally left the room.* □ *Why do I have to writhe under her insults?*

writhe with something **1.** and **writhe in** something [for someone or an animal] to squirm because of something, such as pain. □ *Carl writhed with pain and began to cry.* □ *He was writhing in pain when the paramedics arrived.* **2.** [for something] to support or contain something that is writhing. □ *The pit was writhing with snakes and other horrid things.* □ *The floor of the basement was writhing in spiders and crawly things.*

written in stone Go to **carved in stone**.

*****the **wrong number 1.** *Lit.* an incorrect telephone number. (*Typically: **get** ~; **have** ~; **dial** ~; **give** someone ~.) □ *He got the wrong number and hung up.* □ *When a young child answered, I knew I had the wrong number.* **2.** *Fig.* [a state of being] incorrect, late, inaccurate, etc. (*Typically: **get** ~; **have** ~; **give** someone ~.) □ *Boy, do you have the wrong number! Get with it!* □ *You have missed the boat again. You have the wrong number!*

the **wrong side of the tracks** Go to the **other side of the tracks**.

wrote the book on something *Fig.* to be very authoritative about something; to know enough about something to write the definitive book on it. (Always in past tense.) □ *Ted wrote the book on unemployment. He's been looking for work in three states for two years.* □ *Do I know about misery? I wrote the book on misery!*

*****wrought up** disturbed or excited. (*Wrought* is an old past tense and past participle meaning "worker." *Typically: **be** ~; **get** ~.) □ *She is so wrought up, she can't think.* □ *I am sorry you are so wrought up.*

X marks the spot. This is the exact spot. (Sometimes the speaker will draw an X in the spot while saying this.) □ *This is where the rock struck my car—X marks the spot.* □ *Now, please move that table over here. Yes, right here—X marks the spot.*

X someone or something out† to mark out something printed or in writing, with Xs. □ *Sally X'd the incorrect information out.* □ *Sally X'd out the incorrect information.* □ *You should X Tom out. He's not coming.* □ *Please X out this line of print.*

X'd out 1. eliminated; crossed-out. □ *But the Babbits are X'd out.* □ *Put the X'd out Babbits back where they were.* **2.** *Sl.* killed. (Underworld.) □ *Mr. Big wanted Wilbur X'd out.* □ *He wanted Sam to see that all these punks were X'd out.*

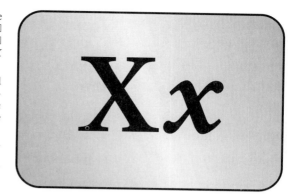

X

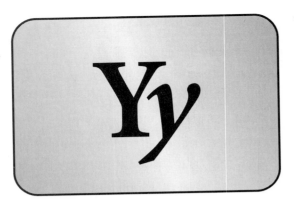

yack one's **head off** *Fig.* to talk a great deal. □ *Jane yacked her head off and ended up with a sore throat.* □ *Don't yack your head off!*

yack something **up**† *Inf.* to talk a great deal [about someone or something]. (The *something* is often *it*.) □ *She yacked the concert up endlessly.* □ *Sally yacked up the concert, trying to get people to attend.* □ *Yack it up and see if you can get people to attend.*

yammer (away) about someone or something to talk endlessly about someone or something. □ *What are you yammering about?* □ *They were yammering away about the state of the economy.*

yank at someone or something to pull or tug at someone or something. □ *Please don't yank at the drapery cord.* □ *Stop yanking at me!*

yank on something to pull or tug on something. □ *Don't yank on my hair!* □ *Yank on this rope to send a signal to the worker on the floor above.*

yank someone **around** *Sl.* to harass someone; to give someone a hard time. □ *Listen, I don't mean to yank you around all the time, but we have to have the drawings by Monday.* □ *Please stop yanking me around.*

yank someone or something† Go to **yank** someone or something **into** something.

yank someone or something **apart**† **1.** to pull, tear, or rip someone or something to pieces. □ *Please don't yank the book apart!* □ *He yanked apart the book!* □ *He threatened to yank his opponent apart.* **2.** to separate people or things. □ *The teacher yanked them apart.* □ *The teacher yanked apart the fighting boys.*

yank someone or something **around** to pull or jerk someone or something around. □ *Don't yank Billy around so. You'll hurt him!* □ *Please don't yank the chairs around. Move them carefully.*

yank someone or something **away**† **(from** someone or something**)** to jerk someone or something away from someone or something. □ *He yanked his hand away from the fire.* □ *Please yank away that rug from the fire before it gets burned.*

yank someone or something **into** something and **yank** someone or something† to jerk or pull someone or something into something. □ *Mary yanked Sally into the car and sped off.* □ *She yanked in the anchor rope and we rowed away.*

yank someone or something **off (of)** something and **yank** someone or something **off**† to jerk someone or something off something. (*Of* is usually retained before pronouns.) □ *She yanked the coffeepot off the counter and ran upstairs.* □ *She yanked off the box lid.*

yank someone or something **out of** something and **yank** someone or something **out**† to pull or jerk someone or something out of something. □ *Sam yanked the turnips out of the ground one by one.* □ *He yanked out the best of the young carrots from the rich soil.*

yank someone's **chain** *Sl.* to harass someone; to give someone a hard time. (As if one were a dog wearing a choker collar, on a leash.) □ *Stop yanking my chain!* □ *Do you really think you can just yank my chain whenever you want?*

yank something **off**† to pull or jerk off something, such as a piece of clothing. □ *She yanked her jacket off.* □ *She yanked off her jacket and threw it on the chair.*

yank something **up**† to pull or jerk something up. □ *He yanked his pants up.* □ *He yanked up his pants and threw on his shirt.*

yap about someone or something to talk casually about someone or something; to gossip or complain about someone or something. □ *Stop yapping about Molly.* □ *Claire is always yapping about her salary.*

yap at someone **1.** *Lit.* [for a small dog] to bark at someone or something. □ *The dog yapped at the cat in great frustration.* □ *I am tired of that dog yapping at me all the time!* **2.** *Fig.* [for someone] to scold or bark at someone shrilly. □ *Don't yap at me. I didn't do it.* □ *Bob yapped at Bill for something he didn't do.*

Ye gods (and little fishes)! *Inf.* What a surprising thing! □ *Ye gods and little fishes! Someone covered my car with broken eggs!* □ *Ye gods! What a rainstorm!*

year after year for many years, one after another. □ *We go to the same place for our vacation year after year.* □ *I seem to earn the same salary year after year.*

year in, year out year after year; for years. □ *I seem to have hay fever year in, year out. I never get over it.* □ *John wears the same old suit, year in, year out.*

yearn for someone or something to long for someone or something; to desire someone or something strongly. □ *Sam sat alone in his room, yearning for Mary.* □ *Mary yearned for a big bowl of high-butterfat ice cream.*

years running Go to **days running**.

yell at someone or something to shout at someone or something, usually in anger. □ *Please don't yell at me.* □ *There is no point in yelling at a cat.*

yell bloody murder Go to **scream bloody murder**.

yell one's **guts out** Go to next.

yell one's **head off** and **yell** one's **guts out 1.** *Fig.* to yell loud and long. □ *I was yelling my head off at the football game.* □ *Stop yelling your guts out and listen to me.* **2.** *Fig.* to complain bitterly and loudly. □ *Some lady is yelling her head off about shoddy workmanship out in the lobby.* □ *I yell my guts out about bad service when I get bad service!*

yell out to cry out; to shout loudly. □ *The pain caused the child to yell out.* □ *I yelled out, but no one heard me.*

yell something **at** someone or something to shout something at someone or something, usually in anger. □ *Please don't yell those things at me.* □ *He stood on the porch, yelling curses at a dog on his lawn.*

yell something **out**† **(at** someone or something**)** to shout something loudly at someone or something. □ *The dictator yelled curses out at the troops.* □ *The director yelled out his disgust at the cast of the play.*

a **yellow streak (down** someone's **back)** a tendency toward cowardice. □ *Tim's got a yellow streak down his back a mile wide.* □ *Get rid of that yellow streak. Show some courage.*

yen for someone or something to long for someone or something. □ *I yen for a great big bowl of highly fattening ice cream.* □ *Frank yenned for Sally.*

Yes indeed(y (do))! *Inf.* Definitely yes! □ *Tom: Will you marry me? Jane: Yes indeedy do, I will!* □ *Charlie: Did your horse win the race? Bill: Yes indeedy!*

Yes siree(, Bob)! *Inf.* Absolutely!; Without a doubt! (Not necessarily said to a male and not necessarily to Bob.) □ *Mary: Do you want some more cake? Tom: Yes siree, Bob!* □ *"That was a fine turkey dinner. Yes siree!" said Uncle Henry.*

Yesterday wouldn't be too soon. Immediately.; Right away. (An answer to the question "When do you want this?") □ *Mary: Mr. Franklin, when do you want this? Fred: Well, yesterday wouldn't be too soon.* □ *Alice: When am I supposed to have this finished? Sue: Yesterday wouldn't be too soon.*

yield someone or something **(over) (to** someone or something**)** to give up someone or something to someone or something. (The *over* is typically used where the phrase is synonymous with *hand over*.) □ *You must yield Tom over to his mother.* □ *Will you yield the right-of-way to the other driver, or not?* □ *Please yield the right-of-way to me.*

yield someone or something **up**† **(to** someone**)** to give someone or something up to someone. □ *He had to yield his daughter up to Claire.* □ *The judge required that Tom yield up his daughter to his ex-wife.* □ *Finally, he yielded up the money.*

yield something **to** someone **1.** to give the right-of-way to someone. □ *You must yield the right-of-way to pedestrians.* □ *You failed to yield the right-of-way to the oncoming car.* **2.** to give up something to someone. □ *The army yielded the territory to the invading army.* □ *We yielded the territory to the government.*

yield to someone **1.** to let someone go ahead; to give someone the right-of-way. □ *Please yield to the next speaker.* □ *She yielded to the next speaker.* **2.** to give in to someone. □ *She found it hard to yield to her husband in an argument.* □ *I will yield to no one.*

a **yoke around** someone's **neck** *Fig.* something that oppresses people; a burden. □ *John's greedy children are a yoke around his neck.* □ *The Smiths have a huge mortgage that has become a yoke around their necks.*

yoke people or things **together** to connect two people together with a yoke; to connect two animals together with a yoke. □ *Todd yoked the oxen together for the parade.* □ *Sam yoked Fred and Tom together so they could pull the load.*

You ain't just whistlin' Dixie. *Rur.* You are right. □ *Tom: Sure is hot today. Bill: Yeah, you ain't just whistlin' Dixie. It's a scorcher.* □ *Charlie: That was a good movie. Jane: You ain't just whistlin' Dixie. It was the best I've ever seen.*

You ain't seen nothing yet! *Rur.* The best, most exciting, or cleverest part is yet to come! (The use of *ain't* is a fixed part of this idiomatic expression.) □ *Alice: Well, the first act was simply divine. Sue: Stick around. You ain't seen nothing yet!* □ *Mary: This part of the city is really beautiful. Bill: You ain't seen nothing yet!*

You (always) give up too eas(il)y. You don't stand up for your rights.; You give up without a fight. □ *Bill: Well, I guess she was right. Bob: No, she was wrong. You always give up too easily.* □ *Bob: I asked her to go out with me Friday, but she said she thought she was busy. Tom: Ask her again. You give up too easy.*

You and what army? Go to next.

You and who else? and **You and what army?** *Inf.* a phrase that responds to a threat by implying that the threat is a weak one. □ *Bill: I'm going to punch you in the nose! Bob: Yeah? You and who else?* □ *Tom: Our team is going to slaughter your team. Bill: You and what army?* □ *Bill: If you don't stop doing that, I'm going to hit you. Tom: You and who else?*

[you are] See the entries beginning with *you're*.

You are more than welcome. 1. You are very welcome to be here. □ *Please make yourself at home. You are more than welcome.* **2.** Your thanks are very gratefully accepted. □ *A: Thank you so much. B: You are more than welcome.*

You are never too old to learn. Go to It is never too late to learn.

You are something else (again)! *Inf.* You are amazing or entertaining! □ *After Sally finished telling her joke, everyone laughed and someone said, "Oh, Sally, you are something else!"* □ *"You are something else again," said Fred, admiring Sue's presentation.*

You are welcome. and **You're welcome.** a polite response to *Thank you.* □ *"Thank you for helping me." "You're welcome."* □ *"Thank you very much!" "You are welcome!"*

You asked for it! 1. You are getting what you requested. □ *The waiter set a huge bowl of ice cream, strawberries, and whipped cream in front of Mary, saying apologetically, "You asked for it!"* □ *Bill: Gee, this escargot stuff is gross! Mary: You asked for it!* **2.** You are getting the punishment you deserve! □ *Bill: The tax people just ordered me to pay a big fine. Bob: The careless way you do your tax forms caused it. You asked for it!* □ *Mother: I'm sorry to have to punish you in this fashion, but you asked for it! Bill: I did not!*

You been keeping busy? Go to (Have you) been keeping busy?

You been keeping cool? Go to (Have you) been keeping cool?

You been keeping out of trouble? Go to (Have you) been keeping out of trouble?

You been okay? Go to (Have you) been okay?

You bet! 1. *Inf.* Yes. □ *Tom: Are you coming to the party? Jane: You bet!* □ *Charlie: May I borrow your hammer?*

Mary: You bet! **2.** *Inf.* You're welcome. □ *Tom: Thank you. Jane: You bet.* □ *Sally: I appreciate it. Mary: You bet.*

You bet your boots! Go to next.

You bet your (sweet) life! and **You bet your boots!; You bet your life!; You bet your (sweet) bippy.** *Inf. Fig.* You can be absolutely certain of something! □ *Mary: Will I need a coat today? Bill: You bet your sweet life! It's colder than an iceberg out there.* □ *Bill: Will you be at the game Saturday? Tom: You bet your boots!*

You betcha! *Inf.* Yes!; You can be sure of it! (Literally, You bet, you.) □ *Will I be there? You betcha.* □ *Can I? You betcha!*

You called? 1. a phrase used when returning a telephone call, meaning "What did you want to talk about when you called before?" □ *Bill (answering the phone): Hello? Bob: This is Bob. You called?* □ *Tom: You called? It's Tom. Mary: Hi, Tom. Yes, I wanted to ask you about these estimates.* **2.** a phrase said by someone who has been summoned into a person's presence. (Often used in jest, in the way a servant might answer an employer.) □ *Mary: Oh, Tom. Come over here a minute. Tom (coming to where Mary is standing): You called?* □ *Tom: Bill! Bill! Over here, Bill, across the street. Bill (panting from running and with mock deference): You called?*

You can bet the farm (on someone or something**).** *Rur.* You can be certain of someone or something. □ *This is a good investment. You can bet the farm on it.* □ *You can bet the farm that Joe is gonna get that job.*

You can catch more flies with honey than with vinegar. *Prov.* It is easier to get what you want by flattering people and being polite to them than by making demands. □ *Jill: This meal is terrible. Let's get the restaurant manager over here and make a scene unless he gives us our money back. Jane: We might have more luck if we ask politely. You can catch more flies with honey than with vinegar.*

You can lead a horse to water, but you can't make it drink. *Prov.* You can present someone with an opportunity, but you cannot force him or her to take advantage of it. □ *Jill: I told Katy about all the jobs that are available at our company, but she hasn't applied for any of them. Jane: You can lead a horse to water, but you can't make it drink.*

You can say that again! and **You said it!** *Inf.* That is true.; You are correct. (The word *that* is emphasized.) □ *Mary: It sure is hot today. Jane: You can say that again!* □ *Bill: This cake is yummy! Bob: You said it!*

You cannot get a quart into a pint pot. *Prov.* You cannot fit too much of something into a space that is too small. □ *That dog is simply too big to get into this kennel. You can't get a quart into a pint pot.* □ *Our refrigerator isn't big enough to fit that watermelon in. You can't get a quart into a pint pot.*

You cannot get blood from a stone. and **You cannot get blood from a turnip.** *Prov.* You cannot get help from an uncharitable person or money from someone who has none. □ *Jerry and James spent two hours trying to convince the old miser to contribute to the children's hospital; finally, James turned to Jerry and said in disgust, "This is hopeless. We can't get blood from a stone."* □ *The*

government can't increase taxes any further—nobody has the money! You can't get blood from a turnip.

You cannot get blood from a turnip. Go to previous.

You cannot have your cake and eat it (too). *Prov.* You cannot enjoy two desirable things at the same time. □ *Jill: There's an apartment across the street from me, much bigger and prettier than mine, and it even costs less. I'd really like to rent it—but I don't want to go to the trouble of moving. Jane: You can't have your cake and eat it too.* □ *Fred: I want to lose weight, but I'm not willing to change the way I eat. Alan: You can't have your cake and eat it.*

You cannot lose what you never had. *Prov.* You should have not lost something if you only wished that you had it to begin with. □ *Bill: I've lost Mary. She's gotten engaged to Tom. Fred: But, Bill, Mary was never your girlfriend. You can't lose what you never had.*

You cannot make a silk purse out of a sow's ear. *Prov.* You cannot make someone more refined than he or she is by nature. □ *I've given up trying to get my cousin to appreciate classical music. You can't make a silk purse out of a sow's ear.*

You cannot make an omelet without breaking eggs. *Prov.* In order to get something good or useful, you must give up something else. □ *Jill: Why do they have to tear down that beautiful old building to build an office park? Jane: You can't make an omelet without breaking eggs.* □ *Alan: We may make more money by raising our prices, but we'll also upset a lot of customers. Fred: You can't make an omelet without breaking eggs.*

You cannot make bricks without straw. *Prov.* You have to have all the necessary materials in order to make something. □ *Ellen: I really wanted to give Fred a birthday party, but none of the people I invited were able to come. Jane: Don't blame yourself. You can't make bricks without straw.*

You cannot please everyone. *Prov. Cliché* No matter what you do, there will always be some people who do not like it. □ *Nancy: My mother wants me to have a big wedding in the church, but my fiancé's mother insists that we should have an informal ceremony. What am I going to do? Jane: Well, you can't please everyone. Just do what you and your fiancé want to do.*

You cannot put new wine in old bottles. *Prov.* You should not try to combine the new with the old. □ *I think it is a mistake for the managers of that traditional art gallery to exhibit modern paintings. You can't put new wine in old bottles.* □ *Doug's attempt to teach ancient Chinese medicine to doctors trained in Western medicine was not a success. "I guess I can't put new wine in old bottles," Doug thought ruefully.*

You cannot serve God and mammon. *Prov.* You cannot both be a good person and dedicate yourself to making money. (Biblical. *Mammon* means riches.) □ *The minister warned the businessman that he could not serve God and mammon, and encouraged him to donate some of his wealth to charity.*

You cannot teach an old dog new tricks. *Prov.* Someone who is used to doing things a certain way cannot change. (Usually not polite to say about the person you are talking to; you can say it about yourself or about a third person.) □ *I've been away from school for fifteen years; I can't go back to college now. You can't teach an old dog new tricks.* □ *Kevin's doctor told him not to eat starchy food anymore, but Kevin still has potatoes with every meal. I guess you can't teach an old dog new tricks.*

(You) can't beat that. and **(You) can't top that.** *Inf.* No one can do better than that. (This *you* represents both personal and impersonal antecedents. That is, it means second person singular or plural, and *anyone*.) □ *Mary: Wow! Look at the size of that lobster! It looks yummy! Bill: Yeah. You can't beat that. I wonder what it's going to cost.* □ *"What a view! Nothing like it anywhere! You can't top this!" said Jeff, admiring his room's ocean view.*

You can't expect me to believe that. and **You don't expect me to believe that.** That is so outrageous that no one could believe it. □ *Bill: My father is running for president. Bob: You can't expect me to believe that.* □ *Jane: Everyone in our family has one extra toe. Mary: You don't expect me to believe that!*

(You) can't fight city hall. *Fig.* There is no way to win in a battle against a bureaucracy. □ *Bill: I guess I'll go ahead and pay the tax bill. Bob: Might as well. You can't fight city hall.* □ *Mary: How did things go at your meeting with the zoning board? Sally: I gave up. Can't fight city hall.*

(You) can't get there from here. a catchphrase said jokingly when someone asks directions to get to a place that can be reached only by a circuitous route. □ *Bill: How far is it to Adamsville? Tom: Adamsville? Oh, that's too bad. You can't get there from here.* □ *"Galesburg? Galesburg, you say?" said the farmer. "By golly, you can't get there from here!"*

You can't mean that! *Inf.* Surely you do not mean what you said! □ *Bill: I hate you! Mary: You can't mean that.* □ *Sally: The cake burned and there's no time to start another before the party. Mary: You can't mean that!*

(You) can't take it with you. *Prov. Cliché* Since you cannot take your wealth with you when you die, you ought to enjoy it while you're alive. □ *Go ahead, splurge a little while you've got it. You can't take it with you.* □ *Henry: Sure, I spent a fortune on this car. Can't take it with you, you know. Rachel: And this way, you can share it with your friends.*

You can't tell a book by its cover. Go to Don't judge a book by its cover.

(You) can't top that. Go to (You) can't beat that.

(You) can't win them all. and **(You) can't win 'em all.** *Inf.* a catch phrase said when someone, including the speaker, has lost in a contest or failed at something. (The *you* is impersonal, meaning *one*, *anyone*. The apostrophe on *'em* is not always used.) □ *Mary: Gee, I came in last again! Jane: Oh, well. You can't win them all.* □ *"Can't win 'em all," muttered Alice as she left the boss's office with nothing accomplished.*

You changed your mind? Go to (Have you) changed your mind?

(You) could have fooled me. *Inf.* I would have thought otherwise.; I would have thought the opposite. □ *Henry: Did you know that this land is among the most productive in the entire state? Jane: You could have fooled me. It looks*

quite barren. □ *John: I really do like Mary. Andy: Could have fooled me. You treat her rather badly sometimes.*

You could have knocked me over with a feather. *Fig.* I was extremely surprised.; I was so surprised that it was as if I was disoriented and could have been knocked over easily. □ *When she told me she was going to get married, you could have knocked me over with a feather.* □ *John: Did you hear that they are going to tear down city hall and build a new one—price tag twelve million dollars? Sally: Yes, and when I heard that, you could have knocked me over with a feather.*

You couldn't (do that)! and **You wouldn't (do that)!** an indication of disbelief that someone might do something. □ *Bill: I'm going to run away from home! Jane: You couldn't!* □ *Bill: I get so mad at my brother, I could just strangle him. Tom: You couldn't do that!*

You doing okay? Go to (Are you) doing okay?

You don't expect me to believe that. Go to You can't expect me to believe that.

You don't get something for nothing. *Prov.* Everything costs something, and anything that appears to be free must be deceptive. □ *Jill: This newspaper ad says we can get a trip to Hawaii for free. Jane: There must be a catch to it somewhere. You don't get something for nothing.*

You don't know the half of it. *Inf.* You really don't know how bad it is.; You might think that what you have heard is bad, but you do not know the whole story. □ *Mary: They say you've been having a bad time at home. Sally: You don't know the half of it.* □ *Sally: The company has no cash, they are losing orders right and left, and the comptroller is cooking the books. Mary: Sounds bad. Sally: You don't know the half of it.*

You don't know where it's been. Do not touch something or put it in your mouth, because you do not know where it has been and what kind of dirt it has picked up. (Most often said to children.) □ *Mother: Don't put that money in your mouth. You don't know where it's been. Bill: Okay.* □ *Take that stick out of your mouth. You don't know where it's been.*

You don't say. 1. *Inf.* a general response to something that someone has said. (Expresses a little polite surprise or interest, but not disbelief.) □ *Bill: I'm starting work on a new job next Monday. Bob: You don't say.* □ *Sally: The Jones boys are keeping a pet snake. Alice: You don't say.* **2.** *Inf.* You have just said something that everybody already knows. □ *Bill: I think I'm beginning to put on a little weight. Jane: You don't say.* □ *John: My goodness, prices are getting high. Sue: You don't say.*

You first. an invitation for someone to precede the speaker. (See the examples.) □ *Bill: Let's try some of this goose liver stuff. Jane: You first.* □ *Bill: The water sure looks cold. Let's jump in. Bob: You first.*

You get what you pay for. *Prov. Cliché* If you do not pay much money for something, it is probably of poor quality.; If you pay well for something, it is more likely to be of good quality. □ *Alan: I was so pleased to find shoes for such a low price, but look, they're falling apart already. Jane: You get what you pay for.* □ *This brand of soup is more expensive, but remember, you get what you pay for.*

Y

777

You got it! 1. *Inf.* I agree to what you asked!; You will get what you want! □ *You want a green one? You got it!* □ *This one? You got it!* **2.** *Inf.* You are right! □ *That's exactly right! You got it!* □ *That's the answer. You got it!*

You got me beat. Go to (It) beats me.

You got me there. *Inf.* I do not know the answer to your question. (Also with subjects other than second person.) □ *You got me there. I don't know.* □ *You got me there. I have no idea what the answer is.*

You got to do what you got to do. and **A man's gotta do what a man's gotta do.** One has to do whatever it is that one feels obliged to do. □ *I know I wouldn't ever agree to that kind of thing, but you got to do what you got to do.*

You have to eat a peck of dirt before you die. *Prov.* No one can escape eating a certain amount of dirt on his or her food.; Everyone must endure a number of unpleasant things in his or her lifetime. (Often said to console someone who has eaten some dirt or had to endure something unpleasant.) □ *Ellen: Oh, no! I forgot to wash this apple before I took a bite out of it. Fred: You have to eat a peck of dirt before you die.*

You hear? Go to (Do) you hear?

You heard someone. Don't argue. You heard your instructions from someone. (The *someone* can be a person's name, a title, or a pronoun.) □ *Andy: You heard the man. Get moving. Henry: Don't rush me!* □ *Bill: What makes her think she can tell me what to do? Bob: She's the boss. Do it! You heard her!*

You just don't get it! *Inf.* You really don't see what people are trying to tell you! (Also with subjects other than second person.) □ *You just don't get it! People avoid you because you offend them.*

You (just) wait (and see)! and **Just (you) wait (and see)!** *Inf.* Wait and see what will happen.; If you wait, you will see that what I predict will be true. □ *John: You'll get what you deserve! Just you wait! Jane: Mind your own business.* □ *Bill: Things will get better. You just wait and see! Sue: Sure, but when?*

(You) (just) watch! *Inf.* Just pay attention to what I do, and you will see that what I said is true! □ *Rachel: I'll get her to change! You just watch! Andy: You'll see I'm right. Sally: Sure, you are.* □ *Bob: Watch! This is the way it's done. Bill: You don't know what you're doing. Bob: Just watch!*

you know an expression placed on the end of a statement for pause or emphasis. (This expression is often overused, in which case it is totally meaningless and irritating.) □ *Tom: Sure, I spent a fortune on this car. Can't take it with you, you know. Rachel: But there are better things to do with it here and now.* □ *Bill: Do you always lock your door? Tom: Usually. There's a lot of theft around here, you know.*

You know what I mean? Go to (Do you) know what I'm saying?

You leaving so soon? Go to (Are you) leaving so soon?

You make a better door than you do a window. *Rur.* I cannot see through you, so move aside. □ *Joe was just standing in front of the TV. "Hey," I said, "You make a better door than you do a window."* □ *Charlie: Isn't this a great view? Jane: You make a better door than you do a window. Let me see.*

You make me laugh! *Inf. Fig.* What you said is totally ridiculous.; You are totally ridiculous. (Compare this with Don't make me laugh!) □ *Bill: I have this plan to make electricity from garbage. Sally: What a dumb idea! You make me laugh!* □ *Bill: I'm really sorry. Give me another chance. I'll never do it again! Jane: You make me laugh!*

You mean to tell me something? Go to (Do) you mean to say something?

You must lose a fly to catch a trout. *Prov.* You have to sacrifice something in order to get what you want. (Implies that what you sacrifice is minor compared to what you will get.) □ *Amy was willing to live cheaply for several years in order to save enough money to buy her own house. She knew that you must lose a fly to catch a trout.*

You never know (what you can do) till you try. *Prov.* Even if you think you are not able to do something, you should try to do it. □ *Jill: Want to go rock-climbing with me this weekend? Jane: Oh, I can't rock-climb. Jill: How do you know? Have you ever tried it? Jane: No, not really. Jill: You don't know what you can do till you try.* □ *Alan: I'll never be able to learn to dance. Jane: You don't know till you try.*

You never miss the water till the well runs dry. *Prov.* People are not grateful for what they have until they lose it. □ *Jill: I never realized what a good friend Jeanie was until she moved away. Jane: You never miss the water till the well runs dry.*

You pays your money and you takes your chance(s). *Prov.* You must resign yourself to taking risks.; Everything costs something, but paying for something does not guarantee that you will get it. (The grammatical errors are intentional.) □ *Customer: Can you guarantee that this washing machine won't break? Salesman: No guarantees. You pays your money and you takes your chances.*

You (really) said a mouthful. *Inf. Fig.* You said exactly what needed to be said.; What you said was very meaningful and had great impact. □ *Bill: Did you hear what I said to her? Jane: Yes. You said a mouthful. Was she mad?* □ *Bill: This is the worst food I have ever eaten. It is either stale, wilted, dry, or soggy! Tom: You said a mouthful!*

You said it! Go to You can say that again!

You scared the crap out of me. Go to You scared the hell out of me.

You scared the devil out of me. Go to next.

You scared the hell out of me. and **You scared the crap out of me.; You scared the dickens out of me.; You scared the devil out of me.; You scared me out of my wits.; You scared the pants off (of) me.** You frightened me very badly. (Also with subjects other than second person. *Of* is usually retained before pronouns.) □ *He scared the hell out of all of us.* □ *She really scared the pants off of me.*

You scratch my back and I'll scratch yours. *Fig.* You do a favor for me and I'll do a favor for you.; If you do something for me that I cannot do for myself, I will do something for you that you cannot do for yourself. □ *I'll grab the box on the top shelf if you will creep under the table* *and pick up my pen. You scratch my back, and I'll scratch yours.*

You think you're so smart! *Inf.* You act as if you know far more than you do. (Also with subjects other than second person.) □ *You think you're so smart! You don't know anything!* □ *Boy! He thinks he's so smart!*

(You) took the words right out of my mouth. *Inf. Fig.* You said exactly what I meant to say before I had a chance to say it, and, therefore, I agree with you very much. □ *Bill: I think she's old enough to know better. Tom: You took the words right out of my mouth.* □ *Mary: This movie is going to put me to sleep. Jane (yawning): You took the words right out of my mouth.*

(You) want a piece of me? *Sl.* Do you want to fight with me? □ *Come on, Wussy. You want a piece of me?*

(You want to) know something? Go to (Do you) want to know something?

You want to make something of it? Go to (Do you) want to make something of it?

[you will] See the entries beginning with *you'll.*

You win some, you lose some. and **You win a few, you lose a few.** *Prov. Cliché* You cannot always succeed. (You can say this when you have not succeeded, to show that you are not discouraged.) □ *Jill: I was sorry to hear that you didn't win your court case. Jane: Well, you win some, you lose some.* □ *Bill: I thought it was terrible that you didn't get a prize in the art contest. Bob: You win a few, you lose a few.*

[you would] See the entries beginning with *you'd.*

You wouldn't dare (to do something)! an exclamation that shows disbelief about something that the speaker has stated an intention of doing. □ *Bill: I'm going to leave school. Tom: You wouldn't dare leave!* □ *Bill: Be quiet or I'll slap you. Jane: You wouldn't dare to slap me!*

You wouldn't (do that)! Go to You couldn't (do that)!

You('d) better believe it! *Inf.* a way of emphasizing a previous statement. □ *Bill: Man, you're the best goalie this team has ever had! Tom: You better believe it!* □ *Bill: This food is so bad. It will probably stunt my growth. Tom: You'd better believe it!*

(You'd) better get moving. an expression encouraging someone to leave. □ *Jane: It's nearly dark. Better get moving. Mary: Okay. I'm leaving right now.* □ *Bob: I'm off. Good night. Bill: Yes, it's late. You'd better get moving.*

You'll be sorry you asked. *Inf.* The answer to the question you just asked is so bad that you will be sorry you asked it. (Compare this with **(Are you) sorry you asked?**) □ *Father: What are your grades going to be like this semester? Sally: You'll be sorry you asked.* □ *Mary: How much did you pay for that lamp? Jane: You'll be sorry you asked.*

You'll get onto it. and **You'll get into it.** *Inf.* Don't worry. You will become more comfortable with this situation soon.; You will catch the spirit of the situation soon. □ *Bill: I just can't seem to do this right. Bob: You'll get into it.* □ *Mary: How long does it take to learn to work this computer? Jane: Don't fret. You'll get onto it.*

You'll get the hang of it. Don't worry. You will learn soon how it is done. □ *Mary: It's harder than I thought to glue these things together. Tom: You'll get the hang of it.* □ *Bill: I can't seem to swing this club the way you showed me. Sally: You'll get the hang of it. Don't worry. Golf is easy.*

You'll never get away with it. You will never succeed with that illegal or outrageous plan. □ *Bill: I have a plan to cheat on the exam. Mary: You'll never get away with it.* □ *Jane: I think I can fool the IRS and save a lot on my taxes. Mary: You'll never get away with it.*

***young at heart** having a youthful spirit no matter what one's age. (*Typically: **act** ~; **be** ~; **keep** someone ~; **stay** ~.) □ *I am over 70 but I still feel young at heart.*

Young men may die, but old men must die. *Prov.* Young people may be killed by accidents or disease, but old people cannot avoid dying for very long, simply because they are old. □ *When Grandfather was so sick, he told us, "Don't feel too bad if I pass on; it's my time. Young men may die, old men must die."* □ *I'm afraid old Mr. Ferris won't live much longer. Young men may die, but old men must die.*

Your guess is as good as mine. *Inf.* I do not know. □ *Jane: Are there any good movies playing tonight? Alan: Your guess is as good as mine.* □ *Jill: How long should we bake this pie? Jane: Your guess is as good as mine.*

Your place or mine? *Inf.* an expression asking someone about whose dwelling should be the site of a rendezvous. (Often associated with a sudden or spontaneous sexual encounter.) □ *Bill: So, do you want to go somewhere? Mary: Your place or mine?* □ *Bill: I was thinking of watching a movie at home. Mary: Okay, I'll rent the movie and we'll watch it at your place.*

Your secret is safe with me. I will not tell your secret to anyone. □ *Don't worry. I won't tell. Your secret's safe with me.* □ *Your secret is safe with me. I will carry it to my grave.*

You're dern tootin'! *Rur.* You are absolutely right! (Never the full form *tooting.*) □ *Tom: Are you really going to take up boxing? Bob: You're dern tootin'!* □ *Father: Do you really want to buy that droopy-looking puppy? Bill: You're dern tootin'!*

You're excused. 1. You may leave the room, the table, etc. (Said in response to **May I be excused?**) □ *Mother: Are you finished, Tom? Tom: Yes, ma'am. Mother: You're excused.* □ *Bill (raising his hand): Can I leave the room? I have to go get my books off my bike. Teacher: You're excused. Bill: Thanks.* **2.** You must leave the room or the premises. (Typically said at the end of a scolding.) □ *Father: I've heard quite enough of this nonsense, Tom. You're excused. Tom: Sorry.* □ *Andy: That is the end of this conversation. You're excused. Bob: But, there's more.* **3.** You are forgiven for belching or for some other breach of strict etiquette. (Said in response to **Excuse me.**) □ *Tom (after belching): Excuse me. Father: You're excused.* □ *Sally: Excuse me for being so noisy. Mother: You're excused.*

You're (just) wasting my time. *Inf.* What you have to say is of no interest to me. □ *Rachel: I've heard enough. You're just wasting my time. Good-bye. Mary: If that's the way you feel about it, good-bye.* □ *Bill: Come on, Bill. I'll show you what I mean. Bill: No, you're wasting my time.*

You're out of your mind! and **You've got to be out of your mind!** *Inf.* You must be crazy for saying or doing that! (Said to someone who has said or done something silly or stupid.) □ *Andy: Go to the Amazon? You're out of your mind! Jane: Maybe so, but doesn't it sound like fun?* □ *Mary: Come on, Jane. Let's go swimming in the river. Jane: Look at that filthy water. Swim in it? You've got to be out of your mind!*

You're telling me! *Inf.* I know all too well the truth of what you are saying. □ *Tom: Man, it's hot today! Bob: You're telling me!* □ *Jane: This food is really terrible. Sally: Wow! You're telling me!*

You're the doctor. *Inf. Fig.* You are in a position to tell me what to do.; I yield to you and your knowledge of this matter. (Usually jocular; the person being addressed is most likely not a physician.) □ *Bill: Eat your dinner, then you'll feel more like playing ball. Get some energy! Tom: Okay, you're the doctor.* □ *Teacher: You'd better study the first two chapters more thoroughly. Bob: You're the doctor.*

You're too much! 1. *Inf.* You are too much of a problem for me. □ *Andy: You're too much! I'm going to report you to the head office! Bob: Go ahead. See if I care.* □ *Bob: Get out! Just go home! You're too much! Andy: What did I do? Bob: You're a pest!* **2.** *Inf.* You are just too funny, clever, entertaining, etc. □ *Alice: Oh, Fred, that was really funny. You're too much! Fred: I do my best.* □ *Sally: What a clever thing to say! You're too much! Andy: Actually, I didn't make it up myself.*

You're welcome. Go to You are welcome.

yours truly 1. a closing phrase at the end of a letter, just before the signature. □ *Yours truly, Tom Jones.* □ *Best wishes from yours truly, Bill Smith.* **2.** oneself; I; me. □

There's nobody here right now but yours truly. □ *Everyone else got up and left the table leaving yours truly to pay the bill.*

Yourself? Go to And you?

Youth must be served. *Prov.* Young people should be allowed to have fun. □ *Don't lecture the young folks because they were out dancing all night. Youth must be served.* □ *I don't know where my daughter gets the energy for school, sports, and a full social life. Youth must be served, I suppose.*

You've got another think coming. You will have to rethink your position. (The second part of an expression something like, "If you think so-and-so, then **you've got another think coming.**" Also with *thing* rather than *think*.) □ *Rachel: If you think I'm going to stand here and listen to your complaining all day, you've got another think coming! Bill: Frankly, I don't care what you do.* □ *Andy: If you think you can get away with it, you've got another think coming! Bob: Get away with what? I didn't do anything!*

(You've) got me stumped. *Inf.* I can't possibly figure out the answer to your question. □ *Bill: How long is the Amazon River? Jane: You've got me stumped.* □ *Bob: Do you know of a book that would interest a retired sea captain? Sally: You've got me stumped.*

You've got to be kidding! *Inf.* This cannot be the truth. Surely you are kidding me! □ *Bob: Sally is getting married. Did you hear? Mary: You've got to be kidding!* □ *Bill: I think I swallowed my gold tooth! Mother: You've got to be kidding!*

You've got to be out of your mind! Go to You're out of your mind!

zeek out *Sl.* to lose control of oneself. □ *I was in a pretty bad state. I almost zeeked out.* □ *Fred zeeked out and had to be calmed down.*

zerked (out) *Sl.* heavily intoxicated on drugs. □ *Gary looked really zerked out, and I thought he was really stoned.* □ *Wilbur gets zerked out every weekend.*

zero in (on someone or something**)** to aim directly at someone or something. □ *The television camera zeroed in on the little boy scratching his head.* □ *The commercial zeroed in on the glass of cola.* □ *Mary is very good about zeroing in on the most important and helpful ideas.*

zero tolerance absolutely no toleration of even the smallest infraction of a rule. □ *Because of the zero tolerance rule, the kindergartner was expelled from school because his mother accidentally left a table knife in his lunch box.*

zigged when one **should've zagged** performed one deed when another deed would have been better; to do something inconsequentially different from another thing. □ *I don't know why she complained. I guess I zigged when I should have zagged.*

zip along to move along very fast. □ *The motorcycle zipped along nicely.* □ *Let's zip along and get there on time.*

Zip it up! Go to Zip (up) your lip!

zip past someone or something to run or move past someone or something very rapidly. □ *The deer zipped past the hunter, who stood there, startled.* □ *The cars zipped past the intersection.*

zip something **on**† to put on a piece of clothing and zip it up. □ *She zipped her jumper on and headed toward the door.* □ *Zip on your jacket and let's go.*

zip something **up**† **1.** to close a zipper. □ *You should zip that zipper up.* □ *You should zip up that zipper.* **2.** to close a garment by zipping a zipper closed. □ *You had better zip your jacket up.* □ *You had better zip up your jacket.* **3.** *Sl.* to close one's mouth. (Fig. on ②.) □ *Zip your mouth up, Fred!* □ *Zip up your mouth, Fred.*

Zip (up) your lip! and **Zip it up!** *Inf.* Be quiet!; Close your mouth and be quiet! □ *"I've heard enough. Zip your lip!" hollered the coach.* □ *Andy: All right, you guys. Shut up! Zip it up! Bob: Sorry. Andy: That's better.*

zone something **as** something to create a particular legally defined area within a governmental or other local area. □ *They zoned this area as a shopping district.* □ *The city council zoned the vacant lot as a park.*

zone something **for** something to specify what can be built or what can be done within a particular legally defined area within a governmental area. □ *Did the council zone this area for business?* □ *They zoned this area for residences.*

zone something **off**† to create a special regulatory zone in an area. □ *The council zoned part of the land off for a park.* □ *They zoned off land for a park.*

zonk out *Sl.* to collapse from exhaustion; to go into a stupor from drugs or exhaustion. □ *I'm gonna go home and zonk out.* □ *I went home after the trip and just zonked out.*

zonk someone **out**† **1.** *Sl.* to make someone tired or exhausted. □ *All the work zonked him out.* □ *She zonked out the team with the long practice.* **2.** *Sl.* to cause some-

one to become intoxicated. □ *The drug zonked Max out totally.* □ *It zonked out Max.*

zonked (out) and **zounked (out)** **1.** *Sl.* drug intoxicated. □ *She's too zonked to drive.* □ *Jed was almost zounked out to unconsciousness.* **2.** *Sl.* exhausted; asleep. □ *She was totally zonked out by the time I got home.* □ *I feel zounked. Good night.*

zoom across (something**)** to run or move across something very fast. □ *The missile zoomed across the sky.* □ *We looked at the sky just as a comet zoomed across.*

zoom along to move along very rapidly. □ *The bus zoomed along rapidly all night long.* □ *Let's zoom along while the road is clear.*

zoom in (on someone or something**)** **1.** and **pan in (on** someone or something**)** to move in to a close-up picture of someone or something, using a zoom lens or a similar lens. □ *The camera zoomed in on the love scene.* □ *The camera operator panned in slowly.* **2.** to fly or move rapidly at someone or something. □ *The hawk zoomed in on the sparrow.* □ *The angry bees zoomed in on Jane and stung her.* □ *When the door opened, the cat zoomed in.* **3.** to concentrate on a matter related to someone or a problem. □ *Let's zoom in on this matter of debt.* □ *She zoomed in and dealt quickly with the problem at hand.*

zoom off to leave in a hurry. □ *Sorry, I have to zoom off.* □ *We will zoom off soon.*

zoom out **1.** *Sl.* to lose control. □ *I nearly zoomed out when I got the news.* □ *Fred zoomed out and started screaming at John.* **2.** Go to pan out.

zoom over someone or something to fly over someone or something at high speed. □ *The plane zoomed over the treetops.* □ *A small bird zoomed over the hikers, shrieking wildly.*

zoom past someone or something to run or move past someone or something very rapidly. □ *The runners zoomed past the spectators.* □ *Our train zoomed past town after town.*

zoom someone or something **(over) to** someone to send something to someone very fast. □ *Please use my car to zoom Molly over to the bank.* □ *Would you zoom this package to the downtown office?*

zoom through (something**)** **1.** to pass through a town or some other location very fast. □ *Don't just zoom through*

Z

these little towns. Stop and explore one or two. □ *We didn't stop. We just zoomed through.* **2.** to work one's way through something very rapidly. □ *She zoomed through the reading assignment and went on to something else.* □ *Jeff can open a book and zoom through in record time.*

zoom up to drive or pull up to a place. □ *A car zoomed up, and seven kids got out.* □ *Let's zoom up to the door and see if she's home.*

zounked (out) Go to zonked (out).

Phrase-Finder Index

This is an index of the words found in the dictionary entries. It helps you find the entry you are seeking by showing you what to look up in the dictionary.

HINTS

1. The index deals only with word FORM and not with word MEANING. Each word on the left tells you what phrase to look up.
2. The word on the left can be found in the phrase on the right. That means you can locate a phrase even if you can only remember or identify a word or two.
3. Identical words on the left may not even share the same meaning. That is not a problem since they are only used for indexing purposes. Meaning is found in the dictionary entries.
4. The words on the left are usually the simplest and most basic form of the words you are looking up, that is, present tense verbs and singular nouns.
5. Look up a major word in the idiom, preferably a verb, and go to the dictionary **entry head** listed in the right-hand column. If that fails, try an adverb, preposition, or other word.

TO THE LEARNER

Use the index to figure out what the boundaries of the target phrase are and to find out how the phrase is listed in the dictionary section. The index allows you to extract the core of the idiomatic expression so you can look up the core of the phrase in the dictionary section.

For example, you hear the sentence "He's always throwing his weight around." and don't understand it. There is no easy way for you to tell how the problematic part of this sentence is listed in this or any other dictionary. Using this index, if you start by looking up the VERB in the sentence, you will find **throw** one's **weight around**, and this is how the form is listed in the dictionary. Simply look up **throw** one's **weight around** in the dictionary.

You can also find the same phrase by looking up the words *weight* or *around* since these words are part of the core of the expression. The expression will not be found under *He* or *always* since these two words are not part of the core. Note that you also can learn what the actual core of the idiom is, so you will be able to use it yourself at a later time.

As you try to find the dictionary entry by using the index, you should first look up the VERB, then an ADVERB or PREPOSITION, then a NOUN or PRONOUN. While there are many nouns and pronouns in the index, most of the nouns and pronouns contained in real-life idioms and phrasal verbs are variables. They belong to *groups* of potential nouns or pronouns that are represented by so (someone), sth (something), or so/sth (someone or something) in this dictionary.

If you are trying to understand "He frequently noises his problems about.", you should first look up *noise*, and you would find **noise** sth **about**, which is the form of the idiom listed in this dictionary. The noun, *problem*, is the variable part of the idiom: **noise** sth **about**.

When you are writing, use the index to find out the correct form of phrasal verbs and prepositional verbs. The variables show where a noun, pronoun, or other form is required, but not exactly which word to use.

TO THE TEACHER

The index provides important lists of the prepositions and adverbs used in phrasal and prepositional verbs. These can be used in lesson preparation. It also provides the quickest way to locate the core form of the idiomatic expressions containing a specific word. The index can be used in making supplementary vocabulary lists that include the phrases that use the words on the lists. Students should be encouraged to consult the index to verify the correct form of phrasal verbs, prepositional verbs, and phrasal-prepositional verbs.

aback taken aback
abandon Abandon hope, all ye who enter here.
abandon abandon oneself to sth
abandon abandon ship
abandon abandon so/sth to so/sth
abandon like rats abandoning a sinking ship
abandon Rats abandon a sinking ship.
abbreviate abbreviate sth to sth
ABCs ABCs of sth
ABCs know one's ABCs
abduct abduct so from so/sth
abet abet so in sth
abet aid and abet so
abeyance hold sth in abeyance
abeyance in abeyance
abhor Nature abhors a vacuum.
abide abide by sth
abide abide with so
ability to the best of one's ability
able able to breathe (easily) again
able able to breathe (freely) again
able able to cut sth
able able to do sth
able able to do sth blindfolded
able able to do sth standing on one's head
able able to do sth with one's eyes closed
able able to fog a mirror
able able to make an event
able able to take a joke
able able to take just so much
able able to take only so much
able not able
able ready, willing, and able
aboard come aboard
aboard get aboard sth
aboard go aboard
aboard take so/sth aboard
aboard Welcome aboard.
abode take up one's abode some place
abound abound in sth
abound abound with so/sth
about about as exciting as watching (the) paint dry
about about one's business
about about to do sth
about advise so about so/sth
about agree (with so) (about so/sth)
about (all) at sea (about sth)
about all tore up (about sth)
about (a)long about a certain time
about approach so about so/sth
about ask about so/sth
about ask around (about so/sth)
about bandy sth about
about beat about the bush
about beef about so/sth
about Better keep still about it.
about bicker (with so) (about so/sth)
about bitch about so/sth
about boast about so/sth
about bother about sth
about bother one's (pretty little) head about so/sth
about brag about so/sth
about brief so about so/sth
about bring sth about
about brood about so/sth
about bruit sth about
about bustle about doing sth
about bustle about some place
about call around (about so/sth)

about call so about sth
about care about so/sth
about care nothing about so/sth
about carp about so/sth
about carp at so (about so/sth)
about carry on (about so/sth)
about carry so/sth about
about catch hell (about so/sth)
about cause qualms (about so/sth)
about caution so about so/sth
about chat about so/sth
about chatter about so/sth
about check with so (about sth)
about chortle about so/sth
about chuckle about so/sth
about come about
about come clean (with so) (about sth)
about come to terms (about so/sth)
about comment about so/sth
about complain about so/sth
about concern oneself about so/sth
about confer with so (about so/sth)
about confuse so about sth
about consult (with) so (about so/sth)
about converse with so (about so/sth)
about correspond with so (about so/sth)
about counsel so about sth
about crazy about so/sth
about create a stink (about sth)
about crow about sth
about cut up (about so/sth)
about dart about
about dawdle about
about daydream about so/sth
about debate (with so) about sth
about deliberate about so/sth
about differ (with so) about sth
about disagree (with so) (about so/sth)
about do an about-face (on so/sth)
about do sth about so/sth
about doesn't know beans (about sth)
about Don't even think about (doing) it.
about Don't even think about it (happening).
about Don't worry (about a thing).
about Don't worry your (pretty little) head about it.
about dream about so/sth
about drone on (about so/sth)
about embarrass so about so/sth
about enlighten so (about so/sth)
about excite so about sth
about exercised about sth
about expostulate about so/sth
about fall out (with so) (about sth)
about feel guilty (about sth)
about feel somehow about so/sth
about feel so out (about so/sth)
about feeling about sth
about fight about so/sth
about fight (with) so/sth (about so/sth)
about find out a thing or two (about so/sth)
about find (sth) out (about so/sth) (from so/sth)
about flit about
about flutter about
about follow so/sth about
about forewarn so about sth
about Forget (about) it!
about forget about so/sth
about fret about so/sth

about front off (about sth)
about fume about so/sth
about fuss about
about generalize about so/sth
about get about
about get hell (about so/sth)
about get into an argument (with so) (about so/sth)
about get one's wits about one
about get on(to) so (about sth)
about go about
about go into a song and dance (about sth)
about go into the same old song and dance about sth
about go on (and on) (about so/sth)
about go to so (about so/sth)
about gossip about so/sth
about gripe (to so/sth) (about so/sth)
about groan about so/sth
about grope (about) (for so/sth)
about grouse about so/sth
about grovel (about) in sth
about grumble about so/sth
about haggle about sth
about halfhearted (about so/sth)
about hassle so about sth
about have a clear conscience (about so/sth)
about have a clue (about sth)
about have a thing about so/sth
about have doubts about so/sth
about have feelings about so/sth
about have so/sth about
about hear about so/sth
about How about a lift?
about How about that!
about How about you?
about How bout them apples?
about hypothesize about sth
about (I have) nothing to complain about.
about idle about
about in a stew (about so/sth)
about in accord (with so/sth) (about so/sth)
about in hot water (with so) (about so/sth)
about in the dark (about so/sth)
about inform so about so/sth
about inkling (about so/sth)
about inquire about so/sth
about It's about time!
about I've heard so much about you.
about jabber about so/sth
about jaw about so/sth
about jest about so/sth
about joke (with so) (about so/sth)
about keen about so/sth
about keep after so (about sth)
about keep at so (about sth)
about keep (going) on about so/sth
about keep on so (about sth)
about keep one's mouth shut (about so/sth)
about keep one's wits about one
about keep quiet (about so/sth)
about keep so in ignorance (about so/sth)
about keep so in the dark (about so/sth)
about keep so/sth about
about Keep your mouth shut (about so/sth).

about keyed up (about sth)
about kick about so/sth
about kid so about so/sth
about knock about (some place) (with so)
about knock about (somewhere)
about knock so/sth about
about know a thing or two (about so/sth)
about know about so/sth
about know as much about sth as a hog knows about Sunday
about know no more about sth than a frog knows about bedsheets
about know one's way about
about lash sth about
about laugh about so/sth
about lay about
about lay down the law (to so) (about sth)
about learn a thing or two (about so/sth)
about learn about so/sth
about lecture at so (about sth)
about lecture ((to) so) about so/sth
about less said (about sth), the better.
about let on (about so/sth)
about let on (to so) (about so/sth)
about Let's talk (about it).
about let so know (about sth)
about level with so (about so/sth)
about lie about
about lie to so (about so/sth)
about litter sth about
about loll about (some place)
about look about (for so/sth)
about mad about so/sth
about make a big deal about sth
about make a (big) stink (about so/sth)
about make a stink (about sth)
about make cracks about so/sth
about Make no bones about it.
about Make no mistake (about it)!
about make one's mind up (about so/sth)
about make overtures about doing sth
about make sth about so/sth
about man about town
about mess about
about millstone about one's neck
about mislead so about sth
about mixed feelings (about so/sth)
about moan about sth
about moon about so/sth
about moralize about so/sth
about move about
about much ado about nothing
about mutter about so/sth
about mutter sth about so/sth
about nag at so (about so/sth)
about needle so about so/sth
about niggle about sth
about no buts about it
about no ifs, ands, or buts (about it)
about no two ways about it
about noise sth about
about nose about (for so/sth)
about not breathe a word (about so/sth)
about not care two hoots about so/sth
about not give a hang about so/sth
about not give two hoots about so/sth
about not know beans (about so/sth)
about not know the first thing about so/sth

about not trouble one's (pretty) (little) head about sth
about nothing to boast about
about nothing to write home about
about notify so about so/sth
about nuts about so/sth
about of a single mind (about so/sth)
about of one mind (about so/sth)
about of two minds (about so/sth)
about on the fence (about sth)
about open up (about so/sth) (with so)
about order so about
about out and about
about peer about
about pester so about so/sth
about play about (with so/sth)
about poke about
about pout about so/sth
about prattle (away) about so/sth
about preach about sth
about protest about so/sth
about prowl about
about pull so about
about push so/sth about
about put a bee in so's bonnet (about so/sth)
about put one's foot down (about so/sth)
about put out (about so/sth)
about putter about
about qualms (about so/sth)
about quarrel (with so) (about so/sth)
about question so about so/sth
about quibble (about so/sth) (with so)
about quip about so/sth
about quiz so about so/sth
about rag so about so/sth
about rail at so (about sth)
about raise a (big) stink (about so/sth)
about raise a hue and cry (about sth)
about raise a stink (about sth)
about ramble on (about so/sth)
about rant and rave (about so/sth)
about rant (at so) about so/sth
about rattle on (about so/sth)
about rave about so/sth
about read about so/sth
about reassure so about sth
about religious about doing sth
about remind so about so/sth
about reminisce about so/sth
about remonstrate (with so) (about so/sth)
about report about so/sth
about ride so about sth
about roam about
about roll about
about rough idea (about sth)
about ruminate about sth
about say sth about so/sth
about scatter sth about
about scold so about sth
about scratch about (for sth)
about second thoughts (about so/sth)
about see a man about a dog
about see about so/sth
about see eye to eye (about so/sth) (with so)
about see so about so/sth
about send one about one's business
about serious about so
about set about doing sth
about set so about sth

about set so's mind at ease (about so/sth)
about shout about so/sth
about Shut up about it.
about sigh about sth
about sit on the fence (about sth)
about So had better keep still about it.
about something about so/sth
about sth to shout about
about sorry about that
about sound off (about sth)
about speak about so/sth
about speak out (about so/sth)
about speak with so (about so/sth)
about speculate about so/sth
about splash about
about splash sth about
about spout off (about so/sth)
about sprawl about
about squabble about so/sth
about squawk about sth
about stay after so (about sth)
about stay in the dark (about so/sth)
about sulk about sth
about swirl about so/sth
about sympathize with so (about so/sth)
about talk about so/sth
about Talk about so/sth!
about talk with so (about so/sth)
about taunt so about sth
about tease so about so/sth
about tell so a thing or two (about so/sth)
about tell so about so/sth
about That's about the size of it.
about theorize about so/sth
about (There is) no doubt about it.
about thing or two (about so/sth)
about think about so/sth
about think twice about so/sth
about tip so off (about so/sth)
about trouble one's head about so/sth
about trouble oneself about so/sth
about trouble so about so/sth
about turn about
about under the gun (about sth)
about (up and) about
about up in the air (about sth)
about update so about so/sth
about wander about
about warn so about so/sth
about We need to talk about sth.
about We were just talking about you.
about weep about so/sth
about What about (doing) sth?
about What about (having) sth?
about What about it?
about What about you?
about What do you know (about that)?
about whine about so/sth
about whisper about so/sth
about wild about so/sth
about wise so up (about so/sth)
about wobble about
about wonder about so/sth
about word with so (about sth)
about worried sick (about so/sth)
about worry about so/sth
about worry oneself about so/sth
about wrangle (with so) (about so/sth)
about write about so/sth
about write so/sth about sth
about yammer (away) about so/sth

about yap about so/sth
about-face about-face (on so/sth)
above above and beyond (sth)
above above average
above above (doing) sth
above above one's bend
above above one's huckleberry
above above par
above above reproach
above above so
above above suspicion
above above the law
above Caesar's wife must be above suspicion.
above cut above average
above cut above sth
above get one's head above water
above go above and beyond one's duty
above go above and beyond (sth)
above go above and beyond the call of duty
above go above so
above head and shoulders above so/sth
above keep one's head above water
above keep oneself above suspicion
above live above so/sth
above marry above oneself
above notch above
above over and above sth
above place so/sth above so/sth
above prize so/sth above so/sth
above put so/sth above so/sth
above rank above so
above rate so/sth above so/sth else
above rise above sth
above set so/sth above so/sth
above stand head and shoulders above so/sth
above tower above so/sth
above tower head and shoulders above so/sth
above value so/sth above so/sth
aboveboard aboveboard
aboveboard honest and aboveboard
aboveboard open and aboveboard
abreast abreast of so/sth
abreast keep abreast of so/sth
abreast stay abreast of so/sth
abscond abscond with so/sth
absence Absence makes the heart grow fonder.
absence conspicuous by one's absence
absence in the absence of so/sth
absence leave of absence
absence made conspicuous by one's absence
absent absent oneself from so/sth
absent absent without leave
absent absent-minded professor
absent go absent without leave
absolute Absolute power corrupts absolutely.
absolutely Absolute power corrupts absolutely.
absolutely Absolutely not!
absolve absolve so from sth
absorb absorb oneself in so/sth
absorb absorb so in(to) sth
absorb absorb sth in(to) sth
absorb absorb sth with sth
abstain abstain from sth
abstain abstain from voting
abstract abstract sth from so/sth

abstract abstract sth from sth
abut abut on sth
abut abut (up) against sth
accede accede to sth
accept accept so as sth
accept accept sth as sth
accept accept the blame for sth
accept I can accept that.
accept I can't accept that.
acceptable acceptable damage
acceptable acceptable losses
access access to so/sth
accident accidentally-on-purpose
accident Accidents will happen.
accident have an accident
acclimate acclimate so or an animal to sth
acclimatize acclimatize so or an animal to sth
accommodate accommodate oneself to sth
accommodate accommodate so with sth
accompany accompanied by sth
accompany accompany so on a journey
accompany accompany so on a musical instrument
accompany accompany so with sth
accomplishment celebrate so for an accomplishment
accord accord with sth
accord in accord (with so/sth) (about so/sth)
accord of one's own accord
accord reach an accord (with so)
accordance in accordance with sth
according according to all accounts
according according to Hoyle
according according to one's own lights
according according to so/sth
according according to sth
according cut one's coat according to one's cloth
account according to all accounts
account account for so/sth
account account for sth
account balance the accounts
account blow-by-blow account
account bring so to account
account by all accounts
account call so to account
account cook the accounts
account give a good account of oneself
account give an account of so/sth (to so)
account hold so accountable (for sth)
account not on any account
account on account
account on any account
account on no account
account on so's account
account square accounts (with so)
account take account of so/sth
account take into account so/sth
account take so/sth into account
account take sth into account
account There is no accounting for taste(s).
account There's no accounting for taste.
account turn sth to good account
accountable hold so accountable (for sth)
accredit accredit sth to so
accrue accrue to so/sth

accuse accuse so of sth
accuse guilty conscience needs no accuser.
accuse He who excuses himself accuses himself.
accuse Never ask pardon before you are accused.
accustom accustom so to so/sth
accustom accustomed to so/sth
accustom grow accustomed to doing sth
accustom grow accustomed to so/sth
ace ace in the hole
ace ace in(to sth)
ace ace out
ace ace so out
ace black as the ace of spades
ace come within an ace of sth
ace have an ace up one's sleeve
ace hold all the aces
ace so's ace in the hole
ace within an ace of (doing) sth
ache ache for so/sth
ache aching heart
ache splitting headache
Achilles Achilles' heel
acid acid test
acknowledge acknowledge so as sth
acknowledge acknowledge so to be right
acknowledge acknowledge sth as sth
acknowledge acknowledge (the) receipt of sth
acorn Great oaks from little acorns grow.
acorn like stealing acorns from a blind pig
acorn Mighty oaks from little acorns grow.
acquaint acquaint so with sth
acquaint acquainted with so
acquaint acquainted with sth
acquaintance (I'm) delighted to make your acquaintance.
acquiesce acquiesce to so/sth
acquire *taste for sth
acquit acquit so of sth
across across the board
across come across
across crawl across sth
across creep across sth
across cut across sth
across dart across sth
across dash across sth
across drop across sth
across drop sth across sth
across edge (one's way) across (sth)
across extend across sth
across ferry so/sth across sth
across flash across sth
across flow across sth
across fly across sth
across get across (sth)
across get so across (in a good way)
across get so/sth across sth
across get sth across (to so)
across glide across sth
across go across (sth)
across go across sth to so/sth
across guide so/sth across (sth)
across inch one's way across sth
across inch oneself across sth
across jump across sth
across lean across so/sth

across pan across to so/sth
across push so/sth across (sth)
across put so across (in a good way)
across put sth across (to so)
across rap so across the knuckles
across run across so/sth
across run across sth
across scuttle across sth
across see so across sth
across send so/sth across (sth)
across skid across sth
across smuggle so/sth across sth
across steam across sth
across streak across sth
across stumble across so/sth
across take so/sth across (sth)
across tear across sth
across throw sth across so/sth
across throw sth across sth
across thunder across sth
across tramp across sth
across travel across sth
across trek across sth
across troop across so/sth
across wade across sth
across walk across sth
across zoom across (sth)
act act as so
act act for so
act act full of oneself
act act high-and-mighty
act act in earnest
act act like a cold fish
act act like oneself again
act act of faith
act act of God
act act of war
act act out
act act sth out
act act tough on so
act act up
act act (up)on sth
act act within one's rights
act act young at heart
act Act your age!
act catch so in the act (of doing sth)
act caught in the act
act clean one's act up
act get in(to) the act
act get one's act together
act go into one's act
act hard act to follow
act in on the act
act in the act (of doing sth)
act It would take an act of Congress to do sth.
act keep an act up
act keep one's act up
act keep up an act
act keep up one's act
act let so in on the act
act put on an act
act read so the riot act
act tough act to follow
action Actions speak louder than words.
action all talk (and no action)
action bit of the action
action bring so/sth into action
action chill so's action
action course of action
action galvanize so into action
action go into action

action out of action
action piece (of the action)
action slice of the action
action spring into action
action suit one's actions to one's words
action swing into action
action take action against so/sth
action take action on so/sth
action where the action is
active on active duty
activity hive of activity
activity hum with activity
actual grounded in (actual) fact
Adam not know so from Adam
adapt adapt so/sth to sth
adapt adapt sth for sth
adapt adapt sth from sth
adapt adapt sth to sth
adapt adapt to sth
add add fuel to the fire
add add fuel to the flame
add add insult to injury
add add sth into sth
add add (sth) on(to) sth
add add (sth) to sth
add add sth together
add add sth up
add add up (to sth)
add add up to the same thing
addict addict so to sth
addition in addition (to sth)
address address comments or remarks to so
address address oneself to so
address address oneself to sth
address address so as a specific title or attribute
address address sth to so
adhere adhere to sth
adieu bid adieu to so/sth
adjourn adjourn for a time
adjourn adjourn to some place
adjust adjust (oneself) to so/sth
adjust adjust sth to sth
adjust readjust to so/sth
administer administer sth to so or an animal
admire admire so for sth
admire admire to do sth
admit admit so (in)to some place
admit admit sth into sth
admit admit sth to so
admit admit to sth
admonish admonish so for sth
ado much ado about nothing
ado without further ado
adopt adopt so as sth
adopt adopt sth as sth
adore adore so for doing sth
adore adore so for having sth
adorn adorn so/sth with sth
adulterate adulterate sth with sth
advance advance sth to so/sth (against sth)
advance advance to(ward) so/sth
advance advance (up)on so/sth
advance advanced in years
advance in advance
advance make advances at so
advance make advances to so
advance on advance notice
advance pay in advance
advance with advance notice
advantage advantage of so

advantage culturally advantaged
advantage show sth to good advantage
advantage take advantage of so
advantage turn sth to one's advantage
advertise advertise for so
advertise advertise sth for a price
advertise advertise sth for sth
advice Nothing is given so freely as advice.
advice sage advice
advise advise against sth
advise advise so about so/sth
advise advise so against doing sth
advise advise so of sth
advise advise so on so/sth
advise take sth under advisement
advisement take sth under advisement
advocate play (the) devil's advocate
aegis under the aegis of so
affair fine state of affairs
affair have an affair (with so)
affair pretty state of affairs
affair settle so's affairs
affair There is a tide in the affairs of men.
affiliate affiliate (so/sth) to so/sth
affiliate affiliate (so/sth) with so/sth
affinity affinity for so/sth
affirmative in the affirmative
affix affix one's signature to sth
affix affix sth to so/sth
afflict afflict so with so
afflict afflict so with sth
afoul fall (a)foul of so/sth
afoul run (a)foul of so/sth
afraid afraid of one's own shadow
afraid 'Fraid not.
afraid 'Fraid so.
afraid fraidy cat
afraid He who rides a tiger is afraid to dismount.
afraid (I'm) afraid not.
afraid (I'm) afraid so.
aft fore and aft
after after a fashion
after After a storm comes a calm.
after after all
after after hours
after after so/sth
after after the fact
after after the fashion of so/sth
after after the style of so/sth
after After while(, crocodile).
after After you.
after ask after so
after chase after so/sth
after chase around after so/sth
after come after so/sth
after day after day
after devil looks after his own.
after flock after so/sth
after follow after the style of so/sth
after follow on (after so/sth)
after get after so
after go after so
after go after so/sth or an animal
after grope after so/sth
after hanker after so/sth
after head out after so/sth or an animal
after hunger after sth
after hunt after so/sth
after If you run after two hares, you will catch neither.

after inquire after so
after It is easy to be wise after the event.
after keep after so (about sth)
after linger on (after so/sth)
after live happily ever after
after live on (after so)
after Lock the stable door after the horse is stolen.
after look after number one
after look after so/sth
after lust after so
after make (out) after so/sth
after man after my own heart
after mop up (after so)
after morning after (the night before)
after much sought after
after name so after so else
after one thing or person after another
after pattern sth after sth
after pick up after so/sth
after pine after so/sth
after pine away (after so/sth)
after race around (after so/sth)
after reach out (after so/sth)
after run after so
after run around after so/sth
after search after so/sth
after see after so/sth
after seek after so/sth
after send after so/sth
after send so after so/sth
after Shut the stable door after the horse has bolted.
after snap back (after sth)
after stay after so (about sth)
after stay after (so/sth)
after stay on (after so/sth)
after strain after sth
after strive after sth
after sweep up after so
after tag along (after so)
after tail after so
after take after so
after take off (after so/sth)
after take out (after so/sth)
after throw good money after bad
after time after time
after trail (along) (after so/sth)
after trot after so
after year after year
afternoon (Good) afternoon.
again able to breathe (easily) again
again able to breathe (freely) again
again act like oneself again
again again and again
again Again(, please).
again (all) over again
again at it again
again back at it (again)
again Call again.
again Can I see you again?
again Come again.
again Could I see you again?
again Do we have to go through all that again?
again Don't make me say it again!
again Don't make me tell you again!
again (every) now and again
again feel like oneself again
again Here we go again.
again How's that again?

again (I) hope to see you again (sometime).
again If at first you don't succeed, try, try again.
again (It's) good to see you (again).
again Let's do this again (sometime).
again Let's not go through all that again.
again May I see you again?
again Not again!
again off again, on again
again on again, off again
again oneself again
again over and over (again)
again Run it by (me) again.
again run sth by (so) (again)
again Run that by (me) again.
again say sth over (and over (again))
again seem like oneself again
again set one on one's feet again
again something else (again)
again Till we meet again.
again time and (time) again
again try so back (again)
again Until we meet again.
again use sth over (again)
again walk on stage and off again
again We must do this again (sometime).
again We'll try again some other time.
again What was the name again?
again Will I see you again?
again You are something else (again)!
again You can say that again!
against abut (up) against sth
against advance sth to so/sth (against sth)
against advise against sth
against advise so against doing sth
against against all odds
against against so/sth
against against so's will
against against the clock
against against the grain
against agitate against so/sth
against ally (oneself) (with so) (against so/sth)
against appeal against sth
against argue against so/sth
against arm (so against so/sth) (with sth)
against balance sth against sth else
against band together (against so/sth)
against bang against so/sth
against bang one's head against a brick wall
against bang sth against so/sth
against bank sth up (against sth)
against bash sth against so/sth
against battle against so/sth
against bear a grudge (against so)
against bear up (against sth)
against beat against so/sth
against beat one's head against the wall
against bias so against so/sth
against break against sth
against bring a charge against so/sth
against brush (up) against so/sth
against build a case (against so)
against bump (up) against so/sth
against bundle (oneself) up (against sth)
against bundle (so) up (against sth)
against butt (up) against so/sth
against campaign against so/sth
against cards are stacked against one

against chalk sth up (against so)
against charge sth against sth
against clamor against so/sth
against clash against sth
against combine sth against so/sth
against come out against so/sth
against come up against so/sth
against compete against so
against compete against sth
against conspire with so (against so/sth)
against contend against so/sth
against counsel so against sth
against count against so
against count sth against so
against cover so/sth against sth
against crusade against so/sth
against crush (up) against so/sth
against cry out (against so/sth)
against cut against the grain
against dash so/sth against so/sth
against dead set against so/sth
against debit sth against so/sth
against decide against so/sth
against declare (oneself) against so/sth
against declare war against so/sth
against defend so/sth against so/sth
against demonstrate against so/sth
against direct sth against so/sth
against discriminate against so/sth
against divide so against so/sth
against draw against an amount of money
against fight against so/sth
against fight against time
against file charges (against so)
against file sth against so
against find against so/sth
against fortify so or an animal (against sth) (with sth)
against fulminate against so/sth
against gather a case (against so)
against get up against so/sth
against go against so/sth
against go against the grain
against go to bat against so
against go up against so
against graze against so/sth
against guarantee against sth
against guarantee sth against sth (for sth)
against guard against so/sth
against harbor sth against so/sth
against have a case (against so)
against have one's heart (dead) set against sth
against have sth against so/sth
against have the cards stacked against one
against have the deck stacked against one
against hedge against sth
against hedge sth against sth
against hit against so/sth
against hold a grudge (against so)
against hold out (against so/sth)
against hold sth against so
against hope against (all) hope
against house divided against itself cannot stand.
against immunize so against sth
against indemnify so/sth against sth
against inoculate so against sth
against institute sth against so/sth
against insulate so/sth against so/sth
against insure against sth

against insure so/sth (against sth) (for sth)
against intrigue (with so) (against so)
against inveigh against so/sth
against jar against so/sth
against keep on (one's) guard (against so/sth)
against kick against so/sth
against knock against so/sth
against knock one's head (up) against a brick wall
against knock sth against sth
against knock (up) against so/sth
against lap (up) against sth
against lash against sth
against launch sth against so/sth
against lay sth against sth
against lead so/sth against so/sth
against lean against so/sth
against lean back (against so/sth)
against lean sth against so/sth
against legislate against sth
against level a charge against so
against lift a hand (against so/sth)
against line so/sth up against sth
against line up against sth
against lobby against sth
against lodge sth against so
against lodge sth against sth
against make sth against so/sth
against march against so/sth
against match so against so/sth against sth else
against measure so against so else or sth against sth else
against measure so up against so/sth
against mental block (against sth)
against militate against sth
against mount sth against so/sth
against murmur against so/sth
against mutiny against so/sth
against nestle (up) against so/sth
against nurse a grudge (against so)
against nuzzle up against so/sth
against odds are against one
against offend against so/sth
against on (one's) guard (against so/sth)
against one's heart is (dead) set against sth
against operate against so/sth
against pin so/sth against sth
against pit so/sth against sth
against place sth up against sth
against play against so/sth
against play both ends (against the middle)
against play so against so else
against play so off against so else
against plot against so/sth
against poison so against so/sth
against preach against so/sth
against prefer sth against so
against prejudice so/sth against so/sth
against preserve so/sth against sth
against press against so/sth
against press charges (against so)
against press sth against so/sth
against prevail against so/sth
against proceed against so/sth
against prop so/sth up (against so/sth)
against protect so/sth against so/sth
against provide against sth
against push so up against the wall
against push sth (up) against so/sth

against push (up) against so/sth
against put so up against so
against race against so/sth
against race against time
against rage against so/sth
against rail against so/sth
against raise a hand (against so/sth)
against raise one's voice against so/sth
against rant against so/sth
against react against so/sth
against reason against sth
against rebel against so/sth
against remain on (one's) guard (against sth)
against rest against so/sth
against rest sth against sth
against retaliate against so/sth
against revolt against so/sth
against rise (up) against so/sth
against rub sth against so/sth
against rub (up) against so/sth
against rule against so/sth
against run against so
against run against the grain
against run one's head against a brick wall
against run up against so/sth
against safeguard against so/sth
against safeguard so/sth against so/sth
against sail against sth
against saw against the grain
against say sth against so/sth
against scheme against so/sth
against score against so/sth
against score sth (up) against so/sth
against secure sth against so/sth or an animal
against security against sth
against see sth against sth
against seek revenge (against so)
against set one's heart against sth
against set so/sth up against so/sth
against set sth against so/sth
against side against so
against sin against so/sth
against slant against sth
against slant sth against so/sth
against slap against so/sth
against slap sth against so/sth
against smear campaign (against so)
against snuggle (up) against so/sth
against speak against so/sth
against speak out (against so/sth)
against speak up (against so/sth)
against squash up against so/sth
against squeeze up against so/sth
against stack against so/sth
against stack the cards (against so/sth)
against stack the deck (against so/sth)
against stand against so/sth
against stand out (against sth)
against stand up against so/sth
against stay on (one's) guard (against so/sth)
against steel so against so/sth
against stick out against sth
against strive against sth
against struggle against so/sth
against stub one's toe against sth
against swear sth out against so
against swim against the current
against swim against the tide
against take a stand (against so/sth)
against take action against so/sth

against take revenge (against so)
against take sides against so/sth
against take up arms (against so/sth)
against team up against so/sth
against testify against so/sth
against thrust so/sth against so/sth
against thud against so/sth
against transgress against so/sth
against turn against so/sth
against turn so/sth against so/sth
against two strikes against one
against unite against so/sth
against unite so against so/sth
against unleash so/sth against so/sth
against up against so/sth
against up against sth
against up against the wall
against vaccinate so or an animal against sth
against vote against so/sth
against wage sth against so/sth
against war against so/sth
against warn so against so/sth
against weigh against so/sth
against weigh sth against so/sth
against weight sth against so/sth
against work against so/sth
against write against so/sth
against write sth against so/sth
age Act your age!
age Age before beauty.
age age of miracles is past.
age age out (of sth)
age come of age
age go on for an age
age in a coon's age
age in an age of years
age in this day and age
age live to the (ripe old) age of sth
age of age
age ripe old age
age tender age of...
age What's your age?
agenda hidden agenda
agitate agitate against so/sth
agitate agitate for sth
agog all agog
agonize agonize (oneself) over so/sth
agree agree to disagree
agree agree to sth
agree agree (up)on so/sth
agree agree with so
agree agree (with so) (about so/sth)
agree agree with sth
agree agree (with sth) (in sth)
agree Birds in their little nests agree.
agree not agree with so
agreement in agreement (with so/sth)
agreement reach an agreement (with so)
agreement sweetheart agreement
aground run aground (on sth)
ah (Ah) shucks!
ahead ahead of one's time
ahead ahead of schedule
ahead ahead (of so/sth)
ahead ahead of sth
ahead ahead of the game
ahead ahead of time
ahead arrive ahead of time
ahead cause lean times (ahead)
ahead come out ahead
ahead cut in (ahead of so/sth)

ahead dead ahead
ahead draw ahead (of so/sth)
ahead finish ahead of schedule
ahead full steam ahead
ahead get ahead (in sth)
ahead get ahead of oneself
ahead Go ahead.
ahead (Go ahead,) make my day!
ahead go ahead (of so/sth)
ahead go ahead (with sth)
ahead keep ahead (of so/sth)
ahead keep ahead of sth
ahead keep ahead of the game
ahead keep one step ahead of so/sth
ahead lean times (ahead)
ahead leave ahead of time
ahead lie ahead of so/sth
ahead look ahead to sth
ahead mean lean times (ahead)
ahead move ahead of so/sth
ahead one jump ahead (of so/sth)
ahead one move ahead (of so/sth)
ahead pull ahead (of so/sth)
ahead push ahead (with sth)
ahead push so/sth ahead of so
ahead push so/sth on (ahead) (of so/sth)
ahead put so/sth ahead of (of so/sth)
ahead quit while one is ahead
ahead remain ahead (of so/sth)
ahead remain ahead of sth
ahead remain ahead of the game
ahead see ahead (of so/sth)
ahead send ahead for sth
ahead send so/sth on (ahead) (of so/sth)
ahead show up ahead of time
ahead stay ahead of sth
ahead stay ahead of the game
ahead stay one step ahead of so/sth
ahead think ahead of one's time
ahead think ahead (to sth)
ahead two jumps ahead of so
ahead walk ahead of so/sth
ahead wire ahead (for sth)
ahold (a)hold of so/sth
ahold catch (a)hold of so/sth
ahold take (a)hold of so/sth
aid aid and abet so
aid aid so in doing sth
aid aid so in sth
aid be in aid of
aid bring sth to so's aid
ail good for what ails you
aim aim for sth
aim aim for the sky
aim Aim for the stars!
aim aim sth at so/sth
aim aim to do sth
aim take aim at so/sth
aim take aim (at so/sth or an animal)
aim We aim to please.
ain't ain't fittin' to roll with a pig
ain't ain't got a grain of sense
ain't ain't got a lick of sense
ain't ain't got the brains God gave a squirrel
ain't ain't got the sense God gave geese
ain't Ain't it the truth?
ain't ain't particular
ain't Church ain't out till they quit singing.
ain't If it ain't chickens, it's feathers.
ain't It ain't fittin'.

ain't like there ain't no tomorrow
ain't That ain't hay.
ain't That ain't no lie.
ain't That ain't the way I heard it.
ain't There ain't no such thing as a free lunch.
ain't (There ain't) nothin' to it.
ain't You ain't just whistlin' Dixie.
ain't You ain't seen nothing yet!
air air
air air one's belly
air air one's dirty linen in public
air air one's grievances
air air one's lungs
air air one's paunch
air air one's pores
air air out
air air sth out
air breath of fresh air
air build castles in the air
air clear the air
air come up for air
air dance on air
air float on air
air free as (the) air
air full of hot air
air gasp for air
air give oneself airs
air gulp for air
air have one's nose in the air
air in midair
air in the air
air keep so/sth hanging (in midair)
air leave so/sth hanging (in midair)
air leave so up in the air
air leave sth up in the air
air light as air
air (little) nip in the air
air off the air
air on the air
air one's nose is in the air
air out of thin air
air pant for air
air pull sth out of thin air
air put on airs
air stick one's nose up in the air
air up in the air (about so/sth)
air vanish into thin air
air walk on air
aisle leave them rolling in the aisles
aisle rolling in the aisles
alarm I don't want to alarm you, but
alcohol have an alcohol problem
alcohol under the influence (of alcohol)
alert alert so to sth
alert on the alert (for so/sth)
alienate alienate so from so/sth
alight alight from sth
alight alight (up)on so/sth
align align oneself with so/sth
align align sth with sth
alike alike as (two) peas in a pod
alike Great minds think alike.
alike look alike
alike share and share alike
alive alive and kicking
alive alive and well
alive alive with people or things
alive Land(s) sakes (alive)!
alive Look alive!
alive more dead than alive
alive Sakes alive!

alive skin so alive
all Abandon hope, all ye who enter here.
all according to all accounts
all after all
all against all odds
all all agog
all all and sundry
all all around Robin Hood's barn
all all at once
all (all) at sea (about sth)
all (all) balled up
all (all) beer and skittles
all all better (now)
all all by one's lonesome
all All cats are gray in the dark.
all all day long
all (all) dolled up
all (all) dressed up
all all dressed up and nowhere to go
all all ears
all all eyes and ears
all (all) for so/sth
all (all) for the best
all all gone
all All good things must (come to an) end.
all all hell broke loose
all (all) het up
all all hours (of the day and night)
all all in
all (all) in one breath
all (all) in the family
all (all) joking aside
all (all) kidding aside
all all kinds of so/sth
all all manner of so/sth
all all my eye (and Betty Martin)
all all night long
all all oak and iron bound
all all of a size
all all of a sudden
all all or nothing
all all over (some place)
all (all) over again
all all over hell and gone
all all over hell and half of Georgia
all all over the earth
all all over the world
all all over town
all all right
all All righty.
all All right(y) already!
all All roads lead to Rome.
all All's fair in love and war.
all All's well that ends well.
all (all) set (to do sth)
all all shook up
all all show and no go
all (all) skin and bones
all all spruced up
all all sweetness and light
all All systems (are) go.
all all talk (and no action)
all All that glistens is not gold.
all All that glitters is not gold.
all All the best to so.
all all the livelong day
all all the marbles
all all the more reason for doing sth
all all the rage
all all the same
all all the time

all all the way
all all there
all all things being equal
all All things must pass.
all all things to all men
all all things to all people
all All things will pass.
all all thumbs
all all to the good
all all told
all all tore up (about sth)
all (all) tuckered out
all all vine and no taters
all all walks of life
all (all) well and good
all all wet
all all wool and a yard wide
all all wool and no shoddy
all All work and no play makes Jack a dull boy.
all all year round
all all-out effort
all all-out war
all and all that jazz
all as all get out
all as bad as all that
all at all
all away from it all
all beggar (all) description
all begin an all-out effort
all big as all outdoors
all blow sth out of (all) proportion
all bring sth all together
all by all accounts
all by all appearances
all by all means
all call (all) the shots
all common thread (to all this)
all Conscience does make cowards of us all.
all cry all the way to the bank
all daddy of them all
all distribute sth (all) around
all Do we have to go through all that again?
all Don't put all your eggs in one basket.
all Don't spend it all in one place.
all Don't that (just) beat all!
all downhill all the way
all drool (all) over so/sth
all end it (all)
all end up with all the marbles
all everything an' all
all Everything's going to be all right.
all Everything will be all right.
all Everything will work out (all right).
all fall (all) over oneself (to do sth)
all fall all over so
all fawn (all) over so
all firing on all cylinders
all first of all
all for all I care
all for all I know
all for all intents and purposes
all for all it's worth
all for (all) one's trouble
all for all practical purposes
all for all so's problems
all for all the world
all from all corners of the world
all get down (on all fours)
all get it (all) together

all get so (all) wrong
all Give it all you've got!
all give up (all) hope
all go all out (for so/sth)
all go all the way (with so)
all God's in his heaven; all's right with the world.
all good time was had by all.
all granddaddy of them all
all grow out of (all) proportion
all Hang it all!
all have all one's marbles
all have it (all) over so/sth (in sth)
all have it all together
all hitting on all cylinders
all hold all the aces
all hold all the cards
all hope against (all) hope
all (I) haven't got all day.
all I hope all goes well.
all I was up all night with a sick friend.
all Idleness is the root of all evil.
all If that don't beat all!
all I'm all ears.
all in (all) good conscience
all in all my born days
all in all probability
all in no time (at all)
all is all
all (It) doesn't bother me at all.
all It is all over with so.
all It's (all) Greek to me.
all It's all over but the shouting.
all It's all so needs.
all (It's) no trouble (at all).
all It's written all over one's face.
all It takes all kinds (to make a world).
all (It) won't bother me at all.
all It'll all come out in the wash.
all jack of all trades
all jack of all trades is a master of none.
all jump all over so
all know all the angles
all know where all the bodies are buried
all laugh all the way to the bank
all least of all
all let it all hang out
all Let's not go through all that again.
all Life isn't all beer and skittles.
all (little) new to (all) this
all lose (all) one's marbles
all love of money is the root of all evil.
all make an all-out effort
all Moderation in all things.
all Money is the root of all evil.
all most of all
all not all sth is cracked up to be
all not all there
all not at all
all Not bad (at all).
all not for all the tea in China
all not have all one's marbles
all Of all things!
all on all fours
all once and for all
all one and all
all out of (all) proportion
all play it for all it's worth
all pour (all) over so/sth
all pull all the stops out
all put all one's eggs in one basket

all ride off in all directions
all romp all over so
all run off in all directions
all run on all cylinders
all shame of it (all)!
all shoot so/sth (all) to hell
all slobber (all) over so/sth
all slosh sth (all) over so/sth
all splash sth (all) over so/sth
all spread all over (some place)
all start an all-out effort
all strew sth (all) over sth
all swarm (all) over so/sth
all tell all
all That (all) depends.
all that beats sth all to pieces
all That's all for so.
all That's all she wrote.
all That's all so needs.
all (the) be-all and (the) end-all
all Things will work out (all right).
all till all hours (of the day and night)
all 'Tis better to have loved and lost than never to have loved at all.
all track sth (all) over sth
all turn out (all right)
all until all hours
all walk all over so/sth
all warts and all
all when all is said and done
all Where have you been all my life?
all Will that be all?
all win all the marbles
all winner take all
all with all one's heart (and soul)
all with all the fixin(g)s
all with all the trimmings
all work out (all right)
all (You) can't win them all.
alley go up a blind alley
alley right down so's alley
alley right up so's alley
alley up a blind alley
alligator Later, alligator.
alligator See you later, alligator.
allocate allocate sth to so/sth
allot allot sth to so/sth
allow allow for so/sth
allow Allow me.
allow allow some elbow room
allow allow so/sth in
allow allow so/sth into a place
allow allow so up (from sth)
allow allow sth for sth
allowance make allowance(s) (for so/sth)
alloy alloy sth with sth
allude allude to so/sth
ally ally oneself to so/sth
ally ally (oneself) (with so) (against so/sth)
almighty almighty dollar
almost (almost) jump out of one's skin
almost almost lost it
aloft take sth aloft
alone go it alone
alone He travels fastest who travels alone.
alone Laugh and the world laughs with you; weep and you weep alone.
alone Leave me alone!
alone leave so/sth alone
alone leave so/sth or some creature alone
alone leave well enough alone

alone let alone so/sth
alone let so/sth alone
alone let so/sth or some creature **alone**
alone let well enough alone
alone Man does not live by bread alone.
along (a)long about a certain time
along along in years
along along similar lines
along along these lines
along along those lines
along along with so/sth
along amble along (sth)
along barrel along
along bounce along
along breeze along
along bring so/sth along (to sth)
along bump along
along buzz along
along carry so along (with so)
along carry so along (with sth)
along carry sth along (with so)
along chug along
along coast along
along come along (with so)
along crawl along sth
along creep along sth
along cut along sth
along dawdle along
along dodder along
along drift along
along ease so/sth along
along flow along
along get along
along go along
along help so along
along How is so getting along?
along hurry so/sth along
along (I) have to be moving along.
along (I) have to move along.
along (I) have to run along.
along (I'm) (just) plugging along.
along inch along (sth)
along inch one's way along sth
along inch oneself along sth
along jog along
along lope along
along lumber along
along make one's way along sth
along move along
along muddle along
along nurse so or an animal along
along nurse sth along
along pass sth along (to so)
along play along (with so/sth)
along plod along
along poke along
along pound along sth
along pour along sth
along puff along
along push along
along push so/sth along
along putt along
along roll along
along run along
along sail along (sth)
along saunter along
along scamper along
along scrape along (on sth)
along scurry along
along send so/sth along
along sing along (with so/sth)
along slide along

along slither along
along snake along
along string along (with so)
along string so along
along struggle along under sth
along struggle along (with so/sth)
along sweep along
along tag along (after so)
along take so/sth along
along tear along
along toddle along
along trail (along) (after so/sth)
along trip along
along trot along
along trudge along
along tumble along
along urge so along
along walk along
along work one's way along sth
along zip along
along zoom along
alongside alongside (of) so/sth
alongside draw (up) alongside so/sth
alongside lay alongside sth
alongside lay sth alongside ((of) sth)
alongside lie alongside ((of) so or an animal)
alongside line up alongside so/sth
alongside pull (up) alongside ((of) so/sth)
aloof aloof from so/sth
aloof keep aloof from so/sth
aloof remain aloof from so/sth
aloof stay aloof from so/sth
alpha alpha and omega
alphabet alphabet soup
already All right(y) already!
also also-ran
also They also serve who only stand and wait.
altar bow to the porcelain altar
alter Circumstances alter cases.
alternate alternate between so and so else
alternate alternate with sth
altogether in the altogether
always always chasing rainbows
always bad penny always turns up.
always bread always falls on the buttered side.
always bully is always a coward.
always customer is always right.
always first step is always the hardest.
always grass is always greener on the other side (of the fence).
always It's always darkest just before the dawn.
always Keep a thing seven years and you'll (always) find a use for it.
always latch string is always out.
always Not always.
always Once a priest, always a priest.
always Once a whore, always a whore.
always rich man's joke is always funny.
always unexpected always happens.
always You (always) give up too eas(il)y.
amalgamate amalgamate sth with sth
amalgamate amalgamate with sth
amble amble along (sth)
ambulance ambulance chaser
amend make amends (to so) (for so/sth)
American American as apple pie

American the American dream
amiss take sth amiss
amok run amok
among apportion sth out (among some people)
among browse among sth
among choose among so/sth
among circulate among so/sth
among count so among sth
among decide among so and so else
among distinguish oneself among so
among distribute sth among so/sth
among include so/sth among sth
among intersperse sth among sth
among list so/sth among sth
among live among so
among number so/sth among sth
among put so/sth among so/sth
among rank among sth
among rank so among sth
among rate so/sth among sth
among ration sth out (among so)
among reckon so/sth among sth
among There is honor among thieves.
among work among so/sth
amount amount to much
amount amount to sth
amount amount to the same thing
amount amount (up) to sth
amount bring an amount of money in
amount clock so speeds of some amount
amount come out at an amount
amount come out to an amount
amount don't amount to a bucket of spit
amount down by some amount
amount draw against an amount of money
amount estimate the cost at some amount
amount fall by some amount
amount front so some amount of money
amount get an amount of money for sth
amount get by (on a small amount of money)
amount get sth for an amount of money
amount hit speeds of some amount
amount live on an amount of money
amount lose some amount of time
amount make (an amount of) headway
amount not amount to a hill of beans
amount out an amount of money
amount pull down (an amount of money)
amount put an amount of time in on sth
amount put sth at an amount
amount reach speeds of some amount
amount set so back (some amount of money)
amount shell out (an amount of money)
amount speeds of some amount
amount start so out at an amount of money
amount take an amount of money for sth
amount throw an amount of light on so/sth
amount to the tune of some amount of money
amuck run amok
amuse amuse so with sth
analysis in the final analysis
analysis in the last analysis
anchor lie at anchor
ancient ancient history
and all my eye (and Betty Martin)
and all talk (and no action)
and and all that jazz
and and change
and And how!
and and so forth

and and so on
and and sth to spare
and and that's a fact
and And that's that.
and and the like
and and them
and and then some
and and this and that
and and those
and and what have you
and And you?
and between you (and) me and the bedpost
and big as life (and twice as ugly)
and bigger than life (and twice as ugly)
and break down (and cry)
and bushel and a peck (and some in a gourd)
and Close only counts in horseshoes (and hand grenades).
and Come 'n' get it!
and could fight a circle-saw (and it a-runnin')
and cross one's heart (and hope to die)
and done 'n' did
and East is East and West is West (and never the twain shall meet).
and Every man for himself (and the devil take the hindmost).
and everything an' all
and eye for an eye (and a tooth for a tooth).
and go on (and on) (about so/sth)
and grow sick (and tired) of so/sth
and Hell's bells (and buckets of blood)!
and Here today, (and) gone tomorrow.
and If ifs and ands were pots and pans (there'd be no work for tinkers' hands).
and It's raining pitchforks (and hammer handles).
and Just (you) wait (and see)!
and large as life (and twice as ugly)
and mad enough to chew nails (and spit rivets)
and many (and many)'s the time
and Marry in haste, (and) repent at leisure.
and no ifs, ands, or buts (about it)
and one's (butter and) egg money
and out of the frying pan (and) into the fire
and over (and done) with
and pitch in (and help) (with sth)
and put wear (and tear) on sth
and say sth over (and over (again))
and sick (and tired) of so/sth
and Speak of the devil (and in he walks).
and Talk of the devil (and he is sure to appear).
and think so hung the moon (and stars)
and turn tail (and run)
and (up and) about
and with all one's heart (and soul)
and Ye gods (and little fishes)!
and You (just) wait (and see)!
angel Fools rush in where angels fear to tread.
anger bristle with anger
anger Do not let the sun go down on your anger.
anger express one's anger

anger fire so with anger
anger flame with anger
anger flash with anger
angle angle for sth
angle angle off (to(ward) sth)
angle know all the angles
angry angry enough to chew nails
angry wax angry
animal administer sth to so or an animal
animal curl up with so or an animal
animal cut at so or an animal
animal do away with so or an animal
animal draw (so's) fire (away) from so/sth or an animal
animal feed sth to so or an animal
animal fix an animal
animal get at so or an animal
animal go after so/sth or an animal
animal grouse at so or an animal
animal have a soft spot (in one's heart) for so or an animal
animal have pity on so or an animal
animal head out after so/sth or an animal
animal hide from so or an animal
animal lam into so or an animal
animal lash into so or an animal
animal lay one's hands on so/sth or an animal
animal leave sth for so or an animal
animal match for so/sth or an animal
animal mate with an animal
animal murmur at so or an animal
animal part so or an animal from so or an animal
animal pin so/sth beneath so/sth or an animal
animal put one's hands on so/sth or an animal
animal put sth on so or an animal
animal secure sth against so/sth or an animal
animal set so or an animal on so or an animal
animal slip up on so/sth or an animal
animal snarl at so/sth or an animal
animal spring (up)on so/sth or an animal
animal take it easy on so/sth or an animal
animal terrify so or an animal out of sth
animal train sth on so/sth or an animal
animal walk away with so or an animal
animal weep for so or an animal
animal whale into so or an animal
animal withhold sth from so or an animal
animal worry an animal out of sth
ankle by ankle express
ankle sprain one's ankle
annex annex sth to sth
annex annex to sth
announce announce (one's support) for so/sth
announce announce sth to so
anoint anoint so with sth
anon ever and anon
another another country heard from
another (another) nail in so's or sth's coffin
another another pair of eyes
another dance to another tune
another Don't give it another thought.
another go at one another tooth and nail
another have another guess coming
another have another think coming
another He who fights and runs away, may live to fight another day.
another horse of another color

another It's six of one, half a dozen of another.
another keep sth for another occasion
another leave sth for another occasion
another not give it another thought
another One good turn deserves another.
another one law for the rich and another for the poor
another One man's loss is another man's gain.
another One man's meat is another man's poison.
another One man's trash is another man's treasure.
another One thing leads to another.
another one thing or person after another
another one way or another
another put another way
another sing another tune
another Tell me another (one)!
another to put it another way
another Tomorrow is another day.
another When one door shuts, another opens.
another (Would you) care for another (one)?
another You've got another think coming.
answer answer back (to so)
answer answer for so
answer answer so back
answer answer so's purpose
answer answer the call
answer answer the door
answer answer to so
answer answer to the description of so
answer answer to the name (of) sth
answer not take no for an answer
answer pat answer
answer soft answer turneth away wrath.
ant ants in one's pants
ante raise the ante
ante up the ante
any any fool thing
any Any friend of so('s) (is a friend of mine).
any any number of so/sth
any any old thing
any any port in a storm
any any Tom, Dick, and Harry
any at any cost
any at any rate
any by any means
any by any stretch of the imagination
any cannot see (any) further than the end of one's nose
any Don't give me any of your lip!
any Don't let it go any further.
any Don't take any wooden nickels.
any Eavesdroppers never hear any good of themselves.
any go to any length
any golden key can open any door.
any in any case
any in any event
any in any way, shape, or form
any Is there any truth to sth?
any (It) doesn't bother me any.
any It's an ill wind that blows nobody (any) good.
any (It) won't bother me any.

any Listeners never hear any good of themselves.
any not any hard feelings
any not going to win any beauty contests
any not on any account
any not see any objection (to sth)
any not under any circumstances
any on any account
any rose by any other name would smell as sweet.
any thing you don't want is dear at any price.
any without any strings attached
anybody It's anybody's guess.
anymore not a kid anymore
anymore Not anymore.
anymore (We) don't see you much around here anymore.
anyone Anyone I know?
anyone Don't breathe a word of this to anyone.
anyone little (hard) work never hurt anyone.
anyone not give anyone the time of day
anything Anything new down your way?
anything Anything you say.
anything can't do anything with so/sth
anything Don't do anything I wouldn't do.
anything If anything can go wrong, it will.
anything if anything should happen
anything If there's anything you need, don't hesitate to ask.
anything If you don't make mistakes, you don't make anything.
anything (Is) anything going on?
anything Is there anything else?
anything not able to make anything out of so/sth
anything not for (anything in) the world
anything not have anything to do with so/sth
anything not have anything to do with sth
anything (Will there be) anything else?
anytime Anytime you are ready.
anytime Come back anytime.
apart come apart
apart draw apart (from so/sth)
apart draw sth apart
apart drift apart (from each other)
apart fall apart (at the seams)
apart fly apart
apart grow apart (from so/sth)
apart grow poles apart
apart grow worlds apart
apart hack so/sth apart
apart keep so/sth apart
apart live apart (from so)
apart live worlds apart
apart pick so/sth apart
apart poles apart
apart pull so apart
apart pull so/sth apart
apart rip so/sth apart
apart set so apart from so else
apart set sth apart from sth else
apart stand apart (from so/sth)

apart take so apart
apart take sth apart
apart tear a place apart
apart tear so apart
apart tear sth apart
apart tell people or things apart
apart tell things apart
apart think worlds apart
apart use your head for more than something to keep your ears apart
apart worlds apart
apart yank so/sth apart
ape go ape (over so/sth)
apologize apologize (to so) (for so)
apparel intimate apparel
appeal appeal against sth
appeal appeal (to a court) (for sth)
appeal appeal to so
appear appear as sth
appear appear at some place
appear appear at some time
appear appear before so
appear appear before sth
appear appear for so
appear appear in court
appear appear in sth
appear appear out of nowhere
appear appear to be rooted to the spot
appear appear to so
appear appear to so that...
appear appear under the name of some name
appear appear (up)on sth
appear *naked eye
appear Talk of the devil (and he is sure to appear).
appearance Appearances can be deceiving.
appearance by all appearances
appearance keep up appearances
appearance make an appearance
appearance put in an appearance (at sth)
append append sth (on)to sth
appertain appertain to sth
appetite get up an appetite
appetite have an appetite for sth
appetite lose one's appetite
appetite whet so's appetite
apple American as apple pie
apple apple a day keeps the doctor away.
apple apple of so's eye
apple apple-polisher
apple apples and oranges
apple Big Apple
apple easy as (apple) pie
apple How bout them apples?
apple How do you like them apples?
apple in apple-pie order
apple motherhood and apple pie
apple put sth in apple-pie order
apple rotten apple
apple rotten apple spoils the barrel.
apple sure as God made little green apples
apple upset the apple cart
application make application (to so/sth) (for sth)
apply apply oneself to sth
apply apply sth to sth
apply apply to so/sth

apply apply (to so/sth) (for sth)
apply apply within
appoint appoint so to sth
appoint at the appointed time
appointment make an appointment (with so)
apportion apportion sth out (among some people)
appraise appraise sth at sth
apprentice apprentice so to so
apprise apprise so of sth
approach approach so about so/sth
appropriate appropriate sth for sth
approval on approval
approve approve of so/sth
april April showers bring May flowers.
apron tied to one's mother's apron strings
arbitrate arbitrate between so and so else
arbitrate arbitrate in a dispute
arch arch (oneself) over
arch arch over so/sth
arch arch sth over so/sth
architect Every man is the architect of his own fortune.
are There aren't enough hours in the day.
area gray area
argue argue against so/sth
argue argue back
argue argue for so/sth
argue argue one's way out of sth
argue argue so down
argue argue so into doing sth
argue argue sth down
argue argue sth out
argue argue (with so) (over so/sth)
argue argue with sth
argue arguing for the sake of arguing
argue arguing for the sake of argument
argue (I) can't argue with that.
argument arguing for the sake of argument
argument get into an argument (with so) (about so/sth)
argument have an argument (with so)
arise arise from sth
arm arm in arm
arm arm (so against so/sth) (with sth)
arm babe in arms
arm break one's arm patting oneself on the back
arm busy as a one-armed paperhanger
arm cost an arm and a leg
arm Forewarned is forearmed.
arm give one's right arm (for so/sth)
arm go arm in arm
arm Governments have long arms.
arm have a good arm
arm keep at arm's length from so/sth
arm keep so/sth at arm's length
arm Kings have long arms.
arm lay down one's arms
arm long arm of the law
arm pay an arm and a leg (for sth)
arm put the arm on so
arm receive so with open arms
arm shot in the arm
arm Stretch your arm no further than your sleeve will reach.
arm stroll arm in arm
arm strong-arm tactics

arm take up arms (against so/sth)
arm twist so's arm
arm up in arms
arm walk arm in arm
arm welcome so with open arms
armed armed and dangerous
armed armed to the teeth
armed busy as a one-armed paperhanger
armor chink in one's armor
army army marches on its stomach.
army You and what army?
around all around Robin Hood's barn
around around so/sth
around (a)round the bend
around (a)round the clock
around ask around (about so/sth)
around bang so/sth around
around bash so/sth around
around bat sth around
around beat around the bush
around been around
around big around as a molasses barrel
around blab sth around
around blue around the gills
around boss so around
around bounce sth around (with so)
around bring so around
around bring sth around (to so/sth)
around bring sth crashing down (around one)
around bum around (with so)
around bustle around
around call around (about so/sth)
around carry so around (with oneself)
around carry sth around (with one)
around cast around for so/sth
around center around so/sth
around chase around after so/sth
around chase so/sth around
around circle around (over so/sth)
around circle around so/sth
around clatter around
around close (in) around so/sth
around clown around (with so)
around cluster around so/sth
around cluster so/sth around so/sth
around coil (itself) around so/sth
around collect around so/sth
around come (a)round
around come around (for a visit)
around come around (to doing sth)
around come around (to some place)
around come around (to visit)
around crash around
around crash down (around so/sth)
around crouch around
around crowd around so/sth
around cruise around in sth
around cut around sth
around dilly-dally (around) with so/sth
around distribute sth (all) around
around drape sth around so/sth
around drive so around sth
around drive so around the bend
around drive sth around sth
around drop around (for sth)
around drop around (sometime)
around edge (one's way) around sth
around enough (sth) to go (a)round
around entwine around so/sth
around entwine sth around so/sth

around every time one turns around
around fart around
around faunch around
around feel around (for so/sth)
around ferry so around
around fiddle around (with so)
around fiddle around (with sth)
around fidget around
around find a way around so/sth
around find one's way (around)
around find one's way around (sth)
around fit around sth
around flap around
around flash sth around
around fling so/sth around
around flip around
around float around
around flock around so/sth
around flop around
around flounder around
around fly around
around fool around
around fool (around) with so/sth
around forage (around) (for sth)
around fuss around
around fuss (around) with so/sth
around futz around
around gad around
around gallivant around
around galumph around
around gather around so/sth
around gather so/sth around (oneself)
around gaze around (at so/sth)
around get around
around get (around) to so/sth
around get so around the table
around glance around (some place)
around go around
around go (a)round in circles
around go (a)round the bend
around goof around
around green around the gills
around grope (around) (for so/sth)
around group so/sth around so/sth
around grub around (for so/sth)
around grub around (in sth)
around guide so around sth
around hack around
around hand sth around
around hang around (some place)
around hang around so/sth
around hang around (with so)
around have been around
around have so around (for sth)
around hell around
around hem and haw (around)
around horse around (with so/sth)
around hover around (so/sth)
around huddle around so/sth
around hurl sth around
around jack around
around jack so around
around jerk around
around jerk so around
around jockey around
around jockey sth around
around jostle so around
around juggle so/sth around
around keep so/sth around
around kick some ass (around)
around kick so/sth around
around kick sth around

around kid around (with so)
around klutz around
around knock around
around know one's way around
around lay around
around leave sth (lying) around
around lie around (some place)
around linger around
around live around so/sth
around loaf around
around loiter around
around loll around
around lollygag (around)
around longest way round is the shortest way home.
around look around (at sth)
around look around for so/sth
around look around (in) some place
around lounge around (some place)
around Love makes the world go round.
around lurk around
around mess around
around mill around
around moist around the edges
around mope around
around move around
around move so/sth around
around muddle around
around noodle around
around nose around (sth)
around orbit (around) so/sth
around other way (a)round
around pace around
around pal around (with so)
around pale around the gills
around pass sth around (to so)
around pass the hat (around) (to so)
around piddle around
around play around (with so/sth)
around poke around
around pop around (for a visit)
around prance around
around pry around
around pull around to sth
around pull so/sth around
around push so around
around push so/sth around
around pussyfoot around
around putter around
around putz around
around race around
around rake sth around
around rally around so/sth
around rat around
around rattle around in sth
around revolve around so/sth
around ring around sth
around rock around
around roll around
around romp around
around root around (for sth)
around route so/sth around sth
around rummage around (somewhere) (for sth)
around run around
around run circles around so
around run rings around so
around runaround
around sail around
around scavenge (around) for so/sth
around scout around (for so/sth)
around screw so around

around screw around with so/sth
around scrounge around (for so/sth)
around see around sth
around see so/sth around sth
around See you around.
around send so/sth around
around serve sth around
around shop around (for sth)
around shove so around
around show so around (some place)
around sit around
around skate around
around skirt around so/sth
around sleep around the clock
around sleep around (with so)
around slide around
around slide sth around
around slink around
around slip around
around slop around
around slop sth around
around slosh around (in sth)
around slosh sth around
around slouch around
around sneak around (some place)
around sneak around so/sth
around snoop around (sth)
around spatter sth around
around spaz around
around spin around
around spread so/sth around
around spread sth around
around stagger around
around stand around
around stick around
around stir sth around
around storm around
around stroll around
around strut around
around swarm around so/sth
around swim around
around swing around (to sth)
around swirl around
around swish around
around switch around
around switch (around) (with so/sth)
around switch so/sth around
around take so around
around take sth around
around talk around sth
around tear around (some place)
around thrash around
around throng around so/sth
around throw one's weight around
around throw so/sth around
around throw so's name around
around tinker (around) (with sth)
around tool around (in sth)
around toss so/sth around
around toss sth around
around tout so/sth around
around trace around sth
around traipse around (some place)
around tuck sth around so/sth
around turn around
around turn sth around
around twine around sth
around twist around
around twist so around one's little finger
around twist so's words (around)
around twist sth around so/sth
around waffle around
around wait (around) (for so/sth)

around walk around
around wallow (around) in sth
around waltz around sth
around wave sth around
around (We) don't see you much around here anymore.
around weave around
around What's going on (around here)?
around What(ever) goes around, comes around.
around wheel around
around wheel so/sth around
around whip around
around whip so/sth around
around whirl around
around whirl so/sth around
around whisk so around
around whisper sth around
around wind around
around wind so around one's little finger
around wind sth around sth
around work around so/sth
around work around to so/sth
around wrap around so/sth
around wrap one's car around sth
around wrap so/sth around sth
around wrap sth around so
around wreathe (itself) around so/sth
around wreathe sth around so/sth
around yank so around
around yank so/sth around
around yoke around so's neck
arouse arouse so from sth
arrange arrange for so to do sth
arrange arrange for sth
arrange arrange some music for sth
arrange arrange sth for some time
arrange arrange sth for so/sth
arrange arrange sth with so/sth
arrangement make arrangements for so
arrangement make arrangements to do sth
arrangement make arrangements (with so) (for sth)
arrangement make the arrangements
arrears in arrears
arrest put so under arrest
arrest under arrest
arrive arrive at a decision
arrive arrive back (some place)
arrive arrive in force
arrive arrive in the (very) nick of time
arrive arrive on a wing and a prayer
arrive arrive on the scene
arrive arrive (some place) at some time
arrive arrive (some place) from some other place
arrive arrive (some place) in sth
arrive arrive some place in a body
arrive arrive (somewhere) at the stroke of some time
arrive arrive (somewhere) (up)on the stroke of some time
arrive arrive (up)on the scene (of sth)
arrive have arrived
arrive *in a body
arrive It is better to travel hopefully than to arrive.
arrow straight as an arrow
arrow swift as an arrow
art Art is long and life is short.

art state of the art
art work of art
article genuine article
artist off artist
artist (rip-)off artist
artist take-off artist
as about as exciting as watching (the) paint dry
as accept so as sth
as accept sth as sth
as acknowledge so as sth
as acknowledge sth as sth
as act as one
as act as so
as address so as a specific title or attribute
as adopt so as sth
as adopt sth as sth
as alike as (two) peas in a pod
as American as apple pie
as appear as sth
as as a duck takes to water
as as a (general) rule
as as a last resort
as As a man sows, so shall he reap.
as as a matter of course
as as a matter of fact
as as a result (of sth)
as as a rule
as as a token (of sth)
as as all get out
as as an aside
as as bad as all that
as as far as anyone knows
as as far as it goes
as as far as possible
as as far as so is concerned
as as far as sth is concerned
as as for so/sth
as as good as one's word
as As I live and breathe!
as as I see it
as as I was saying
as as it is
as as it were
as as long as
as as luck would have it
as as one
as as soon as
as as such
as As the twig is bent, so is the tree inclined.
as as usual
as as we speak
as as well
as As you make your bed, so you must lie (up)on it.
as As you sow, so shall you reap.
as awkward as a bull in a china shop
as awkward as a cow on a crutch
as awkward as a cow on roller skates
as bald as a baby's backside
as bald as a coot
as baleful as death
as be so bold as to do sth
as be that as it may
as big around as a molasses barrel
as big as all outdoors
as big as life (and twice as ugly)
as bigger than life (and twice as ugly)
as black as a skillet
as black as one is painted
as black as pitch
as black as the ace of spades

as blind as a bat
as bold as brass
as bright as a button
as bright as a new pin
as broad as a barn door
as brown as a berry
as business as usual
as busy as a beaver (building a new dam)
as busy as a cranberry merchant (at Thanksgiving)
as busy as a fish peddler in Lent
as busy as a hibernating bear
as busy as a one-armed paperhanger
as busy as Grand Central Station
as busy as popcorn on a skillet
as Can't say (a)s I do(, can't say (a)s I don't).
as cast so as sth
as catch-as-catch-can
as charge sth off as sth
as choose so as sth
as clean as a hound's tooth
as clean as a whistle
as clear as a bell
as clear as crystal
as clear as mud
as clear as vodka
as close as two coats of paint
as cocky as the king of spades
as cold as a welldigger's ass (in January)
as cold as a welldigger's feet (in January)
as cold as a witch's tit
as cold as marble
as come across as so/sth (to so)
as come as no surprise
as come on as sth
as comfortable as an old shoe
as common as an old shoe
as common as dirt
as conceited as a barber's cat
as conceive of so/sth as so/sth
as condemn so as sth
as consider so (as) sth
as construe sth as sth
as cool as a cucumber
as count so/sth as sth
as count sth as sth
as crazy as a betsy bug
as crazy as a loon
as crazy as a peach-orchard boar
as crooked as a barrel of fish hooks
as crooked as a dog's hind leg
as cunning as a fox
as cute as a bug's ear
as dead as a dodo
as dead as a doornail
as deaf as a post
as define sth as sth
as denounce so as sth
as depict so as sth
as deputize so as sth
as describe so/sth as sth
as designate so/sth as sth
as devil is not so black as he is painted.
as different as night and day
as disguise so/sth as so/sth
as dismiss sth as sth
as Do as I say, not as I do.
as do as sth

as Do as you would be done by.
as Do unto others as you would have them do unto you.
as double as so/sth
as double in brass (as sth)
as dress so up (as so/sth)
as dress (up) as so/sth
as drunk as a lord
as drunk as a skunk
as dry as a bone
as dry as dust
as dull as dishwater
as dull as ditchwater
as easy as A, B, C
as easy as (apple) pie
as easy as duck soup
as easy as falling off a log
as easy as rolling off a log
as easy as shooting fish in a barrel
as elect so (as) sth
as emerge (from sth) (as sth)
as employ so as sth
as end up (as) (sth)
as engage so as sth
as Enough is as good as a feast.
as envisage so/sth as so/sth
as envision so as so else
as establish so/sth as so/sth
as evaluate so as sth
as even as we speak
as exciting as watching (the) paint dry
as extol so/sth as sth
as fancy so as so/sth
as fat as a pig
as feature so as sth
as figure so as sth
as finger so as so
as fit as a fiddle
as flat as a board
as flat as a pancake
as flop as sth
as free as a bird
as free as (the) air
as fresh as a daisy
as full as a tick
as funny as a barrel of monkeys
as funny as a crutch
as gaudy as a butterfly
as gentle as a lamb
as give as good as one gets
as go as so/sth
as go down (in history) (as so/sth)
as go so far as to say sth
as good as done
as good as gold
as good as new
as graceful as a swan
as green as grass
as groom so as sth
as gruff as a bear
as had (just) as soon do sth
as hail so as sth
as Handsome is as handsome does.
as happy as a clam (at high tide)
as happy as a clam (in butter sauce)
as happy as a lark
as happy as can be
as hard as a rock
as hard as nails
as hard as stone
as have a mind as sharp as a steel trap
as have so pegged as sth
as high as a kite

as high as the sky
as hoarse as a crow
as hold so/sth up as an example
as honor so as sth
as hot as fire
as hot as hell
as hungry as a bear
as hungry as a hunter
as (I) can't say (as) I do.
as (I) can't say (as) I have.
as I'd (just) as leave do sth
as I'd (just) as soon (as) do sth
as identify so as so
as idolize so/sth as sth
as imagine so/sth as so/sth
as impress so as sth
as in the same boat (as so)
as inaugurate so as sth
as innocent as a lamb
as innocent as a newborn babe
as install so as sth
as intend sth as sth
as interpret sth as sth
as issue sth as sth
as (just) as I expected
as know as much about sth as a hog knows about Sunday
as know so as sth
as know so/sth as sth
as label so/sth as sth
as large as life
as light as a feather
as light as air
as likely as not
as list so as sth
as look as if butter wouldn't melt in one's mouth
as look on so as sth
as look (up)on so/sth as sth
as mad as a hatter
as mad as a hornet
as mad as a March hare
as mad as a wet hen
as mad as hell
as make as if to do sth
as make good as sth
as make it to sth; make it as far as sth
as make so bold as to do sth
as mark sth as sth
as masquerade as so/sth
as may as well
as mean sth as sth
as meek as a lamb
as merry as a cricket
as merry as the day is long
as might as well
as miss is as good as a mile.
as move as one
as Moving three times is as bad as a fire.
as naked as a jaybird
as name so as sth
as neat as a pin
as nod is as good as a wink to a blind horse.
as nominate so as sth
as not as young as one used to be
as Nothing is given so freely as advice.
as nutty as a fruitcake
as obstinate as a mule
as offer sth to so (as sth)
as officiate (as sth) (at sth)
as old as Methuselah

as old as the hills
as ordain so (as) sth
as pale as a ghost
as pale as death
as palm so/sth off (on so) (as so/sth)
as pass as so/sth
as pass so/sth off (on so) (as so/sth)
as pass sth off (as sth)
as pass sth off (on so) (as sth)
as patient as Job
as pawn so/sth off (on so) (as so/sth)
as pay as you go
as peg so as sth
as perceive so/sth as sth
as phony as a three-dollar bill
as picture so as so/sth
as plain as a pikestaff
as plain as day
as play sth as sth
as pleased as Punch
as point to sth as sth
as poor as a church mouse
as portray so as so/sth
as portray so/sth as so
as pose as so
as posture as so/sth
as pretty as a picture
as Pretty is as pretty does.
as proud as a peacock
as prove oneself as sth
as pull together (as a team)
as pure as the driven snow
as put so down as sth bad
as put so/sth down as sth
as qualify as sth
as qualify so as sth
as queer as a three-dollar bill
as quick as a flash
as quick as a wink
as quick as (greased) lightning
as quiet as a (church) mouse
as quiet as the grave
as rank as sth
as rank so/sth as sth
as rate so/sth as sth
as read so/sth as sth
as reappoint so as sth
as receive so as so/sth
as reckon so as so/sth
as recognize so as so/sth
as recommend so as sth
as red as a cherry
as red as a poppy
as red as a rose
as red as a ruby
as red as blood
as regard so/sth as so/sth
as register so as sth
as regular as clockwork
as reinstate so as sth
as remember so as sth
as represent so/sth as sth
as reputation (as a sth)
as respect so as sth
as right as rain
as rose by any other name would smell as sweet.
as run as sth
as same as so/sth
as scarce as hen's teeth
as see so as so/sth
as see so as sth
as see sth as sth else

as select so/sth as sth
as sell so/sth as sth
as serve as a guinea pig
as serve as so/sth
as serve as the driving force (behind so/sth)
as set so/sth up as sth
as set sth down as sth
as sharp as a razor
as sharp as a tack
as show so up as sth
as shrug sth off (as sth)
as sick as a dog
as sign on (with so/sth) (as sth)
as silent as the dead
as silent as the grave
as silly as a goose
as skinny as a beanpole
as slick as a whistle
as slippery as an eel
as slow as molasses in January
as sly as a fox
as smooth as glass
as smooth as silk
as snug as a bug in a rug
as so far as anyone knows
as so far as possible
as so far as so is concerned
as so far as sth is concerned
as so long as
as sober as a judge
as soft as a baby's backside
as soft as a baby's bottom
as soft as down
as soft as silk
as soft as velvet
as solid as a rock
as soon as possible
as sound as a barrel
as sound as a bell
as sound as a dollar
as sound as if
as sour as vinegar
as speak as one
as spot so as sth
as stamp so/sth as sth
as star as so/sth
as start as sth
as start off as so/sth
as start out as sth
as start so in (as sth)
as start so out (as sth)
as steady as a rock
as stiff as a poker
as stigmatize so as sth
as still as death
as straight as an arrow
as strike so as sth
as strong as a horse
as strong as a lion
as strong as an ox
as stubborn as a mule
as succeed as sth
as succeed so as sth
as such as...
as such as it is
as sure as eggs is eggs
as sure as fate
as sure as God made little green apples
as sure as hell
as sure as I'm standing here
as Sure as shooting!

as sure as you live
as swear so in (as sth)
as sweet as honey
as swift as an arrow
as swift as lightning
as swift as the wind
as swift as thought
as take so as so
as take so in as sth
as take sth as sth
as target so/sth as sth
as Them as has, gits.
as There ain't no such thing as a free lunch.
as There's no such thing as a free lunch.
as There's none so blind as those who will not see.
as There's none so deaf as those who will not hear.
as thick as a short plank
as thick as pea soup
as thick as thieves
as thick as two short planks
as tight as a drum
as tight as a tick
as tight as Dick's hatband
as tight as Midas's fist
as tough as an old boot
as tough as old (shoe) leather
as tout so/sth as sth
as train so or an animal as sth
as treat so/sth as sth
as true as steel
as try as I may
as try as I might
as Two can play (at) this game (as well as one).
as ugly as a toad
as ugly as sin
as use so/sth as an excuse
as use so/sth as sth
as vain as a peacock
as value so/sth as sth
as visualize so/sth as so/sth
as volunteer as sth
as warm as toast
as weak as a baby
as weak as a kitten
as When in Rome(, do as the Romans do).
as white as a ghost
as white as a sheet
as white as snow
as white as the driven snow
as wind up (as) sth
as wise as an owl
as wise as Solomon
as without (so much as) a (for or) by your leave
as without so much as doing sth
as work as sth
as work out (as sth)
as worship so as sth
as would as soon do sth as look at you
as would (just) as soon do sth
as write so down as sth
as write so/sth off (as a sth)
as Your guess is as good as mine.
as zone sth as sth
ascertain ascertain sth from so/sth
ascribe ascribe sth to so/sth
ashes rise from the ashes

aside (all) joking aside
aside (all) kidding aside
aside as an aside
aside aside from so/sth
aside brush so/sth aside
aside cast so aside
aside cast sth aside
aside draw (oneself) aside
aside draw so aside
aside elbow so aside
aside fling so/sth aside
aside jostle so aside
aside kick so/sth aside
aside lay sth aside
aside leave sth aside
aside look aside
aside motion so aside
aside move aside
aside nudge so/sth aside
aside place sth aside
aside pull so aside
aside push so/sth aside
aside put sth aside
aside set sth aside
aside stand aside
aside step aside (for so)
aside sweep so/sth aside
aside take so aside
aside throw so/sth aside
aside thrust so/sth aside
aside toss so/sth aside
aside turn so aside
aside turn sth aside
aside wave so/sth aside
ask (Are you) sorry you asked?
ask ask about so/sth
ask ask after so
ask ask around (about so/sth)
ask ask for a knuckle sandwich
ask ask for so/sth
ask ask for sth bad or dire
ask ask for the moon
ask ask for trouble
ask Ask me no questions, I'll tell you no lies.
ask Ask no questions and hear no lies.
ask ask so back
ask ask so down
ask ask so for sth
ask ask so in
ask ask so in(to) some place
ask ask so out (for sth)
ask ask so out (to sth)
ask ask so over
ask ask so to sth
ask ask so up
ask ask sth of so/sth
ask asking price
ask Don't ask.
ask Don't ask me.
ask for the asking
ask (I) couldn't ask for more.
ask I couldn't ask you to do that.
ask If there's anything you need, don't hesitate to ask.
ask If you don't see what you want, please ask (for it).
ask (I'm) sorry you asked (that).
ask (It) doesn't hurt to ask.
ask (It) never hurts to ask.
ask Never ask pardon before you are accused.
ask no questions asked

ask one's for the asking
ask Shoot first, ask questions later.
ask Sorry (that) I asked.
ask You asked for it!
ask You'll be sorry you asked.
askance look askance at so/sth
asleep asleep at the switch
asleep fall asleep
asleep sound asleep
aspersions cast aspersions on so
aspire aspire to sth
ass bust ass out of some place
ass bust (one's) ass (to do sth)
ass cold as a welldigger's ass (in January)
ass couldn't hit a bull in the ass with a bass fiddle
ass doesn't know his ass from a hole in the ground
ass doesn't know his ass from his elbow
ass flat on one's ass
ass get off one's ass
ass get one's ass in gear
ass Get your ass over here!
ass have a corncob up one's ass
ass have one's ass in a sling
ass If a toady frog had wings, he wouldn't bump his ass.
ass In a pig's ass!
ass It will be your ass!
ass kick ass
ass kick in the ass
ass kick some ass (around)
ass kiss so's ass
ass pain in the ass
ass sit on one's ass
ass smart ass
ass tits and ass
ass work one's ass off
assail assail so with sth
assassination character assassination
assault assault and battery
assault assault the ear
assent assent to sth
assess assess sth at sth
assign assign so/sth to so/sth
assign assign sth to so
assimilate assimilate so/sth into sth
assimilate assimilate with some people
assist assist in sth
assist assist (so) at sth
assist assist so in sth
assist assist so with so/sth
assistance come to so's assistance
associate associate oneself with so/sth
associate associate so/sth with so/sth
associate associate with so
assume assume a low profile
assume assume liability for sth
assumption labor under an assumption
assure assure so of sth
assure rest assured
astound astound so with sth
astray best-laid plans of mice and men oft(en) go astray.
astray go astray
astray lead so astray
at act young at heart
at aim sth at so/sth
at all at once
at (all) at sea (about sth)
at appear at some place

at appear at some time
at appraise sth at sth
at arrive at a decision
at arrive (some place) at some time
at arrive (somewhere) at the stroke of some time
at asleep at the switch
at assess sth at sth
at assist (so) at sth
at at a dead end
at at a fast clip
at at a good clip
at at a loss (for words)
at at a moment's notice
at at a premium
at at a set time
at at a sitting
at at a snail's gallop
at at a snail's pace
at at a stretch
at at all
at at an early date
at at an end
at at any cost
at at any rate
at at bay
at at best
at at close range
at at cross-purposes
at at death's door
at at ease
at at every turn
at at face value
at at fault
at at first
at at full blast
at at full speed
at at full strength
at at full throttle
at at full tilt
at at great length
at at half-mast
at at half-staff
at at hand
at at hazard
at at home
at at it again
at at its best
at at large
at at last
at at least
at at leisure
at at length
at at liberty
at at loggerheads (with so)
at at (long) last
at at loose ends
at at most
at at night
at at odds (with so)
at at once
at at one fell swoop
at at one's best
at at one's leisure
at at one's wit's end
at at peace
at at play
at at present
at at random
at at regular intervals
at at rest
at at risk
at at sea

at at sixes and sevens
at at some length
at at some time sharp
at at so
at at so's beck and call
at at so's doorstep
at at so's earliest convenience
at at so's mercy
at at so's request
at at so's service
at at stake
at at that rate
at at the appointed time
at at the bottom of the hour
at at the bottom of the ladder
at at the break of dawn
at at the crack of dawn
at at the drop of a hat
at at the eleventh hour
at at the end of nowhere
at at the end of one's rope
at at the end of one's tether
at at the end of the day
at at the expense of so/sth
at at the forefront (of sth)
at at the height of sth
at at the helm (of sth)
at at the last gasp
at at the last minute
at at the latest
at at the mercy of so
at at (the) most
at at the outset
at at the point of doing sth
at at the present time
at at the rear of sth
at at the same time
at at the top of one's game
at at the top of one's lungs
at at the top of one's voice
at at the top of the hour
at at the (very) outside
at at the wheel
at at (the) worst
at at the zenith of sth
at at this juncture
at at this point (in time)
at at this rate
at at this stage (of the game)
at at times
at at will
at at work
at average out (at sth)
at back at it (again)
at back (at so)
at balk at sth
at bang (away) at sth
at bark at so
at bark sth out at so
at bay at sth
at beat at sth
at bite back (at so/sth)
at blanch at sth
at blaze away (at so/sth)
at blink at sth
at blurt sth out (at so)
at boggle at sth
at bridle at so/sth
at bristle at sth
at burn so at the stake
at burn the candle at both ends
at burst at the seams

at busy as a cranberry merchant (at Thanksgiving)
at buy sth at sth
at call at some place
at carp at so (about so/sth)
at carp at so/sth
at cat can look at a king.
at catch so at a bad time
at catch so at sth
at cavil at so
at chafe at sth
at champ at the bit
at charge at so/sth
at Charity begins at home.
at chatter (away) (at so/sth)
at cheat at sth
at check in (at sth)
at chew (away) at sth
at chip (away) at sth
at chomp at the bit
at clock so/sth at sth
at close at hand
at clutch at so/sth
at clutch at straws
at cock a snook at so
at come apart at the seams
at come at so/sth
at Come in and make yourself at home.
at come out at an amount
at come out at so/sth
at compute sth at sth
at concentrate at some place
at concentrate so/sth at sth
at connive at sth (with so)
at crack at so
at crack at sth
at curse at so/sth
at cut at so or an animal
at cut at sth
at cut one's eyes at so/sth
at cut so off at the pass
at dab at sth
at dabble at sth
at dance at so's wedding
at dart a glance at so/sth
at dart out (of sth) (at so/sth)
at demur at sth
at difficult is done at once; the impossible takes a little longer.
at dig at so/sth
at dine at some place
at direct sth at so/sth
at disappointed at so/sth
at disgusted at so/sth
at dock (sth) at some place
at down-at-the-heels
at draw the line (at sth)
at drive at sth
at drowning man will clutch at a straw.
at eat (away) at so
at eat (away) at sth
at end up at sth
at estimate the cost at some amount
at excel at sth
at explain at great length
at exult at sth
at fall apart (at the seams)
at fall asleep at the switch
at fall (down) at sth
at feel at home
at fetch up at some place
at fight back (at so/sth)

at fire away (at so)
at fire (sth) at so/sth
at fire (sth) back (at so/sth)
at first crack at sth
at flash a smile (at so)
at flash sth at so/sth
at fling oneself at so
at fling sth at so/sth
at fly at so/sth
at foam at the mouth
at freak out (at so/sth)
at frown at so/sth
at fume at so
at fuss at so/sth
at gape at so/sth
at gasp at so/sth
at gawk at so/sth
at gaze around (at so/sth)
at gaze at so/sth
at get at so
at get at sth
at get mad (at sth)
at giggle at so/sth
at give so a crack at sth
at give so a whack at sth
at glance at so/sth
at glance back (at so)
at glance down (at sth)
at glare at so/sth
at glower at so/sth
at gnaw (away) at so
at gnaw (away) at so/sth
at go at a fast clip
at go at a good clip
at go at it hammer and tongs
at go at it tooth and nail
at go at one another tooth and nail
at go at so
at go at so/sth
at go at sth
at go at sth like a boy killing snakes
at go on (at so)
at goggle at so/sth
at grab at so/sth
at grasp at so/sth
at grasping at straws
at grin at so/sth
at grind away (at so)
at grind away (at sth)
at gripe at so
at grope at so/sth
at grouse at so or an animal
at grow disgusted at so/sth
at growl at so/sth
at grumble at so
at guess at sth
at guffaw at so/sth
at hack (away) at so/sth
at hammer (away) at so
at hammer (away) at sth
at happy as a clam (at high tide)
at hard at it
at have a go at sth
at have a whack at sth
at Have at it.
at have at so
at have at sth
at have so's best interest(s) at heart
at have sth at one's fingertips
at He puts his pants on one leg at a time.
at He who would climb the ladder must begin at the bottom.

at head so off at the pass
at head so/sth at so/sth
at heave sth at so/sth
at Here's looking at you.
at hint at sth
at hiss at so/sth
at hit at so/sth
at hit back (at so/sth)
at hit out (at so/sth) (in sth)
at hold so/sth at bay
at hold so/sth at sth
at hold the line (at so/sth)
at honk at so/sth
at hoot at so/sth
at hopeless at doing sth
at howl at so/sth
at hurl insults (at so)
at hurl sth at so/sth
at If at first you don't succeed, try, try again.
at ill at ease
at I'm awful at names.
at I'm terrible at names.
at in (at) one ear and out (of) the other
at in at the kill
at in no time (at all)
at in the right place at the right time
at in the wrong place at the wrong time
at (It) doesn't bother me at all.
at (It's) no trouble (at all).
at (It) won't bother me at all.
at jab at so/sth
at jab sth at so/sth
at jaw at so
at jeer at so/sth
at jest at so/sth
at joined at the hip
at jump at so/sth
at jump at sth
at jump at the opportunity (to do sth)
at keep at arm's length from so/sth
at Keep at it!
at keep at so (about sth)
at keep at sth
at keep (going) on at so/sth
at keep so at sth
at keep so/sth at a distance
at keep so/sth at arm's length
at keep so/sth at bay
at keep so young at heart
at kick at so/sth
at kick back (at so/sth)
at kick out (at so/sth)
at knock at sth
at knock away (at sth)
at know at a glance that...
at know where it's at
at know where sth is at
at labor at sth
at land at some place
at land sth at some place
at lash at so/sth
at lash back (at so/sth)
at lash out (at so/sth)
at laugh at so/sth
at laugh away at so/sth
at lay sth at so's door
at lay sth at so's feet
at leap at so/sth
at leap at the chance (to do sth)
at leap at the opportunity (to do sth)

at leave it at that
at leave so at loose ends
at leave so/sth (at) some place
at lecture at so (about sth)
at leer at so
at let so/sth at so/sth
at level sth at so/sth
at lick at sth
at lie at anchor
at lie at death's door
at Life begins at forty.
at lob sth at so/sth
at look around (at sth)
at look askance at so/sth
at look at so cross-eyed
at look at so/sth
at look at the crux of the matter
at look at the heart of the matter
at Look (at) what the cat dragged in!
at look back (at so/sth)
at look daggers at so
at look down (at so/sth)
at look up at so/sth
at lose at sth
at lose one's temper (at so/sth)
at lose sth at sth
at love at first sight
at Lucky at cards, unlucky in love.
at lunge at so/sth
at lurch at so/sth
at mad (at so/sth)
at maintain sth at sth
at make a face (at so)
at make a grab at so/sth
at make a pass at so
at make a pass at sth
at make advances at so
at make eyes at so
at make faces (at so)
at make good (at sth)
at make oneself at home
at make so mad (at so/sth)
at make so sick at heart
at make sth at so
at Make yourself at home.
at Marry in haste, (and) repent at leisure.
at marvel at so/sth
at more so/sth than one can shake a stick at
at move at a fast clip
at move at a good clip
at murmur at so or an animal
at nag at so (about so/sth)
at near at hand
at nibble at sth
at nibble away at sth
at nip at so/sth
at nod at so
at not at all
at Not bad (at all).
at nothing to be sneezed at
at nothing to sneeze at
at officiate (as sth) (at sth)
at ogle (at) so/sth
at old hand at doing sth
at One cannot be in two places at once.
at out at some place
at pale at sth
at panic at sth
at past master at sth
at peck at sth

at peek at so/sth
at peek out of sth (at so/sth)
at peep at so/sth
at peep out (of sth) (at so/sth)
at peer at so/sth
at peer out at so/sth
at peg away (at sth)
at persevere at sth
at pick at so/sth
at pick at sth
at pitch sth at so/sth
at place so/sth at sth
at place sth at a premium
at play at full blast
at play at sth
at play sth at full blast
at plod away at sth
at pluck at so/sth
at plug away (at sth)
at point at so/sth
at point sth at so/sth
at point the finger at so
at poke at so/sth
at poke fun at so/sth
at poke sth at so/sth
at pound away (at so/sth)
at preach at so
at present so (to so) (at sth)
at preside at sth
at prod at so/sth
at puff (away) at sth
at pull at so
at push at so/sth
at put in a hard day at work
at put in an appearance (at sth)
at put one at (one's) ease
at put so/sth at loose ends
at put so/sth at so's disposal
at put sth at a premium
at put sth at an amount
at put sth at so's door
at quail at so/sth
at question so at great length
at rage at so/sth
at rail at so (about sth)
at rant (at so) about so/sth
at rant at so/sth
at rap at sth
at rate sth at sth
at rebel at so/sth
at recoil at the sight (of so/sth)
at recoil at the thought (of so/sth)
at rejoice at sth
at remain at bay
at remain at some place
at retail at sth
at revolted at so/sth
at roar at so/sth
at rub (away) at sth
at run at a fast clip
at run at a good clip
at run at full blast
at run at so/sth
at run off at the mouth
at run out at so/sth
at run sth at full blast
at rush at so/sth
at scoff at so/sth
at scowl at so/sth
at scratch at sth
at scream at so/sth
at scribble away (at sth)

at see the light (at the end of the tunnel)
at sell at sth
at sell sth at sth
at set so's mind at ease (about so/sth)
at set sth at sth
at shot at so
at sick at heart
at sit at sth
at sit at the feet of so
at slash (out) at so
at slave away (at sth)
at sling sth at so/sth
at smart at sth
at smile at so
at smirk at so/sth
at snap at so
at snap at sth
at snap back (at so)
at snarl at so/sth or an animal
at snatch at so/sth
at sneer at so/sth
at sneeze at so
at sneeze at sth
at sniff at so/sth
at snipe at so/sth
at snort at so/sth
at sore (at so)
at speak at great length
at spell so (at sth)
at spit at so/sth
at spring at so/sth
at spring out at so
at squint at so/sth
at squirt sth at so/sth
at stab at so
at stab at so/sth
at stab at sth
at stab sth at so/sth
at stand at sth
at stare at so/sth
at stare out at so/sth
at start so out at an amount of money
at station so at sth
at stay at some place
at stay at sth
at stay young at heart
at steal a glance at so/sth
at stick at sth
at stop at sth
at storm at so/sth
at strain at gnats and swallow camels
at strain at the leash
at strain away (at sth)
at strike at so/sth
at strike back (at so/sth)
at strike out (at so/sth)
at succeed at sth
at swear at so/sth
at swing at so/sth
at take a crack at sth
at take a dig at so
at take a gander (at so/sth)
at take a go at so
at take a go at sth
at take a jab at so
at take a look at so/sth
at take a poke at so
at take a pop at so
at take a potshot at so/sth
at take a punch at so
at take a shot at so/sth
at take a stab at so

at take a stab at sth
at take a swing at so
at take a swipe at so/sth
at take a try at so
at take a try at sth
at take a whack at sth
at take aim at so/sth
at take aim (at so/sth or an animal)
at take digs at so
at take first crack at sth
at take offense (at so/sth)
at take one at one's word
at take so/sth at face value
at take a crack at so
at take turns ((at) doing sth)
at take umbrage at sth
at talk at so
at tap at sth
at tear at so/sth
at The wolf is at the door.
at thing you don't want is dear at any price.
at thrill at so/sth
at throw a glance at so/sth
at throw insults (at so)
at throw money at sth
at throw oneself at so
at throw oneself at so's feet
at throw oneself at the mercy of some authority
at throw sth at so/sth
at throw sth back at so
at throw the book at so
at thrust sth at so/sth
at thumb one's nose at so/sth
at tilt at windmills
at tip the scales at sth
at 'Tis better to have loved and lost than never to have loved at all.
at toss sth at so/sth
at touch at some place
at trade at some place
at travel at a fast clip
at travel at a good clip
at tremble at sth
at try at so
at try at sth
at try one's hand (at sth)
at try one's luck (at sth)
at tug at so/sth
at tug away (at sth)
at turn one's nose up at so/sth
at Two can play (at) this game (as well as one).
at up and at 'em
at value sth at sth
at wait at sth (for so/sth)
at want first crack at sth
at wave at so
at wave back (at so)
at wear away at so/sth
at weigh in (at sth)
at whack at sth
at What are you driving at?
at When poverty comes in at the door, love flies out of the window.
at When the wolf comes in at the door, love creeps out of the window.
at where it's at
at where so is at
at where so's head is at
at whistle at so/sth
at whittle at sth

at will stop at nothing
at win at sth
at win sth at sth
at wince at sth
at wink at so
at wink at sth
at wonder at so/sth
at work at sth
at work away (at sth)
at work out (at sth)
at would as soon do sth as look at you
at yank at so/sth
at yap at so
at yell at so/sth
at yell sth at so/sth
at yell sth out (at so/sth)
at young at heart
ate dog ate my homework.
atone atone for sth
attach attach oneself to so
attach attach oneself to sth
attach attach to so
attach attach to sth
attach attached to so/sth
attach with no strings attached
attach without any strings attached
attack attack in force
attack attack (of an illness)
attack produce an attack (of an illness)
attack suffer an attack (of an illness)
attend attend to so
attendance take attendance
attention bring so/sth to so's attention
attention bring sth to so's attention
attention call attention to so/sth
attention call so's attention to sth
attention call so to attention
attention call sth to so's attention
attention center of attention
attention come to attention
attention come to so's attention
attention direct so's attention to so/sth
attention draw so's attention to so/sth
attention draw sth to so's attention
attention get so's attention
attention grab so's attention
attention grip so's attention
attention hold so's attention
attention pay attention (to so/sth)
attention rivet so's attention
attention snap to (attention)
attention spring to attention
attest attest to sth
attire attire so in sth
attitude cop an attitude
attitude devil-may-care attitude
attitude have a bad attitude
attitude wait-and-see attitude
attract attract so/sth to so/sth else
attribute address so as a specific title or attribute
attribute attribute sth to so/sth
attune attune so/sth to so/sth else
auction auction sth off
auction come up for auction
auction Dutch auction
auction go up for auction
auction put sth up for auction
auction up for auction
audition audition for sth
audition audition so for sth
augur augur well for so/sth
auspices under the auspices of so

authority throw oneself at the mercy of some authority
authority throw oneself on the mercy of some authority
avail avail oneself of sth
avail of no avail
avail to no avail
available make so/sth available to so
avenge avenge oneself (on so/sth) (for sth)
avenue avenue of escape
average above average
average average out (at sth)
average average sth up
average below average
average cut above average
average on average
average on the average
avert avert sth (away) from so/sth
avoid avoid so/sth like the plague
aw (Aw) shucks!
awagging set tongues (a)wagging
awaken awake(n) from sth
awaken awake(n) so from sth
awaken awake(n) so to sth
awaken awake(n) to sth
award award sth (to so) (for sth)
award award sth to so/sth
away apple a day keeps the doctor away.
away avert sth (away) from so/sth
away away from it all
away away from one's desk
away away (from so/sth)
away back away (from so/sth)
away bang (away) at sth
away barter sth away
away blaze away (at so/sth)
away blow away
away blow so away
away blow so/sth away
away boil sth away
away break away (from so)
away break sth away (from sth)
away breeze away
away bring sth away (from sth)
away brush sth away (from sth)
away burn away
away Burn not your house to fright the mouse away.
away burn sth away
away bury so/sth away (some place)
away call so away (from sth)
away carry so away
away carry so/sth away
away chase so/sth (away) from some place
away chatter (away) (at so/sth)
away chew (away) at sth
away chew sth away
away chip away
away chip (away) at sth
away chip sth away (from sth)
away chuck so/sth away
away chuck sth away
away clear sth away
away come away empty-handed
away come away (from so/sth)
away come away with so
away conduct so away (from so/sth)
away Constant dropping wears away a stone.
away cower (away) from so/sth
away creep away
away cringe away from so/sth

away crumble away
away cut sth away (from sth)
away dash away
away dawdle sth away
away deflect sth away from so/sth
away die away
away do away with oneself
away do away with so or an animal
away do away with sth
away Don't stay away so long.
away drag sth away (from sth)
away drain away
away drain sth away (from sth)
away draw away (from so/sth)
away draw some kind of attention away (from so/sth)
away draw (so's) fire (away) from so/sth or an animal
away dream sth away
away drift away (from so)
away drift away (from sth)
away drive away
away drive so or an animal away (from sth or some place)
away drop away
away dwindle away (to sth)
away ease away (from so/sth)
away eat (away) at so
away eat (away) at sth
away eat sth away
away ebb away
away edge away (from so/sth)
away explain sth away
away face away (from so/sth)
away fade away (into sth)
away faint dead away
away fall away (from so/sth)
away fall away toward sth
away far and away the best
away fiddle sth away
away file sth (away)
away file sth away (from sth)
away fire away (at so)
away flake away (from sth)
away fling so/sth away
away flow away
away flush sth away
away fly away
away fold sth away
away frighten so/sth away
away fritter sth away (on so/sth)
away gamble sth away
away get away
away get carried away
away get so/sth away from so/sth
away give so away (to so)
away give so/sth away
away give sth away (to so)
away give the bride away
away give the game away
away glide away (from so/sth)
gnaw gnaw (away) at so
gnaw gnaw (away) at so/sth
away Go away!
away go away empty-handed
away go away (for sth)
away go away with so/sth
away grab so/sth away (from so/sth)
away grind away (at so)
away grind away (at sth)
away grind sth away
away grow away from so
away grow away from sth

away guide so away from so/sth
away guide sth away (from so/sth)
away hack (away) at so/sth
away hammer (away) at so
away hammer (away) at sth
away He who fights and runs away, may live to fight another day.
away head away from so/sth
away heartbeat away from being sth
away hide so/sth away (some place)
away hire so away (from so/sth)
away hurl sth away (from so/sth)
away hurry away
away idle sth away
away incline away (from so/sth)
away jerk sth away (from so/sth or an animal)
away (just) a stone's throw away (from sth)
away keep away (from so/sth)
away keep so/sth away (from so/sth)
away kick so/sth away
away kiss sth away (from sth)
away knock away (at sth)
away laugh away at so/sth
away laugh sth away
away lay so away
away lay sth away (for so)
away laze sth away
away leach away
away leach sth away (from sth)
away lead so/sth (away) (from so/sth)
away loaf sth away
away lock so/sth away
away loiter sth away
away look away (from so/sth)
away look to be a million miles away
away lure so/sth away (from so/sth)
away make away with so/sth
away melt away
away melt sth away
away million miles away
away moon sth away
away motion so away from so/sth
away move away (from so/sth)
away move so/sth away (from so/sth)
away nibble away at sth
away one's home away from home
away one that got away
away pack sth away
away pass away
away peel sth away (from sth)
away peg away (at sth)
away pick sth away
away piddle sth away
away pine away (after so/sth)
away pipe sth away
away pitch sth away
away plane sth away
away plod away at sth
away plug away (at sth)
away pound away (at so/sth)
away prattle (away) about so/sth
away prune sth away
away puff (away) at sth
away pull away from so/sth
away pull so/sth away from so/sth
away purge sth away
away push (oneself) away (from sth)
away push so/sth (away) (from sth)
away put so away
away put sth away
away rattle away

away remain away (from so/sth)
away ride away
away right away
away rip sth away (from so)
away rip sth away (from sth)
away roar away
away roll away
away roll sth away
away rot away
away rub (away) at sth
away rub sth away
away run away (from so/sth)
away run away with so
away run away with sth
away rust away
away sag away (from sth)
away salt sth away
away scamper away
away scare so/sth away (from so/sth)
away scrape away (from sth)
away scratch sth away
away scribble away (at sth)
away scrub sth away
away scuttle away
away seep away
away send away (for sth)
away send so away
away send so/sth away
away shy away (from so/sth)
away sidle away (from so/sth)
away sign sth away
away slave away (at sth)
away sleep sth away
away slink away
away slip away
away slither away
away slope away from sth
away smooth sth away
away snatch so/sth (away) from so/sth
away sneak away (from some place)
away sock sth away
away soft answer turneth away wrath.
away speed away (from so/sth)
away spirit so/sth away (somewhere)
away sponge sth away
away squander sth away
away square so away
away squared away
away squirrel sth away
away stash sth away
away stay away (from so/sth)
away steal away (from so/sth)
away steer away from so/sth
away step away from one's desk
away stone's throw away
away store sth away
away stow away
away stow sth away
away strain away (at sth)
away stray (away) (from sth)
away stretch away (from sth)
away stretch away to some place
away strip sth away (from so/sth)
away sweep so/sth away
away swerve (away) (from so/sth)
away take away from so/sth
away Take it away!
away take so/sth away (from so/sth)
away take so's breath away
away take sth away (from so/sth)
away tear away (from so/sth)
away tear (oneself) away (from so/sth)
away tear sth away (from so/sth)

away throw sth away
away thrust so/sth away from so/sth
away tick away
away toddle away
away toss so/sth away
away tow so/sth away
away trail away
away trickle away
away trifle sth away (on so/sth)
away trim sth away (from sth)
away tuck sth away
away tug away (at sth)
away turn (away) (from so/sth)
away turn (away) or an animal (away) (from sth)
away up and away
away vanish away
away veer (away) (from so/sth)
away walk away from so/sth
away walk away with so or an animal
away walk away with sth
away wander away (from so/sth)
away warn so away from so/sth
away wash away
away wash so/sth away
away wash sth away
away waste away
away waste sth away
away wave so/sth away (from so/sth)
away wean so (away) from sth
away wear away at so/sth
away wear sth away
away wheedle sth away from so
away wheel so/sth away
away When the cat's away, the mice will play.
away while a period of time away (doing sth)
away whip sth away (from so)
away whisk so/sth away
away whittle sth away
away Wild horses couldn't drag so away (from so).
away will sth away
away win so away (from so/sth)
away wink sth away
away wipe sth away
away wish so/sth away
away wither away
away woo so away (from so/sth)
away work away (at sth)
away wrest so/sth (away) from so/sth
away write away
away yammer (away) about so/sth
away yank so/sth away (from so/sth)
away You'll never get away with it.
awe in awe (of so/sth)
awe stand in awe (of so/sth)
awesome totally awesome
awful I'm awful at names.
awful Thanks awfully.
awkward awkward as a bull in a china shop
awkward awkward as a cow on a crutch
awkward awkward as a cow on roller skates
awkward by main strength and awkwardness
awkward main strength and awkwardness
awkward place so in an awkward position
awkward put so in an awkward position

awkwardness by main strength and awkwardness
awkwardness main strength and awkwardness
awol go AWOL
axe axe
axe get axed
axe have an ax(e) to grind
axe old battle-axe
babe babe in arms
babe babe in the woods
babe innocent as a newborn babe
babe Out of the mouths of babes (oft times come gems).
baby babe in arms
baby babe in the woods
baby bald as a baby's backside
baby Don't throw the baby out with the bathwater.
baby innocent as a newborn babe
baby like taking candy from a baby
baby Out of the mouths of babes (oft times come gems).
baby soft as a baby's backside
baby soft as a baby's bottom
baby throw the baby out with the bath(water)
baby weak as a baby
babysit babysit for so
bachelor son of a bachelor
back answer back (to so)
back answer so back
back argue back
back arrive back (some place)
back ask so back
back back and fill
back back and forth
back back at it (again)
back back (at so)
back back away (from so/sth)
back back down (from so/sth)
back back down (on sth)
back back down (sth)
back back East
back back in(to) (the) harness
back back in(to) circulation
back back into so/sth
back back of the beyond
back back off (from so/sth)
back back on one's feet
back back on track
back back oneself into a corner
back back onto so/sth
back back out (of sth)
back back over so/sth
back back (some place)
back back so for sth
back back so/sth into so/sth
back back so/sth off (from sth)
back back so/sth onto so/sth
back back so/sth out (from sth)
back back so/sth out of sth
back back so/sth up to so/sth
back back so up
back back sth up
back back the wrong horse
back back to basics
back back to square one
back back to the drawing board
back back to the salt mines
back back up
back back-order sth
back back-to-back

back beat so/sth back
back behind so's back
back bend back
back bend so/sth back
back bite back (at so/sth)
back blink one's tears back
back bounce back (from sth)
back bounce sth back and forth
back boys in the back room
back break one's arm patting oneself on the back
back break one's back (to do sth)
back break the back of sth
back bring so back out
back bring so back to reality
back bring so or an animal back to life
back bring so/sth back
back bring sth back
back buy sth back (from so)
back call back
back call so back
back call so/sth back
back call sth (back) in
back carry so back (to some time)
back carry sth back
back cast sth back (some place)
back change back (from sth)
back change back ((in)to so/sth)
back change sth back
back check back (on so/sth)
back check back (with so)
back choke sth back
back chop sth back
back come back
back crawl back to so
back crick in one's back
back cut back
back cut sth back
back date back (to so or some time)
back die back
back double back (on so/sth)
back drift back (to so)
back drift back (to so/sth)
back drive back
back drive so back on sth
back drive so back to so
back drive so/sth back
back drop back
back ease back (on sth)
back echo back to so
back fade back (into sth)
back fall back
back feed sth back into sth
back feed sth back to so
back fight back (at so/sth)
back fight (one's way) back (to sth)
back fire (sth) back (at so/sth)
back fire sth back (to so/sth)
back flash back (on so/sth)
back flash back (to so/sth)
back (flat) on one's back
back fling one's head back
back fling so/sth back
back fold back
back fold sth back
back from way back
back get back (to so) (on sth)
back get back to sth
back Get off my back!
back Get off so's back!
back get one's ears pinned back
back get so/sth back
back get so's back up

back give so a pat on the back
back give so/sth back (to so/sth)
back give so the shirt off one's back
back give sth back (to so) (with interest)
back glance back (at so)
back go back
back go behind so's back
back grow back
back gulp sth back
back hand sth back (to so)
back hang back (from so/sth)
back harder than the back of God's head
back hark(en) back to sth
back have a yellow streak down one's back
back have been to hell and back
back have calluses from patting one's own back
back have eyes in the back of one's head
back have one's back to the wall
back have so back
back head back (some place)
back help so back (to sth)
back hit back (at so/sth)
back hold back (on sth)
back hold so back
back hold so/sth or an animal back (from so/sth)
back hold sth back for a rainy day
back hurry back (to so/sth)
back I'll call back later.
back I'll get back to you (on that).
back in the back
back inch back
back juice sth back
back keep off (of) so's back
back keep so back
back keep so/sth back
back keep so/sth or an animal back (from so/sth)
back keep sth in the back of so's mind
back kick back
back kick sth back (to so/sth)
back knock back a drink
back knock one back
back knock so back (an amount of money)
back knock sth back
back know so/sth like the back of one's hand
back laid back
back lash back (at so/sth)
back lead back (to some place)
back lead so/sth back (to so/sth)
back lean back
back lease sth back
back leave sth in the back of so's mind
back Let me get back to you (on that).
back lie back
back like water off a duck's back
back loll back
back look back (at so/sth)
back make one's way back (to so)
back move back (from so/sth)
back move so/sth back (from sth)
back nail so's ears back
back nail sth back
back nurse so back to health
back on horseback
back on so's back
back on the back burner
back pace back and forth

back pass sth back (to so)
back pat so on the back
back pay so back
back pay sth back (to so)
back peel sth back (from sth)
back pin so's ears back
back pin sth back
back pinch sth back
back place sth back
back play sth back (to so)
back plow sth back into sth
back pop back (for sth)
back pour sth back (in(to sth))
back pull back (from so/sth)
back pull so/sth back (from so/sth)
back push so/sth back (from so/sth)
back put one's back (in)to sth
back put so's back up
back put sth back
back put sth in the back of so's mind
back put sth on the back burner
back reach back (in)to sth
back read sth back (to so)
back rear back
back receive so/sth back
back reel back (from sth)
back refer so back to so/sth
back refer sth back to so/sth
back reflect (back) (up)on so/sth
back rein back on so/sth
back remain in the back of so's mind
back report back (on so/sth)
back report back (to so/sth)
back ring back
back ring so back
back roll back
back roll prices back
back roll sth back
back run back
back run sth back
back scratch so's back
back see so back (to sth)
back send so back for sth
back send so/sth back
back Set a beggar on horseback, and he'll ride to the devil.
back set one (back) on one's feet
back set one back on one's heels
back set so back (some amount of money)
back set sth back
back sink back (into sth)
back sit back
back slip back (to sth)
back slip sth back
back smooth sth back
back snap back (after sth)
back snap back (at so)
back snap back (on so/sth)
back snap sth back
back spring back (to some place)
back stab so in the back
back stand back (from so/sth)
back stand (in) back of so/sth
back start back (to some place)
back stay back (from sth)
back stay in the back of so's mind
back step back (from so/sth)
back step back on so/sth
back straw that broke the camel's back
back strike back (at so/sth)
back sway back and forth
back sweep sth back
back switch back (to sth)

back switch sth back (to sth)
back take one back (to some time)
back take sth back
back talk back (to so)
back think back (on so/sth)
back think back (to sth)
back throw so/sth back
back throw sth back
back throw sth back at so
back thrust so/sth back
back tie sth back
back tilt sth back
back toss so/sth back
back toss sth back and forth
back trace so/sth (back) (to so/sth)
back try so back (again)
back turn back (from some place)
back turn back the clock
back turn one's back (on so/sth)
back turn so/sth back
back turn the clock back
back walk back ((to) sth)
back want so/sth back
back wave back (at so)
back wave so back (from sth)
back welcome so/sth back
back whip back (on so)
back win so/sth back (from so/sth)
back wind back
back wire sth back to so
back with both hands tied behind one's back
back with one hand tied behind one's back
back write back to so
back write sth back to so
back yellow streak (down so's back)
back You scratch my back and I'll scratch yours.
backfire backfire on so
backhanded backhanded compliment
backhanded pay so a backhanded compliment
backroom backroom boys
backseat backseat driver
backseat take a backseat (to so/sth)
backside bald as a baby's backside
backside soft as a baby's backside
backwards bend over backwards (to do sth)
backwards fall over backwards (to do sth)
backwards know sth backwards and forwards
backwards know sth forwards and backwards
backwards lean over backwards (to do sth)
backyard in one's (own) backyard
bacon bring home the bacon
bacon language that would fry bacon
bacon save one's bacon
bacon What's shakin' (bacon)?
bad as bad as all that
bad ask for sth bad or dire
bad bad blood (between people)
bad bad egg
bad bad excuse is better than none.
bad bad hair day
bad Bad money drives out good.
bad Bad news travels fast.
bad bad penny
bad bad time

bad bad times
bad bad-mouth so/sth
bad catch so at a bad time
bad come out badly
bad come to a bad end
bad Fire is a good servant but a bad master.
bad go bad
bad go badly with so/sth
bad go from bad to worse
bad good riddance (to bad rubbish)
bad have a bad attitude
bad have a bad case of the simples
bad have a bad effect (on so/sth)
bad have to do sth so bad one can taste it
bad Hope is a good breakfast but a bad supper.
bad in a bad mood
bad in a bad way
bad in bad faith
bad in bad shape
bad in bad sorts
bad in bad taste
bad in bad (with so)
bad (It's) not half bad.
bad leave a bad taste in so's mouth
bad make the best of a bad job
bad Moving three times is as bad as a fire.
bad need so bad one can taste it
bad Not bad (at all).
bad Nothing so bad but (it) might have been worse.
bad off to a bad start
bad put so in a bad mood
bad so bad one can taste it
bad streak of bad luck
bad string of bad luck
bad (That's) too bad.
bad throw good money after bad
bad want so bad one can taste it
badger badger so into sth
badger badger so/sth to death
badly come out badly
badly go badly with so/sth
bag bag and baggage
bag Bag it!
bag bag of bones
bag bag of tricks
bag bag on so
bag bag some rays
bag Bag that!
bag Bag your face!
bag cat is out of the bag
bag check so's bags through (to some place)
bag doggy bag
bag half in the bag
bag in the bag
bag leave so holding the bag
bag let the cat out of the bag
bag mixed bag
bag put the feed bag on
bag put the nose-bag on
bag tie on the nose-bag
bag whole bag of tricks
baggage bag and baggage
bail bail out (of sth)
bail bail so/sth out
bail bail so out of jail
bail bail sth out
bail jump bail
bail out on bail

bail skip bail
bait bait and switch
bait crow bait
bait Fish or cut bait.
bait rise to the bait
bake bake sth from scratch
bake *from scratch
baker baker's dozen
balance balance of power
balance balance out
balance balance sth against sth else
balance balance sth with sth else
balance balance the accounts
balance catch so off balance
balance hang in the balance
balance in the balance
balance strike a balance (between two things)
balance throw so off balance
balances checks and balances
bald bald as a baby's backside
bald bald as a coot
baleful baleful as death
balk balk at sth
ball ball and chain
ball ball is in so's court
ball ball of fire
ball ball so/sth up
ball ball sth up
ball balls of one's feet
ball behind the eight ball
ball break one's balls to do sth
ball break (so's) balls
ball bust (so's) balls
ball carry the ball
ball connect (with the ball)
ball drop the ball
ball end of the ball game
ball get the ball rolling
ball go under the wrecking ball
ball Great balls of fire!
ball have a ball
ball have so behind the eight ball
ball have sth on the ball
ball have the ball in one's court
ball keep one's eye on the ball
ball keep the ball rolling
ball on the ball
ball pitch so a curve(ball)
ball play ball with so
ball play hardball (with so)
ball political football
ball put balls on sth
ball put so behind the eight ball
ball set the ball rolling
ball start the ball rolling
ball That's the way the ball bounces.
ball whole ball of wax
ball (whole) new ball game
balled (all) balled up
ballistic go ballistic
balloon go over like a lead balloon
balloon send up a trial balloon
balloon trial balloon
ballot stuff the ballot box
ballpark ballpark figure
ballpark in the ballpark
ballpark out of the ballpark
bam wham bam thank you ma'am
ban ban so from sth
bananas go bananas
band band together (against so/sth)
band strike up the band

band tight as Dick's hatband
band to beat the band
bandage bandage so/sth up
bandit make out like a bandit
bandwagon climb on the bandwagon
bandwagon hop on the bandwagon
bandwagon jump on the bandwagon
bandwagon on the bandwagon
bandy bandy sth about
bandy bandy with so
bang bang against so/sth
bang bang (away) at sth
bang (bang) dead to rights
bang bang for the buck
bang bang into so/sth
bang bang on so/sth
bang bang one's head against a brick wall
bang bang so/sth around
bang bang so up
bang bang sth against so/sth
bang bang sth in
bang bang sth into so/sth
bang bang sth out
bang bang sth up
bang bang the drum for so/sth
bang get a bang out of so/sth
bang give so a bang
bang go over with a bang
bang start (off) with a bang
banish banish so/sth from some place
bank bank on sth
bank bank sth up (against sth)
bank break the bank
bank can take it to the bank
bank cry all the way to the bank
bank laugh all the way to the bank
banker banker's hours
banker emptier than a banker's heart
banker keep banker's hours
baptism baptism of fire
bar bar none
bar bar so from some place
bar behind bars
bar Katie bar the door
bar no holds barred
bar put so behind bars
bar raise the bar
barber conceited as a barber's cat
bare bare one's soul (to so)
bare bare one's teeth
bare bare sth
bare bare sth to so
bare bare-bones
bare stand there with one's bare face hanging out
barf barf out
barf barf so out
bargain bargain (for so/sth) (with so)
bargain bargain for sth
bargain bargain on sth
bargain bargain (over so/sth) (with so)
bargain bargaining chip
bargain drive a hard bargain
bargain hold one's end of the bargain up
bargain include sth in the bargain
bargain It takes two to make a bargain.
bargain keep one's end of the bargain up
bargain keep one's side of the bargain

bargain live up to one's end of the bargain
bargain more than one bargained for
bargain seal a bargain
bargain seal the bargain
bargain strike a bargain
bargain throw sth into the bargain
barge barge in (on so/sth)
barge barge in(to some place)
barge barge into so/sth
bark bark at so
bark bark sth out at so
bark bark up the wrong tree
bark barking dog never bites.
bark One's bark is worse than one's bite.
bark Why keep a dog and bark yourself?
barn all around Robin Hood's barn
barn broad as a barn door
barn can't hit the (broad) side of a barn
barn hit the (broad) side of a barn
barn raised in a barn
barn Were you born in a barn?
barred no holds barred
barrel barrel along
barrel barrel in(to some place)
barrel barrel of fun
barrel barrel out (of some place)
barrel big around as a molasses barrel
barrel bottom of the barrel
barrel crooked as a barrel of fish hooks
barrel easy as shooting fish in a barrel
barrel funny as a barrel of monkeys
barrel have so over a barrel
barrel let so have it (with both barrels)
barrel like shooting fish in a barrel
barrel loaded to the barrel
barrel lock, stock, and barrel
barrel more fun than a barrel of monkeys
barrel over a barrel
barrel put so over a barrel
barrel rotten apple spoils the barrel.
barrel scrape the bottom of the barrel
barrel sound as a barrel
barrelhead cash on the barrelhead
barter barter for sth
barter barter sth away
barter barter sth for sth else
barter barter sth off
barter barter with so
base base one's opinion on sth
base base sth (up)on so/sth
base get to first base (with so/sth)
base off base
base reach first base (with so/sth)
base steal a base
base touch base (with so)
base way off (base)
bash bash so/sth around
bash bash sth against so/sth
bash bash sth in
bash bash sth up
basics back to basics
basis on a first-name basis (with so)
bask bask in sth
basket basket case
basket can't carry a tune in a bushel basket
basket Don't put all your eggs in one basket.

basket put all one's eggs in one basket
bass couldn't hit a bull in the ass with a bass fiddle
bastards Don't let the bastards wear you down.
bat bat sth around
bat blind as a bat
bat drive so batty
bat go to bat against so
bat go to bat for so
bat have bats in one's belfry
bat like a bat out of hell
bat not bat an eye
bat not bat an eyelid
bat right off the bat
bat straight off the bat
bat without batting an eye
batch ba(t)ch (it)
bated with bated breath
bath take a bath
bathe bathe so/sth in sth
bathroom go to the bathroom
bathroom use the bathroom
bathwater Don't throw the baby out with the bathwater.
bathwater throw the baby out with the bath(water)
batten batten down the hatches
batter batter so/sth up
batter batter sth down
battery assault and battery
batting without batting an eye
battle battle against so/sth
battle battle for sth
battle battle of the bulge
battle battle royal
battle battle sth out
battle battle (with so) (over so/sth)
battle half the battle
battle old battle-axe
battle uphill battle
batty drive so batty
bawl bawl so out
bawl give so a (good) bawling out
bay at bay
bay bay at sth
bay hold so/sth at bay
bay keep so/sth at bay
bay remain at bay
be *absent without leave
be acknowledge so to be right
be *acquainted with so
be *ahead of sth
be *ahead of the game
be *(all) balled up
be *(all) dolled up
be *(all) dressed up
be *(all) het up
be *all over (some place)
be *(all) set (to do sth)
be *all spruced up
be *(all) tuckered out
be appear to be rooted to the spot
be Appearances can be deceiving.
be *arm in arm
be *asleep at the switch
be *at bay
be *attack (of an illness)
be *away from it all
be *away from one's desk
be *back in (the) harness
be *back in(to) circulation
be *back on one's feet

be *back on track
be Be careful.
be be for doing sth
be be for so/sth
be be game
be be given precedence over so/sth
be Be good.
be Be happy to (do sth).
be be in aid of
be Be just before you're generous.
be Be my guest.
be be one's brother's keeper
be be one's own man
be be one's own master
be Be quiet!
be be so bold as to do sth
be be that as it may
be be the last person (to do sth)
be Be there or be square.
be be too
be *becoming on so
be *before so
be Beggars can't be choosers.
be *behind schedule
be *behind the eight ball
be *best of both worlds
be Better be an old man's darling than a young man's slave.
be Better (be) safe than sorry.
be Better be the head of a dog than the tail of a lion.
be *big picture
be *big send-off
be *black mark beside one's name
be Blessed is he who expects nothing, for he shall never be disappointed.
be *bogged down
be Boys will be boys.
be *bright idea
be *bull in a china shop
be *bum steer
be *by the seat of one's pants
be Caesar's wife must be above suspicion.
be *can of worms
be *carte blanche
be *case of sth
be *cheesed off
be Children should be seen and not heard.
be *chilled to the bone
be *clear of sth
be *clear sailing
be *close to so
be come out to be
be Could I be excused?
be couldn't be happier
be cracked up to be sth
be *crux of the matter
be cut out to be sth
be deem it (to be) necessary
be Do as you would be done by.
be Don't be gone (too) long.
be Don't be too sure.
be door must be either shut or open.
be *down to the last bit of money
be *down to the wire
be *down with a disease
be *down (with so)
be *drawn and quartered
be *earful
be Eat, drink, and be merry, for tomorrow we die.

be *(either) feast or famine
be *end in itself
be *even (with so)
be Everything's going to be all right.
be Everything will be all right.
be Everything will be great.
be Everything will be just fine.
be Everything will be okay.
be Evil be to him who evil thinks.
be far be it from me to do sth
be *fire under so
be fit to be tied
be *for the better
be force to be reckoned with
be *fresh start
be *fresh (with so)
be Glory be!
be *hand in hand
be happy as can be
be *hepped (up)
be *home free
be *household name
be (I) could be better.
be (I) could be worse.
be (I) couldn't be better.
be (I) have to be moving along.
be I must be off.
be I wasn't brought up in the woods to be scared by owls.
be (I'd be) happy to (do sth).
be (I'd) better be going.
be If God did not exist, it would be necessary to invent Him.
be If ifs and ands were pots and pans (there'd be no work for tinkers' hands).
be If you can't be good, be careful.
be If you would be well served, serve yourself.
be If you're born to be hanged, then you'll never be drowned.
be I'll be a monkey's uncle!
be (I'll) be right there.
be (I'll) be right with you.
be (I'll) be seeing you.
be *in a bad mood
be *in a bind
be *in a fix
be *in a huff
be *in a lather
be *in a (pretty) pickle
be *in a rut
be *in (a) single file
be *in a (tight) spot
be *in a tizzy
be *in a vicious circle
be *in a world of one's own
be *in an ivory tower
be *in apple-pie order
be *in bad (with so)
be *in Dutch (with so)
be *in earnest
be *in (good) (with so)
be *in hand
be *in harm's way
be *in on sth
be *in on the act
be *in on the ground floor
be *in order
be *in place
be *in plain language
be *in play
be *in power

be *in so's face
be *in so's good graces
be *in so's hair
be *in so's possession
be *in step (with so)
be *in the back of so's mind
be *in the bag
be *in the balance
be *in the best of health
be *in the clear
be *in the fast lane
be *in the groove
be *in the gutter
be *in the (home)stretch
be *in the mainstream (of sth)
be *in the open
be *in the public eye
be *in touch (with so)
be *in tune with the times
be *in writing
be *infested with sth
be *intimate with so
be *involved (with so)
be *involved with sth
be (It) can't be helped.
be (It) couldn't be better.
be (It) couldn't be helped.
be It is better to be born lucky than rich.
be It is easy to be wise after the event.
be (It's) good to be here.
be (It's) nice to be here.
be It's time we should be going.
be It will be your ass!
be It'll be a cold day in hell when sth happens.
be It'll be a long day in January when sth happens.
be (I've) got to be shoving off.
be Judge not, lest ye be judged.
be Judge not, that ye be not judged.
be *keyed up (about sth)
be *king's ransom
be *knee-deep in sth
be *knee-high by the 4th of July
be *law unto oneself
be leave a lot to be desired
be leave so/sth be
be Let bygones be bygones.
be Let it be.
be let so/sth or some creature be
be *like a ton of bricks
be *like death warmed over
be *like stink
be *like the devil
be *like the dickens
be *like the wind
be *load off one's feet
be *load off one's mind
be *long shot
be look to be a million miles away
be *losing streak
be *lot of nerve
be *lot of promise
be *low profile
be *lucky streak
be make sth out to be sth else
be May I be excused?
be meant to be
be *method in one's madness
be might as well be hung for a sheep as (for) a lamb
be *million miles away

be *mixed up in sth
be *mixed up with so else
be Neither a borrower nor a lender be.
be *(neither) hide nor hair
be not all sth is cracked up to be
be not as young as one used to be
be not what sth is cracked up to be
be nothing to be sneezed at
be *of age
be *off base
be *off campus
be *off course
be *off on a sidetrack
be *off (on sth)
be *off on the wrong foot
be *off one's game
be *off one's rocker
be *off the beaten track
be *off the hook
be *off the wagon
be *off (to a flying start)
be *off (to the side) with so
be *off topic
be *off (work)
be old enough to be so's father
be old enough to be so's mother
be *old warhorse
be *on a diet
be *on a first-name basis (with so)
be *on a fool's errand
be *on a pedestal
be *on a power trip
be *on a silver platter
be *on a string
be *on course
be *on its feet
be *on one's toes
be *on one's way ((to) some place)
be *on so's case
be *on so's heels
be *on so's nerves
be *on so's shoulders
be *on the back burner
be *on the bandwagon
be *on the dot
be *on the fence (about sth)
be *on the front burner
be *on the good side of so
be *on the market
be *on the stick
be *on the telephone
be *on the tip of one's tongue
be *on the wrong side of so
be *on track
be One cannot be in two places at once.
be One cannot love and be wise.
be *one up (on so)
be *oneself again
be *onto a good thing
be *onto so
be *onto sth
be *out and about
be *out from sth
be *out in force
be *out in large numbers
be *out in the cold
be *out in the open
be *out of (all) proportion
be *out of context
be *out of control
be *out of debt
be *out of favor (with so)

be *out of gas
be *out of harm's way
be *out of nowhere
be *out of one's depth
be *out of one's mind
be *out of one's skull
be *out of patience
be *out of place
be *out of practice
be *out of sight
be *out of so's hands
be *out (of sth)
be *out of sync
be *out of the closet
be *out of the frying pan (and) into the fire
be *out of the goodness of one's heart
be *out of the way
be *out of the woodwork
be *out on a limb
be *out-of-bounds
be *over a barrel
be *over (and done) with
be *over so's head
be *over the hill
be *over the wall
be *over (with)
be *paper trail
be *past master at sth
be *physical (with so)
be *poles apart
be *possessed by sth
be *possessed of sth
be powers that be
be Promises are like piecrust, made to be broken.
be prove to be sth
be *putty in so's hands
be *raw deal
be *ready (to do sth)
be *rolling in the aisles
be *root of the problem
be *rooted to sth
be *rooted to the spot
be *rough idea (about sth)
be *run for one's money
be *second nature to so
be *set to do sth
be *sewed up
be *shadow of oneself
be *shock of one's life
be *short end of the stick
be *short with so
be *sick at heart
be *sinking feeling
be *slated for sth
be *slave to sth
be *so bad one can taste it
be So be it.
be *soft on so
be So will be with you in a minute.
be *sth to shout about
be *sore (at so)
be *speeds of some amount
be *spit and image of so
be stand up and be counted
be *start
be *stir-crazy
be *strapped for sth
be *stricken with sth
be *taste of one's own medicine
be That'll be the day!
be (the) be-all and (the) end-all

be There will be hell to pay.
be There will be the devil to pay.
be *thick-skinned
be (Things) could be better.
be (Things) could be worse.
be (Things) couldn't be better.
be (Things) might be better.
be *thin-skinned
be *through the mill
be to be on the safe side
be to be safe
be *tongue-lashing
be *too funny for words
be too good to be true
be *too good to be true
be *too much
be *tough on so
be turn out to be so/sth
be *turning point
be *two strikes against one
be *under a spell
be *under arrest
be *under (close) scrutiny
be *under control
be *under fire
be *under one's belt
be *under pressure
be *under so's thumb
be *under so's wing(s)
be *under way
be *under wraps
be *up a blind alley
be *up against sth
be *up against the wall
be *(up and) about
be *up before so
be *up for auction
be *up for reelection
be *up for sale
be *up for sth
be *up in arms
be *up to here (with sth)
be *up to one's knees
be *up to one's neck (in sth)
be *up to speed
be *up to the minute
be *up with so
be *(up)on so
be *upside-down
be *up-to-date
be (Well,) I'll be!
be *well into sth
be What can't be cured must be endured.
be What must be, must be.
be What's done cannot be undone.
be what so/sth is cracked up to be
be What will be, will be.
be Whatever will be, will be.
be What'll it be?
be Where ignorance is bliss, 'tis folly to be wise.
be *wide of the mark
be will be the death of so/sth (yet)
be Will that be all?
be (Will there be) anything else?
be *with child
be *within earshot (of sth)
be *within one's grasp
be *within range
be *worked up (over sth)
be *worst of sth
be would not be caught dead (doing sth)

be would not be seen dead (doing sth)
be wouldn't want to be in so's shoes
be *wrong number
be *wrought up
be Yesterday wouldn't be too soon.
be You'll be sorry you asked.
be Youth must be served.
be You've got to be kidding!
be You've got to be out of your mind!
bead draw a bead on so/sth
bead get a bead on so/sth
beam Beam me up, Scotty!
beam beam so/sth up (to some place)
beam beam up
beam broad in the beam
beam on the beam
beam steam so's beam
bean doesn't know beans (about sth)
bean down to chili and beans
bean full of beans
bean not amount to a hill of beans
bean not know beans (about so/sth)
bean not worth a hill of beans
bean skinny as a beanpole
bean spill the beans
bear bear a grudge (against so)
bear bear a resemblance to so/sth
bear bear down (on so/sth)
bear bear fruit
bear bear in mind that...
bear bear off (of sth)
bear bear one's cross
bear bear so/sth in mind
bear bear so/sth up
bear bear so up
bear bear sth out
bear bear the blame for sth
bear bear the brunt (of sth)
bear bear up (against sth)
bear bear up (under sth)
bear bear (up)on sth
bear bear watching
bear bear with so/sth
bear Beware of Greeks bearing gifts.
bear busy as a hibernating bear
bear grin and bear it
bear gruff as a bear
bear have a bear by the tail
bear have (some) bearing on sth
bear hot enough to burn a polar bear's butt
bear hungry as a bear
bear loaded for bear
bear more than one can bear
beard beard the lion in his den
bearings one's bearings
bearings tell one one's bearings
beat beat a dead horse
beat beat a (hasty) retreat
beat beat a path to so's door
beat beat about the bush
beat beat against so/sth
beat beat around the bush
beat beat at sth
beat beat down (on so/sth)
beat Beat it!
beat beat on so/sth
beat beat one's brains out (to do sth)
beat beat one's gums
beat beat one's head against the wall
beat beat oneself up
beat beat so down
beat beat so into (doing) sth

beat beat so into sth
beat beat so/sth back
beat beat so/sth off
beat beat so/sth out
beat beat so out
beat beat so's brains out
beat beat so to sth
beat beat so to the punch
beat beat so up
beat beat sth down
beat beat sth into so
beat beat sth into sth
beat beat sth up
beat beat the clock
beat beat the drum for so/sth
beat beat the gun
beat beat the hell out of so
beat beat the (natural) stuffing out of so
beat beat the pants off (of) so
beat beat the rap
beat beat the shit out of so
beat beat the socks off (of) so
beat beat the stuffing out of so
beat beat the tar out of so
beat beat up on so
beat browbeat so into sth
beat Don't that (just) beat all!
beat heartbeat away from being sth
beat (I) can't beat that.
beat If that don't beat a pig a-pecking!
beat If that don't beat all!
beat If you can't beat them, join them.
beat in a heartbeat
beat (It) beats me.
beat (It's) got me beat.
beat march to (the beat of) a different drummer
beat off the beaten path
beat off the beaten track
beat one's heart misses a beat
beat one's heart skips a beat
beat pound a beat
beat take a beating
beat That beats everything!
beat that beats sth all to pieces
beat to the beat the band
beat travel off the beaten path
beat without missing a beat
beat (You) can't beat that.
beat You got me beat.
beauties bevy of beauties
beauty Age before beauty.
beauty Beauty is in the eye of the beholder.
beauty Beauty is only skin-deep.
beauty bevy of beauties
beauty (I've) got to go home and get my beauty sleep.
beauty not going to win any beauty contests
beauty thing of beauty is a joy forever.
beaver busy as a beaver (building a new dam)
beaver eager beaver
beaver work like a beaver
beck at so's beck and call
beckon beckon to so
become become of so/sth
become becoming on so
become *end in itself
become *friends with so
become *household name

become *law unto oneself
become look becoming on so
become *one's own worst enemy
become *oneself again
become *past master at sth
become *putty in so's hands
become *rooted to sth
become *rooted to the spot
become *second nature to so
become *shadow of oneself
become *slave to sth
become *stricken with sth
becoming look becoming on so
bed As you make your bed, so you must lie (up)on it.
bed bed down (for sth)
bed bed down some place
bed bed of roses
bed bed (so/sth) down (some place)
bed bed-and-breakfast
bed Early to bed and early to rise, makes a man healthy, wealthy, and wise.
bed fall out of bed
bed get into bed with so
bed get up on the wrong side of bed
bed go to bed
bed hotbed of sth
bed make one's (own) bed
bed make so's bed (up)
bed make the bed (up)
bed on one's deathbed
bed put so to bed
bed put sth to bed
bed put to bed with a shovel
bed send so to bed
bed should have stood in bed
bed sick in bed
bed take to one's bed
bed tumble into bed
bedeck bedeck so/sth with sth
bedfellows Politics makes strange bedfellows.
bedpost between you (and) me and the bedpost
bedsheets know no more about sth than a frog knows about bedsheets
bee bee in one's bonnet
bee birds and the bees
bee put a bee in so's bonnet (about so/sth)
beef beef about so/sth
beef beef sth up
beef Where's the beef?
beeline make a beeline for so/sth
been been around
been been had
been have been around
been have been to hell and back
been (Have you) been keeping busy?
been (Have you) been keeping cool?
been (Have you) been keeping out of trouble?
been (Have you) been okay?
been How (have) you been?
been How's the world (been) treating you?
been (It) hasn't been easy.
been It's been.
been It's been a slice!
been (It's been) good talking to you.
been (I've) been getting by.
been (I've) been keeping cool.

been (I've) been keeping myself busy.
been (I've) been keeping out of trouble.
been (I've) been okay.
been (I've) been there(, done that).
been (I've) been under the weather.
been (I've) never been better.
been Life's been good (to me).
been moment everyone has been waiting for
been Nothing so bad but (it) might have been worse.
been Things haven't been easy.
been What have you been up to?
been Where have you been all my life?
been Where (have) you been hiding (yourself)?
been Where (have) you been keeping yourself?
been You been keeping busy?
been You been keeping cool?
been You been keeping out of trouble?
been You been okay?
been You don't know where it's been.
beer (all) beer and skittles
beer beer up
beer cry in one's beer
beer I've seen better heads on nickel beers.
beer Life isn't all beer and skittles.
beeswax Mind your own beeswax.
beeswax none of so's beeswax
before Age before beauty.
before appear before so
before appear before sth
before Be just before you're generous.
before before long
before before so
before before so's time
before before you can say Jack Robinson
before before you know it
before bend before sth
before bow before so/sth
before bring so before so/sth
before bring sth before so/sth
before Business before pleasure.
before calm before the storm
before cast (one's) pearls before swine
before come before so/sth
before Coming events cast their shadows before.
before count one's chickens before they hatch
before Cowards die many times before their death(s).
before cringe before so/sth
before cross a bridge before one comes to it
before cry before one is hurt
before dangle sth before so
before darkest hour is just before the dawn.
before Don't count your chickens before they are hatched.
before Don't cry before you are hurt.
before Don't put the cart before the horse.
before Fingers were made before forks.
before go before so
before go on before (so)
before grovel before so/sth

before happen before so's time
before haul so (up) before so/sth
before Haven't I seen you somewhere before?
before It's always darkest just before the dawn.
before kneel down (before so/sth)
before lay sth before so
before lie before so/sth
before Look before you leap.
before lull before the storm
before morning after (the night before)
before Never ask pardon before you are accused.
before occur before so's time
before place so/sth before so/sth
before Pride goes before a fall.
before prostrate oneself before so/sth
before put so/sth before so/sth
before put the cart before the horse
before quail before so/sth
before reed before the wind lives on, while mighty oaks do fall.
before send so before so/sth
before set sth before so/sth or some creature
before Sing before breakfast, you'll cry before night.
before stand up before so
before summon so before so/sth
before swim before so's eyes
before take so/sth before so/sth
before think before doing sth
before think twice (before doing sth)
before up before so
before use sth before sth
before We must learn to walk before we can run.
before You have to eat a peck of dirt before you die.
beg beg for so/sth
beg beg of so
beg beg off (on sth)
beg beg sth from so
beg beg sth of so
beg beg sth off
beg beg the question
beg beg to differ (with so)
beg go begging
beg (I) beg your pardon, but...
beg I'll have to beg off.
begets Love begets love.
beggar beggar (all) description
beggar Beggars can't be choosers.
beggar If wishes were horses, then beggars would ride.
beggar Set a beggar on horseback, and he'll ride to the devil.
begin begin an all-out effort
begin begin by doing sth
begin begin to see daylight
begin begin to see the light
begin begin with so/sth
begin beginning of the end
begin Charity begins at home.
begin He that would the daughter win, must with the mother first begin.
begin He who begins many things, finishes but few.
begin He who would climb the ladder must begin at the bottom.
begin Life begins at forty.
beginner beginner's luck

beginning beginning of the end
beguile beguile so into sth
beguile beguile so out of sth
beguile beguile so with sth
begun Well begun is half done.
behalf in behalf of so
behalf in so's behalf
behalf on behalf of so
behalf on so's behalf
behavior on one's best behavior
behavior time off for good behavior
behind behind bars
behind behind closed doors
behind behind schedule
behind behind so's back
behind behind the eight ball
behind behind the scenes
behind behind the times
behind Behind you!
behind burn one's bridges (behind one)
behind close ranks (behind so/sth)
behind come from behind
behind come (up) from behind
behind die behind the wheel
behind dodge behind sth
behind drag behind
behind drag sth behind one
behind driving force (behind so/sth)
behind drop behind (in sth)
behind drop behind (so/sth)
behind fall behind (in sth)
behind fall behind schedule
behind fall behind (so/sth)
behind fall behind (with sth)
behind go behind so's back
behind hang behind (so/sth)
behind hardly dry behind the ears
behind have so behind the eight ball
behind hide behind so/sth
behind hide so/sth behind sth
behind If two ride on a horse, one must ride behind.
behind lag behind in sth
behind lag behind (so/sth)
behind leave so/sth behind
behind lie behind so/sth
behind line so/sth up behind so/sth
behind line so up behind so/sth
behind line up behind so/sth
behind march behind so/sth
behind not dry behind the ears
behind peek out (from behind so/sth)
behind place so/sth behind so/sth
behind power behind the throne
behind put so behind bars
behind put so behind the eight ball
behind put sth behind one
behind put sth behind so/sth
behind remain behind
behind run behind
behind serve as the driving force (behind so/sth)
behind sit behind so/sth
behind slouch behind sth
behind stand behind so/sth
behind stay behind
behind stop behind so/sth
behind trail behind (so/sth)
behind wet behind the ears
behind with both hands tied behind one's back
behind with one hand tied behind one's back

behold Lo and behold!
behold marvel to behold
beholder Beauty is in the eye of the beholder.
behoove behoove one to do sth
behoove it behooves one to do sth
being all things being equal
being bring sth into being
being come into being
being for the time being
being heartbeat away from being sth
being into being
being other things being equal
bejeebers knock the bejeebers out of so/sth
belabor belabor the point
belch belch out
belch belch sth up
belfry have bats in one's belfry
believe believe in so/sth
believe believe it or not
believe Believe nothing of what you hear, and only half of what you see.
believe believe sth of so
believe Believe you me!
believe Do you expect me to believe that?
believe hard to believe
believe I believe so.
believe I believe we've met.
believe I can't believe (that)!
believe I do believe.
believe I don't believe it!
believe (I) don't believe I've had the pleasure.
believe I don't believe this!
believe lead so to believe sth
believe liar is not believed (even) when he tells the truth.
believe make a believer (out) of so
believe make believe that...
believe not believe one's ears
believe not believe one's eyes
believe Seeing is believing.
believe Would you believe!
believe You can't expect me to believe that.
believe You don't expect me to believe that.
believe You('d) better believe it!
believer make a believer (out) of so
bell bell, book, and candle
bell bells and whistles
bell clear as a bell
bell doesn't have enough sense to bell a cat
bell Hell's bells (and buckets of blood)!
bell ring a bell
bell ring the bell
bell saved by the bell
bell sound as a bell
bell with bells on (one's toes)
bellow bellow sth out
belly air one's belly
belly belly out
belly belly up
belly go belly up
belly growing youth has a wolf in his belly.
belly have a yellow belly
belly turn belly up
bellyful have a bellyful
belong belong to so/sth

belong belong under sth
belong To the victors belong the spoils.
below below average
below below par
below below so
below drop below so/sth
below fall below sth
below go below
below hit so below the belt
below lie below so/sth
below marry below oneself
below notch below (so/sth)
below rate so/sth below so/sth else
below rate sth below sth else
below send so below
below sink below so/sth
below sink below sth
below sit below so/sth
below take so below
belt belt a drink down
belt belt so/sth down
belt belt so up
belt belt sth out
belt belt the grape
belt belt up
belt hit so below the belt
belt pull one's belt in (a notch)
belt rust belt
belt sun belt
belt take one's belt in (a notch)
belt tighten one's belt
belt under one's belt
bench on the bench
bench warm the bench
bend above one's bend
bend (a)round the bend
bend bend back
bend bend before sth
bend bend down
bend bend forward
bend bend in
bend bend one's elbow
bend bend over
bend bend so out of shape
bend bend so's ear
bend bend sth out of shape
bend bend the elbow
bend bend the law
bend bend the rules
bend drive so around the bend
bend fender bender
bend go (a)round the bend
bend on bended knee
bended on bended knee
bender fender bender
beneath beneath contempt
beneath beneath one's dignity
beneath beneath so
beneath beneath sth
beneath fall beneath sth
beneath feel it beneath one (to do sth)
beneath marry beneath oneself
beneath pin so/sth beneath so/sth or an animal
beneath sit beneath sth
benefit benefit by sth
benefit benefit from sth
benefit benefit of the doubt
benefit of benefit (to so)
bent As the twig is bent, so is the tree inclined.
bent bent on doing sth

bent bent out of shape
bent hell-bent for leather
bent hell-bent for somewhere or sth
bequeath bequeath sth to so
bereft bereft of so/sth
berry above one's huckleberry
berry brown as a berry
berry busy as a cranberry merchant (at Thanksgiving)
berry give so the raspberry
berserk go berserk
berth give so/sth a wide berth
beset beset so with sth
beside beside oneself (with sth)
beside beside the point
beside beside the question
beside black mark beside one's name
beside pale beside so/sth
beside set sth beside sth
besiege besiege so/sth with sth
besmirch besmirch so/sth with sth
best (all) for the best
best All the best to so.
best at best
best at its best
best at one's best
best best defense is a good offense.
best best is the enemy of the good.
best best of both worlds
best best of so
best best part of sth
best best things come in small packages.
best best things in life are free.
best best-case scenario
best best-laid plans of mice and men oft(en) go astray.
best bring out the best in so
best come off second best
best do one's (level) best
best East, west, home's best.
best enjoy the best of both worlds
best even in the best of times
best (Even) the best of friends must part.
best Everything will work out for the best.
best Experience is the best teacher.
best far and away the best
best Give my best to so.
best give one's best
best give sth one's best shot
best God takes soonest those he loveth best.
best good is the enemy of the best.
best (had) best do sth
best have so's best interest(s) at heart
best have the best of so/sth
best He who laughs last, laughs best.
best Honesty is the best policy.
best hope for the best
best Hunger is the best sauce.
best in one's (own) (best) interest(s)
best in one's Sunday best
best in the best of health
best live in the best of both worlds
best make the best of a bad job
best make the best of sth
best man's best friend
best old poacher makes the best gamekeeper.
best on one's best behavior
best one's best bib and tucker

best one's best shot
best put one's best foot forward
best Revenge is a dish best served cold.
best so's level best
best Sunday best
best (The) best of luck (to so).
best to the best of one's ability
best to the best of one's knowledge
best with the best will in the world
best work out for the best
bestow bestow sth on so
bet bet on so/sth
bet bet one's bottom dollar
bet bet one's life
bet bet so dollars to doughnuts
bet bet sth on so/sth
bet bet the farm
bet bet with so
bet good bet
bet hedge one's bets
bet (I) wouldn't bet on it.
bet I'd bet money (on it).
bet I('ll) bet
bet sure bet
bet You bet!
bet You bet your boots!
bet You bet your (sweet) life!
bet You betcha!
bet You can bet the farm (on so/sth).
betcha You betcha!
betroth betroth so to so
betsy crazy as a betsy bug
betsy Heavens to Betsy!
better all better (now)
better bad excuse is better than none.
better Better be an old man's darling than a young man's slave.
better Better (be) safe than sorry.
better Better be the head of a dog than the tail of a lion.
better Better keep still about it.
better Better late than never.
better better left unsaid
better Better luck next time.
better better of so
better better off (doing sth)
better better off (somewhere)
better Better the devil you know than the devil you don't know.
better build a better mousetrap
better (damn) sight better
better deserve better from so/sth
better Discretion is the better part of valor.
better do so one better
better Example is better than precept.
better for better or for worse
better for the better
better get better
better go on to a better land
better go (so) one better
better Half a loaf is better than none.
better have seen better days
better (I) could be better.
better (I) couldn't be better.
better (I'd) better be going.
better (I'd) better get moving.
better (I'd) better get on my horse.
better (I'd) better hit the road.
better (It) couldn't be better.
better It is better to be born lucky than rich.

better It is better to give than to receive.
better It is better to travel hopefully than to arrive.
better It is better to wear out than to rust out.
better (It's) better than nothing.
better (I've) (got) better things to do.
better (I've) never been better.
better (I've) seen better.
better I've seen better heads on nickel beers.
better know better (than to do sth)
better less said (about sth), the better.
better notch better than (so/sth)
better one's better half
better Prevention is better than cure.
better so much the better
better So had better keep still about it.
better Something is better than nothing.
better sooner the better.
better take a turn for the better
better (Things) could be better.
better (Things) couldn't be better.
better (Things) might be better.
better think better of so/sth
better think better of sth
better 'Tis better to have loved and lost than never to have loved at all.
better Two heads are better than one.
better You make a better door than you do a window.
better You('d) better believe it!
better (You'd) better get moving.
Betty all my eye (and Betty Martin)
between alternate between so and so else
between arbitrate between so and so else
between bad blood (between people)
between between a rock and a hard place
between between jobs
between between life and death
between between projects
between between so and so else
between between sth and sth else
between between the devil and the deep blue sea
between between you (and) me and the bedpost
between between you and me and these four walls
between betwixt and between
between choose between two people or things
between come between so and so else
between come between sth and sth else
between commute between places
between decide between so and so else
between differentiate between so/sth and so/sth else
between discern between so/sth and so/sth else
between discriminate between so and so else or sth and sth else
between distinguish between so/sth and so/sth else
between distribute sth between so
between divide sth between people or things

between divide sth (up) (between so/sth)
between divided between sth
between divvy sth up (between so)
between draw a line between sth and sth else
between draw the line between sth and sth else
between drive a wedge between so and so else
between drive between sth and sth else
between fall between sth and sth else
between fall between two stools
between few and far between
between fluctuate between so and so else
between fluctuate between sth and sth else
between get between so/sth and so/sth else
between go between so/sth and so/sth else
between hedge between keeps friendship green
between hit so (right) between the eyes
between hover between sth and sth else
between in between
between in the interim (between things)
between insert sth between sth and sth else
between interpose so/sth between people or things
between intersperse sth between sth else
between intervene between so and so else
between judge between so/sth and so/sth else
between mediate between so and so else
between migrate between some place and some place else
between oscillate between so/sth and so/sth else
between ply between sth and sth else
between put some distance between so and oneself or sth
between read between the lines
between run between sth and sth else
between sandwich so/sth between people or things
between slip between the cracks
between split sth between (so and so else)
between stand between so/sth and so/sth else
between step between so/sth and so/sth else
between strike a balance (between two things)
between take the bit between the teeth
between tell the difference between so and so else or sth and sth else
between There is a fine line between sth and sth else.
between There is no love lost (between so and so else).
between torn between so and so else
between vacillate between so and so else or sth and sth else
between vary between so and so else
between vary between sth and sth else

between waver between so and so else
between waver between sth and sth else
between wedge so/sth (in) between people or things
between with one's tail between one's legs
betwixt betwixt and between
betwixt There's many a slip 'twixt the cup and the lip.
bevy bevy of beauties
beware Beware of Greeks bearing gifts.
beware beware of so/sth
beware Let the buyer beware.
beyond above and beyond (sth)
beyond back of the beyond
beyond beyond a reasonable doubt
beyond beyond help
beyond beyond me
beyond beyond measure
beyond beyond one's depth
beyond beyond one's ken
beyond beyond one's means
beyond beyond repair
beyond beyond some emotional response
beyond beyond so/sth
beyond beyond the pale
beyond beyond the shadow of a doubt
beyond beyond words
beyond can't see beyond the end of one's nose
beyond go above and beyond one's duty
beyond go above and beyond (sth)
beyond go above and beyond the call of duty
beyond go beyond so/sth
beyond go beyond sth
beyond great beyond
beyond lie beyond so/sth
beyond live beyond one's means
beyond look beyond so/sth
beyond move beyond so/sth
beyond see beyond sth
bias bias so against so/sth
bias on the bias
bib one's best bib and tucker
Bibles swear on a stack of Bibles
bicker bicker (with so) (about so/sth)
bid bid adieu to so/sth
bid bid sth down
bid bid (sth) for sth
bid bid (sth) on sth
bid bid sth up
bid do so's bidding
bidding do so's bidding
bide bide one's time
big big and bold
big Big Apple
big big around as a molasses barrel
big big as all outdoors
big big as life (and twice as ugly)
big big break
big big bucks
big big drink of water
big big eye
big big frog in a small pond
big big hand for sth
big (big) head
big big man on campus
big big moment
big big of so
big big picture

big big send-off
big big with so
big bigger than life (and twice as ugly)
big bigger they are, the harder they fall.
big biggest frog in the puddle
big biggest toad in the puddle
big bite the big one
big buy the big one
big cut a big swath
big go over big (with so)
big have a big mouth
big have bigger fish to fry
big in a big way
big know the big picture
big Like it's such a big deal!
big Little pitchers have big ears.
big make a big deal about sth
big make a (big) stink (about so/sth)
big make it big
big no big deal
big no biggie
big one's eyes are bigger than one's stomach
big play a big part (in sth)
big play in the big leagues
big raise a (big) stink (about so/sth)
big see the big picture
big show so the big picture
big talk big
big too big for one's britches
big What's the (big) idea?
bigger bigger than life (and twice as ugly)
bigger bigger they are, the harder they fall.
bigger have bigger fish to fry
bigger one's eyes are bigger than one's stomach
biggest biggest frog in the puddle
biggest biggest toad in the puddle
biggie no biggie
bike On your bike!
bilk bilk so out of sth
bill bill so for sth
bill clean bill of health
bill Could I have the bill?
bill fill the bill
bill fit the bill
bill foot the bill (for sth)
bill pad the bill
bill phony as a three-dollar bill
bill queer as a three-dollar bill
bill sell so a bill of goods
billow billow out
bind bind so/sth down
bind bind so/sth together
bind bind so/sth up (in sth)
bind bind so/sth up (with sth)
bind bind so over (to so/sth)
bind bind oneself in a bind
bind in a bind
binge binge and purge
binge go on a binge
bird bird in the hand is worth two in the bush.
bird bird's-eye view
bird birds and the bees
bird Birds in their little nests agree.
bird Birds of a feather flock together.
bird early bird
bird early bird catches the worm.
bird eat like a bird
bird Fine feathers make fine birds.

bird for the birds
bird free as a bird
bird in the catbird seat
bird It's an ill bird that fouls its own nest.
bird kill two birds with one stone
bird little bird told me.
bird naked as a jaybird
bird on the bird
birth give birth to so/sth
birthday in one's birthday suit
biscuit son of a sea biscuit
bit bit much
bit bit of the action
bit bit off
bit blow so/sth to bits
bit champ at the bit
bit chomp at the bit
bit do one's bit
bit Every little bit helps.
bit find so a bit off
bit hair of the dog that bit one
bit If it was a snake it woulda bit you.
bit in a little bit
bit little bit (of sth)
bit not a bit
bit one little bit
bit play a bit part
bit quite a bit
bit take the bit between the teeth
bit take the bit in one's teeth
bitch bitch about so/sth
bitch bitch of a so/sth
bitch bitch so off
bitch bitch so/sth up
bitch son of a bitch
bite bite back (at so/sth)
bite bite into sth
bite bite off more than one can chew
bite bite on so
bite bite on sth
bite bite one's nails
bite bite one's tongue
bite bite so's head off
bite bite sth off
bite bite the big one
bite bite the bullet
bite bite the dust
bite bite the hand that feeds one
bite Bite the ice!
bite bite (to eat)
bite Bite your tongue!
bite bitten by the same bug
bite Don't bite off more than you can chew.
bite Don't make two bites of a cherry.
bite grab a bite (to eat)
bite I'll bite.
bite Once bitten, twice shy.
bite One's bark is worse than one's bite.
bite put the bite on so
bite snakebite medicine
bites barking dog never bites.
bitten bitten by the same bug
bitten Once bitten, twice shy.
bitter bitter pill to swallow
bitter Take the bitter with the sweet.
bitter till the bitter end
bitter to the bitter end
bitty itty-bitty
bitty little bitty
blab blab sth around
blab blab sth out

black black as a skillet
black black as one is painted
black black as pitch
black black as the ace of spades
black black eye
black black mark beside one's name
black black out
black black sheep of the family
black black sth out
black black-and-blue
black devil is not so black as he is painted.
black get sth down (in black and white)
black in black and white
black in the black
black pitch black
black pot is calling the kettle black.
black put sth down in black and white
black set sth down in black and white
black That's the pot calling the kettle black.
blackmail blackmail so into doing sth
blame accept the blame for sth
blame bear the blame for sth
blame blame for sth
blame blame so for sth
blame blame sth on so
blame lay the blame (for sth) on so
blame lay the blame on so/sth
blame place the blame on so/sth (for sth)
blame put the blame on so/sth
blame shoulder the blame for sth
blame take the blame (for doing sth)
blanch blanch at sth
blanch blanch with sth
blanche carte blanche
blank blank check
blank blank sth out
blank draw a blank
blank Fill in the blanks.
blank give so a blank check
blank give so a blank look
blank give so a blank stare
blank one's mind went blank
blanket blanket so/sth with sth
blanket born on the wrong side of the blanket
blanket eyes like two burnt holes in a blanket
blanket wet blanket
blast at full blast
blast blast off (for some place)
blast blast sth off sth else
blast have a blast
blast play at full blast
blast play sth at full blast
blast run at full blast
blast run sth at full blast
blaze blaze a trail
blaze blaze away (at so/sth)
blaze blaze down (on so/sth)
blaze blaze up
blaze blaze with sth
blaze Damn it to blue blazes!
blaze Go to blazes!
bleach bleach sth out
bleed bleed for so
bleed bleed from sth
bleed bleed so white
bleed bleed to death
bleed bleeding heart
bleed on the bleeding edge
bleep bleep sth out

blend blend in (with so/sth)
blend blend in(to sth)
blend blend sth into sth else
blend blend sth together (with sth)
bless Bless one's lucky star.
bless Bless one's stars.
bless bless so/sth with sth
bless blessed event
bless Blessed is he who expects nothing, for he shall never be disappointed.
bless blessing in disguise
bless It is more blessed to give than to receive.
bless thankful for small blessings
bless with my blessing
blessing blessing in disguise
blessing with my blessing
blessings thankful for small blessings
blight blight on the land
blimp blimp out
blimp Have a blimp!
blind blind as a bat
blind blind leading the blind
blind blind luck
blind blind so to sth
blind case of the blind leading the blind
blind go up a blind alley
blind In the country of the blind, the one-eyed man is king.
blind like a blind dog in a meat market
blind like stealing acorns from a blind pig
blind Love is blind.
blind Men are blind in their own cause.
blind nod is as good as a wink to a blind horse.
blind rob so blind
blind There's none so blind as those who will not see.
blind turn a blind eye (to so/sth)
blind up a blind alley
blindfolded able to do sth blindfolded
blink blink at sth
blink blink one's tears back
blink on the blink
bliss bliss out
bliss bliss so out
bliss Ignorance is bliss.
bliss Where ignorance is bliss, 'tis folly to be wise.
blitz blitz so out
blitz blitzed out
block block so/sth in some place
block block so up
block block sth off
block block sth out
block block sth up
block chip off the old block
block go on the block
block knock so's block off
block mental block (against sth)
block new kid on the block
block on the block
block put one's head on the block (for so/sth)
block stumbling block
block writer's block
blood bad blood (between people)
blood blood and guts
blood Blood is thicker than water.

blood blood, sweat, and tears
blood Blood will have blood.
blood Blood will tell.
blood bloody but unbowed
blood blue blood
blood cry bloody murder
blood curdle so's blood
blood draw blood
blood flesh and blood
blood fresh blood
blood get so's blood up
blood have so's blood on one's hands
blood Hell's bells (and buckets of blood)!
blood in cold blood
blood in one's blood
blood in the blood
blood make so's blood boil
blood make so's blood run cold
blood out for blood
blood own flesh and blood
blood red as blood
blood scream bloody murder
blood smell blood
blood (some) new blood
blood sweat blood
blood take so's blood pressure
blood taste blood
blood too rich for so's blood
blood yell bloody murder
blood You cannot get blood from a stone.
blood You cannot get blood from a turnip.
bloody bloody but unbowed
bloody cry bloody murder
bloody scream bloody murder
bloody yell bloody murder
bloom come into bloom
bloom come out (in bloom)
bloom in bloom
bloom late bloomer
bloom out (in bloom)
blossom blossom forth
blossom blossom into sth
blossom blossom out
blossom bring sth into blossom
blossom come into blossom
blossom come out (in blossom)
blossom in blossom
blossom out (in blossom)
blot blot on the landscape
blot blot so/sth out
blot blot so out
blot blot sth out
blow blow a bundle (on so)
blow blow a fuse
blow blow away
blow blow hot and cold
blow blow in
blow blow in(to some place) (from some place)
blow blow into sth
blow Blow it out your ear!
blow blow itself out
blow blow off
blow Blow on it!
blow blow on sth
blow blow one's cookies
blow blow one's cool
blow blow one's cork
blow blow one's fuse
blow blow one's groceries

blow blow one's lid
blow blow one's lines
blow blow (one's) lunch
blow blow one's nose
blow blow one's own horn
blow blow one's stack
blow blow one's top
blow blow over
blow blow so a kiss
blow blow so away
blow blow so off
blow blow so/sth away
blow blow so/sth down
blow *blow so/sth off
blow blow so/sth out of the water
blow blow so/sth over
blow blow so/sth to bits
blow blow so/sth to kingdom come
blow blow so/sth to pieces
blow blow so/sth to smithereens
blow blow so/sth up
blow blow so out
blow blow so over
blow blow so's brains out
blow blow so's cover
blow blow so's doors off
blow blow so's mind
blow blow so to sth
blow blow sth
blow blow sth out
blow blow sth to smithereens
blow blow sth up
blow blow sth wide open
blow blow the joint
blow blow the lid off (sth)
blow blow the whistle (on so)
blow blow up
blow blow-by-blow account
blow blow-by-blow description
blow blown (up)
blow come to blows (over so/sth)
blow have a blowout
blow It blows my mind!
blow It's an ill wind that blows nobody (any) good.
blow land a blow
blow *out of (all) proportion
blow see which way the wind is blowing
blown blown (up)
blowout have a blowout
blue between the devil and the deep blue sea
blue black-and-blue
blue blue around the gills
blue blue blood
blue blue collar
blue blues
blue bolt from the blue
blue burn with a low blue flame
blue come out of a clear blue sky
blue come out of the blue
blue cuss a blue streak
blue Damn it to blue blazes!
blue feel blue
blue in a (blue) funk
blue like a bolt from the blue
blue like a bolt out of the blue
blue once in a blue moon
blue screwed, blued, and tattooed
blue talk a blue streak
blue talk until one is blue in the face
blues blues

bluff bluff one's way out (of sth)
bluff bluff so into sth
bluff bluff so out (of sth)
bluff call so's bluff
blurt blurt sth out (at so)
blush at first blush
blush blush with sth
boar crazy as a peach-orchard boar
board aboveboard
board across the board
board back to the drawing board
board board so or an animal out
board board sth up
board board with so
board flat as a board
board go back to the drawing board
board go by the board
board on board
board room and board
boast boast about so/sth
boast nothing to boast about
boat in the same boat (as so)
boat just off the boat
boat miss the boat
boat rock the boat
bob No siree(, Bob)!
bob Yes siree(, Bob)!
bode bode somehow for so/sth
bodily bodily functions
body arrive some place in a body
body bodily functions
body body politic
body enough to keep body and soul together
body go in a body
body in a body
body keep body and soul together
body know where all the bodies are buried
body leave in a body
body Over my dead body!
body put weight on some part of the body
body reach someplace in a body
body travel in a body
body warm body
bog bog down
bog bogged down
boggle boggle at sth
boggle boggle so's mind
boil boil down to sth
boil boil over
boil boil sth away
boil boil sth down
boil boil sth out
boil boil sth up
boil boil with sth
boil bring so to a boil
boil bring sth to a boil
boil come to a boil
boil have a low boiling point
boil make so's blood boil
boil watched pot never boils.
bold be so bold as to do sth
bold big and bold
bold bold as brass
bold Fortune favors the bold.
bold make so bold as to do sth
bollix bollix sth up
bolster bolster so up
bolster bolster sth up
bolt bolt from the blue
bolt bolt out (of some place)
bolt bolt sth down

bolt get down to the nuts and bolts
bolt like a bolt from the blue
bolt like a bolt out of the blue
bolt make a bolt for so/sth
bolt nuts and bolts
bolt Shut the stable door after the horse has bolted.
bolt sit bolt upright
bomb bomb out (of sth)
bomb bomb so out
bomb bomb sth out
bomb drop a bomb(shell)
bomb explode a bombshell
bombard bombard so/sth with sth
bombard bombard so with questions
bombshell drop a bomb(shell)
bombshell explode a bombshell
bond one's word is one's bond
bone (all) skin and bones
bone bag of bones
bone bare-bones
bone bone of contention
bone bone up (on sth)
bone chilled to the bone
bone crazy bone
bone cut so to the bone
bone cut sth to the bone
bone dry as a bone
bone feel sth in one's bones
bone funny bone
bone Hard words break no bones.
bone have a bone to pick (with so)
bone know sth in one's bones
bone Make no bones about it.
bone nothing but skin and bones
bone pull a boner
bone Sticks and stones may break my bones, but words will never hurt me.
bone work one's fingers to the bone
boner pull a boner
bonkers drive so bonkers
bonnet bee in one's bonnet
bonnet put a bee in so's bonnet (about so/sth)
boo boo so off the stage
boo can't say boo to a goose
booby booby prize
boogie boogie down (to somewhere)
book bell, book, and candle
book book (on) out
book book so on sth
book book so through (to some place)
book book sth up
book by the book
book close the books on so/sth
book coffee-table book
book cook the books
book crack a book
book cuddle up with a (good) book
book curl up (with a (good) book)
book do sth by the book
book Don't judge a book by its cover.
book go by the book
book Good Book
book have one's name inscribed in the book of life
book have one's nose in a book
book hit the books
book in one's book
book (like) an open book
book make book on sth
book Not in my book.
book on the books

book one for the (record) books
book play by the book
book pound the books
book read so like a book
book run sth by the book
book sing from the same hymnbook
book take a leaf out of so's book
book take a page from so's book
book throw the book at so
book use every trick in the book
book wrote the book on sth
book You can't tell a book by its cover.
boom boom out
boom boom sth out
boom lower the boom on so
boondocks camp in the boondocks
boondocks in the boondocks
boondocks live in the boondocks
boondocks stay in the boondocks
boonies camp in the boonies
boonies in the boonies
boost boost so up
boot boot
boot boot so or an animal out
boot boot sth up
boot boot up
boot couldn't pour water out of a boot (if there was instructions on the heel)
boot die in one's boots
boot die with one's boots on
boot quake in one's boots
boot shake in one's boots
boot to boot
boot tough as an old boot
boot You bet your boots!
bootstraps pull oneself up by one's (own) bootstraps
booze booze it up
booze booze up
booze hit the booze
border border (up)on sth
borderline on the borderline
bore bore so stiff
bore bore so to death
bore bore so to tears
bore bore the pants off of so
bore bore through so
bore bore through sth
bore bored silly
bore bored to distraction
bore die of boredom
boredom die of boredom
born born and bred
born born and raised
born born on the wrong side of the blanket
born born out of wedlock
born born with a silver spoon in one's mouth
born If you're born to be hanged, then you'll never be drowned.
born in all my born days
born innocent as a newborn babe
born It is better to be born lucky than rich.
born not born yesterday
born Were you born in a barn?
borrow borrow sth
borrow borrow sth from so
borrow borrow trouble
borrow live on borrowed time
borrow Neither a borrower nor a lender be.

bosom bosom buddy
bosom bosom pal
bosom unbosom oneself to so
boss boss so around
botch botch sth up
both best of both worlds
both both sheets in the wind
both burn the candle at both ends
both can't find one's butt with both hands (in broad daylight)
both cut both ways
both dive in with both feet
both enjoy the best of both worlds
both foot in both camps
both have it both ways
both jump in with both feet
both land (up)on both feet
both let so have it (with both barrels)
both live in the best of both worlds
both make (both) ends meet
both play both ends (against the middle)
both with both hands tied behind one's back
bother bother about sth
bother bother one's (pretty little) head about so/sth
bother bother so with so/sth
bother bother with so/sth
bother Don't bother.
bother Don't bother me!
bother go to the bother (of doing sth)
bother hot and bothered
bother (It) doesn't bother me any.
bother (It) doesn't bother me at all.
bother (It) don't bother me none.
bother (It) won't bother me any.
bother (It) won't bother me at all.
bottle bottle
bottle bottle sth up
bottle chief cook and bottle washer
bottle cork high and bottle deep
bottle crack a bottle open
bottle hit the bottle
bottle You cannot put new wine in old bottles.
bottom at the bottom of the hour
bottom at the bottom of the ladder
bottom bet one's bottom dollar
bottom bottom fell out (of sth)
bottom bottom line
bottom bottom of the barrel
bottom bottom of the heap
bottom bottom out
bottom Bottoms up!
bottom Every tub must stand on its own bottom.
bottom from the bottom of one's heart
bottom from top to bottom
bottom get to the bottom of sth
bottom He who would climb the ladder must begin at the bottom.
bottom hit bottom
bottom hit (rock) bottom
bottom knock the bottom out (of sth)
bottom learn sth from the bottom up
bottom Let every tub stand on its own bottom.
bottom on the bottom rung (of the ladder)
bottom reach (rock) bottom
bottom (rock) bottom

bottom scrape the bottom of the barrel
bottom soft as a baby's bottom
bounce bounce along
bounce bounce back (from sth)
bounce bounce for sth
bounce bounce off ((of) sth)
bounce bounce out (of sth)
bounce bounce sth around (with so)
bounce bounce sth back and forth
bounce bounce sth off (of) so/sth
bounce bounce up and down
bounce That's the way the ball bounces.
bound all oak and iron bound
bound bound and determined
bound bound for somewhere
bound bound hand and foot
bound bound to do sth
bound bound up with so/sth
bound by leaps and bounds
bound duty bound (to do sth)
bound go out-of-bounds
bound increase by leaps and bounds
bound keep (so/sth) within bounds
bound out-of-bounds
bound within bounds
bout How bout them apples?
bow bloody but unbowed
bow bow and scrape
bow bow before so/sth
bow bow down (to so/sth)
bow bow out (of some place)
bow bow out (of sth)
bow bow to so's demands
bow bow to the porcelain altar
bow take a bow
bowel Don't get your bowels in an uproar!
bowel evacuate one's bowels
bowel get one's bowels in an uproar
bowl bowl so over
bowl bowl up
bowl Life is just a bowl of cherries.
box box so in
box box so/sth in
box box so up
box box sth up
box boxed in
box boxed on the table
box boxed (up)
box go home in a box
box open Pandora's box
box stuff the ballot box
box think inside the box
box think outside the box
boy All work and no play makes Jack a dull boy.
boy backroom boys
boy Boy howdy!
boy boys in the back room
boy Boys will be boys.
boy fair-haired boy
boy go at sth like a boy killing snakes
boy good old boy
boy How's my boy?
boy How's the boy?
boy Oh, boy.
boy separate the men from the boys
boy That's my boy.
boy whipping boy
brace brace oneself for sth
brace brace so/sth up

brace brace up
brag brag about so/sth
brain ain't got the brains God gave a
squirrel
brain beat one's brains out (to do sth)
brain beat so's brains out
brain blow so's brains out
brain brain so
brain have one's brain on a leash
brain have so/sth on the brain
brain idle brain is the devil's workshop.
brain pick so's brain(s)
brain rack one's brain(s)
brainwash brainwash so with sth
brake hit the brakes
brake jam the brakes on
brake put the brakes on so
brake put the brakes on sth
brake slam the brakes on
branch branch off (from sth)
branch branch out (from sth)
branch branch out (into sth)
branch hold out the olive branch
brand (brand) spanking new
brass bold as brass
brass brass so off
brass double in brass (as sth)
brass get down to brass tacks
brass top brass
brave brave sth out
brave Fortune favors the brave.
brave None but the brave deserve the
fair.
brave put on a (brave) front
brave put up a (brave) front
breach step in(to the breach)
bread bread always falls on the
buttered side.
bread bread and water
bread Bread is the staff of life.
bread bread-and-butter letter
bread break bread with so
bread Cast one's bread upon the waters.
bread greatest thing since sliced bread
bread know which side one's bread is
buttered on
bread Man does not live by bread
alone.
bread so's bread and butter
breadth by a hair('s breadth)
breadth come within a hair('s breadth)
of so/sth
breadth within a hair('s breadth) of sth
break all hell broke loose
break at the break of dawn
break big break
break break
break break a code
break break a habit
break break a law
break Break a leg!
break break a record
break break a story
break break against sth
break break away (from so)
break break bread with so
break break camp
break break down
break break even
break break for sth
break break free (from so)
break break ground (for sth)
break break in (on so)

break break in (on sth)
break break into a gallop
break break into sth
break break in(to sth or some place)
break break in(to) tears
break Break it up!
break break loose (from so)
break break new ground
break break off (from sth)
break break off (with so)
break break one's arm patting oneself
on the back
break break one's back (to do sth)
break break one's balls to do sth
break break one's habit
break break one's neck (to do sth)
break break one's stride
break break one's word
break break out
break break over sth
break break silence
break break so down
break break so in
break break so/sth of sth
break break (so's) balls
break break so's fall
break break so's heart
break break so's stones
break break so up
break break sth away (from sth)
break break sth down
break break sth free (from sth)
break break sth in
break break sth loose from sth
break break sth off (of) sth
break break sth on sth
break break sth out (of sth)
break break sth to pieces
break break sth to so
break break sth up
break break sth off
break break the back of sth
break break the bank
break break the habit
break break the ice
break break the law
break break the news (to so)
break break the silence
break break the spell
break break through (sth)
break break through (to so/sth)
break break up
break break (up) (into sth)
break break wind
break break with so
break breaking and entering
break breaking point
break broken dreams
break broken reed
break cut so a break
break dead broke
break die of a broken heart
break even break
break flat broke
break Gimme a break!
break Give me a break!
break go broke
break go for broke
break Hard words break no bones.
break Ignorance (of the law) is no
excuse (for breaking it).
break lucky break
break make a break for so/sth

break make or break so
break (nervous) breakdown
break nice break
break Promises are like piecrust, made
to be broken.
break sound like a broken record
break Sticks and stones may break my
bones, but words will never hurt me.
break straw that broke the camel's
back
break take a break
break take one's break
break tough break
break You cannot make an omelet
without breaking eggs.
breakdown (nervous) breakdown
breakfast bed-and-breakfast
breakfast from hell to breakfast
breakfast have so for breakfast
breakfast Hope is a good breakfast
but a bad supper.
breakfast shoot one's breakfast
breakfast Sing before breakfast, you'll
cry before night.
breakfast will eat so for breakfast
breast Hope springs eternal (in the
human breast).
breast make a clean breast of sth (to
so)
breath (all) in one breath
breath breath of fresh air
breath catch one's breath
breath curse so/sth under one's breath
breath curse under one's breath
breath Don't hold your breath.
breath Don't waste your breath.
breath gasp for breath
breath hold one's breath
breath I don't have time to catch my
breath.
breath in the same breath
breath mutter sth under one's breath
breath out of breath
breath save one's breath
breath say sth under one's breath
breath take so's breath away
breath time to catch one's breath
breath under one's breath
breath waste one's breath
breath with bated breath
breath with every (other) breath
breathe able to breathe (easily) again
breathe able to breathe (freely) again
breathe As I live and breathe!
breathe breathe a sigh of relief
breathe breathe down so's neck
breathe breathe easy
breathe breathe in
breathe breathe into sth
breathe breathe one's last
breathe breathe out
breathe breathe sth in
breathe breathe sth into sth
breathe breathe sth (of sth) (to so)
breathe breathe sth out
breathe breathe (up)on so/sth
breathe Don't breathe a word of this
to anyone.
breathe hardly have time to breathe
breathe I don't have time to breathe.
breathe (I) won't breathe a word (of
it).

breathe not breathe a word (about so/sth)
breathe not breathe a word of it
breathe scarcely have time to breathe
bred born and bred
breed born and bred
breed Breeding will tell.
breed Familiarity breeds contempt.
breed Like breeds like.
breeze breeze along
breeze breeze away
breeze breeze in (from some place)
breeze breeze in(to some place)
breeze breeze off
breeze breeze out (of some place)
breeze breeze through (sth)
breeze bright and breezy
breeze fan the breeze
breeze shoot the breeze
breezy bright and breezy
brevity Brevity is the soul of wit.
brew brew a plot
brew brew sth up
brew brew up
brew storm is brewing.
brew suck (some) brew
brew There is trouble brewing.
brew Trouble is brewing.
bribe bribe so into doing sth
brick bang one's head against a brick wall
brick brick sth up
brick bricks and mortar
brick brick(s)-and-mortar
brick built like a brick outhouse
brick drop a brick
brick fall like a ton of bricks
brick few bricks short of a load
brick hit like a ton of bricks
brick hit so like a ton of bricks
brick hit the bricks
brick knock one's head (up) against a brick wall
brick like a ton of bricks
brick one brick shy of a load
brick run one's head against a brick wall
brick three bricks shy of a load
brick two bricks shy of a load
brick You cannot make bricks without straw.
bride give the bride away
bride Happy is the bride that the sun shines on.
bridge bridge over sth
bridge bridge the gap
bridge burn one's bridges (behind one)
bridge burn one's bridges in front of one
bridge cross a bridge before one comes to it
bridge cross that bridge when one comes to it
bridge water under the bridge
bridle bridle at so/sth
brief Brevity is the soul of wit.
brief brief so about so/sth
brief hold no brief for so/sth
brief in brief
bright bright and breezy
bright bright and early
bright bright as a button
bright bright as a new pin
bright bright idea
bright brighten up

bright bright-eyed and bushy-tailed
bright look on the bright side
bright on the bright side
bright One's future looks bright.
brim brim over (with sth)
brim brim with sth
brim brimming with sth
brim filled to the brim
bring April showers bring May flowers.
bring bring a charge against so/sth
bring bring a dog to heel
bring bring a verdict in
bring bring an amount of money in
bring bring down the curtain (on sth)
bring bring home the bacon
bring bring one out of one's shell
bring bring one to one's feet
bring bring one to one's senses
bring bring one to oneself
bring bring out the best in so
bring bring so around
bring bring so back out
bring bring so back to reality
bring bring so before so/sth
bring bring so down
bring bring so in (on sth)
bring bring so into the world
bring bring so on
bring bring so or an animal back to life
bring bring so/sth along (to sth)
bring bring so/sth back
bring bring so/sth forth
bring bring so/sth forward
bring bring so/sth in
bring bring so/sth into action
bring bring so/sth into contact with so/sth
bring bring so/sth into disrepute
bring bring so/sth into line (with so/sth)
bring bring so/sth into prominence
bring bring so/sth in(to) some place
bring bring so/sth into view
bring bring so/sth out
bring bring so/sth to a halt
bring bring so/sth to life
bring bring so/sth to light
bring bring so/sth to so's attention
bring bring so/sth to trial
bring bring so/sth under control
bring bring so/sth under one's control
bring bring so/sth under so/sth
bring bring so/sth up
bring bring so/sth up-to-date
bring bring so/sth within range (of so/sth)
bring bring so out of the closet
bring bring so out (on sth)
bring bring so over from some place
bring bring so over ((to) some place)
bring bring so over to sth
bring bring so through sth
bring bring so to
bring bring so together
bring bring so up for sth
bring bring so up on sth
bring bring so up sharply
bring bring so up short
bring bring so up to speed on so/sth
bring bring so up-to-date (on so/sth)
bring bring sth about
bring bring sth all together
bring bring sth around (to so/sth)
bring bring sth away (from sth)
bring bring sth back
bring bring sth before so/sth

bring bring sth crashing down (around one)
bring bring sth down
bring bring sth home to so
bring bring sth into being
bring bring sth into blossom
bring bring sth into focus
bring bring sth into play
bring bring sth into question
bring bring sth into service
bring bring sth off
bring bring sth on
bring bring sth out
bring bring sth to a boil
bring bring sth to a climax
bring bring sth to a close
bring bring sth to a dead end
bring bring sth to a head
bring bring sth to a standstill
bring bring sth to a successful conclusion
bring bring sth to an end
bring bring sth to fruition
bring bring sth to its feet
bring bring sth to light
bring bring sth to mind
bring bring sth to rest
bring bring sth to so's aid
bring bring sth to so's attention
bring bring sth to the fore
bring bring sth together
bring bring sth up
bring bring sth (up)on oneself
bring bring sth with
bring bring sth within a range
bring bring the house down
bring bring up the rear
bring I wasn't brought up in the woods to be scared by owls.
bring *out in the open
bring *out of the closet
bring That brings me to the (main) point.
bring *up to speed
bring *up to the minute
bring What brings you here?
bring which brings me to the (main) point
bring worth of a thing is what it will bring.
brink drive so to the brink
brink on the brink (of doing sth)
bristle bristle at sth
bristle bristle with anger
bristle bristle with rage
britches too big for one's britches
britches wear the britches (in the family)
broach broach sth with so
broad broad as a barn door
broad broad in the beam
broad broaden out
broad broaden sth out
broad can't find one's butt with both hands (in broad daylight)
broad can't hit the (broad) side of a barn
broad have broad shoulders
broad hit the (broad) side of a barn
broad in broad daylight
broad Travel broadens the mind.
broaden broaden out
broaden broaden sth out

broaden Travel broadens the mind.
broadway on Broadway
broke all hell broke loose
broke dead broke
broke flat broke
broke go broke
broke go for broke
broke straw that broke the camel's back
broken broken dreams
broken broken reed
broken die of a broken heart
broken Promises are like piecrust, made to be broken.
broken sound like a broken record
bronco bust a bronco
brood brood about so/sth
broom New brooms sweep clean.
broomstick jump over the broomstick
broth Too many cooks spoil the broth.
brother Am I my brother's keeper?
brother be one's brother's keeper
brother everybody and his brother
brother I am not my brother's keeper.
brother (soul) brother
brought I wasn't brought up in the woods to be scared by owls.
brow by the sweat of one's brow
brow cause (some) eyebrows to raise
brow cause some raised eyebrows
brow down to a gnat's eyebrow
brow knit one's brow
brow raise a few eyebrows
brow raise some eyebrows
browbeat browbeat so into sth
brown brown as a berry
brown brown out
brown brown so off
brown browned (off)
brown do sth up brown
browse browse among sth
browse browse on sth
browse browse over sth
browse browse through sth
bruise cruising for a bruising
bruit bruit sth about
brunt bear the brunt (of sth)
brush brush by so/sth
brush brush over so/sth
brush brush past so/sth
brush brush so off
brush brush so/sth aside
brush brush sth away (from sth)
brush brush sth down
brush brush sth off so/sth
brush brush sth up
brush brush (up) against so/sth
brush brush up (on sth)
brush brush with death
brush brush-off
brush have a brush with sth
brush tarred with the same brush
brute by brute strength
bubble bubble over
bubble bubble up (through sth)
bubble burst so's bubble
bubble half a bubble off plumb
buck bang for the buck
buck big bucks
buck buck for sth
buck buck so off
buck buck stops here.
buck buck up

buck make a fast buck
buck make a quick buck
buck pass the buck
bucket can't carry a tune in a bucket
bucket don't amount to a bucket of spit
bucket drop in the bucket
bucket For crying in a bucket!
bucket go to hell in a bucket
bucket Hell's bells (and buckets of blood)!
bucket kick the bucket
buckle buckle down (to sth)
buckle buckle so in
buckle buckle so/sth down
buckle buckle so/sth up
buckle buckle under
buckle buckle up
bud bud out
bud budding genius
bud Gather ye rosebuds while ye may.
bud nip sth in the bud
buddy bosom buddy
buddy buddy up (to so)
buddy buddy up (with so)
budget budget sth for so/sth
buff buff sth down
buff buff sth up
buff in the buff
buff sleep in the buff
buffet buffet so/sth from so/sth to so/sth
bug bitten by the same bug
bug bug off
bug bug out
bug bug so
bug crazy as a betsy bug
bug cute as a bug's ear
bug snug as a bug in a rug
buggy buggy whip
buggy go the way of the horse and buggy
buggy horse and buggy
build build a better mousetrap
build build a case (against so)
build build a fire under so
build build castles in Spain
build build castles in the air
build build down
build build one's hopes on so/sth
build build on(to) sth
build build out onto sth
build build so in
build build so into sth
build build so/sth up
build build so up (for sth)
build build sth in
build build sth into sth
build build sth on
build build sth on(to) sth
build build sth out of sth
build build (sth) out over sth
build build (sth) over sth
build build sth to order
build build sth up
build build sth (up)on sth
build build up
build build (up)on sth
build built like a brick outhouse
build busy as a beaver (building a new dam)
build *fire under so
build It is easier to tear down than to build up.

build Rome was not built in a day.
built built like a brick outhouse
built Rome was not built in a day.
bulge battle of the bulge
bulge bulge out
bulge bulge with sth
bulk in bulk
bull awkward as a bull in a china shop
bull bull in a china shop
bull cock-and-bull story
bull couldn't hit a bull in the ass with a bass fiddle
bull full of bull
bull hit the bull's-eye
bull like a bull in a china shop
bull shoot the bull
bull take the bull by the horns
bull throw the bull
bull pen go into the bull pen
bull pen in the bull pen
bulldoze bulldoze into sth
bulldoze bulldoze through sth
bullet bite the bullet
bullet sweat bullets
bully Bully for you!
bully bully is always a coward.
bully bully so into sth
bum bum around (with so)
bum bum out
bum bum's rush
bum bum so out
bum bum sth off so
bum bum steer
bum bummed (out)
bumble bumble through sth
bump bump along
bump bump into so
bump bump so off
bump bump so/sth up
bump Bump that!
bump bump (up) against so/sth
bump goose bumps
bump If a toady frog had wings, he wouldn't bump his ass.
bump If frogs had wheels, they wouldn't bump their butts.
bump Let's bump this place!
bump like a bump on a log
bumper bumper to bumper
bun Get your buns over here!
bunch bunch of fives
bunch bunch so/sth up
bunch bunch up
bunch thanks a bunch
bundle blow a bundle (on so)
bundle bundle from heaven
bundle bundle of joy
bundle bundle of nerves
bundle bundle off
bundle bundle (oneself) up (against sth)
bundle bundle so into sth
bundle bundle so off (to some place)
bundle bundle (so) up (against sth)
bundle bundle so up (in sth)
bundle bundle sth off (to so or some place)
bundle drop a bundle (on so)
bundle drop a bundle (on sth)
bundle lose a bundle
bundle make a bundle
bundle save a bundle (on sth)
bung bung sth in
bung bung sth up
bung bunged up

bungle bungle sth up
bunk bunk down (for the night)
bunk bunk (up) together
bunk bunk (up) with so
bunny dust bunny
bunny quick like a bunny
bunny snow bunny
buoy buoy so/sth up
buoy buoy so up
burden burden so/sth with so/sth
burden burden so with sth
burden unburden oneself to so
burgeon burgeon out
burn burn sth to a crisp
burn burn away
burn burn down
burn burn for so/sth
burn burn (itself) out
burn Burn not your house to fright the mouse away.
burn burn off
burn burn one's bridges (behind one)
burn burn one's bridges in front of one
burn burn (oneself) out
burn burn so at the stake
burn burn so down
burn burn so in effigy
burn burn so out
burn burn so up
burn burn sth away
burn burn sth down
burn burn sth in
burn burn sth into sth
burn burn sth off
burn burn sth out
burn burn sth up
burn burn the candle at both ends
burn burn the midnight oil
burn burn up
burn burn with a low blue flame
burn burn with sth
burn burned to a cinder
burn burned up
burn burning question
burn burnt child dreads the fire.
burn crash and burn
burn do a slow burn
burn eyes like two burnt holes in a blanket
burn fiddle while Rome burns
burn get one's fingers burned
burn have sth to burn
burn hot enough to burn a polar bear's butt
burn If you play with fire, you get burned.
burn keep the home fires burning
burn Money burns a hole in so's pocket.
burn on the back burner
burn on the front burner
burn put sth on the back burner
burn put sth on the front burner
burn slash and burn
burn That (really) burns me (up)!
burner on the back burner
burner on the front burner
burner put sth on the back burner
burner put sth on the front burner
burnt burnt child dreads the fire.
burnt eyes like two burnt holes in a blanket
burr have a burr under one's saddle
burst burst

bury bury one's head in the sand
bury bury oneself in sth
bury bury so/sth away (some place)
bury bury so/sth in sth
bury bury so/sth under sth
bury bury the hatchet
bury dead and buried
bury know where all the bodies are buried
bury Let the dead bury the dead.
bush beat about the bush
bush beat around the bush
bush bird in the hand is worth two in the bush.
bush bush out
bushel bushel and a peck (and some in a gourd)
bushel can't carry a tune in a bushel basket
bushel hide one's light under a bushel
bushy bright-eyed and bushy-tailed
busiest busiest men have the most leisure.
business about one's business
business business
business business as usual
business Business before pleasure.
business do a land-office business
business do business with so
business do one's business
business funny business
business get down to business
business get one's nose out of so's business
business Get your nose out of my business.
business go about one's business
business go out of business
business have no business doing sth
business How's business?
business I'll thank you to mind your own business.
business (I'm just) minding my own business.
business in business
business (It's) none of your business!
business (just) taking care of business
business keep one's nose out of so's business
business Keep your nose out of my business.
business land-office business
business Let's get down to business.
business like nobody's business
business make it one's business to do sth
business mean business
business mind one's own business
business Mind your own business.
business monkey business
business none of so's business
business open for business
business place of business
business Punctuality is the soul of business.
business send one about one's business
business set so up (in business)
business strictly business
business That's show business (for you).
busman busman's holiday
bust bust a bronco
bust bust a gut
bust bust a move

bust bust ass out of some place
bust bust (one's) ass (to do sth)
bust bust one's butt to do sth
bust bust out laughing
bust bust out (of some place)
bust bust (some) suds
bust bust so one
bust bust so out of some place
bust bust (so's) balls
bust bust (so's) stones
bust bust so up
bust bust so wide open
bust bust sth up
bust bust sth wide open
bust bust up
bust bust flat busted
bust Well, bust my buttons!
bustle bustle about doing sth
bustle bustle about some place
bustle bustle around
bustle bustle off
bustle bustle so off
bustle hustle and bustle
busy busiest men have the most leisure.
busy busy as a beaver (building a new dam)
busy busy as a cranberry merchant (at Thanksgiving)
busy busy as a fish peddler in Lent
busy busy as a hibernating bear
busy busy as a one-armed paperhanger
busy busy as Grand Central Station
busy busy as popcorn on a skillet
busy busy oneself with so/sth
busy busy so with so/sth
busy get busy
busy (Have you) been keeping busy?
busy I'm busy.
busy (I've) been keeping myself busy.
busy keep the stork busy
busy You been keeping busy?
busybody I don't want to sound like a busybody, but
but bloody but unbowed
but but for so/sth
but but good
but can't help but do sth
but Christmas comes but once a year.
but Close, but no cigar.
but everything but the kitchen sink
but Fire is a good servant but a bad master.
but gone but not forgotten
but He who begins many things, finishes but few.
but Hope for the best but expect the worst.
but Hope is a good breakfast but a bad supper.
but (I) beg your pardon, but...
but I don't want to alarm you, but
but I don't want to sound like a busybody, but
but I don't want to upset you, but
but (I) would if I could(, but I can't).
but It is not work that kills, but worry.
but It never rains but it pours.
but It's all over but the shouting.
but last but not least
but Little thieves are hanged, but great ones escape.

but Many are called but few are chosen.
but mouse that has but one hole is quickly taken.
but no buts about it
but no ifs, ands, or buts (about it)
but None but the brave deserve the fair.
but nothing but
but Nothing is certain but death and taxes.
but Nothing is certain but the unforeseen.
but Nothing so bad but (it) might have been worse.
but Opportunity knocks but once.
but poor but clean
but sadder but wiser
but separate but equal
but slow but sure
but slowly but surely
but spirit is willing, but the flesh is weak.
but Sticks and stones may break my bones, but words will never hurt me.
but Thanks, but no thanks.
but There but for the grace of God (go I).
but Two is company, (but) three's a crowd.
but You can lead a horse to water, but you can't make it drink.
but Young men may die, but old men must die.
butler The butler did it.
butt bust one's butt to do sth
butt butt in (on so/sth)
butt butt into sth
butt butt of a joke
butt butt out
butt butt (up) against so/sth
butt can't find one's butt with both hands (in broad daylight)
butt get off one's butt
butt hot enough to burn a polar bear's butt
butt If frogs had wheels, they wouldn't bump their butts.
butt kick butt
butt kick in the butt
butter bread always falls on the buttered side.
butter bread-and-butter letter
butter butter so up
butter Butter wouldn't melt (in so's mouth).
butter Fine words butter no parsnips.
butter happy as a clam (in butter sauce)
butter know which side one's bread is buttered on
butter look as if butter wouldn't melt in one's mouth
butter one's (butter and) egg money
butter so's bread and butter
butterfly butterflies in one's stomach
butterfly gaudy as a butterfly
button bright as a button
button button sth down
button button sth up
button button up
button button (up) one's lip
button Dad fetch my buttons!

button hit the panic button
button on the button
button press the panic button
button push the panic button
button Well, bust my buttons!
buttress buttress sth up
buy buy a pig in a poke
buy buy a round (of drinks)
buy buy in(to sth)
buy buy it
buy buy one's way in(to sth)
buy buy one's way out (of sth)
buy buy some food to go
buy buy so off
buy buy so/sth out
buy buy so's wolf ticket
buy buy sth
buy buy sth at sth
buy buy sth back (from so)
buy buy sth for a song
buy buy sth (from so) (for sth)
buy buy sth on credit
buy buy sth on time
buy buy sth out
buy buy sth sight unseen
buy buy sth up
buy buy the big one
buy buy the farm
buy buy the next round (of drinks)
buy buy time
buy buy trouble
buy (Could I) buy you a drink?
buy *for a song
buy Let the buyer beware.
buy not buy sth
buy *to go
buy Why buy a cow when milk is so cheap?
buy Why buy a cow when you can get milk for free?
buzz buzz along
buzz buzz for so
buzz buzz in(to some place)
buzz buzz off
buzz buzz so into a place
buzz buzz with sth
buzz get a buzz out of so/sth
buzz give so a buzz
buzz have a buzz on
buzz What's buzzin' (cousin)?
by abide by sth
by accompanied by sth
by all by one's lonesome
by begin by doing sth
by benefit by sth
by bitten by the same bug
by blow-by-blow account
by blow-by-blow description
by brush by so/sth
by by a hair('s breadth)
by by a mile
by by a show of hands
by by a whisker
by by all accounts
by by all appearances
by by all means
by by and by
by by and large
by by ankle express
by by any means
by by any stretch of the imagination
by by brute strength
by by chance

by by check
by by choice
by by coincidence
by By cracky!
by by day
by by dint of sth
by by fits and starts
by by force of habit
by By godfrey!
by by guess and by golly
by by guess and by gosh
by by hand
by by herself
by by hook or (by) crook
by by itself
by by leaps and bounds
by by main strength and awkwardness
by by means of sth
by by mistake
by by myself
by by night
by by no means
by by oneself
by by ourselves
by by return mail
by by return post
by by rote
by by shank's mare
by by the book
by by the by
by by the day
by by the dozen
by by the dozens
by by the end of the day
by by the handful
by by the hour
by by the month
by by the nape of the neck
by by the numbers
by by the same token
by by the seat of one's pants
by by the skin of one's teeth
by by the sweat of one's brow
by by the unit
by by the way
by by the week
by by the year
by by themselves
by by virtue of sth
by by way of sth
by by word of mouth
by by yourself
by by yourselves
by call so by a name
by catch so by surprise
by cheek by jowl
by come by (some place)
by come by sth
by come by sth honestly
by conspicuous by one's absence
by continue by doing sth
by copy sth out (by hand)
by Could I get by, please?
by creep by
by crushed by sth
by delight so by sth
by Desires are nourished by delays.
by die by one's own hand
by die by sth
by divide by sth
by divide by sth with sth
by Do as you would be done by.
by do somehow by so

by do sth by hand
by do sth by the book
by done by mirrors
by Don't judge a book by its cover.
by down by some amount
by drop by (sometime)
by drop by the wayside
by easy to come by
by edge by (so/sth)
by end up (by) doing sth
by enter (sth) by sth
by escape by the skin of one's teeth
by exceed so/sth by sth
by exemplify sth by sth
by fall by some amount
by fall by the wayside
by finish (sth) by doing sth
by fly by
by fly-by-night
by gain sth by doing sth
by get by (on a shoestring)
by get by (on a small amount of money)
by get by (so/sth)
by get by (with sth)
by get by (without so/sth)
by get so/sth by so/sth
by get the go-by
by give so the go-by
by go by (so/sth)
by go by the board
by go by the book
by go by the name of sth
by go off (by oneself)
by go (somewhere) by shank's mare
by good time was had by all.
by grasp so/sth by sth
by grow knee-high by the 4th of July
by hang by a hair
by hang by a thread
by hang by sth
by hang on by a thread
by hang so by the neck
by has the world by the tail (with a downhill drag)
by have a bear by the tail
by have a tiger by the tail
by have so by so/sth
by have so by sth
by hold by sth
by hold so/sth by sth
by How's by you?
by I wasn't brought up in the woods to be scared by owls.
by identify so/sth by sth
by (I'm) glad you could drop by.
by (I'm) just getting by.
by impress so by sth
by inch by inch
by increase by leaps and bounds
by increase sth by sth
by increment sth by sth
by (I've) been getting by.
by judging by sth
by justify sth by sth
by keep so/sth by so
by keep so by sth
by knee-high by the 4th of July
by know so by sight
by know so/sth by name
by know so/sth by sth
by know sth by heart
by lay sth by
by lead so by sth

by lead so by the nose
by learn by sth
by learn sth by heart
by learn sth by rote
by let so (get) by
by let so get by with sth
by let so pass by
by let so slide by
by let sth slide by
by let sth slip by
by let the chance slip by
by little by little
by live by one's wits
by live by sth
by Live by the sword, die by the sword.
by lose by sth
by made conspicuous by one's absence
by make a living by doing sth
by make it by the seat of one's pants
by Man does not live by bread alone.
by man is known by the company he keeps.
by mean by sth
by miss (sth) by a mile
by multiply by sth
by multiply sth by sth
by not by a long shot
by number off (by sth)
by oblige so by sth
by occupy oneself by sth
by one by one
by pale by comparison
by panic so by sth
by parade by (so)
by pass by (so/sth)
by pass so/sth by
by pay by sth
by place so by so/sth
by play by ear
by play by the book
by play sth by ear
by play-by-play description
by pop by (for a visit)
by possessed by sth
by preface sth by sth
by profit by sth
by pull oneself up by one's (own) bootstraps
by pull so/sth by sth
by punish so by sth
by push (oneself) by (so/sth)
by put off by so/sth
by put so by so/sth
by put sth by
by put upon by so
by recognize so/sth by sth
by reduce sth by sth
by repay so by sth
by replace so/sth by so/sth
by ride by so/sth
by roll by
by rose by any other name would smell as sweet.
by Run it by (me) again.
by run sth by (so) (again)
by run sth by the book
by Run that by (me) again.
by satisfy sth by sth
by saved by the bell
by scrape by (on sth)
by scrape by (sth)
by scrape by (with sth)
by seat so by so/sth

by send sth by sth
by set great store by so/sth
by side by side
by sit by so
by sit idly by
by slide by
by slip by
by squeak by (so/sth)
by squeeze by (so/sth)
by stand by
by stand idly by
by start off (by doing sth)
by stay by so/sth
by step-by-step
by stick by so/sth
by stop by (some place)
by surprise so by sth
by suspend sth by sth
by swear by so/sth
by take so by surprise
by take so/sth by sth
by take so/sth by storm
by take so/sth by surprise
by take the bull by the horns
by tell so/sth by sth
by thoughts to live by
by touched by so/sth
by trail so/sth by sth
by travel by sth
by tree is known by its fruit.
by use sth by sth
by win by a nose
by wind up (by) doing sth
by without (so much as) a (for or) by your leave
by word by word
by words to live by
by You can't tell a book by its cover.
bye Bye for now.
bye Good-bye and good riddance.
bye Good-bye for now.
bye (Good-bye) until then.
bye kiss sth good-bye
bye See ya, bye-bye.
bygones Let bygones be bygones.
byways highways and byways
cab hail a cab
caboodle whole kit and caboodle
cackling He that would have eggs must endure the cackling of hens.
cadge cadge sth from so
Caesar Caesar's wife must be above suspicion.
cage cage so/sth in
cage cage so/sth up (in sth)
cahoots in cahoots (with so)
Cain raise Cain
cajole cajole so into sth
cajole cajole so out of sth
cake cake so/sth with sth
cake eat one's cake and have it too
cake have one's cake and eat it too
cake icing on the cake
cake Let them eat cake.
cake nuttier than a fruitcake
cake nutty as a fruitcake
cake piece of cake
cake sell like hotcakes
cake Shut your cake hole!
cake slice of the cake
cake That takes the cake!
cake You cannot have your cake and eat it (too).

calculate calculate on sth
calculate calculate sth into sth
calf kill the fatted calf
call answer the call
call at so's beck and call
call call a halt to sth
call call a meeting
call call a spade a spade
call Call again.
call call (all) the shots
call call around (about so/sth)
call call at some place
call call attention to so/sth
call call back
call call for so/sth
call call hogs
call call in sick
call call in (to some place)
call call it a day
call call it a night
call call it quits
call Call my service.
call Call no man happy till he dies.
call call of nature
call call on so
call call on sth
call call out (to so)
call call so about sth
call call so away (from sth)
call call so back
call call so by a name
call call so down
call call so forth
call call so forward
call call so in (for sth)
call call so names
call call so on the carpet
call call so or an animal off (so/sth)
call call so/sth back
call call so/sth in
call call so/sth into question
call call so/sth into sth
call call so/sth out
call call so/sth up
call call so out
call call so over (to some place)
call call so's attention to sth
call call so's bluff
call call so to account
call call so to attention
call call so together
call call so up
call call sth (back) in
call call sth down (on so)
call call sth down (to so)
call call sth forth
call call sth in
call call sth off
call call sth out
call call sth square
call call sth to mind
call call sth to so's attention
call call sth up
call call the dogs off
call call the meeting to order
call call (the) roll
call call the shots
call call the tune
call call to so
call call (up)on so
call call (up)on so (for sth)
call call (up)on so (to do sth)
call called to straw

call Can I tell her who's calling?
call can't call one's soul one's own
call close call
call Could I call you?
call Could I have so call you?
call Could I tell him who's calling?
call Don't call us, we'll call you.
call Give me a call.
call give so a call
call go above and beyond the call of duty
call have a close call
call He who pays the piper calls the tune.
call I'll call back later.
call issue a call for sth
call last call (for sth)
call Let's call it a day.
call Many are called but few are chosen.
call May I tell him who's calling?
call no salesman will call
call not able to call one's time one's own
call on call
call pay a call
call place to call one's own
call pot is calling the kettle black.
call put sth in will-call
call taking calls
call Thank you for calling.
call That's the pot calling the kettle black.
call Time to call it a day.
call Time to call it a night.
call tough call
call What number are you calling?
call Who's calling(, please)?
call within calling distance
call You called?
calluses have calluses from patting one's own back
calm After a storm comes a calm.
calm calm before the storm
calm calm down
calm calm so or an animal down
calm cool, calm, and collected
came This is where I came in.
camel straw that broke the camel's back
camel strain at gnats and swallow camels
camp break camp
camp camp in the boondocks
camp camp in the boonies
camp camp it up
camp camp out
camp foot in both camps
camp pitch camp
campaign campaign against so/sth
campaign campaign for so/sth
campaign smear campaign (against so)
camper happy camper
campus big man on campus
campus live off campus
campus move off campus
campus off campus
campus on campus
can Appearances can be deceiving.
can before you can say Jack Robinson
can bite off more than one can chew
can Can do.
can Can I help you?
can Can I leave a message?

can Can I see you again?
can Can I see you in my office?
can Can I speak to so?
can Can I take a message?
can Can I take your order (now)?
can Can I tell her who's calling?
can Can I use your powder room?
can Can it!
can can (just) whistle for sth
can can of worms
can can take it to the bank
can Can we continue this later?
can Can you excuse us, please?
can Can you hold?
can Can you imagine?
can Can you keep a secret?
can cat can look at a king.
can catch-as-catch-can
can Come back when you can stay longer.
can devil can cite Scripture for his own purpose.
can devil can quote Scripture for his own purpose.
can Don't bite off more than you can chew.
can Don't put off for tomorrow what you can do today.
can game that two can play
can golden key can open any door.
can happy as can be
can have to do sth so bad one can taste it
can How can I serve you?
can I can accept that.
can I can live with that.
can (I) can too.
can If anything can go wrong, it will.
can If you don't like it, (you can) lump it.
can Is there some place I can wash up?
can like a can of corn
can live out of cans
can more so/sth than one can shake a stick at
can more than one can bear
can need so bad one can taste it
can Neither can I.
can No can do.
can No man can serve two masters.
can open a can of worms
can quicker than you can say Jack Robinson
can so bad one can taste it
can Those who can, do; those who can't, teach.
can Two can play (at) this game (as well as one).
can want so bad one can taste it
can We must learn to walk before we can run.
can What can I do for you?
can What can I say?
can What can I tell you?
can What else can I do?
can What else can I do for you?
can What more can I do?
can Where can I wash up?
can Why buy a cow when you can get milk for free?
can You can bet the farm (on so/sth).
can You can catch more flies with honey than with vinegar.

can You can lead a horse to water, but you can't make it drink.
can You can say that again!
can You never know (what you can do) till you try.
canary look like the cat that swallowed the canary
cancel cancel each other out
cancel cancel out (of sth)
cancel cancel so out
cancel cancel so's Christmas
cancel cancel sth out
candidate candidate for a pair of wings
candidate look like a candidate for a pair of wings
candidly speaking (quite) candidly
candle bell, book, and candle
candle burn the candle at both ends
candle can't hold a candle to so
candle not hold a candle to so/sth
candy like taking candy from a baby
cannon loose cannon
cannot Beggars can't be choosers.
cannot cannot
cannot can't call one's soul one's own
cannot can't carry a tune
cannot can't do anything with so/sth
cannot can't find one's butt with both hands (in broad daylight)
cannot can't hack it
cannot can't help but do sth
cannot can't hit the (broad) side of a barn
cannot can't hold a candle to so
cannot can't make heads or tails (out) of so/sth
cannot Can't say (a)s I do(, can't say (a)s I don't).
cannot can't say boo to a goose
cannot can't see a hole in a ladder
cannot can't see beyond the end of one's nose
cannot can't see one's hand in front of one's face
cannot can't see straight
cannot can't stand (the sight of) so/sth
cannot can't stomach so/sth
cannot can't wait (for sth (to happen))
cannot can't wait (to do sth)
cannot empty sack cannot stand upright.
cannot He that cannot obey cannot command.
cannot house divided against itself cannot stand.
cannot I can't accept that.
cannot (I) can't argue with that.
cannot (I) can't beat that.
cannot (I) can't believe (that)!
cannot (I) can't complain.
cannot I can't get over sth!
cannot (I) can't help it.
cannot (I) can't rightly say.
cannot (I) can't say (as) I do.
cannot (I) can't say (as) I have.
cannot (I) can't say for sure.
cannot (I) can't say's I do.
cannot (I) can't say's I have.
cannot (I) can't say that I do.
cannot (I) can't say that I have.
cannot (I) can't thank you enough.
cannot (I) can't top that.

cannot (I) would if I could(, but I can't).
cannot If you can't be good, be careful.
cannot If you can't beat them, join them.
cannot If you can't lick 'em, join 'em.
cannot If you can't stand the heat, get out of the kitchen.
cannot (It) can't be helped.
cannot leopard cannot change his spots.
cannot make an offer one cannot refuse
cannot make one an offer one cannot refuse
cannot mill cannot grind with water that is past.
cannot Never make a threat you cannot carry out.
cannot offer one cannot refuse
cannot One cannot be in two places at once.
cannot One cannot love and be wise.
cannot Those who can, do; those who can't, teach.
cannot What can't be cured must be endured.
cannot What's done cannot be undone.
cannot You can lead a horse to water, but you can't make it drink.
cannot You cannot get a quart into a pint pot.
cannot You cannot get blood from a stone.
cannot You cannot get blood from a turnip.
cannot You cannot have your cake and eat it (too).
cannot You cannot lose what you never had.
cannot You cannot make a silk purse out of a sow's ear.
cannot You cannot make an omelet without breaking eggs.
cannot You cannot make bricks without straw.
cannot You cannot please everyone.
cannot You cannot put new wine in old bottles.
cannot You cannot serve God and mammon.
cannot You cannot teach an old dog new tricks.
cannot (You) can't beat that.
cannot You can't expect me to believe that.
cannot (You) can't fight city hall.
cannot (You) can't get there from here.
cannot You can't mean that!
cannot (You) can't take it with you.
cannot You can't tell a book by its cover.
cannot (You) can't top that.
cannot (You) can't win them all.
canoe paddle one's own canoe
cap cap and gown
cap feather in one's cap
cap put a cap on sth
cap put one's thinking cap on
capable capable of doing sth
capacity Genius is an infinite capacity for taking pains.
capitalize capitalize on sth

capitulate capitulate to so/sth
captain captain of industry
capture capture so's imagination
car wrap one's car around sth
card card
card card-carrying member
card cards are stacked against one
card deal the race card
card drawing card
card few cards short of a deck
card few cards shy of a full deck
card have the cards stacked against one
card hold all the cards
card in the cards
card keep one's cards close to one's chest
card keep one's cards close to one's vest
card lay one's cards on the table
card Lucky at cards, unlucky in love.
card play one's cards close to one's chest
card play one's cards right
card play one's cards well
card play one's trump card
card play the race card
card put one's cards on the table
card see sth in the cards
card stack the cards (against so/sth)
card the race card
card use the race card
care care about so/sth
care care for so
care care for sth
care care nothing about so/sth
care care nothing for so/sth
care care to do sth
care could(n't) care less
care devil-may-care attitude
care devil-may-care manner
care didn't care a whit
care didn't care too hard
care (Do you) care if I join you?
care doesn't care who knows it
care don't care a whit
care for all I care
care (I) could(n't) care less.
care I don't care.
care (I) don't care if I do.
care in care of so
care in so's care
care in the care of so
care (just) taking care of business
care leave so/sth in so's care
care leave so/sth in the care of so
care leave so/sth under so's care
care not care two hoots about so/sth
care not have a care in the world
care past caring
care place so/sth in so's care
care place so/sth into the care of so
care place so/sth under so's care
care See if I care!
care Take care.
care take care of number one
care take care of numero uno
care take care of so
care take care of sth
care Take care (of yourself).
care That takes care of that.
care under so's care
care Who cares?
care (Would you) care for another (one)?
care (Would you) care to...?
care (Would you) care to dance?

care (Would you) care to join us?
careful Be careful.
careful careful not to do sth
careful careful (with sth)
careful If you can't be good, be careful.
carnal have carnal knowledge of so
carp carp about so/sth
carp carp at so (about so/sth)
carp carp at so/sth
carpet call so on the carpet
carpet haul so on the carpet
carpet red-carpet treatment
carpet roll out the red carpet (for so)
carpet sweep sth under the carpet
carriage horse and carriage
carry cannot carry a tune
carry can't carry a tune
carry card-carrying member
carry carry (a lot of) weight (with so/sth)
carry carry a secret to the grave
carry carry a torch (for so)
carry carry coals to Newcastle
carry carry on
carry carry one's cross
carry carry one's (own) weight
carry carry over
carry carry so along (with so)
carry carry so along (with sth)
carry carry so around (with oneself)
carry carry so away
carry carry so back (to some time)
carry carry so/sth about
carry carry so/sth away
carry carry so/sth into some place
carry carry so/sth off
carry carry so/sth out
carry carry so/sth over from sth
carry carry so/sth over to sth
carry carry so/sth through sth
carry carry so somewhere
carry carry so through (sth)
carry carry sth along (with so)
carry carry sth around (with one)
carry carry sth back
carry carry sth down
carry carry sth forward
carry carry sth off
carry carry sth on
carry carry sth onto sth
carry carry sth out
carry carry sth over
carry carry sth with
carry carry the ball
carry carry the day
carry carry the torch
carry carry the weight of the world on one's shoulders
carry carry through (on sth)
carry carry weight (with so)
carry cash-and-carry
carry get carried away
carry Never make a threat you cannot carry out.
carry *on so's shoulders
cart cart so/sth off
cart Don't put the cart before the horse.
cart put the cart before the horse
cart upset the apple cart
carte carte blanche

carter more sth than Carter has (liver) pills
carve carve so/sth up
carve carve sth from sth
carve carve sth in
carve carve sth into sth
carve carve sth out
carve carve sth up
carve carved in stone
case basket case
case best-case scenario
case build a case (against so)
case case
case case in point
case case of mistaken identity
case case of sth
case case of the blind leading the blind
case case so/sth out
case case the joint
case Circumstances alter cases.
case gather a case (against so)
case get down to cases
case Get off so's case!
case have a bad case of the simples
case have a case (against so)
case I rest my case.
case in any case
case in case of sth
case in case (sth happens)
case in the case of so/sth
case just in case
case keep off (of) so's case
case keep on so's case
case live out of a suitcase
case look like a case of sth
case make a federal case out of sth
case nut case
case on so's case
case open-and-shut case
case treat a case of sth
case worst-case scenario
cash cash flow problem
cash cash in (on so)
cash Cash is king.
cash Cash is trash.
cash cash money
cash cash on the barrelhead
cash cash on the line
cash cash (one's chips) in
cash cash or credit
cash cash sth in
cash cash-and-carry
cash cold, hard cash
cash pressed for cash
cast cast a spell (on so)
cast cast around for so/sth
cast cast aspersions on so
cast cast doubt(s) (on so/sth)
cast cast in the same mold
cast cast off (from sth)
cast Cast one's bread upon the waters.
cast cast one's eyes down
cast cast one's lot in (with so/sth)
cast cast (one's) pearls before swine
cast cast one's vote
cast cast so as sth
cast cast so aside
cast cast so/sth up
cast cast sth aside
cast cast sth back (some place)
cast cast sth down
cast cast sth off
cast cast the first stone

cast cast-iron stomach
cast Coming events cast their shadows before.
cast die is cast.
cast recast sth in sth
castle build castles in Spain
castle build castles in the air
castle man's home is his castle.
cat All cats are gray in the dark.
cat cat can look at a king.
cat cat has nine lives.
cat cat in gloves catches no mice.
cat cat is out of the bag
cat conceited as a barber's cat
cat Curiosity killed the cat.
cat dead cat on the line
cat doesn't have enough sense to bell a cat
cat Dog my cats!
cat fat cat
cat fraidy cat
cat (Has the) cat got your tongue?
cat in the catbird seat
cat It's raining cats and dogs.
cat let the cat out of the bag
cat Look (at) what the cat dragged in!
cat look like sth the cat dragged in
cat look like the cat that swallowed the canary
cat mad enough to kick a cat
cat not enough room to swing a cat
cat play cat and mouse with so
cat purr like a cat
cat rain cats and dogs
cat shoot the cat
cat sling the cat
cat smiling like a Cheshire cat
cat There's more than one way to skin a cat.
cat When the cat's away, the mice will play.
catapult catapult so/sth into sth
catbird in the catbird seat
catch catch a glimpse of so/sth
catch catch a whiff of sth
catch catch (a)hold of so/sth
catch catch cold
catch catch forty winks
catch catch hell
catch catch it
catch Catch me later.
catch Catch me some other time.
catch catch (on) fire
catch catch on (to sth)
catch catch on (with so)
catch catch one off (one's) guard
catch catch one's breath
catch catch one's death (of cold)
catch catch one with one's pants down
catch catch onto so/sth
catch catch onto sth
catch catch sight of so/sth
catch catch some rays
catch catch some Zs
catch catch so at a bad time
catch catch so at sth
catch catch so by surprise
catch catch so doing sth
catch catch so flat-footed
catch catch so in the act (of doing sth)
catch catch so napping
catch catch so off balance
catch catch so off guard

catch catch so/sth in sth
catch catch so out
catch catch so red-handed
catch catch so's eye
catch catch so up in sth
catch catch so up (on so/sth)
catch catch so up short
catch catch so with sth
catch catch sth
catch catch sth from so
catch catch sth on sth
catch catch sth up in sth
catch catch the devil
catch catch the next wave
catch catch to it
catch catch up (on so/sth)
catch catch up (on sth)
catch catch up (to so/sth)
catch catch up with so
catch catch up with so/sth)
catch catch up (with so/sth)
catch catch wind of sth
catch catch-as-catch-can
catch caught in the act
catch caught in the crossfire
catch caught short
catch caught unaware(s)
catch caught up in sth
catch First catch your hare.
catch I didn't catch the name.
catch I didn't (quite) catch that (last) remark.
catch I don't have time to catch my breath.
catch If you run after two hares, you will catch neither.
catch (I'll) catch you later.
catch (I'll) try to catch you later.
catch (I'll) try to catch you some other time.
catch not let so catch so doing sth
catch not want to catch so doing sth
catch Set a thief to catch a thief.
catch time to catch one's breath
catch *up with so
catch What's the catch?
catch *whiff of sth
catch would not be caught dead (doing sth)
catch You can catch more flies with honey than with vinegar.
catch You must lose a fly to catch a trout.
catches cat in gloves catches no mice.
catches early bird catches the worm.
cater cater to so/sth
caught caught in the act
caught caught in the crossfire
caught caught short
caught caught unaware(s)
caught caught up in sth
caught would not be caught dead (doing sth)
cause cause a commotion
cause cause hard feelings
cause cause lean times (ahead)
cause cause qualms (about so/sth)
cause cause (quite) a stir
cause cause (some) eyebrows to raise
cause cause some raised eyebrows
cause cause (some) tongues to wag
cause give cause for sth
cause have cause to do sth
cause lost cause

cause Men are blind in their own cause.
cause (That causes) no problem.
caution caution so about so/sth
caution throw caution to the wind
cave cave in
cavil cavil at so
cease cease and desist
cease Wonders never cease!
cede cede sth to so
ceiling hit the ceiling
celebrate celebrate so for an accomplishment
cement cement sth on
cement cement sth on(to) sth
cement cement sth together
censure censure so (for sth)
cent He wears a ten-dollar hat on a five-cent head.
cent not worth a red cent
cent put one's two cents(' worth) in
center center around so/sth
center center of attention
center center on so/sth
center center sth on so/sth
center dead center
center off center
center on dead center
central busy as Grand Central Station
century turn of the century
'cept did everything he could 'cept eat us
ceremony Don't stand on ceremony.
ceremony stand on ceremony
certain certain party
certain certain sure
certain Certainly not!
certain dead certain
certain in no uncertain terms
certain make certain of sth
certain Nothing is certain but death and taxes.
certain Nothing is certain but the unforeseen.
certainly Certainly not!
chafe chafe at sth
chaff separate the wheat from the chaff
chain ball and chain
chain chain is no stronger than its weakest link.
chain chain of command
chain chain so or an animal up
chain chain so/sth down
chain chain sth to sth
chain chain sth up
chain weak link (in the chain)
chain yank so's chain
chair grab a chair
chair keep one's chair
chair play first chair
chair Pull up a chair.
chalk chalk sth out
chalk chalk sth up
challenge challenge so on sth
challenge challenge so to sth
challenge hygienically challenged
challenge rise to the challenge
challenge take up the challenge
champ champ at the bit
chance by chance
chance chance sth
chance chance (up)on so/sth

chance chances are
chance fancy so's chances
chance fat chance
chance fighting chance
chance ghost of a chance
chance Give me a chance!
chance last chance (for sth)
chance leap at the chance (to do sth)
chance leave sth to chance
chance let the chance slip by
chance Not a chance!
chance not have a snowball's chance in hell
chance off chance
chance on the off chance
chance once-in-a-lifetime chance
chance slim chance
chance sporting chance
chance stand a chance (of doing sth)
chance take a chance
chance (There is) no chance.
chance when you get a chance
chance You pays your money and you takes your chance(s).
change and change
change change back (from sth)
change change back ((in)to so/sth)
change change hands
change change horses in midstream
change change horses in the middle of the stream
change change into so/sth
change change (of life)
change change of pace
change change of scenery
change change off
change change out of sth
change change over (from so/sth) (to so/sth)
change change places with so
change change so/sth into so/sth
change change so's mind
change change so's tune
change change sth back
change change sth with so
change change the channel
change change the subject
change change to sth
change chunk of change
change Don't change horses in midstream.
change *for the better
change go through the changes
change have a change of heart
change (Have you) changed your mind?
change (I) changed my mind.
change I felt like a penny waiting for change.
change (It's) time for a change.
change leopard cannot change his spots.
change make change (for so) (for sth)
change sea change
change small change
change Times are changing.
change Times change and we with time.
change Times change(, people change).
change You changed your mind?
channel change the channel
channel channel sth in(to sth)

channel channel sth off
channel go through channels
channel go through (the proper) channels
channel work through channels
chapter chapter and verse
character character assassination
character in character
character out of character
character shady character
character suspicious character
charge bring a charge against so/sth
charge charge at so/sth
charge charge down on so/sth
charge charge in(to some place)
charge Charge it to the dust and let the rain settle it.
charge charge (of so/sth)
charge charge off
charge charge out (of some place)
charge charge so/sth (with) sth
charge charge so up
charge charge so with sth
charge charge sth against sth
charge charge (sth) for so
charge charge (sth) for sth
charge charge sth off as sth
charge charge sth on sth
charge charge sth up
charge charged up
charge file charges (against so)
charge get a charge out of so/sth
charge give so a charge
charge in charge (of so/sth)
charge in the charge of so
charge level a charge against so
charge press charges (against so)
charge take charge (of so/sth)
charity Charity begins at home.
charley charley horse
charm charm so with sth
charm charm the pants off so
charm third time's the charm.
chart chart sth out (for so/sth)
chase always chasing rainbows
chase ambulance chaser
chase chase after so/sth
chase chase around after so/sth
chase chase so or an animal in
chase chase so or an animal in(to) some place
chase chase so/sth around
chase chase so/sth (away) from some place
chase chase so/sth down
chase chase so/sth out of some place
chase chase so/sth up
chase cut to the chase
chase give chase (to so/sth)
chase Go chase yourself!
chase lead so on a merry chase
chase send so on a wild-goose chase
chase wild-goose chase
chat chat about so/sth
chatter chatter about so/sth
chatter chatter (away) (at so/sth)
chatter chatter from sth
cheap dirt cheap
cheap Talk is cheap.
cheap Why buy a cow when milk is so cheap?
cheat cheat at sth
cheat cheat on so
cheat cheat so out of sth
cheat Cheats never prosper.

check blank check
check by check
check check back (on so/sth)
check check back (with so)
check check in (at sth)
check check in (on so/sth)
check check in (with so)
check check in(to sth)
check check on so/sth
check check out
check check out (from sth)
check Check, please.
check check to in
check check so/sth off
check check so/sth out
check check so/sth over
check check so/sth through (sth)
check check so's bags through (to some place)
check check sth in
check check sth out
check check that
check check through sth
check check up (on so/sth)
check check with so (about sth)
check checks and balances
check checkup
check cut (so) a check
check give so a blank check
check hold so/sth in check
check honor so's check
check keep so/sth in check
check make a check (out) (to so/sth)
check make a check over to so/sth
check make a check to so/sth
check pick up the check
check rain check (on sth)
check take a rain check (on sth)
checkup checkup
cheek cheek by jowl
cheek tongue-in-cheek
cheek turn the other cheek
cheer cheer for so/sth
cheer cheer so/sth on
cheer cheer so up
cheer cheer up
cheese cheese so off
cheese cheesed off
cheese cut the cheese
cheese Say cheese!
cherry cherry-pick sth
cherry Don't make two bites of a cherry.
cherry Life is just a bowl of cherries.
cherry red as a cherry
Cheshire smiling like a Cheshire cat
chest get sth off one's chest
chest keep one's cards close to one's chest
chest play one's cards close to one's chest
chest put hair on so's chest
chest take the spear (in one's chest)
chew angry enough to chew nails
chew bite off more than one can chew
chew chew (away) at sth
chew chew on so/sth
chew chew one's own tobacco
chew chew one's cud
chew chew so/sth up
chew chew so out
chew chew sth away
chew chew sth off sth
chew chew sth over

chew chew sth up
chew chew the fat
chew chew the rag
chew close chewer and a tight spitter
chew Don't bite off more than you can chew.
chew mad enough to chew nails (and spit rivets)
chicken chicken feed
chicken chicken out (of sth)
chicken chicken out on so
chicken chicken-hearted
chicken chickens come home to roost.
chicken count one's chickens before they hatch
chicken Don't count your chickens before they are hatched.
chicken for chicken feed
chicken go to bed with the chickens
chicken If it ain't chickens, it's feathers.
chicken no spring chicken
chicken run around like a chicken with its head cut off
chide chide so for sth
chief chief cook and bottle washer
chief Too many chiefs and not enough Indians.
child burnt child dreads the fire.
child child is father of the man.
child child's play
child Children and fools tell the truth.
child Children should be seen and not heard.
child devil's children have the devil's luck.
child expecting (a child)
child Heaven protects children(, sailors,) and drunken men.
child It is a wise child that knows its own father.
child Monday's child is fair of face.
child poster child (for sth)
child Spare the rod and spoil the child.
child with child
childhood in one's second childhood
children Children and fools tell the truth.
children Children should be seen and not heard.
children devil's children have the devil's luck.
children Heaven protects children(, sailors,) and drunken men.
chili down to chili and beans
chill chill out
chill chill so's action
chill chilled to the bone
chill put the chill on so
chill take the chill off ((of) a place)
chime chime in (with sth)
chimney smoke like a chimney
chin chin music
chin chuck so under the chin
chin keep one's chin up
chin Keep your chin up.
chin make chin music
chin take it on the chin
chin take sth on the chin
chin wag one's chin
china awkward as a bull in a china shop
china bull in a china shop
china like a bull in a china shop

china not for all the tea in China
chink chink in one's armor
chip bargaining chip
chip cash (one's chips) in
chip chip away
chip chip (away) at sth
chip chip in (on sth) (for so)
chip chip in (with sth) (on sth) (for so)
chip chip off the old block
chip chip on one's shoulder
chip chip sth away (from sth)
chip chip sth in (on sth)
chip chips and dip
chip cow chip
chip in the chips
chip Let the chips fall where they may.
chip when the chips are down
chisel chisel in (on so/sth)
chisel chisel so out of sth
chock chock full of sth
choice by choice
choice Hobson's choice
choir preach to the choir
choke choke on sth
choke choke so off
choke choke so up
choke choke sth back
choke choke sth down
choke choke sth off
choke choke sth up
choke choke up
chomp chomp at the bit
choose Beggars can't be choosers.
choose choose among so/sth
choose choose between two people or things
choose choose from so/sth
choose choose so as sth
choose choose so/sth for sth
choose choose sth for so
choose choose (up) sides
choose Many are called but few are chosen.
choose nothing to choose from
choose pick and choose
chop chop so off
chop chop so/sth (up) (in(to) sth)
chop chop sth back
chop chop sth down
chop chop sth off (of) sth
chop lick one's chops
chord strike a chord (with so)
chortle chortle about so/sth
chortle chortle with sth
chosen Many are called but few are chosen.
chow chow (sth) down
Christmas cancel so's Christmas
Christmas Christmas comes but once a year.
chuck chuck it in
chuck chuck so/sth away
chuck chuck so out of some place
chuck chuck so under the chin
chuck chuck sth away
chuck chuck sth down
chuck chuck sth into sth
chuck chuck sth over sth
chuck chuck sth up
chuckle chuckle about so/sth
chuckle chuckle with sth
chug chug along
chum chum up to so

chum chum up with so
chunk chunk of change
chunk chunk sth
church Church ain't out till they quit singing.
church church key
church nearer the church, the farther from God.
church poor as a church mouse
church quiet as a (church) mouse
churn churn sth out
churn churn sth up
chute down the chute
chute go down the chute
cigar Close, but no cigar.
cinch have sth cinched
cinch It's a (dead) cinch.
cinch lead-pipe cinch
cinder burned to a cinder
circle circle around (over so/sth)
circle circle around so/sth
circle come full circle
circle could fight a circle-saw (and it a-runnin')
circle go (a)round in circles
circle in a vicious circle
circle run circles around so
circle run in circles
circle talk in circles
circulate circulate among so/sth
circulate circulate sth through sth
circulate circulate through sth
circulation back in(to) circulation
circulation out of circulation
circumstances Circumstances alter cases.
circumstances extenuating circumstances
circumstances in reduced circumstances
circumstances not under any circumstances
circumstances under certain circumstances
circumstances under no circumstances
circumstances under normal circumstances
circumstances under the circumstances
circus like a three-ring circus
cite cite so for sth
cite devil can cite Scripture for his own purpose.
city city slicker
city (You) can't fight city hall.
civil Civility costs nothing.
civil keep a civil tongue (in one's head)
civility Civility costs nothing.
claim claim a life
claim claim sth for so/sth
claim claim sth for sth
claim lay claim to sth
claim so's claim to fame
claim stake a claim to so/sth
claim stake out a claim to sth
clam clam up
clam happy as a clam (at high tide)
clam happy as a clam (in butter sauce)
clamber clamber onto sth
clamber clamber up (sth)
clamor clamor against so/sth
clamor clamor for so/sth

clamp clamp down (on so/sth)
clamp clamp sth on(to) sth
clamp put the clamps on so/sth
clap clap eyes on so/sth
clap clap so in(to) some place
clap clap sth on(to) sth
clap clap sth out
clap clap sth together
clash clash against sth
clash clash (with so) (over so/sth)
clash clash with sth
clasp clasp so/sth to sth
class class so/sth with so/sth
class cut class
clatter clatter around
clause grandfather clause
claw claw one's way to the top
claw claw sth off so/sth
claw one's claws are showing
clay have feet of clay
clean clean as a hound's tooth
clean clean as a whistle
clean clean bill of health
clean clean one's act up
clean clean one's plate
clean clean out (of sth)
clean clean so/sth down
clean clean so/sth out of sth
clean clean so/sth up
clean clean so's plow
clean clean sth off
clean clean sth off sth
clean clean sth out
clean clean sweep
clean clean the floor up with so
clean clean up (on sth)
clean clean (up) one's plate
clean clean-cut
clean cleaned out
clean Cleanliness is next to godliness.
clean come clean (with so) (about sth)
clean have clean hands
clean keep one's nose clean
clean make a clean breast of sth (to so)
clean make a clean sweep
clean New brooms sweep clean.
clean poor but clean
clean so clean you could eat off the floor
clean start (off) with a clean slate
clean start (over) with a clean slate
clean take so to the cleaners
clean wipe so's slate clean
clean wipe the slate clean
cleaners take so to the cleaners
cleanliness Cleanliness is next to godliness.
clear clear as a bell
clear clear as crystal
clear clear as mud
clear clear as vodka
clear clear of sth
clear clear off ((of) some place)
clear clear out (of some place)
clear clear sailing
clear clear so of sth
clear clear so/sth out of some place
clear clear so's name
clear clear sth away
clear clear sth for publication
clear clear sth from some place
clear clear sth off sth
clear clear sth up

clear clear sth with so/sth
clear clear the air
clear clear the decks
clear clear the table
clear Clear the way!
clear clear up
clear coast is clear.
clear come out of a clear blue sky
clear Do I make myself (perfectly) clear?
clear free and clear
clear have a clear conscience (about so/sth)
clear Have I made myself clear?
clear (I) read you loud and clear.
clear in the clear
clear jump clear of sth
clear keep clear of sth
clear loud and clear
clear make so's position clear
clear make sth clear to so
clear move clear of sth
clear remain clear of sth
clear see one's way (clear) (to do sth)
clear stand clear of sth
clear stay clear of so/sth
clear steer clear (of so/sth)
cleave cleave to so
click click with so
climax bring sth to a climax
climax come to a climax
climb climb down (from sth)
climb climb on
climb climb on(to) sth
climb climb out (of sth)
climb climb the wall(s)
climb climb up (sth)
climb He who would climb the ladder must begin at the bottom.
climb *on the bandwagon
cling cling to so/sth
cling cling together
clip at a fast clip
clip at a good clip
clip clip so's wings
clip clip sth from sth
clip clip sth on(to) so/sth
clip clip sth out of sth
clip go at a fast clip
clip go at a good clip
clip move at a fast clip
clip move at a good clip
clip run at a fast clip
clip run at a good clip
clip travel at a fast clip
clip travel at a good clip
cloak cloak so/sth in secrecy
cloak cloak-and-dagger
clock against the clock
clock (a)round the clock
clock beat the clock
clock clock in
clock clock out
clock clock so in
clock clock so/sth at sth
clock clock so out
clock clock so at speeds of some amount
clock clock sth up
clock clock-watcher
clock face that could stop a clock
clock homely enough to stop a clock
clock sleep around the clock
clock *speeds of some amount

clock turn back the clock
clock turn the clock back
clockwork go like clockwork
clockwork regular as clockwork
clockwork run like clockwork
clog clog so up
clog clog sth up
clog clog sth with sth
clog clog up
close able to do sth with one's eyes closed
close at close range
close behind closed doors
close bring sth to a close
close close a deal
close close a sale
close close as two coats of paint
close close at hand
close Close, but no cigar.
close close call
close close chewer and a tight spitter
close close down
close close enough for government work
close close enough to use the same toothpick
close close (in) around so/sth
close close in for the kill
close close in (on so/sth)
close close on sth
close close one's eyes to sth
close Close only counts in horseshoes (and hand grenades).
close close ranks
close close shave
close close so/sth down
close close so/sth in (sth)
close close so out of sth
close close so up
close close sth down
close close sth off
close close sth out
close close sth to so
close close sth up
close close the books on so/sth
close close the deal
close close the door on so/sth
close close the door to so/sth
close close the sale
close close to home
close close to so
close close up
close close with so/sth
close closefisted (with money)
close come close (to so/sth)
close come to a close
close draw sth to a close
close draw to a close
close have a close call
close have a close shave
close have so/sth under (close) scrutiny
close keep a close rein on so/sth
close keep a close watch on so/sth
close keep (close) watch (on so/sth)
close keep (close) watch (over so/sth)
close keep one's cards close to one's chest
close keep one's cards close to one's vest
close keep so/sth under (close) scrutiny
close move close to so/sth
close play one's cards close to one's chest
close sit close to so/sth
close stand close to so/sth

close too close for comfort
close under (close) scrutiny
closefisted closefisted (with money)
closet bring so out of the closet
closet closet so with so
closet come out of the closet
closet out of the closet
closet skeleton(s) in the closet
cloth cut from the same cloth
cloth cut one's coat according to one's cloth
cloth cut one's coat to suit one's cloth
cloth make sth up out of whole cloth
cloth man of the cloth
clothe clothe so in sth
clothes Clothes make the man.
clothes not have a stitch of clothes (on)
clothes Sunday-go-to-meeting clothes
clothes wolf in sheep's clothing
clothing wolf in sheep's clothing
cloud cloud over
cloud cloud up
cloud coming up a cloud
cloud Every cloud has a silver lining.
cloud Get your head out of the clouds!
cloud have one's head in the clouds
cloud on cloud nine
cloud under a cloud (of suspicion)
clover in clover
clown clown around (with so)
club Join the club!
clue clue so in (on sth)
clue have a clue (about sth)
clue not a clue
clunk clunk down
clunk clunk sth down
cluster cluster around so/sth
cluster cluster so/sth around so/sth
cluster cluster together
clutch clutch at so/sth
clutch clutch at straws
clutch clutch so/sth to sth
clutch clutch (up)
clutch drowning man will clutch at a straw.
clutch in(to) so's clutches
clutter clutter sth up
coach coach so for sth
coach drive a coach and horses through sth
coal carry coals to Newcastle
coal haul so over the coals
coal rake so over the coals
coalesce coalesce into sth
coast coast along
coast coast is clear.
coast coast-to-coast
coat close as two coats of paint
coat coat and tie
coat coat so/sth with sth
coat cut one's coat according to one's cloth
coat cut one's coat to suit one's cloth
coat hang on so's coattails
coat ride on so's coattails
coattails hang on so's coattails
coax coax so or an animal in(to sth)
coax coax so or an animal out of sth
coax coax so to do sth
cob have a corncob up one's ass
cobble cobble sth up
cobble Let the cobbler stick to his last.

cobbler Let the cobbler stick to his last.
cock cock a snook at so
cock cock of the walk
cock cock-and-bull story
cock coldcock so
cock go off half-cocked
cock knock sth into a cocked hat
cockles warm the cockles of so's heart
cocky cocky as the king of spades
cod send sth C.O.D.
code break a code
coerce coerce so or an animal into sth
coexist coexist with so/sth
coffee coffee and
coffee coffee-table book
coffee Wake up and smell the coffee.
coffin (another) nail in so's or sth's coffin
cogitate cogitate on sth
cohabit cohabit with so
coil coil (itself) around so/sth
coil coil (itself) up
coil coil sth up
coil shuffle off this mortal coil
coin coin a phrase
coin do some fine coin
coincide by coincidence
coincide coincide with sth
coincidence by coincidence
cold act like a cold fish
cold blow hot and cold
cold break out in a cold sweat
cold catch cold
cold catch one's death (of cold)
cold cold as a welldigger's ass (in January)
cold cold as a welldigger's feet (in January)
cold cold as a witch's tit
cold cold as marble
cold cold comfort
cold cold feet
cold cold fish
cold Cold hands, warm heart.
cold cold, hard cash
cold cold shoulder
cold cold sober
cold cold turkey
cold cold-shoulder
cold dash cold water on sth
cold Feed a cold and starve a fever.
cold go cold turkey
cold in a cold sweat
cold in cold blood
cold in cold storage
cold (Is it) cold enough for you?
cold It'll be a cold day in hell when sth happens.
cold keep so or some creature out in the cold
cold knock so cold
cold leave so cold
cold leave so or some creature out in the cold
cold make so's blood run cold
cold out cold
cold out in the cold
cold pour cold water on sth
cold Revenge is a dish best served cold.
cold so cold you could hang meat
cold stone(-cold) sober

cold stop so cold
cold take cold
cold take one's death (of cold)
cold throw cold water on sth
cold coldcock so
collaborate collaborate with so/sth
collapse collapse into sth
collapse collapse under so/sth
collar blue collar
collar collar-and-tie men
collar hot under the collar
collate collate sth with sth
collect collect around so/sth
collect collect (money) for so/sth
collect collect (money) for sth
collect collect on sth
collect collect one's thoughts
collect collect sth from so
collect collect sth up
collect cool, calm, and collected
collect take a collection up (from so) (for so/sth)
collection take a collection up (from so) (for so/sth)
college old college try
collide collide with so/sth
collude collude with so/sth
color color sth in
color come through sth (with flying colors)
color horse of a different color
color horse of another color
color lend color to sth
color person of color
color riot of color
color sail under false colors
color see the color of so's money
color show one's (true) colors
color so's true colors
color with flying colors
Columbia give so Hail Columbia
comb comb sth for so/sth
comb comb sth out of sth
comb comb through sth
comb go over sth with a fine-tooth comb
comb go through sth with a fine-tooth comb
comb run a comb through sth
comb search sth with a fine-tooth comb
combine combine sth against so/sth
combine combine sth with sth
come After a storm comes a calm.
come All good things must (come to an) end.
come best things come in small packages.
come blow so/sth to kingdom come
come chickens come home to roost.
come Christmas comes but once a year.
come come a cropper
come come aboard
come come about
come come across
come come after so/sth
come Come again.
come come along (with so)
come Come and get it!
come come apart
come come (a)round
come come around (for a visit)
come come around (to doing sth)

come come around (to some place)
come come around (to visit)
come come as no surprise
come come at so/sth
come come away empty-handed
come come away (from so/sth)
come come away with so
come come back
come come before so/sth
come come between so and so else
come come between sth and sth else
come come by (some place)
come come by sth
come come by sth honestly
come come clean (with so) (about sth)
come come close (to so/sth)
come come down
come come for so
come come forth
come come forward
come come from behind
come come from far and wide
come come from nowhere
come come from some place
come come from so/sth
come come full circle
come come hell or high water
come come home from some place
come come home (to roost)
come come home to so
come come in
come come (in) on a wing and a prayer
come come into a (small) fortune
come come into being
come come into bloom
come come into blossom
come come into conflict
come come in(to) contact (with so/sth)
come come into effect
come come into existence
come come into fashion
come come into focus
come come in(to) heat
come come into one's or its own
come come into play
come come into power
come come into prominence
come come into season
come come into service
come come into sight
come come into (some) money
come come into so's possession
come come into the world
come come into view
come come Monday
come Come 'n' get it!
come come naturally (to so)
come come of age
come come off
come come on
come come on(to) so/sth
come come out
come come out in favor of so/sth
come come over
come come rain or (come) shine
come come rain or shine
come Come right in.
come come (right) on top of sth
come come short of sth
come come so's way
come come through

come come to
come come together
come come true
come come under sth
come come under the hammer
come come unglued
come come up
come come (up) from behind
come come (up)on so/sth
come come what may
come come with (so/sth)
come come with the territory
come come within a hair('s breadth) of so/sth
come come within an ace of sth
come come within an inch of doing sth
come come within an inch of so/sth
come come within earshot (of sth)
come come within range
come come within sth
come come-hither look
come Coming events cast their shadows before.
come coming out of one's ears
come Coming through(, please).
come coming up a cloud
come Could I come in?
come cross a bridge before one comes to it
come cross that bridge when one comes to it
come doesn't have enough sense to come in out of the rain
come *down with a disease
come dream come true
come easy come, easy go
come easy to come by
come Everything comes to him who waits.
come Everything's coming up roses.
come First come, first served.
come Good things come in small packages.
come Good things come to him who waits.
come (had) known it was coming
come harbinger of things to come
come has come and gone
come have another guess coming
come have another think coming
come have come a long way
come have sth coming (to one)
come How come?
come if push comes to shove
come If the mountain will not come to Mahomet, Mahomet must go to the mountain.
come if (the) worst comes to (the) worst
come (I'm) glad you could come.
come *in so's possession
come It'll all come out in the wash.
come knew it was coming
come know where one is coming from
come March comes in like a lion, and goes out like a lamb.
come Misfortunes never come singly.
come Morning dreams come true.
come not know enough to come in out of the rain
come not know if one is coming or going

come not know whether one is coming or going
come Nothing comes of nothing.
come *of age
come *out in force
come *out in large numbers
come *out in the open
come *out of nowhere
come *out of the closet
come Out of the mouths of babes (oft times come gems).
come *out of the woodwork
come portent of things to come
come sign of things to come
come some creature's time has come
come so's time has come
come They must have seen you coming.
come till kingdom come
come Tomorrow never comes.
come *turning point
come (un)til the cows come home
come *up against sth
come *up before so
come *up for reelection
come *up for sale
come up-and-coming
come (We're) glad you could come.
come What goes up must come down.
come What's coming off?
come what's coming to one
come What(ever) goes around, comes around.
come when it comes right down to it
come when it comes to sth
come when one's ship comes in
come When poverty comes in at the door, love flies out of the window.
come when push comes to shove
come When the wolf comes in at the door, love creeps out of the window.
come where one is coming from
come will come of sth
come *within earshot (of sth)
come *within range
come Won't you come in?
come You've got another think coming.
comeback make a comeback
comedy Cut the comedy!
comeuppance get one's comeuppance
comfort cold comfort
comfort creature comforts
comfort too close for comfort
comfortable comfortable as an old shoe
command chain of command
command have a good command of sth
command He that cannot obey cannot command.
commence commence with so/sth
commend commend so for sth
commend commend so/sth to so/sth
comment comment about so/sth
comment No comment.
commiserate commiserate with so
commission out of commission
commit commit oneself on sth
commit commit oneself to so/sth
commit commit oneself to sth
commit commit so/sth for sth
commit commit so/sth to sth
commit commit sth to memory
commit commit to so

commode commode-hugging drunk
common common as an old shoe
common common as dirt
common common thread (to all this)
common have sth in common (with so/sth)
common in the Common Era
common ounce of common sense is worth a pound of theory.
commotion cause a commotion
commune commune with sth
communicate communicate sth to so
communicate communicate with so
commute commute between places
commute commute from some place
commute commute sth into sth
company Desert and reward seldom keep company.
company keep company (with so)
company keep so company
company man is known by the company he keeps.
company Misery loves company.
company part company (with so)
company Two is company, (but) three's a crowd.
compare compare notes on so/sth
compare compare so/sth to so/sth
compare compare so/sth with so/sth
comparison pale by comparison
compartmentalize compartmentalize sth into sth
compel compel so to do sth
compensate compensate for sth
compensate compensate so for sth
compete compete against so
compete compete against sth
compete compete for so/sth
compete compete in sth
compete compete with so/sth
compile compile sth from sth
complain complain about so/sth
complain complain of sth
complain complain to so
complain (I) can't complain.
complain (I have) nothing to complain about.
compliment backhanded compliment
compliment compliment so on sth
compliment fish for a compliment
compliment left-handed compliment
compliment pay so a backhanded compliment
compliment pay so a compliment
compliment pay so a left-handed compliment
compliment return so's compliment
compliment return the compliment
comply comply with sth
comport comport oneself with some manner
compose composed of sth
compose regain one's composure
composed composed of sth
composure regain one's composure
compound compound sth with sth
compress compress sth into sth
comprise comprised of so/sth
compromise compromise on so/sth (with so)
compromise reach a compromise
compute compute sth at sth
con con so into sth
con con so out of sth

conceal conceal so/sth from so/sth
conceal place of concealment
concealment place of concealment
concede concede sth to so/sth
concede concede to so/sth
conceit conceited as a barber's cat
conceive conceive of so/sth
conceive conceive of so/sth as so/sth
concentrate concentrate at some place
concentrate concentrate so/sth at sth
concentrate concentrate sth on so/sth
concentrate concentrate (up)on so/sth
concern as far as so is concerned
concern as far as sth is concerned
concern concern oneself about so/sth
concern concern so in sth
concern concern so with so/sth
concern so far as so is concerned
concern so far as sth is concerned
concern to whom it may concern
concert in concert (with so)
conclusion bring sth to a successful conclusion
conclusion come to a conclusion
conclusion foregone conclusion
conclusion jump to conclusions
conclusion leap to conclusions
conclusion reach a conclusion
conclusion rush to conclusions
concur concur on so/sth (with so)
condemn condemn so as sth
condemn condemn so for sth
condemn condemn so to sth
condense condense sth (in)to sth
condescend condescend to do sth
condescend condescend to so
condition condition so/sth to sth
condition find sth in mint condition
condition in a delicate condition
condition in an interesting condition
condition in condition
condition in good condition
condition in mint condition
condition in the pink (of condition)
condition keep in good condition
condition out of condition
condition under certain conditions
conduct conduct so away (from so/sth)
conduct conduct so into sth
conduct conduct so out of sth
confederate confederate with so/sth
confer confer on so/sth (with so)
confer confer sth (up)on so
confer confer with so (about so/sth)
confess confess sth to so
confess confess to sth
confess (Open) confession is good for the soul.
confession (Open) confession is good for the soul.
confide confide in so
confide confide sth in so
confidence have confidence in so
confidence take so into one's confidence
confidence vote of confidence
confine confine so or an animal to sth
confine confine so or an animal within sth
confine confine sth to so/sth
confirm confirm so in sth
confiscate confiscate sth from so/sth
conflict come into conflict
conflict conflict with sth

conform conform to sth
conform conform with sth
confront confront so with sth
confuse confuse so about sth
confuse confuse so or an animal with sth
confuse confuse so with so else
confusion throw so/sth into confusion
congratulate congratulate so (up)on sth
congress It would take an act of Congress to do sth.
conjecture conjecture on sth
conjure conjure so/sth up
conk conk off
conk conk out
connect connect so/sth (up) to so/sth
connect connect (up) to sth
connect connect (up) with so/sth
connect connect (with so)
connect connect (with the ball)
connect disconnect so/sth from so/sth
conniption have a conniption (fit)
connive connive at sth (with so)
conquer divide and conquer
consarn Consarn it!
conscience Conscience does make cowards of us all.
conscience guilty conscience needs no accuser.
conscience have a clear conscience (about so/sth)
conscience in (all) good conscience
conscript conscript so into sth
consecrate consecrate so/sth to God
consent consent to sth
consent Silence gives consent.
consequence in consequence (of sth)
consider consider so (as) sth
consider consider so for sth
consideration in consideration of sth
consideration out of consideration (for so/sth)
consign consign sth to so/sth
consignment on consignment
consist consist of so/sth
console console so on sth
console console so with sth
consort consort with so
conspicuous conspicuous by one's absence
conspicuous made conspicuous by one's absence
conspicuous make oneself conspicuous
conspire conspire with so (against so/sth)
constant Constant dropping wears away a stone.
constant in a (constant) state of flux
constrain constrain so from doing sth
construct construct sth from sth
construction under construction
construe construe sth as sth
consult consult (with) so (about so/sth)
contact bring so/sth into contact with so/sth
contact come in(to) contact (with so/sth)
contact contact with so
contact in contact (with so/sth)
contact lose contact with so/sth
contact make contact with so
contaminate contaminate so/sth with sth
contempt beneath contempt
contempt Familiarity breeds contempt.

contempt in contempt (of court)
contend contend against so/sth
contend contend with a problem
contend contend with so (for sth)
content content oneself with so/sth
content contented mind is a perpetual feast.
content to one's heart's content
contention bone of contention
contentment feel a glow of contentment
contest no contest
contest not going to win any beauty contests
context in the context of sth
context lift sth out of context
context out of context
context quote so/sth out of context
context take sth out of context
continental don't give a continental
continue Can we continue this later?
continue continue by doing sth
continue continue one's losing streak
continue continue with sth
continue Could we continue this later?
contract contract sth out
contract contract with so (for sth)
contract put a contract out on so
contradiction contradiction in terms
contrary contrary to sth
contrary on the contrary
contrary to the contrary
contrast contrast so/sth with so/sth else
contrast contrast with so/sth
contribute contribute sth (to so) (for so/sth)
contribute contribute to sth
control bring so/sth under control
control bring so/sth under one's control
control control over so/sth
control control the purse strings
control exercise control over so/sth
control go out of control
control have so/sth under control
control in control of so/sth
control keep so/sth under control
control out of control
control rage out of control
control take control of so/sth
control under control
convalesce convalesce from sth
convenience at so's earliest convenience
converge converge (up)on so/sth
conversation open a conversation
conversation strike up a conversation
converse converse with so (about so/sth)
convert convert from sth ((in)to sth)
convert convert so/sth (from sth) ((in)to sth)
convert preach to the converted
convey convey sth (from so/sth) (to so/sth)
convict convict so of sth
convictions have the courage of one's convictions
convince convince so of sth
convulse convulse so with sth
cook chief cook and bottle washer
cook cook so's goose
cook cook (sth) out
cook cook sth to perfection
cook cook sth up

cook cook the accounts
cook cook the books
cook cook up a storm
cook cooked up
cook cooking with gas
cook Now you're cooking (with gas)!
cook one's goose is cooked
cook Too many cooks spoil the broth.
cook Too many cooks spoil the stew.
cook *up a storm
cook What's cooking?
cookie blow one's cookies
cookie juice and cookies
cookie shoot one's cookies
cookie snap one's cookies
cookie That's the way the cookie crumbles.
cookie toss one's cookies
cookie tough cookie
cookie tough cookies
cool blow one's cool
cool cool as a cucumber
cool cool, calm, and collected
cool cool down
cool Cool it!
cool cool off
cool cool one's heels
cool cool out
cool cool so down
cool cool so out
cool cooled out
cool cooler heads prevail
cool (Have you) been keeping cool?
cool I'm cool.
cool (I've) been keeping cool.
cool keep cool
cool keep one's cool
cool lose one's cool
cool play it cool
cool You been keeping cool?
coon in a coon's age
coop coop so/sth up
coop fly the coop
cooperate cooperate with so (on sth)
co-opt co-opt so into sth
coordinate coordinate sth with sth
coot bald as a coot
cop cop a packet
cop cop a plea
cop cop a squat
cop cop an attitude
cop cop onto sth
cop cop out (of sth)
cop cop out (on so)
cop cop out (on sth)
cop cop some Zs
cop cop sth from so/sth
cope cope with so/sth
copulate copulate with so
copy copy sth down (from so/sth)
copy copy sth out
cordon cordon sth off
core rotten to the core
core to the core
cork blow one's cork
cork cork high and bottle deep
cork cork sth up
cork pop one's cork
corn like a can of corn
corncob have a corncob up one's ass
corner back oneself into a corner
corner corner the market on sth
corner cut corners

corner drive so into a corner
corner from all corners of the world
corner from the four corners of the earth
corner have so in one's corner
corner have so/sth cornered
corner out of the corner of one's eye
corner turn the corner
corral corral so/sth
correct house of correction
correct if my memory serves me correctly
correct stand corrected
correlate correlate sth with sth
correlate correlate with sth
correspond correspond to sth
correspond correspond with so (about so/sth)
corrupt Absolute power corrupts absolutely.
cost at all costs
cost at any cost
cost Civility costs nothing.
cost cost a king's ransom
cost cost a pretty penny
cost cost an arm and a leg
cost cost sth out
cost cost the earth
cost Courtesy costs nothing.
cost estimate the cost at some amount
cost *king's ransom
cotton cotton (on)to so/sth
cotton cotton up to so
cotton in high cotton
cotton in low cotton
cotton in tall cotton
couch couch potato
couch couch sth in sth
cough cough one's head off
cough cough sth out
cough cough sth up
could could do with so/sth
could could fight a circle-saw (and it a-runnin')
could Could I be excused?
could (Could I) buy you a drink?
could Could I call you?
could Could I come in?
could Could I get by, please?
could (Could I) get you something (to drink)?
could (Could I) give you a lift?
could Could I have a lift?
could Could I have a word with you?
could Could I have so call you?
could Could I have the bill?
could Could I help you?
could Could I join you?
could Could I leave a message?
could Could I see you again?
could Could I see you in my office?
could Could I speak to so?
could Could I take a message?
could Could I take your order (now)?
could Could I tell him who's calling?
could Could I use your powder room?
could Could we continue this later?
could Could you excuse us, please?
could Could you hold?
could Could you keep a secret?
could did everything he could 'cept eat us
could face that could stop a clock

could face (that) only a mother could love
could How could you (do sth)?
could (I) could be better.
could (I) could be worse.
could I could eat a horse!
could (I) would if I could(, but I can't).
could if looks could kill
could (I'm) glad you could come.
could (I'm) glad you could drop by.
could might could
could so clean you could eat off the floor
could so cold you could hang meat
could so mad I could scream
could so quiet you could hear a pin drop
could so still you could hear a pin drop
could (Things) could be better.
could (Things) could be worse.
could (We're) glad you could come.
could Who could have thought?
could (You) could have fooled me.
could You could have knocked me over with a feather.
couldn't couldn't be happier
couldn't could(n't) care less
couldn't couldn't hit a bull in the ass with a bass fiddle
couldn't couldn't pour water out of a boot (if there was instructions on the heel)
couldn't (I) couldn't ask for more.
couldn't I couldn't ask you to do that.
couldn't (I) couldn't be better.
couldn't (I) could(n't) care less.
couldn't (I) couldn't help it.
couldn't (It) couldn't be better.
couldn't (It) couldn't be helped.
couldn't (Things) couldn't be better.
couldn't Wild horses couldn't drag so away (from sth).
couldn't You couldn't (do that)!
council Councils of war never fight.
counsel counsel so about sth
counsel counsel so against sth
counsel keep one's own counsel
count Close only counts in horseshoes (and hand grenades).
count count against so
count count down
count count for sth
count count from sth (up) to sth
count count heads
count Count no man happy till he dies.
count count noses
count count off
count count on so/sth
count count one's chickens before they hatch
count count so among sth
count count so in (for sth)
count count so/sth as sth
count count so/sth off
count count so/sth up
count count so out (for sth)
count count sth against so
count count sth as sth
count count sth in
count count sth out
count count up to sth
count count (up)on so/sth
count count with so

count counter so/sth with sth
count counter with sth
count Don't count your chickens before they are hatched.
count down for the count
count Every minute counts.
count Every moment counts.
count go down for the count
count go out for the count
count (!) wouldn't count on it.
count lose count of so/sth
count out for the count
count over the counter
count run counter to sth
count stand up and be counted
count take the (long) count
count under the counter
country another country heard from
country country mile
country Happy is the country which has no history.
country In the country of the blind, the one-eyed man is king.
country prophet is not without honor save in his own country.
country So many countries, so many customs.
couple couple of
couple couple so with so
couple couple sth (on)to sth
couple couple sth together
couple couple sth with sth
couple couple up (with so)
couple couple with so
couple couple with sth
courage Dutch courage
courage get enough courage up (to do sth)
courage get the courage up (to do sth)
courage have the courage of one's convictions
courage pluck up so's courage
courage screw up one's courage
course as a matter of course
course course of action
course course of true love never did run smooth.
course course through sth
course crash course in sth
course drift off course
course in due course
course in the course of time
course of course
course off course
course on course
course par for the course
course run its course
course stay on course
course take a course (in sth)
course take its course
court appear in court
court ball is in so's court
court have the ball in one's court
court in contempt (of court)
court kangaroo court
court laugh sth out of court
court pay court to so
court settle (sth) (out of court)
court stand up in court
court take so to court
courtesy Courtesy costs nothing.
courtesy out of courtesy (to so)
cousin kissing cousins

cousin think so is God's own cousin
cousin What's buzzin' (cousin)?
cover blow so's cover
cover cover a lot of ground
cover cover for so
cover cover so in sth
cover cover so/sth against sth
cover cover so/sth for sth
cover cover so/sth up
cover cover so's tracks (up)
cover cover sth up
cover cover the territory
cover cover the waterfront
cover cover (up) for so
cover Don't judge a book by its cover.
cover duck and cover
cover take cover
cover You can't tell a book by its cover.
cow awkward as a cow on a crutch
cow awkward as a cow on roller skates
cow cow chip
cow cow juice
cow cow paste
cow cow patty
cow cow pie
cow cow so into sth
cow Don't have a cow!
cow Holy cow!
cow sacred cow
cow (un)til the cows come home
cow Why buy a cow when milk is so cheap?
cow Why buy a cow when you can get milk for free?
coward bully is always a coward.
coward Conscience does make cowards of us all.
coward Cowards die many times before their death(s).
coward take the coward's way out
cower cower (away) from so/sth
cower cower down (from sth)
cower cower from sth
cozy cozy up (to so)
crack at the crack of dawn
crack crack a book
crack crack a bottle open
crack crack a joke
crack crack a smile
crack crack at so
crack crack at sth
crack crack down (on so/sth)
crack crack open
crack crack some suds
crack crack so/sth up
crack crack so up
crack crack sth up
crack crack sth (wide) open
crack crack the door (open)
crack crack the window (open)
crack crack under the strain
crack crack up
crack cracked
crack dirty crack
crack fall through the cracks
crack first crack at sth
crack get cracking
crack give so a crack at sth
crack go through the cracks
crack hard nut to crack
crack He that would eat the kernel must crack the nut.
crack make cracks about so/sth

crack not all sth is cracked up to be
crack not what sth is cracked up to be
crack paper over the cracks (in sth)
crack slip between the cracks
crack slip through the cracks
crack take a crack at so
crack take a crack at sth
crack take first crack at sth
crack through the cracks
crack tough nut to crack
crack want first crack at sth
crack what so/sth is cracked up to be
cracky By cracky!
cradle from the cradle to the grave
cradle hand that rocks the cradle rules the world.
cradle rob the cradle
cram cram for a test
cram cram for an examination
cram cram so/sth into sth
cram cram so/sth with so/sth
cramp cramp so's style
cranberry busy as a cranberry merchant (at Thanksgiving)
crank crank so up
crank crank sth out
crank crank sth up
cranny every nook and cranny
crap crap out
crap shoot the crap
crap throw the crap
crap You scared the crap out of me.
crash bring sth crashing down (around one)
crash crash and burn
crash crash around
crash crash course in sth
crash crash down (around so/sth)
crash crash into so/sth
crash crash out (of some place)
crash crash sth together
crash crash through sth
crash crash to the floor
crash crash together
crash crash with so
crave crave to do sth
craw have sth stick in one's craw
crawl crawl across sth
crawl crawl along sth
crawl crawl back to so
crawl crawl in(to sth)
crawl crawl out
crawl crawl over sth
crawl crawling with some kind of creature
crawl crawling with so
crawl make so's flesh crawl
crawl make so's skin crawl
crazy crazy about so/sth
crazy crazy as a betsy bug
crazy crazy as a loon
crazy crazy as a peach-orchard boar
crazy crazy bone
crazy crazy for so/sth
crazy crazy in the head
crazy drive so crazy
crazy go crazy
crazy go stir-crazy
crazy like crazy
crazy make so stir-crazy
crazy stir-crazy
creak creaking door hangs longest.
creak creaking gate hangs longest.
cream cream of the crop

crease crease sth up
create create a scene
create create a stink (about sth)
create create an uproar
creation all over creation
creation hind end of creation
creation in creation
creature creature comforts
credence give credence to so/sth
credit buy sth on credit
credit cash or credit
credit credit (for sth)
credit credit so/sth for sth
credit credit so/sth with sth
credit credit sth to so
credit credit to so/sth
credit deserve credit for sth
credit do credit to so
credit do so credit
credit extend credit (to so or a company)
credit extend so or a company credit
credit Give credit where credit is due.
credit on credit
credit reflect credit (up)on so/sth
credit sell sth on credit
credit take credit for sth
creek God willing and the creek don't rise
creek Lord willing and the creek don't rise
creek up a creek
creek up the creek (without a paddle)
creep creep across sth
creep creep along sth
creep creep away
creep creep by
creep creep in(to) sth
creep creep out (from under so/sth)
creep creep out (of sth)
creep creep out of the woodwork
creep creep over so/sth
creep creep under sth
creep creep up
creep creeps
creep When the wolf comes in at the door, love creeps out of the window.
crib crib sth from so/sth
crick crick in one's back
crick crick in one's neck
cricket It's not cricket.
cricket merry as a cricket
crime Crime doesn't pay.
crime partners in crime
crime Poverty is not a crime.
cringe cringe away from so/sth
cringe cringe before so/sth
crinkle crinkle up
crisp burn sth to a crisp
criticism open oneself to criticism
criticism open to criticism
criticize criticize so for sth
crock crock so/sth up
crocodile After while(, crocodile).
crocodile cry crocodile tears
crocodile shed crocodile tears
crook by hook or (by) crook
crook crooked as a barrel of fish hooks
crook crooked as a dog's hind leg
crop come a cropper
crop cream of the crop
crop crop out
crop crop so/sth out
crop crop up

crop Good seed makes a good crop.
cropper come a cropper
cross at cross-purposes
cross bear one's cross
cross carry one's cross
cross cross a bridge before one comes to it
cross cross from some place to some place
cross cross one's fingers
cross cross one's heart (and hope to die)
cross cross over
cross cross paths (with so)
cross cross so
cross cross so's mind
cross cross so's palm with silver
cross cross so up
cross cross sth with sth
cross cross swords (with so)
cross cross that bridge when one comes to it
cross cross the Rubicon
cross Cross the stream where it is shallowest.
cross Crosses are ladders that lead to heaven.
cross cross-examine so
cross double-cross so
cross have one's wires crossed
cross keep one's fingers crossed (for so/sth)
cross look at so cross-eyed
cross nail so to a cross
cross star-crossed lovers
crossfire caught in the crossfire
crouch crouch around
crouch crouch down
crow crow about sth
crow crow bait
crow crow over sth
crow eat crow
crow hoarse as a crow
crow make so eat crow
crowd crowd around so/sth
crowd crowd in
crowd crowd in(to) some place
crowd crowd so/sth in(to) sth
crowd crowd so/sth out of sth
crowd crowd so/sth together
crowd crowd sth with so/sth
crowd crowd through (sth)
crowd crowd together
crowd far from the madding crowd
crowd follow the crowd
crowd play to the crowd
crowd Two is company, (but) three's a crowd.
crown crown so with sth
crown crown sth with sth
crown Uneasy lies the head that wears a crown.
cruise cruise around in sth
cruise cruising for a bruising
crum crum sth up
crumble crumble away
crumble crumble into sth
crumble crumble sth up (into sth)
crumble crumble up
crumble That's the way the cookie crumbles.
crumped crumped out
crumple crumple sth up
crumple crumple up

crunch crunch so/sth up
crunch crunch sth down
crusade crusade against so/sth
crusade crusade for so/sth
crush crush on so
crush crush so/sth down
crush crush so/sth to sth
crush crush sth in
crush crush sth (in)to sth
crush crush sth out
crush crush sth up
crush crush (up) against so/sth
crush crushed by sth
crust upper crust
crutch awkward as a cow on a crutch
crutch funny as a crutch
crux crux of the matter
crux go to the crux of the matter
crux look at the crux of the matter
cry break down (and cry)
cry burst out crying
cry cry all the way to the bank
cry cry before one is hurt
cry cry bloody murder
cry cry crocodile tears
cry cry for so/sth
cry cry in one's beer
cry cry one's eyes out
cry cry one's heart out
cry cry oneself to sleep
cry cry out (against so/sth)
cry cry out for so/sth
cry cry out (in sth)
cry cry over so/sth
cry cry over spilled milk
cry cry (sth) out (to so or an animal)
cry cry uncle
cry cry wolf
cry crying need (for so/sth)
cry crying shame
cry Don't cry before you are hurt.
cry Don't cry over spilled milk.
cry far cry from sth
cry For crying in a bucket!
cry For crying out loud!
cry hue and cry
cry It's no use crying over spilled milk.
cry raise a hue and cry (about sth)
cry Sing before breakfast, you'll cry before night.
crystal clear as crystal
cucumber cool as a cucumber
cud chew one's cud
cuddle cuddle up (to so/sth)
cuddle cuddle up with a (good) book
cuddle cuddle up (with so)
cue cue so in
cue take one's cue from so
cuff off-the-cuff
cuff put sth on the cuff
cuff speak off-the-cuff
cull cull so/sth out of sth
culminate culminate in sth
culturally culturally advantaged
culturally culturally deprived
culturally culturally disadvantaged
culture culture vulture
cunning cunning as a fox
cup cup one's hands together
cup in one's cups
cup just one's cup of tea
cup My cup runneth over.
cup not one's cup of tea

cup tempest in a teacup
cup There's many a slip 'twixt the cup and the lip.
curdle curdle so's blood
cure cure so of sth
cure cure sth of sth
cure ounce of prevention is worth a pound of cure.
cure Prevention is better than cure.
cure take the cure
cured What can't be cured must be endured.
curiosity Curiosity killed the cat.
curiosity die from curiosity
curiosity die of curiosity
curiosity pique so's curiosity
curl curl so's hair
curl curl sth up
curl curl up and die
curl curl up (in(to) sth
curl curl up (with a (good) book)
curl curl up with so or an animal
curl curly dirt
curl make so's hair curl
currency give currency to sth
current swim against the current
curry curry favor with so
curse curse at so/sth
curse curse so for sth
curse curse so/sth under one's breath
curse curse so/sth with sth
curse curse under one's breath
curse *under one's breath
curtain bring down the curtain (on sth)
curtain curtain sth off
curtain curtains for so/sth
curtain ring the curtain down (on sth)
curtain ring the curtain up
curtsy curtsy to so
curve curve to sth
curve pitch so a curve(ball)
curve throw so a curve
cusp on the cusp (of sth)
cuss cuss a blue streak
cuss cuss so out
custody in custody (of so/sth)
custody remand so (in)to the custody of so
custom So many countries, so many customs.
customer customer is always right.
customer one to a customer
customer slippery customer
customer tough customer
cut able to cut sth
cut clean-cut
cut cut a big swath
cut cut a deal
cut cut a fine figure
cut cut a long story short
cut cut a wide swath
cut cut above average
cut cut above sth
cut cut across sth
cut cut against the grain
cut cut along sth
cut cut and dried
cut cut and paste
cut cut and run
cut cut around sth
cut cut at so or an animal
cut cut at sth
cut cut back

cut cut both ways
cut cut class
cut cut corners
cut cut down (on sth)
cut cut from the same cloth
cut cut in (ahead of so/sth)
cut cut in (on so)
cut cut in (on sth)
cut cut in (with sth)
cut cut in(to sth)
cut Cut it out!
cut cut loose (with sth)
cut cut no ice (with so)
cut cut off
cut cut one's coat according to one's cloth
cut cut one's coat to suit one's cloth
cut cut one's eyes at so/sth
cut cut one's eyeteeth on sth
cut cut one's losses
cut cut one's nose off to spite one's face
cut cut one's (own) throat
cut cut one's wolf loose
cut cut (oneself) loose (from so/sth)
cut cut oneself on sth
cut cut out
cut cut school
cut cut some Zs
cut cut so a break
cut cut (so) a check
cut cut so dead
cut cut so down
cut cut so in (on sth)
cut cut so off at the pass
cut cut so off without a penny
cut cut so/sth loose from sth
cut cut so/sth off (from sth)
cut cut so/sth off (short)
cut cut so/sth out
cut cut so/sth to sth
cut cut so/sth up
cut cut so/sth with sth
cut cut so's water off
cut cut so some slack
cut cut so to ribbons
cut cut so to the bone
cut cut so to the quick
cut cut so up
cut cut sth away (from sth)
cut cut sth back
cut cut sth down
cut cut sth from sth
cut cut sth into sth
cut cut sth off
cut cut sth on sth
cut cut sth out
cut cut sth to the bone
cut cut sth with sth
cut cut teeth
cut cut the cheese
cut Cut the comedy!
cut cut the deadwood out
cut cut the dust
cut Cut the funny stuff!
cut cut the ground out from under so
cut cut the mustard
cut cut the pie up
cut Cut the shit!
cut cut through red tape
cut cut through sth
cut cut to so/sth
cut cut to the chase
cut cut up
cut cut your peaches

cut cutting edge
cut Fish or cut bait.
cut have one's work cut out for one
cut It cuts two ways.
cut (It) don't cut no ice (with so).
cut (It) don't cut no squares (with so).
cut on the cutting edge
cut one's work is cut out for one
cut run around like a chicken with its head cut off
cute cute as a bug's ear
cylinder firing on all cylinders
cylinder hitting on all cylinders
cylinder run on all cylinders
dab dab at sth
dab dab sth off
dab dab sth on(to) sth
dab smack (dab) in the middle
dabble dabble at sth
dabble dabble in sth
dad Dad fetch my buttons!
daddy daddy of them all
daddy granddaddy of them all
dagger cloak-and-dagger
dagger look daggers at so
daily daily dozen
daily daily grind
daisy fresh as a daisy
daisy pushing up (the) daisies
dally dally over sth
dally dally with so
dally dilly-dally (around) with so/sth
dam busy as a beaver (building a new dam)
dam dam sth up
dam water over the dam
damage acceptable damage
damage do so damage
damage What's the damage?
damn Damn it to blue blazes!
damn (damn) sight better
damn damn so/sth with faint praise
damn damn so with sth
damn Damned if you do, damned if you don't.
damn Hot damn!
damn I'm damned if I do and damned if I don't.
damn not give a tinker's damn
damn not worth a damn
damnation Hellfire and damnation!
damp damp off
damp damp sth down
damp dampen so's spirits
damper put a damper on sth
dance dance at so's wedding
dance dance on air
dance dance out of step (with so/sth)
dance dance out of time (with so/sth)
dance dance to a different tune
dance dance to another tune
dance dance to sth
dance dance with death
dance dance with so
dance go into a song and dance (about sth)
dance go into the same old song and dance about sth
dance tap-dance like mad
dance (Would you) care to dance?
dander get so's dander up
dandy fine and dandy
dandy jim-dandy

dang gol dang
dang That's for dang sure!
danger fly into the face of danger
danger fraught with danger
dangerous armed and dangerous
dangerous little knowledge is a dangerous thing.
dangerous on dangerous ground
dangle dangle from sth
dangle dangle sth before so
dangle dangle sth from sth
dangle dangle sth in front of so
danish coffee and Danish
dare dare so (to do sth)
dare You wouldn't dare (to do sth)!
dark All cats are gray in the dark.
dark dark horse
dark dark side of so/sth
dark darken so's door
dark darkest hour is just before the dawn.
dark in the dark (about so/sth)
dark It's always darkest just before the dawn.
dark keep so in the dark (about so/sth)
dark pitch dark
dark shot in the dark
dark stay in the dark (about so/sth)
dark whistle in the dark
darken darken so's door
darkest darkest hour is just before the dawn.
darkest It's always darkest just before the dawn.
darling Better be an old man's darling than a young man's slave.
darn darn tooting
dart dart a glance at so/sth
dart dart about
dart dart across sth
dart dart in and out
dart dart out (of sth) (at so/sth)
dash dash a letter off
dash dash a note off
dash dash across sth
dash dash away
dash dash cold water on sth
dash dash off
dash dash out (for sth)
dash dash over (for sth)
dash dash so/sth against so/sth
dash dash so's hopes
dash dash sth off
dash dash sth to pieces
dash make a dash for so/sth
date at an early date
date bring so/sth up-to-date
date bring so up-to-date (on so/sth)
date date back (to so or some time)
date date from sth
date to date
date update so about so/sth
date up-to-date
daub daub sth on(to) sth
daub daub sth with sth
daughter He that would the daughter win, must with the mother first begin.
daughter Like mother, like daughter.
Davy Davy Jones's locker
Davy go to Davy Jones's locker
dawdle dawdle about
dawdle dawdle along
dawdle dawdle over sth

dawdle dawdle sth away
dawn at the break of dawn
dawn at the crack of dawn
dawn darkest hour is just before the dawn.
dawn dawn (up)on so
dawn from dawn to dusk
dawn It's always darkest just before the dawn.
day all day long
day all hours (of the day and night)
day all in a day's work
day all the livelong day
day apple a day keeps the doctor away.
day at all hours (of the day and night)
day at the end of the day
day bad hair day
day by day
day by the day
day by the end of the day
day call it a day
day carry the day
day day after day
day day and night
day day in and day out
day day late and a dollar short
day day off
day day one
day day person
day days running
day day-tripper
day different as night and day
day dog days
day Don't give up your day job.
day Don't quit your day job.
day Every dog has its day.
day first see the light of day
day for days on end
day for (some) days running
day forever and a day
day from day one
day from day to day
day from this day forward
day from this day on
day (Go ahead,) make my day!
day good old days
day Great day (in the morning)!
day have a field day
day Have a nice day.
day have had its day
day have seen better days
day He who fights and runs away, may live to fight another day.
day hold sth back for a rainy day
day (I) haven't got all day.
day if one's a day
day in all my born days
day in one's salad days
day in this day and age
day It'll be a cold day in hell when sth happens.
day It'll be a long day in January when sth happens.
day keep sth for a rainy day
day late in the day
day Let's call it a day.
day live from day to day
day live out one's days
day make a day of doing sth
day make a day of it
day Make my day!
day merry as the day is long

day night and day
day nine days' wonder
day not give anyone the time of day
day one of these days
day one's days are numbered
day order of the day
day pass the time (of day)
day pass the time of day (with so)
day plain as day
day put in a hard day at work
day put sth aside for a rainy day
day red-letter day
day Rome was not built in a day.
day save (sth) for a rainy day
day save the day
day see the light (of day)
day seven-day wonder
day since day one
day Sufficient unto the day is the evil thereof.
day take the day off
day That'll be the day!
day There aren't enough hours in the day.
day Those were the days.
day three squares (a day)
day till all hours (of the day and night)
day Time to call it a day.
day Tomorrow is another day.
day until all hours (of the day and night)
day win the day
day with each passing day
daydream daydream about so/sth
daylight begin to see daylight
daylight can't find one's butt with both hands (in broad daylight)
daylight daylight robbery
daylight in broad daylight
daylight knock the (living) daylights out of so
daylight scare the living daylights out of so
dead at a dead end
dead (bang) dead to rights
dead beat a dead horse
dead bring sth to a dead end
dead come to a dead end
dead cut so dead
dead dead ahead
dead dead and buried
dead dead and gone
dead dead as a dodo
dead dead as a doornail
dead dead broke
dead dead cat on the line
dead dead center
dead dead certain
dead dead drunk
dead dead duck
dead dead easy
dead dead from the neck up
dead dead giveaway
dead dead in so's or an animal's tracks
dead dead in the water
dead dead letter
dead dead loss
dead dead meat
dead Dead men tell no tales.
dead dead on
dead (dead) ringer (for so)
dead dead serious
dead dead set against so/sth

dead dead to the world
dead dead wrong
dead deaden sth with sth
dead deader than a doornail
dead deadly dull
dead drop dead
dead drop-dead gorgeous
dead faint dead away
dead female of the species is more deadly than the male.
dead flog a dead horse
dead give so up for dead
dead have one's heart (dead) set against sth
dead have so dead to rights
dead in a dead heat
dead It's a (dead) cinch.
dead It's ill waiting for dead men's shoes.
dead knock so dead
dead leave so for dead
dead Let the dead bury the dead.
dead look like a (dead) ringer (for so)
dead more dead than alive
dead Never speak ill of the dead.
dead on dead center
dead one's heart is (dead) set against sth
dead Over my dead body!
dead play dead
dead raise so from the dead
dead reach a dead end
dead rise from the dead
dead roll over and play dead
dead silent as the dead
dead stone dead
dead stop dead in one's tracks
dead stop one or sth dead in one's or sth's tracks
dead take so for dead
dead taken for dead
dead wake the dead
dead would not be caught dead (doing sth)
dead would not be seen dead (doing sth)
deaden deaden sth with sth
deader deader than a doornail
deadline under a deadline
deadwood cut the deadwood out
deaf deaf and dumb
deaf deaf as a post
deaf fall on deaf ears
deaf There's none so deaf as those who will not hear.
deaf turn a deaf ear (to so/sth)
deal close a deal
deal close the deal
deal cut a deal
deal deal in sth
deal deal so in
deal deal so into sth
deal deal so out of sth
deal deal sth out
deal deal the race card
deal deal with so
deal dirty deal
deal done deal
deal great deal
deal It's a deal.
deal Like it's such a big deal!
deal make a big deal about sth
deal make a deal with so
deal no big deal
deal package deal

deal raw deal
deal shady deal
deal square deal
deal strike a deal
deal sweeten (up) the deal
deal sweetheart deal
deal think a great deal of so/sth
deal What's the deal?
deal wheel and deal
dear dear departed
dear Dear John letter
dear Dear me!
dear hang on for dear life
dear thing you don't want is dear at any price.
death at death's door
death badger so/sth to death
death baleful as death
death between life and death
death bleed to death
death bore so to death
death brush with death
death catch one's death (of cold)
death Cowards die many times before their death(s).
death dance with death
death Death is the great leveler.
death death on sth
death die a natural death
death fate worse than death
death feel like death warmed over
death fight to the death
death flog so to death
death freeze to death
death frighten so or an animal to death
death frightened to death
death have a death wish
death kiss of death
death lie at death's door
death like death warmed over
death look like death warmed over
death matter of life and death
death meet one's death
death nickel-and-dime so (to death)
death Nothing is certain but death and taxes.
death pale as death
death put so or some creature to death
death scare so or an animal to death
death scared to death
death send one to one's death
death sick to death (of so/sth)
death sign one's own death warrant
death snatch so from the jaws of death
death snatch so out of the jaws of death
death still as death
death struggle to the death
death take one's death (of cold)
death The wages of sin is death.
death There is a remedy for everything except death.
death thrilled to death
death tickle so to death
death will be the death of so/sth (yet)
deathbed on one's deathbed
debate debate on sth
debate debate (with so) about sth
debit debit sth against so/sth
debit debit sth to so/sth
debit debit sth with sth
debt head over heels in debt
debt in debt

debt out of debt
debt owe so a debt of gratitude
debt pay one's debt (to society)
decay fall into decay
deceive Appearances can be deceiving.
deceive deceive so into sth
deceive deceive so with sth
decide decide against so/sth
decide decide among so and so else
decide decide between so and so else
decide decide for so/sth
decide decide in favor of so/sth
decide decide (up)on so/sth
decision arrive at a decision
decision eleventh-hour decision
decision reach a decision
deck deck so/sth out (in sth)
deck few cards short of a deck
deck few cards shy of a full deck
deck have the deck stacked against one
deck hit the deck
deck not playing with a full deck
deck on deck
deck play with a full deck
deck stack the deck (against so/sth)
decks clear the decks
declare declare (oneself) against so/sth
declare declare (oneself) for so/sth
declare declare war against so/sth
declare I declare (to goodness)!
declare I (do) declare!
decorate decorate so for sth
decorate decorate sth with sth
dedicate dedicate so/sth to so/sth
dedicate rededicate oneself or sth to so/sth
deduce deduce sth from sth
deduct deduct sth from sth else
deed deed sth (over) to so
deem deem it (to be) necessary
deep Beauty is only skin-deep.
deep between the devil and the deep blue sea
deep cork high and bottle deep
deep deep-six so/sth
deep dig deep
deep get in deeper
deep go off the deep end
deep in deep
deep jump off the deep end
deep knee-deep in sth
deep one's deepest sympathy
deep stand knee-deep in sth
deep Still waters run deep.
deepest one's deepest sympathy
deface deface sth with sth
default default on sth
defeat go down in defeat
defeat go down to defeat
defeat snatch victory from the jaws of defeat
defect defect from sth
defect defect to sth
defend defend so/sth against so/sth
defend defend so with sth
defense best defense is a good offense.
defense on the defensive
defense spring to so's defense
defensive on the defensive
defer defer to so/sth (on sth)
defer Hope deferred makes the heart sick.

defer Hope deferred maketh the heart sick.
defiance in defiance (of so/sth)
define define sth as sth
definitely Definitely not!
deflect deflect sth away from so/sth
defraud defraud so out of sth
degenerate degenerate into sth
degree third degree
degree to the nth degree
degree turn one hundred and eighty degrees
degree turn three hundred and sixty degrees
deign deign to do sth
delay Desires are nourished by delays.
delegate delegate so to sth
delegate delegate sth to so
delete delete sth from sth
deliberate deliberate about so/sth
deliberate deliberate on so/sth
deliberate deliberate over so/sth
delicate in a delicate condition
delight delight in so/sth
delight delight so by sth
delight delight so with sth
delight (I'm) delighted to have you (here).
delight (I'm) delighted to make your acquaintance.
delight ravished with delight
delight (We're) delighted to have you (here).
deliver deliver so from so/sth
deliver deliver so of sth
deliver deliver so/sth to so/sth
deliver deliver sth under pressure
deliver deliver sth up to so
deliver signed, sealed, and delivered
deliver stand and deliver
deliver *under pressure
delude delude so into sth
delude delude so with sth
deluge deluge so/sth with sth
delve delve into sth
demand demand sth from so/sth
demand demand sth of so/sth
demand in great demand
demand make demands of so/sth
demand supply and demand
demands bow to so's demands
demonstrate demonstrate against so/sth
demonstrate demonstrate for so/sth
demonstrate demonstrate sth to so
demote demote so from sth (to sth)
demur demur at sth
den beard the lion in his den
den den of iniquity
denial in denial
Denmark Something is rotten in (the state of) Denmark.
denounce denounce so as sth
denounce denounce so for sth
dent dent sth up
dent make a dent in sth
denude denude so/sth of sth
deny deny so/sth to so
depart dear departed
depart depart for some place
depart depart from some place
depart depart this life
depend depend (up)on so/sth

depend That (all) depends.
depict depict so as sth
deplete deplete sth of sth
deport deport so (from some place) (to some other place)
deposit deposit sth in(to) sth
deprive culturally deprived
deprive deprive so of sth
depth beyond one's depth
depth out of one's depth
deputize deputize so as sth
derive derive from sth
derive derive sth from so/sth
derive derive sth from sth
dern gol dern
dern You're dern tootin'!
descend descend from so or some group
descend descend from sth
descend descend into sth
descend descend to sth
descend descend (up)on so/sth
describe describe so/sth as sth
describe describe so/sth to so
description answer to the description of so
description beggar (all) description
description blow-by-blow description
description play-by-play description
desensitize desensitize so to sth
desert desert a sinking ship
desert Desert and reward seldom keep company.
desert desert so/sth for so/sth else
desert desert so/sth to so/sth
desert get one's just deserts
deserve deserve better from so/sth
deserve deserve credit for sth
deserve None but the brave deserve the fair.
deserve One good turn deserves another.
design design sth for so
design design sth for sth
design have designs on so/sth
designate designate so/sth as sth
desire Desires are nourished by delays.
desire gratify so's desires
desire leave a lot to be desired
desist cease and desist
desist desist from sth
desk away from one's desk
desk step away from one's desk
despair despair of sth
despair drive so to despair
despair sink into despair
despair throw one's hands up (in despair)
desperate Desperate diseases must have desperate remedies.
despise despise so for sth
despoil despoil sth of sth
destine destine so for sth
destine destined for some place
detach detach so/sth from so/sth
detail detail so for sth
detail detail so to so/sth
detail down to the last detail
detail go into detail(s)
detail in detail
detect detect sth in sth
deter deter so/sth from sth
determine bound and determined

determine determine the root of the problem
determine *root of the problem
detract detract from so/sth
deuce What the deuce?
develop develop from so/sth (into so/sth)
deviate deviate from sth
device leave one to one's own devices
devil Better the devil you know than the devil you don't know.
devil between the devil and the deep blue sea
devil catch the devil
devil devil
devil devil of a job
devil devil of a time
devil devil's children have the devil's luck.
devil devil's own job
devil devil's own time
devil devil so or an animal for sth
devil Devil take the hindmost.
devil devil-may-care attitude
devil devil-may-care manner
devil Every man for himself (and the devil take the hindmost).
devil fight like the devil
devil for the devil of it
devil full of the devil
devil give the devil her due
devil give the devil his due
devil go to (the devil)
devil have the devil to pay
devil He who sups with the devil should have a long spoon.
devil idle brain is the devil's workshop.
devil like the devil
devil Needs must when the devil drives.
devil play (the) devil's advocate
devil play the devil with sth
devil raise the devil (with so)
devil raise the devil (with sth)
devil Set a beggar on horseback, and he'll ride to the devil.
devil Speak of the devil (and in he walks).
devil Talk of the devil (and he is sure to appear).
devil Tell the truth and shame the devil.
devil There will be the devil to pay.
devil What (in) the devil?
devil What the devil?
devil Who (in) the devil?
devil You scared the devil out of me.
devolve devolve (up)on so/sth
devote devote oneself to so/sth
devote devote so/sth to so/sth
dial dial the wrong number
dial Don't touch that dial!
dial *wrong number
dialogue dialogue with so
diamond diamond in the rough
diapers soil one's diaper(s)
diarrhea diarrhea of the jawbone
diarrhea diarrhea of the mouth
dibs dibs on sth
dibs have dibs on sth
dibs put one's dibs on sth
dice no dice
Dick any Tom, Dick, and Harry
Dick (every) Tom, Dick, and Harry

Dick tight as Dick's hatband
dickens fight like the dickens
dickens like the dickens
dickens raise the dickens (with so/sth)
dickens What (in) the dickens?
dicker dicker with so (for sth)
dictate dictate (sth) to so
did course of true love never did run smooth.
did did everything he could 'cept eat us
did Did you hear?
did done 'n' did
did If God did not exist, it would be necessary to invent Him.
did The butler did it.
diddle diddle so out of sth
diddle diddle sth out of so
diddle diddle with sth
didn't didn't care a whit
didn't didn't care too hard
didn't didn't exchange more than three words with so
didn't didn't invent gunpowder
didn't I didn't catch the name.
didn't I didn't hear you.
didn't I didn't (quite) catch that (last) remark.
die Call no man happy till he dies.
die Count no man happy till he dies.
die Cowards die many times before their death(s).
die cross one's heart (and hope to die)
die curl up and die
die die a natural death
die die away
die die back
die die behind the wheel
die die by one's own hand
die die by sth
die die down
die die for so/sth
die die from curiosity
die die from sth
die die in one's boots
die die in sth
die die is cast.
die die laughing
die die of a broken heart
die die of boredom
die die of curiosity
die die of sth
die die of throat trouble
die die off
die die on so
die die on the vine
die die out
die die with one's boots on
die do or die
die dying to do sth
die dying to know (sth)
die Eat, drink, and be merry, for tomorrow we die.
die good die young.
die Live by the sword, die by the sword.
die Never say die.
die Old habits die hard.
die to die for
die Whom the gods love die young.
die You have to eat a peck of dirt before you die.

die Young men may die, but old men must die.
diet go on a diet
diet on a diet
diet put so on a diet
diet stay on a diet
differ beg to differ (with so)
differ differ from sth
differ differ in sth
differ differ (with so) about sth
differ Tastes differ.
difference (It) makes me no difference.
difference (It) makes no difference to me.
difference make a difference in so/sth
difference make a difference to so
difference make no difference (to so)
difference same difference
difference split the difference
difference tell the difference between so and so else or sth and sth else
difference What difference does it make?
different dance to a different tune
different different as night and day
different Different strokes for different folks.
different horse of a different color
different march to (the beat of) a different drummer
different sing a different tune
differentiate differentiate between so/sth and so/sth else
differentiate differentiate so/sth from so/sth else
difficult difficult is done at once; the impossible takes a little longer.
difficult difficult times
diffuse diffuse sth through sth else
diffuse diffuse through sth
dig dig at so/sth
dig dig deep
dig dig down
dig dig for sth
dig dig in(to sth)
dig dig one's heels in
dig dig one's own grave
dig dig out (of sth)
dig dig some dirt up (on so)
dig dig so/sth in sth
dig dig so/sth out of sth
dig dig so/sth up
dig dig sth into sth
dig dig sth out
dig Dig up!
dig dig up one's tomahawk
dig give so a dig
dig take a dig at so
dig take digs at so
diggety Hot diggety (dog)!
dignity beneath one's dignity
dignity stand on one's dignity
digress digress from sth
dilate dilate on sth
dilemma on the horns of a dilemma
diligence Diligence is the mother of good luck.
dilly dilly-dally (around) with so/sth
dim dim down
dim dim out
dim dim sth down
dim dim sth up

dim take a dim view of so/sth
dime dime a dozen
dime get off the dime
dime nickel-and-dime so (to death)
dime not worth a dime
dime stop on a dime
dime turn on a dime
din din sth into so
dine dine at some place
dine dine in
dine dine off sth
dine dine on sth
dine dine out
dine wine and dine so
ding dinged out
dink dink so off
dinner Dinner is served.
dinner take so out to dinner
dint by dint of sth
dip chips and dip
dip dip into one's savings
dip dip in(to sth)
dip dip sth in(to) sth
dip dip to sth
dip skinny-dip
dire in dire straits
direct direct so's attention to so/sth
direct direct sth against so/sth
direct direct sth at so/sth
direct direct sth to so
direct direct sth to(ward) so/sth
direction go in the right direction
direction ride off in all directions
direction run off in all directions
dirt common as dirt
dirt curly dirt
dirt dig some dirt up (on so)
dirt dirt cheap
dirt dish the dirt
dirt hit pay dirt
dirt take a dirt nap
dirt Throw dirt enough, and some will stick.
dirt You have to eat a peck of dirt before you die.
dirty air one's dirty linen in public
dirty dirty crack
dirty dirty deal
dirty dirty dog
dirty dirty look
dirty dirty old man
dirty dirty one's hands
dirty dirty sth up
dirty dirty word
dirty dirty work
dirty Do not wash your dirty linen in public.
dirty do so dirt(y)
dirty down and dirty
dirty get one's hands dirty
dirty quick and dirty
dirty so's dirty laundry
dirty wash one's dirty linen in public
disabuse disabuse so of sth
disadvantaged culturally disadvantaged
disagree agree to disagree
disagree disagree with so
disagree disagree (with so) (about so/sth)
disappear disappear from sth

disappoint Blessed is he who expects nothing, for he shall never be disappointed.
disappoint disappoint so with so/sth
disappoint disappointed at so/sth
disappointed disappointed in so/sth
disapprove disapprove of so/sth
disaster disaster of epic proportions
disaster spell disaster
disbar disbar so from sth
discern discern between so/sth and so/sth
discern discern so/sth from sth else
discern discern sth from so/sth
discharge discharge so from sth
discharge discharge sth from sth
discharge discharge sth into sth
discipline discipline so for sth
disclose disclose sth to so
disconnect disconnect so/sth from so/sth
discount five-finger discount
discourage discourage so from sth
discourse discourse (up)on so/sth
discretion Discretion is the better part of valor.
discretion ounce of discretion is worth a pound of wit.
discriminate discriminate against so/sth
discriminate discriminate between so and so else or sth and sth else
discuss discuss so/sth with so
disease Desperate diseases must have desperate remedies.
disease disease to please
disease down with a disease
disease expose so or an animal to a disease
disease foot-in-mouth disease
disembark disembark from sth
disengage disengage (oneself) from so/sth
disengage disengage sth from sth
disentangle disentangle so/sth from so/sth
disfavor fall into disfavor
disgrace fall into disgrace
disguise blessing in disguise
disguise disguise so in sth
disguise disguise so/sth as so/sth
disguise in disguise
disgusted disgusted at so/sth
disgusted disgusted with so/sth
disgusted grow disgusted at so/sth
disgusted grow disgusted with so/sth
dish dish on so
dish dish sth out
dish dish the dirt
dish Revenge is a dish best served cold.
dishe do the dishes
dishwater dull as dishwater
disinclined disinclined to do sth
dislodge dislodge so/sth from so/sth
dismiss dismiss so (from sth) (for sth)
dismiss dismiss sth as sth
dismount dismount from sth
dismount He who rides a tiger is afraid to dismount.
disorderly drunk and disorderly
dispatch dispatch so from some place
dispatch dispatch so/sth to so/sth
dispense dispense sth (to so) (from sth)
dispense dispense with so/sth
display display sth to so
disposal put so/sth at so's disposal

dispose dispose of so
disposed ill-disposed to doing sth
disposed well disposed to(ward) so/sth
disposes Man proposes, God disposes.
dispossess dispossess so of sth
dispute dispute sth with so
disqualify disqualify so/sth for sth
disrepute bring so/sth into disrepute
diss dis(s) (on) so
dissatisfy dissatisfied with so/sth
dissatisfy grow dissatisfied with so/sth
dissent dissent from sth
dissociate dissociate oneself from so/sth
dissolve dissolve in sth
dissolve dissolve into sth
dissolve dissolve sth in sth
dissolve dissolve sth into sth
dissuade dissuade so from sth
distance Distance lends enchantment (to the view).
distance distance oneself from so/sth
distance go the distance
distance keep one's distance (from so/sth)
distance keep so/sth at a distance
distance put some distance between so and oneself or sth
distance within calling distance
distance within hailing distance
distance within shouting distance
distance within walking distance
distill distill sth from sth
distinguish distinguish between so/sth and so/sth else
distinguish distinguish oneself among so
distinguish distinguish so/sth from so/sth else
distract distract so from sth
distraction bored to distraction
distraction drive so to distraction
distribute distribute sth (all) around
distribute distribute sth among so/sth
distribute distribute sth between so
distribute distribute sth over sth
distribute distribute sth to so
disuse fall into disuse
ditch last-ditch effort
ditch make last-ditch effort
ditchwater dull as ditchwater
dither in a dither
dive dive in with both feet
dive dive in(to sth)
dive dive off ((of) sth)
dive go into a nosedive
dive take a dive
dive take a nosedive
diverge diverge from sth
diverge diverge to sth
divert divert so/sth from so/sth
divert divert so/sth to so/sth
divert divert sth into sth
divert divert sth onto sth
divest divest so/sth of sth
divide divide and conquer
divide divide by sth
divide divide so against so/sth
divide divide sth between people or things
divide divide sth by sth
divide divide sth fifty-fifty
divide divide sth into sth
divide divide sth (off) (from sth or animals)
divide divide sth (up) (between so/sth)
divide divide sth with so

divide divided between sth
divide divided on so/sth
divide house divided against itself cannot stand.
divide United we stand, divided we fall.
divine To err is human(, to forgive divine).
divorce divorce oneself from sth
divulge divulge sth to so
divvy divvy sth up (between so)
dixie not just whistling Dixie
dixie You ain't just whistlin' Dixie.
do A man's gotta do what a man's gotta do.
do after all is said and done
do (Are you) doing okay?
do Can do.
do can't do anything with so/sth
do Can't say (a)s I do(, can't say (a)s I don't).
do careful not to do sth
do could do with so/sth
do Damned if you do, damned if you don't.
do devil finds work for idle hands to do.
do difficult is done at once; the impossible takes a little longer.
do do a double take
do do a dump on so/sth
do do a fade
do do a flip-flop (on sth)
do do a job on so/sth
do do a land-office business
do do a number on so/sth
do do a one-eighty
do do a slow burn
do do a snow job on so
do do a takeoff on so/sth
do do a three-sixty
do do an about-face (on so/sth)
do do an errand
do Do as I say, not as I do.
do do as sth
do Do as you would be done by.
do do away with oneself
do do away with so or an animal
do do away with sth
do do business with so
do do credit to so
do do dope
do do drugs
do do for so
do do for sth
do (Do) have some more.
do Do I have to paint (you) a picture?
do Do I have to spell it out (for you)?
do Do I make myself (perfectly) clear?
do Do I need to paint you a picture?
do do it
do do justice to sth
do Do not let the sun go down on your anger.
do Do not let the sun go down on your wrath.
do Do not wash your dirty linen in public.
do do one's bit
do do one's business
do do one's duty
do do one's (level) best
do do one's (own) thing

do do one's part
do do one's utmost (to do sth)
do do oneself proud
do do or die
do do's and don'ts
do Do sit down.
do do so
do do some fine coin
do do somehow by so
do do somehow for so
do do so a favor
do do so a good turn
do do so a heap of good
do do so a kindness
do do so a power of good
do do so credit
do do so damage
do do so dirt(y)
do do so (down)
do do so good
do do so in
do do so one better
do do so/sth up
do do so out of sth
do do so over
do do so proud
do do so's bidding
do do so's heart good
do do sth about so/sth
do do sth by hand
do do sth by the book
do do sth from scratch
do do sth hand in hand
do do sth in
do do sth over
do do sth up
do do sth with so/sth
do Do tell.
do do the dishes
do do the honors
do do the trick
do do time
do do too
do Do unto others as you would have them do unto you.
do Do we have to go through all that again?
do Do what?
do do with so/sth
do do without
do (Do you) care if I join you?
do (Do) you eat with that mouth?
do Do you expect me to believe that?
do Do you follow?
do (Do you) get my drift?
do (Do you) get the picture?
do (Do) you hear?
do (Do) you kiss your momma with that mouth?
do (Do you) know what?
do (Do you) know what I mean?
do (Do you) know what I'm saying?
do (Do) you mean to say sth?
do (Do) you mean to tell me sth?
do Do you mind?
do (Do you) mind if...?
do (Do you) mind if I join you?
do Do you read me?
do (Do you) want to know something?
do (Do you) want to make something of it?
do (Do) you want to step outside?
do done and gone

do done by mirrors
do done deal
do done for
do done in
do done 'n' did
do done over
do done to a T
do done to a turn
do done told you
do done with mirrors
do done with so/sth
do Don't do anything I wouldn't do.
do Don't even think about (doing) it.
do Don't put off for tomorrow what you can do today.
do Don't tell me what to do!
do easier said than done
do fine how do you do
do get down to (doing) sth
do get out of (doing) sth
do good as done
do have nothing to do with so/sth
do have sth doing
do have sth to do with sth
do have to do with sth
do How (are) you doing?
do How do you do.
do How do you know?
do How do you like school?
do How do you like that?
do How do you like them apples?
do How do you like this weather?
do How dumb do you think I am?
do How many times do I have to tell you?
do (I) can't say (as) I do.
do (I) can't say's I do.
do (I) can't say that I do.
do I couldn't ask you to do that.
do I do believe.
do I (do) declare!
do (I) don't care if I do.
do (I) don't mind if I do.
do If a thing is worth doing, it's worth doing well.
do If you want a thing done well, do it yourself.
do I'm damned if I do and damned if I don't.
do (I'm) doing okay.
do in thing (to do)
do It will take some doing.
do (I've) been there(, done that).
do I've done my do.
do (I've) (got) better things to do.
do I've got work to do.
do left hand doesn't know what the right hand is doing.
do Let George do it.
do Let's do lunch (sometime).
do Let's do this again (sometime).
do make do (with so/sth)
do Monkey see, monkey do.
do No can do.
do No harm done.
do No sooner said than done
do not have anything to do with so/sth
do not have anything to do with sth
do Nothing doing!
do *out of the goodness of one's heart
do over (and done) with
do reed before the wind lives on, while mighty oaks do fall.

do So do I.
do Suppose I do?
do Supposing I do?
do take some doing
do tell so what to do with sth
do That's a fine how-do-you-do.
do That will do.
do Those who can, do; those who can't, teach.
do Two wrongs do not make a right.
do We must do this again (sometime).
do Well begun is half done.
do Well done!
do We('ll) have to do lunch sometime.
do (Well,) what do you know!
do well-to-do
do What can I do for you?
do What do you know?
do What do you know (about that)?
do What do you know for sure?
do What do you say?
do What do you think?
do What do you think of that?
do What do you think of this weather?
do What do you think you are doing here?
do What do you want me to say?
do What else can I do?
do What else can I do for you?
do What if I do?
do What more can I do?
do What's done cannot be undone.
do What's done is done.
do when all is said and done
do When do we eat?
do When in Rome(, do as the Romans do).
do Where do (you think) you get off?
do Who do you think you are?
do Who do you think you're kidding?
do Who do you think you're talking to?
do Who do you want to speak to?
do Who do you want (to talk to)?
do Will do.
do With whom do you wish to speak?
do woman's work is never done.
do Yes indeed(y (do))!
do You couldn't (do that)!
do You doing okay?
do You got to do what you got to do.
do You make a better door than you do a window.
do You never know (what you can do) till you try.
do You wouldn't (do that)!
doc What's up, doc?
dock dock so/sth for sth
dock dock (sth) at some place
dock dock sth from sth
doctor apple a day keeps the doctor away.
doctor Doctor Livingstone, I presume?
doctor doctor's orders
doctor doctor so up
doctor just what the doctor ordered
doctor spin doctor
doctor You're the doctor.
dodder dodder along
dodge dodge behind sth
dodo dead as a dodo
dodo go the way of the dodo
does Conscience does make cowards of us all.

does Does it work for you?
does Dog does not eat dog.
does Easy does it.
does Handsome is as handsome does.
does How does that grab you?
does Man does not live by bread alone.
does Money does not grow on trees.
does neither does so
does One swallow does not make a summer.
does Pretty is as pretty does.
does That does it!
does What difference does it make?
does What does that prove?
doesn't Crime doesn't pay.
doesn't doesn't care who knows it
doesn't doesn't have enough sense to bell a cat
doesn't doesn't have enough sense to come in out of the rain
doesn't doesn't have the sense God gave geese
doesn't doesn't have the sense God gave him (or her)
doesn't doesn't know beans (about sth)
doesn't doesn't know his ass from a hole in the ground
doesn't doesn't know his ass from his elbow
doesn't (It) doesn't bother me any.
doesn't (It) doesn't bother me at all.
doesn't (It) doesn't hurt to ask.
doesn't It doesn't quite suit me.
doesn't (It) (really) doesn't matter to me.
doesn't left hand doesn't know what the right hand is doing.
doesn't This doesn't quite suit me.
doesn't What one doesn't know won't hurt one.
doesn't What the eye doesn't see, the heart doesn't grieve over.
dog barking dog never bites.
dog Better be the head of a dog than the tail of a lion.
dog bring a dog to heel
dog call the dogs off
dog crooked as a dog's hind leg
dog dirty dog
dog dog and pony show
dog dog ate my homework.
dog dog days
dog Dog does not eat dog.
dog dog in the manger
dog Dog my cats!
dog dog-eat-dog
dog dog-faced liar
dog doggy bag
dog Every dog has its day.
dog go to the dogs
dog hair of the dog that bit one
dog Hot diggety (dog)!
dog I wouldn't wish that on a dog.
dog If you lie down with dogs, you will get up with fleas.
dog It's raining cats and dogs.
dog lead a dog's life
dog Let sleeping dogs lie.
dog like a blind dog in a meat market
dog live a dog's life
dog Love me, love my dog.

dog lucky dog
dog meaner than a junkyard dog (with fourteen sucking pups)
dog put a dog off the scent
dog put on the dog
dog rain cats and dogs
dog see a man about a dog
dog shaggy-dog story
dog shouldn't happen to a dog
dog sick as a dog
dog tail wagging the dog
dog throw so to the dogs
dog Why keep a dog and bark yourself?
dog You cannot teach an old dog new tricks.
doggo lie doggo
doggy doggy bag
doghouse find oneself in the doghouse
doghouse in the doghouse
doghouse put so into the doghouse
doldrums in the doldrums
doldrums put so into the doldrums
dole dole sth out (to so)
dole on the dole
doll (all) dolled up
doll doll so up
dollar almighty dollar
dollar bet one's bottom dollar
dollar bet so dollars to doughnuts
dollar day late and a dollar short
dollar dollar for dollar
dollar feel like a million (dollars)
dollar He wears a ten-dollar hat on a five-cent head.
dollar like a million (dollars)
dollar look like a million dollars
dollar phony as a three-dollar bill
dollar queer as a three-dollar bill
dollar sixty-four-dollar question
dollar sound as a dollar
dominion gain dominion over so/sth
don't Better the devil you know than the devil you don't know.
don't Can't say (a)s I do(, can't say (a)s I don't).
don't Damned if you do, damned if you don't.
don't do's and don'ts
don't don't amount to a bucket of spit
don't Don't ask.
don't Don't ask me.
don't Don't be gone (too) long.
don't Don't be too sure.
don't Don't bite off more than you can chew.
don't Don't bother.
don't Don't bother me!
don't Don't breathe a word of this to anyone.
don't Don't call us, we'll call you.
don't don't care a whit
don't Don't change horses in midstream.
don't Don't count your chickens before they are hatched.
don't Don't cry before you are hurt.
don't Don't cry over spilled milk.
don't Don't do anything I wouldn't do.
don't Don't even look like sth!
don't Don't even think about (doing) it.
don't Don't even think about it (happening).

don't Don't forget to write.
don't Don't get your bowels in an uproar!
don't don't give a continental
don't don't give a hoot (in hell's hollow)
don't Don't give it a (second) thought.
don't Don't give it another thought.
don't Don't give me any of your lip!
don't Don't give me that line!
don't Don't give up!
don't Don't give up the ship!
don't Don't give up without a fight!
don't Don't give up your day job.
don't Don't hand me that (line)!
don't Don't have a cow!
don't don't have a pot to piss in (or a window to throw it out of)
don't Don't hold your breath.
don't Don't I know it!
don't Don't I know you from somewhere?
don't Don't judge a book by its cover.
don't Don't knock it.
don't don't know whether to eat it or rub it on
don't Don't let it go any further.
don't Don't let it out of this room.
don't Don't let so/sth get you down.
don't Don't let the bastards wear you down.
don't Don't look a gift horse in the mouth.
don't Don't make me laugh!
don't Don't make me say it again!
don't Don't make me tell you again!
don't Don't make two bites of a cherry.
don't Don't mention it.
don't Don't mind me.
don't Don't push (me)!
don't Don't put all your eggs in one basket.
don't Don't put off for tomorrow what you can do today.
don't Don't put the cart before the horse.
don't Don't quit trying.
don't Don't quit your day job.
don't Don't rush me!
don't Don't say it!
don't Don't speak too soon.
don't Don't spend it all in one place.
don't Don't stand on ceremony.
don't Don't start (on me)!
don't Don't stay away so long.
don't Don't sweat it!
don't Don't take any wooden nickels.
don't Don't teach your grandmother to suck eggs.
don't Don't tell a soul.
don't Don't tell me what to do!
don't Don't that (just) beat all!
don't Don't throw the baby out with the bathwater.
don't Don't touch that dial!
don't Don't waste my time.
don't Don't waste your breath.
don't Don't waste your time.
don't Don't work too hard.
don't Don't worry (about a thing).
don't Don't worry your (pretty little) head about it.
don't Don't you know it!

don't Don't you wish!
don't God willing and the creek don't rise
don't I don't believe it!
don't (I) don't believe I've had the pleasure.
don't I don't believe this!
don't I don't care.
don't (I) don't care if I do.
don't I don't have time to breathe.
don't I don't have time to catch my breath.
don't I don't know.
don't I don't mean maybe!
don't (I) don't mind if I do.
don't I don't mind telling you (sth).
don't I don't rightly know.
don't (I) don't think so.
don't I don't understand (it).
don't I don't want to alarm you, but
don't I don't want to sound like a busybody, but
don't I don't want to upset you, but
don't I don't want to wear out my welcome.
don't I don't wonder.
don't If at first you don't succeed, try, try again.
don't If that don't beat a pig a-pecking!
don't If that don't beat all!
don't If there's anything you need, don't hesitate to ask.
don't If you don't like it, (you can) lump it.
don't If you don't make mistakes, you don't make anything.
don't If you don't mind!
don't If you don't see what you want, please ask (for it).
don't I'm damned if I do and damned if I don't.
don't (It) don't bother me none.
don't (It) don't cut no ice (with so).
don't (It) don't cut no squares (with so).
don't (It) don't make me no nevermind.
don't Lord willing and the creek don't rise
don't (Please) don't get up.
don't Some people (just) don't know when to quit.
don't Suppose I don't?
don't Supposing I don't?
don't They don't make them like they used to.
don't thing you don't want is dear at any price.
don't (We) don't see you much around here anymore.
don't What if I don't?
don't What you don't know won't hurt you.
don't where the sun don't shine
don't why don't you?
don't You don't expect me to believe that.
don't You don't get something for nothing.
don't You don't know the half of it.
don't You don't know where it's been.
don't You don't say.
don't You just don't get it!

doom doom so/sth to sth
doom doomed to sth
door answer the door
door at death's door
door beat a path to so's door
door behind closed doors
door blow so's doors off
door broad as a barn door
door close the door on so/sth
door close the door to so/sth
door crack the door (open)
door creaking door hangs longest.
door darken so's door
door door must be either shut or open.
door doors open up (to so)
door door-to-door
door from door to door
door get one's foot in the door
door golden key can open any door.
door Katie bar the door
door keep the wolf from the door
door lay sth at so's door
door leave the door open (for sth)
door lie at death's door
door live next door (to so)
door Lock the stable door after the horse is stolen.
door one's next-door neighbor
door open a few doors (for so)
door open some doors (for so)
door open the door to so
door open the door to sth
door put sth at so's door
door see so to the door
door show so (to) the door
door shut the door (up)on so/sth
door Shut the stable door after the horse has bolted.
door slam the door in so's face
door The wolf is at the door.
door When one door shuts, another opens.
door When poverty comes in at the door, love flies out of the window.
door When the wolf comes in at the door, love creeps out of the window.
door You make a better door than you do a window.
doornail dead as a doornail
doornail deader than a doornail
doorstep at so's doorstep
doorstep on so's doorstep
dope do dope
dope dope so or an animal up
dope dope sth out
dope straight dope
dork dork off
dose dose of one's own medicine
dose dose so or an animal with sth
dose go through so like a dose of the salts
dose overdose (so) on sth
doss doss down (for some time)
dot dot sth with sth
dot on the dot
dot see so on the dot
dot show up on the dot
dot sign on the dotted line
dote dote (up)on so/sth
double do a double take
double double as so/sth
double double back (on so/sth)

double double Dutch
double double in brass (as sth)
double double over
double double so over
double double sth over
double double up (on so/sth)
double double up (with laughter)
double double up (with pain)
double double up (with so)
double double whammy
double double-cross so
double double-edged sword
double on the double
double see double
doubt benefit of the doubt
doubt beyond a reasonable doubt
doubt beyond the shadow of a doubt
doubt cast doubt(s) (on so/sth)
doubt doubting Thomas
doubt have doubts about so/sth
doubt I doubt it.
doubt I doubt that.
doubt no doubt
doubt (There is) no doubt about it.
doubt without a doubt
doubt without a shadow of a doubt
doughnuts bet so dollars to doughnuts
douse douse so/sth with sth
dovetail dovetail sth into sth
dovetail dovetail with sth
down Anything new down your way?
down (Are) things getting you down?
down argue so down
down argue sth down
down ask so down
down back down (from so/sth)
down back down (on sth)
down back down (sth)
down batten down the hatches
down batter sth down
down bear down (on so/sth)
down beat down (on so/sth)
down beat so down
down beat sth down
down bed down (for sth)
down bed down some place
down bed (so/sth) down (some place)
down belt a drink down
down belt so/sth down
down bend down
down bid sth down
down bind so/sth down
down blaze down (on so/sth)
down blow so/sth down
down bog down
down bogged down
down boil down to sth
down boil sth down
down bolt sth down
down boogie down (to somewhere)
down bounce up and down
down bow down (to so/sth)
down break down
down break so down
down break sth down
down breathe down so's neck
down bring down the curtain (on sth)
down bring so down
down bring sth crashing down (around one)
down bring sth down
down bring the house down
down brush sth down

down buckle down (to sth)
down buckle so/sth down
down buff sth down
down build down
down bunk down (for the night)
down burn down
down burn so down
down burn sth down
down button sth down
down call so down
down call sth down (on so)
down call sth down (to so)
down calm down
down calm so or an animal down
down carry sth down
down cast one's eyes down
down cast sth down
down catch one with one's pants down
down chain so/sth down
down charge down on so/sth
down chase so/sth down
down choke sth down
down chop sth down
down chow (sth) down
down chuck sth down
down clamp down (on so/sth)
down clean so/sth down
down climb down (from sth)
down close down
down close so/sth down
down close sth down
down clunk down
down clunk sth down
down come down
down cool down
down cool so down
down copy sth down (from so/sth)
down count down
down cower down (from sth)
down crack down (on so/sth)
down crash down (around so/sth)
down crouch down
down crunch sth down
down crush so/sth down
down cut down (on sth)
down cut so down
down cut sth down
down damp sth down
down die down
down dig down
down dim down
down dim sth down
down Do not let the sun go down on your anger.
down Do not let the sun go down on your wrath.
down Do sit down.
down do so (down)
down Don't let so/sth get you down.
down Don't let the bastards wear you down.
down doss down (for some time)
down down and dirty
down down by some amount
down down for sth
down down for the count
down down in the dumps
down down in the mouth
down down on one's luck
down down on so/sth
down down one for the road
down down pat
down down South

down down the chute
down down the drain
down Down the hatch.
down down the little red lane
down down the road
down down the street
down down the tube(s)
down down to a gnat's eyebrow
down down to chili and beans
down down to the last bit of money
down down to the last detail
down down under
down down with a disease
down down (with so)
down Down with so/sth!
down down-and-out
down down-at-the-heels
down down-home
down down-to-earth
down down-to-the-wire
down drag so/sth down
down draw sth down
down dress so down
down dressing-down
down drill down (to sth)
down drink sth down
down drive a price down
down drive down (to some place)
down drive so down (to some place)
down drive sth down (to some place)
down drizzle down (on so/sth)
down drop down
down drop so/sth down
down duck down
down dwindle down (to sth)
down ease so/sth down (from sth)
down face so down
down face sth down
down fade down
down fade sth down
down fall down
down fall (down) at sth
down fasten sth down (to sth)
down fight so/sth down
down fight sth down
down file sth down
down flag so/sth down
down flake down
down fling so/sth down
down flop down
down flop sth down on(to) sth
down flutter down
down force so/sth down
down force sth down
down garbage sth down
down get down
down get (down) off one's high horse
down get so down
down get so/sth down (from sth)
down get so/sth down sth
down get sth down
down glance down (at sth)
down glare down on so/sth
down glue sth down
down go down
down gobble sth down
down grade so down (on sth)
down grind so down
down grind sth down
down grow down (into sth)
down gulp sth down
down gun so or an animal down
down guzzle sth down

down hack sth down
down hammer sth down
down hand sth down from so to so
down hand sth down (to so)
down hands down
down hang down (from so/sth)
down haul sth down
down have a yellow streak down one's back
down have so down
down have sth down to a T
down He that is down need fear no fall.
down help so down (from sth)
down hew sth down
down hold so or an animal down
down hook sth down
down hoot so down
down hose so down
down hose so/sth down
down hound so or an animal down
down howl so down
down hunker down (on sth)
down hunker down to sth
down hunt so/sth down
down hurl so/sth down
down hurry down (to somewhere)
down ice sth down
down If you lie down with dogs, you will get up with fleas.
down It is easier to tear down than to build up.
down jaw so down
down jot sth down
down jump (down) (from sth)
down jump down so's throat
down jump down sth
down keep it down (to a dull roar)
down keep so down
down keep so/sth down
down keep sth down
down Keep your head down.
down kick sth down
down kneel down
down kneel down (before so/sth)
down knock so down a peg (or two)
down knock so down to size
down knock so/sth down
down knock sth down
down knock-down, drag-out fight
down knuckle down (to sth)
down lash down on so/sth
down lash so/sth down
down laugh so/sth down
down lay down
down lay (oneself) down
down lay so down
down lay sth down (on sth)
down lead down to sth
down lead so down (sth)
down lead so down the garden path
down lead so down to sth
down lean down
down leap down (from sth)
down leave sth down
down let down
down let one's guard down
down let one's hair down
down Let's get down to business.
down let so down
down let so/sth down
down level sth down
down lie down

down lift so/sth down (from sth)
down live sth down
down load so/sth down (with so/sth)
down look down (at so/sth)
down look up and down (for so/sth)
down look up and down sth
down mark so down
down mark sth down
down melt down
down melt sth down
down mop sth down
down move down
down move so/sth down
down mow so/sth down
down nail so down (on sth)
down nail sth down
down narrow sth down (to people or things)
down nestle down (in sth)
down note sth down
down nothing down
down *one for the road
down pace up and down
down pack down
down pack sth down
down pad down (some place)
down pare sth down (to sth)
down pass sth down (to so)
down paste sth down
down pat sth down
down pay sth down
down peg sth down
down pelt down (on so/sth)
down pin so down (on sth)
down pin sth down
down pipe down
down place sth down (on sth)
down plane sth down
down plaster one's hair down
down play down to so
down play so/sth down
down plonk sth down
down plump sth down
down plunge down sth
down plunk (oneself) down
down plunk so/sth down
down point down to sth
down pop down (for a visit)
down pound sth down
down pour down (on so/sth)
down pour money down the drain
down press down on so/sth
down price sth down
down pull down (an amount of money)
down pull so down
down pull so or an animal down
down pull sth down
down punch sth down
down push down on sth
down push so/sth down
down put an animal down
down put one's foot down (about so/sth)
down put roots down (some place)
down put so down as sth bad
down put so down (for sth)
down put so/sth down
down put sth down
down quiet down
down quiet so or an animal down
down rain down on so/sth
down rain sth down (on so/sth)
down ram so/sth down so's throat
down ram sth down
down reach down

down reach sth down
down remain down
down render sth down
down ride so or an animal down
down ride sth down
down right down so's alley
down ring the curtain down (on sth)
down rinse so/sth down
down rinse sth down (with sth)
down rip sth down
down roll down
down roll sth down
down round sth down
down rub so or an animal down
down run down
down run it down
down run so/sth down
down run sth down
down sag down
down salt sth down
down sand sth down
down saw sth down
down scale sth down
down scarf sth down
down scoot down (to some place)
down scream down (on so/sth)
down scream so down
down screw sth down
down scribble sth down
down scrub so/sth down
down scrunch down
down scrunch sth down (into sth)
down see so down to sth
down sell so down the river
down send so down for sth
down send so/sth down
down set so down (on(to) sth)
down set so/sth down
down set sth down
down settle down
down shake so down
down shake sth down
down shoot so down in flames
down shoot so/sth or an animal down
down shoot sth down
down shout so/sth down
down shove so/sth down so's throat
down shut down
down shut sth down
down simmer down
down sink down
down sit down
down slam so/sth down
down slam sth down (on(to) sth)
down slap so down
down slap sth down
down sled down sth
down slick sth down
down slide down from sth
down slide down sth
down slim down
down slim so down
down slip down
down slip sth down
down slope down (to sth or some place)
down slope (down) toward sth
down slouch down
down slow down
down sluice sth down
down slump down
down smack so down
down smack sth down (on(to) sth)
down smooth sth down

down snug down (some place)
down snuggle down (into sth)
down snuggle down (with so)
down snuggle down (with sth)
down soap so/sth down
down soft as down
down (so's) ups and downs
down spaz down
down speak down to so
down spell so down
down spiral down
down splash down
down sponge so/sth down
down squash sth down
down stand down
down stare so down
down stay down
down step down (from sth)
down step sth down
down stick sth down
down stoop down
down strap so/sth down
down stream down (on so/sth)
down strike so/sth down
down strike sth down
down strip down
down strip so/sth down to sth
down stuff sth down so's throat
down stuff sth down sth
down suck so/sth down
down swab sth down
down swallow sth down
down sweep down on so/sth
down sweep sth down
down swill sth down
down swoop down (up)on so/sth
down tack sth down
down take so down a notch (or two)
down take so down a peg (or two)
down take so down (to size)
down take so/sth down
down take sth down
down take sth lying down
down talk down to so
down talk so down
down tamp sth down
down tap sth down
down tear down sth
down tear so/sth down
down tear sth down
down thin down
down thin so down
down thin sth down
down throttle sth down
down throw down the gauntlet
down throw sth down
down thrust sth down
down thumbs down
down thump sth down
down tie so down (to so/sth)
down tie so/sth down
down tied down
down tone sth down
down topple down
down topple sth down
down toss sth down
down touch down
down towel so/sth down
down track so/sth down
down trample so/sth down
down trickle down (to so/sth)
down trim (oneself) down
down trim sth down

down tumble down
down tumble so/sth down sth
down turn a place upside down
down turn so down
down turn so/sth upside down
down turn sth down
down turn sth upside down
down turn thumbs down (on so/sth)
down up one side and down the other
down upside-down
down vote so/sth down
down walk down sth
down wash sth down sth
down wash sth down (with sth)
down water sth down
down wear down
down wear so down
down wear sth down
down weigh so down
down weigh so/sth down
down weight so/sth down (with sth)
down wet so/sth down
down What goes up must come down.
down What's going down?
down when it comes right down to it
down when the chips are down
down whittle so down to size
down whittle sth down (to size)
down wind down
down wind sth down
down wipe sth down
down wolf sth down
down work down (the line) (to so/sth)
down work sth down
down write down to so
down write so down as sth
down write sth down
down yellow streak (down so's back)
downgrade downgrade so/sth to sth
downhill downhill all the way
downhill downhill from here on
downhill go downhill
downhill has the world by the tail (with a downhill drag)
downtime downtime
doze doze off (to sleep)
dozen baker's dozen
dozen by the dozen
dozen by the dozens
dozen daily dozen
dozen dime a dozen
dozen It's six of one, half a dozen of another.
dozen nineteen to the dozen
dozen six of one and half a dozen of the other
drabs in dribs and drabs
draft draft so for sth
draft draft so into sth
draft feel a draft
drag drag behind
drag drag on
drag drag (on so)
drag drag (on sth)
drag drag one's feet (on or over sth)
drag drag out
drag drag so in (on sth)
drag drag so/sth down
drag drag so/sth into sth
drag drag so/sth off of so/sth
drag drag so/sth off (to sth)
drag drag so/sth on(to) sth
drag drag so/sth over to so/sth

drag drag so/sth through sth
drag drag so through the mud
drag drag so up
drag drag sth away (from sth)
drag drag sth behind one
drag drag sth out
drag drag sth up
drag dragged out
drag has the world by the tail (with a downhill drag)
drag in drag
drag knock-down, drag-out fight
drag Look (at) what the cat dragged in!
drag look like the cat dragged in
drag take a drag (on sth)
drag Wild horses couldn't drag so away (from sth).
dragoon dragoon so into sth
drain down the drain
drain drain away
drain drain from sth
drain drain out
drain drain so/sth of sth
drain drain sth away (from sth)
drain drain sth from so/sth
drain drain sth of sth
drain drain sth off sth
drain drain sth out of sth
drain go down the drain
drain pour money down the drain
drape drape oneself over sth
drape drape over (sth)
drape drape so/sth in sth
drape drape so/sth with sth
drape drape sth around so/sth
draw back to the drawing board
draw draw a bead on so/sth
draw draw a blank
draw draw a line between sth and sth else
draw draw a line in the sand
draw draw against an amount of money
draw draw ahead (of so/sth)
draw draw apart (from so/sth)
draw draw away (from so/sth)
draw draw blood
draw draw fire from so
draw draw for sth
draw draw in one's horns
draw draw interest
draw draw lots
draw draw near
draw draw on so/sth
draw draw (oneself) aside
draw draw oneself up (to sth)
draw draw people or things together
draw draw some kind of attention away (from so/sth)
draw draw so aside
draw draw so or an animal out of sth
draw draw (so/sth) from sth
draw draw so/sth into sth
draw draw so/sth out of some place
draw draw so/sth to(ward) so/sth
draw draw so out on so/sth
draw draw so's attention to so/sth
draw draw (so's) fire (away) from so/sth or an animal
draw draw so together
draw draw sth apart
draw draw sth down
draw draw sth forth
draw draw sth off (from sth)

draw draw sth out
draw draw sth over so/sth
draw draw sth to
draw draw sth up
draw draw straws for sth
draw draw the line (at sth)
draw draw the line between sth and sth else
draw draw to a close
draw draw up
draw draw (up) alongside so/sth
draw draw upon sth
draw drawing card
draw drawn and quartered
draw drawn like a moth to a flame
draw get the draw on so
draw go back to the drawing board
draw have so drawn and quartered
draw luck of the draw
draw One has to draw the line somewhere.
draw quick on the draw
draw slow on the draw
drawers drop one's drawers
drawn drawn and quartered
drawn drawn like a moth to a flame
drawn have so drawn and quartered
dread burnt child dreads the fire.
dream broken dreams
dream daydream about so/sth
dream dream about so/sth
dream dream come true
dream Dream of a funeral and you hear of a marriage.
dream Dream of a funeral and you hear of a wedding.
dream dream of doing sth
dream dream of so/sth
dream Dream on.
dream dream sth away
dream dream sth up
dream Morning dreams come true.
dream pipe dream
dream the American dream
dream wouldn't dream of doing sth
dredge dredge so/sth up
drench drench so/sth in sth
dress (all) dressed up
dress all dressed up and nowhere to go
dress dress for so
dress dress for sth
dress dress (oneself) up
dress dress so down
dress dress so/sth up
dress dress so up (as so/sth)
dress dress (up) as so/sth
dress dressed to kill
dress dressed to the nines
dress dressed to the teeth
dress dressed (up) fit to kill
dress dressing-down
dribs in dribs and drabs
drift (Do you) get my drift?
drift drift along
drift drift apart (from each other)
drift drift away (from so)
drift drift away (from so/sth)
drift drift back (to so)
drift drift back (to so/sth)
drift drift in(to sth)
drift drift off
drift drift out

drift drift toward so/sth
drift drift with sth
drift get so's drift
drift get the drift of sth
drift if you get my drift
drill drill down (to sth)
drill drill in(to sth)
drill drill so in sth
drill drill sth into so/sth
drill What's the drill?
drink big drink of water
drink buy a round (of drinks)
drink buy the next round (of drinks)
drink (Could I) buy you a drink?
drink (Could I) get you something (to drink)?
drink drink like a fish
drink drink so under the table
drink drink sth down
drink drink sth in
drink drink sth up
drink drink to excess
drink drink to so/sth
drink Drink up!
drink drive so to drink
drink Eat, drink, and be merry, for tomorrow we die.
drink fall in the drink
drink I'll drink to that!
drink in the drink
drink knock back a drink
drink *one for the road
drink tall drink of water
drink throw so in the drink
drink What are you drinking?
drink What would you like to drink?
drink You can lead a horse to water, but you can't make it drink.
drip drip in(to sth)
drip drip sth into sth
drip drip with sth
drive backseat driver
drive Bad money drives out good.
drive drive a coach and horses through sth
drive drive a hard bargain
drive drive a price down
drive drive a price up
drive drive a wedge between so and so else
drive drive at sth
drive drive away
drive drive back
drive drive between sth and sth else
drive drive down (to some place)
drive drive into so/sth
drive drive in(to sth)
drive drive into the middle of nowhere
drive drive off
drive drive on
drive drive one out of one's mind
drive drive out (to some place)
drive drive over (to some place)
drive Drive safely.
drive drive so around sth
drive drive so around the bend
drive drive so back on sth
drive drive so back to so
drive drive so batty
drive drive so bonkers
drive drive so crazy
drive drive so down (to some place)
drive drive so insane

drive drive so into a corner
drive drive so mad
drive drive so nuts
drive drive so on (to sth)
drive drive so or an animal away (from sth or some place)
drive drive so or an animal out of sth
drive drive so/sth back
drive drive so/sth off
drive drive so out
drive drive so to despair
drive drive so to distraction
drive drive so to do sth
drive drive so to drink
drive drive so to the brink
drive drive so to the edge
drive drive so to the wall
drive drive so up the wall
drive drive so up (to some place)
drive drive sth around sth
drive drive sth down (to some place)
drive drive sth home
drive drive sth into so/sth
drive drive sth into sth
drive drive sth into the ground
drive drive through (sth)
drive drive up (to some place)
drive driving force (behind so/sth)
drive for a drive
drive in the driver's seat
drive Needs must when the devil drives.
drive pure as the driven snow
drive serve as the driving force (behind so/sth)
drive Sunday driver
drive take sth for a drive
drive What are you driving at?
drive white as the driven snow
drizzle drizzle down (on so/sth)
drone drone on (about so/sth)
drone drone sth out
drool drool (all) over so/sth
drop at the drop of a hat
drop Constant dropping wears away a stone.
drop drop a bomb(shell)
drop drop a brick
drop drop a bundle (on so)
drop drop a bundle (on sth)
drop drop a hint
drop drop across so/sth
drop drop around (for sth)
drop drop around (sometime)
drop drop away
drop drop back
drop drop behind (in sth)
drop drop behind (so/sth)
drop drop below so/sth
drop drop by (sometime)
drop drop by the wayside
drop drop dead
drop drop down
drop drop everything
drop drop in (on so)
drop drop in one's tracks
drop Drop in sometime.
drop drop in the bucket
drop drop in the ocean
drop drop in (to say hello)
drop Drop it!
drop drop like flies
drop drop names

drop drop off
drop drop one's drawers
drop drop one's teeth
drop drop out of sight
drop drop out (of sth)
drop drop over
drop drop so
drop drop so a few lines
drop drop so a line
drop drop so's name
drop drop sth across sth
drop drop sth on so
drop drop the ball
drop drop the other shoe
drop Drop the subject!
drop drop up (some place)
drop drop-dead gorgeous
drop get the drop on so
drop (I'm) glad you could drop by.
drop not to touch a drop
drop so quiet you could hear a pin drop
drop so still you could hear a pin drop
drop *through the cracks
drop Turn on, tune in, drop out.
drop wait for the other shoe to drop
drove bring so/sth out in droves
drove come out in droves
drove in droves
drove out in droves
drown drown in sth
drown drown one's sorrows
drown drown one's troubles
drown drown so in sth
drown drown so or an animal in sth
drown drown so or an animal out
drown drown so/sth out
drown drowning man will clutch at a straw.
drown If you're born to be hanged, then you'll never be drowned.
drug do drugs
drug drug on the market
drum bang the drum for so/sth
drum beat the drum for so/sth
drum drum on sth
drum drum so out
drum drum sth into so
drum drum sth out
drum drum sth up
drum march to (the beat of) a different drummer
drum tight as a drum
drunk commode-hugging drunk
drunk dead drunk
drunk drunk and disorderly
drunk drunk as a lord
drunk drunk as a skunk
drunk Heaven protects children(, sailors,) and drunken men.
drunk screeching (drunk)
druthers have one's druthers
dry about as exciting as watching (the) paint dry
dry cut and dried
dry dry as a bone
dry dry as dust
dry dry out
dry dry run
dry dry so/sth off
dry dry so out
dry dry sth out
dry dry sth up

dry dry spell
dry dry up
dry dry-gulch so
dry exciting as watching (the) paint dry
dry hang so out to dry
dry hardly dry behind the ears
dry high and dry
dry Keep your powder dry.
dry leave so high and dry
dry not dry behind the ears
dry Put your trust in God, and keep your powder dry.
dry You never miss the water till the well runs dry.
dub dub sth in
dub dub sth over
dub flub the dub
duck as a duck takes to water
duck dead duck
duck duck and cover
duck duck down
duck duck out (of some place)
duck duck out (of sth)
duck duck soup
duck easy as duck soup
duck Fine weather for ducks.
duck get one's ducks in a row
duck lame duck
duck like a sitting duck
duck like water off a duck's back
duck looking like a sitting duck
duck Lord love a duck!
duck Lovely weather for ducks.
duck sitting duck
dude dude (oneself) up
dude duded up
dudgeon in high dudgeon
due Give credit where credit is due.
due give the devil her due
due give the devil his due
due in due course
due in due time
due pay one's dues
duke duke it out
duke duke so out
duke put up one's dukes
dull All work and no play makes Jack a dull boy.
dull deadly dull
dull dull as dishwater
dull dull as ditchwater
dull keep it down (to a dull roar)
dull never a dull moment
dumb deaf and dumb
dumb How dumb do you think I am?
dumb play dumb
dummy dummy up
dump do a dump on so/sth
dump down in the dumps
dump dump a load
dump dump on so/sth
dump dump one's load
dump dump sth on so
dump dumped on
dump Let's dump.
dun dun so for sth
dunk dunk so/sth into sth
dunk slam dunk
duration for the duration
dusk from dawn to dusk
dust bite the dust
dust Charge it to the dust and let the rain settle it.

dust cut the dust
dust dry as dust
dust dust bunny
dust dust kitten
dust dust so off
dust dust so/sth off
dust dust so's pants
dust dust sth out
dust gather dust
dust kiss the dust
dust when the dust settles
dutch double Dutch
dutch Dutch auction
dutch Dutch courage
dutch Dutch treat
dutch Dutch uncle
dutch go Dutch
dutch in Dutch (with so)
duty come on (duty)
duty do one's duty
duty duty bound (to do sth)
duty go above and beyond one's duty
duty go above and beyond the call of duty
duty in the line of duty
duty off duty
duty on active duty
duty on duty
duty relieve one of one's duties
duty shirk one's duty
dwell dwell in an ivory tower
dwell dwell (up)on so/sth
dwell dwell (up)on sth
dwell *in an ivory tower
dwindle dwindle away (to sth)
dwindle dwindle down (to sth)
dye dyed-in-the-wool
dying dying to do sth
dying dying to know (sth)
each cancel each other out
each fall in love (with each other)
each made for each other
each To each his own.
each with each passing day
eager eager beaver
eagle eagle eye
ear all ears
ear all eyes and ears
ear assault the ear
ear bend so's ear
ear Blow it out your ear!
ear coming out of one's ears
ear cute as a bug's ear
ear fall on deaf ears
ear Fields have eyes, and woods have ears.
ear get one's ears pinned back
ear get one's ears set out
ear give (an) ear to so/sth
ear go in one ear and out the other
ear grin from ear to ear
ear hang up (in so's ear)
ear hardly dry behind the ears
ear have an ear for sth
ear have one's ear to the ground
ear I'm all ears.
ear In a pig's ear!
ear in (at) one ear and out (of) the other
ear keep an ear to the ground
ear keep one's ear to the ground
ear lend an ear to so/sth
ear lend your ear to so/sth

ear like tryin' to scratch your ear with your elbow
ear Little pitchers have big ears.
ear lower so's ears
ear music to so's ears
ear nail so's ears back
ear not believe one's ears
ear not dry behind the ears
ear one's ears are red
ear one's ears are ringing
ear pin so's ears back
ear play by ear
ear play sth by ear
ear pound one's ear
ear prick up its ears
ear pull in one's ears
ear ring in so's ears
ear talk so's ear off
ear throw one out on one's ear
ear tin ear
ear turn a deaf ear (to so/sth)
ear up to one's ears (in sth)
ear use your head for more than something to keep your ears apart
ear Walls have ears.
ear wet behind the ears
ear You cannot make a silk purse out of a sow's ear.
earful earful
earliest at so's earliest convenience
early at an early date
early at so's earliest convenience
early bright and early
early early bird
early early bird catches the worm.
early early on
early Early ripe, early rotten.
early Early to bed and early to rise, makes a man healthy, wealthy, and wise.
early gotta get up pretty early in the morning to do sth
earmark earmark sth for so/sth
earn earn one's keep
earn earn one's spurs
earn penny saved is a penny earned.
earnest act in earnest
earnest in earnest
earnest speak in earnest
earshot come within earshot (of sth)
earshot move within earshot (of sth)
earshot out of earshot
earshot within earshot (of sth)
earth all over the earth
earth bring so down to earth
earth come down to earth
earth cost the earth
earth down-to-earth
earth from the four corners of the earth
earth hell on earth
earth like nothing on earth
earth move heaven and earth to do sth
earth no earthly reason
earth on earth
earth paradise (on earth)
earth plummet to earth
earth run so/sth to earth
earth salt of the earth
earth to the ends of the earth
earth Where on (God's green) earth?
earth wipe so/sth off the face of the earth

earthly no earthly reason
ease at ease
ease ease away (from so/sth)
ease ease back (on sth)
ease ease off
ease ease (on) out (of sth)
ease ease so (on) out (of sth)
ease ease so/sth along
ease ease so/sth down (from sth)
ease ease so to out of sth
ease ease up (on so/sth)
ease ill at ease
ease put one at (one's) ease
ease set so's mind at ease (about so/sth)
ease with ease
easier easier said than done
easier It is easier to tear down than to build up.
easily able to breathe (easily) again
easily You (always) give up too eas(il)y.
east back East
east East is East and West is West (and never the twain shall meet).
east East, west, home's best.
easy able to breathe (easily) again
easy breathe easy
easy dead easy
easy easier said than done
easy easy as A, B, C
easy easy as (apple) pie
easy easy as duck soup
easy easy as falling off a log
easy easy as rolling off a log
easy easy as shooting fish in a barrel
easy easy come, easy go
easy Easy does it.
easy easy money
easy easy pickings
easy Easy, there!
easy easy to come by
easy free and easy
easy get off (easy)
easy go easy on so/sth
easy go easy on sth
easy have an easy time of it
easy I'm easy (to please).
easy (It) hasn't been easy.
easy It is easier to tear down than to build up.
easy It is easy to be wise after the event.
easy let so off (easy)
easy on easy street
easy over easy
easy Take it easy.
easy take it easy on so/sth or an animal
easy take it easy on sth
easy take the easy way out
easy take things easy
easy That's easy for you to say.
easy Things haven't been easy.
easy Uneasy lies the head that wears a crown.
easy You (always) give up too eas(il)y.
eat bite (to eat)
eat did everything he could 'cept eat us
eat (Do) you eat with that mouth?
eat dog ate my homework.
eat Dog does not eat dog.
eat dog-eat-dog

eat don't know whether to eat it or rub it on
eat eat (a meal) out
eat eat an animal up
eat eat and run
eat eat (away) at so
eat eat (away) at sth
eat eat crow
eat Eat, drink, and be merry, for tomorrow we die.
eat eat high on the hog
eat eat humble pie
eat eat in
eat eat in(to sth)
eat eat like a bird
eat eat like a horse
eat Eat my shorts!
eat eat one's cake and have it too
eat eat one's fill
eat eat one's hat
eat eat one's heart out
eat eat one's words
eat eat out
eat eat so out
eat eat so's lunch
eat eat so's salt
eat eat so up
eat eat sth away
eat eat sth off
eat eat sth out
eat eat (sth) out of sth
eat eat sth up
eat eat through (sth)
eat Eat to live, not live to eat.
eat Eat up!
eat eat(en) up with sth
eat grab a bite (to eat)
eat have one's cake and eat it too
eat He that would eat the kernel must crack the nut.
eat I could eat a horse!
eat (I) hate to eat and run.
eat I'll eat my hat.
eat Let them eat cake.
eat make so eat crow
eat so clean you could eat off the floor
eat The proof of the pudding is in the eating.
eat What's eating so?
eat When do we eat?
eat will eat so for breakfast
eat You cannot have your cake and eat it (too).
eat You have to eat a peck of dirt before you die.
eaten eat(en) up with sth
eavesdrop eavesdrop on so
eavesdrop eavesdrop on sth
eavesdrop Eavesdroppers never hear any good of themselves.
ebb ebb and flow
ebb ebb away
echo echo back to sth
echo echo with sth
economical economical with the truth
economize economize on sth
edge cutting edge
edge double-edged sword
edge drive so to the edge
edge edge away (from so/sth)
edge edge by (so/sth)
edge edge on so
edge edge (one's way) across (sth)

edge edge (one's way) around sth
edge edge over so
edge edge so out of sth
edge edge sth out
edge edge sth with sth
edge live on the edge
edge moist around the edges
edge on edge
edge on the bleeding edge
edge on the cutting edge
edge on the edge
edge on the leading edge
edge over the edge
edge set so's teeth on edge
edge take the edge off ((of) sth)
edge two-edged sword
edgewise get a word in edgewise
edit edit sth out of sth
educate educate so for sth
educate educate so in sth
eel slippery as an eel
effect come into effect
effect go into effect
effect have a bad effect (on so/sth)
effect have an effect on so/sth
effect in effect
effect or words to that effect
effect put sth into effect
effect something to that effect
effect strain for an effect
effect take effect
effigy burn so in effigy
effigy hang so in effigy
effort A for effort
effort all-out effort
effort begin an all-out effort
effort last-ditch effort
effort make an all-out effort
effort make every effort to do sth
effort make last-ditch effort
effort start an all-out effort
egg bad egg
egg Don't put all your eggs in one basket.
egg Don't teach your grandmother to suck eggs.
egg egg so on
egg Go fry an egg!
egg good egg
egg goose egg
egg have egg on one's face
egg He that would have eggs must endure the cackling of hens.
egg Kill the goose that lays the golden egg(s).
egg lay an egg
egg one's (butter and) egg money
egg put all one's eggs in one basket
egg rotten egg
egg sure as eggs is eggs
egg teach one's grandmother to suck eggs
egg walk on eggs
egg You cannot make an omelet without breaking eggs.
eggshell walk on eggshells
ego stroke so's ego
eight behind the eight ball
eight have so behind the eight ball
eight put so behind the eight ball
eighty do a one-eighty
eighty eighty-six sth

eighty turn one hundred and eighty degrees
either door must be either shut or open.
either (either) feast or famine
eject eject so from some place
eke eke sth out
elaborate elaborate on so/sth
elbow allow some elbow room
elbow bend one's elbow
elbow bend the elbow
elbow doesn't know his ass from his elbow
elbow elbow grease
elbow elbow (one's way) through (sth)
elbow elbow so aside
elbow elbow so out of sth
elbow lift one's elbow
elbow like tryin' to scratch your ear with your elbow
elbow need some elbow room
elbow rub elbows (with so)
elbow some elbow room
elbow use some elbow grease
elect elect so (as) sth
elect elect so to sth
elegant elegant sufficiency
element in one's element
element out of one's element
elephant seeing pink elephants
elephant white elephant
elevate elevate so/sth to sth
eleventh at the eleventh hour
eleventh eleventh-hour decision
elicit elicit sth from so
eliminate eliminate so/sth from sth
elope elope with so
eloquent wax eloquent
else alternate between so and so else
else arbitrate between so and so else
else between so and so else
else between sth and sth else
else come between so and so else
else come between sth and sth else
else confuse so with so else
else decide among so and so else
else decide between so and so else
else differentiate between so/sth and so/sth else
else differentiate so/sth from so/sth else
else discern between so/sth and so/sth else
else discriminate between so and so else or sth and sth else
else distinguish between so/sth and so/sth else
else draw a line between sth and sth else
else draw the line between sth and sth else
else drive a wedge between so and so else
else drive between sth and sth else
else envision so as so else
else equate so to so else
else fall between sth and sth else
else flit from sth to sth else
else fluctuate between so and so else
else fluctuate between sth and sth else
else get between so/sth and so/sth else
else go between so/sth and so/sth else
else hover between sth and sth else
else insert sth between sth and sth else
else interchange so with so else
else intersperse sth between sth else

else intervene between so and so else
else Is there anything else?
else join so with so else
else join sth to sth else
else join sth in with sth else
else judge between so/sth and so/sth else
else make sth out to be sth else
else match so against so else or sth against sth else
else mediate between so and so else
else migrate between some place and some place else
else mingle so with so else
else mistake so for so else
else mistake sth for sth else
else mix so up with so else
else mix sth up with sth else
else mixed up with so else
else name so after so else
else name so for so else
else or else
else oscillate between so/sth and so/sth else
else play so off against so else
else ply between sth and sth else
else rate so/sth below so/sth else
else rate so below sth else
else run between sth and sth else
else segregate so from so else
else segregate sth from sth else
else separate so from so else
else separate sth from sth else
else (So) what else is new?
else something else (again)
else step between so/sth and so/sth else
else sub so for so else
else subordinate so/sth to so/sth else
else substitute so for so else
else tell so from so else
else tell sth from sth else
else tell the difference between so and so else or sth and sth else
else There is a fine line between sth and sth else.
else throw so over for so else
else torn between so and so else
else vacillate between so and so else or sth and sth else
else vacillate between so and so else or sth and sth else
else vary between so and so else
else vary between sth and sth else
else waver between so and so else
else waver between sth and sth else
else What else can I do?
else What else can I do for you?
else (Will there be) anything else?
else You and who else?
else You are something else (again)!
'em If you can't lick 'em, join 'em.
'em Put 'em up!
'em Stick 'em up!
'em up and at 'em
emanate emanate from so/sth
emancipate emancipate so from so/sth
embark embark for some place
embark embark on sth
embarrass embarrass so about so/sth
embarrass embarrass so into doing sth
embarrass embarrass so with sth
embarrass financially embarrassed
embed embed so/sth in sth
embed embed sth in sth

embellish embellish sth with sth
embezzle embezzle sth from so/sth
emblazon emblazon sth on(to) sth
emblazon emblazon sth with sth
embody embody sth in sth
embroil embroil so in sth
emerge emerge (from sth) (as sth)
emigrate emigrate (from some place) (to some place)
emit emit sth (from sth) (into sth)
emotion let one's emotions show
emotional beyond some emotional response
empathize empathize with so/sth
emphasis lay emphasis on sth
employ employ so as sth
employ employ so for sth
employ employ so in sth
empower empower so to do sth
empty come away empty-handed
empty emptier than a banker's heart
empty empty into sth
empty empty sack cannot stand upright.
empty empty so out
empty empty sth into sth
empty empty sth out
empty Empty vessels make the most sound.
empty go away empty-handed
enable enable so to do sth
enamor enamored of so/sth
encase encase so/sth in sth
enchant enchant so with sth
enchantment Distance lends enchantment (to the view).
enchilada whole enchilada
enclose enclose so/sth (with)in sth
encompass encompass so/sth (with)in sth
encourage encourage so in sth
encourage encourage so to do sth
encroach encroach (up)on so/sth
encumber encumber so/sth with so/sth
end All good things must (come to an) end.
end All's well that ends well.
end at a dead end
end at an end
end at loose ends
end at one's wit's end
end at the end of nowhere
end at the end of one's rope
end at the end of one's tether
end at the end of the day
end beginning of the end
end bring sth to a dead end
end bring sth to an end
end burn the candle at both ends
end business end of sth
end by the end of the day
end cannot see (any) further than the end of one's nose
end can't see beyond the end of one's nose
end come out (of) the little end of the horn
end come to a bad end
end come to a dead end
end come to an end
end come to an untimely end
end end in itself
end end in sth
end end it (all)

end end justifies the means.
end End of story.
end end of the ball game
end end of the line
end end of the road
end end sth up
end end up
end end with sth
end for days on end
end for hours on end
end go off the deep end
end hind end
end hind end of creation
end hold one's end of the bargain up
end hold one's end up
end jump off the deep end
end keep one's end of the bargain up
end keep one's end up
end leave some loose ends
end leave so at loose ends
end (little) short on one end
end live up to one's end of the bargain
end living end
end make (both) ends meet
end make so's hair stand on end
end meet one's end
end no end of sth
end not know which end is up
end odds and ends
end play both ends (against the middle)
end put an end to sth
end put so/sth at loose ends
end reach a dead end
end see no further than the end of one's nose
end see the light (at the end of the tunnel)
end short end of the stick
end some loose ends
end (the) be-all and (the) end-all
end till the bitter end
end to the bitter end
end to the ends of the earth
endear endear so to so/sth
endeavor endeavor to do sth
endow endow so/sth with sth
endure He that would have eggs must endure the cackling of hens.
endure What can't be cured must be endured.
enemy best is the enemy of the good.
enemy good is the enemy of the best.
enemy I wouldn't wish that on my worst enemy.
enemy one's own worst enemy
enfold enfold so in sth
enforce enforce sth on so
engage engage in small talk
engage engage so as sth
engage engage so/sth in sth
engage engage so to so
English in plain English
English Queen's English
English say sth in plain English
English write sth in plain English
engorge engorge (itself) on so/sth
engorge engorge (itself) with sth
engrave engrave sth into sth
engrave engrave sth on(to) sth
engrave engrave sth with sth
engrave engraved in stone
engross engross so in sth

engulf engulf so/sth in sth
enjoin enjoin so/sth from sth
enjoin enjoin so to do sth
enjoy enjoy the best of both worlds
enjoy Enjoy your meal.
enlarge enlarge (up)on sth
enlighten enlighten so (about so/sth)
enlist enlist (oneself) for sth
enlist enlist (oneself) in sth
enlist enlist so for sth
enlist enlist so in sth
enmesh enmesh so/sth in sth
enough angry enough to chew nails
enough close enough for government work
enough close enough to use the same toothpick
enough doesn't have enough sense to bell a cat
enough doesn't have enough sense to come in out of the rain
enough enough and some to spare
enough Enough is as good as a feast.
enough Enough is enough.
enough enough (sth) to go (a)round
enough enough sth to plague a saint
enough enough to keep body and soul together
enough get enough courage up (to do sth)
enough get enough guts up (to do sth)
enough get enough nerve up (to do sth)
enough Give so enough rope and he'll hang himself.
enough Good enough.
enough good enough for government work
enough good enough for so/sth
enough have had enough
enough homely enough to stop a clock
enough hot enough to burn a polar bear's butt
enough (I) can't thank you enough.
enough (Is it) cold enough for you?
enough (Is it) hot enough for you?
enough I've had enough of this!
enough leave well enough alone
enough let well enough alone
enough mad enough to chew nails (and spit rivets)
enough mad enough to kick a cat
enough mad enough to spit nails
enough not enough room to swing a cat
enough not know enough to come in out of the rain
enough old enough to be so's father
enough old enough to be so's mother
enough That's enough!
enough That's enough for now.
enough (That's) enough (of this) foolishness!
enough There aren't enough hours in the day.
enough Throw dirt enough, and some will stick.
enough Too many chiefs and not enough Indians.
enough word to the wise (is enough).
enrich enrich so/sth with sth
enroll enroll (so) for sth
enroll enroll (so) in sth
ensconce ensconce oneself in sth

enshrine enshrine so in one's heart
enshrine enshrine so's memory in one's heart
enshrine enshrine sth in sth
ensnare ensnare so/sth in sth
ensue ensue from sth
entangle entangle so/sth in sth
entangle entangle so/sth with sth
enter Abandon hope, all ye who enter here.
enter breaking and entering
enter enter in sth
enter enter into sth
enter enter one's mind
enter enter so/sth in(to) sth
enter enter (sth) by sth
enter enter the fray
enter enter the lists
enter enter (up)on sth
entertain entertain so with sth
enthrall enthrall so with sth
enthusiasm fire so with enthusiasm
entice entice so or an animal into doing sth
entice entice so or an animal into sth
entice entice so or an animal with sth
entirety in its entirety
entirety in their entirety
entitle entitle so to do sth
entomb entomb so or an animal in sth
entrance make an entrance
entrap entrap so (in sth) (with sth)
entreat entreat so to do sth
entrust entrust so/sth to so
entrust entrust so with so/sth
entwine entwine around so/sth
entwine entwine sth around so/sth
enunciate enunciate sth to so
envelop envelop so/sth in so/sth
envelope push the envelope
envisage envisage so/sth as so/sth
envision envision so as so else
envy envy so for so/sth
envy green with envy
epic disaster of epic proportions
equal all things being equal
equal equal so/sth in sth
equal equal to so
equal other things being equal
equal separate but equal
equate equate so/sth with so/sth
equate equate so to so else
equip equip so/sth (with sth) (for sth)
equip equip sth with sth
'er Put 'er there(, pal).
era in the Common Era
erase erase sth from sth
err To err is human(, to forgive divine).
errand do an errand
errand go on a fool's errand
errand go on an errand
errand on a fool's errand
errand run an errand
errand send so (out) on an errand
error rounding error
error trial and error
erupt erupt from sth
erupt erupt into sth
escalate escalate into sth
escalate escalate sth into sth
escape avenue of escape
escape escape by the skin of one's teeth
escape escape (from so/sth) (to some place)

escape escape so's notice
escape Little thieves are hanged, but great ones escape.
escort escort so/sth from sth
escort escort so/sth to sth
essence in essence
essence Time is of the essence.
establish establish so/sth as so/sth
establish establish so/sth in sth
estimate estimate the cost at some amount
estrange estranged from so
etch etch sth in(to) sth
eternal eternal life
eternal eternal triangle
eternal Hope springs eternal (in the human breast).
euchre get euchred out of sth
evacuate evacuate one's bowels
evacuate evacuate so (from sth) (to sth)
evaluate evaluate so as sth
eve on the eve of sth
even break even
even Don't even look like sth!
even Don't even think about (doing) it.
even Don't even think about it (happening).
even Even a worm will turn.
even even as we speak
even even break
even even if it kills me
even even in the best of times
even even sth out
even even sth up
even even steven
even (Even) the best of friends must part.
even even (with so)
even keep on an even keel
even keep sth on an even keel
even land so poor it wouldn't even raise a fuss
even liar is not believed (even) when he tells the truth.
evening evening of life
evening (Good) evening.
evening lady of the evening
evening Thank you for a lovely evening.
event able to make an event
event blessed event
event Coming events cast their shadows before.
event in any event
event in the event of sth
event in the unlikely event of sth
event It is easy to be wise after the event.
ever ever and anon
ever forever and ever
ever live happily ever after
ever more than you('ll ever) know
every at every turn
every Every cloud has a silver lining.
every Every dog has its day.
every every fool thing
every Every horse thinks its own pack heaviest.
every every inch a sth
every Every Jack has his Jill.
every every last one
every Every little bit helps.
every every living soul

every Every man for himself (and the devil take the hindmost).
every Every man has his price.
every Every man is the architect of his own fortune.
every Every man to his taste.
every Every minute counts.
every Every moment counts.
every every mother's son (of them)
every every nook and cranny
every (every) now and again
every (every) now and then
every every other person or thing
every every time one turns around
every (every) Tom, Dick, and Harry
every Every tub must stand on its own bottom.
every every walk of life
every ever(y) which way
every hang on (so's) every word
every How's every little thing?
every Let every man skin his own skunk.
every Let every tub stand on its own bottom.
every make every effort to do sth
every There are tricks in every trade.
every There are two sides to every question.
every There are two sides to every story.
every use every trick in the book
every with every (other) breath
everybody everybody and his brother
everybody everybody and his uncle
everybody Everybody loves a lord.
everyone moment everyone has been waiting for
everyone You cannot please everyone.
everything did everything he could 'cept eat us
everything drop everything
everything everything an' all
everything everything but the kitchen sink
everything Everything comes to him who waits.
everything everything from A to Z
everything everything from soup to nuts
everything everything humanly possible
everything Everything's coming up roses.
everything Everything's going to be all right.
everything Everything will be all right.
everything Everything will be great.
everything Everything will be just fine.
everything Everything will be okay.
everything Everything will work out (all right).
everything Everything will work out for the best.
everything Hold everything!
everything (Is) everything okay?
everything Is that everything?
everything place for everything, and everything in its place.
everything That beats everything!
everything There is a remedy for everything except death.

everything There is a time and a place for everything.
everything with everything (on it)
everywhere here, there, and everywhere
evict evict so from some place
evidence give evidence of sth
evidence much in evidence
evil Evil be to him who evil thinks.
evil Idleness is the root of all evil.
evil lesser of two evils
evil love of money is the root of all evil.
evil Money is the root of all evil.
evil See no evil, hear no evil, speak no evil.
evil Sufficient unto the day is the evil thereof.
evolve evolve (from sth) (into sth)
exact exact sth from so
exam sit for an exam
examination cram for an examination
examine cross-examine so
examine examine so in sth
examine examine so on sth
examine examine so/sth for sth
example Example is better than precept.
example hold so/sth up as an example
example make an example of so
exceed exceed so/sth by sth
exceed exceed so/sth in sth
exceed mills of God grind slowly, yet they grind exceeding small.
excel excel at sth
excel excel in sth
except did everything he could 'cept eat us
except There is a remedy for everything except death.
exception exception proves the rule.
exception make an exception (for so)
exception take exception (to sth)
exercise exercise a firm hand
excerpt excerpt sth from sth
excess do sth to excess
excess drink to excess
exchange didn't exchange more than three words with so
exchange exchange no more than some number of words with so
exchange exchange sth for sth
exchange exchange sth with so
exchange hardly exchange more than some number of words with so
exchange in exchange (for so/sth)
exchange not exchange more than some number of words with so
exchange scarcely exchange more than some number of words with so
excite about as exciting as watching (the) paint dry
excite excite so about sth
excite excite sth in so
excite exciting as watching (the) paint dry
excitement ripple of excitement
excitment burst with excitment
exclude exclude so/sth from sth
excuse bad excuse is better than none.
excuse Can you excuse us, please?
excuse Could I be excused?
excuse Could you excuse us, please?

excuse Excuse me.
excuse Excuse my French.
excuse excuse so
excuse excuse so for sth
excuse excuse so from sth
excuse He who excuses himself accuses himself.
excuse Ignorance (of the law) is no excuse (for breaking it).
excuse May I be excused?
excuse use so/sth as an excuse
excuse Will you excuse us, please?
excuse Would you excuse me?
excuse Would you excuse us, please?
excuse You're excused.
exemplify exemplify sth by sth
exempt exempt so from sth
exercise exercise control over so/sth
exercise exercise power over so/sth
exercise exercise so or an animal in sth
exercise exercised about sth
exercise *firm hand
exhibition make an exhibition of oneself
exhort exhort so to do sth
exile exile so (from sth) (to sth)
exist If God did not exist, it would be necessary to invent Him.
existence come into existence
existence in existence
exit exit (from sth) (to sth)
exorcise exorcise sth out of so
expand expand into sth
expand expand one's horizons
expand expand sth into sth
expand expand (up)on sth
expatiate expatiate on so/sth
expect Blessed is he who expects nothing, for he shall never be disappointed.
expect Do you expect me to believe that?
expect expect so/sth for sth
expect expect sth from so/sth
expect expecting (a child)
expect Hope for the best but expect the worst.
expect I expect.
expect (just) as I expected
expect unexpected always happens.
expect when least expected
expect You can't expect me to believe that.
expect You don't expect me to believe that.
expectant expectant mother
expectation come up to so's expectations
expectation fire so with expectations
expedition fishing expedition
expedition go on a fishing expedition
expel expel so from sth
expel expel sth from sth
expend expend sth for sth
expend expend sth in sth
expend expend sth on so/sth
expense at the expense of so/sth
expense Expense is no object.
expense go to the expense (of doing sth)
expense out-of-pocket expenses
experience Experience is the best teacher.
experience Experience is the father of wisdom.

experience Experience is the mother of wisdom.
experience Experience is the teacher of fools.
experience growth experience
experience learning experience
experiment experiment in sth
experiment experiment (up)on so/sth
experiment experiment with so/sth
explain explain at great length
explain explain oneself
explain explain so/sth to so
explain explain sth away
explode explode a bombshell
explode explode with sth
export export sth to some place
export export sth to so/sth
expose expose so or an animal to a disease
expose expose so/sth to so/sth
expose expose sth or oneself to so/sth
expostulate expostulate about so/sth
expound expound ((up)on so/sth) (to so)
express by ankle express
express express one's anger
express express oneself (to so) (on sth)
express express sth in round figures
express express sth in round numbers
expression if you'll pardon the expression
expropriate expropriate sth (from so/sth) (for so/sth)
expunge expunge sth from sth
expurgate expurgate sth from sth
extend extend across sth
extend extend credit (to so or a company)
extend extend (from sth) (to sth)
extend extend one's sympathy (to so)
extend extend over so/sth
extend extend so or a company credit
extend extend sth to sth
extend extend to so/sth
extent to a great extent
extent to some extent
extenuate extenuating circumstances
extol extol so/sth as sth
extort extort sth from so/sth
extra go the extra mile
extract extract sth from so/sth
extradite extradite so from some place (to some place)
extrapolate extrapolate sth from sth
extreme go from one extreme to the other
extreme go to extremes (to do sth)
extricate extricate so/sth from so/sth
exult exult at sth
exult exult in sth
exult exult over sth
eye able to do sth with one's eyes closed
eye all eyes and ears
eye all my eye (and Betty Martin)
eye another pair of eyes
eye appear to the naked eye
eye apple of so's eye
eye Beauty is in the eye of the beholder.
eye big eye
eye bird's-eye view
eye black eye
eye bright-eyed and bushy-tailed
eye cast one's eyes down
eye catch so's eye

eye clap eyes on so/sth
eye close one's eyes to sth
eye cry one's eyes out
eye cut one's eyes at so/sth
eye eagle eye
eye eye for an eye (and a tooth for a tooth).
eye eye of the hurricane
eye eye of the storm
eye eyes like saucers
eye eyes like two burnt holes in a blanket
eye feast one's eyes ((up)on so/sth)
eye Fields have eyes, and woods have ears.
eye find oneself in the public eye
eye fresh pair of eyes
eye get so's eye
eye give so the eye
eye have a roving eye
eye have an eye for so/sth
eye have eyes in the back of one's head
eye have one's eye on so/sth
eye have one's eye out (for so/sth)
eye have so's eye
eye Here's mud in your eye.
eye hit so (right) between the eyes
eye hit the bull's-eye
eye In a pig's eye!
eye in one's mind's eye
eye In the country of the blind, the one-eyed man is king.
eye in the public eye
eye in the twinkling of an eye
eye in the wink of an eye
eye keep an eye on so/sth
eye keep an eye out (for so/sth)
eye keep one's eye on so/sth
eye keep one's eye on the ball
eye keep one's eyes open (for so/sth)
eye keep one's eye(s) out (for so/sth)
eye keep one's eyes peeled (for so/sth)
eye keep one's weather eye open
eye lay eyes on so/sth
eye look at so cross-eyed
eye look so in the eye
eye look to the naked eye
eye make eyes at so
eye more (to sth) than meets the eye
eye need some shut-eye
eye not bat an eye
eye not believe one's eyes
eye one eye on so/sth
eye one's eyes are bigger than one's stomach
eye only have eyes for so
eye open so's eyes to so/sth
eye out of the corner of one's eye
eye pull the wool over so's eyes
eye put so's eye out
eye run one's eyes over sth
eye see eye to eye (about so/sth) (with so)
eye see with the naked eye
eye set eyes on so/sth
eye shut one's eyes to sth
eye sight for sore eyes
eye some shut-eye
eye stars in one's eyes
eye swim before so's eyes
eye take one's eyes off (of) so/sth
eye turn a blind eye (to so/sth)
eye use some shut-eye

eye visible to the naked eye
eye What the eye doesn't see, the heart doesn't grieve over.
eye with an eye to doing sth
eye with (one's) eyes (wide) open
eye with the naked eye
eye without batting an eye
eyeball eyeball-to-eyeball
eyeball up to one's eyeballs (in sth)
eyebrow cause (some) eyebrows to raise
eyebrow cause some raised eyebrows
eyebrow down to a gnat's eyebrow
eyebrow raise a few eyebrows
eyebrow raise some eyebrows
eyeful eyeful (of so/sth)
eyelid not bat an eyelid
eyeteeth cut one's eyeteeth on sth
eyeteeth give one's eyeteeth (for so/sth)
face at face value
face Bag your face!
face blow up in so's face
face can't see one's hand in front of one's face
face cut one's nose off to spite one's face
face do an about-face (on so/sth)
face dog-faced liar
face face away (from so/sth)
face face off
face face so down
face face so/sth forward
face face (so/sth) into sth
face face so with sth
face face sth down
face face sth head-on
face face sth with sth
face face that could stop a clock
face face (that) only a mother could love
face face (the) facts
face face the music
face face up (to so/sth)
face face-to-face
face fall (flat) on one's face
face feed one's face
face fill one's face
face fling sth up in so's face
face fly in the face of so/sth
face fly into the face of danger
face get out of one's face
face give so a red face
face have egg on one's face
face hide one's face in shame
face I'd rather face a firing squad than do sth.
face in so's face
face It's written all over one's face.
face keep a straight face
face laugh in so's face
face laugh out of the other side of one's face
face look so in the face
face lose face
face make a face (at so)
face make faces (at so)
face mess so's face up
face Monday's child is fair of face.
face not show one's face
face on the face of it
face powder one's face
face put a smile on so's face
face put one's face on

face red in the face
face save (one's) face
face say sth (right) to so's face
face set sth in a type face
face slam the door in so's face
face slap in the face
face smack in the face
face smash so's face in
face soak one's face
face stand there with one's bare face hanging out
face stare so in the face
face straight face
face stuff one's face
face take so/sth at face value
face take sth at face value
face talk until one is blue in the face
face tell one to one's face
face throw sth in(to) so's face
face what's his face
face wipe so/sth off the face of the earth
face wipe sth off (one's face)
fact after the fact
fact and that's a fact
fact as a matter of fact
fact face (the) facts
fact Fact is stranger than fiction.
fact facts of life
fact get down to the facts
fact get the facts straight
fact grounded in (actual) fact
fact have the facts straight
fact in fact
fact in point of fact
fact It's for a fact.
fact known fact
factor fudge factor
fade do a fade
fade fade away (into sth)
fade fade back (into sth)
fade fade down
fade fade from sth
fade fade from view
fade fade into sth
fade fade out
fade fade sth down
fade fade sth in
fade fade sth out
fade fade sth up
fag fag so out
fag fagged out
fail fail in sth
fail fail so on sth
fail sth never fails
fail without fail
faint damn so/sth with faint praise
faint faint dead away
faint faint from sth
faint Faint heart never won fair lady.
faint faint of heart
fair All's fair in love and war.
fair Faint heart never won fair lady.
fair fair and impartial
fair fair and square
fair fair game (for sth)
fair fair shake
fair fair sth out
fair fair to middlin'
fair fair-haired boy
fair fair-weather friend
fair Hoist your sail when the wind is fair.
fair Monday's child is fair of face.

fair No fair!
fair None but the brave deserve the fair.
fair one's fair share
fair play fair
fair Turnabout is fair play.
faith act of faith
faith Faith will move mountains.
faith have faith in so
faith in bad faith
faith in good faith
faith keep faith with so
faith leap of faith
faith Oh, ye of little faith.
faith pin one's faith on so/sth
faith require a leap of faith
faith show good faith
faith take sth on faith
fake fake it
fake fake off
fake fake so out
fall *asleep at the switch
fall at one fell swoop
fall bigger they are, the harder they fall.
fall bottom fell out (of sth)
fall bread always falls on the buttered side.
fall break so's fall
fall easy as falling off a log
fall fall (a)foul of so/sth
fall fall (all) over oneself (to do sth)
fall fall all over so
fall fall apart (at the seams)
fall fall asleep
fall fall away (from so/sth)
fall fall away toward sth
fall fall back
fall fall behind (in sth)
fall fall behind schedule
fall fall behind (so/sth)
fall fall behind (with sth)
fall fall below sth
fall fall beneath sth
fall fall between sth and sth else
fall fall between two stools
fall fall by some amount
fall fall by the wayside
fall fall down
fall fall (down) at sth
fall fall (flat) on one's face
fall fall for so
fall fall for sth
fall fall from grace
fall fall from power
fall fall from so/sth
fall fall head over heels
fall fall heir to sth
fall fall ill
fall fall in
fall fall into a trap
fall fall into decay
fall fall into disfavor
fall fall into disgrace
fall fall into disuse
fall fall in(to) line
fall fall into one's lap
fall fall in(to) place
fall fall into so's trap
fall fall in(to sth)
fall fall in(to step)
fall fall into the gutter
fall fall into the trap
fall fall into the wrong hands

fall fall like a ton of bricks
fall fall off
fall fall on deaf ears
fall fall on hard times
fall fall on one's knees
fall fall on one's sword
fall fall on so's shoulders
fall fall on(to) so/sth
fall fall out
fall fall out (with so)
fall fall outside sth
fall fall over
fall fall overboard
fall fall short
fall fall through
fall fall to
fall fall toward sth
fall fall under so/sth
fall fall under so's spell
fall fall (up)on so
fall fall wide of the mark
fall fall within sth
fall He that is down need fear no fall.
fall How the mighty have fallen.
fall hush fell over so/sth
fall in one fell swoop
fall *in the gutter
fall just fell off the turnip truck
fall Let the chips fall where they may.
fall *like a ton of bricks
fall Little strokes fell great oaks.
fall *off the wagon
fall *on so's shoulders
fall Pride goes before a fall.
fall reed before the wind lives on, while mighty oaks do fall.
fall riding for a fall
fall take a fall
fall take the fall
fall *through the cracks
fall United we stand, divided we fall.
fall *wide of the mark
fallow lie fallow
false false move
false lull so into a false sense of security
false one false move
false sail under false colors
falter falter in sth
fame house of ill fame
fame so's claim to fame
familiar familiar with so/sth
familiar have a familiar ring (to it)
familiar unfamiliar territory
familiarity Familiarity breeds contempt.
familiarize familiarize so with sth
family (all) in the family
family black sheep of the family
family family that prays together stays together.
family get so in a family way
family How's the family?
family How's your family?
family in a family way
family in the family way
family like one of the family
family run in the family
family wear the britches (in the family)
family wear the pants (in the family)
famine (either) feast or famine
famous famous last words
fan fan of so

fan fan out
fan fan sth out
fan fan the breeze
fan fan the flames (of sth)
fan hit the fan
fan when the shit hits the fan
fancy fancy footwork
fancy Fancy meeting you here!
fancy fancy so as so/sth
fancy fancy so's chances
fancy Fancy that!
fancy flight of fancy
fancy footloose and fancy-free
fancy strike so's fancy
fancy suit so's fancy
fancy take a fancy to so/sth
fancy tickle so's fancy
fantastic trip the light fantastic
far as far as anyone knows
far as far as it goes
far as far as possible
far as far as so is concerned
far as far as sth is concerned
far come from far and wide
far far and away the best
far far be it from me to do sth
far far cry from sth
far far from it
far far from the madding crowd
far far gone
far far into the night
far far out
far far-off look
far few and far between
far from far and near
far from near and far
far go so far as to say sth
far go too far
far make it to sth; make it as far as sth
far push so too far
far so far as anyone knows
far so far as possible
far so far as so is concerned
far so far as sth is concerned
far So far, so good.
faraway faraway look
farm bet the farm
farm buy the farm
farm farm so out
farm farm sth out
farm sell the farm
farm You can bet the farm (on so/sth).
fart fart around
farther nearer the church, the farther from God.
fashion after a fashion
fashion after the fashion of so/sth
fashion come into fashion
fashion fashion sth into sth
fashion fashion sth on sth
fashion fashion sth out of sth
fashion go out of fashion
fashion in fashion
fashion out of fashion
fast at a fast clip
fast Bad news travels fast.
fast fast and furious
fast fast friends
fast fast one
fast fast-talk so into sth
fast fast-talk so out of sth
fast get nowhere fast
fast go at a fast clip

fast He travels fastest who travels alone.
fast in the fast lane
fast life in the fast lane
fast live in the fast lane
fast make a fast buck
fast make fast work of so/sth
fast move at a fast clip
fast move in the fast lane
fast on the fast track
fast play fast and loose (with so/sth)
fast pull a fast one
fast run at a fast clip
fast stay in the fast lane
fast thick and fast
fast travel at a fast clip
fasten fasten so/sth (on)to so/sth
fasten fasten sth down (to sth)
fasten fasten sth up
fasten fasten (up)on so/sth
faster faster and faster
fastest He travels fastest who travels alone.
fat chew the fat
fat fat and happy
fat fat and sassy
fat fat as a pig
fat fat cat
fat fat chance
fat fat hit the fire
fat fat is in the fire.
fat fatten so or an animal up (with sth)
fat fatten up (on sth)
fat kill the fatted calf
fat live off the fat of the land
fat suddenly the fat hit the fire
fat then the fat hit the fire
fat till the fat lady sings
fat when the fat hit the fire
fat when the fat lady sings
fat work some fat off
fate fate worse than death
fate leave one to one's fate
fate seal so's fate
fate so's fate is sealed
fate sure as fate
fate turn of fate
fate twist of fate
father child is father of the man.
father Experience is the father of wisdom.
father father sth on so
father It is a wise child that knows its own father.
father like father, like son
father old enough to be so's father
father wish is father to the thought.
fatted kill the fatted calf
fatten fatten so or an animal up (with sth)
fatten fatten up (on sth)
fault at fault
fault fault so (for sth)
fault find fault (with so/sth)
fault generous to a fault
fauna flora and fauna
faunch faunch around
favor come out in favor of so/sth
favor curry favor with so
favor decide in favor of so/sth
favor do so a favor
favor fall out of favor (with so)
favor favor so/sth with sth
favor find favor with so

favor Fortune favors the bold.
favor Fortune favors the brave.
favor go in so's favor
favor go out of favor (with so)
favor in favor of so
favor in favor (of so/sth)
favor in so's favor
favor lose favor (with so)
favor opt in favor of so/sth
favor out of favor (with so)
favor return the favor
favor rule in favor of so/sth
favor Thank God for small favors.
favorite odds-on favorite
fawn fawn (all) over so
fawn fawn (up)on so
fear fear for so/sth
fear Fools rush in where angels fear to tread.
fear for fear of sth
fear He that is down need fear no fall.
fear in fear and trembling
fear never fear
fear put the fear of God in(to) so
feast contented mind is a perpetual feast.
feast (either) feast or famine
feast Enough is as good as a feast.
feast feast one's eyes ((up)on so/sth)
feast feast (up)on sth
feast movable feast
feather Birds of a feather flock together.
feather feather in one's cap
feather feather one's (own) nest
feather Fine feathers make fine birds.
feather fuss and feathers
feather If it ain't chickens, it's feathers.
feather in fine feather
feather knock so over (with a feather)
feather light as a feather
feather ruffle its feathers
feather ruffle so's feathers
feather tar and feather so
feather You could have knocked me over with a feather.
feature feature so as sth
feature feature so in sth
fed fed up (to some degree) (with so/sth)
fed I'm (really) fed up (with so/sth).
federal make a federal case out of sth
feed bite the hand that feeds one
feed chicken feed
feed fed up (to some degree) (with so/sth)
feed Feed a cold and starve a fever.
feed feed off (of) sth
feed feed one's face
feed feed so a line
feed feed so/sth or an animal with sth
feed feed sth back into sth
feed feed sth back to so
feed feed sth into sth
feed feed sth to so
feed feed the kitty
feed feed (up)on so/sth
feed feeding frenzy
feed for chicken feed
feed I'm (really) fed up (with so/sth).
feed put the feed bag on
feed spoon-feed so
feel (Are you) feeling okay?
feel feel a draft
feel feel a glow of contentment

feel feel a glow of happiness
feel feel around (for so/sth)
feel feel at home
feel feel blue
feel feel fit
feel feel for so
feel feel for sth
feel feel free (to do sth)
feel feel guilty (about sth)
feel feel it beneath one (to do sth)
feel feel like a million (dollars)
feel feel like a new person
feel feel like death warmed over
feel feel like doing sth
feel feel like oneself again
feel feel like so/sth
feel feel of sth
feel feel on top of the world
feel feel one's gorge rise
feel feel one's oats
feel feel out of place
feel feel out of sorts
feel feel out of things
feel feel pinched
feel feel somehow about so/sth
feel feel so out (about so/sth)
feel feel so up
feel feel sth in one's bones
feel feel sth with sth
feel feel the pinch
feel feel up to sth
feel feeling about sth
feel feeling (kinda) puny
feel feeling no pain
feel feeling (that sth is the case)
feel gut feeling
feel How (are) you feeling?
feel I just have this feeling.
feel (I'm) feeling okay.
feel *like death warmed over
feel not feel like oneself
feel not feeling oneself
feel *out of place
feel sinking feeling
feeler put out (some) feelers (on so/sth)
feelings cause hard feelings
feelings hard feelings
feelings have feelings about so/sth
feelings hurt so's feelings
feelings mixed feelings (about so/sth)
feelings no hard feelings
feelings not any hard feelings
feet back on one's feet
feet balls of one's feet
feet bring one to one's feet
feet bring sth to its feet
feet cold as a welldigger's feet (in January)
feet cold feet
feet come to one's feet
feet dead on one's feet
feet dive in with both feet
feet drag one's feet (on or over sth)
feet find one's feet
feet get one on one's feet
feet get one's feet wet
feet get some weight off one's feet
feet get to one's feet
feet have feet of clay
feet have one's feet on the ground
feet have two left feet
feet I felt like a penny waiting for change.

feet itchy feet
feet jump in with both feet
feet keep one's feet on the ground
feet keep out from under so's feet
feet keep sth on its feet
feet knock one off one's feet
feet land (up)on both feet
feet land (up)on one's feet
feet lay sth at so's feet
feet let grass grow under one's feet
feet load off one's feet
feet not let the grass grow under one's feet
feet on its feet
feet on one's feet
feet patter of tiny feet
feet put one on one's feet
feet put sth on its feet
feet put one's feet up
feet regain one's feet
feet rise to one's feet
feet run one's feet off
feet set one (back) on one's feet
feet set one on one's feet again
feet sit at the feet of so
feet six feet under
feet spring to one's feet
feet stand on one's (own) two feet
feet sweep one off one's feet
feet take a load off one's feet
feet think on one's feet
feet throw oneself at so's feet
feet vote with one's feet
feet walk so's feet off
felicitations Greetings and felicitations!
fell at one fell swoop
fell bottom fell out (of sth)
fell hush fell over so/sth
fell in one fell swoop
fell just fell off the turnip truck
fell Little strokes fell great oaks.
fellow hale-fellow-well-met
felt I felt like a penny waiting for change.
female female of the species is more deadly than the male.
fence fence an animal in
fence fence so in
fence fence so or an animal out
fence fence so/sth off (from sth)
fence fence sth in
fence Good fences make good neighbors.
fence grass is always greener on the other side (of the fence).
fence mend (one's) fences
fence on the fence (about sth)
fence sit on the fence
fence straddle the fence
fend fend for oneself
fend fend so/sth off
fender fender bender
ferret ferret sth out
ferry ferry so around
ferry ferry so/sth across sth
fess fess up (to sth)
festoon festoon so/sth with sth
fetch Dad fetch my buttons!
fetch fetch sth in
fetch fetch sth out of sth
fetch fetch up
feud feud (with so) (over so/sth)

fever Feed a cold and starve a fever.
fever run a fever
few drop so a few lines
few few and far between
few few bricks short of a load
few few cards short of a deck
few few cards shy of a full deck
few get off a few good ones
few hang a few on
few He who begins many things, finishes but few.
few I have to wash a few things out.
few man of few words
few Many are called but few are chosen.
few open a few doors (for so)
few precious few
few pull a few strings
few quite a few
few raise a few eyebrows
few Win a few, lose a few.
fiction Fact is stranger than fiction.
fiction Truth is stranger than fiction.
fiddle couldn't hit a bull in the ass with a bass fiddle
fiddle fiddle around (with so)
fiddle fiddle around (with sth)
fiddle fiddle sth away
fiddle fiddle while Rome burns
fiddle fiddle with so/sth
fiddle fit as a fiddle
fiddle have more than one string to one's fiddle
fiddle play second fiddle (to so)
fiddle There's many a good tune played on an old fiddle.
fidget fidget around
fidget fidget with sth
field come out of left field
field field questions
field Fields have eyes, and woods have ears.
field have a field day
field level playing field
field level the (playing) field
field order so off the field
field out in left field
field out of left field
field play the field
fifth fifth wheel
fifty divide sth fifty-fifty
fifty fifty-fifty
fifty go fifty-fifty (on sth)
fifty split sth fifty-fifty
fight could fight a circle-saw (and it a-runnin')
fight Councils of war never fight.
fight Don't give up without a fight!
fight fight about so/sth
fight fight against so/sth
fight fight against time
fight fight back (at so/sth)
fight Fight fire with fire.
fight fight for so/sth
fight fight like hell
fight fight like the devil
fight fight like the dickens
fight fight on
fight fight (one's way) back (to sth)
fight fight one's way out (of sth)
fight fight (one's way) through (sth)
fight fight over so/sth
fight fight so/sth down

fight fight so/sth hammer and tongs
fight fight so/sth off
fight fight so/sth tooth and nail
fight fight so/sth with sth
fight fight sth down
fight fight sth out
fight fight sth through (sth)
fight fight the good fight
fight fight to the death
fight fight (with) so or some creature (over so/sth)
fight fight (with) so/sth (about so/sth)
fight fighting chance
fight give up the fight
fight go down fighting
fight He who fights and runs away, may live to fight another day.
fight I won't give up without a fight.
fight knock-down, drag-out fight
fight like fighting snakes
fight pick a fight (with so)
fight put up a fight
fight spoiling for a fight
fight Them's fighting words!
fight throw a fight
fight (You) can't fight city hall.
figure ballpark figure
figure cut a fine figure
figure express sth in round figures
figure figure in sth
figure figure on doing sth
figure figure on so/sth
figure figure out the root of the problem
figure figure so as sth
figure figure so/sth in
figure figure so/sth in((to) sth)
figure figure so/sth out
figure figure sth up
figure flatter one's figure
figure Go figure.
figure in round figures
figure It figures.
figure write sth in round figures
filch filch sth (from so)
file file charges (against so)
file file for sth
file file in((to) sth)
file file out (of sth)
file file past (so/sth)
file file sth against so
file file sth (away)
file file sth away (from sth)
file file sth down
file file sth off ((of) sth)
file file sth with so/sth
file file sth off
file have sth on file
file in (a) single file
file march in (a) single file
file rank and file
file single file
file walk in (a) single file
fill back and fill
fill eat one's fill
fill fill in
fill fill one's face
fill fill out
fill fill so full of lead
fill fill so in (on so/sth)
fill fill so/sth up (with sth)
fill fill so's head with sth
fill fill so's shoes

fill fill sth in
fill fill sth out
fill fill sth to sth
fill fill the bill
fill fill the gap
fill fill up
fill filled to the brim
fill Little and often fills the purse.
fill one's fill of so/sth
fill refill a prescription
fill smoke-filled room
film film over
filter filter in(to some place)
filter filter sth out of sth
filter filter through (sth)
filthy filthy lucre
filthy filthy rich
final final fling
final final say
final final word
final get the final word
final have the final say
final in the final analysis
final one final thing
final one final word
financially financially embarrassed
find can't find one's butt with both hands (in broad daylight)
find devil finds work for idle hands to do.
find find a way around so/sth
find find against so/sth
find find fault (with so/sth)
find find favor with so
find find for so/sth
find find it in one's heart (to do sth)
find find it in oneself (to do sth)
find find its way somewhere
find find (neither) hide nor hair
find find one's feet
find find one's own level
find find one's tongue
find find one's way (around)
find find one's way around (sth)
find find one's way (somewhere)
find find oneself
find find oneself in a bind
find find oneself in a jam
find find oneself in the doghouse
find find oneself in the market (for sth)
find find oneself in the public eye
find find oneself with so/sth
find find oneself without so/sth
find find out a thing or two (about so/sth)
find find so a bit off
find find so a little off
find find so guilty
find find so in
find find so innocent
find find so not guilty
find find so out
find find sth in mint condition
find find sth out
find find (sth) out (about so/sth) (from so/sth)
find find (sth) out the hard way
find find the root of the problem
find find time for so/sth
find Finders keepers(, losers weepers).
find found money
find found sth (up)on sth
find good man is hard to find.

find Keep a thing seven years and you'll (always) find a use for it.
find lost-and-found
find Love will find a way.
find *(neither) hide nor hair
find *one's bearings
find *root of the problem
find Seek and ye shall find.
find Where will I find you?
finder Finders keepers(, losers weepers).
fine Come on in, the water's fine!
fine cut a fine figure
fine do some fine coin
fine Everything will be just fine.
fine fine and dandy
fine Fine feathers make fine birds.
fine fine how do you do
fine fine kettle of fish
fine fine print
fine fine so for sth
fine fine state of affairs
fine Fine weather for ducks.
fine Fine words butter no parsnips.
fine fine-tune sth
fine go over sth with a fine-tooth comb
fine go through sth with a fine-tooth comb
fine in fine feather
fine (It) suits me (fine).
fine not to put too fine a point on it
fine put too fine a point on sth
fine search sth with a fine-tooth comb
fine That's a fine how-do-you-do.
fine (That's) fine with me.
fine There is a fine line between sth and sth else.
finger cross one's fingers
finger finger so as so
finger Fingers were made before forks.
finger five-finger discount
finger get one's fingers burned
finger give so the finger
finger have a finger in the pie
finger have one's finger in too many pies
finger have one's finger(s) in the till
finger have sth at one's fingertips
finger have sticky fingers
finger keep one's finger on the pulse of sth
finger keep one's fingers crossed (for so/sth)
finger lay a finger on so/sth
finger lay the finger on so
finger not lift a finger (to help so)
finger point the finger at so
finger put one's finger on sth
finger put the finger on so
finger run one's fingers through one's hair
finger slip through so's fingers
finger stick to so's fingers
finger twist so around one's little finger
finger wind so around one's little finger
finger work one's fingers to the bone
fingertips have sth at one's fingertips
finish finish ahead of schedule
finish finish so or an animal off
finish finish so/sth off
finish finish so/sth up
finish finish (sth) by doing sth
finish finish (sth) off
finish finish (sth) off with sth

finish finish sth with a lick and a promise
finish finish with sth
finish finishing touch(s)
finish from start to finish
finish Give us the tools, and we will finish the job.
finish He who begins many things, finishes but few.
finish I'm not finished with you.
finish Nice guys finish last.
fink fink on so
fink fink out (on so/sth)
fire add fuel to the fire
fire ball of fire
fire baptism of fire
fire build a fire under so
fire burnt child dreads the fire.
fire catch (on) fire
fire caught in the crossfire
fire draw fire from so
fire draw (so's) fire (away) from so/sth or an animal
fire fat hit the fire
fire fat is in the fire.
fire Fight fire with fire.
fire fire away (at so)
fire Fire is a good servant but a bad master.
fire fire over sth
fire fire so up
fire fire so with anger
fire fire so with enthusiasm
fire fire so with expectations
fire fire (sth) at so/sth
fire fire (sth) back (at so/sth)
fire fire sth back (to so/sth)
fire fire sth into so/sth
fire fire sth off (to so)
fire fire sth up
fire fire under so
fire fire up
fire fire (up)on so/sth
fire fired up
fire firing on all cylinders
fire go out of the frying pan into the fire
fire Great balls of fire!
fire hang fire
fire have too many irons in the fire
fire Hellfire and damnation!
fire hold one's fire
fire hot as fire
fire I'd rather face a firing squad than do sth.
fire If you play with fire, you get burned.
fire jump out of the frying pan into the fire
fire keep the home fires burning
fire light a fire under so
fire like a house on fire
fire Moving three times is as bad as a fire.
fire on fire
fire open fire (on so)
fire open fire (on so/sth)
fire out of the frying pan (and) into the fire
fire play with fire
fire pull sth out of the fire
fire resign under fire
fire set fire to so/sth

fire set so on fire
fire set so/sth on fire
fire set the world on fire
fire spread like wildfire
fire stamp a fire out
fire start a fire under so
fire suddenly the fat hit the fire
fire then the fat hit the fire
fire (There's) no smoke without fire.
fire think under fire
fire under fire
fire when the fat hit the fire
fire Where's the fire?
fire Where there's smoke there's fire.
firm exercise a firm hand
firm firm hand
firm firm sth up
firm firm up
firm keep a firm grip on so/sth
firm need a firm hand
firm take a firm grip on so/sth
firm take a (firm) stand on sth
firm use a firm hand
first at first
first cast the first stone
first first and foremost
first First catch your hare.
first First come, first served.
first first crack at sth
first first hundred years are the hardest.
first First impressions are the most lasting.
first first leg (of a journey)
first first of all
first first off
first first see the light of day
first first step is always the hardest.
first first thing (in the morning)
first First things first.
first firstest with the mostest
first get to first base (with so/sth)
first He that would the daughter win, must with the mother first begin.
first hindside first
first If at first you don't succeed, try, try again.
first in the first instance
first in the first place
first Ladies first.
first love at first sight
first Not if I see you first.
first not know the first thing about so/sth
first of the first water
first on a first-name basis (with so)
first play first chair
first reach first base (with so/sth)
first Self-preservation is the first law of nature.
first Shoot first, ask questions later.
first take first crack at sth
first want first crack at sth
first You first.
firstest firstest with the mostest
fish act like a cold fish
fish busy as a fish peddler in Lent
fish cold fish
fish crooked as a barrel of fish hooks
fish drink like a fish
fish easy as shooting fish in a barrel
fish fine kettle of fish
fish fish for a compliment

fish fish for sth
fish fish in troubled waters
fish Fish or cut bait.
fish fish so/sth out of sth
fish fish sth up
fish fish story
fish fish tale
fish fishing expedition
fish go on a fishing expedition
fish have bigger fish to fry
fish like a fish out of water
fish like shooting fish in a barrel
fish neither fish nor fowl
fish smell fishy
fish There are plenty of (other) fish in the sea.
fish Ye gods (and little fishes)!
fishy smell fishy
fist closefisted (with money)
fist hand over fist
fist rule with an iron fist
fist tight as Midas's fist
fist tightfisted (with money)
fist two-fisted
fit ain't fittin' to roll with a pig
fit by fits and starts
fit dressed (up) fit to kill
fit feel fit
fit fit and trim
fit fit around sth
fit fit as a fiddle
fit fit for a king
fit fit for the gods
fit fit in (somehow) (with sth)
fit fit in (with so/sth)
fit fit in((to) sth)
fit fit like a glove
fit fit so for sth
fit fit so/sth in((to) sth)
fit fit so/sth out (for sth)
fit fit so/sth out (with sth)
fit fit so/sth up (with sth)
fit fit so to a T
fit fit sth on(to) sth
fit fit sth to sth
fit fit sth together
fit fit the bill
fit fit to be tied
fit fit to kill
fit fit together
fit fit with sth
fit fits and starts
fit have a conniption (fit)
fit have a fit
fit hissy (fit)
fit If the shoe fits(, wear it).
fit in fits and starts
fit It ain't fittin'
fit keep fit
fit look fit to kill
fit see fit (to do sth)
fit survival of the fittest
fit think so fit for sth
fit think so/sth fit for so/sth
fit throw a fit
fit with fits and starts
fittest survival of the fittest
fitting ain't fittin' to roll with a pig
fitting It ain't fittin'.
five bunch of fives
five five-finger discount
five Give me five!
five hang five

five He wears a ten-dollar hat on a five-cent head.
five nine-to-five job
five Slip me five!
five slip so five
five take five
fix fix
fix fix an animal
fix fix so/sth up
fix fix so's wagon
fix fix so up (with so)
fix fix so up (with sth)
fix fix sth
fix fix sth for (a meal)
fix fix sth on(to) sth
fix fix sth over
fix fix sth with so
fix fix (up)on so/sth
fix fixed up
fix fixin(g) to do sth
fix How is so fixed for sth?
fix in a fix
fix with all the fixin(g)s
fixings with all the fixin(g)s
fixture regular fixture
fizz fizz up
fizzle fizzle out
flack flack out
flag flag so/sth down
flair have a flair for sth
flake flake away (from sth)
flake flake down
flake flake off ((of) sth)
flake flake out
flake flake sth off
flame add fuel to the flame
flame burn with a low blue flame
flame burst into flame(s)
flame drawn like a moth to a flame
flame fan the flames (of sth)
flame flame up
flame flame with anger
flame flame with lust
flame flame with resentment
flame flame with vengeance
flame go down in flames
flame go up in flames
flame shoot so down in flames
flank flank (up)on so/sth
flap flap around
flap flap one's gums
flap flap one's jaws
flare flare out
flare flare sth out
flare flare up
flash flash a smile (at so)
flash flash across sth
flash flash back (on so/sth)
flash flash back (to so/sth)
flash flash in the pan
flash flash into one's mind
flash flash into view
flash flash off
flash flash on
flash flash out
flash flash sth around
flash flash sth at so/sth
flash flash sth up (some place)
flash flash through one's mind
flash flash with anger
flash flash with recognition
flash in a flash
flash quick as a flash

flat catch so flat-footed
flat fall (flat) on one's face
flat flat as a board
flat flat as a pancake
flat flat broke
flat flat busted
flat flat on one's ass
flat (flat) on one's back
flat flat out
flat flatten so/sth out
flat in no time flat
flat in nothing flat
flat leave so flat
flatter flatter one's figure
flatter Flattery will get you nowhere.
flatter Imitation is the sincerest form of flattery.
flavor flavor food with sth
flea If you lie down with dogs, you will get up with fleas.
flea not hurt a flea
fleck fleck sth with sth
flee flee from so/sth
flee flee to sth
fleet fleet of foot
fleet fleeting glance
flesh flesh and blood
flesh flesh out
flesh flesh sth out (with sth)
flesh in the flesh
flesh make so's flesh crawl
flesh owe so a pound of flesh
flesh own flesh and blood
flesh pay so a pound of flesh
flesh pound of flesh
flesh press (the) flesh
flesh spirit is willing, but the flesh is weak.
flesh take a pound of flesh
flesh thorn in so's flesh
flex flex sth out of shape
flex flexed out of shape
flick flick out
flick flick sth off
flick flick sth on
flick flick sth out
flick flick sth with sth
flick flick through sth
flicker flicker out
flight flight of fancy
flight Have a nice flight.
flight in flight
flight in full flight
flinch flinch from so/sth
fling final fling
fling fling one's head back
fling fling oneself at so
fling fling so/sth around
fling fling so/sth aside
fling fling so/sth away
fling fling so/sth back
fling fling so/sth down
fling fling so/sth out of sth
fling fling sth at so/sth
fling fling sth in(to) sth
fling fling sth off of oneself
fling fling sth off (of) sth
fling fling sth on oneself
fling fling sth up in so's face
fling fling sth up (in sth)
fling fling up
flip do a flip-flop (on sth)
flip flip around

flip flip one's lid
flip flip one's wig
flip flip out
flip flip over
flip flip side
flip flip so for sth
flip flip so off
flip flip so/sth over
flip flip so out
flip flip through sth
flirt flirt with so
flirt flirt with the idea of doing sth
flit flit about
flit flit from person to person
flit flit from sth to sth else
float float a loan
float float around
float float into sth
float float on air
float float through sth
float float (up)on sth
flock Birds of a feather flock together.
flock flock after so/sth
flock flock around so/sth
flock flock in((to) some place)
flock flock to so/sth
flock flock together
flog flog a dead horse
flog flog so to death
flood flood in(to sth)
flood flood out (of sth)
flood flood so/sth out of sth
flood flood so/sth with sth
floor clean the floor up with so
floor crash to the floor
floor floor
floor floor it
floor floor so
floor in on the ground floor
floor let so in on the ground floor
floor mop the floor up with so
floor so clean you could eat off the floor
floor take the floor
floor This is my floor.
floor walk the floor
floor wipe the floor up with so
flop do a flip-flop (on sth)
flop flop around
flop flop as sth
flop flop down
flop flop into sth
flop flop so/sth over
flop flop sth down on(to) sth
flop That's the way the mop flops.
flora flora and fauna
floral floral tribute
flotsam flotsam and jetsam
flounce flounce in(to some place)
flounce flounce out (of some place)
flounder flounder around
flounder flounder through sth
flow cash flow problem
flow ebb and flow
flow flow across sth
flow flow along
flow flow away
flow flow from sth
flow flow (from sth) (to sth)
flow flow in(to sth)
flow flow out (of sth)
flow flow over so/sth
flow flow with sth

flow go with the flow
flow overflow into sth
flow overflow with so/sth
flower April showers bring May flowers.
flub flub sth up
flub flub the dub
flub flub up
fluctuate fluctuate between so and so else
fluctuate fluctuate between sth and sth else
fluctuate fluctuate with sth
fluff fluff one's lines
fluff fluff sth out
fluff fluff sth up
flunk flunk out (of sth)
flunk flunk so out
flush flush so/sth out of some place
flush flush sth away
flush flush with sth
flutter flutter about
flutter flutter down
flutter flutter over so/sth
flux in a (constant) state of flux
flux in flux
fly *by the seat of one's pants
fly come through sth (with flying colors)
fly drop like flies
fly fly across sth
fly fly apart
fly fly around
fly fly at so/sth
fly fly away
fly fly by
fly fly from so/sth (to sth)
fly fly from sth (to sth)
fly fly in
fly fly in the ointment
fly fly into a rage
fly fly into sth
fly fly into the face of danger
fly fly off
fly fly out (of sth)
fly fly over so/sth
fly fly past (so/sth)
fly fly so/sth in(to some place) (from some place)
fly fly so/sth out of sth
fly fly the coop
fly fly to so/sth
fly fly to sth
fly fly up to sth
fly fly-by-night
fly flying high
fly Go fly a kite!
fly got to fly
fly It'll never fly.
fly I've got to fly.
fly I('ve) gotta fly.
fly keep the stork flying
fly let fly with sth
fly like flies to manure
fly make the fur fly
fly (My,) how time flies.
fly no flies on so
fly off (to a flying start)
fly on the fly
fly straighten up and fly right
fly There's no flies on so.
fly time flies (when you're having fun)

fly When poverty comes in at the door, love flies out of the window.
fly with flying colors
fly You can catch more flies with honey than with vinegar.
fly You must lose a fly to catch a trout.
foam foam at the mouth
foam foam up
fob fob so/sth off (on(to) so)
focus bring sth into focus
focus come into focus
focus focus on so/sth
focus focus sth on so/sth
focus go out of focus
focus in focus
focus out of focus
foe friend or foe
fog able to fog a mirror
fog fog over
fog fog sth up
fog fog up
fog foggiest (idea)
fog in a fog
foggiest foggiest (idea)
foist foist so/sth off (on so/sth)
fold fold back
fold fold one's hands
fold fold sth away
fold fold sth back
fold fold sth into sth
fold fold sth over
fold fold sth up
fold fold, spindle, or mutilate
fold fold up
fold folding money
fold unfold into sth
fold unfold sth into sth
folk Different strokes for different folks.
folk (home) folks
folk Idle folk have the least leisure.
follow Do you follow?
follow follow after the style of so/sth
follow follow in so's tracks
follow follow on (after so/sth)
follow follow one's heart
follow follow one's nose
follow follow orders
follow follow so/sth about
follow follow so/sth out
follow follow so's lead
follow follow so up
follow follow sth through
follow follow sth up
follow follow suit
follow follow the crowd
follow follow through (on sth)
follow follow through (with sth)
follow follow up (on so)
follow follow up (on so/sth)
follow follow up (on sth)
follow hard act to follow
follow tough act to follow
folly Where ignorance is bliss, 'tis folly to be wise.
foment foment trouble
fond Absence makes the heart grow fonder.
fond fond of so/sth
food flavor food with sth
food food for thought
fool any fool thing
fool Children and fools tell the truth.

fool every fool thing
fool Experience is the teacher of fools.
fool fool and his money are soon parted.
fool fool around
fool fool (around) with so/sth
fool Fool me once, shame on you; fool me twice, shame on me.
fool fool's paradise
fool fool so into sth
fool Fools rush in where angels fear to tread.
fool go on a fool's errand
fool make a fool (out) of so
fool nobody's fool
fool on a fool's errand
fool penny-wise and pound-foolish
fool play so for a fool
fool play the fool
fool take so for a fool
fool (That's) enough (of this) foolishness!
fool There's no fool like an old fool.
fool (You) could have fooled me.
foolish penny-wise and pound-foolish
foolishness (That's) enough (of this) foolishness!
foot back on one's feet
foot balls of one's feet
foot bound hand and foot
foot bring one to one's feet
foot bring sth to its feet
foot catch so flat-footed
foot cold as a welldigger's feet (in January)
foot cold feet
foot come to one's feet
foot dead on one's feet
foot dive in with both feet
foot drag one's feet (on or over sth)
foot find one's feet
foot fleet of foot
foot foot in both camps
foot foot the bill (for sth)
foot foot-in-mouth disease
foot get one on one's feet
foot get one's feet wet
foot get one's foot in the door
foot get some weight off one's feet
foot get to one's feet
foot have feet of clay
foot have one foot in the grave
foot have one's feet on the ground
foot have the shoe on the other foot
foot have two left feet
foot hotfoot it (off to) somewhere
foot hotfoot it out of somewhere
foot I wouldn't touch it with a ten-foot pole.
foot itchy feet
foot jump in with both feet
foot keep one's feet on the ground
foot keep out from under so's feet
foot keep sth on its feet
foot knock one off one's feet
foot land (up)on both feet
foot land (up)on one's feet
foot lay sth at so's feet
foot let grass grow under one's feet
foot load off one's feet
foot My foot!
foot not let the grass grow under one's feet

foot not set foot somewhere
foot not touch so/sth with a ten-foot pole
foot off on the right foot (with so/sth)
foot off on the wrong foot
foot on foot
foot on its feet
foot on one's feet
foot patter of tiny feet
foot play footsie with so
foot put one foot in front of the other
foot put one on one's feet
foot put one's best foot forward
foot put one's feet up
foot put one's foot down (about so/sth)
foot put one's foot in it
foot put one's foot in one's mouth
foot put sth on its feet
foot regain one's feet
foot rise to one's feet
foot run one's feet off
foot set foot in some place
foot set one (back) on one's feet
foot set one on one's feet again
foot shoe is on the other foot.
foot shoot oneself in the foot
foot sit at the feet of so
foot six feet under
foot spring to one's feet
foot stand on one's (own) two feet
foot start off on the wrong foot
foot step off on the wrong foot
foot stick one's foot in one's mouth
foot sweep one off one's feet
foot take a load off one's feet
foot think on one's feet
foot throw oneself at so's feet
foot vote with one's feet
foot wait on so hand and foot
foot walk so's feet off
foot wouldn't touch so/sth with a ten-foot pole
football political football
foothold foothold (somewhere)
foothold help so get a foothold (somewhere)
footloose footloose and fancy-free
footsie play footsie with so
footwork fancy footwork
for A for effort
for accept the blame for sth
for account for so/sth
for account for sth
for ache for so/sth
for acquire a taste for sth
for act for so
for adapt sth for sth
for adjourn for a time
for admire so for sth
for admonish so for sth
for adore so for doing sth
for adore so for having sth
for advertise for so/sth
for advertise sth for a price
for advertise sth for sth
for affinity for so/sth
for agitate for sth
for aim for sth
for aim for the sky
for Aim for the stars!
for (all) for so/sth
for (all) for the best
for All right for you!

for all the more reason for doing sth
for allow for so/sth
for allow sth for sth
for angle for sth
for announce (one's support) for so/sth
for answer for so
for apologize (to so) (for so)
for appeal (to a court) (for sth)
for appear for so
for apply (to so/sth) (for sth)
for appropriate sth for sth
for (Are you) ready for this?
for argue for so/sth
for arguing for the sake of arguing
for arguing for the sake of argument
for arrange for so to do sth
for arrange for sth
for arrange some music for sth
for arrange sth for some time
for arrange sth for so/sth
for as for so/sth
for ask for a knuckle sandwich
for ask for so/sth
for ask for sth bad or dire
for ask for the moon
for ask for trouble
for ask so for sth
for ask so out (for sth)
for assume liability for sth
for at a loss (for words)
for atone for sth
for audition for sth
for audition so for sth
for augur well for so/sth
for avenge oneself (on so/sth) (for sth)
for award sth (to so) (for sth)
for babysit for so
for back so for sth
for bang for the buck
for bang the drum for so/sth
for bargain (for so/sth) (with so)
for bargain for sth
for barter for sth
for barter sth for sth else
for battle for sth
for be for doing sth
for be for so/sth
for bear the blame for sth
for beat the drum for so/sth
for bed down (for sth)
for beg for so/sth
for bend over backwards (to do sth) (for so)
for bid (sth) for sth
for big hand for sth
for bill so for sth
for blame for sth
for blame so for sth
for blast off (for some place)
for bleed for so
for Blessed is he who expects nothing, for he shall never be disappointed.
for bode somehow for so/sth
for bounce for sth
for bound for somewhere
for brace oneself for sth
for break for sth
for break ground (for sth)
for break sth down (for so)
for bring so up for sth
for buck for sth
for budget sth for so/sth
for build so up (for sth)

for Bully for you!
for bunk down (for the night)
for burn for so/sth
for but for so/sth
for buy sth for a song
for buy sth (from so) (for sth)
for buzz for so
for Bye for now.
for call for so/sth
for call so in (for sth)
for call (up)on so (for sth)
for campaign for so/sth
for can (just) whistle for sth
for candidate for a pair of wings
for cannot see the forest for the trees
for cannot see the wood for the trees
for can't wait (for sth (to happen))
for care for so
for care for sth
for care nothing for so/sth
for carry a torch (for so)
for cash sth in (for sth)
for cast around for so/sth
for celebrate so for an accomplishment
for censure so (for sth)
for charge (sth) for so
for charge (sth) for sth
for chart sth out (for so/sth)
for cheer for so/sth
for chide so for sth
for chip in (on sth) (for so)
for chip in (with sth) (on sth) (for so)
for chip in (on sth) (for so)
for choose so/sth for sth
for choose sth for so
for cite so for sth
for claim sth for so/sth
for claim sth for sth
for clamor for so/sth
for clear sth for publication
for close enough for government work
for close in for the kill
for coach so for sth
for collect (money) for so/sth
for collect (money) for sth
for comb sth for so/sth
for come around (for a visit)
for come for so
for come in for sth
for come out for so/sth
for come through (for so/sth)
for come up for air
for come up for auction
for come up for reelection
for come up for sale
for come up for sth
for commend so for sth
for commit so/sth for sth
for compensate for sth
for compensate so for sth
for compete for so/sth
for condemn so for sth
for consider so for sth
for contend with so (for sth)
for contract with so (for sth)
for contribute sth (to so) (for so/sth)
for count for sth
for count so in (for sth)
for count so out (for sth)
for cover for so
for cover so/sth for sth
for cover (up) for so
for cram for a test

for cram for an examination
for crazy for so/sth
for credit (for sth)
for credit so/sth for sth
for criticize so for sth
for cruising for a bruising
for crusade for so/sth
for cry for so/sth
for cry out for so/sth
for crying need (for so/sth)
for curse so for sth
for curtains for so/sth
for cut out (for some place)
for cut out for so/sth
for cut out for sth
for dash out (for sth)
for dash over (for sth)
for (dead) ringer (for so)
for decide for so/sth
for declare (oneself) for so/sth
for decorate so for sth
for demonstrate for so/sth
for denounce so for sth
for depart for some place
for desert so/sth for so/sth else
for deserve credit for sth
for design sth for so
for design sth for sth
for despise so for sth
for destine so for sth
for destined for sth
for detail so for sth
for devil can cite Scripture for his own purpose.
for devil can quote Scripture for his own purpose.
for devil finds work for idle hands to do.
for devil so or an animal for sth
for dicker with so (for sth)
for die for so/sth
for Different strokes for different folks.
for dig for sth
for discipline so for sth
for dismiss so (from sth) (for sth)
for disqualify so/sth for sth
for do for so
for do for sth
for Do I have to spell it out (for you)?
for do somehow for so
for dock so/sth for sth
for Does it work for you?
for dollar for dollar
for done for
for Don't put off for tomorrow what you can do today.
for doss down (for some time)
for down for sth
for down for the count
for down one for the road
for draft so for sth
for draw for sth
for draw straws for sth
for dress for so
for dress for sth
for drop around (for sth)
for dun so for sth
for earmark sth for so/sth
for Eat, drink, and be merry, for tomorrow we die.
for educate so for sth
for embark for some place
for employ so for sth

for enlist (oneself) for sth
for enlist so for sth
for enroll (so) for sth
for envy so for so/sth
for equip so/sth (with sth) (for sth)
for Every man for himself (and the devil take the hindmost).
for Everything will work out for the best.
for examine so/sth for sth
for exchange sth for sth
for excuse so for sth
for expect so/sth for sth
for expend sth for sth
for expropriate sth (from so/sth) (for so/sth)
for eye for an eye (and a tooth for a tooth).
for fair game (for sth)
for fall for so
for fall for sth
for fault so (for sth)
for fear for so/sth
for feel around (for so/sth)
for feel for so
for feel for sth
for fend for oneself
for fight for so/sth
for file for sth
for fill in (for so/sth)
for find for so/sth
for find oneself in the market (for sth)
for find time for so/sth
for fine so for sth
for Fine weather for ducks.
for fish for a compliment
for fish for sth
for fit for a king
for fit for the gods
for fit so for sth
for fit so/sth out (for sth)
for fix sth for (a meal)
for flip so for sth
for food for thought
for foot the bill (for sth)
for for a drive
for for a lark
for for a living
for for a ride
for for a song
for for a spin
for for a split second
for for all I care
for for all I know
for for all intents and purposes
for for all it's worth
for for (all) one's trouble
for for all practical purposes
for for all so's problems
for for all the world
for for better or for worse
for for chicken feed
for For crying in a bucket!
for For crying out loud!
for for days on end
for for fear of sth
for for free
for for giggles
for for good
for For goodness sake!
for For gosh sake!
for For heaven('s) sake!
for for hours on end

for for instance
for for keeps
for for kicks
for for life
for for miles
for for my money
for for one's (own) part
for for one's (own) sake
for for openers
for for peanuts
for For Pete's sake!
for For pity's sake!
for for real
for for safekeeping
for for sale
for For shame!
for for short
for for (some) days running
for for (some) months running
for for (some) years running
for for so/sth's sake
for for starters
for for sure
for for that matter
for for the asking
for for the better
for for the birds
for for the devil of it
for for the duration
for for the fun of it
for for the good of so/sth
for for the heck of it
for for the hell of it
for for the life of me
for For the love of Mike!
for for the moment
for for the most part
for for the record
for for the sake of so/sth
for for the time being
for For want of a nail the shoe was lost; for want of a shoe the horse was lost; and for want of a horse the man was lost.
for for what(ever) it's worth
for for your information
for forage (around) (for sth)
for forgive so for sth
for fork some money out (for sth)
for front for so/sth
for fumble for sth
for furnish sth for so/sth
for furnish sth for sth
for gasp for air
for gasp for breath
for gear so/sth up (for so/sth)
for gear up for so/sth
for Genius is an infinite capacity for taking pains.
for get an amount of money for sth
for get so up (for sth)
for get sth for an amount of money
for get sth for so
for get sth for sth
for get sth together (for a particular time)
for give cause for sth
for give one's eyeteeth (for so/sth)
for give one's right arm (for so/sth)
for give so/sth up (for lost)
for give so pause (for thought)
for give so tit for tat
for give so up for dead
for give sth for sth

for glutton for punishment
for go all out (for so/sth)
for go along (with so) for the ride
for go away (for sth)
for go down for the count
for go down for the third time
for go for broke
for Go for it!
for go for nothing
for go for so/sth
for go in for sth
for go on for an age
for go out for so/sth
for go out (for sth)
for go out for the count
for go to bat for so
for go up for auction
for good enough for government work
for good enough for so/sth
for good for what ails you
for Good for you!
for Good-bye for now.
for grab for so/sth
for grapple (with so) (for sth)
for grieve for so/sth
for grist for the mill
for groom so for sth
for grope (about) (for sth)
for grope (around) (for sth)
for grounds for sth
for grub around (for so/sth)
for guarantee sth against sth (for sth)
for gulp for air
for gun for so
for hang on for dear life
for hang so for sth
for hard up (for sth)
for have a flair for sth
for have a gift for (doing) sth
for have a head for sth
for have a lot going (for one)
for have a nose for sth
for have a passion for so/sth
for have a penchant for doing sth
for have a soft spot (in one's heart) for so or an animal
for have a thirst for sth
for have (a) use for so/sth
for have a weakness for so/sth
for have an appetite for sth
for have an ear for sth
for have an eye for so/sth
for Have I got something for you!
for have it in for so
for have one's eye out (for so/sth)
for have one's work cut out for one
for have so around (for sth)
for have so for breakfast
for have so over (for sth)
for have so slated for sth
for have so up (for sth)
for have sth for (a meal)
for have sth for so
for have sth for sth
for have sth going (for oneself)
for have sth in store (for so)
for have the hots for so
for have the stomach for sth
for He that would go to sea for pleasure, would go to hell for a pastime.
for head for so/sth
for head for the hills

for head for the last roundup
for head for (the) tall timber
for head out (for sth)
for headed for sth
for hell-bent for leather
for hell-bent for somewhere or sth
for hint for sth
for hit out (for sth or some place)
for hit so up (for sth)
for hold good for so/sth
for hold no brief for so/sth
for hold out (for so/sth)
for hold so accountable (for sth)
for hold so for ransom
for hold so responsible (for sth)
for hold sth back for a rainy day
for hold sth for so
for hold sth in store (for so)
for hold still (for so/sth)
for hold still for sth
for hold terror for so
for hold up (for so/sth)
for hone for so/sth
for honor so for sth
for hope for so
for hope for the best
for How is so fixed for sth?
for hunger for so/sth
for hungry for sth
for hunt for so/sth
for hunt high and low (for so/sth)
for hurt for so/sth
for hurtin' for sth
for (I) can't say for sure.
for (I) couldn't ask for more.
for I felt like a penny waiting for change.
for I'd like (for) you to meet so.
for If ifs and ands were pots and pans (there'd be no work for tinkers' hands).
for if one knows what's good for one
for If you don't see what you want, please ask (for it).
for if you know what's good for you
for If you want peace, (you must) prepare war.
for Ignorance (of the law) is no excuse (for breaking it).
for impeach so for sth
for in exchange (for so/sth)
for in for sth
for in return for (so/sth)
for in some transaction for so
for in store (for so)
for in the market (for sth)
for in the mood (for sth)
for incapacitate so (for sth) (for a period of time)
for indict so for sth
for inquire for so
for insure so/sth (against sth) (for sth)
for intend sth for so/sth
for intercede (for so) (with so/sth)
for interpret for so
for interpret sth for so
for interview so for sth
for interview with so for sth
for invite so over (for sth)
for (Is it) cold enough for you?
for (Is it) hot enough for you?
for issue a call for sth
for It's for a fact.

for It's for you.
for It's ill waiting for dead men's shoes.
for (It's) time for a change.
for (It) works for me.
for itch for sth
for jockey for position
for jump for joy
for Keep a thing seven years and you'll (always) find a use for it.
for keep an eye out (for so/sth)
for keep one's eyes open (for so/sth)
for keep one's eye(s) out (for so/sth)
for keep one's eyes peeled (for so/sth)
for keep one's fingers crossed (for so/sth)
for keep so/sth for so
for keep so/sth in mind (for so/sth)
for keep sth for a rainy day
for keep sth for another occasion
for keep still (for so/sth)
for kick in (on sth) (for so/sth)
for kick oneself (for doing sth)
for kick sth in (on sth) (for so/sth)
for kill for sth
for knock oneself out (to do sth) (for so/sth)
for knock so for a loop
for know one for what one is
for labor for so/sth
for labor for sth
for lack for sth
for last call (for sth)
for last chance (for sth)
for last for sth
for lay down one's life (for so/sth)
for lay for so/sth
for lay sth aside for so/sth
for lay sth away (for so)
for lay sth for so/sth
for lay the blame (for sth) on so
for leap for joy
for leave for some place
for leave oneself wide open for sth
for leave so for dead
for leave sth for another occasion
for leave sth for so or an animal
for leave the door open (for sth)
for leave word for so to do sth
for lecture so for sth
for legislate for sth
for let oneself in for sth
for let so in for sth
for lie in store (for so)
for lie in wait (for so/sth)
for light out (for some place)
for light out (of some place) (for some place)
for like looking for a needle in a haystack
for line so up (for sth)
for line up for sth
for listen for so/sth
for live for so/sth
for live for the moment
for loaded for bear
for lobby for sth
for log so for sth
for long for so/sth
for look about (for so/sth)
for look around for so/sth
for look for so/sth
for look for so/sth high and low
for look for trouble
for look high and low (for so/sth)
for look like a candidate for a pair of wings

for look like a (dead) ringer (for so)
for look none the worse for wear
for look out for number one
for look out for so
for look to so/sth (for sth)
for look up and down (for so/sth)
for Lovely weather for ducks.
for lucky for you
for lunge for so/sth
for lust for sth
for made for each other
for made for so
for made for sth
for make a beeline for so/sth
for make a bolt for so/sth
for make a break for so/sth
for make a dash for so/sth
for make a (kind of) life for oneself
for make a name (for oneself)
for make a pitch (for so/sth)
for make a play (for so)
for make a run for it
for make allowance(s) (for so/sth)
for make amends (to so) (for so/sth)
for make an exception (for so)
for make application (to so/sth) (for sth)
for make arrangements for so
for make arrangements (with so) (for sth)
for make change (for so) (for sth)
for make for somewhere
for make it hot for so
for make life miserable for so
for make (out) for so/sth
for make room (for so/sth)
for make so the scapegoat for sth
for make sth for so/sth
for make time for so/sth
for make tracks (for sth)
for make up for lost time
for make up for so/sth
for make way (for so/sth)
for maneuver for sth
for mark so for life
for match for so/sth or an animal
for mean (for so) to do sth
for mean sth for so/sth
for Mecca for so
for meet the requirements (for sth)
for might as well be hung for a sheep as (for) a lamb
for milk so for sth
for mine for sth
for mistake so for so else
for mistake sth for sth else
for moment everyone has been waiting for
for more than one bargained for
for motion (for) so to do sth
for mourn for so/sth
for move for sth
for move in for the kill
for name so for so else
for name so/sth for so/sth
for No rest for the wicked.
for nominate so for sth
for none the worse for wear
for nose about (for so/sth)
for not able to get sth for love or money
for not able to see the forest for the trees
for not for a moment
for not for all the tea in China

for not for (anything in) the world
for not for hire
for not for love nor money
for Not for my money.
for not for publication
for not long for this world
for not miss sth for love nor money
for not miss sth for the world
for not take no for an answer
for noted for sth
for Nothing for me, thanks.
for obtain sth for so/sth
for offer sth for sth
for on the alert (for so/sth)
for on the lookout (for so/sth)
for on the watch for so/sth
for once and for all
for one for the (record) books
for one for the road
for One hand for oneself and one for the ship.
for one law for the rich and another for the poor
for one's for the asking
for one's work is cut out for one
for only have eyes for so
for open a few doors (for so)
for (Open) confession is good for the soul.
for open for business
for open some doors (for so)
for opt for sth
for out for blood
for out for the count
for out of consideration (for so/sth)
for owe sth (to so) (for sth)
for pan for sth
for pant for air
for pant for so/sth
for par for the course
for Pardon me for living!
for pardon so for sth
for pass for so/sth
for pass for sth
for pave the way (for so/sth) (with sth)
for pay an arm and a leg (for sth)
for pay for sth
for pay so (for sth) (with sth)
for pay sth out (for so/sth)
for pay through the nose (for sth)
for penalize so for sth
for penny for your thoughts!
for persecute so for sth
for petition so/sth for sth
for pick so/sth out (for so/sth)
for pick up so for a song
for pinch so for sth
for pinch-hit for so
for pine for so/sth
for place for everything, and everything in its place.
for place the blame on so/sth (for sth)
for plan for so
for plan for sth
for play for keeps
for play for sth
for play for time
for play it for all it's worth
for play so for a fool
for plead for so
for plead for sth
for pleased for so/sth
for plump for so/sth

for poise oneself for sth
for poised for sth
for pop around (for a visit)
for pop back (for sth)
for pop by (for a visit)
for pop down (for a visit)
for pop for sth
for pop in (for a visit)
for pop over (for a visit)
for pose for so/sth
for poster child (for sth)
for pound for pound
for pray for so/sth
for prepare so for sth
for prepare so/sth for sth
for prescribe sth for so
for prescribe sth for sth
for preserve sth for so/sth
for press for sth
for pressed for cash
for pressed for money
for pressed for time
for probe sth for sth
for procure sth (from so/sth) (for so/sth)
for produce sth for sth
for prospect for sth
for provide for so/sth
for provide sth for so/sth
for psyched up (for sth)
for pull for so/sth
for pump so for sth
for pump so up (for sth)
for punish so for sth
for purchase sth for so
for push for sth
for pushed for money
for pushed for time
for put a plug in (for so/sth)
for put in a good word (for so)
for put in for sth
for put money up (for sth)
for put one's head on the block (for so/sth)
for put so down (for sth)
for put so up (for sth)
for put sth aside for a rainy day
for put sth aside (for sth)
for put sth up for auction
for put sth up for sale
for qualify for sth
for qualify so for sth
for queer for sth
for quest for so/sth
for queue up (for sth)
for race for sth
for race so for sth
for raise money for so/sth
for reach for so/sth
for reach for the sky
for Reach for the stars!
for read for sth
for read so out (for sth)
for rebuke so for sth
for recognize one for what one is
for recognize so/sth for sth
for recognize sth for what it is
for recommend so for sth
for recompense so for sth
for recruit so for sth
for register for sth
for register so for sth
for rehearse for sth
for reimburse so for sth

for remunerate so for sth
for renounce so for sth
for repay so for sth
for report for sth
for reprimand so for sth
for reproach so for sth
for reprove so for sth
for reputation (for doing sth)
for requisition sth for so/sth
for reserve sth for so/sth
for respect so for sth
for rest up (for sth)
for retail for sth
for retool for sth
for retool sth for sth
for return sth for sth
for revere so/sth for sth
for review for sth
for reward so for sth
for riding for a fall
for roll out the red carpet (for so)
for root around (for sth)
for root for so/sth
for rummage around (somewhere) (for sth)
for run for it
for run for one's life
for run for one's money
for run for sth
for run for the hills
for run sth in (for sth)
for rush for sth
for sacrifice so/sth for so/sth
for sail for some place
for same for me.
for save money up (for sth)
for save oneself (for marriage)
for save (sth) for a rainy day
for save sth for so/sth
for save (up) (for sth)
for Say hello to so (for me).
for say sth for sth
for scavenge (around) for so/sth
for scheme for sth
for scold so for sth
for score sth for sth
for scour sth for so/sth
for scout around (for so/sth)
for scramble for so/sth
for scratch about (for sth)
for scream for sth
for scrounge around (for so/sth)
for search for so/sth
for search high and low (for so/sth)
for search so for sth
for search sth for so/sth
for seem pushed for time
for select so/sth for so/sth
for sell sth for a certain price
for sell sth for a song
for send ahead for sth
for send away (for sth)
for send for so/sth
for send in for sth
for send off for sth
for send out (for so/sth)
for send so back for sth
for send so down for sth
for send so for so/sth
for send so in for so
for send so/sth around for so/sth
for send so out (for so/sth)
for sentence so to sth (for sth)
for serve sth for sth

for set for life
for set off (for sth)
for set out (for some place) (from some place)
for set sail for some place
for set sth aside (for so/sth)
for set sth for sth
for set sth out (for so/sth)
for set the stage for sth
for settle for sth
for shift for oneself
for shoot for sth
for shoot for the sky
for shop around (for sth)
for short for sth
for shoulder the blame for sth
for sigh for so
for sight for sore eyes
for sign for so
for sign for sth
for sign so up (for sth)
for sign sth for so
for sign up (for sth)
for signal for so
for signal for sth
for single so/sth out (for sth)
for sit for an exam
for sit for one's portrait
for sit for so
for sit in (for so)
for sit still for sth
for slate so/sth for sth
for slated for sth
for so much for so/sth
for So much for that.
for solicit for so/sth
for solicit so for sth
for speak for itself
for speak for oneself
for speak for so/sth
for speak for themselves
for speak up for so/sth
for speaking for oneself
for spell sth for so
for spend sth for sth
for *split second
for spoiling for a fight
for spoken for
for spring for sth
for square off (for sth)
for square up (for fighting)
for stall for time
for stall so/sth for sth
for stand for sth
for stand in (for so)
for stand still for sth
for stand up for so/sth
for start for some place
for starve for some food
for starve for so/sth
for stay for sth
for stay up (for sth)
for steel oneself for so/sth
for steer sth for sth
for step aside (for so)
for stick one's neck out (for so/sth)
for stick up for so/sth
for sting so for sth
for stop for so
for stop for sth
for stop off (some place) (for a period of time)
for strain for an effect
for strapped for sth

for strike for sth
for strike out for some place
for strip for sth
for strive for sth
for struggle for sth
for struggle with so for sth
for study for sth
for stump for so
for sub for so/sth
for sub so for so else
for substitute for so/sth
for substitute so for so else
for sucker for so/sth
for sue for sth
for sue so for sth
for suffice for so/sth
for suited for sth
for swap so/sth for so/sth else
for sweat for sth
for swim for it
for swim for so/sth
for swing for sth
for tab so for sth
for take a collection up (from so) (for so/sth)
for take a look for so/sth
for take a turn for the better
for take a turn for the worse
for take an amount of money for sth
for take credit for sth
for Take my word for it.
for take off (for some place)
for take one for the road
for take so for a fool
for take so for a ride
for take so for an idiot
for take so for dead
for take so for so/sth
for take so for sth
for take so/sth for granted
for take so's word for sth
for take sth for a drive
for take the blame (for doing sth)
for take the rap (for so)
for take the rap (for sth)
for taken for dead
for tap so (for sth)
for tender sth for sth
for tender sth (to so) (for sth)
for tense up (for sth)
for test for sth
for test so/sth for sth
for testify for so
for Thank God for small favors.
for thank so for sth
for Thank you for a lovely evening.
for Thank you for a lovely time.
for Thank you for calling.
for Thank you for having me.
for Thank you for inviting me.
for Thank you for sharing.
for thankful for small blessings
for Thanks for the lift.
for Thanks for the ride.
for That's all for so.
for That's easy for you to say.
for That's enough for now.
for That's for dang sure!
for That's show business (for you).
for There but for the grace of God (go I).
for There is a remedy for everything except death.

for There is a time and a place for everything.
for There is no accounting for taste(s).
for There is no rest for the weary.
for There's no accounting for taste.
for think for oneself
for think so fit for sth
for think so/sth fit for so/sth
for thirst for sth
for thirsty for sth
for throw a party (for so)
for throw so for a loop
for throw so for a loss
for throw so over for so else
for ticket so for some place
for tie (with so) (for sth)
for Time and tide wait for no man.
for time for so/sth
for time off for good behavior
for to die for
for toil for so
for toil for sth
for toll for so
for too big for one's britches
for too close for comfort
for too funny for words
for too rich for so's blood
for toss (so) for sth
for touch so (up) for sth
for trade so/sth for so/sth
for trade sth in (for sth)
for train for sth
for train so or an animal for sth
for travel for so/sth
for treat so (for sth) (with sth)
for trouble so for sth
for trust so for sth
for try for sth
for try out (for sth)
for try so for sth
for try sth (on) (for size)
for turn out (for sth)
for turn to so/sth (for sth)
for unite for sth
for up for auction
for up for grabs
for up for reelection
for up for sale
for up for sth
for upbraid so for sth
for use so/sth for sth
for use your head for more than a hatrack
for use your head for more than something to keep your ears apart
for utilize so/sth for sth
for value so/sth for sth
for vie (with so) (for so/sth)
for volunteer for sth
for vote for so/sth
for vouch for so/sth
for wait (around) (for so/sth)
for wait at sth (for so/sth)
for wait for the next wave
for wait for the other shoe to drop
for wait up (for so)
for want for nothing
for want for sth
for want so for sth
for want sth for so/sth
for wash up (for sth)
for watch for so/sth
for watch out for so

for weep for joy
for weep for so or an animal
for What can I do for you?
for What do you know for sure?
for What else can I do for you?
for what for
for What's in it for me?
for What's on tap for today?
for What's sauce for the goose is sauce for the gander.
for whistle for so/sth
for Why buy a cow when you can get milk for free?
for will eat so for breakfast
for wire ahead (for sth)
for wire for sth
for wire so/sth for sth
for wish for sth
for with so/sth for some time
for without (so much as) a (for or) by your leave
for witness for so/sth
for word for word
for work for so
for work for sth
for work out for the best
for worse for wear
for (Would you) care for another (one)?
for write away for sth
for write for sth
for write in(to sth) (for sth)
for write off (to so) (for sth)
for write so for sth
for yearn for so/sth
for yen for so/sth
for You asked for it!
for You don't get something for nothing.
for You get what you pay for.
for zone sth for sth
forage forage (around) (for sth)
forbid forbidden fruit
forbid God forbid!
forbid Heaven forbid!
force arrive in force
force attack in force
force by force of habit
force come out in force
force driving force (behind so/sth)
force force so or an animal from sth
force force so/sth down
force force so/sth in(to) sth
force force so/sth off (of) sth
force force so/sth (off) on so
force force so/sth out of sth
force force so/sth through sth
force force so out of office
force force so's hand
force force so to the wall
force force sth down
force force sth through sth
force force sth up
force force to be reckoned with
force go out in force
force in force
force join forces (with so)
force out in force
force serve as the driving force (behind so/sth)
fore bring sth to the fore
fore come to the fore
fore fore and aft

forearmed Forewarned is forearmed.
foreclose foreclose on sth
forefront at the forefront (of sth)
forefront in the forefront (of sth)
foregone foregone conclusion
foremost first and foremost
foresee Nothing is certain but the unforeseen.
forest cannot see the forest for the trees
forest not able to see the forest for the trees
forever forever and a day
forever forever and ever
forever lost and gone forever
forever thing of beauty is a joy forever.
forewarn forewarn so about sth
forewarn Forewarned is forearmed.
forget Don't forget to write.
forget Forget (about) it!
forget forget about so/sth
forget forget one's manners
forget forget oneself
forget Forget you!
forget Forgive and forget.
forget gone but not forgotten
forgive Forgive and forget.
forgive forgive so for sth
forgive To err is human(, to forgive divine).
forgot gone but not forgotten
fork Fingers were made before forks.
fork fork some money out (for sth)
fork fork sth out (to so)
fork fork sth over (to so)
fork speak with a forked tongue
form form an opinion
form form and substance
form form from sth
form form so/sth into sth
form form sth out of sth
form form (up) into sth
form Imitation is the sincerest form of flattery.
form in any way, shape, or form
form in rare form
form in top form
form true to form
fort hold the fort
forth and so forth
forth back and forth
forth blossom forth
forth bounce sth back and forth
forth bring so/sth forth
forth burst forth
forth call so forth
forth call sth forth
forth come forth
forth draw sth forth
forth give forth with sth
forth gush (forth) (from so/sth)
forth hold forth (on so/sth)
forth issue (forth) from some place
forth launch forth on sth
forth launch forth ((up)on sth)
forth lead forth
forth lead so/sth forth
forth pace back and forth
forth pour forth
forth put (sth) forth
forth sally forth
forth set forth on sth
forth set sth forth

forth spring (forth) from so/sth
forth stretch forth (from sth)
forth sway back and forth
forth toss sth back and forth
forth venture forth
fortify fortify so or an animal (against sth) (with sth)
fortune come into a (small) fortune
fortune Every man is the architect of his own fortune.
fortune Fortune favors the bold.
fortune Fortune favors the brave.
fortune small fortune
forty catch forty winks
forty forty winks
forty Life begins at forty.
forty take forty winks
forward bend forward
forward bring so/sth forward
forward call so forward
forward carry sth forward
forward come forward
forward face so/sth forward
forward forward sth from some place (to so or some place)
forward from this day forward
forward go forward with sth
forward inch forward
forward incline forward
forward incline sth forward
forward know sth backwards and forwards
forward know sth forwards and backwards
forward lean forward
forward lean sth forward
forward leap forward
forward look forward to sth
forward lurch forward
forward move forward with sth
forward move so/sth forward
forward pass sth forward
forward pitch forward
forward press forward
forward push forward
forward push so/sth forward
forward put one's best foot forward
forward put so/sth forward
forward put sth forward
forward set sth forward
forward step forward
forward thrust sth forward
forward urge so forward
foul foul one's own nest
foul foul out (of sth)
foul foul play
foul foul so/sth up
foul foul up
foul fouled up
foul It's an ill bird that fouls its own nest.
foul use foul language
found found money
found found sth (up)on sth
found lost-and-found
four between you and me and these four walls
four four sheets in the wind
four from the four corners of the earth
four get down (on all fours)
four on all fours
four sixty-four-dollar question
foursome make up a foursome

fourteen meaner than a junkyard dog (with fourteen sucking pups)
fourth grow knee-high by the 4th of July
fourth knee-high by the 4th of July
fowl neither fish nor fowl
fox cunning as a fox
fox sly as a fox
'fraid 'Fraid so.
fraidy fraidy cat
frame frame sth in sth
frame frame sth out
frame one's frame of mind
frank frankly speaking
frank (speaking) (quite) frankly
fraternize fraternize with so/sth
fraught fraught with danger
fray enter the fray
fray join the fray
fray jump into the fray
frazzle wear so to a frazzle
freak freak out (at so/sth)
freak freak out (on sth)
freak freak out (over so/sth)
freak freak so out
freak freaked (out)
free able to breathe (freely) again
free best things in life are free.
free break free (from so)
free break sth free (from sth)
free feel free (to do sth)
free footloose and fancy-free
free for free
free free and clear
free free and easy
free free as a bird
free free as (the) air
free free gift
free free hand (with so/sth)
free free lunch
free free ride
free free so/sth from so/sth
free free translation
free get free of so/sth
free get off scot-free
free get so/sth free (from so/sth)
free give free rein to so
free go scot-free
free home free
free make free with so
free make free with sth
free Nothing is given so freely as advice.
free set so/sth free (from sth)
free There ain't no such thing as a free lunch.
free There's no such thing as a free lunch.
free Why buy a cow when you can get milk for free?
freedom give one one's freedom
freeze freeze on doing sth
freeze freeze one's tail off
freeze freeze (on)to sth
freeze freeze over
freeze freeze so/sth in one's memory
freeze freeze so/sth to death
freeze freeze so out
freeze freeze so's wages
freeze freeze sth into sth
freeze freeze up
freeze play freeze-out
freeze put the freeze on so

freeze till hell freezes over
freeze until hell freezes over
French Excuse my French.
French Pardon my French.
frenzy feeding frenzy
fresh breath of fresh air
fresh fresh and sweet
fresh fresh as a daisy
fresh fresh blood
fresh fresh out (of sth)
fresh fresh pair of eyes
fresh fresh start
fresh fresh (with so)
fresh freshen so/sth up
fresh freshen up
fresh make a fresh start
fret fret about so/sth
fret Fret not!
fret fret over so/sth
friend Any friend of so('s) (is a friend of mine).
friend (Even) the best of friends must part.
friend fair-weather friend
friend fast friends
friend friend in need is a friend indeed.
friend friend or foe
friend friends with so
friend He that hath a full purse never wanted a friend.
friend hedge between keeps friendship green.
friend I was up all night with a sick friend.
friend Lend your money and lose your friend.
friend make a friend
friend make friends
friend man's best friend
friend Short reckonings make long friends.
friend strike up a friendship
friend user friendly
friend Who's your friend?
friendly user friendly
friendship hedge between keeps friendship green.
friendship strike up a friendship
fright Burn not your house to fright the mouse away.
frighten frighten one out of one's wits
frighten frighten so or an animal in
frighten frighten so or an animal into doing sth
frighten frighten so or an animal into sth
frighten frighten so or an animal to death
frighten frighten so/sth away
frighten frighten so out of a year's growth
frighten frighten the hell out of so
frighten frighten the pants off so
frighten frightened to death
fringe lunatic fringe
fringe on the fringe
fritter fritter sth away (on so/sth)
fritz on the fritz
fro to and fro
fro toing and froing (on sth)
frog big frog in a small pond
frog biggest frog in the puddle
frog frog in one's throat

frog If a toady frog had wings, he wouldn't bump his ass.
frog If frogs had wheels, they wouldn't bump their butts.
frog know no more about sth than a frog knows about bedsheets
frog like herding frogs
from abduct so from so/sth
from absent oneself from so/sth
from absolve so from sth
from abstain from sth
from abstain from voting
from abstract sth from so/sth
from abstract sth from sth
from adapt sth from sth
from alienate so from so/sth
from alight from sth
from allow so up (from sth)
from aloof from so/sth
from another country heard from
from arise from sth
from arouse so from sth
from arrive (some place) from some other place
from ascertain sth from so/sth
from aside from so/sth
from avert sth (away) from so/sth
from awake(n) from sth
from awake(n) so from sth
from away from it all
from away from one's desk
from away (from so/sth)
from back away (from so/sth)
from back down (from so/sth)
from back off (from so/sth)
from back so off (from sth)
from back so/sth out (from sth)
from bake sth from scratch
from ban so from sth
from banish so/sth from some place
from bar so from some place
from beg sth from so
from benefit from sth
from bleed from sth
from blow in (from some place)
from blow in(to some place) (from some place)
from bolt from the blue
from borrow sth from so
from bounce back (from sth)
from branch off (from sth)
from branch out (from sth)
from break away (from so)
from break free (from so)
from break loose (from so)
from break off (from sth)
from break sth away (from sth)
from break sth free (from sth)
from break sth loose from sth
from breeze in (from some place)
from bring so over from some place
from bring sth away (from sth)
from brush sth away (from sth)
from buffet so/sth from so/sth to so/sth
from build so/sth up (from sth)
from bundle from heaven
from buy sth back (from so)
from buy sth (from so) (for sth)
from cadge sth from so
from call so away (from sth)
from carry so/sth over from sth
from carve sth from sth
from cast off (from sth)

from catch sth from so
from change back (from sth)
from change over (from so/sth) (to so/sth)
from chase so/sth (away) from some place
from chatter from sth
from check out (from sth)
from chip sth away (from sth)
from choose from so/sth
from clear sth from some place
from climb down (from sth)
from clip sth from sth
from collect sth from so
from come away (from so/sth)
from come back (from some place)
from come down (from some place)
from come down (from sth)
from come from behind
from come from far and wide
from come from nowhere
from come from some place
from come from so/sth
from come home from some place
from come (up) from behind
from commute from some place
from compile sth from sth
from conceal so/sth from so/sth
from conduct so away (from so/sth)
from confiscate sth from so/sth
from constrain so from doing sth
from construct sth from sth
from convalesce from sth
from convert from sth ((in)to sth)
from convert so/sth (from sth) ((in)to sth)
from convey sth (from sth) (to so/sth)
from cop sth from so/sth
from copy sth down (from so/sth)
from count from sth (up) to sth
from cower (away) from so/sth
from cower down (from sth)
from cower from sth
from crawl out (from under so/sth)
from creep out (from under so/sth)
from crib sth from so/sth
from cringe away from so/sth
from cross from some place to some place
from cut from the same cloth
from cut (oneself) loose (from so/sth)
from cut so/sth loose from sth
from cut so/sth off (from sth)
from cut sth away (from sth)
from cut sth from sth
from cut the ground out from under so
from dangle from sth
from dangle sth from sth
from date from sth
from *day one
from dead from the neck up
from deduce sth from sth
from deduct sth from sth else
from defect from sth
from deflect sth away from so/sth
from delete sth from sth
from deliver so from so/sth
from demand sth from so/sth
from demote so from sth (to sth)
from depart from some place
from deport so (from some place) (to some other place)
from derive from sth
from derive sth from so/sth
from derive sth from sth
from descend from so or some group
from descend from sth

from deserve better from so/sth
from desist from sth
from detach so/sth from so/sth
from deter so/sth from sth
from detract from so/sth
from develop from so/sth (into so/sth)
from deviate from sth
from die from curiosity
from die from sth
from differ from sth
from differentiate so/sth from so/sth else
from digress from sth
from disappear from sth
from disbar so from sth
from discern so/sth from sth else
from discern sth from so/sth else
from discharge so from sth
from discharge sth from sth
from disconnect so/sth from so/sth
from discourage so from sth
from disembark from sth
from disengage (oneself) from so/sth
from disengage sth from sth
from disentangle sth from so/sth
from dislodge so/sth from so/sth
from dismiss so (from sth) (for sth)
from dismount from sth
from dispatch so from some place
from dispense sth (to so) (from sth)
from dissent from sth
from dissociate oneself from so/sth
from dissuade so from sth
from distance oneself from so/sth
from distill sth from sth
from distinguish so/sth from so/sth else
from distract so from sth
from diverge from sth
from divert so/sth from so/sth
from divide sth (off) (from sth or animals)
from divorce oneself from sth
from do sth from scratch
from dock sth from sth
from doesn't know his ass from a hole in the ground
from doesn't know his ass from his elbow
from Don't I know you from somewhere?
from downhill from here on
from drag sth away (from sth)
from drain from sth
from drain sth away (from sth)
from drain sth from so/sth
from draw apart (from so/sth)
from draw away (from so/sth)
from draw fire from so
from draw some kind of attention away (from so/sth)
from draw (so/sth) from sth
from draw (so's) fire (away) from so/sth or an animal
from draw sth off (from sth)
from drift apart (from each other)
from drift away (from so)
from drift away (from so/sth)
from drive so or an animal away (from sth or some place)
from drop so/sth from sth
from ease away (from so/sth)
from ease off (from so/sth)
from ease so/sth down (from sth)
from edge away (from so/sth)
from eject so from some place

from elicit sth from so
from eliminate so/sth from sth
from emanate from so/sth
from emancipate so from so/sth
from embezzle sth from so/sth
from emerge (from sth) (as sth)
from emigrate (from some place) (to some place)
from emit sth (from sth) (into sth)
from enjoin so/sth from sth
from ensue from sth
from erase sth from sth
from erupt from sth
from escape (from so/sth) (to some place)
from escort so/sth from sth
from estranged from so
from evacuate so (from sth) (to sth)
from everything from A to Z
from everything from soup to nuts
from evict so from some place
from evolve (from sth) (into sth)
from exact sth from so
from excerpt sth from sth
from exclude so/sth from sth
from excuse so from sth
from exempt so from sth
from exile so (from sth) (to sth)
from exit (from sth) (to sth)
from expect sth from so/sth
from expel so from sth
from expel sth from sth
from expropriate sth (from so/sth) (for so/sth)
from expunge sth from sth
from expurgate sth from sth
from extend (from sth) (to sth)
from extort sth from so/sth
from extract sth from so/sth
from extradite so from some place (to some place)
from extrapolate sth from sth
from extricate so/sth from so/sth
from face away (from so/sth)
from fade from sth
from fade from view
from faint from sth
from fall away (from so/sth)
from fall from grace
from fall from power
from fall from sth
from fan out (from some place)
from far be it from me to do sth
from far cry from sth
from far from it
from far from the madding crowd
from fence so/sth off (from sth)
from ferret sth out (from sth)
from filch sth (from so)
from file sth away (from sth)
from find (sth) out (about so/sth) (from so/sth)
from flake away (from so/sth)
from flee from so/sth
from flinch from so/sth
from flit from person to person
from flit from sth to sth else
from flow from sth
from flow (from sth) (to sth)
from fly from so/sth (to so)
from fly from sth (to sth)
from fly so/sth in(to some place) (from some place)
from force so or an animal from sth

from form from sth
from forward sth from some place (to so or some place)
from free so/sth from so/sth
from from A to Z
from from all corners of the world
from from dawn to dusk
from from day one
from from day to day
from from door to door
from from far and near
from from giddy-up to whoa
from from hand to hand
from from head to toe
from from hell to breakfast
from from here on (in)
from from here till next Tuesday
from from Missouri
from from my perspective
from from near and far
from from overseas
from from pillar to post
from from rags to riches
from from scratch
from from sea to shining sea
from from side to side
from from start to finish
from from stem to stern
from from the bottom of one's heart
from from the cradle to the grave
from from the four corners of the earth
from from (the) git-go
from from the ground up
from from the heart
from from the old school
from from the outset
from from the sublime to the ridiculous
from from the top
from from the word go
from from this day forward
from from this day on
from from time to time
from from tip to toe
from from top to bottom
from from way back
from from where I stand
from gain from sth
from gain sth from sth
from gather sth from so
from gather sth from sth
from generalize from sth
from get a rise from so
from get away (from so/sth)
from get down (from sth)
from get one's kicks (from so/sth)
from get so/sth away from so/sth
from get so/sth down (from sth)
from get so/sth free (from so/sth)
from get sth from so/sth
from get sth straight from the horse's mouth
from get up (from sth)
from glean sth from sth
from glide away (from so/sth)
from go from bad to worse
from go from one extreme to the other
from go out from sth
from grab so/sth away (from so/sth)
from graduate (from sth)
from Great oaks from little acorns grow.
from grin from ear to ear

from grow apart (from so/sth)
from grow away from so
from grow away from sth
from grow from sth
from grow sth from sth
from guard so/sth from so/sth
from guide so away from so/sth
from guide sth away (from so/sth)
from gush (forth) (from so/sth)
from hail from some place
from hand sth down from so to so
from hang back (from so/sth)
from hang down (from so/sth)
from hang from sth
from hang so/sth from sth
from haul sth (from some place) to some place
from haul sth up (from sth)
from have calluses from patting one's own back
from head away from so/sth
from hear from so/sth
from hear word (from so/sth)
from heartbeat away from being sth
from help so down (from sth)
from help so up (from sth)
from hide from so or an animal
from hide out (from so/sth)
from hinder so from sth
from hire so away (from so/sth)
from hold off (from) doing sth
from hold so/sth or an animal back (from so/sth)
from hound so from some place
from hurl sth away (from so/sth)
from immigrate (in)to some place (from some place)
from import sth (from sth) ((in)to sth)
from incline away (from so/sth)
from increase sth (from sth) (to sth)
from infer sth from sth
from inherit sth from so
from inhibit so from doing sth
from inhibit sth from doing sth
from isolate so/sth from so/sth
from issue (forth) from some place
from issue from sth
from jerk sth away (from so/sth or an animal)
from jet (from some place) (to some place)
from jet from sth
from jump (down) (from sth)
from jump from sth to sth
from jump up (from sth)
from (just) a stone's throw away (from sth)
from (just) a stone's throw (from sth)
from jut out (from sth)
from keep aloof from so/sth
from keep at arm's length from so/sth
from keep away (from so/sth)
from keep from sth
from keep one's distance (from so/sth)
from keep out from under so's feet
from keep so from doing sth
from keep so from so/sth
from keep so/sth away (from so/sth)
from keep so/sth from doing sth
from keep so/sth or an animal back (from so/sth)
from keep sth from so
from keep the wolf from the door
from kiss sth away (from sth)

from knock the props out from under so
from know from sth
from know shit from Shinola
from know so from so
from know sth from memory
from know sth from sth
from know where one is coming from
from lapse from grace
from last (from sth) until sth
from lay off ((from) sth)
from lay so off (from sth)
from leach sth away (from sth)
from lead so/sth (away) (from so/sth)
from leap down (from sth)
from learn from so/sth
from learn sth from so/sth
from learn sth from the bottom up
from lease sth from so
from liberate so/sth from so/sth
from lift so/sth down (from sth)
from lift sth from so/sth
from like a bolt from the blue
from like stealing acorns from a blind pig
from like taking candy from a baby
from live apart (from so)
from live from day to day
from live from hand to mouth
from look away (from so/sth)
from look up (from sth)
from lure so/sth away (from so/sth)
from made from the same mold
from mail sth from some place
from make a living from sth
from make sth from scratch
from make sth from sth
from make sth up from sth
from manna from heaven
from march (from some place) (to some place)
from Mighty oaks from little acorns grow.
from migrate (from some place) (to some place)
from money from home
from mooch (sth) from so
from motion so away from so/sth
from move away (from so/sth)
from move back (from so/sth)
from move (from some place) (to some place)
from move off (from so/sth)
from move out (from under so/sth)
from move so/sth away (from so/sth)
from move so/sth back (from so/sth)
from move so/sth off ((from) so/sth)
from nearer the church, the farther from God.
from not know from nothing
from not know so from Adam
from nothing to choose from
from obliterate so/sth from sth
from omit so/sth from sth
from on loan (from so/sth)
from one's home away from home
from ooze (out) (from so/sth)
from operate from sth
from order sth from so/sth
from originate from sth
from oust so from sth
from out from sth
from out (from under so/sth)

from part from so
from part so or an animal from so or an animal
from pass from sth
from peek out (from behind so/sth)
from peek out (from underneath so/sth)
from peel off (from sth)
from peel sth away (from sth)
from peel sth back (from sth)
from perish from sth
from pick so/sth from so/sth
from pilfer from so/sth
from pilfer sth from so/sth
from pinch sth from so/sth
from pipe sth from some place (to some place)
from pluck sth from so/sth
from plunge from sth
from preclude so/sth from sth
from preserve so/sth from so/sth
from prevent so from doing sth
from proceed (from sth) (to sth)
from procure sth (from sth) (for so/sth)
from produce sth from sth
from prohibit so from sth
from prohibit sth from sth
from promote so (from sth) (to sth)
from prosper from sth
from protrude from so/sth
from pry sth from so
from pry sth from sth
from pull away from so/sth
from pull back (from so/sth)
from pull so/sth away from so/sth
from pull so/sth back (from so/sth)
from pull the rug out (from under so)
from purge so/sth from sth
from push (oneself) away (from sth)
from push so/sth (away) (from so/sth)
from push so/sth back (from so/sth)
from quote (sth) from so/sth
from radiate from so/sth
from raise so from sth
from raise so from the dead
from raise so or an animal from sth
from range from sth to sth
from read from sth
from read from the same page
from realize sth from sth
from reap sth from sth
from rebound from sth
from recall so from sth
from recall so/sth from sth
from recede from sth
from receive sth from some place
from receive sth from so
from receive word (from so/sth)
from reclaim so/sth from so/sth
from recoil from so/sth
from reconstruct sth from sth
from record sth from sth
from recoup sth from so/sth
from recover from so/sth
from recover from sth
from recover sth from so/sth
from recruit so from sth
from recuperate from sth
from reduce sth from sth to sth
from reel back (from sth)
from refrain from sth
from regain sth from so/sth
from release so/sth from sth
from remain aloof from so/sth
from remain away (from so/sth)

from remove so from sth
from remove so/sth from so/sth
from rend sth from so/sth
from rent sth from so
from repel so from sth
from reproduce sth from sth
from repulse so/sth from sth
from request sth from so
from require sth from so
from requisition sth from so/sth
from rescue so/sth from so/sth
from resign from sth
from rest from sth
from rest up (from sth)
from restrain so from sth
from result from sth
from resurrect so/sth from sth
from retire from sth
from retire so/sth from sth
from retreat (from sth) (to some place)
from retrieve so/sth from some place
from retrieve sth from so
from return from some place
from rip sth away (from so)
from rip sth away (from sth)
from rise from so/sth
from rise from the ashes
from rise from the dead
from rise from the grave
from rise from the ranks
from rouse so from sth
from run away (from so/sth)
from run from so/sth
from run from sth to sth
from rush off (from some place)
from sag away (from sth)
from sail from some place to some place else
from salvage sth from sth
from save so/sth from so/sth
from scare so/sth away (from so/sth)
from scrape sth away (from sth)
from scratch sth from sth
from screen so/sth (off) (from so/sth)
from seal sth off from so/sth
from secede from sth
from seduce so from sth
from seek sth from so/sth
from segregate so from so else
from segregate sth from sth else
from select from so/sth
from select so from sth
from send so from pillar to post
from send sth from sth
from separate off (from sth)
from separate so from so else
from separate sth from sth else
from separate sth off from sth
from separate the men from the boys
from separate the wheat from the chaff
from set out (for some place) (from some place)
from set so apart from so else
from set so/sth free (from sth)
from set sth apart from sth else
from set sth back from sth else
from shoot from the hip
from shuttle so/sth from person to person
from shy away (from so/sth)
from sidle away (from so/sth)
from sift sth from sth
from sing from the same hymnbook

from siphon sth off (from sth)
from slide down from sth
from slip from sth
from slope away from sth
from smart from sth
from snatch so from the jaws of death
from snatch so/sth (away) from so/sth
from snatch victory from the jaws of defeat
from sneak away (from some place)
from so/sth from hell
from speak from sth
from speed away (from so/sth)
from split off (from sth)
from sponge sth from so
from sponge sth from sth
from spout from sth
from spring (forth) from so/sth
from squeeze sth from sth
from squirt from sth
from stagger from sth
from stand apart (from so/sth)
from stand back (from so/sth)
from stand off from so/sth
from stand out (from so/sth)
from stand out (from sth)
from start from scratch
from start from some place
from start off from some place
from stay aloof from so/sth
from stay away (from so/sth)
from stay back (from sth)
from steal away (from so/sth)
from steal from so/sth
from steal sth from so/sth
from steer away from so/sth
from stem from sth
from step away from one's desk
from step back (from so/sth)
from step down (from sth)
from stick out (from so/sth)
from stop so from doing sth
from (straight) from the horse's mouth
from straight from the shoulder
from stray (away) (from sth)
from stretch away (from sth)
from stretch forth (from sth)
from (strictly) from hunger
from strike so/sth from sth
from strip sth away (from so/sth)
from subtract sth from sth else
from suck sth from sth
from suffer from sth
from supply sth (to so/sth) (from sth)
from suspend so from sth
from suspend so/sth from sth
from sway from side to side
from sweep in (from some place)
from swerve (away) (from so/sth)
from swing from sth
from switch from so to so else
from switch from sth to sth else
from switch sth (from sth) (in)to sth
from take a collection up (from so) (for so/sth)
from take a page from so's book
from take away from so/sth
from take heart (from sth)
from Take it from me!
from take it from the top
from take off from sth
from take off from work
from take one's cue from so

from take over (from so)
from take ((some) time) off from work
from take so/sth away (from so/sth)
from take sth away (from so/sth)
from take sth back (from so)
from take sth from so
from take sth from sth
from tear away (from so/sth)
from tear loose (from so/sth)
from tear off (from so/sth)
from tear (oneself) away (from so/sth)
from tear so or some animal limb from limb
from tear sth away (from so/sth)
from tear sth from sth
from tell shit from Shinola
from tell so from so else
from tell sth from sth
from thrust so/sth away from so/sth
from trade up from sth
from transcribe sth from so/sth
from transfer so/sth (from some place) (to some place)
from transfer sth (from so) (to so else)
from transform so/sth (from so/sth) (in)to so/sth
from translate sth (from sth) ((in)to sth)
from transliterate sth (from sth) ((in)to sth)
from transmit sth (from some place) (to some place)
from transmute sth (from sth) ((in)to sth)
from transport so/sth (from some place) (to some place)
from transpose sth (from sth) ((in)to sth)
from tremble from sth
from trim sth away (from sth)
from trim sth from sth
from tumble from sth
from turn (away) (from so/sth)
from turn back (from some place)
from turn so or an animal (away) (from sth)
from unload sth from sth
from uproot so from some place
from uproot sth from some place
from vacuum sth up (from sth)
from vanish from sth
from vary (from sth) (in sth)
from vary from sth to sth
from veer (away) (from so/sth)
from veer off (from so/sth)
from visit from the stork
from wake so (up) from sth
from wake (up) from sth
from walk away from so/sth
from wall sth off (from so/sth)
from wander away (from so/sth)
from wander from sth
from wander off (from so/sth)
from wangle sth from so
from warn so away from so/sth
from wave so back (from sth)
from wave so/sth away (from so/sth)
from wean so (away) from sth
from weave sth from sth
from well up (from sth)
from wheedle sth away from so
from where one is coming from
from whip sth away (from so)
from Wild horses couldn't drag so away (from sth).
from win so away (from so/sth)
from win so/sth back (from so/sth)
from withdraw from sth

from withdraw so from sth
from withdraw sth from so/sth
from withhold sth from so or an animal
from woo so away (from so/sth)
from word (from so/sth)
from wrench sth from so
from wrest so/sth (away) from so/sth
from wrestle sth from so
from wring sth from sth
from yank so/sth away (from so/sth)
from You cannot get blood from a stone.
from You cannot get blood from a turnip.
from (You) can't get there from here.
front at the forefront (of sth)
front burn one's bridges in front of one
front can't see one's hand in front of one's face
front dangle sth in front of so
front front for so/sth
front front off (about sth)
front front on sth
front front so some amount of money
front front-runner
front in the forefront (of sth)
front on the front burner
front out front
front parade so/sth in front of so/sth
front pull (out) in front of so/sth
front put on a (brave) front
front put one foot in front of the other
front put sth on the front burner
front put up a (brave) front
front up front
frost frost over
frost frosted (over)
froth froth sth up
froth froth up
frown frown at so/sth
frown frown on so/sth
fruit bear fruit
fruit forbidden fruit
fruit fruits of one's labor(s)
fruit low-hanging fruit
fruit Stolen fruit is sweetest.
fruit tree is known by its fruit.
fruitcake nuttier than a fruitcake
fruitcake nutty as a fruitcake
fruition bring sth to fruition
fruition come to fruition
fry fry sth up
fry Go fry an egg!
fry go out of the frying pan into the fire
fry have bigger fish to fry
fry jump out of the frying pan into the fire
fry language that would fry bacon
fry out of the frying pan (and) into the fire
fry small fry
fuck Fuck you!
fuck What the fuck?
fudge fudge factor
fuel add fuel to the fire
fuel add fuel to the flame
fuel fuel sth (up)
fuel fuel up
fuel take fuel on
full act full of oneself
full at full blast
full at full speed
full at full strength

full at full throttle
full at full tilt
full chock full of sth
full come full circle
full few cards shy of a full deck
full fill so full of lead
full full as a tick
full full of beans
full full of bull
full full of holes
full full of hot air
full full of Old Nick
full full of oneself
full full of prunes
full full of the devil
full full plate
full full steam ahead
full full up
full get up a (full) head of steam
full have one's hands full (with so/sth)
full He that hath a full purse never wanted a friend.
full in full flight
full in full swing
full mouth full of South
full move into full swing
full not playing with a full deck
full play at full blast
full play sth at full blast
full play with a full deck
full run at full blast
full run sth at full blast
full shot full of holes
full woods are full of so/sth
fulminate fulminate against so/sth
fumble fumble for sth
fume fume about so/sth
fume fume at so
fun barrel of fun
fun for the fun of it
fun fun and games
fun have fun
fun make fun of so/sth
fun more fun than a barrel of monkeys
fun poke fun at so/sth
fun time flies (when you're having fun)
function bodily functions
funeral Dream of a funeral and you hear of a marriage.
funeral Dream of a funeral and you hear of a wedding.
funeral It's your funeral.
funk funked out
funk in a (blue) funk
funny Cut the funny stuff!
funny funny as a barrel of monkeys
funny funny as a crutch
funny funny bone
funny funny business
funny funny ha-ha
funny funny money
funny funny peculiar
funny rich man's joke is always funny.
funny strike so funny
funny That's funny.
funny too funny for words
fur fur piece
fur make the fur fly
fur rub so('s fur) the wrong way
furious fast and furious
furnish furnish sth for so/sth
furnish furnish sth for sth

further cannot see (any) further than the end of one's nose
further Don't let it go any further.
further see no further than the end of one's nose
further Stretch your arm no further than your sleeve will reach.
further without further ado
furtive furtive glance
fury Hell hath no fury like a woman scorned.
fuse blow a fuse
fuse blow one's fuse
fuse fuse sth with sth
fuse fuse with sth
fuss fuss about
fuss fuss and feathers
fuss fuss around
fuss fuss (around) with so/sth
fuss fuss at so/sth
fuss fuss over so/sth
fuss kick up a fuss
fuss land so poor it wouldn't even raise a fuss
fuss make a fuss (over so/sth)
future in the near future
future One's future looks bright.
futz futz around
futz futz sth up
gab gab up a storm
gab have the gift of gab
gab *up a storm
gad gad around
gag gag on sth
gain gain dominion over so/sth
gain gain from sth
gain gain ground
gain gain in sth
gain gain on so/sth
gain gain sth by doing sth
gain gain sth from sth
gain ill-gotten gains
gain No pain, no gain.
gain Nothing ventured, nothing gained.
gain One man's loss is another man's gain.
gain *perspective on sth
gall have the gall to do sth
gallery play to the gallery
gallivant gallivant around
gallop at a snail's gallop
gallop break into a gallop
gallop gallop through sth
galumph galumph around
galvanize galvanize so into action
gambit opening gambit
gamble gamble on so/sth
gamble gamble sth away
game ahead of the game
game at the top of one's game
game at this stage (of the game)
game be game
game end of the ball game
game fair game (for sth)
game fun and games
game game is up.
game game that two can play
game give the game away
game keep ahead of the game
game name of the game
game off one's game
game play games (with so)
game put one off one's game

game remain ahead of the game
game stay ahead of the game
game throw a game
game throw one off one's game
game Two can play (at) this game (as well as one).
game (whole) new ball game
gamekeeper old poacher makes the best gamekeeper.
gamut run the gamut
gander take a gander (at so/sth)
gander What's sauce for the goose is sauce for the gander.
gang gang up (on so)
gangbusters come on like gangbusters
gangbusters like gangbusters
gap bridge the gap
gap fill the gap
gape gape at so/sth
garb garb so in sth
garbage Garbage in, garbage out.
garbage garbage sth down
garden lead so down the garden path
garden lead so up the garden path
garner garner sth in
garnish garnish sth with sth
gas cooking with gas
gas gas sth up
gas gas up
gas gassed (up)
gas Now you're cooking (with gas)!
gas out of gas
gas pass gas
gas run out of gas
gas step on the gas
gasp at the last gasp
gasp gasp at so/sth
gasp gasp for air
gasp gasp for breath
gasp gasp sth out
gate creaking gate hangs longest.
gate get the gate
gate give so the gate
gather gather a case (against so)
gather gather around so/sth
gather gather dust
gather gather so into sth
gather gather so/sth around (oneself)
gather gather so/sth to oneself
gather gather so/sth together
gather gather sth from so
gather gather sth from sth
gather gather sth in
gather gather sth up
gather gather together
gather Gather ye rosebuds while ye may.
gather rolling stone gathers no moss.
gaudy gaudy as a butterfly
gauntlet run the gauntlet
gauntlet throw down the gauntlet
gave ain't got the brains God gave a squirrel
gave ain't got the sense God gave geese
gave doesn't have the sense God gave geese
gave doesn't have the sense God gave him (or her)
gawk gawk at so/sth
gaze gaze around (at so/sth)
gaze gaze at so/sth
gaze gaze on so/sth

gaze gaze out on sth
gaze rivet one's gaze on so/sth
gaze steely gaze
gear gear so/sth up (for so/sth)
gear gear sth to so/sth
gear gear up for so/sth
gear get one's ass in gear
gear get one's tail in gear
gear in high gear
gear move into high gear
gear swing into high gear
geese ain't got the sense God gave geese
geese doesn't have the sense God gave geese
gem Out of the mouths of babes (oft times come gems).
general as a (general) rule
general in general
generalize generalize about so/sth
generalize generalize from sth
generalize generalize on so/sth
generation Generation X
generous Be just before you're generous.
generous generous to a fault
genius budding genius
genius Genius is an infinite capacity for taking pains.
genius Genius is ten percent inspiration and ninety percent perspiration.
genius stroke of genius
gentle gentle as a lamb
genuine genuine article
george Let George do it.
Georgia all over hell and half of Georgia
gesture token gesture
get *A for effort
get A man's gotta do what a man's gotta do.
get *acquainted with so
get *advantage of so
get *ahead of sth
get *ahead of the game
get ain't got a grain of sense
get ain't got a lick of sense
get ain't got the brains God gave a squirrel
get ain't got the sense God gave geese
get *air
get *(all) balled up
get *(all) dolled up
get *(all) dressed up
get *(all) het up
get *(all) set (to do sth)
get *all spruced up
get *all the marbles
get *(all) tuckered out
get *ants in one's pants
get (Are) things getting you down?
get as all get out
get *away from it all
get *back (at so)
get *back in (the) harness
get *back in(to) circulation
get *back on one's feet
get *back on track
get *bee in one's bonnet
get *behind schedule
get *behind the eight ball
get *benefit of the doubt

get *better of so
get *big eye
get *big hand for sth
get *(big) head
get *big picture
get *big send-off
get *bite (to eat)
get *black mark beside one's name
get *blame for sth
get *bogged down
get *boot
get *break
get *bright idea
get *brush-off
get *bum's rush
get *bum steer
get *business
get *butterflies in one's stomach
get *carte blanche
get *case of sth
get *charley horse
get *checkup
get *cheesed off
get *chilled to the bone
get *chip on one's shoulder
get *clean bill of health
get *clear of sth
get *close to so
get *cold feet
get *cold shoulder
get Come and get it!
get Come 'n' get it!
get Could I get by, please?
get (Could I) get you something (to drink)?
get *credit (for sth)
get *creeps
get *crux of the matter
get *day off
get *devil
get *dirty look
get (Do you) get my drift?
get (Do you) get the picture?
get Don't get your bowels in an uproar!
get Don't let so/sth get you down.
get *down pat
get *down to the last bit of money
get *down to the wire
get *down with a disease
get *down (with so)
get *earful
get *even break
get *even (with so)
get *fair shake
get *feel for sth
get *first crack at sth
get *fix on sth
get *fix
get Flattery will get you nowhere.
get *floor
get *foothold (somewhere)
get *for a song
get *fresh start
get *fresh (with so)
get *frog in one's throat
get get a bang out of so/sth
get get a bead on so/sth
get get a buzz out of so/sth
get get a charge out of so/sth
get get a hurry on
get get a kick out of so/sth
get get a laugh
get Get a life!

get get a load of so/sth
get get a lot of mileage out of sth
get get a move on
get get a rise from so
get get a say (in sth)
get get a (sound) grasp of sth
get get a ticket
get get a weight off one's mind
get get a word in edgewise
get get aboard
get get about
get get across (sth)
get get after so
get get ahead (in sth)
get get ahead of oneself
get get along
get get an amount of money **for** sth
get get around
get get (around) to so/sth
get get at so
get get at sth
get get away
get get axed
get get back (to so) (on sth)
get get back to sth
get get better
get get between so/sth **and** so/sth else
get get busy
get get by (on a shoestring)
get get by (on a small amount of money)
get get by (so/sth)
get get by (with sth)
get get by (without so/sth)
get get carried away
get get cracking
get get down
get get (down) off one's high horse
get get enough courage up (to do sth)
get get enough guts up (to do sth)
get get enough nerve up (to do sth)
get get euchred out of sth
get get free of so/sth
get get going
get get hell (about so/sth)
get get hip to so/sth
get get home to so/sth
get get in deeper
get get inside sth
get get into a mess
get get into an argument (with so) (about so/sth)
get get into bed with so
get get into one's stride
get get into sth
get get in(to) the act
get get in(to) the swing of things
get get it
get get laid
get get lost
get get mad (at sth)
get get married
get get moving
get get nowhere fast
get get off
get get on
get get one on one's feet
get get one right here
get get one's act together
get get one's ass in gear
get get one's bowels in an uproar
get get one's comeuppance
get get one's ducks in a row
get get one's ears pinned back

get get one's ears set out
get get one's feet wet
get get one's fingers burned
get get one's foot in the door
get get one's hands dirty
get get one's head above water
get get one's head together
get get one's hooks in(to) so/sth
get get one's just deserts
get get one's just reward(s)
get get one's kicks (from so/sth)
get get one's knuckles rapped
get get one's lumps
get get one's nose out of joint
get get one's nose out of so's business
get get one's rocks off (on sth)
get get one's shit together
get get one's stuff together
get get one's tail in gear
get get one's teeth into sth
get get one's ticket punched
get get one's wits about one
get get (oneself) into a stew (over so/sth)
get get oneself up
get get on(to) so (about sth)
get get on(to) the (tele)phone
get get out
get get (out) while the gettin(g)'s good
get Get over it!
get get over so/sth
get get over sth
get get over (to some place)
get get past (so/sth)
get Get real!
get get religion
get get right on sth
get get rolling
get get screwed
get Get serious!
get get shed of so/sth
get get shut of so/sth
get get smart (with so)
get get some kind of mileage out of sth
get get (some) steam up
get get some weight off one's feet
get get so across (in a good way)
get get so (all) wrong
get get so around the table
get get so down
get get so going
get get so in a family way
get get so in(to) sth
get get so off
get get so on(to) so/sth
get get so/sth across sth
get get so/sth away from so/sth
get get so/sth back
get get so/sth by so/sth
get get so/sth down (from sth)
get get so/sth down sth
get get so/sth free (from so/sth)
get get so/sth in(to) sth
get get so/sth off so/sth
get get so/sth out of one's mind
get get so/sth out of one's sight
get get so/sth out of so/sth
get get so/sth through (to so/sth)
get get so/sth together
get get so out of a jam
get get so out of one's hair
get get so's attention
get get so's back up
get get so's blood up

get get so's dander up
get get so's drift
get get so's eye
get get so's goat
get get so's hackles up
get get so's Irish up
get get so through sth
get get so through (to so/sth)
get get so up
get get sth
get get sth across (to so)
get get sth down
get get sth for an amount of money
get get sth for so
get get sth for sth
get get sth from so/sth
get get sth going with so
get get sth home to so/sth
get get sth into a mess
get get sth in(to) so
get get sth into so's thick head
get get sth in(to) sth
get get sth off
get get sth out
get get sth over (to so)
get get sth past (so/sth)
get get sth straight
get get sth through so's thick skull
get get sth to so
get get sth together (for a particular time)
get get sth up
get get sth wrapped up
get get started on sth
get get the ball rolling
get get the courage up (to do sth)
get get the draw on so
get get the drift of sth
get get the drop on so
get get the facts straight
get get the final word
get get the gate
get get the go-by
get get the hell out (of here)
get get the kinks (ironed) out
get get the lead out
get Get the message?
get get the most out of so/sth
get Get the picture?
get get the point (of sth)
get get the shaft
get get the show on the road
get get the spunk up (to do sth)
get get the word
get get the wrinkles out (of sth)
get get through (sth)
get get through (to so)
get get through (to sth)
get get through (with so/sth)
get get to first base (with so/sth)
get get to one's feet
get get to so
get get to sth
get get to the bottom of sth
get get to the point (of sth)
get get to the top (of sth)
get get together (with so) (on so/sth)
get get tough (with so)
get get under so's skin
get get under sth
get get up
get get well
get get wet
get get wind of sth

get get with it
get get with sth
get get with the program
get Get your ass over here!
get Get your buns over here!
get Get your head out of the clouds!
get Get your nose out of my business.
get give as good as one gets
get Give it all you've got!
get *glad hand
get *(good) working over
get *goods on so
get *goose bumps
get got to fly
get gotta get up pretty early in the morning to do sth
get *gray hair(s)
get *grip on oneself
get *grip on sth
get *hand in sth
get *hand with sth
get *handle on sth
get *hang of sth
get *hard sell
get *hard time
get (Has the) cat got your tongue?
get have (got) a glow on
get Have I got something for you!
get have to get married
get He will get his.
get *head start (on so)
get *head start (on sth)
get *hell
get help so get a foothold (somewhere)
get help so or an animal (get) over sth
get *helping hand
get *hepped (up)
get *high sign
get *hold on so
get *home free
get How are you getting on?
get How is so getting along?
get I can't get over sth!
get (I) haven't got all day.
get (I'd) better get moving.
get (I'd) better get on my horse.
get if the going gets tough
get If you can't stand the heat, get out of the kitchen.
get if you get my drift
get If you lie down with dogs, you will get up with fleas.
get If you play with fire, you get burned.
get I'll get back to you (on that).
get I'll get right on it.
get ill-gotten gains
get (I'm) just getting by.
get *in a bad mood
get *in a bind
get *in a fix
get *in a huff
get *in a lather
get *in a (pretty) pickle
get *in a rut
get *in (a) single file
get *in a (tight) spot
get *in a tizzy
get *in a vicious circle
get *in bad (with so)
get *in Dutch (with so)
get *in (good) (with so)
get *in harm's way

get *in on sth
get *in on the act
get *in on the ground floor
get *in power
get *in so's face
get *in so's good graces
get *in so's hair
get *in so's possession
get *in step (with so)
get *in the best of health
get *in the clear
get *in the groove
get *in the (home)stretch
get *in the mainstream (of sth)
get *in the open
get *in the public eye
get *in touch (with so)
get *in tune with the times
get *infested with sth
get *inkling (of sth)
get *inside track
get *intimate with so
get *involved (with so)
get *involved with sth
get (It's) got me beat.
get It takes (some) getting used to.
get *itch for sth
get *itch to do sth
get *itchy feet
get *itchy palm
get (I've) been getting by.
get (I've) (got) better things to do.
get (I've) got to be shoving off.
get I've got to fly.
get (I've) got to get moving.
get (I've) got to go.
get (I've) got to go home and get my beauty sleep.
get (I've) got to hit the road.
get (I've) got to run.
get (I've) got to shove off.
get (I've) got to split.
get (I've) got to take off.
get I've got work to do.
get I('ve) gotta fly.
get *jump on so
get *keyed up (about sth)
get *knee-deep in sth
get *knuckle sandwich
get *last laugh (on so)
get *last word
get *leg up on so
get *leg up
get Let me get back to you (on that).
get Let's get down to business.
get Let's get out of here.
get Let's get together (sometime).
get let so (get) by
get let so get by with sth
get let so (get) off (sth)
get let so get on with sth
get let so (get) past
get let so or an animal (get) out (of sth)
get let sth (get) out
get *licking
get *load off one's feet
get *load off one's mind
get *mental block (against sth)
get *mixed up in sth
get *mixed up with so else
get more you get, the more you want.
get *nod

get not able to get sth for love or money
get not get one's hopes up
get *off base
get *off course
get *off on a sidetrack
get *off (on sth)
get *off on the wrong foot
get *off the beaten track
get *off the hook
get *off (to a flying start)
get *off topic
get *off (work)
get *(old) heave-ho
get *on a first-name basis (with so)
get *on course
get *on its feet
get *on one's way ((to) some place)
get *on so's case
get *on so's nerves
get *on the bandwagon
get *on the dot
get *on the good side of so
get *on the stick
get *on the telephone
get *on the wrong side of so
get *on track
get on your mark, get set, go
get *one's bearings
get *one's money's worth
get *one's (own) way
get *one's say
get *one's sea legs
get *one's second wind
get *one's start
get *one's walking papers
get one that got away
get *one up (on so)
get *onto a good thing
get *onto so
get *onto sth
get *out and about
get *out from sth
get *out in the open
get *out of debt
get *out of favor (with so)
get *out of harm's way
get *out of one's depth
get *out of practice
get *out (of sth)
get *out of sync
get *out of the frying pan (and) into the fire
get *out of the way
get *out on a limb
get out to get so
get *out-of-bounds
get *over a barrel
get *over (and done) with
get *over (with)
get *physical (with so)
get play hard to get
get (Please) don't get up.
get *raw deal
get *ready (to do sth)
get (real) go-getter
get *red-carpet treatment
get *reputation (as a sth)
get *reputation (for doing sth)
get *right-of-way
get *root of the problem
get *runaround
get *sack

get *set to do sth
get She will get hers.
get *shellacking
get *shock of one's life
get *short end of the stick
get *short with so
get *sinking feeling
get *slap on the wrist
get *soft on so
get *(solid) grasp of sth
get *some elbow room
get *some shut-eye
get Something's got to give.
get *sore (at so)
get squeaking wheel gets the oil.
get *start
get *strapped for sth
get *swelled head
get *taste for sth
get *taste of one's own medicine
get tell so where to get off
get Them as has, gits.
get *third degree
get *time off for good behavior
get *time off
get *time to catch one's breath
get *to go
get *tongue-lashing
get *too funny for words
get *too good to be true
get *too much
get *tough on so
get *under control
get *under one's belt
get *under pressure
get *under so's thumb
get *under so's wing(s)
get *under way
get *up against the wall
get *(up and) about
get *up for sth
get *up in arms
get *up to here (with sth)
get *up to one's knees
get *up to one's neck (in sth)
get *up to speed
get *up with so
get *upper hand (on so)
get *upside-down
get *up-to-date
get *voice (in sth)
get *well into sth
get *what for
get *what's coming to one
get What's got(ten) into so?
get What you see is what you get.
get when the going gets tough
get When the going gets tough, the tough get going.
get when you get a chance
get when you get a minute
get Where do (you think) you get off?
get *wherewithal (to do sth)
get *whiff of sth
get Why buy a cow when you can get milk for free?
get *with child
get *within one's grasp
get *within range
get *word with so (about sth)
get *worked up (over sth)
get *works
get *worst of sth

get *wrought up
get You cannot get a quart into a pint pot.
get You cannot get blood from a stone.
get You cannot get blood from a turnip.
get (You) can't get there from here.
get You don't get something for nothing.
get You get what you pay for.
get You got it!
get You got me beat.
get You got me there.
get You got to do what you got to do.
get You just don't get it!
get (You'd) better get moving.
get You'll get onto it.
get You'll get the hang of it.
get You'll never get away with it.
get You've got another think coming.
get (You've) got me stumped.
get You've got to be kidding!
get You've got to be out of your mind!
ghost ghost of a chance
ghost give up the ghost
ghost pale as a ghost
ghost white as a ghost
giant sleeping giant
giddy from giddy-up to whoa
gift Beware of Greeks bearing gifts.
gift Don't look a gift horse in the mouth.
gift free gift
gift God's gift (to women)
gift have a gift for (doing) sth
gift have the gift of gab
gift look a gift horse in the mouth
giggle for giggles
giggle giggle at so/sth
gild gild the lily
gill blue around the gills
gill green around the gills
gill loaded to the gills
gill pale around the gills
gimme Gimme a break!
gird gird up one's loins
girl That's my girl.
git from (the) git-go
gitalong have a hitch in one's gitalong
gits Them as has, gits.
give be given precedence over so/sth
give *big eye
give *big hand for sth
give *big send-off
give *blame for sth
give *boot
give *break
give *bright idea
give *brush-off
give *bum steer
give *business
give busy as a cranberry merchant (at Thanksgiving)
give *chip on one's shoulder
give *clean bill of health
give *cold shoulder
give (Could I) give you a lift?
give *credit (for sth)
give *creeps
give *day off
give *devil
give *dirty look
give don't give a continental
give don't give a hoot (in hell's hollow)

give Don't give it a (second) thought.
give Don't give it another thought.
give Don't give me any of your lip!
give Don't give me that line!
give Don't give up!
give Don't give up the ship!
give Don't give up without a fight!
give Don't give up your day job.
give *earful
give *even break
give *fair shake
give *feel for sth
give Gimme a break!
give give a good account of oneself
give give a little
give give an account of so/sth (to so)
give give (an) ear to so/sth
give give as good as one gets
give give birth to so/sth
give give cause for sth
give give chase (to so/sth)
give give credence to so/sth
give Give credit where credit is due.
give give currency to sth
give give evidence of sth
give give forth with sth
give give free rein to so
give give ground
give Give her the gun.
give give in
give Give it a rest!
give Give it all you've got!
give Give it the gun.
give Give it time.
give give it to so (straight)
give Give it up!
give Give me a break!
give Give me a call.
give Give me a chance!
give Give me a rest!
give Give me a ring.
give Give me five!
give Give my best to so.
give give of oneself
give give one one's freedom
give give one's best
give give one's eyeteeth (for so/sth)
give give (one's) notice
give give one's right arm (for so/sth)
give give oneself airs
give give oneself over to so/sth
give give oneself up (to so/sth)
give give out
give give (out) with sth
give give rise to sth
give give some thought to sth
give give so a bang
give give so a blank check
give give so a blank look
give give so a blank stare
give give so a buzz
give give so a call
give give so a charge
give give so a crack at sth
give give so a dig
give give so a (good) bawling out
give give so a kick
give give so a lift
give give so a line
give give so a pain
give give so a pat on the back
give give so a piece of one's mind
give give so a red face

give give so a ride
give give so a ring
give give so a whack at sth
give Give so an inch and he'll take a mile.
give Give so an inch and he'll take a yard.
give give so away (to so)
give Give so enough rope and he'll hang himself.
give give so Hail Columbia
give give so no quarter
give give so odds that...
give give so/sth a wide berth
give give so/sth away
give give so/sth back (to so/sth)
give give so/sth up (for lost)
give give so/sth up (to so)
give give so pause (for thought)
give give so some lip
give give so some skin
give give so some sugar
give give so static
give give so the eye
give give so the finger
give give so the gate
give give so the go-by
give give so the raspberry
give give so the shaft
give give so the shirt off one's back
give give so the slip
give give so tit for tat
give give so to understand sth
give give so up for dead
give give sth a go
give give sth a shot
give give sth a try
give give sth a whirl
give give sth away (to so)
give give sth back (to so) (with interest)
give give sth for sth
give give sth off
give give sth one's best shot
give give sth out
give give sth over (to so/sth)
give give sth to so
give give sth under (the) threat of sth
give give sth up
give give teeth to sth
give give the bride away
give give the devil her due
give give the devil his due
give give the game away
give give the lie to sth
give give up
give Give us the tools, and we will finish the job.
give give vent to sth
give give voice to sth
give give way to so/sth
give give weight to sth
give give with sth
give given to doing sth
give given to understand
give *glad hand
give *(good) working over
give *goose bumps
give *gray hair(s)
give *hand in sth
give *hand with sth
give *handle on sth
give *hard sell
give *hard time

give He gives twice who gives quickly.
give *hell
give *helping hand
give *high sign
give I won't give up without a fight.
give It is better to give than to receive.
give It is more blessed to give than to receive.
give *knuckle sandwich
give *lick and a promise
give *licking
give lot of give-and-take
give *lump in one's throat
give *nod
give not give a hang about so/sth
give not give a tinker's damn
give not give anyone the time of day
give not give it another thought
give not give two hoots about so/sth
give Nothing is given so freely as advice.
give *(old) heave-ho
give *on a silver platter
give *once-over
give *one's money's worth
give *one's (own) way
give *one's start
give *one's walking papers
give *out
give *perspective on sth
give *pound of flesh
give *raw deal
give *red-carpet treatment
give *reputation (as a sth)
give *reputation (for doing sth)
give *right-of-way
give *rough idea (about sth)
give *run for one's money
give *runaround
give *sack
give *shellacking
give *shock of one's life
give *short end of the stick
give Silence gives consent.
give *slap on the wrist
give *some elbow room
give Something's got to give.
give *start
give *swelled head
give *taste for sth
give *taste of one's own medicine
give *third degree
give *time off
give *time to catch one's breath
give *tongue-lashing
give *try at so
give *try at sth
give *upper hand (on so)
give *voice (in sth)
give *what for
give What gives?
give *what's coming to one
give *wherewithal (to do sth)
give *whiff of sth
give *works
give *worst of sth
give *wrong number
give You (always) give up too eas(il)y.
giveaway dead giveaway
glad Am I glad to see you!
glad glad hand
glad (I'm) glad to hear it.
glad (I'm) glad you could come.

glad (I'm) glad you could drop by.
glad (I'm) (very) glad to meet you.
glad (We're) glad you could come.
glance at first glance
glance dart a glance at so/sth
glance fleeting glance
glance furtive glance
glance glance around (some place)
glance glance at so/sth
glance glance back (at so)
glance glance down (at sth)
glance glance off (so/sth)
glance glance over so/sth
glance glance through sth
glance know at a glance that...
glance steal a glance at so/sth
glance throw a glance at so/sth
glare glare at so/sth
glare glare down on so/sth
glare rivet one's glare on so/sth
glass glass sth in
glass have a glass jaw
glass People who live in glass houses shouldn't throw stones.
glass raise one's glass to so/sth
glass smooth as glass
glaze glaze over
gleam gleam with sth
glean glean sth from sth
glide glide across sth
glide glide away (from so/sth)
glimmer not a glimmer (of an idea)
glimpse catch a glimpse of so/sth
glint glint with sth
glisten All that glistens is not gold.
glisten glisten with sth
glitter All that glitters is not gold.
glitter glitter with sth
gloat gloat over sth
glory Glory be!
glory glory in sth
glory in one's glory
glory send so to glory
gloss gloss over sth
glove fit like a glove
glove gloves are off.
glove hand in glove (with so)
glove handle so with kid gloves
glove rule with a velvet glove
glove take one's gloves off
gloves cat in gloves catches no mice.
glow feel a glow of contentment
glow feel a glow of happiness
glow glow with sth
glow have (got) a glow on
glow in glowing terms
glower glower at so/sth
glue glue sth down
glue glue sth on(to) sth
glue glue sth together
glue glued to so/sth
glued come unglued
glut glut on the market
glut glut so/sth with sth
glutton glutton for punishment
gnash gnash one's teeth
gnash gnashing of teeth
gnat down to a gnat's eyebrow
gnat strain at gnats and swallow camels
gnaw gnaw (away) at so
gnaw gnaw (away) at so/sth
gnaw gnaw on sth

go *about one's business
go *absent without leave
go *against the grain
go all dressed up and nowhere to go
go all gone
go all over hell and gone
go all show and no go
go All systems (are) go.
go (Are you) going my way?
go *arm in arm
go as far as it goes
go *at a fast clip
go *at a good clip
go *before so
go best-laid plans of mice and men oft(en) go astray.
go buy some food to go
go *by the book
go dead and gone
go Do not let the sun go down on your anger.
go Do not let the sun go down on your wrath.
go Do we have to go through all that again?
go done and gone
go Don't be gone (too) long.
go Don't let it go any further.
go easy come, easy go
go enough (sth) to go (a)round
go Everything's going to be all right.
go far gone
go *for a spin
go from (the) git-go
go from the word go
go get going
go get so going
go get sth going with so
go get the go-by
go give so the go-by
go give sth a go
go go a long way toward doing sth
go go a mile a minute
go go aboard
go go about
go go above and beyond one's duty
go go above and beyond (sth)
go go above and beyond the call of duty
go go above so
go go absent without leave
go go across (sth)
go go across sth to so/sth
go go after so
go go after so/sth or an animal
go go against so/sth
go go against the grain
go Go ahead.
go (Go ahead,) make my day!
go go ahead (of so/sth)
go go ahead (with sth)
go go all out (for so/sth)
go go all the way (with so)
go go along
go go ape (over so/sth)
go go arm in arm
go go around
go go (a)round in circles
go go (a)round the bend
go go as so/sth
go go astray
go go at a fast clip
go go at a good clip

go go at it hammer and tongs
go go at it tooth and nail
go go at one another tooth and nail
go go at so
go go at so/sth
go go at sth
go go at sth like a boy killing snakes
go Go away!
go go away empty-handed
go go away (for sth)
go go away with so/sth
go go AWOL
go go back
go go bad
go go badly with so/sth
go go ballistic
go go bananas
go go before so
go go begging
go go behind so's back
go go belly up
go go below
go go berserk
go go between so/sth and so/sth else
go go beyond so/sth
go go beyond sth
go go broke
go go by (so/sth)
go go by the board
go go by the book
go go by the name of sth
go Go chase yourself!
go go cold turkey
go go crazy
go go down
go go downhill
go go Dutch
go go easy on so/sth
go go easy on sth
go go fifty-fifty (on sth)
go Go figure.
go Go fly a kite!
go go for broke
go Go for it!
go go for nothing
go go for so/sth
go go forward with sth
go go from bad to worse
go go from one extreme to the other
go Go fry an egg!
go go hand in hand
go go haywire
go go hog wild
go go home in a box
go go home to mama
go go hungry
go go in
go go into a huddle
go go into a nosedive
go go into a song and dance (about sth)
go go into a tailspin
go go into action
go go into detail(s)
go go into effect
go go into heat
go go into hiding
go go into hock
go go into one's act
go go into orbit
go go into service
go go into sth
go go into the bull pen
go go into the red

go go into the same old song and dance about sth
go go into the service
go go it alone
go Go jump in the lake!
go go like clockwork
go go like stink
go go like the wind
go go near (to) so/sth
go go nuts
go go off
go Go on.
go go on a binge
go go on a diet
go go on a fishing expedition
go go on a fool's errand
go go on a power trip
go go on a rampage
go go on an errand
go go on and on
go go on (and on) (about so/sth)
go go on (at so)
go go on before (so)
go go on doing sth
go go on for an age
go go on sth
go go on the block
go go on to a better land
go go on to sth
go go on tour
go go on with sth
go Go on (with you)!
go go out
go go (out) on strike
go go over
go go overboard
go go past so/sth
go go past sth
go go places
go Go play in the traffic.
go go postal
go go public (with sth)
go go (right) through so
go go scot-free
go go sky-high
go go so far as to say sth
go go (so) one better
go go (somewhere) by shank's mare
go go sour
go go South
go go stag
go go steady with so
go go stir-crazy
go go straight
go go (straight) to the top
go go the distance
go go the extra mile
go go the limit
go go the way of the dodo
go go the way of the horse and buggy
go go there
go go through
go Go to!
go go to any length
go go to bat against so
go go to bat for so
go go to bed
go Go to blazes!
go go to Davy Jones's locker
go go to extremes (to do sth)
go go to great lengths (to do sth)
go go to hell
go go to it

go go to one's (just) reward
go go to pieces
go go to pot
go go to press
go go to rack and ruin
go go to sea
go go to seed
go go to so (about so/sth)
go go to so/sth
go go to so's head
go go to the bathroom
go go to the bother (of doing sth)
go go to the crux of the matter
go go to (the devil)
go go to the dogs
go go to the expense (of doing sth)
go go to the heart of the matter
go go to the lavatory
go go to the limit
go go to the polls
go go to the root of the matter
go go to the toilet
go go to the trouble (of doing sth)
go go to the wall (on sth)
go go to town
go go to trial
go go to war (over so/sth)
go go to waste
go go to work (on so/sth)
go go to wrack and ruin
go Go to your room!
go go together
go go too far
go go toward so/sth
go go under
go go up
go go well with so/sth
go go whole hog
go go wild
go go window-shopping
go go with it
go go with so
go go with (so/sth)
go go with sth
go go with the flow
go go with the territory
go go with the tide
go go without
go go wrong
go going, going, gone
go going great guns
go going on
go going rate
go going strong
go going to tattle
go going to tell
go gone but not forgotten
go gone goose
go gone on
go gone to meet one's maker
go gone with the wind
go Good going!
go good to go
go *hand in hand
go has come and gone
go have a go at sth
go have a good thing going
go have a lot going (for one)
go have a thing going (with so)
go have one's heart go out to so
go have some food to go
go have sth going (for oneself)
go have something going (with so)

go have to go some (to do sth)
go He that would go to sea for pleasure, would go to hell for a pastime.
go heavy going
go Here goes nothing.
go Here (it) goes.
go Here today, (and) gone tomorrow.
go Here we go again.
go Here you go.
go How goes it?
go How goes it (with you)?
go How's it going?
go How're things going?
go (I) have to go now.
go I hope all goes well.
go (I) really must go.
go (I'd) better be going.
go If anything can go wrong, it will.
go if the going gets tough
go If the mountain will not come to Mahomet, Mahomet must go to the mountain.
go I'll (have to) let you go.
go I'm gone.
go *in a body
go (Is) anything going on?
go (It) just goes to show (you) (sth).
go (It) (just) goes without saying.
go (It's) time to go.
go It's time we should be going.
go (I've) got to go.
go (I've) got to go home and get my beauty sleep.
go keep (going) on about so/sth
go keep (going) on at so/sth
go keep so/sth going
go leave go of so/sth
go let go of so/sth
go let go (with sth)
go Let it go.
go let oneself go
go Let's go somewhere where it's (more) quiet.
go Let's not go through all that again.
go let so go
go like it was going out of style
go *like stink
go *like the devil
go *like the dickens
go long gone
go lost and gone forever
go Love makes the world go round.
go make a go of sth
go March comes in like a lion, and goes out like a lamb.
go *mile a minute
go Nice going!
go no go
go not able to go on
go not going to win any beauty contests
go not know if one is coming or going
go not know whether one is coming or going
go *off course
go *off one's rocker
go off so/sth goes
go *off (to the side) with so
go *on a diet
go *on a fool's errand
go *on a power trip
go on the go

go on your mark, get set, go
go one's heart goes out to so
go only way to go
go order some food to go
go *out in force
go *out of control
go *out of one's mind
go *out of one's skull
go *out on a limb
go *over so's head
go *over the hill
go *over the wall
go pay as you go
go Pride goes before a fall.
go rarin' to go
go ready, set, go
go (real) go-getter
go slow going
go So it goes.
go spend money like it's going out of style
go *stir-crazy
go Sunday-go-to-meeting clothes
go take a go at so
go take a go at sth
go That's (just) the way it goes.
go (That's the) way to go!
go There but for the grace of God (go I).
go There you go.
go *through the cracks
go *through the mill
go to go
go to hell and gone
go touch-and-go
go tough going
go *up a blind alley
go *up against sth
go *up for auction
go What goes up must come down.
go What's going down?
go What's going on (around here)?
go What(ever) goes around, comes around.
go when the going gets tough
go When the going gets tough, the tough get going.
goad goad so into sth
goad goad so on
goal fall short of one's goal(s)
goat get so's goat
goat make so the scapegoat for sth
gobble gobble so/sth up
gobble gobble sth down
gobble gobble sth up
God act of God
God ain't got the brains God gave a squirrel
God ain't got the sense God gave geese
God consecrate so/sth to God
God doesn't have the sense God gave geese
God doesn't have the sense God gave him (or her)
god fit for the gods
God God forbid!
God God helps them that help themselves.
God God only knows!
God God rest so's soul.
God God's gift (to women)

God God takes soonest those he loveth best.
God God willing.
God God willing and the creek don't rise
god gods send nuts to those who have no teeth.
God harder than the back of God's head
God Honest to God.
God If God did not exist, it would be necessary to invent Him.
God Man proposes, God disposes.
God mills of God grind slowly, yet they grind exceeding small.
God nearer the church, the farther from God.
god pray to the porcelain god
God put the fear of God in(to) so
God Put your trust in God, and keep your powder dry.
God So help me(, God)!
God sure as God made little green apples
god Take the goods the gods provide.
God Thank God for small favors.
God There but for the grace of God (go I).
God think so is God's own cousin
God Where on (God's green) earth?
god Whom the gods love die young.
god Ye gods (and little fishes)!
God You cannot serve God and mammon.
godfrey By godfrey!
godliness Cleanliness is next to godliness.
Gods God's in his heaven; all's right with the world.
goggle goggle at so/sth
gol gol dang
gol gol dern
gold All that glistens is not gold.
gold All that glitters is not gold.
gold gold mine of information
gold good as gold
gold have a heart of gold
gold pot of gold
gold sitting on a gold mine
gold worth its weight in gold
golden golden key can open any door.
golden golden opportunity
golden Kill the goose that lays the golden egg(s).
golden Silence is golden.
golly by guess and by golly
golly Good golly, Miss Molly!
goner goner
good All good things must (come to an) end.
good all in good time
good all to the good
good (all) well and good
good as good as one's word
good at a good clip
good Bad money drives out good.
good Be good.
good best defense is a good offense.
good best is the enemy of the good.
good but good
good come to no good
good cuddle up with a (good) book
good curl up (with a (good) book)

good Diligence is the mother of good luck.
good do so a good turn
good do so a heap of good
good do so a power of good
good do so good
good do so's heart good
good Eavesdroppers never hear any good of themselves.
good Enough is as good as a feast.
good fight the good fight
good Fire is a good servant but a bad master.
good for good
good For goodness sake!
good for the good of so/sth
good get off a few good ones
good get (out) while the gettin(g)'s good
good get so across (in a good way)
good give a good account of oneself
good give as good as one gets
good give so a (good) bawling out
good go at a good clip
good (Good) afternoon.
good good and sth
good good as done
good good as gold
good good as new
good good bet
good Good Book
good good die young.
good good egg
good Good enough.
good good enough for government work
good good enough for so/sth
good (Good) evening.
good Good fences make good neighbors.
good good for what ails you
good Good for you!
good Good going!
good Good golly, Miss Molly!
good (good) grasp of sth
good Good grief!
good (Good) heavens!
good good husband makes a good wife.
good good is the enemy of the best.
good good Jack makes a good Jill.
good Good job!
good Good luck!
good good man is hard to find.
good good many
good Good men are scarce.
good (Good) morning.
good (Good) night.
good good old boy
good good old days
good good riddance (to bad rubbish)
good Good seed makes a good crop.
good good sport
good Good things come in small packages.
good Good things come to him who waits.
good good time was had by all.
good good to go
good (good) working over
good Good-bye and good riddance.
good Good-bye for now.
good (Good-bye) until then.

good goods on so
good have a good arm
good have a good command of sth
good have a good head on one's shoulders
good have a (good) mind to do sth
good Have a good one.
good have a good thing going
good Have a good time.
good Have a good trip.
good have a (good) working over
good (have) never had it so good
good have too much of a good thing
good hold good for so/sth
good Honest to goodness.
good Hope is a good breakfast but a bad supper.
good I declare (to goodness)!
good (I) had a good time.
good I must say good night.
good if one knows what's good for one
good If you can't be good, be careful.
good if you know what's good for you
good in (all) good conscience
good in good condition
good in good faith
good in good hands
good in good repair
good in good shape
good in good spirits
good in good time
good in (good) (with so)
good in so's good graces
good It's an ill wind that blows nobody (any) good.
good (It's been) good talking to you.
good (It's) good to be here.
good (It's) good to have you here.
good (It's) good to hear your voice.
good (It's) good to see you (again).
good keep good time
good keep in good condition
good keep in good shape
good keep in good with so
good keep on the good side of so
good Keep up the good work.
good kiss sth good-bye
good Life's been good (to me).
good Listeners never hear any good of themselves.
good look good on paper
good make good as sth
good make good (at sth)
good make good money
good make good on sth
good make good time
good make (good) use of sth
good make so look good
good make sth good
good miss is as good as a mile.
good move at a good clip
good (My) goodness (gracious)!
good No news is good news.
good nod is as good as a wink to a blind horse.
good off to a good start (with so/sth)
good on good terms (with so)
good on so's good side
good on the good side of so
good One good turn deserves another.
good onto a good thing
good (Open) confession is good for the soul.

good out of the goodness of one's heart
good picture of (good) health
good put in a good word (for so)
good put so across (in a good way)
good put sth to (good) use
good road to hell is paved with good intentions.
good run at a good clip
good run the good race
good sell so a bill of goods
good show good faith
good show sth to good advantage
good So far, so good.
good so's word is good
good stand so in good stead
good stay on the good side of so
good streak of good luck
good string of good luck
good Take the goods the gods provide.
good Thank goodness!
good There's many a good tune played on an old fiddle.
good throw good money after bad
good time off for good behavior
good too good to be true
good too much of a good thing
good travel at a good clip
good turn sth to good account
good twelve good men and true
good up to no good
good Very good.
good What's the good of sth?
good What's the (good) word?
good when one is good and ready
good Your guess is as good as mine.
goodness For goodness sake!
goodness Honest to goodness.
goodness I declare (to goodness)!
goodness (My) goodness (gracious)!
goodness out of the goodness of one's heart
goodness Thank goodness!
goof goof around
goof goof off
goof goof on so
goof goof so/sth up
goof goof up (on sth)
goof goofed (up)
goose ain't got the sense God gave geese
goose can't say boo to a goose
goose cook so's goose
goose doesn't have the sense God gave geese
goose gone goose
goose goose bumps
goose goose egg
goose goose pimples
goose Kill the goose that lays the golden egg(s).
goose one's goose is cooked
goose send so on a wild-goose chase
goose silly as a goose
goose What's sauce for the goose is sauce for the gander.
goose wild-goose chase
gorge feel one's gorge rise
gorge gorge oneself on sth
gorge gorge so/sth with sth
gorge make so's gorge rise
gorgeous drop-dead gorgeous
gork gorked (out)
gosh by guess and by gosh

gosh For gosh sake!
goshen Land o' Goshen!
gospel gospel truth
gossip gossip about so/sth
got A man's gotta do what a man's gotta do.
got ain't got a grain of sense
got ain't got a lick of sense
got ain't got the brains God gave a squirrel
got ain't got the sense God gave geese
got Give it all you've got!
got got to fly
got gotta get up pretty early in the morning to do sth
got (Has the) cat got your tongue?
got have (got) a glow on
got Have I got something for you!
got (I) haven't got all day.
got (It's) got me beat.
got (I've) (got) better things to do.
got (I've) got to be shoving off.
got I've got to fly.
got (I've) got to get moving.
got (I've) got to go.
got (I've) got to go home and get my beauty sleep.
got (I've) got to hit the road.
got (I've) got to run.
got (I've) got to shove off.
got (I've) got to split.
got (I've) got to take off.
got I've got work to do.
got I('ve) gotta fly.
got one that got away
got Something's got to give.
got You got it!
got You got me beat.
got You got me there.
got You got to do what you got to do.
got You've got another think coming.
got (You've) got me stumped.
got You've got to be kidding!
got You've got to be out of your mind!
gotta A man's gotta do what a man's gotta do.
gotta gotta get up pretty early in the morning to do sth
gotta I('ve) gotta fly.
gotten ill-gotten gains
gotten What's got(ten) into so?
gouge gouge sth out
gourd bushel and a peck (and some in a gourd)
government close enough for government work
government good enough for government work
government Governments have long arms.
gown cap and gown
gown town-and-gown
grab grab a bite (to eat)
grab grab a chair
grab grab a seat
grab grab at so/sth
grab grab for so/sth
grab grab on(to so/sth)
grab grab so/sth away (from so/sth)
grab grab so's attention
grab How does that grab you?
grab make a grab at so/sth
grabs up for grabs

grace fall from grace
grace grace so/sth with one's presence
grace grace sth with sth
grace lapse from grace
grace saving grace
grace say grace
grace There but for the grace of God (go I).
graced graced with sth
graceful graceful as a swan
graces in so's good graces
gracious gracious plenty
gracious (My) goodness (gracious)!
grade grade so down (on sth)
grade make the grade
grade upgrade so/sth to sth
graduate graduate (from sth)
graduate graduate (in sth) (with sth)
graft graft sth on(to) sth
grain against the grain
grain ain't got a grain of sense
grain cut against the grain
grain go against the grain
grain grain of truth
grain run against the grain
grain saw against the grain
grand busy as Grand Central Station
granddaddy granddaddy of them all
grandfather grandfather clause
grandfather grandfather so/sth in
grandmother Don't teach your grandmother to suck eggs.
grandmother teach one's grandmother to suck eggs
grant grant so no quarter
grant grant sth to so
grant take so/sth for granted
grape belt the grape
grape sour grapes
graph graph sth out
grapple grapple (with so) (for sth)
grapple grapple with sth
grasp get a (sound) grasp of sth
grasp (good) grasp of sth
grasp grasp at so/sth
grasp grasp so/sth by sth
grasp grasping at straws
grasp have a (sound) grasp of sth
grasp (solid) grasp of sth
grasp (sound) grasp of sth
grasp within one's grasp
grasp within so's grasp
grass grass is always greener on the other side (of the fence).
grass grass widow
grass green as grass
grass let grass grow under one's feet
grass not let the grass grow under one's feet
grass snake in the grass
grasshopper knee-high to a grasshopper
grasshopper since so was knee-high to a grasshopper
grate grate on so
grate grate on so('s nerves)
grate grate on sth
gratify gratify so's desires
gratitude owe so a debt of gratitude
grave carry a secret to the grave
grave dig one's own grave
grave from the cradle to the grave
grave have one foot in the grave

grave quiet as the grave
grave rise from the grave
grave roll (over) in one's grave
grave silent as the grave
grave swear on one's mother's grave
grave take it to one's grave
grave turn (over) in one's grave
gravitate gravitate to(ward) so/sth
gravy rest is gravy.
gravy ride the gravy train
gray All cats are gray in the dark.
gray gray area
gray gray hair(s)
gray gray matter
graze graze against so/sth
graze graze on sth
grease elbow grease
grease grease so's palm
grease grease the skids
grease greasy spoon
grease like greased lightning
grease quick as (greased) lightning
grease use some elbow grease
greasy greasy spoon
great at great length
great Death is the great leveler.
great Everything will be great.
great explain at great length
great go to great lengths (to do sth)
great going great guns
great Great balls of fire!
great great beyond
great Great day (in the morning)!
great great deal
great Great minds think alike.
great Great oaks from little acorns grow.
great Great Scott!
great great unwashed
great greater the truth, the greater the libel.
great greatest thing since indoor plumbing
great greatest thing since sliced bread
great in great demand
great in great haste
great Little strokes fell great oaks.
great Little thieves are hanged, but great ones escape.
great make a great show of sth
great no great shakes
great question so at great length
great set great store by so/sth
great speak at great length
great take (great) pains (to do sth)
great think a great deal of so/sth
great Time is a great healer.
great to a great extent
Greek Beware of Greeks bearing gifts.
Greek Greek to so
Greek It's (all) Greek to me.
green grass is always greener on the other side (of the fence).
green green around the gills
green green as grass
green green stuff
green green with envy
green have a green thumb
green hedge between keeps friendship green.
green sure as God made little green apples
green Where on (God's green) earth?

greet greet so/sth with sth
greet Greetings and felicitations!
greetings Greetings and felicitations!
grenade Close only counts in horseshoes (and hand grenades).
grief come to grief
grief Good grief!
grievance air one's grievances
grieve grieve for so/sth
grieve grieve over so/sth
grieve What the eye doesn't see, the heart doesn't grieve over.
grim grim reaper
grin grin and bear it
grin grin at so/sth
grin grin from ear to ear
grind daily grind
grind grind away (at so)
grind grind away (at sth)
grind grind on
grind grind so down
grind grind sth away
grind grind sth down
grind grind sth into sth
grind grind sth out
grind grind sth to sth
grind grind sth together
grind grind sth up
grind grind to a halt
grind have an ax(e) to grind
grind mill cannot grind with water that is past.
grind mills of God grind slowly, yet they grind exceeding small.
grindstone keep one's nose to the grindstone
grindstone put one's nose to the grindstone
grip grip on oneself
grip grip on sth
grip grip so's attention
grip keep a firm grip on so/sth
grip keep a tight grip on so/sth
grip lose one's grip on so/sth
grip take a firm grip on so/sth
gripe gripe at so
gripe gripe one's soul
gripe gripe (to so/sth) (about so/sth)
grips come to grips with so/sth
grist grist for the mill
grit get down to the nitty-gritty
grit grit one's teeth
gritty get down to the nitty-gritty
groan groan about so/sth
groan groan sth out
groan groan under sth
groan groan with sth
groceries blow one's groceries
gronk gronk (out)
groom groom so as sth
groom groom so for sth
groove groove on so/sth
groove in the groove
grope grope (about) (for so/sth)
grope grope after so/sth
grope grope (around) (for so/sth)
grope grope at so/sth
gross gross so out
gross So gross!
ground break ground (for sth)
ground break new ground
ground cover a lot of ground

ground cut the ground out from under so
ground doesn't know his ass from a hole in the ground
ground drive sth into the ground
ground from the ground up
ground gain ground
ground get sth off the ground
ground give ground
ground ground so in sth
ground ground sth on sth
ground grounded in (actual) fact
ground grounds for sth
ground have one's ear to the ground
ground have one's feet on the ground
ground hit the ground running
ground hold one's ground
ground in on the ground floor
ground keep an ear to the ground
ground keep one's ear to the ground
ground keep one's feet on the ground
ground let so in on the ground floor
ground level sth to the ground
ground lose ground (to so/sth)
ground middle ground
ground on dangerous ground
ground on moral grounds
ground on shaky ground
ground one's old stamping ground
ground raze sth to the ground
ground riveted to the ground
ground run sth into the ground
ground shift one's ground
ground stand one's ground
ground worship the ground so walks on
group group so/sth around so/sth
group group so/sth together
group group sth under sth
grouse grouse about so/sth
grouse grouse at so or an animal
grovel grovel (about) in sth
grovel grovel before so/sth
grovel grovel to so
grow Absence makes the heart grow fonder.
grow Great oaks from little acorns grow.
grow grow accustomed to doing sth
grow grow accustomed to so/sth
grow grow apart (from so/sth)
grow grow away from so
grow grow away from sth
grow grow back
grow grow disgusted at so/sth
grow grow disgusted with so/sth
grow grow dissatisfied with so/sth
grow grow down (into sth)
grow grow from sth
grow grow in sth
grow grow into sth
grow grow knee-high by the 4th of July
grow grow on so
grow grow out
grow grow over sth
grow grow poles apart
grow grow sick (and tired) of so/sth
grow grow soft on so
grow grow sth from sth
grow grow thick-skinned
grow grow thin-skinned
grow grow to do sth
grow grow together

grow grow up
grow grow worlds apart
grow growing youth has a wolf in his belly.
grow have growing pains
grow *knee-high by the 4th of July
grow let grass grow under one's feet
grow Mighty oaks from little acorns grow.
grow Money does not grow on trees.
grow not grow on trees
grow not let the grass grow under one's feet
grow *out of (all) proportion
grow *poles apart
grow *thick-skinned
grow *thin-skinned
growl growl at so/sth
growl growl sth out
growth frighten so out of a year's growth
growth growth experience
growth growth opportunity
grub grub around (for so/sth)
grub grub around (in sth)
grudge bear a grudge (against so)
grudge hold a grudge (against so)
grudge nurse a grudge (against so)
gruff gruff as a bear
grumble grumble about so/sth
grumble grumble at so
grunt grunt sth out
grunt grunt work
guarantee guarantee against sth
guarantee guarantee sth against sth (for sth)
guard catch one off (one's) guard
guard catch so off guard
guard guard against so/sth
guard guard so/sth from so/sth
guard keep on (one's) guard (against so/sth)
guard let one's guard down
guard on (one's) guard (against so/sth)
guard put one on one's guard
guard remain on (one's) guard (against so/sth)
guard safeguard against so/sth
guard safeguard so/sth against so/sth
guard stay on (one's) guard (against so/sth)
guess by guess and by golly
guess by guess and by gosh
guess guess at sth
guess Guess what!
guess have another guess coming
guess hazard a guess
guess I guess.
guess It's anybody's guess.
guess make a guess
guess never would have guessed
guess second-guess so
guess take a guess
guess Your guess is as good as mine.
guest Be my guest.
guest guest of honor
guffaw guffaw at so/sth
guide guide so around sth
guide guide so away from so/sth
guide guide so/sth across (sth)
guide guide sth away (from so/sth)
guilt feel guilty (about sth)
guilt find so guilty

guilt find so not guilty
guilt guilty conscience needs no accuser.
guilt lay a guilt trip on so
guilt plead guilty to sth
guinea serve as a guinea pig
gulch dry-gulch so
gulp gulp for air
gulp gulp sth back
gulp gulp sth down
gum beat one's gums
gum flap one's gums
gum gum sth up
gun beat the gun
gun Give her the gun.
gun Give it the gun.
gun going great guns
gun gun for so
gun gun so or an animal down
gun jump the gun
gun pull a gun (on so)
gun shotgun wedding
gun smoking gun
gun son of a gun
gun stick to one's guns
gun under the gun (about sth)
gunpowder didn't invent gunpowder
gush gush (forth) (from so/sth)
gush gush over so/sth
gush gush with sth
gussy gussied up
gussy gussy so/sth up
gut blood and guts
gut bust a gut
gut get enough guts up (to do sth)
gut gut feeling
gut gut reaction
gut gut response
gut hate so's guts
gut kick in the guts
gut my gut tells me (that)
gut spew one's guts (out)
gut spill one's guts
gut split a gut
gut yell one's guts out
gutter fall into the gutter
gutter have one's mind in the gutter
gutter in the gutter
gutter put so into the gutter
guy Mr. Nice Guy
guy Nice guys finish last.
guy regular guy
guy smart guy
guy tough guy
guzzle guzzle sth down
gyp gyp so out of sth
habit break a habit
habit break one's habit
habit break the habit
habit by force of habit
habit kick a habit
habit kick the habit
habit knock the habit
habit make a habit of sth
habit Old habits die hard.
habit shake a habit
habit shake the habit
habituate habituate so to so/sth
hack can't hack it
hack hack around
hack hack (away) at so/sth
hack hack one's way through sth

hack hack so (off)
hack hack so/sth apart
hack hack sth
hack hack sth down
hack hack sth off
hack hack sth out of sth
hack hack sth to sth
hack hack sth up
hack hacked (off)
hackle get so's hackles up
had been had
had good time was had by all.
had (had) best do sth
had had (just) as soon do sth
had (had) known it was coming
had had rather do sth
had had sooner do sth
had hadn't oughta
had have had enough
had have had it (up to here)
had have had its day
had (have) never had it so good
had (I) don't believe I've had the pleasure.
had (I) had a good time.
had I had a lovely time.
had (I) had a nice time.
had If a toady frog had wings, he wouldn't bump his ass.
had If frogs had wheels, they wouldn't bump their butts.
had I've had a lovely time.
had I've had enough of this!
had I've had it up to here (with so/sth).
had So had better keep still about it.
had was had
had We had a lovely time.
had We've had a lovely time.
had You cannot lose what you never had.
haggle haggle about sth
haggle haggle (with so) over so/sth
ha-ha funny ha-ha
hail give so Hail Columbia
hail hail a cab
hail hail a taxi
hail hail from some place
hail hail so as sth
hail within hailing distance
hair bad hair day
hair by a hair('s breadth)
hair come within a hair('s breadth) of so/sth
hair curl so's hair
hair fair-haired boy
hair find (neither) hide nor hair
hair get out of so's hair
hair get so out of one's hair
hair gray hair(s)
hair hair and hide(, horns and tallow)
hair hair of the dog that bit one
hair hang by a hair
hair in so's hair
hair let one's hair down
hair make so's hair curl
hair make so's hair stand on end
hair (neither) hide nor hair
hair part so's hair
hair plaster one's hair down
hair put hair on so's chest
hair put one's hair up
hair run one's fingers through one's hair
hair run one's hand through one's hair

hair see (neither) hide nor hair
hair split hairs
hair tear one's hair (out)
hair within a hair('s breadth) of sth
hale hale and hearty
hale hale-fellow-well-met
half all over hell and half of Georgia
half at half-mast
half at half-staff
half Believe nothing of what you hear, and only half of what you see.
half go off half-cocked
half half a bubble off plumb
half Half a loaf is better than none.
half half in the bag
half half the battle
half half the time
half Half the truth is often a whole lie.
half Half the world knows not how the other half lives.
half half under
half have half a mind to do sth
half have half a notion to do sth
half how the other half lives
half howdy and a half
half (It's) not half bad.
half It's six of one, half a dozen of another.
half one's better half
half rip sth in half
half six of one and half a dozen of the other
half trouble shared is a trouble halved.
half Well begun is half done.
half without half trying
half You don't know the half of it.
halfhearted halfhearted (about so/sth)
halfway meet so halfway
hall (You) can't fight city hall.
halloo Never halloo till you are out of the woods.
halt bring so/sth to a halt
halt call a halt to sth
halt come to a halt
halt grind to a halt
halved trouble shared is a trouble halved.
ham ham sth up
hamburger make hamburger (out) of so
hammer come under the hammer
hammer fight so/sth hammer and tongs
hammer go at it hammer and tongs
hammer go under the hammer
hammer hammer (away) at so
hammer hammer (away) at sth
hammer hammer on so/sth
hammer hammer sth down
hammer hammer sth home
hammer hammer sth into sth
hammer hammer sth onto sth
hammer hammer sth out
hammer It's raining pitchforks (and hammer handles).
Hancock one's John Hancock
hand at hand
hand big hand for sth
hand bird in the hand is worth two in the bush.
hand bite the hand that feeds one
hand bound hand and foot
hand by a show of hands
hand by hand

hand can't find one's butt with both hands (in broad daylight)
hand can't see one's hand in front of one's face
hand catch so red-handed
hand change hands
hand close at hand
hand Close only counts in horseshoes (and hand grenades).
hand Cold hands, warm heart.
hand come away empty-handed
hand come in handy
hand copy sth out (by hand)
hand cup one's hands together
hand devil finds work for idle hands to do.
hand die by one's own hand
hand dirty one's hands
hand do sth by hand
hand do sth hand in hand
hand Don't hand me that (line)!
hand eat out of so's hand
hand exercise a firm hand
hand fall into the wrong hands
hand firm hand
hand fold one's hands
hand force so's hand
hand free hand (with so/sth)
hand from hand to hand
hand get one's hands dirty
hand glad hand
hand go away empty-handed
hand go hand in hand
hand hand in glove (with so)
hand hand in hand
hand hand in sth
hand Hand it over.
hand hand over fist
hand hand over hand
hand hand so/sth over (to so/sth)
hand hand so sth
hand hand sth around
hand hand sth back (to so)
hand hand sth down from so to so
hand hand sth down (to so)
hand hand sth in
hand hand sth in (to so)
hand hand sth off (to so)
hand hand sth on (to so/sth)
hand hand sth out (to so)
hand hand sth over
hand hand sth to so
hand hand sth up (to so)
hand hand that rocks the cradle rules the world.
hand hand with sth
hand hands down
hand Hands off!
hand Hands up!
hand have clean hands
hand have one's hand in sth
hand have one's hand in the till
hand have one's hands full (with so/sth)
hand have one's hands tied
hand have so/sth in one's hands
hand have so/sth on one's hands
hand have so/sth (well) in hand
hand have so's blood on one's hands
hand have sth in hand
hand have to hand it to so
hand have (too much) time on one's hands
hand helping hand

hand hold so's hand
hand If ifs and ands were pots and pans (there'd be no work for tinkers' hands).
hand in good hands
hand in hand
hand join hands
hand keep on the left(-hand) side (of sth)
hand keep on the right(-hand) side (of sth)
hand keep one's hand in (sth)
hand keep one's hands off (sth)
hand keep one's hands to oneself
hand know so/sth like the back of one's hand
hand know so/sth like the palm of one's hand
hand lay one's hands on so/sth or an animal
hand leave so/sth in one's hands
hand left hand doesn't know what the right hand is doing.
hand left-handed compliment
hand lend a hand (to so)
hand lend (so) a hand
hand lend so a hand with sth
hand lift a hand (against so/sth)
hand live from hand to mouth
hand Many hands make light work.
hand near at hand
hand need a firm hand
hand need a helping hand
hand not lift a hand (to help so)
hand offer a helping hand
hand old hand at doing sth
hand on (the) one hand
hand on the other hand
hand One hand for oneself and one for the ship.
hand out of hand
hand out of so's hands
hand pay so a backhanded compliment
hand pay so a left-handed compliment
hand play into so's hands
hand pull sth out of so's hands
hand put one's hand to the plow
hand put one's hand up
hand put one's hands on so/sth or an animal
hand putty in so's hands
hand raise a hand (against so/sth)
hand reject so/sth out of hand
hand run one's hand through one's hair
hand second hand
hand seem like putty in so's hands
hand shake hands
hand shake (hands) on sth
hand shake so's hand
hand show of hands
hand show one's hand
hand sit hand in hand
hand sit on its hands
hand sit on one's hands
hand sit on their hands
hand soil one's hands
hand so's hands are tied
hand take a hand in sth
hand take one's hands off (of) so/sth
hand take so in hand
hand take so/sth off so's hands
hand take so's life in one's hands
hand take sth out of so's hands
hand take the law into one's own hands
hand throw one's hands up (in despair)

hand throw one's hands up in horror
hand tie so's hands
hand Time hangs heavy on so's hands.
hand tip one's hand
hand try one's hand (at sth)
hand turn one's hand to sth
hand upper hand (on so)
hand use a firm hand
hand wait on so hand and foot
hand walk hand in hand
hand wash one's hands of so/sth
hand well in hand
hand with both hands tied behind one's back
hand (with) hat in hand
hand with one hand tied behind one's back
handful by the handful
handful handful
handle fly off the handle
handle handle on sth
handle handle so with kid gloves
handle It's raining pitchforks (and hammer handles).
handle postage and handling
handle shipping and handling
handsome Handsome is as handsome does.
handwriting read the handwriting on the wall
handwriting see the (hand)writing on the wall
handy come in handy
hang busy as a one-armed paperhanger
hang creaking door hangs longest.
hang creaking gate hangs longest.
hang Give so enough rope and he'll hang himself.
hang hang a few on
hang hang a huey
hang hang a left
hang hang a louie
hang hang a ralph
hang hang a right
hang hang around (some place)
hang hang around so/sth
hang hang around (with so)
hang hang back (from so/sth)
hang hang behind (so/sth)
hang hang by a hair
hang hang by a thread
hang hang by sth
hang hang down (from so/sth)
hang hang fire
hang hang five
hang hang from sth
hang hang in the balance
hang Hang in there.
hang Hang it all!
hang hang it up
hang hang loose
hang hang of sth
hang hang off
hang hang on
hang hang one on
hang hang one's hat (up) somewhere
hang hang out (of sth)
hang hang out (some place)
hang hang out (with so/sth)
hang hang over so/sth
hang hang over so('s head)
hang hang so by the neck

hang hang so for sth
hang hang so in effigy
hang hang so/sth from sth
hang hang so/sth with sth
hang hang so/sth out to dry
hang hang sth on so
hang hang sth out (of sth)
hang hang sth over so/sth
hang hang sth up
hang hang ten
hang hang together
hang hang tough (on sth)
hang hang up
hang hang with so
hang have sth hanging over one's head
hang have sth hung up and salted
hang hung up (on so/sth)
hang If you're born to be hanged, then you'll never be drowned.
hang *in the balance
hang keep so/sth hanging (in midair)
hang leave so/sth hanging (in midair)
hang let it all hang out
hang Little thieves are hanged, but great ones escape.
hang low-hanging fruit
hang might as well be hung for a sheep as (for) a lamb
hang not give a hang about so/sth
hang so cold you could hang meat
hang somewhere to hang (up) one's hat
hang stand there with one's bare face hanging out
hang teach so the hang of sth
hang thereby hangs a tale
hang think so hung the moon (and stars)
hang Time hangs heavy on so's hands.
hang You'll get the hang of it.
hanker hanker after so/sth
happen Accidents will happen.
happen Don't even think about it (happening).
happen happen before so's time
happen happen in the (very) nick of time
happen happen to so/sth
happen happen (up)on so/sth
happen if anything should happen
happen no matter what (happens)
happen Shit happens.
happen shouldn't happen to a dog
happen unexpected always happens.
happen What happened?
happen What's happ(ening)?
happiness feel a glow of happiness
happy Be happy to (do sth).
happy Call no man happy till he dies.
happy couldn't be happier
happy Count no man happy till he dies.
happy fat and happy
happy feel a glow of happiness
happy happy as a clam (at high tide)
happy happy as a clam (in butter sauce)
happy happy as a lark
happy happy as can be
happy happy camper
happy happy hour
happy Happy is the bride that the sun shines on.

happy Happy is the country which has no history.
happy hit a happy medium
happy (I'd be) happy to (do sth).
happy live happily ever after
happy strike a happy medium
harbinger harbinger of things to come
harbor harbor sth against so/sth
hard between a rock and a hard place
hard cause hard feelings
hard cold, hard cash
hard come down (hard) (on so/sth)
hard didn't care too hard
hard do sth the hard way
hard Don't work too hard.
hard drive a hard bargain
hard fall on hard times
hard find (sth) out the hard way
hard first hundred years are the hardest.
hard first step is always the hardest.
hard good man is hard to find.
hard hard act to follow
hard hard as a rock
hard hard as nails
hard hard as stone
hard hard at sth
hard hard feelings
hard hard nut to crack
hard hard of hearing
hard hard on so's heels
hard hard on so
hard hard put (to do sth)
hard hard row to hoe
hard hard sell
hard hard sledding
hard hard time
hard hard times
hard hard to believe
hard hard to swallow
hard hard to take
hard hard up (for sth)
hard Hard words break no bones.
hard hardly dry behind the ears
hard hardly exchange more than some number of words with so
hard hardly have time to breathe
hard hardly have time to think
hard hard-nosed
hard hit so hard
hard learn (sth) the hard way
hard little (hard) work never hurt anyone.
hard no hard feelings
hard not any hard feelings
hard Old habits die hard.
hard *on so's heels
hard play hard to get
hard put in a hard day at work
hard put the hard word on so
hard school of hard knocks
hard take a hard line (with so)
hardball play hardball (with so)
harden harden oneself to sth
harden harden sth off
harden harden sth up
harder bigger they are, the harder they fall.
harder harder than the back of God's head
hardly hardly dry behind the ears
hardly hardly exchange more than some number of words with so

hardly hardly have time to breathe
hardly hardly have time to think
hare First catch your hare.
hare If you run after two hares, you will catch neither.
hare mad as a March hare
hare run with the hare and hunt with the hounds
hark hark(en) back to sth
harm come to harm
harm in harm's way
harm No harm done.
harm out of harm's way
harm put so in harm's way
harmonize harmonize with so/sth
harmony in harmony (with so/sth)
harness back in(to) (the) harness
harness harness an animal up
harness harness so or an animal to sth
harp harp on so/sth
harp keep harping on sth
harry any Tom, Dick, and Harry
harry (every) Tom, Dick, and Harry
has cat has nine lives.
has Every cloud has a silver lining.
has Every dog has its day.
has Every Jack has his Jill.
has Every man has his price.
has growing youth has a wolf in his belly.
has Happy is the country which has no history.
has has come and gone
has (Has the) cat got your tongue?
has has the world by the tail (with a downhill drag)
has It has so's name on it.
has (It) hasn't been easy.
has It is a long lane that has no turning.
has moment everyone has been waiting for
has more sth than Carter has (liver) pills
has mouse that has but one hole is quickly taken.
has One has to draw the line somewhere.
has price one has to pay
has rumor has it that...
has Shut the stable door after the horse has bolted.
has some creature's time has come
has so's time has come
has Them as has, gits.
has worm (has) turned.
hash hash sth over (with so)
hash hash sth up
hash settle so's hash
hassle hassle so about sth
haste beat a (hasty) retreat
haste Haste makes waste.
haste in great haste
haste Make haste slowly.
haste Marry in haste, (and) repent at leisure.
haste More haste, less speed.
hasty beat a (hasty) retreat
hat at the drop of a hat
hat eat one's hat
hat Hang on to your hat!
hat hang one's hat (up) somewhere
hat hats off to so/sth

hat He wears a ten-dollar hat on a five-cent head.
hat Here's your hat, what's your hurry?
hat Hold on to your hat!
hat I'll eat my hat.
hat keep sth under one's hat
hat knock sth into a cocked hat
hat mad as a hatter
hat old hat
hat pass the hat (around) (to so)
hat pull sth out of a hat
hat somewhere to hang (up) one's hat
hat take off one's hat (to so)
hat take one's hat off to so
hat talk through one's hat
hat throw one's hat in the ring
hat toss one's hat into the ring
hat wear more than one hat
hat wear two hats
hat (with) hat in hand
hatband tight as Dick's hatband
hatch batten down the hatches
hatch count one's chickens before they hatch
hatch Don't count your chickens before they are hatched.
hatch Down the hatch.
hatch hatch an animal out
hatchet bury the hatchet
hatchet hatchet man
hate hate so/sth like sin
hate hate so's guts
hate (I) hate to eat and run.
hate love-hate relationship
hate pet hate
hath He that hath a full purse never wanted a friend.
hath Hell hath no fury like a woman scorned.
hatrack use your head for more than a hatrack
hatter mad as a hatter
haul haul off and do sth
haul haul so in
haul haul so on the carpet
haul haul so/sth over to sth
haul haul so over the coals
haul haul so (up) before so/sth
haul haul sth down
haul haul sth (from some place) to some place
haul haul sth up (from sth)
haul haul up (somewhere)
haul in the long haul
haul in the short haul
haul over the long haul
haul over the short haul
haunt come back to haunt one
haunt return to haunt one
have not Haven't I seen you somewhere before?
have not (I) haven't got all day.
have not (I) haven't seen you in a long time.
have not (I) haven't seen you in a month of Sundays.
have not Things haven't been easy.
have *advantage of so
have *all the marbles
have and what have you
have *ants in one's pants
have as luck would have it
have *attack (of an illness)
have *bee in one's bonnet

have been had
have *benefit of the doubt
have *best of both worlds
have *better of so
have *bite (to eat)
have *black mark beside one's name
have Blood will have blood.
have *blues
have *break
have busiest men have the most leisure.
have *butterflies in one's stomach
have *carte blanche
have *case of sth
have cat has nine lives.
have *charley horse
have *checkup
have *chip on one's shoulder
have *clear sailing
have *cold feet
have *contact with so
have Could I have a lift?
have Could I have a word with you?
have Could I have so call you?
have Could I have the bill?
have *creeps
have *crush on so
have *day off
have Desperate diseases must have desperate remedies.
have devil's children have the devil's luck.
have (Do) have some more.
have Do I have to paint (you) a picture?
have Do I have to spell it out (for you)?
have Do unto others as you would have them do unto you.
have Do we have to go through all that again?
have doesn't have enough sense to bell a cat
have doesn't have enough sense to come in out of the rain
have doesn't have the sense God gave geese
have doesn't have the sense God gave him (or her)
have Don't have a cow!
have don't have a pot to piss in (or a window to throw it out of)
have *down pat
have eat one's cake and have it too
have *(either) feast or famine
have Every cloud has a silver lining.
have Every dog has its day.
have Every Jack has his Jill.
have Every man has his price.
have *feel of sth
have *feeling (that sth is the case)
have Fields have eyes, and woods have ears.
have *first crack at sth
have *fix on sth
have *floor
have *foot in both camps
have *foothold (somewhere)
have *fresh start
have *frog in one's throat
have gods send nuts to those who have no teeth.
have good time was had by all.

have *goods on so
have *goose bumps
have Governments have long arms.
have *gray hair(s)
have *grip on oneself
have *grip on sth
have growing youth has a wolf in his belly.
have (had) best do sth
have had (just) as soon do sth
have (had) known it was coming
have had rather do sth
have had sooner do sth
have hadn't oughta
have *hand in sth
have *hand with sth
have *handle on sth
have *hang of sth
have Happy is the country which has no history.
have *hard feelings
have hardly have time to breathe
have hardly have time to think
have has come and gone
have (Has the) cat got your tongue?
have has the world by the tail (with a downhill drag)
have have a bad attitude
have have a bad case of the simples
have have a bad effect (on so/sth)
have have a ball
have have a bear by the tail
have have a bellyful
have have a big mouth
have have a blast
have Have a blimp!
have have a blowout
have have a bone to pick (with so)
have have a brush with sth
have have a burr under one's saddle
have have a buzz on
have have a case (against so)
have have a change of heart
have have a clear conscience (about so/sth)
have have a close call
have have a close shave
have have a clue (about sth)
have have a conniption (fit)
have have a corncob up one's ass
have have a death wish
have have a familiar ring (to it)
have have a field day
have have a finger in the pie
have have a fit
have have a flair for sth
have have a gift for (doing) sth
have have a glass jaw
have have a go at sth
have have a good arm
have have a good command of sth
have have a good head on one's shoulders
have have a (good) mind to do sth
have Have a good one.
have have a good thing going
have Have a good time.
have Have a good trip.
have have a (good) working over
have have a green thumb
have have a head for sth
have have a heart
have have a heart-to-heart (talk)

have have a hidden talent
have have a hitch in one's gitalong
have have a hunch (that sth is the case)
have have a keen interest in sth
have have a kick to it
have have a load on
have have a lot going (for one)
have have a lot on one's mind
have have a low boiling point
have have a mind as sharp as a steel trap
have have a mind of one's own
have have a mind to
have have a near miss
have Have a nice day.
have Have a nice flight.
have have a nose for sth
have have a one-track mind
have have a passion for so/sth
have have a penchant for doing sth
have have a place in sth
have have a rare old time
have have a rough time (of it)
have have a roving eye
have have a run of sth
have have a run-in (with so/sth)
have Have a safe journey.
have have a score to settle (with so)
have have a scrape (with so/sth)
have have a screw loose
have have a seat
have have a set-to (with so)
have have a soft spot (in one's heart) for so or an animal
have have a (sound) grasp of sth
have have a spaz
have have a stake in sth
have have a stroke
have have a sweet tooth
have have a thing about so/sth
have have a thing going (with so)
have have a thirst for sth
have have a tiger by the tail
have have (a) use for so/sth
have have a way with so/sth
have have a way with words
have have a weakness for so/sth
have have a weight problem
have have a whack at sth
have have a whale of a time
have have a yellow belly
have have a yellow streak down one's back
have have all one's marbles
have have an accident
have have an ace up one's sleeve
have have an affair (with so)
have have an alcohol problem
have have an appetite for sth
have have an argument (with so)
have have an ax(e) to grind
have have an ear for sth
have have an easy time of it
have have an effect on so/sth
have have an eye for so/sth
have have an impact on so/sth
have have another guess coming
have have another think coming
have have arrived
have Have at it.
have have at so
have have at sth

have have bats in one's belfry
have have been around
have have been to hell and back
have have bigger fish to fry
have have broad shoulders
have have calluses from patting one's own back
have have carnal knowledge of so
have have cause to do sth
have have clean hands
have have come a long way
have have confidence in so
have have designs on so/sth
have have dibs on sth
have have doubts about so/sth
have have egg on one's face
have have eyes in the back of one's head
have have faith in so
have have feelings about so/sth
have have feet of clay
have have fun
have have (got) a glow on
have have growing pains
have have had enough
have have had it (up to here)
have have had its day
have have half a mind to do sth
have have half a notion to do sth
have have hell to pay
have have hidden talents
have have (high) hopes of sth
have Have I got something for you!
have Have I made myself clear?
have have intimate relations with so
have have it (all) over so/sth (in sth)
have have it all together
have have it both ways
have have it in for so
have have it in one to do sth
have have it made
have Have it your way.
have have just one oar in the water
have have kittens
have have more luck than sense
have have more than one string to one's fiddle
have have neither rhyme nor reason
have (have) never had it so good
have have no business doing sth
have have no staying power
have have no truck with sth
have have none of sth
have have nothing on so
have have nothing to do with so/sth
have have one foot in the grave
have have one in the oven
have have one's ass in a sling
have have one's back to the wall
have have one's brain on a leash
have have one's cake and eat it too
have have one's druthers
have have one's ear to the ground
have have one's eye on so/sth
have have one's eye out (for so/sth)
have have one's feet on the ground
have have one's finger in too many pies
have have one's finger(s) in the till
have have one's hand in sth
have have one's hand in the till
have have one's hands full (with so/sth)
have have one's hands tied
have have one's head in the clouds

have have one's head in the sand
have have one's heart (dead) set against sth
have have one's heart go out to so
have have one's heart in one's mouth
have have one's heart in the right place
have have one's heart on one's sleeve
have have one's heart set on sth
have have one's heart stand still
have have one's luck run out
have have one's mind in the gutter
have have one's name inscribed in the book of life
have have one's nose in a book
have have one's nose in the air
have have one's nose out of joint
have have one's rathers
have have one's shoulder to the wheel
have have one's way with so
have have one's wires crossed
have have one's words stick in one's throat
have have one's work cut out for one
have have one too many
have have oneself sth
have have pity on so or an animal
have have pull with so
have have recourse to sth
have have relations with so
have have rocks in one's head
have have seen better days
have have so
have have (some) bearing on sth
have have some food to go
have have (some) time to kill
have have so around (for sth)
have have so back
have have so behind the eight ball
have have so by so/sth
have have so by sth
have have so dead to rights
have have so down
have have so drawn and quartered
have have so for breakfast
have have so in
have have so on a string
have have so on the string
have have so/sth about
have have so/sth cornered
have have so/sth in mind
have have so/sth in one's hands
have have so/sth in one's sights
have have so/sth in tow
have have so/sth on one's hands
have have so/sth on one's mind
have have so/sth on the brain
have have so/sth on track
have have so/sth under (close) scrutiny
have have so/sth under control
have have so/sth (well) in hand
have have so over a barrel
have have so over (for sth)
have have so pegged as sth
have have so's best interest(s) at heart
have have so's blood on one's hands
have have so's eye
have have so's hide
have have so slated for sth
have have so slated to do sth
have have so under a spell
have have so under one's spell
have have so under so's thumb
have have so under so's wing(s)

have have so up (for sth)
have have sth against so/sth
have have sth at one's fingertips
have have sth cinched
have have sth coming (to one)
have have sth doing
have have sth down to a T
have have sth for (a meal)
have have sth for so
have have sth for sth
have have sth going (for oneself)
have have something going (with so)
have have sth hanging over one's head
have have sth hung up and salted
have have sth in common (with so/sth)
have have sth in hand
have have sth in stock
have have sth in store (for so)
have have sth made
have have sth on
have have sth out
have have sth stick in one's craw
have have sth to burn
have have sth to do with sth
have have sth to spare
have have sth up one's sleeve
have have sth wrapped up
have have sticky fingers
have have the ball in one's court
have have the best of so/sth
have have the cards stacked against one
have have the courage of one's convictions
have have the deck stacked against one
have have the devil to pay
have have the facts straight
have have the final say
have have the gall to do sth
have have the gift of gab
have have the hots for so
have have the makings of sth
have have the Midas touch
have have the mullygrubs
have have the patience of a saint
have have the patience of Job
have have the presence of mind to do sth
have have the shoe on the other foot
have have the stomach for sth
have have the time of one's life
have have to do sth so bad one can taste it
have have to do with sth
have have to get married
have have to go some (to do sth)
have have to hand it to so
have have to live with sth
have have too
have have (too much) time on one's hands
have have two left feet
have have what it takes
have have words
have (Have you) been keeping busy?
have (Have you) been keeping cool?
have (Have you) been keeping out of trouble?
have (Have you) been okay?
have (Have you) changed your mind?
have Have you heard?
have Have you met so?
have He that would have eggs must endure the cackling of hens.

have He who sups with the devil should have a long spoon.
have *head start (on so)
have *head start (on sth)
have *hold on so
have How (have) you been?
have How many times do I have to tell you?
have How the mighty have fallen.
have (I) can't say (as) I have.
have (I) can't say's I have.
have (I) can't say that I have.
have (I) don't believe I've had the pleasure.
have I don't have time to breathe.
have I don't have time to catch my breath.
have (I) had a good time.
have I had a lovely time.
have (I) had a nice time.
have (I have) no problem with that.
have (I have) nothing to complain about.
have (I) have to be moving along.
have (I) have to go now.
have (I) have to move along.
have (I) have to push off.
have (I) have to run along.
have (I) have to shove off.
have I have to wash a few things out.
have I just have this feeling.
have I'd like (to have) a word with you.
have Idle folk have the least leisure.
have Idle people have the least leisure.
have If a toady frog had wings, he wouldn't bump his ass.
have If frogs had wheels, they wouldn't bump their butts.
have I'll have the same.
have I'll have to beg off.
have I'll (have to) let you go.
have (I'm) delighted to have you (here).
have (I'm) having a wonderful time; wish you were here.
have I'm having quite a time.
have (I'm) having the time of my life.
have *in hand
have *in the back of so's mind
have *in the bag
have *in (with so)
have *in writing
have *inkling (of sth)
have *inside track
have It has so's name on it.
have (It) hasn't been easy.
have It is a long lane that has no turning.
have (It's) good to have you here.
have (It's) nice to have you here.
have *itch for sth
have *itch to do sth
have *itchy feet
have *itchy palm
have I've had a lovely time.
have I've had enough of this!
have I've had it up to here (with so/sth).
have *jump on so
have Kings have long arms.
have *last laugh (on so)
have *last word
have *lean times (ahead)

have *leg up on so
have *leg up
have Let me have it!
have Let's have it!
have let so have it (with both barrels)
have Little pitchers have big ears.
have *look-see
have *losing streak
have *lot of nerve
have *lot of promise
have *low profile
have *lucky streak
have *lump in one's throat
have *mental block (against sth)
have *method in one's madness
have moment everyone has been waiting for
have more sth than Carter has (liver) pills
have more you have, the more you want.
have mouse that has but one hole is quickly taken.
have *neither rhyme nor reason
have never would have guessed
have Nice place you have here.
have Nice weather we're having.
have No more than I have to.
have not have a care in the world
have not have a leg to stand on
have not have a snowball's chance in hell
have not have a stitch of clothes (on)
have not have all one's marbles
have not have anything to do with so/sth
have not have anything to do with sth
have not have the heart to do sth
have Nothing so bad but (it) might have been worse.
have *on a string
have *on so's shoulders
have *on the tip of one's tongue
have *one for the road
have One has to draw the line somewhere.
have *one's bearings
have *one's say
have *one's sea legs
have *one's second wind
have *one's start
have only have eyes for so
have *open mind
have *out
have *over (and done) with
have *paper trail
have *perspective on sth
have *price on one's head
have price one has to pay
have *reputation (as a sth)
have *reputation (for doing sth)
have *right to do sth
have *right to sth
have *right-of-way
have *rolling in the aisles
have *rough idea (about sth)
have rumor has it that...
have scarcely have time to breathe
have *sewed up
have should have stood in bed
have Shrouds have no pockets.
have Shut the stable door after the horse has bolted.

have *sinking feeling
have *slated for sth
have *slated to do sth
have *so bad one can taste it
have *(solid) grasp of sth
have some creature's time has come
have *some elbow room
have *some loose ends
have So had better keep still about it.
have so's time has come
have *sth to shout about
have *stars in one's eyes
have *start
have *straight face
have *swelled head
have *taste for sth
have Thank you for having me.
have Them as has, gits.
have They must have seen you coming.
have time flies (when you're having fun)
have *time off for good behavior
have *time off
have *time to catch one's breath
have 'Tis better to have loved and lost than never to have loved at all.
have *to go
have to have a hollow leg
have *try at so
have *try at sth
have *two strikes against one
have *under a spell
have *under arrest
have *under (close) scrutiny
have *under control
have *under one's belt
have *under so's thumb
have *under so's wing(s)
have *under way
have *under wraps
have *upper hand (on so)
have *vested interest in sth
have *voice (in sth)
have Walls have ears.
have was had
have We had a lovely time.
have We('ll) have to do lunch sometime.
have (We're) delighted to have you (here).
have We've had a lovely time.
have What are you having?
have What have you been up to?
have Where have you been all my life?
have Where (have) you been hiding (yourself)?
have Where (have) you been keeping yourself?
have *wherewithal (to do sth)
have *whiff of sth
have Who could have thought?
have Who would have thought?
have *word with so (about sth)
have worm (has) turned.
have would like (to have) so/sth
have You cannot have your cake and eat it (too).
have You cannot lose what you never had.
have (You) could have fooled me.
have You could have knocked me over with a feather.

have You have to eat a peck of dirt before you die.
havoc play havoc with so/sth
havoc raise havoc with so/sth
havoc wreak havoc (with sth)
haw hem and haw (around)
hawk watch so/sth like a hawk
hay hit the hay
hay Make hay while the sun shines.
hay That ain't hay.
haystack like looking for a needle in a haystack
haywire go haywire
hazard at hazard
hazard hazard a guess
hazard hazard an opinion
he As a man sows, so shall he reap.
he Blessed is he who expects nothing, for he shall never be disappointed.
he Call no man happy till he dies.
he Count no man happy till he dies.
he devil is not so black as he is painted.
he did everything he could 'cept eat us
he God takes soonest those he loveth best.
he He gives twice who gives quickly.
he He lives long who lives well.
he He puts his pants on one leg at a time.
he He that cannot obey cannot command.
he He that hath a full purse never wanted a friend.
he He that is down need fear no fall.
he He that would eat the kernel must crack the nut.
he He that would go to sea for pleasure, would go to hell for a pastime.
he He that would have eggs must endure the cackling of hens.
he He that would the daughter win, must with the mother first begin.
he He travels fastest who travels alone.
he He wears a ten-dollar hat on a five-cent head.
he He who begins many things, finishes but few.
he He who excuses himself accuses himself.
he He who fights and runs away, may live to fight another day.
he He who hesitates is lost.
he He who laughs last, laughs best.
he He who laughs last, laughs longest.
he He who pays the piper calls the tune.
he He who rides a tiger is afraid to dismount.
he He who sups with the devil should have a long spoon.
he He who would climb the ladder must begin at the bottom.
he He will get his.
he If a toady frog had wings, he wouldn't bump his ass.
he liar is not believed (even) when he tells the truth.
he man is known by the company he keeps.
he Set a beggar on horseback, and he'll ride to the devil.

he Speak of the devil (and in he walks).

he Talk of the devil (and he is sure to appear).

head able to do sth standing on one's head

head bang one's head against a brick wall

head beat one's head against the wall

head Better be the head of a dog than the tail of a lion.

head (big) head

head bite so's head off

head bother one's (pretty little) head about so/sth

head bring sth down on one('s head)

head bring sth to a head

head bury one's head in the sand

head can't make heads or tails (out) of so/sth

head come to a head

head come up heads

head cooler heads prevail

head cough one's head off

head count heads

head crazy in the head

head Don't worry your (pretty little) head about it.

head face sth head-on

head fall head over heels

head fill so's head with sth

head fling one's head back

head from head to toe

head get one's head above water

head get one's head together

head get sth into so's thick head

head get up a (full) head of steam

head Get your head out of the clouds!

head go out of one's head

head go over so's head

head go to so's head

head hang over so('s head)

head harder than the back of God's head

head have a good head on one's shoulders

head have a head for sth

head have eyes in the back of one's head

head have one's head in the clouds

head have one's head in the sand

head have rocks in one's head

head have sth hanging over one's head

head He wears a ten-dollar hat on a five-cent head.

head head

head head and shoulders above so/sth

head head away from so/sth

head head back (some place)

head head for so/sth

head head for the hills

head head for the last roundup

head head for (the) tall timber

head head in(to sth)

head head on

head head out after so/sth or an animal

head head out (for sth)

head head over heels in debt

head head over heels in love (with so)

head head so off at the pass

head head so/sth at so/sth

head head so/sth into so/sth

head head so/sth off

head head sth out

head head sth up

head head South

head head start (on so)

head head toward so/sth

head headed for sth

head heads or tails

head Heads up!

head heads will roll

head hide one's head in the sand

head hit the nail (right) on the head

head hold one's head up

head hold sth over so('s head)

head in over one's head (with so/sth)

head I've seen better heads on nickel beers.

head keep a civil tongue (in one's head)

head keep one's head

head Keep your head down.

head knock one's head (up) against a brick wall

head knock some heads together

head laugh one's head off

head lose one's head (over so/sth)

head make heads or tails of so/sth

head make so's head spin

head make so's head swim

head need sth like a hole in the head

head not able to make head or tail of sth

head not trouble one's (pretty) (little) head about sth

head on so's head

head out of one's head

head over so's head

head pass over so's head

head place a price on one's head

head pound so's head in

head price on one's head

head put a price on one's head

head put ideas into so's head

head put one in over one's head

head put one's head on the block (for so/sth)

head put people's heads together

head put sth in(to) so's head

head rear its ugly head

head (right) off the top of one's head

head run around like a chicken with its head cut off

head run one's head against a brick wall

head snap so's head off

head soft in the head

head stand head and shoulders above so/sth

head stand on one's head

head stand sth on its head

head still tongue makes a wise head.

head stuff so's head with sth

head swelled head

head take so's head off

head take sth into one's head

head talk one's head off

head talk over so's head

head talk so's head off

head touched (in the head)

head tower head and shoulders above so/sth

head trouble one's head about so/sth

head turn so's head

head Two heads are better than one.

head Uneasy lies the head that wears a crown.

head use one's head

head use your head for more than a hatrack

head use your head for more than something to keep your ears apart

head where so's head is at

head yack one's head off

head yell one's head off

headache splitting headache

headway make (an amount of) headway

heal heal over

heal heal so of sth

heal heal up

heal Physician, heal thyself.

heal Time is a great healer.

health clean bill of health

health Early to bed and early to rise, makes a man healthy, wealthy, and wise.

health in the best of health

health in the pink (of health)

health nurse so back to health

health picture of (good) health

heap bottom of the heap

heap do so a heap of good

heap heap of sth

heap heap sight

heap heap sth up

heap heap sth (up)on so/sth

heap heap sth with sth

heap top of the heap

heap whole heap more

hear Ask no questions and hear no lies.

hear Believe nothing of what you hear, and only half of what you see.

hear Did you hear?

hear (Do) you hear?

hear Dream of a funeral and you hear of a marriage.

hear Dream of a funeral and you hear of a wedding.

hear Eavesdroppers never hear any good of themselves.

hear hard of hearing

hear hear a peep out of so

hear hear about so/sth

hear hear from so/sth

hear hear of so/sth

hear hear so out

hear hear sth through

hear hear word (from so/sth)

hear hearing impaired

hear I didn't hear you.

hear I hear what you're saying.

hear I hear you.

hear (I'm) glad to hear it.

hear (I'm) sorry to hear that.

hear (It's) good to hear your voice.

hear like to hear oneself talk

hear Listeners never hear any good of themselves.

hear Now hear this!

hear See no evil, hear no evil, speak no evil.

hear so quiet you could hear a pin drop

hear so still you could hear a pin drop

hear talk to hear one's own voice

hear There's none so deaf as those who will not hear.

hear will not hear of sth

hear You hear?

heard another country heard from
heard Children should be seen and not heard.
heard Have you heard?
heard (I) never heard of such a thing!
heard I've heard so much about you.
heard make oneself heard
heard That ain't the way I heard it.
heard You heard so.
hearken hearken to so/sth
heart Absence makes the heart grow fonder.
heart aching heart
heart act young at heart
heart bleeding heart
heart break so's heart
heart chicken-hearted
heart Cold hands, warm heart.
heart cross one's heart (and hope to die)
heart cry one's heart out
heart die of a broken heart
heart do so's heart good
heart eat one's heart out
heart emptier than a banker's heart
heart enshrine so in one's heart
heart enshrine so's memory in one's heart
heart Faint heart never won fair lady.
heart faint of heart
heart find it in one's heart (to do sth)
heart follow one's heart
heart from the bottom of one's heart
heart from the heart
heart go to the heart of the matter
heart hale and hearty
heart halfhearted (about so/sth)
heart have a change of heart
heart have a heart
heart have a heart-to-heart (talk)
heart have a soft spot (in one's heart) for so or an animal
heart have one's heart (dead) set against sth
heart have one's heart go out to so
heart have one's heart in one's mouth
heart have one's heart in the right place
heart have one's heart on one's sleeve
heart have one's heart set on sth
heart have one's heart stand still
heart have so's best interest(s) at heart
heart heart and soul
heart heart of the matter
heart heavy purse makes a light heart.
heart Home is where the heart is.
heart Hope deferred makes the heart sick.
heart Hope deferred maketh the heart sick.
heart It is a poor heart that never rejoices.
heart keep so young at heart
heart know sth by heart
heart learn sth by heart
heart light purse makes a heavy heart.
heart look at the heart of the matter
heart lose heart
heart make so sick at heart
heart man after my own heart
heart not have the heart to do sth
heart one's heart goes out to so
heart one's heart is (dead) set against sth

heart one's heart is in one's mouth
heart one's heart is in the right place
heart one's heart is set on sth
heart one's heart misses a beat
heart one's heart skips a beat
heart one's heart stands still
heart open one's heart to so/sth
heart out of the goodness of one's heart
heart play one's heart out
heart pour one's heart out to so
heart put one's heart (and soul) into sth
heart set one's heart against sth
heart set one's heart on so/sth
heart sick at heart
heart sing one's heart out
heart sob one's heart out
heart stay young at heart
heart steal so's heart
heart take heart (from sth)
heart take so or an animal into one's heart
heart take sth to heart
heart to one's heart's content
heart warm the cockles of so's heart
heart way to a man's heart is through his stomach.
heart wear one's heart on one's sleeve
heart What the eye doesn't see, the heart doesn't grieve over.
heart win so's heart
heart win the heart of so
heart with a heavy heart
heart with all one's heart (and soul)
heart young at heart
heartbeat heartbeat away from being sth
heartbeat in a heartbeat
heartstrings play on so's heartstrings
hearty hale and hearty
heat (all) het up
heat come in(to) heat
heat go into heat
heat heat so up
heat heat sth up (to sth)
heat heat up
heat If you can't stand the heat, get out of the kitchen.
heat in a dead heat
heat in heat
heat It's not the heat, it's the humidity.
heat put the heat on
heat take some heat
heat take the heat
heat turn the heat up (on so)
heat turn up the heat (on so/sth)
heave heave in(to) sight
heave heave sth at so/sth
heave heave sth up
heave heave to
heave (old) heave-ho
heaven bundle from heaven
heaven Crosses are ladders that lead to heaven.
heaven For heaven('s) sake!
heaven God's in his heaven; all's right with the world.
heaven (Good) heavens!
heaven Heaven forbid!
heaven Heaven help us!
heaven Heaven protects children(, sailors,) and drunken men.
heaven Heavens to Betsy!
heaven in heaven
heaven in hog heaven

heaven in seventh heaven
heaven manna from heaven
heaven marriage made in heaven
heaven Marriages are made in heaven.
heaven match made in heaven
heaven move heaven and earth to do sth
heaven (My) heavens!
heaven smell to (high) heaven
heaven stink to high heaven
heaven Thank heavens!
heaven the heavens opened
heaviest Every horse thinks its own pack heaviest.
heavy Every horse thinks its own pack heaviest.
heavy heavy going
heavy heavy into so/sth
heavy heavy purse makes a light heart.
heavy hot and heavy
heavy lay a (heavy) trip on so
heavy light purse makes a heavy heart.
heavy play the heavy
heavy Time hangs heavy on so's hands.
heavy with a heavy heart
heck for the heck of it
heck What the heck!
hedge hedge against sth
hedge hedge between keeps friendship green.
hedge hedge one's bets
hedge hedge so in
hedge hedge so/sth in
hedge hedge sth against sth
heed pay heed to so
heed take heed (of so/sth)
heel Achilles' heel
heel bring a dog to heel
heel bring so to heel
heel cool one's heels
heel couldn't pour water out of a boot (if there was instructions on the heel)
heel dig one's heels in
heel down-at-the-heels
heel fall head over heels
heel hard on so's heels
heel head over heels in debt
heel head over heels in love (with so)
heel hot on so's heels
heel kick one's heels up
heel on so's heels
heel on the heels of sth
heel right on so's heels
heel set one back on one's heels
heel take to one's heels
heel well-heeled
height at the height of sth
heir fall heir to sth
heist heist so/sth (up)
hell all hell broke loose
hell all over hell and gone
hell all over hell and half of Georgia
hell beat the hell out of so
hell catch hell
hell come hell or high water
hell don't give a hoot (in hell's hollow)
hell fight like hell
hell for the hell of it
hell frighten the hell out of so
hell from hell to breakfast
hell get hell (about so/sth)
hell get the hell out (of here)
hell go to hell

hell have been to hell and back
hell have hell to pay
hell He that would go to sea for pleasure, would go to hell for a pastime.
hell hell
hell hell of a mess
hell hell of a note
hell hell of a so/sth
hell Hell's bells (and buckets of blood)!
hell hell-bent for leather
hell hell-bent for somewhere or sth
hell helluva so/sth
hell hot as hell
hell It'll be a cold day in hell when sth happens.
hell knock the hell out of so/sth
hell like a bat out of hell
hell like hell
hell mad as hell
hell not a hope in hell
hell not have a snowball's chance in hell
hell play hell with so/sth
hell quicker than hell
hell raise hell (with sth)
hell road to hell is paved with good intentions.
hell shoot so/sth (all) to hell
hell so/sth from hell
hell sure as hell
hell The hell you say!
hell There will be hell to pay.
hell through hell and high water
hell till hell freezes over
hell to hell and gone
hell (To) hell with that!
hell until hell freezes over
hell What (in) the hell?
hell What the hell?
hell Who (in) the hell?
hell You scared the hell out of me.
hellfire Hellfire and damnation!
hello drop in (to say hello)
hello Say hello to so (for me).
helluva helluva so/sth
helm at the helm (of sth)
help beyond help
help Can I help you?
help cannot help doing sth
help can't help but do sth
help Could I help you?
help Every little bit helps.
help God helps them that help themselves.
help Heaven help us!
help help oneself (to sth)
help help out some place
help help out (with sth)
help help so along
help help so back (to sth)
help help so down (from sth)
help help so get a foothold (somewhere)
help help so in sth
help help so in(to sth)
help help so off (of) sth
help help so off with sth
help help so on with sth
help help so or an animal (get) over sth
help help so or an animal out (of sth)
help help so/sth out with so/sth
help help so/sth with so/sth
help help (so) out

help help so up (from sth)
help Help yourself.
help helping hand
help How may I help you?
help (I) can't help it.
help (I) couldn't help it.
help (It) can't be helped.
help (It) couldn't be helped.
help May I help you?
help need a helping hand
help not able to help sth
help not lift a finger (to help so)
help not lift a hand (to help so)
help offer a helping hand
help pitch in (and help) (with sth)
help seek professional help
help So help me(, God)!
hem hem and haw (around)
hem hem so/sth in
hen He that would have eggs must endure the cackling of hens.
hen mad as a wet hen
hen scarce as hen's teeth
hen scarcer than hen's teeth
Henry one's John Henry
hepped hepped (up)
her Can I tell her who's calling?
her doesn't have the sense God gave him (or her)
her Give her the gun.
her give the devil her due
her Let her rip!
her Put 'er there(, pal).
her She will get hers.
herd herd so/sth together
herd like herding frogs
herd ride herd on so/sth
here Abandon hope, all ye who enter here.
here buck stops here.
here downhill from here on
here Fancy meeting you here!
here from here on (in)
here from here till next Tuesday
here get one right here
here Get out (of here)!
here get the hell out (of here)
here Get your ass over here!
here Get your buns over here!
here have had it (up to here)
here here and now
here here and there
here Here goes nothing.
here Here (it) goes.
here Here's looking at you.
here Here's mud in your eye.
here Here's to so/sth.
here Here's to you.
here Here's your hat, what's your hurry?
here here, there, and everywhere
here Here today, (and) gone tomorrow.
here Here we go again.
here Here you go.
here (I) never thought I'd see you here!
here (I'm) delighted to have you (here).
here (I'm) having a wonderful time; wish you were here.
here I'm out of here.
here (It's) good to be here.
here (It's) good to have you here.

here (It's) nice to be here.
here (It's) nice to have you here.
here I've had it up to here (with so/sth).
here Let's get out of here.
here look here
here Look who's here!
here neither here nor there
here Nice place you have here.
here Same here.
here sure as I'm standing here
here this here
here Today here, tomorrow the world.
here up to here (with sth)
here (We) don't see you much around here anymore.
here (We're) delighted to have you (here).
here What brings you here?
here What do you think you are doing here?
here What's going on (around here)?
here (You) can't get there from here.
hero unsung hero
herring red herring
herself by herself
hesitate He who hesitates is lost.
hesitate hesitate over sth
hesitate If there's anything you need, don't hesitate to ask.
hess mell of a hess
het (all) het up
hew hew sth down
hew hew sth out of sth
hew hew to sth
hibernate busy as a hibernating bear
hide find (neither) hide nor hair
hide go into hiding
hide hair and hide(, horns and tallow)
hide have a hidden talent
hide have hidden talents
hide have so's hide
hide hidden agenda
hide hide behind so/sth
hide hide from so or an animal
hide hide one's face in shame
hide hide one's head in the sand
hide hide one's light under a bushel
hide hide out (from so/sth)
hide hide so/sth away (some place)
hide hide so/sth behind sth
hide hide sth in sth
hide nail so('s hide) to the wall
hide (neither) hide nor hair
hide see (neither) hide nor hair
hide tan so's hide
hide Where (have) you been hiding (yourself)?
high act high-and-mighty
high come hell or high water
high cork high and bottle deep
high eat high on the hog
high flying high
high get (down) off one's high horse
high go sky-high
high grow knee-high by the 4th of July
high happy as a clam (at high tide)
high have (high) hopes of sth
high high and dry
high high as a kite
high high as the sky
high high man on the totem pole
high high on sth
high high roller

high high sign
high high-and-mighty
high high-pressure so into sth
high hit the high spots
high hold so/sth in high regard
high hunt high and low (for so/sth)
high in high cotton
high in high dudgeon
high in high gear
high in (high) hopes of sth
high it's high time
high knee-high by the 4th of July
high knee-high to a grasshopper
high knee-high to a jackrabbit
high leave so high and dry
high like hell and high lightning
high live high off the hog
high look for so/sth high and low
high look high and low (for so/sth)
high (lord) high muck-a-muck
high move into high gear
high on one's high horse
high running high
high search high and low (for so/sth)
high seem high and mighty
high since so was knee-high to a grasshopper
high smell to (high) heaven
high speak highly of so/sth
high stink to high heaven
high swing into high gear
high think highly of so/sth
high through hell and high water
hightail hightail it out of somewhere
highway highway robbery
highway highways and byways
hike hike sth up
hike take a hike
hill go over the hill
hill head for the hills
hill make a mountain out of a molehill
hill not amount to a hill of beans
hill not worth a hill of beans
hill old as the hills
hill over the hill
hill run for the hills
hill take to the hills
hill uphill battle
Hill What in (the) Sam Hill?
him Could I tell him who's calling?
him doesn't have the sense God gave him (or her)
him Everything comes to him who waits.
him Evil be to him who evil thinks.
him Good things come to him who waits.
him If God did not exist, it would be necessary to invent Him.
him May I tell him who's calling?
himself Every man for himself (and the devil take the hindmost).
himself He who excuses himself accuses himself.
hind crooked as a dog's hind leg
hind get up on one's hind legs
hind hind end
hind hind end of creation
hind suck so's hind tit
hinder hinder so from sth
hindmost Devil take the hindmost.
hindmost Every man for himself (and the devil take the hindmost).

hindside hindside first
hindsight in hindsight
hinge hinge (up)on so/sth
hint drop a hint
hint hint at sth
hint hint for sth
hint hint sth to so
hint take a hint
hip get hip to so/sth
hip hip to so/sth
hip joined at the hip
hip shoot from the hip
hire hire so away (from so/sth)
hire hire so/sth out
hire not for hire
his beard the lion in his den
his devil can cite Scripture for his own purpose.
his devil can quote Scripture for his own purpose.
his devil looks after his own.
his doesn't know his ass from a hole in the ground
his doesn't know his ass from his elbow
his Every Jack has his Jill.
his Every man has his price.
his Every man is the architect of his own fortune.
his Every man to his taste.
his everybody and his brother
his everybody and his uncle
his fool and his money are soon parted.
his give the devil his due
his God's in his heaven; all's right with the world.
his growing youth has a wolf in his belly.
his He puts his pants on one leg at a time.
his He will get his.
his If a toady frog had wings, he wouldn't bump his ass.
his leopard cannot change his spots.
his Let every man skin his own skunk.
his Let the cobbler stick to his last.
his man's home is his castle.
his prophet is not without honor save in his own country.
his To each his own.
his way to a man's heart is through his stomach.
his what's his face
his what's his name
hiss hiss at so/sth
hiss hiss so off ((of) the stage)
hiss hiss sth out
hissy hissy (fit)
history ancient history
history go down (in history) (as so/sth)
history Happy is the country which has no history.
history History repeats itself.
history I'm history.
history rest is history.
hit can't hit the (broad) side of a barn
hit couldn't hit a bull in the ass with a bass fiddle
hit fat hit the fire
hit hit a happy medium
hit hit a plateau
hit hit a snag

hit hit a sour note
hit hit against so/sth
hit hit and miss
hit hit at so/sth
hit hit back (at so/sth)
hit hit bottom
hit hit home
hit hit it off (with so)
hit hit like a ton of bricks
hit hit on so
hit hit on sth
hit hit one's stride
hit hit one where one lives
hit hit or miss
hit hit out (at so/sth) (in sth)
hit hit out (for sth or some place)
hit hit pay dirt
hit hit (rock) bottom
hit hit so
hit hit so below the belt
hit hit so hard
hit hit so in sth
hit hit so like a ton of bricks
hit hit so (right) between the eyes
hit hit so up (for sth)
hit hit so with sth
hit hit sth off
hit hit speeds of some amount
hit hit the books
hit hit the booze
hit hit the bottle
hit hit the brakes
hit hit the bricks
hit hit the (broad) side of a barn
hit hit the bull's-eye
hit hit the ceiling
hit hit the deck
hit hit the fan
hit hit the ground running
hit hit the hay
hit hit the high spots
hit hit the jackpot
hit hit the nail (right) on the head
hit hit the panic button
hit hit the pavement
hit hit the road
hit hit the roof
hit hit the sack
hit hit the skids
hit hit the spot
hit hit the trail
hit hit town
hit hit (up)on so/sth
hit hitting on all cylinders
hit (I'd) better hit the road.
hit (It's) time to hit the road.
hit (I've) got to hit the road.
hit *like a ton of bricks
hit make a hit with so
hit pinch-hit for so
hit *(rock) bottom
hit smash hit
hit *speeds of some amount
hit suddenly the fat hit the fire
hit then the fat hit the fire
hit when the fat hit the fire
hit when the shit hits the fan
hitch have a hitch in one's gitalong
hitch hitch a ride
hitch hitch so/sth (up) (to sth)
hitch Hitch your wagon to a star.
hitch without a hitch
hither come-hither look

hither hither, thither, and yon
hive hive of activity
ho gung ho
ho (old) heave-ho
hoard hoard sth up
hoarse hoarse as a crow
hob play hob with so/sth
hob raise hob with so/sth
hobnob hobnob with so/sth
Hobson's Hobson's choice
hock go into hock
hock in hock
hock out of hock
hoe hard row to hoe
hoe hoe one's own row
hoe tough row to hoe
hog call hogs
hog eat high on the hog
hog go hog wild
hog go whole hog
hog hog wild
hog in hog heaven
hog know as much about sth as a hog knows about Sunday
hog live high off the hog
hog road hog
hoist hoist with one's own petard
hoist Hoist your sail when the wind is fair.
hold Can you hold?
hold can't hold a candle to so
hold Could you hold?
hold Don't hold your breath.
hold foothold (somewhere)
hold help so get a foothold (somewhere)
hold hold a grudge (against so)
hold hold a meeting
hold hold all the aces
hold hold all the cards
hold hold back (on sth)
hold hold by sth
hold Hold everything!
hold hold forth (on so/sth)
hold hold good for so/sth
hold Hold it!
hold hold no brief for so/sth
hold hold off (from) doing sth
hold hold off (on so/sth)
hold hold on
hold hold on so
hold hold on sth
hold hold (on) tight
hold hold one's breath
hold hold one's end of the bargain up
hold hold one's end up
hold hold one's fire
hold hold one's ground
hold hold one's head up
hold hold one's liquor
hold hold one's mouth the right way
hold hold one's nose
hold hold one's own
hold hold one's peace
hold hold one's temper
hold hold one's tongue
hold hold oneself together
hold hold out (against so/sth)
hold hold out (for so/sth)
hold hold out the olive branch
hold Hold, please.
hold hold so accountable (for sth)
hold hold so back
hold hold so for ransom

hold hold so hostage
hold hold so or an animal down
hold hold so/sth at bay
hold hold so/sth at sth
hold hold so/sth by sth
hold hold so/sth in check
hold hold so/sth in high regard
hold hold so/sth in low regard
hold hold so/sth in reserve
hold hold so/sth off
hold hold so/sth or an animal back (from so/sth)
hold hold so/sth out (of sth)
hold hold so/sth over
hold hold so/sth still
hold hold so/sth together
hold hold so/sth up
hold hold so responsible (for sth)
hold hold so's attention
hold hold so's hand
hold hold so to sth
hold hold so under so's thumb
hold hold so up to sth
hold hold sth against so
hold hold sth back for a rainy day
hold hold sth for so
hold hold sth in
hold hold sth in abeyance
hold hold sth in store (for so)
hold hold sth inside ((of) one(self))
hold hold (sth) out on so/sth
hold hold sth out (to so)
hold hold sth over so('s head)
hold hold sth together
hold Hold still.
hold hold terror for so
hold hold the fort
hold hold the line (at so/sth)
hold Hold the phone.
hold hold the purse strings
hold Hold the wire(, please).
hold hold together
hold hold true
hold hold under wraps
hold hold up
hold Hold your horses!
hold Hold your tater!
hold Hold your tongue!
hold household name
hold household word
hold lay hold of so/sth
hold leave so holding the bag
hold lose one's hold on so/sth
hold no holds barred
hold not hold a candle to so/sth
hold not hold a stick to so/sth
hold not hold water
hold not hold with sth
hold on hold
hold Please hold.
hold put a hold on sth
hold put so on hold
hold put so/sth on hold
hold put sth on hold
hold relax one's hold on so/sth
hold take hold of so/sth
hold *under so's thumb
hold *under wraps
hold Will you hold?
hold won't hold water
hole ace in the hole
hole can't see a hole in a ladder

hole doesn't know his ass from a hole in the ground
hole eyes like two burnt holes in a blanket
hole full of holes
hole go in the hole
hole hole in one
hole hole in the wall
hole hole up (somewhere)
hole in the hole
hole Money burns a hole in so's pocket.
hole mouse that has but one hole is quickly taken.
hole need sth like a hole in the head
hole out of the hole
hole pick holes in sth
hole poke a hole in sth
hole punch a hole in sth
hole put so in the hole
hole shot full of holes
hole Shut your cake hole!
hole so's ace in the hole
hole square peg in a round hole
hole watering hole
holiday busman's holiday
holiday hell on a holiday
holler holler sth out
holler holler uncle
holler hoot and holler
holler two (w)hoops and a holler
hollow don't give a hoot (in hell's hollow)
hollow hollow sth out
hollow to have a hollow leg
holy Holy cow!
holy holy Joe
holy Holy mackerel!
holy Holy moley!
homage pay homage to so/sth
home at home
home bring home the bacon
home bring sth home to so
home Charity begins at home.
home chickens come home to roost.
home close to home
home come home from some place
home come home (to roost)
home come home to so
home Come in and make yourself at home.
home down-home
home drive sth home
home East, west, home's best.
home eat so out of house and home
home feel at home
home get home to so/sth
home get sth home to so/sth
home go home in a box
home go home to mama
home hammer sth home
home hit home
home (home) folks
home home free
home home in (on so/sth)
home Home is where the heart is.
home home on(to sth)
home homely enough to stop a clock
home (I've) got to go home and get my beauty sleep.
home keep the home fires burning
home longest way round is the shortest way home.
home make oneself at home

home Make yourself at home.
home man's home is his castle.
home Men make houses, women make homes.
home money from home
home nothing to write home about
home one's home away from home
home see so home
home strike home
home take sth home (with oneself)
home There's no place like home.
home There's nobody home.
home (un)til the cows come home
home woman's place is in the home.
homestretch in the (home)stretch
homework dog ate my homework.
hone hone for so/sth
honest come by sth honestly
honest honest and aboveboard
honest Honest to God.
honest Honest to goodness.
honest Honest to Pete.
honest Honesty is the best policy.
honest keep so honest
honest make an honest woman of so
honey sweet as honey
honey sweeter than honey
honey You can catch more flies with honey than with vinegar.
honeymoon honeymoon is over.
honk honk at so/sth
honor do the honors
honor guest of honor
honor honor so as sth
honor honor so for sth
honor honor so's check
honor honor so with sth
honor in honor of so/sth
honor on one's honor
honor prophet is not without honor save in his own country.
honor put one on one's honor
honor so's word of honor
honor There is honor among thieves.
hooch hooched (up)
hood all around Robin Hood's barn
hood look under the hood
hoodwink hoodwink so into sth
hoodwink hoodwink so out of sth
hoof hoof it
hook by hook or (by) crook
hook crooked as a barrel of fish hooks
hook get one's hooks in(to) so/sth
hook hook in(to sth)
hook hook, line, and sinker
hook hook oneself on so/sth
hook hook so on sth
hook hook so/sth up (to so/sth)
hook hook so up (with so)
hook hook sth down
hook hook sth into sth
hook hook sth on(to so/sth)
hook hook sth up
hook hook up with so
hook hooked on sth
hook let so off the hook
hook off the hook
hook on one's own hook
hook ring off the hook
hook swallow sth hook, line, and sinker
hooky play hooky
hoop jump through a hoop

hoot don't give a hoot (in hell's hollow)
hoot hoot and holler
hoot hoot at so/sth
hoot hoot so down
hoot hoot so off the stage
hoot not care two hoots about so/sth
hoot not give two hoots about so/sth
hop hop in(to sth)
hop hop off ((of) sth)
hop hop on the bandwagon
hop hop on(to sth)
hop hop, skip, and a jump
hop hop up
hop Hop to it!
hop hop up (to so/sth)
hop hopped up
hop hopping mad
hop in the hopper
hop *on the bandwagon
hope Abandon hope, all ye who enter here.
hope build one's hopes on so/sth
hope cross one's heart (and hope to die)
hope dash so's hopes
hope give up (all) hope
hope have (high) hopes of sth
hope hope against (all) hope
hope Hope deferred makes the heart sick.
hope Hope deferred maketh the heart sick.
hope hope for sth
hope hope for the best
hope Hope is a good breakfast but a bad supper.
hope Hope springs eternal (in the human breast).
hope hopeless at doing sth
hope I hope all goes well.
hope (I) hope not.
hope (I) hope so.
hope (I) hope to see you again (sometime).
hope in (high) hopes of sth
hope It is better to travel hopefully than to arrive.
hope live in hope(s) of sth
hope not a hope in hell
hope not get one's hopes up
hope pin one's hopes on so/sth
hope set one's hopes on so/sth
hope Where there's life there's hope.
hope While there's life there's hope.
hopper in the hopper
horizon expand one's horizons
horizon loom large (on the horizon)
horizon on the horizon
horn blow one's own horn
horn come out (of) the little end of the horn
horn draw in one's horns
horn hair and hide(, horns and tallow)
horn horn in (on so)
horn horn in (on sth)
horn lock horns (with so)
horn on the horns of a dilemma
horn pull in one's horns
horn take the bull by the horns
horn toot one's own horn
hornet mad as a hornet
hornet stir up a hornet's nest

horror in horror
horror throw one's hands up in horror
horse back the wrong horse
horse beat a dead horse
horse change horses in midstream
horse change horses in the middle of the stream
horse charley horse
horse dark horse
horse Don't change horses in midstream.
horse Don't look a gift horse in the mouth.
horse Don't put the cart before the horse.
horse drive a coach and horses through sth
horse eat like a horse
horse Every horse thinks its own pack heaviest.
horse flog a dead horse
horse For want of a nail the shoe was lost; for want of a shoe the horse was lost; and for want of a horse the man was lost.
horse get (down) off one's high horse
horse get on one's horse
horse get sth straight from the horse's mouth
horse go the way of the horse and buggy
horse Hold your horses!
horse horse and buggy
horse horse and carriage
horse horse around (with so/sth)
horse horse of a different color
horse horse of another color
horse horse sense
horse I could eat a horse!
horse (I'd) better get on my horse.
horse If two ride on a horse, one must ride behind.
horse If wishes were horses, then beggars would ride.
horse Lock the stable door after the horse is stolen.
horse look a gift horse in the mouth
horse nod is as good as a wink to a blind horse.
horse on one's high horse
horse one-horse town
horse play the horses
horse put a horse out to pasture
horse put the cart before the horse
horse Shut the stable door after the horse has bolted.
horse (straight) from the horse's mouth
horse strong as a horse
horse Wild horses couldn't drag so away (from sth).
horse You can lead a horse to water, but you can't make it drink.
horseback on horseback
horseshoe Close only counts in horseshoes (and hand grenades).
hose hose so down
hose hose so/sth down
hospital rush so to the hospital
hostage hold so hostage
hostage take so hostage
hot blow hot and cold
hot drop so/sth like a hot potato

hot full of hot air
hot have the hots for so
hot hot and bothered
hot hot and heavy
hot hot as fire
hot hot as hell
hot Hot damn!
hot Hot diggety (dog)!
hot hot enough to burn a polar bear's butt
hot hot off the press
hot hot on so's heels
hot hot on sth
hot hot on the trail (of so/sth or some creature)
hot hot ticket
hot hot under the collar
hot Hot ziggety!
hot in hot water (with so) (about so/sth)
hot in the hot seat
hot (Is it) hot enough for you?
hot make it hot for so
hot not so hot
hot *on so's heels
hot on the hot seat
hot piping hot
hot Strike while the iron is hot.
hotbed hotbed of sth
hotcake sell like hotcakes
hotfoot hotfoot it (off to) somewhere
hotfoot hotfoot it out of somewhere
hound clean as a hound's tooth
hound hound so from some place
hound hound so or an animal **down**
hound hound so out (of sth or some place)
hound hound sth out of so
hound run with the hare and hunt with the hounds
hour after hours
hour all hours (of the day and night)
hour at all hours (of the day and night)
hour at the bottom of the hour
hour at the eleventh hour
hour at the top of the hour
hour banker's hours
hour by the hour
hour darkest hour is just before the dawn.
hour eleventh-hour decision
hour for hours on end
hour happy hour
hour keep banker's hours
hour keep late hours
hour on the hour
hour rush hour
hour small hours (of the night)
hour There aren't enough hours in the day.
hour till all hours (of the day and night)
hour until all hours
hour wee hours (of the night)
house bring the house down
house Burn not your house to fright the mouse away.
house eat so out of house and home
house end up in the poorhouse
house find oneself in the doghouse
house house divided against itself cannot stand.
house house moss
house house of correction
house house of ill fame

house house of ill repute
house in the doghouse
house in the poorhouse
house keep house
house like a house on fire
house live in the poorhouse
house Men make houses, women make homes.
house My house is your house.
house on the house
house Our house is your house.
house People who live in glass houses shouldn't throw stones.
house put one's house in order
house put one's own house in order
house put so into the doghouse
house set one's house in order
house Welcome to our house.
household household name
household household word
hover hover around (so/sth)
hover hover between sth and sth else
hover hover over so/sth
how And how!
how fine how do you do
how Half the world knows not how the other half lives.
how How about a lift?
how How about that!
how How about you?
how How (are) you doing?
how How (are) you feeling?
how How are you getting on?
how How bout them apples?
how How can I serve you?
how How come?
how How could you (do sth)?
how How do you do.
how How do you know?
how How do you like school?
how How do you like that?
how How do you like them apples?
how How do you like this weather?
how How does that grab you?
how How dumb do you think I am?
how How goes it?
how How goes it (with you)?
how How (have) you been?
how How is so fixed for sth?
how How is so getting along?
how How is so making out?
how How many times do I have to tell you?
how How may I help you?
how How's business?
how How's by you?
how How's every little thing?
how How's it going?
how How's (it) with you?
how How's my boy?
how How's that again?
how How's the boy?
how How's the family?
how How's the wife?
how How's the world (been) treating you?
how How's tricks?
how How's your family?
how How should I know?
how How so?
how How the mighty have fallen.
how how the other half lives
how How will I know you?

how How will I recognize you?
how How're things going?
how How're things (with you)?
how (My,) how time flies.
how no matter how you slice it
how That's a fine how-do-you-do.
howdy Boy howdy!
howdy howdy and a half
howl howl at so/sth
howl howl so down
howl howl with sth
hoyle according to Hoyle
huckleberry above one's huckleberry
huddle go into a huddle
huddle huddle around so/sth
huddle huddle so together
huddle huddle (up) (together)
hue hue and cry
hue raise a hue and cry (about sth)
huey hang a huey
huff huff and puff
huff in a huff
hug commode-hugging drunk
hum hum with activity
human everything humanly possible
human Hope springs eternal (in the human breast).
human milk of human kindness
human To err is human(, to forgive divine).
humble eat humble pie
humble in my humble opinion
humidity It's not the heat, it's the humidity.
humor sense of humor
hump over the hump
hunch have a hunch (that sth is the case)
hunch hunch over
hunch hunch sth up
hunch hunch up
hundred first hundred years are the hardest.
hundred one in a hundred
hundred turn one hundred and eighty degrees
hundred turn three hundred and sixty degrees
hung have sth hung up and salted
hung hung up (on so/sth)
hung might as well be hung for a sheep as (for) a lamb
hung think so hung the moon (and stars)
hunger hunger after sth
hunger hunger for so/sth
hunger Hunger is the best sauce.
hunger (strictly) from hunger
hungry go hungry
hungry hungry as a bear
hungry hungry as a hunter
hungry hungry for sth
hunker hunker down (on sth)
hunker hunker down to sth
hunt hunt after so/sth
hunt hunt for so/sth
hunt hunt high and low (for so/sth)
hunt hunt so/sth down
hunt hunt so/sth out
hunt hunt so/sth up
hunt hunt through sth
hunt run with the hare and hunt with the hounds
hunter hungry as a hunter

hurl hurl insults (at so)
hurl hurl so/sth at so/sth
hurl hurl so/sth down
hurl hurl so/sth into sth
hurl hurl so/sth out (of some place)
hurl hurl sth around
hurl hurl sth away (from so/sth)
hurrah last hurrah
hurricane eye of the hurricane
hurry get a hurry on
hurry Here's your hat, what's your hurry?
hurry hurry away
hurry hurry back (to so/sth)
hurry hurry down (to somewhere)
hurry hurry off
hurry hurry on
hurry hurry one on one's way
hurry hurry so/sth along
hurry hurry so/sth in(to sth)
hurry hurry so/sth up
hurry hurry up
hurt cry before one is hurt
hurt Don't cry before you are hurt.
hurt hurt for so/sth
hurt hurt so's feelings
hurt hurtin' for sth
hurt (It) doesn't hurt to ask.
hurt (It) never hurts to ask.
hurt little (hard) work never hurt anyone.
hurt not hurt a flea
hurt Sticks and stones may break my bones, but words will never hurt me.
hurt What one doesn't know won't hurt one.
hurt What you don't know won't hurt you.
hurtle hurtle through sth
husband good husband makes a good wife.
hush hush fell over so/sth
hush hush money
hush hush so up
hush hush sth up
hush hush up
hush Hush your mouth!
hustle hustle and bustle
hustle hustle up
Hyde Jekyll and Hyde
hygienically hygienically challenged
hymnbook sing from the same hymnbook
hype hype so/sth (up)
hypothesize hypothesize about sth
hypothesize hypothesize on sth
I Am I glad to see you!
I Am I my brother's keeper?
I Am I right?
I Anyone I know?
I As I live and breathe!
I as I see it
I as I was saying
I Ask me no questions, I'll tell you no lies.
I Can I help you?
I Can I leave a message?
I Can I see you again?
I Can I see you in my office?
I Can I speak to so?
I Can I take a message?
I Can I take your order (now)?
I Can I tell her who's calling?

I Can I use your powder room?
I Can't say (a)s I do(, can't say (a)s I don't).
I Could I be excused?
I (Could I) buy you a drink?
I Could I call you?
I Could I come in?
I Could I get by, please?
I (Could I) get you something (to drink)?
I (Could I) give you a lift?
I Could I have a lift?
I Could I have a word with you?
I Could I have so call you?
I Could I have the bill?
I Could I help you?
I Could I join you?
I Could I leave a message?
I Could I see you again?
I Could I see you in my office?
I Could I speak to so?
I Could I take a message?
I Could I take your order (now)?
I Could I tell him who's calling?
I Could I use your powder room?
I Do as I say, not as I do.
I Do I have to paint (you) a picture?
I Do I have to spell it out (for you)?
I Do I make myself (perfectly) clear?
I Do I need to paint you a picture?
I (Do you) care if I join you?
I (Do you) know what I mean?
I (Do you) know what I'm saying?
I (Do you) mind if I join you?
I Doctor Livingstone, I presume?
I Don't do anything I wouldn't do.
I Don't I know it!
I Don't I know you from somewhere?
I for all I care
I for all I know
I from where I stand
I Have I got something for you!
I Have I made myself clear?
I Haven't I seen you somewhere before?
I How can I serve you?
I How dumb do you think I am?
I How many times do I have to tell you?
I How may I help you?
I How should I know?
I How will I know you?
I How will I recognize you?
I I am not my brother's keeper.
I I am so sure!
I (I) beg your pardon, but...
I I believe so.
I I believe we've met.
I I can accept that.
I I can live with that.
I (I) can too.
I I can't accept that.
I (I) can't argue with that.
I (I) can't beat that.
I I can't believe (that)!
I (I) can't complain.
I I can't get over sth!
I (I) can't help it.
I (I) can't rightly say.
I (I) can't say (as) I do.
I (I) can't say (as) I have.
I (I) can't say for sure.
I (I) can't say's I do.

I (I) can't say's I have.
I (I) can't say that I do.
I (I) can't say that I have.
I (I) can't thank you enough.
I (I) can't top that.
I (I) changed my mind.
I (I) could be better.
I (I) could be worse.
I I could eat a horse!
I (I) couldn't ask for more.
I I couldn't ask you to do that.
I (I) could(n't) care less.
I (I) couldn't help it.
I I declare (to goodness)!
I I didn't catch the name.
I I didn't hear you.
I I didn't (quite) catch that (last) remark.
I I do believe.
I I (do) declare!
I I don't believe it!
I (I) don't believe I've had the pleasure.
I I don't believe this!
I I don't care.
I (I) don't care if I do.
I I don't have time to breathe.
I I don't have time to catch my breath.
I I don't know.
I I don't mean maybe!
I (I) don't mind if I do.
I I don't mind telling you (sth).
I I don't rightly know.
I (I) don't think so.
I I don't understand (it).
I I don't want to alarm you, but
I I don't want to sound like a busybody, but
I I don't want to upset you, but
I I don't want to wear out my welcome.
I I don't wonder.
I I doubt it.
I I doubt that.
I I expect.
I I felt like a penny waiting for change.
I I guess.
I (I) had a good time.
I I had a lovely time.
I (I) had a nice time.
I (I) hate to eat and run.
I (I have) no problem with that.
I (I have) nothing to complain about.
I (I) have to be moving along.
I (I) have to go now.
I (I) have to move along.
I (I) have to push off.
I (I) have to run along.
I (I) have to shove off.
I I have to wash a few things out.
I (I) haven't got all day.
I (I) haven't seen you in a long time.
I (I) haven't seen you in a month of Sundays.
I I hear what you're saying.
I I hear you.
I I hope all goes well.
I (I) hope not.
I (I) hope so.
I (I) hope to see you again (sometime).
I I just have this feeling.
I (I) just want(ed) to mention sth.
I (I) just want(ed) to say sth.
I I kid you not.

I I know (just) what you mean.
I (I) love it!
I I must be off.
I I must say good night.
I I need it yesterday.
I (I) never heard of such a thing!
I (I) never thought I'd see you here!
I I owe you one.
I I promise you!
I (I) read you loud and clear.
I (I) really must go.
I I rest my case.
I I spoke out of turn.
I I spoke too soon.
I I suppose.
I I suspect.
I I swan!
I I think not.
I I think so.
I (I was) just wondering.
I I was up all night with a sick friend.
I I wasn't brought up in the woods to be scared by owls.
I I wish I'd said that.
I (I) wonder if
I (I) won't breathe a word (of it).
I I won't give up without a fight.
I (I) won't tell a soul.
I (I) would if I could(, but I can't).
I I would like you to meet so.
I (I) wouldn't bet on it.
I (I) wouldn't count on it.
I (I) wouldn't if I were you.
I (I) wouldn't know.
I I wouldn't touch it with a ten-foot pole.
I I wouldn't wish that on a dog.
I I wouldn't wish that on my worst enemy.
I (I'd be) happy to (do sth).
I I'd bet money (on it).
I (I'd) better be going.
I (I'd) better get moving.
I (I'd) better get on my horse.
I (I'd) better hit the road.
I I'd (just) as leave do sth
I I'd (just) as soon (as) do sth
I I'd like (for) you to meet so.
I I'd like (to have) a word with you.
I I'd like to speak to so, please.
I I'd rather face a firing squad than do sth
I if I were you
I if I've told you once, I've told you a thousand times
I I'll be a monkey's uncle!
I (I'll) be right there.
I (I'll) be right with you.
I (I'll) be seeing you.
I I('ll) bet
I I'll bite.
I I'll call back later.
I (I'll) catch you later.
I I'll drink to that!
I I'll eat my hat.
I I'll get back to you (on that).
I I'll get right on it.
I I'll have the same.
I I'll have to beg off.
I I'll (have to) let you go.
I I'll look you up when I'm in town.
I I'll put a stop to that.
I (I'll) see you in a little while.
I I'll see you later.

I (I'll) see you next year.
I (I'll) see you (real) soon.
I (I'll) see you then.
I (I'll) see you tomorrow.
I (I'll) talk to you soon.
I I'll thank you to keep your opinions to yourself.
I I'll thank you to mind your own business.
I (I'll) try to catch you later.
I (I'll) try to catch you some other time.
I (I'm) afraid not.
I (I'm) afraid so.
I I'm all ears.
I I'm awful at names.
I I'm busy.
I I'm cool.
I I'm damned if I do and damned if I don't.
I (I'm) delighted to have you (here).
I (I'm) delighted to make your acquaintance.
I (I'm) doing okay.
I I'm easy (to please).
I (I'm) feeling okay.
I (I'm) glad to hear it.
I (I'm) glad you could come.
I (I'm) glad you could drop by.
I I'm gone.
I (I'm) having a wonderful time; wish you were here.
I I'm having quite a time.
I (I'm) having the time of my life.
I I'm history.
I (I'm) just getting by.
I I'm just looking.
I (I'm just) minding my own business.
I (I'm) (just) plugging along.
I (I'm) (just) thinking out loud.
I I'm like you
I I'm listening.
I I'm not finished with you.
I I'm not kidding.
I I'm not surprised.
I I'm off.
I I'm only looking.
I I'm out of here.
I (I'm) pleased to meet you.
I (I'm) (really) fed up (with so/sth).
I (I'm) sorry.
I (I'm) sorry to hear that.
I (I'm) sorry you asked (that).
I I'm speechless.
I I'm terrible at names.
I (I'm) (very) glad to meet you.
I I'm with you.
I Is there some place I can wash up?
I (I've) been getting by.
I (I've) been keeping cool.
I (I've) been keeping myself busy.
I (I've) been keeping out of trouble.
I (I've) been okay.
I (I've) been there(, done that).
I (I've) been under the weather.
I I've done my do.
I (I've) (got) better things to do.
I (I've) got to be shoving off.
I I've got to fly.
I (I've) got to get moving.
I (I've) got to go.
I (I've) got to go home and get my beauty sleep.
I (I've) got to hit the road.

I (I've) got to run.
I (I've) got to shove off.
I (I've) got to split.
I (I've) got to take off.
I I've got work to do.
I I('ve) gotta fly.
I I've had a lovely time.
I I've had enough of this!
I I've had it up to here (with so/sth).
I I've heard so much about you.
I (I've) never been better.
I (I've) seen better.
I I've seen better heads on nickel beers.
I (I've) seen worse.
I (just) as I expected
I like I was saying
I Likewise(, I'm sure).
I Lord knows I've tried.
I May I be excused?
I May I help you?
I May I see you again?
I May I speak to so?
I May I take a message?
I May I take your order (now)?
I May I tell him who's calling?
I May I use your powder room?
I need I remind you that...
I Need I say more?
I Neither can I.
I No more than I have to.
I Not if I see you first.
I Not if I see you sooner.
I (Now,) where was I?
I See if I care!
I So do I.
I so mad I could scream
I Sorry (that) I asked.
I Suppose I do?
I Suppose I don't?
I Supposing I do?
I Supposing I don't?
I sure as I'm standing here
I That ain't the way I heard it.
I That's what I say.
I the way I see it
I There but for the grace of God (go I).
I This is where I came in.
I try as I may
I try as I might
I (Well,) I never!
I (Well,) I'll be!
I What can I do for you?
I What can I say?
I What can I tell you?
I What else can I do?
I What else can I do for you?
I What if I do?
I What if I don't?
I What more can I do?
I Where can I wash up?
I Where will I find you?
I Will I see you again?
I You know what I mean?
I You scratch my back and I'll scratch yours.
ice Bite the ice!
ice break the ice
ice cut no ice (with so)
ice ice over
ice ice sth down
ice ice sth up
ice ice up

ice icing on the cake
ice (It) don't cut no ice (with so).
ice on ice
ice on thin ice
ice put so/sth on ice
ice skate on thin ice
ice stink on ice
ice walk on thin ice
iceberg tip of the iceberg
icing icing on the cake
idea bright idea
idea flirt with the idea of doing sth
idea foggiest (idea)
idea not a glimmer (of an idea)
idea put ideas into so's head
idea rough idea (about sth)
idea The very idea!
idea What's the (big) idea?
identify identify (oneself) with so/sth
identify identify so as so
identify identify so/sth by sth
identify identify so/sth with so/sth
identity case of mistaken identity
idiot take so for an idiot
idle devil finds work for idle hands to do.
idle idle about
idle idle brain is the devil's workshop.
idle Idle folk have the least leisure.
idle Idle people have the least leisure.
idle idle sth away
idle Idleness is the root of all evil.
idleness Idleness is the root of all evil.
idly sit idly by
idly stand idly by
idolize idolize so/sth as sth
if couldn't pour water out of a boot (if there was instructions on the heel)
if Damned if you do, damned if you don't.
if (Do you) care if I join you?
if (Do you) mind if...?
if (Do you) mind if I join you?
if even if it kills me
if (I) don't care if I do.
if (I) don't mind if I do.
if (I) wonder if
if (I) would if I could(, but I can't).
if (I) wouldn't if I were you.
if If a thing is worth doing, it's worth doing well.
if If a toady frog had wings, he wouldn't bump his ass.
if If anything can go wrong, it will.
if if anything should happen
if If at first you don't succeed, try, try again.
if If frogs had wheels, they wouldn't bump their butts.
if If God did not exist, it would be necessary to invent Him.
if if I were you
if If ifs and ands were pots and pans (there'd be no work for tinkers' hands).
if If it ain't chickens, it's feathers.
if If it was a snake it woulda bit you.
if if I've told you once, I've told you a thousand times
if if looks could kill
if if my memory serves me correctly
if if not
if if one knows what's good for one

if if one's a day
if if push comes to shove
if if so
if If that don't beat a pig a-pecking!
if If that don't beat all!
if if the going gets tough
if If the mountain will not come to Mahomet, Mahomet must go to the mountain.
if If the shoe fits(, wear it).
if if the truth were known
if if (the) worst comes to (the) worst
if If there's anything you need, don't hesitate to ask.
if If two ride on a horse, one must ride behind.
if If wishes were horses, then beggars would ride.
if If you can't be good, be careful.
if If you can't beat them, join them.
if If you can't lick 'em, join 'em.
if If you can't stand the heat, get out of the kitchen.
if If you don't like it, (you can) lump it.
if If you don't make mistakes, you don't make anything.
if If you don't mind!
if If you don't see what you want, please ask (for it).
if if you get my drift
if if you know what's good for you
if If you lie down with dogs, you will get up with fleas.
if if you must
if If you play with fire, you get burned.
if if you please
if If you run after two hares, you will catch neither.
if If you want a thing done well, do it yourself.
if If you want peace, (you must) prepare for war.
if If you would be well served, serve yourself.
if if you would(, please)
if if you'll pardon the expression
if If you're born to be hanged, then you'll never be drowned.
if if you've a mind to do sth
if I'm damned if I do and damned if I don't.
if look as if butter wouldn't melt in one's mouth
if make as if to do sth
if Mind if...?
if no ifs, ands, or buts (about it)
if Not if I see you first.
if Not if I see you sooner.
if not know if one is coming or going
if See if I care!
if sound as if
if What if...?
if What would you say if...?
ignorance Ignorance is bliss.
ignorance Ignorance (of the law) is no excuse (for breaking it).
ignorance keep so in ignorance (about so/sth)
ignorance Where ignorance is bliss, 'tis folly to be wise.
ignorant play ignorant
ill fall ill
ill house of ill fame

ill house of ill repute
ill ill at ease
ill ill will
ill ill-disposed to doing sth
ill ill-gotten gains
ill It's an ill bird that fouls its own nest.
ill It's an ill wind that blows nobody (any) good.
ill It's ill waiting for dead men's shoes.
ill Never speak ill of the dead.
ill speak ill of so
ill take ill
ill woman of ill repute
illuminate illuminate sth with sth
illustrate illustrate sth with sth
image spit and image of so
image spitting image of so
imagination by any stretch of the imagination
imagination capture so's imagination
imagine Can you imagine?
imagine imagine so/sth as so/sth
imagine Imagine that!
imbue imbue so with sth
imitation Imitation is the sincerest form of flattery.
immediate immediate occupancy
immemorial since time immemorial
immerse immerse so/sth in sth
immigrate immigrate (in)to some place (from some place)
immunize immunize so against sth
impact have an impact on so/sth
impact impact (up)on so/sth
impact upon impact
impair hearing impaired
impair visually impaired
impale impale so/sth on sth
impart impart sth to so/sth
impartial fair and impartial
impasse come to an impasse
impasse reach an impasse
impeach impeach so for sth
impinge impinge (up)on so/sth
implant implant sth in(to) so/sth
implicate implicate so (in sth)
import import sth (from sth) ((in)to sth)
important important milestone in so's life
impose impose sth (up)on so
impose impose (up)on so
impose superimpose sth on(to) so/sth
impossible difficult is done at once; the impossible takes a little longer.
impregnate impregnate sth with sth
impress impress so as sth
impress impress so by sth
impress impress so with so/sth
impress impress sth into sth
impress impress sth (up)on so
impress impress sth (up)on sth
impression First impressions are the most lasting.
impression leave an impression (on so)
impression leave so with an impression
impression make an impression on so
imprint imprint sth into sth
imprint imprint sth on(to) sth
imprint imprint sth with sth
imprison imprison so in sth
improve improve (up)on sth

901

improvise improvise on sth
impulse on impulse
impunity with impunity
impute impute sth to so/sth
in abet so in sth
in abound in sth
in absorb oneself in so/sth
in ace in the hole
in act in earnest
in advanced in years
in agree (with sth) (in sth)
in aid so in doing sth
in aid so in sth
in air one's dirty linen in public
in alike as (two) peas in a pod
in All cats are gray in the dark.
in all in
in (all) in one breath
in (all) in the family
in All's fair in love and war.
in allow so/sth in
in along in years
in (another) nail in so's or sth's coffin
in ants in one's pants
in any port in a storm
in appear in court
in appear in sth
in arbitrate in a dispute
in arm in arm
in arrive in force
in arrive in the (very) nick of time
in arrive (some place) in sth
in arrive some place in a body
in ask so in
in assist in sth
in assist so in sth
in at this point (in time)
in attack in force
in attire so in sth
in awkward as a bull in a china shop
in babe in arms
in babe in the woods
in back in(to) (the) harness
in ball is in so's court
in bang sth in
in barge in (on so/sth)
in bash sth in
in bask in sth
in bathe so/sth in sth
in be in aid of
in bear in mind that...
in bear so/sth in mind
in beard the lion in his den
in Beauty is in the eye of the beholder.
in bee in one's bonnet
in believe in so/sth
in bend in
in best things come in small packages.
in best things in life are free.
in big frog in a small pond
in biggest frog in the puddle
in biggest toad in the puddle
in bind so/sth up (in sth)
in bird in the hand is worth two in the bush.
in Birds in their little nests agree.
in blend in (with so/sth)
in blessing in disguise
in block so/sth in some place
in blow in
in blow up in so's face
in born with a silver spoon in one's mouth

in both sheets in the wind
in box so in
in box so/sth in
in boxed in
in boys in the back room
in break in (on so)
in break in (on sth)
in break out in a cold sweat
in break out in a rash
in break out (in pimples)
in break so in
in break sth in
in breathe in
in breathe in
in breeze in (from some place)
in bring a verdict in
in bring an amount of money in
in bring out the best in so
in bring so in (on sth)
in bring so/sth in
in bring so/sth out in droves
in bring sth out (in so)
in bring sth out in the open
in broad in the beam
in buckle so in
in build castles in Spain
in build castles in the air
in build so in
in build sth in
in bull in a china shop
in bundle so up (in sth)
in bung sth in
in burn one's bridges in front of one
in burn so in effigy
in burn sth in
in burst in (on so/sth)
in burst in ((up)on so/sth)
in burst in (with sth)
in bury one's head in the sand
in bury oneself in sth
in bury so/sth in sth
in bushel and a peck (and some in a gourd)
in busy as a fish peddler in Lent
in butt in (on so/sth)
in Butter wouldn't melt (in so's mouth).
in butterflies in one's stomach
in buy a pig in a poke
in cage so/sth in
in cage so/sth up (in sth)
in call in sick
in call in (to some place)
in call so in (for sth)
in call so/sth in
in call sth (back) in
in call sth in
in camp in the boondocks
in camp in the boonies
in Can I see you in my office?
in can't carry a tune in a bucket
in can't carry a tune in a bushel basket
in can't carry a tune in a paper sack
in can't find one's butt with both hands (in broad daylight)
in can't see a hole in a ladder
in can't see one's hand in front of one's face
in carve sth in
in carved in stone
in case in point
in cash in (on sth)
in cash (one's chips) in
in cash sth in

in cast in the same mold
in cast one's lot in (with so/sth)
in cat in gloves catches no mice.
in catch so in the act (of doing sth)
in catch so/sth in sth
in catch so up in sth
in catch sth up in sth
in caught in the act
in caught in the crossfire
in caught up in sth
in cave in
in change horses in midstream
in change horses in the middle of the stream
in chase so or an animal in
in check in (at sth)
in check in (on so/sth)
in check in (with so)
in check so in
in check sth in
in chime in (with sth)
in chink in one's armor
in chip in (on sth) (for so)
in chip in (with sth) (on sth) (for so)
in chip sth in (on sth)
in chisel in (on so/sth)
in chuck it in
in cloak so/sth in secrecy
in clock in
in clock so in
in close (in) around so/sth
in close in for the kill
in close in (on so/sth)
in Close only counts in horseshoes (and hand grenades).
in close so/sth in (sth)
in clothe so in sth
in clue so in (on sth)
in cold as a welldigger's ass (in January)
in cold as a welldigger's feet (in January)
in color sth in
in come down in the world
in come in
in come (in) on a wing and a prayer
in Come (on) in.
in Come on in, the water's fine!
in come out (in bloom)
in come out (in blossom)
in come out in droves
in come out in favor of so/sth
in come out in force
in come out in large numbers
in come out in sth
in come out in the open
in come out in the wash
in Come right in.
in come up in the world
in compete in sth
in concern so in sth
in confide in so
in confide sth in so
in confirm so in sth
in contradiction in terms
in couch sth in sth
in Could I come in?
in Could I see you in my office?
in couldn't hit a bull in the ass with a bass fiddle
in count so in (for sth)
in count sth in
in cover so in sth

in crash course in sth
in crazy in the head
in crick in one's back
in crick in one's neck
in crowd in
in cruise around in sth
in crush sth in
in cry in one's beer
in cry out (in sth)
in cue so in
in culminate in sth
in cut in (ahead of so/sth)
in cut in (on so)
in cut in (on sth)
in cut in (with sth)
in cut so in (on sth)
in dabble in sth
in dangle sth in front of so
in dart in and out
in day in and day out
in dead in so's or an animal's tracks
in dead in the water
in deal in sth
in deal so in
in decide in favor of so/sth
in deck so/sth out (in sth)
in delight in so/sth
in detect sth in
in diamond in the rough
in die in one's boots
in die in sth
in differ in sth
in dig one's heels in
in dig so/sth in sth
in dine in
in disguise so in sth
in disappointed in so/sth
in dissolve in sth
in dissolve sth in sth
in dive in with both feet
in Do not wash your dirty linen in public.
in do so in
in do sth hand in hand
in do sth in
in doesn't have enough sense to come in out of the rain
in doesn't know his ass from a hole in the ground
in dog in the manger
in done in
in Don't change horses in midstream.
in Don't get your bowels in an uproar!
in don't give a hoot (in hell's hollow)
in don't have a pot to piss in (or a window to throw it out of)
in Don't look a gift horse in the mouth.
in Don't put all your eggs in one basket.
in Don't spend it all in one place.
in double in brass (as sth)
in down in the dumps
in down in the mouth
in drag so in (on sth)
in drape so/sth in sth
in draw a line in the sand
in draw in one's horns
in drench so/sth in sth
in dress so/sth up (in sth)
in drill so in sth
in drink sth in
in drop behind (in sth)
in drop in (on so)

in drop in one's tracks
in Drop in sometime.
in drop in the bucket
in drop in the ocean
in drop in (to say hello)
in drown in sth
in drown so in sth
in drown so or an animal in sth
in dub sth in
in dwell in an ivory tower
in dyed-in-the-wool
in easy as shooting fish in a barrel
in eat in
in educate so in sth
in embed so/sth in sth
in embed sth in sth
in embody sth in sth
in embroil so in sth
in employ so in sth
in encase so in sth
in encourage so in sth
in end in itself
in end in sth
in end up in the poorhouse
in enfold so in sth
in engage in small talk
in engage so/sth in sth
in engraved in stone
in engross so in sth
in engulf so/sth in sth
in enlist oneself in sth
in enlist so in sth
in enmesh so/sth in sth
in enroll (so) in sth
in ensconce oneself in sth
in enshrine so in one's heart
in enshrine so's memory in one's heart
in enshrine sth in sth
in ensnare so/sth in sth
in entangle so/sth in sth
in enter in sth
in entomb so or an animal in sth
in entrap so (in sth) (with sth)
in envelop so/sth in so/sth
in equal so/sth in sth
in establish so/sth in sth
in even in the best of times
in examine so in sth
in exceed so/sth in sth
in excel in sth
in excite sth in so
in exercise so or an animal in sth
in expend sth in sth
in experiment in sth
in express sth in round figures
in express sth in round numbers
in exult in sth
in eyes like two burnt holes in a blanket
in fade sth in
in fail in sth
in fall behind (in sth)
in fall head over heels in love (with so)
in fall in
in falter in sth
in fat is in the fire.
in feather in one's cap
in feature so in sth
in feel sth in one's bones
in fence an animal in
in fence so in
in fence sth in
in fetch sth in

in figure in sth
in figure so/sth in
in fill in
in fill so in (on so/sth)
in fill sth in
in find it in one's heart (to do sth)
in find it in oneself (to do sth)
in find oneself in a bind
in find oneself in a jam
in find oneself in the doghouse
in find oneself in the market (for sth)
in find oneself in the public eye
in find so in
in find sth in mint condition
in first thing (in the morning)
in fish in troubled waters
in fit in (somehow) (with sth)
in fit in (with so/sth)
in flash in the pan
in fling sth up in so's face
in fling sth up (in sth)
in fly in
in fly in the ointment
in follow in so's tracks
in Fools rush in where angels fear to tread.
in foot in both camps
in foot-in-mouth disease
in For crying in a bucket!
in four sheets in the wind
in frame sth in sth
in freeze so/sth in one's memory
in friend in need is a friend indeed.
in frighten so or an animal in
in frog in one's throat
in from here on (in)
in gain in sth
in garb so in sth
in Garbage in, garbage out.
in garner sth in
in gather sth in
in get a say (in sth)
in get a word in edgewise
in get ahead (in sth)
in get in deeper
in get it in the neck
in get on (in years)
in get one's ass in gear
in get one's bowels in an uproar
in get one's ducks in a row
in get one's foot in the door
in get one's tail in gear
in get so across (in a good way)
in get so in a family way
in get sth down (in black and white)
in give in
in glass sth in
in glory in sth
in go arm in arm
in go (a)round in circles
in go down in defeat
in go down in flames
in go down (in history) (as so/sth)
in go hand in hand
in go home in a box
in go in
in Go jump in the lake!
in go out in force
in go out in search of so/sth
in Go play in the traffic.
in go to hell in a bucket
in go up in flames
in go up in smoke

in God's in his heaven; all's right with the world.
in Good things come in small packages.
in gotta get up pretty early in the morning to do sth
in graduate (in sth) (with sth)
in grandfather so/sth in
in Great day (in the morning)!
in ground so in sth
in grounded in (actual) fact
in grovel (about) in sth
in grow in sth
in growing youth has a wolf in his belly.
in grub around (in sth)
in half in the bag
in hand in glove (with so)
in hand in hand
in hand in sth
in hand sth in
in hand sth in (to so)
in hang in the balance
in Hang in there.
in hang so in effigy
in hang up (in so's ear)
in happen in the (very) nick of time
in happy as a clam (in butter sauce)
in haul so in
in have a finger in the pie
in have a hitch in one's gitalong
in have a keen interest in sth
in have a place in sth
in have a run-in (with so/sth)
in have a soft spot (in one's heart) for so or an animal
in have a stake in sth
in have bats in one's belfry
in have confidence in so
in have eyes in the back of one's head
in have faith in so
in have it (all) over so/sth (in sth)
in have it in for so
in have it in one to do sth
in have it made in the shade
in have just one oar in the water
in have one foot in the grave
in have one in the oven
in have one's ass in a sling
in have one's finger in too many pies
in have one's finger(s) in the till
in have one's hand in sth
in have one's hand in the till
in have one's head in the clouds
in have one's head in the sand
in have one's heart in one's mouth
in have one's heart in the right place
in have one's mind in the gutter
in have one's name inscribed in the book of life
in have one's nose in a book
in have one's nose in the air
in have one's words stick in one's throat
in have rocks in one's head
in have so in
in have so/sth in mind
in have so/sth in one's hands
in have so/sth in one's sights
in have so/sth in tow
in have so/sth (well) in hand
in have sth in common (with so/sth)
in have sth in hand
in have sth in stock

in have sth in store (for so)
in have sth stick in one's craw
in have the ball in one's court
in have too many irons in the fire
in head over heels in debt
in head over heels in love (with so)
in hedge so in
in hedge so/sth in
in help so in sth
in hem so/sth in
in Here's mud in your eye.
in hide one's face in shame
in hide one's head in the sand
in hide sth in sth
in hit out (at so/sth) (in sth)
in hit so in sth
in hold so/sth in check
in hold so/sth in high regard
in hold so/sth in low regard
in hold so/sth in reserve
in hold sth in
in hold sth in abeyance
in hold sth in store (for so)
in hole in one
in hole in the wall
in home in (on so/sth)
in Hope springs eternal (in the human breast).
in horn in (on so)
in horn in (on sth)
in (I) haven't seen you in a long time.
in (I) haven't seen you in a month of Sundays.
in I wasn't brought up in the woods to be scared by owls.
in I'll look you up when I'm in town.
in (I'll) see you in a little while.
in immerse so/sth in sth
in implicate so (in sth)
in important milestone in so's life
in imprison so in sth
in in a bad mood
in in a bad way
in in a big way
in in a bind
in in a (blue) funk
in in a body
in in a cold sweat
in in a (constant) state of flux
in in a coon's age
in in a dead heat
in in a delicate condition
in in a dither
in in a family way
in in a fix
in in a flash
in in a fog
in in a heartbeat
in in a huff
in in a jam
in in a jiffy
in in a lather
in in a little bit
in in a mad rush
in in a month of Sundays
in in a nutshell
in In a pig's ass!
in In a pig's ear!
in In a pig's eye!
in in a pinch
in in a pique
in in a (pretty) pickle
in in a quandary

in in a rut
in in a sense
in in (a) shambles
in in (a) single file
in in a snit
in in a split second
in in a stage whisper
in in a stew (about so/sth)
in in a stupor
in in a (tight) spot
in in a tizzy
in in a twit
in in a twitter
in in a vicious circle
in in a word
in in a world of one's own
in in abeyance
in in accord (with so/sth) (about so/sth)
in in accordance with sth
in in addition (to sth)
in in advance
in in agreement (with so/sth)
in in (all) good conscience
in in all my born days
in in all probability
in in an age of years
in in an interesting condition
in in an ivory tower
in in and of itself
in in any case
in in any event
in in any way, shape, or form
in in apple-pie order
in in arrears
in in (at) one ear and out (of) the other
in in at the kill
in in awe (of so/sth)
in in bad faith
in in bad shape
in in bad sorts
in in bad taste
in in bad (with so)
in in behalf of so
in in between
in in black and white
in in bloom
in in blossom
in in brief
in in broad daylight
in in bulk
in in business
in in cahoots (with so)
in in care of so
in in case of sth
in in case (sth happens)
in in character
in in charge (of so/sth)
in in clover
in in cold blood
in in cold storage
in in concert (with so)
in in condition
in in consequence (of sth)
in in consideration of sth
in in contact (with so/sth)
in in contempt (of court)
in in control of so/sth
in in creation
in in custody (of so/sth)
in in debt
in in deep
in in defiance (of so/sth)

in in denial
in in detail
in in dire straits
in in disguise
in in drag
in in dribs and drabs
in in droves
in in due course
in in due time
in in Dutch (with so)
in in earnest
in in effect
in in essence
in in exchange (for so/sth)
in in existence
in in fact
in in fashion
in in favor of so
in in favor (of so/sth)
in in fear and trembling
in in fine feather
in in fits and starts
in in flight
in in flux
in in focus
in in for sth
in in force
in in full flight
in in full swing
in in general
in in glowing terms
in in good condition
in in good faith
in in good hands
in in good repair
in in good shape
in in good spirits
in in good time
in in (good) (with so)
in in great demand
in in great haste
in in hand
in in harm's way
in in harmony (with so/sth)
in in heat
in in heaven
in in high cotton
in in high dudgeon
in in high gear
in in (high) hopes of sth
in in hindsight
in in hock
in in hog heaven
in in honor of so/sth
in in horror
in in hot water (with so) (about so/sth)
in in ink
in in its entirety
in in its prime
in in jeopardy
in in (just) a minute
in in (just) a second
in in keeping (with sth)
in in kind
in in labor
in in league (with so)
in in less than no time
in in lieu of sth
in In like a lion, out like a lamb.
in in limbo
in in line
in in love (with so/sth)
in in low cotton

in in luck
in in many respects
in in marching order
in in memory of so
in in midair
in in mint condition
in in my humble opinion
in in my opinion
in in my view
in in name only
in in need (of sth)
in in neutral
in in no mood to do sth
in in no time (at all)
in in no time flat
in in no uncertain terms
in in nothing flat
in in on sth
in in on the act
in in on the ground floor
in in on the kill
in in one fell swoop
in in one's birthday suit
in in one's blood
in in one's book
in in one's cups
in in one's element
in in one's glory
in in one's mind's eye
in in one's opinion
in in one's or its prime
in in one's (own) backyard
in in one's (own) (best) interest(s)
in in one's own way
in in one's right mind
in in one's salad days
in in one's second childhood
in in one's spare time
in in one's Sunday best
in in opposition (to so/sth)
in in orbit
in in order
in in other words
in in over one's head (with so/sth)
in in park
in in part
in in particular
in in passing
in in pencil
in in perpetuity
in in person
in in perspective
in in place
in in plain English
in in plain language
in in play
in in point of fact
in in poor taste
in in power
in in practice
in in press
in in print
in in private
in in progress
in in proportion
in in public
in in pursuit of sth
in in quest of so/sth
in in rags
in in rare form
in in reality
in in receipt of sth
in in recent memory

in in reduced circumstances
in in reference to so/sth
in in regard to so/sth
in in rehearsal
in in relation to so/sth
in in remission
in in retrospect
in in return for (so/sth)
in in round figures
in in round numbers
in in ruins
in in search of so/sth
in in season
in in secret
in in service
in in session
in in seventh heaven
in in shape
in in short
in in sight
in in so many words
in in some neck of the woods
in in some respects
in in some transaction for so
in in so else's place
in in so else's shoes
in in so's behalf
in in so's care
in in so's face
in in so's favor
in in so's good graces
in in so's hair
in in so's name
in in so's or sth's way
in in so's possession
in in so's prayers
in in spades
in in spite of so/sth
in in step (with so)
in in step (with so/sth)
in in step (with sth)
in in stitches
in in stock
in in storage
in in store (for so)
in in style
in in surgery
in in tall cotton
in in tandem
in in tatters
in in terms of sth
in in the absence of so/sth
in in the act (of doing sth)
in in the affirmative
in in the air
in in the altogether
in in the back
in in the bag
in in the balance
in in the ballpark
in in the best of health
in in the black
in in the blood
in in the boondocks
in in the boonies
in in the buff
in in the bull pen
in in the cards
in in the care of so
in in the case of so/sth
in in the catbird seat
in in the C.E.
in in the charge of so

in in the chips
in in the clear
in in the Common Era
in in the context of sth
in In the country of the blind, the one-eyed man is king.
in in the course of time
in in the dark (about so/sth)
in in the doghouse
in in the doldrums
in in the drink
in in the driver's seat
in in the event of sth
in in the family way
in in the fast lane
in in the final analysis
in in the first instance
in in the first place
in in the flesh
in in the forefront (of sth)
in in the groove
in in the gutter
in in the hole
in in the (home)stretch
in in the hopper
in in the hot seat
in in the interest of saving time
in in the interest of so/sth
in in the interim (between things)
in in the know
in in the lap of luxury
in in the last analysis
in in the laundry
in in (the) light of sth
in in the limelight
in in the line of duty
in in the long haul
in in the long run
in in the loop
in in the main
in in the mainstream (of sth)
in in the making
in in the market (for sth)
in in the meantime
in in the middle of nowhere
in in the money
in in the mood (for sth)
in in the near future
in in the nude
in in the offing
in in the open
in in the picture
in in the pink (of condition)
in in the pink (of health)
in in the pipeline
in in the poorhouse
in in the prime of life
in in the public eye
in in the raw
in in the rear
in in the red
in in the right
in in the road
in in the running
in in the same boat (as so)
in in the same breath
in in the second place
in in the short haul
in in the short run
in in the soup
in in the spotlight
in in the swim of things
in in the trust of so

in in the twinkling of an eye
in in the unlikely event of sth
in in the (very) nick of time
in in the wake of sth
in in the way of so('s plans)
in in the way of so/sth
in in the way of sth
in in the wind
in in the wink of an eye
in in the works
in in the world
in in the worst way
in in the wrong
in in their entirety
in in theory
in in there
in in these parts
in in thing (to do)
in ins and outs (of sth)
in in this day and age
in in those parts
in in time
in in times past
in in top form
in in touch (with so)
in in touch with so/sth
in in tow
in in transit
in in triplicate
in in trouble
in in tune
in in turn
in in two shakes of a lamb's tail
in in unison
in in use
in in vain
in in view of sth
in in vogue
in in with so
in in (with so)
in in writing
in incarcerate so in sth
in include so in (sth)
in include sth in the bargain
in increase in sth
in induce labor in so
in indulge in sth
in ink sth in
in inspire sth in so
in install sth in so/sth
in instruct so in sth
in instrumental in doing sth
in inter so in sth
in interest so in so/sth
in interest so in sth
in interfere in sth
in intern so in sth
in intervene in sth
in invest in so/sth
in invest so's time in sth
in invest sth in so/sth
in involve so in sth
in It'll all come out in the wash.
in It'll be a cold day in hell when sth happens.
in It'll be a long day in January when sth happens.
in jab so in sth
in join in (with so)
in join in ((with) sth)
in jump in with both feet
in just in case
in just in time

in keep a civil tongue (in one's head)
in keep in good condition
in keep in good shape
in keep in good with so
in keep in step (with so)
in Keep in there!
in Keep in touch.
in keep in touch (with so)
in keep in touch (with so/sth)
in keep in training
in keep (it) in mind that
in keep one in one's place
in keep one's hand in (sth)
in keep people straight (in one's mind)
in keep so in (a state of) suspense
in keep so in ignorance (about so/sth)
in keep so in sight
in keep so in stitches
in keep so in the dark (about so/sth)
in keep so in the picture
in keep so or an animal in
in keep so or some creature out in the cold
in keep so/sth hanging (in midair)
in keep so/sth in check
in keep so/sth in mind
in keep so/sth in order
in keep so/sth in reserve
in keep so/sth in some place
in keep so/sth in with so/sth
in keep sth in
in keep things straight (in one's mind)
in kick in (on sth) (for so/sth)
in kick in the ass
in kick in the butt
in kick in the guts
in kick in the (seat of the) pants
in kick in the teeth
in kick sth in
in knee-deep in sth
in knocked in
in know sth in one's bones
in lag behind in sth
in land in sth
in land so in sth
in languish in some place
in late in life
in late in the day
in laugh in so's face
in lay in ruins
in lay so out in lavender
in lay sth in
in leave a bad taste in so's mouth
in leave in a body
in leave so in peace
in leave so in the lurch
in leave so or some creature out in the cold
in leave so/sth hanging (in midair)
in leave so/sth in one's hands
in leave so/sth in so's care
in leave so/sth in (sth)
in leave so/sth in the care of so
in leave so/sth in the trust of so
in leave so up in the air
in leave sth in limbo
in leave sth in ruins
in leave sth in the back of so's mind
in leave sth up in the air
in leave them rolling in the aisles
in legend in one's own (life)time
in let oneself in for sth
in let so in for sth
in let so in on sth
in let so in on the act

in let so in on the ground floor
in lie in
in lie out (in sth)
in life in the fast lane
in like a blind dog in a meat market
in like a bull in a china shop
in like looking for a needle in a haystack
in like shooting fish in a barrel
in like (two) peas in a pod
in line so/sth up (in sth)
in listen in (on so/sth)
in (little) nip in the air
in live in
in lock in on so/sth
in lock so or an animal (up) in (sth)
in lock sth in sth
in lodge sth in sth
in long in the tooth
in look a gift horse in the mouth
in look around (in) some place
in look as if butter wouldn't melt in one's mouth
in Look (at) what the cat dragged in!
in look in (on so/sth)
in look like sth the cat dragged in
in Look me up when you're in town.
in look so in the eye
in look so in the face
in lose oneself in so/sth
in lose sth in sth
in lost in sth
in Lucky at cards, unlucky in love.
in lump in one's throat
in lure so/sth in to sth
in luxuriate in sth
in maintain so in sth
in major in sth
in make a dent in sth
in make a difference in so/sth
in make one's way in the world
in make sth in sth
in man in the street
in Many a true word is spoken in jest.
in March comes in like a lion, and goes out like a lamb.
in march in (a) single file
in march in step (with so)
in mark sth in
in marriage made in heaven
in Marriages are made in heaven.
in Marry in haste, (and) repent at leisure.
in match made in heaven
in match so/sth in sth
in meddle in sth
in melt in one's mouth
in melt in sth
in Men are blind in their own cause.
in mention so/sth in passing
in mention so/sth in sth
in method in one's madness
in milestone in so's life
in mingle in (with so)
in minor in sth
in misplace one's trust (in so)
in mission in life
in mix in (with so/sth)
in mix so up in sth
in mixed up in sth
in model sth in sth
in Moderation in all things.
in Money burns a hole in so's pocket.

in move in for the kill
in move in (on so)
in move in (on so/sth)
in move in the fast lane
in move in with so
in move up in the world
in much in evidence
in muscle in (on so/sth)
in need sth like a hole in the head
in nest in sth
in nestle down (in sth)
in Never in a thousand years!
in never in my life
in nip sth in the bud
in no point in sth
in not a hope in hell
in not for all the tea in China
in not for (anything in) the world
in not have a care in the world
in not have a snowball's chance in hell
in Not in a thousand years!
in Not in my book.
in not in the least
in not in the same league with so/sth
in not know enough to come in out of the rain
in not put (a lot) of stock in sth
in not take stock in sth
in number in sth
in on in years
in once in a blue moon
in once-in-a-lifetime chance
in once-in-a-lifetime opportunity
in One cannot be in two places at once.
in one in a hundred
in one in a thousand
in one's heart is in one's mouth
in one's heart is in the right place
in one's nose is in the air
in opt in favor of so/sth
in order sth in
in originate in sth
in out (in bloom)
in out (in blossom)
in out in droves
in out in force
in out in large numbers
in out in left field
in out in the cold
in out in the open
in pack it in
in pack so/sth in
in pack so/sth (in) like sardines
in pack sth in sth
in pack sth up (in sth)
in pack them in
in packed (in) like sardines
in pain in the ass
in pain in the neck
in pain in the rear
in paint sth in
in pan in (on so/sth)
in paper over the cracks (in sth)
in parade so/sth in front of so/sth
in part in sth
in partake in sth
in participate (in sth) (with so/sth)
in partners in crime
in pass in review
in pass sth in (to so)
in pay in advance
in peek in (on so/sth)

in pen so or an animal in (some place)
in pencil so/sth in
in People who live in glass houses shouldn't throw stones.
in perish in sth
in persevere in sth
in persist in doing sth
in phone in (to so/sth)
in phone sth in (to so/sth)
in pick holes in sth
in picture so in sth
in pie in the sky
in pitch in (and help) (with sth)
in place for everything, and everything in its place.
in place one's trust in so/sth
in place so in an awkward position
in place so/sth in jeopardy
in place so/sth in so's care
in place so/sth in the trust of so
in place sth in sth
in plant sth in sth
in play a big part (in sth)
in play a large part (in sth)
in play a part in sth
in play a role in sth
in play in sth
in play in the big leagues
in plow sth in
in poke a hole in sth
in poke about (in sth)
in poke around (in sth)
in poke so in sth
in pop in (for a visit)
in pound so's head in
in pound sth in
in pride oneself in sth
in print sth in sth
in proof is in the pudding.
in prophet is not without honor save in his own country.
in pull in one's ears
in pull in one's horns
in pull in some place
in pull one's belt in (a notch)
in pull (out) in front of so/sth
in pull so in
in punch a hole in sth
in punch in
in punch so in sth
in punch sth in
in push so/sth about in sth
in push so/sth around in sth
in push sth in
in put a bee in so's bonnet (about so/sth)
in put a plug in (for so/sth)
in Put a sock in it!
in put all one's eggs in one basket
in put an amount of time in on sth
in put in a good word (for so)
in put in a hard day at work
in put in an appearance (at sth)
in put in for sth
in put in some place
in put one foot in front of the other
in put one in one's place
in put one in over one's head
in put one's foot in it
in put one's foot in one's mouth
in put one's house in order
in put one's nose in (where it's not wanted)
in put one's oar in

in put one's own house in order
in put one's trust in so/sth
in put one's two cents(' worth) in
in put oneself in so else's place
in put so across (in a good way)
in put so in
in put so or some creature out in the cold
in put so/sth in
in put sth back in play
in put sth down in black and white
in put sth in
in Put that in your pipe and smoke it!
in Put your trust in God, and keep your powder dry.
in putty in so's hands
in quake in one's boots
in rain in on so/sth
in raised in a barn
in rake sth in
in rattle around in sth
in reach some place in a body
in reach sth in the (very) nick of time
in read sth in sth
in recast sth in sth
in record sth in sth
in red in the face
in reef a sail in
in reel sth in
in reflected in sth
in register in sth
in register so in sth
in rein so/sth in
in reinstate so in sth
in rejoice in so/sth
in relocate so/sth in sth
in remain in limbo
in remain in (sth)
in remain in the back of so's mind
in remain in touch (with so/sth)
in remember so in one's will
in report in
in repose in sth
in represent so in sth
in resemble so/sth in sth
in reside in some place
in reside in so/sth
in rest in peace
in rest in sth
in rest in so/sth
in restore so's trust in sth
in result in sth
in revel in sth
in rich in sth
in ride off in all directions
in rig so/sth out (in sth)
in right in the kisser
in ring in so's ears
in ring in so's mind
in ring in the new year
in rip sth in half
in rip sth in two
in rise in sth
in rival so in sth
in roll in
in roll (oneself) up in sth
in roll (over) in one's grave
in roll so/sth (up) in sth
in roll sth in
in rolling in it
in rolling in money
in rolling in sth
in rolling in the aisles
in Rome was not built in a day.

in root sth in sth
in rooted in sth
in rope so in
in rough sth in
in rub salt in a wound
in rub so's nose in it
in rub sth in
in rule in favor of so/sth
in run in circles
in run in sth
in run in the family
in run off in all directions
in run so in
in run sth in
in safety in numbers
in save so in the (very) nick of time
in say (in sth)
in say sth in a roundabout way
in say sth in plain English
in say sth in plain language
in school so in sth
in see so/sth in a new light
in see sth in so/sth
in see sth in the cards
in seem like putty in so's hands
in send in for sth
in send so in
in serve sth in sth
in set foot in some place
in set in
in set one's house in order
in set so up (in business)
in set sth down in black and white
in set sth in
in settle in
in shake in one's boots
in ships that pass in the night
in shoot oneself in the foot
in shoot so down in flames
in shot in the arm
in shot in the dark
in should have stood in bed
in shroud so/sth in sth
in sick in bed
in sign in
in sign so in
in sign sth in
in sink in
in sit hand in hand
in sit in (for so)
in sit in judgment (up)on so/sth
in sit in (on sth)
in skeleton(s) in the closet
in sketch sth in
in slam the door in so's face
in slap in the face
in slap so in sth
in sleep in
in slip in (some place)
in slosh around (in sth)
in slouch down (in sth)
in slow as molasses in January
in slower than molasses in January
in smack (dab) in the middle
in smack in the face
in smash so's face in
in smash sth in
in snake in the grass
in snow so/sth in
in snowed in
in snug as a bug in a rug
in soak sth in sth
in sock so/sth in

in socked in
in soft in the head
in so's ace in the hole
in So will be with you in a minute.
in Something is rotten in (the state of) Denmark.
in (somewhere) in the neighborhood of sth
in speak in earnest
in Speak of the devil (and in he walks).
in specialize in sth
in speculate in sth
in spend time in sth
in split in sth
in *split second
in square peg in a round hole
in squash sth in
in stab so in sth
in stab so in the back
in stand in awe (of so/sth)
in stand (in) back of so/sth
in stand in (for so)
in stand in so's way
in stand knee-deep in sth
in stand so in good stead
in stand up in court
in star in sth
in stare so in the face
in stars in one's eyes
in start in on so/sth
in start so in (as sth)
in start so up (in sth)
in stash sth in sth
in stave in
in stay in limbo
in stay in (sth)
in stay in the back of so's mind
in stay in the boondocks
in stay in the dark (about so/sth)
in stay in the fast lane
in stay in touch (with so/sth)
in steep so in sth
in steep sth in sth
in step in sth
in stew in one's own juice
in stick in so's mind
in stick in sth
in stick one's foot in one's mouth
in stick one's nose in (where it's not wanted)
in stick one's nose up in the air
in stick one's oar in
in stick-in-the-mud
in stir sth in
in stitch in time saves nine.
in stock in trade
in stop dead in one's tracks
in stop in (some place)
in stop one or sth dead in one's or sth's tracks
in store sth in sth
in strip sth in
in stroll arm in arm
in (stuck) in a rut
in stuck in traffic
in Stuff a sock in it!
in submerge so/sth in sth
in succeed in sth
in suck so in
in suck sth in
in surpass so/sth in sth
in sustain so in sth
in swathe so/sth in sth
in swear so in (as sth)

in sweep in (from some place)
in swim in sth
in swimming in sth
in take a course (in sth)
in take a hand in sth
in Take a running jump (in the lake)!
in take an interest in so/sth
in take no stock in sth
in take one's belt in (a notch)
in take part (in sth)
in take pride in so/sth
in take refuge in sth
in take solace (in sth)
in take so in
in take so or an animal in
in take so's life in one's hands
in take sth in
in take sth out in trade
in take the bit in one's teeth
in take the spear (in one's chest)
in tale never loses in the telling.
in talk in circles
in talk until one is blue in the face
in telephone sth in (to so)
in tempest in a teacup
in tempest in a teapot
in test so in sth
in The proof of the pudding is in the eating.
in There are plenty of (other) fish in the sea.
in There are tricks in every trade.
in There aren't enough hours in the day.
in There is a tide in the affairs of men.
in There is safety in numbers.
in There's many a true word spoken in jest.
in This is where I came in.
in thorn in so's flesh
in thorn in so's side
in three sheets in the wind
in throw a monkey wrench in the works
in throw in the sponge
in throw in the towel
in throw in with so
in throw one's hands up (in despair)
in throw one's hands up in horror
in throw one's hat in the ring
in throw so in the drink
in throw so/sth in
in throw sth in
in tie in (with so/sth)
in tie in with sth
in tie so (up) in knots
in tie sth in a knot
in time in
in time so in
in tongue-in-cheek
in tool around (in sth)
in toss in the sponge
in touched (in the head)
in trade sth in (for sth)
in traffic in sth
in train so in sth
in transcribe sth in sth
in trap so in sth
in trap so/sth in sth
in travel in a body
in trust in so/sth
in tune in (on so/sth)
in tune in (to sth)

in tune sth in
in tuned in
in turn in
in Turn on, tune in, drop out.
in turn (over) in one's grave
in turn so/sth in (to so/sth)
in turn sth over in one's mind
in twist (slowly) in the wind
in unite in sth
in unite so in sth
in up in arms
in up in the air (about so/sth)
in up in years
in up to one's ears (in sth)
in up to one's eyeballs (in sth)
in up to one's neck (in sth)
in use every trick in the book
in vary (from sth) (in sth)
in vest sth in so/sth
in vested interest in sth
in voice (in sth)
in waiting in the wings
in walk arm in arm
in walk hand in hand
in walk in (a) single file
in walk in on so/sth
in walk right in
in wall so/sth in
in wallow (around) in sth
in wallow in sth
in want so/sth in sth
in wash one's dirty linen in public
in weak link (in the chain)
in wear the britches (in the family)
in wear the pants (in the family)
in weave in and out (of sth)
in wedge so/sth (in) between people or things
in week in, week out
in weigh in (at sth)
in well in hand
in well up in years
in welter in sth
in Were you born in a barn?
in What (in) the devil?
in What (in) the dickens?
in What (in) the hell?
in What in (the) Sam Hill?
in What's in a name?
in What's in it for me?
in When in Rome(, do as the Romans do).
in when one's ship comes in
in When poverty comes in at the door, love flies out of the window.
in When the wolf comes in at the door, love creeps out of the window.
in Where in the world...?
in whistle in the dark
in Who (in) the devil?
in Who (in) the hell?
in wide place in the road
in wind sth in
in wire sth in
in (with) hat in hand
in with the best will in the world
in With you in a minute.
in wolf in sheep's clothing
in woman's place is in the home.
in Won't you come in?
in work in an ivory tower
in worth its weight in gold
in wouldn't want to be in so's shoes

in wrap so/sth (up) (in sth)
in wrapped up in so/sth
in wreathe so/sth in sth
in write so in (on sth)
in write sth in
in writhe in sth
in written in stone
in year in, year out
in You cannot put new wine in old bottles.
in zero in (on so/sth)
in zoom in (on so/sth)
inaugurate inaugurate so as sth
incapacitate incapacitate so (for sth) (for a period of time)
incarcerate incarcerate so in sth
inch come within an inch of doing sth
inch come within an inch of so/sth
inch every inch a sth
inch Give so an inch and he'll take a mile.
inch Give so an inch and he'll take a yard.
inch inch along (sth)
inch inch back
inch inch by inch
inch inch forward
inch inch one's way across sth
inch inch one's way along sth
inch inch oneself across sth
inch inch oneself along sth
inch inch over
inch within an inch of one's life
incite incite so to sth
incline As the twig is bent, so is the tree inclined.
incline incline away (from so/sth)
incline incline forward
incline incline sth forward
incline incline toward so/sth
incline inclined to do sth
inclined disinclined to do sth
include include so in (sth)
include include so/sth among sth
include include so out (of sth)
include include sth in the bargain
incorporate incorporate so/sth in(to) sth
increase increase by leaps and bounds
increase increase in sth
increase increase sth by sth
increase increase sth (from sth) (to sth)
increment increment sth by sth
inculcate inculcate so with sth
inculcate inculcate sth in(to) so
incumbent incumbent (up)on so to do sth
indeed friend in need is a friend indeed.
indeed Yes indeed(y (do))!
indemnify indemnify so/sth against sth
Indian Too many chiefs and not enough Indians.
indicate indicate sth to so
indict indict so for sth
indispensable No one is indispensable.
indoctrinate indoctrinate so into sth
indoctrinate indoctrinate so with sth
indoor greatest thing since indoor plumbing
induce induce labor in so
induct induct so into sth
indulge indulge in sth

indulge indulge so with sth
industry captain of industry
infatuate infatuated with so/sth
infect infect so with sth
infer infer sth from so
infest infested with sth
infiltrate infiltrate into sth
infinite Genius is an infinite capacity for taking pains.
inflate inflate sth with sth
inflict inflict so (up)on so
inflict inflict sth (up)on so/sth
influence under the influence (of alcohol)
inform inform on so
inform inform so about so/sth
inform inform so of sth
inform inform so on so
information for your information
information gold mine of information
information inside information
information mine of information
infringe infringe (up)on sth
infuse infuse so with sth
infuse infuse sth into so
infuse infuse sth into sth
infuse infuse sth with sth
ingratiate ingratiate oneself into sth
ingratiate ingratiate oneself with so
inherit inherit sth from so
inhibit inhibit so from doing sth
inhibit inhibit sth from doing sth
inhumanity man's inhumanity to man
iniquity den of iniquity
initiate initiate so into sth
initiative take the initiative (to do sth)
inject inject sth into so/sth or some creature
inject inject sth into sth
injury add insult to injury
ink in ink
ink ink sth in
ink red ink
inkling inkling (about so/sth)
inkling inkling (of sth)
inlay inlay sth with sth
innocent find so innocent
innocent innocent as a lamb
innocent innocent as a newborn babe
innocent play innocent
inoculate inoculate so against sth
inoculate inoculate so with sth
inquire inquire about so/sth
inquire inquire after so
inquire inquire for so
inquire inquire into sth
inquire inquire sth of so
inquire inquire within
inroad make inroads into sth
insane drive so insane
inscribe have one's name inscribed in the book of life
inscribe inscribe sth into sth
inscribe inscribe sth on(to) sth
inscribe inscribe sth with sth
insert insert sth between sth and sth else
insert insert sth in(to) sth
inside get inside sth
inside hold sth inside ((of) one(self))
inside inside a week
inside inside information
inside inside job
inside inside joke
inside inside story

inside inside track
inside keep inside ((of) sth)
inside keep sth inside ((of) one(self))
inside know sth inside out
inside put so in(side) (sth)
inside put sth in((side) so/sth)
inside step inside (some place)
inside take so/sth or an animal in(side)
inside think inside the box
inside turn some place inside out
inside turn so/sth inside out
inside well up (inside so)
insinuate insinuate oneself into sth
insinuate insinuate sth to so
insist insist (up)on sth
inspiration Genius is ten percent inspiration and ninety percent perspiration.
inspire inspire so with sth
inspire inspire sth in so
install install so as sth
install install sth in sth
instance for instance
instance in the first instance
instigate instigate so to do sth
instill instill so with sth
instill instill sth in(to) so
instill instill sth in(to) sth
instinct killer instinct
institute institute sth against so/sth
instruct instruct so in sth
instruction couldn't pour water out of a boot (if there was instructions on the heel)
instrumental instrumental in doing sth
insulate insulate so/sth against so/sth
insult add insult to injury
insult hurl insults (at so)
insult throw insults (at so)
insult trade insults (with so)
insure insure against sth
insure insure so/sth (against sth) (for sth)
insure insure so/sth with sth
integrate integrate so/sth into sth
integrate integrate so with so
integrate integrate sth with sth
intend intend sth as sth
intend intend sth for so/sth
intent for all intents and purposes
intent intent on doing sth
intention road to hell is paved with good intentions.
inter inter so in sth
interact interact with so
interact interact with sth
intercede intercede (for so) (with so/sth)
interchange interchange so with so else
interchange interchange sth with sth
interest draw interest
interest give sth back (to so) (with interest)
interest have a keen interest in sth
interest have so's best interest(s) at heart
interest in an interesting condition
interest in one's (own) (best) interest(s)
interest in the interest of saving time
interest in the interest of so/sth
interest interest so in so/sth
interest interest so in sth
interest of interest (to so)
interest pique so's interest

interest take an interest in so/sth
interest vested interest in sth
interface interface so/sth with so/sth
interface interface with so/sth
interfere interfere in sth
interfere interfere with so/sth
interim in the interim (between things)
interject interject so into sth
interject interject sth into sth
interlace interlace sth with sth
intermarry intermarry with so
intermingle intermingle sth with sth
intermingle intermingle with so
intern intern so in sth
interpose interpose so/sth between people or things
interpose interpose sth in(to) sth
interpret interpret for so
interpret interpret sth as sth
interpret interpret sth for so
intersperse intersperse sth among sth
intersperse intersperse sth between sth else
intersperse intersperse sth throughout sth
intersperse intersperse sth with sth
intertwine intertwine sth with sth
intertwine intertwine with sth
interval at regular intervals
intervene intervene between so and so else
intervene intervene in sth
intervene intervene with so/sth
interview interview so for sth
interview interview with so for sth
intimate have intimate relations with so
intimate intimate apparel
intimate intimate sth to so
intimate intimate with so
intimidate intimidate so into sth
intimidate intimidate so with sth
into absorb so in(to) sth
into absorb sth in(to) sth
into ace in(to sth)
into add sth into sth
into admit so (in)to some place
into admit sth into sth
into allow so/sth into a place
into argue so into doing sth
into ask so in(to) some place
into assimilate so/sth into sth
into back in(to) circulation
into back into so/sth
into back oneself into a corner
into back so/sth into so/sth
into badger so into sth
into bang into so/sth
into bang sth into so/sth
into barge in(to some place)
into barge into so/sth
into barrel in(to some place)
into beat so into (doing) sth
into beat so into sth
into beat sth into so
into beat sth into so
into beguile so into sth
into bite into sth
into blackmail so into doing sth
into blend in(to sth)
into blend sth into sth else
into blossom into sth

into blow in(to some place) (from some place)
into blow into sth
into bluff so into sth
into branch out (into sth)
into break into a gallop
into break into sth
into break in(to sth or some place)
into break in(to) tears
into break out in(to) tears
into break sth down (into sth)
into break sth up (into sth)
into break (up) (into sth)
into breathe into sth
into breathe sth into sth
into breeze in(to some place)
into bribe so into doing sth
into bring so into the world
into bring so/sth into action
into bring so/sth into contact with so/sth
into bring so/sth into disrepute
into bring so/sth into line (with so/sth)
into bring so/sth into prominence
into bring so/sth in(to) some place
into bring so/sth into view
into bring sth into being
into bring sth into blossom
into bring sth into focus
into bring sth into play
into bring sth into question
into bring sth into service
into browbeat so into sth
into build so into sth
into build so/sth up (into so/sth)
into build sth into sth
into bulldoze into sth
into bully so into sth
into bump into so
into bundle so into sth
into burn sth into sth
into burst into flame(s)
into burst into sight
into burst in(to some place)
into burst into sth
into burst into tears
into burst out into sth
into butt into sth
into buy in(to sth)
into buy one's way in(to sth)
into buzz in(to some place)
into buzz so into a place
into cajole so into sth
into calculate sth into sth
into call so/sth into question
into call so/sth into sth
into carry so/sth into some place
into carve sth into sth
into catapult so/sth into sth
into change back ((in)to so/sth)
into change into so/sth
into change so/sth into so/sth
into channel sth in(to sth)
into charge in(to some place)
into chase so or an animal in(to) some place
into check in(to sth)
into chop so/sth (up) (in(to) sth)
into chuck sth into sth
into clap so in(to) some place
into coalesce into sth
into coax so or an animal in(to sth)
into coerce so or an animal into sth
into coil (itself) up into sth
into collapse into sth

into come into a (small) fortune
into come into being
into come into bloom
into come into blossom
into come into conflict
into come in(to) contact (with so/sth)
into come into effect
into come into existence
into come into fashion
into come into focus
into come in(to) heat
into come into one's or its own
into come into play
into come into power
into come into prominence
into come into season
into come into service
into come into sight
into come into (some) money
into come into so's possession
into come into the world
into come into view
into come out in(to) the open
into commute sth into sth
into compartmentalize sth into sth
into compress sth into sth
into con so into sth
into condense sth (in)to sth
into conduct so into sth
into conscript so into sth
into convert from sth ((in)to sth)
into convert so/sth (from sth) ((in)to sth)
into co-opt so into sth
into cow so into sth
into cram so/sth into sth
into crash into so/sth
into crawl in(to sth)
into creep in(to sth)
into cross over into some place
into crowd in(to) some place
into crowd so/sth in(to) sth
into crumble into sth
into crumble sth up (into sth)
into crush sth (in)to sth
into crush sth up (into sth)
into curl up (in(to) sth)
into cut in(to sth)
into cut sth into sth
into deal so into sth
into deceive so into sth
into degenerate into sth
into delude so into sth
into delve into sth
into deposit sth in(to) sth
into descend into sth
into develop from so/sth (into so/sth)
into dig in(to sth)
into dig sth into sth
into din sth into so
into dip into one's savings
into dip in(to sth)
into dip sth in(to) sth
into discharge sth into sth
into dissolve into sth
into dissolve sth into sth
into dive in(to sth)
into divert sth into sth
into divide sth into sth
into dovetail sth into sth
into draft so into sth
into drag so/sth into sth
into dragoon so into sth
into draw so/sth into sth

into drift in(to sth)
into drill in(to sth)
into drill sth into so/sth
into drip in(to sth)
into drip sth into sth
into drive into so/sth
into drive in(to sth)
into drive into the middle of nowhere
into drive so into a corner
into drive sth into so/sth
into drive sth into sth
into drive sth into the ground
into drop so/sth into sth
into drum sth into so
into dunk so/sth into sth
into eat in(to sth)
into embarrass so into doing sth
into emit sth (from sth) (into sth)
into empty into sth
into empty sth into sth
into engrave sth into sth
into enter into sth
into enter so/sth in(to) sth
into entice so or an animal into doing sth
into entice so or an animal into sth
into erupt into sth
into escalate into sth
into escalate sth into sth
into etch sth in(to) sth
into evolve (from sth) (into sth)
into expand into sth
into expand sth into sth
into face (so/sth) into sth
into fade away (into sth)
into fade back (into sth)
into fade into sth
into fall into a trap
into fall into decay
into fall into disfavor
into fall into disgrace
into fall into disuse
into fall in(to) line
into fall in(to) one's lap
into fall in(to) place
into fall into so's trap
into fall in(to sth)
into fall in(to step)
into fall into the gutter
into fall into the trap
into fall into the wrong hands
into far into the night
into fashion sth into sth
into fast-talk so into sth
into feed sth back into sth
into feed sth into sth
into figure so/sth in((to) sth)
into file in((to) sth)
into filter in(to some place)
into fire sth into so/sth
into fit in((to) sth)
into fit so/sth in((to) sth)
into flash into one's mind
into flash into view
into fling sth in(to) sth
into float into sth
into flock in((to) some place)
into flood in(to sth)
into flop into sth
into flounce in(to some place)
into flow in(to sth)
into fly into a rage
into fly into sth
into fly into the face of danger

into fly so/sth in(to some place) (from some place)
into fold sth into sth
into fool so into sth
into force so/sth in(to) sth
into form so/sth into sth
into form (up) into sth
into freeze sth into sth
into frighten so or an animal **into** doing sth
into frighten so or an animal **into** sth
into galvanize so into action
into gather so into sth
into get into a mess
into get into an argument (with so) (about so/sth)
into get into bed with so
into get into one's stride
into get into sth
into get in(to) the act
into get in(to) the swing of things
into get one's hooks in(to) so/sth
into get one's teeth into sth
into get (oneself) into a stew (over so/sth)
into get so in(to) sth
into get so/sth in(to) sth
into get sth into a mess
into get sth in(to) so
into get sth into so's thick head
into get sth in(to) sth
into go into a huddle
into go into a nosedive
into go into a song and dance (about sth)
into go into a tailspin
into go into action
into go into detail(s)
into go into effect
into go into heat
into go into hiding
into go into hock
into go into one's act
into go into orbit
into go into service
into go into sth
into go into the bull pen
into go into the red
into go into the same old song and dance about sth
into go into the service
into go off (into sth)
into go out of the frying pan into the fire
into goad so into sth
into grind sth into sth
into grow down (into sth)
into grow into sth
into grow up into so/sth
into hammer sth into sth
into head in(to sth)
into head so/sth into so/sth
into heave in(to) sight
into heavy into so/sth
into help so in(to sth)
into high-pressure so into sth
into hoodwink so into sth
into hook in(to sth)
into hook sth into sth
into hop in(to sth)
into hurl so/sth into sth
into hurry so/sth in(to sth)
into immigrate (in)to some place (from some place)
into implant sth in(to) so/sth

into import sth (from sth) ((in)to sth)
into impress sth into sth
into imprint sth into sth
into incorporate so/sth in(to) sth
into inculcate sth in(to) so
into indoctrinate so into sth
into induct so into sth
into infiltrate into sth
into infuse sth into so
into infuse sth into sth
into ingratiate oneself into sth
into initiate so into sth
into inject sth into so/sth or some creature
into inject sth into sth
into inquire into sth
into inscribe sth into sth
into insert sth in(to) sth
into insinuate oneself into sth
into instill sth in(to) so
into instill sth in(to) sth
into integrate so/sth into sth
into interject so into sth
into interject sth into sth
into interpose sth in(to) sth
into intimidate so into sth
into in(to) a jam
into into being
into in(to) so's clutches
into introduce so into sth
into introduce sth into sth
into intrude into sth
into intrude oneself into sth
into inveigle so into sth
into invite so into some place
into jab sth into sth
into jam so/sth in((to) sth)
into jockey so/sth into position
into jump in((to) sth)
into jump into the fray
into jump out of the frying pan into the fire
into jut out (into sth)
into knock some sense into so
into knock so into sth
into knock sth into a cocked hat
into lace into so/sth
into lace so into sth
into lam into so or an animal
into lapse into sth
into lash into so or an animal
into lash into sth
into launch into sth
into lay into so/sth
into lay so/sth in(to) sth
into leach in(to sth)
into lead in(to sth)
into lead so into sth
into leak in(to sth)
into lean in(to sth)
into let so/sth into sth
into lick so/sth into shape
into lick sth into shape
into light into so/sth
into line up in(to) sth
into load into sth
into load so/sth into sth
into look into sth
into luck into sth
into lull so into a false sense of security
into make inroads into sth
into make so/sth into sth
into maneuver so into sth
into marry into sth

into melt into sth
into melt sth into sth
into merge in(to sth)
into merge so/sth into sth
into metamorphose into sth
into mix so/sth into sth
into move into full swing
into move into high gear
into move in(to sth)
into move so/sth into sth
into move up into sth
into mushroom into sth
into nail sth into sth
into nose in(to sth)
into open into sth
into opt in(to sth)
into order so in(to sth)
into out of the frying pan (and) into the fire
into overflow into sth
into pack so/sth into sth
into parlay sth into sth
into partition sth into sth
into pass into sth
into pay into sth
into pay sth into sth
into peek in(to sth)
into peep in(to sth)
into peer in(to sth)
into penetrate into so/sth
into permit so into sth
into pester so into sth
into phase so/sth into sth
into pile in(to sth)
into pile so into sth
into pilot sth into sth
into pipe sth into some place
into pitch sth into sth
into place so/sth into the care of so
into play into so's hands
into plow into so/sth
into plow sth back into sth
into plug (oneself) in(to sth)
into plug sth into sth
into plunge in(to sth)
into plunge sth into so/sth
into poke one's nose in(to sth)
into poke sth into sth
into polarize sth into sth
into pop in(to sth)
into pop sth into sth
into pound sth into so
into pour in(to sth)
into pour oneself into sth
into pour sth back (in(to sth))
into pour sth into sth
into precipitate into sth
into precipitate sth into sth
into press so/sth into service
into press sth into sth
into pressure so into sth
into probe into sth
into prod so into sth
into project sth into sth
into provoke so into sth
into pry into sth
into puff up (into sth)
into pull in(to some place)
into pull so into a place
into pull so into sth
into pull so/sth into sth
into pump sth into so/sth
into punch sth into sth

into push so into sth
into push so/sth into so/sth
into push so/sth or an animal **into** sth
into put ideas into so's head
into put one's back (in)to sth
into put one's heart (and soul) into sth
into put some teeth into sth
into put so into power
into put so into the doghouse
into put so into the doldrums
into put so into the gutter
into put so/sth in(to) jeopardy
into put so/sth into order
into put so/sth into sth
into put so/sth into the middle of nowhere
into put sth into effect
into put sth into orbit
into put sth in(to) order
into put sth into perspective
into put sth into place
into put sth into practice
into put sth in(to) print
into put sth in(to) service
into put sth in(to) so's head
into put sth into use
into put sth into words
into put teeth in(to) sth
into put the fear of God in(to) so
into put words in(to) so's mouth
into race into so/sth
into race into sth
into railroad so into sth
into ram into so/sth
into ram sth into so/sth
into reach back (in)to sth
into reach in(to) sth
into reach out into sth
into read sth into sth
into receive so into sth
into reckon so/sth into sth
into recruit so into sth
into relapse into sth
into relax into sth
into remand so (in)to the custody of so
into rend sth into sth
into render sth in(to) sth
into research into so/sth
into retire (in)to sth
into rip into so/sth
into ripen into sth
into rocket (in)to sth
into rocket sth into sth
into roll in(to some place)
into roll sth up (into sth)
into rope so into doing sth
into rope so into sth
into rub sth into sth
into run into a stone wall
into run into so
into run in(to sth)
into run so/sth into sth
into run sth into sth
into run sth into the ground
into rush in(to sth)
into rush so into sth
into rush so/sth into sth
into rush sth into print
into sail into so
into sail in(to sth)
into saw into sth
into saw sth (up) (in(to) sth)
into screw sth into sth

into scrunch down into sth
into scrunch sth down (into sth)
into see so into sth
into see sth into sth
into segregate so/sth or an animal **into** sth
into segue into sth
into send so into a state or condition
into send so into sth
into send sth into sth
into separate so/sth into sth
into set sth into sth
into show so into somewhere
into sink back (into sth)
into sink into despair
into sink into oblivion
into sink one's teeth into sth
into sink sth in(to) so/sth
into skid into so/sth
into slam into so/sth
into slice in(to sth)
into slide into sth
into slide sth into sth
into slink in(to sth)
into slip in(to sth)
into slip sth in(to) sth
into slump down in(to) sth
into smash into sth
into smuggle so/sth into some place
into snap into sth
into snap sth into sth
into sneak in(to some place)
into sneeze into sth
into snoop into sth
into snowball into sth
into snuggle down (into sth)
into soak in(to sth)
into spill (out) into sth
into spill (over) into sth
into spit sth in(to) sth
into split so/sth up (into sth)
into split sth into sth
into spring into action
into squash sth into sth
into squeeze so/sth into sth
into squirm in(to sth)
into stagger in(to some place)
into stalk in(to some place)
into stampede in(to some place)
into stampede so/sth into sth
into stare into sth
into starve so or an animal **into** sth
into steam in((to) sth)
into steer into sth
into step in(to some place)
into step into so's shoes
into step into sth
into step in(to the breach)
into step out into sth
into stick one's nose in(to) sth
into stick sth into so/sth
into stimulate so or an animal **into** sth
into stir so (in)to sth
into stir sth into sth
into storm in(to some place)
into strap so/sth in(to) sth
into stray in(to sth)
into stream in(to sth)
into stride in(to some place)
into strike sth into sth
into strut in(to some place)
into stuff so/sth into so/sth
into stumble into so/sth
into subdivide sth into sth

into suck so/sth into sth
into sucker so into sth
into surge in(to sth)
into swarm in(to sth)
into sweep in(to some place)
into sweep so into sth
into sweep sth into sth
into swerve into so/sth
into swim into sth
into swing into action
into swing into high gear
into swing into sth
into switch into sth
into switch sth (from sth) (in)to sth
into take into account so/sth
into take so into one's confidence
into take so or an animal **into** one's heart
into take so/sth into account
into take sth into account
into take sth into one's head
into take sth into some place
into take the law into one's own hands
into talk so into (doing) sth
into tap sth into sth
into taunt so into sth
into tear into some place
into tear into so
into tear into sth
into tease so into doing sth
into telescope sth into sth
into tempt so into sth
into terrify so into sth
into terrorize so into sth
into throng in(to sth)
into throw oneself into sth
into throw so/sth into confusion
into throw so/sth into sth
into throw sth into sharp relief
into throw sth in(to) so's face
into throw sth into the bargain
into thrust sth into so/sth
into thud into so/sth
into tie in(to sth)
into tie so/sth into sth
into torment so into doing sth
into torture so into sth
into toss one's hat into the ring
into toss sth into sth
into tow so/sth into sth
into track sth into some place
into translate sth (from sth) ((in)to sth)
into transliterate sth (from sth) ((in)to sth)
into transmute sth (from sth) ((in)to sth)
into transpose sth (from sth) ((in)to sth)
into trap so into sth
into trick so into (doing) sth
into trickle in(to sth)
into troop in(to sth)
into tuck into sth
into tuck so in(to) sth
into tuck sth in(to) sth
into tumble into bed
into tumble into so/sth
into turn in((to) some place)
into turn into so/sth
into turn so/sth into so/sth
into twist sth into sth
into type sth into sth
into unfold into sth
into unfold sth into sth
into unify so/sth into sth
into unite so/sth into sth

into usher so/sth **into** some place
into vanish **into** sth
into vanish **into** thin air
into vault **into** sth
into verge **into** sth
into vote so **into** sth
into vote sth **into** law
into wade in(to sth)
into walk in(to sth)
into walk (right) **into** a trap
into walk (right) **into** so/sth
into waltz in(to some place)
into wander in(to sth)
into want in((to) sth)
into weave sth **into** sth
into welcome so **into** sth
into well **into** sth
into whale **into** so or an animal
into What's got(ten) **into** so?
into wheedle so **into** sth
into wheel so/sth **into** sth
into whip **into** sth
into whip so **into** a state
into whip so **into** doing sth
into whip so/sth **into** shape
into whip sth **into** shape
into whip sth **into** sth
into wind **into** sth
into wind sth (up) (**into** sth)
into wired **into** so/sth
into withdraw **into** oneself
into withdraw **into** sth
into withdraw sth **into** sth
into work (one's way) **into** sth
into work oneself (up) **into** a lather
into work oneself up **into** sth
into work so/sth **into** sth
into work sth down (**into** sth)
into work sth **into** sth
into work sth up **into** sth
into worm (one's way) in(to sth)
into wrestle sth **into** sth
into wriggle in(to sth)
into write in(to sth) (for sth)
into write sth **into** sth
into yank so/sth **into** sth
into You cannot get a quart **into** a pint pot.
intoxicate intoxicate so with so/sth
intoxicate intoxicate so with sth
intrigue intrigue so with so/sth
intrigue intrigue (with so) (against so)
introduce introduce so **into** sth
introduce introduce so to so
introduce introduce sth **into** sth
intrude intrude **into** sth
intrude intrude oneself **into** sth
intrude intrude (up)on so/sth
inundate inundate so/sth with sth
inure inure so/sth to sth
invasion invasion of (so's) privacy
inveigh inveigh against so/sth
inveigle inveigle so **into** sth
inveigle inveigle so out of sth
inveigle inveigle sth out of so
invent didn't invent gunpowder
invent If God did not exist, it would be necessary to invent Him.
invent Necessity is the mother of invention.
invent reinvent the wheel
invention Necessity is the mother of invention.

inventory take inventory
invest invest in so/sth
invest invest so's time in sth
invest invest so with sth
invest invest sth in so/sth
invite invite so **into** some place
invite invite so out
invite invite so over (for sth)
invite invite so to sth
invite Thank you for inviting me.
invoke invoke sth (up)on so/sth
involve involve so in sth
involve involve so with so/sth
involve involved (with so)
involve involved with sth
iota not one iota
Irish get so's Irish up
Irish the luck of the Irish
iron all oak and iron bound
iron cast-iron stomach
iron get the kinks (ironed) out
iron have too many irons in the fire
iron iron sth out
iron pump (some) iron
iron rule with an iron fist
iron Strike while the iron is hot.
is after all is said and done
is age of miracles is past.
is All that glistens is not gold.
is All that glitters is not gold.
is Any friend of so('s) (is a friend of mine).
is Art is long and life is short.
is as far as so is concerned
is as far as sth is concerned
is as it is
is As the twig is bent, so is the tree inclined.
is bad excuse is better than none.
is ball is in so's court
is Beauty is in the eye of the beholder.
is Beauty is only skin-deep.
is best defense is a good offense.
is best is the enemy of the good.
is bird in the hand is worth two in the bush.
is black as one is painted
is Blessed is he who expects nothing, for he shall never be disappointed.
is Blood is thicker than water.
is Bread is the staff of life.
is Brevity is the soul of wit.
is bully is always a coward.
is Cash is king.
is Cash is trash.
is cat is out of the bag
is chain is no stronger than its weakest link.
is child is father of the man.
is Cleanliness is next to godliness.
is coast is clear.
is contented mind is a perpetual feast.
is Cross the stream where it is shallowest.
is cry before one is hurt
is customer is always right.
is darkest hour is just before the dawn.
is Death is the great leveler.
is devil is not so black as he is painted.
is die is cast.
is difficult is done at once; the impossible takes a little longer.
is Diligence is the mother of good luck.

is Dinner is served.
is Discretion is the better part of valor.
is East is East and West is West (and never the twain shall meet).
is Enough is as good as a feast.
is Enough is enough.
is Every man is the architect of his own fortune.
is Example is better than precept.
is Expense is no object.
is Experience is the best teacher.
is Experience is the father of wisdom.
is Experience is the mother of wisdom.
is Experience is the teacher of fools.
is Fact is stranger than fiction.
is fat is in the fire.
is feeling (that sth is the case)
is female of the species is more deadly than the male.
is Fire is a good servant but a bad master.
is first step is always the hardest.
is Forewarned is forearmed.
is friend in need is a friend indeed.
is From the sublime to the ridiculous is only a step.
is game is up.
is Genius is an infinite capacity for taking pains.
is Genius is ten percent inspiration and ninety percent perspiration.
is Give credit where credit is due.
is good is the enemy of the best.
is good man is hard to find.
is grass is always greener on the other side (of the fence).
is Half a loaf is better than none.
is Half the truth is often a whole lie.
is Handsome is as handsome does.
is Happy is the bride that the sun shines on.
is Happy is the country which has no history.
is have a hunch (that sth is the case)
is He that is down need fear no fall.
is He who hesitates is lost.
is He who rides a tiger is afraid to dismount.
is Hoist your sail when the wind is fair.
is Home is where the heart is.
is Honesty is the best policy.
is honeymoon is over.
is Hope is a good breakfast but a bad supper.
is How is so fixed for sth?
is How is so getting along?
is How is so making out?
is Hunger is the best sauce.
is idle brain is the devil's workshop.
is Idleness is the root of all evil.
is If a thing is worth doing, it's worth doing well.
is Ignorance is bliss.
is Ignorance (of the law) is no excuse (for breaking it).
is Imitation is the sincerest form of flattery.
is In the country of the blind, the one-eyed man is king.
is is all
is (Is) anything going on?
is (Is) everything okay?
is (Is it) cold enough for you?

is (Is it) hot enough for you?
is Is so there?
is Is that everything?
is Is that right?
is Is that so?
is Is there any truth to sth?
is Is there anything else?
is Is there some place I can wash up?
is (Is) this (seat) taken?
is It is a long lane that has no turning.
is It is a poor heart that never rejoices.
is It is a wise child that knows its own father.
is It is all over with so.
is It is better to be born lucky than rich.
is It is better to give than to receive.
is It is better to travel hopefully than to arrive.
is It is better to wear out than to rust out.
is It is easier to tear down than to build up.
is It is easy to be wise after the event.
is It is more blessed to give than to receive.
is It is never too late to learn.
is It is never too late to mend.
is It is not work that kills, but worry.
is It is the pace that kills.
is It isn't worth it.
is It isn't worth the trouble.
is jack of all trades is a master of none.
is jig is up.
is joke is on so.
is jury is still out on so/sth.
is know one for what one is
is know when one is not wanted
is know where one is coming from
is know where sth is at
is know which is which
is know which side one's bread is buttered on
is Knowledge is power.
is latch string is always out.
is left hand doesn't know what the right hand is doing.
is Less is more.
is liar is not believed (even) when he tells the truth.
is Life is just a bowl of cherries.
is Life is short and time is swift.
is Life is too short.
is Life isn't all beer and skittles.
is little knowledge is a dangerous thing.
is Lock the stable door after the horse is stolen.
is longest way round is the shortest way home.
is Love is blind.
is love of money is the root of all evil.
is man is known by the company he keeps.
is man's home is his castle.
is Many a true word is spoken in jest.
is merry as the day is long
is mill cannot grind with water that is past.
is miss is as good as a mile.
is Monday's child is fair of face.
is Money is no object.
is Money is power.
is Money is the root of all evil.

is mouse that has but one hole is quickly taken.
is Moving three times is as bad as a fire.
is My house is your house.
is Necessity is the mother of invention.
is No news is good news.
is No one is indispensable.
is nod is as good as a wink to a blind horse.
is not all sth is cracked up to be
is not know if one is coming or going
is not know whether one is coming or going
is not know which end is up
is not what sth is cracked up to be
is Nothing is certain but death and taxes.
is Nothing is certain but the unforeseen.
is Nothing is given so freely as advice.
is One man's loss is another man's gain.
is One man's meat is another man's poison.
is One man's trash is another man's treasure.
is One of these days is none of these days.
is One's bark is worse than one's bite.
is one's goose is cooked
is one's heart is (dead) set against sth
is one's heart is in one's mouth
is one's heart is in the right place
is one's heart is set on sth
is one's name is mud
is one's nose is in the air
is one's number is up
is one's word is one's bond
is one's work is cut out for one
is (Open) confession is good for the soul.
is ounce of common sense is worth a pound of theory.
is ounce of discretion is worth a pound of wit.
is ounce of prevention is worth a pound of cure.
is Our house is your house.
is Patience is a virtue.
is pen is mightier than the sword.
is penny saved is a penny earned.
is picture is worth a thousand words.
is Possession is nine-tenths of the law.
is pot is calling the kettle black.
is Poverty is no sin.
is Poverty is not a crime.
is Pretty is as pretty does.
is Prevention is better than cure.
is Procrastination is the thief of time.
is proof is in the pudding.
is prophet is not without honor save in his own country.
is Punctuality is the soul of business.
is Put your money where your mouth is!
is quit while one is ahead
is recognize one for what one is
is recognize sth for what it is
is rest is gravy.
is rest is history.
is Revenge is a dish best served cold.
is Revenge is sweet.

is rich man's joke is always funny.
is road to hell is paved with good intentions.
is see (to it) that sth is done
is see which way the wind is blowing
is Seeing is believing.
is Self-praise is no recommendation.
is Self-preservation is the first law of nature.
is shoe is on the other foot.
is Silence is golden.
is so far as so is concerned
is so far as sth is concerned
is (So) what else is new?
is So/sth is supposed to.
is so's fate is sealed
is so's point is well taken
is so's word is good
is Something is better than nothing.
is sth is killing so
is Something is rotten in (the state of) Denmark.
is spirit is willing, but the flesh is weak.
is Stolen fruit is sweetest.
is storm is brewing.
is Strike while the iron is hot.
is such as it is
is Such is life!
is Sufficient unto the day is the evil thereof.
is sure as eggs is eggs
is Talk is cheap.
is Talk of the devil (and he is sure to appear).
is talk until one is blue in the face
is Tell it like it is.
is tell which is which
is The proof of the pudding is in the eating.
is The wages of sin is death.
is The wolf is at the door.
is There is a fine line between sth and sth else.
is There is a remedy for everything except death.
is There is a tide in the affairs of men.
is There is a time and a place for everything.
is There is honor among thieves.
is There is no accounting for taste(s).
is (There is) no chance.
is there is no doing sth
is (There is) no doubt about it.
is There is no love lost (between so and so else).
is (There is) no need (to).
is There is no pleasure without pain.
is There is no rest for the weary.
is There is no royal road to learning.
is There is nothing new under the sun.
is There is safety in numbers.
is There is trouble brewing.
is thing of beauty is a joy forever.
is thing you don't want is dear at any price.
is think so is God's own cousin
is This is it.
is This is my floor.
is This is where I came in.
is This one is on so.
is Time is a great healer.
is Time is money.
is Time is of the essence.

is time is ripe.
is Time is up.
is To err is human(, to forgive divine).
is Tomorrow is another day.
is tree is known by its fruit.
is Trouble is brewing.
is trouble shared is a trouble halved.
is Truth is stranger than fiction.
is Turnabout is fair play.
is Two is company, (but) three's a crowd.
is Union is strength.
is Variety is the spice of life.
is Virtue is its own reward.
is way to a man's heart is through his stomach.
is Well begun is half done.
is What is it?
is What's done is done.
is What's sauce for the goose is sauce for the gander.
is What's yours is mine, and what's mine is mine.
is what so/sth is cracked up to be
is What you see is what you get.
is when all is said and done
is when one is good and ready
is when the time is ripe
is Where ignorance is bliss, 'tis folly to be wise.
is Where is the restroom?
is where one is coming from
is where so is at
is where so's head is at
is where the action is
is Who is it?
is Who is this?
is Why buy a cow when milk is so cheap?
is wish is father to the thought.
is Woe is me!
is woman's place is in the home.
is woman's work is never done.
is word (once) spoken is past recalling.
is word to the wise (is enough).
is world is one's oyster.
is worth of a thing is what it will bring.
is Your guess is as good as mine.
is Your secret is safe with me.
island maroon so on an island
isolate isolate so/sth from so/sth
issue issue a call for sth
issue issue (forth) from some place
issue issue from sth
issue issue so with sth
issue issue sth as sth
issue issue sth to so
issue make an issue of so/sth
issue reissue sth to so
issue take issue with so
issue take issue with sth
it Ain't it the truth?
it almost lost it
it as far as it goes
it as I see it
it as it is
it as it were
it as luck would have it
it As you make your bed, so you must lie (up)on it.
it at it again
it away from it all
it back at it (again)

it Bag it!
it ba(t)ch (it)
it be that as it may
it Beat it!
it before you know it
it believe it or not
it Better keep still about it.
it Blow it out your ear!
it Blow on it!
it booze it up
it Break it up!
it buy it
it call it a day
it call it a night
it call it quits
it camp it up
it Can it!
it can take it to the bank
it can't hack it
it catch it
it catch to it
it Charge it to the dust and let the rain settle it.
it chuck it in
it Come and get it!
it Come 'n' get it!
it Come off it!
it come to think of it
it Consarn it!
it Cool it!
it could fight a circle-saw (and it a-runnin')
it cross a bridge before one comes to it
it cross that bridge when one comes to it
it Cross the stream where it is shallowest.
it Cut it out!
it Damn it to blue blazes!
it deem it (to be) necessary
it Do I have to spell it out (for you)?
it do it
it (Do you) want to make something of it?
it Does it work for you?
it doesn't care who knows it
it Don't even think about (doing) it.
it Don't even think about it (happening).
it Don't give it a (second) thought.
it Don't give it another thought.
it don't have a pot to piss in (or a window to throw it out of)
it Don't I know it!
it Don't knock it.
it don't know whether to eat it or rub it on
it Don't let it go any further.
it Don't let it out of this room.
it Don't make me say it again!
it Don't mention it.
it Don't say it!
it Don't spend it all in one place.
it Don't sweat it!
it Don't worry your (pretty little) head about it.
it Don't you know it!
it Drop it!
it duke it out
it Easy does it.
it eat one's cake and have it too
it end it (all)
it even if it kills me

it fake it
it far be it from me to do sth
it far from it
it feel it beneath one (to do sth)
it find it in one's heart (to do sth)
it find it in oneself (to do sth)
it floor it
it for all it's worth
it for the devil of it
it for the fun of it
it for the heck of it
it for the hell of it
it for what(ever) it's worth
it Forget (about) it!
it get it
it Get off it!
it Get out with it!
it Get over it!
it get with it
it Give it a rest!
it Give it all you've got!
it Give it the gun.
it Give it time.
it give it to so (straight)
it Give it up!
it go at it hammer and tongs
it go at it tooth and nail
it Go for it!
it go it alone
it go to it
it go with it
it grin and bear it
it (had) known it was coming
it Hand it over.
it Hang it all!
it hang it up
it have a familiar ring (to it)
it have a kick to it
it have a rough time (of it)
it have an easy time of it
it Have at it.
it have had it (up to here)
it have it (all) over so/sth (in sth)
it have it all together
it have it both ways
it have it in for so
it have it in one to do sth
it have it made
it Have it your way.
it (have) never had it so good
it have one's cake and eat it too
it have to do sth so bad one can taste it
it have to hand it to so
it have what it takes
it Here (it) goes.
it hightail it out of somewhere
it hit it off (with so)
it Hold it!
it hoof it
it Hop to it!
it hotfoot it (off to) somewhere
it hotfoot it out of somewhere
it How goes it?
it How goes it (with you)?
it How's it going?
it How's (it) with you?
it (I) can't help it.
it (I) couldn't help it.
it I don't believe it!
it I don't understand (it).
it I doubt it.
it (I) love it!
it I need it yesterday.

it (I) won't breathe a word (of it).
it (I) wouldn't bet on it.
it (I) wouldn't count on it.
it I wouldn't touch it with a ten-foot pole.
it I'd bet money (on it).
it If a thing is worth doing, it's worth doing well.
it If anything can go wrong, it will.
it If God did not exist, it would be necessary to invent Him.
it If it ain't chickens, it's feathers.
it If it was a snake it woulda bit you.
it If the shoe fits(, wear it).
it If you don't like it, (you can) lump it.
it If you don't see what you want, please ask (for it).
it If you want a thing done well, do it yourself.
it Ignorance (of the law) is no excuse (for breaking it).
it I'll get right on it.
it (I'm) glad to hear it.
it (Is it) cold enough for you?
it (Is it) hot enough for you?
it It ain't fittin'.
it (It) beats me.
it it behooves one to do sth
it It blows my mind!
it (It) can't be helped.
it (It) couldn't be better.
it (It) couldn't be helped.
it It cuts two ways.
it (It) doesn't bother me any.
it (It) doesn't bother me at all.
it (It) doesn't hurt to ask.
it It doesn't quite suit me.
it (It) don't bother me none.
it (It) don't cut no ice (with so).
it (It) don't cut no squares (with so).
it (It) don't make me no nevermind.
it It figures.
it It has so's name on it.
it (It) hasn't been easy.
it It is a long lane that has no turning.
it It is a poor heart that never rejoices.
it It is a wise child that knows its own father.
it It is all over with so.
it It is better to be born lucky than rich.
it It is better to give than to receive.
it It is better to travel hopefully than to arrive.
it It is better to wear out than to rust out.
it It is easier to tear down than to build up.
it It is easy to be wise after the event.
it It is more blessed to give than to receive.
it It is never too late to learn.
it It is never too late to mend.
it It is not work that kills, but worry.
it It is the pace that kills.
it It isn't worth it.
it It isn't worth the trouble.
it (It) just goes to show (you) (sth).
it (It) (just) goes without saying.
it (It) makes me no difference.
it (It) makes no difference to me.
it (It) never hurts to ask.
it It never rains but it pours.
it It (only) stands to reason.

it (It) (really) doesn't matter to me.
it It's a (dead) cinch.
it It's a deal.
it It's a jungle out there.
it It's a snap.
it It's a toss-up.
it It's about time!
it It's (all) Greek to me.
it It's all over but the shouting.
it It's all so needs.
it It's always darkest just before the dawn.
it It's an ill bird that fouls its own nest.
it It's an ill wind that blows nobody (any) good.
it It's anybody's guess.
it It's been.
it It's been a slice!
it (It's been) good talking to you.
it (It's) better than nothing.
it It's for a fact.
it It's for you.
it (It's) good to be here.
it (It's) good to have you here.
it (It's) good to hear your voice.
it (It's) good to see you (again).
it (It's) got me beat.
it it's high time
it It's ill waiting for dead men's shoes.
it It's just one of those things.
it (It's) just what you need.
it (It's) nice to be here.
it (It's) nice to have you here.
it (It's) nice to meet you.
it (It's) nice to see you.
it (It's) no picnic!
it (It's) no trouble (at all).
it It's no use crying over spilled milk.
it (It's) none of your business!
it It's not cricket.
it (It's) not half bad.
it It's not kosher.
it It's not over till it's over.
it (It's) not supposed to.
it It's not the heat, it's the humidity.
it It's on me.
it It's raining cats and dogs.
it It's raining pitchforks (and hammer handles).
it It's six of one, half a dozen of another.
it (It's) time for a change.
it (It's) time to go.
it (It's) time to hit the road.
it (It's) time to run.
it (It's) time to shove off.
it (It's) time to split.
it It's time we should be going.
it It's written all over one's face.
it It's you!
it It's your funeral.
it It's your move.
it It's your turn.
it it strikes me that
it It sucks.
it (It) suits me (fine).
it It takes all kinds (to make a world).
it It takes money to make money.
it (It) takes one to know one.
it It takes (some) getting used to.
it It takes two to make a bargain.
it It takes two to make a quarrel.
it (It) takes two to tango.

it It will be your ass!
it It will take some doing.
it (It) won't bother me any.
it (It) won't bother me at all.
it It won't wash!
it (It) works for me.
it It would take an act of Congress to do sth
it It'll all come out in the wash.
it It'll be a cold day in hell when sth happens.
it It'll be a long day in January when sth happens.
it It'll never fly.
it I've had it up to here (with so/sth).
it Keep a thing seven years and you'll (always) find a use for it.
it Keep at it!
it keep it down (to a dull roar)
it keep (it) in mind that
it Keep it up!
it knew it was coming
it Knock it off!
it know where it's at
it land so poor it wouldn't even raise a fuss
it lay it on the line
it lay it on thick
it lay it on with a trowel
it leave it at that
it leave it to so
it leave so to it
it Let George do it.
it let it all hang out
it Let it be.
it Let it go.
it Let it roll!
it Let me have it!
it Let's call it a day.
it Let's go somewhere where it's (more) quiet.
it Let's have it!
it Let's shake on it.
it Let's talk (about it).
it let so have it (with both barrels)
it Like it or lump it!
it Like it's such a big deal!
it like it was going out of style
it live it up
it long and the short of it
it lord it over so
it lose it
it Lump it!
it make a day of it
it make a night of it
it make a run for it
it make it
it Make no bones about it.
it Make no mistake (about it)!
it mix it up (with so)
it need so bad one can taste it
it no buts about it
it no ifs, ands, or buts (about it)
it no matter how you slice it
it no two ways about it
it not breathe a word of it
it not give it another thought
it not put it past so
it not to put too fine a point on it
it not with it
it not worth the paper it's printed on
it not worth the paper it's written on

it Nothing so bad but (it) might have been worse.
it Nothing to it!
it on the face of it
it out of it
it pack it in
it park it (somewhere)
it play it cool
it play it for all it's worth
it play it safe
it pour it on thick
it Put a sock in it!
it put it on the line
it put one's foot in it
it put one's nose in (where it's not wanted)
it Put that in your pipe and smoke it!
it put to it
it read it and weep
it recognize sth for what it is
it rolling in it
it rough it
it rub so's nose in it
it rumor has it that...
it run for it
it Run it by (me) again.
it run it down
it Save it!
it see (to it) that sth is done
it Shake it (up)!
it shame of it (all)!
it shank it
it short and the long of it
it Shut up about it.
it Skip it!
it slug it out
it Snap it up!
it Snap to it!
it so bad one can taste it
it So be it.
it So it goes.
it sock it to so
it So had better keep still about it.
it spend money like it's going out of style
it spread it on thick
it step on it
it stick it to so
it stick one's nose in (where it's not wanted)
it Stick with it.
it stretch it
it strike it rich
it Stuff a sock in it!
it such as it is
it swim for it
it take it
it Take my word for it.
it Tell it like it is.
it Tell it to the marines!
it That ain't the way I heard it.
it That does it!
it That's about the size of it.
it That's it!
it That's (just) the way it goes.
it That's more like it.
it That tears it!
it The butler did it.
it the way I see it
it (There ain't) nothin' to it.
it (There is) no doubt about it.
it (There's) nothing to it!
it Think nothing of it.

it This is it.
it tie it on
it Time to call it a day.
it Time to call it a night.
it 'Tis better to have loved and lost than never to have loved at all.
it to put it another way
it to put it mildly
it to whom it may concern
it Wanna make sumpin' of it?
it want so bad one can taste it
it Want to make something of it?
it Watch it!
it way it plays
it What about it?
it What difference does it make?
it What is it?
it What of it?
it What's in it for me?
it What's it to you?
it What'll it be?
it when it comes right down to it
it when it comes to sth
it Where ignorance is bliss, 'tis folly to be wise.
it where it's at
it Who is it?
it Who was it?
it whoop it up
it wing it
it Wipe it off!
it with everything (on it)
it with it
it worth of a thing is what it will bring.
it You asked for it!
it You can lead a horse to water, but you can't make it drink.
it You cannot have your cake and eat it (too).
it (You) can't take it with you.
it You don't know the half of it.
it You don't know where it's been.
it You got it!
it You just don't get it!
it You said it!
it You want to make something of it?
it You('d) better believe it!
it You'll get onto it.
it You'll get the hang of it.
it You'll never get away with it.
it Zip it up!
itch itch for sth
itch itch to do sth
itch itching palm
itch itchy feet
itch itchy palm
itch seven-year itch
itself blow itself out
itself burn (itself) out
itself by itself
itself coil (itself) around so/sth
itself coil (itself) up
itself end in itself
itself engorge (itself) on so/sth
itself engorge (itself) with sth
itself History repeats itself.
itself house divided against itself cannot stand.
itself in and of itself
itself speak for itself
itself suggest itself to so
itself work itself out
itself wreathe (itself) around so/sth

itty itty-bitty
ivory dwell in an ivory tower
ivory in an ivory tower
ivory live in an ivory tower
ivory tickle the ivories
ivory work in an ivory tower
jab jab at so/sth
jab jab so in sth
jab jab so with sth
jab jab sth at so/sth
jab jab sth into sth
jab jab sth out
jab take a jab at so
jabber jabber about so/sth
jack All work and no play makes Jack a dull boy.
jack before you can say Jack Robinson
jack Every Jack has his Jill.
jack good Jack makes a good Jill.
jack jack around
jack jack of all trades
jack jack of all trades is a master of none.
jack jack so around
jack jack so up
jack jack sth up
jack jacked (out)
jack quicker than you can say Jack Robinson
jackpot hit the jackpot
jackrabbit knee-high to a jackrabbit
jail bail so out of jail
jam find oneself in a jam
jam get out of a jam
jam get so out of a jam
jam in a jam
jam in(to) a jam
jam jam session
jam jam so/sth in((to) sth)
jam jam so/sth together
jam jam sth together
jam jam sth up
jam jam sth (up) with sth
jam jam the brakes on
jam jam with so
jam traffic jam
jangle jangle on sth
January cold as a welldigger's ass (in January)
January cold as a welldigger's feet (in January)
January It'll be a long day in January when sth happens.
January slow as molasses in January
January slower than molasses in January
jar jar against so/sth
jar jar on so/sth
jaw flap one's jaws
jaw have a glass jaw
jaw jaw about so/sth
jaw jaw at so
jaw jaw so down
jaw snatch so from the jaws of death
jaw snatch so out of the jaws of death
jaw snatch victory from the jaws of defeat
jawbone diarrhea of the jawbone
jaybird naked as a jaybird
jazz and all that jazz
jazz jazz so/sth up
jazz jazzed (up)
jeer jeer at so/sth

Jekyll Jekyll and Hyde
jeopardy in jeopardy
jeopardy place so/sth in jeopardy
jeopardy put so/sth in(to) jeopardy
jerk jerk around
jerk jerk so around
jerk jerk so/sth out of sth
jerk jerk so over
jerk jerk sth away (from so/sth or an animal)
jerk jerk sth off
jerk jerk sth out of so/sth
jerk jerk sth up
jerk knee-jerk reaction
jest jest about so/sth
jest jest at so/sth
jest jest with so
jest Many a true word is spoken in jest.
jest There's many a true word spoken in jest.
jet jet (from some place) (to some place)
jet jet from sth
jetsam flotsam and jetsam
jibe jibe with sth
jiffy in a jiffy
jig jig is up.
Jill Every Jack has his Jill.
Jill good Jack makes a good Jill.
jim jim-dandy
jimmy jimmy sth up
job between jobs
job come to the job with sth
job devil of a job
job devil's own job
job do a job on so/sth
job do a snow job on so
job Don't give up your day job.
job Don't quit your day job.
job fall down on the job
job Give us the tools, and we will finish the job.
job Good job!
Job have the patience of Job
job lay down on the job
job inside job
job lie down on the job
job make the best of a bad job
job Nice job!
job nine-to-five job
job on the job
job patient as Job
job pull a job
job put-up job
job snow job
job walk off the job
jockey jockey around
jockey jockey for position
jockey jockey so/sth into position
jockey jockey sth around
Joe holy Joe
jog jog along
jog jog so's memory
jog jog to the right or left
John Dear John letter
John one's John Hancock
John one's John Henry
join Could I join you?
join (Do you) care if I join you?
join (Do you) mind if I join you?
join If you can't beat them, join them.
join If you can't lick 'em, join 'em.
join join forces (with so)
join join hands

join join in (with so)
join join in ((with) sth)
join join so with so else
join join sth and sth else together
join join sth to sth else
join join sth with sth else
join Join the club!
join join the fray
join join up
join join (up) with so/sth
join join with so
join joined at the hip
join (Would you) care to join us?
joint blow the joint
joint case the joint
joint get one's nose out of joint
joint have one's nose out of joint
joint put one's nose out of joint
joint put so's nose out of joint
joke able to take a joke
joke (all) joking aside
joke butt of a joke
joke crack a joke
joke inside joke
joke joke is on so.
joke joke (with so) (about so/sth)
joke no joke
joke play a joke on so
joke rich man's joke is always funny.
joke standing joke
jolt jolt so out of sth
jolt jolt to a start
jolt jolt to a stop
Jones Davy Jones's locker
Jones go to Davy Jones's locker
Jones keep up with the Joneses
José No way, José!
jostle jostle so around
jostle jostle so aside
jostle jostle with so
jot jot sth down
journey Have a safe journey.
jowl cheek by jowl
joy bundle of joy
joy burst with joy
joy jump for joy
joy leap for joy
joy pride and joy
joy thing of beauty is a joy forever.
joy weep for joy
judge Don't judge a book by its cover.
judge judge between so/sth and so/sth else
judge Judge not, lest ye be judged.
judge Judge not, that ye be not judged.
judge judge one on one's own merits
judge judge sth on its own merits
judge judging by sth
judge pass judgment (on so/sth)
judge sit in judgment (up)on so/sth
judge sober as a judge
judgment pass judgment (on so/sth)
judgment sit in judgment (up)on so/sth
jug jugged (up)
juggle juggle so/sth around
juice cow juice
juice juice and cookies
juice juice sth back
juice juice sth up
juice juice up
juice stew in one's own juice
July grow knee-high by the 4th of July
July knee-high by the 4th of July

jumble jumble so/sth together
jumble jumble sth together
jumble jumble sth up
jump (almost) jump out of one's skin
jump Go jump in the lake!
jump hop, skip, and a jump
jump jump across sth
jump jump all over so
jump jump at so/sth
jump jump at sth
jump jump at the opportunity (to do sth)
jump jump bail
jump jump clear of sth
jump jump (down) (from sth)
jump jump down so's throat
jump jump down sth
jump jump for joy
jump jump from sth to sth
jump jump in with both feet
jump jump in((to) sth)
jump jump into the fray
jump jump off ((of) sth)
jump jump off the deep end
jump jump on so
jump jump on so/sth
jump jump on the bandwagon
jump jump on((to) sth)
jump jump out of sth
jump jump out of the frying pan into the fire
jump jump over sth
jump jump over the broomstick
jump jump ship
jump jump the gun
jump jump the track
jump jump through a hoop
jump jump to conclusions
jump jump up (from sth)
jump jump up (on so/sth)
jump jump up (to sth)
jump jump with sth
jump jumping-off place
jump jumping-off point
jump nearly jump out of one's skin
jump *on the bandwagon
jump one jump ahead (of so/sth)
jump Take a running jump (in the lake)!
jump two jumps ahead of so
juncture at this juncture
jungle It's a jungle out there.
junk junk mail
junkyard meaner than a junkyard dog (with fourteen sucking pups)
jury jury is still out on so/sth.
just able to take just so much
just Be just before you're generous.
just can (just) whistle for sth
just darkest hour is just before the dawn.
just Don't that (just) beat all!
just Everything will be just fine.
just get one's just deserts
just get one's just reward(s)
just go to one's (just) reward
just had (just) as soon do sth
just have just one oar in the water
just I just have this feeling.
just (I) just want(ed) to mention sth.
just (I) just want(ed) to say sth.
just I know (just) what you mean.
just (I was) just wondering.

just I'd (just) as leave do sth
just I'd (just) as soon (as) do sth
just (I'm) just getting by.
just I'm just looking.
just (I'm just) minding my own business.
just (I'm) (just) plugging along.
just (I'm) (just) thinking out loud.
just in (just) a minute
just in (just) a second
just (It) just goes to show (you) (sth).
just (It) (just) goes without saying.
just It's always darkest just before the dawn.
just It's just one of those things.
just (It's) just what you need.
just just a minute
just (just) a stone's throw away (from sth)
just (just) a stone's throw (from sth)
just (just) as I expected
just just fell off the turnip truck
just just in case
just just in time
just just let me say
just just like that
just just off the boat
just just one's cup of tea
just just passing through
just just so
just (just) taking care of business
just just the same
just just the ticket
just just what the doctor ordered
just Just (you) wait (and see)!
just let me (just) say
just Life is just a bowl of cherries.
just not just whistling Dixie
just Some people (just) don't know when to quit.
just That's (just) the way it goes.
just That's (just) too much!
just That's just what you need.
just We were just talking about you.
just would (just) as soon do sth
just You ain't just whistlin' Dixie.
just You just don't get it!
just You (just) wait (and see)!
just (You) (just) watch!
just You're (just) wasting my time.
justice bring so to justice
justice do justice to sth
justice miscarriage of justice
justice poetic justice
justice travesty of justice
justify end justifies the means.
justify justify sth by sth
justify justify sth to so
jut jut out (from sth)
jut jut out (into sth)
jut jut out (over sth)
juxtapose juxtapose so/sth to so/sth
kangaroo kangaroo court
Katie Katie bar the door
keel keel over
keel keel sth over
keel keep on an even keel
keel keep sth on an even keel
keen have a keen interest in sth
keen keen about sth
keen keen on doing sth
keen keen on so/sth
keep Am I my brother's keeper?

keep apple a day keeps the doctor away.
keep be one's brother's keeper
keep Better keep still about it.
keep Can you keep a secret?
keep Could you keep a secret?
keep Desert and reward seldom keep company.
keep earn one's keep
keep enough to keep body and soul together
keep Finders keepers(, losers weepers).
keep for keeps
keep for safekeeping
keep (Have you) been keeping busy?
keep (Have you) been keeping cool?
keep (Have you) been keeping out of trouble?
keep hedge between keeps friendship green.
keep I am not my brother's keeper.
keep I'll thank you to keep your opinions to yourself.
keep in keeping (with sth)
keep (I've) been keeping cool.
keep (I've) been keeping myself busy.
keep (I've) been keeping out of trouble.
keep keep a civil tongue (in one's head)
keep keep a close rein on so/sth
keep keep a close watch on so/sth
keep keep a firm grip on so/sth
keep keep a lid on sth
keep keep a low profile
keep keep a promise
keep keep a secret
keep Keep a stiff upper lip.
keep keep a straight face
keep Keep a thing seven years and you'll (always) find a use for it.
keep keep a tight grip on so/sth
keep keep a tight rein on so/sth
keep keep abreast of so/sth
keep keep after so (about sth)
keep keep ahead (of so/sth)
keep keep ahead of sth
keep keep ahead of the game
keep keep aloof from so/sth
keep keep an act up
keep keep an ear to the ground
keep keep an eye on so/sth
keep keep an eye out (for so/sth)
keep keep an open mind
keep keep at arm's length from so/sth
keep Keep at it!
keep keep at so (about sth)
keep keep at sth
keep keep away (from so/sth)
keep keep banker's hours
keep keep body and soul together
keep keep clear of sth
keep keep (close) watch (on so/sth)
keep keep (close) watch (over so/sth)
keep keep company (with so)
keep keep cool
keep keep faith with so
keep keep fit
keep keep from sth
keep keep (going) on about so/sth
keep keep (going) on at so/sth
keep keep good time
keep keep harping on sth

keep keep house
keep keep in good condition
keep keep in good shape
keep keep in good with so
keep keep in step (with so)
keep Keep in there!
keep Keep in touch.
keep keep in touch (with so)
keep keep in touch (with so/sth)
keep keep in training
keep keep inside ((of) sth)
keep keep it down (to a dull roar)
keep keep (it) in mind that
keep Keep it up!
keep keep late hours
keep keep off (of) so's back
keep keep off (of) so's case
keep keep off ((of) sth)
keep keep on
keep keep on keeping on
keep Keep (on) trying.
keep keep one in one's place
keep keep one on one's toes
keep keep one's act up
keep keep one's cards close to one's chest
keep keep one's cards close to one's vest
keep keep one's chair
keep keep one's chin up
keep keep one's cool
keep keep one's distance (from so/sth)
keep keep one's ear to the ground
keep keep one's end of the bargain up
keep keep one's end up
keep keep one's eye on so/sth
keep keep one's eye on the ball
keep keep one's eyes open (for so/sth)
keep keep one's eye(s) out (for so/sth)
keep keep one's eyes peeled (for so/sth)
keep keep one's feet on the ground
keep keep one's finger on the pulse of sth
keep keep one's fingers crossed (for so/sth)
keep keep one's hand in (sth)
keep keep one's hands off (sth)
keep keep one's hands to oneself
keep keep one's head
keep keep one's mind on so/sth
keep keep one's mouth shut (about so/sth)
keep keep one's nose clean
keep keep one's nose out of so's business
keep keep one's nose out of sth
keep keep one's nose to the grindstone
keep keep one's opinions to oneself
keep keep one's own counsel
keep keep one's pants on
keep keep one's place
keep keep one's promise
keep keep one's seat
keep keep one's shirt on
keep keep one's shoulder to the wheel
keep keep one's side of the bargain
keep keep one's temper
keep keep one's weather eye open
keep keep one's wits about one
keep keep one's word
keep keep one step ahead of so/sth
keep keep oneself above suspicion
keep keep oneself to oneself
keep keep out from under so's feet

keep Keep out of my way.
keep keep out of sight
keep keep out (of sth)
keep Keep out of this!
keep keep pace (with so/sth)
keep keep people straight (in one's mind)
keep keep quiet (about so/sth)
keep keep sight of so/sth
keep Keep smiling.
keep keep so at sth
keep keep so back
keep keep so company
keep keep so down
keep keep so from doing sth
keep keep so from so/sth
keep keep so honest
keep keep so in (a state of) suspense
keep keep so in ignorance (about so/sth)
keep keep so in sight
keep keep so in stitches
keep keep so in the dark (about so/sth)
keep keep so in the picture
keep keep so on
keep keep so on a string
keep keep so on (sth)
keep keep so on tenterhooks
keep keep so or an animal in
keep keep so or some creature out in the cold
keep keep so/sth about
keep keep so/sth apart
keep keep so/sth around
keep keep so/sth at a distance
keep keep so/sth at arm's length
keep keep so/sth at bay
keep keep so/sth away (from so/sth)
keep keep so/sth back
keep keep so/sth by so
keep keep so/sth down
keep keep so/sth for so
keep keep so/sth from doing sth
keep keep so/sth going
keep keep so/sth hanging (in midair)
keep keep so/sth in check
keep keep so/sth in mind
keep keep so/sth in order
keep keep so/sth in reserve
keep keep so/sth in some place
keep keep so/sth in with so/sth
keep keep so/sth off
keep keep so/sth on (the) (right) track
keep keep so/sth on track
keep keep so/sth out (of sth)
keep keep so/sth out of the way
keep keep so/sth quiet
keep keep so/sth still
keep keep so/sth together
keep keep so/sth under (close) scrutiny
keep keep so/sth under control
keep keep so/sth under sth
keep keep (so/sth) within bounds
keep keep so posted
keep keep so/sth or an animal back (from so/sth)
keep keep so under so's thumb
keep keep so up
keep keep so young at heart
keep keep sth by
keep keep sth down
keep keep sth for a rainy day
keep keep sth for another occasion
keep keep sth from so
keep keep sth in

keep keep sth inside ((of) one(self))
keep keep sth of so's or sth's
keep keep sth on
keep keep sth quiet
keep keep sth still
keep keep sth to a minimum
keep keep sth to oneself
keep keep sth under one's hat
keep keep sth under wraps
keep keep sth until some time
keep keep sth up
keep keep sth with so
keep Keep still.
keep keep tab(s) (on so/sth)
keep keep the ball rolling
keep keep the home fires burning
keep keep the stork busy
keep keep the stork flying
keep keep the wolf from the door
keep keep things straight (in one's mind)
keep Keep this to yourself.
keep keep time
keep keep to oneself
keep keep to sth
keep keep to the straight and narrow
keep keep together
keep keep track (of so/sth)
keep keep under sth
keep keep under wraps
keep keep up an act
keep keep up appearances
keep keep up one's act
keep Keep up the good work.
keep keep up (with so/sth)
keep keep up with the Joneses
keep keep up with the times
keep keep watch on so/sth
keep keep watch over so/sth
keep keep within sth
keep Keep your chin up.
keep Keep your head down.
keep Keep your mouth shut (about so/sth).
keep Keep your nose out of my business.
keep Keep your opinions to yourself!
keep Keep your pants on!
keep Keep your powder dry.
keep Keep your shirt on!
keep Keep your shop and your shop will keep you.
keep *low profile
keep man is known by the company he keeps.
keep old poacher makes the best gamekeeper.
keep *on one's toes
keep *open mind
keep *out in the cold
keep out of keeping (with sth)
keep *out of sight
keep play for keeps
keep Put your trust in God, and keep your powder dry.
keep So had better keep still about it.
keep *straight face
keep *under (close) scrutiny
keep *under control
keep *under so's thumb
keep *under wraps
keep use your head for more than something to keep your ears apart
keep What's keeping so?

keep Where (have) you been keeping yourself?
keep Why keep a dog and bark yourself?
keep You been keeping busy?
keep You been keeping cool?
keep You been keeping out of trouble?
keeper Am I my brother's keeper?
keeper be one's brother's keeper
keeper Finders keepers(, losers weepers).
keeper I am not my brother's keeper.
keg sitting on a powder keg
ken beyond one's ken
kernel He that would eat the kernel must crack the nut.
kettle fine kettle of fish
kettle pot is calling the kettle black.
kettle That's the pot calling the kettle black.
key church key
key golden key can open any door.
key key so up
key key to success
key keyed up (about sth)
key modulate to a (different) key
key off-key
kibosh put the kibosh on so/sth
kick alive and kicking
kick for kicks
kick get a kick out of so/sth
kick get one's kicks (from so/sth)
kick give so a kick
kick have a kick to it
kick kick a habit
kick kick about so/sth
kick kick against so/sth
kick kick around
kick kick ass
kick kick at so/sth
kick kick back
kick kick butt
kick kick in (on sth) (for so/sth)
kick kick in the ass
kick kick in the butt
kick kick in the guts
kick kick in the (seat of the) pants
kick kick in the teeth
kick kick like a mule
kick kick like a steer
kick kick off
kick kick one's heels up
kick kick oneself (for doing sth)
kick kick out (at so/sth)
kick kick over
kick kick some ass (around)
kick kick so or an animal out
kick kick so/sth around
kick kick so/sth aside
kick kick so/sth away
kick kick sth around
kick kick sth back (to so/sth)
kick kick sth down
kick kick sth in
kick kick sth off
kick kick sth out of sth
kick kick the bucket
kick kick the habit
kick kick the (natural) stuffing out of so
kick kick up
kick mad enough to kick a cat
kick *up a storm
kid (all) kidding aside

kid handle so with kid gloves
kid I kid you not.
kid I'm not kidding.
kid kid around (with so)
kid kid's stuff
kid kid so about so/sth
kid like a kid with a new toy
kid new kid on the block
kid No kidding!
kid not a kid anymore
kid snotnose(d) (kid)
kid Who do you think you're kidding?
kid You've got to be kidding!
kill close in for the kill
kill Curiosity killed the cat.
kill dressed to kill
kill dressed (up) fit to kill
kill even if it kills me
kill fit to kill
kill go at sth like a boy killing snakes
kill have (some) time to kill
kill if looks could kill
kill in at the kill
kill in on the kill
kill It is not work that kills, but worry.
kill It is the pace that kills.
kill kill for sth
kill kill so or an animal off
kill kill so with kindness
kill kill the fatted calf
kill Kill the goose that lays the golden egg(s).
kill kill time
kill kill two birds with one stone
kill killed outright
kill killer instinct
kill look fit to kill
kill make a killing
kill move in for the kill
kill sth is killing so
kilter get off kilter
kilter go off kilter
kilter go out of kilter
kilter knock sth off kilter
kilter knock sth out of kilter
kilter off-kilter
kilter out of kilter
kimono open (up) one's kimono
kin kith and kin
kin one's next of kin
kind all kinds of so/sth
kind do so a kindness
kind feeling (kinda) puny
kind in kind
kind It takes all kinds (to make a world).
kind kill so with kindness
kind Kind of.
kind kind of sth
kind milk of human kindness
kind nothing of the kind
kind take kindly to sth
kind Thank you kindly.
kind two of a kind
kindness do so a kindness
kindness kill so with kindness
kindness milk of human kindness
king Cash is king.
king cat can look at a king.
king cocky as the king of spades
king cost a king's ransom
king fit for a king

king In the country of the blind, the one-eyed man is king.
king king's ransom
king Kings have long arms.
king pay a king's ransom
king spend a king's ransom
king sport of kings
kingdom blow so/sth to kingdom come
kingdom till kingdom come
kink get the kinks (ironed) out
kink kink up
kiss blow so a kiss
kiss (Do) you kiss your momma with that mouth?
kiss kiss and make up
kiss kiss and tell
kiss kiss of death
kiss kiss off
kiss kiss so off
kiss kiss so on sth
kiss kiss so/sth off
kiss kiss so's ass
kiss kiss sth away (from sth)
kiss kiss sth good-bye
kiss kiss the dust
kiss kiss up to so
kiss kissing cousins
kiss right in the kisser
kiss sealed with a kiss
kisser right in the kisser
kit whole kit and caboodle
kitchen everything but the kitchen sink
kitchen If you can't stand the heat, get out of the kitchen.
kite Go fly a kite!
kite high as a kite
kith kith and kin
kitten dust kitten
kitten feed the kitty
kitten have kittens
kitten purr like a kitten
kitten weak as a kitten
kitty feed the kitty
klutz klutz around
knee fall on one's knees
knee fall to one's knees
knee go down on one's knees
knee grow knee-high by the 4th of July
knee knee-deep in sth
knee knee-high by the 4th of July
knee knee-high to a grasshopper
knee knee-high to a jackrabbit
knee knee-jerk reaction
knee knock one's knees together
knee on bended knee
knee since so was knee-high to a grasshopper
knee stand knee-deep in sth
knee up to one's knees
kneel kneel down
kneel kneel down (before so/sth)
knew knew it was coming
knife go under the knife
knife pull a knife (on so)
knit knit one's brow
knit knit sth together
knit knit together
knock Don't knock it.
knock knock about (some place) (with so)
knock knock about (somewhere)
knock knock against so/sth
knock knock around

knock knock at sth
knock knock away (at sth)
knock knock back a drink
knock Knock it off!
knock knock off (doing sth)
knock knock off (work)
knock knock on sth
knock knock on wood
knock knock one back
knock knock one off one's feet
knock knock one over
knock knock one's head (up) against a brick wall
knock knock one's knees together
knock knock oneself out (to do sth) (for so/sth)
knock knock over sth
knock knock some heads together
knock knock some sense into so
knock knock so back (an amount of money)
knock knock so cold
knock knock so dead
knock knock so down a peg (or two)
knock knock so down to size
knock knock so for a loop
knock knock so into sth
knock knock so off
knock knock so/sth about
knock knock so/sth down
knock knock so/sth over
knock knock so out
knock knock so over (with a feather)
knock knock so's block off
knock knock so's socks off
knock knock so some skin
knock knock so up
knock knock sth against sth
knock knock sth back
knock knock sth down
knock knock sth into a cocked hat
knock knock sth off
knock knock sth out
knock knock sth over
knock knock sth to so
knock knock sth together
knock knock the bejeebers out of so/sth
knock knock the bottom out (of sth)
knock knock the habit
knock knock the hell out of so/sth
knock knock the (living) daylights out of so
knock knock the props out from under so
knock knock the stuffing out of so
knock knock the wind out of so's sails
knock knock through sth
knock knock (up) against so/sth
knock knock-down, drag-out fight
knock knocked in
knock knocked out
knock knocked up
knock Opportunity knocks but once.
knock school of hard knocks
knock You could have knocked me over with a feather.
knot knot sth together
knot tie so (up) in knots
knot tie sth in a knot
knot tie the knot
know Anyone I know?
know as far as anyone knows
know before you know it

know Better the devil you know than the devil you don't know.
know (Do you) know what?
know (Do you) know what I mean?
know (Do you) know what I'm saying?
know (Do you) want to know something?
know doesn't care who knows it
know doesn't know beans (about sth)
know doesn't know his ass from a hole in the ground
know doesn't know his ass from his elbow
know Don't I know it!
know Don't I know you from somewhere?
know don't know whether to eat it or rub it on
know Don't you know it!
know dying to know (sth)
know for all I know
know God only knows!
know (had) known it was coming
know Half the world knows not how the other half lives.
know How do you know?
know How should I know?
know How will I know you?
know I don't know.
know I don't rightly know.
know I know (just) what you mean.
know (I) wouldn't know.
know if one knows what's good for one
know if the truth were known
know if you know what's good for you
know in the know
know It is a wise child that knows its own father.
know (It) takes one to know one.
know know a thing or two (about so/sth)
know know a trick or two
know know about so/sth
know know all the angles
know know as much about sth as a hog knows about Sunday
know know at a glance that...
know know better (than to do sth)
know know from sth
know know no more about sth than a frog knows about bedsheets
know know of so/sth
know know one for what one is
know know one's ABCs
know know one's onions
know know one's place
know know one's stuff
know know one's way about
know know one's way around
know know shit from Shinola
know know so as so
know know so by sight
know know so from so
know know so/sth as sth
know know so/sth by name
know know so/sth by sth
know know so/sth like the back of one's hand
know know so/sth like the palm of one's hand
know know sth backwards and forwards
know know sth by heart

know know sth forwards and backwards
know know sth from memory
know know sth from sth
know know sth in one's bones
know know sth inside out
know know sth only too well
know know sth through and through
know know the big picture
know know the ropes
know know the score
know know the tricks of the trade
know Know thyself.
know Know what?
know know what's what
know know when one is not wanted
know know where all the bodies are buried
know know where it's at
know know where one is coming from
know know where so stands (on so/sth)
know know where sth is at
know know whereof one speaks
know know which is which
know know which side one's bread is buttered on
know known fact
know known quantity
know left hand doesn't know what the right hand is doing.
know let so know (about sth)
know like, you know
know Lord knows I've tried.
know man is known by the company he keeps.
know more than you('ll ever) know
know Necessity knows no law.
know not know beans (about so/sth)
know not know enough to come in out of the rain
know not know from nothing
know not know if one is coming or going
know not know one's own strength
know not know so from Adam
know not know the first thing about so/sth
know not know what to make of so/sth
know not know where to turn
know not know whether one is coming or going
know not know which end is up
know not know which way to turn
know *ropes
know so far as anyone knows
know Some people (just) don't know when to quit.
know (the) Lord only knows
know tree is known by its fruit.
know *tricks of the trade
know (Well,) what do you know!
know What do you know?
know What do you know (about that)?
know What do you know for sure?
know What one doesn't know won't hurt one.
know What's (there) to know?
know What you don't know won't hurt you.
know Who knows?
know You don't know the half of it.
know You don't know where it's been.
know you know

know You never know (what you can do) till you try.
know (You want to) know something?
knowledge have carnal knowledge of so
knowledge Knowledge is power.
knowledge little knowledge is a dangerous thing.
knowledge to the best of one's knowledge
known (had) known it was coming
known if the truth were known
known known fact
known known quantity
known man is known by the company he keeps.
known tree is known by its fruit.
knuckle ask for a knuckle sandwich
knuckle get one's knuckles rapped
knuckle knuckle down (to sth)
knuckle knuckle sandwich
knuckle knuckle under (to so/sth)
knuckle rap so across the knuckles
knuckle want a knuckle sandwich
knuckle white knuckle sth
kosher It's not kosher.
kowtow kowtow to so/sth
label label so/sth as sth
label label so/sth with sth
labor fruits of one's labor(s)
labor in labor
labor induce labor in so
labor labor at sth
labor labor for so/sth
labor labor for sth
labor labor of love
labor labor over so/sth
labor labor under an assumption
lace lace into so/sth
lace lace so into sth
lace lace so up
lace lace sth up
lace lace sth with sth
lack lack for sth
ladder at the bottom of the ladder
ladder can't see a hole in a ladder
ladder Crosses are ladders that lead to heaven.
ladder He who would climb the ladder must begin at the bottom.
ladder on the bottom rung (of the ladder)
ladies Ladies first.
ladle ladle sth out of sth
ladle ladle sth up
lady Faint heart never won fair lady.
lady Ladies first.
lady ladies' man
lady lady of the evening
lady till the fat lady sings
lady when the fat lady sings
lag lag behind in sth
lag lag behind (so/sth)
laid best-laid plans of mice and men oft(en) go astray.
laid get laid
laid laid back
laid laid out
laid laid up
lake Go jump in the lake!
lake Take a running jump (in the lake)!
lam lam into so or an animal
lam on the lam

lam take it on the lam
lamb gentle as a lamb
lamb In like a lion, out like a lamb.
lamb in two shakes of a lamb's tail
lamb innocent as a lamb
lamb like a lamb to the slaughter
lamb like lambs to the slaughter
lamb March comes in like a lion, and goes out like a lamb.
lamb meek as a lamb
lamb might as well be hung for a sheep as (for) a lamb
lamb two shakes of a lamb's tail
lame lame duck
lament lament over so/sth
land blight on the land
land do a land-office business
land go on to a better land
land land a blow
land land a job
land land at some place
land land in sth
land Land o' Goshen!
land land of Nod
land land so poor it wouldn't even raise a fuss
land land so in sth
land land sth at some place
land land too poor to raise a racket on
land land up somehow
land land (up)on both feet
land land (up)on one's feet
land land (up)on so/sth
land land-office business
land Land(s) sakes (alive)!
land lay of the land
land live off the fat of the land
land live off the land
land on land
landscape blot on the landscape
landslide landslide victory
lane down the little red lane
lane in the fast lane
lane It is a long lane that has no turning.
lane life in the fast lane
lane live in the fast lane
lane move in the fast lane
lane stay in the fast lane
language in plain language
language language that would fry bacon
language say sth in plain language
language speak so's language
language speak the same language
language use foul language
language use strong language
languish languish in some place
languish languish over so/sth
lap fall into one's lap
lap in the lap of luxury
lap lap of luxury
lap lap over (sth)
lap lap sth up
lap lap (up) against sth
lap Make a lap!
lapse lapse from grace
lapse lapse into sth
lard tub of lard
large at large
large by and large
large come out in large numbers
large large as life

large larger than life
large live large
large loom large (on the horizon)
large out in large numbers
large play a large part (in sth)
lark for a lark
lark happy as a lark
lark on a lark
lash lash against sth
lash lash at so/sth
lash lash back (at so/sth)
lash lash down on so/sth
lash lash into so or an animal
lash lash into sth
lash lash out (at so/sth)
lash lash so/sth down
lash lash so/sth to sth
lash lash sth about
lash lash sth together
lash tongue-lashing
last as a last resort
last at last
last at (long) last
last at the last gasp
last at the last minute
last be the last person (to do sth)
last breathe one's last
last down to the last bit of money
last down to the last detail
last every last one
last famous last words
last First impressions are the most lasting.
last He who laughs last, laughs best.
last He who laughs last, laughs longest.
last head for the last roundup
last I didn't (quite) catch that (last) remark.
last in the last analysis
last last but not least
last last call (for sth)
last last chance (for sth)
last last for sth
last last (from sth) until sth
last last hurrah
last last laugh (on so)
last last out
last last roundup
last last sth out
last last straw
last last will and testament
last last word
last last-ditch effort
last Let the cobbler stick to his last.
last make last-ditch effort
last Nice guys finish last.
last on so's or sth's last legs
last one's last resting place
last pay so's last respects (to so)
last see the last of so/sth
last seem like the last person
last to the last
last very last
latch latch on(to so)
latch latch onto sth
latch latch string is always out.
late at the latest
late Better late than never.
late day late and a dollar short
late It is never too late to learn.
late It is never too late to mend.
late keep late hours

late late bloomer
late late in life
late late in the day
late late unpleasantness
late of late
late stay up late
late too little, too late
later Can we continue this later?
later Catch me later.
later Could we continue this later?
later I'll call back later.
later (I'll) catch you later.
later I'll see you later.
later (I'll) try to catch you later.
later Later, alligator.
later Perhaps a little later.
later (See you) later.
later See you later, alligator.
later Shoot first, ask questions later.
later sooner or later
latest at the latest
lather in a lather
lather lather sth up
lather lather up
lather work oneself (up) into a lather
laugh burst out laughing
laugh bust out laughing
laugh die laughing
laugh Don't make me laugh!
laugh get a laugh
laugh He who laughs last, laughs best.
laugh He who laughs last, laughs longest.
laugh last laugh (on so)
laugh laugh about so/sth
laugh laugh all the way to the bank
laugh Laugh and the world laughs with you; weep and you weep alone.
laugh laugh at so/sth
laugh laugh away at so/sth
laugh laugh in so's face
laugh laugh one's head off
laugh laugh oneself out of sth
laugh laugh oneself silly
laugh laugh out of the other side of one's face
laugh laugh out of the other side of one's mouth
laugh laugh so off the stage
laugh laugh so/sth down
laugh laugh so out of sth
laugh laugh sth away
laugh laugh sth off
laugh laugh sth out of court
laugh laugh up one's sleeve
laugh laugh with sth
laugh no laughing matter
laugh You make me laugh!
laugh laughingstock
laughingstock make a laughingstock of oneself or sth
laughingstock make oneself or sth a laughingstock
laughter double up (with laughter)
laughter split one's sides (with laughter)
launch launch forth on sth
launch launch forth ((up)on sth)
launch launch into sth
launch launch (one's lunch)
launch launch out on sth
launch launch sth against so/sth
laundry in the laundry

laundry so's dirty laundry
laurels look to one's laurels
laurels rest on one's laurels
lavatory go to the lavatory
lavender lay so out in lavender
lavish lavish sth (up)on so
law above the law
law bend the law
law break a law
law break the law
law Ignorance (of the law) is no excuse (for breaking it).
law law unto oneself
law lay down the law (to so) (about sth)
law long arm of the law
law Necessity knows no law.
law one law for the rich and another for the poor
law Possession is nine-tenths of the law.
law Self-preservation is the first law of nature.
law take the law into one's own hands
law vote sth into law
lay best-laid plans of mice and men oft(en) go astray.
lay get laid
lay Kill the goose that lays the golden egg(s).
lay laid back
lay laid out
lay laid up
lay lay a finger on so/sth
lay lay a guilt trip on so
lay lay a (heavy) trip on so
lay lay about
lay lay alongside sth
lay lay an egg
lay lay around
lay lay claim to sth
lay lay down
lay lay emphasis on sth
lay lay eyes on so/sth
lay lay for so/sth
lay lay hold of so/sth
lay lay in ruins
lay lay into so/sth
lay lay it on the line
lay lay it on thick
lay lay it on with a trowel
lay lay low
lay lay of the land
lay lay off ((from) sth)
lay lay off ((of) so/sth)
lay lay off (so/sth)
lay lay one on
lay lay one's cards on the table
lay lay one's hands on so/sth or an animal
lay lay (oneself) down
lay lay over (some place)
lay lay (some) rubber
lay lay some sweet lines on so
lay lay so away
lay lay so down
lay lay so off (from sth)
lay lay so/sth in(to) sth
lay lay so out
lay lay so to rest
lay lay so up
lay lay sth against sth
lay lay sth alongside ((of) sth)
lay lay sth aside
lay lay sth at so's door

lay lay sth at so's feet
lay lay sth away (for so)
lay lay sth before so
lay lay sth by
lay lay sth down (on sth)
lay lay sth for so/sth
lay lay sth in
lay lay sth on
lay lay sth out
lay lay sth over so/sth
lay lay sth to rest
lay lay sth to sth
lay lay sth to waste
lay lay sth together
lay lay sth under sth
lay lay sth up
lay lay stress on sth
lay lay the blame (for sth) on so
lay lay the blame on so/sth
lay lay the finger on so
lay lay to
lay lay waste to sth
layaway put sth in layaway
laze laze sth away
leach leach away
leach leach in(to sth)
leach leach out of sth
leach leach sth away (from sth)
lead All roads lead to Rome.
lead blind leading the blind
lead case of the blind leading the blind
lead Crosses are ladders that lead to heaven.
lead fill so full of lead
lead follow so's lead
lead get the lead out
lead go over like a lead balloon
lead lead a dog's life
lead lead back (to some place)
lead lead down to sth
lead lead forth
lead lead in(to sth)
lead lead off
lead lead on
lead lead so astray
lead lead so by sth
lead lead so by the nose
lead lead so down (sth)
lead lead so down the garden path
lead lead so down to sth
lead lead so into sth
lead lead so on
lead lead so or an animal out of sth
lead lead so or an animal to sth
lead lead so/sth against so/sth
lead lead so/sth (away) (from so/sth)
lead lead so/sth back (to so/sth)
lead lead so/sth forth
lead lead so/sth off
lead lead so to believe sth
lead lead so to to do sth
lead lead so up sth
lead lead so up the garden path
lead lead the life of Riley
lead lead the way
lead lead up to sth
lead lead with so/sth
lead lead with sth
lead leading question
lead lead-pipe cinch
lead on the leading edge
lead One thing leads to another.
lead shake the lead out

lead You can lead a horse to water, but you can't make it drink.
leaf leaf out
leaf leaf through sth
leaf take a leaf out of so's book
leaf turn over a new leaf
league in league (with so)
league not in the same league with so/sth
league play in the big leagues
leak leak in(to sth)
leak leak out
leak leak sth (out)
leak leak sth to so
leak leak through sth
leak take a leak
lean cause lean times (ahead)
lean lean across so/sth
lean lean against so/sth
lean lean and mean
lean lean back
lean lean down
lean lean forward
lean lean in(to sth)
lean lean on so
lean lean out of sth
lean lean over
lean lean sth against so/sth
lean lean sth forward
lean lean times (ahead)
lean lean toward doing sth
lean lean toward so/sth
lean mean lean times (ahead)
leap by leaps and bounds
leap increase by leaps and bounds
leap leap at so/sth
leap leap at the chance (to do sth)
leap leap at the opportunity (to do sth)
leap leap down (from sth)
leap leap for joy
leap leap forward
leap leap of faith
leap leap out (of sth)
leap leap over sth
leap leap to conclusions
leap leap up
leap Look before you leap.
leap require a leap of faith
learn It is never too late to learn.
learn learn a thing or two (about so/sth)
learn learn about so
learn learn by sth
learn learn from so/sth
learn learn of so/sth
learn learn sth by heart
learn learn sth by rote
learn learn sth from so/sth
learn learn sth from the bottom up
learn learn (sth) the hard way
learn learn the ropes
learn learn the tricks of the trade
learn learn to live with sth
learn learning experience
learn live and learn
learn *ropes
learn There is no royal road to learning.
learn *tricks of the trade
learn We must learn to walk before we can run.
learn You are never too old to learn.
lease lease sth back
lease lease sth from so

lease lease sth (out) to so
lease new lease on life
leash have one's brain on a leash
leash on a tight leash
leash strain at the leash
leash unleash so/sth **against** so/sth
leash unleash so/sth (up)on so/sth
least at least
least Idle folk have the least leisure.
least Idle people have the least leisure.
least last but not least
least least little thing
least least of all
least line of least resistance
least not in the least
least path of least resistance
least to say the least
least when least expected
leather hell-bent for leather
leather tough as old (shoe) leather
leave absent without leave
leave (Are you) leaving so soon?
leave Can I leave a message?
leave Could I leave a message?
leave go absent without leave
leave I'd (just) as leave do sth
leave leave a bad taste in so's mouth
leave leave a lot to be desired
leave leave a paper trail
leave leave a sinking ship
leave leave ahead of time
leave leave an impression (on so)
leave leave for some place
leave leave go of so/sth
leave leave in a body
leave leave it at that
leave leave it to so
leave Leave me alone!
leave leave no stone unturned
leave leave of absence
leave leave off sth
leave leave one's mark on so
leave leave one to one's fate
leave leave one to one's own devices
leave leave one to one's own resources
leave leave oneself wide open for sth
leave leave some loose ends
leave leave so at loose ends
leave leave so cold
leave leave so flat
leave leave so for dead
leave leave so high and dry
leave leave so holding the bag
leave leave so in peace
leave leave so in the lurch
leave leave so or some creature out in the cold
leave leave so/sth alone
leave leave so/sth (at) some place
leave leave so/sth be
leave leave so/sth behind
leave leave so/sth hanging (in midair)
leave leave so/sth in one's hands
leave leave so/sth in so's care
leave leave so/sth in (sth)
leave leave so/sth in the care of so
leave leave so/sth in the trust of so
leave leave so/sth out of sth
leave leave so/sth to so
leave leave so/sth under so's care
leave leave so/sth with so/sth
leave leave so sitting pretty
leave leave so/sth or some creature **alone**

leave leave so to it
leave leave so up in the air
leave leave so with an impression
leave leave sth aside
leave leave sth down
leave leave sth for another occasion
leave leave sth for so or an animal
leave leave sth in limbo
leave leave sth in ruins
leave leave sth in the back of so's mind
leave leave sth (lying) around
leave leave sth on
leave leave sth open
leave leave sth to chance
leave leave sth to so
leave leave sth up
leave leave the door open (for sth)
leave leave the room
leave leave them rolling in the aisles
leave leave well enough alone
leave leave with so
leave leave word for so to do sth
leave leave word (with so)
leave make like a tree and leave
leave *on so's shoulders
leave *on the back burner
leave *out in the cold
leave *paper trail
leave *some loose ends
leave Take it or leave it.
leave take leave of one's senses
leave take leave of so/sth
leave take (one's) leave (of so)
leave without (so much as) a (for or) by your leave
leave You leaving so soon?
lecture lecture at so (about sth)
lecture lecture so for sth
lecture lecture ((to) so) about so/sth
leer leer at so
left better left unsaid
left come out of left field
left hang a left
left have two left feet
left jog to the right or left
left keep on the left(-hand) side (of sth)
left left and right
left left hand doesn't know what the right hand is doing.
left left-handed compliment
left out in left field
left out of left field
left pay so a left-handed compliment
left right and left
left take up where one left off
leg Break a leg!
leg cost an arm and a leg
leg crooked as a dog's hind leg
leg first leg (of a journey)
leg get up on one's hind legs
leg He puts his pants on one leg at a time.
leg leg up
leg legwork
leg not have a leg to stand on
leg on so's or sth's last legs
leg one's sea legs
leg pay an arm and a leg (for sth)
leg pull so's leg
leg shake a leg
leg stretch one's legs
leg to have a hollow leg

leg with one's tail between one's legs
legend legend in one's own (life)time
legend urban legend
legislate legislate against sth
legislate legislate for sth
leisure at leisure
leisure at one's leisure
leisure busiest men have the most leisure.
leisure Idle folk have the least leisure.
leisure Idle people have the least leisure.
leisure Marry in haste, (and) repent at leisure.
lend Distance lends enchantment (to the view).
lend lend a hand (to so)
lend lend an ear to so/sth
lend lend color to sth
lend lend oneself or itself to sth
lend lend (so) a hand
lend lend so a hand with sth
lend lend sth out (to so)
lend lend sth to so
lend lend your ear to so/sth
lend Lend your money and lose your friend.
lender Neither a borrower nor a lender be.
length at great length
length at length
length at some length
length explain at great length
length go to any length
length go to great lengths (to do sth)
length keep at arm's length from so/sth
length keep so/sth at arm's length
length lengthen out
length question so at great length
length speak at great length
lengthen lengthen out
lent busy as a fish peddler in Lent
leopard leopard cannot change his spots.
less could(n't) care less
less (I) could(n't) care less.
less in less than no time
less Less is more.
less less said (about sth), the better.
less less than pleased
less lesser (of the two)
less lesser of two evils
less More haste, less speed.
less more or less
lesser lesser (of the two)
lesser lesser of two evils
lesson teach so a lesson
lest Judge not, lest ye be judged.
let Charge it to the dust and let the rain settle it.
let Do not let the sun go down on your anger.
let Do not let the sun go down on your wrath.
let Don't let it go any further.
let Don't let it out of this room.
let Don't let so/sth get you down.
let Don't let the bastards wear you down.
let I'll (have to) let you go.
let just let me say
let let alone so/sth
let Let bygones be bygones.

let let down
let Let every man skin his own skunk.
let Let every tub stand on its own bottom.
let let fly with sth
let Let George do it.
let let go of so/sth
let let go (with sth)
let let grass grow under one's feet
let Let her rip!
let let it all hang out
let Let it be.
let Let it go.
let Let it roll!
let let loose of so/sth
let let loose (with sth)
let Let me get back to you (on that).
let Let me have it!
let let me (just) say
let let off (some) steam
let let on (about so/sth)
let let on sth
let let on (to so) (about so/sth)
let let one's emotions show
let let one's guard down
let let one's hair down
let let oneself go
let let oneself in for sth
let let out
let Let's bump this place!
let Let's call it a day.
let Let's do lunch (sometime).
let Let's do this again (sometime).
let Let's dump.
let Let's get down to business.
let Let's get out of here.
let Let's get together (sometime).
let Let's go somewhere where it's (more) quiet.
let Let's have it!
let Let's not go through all that again.
let Let's rock and roll!
let let's say
let Let's shake on it.
let Let's talk (about it).
let Let sleeping dogs lie.
let let so down
let let so (get) by
let let so get by with sth
let let so (get) off (sth)
let let so get on with sth
let let so (get) past
let let so go
let let so have it (with both barrels)
let let so in for sth
let let so in on sth
let let so in on the act
let let so in on the ground floor
let let so know (about sth)
let let so off
let let so or an animal (get) out (of sth)
let let so or an animal out of sth
let let so/sth alone
let let so/sth at so/sth
let let so/sth down
let let so/sth into sth
let let so/sth through (sth)
let let so pass by
let let so slide by
let let so/sth or some creature alone
let let so/sth or some creature be
let let sth (get) out
let let sth off

let let sth out
let let sth pass
let let sth ride
let let sth slide
let let sth slip by
let let sth slip (out)
let Let the buyer beware.
let let the cat out of the bag
let let the chance slip by
let Let the chips fall where they may.
let Let the cobbler stick to his last.
let Let the dead bury the dead.
let Let them eat cake.
let let things slide
let let up
let Let us do sth.
let let well enough alone
let live and let live
let not let so catch so doing sth
let not let the grass grow under one's feet
let sit back and let sth happen
letter bread-and-butter letter
letter dash a letter off
letter dead letter
letter Dear John letter
letter red-letter day
letter to the letter
level at sea level
level Death is the great leveler.
level do one's (level) best
level find one's own level
level level a charge against so
level level off
level level out
level level playing field
level level sth at so/sth
level level sth down
level level sth off
level level sth out
level level sth to the ground
level level sth up
level level the (playing) field
level level with so (about so/sth)
level lower oneself to some level
level on the level
level so's level best
level (strictly) on the level
leveler Death is the great leveler.
levy levy sth (up)on so/sth
liability assume liability for sth
liar dog-faced liar
liar liar is not believed (even) when he tells the truth.
libel greater the truth, the greater the libel.
liberate liberate so/sth from so/sth
liberty at liberty
liberty take liberties with so/sth
liberty take the liberty of doing sth
license license to do sth
license poetic license
lick ain't got a lick of sense
lick finish sth with a lick and a promise
lick If you can't lick 'em, join 'em.
lick lick and a promise
lick lick at sth
lick lick of work
lick lick one's chops
lick lick one's lips
lick lick one's wounds
lick lick so/sth into shape
lick lick sth into shape

lick lick sth off (of) sth
lick lick sth up
lick licking
lick take a licking
lid blow one's lid
lid blow the lid off (sth)
lid flip one's lid
lid keep a lid on sth
lid lid on sth
lid not bat an eyelid
lid put a lid on sth
lid take the lid off (of) sth
lie As you make your bed, so you must lie (up)on it.
lie Ask me no questions, I'll tell you no lies.
lie Ask no questions and hear no lies.
lie give the lie to sth
lie Half the truth is often a whole lie.
lie If you lie down with dogs, you will get up with fleas.
lie leave sth (lying) around
lie Let sleeping dogs lie.
lie lie about
lie lie ahead of so/sth
lie lie alongside ((of) so or an animal)
lie lie around (some place)
lie lie at anchor
lie lie at death's door
lie lie back
lie lie before so/sth
lie lie behind so/sth
lie lie below so/sth
lie lie beyond so/sth
lie lie doggo
lie lie down
lie lie fallow
lie lie in
lie lie like a rug
lie lie low
lie lie out (in sth)
lie lie through one's teeth
lie lie to so (about so/sth)
lie lie (up)on so
lie lie with so
lie lie within sth
lie little white lie
lie No lie?
lie pack of lies
lie take sth lying down
lie That ain't no lie.
lie Uneasy lies the head that wears a crown.
lie *(up)on so
lieu in lieu of sth
life all walks of life
life Art is long and life is short.
life best things in life are free.
life bet one's life
life between life and death
life big as life (and twice as ugly)
life bigger than life (and twice as ugly)
life Bread is the staff of life.
life bring so or an animal back to life
life bring so/sth to life
life bring sth back to life
life change (of life)
life claim a life
life come to life
life depart this life
life eternal life
life evening of life
life every walk of life

life facts of life
life for life
life for the life of me
life Get a life!
life get out with one's life
life hang on for dear life
life have one's name inscribed in the book of life
life have the time of one's life
life (I'm) having the time of my life.
life important milestone in so's life
life in the prime of life
life large as life
life larger than life
life late in life
life lay down one's life (for so/sth)
life lead a dog's life
life lead the life of Riley
life Life begins at forty.
life life in the fast lane
life Life is just a bowl of cherries.
life Life is short and time is swift.
life Life is too short.
life Life isn't all beer and skittles.
life life of the party
life Life's been good (to me).
life live a dog's life
life live a life of sth
life live the life of Riley
life make a (kind of) life for oneself
life make life miserable for so
life mark so for life
life matter of life and death
life milestone in so's life
life mission in life
life never in my life
life new lease on life
life one's way of life
life pester the life out of so
life run for one's life
life seamy side of life
life set for life
life shock of one's life
life spring to life
life Such is life!
life take one's own life
life take so's life
life Variety is the spice of life.
life Where have you been all my life?
life Where there's life there's hope.
life While there's life there's hope.
life within an inch of one's life
life You bet your (sweet) life!
lifetime legend in one's own (life)time
lifetime once-in-a-lifetime chance
lifetime once-in-a-lifetime opportunity
lift (Could I) give you a lift?
lift Could I have a lift?
lift give so a lift
lift How about a lift?
lift lift a hand (against so/sth)
lift lift off
lift lift one's elbow
lift lift so/sth down (from sth)
lift lift so/sth up
lift lift so's spirits
lift lift sth from so/sth
lift lift sth off (of) so/sth
lift lift sth out of context
lift lift up
lift not lift a finger (to help so)
lift not lift a hand (to help so)
lift Thanks for the lift.

light according to one's own lights
light all sweetness and light
light at first light
light begin to see daylight
light begin to see the light
light bring so/sth to light
light bring sth to light
light can't find one's butt with both hands (in broad daylight)
light come to light
light daylight robbery
light first see the light of day
light get off (lightly)
light heavy purse makes a light heart.
light hide one's light under a bushel
light in broad daylight
light in (the) light of sth
light in the limelight
light in the spotlight
light light a fire under so
light light as a feather
light light as air
light light into so/sth
light light out (for some place)
light light out (of some place) (for some place)
light light purse makes a heavy heart.
light light so/sth up
light light sth up
light light sth with sth
light light up
light light (up)on so/sth
light lighten sth up
light lighten up
light make light of sth
light Many hands make light work.
light once-over-lightly
light out like a light
light punch so's lights out
light run a red light
light see so/sth in a new light
light see the light
light shed (some) light on sth
light steal the spotlight
light throw an amount of light on so/sth
light throw (some) light on sth
light trip the light fantastic
lighten lighten sth up
lighten lighten up
lightly get off (lightly)
lightly once-over-lightly
lightning Lightning never strikes (the same place) twice.
lightning like greased lightning
lightning like hell and high lightning
lightning quick as (greased) lightning
lightning swift as lightning
like act like a cold fish
like act like oneself again
like and the like
like avoid so/sth like the plague
like built like a brick outhouse
like *bull in a china shop
like come across like so/sth (to so)
like come on like gangbusters
like come out smelling like a rose
like come up smelling like a rose
like Don't even look like sth!
like drawn like a moth to a flame
like drink like a fish
like drop like flies
like drop so/sth like a hot potato
like eat like a bird

like eat like a horse
like eyes like saucers
like eyes like two burnt holes in a blanket
like fall like a ton of bricks
like feel like a million (dollars)
like feel like a new person
like feel like death warmed over
like feel like doing sth
like feel like oneself again
like feel like so/sth
like fight like hell
like fight like the devil
like fight like the dickens
like fit like a glove
like go at sth like a boy killing snakes
like go like clockwork
like go like stink
like go like the wind
like go over like a lead balloon
like go through so like a dose of the salts
like hate so/sth like sin
like Hell hath no fury like a woman scorned.
like hit like a ton of bricks
like hit so like a ton of bricks
like How do you like school?
like How do you like that?
like How do you like them apples?
like How do you like this weather?
like I don't want to sound like a busybody, but
like I felt like a penny waiting for change.
like I would like you to meet so.
like I'd like (for) you to meet so.
like I'd like (to have) a word with you.
like I'd like to speak to so, please.
like If you don't like it, (you can) lump it.
like I'm like you
like In like a lion, out like a lamb.
like just like that
like kick like a mule
like kick like a steer
like know so/sth like the back of one's hand
like know so/sth like the palm of one's hand
like lie like a rug
like like a bat out of hell
like like a blind dog in a meat market
like like a bolt from the blue
like like a bolt out of the blue
like like a bull in a china shop
like like a bump on a log
like like a can of corn
like like a fish out of water
like like a house on fire
like like a kid with a new toy
like like a lamb to the slaughter
like like a million (dollars)
like like a sitting duck
like like a three-ring circus
like like a ton of bricks
like (like) an open book
like Like breeds like.
like like crazy
like like death warmed over
like like father, like son
like like fighting snakes
like like flies to manure

like like gangbusters
like like greased lightning
like like hell
like like herding frogs
like like I was saying
like Like it or lump it!
like Like it's such a big deal!
like like it was going out of style
like like lambs to the slaughter
like like looking for a needle in a haystack
like like mad
like Like mother, like daughter.
like like nobody's business
like like nothing on earth
like like one of the family
like like pigs to the slaughter
like like rats abandoning a sinking ship
like like shooting fish in a barrel
like like stealing acorns from a blind pig
like like stink
like like taking candy from a baby
like like the devil
like like the dickens
like like the wind
like like there ain't no tomorrow
like like there's no tomorrow
like like to
like like tryin' to scratch your ear with your elbow
like like (two) peas in a pod
like like water off a duck's back
like like, you know
like likely as not
like liken so/sth to so/sth
like likes of so/sth
like live like a marked man
like look like a candidate for a pair of wings
like look like a case of sth
like look like a (dead) ringer (for so)
like look like a million dollars
like look like a saddle on a sow
like look like death warmed over
like look like so/sth
like look like sth
like look like sth the cat dragged in
like look like the cat that swallowed the canary
like looking like a sitting duck
like make like a tree and leave
like make like so/sth
like make out like a bandit
like make (out) like sth
like March comes in like a lion, and goes out like a lamb.
like move like stink
like move like the wind
like need sth like a hole in the head
like not feel like oneself
like Not likely.
like Nothing succeeds like success.
like off like a shot
like out like a light
like pack so/sth (in) like sardines
like packed (in) like sardines
like play like so/sth
like Promises are like piecrust, made to be broken.
like purr like a cat
like purr like a kitten
like quick like a bunny

like read so like a book
like run around like a chicken with its head cut off
like run like clockwork
like run like stink
like run like the wind
like seem like a long shot
like seem like oneself again
like seem like putty in so's hands
like seem like so/sth
like seem like the last person
like sell like hotcakes
like sleep like a log
like smell like a rose
like smiling like a Cheshire cat
like smoke like a chimney
like sound like
like spend money like it's going out of style
like spend money like there's no tomorrow
like spread like wildfire
like stick out like a sore thumb
like swear like a trooper
like swim like stink
like take a liking to so/sth
like take it like a man
like talk like a nut
like tap-dance like mad
like taste like more
like taste like sth
like Tell it like it is.
like That's more like it.
like There's no fool like an old fool.
like There's no place like home.
like (There's) no time like the present.
like They don't make them like they used to.
like to so's liking
like treat so/sth like so/sth
like watch so/sth like a hawk
like What would you like to drink?
like work like a beaver
like would like (to have) so/sth
likely in the unlikely event of sth
likely likely as not
likely Not likely.
liken liken so/sth to so/sth
likewise Likewise(, I'm sure).
lily gild the lily
limb go out on a limb
limb out on a limb
limb put so out on a limb
limb tear so or some animal limb from limb
limber limber so/sth up
limbo in limbo
limbo leave sth in limbo
limbo put sth in limbo
limbo remain in limbo
limbo stay in limbo
limelight in the limelight
limit go the limit
limit go to the limit
limit limit so to sth
limit limit sth to sth
limit off-limits
limit sky's the limit.
limit within limits
line along similar lines
line along these lines
line along those lines
line blow one's lines
line bottom line

line bring so/sth into line (with so/sth)
line cash on the line
line dead cat on the line
line Don't give me that line!
line Don't hand me that (line)!
line draw a line between sth and sth else
line draw a line in the sand
line draw the line (at sth)
line draw the line between sth and sth else
line drop so a few lines
line drop so a line
line end of the line
line Every cloud has a silver lining.
line fall in(to) line
line feed so a line
line fluff one's lines
line give so a line
line go down the line
line hold the line (at so/sth)
line hook, line, and sinker
line in line
line in the line of duty
line keep so or an animal in line
line lay it on the line
line lay some sweet lines on so
line line of least resistance
line line on so/sth
line line one's own pocket(s)
line line so/sth up
line line so up behind so/sth
line line so up (for sth)
line line so up (with so)
line line sth with sth
line line up
line muff one's lines
line off-line
line One has to draw the line somewhere.
line online
line out of line (with sth)
line party line
line put it on the line
line put one's neck on the line
line put some sweet lines on so
line read between the lines
line run down some lines
line sign on the dotted line
line step out of line
line swallow sth hook, line, and sinker
line take a hard line (with so)
line There is a fine line between sth and sth else.
line toe the line
line under a deadline
line Who's on the line?
line work down (the line) (to so/sth)
linen air one's dirty linen in public
linen Do not wash your dirty linen in public.
linen wash one's dirty linen in public
linger linger around
linger linger on
linger linger over sth
lining Every cloud has a silver lining.
link chain is no stronger than its weakest link.
link link so/sth to so/sth
link link so/sth up (to sth)
link link so/sth with so/sth
link link up to so/sth
link weak link (in the chain)
lion beard the lion in his den

lion Better be the head of a dog than the tail of a lion.
lion In like a lion, out like a lamb.
lion lion's share of sth
lion March comes in like a lion, and goes out like a lamb.
lion strong as a lion
lip button (up) one's lip
lip Don't give me any of your lip!
lip give so some lip
lip Keep a stiff upper lip.
lip lick one's lips
lip Loose lips sink ships.
lip My lips are sealed.
lip None of your lip!
lip pay lip service (to sth)
lip Read my lips!
lip read so's lips
lip There's many a slip 'twixt the cup and the lip.
lip Watch my lips!
lip Zip (up) your lip!
liquor hold one's liquor
liquor liquor so up
liquor liquor up
list enter the lists
list list so as sth
list list so/sth among sth
list list so/sth off
list list to a direction
list on the waiting list
list shopping list
list sucker list
list wish list
listen I'm listening.
listen listen for so/sth
listen listen in (on so/sth)
listen listen to reason
listen listen to so/sth
listen listen up
listen Listeners never hear any good of themselves.
listen stop, look, and listen
litmus litmus test
litter litter sth about
litter litter sth up
litter runt of the litter
little Birds in their little nests agree.
little bother one's (pretty little) head about so/sth
little come out (of) the little end of the horn
little difficult is done at once; the impossible takes a little longer.
little Don't worry your (pretty little) head about it.
little down the little red lane
little Every little bit helps.
little find so a little off
little give a little
little Great oaks from little acorns grow.
little How's every little thing?
little (I'll) see you in a little while.
little in a little bit
little least little thing
little Little and often fills the purse.
little little bird told me.
little little bit (of sth)
little little bitty
little little by little
little little (hard) work never hurt anyone.

little little knowledge is a dangerous thing.
little (little) new to (all) this
little (little) nip in the air
little little off
little little old so/sth
little Little pitchers have big ears.
little little pricey
little little shaver
little (little) short on one end
little little steep
little Little strokes fell great oaks.
little Little thieves are hanged, but great ones escape.
little Little things please little minds.
little little white lie
little make little of so/sth
little Mighty oaks from little acorns grow.
little not trouble one's (pretty) (little) head about sth
little Oh, ye of little faith.
little one little bit
little Perhaps a little later.
little precious little
little sure as God made little green apples
little think little of so/sth
little too little, too late
little twist so around one's little finger
little wind so around one's little finger
little Ye gods (and little fishes)!
live all the way live
live As I live and breathe!
live cat has nine lives.
live Eat to live, not live to eat.
live every living soul
live for a living
live Half the world knows not how the other half lives.
live have to live with sth
live He lives long who lives well.
live He who fights and runs away, may live to fight another day.
live hit one where one lives
live how the other half lives
live I can live with that.
live *in a world of one's own
live *in an ivory tower
live *in the fast lane
live knock the (living) daylights out of so
live learn to live with sth
live live a dog's life
live live a life of sth
live live above so/sth
live live among so
live live and learn
live live and let live
live live apart (from so)
live live around so/sth
live live beyond one's means
live live by one's wits
live live by sth
live Live by the sword, die by the sword.
live live for so/sth
live live for the moment
live live from day to day
live live from hand to mouth
live live happily ever after
live live high off the hog
live live in

live live it up
live live large
live live like a marked man
live live next door (to so)
live live off campus
live live off (of) so/sth
live live off the fat of the land
live live off the land
live live on (after so)
live live on (after so/sth)
live live on an amount of money
live live on borrowed time
live live on one's own
live live on so
live live on the edge
live live out of a suitcase
live live out of cans
live live out one's days
live live over so/sth
live live sth down
live live sth out
live live sth over
live live the life of Riley
live live through sth
live live to do sth
live live to the (ripe old) age of sth
live live together
live live (together) with so
live live under so/sth
live live under sth (negative)
live live under the same roof (with so)
live live up to one's end of the bargain
live live up to sth
live live with so
live live with sth
live live within one's means
live live within sth
live live without sth
live live worlds apart
live liven sth up
live living end
live make a living by doing sth
live make a living from sth
live Man does not live by bread alone.
live not a living soul
live not tell a (living) soul
live *off campus
live Pardon me for living!
live People who live in glass houses shouldn't throw stones.
live reed before the wind lives on, while mighty oaks do fall.
live scare the living daylights out of so
live sure as you live
live thoughts to live by
live where so lives
live words to live by
livelong all the livelong day
liven liven sth up
liver more sth than Carter has (liver) pills
Livingstone Doctor Livingstone, I presume?
lo Lo and behold!
load dump a load
load dump one's load
load few bricks short of a load
load get a load of so/sth
load have a load on
load load into sth
load load off one's feet
load load off one's mind
load load so/sth down (with so/sth)

load load so/sth into sth
load load so/sth up (with so/sth)
load load sth onto so/sth
load load sth with sth
load load up (with sth)
load loaded for bear
load loaded to the barrel
load loaded to the gills
load one brick shy of a load
load take a load off (of) so's mind
load take a load off one's feet
load Thanks loads.
load three bricks shy of a load
load two bricks shy of a load
load unload so/sth on(to) so
load unload sth from sth
loaf Half a loaf is better than none.
loaf loaf around
loaf loaf sth away
loan float a loan
loan loan sth to so
loan on loan (from so/sth)
loan take out a loan
lob lob sth at so/sth
lobby lobby against sth
lobby lobby for sth
local local yokel
location on location
lock lock horns (with so)
lock lock in on so/sth
lock lock on(to so/sth)
lock lock so or an animal (up) in (sth)
lock lock so/sth away
lock lock so/sth out of sth
lock lock so/sth up (somewhere)
lock lock sth in
lock lock sth onto so/sth
lock lock, stock, and barrel
lock Lock the stable door after the horse is stolen.
lock pick a lock
locker Davy Jones's locker
locker go to Davy Jones's locker
locker send so to the locker room
loco plumb loco
lodge lodge so with so
lodge lodge sth against so
lodge lodge sth against sth
lodge lodge sth in sth
lodge lodge with so
log easy as falling off a log
log easy as rolling off a log
log like a bump on a log
log log off
log log on
log log out
log log so for sth
log log so off
log log so on (to sth)
log log so out
log log sth up
log sleep like a log
loggerheads at loggerheads (with so)
loins gird up one's loins
loiter loiter around
loiter loiter over sth
loiter loiter sth away
loll loll about (some place)
loll loll around
loll loll back
loll loll out
lollygag lollygag (around)
lonesome all by one's lonesome

long all day long
long all night long
long Art is long and life is short.
long as long as
long at (long) last
long before long
long Come back when you can stay longer.
long creaking door hangs longest.
long creaking gate hangs longest.
long cut a long story short
long difficult is done at once; the impossible takes a little longer.
long Don't be gone (too) long.
long Don't stay away so long.
long go a long way toward doing sth
long Governments have long arms.
long have come a long way
long He lives long who lives well.
long He who laughs last, laughs longest.
long He who sups with the devil should have a long spoon.
long (I) haven't seen you in a long time.
long in the long haul
long in the long run
long It is a long lane that has no turning.
long It'll be a long day in January when sth happens.
long Kings have long arms.
long long and the short of it
long long arm of the law
long long for so/sth
long long gone
long long in the tooth
long long shot
long long story short
long Long time no see.
long longest way round is the shortest way home.
long make a long story short
long merry as the day is long
long not by a long shot
long not long for this world
long over the long haul
long seem like a long shot
long short and the long of it
long Short reckonings make long friends.
long So long.
long so long as
long Take a long walk off a short pier.
long take the (long) count
longer Come back when you can stay longer.
longer difficult is done at once; the impossible takes a little longer.
longest creaking door hangs longest.
longest creaking gate hangs longest.
longest He who laughs last, laughs longest.
longest longest way round is the shortest way home.
look *becoming on so
look cat can look at a king.
look come-hither look
look devil looks after his own.
look dirty look
look Don't even look like sth!
look Don't look a gift horse in the mouth.

look faraway look
look far-off look
look give so a blank look
look Here's looking at you.
look if looks could kill
look I'll look you up when I'm in town.
look I'm just looking.
look I'm only looking.
look *like death warmed over
look like looking for a needle in a haystack
look look a gift horse in the mouth
look look about (for so/sth)
look look after number one
look look after so/sth
look look ahead to sth
look look alike
look Look alive!
look look around (at sth)
look look around for so/sth
look look around (in) some place
look look as if butter wouldn't melt in one's mouth
look look aside
look look askance at so/sth
look look at so cross-eyed
look look at so/sth
look look at the crux of the matter
look look at the heart of the matter
look Look (at) what the cat dragged in!
look look away (from so/sth)
look look back (at so/sth)
look look becoming on so
look Look before you leap.
look look beyond so/sth
look look daggers at so
look look down (at so/sth)
look look fit to kill
look look for so/sth
look look for so/sth high and low
look look for trouble
look look forward to sth
look look good on paper
look look here
look look high and low (for so/sth)
look look in (on so/sth)
look look into sth
look look like a candidate for a pair of wings
look look like a case of sth
look look like a (dead) ringer (for so)
look look like a million dollars
look look like a saddle on a sow
look look like death warmed over
look look like so/sth
look look like sth
look look like sth the cat dragged in
look look like the cat that swallowed the canary
look Look me up when you're in town.
look look none the worse for wear
look look on
look look out
look look (out) on(to) sth
look look so in the eye
look look so in the face
look look so/sth over
look look so/sth up
look look the other way
look look through sth
look look to be a million miles away
look look to one's laurels
look look to so/sth (for sth)

look look to the naked eye
look look toward so/sth
look look under the hood
look look up
look look (up)on so/sth as sth
look look (up)on so/sth with sth
look Look who's here!
look Look who's talking!
look looking like a sitting duck
look looking over one's shoulder
look make so look good
look make so look ridiculous
look One's future looks bright.
look *spit and image of so
look stop, look, and listen
look take a look at so/sth
look take a look for so/sth
look Things are looking up.
look would as soon do sth as look at you
lookout on the lookout (for so/sth)
look-see look-see
loom loom large (on the horizon)
loom loom out of sth
loom loom up
loon crazy as a loon
loop in the loop
loop knock so for a loop
loop throw so for a loop
loose all hell broke loose
loose at loose ends
loose break loose (from so)
loose break sth loose from sth
loose cut loose (with sth)
loose cut one's wolf loose
loose cut (oneself) loose (from so/sth)
loose cut so/sth loose from sth
loose footloose and fancy-free
loose hang loose
loose have a screw loose
loose leave some loose ends
loose leave so at loose ends
loose let loose of so/sth
loose let loose (with sth)
loose loose cannon
loose Loose lips sink ships.
loose loose translation
loose loosen so/sth up
loose loosen so up
loose loosen up
loose on the loose
loose play fast and loose (with so/sth)
loose put so/sth at loose ends
loose some loose ends
loose stay loose
loose tear loose (from so/sth)
loosen loosen so/sth up
loosen loosen so up
loosen loosen up
lop lop sth off (of) sth
lope lope along
lord drunk as a lord
lord Everybody loves a lord.
lord (lord) high muck-a-muck
lord lord it over so
lord Lord knows I've tried.
lord Lord love a duck!
lord Lord willing and the creek don't rise
lord (the) Lord only knows
lose continue one's losing streak
lose Finders keepers(, losers weepers).
lose Lend your money and lose your friend.

lose lose a bundle
lose lose (all) one's marbles
lose lose at sth
lose lose by sth
lose lose contact with so/sth
lose lose count of so/sth
lose lose face
lose lose favor (with so)
lose lose ground (to so/sth)
lose lose heart
lose lose it
lose lose money on sth
lose lose one's appetite
lose lose one's cool
lose lose one's grip on so/sth
lose lose one's head (over so/sth)
lose lose one's hold on so/sth
lose lose one's lunch
lose lose one's reason
lose lose one's shirt
lose lose one's temper (at so/sth)
lose lose one's touch (with so/sth)
lose lose one's train of thought
lose lose oneself in so/sth
lose lose out
lose lose patience (with so/sth)
lose lose sight of so/sth
lose lose sleep over so/sth
lose lose some amount of time
lose lose sth at sth
lose lose sth in sth
lose lose sth to so
lose lose the use of sth
lose lose to so/sth
lose lose touch with reality
lose lose touch with so/sth
lose lose trace of so/sth
lose lose track (of so/sth)
lose losing streak
lose *one's bearings
lose stand to lose sth
lose tale never loses in the telling.
lose two-time loser
lose Win a few, lose a few.
lose You cannot lose what you never had.
lose You must lose a fly to catch a trout.
lose You win some, you lose some.
loser Finders keepers(, losers weepers).
loser two-time loser
loss acceptable losses
loss at a loss (for words)
loss cut one's losses
loss dead loss
loss One man's loss is another man's gain.
loss throw so for a loss
lost almost lost it
lost For want of a nail the shoe was lost; for want of a shoe the horse was lost; and for want of a horse the man was lost.
lost get lost
lost give so up (for lost)
lost He who hesitates is lost.
lost lost and gone forever
lost lost cause
lost lost in sth
lost lost on so
lost lost without so/sth
lost lost-and-found

lost make up for lost time
lost There is no love lost (between so and so else).
lost 'Tis better to have loved and lost than never to have loved at all.
lot carry (a lot of) weight (with so/sth)
lot cast one's lot in (with so/sth)
lot cover a lot of ground
lot get a lot of mileage out of sth
lot have a lot going (for one)
lot have a lot on one's mind
lot leave a lot to be desired
lot lot of give-and-take
lot lot of nerve
lot lot of promise
lot lot of so/sth
lot Lots of luck!
lot lots of people or things
lot not put a (lot) of stock in sth
lot quite a lot
lot show a lot of promise
lot take a lot of nerve
lot take a lot off (of) so's mind
lot take a lot out of so
lot Thank you a lot.
lot Thanks (a lot).
lot think a lot of so/sth
lots draw lots
loud Actions speak louder than words.
loud For crying out loud!
loud (I) read you loud and clear.
loud (I'm) (just) thinking out loud.
loud loud and clear
loud say sth out loud
loud think out loud
louie hang a louie
lounge lounge around (some place)
louse louse so/sth up
lousy lousy with so/sth
love All's fair in love and war.
love course of true love never did run smooth.
love Everybody loves a lord.
love face (that) only a mother could love
love fall head over heels in love (with so)
love fall in love (with each other)
love fall in love (with so)
love fall in love (with sth)
love fall out of love (with so)
love For the love of Mike!
love God takes soonest those he loveth best.
love head over heels in love (with so)
love I had a lovely time.
love (I) love it!
love in love (with so/sth)
love I've had a lovely time.
love labor of love
love Lord love a duck!
love love at first sight
love Love begets love.
love Love is blind.
love Love makes the world go round.
love Love me, love my dog.
love love of money is the root of all evil.
love Love will find a way.
love Love you!
love love-hate relationship
love Lovely weather for ducks.
love Lucky at cards, unlucky in love.

love make love (to so)
love Misery loves company.
love not able to get sth for love or money
love not for love nor money
love not miss sth for love nor money
love One cannot love and be wise.
love puppy love
love star-crossed lovers
love Thank you for a lovely evening.
love Thank you for a lovely time.
love There is no love lost (between so and so else).
love 'Tis better to have loved and lost than never to have loved at all.
love We had a lovely time.
love We've had a lovely time.
love When poverty comes in at the door, love flies out of the window.
love When the wolf comes in at the door, love creeps out of the window.
love Whom the gods love die young.
lovely I've had a lovely time.
lovely Lovely weather for ducks.
lovely Thank you for a lovely evening.
lovely Thank you for a lovely time.
lovely We had a lovely time.
lovely We've had a lovely time.
lover star-crossed lovers
loveth God takes soonest those he loveth best.
low assume a low profile
low burn with a low blue flame
low have a low boiling point
low hold so/sth in low regard
low hunt high and low (for so/sth)
low in low cotton
low keep a low profile
low lay low
low lie low
low look for so/sth high and low
low look high and low (for so/sth)
low low man on the totem pole
low low profile
low lower one's sights
low lower one's voice
low lower oneself to some level
low lower so's ears
low lower so's spirits
low lower the boom on so
low low-hanging fruit
low run low (on sth)
low search high and low (for so/sth)
low straight low
lowdown lowdown (on so/sth)
lower lower one's sights
lower lower one's voice
lower lower oneself to some level
lower lower so's ears
lower lower so's spirits
lower lower the boom on so
luck as luck would have it
luck beginner's luck
luck Better luck next time.
luck Bless one's lucky star.
luck blind luck
luck devil's children have the devil's luck.
luck Diligence is the mother of good luck.
luck down on one's luck
luck Good luck!
luck have more luck than sense

luck have one's luck run out
luck in luck
luck It is better to be born lucky than rich.
luck Lots of luck!
luck luck into sth
luck luck of the draw
luck luck out
luck Lucky at cards, unlucky in love.
luck lucky break
luck lucky dog
luck lucky for you
luck lucky streak
luck one's luck runs out
luck out of luck
luck press one's luck
luck pure luck
luck push one's luck
luck rotten luck
luck streak of bad luck
luck streak of good luck
luck streak of luck
luck string of bad luck
luck string of good luck
luck stroke of luck
luck thank one's lucky stars
luck (The) best of luck (to so).
luck the luck of the Irish
luck tough luck
luck try one's luck (at sth)
lucky Bless one's lucky star.
lucky It is better to be born lucky than rich.
lucky Lucky at cards, unlucky in love.
lucky lucky break
lucky lucky dog
lucky lucky for you
lucky lucky streak
lucky thank one's lucky stars
lucre filthy lucre
lull lull before the storm
lull lull so into a false sense of security
lull lull so or an animal to sleep
lumber lumber along
lumber lumber off
lump get one's lumps
lump If you don't like it, (you can) lump it.
lump Like it or lump it!
lump lump in one's throat
lump Lump it!
lump lump so and so else together
lump take one's lumps
lunatic lunatic fringe
lunch blow (one's) lunch
lunch eat so's lunch
lunch free lunch
lunch launch (one's lunch)
lunch Let's do lunch (sometime).
lunch lose one's lunch
lunch lunch off sth
lunch lunch out
lunch out to lunch
lunch There ain't no such thing as a free lunch.
lunch There's no such thing as a free lunch.
lunch We('ll) have to do lunch sometime.
lung air one's lungs
lung at the top of one's lungs
lunge lunge at so/sth
lunge lunge for so/sth

lurch leave so in the lurch
lurch lurch at so/sth
lurch lurch forward
lure lure so/sth away (from so/sth)
lure lure so/sth in to sth
lurk lurk around
lust flame with lust
lust lust after so
lust lust for sth
luxuriate luxuriate in sth
luxury in the lap of luxury
luxury lap of luxury
lying leave sth (lying) around
lying take sth lying down
ma'am wham bam thank you ma'am
mackerel Holy mackerel!
mad drive so mad
mad far from the madding crowd
mad get mad (at sth)
mad hopping mad
mad in a mad rush
mad like mad
mad mad about so/sth
mad mad as a hatter
mad mad as a hornet
mad mad as a March hare
mad mad as a wet hen
mad mad as hell
mad mad (at so/sth)
mad mad enough to chew nails (and spit rivets)
mad mad enough to kick a cat
mad mad enough to spit nails
mad make so mad (at so/sth)
mad method in one's madness
mad so mad I could scream
mad stark raving mad
mad steaming (mad)
mad tap-dance like mad
madam wham bam thank you ma'am
madding far from the madding crowd
made Fingers were made before forks.
made Have I made myself clear?
made have it made
made have sth made
made made conspicuous by one's absence
made made for each other
made made for so
made made for sth
made made from the same mold
made made to measure
made made to order
made marriage made in heaven
made Marriages are made in heaven.
made match made in heaven
made not made of money
made Promises are like piecrust, made to be broken.
made sure as God made little green apples
madness method in one's madness
Mahomet If the mountain will not come to Mahomet, Mahomet must go to the mountain.
maiden maiden voyage
mail by return mail
mail junk mail
mail mail sth from some place
mail mail sth to so

main by main strength and awkwardness
main in the main
main main strength and awkwardness
main might and main
main That brings me to the (main) point.
main which brings me to the (main) point
mainstream in the mainstream (of sth)
maintain maintain so in sth
maintain maintain sth at sth
major major in sth
make able to make an event
make Absence makes the heart grow fonder.
make All work and no play makes Jack a dull boy.
make *all-out effort
make As you make your bed, so you must lie (up)on it.
make can't make heads or tails (out) of so/sth
make Clothes make the man.
make Come in and make yourself at home.
make Conscience does make cowards of us all.
make *contact with so
make Do I make myself (perfectly) clear?
make (Do you) want to make something of it?
make Don't make me laugh!
make Don't make me say it again!
make Don't make me tell you again!
make Don't make two bites of a cherry.
make Early to bed and early to rise, makes a man healthy, wealthy, and wise.
make Empty vessels make the most sound.
make Fine feathers make fine birds.
make Fingers were made before forks.
make *from scratch
make (Go ahead,) make my day!
make gone to meet one's maker
make Good fences make good neighbors.
make good husband makes a good wife.
make Good Jack makes a good Jill.
make Good seed makes a good crop.
make Haste makes waste.
make Have I made myself clear?
make have it made
make have sth made
make have the makings of sth
make heavy purse makes a light heart.
make Hope deferred makes the heart sick.
make Hope deferred maketh the heart sick.
make How is so making out?
make If you don't make mistakes, you don't make anything.
make (I'm) delighted to make your acquaintance.
make in the making
make (It) don't make me no nevermind.
make (It) makes me no difference.

make (It) makes no difference to me.
make It takes all kinds (to make a world).
make It takes money to make money.
make It takes two to make a bargain.
make It takes two to make a quarrel.
make kiss and make up
make *last-ditch effort
make *leap of faith
make light purse makes a heavy heart.
make Love makes the world go round.
make made conspicuous by one's absence
make made for each other
make made for so
make made for sth
make made from the same mold
make made to measure
make made to order
make make a beeline for so/sth
make make a believer (out) of so
make make a big deal about sth
make make a (big) stink (about so/sth)
make make a bolt for so/sth
make make a break for so/sth
make make a bundle
make make a check (out) (to so/sth)
make make a check over to so/sth
make make a check to so/sth
make make a clean breast of sth (to so)
make make a clean sweep
make make a comeback
make make a dash for so/sth
make make a day of doing sth
make make a day of it
make make a deal with so
make make a dent in sth
make make a difference in so/sth
make make a difference to so
make make a face (at so)
make make a fast buck
make make a federal case out of sth
make make a fool (out) of so
make make a fresh start
make make a friend
make make a fuss (over so/sth)
make make a go of sth
make make a grab at so/sth
make make a great show of sth
make make a guess
make make a habit of sth
make make a hit with so
make make a killing
make make a (kind of) life for oneself
make Make a lap!
make make a laughingstock of oneself or sth
make make a living by doing sth
make make a living from sth
make make a long story short
make make a man of so
make make a meal of sth
make make a mental note of sth
make make a mess of sth
make make a mistake
make make a mockery of sth
make make a monkey (out) of so
make make a mountain out of a molehill
make make a move on so
make make a name (for oneself)
make make a night of it
make make a note of sth

make make a nuisance of oneself
make make a paper trail
make make a pass at so
make make a pass at sth
make make a pig of oneself
make make a pile
make make a pitch (for so/sth)
make make a play (for so)
make make a point
make make a practice of sth
make make a quick buck
make make a reservation
make make a run for it
make make a scene
make make a secret of sth
make make a start on sth
make make a stink (about sth)
make make a virtue of necessity
make make advances at so
make make advances to so
make make allowance(s) (for so/sth)
make make amends (to so) (for so/sth)
make make an all-out effort
make make (an amount of) headway
make make an appearance
make make an appointment (with so)
make make an entrance
make make an example of so
make make an exception (for so)
make make an exhibition of oneself
make make an honest woman of so
make make an impression on so
make make an issue of so/sth
make make an offer one cannot refuse
make make an uproar
make make application (to so/sth) (for sth)
make make arrangements for so
make make arrangements to do sth
make make arrangements (with so) (for sth)
make make as if to do sth
make make away with so/sth
make make believe that...
make make book on sth
make make (both) ends meet
make make certain of sth
make make change (for so) (for sth)
make make chin music
make make contact with so
make make cracks about so/sth
make make demands of so/sth
make make do (with so/sth)
make make every effort to do sth
make make eyes at so
make make faces (at so)
make make fast work of so/sth
make make for somewhere
make make free with so
make make free with sth
make make friends
make make fun of so/sth
make make good as sth
make make good (at sth)
make make good money
make make good on sth
make make good time
make make (good) use of sth
make make hamburger (out) of so
make Make haste slowly.
make Make hay while the sun shines.
make make heads or tails of so/sth
make make inroads into sth

make make it
make make last-ditch effort
make make life miserable for so
make make light of sth
make make like a tree and leave
make make like so/sth
make make little of so/sth
make make love (to so)
make make mention of so/sth
make make merry
make make mincemeat (out) of so
make Make mine sth.
make make mischief
make make money on sth
make Make my day!
make Make no bones about it.
make make no difference (to so)
make Make no mistake (about it)!
make make nonsense of sth
make make nothing of sth
make make off with so/sth
make make one an offer one cannot refuse
make make one's mark
make make one's mind up (about so/sth)
make make one's money stretch
make make one's (own) bed
make make (one's) peace with so
make make one's way along sth
make make one's way back (to sth)
make make one's way in the world
make make one's way through sth
make make oneself at home
make make oneself conspicuous
make make oneself heard
make make oneself miserable
make make oneself or sth a laughingstock
make make oneself scarce
make make (oneself) up
make make or break so
make make (out) after so/sth
make make (out) for so/sth
make make out like a bandit
make make (out) like sth
make make out that...
make make out (with so)
make make out (with so/sth)
make make overtures about doing sth
make make points (with so)
make make reservations
make make room (for so/sth)
make make sense
make make short work of so/sth
make make so bold as to do sth
make make (some) sense (out) of so/sth
make make so
make make so an offer
make make so eat crow
make make so look good
make make so look ridiculous
make make so mad (at so/sth)
make make so over
make make so's bed (up)
make make so's blood boil
make make so's blood run cold
make make so's flesh crawl
make make so's gorge rise
make make so's hair curl
make make so's hair stand on end
make make so's head spin
make make so's head swim
make make so's mind up
make make so's mouth water

make make so's position clear
make make so's skin crawl
make make so sick
make make so stir crazy
make make so the scapegoat for sth
make make so up
make make sth
make make sth a practice
make make sth about so/sth
make make sth against so/sth
make make sth at so
make make sth clear to so
make make sth for so/sth
make make sth from scratch
make make sth from sth
make make sth good
make make sth in sth
make make sth of so/sth
make make sth of sth
make make sth off (of) so/sth
make make sth out
make make sth (out) of sth
make make sth over
make make sth right
make make sth to order
make make sth up
make make sth with sth
make make sure (of sth)
make make the arrangements
make make the bed (up)
make make the best of a bad job
make make the best of sth
make make the fur fly
make make the grade
make make the most of sth
make make the scene
make make the team
make make time for so/sth
make make time (with so)
make make (too) much of so/sth
make make tracks (for sth)
make make trouble
make make up
make make use of so/sth
make make war (on so/sth)
make make water
make make waves
make make way
make make with sth
make Make your mind up.
make Make yourself at home.
make Many hands make light work.
make marriage made in heaven
make Marriages are made in heaven.
make match made in heaven
make Men make houses, women make homes.
make Might makes right.
make Never make a threat you cannot carry out.
make not able to make anything out of so/sth
make not able to make head or tail of sth
make not know what to make of so/sth
make not made of money
make *offer one cannot refuse
make old poacher makes the best gamekeeper.
make on the make
make One swallow does not make a summer.
make Opportunity makes a thief.

make *paper trail
make Politics makes strange bedfellows.
make Practice makes perfect.
make Promises are like piecrust, made to be broken.
make put the make on so
make run a make on so
make Short reckonings make long friends.
make still tongue makes a wise head.
make sure as God made little green apples
make That makes two of us.
make They don't make them like they used to.
make Two wrongs do not make a right.
make Wanna make sumpin' of it?
make Want to make something of it?
make What difference does it make?
make what makes so tick
make what makes sth tick
make What makes you think so?
make You can lead a horse to water, but you can't make it drink.
make You cannot make a silk purse out of a sow's ear.
make You cannot make an omelet without breaking eggs.
make You cannot make bricks without straw.
make You make a better door than you do a window.
make You make me laugh!
make You want to make something of it?
maketh Hope deferred maketh the heart sick.
male female of the species is more deadly than the male.
mama go home to mama
mammon You cannot serve God and mammon.
man A man's gotta do what a man's gotta do.
man all things to all men
man As a man sows, so shall he reap.
man be one's own man
man best-laid plans of mice and men oft(en) go astray.
man Better be an old man's darling than a young man's slave.
man big man on campus
man busiest men have the most leisure.
man Call no man happy till he dies.
man child is father of the man.
man Clothes make the man.
man collar-and-tie men
man Count no man happy till he dies.
man Dead men tell no tales.
man dirty old man
man drowning man will clutch at a straw.
man Early to bed and early to rise, makes a man healthy, wealthy, and wise.
man Every man for himself (and the devil take the hindmost).
man Every man has his price.
man Every man is the architect of his own fortune.
man Every man to his taste.

man For want of a nail the shoe was lost; for want of a shoe the horse was lost; and for want of a horse the man was lost.
man good man is hard to find.
man Good men are scarce.
man hatchet man
man Heaven protects children(, sailors,) and drunken men.
man high man on the totem pole
man In the country of the blind, the one-eyed man is king.
man It's ill waiting for dead men's shoes.
man ladies' man
man Let every man skin his own skunk.
man live like a marked man
man low man on the totem pole
man make a man of so
man man about town
man man after my own heart
man Man does not live by bread alone.
man man in the street
man man is known by the company he keeps.
man man of few words
man man of the cloth
man Man proposes, God disposes.
man man's best friend
man man's home is his castle.
man man's inhumanity to man
man marked man
man Men are blind in their own cause.
man Men make houses, women make homes.
man No man can serve two masters.
man odd man out
man One man's loss is another man's gain.
man One man's meat is another man's poison.
man One man's trash is another man's treasure.
man one-man show
man rich man's joke is always funny.
man see a man about a dog
man separate the men from the boys
man So's your old man!
man stick man
man straight man
man straw man
man take it like a man
man There is a tide in the affairs of men.
man Time and tide wait for no man.
man twelve good men and true
man way to a man's heart is through his stomach.
man Young men may die, but old men must die.
manage manage with so/sth
manage manage without so/sth
maneuver maneuver for sth
maneuver maneuver so into sth
maneuver maneuver so out of sth
manger dog in the manger
manna manna from heaven
manner all manner of so/sth
manner comport oneself with some manner
manner devil-may-care manner
manner forget one's manners
manner Other times, other manners.

manure like flies to manure
many at least so many
many Cowards die many times before their death(s).
many good many
many have one too many
many have one's finger in too many pies
many have too many irons in the fire
many He who begins many things, finishes but few.
many How many times do I have to tell you?
many in many respects
many in so many words
many Many a true word is spoken in jest.
many many (and many)'s the time
many Many are called but few are chosen.
many Many hands make light work.
many one too many
many So many countries, so many customs.
many There's many a good tune played on an old fiddle.
many There's many a slip 'twixt the cup and the lip.
many There's many a true word spoken in jest.
many Too many chiefs and not enough Indians.
many Too many cooks spoil the broth.
many Too many cooks spoil the stew.
map map sth out
map put sth on the map
mar mar sth up
marble all the marbles
marble cold as marble
marble end up with all the marbles
marble have all one's marbles
marble lose (all) one's marbles
marble not have all one's marbles
marble win all the marbles
march army marches on its stomach.
march *in (a) single file
march in marching order
March mad as a March hare
march march against so/sth
march march behind so/sth
March March comes in like a lion, and goes out like a lamb.
march march (from some place) (to some place)
march march in (a) single file
march march in step (with so)
march march on
march march out of time (with so/sth)
march march past so/sth
march march to (the beat of) a different drummer
march steal a march on so/sth
mare by shank's mare
mare go (somewhere) by shank's mare
mare shank's mare
marine Tell it to the marines!
mark black mark beside one's name
mark fall wide of the mark
mark leave one's mark on so
mark make one's mark
mark mark my word(s)
mark mark so down
mark mark so for life
mark mark so/sth off

mark mark so/sth out
mark mark so/sth with sth
mark mark sth as sth
mark mark sth down
mark mark sth in
mark mark sth up
mark mark time
mark marked man
mark off the mark
mark on the mark
mark on your mark, get set, go
mark quick off the mark
mark slow off the mark
mark toe the mark
mark wide of the mark
mark X marks the spot.
market corner the market on sth
market drug on the market
market find oneself in the market (for sth)
market glut on the market
market in the market (for sth)
market like a blind dog in a meat market
market on the market
market play the (stock) market
market price so/sth out of the market
market put sth on the market
maroon maroon so on an island
marriage Dream of a funeral and you hear of a marriage.
marriage marriage made in heaven
marriage Marriages are made in heaven.
marriage save oneself (for marriage)
married get married
married have to get married
marry get married
marry have to get married
marry marry above oneself
marry marry below oneself
marry marry beneath oneself
marry Marry in haste, (and) repent at leisure.
marry marry into sth
marry marry one's way out of sth
marry marry so off (to so)
marry marry up (with so)
marshal marshal so/sth together
martin all my eye (and Betty Martin)
marvel marvel at so/sth
marvel marvel to behold
mash mash on sth
mash mash sth up
mash mash sth with sth
mask mask sth out
masquerade masquerade as so/sth
mast at half-mast
master be one's own master
master Fire is a good servant but a bad master.
master jack of all trades is a master of none.
master No man can serve two masters.
master past master at sth
match match for so/sth or an animal
match match made in heaven
match match so against so else or sth against sth else
match match so/sth in sth
match match so (up) (with so)
match match up

match match wits (with so)
match meet one's match
match mix and match
match strike a match
match whole shooting match
mate mate so with so
mate mate with an animal
mate mate with so
materialize materialize out of nowhere
materialize *out of nowhere
matter as a matter of course
matter as a matter of fact
matter crux of the matter
matter for that matter
matter go to the crux of the matter
matter go to the heart of the matter
matter go to the root of the matter
matter gray matter
matter heart of the matter
matter (It) (really) doesn't matter to me.
matter look at the crux of the matter
matter look at the heart of the matter
matter matter of life and death
matter matter of opinion
matter matter to so
matter mind over matter
matter no laughing matter
matter no matter how you slice it
matter no matter what (happens)
matter root of the matter
matter What's the matter (with you)?
mature of mature years
max max out
max maxed out
max to the max
may April showers bring May flowers.
may be that as it may
may come what may
may devil-may-care attitude
may devil-may-care manner
may Gather ye rosebuds while ye may.
may He who fights and runs away, may live to fight another day.
may How may I help you?
may Let the chips fall where they may.
may may as well
may May I be excused?
may May I help you?
may May I see you again?
may May I speak to so?
may May I take a message?
may May I take your order (now)?
may May I tell him who's calling?
may May I use your powder room?
may Sticks and stones may break my bones, but words will never hurt me.
may to whom it may concern
may try as I may
may Young men may die, but old men must die.
maybe I don't mean maybe!
maybe Maybe some other time.
McCoy real McCoy
me Allow me.
me Ask me no questions, I'll tell you no lies.
me Beam me up, Scotty!
me Believe you me!
me between you (and) me and the bedpost

me between you and me and these four walls
me beyond me
me Catch me later.
me Catch me some other time.
me Dear me!
me Do you expect me to believe that?
me (Do) you mean to tell me sth?
me Do you read me?
me Don't ask me.
me Don't bother me!
me Don't give me any of your lip!
me Don't give me that line!
me Don't hand me that (line)!
me Don't make me laugh!
me Don't make me say it again!
me Don't make me tell you again!
me Don't mind me.
me Don't push (me)!
me Don't rush me!
me Don't start (on me)!
me Don't tell me what to do!
me even if it kills me
me Excuse me.
me far be it from me to do sth
me Fool me once, shame on you; fool me twice, shame on me.
me for the life of me
me Give me a break!
me Give me a call.
me Give me a chance!
me Give me a rest!
me Give me a ring.
me Give me five!
me if my memory serves me correctly
me (It) beats me.
me (It) doesn't bother me any.
me (It) doesn't bother me at all.
me It doesn't quite suit me.
me (It) don't bother me none.
me (It) don't make me no nevermind.
me (It) makes me no difference.
me (It) makes no difference to me.
me (It) (really) doesn't matter to me.
me It's (all) Greek to me.
me (It's) got me beat.
me It's on me.
me it strikes me that
me (It) suits me (fine).
me (It) won't bother me any.
me (It) won't bother me at all.
me (It) works for me.
me just let me say
me Leave me alone!
me Let me get back to you (on that).
me Let me have it!
me let me (just) say
me Life's been good (to me).
me little bird told me.
me Look me up when you're in town.
me Love me, love my dog.
me my gut tells me (that)
me need a pick-me-up
me Nothing for me, thanks.
me Pardon (me).
me Pardon me for living!
me Permit me.
me Remember me to so.
me Run it by (me) again.
me Run that by (me) again.
me same for me.
me Say hello to so (for me).
me Says me!

me Search me.
me Sez me!
me Skin me!
me Slip me five!
me So help me(, God)!
me So, sue me.
me Sticks and stones may break my bones, but words will never hurt me.
me Take it from me!
me Tell me another (one)!
me Thank you for having me.
me Thank you for inviting me.
me That brings me to the (main) point.
me That (really) burns me (up)!
me That's a new one on me!
me (That's) fine with me.
me That's news to me.
me This doesn't quite suit me.
me Trust me!
me Try me.
me want a pick-me-up
me Want a piece of me?
me What do you want me to say?
me What's in it for me?
me which brings me to the (main) point
me Woe is me!
me Would you excuse me?
me You can't expect me to believe that.
me (You) could have fooled me.
me You could have knocked me over with a feather.
me You don't expect me to believe that.
me You got me beat.
me You got me there.
me You make me laugh!
me You mean to tell me sth?
me You scared the crap out of me.
me You scared the devil out of me.
me You scared the hell out of me.
me (You) want a piece of me?
me Your secret is safe with me.
me You're telling me!
me (You've) got me stumped.
meal eat (a meal) out
meal Enjoy your meal.
meal fix sth for (a meal)
meal have sth for (a meal)
meal make a meal of sth
meal square (meal)
mean beyond one's means
mean by all means
mean by any means
mean by means of sth
mean by no means
mean (Do you) know what I mean?
mean (Do) you mean to say sth?
mean (Do) you mean to tell me sth?
mean end justifies the means.
mean I don't mean maybe!
mean I know (just) what you mean.
mean lean and mean
mean live beyond one's means
mean live within one's means
mean mean business
mean mean by sth
mean mean (for so) to do sth
mean mean lean times (ahead)
mean mean no offense
mean mean nothing (to so)
mean mean sth as sth

mean mean sth for so/sth
mean mean sth (to so)
mean mean streak
mean mean to (do sth)
mean mean well
mean meaner than a junkyard dog (with fourteen sucking pups)
mean meant to be
mean No offense meant.
mean take on a new meaning
mean You can't mean that!
mean You know what I mean?
mean You mean to tell me sth?
meant meant to be
meant No offense meant.
meantime in the meantime
measure beyond measure
measure for good measure
measure made to measure
measure measure so against so else or sth against sth else
measure measure so up against so/sth
measure measure sth off
measure measure sth out
measure measure up (to so/sth)
meat dead meat
meat like a blind dog in a meat market
meat One man's meat is another man's poison.
meat so cold you could hang meat
Mecca Mecca for so
meddle meddle in sth
meddle meddle with so/sth
mediate mediate between so and so else
medicate on medication
medication on medication
medicine dose of one's own medicine
medicine snakebite medicine
medicine take one's medicine
medicine taste of one's own medicine
meditate meditate on so/sth
medium hit a happy medium
medium strike a happy medium
meek meek as a lamb
meet call a meeting
meet call the meeting to order
meet East is East and West is West (and never the twain shall meet).
meet Fancy meeting you here!
meet gone to meet one's maker
meet hold a meeting
meet I would like you to meet so.
meet I'd like (for) you to meet so.
meet (I'm) pleased to meet you.
meet (I'm) (very) glad to meet you.
meet (It's) nice to meet you.
meet make (both) ends meet
meet meet one's death
meet meet one's end
meet meet one's match
meet meet one's Waterloo
meet meet so halfway
meet meet the requirements (for sth)
meet meet up with so/sth
meet meet with so
meet meet with sth
meet meeting of the minds
meet more (to sth) than meets the eye
meet Nice meeting you.
meet Sunday-go-to-meeting clothes
meet Till we meet again.
meet Until we meet again.
meet where the rubber meets the road

meeting call a meeting
meeting call the meeting to order
meeting meeting of the minds
mell mell of a hess
mellow mellow out
melt Butter wouldn't melt (in so's mouth).
melt look as if butter wouldn't melt in one's mouth
melt melt away
melt melt down
melt melt in one's mouth
melt melt in sth
melt melt into sth
melt melt sth away
melt melt sth down
melt melt sth into sth
member card-carrying member
memory commit sth to memory
memory enshrine so's memory in one's heart
memory freeze so/sth in one's memory
memory if my memory serves me correctly
memory in memory of so
memory in recent memory
memory jog so's memory
memory know sth from memory
men all things to all men
men best-laid plans of mice and men oft(en) go astray.
men busiest men have the most leisure
men collar-and-tie men
men Dead men tell no tales.
men Good men are scarce.
men Heaven protects children(, sailors,) and drunken men.
men It's ill waiting for dead men's shoes.
men Men are blind in their own cause.
men Men make houses, women make homes.
men separate the men from the boys
men There is a tide in the affairs of men.
men twelve good men and true
men Young men may die, but old men must die.
mend It is never too late to mend.
mend mend (one's) fences
mend mend one's ways
mend on the mend
mental make a mental note of sth
mental mental block (against sth)
mention Don't mention it.
mention (I) just want(ed) to mention sth.
mention make mention of so/sth
mention mention so/sth in passing
mention mention so/sth in sth
mention mention sth to so
mention not worth mentioning
merchant busy as a cranberry merchant (at Thanksgiving)
mercy at so's mercy
mercy at the mercy of so
mercy throw oneself at the mercy of some authority
mercy throw oneself on the mercy of some authority
mere mere trifle
merge merge in(to sth)

merge merge so/sth into sth
merge merge sth with sth
merge merge with so/sth
merit judge one on one's own merits
merit judge sth on its own merits
merry Eat, drink, and be merry, for tomorrow we die.
merry lead so on a merry chase
merry make merry
merry merry as a cricket
merry merry as the day is long
merry more the merrier
mesh mesh together
mesh mesh with sth
mess get into a mess
mess get out of a mess
mess get sth into a mess
mess hell of a mess
mess make a mess of sth
mess mess about
mess mess around
mess mess so over
mess mess so's face up
mess mess so up
mess mess sth up
mess mess up
mess mess with so/sth
mess messed up
mess (whole) mess of so/sth
message Can I leave a message?
message Can I take a message?
message Could I leave a message?
message Could I take a message?
message Get the message?
message May I take a message?
met hale-fellow-well-met
met Have you met so?
met I believe we've met.
metal put the pedal to the metal
metamorphose metamorphose into sth
mete mete sth out
method method in one's madness
methuselah old as Methuselah
mice best-laid plans of mice and men oft(en) go astray.
mice cat in gloves catches no mice.
mice When the cat's away, the mice will play.
Mickey slip so a Mickey
midair in midair
midair keep so/sth hanging (in midair)
midair leave so/sth hanging (in midair)
Midas have the Midas touch
Midas tight as Midas's fist
middle change horses in the middle of the stream
middle drive into the middle of nowhere
middle in the middle of nowhere
middle middle ground
middle middle of nowhere
middle play both ends (against the middle)
middle put so/sth into the middle of nowhere
middle smack (dab) in the middle
middling fair to middlin'
midnight burn the midnight oil
midstream change horses in midstream
midstream Don't change horses in midstream.
might might and main

might might as well
might might could
might Might makes right.
might Nothing so bad but (it) might have been worse.
might (Things) might be better.
might try as I might
mighty act high-and-mighty
mighty high-and-mighty
mighty How the mighty have fallen.
mighty might(y) nigh
mighty Mighty oaks from little acorns grow.
mighty pen is mightier than the sword.
mighty reed before the wind lives on, while mighty oaks do fall.
mighty seem high and mighty
migrate migrate between some place and some place else
migrate migrate (from some place) (to some place)
mike For the love of Mike!
mild to put it mildly
mile by a mile
mile country mile
mile for miles
mile Give so an inch and he'll take a mile.
mile go a mile a minute
mile go the extra mile
mile mile a minute
mile million miles away
mile miss is as good as a mile.
mile miss (sth) by a mile.
mile move a mile a minute
mile stick out a mile
mile talk a mile a minute
mile travel a mile a minute
mileage get a lot of mileage out of sth
mileage get some kind of mileage out of sth
miles look to be a million miles away
milestone important milestone in so's life
milestone milestone in so's life
militate militate against sth
milk cry over spilled milk
milk Don't cry over spilled milk.
milk It's no use crying over spilled milk.
milk milk of human kindness
milk milk so for sth
milk Why buy a cow when milk is so cheap?
milk Why buy a cow when you can get milk for free?
mill go through the mill
mill grist for the mill
mill mill around
mill mill cannot grind with water that is past.
mill mills of God grind slowly, yet they grind exceeding small.
mill put so through the mill
mill run-of-the-mill
mill send so through the mill
mill through the mill
million feel like a million (dollars)
million like a million (dollars)
million look like a million dollars
million look to be a million miles away
million million miles away
million Thanks a million.

millstone millstone about one's neck
mince mince (one's) words
mincemeat make mincemeat (out) of so
mind absent-minded professor
mind bear in mind that...
mind bear so/sth in mind
mind blow so's mind
mind boggle so's mind
mind bring sth to mind
mind call sth to mind
mind change so's mind
mind come to mind
mind contented mind is a perpetual feast.
mind cross so's mind
mind Do you mind?
mind (Do you) mind if...?
mind (Do you) mind if I join you?
mind Don't mind me.
mind drive one out of one's mind
mind enter one's mind
mind flash into one's mind
mind flash through one's mind
mind get a weight off one's mind
mind get so/sth out of one's mind
mind give so a piece of one's mind
mind go out of one's mind
mind Great minds think alike.
mind have a (good) mind to do sth
mind have a lot on one's mind
mind have a mind as sharp as a steel trap
mind have a mind of one's own
mind have a mind to
mind have a one-track mind
mind have half a mind to do sth
mind have one's mind in the gutter
mind have so/sth in mind
mind have so/sth on one's mind
mind have the presence of mind to do sth
mind (Have you) changed your mind?
mind (I) changed my mind.
mind (I) don't mind if I do.
mind I don't mind telling you (sth).
mind If you don't mind!
mind if you've a mind to do sth
mind I'll thank you to mind your own business.
mind (I'm just) minding my own business.
mind in one's mind's eye
mind in one's right mind
mind in the back of so's mind
mind It blows my mind!
mind (It) don't make me no nevermind.
mind keep an open mind
mind keep (it) in mind that
mind keep one's mind on so/sth
mind keep people straight (in one's mind)
mind keep so/sth in mind
mind keep sth in the back of so's mind
mind keep things straight (in one's mind)
mind leave sth in the back of so's mind
mind Little things please little minds.
mind load off one's mind
mind make one's mind up (about so/sth)
mind make so's mind up
mind Make your mind up.
mind meeting of the minds
mind Mind if...?

mind mind one's own business
mind mind one's p's and q's
mind mind over matter
mind mind the store
mind mind you
mind Mind your own beeswax.
mind Mind your own business.
mind Never mind!
mind of a single mind (about so/sth)
mind of one mind (about so/sth)
mind of two minds (about so/sth)
mind on one's mind
mind one's frame of mind
mind one's mind went blank
mind one-track mind
mind open mind
mind out of one's mind
mind Out of sight, out of mind.
mind pass through so's mind
mind peace of mind
mind put one's mind to sth
mind put so in mind of so/sth
mind put so/sth out of one's mind
mind put sth in the back of so's mind
mind read so's mind
mind recall sth to mind
mind remain in the back of so's mind
mind ring in so's mind
mind scare one out of one's mind
mind set one's mind on so/sth
mind set one's mind to sth
mind set so's mind at ease (about so/sth)
mind slip one's mind
mind Small things please small minds.
mind speak one's mind
mind state of mind
mind stay in the back of so's mind
mind stick in so's mind
mind take a load off (of) so's mind
mind take a lot off (of) so's mind
mind take a weight off one's mind
mind Travel broadens the mind.
mind turn sth over in one's mind
mind weigh on so's mind
mind weight off one's mind
mind You changed your mind?
mind You're out of your mind!
mind You've got to be out of your mind!
mine Any friend of so('s) (is a friend of mine).
mine back to the salt mines
mine go back to the salt mines
mine gold mine of information
mine Make mine sth.
mine mine for sth
mine mine of information
mine sitting on a gold mine
mine What's yours is mine, and what's mine is mine.
mine Your guess is as good as mine.
mine Your place or mine?
mingle mingle in (with so)
mingle mingle so with so else
mingle mingle with so
minimum keep sth to a minimum
minister minister to so/sth
minor minor in sth
mint find sth in mint condition
mint in mint condition
minute at the last minute
minute bring sth up to the minute
minute Every minute counts.

minute go a mile a minute
minute Hold on (a minute)!
minute in (just) a minute
minute just a minute
minute mile a minute
minute minute sth happens
minute move a mile a minute
minute So will be with you in a minute.
minute talk a mile a minute
minute travel a mile a minute
minute up-to-the-minute
minute Wait up (a minute)!
minute when you get a minute
minute With you in a minute.
miracle age of miracles is past.
mirror able to fog a mirror
mirror done by mirrors
mirror done with mirrors
mirror smoke and mirrors
miscarriage miscarriage of justice
mischief make mischief
miserable make life miserable for so
miserable make oneself miserable
misery Misery loves company.
misery put one out of (one's) misery
misery put some creature out of its misery
misfortune Misfortunes never come singly.
mislead mislead so about sth
misplace misplace one's trust (in so)
miss Good golly, Miss Molly!
miss have a near miss
miss hit and miss
miss hit or miss
miss miss a trick
miss miss is as good as a mile.
miss miss out (on sth)
miss miss (sth) by a mile
miss miss the boat
miss miss the point
miss not miss a thing
miss not miss much
miss not miss sth for love nor money
miss not miss sth for the world
miss one's heart misses a beat
miss without missing a beat
miss You never miss the water till the well runs dry.
mission mission in life
Missouri from Missouri
mist mist over
mist mist up
mistake by mistake
mistake case of mistaken identity
mistake If you don't make mistakes, you don't make anything.
mistake make a mistake
mistake Make no mistake (about it)!
mistake mistake so for so else
mistake mistake sth for sth else
mix mix and match
mix mix in (with so/sth)
mix mix it up (with so)
mix mix so/sth into sth
mix mix so up
mix mix sth up
mix mix with so/sth
mix mix with sth
mix mixed bag
mix mixed feelings (about so/sth)
mix mixed up in sth
mix mixed up with so else
moan moan about sth

moan moan sth out
moan moan with sth
mock make a mockery of sth
mock mock sth up
mockery make a mockery of sth
model model so on so
model model sth in sth
model model sth on sth
moderation Moderation in all things.
modulate modulate to a (different) key
moist moist around the edges
molasses big around as a molasses barrel
molasses slow as molasses in January
molasses slower than molasses in January
mold cast in the same mold
mold made from the same mold
mold mold sth out of sth
molehill make a mountain out of a molehill
Moley Holy moley!
Molly Good golly, Miss Molly!
moment at a moment's notice
moment big moment
moment Every moment counts.
moment for the moment
moment live for the moment
moment moment everyone has been waiting for
moment moment of truth
moment never a dull moment
moment not a moment to spare
moment not for a moment
moment on a moment's notice
moment on the spur of the moment
moment One moment, please.
moment without a moment to spare
momma (Do) you kiss your momma with that mouth?
Monday come Monday
Monday Monday's child is fair of face.
money Bad money drives out good.
money cash money
money closefisted (with money)
money collect (money) for so/sth
money collect (money) for sth
money come into (some) money
money easy money
money folding money
money fool and his money are soon parted.
money for my money
money found money
money funny money
money hush money
money I'd bet money (on it).
money in the money
money It takes money to make money.
money Lend your money and lose your friend.
money lose money on sth
money love of money is the root of all evil.
money make good money
money make money on sth
money make one's money stretch
money Money burns a hole in so's pocket.
money Money does not grow on trees.
money money from home
money Money is no object.
money Money is power.

money Money is the root of all evil.
money Money talks.
money not able to get sth for love or money
money not for love nor money
money Not for my money.
money not made of money
money not miss sth for love nor money
money on the money
money one's (butter and) egg money
money one's money's worth
money pour money down the drain
money pressed for money
money pushed for money
money put money up (for sth)
money put one's money on so/sth (to do sth)
money Put your money where your mouth is!
money raise money for so/sth
money rolling in money
money run for one's money
money save (money) on sth
money save (money) toward sth
money save money up (for sth)
money see the color of so's money
money smart money
money soft money
money spend money like it's going out of style
money spend money like there's no tomorrow
money spending money
money stretch one's money
money throw good money after bad
money throw money at sth
money tightfisted (with money)
money Time is money.
money You pays your money and you takes your chance(s).
monkey funny as a barrel of monkeys
monkey I'll be a monkey's uncle!
monkey make a monkey (out) of so
monkey monkey business
monkey Monkey see, monkey do.
monkey monkey suit
monkey monkey with so/sth
monkey more fun than a barrel of monkeys
monkey throw a monkey wrench in the works
month by the month
month for (some) months running
month (I) haven't seen you in a month of Sundays.
month in a month of Sundays
month months running
mooch mooch (sth) from so
mood in a bad mood
mood in no mood to do sth
mood in the mood (for sth)
mood put so in a bad mood
moon ask for the moon
moon honeymoon is over.
moon moon about so/sth
moon moon sth away
moon once in a blue moon
moon promise so the moon
moon promise the moon (to so)
moon think so hung the moon (and stars)
mop mop sth down
mop mop sth off

mop mop sth up
mop mop the floor up with so
mop mop up (after so/sth)
mop mopping-up operation
mop That's the way the mop flops.
mope mope around
moral on moral grounds
moralize moralize about so/sth
more all the more reason for doing sth
more bite off more than one can chew
more didn't exchange more than three words with so
more (Do) have some more.
more Don't bite off more than you can chew.
more exchange no more than some number of words with so
more female of the species is more deadly than the male.
more hardly exchange more than some number of words with so
more have more luck than sense
more have more than one string to one's fiddle
more (I) couldn't ask for more.
more It is more blessed to give than to receive.
more know no more about sth than a frog knows about bedsheets
more Less is more.
more Let's go somewhere where it's (more) quiet.
more more and more
more more dead than alive
more more fun than a barrel of monkeys
more More haste, less speed.
more more often than not
more more or less
more More power to you!
more more's the pity
more more so/sth than one can shake a stick at
more more sth than Carter has (liver) pills
more more than one bargained for
more more than one can bear
more more than you('ll ever) know
more more the merrier
more more (to sth) than meets the eye
more more you get, the more you want.
more more you have, the more you want.
more Need I say more?
more No more than I have to.
more not exchange more than some number of words with so
more once more
more one more time
more Say no more.
more scarcely exchange more than some number of words with so
more taste like more
more That's more like it.
more There's more than one way to skin a cat.
more use your head for more than a hatrack
more use your head for more than something to keep your ears apart
more wear more than one hat
more What more can I do?

more whole heap more
more You are more than welcome.
more You can catch more flies with honey than with vinegar.
morning first thing (in the morning)
morning (Good) morning.
morning gotta get up pretty early in the morning to do sth
morning Great day (in the morning)!
morning morning after (the night before)
morning Morning dreams come true.
mortal shuffle off this mortal coil
mortar bricks and mortar
mortar brick(s)-and-mortar
moss house moss
moss rolling stone gathers no moss.
most at most
most at (the) most
most busiest men have the most leisure.
most Devil take the hindmost.
most Empty vessels make the most sound.
most Every man for himself (and the devil take the hindmost).
most First impressions are the most lasting.
most for the most part
most get the most out of so/sth
most make the most of sth
most most of all
mostest firstest with the mostest
moth drawn like a moth to a flame
mothball bring sth out of mothballs
mothball put sth in mothballs
mother Diligence is the mother of good luck.
mother every mother's son (of them)
mother expectant mother
mother Experience is the mother of wisdom.
mother face (that) only a mother could love
mother He that would the daughter win, must with the mother first begin.
mother Like mother, like daughter.
mother Necessity is the mother of invention.
mother old enough to be so's mother
mother swear on one's mother's grave
mother tied to one's mother's apron strings
motherhood motherhood and apple pie
motion go through the motions
motion motion (for) so to do sth
motion motion so aside
motion motion so away from so/sth
motion motion so to one side
motion motion to so
motion set sth in motion
motion table a motion
mound mound sth up
mount mount sth against so/sth
mount mount sth on sth
mount mount up
mountain Faith will move mountains.
mountain If the mountain will not come to Mahomet, Mahomet must go to the mountain.
mountain make a mountain out of a molehill

mourn mourn for so/sth
mouse Burn not your house to fright the mouse away.
mouse mouse that has but one hole is quickly taken.
mouse play cat and mouse with so
mouse poor as a church mouse
mouse quiet as a (church) mouse
mousetrap build a better mousetrap
mouth bad-mouth so/sth
mouth born with a silver spoon in one's mouth
mouth Butter wouldn't melt (in so's mouth).
mouth by word of mouth
mouth diarrhea of the mouth
mouth (Do) you eat with that mouth?
mouth (Do) you kiss your momma with that mouth?
mouth Don't look a gift horse in the mouth.
mouth down in the mouth
mouth foam at the mouth
mouth foot-in-mouth disease
mouth get sth straight from the horse's mouth
mouth have a big mouth
mouth have one's heart in one's mouth
mouth hold one's mouth the right way
mouth Hush your mouth!
mouth keep one's mouth shut (about so/sth)
mouth Keep your mouth shut (about so/sth).
mouth laugh out of the other side of one's mouth
mouth leave a bad taste in so's mouth
mouth live from hand to mouth
mouth look a gift horse in the mouth
mouth look as if butter wouldn't melt in one's mouth
mouth make so's mouth water
mouth melt in one's mouth
mouth mouth full of South
mouth mouth off
mouth mouth on so
mouth not open one's mouth
mouth one's heart is in one's mouth
mouth Out of the mouths of babes (oft times come gems).
mouth put one's foot in one's mouth
mouth put words in(to) so's mouth
mouth Put your money where your mouth is!
mouth rinse so's mouth out (with soap)
mouth run off at the mouth
mouth shoot one's mouth off
mouth smart mouth
mouth stick one's foot in one's mouth
mouth (straight) from the horse's mouth
mouth take the words out of so's mouth
mouth Watch your mouth!
mouth Well, shut my mouth!
mouth (You) took the words right out of my mouth.
mouthful say a mouthful
mouthful You (really) said a mouthful.
movable movable feast
move bust a move
move Faith will move mountains.
move false move

move get a move on
move get moving
move (I) have to be moving along.
move (I) have to move along.
move (I'd) better get moving.
move *in the fast lane
move It's your move.
move (I've) got to get moving.
move *like stink
move make a move on so
move *mile a minute
move movable feast
move move a mile a minute
move move about
move move ahead of so/sth
move move along
move move around
move move as one
move move aside
move move at a fast clip
move move at a good clip
move move away (from so/sth)
move move back (from so/sth)
move move beyond so/sth
move move clear of sth
move move close to so/sth
move move down
move move for sth
move move forward with sth
move move (from some place) (to some place)
move move heaven and earth to do sth
move move in for the kill
move move in (on so)
move move in (on so/sth)
move move in the fast lane
move move in with so
move move into full swing
move move into high gear
move move in(to sth)
move move like stink
move move like the wind
move move off campus
move move off (from so/sth)
move move off (to the side) with so
move move on
move move out (from under so/sth)
move move out (of some place)
move move over
move move so/sth around
move move so/sth away (from so/sth)
move move so/sth back (from so/sth)
move move so/sth down
move move so/sth forward
move move so/sth into sth
move move so/sth off ((from) so/sth)
move move so/sth on
move move so/sth out (of some place)
move move so/sth out of the way
move move so/sth over
move move so/sth to sth
move move so/sth up
move move so to tears
move move so up
move move to some place
move move toward so/sth
move move up
move move within earshot (of sth)
move move within range
move movers and shakers
move Moving three times is as bad as a fire.
move not move a muscle

move *off campus
move on the move
move one false move
move one move ahead (of so/sth)
move prime mover
move put the moves on so
move *within earshot (of sth)
move *within range
move (You'd) better get moving.
mover movers and shakers
mover prime mover
mow mow so/sth down
Mr. Mr. Nice Guy
Mr. Mr. Right
much able to take just so much
much able to take only so much
much amount to much
much bit much
much come to much
much have too much of a good thing
much have too much on one's plate
much have (too much) time on one's hands
much I've heard so much about you.
much know as much about sth as a hog knows about Sunday
much make (too) much of so/sth
much much ado about nothing
much much in evidence
much Much obliged.
much much of a muchness
much much sought after
much not miss much
much Not (too) much.
much Nothing much.
much so much for so/sth
much So much for that.
much so much the better
much take too much on
much Thank you so much.
much Thank you very much.
much That's (just) too much!
much think much of so/sth
much too much
much (We) don't see you much around here anymore.
much without (so much as) a (for or) by your leave
much without so much as doing sth
much You're too much!
muchness much of a muchness
muck (lord) high muck-a-muck
muck muck sth up
mud clear as mud
mud drag so through the mud
mud Here's mud in your eye.
mud one's name is mud
mud stick-in-the-mud
muddle muddle along
muddle muddle around
muddle muddle sth up
muddle muddle through (sth)
muddle muddled (up)
muddy muddy sth up
muddy muddy the water
muff muff one's lines
muffle muffle sth up
mulct mulct sth out of so
mule kick like a mule
mule obstinate as a mule
mule stubborn as a mule
mull mull sth over
mullygrub have the mullygrubs

multiply multiply by sth
multiply multiply sth by sth
multitude multitude of sins
mum Mum's the word.
munch munch out
mung mung sth up
murder cry bloody murder
murder get away with murder
murder murder on sth
murder Murder will out.
murder scream bloody murder
murder yell bloody murder
murmur murmur against so/sth
murmur murmur at so or an animal
muscle muscle in (on so/sth)
muscle muscle so out of sth
muscle not move a muscle
muscle pull a muscle
muse muse over so/sth
mushroom mushroom into sth
music chin music
music face the music
music make chin music
music music to so's ears
music set sth to music
music Stop the music!
muss muss so/sth up
must All good things must (come to an) end.
must All things must pass.
must As you make your bed, so you must lie (up)on it.
must Caesar's wife must be above suspicion.
must Desperate diseases must have desperate remedies.
must door must be either shut or open.
must (Even) the best of friends must part.
must Every tub must stand on its own bottom.
must He that would eat the kernel must crack the nut.
must He that would have eggs must endure the cackling of hens.
must He that would the daughter win, must with the mother first begin.
must He who would climb the ladder must begin at the bottom.
must I must be off.
must I must say good night.
must (I) really must go.
must If the mountain will not come to Mahomet, Mahomet must go to the mountain.
must If two ride on a horse, one must ride behind.
must if you must
must If you want peace, (you must) prepare for war.
must Needs must when the devil drives.
must They must have seen you coming.
must We must do this again (sometime).
must We must learn to walk before we can run.
must What can't be cured must be endured.
must What goes up must come down.
must What must be, must be.

must You must lose a fly to catch a trout.
must Young men may die, but old men must die.
must Youth must be served.
mustard cut the mustard
muster muster out of sth
muster muster sth up
muster pass muster
mutilate fold, spindle, or mutilate
mutiny mutiny against so/sth
mutter mutter about so/sth
mutter mutter sth about so/sth
mutter mutter sth under one's breath
mutter *under one's breath
my all my eye (and Betty Martin)
my Am I my brother's keeper?
my (Are you) going my way?
my Be my guest.
my Call my service.
my Can I see you in my office?
my Could I see you in my office?
my Dad fetch my buttons!
my (Do you) get my drift?
my dog ate my homework.
my Dog my cats!
my Don't waste my time.
my Eat my shorts!
my Excuse my French.
my for my money
my from my perspective
my Get off my back!
my Get out of my sight!
my Get your nose out of my business.
my Give my best to so.
my (Go ahead,) make my day!
my How's my boy?
my I am not my brother's keeper.
my (I) changed my mind.
my I don't have time to catch my breath.
my I don't want to wear out my welcome.
my I rest my case.
my I wouldn't wish that on my worst enemy.
my (I'd) better get on my horse.
my if my memory serves me correctly
my if you get my drift
my I'll eat my hat.
my (I'm) having the time of my life.
my (I'm just) minding my own business.
my in all my born days
my in my humble opinion
my in my opinion
my in my view
my It blows my mind!
my I've done my do.
my (I've) got to go home and get my beauty sleep.
my Keep out of my way.
my Keep your nose out of my business.
my Love me, love my dog.
my Make my day!
my man after my own heart
my mark my word(s)
my My cup runneth over.
my My foot!
my (My) goodness (gracious)!
my my gut tells me (that)
my (My) heavens!
my My house is your house.

my (My,) how time flies.
my My lips are sealed.
my My(, my).
my my one and only
my My pleasure.
my never in my life
my Not for my money.
my Not in my book.
my Over my dead body!
my Pardon my French.
my Read my lips!
my Stay out of my way.
my Sticks and stones may break my bones, but words will never hurt me.
my Take my word for it.
my That's my boy.
my That's my girl.
my This is my floor.
my Watch my lips!
my Well, bust my buttons!
my Well, shut my mouth!
my Where have you been all my life?
my with my blessing
my You scratch my back and I'll scratch yours.
my (You) took the words right out of my mouth.
my You're (just) wasting my time.
myself by myself
myself Do I make myself (perfectly) clear?
myself Have I made myself clear?
myself (I've) been keeping myself busy.
'n' Come 'n' get it!
'n' done 'n' did
nag nag at so (about so/sth)
nail angry enough to chew nails
nail (another) nail in so's or sth's coffin
nail bite one's nails
nail dead as a doornail
nail deader than a doornail
nail fight so/sth tooth and nail
nail For want of a nail the shoe was lost; for want of a shoe the horse was lost; and for want of a horse the man was lost.
nail go at it tooth and nail
nail go at one another tooth and nail
nail hard as nails
nail hit the nail (right) on the head
nail mad enough to chew nails (and spit rivets)
nail mad enough to spit nails
nail nail so down (on sth)
nail nail so's ears back
nail nail so('s hide) to the wall
nail nail so to a cross
nail nail sth back
nail nail sth down
nail nail sth into sth
nail nail sth onto sth
nail nail sth up
nail throw up one's toenails
nail thumbnail sketch
naked appear to the naked eye
naked look to the naked eye
naked naked as a jaybird
naked naked eye
naked naked truth
naked see with the naked eye
naked visible to the naked eye
naked with the naked eye

name answer to the name (of) sth
name appear under the name of some name
name black mark beside one's name
name call so by a name
name call so names
name clear so's name
name drop names
name drop so's name
name go by the name of sth
name go under the name of sth
name have one's name inscribed in the book of life
name household name
name I didn't catch the name.
name I'm awful at names.
name I'm terrible at names.
name in name only
name in so's name
name It has so's name on it.
name know so/sth by name
name make a name (for oneself)
name name of the game
name name so after so else
name name so as sth
name name so for so else
name name so/sth for so/sth
name Name your poison.
name on a first-name basis (with so)
name one's name is mud
name rose by any other name would smell as sweet.
name take names
name throw so's name around
name what's his name
name What's in a name?
name What was the name again?
name worthy of the name
nap catch so napping
nap take a dirt nap
nap take a nap
nape by the nape of the neck
narrow keep to the straight and narrow
narrow narrow sth down (to people or things)
narrow narrow squeak
narrow straight and narrow
natural beat the (natural) stuffing out of so
natural come naturally (to so)
natural die a natural death
natural kick the (natural) stuffing out of so
nature answer the call (of nature)
nature call of nature
nature Nature abhors a vacuum.
nature nature stop
nature second nature to so
nature Self-preservation is the first law of nature.
naught come to naught
nause nause so out
near draw near
near from far and near
near from near and far
near go near (to) so/sth
near have a near miss
near in the near future
near near at hand
near nearer the church, the farther from God.
near nearly jump out of one's skin

near nowhere near
nearly nearly jump out of one's skin
neat neat as a pin
necessary deem it (to be) necessary
necessary If God did not exist, it would be necessary to invent Him.
necessity make a virtue of necessity
necessity Necessity is the mother of invention.
necessity Necessity knows no law.
necessity out of necessity
neck break one's neck (to do sth)
neck breathe down so's neck
neck by the nape of the neck
neck crick in one's neck
neck dead from the neck up
neck get it in the neck
neck hang so by the neck
neck in some neck of the woods
neck millstone about one's neck
neck neck and neck
neck neck with so
neck pain in the neck
neck put one's neck on the line
neck risk one's neck (to do sth)
neck save so's neck
neck stick one's neck out (for so/sth)
neck up to one's neck (in sth)
neck yoke around so's neck
need crying need (for so/sth)
need Do I need to paint you a picture?
need need (to be) done
need *firm hand
need *fix
need friend in need is a friend indeed.
need guilty conscience needs no accuser.
need He that is down need fear no fall.
need I need it yesterday.
need If there's anything you need, don't hesitate to ask.
need in need (of sth)
need It's all so needs.
need (It's) just what you need.
need need a firm hand
need need a helping hand
need need a pick-me-up
need need I remind you that...
need Need I say more?
need need so bad one can taste it
need need some elbow room
need need some shut-eye
need need sth like a hole in the head
need need sth yesterday
need Needless to say
need Needs must when the devil drives.
need *so bad one can taste it
need *some elbow room
need *some shut-eye
need That's all so needs.
need That's just what you need.
need (There is) no need (to).
need We need to talk about sth.
needle like looking for a needle in a haystack
needle needle so about so/sth
needle on pins and needles
needle pins and needles
needless needless to say
neglect neglect to do sth
negotiate negotiate (with so/sth) (over so/sth)

neighbor Good fences make good neighbors.
neighbor neighbor on sth
neighbor one's next-door neighbor
neighborhood (somewhere) in the neighborhood of sth
neither find (neither) hide nor hair
neither have neither rhyme nor reason
neither If you run after two hares, you will catch neither.
neither Neither a borrower nor a lender be.
neither Neither can I.
neither neither does so
neither neither fish nor fowl
neither neither here nor there
neither (neither) hide nor hair
neither neither rhyme nor reason
neither see (neither) hide nor hair
Nellie Whoa, Nellie!
nerve bundle of nerves
nerve get enough nerve up (to do sth)
nerve grate on so('s nerves)
nerve lot of nerve
nerve nerves of steel
nerve on so's nerves
nerve take a lot of nerve
nerve What (a) nerve!
nervous (nervous) breakdown
nest Birds in their little nests agree.
nest feather one's (own) nest
nest foul one's own nest
nest It's an ill bird that fouls its own nest.
nest nest in sth
nest nest together
nest stir up a hornet's nest
nest turkey's nest
nestle nestle down (in sth)
nestle nestle (up) against so/sth
net surf the Net
neutral in neutral
never barking dog never bites.
never Better late than never.
never Blessed is he who expects nothing, for he shall never be disappointed.
never Cheats never prosper.
never Councils of war never fight.
never course of true love never did run smooth.
never East is East and West is West (and never the twain shall meet).
never Eavesdroppers never hear any good of themselves.
never Faint heart never won fair lady.
never (have) never had it so good
never He that hath a full purse never wanted a friend.
never (I) never heard of such a thing!
never (I) never thought I'd see you here!
never If you're born to be hanged, then you'll never be drowned.
never It is a poor heart that never rejoices.
never It is never too late to learn.
never It is never too late to mend.
never (It) never hurts to ask.
never It never rains but it pours.
never It'll never fly.
never (I've) never been better.

never Lightning never strikes (the same place) twice.
never Listeners never hear any good of themselves.
never little (hard) work never hurt anyone.
never Misfortunes never come singly.
never never a dull moment
never Never ask pardon before you are accused.
never never fear
never Never halloo till you are out of the woods.
never Never in a thousand years!
never never in my life
never Never make a threat you cannot carry out.
never Never mind!
never Never say die.
never Never speak ill of the dead.
never Never tell tales out of school.
never Never trouble trouble till trouble troubles you.
never never would have guessed
never now or never
never sth never fails
never Sticks and stones may break my bones, but words will never hurt me.
never tale never loses in the telling.
never 'Tis better to have loved and lost than never to have loved at all.
never Tomorrow never comes.
never watched pot never boils.
never (Well,) I never!
never woman's work is never done.
never Wonders never cease!
never You are never too old to learn.
never You cannot lose what you never had.
never You never know (what you can do) till you try.
never You never miss the water till the well runs dry.
never You'll never get away with it.
nevermind (It) don't make me no nevermind.
new Anything new down your way?
new Bad news travels fast.
new (brand) spanking new
new break new ground
new break the news (to so)
new bright as a new pin
new busy as a beaver (building a new dam)
new feel like a new person
new good as new
new like a kid with a new toy
new (little) new to (all) this
new New brooms sweep clean.
new new kid on the block
new new lease on life
new new one on so
new ring in the new year
new see so/sth in a new light
new (So) what else is new?
new (some) new blood
new take a new turn
new take on a new meaning
new take on a new significance
new That's a new one on me!
new There is nothing new under the sun.
new turn over a new leaf

new What's new?
new What's new with you?
new (whole) new ball game
new You cannot put new wine in old bottles.
new You cannot teach an old dog new tricks.
newborn innocent as a newborn babe
Newcastle carry coals to Newcastle
news No news is good news.
news That's news to me.
next Better luck next time.
next buy the next round (of drinks)
next catch the next wave
next Cleanliness is next to godliness.
next from here till next Tuesday
next (I'll) see you next year.
next live next door (to so)
next Next question.
next next to nothing
next next to so/sth
next next world
next one's next of kin
next one's next-door neighbor
next place so/sth next to so/sth
next Till next time.
next wait for the next wave
nibble nibble at sth
nibble nibble away at sth
nice Have a nice day.
nice Have a nice flight.
nice (I) had a nice time.
nice (It's) nice to be here.
nice (It's) nice to have you here.
nice (It's) nice to meet you.
nice (It's) nice to see you.
nice Mr. Nice Guy
nice nice and some quality
nice nice break
nice Nice going!
nice Nice guys finish last.
nice Nice job!
nice Nice meeting you.
nice Nice place you have here.
nice Nice weather we're having.
nick arrive in the (very) nick of time
nick full of Old Nick
nick happen in the (very) nick of time
nick in the (very) nick of time
nick nick sth up
nick reach sth in the (very) nick of time
nick save so in the (very) nick of time
nickel Don't take any wooden nickels.
nickel I've seen better heads on nickel beers.
nickel nickel-and-dime so (to death)
niggle niggle about sth
niggle niggle (over sth) (with so)
nigh might(y) nigh
night all hours (of the day and night)
night all night long
night at all hours (of the day and night)
night at night
night bunk down (for the night)
night burn the midnight oil
night by night
night call it a night
night day and night
night different as night and day
night far into the night
night fly-by-night

night (Good) night.
night I must say good night.
night I was up all night with a sick friend.
night make a night of it
night morning after (the night before)
night night and day
night night on the town
night night owl
night night person
night one-night stand
night Saturday night special
night ships that pass in the night
night Sing before breakfast, you'll cry before night.
night small hours (of the night)
night till all hours (of the day and night)
night Time to call it a night.
night until all hours (of the day and night)
night wee hours (of the night)
nine cat has nine lives.
nine dressed to the nines
nine Genius is ten percent inspiration and ninety percent perspiration.
nine nine days' wonder
nine nine times out of ten
nine nine-to-five job
nine on cloud nine
nine Possession is nine-tenths of the law.
nine stitch in time saves nine.
nine whole nine yards
nineteen nineteen to the dozen
ninety Genius is ten percent inspiration and ninety percent perspiration.
nip (little) nip in the air
nip nip and tuck
nip nip at so/sth
nip nip sth in the bud
nip nip sth off (of) sth
nitty get down to the nitty-gritty
no all show and no go
no all talk (and no action)
no all vine and no taters
no all wool and no shoddy
no All work and no play makes Jack a dull boy.
no Ask me no questions, I'll tell you no lies.
no Ask no questions and hear no lies.
no by no means
no Call no man happy till he dies.
no cat in gloves catches no mice.
no chain is no stronger than its weakest link.
no Close, but no cigar.
no come as no surprise
no come to no good
no Count no man happy till he dies.
no cut no ice (with so)
no Dead men tell no tales.
no exchange no more than some number of words with so
no Expense is no object.
no feeling no pain
no Fine words butter no parsnips.
no give so no quarter
no gods send nuts to those who have no teeth.
no grant so no quarter

no guilty conscience needs no accuser.
no Happy is the country which has no history.
no Hard words break no bones.
no have no business doing sth
no have no staying power
no have no truck with sth
no He that is down need fear no fall.
no Hell hath no fury like a woman scorned.
no hold no brief for so/sth
no (I have) no problem with that.
no If ifs and ands were pots and pans (there'd be no work for tinkers' hands).
no Ignorance (of the law) is no excuse (for breaking it).
no in less than no time
no in no mood to do sth
no in no time (at all)
no in no time flat
no in no uncertain terms
no (It) don't cut no ice (with so).
no (It) don't cut no squares (with so).
no (It) don't make me no nevermind.
no It is a long lane that has no turning.
no (It) makes me no difference.
no (It) makes no difference to me.
no It's no picnic!
no (It's) no trouble (at all).
no It's no use crying over spilled milk.
no know no more about sth than a frog knows about bedsheets
no leave no stone unturned
no like there ain't no tomorrow
no like there's no tomorrow
no Long time no see.
no Make no bones about it.
no make no difference (to so)
no Make no mistake (about it)!
no mean no offense
no Money is no object.
no Necessity knows no law.
no no big deal
no no biggie
no no buts about it
no No can do.
no No comment.
no no contest
no no dice
no no doubt
no no earthly reason
no no end of sth
no No fair!
no no flies on so
no no go
no no great shakes
no no hard feelings
no No harm done.
no no holds barred
no no ifs, ands, or buts (about it)
no no joke
no No kidding!
no no laughing matter
no No lie?
no No man can serve two masters.
no no matter how you slice it
no no matter what (happens)
no No more than I have to.
no No news is good news.
no No, no, a thousand times no!
no no nonsense
no No offense meant.

no No offense taken.
no No one is indispensable.
no No pain, no gain.
no no point in sth
no no problem
no no questions asked
no No rest for the wicked.
no no sale
no no salesman will call
no no shortage of sth
no No siree(, Bob)!
no no skin off so's nose
no no skin off so's teeth
no no soap
no no sooner said than done
no no spring chicken
no no stress
no no sweat
no No, thank you.
no no thanks to you
no no trespassing
no no two ways about it
no No way!
no No way, José!
no no wonder
no not take no for an answer
no no-win situation
no of no avail
no on no account
no point of no return
no Poverty is no sin.
no rolling stone gathers no moss.
no Say no more.
no See no evil, hear no evil, speak no evil.
no see no further than the end of one's nose
no see no objection (to sth)
no Self-praise is no recommendation.
no Shrouds have no pockets.
no spend money like there's no tomorrow
no Stretch your arm no further than your sleeve will reach.
no take no prisoners
no take no stock in sth
no Thanks, but no thanks.
no That ain't no lie.
no (That causes) no problem.
no There ain't no such thing as a free lunch.
no There is no accounting for taste(s).
no (There is) no chance.
no there is no doing sth
no (There is) no doubt about it.
no There is no love lost (between so and so else).
no (There is) no need (to).
no There is no pleasure without pain.
no There is no rest for the weary.
no There is no royal road to learning.
no There's no accounting for taste.
no There's no flies on so.
no There's no fool like an old fool.
no There's no place like home.
no There's no rose without a thorn.
no (There's) no smoke without fire.
no There's no such thing as a free lunch.
no (There's) no time like the present.
no (There's) no way to tell.
no Time and tide wait for no man.
no to no avail

no under no circumstances
no up to no good
no with no strings attached
nobody It's an ill wind that blows nobody (any) good.
nobody like nobody's business
nobody nobody's fool
nobody There's nobody home.
nod land of Nod
nod nod
nod nod at so
nod nod is as good as a wink to a blind horse.
nod nod off
noggin use one's noggin
noise noise sth about
nominate nominate so as sth
nominate nominate so for sth
nominate nominate so to sth
none bad excuse is better than none.
none bar none
none Half a loaf is better than none.
none have none of sth
none (It) don't bother me none.
none (It's) none of your business!
none jack of all trades is a master of none.
none look none the worse for wear
none None but the brave deserve the fair.
none none of so's beeswax
none none of so's business
none None of your lip!
none none other than
none none the wiser
none none the worse for wear
none none too sth
none One of these days is none of these days.
none second to none
none There's none so blind as those who will not see.
none There's none so deaf as those who will not hear.
nonsense make nonsense of sth
nonsense no nonsense
nonsense stuff and nonsense
noodle noodle around
noodle noodle over sth
noodle use one's noodle
nook every nook and cranny
nor find (neither) hide nor hair
nor have neither rhyme nor reason
nor Neither a borrower nor a lender be.
nor neither fish nor fowl
nor neither here nor there
nor (neither) hide nor hair
nor neither rhyme nor reason
nor not for love nor money
nor not miss sth for love nor money
nor see (neither) hide nor hair
normal under normal circumstances
north up North
nose blow one's nose
nose cannot see (any) further than the end of one's nose
nose can't see beyond the end of one's nose
nose count noses
nose cut one's nose off to spite one's face
nose follow one's nose
nose get one's nose out of joint

nose get one's nose out of so's business
nose Get your nose out of my business.
nose hard-nosed
nose have a nose for sth
nose have one's nose in a book
nose have one's nose in the air
nose have one's nose out of joint
nose hold one's nose
nose keep one's nose clean
nose keep one's nose out of so's business
nose keep one's nose out of sth
nose keep one's nose to the grindstone
nose Keep your nose out of my business.
nose lead so by the nose
nose no skin off so's nose
nose nose about (for so/sth)
nose nose around (sth)
nose nose in(to sth)
nose nose out (of sth)
nose nose so or a group out
nose nose sth out of sth
nose nose sth (out) (onto sth)
nose on the nose
nose one's nose is in the air
nose pay through the nose (for sth)
nose poke one's nose in(to sth)
nose powder one's nose
nose put one's nose in (where it's not wanted)
nose put one's nose out of joint
nose put one's nose to the grindstone
nose put so's nose out of joint
nose (right) under so's (very) nose
nose rub so's nose in it
nose see no further than the end of one's nose
nose snotnose(d) (kid)
nose stick one's nose in (where it's not wanted)
nose stick one's nose in(to sth)
nose stick one's nose up in the air
nose take it on the nose
nose thumb one's nose at so/sth
nose turn one's nose up at so/sth
nose win by a nose
nose-bag put the nose-bag on
nose-bag tie on the nose-bag
nosedive go into a nosedive
nosedive take a nosedive
nosh nosh on sth
not Absolutely not!
not All that glistens is not gold.
not All that glitters is not gold.
not believe it or not
not Burn not your house to fright the mouse away.
not careful not to do sth
not Certainly not!
not Children should be seen and not heard.
not Definitely not!
not devil is not so black as he is painted.
not Do as I say, not as I do.
not Do not let the sun go down on your anger.
not Do not let the sun go down on your wrath.
not Do not wash your dirty linen in public.

not Dog does not eat dog.
not Eat to live, not live to eat.
not find so not guilty
not 'Fraid not.
not Fret not!
not gone but not forgotten
not Half the world knows not how the other half lives.
not I am not my brother's keeper.
not I expect not.
not I guess not.
not (I) hope not.
not I kid you not.
not I suppose not.
not I suspect not.
not I think not.
not If God did not exist, it would be necessary to invent Him.
not if not
not If the mountain will not come to Mahomet, Mahomet must go to the mountain.
not (I'm) afraid not.
not I'm not finished with you.
not I'm not kidding.
not I'm not surprised.
not It is not work that kills, but worry.
not It's not cricket.
not (It's) not half bad.
not It's not kosher.
not (It's) not supposed to.
not It's not the heat, it's the humidity.
not Judge not, lest ye be judged.
not Judge not, that ye be not judged.
not know when one is not wanted
not last but not least
not Let's not go through all that again.
not liar is not believed (even) when he tells the truth.
not likely as not
not Man does not live by bread alone.
not Money does not grow on trees.
not more often than not
not not a bit
not Not a chance!
not not a clue
not not a glimmer (of an idea)
not not a hope in hell
not not a kid anymore
not not a living soul
not not a moment to spare
not not able
not Not again!
not not agree with so
not not all sth is cracked up to be
not not all there
not Not always.
not not amount to a hill of beans
not not any hard feelings
not Not anymore.
not not as young as one used to be
not not at all
not Not bad (at all).
not not bat an eye
not not bat an eyelid
not not believe one's ears
not not believe one's eyes
not not born yesterday
not not breathe a word (about so/sth)
not not breathe a word of it
not not buy sth
not not by a long shot

not not care two hoots about so/sth
not not dry behind the ears
not not enough room to swing a cat
not not exchange more than some number of words with so
not not feel like oneself
not not feeling oneself
not not for a moment
not not for all the tea in China
not not for (anything in) the world
not not for hire
not not for love nor money
not Not for my money.
not not for publication
not not get one's hopes up
not not give a hang about so/sth
not not give a tinker's damn
not not give anyone the time of day
not not give it another thought
not not give two hoots about so/sth
not not going to win any beauty contests
not not grow on trees
not not have a care in the world
not not have a leg to stand on
not not have a snowball's chance in hell
not not have a stitch of clothes (on)
not not have all one's marbles
not not have anything to do with so/sth
not not have anything to do with sth
not not have the heart to do sth
not not hold a candle to so/sth
not not hold a stick to so/sth
not not hold water
not not hold with sth
not not hurt a flea
not Not if I see you first.
not Not if I see you sooner.
not Not in a thousand years!
not not in my book.
not not in the least
not not in the same league with so/sth
not not just whistling Dixie
not not know beans (about so/sth)
not not know enough to come in out of the rain
not not know from nothing
not not know if one is coming or going
not not know one's own strength
not not know so from Adam
not not know the first thing about so/sth
not not know what to make of so/sth
not not know where to turn
not not know whether one is coming or going
not not know which end is up
not not know which way to turn
not not let so catch so doing sth
not not let the grass grow under one's feet
not not lift a finger (to help so)
not not lift a hand (to help so)
not Not likely.
not not long for this world
not not made of money
not not miss a thing
not not miss much
not not miss sth for love nor money
not not miss sth for the world
not not move a muscle
not not on any account
not not one iota

not not one's cup of tea
not not one's place
not not open one's mouth
not not playing with a full deck
not not put (a lot) of stock in sth
not not put it past so
not Not right now, thanks.
not not see any objection (to sth)
not not set foot somewhere
not not shed a tear
not not show one's face
not not sleep a wink
not not so hot
not not take no for an answer
not not take stock in sth
not not tell a (living) soul
not not to put too fine a point on it
not not to touch a drop
not Not to worry.
not Not (too) much.
not not too shabby
not not touch so/sth with a ten-foot pole
not not trouble one's (pretty) (little) head about sth
not not under any circumstances
not not up to scratch
not not up to snuff
not not utter a word
not not want to catch so doing sth
not not what sth is cracked up to be
not not with it
not not worth a damn
not not worth a dime
not not worth a hill of beans
not not worth a red cent
not not worth mentioning
not not worth one's while
not not worth the paper it's printed on
not not worth the paper it's written on
not not worth the trouble
not One swallow does not make a summer.
not Poverty is not a crime.
not prophet is not without honor save in his own country.
not put one's nose in (where it's not wanted)
not Rome was not built in a day.
not (So's) not supposed to.
not stick one's nose in (where it's not wanted)
not There's none so blind as those who will not see.
not There's none so deaf as those who will not hear.
not Too many chiefs and not enough Indians.
not Two wrongs do not make a right.
not Waste not, want not.
not whether or not
not Why not?
not will not hear of sth
not would not be caught dead (doing sth)
not would not be seen dead (doing sth)
notch notch above
notch notch below (so/sth)
notch notch better than (so/sth)
notch notch sth up
notch pull one's belt in (a notch)
notch take one's belt in (a notch)
notch take so down a notch (or two)
notch top notch
note dash a note off

947

note hell of a note
note hit a sour note
note make a mental note of sth
note make a note of sth
note note sth down
note so of note
note strike a sour note
note strike the right note
note take note of so/sth
noted noted for sth
notes compare notes on so/sth
notes swap notes (on so/sth)
nother whole nother thing
nothin' (there ain't) nothin' to it
nothing all or nothing
nothing Believe nothing of what you hear, and only half of what you see.
nothing Blessed is he who expects nothing, for he shall never be disappointed.
nothing care nothing about so/sth
nothing care nothing for so/sth
nothing Civility costs nothing.
nothing come to nothing
nothing Courtesy costs nothing.
nothing go for nothing
nothing have nothing on so
nothing have nothing to do with so/sth
nothing Here goes nothing.
nothing (I have) nothing to complain about.
nothing in nothing flat
nothing (It's) better than nothing.
nothing like nothing on earth
nothing make nothing of sth
nothing make sth out of nothing
nothing mean nothing (to so)
nothing much ado about nothing
nothing next to nothing
nothing not know from nothing
nothing nothing but
nothing Nothing comes of nothing.
nothing Nothing doing!
nothing nothing down
nothing Nothing for me, thanks.
nothing Nothing is certain but death and taxes.
nothing Nothing is certain but the unforeseen.
nothing Nothing is given so freely as advice.
nothing Nothing much.
nothing nothing of the kind
nothing nothing short of sth
nothing Nothing so bad but (it) might have been worse.
nothing Nothing succeeds like success.
nothing nothing to be sneezed at
nothing nothing to boast about
nothing nothing to choose from
nothing Nothing to it!
nothing nothing to sneeze at
nothing nothing to speak of
nothing nothing to write home about
nothing nothing upstairs
nothing Nothing ventured, nothing gained.
nothing Something is better than nothing.
nothing sweet nothings
nothing There is nothing new under the sun.
nothing (There's) nothing to it!

nothing think nothing of doing sth
nothing Think nothing of it.
nothing think nothing of so/sth
nothing to say nothing of so/sth
nothing want for nothing
nothing will stop at nothing
nothing You ain't seen nothing yet!
nothing You don't get something for nothing.
notice at a moment's notice
notice come to so's notice
notice escape so's notice
notice give (one's) notice
notice on a moment's notice
notice on advance notice
notice on short notice
notice serve notice (on so)
notice sit up and take notice
notice take notice of so/sth
notice with advance notice
notify notify so about so/sth
notify notify so of sth
notion have half a notion to do sth
nourish Desires are nourished by delays.
now all better (now)
now Bye for now.
now Can I take your order (now)?
now Could I take your order (now)?
now (every) now and again
now (every) now and then
now Good-bye for now.
now here and now
now (I) have to go now.
now May I take your order (now)?
now Not right now, thanks.
now now and then
now Now hear this!
now now, now
now now or never
now now then
now Now what?
now (Now,) where was I?
now Now you're cooking (with gas)!
now Now you're talking!
now right now
now That's enough for now.
now What now?
nowhere all dressed up and nowhere to go
nowhere appear out of nowhere
nowhere at the end of nowhere
nowhere come from nowhere
nowhere come out of nowhere
nowhere drive into the middle of nowhere
nowhere Flattery will get you nowhere.
nowhere get nowhere fast
nowhere in the middle of nowhere
nowhere materialize out of nowhere
nowhere middle of nowhere
nowhere nowhere near
nowhere out of nowhere
nowhere put so/sth into the middle of nowhere
nth to the nth degree
nude denude so/sth of sth
nude in the nude
nudge nudge so/sth aside
nuisance make a nuisance of oneself
null null and void
number any number of so/sth

number by the numbers
number come out in large numbers
number dial the wrong number
number do a number on so/sth
number express sth in round numbers
number in round numbers
number look after number one
number look out for number one
number number in sth
number number of things or people
number number off (by sth)
number number so/sth among sth
number number so with sth
number one's days are numbered
number one's number is up
number out in large numbers
number quite a number
number safety in numbers
number take care of number one
number There is safety in numbers.
number What number are you calling?
number wrong number
numero take care of numero uno
nurse nurse a grudge (against so)
nurse nurse so back to health
nurse nurse so or an animal along
nurse nurse so through (sth)
nurse nurse sth along
nut drive so nuts
nut everything from soup to nuts
nut get down to the nuts and bolts
nut go nuts
nut gods send nuts to those who have no teeth.
nut hard nut to crack
nut He that would eat the kernel must crack the nut.
nut nut case
nut nut up
nut nuts about so/sth
nut nuts and bolts
nut Nuts to you!
nut off one's nut
nut talk like a nut
nut tough nut to crack
nutshell in a nutshell
nutshell put sth in a nutshell
nuttier nuttier than a fruitcake
nutty nutty as a fruitcake
nuzzle nuzzle up against so/sth
o' Land o' Goshen!
oak all oak and iron bound
oak Great oaks from little acorns grow.
oak Little strokes fell great oaks.
oak Mighty oaks from little acorns grow.
oak reed before the wind lives on, while mighty oaks do fall.
oar have just one oar in the water
oar put one's oar in
oar stick one's oar in
oat feel one's oats
oat sow one's wild oats
oath take an oath
oath under oath
obey He that cannot obey cannot command.
object Expense is no object.
object Money is no object.
object not see any objection (to sth)
object object to so/sth
object raise (an) objection (to so/sth)
object see no objection (to sth)

objection not see any objection (to sth)
objection raise (an) objection (to so/sth)
objection see no objection (to sth)
obligate obligate so to so/sth
oblige Much obliged.
oblige oblige so by sth
oblige oblige so to do sth
oblige oblige so with sth
obliterate obliterate so/sth from sth
oblivion sink into oblivion
obsess obsessed with so/sth
obstinate obstinate as a mule
obtain obtain sth for so/sth
occasion keep sth for another occasion
occasion leave sth for another occasion
occasion on occasion
occasion rise to the occasion
occupancy immediate occupancy
occupy occupy oneself by sth
occupy occupy so with sth
occur occur before so's time
occur occur to so
ocean drop in the ocean
ocean oceans of so/sth
odd against all odds
odd at odds (with so)
odd give so odds that...
odd odd man out
odd odd sth
odd odds and ends
odd odds are against one
odd odds-on favorite
odor odor of sanctity
of ABCs of sth
of abreast of so/sth
of accuse so of sth
of ace out (of sth)
of acknowledge (the) receipt of sth
of acquit so of sth
of act full of oneself
of act of faith
of act of God
of act of war
of advantage of so
of advise so of sth
of afraid of one's own shadow
of after the fashion of so/sth
of after the style of so/sth
of age of miracles is past.
of age out (of sth)
of ahead of one's time
of ahead of schedule
of ahead (of so/sth)
of ahead of sth
of ahead of the game
of ahead of time
of (a)hold of so/sth
of ain't got a grain of sense
of ain't got a lick of sense
of all hours (of the day and night)
of all kinds of so/sth
of all manner of so/sth
of all of a size
of all of a sudden
of all over hell and half of Georgia
of all walks of life
of (almost) jump out of one's skin
of alongside (of) so/sth
of another pair of eyes
of answer the call (of nature)
of answer to the description of so

of answer to the name (of) sth
of Any friend of so('s) (is a friend of mine).
of any number of so/sth
of appear out of nowhere
of appear under the name of some name
of apple of so's eye
of apprise so of sth
of approve of so/sth
of argue one's way out of sth
of arguing for the sake of arguing
of arguing for the sake of argument
of arrive ahead of time
of arrive in the (very) nick of time
of arrive (somewhere) at the stroke of some time
of arrive (somewhere) (up)on the stroke of some time
of arrive (up)on the scene (of sth)
of as a matter of course
of as a matter of fact
of as a result (of sth)
of as a token (of sth)
of ask sth of so/sth
of assure so of sth
of at all hours (of the day and night)
of at the bottom of the hour
of at the bottom of the ladder
of at the break of dawn
of at the crack of dawn
of at the drop of a hat
of at the end of nowhere
of at the end of one's rope
of at the end of one's tether
of at the end of the day
of at the expense of so/sth
of at the forefront (of sth)
of at the height of sth
of at the helm (of sth)
of at the mercy of so
of at the point of doing sth
of at the rear of sth
of at the top of one's game
of at the top of one's lungs
of at the top of one's voice
of at the top of the hour
of at the zenith of sth
of at this stage (of the game)
of attack (of an illness)
of avail oneself of sth
of avenue of escape
of back of the beyond
of back out (of sth)
of back so/sth out of sth
of bag of bones
of bag of tricks
of bail out (of sth)
of bail so out of jail
of balance of power
of ball of fire
of balls of one's feet
of baptism of fire
of barrel of fun
of barrel out (of some place)
of battle of the bulge
of be in aid of
of bear off (of sth)
of bear the brunt (of sth)
of beat the hell out of so
of beat the (natural) stuffing out of so
of beat the pants off (of) so
of beat the shit out of so
of beat the socks off (of) so

of beat the stuffing out of so
of beat the tar out of so
of Beauty is in the eye of the beholder.
of become of so/sth
of bed of roses
of beg of so
of beg sth of so
of beginning of the end
of beguile so out of sth
of Believe nothing of what you hear, and only half of what you see.
of believe sth of so
of bend so out of shape
of bend sth out of shape
of benefit of the doubt
of bent out of shape
of bereft of so/sth
of best is the enemy of the good.
of best of both worlds
of best of so
of best part of sth
of best-laid plans of mice and men oft(en) go astray.
of Better be the head of a dog than the tail of a lion.
of better of so
of bevy of beauties
of Beware of Greeks bearing gifts.
of beware of so/sth
of beyond the shadow of a doubt
of big drink of water
of big of so
of bilk so out of sth
of Birds of a feather flock together.
of bit of the action
of bitch of a so/sth
of black as the ace of spades
of black sheep of the family
of blow so/sth out of the water
of blow sth out of (all) proportion
of bluff one's way out (of sth)
of bluff so out (of sth)
of boil sth out of so
of bolt out (of some place)
of bomb out (of sth)
of bone of contention
of bore the pants off of so
of born on the wrong side of the blanket
of born out of wedlock
of bottom fell out (of sth)
of bottom of the barrel
of bottom of the heap
of bounce off ((of) sth)
of bounce out (of sth)
of bounce sth off (of) so/sth
of bow out (of some place)
of bow out (of sth)
of Bread is the staff of life.
of break out (of sth)
of break so/sth of sth
of break sth off (of) sth
of break sth out (of sth)
of break the back of sth
of breath of fresh air
of breathe a sigh of relief
of breathe sth (of sth) (to so)
of breeze out (of some place)
of Brevity is the soul of wit.
of bring one out of one's shell
of bring so/sth out of sth
of bring so/sth out of the woodwork
of bring so/sth within range (of so/sth)

of bring so out of the closet
of bring sth out of mothballs
of bring sth out of so
of build sth out of sth
of bunch of fives
of bundle of joy
of bundle of nerves
of burn one's bridges in front of one
of burn so out of sth
of burst out (of some place)
of burst out (of sth)
of business end of sth
of bust ass out of some place
of bust out (of some place)
of bust so out of some place
of butt of a joke
of buy a round (of drinks)
of buy one's way out (of sth)
of buy the next round (of drinks)
of by a show of hands
of by all means of sth
of by any stretch of the imagination
of by dint of sth
of by force of habit
of by means of sth
of by the end of the day
of by the nape of the neck
of by the seat of one's pants
of by the skin of one's teeth
of by the sweat of one's brow
of by virtue of sth
of by way of sth
of by word of mouth
of cajole so out of sth
of call of nature
of can of worms
of cancel out (of sth)
of cancel so out of sth
of candidate for a pair of wings
of cannot see (any) further than the end of one's nose
of can't hit the (broad) side of a barn
of can't make heads or tails (out) of so/sth
of can't see beyond the end of one's nose
of can't see one's hand in front of one's face
of can't stand (the sight of) so/sth
of capable of doing sth
of captain of industry
of carry (a lot of) weight (with so/sth)
of carry the weight of the world on one's shoulders
of carve sth out (of sth)
of case of mistaken identity
of case of sth
of case of the blind leading the blind
of cat is out of the bag
of catch a glimpse of so/sth
of catch a whiff of sth
of catch (a)hold of so/sth
of catch one's death (of cold)
of catch sight of so/sth
of catch so in the act (of doing sth)
of catch wind of sth
of center of attention
of chain of command
of change horses in the middle of the stream
of change (of life)
of change of pace
of change of scenery

of change out of sth
of charge (of so/sth)
of charge out (of some place)
of chase so/sth out of some place
of cheat so out of sth
of check out (of sth)
of check so/sth out (of sth)
of chicken out (of sth)
of child is father of the man.
of chisel so out of sth
of chock full of sth
of chop sth off (of) sth
of chuck so out of some place
of chunk of change
of clean bill of health
of clean out (of sth)
of clean so/sth out of sth
of clear of sth
of clear off ((of) some place)
of clear out (of some place)
of clear so of sth
of clear so/sth out of some place
of climb out (of sth)
of clip sth out of sth
of clock so at speeds of some amount
of close as two coats of paint
of close so out of sth
of coax so or an animal out of sth
of cock of the walk
of cocky as the king of spades
of comb sth out of sth
of come in out of the rain
of come of age
of come off ((of) sth)
of come out in favor of so/sth
of come out of a clear blue sky
of come out of left field
of come out of nowhere
of come out of one's shell
of come out (of so/sth)
of come out (of sth)
of come out of the blue
of come out of the closet
of come out (of) the little end of the horn
of come out of the woodwork
of come (right) on top of sth
of come short of sth
of come to think of it
of come within a hair('s breadth) of so/sth
of come within an ace of sth
of come within an inch of doing sth
of come within an inch of so/sth
of come within earshot (of sth)
of come within range (of sth)
of coming out of one's ears
of complain of sth
of composed of sth
of comprised of so/sth
of con so out of sth
of conceive of so/sth
of conceive of so/sth as so/sth
of conduct so out of sth
of Conscience does make cowards of us all.
of consist of so/sth
of convict so of sth
of convince so of sth
of cop out (of sth)
of copy sth out of sth
of couldn't pour water out of a boot (if there was instructions on the heel)

of Councils of war never fight.
of couple of
of course of action
of course of true love never did run smooth.
of cover a lot of ground
of crap out (of sth)
of crap out (of sth) (on so)
of crash out (of some place)
of crawl out (of sth)
of cream of the crop
of creep out (of sth)
of creep out of the woodwork
of crooked as a barrel of fish hooks
of cross so/sth off (of) sth
of crowd so/sth out of sth
of crush sth out of so/sth
of crux of the matter
of cull so/sth out of sth
of cure so of sth
of cure sth of sth
of cut in (ahead of so/sth)
of cut sth out of sth
of dab sth off (of) sth
of daddy of them all
of dance out of step (with so/sth)
of dance out of time (with so/sth)
of dangle sth in front of so
of dark side of so/sth
of dart out (of sth) (at so/sth)
of deal so out of sth
of decide in favor of so/sth
of defraud so out of sth
of deliver so of sth
of demand sth of so/sth
of denude so/sth of sth
of deplete sth of sth
of deprive so of sth
of despair of sth
of despoil sth of sth
of determine the root of the problem
of devil of a job
of devil of a time
of diarrhea of the jawbone
of diarrhea of the mouth
of diddle so out of sth
of diddle sth out of so
of die of a broken heart
of die of boredom
of die of curiosity
of die of sth
of die of throat trouble
of dig out (of sth)
of dig so/sth out of sth
of Diligence is the mother of good luck.
of disabuse so of sth
of disapprove of so/sth
of disaster of epic proportions
of Discretion is the better part of valor.
of dispose of so
of dispossess so of sth
of dive off ((of) sth)
of divest so/sth of sth
of do so a heap of good
of do so a power of good
of do so out of sth
of (Do you) want to make something of it?
of doesn't have enough sense to come in out of the rain
of don't amount to a bucket of spit

of Don't breathe a word of this to anyone.
of Don't give me any of your lip!
of don't have a pot to piss in (or a window to throw it out of)
of Don't let it out of this room.
of Don't make two bites of a cherry.
of dose of one's own medicine
of drag so/sth off of so/sth
of drag sth out of so
of drain so/sth of sth
of drain sth of so
of drain sth out of sth
of draw ahead (of so/sth)
of draw so or an animal out of sth
of draw so/sth out of some place
of draw sth out of so
of Dream of a funeral and you hear of a marriage.
of Dream of a funeral and you hear of a wedding.
of dream of doing sth
of dream of so/sth
of drive into the middle of nowhere
of drive one out of one's mind
of drive so or an animal out of sth
of drive so out of office
of drop out of sight
of drop out (of sth)
of drop so/sth out of sth
of drum so out of sth
of duck out (of some place)
of duck out (of sth)
of ease (on) out (of sth)
of ease so (on) out (of sth)
of ease so out of sth
of eat out of so's hand
of eat so out of house and home
of eat sth off (of) sth
of eat (sth) out of sth
of Eavesdroppers never hear any good of themselves.
of edge so out of sth
of edge sth out of sth
of edit sth out of sth
of elbow so out of sth
of enamored of so/sth
of End of story.
of end of the ball game
of end of the line
of end of the road
of end up with the short end of the stick
of enjoy the best of both worlds
of escape by the skin of one's teeth
of even in the best of times
of (Even) the best of friends must part.
of evening of life
of Every man is the architect of his own fortune.
of every mother's son (of them)
of every walk of life
of exorcise sth out of so
of Experience is the father of wisdom.
of Experience is the mother of wisdom.
of Experience is the teacher of fools.
of eye of the hurricane
of eye of the storm
of eyeful (of so/sth)
of facts of life
of faint of heart
of fake so out of sth
of fall (a)foul of so/sth

of fall like a ton of bricks
of fall off (of) sth
of fall out of bed
of fall out of favor (with so)
of fall out of love (with so)
of fall out (of sth)
of fall short of one's goal(s)
of fall wide of the mark
of fan of so
of fan the flames (of sth)
of fashion sth out of sth
of fast-talk so out of sth
of feed off (of) sth
of feel a glow of contentment
of feel a glow of happiness
of feel of sth
of feel on top of the world
of feel out of place
of feel out of sorts
of feel out of things
of female of the species is more deadly than the male.
of ferret sth out of so/sth
of fetch sth out of sth
of few bricks short of a load
of few cards short of a deck
of few cards shy of a full deck
of fight one's way out (of sth)
of figure out the root of the problem
of file out (of sth)
of file sth off ((of) sth)
of fill so full of lead
of filter sth out of sth
of find the root of the problem
of fine kettle of fish
of fine state of affairs
of finish ahead of schedule
of first leg (of a journey)
of first of all
of first see the light of day
of fish so/sth out of sth
of fish sth up out of sth
of flake off ((of) sth)
of flake sth off of sth
of fleet of foot
of flex sth out of shape
of flexed out of shape
of flight of fancy
of fling so/sth out of sth
of fling sth off of oneself
of fling sth out (of) sth
of flirt with the idea of doing sth
of flood out (of sth)
of flood so/sth out of sth
of flounce out (of some place)
of flow out (of sth)
of flunk out (of sth)
of flush so/sth out of some place
of fly by the seat of one's pants
of fly in the face of so/sth
of fly in the teeth of so/sth
of fly into the face of danger
of fly out (of sth)
of fly so/sth out of sth
of follow after the style of so/sth
of fond of so/sth
of for fear of sth
of for the devil of it
of for the fun of it
of for the good of so/sth
of for the heck of it
of for the hell of it
of for the life of me

of For the love of Mike!
of for the sake of so/sth
of For want of a nail the shoe was lost; for want of a shoe the horse was lost; and for want of a horse the man was lost.
of force so/sth off (of) sth
of force so/sth out of sth
of force so out of office
of form sth out of sth
of foul out (of sth)
of fresh out (of sth)
of fresh pair of eyes
of frighten one out of one's wits
of frighten so out of a year's growth
of frighten the hell out of so
of from all corners of the world
of from the bottom of one's heart
of from the four corners of the earth
of fruits of one's labor(s)
of full of beans
of full of bull
of full of holes
of full of hot air
of full of Old Nick
of full of oneself
of full of prunes
of full of the devil
of funny as a barrel of monkeys
of get a bang out of so/sth
of get a buzz out of so/sth
of get a charge out of so/sth
of get a kick out of so/sth
of get a load of so/sth
of get a lot of mileage out of sth
of get a (sound) grasp of sth
of get ahead of oneself
of get euchred out of sth
of get free of so/sth
of get in(to) the swing of things
of get off (of) so/sth
of get off (of) sth
of get on the track of so/sth
of get one's nose out of joint
of get one's nose out of so's business
of get out of a jam
of get out of a mess
of get out of (doing) sth
of Get out (of here)!
of Get out of my sight!
of get out of one's face
of get out of so's hair
of get out of the road
of get out of time (with so/sth)
of Get out of town!
of get out of wind
of get shed of so/sth
of get shut of so/sth
of get some kind of mileage out of sth
of get so/sth out of one's mind
of get so/sth out of one's sight
of get so/sth out of so/sth
of get so out of a jam
of get so out of one's hair
of get sth out of one's system
of get sth out of so
of get sth out (of so/sth)
of get sth out of sth
of get the drift of sth
of get the hell out (of here)
of get the most out of so/sth
of get the point (of sth)
of get the wrinkles out (of sth)

of get to the bottom of sth
of get to the point (of sth)
of get to the top (of sth)
of get up a (full) head of steam
of get up (off (of) sth)
of get up on the wrong side of bed
of get wind of sth
of Get your head out of the clouds!
of Get your nose out of my business.
of ghost of a chance
of give a good account of oneself
of give an account of so/sth (to so)
of give evidence of sth
of give of oneself
of give so a piece of one's mind
of give sth under (the) threat of sth
of gnashing of teeth
of go above and beyond the call of duty
of go ahead (of so/sth)
of go by the name of sth
of go in and out (of sth)
of go out in search of so/sth
of go out of business
of go out of control
of go out of fashion
of go out of favor (with so)
of go out of focus
of go out of kilter
of go out of one's head
of go out of one's mind
of go out of one's senses
of go out of one's skull
of go out of one's way (to do sth)
of go out of practice
of go out of service
of go out of sight
of go out (of sth)
of go out of style
of go out of the frying pan into the fire
of go out-of-bounds
of go the way of the dodo
of go the way of the horse and buggy
of go through so like a dose of the salts
of go to the bother (of doing sth)
of go to the crux of the matter
of go to the expense (of doing sth)
of go to the heart of the matter
of go to the root of the matter
of go to the trouble (of doing sth)
of go under the name of sth
of gold mine of information
of (good) grasp of sth
of good is the enemy of the best.
of gouge sth out of so
of gouge sth out of sth
of grain of truth
of granddaddy of them all
of grass is always greener on the other side (of the fence).
of Great balls of fire!
of grow knee-high by the 4th of July
of grow out of (all) proportion
of grow out of sth
of grow sick (and tired) of so/sth
of guest of honor
of gyp so out of sth
of hack sth out of sth
of hair of the dog that bit one
of hang of sth
of hang out (of sth)
of hang sth out (of sth)
of happen in the (very) nick of time

of harbinger of things to come
of hard of hearing
of harder than the back of God's head
of have a bad case of the simples
of have a change of heart
of have a good command of sth
of have a heart of gold
of have a heart of stone
of have a mind of one's own
of have a rough time (of it)
of have a run of sth
of have a (sound) grasp of sth
of have a whale of a time
of have an easy time of it
of have carnal knowledge of so
of have eyes in the back of one's head
of have feet of clay
of have (high) hopes of sth
of have none of sth
of have one's name inscribed in the book of life
of have one's nose out of joint
of have the best of so/sth
of have the courage of one's convictions
of have the gift of gab
of have the makings of sth
of have the patience of a saint
of have the patience of Job
of have the presence of mind to do sth
of have the time of one's life
of have too much of a good thing
of (Have you) been keeping out of trouble?
of He that would have eggs must endure the cackling of hens.
of heal so of sth
of heap of sth
of hear a peep out of so
of hear of so/sth
of heart of the matter
of hell of a mess
of hell of a note
of hell of a so/sth
of Hell's bells (and buckets of blood)!
of help so off (of) sth
of help so or an animal out (of sth)
of hew sth out of sth
of hightail it out of somewhere
of hind end of creation
of hiss so off ((of) the stage)
of hit like a ton of bricks
of hit so like a ton of bricks
of hit speeds of some amount
of hit the (broad) side of a barn
of hive of activity
of hold one's end of the bargain up
of hold so/sth out (of sth)
of hold sth inside ((of) one(self))
of hoodwink so out of sth
of hop off ((of) sth)
of horse of a different color
of horse of another color
of hot on the trail (of so/sth or some creature)
of hotbed of sth
of hotfoot it out of somewhere
of hound so out (of sth or some place)
of hound sth out of so
of house of correction
of house of ill fame
of house of ill repute
of hurl so/sth out (of some place)
of (I) haven't seen you in a month of Sundays.

of (I) never heard of such a thing!
of I spoke out of turn.
of (I) won't breathe a word (of it).
of Idleness is the root of all evil.
of If you can't stand the heat, get out of the kitchen.
of Ignorance (of the law) is no excuse (for breaking it).
of (I'm) having the time of my life.
of I'm out of here.
of Imitation is the sincerest form of flattery.
of in a (constant) state of flux
of in a month of Sundays
of in a world of one's own
of in an age of years
of in and of itself
of in (at) one ear and out (of) the other
of in awe (of so/sth)
of in behalf of so
of in care of so
of in case of sth
of in charge (of so/sth)
of in consequence (of sth)
of in consideration of sth
of in contempt (of court)
of in control of so/sth
of in custody (of so/sth)
of in defiance (of so/sth)
of in favor of so
of in favor (of so/sth)
of in (high) hopes of sth
of in honor of so/sth
of in lieu of sth
of in memory of so
of in need (of sth)
of in place of so/sth
of in point of fact
of in pursuit of sth
of in quest of so/sth
of in receipt of sth
of in search of so/sth
of in some neck of the woods
of in spite of so/sth
of in terms of sth
of in the absence of so/sth
of in the act (of doing sth)
of in the back of so's mind
of in the best of health
of in the care of so
of in the case of so/sth
of in the charge of so
of in the context of sth
of In the country of the blind, the one-eyed man is king.
of in the course of time
of in the event of sth
of in the forefront (of sth)
of in the interest of saving time
of in the interest of so/sth
of in the lap of luxury
of in (the) light of sth
of in the line of duty
of in the mainstream (of sth)
of in the middle of nowhere
of in the pink (of condition)
of in the pink (of health)
of in the prime of life
of in the swim of things
of in the trust of so
of in the twinkling of an eye
of in the unlikely event of sth

of in the (very) nick of time
of in the wake of sth
of in the way of so('s plans)
of in the way of so/sth
of in the way of sth
of in the wink of an eye
of in two shakes of a lamb's tail
of in view of sth
of include so out (of sth)
of inform so of sth
of inkling (of sth)
of inquire sth of so
of ins and outs (of sth)
of invasion of (so's) privacy
of inveigle so out of sth
of inveigle sth out of so
of It's just one of those things.
of (It's) none of your business!
of It's six of one, half a dozen of another.
of It would take an act of Congress to do sth.
of (I've) been keeping out of trouble.
of I've had enough of this!
of jack of all trades
of jack of all trades is a master of none.
of jerk so/sth out of sth
of jerk sth off (of) so/sth
of jerk sth out of so/sth
of jolt so out of sth
of jump clear of sth
of jump off ((of) sth)
of jump out of sth
of jump out of the frying pan into the fire
of just one's cup of tea
of (just) taking care of business
of keep abreast of so/sth
of keep ahead (of so/sth)
of keep ahead of sth
of keep ahead of the game
of keep clear of sth
of keep inside ((of) sth)
of keep off (of) so's back
of keep off (of) so's case
of keep off ((of) sth)
of keep on the good side of so
of keep on the left(-hand) side (of sth)
of keep on the right side of so
of keep on the right(-hand) side (of sth)
of keep on top (of so/sth)
of keep one's end of the bargain up
of keep one's finger on the pulse of sth
of keep one's nose out of so's business
of keep one's nose out of sth
of keep one's side of the bargain
of keep one step ahead of so/sth
of Keep out of my way.
of keep out of sight
of keep out (of sth)
of Keep out of this!
of keep sight of so/sth
of keep so in (a state of) suspense
of keep so/sth off ((of) so/sth)
of keep so/sth out (of sth)
of keep so/sth out of the way
of keep sth in the back of so's mind
of keep sth inside ((of) one(self))
of keep sth of so's or sth's
of keep track (of so/sth)
of Keep your nose out of my business.
of kick in the (seat of the) pants

of kick sth off (of) so/sth
of kick sth out of sth
of kick the (natural) stuffing out of so
of Kind of.
of kind of sth
of kiss of death
of knee-high by the 4th of July
of knock sth off (of) so/sth
of knock sth out of kilter
of knock sth out of place
of knock sth out of so
of knock sth out of sth
of knock the bejeebers out of so/sth
of knock the bottom out (of sth)
of knock the hell out of so/sth
of knock the (living) daylights out of so
of knock the stuffing out of so
of knock the wind out of so's sails
of know of so/sth
of know so/sth like the back of one's hand
of know so/sth like the palm of one's hand
of know the tricks of the trade
of labor of love
of ladle sth out of sth
of lady of the evening
of Land o' Goshen!
of land of Nod
of lap of luxury
of laugh oneself out of sth
of laugh out of the other side of one's face
of laugh out of the other side of one's mouth
of laugh so out of sth
of laugh sth out of court
of lay hold of so/sth
of lay of the land
of lay off ((of) so/sth)
of lay sth alongside ((of) sth)
of leach out of sth
of lead so or an animal out of sth
of lead the life of Riley
of leak out (of sth)
of lean out of sth
of leap of faith
of leap out (of sth)
of learn of so/sth
of learn the tricks of the trade
of least of all
of leave ahead of time
of leave go of so/sth
of leave of absence
of leave so/sth in the care of so
of leave so/sth in the trust of so
of leave so out of sth
of leave sth in the back of so's mind
of lesser (of the two)
of lesser of two evils
of let go of so/sth
of let loose of so/sth
of Let's get out of here.
of let so or an animal (get) out (of sth)
of let so or an animal out of sth
of let the cat out of the bag
of lick of work
of lick sth off (of) sth
of lie ahead of so/sth
of lie alongside ((of) so or an animal)
of Life is just a bowl of cherries.
of life of the party
of lift sth off (of) so/sth
of lift sth out of context

of light out (of some place) (for some place)
of like a bat out of hell
of like a bolt out of the blue
of like a can of corn
of like a fish out of water
of like a ton of bricks
of like it was going out of style
of like one of the family
of likes of so/sth
of line of least resistance
of lion's share of sth
of Listeners never hear any good of themselves.
of little bit (of sth)
of live a life of sth
of live in a world of one's own
of live in hope(s) of sth
of live in the best of both worlds
of live off (of) so/sth
of live off the fat of the land
of live out of a suitcase
of live out of cans
of live the life of Riley
of live to the (ripe old) age of sth
of live up to one's end of the bargain
of lock so/sth out of sth
of long and the short of it
of long arm of the law
of look at the crux of the matter
of look at the heart of the matter
of look like a candidate for a pair of wings
of look like a case of sth
of look out (of) sth
of loom out of sth
of lop sth off (of) sth
of lose count of so/sth
of lose one's train of thought
of lose sight of so/sth
of lose the use of sth
of lose trace of so/sth
of lose track (of so/sth)
of lot of give-and-take
of lot of nerve
of lot of promise
of lot of so/sth
of Lots of luck!
of lots of people or things
of love of money is the root of all evil.
of luck of the draw
of luck out of sth
of lull so into a false sense of security
of make a believer (out) of so
of make a clean breast of sth (to so)
of make a day of doing sth
of make a day of it
of make a federal case out of sth
of make a fool (out) of so
of make a go of sth
of make a great show of sth
of make a habit of sth
of make a laughingstock of oneself or sth
of make a man of so
of make a meal of sth
of make a mental note of sth
of make a mess of sth
of make a mockery of sth
of make a monkey (out) of so
of make a mountain out of a molehill
of make a night of it
of make a note of sth
of make a nuisance of oneself
of make a pig of oneself

of make a point of doing sth
of make a point of so/sth
of make a practice of sth
of make a secret of sth
of make a virtue of necessity
of make an example of so
of make an exhibition of oneself
of make an honest woman of so
of make an issue of so/sth
of make certain of sth
of make demands of so/sth
of make fast work of so/sth
of make fun of so/sth
of make (good) use of sth
of make hamburger (out) of so
of make heads or tails of so/sth
of make it by the seat of one's pants
of make light of sth
of make little of so/sth
of make mention of so/sth
of make mincemeat (out) of so
of make nonsense of sth
of make nothing of sth
of make short work of so/sth
of make (some) sense (out) of so/sth
of make sth of so/sth
of make sth of sth
of make sth off (of) so/sth
of make sth out of nothing
of make sth (out) of sth
of make sth up out of whole cloth
of make sure (of sth)
of make the best of a bad job
of make the best of sth
of make the most of sth
of make (too) much of so/sth
of make use of so/sth
of man of few words
of man of the cloth
of maneuver so out of sth
of march out of time (with so/sth)
of march to (the beat of) a different drummer
of marry one's way out of sth
of materialize out of nowhere
of matter of life and death
of matter of opinion
of meeting of the minds
of mell of a hess
of middle of nowhere
of milk of human kindness
of mills of God grind slowly, yet they grind exceeding small.
of mine of information
of miscarriage of justice
of mold sth out of sth
of moment of truth
of Monday's child is fair of face.
of Money is the root of all evil.
of more fun than a barrel of monkeys
of most of all
of mouth full of South
of move ahead of so/sth
of move clear of sth
of move out (of some place)
of move so/sth out (of some place)
of move so/sth out of the way
of move within earshot (of sth)
of move within range (of sth)
of much of a muchness
of mulct sth out of so
of multitude of sins
of muscle so out of sth

of muster out of sth
of name of the game
of nearly jump out of one's skin
of Necessity is the mother of invention.
of nerves of steel
of Never halloo till you are out of the woods.
of Never speak ill of the dead.
of Never tell tales out of school.
of nine times out of ten
of nip sth off (of) sth
of no end of sth
of no shortage of sth
of none of so's beeswax
of none of so's business
of None of your lip!
of nose out (of sth)
of nose sth out of sth
of not a glimmer (of an idea)
of not able to make anything out of so/sth
of not able to make head or tail of sth
of not amount to a hill of beans
of not breathe a word of it
of not give anyone the time of day
of not have a stitch of clothes (on)
of not know enough to come in out of the rain
of not know what to make of so/sth
of not made of money
of not one's cup of tea
of not put (a lot) of stock in sth
of not worth a hill of beans
of Nothing comes of nothing.
of nothing of the kind
of nothing short of sth
of nothing to speak of
of notify so of sth
of number of things or people
of oceans of so/sth
of odor of sanctity
of of a single mind (about so/sth)
of of age
of Of all things!
of of benefit (to so)
of of course
of of interest (to so)
of of late
of of mature years
of of no avail
of of one mind (about so/sth)
of of one's own accord
of of service (to so)
of of the first water
of of the old school
of of the persuasion that...
of of two minds (about so/sth)
of Oh, ye of little faith.
of on behalf of so
of on the bottom rung (of the ladder)
of on the brink (of doing sth)
of on the cusp (of sth)
of on the edge of one's seat
of on the eve of sth
of on the face of it
of on the good side of so
of on the heels of sth
of on the horns of a dilemma
of on the point of doing sth
of on the spur of the moment
of on the strength of sth
of on the tip of one's tongue
of on the track of so/sth

of on the trail of so/sth
of on the verge of doing sth
of on the wrong side of so
of on top of sth
of on top of the world
of one brick shy of a load
of one jump ahead (of so/sth)
of one move ahead (of so/sth)
of one of these days
of one's fill of so/sth
of one's frame of mind
of one's next of kin
of one's way of life
of one sandwich short of a picnic
of open a can of worms
of opt in favor of so/sth
of opt out (of sth)
of order of the day
of order so off ((of) sth)
of order so out of some place
of other side of the tracks
of ounce of common sense is worth a pound of theory.
of ounce of discretion is worth a pound of wit.
of ounce of prevention is worth a pound of cure.
of out of action
of out of (all) proportion
of out of breath
of out of character
of out of circulation
of out of commission
of out of condition
of out of consideration (for so/sth)
of out of context
of out of control
of out of courtesy (to so)
of out of debt
of out of earshot
of out of fashion
of out of favor (with so)
of out of focus
of out of gas
of out of hand
of out of harm's way
of out of hock
of out of it
of out of keeping (with sth)
of out of kilter
of out of left field
of out of line (with sth)
of out of luck
of out of necessity
of out of nowhere
of out of one's depth
of out of one's element
of out of one's head
of out of one's mind
of out of one's skull
of out of one's way
of out of order
of out of patience
of out of place
of out of practice
of out of print
of out of proportion
of out of reach
of out of season
of out of service
of out of shape
of out of sight
of Out of sight, out of mind.

of out of so's hands
of out of so's way
of out (of sth)
of out of sorts
of out of spite
of out of step (with so/sth)
of out of stock
of out of style
of out of sync
of out of the ballpark
of out of the closet
of out of the corner of one's eye
of out of the frying pan (and) into the fire
of out of the goodness of one's heart
of out of the hole
of Out of the mouths of babes (oft times come gems).
of out of the ordinary
of out of the picture
of out of the question
of out of the red
of out of the running
of out of the swim of things
of out of the way
of out (of) the window
of out of the woods
of out of the woodwork
of out of thin air
of out of this world
of out of time (with so/sth)
of out of touch (with so/sth)
of out of town
of out of tune (with so/sth)
of out of turn
of out of w(h)ack
of out of wind
of out of work
of out-of-bounds
of out-of-pocket expenses
of outside of sth
of owe so a debt of gratitude
of owe so a pound of flesh
of pack of lies
of parade so/sth in front of so/sth
of pare sth off (of) sth
of partake of sth
of particulars of sth
of parting of the ways
of pass the time (of day)
of pass the time of day (with so)
of path of least resistance
of patter of tiny feet
of pay so a pound of flesh
of peace of mind
of peek out of sth (at so/sth)
of peel off ((of) sth)
of peel sth off ((of) sth)
of peep out (of sth) (at so/sth)
of permit so out (of sth)
of person of color
of persuade so of sth
of pester so out of sth
of pester the life out of so
of phase so/sth out of sth
of pick of sth
of pick so/sth off (of) so/sth
of pick so/sth out of sth
of pick up the pieces (of sth)
of picture of (good) health
of piece of cake
of piece (of the action)
of pile out (of sth)

of pillar of strength
of pillar of support
of pilot sth out of sth
of pinch sth off (of) sth
of pit of one's stomach
of pitch so/sth out (of) sth
of place of business
of place of concealment
of place so/sth in the trust of so
of place so/sth into the care of so
of plenty of sth
of pluck sth off (of) so/sth
of pluck sth out of sth
of pocket of resistance
of point of no return
of point of view
of poke out (of sth)
of poke sth out of sth
of pop out (of sth)
of pop sth out of sth
of portent of things to come
of possessed of sth
of Possession is nine-tenths of the law.
of pot of gold
of pound of flesh
of pour out (of sth)
of pour sth off (of) sth
of press sth out of sth
of pretty state of affairs
of price so/sth out of the market
of Procrastination is the thief of time.
of produce an attack (of an illness)
of prune sth of sth
of prune sth off (of) sth
of pry sth off (of) sth
of pry sth out of so
of pry sth out (of sth)
of pull ahead (of so/sth)
of pull so/sth ahead (of so/sth)
of pull out (of sth)
of pull sth out of a hat
of pull sth out of so
of pull sth out of so's hands
of pull sth out of the fire
of pull sth out of thin air
of pull sth up (out of sth)
of pull (up) alongside ((of) so/sth)
of pump sth out of so/sth
of punch sth out of sth
of Punctuality is the soul of business.
of purge so/sth of so/sth
of push so/sth ahead of so
of push so/sth off (of) so/sth
of push so/sth on (ahead) (of so/sth)
of push so/sth out of sth
of put one foot in front of the other
of put one out of (one's) misery
of put one's nose out of joint
of put some creature out of its misery
of put so in mind of so/sth
of put so off (of) sth
of put so or an animal out of sth
of put so/sth ahead (of so/sth)
of put so/sth into the middle of nowhere
of put so/sth out of one's mind
of put so/sth out of the way
of put so out of the way
of put so's nose out of joint
of put sth in the back of so's mind
of put sth in the way of so/sth
of put the fear of God in(to) so
of question of sth
of quiz out (of sth)

of quote so/sth out of context
of rage out of control
of raise so/sth to the surface (of sth)
of rake sth off (of) sth
of rake sth out of sth
of reach sth in the (very) nick of time
of reach speeds of some amount
of read of so/sth (somewhere)
of read so out of sth
of read (so) sth out of sth
of reality of the situation
of reassure so of sth
of recoil at the sight (of so/sth)
of recoil at the thought (of so/sth)
of reek of sth
of regardless of sth
of reject so/sth out of hand
of relieve one of one's duties
of relieve so of sth
of remain ahead (of so/sth)
of remain ahead of sth
of remain ahead of the game
of remain clear of sth
of remain in the back of so's mind
of remand so (in)to the custody of so
of remind so of so/sth
of reminiscent of so/sth
of request sth of so
of require a leap of faith
of require sth of so
of rid of so/sth
of rid oneself or sth of so/sth
of ride out (of some place)
of (right) off the top of one's head
of right-of-way
of rinse sth out of sth
of riot of color
of rip sth off (of) so/sth
of rip sth out of so/sth
of ripple of excitement
of ripple of protest
of risk of rain
of risk of showers
of risk of thunder(storms)
of rob so of sth
of roll sth off (of) so/sth
of root of the matter
of root of the problem
of root so/sth out of sth
of rouse so out of sth
of roust so out of sth
of rout so/sth out of some place
of rub off ((of) sth)
of rub sth off (of) sth
of ruin of so/sth
of rule in favor of so/sth
of rule of thumb
of run a risk (of sth)
of run (a)foul of so/sth
of run out of gas
of run out of patience
of run out of some place
of run out (of sth)
of run out of steam
of run out of time
of run short (of sth)
of run so/sth off (of) sth
of run so/sth out of sth
of run sth out of sth
of run the risk (of sth)
of run-of-the-mill
of runt of the litter
of rush out (of sth)

of rush so/sth out of sth
of salt of the earth
of sands of time
of save so in the (very) nick of time
of savor of sth
of saw sth off (of) sth
of scare one out of one's mind
of scare one out of one's wits
of scare so or an animal out of sth
of scare so out of sth
of scare sth out of so
of scare the living daylights out of so
of scare the pants off (of) so
of scare the wits out of so
of school of hard knocks
of school of thought
of scoop sth out of sth
of scour sth off (of) sth
of scour sth out of sth
of scrape sth off (of) so/sth
of scrape sth out of sth
of scrape the bottom of the barrel
of screen so/sth out of sth
of screw so out of sth
of scrub sth off (of) sth
of scrub sth out of sth
of seamy side of life
of see ahead (of so/sth)
of see no further than the end of one's nose
of see so out (of sth)
of see sth of so/sth
of see the color of so's money
of see the last of so/sth
of see the light (at the end of the tunnel)
of see the light (of day)
of seem out of place
of seep out (of sth)
of Self-preservation is the first law of nature.
of sell so a bill of goods
of send so/sth on (ahead) (of so/sth)
of send so out of sth
of sense of humor
of separate sth out of sth
of set of pipes
of set of wheels
of settle (sth) (out of court)
of shades of so/sth
of shadow of oneself
of shame of it (all)!
of shock of one's life
of short and the long of it
of short end of the stick
of short of sth
of shot full of holes
of show a lot of promise
of show of hands
of show signs of sth
of show so out (of sth)
of show so the tricks of the trade
of show up ahead of time
of sick (and tired) of so/sth
of sick to death (of so/sth)
of sift sth out of sth
of sign of the times
of sign of things to come
of sign so out of some place
of sign sth out of some place
of sing of so/sth
of sing the praises of so/sth
of sit at the feet of so

of (sitting) on top of the world
of six of one and half a dozen of the other
of skim sth off (of) sth
of slice of the action
of slice of the cake
of slide out of sth
of slide sth out of sth
of slink out (of some place)
of slip of the tongue
of slip off ((of) so/sth)
of slip out (of sth)
of slop out (of sth)
of smack of sth
of small hours (of the night)
of smash out of sth
of smell of sth
of smoke so/sth or an animal out of sth
of smuggle so/sth out of some place
of snack off (of) sth
of snap out of sth
of snap sth out of sth
of snatch so from the jaws of death
of snatch so out of the jaws of death
of snatch sth out of sth
of snatch victory from the jaws of defeat
of sneak out (of some place)
of snip sth off (of) sth
of soak sth off (of) sth
of soak sth out of sth
of (solid) grasp of sth
of so of note
of so's train of thought
of so's word of honor
of Something is rotten in (the state of) Denmark.
of sth of sorts
of something of the sort
of (somewhere) in the neighborhood of sth
of son of a bachelor
of son of a bitch
of son of a gun
of son of a sea biscuit
of Sort of.
of sort of sth
of (sound) grasp of sth
of speak highly of so/sth
of speak ill of so
of speak of so/sth
of Speak of the devil (and in he walks).
of speak out of turn
of spear sth out (of sth)
of speeds of some amount
of spend money like it's going out of style
of spill out (of sth)
of spin sth out of sth
of spit and image of so
of spitting image of so
of splinter off ((of) sth)
of split sth off (of) sth
of sponge sth off of so/sth
of sport of kings
of spring out of sth
of spurt out (of so/sth)
of squeeze sth out of sth
of squint out of sth
of squirm out (of sth)
of squirt out (of so/sth)
of squirt sth out of sth
of stagger out (of some place)

of stalk out of some place
of stamp sth out of so/sth
of stampede out of some place
of stand a chance (of doing sth)
of stand clear of sth
of stand in awe (of so/sth)
of stand (in) back of so/sth
of stand outside ((of) sth)
of stand the test of time
of startle so out of sth
of starve so or an animal out of some place
of state of mind
of state of the art
of stay abreast of so/sth
of stay ahead of sth
of stay ahead of the game
of stay clear of so/sth
of stay in the back of so's mind
of stay on the good side of so
of stay on top of so/sth
of stay one step ahead of so/sth
of Stay out of my way.
of stay out of sight
of stay out (of sth)
of Stay out of this!
of steal out of some place
of steam out (of some place)
of steam sth off (of) sth
of steam sth out of sth
of steer clear (of so/sth)
of step off (of) sth
of step out of line
of step out (of sth)
of stick out (of so/sth)
of stop off (some place) (for a period of time)
of stop short of a place
of stop short of doing sth
of storm out (of some place)
of strain sth off of sth
of streak of bad luck
of streak of good luck
of streak of luck
of stride out of some place
of strike sth off (of) so/sth
of string of bad luck
of string of good luck
of strip so/sth of sth
of strip sth off (of) so/sth
of stroke of genius
of stroke of luck
of strut out of some place
of sue the pants off (of) so
of suffer an attack (of an illness)
of suggestive of sth
of surge out (of sth)
of survival of the fittest
of suspect so of sth
of swab sth out of sth
of swarm out of sth
of swear on a stack of Bibles
of sweat sth out of so
of sweep out of some place
of sweep so/sth out of sth
of sweep sth off (of) sth
of swindle so out of sth
of swish sth off (of) so/sth
of take a dim view of so/sth
of take a leaf out of so's book
of take a load off (of) so's mind
of take a lot of nerve
of take a lot off (of) so's mind
of take a lot out of so
of take a pound of flesh

of take a whiff of sth
of take account of so/sth
of take advantage of so
of take (a)hold of so/sth
of take care of number one
of take care of numero uno
of take care of so
of take care of sth
of Take care (of yourself).
of take charge (of so/sth)
of take control of so/sth
of take heed (of so/sth)
of take hold of so/sth
of take leave of one's senses
of take leave of so/sth
of take note of so/sth
of take notice of so/sth
of take one's death (of cold)
of take one's eyes off (of) so/sth
of take one's hands off (of) so/sth
of take (one's) leave (of so)
of take one's pick of so/sth
of take possession (of sth)
of take so/sth out of sth
of take sth out of context
of take sth out of so
of take sth out of so's hands
of take sth with a pinch of salt
of take stock (of sth)
of take the chill off ((of) a place)
of take the edge off ((of) sth)
of take the heat off (of) so/sth
of take the liberty of doing sth
of take the lid off (of) sth
of take the pulse of sth
of take the starch out of so
of take the stuffing out of so
of take the wind out of so's sails
of take the words out of so's mouth
of take years off (of) so/sth
of tale of woe
of talk of a place
of talk of so/sth
of Talk of the devil (and he is sure to appear).
of talk one's way out of sth
of talk so out of doing sth
of talk so out of sth
of tall drink of water
of taste of one's own medicine
of taste of sth
of teach so the hang of sth
of teach so the tricks of the trade
of tear out (of some place)
of tear sth off (of) so/sth
of tear sth out of sth
of tease sth out of sth
of tell of so/sth
of tell tales out of school
of tender age of...
of terrify so or an animal out of sth
of test out (of sth)
of That makes two of us.
of That's about the size of it.
of (That's) enough (of this) foolishness!
of That takes care of that.
of (The) best of luck (to so).
of the luck of the Irish
of The proof of the pudding is in the eating.
of The wages of sin is death.

of There are plenty of (other) fish in the sea.
of There but for the grace of God (go I).
of There is a tide in the affairs of men.
of thing of beauty is a joy forever.
of think a great deal of so/sth
of think a lot of so/sth
of think ahead of one's time
of think better of so/sth
of think better of sth
of think highly of so/sth
of think little of so/sth
of think much of so/sth
of think nothing of doing sth
of Think nothing of it.
of think nothing of so/sth
of think of so/sth
of think sth of so/sth
of think the world of so/sth
of (this) vale of tears
of thrash sth out of so
of three bricks shy of a load
of throng out (of sth)
of throw oneself at the mercy of some authority
of throw oneself on the mercy of some authority
of throw so or an animal off (of) sth
of throw so/sth off (of) sth
of throw so/sth out of sth
of throw so out of sth
of till all hours (of the day and night)
of Time is of the essence.
of tip of the iceberg
of tire of so/sth
of to say nothing of so/sth
of to so's way of thinking
of to the best of one's ability
of to the best of one's knowledge
of to the ends of the earth
of to the tune of some amount of money
of tons of sth
of too much of a good thing
of top of the heap
of topple off (of) sth
of toss so/sth off (of) sth
of toss so/sth out of sth
of touch of sth
of tow so/sth out (of some place)
of tower of strength
of travesty of justice
of treat a case of sth
of trick so out of sth
of trickle out (of sth)
of tricks of the trade
of trim sth off (of) so/sth
of tub of lard
of tumble out of sth
of turn of fate
of turn of the century
of turn so or an animal out of sth
of tweak sth off (of) so/sth
of twist of fate
of twist sth off (of) sth
of twist sth out of sth
of two bricks shy of a load
of two jumps ahead of so
of two of a kind
of two shakes of a lamb's tail
of under a cloud (of suspicion)
of under the aegis of so
of under the auspices of so

of under the influence (of alcohol)
of until all hours (of the day and night)
of upshot of sth
of usher so/sth out of some place
of Variety is the spice of life.
of venture out ((of) sth)
of (very) picture of sth
of villain of the piece
of vindicate so of sth
of vote of confidence
of vote of thanks
of vote so out of sth
of walk ahead of so/sth
of walk out (of sth)
of wangle out of sth
of Wanna make sumpin' of it?
of Want a piece of me?
of want off ((of) sth)
of want out (of sth)
of want so/sth out of sth
of Want to make something of it?
of warm the cockles of so's heart
of warn so of sth
of wash off ((of) so/sth)
of wash one's hands of so/sth
of wash so out of sth
of wash sth of sth
of wash sth off (of) so/sth
of wash sth out of sth
of waste of space
of wealth of sth
of wear off ((of) sth)
of wear sth off (of) sth
of weary of so/sth
of weasel out (of sth)
of weave in and out (of sth)
of wee hours (of the night)
of well out (of sth)
of well out(side) of sth
of well up (out of sth)
of whale the tar out of so
of What do you think of that?
of What do you think of this weather?
of What of it?
of What's the good of sth?
of wheel so/sth out of sth
of When poverty comes in at the door, love flies out of the window.
of When the wolf comes in at the door, love creeps out of the window.
of whiff of sth
of whisk sth off (of) so/sth
of whittle sth out of sth
of whole bag of tricks
of whole ball of wax
of (whole) mess of so/sth
of whys and wherefores of sth
of wide of the mark
of wiggle out of sth
of will be the death of so/sth (yet)
of will come of sth
of will not hear of sth
of wimp out (of sth)
of win the heart of so
of window of opportunity
of wipe so/sth off the face of the earth
of within a hair('s breadth) of sth
of within a stone's throw (of sth)
of within an ace of (doing) sth
of within an inch of one's life
of within earshot (of sth)
of without a shadow of a doubt
of woman of ill repute

of woods are full of so/sth
of work of art
of work sth out of sth
of worm (one's way) out (of sth)
of worm sth out of so
of worry an animal out of sth
of worry sth out of so
of worst of sth
of worth of a thing is what it will bring.
of worthy of the name
of wouldn't dream of doing sth
of wrench sth off (of) so/sth
of wrench sth out of sth
of wrest sth off (of) sth
of wriggle out (of sth)
of wring sth out of so
of wring sth out of sth
of write of so/sth
of wrong side of the tracks
of yank so/sth off (of) sth
of yank so/sth out of sth
of You been keeping out of trouble?
of You cannot make a silk purse out of a sow's ear.
of You don't know the half of it.
of You have to eat a peck of dirt before you die.
of You scared the crap out of me.
of You scared the devil out of me.
of You scared the hell out of me.
of (You) took the words right out of my mouth.
of (You) want a piece of me?
of You want to make something of it?
of You'll get the hang of it.
of You're out of your mind!
of You've got to be out of your mind!
off angle off (to(ward) sth)
off auction sth off
off back off (from so/sth)
off back so/sth off (from sth)
off barter sth off
off bear off (of sth)
off beat so/sth off
off beat the pants off (of) so
off beat the socks off (of) so
off beg off (on sth)
off beg sth off
off better off (doing sth)
off better off (somewhere)
off big send-off
off bit off
off bitch so off
off bite off more than one can chew
off bite so's head off
off bite sth off
off blast off (for some place)
off blast sth off sth else
off block sth off
off blow off
off blow so off
off blow so/sth off
off blow so's doors off
off blow the lid off (sth)
off boo so off the stage
off bore the pants off of so
off bounce off ((of) sth)
off bounce sth off (of) so/sth
off branch off (from sth)
off brass so off
off break off (from sth)
off break off (with so)
off break sth off (of) sth

off break sth off
off breeze off
off bring sth off
off brown so off
off browned (off)
off brush so off
off brush sth off so/sth
off brush-off
off buck so off
off bug off
off bum sth off so
off bump so off
off bundle off
off bundle so off (to some place)
off bundle sth off (to so or some place)
off burn off
off burn sth off
off bustle off
off bustle so off
off buy so off
off buzz off
off call so or an animal off (so/sth)
off call sth off
off call the dogs off
off carry so/sth off
off carry sth off
off cart so/sth off
off cast off (from sth)
off cast sth off
off catch one off (one's) guard
off catch so off balance
off catch so off guard
off change off
off channel sth off
off charge off
off charge sth off as sth
off charm the pants off so
off check so/sth off
off cheese off
off cheesed off
off chew sth off sth
off chip off the old block
off choke so off
off choke sth off
off chop so off
off chop sth off (of) sth
off claw sth off so/sth
off clean sth off
off clean sth off sth
off clear off ((of) some place)
off clear sth off sth
off close sth off
off come off
off conk off
off cool off
off cordon sth off
off cough one's head off
off count off
off count so/sth off
off cross so/sth off (of) sth
off curtain sth off
off cut off
off cut one's nose off to spite one's face
off cut so off at the pass
off cut so off without a penny
off cut so/sth off (from sth)
off cut so/sth off (short)
off cut so's water off
off cut sth off
off dab sth off
off damp off
off dash a letter off
off dash a note off

off dash off
off dash sth off
off day off
off die off
off dine off sth
off dink so off
off dive off ((of) sth)
off divide sth (off) (from sth or animals)
off do a takeoff on so/sth
off Don't bite off more than you can chew.
off Don't put off for tomorrow what you can do today.
off dork off
off doze off (to sleep)
off drag so/sth off of so/sth
off drag so/sth off (to so/sth)
off drain sth off sth
off draw sth off (from sth)
off drift off
off drive off
off drive so/sth off
off drop off
off drop so/sth off
off dry so/sth off
off dust so off
off dust so/sth off
off ease off
off easy as falling off a log
off easy as rolling off a log
off eat sth off
off face off
off fake off
off fall off
off far-off look
off feed off (of) sth
off fence so/sth off (from sth)
off fend so/sth off
off fight so/sth off
off file sth off ((of) sth)
off file sth off
off find so a bit off
off find so a little off
off finish so or an animal off
off finish so/sth off
off finish (sth) off
off finish (sth) off with sth
off fire sth off (to so)
off first off
off flake off ((of) sth)
off flake sth off
off flash off
off flick sth off
off fling sth off of oneself
off fling sth off (of) sth
off flip so off
off fly off
off fob so/sth off (on(to) so)
off foist so/sth off (on so/sth)
off force so/sth off (of) sth
off force so/sth (off) on so
off freeze one's tail off
off frighten the pants off so
off front off (about sth)
off get a weight off one's mind
off get (down) off one's high horse
off get it off
off get off
off get one's rocks off (on sth)
off get some weight off one's feet
off get so off
off get so/sth off so/sth
off get sth off

off get up (off (of) sth)
off give so the shirt off one's back
off give sth off
off glance off (so/sth)
off gloves are off.
off go off
off goof off
off hack so (off)
off hack sth off
off hacked (off)
off half a bubble off plumb
off hand sth off (to so)
off Hands off!
off hang off
off harden sth off
off hats off to so/sth
off haul off and do sth
off head so off at the pass
off head so/sth off
off help so off (of) sth
off help so off with sth
off hiss so off ((of) the stage)
off hit it off (with so)
off hit sth off
off hold off (from) doing sth
off hold off (on so/sth)
off hold so/sth off
off hoot so off the stage
off hop off ((of) sth)
off hot off the press
off hotfoot it (off to) somewhere
off hurry off
off (I) have to push off.
off (I) have to shove off.
off I must be off.
off I'll have to beg off.
off I'm off.
off in the offing
off (It's) time to shove off.
off (I've) got to be shoving off.
off (I've) got to shove off.
off (I've) got to take off.
off jerk sth off
off jump off ((of) sth)
off jump off the deep end
off jumping-off place
off jumping-off point
off just fell off the turnip truck
off just off the boat
off keep off (of) so's back
off keep off (of) so's case
off keep off ((of) sth)
off keep one's hands off (sth)
off keep so/sth off
off kick off
off kick sth off
off kill so or an animal off
off kiss off
off kiss so off
off kiss so/sth off
off Knock it off!
off knock off (doing sth)
off knock off (work)
off knock one off one's feet
off knock so off
off knock so's block off
off knock so's socks off
off knock sth off
off laugh one's head off
off laugh so off the stage
off laugh sth off
off lay off ((from) sth)
off lay off ((of) so/sth)

off lay off (so/sth)
off lay so off (from sth)
off lead off
off lead so/sth off
off leave off sth
off let off (some) steam
off let so (get) off (sth)
off let so off
off let sth off
off level off
off level sth off
off lick sth off (of) sth
off lift off
off lift sth off (of) so/sth
off like water off a duck's back
off list so/sth off
off little off
off live high off the hog
off live off campus
off live off (of) so/sth
off live off the fat of the land
off live off the land
off load off one's feet
off load off one's mind
off log off
off log so off
off lop sth off (of) sth
off lumber off
off lunch off sth
off make off with so/sth
off make sth off (of) so/sth
off mark so/sth off
off marry so off (to so)
off measure sth off
off mop sth off
off mouth off
off move off campus
off move off (from so/sth)
off move off (to the side) with so
off move so/sth off ((from) so/sth)
off nip sth off (of) sth
off no skin off so's nose
off no skin off so's teeth
off nod off
off number off (by sth)
off off again, on again
off off and on
off off and running
off off artist
off off base
off off campus
off off center
off off chance
off off course
off off duty
off off like a shot
off off on a sidetrack
off off on so/sth
off off (on sth)
off off on the right foot (with so/sth)
off off on the wrong foot
off off one's game
off off one's nut
off off one's rocker
off off one's trolley
off off season
off off so/sth goes
off off the air
off off the beaten path
off off the beaten track
off off the hook
off off the mark
off off the record

off off the shelf
off off the subject
off off the track
off off the wagon
off off to a bad start
off off (to a flying start)
off off to a good start (with so/sth)
off off to a running start
off off to one side
off off to the races
off off (to the side) with so
off off topic
off Off with you!
off off (work)
off off-key
off off-kilter
off off-limits
off off-line
off off-the-cuff
off off-the-wall
off on again, off again
off on and off
off on the off chance
off order so off ((of) sth)
off order so off the field
off pace sth off
off pack so off (to so/sth)
off pack sth off (to so/sth)
off pair off
off palm so/sth off (on so) (as so/sth)
off pare sth off (of) sth
off pass so/sth off (on so) (as so/sth)
off pass sth off
off pawn so/sth off (on so) (as so/sth)
off pay off
off pay so off
off pay sth off
off peel off (from sth)
off peel off ((of) sth)
off peel sth off ((of) sth)
off pension so off
off pick so/sth off
off pile off (sth)
off pinch sth off
off piss so off
off pissed (off)
off plane sth off
off play so off against so else
off play sth off
off pluck sth off (of) so/sth
off polish sth off
off pop off
off pop so off
off pour sth off (of) sth
off prune sth off (of) sth
off pry sth off (of) sth
off pull off (sth)
off pull sth off
off push off
off push (oneself) off (on sth)
off push so/sth off (of) so/sth
off push sth off on(to) so
off put a dog off the scent
off put off by so/sth
off put one off one's game
off put one off one's stride
off put so off
off put sth off
off quick off the mark
off raffle sth off
off rake sth off
off rattle sth off

off read sth off
off reel sth off
off ricochet off sth
off ride off
off right off the bat
off (right) off the top of one's head
off ring off the hook
off rinse so/sth off
off rip off
off rip so off
off rip sth off
off (rip-)off artist
off roll off (so/sth)
off roll sth off (of) so/sth
off rope sth off
off rot off
off round off to sth
off round sth off
off rub off ((of) sth)
off rub off (on so)
off rub off on(to) so/sth
off rub sth off (of) sth
off run around like a chicken with its head cut off
off run off
off run one's feet off
off run so/sth off (of) sth
off run sth off
off rush off (from some place)
off rush sth off (to so/sth)
off saw sth off (of) sth
off scare so or an animal off
off scare the pants off (of) so
off scour sth off (of) sth
off scrape sth off (of) so/sth
off screen so/sth (off) (from so/sth)
off screw off
off scrub so/sth off
off scrub sth off (of) sth
off seal sth off from so/sth
off see so off
off sell sth off
off send off for sth
off send so off
off send sth off (to so/sth)
off separate off (from sth)
off separate sth off from sth
off set off (for sth)
off set off on sth
off set so off
off set sth off
off shag (off)
off shake a disease or illness off
off shake so/sth off
off shake sth off
off shoot one's mouth off
off shove off
off show off
off show so/sth off
off shrug sth off (as sth)
off shuck sth off
off shuffle off this mortal coil
off sign off
off siphon sth off (from sth)
off skim sth off (of) sth
off skip off (with sth)
off slack off
off sleep sth off
off slice sth off
off slink off
off slip off
off slip sth off
off slough sth off

off slow off the mark
off sluff (off)
off snack off (of) sth
off snap so's head off
off snap sth off
off snip sth off
off so clean you could eat off the floor
off soak sth off (of) sth
off sound off
off spark sth off
off speak off-the-cuff
off spiel off
off spin off
off spin sth off
off spirit so/sth off (to some place)
off splinter off ((of) sth)
off split off (from sth)
off split sth off (of) sth
off sponge sth off of so/sth
off spout off (about so/sth)
off square off (for sth)
off square sth off
off stake sth off
off stall so/sth off
off stand off from so/sth
off stand off some place
off stand so/sth off
off start off
off start (off) with a bang
off start (off) with a clean slate
off start (off) with so/sth
off start so off (on sth)
off stave so/sth off
off stave sth off
off stay off (sth)
off steal sth off so
off steam sth off (of) sth
off step off
off step sth off
off stop off (some place) (for a period of time)
off straight off
off strain sth off of sth
off strike sth off (of) so/sth
off strip sth off (of) so/sth
off sue the pants off (of) so
off swear off (sth)
off sweat sth off
off sweep off
off sweep one off one's feet
off sweep sth off (of) sth
off swish sth off (of) sth
off switch off
off switch so/sth off
off tail off
off take a load off (of) so's mind
off take a load off one's feet
off Take a long walk off a short pier.
off take a lot off (of) so's mind
off take a weight off one's mind
off take off
off take one's eyes off (of) so/sth
off take one's gloves off
off take one's hands off (of) so/sth
off take one's hat off to so
off take oneself off some place
off take (some) time off
off take ((some) time) off from work
off take so off
off take so/sth off
off take so's head off
off take sth off
off take the chill off ((of) a place)
off take the day off

off take the edge off ((of) sth)
off take the heat off (of) so/sth
off take the lid off (of) sth
off take up where one left off
off take years off (of) so/sth
off take-off artist
off talk one's head off
off talk so's ear off
off talk so's head off
off taper off (doing sth)
off tear off (from so/sth)
off tear sth off (of) so/sth
off tee off
off tee so off
off teed off
off tell so off
off tell so where to get off
off throw one off one's game
off throw so off
off throw so or an animal off (of) sth
off throw so/sth off (of) sth
off throw sth off
off tick so off
off ticked (off)
off tie sth off
off time off
off tip so off (about so/sth)
off toddle off
off top sth off
off topple off (of) sth
off toss so/sth off (of) sth
off toss sth off
off touch so/sth off
off towel so/sth off
off trade sth off
off trail off
off travel off the beaten path
off trigger so off
off trigger sth off
off trim sth off (of) so/sth
off turn off
off turn so off
off turn so's water off
off turn sth off
off turned off
off tweak sth off (of) so/sth
off twist sth off (of) sth
off veer off (from so/sth)
off walk off
off walk on stage and off again
off walk so's feet off
off wall so/sth off
off wall sth off (from so/sth)
off waltz off
off wander off (from so/sth)
off want off ((of) sth)
off ward so/sth off
off warn so off
off wash off ((of) so/sth)
off wash so/sth off
off wash sth off (of) so/sth
off wave so/sth off
off way off (base)
off wear off
off wear sth off (of) sth
off weight off one's mind
off whack sth off
off What's coming off?
off wheel so/sth off
off Where do (you think) you get off?
off whip sth off
off whip sth written off to so
off whisk so or an animal off

off whisk so/sth off (to sth)
off whisk sth off (of) so/sth
off wind sth off
off Wipe it off!
off wipe so/sth off
off wipe so/sth (off) (with sth)
off wipe sth off
off wipe sth (off) (on sth)
off wish so/sth (off) on so
off work one's ass off
off work one's tail off
off work some fat off
off work some weight off
off work sth off
off wrench sth off (of) so/sth
off wrest sth off (of) sth
off write off (to so) (for sth)
off write so/sth off
off write sth off
off yack one's head off
off yank so/sth off (of) sth
off yank sth off
off yell one's head off
off zone sth off
off zoom off
offend offend against so/sth
offend offend so with sth
offense best defense is a good offense.
offense mean no offense
offense No offense meant.
offense No offense taken.
offense take offense (at so/sth)
offer make an offer one cannot refuse
offer make one an offer one cannot refuse
offer make so an offer
offer offer a helping hand
offer offer one cannot refuse
offer offer sth for sth
offer offer sth to so (as sth)
offer offer sth up (to so/sth)
office Can I see you in my office?
office Could I see you in my office?
office do a land-office business
office drive so out of office
office force so out of office
office land-office business
office take office
officiate officiate (as sth) (at sth)
offing in the offing
oft Out of the mouths of babes (oft times come gems).
often best-laid plans of mice and men oft(en) go astray.
often Half the truth is often a whole lie.
often Little and often fills the purse.
often more often than not
often Out of the mouths of babes (oft times come gems).
ogle ogle (at) so/sth
oh Oh, boy.
oh Oh, sure (so/sth will)!
oh Oh, ye of little faith.
oh Oh, yeah?
oil burn the midnight oil
oil oil so's palm
oil pour oil on troubled water(s)
oil squeaking wheel gets the oil.
oink oink out
ointment fly in the ointment
okay (Are you) doing okay?

okay (Are you) feeling okay?
okay Everything will be okay.
okay (Have you) been okay?
okay (I'm) doing okay.
okay (I'm) feeling okay.
okay (Is) everything okay?
okay (I've) been okay.
okay You been okay?
okay You doing okay?
ol' same o(l)' same o(l)'
old any old thing
old Better be an old man's darling than a young man's slave.
old chip off the old block
old comfortable as an old shoe
old common as an old shoe
old dirty old man
old from the old school
old full of Old Nick
old go into the same old song and dance about sth
old good old boy
old good old days
old have a rare old time
old little old so/sth
old live to the (ripe old) age of sth
old of the old school
old old as Methuselah
old old as the hills
old old battle-axe
old old college try
old old enough to be so's father
old old enough to be so's mother
old Old habits die hard.
old old hand at doing sth
old old hat
old (old) heave-ho
old old one-two
old old poacher makes the best gamekeeper.
old old warhorse
old old wives' tale
old one's old stamping ground
old perform an old warhorse
old play an old warhorse
old ring out the old
old ripe old age
old same o(l)' same o(l)'
old same old story
old So's your old man!
old There's many a good tune played on an old fiddle.
old There's no fool like an old fool.
old tough as an old boot
old tough as old (shoe) leather
old You are never too old to learn.
old You cannot put new wine in old bottles.
old You cannot teach an old dog new tricks.
old Young men may die, but old men must die.
olive hold out the olive branch
omega alpha and omega
omelet You cannot make an omelet without breaking eggs.
omit omit so/sth from sth
on able to do sth standing on one's head
on about-face (on so/sth)
on abut on sth
on accidentally-on-purpose
on accompany so on a journey
on accompany so on a musical instrument

on act tough on so
on advise so on so/sth
on and so on
on army marches on its stomach.
on arrive on a wing and a prayer
on arrive on the scene
on avenge oneself (on so/sth) (for sth)
on awkward as a cow on a crutch
on awkward as a cow on roller skates
on back down (on sth)
on back on one's feet
on back on track
on backfire on so
on bag on so
on bang on so/sth
on bank on sth
on bargain on sth
on barge in (on so/sth)
on base one's opinion on sth
on bear down (on so/sth)
on beat down (on so/sth)
on beat on so/sth
on beat up on so
on becoming on so
on beg off (on sth)
on bent on doing sth
on bestow sth on so
on bet on so/sth
on bet sth on so/sth
on bid (sth) on sth
on big man on campus
on bite on so
on bite on sth
on blame sth on so
on blaze down (on so/sth)
on blight on the land
on blot on the landscape
on blow a bundle (on so)
on Blow on it!
on blow on sth
on blow the whistle (on so)
on bone up (on sth)
on book (on) out
on book so on sth
on born on the wrong side of the blanket
on boxed on the table
on bread always falls on the buttered side.
on break in (on so)
on break in (on sth)
on break one's arm patting oneself on the back
on break sth on sth
on bring down the curtain (on sth)
on bring so in (on sth)
on bring so on
on bring so out (on sth)
on bring so up on sth
on bring so up to speed on so/sth
on bring so up-to-date (on so/sth)
on bring sth down on one('s head)
on bring sth on
on browse on sth
on brush up (on sth)
on build one's hopes on so/sth
on build sth on
on burst in (on so/sth)
on busy as popcorn on a skillet
on butt in (on so/sth)
on buy sth on credit
on buy sth on time
on calculate on sth

on call on so
on call on sth
on call so on the carpet
on call sth down (on so)
on capitalize on sth
on carry on
on carry sth on
on carry the weight of the world on one's shoulders
on carry through (on sth)
on cash in (on sth)
on cash on the barrelhead
on cash on the line
on cast a spell (on so)
on cast aspersions on so
on cast doubt(s) (on so/sth)
on catch (on) fire
on catch on (to sth)
on catch on (with so)
on catch so up (on so/sth)
on catch sth on sth
on catch up (on so/sth)
on catch up (on sth)
on cement sth on
on center on so/sth
on center on so/sth
on challenge so on sth
on charge down on so/sth
on charge sth on sth
on cheat on so
on check back (on so/sth)
on check in (on so/sth)
on check on so/sth
on check up (on so/sth)
on cheer so/sth on
on chew on so/sth
on chicken out on so
on chip in (on sth)
on chip in (with sth) (on sth) (for so)
on chip on one's shoulder
on chip sth in (on sth)
on chisel in (on so/sth)
on choke on sth
on clamp down (on so/sth)
on clap eyes on so/sth
on clean up (on sth)
on climb on
on close in (on so/sth)
on close on sth
on close the books on so/sth
on close the door on so/sth
on clue so in (on sth)
on cogitate on sth
on collect on sth
on come down (hard) (on so/sth)
on come (in) on a wing and a prayer
on come in on sth
on come on
on Come (on) in.
on come out on sth
on come out on top
on come (right) on top of sth
on come together (on sth)
on commit oneself on sth
on compare notes on so/sth
on compliment so on sth
on compromise on so/sth (with so)
on concentrate sth on so/sth
on concur on so/sth (with so)
on confer on so/sth (with so)
on conjecture on sth
on console so on sth
on cooperate with so (on sth)

on cop out (on so)
on cop out (on sth)
on corner the market on sth
on couldn't pour water out of a boot (if there was instructions on the heel)
on count on so/sth
on crack down (on so/sth)
on crap out (of sth) (on so)
on creep up on so/sth
on crowd in (on so/sth)
on crush on so
on cut back (on sth)
on cut down (on sth)
on cut in (on so)
on cut in (on sth)
on cut one's eyeteeth on sth
on cut oneself on sth
on cut so in (on sth)
on cut sth on sth
on dance on air
on dash cold water on sth
on dead cat on the line
on dead on
on death on sth
on debate on sth
on default on sth
on defer to so/sth (on sth)
on deliberate on so/sth
on die on so
on die on the vine
on die with one's boots on
on dig some dirt up (on so)
on dilate on sth
on dine on sth
on dish on so
on dis(s) (on) so
on divided on so/sth
on do a dump on so/sth
on do a flip-flop (on sth)
on do a job on so/sth
on do a number on so/sth
on do a snow job on so
on do a takeoff on so/sth
on do an about-face (on so/sth)
on Do not let the sun go down on your anger.
on Do not let the sun go down on your wrath.
on don't know whether to eat it or rub it on
on Don't stand on ceremony.
on Don't start (on me)!
on double back (on so/sth)
on double up (on so/sth)
on down on one's luck
on down on so
on downhill from here on
on drag on
on drag (on so)
on drag (on sth)
on drag one's feet (on or over sth)
on drag so in (on sth)
on draw a bead on so/sth
on draw on sth
on draw so out on so/sth
on Dream on.
on drive on
on drive so back on sth
on drive so on (to sth)
on drizzle down (on so/sth)
on drone on (about so/sth)
on drop a bundle (on so)

on drop a bundle (on sth)
on drop down (on so/sth)
on drop in (on so)
on drop so/sth on so/sth
on drop sth on so
on drug on the market
on drum on sth
on dump on so/sth
on dump sth on so
on dumped on
on early on
on ease back (on sth)
on ease off (on so/sth)
on ease (on) out (of sth)
on ease so (on) out (of sth)
on ease up (on so/sth)
on eat high on the hog
on eavesdrop on so
on eavesdrop on sth
on economize on sth
on edge on so
on egg so on
on elaborate on so/sth
on embark on sth
on enforce sth on so
on engorge (itself) on so/sth
on Every tub must stand on its own bottom.
on examine so on sth
on expatiate on so/sth
on expend sth on so/sth
on express oneself (to so) (on sth)
on face sth head-on
on fail so on sth
on fall down on so/sth
on fall down on the job
on fall (flat) on one's face
on fall in on so/sth
on fall on deaf ears
on fall on hard times
on fall on one's knees
on fall on one's sword
on fall on so's shoulders
on fashion sth on sth
on father sth on so
on fatten up (on sth)
on feel on top of the world
on fight on
on figure on doing sth
on figure on so/sth
on figure so/sth in (on sth)
on fill so in (on so/sth)
on fink on so
on fink out (on so/sth)
on firing on all cylinders
on fix on sth
on flash back (on so/sth)
on flash on
on flat on one's ass
on (flat) on one's back
on flick sth on
on fling sth on oneself
on float on air
on focus on so/sth
on focus sth on so/sth
on foist so/sth off (on so/sth)
on follow on (after so/sth)
on follow through (on sth)
on follow up (on so)
on follow up (on so/sth)
on follow up (on sth)
on Fool me once, shame on you; fool me twice, shame on me.

on for days on end
on for hours on end
on force so/sth (off) on so
on foreclose on sth
on freak out (on sth)
on freeze on doing sth
on fritter sth away (on so/sth)
on from here on (in)
on from this day on
on front on sth
on frown on so/sth
on gag on sth
on gain on so/sth
on gamble on so/sth
on gang up (on so)
on gaze on so/sth
on gaze out on sth
on generalize on so/sth
on get a bead on so/sth
on get a hurry on
on get a move on
on get along (on a shoestring)
on get along on sth
on get back (to so) (on sth)
on get by (on a shoestring)
on get by (on a small amount of money)
on get down (on all fours)
on get it on
on get on
on get one on one's feet
on get one's rocks off (on sth)
on get right on sth
on get sth down (on paper)
on get started on sth
on get the draw on so
on get the drop on so
on get the show on the road
on get together (with so) (on so/sth)
on get up on one's hind legs
on get up on the wrong side of bed
on give so a pat on the back
on give up (on so/sth)
on glare down on so/sth
on glut on the market
on gnaw on sth
on go back on one's promise
on go back on one's word
on go down on one's knees
on go easy on so/sth
on go easy on sth
on go fifty-fifty (on sth)
on go in with so (on sth)
on go off on a tangent
on go off on so
on Go on.
on go on a binge
on go on a diet
on go on a fishing expedition
on go on a fool's errand
on go on a power trip
on go on a rampage
on go on an errand
on go on and on
on go on (and on) (about so/sth)
on go on (at so)
on go on before (so)
on go on doing sth
on go on for an age
on go on sth
on go on the block
on go on to a better land
on go on to sth
on go on tour

on go on with sth
on Go on (with you)!
on go out on a limb
on go (out) on strike
on go to the wall (on sth)
on go to work (on so/sth)
on goad so on
on going on
on gone on
on goods on so
on goof on so
on goof up (on sth)
on gorge oneself on sth
on grade so down (on sth)
on grass is always greener on the other side (of the fence).
on grate on so
on grate on so('s nerves)
on grate on sth
on graze on sth
on grind on
on grip on oneself
on grip on sth
on groove on so/sth
on ground sth on sth
on grow on so
on grow soft on so
on hammer on so/sth
on hand sth on (to so/sth)
on handle on sth
on hang a few on
on hang on
on hang one on
on hang sth on so
on hang tough (on sth)
on hang up (on so/sth)
on Happy is the bride that the sun shines on.
on hard on so's heels
on hard on so
on harp on so/sth
on haul so on the carpet
on have a bad effect (on so/sth)
on have a buzz on
on have a good head on one's shoulders
on have a load on
on have a lot on one's mind
on have an effect on so/sth
on have an impact on so/sth
on have designs on so/sth
on have dibs on sth
on have egg on one's face
on have (got) a glow on
on have nothing on so
on have one's brain on a leash
on have one's eye on so/sth
on have one's feet on the ground
on have one's heart on one's sleeve
on have one's heart set on sth
on have pity on so or an animal
on have (some) bearing on sth
on have so on a string
on have so on the string
on have so/sth on one's hands
on have so/sth on one's mind
on have so/sth on the brain
on have so/sth on track
on have so's blood on one's hands
on have sth on
on have the shoe on the other foot
on have too much on one's plate
on have (too much) time on one's hands

on He puts his pants on one leg at a time.
on He wears a ten-dollar hat on a five-cent head.
on head on
on head start (on so)
on head start (on sth)
on hell on a holiday
on hell on earth
on help so on with sth
on high man on the totem pole
on high on sth
on hit on so
on hit on sth
on hit so or an animal on sth
on hit the nail (right) on the head
on hitting on all cylinders
on hold back (on sth)
on hold forth (on so/sth)
on hold off (on so/sth)
on hold on
on hold on so
on hold on sth
on hold (on) tight
on hold (sth) out on so/sth
on hold up (on so/sth)
on home in (on so/sth)
on hook oneself on so/sth
on hook so on sth
on hooked on sth
on hop on the bandwagon
on horn in (on so)
on horn in (on sth)
on hot on so's heels
on hot on sth
on hot on the trail (of so/sth or some creature)
on How are you getting on?
on hung up (on so/sth)
on hunker down (on sth)
on hurry on
on hurry one on one's way
on hypothesize on sth
on (I) wouldn't bet on it.
on (I) wouldn't count on it.
on I wouldn't wish that on a dog.
on I wouldn't wish that on my worst enemy.
on icing on the cake
on I'd bet money (on it).
on (I'd) better get on my horse.
on If two ride on a horse, one must ride behind.
on I'll get back to you (on that).
on I'll get right on it.
on impale so/sth on sth
on improvise on sth
on in on sth
on in on the act
on in on the ground floor
on in on the kill
on inform on so
on inform so on so
on intent on doing sth
on (Is) anything going on?
on It has so's name on it.
on It's on me.
on I've seen better heads on nickel beers.
on jam the brakes on
on jangle on sth
on jar on so/sth
on joke is on so.

on judge one on one's own merits
on judge sth on its own merits
on jump on so
on jump on the bandwagon
on jump up (on so/sth)
on jury is still out on so/sth.
on keen on doing sth
on keen on so/sth
on keep a close rein on so/sth
on keep a close watch on so/sth
on keep a firm grip on so/sth
on keep a lid on sth
on keep a tight grip on so/sth
on keep a tight rein on so/sth
on keep an eye on so/sth
on keep (close) watch (on so/sth)
on keep (going) on about so/sth
on keep (going) on at so/sth
on keep harping on sth
on keep on
on Keep (on) trying.
on keep one on one's toes
on keep one's eye on so/sth
on keep one's eye on the ball
on keep one's feet on the ground
on keep one's finger on the pulse of sth
on keep one's mind on so/sth
on keep one's pants on
on keep one's shirt on
on keep so on
on keep so on a string
on keep so on (sth)
on keep so on tenterhooks
on keep so/sth on (the) (right) track
on keep so/sth on track
on keep sth on
on keep tab(s) (on so/sth)
on keep watch on so/sth
on Keep your pants on!
on Keep your shirt on!
on kick in (on sth) (for so/sth)
on kick sth in (on sth) (for so/sth)
on kiss so on sth
on knock on so
on knock on wood
on know where so stands (on so/sth)
on know which side one's bread is buttered on
on land too poor to raise a racket on
on lash down on so/sth
on last laugh (on so)
on launch forth on sth
on launch out on sth
on lay a finger on so/sth
on lay a guilt trip on so
on lay a (heavy) trip on so
on lay down on the job
on lay emphasis on sth
on lay eyes on so/sth
on lay it on the line
on lay it on thick
on lay it on with a trowel
on lay one on
on lay one's cards on the table
on lay one's hands on so/sth or an animal
on lay some sweet lines on so
on lay sth down (on sth)
on lay sth on
on lay sth out on so/sth
on lay stress on sth
on lay the blame (for sth) on so
on lay the blame on so/sth
on lay the finger on so

on lead on
on lead so on
on lean back (on so/sth)
on lean on so
on leave an impression (on so)
on leave one's mark on so
on leave sth on
on leg up on so
on Let every tub stand on its own bottom.
on Let me get back to you (on that).
on let on (about so/sth)
on let on sth
on let on (to so) (about so/sth)
on Let's shake on it.
on let so get on with sth
on let so in on sth
on let so in on the act
on let so in on the ground floor
on let up (on so/sth)
on lid on sth
on lie down on sth
on lie down on the job
on lighten up (on so/sth)
on like a bump on a log
on like a house on fire
on like nothing on earth
on line on so
on line so/sth up on sth
on line up on sth
on linger on
on listen in (on so/sth)
on (little) short on one end
on live on (after so)
on live on (after so/sth)
on live on an amount of money
on live on borrowed time
on live on one's own
on live on sth
on live on the edge
on lock in on so/sth
on log on
on log so on (to sth)
on look becoming on so
on look good on paper
on look in (on so/sth)
on look like a saddle on a sow
on look on
on loom large (on the horizon)
on lose money on sth
on lose one's grip on so/sth
on lose one's hold on so/sth
on lost on so
on low man on the totem pole
on lowdown (on so/sth)
on lower the boom on so
on make a move on so
on make a start on sth
on make an impression on so
on make book on sth
on make good on sth
on make money on sth
on make so's hair stand on end
on make war (on so/sth)
on march on
on maroon so on an island
on mash on sth
on meditate on so/sth
on miss out (on sth)
on model so on so
on model sth on sth
on Money does not grow on trees.
on mount sth on sth

on mouth on so
on move in (on so)
on move in (on so/sth)
on move on
on move so/sth on
on murder on sth
on muscle in (on so/sth)
on nail so down (on sth)
on neighbor on sth
on new kid on the block
on new lease on life
on new one on so
on night on the town
on no flies on so
on nosh on sth
on not able to go on
on not grow on trees
on not have a leg to stand on
on not have a stitch of clothes (on)
on not on any account
on not to put too fine a point on it
on not worth the paper it's printed on
on not worth the paper it's written on
on odds-on favorite
on off again, on again
on off and on
on off on a sidetrack
on off on so
on off (on sth)
on off on the right foot (with so/sth)
on off on the wrong foot
on on a diet
on on a first-name basis (with so)
on on a fool's errand
on on a lark
on on a moment's notice
on on a pedestal
on on a power trip
on on a roll
on on a shoestring
on on a silver platter
on on a string
on on a tight leash
on on a wing and a prayer
on on account
on on active duty
on on advance notice
on on again, off again
on on all fours
on on and off
on on any account
on on approval
on on average
on on behalf of so
on on bended knee
on on board
on on Broadway
on on call
on on campus
on on cloud nine
on on consignment
on on course
on on credit
on on dangerous ground
on on dead center
on on deck
on on duty
on on earth
on on easy street
on on edge
on on fire
on on foot
on on good terms (with so)

on on hold
on on horseback
on on ice
on on impulse
on on in years
on on its feet
on on land
on on loan (from so/sth)
on on location
on on medication
on on moral grounds
on on no account
on on occasion
on on one's best behavior
on on one's deathbed
on on one's feet
on on (one's) guard (against so/sth)
on on one's high horse
on on one's honor
on on one's mind
on on one's own
on on one's person
on on one's toes
on on one's way ((to) some place)
on on one's way (to sth or some place)
on on order
on on par (with so/sth)
on on pins and needles
on on probation
on on purpose
on on record
on on sale
on on schedule
on on second thought
on on shaky ground
on on short notice
on on so/sth
on on so's account
on on so's back
on on so's behalf
on on so's case
on on so's doorstep
on on so's good side
on on so's head
on on so's heels
on on so's nerves
on on so's or sth's last legs
on on so's say-so
on on so's shoulders
on on so's tail
on on so's watch
on on so's wrong side
on on sth
on on speaking terms (with so)
on on spec
on on standby
on on tap
on on target
on on the air
on on the alert (for so/sth)
on on the average
on on the back burner
on on the ball
on on the bandwagon
on on the beam
on on the bench
on on the bias
on on the bird
on on the bleeding edge
on on the blink
on on the block
on on the books
on on the borderline

on on the bottom rung (of the ladder)
on on the bright side
on on the brink (of doing sth)
on on the button
on on the contrary
on on the cusp (of sth)
on on the cutting edge
on on the defensive
on on the dole
on on the dot
on on the double
on on the edge
on on the eve of sth
on on the face of it
on on the fast track
on on the fence (about sth)
on on the fly
on on the fringe
on on the fritz
on on the front burner
on on the go
on on the good side of so
on on the heels of sth
on on the horizon
on on the horns of a dilemma
on on the hot seat
on on the hour
on on the house
on on the job
on on the lam
on on the leading edge
on on the level
on on the lookout (for so/sth)
on on the loose
on on the make
on on the mark
on on the market
on on the mend
on on the money
on on the move
on on the nose
on on the off chance
on on (the) one hand
on on the other hand
on on the outs (with so)
on on the phone
on on the pill
on on the point of doing sth
on on the prowl
on on the QT
on on the rag
on on the right track
on on the rise
on on the road
on on the rocks
on on the run
on on the safe side
on on the same wavelength
on on the sauce
on on the scene
on on the shelf
on on the side
on on the skids
on on the sly
on on the spot
on on the spur of the moment
on on the stick
on on the street
on on the strength of sth
on on the table
on on the take
on on the telephone
on on the throne

on on the tip of one's tongue
on on the track of so/sth
on on the trail of so/sth
on on the up-and-up
on on the verge of doing sth
on on the wagon
on on the waiting list
on on the wane
on on the warpath
on on the watch for so/sth
on on the way (to sth or some place)
on on the whole
on on the wing
on on the (witness) stand
on on the wrong side of so
on on the wrong track
on on thin ice
on on time
on on tiptoe
on on top of sth
on on top of the world
on on track
on on trial
on on vacation
on on view
on on with so
on On your bike!
on on your mark, get set, go
on one eye on so/sth
on one's heart is set on sth
on one up (on so)
on open fire (on so)
on open fire (on so/sth)
on open season (on some creature)
on open season (on so)
on open up (on so/sth or an animal)
on operate on so
on operate on sth
on out on a limb
on out on bail
on (out) on parole
on (out) on patrol
on out (on strike)
on out on the town
on overdose (so) on sth
on paint on sth
on palm so/sth off (on so) (as so/sth)
on pan in (on so/sth)
on paradise (on earth)
on pass judgment (on so/sth)
on pass on
on pass sentence on so
on pass so on (to so)
on pass so/sth off (on so) (as so/sth)
on pass sth off (on so) (as sth)
on pass sth on
on paste sth on so
on pat so on the back
on pat so/sth on sth
on pattern sth on sth
on pawn so/sth off (on so) (as so/sth)
on pay a call on so
on pay on sth
on peek in (on so/sth)
on pelt down (on so/sth)
on perch on sth
on perch so/sth on sth
on perform sth on so/sth
on perspective on sth
on pick on somebody your own size
on pick on so/sth
on pick on someone your own size
on pick up on sth

on pig out (on sth)
on pile the work on (so)
on pin one's faith on so/sth
on pin one's hopes on so/sth
on pin so down (on sth)
on pin sth on so
on pivot on sth
on place a price on one's head
on place a strain on so/sth
on place so on a pedestal
on place so/sth on so/sth
on place sth down (on sth)
on place the blame on so/sth (for sth)
on plan on so
on plan on sth
on plant sth on so
on play a joke on so
on play a prank on so
on play a trick on so
on play on
on play sth on so/sth
on play tricks on so
on plot sth on sth
on pontificate on sth
on pop so on sth
on pork out (on sth)
on post sth on sth
on pound on so/sth
on pound sth on so/sth
on pour cold water on sth
on pour down (on so/sth)
on pour it on thick
on pour oil on troubled water(s)
on pox on so/sth!
on present sth on a silver platter
on press down on so/sth
on press on sth
on press sth on
on prey on sth
on price on one's head
on pronounce sth on so/sth
on pull a gun (on so)
on pull a knife (on so)
on pull a stunt (on so)
on pull a trick (on so)
on pull on sth
on pull one over on so
on pull rank (on so)
on pull sth on
on pull the plug (on so)
on pull the plug (on sth)
on punch so on sth
on push down on sth
on push on so/sth
on push on (to sth)
on push on (with sth)
on push (oneself) off (on sth)
on push so/sth on (ahead) (of so/sth)
on push up on sth
on put a cap on sth
on put a contract out on so
on put a damper on sth
on put a hold on sth
on put a lid on sth
on put a premium on sth
on put a price on one's head
on put a smile on so's face
on put a spin on sth
on put a strain on so/sth
on put an amount of time **in** on sth
on put balls on sth
on put hair on so's chest
on put it on the line

on put on
on put one on one's feet
on put one on one's guard
on put one on one's honor
on put one over on so
on put one's cards on the table
on put one's dibs on sth
on put one's face on
on put one's finger on sth
on put one's hands on so/sth or an animal
on put one's head on the block (for so/sth)
on put one's money on so/sth (to do sth)
on put one's neck on the line
on put one's thinking cap on
on put out a warrant (on so)
on put out (some) feelers (on so/sth)
on put pressure on sth
on put some sweet lines on so
on put (some) years on so/sth
on put so on
on put so/sth on hold
on put so/sth on ice
on put so/sth on sth
on put so/sth on track
on put so out on a limb
on put sth back on track
on put sth on
on put sth over on so
on put the arm on so
on put the bite on so
on put the blame on so/sth
on put the brakes on so
on put the brakes on sth
on put the chill on so
on put the clamps on so/sth
on put the feed bag on
on put the finger on so
on put the freeze on so
on put the hard word on so
on put the heat on
on put the kibosh on so/sth
on put the make on so
on put the moves on so
on put the nose-bag on
on put (the) pressure on so (to do sth)
on put the screws on (so)
on put the skids on (sth)
on put the squeeze on so
on put the touch on so
on put too fine a point on sth
on put wear (and tear) on sth
on put weight on
on quick on the draw
on quick on the trigger
on quick on the uptake
on quit on so
on quiz so on so/sth
on rag on so
on rain check (on sth)
on rain down on so/sth
on rain in on so/sth
on rain on so's parade
on rain sth down (on so/sth)
on rake on so
on ramble on
on rank on so
on rap on sth
on rap sth out (on sth)
on rat on so
on rattle on (about so/sth)
on read on
on read the handwriting on the wall

on read up (on so/sth)
on record sth on sth
on redound on so
on reed before the wind lives on, while mighty oaks do fall.
on register on sth
on rein back on so/sth
on relax one's hold on so/sth
on reliance on so/sth
on remain on
on renege on sth
on report back (on so/sth)
on rest on one's laurels
on retire on sth
on ride herd on so/sth
on ride on
on ride up (on so)
on Right on!
on right on so's heels
on right on time
on ring the curtain down (on sth)
on rip on so
on risk sth on so/sth
on rivet one's gaze on so/sth
on rivet one's glare on so/sth
on roll on
on romp on so
on rotate on sth
on rub off (on so)
on rule on sth
on ruminate on sth
on run a make on so
on run aground (on sth)
on run low (on sth)
on run on
on run on so
on run out (on so)
on rush on sth
on save a bundle (on sth)
on save (money) on sth
on scope (on) so
on scrape along (on sth)
on scrape by (on sth)
on scream down (on so/sth)
on scrimp on sth
on see so on the dot
on see the (hand)writing on the wall
on sell so on sth
on sell sth on credit
on send so on a wild-goose chase
on send so/sth on (ahead) (of so/sth)
on send so (out) on an errand
on serve notice (on so)
on serve on sth
on serve sth on a silver platter
on serve sth on so
on Set a beggar on horseback, and he'll ride to the devil.
on set eyes on so/sth
on set forth on sth
on set off on sth
on set one (back) on one's feet
on set one back on one's heels
on set one on one's feet again
on set one's heart on so/sth
on set one's hopes on so/sth
on set one's mind on so/sth
on set one's sights on so/sth
on set out on one's own
on set out (on sth)
on set so on fire
on set so or an animal **on** so or an animal
on set so/sth on fire

on set so/sth on track
on set so's teeth on edge
on set the world on fire
on set to work (on so/sth)
on settle on sth
on shake (hands) on sth
on Shame on you!
on shed (some) light on sth
on shoe is on the other foot.
on show up on the dot
on sign off on sth
on sign on
on sign so on
on sit down on sth
on sit in (on sth)
on sit on its hands
on sit on one's ass
on sit on one's hands
on sit on so/sth
on sit on the fence
on sit on their hands
on sitting on a gold mine
on sitting on a powder keg
on (sitting) on top of the world
on skate on sth
on skate on thin ice
on skimp on sth
on skip out (on so/sth)
on slack up (on sth)
on slam the brakes on
on slap on the wrist
on slap so on sth
on slap so on the wrist
on slap sth on
on sleep on sth
on slip on sth
on slip one over on so/sth
on slip sth on
on slip something over on so/sth
on slip up on so/sth or an animal
on slip up on sth
on slow on the draw
on slow on the uptake
on smile on so/sth
on snap back (on so/sth)
on snap sth on
on sneak up on so/sth
on sneeze on so/sth
on snitch on so
on soft on so
on soften one's stance (on so/sth)
on sold on so/sth
on Soup's on!
on spatter on so/sth
on speak out (on sth)
on speculate on sth
on spend sth on so/sth
on splash on sth
on splurge on so/sth
on spread it on thick
on spread sth on
on spring sth on so
on spur so on
on squander sth on so/sth
on squeal (on so) (to so)
on stake one's reputation on so/sth
on stamp on so/sth
on stand on ceremony
on stand on one's dignity
on stand on one's head
on stand on one's (own) two feet
on stand on sth
on stand pat (on sth)

on stand sth on its head
on start in on so/sth
on start off (on sth)
on start off on the wrong foot
on start on so/sth
on start out (on sth)
on start so off (on sth)
on stay on a diet
on stay on (after so/sth)
on stay on course
on stay on (one's) guard (against so/sth)
on stay on one's toes
on stay on (some place)
on stay on sth
on stay on the good side of so
on stay on top of so/sth
on steal a march on so/sth
on steal up on so/sth
on step back on so/sth
on step off on the wrong foot
on step on it
on step on so/sth
on step on so's toes
on step on the gas
on step out (on so)
on stink on ice
on stock up (on sth)
on stoked on so/sth
on stomp on so
on stool (on so)
on stop on a dime
on stop on sth
on strand so on sth
on stream down (on so/sth)
on strew sth on so/sth
on (strictly) on the level
on (strictly) on the up-and-up
on strike out on one's own
on strike so/sth on sth
on struggle on with sth
on strum sth on sth
on stuck on so/sth
on stuck on sth
on study up on so/sth
on stumble on so/sth
on subsist on sth
on swap notes (on so/sth)
on swear on a stack of Bibles
on swear on one's mother's grave
on sweep down on so/sth
on sweet on so
on switch on
on switch sth on
on switched on
on take a bath (on sth)
on take a chance on so/sth
on take a drag (on sth)
on take a firm grip on so/sth
on take a (firm) stand on sth
on take a rain check (on sth)
on take action on so/sth
on take fuel on
on take it easy on so/sth or an animal
on take it easy on sth
on take it on the chin
on take it on the lam
on take it on the nose
on take it out on so/sth
on take off (on sth)
on take on a new meaning
on take on a new significance
on take on (so)
on take pity (on so or an animal)

on take (quite) a toll (on so/sth)
on take so on
on take so/sth on
on take so's word on sth
on take so up on sth
on take sth on faith
on take sth on the chin
on take sth on trust
on take sth out on so/sth
on take too much on
on talk on
on tank up (on sth)
on tap on sth
on tap so/sth on sth
on tattle (on so) (to so)
on tear sth on sth
on tell on so
on tell so on so
on That's a new one on me!
on theorize on sth
on There's many a good tune played on an old fiddle.
on There's no flies on so.
on thin on top
on think back (on so/sth)
on think on one's feet
on think the sun rises and sets on so
on This one is on so.
on throw an amount of light on so/sth
on throw cold water on sth
on throw one out on one's ear
on throw oneself on the mercy of some authority
on throw (some) light on sth
on throw sth away on so/sth
on throw sth on so/sth
on thump on so/sth
on thump sth out (on the piano)
on tie it on
on tie on the nose-bag
on tie one on
on Time hangs heavy on so's hands.
on to be on the safe side
on toing and froing (on sth)
on touch on sth
on tough on so
on trade on sth
on train one's sights on sth
on train so on sth
on train sth on so/sth or an animal
on travel on sth
on tread on so's toes
on trifle sth away (on so/sth)
on trip on so/sth
on try sth (on) (for size)
on try sth on with so
on try sth out on so
on tune in (on so/sth)
on turn on
on Turn on, tune in, drop out.
on turn one's back (on so/sth)
on turn so on
on turn sth on
on turn the heat up (on so)
on turn the tables (on so)
on turn thumbs down (on so/sth)
on turn thumbs up (on so/sth)
on turn up the heat (on so/sth)
on up on so/sth
on upper hand (on so)
on wager on so/sth
on wager sth on so/sth
on wait on so hand and foot

on wait (on) tables
on walk in on so/sth
on walk on
on walk out (on so)
on walk out (on sth)
on want sth on a silver platter
on waste sth on so/sth
on wave so/sth on
on wear and tear (on sth)
on wear on (for a period of time)
on wear on so
on wear one's heart on one's sleeve
on weigh on so's mind
on welsh on so
on welsh on sth (with so)
on What's going on (around here)?
on What's on tap for today?
on Whatever turns you on.
on Where on (God's green) earth?
on whip back (on so)
on whip so/sth on
on Who's on the line?
on Who's on the phone?
on wipe sth (off) (on sth)
on wish so/sth (off) on so
on with bells on (one's toes)
on with everything (on it)
on wither on the vine
on work on so
on work on sth
on worship the ground so walks on
on write on and on
on write so in (on sth)
on write sth off (on one's taxes)
on wrote the book on sth
on yank on sth
on You can bet the farm (on so/sth).
on zero in (on so/sth)
on zip sth on
on zoom in (on so/sth)
once all at once
once at once
once Christmas comes but once a year.
once difficult is done at once; the impossible takes a little longer.
once Fool me once, shame on you; fool me twice, shame on me.
once if I've told you once, I've told you a thousand times
once Once a priest, always a priest.
once Once a whore, always a whore.
once once and for all
once Once bitten, twice shy.
once once in a blue moon
once once more
once once upon a time
once once-in-a-lifetime chance
once once-in-a-lifetime opportunity
once once-over
once once-over-lightly
once One cannot be in two places at once.
once Opportunity knocks but once.
once word (once) spoken is past recalling.
one act as one
one (all) in one breath
one all in one piece
one at one fell swoop
one back to square one
one bite the big one
one bust so one
one busy as a one-armed paperhanger

one buy the big one
one day one
one do a one-eighty
one do so one better
one Don't put all your eggs in one basket.
one Don't spend it all in one place.
one down one for the road
one every last one
one fast one
one from day one
one get off a few good ones
one go at one another tooth and nail
one go back to square one
one go from one extreme to the other
one go in one ear and out the other
one go (so) one better
one hang one on
one Have a good one.
one have a one-track mind
one have just one oar in the water
one have more than one string to one's fiddle
one have one foot in the grave
one have one in the oven
one have one too many
one He puts his pants on one leg at a time.
one hole in one
one If two ride on a horse, one must ride behind.
one in (at) one ear and out (of) the other
one in one fell swoop
one In the country of the blind, the one-eyed man is king.
one It's just one of those things.
one It's six of one, half a dozen of another.
one (It) takes one to know one.
one kill two birds with one stone
one knock one back
one knock one over
one lay one on
one like one of the family
one (little) short on one end
one Little thieves are hanged, but great ones escape.
one look after number one
one look out for number one
one motion so to one side
one mouse that has but one hole is quickly taken.
one my one and only
one new one on so
one No one is indispensable.
one not one iota
one of one mind (about so/sth)
one off to one side
one old one-two
one on (the) one hand
one one and all
one one and only
one one and the same
one one brick shy of a load
one one by one
one One cannot be in two places at once.
one One cannot love and be wise.
one one eye on so/sth
one one false move
one one final thing
one one final word

one one for the (record) books
one one for the road
one One good turn deserves another.
one One hand for oneself and one for the ship.
one One has to draw the line somewhere.
one one in a hundred
one one in a thousand
one one jump ahead (of so/sth)
one one law for the rich and another for the poor
one one little bit
one One man's loss is another man's gain.
one One man's meat is another man's poison.
one One man's trash is another man's treasure.
one One moment, please.
one one more time
one one move ahead (of so/sth)
one one of these days
one one sandwich short of a picnic
one One swallow does not make a summer.
one one that got away
one One thing leads to another.
one one thing or person after another
one one to a customer
one one too many
one one up (on so)
one one way or another
one one-horse town
one one-man show
one one-night stand
one one-track mind
one paste so one
one pull a fast one
one pull one over on so
one put all one's eggs in one basket
one put one foot in front of the other
one put one over on so
one since day one
one six of one and half a dozen of the other
one slip one over on so/sth
one speak as one
one take care of number one
one take one for the road
one take so to one side
one Tell me another (one)!
one That's a new one on me!
one There's more than one way to skin a cat.
one This one is on so.
one tie one on
one turn one hundred and eighty degrees
one Two can play (at) this game (as well as one).
one Two heads are better than one.
one up one side and down the other
one wear more than one hat
one When one door shuts, another opens.
one with one hand tied behind one's back
one (Would you) care for another (one)?
oneself break one's arm patting oneself on the back
oneself by oneself

oneself make a (kind of) life for oneself
onion know one's onions
online online
only able to take only so much
only Beauty is only skin-deep.
only Believe nothing of what you hear, and only half of what you see.
only Close only counts in horseshoes (and hand grenades).
only face (that) only a mother could love
only From the sublime to the ridiculous is only a step.
only God only knows!
only I'm only looking.
only in name only
only It (only) stands to reason.
only know sth only too well
only my one and only
only one and only
only only have eyes for so
only (Only) time will tell.
only only way to go
only (the) Lord only knows
only They also serve who only stand and wait.
onto add (sth) on(to) sth
onto append sth (on)to sth
onto back onto so/sth
onto back so/sth onto so/sth
onto build on(to) sth
onto build out onto sth
onto build sth onto sth
onto burst onto the scene
onto carry sth onto sth
onto catch onto so/sth
onto catch onto sth
onto cement sth on(to) sth
onto clamber onto sth
onto clamp sth on(to) sth
onto clap sth on(to) sth
onto climb on(to) sth
onto clip sth on(to) so/sth
onto come on(to) so/sth
onto cop onto sth
onto cotton (on)to so/sth
onto couple sth (on)to sth
onto dab sth on(to) sth
onto daub sth on(to) sth
onto divert sth onto sth
onto drag so/sth on(to) sth
onto emblazon sth on(to) sth
onto engrave sth on(to) sth
onto face on(to) sth
onto fall back on(to) so/sth
onto fall on(to) so/sth
onto fasten so/sth (on)to so/sth
onto fit sth on(to) sth
onto fix sth on(to) sth
onto flop sth down on(to) sth
onto fob so/sth off (on(to) so)
onto freeze (on)to sth
onto get on(to) so (about sth)
onto get on(to) the (tele)phone
onto get so on(to) so/sth
onto glue sth on(to) sth
onto grab on(to) so/sth)
onto graft sth on(to) sth
onto hammer sth onto sth
onto home on(to) sth
onto hook sth on(to) so/sth)
onto hop on(to) sth)
onto imprint sth on(to) sth

onto inscribe sth on(to) sth
onto jump on((to) sth)
onto latch on(to) so)
onto latch onto sth
onto load sth onto so/sth
onto lock on(to) so/sth)
onto lock sth onto so/sth
onto look (out) on(to) sth
onto nail sth onto sth
onto nose sth (out) (onto sth)
onto onto a good thing
onto onto so
onto onto sth
onto open (out) on(to) sth
onto paint sth onto sth
onto pile on((to) so/sth)
onto pile so/sth on(to) sth
onto pin sth (on)to sth
onto pin sth up on(to) sth
onto plaster sth onto sth
onto pop sth on(to) sth
onto pour sth on(to) sth
onto pour sth out on(to) so/sth
onto press sth onto sth
onto project sth onto so
onto project sth on(to) so/sth
onto push sth off on(to) so
onto put so onto so/sth
onto rivet sth on(to) sth
onto roll sth onto sth
onto rub off on(to) so/sth
onto rub sth onto sth
onto run sth onto sth
onto screw sth (on)(to sth)
onto seize onto so/sth
onto set so down (on(to) sth)
onto slam sth down (on(to) sth)
onto slap sth onto so/sth
onto slop sth on(to) so/sth
onto slosh sth on(to) so/sth
onto smack sth down (on(to) sth)
onto smear sth on(to) so/sth
onto smooth sth onto so/sth
onto spatter sth on(to) so/sth
onto spill over on(to) so/sth
onto spit sth on(to) sth
onto splash sth on(to) so/sth
onto spray sth onto so/sth
onto spread sth onto sth
onto sprinkle sth on(to) so/sth
onto stamp sth onto sth
onto stick sth on(to) so/sth
onto stitch sth onto sth
onto strap sth onto so/sth
onto stray onto sth
onto suffix sth onto sth
onto superimpose sth on(to) so/sth
onto tack sth onto sth
onto throw so/sth on(to) sth
onto tie sth onto so/sth
onto tighten sth on(to) sth
onto turn off (sth) onto sth
onto turn onto sth
onto unload so/sth on(to) so
onto vote so on(to) sth)
onto wind sth onto sth
onto You'll get onto it.
onward press on(ward)
ooze ooze (out) (from so/sth)
ooze ooze with sth
open blow sth wide open
open bring sth out in the open
open bust so wide open

open bust sth wide open
open *can of worms
open come out in the open
open come out in(to) the open
open crack a bottle open
open crack open
open crack sth (wide) open
open crack the door (open)
open crack the window (open)
open door must be either shut or open.
open doors open up (to so)
open for openers
open golden key can open any door.
open in the open
open keep an open mind
open keep one's eyes open (for so/sth)
open keep one's weather eye open
open leave oneself wide open for sth
open leave sth open
open leave the door open (for sth)
open (like) an open book
open not open one's mouth
open open a can of worms
open open a conversation
open open a few doors (for so)
open open and aboveboard
open (Open) confession is good for the soul.
open open fire (on so)
open open fire (on so/sth)
open open for business
open open into sth
open open mind
open open one's heart to so/sth
open open oneself to criticism
open open (out) on(to) sth
open open Pandora's box
open open season (on some creature)
open open season (on so)
open open secret
open open some doors (for so)
open open so's eyes to so/sth
open open so up
open open sth out
open open sth up
open open the door to so
open open the door to sth
open open to criticism
open open to question
open open to sth
open open up
open open (up) one's kimono
open open with so/sth
open open-and-shut case
open opening gambit
open out in the open
open put sth in the open
open receive so with open arms
open the heavens opened
open welcome so with open arms
open When one door shuts, another opens.
open wide open
open with (one's) eyes (wide) open
openers for openers
operate operate against so/sth
operate operate from sth
operate operate on so
operate operate on sth
operation mopping-up operation
opinion base one's opinion on sth
opinion form an opinion

opinion hazard an opinion
opinion I'll thank you to keep your opinions to yourself.
opinion in my humble opinion
opinion in my opinion
opinion in one's opinion
opinion keep one's opinions to oneself
opinion Keep your opinions to yourself!
opinion matter of opinion
opportunity golden opportunity
opportunity growth opportunity
opportunity jump at the opportunity (to do sth)
opportunity leap at the opportunity (to do sth)
opportunity once-in-a-lifetime opportunity
opportunity Opportunity knocks but once.
opportunity Opportunity makes a thief.
opportunity photo op(portunity)
opportunity seize the opportunity
opportunity window of opportunity
oppose opposed to sth
opposite opposite sex
opposition in opposition (to so/sth)
opt co-opt so into sth
opt opt for sth
opt opt in favor of so/sth
opt opt in(to sth)
opt opt out (of sth)
oranges apples and oranges
orbit go into orbit
orbit in orbit
orbit orbit (around) so/sth
orbit put sth into orbit
orchard crazy as a peach-orchard boar
ordain ordain so (as) sth
order (Are you) ready to order?
order back-order sth
order build sth to order
order call a meeting to order
order call the meeting to order
order Can I take your order (now)?
order Could I take your order (now)?
order doctor's orders
order follow orders
order in apple-pie order
order in marching order
order in order
order in short order
order just what the doctor ordered
order keep so/sth in order
order made to order
order make sth to order
order May I take your order (now)?
order on order
order order of the day
order order some food to go
order order so about
order order so in(to sth)
order order so off ((of) sth)
order order so off the field
order order so out of some place
order order sth from so/sth
order order sth in
order out of order
order place an order
order put one's house in order
order put one's own house in order
order put so/sth into order

order put sth in apple-pie order
order put sth in order
order put sth in(to) order
order set one's house in order
order tall order
order *to go
ordinary out of the ordinary
orient orient so to sth
originate originate from sth
originate originate in sth
originate originate with so/sth
ornament ornament sth with sth
oscillate oscillate between so/sth and so/sth
other cancel each other out
other Catch me some other time.
other Do unto others as you would have them do unto you.
other drop the other shoe
other every other person or thing
other fall in love (with each other)
other go from one extreme to the other
other go in one ear and out the other
other grass is always greener on the other side (of the fence).
other Half the world knows not how the other half lives.
other have the shoe on the other foot.
other how the other half lives
other (I'll) try to catch you some other time.
other in (at) one ear and out (of) the other
other in other words
other laugh out of the other side of one's face
other laugh out of the other side of one's mouth
other look the other way
other made for each other
other Maybe some other time.
other none other than
other on the other hand
other other place
other other side of the tracks
other other things being equal
other Other times, other manners.
other other way (a)round
other put one foot in front of the other
other rose by any other name would smell as sweet.
other shoe is on the other foot.
other six of one and half a dozen of the other
other something or other
other There are plenty of (other) fish in the sea.
other turn the other cheek
other turn the other way
other up one side and down the other
other wait for the other shoe to drop
other We'll try again some other time.
other with every (other) breath
ought hadn't oughta
oughta hadn't oughta
ounce ounce of common sense is worth a pound of theory.
ounce ounce of discretion is worth a pound of wit.
ounce ounce of prevention is worth a pound of cure.
our Our house is your house.

our Welcome to our house.
ourselves by ourselves
oust oust so from sth
out ace out
out ace so out
out act out
out act sth out
out age out (of sth)
out air out
out air sth out
out (all) tuckered out
out all-out effort
out all-out war
out (almost) jump out of one's skin
out appear out of nowhere
out apportion sth out (among some people)
out argue one's way out of sth
out argue sth out
out as all get out
out ask so out (for sth)
out ask so out (to sth)
out average out (at sth)
out back out (of sth)
out back so/sth out (from sth)
out back so/sth out of sth
out Bad money drives out good.
out bail out (of sth)
out bail so/sth out
out bail so out of jail
out bail sth out
out balance out
out bang so out
out barf out
out barf so out
out bark sth out at so
out barrel out (of some place)
out battle sth out
out bawl so out
out bear sth out
out beat one's brains out (to do sth)
out beat so/sth out
out beat so out
out beat so's brains out
out beat the hell out of so
out beat the (natural) stuffing out of so
out beat the shit out of so
out beat the stuffing out of so
out beat the tar out of so
out begin an all-out effort
out beguile so out of sth
out belch out
out bellow sth out
out belly out
out belt sth out
out bend so out of shape
out bend sth out of shape
out bent out of shape
out bilk so out of sth
out billow out
out blab sth out
out black out
out black sth out
out blank sth out
out bleach sth out
out bleep sth out
out blimp out
out bliss out
out bliss so out
out blitz so out
out blitzed out
out block sth out
out blossom out

out blot so/sth out
out blot so out
out blot sth out
out Blow it out your ear!
out blow itself out
out blow so/sth out of the water
out blow so out
out blow so's brains out
out blow sth out
out bluff one's way out (of sth)
out bluff so out (of sth)
out blurt sth out (at so)
out board so or an animal out
out boil sth out
out bolt out (of some place)
out bomb out (of sth)
out bomb so out
out bomb sth out
out book (on) out
out boom out
out boom sth out
out boot so or an animal out
out born out of wedlock
out bottom fell out (of sth)
out bottom out
out bounce out (of sth)
out bow out (of some place)
out bow out (of sth)
out branch out (from sth)
out branch out (into sth)
out brave sth out
out break out
out break sth out (of sth)
out breathe out
out breathe sth out
out breeze out (of some place)
out bring one out of one's shell
out bring out the best in so
out bring so back out
out bring so/sth out
out bring so out of the closet
out bring so out (on sth)
out bring sth out
out broaden out
out broaden sth out
out brown out
out bud out
out bug out
out build out onto sth
out build sth out of sth
out build (sth) out over sth
out bulge out
out bum out
out bum so out
out bummed (out)
out burgeon out
out burn (itself) out
out burn (oneself) out
out burn so out
out burn sth out
out burst out
out bush out
out bust ass out of some place
out bust out laughing
out bust out (of some place)
out bust so out of some place
out butt out
out buy one's way out (of sth)
out buy so/sth out
out buy sth out
out cajole so out of sth
out call out (to so)
out call so/sth out

out call so out
out call sth out
out camp out
out cancel each other out
out cancel out (of sth)
out cancel so out
out cancel sth out
out can't make heads or tails (out) of so/sth
out carry so/sth out
out carry sth out
out carve sth out
out case so/sth out
out cat is out of the bag
out catch so out
out chalk sth out
out change out of sth
out charge out (of some place)
out chart sth out (for so/sth)
out chase so/sth out of some place
out cheat so out of sth
out check out
out check out (from sth)
out check so/sth out
out check sth out
out chew so out
out chicken out (of sth)
out chicken out on so
out chill out
out chisel so out of sth
out chuck so out of some place
out Church ain't out till they quit singing.
out churn sth out
out clap sth out
out clean out (of sth)
out clean so/sth out of sth
out clean sth out
out cleaned out
out clear out (of some place)
out clear so/sth out of some place
out climb out (of sth)
out clip sth out of sth
out clock out
out clock so out
out close so out of sth
out close sth out
out coax so or an animal out of sth
out comb sth out of sth
out come in out of the rain
out come out
out coming out of one's ears
out con so out of sth
out conduct so out of sth
out conk out
out contract sth out
out cook (sth) out
out cool out
out cool so out
out cooled out
out cop out (of sth)
out cop out (on so)
out cop out (on sth)
out copy sth out
out cost sth out
out cough sth out
out couldn't pour water out of a boot (if there was instructions on the heel)
out count so out (for sth)
out count sth out
out crank sth out
out crap out
out crash out (of some place)

out crawl out
out creep out (from under so/sth)
out creep out (of sth)
out creep out of the woodwork
out crop out
out crop so/sth out
out cross so/sth out
out crowd so/sth out of sth
out crumped out
out crush sth out
out cry one's eyes out
out cry one's heart out
out cry out (against so/sth)
out cry out for so/sth
out cry out (in sth)
out cry (sth) out (to so or an animal)
out cull so/sth out of sth
out cuss so out
out Cut it out!
out cut out
out cut so/sth out
out cut sth out
out cut the deadwood out
out cut the ground out from under so
out dance out of step (with so/sth)
out dance out of time (with so/sth)
out dart in and out
out dart out (of sth) (at so/sth)
out dash out (for sth)
out day in and day out
out deal so out of sth
out deal sth out
out deck so/sth out (in sth)
out defraud so out of sth
out diddle so out of sth
out diddle sth out of so
out die out
out dig out (of sth)
out dig so/sth out of sth
out dig sth out
out dim out
out dine out
out dinged out
out dish sth out
out Do I have to spell it out (for you)?
out do so out of sth
out doesn't have enough sense to come in out of the rain
out dole sth out (to so)
out don't have a pot to piss in (or a window to throw it out of)
out Don't let it out of this room.
out Don't throw the baby out with the bathwater.
out dope sth out
out down-and-out
out drag out
out drag sth out
out dragged out
out drain out
out drain sth out of sth
out draw so or an animal out of sth
out draw so/sth out of some place
out draw so out on so/sth
out draw sth out
out drift out
out drive one out of one's mind
out drive out (to some place)
out drive so or an animal out of sth
out drive so out
out drone sth out
out drop out of sight
out drop out (of sth)

out drop so/sth out of sth
out drown so or an animal out
out drown so/sth out
out drum so out
out drum sth out
out dry out
out dry so out
out dry sth out
out duck out (of some place)
out duck out (of sth)
out duke it out
out duke so out
out dust sth out
out ease (on) out (of sth)
out ease so (on) out (of sth)
out ease so out of sth
out eat (a meal) out
out eat one's heart out
out eat out
out eat so out
out eat sth out
out eat (sth) out of sth
out edge so out of sth
out edge sth out
out edit sth out of sth
out eke sth out
out elbow so out of sth
out empty so out
out empty sth out
out even sth out
out Everything will work out (all right).
out Everything will work out for the best.
out exorcise sth out of so
out fade out
out fade sth out
out fag so out
out fagged out
out fair sth out
out fake so out
out fall out
out fan out
out fan sth out
out far out
out farm so out
out farm sth out
out fashion sth out of sth
out fast-talk so out of sth
out feel out of place
out feel out of sorts
out feel out of things
out feel so out (about so/sth)
out fence so or an animal out
out ferret sth out
out fetch sth out of sth
out fight one's way out (of sth)
out fight sth out
out figure out the root of the problem
out figure so/sth out
out file out (of sth)
out fill sth out
out fill out
out filter sth out of sth
out find out a thing or two (about so/sth)
out find so out
out find sth out
out find (sth) out (about so/sth) (from so/sth)
out find (sth) out the hard way
out fink out (on so/sth)
out fish so/sth out of sth
out fish sth up out of sth

out fit so/sth out (for sth)
out fit so/sth out (with sth)
out fizzle out
out flack out
out flake out
out flare out
out flare sth out
out flash out
out flat out
out flatten so/sth out
out flesh out
out flesh sth out (with sth)
out flex sth out of shape
out flexed out of shape
out flick out
out flick sth out
out flicker out
out fling so/sth out of sth
out flip out
out flip so out
out flood out (of sth)
out flood so/sth out of sth
out flounce out (of some place)
out flow out (of sth)
out fluff sth out
out flunk out (of sth)
out flunk so out
out flush so/sth out of some place
out fly out (of sth)
out fly so/sth out of sth
out follow so/sth out
out For crying out loud!
out force so/sth out of sth
out force so out of office
out fork some money out (for sth)
out fork sth out (to so)
out form sth out of sth
out foul out (of sth)
out frame sth out
out freak out (at so/sth)
out freak out (on sth)
out freak out (over so/sth)
out freak so out
out freaked (out)
out freeze so out
out fresh out (of sth)
out frighten one out of one's wits
out frighten so out of a year's growth
out frighten the hell out of so
out funked out
out Garbage in, garbage out.
out gasp sth out
out gaze out on sth
out get a bang out of so/sth
out get a buzz out of so/sth
out get a charge out of so/sth
out get a kick out of so/sth
out get a lot of mileage out of sth
out get euchred out of sth
out get it out
out get one's ears set out
out get one's nose out of joint
out get one's nose out of so's business
out get out
out get (out) while the gettin(g)'s good
out get some kind of mileage out of sth
out get so/sth out of one's mind
out get so/sth out of one's sight
out get so/sth out of so/sth
out get so out of a jam
out get so out of one's hair
out get sth out

out get the hell out (of here)
out get the kinks (ironed) out
out get the lead out
out get the most out of so/sth
out get the wrinkles out (of sth)
out Get your head out of the clouds!
out Get your nose out of my business.
out give out
out give (out) with sth
out give so a (good) bawling out
out give sth out
out go all out (for so/sth)
out go in and out (of sth)
out go in one ear and out the other
out go out
out go (out) on strike
out gorked (out)
out gouge sth out
out graph sth out
out grind sth out
out groan sth out
out gronk (out)
out gross so out
out grow out
out growl sth out
out grunt sth out
out gyp so out of sth
out hack sth out of sth
out hammer sth out
out hand sth out (to so)
out hang out (of sth)
out hang out (some place)
out hang out (with so/sth)
out hang so out to dry
out hang sth out (of sth)
out hatch an animal out
out have one's eye out (for so/sth)
out have one's heart go out to so
out have one's luck run out
out have one's nose out of joint
out have one's work cut out for one
out have sth out
out (Have you) been keeping out of trouble?
out head out after so/sth or an animal
out head out (for sth)
out head sth out
out hear a peep out of so
out hear so out
out help out some place
out help out (with sth)
out help so or an animal out (of sth)
out help so/sth out with so/sth
out help (so) out
out hew sth out of sth
out hide out (from so/sth)
out hightail it out of somewhere
out hire so/sth out
out hiss sth out
out hit out (at so/sth) (in sth)
out hit out (for sth or some place)
out hold out (against so/sth)
out hold out (for so/sth)
out hold out the olive branch
out hold so/sth out (of sth)
out hold (sth) out on so/sth
out hold sth out (to so)
out holler sth out
out hollow sth out
out hoodwink so out of sth
out hotfoot it out of somewhere
out hound so out (of sth or some place)
out hound sth out of so

out How is so making out?
out hunt so/sth out
out hurl so/sth out (of some place)
out I don't want to wear out my welcome.
out I have to wash a few things out.
out I spoke out of turn.
out If you can't stand the heat, get out of the kitchen.
out (I'm) (just) thinking out loud.
out I'm out of here.
out in (at) one ear and out (of) the other
out In like a lion, out like a lamb.
out include so out (of sth)
out ins and outs (of sth)
out inveigle so out of sth
out inveigle sth out of so
out invite so out
out iron sth out
out It is better to wear out than to rust out.
out It's a jungle out there.
out It'll all come out in the wash.
out (I've) been keeping out of trouble.
out jab sth out
out jacked (out)
out jerk so/sth out of sth
out jerk sth out of so/sth
out jolt so out of sth
out jump out of sth
out jump out of the frying pan into the fire
out jury is still out on so/sth.
out jut out (from sth)
out jut out (into sth)
out jut out (over so/sth)
out keep an eye out (for so/sth)
out keep one's eye(s) out (for so/sth)
out keep one's nose out of so's business
out keep one's nose out of sth
out keep out from under so's feet
out Keep out of my way.
out keep out of sight
out keep out (of sth)
out Keep out of this!
out keep so or some creature out in the cold
out keep so/sth out (of sth)
out keep so/sth out of the way
out Keep your nose out of my business.
out kick out (at so/sth)
out kick so or an animal out
out kick sth out of sth
out kick the (natural) stuffing out of so
out knock oneself out (to do sth) (for so/sth)
out knock so out
out knock sth out
out knock the bejeebers out of so/sth
out knock the bottom out (of sth)
out knock the hell out of so/sth
out knock the (living) daylights out of so
out knock the props out from under so
out knock the stuffing out of so
out knock the wind out of so's sails
out knock-down, drag-out fight
out knocked out
out know sth inside out
out ladle sth out of sth
out laid out
out lash out (at so/sth)
out last out

out last sth out
out latch string is always out.
out laugh oneself out of sth
out laugh out of the other side of one's face
out laugh out of the other side of one's mouth
out laugh so out of sth
out laugh sth out of court
out launch out on sth
out lay so out
out lay sth out
out leach out of sth
out lead so or an animal out of sth
out leaf out
out leak out
out leak sth (out)
out lean out of sth
out leap out (of sth)
out lease sth (out) to so
out leave so or some creature out in the cold
out leave so/sth out of sth
out lend sth out (to so)
out lengthen out
out let it all hang out
out let so or an animal (get) out (of sth)
out let so or an animal out of sth
out let sth (get) out
out let sth out
out let sth slip (out)
out let the cat out of the bag
out level out
out level sth out
out lie out (in sth)
out lift sth out of context
out light out (for some place)
out light out (of some place) (for some place)
out like a bat out of hell
out like a bolt out of the blue
out like a fish out of water
out like it was going out of style
out live out of a suitcase
out live out of cans
out live out one's days
out live sth out
out lock so/sth out of sth
out log out
out log so out
out loll out
out look out
out look (out) on(to) sth
out loom out of sth
out lose out
out luck out
out lunch out
out make a believer (out) of so
out make a check (out) (to so/sth)
out make a federal case out of sth
out make a fool (out) of so
out make a monkey (out) of so
out make a mountain out of a molehill
out make an all-out effort
out make hamburger (out) of so
out make mincemeat (out) of so
out make (out) after so/sth
out make (out) for so/sth
out make out like a bandit
out make (out) like sth
out make out that...
out make out (with so)
out make out (with so/sth)

out make (some) sense (out) of so/sth
out make sth out
out make sth (out) of sth
out make sth up out of whole cloth
out maneuver so out of sth
out map sth out
out March comes in like a lion, and goes out like a lamb.
out march out of time (with so/sth)
out mark so/sth out
out marry one's way out of sth
out mask sth out
out materialize out of nowhere
out max out
out maxed out
out measure sth out
out mellow out
out mete sth out
out miss out (on sth)
out moan sth out
out mold sth out of sth
out move out (from under so/sth)
out move out (of some place)
out move so/sth out (of some place)
out move so/sth out of the way
out mulct sth out of so
out munch out
out Murder will out.
out muscle so out of sth
out muster out of sth
out nause so out
out nearly jump out of one's skin
out Never halloo till you are out of the woods.
out Never make a threat you cannot carry out.
out Never tell tales out of school.
out nine times out of ten
out nose out (of sth)
out nose so or a group out
out nose sth out of sth
out nose sth (out) (onto sth)
out not able to make anything out of so/sth
out not know enough to come in out of the rain
out odd man out
out oink out
out on the lookout (for so/sth)
out on the outs (with so)
out one's heart goes out to so
out one's luck runs out
out one's work is cut out for one
out ooze (out) (from so/sth)
out open (out) on(to) sth
out open sth out
out opt out (of sth)
out order so out of some place
out out
out out an amount of money
out out and about
out out at some place
out out cold
out out for blood
out out for the count
out out from sth
out out (from under so/sth)
out out front
out out (in bloom)
out out (in blossom)
out out in droves
out out in force
out out in large numbers

out out in left field
out out in the cold
out out in the open
out out like a light
out out of action
out out of (all) proportion
out out of breath
out out of character
out out of circulation
out out of commission
out out of condition
out out of consideration (for so/sth)
out out of context
out out of control
out out of courtesy (to so)
out out of debt
out out of earshot
out out of fashion
out out of favor (with so)
out out of focus
out out of gas
out out of hand
out out of harm's way
out out of hock
out out of it
out out of keeping (with sth)
out out of kilter
out out of left field
out out of line (with sth)
out out of luck
out out of necessity
out out of nowhere
out out of one's depth
out out of one's element
out out of one's head
out out of one's mind
out out of one's skull
out out of one's way
out out of order
out out of patience
out out of place
out out of practice
out out of print
out out of proportion
out out of reach
out out of season
out out of service
out out of shape
out out of sight
out Out of sight, out of mind.
out out of so's hands
out out of so's way
out out of (of) sth)
out out of sorts
out out of spite
out out of step (with so/sth)
out out of stock
out out of style
out out of sync
out out of the ballpark
out out of the closet
out out of the corner of one's eye
out out of the frying pan (and) into the fire
out out of the goodness of one's heart
out out of the hole
out Out of the mouths of babes (oft times come gems).
out out of the ordinary
out out of the picture
out out of the question
out out of the red
out out of the running

out out of the swim of things
out out of the way
out out (of) the window
out out of the woods
out out of the woodwork
out out of thin air
out out of this world
out out of time (with so/sth)
out out of touch (with so/sth)
out out of town
out out of tune (with so/sth)
out out of turn
out out of w(h)ack
out out of wind
out out of work
out out on a limb
out out on bail
out (out) on parole
out (out) on patrol
out out (on strike)
out out on the town
out Out, please.
out out to (a meal)
out out to get so
out out to lunch
out out to win
out out West
out out-of-bounds
out out-of-pocket expenses
out Over and out.
out pace sth out
out pad out
out pad sth out
out paint sth out
out pan out
out pant sth out
out parade so or an animal out
out parcel so/sth out
out pass out
out pass sth out (to so)
out pay sth out
out peal out
out peek out (from behind so/sth)
out peek out (from underneath so/sth)
out peek out of sth (at so/sth)
out peel out
out peep out (of sth) (at so/sth)
out peer out at so/sth
out peg out
out permit so out (of sth)
out pester so out of sth
out pester the life out of so
out peter out
out phase so/sth out of sth
out pick so/sth out
out piece sth out
out pig out (on sth)
out pile out (of sth)
out pilot sth out of sth
out pitch so/sth out (of) sth
out pitch sth out
out plan sth out
out play freeze-out
out play one's heart out
out play out
out play sth out
out played out
out plot sth out
out pluck sth out of sth
out point so/sth out
out poke out (of sth)
out poke sth out of sth
out pooch out

out poop out
out poop so/sth out
out pooped (out)
out pop out (of sth)
out pop sth out of sth
out pork out (on sth)
out portion sth out
out pound sth out
out pour one's heart out to so
out pour out (of sth)
out pour out one's soul
out pour sth out on(to) so/sth
out press sth out of sth
out price so/sth out of the market
out price sth out
out print sth out
out pry sth out of so
out pry sth out (of sth)
out psych out
out psych so out
out psyched (out)
out puff out
out puff sth out
out pull all the stops out
out pull (out) in front of so/sth
out pull out (of sth)
out pull sth out
out pull sth up (out of sth)
out pull the rug out (from under so)
out pump sth out of so/sth
out punch out
out punch so out
out punch so's lights out
out punch sth out of sth
out punk out
out push out
out push so/sth out of sth
out put a contract out on so
out put a horse out to pasture
out put an animal out
out put one out of (one's) misery
out put one's nose out of joint
out put oneself out
out put out
out put some creature out of its misery
out put so or an animal out of sth
out put so or some creature out in the cold
out put so/sth out of one's mind
out put so/sth out of the way
out put so out
out put so's eye out
out put so's nose out of joint
out put sth out
out puzzle sth out
out quiz out (of sth)
out quote so/sth out of context
out rack out
out rag out
out rage out of control
out rain sth out
out rake sth out of sth
out rank so (out)
out rap sth out (on sth)
out rasp sth out
out rat out
out ration sth out (among so)
out raunch so out
out reach out
out read so out (for sth)
out read so out of sth
out read (so) sth out of sth
out read sth out
out ream so out

out ream sth out
out reason sth out
out reject so/sth out of hand
out rent sth (out) (to so)
out ride out (of some place)
out ride sth out
out rig so/sth out (in sth)
out ring out
out rinse so's mouth out (with soap)
out rinse sth out
out rip sth out of so/sth
out roar sth out
out roll out the red carpet (for so)
out roll sth out
out root so/sth out of sth
out root sth out
out rot out
out rough sth out
out round sth out
out rouse so out of sth
out roust so out of sth
out rout so/sth out of some place
out row (so/sth) out to sth
out rub so out
out rub sth out
out rule so/sth out
out run out at so/sth
out run out of gas
out run out of patience
out run out of some place
out run out (of sth)
out run out of steam
out run out of time
out run out (on so)
out run so/sth out of sth
out run sth out of sth
out rush out (of sth)
out rush so/sth out of sth
out rust out
out sack out
out sacked out
out say sth out loud
out scare one out of one's mind
out scare one out of one's wits
out scare so or an animal out
out scare so out of sth
out scare sth out of so
out scare the living daylights out of so
out scare the wits out of so
out scarf out
out schiz(z) out
out scoop sth out of sth
out scope so/sth out
out scour sth out
out scout so/sth out
out scrape sth out
out scratch so/sth out
out scream sth out
out screen so/sth out of sth
out screw so out of sth
out scrub sth out
out scuzz so out
out search so/sth out
out see so out (of sth)
out seek so/sth out
out seem out of place
out seep out (of sth)
out sell out
out sell so out
out sell sth out
out send out (for so/sth)
out send so out
out send so (out) on an errand

out separate sth out of sth
out serve sth out
out set out (for some place) (from some place)
out set out on one's own
out set out (on sth)
out set out to do sth
out set sth out (for so/sth)
out settle (sth) (out of court)
out shagged out
out shake sth out
out shake the lead out
out Shape up or ship out.
out shell out (an amount of money)
out shoot sth out
out show so out (of sth)
out shut so/sth out
out sift sth out of sth
out sign out
out sign so out of some place
out sign sth out of some place
out sing one's heart out
out sing out
out sing sth out
out single so/sth out (for sth)
out sit out
out sit sth out
out sketch sth out
out skip (out)
out skip out (on so/sth)
out skip out with sth
out slash (out) at so
out sleep out
out slide out of sth
out slide sth out of sth
out sling sth out
out slink out (of some place)
out slip out
out slop out (of sth)
out slug it out
out sluice sth out
out smash out of sth
out smell so/sth or an animal out
out smoke so/sth or an animal out of sth
out smooth sth out
out smuggle so/sth out of some place
out snap out of sth
out snap sth out of sth
out snarl sth out
out snatch so out of the jaws of death
out snatch sth out of sth
out sneak out (of some place)
out sniff so/sth out
out snuff so out
out snuff sth out
out soak sth out of sth
out sob one's heart out
out sob sth out
out sold out
out sort oneself out
out sort sth out
out sound so out
out sound sth out
out space out
out space so out
out spaced (out)
out spaz out
out speak out
out spear sth out (of sth)
out spell sth out
out spend money like it's going out of style
out spew one's guts (out)

out spew sth out
out spiffed out
out spill (out) into sth
out spill out (of sth)
out spin out
out spin sth out
out spit sth out
out splay out
out spoon sth out
out spout sth out
out sprawl out
out spread out
out spread sth out
out spring out at so
out spring out of sth
out spurt out (of so/sth)
out spurt sth out
out sputter out
out sputter sth out
out squeeze sth out of sth
out squiff out
out squint out of sth
out squirm out (of sth)
out squirt out (of so/sth)
out squirt sth out of sth
out stagger out (of some place)
out stake out a claim to sth
out stake so/sth out
out stalk out of some place
out stammer sth out
out stamp a fire out
out stamp so out
out stamp sth out
out stampede out of some place
out stand out (against so/sth)
out stand out (from so/sth)
out stand out (from sth)
out stand there with one's bare face hanging out
out stare out at so/sth
out start an all-out effort
out start out
out start so out (as sth)
out start so out at an amount of money
out startle so out of sth
out starve so or an animal out of some place
out Stay out of my way.
out stay out of sight
out stay out (of sth)
out Stay out of this!
out steal out of some place
out steam out (of some place)
out steam sth out of sth
out step out into sth
out step out of line
out step out (of sth)
out step out (on so)
out stick one's neck out (for so/sth)
out stick one's tongue out
out stick out
out stick sth out
out stoked out
out storm out (of some place)
out straight out
out straighten out
out straighten so out
out straighten sth out
out stretch out
out stretch so/sth out
out stretch sth out (to so/sth)
out stride out of some place
out strike out
out strike sth out

out string sth out
out strung out
out strut out of some place
out stub sth out
out surge out (of sth)
out suss so out
out swab sth out
out swarm out of sth
out swear sth out against so
out sweat sth out
out sweep out of some place
out sweep so/sth out of sth
out sweep sth out
out swell out
out swindle so out of sth
out switch sth out
out tag so out
out take a leaf out of so's book
out take a lot out of so
out take it out on so/sth
out take out a loan
out take out (after so/sth)
out take so/sth out of sth
out take so out
out take sth out
out take the coward's way out
out take the easy way out
out take the starch out of so
out take the stuffing out of so
out take the wind out of so's **sails**
out take the words out of so's mouth
out take time out
out talk one's way out of sth
out talk oneself out
out talk so out of doing sth
out talk so out of sth
out talk sth out
out talked out
out tap out
out tap sth out
out tear one's **hair** (out)
out tear out (of some place)
out tear sth out of sth
out tease sth out
out tell tales out of school
out terrify so or an animal out of sth
out test out (of sth)
out test sth out
out thaw out
out thaw so/sth out
out thin out
out thin sth out
out Things will work out (all right).
out think out loud
out think sth out
out thrash sth out
out Three strikes and you are out.
out throng out (of sth)
out throw one out on one's ear
out throw so/sth out of sth
out throw so out of sth
out throw the baby out with the bath(water)
out thrust out
out thump sth out (on the piano)
out thunder sth out
out Time (out)!
out time out
out time so out
out tire out
out tire so out
out toss so/sth out of sth
out tough sth out

out tow so/sth out (of some place)
out tow so/sth out (to sth)
out trample sth out
out trick so out of sth
out trickle out (of sth)
out trot so/sth out
out trot sth out
out truth will out.
out try one's **wings** (out)
out try out (for sth)
out try so/sth out
out try sth out on so
out tucker so out
out tumble out of sth
out tune out
out tune so/sth out
out Turn on, tune in, drop out.
out turn out
out turn some place inside out
out turn so or an animal out of sth
out turn so/sth inside out
out turn so out
out turn sth out
out twist sth out of sth
out type sth out
out usher so/sth out of some place
out vacuum sth out
out veg out
out vegged out
out venture out ((of) sth)
out vomit sth out
out vote so out of sth
out wait sth out
out walk out (of sth)
out walk out (on so)
out walk out (on sth)
out walk out with so
out walk so out
out wangle out of sth
out want out (of sth)
out want so/sth out of sth
out wash out
out wash so out
out wash sth out
out washed out
out watch out for so
out way out
out wear out
out wear so out
out wear sth out
out weasel out (of sth)
out weave in and out (of sth)
out weed so/sth out
out week in, week out
out weigh sth out
out weird out
out weirded out
out well out (of sth)
out well up (out of sth)
out whacked (out)
out whale the tar out of so
out wheel so/sth out of sth
out wheeze sth out
out When poverty comes in at the door, love flies out of the window.
out When the wolf comes in at the door, love creeps out of the window.
out whine sth out
out whip sth out
out whittle sth out of sth
out wig out
out wiggle out of sth
out wimp out (of sth)

out win (out) (over so/sth)
out wipe out
out wipe so out
out wipe sth out
out work itself out
out work out
out work sth out of sth
out work sth out (with so)
out work things out
out worm (one's **way**) out (of sth)
out worm sth out of so
out worry an animal out of sth
out worry sth out of so
out wrench sth out of sth
out wriggle out (of sth)
out wring sth out
out write sth out
out X so/sth out
out X'd out
out yank so/sth out of sth
out year in, year out
out yell one's guts out
out yell out
out yell sth out (at so/sth)
out You been keeping out of trouble?
out You cannot make a silk purse out of a sow's ear.
out You scared the crap out of me.
out You scared the devil out of me.
out You scared the hell out of me.
out (You) took the words right out of my mouth.
out You're out of your mind!
out You've got to be out of your mind!
out zeek out
out zerked (out)
out zonk out
out zonk so out
out zonked (out)
out zoom out
out zounked (out)
outdoor big as all outdoors
outhouse built like a brick outhouse
outright killed outright
outset at the outset
outset from the outset
outside at the (very) outside
outside (Do) you want to step outside?
outside fall outside sth
outside outside of sth
outside stand outside ((of) sth)
outside step outside
outside think outside the box
outside well out(side) of sth
oven have one in the oven
over agonize (oneself) over so/sth
over all over
over (all) over again
over arch (oneself) over
over arch over so/sth
over arch sth over so/sth
over argue (with so) (over so/sth)
over ask so over
over back over so/sth
over bargain (over so/sth) (with so)
over battle (with so) (over so/sth)
over be given precedence over so/sth
over bend over
over bind so over (to so/sth)
over blow over
over blow so/sth over
over blow so over

over boil over
over bowl so over
over break over sth
over bridge over sth
over brim over (with sth)
over bring so over from some place
over bring so over ((to) some place)
over bring so over to sth
over browse over sth
over brush over so/sth
over bubble over
over build (sth) out over sth
over build (sth) over sth
over call so over (to some place)
over carry over
over carry so/sth over from sth
over carry so/sth over to sth
over carry sth over
over change over (from so/sth) (to so/sth)
over check so/sth over
over chew sth over
over chuck sth over sth
over circle around (over so/sth)
over clash (with so) (over so/sth)
over cloud over
over come over
over come to blows (over so/sth)
over control over so/sth
over crawl over sth
over creep over so/sth
over cross over
over crow over sth
over cry over so/sth
over cry over spilled milk
over dally over sth
over dash over (for sth)
over dawdle over sth
over deed sth (over) to so
over deliberate over so/sth
over distribute sth over sth
over do so over
over do sth over
over done over
over Don't cry over spilled milk.
over double over
over double so over
over double sth over
over drag one's feet (on or over sth)
over drag so/sth over to so/sth
over drape oneself over sth
over drape over (sth)
over draw sth over so/sth
over drive over (to some place)
over drool (all) over so/sth
over drop over
over dub sth over
over edge over so
over exercise control over so/sth
over exercise power over so/sth
over extend over so/sth
over exult over sth
over fall (all) over oneself (to do sth)
over fall all over so
over fall head over heels
over fall out (with so) (over sth)
over fall over
over fawn (all) over so
over feel like death warmed over
over feud (with so) (over so/sth)
over fight over so/sth
over fight (with) so or some creature (over so/sth)
over film over

over fire over sth
over fix sth over
over flip over
over flip so/sth over
over flop so/sth over
over flow over so/sth
over flutter over so/sth
over fly over so/sth
over fog over
over fold sth over
over fork sth over (to so)
over freak out (over so/sth)
over freeze over
over fret over so/sth
over frost over
over frosted (over)
over fuss over so/sth
over gain dominion over so/sth
over Get over it!
over get over so/sth
over get over sth
over get over (to some place)
over get sth over (to so)
over Get your ass over here!
over Get your buns over here!
over give oneself over to so/sth
over give sth over (to so/sth)
over glance over so/sth
over glaze over
over gloat over sth
over gloss over sth
over go ape (over so/sth)
over go over
over go to war (over so/sth)
over (good) working over
over grieve over so/sth
over grow over sth
over gush over so/sth
over haggle (with so) over so/sth
over Hand it over.
over hand over fist
over hand over hand
over hand so/sth over (to so/sth)
over hand sth over
over hang over so/sth
over hang over so('s head)
over hang sth over so/sth
over hash sth over (with so)
over haul so/sth over to so
over haul so over the coals
over have a (good) working over
over have it (all) over so/sth (in sth)
over have so over a barrel
over have so over (for sth)
over have sth hanging over one's head
over have words with so (over so/sth)
over head over heels in debt
over head over heels in love (with so)
over heal over
over help so or an animal (get) over sth
over hesitate over sth
over hold so/sth over
over hold sth over so('s head)
over honeymoon is over.
over hover over so/sth
over hunch over
over hush fell over so/sth
over I can't get over sth!
over ice over
over in over one's head (with so/sth)
over inch over
over invite so over (for sth)

over It is all over with so.
over It's all over but the shouting.
over It's no use crying over spilled milk.
over It's not over till it's over.
over It's written all over one's face.
over jerk so over
over jump all over so
over jump off the deep end (over so/sth)
over jump over sth
over jump over the broomstick
over jut out (over so/sth)
over keel over
over keel sth over
over keep (close) watch (over so/sth)
over keep watch over so/sth
over kick over
over knock one over
over knock over sth
over knock so/sth over
over knock so over (with a feather)
over knock sth over
over labor over so/sth
over lament over so/sth
over languish over so/sth
over lap over (sth)
over lay over (some place)
over lay sth over so/sth
over lean over
over leap over sth
over like death warmed over
over linger over sth
over live over so/sth
over live sth over
over loiter over sth
over look like death warmed over
over look so/sth over
over looking over one's shoulder
over lord it over so
over lose one's head (over so/sth)
over lose sleep over so/sth
over make a check over to so/sth
over make a fuss (over so/sth)
over make so over
over make sth over
over mess so over
over mind over matter
over mist over
over move over
over move so/sth over
over mull sth over
over muse over so/sth
over My cup runneth over.
over negotiate (with so/sth) (over so/sth)
over niggle (over sth) (with so)
over noodle over sth
over once-over
over once-over-lightly
over over a barrel
over over and above sth
over over (and done) with
over Over and out.
over over and over (again)
over over easy
over Over my dead body!
over over so's head
over over the counter
over over the edge
over over the hill
over over the hump
over over the long haul
over over the short haul

over over the top
over over the wall
over over (with)
over paint over sth
over pan over so/sth
over paper over sth
over paper over sth
over paper over the cracks (in sth)
over part over sth
over party's over.
over pass over (so/sth)
over pass over so's head
over pass sth over (to so)
over peek over sth
over peep over sth
over peer over sth
over pick sth over
over picked over
over pine over so/sth
over pitch so/sth over sth
over plank over sth
over plaster over sth
over play sth over
over poise over so/sth
over pop over (for a visit)
over pore over sth
over pour (all) over so/sth
over pour sth over so/sth
over pray over sth
over precedence over so/sth
over preside over sth
over pull one over on so
over pull over (to sth)
over pull so/sth over (to sth)
over pull sth down over so/sth
over pull sth over so/sth
over pull the wool over so's eyes
over push so/sth over
over put one in over one's head
over put one over on so
over put so/sth over
over put so over a barrel
over put sth over
over puzzle over so/sth
over quarrel (with so) (over so/sth)
over quit over so/sth
over rage over so/sth
over rake so over the coals
over range over sth
over rave over so/sth
over read sth over
over reign over so/sth
over rejoice over sth
over relinquish sth over so
over remand so over to so
over retain sth over so/sth
over rhapsodize over so/sth
over ride over so/sth
over ride roughshod over so/sth
over roll over
over roll (over) in one's grave
over roll so/sth over
over roll sth over
over romp all over so
over roof sth over
over rub sth over sth
over rule over so/sth
over run back over sth
over run one's eye over sth
over run over
over run roughshod over so/sth
over run sth over to so/sth
over say sth over (and over (again))
over scab over

over scar over
over scoot over
over screw so over
over see over sth
over send so over (to) some place
over send sth over ((to) some place)
over set sth over sth
over sign sth over (to so)
over skate over sth
over skim over sth
over skip over so/sth
over slave over sth
over sled over sth
over sleep over (with so) (some place)
over slide over sth
over slip one over on so/sth
over slip something over on so/sth
over slip sth over sth
over slobber (all) over so/sth
over slobber over so/sth
over slobber over sth
over slop over
over slop sth over sth
over slosh over
over slosh sth (all) over so/sth
over slouch over
over slump over
over slur over sth
over sorrow over so/sth
over spill over
over spill (over) into sth
over splash over
over splash sth (all) over so/sth
over spread all over (some place)
over spread over so/sth
over spread sth over so/sth
over squabble over so/sth
over stand over so/sth
over start over
over start (over) with a clean slate
over start so over
over stay over (somewhere)
over steal over so/sth
over step over so/sth
over step over (to) some place
over stoop over
over stop over (some place)
over strew sth (all) over sth
over strew sth over so/sth
over strike over sth
over stumble over so/sth
over swarm (all) over so/sth
over sweep over so
over switch over (to so/sth)
over switch so/sth over to sth
over switch sth over (to sth)
over swoon over so/sth
over take over (from so)
over take pains over sth
over take precedence over so/sth
over take so/sth over
over take sth over
over talk over so's head
over talk over sth
over talk so/sth over (with so)
over talk sth over
over tangle with so/sth (over so/sth)
over think sth over
over throw so/sth over so/sth
over throw so over
over tide so over (until sth)
over till hell freezes over
over tip over

over tip so over
over tip sth over
over toil over so/sth
over topple over
over tower over so/sth
over trace over sth
over track sth (all) over sth
over trail over sth
over traipse over
over travel over sth
over triumph over so/sth
over tumble over
over turn over
over turn (over) in one's grave
over turn so/sth over
over turn sth over in one's mind
over type over sth
over until hell freezes over
over use sth over (again)
over vault over so/sth
over walk all over so/sth
over walk over (to so/sth)
over walk so over to so/sth
over war over so/sth
over warm sth over
over warmed over
over wash over so
over watch over so/sth
over water over the dam
over (way) over there
over weep over so/sth
over well over
over What the eye doesn't see, the heart doesn't grieve over.
over whip sth over (to so)
over win (out) (over so/sth)
over win so over (to sth)
over winter over (some place)
over work so/sth over
over work so over
over work sth down (over sth)
over work sth over
over worked up (over sth)
over worry over so/sth
over wrangle (with so) (over so/sth)
over yield so/sth (over) (to so/sth)
over You could have knocked me over with a feather.
over zoom over so/sth
over zoom so/sth (over) to so
overboard fall overboard
overboard go overboard
overboard wash overboard
overboard wash so/sth overboard
overdose overdose (so) on sth
overflow overflow into sth
overflow overflow with so/sth
overseas from overseas
overture make overtures about doing sth
owe I owe you one.
owe owe so a debt of gratitude
owe owe so a pound of flesh
owe owe sth (to so) (for sth)
owe owing to
owe *pound of flesh
owl I wasn't brought up in the woods to be scared by owls.
owl night owl
owl wise as an owl
own according to one's own lights
own afraid of one's own shadow
own be one's own man
own be one's own master

own blow one's own horn
own can't call one's soul one's own
own carry one's (own) weight
own chew one's own tobacco
own come into one's or its own
own cut one's (own) throat
own devil can cite Scripture for his own purpose.
own devil can quote Scripture for his own purpose.
own devil looks after his own.
own devil's own job
own devil's own time
own die by one's own hand
own dig one's own grave
own do one's (own) thing
own dose of one's own medicine
own Every horse thinks its own pack heaviest.
own Every man is the architect of his own fortune.
own Every tub must stand on its own bottom.
own feather one's (own) nest
own find one's own level
own for one's (own) part
own for one's (own) sake
own foul one's own nest
own have a mind of one's own
own have calluses from patting one's own back
own hoe one's own row
own hoist with one's own petard
own hold one's own
own I'll thank you to mind your own business.
own (I'm just) minding my own business.
own in a world of one's own
own in one's (own) backyard
own in one's (own) (best) interest(s)
own in one's own way
own It is a wise child that knows its own father.
own It's an ill bird that fouls its own nest.
own judge one on one's own merits
own judge sth on its own merits
own keep one's own counsel
own leave one to one's own devices
own leave one to one's own resources
own legend in one's own (life)time
own Let every man skin his own skunk.
own Let every tub stand on its own bottom.
own line one's own pocket(s)
own live in a world of one's own
own live on one's own
own make one's (own) bed
own man after my own heart
own Men are blind in their own cause.
own mind one's own business
own Mind your own beeswax.
own Mind your own business.
own not able to call one's time one's own
own not know one's own strength
own of one's own accord
own on one's own
own one's (own) way
own one's (own) way (with so/sth)
own one's own worst enemy
own own flesh and blood

own own up to so
own own up (to sth)
own paddle one's own canoe
own pay one's own way
own pick on somebody your own size
own pick on someone your own size
own place to call one's own
own prophet is not without honor save in his own country.
own pull one's (own) weight
own pull oneself up by one's (own) bootstraps
own put one's own house in order
own set one's (own) price
own set out on one's own
own sign one's own death warrant
own stand on one's (own) two feet
own stew in one's own juice
own strike out on one's own
own take one's own life
own take the law into one's own hands
own talk to hear one's own voice
own taste of one's own medicine
own tell its own story
own tell its own tale
own think so is God's own cousin
own To each his own.
own toot one's own horn
own under one's own steam
own Virtue is its own reward.
ox strong as an ox
oyster world is one's oyster.
P mind one's p's and q's
pace at a snail's pace
pace change of pace
pace It is the pace that kills.
pace keep pace (with so/sth)
pace pace around
pace pace back and forth
pace pace sth off
pace pace sth out
pace pace up and down
pace pick up the pace
pace put one through one's paces
pace put sth through its paces
pack Every horse thinks its own pack heaviest.
pack pack a punch
pack pack a wallop
pack pack down
pack pack it in
pack pack of lies
pack pack so off (to so/sth)
pack pack so/sth in
pack pack so/sth (in) like sardines
pack pack so/sth into sth
pack pack so/sth together
pack pack sth away
pack pack sth down
pack pack sth in sth
pack pack sth off (to so/sth)
pack pack sth up (in sth)
pack pack them in
pack pack up
pack send so packing
package best things come in small packages.
package Good things come in small packages.
package package deal
packet cop a packet
pad pad down (some place)
pad pad out

pad pad sth out
pad pad the bill
paddle paddle one's own canoe
paddle up the creek (without a paddle)
page read from the same page
page take a page from so's book
paid put paid to sth
pain double up (with pain)
pain feeling no pain
pain Genius is an infinite capacity for taking pains.
pain give so a pain
pain have growing pains
pain No pain, no gain.
pain pain in the ass
pain pain in the neck
pain pain in the rear
pain racked with pain
pain royal pain
pain share so's pain
pain take (great) pains (to do sth)
pain take pains over sth
pain take pains with so/sth
pain There is no pleasure without pain.
paint about as exciting as watching (the) paint dry
paint black as one is painted
paint close as two coats of paint
paint devil is not so black as he is painted.
paint Do I have to paint (you) a picture?
paint Do I need to paint you a picture?
paint exciting as watching (the) paint dry
paint paint on sth
paint paint over sth
paint paint sth in
paint paint sth onto sth
paint paint sth out
paint paint the town (red)
pair another pair of eyes
pair candidate for a pair of wings
pair fresh pair of eyes
pair look like a candidate for a pair of wings
pair pair off
pair pair up (with so)
pal bosom pal
pal pal around (with so)
pal pal up (with so)
pal pally (with so)
pal Put 'er there(, pal).
pale beyond the pale
pale pale around the gills
pale pale as a ghost
pale pale as death
pale pale at sth
pale pale beside so/sth
pale pale by comparison
pally pally (with so)
palm cross so's palm with silver
palm grease so's palm
palm itching palm
palm itchy palm
palm know so/sth like the palm of one's hand
palm oil so's palm
palm palm so/sth off (on so) (as so/sth)
pan flash in the pan
pan go out of the frying pan into the fire

pan If ifs and ands were pots and pans (there'd be no work for tinkers' hands).
pan jump out of the frying pan into the fire
pan out of the frying pan (and) into the fire
pan pan across to so/sth
pan pan for sth
pan pan in (on so/sth)
pan pan out
pan pan over so/sth
pancake flat as a pancake
pander pander to so/sth
Pandora open Pandora's box
panic hit the panic button
panic panic at sth
panic panic so by sth
panic press the panic button
panic push the panic button
pant ants in one's pants
pant beat the pants off (of) so
pant bore the pants off of so
pant by the seat of one's pants
pant catch one with one's pants down
pant charm the pants off so
pant dust so's pants
pant fly by the seat of one's pants
pant frighten the pants off so
pant He puts his pants on one leg at a time.
pant keep one's pants on
pant Keep your pants on!
pant kick in the (seat of the) pants
pant make it by the seat of one's pants
pant pant for air
pant pant for so/sth
pant pant sth out
pant scare the pants off (of) so
pant sue the pants off (of) so
pant wear the pants (in the family)
paper can't carry a tune in a paper sack
paper get sth down (on paper)
paper leave a paper trail
paper look good on paper
paper make a paper trail
paper not worth the paper it's printed on
paper not worth the paper it's written on
paper one's walking papers
paper paper over sth
paper paper over the cracks (in sth)
paper paper trail
paper put sth on paper
paperhanger busy as a one-armed paperhanger
par above par
par below par
par on par (with so/sth)
par par for the course
par up to par
parade parade by (so)
parade parade so or an animal out
parade parade so/sth in front of so/sth
parade rain on so's parade
paradise fool's paradise
paradise paradise (on earth)
parcel parcel so/sth out
parcel parcel sth up
parcel part and parcel
pardon (I) beg your pardon, but...

pardon if you'll pardon the expression
pardon Never ask pardon before you are accused.
pardon Pardon (me).
pardon Pardon me for living!
pardon Pardon my French.
pardon pardon so for sth
pare pare sth down (to sth)
pare pare sth off (of) sth
park ballpark figure
park in park
park in the ballpark
park out of the ballpark
park park it (somewhere)
parlay parlay sth into sth
parley parley with so
parole (out) on parole
parry thrust and parry
parsnip Fine words butter no parsnips.
part best part of sth
part Discretion is the better part of valor.
part do one's part
part (Even) the best of friends must part.
part fool and his money are soon parted.
part for one's (own) part
part for the most part
part in part
part in these parts
part in those parts
part part and parcel
part part company (with so)
part part from so
part part in sth
part part over sth
part part or an animal from so or an animal
part part so's hair
part part so's part
part part with so/sth
part parting of the ways
part play a big part (in sth)
part play a bit part
part play a large part (in sth)
part play a part in sth
part take part (in sth)
part take so's part
partake partake in sth
partake partake of sth
partial partial to so/sth
partial partially sighted
partially partially sighted
participate participate (in sth) (with so/sth)
particular ain't particular
particular in particular
particular particulars of sth
partition partition sth into sth
partition partition sth off
partner partners in crime
party certain party
party life of the party
party party line
party party's over.
party party to sth
party responsible party
party throw a party (for so)
pass All things must pass.
pass All things will pass.
pass come to a pretty pass
pass come to pass
pass cut so off at the pass
pass head so off at the pass

pass in passing
pass just passing through
pass let so pass by
pass let sth pass
pass make a pass at so
pass make a pass at sth
pass mention so/sth in passing
pass *over so's head
pass pass as so/sth
pass pass away
pass pass by (so/sth)
pass pass for so/sth
pass pass for sth
pass pass from sth
pass pass gas
pass pass in review
pass pass into sth
pass pass judgment (on so/sth)
pass pass muster
pass pass on
pass pass out
pass pass over (so/sth)
pass pass over so's head
pass pass sentence on so
pass pass so on (to so)
pass pass so/sth by
pass pass so/sth off (on so) (as so/sth)
pass pass so/sth up
pass pass sth along (to so)
pass pass sth around (to so)
pass pass sth back (to so)
pass pass sth down (to so)
pass pass sth forward
pass pass sth in (to so)
pass pass sth off
pass pass sth on
pass pass sth out (to so)
pass pass sth over (to so)
pass pass sth to so
pass pass the buck
pass pass the hat (around) (to so)
pass pass the time (of day)
pass pass the time of day (with so)
pass pass through so
pass pass through so's mind
pass pass through sth
pass pass under sth
pass ships that pass in the night
pass with each passing day
passion have a passion for so/sth
passport passport to sth
past age of miracles is past.
past brush past so/sth
past file past (so/sth)
past fly past (so/sth)
past get past (so/sth)
past get sth past (so/sth)
past go past so/sth
past go past sth
past in times past
past let so (get) past
past live in the past
past march past so/sth
past mill cannot grind with water that is past.
past not put it past so
past past caring
past past master at sth
past past so's or sth's prime
past push past (so/sth)
past slip past so/sth
past slip so/sth past so/sth
past smuggle so/sth past (so/sth)

past thunder past so/sth
past whiz past so/sth
past word (once) spoken is past recalling.
past zip past so/sth
past zoom past so/sth
paste cow paste
paste cut and paste
paste paste so one
paste paste sth down
paste paste sth on so
paste paste sth up
pastime He that would go to sea for pleasure, would go to hell for a pastime.
pasture put a horse out to pasture
pasture put so out to pasture
pat break one's arm patting oneself on the back
pat down pat
pat give so a pat on the back
pat have calluses from patting one's own back
pat pat answer
pat pat so on the back
pat pat so/sth on sth
pat pat sth down
pat stand pat (on sth)
patch patch a quarrel up
patch patch so up
patch patch sth together (with sth)
patch patch sth up
path beat a path to so's door
path cross paths (with so)
path lead so down the garden path
path lead so up the garden path
path off the beaten path
path path of least resistance
path primrose path
path travel off the beaten path
patience have the patience of a saint
patience have the patience of Job
patience lose patience (with so/sth)
patience out of patience
patience Patience is a virtue.
patience run out of patience
patience try so's patience
patient patient as Job
patrol (out) on patrol
patter patter of tiny feet
pattern pattern sth after sth
pattern pattern sth on sth
patty cow patty
Paul rob Peter to pay Paul
paunch air one's paunch
pause give so pause (for thought)
pave pave the way (for so/sth) (with sth)
pave road to hell is paved with good intentions.
pavement hit the pavement
pavement pound the pavement
pawn pawn so/sth off (on so) (as so/sth)
pay Crime doesn't pay.
pay have hell to pay
pay have the devil to pay
pay He who pays the piper calls the tune.
pay hit pay dirt
pay *king's ransom
pay pay a call
pay pay a king's ransom
pay pay a visit to so/sth
pay pay an arm and a leg (for sth)

pay pay as you go
pay pay attention (to so/sth)
pay pay by sth
pay pay court to so
pay pay for sth
pay pay heed to so
pay pay homage to so/sth
pay pay in advance
pay pay into sth
pay pay lip service (to sth)
pay pay off
pay pay on sth
pay pay one's debt (to society)
pay pay one's dues
pay pay one's last respects (to so)
pay pay one's own way
pay pay so a backhanded compliment
pay pay so a compliment
pay pay so a left-handed compliment
pay pay so a pound of flesh
pay pay so back
pay pay so (for sth) (with sth)
pay pay so off
pay pay (so/sth) a visit
pay pay so respect
pay pay so's way
pay pay sth back (to so)
pay pay sth down
pay pay sth into sth
pay pay sth off
pay pay sth out
pay pay sth up
pay pay the penalty
pay pay the piper
pay pay the price
pay pay through sth
pay pay through the nose (for sth)
pay pay to do sth
pay pay tribute to so/sth
pay pay up
pay *pound of flesh
pay price one has to pay
pay put paid to sth
pay rob Peter to pay Paul
pay There will be hell to pay.
pay There will be the devil to pay.
pay You get what you pay for.
pay You pays your money and you takes your chance(s).
pea alike as (two) peas in a pod
pea like (two) peas in a pod
pea thick as pea soup
peace at peace
peace hold one's peace
peace If you want peace, (you must) prepare for war.
peace leave so in peace
peace make (one's) peace with so
peace peace of mind
peace rest in peace
peach crazy as a peach-orchard boar
peach cut your peaches
peacock proud as a peacock
peacock vain as a peacock
peal peal out
peanut for peanuts
pearl cast (one's) pearls before swine
peck bushel and a peck (and some in a gourd)
peck If that don't beat a pig a-pecking!
peck peck at sth
peck peck sth up

peck You have to eat a peck of dirt before you die.
peculiar funny peculiar
pedal put the pedal to the metal
pedal soft-pedal sth
peddler busy as a fish peddler in Lent
pedestal on a pedestal
pedestal place so on a pedestal
pedestal put so on a pedestal
peek peek at so/sth
peek peek in (on so/sth)
peek peek in(to sth)
peek peek out (from behind so/sth)
peek peek out (from underneath so/sth)
peek peek out of sth (at so/sth)
peek peek over sth
peek peek through (sth)
peek peek under sth
peel keep one's eyes peeled (for so/sth)
peel peel off (from sth)
peel peel off ((of) sth)
peel peel out
peel peel sth away (from sth)
peel peel sth back (from sth)
peel peel sth off ((of) sth)
peep hear a peep out of so
peep peep
peep peep at so/sth
peep peep in(to sth)
peep peep out (of sth) (at so/sth)
peep peep over sth
peep peep through sth
peep peep under sth
peer peer about
peer peer at so/sth
peer peer in(to sth)
peer peer out at so/sth
peer peer over sth
peer peer through sth
peer peer under sth
peeve pet peeve
peg have so pegged as sth
peg knock so down a peg (or two)
peg peg away (at sth)
peg peg out
peg peg so as sth
peg peg sth down
peg square peg in a round hole
peg take so down a peg (or two)
pelt pelt down (on so/sth)
pelt pelt so/sth with sth
pen go into the bull pen
pen in the bull pen
pen pen is mightier than the sword.
pen pen so or an animal in (some place)
pen pen so or an animal up
penalize penalize so for sth
penalty pay the penalty
penchant have a penchant for doing sth
pencil in pencil
pencil pencil so/sth in
penetrate penetrate into so/sth
penetrate penetrate sth with sth
penetrate penetrate through sth
penny bad penny
penny cost a pretty penny
penny cut so off without a penny
penny I felt like a penny waiting for change.
penny penny for your thoughts!
penny penny saved is a penny earned.
penny penny-wise and pound-foolish
pension pension so off

people all things to all people
people Idle people have the least leisure.
people people sth with so
people People who live in glass houses shouldn't throw stones.
people Some people (just) don't know when to quit.
people split people up
people Times change(, people change).
pep pep so/sth up
pepper pepper so/sth with sth
perceive perceive so/sth as sth
percent Genius is ten percent inspiration and ninety percent perspiration.
perch perch on sth
perch perch so/sth on sth
percolate percolate through sth
perfect cook sth to perfection
perfect perfect stranger
perfect picture perfect
perfect Practice makes perfect.
perfection cook sth to perfection
perfectly Do I make myself (perfectly) clear?
perform *old warhorse
perform perform an old warhorse
perform perform sth on so/sth
perhaps Perhaps a little later.
perish perish from sth
perish perish in sth
perish Perish the thought.
perish perish with sth
perish publish or perish
perk perk so up
perk perk sth up
perk perk up
permeate permeate sth with sth
permeate permeate through sth
permit Permit me.
permit permit so into sth
permit permit so out (of sth)
permit permit so through (sth)
permit permit so up (sth)
permit permit so up to sth
permit weather permitting
perpetual contented mind is a perpetual feast.
perpetuity in perpetuity
persecute persecute so for sth
persevere persevere at sth
persevere persevere in sth
persevere persevere with sth
persist persist in doing sth
persist persist with sth
person be the last person (to do sth)
person day person
person feel like a new person
person flit from person to person
person have sth on one('s person)
person in person
person night person
person on one's person
person person of color
person seem like the last person
person shuttle so/sth from person to person
personally take sth personally
perspective from my perspective
perspective in perspective
perspective perspective on sth

perspective put sth into perspective
perspiration Genius is ten percent inspiration and ninety percent perspiration.
persuade persuade so of sth
persuade persuade so to do sth
persuasion of the persuasion that...
pertain pertain to so/sth
pester pester so about so/sth
pester pester so into sth
pester pester so out of sth
pester pester so with sth
pester pester the life out of so
pet pet hate
pet pet peeve
pet teacher's pet
petard hoist with one's own petard
Pete For Pete's sake!
Pete Honest to Pete.
peter peter out
Peter rob Peter to pay Paul
petition petition so/sth for sth
phase phase so/sth into sth
phase phase so/sth out of sth
phone get on the phone
phone Hold the phone.
phone on the phone
phone phone in (to so/sth)
phone phone so up
phone phone sth in (to so/sth)
phone Who's on the phone?
phony phony as a three-dollar bill
photo photo op(portunity)
phrase coin a phrase
physical physical (with so)
physician Physician, heal thyself.
piano thump sth out (on the piano)
pick cherry-pick sth
pick close enough to use the same toothpick
pick easy pickings
pick have a bone to pick (with so)
pick need a pick-me-up
pick pick a fight (with so)
pick pick a lock
pick pick a quarrel (with so)
pick pick and choose
pick pick at so/sth
pick pick at sth
pick pick holes in sth
pick pick of sth
pick pick on somebody your own size
pick pick on so/sth
pick pick on someone your own size
pick pick one's way through sth
pick pick so/sth apart
pick pick so/sth from so/sth
pick pick so/sth off
pick pick so/sth out
pick pick so/sth to pieces
pick pick so's brain(s)
pick pick so up
pick pick sth away
pick pick sth over
pick pick sth to pieces
pick pick sth up
pick pick up
pick picked over
pick take one's pick of so/sth
pick want a pick-me-up
pickle in a (pretty) pickle
pickle pretty pickle
picnic It's no picnic!

picnic one sandwich short of a picnic
picture big picture
picture Do I have to paint (you) a picture?
picture Do I need to paint you a picture?
picture (Do you) get the picture?
picture Get the picture?
picture in the picture
picture keep so in the picture
picture know the big picture
picture out of the picture
picture picture is worth a thousand words.
picture picture of (good) health
picture picture perfect
picture picture so as sth
picture picture so in sth
picture pretty as a picture
picture put so in the picture
picture see the big picture
picture show so the big picture
picture (very) picture of sth
piddle piddle around
piddle piddle sth away
pie American as apple pie
pie cow pie
pie cut the pie up
pie easy as (apple) pie
pie eat humble pie
pie have a finger in the pie
pie have one's finger in too many pies
pie in apple-pie order
pie motherhood and apple pie
pie pie in the sky
pie put sth in apple-pie order
piece all in one piece
piece blow so/sth to pieces
piece break sth to pieces
piece dash sth to pieces
piece down the road a piece
piece fall to pieces
piece fur piece
piece give so a piece of one's mind
piece go to pieces
piece pick so/sth to pieces
piece pick sth to pieces
piece pick up the pieces (of sth)
piece piece of cake
piece piece (of the action)
piece piece sth out
piece piece sth together
piece pull so/sth to pieces
piece say one's piece
piece speak one's piece
piece take sth to pieces
piece tear so/sth to pieces
piece that beats sth all to pieces
piece thrill so to pieces
piece thrilled to pieces
piece tickle so to pieces
piece villain of the piece
piece Want a piece of me?
piece (You) want a piece of me?
piecrust Promises are like piecrust, made to be broken.
pier Take a long walk off a short pier.
pierce pierce through sth
pierce piercing scream
pig ain't fittin' to roll with a pig
pig buy a pig in a poke
pig fat as a pig
pig If that don't beat a pig a-pecking!

pig In a pig's ass!
pig In a pig's ear!
pig In a pig's eye!
pig like pigs to the slaughter
pig like stealing acorns from a blind pig
pig make a pig of oneself
pig pig out (on sth)
pig serve as a guinea pig
pigeon stool (pigeon)
pikestaff plain as a pikestaff
pile make a pile
pile pile in(to sth)
pile pile off (sth)
pile pile on((to) so/sth)
pile pile out (of sth)
pile pile so into sth
pile pile so/sth on(to) so/sth
pile pile sth up
pile pile the work on (so)
pile pile up
pilfer pilfer from so/sth
pilfer pilfer sth from so/sth
pill bitter pill to swallow
pill on the pill
pillar from pillar to post
pillar pillar of strength
pillar pillar of support
pillar send so from pillar to post
pills more sth than Carter has (liver) pills
pilot pilot so/sth through (sth)
pilot pilot sth into sth
pilot pilot sth out of sth
pimple break out (in pimples)
pimple goose pimples
pin bright as a new pin
pin get one's ears pinned back
pin neat as a pin
pin on pins and needles
pin pin one's faith on so/sth
pin pin one's hopes on so/sth
pin pin so down (on sth)
pin pin so/sth against sth
pin pin so/sth beneath so/sth or an animal
pin pin so/sth under so/sth
pin pin so's ears back
pin pin sth back
pin pin sth down
pin pin sth on so
pin pin sth (on)to sth
pin pin sth up
pin pins and needles
pin so quiet you could hear a pin drop
pin so still you could hear a pin drop
pinch feel pinched
pinch feel the pinch
pinch in a pinch
pinch pinch and scrape
pinch pinch so for sth
pinch pinch sth back
pinch pinch sth from so/sth
pinch pinch sth off
pinch pinch-hit for so
pinch take sth with a pinch of salt
pine pine after so/sth
pine pine away (after so/sth)
pine pine for so/sth
pine pine over so/sth
pink in the pink (of condition)
pink in the pink (of health)
pink seeing pink elephants
pink seeing pink spiders
pink tickle so pink

pink tickled pink
pint You cannot get a quart into a pint pot.
pip pipped (up)
pipe lead-pipe cinch
pipe pipe down
pipe pipe dream
pipe pipe sth away
pipe pipe sth from some place (to some place)
pipe pipe sth into some place
pipe pipe up (with sth)
pipe piping hot
pipe Put that in your pipe and smoke it!
pipe set of pipes
pipeline in the pipeline
piper He who pays the piper calls the tune.
piper pay the piper
pique in a pique
pique pique so's curiosity
pique pique so's interest
piss don't have a pot to piss in (or a window to throw it out of)
piss piss so off
piss pissed (off)
pit pit of one's stomach
pit pit one's shoulder to the wheel
pit pit so/sth against so/sth
pitch black as pitch
pitch in there pitching
pitch make a pitch (for so/sth)
pitch pitch a tent
pitch pitch black
pitch pitch camp
pitch pitch dark
pitch pitch forward
pitch pitch in (and help) (with sth)
pitch pitch so a curve(ball)
pitch pitch so/sth out (of) sth
pitch pitch so/sth over sth
pitch pitch sth at so/sth
pitch pitch sth away
pitch pitch sth into sth
pitch pitch sth out
pitch pitch (the) woo
pitcher Little pitchers have big ears.
pitchfork It's raining pitchforks (and hammer handles).
pity For pity's sake!
pity have pity on so or an animal
pity more's the pity
pity take pity (on so or an animal)
pity What a pity!
pivot pivot on sth
place adjourn to some place
place admit so (in)to some place
place allow so/sth into a place
place appear at some place
place arrive (some place) from some other place
place ask so in(to) some place
place banish so/sth from some place
place bar so from some place
place between a rock and a hard place
place bring so/sth in(to) some place
place bring so over from some place
place bust ass out of some place
place bust so out of some place
place bustle about some place
place buzz so into a place
place call at some place
place change places with so

place chase so or an animal in(to) some place
place chase so/sth (away) from some place
place chase so/sth out of some place
place chuck so out of some place
place clap so in(to) some place
place clear so/sth out of some place
place come from some place
place cross from some place to some place
place crowd in(to) some place
place dispatch so from some place
place Don't spend it all in one place.
place draw so/sth out of some place
place eject so from some place
place evict so from some place
place fall in(to) place
place feel out of place
place flush so/sth out of some place
place go places
place haul sth (from some place) to some place
place have a place in sth
place have one's heart in the right place
place hound so from some place
place in place
place in so else's place
place in the first place
place in the right place at the right time
place in the second place
place in the wrong place at the wrong time
place Is there some place I can wash up?
place jumping-off place
place keep one in one's place
place keep one's place
place knock sth out of place
place know one's place
place Let's bump this place!
place Lightning never strikes (the same place) twice.
place migrate between some place and some place else
place Nice place you have here.
place not one's place
place One cannot be in two places at once.
place one's heart is in the right place
place one's last resting place
place order so out of some place
place other place
place out at some place
place out of place
place place a price on one's head
place place a strain on so/sth
place place an order
place place for everything, and everything in its place.
place place of business
place place of concealment
place place one's trust in so/sth
place place so
place place so by so/sth
place place so in an awkward position
place place so on a pedestal
place place so with so/sth
place place sth aside
place place sth at a premium
place place sth back
place place sth down (on sth)
place place sth in sth
place place sth under so/sth
place place sth up against sth

place place sth with so/sth
place place the blame on so/sth (for sth)
place place to call one's own
place pull so into a place
place put one in one's place
place put oneself in so else's place
place put sth into place
place quit a place
place race so to some place
place repatriate so to some place
place rout so/sth out of some place
place run up to some place
place see so to some place
place seem out of place
place send so over (to) some place
place set foot in some place
place set sth in a place
place shoot a place up
place sign so out of some place
place sign sth out of some place
place smuggle so/sth into some place
place smuggle so/sth out of some place
place starve so or an animal out of some place
place stop short of a place
place stranger to sth or some place
place take oneself off some place
place take place
place take sth into some place
place talk of a place
place There is a time and a place for everything.
place There's no place like home.
place ticket so for some place
place track sth into some place
place uproot so from some place
place usher so/sth into some place
place usher so/sth out of some place
place wide place in the road
place woman's place is in the home.
place Your place or mine?
plague avoid so/sth like the plague
plague enough sth to plague a saint
plague plague so/sth with sth
plain in plain English
plain in plain language
plain plain and simple
plain plain as a pikestaff
plain plain as day
plain put sth plainly
plain say sth in plain English
plain say sth in plain language
plain write sth in plain English
plan best-laid plans of mice and men oft(en) go astray.
plan in the way of so('s plans)
plan plan for so
plan plan for sth
plan plan on so
plan plan on sth
plan plan sth out
plan upset so's plans
plane plane sth away
plane plane sth down
plane plane sth off
plank plank over sth
plank thick as a short plank
plank thick as two short planks
plank walk the plank
plant plant sth in sth
plant plant sth on so
plaster plaster one's hair down
plaster plaster over sth
plaster plaster sth onto sth

plaster plaster sth up
plaster plaster sth with sth
plate clean one's plate
plate clean (up) one's plate
plate full plate
plate have too much on one's plate
plate step up to the plate
plateau hit a plateau
platter on a silver platter
platter present sth on a silver platter
platter serve sth on a silver platter
platter want sth on a silver platter
play All work and no play makes Jack a dull boy.
play at play
play bring sth into play
play child's play
play come into play
play foul play
play game that two can play
play Go play in the traffic.
play If you play with fire you get burned.
play in play
play level playing field
play level the (playing) field
play make a play (for so)
play not playing with a full deck
play *old warhorse
play play a big part (in sth)
play play a bit part
play play a joke on so
play play a large part (in sth)
play play a part in sth
play play a prank on so
play play a role in sth
play play a trick on so
play play about (with so/sth)
play play against so/sth
play play along (with so/sth)
play play an old warhorse
play play around (with so/sth)
play play at full blast
play play at sth
play play ball with so
play play both ends (against the middle)
play play by ear
play play by the book
play play cat and mouse with so
play play dead
play play down to so
play play dumb
play play fair
play play fast and loose (with so/sth)
play play first chair
play play footsie with so
play play for keeps
play play for sth
play play for time
play play freeze-out
play play games (with so)
play play hard to get
play play hardball (with so)
play play havoc with so/sth
play play hell with so/sth
play play hob with so/sth
play play hooky
play play ignorant
play play in sth
play play in the big leagues
play play innocent
play play into so's hands

play play it cool
play play it for all it's worth
play play it safe
play play like so/sth
play play on
play play one's cards close to one's chest
play play one's cards right
play play one's cards well
play play one's heart out
play play one's trump card
play play out
play play politics
play play possum
play play second fiddle (to so)
play play so against so else
play play so for a fool
play play so off against so else
play play so/sth down
play play so/sth up
play play sth as sth
play play sth at full blast
play play sth back (to so)
play play sth by ear
play play sth off
play play sth on so/sth
play play sth out
play play sth over
play play sth through
play play sth up
play play sth with so/sth
play play (the) devil's advocate
play play the devil with sth
play play the field
play play the fool
play play the heavy
play play the horses
play play the ponies
play play the race card
play play the (stock) market
play play through
play play to so/sth
play play to the crowd
play play to the gallery
play play tricks on so
play play up to so
play play (up)on sth
play play with a full deck
play play with fire
play play with so/sth
play play-by-play description
play played out
play power play
play put sth back in play
play put sth in play
play roll over and play dead
play team player
play *the race card
play There's many a good tune played on an old fiddle.
play Turnabout is fair play.
play Two can play (at) this game (as well as one).
play way it plays
play When the cat's away, the mice will play.
plea cop a plea
plead plead for so
plead plead for sth
plead plead guilty to sth
plead plead to sth
plead plead with so
please Again(, please).
please Can you excuse us, please?

please Check, please.
please Coming through(, please).
please Could I get by, please?
please Could you excuse us, please?
please disease to please
please Hold, please.
please Hold the wire(, please).
please I'd like to speak to so, please.
please If you don't see what you want, please ask (for it).
please if you please
please if you would(, please)
please I'm easy (to please).
please (I'm) pleased to meet you.
please less than pleased
please Little things please little minds.
please One moment, please.
please Out, please.
please (Please) don't get up.
please Please hold.
please please oneself
please pleased as Punch
please pleased for so/sth
please pleased with so/sth
please Pretty please?
please Small things please small minds.
please We aim to please.
please Who's calling(, please)?
please Will you excuse us, please?
please Would you excuse us, please?
please Would you please?
please You cannot please everyone.
pleasure Business before pleasure.
pleasure He that would go to sea for pleasure, would go to hell for a pastime.
pleasure (I) don't believe I've had the pleasure.
pleasure My pleasure.
pleasure Stolen pleasures are sweetest.
pleasure There is no pleasure without pain.
pleasure With pleasure.
pledge pledge sth to so
pledge take the pledge
plenty gracious plenty
plenty plenty of sth
plenty There are plenty of (other) fish in the sea.
plight plight one's troth to so
plod plod along
plod plod away at sth
plod plod through sth
plonk plonk sth down
plot brew a plot
plot plot against so/sth
plot plot sth on sth
plot plot sth out
plot plot thickens.
plot plot with so
plow clean so's plow
plow plow into so/sth
plow plow sth back into sth
plow plow sth in
plow plow sth under (sth)
plow plow sth up
plow plow through sth
plow put one's hand to the plow
pluck pluck at so/sth
pluck pluck sth from so/sth
pluck pluck sth off (of) so/sth

pluck pluck sth out of sth
pluck pluck up so's courage
plug (I'm) (just) plugging along.
plug plug away (at sth)
plug plug (oneself) in(to sth)
plug plug sth into sth
plug plug sth up
plug pull the plug (on so)
plug pull the plug (on sth)
plug put a plug in (for so/sth)
plumb half a bubble off plumb
plumb plumb loco
plumbing check out the plumbing
plumbing greatest thing since indoor plumbing
plumbing visit the plumbing
plummet plummet to earth
plummet plummet to sth
plump plump for so/sth
plump plump sth down
plump plump sth up
plunge plunge down sth
plunge plunge from sth
plunge plunge in(to sth)
plunge plunge sth into so/sth
plunge plunge to sth
plunge take the plunge
plunk plunk (oneself) down
plunk plunk so/sth down
ply ply between sth and sth else
ply ply so with sth
poacher old poacher makes the best gamekeeper.
pock pock sth with sth
pocket have so in one's pocket
pocket line one's own pocket(s)
pocket Money burns a hole in so's pocket.
pocket out-of-pocket expenses
pocket pocket of resistance
pocket Shrouds have no pockets.
pod alike as (two) peas in a pod
pod like (two) peas in a pod
poetic poetic justice
poetic poetic license
poetic wax poetic
point at the point of doing sth
point at this point (in time)
point belabor the point
point beside the point
point breaking point
point case in point
point come to a turning point
point come to the point
point get the point (of sth)
point get to the point (of sth)
point have a low boiling point
point in point of fact
point jumping-off point
point make a point
point make points (with so)
point miss the point
point no point in sth
point not to put too fine a point on it
point on the point of doing sth
point point at so/sth
point point down to sth
point point of no return
point point of view
point point so/sth out
point point sth at so/sth
point point sth up
point point the finger at so

point point to so/sth
point point to sth
point point to sth as sth
point point toward so/sth
point put too fine a point on sth
point reach a turning point
point selling point
point so's point is well taken
point stretch a point
point stretch the point
point That brings me to the (main) point.
point touch a sore point
point turning point
point which brings me to the (main) point
poise poise oneself for sth
poise poise over so/sth
poise poised for sth
poise poised to do sth
poison Name your poison.
poison One man's meat is another man's poison.
poison poison so against so/sth
poison poison so or an animal with sth
poison poison sth with sth
poke buy a pig in a poke
poke poke a hole in sth
poke poke about
poke poke along
poke poke around
poke poke at so/sth
poke poke fun at so/sth
poke poke one's nose in(to sth)
poke poke out (of sth)
poke poke so in sth
poke poke sth at so/sth
poke poke sth into sth
poke poke sth out of sth
poke poke sth through so/sth
poke poke through (sth)
poke take a poke at so
poker stiff as a poker
polar hot enough to burn a polar bear's butt
polarize polarize sth into sth
pole grow poles apart
pole high man on the totem pole
pole I wouldn't touch it with a ten-foot pole.
pole low man on the totem pole
pole not touch so/sth with a ten-foot pole
pole poles apart
pole skinny as a beanpole
pole up the pole
pole wouldn't touch so/sth with a ten-foot pole
policy Honesty is the best policy.
polish apple-polisher
polish polish sth off
polish polish sth up
polish spit and polish
politic body politic
politic play politics
politic Politics makes strange bedfellows.
political political football
poll go to the polls
pollute pollute sth with sth
pond big frog in a small pond
ponder ponder (up)on sth
pontificate pontificate on sth

pony dog and pony show
pony play the ponies
pooch pooch out
poop poop out
poop poop so/sth out
poop pooped (out)
poor in poor taste
poor It is a poor heart that never rejoices.
poor land so poor it wouldn't even raise a fuss
poor land too poor to raise a racket on
poor one law for the rich and another for the poor
poor poor as a church mouse
poor poor but clean
poorhouse end up in the poorhouse
poorhouse in the poorhouse
poorhouse live in the poorhouse
pop pop around (for a visit)
pop pop back (for sth)
pop pop by (for a visit)
pop pop down (for a visit)
pop pop for sth
pop pop in (for a visit)
pop pop in(to sth)
pop pop off
pop pop one's cork
pop pop out (of sth)
pop pop over (for a visit)
pop pop (some) tops
pop pop so off
pop pop so on sth
pop pop sth into sth
pop pop sth on(to) sth
pop pop sth out of sth
pop pop sth up
pop pop the question
pop pop up
pop take a pop at so
pop What's poppin'?
popcorn busy as popcorn on a skillet
poppy red as a poppy
porcelain bow to the porcelain altar
porcelain pray to the porcelain god
pore air one's pores
pore pore over sth
pork pork out (on sth)
port any port in a storm
portent portent of things to come
portion portion sth out
portrait sit for one's portrait
portray portray so as so/sth
portray portray so/sth as so
pose pose a question
pose pose as so
pose pose for so/sth
pose strike a pose
position come to the position with sth
position jockey for position
position jockey so/sth into position
position make so's position clear
position place so in an awkward position
position put so in an awkward position
possess possessed by sth
possess possessed of sth
possession come into so's possession
possession in so's possession
possession Possession is nine-tenths of the law.
possession take possession (of sth)
possible as far as possible

possible everything humanly possible
possible so far as possible
possible soon as possible
possum play possum
post by return post
post deaf as a post
post from pillar to post
post keep so posted
post post so somewhere
post post sth on sth
post post sth to so
post post sth up
post send so from pillar to post
postage postage and handling
postal go postal
poster poster child (for sth)
postpone postpone sth until sth
posture posture as so/sth
pot don't have a pot to piss in (or a window to throw it out of)
pot go to pot
pot hit the jackpot
pot If ifs and ands were pots and pans (there'd be no work for tinkers' hands).
pot pot is calling the kettle black.
pot pot of gold
pot pot sth up
pot sweeten the pot
pot tempest in a teapot
pot That's the pot calling the kettle black.
pot watched pot never boils.
pot You cannot get a quart into a pint pot.
potato couch potato
potato drop so/sth like a hot potato
potato small potatoes
potential realize one's potential
potshot take a potshot at so/sth
pounce pounce (up)on so/sth
pound ounce of common sense is worth a pound of theory.
pound ounce of discretion is worth a pound of wit.
pound ounce of prevention is worth a pound of cure.
pound owe so a pound of flesh
pound pay so a pound of flesh
pound penny-wise and pound-foolish
pound pound a beat
pound pound along sth
pound pound away (at so/sth)
pound pound for pound
pound pound of flesh
pound pound on so/sth
pound pound one's ear
pound pound so's head in
pound pound sth down
pound pound sth in
pound pound sth into so
pound pound sth on so/sth
pound pound sth out
pound pound sth up
pound pound the books
pound pound the pavement
pound take a pound of flesh
pour couldn't pour water out of a boot (if there was instructions on the heel)
pour It never rains but it pours.
pour pour (all) over so/sth
pour pour along sth
pour pour cold water on sth

pour pour down (on so/sth)
pour pour forth
pour pour in(to sth)
pour pour it on thick
pour pour money down the drain
pour pour oil on troubled water(s)
pour pour one's heart out to so
pour pour oneself into sth
pour pour out (of sth)
pour pour out one's soul
pour pour sth back (in(to sth))
pour pour sth into sth
pour pour sth off (of) sth
pour pour sth on(to) sth
pour pour sth out on(to) so/sth
pour pour sth over so/sth
pour pour sth through sth
pour pour through sth
pour pour with rain
pour pouring rain
pout pout about sth
poverty Poverty is no sin.
poverty Poverty is not a crime.
poverty When poverty comes in at the door, love flies out of the window.
powder Can I use your powder room?
powder Could I use your powder room?
powder Keep your powder dry.
powder May I use your powder room?
powder powder one's face
powder powder one's nose
powder powder up
powder Put your trust in God, and keep your powder dry.
powder sitting on a powder keg
powder take a powder
power Absolute power corrupts absolutely.
power balance of power
power come into power
power do so a power of good
power exercise power over so/sth
power fall from power
power go on a power trip
power have no staying power
power in power
power Knowledge is power.
power Money is power.
power More power to you!
power on a power trip
power power behind the throne
power power play
power power sth up
power power sth with sth
power power up
power powers that be
power put so into power
pox pox on so/sth!
practical for all practical purposes
practice go out of practice
practice in practice
practice make a practice of sth
practice make sth a practice
practice out of practice
practice Practice makes perfect.
practice practice (up)on so/sth
practice Practice what you preach.
practice put sth into practice
praise damn so/sth with faint praise
praise praise so/sth to the skies
praise Self-praise is no recommendation.

praise sing so's or sth's praises
praise sing the praises of so/sth
prance prance around
prank play a prank on so
prattle prattle (away) about so/sth
pray family that prays together stays together.
pray pray for so/sth
pray pray over sth
pray pray to so/sth
pray pray to the porcelain god
prayer arrive on a wing and a prayer
prayer come (in) on a wing and a prayer
prayer in so's prayers
prayer on a wing and a prayer
preach Practice what you preach.
preach preach about sth
preach preach against so/sth
preach preach at so
preach preach to so
preach preach to the choir
preach preach to the converted
precedence be given precedence over so/sth
precedence precedence over so/sth
precedence take precedence over so/sth
precedent set a precedent
precept Example is better than precept.
precious precious few
precious precious little
precipitate precipitate into sth
precipitate precipitate sth into sth
preclude preclude so/sth from sth
predicate predicate sth (up)on sth
predispose predispose so/sth to(ward) sth
preface preface sth by sth
preface preface sth with sth
prefer prefer so/sth to so/sth else
prefer prefer sth against so
prefix prefix sth to sth
prejudice prejudice so/sth against so/sth
prelude prelude to sth
premium at a premium
premium place sth at a premium
premium put a premium on sth
premium put sth at a premium
prepare Hope for the best and prepare for the worst.
prepare If you want peace, (you must) prepare for war.
prepare prepare so for sth
prepare prepare so/sth for sth
prescribe prescribe sth for so
prescribe prescribe sth for sth
prescription refill a prescription
presence grace so/sth with one's presence
presence have the presence of mind to do sth
present at present
present at the present time
present live in the present
present *on a silver platter
present present so (to so) (at sth)
present present so with sth
present present sth on a silver platter
present present sth to so
present (There's) no time like the present.

preservation Self-preservation is the first law of nature.
preserve preserve so/sth against sth
preserve preserve so/sth from so/sth
preserve preserve sth for so/sth
preside preside at sth
preside preside over sth
press go to press
press hot off the press
press in press
press press against so/sth
press press charges (against so)
press press down on so/sth
press press for sth
press press forward
press press on sth
press press one's luck
press press on(ward)
press press sth into service
press press so to the wall
press press sth against so/sth
press press sth into sth
press press sth on
press press sth onto sth
press press sth out of sth
press press sth together
press press sth (up)on so
press press (the) flesh
press press the panic button
press press (up)on so/sth
press pressed for cash
press pressed for money
press pressed for time
press Stop the presses!
pressure deliver sth under pressure
pressure high-pressure so into sth
pressure pressure so into sth
pressure put pressure on sth
pressure put sth under pressure
pressure put (the) pressure on so (to do sth)
pressure take so's blood pressure
pressure under pressure
presume Doctor Livingstone, I presume?
presume presume (up)on so/sth
pretend pretend to sth
pretty bother one's (pretty little) head about sth
pretty come to a pretty pass
pretty cost a pretty penny
pretty Don't worry your (pretty little) head about it.
pretty gotta get up pretty early in the morning to do sth
pretty in a (pretty) pickle
pretty leave so sitting pretty
pretty not trouble one's (pretty) (little) head about sth
pretty pretty as a picture
pretty Pretty is as pretty does.
pretty pretty oneself or sth up
pretty pretty pickle
pretty Pretty please?
pretty pretty state of affairs
pretty sitting pretty
prevail cooler heads prevail
prevail prevail against so/sth
prevail prevail (up)on so/sth (to do sth)
prevent prevent so from doing sth
prevent take steps (to prevent sth)
prevention ounce of prevention is worth a pound of cure.

prevention Prevention is better than cure.
prey prey on sth
prey prey (up)on so/sth
price asking price
price Every man has his price.
price little pricey
price pay the price
price place a price on one's head
price price on one's head
price price one has to pay
price price so/sth out of the market
price price sth down
price price sth out
price price sth up
price put a price on one's head
price quote a price
price roll prices back
price set one's (own) price
price thing you don't want is dear at any price.
price What price sth?
pricey little pricey
prick prick up its ears
pride burst with pride
pride pride and joy
pride Pride goes before a fall.
pride pride oneself in sth
pride swallow one's pride
pride take pride in so/sth
priest Once a priest, always a priest.
prime in its prime
prime in one's or its prime
prime in the prime of life
prime past so's or sth's prime
prime prime mover
prime prime sth with sth
primp primp (oneself) up
primrose primrose path
print fine print
print in print
print not worth the paper it's printed on
print out of print
print print sth in sth
print print sth out
print print sth up
print put sth in(to) print
print rush sth into print
print small print
prisoner take no prisoners
privacy invasion of (so's) privacy
private in private
privy privy to sth
prize booby prize
prize prize so/sth above so/sth
probability in all probability
probation on probation
probe probe into sth
probe probe sth for sth
problem cash flow problem
problem determine the root of the problem
problem figure out the root of the problem
problem find the root of the problem
problem for all so's problems
problem have a weight problem
problem have an alcohol problem
problem (I have) no problem with that.
problem no problem
problem root of the problem

987

problem (That causes) no problem.
problem What's the problem?
proceed proceed against so/sth
proceed proceed (from sth) (to sth)
proceed proceed with sth
procrastination Procrastination is the thief of time.
procure procure sth (from so/sth) (for so/sth)
prod prod at so/sth
prod prod so into sth
produce produce an attack (of an illness)
produce produce sth for sth
produce produce sth from sth
professional seek professional help
professor absent-minded professor
profile assume a low profile
profile keep a low profile
profile low profile
profit profit by sth
profit turn a profit
program get with the program
progress in progress
progress progress to sth
progress progress toward sth
progress progress with sth
prohibit prohibit so from sth
prohibit prohibit sth from sth
project between projects
project project into sth
project project sth onto so
project project sth on(to) so/sth
prominence bring so/sth into prominence
prominence come into prominence
promise finish sth with a lick and a promise
promise go back on one's promise
promise I promise you!
promise keep a promise
promise keep one's promise
promise lick and a promise
promise lot of promise
promise promise so the moon
promise promise sth to so
promise promise the moon (to so)
promise Promises are like piecrust, made to be broken.
promise show a lot of promise
promote promote so (from sth) (to sth)
prone prone to sth
pronounce pronounce sth on so/sth
proof proof is in the pudding.
proof The proof of the pudding is in the eating.
prop knock the props out from under so
prop prop so/sth up (against so/sth)
proper go through (the proper) channels
prophet prophet is not without honor save in his own country.
proportion blow sth out of (all) proportion
proportion grow out of (all) proportion
proportion in proportion
proportion out of (all) proportion
proportion out of proportion
proportion disaster of epic proportions
propose Man proposes, God disposes.
propose propose a toast

propose propose sth to so
propose propose to so
prospect prospect for sth
prosper Cheats never prosper.
prosper prosper from sth
prostrate prostrate oneself before so/sth
protect Heaven protects children(, sailors,) and drunken men.
protect protect so/sth against so/sth
protest protest about so/sth
protest ripple of protest
protrude protrude from so/sth
proud do oneself proud
proud do so proud
proud proud as a peacock
prove exception proves the rule.
prove prove oneself as sth
prove prove sth to so
prove prove to be sth
prove What does that prove?
provide provide against sth
provide provide for so/sth
provide provide so with sth
provide provide sth for so/sth
provide provide sth under sth
provide provided that
provide Take the goods the gods provide.
provoke provoke so into sth
prowl on the prowl
prowl prowl about
prune full of prunes
prune prune sth away
prune prune sth of sth
prune prune sth off (of) sth
pry pry around
pry pry into sth
pry pry sth from so
pry pry sth from sth
pry pry sth off (of) sth
pry pry sth out of so
pry pry sth out (of sth)
pry pry sth up
psych psych out
psych psych so out
psych psych so up
psych psych up
psych psyched (out)
psych psyched (up)
psych psyched up (for sth)
public air one's dirty linen in public
public Do not wash your dirty linen in public.
public find oneself in the public eye
public go public (with sth)
public in public
public in the public eye
public take sth public
public wash one's dirty linen in public
publication clear sth for publication
publication not for publication
publish publish or perish
pucker pucker sth up
pucker pucker up
pudding proof is in the pudding.
pudding The proof of the pudding is in the eating.
puddle biggest frog in the puddle
puddle biggest toad in the puddle
puff huff and puff
puff puff along
puff puff (away) at sth
puff puff out

puff puff so/sth up
puff puff sth out
puff puff up
pull have pull with so
pull *out of so's hands
pull pull a boner
pull pull a fast one
pull pull a few strings
pull pull a gun (on so)
pull pull a job
pull pull a knife (on so)
pull pull a muscle
pull pull a stunt (on so)
pull pull a trick (on so)
pull pull ahead (of so/sth)
pull pull all the stops out
pull pull around to sth
pull pull at so
pull pull away from so/sth
pull pull back (from so/sth)
pull pull down (an amount of money)
pull pull for so/sth
pull pull in one's ears
pull pull in one's horns
pull pull in some place
pull pull in(to some place)
pull pull off (sth)
pull pull on sth
pull pull one over on so
pull pull one's belt in (a notch)
pull pull one's (own) weight
pull pull one's punches
pull pull oneself together
pull pull oneself up by one's (own) bootstraps
pull pull (out) in front of so/sth
pull pull out (of sth)
pull pull over (to sth)
pull pull rank (on so)
pull pull (some) strings
pull pull so about
pull pull so apart
pull pull so aside
pull pull so down
pull pull so in
pull pull so into a place
pull pull so into sth
pull pull so or an animal down
pull pull so or an animal through (sth)
pull pull so/sth apart
pull pull so/sth around
pull pull so/sth away from so/sth
pull pull so/sth back (from so/sth)
pull pull so/sth by sth
pull pull so/sth into sth
pull pull so/sth over (to sth)
pull pull so/sth to pieces
pull pull so/sth under
pull pull so/sth up
pull pull so's leg
pull pull so's or sth's teeth
pull pull so through (sth)
pull pull so up short
pull pull sth down
pull pull sth off
pull pull sth on
pull pull sth out
pull pull sth over so/sth
pull pull sth to
pull pull sth together
pull pull sth toward oneself
pull pull sth up
pull pull the plug (on so)

pull pull the plug (on sth)
pull pull the rug out (from under so)
pull pull the wool over so's eyes
pull pull through (sth)
pull pull together (as a team)
pull Pull up a chair.
pull pull (up) alongside ((of) so/sth)
pull pull up (somewhere)
pull pull up stakes
pull pull up to sth
pulse keep one's finger on the pulse of sth
pulse pulse through so/sth
pulse take so's pulse
pulse take the pulse of sth
pump pump (some) iron
pump pump so for sth
pump pump so up (for sth)
pump pump sth into so/sth
pump pump sth out of so/sth
pump pump sth through sth
pump pump sth up
pump pumped (up)
pumpkin some pumpkins
punch beat so to the punch
punch get one's ticket punched
punch pack a punch
Punch pleased as Punch
punch pull one's punches
punch punch a hole in sth
punch punch in
punch punch out
punch punch so in sth
punch punch so on sth
punch punch so out
punch punch so's lights out
punch punch sth down
punch punch sth in
punch punch sth into sth
punch punch sth out of sth
punch punch sth up
punch roll with the punches
punch take a punch at so
punch telegraph one's punches
punch throw a punch
punctuality Punctuality is the soul of business.
punctuate punctuate sth with sth
punish punish so by sth
punish punish so for sth
punish punish so with sth
punishment glutton for punishment
punk punk out
puny feeling (kinda) puny
pup meaner than a junkyard dog (with fourteen sucking pups)
puppy puppy love
purchase purchase sth for so
pure pure and simple
pure pure as the driven snow
pure pure luck
purge binge and purge
purge purge so/sth from sth
purge purge so/sth of so/sth
purge purge sth away
purpose accidentally-on-purpose
purpose answer so's purpose
purpose at cross-purposes
purpose devil can cite Scripture for his own purpose.
purpose devil can quote Scripture for his own purpose.
purpose for all intents and purposes

purpose for all practical purposes
purpose on purpose
purpose serve a (useful) purpose
purpose serve so's purpose
purr purr like a cat
purr purr like a kitten
purse control the purse strings
purse He that hath a full purse never wanted a friend.
purse heavy purse makes a light heart.
purse hold the purse strings
purse light purse makes a heavy heart.
purse Little and often fills the purse.
purse purse sth up
purse You cannot make a silk purse out of a sow's ear.
pursuit in pursuit of sth
push Don't push (me)!
push (I) have to push off.
push if push comes to shove
push push ahead (with sth)
push push along
push push at so/sth
push push down on sth
push push for sth
push push forward
push push off
push push on so/sth
push push on (to sth)
push push on (with sth)
push push one's luck
push push (oneself) away (from sth)
push push (oneself) by (so/sth)
push push (oneself) off (on sth)
push push out
push push past (so/sth)
push push so around
push push so into sth
push push so/sth about
push push so/sth across (sth)
push push so/sth ahead of so
push push so/sth along
push push so/sth around
push push so/sth aside
push push so/sth (away) (from so/sth)
push push so/sth back (from so/sth)
push push so/sth down
push push so/sth forward
push push so/sth into so/sth
push push so/sth off (of) so/sth
push push so/sth on (ahead) (of so/sth)
push push so/sth or an animal into sth
push push so/sth out of sth
push push so/sth over
push push so/sth to so/sth
push push so/sth toward so/sth
push push so/sth up
push push so to sth
push push so to the wall
push push so too far
push push so up against the wall
push push sth in
push push sth off on(to) so
push push sth through (sth)
push push sth to
push push sth (up) against so/sth
push push the envelope
push push the panic button
push push through (sth)
push push toward so/sth
push push (up) against so/sth
push push up on sth
push pushed for money

push pushed for time
push pushing up (the) daisies
push seem pushed for time
push *up against the wall
push when push comes to shove
pussyfoot pussyfoot around
put Don't put all your eggs in one basket.
put Don't put off for tomorrow what you can do today.
put Don't put the cart before the horse.
put hard put (to do sth)
put He puts his pants on one leg at a time.
put I'll put a stop to that.
put *in apple-pie order
put *in harm's way
put *in order
put *in perspective
put *in place
put *in plain language
put *in play
put *in the gutter
put *in writing
put *lid on sth
put not put (a lot) of stock in sth
put not put it past so
put not to put too fine a point on it
put *off one's game
put *on a pedestal
put *on so's shoulders
put *on the back burner
put *on the front burner
put *on the market
put *out in the cold
put put a bee in so's bonnet (about so/sth)
put put a cap on sth
put put a contract out on so
put put a damper on sth
put put a dog off the scent
put put a hold on sth
put put a horse out to pasture
put put a lid on sth
put put a plug in (for so/sth)
put put a premium on sth
put put a price on one's head
put put a smile on so's face
put Put a sock in it!
put put a spin on sth
put put a stop to sth
put put a strain on so/sth
put put all one's eggs in one basket
put put an amount of time in on sth
put put an animal down
put put an animal out
put put an end to sth
put put another way
put put balls on sth
put Put 'em up!
put Put 'er there(, pal).
put put hair on so's chest
put put ideas into so's head
put put in a good word (for so)
put put in a hard day at work
put put in an appearance (at sth)
put put in for sth
put put in some place
put put it on the line
put put money up (for sth)
put put off by so/sth
put put on

put put one at (one's) ease
put put one foot in front of the other
put put one in one's place
put put one in over one's head
put put one off one's game
put put one off one's stride
put put one on one's feet
put put one on one's guard
put put one on one's honor
put put one out of (one's) misery
put put one over on so
put put one's back (in)to sth
put put one's best foot forward
put put one's cards on the table
put put one's dibs on sth
put put one's face on
put put one's feet up
put put one's finger on sth
put put one's foot down (about so/sth)
put put one's foot in it
put put one's foot in one's mouth
put put one's hair up
put put one's hand to the plow
put put one's hand up
put put one's hands on so/sth or an animal
put put one's head on the block (for so/sth)
put put one's heart (and soul) into sth
put put one's house in order
put put one's mind to sth
put put one's money on so/sth (to do sth)
put put one's neck on the line
put put one's nose in (where it's not wanted)
put put one's nose out of joint
put put one's nose to the grindstone
put put one's oar in
put put one's own house in order
put put one's thinking cap on
put put one's trust in so/sth
put put one's two cents(' worth) in
put put one through one's paces
put put oneself in so else's place
put put oneself out
put put out
put put paid to sth
put put people or things together
put put people's heads together
put put pressure on sth
put put roots down (some place)
put put some creature out of its misery
put put some distance between so and oneself or sth
put put some sweet lines on so
put put some teeth into sth
put put (some) years on so/sth
put put so across (in a good way)
put put so away
put put so behind bars
put put so behind the eight ball
put put so by so/sth
put put so down as sth bad
put put so down (for sth)
put put so in
put put so in(side) (sth)
put put so into power
put put so into the doghouse
put put so into the doldrums
put put so into the gutter
put put so off
put put so on
put put so onto so/sth
put put so or an animal out of sth

put put so or an animal to sleep
put put so or some creature to death
put put so or some creature out in the cold
put put so/sth above so/sth
put put so/sth ahead (of so/sth)
put put so/sth among so/sth
put put so/sth at loose ends
put put so/sth at so's disposal
put put so/sth before so/sth
put put so/sth down
put put so/sth forward
put put so/sth in
put put so/sth in(to) jeopardy
put put so/sth into order
put put so/sth into sth
put put so/sth into the middle of nowhere
put put so/sth on hold
put put so/sth on ice
put put so/sth on sth
put put so/sth on track
put put so/sth out of one's mind
put put so/sth out of the way
put put so/sth over
put put so/sth through (to so)
put put so/sth to the test
put put so/sth under sth
put put so/sth with so
put put so out
put put so over a barrel
put put so's back up
put put so's eye out
put put so's nose out of joint
put put so through sth
put put so through the mill
put put so through the wringer
put put so to bed
put put so to shame
put put so to sleep
put put so under
put put so up
put put so wise to so/sth
put put sth across (to so)
put put sth aside
put put sth at a premium
put put sth at an amount
put put sth at so's door
put put sth away
put put sth back
put put sth behind one
put put sth behind so/sth
put put sth by
put put sth down
put put (sth) forth
put put sth forward
put put sth in
put put sth in((side) so/sth)
put put sth into effect
put put sth into orbit
put put sth in(to) order
put put sth into perspective
put put sth into place
put put sth into practice
put put sth in(to) print
put put sth in(to) service
put put sth in(to) so's head
put put sth into use
put put sth into words
put put sth off
put put sth on
put put sth out
put put sth over
put put sth plainly

put put sth right
put put sth straight
put put sth through its paces
put put sth to bed
put put sth to (good) use
put put sth to rest
put put sth together
put put sth under pressure
put put sth up
put put teeth in(to) sth
put Put that in your pipe and smoke it!
put put the arm on so
put put the bite on so
put put the blame on so/sth
put put the brakes on so
put put the brakes on sth
put put the cart before the horse
put put the chill on so
put put the clamps on so/sth
put put the fear of God in(to) so
put put the feed bag on
put put the finger on so
put put the freeze on so
put put the hard word on so
put put the heat on
put put the kibosh on so/sth
put put the make on so
put put the moves on so
put put the nose-bag on
put put the pedal to the metal
put put (the) pressure on so (to do sth)
put put the screws on (so)
put put the skids on (sth)
put put the skids under so/sth
put put the squeeze on so
put put the touch on so
put put to bed with a shovel
put put to it
put put too fine a point on sth
put put two and two together
put put up a (brave) front
put put up a fight
put put up a struggle
put put up one's dukes
put Put up or shut up!
put put up with so/sth
put put upon by so
put put wear (and tear) on sth
put put weight on
put put words in(to) so's mouth
put Put your money where your mouth is!
put Put your trust in God, and keep your powder dry.
put put-up job
put stay put
put *through the mill
put to put it another way
put to put it mildly
put *under a spell
put *under arrest
put *under pressure
put *up for auction
put *up for sale
put You cannot put new wine in old bottles.
putt putt along
putter putter about
putter putter around
putty putty in so's hands
putty seem like putty in so's hands
putz putz around
puzzle puzzle over so/sth

puzzle puzzle sth out
Q mind one's p's and q's
QT on the QT
quail quail at so/sth
quail quail before so/sth
quake quake in one's boots
quake quake with sth
qualify qualify as sth
qualify qualify for sth
qualify qualify so as sth
qualify qualify so for sth
quality quality time
qualm cause qualms (about so/sth)
qualm qualms (about so/sth)
quandary in a quandary
quantity known quantity
quantity unknown quantity
quarrel It takes two to make a quarrel.
quarrel patch a quarrel up
quarrel pick a quarrel (with so)
quarrel quarrel (with so) (about so/sth)
quarrel quarrel (with so) (over so/sth)
quarrel quarrel with sth
quart You cannot get a quart into a pint pot.
quarter drawn and quartered
quarter give so no quarter
quarter grant so no quarter
quarter have so drawn and quartered
Queen Queen's English
queer queer as a three-dollar bill
queer queer for sth
quest in quest of so/sth
quest quest for so/sth
question Ask me no questions, I'll tell you no lies.
question Ask no questions and hear no lies.
question beg the question
question beside the question
question bombard so with questions
question bring sth into question
question burning question
question call so/sth into question
question field questions
question leading question
question Next question.
question no questions asked
question open to question
question out of the question
question pop the question
question pose a question
question question of sth
question question so about so/sth
question question so at great length
question Shoot first, ask questions later.
question sixty-four-dollar question
question There are two sides to every question.
question without question
queue queue up (for sth)
quibble quibble (about so/sth) (with so)
quick cut so to the quick
quick He gives twice who gives quickly.
quick make a quick buck
quick mouse that has but one hole is quickly taken.
quick quick and dirty
quick quick as a flash
quick quick as a wink
quick quick as (greased) lightning

quick quick like a bunny
quick quick off the mark
quick quick on the draw
quick quick on the trigger
quick quick on the uptake
quick quick study
quick quick temper
quick quicker than hell
quick quicker than you can say Jack Robinson
quiet Be quiet!
quiet keep quiet (about so/sth)
quiet keep so/sth quiet
quiet keep sth quiet
quiet Let's go somewhere where it's (more) quiet.
quiet quiet as a (church) mouse
quiet quiet as the grave
quiet quiet down
quiet quiet so or an animal down
quiet so quiet you could hear a pin drop
quip quip about so/sth
quit Church ain't out till they quit singing.
quit Don't quit trying.
quit Don't quit your day job.
quit quit a place
quit quit on so
quit quit over so/sth
quit quit while one is ahead
quit Some people (just) don't know when to quit.
quite cause (quite) a stir
quite I didn't (quite) catch that (last) remark.
quite I'm having quite a time.
quite It doesn't quite suit me.
quite quite a bit
quite quite a few
quite quite a lot
quite quite a number
quite quite a sth
quite quite something
quite speaking (quite) candidly
quite (speaking) (quite) frankly
quite take (quite) a toll (on so/sth)
quite This doesn't quite suit me.
quits call it quits
quiver quiver with sth
quiz quiz out (of sth)
quiz quiz so about so/sth
quiz quiz so on so/sth
quote devil can quote Scripture for his own purpose.
quote put sth in quotes
quote quote a price
quote quote so/sth out of context
quote quote (sth) from so/sth
quote quote, unquote
rabbit knee-high to a jackrabbit
raccoon in a coon's age
race deal the race card
race off to the races
race play the race card
race race against so/sth
race race against time
race race around
race race for so
race race into so/sth
race race into sth
race race so for sth

race race so to some place
race race through so/sth
race race through sth
race race to so/sth
race race up to so/sth
race race with so/sth
race rat race
race run the good race
race Slow and steady wins the race.
race the race card
race tight race
race use the race card
rack go to rack and ruin
rack rack one's brain(s)
rack rack out
rack rack sth up
rack racked with pain
rack use your head for more than a hatrack
racket land too poor to raise a racket on
radiate radiate from so/sth
raffle raffle sth off
rag chew the rag
rag from rags to riches
rag in rags
rag on the rag
rag rag on so
rag rag out
rag rag so about so/sth
rag run so ragged
rag talk so ragged
rage all the rage
rage bristle with rage
rage fly into a rage
rage rage against so/sth
rage rage at so/sth
rage rage out of control
rage rage over so/sth
rage rage through sth
ragged run so ragged
ragged talk so ragged
rail rail against so/sth
rail rail at so (about sth)
railroad railroad so into sth
railroad railroad sth through (sth)
rain Charge it to the dust and let the rain settle it.
rain come in out of the rain
rain come rain or (come) shine
rain come rain or shine
rain doesn't have enough sense to come in out of the rain
rain hold sth back for a rainy day
rain It never rains but it pours.
rain It's raining cats and dogs.
rain It's raining pitchforks (and hammer handles).
rain keep sth for a rainy day
rain not know enough to come in out of the rain
rain pour with rain
rain pouring rain
rain put sth aside for a rainy day
rain rain cats and dogs
rain rain check (on sth)
rain rain down on so/sth
rain rain in on so/sth
rain rain on so's parade
rain rain or shine
rain rain sth down (on so/sth)
rain rain sth out
rain rain (up)on so/sth

rain right as rain
rain risk of rain
rain save (sth) for a rainy day
rain take a rain check (on sth)
rainbow always chasing rainbows
rainy hold sth back for a rainy day
rainy keep sth for a rainy day
rainy put sth aside for a rainy day
rainy save (sth) for a rainy day
raise born and raised
raise cause (some) eyebrows to raise
raise cause some raised eyebrows
raise land so poor it wouldn't even
 raise a fuss
raise land too poor to raise a racket on
raise raise a (big) stink (about so/sth)
raise raise a few eyebrows
raise raise a hand (against so/sth)
raise raise a hue and cry (about sth)
raise raise a stink (about sth)
raise raise (an) objection (to so/sth)
raise raise Cain
raise raise havoc with so/sth
raise raise hell (with sth)
raise raise hob with so/sth
raise raise money for so/sth
raise raise one's glass to so/sth
raise raise one's sights
raise raise one's voice against so/sth
raise raise one's voice (to so)
raise raise some eyebrows
raise raise so from sth
raise raise so from the dead
raise raise so or an animal from sth
raise raise so/sth to sth
raise raise so/sth to the surface (of sth)
raise raise so/sth up
raise raise so's spirits
raise raise so to sth
raise raise sth with so
raise raise the ante
raise raise the bar
raise raise the devil (with so)
raise raise the devil (with sth)
raise raise the dickens (with so/sth)
raise raise up
raise raised in a barn
rake rake on so
rake rake so over the coals
rake rake sth around
rake rake sth in
rake rake sth off
rake rake sth out of sth
rake rake sth up
rake rake through sth
rally rally around so/sth
rally rally to so/sth
ralph hang a ralph
ralph ralph sth up
ram ram into so/sth
ram ram so/sth down so's throat
ram ram sth down
ram ram sth into so/sth
ram ram sth through (sth)
ram ram through sth
ramble ramble on
rampage go on a rampage
rampant run rampant
ran also-ran
random at random
range at close range
range bring so/sth within range (of so/sth)
range bring sth within a range

range come within range
range move within range
range range from sth to sth
range range over sth
range within range
rank close ranks
rank come up through the ranks
rank pull rank (on so)
rank rank above so
rank rank among sth
rank rank and file
rank rank as sth
rank rank on so
rank rank so among sth
rank rank so/sth as sth
rank rank so (out)
rank rank so with so
rank rank with so/sth
rank rise from the ranks
ransom cost a king's ransom
ransom hold so for ransom
ransom king's ransom
ransom pay a king's ransom
ransom spend a king's ransom
rant rant against so/sth
rant rant and rave (about so/sth)
rant rant (at so) about so/sth
rant rant at so/sth
rap beat the rap
rap get one's knuckles rapped
rap rap at sth
rap rap on sth
rap rap so across the knuckles
rap rap sth out (on sth)
rap rap with so
rap take the rap (for so)
rap take the rap (for sth)
rare have a rare old time
rare in rare form
rare rarin' to go
raring rarin' to go
rash break out in a rash
rasp rasp sth out
raspberry give so the raspberry
rat like rats abandoning a sinking ship
rat rat around
rat rat on so
rat rat out
rat rat race
rat Rats abandon a sinking ship.
rat rug rat
rat smell a rat
rate at any rate
rate at that rate
rate at this rate
rate going rate
rate rate so/sth above so/sth else
rate rate so/sth among sth
rate rate so/sth as sth
rate rate so/sth below so/sth else
rate rate so/sth with so/sth else
rate rate sth at sth
rate rate sth below sth else
rate rate with so
rather had rather do sth
rather have one's rathers
rather I'd rather face a firing squad
 than do sth
rather would rather
ration ration sth out (among so)
rattle rattle around in sth
rattle rattle away
rattle rattle its saber

rattle rattle on (about so/sth)
rattle rattle one's saber
rattle rattle sth off
rattle slightly rattled
raunch raunch so out
rave rant and rave (about so/sth)
rave rave about so/sth
rave rave over so/sth
rave stark raving mad
ravish ravished with delight
raw in the raw
raw raw deal
raw raw recruit
ray bag some rays
ray catch some rays
raze raze sth to the ground
razor sharp as a razor
reach out of reach
reach reach a compromise
reach reach a conclusion
reach reach a dead end
reach reach a decision
reach reach a turning point
reach reach an accord (with so)
reach reach an agreement (with so)
reach reach an impasse
reach reach an understanding with so
reach reach back (in)to sth
reach reach down
reach reach first base (with so/sth)
reach reach for so/sth
reach reach for the sky
reach Reach for the stars!
reach reach in(to sth)
reach reach one's stride
reach reach out
reach reach (rock) bottom
reach reach so
reach reach some place in a body
reach reach sth down
reach reach sth in the (very) nick of
 time
reach reach sth up to so
reach reach speeds of some amount
reach reach to sth
reach reach toward so/sth
reach *speeds of some amount
reach Stretch your arm no further than
 your sleeve will reach.
reach *turning point
reach within so's reach
react react against so/sth
react react to so/sth
reaction gut reaction
reaction knee-jerk reaction
read Do you read me?
read (I) read you loud and clear.
read read about so/sth
read read between the lines
read read for so
read read from sth
read read from the same page
read read it and weep
read Read my lips!
read read of so/sth (somewhere)
read read on
read read one one's rights
read read oneself to sleep
read read so like a book
read read so/sth as sth
read read so out (for sth)
read read so out of sth
read read so's lips

read read so's mind
read read (so) sth out of sth
read read so the riot act
read read sth back (to so)
read read sth in sth
read read sth into sth
read read sth off
read read sth out
read read sth over
read read sth through
read read (sth) to so
read read the handwriting on the wall
read read up (on so/sth)
readjust readjust to so/sth
ready Anytime you are ready.
ready (Are you) ready for this?
ready (Are you) ready to order?
ready ready, set, go
ready ready (to do sth)
ready ready, willing, and able
ready rough-and-ready
ready when one is good and ready
real for real
real Get real!
real (I) really must go.
real (I'll) see you (real) soon.
real I'm (really) fed up (with so/sth).
real (It) (really) doesn't matter to me.
real (real) go-getter
real real McCoy
real real thing
real That (really) burns me (up)!
real You (really) said a mouthful.
reality bring so back to reality
reality in reality
reality lose touch with reality
reality reality of the situation
reality virtual reality
realize realize one's potential
realize realize sth from sth
really (I) really must go.
really I'm (really) fed up (with so/sth).
really (It) (really) doesn't matter to me.
really That (really) burns me (up)!
really You (really) said a mouthful.
ream ream so out
ream ream sth out
reap As a man sows, so shall he reap.
reap As you sow, so shall you reap.
reap grim reaper
reap reap sth from sth
reap Sow the wind and reap the whirlwind.
reaper grim reaper
reappoint reappoint so as sth
rear at the rear of sth
rear bring up the rear
rear get off one's rear
rear in the rear
rear pain in the rear
rear rear back
rear rear its ugly head
rear rear up
reason all the more reason for doing sth
reason beyond a reasonable doubt
reason have neither rhyme nor reason
reason It (only) stands to reason.
reason listen to reason
reason lose one's reason
reason neither rhyme nor reason
reason no earthly reason
reason reason against sth

reason reason sth out
reason reason with so
reason stand to reason
reason within reason
reason without rhyme or reason
reasonable beyond a reasonable doubt
reassign reassign so to sth
reassure reassure so about sth
reassure reassure so of sth
rebel rebel against so/sth
rebel rebel at so/sth
rebound rebound from sth
rebuke rebuke so for sth
recall recall so from sth
recall recall so/sth from sth
recall recall sth to mind
recall recall sth to so
recall word (once) spoken is past recalling.
recast recast sth in sth
recede recede from sth
receipt acknowledge (the) receipt of sth
receipt in receipt of sth
receive It is better to give than to receive.
receive It is more blessed to give than to receive.
receive receive so as so/sth
receive receive so into sth
receive receive so/sth back
receive receive so with open arms
receive receive sth from some place
receive receive sth from so
receive receive word (from so/sth)
recent in recent memory
reckon force to be reckoned with
reckon reckon so as so/sth
reckon reckon so/sth among sth
reckon reckon so/sth into sth
reckon reckon with so/sth
reckon reckon without so
reckon Short reckonings make long friends.
reckoning Short reckonings make long friends.
reclaim reclaim so/sth from so/sth
recognition flash with recognition
recognize flash with recognition
recognize How will I recognize you?
recognize recognize one for what one is
recognize recognize so as so/sth
recognize recognize so/sth by sth
recognize recognize so/sth for sth
recognize recognize sth for what it is
recoil recoil at the sight (of so/sth)
recoil recoil at the thought (of so/sth)
recoil recoil from so/sth
recommend recommend so as sth
recommend recommend so for sth
recommend recommend so/sth to so
recommend Self-praise is no recommendation.
recommendation Self-praise is no recommendation.
recompense recompense so for sth
reconcile reconcile oneself to sth
reconcile reconcile sth with sth
reconstruct reconstruct sth from sth
record break a record
record for the record
record off the record

record on record
record one for the (record) books
record record sth from sth
record record sth in sth
record record sth on sth
record set the record straight
record sound like a broken record
recount recount sth to so
recoup recoup sth from so/sth
recourse have recourse to sth
recover recover from so/sth
recover recover from sth
recover recover sth from so/sth
recovery on the road to recovery
recruit raw recruit
recruit recruit so for sth
recruit recruit so from sth
recruit recruit so into sth
recuperate recuperate from sth
red catch so red-handed
red cut through red tape
red down the little red lane
red give so a red face
red go into the red
red in the red
red not worth a red cent
red one's ears are red
red out of the red
red paint the town (red)
red red as a cherry
red red as a poppy
red red as a rose
red red as a ruby
red red as blood
red red herring
red red in the face
red red ink
red red tape
red red-carpet treatment
red red-letter day
red roll out the red carpet (for so)
red run a red light
red see red
rededicate rededicate oneself or sth to so/sth
redound redound on so
reduce in reduced circumstances
reduce reduce so to silence
reduce reduce so to tears
reduce reduce sth by sth
reduce reduce sth from sth to sth
reduce reduced to doing sth
reed broken reed
reed reed before the wind lives on, while mighty oaks do fall.
reef reef a sail in
reek reek of sth
reek reek with sth
reel reel back (from sth)
reel reel sth in
reel reel sth off
reel reel under sth
reelection come up for reelection
reelection up for reelection
refer refer so back to so/sth
refer refer so to so/sth
refer refer sth back to so/sth
refer refer to so/sth
reference in reference to so/sth
reference with reference to so/sth
refill refill a prescription
reflect reflect (back) (up)on so/sth
reflect reflect credit (up)on so/sth

reflect reflected in sth
refrain refrain from sth
refresh refresh so with sth
refresh refresh sth with sth
refuge take refuge in sth
refund refund sth to so
refuse make an offer one cannot refuse
refuse make one an offer one cannot refuse
refuse offer one cannot refuse
refuse refuse sth to so
refuse refuse to do sth
regain regain one's composure
regain regain one's feet
regain regain sth from so/sth
regale regale so with sth
regard hold so/sth in high regard
regard hold so/sth in low regard
regard in regard to so/sth
regard regard so/sth as so/sth
regard regard so/sth with sth
regard regardless of sth
regard with regard to so/sth
regardless regardless of sth
register register for sth
register register in sth
register register on sth
register register so as sth
register register so for sth
register register so in sth
register register sth with so/sth
register register with so
regress regress to sth
regular at regular intervals
regular regular as clockwork
regular regular fixture
regular regular guy
rehearsal in rehearsal
rehearse rehearse for sth
reign reign over so/sth
reimburse reimburse so for sth
reimburse reimburse sth to so
rein give free rein to so
rein keep a close rein on so/sth
rein keep a tight rein on so/sth
rein rein back on so/sth
rein rein so/sth in
rein rein sth up
rein rein up
reinforce reinforce so/sth with sth
reinstate reinstate so as sth
reinstate reinstate so in sth
reinvent reinvent the wheel
reissue reissue sth to so
reject reject so/sth out of hand
rejoice It is a poor heart that never rejoices.
rejoice rejoice at sth
rejoice rejoice in so/sth
rejoice rejoice over sth
relapse relapse into sth
relate relate sth to so
relate relate sth to sth
relate relate to so/sth
relate related to so
relation have intimate relations with so
relation have relations with so
relation in relation to so/sth
relation love-hate relationship
relationship love-hate relationship
relative relative to so/sth
relax relax into sth
relax relax one's hold on so/sth

relay relay sth to so
release release so/sth from sth
release release so to so
relegate relegate so to so/sth
reliance reliance on so/sth
relief breathe a sigh of relief
relief throw sth into sharp relief
relieve relieve one of one's duties
relieve relieve oneself
relieve relieve so of sth
religion get religion
religious religious about doing sth
relinquish relinquish sth over so
relinquish relinquish sth to so/sth
relish with relish
relocate relocate so/sth in sth
reluctant reluctant to do sth
rely rely (up)on so/sth
remain *at bay
remain remain ahead (of so/sth)
remain remain ahead of sth
remain remain ahead of the game
remain remain aloof from so/sth
remain remain at bay
remain remain at some place
remain remain away (from so/sth)
remain remain behind
remain remain clear of sth
remain remain down
remain remain in limbo
remain remain in (sth)
remain remain in the back of so's mind
remain remain in touch (with so/sth)
remain remain on
remain remain together
remain remain under sth
remain remain up
remain remain within (sth)
remand remand so (in)to the custody of so
remand remand so over to so
remark I didn't (quite) catch that (last) remark.
remark remark (up)on so/sth
remedy Desperate diseases must have desperate remedies.
remedy There is a remedy for everything except death.
remember Remember me to so.
remember remember so as sth
remember remember so in one's will
remember remember so to so
remember Remember to write.
remind need I remind you that...
remind remind so about so/sth
remind remind so of so/sth
reminisce reminisce about so/sth
reminisce reminisce with so
reminiscent reminiscent of so/sth
remission in remission
remit remit sth to so/sth
remonstrate remonstrate (with so) (about so/sth)
remove remove so from sth
remove remove so/sth from so/sth
remunerate remunerate so for sth
rend rend sth from so/sth
rend rend sth into sth
render render sth down
render render sth in(to) sth
render render sth to so/sth
renege renege on sth
renounce renounce so for sth

rent rent sth from so
rent rent sth (out) (to so)
repair beyond repair
repair in good repair
repair repair to some place
repatriate repatriate so to some place
repay repay so by sth
repay repay so for sth
repay repay so with sth
repeat History repeats itself.
repel repel so from sth
repent Marry in haste, (and) repent at leisure.
replace replace so/sth by so/sth
replenish replenish sth with sth
reply reply to so/sth
report report about so/sth
report report back (on so/sth)
report report back (to so/sth)
report report for sth
report report in
report report sth to so
report report to so/sth
report report (up)on so/sth
repose repose in sth
repose repose (up)on sth
represent represent so in sth
represent represent so/sth as sth
represent represent sth to so
reprimand reprimand so for sth
reproach above reproach
reproach reproach so for sth
reproach reproach so with sth
reproduce reproduce sth from sth
reprove reprove so for sth
repulse repulse so/sth from sth
reputation reputation (as a sth)
reputation reputation (for doing sth)
reputation stake one's reputation on so/sth
repute house of ill repute
repute woman of ill repute
reputed reputed to
request at so's request
request request so to do sth
request request sth from so
request request sth of so
require require a leap of faith
require require sth from so
require require sth of so
requirement meet the requirements (for sth)
requisition requisition sth for so/sth
requisition requisition sth from so/sth
rescue come to so's or sth's rescue
rescue rescue so/sth from so/sth
research research into so/sth
resemblance bear a resemblance to so/sth
resemble resemble so/sth in sth
resentment flame with resentment
reservation make a reservation
reservation make reservations
reserve hold so/sth in reserve
reserve keep so/sth in reserve
reserve reserve sth for so/sth
reside reside in some place
reside reside in so/sth
residence take up residence some place
resign resign from sth
resign resign oneself to sth
resign resign under fire
resign *under fire

resistance line of least resistance
resistance path of least resistance
resistance pocket of resistance
resonate resonate with so
resort as a last resort
resort resort to sth
resound resound through(out) sth
resound resound with sth
resource leave one to one's own resources
respect in many respects
respect in some respects
respect pay one's last respects (to so)
respect pay so respect
respect respect so as sth
respect respect so for sth
respect with respect to so/sth
respond respond to so/sth
response gut response
responsible hold so responsible (for sth)
responsible responsible party
rest at rest
rest bring sth to rest
rest come to rest
rest Give it a rest!
rest Give me a rest!
rest God rest so's soul.
rest I rest my case.
rest lay so to rest
rest lay sth to rest
rest No rest for the wicked.
rest one's last resting place
rest put sth to rest
rest rest against so/sth
rest rest assured
rest rest from sth
rest rest in peace
rest rest in sth
rest rest is gravy.
rest rest is history.
rest rest on one's laurels
rest rest sth against sth
rest rest sth in so/sth
rest rest up (for sth)
rest rest up (from sth)
rest rest (up)on sth
rest rest with so/sth
rest There is no rest for the weary.
restore restore so's trust in sth
restore restore sth to so
restore restore sth to sth
restrain restrain so from sth
restrict restrict so/sth to so/sth
restroom Where is the restroom?
result as a result (of sth)
result result from sth
result result in sth
resurrect resurrect so/sth from sth
retail retail at sth
retail retail for sth
retail retail sth to so
retain retain sth over so/sth
retaliate retaliate against so/sth
retire retire from sth
retire retire (in)to sth
retire retire on sth
retire retire so/sth from sth
retire retire to some place
retool retool for sth
retool retool sth for sth
retreat beat a (hasty) retreat
retreat retreat (from sth) (to some place)

retrieve retrieve so/sth from some place
retrieve retrieve sth from so
retrospect in retrospect
return by return mail
return by return post
return in return for (so/sth)
return point of no return
return return so/sth to so
return return so's compliment
return return sth for sth
return return the compliment
return return the favor
return return to haunt one
return return to some place
return return with sth
reunite reunite so/sth with so/sth
rev rev sth up
rev rev up
reveal reveal so/sth to so
revel revel in sth
revenge Revenge is a dish best served cold.
revenge Revenge is sweet.
revenge revenge oneself (up)on so/sth
revenge seek revenge (against so)
revenge take revenge (against so)
reverberate reverberate through sth
reverberate reverberate throughout sth
reverberate reverberate with sth
revere revere so/sth for sth
revert revert to so/sth
review pass in review
review review for sth
revolt revolt against so/sth
revolted revolted at so/sth
revolve revolve around so/sth
reward Desert and reward seldom keep company.
reward get one's just reward(s)
reward go to one's (just) reward
reward reward so for sth
reward reward so with sth
reward Virtue is its own reward.
rhapsodize rhapsodize over so/sth
rhyme have neither rhyme nor reason
rhyme neither rhyme nor reason
rhyme rhyme sth with sth
rhyme rhyme with sth
rhyme run one's rhymes
rhyme without rhyme or reason
rib stick to one's ribs
ribbon cut so to ribbons
rich filthy rich
rich from rags to riches
rich It is better to be born lucky than rich.
rich one law for the rich and another for the poor
rich rich in sth
rich rich man's joke is always funny.
rich rich with sth
rich stinking rich
rich strike it rich
rich too rich for so's blood
riches from rags to riches
ricochet ricochet off sth
rid good riddance (to bad rubbish)
rid good-bye and good riddance
rid rid of so/sth
rid rid oneself or sth of so/sth
riddance good riddance (to bad rubbish)

riddance Good-bye and good riddance.
riddle riddle so/sth with sth
ride for a ride
ride free ride
ride give so a ride
ride go along (with so) for the ride
ride He who rides a tiger is afraid to dismount.
ride hitch a ride
ride If two ride on a horse, one must ride behind.
ride If wishes were horses, then beggars would ride.
ride let sth ride
ride ride away
ride ride by so/sth
ride ride herd on so/sth
ride ride off
ride ride on
ride ride out (of some place)
ride ride over so/sth
ride ride roughshod over so/sth
ride ride so about sth
ride ride so or an animal down
ride ride sth down
ride ride sth out
ride ride the gravy train
ride ride to some place
ride ride up (on so)
ride ride (up)on so/sth
ride ride with so
ride riding for a fall
ride Set a beggar on horseback, and he'll ride to the devil.
ride take so for a ride
ride Thanks for the ride.
ride thumb a ride
ridicule from the sublime to the ridiculous
ridicule hold so/sth up to ridicule
ridicule make so look ridiculous
ridiculous from the sublime to the ridiculous
ridiculous make so look ridiculous
rifle rifle through sth
rig rig so/sth out (in sth)
rig rig sth up
right acknowledge so to be right
right act within one's rights
right all right
right All righty.
right All right(y) already!
right Am I right?
right (bang) dead to rights
right Come right in.
right come (right) on top of sth
right customer is always right.
right Everything's going to be all right.
right Everything will be all right.
right Everything will work out (all right).
right get one right here
right get right on sth
right give one's right arm (for so/sth)
right go in the right direction
right go (right) through so
right God's in his heaven; all's right with the world.
right hang a right
right have one's heart in the right place
right have so dead to rights
right hit so (right) between the eyes

right hit the nail (right) on the head
right hold one's mouth the right way
right (I) can't rightly say.
right I don't rightly know.
right (I'll) be right there.
right (I'll) be right with you.
right I'll get right on it.
right in one's right mind
right in the right
right Is that right?
right jog to the right or left
right keep on the right side of so
right keep on the right(-hand) side (of sth)
right keep so/sth on (the) (right) track
right left and right
right left hand doesn't know what the right hand is doing.
right make sth right
right Might makes right.
right Mr. Right
right Not right now, thanks.
right off on the right foot (with so/sth)
right *on so's heels
right on the right track
right one's heart is in the right place
right play one's cards right
right put sth right
right read one one's rights
right right and left
right right as rain
right right at a certain time
right right away
right right down so's alley
right right in the kisser
right right now
right right off the bat
right (right) off the top of one's head
right Right on!
right right on so's heels
right right on time
right right side up
right right stuff
right right to do sth
right right to sth
right (right) under so's (very) nose
right right up so's alley
right right-of-way
right sail (right) through sth
right say sth (right) to so's face
right serve so right
right set sth right
right sit right with so
right step right up
right straighten up and fly right
right strike the right note
right Things will work out (all right).
right turn out (all right)
right Two wrongs do not make a right.
right walk right in
right walk (right) into a trap
right walk (right) into so/sth
right walk right up (to so/sth)
right when it comes right down to it
right whiz (right) through sth
right within one's rights
right work out (all right)
right (You) took the words right out of my mouth.
rightly (I) can't rightly say.
rightly I don't rightly know.
righty All righty.
righty All right(y) already!

rile rile so up
Riley lead the life of Riley
Riley live the life of Riley
ring (dead) ringer (for so)
ring Give me a ring.
ring give so a ring
ring have a familiar ring (to it)
ring like a three-ring circus
ring look like a (dead) ringer (for so)
ring one's ears are ringing
ring ring a bell
ring ring around sth
ring ring back
ring ring in so's ears
ring ring in so's mind
ring ring in the new year
ring ring off the hook
ring ring out
ring ring so back
ring ring so up
ring ring sth up
ring ring the bell
ring ring the curtain down (on sth)
ring ring the curtain up
ring ring true
ring ring with sth
ring run rings around so
ring throw one's hat in the ring
ring toss one's hat into the ring
ringer (dead) ringer (for so)
ringer look like a (dead) ringer (for so)
rinse rinse so/sth down
rinse rinse so/sth off
rinse rinse so's mouth out (with soap)
rinse rinse sth down (with sth)
rinse rinse sth out
rinse rinse sth with sth
riot read so the riot act
riot riot of color
riot run riot
rip Let her rip!
rip rip into so/sth
rip rip off
rip rip on so
rip rip so off
rip rip so/sth apart
rip rip so/sth to sth
rip rip so/sth up
rip rip sth away (from so)
rip rip sth away (from sth)
rip rip sth down
rip rip sth in half
rip rip sth in two
rip rip sth off
rip rip sth out of so/sth
rip rip sth up
rip (rip-)off artist
rip ripsnorter
ripe Early ripe, early rotten.
ripe live to the (ripe old) age of sth
ripe ripe old age
ripe ripen into sth
ripe Soon ripe, soon rotten.
ripe time is ripe.
ripe when the time is ripe
ripple ripple of excitement
ripple ripple of protest
ripple ripple through sth
rise Early to bed and early to rise, makes a man healthy, wealthy, and wise.
rise feel one's gorge rise
rise get a rise from so

rise give rise to sth
rise God willing and the creek don't rise
rise Lord willing and the creek don't rise
rise make so's gorge rise
rise on the rise
rise rise above sth
rise Rise and shine!
rise rise from so/sth
rise rise from the ashes
rise rise from the dead
rise rise from the grave
rise rise from the ranks
rise rise in sth
rise rise to one's feet
rise rise to the bait
rise rise to the challenge
rise rise to the occasion
rise rise to the top
rise rise up
rise rise (up) against so/sth
rise think the sun rises and sets on so
risk at risk
risk risk of rain
risk risk of showers
risk risk of thunder(storms)
risk risk one's neck (to do sth)
risk risk sth on so/sth
risk run a risk (of sth)
risk run the risk (of sth)
risk take a risk
ritz put on the ritz
rival rival so in sth
river sail up a river
river sell so down the river
river send so up (the river)
river up the river
rivet mad enough to chew nails (and spit rivets)
rivet rivet one's gaze on so/sth
rivet rivet one's glare on so/sth
rivet rivet so's attention
rivet rivet sth on(to) sth
rivet riveted to the ground
road All roads lead to Rome.
road down one for the road
road down the road
road end of the road
road get out of the road
road get the show on the road
road hit the road
road (I'd) better hit the road.
road in the road
road (It's) time to hit the road.
road (I've) got to hit the road.
road on the road
road one for the road
road road hog
road road to hell is paved with good intentions.
road rocky road
road smack the road
road take one for the road
road There is no royal road to learning.
road where the rubber meets the road
road wide place in the road
roam roam about
roar keep it down (to a dull roar)
roar roar at so/sth
roar roar away
roar roar sth out
rob daylight robbery

rob highway robbery
rob rob Peter to pay Paul
rob rob so blind
rob rob so of sth
rob rob the cradle
robbery daylight robbery
robbery highway robbery
robin all around Robin Hood's barn
Robinson before you can say Jack Robinson
Robinson quicker than you can say Jack Robinson
rock between a rock and a hard place
rock get one's rocks off (on sth)
rock hand that rocks the cradle rules the world.
rock hard as a rock
rock have rocks in one's head
rock hit (rock) bottom
rock Let's rock and roll!
rock on the rocks
rock reach (rock) bottom
rock rock around
rock (rock) bottom
rock rock so to sth
rock rock the boat
rock rocky road
rock solid as a rock
rock steady as a rock
rocker off one's rocker
rocket rocket (in)to sth
rocket rocket sth into sth
rocky rocky road
rod Spare the rod and spoil the child.
Roger Roger (wilco).
role play a role in sth
roll ain't fittin' to roll with a pig
roll awkward as a cow on roller skates
roll call (the) roll
roll easy as rolling off a log
roll get rolling
roll get the ball rolling
roll heads will roll
roll high roller
roll keep the ball rolling
roll leave them rolling in the aisles
roll Let it roll!
roll Let's rock and roll!
roll on a roll
roll roll about
roll roll along
roll roll around
roll roll away
roll roll back
roll roll by
roll roll down
roll roll in
roll roll in(to some place)
roll roll off (so/sth)
roll roll on
roll roll one's sleeves up
roll roll (oneself) up in sth
roll roll out the red carpet (for so)
roll roll over
roll roll (over) in one's grave
roll roll prices back
roll roll so/sth over
roll roll so/sth (up) in sth
roll roll sth away
roll roll sth back
roll roll sth down
roll roll sth in
roll roll sth off (of) so/sth

roll roll sth onto sth
roll roll sth out
roll roll sth over
roll roll sth to so/sth
roll roll sth up
roll roll with the punches
roll rolling in it
roll rolling in money
roll rolling in sth
roll rolling in the aisles
roll rolling stone gathers no moss.
roll set the ball rolling
roll start the ball rolling
roll take (the) roll
roller awkward as a cow on roller skates
roller high roller
Roman When in Rome(, do as the Romans do).
Rome All roads lead to Rome.
Rome fiddle while Rome burns
Rome Rome was not built in a day.
Rome When in Rome(, do as the Romans do).
romp romp all over so
romp romp around
romp romp on so
romp romp through sth
roof go through the roof
roof hit the roof
roof live under the same roof (with so)
roof roof sth over
room allow some elbow room
room boys in the back room
room Can I use your powder room?
room Could I use your powder room?
room Don't let it out of this room.
room Go to your room!
room leave the room
room make room (for so/sth)
room May I use your powder room?
room need some elbow room
room not enough room to swing a cat
room room and board
room room together
room room with so
room send so to the locker room
room smoke-filled room
room some elbow room
room take up room
roost chickens come home to roost.
roost come home (to roost)
roost rule the roost
root appear to be rooted to the spot
root determine the root of the problem
root figure out the root of the problem
root find the root of the problem
root go to the root of the matter
root Idleness is the root of all evil.
root love of money is the root of all evil.
root Money is the root of all evil.
root put roots down (some place)
root root around (for sth)
root root for so/sth
root root of the matter
root root of the problem
root root so/sth out of sth
root root sth in sth
root root sth out
root root sth up
root rooted in sth
root rooted to sth

root rooted to the spot
root take root
rope at the end of one's rope
rope Give so enough rope and he'll hang himself.
rope know the ropes
rope learn the ropes
rope rope so in
rope rope so into doing sth
rope rope so into sth
rope rope so or an animal up
rope rope sth off
rope rope sth together
rope ropes
rope show so the ropes
rope skip rope
rope walk a tightrope
rose bed of roses
rose come out smelling like a rose
rose come up smelling like a rose
rose Everything's coming up roses.
rose primrose path
rose red as a rose
rose rose by any other name would smell as sweet.
rose smell like a rose
rose There's no rose without a thorn.
rosebud Gather ye rosebuds while ye may.
rot Early ripe, early rotten.
rot rot away
rot rot off
rot rot out
rot rotten apple
rot rotten apple spoils the barrel.
rot rotten egg
rot rotten luck
rot rotten to the core
rot Something is rotten in (the state of) Denmark.
rot Soon ripe, soon rotten.
rot spoiled rotten
rotate rotate on sth
rote by rote
rote learn sth by rote
rotten Early ripe, early rotten.
rotten rotten apple
rotten rotten apple spoils the barrel.
rotten rotten egg
rotten rotten luck
rotten rotten to the core
rotten Something is rotten in (the state of) Denmark.
rotten Soon ripe, soon rotten.
rotten spoiled rotten
rough diamond in the rough
rough have a rough time (of it)
rough rough idea (about sth)
rough rough it
rough rough so up
rough rough sth in
rough rough sth out
rough rough sth up
rough rough stuff
rough rough time
rough rough-and-ready
rough rough-and-tumble
rough Take the rough with the smooth.
roughshod ride roughshod over so/sth
roughshod run roughshod over so/sth
round all year round
round buy a round (of drinks)
round buy the next round (of drinks)

round express sth in round figures
round express sth in round numbers
round in round figures
round in round numbers
round longest way round is the shortest way home.
round Love makes the world go round.
round round off to sth
round round so/sth up
round round sth down
round round sth off
round round sth out
round round sth up
round round up to sth
round rounding error
round round-trip ticket
round square peg in a round hole
round write sth in round figures
roundabout say sth in a roundabout way
roundup head for the last roundup
roundup last roundup
rouse rouse so from sth
rouse rouse so out of sth
rouse rouse so to sth
roust roust so out of sth
rout rout so/sth out of some place
route route so/sth around sth
route route sth to so
rove have a roving eye
row get one's ducks in a row
row hard row to hoe
row hoe one's own row
row kick up a row
row row (so/sth) out to sth
row tough row to hoe
royal battle royal
royal royal pain
royal royal treatment
royal There is no royal road to learning.
rub don't know whether to eat it or rub it on
rub rub (away) at sth
rub rub elbows (with so)
rub rub off ((of) sth)
rub rub off (on so)
rub rub off on(to) so/sth
rub rub salt in a wound
rub rub shoulders with so
rub rub so or an animal down
rub rub so/sth with sth
rub rub so out
rub rub so('s fur) the wrong way
rub rub so's nose in it
rub rub sth against so/sth
rub rub sth away
rub rub sth in
rub rub sth into sth
rub rub sth off (of) sth
rub rub sth onto sth
rub rub sth out
rub rub sth over sth
rub rub sth together
rub rub sth up
rub rub (up) against so/sth
rubber lay (some) rubber
rubber where the rubber meets the road
rubbish good riddance (to bad rubbish)
Rubicon cross the Rubicon
ruby red as a ruby

ruffle ruffle its feathers
ruffle ruffle so's feathers
ruffle ruffle sth up
rug lie like a rug
rug pull the rug out (from under so)
rug rug rat
rug snug as a bug in a rug
ruin go to rack and ruin
ruin go to wrack and ruin
ruin in ruins
ruin lay in ruins
ruin leave sth in ruins
ruin lie in ruins
ruin ruin of so/sth
ruin wrack and ruin
rule as a (general) rule
rule as a rule
rule bend the rules
rule exception proves the rule.
rule hand that rocks the cradle rules the world.
rule rule against so/sth
rule rule in favor of so/sth
rule rule of thumb
rule rule on sth
rule rule over so/sth
rule rule so/sth out
rule rule the roost
rule rule with a velvet glove
rule rule with an iron fist
ruminate ruminate about sth
ruminate ruminate on sth
rummage rummage around (somewhere) (for sth)
rummage rummage through sth
rumor rumor has it that...
rump rump session
rumple rumple so/sth up
run also-ran
run could fight a circle-saw (and it a-runnin')
run course of true love never did run smooth.
run cut and run
run days running
run dry run
run eat and run
run for (some) days running
run for (some) months running
run for (some) years running
run front-runner
run have a run of sth
run have a run-in (with so/sth)
run have one's luck run out
run He who fights and runs away, may live to fight another day.
run hit the ground running
run (I) hate to eat and run.
run (I) have to run along.
run If you run after two hares, you will catch neither.
run in the long run
run in the running
run in the short run
run (It's) time to run.
run (I've) got to run.
run *like stink
run *like the devil
run *like the wind
run make a run for it
run make so's blood run cold
run months running
run My cup runneth over.

run off and running
run off to a running start
run on the run
run one's luck runs out
run *out of gas
run *out of patience
run *out (of sth)
run out of the running
run run a comb through sth
run run a fever
run run a make on so
run run a red light
run run a risk (of sth)
run run a tab
run run a taut ship
run run a temperature
run run a tight ship
run run across so/sth
run run across sth
run run (a)foul of so/sth
run run after so
run run against so
run run against the grain
run run aground (on sth)
run run along
run run amok
run run amuck
run run an errand
run run around
run run as sth
run run at a fast clip
run run at a good clip
run run at full blast
run run at so/sth
run run away (from so/sth)
run run away with so
run run away with sth
run run back
run run behind
run run between sth and sth else
run run circles around so
run run counter to sth
run run down
run run for it
run run for one's life
run run for one's money
run run for sth
run run for the hills
run run from so/sth
run run from sth to sth
run run in circles
run run in sth
run run in the family
run run into a stone wall
run run into so
run run in(to sth)
run Run it by (me) again.
run run it down
run run its course
run run like clockwork
run run like stink
run run like the wind
run run low (on sth)
run run off
run run on
run run on sth
run run one's eye over sth
run run one's feet off
run run one's fingers through one's hair
run run one's hand through one's hair
run run one's head against a brick wall
run run one's rhymes
run run out at so/sth

run run out of gas
run run out of patience
run run out of some place
run run out (of sth)
run run out of steam
run run out of time
run run out (on so)
run run over
run run rampant
run run rings around so
run run riot
run run roughshod over so/sth
run run scared
run run short (of sth)
run run so in
run run so/sth down
run run so/sth into sth
run run so/sth off (of) sth
run run so/sth out of sth
run run so/sth to earth
run run so/sth to sth
run run so ragged
run run so through sth
run run so through (with sth)
run run sth at full blast
run run sth back
run run sth by (so) (again)
run run sth by the book
run run sth down
run run sth in
run run sth into sth
run run sth into the ground
run run sth off
run run sth onto sth
run run sth out of sth
run run sth over to so/sth
run run sth through sth
run run sth up
run Run that by (me) again.
run run the gamut
run run the gauntlet
run run the good race
run run the risk (of sth)
run run the show
run run through sth
run run to seed
run run to so/sth
run run to sth
run run up against so/sth
run run up to some place
run run up (to so/sth)
run run wild
run run with so/sth
run run with sth
run run with the hare and hunt with the hounds
run running high
run run-of-the-mill
run Still waters run deep.
run Take a running jump (in the lake)!
run turn tail (and run)
run *up against sth
run up and running
run We must learn to walk before we can run.
run weeks running
run years running
run You never miss the water till the well runs dry.
runaround runaround
rung on the bottom rung (of the ladder)
runner front-runner

runneth My cup runneth over.
running could fight a circle-saw (and it a-runnin')
running days running
running for (some) days running
running for (some) months running
running for (some) years running
running hit the ground running
running in the running
running months running
running off and running
running off to a running start
running out of the running
running running high
running Take a running jump (in the lake)!
running up and running
running weeks running
running years running
runt runt of the litter
rush bum's rush
rush Don't rush me!
rush Fools rush in where angels fear to tread.
rush in a mad rush
rush rush at so/sth
rush rush for sth
rush rush hour
rush rush in(to sth)
rush rush off (from some place)
rush rush on sth
rush rush out (of sth)
rush rush so into sth
rush rush so/sth into sth
rush rush so/sth out of sth
rush rush so to the hospital
rush rush sth into print
rush rush sth off (to so/sth)
rush rush sth through (sth)
rush rush through sth
rush rush to conclusions
rush rush to so/sth
rust It is better to wear out than to rust out.
rust rust away
rust rust belt
rust rust out
rustle rustle sth up
rut in a rut
rut (stuck) in a rut
saber rattle its saber
saber rattle one's saber
sack can't carry a tune in a paper sack
sack empty sack cannot stand upright.
sack hit the sack
sack sack
sack sack out
sack sack sth up
sack sacked out
sacred sacred cow
sacrifice sacrifice so/sth for so/sth
sacrifice sacrifice so/sth to so/sth
sad sad sight
sadder sadder but wiser
saddle have a burr under one's saddle
saddle look like a saddle on a sow
saddle saddle an animal up
saddle saddle so with so/sth
saddle saddle up
saddle saddled with so/sth
safe Better (be) safe than sorry.
safe Have a safe journey.
safe Have a safe trip.

safe on the safe side
safe play it safe
safe safe and sound
safe safety in numbers
safe There is safety in numbers.
safe to be on the safe side
safe to be safe
safe Your secret is safe with me.
safeguard safeguard against so/sth
safeguard safeguard so/sth against so/sth
safekeeping for safekeeping
safely Drive safely.
safety safety in numbers
safety There is safety in numbers.
sag sag away (from sth)
sag sag down
sag sag under sth
sage sage advice
said after all is said and done
said easier said than done
said I wish I'd said that.
said less said (about sth), the better.
said no sooner said than done
said Well said.
said What so said.
said when all is said and done
said You (really) said a mouthful.
said You said it!
sail clear sailing
sail Hoist your sail when the wind is fair.
sail knock the wind out of so's sails
sail sail against sth
sail sail along (sth)
sail sail around
sail sail for some place
sail sail from some place to some place else
sail sail into so
sail sail in(to sth)
sail sail (right) through sth
sail sail under false colors
sail sail up a river
sail set sail for some place
sail smooth sailing
sail take the wind out of so's sails
sailor Heaven protects children(, sailors,) and drunken men.
saint enough sth to plague a saint
saint have the patience of a saint
sake arguing for the sake of arguing
sake arguing for the sake of argument
sake For goodness sake!
sake For gosh sake!
sake For heaven('s) sake!
sake for one's (own) sake
sake For Pete's sake!
sake For pity's sake!
sake for so/sth's sake
sake for the sake of so/sth
sake Land(s) sakes (alive)!
sake Sakes alive!
salad in one's salad days
salad toss a salad
sale close a sale
sale close the sale
sale come up for sale
sale for sale
sale no sale
sale on sale
sale put sth up for sale
sale up for sale
salesman no salesman will call
sally sally forth

salt back to the salt mines
salt eat so's salt
salt go back to the salt mines
salt go through so like a dose of the salts
salt have sth hung up and salted
salt rub salt in a wound
salt salt of the earth
salt salt sth away
salt salt sth down
salt salt sth with sth
salt take sth with a pinch of salt
salt worth one's salt
salute salute so with sth
salvage salvage sth from so/sth
Sam What in (the) Sam Hill?
same add up to the same thing
same all the same
same amount to the same thing
same at the same time
same bitten by the same bug
same by the same token
same cast in the same mold
same close enough to use the same toothpick
same come to the same thing
same cut from the same cloth
same go into the same old song and dance about sth
same I'll have the same.
same in the same boat (as so)
same in the same breath
same just the same
same Lightning never strikes (the same place) twice.
same live under the same roof (with so)
same made from the same mold
same not in the same league with so/sth
same on the same wavelength
same one and the same
same read from the same page
same same as so/sth
same same difference
same same for me.
same Same here.
same same o(l)' same o(l)'
same same old story
same same to you.
same sing from the same hymnbook
same speak the same language
same tarred with the same brush
sanctity odor of sanctity
sand bury one's head in the sand
sand draw a line in the sand
sand have one's head in the sand
sand hide one's head in the sand
sand sand sth down
sand sands of time
sandwich ask for a knuckle sandwich
sandwich knuckle sandwich
sandwich one sandwich short of a picnic
sandwich sandwich so/sth between people or things
sandwich want a knuckle sandwich
sardine pack so/sth (in) like sardines
sardine packed (in) like sardines
sassy fat and sassy
satiate satiate so or an animal with sth
satisfy satisfy so or an animal with sth
satisfy satisfy sth by sth
saturate saturate so/sth with sth

Saturday Saturday night special
sauce happy as a clam (in butter sauce)
sauce Hunger is the best sauce.
sauce on the sauce
sauce What's sauce for the goose is sauce for the gander.
saucer eyes like saucers
saunter saunter along
save dip into one's savings
save in the interest of saving time
save penny saved is a penny earned.
save prophet is not without honor save in his own country.
save save a bundle (on sth)
save Save it!
save save (money) on sth
save save (money) toward sth
save save money up (for sth)
save save one's bacon
save save one's breath
save save (one's) face
save save oneself (for marriage)
save save so in the (very) nick of time
save save so/sth from so/sth
save save so's neck
save save so's skin
save save (sth) for a rainy day
save save sth for so/sth
save save sth up
save save the day
save save (up) (for sth)
save saved by the bell
save saving grace
save scrimp and save
save stitch in time saves nine.
savor savor of sth
saw could fight a circle-saw (and it a-runnin')
saw saw against the grain
saw saw into sth
saw saw sth down
saw saw sth off (of) sth
saw saw sth (up) (in(to) sth)
saw saw through sth
say after all is said and done
say Anything you say.
say as I was saying
say before you can say Jack Robinson
say better left unsaid
say Can't say (a)s I do(, can't say (a)s I don't).
say can't say boo to a goose
say Do as I say, not as I do.
say (Do you) know what I'm saying?
say (Do) you mean to say sth?
say Don't make me say it again!
say Don't say it!
say drop in (to say hello)
say easier said than done
say final say
say get a say (in sth)
say go so far as to say sth
say have the final say
say (I) can't rightly say.
say (I) can't say (as) I do.
say (I) can't say (as) I have.
say (I) can't say for sure.
say (I) can't say's I do.
say (I) can't say's I have.
say (I) can't say that I do.
say (I) can't say that I have.
say I hear what you're saying.

say (I) just want(ed) to say sth.
say I must say good night.
say I wish I'd said that.
say *in plain language
say (It) (just) goes without saying.
say just let me say
say less said (about sth), the better.
say let me (just) say
say let's say
say like I was saying
say Need I say more?
say needless to say
say Never say die.
say No sooner said than done
say on so's say-so
say one's say
say quicker than you can say Jack Robinson
say say a mouthful
say Say cheese!
say say grace
say Say hello to so (for me).
say say (in sth)
say Say no more.
say say one's piece
say say sth about so/sth
say say sth against so/sth
say say sth for sth
say say sth in a roundabout way
say say sth in plain English
say say sth in plain language
say say sth out loud
say say sth over (and over (again))
say say sth (right) to so's face
say say sth to oneself
say say sth to so
say say sth to sth
say say sth under one's breath
say say that...
say say the word
say say uncle
say Say what?
say Say when.
say Says me!
say Says who?
say Says you!
say Smile when you say that.
say That's easy for you to say.
say That's what I say.
say The hell you say!
say to say nothing of so/sth
say to say the least
say *under one's breath
say Well said.
say What can I say?
say What do you say?
say What do you want me to say?
say What say?
say What so said.
say What would you say if...?
say when all is said and done
say You can say that again!
say You don't say.
say You (really) said a mouthful.
say You said it!
scab scab over
scale scale sth down
scale scale sth to sth
scale tip the scales at sth
scam What's the scam?
scamper scamper along
scamper scamper away

scapegoat make so the scapegoat for sth
scar scar over
scarce Good men are scarce.
scarce make oneself scarce
scarce scarce as hen's teeth
scarce scarcely exchange more than some number of words with so
scarce scarcely have time to breathe
scarce scarcer than hen's teeth
scarcely scarcely exchange more than some number of words with so
scarcely scarcely have time to breathe
scare I wasn't brought up in the woods to be scared by owls.
scare run scared
scare scare one out of one's mind
scare scare one out of one's wits
scare scare so or an animal off
scare scare so or an animal out
scare scare so or an animal to death
scare scare so/sth away (from so/sth)
scare scare so/sth up
scare scare so out of sth
scare scare so stiff
scare scare sth out of so
scare scare the living daylights out of so
scare scare the pants off (of) so
scare scare the wits out of so
scare scared silly
scare scared stiff
scare scared to death
scare You scared the crap out of me.
scare You scared the devil out of me.
scare You scared the hell out of me.
scarf scarf out
scarf scarf sth down
scatter scatter sth about
scavenge scavenge (around) for so/sth
scenario best-case scenario
scenario worst-case scenario
scene arrive on the scene
scene arrive (up)on the scene (of sth)
scene behind the scenes
scene burst onto the scene
scene burst (up)on the scene
scene come on the scene
scene create a scene
scene make a scene
scene make the scene
scene on the scene
scenery change of scenery
scent put a dog off the scent
scent put so off the scent
schedule ahead of schedule
schedule behind schedule
schedule fall behind schedule
schedule finish ahead of schedule
schedule on schedule
scheme scheme against so/sth
scheme scheme for sth
schizz schiz(z) out
school cut school
school from the old school
school How do you like school?
school Never tell tales out of school.
school of the old school
school school of hard knocks
school school of thought
school school so in sth
school tell tales out of school
scoff scoff at so/sth

scold scold so about sth
scold scold so for sth
scoop scoop sth out of sth
scoop scoop sth up
scoop What's the scoop?
scoot scoot down (to some place)
scoot scoot over
scope scope (on) so
scope scope so/sth out
score have a score to settle (with so)
score know the score
score score against so/sth
score score for sth
score score sth (up) against so/sth
score score with so or a group
score settle a score with so
score settle the score (with so)
scorn Hell hath no fury like a woman scorned.
scorn hold so/sth up to scorn
scot get off scot-free
scot go scot-free
Scott Great Scott!
Scotty Beam me up, Scotty!
scour scour sth for so/sth
scour scour sth off (of) sth
scour scour sth out
scout scout around (for so/sth)
scout scout so/sth out
scout scout so/sth up
scowl scowl at so/sth
scramble scramble for so/sth
scrape bow and scrape
scrape have a scrape (with so/sth)
scrape pinch and scrape
scrape scrape along (on sth)
scrape scrape by (on sth)
scrape scrape by (sth)
scrape scrape by (with sth)
scrape scrape so/sth together
scrape scrape sth away (from sth)
scrape scrape sth off (of) so/sth
scrape scrape sth out
scrape scrape sth together
scrape scrape the bottom of the barrel
scrape scrape through (sth)
scratch bake sth from scratch
scratch do sth from scratch
scratch from scratch
scratch like tryin' to scratch your ear with your elbow
scratch make sth from scratch
scratch not up to scratch
scratch scratch about (for sth)
scratch scratch at sth
scratch scratch so/sth from sth
scratch scratch so/sth out
scratch scratch so/sth up
scratch scratch so's back
scratch scratch sth away
scratch scratch the surface
scratch start from scratch
scratch You scratch my back and I'll scratch yours.
scream *like the dickens
scream piercing scream
scream scream at so/sth
scream scream bloody murder
scream scream down (on so/sth)
scream scream for sth
scream scream so down
scream scream sth out
scream scream with sth

scream so mad I could scream
screech screeching (drunk)
screen screen so/sth (off) (from so/sth)
screen screen so/sth out of sth
screw get screwed
screw have a screw loose
screw put the screws on (so)
screw screw around
screw screw off
screw screw so around
screw screw so/sth up
screw screw so out of sth
screw screw so over
screw screw so up
screw screw sth down
screw screw sth into sth
screw screw sth (on)(to sth)
screw screw sth up
screw screw up
screw screwed, blued, and tattooed
screw screwed up
scribble scribble away (at sth)
scribble scribble sth down
scrimp scrimp and save
scrimp scrimp on sth
scripture devil can cite Scripture for his own purpose.
scripture devil can quote Scripture for his own purpose.
scrounge scrounge around (for so/sth)
scrounge scrounge so/sth up
scrub scrub so/sth down
scrub scrub so/sth off
scrub scrub sth away
scrub scrub sth off (of) sth
scrub scrub sth out
scrub scrub up
scrunch scrunch down
scrunch scrunch sth down (into sth)
scrunch scrunch sth up
scrutiny have so/sth under (close) scrutiny
scrutiny keep so/sth under (close) scrutiny
scrutiny under (close) scrutiny
scuff scuff sth up
scuffle scuffle with so
scurry scurry along
scuttle scuttle across sth
scuttle scuttle away
scuzz scuzz so out
sea (all) at sea (about sth)
sea at sea
sea between the devil and the deep blue sea
sea from overseas
sea from sea to shining sea
sea go to sea
sea He that would go to sea for pleasure, would go to hell for a pastime.
sea one's sea legs
sea sea change
sea son of a sea biscuit
sea There are plenty of (other) fish in the sea.
seal My lips are sealed.
seal seal a bargain
seal seal so's fate
seal seal sth off from so/sth
seal seal sth (up) (with sth)
seal seal the bargain
seal sealed (up)

seal sealed with a kiss
seal signed, sealed, and delivered
seal so's fate is sealed
seam burst at the seams
seam come apart at the seams
seam fall apart (at the seams)
seam seam sth with sth
seamy seamy side of life
search go out in search of so/sth
search in search of so/sth
search search after so/sth
search search for so/sth
search search high and low (for so/sth)
search Search me.
search search so for sth
search search so/sth out
search search sth for so/sth
search search sth with a fine-tooth comb
search search through sth
season come into season
season in season
season off season
season open season (on some creature)
season open season (on so)
season out of season
season season sth with sth
seat by the seat of one's pants
seat fly by the seat of one's pants
seat grab a seat
seat have a seat
seat in the catbird seat
seat in the driver's seat
seat in the hot seat
seat (Is) this (seat) taken?
seat keep one's seat
seat kick in the (seat of the) pants
seat make it by the seat of one's pants
seat on the edge of one's seat
seat on the hot seat
seat seat so by so/sth
seat show one to one's seat
seat show so to a seat
seat take a backseat (to so/sth)
seat Take your seat.
secede secede from sth
second come off second best
second Don't give it a (second) thought.
second for a split second
second in a split second
second in (just) a second
second in one's second childhood
second in the second place
second on second thought
second one's second wind
second play second fiddle (to so)
second second hand
second second nature to so
second second thoughts (about so/sth)
second second to none
second second-guess so
second split second
secrecy cloak so/sth in secrecy
secret Can you keep a secret?
secret carry a secret to the grave
secret cloak so/sth in secrecy
secret Could you keep a secret?
secret in secret
secret keep a secret
secret make a secret of sth
secret open secret
secret trade secret

secret Your secret is safe with me.
secure lull so into a false sense of security
secure secure sth against so/sth or an animal
secure security against sth
security lull so into a false sense of security
seduce seduce so from sth
see Am I glad to see you!
see as I see it
see begin to see daylight
see begin to see the light
see Believe nothing of what you hear, and only half of what you see.
see buy sth sight unseen
see Can I see you again?
see Can I see you in my office?
see cannot see (any) further than the end of one's nose
see cannot see the forest for the trees
see cannot see the wood for the trees
see can't see a hole in a ladder
see can't see beyond the end of one's nose
see can't see one's hand in front of one's face
see can't see straight
see Children should be seen and not heard.
see Come back and see us.
see Could I see you again?
see Could I see you in my office?
see first see the light of day
see have seen better days
see Haven't I seen you somewhere before?
see (I) haven't seen you in a long time.
see (I) haven't seen you in a month of Sundays.
see (I) hope to see you again (sometime).
see (I) never thought I'd see you here!
see If you don't see what you want, please ask (for it).
see (I'll) be seeing you.
see (I'll) see you in a little while.
see I'll see you later.
see (I'll) see you next year.
see (I'll) see you (real) soon.
see (I'll) see you then.
see (I'll) see you tomorrow.
see (It's) good to see you (again).
see (It's) nice to see you.
see (I've) seen better.
see I've seen better heads on nickel beers.
see (I've) seen worse.
see Just (you) wait (and see)!
see Long time no see.
see look-see
see May I see you again?
see Monkey see, monkey do.
see *(neither) hide nor hair
see not able to see the forest for the trees
see Not if I see you first.
see Not if I see you sooner.
see not see any objection (to sth)
see *on the dot
see see a man about a dog
see see about so/sth
see see after so/sth
see see ahead (of so/sth)

see see around sth
see see beyond sth
see see double
see see eye to eye (about so/sth) (with so)
see see fit (to do sth)
see See if I care!
see see (neither) hide nor hair
see See no evil, hear no evil, speak no evil.
see see no further than the end of one's nose
see see no objection (to sth)
see see one's way (clear) (to do sth)
see see over sth
see see red
see see so about so/sth
see see so across sth
see see so as so/sth
see see so as sth
see see so back (to sth)
see see so down to sth
see see so home
see see so into sth
see see so off
see see so on the dot
see see so/sth around sth
see see so/sth in a new light
see see so out (of sth)
see see so to some place
see see so to sth
see see so to the door
see see so up to sth
see see sth against sth
see see sth as sth else
see see sth in so/sth
see see sth in the cards
see see sth of so/sth
see see sth through
see see stars
see see the big picture
see see the color of so's money
see see the (hand)writing on the wall
see see the last of so/sth
see see the light
see see the sights
see see through so/sth
see see (to it) that sth is done
see see to so/sth
see see which way the wind is blowing
see see with the naked eye
see See ya.
see See ya, bye-bye.
see See you.
see See you around.
see (See you) later.
see See you later, alligator.
see Seeing is believing.
see seeing pink elephants
see seeing pink spiders
see seeing snakes
see seeing that...
see seeing things
see the way I see it
see There's none so blind as those who will not see.
see They must have seen you coming.
see wait-and-see attitude
see (We) don't see you much around here anymore.
see What the eye doesn't see, the heart doesn't grieve over.
see What you see is what you get.

see Will I see you again?
see would not be seen dead (doing sth)
see You ain't seen nothing yet!
see You (just) wait (and see)!
seed go to seed
seed Good seed makes a good crop.
seed run to seed
seek much sought after
seek seek after so/sth
seek Seek and ye shall find.
seek seek professional help
seek seek revenge (against so)
seek seek so/sth out
seek seek sth from so/sth
seem *million miles away
seem *out of place
seem seem high-and-mighty
seem seem like a long shot
seem seem like oneself again
seem seem like putty in so's hands
seem seem like so/sth
seem seem like the last person
seem seem out of place
seem seem pushed for time
seem Things are seldom what they seem.
seen Children should be seen and not heard.
seen have seen better days
seen Haven't I seen you somewhere before?
seen (I) haven't seen you in a long time.
seen (I) haven't seen you in a month of Sundays.
seen (I've) seen better.
seen I've seen better heads on nickel beers.
seen (I've) seen worse.
seen They must have seen you coming.
seen would not be seen dead (doing sth)
seen You ain't seen nothing yet!
seep seep away
seep seep in(to sth)
seep seep out (of sth)
seep seep through sth
seethe seethe with so/sth
seethe seethe with sth
segregate segregate so from so else
segregate segregate so/sth or an animal into sth
segregate segregate sth from sth else
segue segue into sth
seize seize onto so/sth
seize seize so/sth with sth
seize seize sth up
seize seize the opportunity
seize seize up
seize seize (up)on sth
seize seized with sth
seldom Desert and reward seldom keep company.
seldom Things are seldom what they seem.
select select from so/sth
select select so from sth
select select so/sth as sth
select select so/sth for so/sth
self by herself
self Every man for himself (and the devil take the hindmost).
self He who excuses himself accuses himself.

self Self-praise is no recommendation.
self Self-preservation is the first law of nature.
sell hard sell
sell sell at sth
sell sell like hotcakes
sell sell out
sell sell so a bill of goods
sell sell so down the river
sell sell so on sth
sell sell so/sth as sth
sell sell so/sth short
sell sell so out
sell sell sth at sth
sell sell sth for a certain price
sell sell sth for a song
sell sell sth off
sell sell sth on credit
sell sell sth out
sell sell the farm
sell selling point
sell soft sell
send big send-off
send gods send nuts to those who have no teeth.
send send after so/sth
send send ahead for sth
send send away (for sth)
send send for so/sth
send send in for sth
send send off for sth
send send one about one's business
send send one to one's death
send send out (for so/sth)
send send so after so/sth
send send so away
send send so back for sth
send send so before so/sth
send send so below
send send so down for sth
send send so for so/sth
send send so from pillar to post
send send so in
send send so into a state or condition
send send so into sth
send send so off
send send so on a wild-goose chase
send send so/sth across (sth)
send send so/sth along
send send so/sth around
send send so/sth away
send send so/sth back
send send so/sth down
send send so/sth on (ahead) (of so/sth)
send send so/sth under sth
send send so/sth up
send send so out
send send so (out) on an errand
send send so over (to) some place
send send so packing
send send so through the mill
send send so to bed
send send so to glory
send send so to the locker room
send send so to the showers
send send so up
send send sth by sth
send send sth C.O.D.
send send sth from sth
send send sth into sth
send send sth off (to so/sth)
send send sth over ((to) some place)
send send sth to so/sth

send send up a trial balloon
send send word to so
send *through the mill
sense ain't got a grain of sense
sense ain't got a lick of sense
sense ain't got the sense God gave geese
sense bring one to one's senses
sense come to one's senses
sense doesn't have enough sense to bell a cat
sense doesn't have enough sense to come in out of the rain
sense doesn't have the sense God gave geese
sense doesn't have the sense God gave him (or her)
sense go out of one's senses
sense have more luck than sense
sense horse sense
sense in a sense
sense knock some sense into so
sense lull so into a false sense of security
sense make sense
sense make (some) sense (out) of so/sth
sense ounce of common sense is worth a pound of theory.
sense sense of humor
sense sixth sense
sense take leave of one's senses
sensitize sensitize so to sth
sentence pass sentence on so
sentence sentence so to sth (for sth)
separate separate but equal
separate separate off (from sth)
separate separate so from so else
separate separate so/sth into sth
separate separate sth from sth else
separate separate sth off from sth
separate separate sth out of sth
separate separate the men from the boys
separate separate the wheat from the chaff
serious dead serious
serious Get serious!
serious serious about so
servant Fire is a good servant but a bad master.
serve Dinner is served.
serve First come, first served.
serve How can I serve you?
serve if my memory serves me correctly
serve If you would be well served, serve yourself.
serve No man can serve two masters.
serve *on a silver platter
serve Revenge is a dish best served cold.
serve serve a (useful) purpose
serve serve as a guinea pig
serve serve as so/sth
serve serve as the driving force (behind so/sth)
serve serve notice (on so)
serve serve on sth
serve serve so right
serve serve so's purpose
serve serve so with sth
serve serve sth around

serve serve sth for sth
serve serve sth in sth
serve serve sth on a silver platter
serve serve sth on so
serve serve sth out
serve serve sth to so
serve serve sth up
serve serve time
serve serve under so/sth
serve serve with so
serve They also serve who only stand and wait.
serve You cannot serve God and mammon.
serve Youth must be served.
service at so's service
service bring sth into service
service Call my service.
service come into service
service go into service
service go into the service
service go out of service
service in service
service of service (to so)
service out of service
service pay lip service (to sth)
service press so/sth into service
service put sth in(to) service
session in session
session jam session
session rump session
set (all) set (to do sth)
set at a set time
set dead set against so/sth
set get one's ears set out
set have a set-to (with so)
set have one's heart (dead) set against sth
set have one's heart set on sth
set not set foot somewhere
set on your mark, get set, go
set one's heart is (dead) set against sth
set one's heart is set on sth
set ready, set, go
set Set a beggar on horseback, and he'll ride to the devil.
set set a precedent
set Set a thief to catch a thief.
set set a trap
set set about doing sth
set set eyes on so/sth
set set fire to so/sth
set set foot in some place
set set for life
set set forth on sth
set set great store by so/sth
set set in
set set of pipes
set set of wheels
set set off (for sth)
set set off on sth
set set one (back) on one's feet
set set one back on one's heels
set set one on one's feet again
set set one's heart against sth
set set one's heart on so/sth
set set one's hopes on so/sth
set set one's house in order
set set one's mind on so/sth
set set one's mind to sth
set set one's (own) price
set set one's sights on so/sth

set set out (for some place) (from some place)
set set out on one's own
set set out (on sth)
set set out to do sth
set set sail for some place
set set so about sth
set set so apart from so else
set set so back (some amount of money)
set set so down (on(to) sth)
set set so off
set set so on fire
set set so or an animal on so or an animal
set set so/sth above so/sth
set set so/sth down
set set so/sth free (from sth)
set set so/sth on fire
set set so/sth on track
set set so/sth to work
set set so/sth up against so/sth
set set so/sth up as sth
set set so's mind at ease (about so/sth)
set set so's teeth on edge
set set so straight
set set so up
set set sth against so/sth
set set sth apart from sth else
set set sth aside
set set sth at sth
set set sth back
set set sth before so/sth or some creature
set set sth beside sth
set set sth down
set set sth for sth
set set sth forth
set set sth forward
set set sth in
set set sth into sth
set set sth off
set set sth out (for so/sth)
set set sth over sth
set set sth right
set set sth straight
set set sth to music
set set sth up
set set sth (up)on sth
set set the ball rolling
set set the record straight
set set the stage for sth
set set the table
set set the world on fire
set set to
set set tongues (a-)wagging
set set type
set set up shop somewhere
set set upon so/sth
set think the sun rises and sets on so
setback suffer a setback
settle Charge it to the dust and let the rain settle it.
settle have a score to settle (with so)
settle settle a score with so
settle settle down
settle settle for sth
settle settle in
settle settle on sth
settle settle so's affairs
settle settle so's hash
settle settle (sth) (out of court)
settle settle the score (with so)
settle settle up with so
settle when the dust settles
seven at sixes and sevens

seven in seventh heaven
seven Keep a thing seven years and you'll (always) find a use for it.
seven seven-day wonder
seven seven-year itch
seventh in seventh heaven
sever sever ties with so
sew sew so/sth up
sew sewed up
sex opposite sex
sez Sez me!
sez Sez who?
shabby not too shabby
shack shack up (with so)
shackle shackle so with sth
shade have it made in the shade
shade shades of so/sth
shadow afraid of one's own shadow
shadow beyond the shadow of a doubt
shadow Coming events cast their shadows before.
shadow shadow of oneself
shadow without a shadow of a doubt
shady shady character
shady shady deal
shaft get the shaft
shaft give so the shaft
shag shag (off)
shag shagged out
shag shaggy-dog story
shaggy shaggy-dog story
shake all shook up
shake fair shake
shake in two shakes of a lamb's tail
shake Let's shake on it.
shake more so/sth than one can shake a stick at
shake movers and shakers
shake no great shakes
shake on shaky ground
shake shake a disease or illness off
shake shake a habit
shake shake a leg
shake shake hands
shake shake (hands) on sth
shake shake in one's boots
shake Shake it (up)!
shake shake so down
shake shake so/sth off
shake shake so/sth up
shake shake so's hand
shake shake so up
shake shake sth down
shake shake sth off
shake shake sth out
shake shake sth up
shake shake the habit
shake shake the lead out
shake shook up
shake two shakes of a lamb's tail
shake What's shakin' (bacon)?
shaker movers and shakers
shaking What's shakin' (bacon)?
shaky on shaky ground
shall As a man sows, so shall he reap.
shall As you sow, so shall you reap.
shall Blessed is he who expects nothing, for he shall never be disappointed.
shall East is East and West is West (and never the twain shall meet).
shall Seek and ye shall find.

shallow Cross the stream where it is shallowest.
shambles in (a) shambles
shame crying shame
shame Fool me once, shame on you; fool me twice, shame on me.
shame For shame!
shame hide one's face in shame
shame put so to shame
shame shame of it (all)!
shame Shame on you!
shame Tell the truth and shame the devil.
shame What a shame!
shank by shank's mare
shank go (somewhere) by shank's mare
shank shank it
shank shank's mare
shape bend so out of shape
shape bend sth out of shape
shape bent out of shape
shape flex sth out of shape
shape flexed out of shape
shape in any way, shape, or form
shape in bad shape
shape in good shape
shape in shape
shape keep in good shape
shape lick so/sth into shape
shape lick sth into shape
shape out of shape
shape shape so up
shape shape up
shape take shape
shape whip so/sth into shape
shape whip sth into shape
share lion's share of sth
share one's fair share
share share and share alike
share share so's pain
share share so's sorrow
share Thank you for sharing.
share trouble shared is a trouble halved.
sharp at some time sharp
sharp bring so up sharply
sharp have a mind as sharp as a steel trap
sharp sharp as a razor
sharp sharp as a tack
sharp sharp tongue
sharp sharp wit
sharp throw sth into sharp relief
shave close shave
shave have a close shave
shave little shaver
she She will get hers.
she That's all she wrote.
she That's what she wrote.
shebang whole shebang
shed get shed of so/sth
shed not shed a tear
shed shed crocodile tears
shed shed (some) light on sth
sheep black sheep of the family
sheep might as well be hung for a sheep as (for) a lamb
sheep wolf in sheep's clothing
sheet both sheets in the wind
sheet four sheets in the wind
sheet know no more about sth than a frog knows about bedsheets
sheet three sheets in the wind

sheet two sheets to the wind
sheet white as a sheet
shelf off the shelf
shelf on the shelf
shell bring one out of one's shell
shell come out of one's shell
shell shell out (an amount of money)
shell walk on eggshells
shellac shellacking
shift shift for oneself
shift shift one's ground
shift stick shift
shine come rain or (come) shine
shine come rain or shine
shine from sea to shining sea
shine Happy is the bride that the sun shines on.
shine Make hay while the sun shines.
shine rain or shine
shine Rise and shine!
shine shine up to so
shine take a shine to so/sth
shine where the sun don't shine
Shinola know shit from Shinola
Shinola tell shit from Shinola
ship abandon ship
ship desert a sinking ship
ship Don't give up the ship!
ship jump ship
ship leave a sinking ship
ship like rats abandoning a sinking ship
ship Loose lips sink ships.
ship One hand for oneself and one for the ship.
ship Rats abandon a sinking ship.
ship run a taut ship
ship run a tight ship
ship Shape up or ship out.
ship shipping and handling
ship ships that pass in the night
ship when one's ship comes in
shirk shirk one's duty
shirt give so the shirt off one's back
shirt keep one's shirt on
shirt Keep your shirt on!
shirt lose one's shirt
shit beat the shit out of so
shit Cut the shit!
shit get one's shit together
shit know shit from Shinola
shit Shit happens.
shit shoot the shit
shit tell shit from Shinola
shit when the shit hits the fan
shock shock of one's life
shoddy all wool and no shoddy
shoe Close only counts in horseshoes (and hand grenades).
shoe comfortable as an old shoe
shoe common as an old shoe
shoe drop the other shoe
shoe fill so's shoes
shoe For want of a nail the shoe was lost; for want of a shoe the horse was lost; and for want of a horse the man was lost.
shoe have the shoe on the other foot
shoe If the shoe fits(, wear it).
shoe in so else's shoes
shoe It's ill waiting for dead men's shoes.
shoe shoe is on the other foot.

shoe step into so's shoes
shoe tough as old (shoe) leather
shoe wait for the other shoe to drop
shoe wouldn't want to be in so's shoes
shoestring get along (on a shoestring)
shoestring get by (on a shoestring)
shoestring on a shoestring
shook all shook up
shook shook up
shoot easy as shooting fish in a barrel
shoot like shooting fish in a barrel
shoot shoot a place up
shoot Shoot first, ask questions later.
shoot shoot for sth
shoot shoot for the sky
shoot shoot from the hip
shoot shoot one's breakfast
shoot shoot one's cookies
shoot shoot one's mouth off
shoot shoot one's supper
shoot shoot one's wad
shoot shoot oneself in the foot
shoot shoot so down in flames
shoot shoot so/sth (all) to hell
shoot shoot so/sth or an animal down
shoot shoot sth down
shoot shoot sth out
shoot shoot the breeze
shoot shoot the bull
shoot shoot the cat
shoot shoot the crap
shoot shoot the shit
shoot shoot the works
shoot shoot up
shoot straight shooter
shoot Sure as shooting!
shoot whole shooting match
shop awkward as a bull in a china shop
shop bull in a china shop
shop close up shop
shop go window-shopping
shop idle brain is the devil's workshop.
shop Keep your shop and your shop will keep you.
shop like a bull in a china shop
shop set up shop somewhere
shop shop around (for sth)
shop shopping list
shop talk shop
shore shore so up
shore shore sth up
short Art is long and life is short.
short bring so up short
short catch so up short
short caught short
short come short of sth
short cut a long story short
short cut so/sth off (short)
short day late and a dollar short
short Eat my shorts!
short end up with the short end of the stick
short fall short
short few bricks short of a load
short few cards short of a deck
short for short
short in short
short in the short haul
short in the short run
short Life is short and time is swift.
short Life is too short.
short (little) short on one end

short long and the short of it
short long story short
short longest way round is the shortest way home.
short make a long story short
short make short work of so/sth
short no shortage of sth
short nothing short of sth
short on short notice
short one sandwich short of a picnic
short over the short haul
short pull so up short
short run short (of sth)
short sell so/sth short
short short and sweet
short short and the long of it
short short end of the stick
short short for sth
short short of sth
short Short reckonings make long friends.
short short shrift
short short temper
short short with so
short stop short of a place
short stop short of doing sth
short Take a long walk off a short pier.
short thick as a short plank
short thick as two short planks
shortage no shortage of sth
shortest longest way round is the shortest way home.
shot call (all) the shots
shot call the shots
shot give sth a shot
shot give sth one's best shot
shot long shot
shot not by a long shot
shot off like a shot
shot one's best shot
shot seem like a long shot
shot shot at so
shot shot full of holes
shot shot in the arm
shot shot in the dark
shot shot through with sth
shot take a potshot at so/sth
shot take a shot at so/sth
shotgun shotgun wedding
should Children should be seen and not heard.
should He who sups with the devil should have a long spoon.
should How should I know?
should if anything should happen
should It's time we should be going.
should People who live in glass houses shouldn't throw stones.
should should have stood in bed
should shouldn't happen to a dog
should zigged when one should've zagged
shoulder carry sth on so's shoulders
shoulder carry the weight of the world on one's shoulders
shoulder chip on one's shoulder
shoulder cold shoulder
shoulder cold-shoulder
shoulder fall on so's shoulders
shoulder have a good head on one's shoulders
shoulder have broad shoulders

shoulder have one's shoulder to the wheel
shoulder head and shoulders above so/sth
shoulder keep one's shoulder to the wheel
shoulder leave sth on so's shoulders
shoulder looking over one's shoulder
shoulder on so's shoulders
shoulder pit one's shoulder to the wheel
shoulder put sth on so's shoulders
shoulder rub shoulders with so
shoulder shoulder the blame for sth
shoulder shoulder to shoulder
shoulder stand head and shoulders above so/sth
shoulder straight from the shoulder
shoulder tower head and shoulders above so/sth
shout It's all over but the shouting.
shout shout about so/sth
shout shout so/sth down
shout sth to shout about
shout within shouting distance
shove (I) have to shove off.
shove if push comes to shove
shove (It's) time to shove off.
shove (I've) got to be shoving off.
shove (I've) got to shove off.
shove shove off
shove shove one's way somewhere
shove shove so around
shove shove so/sth down so's throat
shove when push comes to shove
shovel put so to bed with a shovel
shovel put to bed with a shovel
show all show and no go
show by a show of hands
show dog and pony show
show get the show on the road
show (It) just goes to show (you) (sth).
show let one's emotions show
show make a great show of sth
show not show one's face
show *on the dot
show one's claws are showing
show one-man show
show *ropes
show run the show
show show a lot of promise
show show and tell
show show good faith
show show of hands
show show off
show show one's hand
show show one's teeth
show show one's (true) colors
show show one to one's seat
show show signs of sth
show show so around (some place)
show show so into somewhere
show show so one's stuff
show show so/sth off
show show so out (of sth)
show show so the big picture
show show so the ropes
show show so the tricks of the trade
show show so to a seat
show show so (to) the door
show show so up
show show sth to good advantage
show show up

show steal the show
show That's show business (for you).
show *tricks of the trade
shower April showers bring May flowers.
shower risk of showers
shower send so to the showers
shower shower so/sth with sth
shower take a shower
shrift short shrift
shrink shrinking violet
shroud shroud so/sth in sth
shroud Shrouds have no pockets.
shrug shrug sth off (as sth)
shuck (Ah) shucks!
shuck (Aw) shucks!
shuck shuck sth off
shuffle shuffle off this mortal coil
shush shush (up)
shut door must be either shut or open.
shut get shut of so/sth
shut keep one's mouth shut (about so/sth)
shut Keep your mouth shut (about so/sth).
shut need some shut-eye
shut open-and-shut case
shut Put up or shut up!
shut shut down
shut shut one's eyes to sth
shut shut so/sth out
shut shut so up
shut shut sth down
shut shut the door (up)on so/sth
shut Shut the stable door after the horse has bolted.
shut Shut up!
shut Shut up about it.
shut Shut your cake hole!
shut some shut-eye
shut use some shut-eye
shut Well, shut my mouth!
shut When one door shuts, another opens.
shuttle shuttle so/sth from person to person
shy few cards shy of a full deck
shy Once bitten, twice shy.
shy one brick shy of a load
shy shy away (from so/sth)
shy three bricks shy of a load
shy two bricks shy of a load
sick call in sick
sick grow sick (and tired) of so/sth
sick Hope deferred makes the heart sick.
sick Hope deferred maketh the heart sick.
sick I was up all night with a sick friend.
sick make so sick
sick report in sick
sick sick (and tired) of so/sth
sick sick as a dog
sick sick at heart
sick sick in bed
sick sick to death (of so/sth)
sick sick (up)
sick take sick
sick worried sick (about so/sth)
side born on the wrong side of the blanket

side bread always falls on the buttered side.
side can't hit the (broad) side of a barn
side choose (up) sides
side dark side of so/sth
side flip side
side from side to side
side get up on the wrong side of bed
side go off (to the side) with so
side grass is always greener on the other side (of the fence).
side hindside first
side hit the (broad) side of a barn
side keep on the good side of so
side keep on the left(-hand) side (of sth)
side keep on the right side of so
side keep on the right(-hand) side (of sth)
side keep one's side of the bargain
side know which side one's bread is buttered on
side laugh out of the other side of one's face
side laugh out of the other side of one's mouth
side look on the bright side
side motion so to one side
side move off (to the side) with so
side off to one side
side off (to the side) with so
side on so's good side
side on so's wrong side
side on the bright side
side on the good side of so
side on the safe side
side on the side
side on the wrong side of so
side other side of the tracks
side right side up
side seamy side of life
side side against so
side side by side
side side with so
side split one's sides (with laughter)
side stay on the good side of so
side step off (to the side) with so
side sunny-side up
side sway from side to side
side take sides
side take so to one side
side There are two sides to every question.
side There are two sides to every story.
side thorn in so's side
side to be on the safe side
side up one side and down the other
side wrong side of the tracks
sidetrack off on a sidetrack
sidle sidle away (from so/sth)
sidle sidle up (to so/sth)
sift sift sth from sth
sift sift sth out of sth
sift sift sth through sth
sift sift through sth
sigh breathe a sigh of relief
sigh sigh about sth
sigh sigh for so
sight burst into sight
sight buy sth sight unseen
sight can't stand (the sight of) so/sth
sight catch sight of so/sth

sight come into sight
sight (damn) sight better
sight drop out of sight
sight get so/sth out of one's sight
sight go out of sight
sight have so/sth in one's sights
sight heap sight
sight heave in(to) sight
sight in sight
sight keep out of sight
sight keep sight of so/sth
sight keep so in sight
sight know so by sight
sight lose sight of so/sth
sight love at first sight
sight lower one's sights
sight out of sight
sight Out of sight, out of mind.
sight partially sighted
sight raise one's sights
sight recoil at the sight (of so/sth)
sight sad sight
sight see the sights
sight set one's sights on so/sth
sight sight for sore eyes
sight sorry sight
sight stay out of sight
sight train one's sights on sth
sign high sign
sign show signs of sth
sign sign for so
sign sign for sth
sign sign in
sign sign of the times
sign sign of things to come
sign sign off
sign sign on
sign sign one's own death warrant
sign sign out
sign sign so in
sign sign so on
sign sign so out of some place
sign sign so up (for sth)
sign sign so up (with so/sth)
sign sign sth away
sign sign sth for so
sign sign sth in
sign sign sth out of some place
sign sign sth over (to so)
sign sign up (for sth)
sign sign up (with so/sth)
sign signed, sealed, and delivered
signal signal for so
signal signal for sth
signal signal (to) so (to do sth)
signature affix one's signature to sth
significance take on a new significance
silence break silence
silence break the silence
silence reduce so to silence
silence Silence gives consent.
silence Silence is golden.
silent silent as the dead
silent silent as the grave
silent strong, silent type
silk smooth as silk
silk soft as silk
silk You cannot make a silk purse out of a sow's ear.
silly bored silly
silly laugh oneself silly
silly scared silly

silly silly as a goose
silt silt up
silver born with a silver spoon in one's mouth
silver cross so's palm with silver
silver Every cloud has a silver lining.
silver on a silver platter
silver present sth on a silver platter
silver serve sth on a silver platter
silver want sth on a silver platter
similar along similar lines
simmer simmer down
simple have a bad case of the simples
simple plain and simple
simple pure and simple
sin hate so/sth like sin
sin live in sin
sin multitude of sins
sin Poverty is no sin.
sin sin against so/sth
sin The wages of sin is death.
sin ugly as sin
since *day one
since greatest thing since indoor plumbing
since greatest thing since sliced bread
since since day one
since since so was knee-high to a grasshopper
since since time immemorial
since Since when?
sincerest Imitation is the sincerest form of flattery.
sing Church ain't out till they quit singing.
sing lay low and sing small
sing sing a different tune
sing sing along (with so/sth)
sing sing another tune
sing Sing before breakfast, you'll cry before night.
sing sing from the same hymnbook
sing sing of so/sth
sing sing one's heart out
sing sing out
sing sing so's or sth's praises
sing sing so to sleep
sing sing sth out
sing sing the praises of so/sth
sing sing to so/sth
sing sing together
sing sing up a storm
sing till the fat lady sings
sing *up a storm
sing when the fat lady sings
single in (a) single file
single march in (a) single file
single Misfortunes never come singly.
single of a single mind (about so/sth)
single single file
single single so/sth out (for sth)
single walk in (a) single file
singly Misfortunes never come singly.
sink desert a sinking ship
sink everything but the kitchen sink
sink hook, line, and sinker
sink leave a sinking ship
sink like rats abandoning a sinking ship
sink Loose lips sink ships.
sink Rats abandon a sinking ship.
sink sink back (into sth)
sink sink below so/sth
sink sink below sth

sink sink down
sink sink in
sink sink into despair
sink sink into oblivion
sink sink one's teeth into sth
sink sink or swim
sink sink sth in(to) so/sth
sink sink to (doing) sth
sink sink under (sth)
sink sinking feeling
sink swallow sth hook, line, and sinker
sinker hook, line, and sinker
sinker swallow sth hook, line, and sinker
siphon siphon sth off (from sth)
siree No siree(, Bob)!
siree Yes siree(, Bob)!
sister (soul) sister
sister weak sister
sit at a sitting
sit Come in and sit a spell.
sit Do sit down.
sit leave so sitting pretty
sit like a sitting duck
sit looking like a sitting duck
sit *on the fence (about sth)
sit sit around
sit sit at sth
sit sit at the feet of so
sit sit back
sit sit behind so/sth
sit sit below so/sth
sit sit beneath sth
sit sit bolt upright
sit sit by so
sit sit close to so/sth
sit sit down
sit sit for an exam
sit sit for one's portrait
sit sit for so
sit sit hand in hand
sit sit idly by
sit sit in (for so)
sit sit in judgment (up)on so/sth
sit sit in (on sth)
sit sit on its hands
sit sit on one's ass
sit sit on one's hands
sit sit on so/sth
sit sit on the fence
sit sit on their hands
sit sit out
sit sit right with so
sit sit sth out
sit sit still for sth
sit sit through sth
sit sit tight
sit sit up
sit sit well with so
sit sit with so
sit sitting duck
sit sitting on a gold mine
sit sitting on a powder keg
sit (sitting) on top of the world
sit sitting pretty
situation no-win situation
situation reality of the situation
six at sixes and sevens
six deep-six so/sth
six eighty-six sth
six It's six of one, half a dozen of another.
six six feet under

six six of one and half a dozen of the other
six sixth sense
sixth sixth sense
sixty do a three-sixty
sixty sixty-four-dollar question
sixty turn three hundred and sixty degrees
size all of a size
size beat so down to size
size cut so down (to size)
size knock so down to size
size pick on somebody your own size
size pick on someone your own size
size size so/sth up
size take so down (to size)
size That's about the size of it.
size try sth (on) (for size)
size whittle so down to size
size whittle sth down (to size)
skate awkward as a cow on roller skates
skate skate around
skate skate on sth
skate skate on thin ice
skate skate over sth
skeleton skeleton(s) in the closet
sketch sketch sth in
sketch sketch sth out
sketch thumbnail sketch
skid grease the skids
skid hit the skids
skid on the skids
skid put the skids on (sth)
skid skid across sth
skid skid into so/sth
skid put the skids under sth or so
skies praise so/sth to the skies
skillet black as a skillet
skillet busy as popcorn on a skillet
skim skim over sth
skim skim sth off (of) sth
skim skim through sth
skimp skimp on sth
skin (all) skin and bones
skin (almost) jump out of one's skin
skin Beauty is only skin-deep.
skin by the skin of one's teeth
skin escape by the skin of one's teeth
skin get under so's skin
skin give so some skin
skin grow thick-skinned
skin grow thin-skinned
skin knock so some skin
skin Let every man skin his own skunk.
skin make so's skin crawl
skin nearly jump out of one's skin
skin no skin off so's nose
skin no skin off so's teeth
skin nothing but skin and bones
skin save so's skin
skin Skin me!
skin skin so alive
skin soak so to the skin
skin soaked to the skin
skin There's more than one way to skin a cat.
skin thick-skinned
skin thin-skinned
skinny skinny as a beanpole
skinny skinny-dip
skip hop, skip, and a jump
skip one's heart skips a beat

skip skip bail
skip Skip it!
skip skip off (with sth)
skip skip (out)
skip skip out (on so/sth)
skip skip out with sth
skip skip over so/sth
skip skip rope
skip skip through sth
skirmish skirmish with so/sth
skirt skirt around so/sth
skittles (all) beer and skittles
skittles Life isn't all beer and skittles.
skull get sth through so's thick skull
skull go out of one's skull
skull out of one's skull
skunk drunk as a skunk
skunk Let every man skin his own skunk.
sky aim for the sky
sky come out of a clear blue sky
sky go sky-high
sky high as the sky
sky pie in the sky
sky praise so/sth to the skies
sky reach for the sky
sky shoot for the sky
sky sky's the limit.
slack cut so some slack
slack slack off
slack slack up (on sth)
slack take the slack up
slam slam dunk
slam slam into so/sth
slam slam so/sth down
slam slam sth down (on(to) sth)
slam slam the brakes on
slam slam the door in so's face
slant slant against sth
slant slant sth against so/sth
slant slant sth toward so/sth
slant slant toward so/sth
slap slap against so/sth
slap slap in the face
slap slap on the wrist
slap slap so down
slap slap so in sth
slap slap so on sth
slap slap so on the wrist
slap slap sth against so/sth
slap slap sth down
slap slap sth on
slap slap sth onto so/sth
slap slap sth together
slash slash and burn
slash slash (out) at so
slate have so slated for sth
slate have so slated to do sth
slate slate so/sth for sth
slate slated for sth
slate slated to do sth
slate start (off) with a clean slate
slate start (over) with a clean slate
slate wipe so's slate clean
slate wipe the slate clean
slaughter like a lamb to the slaughter
slaughter like lambs to the slaughter
slaughter like pigs to the slaughter
slave Better be an old man's darling than a young man's slave.
slave slave away (at sth)
slave slave over sth
slave slave to sth

sled hard sledding
sled sled down sth
sled sled over sth
sled tough sledding
sleep cry oneself to sleep
sleep doze off (to sleep)
sleep drift off to sleep
sleep drop off (to sleep)
sleep get off to sleep
sleep (I've) got to go home and get my beauty sleep.
sleep Let sleeping dogs lie.
sleep lose sleep over so/sth
sleep lull so or an animal to sleep
sleep not sleep a wink
sleep put so or an animal to sleep
sleep put so to sleep
sleep read oneself to sleep
sleep sing so to sleep
sleep sleep around the clock
sleep sleep around (with so)
sleep sleep in
sleep sleep like a log
sleep sleep on sth
sleep sleep out
sleep sleep over (with so) (some place)
sleep sleep sth away
sleep sleep sth off
sleep sleep through sth
sleep sleep tight
sleep sleep together
sleep sleep with so
sleep sleeping giant
sleep sob oneself to sleep
sleeve have an ace up one's sleeve
sleeve have one's heart on one's sleeve
sleeve have sth up one's sleeve
sleeve laugh up one's sleeve
sleeve roll one's sleeves up
sleeve Stretch your arm no further than your sleeve will reach.
sleeve wear one's heart on one's sleeve
slice greatest thing since sliced bread
slice It's been a slice!
slice no matter how you slice it
slice slice in(to sth)
slice slice of the action
slice slice of the cake
slice slice so/sth up
slice slice sth off
slice slice through sth
slick city slicker
slick slick as a whistle
slick slick sth down
slick slick sth up
slicker city slicker
slide let so slide by
slide let sth slide
slide let things slide
slide slide along
slide slide around
slide slide by
slide slide down from sth
slide slide down sth
slide slide into sth
slide slide out of sth
slide slide over sth
slide slide sth around
slide slide sth into sth
slide slide sth out of sth
slightly slightly rattled
slim slim chance
slim slim down

slim slim so down
sling have one's ass in a sling
sling sling sth at so/sth
sling sling sth out
sling sling the cat
slink slink around
slink slink away
slink slink in(to sth)
slink slink off
slink slink out (of some place)
slip give so the slip
slip let sth slip by
slip let sth slip (out)
slip let the chance slip by
slip slip around
slip slip away
slip slip back (to so/sth)
slip slip between the cracks
slip slip by
slip slip down
slip slip from sth
slip slip in (some place)
slip slip in(to sth)
slip Slip me five!
slip slip of the tongue
slip slip off
slip slip on sth
slip slip one over on so/sth
slip slip one's mind
slip slip one's trolley
slip slip out
slip slip past so/sth
slip slip so a Mickey
slip slip so five
slip slip so/sth past so/sth
slip slip sth back
slip slip sth down
slip slip sth in(to) sth
slip slip sth off
slip slip sth on
slip slip something over on so/sth
slip slip sth over so/sth
slip slip sth through (sth)
slip slip through so's fingers
slip slip through sth
slip slip through the cracks
slip slip up
slip slippery as an eel
slip slippery customer
slip slippery slope
slip There's many a slip 'twixt the cup and the lip.
slip *through the cracks
slippery slippery as an eel
slippery slippery customer
slippery slippery slope
slither slither along
slither slither away
slob slob up
slobber slobber (all) over so/sth
slobber slobber over so/sth
slobber slobber over sth
slog slog through sth
slop slop around
slop slop out (of sth)
slop slop over
slop slop sth around
slop slop sth on(to) so/sth
slop slop sth over sth
slope slippery slope
slope slope away from sth
slope slope down (to sth or some place)
slope slope (down) toward sth

slope slope up (to sth)
slosh slosh around (in sth)
slosh slosh over
slosh slosh sth (all) over so/sth
slosh slosh sth around
slosh slosh sth on(to) so/sth
slosh slosh through sth
slouch slouch around
slouch slouch behind sth
slouch slouch down
slouch slouch over
slough slough sth off
slow do a slow burn
slow Make haste slowly.
slow mills of God grind slowly, yet they grind exceeding small.
slow Slow and steady wins the race.
slow slow as molasses in January
slow slow but sure
slow slow down
slow slow going
slow slow off the mark
slow slow on the draw
slow slow on the uptake
slow slow so/sth up
slow slow study
slow slow up
slow slowly but surely
slow take it slow
slow twist (slowly) in the wind
slower slower and slower
slower slower than molasses in January
slowly Make haste slowly.
slowly mills of God grind slowly, yet they grind exceeding small.
slowly slowly but surely
slowly twist (slowly) in the wind
sluff sluff (off)
slug slug it out
sluice sluice sth down
sluice sluice sth out
slump slump down
slump slump over
slur slur over sth
slush slush up
slut slut's wool
sly on the sly
sly sly as a fox
smack smack (dab) in the middle
smack smack in the face
smack smack of sth
smack smack so down
smack smack sth down (on(to) sth)
smack smack the road
small best things come in small packages.
small big frog in a small pond
small come into a (small) fortune
small engage in small talk
small Good things come in small packages.
small lay low and sing small
small mills of God grind slowly, yet they grind exceeding small.
small small change
small small fortune
small small fry
small small hours (of the night)
small small potatoes
small small print
small Small things please small minds.
small Thank God for small favors.

small thankful for small blessings
smart get smart (with so)
smart smart ass
smart smart at sth
smart smart from sth
smart smart guy
smart smart money
smart smart mouth
smart smart under sth
smart You think you're so smart!
smarten smarten up
smash smash hit
smash smash into sth
smash smash out of sth
smash smash so's face in
smash smash sth in
smash smash sth up
smash smash through sth
smear smear campaign (against so)
smear smear so/sth with sth
smear smear sth on(to) so/sth
smell come out smelling like a rose
smell come up smelling like a rose
smell rose by any other name would smell as sweet.
smell smell a rat
smell smell blood
smell smell fishy
smell smell like a rose
smell smell of sth
smell smell so/sth or an animal out
smell smell sth up
smell smell to (high) heaven
smell Wake up and smell the coffee.
smile crack a smile
smile flash a smile (at so)
smile Keep smiling.
smile put a smile on so's face
smile smile at so
smile smile on so/sth
smile smile (up)on so/sth
smile Smile when you say that.
smile smiling like a Cheshire cat
smirk smirk at so/sth
smite smite so with sth
smithereens blow so/sth to smithereens
smithereens blow sth to smithereens
smoke go up in smoke
smoke Put that in your pipe and smoke it!
smoke smoke and mirrors
smoke smoke like a chimney
smoke smoke so/sth or an animal out of sth
smoke smoke sth up
smoke smoke-filled room
smoke smoking gun
smoke (There's) no smoke without fire.
smoke Where there's smoke there's fire.
smooth course of true love never did run smooth.
smooth smooth as glass
smooth smooth as silk
smooth smooth sailing
smooth smooth sth away
smooth smooth sth back
smooth smooth sth down
smooth smooth sth onto so/sth
smooth smooth sth out
smooth Take the rough with the smooth.
smother smother so/sth with sth

smuggle smuggle so/sth across sth
smuggle smuggle so/sth into some place
smuggle smuggle so/sth out of some place
smuggle smuggle so/sth past (so/sth)
smuggle smuggle so/sth through (sth)
snack snack off (of) sth
snag hit a snag
snail at a snail's gallop
snail at a snail's pace
snake go at sth like a boy killing snakes
snake If it was a snake it woulda bit you.
snake like fighting snakes
snake seeing snakes
snake snake along
snake snake in the grass
snakebite snakebite medicine
snap It's a snap.
snap Make it snappy!
snap snap at so
snap snap at sth
snap snap back (after sth)
snap snap back (at so)
snap snap back (on so/sth)
snap snap into sth
snap Snap it up!
snap snap one's cookies
snap snap out of sth
snap snap so's head off
snap snap sth back
snap snap sth into sth
snap snap sth off
snap snap sth on
snap snap sth out of sth
snap snap sth up
snap snap to (attention)
snap Snap to it!
snappy Make it snappy!
snarl snarl at so/sth or an animal
snarl snarl so/sth up
snarl snarl sth out
snatch snatch at so/sth
snatch snatch so from the jaws of death
snatch snatch so/sth (away) from so/sth
snatch snatch so out of the jaws of death
snatch snatch sth out of sth
snatch snatch sth up
snatch snatch victory from the jaws of defeat
snazz snazz sth up
sneak sneak around (some place)
sneak sneak around so/sth
sneak sneak away (from some place)
sneak sneak in(to some place)
sneak sneak out (of some place)
sneak sneak up on so/sth
sneak sneak up to so/sth
sneer sneer at so/sth
sneeze nothing to be sneezed at
sneeze nothing to sneeze at
sneeze sneeze at so
sneeze sneeze at sth
sneeze sneeze into sth
sneeze sneeze on so/sth
sniff sniff at so/sth
sniff sniff so/sth out
snip snip sth off
snipe snipe at so/sth
snit in a snit
snitch snitch on so
snook cock a snook at so

snoop snoop around (sth)
snoop snoop into sth
snort ripsnorter
snort snort at so/sth
snotnosed snotnose(d) (kid)
snow do a snow job on so
snow pure as the driven snow
snow snow bunny
snow snow job
snow snow so/sth in
snow snow so/sth under with sth
snow snowed in
snow snowed under
snow white as snow
snow white as the driven snow
snowball not have a snowball's chance in hell
snowball snowball into sth
snuff not up to snuff
snuff snuff so out
snuff snuff sth out
snuff up to snuff
snug snug as a bug in a rug
snug snug down (some place)
snuggle snuggle down (into sth)
snuggle snuggle down (with so)
snuggle snuggle down (with sth)
snuggle snuggle (up) against so/sth
snuggle snuggle up (to so/sth)
so able to take just so much
so able to take only so much
so and so forth
so and so on
so (Are you) leaving so soon?
so As a man sows, so shall he reap.
so As the twig is bent, so is the tree inclined.
so As you make your bed, so you must lie (up)on it.
so As you sow, so shall you reap.
so be so bold as to do sth
so devil is not so black as he is painted.
so do so
so Don't stay away so long.
so 'Fraid so.
so go so far as to say sth
so (have) never had it so good
so have so
so have to do sth so bad one can taste it
so How so?
so I am so sure!
so I believe so.
so (I) don't think so.
so I expect (so).
so I guess (so).
so (I) hope so.
so I suppose (so).
so I suspect (so).
so I think so.
so if so
so (I'm) afraid so.
so in so many words
so Is that so?
so I've heard so much about you.
so just so
so land so poor it wouldn't even raise a fuss
so make so bold as to do sth
so need so bad one can taste it
so not so hot
so Nothing is given so freely as advice.

so Nothing so bad but (it) might have been worse.
so on so's say-so
so so bad one can taste it
so So be it.
so so clean you could eat off the floor
so so cold you could hang meat
so So do I.
so so far as anyone knows
so so far as possible
so so far as so is concerned
so so far as sth is concerned
so So far, so good.
so So gross!
so So help me(, God)!
so So it goes.
so So long.
so so long as
so so mad I could scream
so So many countries, so many customs.
so so much for so/sth
so So much for that.
so so much the better
so so quiet you could hear a pin drop
so So's your old man!
so so soon
so so still you could hear a pin drop
so So, sue me.
so so to speak
so So (what)?
so (So) what else is new?
so so-and-so
so take on (so)
so Thank you so much.
so There's none so blind as those who will not see.
so There's none so deaf as those who will not hear.
so want so bad one can taste it
so What makes you think so?
so Why buy a cow when milk is so cheap?
so without (so much as) a (for or) by your leave
so without so much as doing sth
so You leaving so soon?
so You think you're so smart!
soak soak in(to sth)
soak soak one's face
soak soak so/sth with sth
soak soak so to the skin
soak soak sth in sth
soak soak sth off (of) sth
soak soak sth out of sth
soak soak sth up
soak soak through sth
soak soaked to the skin
soap no soap
soap rinse so's mouth out (with soap)
soap soap so/sth down
soap soft soap
sob sob one's heart out
sob sob oneself to sleep
sob sob sth out
sob sob sth to so
sob sob story
sober cold sober
sober sober as a judge
sober sober so up
sober sober up
sober stone(-cold) sober
society pay one's debt (to society)

sock beat the socks off (of) so
sock knock so's socks off
sock Put a sock in it!
sock sock it to so
sock sock so/sth in
sock sock sth away
sock socked in
sock Stuff a sock in it!
soft grow soft on so
soft have a soft spot (in one's heart) for so or an animal
soft soft answer turneth away wrath.
soft soft as a baby's backside
soft soft as a baby's bottom
soft soft as down
soft soft as silk
soft soft as velvet
soft soft in the head
soft soft money
soft soft on so
soft soft sell
soft soft soap
soft soft touch
soft soften one's stance (on so/sth)
soft soften so up
soft soften sth up
soft soften up
soft soft-pedal sth
soft walk soft
soil soil one's diaper(s)
soil soil one's hands
solace take solace (in sth)
sold sold on so/sth
sold sold out
solicit solicit for so/sth
solicit solicit so for sth
solid solid as a rock
solid (solid) grasp of sth
Solomon wise as Solomon
some allow some elbow room
some and then some
some at some length
some bag some rays
some blow off (some) steam
some bushel and a peck (and some in a gourd)
some bust (some) suds
some Catch me some other time.
some catch some rays
some catch some Zs
some cause (some) eyebrows to raise
some cause some raised eyebrows
some cause (some) tongues to wag
some come into (some) money
some cop some Zs
some crack some suds
some cut some Zs
some cut so some slack
some dig some dirt up (on so)
some (Do) have some more.
some do some fine coin
some enough and some to spare
some get (some) steam up
some get some weight off one's feet
some give some thought to sth
some give so some lip
some give so some skin
some give so some sugar
some have (some) time to kill
some have to go some (to do sth)
some (I'll) try to catch you some other time.
some in some respects

some Is there some place I can wash up?
some It takes (some) getting used to.
some It will take some doing.
some kick some ass (around)
some knock some heads together
some knock some sense into so
some knock so some skin
some lay (some) rubber
some lay some sweet lines on so
some leave some loose ends
some let off (some) steam
some make (some) sense (out) of so/sth
some Maybe some other time.
some need some elbow room
some need some shut-eye
some open some doors (for so)
some pop (some) tops
some pull (some) strings
some pump (some) iron
some put out (some) feelers (on so/sth)
some put some distance between so and oneself or sth
some put some sweet lines on so
some put some teeth into sth
some run down some lines
some shed (some) light on sth
some some elbow room
some some loose ends
some (some) new blood
some Some people (just) don't know when to quit.
some some pumpkins
some some shut-eye
some suck (some) brew
some suck (some) suds
some take some doing
some take some heat
some take (some) time off
some take ((some) time) off from work
some Throw dirt enough, and some will stick.
some throw (some) light on sth
some to some extent
some use some elbow grease
some use some shut-eye
some We'll try again some other time.
some work some fat off
some work some weight off
some You win some, you lose some.
somebody pick on somebody your own size
somehow carry on somehow
someone pick on someone your own size
something (Could I) get you something (to drink)?
something (Do you) want to know something?
something (Do you) want to make something of it?
something have something going (with so)
something something else (again)
something Something is better than nothing.
something Something is rotten in (the state of) Denmark.
something something of the sort
something something or other
something Something's got to give.
something something's up

something something to that effect
something Wanna make sumpin' of it?
something Want to make something of it?
something You are something else (again)!
something You don't get something for nothing.
something (You want to) know something?
something You want to make something of it?
sometime (I) hope to see you again (sometime).
son every mother's son (of them)
son like father, like son
son son of a bachelor
son son of a bitch
son son of a gun
son son of a sea biscuit
song buy sth for a song
song for a song
song go into a song and dance (about sth)
song go into the same old song and dance about sth
song pick up so for a song
song sell sth for a song
song swan song
soon (Are you) leaving so soon?
soon as soon as
soon Don't speak too soon.
soon fool and his money are soon parted.
soon God takes soonest those he loveth best.
soon had (just) as soon do sth
soon had sooner do sth
soon I spoke too soon.
soon I'd (just) as soon (as) do sth
soon (I'll) see you (real) soon.
soon (I'll) talk to you soon.
soon no sooner said than done
soon Not if I see you sooner.
soon so soon
soon soon as possible
soon Soon ripe, soon rotten.
soon sooner or later
soon Sooner than you think.
soon sooner the better.
soon would as soon do sth as look at you
soon would (just) as soon do sth
soon Yesterday wouldn't be too soon.
soon You leaving so soon?
sooner had sooner do sth
sooner no sooner said than done
sooner Not if I see you sooner.
sooner sooner or later
sooner Sooner than you think.
sooner sooner the better.
soonest God takes soonest those he loveth best.
sop sop sth up
sop sopping (wet)
sore sight for sore eyes
sore sore (at so)
sore stick out like a sore thumb
sore touch a sore point
sore touch a sore spot
sorrow drown one's sorrows
sorrow share so's sorrow
sorrow sorrow over so/sth

sorry (Are you) sorry you asked?
sorry Better (be) safe than sorry.
sorry (I'm) sorry.
sorry (I'm) sorry to hear that.
sorry (I'm) sorry you asked (that).
sorry sorry about that
sorry sorry sight
sorry Sorry (that) I asked.
sorry You'll be sorry you asked.
sort feel out of sorts
sort in bad sorts
sort out of sorts
sort sth of sorts
sort something of the sort
sort Sort of.
sort sort of sth
sort sort oneself out
sort sort sth out
sought much sought after
soul bare one's soul (to so)
soul Brevity is the soul of wit.
soul can't call one's soul one's own
soul Don't tell a soul.
soul enough to keep body and soul together
soul every living soul
soul God rest so's soul.
soul gripe one's soul
soul heart and soul
soul (I) won't tell a soul.
soul keep body and soul together
soul not a living soul
soul not tell a (living) soul
soul (Open) confession is good for the soul.
soul pour out one's soul
soul Punctuality is the soul of business.
soul put one's heart (and soul) into sth
soul (soul) brother
soul (soul) sister
soul with all one's heart (and soul)
sound Empty vessels make the most sound.
sound get a (sound) grasp of sth
sound have a (sound) grasp of sth
sound I don't want to sound like a busybody, but
sound safe and sound
sound sound as a barrel
sound sound as a bell
sound sound as a dollar
sound sound as if
sound sound asleep
sound (sound) grasp of sth
sound sound like
sound sound off
sound sound so out
sound sound sth out
soup alphabet soup
soup duck soup
soup easy as duck soup
soup everything from soup to nuts
soup in the soup
soup Soup's on!
soup soup sth up
soup souped up
soup thick as pea soup
sour go sour
sour hit a sour note
sour sour as vinegar
sour sour grapes
sour strike a sour note

sour sweet and sour
south down South
south go South
south head South
south mouth full of South
sow As a man sows, so shall he reap.
sow As you sow, so shall you reap.
sow look like a saddle on a sow
sow sow one's wild oats
sow Sow the wind and reap the whirlwind.
sow You cannot make a silk purse out of a sow's ear.
space space out
space space so out
space spaced (out)
space take up space
space waste of space
spade black as the ace of spades
spade call a spade a spade
spade cocky as the king of spades
spade in spades
spade spade sth up
Spain build castles in Spain
spank (brand) spanking new
spar spar with so
spare and sth to spare
spare enough and some to spare
spare have sth to spare
spare in one's spare time
spare not a moment to spare
spare spare so sth
spare Spare the rod and spoil the child.
spare spare tire
spare with sth to spare
spare without a moment to spare
spark spark sth off
sparkle sparkle with sth
spatter spatter on so/sth
spatter spatter so/sth up
spatter spatter so/sth with sth
spatter spatter sth around
spatter spatter sth on(to) so/sth
spaz have a spaz
spaz spaz around
spaz spaz down
spaz spaz out
speak Actions speak louder than words.
speak as we speak
speak *at great length
speak Can I speak to so?
speak Could I speak to so?
speak Don't speak too soon.
speak even as we speak
speak frankly speaking
speak I spoke out of turn.
speak I spoke too soon.
speak I'd like to speak to so, please.
speak *in earnest
speak know whereof one speaks
speak Many a true word is spoken in jest.
speak May I speak to so?
speak Never speak ill of the dead.
speak nothing to speak of
speak on speaking terms (with so)
speak See no evil, hear no evil, speak no evil.
speak so to speak
speak speak about so/sth
speak speak against so/sth

speak speak as one
speak speak at great length
speak speak down to so
speak speak for itself
speak speak for oneself
speak speak for so/sth
speak speak for themselves
speak speak from sth
speak speak highly of so/sth
speak speak ill of so
speak speak in earnest
speak speak of so/sth
speak Speak of the devil (and in he walks).
speak speak off-the-cuff
speak speak one's mind
speak speak one's piece
speak speak out
speak speak so's language
speak speak the same language
speak speak to so
speak speak to sth
speak speak up
speak speak (up)on sth
speak speak volumes
speak speak with a forked tongue
speak speak with so (about so/sth)
speak speaking for oneself
speak speaking (quite) candidly
speak (speaking) (quite) frankly
speak spoken for
speak There's many a true word spoken in jest.
speak Who do you want to speak to?
speak With whom do you wish to speak?
speak word (once) spoken is past recalling.
spear spear sth out (of sth)
spear take the spear (in one's chest)
spec on spec
special Saturday night special
specialize specialize in sth
species female of the species is more deadly than the male.
speculate speculate about so/sth
speculate speculate in sth
speculate speculate on sth
speech I'm speechless.
speechless I'm speechless.
speed at full speed
speed bring so up to speed on so/sth
speed bring sth up to speed
speed clock so at speeds of some amount
speed hit speeds of some amount
speed More haste, less speed.
speed pick up speed
speed reach speeds of some amount
speed speed away (from so/sth)
speed speed so/sth up
speed speed up
speed speeds of some amount
speed up to speed
spell break the spell
spell cast a spell (on so)
spell Come in and sit a spell.
spell Do I have to spell it out (for you)?
spell dry spell
spell fall under so's spell
spell have so in one's spell
spell have so under a spell
spell have so under one's spell

spell put so under a spell
spell spell disaster
spell spell so (at sth)
spell spell so down
spell spell sth for so
spell spell sth out
spell spell trouble
spell under a spell
spend Don't spend it all in one place.
spend *king's ransom
spend spend a king's ransom
spend spend money like it's going out of style
spend spend money like there's no tomorrow
spend spend sth for sth
spend spend sth on so/sth
spend spend time in sth
spend spending money
spend tax-and-spend
spew spew one's guts (out)
spew spew sth out
spew spew sth up
spice spice sth up
spice Variety is the spice of life.
spider seeing pink spiders
spiel spiel sth off
spiff spiff sth up
spiff spiffed out
spiff spiffed up
spill cry over spilled milk
spill Don't cry over spilled milk.
spill It's no use crying over spilled milk.
spill spill one's guts
spill spill (out) into sth
spill spill out (of sth)
spill spill over
spill spill (over) into sth
spill spill the beans
spill spill the works
spill take a spill
spin for a spin
spin go into a tailspin
spin make so's head spin
spin put a spin on sth
spin spin a yarn
spin spin around
spin spin doctor
spin spin off
spin spin one's wheels
spin spin out
spin spin sth off
spin spin sth out
spindle fold, spindle, or mutilate
spiral spiral down
spiral spiral up
spirit dampen so's spirits
spirit in good spirits
spirit lift so's spirits
spirit lower so's spirits
spirit raise so's spirits
spirit spirit is willing, but the flesh is weak.
spirit spirit so/sth away (somewhere)
spirit spirit so/sth off (to some place)
spirit That's the spirit!
spit close chewer and a tight spitter
spit don't amount to a bucket of spit
spit mad enough to chew nails (and spit rivets)
spit mad enough to spit nails
spit spit and image of so
spit spit and polish

spit spit at so/sth
spit spit sth in(to) sth
spit spit sth on(to) sth
spit spit sth out
spit spit sth up
spit spit up
spit spit (up)on so/sth
spit spitting image of so
spite cut one's nose off to spite one's face
spite in spite of so/sth
spite out of spite
spitter close chewer and a tight spitter
spitting spitting image of so
splash splash about
splash splash down
splash splash on so/sth
splash splash over
splash splash so/sth up
splash splash so/sth with sth
splash splash sth about
splash splash sth (all) over so/sth
splash splash sth on(to) so/sth
splatter splatter so/sth up
splay splay out
spleen vent one's spleen
splice splice so (in)to sth
splice splice sth together
splinter splinter off ((of) sth)
split for a split second
split in a split second
split (It's) time to split.
split (I've) got to split.
split split a gut
split split hairs
split split in sth
split split off (from sth)
split split one's sides (with laughter)
split split people up
split split second
split split so/sth up (into sth)
split split so/sth with so/sth
split split sth between (so and so else)
split split sth fifty-fifty
split split sth into sth
split split sth off (of) sth
split split the difference
split split up (with so)
split splitting headache
split vote a split ticket
splurge splurge on so/sth
spoil rotten apple spoils the barrel.
spoil Spare the rod and spoil the child.
spoil spoiled rotten
spoil spoiling for a fight
spoil To the victors belong the spoils.
spoil Too many cooks spoil the broth.
spoil Too many cooks spoil the stew.
spoke I spoke out of turn.
spoke I spoke too soon.
spoken Many a true word is spoken in jest.
spoken spoken for
spoken There's many a true word spoken in jest.
spoken word (once) spoken is past recalling.
sponge sponge so/sth down
sponge sponge sth away
sponge sponge sth from so
sponge sponge sth from sth
sponge sponge sth off of so/sth
sponge sponge sth up
sponge throw in the sponge

sponge toss in the sponge
spook spook so/sth
spoon born with a silver spoon in one's mouth
spoon greasy spoon
spoon He who sups with the devil should have a long spoon.
spoon spoon sth out
spoon spoon sth up
spoon spoon-feed so
sport good sport
sport sport of kings
sport sport with so/sth
sport sporting chance
spot appear to be rooted to the spot
spot have a soft spot (in one's heart) for so or an animal
spot hit the high spots
spot hit the spot
spot in a (tight) spot
spot leopard cannot change his spots.
spot on the spot
spot put so on the spot
spot rooted to the spot
spot spot so as sth
spot spot so (sth)
spot touch a sore spot
spot X marks the spot.
spotlight in the spotlight
spotlight steal the spotlight
spout spout from sth
spout spout off (about so/sth)
spout spout sth out
sprain sprain one's ankle
sprawl sprawl about
sprawl sprawl out
spray spray so/sth with sth
spray spray sth onto so/sth
spread *all over (some place)
spread spread all over (some place)
spread spread it on thick
spread spread like wildfire
spread spread oneself too thin
spread spread out
spread spread over so/sth
spread spread so/sth around
spread spread sth around
spread spread sth on
spread spread sth onto sth
spread spread sth out
spread spread sth over so/sth
spread spread sth under so/sth
spread spread sth with sth
spread spread the word
spread spread to so/sth
spring Hope springs eternal (in the human breast).
spring no spring chicken
spring spring at so/sth
spring spring back (to some place)
spring spring for sth
spring spring (forth) from so/sth
spring spring into action
spring spring out at so
spring spring out of sth
spring spring sth on so
spring spring to attention
spring spring to life
spring spring to one's feet
spring spring to so's defense
spring spring up
spring spring (up)on so/sth or an animal
sprinkle sprinkle so/sth with sth

sprinkle sprinkle sth on(to) so/sth
sprout sprout up
sprout sprout wings
spruce all spruced up
spruce spruce so/sth up
spunk get the spunk up (to do sth)
spur earn one's spurs
spur on the spur of the moment
spur spur so on
spurt spurt out (of so/sth)
spurt spurt sth out
sputter sputter out
sputter sputter sth out
spy spy (up)on so/sth
squabble squabble about so/sth
squabble squabble over so/sth
squabble squabble with so
squabble squabble with sth
squad I'd rather face a firing squad than do sth
squander squander sth away
squander squander sth on so/sth
square back to square one
square Be there or be square.
square call sth square
square fair and square
square go back to square one
square (It) don't cut no squares (with so).
square square accounts (with so)
square square deal
square square (meal)
square square off (for sth)
square square peg in a round hole
square square so away
square square sth off
square square sth up
square square sth with so
square square up (for fighting)
square square up to so/sth
square square up with so
square square with so
square square with sth
square squared away
square three squares (a day)
squash squash so/sth up
squash squash sth down
squash squash sth in
squash squash sth into sth
squash squash up against so/sth
squat cop a squat
squawk squawk about sth
squeak narrow squeak
squeak squeak by (so/sth)
squeak squeak sth through
squeak squeak through (sth)
squeak squeaking wheel gets the oil.
squeal squeal (on so) (to so)
squeal squeal with sth
squeeze put the squeeze on so
squeeze squeeze by (so/sth)
squeeze squeeze so/sth into sth
squeeze squeeze so/sth through (sth)
squeeze squeeze so/sth together
squeeze squeeze so/sth up
squeeze squeeze sth from sth
squeeze squeeze sth out of sth
squeeze squeeze (themselves) together
squeeze squeeze (themselves) up
squeeze squeeze through sth
squeeze squeeze up against so/sth
squiff squiff out

squint squint at so/sth
squint squint out of sth
squirm squirm in(to) sth
squirm squirm out (of sth)
squirm squirm with sth
squirrel ain't got the brains God gave a squirrel
squirrel squirrel sth away
squirt squirt from sth
squirt squirt out (of so/sth)
squirt squirt sth at so/sth
squirt squirt sth out of sth
stab stab at so
stab stab at so/sth
stab stab at sth
stab stab so in sth
stab stab so in the back
stab stab sth at so/sth
stab take a stab at so
stab take a stab at sth
stable Lock the stable door after the horse is stolen.
stable Shut the stable door after the horse has bolted.
stack blow one's stack
stack cards are stacked against one
stack have the cards stacked against one
stack have the deck stacked against one
stack stack sth against so/sth
stack stack sth up
stack stack the cards (against so/sth)
stack stack the deck (against so/sth)
stack stack up
stack swear on a stack of Bibles
staff at half-staff
staff Bread is the staff of life.
stag go stag
stage at this stage (of the game)
stage boo so off the stage
stage hiss so off ((of) the stage)
stage hoot so off the stage
stage in a stage whisper
stage laugh so off the stage
stage set the stage for sth
stage take the stage
stage walk on stage and off again
stagger stagger around
stagger stagger from sth
stagger stagger in(to some place)
stagger stagger out (of some place)
stagger stagger under sth
stain stain sth with sth
stair nothing upstairs
stake at stake
stake burn so at the stake
stake have a stake in sth
stake pull up stakes
stake stake a claim to so/sth
stake stake one's reputation on so/sth
stake stake out a claim to sth
stake stake so/sth out
stake stake so to sth
stake stake sth off
stake up stakes
stalk stalk in(to some place)
stalk stalk out of some place
stall stall for time
stall stall so/sth for sth
stall stall so/sth off
stammer stammer sth out
stamp stamp a fire out
stamp stamp on so/sth

stamp stamp so/sth as sth
stamp stamp so/sth with sth
stamp stamp so out
stamp stamp sth onto sth
stamp stamp sth out
stamp stamp sth (up)on so/sth
stampede stampede in(to some place)
stampede stampede out of some place
stampede stampede so/sth into sth
stamping one's old stamping ground
stance soften one's stance (on so/sth)
stand able to do sth standing on one's head
stand can't stand (the sight of) so/sth
stand Don't stand on ceremony.
stand empty sack cannot stand upright.
stand Every tub must stand on its own bottom.
stand from where I stand
stand have one's heart stand still
stand house divided against itself cannot stand.
stand If you can't stand the heat, get out of the kitchen.
stand It (only) stands to reason.
stand know where so stands (on so/sth)
stand Let every tub stand on its own bottom.
stand make so's hair stand on end
stand not have a leg to stand on
stand on the (witness) stand
stand one's heart stands still
stand one-night stand
stand stand a chance (of doing sth)
stand stand against so/sth
stand stand and deliver
stand stand apart (from so/sth)
stand stand around
stand stand aside
stand stand at sth
stand stand back (from so/sth)
stand stand behind so/sth
stand stand between so/sth and so/sth else
stand stand by
stand stand clear of sth
stand stand close to so/sth
stand stand corrected
stand stand down
stand stand for sth
stand stand head and shoulders above so/sth
stand stand idly by
stand stand in awe (of so/sth)
stand stand (in) back of so/sth
stand stand in (for so)
stand stand in so's way
stand stand knee-deep in sth
stand stand off from so/sth
stand stand off some place
stand stand on ceremony
stand stand on one's dignity
stand stand on one's head
stand stand on one's (own) two feet
stand stand on sth
stand stand one's ground
stand stand out (against so/sth)
stand stand out (from so/sth)
stand stand out (from sth)
stand stand outside ((of) sth)
stand stand over so/sth
stand stand pat (on sth)
stand stand so in good stead

stand stand so/sth off
stand stand so to a treat
stand stand so up
stand stand sth on its head
stand stand still for sth
stand stand tall
stand stand the test of time
stand stand there with one's bare face hanging out
stand stand to lose sth
stand stand to reason
stand stand together
stand stand trial
stand stand up
stand stand (up)on so/sth
stand stand well with so
stand stand with so
stand standing joke
stand sure as I'm standing here
stand take a (firm) stand on sth
stand take a stand (against so/sth)
stand take the stand
stand They also serve who only stand and wait.
stand United we stand, divided we fall.
standard come up to so's standards
standby on standby
standstill bring sth to a standstill
standstill come to a standstill
star Bless one's lucky star.
star Hitch your wagon to a star.
star star as so/sth
star star in sth
star star-crossed lovers
starch take the starch out of so
stare give so a blank stare
stare stare at so/sth
stare stare into sth
stare stare out at so/sth
stare stare so down
stare stare so in the face
stark stark raving mad
stars Aim for the stars!
stars Bless one's stars.
stars Reach for the stars!
stars see stars
stars stars in one's eyes
stars thank one's lucky stars
stars think so hung the moon (and stars)
start by fits and starts
start Don't start (on me)!
start fits and starts
start for starters
start fresh start
start *from scratch
start from start to finish
start get started on sth
start head start (on so)
start head start (on sth)
start in fits and starts
start jolt to a start
start make a fresh start
start make a start on sth
start off to a bad start
start off (to a flying start)
start off to a good start (with so/sth)
start off to a running start
start one's start
start start
start start a fire under so
start start an all-out effort

start start as sth
start start back (to some place)
start start for some place
start start from scratch
start start from some place
start start in on so/sth
start start off
start start (off) with a bang
start start (off) with a clean slate
start start (off) with so/sth
start start on so/sth
start start out
start start over
start start (over) with a clean slate
start start so in (as sth)
start start so off (on sth)
start start so out (as sth)
start start so out at an amount of money
start start so over
start start so up (in sth)
start start sth
start start sth up
start start the ball rolling
start start up
start with fits and starts
starters for starters
startle startle so out of sth
starve Feed a cold and starve a fever.
starve starve for some food
starve starve for so/sth
starve starve so or an animal into sth
starve starve so or an animal out of some place
stash stash sth away
stash stash sth in sth
state fine state of affairs
state in a (constant) state of flux
state keep so in (a state of) suspense
state lie in state
state pretty state of affairs
state Something is rotten in (the state of) Denmark.
state state of mind
state state of the art
static give so static
station busy as Grand Central Station
station station so at sth
stave stave so/sth off
stave stave sth in
stave stave sth off
stay Come back when you can stay longer.
stay Don't stay away so long.
stay family that prays together stays together.
stay have no staying power
stay *in the fast lane
stay *on one's toes
stay *out of sight
stay stay abreast of so/sth
stay stay after so (about sth)
stay stay after (so/sth)
stay stay ahead of sth
stay stay ahead of the game
stay stay aloof from so/sth
stay stay at some place
stay stay at sth
stay stay away (from so/sth)
stay stay back (from sth)
stay stay behind
stay stay by so/sth
stay stay clear of so/sth
stay stay down

stay stay for sth
stay stay in limbo
stay stay in (sth)
stay stay in the back of so's mind
stay stay in the boondocks
stay stay in the dark (about so/sth)
stay stay in the fast lane
stay stay in touch (with so/sth)
stay stay loose
stay stay off (sth)
stay stay on a diet
stay stay on (after so/sth)
stay stay on course
stay stay on (one's) guard (against so/sth)
stay stay on one's toes
stay stay on (some place)
stay stay on sth
stay stay on the good side of so
stay stay on top of so/sth
stay stay one step ahead of so/sth
stay Stay out of my way.
stay stay out of sight
stay stay out (of sth)
stay Stay out of this!
stay stay over (somewhere)
stay stay put
stay stay to sth
stay stay under (sth)
stay stay up (for sth)
stay stay up late
stay stay up until a particular time
stay stay with so/sth
stay stay within sth
stay stay young at heart
stead stand so in good stead
steady go steady with so
steady Slow and steady wins the race.
steady steady as a rock
steal like stealing acorns from a blind pig
steal Lock the stable door after the horse is stolen.
steal steal a base
steal steal a glance at so/sth
steal steal a march on so/sth
steal steal away (from so/sth)
steal steal from so/sth
steal steal out of some place
steal steal over so/sth
steal steal so's heart
steal steal so's thunder
steal steal sth from so/sth
steal steal sth off so
steal steal the show
steal steal the spotlight
steal steal up on so/sth
steal Stolen fruit is sweetest.
steal Stolen pleasures are sweetest.
steam blow off (some) steam
steam full steam ahead
steam get (some) steam up
steam get up a (full) head of steam
steam let off (some) steam
steam run out of steam
steam steam across sth
steam steam in((to) sth)
steam steam out (of some place)
steam steam so's beam
steam steam so up
steam steam sth off (of) sth
steam steam sth out of sth
steam steam sth up
steam steam up

steam steamed (up)
steam steaming (mad)
steam under one's own steam
steel have a mind as sharp as a steel trap
steel nerves of steel
steel steel oneself for so/sth
steel steel so against so/sth
steel steely gaze
steel true as steel
steely steely gaze
steep little steep
steep steep so in sth
steep steep sth in sth
steer bum steer
steer kick like a steer
steer steer away from sth
steer steer clear (of so/sth)
steer steer into sth
steer steer so/sth through sth
steer steer sth for sth
steer steer sth toward so/sth
steer steer through sth
steer steer toward so/sth
stem from stem to stern
stem stem from sth
step at so's doorstep
step *away from one's desk
step dance out of step (with so/sth)
step (Do) you want to step outside?
step fall in(to step)
step first step is always the hardest.
step From the sublime to the ridiculous is only a step.
step in step (with so)
step in step (with so/sth)
step in step (with sth)
step keep in step (with so)
step keep one step ahead of so/sth
step march in step (with so)
step on so's doorstep
step out of step (with so/sth)
step stay one step ahead of so/sth
step step aside (for so)
step step away from one's desk
step step back (from so/sth)
step step back on so/sth
step step between so/sth and so/sth else
step step down (from sth)
step step forward
step step in sth
step step inside (some place)
step step in(to some place)
step step into so's shoes
step step into sth
step step in(to the breach)
step step off
step step on it
step step on so/sth
step step on so's toes
step step on the gas
step step out into sth
step step out of line
step step out (of sth)
step step out (on so)
step step outside
step step over so/sth
step step over (to) some place
step step right up
step step sth down
step step sth off
step step sth up
step step up

step step-by-step
step take steps (to prevent sth)
step watch one's step
stern from stem to stern
steven even steven
stew get (oneself) into a stew (over so/sth)
stew in a stew (about so/sth)
stew stew in one's own juice
stew Too many cooks spoil the stew.
stick end up with the short end of the stick
stick have one's words stick in one's throat
stick have sth stick in one's craw
stick have sticky fingers
stick Let the cobbler stick to his last.
stick more so/sth than one can shake a stick at
stick not hold a stick to so/sth
stick on the stick
stick short end of the stick
stick stick around
stick stick at sth
stick stick by so/sth
stick Stick 'em up!
stick stick in so's mind
stick stick in sth
stick stick it to so
stick stick man
stick stick one's foot in one's mouth
stick stick one's neck out (for so/sth)
stick stick one's nose in (where it's not wanted)
stick stick one's nose in(to sth)
stick stick one's nose up in the air
stick stick one's oar in
stick stick one's tongue out
stick stick out
stick stick shift
stick stick so/sth up
stick stick so with so/sth
stick stick sth down
stick stick sth into so/sth
stick stick sth on(to) so/sth
stick stick sth out
stick stick sth through so/sth
stick stick sth together
stick stick sth up
stick stick to one's guns
stick stick to one's ribs
stick stick to so/sth
stick stick to so's fingers
stick stick together
stick stick up
stick Stick with it.
stick stick with so/sth
stick stick-in-the-mud
stick Sticks and stones may break my bones, but words will never hurt me.
stick Throw dirt enough, and some will stick.
sticky have sticky fingers
stiff bore so stiff
stiff Keep a stiff upper lip.
stiff scare so stiff
stiff scared stiff
stiff stiff as a poker
stiff stiffen sth up
stiff stiffen up
stiff working stiff
stiffen stiffen sth up
stiffen stiffen up

stigmatize stigmatize so as sth
still Better keep still about it.
still have one's heart stand still
still hold so/sth still
still Hold still.
still jury is still out on so/sth.
still keep so/sth still
still keep sth still
still Keep still.
still one's heart stands still
still sit still for sth
still so still you could hear a pin drop
still So had better keep still about it.
still stand still for sth
still still as death
still still tongue makes a wise head.
still Still waters run deep.
stimulate stimulate so or an animal into sth
sting sting so for sth
sting sting so with sth
stink create a stink (about sth)
stink go like stink
stink like stink
stink make a (big) stink (about so/sth)
stink make a stink (about sth)
stink move like stink
stink raise a (big) stink (about so/sth)
stink raise a stink (about sth)
stink run like stink
stink stink on ice
stink stink sth up
stink stink to high heaven
stink stink with sth
stink stinking rich
stink stinking with sth
stink swim like stink
stir cause (quite) a stir
stir go stir-crazy
stir make so stir-crazy
stir stir so (in)to sth
stir stir so up
stir stir sth around
stir stir sth in
stir stir sth into sth
stir stir sth up
stir stir up a hornet's nest
stir stir-crazy
stitch in stitches
stitch keep so in stitches
stitch not have a stitch of clothes (on)
stitch stitch in time saves nine.
stitch stitch sth onto sth
stitch stitch sth up
stock have sth in stock
stock in stock
stock laughingstock
stock lock, stock, and barrel
stock not put (a lot) of stock in sth
stock not take stock in sth
stock out of stock
stock play the (stock) market
stock stock in trade
stock stock sth (up) with sth
stock stock up (on sth)
stock stock up (with sth)
stock take no stock in sth
stock take stock (of sth)
stoke stoke sth up
stoke stoked on so/sth
stoke stoked out
stolen Lock the stable door after the horse is stolen.
stolen Stolen fruit is sweetest.

stolen Stolen pleasures are sweetest.
stomach army marches on its stomach.
stomach butterflies in one's stomach
stomach cannot stomach so/sth
stomach can't stomach so/sth
stomach cast-iron stomach
stomach have the stomach for sth
stomach not able to stomach so/sth
stomach one's eyes are bigger than one's stomach
stomach pit of one's stomach
stomach turn so's stomach
stomach way to a man's heart is through his stomach
stomp stomp on so
stone break so's stones
stone bust (so's) stones
stone carve sth in stone
stone carved in stone
stone cast the first stone
stone Constant dropping wears away a stone.
stone engraved in stone
stone hard as stone
stone have a heart of stone
stone (just) a stone's throw away (from sth)
stone (just) a stone's throw (from sth)
stone keep one's nose to the grindstone
stone kill two birds with one stone
stone leave no stone unturned
stone People who live in glass houses shouldn't throw stones.
stone put one's nose to the grindstone
stone rolling stone gathers no moss.
stone run into a stone wall
stone Sticks and stones may break my bones, but words will never hurt me.
stone stone(-cold) sober
stone stone dead
stone stone's throw away
stone within a stone's throw (of sth)
stone written in stone
stone You cannot get blood from a stone.
stood should have stood in bed
stool fall between two stools
stool stool (on so)
stool stool (pigeon)
stoop stoop down
stoop stoop over
stoop stoop to doing sth
stop buck stops here.
stop come to a stop
stop face that could stop a clock
stop homely enough to stop a clock
stop I'll put a stop to that.
stop jolt to a stop
stop nature stop
stop pull all the stops out
stop put a stop to sth
stop stop at sth
stop stop behind so/sth
stop stop by (some place)
stop stop dead in one's tracks
stop stop for so
stop stop for sth
stop stop in (some place)
stop stop, look, and listen
stop stop off (some place) (for a period of time)
stop stop on a dime

stop stop on sth
stop stop one or sth dead in one's or sth's tracks
stop stop over (some place)
stop stop short of a place
stop stop short of doing sth
stop stop so cold
stop stop so from doing sth
stop stop sth up (with sth)
stop Stop the music!
stop Stop the presses!
stop stop up
stop will stop at nothing
storage in cold storage
storage in storage
store have sth in store (for so)
store hold sth in store (for so)
store in cold storage
store in storage
store in store (for so)
store lie in store (for so)
store mind the store
store set great store by so/sth
store store sth away
store store sth in sth
store store sth up
store watch the store
stork keep the stork busy
stork keep the stork flying
stork visit from the stork
storm After a storm comes a calm.
storm any port in a storm
storm calm before the storm
storm come up a storm
storm cook up a storm
storm eye of the storm
storm gab up a storm
storm kick up a storm
storm lull before the storm
storm risk of thunder(storms)
storm sing up a storm
storm storm around
storm storm at so/sth
storm storm in(to some place)
storm storm out (of some place)
storm take so/sth by storm
storm talk up a storm
storm up a storm
storm weather the storm
story break a story
story cock-and-bull story
story cut a long story short
story End of story.
story fish story
story inside story
story long story short
story make a long story short
story same old story
story shaggy-dog story
story sob story
story tell its own story
story There are two sides to every story.
story top story
story upper story
stow stow away
stow stow sth away
straddle straddle the fence
straight can't see straight
straight get sth straight
straight get the facts straight
straight give it to so (straight)

straight go straight
straight go (straight) to the top
straight have the facts straight
straight keep a straight face
straight keep people straight (in one's mind)
straight keep things straight (in one's mind)
straight keep to the straight and narrow
straight put sth straight
straight set so straight
straight set sth straight
straight set the record straight
straight straight and narrow
straight straight as an arrow
straight straight dope
straight straight face
straight (straight) from the horse's mouth
straight straight from the shoulder
straight straight low
straight straight man
straight straight off
straight straight out
straight straight shooter
straight straight talk
straight straight up
straight straightaway
straight straighten out
straight straighten so/sth up
straight straighten so out
straight straighten sth out
straight straighten up
straight think straight
straight vote a straight ticket
straightaway straightaway
straighten straighten out
straighten straighten so/sth up
straighten straighten so out
straighten straighten sth out
straighten straighten up
strain crack under the strain
strain place a strain on so/sth
strain put a strain on so/sth
strain strain after sth
strain strain at gnats and swallow camels
strain strain at the leash
strain strain away (at sth)
strain strain for an effect
strain strain sth off of sth
strain strain sth through sth
straits in dire straits
strand strand so on sth
strange Politics makes strange bedfellows.
stranger Fact is stranger than fiction.
stranger perfect stranger
stranger stranger to sth or some place
stranger total stranger
stranger Truth is stranger than fiction.
strap strap so/sth down
strap strap so/sth in(to) sth
strap strap sth onto so/sth
strap strapped for sth
straw called to straw
straw clutch at straws
straw draw straws for sth
straw drowning man will clutch at a straw.
straw grasping at straws
straw last straw

straw straw man
straw straw that broke the camel's back
straw You cannot make bricks without straw.
stray stray (away) (from sth)
stray stray in(to sth)
stray stray onto sth
streak continue one's losing streak
streak cuss a blue streak
streak have a yellow streak down one's back
streak losing streak
streak lucky streak
streak mean streak
streak streak across sth
streak streak of bad luck
streak streak of good luck
streak streak of luck
streak talk a blue streak
streak yellow streak (down so's back)
stream change horses in midstream
stream change horses in the middle of the stream
stream Cross the stream where it is shallowest.
stream Don't change horses in midstream.
stream in the mainstream (of sth)
stream stream down (on so/sth)
stream stream in(to sth)
street down the street
street man in the street
street on easy street
street on the street
street put sth on the street
street take it to the street
street two-way street
strength at full strength
strength by brute strength
strength by main strength and awkwardness
strength main strength and awkwardness
strength not know one's own strength
strength on the strength of sth
strength pillar of strength
strength tower of strength
strength Union is strength.
stress lay stress on sth
stress no stress
stretch at a stretch
stretch by any stretch of the imagination
stretch down the road a stretch
stretch in the (home)stretch
stretch make one's money stretch
stretch stretch a point
stretch stretch away (from sth)
stretch stretch away to some place
stretch stretch forth (from sth)
stretch stretch it
stretch stretch one's legs
stretch stretch one's money
stretch stretch out
stretch stretch so/sth out
stretch stretch sth out (to so/sth)
stretch stretch the point
stretch stretch the truth
stretch Stretch your arm no further than your sleeve will reach.
strew strew sth (all) over sth
strew strew sth on so/sth

strew strew sth over so/sth
strew strew sth with sth
stricken stricken with sth
strictly strictly business
strictly (strictly) from hunger
strictly (strictly) on the level
strictly (strictly) on the up-and-up
stride break one's stride
stride get into one's stride
stride hit one's stride
stride put one off one's stride
stride reach one's stride
stride stride in(to some place)
stride stride out of some place
stride take sth in (one's) stride
strike go (out) on strike
strike it strikes me that
strike Lightning never strikes (the same place) twice.
strike out (on strike)
strike strike a balance (between two things)
strike strike a bargain
strike strike a chord (with so)
strike strike a deal
strike strike a happy medium
strike strike a match
strike strike a pose
strike strike a sour note
strike strike at so/sth
strike strike back (at so/sth)
strike strike for sth
strike strike home
strike strike it rich
strike strike out
strike strike over sth
strike strike so as sth
strike strike so funny
strike strike so/sth down
strike strike so/sth from sth
strike strike so/sth on sth
strike strike so/sth with sth
strike strike so's fancy
strike strike sth down
strike strike sth into sth
strike strike sth off (of) so/sth
strike strike sth out
strike strike sth up
strike strike sth (up)on sth
strike strike the right note
strike strike up a conversation
strike strike up a friendship
strike strike up the band
strike Strike while the iron is hot.
strike Three strikes and you are out.
strike two strikes against one
string control the purse strings
string get along (on a shoestring)
string get by (on a shoestring)
string have more than one string to one's fiddle
string have so on a string
string have so on the string
string hold the purse strings
string keep so on a string
string latch string is always out.
string on a shoestring
string on a string
string play on so's heartstrings
string pull a few strings
string pull (some) strings
string string along (with so)
string string of bad luck

string string of good luck
string string so along
string string so up
string string sth out
string string sth together
string strung out
string tied to one's mother's apron strings
string with no strings attached
string without any strings attached
strip strip down
strip strip for sth
strip strip so/sth down to sth
strip strip so/sth of sth
strip strip sth away (from so/sth)
strip strip sth in
strip strip sth off (of) so/sth
strip strip to sth
strive strive after sth
strive strive against sth
strive strive for sth
strive strive to do sth
strive strive toward sth
stroke arrive (somewhere) at the stroke of some time
stroke arrive (somewhere) (up)on the stroke of some time
stroke Different strokes for different folks.
stroke have a stroke
stroke Little strokes fell great oaks.
stroke stroke of genius
stroke stroke of luck
stroke stroke so's ego
stroll stroll arm in arm
stroll stroll around
stroll stroll through sth
strong chain is no stronger than its weakest link.
strong come on strong
strong going strong
strong strong as a horse
strong strong as a lion
strong strong as an ox
strong strong, silent type
strong strong-arm tactics
strong use strong language
struggle give up the struggle
struggle put up a struggle
struggle struggle against so/sth
struggle struggle along under sth
struggle struggle along (with so/sth)
struggle struggle for sth
struggle struggle on with sth
struggle struggle through (sth)
struggle struggle to do sth
struggle struggle to the death
struggle struggle with so for sth
struggle struggle with so/sth
strum strum sth on sth
strung strung out
strut strut around
strut strut in(to some place)
strut strut one's stuff
strut strut out of some place
stub stub one's toe against sth
stub stub sth out
stubborn stubborn as a mule
stuck (stuck) in a rut
stuck stuck in traffic
stuck stuck on so/sth
stuck stuck on sth
stuck stuck with so/sth

study quick study
study slow study
study study for sth
study study up on so/sth
stuff beat the (natural) stuffing out of so
stuff beat the stuffing out of so
stuff Cut the funny stuff!
stuff get one's stuff together
stuff green stuff
stuff kick the (natural) stuffing out of so
stuff kid's stuff
stuff knock the stuffing out of so
stuff know one's stuff
stuff right stuff
stuff rough stuff
stuff show so one's stuff
stuff strut one's stuff
stuff Stuff a sock in it!
stuff stuff and nonsense
stuff stuff one's face
stuff stuff so/sth into so/sth
stuff stuff so/sth with sth
stuff stuff so's head with sth
stuff stuff sth down so's throat
stuff stuff sth down sth
stuff stuff sth up
stuff stuff the ballot box
stuff take the stuffing out of so
stuff That's the stuff!
stumble stumble across so/sth
stumble stumble into so/sth
stumble stumble on so/sth
stumble stumble over so/sth
stumble stumble through sth
stumble stumble (up)on so/sth
stumble stumbling block
stump stump for so
stump stump so
stump (You've) got me stumped.
stunt pull a stunt (on so)
stupor in a stupor
style after the style of so/sth
style cramp so's style
style follow after the style of so/sth
style go out of style
style in style
style like it was going out of style
style out of style
style spend money like it's going out of style
sub sub for so/sth
sub sub so for so else
subdivide subdivide sth into sth
subject change the subject
subject Drop the subject!
subject off the subject
subject subject so/sth to sth
subject subject to sth
subjugate subjugate so to so
sublime from the sublime to the ridiculous
submerge submerge so/sth in sth
submerge submerge so/sth under sth
submit submit so/sth to sth
submit submit to sth
subordinate subordinate so/sth to so/sth else
subpoena subpoena so to do sth
subscribe subscribe to sth
subsist subsist on sth
substance form and substance

substance sum and substance
substitute substitute for so/sth
substitute substitute so for so else
subtract subtract sth from sth else
succeed If at first you don't succeed, try, try again.
succeed Nothing succeeds like success.
succeed succeed as sth
succeed succeed at sth
succeed succeed in sth
succeed succeed so as sth
succeed succeed to sth
success bring sth to a successful conclusion
success key to success
success Nothing succeeds like success.
successful bring sth to a successful conclusion
succumb succumb to sth
such as such
such (I) never heard of such a thing!
such Like it's such a big deal!
such such and such
such such as...
such such as it is
such Such is life!
such There ain't no such thing as a free lunch.
such There's no such thing as a free lunch.
suck Don't teach your grandmother to suck eggs.
suck It sucks.
suck meaner than a junkyard dog (with fourteen sucking pups)
suck suck (some) brew
suck suck (some) suds
suck suck so in
suck suck so/sth down
suck suck so/sth into sth
suck suck so/sth under
suck suck so's hind tit
suck suck sth from sth
suck suck sth in
suck suck sth up
suck suck up to so
suck teach one's grandmother to suck eggs
suck That sucks.
sucker sucker for so/sth
sucker sucker list
sucker sucker so into sth
sudden all of a sudden
sudden suddenly the fat hit the fire
suds bust (some) suds
suds crack some suds
suds suck (some) suds
sue So, sue me.
sue sue for sth
sue sue so for sth
sue sue the pants off (of) so
suffer suffer a setback
suffer suffer an attack (of an illness)
suffer suffer from sth
suffer suffer under so
suffice suffice for so/sth
sufficiency elegant sufficiency
sufficient Sufficient unto the day is the evil thereof.
suffix suffix sth onto sth
suffuse suffuse sth with sth
sugar give so some sugar

suggest suggest itself to so
suggest suggest sth to so
suggestive suggestive of sth
suit cut one's coat to suit one's cloth
suit follow suit
suit in one's birthday suit
suit It doesn't quite suit me.
suit (It) suits me (fine).
suit monkey suit
suit suit one's actions to one's words
suit suit oneself
suit suit (oneself) up
suit suit so/sth to sth
suit suit so's fancy
suit suit so to a T
suit Suit yourself.
suit This doesn't quite suit me.
suitcase live out of a suitcase
suite suited for sth
suite tout suite!
sulk sulk about so/sth
sum sum and substance
sum sum (sth) up
summer One swallow does not make a summer.
summon summon so before so/sth
summon summon so to so/sth
summon summon sth up
sumpin' Wanna make sumpin' of it?
sun Do not let the sun go down on your anger.
sun Do not let the sun go down on your wrath.
sun go to bed with the sun
sun Happy is the bride that the sun shines on.
sun Make hay while the sun shines.
sun sun belt
sun sunny-side up
sun There is nothing new under the sun.
sun think the sun rises and sets on so
sun under the sun
sun where the sun don't shine
Sunday (I) haven't seen you in a month of Sundays.
Sunday in a month of Sundays
Sunday in one's Sunday best
Sunday know as much about sth as a hog knows about Sunday
Sunday Sunday best
Sunday Sunday driver
Sunday Sunday-go-to-meeting clothes
sundry all and sundry
sunny sunny-side up
sunset one's sunset years
sup He who sups with the devil should have a long spoon.
superimpose superimpose sth on(to) so/sth
supper Hope is a good breakfast but a bad supper.
supper shoot one's supper
supply in short supply
supply supply and demand
supply supply so/sth with sth
supply supply sth (to so/sth) (from sth)
support announce (one's support) for so/sth
support pillar of support
suppose I suppose
suppose (It's) not supposed to.
suppose So/sth is supposed to.

suppose (So's) not supposed to.
suppose Suppose I do?
suppose Suppose I don't?
suppose Supposed to.
suppose supposed to do sth
suppose Supposing I do?
suppose Supposing I don't?
sure certain sure
sure Don't be too sure.
sure for sure
sure I am so sure!
sure (I) can't say for sure.
sure Likewise(, I'm sure).
sure make sure (of sth)
sure Oh, sure (so/sth will)!
sure slow but sure
sure slowly but surely
sure sure as eggs is eggs
sure sure as fate
sure sure as God made little green apples
sure sure as hell
sure sure as I'm standing here
sure Sure as shooting!
sure sure as you live
sure sure bet
sure Sure thing.
sure swift and sure
sure Talk of the devil (and he is sure to appear).
sure That's for dang sure!
sure What do you know for sure?
surely slowly but surely
surf surf and turf
surf surf the Net
surface raise so/sth to the surface (of sth)
surface scratch the surface
surge surge in(to sth)
surge surge out (of sth)
surge surge up
surgery in surgery
surpass surpass so/sth in sth
surprise catch so by surprise
surprise come as no surprise
surprise I'm not surprised.
surprise surprise so by sth
surprise surprise so with sth
surprise take so by surprise
surprise take so/sth by surprise
surrender surrender so/sth to so/sth
surrender surrender to so/sth
surround surround so/sth with so/sth
survival survival of the fittest
susceptible susceptible to sth
suspect I suspect.
suspect suspect so of sth
suspend suspend so from sth
suspend suspend so/sth from sth
suspend suspend sth by sth
suspense keep so in (a state of) suspense
suspicion above suspicion
suspicion Caesar's wife must be above suspicion.
suspicion keep oneself above suspicion
suspicion under a cloud (of suspicion)
suspicious suspicious character
suss suss so out
sustain sustain so in sth
swab swab sth down
swab swab sth out
swallow bitter pill to swallow

swallow hard to swallow
swallow look like the cat that swallowed the canary
swallow One swallow does not make a summer.
swallow strain at gnats and swallow camels
swallow swallow one's pride
swallow swallow so/sth up
swallow swallow sth down
swallow swallow sth hook, line, and sinker
swamp swamp so/sth with sth
swan graceful as a swan
swan I swan!
swan swan song
swap swap notes (on so/sth)
swap swap so/sth for so/sth else
swap swap so/sth with so
swap swap with so
swarm swarm (all) over so/sth
swarm swarm around so/sth
swarm swarm in(to sth)
swarm swarm out of sth
swarm swarm through sth
swarm swarm with so/sth
swath cut a big swath
swath cut a wide swath
swathe swathe so/sth in sth
swathe swathe so/sth with sth
sway sway back and forth
sway sway from side to side
sway sway so to sth
swear swear at so/sth
swear swear by so/sth
swear swear like a trooper
swear swear off (sth)
swear swear on a stack of Bibles
swear swear on one's mother's grave
swear swear so in (as sth)
swear swear so to sth
swear swear sth out against so
swear swear sth to so
swear swear to sth
swear swear (up)on so/sth
sweat blood, sweat, and tears
sweat break out in a cold sweat
sweat by the sweat of one's brow
sweat Don't sweat it!
sweat in a cold sweat
sweat no sweat
sweat sweat blood
sweat sweat bullets
sweat sweat for sth
sweat sweat sth off
sweat sweat sth out
sweat work up a sweat
sweep clean sweep
sweep make a clean sweep
sweep New brooms sweep clean.
sweep sweep along
sweep sweep down on so/sth
sweep sweep in (from some place)
sweep sweep in(to some place)
sweep sweep off
sweep sweep one off one's feet
sweep sweep out of some place
sweep sweep over so
sweep sweep so into sth
sweep sweep so/sth aside
sweep sweep so/sth away
sweep sweep so/sth out of sth
sweep sweep sth back

sweep sweep sth down
sweep sweep sth into sth
sweep sweep sth off (of) sth
sweep sweep sth out
sweep sweep sth under the carpet
sweep sweep sth up
sweep sweep through (sth)
sweep sweep up
sweet all sweetness and light
sweet fresh and sweet
sweet have a sweet tooth
sweet lay some sweet lines on so
sweet put some sweet lines on so
sweet Revenge is sweet.
sweet rose by any other name would smell as sweet.
sweet short and sweet
sweet Stolen fruit is sweetest.
sweet Stolen pleasures are sweetest.
sweet sweet and sour
sweet sweet as honey
sweet sweet nothings
sweet sweet on so
sweet sweeten so up
sweet sweeten sth up
sweet sweeten the pot
sweet sweeten (up) the deal
sweet sweeter than honey
sweet sweet-talk so
sweet Take the bitter with the sweet.
sweet You bet your (sweet) life!
sweetheart sweetheart agreement
sweetheart sweetheart deal
swell swell out
swell swell up
swell swell with sth
swell swelled head
swerve swerve (away) (from so/sth)
swerve swerve into so/sth
swift Life is short and time is swift.
swift swift and sure
swift swift as an arrow
swift swift as lightning
swift swift as the wind
swift swift as thought
swill swill sth down
swim in the swim of things
swim make so's head swim
swim out of the swim of things
swim sink or swim
swim swim against the current
swim swim against the tide
swim swim around
swim swim before so's eyes
swim swim for it
swim swim for so/sth
swim swim in sth
swim swim into sth
swim swim like stink
swim swim toward so/sth
swim swim with sth
swim swimming in sth
swim swimming with so/sth
swindle swindle so out of sth
swine cast (one's) pearls before swine
swing get in(to) the swing of things
swing in full swing
swing move into full swing
swing not enough room to swing a cat
swing swing around (to sth)
swing swing at so/sth
swing swing for sth
swing swing from sth

swing swing into action
swing swing into high gear
swing swing into sth
swing swing sth
swing swing to sth
swing swing with so/sth
swing take a swing at so
swipe take a swipe at so/sth
swirl swirl about so/sth
swirl swirl around
swish swish around
swish swish sth off (of) so/sth
switch asleep at the switch
switch bait and switch
switch fall asleep at the switch
switch switch around
switch switch (around) (with so/sth)
switch switch back (to sth)
switch switch from so to so else
switch switch from sth to sth else
switch switch into sth
switch switch off
switch switch on
switch switch over (to so/sth)
switch switch so/sth around
switch switch so/sth off
switch switch so/sth over to sth
switch switch so/sth through
switch switch sth back (to sth)
switch switch sth (from sth) (in)to sth
switch switch sth on
switch switch sth out
switch switch sth over (to sth)
switch switch sth to sth else
switch switch to sth
switch switched on
swoon swoon over so/sth
swoop at one fell swoop
swoop in one fell swoop
swoop swoop down (up)on so/sth
sword cross swords (with so)
sword double-edged sword
sword Live by the sword, die by the sword.
sword pen is mightier than the sword.
sword two-edged sword
sympathize sympathize with so (about so/sth)
sympathy extend one's sympathy (to so)
sympathy one's deepest sympathy
sync out of sync
synchronize synchronize sth with sth else
system All systems (are) go.
system get sth out of one's system
T done to a T
T fit so to a T
T have sth down to a T
T suit so to a T
tab keep tab(s) (on so/sth)
tab pick up the tab
tab run a tab
tab tab so for sth
table boxed on the table
table clear the table
table coffee-table book
table drink so under the table
table get so around the table
table lay one's cards on the table
table on the table
table put one's cards on the table
table set the table
table table a motion

table turn the tables (on so)
table under the table
table wait (on) tables
tack get down to brass tacks
tack sharp as a tack
tack tack sth down
tack tack sth onto sth
tack tack sth up
tactic strong-arm tactics
tag tag along (after so)
tag tag so out
tail Better be the head of a dog than the tail of a lion.
tail bright-eyed and bushy-tailed
tail can't make heads or tails (out) of so/sth
tail come up tails
tail freeze one's tail off
tail get off so's tail
tail get one's tail in gear
tail has the world by the tail (with a downhill drag)
tail have a bear by the tail
tail have a tiger by the tail
tail heads or tails
tail hightail it out of somewhere
tail in two shakes of a lamb's tail
tail make heads or tails of so/sth
tail not able to make head or tail of sth
tail on so's tail
tail tail after so
tail tail off
tail tail wagging the dog
tail turn tail (and run)
tail two shakes of a lamb's tail
tail with one's tail between one's legs
tail work one's tail off
tailor tailor so/sth to so/sth
tailspin go into a tailspin
taint taint sth with sth
take able to take a joke
take able to take just so much
take able to take only so much
take *all the marbles
take as a duck takes to water
take *blame for sth
take Can I take a message?
take Can I take your order (now)?
take can take it to the bank
take Could I take a message?
take Could I take your order (now)?
take Devil take the hindmost.
take difficult is done at once; the impossible takes a little longer.
take do a double take
take Don't take any wooden nickels.
take Every man for himself (and the devil take the hindmost).
take *firm hand
take Genius is an infinite capacity for taking pains.
take Give so an inch and he'll take a mile.
take Give so an inch and he'll take a yard.
take God takes soonest those he loveth best.
take hard to take
take have what it takes
take (Is) this (seat) taken?
take It takes all kinds (to make a world).
take It takes money to make money.

take (It) takes one to know one.
take It takes (some) getting used to.
take It takes two to make a bargain.
take It takes two to make a quarrel.
take (It) takes two to tango.
take It will take some doing.
take It would take an act of Congress to do sth.
take (I've) got to take off.
take (just) taking care of business
take like taking candy from a baby
take *load off one's feet
take *load off one's mind
take *long shot
take *look-see
take lot of give-and-take
take *lot of nerve
take May I take a message?
take May I take your order (now)?
take mouse that has but one hole is quickly taken.
take No offense taken.
take not take no for an answer
take not take stock in sth
take on the take
take *one for the road
take *out of context
take *out of so's hands
take *peep
take *pound of flesh
take quick on the uptake
take *shellacking
take sit up and take notice
take slow on the uptake
take *some loose ends
take so's point is well taken
take take a backseat (to so/sth)
take take a bath
take take a beating
take take a bow
take take a break
take take a chance
take take a collection up (from so) (for so/sth)
take take a course (in sth)
take take a crack at so
take take a crack at sth
take take a dig at so
take take a dim view of so/sth
take take a dirt nap
take take a dive
take take a drag (on sth)
take take a fall
take take a fancy to so/sth
take take a firm grip on so/sth
take take a (firm) stand on sth
take take a gander (at so/sth)
take take a go at so
take take a go at sth
take take a guess
take take a hand in sth
take take a hard line (with so)
take take a hike
take take a hint
take take a jab at so
take take a leaf out of so's book
take take a leak
take take a licking
take take a liking to so/sth
take take a load off (of) so's mind
take take a load off one's feet
take Take a long walk off a short pier.
take take a look at so/sth

take take a look for so/sth
take take a lot of nerve
take take a lot off (of) so's mind
take take a lot out of so
take take a nap
take take a new turn
take take a nosedive
take take a page from so's book
take take a poke at so
take take a pop at so
take take a potshot at so/sth
take take a pound of flesh
take take a powder
take take a punch at so
take take a rain check (on sth)
take take a risk
take Take a running jump (in the lake)!
take take a shine to so/sth
take take a shot at so/sth
take take a shower
take take a spill
take take a stab at so
take take a stab at sth
take take a stand (against so/sth)
take take a swing at so
take take a swipe at so/sth
take take a try at so
take take a try at sth
take take a turn for the better
take take a turn for the worse
take take a vacation
take take a walk
take take a weight off one's mind
take take a whack at sth
take take a whiff of sth
take take account of so/sth
take take action against so/sth
take take action on so/sth
take take advantage of so
take take after so
take take (a)hold of so/sth
take take aim at so/sth
take take aim (at so/sth or an animal)
take take an amount of money for sth
take take an interest in so/sth
take take an oath
take take attendance
take take away from so/sth
take Take care.
take take care of number one
take take care of numero uno
take take care of so
take take care of sth
take Take care (of yourself).
take take charge (of so/sth)
take take cold
take take control of so/sth
take take cover
take take credit for sth
take take digs at so
take take effect
take take exception (to sth)
take take first crack at sth
take take five
take take forty winks
take take fuel on
take take (great) pains (to do sth)
take take heart (from sth)
take take heed (from sth)
take take hold of so/sth
take take ill
take take into account so/sth
take take inventory

take take issue with so
take take issue with sth
take take it
take take its course
take take kindly to sth
take take leave of one's senses
take take leave of so/sth
take take liberties with so/sth
take Take my word for it.
take take names
take take no prisoners
take take no stock in sth
take take note of so/sth
take take notice of so/sth
take take off
take take offense (at so/sth)
take take office
take take on a new meaning
take take on a new significance
take take on (so)
take take one at one's word
take take one back (to some time)
take take one for the road
take take one's belt in (a notch)
take take one's break
take take one's cue from so
take take one's death (of cold)
take take one's eyes off (of) so/sth
take take one's gloves off
take take one's hands off (of) so/sth
take take one's hat off to so
take take (one's) leave (of so)
take take one's lumps
take take one's medicine
take take one's own life
take take one's pick of so/sth
take take one's time
take take one's turn
take take oneself off some place
take take out a loan
take take out (after so/sth)
take take over (from so)
take take pains over sth
take take pains with so/sth
take take part (in sth)
take take pity (on so or an animal)
take take place
take take possession (of sth)
take take precedence over so/sth
take take pride in so/sth
take take (quite) a toll (on so/sth)
take take refuge in sth
take take revenge (against so)
take take root
take take shape
take take sick
take take sides
take take solace (in sth)
take take some doing
take take some heat
take take (some) time off
take take ((some) time) off from work
take take so apart
take take so around
take take so as so
take take so aside
take take so below
take take so by surprise
take take so down a notch (or two)
take take so down a peg (or two)
take take so down (to size)
take take so for a fool
take take so for a ride

take take so for an idiot
take take so for dead
take take so for so/sth
take take so for sth
take take so hostage
take take so in
take take so into one's confidence
take take so off
take take so on
take take so or an animal in
take take so or an animal into one's heart
take take so/sth aboard
take take so/sth across (sth)
take take so/sth along
take take so/sth at face value
take take so/sth away (from so/sth)
take take so/sth before so/sth
take take so/sth by sth
take take so/sth by storm
take take so/sth by surprise
take take so/sth down
take take so/sth for granted
take take so/sth into account
take take so/sth off
take take so/sth on
take take so/sth out of sth
take take so/sth over
take take so/sth with one
take take so/sth wrong
take take so out
take take so's blood pressure
take take so's breath away
take take so's head off
take take so's life
take take so's part
take take so's pulse
take take so's temperature
take take so's word for sth
take take so's word on sth
take take so/sth or an animal in(side)
take take so through (sth)
take take so to court
take take so to one side
take take so to task
take take so to the cleaners
take take so under so's wing(s)
take take so up
take take sth
take take sth aloft
take take sth amiss
take take sth apart
take take sth around
take take sth as sth
take take sth at face value
take take sth away (from so/sth)
take take sth back
take take sth down
take take sth for a drive
take take sth from so
take take sth from sth
take take sth home (with oneself)
take take sth in
take take sth into account
take take sth into one's head
take take sth into some place
take take sth lying down
take take sth off
take take sth on faith
take take sth on the chin
take take sth on trust
take take sth out
take take sth over
take take sth personally

take take sth public
take take sth the wrong way
take take sth to heart
take take sth to pieces
take take sth to so/sth
take take sth under advisement
take take sth up
take take sth (up)on oneself
take take sth with a pinch of salt
take take sth with one
take take sth with sth
take take steps (to prevent sth)
take take stock (of sth)
take take the bit between the teeth
take take the bit in one's teeth
take Take the bitter with the sweet.
take take the blame (for doing sth)
take take the bull by the horns
take take the chill off ((of) a place)
take take the coward's way out
take take the cure
take take the day off
take take the easy way out
take take the edge off ((of) sth)
take take the fall
take take the floor
take Take the goods the gods provide.
take take the heat
take take the initiative (to do sth)
take take the law into one's own hands
take take the liberty of doing sth
take take the lid off (of) sth
take take the (long) count
take take the pledge
take take the plunge
take take the pulse of sth
take take the rap (for so)
take take the rap (for sth)
take take (the) roll
take Take the rough with the smooth.
take take the slack up
take take the spear (in one's chest)
take take the stage
take take the stand
take take the starch out of so
take take the stuffing out of so
take take the trouble (to do sth)
take take the wind out of so's sails
take take the words out of so's mouth
take take things easy
take take time out
take take to one's bed
take take to one's heels
take take to so/sth
take take to the hills
take take too much on
take take turns ((at) doing sth)
take take turns with so
take take turns (with sth)
take take umbrage at sth
take take up arms (against so/sth)
take take up one's abode some place
take take up residence some place
take take up room
take take up (so's) time
take take up space
take take up the challenge
take take up where one left off
take take up with so
take take years off (of) so/sth
take Take your seat.
take taken aback
take taken for dead

take taken with so/sth
take take-off artist
take taking calls
take That takes care of that.
take That takes the cake!
take *time off
take *try at so
take *try at sth
take *under so's wing(s)
take undertake to do sth
take *whiff of sth
take winner take all
take (You) can't take it with you.
take You pays your money and you takes your chance(s).
takeoff do a takeoff on so/sth
tale Dead men tell no tales.
tale fish tale
tale Never tell tales out of school.
tale old wives' tale
tale tale never loses in the telling.
tale tale of woe
tale tell its own tale
tale tell tales out of school
tale thereby hangs a tale
talent have a hidden talent
talent have hidden talents
talk all talk (and no action)
talk engage in small talk
talk fast-talk so into sth
talk fast-talk so out of sth
talk have a heart-to-heart (talk)
talk (I'll) talk to you soon.
talk (It's been) good talking to you.
talk Let's talk (about it).
talk like to hear oneself talk
talk Look who's talking!
talk *mile a minute
talk Money talks.
talk Now you're talking!
talk straight talk
talk sweet-talk so
talk talk a blue streak
talk talk a mile a minute
talk talk about so/sth
talk Talk about so/sth!
talk talk around sth
talk talk at so
talk talk back (to so)
talk talk big
talk talk down to so
talk talk in circles
talk Talk is cheap.
talk talk like a nut
talk talk of a place
talk talk of so/sth
talk Talk of the devil (and he is sure to appear).
talk talk on
talk talk one's head off
talk talk one's way out of sth
talk talk oneself out
talk talk over so's head
talk talk over sth
talk talk shop
talk talk so down
talk talk so into (doing) sth
talk talk so/sth over (with so)
talk talk so/sth up
talk talk so out of doing sth
talk talk so out of sth
talk talk so ragged
talk talk so's ear off

talk talk so's head off
talk talk sth out
talk talk sth over
talk talk sth through
talk talk sth up
talk talk through one's hat
talk talk to hear one's own voice
talk talk to so
talk talk turkey
talk talk until one is blue in the face
talk talk up a storm
talk talk with so (about so/sth)
talk talked out
talk *up a storm
talk We need to talk about sth.
talk We were just talking about you.
talk Who do you think you're talking to?
talk Who do you want (to talk to)?
tall head for (the) tall timber
tall in tall cotton
tall stand tall
tall tall drink of water
tall tall order
tall tall timber(s)
tall walk tall
tallow hair and hide(, horns and tallow)
tally tally sth up
tally tally with sth
tamp tamp sth down
tamper tamper with so/sth
tan tan so's hide
tandem in tandem
tangent go off on a tangent
tangle tangle so/sth up
tangle tangle with so/sth (over so/sth)
tango (It) takes two to tango.
tank tank up (on sth)
tantrum throw a tantrum
tap on tap
tap tap at sth
tap tap on sth
tap tap out
tap tap so (for sth)
tap tap so/sth on sth
tap *tap sth down
tap tap sth into sth
tap tap sth out
tap tap sth with sth
tap tap-dance like mad
tap What's on tap for today?
tape cut through red tape
tape red tape
taper taper off (doing sth)
tar beat the tar out of so
tar tar and feather so
tar tarred with the same brush
tar whale the tar out of so
target on target
target target so/sth as sth
task come to the task with sth
task take so to task
taste acquire a taste for sth
taste Every man to his taste.
taste have to do sth so bad one can taste it
taste in bad taste
taste in poor taste
taste leave a bad taste in so's mouth
taste need so bad one can taste it
taste so bad one can taste it
taste taste blood

taste taste like more
taste taste like sth
taste taste of one's own medicine
taste taste of sth
taste taste of sth
taste Tastes differ.
taste There is no accounting for taste(s).
taste There's no accounting for taste.
taste want so bad one can taste it
tat give so tit for tat
tater all vine and no taters
tater Hold your tater!
tatter in tatters
tattle going to tattle
tattle tattle (on so) (to so)
tattoo screwed, blued, and tattooed
taunt taunt so about sth
taunt taunt so into sth
taunt taunt so with sth
taut run a taut ship
tax Nothing is certain but death and taxes.
tax tax so/sth with sth
tax tax-and-spend
tax write sth off (on one's taxes)
taxi hail a taxi
tea just one's cup of tea
tea not for all the tea in China
tea not one's cup of tea
teach Don't teach your grandmother to suck eggs.
teach teach one's grandmother to suck eggs
teach teach so a lesson
teach teach so the hang of sth
teach teach so the tricks of the trade
teach That'll teach so!
teach Those who can, do; those who can't, teach.
teach *tricks of the trade
teach You cannot teach an old dog new tricks.
teacher Experience is the best teacher.
teacher Experience is the teacher of fools.
teacher teacher's pet
teacup tempest in a teacup
team make the team
team pull together (as a team)
team team player
team team up against so/sth
team team up (with so)
team *up against sth
teapot tempest in a teapot
tear all tore up (about sth)
tear blink one's tears back
tear blood, sweat, and tears
tear bore so to tears
tear break in(to) tears
tear break out in(to) tears
tear burst into tears
tear cry crocodile tears
tear It is easier to tear down than to build up.
tear move so to tears
tear not shed a tear
tear put wear (and tear) on sth
tear reduce so to tears
tear shed crocodile tears
tear tear a place apart
tear tear across sth
tear tear along

tear tear around (some place)
tear tear at so/sth
tear tear away (from so/sth)
tear tear down sth
tear tear into some place
tear tear into so
tear tear into sth
tear tear loose (from so/sth)
tear tear off (from so/sth)
tear tear one's hair (out)
tear tear (oneself) away (from so/sth)
tear tear out (of some place)
tear tear so apart
tear tear so or some animal limb from limb
tear tear so/sth down
tear tear so/sth to pieces
tear tear so up
tear tear sth apart
tear tear sth away (from so/sth)
tear tear sth down
tear tear sth from sth
tear tear sth off (of) so/sth
tear tear sth on sth
tear tear sth out of sth
tear tear sth up
tear That tears it!
tear (this) vale of tears
tear tore (up)
tear torn between so and so else
tear torn (up)
tear wear and tear (on sth)
tease tease so about so/sth
tease tease so into doing sth
tease tease sth out
tee tee off
tee tee so off
tee teed off
tee teed (up)
teem teem with so/sth
teeth armed to the teeth
teeth bare one's teeth
teeth by the skin of one's teeth
teeth cut teeth
teeth dressed to the teeth
teeth drop one's teeth
teeth escape by the skin of one's teeth
teeth fly in the teeth of so/sth
teeth get one's teeth into sth
teeth give teeth to sth
teeth gnash one's teeth
teeth gnashing of teeth
teeth gods send nuts to those who have no teeth.
teeth grit one's teeth
teeth kick in the teeth
teeth lie through one's teeth
teeth no skin off so's teeth
teeth pull so's or sth's teeth
teeth put some teeth into sth
teeth put teeth in(to) sth
teeth scarce as hen's teeth
teeth scarcer than hen's teeth
teeth set so's teeth on edge
teeth show one's teeth
teeth sink one's teeth into sth
teeth take the bit between the teeth
teeth take the bit in one's teeth
teeth teething troubles
telegraph telegraph one's punches
telephone get on(to) the (tele)phone
telephone on the telephone
telephone telephone sth in (to so)
telescope telescope into sth

tell all told
tell Ask me no questions, I'll tell you no lies.
tell Blood will tell.
tell Breeding will tell.
tell Can I tell her who's calling?
tell Children and fools tell the truth.
tell Could I tell him who's calling?
tell Dead men tell no tales.
tell Do tell.
tell (Do) you mean to tell me sth?
tell done told you
tell Don't make me tell you again!
tell Don't tell a soul.
tell Don't tell me what to do!
tell going to tell
tell How many times do I have to tell you?
tell I don't mind telling you (sth).
tell (I) won't tell a soul.
tell if I've told you once, I've told you a thousand times
tell kiss and tell
tell liar is not believed (even) when he tells the truth.
tell little bird told me.
tell May I tell him who's calling?
tell my gut tells me (that)
tell Never tell tales out of school.
tell not tell a (living) soul
tell (Only) time will tell.
tell show and tell
tell tale never loses in the telling.
tell tell all
tell Tell it like it is.
tell Tell it to the marines!
tell tell its own story
tell tell its own tale
tell Tell me another (one)!
tell tell of so/sth
tell tell on so
tell tell one one's bearings
tell tell one to one's face
tell tell people or things apart
tell tell shit from Shinola
tell tell so a thing or two (about so/sth)
tell tell so about so/sth
tell tell so from so else
tell tell so off
tell tell so on so
tell tell so/sth by sth
tell tell so what to do with sth
tell tell so where to get off
tell tell sth from sth
tell tell sth to so
tell tell tales out of school
tell tell the difference between so and so else or sth and sth else
tell Tell the truth and shame the devil.
tell tell the (whole) world
tell tell things apart
tell tell time
tell tell which is which
tell (There's) no way to tell.
tell Time will tell.
tell What can I tell you?
tell You can't tell a book by its cover.
tell You mean to tell me sth?
tell You're telling me!
temper hold one's temper
temper keep one's temper
temper lose one's temper (at so/sth)
temper quick temper

temper short temper
temper temper sth with sth
temperature run a temperature
temperature take so's temperature
tempest tempest in a teacup
tempest tempest in a teapot
tempt tempt so into sth
tempt tempt so to do sth
tempt tempt so with sth
ten Genius is ten percent inspiration and ninety percent perspiration.
ten hang ten
ten He wears a ten-dollar hat on a five-cent head.
ten I wouldn't touch it with a ten-foot pole.
ten nine times out of ten
ten not touch so/sth with a ten-foot pole
ten wouldn't touch so/sth with a ten-foot pole
tend tend to do sth
tend tend toward sth
tender tender age of...
tender tender sth for sth
tender tender sth (to so) (for sth)
tense tense up (for sth)
tent pitch a tent
tenterhooks keep so on tenterhooks
tenths Possession is nine-tenths of the law.
term come to terms (about so/sth)
term come to terms (with so/sth)
term contradiction in terms
term in glowing terms
term in no uncertain terms
term in terms of sth
term on good terms (with so)
term on speaking terms (with so)
terrible I'm terrible at names.
terrify terrify so into sth
terrify terrify so or an animal out of sth
territory come with the territory
territory cover the territory
territory go with the territory
territory unfamiliar territory
terror hold terror for so
terrorize terrorize so into sth
test acid test
test cram for a test
test litmus test
test put so/sth to the test
test stand the test of time
test test for sth
test test out (of sth)
test test so in sth
test test so/sth for sth
test test sth out
testament last will and testament
testify testify against so/sth
testify testify for so
testify testify to sth
tether at the end of one's tether
than Actions speak louder than words.
than bad excuse is better than none.
than Better be an old man's darling than a young man's slave.
than Better (be) safe than sorry.
than Better be the head of a dog than the tail of a lion.
than Better late than never.
than Better the devil you know than the devil you don't know.

than bigger than life (and twice as ugly)
than bite off more than one can chew
than Blood is thicker than water.
than cannot see (any) further than the end of one's nose
than chain is no stronger than its weakest link.
than deader than a doornail
than didn't exchange more than three words with so
than Don't bite off more than you can chew.
than easier said than done
than emptier than a banker's heart
than Example is better than precept.
than exchange no more than some number of words with so
than Fact is stranger than fiction.
than fate worse than death
than female of the species is more deadly than the male.
than Half a loaf is better than none.
than harder than the back of God's head
than hardly exchange more than some number of words with so
than have more luck than sense
than have more than one string to one's fiddle
than I'd rather face a firing squad than do sth
than in less than no time
than It is better to be born lucky than rich.
than It is better to give than to receive.
than It is better to travel hopefully than to arrive.
than It is better to wear out than to rust out.
than It is easier to tear down than to build up.
than It is more blessed to give than to receive.
than (It's) better than nothing.
than know better (than to do sth)
than know no more about sth than a frog knows about bedsheets
than larger than life
than less than pleased
than meaner than a junkyard dog (with fourteen sucking pups)
than more dead than alive
than more fun than a barrel of monkeys
than more often than not
than more so/sth than one can shake a stick at
than more sth than Carter has (liver) pills
than more than one bargained for
than more than one can bear
than more than you('ll ever) know
than more (to sth) than meets the eye
than No more than I have to.
than no sooner said than done
than none other than
than not exchange more than some number of words with so
than notch better than (so/sth)
than nuttier than a fruitcake
than One's bark is worse than one's bite.

than one's eyes are bigger than one's stomach
than pen is mightier than the sword.
than Prevention is better than cure.
than quicker than hell
than quicker than you can say Jack Robinson
than scarcely exchange more than some number of words with so
than scarcer than hen's teeth
than see no further than the end of one's nose
than slower than molasses in January
than Something is better than nothing.
than Sooner than you think.
than Stretch your arm no further than your sleeve will reach.
than sweeter than honey
than There's more than one way to skin a cat.
than 'Tis better to have loved and lost than never to have loved at all.
than Truth is stranger than fiction.
than Two heads are better than one.
than use your head for more than a hatrack
than use your head for more than something to keep your ears apart
than wear more than one hat
than You are more than welcome.
than You can catch more flies with honey than with vinegar.
than You make a better door than you do a window.
thank (I) can't thank you enough.
thank I'll thank you to keep your opinions to yourself.
thank I'll thank you to mind your own business.
thank No, thank you.
thank no thanks to you
thank Not right now, thanks.
thank Nothing for me, thanks.
thank Thank God for small favors.
thank Thank goodness!
thank Thank heavens!
thank thank one's lucky stars
thank thank so for sth
thank Thank you.
thank Thank you a lot.
thank Thank you for a lovely evening.
thank Thank you for a lovely time.
thank Thank you for calling.
thank Thank you for having me.
thank Thank you for inviting me.
thank Thank you for sharing.
thank Thank you kindly.
thank Thank you so much.
thank Thank you very much.
thank thankful for small blessings
thank thanks a bunch
thank Thanks (a lot).
thank Thanks a million.
thank Thanks awfully.
thank Thanks, but no thanks.
thank Thanks for the lift.
thank Thanks for the ride.
thank Thanks loads.
thank thanks to so/sth
thank vote of thanks
thank wham bam thank you ma'am
Thanksgiving busy as a cranberry merchant (at Thanksgiving)

that All's well that ends well.
that All that glistens is not gold.
that All that glitters is not gold.
that and all that jazz
that and that's a fact
that And that's that.
that and this and that
that appear to so that...
that as bad as all that
that at that rate
that Bag that!
that be that as it may
that bear in mind that...
that bite the hand that feeds one
that Bump that!
that check that
that cross that bridge when one comes to it
that Crosses are ladders that lead to heaven.
that Do we have to go through all that again?
that (Do) you eat with that mouth?
that Do you expect me to believe that?
that (Do) you kiss your momma with that mouth?
that Don't give me that line!
that Don't hand me that (line)!
that Don't that (just) beat all!
that Don't touch that dial!
that face that could stop a clock
that face (that) only a mother could love
that family that prays together stays together.
that Fancy that!
that feeling (that sth is the case)
that for that matter
that game that two can play
that give so odds that...
that God helps them that help themselves.
that hair of the dog that bit one
that hand that rocks the cradle rules the world.
that Happy is the bride that the sun shines on.
that have a hunch (that sth is the case)
that He that cannot obey cannot command.
that He that hath a full purse never wanted a friend.
that He that is down need fear no fall.
that He that would eat the kernel must crack the nut.
that He that would go to sea for pleasure, would go to hell for a pastime.
that He that would have eggs must endure the cackling of hens.
that He that would the daughter win, must with the mother first begin.
that How about that!
that How do you like that?
that How does that grab you?
that How's that again?
that I can accept that.
that I can live with that.
that I can't accept that.
that (I) can't argue with that.
that (I) can't beat that.
that I can't believe (that)!
that (I) can't say that I do.

that (I) can't say that I have.
that (I) can't top that.
that I couldn't ask you to do that.
that I didn't (quite) catch that (last) remark.
that I doubt that.
that (I have) no problem with that.
that I wish I'd said that.
that I wouldn't wish that on a dog.
that I wouldn't wish that on my worst enemy.
that If that don't beat a pig a-pecking!
that If that don't beat all!
that I'll drink to that!
that I'll get back to you (on that).
that I'll put a stop to that.
that (I'm) sorry to hear that.
that (I'm) sorry you asked (that).
that Imagine that!
that Is that everything?
that Is that right?
that Is that so?
that It is a long lane that has no turning.
that It is a poor heart that never rejoices.
that It is a wise child that knows its own father.
that It is not work that kills, but worry.
that It is the pace that kills.
that It's an ill bird that fouls its own nest.
that It's an ill wind that blows nobody (any) good.
that it strikes me that
that (I've) been there(, done that).
that Judge not, that ye be not judged.
that just like that
that keep (it) in mind that
that Kill the goose that lays the golden egg(s).
that know at a glance that...
that language that would fry bacon
that leave it at that
that Let me get back to you (on that).
that Let's not go through all that again.
that look like the cat that swallowed the canary
that make believe that...
that make out that...
that mill cannot grind with water that is past.
that mouse that has but one hole is quickly taken.
that my gut tells me (that)
that need I remind you that...
that of the persuasion that...
that one that got away
that or words to that effect
that powers that be
that provided that
that Put that in your pipe and smoke it!
that rumor has it that...
that Run that by (me) again.
that say that...
that see (to it) that sth is done
that seeing that...
that ships that pass in the night
that Smile when you say that.
that So much for that.
that something to that effect
that sorry about that

that Sorry (that) I asked.
that straw that broke the camel's back
that take it that...
that That ain't hay.
that That ain't no lie.
that That ain't the way I heard it.
that That (all) depends.
that That beats everything!
that that beats sth all to pieces
that That brings me to the (main) point.
that (That causes) no problem.
that That does it!
that That makes two of us.
that That (really) burns me (up)!
that That's a fine how-do-you-do.
that That's a new one on me!
that That's about the size of it.
that That's all for so.
that That's all she wrote.
that That's all so needs.
that That's easy for you to say.
that That's enough!
that That's enough for now.
that (That's) enough (of this) foolishness!
that (That's) fine with me.
that That's for dang sure!
that That's funny.
that That's it!
that That's (just) the way it goes.
that That's (just) too much!
that That's just what you need.
that That's more like it.
that That's my boy.
that That's my girl.
that That's news to me.
that That's show business (for you).
that That's that!
that That's the pot calling the kettle black.
that That's the spirit!
that That's the stuff!
that That's the ticket!
that That's the way the ball bounces.
that That's the way the cookie crumbles.
that That's the way the mop flops.
that (That's the) way to go!
that (That's) too bad.
that That's what I say.
that That's what she wrote.
that that's why!
that That sucks.
that That takes care of that.
that That takes the cake!
that That tears it!
that that there
that that very thing
that That will do.
that That'll be the day!
that That'll teach so!
that They went that a'way.
that this a-way and that a-way
that (To) hell with that!
that turn out (that)
that Uneasy lies the head that wears a crown.
that What do you know (about that)?
that What do you think of that?
that What does that prove?
that What's that?
that Will that be all?

that You can say that again!
that (You) can't beat that.
that You can't expect me to believe that.
that You can't mean that!
that (You) can't top that.
that You couldn't (do that)!
that You don't expect me to believe that.
that You wouldn't (do that)!
thaw thaw out
thaw thaw so/sth out
their Birds in their little nests agree.
their Coming events cast their shadows before.
their Cowards die many times before their death(s).
their If frogs had wheels, they wouldn't bump their butts.
their in their entirety
their Men are blind in their own cause.
their sit on their hands
them and them
them daddy of them all
them Do unto others as you would have them do unto you.
them every mother's son (of them)
them God helps them that help themselves.
them granddaddy of them all
them How bout them apples?
them How do you like them apples?
them If you can't beat them, join them.
them If you can't lick 'em, join 'em.
them leave them rolling in the aisles
them Let them eat cake.
them pack them in
them Put 'em up!
them Stick 'em up!
them Them as has, gits.
them Them's fighting words!
them They don't make them like they used to.
them up and at 'em
them (You) can't win them all.
themselves by themselves
themselves Eavesdroppers never hear any good of themselves.
themselves God helps them that help themselves.
themselves Listeners never hear any good of themselves.
themselves speak for themselves
themselves squeeze (themselves) together
themselves squeeze (themselves) up
then and then some
then (every) now and then
then *fat hit the fire
then (Good-bye) until then.
then If wishes were horses, then beggars would ride.
then If you're born to be hanged, then you'll never be drowned.
then (I'll) see you then.
then now and then
then now then
then then and there
then then the fat hit the fire
theorize theorize about so/sth
theorize theorize on sth
theory in theory

theory ounce of common sense is worth a pound of theory.
there all there
there Be there or be square.
there couldn't pour water out of a boot (if there was instructions on the heel)
there Easy, there!
there go there
there Hang in there.
there here and there
there here, there, and everywhere
there If ifs and ands were pots and pans (there'd be no work for tinkers' hands).
there If there's anything you need, don't hesitate to ask.
there (I'll) be right there.
there in there
there Is so there?
there Is there any truth to sth?
there Is there anything else?
there Is there some place I can wash up?
there It's a jungle out there.
there (I've) been there(, done that).
there Keep in there!
there like there ain't no tomorrow
there like there's no tomorrow
there neither here nor there
there not all there
there Put 'er there(, pal).
there spend money like there's no tomorrow
there stand there with one's bare face hanging out
there that there
there then and there
there There ain't no such thing as a free lunch.
there (There ain't) nothin' to it.
there There are plenty of (other) fish in the sea.
there There are tricks in every trade.
there There are two sides to every question.
there There are two sides to every story.
there There aren't enough hours in the day.
there There but for the grace of God (go I).
there There is a fine line between sth and sth else.
there There is a remedy for everything except death.
there There is a tide in the affairs of men.
there There is a time and a place for everything.
there There is honor among thieves.
there There is no accounting for taste(s).
there (There is) no chance.
there there is no doing sth
there (There is) no doubt about it.
there There is no love lost (between so and so else).
there (There is) no need (to).
there There is no pleasure without pain.
there There is no rest for the weary.

there There is no royal road to learning.
there There is nothing new under the sun.
there There is safety in numbers.
there There is trouble brewing.
there There's many a good tune played on an old fiddle.
there There's many a slip 'twixt the cup and the lip.
there There's many a true word spoken in jest.
there There's more than one way to skin a cat.
there There's no accounting for taste.
there There's no flies on so.
there There's no fool like an old fool.
there There's no place like home.
there There's no rose without a thorn.
there (There's) no smoke without fire.
there There's no such thing as a free lunch.
there (There's) no time like the present.
there (There's) no way to tell.
there There's nobody home.
there There's none so blind as those who will not see.
there There's none so deaf as those who will not hear.
there (There's) nothing to it!
there There, there.
there There will be hell to pay.
there There will be the devil to pay.
there There you are.
there There you go.
there (way) over there
there What's (there) to know?
there Where there's a will, there's a way.
there Where there's life there's hope.
there Where there's smoke there's fire.
there While there's life there's hope.
there Who's there?
there (Will there be) anything else?
there (You) can't get there from here.
there You got me there.
thereby thereby hangs a tale
thereof Sufficient unto the day is the evil thereof.
these along these lines
these between you and me and these four walls
these in these parts
these one of these days
they bigger they are, the harder they fall.
they Church ain't out till they quit singing.
they count one's chickens before they hatch
they Don't count your chickens before they are hatched.
they If frogs had wheels, they wouldn't bump their butts.
they Let the chips fall where they may.
they mills of God grind slowly, yet they grind exceeding small.
they They also serve who only stand and wait.
they They don't make them like they used to.
they They must have seen you coming.

they They went that a'way.
they Things are seldom what they seem.
thick Blood is thicker than water.
thick get sth into so's thick head
thick get sth through so's thick skull
thick grow thick-skinned
thick lay it on thick
thick plot thickens.
thick pour it on thick
thick spread it on thick
thick spread sth on thick
thick thick and fast
thick thick as a short plank
thick thick as pea soup
thick thick as thieves
thick thick as two short planks
thick thicken sth up
thick thick-skinned
thick through thick and thin
thicken plot thickens.
thicken thicken sth up
thief Little thieves are hanged, but great ones escape.
thief Opportunity makes a thief.
thief Procrastination is the thief of time.
thief Set a thief to catch a thief.
thief There is honor among thieves.
thief thick as thieves
thieves Little thieves are hanged, but great ones escape.
thieves There is honor among thieves.
thieves thick as thieves
thin grow thin-skinned
thin on thin ice
thin out of thin air
thin pull sth out of thin air
thin skate on thin ice
thin spread oneself too thin
thin thin on top
thin thin out
thin thin so down
thin thin sth down
thin thin down
thin thin-skinned
thin through thick and thin
thin vanish into thin air
thin walk on thin ice
thing add up to the same thing
thing All good things must (come to an) end.
thing all things being equal
thing All things must pass.
thing all things to all men
thing all things to all people
thing All things will pass.
thing amount to the same thing
thing any fool thing
thing any old thing
thing (Are) things getting you down?
thing best things come in small packages.
thing best things in life are free.
thing come to the same thing
thing do one's (own) thing
thing Don't worry (about a thing).
thing every fool thing
thing feel out of things
thing find out a thing or two (about so/sth)
thing first thing (in the morning)
thing First things first.

thing get in(to) the swing of things
thing Good things come in small packages.
thing Good things come to him who waits.
thing greatest thing since indoor plumbing
thing greatest thing since sliced bread
thing harbinger of things to come
thing have a good thing going
thing have a thing about so/sth
thing have a thing going (with so)
thing have too much of a good thing
thing He who begins many things, finishes but few.
thing How's every little thing?
thing How're things going?
thing How're things (with you)?
thing I have to wash a few things out.
thing (I) never heard of such a thing!
thing If a thing is worth doing, it's worth doing well.
thing If you want a thing done well, do it yourself.
thing in the swim of things
thing in thing (to do)
thing It's just one of those things.
thing (I've) (got) better things to do.
thing Keep a thing seven years and you'll (always) find a use for it.
thing know a thing or two (about so/sth)
thing learn a thing or two (about so/sth)
thing least little thing
thing let things slide
thing little knowledge is a dangerous thing.
thing Little things please little minds.
thing Moderation in all things.
thing not know the first thing about so/sth
thing not miss a thing
thing Of all things!
thing one final thing
thing One thing leads to another.
thing onto a good thing
thing other things being equal
thing out of the swim of things
thing portent of things to come
thing real thing
thing seeing things
thing sign of things to come
thing Small things please small minds.
thing Sure thing.
thing take things easy
thing tell so a thing or two (about so/sth)
thing that very thing
thing There ain't no such thing as a free lunch.
thing There's no such thing as a free lunch.
thing thing of beauty is a joy forever.
thing thing or two (about so/sth)
thing thing you don't want is dear at any price.
thing Things are looking up.
thing Things are seldom what they seem.
thing (Things) could be better.
thing (Things) could be worse.
thing (Things) couldn't be better.
thing Things haven't been easy.
thing (Things) might be better.
thing Things will work out (all right).

thing too much of a good thing
thing very thing
thing whole nother thing
thing work things out
thing worth of a thing is what it will bring.
think come to think of it
think Don't even think about (doing) it.
think Don't even think about it (happening).
think Every horse thinks its own pack heaviest.
think Evil be to him who evil thinks.
think Great minds think alike.
think hardly have time to think
think have another think coming
think How dumb do you think I am?
think (I) don't think so.
think I think not.
think I think so.
think (I'm) (just) thinking out loud.
think put one's thinking cap on
think Sooner than you think.
think think a great deal of so/sth
think think a lot of so/sth
think think about so/sth
think think ahead of one's time
think think ahead (to sth)
think think back (on so/sth)
think think back (to sth)
think think before doing sth
think think better of so/sth
think think better of sth
think think for oneself
think think highly of so/sth
think think inside the box
think think little of so/sth
think think much of so/sth
think think nothing of doing sth
think Think nothing of it.
think think nothing of so/sth
think think of so/sth
think think on one's feet
think think out loud
think think outside the box
think think so fit for sth
think think so hung the moon (and stars)
think think so is God's own cousin
think think so/sth fit for so/sth
think think sth of so/sth
think think sth out
think think sth over
think think sth through
think think sth up
think think straight
think think the sun rises and sets on so
think think the world of so/sth
think think to do sth
think think twice about so/sth
think think twice (before doing sth)
think think under fire
think think (up)on so/sth
think think worlds apart
think to so's way of thinking
think *under fire
think What do you think?
think What do you think of that?
think What do you think of this weather?
think What do you think you are doing here?

think What makes you think so?
think Where do (you think) you get off?
think Who do you think you are?
think Who do you think you're kidding?
think Who do you think you're talking to?
think wishful thinking
think You think you're so smart!
think You've got another think coming.
third go down for the third time
third third degree
third third time's the charm.
thirst get up a thirst
thirst have a thirst for sth
thirst thirst for sth
thirst thirsty for sth
thirst work up a thirst
thirsty thirsty for sth
this and this and that
this (Are you) ready for this?
this at this juncture
this at this point (in time)
this at this rate
this at this stage (of the game)
this Can we continue this later?
this come to this
this common thread (to all this)
this Could we continue this later?
this depart this life
this Don't breathe a word of this to anyone.
this Don't let it out of this room.
this from this day forward
this from this day on
this How do you like this weather?
this I don't believe this!
this I just have this feeling.
this in this day and age
this (Is) this (seat) taken?
this I've had enough of this!
this Keep out of this!
this Keep this to yourself.
this Let's bump this place!
this Let's do this again (sometime).
this (little) new to (all) this
this not long for this world
this Now hear this!
this out of this world
this shuffle off this mortal coil
this Stay out of this!
this (That's) enough (of this) foolishness!
this this a-way and that a-way
this This doesn't quite suit me.
this this here
this This is it.
this This is my floor.
this This is where I came in.
this This one is on so.
this (this) vale of tears
this Two can play (at) this game (as well as one).
this We must do this again (sometime).
this What do you think of this weather?
this Who is this?
thither hither, thither, and yon
thither thither and yon
Thomas doubting Thomas
thorn There's no rose without a thorn.
thorn thorn in so's flesh
thorn thorn in so's side

those along those lines
those and those
those God takes soonest those he loveth best.
those gods send nuts to those who have no teeth.
those in those parts
those It's just one of those things.
those There's none so blind as those who will not see.
those There's none so deaf as those who will not hear.
those Those were the days.
those Those who can, do; those who can't, teach.
thought collect one's thoughts
thought Don't give it a (second) thought.
thought Don't give it another thought.
thought food for thought
thought give some thought to sth
thought give so pause (for thought)
thought (I) never thought I'd see you here!
thought lose one's train of thought
thought not give it another thought
thought on second thought
thought penny for your thoughts!
thought Perish the thought.
thought recoil at the thought (of so/sth)
thought school of thought
thought second thoughts (about so/sth)
thought so's train of thought
thought swift as thought
thought thoughts to live by
thought Who could have thought?
thought Who would have thought?
thought wish is father to the thought.
thousand if I've told you once, I've told you a thousand times
thousand Never in a thousand years!
thousand No, no, a thousand times no!
thousand Not in a thousand years!
thousand one in a thousand
thousand picture is worth a thousand words.
thrash thrash around
thrash thrash sth out
thread common thread (to all this)
thread hang by a thread
thread hang on by a thread
thread thread one's way through sth
thread thread through sth
threat give sth under (the) threat of sth
threat Never make a threat you cannot carry out.
threat threaten so with so/sth
three didn't exchange more than three words with so
three do a three-sixty
three like a three-ring circus
three Moving three times is as bad as a fire.
three phony as a three-dollar bill
three queer as a three-dollar bill
three three bricks shy of a load
three three sheets in the wind
three three squares (a day)
three Three strikes and you are out.
three turn three hundred and sixty degrees

three Two is company, (but) three's a crowd.
thrill thrill at so/sth
thrill thrill so to pieces
thrill thrill so with sth
thrill thrill to sth
thrill thrilled to death
thrill thrilled to pieces
thrive thrive (up)on sth
throat cut one's (own) throat
throat die of throat trouble
throat force so/sth down so's throat
throat frog in one's throat
throat have one's words stick in one's throat
throat jump down so's throat
throat lump in one's throat
throat ram so/sth down so's throat
throat shove so/sth down so's throat
throat stuff sth down so's throat
throne on the throne
throne power behind the throne
throng throng around so/sth
throng throng in(to sth)
throng throng out (of sth)
throttle at full throttle
throttle throttle sth down
through book so through (to some place)
through bore through so
through bore through sth
through break through (sth)
through break through (to so/sth)
through breeze through (sth)
through bring so through sth
through browse through sth
through bubble up (through sth)
through bulldoze through sth
through bumble through sth
through burst through sth
through carry so/sth through sth
through carry so through (sth)
through carry through (on sth)
through check so/sth through (sth)
through check so's bags through (to some place)
through check through sth
through circulate sth through sth
through circulate through sth
through comb through sth
through come through
through come up through the ranks
through Coming through(, please).
through course through sth
through crash through sth
through crowd through (sth)
through cut through red tape
through cut through sth
through diffuse sth through sth else
through diffuse through sth
through Do we have to go through all that again?
through drag so/sth through sth
through drag so through the mud
through drive a coach and horses through sth
through drive through (sth)
through eat through (sth)
through elbow (one's way) through (sth)
through fall through
through fight (one's way) through (sth)
through fight sth through (sth)
through filter through (sth)
through flash through one's mind

through flick through sth
through flip through sth
through float through sth
through flounder through sth
through follow sth through
through follow through (on sth)
through follow through (with sth)
through force so/sth through sth
through force sth through sth
through gallop through sth
through get so/sth through (to so/sth)
through get so through sth
through get so through (to so/sth)
through get sth through so's thick skull
through get through (sth)
through get through (to so)
through get through (to sth)
through get through (with so/sth)
through glance through sth
through go (right) through so
through go through
through hack one's way through sth
through hear sth through
through hunt through sth
through hurtle through sth
through jump through a hoop
through just passing through
through knock through sth
through know sth through and through
through leaf through sth
through leak through sth
through Let's not go through all that again.
through let so/sth through (sth)
through lie through one's teeth
through live through sth
through look through sth
through make one's way through sth
through move up through sth
through muddle through (sth)
through nurse so through (sth)
through pass through so
through pass through so's mind
through pass through sth
through pay through sth
through pay through the nose (for sth)
through peek through (sth)
through peep through sth
through peer through sth
through penetrate through sth
through percolate through sth
through permeate through sth
through permit so through (sth)
through pick one's way through sth
through pierce through sth
through pilot so/sth through (sth)
through play sth through
through play through
through plod through sth
through plow through sth
through poke sth through so/sth
through poke through (sth)
through pour sth through sth
through pour through sth
through pull so or an animal through (sth)
through pull so through (sth)
through pull through (sth)
through pulse through so/sth
through pump sth through sth
through push sth through (sth)
through push through (sth)
through put one through one's paces
through put so/sth through (to so)

through put so through sth
through put so through the mill
through put so through the wringer
through put sth through its paces
through race through so/sth
through race through sth
through rage through sth
through railroad sth through (sth)
through rake through sth
through ram sth through (sth)
through ram through sth
through read sth through
through reverberate through sth
through rifle through sth
through ripple through sth
through romp through sth
through rummage through sth
through run a comb through sth
through run one's fingers through one's hair
through run one's hand through one's hair
through run so through sth
through run so through (with sth)
through run sth through sth
through run through sth
through rush sth through (sth)
through rush through sth
through sail (right) through sth
through saw through sth
through scrape through (sth)
through search through sth
through see sth through
through see through so/sth
through seep through sth
through send so through the mill
through shot through with sth
through sift sth through sth
through sift through sth
through sit through sth
through skim through sth
through skip through sth
through sleep through sth
through slice through sth
through slip sth through (sth)
through slip through so's fingers
through slip through sth
through slip through the cracks
through slog through sth
through slosh through sth
through smash through sth
through smuggle so/sth through (sth)
through soak through sth
through squeak sth through
through squeak through (sth)
through squeeze so/sth through (sth)
through squeeze through sth
through steer so/sth through sth
through steer through sth
through stick sth through so/sth
through strain sth through sth
through stroll through sth
through struggle through (sth)
through stumble through sth
through swarm through sth
through sweep through (sth)
through switch so/sth through
through take so through (sth)
through talk sth through
through talk through one's hat
through think sth through
through thread one's way through sth
through thread through sth

through through and through
through through hell and high water
through through the cracks
through through the mill
through through thick and thin
through through with so/sth
through thrust so/sth through sth
through thrust through sth
through thrust up through sth
through thumb through sth
through tramp through sth
through travel through sth
through trickle through (sth)
through trudge through sth
through tunnel through sth
through vote sth through
through wade through sth
through walk so through sth
through walk through sth
through waltz through sth
through way to a man's heart is through his stomach.
through wear through sth
through weave through sth
through whip through sth
through whiz (right) through sth
through win through sth
through wind through sth
through work (one's way) through sth
through work sth through (sth)
through work through channels
through worry through sth
through zoom through (sth)
throughout intersperse sth throughout sth
throughout resound through(out) sth
throughout reverberate throughout sth
throw don't have a pot to piss in (or a window to throw it out of)
throw Don't throw the baby out with the bathwater.
throw (just) a stone's throw away (from sth)
throw (just) a stone's throw (from sth)
throw *off one's game
throw People who live in glass houses shouldn't throw stones.
throw stone's throw away
throw throw a fight
throw throw a fit
throw throw a game
throw throw a glance at so/sth
throw throw a monkey wrench in the works
throw throw a party (for so)
throw throw a punch
throw throw a tantrum
throw throw an amount of light on so/sth
throw throw caution to the wind
throw throw cold water on sth
throw Throw dirt enough, and some will stick.
throw throw down the gauntlet
throw throw good money after bad
throw throw in the sponge
throw throw in the towel
throw throw in with so
throw throw insults (at so)
throw throw money at sth
throw throw one off one's game
throw throw one out on one's ear
throw throw one's hands up (in despair)
throw throw one's hands up in horror

throw throw one's hat in the ring
throw throw one's voice
throw throw one's weight around
throw throw oneself at so
throw throw oneself at so's feet
throw throw oneself at the mercy of some authority
throw throw oneself into sth
throw throw oneself on the mercy of some authority
throw throw people together
throw throw (some) light on sth
throw throw so
throw throw so a curve
throw throw so for a loop
throw throw so for a loss
throw throw so in the drink
throw throw so off
throw throw so out of sth
throw throw so over
throw throw so's name around
throw throw so to the dogs
throw throw so to the wolves
throw throw sth across so/sth
throw throw sth across sth
throw throw sth at so/sth
throw throw sth away
throw throw sth back
throw throw sth back at so
throw throw sth down
throw throw sth in
throw throw sth into sharp relief
throw throw sth in(to) so's face
throw throw sth into the bargain
throw throw sth off
throw throw sth on so/sth
throw throw sth to so/sth
throw throw sth together
throw throw sth up
throw throw the baby out with the bath(water)
throw throw the book at so
throw throw the bull
throw throw the crap
throw throw up
throw within a stone's throw (of sth)
thrust thrust and parry
thrust thrust out
thrust thrust so/sth against so/sth
thrust thrust so/sth aside
thrust thrust so/sth away from so/sth
thrust thrust so/sth back
thrust thrust so/sth through sth
thrust thrust sth at so/sth
thrust thrust sth down
thrust thrust sth forward
thrust thrust sth into so/sth
thrust thrust through sth
thrust thrust up through sth
thud thud against so/sth
thud thud into so/sth
thumb all thumbs
thumb have a green thumb
thumb have so under so's thumb
thumb hold so under so's thumb
thumb keep so under so's thumb
thumb rule of thumb
thumb stick out like a sore thumb
thumb thumb a ride
thumb thumb one's nose at so/sth
thumb thumb through sth
thumb thumbs down
thumb thumbs up

thumb turn thumbs down (on so/sth)
thumb turn thumbs up (on so/sth)
thumb twiddle one's thumbs
thumb under so's thumb
thumbnail thumbnail sketch
thump thump on so/sth
thump thump sth down
thump thump sth out (on the piano)
thunder steal so's thunder
thunder thunder across sth
thunder thunder past so/sth
thunder thunder sth out
thunderstorm risk of thunder(storms)
thyself Know thyself.
thyself Physician, heal thyself.
tick full as a tick
tick make so/sth tick
tick tick away
tick tick so off
tick ticked (off)
tick tight as a tick
tick what makes so tick
tick what makes sth tick
ticket buy so's wolf ticket
ticket get a ticket
ticket get one's ticket punched
ticket hot ticket
ticket just the ticket
ticket round-trip ticket
ticket That's the ticket!
ticket ticket so for some place
ticket vote a split ticket
ticket vote a straight ticket
tickle tickle so pink
tickle tickle so's fancy
tickle tickle so to death
tickle tickle so to pieces
tickle tickle the ivories
tickle tickled pink
tide go with the tide
tide happy as a clam (at high tide)
tide swim against the tide
tide There is a tide in the affairs of men.
tide tide so over (until sth)
tide tide turned
tide Time and tide wait for no man.
tide turn the tide
tidy tidy sth up
tidy tidy up
tie coat and tie
tie collar-and-tie men
tie fit to be tied
tie have one's hands tied
tie sever ties with so
tie *some loose ends
tie so's hands are tied
tie tie in (with so/sth)
tie tie in with sth
tie tie in(to sth)
tie tie it on
tie tie on the nose-bag
tie tie one on
tie tie so down (to so/sth)
tie tie so/sth down
tie tie so/sth into sth
tie tie so/sth to sth
tie tie so/sth up
tie tie so's hands
tie tie so to sth
tie tie so (up) in knots
tie tie sth back
tie tie sth in a knot

tie tie sth off
tie tie sth onto so/sth
tie tie sth up
tie tie the knot
tie tie traffic up
tie tie up (some place)
tie tie (with so) (for sth)
tie tied down
tie tied to one's mother's apron strings
tie tied up
tie with both hands tied behind one's back
tie with one hand tied behind one's back
tiger have a tiger by the tail
tiger He who rides a tiger is afraid to dismount.
tight close chewer and a tight spitter
tight hold (on) tight
tight in a (tight) spot
tight keep a tight grip on so/sth
tight keep a tight rein on so/sth
tight on a tight leash
tight run a tight ship
tight sit tight
tight sleep tight
tight tight as a drum
tight tight as a tick
tight tight as Dick's hatband
tight tight as Midas's fist
tight tight race
tight tighten one's belt
tight tighten sth on(to) sth
tight tighten sth up
tight tighten up
tighten tighten one's belt
tighten tighten sth on(to) sth
tighten tighten sth up
tighten tighten up
tightfisted tightfisted (with money)
tightrope walk a tightrope
till Call no man happy till he dies.
till Church ain't out till they quit singing.
till Count no man happy till he dies.
till from here till next Tuesday
till have one's finger(s) in the till
till have one's hand in the till
till It's not over till it's over.
till Never halloo till you are out of the woods.
till Never trouble trouble till trouble troubles you.
till till all hours (of the day and night)
till till hell freezes over
till till kingdom come
till Till next time.
till till the bitter end
till till the fat lady sings
till Till we meet again.
till You never know (what you can do) till you try.
till You never miss the water till the well runs dry.
tilt at full tilt
tilt tilt at windmills
tilt tilt sth back
tilt tilt to sth
tilt tilt toward so/sth
timber head for (the) tall timber
timber tall timber(s)
time ahead of one's time
time ahead of time

time all in good time
time all the time
time arrive ahead of time
time arrive in the (very) nick of time
time at a set time
time at all times
time at the appointed time
time at the present time
time at the same time
time at this point (in time)
time at times
time bad time
time bad times
time before so's time
time behind the times
time Better luck next time.
time bide one's time
time buy sth on time
time buy time
time Catch me some other time.
time catch so at a bad time
time cause lean times (ahead)
time Cowards die many times before their death(s).
time dance out of time (with so/sth)
time devil of a time
time devil's own time
time difficult times
time do time
time Don't waste my time.
time Don't waste your time.
time downtime
time even in the best of times
time every time one turns around
time fall on hard times
time fight against time
time find time for so/sth
time for the time being
time from time to time
time get out of time (with so/sth)
time Give it time.
time go down for the third time
time good time was had by all.
time half the time
time happen before so's time
time happen in the (very) nick of time
time hard time
time hard times
time hardly have time to breathe
time hardly have time to think
time Have a good time.
time have a rare old time
time have a rough time (of it)
time have a whale of a time
time have an easy time of it
time have (some) time to kill
time have the time of one's life
time have (too much) time on one's hands
time He puts his pants on one leg at a time.
time How many times do I have to tell you?
time I don't have time to breathe.
time I don't have time to catch my breath.
time (I) had a good time.
time I had a lovely time.
time (I) had a nice time.
time (I) haven't seen you in a long time.
time if I've told you once, I've told you a thousand times

time (I'll) try to catch you some other time.
time (I'm) having a wonderful time; wish you were here.
time I'm having quite a time.
time (I'm) having the time of my life.
time in due time
time in good time
time in less than no time
time in no time (at all)
time in no time flat
time in one's spare time
time in the course of time
time in the interest of saving time
time in the meantime
time in the right place at the right time
time in the (very) nick of time
time in the wrong place at the wrong time
time in time
time in times past
time in tune with the times
time invest so's time in sth
time It's about time!
time it's high time
time (It's) time for a change.
time (It's) time to go.
time (It's) time to hit the road.
time (It's) time to run.
time (It's) time to shove off.
time (It's) time to split.
time It's time we should be going.
time I've had a lovely time.
time just in time
time keep good time
time keep time
time keep up with the times
time kill time
time lean times (ahead)
time leave ahead of time
time legend in one's own (life)time
time Life is short and time is swift.
time live on borrowed time
time Long time no see.
time lose some amount of time
time make good time
time make time for so/sth
time make time (with so)
time make up for lost time
time many (and many)'s the time
time march out of time (with so/sth)
time mark time
time Maybe some other time.
time mean lean times (ahead)
time Moving three times is as bad as a fire.
time (My,) how time flies.
time nine times out of ten
time No, a thousand times no!
time not able to call one's time one's own
time not give anyone the time of day
time occur before so's time
time on one's own time
time on time
time once upon a time
time once-in-a-lifetime chance
time once-in-a-lifetime opportunity
time one more time
time (Only) time will tell.
time Other times, other manners.
time Out of the mouths of babes (oft times come gems).
time out of time (with so/sth)

time pass the time (of day)
time pass the time of day (with so)
time play for time
time pressed for time
time Procrastination is the thief of time.
time pushed for time
time quality time
time race against time
time reach sth in the (very) nick of time
time right on time
time rough time
time run out of time
time sands of time
time save so in the (very) nick of time
time scarcely have time to breathe
time seem pushed for time
time serve time
time show up ahead of time
time sign of the times
time since time immemorial
time some creature's time has come
time so's time has come
time spend time in sth
time stall for time
time stand the test of time
time stitch in time saves nine.
time take one's time
time take (some) time off
time take ((some) time) off from work
time take time out
time take up (so's) time
time tell time
time Thank you for a lovely time.
time There is a time and a place for everything.
time (There's) no time like the present.
time think ahead of one's time
time third time's the charm.
time Till next time.
time time after time
time Time and tide wait for no man.
time time and (time) again
time time flies (when you're having fun)
time time for so/sth
time Time hangs heavy on so's hands.
time time in
time Time is a great healer.
time Time is money.
time Time is of the essence.
time time is ripe.
time Time is up.
time time off
time Time (out)!
time time out
time time's a-wastin'
time time so in
time time so out
time Time to call it a day.
time Time to call it a night.
time time to catch one's breath
time time was (when)
time Time will tell.
time Time works wonders.
time Times are changing.
time Times change and we with time.
time Times change(, people change).
time tough times
time trying times
time two-time loser
time two-time so
time We had a lovely time.

time We'll try again some other time.
time We've had a lovely time.
time when the time is ripe
time You're (just) wasting my time.
timely come to an untimely end
tin tin ear
tinge tinge sth with sth
tinker If ifs and ands were pots and pans (there'd be no work for tinkers' hands).
tinker not give a tinker's damn
tinker tinker (around) (with sth)
tiny patter of tiny feet
tip from tip to toe
tip have sth at one's fingertips
tip on the tip of one's tongue
tip tip of the iceberg
tip tip one's hand
tip tip over
tip tip so off (about so/sth)
tip tip so over
tip tip so with sth
tip tip sth over
tip tip sth up
tip tip the scales at sth
tiptoe on tiptoe
tire grow sick (and tired) of so/sth
tire sick (and tired) of so/sth
tire spare tire
tire tire of so/sth
tire tire out
tire tire so out
'tis 'Tis better to have loved and lost than never to have loved at all.
'tis Where ignorance is bliss, 'tis folly to be wise.
tit cold as a witch's tit
tit give so tit for tat
tit suck so's hind tit
tit tits and ass
tizzy in a tizzy
to abandon oneself to sth
to abandon so/sth to so/sth
to abbreviate sth to sth
to able to breathe (easily) again
to able to breathe (freely) again
to able to cut sth
to able to do sth
to able to do sth blindfolded
to able to do sth standing on one's head
to able to do sth with one's eyes closed
to able to fog a mirror
to able to make an event
to able to take a joke
to able to take just so much
to able to take only so much
to about to do sth
to accede to sth
to access to so/sth
to acclimate so or an animal to sth
to acclimatize so or an animal to sth
to accommodate oneself to sth
to according to all accounts
to according to Hoyle
to according to one's own lights
to according to so/sth
to according to sth
to accredit sth to so
to accrue to so/sth
to accustom so to so/sth
to accustomed to so/sth
to acknowledge so to be right
to acquiesce to so/sth

to adapt so/sth to sth
to adapt sth to sth
to adapt to sth
to add fuel to the fire
to add fuel to the flame
to add insult to injury
to add (sth) to sth
to add up (to sth)
to add up to the same thing
to addict so to sth
to address comments or remarks to so
to address oneself to so
to address oneself to sth
to address sth to so
to adhere to sth
to adjourn to some place
to adjust (oneself) to so/sth
to adjust sth to sth
to administer sth to so or an animal
to admire to do sth
to admit sth to so
to admit to sth
to advance sth to so/sth (against sth)
to affiliate (so/sth) to so/sth
to affix one's signature to sth
to affix sth to so/sth
to agree to disagree
to agree to sth
to aim to do sth
to ain't fittin' to roll with a pig
to alert so to sth
to all dressed up and nowhere to go
to All good things must (come to an) end.
to All roads lead to Rome.
to (all) set (to do sth)
to All the best to so.
to all the same (to so)
to all things to all men
to all things to all people
to all to the good
to allocate sth to so/sth
to allot sth to so/sth
to allude to so/sth
to ally oneself to so/sth
to Am I glad to see you!
to amount to much
to amount to sth
to amount to the same thing
to amount (up) to sth
to and sth to spare
to angry enough to chew nails
to annex sth to sth
to annex to sth
to announce sth to so
to answer back (to so)
to answer to so
to answer to the description of so
to answer to the name (of) sth
to apologize (to so) (for so)
to appeal (to a court) (for sth)
to appeal to so
to appear to be rooted to the spot
to appear to so
to appear to so that...
to appear to the naked eye
to appertain to sth
to apply oneself to sth
to apply sth to sth
to apply to so/sth
to apply (to so/sth) (for sth)
to appoint so to sth
to apprentice so to so

to (Are you) ready to order?
to armed to the teeth
to arrange for so to do sth
to as a duck takes to water
to ascribe sth to so/sth
to ask so out (to sth)
to ask so to sth
to aspire to sth
to assent to sth
to assign so/sth to so/sth
to assign sth to so
to attach oneself to so
to attach oneself to sth
to attach to so
to attach to sth
to attached to so/sth
to attend to so
to attest to sth
to attract so/sth to so/sth else
to attribute sth to so/sth
to attune so/sth to so/sth else
to awake(n) so to sth
to awake(n) to sth
to award sth (to so) (for sth)
to award sth to so/sth
to back so/sth up to so/sth
to back to basics
to back to square one
to back to the drawing board
to back to the salt mines
to back up (to so/sth)
to back up (to sth)
to back-to-back
to badger so/sth to death
to (bang) dead to rights
to bare one's soul (to so)
to bare sth to so
to Be happy to (do sth).
to be so bold as to do sth
to be the last person (to do sth)
to beam so/sth up (to some place)
to bear a resemblance to so/sth
to beat a path to so's door
to beat one's brains out (to do sth)
to beat so down to size
to beat so to sth
to beat so to the punch
to beckon to so
to beg to differ (with so)
to begin to see daylight
to begin to see the light
to behoove one to do sth
to belly up (to sth)
to belong to so/sth
to bend over backwards (to do sth)
to bequeath sth to so
to bet so dollars to doughnuts
to betroth so to so
to bid adieu to so/sth
to bind so over (to so/sth)
to bite (to eat)
to bitter pill to swallow
to bleed to death
to blind so to sth
to blow so/sth to bits
to blow so/sth to kingdom come
to blow so/sth to pieces
to blow so/sth to smithereens
to blow so to sth
to boil down to sth
to boogie down (to somewhere)
to book so through (to some place)
to bore so to death

to bore so to tears
to bored to distraction
to bound to do sth
to bow down (to so/sth)
to bow to so's demands
to bow to the porcelain altar
to break one's back (to do sth)
to break one's balls to do sth
to break one's neck (to do sth)
to break sth to pieces
to break sth to so
to break the news (to so)
to break through (to so/sth)
to breathe sth (of sth) (to so)
to bring a dog to heel
to bring one to one's feet
to bring one to one's senses
to bring one to oneself
to bring so back to reality
to bring so down to earth
to bring so or an animal back to life
to bring so/sth along (to sth)
to bring so/sth to a halt
to bring so/sth to life
to bring so/sth to light
to bring so/sth to so's attention
to bring so/sth to trial
to bring so/sth up to sth
to bring so/sth up-to-date
to bring so over ((to) some place)
to bring so over to sth
to bring so to
to bring so up to speed on so/sth
to bring so up-to-date (on so/sth)
to bring sth around (to so/sth)
to bring sth back to life
to bring sth back (to so)
to bring sth down to sth
to bring sth home to so
to bring sth to a boil
to bring sth to a climax
to bring sth to a close
to bring sth to a dead end
to bring sth to a head
to bring sth to a standstill
to bring sth to a successful conclusion
to bring sth to an end
to bring sth to fruition
to bring sth to its feet
to bring sth to light
to bring sth to mind
to bring sth to rest
to bring sth to so's aid
to bring sth to so's attention
to bring sth to the fore
to bring sth up to speed
to bring sth up to the minute
to buckle down (to sth)
to buddy up (to so)
to buffet so/sth from so/sth to so/sth
to build sth to order
to build up to sth
to bumper to bumper
to bundle so off (to some place)
to bundle sth off (to so or some place)
to burn to a crisp
to Burn not your house to fright the mouse away.
to burned to a cinder
to bust a gut (to do sth)
to bust (one's) ass (to do sth)
to bust one's butt to do sth
to buy some food to go

to call a halt to sth
to call a meeting to order
to call attention to so/sth
to call in (to some place)
to call out (to so)
to call so over (to some place)
to call so's attention to sth
to call so to account
to call so to attention
to call sth down (to so)
to call sth to mind
to call sth to so's attention
to call the meeting to order
to call to so
to call (up)on so (to do sth)
to called to straw
to Can I speak to so?
to can take it to the bank
to can't hold a candle to so
to can't say boo to a goose
to can't wait (for sth (to happen))
to capitulate to so/sth
to care to do sth
to careful not to do sth
to carry a secret to the grave
to carry coals to Newcastle
to carry on (to so)
to carry over (to sth)
to carry so back (to some time)
to carry so/sth over to sth
to carry sth over (until some time)
to catch on (to sth)
to catch to it
to catch up (to so/sth)
to cater to so/sth
to cause (some) eyebrows to raise
to cause (some) tongues to wag
to cave in (to so/sth)
to cede sth to so
to chain sth to sth
to chalk sth up (to sth)
to challenge so to sth
to change over (from so/sth) (to so/sth)
to change to sth
to Charge it to the dust and let the rain settle it.
to charge sth up to so/sth
to check so's bags through (to some place)
to chickens come home to roost.
to chilled to the bone
to chum up to so
to clasp so/sth to sth
to claw one's way to the top
to Cleanliness is next to godliness.
to cleave to so
to cling to so/sth
to close enough to use the same toothpick
to close one's eyes to sth
to close sth to so
to close the door to so/sth
to close to home
to close to so
to clutch so/sth to sth
to coast-to-coast
to coax so to do sth
to come across as so/sth (to so)
to come across like so/sth (to so)
to come across (to sth)
to come around (to doing sth)
to come around (to some place)
to come back to haunt one
to come back (to so)

to come back (to so/sth)
to come close (to so/sth)
to come down to earth
to come down to some place
to come down to sth
to come home (to roost)
to come home to so
to come naturally (to so)
to come on (to so)
to come out to an amount
to come out to be
to come to
to come up to so's expectations
to come up to so's standards
to commend so/sth to so/sth
to commit oneself to so/sth
to commit oneself to sth
to commit so/sth to sth
to commit sth to memory
to commit to so
to common thread (to all this)
to communicate sth to so
to compare so/sth to so/sth
to compel so to do sth
to complain to so
to concede sth to so
to concede to so/sth
to condemn so to sth
to condescend to do sth
to condescend to so
to condition so/sth to sth
to confess sth to so
to confess to sth
to confine so or an animal to sth
to confine sth to so/sth
to conform to sth
to connect so/sth (up) to so/sth
to connect (up) to sth
to consecrate so/sth to God
to consent to sth
to consign sth to so/sth
to contrary to sth
to contribute sth (to so) (for so/sth)
to contribute to sth
to convey sth (from so/sth) (to so/sth)
to cook sth to perfection
to correspond to sth
to cotton up to so
to (Could I) get you something (to drink)?
to Could I speak to so?
to count from sth (up) to sth
to count up to sth
to cozy up (to so)
to cracked up to be sth
to crash to the floor
to crave to do sth
to crawl back to so
to credit sth to so/sth
to credit to so/sth
to cross a bridge before one comes to it
to cross from some place to some place
to cross one's heart (and hope to die)
to cross that bridge when one comes to it
to Crosses are ladders that lead to heaven.
to crush so/sth to sth
to cry all the way to the bank
to cry oneself to sleep
to cry (sth) out (to so or an animal)
to cuddle up (to so/sth)
to curtsy to so

to curve to sth
to cut back to so/sth
to cut one's coat according to one's cloth
to cut one's coat to suit one's cloth
to cut one's nose off to spite one's face
to cut out to be sth
to cut so down (to size)
to cut so/sth to sth
to cut so to ribbons
to cut so to the bone
to cut so to the quick
to cut sth down to sth
to cut sth to the bone
to cut to so/sth
to cut to the chase
to Damn it to blue blazes!
to dance to a different tune
to dance to another tune
to dance to sth
to dare so (to do sth)
to dash sth to pieces
to date back (to so or some time)
to dead to the world
to debit sth to so/sth
to dedicate so/sth to so/sth
to deed sth (over) to so
to deem it (to be) necessary
to defect to sth
to defer to so/sth (on sth)
to deign to do sth
to delegate so to sth
to delegate sth to so
to deliver so/sth to so/sth
to deliver sth up to so
to demonstrate sth to so
to demote so from sth (to sth)
to deny so/sth to so
to deport so (from some place) (to some other place)
to descend to sth
to describe so/sth to so
to desensitize so to sth
to desert so/sth to so/sth
to detail so to sth
to devil finds work for idle hands to do.
to devote oneself to so/sth
to devote so/sth to so/sth
to dictate (sth) to so
to dip to sth
to direct so's attention to so/sth
to direct sth to so
to disclose sth to so
to disease to please
to disinclined to do sth
to dispatch so/sth to so/sth
to dispense sth (to so) (from sth)
to display sth to so
to Distance lends enchantment (to the view).
to distribute sth to so
to diverge to sth
to divert so/sth to so/sth
to divulge sth to so
to do credit to so
to Do I have to paint (you) a picture?
to Do I have to spell it out (for you)?
to Do I need to paint you a picture?
to do justice to sth
to do one's utmost (to do sth)
to do sth to excess
to Do we have to go through all that again?
to Do you expect me to believe that?

to (Do) you mean to say sth?
to (Do) you mean to tell me sth?
to (Do you) want to know something?
to (Do you) want to make something of it?
to (Do) you want to step outside?
to doesn't have enough sense to bell a cat
to doesn't have enough sense to come in out of the rain
to dole sth out (to so)
to done to a T
to done to a turn
to don't amount to a bucket of spit
to Don't breathe a word of this to anyone.
to Don't forget to write.
to don't have a pot to piss in (or a window to throw it out of)
to don't know whether to eat it or rub it on
to Don't teach your grandmother to suck eggs.
to Don't tell me what to do!
to doom so/sth to sth
to doomed to sth
to doors open up (to so)
to door-to-door
to down to a gnat's eyebrow
to down to chili and beans
to down to the last bit of money
to down to the last detail
to downgrade so/sth to sth
to down-to-earth
to down-to-the-wire
to doze off (to sleep)
to drag so/sth off (to so/sth)
to drag so/sth over to so/sth
to draw oneself up (to sth)
to draw so's attention to so/sth
to draw sth to
to draw to a close
to drawn like a moth to a flame
to dressed to kill
to dressed to the nines
to dressed to the teeth
to dressed (up) fit to kill
to drift back (to so)
to drift back (to sth)
to drift off to sleep
to drill down (to sth)
to drink to excess
to drink to so/sth
to drive down (to some place)
to drive out (to some place)
to drive over (to some place)
to drive so back to so
to drive so down (to some place)
to drive so on (to sth)
to drive so to despair
to drive so to distraction
to drive so to do sth
to drive so to drink
to drive so to the brink
to drive so to the edge
to drive so to the wall
to drive so up (to some place)
to drive sth down (to some place)
to drive up (to some place)
to drop in (to say hello)
to drop off (to sleep)
to duty bound (to do sth)
to dwindle away (to sth)

to dwindle down (to sth)
to dying to do sth
to dying to know (sth)
to Early to bed and early to rise, makes a man healthy, wealthy, and wise.
to easy to come by
to Eat to live, not live to eat.
to echo back to sth
to elect so to sth
to elevate so/sth to sth
to emigrate (from some place) (to some place)
to empower so to do sth
to enable so to do sth
to encourage so to do sth
to endear so to so/sth
to endeavor to do sth
to engage so to so
to enjoin so to do sth
to enough and some to spare
to enough (sth) to go (a)round
to enough sth to plague a saint
to enough to keep body and soul together
to entitle so to do sth
to entreat so to do sth
to entrust so/sth to sth
to enunciate sth to so
to equal to so
to equate so to so else
to escape (from so/sth) (to some place)
to escort so/sth to sth
to evacuate so (from sth) (to sth)
to Every man to his taste.
to Everything comes to him who waits.
to everything from A to Z
to everything from soup to nuts
to Everything's going to be all right.
to Evil be to him who evil thinks.
to exhort so to do sth
to exile so (from sth) (to sth)
to exit (from sth) (to sth)
to explain so/sth to so
to export sth to some place
to export sth to so/sth
to expose so or an animal to a disease
to expose so/sth to so/sth
to expose sth or oneself to so/sth
to expound ((up)on so/sth) (to so)
to express oneself (to so) (on sth)
to extend credit (to so or a company)
to extend (from sth) (to sth)
to extend one's sympathy (to so)
to extend sth to sth
to extend to so/sth
to extradite so from some place (to some place)
to eyeball-to-eyeball
to face up (to so/sth)
to face-to-face
to fair to middlin'
to fall (all) over oneself (to do sth)
to fall heir to sth
to fall over backwards (to do sth)
to fall to
to far be it from me to do sth
to fasten sth down (to sth)
to fed up (to some degree) (with so/sth)
to feed sth back to so
to feed so to so
to feel free (to do sth)
to feel it beneath one (to do sth)
to feel up to sth

to fess up (to sth)
to fight (one's way) back (to sth)
to fight to the death
to fill sth to sth
to filled to the brim
to find it in one's heart (to do sth)
to find it in oneself (to do sth)
to fire sth back (to so/sth)
to fire sth off (to so)
to fit so to a T
to fit sth to sth
to fit to be tied
to fit to kill
to fixin(g) to do sth
to flash back (to so/sth)
to flee to sth
to flit from person to person
to flit from sth to sth else
to flock to so/sth
to flog so to death
to flow (from sth) (to sth)
to fly from so/sth (to sth)
to fly from sth (to sth)
to fly to so/sth
to fly to sth
to fly up to sth
to Fools rush in where angels fear to tread.
to force so to the wall
to force to be reckoned with
to fork sth out (to so)
to fork sth over (to so)
to forward sth from some place (to so or some place)
to freeze so/sth to death
to frighten so or an animal to death
to frightened to death
to from A to Z
to from dawn to dusk
to from day to day
to from door to door
to from giddy-up to whoa
to from hand to hand
to from head to toe
to from hell to breakfast
to from pillar to post
to from rags to riches
to from sea to shining sea
to from side to side
to from start to finish
to from stem to stern
to from the cradle to the grave
to from the sublime to the ridiculous
to from time to time
to from tip to toe
to from top to bottom
to gather so/sth to oneself
to gear sth to so/sth
to generous to a fault
to get around to doing sth
to get (around) to so/sth
to get back (to so) (on sth)
to get back to sth
to get down to brass tacks
to get down to business
to get down to cases
to get down to (doing) sth
to get down to the facts
to get down to the nitty-gritty
to get down to the nuts and bolts
to get down to work
to get enough courage up (to do sth)
to get enough guts up (to do sth)

to get enough nerve up (to do sth)
to get hip to so/sth
to get home to so/sth
to get off to sleep
to get off (to sth)
to get over (to some place)
to get so/sth through (to so/sth)
to get so through (to so/sth)
to get sth across (to so)
to get sth home to so/sth
to get sth off (to so/sth)
to get sth over (to so)
to get sth to so
to get the courage up (to do sth)
to get the spunk up (to do sth)
to get through (to so)
to get through (to sth)
to get to first base (with so/sth)
to get to one's feet
to get to so
to get to sth
to get to the bottom of sth
to get to the point (of sth)
to get to the top (of sth)
to get up to sth
to give an account of so/sth (to so)
to give (an) ear to so/sth
to give birth to so/sth
to give chase (to so/sth)
to give credence to so/sth
to give currency to sth
to give free rein to so
to give in (to so/sth)
to give it to so (straight)
to Give my best to so.
to give oneself over to so/sth
to give oneself up (to so/sth)
to give rise to sth
to give some thought to sth
to give so away (to so)
to give so/sth back (to so/sth)
to give so/sth up (to so)
to give so to understand sth
to give sth away (to so)
to give sth back (to so) (with interest)
to give sth over (to so/sth)
to give sth to so
to give teeth to sth
to give the lie to sth
to give vent to sth
to give voice to sth
to give way to so/sth
to give weight to sth
to given to doing sth
to given to understand
to glued to so/sth
to go across sth to so/sth
to go back to so/sth
to go back to square one
to go back to the drawing board
to go back to the salt mines
to go down to defeat
to go down to so/sth
to go down to sth
to go from bad to worse
to go from one extreme to the other
to go home to mama
to go near (to) so/sth
to go off (to the side) with so
to go on to a better land
to go on to sth
to go out of one's way (to do sth)
to go out to so

to go over to some place
to go so far as to say sth
to go (straight) to the top
to Go to!
to go to any length
to go to bat against so
to go to bat for so
to go to bed
to Go to blazes!
to go to Davy Jones's locker
to go to extremes (to do sth)
to go to great lengths (to do sth)
to go to hell
to go to it
to go to one's (just) reward
to go to pieces
to go to pot
to go to press
to go to rack and ruin
to go to sea
to go to seed
to go to so (about so/sth)
to go to so/sth
to go to so's head
to go to the bathroom
to go to the bother (of doing sth)
to go to the crux of the matter
to go to (the devil)
to go to the dogs
to go to the expense (of doing sth)
to go to the heart of the matter
to go to the lavatory
to go to the limit
to go to the polls
to go to the root of the matter
to go to the toilet
to go to the trouble (of doing sth)
to go to the wall (on sth)
to go to town
to go to trial
to go to war (over so/sth)
to go to waste
to go to work (on so/sth)
to go to wrack and ruin
to Go to your room!
to go up to so/sth
to God's gift (to women)
to gods send nuts to those who have no teeth.
to going to tattle
to going to tell
to gone to meet one's maker
to good man is hard to find.
to good riddance (to bad rubbish)
to Good things come to him who waits.
to good to go
to got to fly
to gotta get up pretty early in the morning to do sth
to grab a bite (to eat)
to grant sth to so
to Greek to so
to grin from ear to ear
to grind sth to sth
to grind to a halt
to gripe (to so/sth) (about so/sth)
to grovel to so
to grow accustomed to doing sth
to grow accustomed to so/sth
to grow to do sth
to habituate so to so/sth
to hack sth to sth

to hand so/sth over (to so/sth)
to hand sth back (to so)
to hand sth down from so to so
to hand sth down (to so)
to hand sth in (to so)
to hand sth off (to so)
to hand sth on (to so/sth)
to hand sth out (to so)
to hand sth to so
to hand sth up (to so)
to hang on (to so/sth)
to Hang on to your hat!
to hang so out to dry
to happen to so/sth
to harbinger of things to come
to hard act to follow
to hard nut to crack
to hard put (to do sth)
to hard row to hoe
to hard to believe
to hard to swallow
to hard to take
to harden oneself to sth
to hardly have time to breathe
to hardly have time to think
to hark(en) back to sth
to harness so or an animal to sth
to hats off to so/sth
to haul so/sth over to sth
to haul sth (from some place) to some place
to have a bone to pick (with so)
to have a familiar ring (to it)
to have a (good) mind to do sth
to have a heart-to-heart (talk)
to have a kick to it
to have a mind to
to have a score to settle (with so)
to have a set-to (with so)
to have an ax(e) to grind
to have been to hell and back
to have bigger fish to fry
to have cause to do sth
to have had it (up to here)
to have half a mind to do sth
to have half a notion to do sth
to have hell to pay
to have it in one to do sth
to have more than one string to one's fiddle
to have nothing to do with so/sth
to have one's back to the wall
to have one's ear to the ground
to have one's heart go out to so
to have one's shoulder to the wheel
to have recourse to sth
to have some food to go
to have (some) time to kill
to have so dead to rights
to have so slated to do sth
to have sth coming (to one)
to have sth down to a T
to have sth to burn
to have sth to do with sth
to have sth to spare
to have the devil to pay
to have the gall to do sth
to have the presence of mind to do sth
to have to do sth so bad one can taste it
to have to do with sth
to have to get married
to have to go some (to do sth)
to have to hand it to so
to have to live with sth

to He that would go to sea for pleasure, would go to hell for a pastime.
to He who fights and runs away, may live to fight another day.
to He who rides a tiger is afraid to dismount.
to hearken to so/sth
to heat sth up (to sth)
to heave to
to Heavens to Betsy!
to help oneself (to sth)
to help so back (to sth)
to Here's to so.
to Here's to you.
to hew to sth
to hint sth to so
to hip to so/sth
to hitch so/sth (up) (to sth)
to Hitch your wagon to a star.
to hold on (to so/sth)
to Hold on to your hat!
to hold so/sth up to ridicule
to hold so/sth up to scorn
to hold so to sth
to hold so up to sth
to hold sth out (to so)
to homely enough to stop a clock
to Honest to God.
to Honest to goodness.
to Honest to Pete.
to hook so/sth up (to so/sth)
to Hop to it!
to hop up (to so/sth)
to hot enough to burn a polar bear's butt
to hotfoot it (off to) somewhere
to How many times do I have to tell you?
to hunker down to sth
to hurry back (to so/sth)
to hurry down (to somewhere)
to I couldn't ask you to do that.
to I declare (to goodness)!
to I don't have time to breathe.
to I don't have time to catch my breath.
to I don't want to alarm you, but
to I don't want to sound like a busybody, but
to I don't want to upset you, but
to I don't want to wear out my welcome.
to (I) hate to eat and run.
to (I have) nothing to complain about.
to (I) have to be moving along.
to (I) have to go now.
to (I) have to move along.
to (I) have to push off.
to (I) have to run along.
to (I) have to shove off.
to I have to wash a few things out.
to (I) hope to see you again (sometime).
to (I) just want(ed) to mention sth.
to (I) just want(ed) to say sth.
to I wasn't brought up in the woods to be scared by owls.
to I would like you to meet so.
to (I'd be) happy to (do sth).
to I'd like (for) you to meet so.
to I'd like (to have) a word with you.
to I'd like to speak to so, please.

to If God did not exist, it would be necessary to invent Him.
to if push comes to shove
to If the mountain will not come to Mahomet, Mahomet must go to the mountain.
to if (the) worst comes to (the) worst
to If there's anything you need, don't hesitate to ask.
to If you're born to be hanged, then you'll never be drowned.
to if you've a mind to do sth
to I'll drink to that!
to I'll get back to you (on that).
to I'll have to beg off.
to I'll (have to) let you go
to I'll put a stop to that.
to (I'll) talk to you soon.
to I'll thank you to keep your opinions to yourself.
to I'll thank you to mind your own business.
to (I'll) try to catch you later.
to (I'll) try to catch you some other time.
to ill-disposed to doing sth
to (I'm) delighted to have you (here).
to (I'm) delighted to make your acquaintance.
to I'm easy (to please).
to (I'm) glad to hear it.
to (I'm) pleased to meet you.
to (I'm) sorry to hear that.
to (I'm) (very) glad to meet you.
to impart sth to so/sth
to impute sth to so/sth
to in addition (to sth)
to in no mood to do sth
to in opposition (to so/sth)
to in order to do sth
to in reference to so/sth
to in regard to so/sth
to in relation to so/sth
to in thing (to do)
to incite so to sth
to inclined to do sth
to increase sth (from sth) (to sth)
to incumbent (up)on so to do sth
to indicate sth to so
to insinuate sth to so
to instigate so to do sth
to intimate sth to so
to introduce so to so
to inure so to sth
to invite so to sth
to Is there any truth to sth?
to issue sth to so
to it behooves one to do sth
to (It) doesn't hurt to ask.
to It is better to be born lucky than rich.
to It is better to give than to receive.
to It is better to travel hopefully than to arrive.
to It is better to wear out than to rust out.
to It is easier to tear down than to build up.
to It is easy to be wise after the event.
to It is more blessed to give than to receive.
to It is never too late to learn.
to It is never too late to mend.

to (It) just goes to show (you) (sth).
to (It) makes no difference to me.
to (It) never hurts to ask.
to It (only) stands to reason.
to (It) (really) doesn't matter to me.
to It's (all) Greek to me.
to (It's been) good talking to you.
to (It's) good to be here.
to (It's) good to have you here.
to (It's) good to hear your voice.
to (It's) good to see you (again).
to (It's) nice to be here.
to (It's) nice to have you here.
to (It's) nice to meet you.
to (It's) nice to see you.
to (It's) not supposed to.
to (It's) time to go.
to (It's) time to hit the road.
to (It's) time to run.
to (It's) time to shove off.
to (It's) time to split.
to It takes all kinds (to make a world).
to It takes money to make money.
to (It) takes one to know one.
to It takes (some) getting used to.
to It takes two to make a bargain.
to It takes two to make a quarrel.
to (It) takes two to tango.
to It would take an act of Congress to do sth.
to itch to do sth
to (I've) (got) better things to do.
to (I've) got to be shoving off.
to I've got to fly.
to (I've) got to get moving.
to (I've) got to go.
to (I've) got to go home and get my beauty sleep.
to (I've) got to hit the road.
to (I've) got to run.
to (I've) got to shove off.
to (I've) got to split.
to (I've) got to take off.
to I've got work to do.
to I've had it up to here (with so/sth).
to jet (from some place) (to some place)
to jog to the right or left
to join sth to sth else
to jolt to a start
to jolt to a stop
to jump at the opportunity (to do sth)
to jump from sth to sth
to jump to conclusions
to jump up (to sth)
to just the same (to so)
to justify sth to so
to juxtapose so/sth to so/sth
to keep an ear to the ground
to keep it down (to a dull roar)
to keep one's cards close to one's chest
to keep one's cards close to one's vest
to keep one's ear to the ground
to keep one's hands to oneself
to keep one's nose to the grindstone
to keep one's opinions to oneself
to keep one's shoulder to the wheel
to keep oneself to oneself
to keep sth to a minimum
to keep sth to oneself
to Keep this to yourself.
to keep to oneself
to keep to sth
to keep to the straight and narrow

to Keep your opinions to yourself!
to key to success
to kick sth back (to so/sth)
to kiss up to so
to knee-high to a grasshopper
to knee-high to a jackrabbit
to knock oneself out (to do sth) (for so/sth)
to knock so down to size
to knock sth to so
to know better (than to do sth)
to knuckle down (to sth)
to knuckle under (to so/sth)
to kowtow to so/sth
to land too poor to raise a racket on
to lash so/sth to sth
to laugh all the way to the bank
to lay claim to sth
to lay down the law (to so) (about sth)
to lay so to rest
to lay sth to rest
to lay sth to sth
to lay sth to waste
to lay to
to lay waste to sth
to lead back (to some place)
to lead down to sth
to lead so down to sth
to lead so or an animal to sth
to lead so/sth back (to so/sth)
to lead so to believe sth
to lead so to do sth
to lead up to sth
to leak sth to so
to lean over backwards (to do sth)
to leap at the chance (to do sth)
to leap at the opportunity (to do sth)
to leap to conclusions
to learn to live with sth
to lease sth (out) to so
to leave a lot to be desired
to leave it to so
to leave one to one's fate
to leave one to one's own devices
to leave one to one's own resources
to leave so/sth to so
to leave so to it
to leave sth to chance
to leave sth to so
to leave sth up to so/sth
to leave word for so to do sth
to lecture ((to) so) about so/sth
to lend a hand (to so)
to lend an ear to so/sth
to lend color to sth
to lend oneself or itself to sth
to lend sth out (to so)
to lend sth to so
to lend your ear to so/sth
to Let me get back to you (on that).
to let on (to so) (about so/sth)
to Let's get down to business.
to let sth out (to so)
to Let the cobbler stick to his last.
to level sth to the ground
to license to do sth
to lie about so/sth (to so)
to lie to so (about so/sth)
to Life's been good (to me).
to like a lamb to the slaughter
to like flies to manure
to like lambs to the slaughter
to like pigs to the slaughter
to like to

to like tryin' to scratch your ear with your elbow
to liken so/sth to so/sth
to limit so to sth
to limit sth to so
to link so/sth to so/sth
to link so/sth up (to sth)
to link up to so/sth
to list to a direction
to listen to reason
to listen to so/sth
to (little) new to (all) this
to live from day to day
to live from hand to mouth
to live next door (to so)
to live to do sth
to live to the (ripe old) age of sth
to live up to one's end of the bargain
to live up to sth
to loaded to the barrel
to loaded to the gills
to loan sth to so
to log so on (to sth)
to look ahead to sth
to look fit to kill
to look forward to sth
to look to be a million miles away
to look to one's laurels
to look to so/sth (for sth)
to look to the naked eye
to look up to so
to lose ground (to so/sth)
to lose out to so/sth
to lose sth to so
to lose to so/sth
to lower oneself to some level
to lull so or an animal to sleep
to lure so/sth in to sth
to mad enough to chew nails (and spit rivets)
to mad enough to kick a cat
to mad enough to spit nails
to made to measure
to made to order
to mail sth to so
to make a check (out) (to so/sth)
to make a check over to so/sth
to make a check to so/sth
to make a clean breast of sth (to so)
to make a difference to so
to make advances to so
to make amends (to so) (for so/sth)
to make application (to so/sth) (for sth)
to make arrangements to do sth
to make as if to do sth
to make every effort to do sth
to make it one's business to do sth
to make it (to) some place
to make it to sth
to make love (to so)
to make no difference (to so)
to make one's way back (to sth)
to make so bold as to do sth
to make so/sth available to so
to make sth clear to so
to make sth out to be sth else
to make sth to order
to make sth up to so
to make up (to so)
to man's inhumanity to man
to march (from some place) (to some place)
to march to (the beat of) a different drummer

to marry so off (to so)
to marvel to behold
to match up to sth
to matter to so
to May I speak to so?
to mean (for so) to do sth
to mean nothing (to so)
to mean sth (to so)
to mean to (do sth)
to meant to be
to measure up (to so/sth)
to mention sth to so
to migrate (from some place) (to some place)
to minister to so/sth
to modulate to a (different) key
to More power to you!
to more (to sth) than meets the eye
to motion (for) so to do sth
to motion so to one side
to motion to so
to move close to so/sth
to move (from some place) (to some place)
to move heaven and earth to do sth
to move off (to the side) with so
to move on (to sth)
to move so/sth to sth
to move so to tears
to move to some place
to move up (to sth)
to music to so's ears
to nail so('s hide) to the wall
to nail so to a cross
to narrow sth down (to people or things)
to needless to say
to neglect to do sth
to next to nothing
to next to so/sth
to nickel-and-dime so (to death)
to nineteen to the dozen
to nine-to-five job
to No more than I have to.
to no thanks to you
to nod is as good as a wink to a blind horse.
to nominate so to sth
to not a moment to spare
to not able to call one's time one's own
to not able to get sth for love or money
to not able to go on
to not able to help sth
to not able to make anything out of so/sth
to not able to make head or tail of sth
to not able to see the forest for the trees
to not able to stomach so/sth
to not able to wait
to not all sth is cracked up to be
to not amount to a hill of beans
to not as young as one used to be
to not enough room to swing a cat
to not going to win any beauty contests
to not have a leg to stand on
to not have anything to do with so/sth
to not have anything to do with sth
to not have the heart to do sth
to not hold a candle to so/sth
to not hold a stick to so/sth
to not know enough to come in out of the rain
to not know what to make of so/sth
to not know where to turn

to not know which way to turn
to not lift a finger (to help so)
to not lift a hand (to help so)
to not see any objection (to sth)
to not to put too fine a point on it
to not to touch a drop
to Not to worry.
to not up to scratch
to not up to snuff
to not want to catch so doing sth
to not what sth is cracked up to be
to nothing to be sneezed at
to nothing to boast about
to nothing to choose from
to Nothing to it!
to nothing to sneeze at
to nothing to speak of
to nothing to write home about
to nurse so back to health
to Nuts to you!
to object to so/sth
to obligate so to so/sth
to oblige so to do sth
to occur to so
to of benefit (to so)
to of interest (to so)
to of service (to so)
to off to a bad start
to off (to a flying start)
to off to a good start (with so/sth)
to off to a running start
to off to one side
to off to the races
to off (to the side) with so
to offer sth to so (as sth)
to offer sth up (to so/sth)
to old enough to be so's father
to old enough to be so's mother
to on one's way ((to) some place)
to on one's way (to sth or some place)
to on the road to recovery
to on the way (to sth or some place)
to One has to draw the line somewhere.
to one's heart goes out to so
to One thing leads to another.
to one to a customer
to only way to go
to open one's heart to so/sth
to open oneself to criticism
to open so's eyes to so/sth
to open sth up (to so)
to open the door to so
to open the door to sth
to open to criticism
to open to question
to open to so
to open up (to so)
to open up to sth
to opposed to sth
to or words to that effect
to order some food to go
to orient so to sth
to out of courtesy (to so)
to out to (a meal)
to out to get so
to out to lunch
to out to win
to owe sth (to so) (for sth)
to owing to
to own up to so
to own up (to sth)
to pack so off (to so/sth)

to pack sth off (to so/sth)
to pan across to so/sth
to pander to so/sth
to pare sth down (to sth)
to partial to so/sth
to party to sth
to pass so on (to so)
to pass sth along (to so)
to pass sth around (to so)
to pass sth back (to so)
to pass sth down (to so)
to pass sth in (to so)
to pass sth on (to so)
to pass sth out (to so)
to pass sth over (to so)
to pass sth to so
to pass the hat (around) (to so)
to passport to sth
to pay a visit to so/sth
to pay attention (to so/sth)
to pay court to so
to pay heed to so
to pay homage to so/sth
to pay lip service (to sth)
to pay one's debt (to society)
to pay one's last respects (to so)
to pay sth back (to so)
to pay sth out (to so)
to pay to do sth
to pay tribute to so/sth
to permit so up to sth
to persuade so to do sth
to pertain to so/sth
to phone in (to so/sth)
to phone sth in (to so/sth)
to pick so/sth to pieces
to pick sth to pieces
to pipe sth from some place (to some place)
to pit one's shoulder to the wheel
to place so/sth next to so/sth
to place to call one's own
to play down to so
to play hard to get
to play one's cards close to one's chest
to play second fiddle (to so)
to play sth back (to so)
to play to so/sth
to play to the crowd
to play to the gallery
to play up to so
to plead guilty to sth
to plead to sth
to pledge sth to so
to plight one's troth to so
to plummet to earth
to plummet to sth
to plunge to sth
to point down to sth
to point to so/sth
to point to sth
to point to sth as sth
to poised to do sth
to portent of things to come
to post sth to so
to pour one's heart out to so
to praise so/sth to the skies
to pray to so/sth
to pray to the porcelain god
to preach to so
to preach to the choir
to preach to the converted
to prefer so/sth to so/sth else
to prefix sth to sth

to prelude to sth
to present so (to so) (at sth)
to present sth to so
to press so to the wall
to pretend to sth
to prevail (up)on so/sth (to do sth)
to price one has to pay
to privy to sth
to proceed (from sth) (to sth)
to progress to sth
to promise sth to so
to promise the moon (to so)
to Promises are like piecrust, made to be broken.
to promote so (from sth) (to sth)
to prone to sth
to propose sth to so
to propose to so
to prove sth to so
to prove to be sth
to pull around to sth
to pull over (to sth)
to pull so/sth over (to sth)
to pull so/sth to pieces
to pull sth to
to pull sth up to sth
to pull up to sth
to push on (to sth)
to push so/sth to so/sth
to push so to sth
to push so to the wall
to push sth to
to put a horse out to pasture
to put a stop to sth
to put an end to sth
to put one's hand to the plow
to put one's mind to sth
to put one's money on so/sth (to do sth)
to put one's nose to the grindstone
to put paid to sth
to put so or an animal to sleep
to put so or some creature to death
to put so/sth through (to so)
to put so/sth to the test
to put so out to pasture
to put so to bed
to put so to shame
to put so to sleep
to put so up to sth
to put so wise to so/sth
to put sth across (to so)
to put sth down to sth
to put sth to bed
to put sth to (good) use
to put sth to rest
to put the pedal to the metal
to put (the) pressure on so (to do sth)
to put to bed with a shovel
to put to it
to race so to some place
to race to so/sth
to race up to so/sth
to raise (an) objection (to so/sth)
to raise one's glass to so/sth
to raise one's voice (to so)
to raise so/sth to the surface (of sth)
to raise so to sth
to rally to so/sth
to range from sth to sth
to rarin' to go
to raze sth to the ground
to reach out to so

to reach sth up to so
to reach to sth
to react to so/sth
to read oneself to sleep
to read sth back (to so)
to read (sth) to so
to readjust to so/sth
to ready (to do sth)
to reassign so to sth
to recall sth to mind
to recall sth to so
to recommend so/sth to so
to reconcile oneself to sth
to recount sth to so
to rededicate oneself or sth to so/sth
to reduce so to silence
to reduce so to tears
to reduce sth from sth to sth
to reduced to doing sth
to refer so back to so/sth
to refer so to so/sth
to refer sth back to so/sth
to refer to so/sth
to refund sth to so
to refuse sth to so
to refuse to do sth
to regress to sth
to reimburse sth to so
to reissue sth to so
to relate sth to so
to relate sth to sth
to relate to so/sth
to related to so
to relative to so/sth
to relay sth to so
to release so to so
to relegate so to so/sth
to relinquish sth to so/sth
to reluctant to do sth
to remand so over to so
to Remember me to so.
to remember so to so
to Remember to write.
to remit sth to so/sth
to render sth to so/sth
to rent sth (out) (to so)
to repair to some place
to repatriate so to some place
to reply to so/sth
to report back (to so/sth)
to report sth to so
to report to so/sth
to represent sth to so
to reputed to
to request so to do sth
to resign oneself to sth
to resort to sth
to respond to so/sth
to restore sth to so
to restore sth to sth
to restrict so/sth to so/sth
to retail sth to so
to retire to some place
to retreat (from sth) (to some place)
to return so to so
to return to haunt one
to return to some place
to reveal so/sth to so
to revert to so/sth
to ride to some place
to right to do sth
to right to sth
to rip so/sth to sth

to rise to one's feet
to rise to the bait
to rise to the challenge
to rise to the occasion
to rise to the top
to risk one's neck (to do sth)
to riveted to the ground
to road to hell is paved with good intentions.
to rob Peter to pay Paul
to rock so to sth
to roll sth to so/sth
to rooted to sth
to rooted to the spot
to rotten to the core
to round off to sth
to round up to sth
to rouse so to sth
to route sth to so
to row (so/sth) out to sth
to run back to so/sth
to run counter to sth
to run down to some place
to run down to so/sth
to run from sth to sth
to run over to sth
to run so/sth to earth
to run so/sth to sth
to run sth over to so/sth
to run to seed
to run to so/sth
to run to sth
to run up to some place
to run up (to so/sth)
to rush so to the hospital
to rush sth off (to so/sth)
to rush to conclusions
to rush to so/sth
to sacrifice so/sth to so/sth
to sail from some place to some place else
to same to you.
to Say hello to so (for me).
to say sth (right) to so's face
to say sth to oneself
to say sth to so
to say sth to sth
to scale sth to sth
to scarcely have time to breathe
to scare so or an animal to death
to scared to death
to scoot down (to some place)
to scoot over to so/sth
to second nature to so
to second to none
to see eye to eye (about so/sth) (with so)
to see fit (to do sth)
to see no objection (to sth)
to see one's way (clear) (to do sth)
to see so back (to sth)
to see so down to sth
to see so to some place
to see so to sth
to see so to the door
to see so up to sth
to see (to it) that sth is done
to see to so/sth
to sell out (to so)
to send one to one's death
to send so from pillar to post
to send so off (to sth)
to send so over (to) some place
to send so to bed
to send so to glory

to send so to the locker room
to send so to the showers
to send sth off (to so/sth)
to send sth over ((to) some place)
to send sth to so/sth
to send word to so
to sensitize so to sth
to sentence so to sth (for sth)
to serve sth to so
to Set a beggar on horseback, and he'll ride to the devil.
to Set a thief to catch a thief.
to set fire to so/sth
to set one's mind to sth
to set out to do sth
to set so/sth to work
to set sth down to sth
to set sth to music
to set to
to shine up to so
to shoot so/sth (all) to hell
to shoulder to shoulder
to shouldn't happen to a dog
to show one to one's seat
to show so to a seat
to show so (to) the door
to show sth to good advantage
to shut one's eyes to sth
to shuttle so/sth from person to person
to sick to death (of so/sth)
to sidle up (to so/sth)
to sign of things to come
to sign sth over (to so)
to signal (to) so (to do sth)
to since so was knee-high to a grasshopper
to sing so to sleep
to sing to so/sth
to sink to (doing) sth
to sit close to so/sth
to sit down to sth
to slated to do sth
to slave to sth
to slip back (to so/sth)
to slip off (to some place)
to slope down (to sth or some place)
to slope up (to sth)
to smell to (high) heaven
to snap to (attention)
to Snap to it!
to sneak up to so/sth
to snuggle up (to so/sth)
to so to speak
to soak so to the skin
to soaked to the skin
to sob oneself to sleep
to sob sth to so
to sock it to so
to Some people (just) don't know when to quit.
to So/sth is supposed to.
to so's claim to fame
to (So's) not supposed to.
to Something's got to give.
to sth to shout about
to something to that effect
to somewhere to hang (up) one's hat
to speak down to so
to speak to so
to speak to sth
to spirit so/sth off (to some place)
to splice sth (in)to sth
to spread to so/sth

to spring back (to some place)
to spring to attention
to spring to life
to spring to one's feet
to spring to so's defense
to square up to so/sth
to squeal (on so) (to so)
to stack up to so/sth
to stake a claim to so/sth
to stake out a claim to sth
to stake so to sth
to stand close to so/sth
to stand so to a treat
to stand to lose sth
to stand to reason
to stand up to so/sth
to start back (to some place)
to stay to sth
to step off (to the side) with so
to step over (to) some place
to step up to sth
to step up to the plate
to stick it to so
to stick sth out to so
to stick to one's guns
to stick to one's ribs
to stick to so/sth
to stick to so's fingers
to stink to high heaven
to stoop to doing sth
to stranger to sth or some place
to stretch away to some place
to stretch out to so/sth
to stretch sth out (to so/sth)
to strip so/sth down to sth
to strip to sth
to strive to do sth
to struggle to do sth
to struggle to the death
to subject so/sth to sth
to subject to sth
to subjugate so to so
to submit so/sth to sth
to submit to sth
to subordinate so/sth to so/sth else
to subpoena so to do sth
to subscribe to sth
to succeed to sth
to succumb to sth
to suck up to so
to suggest itself to so
to suggest sth to so
to suit one's actions to one's words
to suit so/sth to sth
to suit so to a T
to summon so to so/sth
to Sunday-go-to-meeting clothes
to supply sth (to so/sth) (from sth)
to Supposed to.
to supposed to do sth
to surrender so/sth to so/sth
to surrender to so/sth
to susceptible to sth
to sway from side to side
to sway so to sth
to swear so to sth
to swear sth to so
to swear to sth
to swing around (to sth)
to swing to sth
to switch back (to sth)
to switch from so to so else
to switch from sth to sth else

to switch over (to so/sth)
to switch so/sth over to sth
to switch sth back (to sth)
to switch sth over (to sth)
to switch sth to sth else
to switch to sth
to tailor so/sth to so/sth
to take a backseat (to so/sth)
to take a fancy to so/sth
to take a liking to so/sth
to take a shine to so/sth
to take exception (to sth)
to take (great) pains (to do sth)
to take it to one's grave
to take it to the street
to take it upon oneself to do sth
to take kindly to sth
to take off one's hat (to so)
to take one back (to some time)
to take one's hat off to so
to take so down (to size)
to take so/sth over (to so/sth)
to take so out to dinner
to take so to court
to take so to one side
to take so to task
to take so to the cleaners
to take sth back to so/sth
to take sth to heart
to take sth to pieces
to take sth to so/sth
to take sth up to so
to take steps (to prevent sth)
to take the initiative (to do sth)
to take the trouble (to do sth)
to take to one's bed
to take to one's heels
to take to so/sth
to take to the hills
to talk back (to so)
to talk down to so
to Talk of the devil (and he is sure to appear).
to talk to hear one's own voice
to talk to so
to tattle (on so) (to so)
to teach one's grandmother to suck eggs
to tear so/sth to pieces
to telephone sth in (to so)
to Tell it to the marines!
to tell one to one's face
to tell so what to do with sth
to tell so where to get off
to tell sth to so
to tempt so to do sth
to tend to do sth
to tender sth (to so) (for sth)
to testify to sth
to thanks to so/sth
to that beats sth all to pieces
to That brings me to the (main) point.
to That's easy for you to say.
to That's news to me.
to (That's the) way to go!
to (The) best of luck (to so).
to (There ain't) nothin' to it.
to There are two sides to every question.
to There are two sides to every story.
to (There is) no need (to).
to There is no royal road to learning.
to There's more than one way to skin a cat.

to (There's) no way to tell.
to (There's) nothing to it!
to There will be hell to pay.
to There will be the devil to pay.
to They don't make them like they used to.
to think ahead (to sth)
to think back (to sth)
to think to do sth
to thoughts to live by
to thrill so to pieces
to thrill to sth
to thrilled to death
to thrilled to pieces
to throw caution to the wind
to throw so to the dogs
to throw so to the wolves
to throw sth back to so
to throw sth to so/sth
to throw sth up to so
to tickle so to death
to tickle so to pieces
to tie so down (to so/sth)
to tie so/sth to sth
to tie so to sth
to tied to one's mother's apron strings
to tilt to sth
to Time to call it a day.
to Time to call it a night.
to time to catch one's breath
to 'Tis better to have loved and lost than never to have loved at all.
to to a great extent
to to and fro
to to be on the safe side
to to be safe
to to beat the band
to to boot
to to date
to to die for
to To each his own.
to To err is human(, to forgive divine).
to to go
to to have a hollow leg
to to hell and gone
to (To) hell with that!
to to no avail
to to one's heart's content
to to put it another way
to to put it mildly
to to say nothing of so/sth
to to say the least
to to some extent
to to so's liking
to to so's way of thinking
to to the best of one's ability
to to the best of one's knowledge
to to the bitter end
to to the contrary
to to the core
to to the ends of the earth
to to the last
to to the letter
to to the max
to to the nth degree
to to the tune of some amount of money
to To the victors belong the spoils.
to to whom it may concern
to to wit
to toady (up) to so
to toing and froing (on sth)
to too good to be true
to touch sth to sth

to tough act to follow
to tough nut to crack
to tough row to hoe
to tow so/sth out (to so)
to trace so/sth (back) (to so/sth)
to trade up (to sth)
to train up to sth
to trample so/sth to sth
to transfer so/sth (from some place) (to some place)
to transfer so/sth to so
to transfer sth (from so) (to so else)
to transfer to sth
to transmit sth (from some place) (to some place)
to transmit sth to so/sth
to transport so/sth (from some place) (to some place)
to treat so to sth
to trek to some place
to trickle down (to so/sth)
to trouble oneself (to do sth)
to trouble so to do sth
to true to form
to true to one's word
to trust so/sth to so
to trust so to do sth
to tune in (to sth)
to turn a blind eye (to so/sth)
to turn a deaf ear (to so/sth)
to turn one's hand to sth
to turn out to be so/sth
to turn so/sth in (to so/sth)
to turn so/sth over to so/sth
to turn so/sth to sth
to turn sth to good account
to turn sth to one's advantage
to turn to
to two sheets to the wind
to unaccustomed to so/sth
to unbosom oneself to so
to unburden oneself to so
to undertake to do sth
to up to doing sth
to up to here (with sth)
to up to no good
to up to one's ears (in sth)
to up to one's eyeballs (in sth)
to up to one's knees
to up to one's neck (in sth)
to up to par
to up to snuff
to up to so/sth
to up to sth
to up to speed
to up to the minute
to upgrade so/sth to sth
to upgrade to sth
to up-to-date
to up-to-the-minute
to urge so to do sth
to use your head for more than something to keep your ears apart
to used to do sth
to used to so/sth
to usher so to sth
to vary from sth to sth
to visible to the naked eye
to wait for the other shoe to drop
to wake so up (to sth)
to wake (up) to sth
to walk back ((to) sth)
to walk over (to so/sth)

to walk right up (to so/sth)
to walk so over to so/sth
to walk up to so/sth
to wall-to-wall (with) sth
to waltz up (to so)
to Want to make something of it?
to warm up to so/sth
to wave to so
to way to a man's heart is through his stomach.
to We aim to please.
to We must learn to walk before we can run.
to We need to talk about sth.
to wear so to a frazzle
to wed so to so
to wed so to sth
to wed(ded) to so
to wedded to sth
to welcome so to sth
to welcome so to do sth
to Welcome to our house.
to We('ll) have to do lunch sometime.
to well-to-do
to (We're) delighted to have you (here).
to What do you want me to say?
to What have you been up to?
to what's coming to one
to What's it to you?
to What's (there) to know?
to what so/sth is cracked up to be
to What would you like to drink?
to when it comes right down to it
to when it comes to sth
to when push comes to shove
to Where ignorance is bliss, 'tis folly to be wise.
to wherewithal (to do sth)
to which brings me to the (main) point
to whip sth over (to so)
to whip sth written off to so
to whisk so/sth off (to sth)
to whittle so down to size
to whittle sth down (to size)
to Who do you think you're talking to?
to Who do you want to speak to?
to Who do you want (to talk to)?
to will sth to so
to win so over (to sth)
to wire sth back to so
to wise to so/sth
to wise up (to so/sth)
to wish is father to the thought.
to with a view to doing sth
to with an eye to doing sth
to with reference to so/sth
to with regard to so/sth
to with respect to so/sth
to with sth to spare
to With whom do you wish to speak?
to without a moment to spare
to witness to sth
to woman to woman
to word to the wise
to words to live by
to work around to so/sth
to work down (the line) (to so/sth)
to work one's fingers to the bone
to work one's way up (to sth)
to work oneself up (to sth)
to work so/sth to so/sth
to work up to sth

to would like (to have) so/sth
to (Would you) care to...?
to (Would you) care to dance?
to (Would you) care to join us?
to wouldn't want to be in so's shoes
to write back to so
to write down to so
to write off (to so) (for sth)
to write sth back to so
to write sth to so
to write sth to sth
to write to so
to yield so/sth (over) (to so/sth)
to yield so/sth up (to so)
to yield sth to so
to yield to so
to You are never too old to learn.
to You can lead a horse to water, but you can't make it drink.
to You can't expect me to believe that.
to You don't expect me to believe that.
to You got to do what you got to do.
to You have to eat a peck of dirt before you die.
to You mean to tell me sth?
to You must lose a fly to catch a trout.
to (You want to) know something?
to You want to make something of it?
to You wouldn't dare (to do sth)!
to You've got to be kidding!
to You've got to be out of your mind!
to zoom so/sth (over) to so
toad biggest toad in the puddle
toad If a toady frog had wings, he wouldn't bump his ass.
toad toady (up) to so
toad ugly as a toad
toady If a toady frog had wings, he wouldn't bump his ass.
toady toady (up) to so
toast propose a toast
toast warm as toast
tobacco chew one's own tobacco
today Don't put off for tomorrow what you can do today.
today Here today, (and) gone tomorrow.
today Today here, tomorrow the world.
today What's on tap for today?
toddle toddle along
toddle toddle away
toddle toddle off
toe from head to toe
toe from tip to toe
toe keep on one's toes
toe keep one on one's toes
toe on one's toes
toe on tiptoe
toe stay on one's toes
toe step on so's toes
toe stub one's toe against sth
toe toe the line
toe toe the mark
toe tread on so's toes
toe turn up one's toes
toe with bells on (one's toes)
toenail throw up one's toenails
together add sth together
together band together (against so/sth)
together bind so/sth together
together Birds of a feather flock together.
together blend sth together (with sth)

together bring so together
together bring sth all together
together bring sth together
together bunk (up) together
together call so together
together cement sth together
together clap sth together
together cling together
together cluster together
together come together
together couple sth together
together crash sth together
together crash together
together crowd so/sth together
together crowd together
together cup one's hands together
together draw people or things together
together draw so together
together enough to keep body and soul together
together family that prays together stays together.
together fit sth together
together fit together
together flock together
together gather so/sth together
together gather together
together get it (all) together
together get one's act together
together get one's head together
together get one's shit together
together get one's stuff together
together get so/sth together
together get sth together (for a particular time)
together get together (with so) (on so/sth)
together glue sth together
together go together
together grind sth together
together group so/sth together
together grow together
together hang together
together have it all together
together herd so/sth together
together hold oneself together
together hold so/sth together
together hold sth together
together hold together
together huddle so together
together huddle (up) (together)
together jam so/sth together
together jam sth together
together join sth and sth else together
together jumble so/sth together
together jumble sth together
together keep body and soul together
together keep so/sth together
together keep together
together knit sth together
together knit together
together knock one's knees together
together knock some heads together
together knock sth together
together knot sth together
together lash sth together
together lay sth together
together Let's get together (sometime).
together live together
together live (together) with so
together lump so and so else together
together marshal so/sth together
together mesh together

together nest together
together pack so/sth together
together patch sth together (with sth)
together piece sth together
together press sth together
together pull oneself together
together pull sth together
together pull together (as a team)
together put people or things together
together put people's heads together
together put sth together
together put two and two together
together remain together
together room together
together rope sth together
together rub sth together
together scrape so/sth together
together scrape sth together
together sing together
together slap sth together
together sleep together
together splice sth together
together squeeze so/sth together
together squeeze (themselves) together
together stand together
together stick sth together
together stick together
together string sth together
together throw people together
together throw sth together
together toss sth together
together unite so/sth (together)
together walk together
together weld so and so else together
together weld sth and sth else together
together wire sth together
together work together
together yoke people or things together
toil toil for so
toil toil for sth
toil toil over so/sth
toil toil up sth
toilet go to the toilet
toilet use the toilet
toing toing and froing (on sth)
token as a token (of sth)
token by the same token
token token gesture
told all told
told done told you
told if I've told you once, I've told you a thousand times
told little bird told me.
tolerable tol(er)able (well)
tolerance zero tolerance
toll take (quite) a toll (on so/sth)
toll toll for so
Tom any Tom, Dick, and Harry
Tom (every) Tom, Dick, and Harry
tomahawk dig up one's tomahawk
tomorrow Don't put off for tomorrow what you can do today.
tomorrow Eat, drink, and be merry, for tomorrow we die.
tomorrow Here today, (and) gone tomorrow.
tomorrow (I'll) see you tomorrow.
tomorrow like there ain't no tomorrow
tomorrow like there's no tomorrow
tomorrow spend money like there's no tomorrow

tomorrow Today here, tomorrow the world.
tomorrow Tomorrow is another day.
tomorrow Tomorrow never comes.
ton fall like a ton of bricks
ton hit like a ton of bricks
ton hit so like a ton of bricks
ton like a ton of bricks
ton tons of sth
tone tone so/sth up
tone tone sth down
tong fight so/sth hammer and tongs
tong go at it hammer and tongs
tongue bite one's tongue
tongue Bite your tongue!
tongue cause (some) tongues to wag
tongue find one's tongue
tongue (Has the) cat got your tongue?
tongue hold one's tongue
tongue Hold your tongue!
tongue keep a civil tongue (in one's head)
tongue on the tip of one's tongue
tongue set tongues (a)wagging
tongue sharp tongue
tongue slip of the tongue
tongue speak with a forked tongue
tongue stick one's tongue out
tongue still tongue makes a wise head.
tongue tongue-in-cheek
tongue tongue-lashing
too be too
too didn't care too hard
too do too
too Don't be gone (too) long.
too Don't be too sure.
too Don't speak too soon.
too Don't work too hard.
too eat one's cake and have it too
too go too far
too have one's cake and eat it too
too have one's finger in too many pies
too have one too many
too have too
too have (too much) time on one's hands
too (I) can too.
too I spoke too soon.
too It is never too late to learn.
too It is never too late to mend.
too know sth only too well
too land too poor to raise a racket on
too Life is too short.
too make (too) much of so/sth
too none too sth
too not to put too fine a point on it
too Not (too) much.
too not too shabby
too one too many
too push so too far
too put too fine a point on sth
too spread oneself too thin
too take too much on
too That's (just) too much!
too (That's) too bad.
too too big for one's britches
too too close for comfort
too too funny for words
too too good to be true
too too little, too late
too Too many chiefs and not enough Indians.

too Too many cooks spoil the broth.
too Too many cooks spoil the stew.
too too much
too too rich for so's blood
too Yesterday wouldn't be too soon.
too You (always) give up too eas(il)y.
too You are never too old to learn.
too You cannot have your cake and eat it (too).
too You're too much!
took (You) took the words right out of my mouth.
tool Give us the tools, and we will finish the job.
tool tool around (in sth)
tool tool sth up
tool tool up
toot darn tooting
toot toot one's own horn
toot You're dern tootin'!
tooth armed to the teeth
tooth bare one's teeth
tooth by the skin of one's teeth
tooth clean as a hound's tooth
tooth cut one's eyeteeth on sth
tooth cut teeth
tooth dressed to the teeth
tooth drop one's teeth
tooth escape by the skin of one's teeth
tooth eye for an eye (and a tooth for a tooth).
tooth fight so/sth tooth and nail
tooth fly in the teeth of so/sth
tooth get one's teeth into sth
tooth give one's eyeteeth (for so/sth)
tooth give teeth to sth
tooth gnash one's teeth
tooth gnashing of teeth
tooth go at it tooth and nail
tooth go at one another tooth and nail
tooth go over sth with a fine-tooth comb
tooth go through sth with a fine-tooth comb
tooth gods send nuts to those who have no teeth.
tooth grit one's teeth
tooth have a sweet tooth
tooth kick in the teeth
tooth lie through one's teeth
tooth long in the tooth
tooth no skin off so's teeth
tooth pull so's or sth's teeth
tooth put some teeth into sth
tooth put teeth in(to) sth
tooth scarce as hen's teeth
tooth scarcer than hen's teeth
tooth search sth with a fine-tooth comb
tooth set so's teeth on edge
tooth show one's teeth
tooth sink one's teeth into sth
tooth take the bit between the teeth
tooth take the bit in one's teeth
tooth teething troubles
toothpick close enough to use the same toothpick
top at the top of one's game
top at the top of one's lungs
top at the top of one's voice
top at the top of the hour
top blow one's top
top claw one's way to the top
top come out on top

top come (right) on top of sth
top feel on top of the world
top from the top
top from top to bottom
top get to the top (of sth)
top go (straight) to the top
top (I) can't top that.
top in top form
top keep on top (of so/sth)
top on top of sth
top on top of the world
top over the top
top pop (some) tops
top (right) off the top of one's head
top rise to the top
top (sitting) on top of the world
top stay on top of so/sth
top take it from the top
top thin on top
top top brass
top top notch
top top of the heap
top top so/sth
top top sth off
top top sth up
top top sth with sth
top top story
top (You) can't top that.
topic off topic
topple topple down
topple topple off (of) sth
topple topple over
topple topple sth down
torch carry a torch (for so)
torch carry the torch
tore all tore up (about sth)
tore tore (up)
torment torment so into doing sth
torn torn between so and so else
torn torn (up)
torture torture so into sth
toss It's a toss-up.
toss toss a salad
toss toss in the sponge
toss toss one's cookies
toss toss one's hat into the ring
toss toss (so) for sth
toss toss so/sth around
toss toss so/sth aside
toss toss so/sth away
toss toss so/sth back
toss toss so/sth off (of) sth
toss toss so/sth out of sth
toss toss sth
total total sth up
total total stranger
total totally awesome
tote tote sth up
totem high man on the totem pole
totem low man on the totem pole
touch Don't touch that dial!
touch finishing touch(es)
touch have the Midas touch
touch I wouldn't touch it with a ten-foot pole.
touch in touch (with so)
touch in touch with so/sth
touch Keep in touch.
touch keep in touch (with so)
touch keep in touch (with so/sth)
touch lose one's touch (with so/sth)
touch lose touch with reality
touch lose touch with so/sth

touch not to touch a drop
touch not touch so/sth with a ten-foot pole
touch out of touch (with so/sth)
touch put so in touch with so/sth
touch put the touch on so
touch remain in touch (with so/sth)
touch soft touch
touch stay in touch (with so/sth)
touch touch a sore point
touch touch a sore spot
touch touch at some place
touch touch base (with so)
touch touch down
touch touch of sth
touch touch on sth
touch touch so/sth off
touch touch so/sth with sth
touch touch so (up) for sth
touch touch sth to sth
touch touch sth up
touch touch (up)on sth
touch touch-and-go
touch touched by so/sth
touch touched (in the head)
touch wouldn't touch so/sth with a ten-foot pole
tough act tough on so
tough get tough (with so)
tough hang tough (on sth)
tough if the going gets tough
tough tough act to follow
tough tough as an old boot
tough tough as old (shoe) leather
tough tough break
tough tough call
tough tough cookie
tough tough cookies
tough tough customer
tough tough going
tough tough guy
tough tough luck
tough tough nut to crack
tough tough on so
tough tough row to hoe
tough tough sledding
tough tough sth out
tough tough times
tough toughen so/sth up
tough toughen up
tough when the going gets tough
tough When the going gets tough, the tough get going.
tour go on tour
tout tout so/sth around
tout tout so/sth as sth
tout tout suite!
tow have so/sth in tow
tow in tow
tow tow so/sth away
tow tow so/sth into sth
tow tow so/sth out (of some place)
tow tow so/sth out (to sth)
toward advance to(ward) so/sth
toward angle off (to(ward) sth)
toward direct sth to(ward) so/sth
toward draw so/sth to(ward) so/sth
toward drift toward so/sth
toward fall away toward sth
toward fall toward sth
toward go a long way toward doing sth
toward go toward so/sth
toward gravitate to(ward) so/sth

toward head toward so/sth
toward incline toward so/sth
toward lean toward doing sth
toward lean toward so/sth
toward look toward so/sth
toward move toward so/sth
toward point toward so/sth
toward predispose so/sth to(ward) sth
toward progress toward sth
toward pull sth toward oneself
toward push so/sth toward so/sth
toward push toward so/sth
toward reach toward so/sth
toward save (money) toward sth
toward slant sth toward so/sth
toward slant toward so/sth
toward slope (down) toward sth
toward steer sth toward so/sth
toward steer toward so/sth
toward strive toward sth
toward swim toward so/sth
toward tend toward sth
toward tilt toward so/sth
toward trend toward sth
toward turn so/sth toward so/sth
toward veer toward so/sth
toward well disposed to(ward) so/sth
toward work toward sth
towel throw in the towel
towel towel so/sth down
towel towel so/sth off
tower dwell in an ivory tower
tower in an ivory tower
tower live in an ivory tower
tower tower above so/sth
tower tower head and shoulders above so/sth
tower tower of strength
tower tower over so/sth
tower work in an ivory tower
town all over town
town Get out of town!
town go to town
town hit town
town I'll look you up when I'm in town.
town Look me up when you're in town.
town man about town
town night on the town
town one-horse town
town out of town
town out on the town
town paint the town (red)
town town-and-gown
toy like a kid with a new toy
toy toy with so
toy toy with sth
trace kick over the traces
trace lose trace of so/sth
trace trace around sth
trace trace over sth
trace trace so/sth (back) (to so/sth)
track back on track
track cover so's tracks (up)
track dead in so's or an animal's tracks
track drop in one's tracks
track follow in so's tracks
track get on the track of so/sth
track have a one-track mind
track have so/sth on track
track inside track
track jump the track

track keep on (the) track
track keep so/sth on (the) (right) track
track keep so/sth on track
track keep track (of so/sth)
track lose track (of so/sth)
track make tracks (for sth)
track off on a sidetrack
track off the beaten track
track off the track
track on the fast track
track on the right track
track on the track of so/sth
track on the wrong track
track on track
track one-track mind
track other side of the tracks
track put so off the track
track put so/sth on track
track put sth back on track
track set so/sth on track
track stop dead in one's tracks
track stop one or sth dead in one's or sth's tracks
track throw so off the track
track track so/sth down
track track sth (all) over sth
track track sth into some place
track track sth up
track wrong side of the tracks
trade jack of all trades
trade jack of all trades is a master of none.
trade know the tricks of the trade
trade learn the tricks of the trade
trade show so the tricks of the trade
trade stock in trade
trade take sth out in trade
trade teach so the tricks of the trade
trade There are tricks in every trade.
trade trade at some place
trade trade insults (with so)
trade trade on sth
trade trade secret
trade trade so/sth for so/sth
trade trade sth in (for sth)
trade trade sth off
trade trade sth with so
trade trade up from sth
trade trade up (to sth)
trade trade with so/sth
trade tricks of the trade
traffic Go play in the traffic.
traffic stuck in traffic
traffic tie traffic up
traffic traffic in sth
traffic traffic jam
trail blaze a trail
trail hit the trail
trail hot on the trail (of so/sth or some creature)
trail leave a paper trail
trail make a paper trail
trail on the trail of so/sth
trail paper trail
trail put so off the trail
trail throw so off the trail
trail trail (along) (after so/sth)
trail trail away
trail trail behind (so/sth)
trail trail off
trail trail over sth
trail trail so/sth by sth
train keep in training

train lose one's train of thought
train ride the gravy train
train so's train of thought
train train for sth
train train one's sights on sth
train train so in sth
train train so on sth
train train so or an animal as sth
train train so or an animal for sth
train train sth on so/sth or an animal
train train up to sth
traipse traipse around (some place)
traipse traipse over
tramp tramp across sth
tramp tramp through sth
trample trample so/sth down
trample trample so/sth to sth
trample trample sth out
trample trample (up)on so/sth
transcribe transcribe sth from so/sth
transcribe transcribe sth in sth
transfer transfer so/sth (from some place) (to some place)
transfer transfer so/sth to so
transfer transfer sth (from so) (to so else)
transfer transfer to sth
transform transform so/sth (from sth) (in)to so/sth
transgress transgress against so/sth
transit in transit
translate translate sth (from sth) ((in)to sth)
translation free translation
translation loose translation
transliterate transliterate sth (from sth) ((in)to sth)
transmit transmit sth (from some place) (to some place)
transmit transmit sth to so/sth
transmute transmute sth (from sth) ((in)to sth)
transport transport so/sth (from some place) (to some place)
transpose transpose sth (from sth) ((in)to sth)
trap build a better mousetrap
trap fall into a trap
trap fall into so's trap
trap fall into the trap
trap have a mind as sharp as a steel trap
trap set a trap
trap trap so in sth
trap trap so into sth
trap trap so/sth in sth
trap walk (right) into a trap
trash Cash is trash.
trash One man's trash is another man's treasure.
travel Bad news travels fast.
travel He travels fastest who travels alone.
travel It is better to travel hopefully than to arrive.
travel *mile a minute
travel travel a mile a minute
travel travel across sth
travel travel at a fast clip
travel travel at a good clip
travel Travel broadens the mind.
travel travel by sth
travel travel for so/sth
travel travel in a body

travel travel off the beaten path
travel travel on sth
travel travel over sth
travel travel through sth
travel travel with so
travel travel with sth
travesty travesty of justice
tread Fools rush in where angels fear to tread.
tread tread on so's toes
tread tread (up)on so/sth
treasure One man's trash is another man's treasure.
treat Dutch treat
treat How's the world (been) treating you?
treat stand so to a treat
treat treat a case of sth
treat treat so (for sth) (with sth)
treat treat so/sth as sth
treat treat so/sth like so/sth
treat treat so to sth
treat Trick or treat!
treatment red-carpet treatment
treatment royal treatment
tree As the twig is bent, so is the tree inclined.
tree bark up the wrong tree
tree cannot see the forest for the trees
tree cannot see the wood for the trees
tree make like a tree and leave
tree Money does not grow on trees.
tree not able to see the forest for the trees
tree not grow on trees
tree tree is known by its fruit.
tree up a tree
trek trek across sth
trek trek to some place
tremble in fear and trembling
tremble tremble at sth
tremble tremble from sth
tremble tremble with sth
trend trend toward sth
trespass no trespassing
trespass trespass (up)on sth
trial bring so/sth to trial
trial go to trial
trial on trial
trial send up a trial balloon
trial stand trial
trial trial and error
trial trial balloon
trial trials and tribulations
triangle eternal triangle
tribulation trials and tribulations
tribute floral tribute
tribute pay tribute to so/sth
trick bag of tricks
trick do the trick
trick How's tricks?
trick know a trick or two
trick know the tricks of the trade
trick learn the tricks of the trade
trick miss a trick
trick play a trick on so
trick play tricks on so
trick pull a trick (on so)
trick show so the tricks of the trade
trick teach so the tricks of the trade
trick There are tricks in every trade.
trick Trick or treat!
trick trick so into (doing) sth

trick trick so out of sth
trick tricks of the trade
trick turn a trick
trick use every trick in the book
trick whole bag of tricks
trick You cannot teach an old dog new tricks.
trickle trickle away
trickle trickle down (to so/sth)
trickle trickle in(to sth)
trickle trickle out (of sth)
trickle trickle through (sth)
tried Lord knows I've tried.
tried tried and true
trifle mere trifle
trifle trifle sth away (on so/sth)
trifle trifle with so/sth
trigger quick on the trigger
trigger trigger so off
trigger trigger sth off
trim fit and trim
trim trim (oneself) down
trim trim sth away (from sth)
trim trim sth down
trim trim sth from sth
trim trim sth off (of) so/sth
trim trim sth with sth
trim with all the trimmings
trimming with all the trimmings
trip day-tripper
trip go on a power trip
trip Have a good trip.
trip Have a safe trip.
trip lay a guilt trip on so
trip lay a (heavy) trip on so
trip on a power trip
trip round-trip ticket
trip trip along
trip trip on so/sth
trip trip so up
trip trip the light fantastic
triplicate in triplicate
tripper day-tripper
triumph triumph over so/sth
trolley off one's trolley
trolley slip one's trolley
troop swear like a trooper
troop troop across so/sth
troop troop in(to sth)
trooper swear like a trooper
trot trot after so
trot trot along
trot trot so/sth out
trot trot sth out
troth plight one's troth to so
trouble ask for trouble
trouble borrow trouble
trouble buy trouble
trouble die of throat trouble
trouble drown one's troubles
trouble fish in troubled waters
trouble foment trouble
trouble for (all) one's trouble
trouble go to the trouble (of doing sth)
trouble (Have you) been keeping out of trouble?
trouble in trouble
trouble It isn't worth the trouble.
trouble (It's) no trouble (at all).
trouble (I've) been keeping out of trouble.
trouble look for trouble
trouble make trouble

trouble Never trouble trouble till trouble troubles you.
trouble not trouble one's (pretty) (little) head about sth
trouble not worth the trouble
trouble pour oil on troubled water(s)
trouble spell trouble
trouble take the trouble (to do sth)
trouble teething troubles
trouble There is trouble brewing.
trouble Trouble is brewing.
trouble trouble one's head about so/sth
trouble trouble oneself about so/sth
trouble trouble oneself (to do sth)
trouble trouble shared is a trouble halved.
trouble trouble so about so/sth
trouble trouble so for sth
trouble trouble so to do sth
trouble trouble so with sth
trouble You been keeping out of trouble?
trout You must lose a fly to catch a trout.
trowel lay it on with a trowel
truck have no truck with sth
truck just fell off the turnip truck
truck keep on trucking
trudge trudge along
trudge trudge through sth
true come true
true course of true love never did run smooth.
true dream come true
true hold true
true Many a true word is spoken in jest.
true Morning dreams come true.
true ring true
true show one's (true) colors
true so's true colors
true There's many a true word spoken in jest.
true too good to be true
true tried and true
true true as steel
true true sth up
true true to form
true true to one's word
true twelve good men and true
truly yours truly
trump play one's trump card
trump trump sth up
trump trumped up
truss truss so/sth up
trust in the trust of so
trust leave so/sth in the trust of so
trust misplace one's trust (in so)
trust place one's trust in so/sth
trust place so/sth in the trust of so
trust put one's trust in so/sth
trust Put your trust in God, and keep your powder dry.
trust restore so's trust in sth
trust take sth on trust
trust trust in so/sth
trust Trust me!
trust trust so for sth
trust trust so/sth to so
trust trust so to do sth
trust trust so with so/sth
truth Ain't it the truth?
truth Children and fools tell the truth.

truth economical with the truth
truth gospel truth
truth grain of truth
truth greater the truth, the greater the libel.
truth Half the truth is often a whole lie.
truth if the truth were known
truth Is there any truth to sth?
truth liar is not believed (even) when he tells the truth.
truth moment of truth
truth naked truth
truth stretch the truth
truth Tell the truth and shame the devil.
truth Truth is stranger than fiction.
truth truth will out.
try Don't quit trying.
try give sth a try
try If at first you don't succeed, try, try again.
try (I'll) try to catch you later.
try (I'll) try to catch you some other time.
try Keep (on) trying.
try like tryin' to scratch your ear with your elbow
try Lord knows I've tried.
try old college try
try take a try at so
try take a try at sth
try tried and true
try try as I may
try try as I might
try try at so
try try at sth
try try for sth
try Try me.
try try one's hand (at sth)
try try one's luck (at sth)
try try one's wings (out)
try try out (for sth)
try try so back (again)
try try so for sth
try try so/sth out
try try so's patience
try try sth (on) (for size)
try try sth on with so
try try sth out on so
try trying times
try We'll try again some other time.
try without half trying
try You never know (what you can do) till you try.
tub Every tub must stand on its own bottom.
tub Let every tub stand on its own bottom.
tub tub of lard
tube down the tube(s)
tube go down the tube(s)
tuck nip and tuck
tuck tuck into sth
tuck tuck so in(to) sth
tuck tuck sth around so/sth
tuck tuck sth away
tuck tuck sth in(to) sth
tuck tuck sth up
tucker (all) tuckered out
tucker one's best bib and tucker
tucker tucker so out
Tuesday from here till next Tuesday

tug tug at so/sth
tug tug away (at sth)
tumble rough-and-tumble
tumble tumble along
tumble tumble down
tumble tumble from sth
tumble tumble into bed
tumble tumble into so/sth
tumble tumble out of sth
tumble tumble over
tumble tumble so/sth down sth
tune call the tune
tune cannot carry a tune
tune can't carry a tune
tune change so's tune
tune dance to a different tune
tune dance to another tune
tune fine-tune sth
tune He who pays the piper calls the tune.
tune in tune
tune out of tune (with so/sth)
tune sing a different tune
tune sing another tune
tune There's many a good tune played on an old fiddle.
tune to the tune of some amount of money
tune tune in (on so/sth)
tune tune in (to sth)
tune tune out
tune tune so/sth out
tune tune sth in
tune tune sth up
tune tune up
tune tuned in
tune Turn on, tune in, drop out.
tunnel see the light (at the end of the tunnel)
tunnel tunnel through sth
tunnel tunnel under so/sth
tunnel tunnel vision
turf surf and turf
turkey cold turkey
turkey go cold turkey
turkey talk turkey
turkey turkey's nest
turn at every turn
turn bad penny always turns up.
turn come to a turning point
turn do so a good turn
turn done to a turn
turn Even a worm will turn.
turn every time one turns around
turn I spoke out of turn.
turn in turn
turn It is a long lane that has no turning.
turn It's your turn.
turn leave no stone unturned
turn not know where to turn
turn not know which way to turn
turn One good turn deserves another.
turn out of turn
turn reach a turning point
turn soft answer turneth away wrath.
turn speak out of turn
turn take a new turn
turn take a turn for the better
turn take a turn for the worse
turn take one's turn
turn take turns ((at) doing sth)
turn take turns with so
turn take turns (with sth)

turn tide turned
turn turn a blind eye (to so/sth)
turn turn a deaf ear (to so/sth)
turn turn a place upside down
turn turn a profit
turn turn a trick
turn turn about
turn turn against so/sth
turn turn around
turn turn (away) (from so/sth)
turn turn back (from some place)
turn turn back the clock
turn turn belly up
turn turn in
turn turn in((to) some place)
turn turn into so/sth
turn turn of fate
turn turn of the century
turn turn off
turn turn on
turn Turn on, tune in, drop out.
turn turn one's back (on so/sth)
turn turn one's hand to sth
turn turn one's nose up at so/sth
turn turn one hundred and eighty degrees
turn turn onto sth
turn turn out
turn turn over
turn turn (over) in one's grave
turn turn some place inside out
turn turn so aside
turn turn so down
turn turn so off
turn turn so on
turn turn so or an animal (away) (from sth)
turn turn so or an animal out of sth
turn turn so/sth against so/sth
turn turn so/sth back
turn turn so/sth in (to so/sth)
turn turn so/sth inside out
turn turn so/sth into so/sth
turn turn so/sth over
turn turn so/sth to sth
turn turn so/sth toward so/sth
turn turn so/sth up
turn turn so/sth upside down
turn turn so out
turn turn so's head
turn turn so's stomach
turn turn so's water off
turn turn sth around
turn turn sth aside
turn turn sth down
turn turn sth off
turn turn sth on
turn turn sth out
turn turn sth over in one's mind
turn turn sth to good account
turn turn sth to one's advantage
turn turn sth under (sth)
turn turn sth up
turn turn sth upside down
turn turn tail (and run)
turn turn the clock back
turn turn the corner
turn turn the heat up (on so)
turn turn the other cheek
turn turn the other way
turn turn the tables (on so)
turn turn the tide
turn turn three hundred and sixty degrees

turn turn thumbs down (on so/sth)
turn turn thumbs up (on so/sth)
turn turn to
turn turn turtle
turn turn up
turn turn (up)on so/sth
turn turned off
turn turning point
turn wait one's turn
turn Whatever turns you on.
turn worm (has) turned.
turnabout Turnabout is fair play.
turneth soft answer turneth away wrath.
turnip just fell off the turnip truck
turnip You cannot get blood from a turnip.
turtle turn turtle
tussle tussle with so/sth
twain East is East and West is West (and never the twain shall meet).
tweak tweak sth off (of)
twelve twelve good men and true
twice big as life (and twice as ugly)
twice bigger than life (and twice as ugly)
twice Fool me once, shame on you; fool me twice, shame on me.
twice He gives twice who gives quickly.
twice large as life (and twice as ugly)
twice Lightning never strikes (the same place) twice.
twice Once bitten, twice shy.
twice think twice about so/sth
twice think twice (before doing sth)
twiddle twiddle one's thumbs
twiddle twiddle with sth
twig As the twig is bent, so is the tree inclined.
twilight twilight years
twine twine around sth
twinkle in the twinkling of an eye
twinkle twinkle with sth
twist twist around
twist twist of fate
twist twist (slowly) in the wind
twist twist so around one's little finger
twist twist so's arm
twist twist so's words (around)
twist twist sth around so/sth
twist twist sth into sth
twist twist sth off (of) sth
twist twist sth out of sth
twist twist up
twit in a twit
twitter in a twitter
'twixt There's many a slip 'twixt the cup and the lip.
two alike as (two) peas in a pod
two bird in the hand is worth two in the bush.
two close as two coats of paint
two Don't make two bites of a cherry.
two eyes like two burnt holes in a blanket
two fall between two stools
two find out a thing or two (about so/sth)
two game that two can play
two have two left feet
two If two ride on a horse, one must ride behind.

two If you run after two hares, you will catch neither.
two in two shakes of a lamb's tail
two It cuts two ways.
two It takes two to make a bargain.
two It takes two to make a quarrel.
two (It) takes two to tango.
two kill two birds with one stone
two knock so down a peg (or two)
two know a thing or two (about so/sth)
two know a trick or two
two learn a thing or two (about so/sth)
two lesser (of the two)
two lesser of two evils
two like (two) peas in a pod
two Make it two.
two No man can serve two masters.
two no two ways about it
two not care two hoots about so/sth
two not give two hoots about so/sth
two of two minds (about so/sth)
two old one-two
two One cannot be in two places at once.
two put one's two cents(' worth) in
two put two and two together
two rip sth in two
two stand on one's (own) two feet
two take so down a notch (or two)
two take so down a peg (or two)
two tell so a thing or two (about so/sth)
two That makes two of us.
two There are two sides to every question.
two There are two sides to every story.
two thick as two short planks
two thing or two (about so/sth)
two two bricks shy of a load
two Two can play (at) this game (as well as one).
two Two heads are better than one.
two Two is company, (but) three's a crowd.
two two jumps ahead of so
two two of a kind
two two shakes of a lamb's tail
two two sheets to the wind
two two strikes against one
two two (w)hoops and a holler
two Two wrongs do not make a right.
two two-edged sword
two two-fisted
two two-time loser
two two-time so
two two-way street
two wear two hats
type set type
type strong, silent type
type type over sth
type type sth into sth
type type sth out
type type sth up
ugly big as life (and twice as ugly)
ugly bigger than life (and twice as ugly)
ugly large as life (and twice as ugly)
ugly rear its ugly head
ugly ugly as a toad
ugly ugly as sin
umbrage take umbrage at sth
unaccustomed unaccustomed to so/sth
unaware caught unaware(s)
unbosom unbosom oneself to so

unbowed bloody but unbowed
unburden unburden oneself to so
uncertain in no uncertain terms
uncle cry uncle
uncle Dutch uncle
uncle everybody and his uncle
uncle holler uncle
uncle I'll be a monkey's uncle!
uncle say uncle
under appear under the name of some name
under bear up (under sth)
under belong under sth
under bring so/sth under control
under bring so/sth under one's control
under bring so/sth under so/sth
under buckle under
under build a fire under so
under bury so/sth under sth
under chuck so under the chin
under collapse under so/sth
under come under sth
under come under the hammer
under crack under the strain
under crawl out (from under so/sth)
under creep out (from under so/sth)
under creep under sth
under curse so/sth under one's breath
under curse under one's breath
under cut the ground out from under so
under deliver sth under pressure
under down under
under drink so under the table
under fall under so/sth
under fall under so's spell
under fire under so
under get under so's skin
under get under sth
under give sth under (the) threat of sth
under go under
under groan under sth
under group sth under sth
under half under
under have a burr under one's saddle
under have so/sth under (close) scrutiny
under have so/sth under control
under have so under a spell
under have so under one's spell
under have so under so's thumb
under have so under so's wing(s)
under hide one's light under a bushel
under hold so under so's thumb
under hold under wraps
under hot under the collar
under (I've) been under the weather.
under keep out from under so's feet
under keep so/sth under (close) scrutiny
under keep so/sth under control
under keep so/sth under sth
under keep so under so's thumb
under keep sth under one's hat
under keep sth under wraps
under keep under sth
under keep under wraps
under knock the props out from under so
under knuckle under (to so/sth)
under labor under an assumption
under lay sth under sth
under leave so/sth under so's care
under let grass grow under one's feet
under lie down under sth

under light a fire under so
under live under so/sth
under live under sth (negative)
under live under the same roof (with so)
under look under the hood
under move out (from under so/sth)
under mutter sth under one's breath
under not let the grass grow under one's feet
under not under any circumstances
under out (from under so/sth)
under pass under sth
under peek under sth
under peep under sth
under peer under sth
under pin so/sth under so/sth
under place so/sth under so's care
under place so/sth under so/sth
under plow sth under (sth)
under provide sth under sth
under pull so/sth under
under pull the rug out (from under so)
under put sth under so/sth
under put so under
under put sth under pressure
under put the skids under so/sth
under reel under sth
under remain under sth
under resign under fire
under (right) under so's (very) nose
under sag under sth
under sail under false colors
under say sth under one's breath
under send so/sth under sth
under serve so under so/sth
under sink under (sth)
under six feet under
under smart under sth
under snow so/sth under with sth
under snowed under
under spread sth under so/sth
under stagger under sth
under start a fire under so
under stay under (sth)
under struggle along under sth
under submerge so/sth under sth
under suck so/sth under
under suffer under so
under sweep sth under the carpet
under take so under so's wing(s)
under take sth under advisement
under There is nothing new under the sun.
under think under fire
under tuck sth up (under sth)
under tunnel under sth
under turn sth under (sth)
under under a cloud (of suspicion)
under under a deadline
under under a spell
under under arrest
under under certain circumstances
under under certain conditions
under under (close) scrutiny
under under construction
under under control
under under fire
under under no circumstances
under under normal circumstances
under under oath
under under one's belt
under under one's breath

under under one's own steam
under under pressure
under under so's care
under under so's thumb
under under so's wing(s)
under under the aegis of so
under under the auspices of so
under under the circumstances
under under the counter
under under the gun (about sth)
under under the influence (of alcohol)
under under the sun
under under the table
under under the weather
under under the wire
under under way
under under wraps
under water under the bridge
under work sth under sth
under work under so
under work under sth
under writhe under sth
underneath peek out (from underneath so/sth)
understand come to an understanding (with so)
understand give so to understand sth
understand given to understand
understand I don't understand (it).
understand reach an understanding with so
undertake undertake to do sth
undo What's done cannot be undone.
undone What's done cannot be undone.
uneasy Uneasy lies the head that wears a crown.
unexpected unexpected always happens.
unfamiliar unfamiliar territory
unfold unfold into sth
unfold unfold sth into sth
unforeseen Nothing is certain but the unforeseen.
unglued come unglued
unify unify so/sth into sth
union Union is strength.
unison in unison
unite unite against so/sth
unite unite for sth
unite unite in sth
unite unite so against so/sth
unite unite so in sth
unite unite so/sth into sth
unite unite so/sth (together)
unite unite so/sth with so/sth
unite unite with so
unite United we stand, divided we fall.
unknown unknown quantity
unleash unleash so/sth against so/sth
unleash unleash so/sth (up)on so/sth
unlikely in the unlikely event of sth
unload unload so/sth on(to) so
unload unload sth from sth
unlucky Lucky at cards, unlucky in love.
uno take care of numero uno
unpleasantness late unpleasantness
unquote quote, unquote
unsaid better left unsaid
unseen buy sth sight unseen
unsung unsung hero
until *all hours (of the day and night)

until Call no man happy till he dies.
until carry sth over (until some time)
until Church ain't out till they quit singing.
until Count no man happy till he dies.
until from here till next Tuesday
until (Good-bye) until then.
until It's not over till it's over.
until keep sth until some time
until last (from sth) until sth
until make it (until sth)
until Never halloo till you are out of the woods.
until Never trouble trouble till trouble troubles you.
until postpone sth until sth
until stay up until a particular time
until talk until one is blue in the face
until tide so over (until sth)
until till all hours (of the day and night)
until till hell freezes over
until till kingdom come
until Till next time.
until till the bitter end
until till the fat lady sings
until Till we meet again.
until until all hours
until until hell freezes over
until (un)til the cows come home
until Until we meet again.
until wait up (until sth)
until You never know (what you can do) till you try.
until You never miss the water till the well runs dry.
untimely come to an untimely end
unto Do unto others as you would have them do unto you.
unto law unto oneself
unto Sufficient unto the day is the evil thereof.
unturned leave no stone unturned
unwashed great unwashed
up abut (up) against sth
up act up
up add sth up
up add up (to sth)
up add up to the same thing
up (all) balled up
up (all) dolled up
up (all) dressed up
up all dressed up and nowhere to go
up (all) het up
up all shook up
up all spruced up
up all tore up (about sth)
up allow so up (from sth)
up amount (up) to sth
up ask so up
up average sth up
up back so/sth up to so/sth
up back so up
up back sth up
up back up
up bad penny always turns up.
up ball so/sth up
up ball sth up
up bandage so/sth up
up bang so up
up bang sth up
up bank sth up (against sth)
up bark up the wrong tree

up bash sth up
up batter so/sth up
up Beam me up, Scotty!
up beam so/sth up (to some place)
up beam up
up bear so/sth up
up bear so up
up bear up (against sth)
up bear up (under sth)
up beat oneself up
up beat so up
up beat sth up
up beat up on so
up beef sth up
up beer up
up belch sth up
up belly up
up belt so up
up belt up
up bid sth up
up bind so/sth up (in sth)
up bind so/sth up (with sth)
up bitch so/sth up
up blaze up
up block so up
up block sth up
up blow so/sth up
up blow sth up
up blow up
up blown (up)
up board sth up
up boil sth up
up bollix sth up
up bolster so up
up bolster sth up
up bone up (on sth)
up book sth up
up boost so up
up boot sth up
up boot up
up booze it up
up booze up
up botch sth up
up bottle sth up
up Bottoms up!
up bounce up and down
up bound up with so/sth
up bowl up
up box so up
up box sth up
up boxed (up)
up brace so/sth up
up brace up
up Break it up!
up break so up
up break sth up
up break up
up break (up) (into sth)
up brew so up
up brew up
up brick sth up
up brighten up
up bring so/sth up
up bring so/sth up-to-date
up bring so up for sth
up bring so up on sth
up bring so up sharply
up bring so up short
up bring so up to speed on so/sth
up bring so up-to-date (on so/sth)
up bring sth up
up bring up the rear
up brush sth up

up brush (up) against so/sth
up brush up (on sth)
up bubble up (through sth)
up buck up
up buckle so/sth up
up buckle up
up buddy up (to so)
up buddy up (with so)
up buff sth up
up build so/sth up
up build so up (for sth)
up build sth up
up build up
up bump so/sth up
up bump (up) against so/sth
up bunch so/sth up
up bunch up
up bundle (oneself) up (against sth)
up bundle so up (against sth)
up bundle so up (in sth)
up bung sth up
up bunged up
up bungle sth up
up bunk (up) together
up bunk (up) with so
up buoy so/sth up
up buoy so up
up burn so up
up burn sth up
up burn up
up burned up
up bust so up
up bust sth up
up bust up
up butt (up) against so/sth
up butter so up
up button sth up
up button up
up button (up) one's lip
up buttress sth up
up buy sth up
up cage so/sth up (in sth)
up call so/sth up
up call so up
up call sth up
up camp it up
up carve so/sth up
up carve sth up
up cast so/sth up
up catch so up in sth
up catch so up (on so/sth)
up catch so up short
up catch sth up in sth
up catch up (on so/sth)
up catch up (on sth)
up catch up (to so/sth)
up catch up with so
up catch up (with so/sth)
up caught up in sth
up chain so or an animal up
up chain sth up
up chalk sth up
up charge so up
up charge sth up
up charged up
up chase so/sth up
up check up (on so/sth)
up cheer so up
up cheer up
up chew so/sth up
up chew sth up
up choke so up
up choke sth up

up choke up
up choose (up) sides
up chop so/sth (up) (in(to) sth)
up chuck sth up
up chum up to so
up chum up with so
up churn sth up
up clam up
up clamber up (sth)
up clean one's act up
up clean so/sth up
up clean the floor up with so
up clean up (on sth)
up clean (up) one's plate
up clear sth up
up clear up
up climb up (sth)
up clock sth up
up clog so up
up clog sth up
up clog up
up close so up
up close sth up
up close up
up cloud up
up clutch (up)
up clutter sth up
up cobble sth up
up coil (itself) up
up coil sth up
up collect sth up
up come up
up come (up) from behind
up coming up a cloud
up conjure sth up
up connect so/sth (up) to so/sth
up connect (up) to sth
up connect (up) with so/sth
up cook sth up
up cook up a storm
up cooked up
up coop so/sth up
up cork sth up
up cotton up to so
up cough sth up
up count from sth (up) to sth
up count so/sth up
up count up to sth
up couple up (with so)
up cover so/sth up
up cover so's tracks (up)
up cover sth up
up cover (up) for so
up cozy up (to so)
up crack so/sth up
up crack so up
up crack sth up
up crack up
up cracked up to be sth
up crank so up
up crank sth up
up crease sth up
up creep up
up crinkle up
up crock so/sth up
up crop up
up cross so up
up crum sth up
up crumble sth up (into sth)
up crumble up
up crumple sth up
up crumple up
up crunch so/sth up

up crush sth up
up crush (up) against so/sth
up cuddle up (to so/sth)
up cuddle up with a (good) book
up cuddle up (with so)
up curl sth up
up curl up and die
up curl up (in(to) sth)
up curl up (with a (good) book)
up curl up with so or an animal
up cut so/sth up
up cut so up
up cut the pie up
up cut up
up dam sth up
up dead from the neck up
up deliver sth up to so
up dent sth up
up dig some dirt up (on so)
up dig so/sth up
up Dig up!
up dig up one's tomahawk
up dim sth up
up dirty sth up
up divide sth (up) (between so/sth)
up divvy sth up (between so)
up do so/sth up
up do sth up
up doctor so up
up doll so up
up Don't give up!
up Don't give up the ship!
up Don't give up without a fight!
up Don't give up your day job.
up doors open up (to so)
up dope so or an animal up
up double up (on so/sth)
up double up (with laughter)
up double up (with pain)
up double up (with so)
up drag so up
up drag sth up
up draw oneself up (to sth)
up draw sth up
up draw up
up draw (up) alongside so/sth
up dream sth up
up dredge so/sth up
up dress (oneself) up
up dress sth up
up dress so up (as so/sth)
up dress (up) as so/sth
up dressed (up) fit to kill
up drink sth up
up Drink up!
up drive a price up
up drive so up the wall
up drive so up (to some place)
up drive up (to some place)
up drop up (some place)
up drum sth up
up dry sth up
up dry up
up dude (oneself) up
up duded up
up dummy up
up ease up (on so/sth)
up eat an animal up
up eat so up
up eat sth up
up Eat up!
up eat(en) up with sth
up end sth up

up end up
up even sth up
up Everything's coming up roses.
up face up (to so/sth)
up fade sth up
up fasten sth up
up fatten so or an animal up (with sth)
up fatten up (on sth)
up fed up (to some degree) (with so/sth)
up feel so up
up feel up to sth
up fess up (to sth)
up fetch up
up figure sth up
up fill so/sth up (with sth)
up fill up
up finish so/sth up
up fire so up
up fire sth up
up fire up
up fired up
up firm sth up
up firm up
up fish sth up
up fit so/sth up (with sth)
up fix so/sth up
up fix so up (with so)
up fix so up (with sth)
up fixed up
up fizz up
up flame up
up flare up
up flash sth up (some place)
up fling sth up in so's face
up fling sth up (in sth)
up fling up
up flub sth up
up flub up
up fluff sth up
up fly up to sth
up foam up
up fog sth up
up fog up
up fold sth up
up fold up
up follow so up
up follow sth up
up follow up (on so)
up follow up (on so/sth)
up follow up (on sth)
up force sth up
up form (up) into sth
up foul so/sth up
up foul up
up fouled up
up freeze up
up freshen so/sth up
up freshen up
up from giddy-up to whoa
up from the ground up
up froth sth up
up froth up
up fry sth up
up fuel sth (up)
up fuel up
up full up
up futz sth up
up gab up a storm
up game is up.
up gang up (on so)
up gas sth up
up gas up
up gassed (up)

up gather sth up
up gear so/sth up (for so/sth)
up gear up for so/sth
up get enough courage up (to do sth)
up get enough guts up (to do sth)
up get enough nerve up (to do sth)
up get oneself up
up get (some) steam up
up get so's back up
up get so's blood up
up get so's dander up
up get so's hackles up
up get so's Irish up
up get so up
up get sth up
up get sth wrapped up
up get the courage up (to do sth)
up get the spunk up (to do sth)
up get up
up gird up one's loins
up Give it up!
up give oneself up (to so/sth)
up give so/sth up (for lost)
up give so/sth up (to so)
up give so up for dead
up give sth up
up give up
up go belly up
up go up
up gobble so/sth up
up gobble sth up
up goof so/sth up
up goof up (on sth)
up goofed (up)
up gotta get up pretty early in the morning to do sth
up grind sth up
up grow up
up gum sth up
up gussied up
up gussy so/sth up
up hack sth up
up ham sth up
up hand sth up (to so)
up Hands up!
up hang it up
up hang one's hat (up) somewhere
up hang sth up
up hang up
up hard up (for sth)
up harden sth up
up harness an animal up
up hash sth up
up haul so (up) before so/sth
up haul sth up (from sth)
up haul up (somewhere)
up have a corncob up one's ass
up have an ace up one's sleeve
up have had it (up to here)
up have so up (for sth)
up have sth hung up and salted
up have sth up one's sleeve
up have sth wrapped up
up head for the last roundup
up head sth up
up Heads up!
up heal up
up heap sth up
up heat so up
up heat sth up (to sth)
up heat up
up heave sth up
up heist so/sth (up)

up help so up (from sth)
up hepped (up)
up hike sth up
up hit so up (for sth)
up hitch so/sth (up) (to sth)
up hoard sth up
up hold one's end of the bargain up
up hold one's end up
up hold one's head up
up hold so/sth up
up hold so up to sth
up hold up
up hole up (somewhere)
up hooched (up)
up hook so/sth up (to so/sth)
up hook so up (with so)
up hook sth up
up hook up with so
up hop sth up
up hop up (to so/sth)
up hopped up
up huddle (up) (together)
up hunch sth up
up hunch up
up hung up (on so/sth)
up hunt so/sth up
up hurry so/sth up
up hurry up
up hush so up
up hush sth up
up hush up
up hustle up
up hype so/sth (up)
up I was up all night with a sick friend.
up I wasn't brought up in the woods to be scared by owls.
up I won't give up without a fight.
up ice sth up
up ice up
up If you lie down with dogs, you will get up with fleas.
up I'll look you up when I'm in town.
up I'm (really) fed up (with so/sth).
up Is there some place I can wash up?
up It is easier to tear down than to build up.
up It's a toss-up.
up I've had it up to here (with so/sth).
up jack so up
up jack sth up
up jam sth up
up jam sth (up) with sth
up jazz so/sth up
up jazzed (up)
up jerk sth up
up jig is up.
up jimmy sth up
up join up
up join (up) with so/sth
up jugged (up)
up juice sth up
up juice up
up jumble sth up
up jump up (from sth)
up jump up (on so/sth)
up jump up (to sth)
up keep an act up
up Keep it up!
up keep one's act up
up keep one's chin up
up keep one's end of the bargain up
up keep one's end up
up keep so up

up keep sth up
up keep up an act
up keep up appearances
up keep up one's act
up Keep up the good work.
up keep up (with so/sth)
up keep up with the Joneses
up keep up with the times
up Keep your chin up.
up key so up
up keyed up (about sth)
up kick one's heels up
up kick up
up kink up
up kiss and make up
up kiss up to so
up knock one's head (up) against a brick wall
up knock so up
up knock (up) against so/sth
up knocked up
up lace so up
up lace sth up
up ladle sth up
up laid up
up land up somehow
up lap sth up
up lap (up) against sth
up last roundup
up lather sth up
up lather up
up laugh up one's sleeve
up lay so up
up lay sth up
up lead so up sth
up lead so up the garden path
up lead up to sth
up leap up
up learn sth from the bottom up
up leave so up in the air
up leave sth up
up leg up
up let up
up level sth up
up lick sth up
up lift so/sth up
up lift up
up light so/sth up
up light sth up
up light up
up lighten sth up
up lighten up
up limber so/sth up
up line so/sth up
up line so up behind so/sth
up line so up (for sth)
up line so up (with so)
up line up
up link so/sth up (to sth)
up link up to so/sth
up liquor so up
up liquor up
up listen up
up litter sth up
up live it up
up live up to one's end of the bargain
up live up to sth
up liven sth up
up load so/sth up (with so/sth)
up load up (with sth)
up lock so or an animal (up) in (sth)
up lock so/sth up (somewhere)
up log sth up

up Look me up when you're in town.
up look so/sth up
up look up
up loom up
up loosen so/sth up
up loosen so up
up loosen up
up louse so/sth up
up make one's mind up (about so/sth)
up make (oneself) up
up make so's bed (up)
up make so's mind up
up make so up
up make sth up
up make the bed (up)
up make up
up Make your mind up.
up mar sth up
up mark sth up
up marry up (with so)
up mash sth up
up match so (up) (with so)
up match up
up measure so up against so/sth
up measure up (to so/sth)
up meet up with so/sth
up mess so's face up
up mess so up
up mess sth up
up mess up
up messed up
up mist up
up mix it up (with so)
up mix so up
up mix sth up
up mixed up in sth
up mixed up with so else
up mock sth up
up mop sth up
up mop the floor up with so
up mop up (after so/sth)
up mopping-up operation
up mound sth up
up mount up
up move so/sth up
up move so up
up move up
up muck sth up
up muddle sth up
up muddled (up)
up muddy sth up
up muffle sth up
up mung sth up
up muss so/sth up
up muster sth up
up nail sth up
up need a pick-me-up
up nestle (up) against so/sth
up nick sth up
up not all sth is cracked up to be
up not get one's hopes up
up not know which end is up
up not up to scratch
up not up to snuff
up not what sth is cracked up to be
up notch sth up
up nut up
up nuzzle up against so/sth
up offer sth up (to so/sth)
up on the up-and-up
up one's number is up
up one up (on so)
up open so up

up open sth up
up open up
up open (up) one's kimono
up own up to so
up own up (to sth)
up pace up and down
up pack sth up (in sth)
up pack up
up pair up (with so)
up pal up (with so)
up parcel sth up
up pass so/sth up
up paste sth up
up patch a quarrel up
up patch so up
up patch sth up
up pay sth up
up pay up
up peck sth up
up pen so or an animal up
up pep so/sth up
up perk so up
up perk sth up
up perk up
up permit so up (sth)
up permit so up to sth
up phone so up
up pick so up
up pick sth up
up pick up
up pile sth up
up pile up
up pin sth up
up pipe up (with sth)
up pipped (up)
up place sth up against sth
up plaster sth up
up play so/sth up
up play sth up
up play up to so
up (Please) don't get up.
up plow sth up
up pluck up so's courage
up plug sth up
up plump sth up
up point sth up
up polish sth up
up pop sth up
up pop up
up post sth up
up pot sth up
up pound sth up
up powder up
up power sth up
up power up
up pretty oneself or sth up
up price sth up
up prick up its ears
up primp (oneself) up
up print sth up
up prop so/sth up (against so/sth)
up pry sth up
up psych so up
up psych up
up psyched (up)
up psyched up (for sth)
up pucker sth up
up pucker up
up puff so/sth up
up puff up
up pull oneself up by one's (own) bootstraps
up pull so/sth up

up pull so up short
up pull sth up
up Pull up a chair.
up pull (up) alongside ((of) so/sth)
up pull up (somewhere)
up pull up stakes
up pull up to sth
up pump so up (for sth)
up pump sth up
up pumped (up)
up punch sth up
up purse sth up
up push so/sth up
up push so up against the wall
up push sth (up) against so/sth
up push (up) against so/sth
up push up on sth
up pushing up (the) daisies
up Put 'em up!
up put money up (for sth)
up put one's feet up
up put one's hair up
up put one's hand up
up put so's back up
up put so up
up put sth up
up put up a (brave) front
up put up a fight
up put up a struggle
up put up one's dukes
up Put up or shut up!
up put up with so/sth
up put-up job
up queue up (for sth)
up race up to so/sth
up rack sth up
up raise so/sth up
up raise up
up rake sth up
up ralph sth up
up reach sth up to so
up read up (on so/sth)
up rear up
up rein sth up
up rein up
up remain up
up rest up (for sth)
up rest up (from sth)
up rev sth up
up rev up
up ride up (on so)
up rig sth up
up right side up
up right up so's alley
up rile so up
up ring so up
up ring sth up
up ring the curtain up
up rip so/sth up
up rip sth up
up rise up
up rise (up) against so/sth
up roll one's sleeves up
up roll (oneself) up in sth
up roll so/sth (up) in sth
up roll sth up
up root sth up
up rope so or an animal up
up rough so up
up rough sth up
up round so/sth up
up round sth up
up round up to sth

up rub sth up
up rub (up) against so/sth
up ruffle sth up
up rumple so/sth up
up run sth up
up run up against so/sth
up run up to some place
up run up (to so/sth)
up rustle sth up
up sack sth up
up saddle an animal up
up saddle up
up sail up a river
up save money up (for sth)
up save sth up
up save (up) (for sth)
up saw sth (up) (in(to) sth)
up scare so/sth up
up scoop sth up
up score sth (up) against so/sth
up scout so/sth up
up scratch so/sth up
up screw so/sth up
up screw so up
up screw sth up
up screw up
up screwed up
up scrounge so/sth up
up scrub up
up scrunch sth up
up scuff sth up
up seal sth (up) (with sth)
up sealed (up)
up see so up to sth
up seize sth up
up seize up
up send so/sth up
up send so up
up send up a trial balloon
up serve sth up
up set so/sth up against so/sth
up set so/sth up as sth
up set so up
up set sth up
up set up shop somewhere
up settle up with so
up sew so/sth up
up sewed up
up shack up (with so)
up Shake it (up)!
up shake so/sth up
up shake so up
up shake sth up
up shape so up
up shape up
up shine up to so
up shook up
up shoot a place up
up shoot up
up shore so up
up shore sth up
up show so up
up show up
up shush (up)
up shut so up
up Shut up!
up Shut up about it.
up sick (up)
up sidle up (to so/sth)
up sign so up (for sth)
up sign so up (with so/sth)
up sign up (for sth)
up sign (up) with so/sth

up silt up
up sing up a storm
up sit up
up size so/sth up
up slack up (on sth)
up slice so/sth up
up slick sth up
up slip up
up slob up
up slope up (to sth)
up slow so/sth up
up slow up
up slush up
up smarten up
up smash sth up
up smell sth up
up smoke sth up
up Snap it up!
up snap sth up
up snarl so/sth up
up snatch sth up
up snazz sth up
up sneak up on so/sth
up sneak up to so/sth
up snuggle (up) against so/sth
up snuggle up (to so/sth)
up soak sth up
up sober so up
up sober up
up soften so up
up soften sth up
up soften up
up (so's) ups and downs
up something's up
up somewhere to hang (up) one's hat
up sop so up
up soup sth up
up souped up
up spade sth up
up spatter so/sth up
up speak up
up speed so/sth up
up speed up
up spew sth up
up spice sth up
up spiff sth up
up spiffed up
up spiral up
up spit sth up
up spit up
up splash so/sth up
up splatter so/sth up
up split people up
up split so/sth up (into sth)
up split up (with so)
up sponge sth up
up spoon sth up
up spring up
up sprout up
up spruce so/sth up
up square sth up
up square up (for fighting)
up square up to so/sth
up square up with so
up squash so/sth up
up squash up against so/sth
up squeeze so/sth up
up squeeze (themselves) up
up squeeze up against so/sth
up stack sth up
up stack up
up stand so up
up stand up

up start so up (in sth)
up start sth up
up start up
up stay up (for sth)
up stay up late
up stay up until a particular time
up steal up on so/sth
up steam so up
up steam sth up
up steam up
up steamed (up)
up step right up
up step sth up
up step up
up Stick 'em up!
up stick one's nose up in the air
up stick so/sth up
up stick sth up
up stick up
up stiffen sth up
up stiffen up
up stink sth up
up stir so up
up stir sth up
up stir up a hornet's nest
up stitch sth up
up stock sth (up) with sth
up stock up (on sth)
up stock up (with sth)
up stoke sth up
up stop sth up (with sth)
up stop up
up store sth up
up straight up
up straighten so/sth up
up straighten up
up (strictly) on the up-and-up
up strike sth up
up strike up a conversation
up strike up a friendship
up strike up the band
up string so up
up study up on so/sth
up stuff sth up
up suck sth up
up suck up to so
up suit (oneself) up
up sum (sth) up
up summon sth up
up sunny-side up
up surge up
up swallow so/sth up
up sweep sth up
up sweep up
up sweeten so up
up sweeten sth up
up sweeten (up) the deal
up swell up
up tack sth up
up take a collection up (from so) (for so/sth)
up take so up
up take sth up
up take the slack up
up take up arms (against so/sth)
up take up one's abode some place
up take up residence some place
up take up room
up take up (so's) time
up take up space
up take up the challenge
up take up where one left off
up take up with so

up talk so/sth up
up talk sth up
up talk up a storm
up tally sth up
up tangle so/sth up
up tank up (on sth)
up team up against so/sth
up team up (with so)
up tear so up
up tear sth up
up teed (up)
up tense up (for sth)
up That (really) burns me (up)!
up thicken sth up
up Things are looking up.
up think sth up
up throw one's hands up (in despair)
up throw one's hands up in horror
up throw sth up
up throw up
up thrust up through sth
up thumbs up
up tidy sth up
up tidy up
up tie so/sth up
up tie so (up) in knots
up tie sth up
up tie traffic up
up tie up (some place)
up tied up
up tighten sth up
up tighten up
up Time is up.
up tip sth up
up toady (up) to so
up toil up sth
up tone so/sth up
up tool sth up
up tool up
up top sth up
up tore (up)
up torn (up)
up toss sth up
up total sth up
up tote sth up
up touch so (up) for sth
up touch sth up
up toughen so/sth up
up toughen up
up track sth up
up trade up from sth
up trade up (to sth)
up train up to sth
up trip so up
up true sth up
up trump sth up
up trumped up
up truss so/sth up
up tuck sth up
up tune sth up
up tune up
up turn belly up
up turn one's nose up at so/sth
up turn so/sth up
up turn sth up
up turn the heat up (on so)
up turn thumbs up (on so/sth)
up turn up
up twist up
up type sth up
up up a blind alley
up up a creek
up up a storm

up up a tree
up up against so/sth
up up against sth
up up against the wall
up (up and) about
up up and at 'em
up up and away
up up and did sth
up up and running
up up before so
up up for auction
up up for grabs
up up for reelection
up up for sale
up up for sth
up up front
up up in arms
up up in the air (about so/sth)
up up in years
up up North
up up on so/sth
up up one side and down the other
up up stakes
up up the ante
up up the creek (without a paddle)
up up the pole
up up the river
up up the wall
up up to doing sth
up up to here (with sth)
up up to no good
up up to one's ears (in sth)
up up to one's eyeballs (in sth)
up up to one's knees
up up to one's neck (in sth)
up up to par
up up to snuff
up up to so/sth
up up to sth
up up to speed
up up to the minute
up up with so
up up-and-coming
up up-to-date
up up-to-the-minute
up use so up
up use sth up
up vacuum sth up (from sth)
up vomit sth up
up Wait up (a minute)!
up wait up (for so/sth)
up wait up (until sth)
up wake so or an animal up
up wake so (up) from sth
up wake so up (to sth)
up wake up
up wake (up) from sth
up wake (up) to sth
up walk right up (to so/sth)
up walk up sth
up walk up to so/sth
up wall sth up
up waltz up (to so)
up want a pick-me-up
up warm so/sth up
up warm so up
up warm up
up wash so/sth up
up wash so up
up wash up (for sth)
up washed up
up weigh sth up
up well up (from sth)

up well up in years
up well up (inside so)
up well up (out of sth)
up well up with sth
up whack so/sth up
up whack sth up
up What goes up must come down.
up What have you been up to?
up What's up?
up What's up, doc?
up what so/sth is cracked up to be
up Where can I wash up?
up whip so up
up whip sth up
up whoop it up
up wind so up
up wind sth up
up wind sth (up) (into sth)
up wind up (as) sth
up wind up (by) doing sth
up wind up somehow
up wind up (somewhere)
up wind up with so/sth
up wipe sth up
up wipe the floor up with so
up wire sth up
up wise so up (about so/sth)
up wise up (to so/sth)
up wither up
up work one's way up (to sth)
up work oneself up
up work oneself (up) into a lather
up work so up
up work sth up
up work up a sweat
up work up a thirst
up work up to sth
up worked up (over sth)
up wrap so/sth (up) (in sth)
up wrap so/sth (up) (with sth)
up wrap sth up
up wrapped up
up wrinkle sth up
up wrinkle up
up write so/sth up
up write sth up
up wrought up
up yack sth up
up yank sth up
up yield so/sth up (to so)
up You (always) give up too eas(il)y.
up Zip it up!
up zip sth up
up Zip (up) your lip!
up zoom up
upbraid upbraid so for sth
update update so about so/sth
upgrade upgrade so/sth to sth
upgrade upgrade to sth
uphill uphill battle
upon act (up)on sth
upon advance (up)on so/sth
upon agree (up)on so/sth
upon alight (up)on so/sth
upon appear (up)on sth
upon arrive (somewhere) (up)on the stroke of some time
upon arrive (up)on the scene (of sth)
upon As you make your bed, so you must lie (up)on it.
upon base sth (up)on so/sth
upon bear (up)on sth
upon border (up)on sth

upon breathe (up)on so/sth
upon bring sth (up)on oneself
upon build sth (up)on sth
upon build (up)on sth
upon burst in ((up)on so/sth)
upon burst (up)on so
upon burst (up)on the scene
upon call (up)on so
upon call (up)on so (for sth)
upon call (up)on so (to do sth)
upon Cast one's bread upon the waters.
upon chance (up)on so/sth
upon come (up)on so/sth
upon concentrate (up)on so/sth
upon confer sth (up)on so
upon congratulate so (up)on sth
upon converge (up)on so/sth
upon count (up)on so/sth
upon dawn (up)on so
upon decide (up)on so/sth
upon depend (up)on so/sth
upon descend (up)on so/sth
upon devolve (up)on so/sth
upon discourse (up)on so/sth
upon dote (up)on so/sth
upon draw upon sth
upon dwell (up)on so/sth
upon dwell (up)on sth
upon encroach (up)on so/sth
upon enlarge (up)on sth
upon enter (up)on sth
upon expand (up)on sth
upon experiment (up)on so/sth
upon expound ((up)on so/sth) (to so)
upon fall (up)on so
upon fasten (up)on so/sth
upon fawn (up)on so
upon feast one's eyes ((up)on so/sth)
upon feast (up)on sth
upon feed (up)on so/sth
upon fire (up)on so/sth
upon fix (up)on so/sth
upon flank (up)on so/sth
upon float (up)on sth
upon found sth (up)on sth
upon happen (up)on so/sth
upon heap sth (up)on so/sth
upon hinge (up)on so/sth
upon hit (up)on so/sth
upon impact (up)on so/sth
upon impinge (up)on so/sth
upon impose sth (up)on so
upon impose (up)on so
upon impress sth (up)on so
upon impress sth (up)on sth
upon improve (up)on sth
upon incumbent (up)on so to do sth
upon inflict so (up)on so
upon inflict sth (up)on so/sth
upon infringe (up)on sth
upon insist (up)on sth
upon intrude (up)on so/sth
upon invoke sth (up)on so/sth
upon land (up)on both feet
upon land (up)on one's feet
upon land (up)on sth
upon launch forth ((up)on sth)
upon lavish sth (up)on so
upon levy sth (up)on so/sth
upon lie (up)on so
upon light (up)on so/sth
upon look (up)on so/sth as sth
upon look (up)on so/sth with sth

upon once upon a time
upon play (up)on sth
upon ponder (up)on sth
upon pounce (up)on so/sth
upon practice (up)on so/sth
upon predicate sth (up)on sth
upon press sth (up)on so
upon press (up)on so/sth
upon presume (up)on so/sth
upon prevail (up)on so/sth (to do sth)
upon prey (up)on so/sth
upon put upon by so
upon rain (up)on so/sth
upon reflect (back) (up)on so/sth
upon reflect credit (up)on so/sth
upon rely (up)on so/sth
upon remark (up)on so/sth
upon report (up)on so/sth
upon repose (up)on sth
upon rest (up)on sth
upon revenge oneself (up)on so/sth
upon ride (up)on so/sth
upon seize (up)on sth
upon set sth (up)on sth
upon set upon so/sth
upon shut the door (up)on so/sth
upon sit in judgment (up)on so/sth
upon smile (up)on so/sth
upon speak (up)on sth
upon spit (up)on so/sth
upon spring (up)on so/sth or an animal
upon spy (up)on so/sth
upon stamp sth (up)on so/sth
upon stand (up)on so/sth
upon strike sth (up)on sth
upon stumble (up)on so/sth
upon swear (up)on so/sth
upon swoop down (up)on so/sth
upon take it upon oneself to do sth
upon take sth (up)on oneself
upon think (up)on so/sth
upon thrive (up)on sth
upon touch (up)on sth
upon trample (up)on so/sth
upon tread (up)on so/sth
upon trespass (up)on sth
upon turn in (up)on oneself
upon turn (up)on so/sth
upon unleash so/sth (up)on so/sth
upon upon impact
upon (up)on so
upon urge sth (up)on so
upon vent sth (up)on so/sth
upon venture (up)on so/sth
upon verge (up)on sth
upon visit sth (up)on so
upon vote (up)on so/sth
upon wait (up)on so
upon wear sth (up)on sth
upon wear (up)on so
upon wear (up)on so
upon weigh (up)on so
upon work (up)on sth
upon wreak sth (up)on so/sth
upon wreak vengeance (up)on so/sth
upon write so/sth on
upper Keep a stiff upper lip.
upper upper crust
upper upper hand (on so)
upper upper story
upright empty sack cannot stand upright.
upright sit bolt upright

uproar create an uproar
uproar Don't get your bowels in an uproar!
uproar get one's bowels in an uproar
uproar make an uproar
uproot uproot so from some place
uproot uproot sth from some place
upset I don't want to upset you, but
upset upset so's plans
upset upset the apple cart
upshot upshot of sth
upside turn a place upside down
upside turn so/sth upside down
upside turn sth upside down
upside upside-down
upstairs nothing upstairs
uptake quick on the uptake
uptake slow on the uptake
urban urban legend
urge urge so along
urge urge so forward
urge urge so to do sth
urge urge sth (up)on so
us Can you excuse us, please?
us Come back and see us.
us Conscience does make cowards of us all.
us Could you excuse us, please?
us did everything he could 'cept eat us
us Don't call us, we'll call you.
us Give us the tools, and we will finish the job.
us Heaven help us!
us Let us do sth.
us That makes two of us.
us Will you excuse us, please?
us (Would you) care to join us?
us Would you excuse us, please?
use Can I use your powder room?
use close enough to use the same toothpick
use come in useful
use Could I use your powder room?
use *firm hand
use have (a) use for so/sth
use in use
use It's no use crying over spilled milk.
use It takes (some) getting used to.
use Keep a thing seven years and you'll (always) find a use for it.
use lose the use of sth
use make (good) use of sth
use make use of so/sth
use May I use your powder room?
use not as young as one used to be
use put sth into use
use put sth to (good) use
use serve a (useful) purpose
use *some shut-eye
use They don't make them like they used to.
use use a firm hand
use use every trick in the book
use use foul language
use use one's head
use use one's noggin
use use one's noodle
use use some elbow grease
use use some shut-eye
use use so/sth as an excuse
use use so/sth as sth
use use so/sth for sth

use use so up
use use sth before sth
use use sth by sth
use use sth over (again)
use use sth up
use use sth with sth
use use strong language
use use the bathroom
use use the race card
use use the toilet
use use your head for more than a hatrack
use use your head for more than something to keep your ears apart
use used to do sth
use used to so/sth
use user friendly
used It takes (some) getting used to.
used not as young as one used to be
used They don't make them like they used to.
used used to do sth
used used to so/sth
useful come in useful
useful serve a (useful) purpose
usher usher so/sth into some place
usher usher so/sth out of some place
usher usher so to sth
usual as usual
usual business as usual
utilize utilize so/sth for sth
utmost do one's utmost (to do sth)
utter not utter a word
vacation on vacation
vacation take a vacation
vaccinate vaccinate so or an animal against sth
vaccinate vaccinate so or an animal with sth
vacillate vacillate between so and so else or sth and sth else
vacuum Nature abhors a vacuum.
vacuum vacuum sth out
vacuum vacuum sth up (from sth)
vain in vain
vain vain as a peacock
vale (this) vale of tears
valor Discretion is the better part of valor.
value at face value
value take so/sth at face value
value take sth at face value
value value so/sth above so/sth
value value so/sth as sth
value value so/sth for sth
value value sth at sth
vanish vanish away
vanish vanish from sth
vanish vanish into sth
vanish vanish into thin air
variety Variety is the spice of life.
vary vary between so and so else
vary vary between sth and sth else
vary vary (from sth) (in sth)
vary vary from sth to sth
vary vary with sth
vault vault into sth
vault vault over sth
veer veer (away) (from so/sth)
veer veer off (from so/sth)
veer veer toward so/sth
veg veg out
veg vegged out
velvet rule with a velvet glove

velvet soft as velvet
vengeance do sth with a vengeance
vengeance flame with vengeance
vengeance with a vengeance
vengeance wreak vengeance (up)on so/sth
vent give vent to sth
vent vent one's spleen
vent vent sth (up)on so/sth
venture Nothing ventured, nothing gained.
venture venture forth
venture venture out ((of) sth)
venture venture (up)on so/sth
verdict bring a verdict in
verge on the verge of doing sth
verge verge into sth
verge verge (up)on sth
verify verify sth with so
verse chapter and verse
very arrive in the (very) nick of time
very at the (very) outside
very happen in the (very) nick of time
very (I'm) (very) glad to meet you.
very in the (very) nick of time
very reach sth in the (very) nick of time
very (right) under so's (very) nose
very save so in the (very) nick of time
very Thank you very much.
very that very thing
very The very idea!
very Very good.
very very last
very (very) picture of sth
very very thing
vessel Empty vessels make the most sound.
vest keep one's cards close to one's vest
vest vest so with sth
vest vest sth in so/sth
vest vested interest in sth
vicious in a vicious circle
victor To the victors belong the spoils.
victory landslide victory
victory snatch victory from the jaws of defeat
vie vie (with so) (for so/sth)
view bird's-eye view
view bring so/sth into view
view come into view
view Distance lends enchantment (to the view).
view fade from view
view flash into view
view in my view
view in view of sth
view on view
view point of view
view take a dim view of so/sth
view with a view to doing sth
vigor vim and vigor
villain villain of the piece
vim vim and vigor
vindicate vindicate so of sth
vine all vine and no taters
vine die on the vine
vine wither on the vine
vinegar sour as vinegar
vinegar You can catch more flies with honey than with vinegar.
violet shrinking violet
virtual virtual reality
virtue by virtue of sth

virtue make a virtue of necessity
virtue Patience is a virtue.
virtue Virtue is its own reward.
visible visible to the naked eye
vision tunnel vision
visit come around (for a visit)
visit come around (to visit)
visit pay a visit to so/sth
visit pay (so/sth) a visit
visit pop around (for a visit)
visit pop by (for a visit)
visit pop down (for a visit)
visit pop in (for a visit)
visit pop over (for a visit)
visit visit from the stork
visit visit sth (up)on so
visit visit the plumbing
visit visit with so
visualize visualize so/sth as so/sth
visually visually impaired
vodka clear as vodka
vogue in vogue
voice at the top of one's voice
voice give voice to sth
voice (It's) good to hear your voice.
voice lower one's voice
voice raise one's voice against so/sth
voice raise one's voice (to so)
voice talk to hear one's own voice
voice throw one's voice
voice voice (in sth)
void null and void
volume speak volumes
volunteer volunteer as sth
volunteer volunteer for sth
vomit vomit sth out
vomit vomit sth up
vote abstain from voting
vote cast one's vote
vote vote a split ticket
vote vote a straight ticket
vote vote against so/sth
vote vote for so/sth
vote vote of confidence
vote vote of thanks
vote vote so into sth
vote vote so on(to sth)
vote vote so/sth down
vote vote so out of sth
vote vote sth into law
vote vote sth through
vote vote (up)on so/sth
vote vote with one's feet
vouch vouch for so/sth
voyage maiden voyage
vulture culture vulture
wad shoot one's wad
wade wade across sth
wade wade in(to sth)
wade wade through sth
waffle waffle around
wag cause (some) tongues to wag
wag tail wagging the dog
wag wag one's chin
wage freeze so's wages
wage The wages of sin is death.
wage wage sth against so/sth
wager wager on so/sth
wager wager sth on so/sth
wagon fall off the wagon
wagon fix so's wagon
wagon Hitch your wagon to a star.
wagon off the wagon

wagon on the wagon
wait can't wait (for sth (to happen))
wait can't wait (to do sth)
wait Everything comes to him who waits.
wait Good things come to him who waits.
wait hurry up and wait
wait I felt like a penny waiting for change.
wait It's ill waiting for dead men's shoes.
wait Just (you) wait (and see)!
wait lie in wait (for so/sth)
wait moment everyone has been waiting for
wait not able to wait
wait on the waiting list
wait They also serve who only stand and wait.
wait Time and tide wait for no man.
wait wait (around) (for so/sth)
wait wait at sth (for so/sth)
wait wait for the next wave
wait wait for the other shoe to drop
wait wait on so hand and foot
wait wait (on) tables
wait wait one's turn
wait wait sth out
wait Wait up (a minute)!
wait wait up (for so/sth)
wait wait up (until sth)
wait wait (up)on so
wait wait-and-see attitude
wait waiting in the wings
wait You (just) wait (and see)!
wake awake(n) from sth
wake awake(n) so from sth
wake awake(n) so to sth
wake awake(n) to sth
wake in the wake of sth
wake wake so or an animal up
wake wake so (up) from sth
wake wake so up (to sth)
wake wake the dead
wake wake up
wake wake (up) from sth
wake wake (up) to sth
walk all walks of life
walk cock of the walk
walk every walk of life
walk *in (a) single file
walk one's walking papers
walk Speak of the devil (and in he walks).
walk Take a long walk off a short pier.
walk take a walk
walk walk a tightrope
walk walk across sth
walk walk ahead of so/sth
walk walk all over so/sth
walk walk along
walk walk arm in arm
walk walk around
walk walk away from so/sth
walk walk away with so or an animal
walk walk away with sth
walk walk back ((to) sth)
walk walk down sth
walk walk hand in hand
walk walk in (a) single file
walk walk in on so/sth
walk walk in(to sth)

walk walk off
walk walk on
walk walk out (of sth)
walk walk out (on so)
walk walk out (on sth)
walk walk out with so
walk walk over (to so/sth)
walk walk right in
walk walk (right) into a trap
walk walk (right) into so/sth
walk walk right up (to so/sth)
walk walk soft
walk walk so out
walk walk so over to so/sth
walk walk so's feet off
walk walk so through sth
walk walk tall
walk walk the floor
walk walk the plank
walk walk through sth
walk walk together
walk walk up sth
walk walk up to so/sth
walk walk with so
walk walk with sth
walk We must learn to walk before we can run.
walk within walking distance
walk worship the ground so walks on
wall bang one's head against a brick wall
wall beat one's head against the wall
wall between you and me and these four walls
wall climb the wall(s)
wall drive so to the wall
wall drive so up the wall
wall force so to the wall
wall go over the wall
wall go to the wall (on sth)
wall go up the wall
wall have one's back to the wall
wall hole in the wall
wall knock one's head (up) against a brick wall
wall nail so('s hide) to the wall
wall off-the-wall
wall over the wall
wall press so to the wall
wall push so to the wall
wall push so up against the wall
wall read the handwriting on the wall
wall run into a stone wall
wall run one's head against a brick wall
wall see the (hand)writing on the wall
wall send so up the wall
wall up against the wall
wall up the wall
wall wall so/sth in
wall wall so/sth off
wall wall sth off (from so/sth)
wall wall sth up
wall Walls have ears.
wall wall-to-wall (with) sth
wallop pack a wallop
wallow wallow (around) in sth
wallow wallow in sth
waltz waltz around sth
waltz waltz in(to some place)
waltz waltz off
waltz waltz through sth
waltz waltz up (to so)
wander wander about

wander wander away (from so/sth)
wander wander from sth
wander wander in(to sth)
wander wander off (from so/sth)
wane on the wane
wane wax and wane
wangle wangle out of sth
wangle wangle sth from so
wanna Wanna make sumpin' of it?
want (Do you) want to know something?
want (Do you) want to make something of it?
want (Do) you want to step outside?
want For want of a nail the shoe was lost; for want of a shoe the horse was lost; and for want of a horse the man was lost.
want He that hath a full purse never wanted a friend.
want I don't want to alarm you, but
want I don't want to sound like a busybody, but
want I don't want to upset you, but
want I don't want to wear out my welcome.
want (I) just want(ed) to mention sth.
want (I) just want(ed) to say sth.
want If you don't see what you want, please ask (for it).
want If you want a thing done well, do it yourself.
want If you want peace, (you must) prepare for war.
want know when one is not wanted
want more you get, the more you want.
want more you have, the more you want.
want not want to catch so doing sth
want *on a silver platter
want put one's nose in (where it's not wanted)
want *so bad one can taste it
want stick one's nose in (where it's not wanted)
want thing you don't want is dear at any price.
want Wanna make sumpin' of it?
want want a knuckle sandwich
want want a pick-me-up
want Want a piece of me?
want want first crack at sth
want want for nothing
want want for sth
want want in((to) sth)
want want off ((of) sth)
want want out (of sth)
want want so bad one can taste it
want want so for sth
want want so/sth back
want want so/sth in sth
want want so/sth out of sth
want want sth for so/sth
want want sth on a silver platter
want Want to make something of it?
want Waste not, want not.
want What do you want me to say?
want Who do you want to speak to?
want Who do you want (to talk to)?
want wouldn't want to be in so's shoes
want (You) want a piece of me?
want (You want to) know something?

want You want to make something of it?
war act of war
war All's fair in love and war.
war all-out war
war Councils of war never fight.
war declare war against so/sth
war go to war (over so/sth)
war If you want peace, (you must) prepare for war.
war make war (on so/sth)
war war against so/sth
war war over so/sth
war war with so
ward ward so/sth off
warhorse old warhorse
warhorse perform an old warhorse
warhorse play an old warhorse
warm Cold hands, warm heart.
warm feel like death warmed over
warm like death warmed over
warm look like death warmed over
warm warm as toast
warm warm body
warm warm so/sth up
warm warm so up
warm warm sth over
warm warm the bench
warm warm the cockles of so's heart
warm warm up
warm warmed over
warn warn so about so/sth
warn warn so against so/sth
warn warn so away from so/sth
warn warn so of sth
warn warn so off
warpath on the warpath
warrant put out a warrant (on so)
warrant sign one's own death warrant
wart warts and all
wart worrywart
was as I was saying
was couldn't pour water out of a boot (if there was instructions on the heel)
was For want of a nail the shoe was lost; for want of a shoe the horse was lost; and for want of a horse the man was lost.
was good time was had by all.
was (had) known it was coming
was (I was) just wondering.
was I was up all night with a sick friend.
was I wasn't brought up in the woods to be scared by owls.
was If it was a snake it woulda bit you.
was knew it was coming
was like I was saying
was like it was going out of style
was (Now,) where was I?
was Rome was not built in a day.
was since so was knee-high to a grasshopper
was time was (when)
was was had
was What was the name again?
was Who was it?
wash chief cook and bottle washer
wash come out in the wash
wash Do not wash your dirty linen in public.
wash great unwashed
wash I have to wash a few things out.

wash Is there some place I can wash up?
wash It won't wash!
wash It'll all come out in the wash.
wash wash away
wash wash off ((of) so/sth)
wash wash one's dirty linen in public
wash wash one's hands of so/sth
wash wash out
wash wash over so
wash wash overboard
wash wash so/sth away
wash wash so/sth off
wash wash so/sth overboard
wash wash so/sth up
wash wash so out
wash wash so up
wash wash sth away
wash wash sth down sth
wash wash sth down (with sth)
wash wash sth of sth
wash wash sth off (of) so/sth
wash wash sth out
wash wash up (for sth)
wash washed out
wash washed up
wash Where can I wash up?
waste Don't waste my time.
waste Don't waste your breath.
waste Don't waste your time.
waste go to waste
waste Haste makes waste.
waste lay sth to waste
waste lay waste to sth
waste time's a-wastin'
waste waste away
waste Waste not, want not.
waste waste of space
waste waste one's breath
waste waste so
waste waste sth away
waste waste sth on so/sth
waste You're (just) wasting my time.
wasting time's a-wastin'
watch about as exciting as watching (the) paint dry
watch bear watching
watch clock-watcher
watch exciting as watching (the) paint dry
watch keep a close watch on so/sth
watch keep (close) watch (on so/sth)
watch keep (close) watch (over so/sth)
watch keep watch on so/sth
watch keep watch over so/sth
watch on so's watch
watch on the watch for so/sth
watch watch for so/sth
watch Watch it!
watch Watch my lips!
watch watch one's step
watch watch out for so
watch watch over so/sth
watch watch so/sth like a hawk
watch watch the store
watch Watch your mouth!
watch watched pot never boils.
watch (You) (just) watch!
water as a duck takes to water
water big drink of water
water Blood is thicker than water.
water blow so/sth out of the water
water bread and water

water come hell or high water
water Come on in, the water's fine!
water couldn't pour water out of a boot (if there was instructions on the heel)
water cut so's water off
water dash cold water on sth
water dead in the water
water dull as dishwater
water dull as ditchwater
water fish in troubled waters
water get one's head above water
water have just one oar in the water
water in deep water
water in hot water (with so) (about so/sth)
water keep one's head above water
water like a fish out of water
water like water off a duck's back
water make so's mouth water
water make water
water mill cannot grind with water that is past.
water muddy the water
water not hold water
water of the first water
water pour cold water on sth
water pour oil on troubled water(s)
water Still waters run deep.
water tall drink of water
water through hell and high water
water throw cold water on sth
water turn on the waterworks
water turn so's water off
water water over the dam
water water sth down
water water under the bridge
water watering hole
water Cast one's bread upon the waters.
water won't hold water
water You can lead a horse to water, but you can't make it drink.
water You never miss the water till the well runs dry.
waterfront cover the waterfront
waterworks turn on the waterworks
wave catch the next wave
wave make waves
wave wait for the next wave
wave wave at so
wave wave back (at so)
wave wave so back (from sth)
wave wave so/sth aside
wave wave so/sth away (from so/sth)
wave wave so/sth off
wave wave so/sth on
wave wave sth around
wave wave to so
wavelength on the same wavelength
waver waver between so and so else
waver waver between sth and sth else
wax mind your own beeswax
wax none of so's beeswax
wax wax and wane
wax wax angry
wax wax eloquent
wax wax poetic
wax wax wroth
wax whole ball of wax
way all the way
way Anything new down your way?
way (Are you) going my way?
way argue one's way out of sth

way bluff one's way out (of sth)
way buy one's way in(to sth)
way buy one's way out (of sth)
way by the way
way by way of sth
way claw one's way to the top
way Clear the way!
way come so's way
way cry all the way to the bank
way cut both ways
way do sth the hard way
way downhill all the way
way edge (one's way) across (sth)
way edge (one's way) around sth
way elbow (one's way) through (sth)
way ever(y) which way
way fight (one's way) back (to sth)
way fight one's way out (of sth)
way fight (one's way) through (sth)
way find a way around so/sth
way find its way somewhere
way find one's way (around)
way find one's way around (sth)
way find one's way (somewhere)
way find (sth) out the hard way
way from way back
way get so across (in a good way)
way get so in a family way
way give way to so/sth
way go a long way toward doing sth
way go all the way (with so)
way go out of one's way (to do sth)
way go the way of the dodo
way go the way of the horse and buggy
way hack one's way through sth
way have a way with so/sth
way have a way with words
way have come a long way
way have it both ways
way Have it your way.
way have one's way with so
way hold one's mouth the right way
way hurry one on one's way
way in a bad way
way in a big way
way in a family way
way in any way, shape, or form
way in harm's way
way in one's own way
way in so's or sth's way
way in the family way
way in the way of so('s plans)
way in the way of so/sth
way in the way of sth
way in the worst way
way inch one's way across sth
way inch one's way along sth
way It cuts two ways.
way Keep out of my way.
way keep so/sth out of the way
way know one's way about
way know one's way around
way laugh all the way to the bank
way lead the way
way learn (sth) the hard way
way longest way round is the shortest way home.
way look the other way
way Love will find a way.
way make (an amount of) headway
way make one's way along sth
way make one's way back (to sth)

way make one's way in the world
way make one's way through sth
way make way
way marry one's way out of sth
way mend one's ways
way move so/sth out of the way
way no two ways about it
way No way!
way No way, José!
way not know which way to turn
way on one's way ((to) some place)
way on one's way (to sth or some place)
way on the way (to sth or some place)
way one's (own) way
way one's (own) way (with so/sth)
way one's way of life
way one way or another
way only way to go
way other way (a)round
way out of harm's way
way out of one's way
way out of so's way
way out of the way
way parting of the ways
way pave the way (for so/sth) (with sth)
way pay one's own way
way pay so's way
way pick one's way through sth
way put another way
way put so across (in a good way)
way put so in harm's way
way put so out of the way
way put sth in the way of so/sth
way right-of-way
way rub so('s fur) the wrong way
way say sth in a roundabout way
way see one's way (clear) (to do sth)
way see which way the wind is blowing
way set in one's ways
way shove one's way somewhere
way stand in so's way
way Stay out of my way.
way take sth the wrong way
way take the coward's way out
way take the easy way out
way talk one's way out of sth
way That ain't the way I heard it.
way That's (just) the way it goes.
way That's the way the ball bounces.
way That's the way the cookie crumbles.
way That's the way the mop flops.
way (That's the) way to go!
way the way I see it
way There's more than one way to skin a cat.
way (There's) no way to tell.
way They went that a'way.
way this a-way and that a-way
way thread one's way through sth
way to put it another way
way to so's way of thinking
way turn the other way
way two-way street
way under way
way way it plays
way way off (base)
way way out
way (way) over there
way way to a man's heart is through his stomach.

way Where there's a will, there's a way.
way work one's way along sth
way work (one's way) into sth
way work (one's way) through sth
way work one's way up (to sth)
way worm (one's way) in(to sth)
way worm (one's way) out (of sth)
wayside drop by the wayside
wayside fall by the wayside
we as we speak
we Can we continue this later?
we Could we continue this later?
we Do we have to go through all that again?
we Don't call us, we'll call you.
we Eat, drink, and be merry, for tomorrow we die.
we even as we speak
we Give us the tools, and we will finish the job.
we Here we go again.
we I believe we've met.
we It's time we should be going.
we Nice weather we're having.
we Till we meet again.
we Times change and we with time.
we United we stand, divided we fall.
we Until we meet again.
we We aim to please.
we (We) don't see you much around here anymore.
we We had a lovely time.
we We must do this again (sometime).
we We must learn to walk before we can run.
we We need to talk about sth.
we We were just talking about you.
we We('ll) have to do lunch sometime.
we We'll try again some other time.
we (We're) delighted to have you (here).
we (We're) glad you could come.
we We've had a lovely time.
we When do we eat?
weak chain is no stronger than its weakest link.
weak have a weakness for so/sth
weak spirit is willing, but the flesh is weak.
weak weak as a baby
weak weak as a kitten
weak weak link (in the chain)
weak weak sister
weakest chain is no stronger than its weakest link.
wealth Early to bed and early to rise, makes a man healthy, wealthy, and wise.
wealth wealth of sth
wean wean so (away) from sth
wear Constant dropping wears away a stone.
wear Don't let the bastards wear you down.
wear He wears a ten-dollar hat on a five-cent head.
wear I don't want to wear out my welcome.
wear If the shoe fits(, wear it).
wear It is better to wear out than to rust out.
wear look none the worse for wear
wear none the worse for wear

wear put wear (and tear) on sth
wear Uneasy lies the head that wears a crown.
wear wear and tear (on sth)
wear wear away at so/sth
wear wear down
wear wear more than one hat
wear wear off
wear wear on (for a period of time)
wear wear on so
wear wear one's heart on one's sleeve
wear wear out
wear wear so down
wear wear so out
wear wear so to a frazzle
wear wear sth away
wear wear sth down
wear wear sth off (of) sth
wear wear sth out
wear wear sth (up)on sth
wear wear the britches (in the family)
wear wear the pants (in the family)
wear wear through sth
wear wear two hats
wear wear (up)on so
wear wear (up)on sth
wear worse for wear
weary There is no rest for the weary.
weary weary of so/sth
weary weary so with sth
weasel weasel out (of sth)
weather fair-weather friend
weather Fine weather for ducks.
weather How do you like this weather?
weather (I've) been under the weather.
weather keep one's weather eye open
weather Lovely weather for ducks.
weather Nice weather we're having.
weather under the weather
weather weather permitting
weather weather the storm
weather What do you think of this weather?
weave weave around
weave weave in and out (of sth)
weave weave sth from sth
weave weave sth into sth
weave weave through sth
wed wed so to so
wed wed so to sth
wed wedded to sth
wedded wed(ded) to so
wedding dance at so's wedding
wedding Dream of a funeral and you hear of a wedding.
wedding shotgun wedding
wedge drive a wedge between so and so else
wedge wedge so/sth (in) between people or things
wedlock born out of wedlock
wee wee hours (of the night)
weed weed so/sth out
week by the week
week inside a week
week week in, week out
week weeks running
weep Finders keepers(, losers weepers).
weep Laugh and the world laughs with you; weep and you weep alone.

weep read it and weep
weep weep about so/sth
weep weep for joy
weep weep for so or an animal
weep weep over so/sth
weepers Finders keepers(, losers weepers).
weigh weigh against so/sth
weigh weigh in (at sth)
weigh weigh on so's mind
weigh weigh so down
weigh weigh so/sth down
weigh weigh so's words
weigh weigh sth against sth
weigh weigh sth out
weigh weigh sth up
weigh weigh (up)on so
weight carry (a lot of) weight (with so/sth)
weight carry one's (own) weight
weight carry the weight of the world on one's shoulders
weight carry weight (with so)
weight get a weight off one's mind
weight get some weight off one's feet
weight give weight to sth
weight have a weight problem
weight pull one's (own) weight
weight put on weight
weight put weight on
weight take a weight off one's mind
weight throw one's weight around
weight weight off one's mind
weight weight so/sth down (with sth)
weight weight sth against so/sth
weight work some weight off
weight worth its weight in gold
weird weird out
weird weirded out
welcome I don't want to wear out my welcome.
welcome wear out one's welcome
welcome Welcome aboard.
welcome welcome so into sth
welcome welcome so/sth back
welcome welcome so to sth
welcome welcome so with open arms
welcome welcome so with sth
welcome welcome to do sth
welcome Welcome to our house.
welcome You are more than welcome.
welcome You are welcome.
welcome You're welcome.
weld weld so and so else together
weld weld sth and sth else together
well alive and well
well All's well that ends well.
well (all) well and good
well as well
well augur well for so/sth
well come out well
well get well
well go over (well)
well go well with so/sth
well hale-fellow-well-met
well have so/sth (well) in hand
well He lives long who lives well.
well I hope all goes well.
well If a thing is worth doing, it's worth doing well.
well If you want a thing done well, do it yourself.

well If you would be well served, serve yourself.
well know sth only too well
well leave well enough alone
well let well enough alone
well may as well
well mean well
well might as well
well play one's cards well
well sit well with so
well so's point is well taken
well stand well with so
well tol(er)able (well)
well Two can play (at) this game (as well as one).
well Well begun is half done.
well Well, bust my buttons!
well well disposed to(ward) so/sth
well Well done!
well (Well,) I never!
well (Well,) I'll be!
well well in hand
well well into sth
well well out (of sth)
well well out(side) of sth
well well over
well Well said.
well Well, shut my mouth!
well well up (from sth)
well well up in years
well well up (inside so)
well well up (out of sth)
well well up with sth
well (Well,) what do you know!
well well-heeled
well well-to-do
well You never miss the water till the well runs dry.
welldigger cold as a welldigger's ass (in January)
welldigger cold as a welldigger's feet (in January)
welsh welsh on so
welsh welsh on sth (with so)
welter welter in sth
went one's mind went blank
went They went that a'way.
were as it were
were Fingers were made before forks.
were (I) wouldn't if I were you.
were if I were you
were If ifs and ands were pots and pans (there'd be no work for tinkers' hands).
were if the truth were known
were If wishes were horses, then beggars would ride.
were (I'm) having a wonderful time; wish you were here.
were Those were the days.
were We were just talking about you.
were Were you born in a barn?
west East is East and West is West (and never the twain shall meet).
west East, west, home's best.
west out West
wet all wet
wet get one's feet wet
wet get wet
wet mad as a wet hen
wet sopping (wet)
wet wet behind the ears
wet wet blanket

wet wet one's whistle
wet wet so/sth down
whack give so a whack at sth
whack have a whack at sth
whack out of w(h)ack
whack take a whack at sth
whack whack at sth
whack whack so/sth up
whack whack sth off
whack whack sth up
whack whacked (out)
whale have a whale of a time
whale whale into so or an animal
whale whale the tar out of so
wham wham bam thank you ma'am
whammy double whammy
what A man's gotta do what a man's gotta do.
what and what have you
what Believe nothing of what you hear, and only half of what you see.
what come what may
what Do what?
what (Do you) know what?
what (Do you) know what I mean?
what (Do you) know what I'm saying?
what Don't put off for tomorrow what you can do today.
what Don't tell me what to do!
what good for what ails you
what Guess what!
what have what it takes
what Here's your hat, what's your hurry?
what I hear what you're saying.
what I know (just) what you mean.
what if one knows what's good for one
what If you don't see what you want, please ask (for it).
what if you know what's good for you
what (It's) just what you need.
what just what the doctor ordered
what know one for what one is
what Know what?
what know what's what
what left hand doesn't know what the right hand is doing.
what Look (at) what the cat dragged in!
what no matter what (happens)
what not know what to make of so/sth
what not what sth is cracked up to be
what Now what?
what or what?
what Practice what you preach.
what recognize one for what one is
what recognize sth for what it is
what Say what?
what So (what)?
what (So) what else is new?
what tell so what to do with sth
what That's just what you need.
what That's what I say.
what That's what she wrote.
what Things are seldom what they seem.
what (Well,) what do you know!
what What (a) nerve!
what What a pity!
what What a shame!
what What about (doing) sth?
what What about (having) sth?
what What about it?

what What about you?
what What are you drinking?
what What are you driving at?
what What are you having?
what What brings you here?
what What can I do for you?
what What can I say?
what What can I tell you?
what What can't be cured must be endured.
what What difference does it make?
what What do you know?
what What do you know (about that)?
what What do you know for sure?
what What do you say?
what What do you think?
what What do you think of that?
what What do you think of this weather?
what What do you think you are doing here?
what What do you want me to say?
what What does that prove?
what What else can I do?
what What else can I do for you?
what what for
what What gives?
what What goes up must come down.
what What happened?
what What have you been up to?
what What if...?
what What (in) the devil?
what What (in) the dickens?
what What (in) the hell?
what What in (the) Sam Hill?
what What is it?
what what makes so tick
what what makes sth tick
what What makes you think so?
what What more can I do?
what What must be, must be.
what What now?
what What number are you calling?
what What of it?
what What one doesn't know won't hurt one.
what What price sth?
what What's buzzin' (cousin)?
what What's coming off?
what what's coming to one
what What's cooking?
what What's done cannot be undone.
what What's done is done.
what What's eating so?
what What's going down?
what What's going on (around here)?
what What's got(ten) into so?
what What's happ(ening)?
what what's his face
what what's his name
what What's in a name?
what What's in it for me?
what What's it to you?
what What's keeping so?
what What's new?
what What's new with you?
what What's on tap for today?
what What's poppin'?
what What's sauce for the goose is sauce for the gander.
what What's shakin' (bacon)?
what What's that?
what What's the (big) idea?

what What's the catch?
what What's the damage?
what What's the deal?
what What's the drill?
what What's the good of sth?
what What's the (good) word?
what What's the matter (with you)?
what What's the problem?
what What's the scam?
what What's the scoop?
what What's (there) to know?
what What's up?
what What's up, doc?
what What's with so/sth?
what What's wrong?
what What's your age?
what What's yours?
what What's yours is mine, and what's mine is mine.
what What say?
what what so/sth is cracked up to be
what What so said.
what What the deuce?
what What the devil?
what What the eye doesn't see, the heart doesn't grieve over.
what What the fuck?
what What the heck!
what What the hell?
what What was the name again?
what What will be, will be.
what what with sth
what What would you like to drink?
what What would you say if...?
what What you don't know won't hurt you.
what What you see is what you get.
what What'll it be?
what worth of a thing is what it will bring.
what You and what army?
what You cannot lose what you never had.
what You get what you pay for.
what You got to do what you got to do.
what You know what I mean?
what You never know (what you can do) till you try.
whatever for what(ever) it's worth
whatever What(ever) goes around, comes around.
whatever Whatever turns you on.
whatever Whatever will be, will be.
wheat separate the wheat from the chaff
wheedle wheedle so into sth
wheedle wheedle sth away from so
wheel at the wheel
wheel die behind the wheel
wheel fifth wheel
wheel have one's shoulder to the wheel
wheel If frogs had wheels, they wouldn't bump their butts.
wheel keep one's shoulder to the wheel
wheel pit one's shoulder to the wheel
wheel reinvent the wheel
wheel set of wheels
wheel spin one's wheels
wheel squeaking wheel gets the oil.
wheel wheel and deal
wheel wheel around
wheel wheel so/sth around

wheel wheel so/sth away
wheel wheel so/sth into sth
wheel wheel so/sth off
wheel wheel so/sth out of sth
wheeze wheeze sth out
when Come back when you can stay longer.
when cross that bridge when one comes to it
when *fat hit the fire
when Hoist your sail when the wind is fair.
when I'll look you up when I'm in town.
when It'll be a cold day in hell when sth happens.
when It'll be a long day in January when sth happens.
when know when one is not wanted
when liar is not believed (even) when he tells the truth.
when Look me up when you're in town.
when Needs must when the devil drives.
when Say when.
when Since when?
when Smile when you say that.
when Some people (just) don't know when to quit.
when time flies (when you're having fun)
when time was (when)
when when all is said and done
when When do we eat?
when When in Rome(, do as the Romans do).
when when it comes right down to it
when when it comes to sth
when when least expected
when When one door shuts, another opens.
when when one is good and ready
when when one's ship comes in
when When poverty comes in at the door, love flies out of the window.
when when push comes to shove
when When the cat's away, the mice will play.
when when the chips are down
when when the dust settles
when when the fat hit the fire
when when the fat lady sings
when when the going gets tough
when When the going gets tough, the tough get going.
when when the shit hits the fan
when when the time is ripe
when When the wolf comes in at the door, love creeps out of the window.
when when you get a chance
when when you get a minute
when Why buy a cow when milk is so cheap?
when Why buy a cow when you can get milk for free?
when zigged when one should've zagged
where Cross the stream where it is shallowest.
where Fools rush in where angels fear to tread.
where from where I stand

where Give credit where credit is due.
where hit one where one lives
where Home is where the heart is.
where know where all the bodies are buried
where know where it's at
where know where one is coming from
where know where so stands (on so/sth)
where know where sth is at
where Let's go somewhere where it's (more) quiet.
where Let the chips fall where they may.
where not know where to turn
where (Now,) where was I?
where put one's nose in (where it's not wanted)
where Put your money where your mouth is!
where stick one's nose in (where it's not wanted)
where take up where one left off
where tell so where to get off
where This is where I came in.
where Where can I wash up?
where Where do (you think) you get off?
where Where have you been all my life?
where Where (have) you been hiding (yourself)?
where Where (have) you been keeping yourself?
where Where ignorance is bliss, 'tis folly to be wise.
where Where in the world...?
where Where is the restroom?
where where it's at
where Where on (God's green) earth?
where where one is coming from
where Where's the beef?
where Where's the fire?
where where so is at
where where so lives
where where so's head is at
where where the action is
where where the rubber meets the road
where where the sun don't shine
where Where there's a will, there's a way.
where Where there's life there's hope.
where Where there's smoke there's fire.
where Where will I find you?
where You don't know where it's been.
wherefore whys and wherefores of sth
whereof know whereof one speaks
wherewithal wherewithal (to do sth)
whet whet so's appetite
whether don't know whether to eat it or rub it on
whether not know whether one is coming or going
whether whether or not
which ever(y) which way
which Happy is the country which has no history.
which know which is which
which know which side one's bread is buttered on
which not know which end is up
which not know which way to turn

which see which way the wind is blowing
which tell which is which
which which brings me to the (main) point
whiff catch a whiff of sth
whiff take a whiff of sth
whiff whiff of sth
while After while(, crocodile).
while fiddle while Rome burns
while Gather ye rosebuds while ye may.
while get (out) while the gettin(g)'s good
while (I'll) see you in a little while.
while Make hay while the sun shines.
while make it worth so's while
while not worth one's while
while quit while one is ahead
while reed before the wind lives on, while mighty oaks do fall.
while Strike while the iron is hot.
while while a period of time away (doing sth)
while While there's life there's hope.
while worth so's while
whine whine about so/sth
whine whine sth out
whip buggy whip
whip whip around
whip whip back (on so)
whip whip into sth
whip whip so into a state
whip whip so into doing sth
whip whip so/sth around
whip whip so/sth into shape
whip whip so/sth on
whip whip so up
whip whip sth away (from so)
whip whip sth into shape
whip whip sth into sth
whip whip sth off
whip whip sth out
whip whip sth over (to so)
whip whip sth up
whip whip sth written off to so
whip whip through sth
whip whipping boy
whirl give sth a whirl
whirl whirl around
whirl whirl so/sth around
whirlwind Sow the wind and reap the whirlwind.
whisk whisk so around
whisk whisk so or an animal off
whisk whisk so/sth away
whisk whisk so/sth off (to sth)
whisk whisk sth off (of) so/sth
whisker by a whisker
whisper in a stage whisper
whisper whisper about so/sth
whisper whisper sth around
whistle bells and whistles
whistle blow the whistle (on so)
whistle can (just) whistle for sth
whistle clean as a whistle
whistle not just whistling Dixie
whistle slick as a whistle
whistle wet one's whistle
whistle whistle at so/sth
whistle whistle for so/sth
whistle whistle in the dark
whistle You ain't just whistlin' Dixie.
whistling not just whistling Dixie

whistling You ain't just whistlin' Dixie.
whit didn't care a whit
whit don't care a whit
white bleed so white
white get sth down (in black and white)
white in black and white
white little white lie
white put sth down in black and white
white set sth down in black and white
white white as a ghost
white white as a sheet
white white as snow
white white as the driven snow
white white elephant
white white knuckle sth
whittle whittle at sth
whittle whittle so down to size
whittle whittle sth away
whittle whittle sth down (to size)
whittle whittle sth out of sth
whiz whiz past so/sth
whiz whiz (right) through sth
who Abandon hope, all ye who enter here.
who Blessed is he who expects nothing, for he shall never be disappointed.
who Can I tell her who's calling?
who Could I tell him who's calling?
who doesn't care who knows it
who Everything comes to him who waits.
who Evil be to him who evil thinks.
who gods send nuts to those who have no teeth.
who Good things come to him who waits.
who He gives twice who gives quickly.
who He lives long who lives well.
who He travels fastest who travels alone.
who He who begins many things, finishes but few.
who He who excuses himself accuses himself.
who He who fights and runs away, may live to fight another day.
who He who hesitates is lost.
who He who laughs last, laughs best.
who He who laughs last, laughs longest.
who He who pays the piper calls the tune.
who He who rides a tiger is afraid to dismount.
who He who sups with the devil should have a long spoon.
who He who would climb the ladder must begin at the bottom.
who Look who's here!
who Look who's talking!
who May I tell him who's calling?
who People who live in glass houses shouldn't throw stones.
who Says who?
who Sez who?
who There's none so blind as those who will not see.
who There's none so deaf as those who will not hear.
who They also serve who only stand and wait.

who Those who can, do; those who can't, teach.
who Who cares?
who Who could have thought?
who Who do you think you are?
who Who do you think you're kidding?
who Who do you think you're talking to?
who Who do you want to speak to?
who Who do you want (to talk to)?
who Who (in) the devil?
who Who (in) the hell?
who Who is it?
who Who is this?
who Who knows?
who Who's calling(, please)?
who Who's on the line?
who Who's on the phone?
who Who's there?
who Who's your friend?
who Who was it?
who Who would have thought?
who You and who else?
whoa from giddy-up to whoa
whoa Whoa, Nellie!
whole go whole hog
whole Half the truth is often a whole lie.
whole make sth up out of whole cloth
whole on the whole
whole tell the (whole) world
whole whole bag of tricks
whole whole ball of wax
whole whole enchilada
whole whole heap more
whole whole kit and caboodle
whole (whole) mess of so/sth
whole (whole) new ball game
whole whole nine yards
whole whole nother thing
whole whole shebang
whole whole shooting match
whole whole wide world
whole whole works
whom to whom it may concern
whom Whom the gods love die young.
whom With whom do you wish to speak?
whoop two (w)hoops and a holler
whoop whoop it up
whore Once a whore, always a whore.
why that's why!
why Why buy a cow when milk is so cheap?
why Why buy a cow when you can get milk for free?
why why don't you?
why Why keep a dog and bark yourself?
why Why not?
why whys and wherefores of sth
wicked No rest for the wicked.
wide all wool and a yard wide
wide blow sth wide open
wide bust so wide open
wide bust sth wide open
wide come from far and wide
wide crack sth (wide) open
wide cut a wide swath
wide fall wide of the mark
wide give so/sth a wide berth
wide leave oneself wide open for sth
wide whole wide world

wide wide of the mark
wide wide open
wide wide place in the road
wide with (one's) eyes (wide) open
widow grass widow
wife Caesar's wife must be above suspicion.
wife good husband makes a good wife.
wife How's the wife?
wife old wives' tale
wig flip one's wig
wig wig out
wiggle wiggle out of sth
wilco Roger (wilco).
wild go hog wild
wild go wild
wild hog wild
wild run wild
wild send so on a wild-goose chase
wild sow one's wild oats
wild wild about so/sth
wild wild and woolly
wild Wild horses couldn't drag so away (from sth).
wild wild-goose chase
wildfire spread like wildfire
will not (I) won't breathe a word (of it).
will not I won't give up without a fight.
will not (I) won't tell a soul.
will not (It) won't bother me any.
will not (It) won't bother me at all.
will not It won't wash!
will not What one doesn't know won't hurt one.
will not What you don't know won't hurt you.
will not won't hold water
will not Won't you come in?
will Accidents will happen.
will against so's will
will All things will pass.
will at will
will Blood will have blood.
will Blood will tell.
will Boys will be boys.
will Breeding will tell.
will drowning man will clutch at a straw.
will Even a worm will turn.
will Everything will be all right.
will Everything will be great.
will Everything will be just fine.
will Everything will be okay.
will Everything will work out (all right).
will Everything will work out for the best.
will Faith will move mountains.
will Flattery will get you nowhere.
will Give us the tools, and we will finish the job.
will He will get his.
will heads will roll
will How will I know you?
will How will I recognize you?
will If anything can go wrong, it will.
will If the mountain will not come to Mahomet, Mahomet must go to the mountain.
will If you lie down with dogs, you will get up with fleas.

will If you run after two hares, you will catch neither.
will ill will
will It will be your ass!
will It will take some doing.
will Keep your shop and your shop will keep you.
will last will and testament
will Love will find a way.
will Murder will out.
will no salesman will call
will Oh, sure (so/sth will)!
will (Only) time will tell.
will put sth in will-call
will remember so in one's will
will She will get hers.
will So will be with you in a minute.
will Sticks and stones may break my bones, but words will never hurt me.
will Stretch your arm no further than your sleeve will reach.
will That will do.
will There's none so blind as those who will not see.
will There's none so deaf as those who will not hear.
will There will be hell to pay.
will There will be the devil to pay.
will Things will work out (all right).
will Throw dirt enough, and some will stick.
will Time will tell.
will truth will out.
will What will be, will be.
will Whatever will be, will be.
will When the cat's away, the mice will play.
will Where there's a will, there's a way.
will Where will I find you?
will will be the death of so/sth (yet)
will will come of sth
will Will do.
will will eat so for breakfast
will Will I see you again?
will will not hear of sth
will will sth away
will will sth to so
will will stop at nothing
will Will that be all?
will (Will there be) anything else?
will Will you excuse us, please?
will Will you hold?
will with a will
will with the best will in the world
will worth of a thing is what it will bring.
willing God willing.
willing God willing and the creek don't rise
willing Lord willing and the creek don't rise
willing ready, willing, and able
willing spirit is willing, but the flesh is weak.
wimp wimp out (of sth)
win Faint heart never won fair lady.
win He that would the daughter win, must with the mother first begin.
win not going to win any beauty contests
win no-win situation
win out to win
win Slow and steady wins the race.

win Win a few, lose a few.
win win all the marbles
win win at sth
win win by a nose
win win (out) (over so/sth)
win win so away (from so/sth)
win win so/sth back (from so/sth)
win win so over (to sth)
win win so's heart
win win sth at sth
win win the day
win win the heart of so
win win through sth
win winner take all
win (You) can't win them all.
win You win some, you lose some.
wince wince at sth
wind both sheets in the wind
wind break wind
wind catch wind of sth
wind four sheets in the wind
wind get out of wind
wind get wind of sth
wind go like the wind
wind gone with the wind
wind Hoist your sail when the wind is fair.
wind in the wind
wind It's an ill wind that blows nobody (any) good.
wind knock the wind out of so's sails
wind like the wind
wind move like the wind
wind one's second wind
wind out of wind
wind reed before the wind lives on, while mighty oaks do fall.
wind run like the wind
wind see which way the wind is blowing
wind Sow the wind and reap the whirlwind.
wind swift as the wind
wind take the wind out of so's sails
wind three sheets in the wind
wind throw caution to the wind
wind twist (slowly) in the wind
wind two sheets to the wind
wind wind around
wind wind back
wind wind down
wind wind into sth
wind wind so around one's little finger
wind wind so up
wind wind sth around sth
wind wind sth down
wind wind sth in
wind wind sth off
wind wind sth onto sth
wind wind sth up
wind wind sth (up) (into sth)
wind wind through sth
wind wind up (as) sth
wind wind up (by) doing sth
wind wind up somehow
wind wind up (somewhere)
wind wind up with so/sth
windmill tilt at windmills
window crack the window (open)
window don't have a pot to piss in (or a window to throw it out of)
window go window-shopping
window out (of) the window

window When poverty comes in at the door, love flies out of the window.
window When the wolf comes in at the door, love creeps out of the window.
window window of opportunity
window You make a better door than you do a window.
wine wine and dine so
wine You cannot put new wine in old bottles.
wing arrive on a wing and a prayer
wing candidate for a pair of wings
wing clip so's wings
wing come (in) on a wing and a prayer
wing have so under so's wing(s)
wing If a toady frog had wings, he wouldn't bump his ass.
wing look like a candidate for a pair of wings
wing on a wing and a prayer
wing on the wing
wing sprout wings
wing take so under so's wing(s)
wing try one's wings (out)
wing under so's wing(s)
wing waiting in the wings
wing wing it
wink catch forty winks
wink forty winks
wink hoodwink so into sth
wink hoodwink so out of sth
wink in the wink of an eye
wink nod is as good as a wink to a blind horse.
wink not sleep a wink
wink quick as a wink
wink take forty winks
wink wink at so
wink wink at sth
wink wink sth away
winner winner take all
winter winter over (some place)
wipe Wipe it off!
wipe wipe out
wipe wipe so/sth off
wipe wipe so/sth (off) (with sth)
wipe wipe so out
wipe wipe so's slate clean
wipe wipe sth away
wipe wipe sth down
wipe wipe sth off
wipe wipe sth (off) (on sth)
wipe wipe sth out
wipe wipe sth up
wipe wipe the floor up with so
wipe wipe the slate clean
wire down-to-the-wire
wire have one's wires crossed
wire Hold the wire(, please).
wire under the wire
wire wire ahead (for sth)
wire wire for sth
wire wire so/sth for sth
wire wire sth back to so
wire wire sth in
wire wire sth together
wire wire sth up
wire wired into so/sth
wisdom Experience is the father of wisdom.
wisdom Experience is the mother of wisdom.

wise Early to bed and early to rise, makes a man healthy, wealthy, and wise.
wise It is a wise child that knows its own father.
wise It is easy to be wise after the event.
wise none the wiser
wise One cannot love and be wise.
wise penny-wise and pound-foolish
wise put so wise to so/sth
wise sadder but wiser
wise still tongue makes a wise head.
wise Where ignorance is bliss, 'tis folly to be wise.
wise wise as an owl
wise wise as Solomon
wise wise so up (about so/sth)
wise wise to so/sth
wise wise up (to so/sth)
wise word to the wise
wish Don't you wish!
wish have a death wish
wish I wish I'd said that.
wish I wouldn't wish that on a dog.
wish I wouldn't wish that on my worst enemy.
wish If wishes were horses, then beggars would ride.
wish (I'm) having a wonderful time; wish you were here.
wish wish for so/sth
wish wish is father to the thought.
wish wish list
wish wish so/sth away
wish wish so/sth (off) on so
wish With whom do you wish to speak?
wishful wishful thinking
wit at one's wit's end
wit Brevity is the soul of wit.
wit frighten one out of one's wits
wit get one's wits about one
wit keep one's wits about one
wit live by one's wits
wit match wits (with so)
wit ounce of discretion is worth a pound of wit.
wit scare one out of one's wits
wit scare the wits out of so
wit sharp wit
wit to wit
witch cold as a witch's tit
with abide with so
with able to do sth with one's eyes closed
with abound with so/sth
with abscond with so/sth
with absorb sth with sth
with accommodate so with sth
with accompany so with sth
with accord with sth
with acquaint so with sth
with acquainted with so
with acquainted with sth
with adorn so/sth with sth
with adulterate sth with sth
with affiliate (so/sth) with so/sth
with afflict so with so
with afflict so with sth
with agree with so
with agree (with so) (about so/sth)
with agree with sth
with agree (with sth) (in sth)

with ain't fittin' to roll with a pig
with align oneself with so/sth
with align sth with sth
with alive with people or things
with all right with so
with alloy sth with sth
with ally (oneself) (with so) (against so/sth)
with along with so/sth
with alternate with sth
with amalgamate sth with sth
with amalgamate with sth
with amuse so with sth
with anoint so with sth
with argue (with so) (over so/sth)
with argue with sth
with arm (so against so/sth) (with sth)
with arrange sth with so/sth
with assail so with sth
with assimilate with some people
with assist so with so/sth
with associate oneself with so/sth
with associate so/sth with so/sth
with associate with so
with astound so with sth
with at home with so/sth
with at loggerheads (with so)
with at odds (with so)
with balance sth with sth else
with bandy with so
with bargain (for so/sth) (with so)
with bargain (over so/sth) (with so)
with barter with so
with battle (with so) (over so/sth)
with bear with so/sth
with bedeck so/sth with sth
with beg to differ (with so)
with begin with so/sth
with beguile so with sth
with beset so with sth
with beside oneself (with sth)
with besiege so/sth with sth
with besmirch so/sth with sth
with bet with so
with bicker (with so) (about so/sth)
with big with so
with bind so/sth up (with sth)
with blanch with sth
with blanket so/sth with sth
with blaze with sth
with blend in (with so/sth)
with blend sth together (with sth)
with bless so/sth with sth
with blush with sth
with board with so
with boil over (with sth)
with boil with sth
with bombard so/sth with sth
with bombard so with questions
with born with a silver spoon in one's mouth
with bother so with so/sth
with bother with so/sth
with bounce sth around (with so)
with bound up with so/sth
with brainwash so with sth
with break bread with so
with break off (with so)
with break out (with a rash)
with break out with sth
with break up (with so)
with break with so
with brim over (with sth)

with brim with sth
with brimming with sth
with bring so/sth into contact with so/sth
with bring so/sth into line (with so/sth)
with bring sth with
with bristle with anger
with bristle with rage
with broach sth with so
with brush with death
with buddy up (with so)
with bulge with sth
with bum around (with so)
with bunk (up) with so
with burden so/sth with so/sth
with burden so with sth
with burn with a low blue flame
with burn with sth
with burst in (with sth)
with burst out with sth
with burst with excitment
with burst with joy
with burst with pride
with busy oneself with so/sth
with busy so with so/sth
with buzz with sth
with cake so/sth with sth
with can't do anything with so/sth
with can't find one's butt with both hands (in broad daylight)
with careful (with sth)
with carry (a lot of) weight (with so/sth)
with carry on (with so)
with carry on (with sth)
with carry so along (with so)
with carry so along (with sth)
with carry so around (with oneself)
with carry sth along (with so)
with carry sth around (with one)
with carry sth with
with carry weight (with so)
with cast one's lot in (with so/sth)
with catch on (with so)
with catch one with one's pants down
with catch so with sth
with catch up with so
with catch up (with so/sth)
with change places with so
with change sth with so
with charge so/sth (with) sth
with charge so with sth
with charm so with sth
with check back (with so)
with check in (with so)
with check with so (about sth)
with chime in (with sth)
with chip in (with sth) (on sth) (for so)
with chortle with sth
with chuckle with sth
with chum up with so
with clash (with so) (over so/sth)
with clash with sth
with class so/sth with so/sth
with clean the floor up with so
with clear sth with so/sth
with click with so
with clog sth with sth
with close ranks (with so)
with close with so/sth
with closefisted (with money)
with closet so with so
with clown around (with so)
with coat so/sth with sth
with coexist with so/sth

with cohabit with so
with coincide with sth
with collaborate with so/sth
with collate sth with sth
with collide with so/sth
with collude with so/sth
with combine sth with sth
with come across (with sth)
with come along (with so)
with come away with so
with come clean (with so) (about sth)
with come down with sth
with come forward (with sth)
with come in(to) contact (with so/sth)
with come out in(to) the open with sth
with come out with sth
with come through sth (with flying colors)
with come through (with sth)
with come to an understanding (with so)
with come to grips with so/sth
with come to terms (with so/sth)
with come to the job with sth
with come to the position with sth
with come to the task with sth
with come up with so/sth
with come with (so/sth)
with come with the territory
with commence with so/sth
with commiserate with so
with commune with sth
with communicate with so
with compare so/sth with so/sth
with compete with so/sth
with comply with sth
with comport oneself with some manner
with compound sth with sth
with concern so with sth
with concur on so/sth (with so)
with confederate with so/sth
with confer on so/sth (with so)
with confer with so (about so/sth)
with conflict with sth
with conform with sth
with confront so with sth
with confuse so or an animal with sth
with confuse so with so else
with connect (up) with so/sth
with connect (with so)
with connect (with the ball)
with connive at sth (with so)
with console so with sth
with consort with so
with conspire with so (against so/sth)
with consult (with) so (about so/sth)
with contact with so
with contaminate so/sth with sth
with contend with a problem
with contend with so (for sth)
with content oneself with sth
with continue with sth
with contract with so (for sth)
with contrast so/sth with so/sth else
with contrast with sth
with converse with so (about so/sth)
with convulse so with sth
with cook so up (with so)
with cooking with gas
with cooperate with so (on sth)
with coordinate sth with sth
with cope with so/sth

with copulate with so
with correlate sth with sth
with correlate with sth
with correspond with so (about so/sth)
with could do with so/sth
with Could I have a word with you?
with couldn't hit a bull in the ass with a bass fiddle
with count with so
with counter so/sth with sth
with counter with sth
with couple so with so
with couple sth with sth
with couple up (with so)
with couple with so
with couple with sth
with cram so/sth with so/sth
with crash with so
with crawling with some kind of creature
with crawling with so
with credit so/sth with sth
with cross paths (with so)
with cross so's palm with silver
with cross with so
with cross swords (with so)
with crowd sth with so/sth
with crown so with sth
with crown sth with sth
with cuddle up with a (good) book
with cuddle up (with so)
with curl up (with a (good) book
with curl up with so or an animal
with curry favor with so
with curse so/sth with sth
with cut in (with sth)
with cut loose (with sth)
with cut no ice (with so)
with cut so/sth with sth
with cut sth with sth
with dally with so
with damn so/sth with faint praise
with damn so with sth
with dance out of step (with so/sth)
with dance out of time (with so/sth)
with dance with death
with dance with so
with daub sth with sth
with deaden sth with sth
with deal with so
with debate (with so) about sth
with debit sth with sth
with deceive so with sth
with decorate sth with sth
with deface sth with sth
with defend so with sth
with delight so with sth
with delude so with sth
with deluge so/sth with sth
with dialogue with so
with dicker with so (for sth)
with diddle with so
with didn't exchange more than three words with so
with die with one's boots on
with differ (with so) about sth
with dilly-dally (around) with so/sth
with disagree with so
with disagree (with so) (about so/sth)
with disappoint so with so/sth
with discuss so/sth with so
with disgusted with so/sth
with dispense with so/sth
with dispute sth with so

with dissatisfied with so/sth
with dive in with both feet
with divide sth with so
with do away with oneself
with do away with so or an animal
with do away with sth
with do business with so
with do sth with a vengeance
with do sth with so/sth
with do with so/sth
with (Do) you eat with that mouth?
with (Do) you kiss your momma with that mouth?
with done with mirrors
with done with so/sth
with Don't throw the baby out with the bathwater.
with dose so or an animal with sth
with dot sth with sth
with double up (with laughter)
with double up (with pain)
with double up (with so)
with douse so/sth with sth
with dovetail with sth
with down with a disease
with down (with so)
with Down with so/sth!
with drape so/sth with sth
with drift with sth
with drip with sth
with eat(en) up with sth
with echo with sth
with economical with the truth
with edge sth with sth
with elope with so
with embarrass so with sth
with embellish sth with sth
with emblazon sth with sth
with empathize with so/sth
with enchant so with sth
with encumber so/sth with so/sth
with end up with all the marbles
with end up with so/sth
with end up with the short end of the stick
with end with sth
with endow so/sth with sth
with engorge (itself) with sth
with engrave sth with sth
with enrich so/sth with sth
with entangle so/sth with sth
with entertain so with sth
with enthrall so with sth
with entice so or an animal with sth
with entrap so (in sth) (with sth)
with entrust so with so/sth
with equate so/sth with so/sth
with equip so/sth (with sth) (for sth)
with equip sth with sth
with even (with so)
with exchange no more than some number of words with so
with exchange sth with so
with experiment with so/sth
with explode with sth
with face so with sth
with face sth with sth
with fall behind (with sth)
with fall head over heels in love (with so)
with fall in love (with each other)
with fall in love (with so)
with fall in love (with sth)

with fall in with so/sth
with fall in with sth
with fall out of favor (with so)
with fall out of love (with so)
with fall out (with so) (about sth)
with fall out (with so) (over sth)
with familiar with so/sth
with familiarize so with sth
with fatten so or an animal up (with sth)
with favor so/sth with sth
with fed up (to some degree) (with so/sth)
with feed so/sth or an animal with sth
with feel sth with sth
with festoon so/sth with sth
with feud (with so) (over so/sth)
with fiddle around (with so)
with fiddle around (with sth)
with fiddle with so/sth
with fidget with sth
with Fight fire with fire.
with fight so/sth with sth
with fight (with) so or some creature (over so/sth)
with fight (with) so/sth (about so/sth)
with file sth with so/sth
with fill so/sth up (with sth)
with fill so's head with sth
with find fault (with so/sth)
with find favor with so
with find oneself with so/sth
with finish (sth) off with sth
with finish sth with a lick and a promise
with finish with sth
with fire so with anger
with fire so with enthusiasm
with fire so with expectations
with firstest with the mostest
with fit in (somehow) (with sth)
with fit in (with so/sth)
with fit so/sth out (with sth)
with fit so/sth up (with sth)
with fit with sth
with fix so up (with so)
with fix so up (with sth)
with fix sth with so
with flame with anger
with flame with lust
with flame with resentment
with flame with vengeance
with flash with anger
with flash with recognition
with flavor food with sth
with fleck sth with sth
with flesh sth out (with sth)
with flick sth with sth
with flirt with so
with flirt with the idea of doing sth
with flood so/sth with sth
with flow with sth
with fluctuate with sth
with flush with sth
with fly off with so/sth
with follow through (with sth)
with fool (around) with so/sth
with force to be reckoned with
with fortify so or an animal (against sth) (with sth)
with fraternize with so/sth
with fraught with danger
with free hand (with so/sth)
with fresh (with so)
with friends with so
with fuse sth with sth

with fuse with sth
with fuss (around) with so/sth
with garnish sth with sth
with Get along with you!
with get away with murder
with get away with so
with get away with sth
with get by (with sth)
with get into an argument (with so) (about so/sth)
with get into bed with so
with get it off with so
with get off (with sth)
with get on (with so)
with get on with sth
with get out of time (with so/sth)
with Get out with it!
with get out with one's life
with get smart (with so)
with get sth going with so
with get through (with so/sth)
with get to first base (with so/sth)
with get together (with so) (on so/sth)
with get tough (with so)
with get with it
with get with sth
with get with the program
with give forth with sth
with give (out) with sth
with give sth back (to so) (with interest)
with give with sth
with gleam with sth
with glint with sth
with glisten with sth
with glitter with sth
with glow with sth
with glut so/sth with sth
with go about with so/sth
with go ahead (with sth)
with go all the way (with so)
with go along (with so) for the ride
with go along with so/sth
with go around (with so)
with go around with so/sth
with go away with so/sth
with go badly with so/sth
with go down with sth
with go forward with sth
with go in with so (on sth)
with go off (to the side) with so
with go off (with so)
with go on with sth
with Go on (with you)!
with go out of favor (with so)
with go out (with so)
with go out with sth
with go over big (with so)
with go over sth with a fine-tooth comb
with go over sth (with so)
with go over with a bang
with go public (with sth)
with go steady with so
with go through sth with a fine-tooth comb
with go through with sth
with go to bed (with so)
with go to bed with the chickens
with go to bed with the sun
with go to press with sth
with go well with so/sth
with go with it
with go with so
with go with (so/sth)

with go with sth
with go with the flow
with go with the territory
with go with the tide
with God's in his heaven; all's right with the world.
with gone with the wind
with gorge so/sth with sth
with grace so/sth with one's presence
with grace sth with sth
with graced with sth
with graduate (in sth) (with sth)
with grapple (with so) (for sth)
with grapple with sth
with green with envy
with greet so/sth with sth
with groan with sth
with grow disgusted with so/sth
with grow dissatisfied with so/sth
with gush with sth
with haggle (with so) over so/sth
with hand in glove (with so)
with hand with sth
with handle so with kid gloves
with hang around (with so)
with hang out (with so/sth)
with hang so/sth with sth
with hang with so
with hardly exchange more than some number of words with so
with harmonize with so/sth
with has the world by the tail (with a downhill drag)
with hash sth over (with so)
with have a bone to pick (with so)
with have a brush with sth
with have a run-in (with so/sth)
with have a score to settle (with so)
with have a scrape (with so/sth)
with have a set-to (with so)
with have a thing going (with so)
with have a way with so/sth
with have a way with words
with have an affair (with so)
with have an argument (with so)
with have intimate relations with so
with have no truck with sth
with have nothing to do with so/sth
with have one's hands full (with so/sth)
with have one's way with so
with have pull with so
with have relations with so
with have something going (with so)
with have sth in common (with so/sth)
with have sth out (with so)
with have sth to do with sth
with have to do with sth
with have to live with sth
with have words with so (over so/sth)
with He that would the daughter win, must with the mother first begin.
with He who sups with the devil should have a long spoon.
with head over heels in love (with so)
with heap sth with sth
with help out (with sth)
with help so off with sth
with help so on with sth
with help so/sth out with so/sth
with help so/sth with so/sth
with hit it off (with so)
with hit so with sth
with hobnob with so/sth

with hoist with one's own petard
with honor so with sth
with hook so up (with so)
with hook up with so
with horse around (with so/sth)
with How goes it (with you)?
with How's (it) with you?
with How're things (with you)?
with hum with activity
with I can live with that.
with (I) can't argue with that.
with (I have) no problem with that.
with I was up all night with a sick friend.
with I wouldn't touch it with a ten-foot pole.
with I'd like (to have) a word with you.
with identify (oneself) with so/sth
with identify sth with so/sth
with If you lie down with dogs, you will get up with fleas.
with If you play with fire, you get burned.
with (I'll) be right with you.
with illuminate sth with sth
with illustrate sth with sth
with I'm not finished with you.
with I'm (really) fed up (with so/sth).
with I'm with you.
with imbue so with sth
with impregnate sth with sth
with impress so with so/sth
with imprint sth with sth
with in accord (with so/sth) (about so/sth)
with in accordance with sth
with in agreement (with so/sth)
with in bad (with so)
with in cahoots (with so)
with in concert (with so)
with in contact (with so/sth)
with in Dutch (with so)
with in (good) (with so)
with in harmony (with so/sth)
with in hot water (with so) (about so/sth)
with in keeping (with sth)
with in league (with so)
with in line with sth
with in love (with so/sth)
with in over one's head (with so/sth)
with in step (with so)
with in step (with so/sth)
with in step (with sth)
with in time (with sth)
with in touch (with so)
with in touch with so/sth
with in tune with so/sth
with in tune with the times
with in with so
with in (with so)
with inculcate so with sth
with indoctrinate so with sth
with indulge so with sth
with infatuated with so/sth
with infect so with sth
with infested with sth
with inflate sth with sth
with infuse so with sth
with infuse sth with sth
with ingratiate oneself with so
with inlay sth with sth
with inoculate so with sth

with inscribe sth with sth
with inspire so with sth
with instill so with sth
with insure so/sth with sth
with integrate so with so
with integrate sth with sth
with interact with so
with interact with sth
with intercede (for so) (with so/sth)
with interchange so with so else
with interchange sth with sth
with interface so/sth with so/sth
with interface with so/sth
with interfere with so/sth
with interlace sth with sth
with intermarry with so
with intermingle sth with sth
with intermingle with so
with intersperse sth with sth
with intertwine sth with sth
with intertwine with sth
with intervene with so/sth
with interview with so for sth
with intimate with so
with intimidate so with sth
with intoxicate so with so/sth
with intoxicate so with sth
with intrigue with so
with intrigue (with so) (against so)
with inundate so/sth with sth
with invest so with sth
with involve so with so/sth
with involved (with so)
with involved with sth
with issue so with sth
with (It) don't cut no ice (with so).
with (It) don't cut no squares (with so).
with It is all over with so.
with I've had it up to here (with so/sth).
with jab so with sth
with jam sth (up) with sth
with jam with so
with jest with so
with jibe with sth
with join forces (with so)
with join in (with so)
with join in (with) sth
with join so with so else
with join sth with sth else
with join (up) with so/sth
with join with so
with joke (with so) (about so/sth)
with jostle with so
with jump in with both feet
with jump with sth
with keep company (with so)
with keep faith with so
with keep in good with so
with keep in step (with so)
with keep in touch (with so)
with keep in touch (with so/sth)
with keep on with sth
with keep pace (with so/sth)
with keep so/sth in with so/sth
with keep sth with so
with keep up (with so/sth)
with keep up with the Joneses
with keep up with the times
with kid around (with so)
with kill so with kindness
with kill two birds with one stone
with knock about (some place) (with so)
with knock around (some place) (with so)

with knock so over (with a feather)
with label so/sth with sth
with lace sth with sth
with Laugh and the world laughs with you; weep and you weep alone.
with laugh with sth
with lay it on with a trowel
with lead off (with so/sth)
with lead with so/sth
with lead with sth
with learn to live with sth
with leave so/sth with so/sth
with leave so with an impression
with leave with so
with leave word (with so)
with lend so a hand with sth
with let fly with sth
with let go (with sth)
with let loose (with sth)
with let out (with) sth
with let so get by with sth
with let so get on with sth
with let so have it (with both barrels)
with level with so (about so/sth)
with lie with so
with light sth with sth
with like a kid with a new toy
with like tryin' to scratch your ear with your elbow
with line so/sth up with so/sth
with line so/sth up with sth
with line so up (with so)
with line sth with sth
with line up with so
with link so/sth with so/sth
with live in (with so)
with live (together) with so
with live under the same roof (with so)
with live with so
with live with sth
with load so/sth down (with so/sth)
with load so/sth up (with so/sth)
with load sth with sth
with load up (with sth)
with lock horns (with so)
with lodge so with so
with lodge with so
with look on (with so)
with look (up)on so/sth with sth
with lose contact with so/sth
with lose favor (with so)
with lose one's touch (with so/sth)
with lose patience (with so/sth)
with lose touch with reality
with lose touch with so/sth
with lousy with so/sth
with make a deal with so
with make a hit with so
with make an appointment (with so)
with make arrangements (with so) (for sth)
with make away with so/sth
with make contact with so
with make do (with so/sth)
with make free with so
with make free with sth
with make friends with so
with make off with so/sth
with make (one's) peace with so
with make out (with so)
with make out (with so/sth)
with make points (with so)
with make sth with sth

with make time (with so)
with make up (with so)
with make with sth
with manage with so/sth
with march in step (with so)
with march out of time (with so/sth)
with mark so/sth with sth
with marry up (with so)
with mash sth with sth
with match so (up) (with so)
with match wits (with so)
with mate so with so
with mate with an animal
with mate with so
with meaner than a junkyard dog (with fourteen sucking pups)
with meddle with so
with meet up with so/sth
with meet with so
with meet with sth
with merge sth with sth
with merge with so/sth
with mesh with sth
with mess about (with sth)
with mess around (with sth)
with mess with so/sth
with mill cannot grind with water that is past.
with mingle in (with so)
with mingle so with so else
with mingle with so
with mix in (with so/sth)
with mix it up (with so)
with mix so up with so else
with mix sth up (with sth)
with mix sth up with sth else
with mix with so/sth
with mix with sth
with mixed up with so else
with moan with sth
with monkey with so/sth
with mop up with sth
with mop the floor up with so
with move forward with sth
with move in with so
with move off (to the side) with so
with neck with so
with negotiate (with so/sth) (over so/sth)
with niggle (over sth) (with so)
with not agree with so
with not exchange more than some number of words with so
with not have anything to do with so/sth
with not have anything to do with sth
with not hold with sth
with not in the same league with so/sth
with not playing with a full deck
with not touch so/sth with a ten-foot pole
with not with it
with Now you're cooking (with gas)!
with number so with sth
with oblige so with sth
with obsessed with so/sth
with occupy so with sth
with off on the right foot (with so/sth)
with off to a good start (with so/sth)
with off (to the side) with so
with Off with you!
with offend so with sth
with on a first-name basis (with so)
with on good terms (with so)
with on par (with so/sth)

with on speaking terms (with so)
with on the outs (with so)
with on with so
with one's (own) way (with so/sth)
with ooze with sth
with open up (about so/sth) (with so)
with open up (with so)
with open with so
with originate with so/sth
with ornament sth with sth
with out of favor (with so)
with out of keeping (with sth)
with out of line (with sth)
with out of step (with so/sth)
with out of time (with so/sth)
with out of touch (with so/sth)
with out of tune (with so/sth)
with over (and done) with
with over (with)
with overflow with so/sth
with pair up (with so)
with pal around (with so)
with pal up (with so)
with pally (with so)
with parley with so
with part company (with so)
with part with so/sth
with participate (in sth) (with so/sth)
with pass the time of day (with so)
with patch sth together (with sth)
with pave the way (for so/sth) (with sth)
with pay so (for sth) (with sth)
with pelt so/sth with sth
with penetrate sth with sth
with people sth with so
with pepper so/sth with sth
with perish with sth
with permeate sth with sth
with persevere with sth
with persist with sth
with pester so with sth
with physical (with so)
with pick a fight (with so)
with pick a quarrel (with so)
with pipe up (with sth)
with pitch in (and help) (with sth)
with place so with so/sth
with place sth with so/sth
with plague so/sth with sth
with plaster sth with sth
with play about (with so/sth)
with play along (with so/sth)
with play around (with so/sth)
with play ball with so
with play cat and mouse with so
with play fast and loose (with so/sth)
with play footsie with so
with play games (with so)
with play hardball (with so)
with play havoc with so/sth
with play hell with so/sth
with play hob with so/sth
with play in with so/sth
with play the devil with sth
with play with a full deck
with play with fire
with play with so/sth
with plead with so
with pleased with so/sth
with plot with so
with ply so with sth
with pock sth with sth
with poison so or an animal **with** sth

with poison sth with sth
with pollute sth with sth
with pour with rain
with power sth with sth
with preface sth with sth
with present so with sth
with prime sth with sth
with proceed with sth
with progress with sth
with provide so with sth
with punctuate sth with sth
with punish so with sth
with push ahead (with sth)
with push on (with sth)
with put so in touch with so/sth
with put so/sth with so
with put so up with so
with put to bed with a shovel
with put up with so/sth
with quake with sth
with quarrel (with so) (about so/sth)
with quarrel (with so) (over so/sth)
with quarrel with sth
with quibble (about so/sth) (with so)
with quiver with sth
with race with so/sth
with racked with pain
with raise havoc with so/sth
with raise hell (with sth)
with raise hob with so/sth
with raise sth with so
with raise the devil (with so)
with raise the devil (with sth)
with raise the dickens (with so/sth)
with rank so with so
with rank with so/sth
with rap with so
with rate so/sth with so/sth else
with rate with so
with ravished with delight
with reach an accord (with so)
with reach an agreement (with so)
with reach an understanding with so
with reach first base (with so/sth)
with reason with so
with receive so with open arms
with reckon with so/sth
with reconcile sth with sth
with reek with sth
with refresh so with sth
with refresh sth with sth
with regale so with sth
with regard so/sth with sth
with register sth with so/sth
with register with so
with reinforce so/sth with sth
with remain in touch (with so/sth)
with reminisce with so
with remonstrate (with so) (about so/sth)
with repay so with sth
with replenish sth with sth
with reproach so with sth
with resonate with so
with resound with sth
with rest with so/sth
with return with sth
with reunite so/sth with so/sth
with reverberate with sth
with reward so with sth
with rhyme sth with sth
with rhyme with sth
with rich with sth

with riddle so/sth with sth
with ride with so
with ring with sth
with rinse so's mouth out (with soap)
with rinse sth down (with sth)
with rinse sth with sth
with road to hell is paved with good intentions.
with roll with the punches
with room with so
with round sth off (with sth)
with rub elbows (with so)
with rub shoulders with so
with rub so/sth with sth
with rule with a velvet glove
with rule with an iron fist
with run around like a chicken with its head cut off
with run around with so
with run away with so
with run away with sth
with run off (with so)
with run off with so/sth
with run over sth with so
with run over with sth
with run so through (with sth)
with run with so
with run with sth
with run with the hare and hunt with the hounds
with saddle so with so/sth
with saddled with so/sth
with salt sth with sth
with salute so with sth
with satiate so or an animal with sth
with satisfy so or an animal with sth
with saturate so/sth with sth
with scarcely exchange more than some number of words with so
with score with so or a group
with scrape by (with sth)
with scream with sth
with screw around with so/sth
with scuffle with so
with seal sth (up) (with sth)
with sealed with a kiss
with seam sth with sth
with search with a fine-tooth comb
with season sth with sth
with see eye to eye (about so/sth) (with so)
with see with the naked eye
with seethe with so/sth
with seethe with sth
with seize so/sth with sth
with seized with sth
with send so away with sth
with serve so with sth
with serve with so
with set sth up (with so)
with settle a score with so
with settle the score (with so)
with settle up with so
with sever ties with so
with shack up (with so)
with shackle so with sth
with shake hands (with so)
with short with so
with shot through with sth
with shower so/sth with sth
with side with so
with sign on (with so/sth) (as sth)
with sign so up (with so/sth)

with sign (up) with so/sth
with sing along (with so/sth)
with sit right with so
with sit up with so
with sit well with so
with sit with so
with skip off (with sth)
with skip out with sth
with skirmish with so/sth
with sleep around (with so)
with sleep over (with so) (some place)
with sleep with so
with smear so/sth with sth
with smite so with sth
with smother so/sth with sth
with snow so/sth under with sth
with snuggle down (with so)
with snuggle down (with sth)
with soak so/sth with sth
with So will be with you in a minute.
with spar with so
with sparkle with sth
with spatter so/sth with sth
with speak with a forked tongue
with speak with so (about so/sth)
with splash so/sth with sth
with split one's sides (with laughter)
with split so/sth with sth
with split up (with so)
with sport with so/sth
with spray so/sth with sth
with spread sth with sth
with sprinkle so/sth with sth
with squabble with so
with squabble with sth
with square accounts (with so)
with square up with so
with square with so
with square with so
with squeal with sth
with squirm with sth
with stain sth with sth
with stamp so/sth with sth
with stand there with one's bare face hanging out
with stand up with so
with stand well with so
with stand with so
with start (off) with a bang
with start (off) with a clean slate
with start (off) with so/sth
with start out with so
with start (over) with a clean slate
with start sth up with sth
with start up with so/sth
with stay in touch (with so/sth)
with stay with so/sth
with step off (to the side) with so
with stick so with so/sth
with Stick with it.
with stick with so/sth
with sting so with sth
with stink with sth
with stinking with sth
with stock sth (up) with sth
with stock up (with sth)
with stop sth up (with sth)
with strew sth with sth
with stricken with sth
with strike a chord (with so)
with strike home with so
with strike so/sth with sth

with string along (with so)
with struggle along (with so/sth)
with struggle on with sth
with struggle with so for sth
with struggle with so/sth
with stuck with so/sth
with stuff so/sth with sth
with stuff so's head with sth
with suffuse sth with sth
with supply so/sth with sth
with surprise so with sth
with surround so/sth with so/sth
with swamp so/sth with sth
with swap so/sth with so
with swap with so
with swarm with so/sth
with swathe so/sth with sth
with swell with sth
with swim with sth
with swimming with so/sth
with swing with so/sth
with switch (around) (with so/sth)
with sympathize with so (about so/sth)
with synchronize sth with sth else
with taint sth with sth
with take a hard line (with so)
with take issue with so
with take issue with sth
with take it with one
with take liberties with so/sth
with take pains with so/sth
with take so/sth with one
with take sth home (with oneself)
with take sth up (with so)
with take sth with a pinch of salt
with take sth with one
with take sth with sth
with Take the bitter with the sweet.
with Take the rough with the smooth.
with take turns with so
with take turns (with sth)
with take up with so
with taken with so/sth
with talk so/sth over (with so)
with talk with so (about so/sth)
with tally with sth
with tamper with so/sth
with tangle with so/sth (over so/sth)
with tap sth with sth
with tarred with the same brush
with taunt so with sth
with tax so/sth with sth
with team up (with so)
with teem with so/sth
with tell so what to do with sth
with temper sth with sth
with tempt so with sth
with (That's) fine with me.
with threaten so with so/sth
with thrill so with sth
with through with so/sth
with throw in with so
with throw the baby out with the bath(water)
with tie in (with so/sth)
with tie in with sth
with tie (with so) (for sth)
with tightfisted (with money)
with Times change and we with time.
with tinge with sth
with tinker (around) (with sth)
with tip so with sth
with (To) hell with that!

with top sth off (with sth)
with top sth with sth
with touch base (with so)
with touch so/sth with sth
with toy with so
with toy with sth
with trade insults (with so)
with trade sth with so
with trade with so/sth
with travel with so
with travel with sth
with treat so (for sth) (with sth)
with tremble with sth
with trifle with so/sth
with trim sth with sth
with trouble so with sth
with trust so with so/sth
with try sth on with so
with tussle with so/sth
with twiddle with sth
with twinkle with sth
with unite with so/sth with so/sth
with unite with so
with up to here (with sth)
with up with so
with use sth with sth
with vaccinate so or an animal with sth
with vary with sth
with verify sth with so
with vest so with sth
with vie (with so) (for so/sth)
with visit with so
with vote with one's feet
with walk away with so or an animal
with walk away with sth
with walk off with sth
with walk out with so
with walk with so
with walk with sth
with wall-to-wall (with) sth
with waltz off (with sth)
with war with so
with wash sth down (with sth)
with weary so with sth
with weight so/sth down (with sth)
with welcome so with open arms
with welcome so with sth
with well up with sth
with welsh on sth (with so)
with What's new with you?
with What's the matter (with you)?
with What's with so/sth?
with what with sth
with wind up with so/sth
with wipe so/sth (off) (with sth)
with wipe the floor up with so
with with a heavy heart
with with a vengeance
with with a view to doing sth
with with a will
with with advance notice
with with all one's heart (and soul)
with with all the fixin(g)s
with with all the trimmings
with with an eye to doing sth
with with bated breath
with with bells on (one's toes)
with with both hands tied behind one's back
with with child
with with each passing day
with with ease
with with every (other) breath

with with everything (on it)
with with fits and starts
with with flying colors
with (with) hat in hand
with with impunity
with with it
with with my blessing
with with no strings attached
with with one hand tied behind one's back
with with (one's) eyes (wide) open
with with one's tail between one's legs
with With or without?
with With pleasure.
with with reference to so/sth
with with regard to so/sth
with with relish
with with respect to so/sth
with with so/sth for some time
with with sth to spare
with with the best will in the world
with with the naked eye
with With whom do you wish to speak?
with With you in a minute.
with word with so (about sth)
with work sth out (with so)
with work with so/sth
with work wonders (with so/sth)
with wouldn't touch so/sth with a ten-foot pole
with wrangle (with so) (about so/sth)
with wrangle (with so) (over so/sth)
with wrap so/sth (up) (with sth)
with wrapped up (with so/sth)
with wreak havoc (with sth)
with wrestle with so
with wrestle with sth
with writhe with sth
with You can catch more flies with honey than with vinegar.
with (You) can't take it with you.
with You could have knocked me over with a feather.
with You'll never get away with it.
with Your secret is safe with me.
withdraw withdraw from sth
withdraw withdraw into oneself
withdraw withdraw into sth
withdraw withdraw so from sth
withdraw withdraw sth from so/sth
withdraw withdraw sth into sth
wither wither away
wither wither on the vine
wither wither up
withhold withhold sth from so or an animal
within act within one's rights
within apply within
within bring so/sth within range (of so/sth)
within bring sth within a range
within come within a hair('s breadth) of so/sth
within come within an ace of sth
within come within an inch of doing sth
within come within an inch of so/sth
within come within earshot (of sth)
within come within range
within come within sth
within confine so or an animal within sth
within enclose so/sth (with)in sth
within encompass so/sth (with)in sth
within fall within sth

within inquire within
within keep (so/sth) within bounds
within keep within sth
within lie within sth
within live within one's means
within live within sth
within move within earshot (of sth)
within move within range
within remain within (sth)
within stay within sth
within within a hair('s breadth) of sth
within within a stone's throw (of sth)
within within an ace of (doing) sth
within within an inch of one's life
within within bounds
within within calling distance
within within earshot (of sth)
within within hailing distance
within within limits
within within one's grasp
within within one's rights
within within range
within within reason
within within shouting distance
within within so's grasp
within within so's reach
within within walking distance
without absent without leave
without carry on without so/sth
without cut so off without a penny
without do without
without Don't give up without a fight!
without find oneself without so/sth
without get along without (so/sth)
without get by (without so/sth)
without get on (without so/sth)
without go absent without leave
without go without
without I won't give up without a fight.
without (It) (just) goes without saying.
without live without sth
without lost without so/sth
without manage without so/sth
without prophet is not without honor save in his own country.
without reckon without so
without There is no pleasure without pain.
without There's no rose without a thorn.
without (There's) no smoke without fire.
without up the creek (without a paddle)
without With or without?
without without a doubt
without without a hitch
without without a moment to spare
without without a shadow of a doubt
without without any strings attached
without without batting an eye
without without fail
without without further ado
without without half trying
without without missing a beat
without without question
without without rhyme or reason
without without (so much as) a (for or) by your leave
without without so much as doing sth
without You cannot make an omelet without breaking eggs.

without You cannot make bricks without straw.
witness on the (witness) stand
witness witness for so/sth
witness witness to sth
wives old wives' tale
wobble wobble about
woe tale of woe
woe Woe is me!
wolf buy so's wolf ticket
wolf cry wolf
wolf cut one's wolf loose
wolf growing youth has a wolf in his belly.
wolf keep the wolf from the door
wolf The wolf is at the door.
wolf throw so to the wolves
wolf When the wolf comes in at the door, love creeps out of the window.
wolf wolf in sheep's clothing
wolf wolf sth down
woman God's gift (to women)
woman Hell hath no fury like a woman scorned.
woman make an honest woman of so
woman Men make houses, women make homes.
woman woman of ill repute
woman woman's place is in the home.
woman woman's work is never done.
woman woman to woman
women God's gift (to women)
women Men make houses, women make homes.
won Faint heart never won fair lady.
wonder I don't wonder.
wonder (I was) just wondering.
wonder (I) wonder if
wonder nine days' wonder
wonder no wonder
wonder seven-day wonder
wonder Time works wonders.
wonder wonder about so/sth
wonder wonder at so/sth
wonder Wonders never cease!
wonder work wonders (with so/sth)
wonderful (I'm) having a wonderful time; wish you were here.
woo pitch (the) woo
woo woo so away (from so/sth)
wood babe in the woods
wood cannot see the wood for the trees
wood cut the deadwood out
wood Fields have eyes, and woods have ears.
wood I wasn't brought up in the woods to be scared by owls.
wood in some neck of the woods
wood knock on wood
wood Never halloo till you are out of the woods.
wood out of the woods
wood woods are full of so/sth
wooden Don't take any wooden nickels.
woodwork bring so/sth out of the woodwork
woodwork come out of the woodwork
woodwork creep out of the woodwork
woodwork out of the woodwork
wool all wool and a yard wide
wool all wool and no shoddy

wool dyed-in-the-wool
wool pull the wool over so's eyes
wool slut's wool
woolly wild and woolly
word Actions speak louder than words.
word as good as one's word
word at a loss (for words)
word beyond words
word break one's word
word by word of mouth
word Could I have a word with you?
word didn't exchange more than three words with so
word dirty word
word Don't breathe a word of this to anyone.
word eat one's words
word exchange no more than some number of words with so
word famous last words
word final word
word Fine words butter no parsnips.
word from the word go
word get a word in edgewise
word get the final word
word get the word
word go back on one's word
word hang on (so's) every word
word Hard words break no bones.
word hardly exchange more than some number of words with so
word have a way with words
word have one's words stick in one's throat
word have words
word hear word (from so/sth)
word household word
word (I) won't breathe a word (of it)
word I'd like (to have) a word with you.
word in a word
word in other words
word in so many words
word keep one's word
word last word
word leave word for so to do sth
word leave word (with so)
word man of few words
word Many a true word is spoken in jest.
word mark my word(s)
word mince (one's) words
word Mum's the word.
word not breathe a word (about so/sth)
word not breathe a word of it
word not exchange more than some number of words with so
word not utter a word
word one final word
word one's word is one's bond
word or words to that effect
word picture is worth a thousand words.
word put in a good word (for so)
word put sth into words
word put the hard word on so
word put words in(to) so's mouth
word receive word (from so/sth)
word say the word
word scarcely exchange more than some number of words with so
word send word to so
word so's word is good

word so's word of honor
word spread the word
word Sticks and stones may break my bones, but words will never hurt me.
word suit one's actions to one's words
word Take my word for it.
word take one at one's word
word take so's word for sth
word take so's word on sth
word take the words out of so's mouth
word Them's fighting words!
word There's many a true word spoken in jest.
word too funny for words
word true to one's word
word twist so's words (around)
word weigh so's words
word What's the (good) word?
word word by word
word word for word
word word (from so/sth)
word word (once) spoken is past recalling.
word word to the wise
word word with so (about sth)
word words to live by
word (You) took the words right out of my mouth.
work all in a day's work
work All work and no play makes Jack a dull boy.
work at work
work close enough for government work
work devil finds work for idle hands to do.
work dirty work
work Does it work for you?
work dog ate my homework.
work Don't work too hard.
work Everything will work out (all right).
work Everything will work out for the best.
work fancy footwork
work get down to work
work go like clockwork
work go to work (on so/sth)
work good enough for government work
work (good) working over
work grunt work
work have a (good) working over
work have one's work cut out for one
work If ifs and ands were pots and pans (there'd be no work for tinkers' hands).
work *in an ivory tower
work in the works
work It is not work that kills, but worry.
work (It) works for me.
work I've got work to do.
work Keep up the good work.
work knock off (work)
work lick of work
work little (hard) work never hurt anyone.
work make fast work of so/sth
work make short work of so/sth
work Many hands make light work.
work off (work)
work one's work is cut out for one

work out of work
work pile the work on (so)
work put in a hard day at work
work regular as clockwork
work run like clockwork
work set so/sth to work
work set to work (on so/sth)
work shoot the works
work spill the works
work take off from work
work take ((some) time) off from work
work Things will work out (all right).
work throw a monkey wrench in the works
work Time works wonders.
work whole works
work woman's work is never done.
work work against so/sth
work work among so/sth
work work around so/sth
work work around to so/sth
work work as sth
work work at sth
work work away (at sth)
work work down (the line) (to so/sth)
work work for so
work work for sth
work work in an ivory tower
work work itself out
work work like a beaver
work work of art
work work on so
work work on sth
work work one's ass off
work work one's fingers to the bone
work work one's tail off
work work one's way along sth
work work (one's way) into sth
work work (one's way) through sth
work work one's way up (to sth)
work work oneself up
work work oneself (up) into a lather
work work out
work work some fat off
work work some weight off
work work so/sth into sth
work work so/sth over
work work so/sth to so/sth
work work so over
work work so up
work work sth down
work work sth into sth
work work sth off
work work sth out of sth
work work sth out (with so)
work work sth over
work work sth through (sth)
work work sth under sth
work work sth up
work work things out
work work through channels
work work together
work work toward sth
work work under so
work work under sth
work work up a sweat
work work up a thirst
work work up to sth
work work (up)on sth
work work with so/sth
work work wonders (with so/sth)
work worked up (over sth)
work working stiff

work works
workshop idle brain is the devil's workshop.
world all over the world
world best of both worlds
world bring so into the world
world carry the weight of the world on one's shoulders
world come down in the world
world come into the world
world come up in the world
world dead to the world
world enjoy the best of both worlds
world feel on top of the world
world for all the world
world from all corners of the world
world God's in his heaven; all's right with the world.
world grow worlds apart
world Half the world knows not how the other half lives.
world hand that rocks the cradle rules the world.
world has the world by the tail (with a downhill drag)
world How's the world (been) treating you?
world in a world of one's own
world in the world
world It takes all kinds (to make a world).
world Laugh and the world laughs with you; weep and you weep alone.
world live in a world of one's own
world live in the best of both worlds
world live worlds apart
world Love makes the world go round.
world make one's way in the world
world move up in the world
world next world
world not for (anything in) the world
world not have a care in the world
world not long for this world
world not miss sth for the world
world on top of the world
world out of this world
world set the world on fire
world (sitting) on top of the world
world tell the (whole) world
world think the world of so/sth
world think worlds apart
world Today here, tomorrow the world.
world Where in the world...?
world whole wide world
world with the best will in the world
world world is one's oyster.
world worlds apart
worm can of worms
worm early bird catches the worm.
worm Even a worm will turn.
worm open a can of worms
worm worm (has) turned.
worm worm (one's way) in(to sth)
worm worm (one's way) out (of sth)
worm worm sth out of so
worry Don't worry (about a thing).
worry Don't worry your (pretty little) head about it.
worry It is not work that kills, but worry.
worry Not to worry.
worry worried sick (about so/sth)
worry worry about so/sth

worry worry an animal out of sth
worry worry oneself about so/sth
worry worry over so/sth
worry worry sth out of so
worry worry through sth
worry worrywart
worse fate worse than death
worse for better or for worse
worse go from bad to worse
worse (I) could be worse.
worse (I've) seen worse.
worse look none the worse for wear
worse none the worse for wear
worse Nothing so bad but (it) might have been worse.
worse One's bark is worse than one's bite.
worse take a turn for the worse
worse (Things) could be worse.
worse worse for wear
worship worship so as sth
worship worship the ground so walks on
worst at (the) worst
worst Hope for the best and prepare for the worst.
worst Hope for the best but expect the worst.
worst I wouldn't wish that on my worst enemy.
worst if (the) worst comes to (the) worst
worst in the worst way
worst one's own worst enemy
worst worst of sth
worst worst-case scenario
worth bird in the hand is worth two in the bush.
worth for all it's worth
worth for what(ever) it's worth
worth If a thing is worth doing, it's worth doing well.
worth It isn't worth it.
worth It isn't worth the trouble.
worth make it worth so's while
worth not worth a damn
worth not worth a dime
worth not worth a hill of beans
worth not worth a red cent
worth not worth mentioning
worth not worth one's while
worth not worth the paper it's printed on
worth not worth the paper it's written on
worth not worth the trouble
worth one's money's worth
worth ounce of common sense is worth a pound of theory.
worth ounce of discretion is worth a pound of wit.
worth ounce of prevention is worth a pound of cure.
worth picture is worth a thousand words.
worth play it for all it's worth
worth put one's two cents(' worth) in
worth worth its weight in gold
worth worth of a thing is what it will bring.
worth worth one's salt
worth worth so's while
worth worthy of the name

worthy worthy of the name
would as luck would have it
would Do as you would be done by.
would Do unto others as you would have them do unto you.
would He that would eat the kernel must crack the nut.
would He that would go to sea for pleasure, would go to hell for a pastime.
would He that would have eggs must endure the cackling of hens.
would He that would the daughter win, must with the mother first begin.
would He who would climb the ladder must begin at the bottom.
would (I) would if I could(, but I can't).
would I would like you to meet so.
would If God did not exist, it would be necessary to invent Him.
would If it was a snake it woulda bit you.
would If wishes were horses, then beggars would ride.
would If you would be well served, serve yourself.
would if you would(, please)
would It would take an act of Congress to do sth.
would language that would fry bacon
would never would have guessed
would rose by any other name would smell as sweet.
would What would you like to drink?
would What would you say if...?
would Who would have thought?
would would as soon do sth as look at you
would would (just) as soon do sth
would would like (to have) so/sth
would would not be caught dead (doing sth)
would would not be seen dead (doing sth)
would would rather
would Would you believe!
would (Would you) care for another (one)?
would (Would you) care to...?
would (Would you) care to dance?
would (Would you) care to join us?
would Would you excuse me?
would Would you excuse us, please?
would Would you please?
wouldn't Butter wouldn't melt (in so's mouth).
wouldn't Don't do anything I wouldn't do.
wouldn't (I) wouldn't bet on it.
wouldn't (I) wouldn't count on it.
wouldn't (I) wouldn't if I were you.
wouldn't (I) wouldn't know.
wouldn't I wouldn't touch it with a ten-foot pole.
wouldn't I wouldn't wish that on a dog.
wouldn't I wouldn't wish that on my worst enemy.
wouldn't If a toady frog had wings, he wouldn't bump his ass.
wouldn't If frogs had wheels, they wouldn't bump their butts.

wouldn't land so poor it wouldn't even raise a fuss
wouldn't look as if butter wouldn't melt in one's mouth
wouldn't wouldn't dream of doing sth
wouldn't wouldn't touch so/sth with a ten-foot pole
wouldn't wouldn't want to be in so's shoes
wouldn't Yesterday wouldn't be too soon.
wouldn't You wouldn't dare (to do sth)!
wouldn't You wouldn't (do that)!
wound lick one's wounds
wound rub salt in a wound
wrack go to wrack and ruin
wrack wrack and ruin
wrangle wrangle (with so) (about so/sth)
wrangle wrangle (with so) (over so/sth)
wrap get sth wrapped up
wrap have sth wrapped up
wrap hold under wraps
wrap keep sth under wraps
wrap keep under wraps
wrap under wraps
wrap wrap around so/sth
wrap wrap one's car around sth
wrap wrap so/sth around sth
wrap wrap so/sth (up) (in sth)
wrap wrap so/sth (up) (with sth)
wrap wrap sth around so
wrap wrap sth up
wrap wrapped up
wrath Do not let the sun go down on your wrath.
wrath soft answer turneth away wrath.
wreak wreak havoc (with sth)
wreak wreak sth (up)on so/sth
wreak wreak vengeance (up)on so/sth
wreathe wreathe (itself) around so/sth
wreathe wreathe so/sth in sth
wreathe wreathe sth around so/sth
wreck go under the wrecking ball
wrench throw a monkey wrench in the works
wrench wrench sth from so
wrench wrench sth off (of) so/sth
wrench wrench sth out of sth
wrest wrest so/sth (away) from so/sth
wrest wrest sth off (of) sth
wrestle wrestle sth from so
wrestle wrestle sth into sth
wrestle wrestle with so
wrestle wrestle with sth
wriggle wriggle in(to sth)
wriggle wriggle out (of sth)
wring wring sth from sth
wring wring sth out
wringer put so through the wringer
wrinkle get the wrinkles out (of sth)
wrinkle wrinkle sth up
wrinkle wrinkle up
wrist slap on the wrist
wrist slap so on the wrist
write Don't forget to write.
write *in plain language
write in writing
write It's written all over one's face.
write not worth the paper it's written on
write nothing to write home about
write put so in writing
write read the handwriting on the wall

write Remember to write.
write see the (hand)writing on the wall
write That's all she wrote.
write That's what she wrote.
write write about so/sth
write write against so/sth
write write away
write write back to so
write write down to so
write write for sth
write write in(to sth) (for sth)
write write of so/sth
write write off (to so) (for sth)
write write on and on
write write so down as sth
write write so for sth
write write so in (on sth)
write write so/sth about sth
write write so/sth off
write write so/sth up
write write sth against so/sth
write write sth back to so
write write sth down
write write sth in
write write sth into sth
write write sth off
write write sth out
write write sth to so
write write sth to sth
write write sth up
write write to so
write write (up)on so/sth
write writer's block
write written in stone
write wrote the book on sth
writhe writhe in sth
writhe writhe under sth
writhe writhe with sth
written It's written all over one's face.
written not worth the paper it's written on
written written in stone
wrong back the wrong horse
wrong bark up the wrong tree
wrong born on the wrong side of the blanket
wrong dead wrong
wrong dial the wrong number
wrong fall into the wrong hands
wrong get it wrong
wrong get so (all) wrong
wrong get up on the wrong side of bed
wrong go wrong
wrong If anything can go wrong, it will.
wrong in the wrong
wrong off on the wrong foot
wrong on so's wrong side
wrong on the wrong side of so
wrong on the wrong track
wrong rub so('s fur) the wrong way
wrong start off on the wrong foot
wrong step off on the wrong foot
wrong take so/sth wrong
wrong take sth the wrong way
wrong Two wrongs do not make a right.
wrong What's wrong?
wrong wrong number
wrong wrong side of the tracks
wrote That's all she wrote.
wrote That's what she wrote.

wrote wrote the book on sth
wroth wax wroth
wrought wrought up
X Generation X
X X marks the spot.
X X so/sth out
X X'd out
ya See ya.
ya See ya, bye-bye.
yack yack one's head off
yack yack sth up
yammer yammer (away) about so/sth
yank yank at so/sth
yank yank on sth
yank yank so around
yank yank so/sth
yank yank so's chain
yank yank sth off
yank yank sth up
yap yap about so/sth
yap yap at so
yard all wool and a yard wide
yard Give so an inch and he'll take a yard.
yard meaner than a junkyard dog (with fourteen sucking pups)
yard whole nine yards
yarn spin a yarn
ye Abandon hope, all ye who enter here.
ye Gather ye rosebuds while ye may.
ye Judge not, lest ye be judged.
ye Judge not, that ye be not judged.
ye Oh, ye of little faith.
ye Seek and ye shall find.
ye Ye gods (and little fishes)!
yeah Oh, yeah?
year advanced in years
year all year round
year along in years
year by the year
year Christmas comes but once a year.
year first hundred years are the hardest.
year for (some) years running
year frighten so out of a year's growth
year get on (in years)
year (I'll) see you next year.
year in an age of years
year Keep a thing seven years and you'll (always) find a use for it.
year Never in a thousand years!
year Not in a thousand years!
year of mature years
year on in years
year one's sunset years
year put (some) years on so/sth
year ring in the new year
year seven-year itch
year take years off (of) so/sth
year twilight years
year up in years
year well up in years
year year after year
year year in, year out
year years running
yearn yearn for so/sth
yell yell at so/sth
yell yell bloody murder
yell yell one's guts out
yell yell one's head off
yell yell out
yell yell sth at so/sth

yell yell sth out (at so/sth)
yellow have a yellow belly
yellow have a yellow streak down one's back
yellow yellow streak (down so's back)
yen yen for so/sth
yes Yes indeed(y (do))!
yes Yes siree(, Bob)!
yesterday I need it yesterday.
yesterday need sth yesterday
yesterday not born yesterday
yesterday Yesterday wouldn't be too soon.
yet mills of God grind slowly, yet they grind exceeding small.
yet will be the death of so/sth (yet)
yet You ain't seen nothing yet!
yield *right-of-way
yield yield so/sth (over) (to so/sth)
yield yield so/sth up (to so)
yield yield sth to so
yield yield to so
yoke yoke around so's neck
yoke yoke people or things together
yokel local yokel
yon hither, thither, and yon
yon thither and yon
you After you.
you All right for you!
you Am I glad to see you!
you and what have you
you And you?
you Anything you say.
you Anytime you are ready.
you (Are) things getting you down?
you (Are you) doing okay?
you (Are you) feeling okay?
you (Are you) going my way?
you (Are you) leaving so soon?
you (Are you) ready for this?
you (Are you) ready to order?
you (Are you) sorry you asked?
you As you make your bed, so you must lie (up)on it.
you As you sow, so shall you reap.
you Ask me no questions, I'll tell you no lies.
you Be just before you're generous.
you before you can say Jack Robinson
you before you know it
you Behind you!
you Believe nothing of what you hear, and only half of what you see.
you Believe you me!
you Better the devil you know than the devil you don't know.
you between you (and) me and the bedpost
you between you and me and these four walls
you Bully for you!
you Can I help you?
you Can I see you again?
you Can I see you in my office?
you Can you excuse us, please?
you Can you hold?
you Can you imagine?
you Can you keep a secret?
you Come back when you can stay longer.
you (Could I) buy you a drink?
you Could I call you?

you (Could I) get you something (to drink)?

you (Could I) give you a lift?

you Could I have a word with you?

you Could I have so call you?

you Could I help you?

you Could I join you?

you Could I see you again?

you Could I see you in my office?

you Could you excuse us, please?

you Could you hold?

you Could you keep a secret?

you Damned if you do, damned if you don't.

you Did you hear?

you Do as you would be done by.

you Do I have to paint (you) a picture?

you Do I have to spell it out (for you)?

you Do I need to paint you a picture?

you Do unto others as you would have them do unto you.

you (Do you) care if I join you?

you (Do) you eat with that mouth?

you Do you expect me to believe that?

you Do you follow?

you (Do you) get my drift?

you (Do you) get the picture?

you (Do) you hear?

you (Do) you kiss your momma with that mouth?

you (Do you) know what?

you (Do you) know what I mean?

you (Do you) know what I'm saying?

you (Do) you mean to say sth?

you (Do) you mean to tell me sth?

you Do you mind?

you (Do you) mind if...?

you (Do you) mind if I join you?

you Do you read me?

you (Do you) want to know something?

you (Do you) want to make something of it?

you (Do) you want to step outside?

you Does it work for you?

you done told you

you Don't bite off more than you can chew.

you Don't call us, we'll call you.

you Don't cry before you are hurt.

you Don't I know you from somewhere?

you Don't let so/sth get you down.

you Don't let the bastards wear you down.

you Don't make me tell you again!

you Don't put off for tomorrow what you can do today.

you Don't you know it!

you Don't you wish!

you Dream of a funeral and you hear of a marriage.

you Dream of a funeral and you hear of a wedding.

you Fancy meeting you here!

you fine how do you do

you Flattery will get you nowhere.

you Fool me once, shame on you; fool me twice, shame on me.

you Forget you!

you Fuck you!

you Get along with you!

you Give it all you've got!

you Go on (with you)!

you good for what ails you

you Good for you!

you Have I got something for you!

you (Have you) been keeping busy?

you (Have you) been keeping cool?

you (Have you) been keeping out of trouble?

you (Have you) been okay?

you (Have you) changed your mind?

you Have you heard?

you Have you met so?

you Haven't I seen you somewhere before?

you Here's looking at you.

you Here's to you.

you Here you go.

you How about you?

you How (are) you doing?

you How (are) you feeling?

you How are you getting on?

you How can I serve you?

you How could you (do sth)?

you How do you do.

you How do you know?

you How do you like school?

you How do you like that?

you How do you like them apples?

you How do you like this weather?

you How does that grab you?

you How dumb do you think I am?

you How goes it (with you)?

you How (have) you been?

you How many times do I have to tell you?

you How may I help you?

you How's by you?

you How's (it) with you?

you How's the world (been) treating you?

you How will I know you?

you How will I recognize you?

you How're things (with you)?

you (I) can't thank you enough.

you I couldn't ask you to do that.

you I didn't hear you.

you I don't mind telling you (sth).

you I don't want to alarm you, but

you I don't want to upset you, but

you (I) haven't seen you in a long time.

you (I) haven't seen you in a month of Sundays.

you I hear what you're saying.

you I hear you.

you (I) hope to see you again (sometime).

you I kid you not.

you I know (just) what you mean.

you (I) never thought I'd see you here!

you I owe you one.

you I promise you!

you (I) read you loud and clear.

you I would like you to meet so.

you (I) wouldn't if I were you.

you I'd like (for) you to meet so.

you I'd like (to have) a word with you.

you If at first you don't succeed, try, try again.

you if I were you

you If it was a snake it woulda bit you.

you if I've told you once, I've told you a thousand times

you If there's anything you need, don't hesitate to ask.

you If you can't be good, be careful.

you If you can't beat them, join them.

you If you can't lick 'em, join 'em.

you If you can't stand the heat, get out of the kitchen.

you If you don't like it, (you can) lump it.

you If you don't make mistakes, you don't make anything.

you If you don't mind!

you If you don't see what you want, please ask (for it).

you if you get my drift

you if you know what's good for you

you If you lie down with dogs, you will get up with fleas.

you if you must

you If you play with fire, you get burned.

you if you please

you If you run after two hares, you will catch neither.

you If you want a thing done well, do it yourself.

you If you want peace, (you must) prepare for war.

you If you would be well served, serve yourself.

you if you would(, please)

you if you'll pardon the expression

you If you're born to be hanged, then you'll never be drowned.

you if you've a mind to do sth

you (I'll) be right with you.

you (I'll) be seeing you.

you (I'll) catch you later.

you I'll get back to you (on that).

you I'll (have to) let you go.

you I'll look you up when I'm in town.

you (I'll) see you in a little while.

you I'll see you later.

you (I'll) see you next year.

you (I'll) see you (real) soon.

you (I'll) see you then.

you (I'll) see you tomorrow.

you (I'll) talk to you soon.

you I'll thank you to keep your opinions to yourself.

you I'll thank you to mind your own business.

you (I'll) try to catch you later.

you (I'll) try to catch you some other time.

you (I'm) delighted to have you (here).

you (I'm) glad you could come.

you (I'm) glad you could drop by.

you (I'm) having a wonderful time; wish you were here.

you I'm like you

you I'm not finished with you.

you (I'm) pleased to meet you.

you (I'm) sorry you asked (that).

you (I'm) (very) glad to meet you.

you I'm with you.

you (Is it) cold enough for you?

you (Is it) hot enough for you?

you (It) just goes to show (you) (sth).

you (It's been) good talking to you.

you It's for you.

you (It's) good to have you here.

you (It's) good to see you (again).

you (It's) just what you need.
you (It's) nice to have you here.
you (It's) nice to meet you.
you (It's) nice to see you.
you It's you!
you I've heard so much about you.
you Just (you) wait (and see)!
you Keep a thing seven years and you'll (always) find a use for it.
you Keep your shop and your shop will keep you.
you Laugh and the world laughs with you; weep and you weep alone.
you Let me get back to you (on that).
you like, you know
you Look before you leap.
you Look me up when you're in town.
you Love you!
you lucky for you
you May I help you?
you May I see you again?
you mind you
you More power to you!
you more than you('ll ever) know
you more you get, the more you want.
you more you have, the more you want.
you need I remind you that...
you Never ask pardon before you are accused.
you Never halloo till you are out of the woods.
you Never make a threat you cannot carry out.
you Never trouble trouble till trouble troubles you.
you Nice meeting you.
you Nice place you have here.
you no matter how you slice it
you No, thank you.
you no thanks to you
you Not if I see you first.
you Not if I see you sooner.
you Now you're cooking (with gas)!
you Now you're talking!
you Nuts to you!
you Off with you!
you pay as you go
you Practice what you preach.
you quicker than you can say Jack Robinson
you same to you.
you Says you!
you See ya.
you See ya, bye-bye.
you See you.
you See you around.
you (See you) later.
you See you later, alligator.
you Shame on you!
you Sing before breakfast, you'll cry before night.
you Smile when you say that.
you so clean you could eat off the floor
you so cold you could hang meat
you so quiet you could hear a pin drop
you so still you could hear a pin drop
you So will be with you in a minute.
you Sooner than you think.
you sure as you live
you Thank you.
you Thank you a lot.
you Thank you for a lovely evening.

you Thank you for a lovely time.
you Thank you for calling.
you Thank you for having me.
you Thank you for inviting me.
you Thank you for sharing.
you Thank you kindly.
you Thank you so much.
you Thank you very much.
you That's a fine how-do-you-do.
you That's easy for you to say.
you That's just what you need.
you That's show business (for you).
you The hell you say!
you There you are.
you There you go.
you They must have seen you coming.
you thing you don't want is dear at any price.
you Three strikes and you are out.
you time flies (when you're having fun)
you (We) don't see you much around here anymore.
you We were just talking about you.
you (Well,) what do you know!
you (We're) delighted to have you (here).
you (We're) glad you could come.
you Were you born in a barn?
you wham bam thank you ma'am
you What about you?
you What are you drinking?
you What are you driving at?
you What are you having?
you What brings you here?
you What can I do for you?
you What can I tell you?
you What do you know?
you What do you know (about that)?
you What do you know for sure?
you What do you say?
you What do you think?
you What do you think of that?
you What do you think of this weather?
you What do you think you are doing here?
you What do you want me to say?
you What else can I do for you?
you What have you been up to?
you What makes you think so?
you What number are you calling?
you What's it to you?
you What's new with you?
you What's the matter (with you)?
you What would you like to drink?
you What would you say if...?
you What you don't know won't hurt you.
you What you see is what you get.
you Whatever turns you on.
you when you get a chance
you when you get a minute
you Where do (you think) you get off?
you Where have you been all my life?
you Where (have) you been hiding (yourself)?
you Where (have) you been keeping yourself?
you Where will I find you?
you Who do you think you are?
you Who do you think you're kidding?
you Who do you think you're talking to?

you Who do you want to speak to?
you Who do you want (to talk to)?
you Why buy a cow when you can get milk for free?
you why don't you?
you Will I see you again?
you Will you excuse us, please?
you Will you hold?
you With whom do you wish to speak?
you With you in a minute.
you Won't you come in?
you would as soon do sth as look at you
you Would you believe!
you (Would you) care for another (one)?
you (Would you) care to...?
you (Would you) care to dance?
you (Would you) care to join us?
you Would you excuse me?
you Would you excuse us, please?
you Would you please?
you You ain't just whistlin' Dixie.
you You ain't seen nothing yet!
you You (always) give up too eas(il)y.
you You and what army?
you You and who else?
you You are more than welcome.
you You are never too old to learn.
you You are something else (again)!
you You are welcome.
you You asked for it!
you You been keeping busy?
you You been keeping cool?
you You been keeping out of trouble?
you You been okay?
you You bet!
you You bet your boots!
you You bet your (sweet) life!
you You betcha!
you You called?
you You can bet the farm (on so/sth).
you You can catch more flies with honey than with vinegar.
you You can lead a horse to water, but you can't make it drink.
you You can say that again!
you You cannot get a quart into a pint pot.
you You cannot get blood from a stone.
you You cannot get blood from a turnip.
you You cannot have your cake and eat it (too).
you You cannot lose what you never had.
you You cannot make a silk purse out of a sow's ear.
you You cannot make an omelet without breaking eggs.
you You cannot make bricks without straw.
you You cannot please everyone.
you You cannot put new wine in old bottles.
you You cannot serve God and mammon.
you You cannot teach an old dog new tricks.
you (You) can't beat that.
you You can't expect me to believe that.
you (You) can't fight city hall.

you (You) can't get there from here.
you You can't mean that!
you (You) can't take it with you.
you You can't tell a book by its cover.
you (You) can't top that.
you (You) can't win them all.
you You changed your mind?
you (You) could have fooled me.
you You could have knocked me over with a feather.
you You couldn't (do that)!
you You doing okay?
you You don't expect me to believe that.
you You don't get something for nothing.
you You don't know the half of it.
you You don't know where it's been.
you You don't say.
you You first.
you You get what you pay for.
you You got it!
you You got me beat.
you You got me there.
you You got to do what you got to do.
you You have to eat a peck of dirt before you die.
you You hear?
you You heard so.
you You just don't get it!
you You (just) wait (and see)!
you (You) (just) watch!
you you know
you You leaving so soon?
you You make a better door than you do a window.
you You make me laugh!
you You mean to tell me sth?
you You must lose a fly to catch a trout.
you You never know (what you can do) till you try.
you You never miss the water till the well runs dry.
you You pays your money and you takes your chance(s).
you You (really) said a mouthful.
you You said it!
you You scared the crap out of me.
you You scared the devil out of me.
you You scared the hell out of me.
you You scratch my back and I'll scratch yours.
you You think you're so smart!
you (You) took the words right out of my mouth.
you (You) want a piece of me?
you (You want to) know something?
you You want to make something of it?
you You win some, you lose some.
you You wouldn't dare (to do sth)!
you You wouldn't (do that)!
you You('d) better believe it!
you (You'd) better get moving.
you You'll be sorry you asked.
you You'll get onto it.
you You'll get the hang of it.
you You'll never get away with it.
you You're dern tootin'!
you You're excused.
you You're (just) wasting my time.
you You're out of your mind!
you You're telling me!

you You're the doctor.
you You're too much!
you You're welcome.
you You've got another think coming.
you (You've) got me stumped.
you You've got to be kidding!
you You've got to be out of your mind!
young act young at heart
young Better be an old man's darling than a young man's slave.
young good die young.
young keep so young at heart
young not as young as one used to be
young stay young at heart
young Whom the gods love die young.
young young at heart
young Young men may die, but old men must die.
your Act your age!
your Anything new down your way?
your As you make your bed, so you must lie (up)on it.
your Bag your face!
your Bite your tongue!
your Blow it out your ear!
your Burn not your house to fright the mouse away.
your Can I take your order (now)?
your Can I use your powder room?
your Could I take your order (now)?
your Could I use your powder room?
your cut your peaches
your Do not let the sun go down on your anger.
your Do not let the sun go down on your wrath.
your Do not wash your dirty linen in public.
your (Do) you kiss your momma with that mouth?
your Don't count your chickens before they are hatched.
your Don't get your bowels in an uproar!
your Don't give me any of your lip!
your Don't give up your day job.
your Don't hold your breath.
your Don't put all your eggs in one basket.
your Don't quit your day job.
your Don't teach your grandmother to suck eggs.
your Don't waste your breath.
your Don't waste your time.
your Don't worry your (pretty little) head about it.
your Enjoy your meal.
your First catch your hare.
your for your information
your Get your ass over here!
your Get your buns over here!
your Get your head out of the clouds!
your Get your nose out of my business.
your Go to your room!
your Hang on to your hat!
your (Has the) cat got your tongue?
your Have it your way.
your (Have you) changed your mind?
your Here's mud in your eye.
your Here's your hat, what's your hurry?
your Hitch your wagon to a star.

your Hoist your sail when the wind is fair.
your Hold on to your hat!
your Hold your horses!
your Hold your tater!
your Hold your tongue!
your How's your family?
your Hush your mouth!
your (I) beg your pardon, but...
your I'll thank you to keep your opinions to yourself.
your I'll thank you to mind your own business.
your (I'm) delighted to make your acquaintance.
your (It's) good to hear your voice.
your (It's) none of your business!
your It's your funeral.
your It's your move.
your It's your turn.
your It will be your ass!
your Keep your chin up.
your Keep your head down.
your Keep your mouth shut (about so/sth).
your Keep your nose out of my business.
your Keep your opinions to yourself!
your Keep your pants on!
your Keep your powder dry.
your Keep your shirt on!
your Keep your shop and your shop will keep you.
your lend your ear to so/sth
your Lend your money and lose your friend.
your like tryin' to scratch your ear with your elbow
your Make your mind up.
your May I take your order (now)?
your May I use your powder room?
your Mind your own beeswax.
your Mind your own business.
your My house is your house.
your Name your poison.
your None of your lip!
your On your bike!
your on your mark, get set, go
your Our house is your house.
your penny for your thoughts!
your pick on somebody your own size
your pick on someone your own size
your Put that in your pipe and smoke it!
your Put your money where your mouth is!
your Put your trust in God, and keep your powder dry.
your Shut your cake hole!
your So's your old man!
your Stretch your arm no further than your sleeve will reach.
your Take your seat.
your use your head for more than a hatrack
your use your head for more than something to keep your ears apart
your Watch your mouth!
your What's your age?
your What's yours?
your What's yours is mine, and what's mine is mine.
your Who's your friend?

your without (so much as) a (for or) by your leave
your You bet your boots!
your You bet your (sweet) life!
your You cannot have your cake and eat it (too).
your You changed your mind?
your You pays your money and you takes your chance(s).
your You scratch my back and I'll scratch yours.
your Your guess is as good as mine.
your Your place or mine?
your Your secret is safe with me.
your You're out of your mind!
your yours truly
your You've got to be out of your mind!
your Zip (up) your lip!
yourself by yourself
yourself Come in and make yourself at home.
yourself Go chase yourself!
yourself Help yourself.
yourself If you want a thing done well, do it yourself.
yourself If you would be well served, serve yourself.

yourself I'll thank you to keep your opinions to yourself.
yourself Keep this to yourself.
yourself Keep your opinions to yourself!
yourself Make yourself at home.
yourself Suit yourself.
yourself Take care (of yourself).
yourself Where (have) you been hiding (yourself)?
yourself Where (have) you been keeping yourself?
yourself Why keep a dog and bark yourself?
yourself Yourself?
yourselves by yourselves
youth growing youth has a wolf in his belly.
youth Youth must be served.
Z catch some Zs
Z cop some Zs
Z cut some Zs
Z everything from A to Z
Z from A to Z
zagged zigged when one should've zagged
zeek zeek out
zenith at the zenith of sth
zerked zerked (out)

zero zero in (on so/sth)
zero zero tolerance
zigged zigged when one should've zagged
ziggety Hot ziggety!
zip zip along
zip Zip it up!
zip zip past so/sth
zip zip sth on
zip zip sth up
zip Zip (up) your lip!
zone zone sth as sth
zone zone sth for sth
zone zone sth off
zonk zonk out
zonk zonk so out
zonk zonked (out)
zoom zoom across (sth)
zoom zoom along
zoom zoom in (on so/sth)
zoom zoom off
zoom zoom out
zoom zoom over so/sth
zoom zoom past so/sth
zoom zoom so/sth (over) to so
zoom zoom through (sth)
zoom zoom up
zounk zounked (out)